D1609049
Sadler's Wells
BLACK MARY HOLE
ST. JOHN'S STREET
OLD STREET ROAD
GRAY'S INN LANE
Clerkenwell Green
GOLDEN LANE
Bunhill Fields
Cemetery
SHOREDITCH
Charterhouse
ALDERSGATE ST.
Finsbury Square
Gray's Inn
West Smithfield
St. Giles Cripplegate
HOLBORN
Holborn Hill
CHANCERY LANE
Barbers' Hall
LONDON WALL
Moor Fields
Lincoln's Inn
FLEET MARKET
Newgate
Christ's Hospital
Bethlehem Hospital
BISHOPSGATE STREET
Duke's Theatre
Gough Sq.
NEWGATE STREET
Guildhall
Royal Society
Clifford's Inn
Cheshire Cheese Tavern
Old Bailey
Fleet
Stationers'
Temple Bar
FLEET S
Mitre Tavern
Clement's Church
St. Bride's Church
Royal Exchange
St. Botolph's Church
St. Paul's
STREET
House
LOMBARD ST.
LEADENHALL ST.
Somerset House
Blackfriars
Doctors' Commons
Lloyd's Coffee-house
The Temple
THAMES STREET
St. Olave's Church
Navy Office
THE RIVER THAMES
BLACKFRIARS BRIDGE
The Monument
Tower Hill
The Tower
THE BANKSIDE
LONDON BRIDGE
Cuper's Gardens
ST. GEORGE'S RD.
Southwark Cathedral
St. Thomas' Hospital
PICKLE HERRING ST.
BOROUGH HIGH ST.
Marshalsea Prison
BERMONDSLEY ST.
LAMBETH MARSH
MINT
King's Bench Prison
RUSSELL ST.
NEW ROAD
LONG LANE
KENT STREET
PROSPECT PLACE
THE GRANGE WALK
Union Crescent
Map by Harold K. Faye

The College Survey of English Literature

REVISED, SHORTER EDITION

ALEXANDER M. WITHERSPOON *Yale University*

GENERAL EDITOR

B. J. WHITING *Harvard University*

FRED B. MILLETT *Wesleyan University*

ODELL SHEPARD

ARTHUR PALMER HUDSON *The University of North Carolina*

EDWARD WAGENKNECHT *Boston University*

LOUIS UNTERMEYER

HARCOURT, BRACE & WORLD, INC.

New York, Chicago, San Francisco, Atlanta

Frontispiece photograph of the entrance to St. John's College, Cambridge University, by J. Gordon Miller from Black Star.

PRINTED IN THE UNITED STATES OF AMERICA

Preface to the Revised Edition

After its first decade, *The College Survey of English Literature* appears in a new, revised edition. The wide use of the book in college English courses has confirmed the editors and publishers in their original concept of the nature, purpose, and scope of an anthology for the survey course. Now, as when it was first published, *The College Survey* is designed primarily to introduce the student to the most important and enduring work of the principal writers in each period of English literature. While the editors remain firm in their belief that first and last there can be no substitute for the literature itself, they continue to provide those relevant background materials without which the student would have difficulty in orienting himself to the literary and intellectual climate of each century.

A guiding principle in the publishers' plan for the first edition of *The College Survey of English Literature*, and one that has attracted much favorable comment, was to enlist the services of a specialist for each of the main periods. It has now been the chief responsibility of the revising editor to unify and consolidate the work of those seven original editors. He has made every effort to perform this act of co-ordination with no sacrifice of the distinctive insights of his associates in their particular periods. Indeed, a continuing source of strength in *The College Survey* should be the variety of minds, all working in chosen fields with materials congenial to them, that have gone into its making.

The present edition embodies a careful revision of the original edition in the light of the experience of students and teachers who have used it during the past ten years, and with attention to the literary developments of the decade. An examination of the contents of the volume will reveal that the revised version of *The College Survey, Shorter Edition*, has increased the emphasis on major works of major writers, and, in order to permit intensive study of these authors and a wide choice among their writings, it includes an even more generous representation of their works than is commonly required in survey courses. To convey more adequately an impression of the richness and variety of English literature and of its backgrounds, many authors and selections have also been included that are not properly termed "major" but that justify their presence here by their intrinsic merit.

Like the original work, this revised edition has been prepared with the special needs of two kinds of courses in mind: first, the year course which intends to examine closely the work of a relatively small number of major writers in their proper perspective; secondly, the briefer survey course which attempts to introduce the student to the general field of English literature.

Freshness in point of view has been constantly sought in the revision. A cursory survey of the volume will disclose many additions and improvements in the presentation of authors and works. In the Early Period several important alterations will be noted: *Beowulf* is now given in the verse translation by F. B. Gummere; *Sir Gawain and the Green Knight* in the verse translation by Theodore Howard Banks; and *Piers Plowman* in the verse translation by Henry W. Wells. An additional tale, that of the Friar, has been included in the selection from Chaucer's *Canterbury Tales.*

The Elizabethan section has been enriched by the last scene of Marlowe's *Dr. Faustus*, by Spenser's *Prothalamion*, by further sonnets of Shakespeare and Spenser, and by additional lyrics of their contemporaries. In the Seventeenth Century section Donne has received generous reinforcement; Milton's *Paradise Lost* is now represented by the whole of Books I and II, by the climactic passages of Book IX, and the closing lines of Book XII, together with the Arguments of all twelve books. The selections from Dryden have also been augmented: *Mac Flecknoe* is now given in its entirety, and a portion of *The Hind and the Panther* has been included.

New items among the offerings from the Eighteenth Century include Pope's *Epistle to Dr. Arbuthnot* and some characteristic passages from *Boswell's London Journal, 1762–1763*, which was given to the public for the first time in 1950. The selections from the works of Swift, Thomson, Johnson, Goldsmith, and Blake have been freshened and adjusted to the needs of the survey course. Similarly, the contents of the Romantic and the Victorian periods have been refurbished and improved. Wordsworth's *The Prelude* and Shelley's *Prometheus Unbound* are represented more fully, and selections from Byron's letters are included; the poetry of Matthew Arnold and Gerard Manley Hopkins appears at greater length and to better advantage.

Of special interest and value is the greatly enlarged representation of the poetry and prose of the Twentieth Century, which provides a generous panorama of contemporary English literature. To enrich the poetry section, important poems of Eliot, Auden, and Dylan Thomas are now included, and the quantity of material from the work of Hardy, Yeats, Housman, Masefield, and Spender has been conspicuously increased. Throughout the volume an endeavor has been made to obtain a better balance between poetry and prose than is ordinarily available, and the variety of the poetry is matched by that of the prose, which includes essays of many kinds, historical and biographical sketches, portraits, literary criticism, and short stories. Appearing for the first time in any college anthology are the selections, new in this edition, from the prose of Conrad, E. M. Forster, Virginia Woolf, D. H. Lawrence, and Aldous Huxley.

The texts used in *The College Survey* are uniformly those of standard editions. From the Romantic Period on, the spelling, capitalization, and punctuation of the texts are, in general, those of editions approved by the author or accepted as authentic by the readers of his time. Since printing practices were extremely varied before 1800, the capitalization, punctuation, and spelling of the selections up to the Romantic Period follow the best modern versions consistent with the flavor of the period in which the selections appeared. The arrangement of authors is based on the dates when they flourished rather than on strict chronology.

In the preparation of the introductions and notes, the needs of the average student have been kept constantly in mind. A conscientious and careful effort has been made to steer a middle course between explaining the obvious on one hand and failing to supply necessary information on the other, to the end of giving effective help to the average sophomore reader without cluttering up his thought with esoteric information. The editorial equipment in general, and particularly in the Twentieth Century section, attempts to provide relevant background materials for an intelligent reading of the authors included, while leaving critical interpretation to the individual instructor. The period introductions together constitute a ninety-thousand word historical interpretation of the development of English literature. Many notes, particularly of a geographical or historical nature, which might have been added, have been omitted in the belief, and with the concurring judgment of many instructors, that they are not necessary to the understanding of what may be an allusive but sufficiently clear piece of writing. In general, the introductions and notes are not designed to do the work of either the instructor or the student, or to supplant the college library.

An admired feature of the original *College Survey*, widely imitated in anthologies appearing through the decade, was the inclusion of a generous but not distractingly profuse selection of photographs, portraits, works of art, and manuscript and title pages illustrating the literature and life of each period. The heightened quality of the illustrations in this revised edition will be readily noted, as will the increased teaching utility made possible by the inclusion of more detailed running captions. Here, and also in the preparation of new end paper maps, the aim has been to combine practical usefulness with attractive decorative effect. The front end paper map of London, prepared by Harold K. Faye, has been adapted from *A New Pocket Plan of the Cities of London and Westminster with the Borough of Southwark* (1798), which was generously made available by Mr. Alexander O. Vietor, Curator of Maps in the Yale University Library.

The richly ornamented Renaissance gateway of St. John's College, Cambridge, shown in the frontispiece, was built in the early sixteenth century at the bidding of Lady Margaret of Beaufort, mother of Henry VII. Above the archway to the left appears a large Tudor rose, and the sculptured background is spangled with marguerites (daisies) in honor of the college's foundress. Antelopes support the royal Tudor arms.

The lists of "Suggestions for Further Reading" at the ends of the different periods have been included for the benefit of the student rather than for the scholar. They have been thoroughly revised and brought up to date, and offer helpful suggestions for the student who wishes to do further reading on his own. The books listed are in most well-equipped college libraries. A chapter on "Poetic Forms and Patterns" by Mr. Untermeyer has been added to the revised edition and, following it, a chronological list of the English rulers.

From the beginning, the process of revision of *The College Survey* has been carried forward in consultation with teachers and students who have used or plan to use the anthology. To all who have generously offered criticism, comments, and suggestions the general editor tenders his sincere thanks. Among those who have gone to considerable pains in making suggestions for improvements, he is specially indebted to the following: Professor Paul A. Brown (Temple University), Professor Francis X. Connolly (Fordham University), Professor R. K. Gordon (University of Alberta), Professor Sherman M. Kuhn (University of Michigan), Professor J. S. Moffatt, Jr. (Washington and Lee University), Professor Ruth Mohl (Brooklyn College), Professor Frank G. Nelson (William Jewell College), Professor David Novarr (Cornell University), Professor Robert A. Pratt (Queens College), Professor C. J. Reynolds (University of Maine), Professor Andrew T. Smithberger (University of Notre Dame), and Professor Clarence R. Tracy (University of Saskatchewan). To my friend, Mr. S. Gorley Putt, British representative of the Commonwealth Fund, and formerly of The Queen's University of Belfast and of University College, Exeter, who is largely responsible for the introduction to the Eighteenth Century section, a special debt of thanks is due and is hereby gratefully acknowledged.

A. M. W.

New Haven, Connecticut
February 1, 1951.

CONTENTS

THE SIXTEENTH CENTURY

THE SEVENTEENTH CENTURY

THE EIGHTEENTH CENTURY

THE ROMANTIC PERIOD

THE VICTORIAN PERIOD

THE TWENTIETH CENTURY

GENERAL BIBLIOGRAPHY

This brief list should be supplemented by the lists of books mentioned in the introductions to the different periods and authors, as well as by the bibliographies at the end of each period.

BIBLIOGRAPHICAL AIDS

The Cambridge Bibliography of English Literature, F. W. Bateson, ed., Macmillan, 1941. A monumental and standard bibliographical work dealing with all periods and phases of English literature.

A Concise Bibliography for Students of English, A. G. Kennedy, ed., Stanford University Press, 1940.

A Bibliographical Manual for Students of the Language and Literature of England and the United States. A Short-Title List, compiled by John W. Spargo, Packard, Chicago, 1941.

HISTORICAL BACKGROUND

The Oxford History of England, G. N. Clark, ed., Oxford University Press, 1934—. A monumental history of England, to be completed in fourteen volumes, each an independent book, the whole forming a continuous history of England from the Roman period to the present century. Eight volumes have been published and will be referred to under the respective periods.

Albion, R. G. *A History of England and the British Empire*, Ginn, 1937. Particularly valuable for students of political and economic history.

Hinchman, W. S. *England: A Short Account of Its Life and Culture*, Little, Brown, 1941. An admirable and spirited introduction, for American students, to English thought and civilization.

Lunt, W. E. *History of England*, 3rd ed., Harper, 1946. An excellent history, specially written for the American college student, of the civilization in which our own takes root.

Trevelyan, G. M. *English Social History: A Survey of Six Centuries from Chaucer to Queen Victoria*, Longmans, 1946. An eminently scholarly and eminently readable narrative. A new edition, in four illustrated volumes, will be referred to under the periods represented.

—— *History of England*, Longmans, 1926. One of the best and most readable one-volume histories of England, by one of England's most distinguished historians.

Wingfield-Stratford, Esmé. *The History of British Civilization*, 2 vols., Harcourt, Brace, 1933. An excellent survey.

THE ENGLISH LANGUAGE

Barfield, Owen. *History in English Words*, Doran, 1926. An informative and stimulating study of the historical significance of many of the words we use daily.

Baugh, A. C. *A History of the English Language*, Appleton-Century, 1935. The most up-to-date, systematic, clear, and usable book on the subject.

Greenough, J. B., and Kittredge, G. L. *Words and Their Ways in English Speech*, Macmillan, 1923. A fascinating volume full of striking and unusual information about the English vocabulary.

Krapp, G. P. *The English Language in America*, 2 vols., Century, 1925. Learned and entertaining; the first volume is of particular interest to the general student of English.

Mencken, H. L. *The American Language: An Inquiry into the Development of English in the United States*, rev. ed., Knopf, 1943. *Supplement I–II*, 1945–1948. Full of instruction and humor for any student of English.

Weekley, Ernest. *Concise Etymological Dictionary of Modern English*, Dutton, 1924. Invaluable for those who are interested in the origins and changes in meaning of the words they use and read.

Williams, Margaret. *Word-Hoard*, Sheed and Ward, 1940. Another delightful volume for the student of literature and words.

HISTORIES OF ENGLISH LITERATURE

The Oxford History of English Literature, F. P. Wilson and Bonamy Dobrée, eds., Oxford University Press, 1945—. A definitive and scholarly history which will appear in several volumes, some of them in two parts, the whole forming a continuous history. Designed for both the scholar and the general reader, and taking into consideration the other arts, philosophy, social ideas, etc. Separate volumes will be referred to under the respective periods.

The Cambridge History of English Literature, rev. ed., A. W. Ward and A. R. Waller, eds., 15 vols., Macmillan, 1933. Standard accounts of periods and authors, not always well integrated.

Baugh, A. C., ed., *A Literary History of England*, Appleton-Century-Crofts, 1948. A distinguished and comprehensive history of English literature by five American scholars. Up-to-date in scholarship. Readable and judicious in critical comments.

Legouis, Emile, and Cazamian, Louis. *A History of English Literature*, rev. ed., translated from the French, Macmillan, 1948. One of the best histories of the literature, and particularly valuable as representing the perspective and criticism of two distinguished French scholars of English.

Sampson, George. *The Concise Cambridge History of English Literature*, Macmillan, 1941. Altogether the best shorter history of the literature. The author has extracted the essence of the fifteen volumes of the original history noted above. Vivid and definite in language, concrete in illustration, and precise in detail.

HANDBOOKS, DICTIONARIES, ETC.

Annals of English Literature, 1475–1925, compiled by J. C. Ghosh and E. G. Withycombe, Oxford University Press, 1935. A list of the principal publications of each year, together with an alphabetical index of authors and their works. An invaluable compilation, designed "to show what books people were reading at any time, and with what rivals and candidates for literary fame each had to reckon."

The Oxford Companion to English Literature, by Sir Paul Harvey, Oxford University Press, 1932, 1937. A valuable compendium of information relating to authors, proper names, allusions, etc., commonly met with in English literature.

A Handbook to Literature, with an Outline of Literary History, English and American, by W. F. Thrall and Addison Hibbard, Odyssey Press, 1936. A very convenient and useful book for the college student, containing a dictionary of the most important facts and terms relating to literature and literary studies.

The Reader's Encyclopedia, by William Rose Benét, Crowell, 1948. A one-volume work of references, arranged alphabetically, to almost everything pertaining to the history, literature, and art of England, America, and the world.

The Oxford Classical Dictionary, Sir Paul Harvey and others, eds., Oxford University Press, 1949. The most thorough compendium in one volume of information on all aspects of classical civilization—geography, history, literature, mythology, philosophy, etc., with bibliographies.

A Smaller Classical Dictionary, E. H. Blakeney, ed., Everyman's Library, Dutton, 1923. The most useful and inexpensive of smaller dictionaries relating to all aspects of classical civilization.

A Mapbook of English Literature, by J. D. Briscoe, R. L. Sharp, and M. E. Borish, Holt, 1936. An inexpensive and exceedingly useful book of maps, charts, and guides, which indicate clearly the places where the literature was created, where authors lived, and where they laid their scenes.

THE EARLY PERIOD

PLATE I

A A TENTH-CENTURY ANGLO-SAXON MAP OF THE WORLD (*Map Division, New York Public Library*)

The original in the British Museum is prefixed to a geography, the *Periegesis* (description of the habitable world) by the Greek geographer, Dionysius. The *Periegesis* was translated into Latin by Priscian, a grammarian of the fifth century, and became a popular school text in the Middle Ages.

Medieval maps were illustrations of the geography of Holy Writ rather than attempts to present accurate geographical knowledge. The inhabited world was divided into three symmetrical parts, with Asia occupying one half; Europe and Africa, the other half. The larger size of Asia was attributed to the fact that, according to the Old Testament, it was the portion of Shem, the first born of Noah. At the center of the medieval world was Jerusalem. At the eastern extremity, which was placed at the top of the map, medieval cartographers usually put the terrestrial paradise in which man first lived. (The Anglo-Saxon map is exceptional in showing an island, probably Ceylon, instead of the earthly paradise.) The western limit of the world was marked by the Pillars of Hercules. (See the bottom, center, of the map.) Around this limited area flowed the ocean, of which only a narrow band, like a river, was shown.

B STONEHENGE (*Culver*)

The origin and purpose of this great prehistoric stone monument on Salisbury Plain remains an archaeological mystery, but it is generally agreed today that the great stones were erected in the late Bronze Age or Early Iron Age of England's history, by the Celtic inhabitants who preceded the Anglo-Saxons on the island. Stonehenge probably served either as a temple for sun worship or as a tomb for some great chieftain. The ingenuity of the Celts in erecting it can be realized only when one considers that each of the stones stands about 13½ feet above ground, goes down 4½ feet into the ground, and weighs about twenty-six tons.

The earliest mention of Stonehenge in literature is in Geoffrey of Monmouth's *History of the Kings of Britain.* Geoffrey attributes the building of the monument to the Britons in the fifth century. According to his account, the wizard Merlin transplanted the Giants' Dance from Kildare, Ireland, to Salisbury Plain as a memorial to the men killed in the defeat of Hengist, the Jutish invader.

PLATE II

A A SECTION OF THE BAYEUX TAPESTRY, SHOWING PART OF THE BATTLE OF HASTINGS (*Bayeux*)

This monumental example of the medieval art of tapestry making, 215 feet long, tells the story of the Norman Conquest from the visit of the Saxon king Harold to William of Normandy in 1064 to the end of the Battle of Hastings. The section shown here provides an excellent picture of medieval warfare, which was carried on by comparatively small groups of armored cavalry, armed with lances and battle-axes, and supported by archers. Sometimes, as in this picture, the cavalry dismounted and formed ranks to meet the enemy's charge.

For a long time, it was thought that the Bayeux Tapestry was embroidered by Queen Matilda, the wife of William the Conqueror, but this story has proved to be merely a legend, and some authorities would not assign to the Tapestry a date earlier than the twelfth century. Whatever the date of its making, the Tapestry is a valuable record of an important historical event, and, equally important, a highly imaginative example of one of the most popular medieval art forms.

B SALISBURY CATHEDRAL, A SOUTHWEST VIEW ACROSS THE LAWNS OF THE CLOSE (*Black Star*)

The persistence and dedication of medieval builders had no finer result than Salisbury, begun in 1220 and not completed until the middle of the fourteenth century. Despite the "improvements" of eighteenth and nineteenth-century restorers, Salisbury, with the tallest and most beautiful spire in the country, remains one of the finest examples in England of the Early English style of Gothic architecture. The seventeenth-century divine and poet, George Herbert, often used to walk to Salisbury from his little country church and listen there to the music rising between the slender soaring arches of the cathedral's great nave.

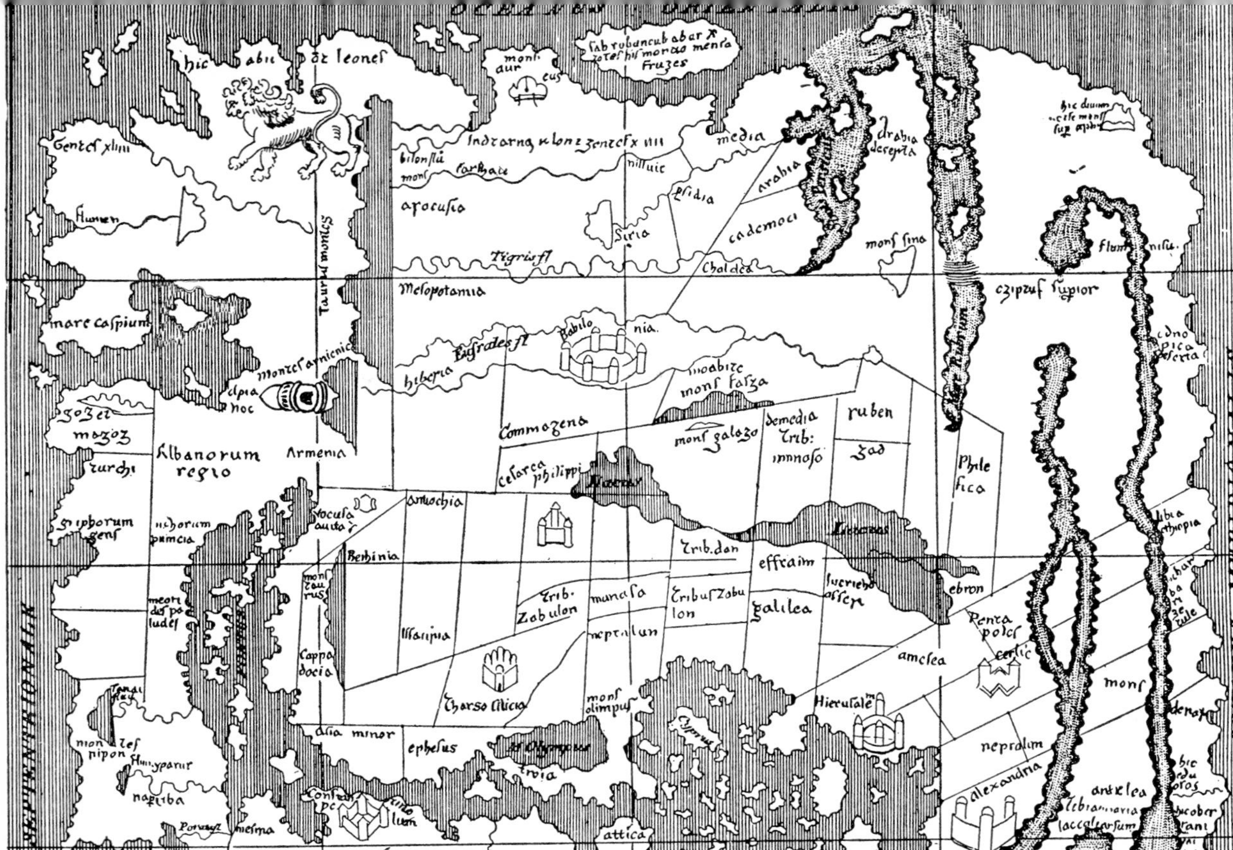

MARE SEPTENTRIONALE
OCEANUS MERIDIONALIS
OCEANUS OCCIDENTALIS
MARE ATLANTICUM
mare caspium
Mesopotamia
Armenia
Albanorum regio
Tracia
attica
macedonia
Roma
alexandria
Hispania
Britannia
Hibernia

A

B

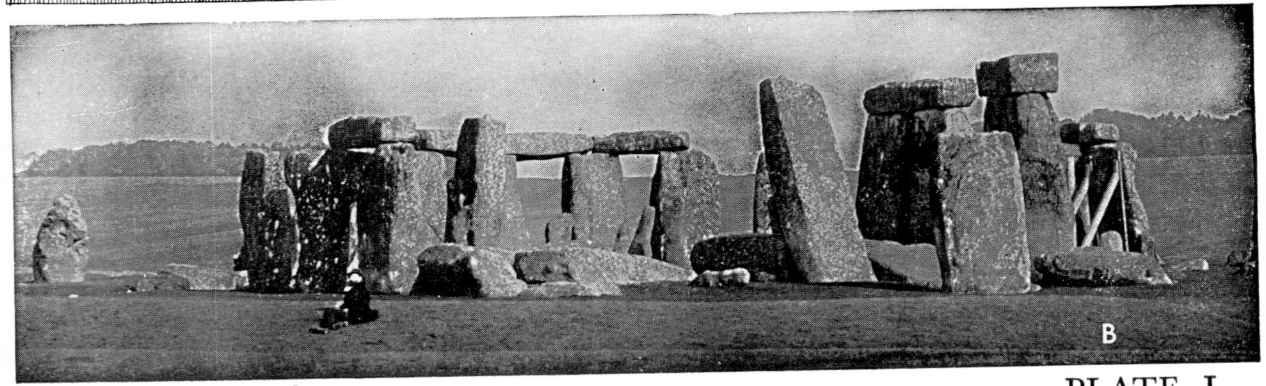

PLATE I

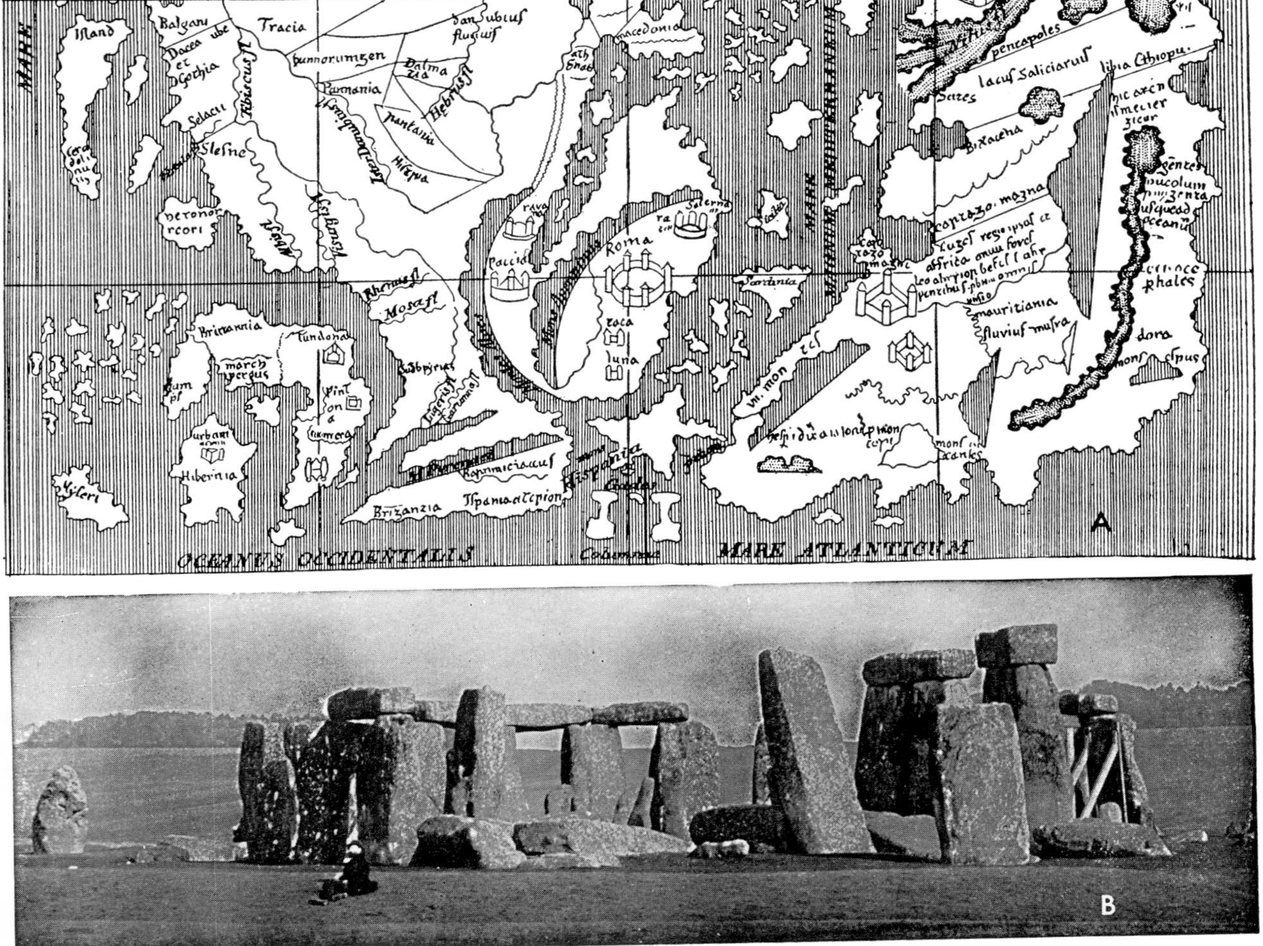

PLATE II

A

B

C

PLATE III

A

V.

Stræt wæs stan fah stig wisode gumum
æt gædere guð byrne scan heard
hond locen hring iren scir song in sear
wum þa hie to sele furðum in hyra gry
re geat wum gangan cwomon setton
sæme þe side scyldas rondas regn heard
wið þæs recedes weal. bugon þa to bence
byrnan hringdon guð searo gumena
garas stodon sæ manna searo samod
æt gædere æsc holt ufan græg wæs se
iren þreat wæpnum gewurþad þa ðær
wlonc hæleð oret mecgas æfter hæle
þum frægn. hwanon ferigeað ge fæt
te scyldas græge syrcan ⁊ grim helmas
here sceafta heap ic eom hroð gares
ar ⁊ ombiht. ne seah ic elþeodige þus
manige men modiglicran. wen ic þ ge for
wlenco nalles for wræc siðum. ac for hige

B

book of kyng Arthur & of his noble knyghtes of the rounde table / that whan they were hole togyders there was euer an C and xl / and here is the ende of the deth of Arthur / I praye you all Jentyl men and Jentyl wymmen that redeth this book of Arthur and his knyghtes from the begynnyng to the endynge / praye for me whyle I am on lyue that god sende me good delyueraunce / & whan I am deed I praye you all praye for my soule / for this book was ended the ix yere of the reygne of kyng edward the fourth / by syr Thomas Maleore knyght as Ihesu helpe hym for hys grete myght / as he is the seruaunt of Ihesu bothe day and nyght /

¶Thus endeth thys noble and Ioyous book entytled le morte Darthur / Notwythstondyng it treateth of the byrth / lyf / and actes of the sayd kyng Arthur / of his noble knyghtes of the rounde table / theyr meruayllous enquestes and aduentures / thachyeuyng of the sangreal / & in thende the dolorous deth & departyng out of thys world of them al / Whiche book was reduced in to englysshe by syr Thomas Malory knyght as afore is sayd / and by me deuyded in to xxi bookes chaptyred and enprynted / and fynysshed in thabbey Westmestre the last day of Juyl the yere of our lord / M / CCCC / lxxxv /

¶ Caxton me fieri fecit

C

D

PLATE IV

C INTERIOR OF A FOURTEENTH-CENTURY HALL (*Courtesy of the Metropolitan Museum of Art*)

The great hall was the central living unit in the medieval castle. In this reconstruction of the hall in Penshurst Castle, Kent, the servants are grouped around the central fire while the lord and lady dine on a dais, entertained by a jester who lies on a bear rug at left. Note the absence of a chimney (the smoke either went out through a hole in the roof or stayed in the room). The tapestries lining the walls served a practical as well as a decorative purpose—they helped to moderate a little the chill of the stone walls. A comparison of this hall with the description of Heorot in *Beowulf* shows that, even by Chaucer's time, the basic architectural living unit was not much different from that of the Anglo-Saxons, although the wooden buildings had been replaced by stone castles. In fact, the great hall remained a central feature of English homes through the Elizabethan period.

D TOWER OF LONDON (*Raymond Buckley*)

The Normans brought castle architecture to England, and a number of their stone fortresses still exist, in whole or in part. The best known of these is the Tower of London, reputedly built on the site of an old Roman fortress by William the Conqueror, although only a small part of the existing structure dates back to the eleventh century. The Tower, as it stands today on the bank of the Thames, consists of a double wall, the inner one having thirteen towers and the outer one, six towers surrounded by a moat. In the central rectangle are barracks; the White Tower (the oldest part of the building); the Chapel of St. Peter ad Vincula in which are buried Queen Anne, Queen Katharine, the Duke of Somerset, and the Duke of Northumberland (all beheaded); and the site of the execution block where so many notables met their deaths. Among the distinguished prisoners of the Tower were Queen Elizabeth (while she was still a princess), Sir Walter Ralegh, Sir Thomas More, Lady Jane Grey, Bishop Fisher, and many Catholics who died for their faith during the sixteenth century.

While the Tower is known chiefly as a prison, it was also a royal residence up until the civil wars of the seventeenth century when the palace building was destroyed by Cromwell. It was customary for the monarchs of England to lodge in the Tower before their coronation and to proceed from there, through the city, to be crowned in Westminster.

PLATE III

A THE SIXTH TAPESTRY IN THE SERIES KNOWN AS THE HUNT OF THE UNICORN (*Courtesy of the Metropolitan Museum of Art, the Cloisters Collection*)

Only a few series of medieval tapestries have survived the vicissitudes of time, wars, and revolutions, and the Unicorn Series is one of the finest of these. Woven for the marriage of Anne of Brittany to Louis XII of France in 1499, it represents the final flowering of the art of medieval tapestry making and combines, in an interesting fashion, the secular and religious symbolism of the unicorn.

In the scene reproduced here the unicorn appears twice—in the upper left-hand corner of the tapestry he is wounded and captured, and in the center of the tapestry he is brought before Anne and Louis at their castle. The royal couple are standing arm in arm. Note the abundance of realistic detail in the scene. More than one hundred different kinds of plants have been counted in the series as a whole, of which eighty have been identified—an evidence of the skill and infinite patience of the medieval tapestry makers.

The unicorn, the central figure in the six tapestries, is a figure of complex meaning in medieval legend. In religious allegory he stood for the figure of the risen Christ; the virgin, by whose power only he could be captured, represented the Virgin Mary; and the huntsman who sought him, the Angel Gabriel. On the secular level, the unicorn came to be associated, through the power of the virgin over him, with the doctrine of courtly love, and his capture symbolized marriage. In still another area of thought, the horn of the unicorn was said to have magical properties for absorbing poison, and powdered unicorn horn was a supposed ingredient of many medieval medicines.

B JOHN BALL PREACHING TO SOLDIERS

This illustration of an incident in the Peasants' Revolt of 1381 comes from a fifteenth-century manuscript of the *Chronicles* of Jean Froissart. Froissart, a contemporary observer of the Revolt, gives us a vivid picture of the poor priest, John Ball, who might be considered one of the first champions of the rights of the common man—or an early example of a rabble-rouser, depending on one's point of view.

"A crazy priest in the county of Kent, called John

Ball, who, for his absurd preaching, had been thrice confined in the prison of the archbishop of Canterbury, was greatly instrumental in inflaming them [i.e., the peasants] with those ideas. He was accustomed, every Sunday after mass, as the people were coming out of the church, to preach to them in the market place and assemble a crowd around him; to whom he would say,—'My good friends, things cannot go on well in England, or ever will until every thing shall be in common; when there shall neither be vassal nor lord, and all distinctions levelled. . . . Are we not all descended from the same parents, Adam and Eve? . . . They [the nobles] are clothed in velvets and rich stuffs . . . while we are forced to wear poor cloth. . . . We are called slaves; and, if we do not perform our services, we are beaten. . . . Let us go to the king, who is young, and remonstrate with him on our servitude, telling him we must have it otherwise, or that we shall find a remedy for it ourselves.'" (Johnes' translation of the *Chronicles*)

C A LATE MEDIEVAL SCRIPTORIUM (*Bettmann Archive*)

A room, known as the scriptorium, was set aside in monasteries for the purpose of writing and copying manuscripts. Here, the monk in charge is dictating to two assistants. The first printers designed their types in imitation of the formalized calligraphy of the scribes, and, therefore, early books often closely resemble handwritten manuscripts.

PLATE IV

A GEOFFREY CHAUCER, THE SEDDON PORTRAIT (*Fogg Museum, Harvard University*)

None of the existing portraits of Chaucer were painted from life, and most of them, like this one, seem to have been based on the portrait which Occleve, Chaucer's disciple, inserted in the manuscript of his *Regement of Princes*. The Occleve portrait was made several years after Chaucer's death.

The fullest description of himself that Chaucer has left us is part of the speech of Harry Bailly in the Prologue to the "Tale of Sir Thopas." Chaucer is obviously poking fun at himself with great good humor when he has Harry say:

. . . "What man artow?" quod he;
"Thou lookest as thou woldest fynde an hare,
For evere upon the ground I se thee stare.
"Approche neer, and looke up murily.
Now war yow, sires, and lat this man have place!
He in the waast is shape as wel as I;
This were a popet in an arm t'embrace
For any womman, smal and fair of face.
He semeth elvyssh by his contenaunce,
For unto no wight dooth he daliaunce."

B A PAGE FROM THE ONLY EXISTING MANUSCRIPT OF BEOWULF (*British Museum*)

C THE LAST PAGE OF THE CAXTON EDITION OF MALORY'S MORTE DARTHUR (*Courtesy of the Pierpont Morgan Library*)

In the Epilogue to his first printed work, a translation of LeFevre's *Recueil des histoires de Troies*, Caxton tells us how he came to learn the new art:

"Forasmuch as in the writing of the same my pen is worn, mine hand weary & not steadfast, mine eyen dimmed with over much looking on the white paper, and my courage not so prone and ready to labour as hit hath been, and that age creepeth on me dayly and feebleth all my body and also because I have promised to diverse gentlemen and to my friends to address to hem as hastily as I might this said book, therefore I have practised and lerned at my great charge & dispense to ordeyne this said book in print after the manner and form as ye may here see, and is not written with pen and ink as other books ben, to thende that every man may have them at ones, for all the books of this story named the Recule of the historyes of Troyes thus emprinted as ye here see were begonne in one day & also finished in one day." (Quoted in *The Golden Book* by Douglas McMurtrie)

D VIRGIN AND CHILD, FOURTEENTH-CENTURY ILE-DE-FRANCE SCHOOL (*Metropolitan Museum of Art*)

Henry Adams, in his *Mont St. Michel and Chartres*, describes the extent and depth of the devotion to the Virgin in medieval society:

"These people knew the Virgin as well as they knew their own mothers; every jewel in her crown . . . every expression on the perfectly familiar features of her grave, imperial face . . . repeated over and over again, in stone, glass, ivory, enamel, wood, . . . the Virgin was as familiar to every one of them as the sun or the seasons. . . ."

The Early Period

PART I. THE OLD ENGLISH ERA

Britain before the English

THE daylight of history breaks upon the island of Britain half a century before the birth of Christ, with the invasion of the Romans under Julius Caesar. About eighteen hundred years before Caesar, however, groups of invaders from the coasts of Spain, France, and the Low Countries established themselves in Britain, and to them we owe the various monuments which culminated in such impressive structures as Stonehenge. In the sixth century B.C., during the Iron Age, the Celts, coming from Central Europe, first appeared on the island. There were two waves of Celtic invasion: one, the Goidelic (Gaelic), which went directly to Ireland, and the other, the Brythonic (British), which came to Britain. In the first century B.C., a third group of Celtic invaders consisted of members of the Belgic tribes (partly Germanic in stock) on whom Roman pressure was becoming intolerable.

Early British culture followed Continental developments, inevitably with a conspicuous time lag. The basic economy was agricultural, but since most of the island was heavily wooded, farming was confined to the open upland slopes of the south and west. The usual domestic animals were found. Soil was originally broken by a light scratch plow; the Belgic Celts seem to have been the first to use a plow of sufficient weight to clear and cultivate the heavier and more fertile soil of the valleys. After the family, the ordinary human unit was the village or town tribe, sometimes, as in the larger fortified hill towns, of considerable size. We have no information concerning the earlier governmental and social institutions, but the Belgic Celts brought the tribal organization of Gaul. The very frequent presence of certain articles in the early graves indicates a belief in immortality. The Celtic priests, known as Druids, were a powerful class whose cult probably originated in Britain, if indeed it was not centered there. The Druids had peculiar rites and customs; they seem to have practiced human sacrifice, and they believed in immortality and transmigration.

The Roman invasion was in two parts: first, the raids made by Julius Caesar in 54 and 53 B.C., which were followed by nearly a hundred years of British independence; and second, the conquest, which began in A.D. 43, under the Emperor Claudius. This final Roman invasion arose from the inevitable need of a great predatory military state to extend its frontiers until no more remain. From the middle of the first century after Christ on until the first quarter of the fifth, Britain was part of the Roman world. It is important to remember that the Roman occupation of Britain lasted for a long period of time, equal to that extending from the discovery of America by Columbus to the election of Abraham Lincoln, or, in English literary annals, from the composition of Sir Thomas Malory's *Morte Darthur* to that of Tennyson's *Idylls of the King*. Romanization was extensive, and appeared in the growth of town life, the development of the system of villas (large, often self-sufficient estates of which the most characteristic feature was the manor house surrounded by slave huts), and the building of hundreds of miles of well-paved roads, portions of which still survive, and the lines of which are still followed in most modern arterial highways. Roman civilization did not, however, take root in Britain as it did in Gaul, and in general the Romans occupied a land whose inhabitants remained British.

Although Britain was never among the well-to-do sections of the Roman Empire, the southern and central sections of the island constituted a peaceful province and enjoyed a reasonable prosperity (based on the export of grain and metals) until the economic troubles and the further invasions of the fourth century. The presence of unconquered tribes in the Scottish highlands made strong garrisons constantly necessary. The great northern wall, built by the Emperor Hadrian from the Solway Firth to the North Sea, and the wall of the Emperor Antoninus Pius, still farther north in Scotland, held the wild tribes back effectively for a while. But opportunities to break through were eventually given them by governmental disorders, notably the folly of many Roman and Romano-British leaders who took their forces to the Continent in fruitless efforts to seize imperial power. There were also raids from Ireland, in one of which the youthful Patrick, later to become Ireland's patron saint, was carried away to be a slave in the land of his future triumph. Even more threatening for the Romano-British future were the increasing numbers of Frankish and Saxon pirates who struck from across the Channel and the North Sea. The hard-pressed government in Rome found it increasingly difficult to aid the beleaguered province, and finally in 410 the Emperor Honorius was forced to tell his British subjects that henceforth they were at liberty to defend themselves.

The English Invasions

The conquest of Britain by the invaders whom we now call English is described in a brief and picturesque fashion in the *Anglo-Saxon Chronicle*. Drawing its information from the Venerable Bede, the English historian of the eighth century, it tells us that in the year 449 a British king invited two Germanic chieftains, Hengist and Horsa, to come to Britain as mercenary soldiers against the marauding Picts from the north of the island. The visitors were eminently successful in battle, but shortly, having perceived "the sluggishness of the Britons and the excellence of the land," they sent home for reinforcements. Then "there came men from three German tribes, the Old Saxons, the Angles, and the Jutes," and their descendants became in due time the English.

Unfortunately modern historians cannot accept this succinct account at its face value. The English conquest of Britain was very nearly the last of those extensive mass migrations from the north of Europe which accompanied and hastened the breakup of the Roman Empire. Despite all that the Romano-Britons could do, by the middle of the fifth century numerous groups of Germans had come to Britain to stay.

These Germanic tribes—and to those listed in the *Chronicle* we must add a few Frisians and fewer Franks—had a number of things in common. They all came from the coastal area on one side or the other of the Danish Peninsula or from the lower part of that peninsula. Linguistically they were of the Low German branch of the West Germanic dialect. (It is from the other branch of West Germanic —High German—that modern literary German has developed.) In the main they were a simple farmer and fisher folk. The piratical expeditions which we associate almost exclusively with their way of life probably supplied no more than incidental luxuries, while the ordinary means of existence were wrested with heavy labor from the soil and the sea.

Thanks to the tenacity of the peat bogs, there exist even today the scanty remains of a few of these linguistic ancestors of ours attired in their habit as they lived. Their trousers, belt holes and all, are singularly modern in appearance. They also wore linen tunics, often bolstered with fur against the cold. Their armor and arms, many of Roman origin or fashioned on Roman models, have survived and prove that these people were well equipped in the materials of war.

Many of their gods were only local divinities inseparably attached to particular shrines, but the various tribes had some deities in common, and by the fourth century Woden (Odin) had driven Thunor (Thor) from his place as chief god. Thor was the fighting farmers' god, a simple giant-killer likely to attract the common people. Woden was a clever god who invented runes,[1] went about in disguise, and appeared as a somewhat gloomy, one-eyed solver of difficulties in mainly aristocratic circles.

The first social unit was the family, which developed inevitably into the clan. The spirit of the *comitatus* (strong feeling of loyalty to the chieftain) is marked in English literature and history. It is well illustrated in *Beowulf* (page 32) and in the act of Harold's house carls dying round their lord at Hastings. As for the larger aspects of government, the Continental Angles had at least one powerful king, Offa; about the Saxons we are by no means so sure, as there is evidence they had many minor local leaders. There was doubtless co-operation and local leeway, but our ancestors were not considerate enough to leave any records of the methods of government by which they conducted their affairs.

Our knowledge of the course of the English conquest of Britain is inferential and often confused. The invasion was actually in two chapters, in the first of which the invaders swept back and forth across the island, seeking only plunder and leaving behind them a trail of sacked towns and burning villas. Because their sole aim was immediate gain, they could strike lightning blows at the weakest and richest points, while the Britons, bound to their individual localities by tradition and inertia, were able to put up at best only the sterile and limited resistance of self-preservation. The second chapter, however, shows a consolidation of British forces, and in it we seem to find the Britons rather more than holding their own. With this period we associate the name of Arthur, who—if he existed at all —was apparently a military leader of less than royal rank, at the head of a mobile fighting force. The course of the invasion, although slowed down, could not be checked, and when in the sixth century we first get a reasonably clear view of the situation, we find the so-called lowland zone occupied by at least ten English kingdoms of varying sizes, of which the most important were, or were to be, Kent, Northumbria, Mercia, and Wessex. Around them on the west and north from Cornwall to the land of the Picts stretched a line of Celtic kingdoms, the gradual assimilation of which by the English was not to be completed until the seventeenth century.

It was formerly assumed that those Britons who did not escape to the Celtic kingdoms of the highland zone, or across the Channel to Gaul, were massacred. But, it is now believed that a very considerable number of Britons survived as slaves, or subtenants nearly on the level of slaves, to be ultimately absorbed into the largely Germanic population. The next few centuries of English history saw the steady growth of the larger English kingdoms at the expense of the Celts or their smaller Germanic neighbors, and a shift of political supremacy from Northumbria to Mercia and finally to Wessex.

The Danes and Alfred

Since it would be too much to attempt to trace in detail here the tangled course of Anglo-Saxon political history before the accession of Alfred (871), only the main facts will follow. After the short-lived leadership of Kent at the end of the sixth century, which was due largely to the wisdom and diplomatic skill of its ruler, Aethelbert,[2] the spasmodically united Northumbrian kingdoms of Bernicia and Deira had a long, though fitful, period of political supremacy. The eighth century saw Northumbria lapse into virtual anarchy, from which it never recovered, while in the meantime two long-lived and gifted kings brought Mercia to its period of greatness. In the ninth century the leadership passed to the hitherto obscure kingdom of Wessex, whose energetic King Ecgbert had assumed the overlordship of England and much of Wales by 830. But a new wave of invaders from Denmark and Norway—beginning as early as 787—made the leadership of Wessex a painful and almost empty matter. Towards the end of the eighth century there were disastrous raids in the north, during which the Danes burned Lindisfarne, sacred to Aidan and Cuthbert, and sacked the monastery at Jarrow, where Bede had lived his long and fruitful life.

The Danes and Norwegians were the last of the Germanic peoples to invade Britain from their northern homes. These Vikings were a tough, hard, aggressive lot, but not without interest in the arts, and they boasted an unwritten literature as tough as themselves and in some ways brilliant. They were careless of human life, risking their own existences at the drop of a sword or spear, massacring hundreds, even thousands, of captured foes as a blood sacrifice to Odin; wily in battle, merciless in victory, and blandly treacherous in defeat. Like their cousins the Anglo-Saxons, they came first as pirati-

[1] Runes were the characters of the alphabet of the ancient Germanic peoples. They consisted of perpendicular and oblique, and a few curved, lines. They were used for inscriptions indicating the ownership of property, for purposes of divination, for magic healing, and, in some late instances, for literary composition.

[2] For the chronology of the English rulers, see p. 134.

cal plunderers and later became invaders and settlers. Unlike the Anglo-Saxons, they did not devote their attention solely to England. Ireland and Western Scotland absorbed most of their energies during the period when Ecgbert was establishing the overlordship of Wessex. By 871, when Alfred ascended a far from stable throne in Wessex, the Danes had made Northumbria and East Anglia their own, terrified and partly occupied the remnants of Mercia, and were forcing Wessex into a long series of inglorious and unsuccessful efforts to buy even a temporary peace.

Alfred was the first king of the English to be acclaimed as truly great by tradition and history, and it is doubtful whether any subsequent monarch fares as well in the people's judgment. From his boyhood Alfred was the bookish—that is, literate—member of his family, but the days of trial found him the only real heir of Ecgbert. Our literary emphasis makes us picture Alfred too much as the king of letters, the pallid scholar rising reluctantly from his manuscripts to kill a book-destroying Dane. Despite a predilection for learning, despite the lifelong ill-health which hounded every one of his father's sons, Alfred was the greatest strategist, the most canny diplomat, and well-nigh the bravest fighter of all the long line of English rulers in whose veins has flowed—and, however diluted, still flows—the blood of the Wessex kings. Alfred's genuine greatness shines forth nowhere more radiantly than in those horrible months when he was forced to lurk, almost alone, in the misty, dismal swamps of Somersetshire. He had trust in his star, in the integrity of his faith, in the loyalty of his folk, and in the future of his land. In no one of these things was he mistaken, and in seven years he brought about the miracle of excluding the Danes from that part of England which lies south of a line drawn from the mouth of Thames to Chester, where the river Dee runs downward to the Irish Sea. Alfred and Guthrum, temporarily ruler of the unruly Scandinavians, came to terms in 878 in the so-called Peace of Wedmore, which meant one overwhelming thing: English England was to survive.

Apart from a few relatively minor disturbances, Alfred was able to devote the remainder of his reign to the political and intellectual betterment of his realm. He possessed singularly clear foresight in governmental matters. He saw and observed the wisdom of preserving local autonomy in the sections of his kingdom other than his own Wessex. As a practical measure of defense he created a series of boroughs (towns) at strategic points. Here we are probably justified in finding the origin of organized town life in England. The earlier English had not perceived the advantages of Romano-British urban centers, nor did their manner of existence lend itself to closely settled areas. The older English unit was the tun (modern English town); that is, a central hall where communal life was carried out and where the unmarried retainers slept, the hall surrounded by smaller and more private residences, sheds, and barns, and the whole shut in by a palisade which sometimes had the added protection of a ditch (moat). The tun might well be the nucleus for the huts of serfs and slaves, who in times of trouble fled to the safety of the stockade. By discreet use of public lands Alfred strengthened patriotic and competent noblemen as focal points of local rule and, what is historically even more important, he made use of foreign craftsmen to create an effective English navy. In the later years of his reign, which ended in 901, he successfully held off an invasion from the mainland.

Alfred's heirs brought considerable sections of Danish England back under English rule, until Aethelstan—at least after the battle of Brunanburh in 937, where he defeated a miscellaneous but ferocious confederacy of Danes, Scots, and Welsh—was generally recognized at home and on the Continent as "*Rex totius Britanniae.*" Under Aethelstan's successors, however, internal dissension, weakness, and cowardice, desire for private privilege and personal immunity had by 1016 subjected the unhappy English to a renewed and even more fateful series of Scandinavian raids. Then Canute the Dane, lord of an Anglo-Scandinavian empire, reigned over England for nineteen years, and proved himself a devoted ruler of his adopted country, the last able and successful king of England before the final invasion by the Normans in 1066.

The Growth of Christianity

Another series of invasions of a very different sort had been begun even before the Roman legions had left the island—the activities of Christian missionaries. The Christian church in Roman Britain was not very large, but it was large enough to share in the persecutions by the Empire, and it provided the first British martyr, St. Alban. Of a Christian family of Roman citizenship in the west of Britain came also St. Patrick, the apostle of Ireland. Christianity was sufficiently rooted in Britain to survive among the Welsh even after every other Roman institution had disappeared, because, as Professor Trevelyan says, "after the departure of the Roman generals and officials, the Christian missionaries alone, among the emissaries of civilization, did not desert the Britons in their day of trouble." [3]

The early history of Christianity in Britain is closely interwoven with that of the church in Ireland. About the year 563 St. Columba with several companions came to Iona, an island off the west coast of Scotland, and began the process of evangelizing Scotland. Within a generation northern Scotland was entirely Christian, and Columba's abbey on Iona had become a strong center of the faith. In the following century came the first great Irish missionary to England, the saintly Aidan, at the request of King Oswald of Northumbria. To this simple, pious monk, who was as zealous for the salvation of a peasant as for that of a king, Oswald gave Lindisfarne (Holy Island) off the east coast. The church and monastery built there in 635 by St. Aidan constituted the first establishment of Irish Christianity in England, and before the century had closed, it had produced the great St. Cuthbert.

In the case of Christianity as in that of the other invasions of Britain, it was from the Continent that the chief impact was to come. In 597 a Roman monk, Augustine, was sent with a band of fellow missionaries by Pope Gregory the Great to convert the pagan English. They were well received by King Aethelbert of Kent, who had married the daughter of the Christian Frankish king of Paris, and had permitted his wife to practice her Christian faith in Canterbury, his capital. The king was converted and gave Augustine and his monks land at Canterbury. The whole of Kent became Christian speedily and without opposition, and the missionaries were likewise successful farther afield in Northumbria. The people as a whole took to the new faith with passivity, if not with enthusiasm. During the first century or so the English showed a disconcerting tendency to apostasy, but they did not fight Christianity. One may plausibly explain this on the grounds that Germanic heathenism, bound as it was to sacred places and local shrines, did not lend itself to transportation. The Christian missionaries, in other words, had to contend not with a flourishing rival faith but rather with a somewhat wearied agnosticism.

Augustine established in England the diocesan organization of the Roman Church, which was to prevail in the years to come. The various dioceses were to be strictly controlled by bishops. The head of the English Church was the Bishop, soon the Archbishop, of Canterbury, who in turn was directly responsible to Rome.

The Irish Church, cut off almost completely from the rest of the Christian world, differed from the Roman Church in several matters. Its organization was monastic rather than diocesan. The two churches differed also in their manner of computing the date of Easter and with respect to the making of the tonsure, the shaving of part of the head of a priest or monk as a sign of dedication to the priesthood or initiation into holy orders. Augustine and his successors at Canterbury refused to compromise with the customs of the Irish Church, and the rivalry between the two branches of Christianity in Britain came inevitably to a head. In 664, Oswy, King of Northumbria and the greatest monarch in England, called a synod to settle the differences at the abbey of Whitby in Yorkshire. The result was at first by no means certain, but Oswy settled the matter effectually by declaring in favor of the Roman side.

The importance of the complete shift to Rome does not require emphasis. It brought an infant church and an infant civilization into firm and lasting contact with the wellspring and reservoir of faith and civilization on the Continent. Aside from pure religion, the greatest value of the church lay in the field of education. Augustine had established a school at Canterbury, but it was only in 669 with the coming of Theodore of Tarsus, the great organizer and administrator of the early English Church, and his coadjutor Hadrian, that it took genuine stature as an institution of higher ecclesiastical learning. Latin, of course, was the basic language in instruction, but Greek, still used in some of the services, was taught, and Hebrew was not unknown to the more advanced scholars. Naturally enough, the chanting of the services demanded that great emphasis be laid on music. Masons, master builders, and workers in stained glass were imported from the Continent, yet the remains of Old English architecture are few and disappointing. Far more important for literary development was the importation of manuscripts, which, while largely religious in character, contained a valuable admixture of classical literary material. Journeys to the Continent, especially to Rome, were frequent, and introduced a wholesome leaven of cosmopolitan culture. The pilgrims included laymen as well as clerics, and apparently a not inconsiderable number of women, and English culture was greatly enriched by the craftsmen, the books, and the relics they brought back with them. Indeed, by the eighth century England had produced, in Northumbria, at least, a civilization that was unsurpassed in Latin Christendom.

[3] G. M. Trevelyan, *History of England*, Longmans, Green, 1928, p. 28.

The church also came to play an important role in strictly governmental affairs. It held itself to be a power apart from, at least equal and, in some respects, superior to, secular authority. As such it favored the codification and writing down of laws, the survey and regularization of landholdings, and the systematization of taxes and tithes. Naturally enough, the mere ability to read and write made clerics invaluable to kings and nobles and gave them rich opportunities to advance and secure their desires. While the church was growing more powerful, secular authority was also growing stronger as one national state gradually took the place of several small, weak, and poor kingdoms, and the opposition of a stubborn state to a proud church arose early in England.

Pre-Christian Poetry

Most so-called primitive races possess an oral literature which is transmitted by word of mouth from generation to generation. The Anglo-Saxons were no exception to this rule, and they brought with them to Britain the rich traditions of the Germanic peoples, with their stirring tales—already crystallized into poetic form—of gods and heroes. These legends constitute the beginning of English literature. That relatively little of this older story-material survives is due in part to the long, troublous period intervening between the coming of the English and the establishment of a written tradition, in part to Christian expurgation and substitution, and in part to the vicissitudes which befell Old English manuscripts, vicissitudes ranging in time from the Danish invasions to the dissolution of the monasteries under Henry VIII. The amazing thing, actually, is that we have as much as we do.

With the coming of Christianity this Old English literature received its first chance of preservation by being committed to writing. However much the English loved and however long they remembered their traditional lays, the mechanical aid of an alphabet was necessary for survival through the centuries. The missionaries brought an alphabet; in addition they early established scriptoria in which copying, and even composition, went on incessantly. Since the manuscripts of Old English poetry were written or revised by clerics or by persons who were influenced by clerics, the substance and coloring of the old pagan poetry was profoundly affected by Christian thought. We could hardly expect that pagan poetry, glorifying the old way of life, presenting heathen customs and emphasizing gods whom the Christian considered at best the Devil's first cousins, should meet with Christian approval and win preservation at Christian hands. That so much of the older pagan material was preserved, and so much that is characteristic of the older days escaped expurgation, is a testimony both to the vigor of the paganism which produced the poetry and to the literary and artistic sense of the Christian editors. Perhaps, too, the stirring episodes of the old stories were of interest to the Christian scribes in their moments of relaxation.

The poet who composed and related the legends of the heroes was the gleeman or *scop*, a prominent and respected figure in Germanic life. He was indispensable as professional entertainer at the king's court where at feasts he recited or chanted the traditional poems, and he could compose more or less extemporaneously on subjects new as well as old. He needed a good memory, a ready wit, and the ability to apply old formulas to new events. Delivery counted much, no doubt, but matter more, and the poems he composed were chiefly narrative. The scop was, of course, in evidence elsewhere than in the king's or noble's household, and, in less fortunate circumstances, as a wandering minstrel he went about the land carrying his stock of songs, improvising fresh and appropriate details, and collecting new legends.

Old English poetry is, with few exceptions, composed in one kind of verse. Unlike most modern verse, it employed not end-rhyme but initial rhyme or alliteration ("apt alliteration's artful aid"), an ancient device known to almost all literatures but employed systematically chiefly by the Germanic peoples. The line, which ordinarily has four feet, is divided in the middle by a marked pause. Normally there are three chief words in the line, two in the first part and one in the second, beginning with the same consonant, and on these the chief emphasis naturally falls. Each line contains a varying number of unaccented and unalliterated words. The opening lines of *Beowulf* (page 15) will illustrate the structure and nature of Old English verse. It is easy to see how in this alliterative structure one word suggested another, and how by such a device the song was more easily recited extemporaneously and retained in the memory, and so handed down for generations before being committed to writing. After the Norman Conquest alliteration ceased to be a distinctive feature of English verse, and, indeed, English literature and the very language itself survived only in some provincial corners of the land. With the coming of the Normans, alliterative verse was superseded by verse with end-rhymes. Alliterative verse appears only infrequently thereafter, as in the fourteenth-century poem, *The Vision of Piers Plowman* (page 86), and in the stirring description of the tournament in Chaucer's *Knight's Tale*. The alliterative principle is, however, still dear to the hearts of Anglo-Saxon people, and in both literary and colloquial usage, as well as in proverbial lore, one finds such phrases as *changes and chances*, *devices and desires*, *friend and foe*, *mice and men*, *to have and to hold*, *kith and kin*, *time and tide*. Many a later English writer in prose as well as poetry finds himself, in a pitch of excitement, instinctively expressing his emotion in the alliterative accents of our first poets. Thus Carlyle, in his *French Revolution*, describes the inflamed citizens as "baring their breasts to the battle-hail," and cries to the old soldier Louis Tournay as he smites the outer drawbridge chain of the Bastille: "Never, over nave or felloe, did thy axe strike such a stroke."

The greatest monument of Old English heroic poetry, indeed, in some respects, the greatest monument of Germanic poetry, and the only full-length heroic epic that has come down to us, is *Beowulf*. This poem is discussed more particularly in the introduction to it (page 14). Here we need only note that the plot, part folk tale, part heroic legend, has nothing English about it. It originated on the Continent, and it contains the heroic legendary material that was shared by all Germanic peoples. As such it is invaluable for the light it throws on the primitive life and ideals of these peoples throughout northwestern Europe. In *Beowulf* and in the Norse sagas western Europe accomplished a kind of heroic poetry that was truly its own, and, except for a few possible echoes of Virgil's *Aeneid* in *Beowulf*, without any influence from Greece and Rome—without also, it may be added, the Mediterranean mellowness and the generous enjoyment of life reflected in the *Iliad* and *Odyssey*. If in substance and general spirit and ideals *Beowulf* is not more English than it is German or Scandinavian, nevertheless the style of the poem and the Christian element in it could not have been found anywhere in the northern Germanic world except England at the time of the composition of the poem in Northumbria.

Beowulf is only one of perhaps a large number of heroic poems once in existence on the Continent, and in *Beowulf* itself there are numerous allusions to earlier heroes. The few fragments of older poetry other than *Beowulf* that have survived indicate something of the possible wealth of Old English poetic themes. The poem *Widsith* ("Far Journey"), which was probably composed in the sixth century, and is perhaps the oldest poem in English, is in effect a catalogue, perhaps a reminder, of the heroes about whom a bard might sing. In it we find named some seventy peoples—a few of them sufficiently Biblical and classical to be the result of interpolation—and nearly as many heroes. When we turn from this imposing list to the remnants of Old English heroic verse, we become aware at once of what our loss has been. Apart from a few names scattered here and there, in works to which they are merely incidental, we find little enough that has survived. In the very early lyric poem *Deor* there are also references to stories once well known which have completely perished. In addition there are two brief fragments, one of which, *The Fight at Finnsburg*, supplements, or is supplemented by, a passage in *Beowulf*. The second fragment, *Waldere*, is really two fragments from what was apparently a poem of considerable length, and tells the story of the escape from the court of Attila, king of the Huns, of Walter of Aquitaine and his betrothed Hildegund, a Burgundian princess. The Old English fragments would give us no notion of the story, which, however, was well known on the Continent and is told in a spirited Latin poem, the *Waltharius*.

The scops to whom we owe the vigorous narrative poetry mentioned above were gifted also in the composition of lyric verse. One of the oldest and most beautiful of the surviving lyrics has just been mentioned: the elegiac song of Deor, the lament of a minstrel who has been supplanted in his lord's favor by a rival singer. The poem is of special interest both for its often tantalizing references to Germanic poetic traditions and for the systematic use of a refrain. Only one other example of the use of this device in Old English poetry has survived. From perhaps the eighth century comes a dramatic lyric, *The Wanderer*, the lament of an exiled retainer for the good old days of his dead lord. Notable in the poem are the almost purely pagan concept of an inescapable and crushing Fate (Wyrd), the sentiment of great respect and love for his lord and the sense of utter dependence on him, and the feeling for nature as evinced in the description of stormy weather at sea. Of the same period, and displaying even greater interest in the sea, with its perils and its fascinations, is *The Seafarer*. Another beautiful lyric, *The Ruin*, survives in a mutilated text, and, like most of the other elegies, expresses, amid the change and decay of the present, a lament for vanished happiness.

Early Old English poetry was all composed in one of the two Anglian dialects, those of Northumbria and Mercia, and was largely Northumbrian. With the Danish invasions Northumbria's supremacy waned and her growing literature was destroyed.

Few of the numerous Northumbrian compositions have survived in the original northern dialect. As the kingdom of Wessex rose to power in the south, it offered a refuge to literature and preserved from oblivion some of the earlier compositions of Northumbria. The overwhelming bulk of Old English writings has, therefore, been transmitted to us in the West Saxon dialect of Wessex, into which the older poetry had been "translated," and thus we have only copies of the original.

Christian Poetry

The elegiac poems to which reference has been made are largely non-Christian in spirit if not altogether in substance, but much Old English poetry is so permeated with Christian sentiments as to make any differentiation between pagan and Christian an almost futile formality. We have seen that most Old English poetry was first committed to writing by Christian scribes, and the poems of Continental origin, the stories of which evolved in pagan surroundings, were often given a Christian coloring in England. *Beowulf* is an intrinsically Christian poem, even the *Waldere* fragments contain Christian touches, and the Old English charms, which are in essence folk poetry of a somewhat sophisticated nature, are an almost inextricable mixture of heathen and Christian. The tinting, however, was not all in one direction. Old English verse of Christian or even of classical origin is often surprisingly heroic and pagan in spirit. We are naturally impressed when the Germanic demigod Welund (Wayland) turns up in an English version of the *De Consolatione Philosophiae* by the Roman philosopher Boethius, but pagan elements in strictly Christian verse, though less spectacular, are really more significant. Two poems of the tenth century, *The Battle of Brunanburh* and *The Battle of Maldon*, contain a few passing references to the Christian God, but they are in the vigorous and creative spirit of the old heroic poetry, and pagan rather than Christian virtues are celebrated.

We know two Old English Christian poets by name. The earlier of these is Caedmon, of the latter half of the seventh century, and of him we know only what the Venerable Bede tells us in his *Ecclesiastical History*—the story of how the humble old cowherd, vexed and ashamed because of his inability to sing impromptu verses to the harp, was divinely inspired to sing of the Creation. Caedmon's hymn has been rendered into modern English as follows by Professor Albert S. Cook:

"Now must we hymn the Master of heaven,
The might of the Maker, the deeds of the Father,
The thought of His heart. He, Lord everlasting,
Established of old the source of all wonders:
Creator all-holy, He hung the bright heaven,
A roof high upreared, o'er the children of men;
The King of mankind then created for mortals
The world in its beauty, the earth spread beneath them,
He, Lord everlasting, omnipotent God." [4]

Of Caedmon's authentic works we have only the nine lines of his hymn of the Creation, preserved by Bede in its original Northumbrian form and translated into the West Saxon dialect by King Alfred in his translation of Bede's *History*. Caedmon's hymn is important as being the earliest extant verse of English origin. The poems we have been considering had their origin on the mainland before the invasion of Britain. The calm, devout, Christian tone of Caedmon's hymn contrasts sharply with the pagan and warlike spirit of the older heroic poetry. It has been called the first indigenous bud of that tree of England's poetry which was afterwards to blossom out into such luxuriance in Spenser's *Faerie Queene*, and grow on into still higher regions and sublimer beauty in the *Paradise Lost* of Milton.

Of the poems formerly, but no longer, ascribed to Caedmon, but which may well have sprung from the school of Biblical paraphrase which he inaugurated, two deserve mention. *Genesis* is really two poems, one inserted bodily into the other. This interpolation, denominated *Genesis B*, is a translation or adaptation from Old Saxon and could not have been written before the time of Alfred. It deals with the revolt and fall of Satan and contains some of the best passages in Old English Christian poetry. *Genesis A*, while a far less meritorious piece, contains vivid battle scenes which exhibit the Germanic taste evident in much Old English Christian poetry. *Exodus* has been often called a little epic, almost as much Germanic as Christian. The poem deals with the crossing of the Red Sea, and the author describes the fate of the unhappy Egyptians with a zest which still moves the reader.

When we come to Cynewulf, second of the Old English Christian poets, who probably flourished in the second half of the eighth century, we find a situation quite opposite to that of Caedmon: we know little or nothing of the poet's life and a good deal about his poems. Cynewulf had the convenient

[4] Albert S. Cook and C. B. Tinker, *Select Translations From Old English Poetry*, Ginn and Company, 1902, p. 77.

habit of signing his name (by the insertion of letters from the old runic alphabet) near the end of his works. Thus we know that he wrote *Juliana*, *The Fates of the Apostles*, *Elene*, and at least the middle portion of *Christ*. Cynewulf's poems afford clear proof that he came later than the author of the Caedmonian pieces (except *Genesis B*). He was a man trained in religious scholarship, primarily interested in non-Biblical Christian literature, and far more subjective than any of his predecessors. War was of little interest to him, but the sea exercised an enormous fascination upon his imagination. Among the poems sometimes ascribed to Cynewulf is *Andreas*, an account of St. Andrew's trip to aid St. Matthew among the Mermedonians. No other Old English poem, not even *The Seafarer*, treats the sea so well, and, in addition, the feeling of Christ's disciples toward their Master is as purely that of the members of the heroic comitatus as anything we find in *Beowulf* or *The Battle of Maldon*. Also ascribed to Cynewulf, *The Dream of the Rood*, in many respects the high-water mark of Old English Christian poetic endeavor, glows with genuine and touching spirituality.

Old English Prose

The prose writings of the Old English period are, inevitably, later and of considerably less interest than the poetry. Most of the earlier prose is in Latin and is the work of priests, and of the earlier priestly writers the greatest is the Venerable Bede, who died in 735. Of Bede's many works, and they include scientific studies as well as religious and theological treatises, the most important, both for its literary qualities and its invaluable information about its author's times, is his *Ecclesiastical History of the English Nation*. The gentleness of the author's nature and the spiritual quality of his mind are reflected throughout the work. Bede is the chief representative of the eighth century renaissance in England which came in the wake of the education introduced by the Christian missionaries.

It is to King Alfred that we owe the Old English translation of Bede's Latin history as well as a great many other prose works. In the literary and intellectual realm, as in military and political affairs, Alfred's pre-eminence is unquestioned, and posterity has never doubted his right to the title of Alfred the Great. Among the works besides Bede's history which he translated, or directed the translation of, were the *Pastoral Care* of Pope Gregory the Great, a guidebook for the clergy; the *Consolation of Philosophy* by Boethius; and Orosius's *History of the World*. It is chiefly to Alfred that we owe the *Anglo-Saxon Chronicle*, which is a revision of an older chronicle history of England and a year-by-year record of current events, with invaluable bits of narrative interspersed.

In the century following Alfred's death in 901 came two other notable prose writers, the churchmen Aelfric and Wulfstan. Aelfric has been called the father of English vernacular literature. His sermons and homilies and *Lives of the Saints* are the most important of his English works, but of greater interest to most modern readers is the Latin colloquy which he composed to assist boys in a monastic school in learning to speak Latin. A contemporary version of the colloquy in Old English (perhaps Aelfric's own) has survived and provides an amusing and informative series of conversations on the occupations of the times. Of Wulfstan, who became Archbishop of York at the beginning of the eleventh century, we have only a few sermons and homilies, oratorical in style, and prophesying doom. The approaching end of the world which he preached did indeed come speedily for the Old English world of which he was the last literary representative. The distinctive qualities of Old English prose had already begun to pass as the styles of such writers as Aelfric and Wulfstan approached more and more nearly to that of Latin prose, and their compositions contrast strikingly with Alfred's simple undecorated writing. In the work of the three writers we see such variety as Old English prose was capable of, and also see proof of the fact that, in the earliest English prose as in the latest, simplicity and unaffectedness of style are the qualities most likely to cause a book to come home to men's business and bosoms and be longest remembered.

Beowulf

About the year 1000 two scribes copied a manuscript in which were brought together three prose works and also the two poems, *Beowulf* and *Judith.* This manuscript, now in the British Museum under the name of Cotton Vitellius A. XV, is probably the most valuable single treasure of English literary history, and that because it contains the *Beowulf,* which is not only our sole Old English epic but also by many centuries the first great literary work to be preserved in any of the vernacular languages of Europe. For five hundred years and more the manuscript doubtless remained in some ecclesiastical library until the time of the dissolution of the monasteries in the thirties of the sixteenth century. While untold thousands of other manuscripts suffered immediate destruction or the humiliation of being used to wrap fish or butter, this one was preserved, probably not because of anyone's appreciation of its actual value, but because of current theological and antiquarian interests which were leading to a gradual rediscovery of the Old English language and literature.

Lawrence Nowell, the earliest compiler of an Old English dictionary, would appear to have had it in his possession in 1563, and it subsequently passed into the hands of Sir Robert Cotton, who died in 1631. In 1700 one of Sir Robert's descendants presented it, with the rest of the family's priceless collection, to the British government. The manuscript narrowly escaped burning in 1731 in a fire which consumed many of its companions; as it was it suffered a scorching which, for want of proper attention, resulted in the breaking away of a number of the margins, with a consequent loss or mutilation of words and letters. The first printed edition of the poem was brought out in 1815 by an Icelander living in Denmark, Grimur Thorkelin. Ironically enough, he had been nearly ready to publish his work when the English bombardment of Copenhagen in 1807 burned his home and destroyed much of his material. The first English edition appeared in 1833. Since then there have been numerous editions and translations and innumerable studies, many of which, notably those which maintained multiple authorship of the poem, are as dead as the scholars who wrote them.

The *Beowulf* is an epic poem, and may properly be called a "folk epic" or "popular epic." Such designation is justified since the poem originated in folk composition and is the result of evolution, even though it received its present form at the hands of some one unknown poet. Despite the relative lateness of the manuscript and the fact that the language of the poem as we have it is predominantly West Saxon, the original was composed probably in the first half of the eighth century in an Anglian dialect, almost certainly Northumbrian. Of the hero of the poem it must be said that there is no external evidence about his existence. He is represented as a Geat, and we are not sure who the Geats were. They may have been the Jutes, the inhabitants of Jutland, but were more likely a tribe in southern Sweden. The adventures related in the poem are the stuff of legend rather than history.

The story, which concerns two widely separated episodes in the life of its hero, is simple enough: Beowulf, a youthful prince of the Geats, goes to Denmark and there kills two monsters, one in the king's hall and the other in an underwater lair. Later he becomes king of the Geats, and in his old age is killed while slaying a dragon which is ravaging his land. By means of an expansive treatment, frequent digressions (taking up some seven hundred lines), many speeches (ranging from four to one hundred sixty lines and using over thirteen hundred lines in all), descriptions, reflections, and moralization, the poet has spun his material out to cover nearly thirty-two hundred lines. Obviously this is no direct narrative, and the use of reminiscence and prophecy, coupled with various stylistic devices, will often make the reader feel that the last thing the author is attempting is to advance his story in a swift, lucid, and logical fashion. Indeed, the reader who feels this will probably be correct, for it is not merely the story element which makes *Beowulf* a great poem. Perhaps the most interesting of the stylistic devices employed is the use of the kenning, a highly metaphorical phrase used to describe a simple thing, as when the sea is referred to as the whale-path, or the sun as the candle of the skies.

A widely spread folk tale, usually called "The Bear's Son Tale," was attached in Northern Europe to a lad called Beowulf, whose very name, "bee-wolf," is a kenning for "bear." There are numerous analogues to the story, the most striking of which occur in the lively Icelandic saga of *Grettir the Strong* (translated by G. A. Highet, Everyman's Library; see especially pages 86–100, and 170–77). Later Beowulf was made into a prince, the folk tale was lifted bodily to a historical or pseudo-historical setting, and the whole was finally worked into an epic, with the emphasis on the noble character of the hero rather than on bold deeds alone. Character analysis is one of the author's chief preoccupations. As Friedrich Klaeber remarks: "He is ever ready to analyze the thoughts and feelings of Beowulf and Hrothgar, the Danes and the Geats, Grendel and his kind, even down to the sea-monsters and birds of prey. Their intentions, resolutions, expectations, hopes, fears, longings, rejoicings, and mental sufferings engage his constant attention. In a moment of intensest action, such as the combat with Grendel, the state of mind of the characters is carefully taken note of." [1]

The mingling of heathen and Christian elements is a matter which has long interested students of the poem. We have here an old pagan story retold by a Christian poet and, almost inevitably, certain heathen traces remain. Among these are the frequent references to Wyrd or Fate and the account of the fashion in which the Danes are said to have tried to ward off the sudden attacks of Grendel: "Sometimes they offered sacrifices at the heathen temples, begged with words that the slayer of demons would aid them against the great calamity. Such was their custom, the hope of the heathen." There are also the references to burning the dead, especially the striking and full account of Beowulf's funeral rites. All these things are truly pagan, but there is no possibility that, as was formerly held, the Christian elements are later additions to the text. Christianity, although not of the profoundly theological kind, is part of the essence of the poem.

In judging the *Beowulf*, there is no need to look upon this oldest epic narrative in any modern European tongue with uncritical enthusiasm, nor should the poem's apparent defects lead to an attitude of unappreciative scorn. It must be admitted that the *Beowulf* as an epic is not in structure or design the equal of the *Iliad* or the *Odyssey*, but it is a genuine poem, with a very real unity of its own, and not a random collection of rough and primitive ballads. It was written by an artist of no mean skill, although his material is not always to our taste or his methods always our methods. We may not fancy his continual allusions to other stories, but that is because we do not understand the references, and this very allusiveness must have given the greatest pleasure of association to the poem's original hearers or readers. Again, the modern reader does not always take kindly to the poet's sententiousness and moralizations, but here one may venture to suggest that great literature, of whatever age or land, has seldom been devoid of ethical significance and expression. The author of the *Beowulf* had an almost complete mastery over his verse form and a great talent for powerful statement and vivid description. There is, as example, Hrothgar's masterful picture of the mere in which Grendel's mother lived, and the subsequent first-hand account of it is almost as good. One has only to read the passage telling of Grendel's visit to Heorot to understand the poet's skill in building up an effect.

Above all, the poem is idealistic, and here Christianity has had a profound effect on the pagan reality. Beowulf is no bloodthirsty Viking or mad berserker, but one of the first great Christian heroes. His life is one of bravery and justice, and his death illustrates the conduct of the perfect king, as well as that of the perfect retainer, and this is the climax and the lesson of the poem, basically pagan and of the North, but somehow restrained, purified, and ennobled.

The characteristic qualities of the Old English language and verse are illustrated in the opening lines of the poem with their proper divisions and their alliterating syllables, as follows:

"Hwaet, we Gar-Dena   in geardagum
þeodcyninga   þrym gefrunon,
Hu þa æþelingas   ellen fremedon!
Oft Scyld Scefing   sceaþena þreatum
Monegum mægþum   meodosetla ofteah,
Egsode eorlas,   syþþan ærest wearð
Feasceaft funden;   he þæs frofre gebad,
Weox under wolcnum,   weorðmyndum þah,
Oð þæt him æghwylc   þara ymbsittendra
Ofer hronrade   hyran scolde,
Gomban gyldan;   þæt wæs god cyning!" [2]

An admirable book for the beginner is William W. Lawrence's *Beowulf and Epic Tradition*, Harvard University Press, 1928, while the more advanced student will turn to R. W. Chambers's *Beowulf*, 2d ed., Macmillan, 1932, and to Charles W. Kennedy's *The Earliest English Poetry: A Critical Survey*, Oxford

[1] *Beowulf*, ed. by Friedrich Klaeber, 3d ed., Heath, 1936, pages lviii–lix.

[2] In Old English every syllable is pronounced, and a word is normally accented on the first syllable. The characters þ and ð represent the sound of *th*. The pronunciation of the vowels follows in general that in the Continental languages. The pronunciation of the consonants is approximately the same as in Modern English, with a few exceptions. *C* before *y* (as in *cyning*) is pronounced as *k*. *G* is hard except before *e* and *i*, when it has the sound of a roughened guttural *y*. *Sc* should probably be pronounced as *sh*. *Y* as a vowel (as in *cyning*) is pronounced approximately as *i* in *king*. The ligature *æ* when short (as in *hwæt*, *æþelingas*, *þæs*, *þæt*, *wæs*) is pronounced as *a* in *man;* when long (as in *mægþum*, *ærest*, *æghwylc*) it is pronounced as *a* in *mane*. The digraphs *ea* and *eo* have the value of diphthongs, with the stress on *e*, which is short as in *men*.

University Press, 1943, pages 53–100. The definitive edition of the original text is that by Friedrich Klaeber, already referred to, which contains acute and rewarding criticism of the poem. The translation given below is by F. B. Gummere, in his *The Oldest English Epic*, 1909, which is reprinted by permission of the publishers, The Macmillan Company of New York.

BEOWULF

[Prologue: Of Scyld, the Founder of the Danish Royal House]

Lo, praise of the prowess of people-kings
of spear-armed Danes, in days long sped,
we have heard, and what honor the athelings won!
Oft Scyld the Scefing from squadroned foes,
from many a tribe, the mead-bench tore,
awing the earls. Since erst he lay
friendless, a foundling, fate repaid him:
for he waxed under welkin, in wealth he throve,
till before him the folk, both far and near,
who house by the whale-path, heard his mandate,
gave him gifts: a good king he!
To him an heir was afterward born,
a son in his halls, whom heaven sent
to favor the folk, feeling their woe
that erst they had lacked an earl for leader
so long a while; the Lord endowed him,
the Wielder-of-Wonder, with world's renown.
Famed was this Beowulf: far flew the boast of him,
son of Scyld, in the Scandian lands.
So becomes it a youth to quit him well
with his father's friends, by fee and gift,
that to aid him, agèd, in after days,
come warriors willing, should war draw nigh,
liegemen loyal: by lauded deeds
shall an earl have honor in every clan.
Forth he fared at the fated moment,
sturdy Scyld to the shelter of God.
Then they bore him over to ocean's billow,
loving clansmen, as late he charged them,
while wielded words the winsome Scyld,
the leader belovèd who long had ruled.
In the roadstead rocked a ring-dight vessel,

3. athelings, princes. **4. Scyld** (that is "Shield") **the Scefing,** son of Scef (that is, "Sheaf"). **5. the mead-bench tore,** that is, he subjugated them. **10. the whale-path,** the sea; the first of the many kennings in the poem. **18. Beowulf.** Not the hero of the poem, but an earlier Danish prince of the same name, or of a similar name which has been made identical with that of the hero by poet or scribe under the influence of Beowulf the Geat. **32. a ring-dight vessel,** probably the ship in which as a child he had drifted ashore (see lines 44–46 below).

ice-flecked, outbound, atheling's barge:
there laid they down their darling lord
on the breast of the boat, the breaker-of-rings,
by the mast the mighty one. Many a treasure
fetched from far was freighted with him.
No ship have I known so nobly dight
with weapons of war and weeds of battle,
with breastplate and blade: on his bosom lay
a heapèd hoard that hence should go
far o'er the flood with him floating away.
No less these loaded the lordly gifts,
thanes' huge treasure, than those had done
who in former time forth had sent him
sole on the seas, a suckling child.
High o'er his head they hoist the standard,
a gold-wove banner; let billows take him,
gave him to ocean. Grave were their spirits,
mournful their mood. No man is able
to say in sooth, no son of the halls,
no hero 'neath heaven,—who harbored that freight!

[Part One: Beowulf and the Monster Grendel]

I

Now Beowulf bode in the burg of the Scyldings,
leader belovèd, and long he ruled
in fame with all folk, since his father had gone
away from the world, till awoke an heir,
haughty Healfdene, who held through life,
sage and sturdy, the Scyldings glad.
Then, one after one, there woke to him,
to the chieftain of clansmen, children four:
Heorogar, then Hrothgar, then Halga brave;
and I heard that —— was ——'s queen,
the Heathoscylfing's helpmate dear.
To Hrothgar was given such glory of war,
such honor of combat, that all his kin
obeyed him gladly till great grew his band
of youthful comrades. It came in his mind
to bid his henchmen a hall uprear,
a master mead-house, mightier far
than ever was seen by the sons of earth,
and within it, then, to old and young
he would all allot that the Lord had sent him,
save only the land and the lives of his men.

39. weeds, garments. **49. gave him to ocean.** Sea-burials of this sort were not unusual among northern Germanic peoples. **1. Beowulf . . . of the Scyldings.** This is still the earlier Beowulf of the Prologue, prince of the Scyldings (Danes). **10. —— was ——'s queen.** The manuscript is imperfect here. **11. the Heathoscylfing's helpmate,** the wife of the Battle-Scylfing (that is, the king of the Swedes). **21. save only . . . men.** The limitations of the arbitrary power of a Germanic prince are here admirably suggested.

Wide, I heard, was the work commanded,
for many a tribe this mid-earth round,
to fashion the folkstead. It fell, as he ordered,
in rapid achievement that ready it stood there,
of halls the noblest: Heorot he named it
whose message had might in many a land.
Not reckless of promise, the rings he dealt,
treasure at banquet: there towered the hall,
high, gabled wide, the hot surge waiting
of furious flame. Nor far was that day
when father and son-in-law stood in feud
for warfare and hatred that woke again.
With envy and anger an evil spirit
endured the dole in his dark abode,
that he heard each day the din of revel
high in the hall: there harps rang out,
clear song of the singer. He sang who knew
tales of the early time of man,
how the Almighty made the earth,
fairest fields enfolded by water,
set, triumphant, sun and moon
for a light to lighten the land-dwellers,
and braided bright the breast of earth
with limbs and leaves, made life for all
of mortal beings that breathe and move.
So lived the clansmen in cheer and revel
a winsome life, till one began
to fashion evils, that fiend of hell.
Grendel this monster grim was called,
march-riever mighty, in moorland living,
in fen and fastness; fief of the giants
the hapless wight a while had kept
since the Creator his exile doomed.
On kin of Cain was the killing avenged
by sovran God for slaughtered Abel.
Ill fared his feud, and far was he driven,
for the slaughter's sake, from sight of men.
Of Cain awoke all that woful breed,
Etins and elves and evil-spirits,
as well as the giants that warred with God
weary while: but their wage was paid them!

22. I heard. Here, as often, the poet alludes to his dependence on authority and information received. **26. Heorot,** that is, Hart Hall, so called because of the stags' antlers which surmounted the gables of the building. **29. treasure at banquet.** The prescribed generosity of the chieftain is alluded to again and again. **31–32. furious flame . . . stood in feud.** Hrothgar's daughter, Freawaru, was married to Ingeld, a prince of the Heathobards, in what was destined to be a vain attempt to end a feud of long standing between the two tribes. The ultimate result was the burning of Heorot. **34. an evil spirit,** the monster Grendel, the details of whose physical appearance are left to the audience's imagination. **38. He sang.** A minstrel sang a poem similar to Caedmon's hymn; see page 12. **51. march-riever,** border-raider. **52–53. fief . . . had kept,** that is, he had inhabited the land of the giants (or monsters). **55. Cain,** an interesting Biblical allusion; see Genesis 4:1–16. **57. his,** Cain's. **60. Etins,** giants.

Went he forth to find at fall of night
that haughty house, and heed wherever
the Ring-Danes, outrevelled, to rest had gone.
Found within it the atheling band
asleep after feasting and fearless of sorrow,
of human hardship. Unhallowed wight,
grim and greedy, he grasped betimes,
wrathful, reckless, from resting-places,
thirty of the thanes, and thence he rushed
fain of his fell spoil, faring homeward,
laden with slaughter, his lair to seek.
Then at the dawning, as day was breaking,
the might of Grendel to men was known;
then after wassail was wail uplifted,
loud moan in the morn. The mighty chief,
atheling excellent, unblithe sat,
labored in woe for the loss of his thanes,
when once had been traced the trail of the fiend,
spirit accurst: too cruel that sorrow,
too long, too loathsome. Not late the respite;
with night returning, anew began
ruthless murder; he recked no whit,
firm in his guilt, of the feud and crime.
They were easy to find who elsewhere sought
in room remote their rest at night,
bed in the bowers, when that bale was shown,
was seen in sooth, with surest token,—
the hall-thane's hate. Such held themselves
far and fast who the fiend outran!
Thus ruled unrighteous and raged his fill
one against all; until empty stood
that lordly building, and long it bode so.
Twelve years' tide the trouble he bore,
sovran of Scyldings, sorrows in plenty,
boundless cares. There came unhidden
tidings true to the tribes of men,
in sorrowful songs, how ceaselessly Grendel
harassed Hrothgar, what hate he bore him,
what murder and massacre, many a year,
feud unfading,—refused consent
to deal with any of Daneland's earls,
make pact of peace, or compound for gold:
still less did the wise men ween to get

22. he, Grendel. **24. They were easy to find,** a good example of litotes, or artistic understatement. Such remarks often seem an expression of grim Anglo-Saxon humor, but we cannot be sure that they were always humorously intended. **28. hall-thane's,** Grendel's. **33. tide,** time. **34. sovran of Scyldings,** Hrothgar. **37. songs,** a highly interesting reference to the composition and circulation of topical ballads. **42. compound for gold.** Grendel had no intention of paying the conventional and legal wergeld (fine) which a murderer, or his family, was obligated to pay to the family of the victim.

great fee for the feud from his fiendish hands.
But the evil one ambushed old and young,
death-shadow dark, and dogged them still,
lured, and lurked in the livelong night
of misty moorlands: men may say not
where the haunts of these Hell-Runes be.
Such heaping of horrors the hater of men,
lonely roamer, wrought unceasing.
harassings heavy. O'er Heorot he lorded,
gold-bright hall, in gloomy nights;
and ne'er could the prince approach his throne,
—'twas judgment of God,—or have joy in his hall.
Sore was the sorrow to Scyldings'-friend,
heart-rending misery. Many nobles
sat assembled, and searched out counsel
how it were best for bold-hearted men
against harassing terror to try their hand.
Whiles they vowed in their heathen fanes
altar-offerings, asked with words
that the slayer-of-souls would succor give them
for the pain of their people. Their practice this,
their heathen hope; 'twas Hell they thought of
in mood of their mind. Almighty they knew not,
Doomsman of Deeds and dreadful Lord,
nor Heaven's-Helmet heeded they ever,
Wielder-of-Wonder.—Woe for that man
who in harm and hatred hales his soul
to fiery embraces;—nor favor nor change
awaits he ever. But well for him
that after death-day may draw to his Lord,
and friendship find in the Father's arms!

3

Thus seethed unceasing the son of Healfdene
with the woe of these days; not wisest men
assuaged his sorrow; too sore the anguish,
loathly and long, that lay on his folk,
most baneful of burdens and bales of the night.

This heard in his home Hygelac's thane,
great among Geats, of Grendel's doings.
He was the mightiest man of valor
in that same day of this our life,
stalwart and stately. A stout wave-walker
he bade make ready. Yon battle-king, said he,
far o'er the swan-road he fain would seek,
the noble monarch who needed men!
The prince's journey by prudent folk
was little blamed, though they loved him dear;
they whetted the hero, and hailed good omens.
And now the bold one from bands of Geats
comrades chose, the keenest of warriors
e'er he could find; with fourteen men
the sea-wood he sought, and, sailor proved,
led them on to the land's confines.

Time had now flown; afloat was the ship,
boat under bluff. On board they climbed,
warriors ready; waves were churning
sea with sand; the sailors bore
on the breast of the bark their bright array,
their mail and weapons: the men pushed off,
on its willing way, the well-braced craft.
Then moved o'er the waters by might of the wind
the bark like a bird with breast of foam,
till in season due, on the second day,
the curvèd prow such course had run
that sailors now could see the land,
sea-cliffs shining, steep high hills,
headlands broad. Their haven was found,
their journey ended. Up then quickly
the Weders' clansmen climbed ashore,
anchored their sea-wood, with armor clashing
and gear of battle: God they thanked
for passing in peace o'er the paths of the sea.

Now saw from the cliff a Scylding clansman,
a warden that watched the water-side,
how they bore o'er the gangway glittering shields,
war-gear in readiness; wonder seized him
to know what manner of men they were.
Straight to the strand his steed he rode,
Hrothgar's henchman; with hand of might
he shook his spear, and spake in parley.
"Who are ye, then, ye armèd men,
mailèd folk, that yon mighty vessel
have urged thus over the ocean ways,
here o'er the waters? A warden I,
sentinel set o'er the sea-march here,
lest any foe to the folk of Danes
with harrying fleet should harm the land.
No aliens ever at ease thus bore them,
linden-wielders: yet word-of-leave
clearly ye lack from clansmen here,
my folk's agreement.—A greater ne'er saw I
of warriors in world than is one of you,—
yon hero in harness! No henchman he
worthied by weapons, if witness his features,
his peerless presence! I pray you, though, tell

49. Hell-Runes, sorcerers of hell. **61. heathen fanes.** The pagan setting of the original story is preserved here in striking fashion. **63. slayer-of-souls.** Probably a Christian reference to the devil, but perhaps to a heathen god. **1. son of Healfdene,** Hrothgar. **6. Hygelac's thane.** Beowulf, the hero of the poem, was the chief thane of Hygelac, king of the Geats, presumably inhabitants of southern Sweden. **10. wave-walker,** a kenning for "ship." **12. swan-road,** another kenning for "sea."

16. hailed good omens. Another Christian reference to heathen practices. **20. sea-wood,** ship. **37. the Weders',** the Geats'. **57. linden-wielders,** shield-bearers.

your folk and home, lest hence ye fare
suspect to wander your way as spies
in Danish land. Now, dwellers afar,
ocean-travellers, take from me
simple advice: the sooner the better
I hear of the country whence ye came."

4

To him the stateliest spake in answer;
the warriors' leader his word-hoard unlocked:—
"We are by kin of the clan of Geats,
and Hygelac's own hearth-fellows we.
To folk afar was my father known,
noble atheling, Ecgtheow named.
Full of winters, he fared away
agèd from earth; he is honored still
through width of the world by wise men all.
To thy lord and liege in loyal mood
we hasten hither, to Healfdene's son,
people-protector: be pleased to advise us!
To that mighty-one come we on mickle errand,
to the lord of the Danes; nor deem I right
that aught be hidden. We hear—thou knowest
if sooth it is—the saying of men,
that amid the Scyldings a scathing monster,
dark ill-doer, in dusky nights
shows terrific his rage unmatched,
hatred and murder. To Hrothgar I
in greatness of soul would succor bring,
so the Wise-and-Brave may worst his foes,—
if ever the end of ills is fated,
of cruel contest, if cure shall follow,
and the boiling care-waves cooler grow;
else ever afterward anguish-days
he shall suffer in sorrow while stands in place
high on its hill that house unpeered."
Astride his steed, the strand-ward answered,
clansman unquailing: "The keen-souled thane
must be skilled to sever and sunder duly
words and works, if he well intends.
I gather, this band is graciously bent
to the Scyldings' master. March, then, bearing
weapons and weeds the way I show you.
I will bid my men your boat meanwhile
to guard for fear lest foemen come,—
your new-tarred ship by shore of ocean
faithfully watching till once again
it waft o'er the waters those well-loved thanes,
—winding-necked wood,—to Weders' bounds,
heroes such as the hest of fate
shall succor and save from the shock of war."
They bent them to march,—the boat lay still,
fettered by cable and fast at anchor,
broad-bosomed ship.—Then shone the boars
over the cheek-guard; chased with gold,
keen and gleaming, guard it kept
o'er the man of war, as marched along
heroes in haste, till the hall they saw,
broad of gable and bright with gold:
that was the fairest, 'mid folk of earth,
of houses 'neath heaven, where Hrothgar lived,
and the gleam of it lightened o'er lands afar.
The sturdy shieldsman showed that bright
burg-of-the-boldest; bade them go
straightway thither; his steed then turned,
hardy hero, and hailed them thus:—
"'Tis time that I fare from you. Father Almighty
in grace and mercy guard you well,
safe in your seekings. Seaward I go.
'Gainst hostile warriors hold my watch."

5

Stone-bright the street: it showed the way
to the crowd of clansmen. Corselets glistened
hand-forged, hard; on their harness bright
the steel ring sang, as they strode along
in mail of battle, and marched to the hall.
There, weary of ocean, the wall along
they set their bucklers, their broad shields, down,
and bowed them to bench: the breastplates clanged,
war-gear of men; their weapons stacked,
spears of the seafarers stood together,
gray-tipped ash: that iron band
was worthily weaponed!—A warrior proud
asked of the heroes their home and kin.
"Whence, now, bear ye burnished shields,
harness gray and helmets grim,
spears in multitude? Messenger, I,
Hrothgar's herald! Heroes so many
ne'er met I as strangers of mood so strong.
'Tis plain that for prowess, not plunged into exile,
for high-hearted valor, Hrothgar ye seek!"
Him the sturdy-in-war bespake with words,
proud earl of the Weders answer made,
hardy 'neath helmet:—"Hygelac's, we,
fellows at board; I am Beowulf named.
I am seeking to say to the son of Healfdene
this mission of mine, to thy master-lord,
the doughty prince, if he deign at all

1. the stateliest, Beowulf. **22. the Wise-and-Brave,** Hrothgar. **30-32. keen-souled . . . words and works,** another example of the poet's beloved sententiousness.

46. the boars, that is, the images of boars on the crests of the helmets. **1. Stone-bright the street,** probably inspired by the paved roads which the Romans had built in Britain. **3. harness,** armor.

grace that we greet him, the good one, now."
Wulfgar spake, the Wendles' chieftain,
whose might of mind to many was known,
his courage and counsel: "The king of Danes,
the Scyldings' friend, I fain will tell,
the Breaker-of-Rings, as the boon thou askest,
the famèd prince, of thy faring hither,
and, swiftly after, such answer bring
as the doughty monarch may deign to give."
Hied then in haste to where Hrothgar sat
white-haired and old, his earls about him,
till the stout thane stood at the shoulder there
of the Danish king: good courtier he!
Wulfgar spake to his winsome lord:—
"Hither have fared to thee far-come men
o'er the paths of ocean, people of Geatland;
and the stateliest there by his sturdy band
is Beowulf named. This boon they seek,
that they, my master, may with thee
have speech at will: nor spurn their prayer
to give them hearing, gracious Hrothgar!
In weeds of the warrior worthy they,
methinks, of our liking; their leader most surely,
a hero that hither his henchmen has led."

6

Hrothgar answered, helmet of Scyldings:—
"I knew him of yore in his youthful days;
his agèd father was Ecgtheow named,
to whom, at home, gave Hrethel the Geat
his only daughter. Their offspring bold
fares hither to seek the steadfast friend.
And seamen, too, have said me this,—
who carried my gifts to the Geatish court,
thither for thanks,—he has thirty men's
heft of grasp in the gripe of his hand,
the bold-in-battle. Blessèd God
out of his mercy this man hath sent
to Danes of the West, as I ween indeed,
against horror of Grendel. I hope to give
the good youth gold for his gallant thought.
Be thou in haste, and bid them hither,
clan of kinsmen, to come before me;
and add this word,—they are welcome guests
to folk of the Danes."
[To the door of the hall
Wulfgar went] and the word declared:—

29. the Wendles' chieftain. The Wendles or Vandals were the East-Germanic people that occupied Spain and northern Africa. **40. good courtier he!** Note here and elsewhere the importance attached to etiquette and proper procedure. **4. Hrethel,** father of Beowulf's mother and of his uncle Hygelac, king of the Geats. **9–10. thirty men's heft of grasp,** an important characteristic of the hero Beowulf.

"To you this message my master sends.
East-Danes' king, that your kin he knows,
hardy heroes, and hails you all
welcome hither o'er waves of the sea!
Ye may wend your way in war-attire,
and under helmets Hrothgar greet;
but let here the battle-shields bide your parley,
and wooden war-shafts wait its end."
Uprose the mighty one, ringed with his men,
brave band of thanes: some bode without,
battle-gear guarding, as bade the chief.
Then hied that troop where the herald led them,
under Heorot's roof: [the hero strode,]
hardy 'neath helm, till the hearth he neared.
Beowulf spake,—his breastplate gleamed,
war-net woven by wit of the smith:—
"Thou Hrothgar, hail! Hygelac's I,
kinsman and follower. Fame a-plenty
have I gained in youth! These Grendel deeds
I heard in my home-land heralded clear.
Seafarers say how stands this hall,
of buildings best, for your band of thanes
empty and idle, when evening sun
in the harbor of heaven is hidden away.
So my vassals advised me well,—
brave and wise, the best of men,—
O sovran Hrothgar, to seek thee here,
for my nerve and my might they knew full well.
Themselves had seen me from slaughter come
blood-flecked from foes, where five I bound,
and that wild brood worsted. I' the waves I slew
nicors by night, in need and peril
avenging the Weders, whose woe they sought,—
crushing the grim ones. Grendel now,
monster cruel, be mine to quell
in single battle! So, from thee,
thou sovran of the Shining-Danes,
Scyldings'-bulwark, a boon I seek,—
and, Friend-of-the-folk, refuse it not,
O Warriors'-shield, now I've wandered far,—
that I alone with my liegemen here,
this hardy band, may Heorot purge!
More I hear, that the monster dire,
in his wanton mood, of weapons recks not;
hence shall I scorn—so Hygelac stay,
king of my kindred, kind to me!—
brand or buckler to bear in the fight,
gold-colored targe; but with gripe alone
must I front the fiend and fight for life,
foe against foe. Then faith be his

38. Fame a-plenty. This naïve boasting is thoroughly in the heroic tradition. **52. nicors,** sea-monsters. **64. weapons.** Beowulf is to learn later that Grendel is impervious to weapons; see page 25. Here, in chivalric manner, he offers to meet him on equal terms.

in the doom of the Lord whom death shall take.
Fain, I ween, if the fight he win,
in this hall of gold my Geatish band
will he fearless eat,—as oft before,—
my noblest thanes. Nor need'st thou then
to hide my head; for his shall I be,
dyed in gore, if death must take me;
and my blood-covered body he'll bear as prey,
ruthless devour it, the roamer-lonely,
with my life-blood redden his lair in the fen:
no further for me need'st food prepare!
To Hygelac send, if Hild should take me,
best of war-weeds, warding my breast,
armor excellent, heirloom of Hrethel
and work of Wayland. Fares Wyrd as she must."

7

Hrothgar spake, the Scyldings'-helmet:—
"For fight defensive, Friend my Beowulf,
to succor and save, thou hast sought us here.
Thy father's combat a feud enkindled,
when Heatholaf with hand he slew
among the Wylfings; his Weder kin
for horror of fighting feared to hold him.
Fleeing, he sought our South-Dane folk,
over surge of ocean the Honor-Scyldings,
when first I was ruling the folk of Danes,
wielded, youthful, this widespread realm,
this hoard-hold of heroes. Heorogar was dead,
my elder brother, had breathed his last,
Healfdene's bairn: he was better than I!
Straightway the feud with fee I settled,
to the Wylfings sent, o'er watery ridges,
treasures olden: oaths he swore me.
Sore is my soul to say to any
of the race of man what ruth for me
in Heorot Grendel with hate hath wrought,
what sudden harryings. Hall-folk fail me,
my warriors wane; for Wyrd hath swept them
into Grendel's grasp. But God is able
this deadly foe from his deeds to turn!
Boasted full oft, as my beer they drank,
earls o'er the ale-cup, armèd men,
that they would bide in the beer-hall here,
Grendel's attack with terror of blades.
Then was this mead-house at morning tide
dyed with gore, when the daylight broke,
all the boards of the benches blood-besprinkled,
gory the hall: I had heroes the less,
doughty dear-ones that death had reft.
—But sit to the banquet, unbind thy words,
hardy hero, as heart shall prompt thee."
Gathered together, the Geatish men
in the banquet-hall on bench assigned,
sturdy-spirited, sat them down,
hardy-hearted. A henchman attended,
carried the carven cup in hand,
served the clear mead. Oft minstrels sang
blithe in Heorot. Heroes reveled,
no dearth of warriors, Weder and Dane.

71. doom, judgment. **75–76. Nor need'st . . . head.** "There will be no need to conduct funeral rites for me." **82. Hild,** Battle. **85. Wayland,** the god of metal-working who in Germanic tradition occupies a place comparable to that of Hephaestos-Vulcan in classical lore. **Wyrd,** Fate. The pagan fatalism of the poem is evident throughout. **2. For fight defensive,** a reference to Hrothgar's service to Beowulf's father, Ecgtheow. Gratitude for this kindness was one of the factors involved in Beowulf's attempt to rid Heorot of Grendel. **6. his Weder kin,** the Geats. **15. with fee,** that is, by paying blood-money to the Wylfings. **17. oaths he swore.** Ecgtheow, apparently, swore to maintain peace in the future. **21. Hall-folk,** the king's retinue of warriors.

8

Unferth spake, the son of Ecglaf,
who sat at the feet of the Scyldings' lord,
unbound the battle-runes.—Beowulf's quest,
sturdy seafarer's, sorely galled him;
ever he envied that other men
should more achieve in middle-earth
of fame under heaven than he himself.—
"Art thou that Beowulf, Breca's rival,
who emulous swam on the open sea,
when for pride the pair of you proved the floods,
and wantonly dared in waters deep
to risk your lives? No living man,
or lief or loath, from your labor dire
could you dissuade, from swimming the main.
Ocean-tides with your arms ye covered,
with strenuous hands the sea-streets measured,
swam o'er the waters. Winter's storm
rolled the rough waves. In realm of sea
a sennight strove ye. In swimming he topped thee,
had more of main! Him at morning-tide
billows bore to the Battling-Raemas,
whence he hied to his home so dear,
beloved of his liegemen, to land of Brondings,
fastness fair, where his folk he ruled,

1. Unferth, a prominent orator and person at the Danish court. He was probably expected to make a flattering speech of welcome to Beowulf; thus his insulting and envious remarks are all the more startling. **9. swam on the open sea.** This youthful adventure of Beowulf's, told in one way by Unferth and in another by the hero, illustrates the poet's method of adding to our information by means of "flashbacks." **19. sennight,** seven nights. **21. Battling-Raemas,** a tribe who probably lived in what is now Romerike, north of Oslo. **23. Brondings.** Breca and his Brondings are mentioned in the Old English poem *Widsith.*

town and treasure. In triumph o'er thee
Beanstan's bairn his boast achieved.
So ween I for thee a worse adventure
—though in buffet of battle thou brave hast been,
in struggle grim,—if Grendel's approach
thou dar'st await through the watch of night!"

Beowulf spake, bairn of Ecgtheow:—
"What a deal hast uttered, dear my Unferth,
drunken with beer, of Breca now,
told of his triumph! Truth I claim it,
that I had more of might in the sea
than any man else, more ocean-endurance.
We twain had talked, in time of youth,
and made our boast,—we were merely boys,
striplings still,—to stake our lives
far at sea: and so we performed it.
Naked swords, as we swam along,
we held in hand, with hope to guard us
against the whales. Not a whit from me
could he float afar o'er the flood of waves,
haste o'er the billows; nor him I abandoned.
Together we twain on the tides abode
five nights full till the flood divided us,
churning waves and chillest weather,
darkling night, and the northern wind
ruthless rushed on us: rough was the surge.
Now the wrath of the sea-fish rose apace;
yet me 'gainst the monsters my mailèd coat,
hard and hand-linked, help afforded,—
battle-sark braided my breast to ward,
garnished with gold. There grasped me firm
and haled me to bottom the hated foe,
with grimmest gripe. 'Twas granted me, though,
to pierce the monster with point of sword,
with blade of battle: huge beast of the sea
was whelmed by the hurly through hand of mine.

9

"Me thus often the evil monsters
thronging threatened. With thrust of my sword,
the darling, I dealt them due return!
Nowise had they bliss from their booty then
to devour their victim, vengeful creatures,
seated to banquet at bottom of sea;
but at break of day, by my brand sore hurt,
on the edge of ocean up they lay,
put to sleep by the sword. And since, by them
on the fathomless sea-ways sailor-folk
are never molested.—Light from east,
came bright God's beacon; the billows sank,
so that I saw the sea-cliffs high,
windy walls. For Wyrd oft saveth
earl undoomed if he doughty be!
And so it came that I killed with my sword
nine of the nicors. Of night-fought battles
ne'er heard I a harder 'neath heaven's dome,
nor adrift on the deep a more desolate man!
Yet I came unharmed from that hostile clutch,
though spent with swimming. The sea upbore me,
flood of the tide, on Finnish land,
the welling waters. Nowise of thee
have I heard men tell such terror of falchions,
bitter battle. Breca ne'er yet,
not one of you pair, in the play of war
such daring deed has done at all
with bloody brand,—I boast not of it!—
though thou wast the bane of thy brethren dear,
thy closest kin, whence curse of hell
awaits thee, well as thy wit may serve!
For I say in sooth, thou son of Ecglaf,
never had Grendel these grim deeds wrought,
monster dire, on thy master dear,
in Heorot such havoc, if heart of thine
were as battle-bold as thy boast is loud!
But he has found no feud will happen;
from sword-clash dread of your Danish clan
he vaunts him safe, from the Victor-Scyldings.
He forces pledges, favors none
of the land of Danes, but lustily murders,
fights and feasts, nor feud he dreads
from Spear-Dane men. But speedily now
shall I prove him the prowess and pride of the Geats,
shall bid him battle. Blithe to mead
go he that listeth, when light of dawn
this morrow morning o'er men of earth,
ether-robed sun from the south shall beam!"

Joyous then was the Jewel-giver,
hoar-haired, war-brave; help awaited
the Bright-Danes' prince, from Beowulf hearing,
folk's good shepherd, such firm resolve.
Then was laughter of liegemen loud resounding
with winsome words. Came Wealhtheow forth,

26. Beanstan's bairn, Breca. **54. battle-sark,** coat of mail. **60. hurly,** hurly-burly, commotion.

14–15. Wyrd . . . doughty be! An early version of "Trust in God and keep your powder dry." **22. Finnish land.** This is interpreted as meaning northern Norway, the land of the Lapps. **29. the bane of thy brethren dear.** Beowulf's charge that Unferth has murdered his nearest kinsmen is a serious accusation, and one wonders how a person guilty of a crime unforgivable among the Germanic peoples could have held a place of honor. A later passage in the poem indicates that Beowulf may here be simply overemphasizing Unferth's failure to protect his relatives in battle. **54. Wealhtheow.** The first element in "Wealhtheow" means "foreign," even specifically "Celtic," and the second means "captive," but the original sense of the word need not be applied literally to Hrothgar's queen.

queen of Hrothgar, heedful of courtesy,
gold-decked, greeting the guests in hall;
and the high-born lady handed the cup
first to the East-Danes' heir and warden,
bade him be blithe at the beer-carouse,
the land's beloved one. Lustily took he
banquet and beaker, battle-famed king.
Through the hall then went the Helmings' Lady,
to younger and older everywhere
carried the cup, till came the moment
when the ring-graced queen, the royal-hearted,
to Beowulf bore the beaker of mead.
She greeted the Geats' lord, God she thanked
in wisdom's words, that her will was granted,
that at last on a hero her hope could lean
for comfort in terrors. The cup he took,
hardy-in-war, from Wealhtheow's hand,
and answer uttered the eager-for-combat.
Beowulf spake, bairn of Ecgtheow:—
"This was my thought, when my thanes and I
bent to the ocean and entered our boat,
that I would work the will of your people
fully, or fighting fall in death,
in fiend's gripe fast. I am firm to do
an earl's brave deed, or end the days
of this life of mine in the mead-hall here."
Well these words to the woman seemed,
Beowulf's battle-boast.—Bright with gold
the stately dame by her spouse sat down.
Again, as erst, began in hall
warriors' wassail and words of power,
the proud-band's revel, till presently
the son of Healfdene hastened to seek
rest for the night; he knew there waited
fight for the fiend in that festal hall,
when the sheen of the sun they saw no more,
and dusk of night sank darkling nigh,
and shadowy shapes came striding on,
wan under welkin. The warriors rose.
Man to man, he made harangue,
Hrothgar to Beowulf, bade him hail,
let him wield the wine hall: a word he added:—
"Never to any man erst I trusted,
since I could heave up hand and shield,
this noble Dane-Hall, till now to thee.
Have now and hold this house unpeered;
remember thy glory; thy might declare;
watch for the foe! No wish shall fail thee
if thou bidest the battle with bold-won life."

62. the Helmings' Lady. Wealhtheow was of the Helmings, probably a Celtic tribe. **84. as erst,** as in the good old days before the coming of Grendel. Beowulf's confidence and the queen's cup have restored the courage of the Danes.

10

Then Hrothgar went with his hero-train,
defence-of-Scyldings, forth from hall;
fain would the war-lord Wealhtheow seek,
couch of his queen. The King-of-Glory
against this Grendel a guard had set,
so heroes heard, a hall-defender,
who warded the monarch and watched for the monster.
In truth, the Geats' prince gladly trusted
his mettle, his might, the mercy of God!
Cast off then his corselet of iron,
helmet from head; to his henchman gave,—
choicest of weapons,—the well-chased sword,
bidding him guard the gear of battle.
Spake then his Vaunt the valiant man,
Beowulf Geat, ere the bed he sought:—
"Of force in fight no feebler I count me,
in grim war-deeds, than Grendel deems him.
Not with the sword, then, to sleep of death
his life will I give, though it lie in my power.
No skill is his to strike against me,
my shield to hew though he hardy be,
bold in battle; we both, this night,
shall spurn the sword, if he seek me here,
unweaponed, for war. Let wisest God,
sacred Lord, on which side soever
doom decree as he deemeth right."
Reclined then the chieftain, and cheek-pillows held
the head of the earl, while all about him
seamen hardy on hall-beds sank.
None of them thought that thence their steps
to the folk and fastness that fostered them,
to the land they loved, would lead them back!
Full well they wist that on warriors many
battle-death seized, in the banquet-hall,
of Danish clan. But comfort and help,
war-weal weaving, to Weder folk
the Master gave, that, by might of one,
over their enemy all prevailed,
by single strength. In sooth 'tis told
that highest God o'er human kind
hath wielded ever!—Thro' wan night striding,
came the walker-in-shadow. Warriors slept
whose hest was to guard the gabled hall,—

2. forth from hall. Even when Heorot was unthreatened, the king would normally sleep in a smaller separate dwelling. **6. hall-defender,** Beowulf. **14. Spake then his Vaunt.** Since Grendel's coming is expected to be without warning, Beowulf delivers his epic "vaunt" or boast before he goes to bed. **18. Not with the sword.** As Hrothgar has made clear (Section 6, lines 9 and 10), Beowulf's strength lies in "the gripe of his hand." **37–39. the Master gave . . . by single strength.** The maintenance of suspense is of little concern to our poet.

all save one. 'Twas widely known
that against God's will the ghostly ravager
him could not hurl to haunts of darkness;
wakeful, ready, with warrior's wrath,
bold he bided the battle's issue.

11

Then from the moorland, by misty crags,
with God's wrath laden, Grendel came.
The monster was minded of mankind now
sundry to seize in the stately house.
Under welkin he walked, till the wine-palace there,
gold-hall of men, he gladly discerned,
flashing with fretwork. Not first time, this,
that he the home of Hrothgar sought,—
yet ne'er in his life-day, late or early,
such hardy heroes, such hall-thanes, found!
To the house the warrior walked apace,
parted from peace; the portal opened,
though with forged bolts fast, when his fists had struck it,
and baleful he burst in his blatant rage,
the house's mouth. All hastily, then,
o'er fair-paved floor the fiend trod on,
ireful he strode; there streamed from his eyes
fearful flashes, like flame to see.
He spied in hall the hero-band,
kin and clansmen clustered asleep,
hardy liegemen. Then laughed his heart;
for the monster was minded, ere morn should dawn,
savage, to sever the soul of each,
life from body, since lusty banquet
waited his will! But Wyrd forbade him
to seize any more of men of earth
after that evening. Eagerly watched
Hygelac's kinsman his cursèd foe,
how he would fare in fell attack.
Not that the monster was minded to pause!
Straightway he seized a sleeping warrior
for the first, and tore him fiercely asunder,
the bone-frame bit, drank blood in streams,
swallowed him piecemeal: swiftly thus
the lifeless corse was clear devoured,
e'en feet and hands. Then farther he hied;
for the hardy hero with hand he grasped,
felt for the foe with fiendish claw,
for the hero reclining,—who clutched it boldly,
prompt to answer, propped on his arm.
Soon then saw that shepherd-of-evils
that never he met in this middle-world,
in the ways of earth, another wight
with heavier hand-gripe; at heart he feared,
sorrowed in soul,—none the sooner escaped!
Fain would he flee, his fastness seek,
the den of devils: no doings now
such as oft he had done in days of old!
Then bethought him the hardy Hygelac-thane
of his boast at evening: up he bounded,
grasped firm his foe, whose fingers cracked.
The fiend made off, but the earl close followed.
The monster meant—if he might at all—
to fling himself free, and far away
fly to the fens,—knew his fingers' power
in the gripe of the grim one. Gruesome march
to Heorot this monster of harm had made!
Din filled the room; the Danes were bereft,
castle-dwellers and clansmen all,
earls, of their ale. Angry were both
those savage hall-guards: the house resounded.
Wonder it was the wine-hall firm
in the strain of their struggle stood, to earth
the fair house fell not; too fast it was
within and without by its iron bands
craftily clamped; though there crashed from sill
many a mead-bench—men have told me—
gay with gold, where the grim foes wrestled.
So well had weened the wisest Scyldings
that not ever at all might any man
that bone-decked, brave house break asunder,
crush by craft,—unless clasp of fire
in smoke engulfed it.—Again uprose
din redoubled. Danes of the North
with fear and frenzy were filled, each one,
who from the wall that wailing heard,
God's foe sounding his grisly song,
cry of the conquered, clamorous pain
from captive of hell. Too closely held him
he who of men in might was strongest
in that same day of this our life.

12

Not in any wise would the earls'-defence
suffer that slaughterous stranger to live,
useless deeming his days and years
to men on earth. Now many an earl
of Beowulf brandished blade ancestral,

46. him, Beowulf. **11. warrior.** Grendel and his mother, however monstrous, are often referred to as human beings. **12. parted from peace,** doomed to hell. **28. Hygelac's kinsman,** Beowulf. **31. sleeping warrior.** The warrior's name, as we learn later, is Hondscio.

47. den of devils. Grendel's lair is thought of as evil enough to be a fitting home for devils, or else Grendel and his mother are identified with the fiends. **56. grim one,** Beowulf. **61. hall-guards,** Beowulf and Grendel. **71. bone-decked,** a reference to the antlers which gave the hall its name. **72–73. unless . . . engulfed it,** an anticipation of the fate of Heorot; see page 17, Section 1.

fain the life of their lord to shield,
their praisèd prince, if power were theirs;
never they knew,—as they neared the foe,
hardy-hearted heroes of war,
aiming their swords on every side
the accursed to kill,—no keenest blade,
no fairest of falchions fashioned on earth,
could harm or hurt that hideous fiend!
He was safe, by his spells, from sword of battle,
from edge of iron. Yet his end and parting
on that same day of this our life
woful should be, and his wandering soul
far off flit to the fiends' domain.
Soon he found, who in former days,
harmful in heart and hated of God,
on many a man such murder wrought,
that the frame of his body failed him now.
For him the keen-souled kinsman of Hygelac
held in hand; hateful alive
was each to other. The outlaw dire
took mortal hurt; a mighty wound
showed on his shoulder, and sinews cracked,
and the bone-frame burst. To Beowulf now
the glory was given, and Grendel thence
death-sick his den in the dark moor sought,
noisome abode: he knew too well
that here was the last of life, an end
of his days on earth.—To all the Danes
by that bloody battle the boon had come.
From ravage had rescued the roving stranger
Hrothgar's hall; the hardy and wise one
had purged it anew. His night-work pleased him,
his deed and its honor. To Eastern Danes
had the valiant Geat his vaunt made good,
all their sorrow and ills assuaged,
their bale of battle borne so long,
and all the dole they erst endured,
pain a-plenty.—'Twas proof of this,
when the hardy-in-fight a hand laid down,
arm and shoulder,—all, indeed,
of Grendel's gripe,—'neath the gabled roof.

[Sections 13–18 tell of the rejoicing of the Danes after the routing of Grendel. A great feast is held at Heorot, at which Hrothgar and his queen give presents to Beowulf and his men. After the feast the warriors prepare for a night's rest.]

19

Then sank they to sleep. With sorrow one bought
his rest of the evening,—as ofttime had happened
when Grendel guarded that golden hall,
evil wrought, till his end drew nigh,
slaughter for sins. 'Twas seen and told
how an avenger survived the fiend,
as was learned afar. The livelong time
after that grim fight, Grendel's mother,
monster of women, mourned her woe.
She was doomed to dwell in the dreary waters,
cold sea-courses, since Cain cut down
with edge of the sword his only brother,
his father's offspring: outlawed he fled,
marked with murder, from men's delights,
warded the wilds.—There woke from him
such fate-sent ghosts as Grendel, who,
war-wolf horrid, at Heorot found
a warrior watching and waiting the fray,
with whom the grisly one grappled amain.
But the man remembered his mighty power,
the glorious gift that God had sent him,
in his Maker's mercy put his trust
for comfort and help: so he conquered the foe,
felled the fiend, who fled abject,
reft of joy, to the realms of death,
mankind's foe. And his mother now,
gloomy and grim, would go that quest
of sorrow, the death of her son to avenge.
To Heorot came she, where helmeted Danes
slept in the hall. Too soon came back
old ills of the earls, when in she burst,
the mother of Grendel. Less grim, though, that terror,
e'en as terror of woman in war is less,
might of maid, than of men in arms
when, hammer-forgèd, the falchion hard,
sword gore-stained, through swine of the helm,
crested, with keen blade carves amain.
Then was in hall the hard-edge drawn,
the swords on the settles, and shields a-many
firm held in hand: nor helmet minded
nor harness of mail, whom that horror seized.

Haste was hers; she would hie afar
and save her life when the liegemen saw her.
Yet a single atheling up she seized
fast and firm, as she fled to the moor.
He was for Hrothgar of heroes the dearest,
of trusty vassals betwixt the seas,
whom she killed on his couch, a clansman famous,
in battle brave.—Nor was Beowulf there;
another house had been held apart,
after giving of gold, for the Geat renowned.—
Uproar filled Heorot; the hand all had viewed,
blood-flecked, she bore with her; bale was returned,
dole in the dwellings: 'twas dire exchange
where Dane and Geat were doomed to give
the lives of loved ones. Long-tried king,

36. swine of the helm. See page 19, Section 4, line 46, and note. **52. the hand,** Grendel's arm.

the hoary hero, at heart was sad
when he knew his noble no more lived,
and dead indeed was his dearest thane.
To his bower was Beowulf brought in haste,
dauntless victor. As daylight broke,
along with his earls the atheling lord,
with his clansmen, came, where the king abode
waiting to see if the Wielder-of-All
would turn this tale of trouble and woe.
Strode o'er floor the famed-in-strife,
with his hand-companions,—the hall resounded,—
wishing to greet the wise old king,
Ingwines' lord; he asked if the night
had passed in peace to the prince's mind.

20

Hrothgar spake, helmet-of-Scyldings:—
"Ask not of pleasure! Pain is renewed
to Danish folk. Dead is Aeschere,
of Yrmenlaf the elder brother,
my sage adviser and stay in council,
shoulder-comrade in stress of fight
when warriors clashed and we warded our heads,
hewed the helm-boars: hero famed
should be every earl as Aeschere was!
But here in Heorot a hand hath slain him
of wandering death-sprite. I wot not whither,
proud of the prey, her path she took,
fain of her fill. The feud she avenged
that yesternight, unyieldingly,
Grendel in grimmest grasp thou killedst,—
seeing how long these liegemen mine
he ruined and ravaged. Reft of life,
in arms he fell. Now another comes
keen and cruel, her kin to avenge,
faring far in feud of blood:
so that many a thane shall think, who e'er
sorrows in soul for that sharer of rings,
this is hardest of heart-bales. The hand lies low
that once was willing each wish to please.
Land-dwellers here and liegemen mine,
who house by those parts, I have heard relate
that such a pair they have sometimes seen,
march-stalkers mighty the moorland haunting,
wandering spirits: one of them seemed,
so far as my folk could fairly judge,
of womankind; and one, accursed,
in man's guise trod the misery-track
of exile, though huger than human bulk.
Grendel in days long gone they named him,
folk of the land; his father they knew not,
nor any brood that was born to him
of treacherous spirits. Untrod is their home;
by wolf-cliffs haunt they and windy headlands,
fenways fearful, where flows the stream
from mountains gliding to gloom of the rocks,
underground flood. Not far is it hence
in measure of miles that the mere expands,
and o'er it the frost-bound forest hanging,
sturdily rooted, shadows the wave.
By night is a wonder weird to see,
fire on the waters. So wise lived none
of the sons of men, to search those depths!
Nay, though the heath-rover, harried by dogs,
the horn-proud hart, this holt should seek,
long distance driven, his dear life first
on the brink he yields ere he brave the plunge
to hide his head: 'tis no happy place!
Thence the welter of waters washes up
wan to welkin when winds bestir
evil storms, and air grows dusk,
and the heavens weep. Now is help once more
with thee alone! The land thou knowst not,
place of fear, where thou findest out
the sin-flecked being. Seek if thou dare!
I will reward thee, for waging this fight,
with ancient treasure, as erst I did,
with winding gold, if thou winnest back."

21

Beowulf spake, bairn of Ecgtheow:
"Sorrow not, sage! It beseems us better
friends to avenge than fruitlessly mourn them.
Each of us all must his end abide
in the ways of the world; so win who may
glory ere death! When his days are told,
that is the warrior's worthiest doom.
Rise, O realm-warder! Ride we anon,
and mark the trail of the mother of Grendel.
No harbor shall hide her—heed my promise!—
enfolding of field or forested mountain
or floor of the flood, let her flee where she will!
But thou this day endure in patience,
as I ween thou wilt, thy woes each one."
Leaped up the graybeard: God he thanked,
mighty Lord, for the man's brave words.
For Hrothgar soon a horse was saddled,
wave-maned steed. The sovran wise
stately rode on; his shield-armed men
followed in force. The footprints led
along the woodland, widely seen,

69. Ingwines' lord, lord of the Danes. **69–70. if the night . . . mind,** a pricelessly inappropriate morning's greeting by an innocent guest. **14. yesternight,** night before last. **22. sharer of rings.** This suggests that Aeschere was a chief in his own right.

a path o'er the plain, where she passed, and trod
the murky moor; of men-at-arms
she bore the bravest and best one, dead,
him who with Hrothgar the homestead ruled.
On then went the atheling-born
o'er stone-cliffs steep and strait defiles,
narrow passes and unknown ways,
headlands sheer, and the haunts of the nicors.
Foremost he fared, a few at his side
of the wiser men, the ways to scan,
till he found in a flash the forested hill
hanging over the hoary rock,
a woful wood: the waves below
were dyed in blood. The Danish men
had sorrow of soul, and for Scyldings all,
for many a hero, 'twas hard to bear,
ill for earls, when Aeschere's head
they found by the flood on the foreland there.
Waves were welling, the warriors saw,
hot with blood; but the horn sang oft
battle-song bold. The band sat down,
and watched on the water worm-like things,
sea-dragons strange that sounded the deep,
and nicors that lay on the ledge of the ness
—such as oft essay at hour of morn
on the road-of-sails their ruthless quest,—
and sea-snakes and monsters. These started away,
swollen and savage that song to hear,
that war-horn's blast. The warden of Geats,
with bolt from bow, then balked of life,
of wave-work, one monster; amid its heart
went the keen war-shaft; in water it seemed
less doughty in swimming whom death had seized.
Swift on the billows, with boar-spears well
hooked and barbed, it was hard beset,
done to death and dragged on the headland,
wave-roamer wondrous. Warriors viewed the grisly guest.

Then girt him Beowulf
in martial mail, nor mourned for his life.
His breastplate broad and bright of hues,
woven by hand, should the waters try;
well could it ward the warrior's body
that battle should break on his breast in vain
nor harm his heart by the hand of a foe.
And the helmet white that his head protected
was destined to dare the deeps of the flood,
through wave-whirl win: 'twas wound with chains,
decked with gold, as in days of yore
the weapon-smith worked it wondrously,
with swine-forms set it, that swords nowise,
brandished in battle, could bite that helm.
Nor was that the meanest of mighty helps
which Hrothgar's orator offered at need:
"Hrunting" they named the hilted sword,
of old-time heirlooms easily first;
iron was its edge, all etched with poison,
with battle-blood hardened, nor blenched it at fight
in hero's hand who held it ever,
on paths of peril prepared to go
to folkstead of foes. Not first time this
it was destined to do a daring task.
For he bore not in mind, the bairn of Ecglaf
sturdy and strong, that speech he had made,
drunk with wine, now this weapon he lent
to a stouter swordsman. Himself, though, durst not
under welter of waters wager his life
as loyal liegeman. So lost he his glory,
honor of earls. With the other not so,
who girded him now for the grim encounter.

22

Beowulf spake, bairn of Ecgtheow:—
"Have mind, thou honored offspring of Healfdene,
gold-friend of men, now I go on this quest,
sovran wise, what once was said:
if in thy cause it came that I
should lose my life, thou wouldst loyal bide
to me, though fallen, in father's place!
Be guardian, thou, to this group of my thanes,
my warrior-friends, if War should seize me;
and the goodly gifts thou gavest me,
Hrothgar beloved, to Hygelac send!
Geatland's king may ken by the gold,
Hrethel's son see, when he stares at the treasure,
that I got me a friend for goodness famed,
and joyed while I could in my jewel-bestower.
And let Unferth wield this wondrous sword,
earl far-honored, this heirloom precious,
hard of edge: with Hrunting I
seek doom of glory, or Death shall take me."

After these words the Weder-Geat lord
boldly hastened, biding never
answer at all: and ocean floods
closed o'er the hero. Long while of the day
fled ere he felt the floor of the sea.
Soon found the fiend who the flood-domain

45. **ness,** cliff. 50. **warden of Geats,** Beowulf. 71. **swine-forms,** round the crown of the helmet.

74. **orator,** Unferth, whose attitude towards Beowulf has changed since his opening speech. 81. **folkstead,** meeting-place. 83. **bairn of Ecglaf,** Unferth. 88. **lost . . . glory.** The poet finds it hard to forgive Unferth, even after his obvious amendment. 13. **Hrethel's son,** Hygelac. 16. **wondrous sword,** presumably Beowulf's own sword, Naegling, which he is leaving behind.

sword-hungry held these hundred winters,
greedy and grim, that some guest from above,
some man, was raiding her monster-realm.
She grasped out for him with grisly claws,
and the warrior seized; yet scathed she not
his body hale; the breastplate hindered,
as she strove to shatter the sark of war,
the linkèd harness, with loathsome hand.
Then bore this brine-wolf, when bottom she touched,
the lord of rings to the lair she haunted,
whiles vainly he strove, though his valor held,
weapon to wield against wondrous monsters
that sore beset him; sea-beasts many
tried with fierce tusks to tear his mail,
and swarmed on the stranger. But soon he marked
he was now in some hall, he knew not which,
where water never could work him harm,
nor through the roof could reach him ever
fangs of the flood. Firelight he saw,
beams of a blaze that brightly shone.
Then the warrior was ware of that wolf-of-the-deep,
mere-wife monstrous. For mighty stroke
he swung his blade, and the blow withheld not.
Then sang on her head that seemly blade
its war-song wild. But the warrior found
the light-of-battle was loath to bite,
to harm the heart: its hard edge failed
the noble at need, yet had known of old
strife hand to hand, and had helmets cloven,
doomed men's fighting-gear. First time, this,
for the gleaming blade that its glory fell.
  Firm still stood, nor failed in valor,
heedful of high deeds, Hygelac's kinsman;
flung away fretted sword, featly jewelled,
the angry earl; on earth it lay
steel-edged and stiff. His strength he trusted,
hand-gripe of might. So man shall do
whenever in war he weens to earn him
lasting fame, nor fears for his life!
Seized then by shoulder, shrank not from combat,
the Geatish war-prince Grendel's mother.
Flung then the fierce one, filled with wrath,
his deadly foe, that she fell to ground.
Swift on her part she paid him back
with grisly grasp, and grappled with him.
Spent with struggle, stumbled the warrior,
fiercest of fighting-men, fell adown.
On the hall-guest she hurled herself, hent her short sword,
broad and brown-edged, the bairn to avenge,
the sole-born son.—On his shoulder lay
braided breast-mail, barring death,
withstanding entrance of edge or blade.
Life would have ended for Ecgtheow's son,
under wide earth for that earl of Geats,
had his armor of war not aided him,
battle-net hard, and holy God
wielded the victory, wisest Maker.
The Lord of Heaven allowed his cause;
and easily rose the earl erect.

51. **light-of-battle,** a kenning for "sword." 52. **its hard edge failed.** Like Grendel, his mother is impervious to ordinary weapons. 73. **hent,** seized.

23

'Mid the battle-gear saw he a blade triumphant,
old-sword of Eotens, with edge of proof,
warriors' heirloom, weapon unmatched,
—save only 'twas more than other men
to bandy-of-battle could bear at all—
as the giants had wrought it, ready and keen.
Seized then its chain-hilt the Scyldings' chieftain,
bold and battle-grim, brandished the sword,
reckless of life, and so wrathfully smote
that it gripped her neck and grasped her hard,
her bone-rings breaking: the blade pierced through
that fated-one's flesh: to floor she sank.
Bloody the blade: he was blithe of his deed.
Then blazed forth light. 'Twas bright within
as when from the sky there shines unclouded
heaven's candle. The hall he scanned.
By the wall then went he; his weapon raised
high by its hilts the Hygelac-thane,
angry and eager. That edge was not useless
to the warrior now. He wished with speed
Grendel to guerdon for grim raids many,
for the war he waged on Western-Danes
oftener far than an only time,
when of Hrothgar's hearth-companions
he slew in slumber, in sleep devoured,
fifteen men of the folk of Danes,
and as many others outward bore,
his horrible prey. Well paid for that
the wrathful prince! For now prone he saw
Grendel stretched there, spent with war,
spoiled of life, so scathed had left him
Heorot's battle. The body sprang far
when after death it endured the blow,
sword-stroke savage, that severed its head.
  Soon, then, saw the sage companions
who waited with Hrothgar, watching the flood,
that the tossing waters turbid grew,
blood-stained the mere. Old men together,
hoary-haired, of the hero spake;
the warrior would not, they weened, again,
proud of conquest, come to seek

2. **Eotens,** giants.

their mighty master. To many it seemed
the wolf-of-the-waves had won his life.
The ninth hour came. The noble Scyldings
left the headland; homeward went
the gold-friend of men. But the guests sat on,
stared at the surges, sick in heart,
and wished, yet weened not, their winsome lord
again to see.

Now that sword began,
from blood of the fight, in battle-droppings,
war-blade, to wane: 'twas a wondrous thing
that all of it melted as ice is wont
when frosty fetters the Father loosens,
unwinds the wave-bonds, wielding all
seasons and times: the true God he!
Nor took from that dwelling the duke of the Geats
precious things, though a plenty he saw,
save only the head and that hilt withal
blazoned with jewels: the blade had melted,
burned was the bright sword, her blood was so hot,
so poisoned the hell-sprite who perished within there.
Soon he was swimming who safe saw in combat
downfall of demons; up-dove through the flood.
The clashing waters were cleansèd now,
waste of waves, where the wandering fiend
her life-days left and this lapsing world.
Swam then to strand the sailors' refuge,
sturdy-in-spirit, of sea-booty glad,
of burden brave he bore with him.
Went then to greet him, and God they thanked,
the thane-band choice of their chieftain blithe,
that safe and sound they could see him again.
Soon from the hardy one helmet and armor
deftly they doffed: now drowsed the mere,
water 'neath welkin, with war-blood stained.
Forth they fared by the footpaths thence,
merry at heart the highways measured,
well-known roads. Courageous men
carried the head from the cliff by the sea,
an arduous task for all the band,
the firm in fight, since four were needed
on the shaft-of-slaughter strenuously
to bear to the gold-hall Grendel's head.
So presently to the palace there
foemen fearless, fourteen Geats,
marching came. Their master-of-clan
mighty amid them the meadow-ways trod.
Strode then within the sovran thane
fearless in fight, of fame renowned,
hardy hero, Hrothgar to greet.
And next by the hair into hall was borne
Grendel's head, where the henchmen were drinking,
an awe to clan and queen alike,
a monster of marvel: the men looked on.

44. The ninth hour, 3 P.M. **46. gold-friend,** Hrothgar. **the guests,** the Geats.

[Sections 24–31 describe Beowulf's account of his adventure, the farewells of Beowulf and Hrothgar, the exchange of gifts, the return of the Geats to their country, and the reception and rewarding of Beowulf by Hygelac.]

[Part Two: Beowulf and the Fire-Dragon]

31

. . . Now further it fell with the flight of years,
with harryings horrid, that Hygelac perished,
and Heardred, too, by hewing of swords
under the shield-wall slaughtered lay,
when him at the van of his victor-folk
sought hardy heroes, Heatho-Scylfings,
in arms o'erwhelming Hereric's nephew.
Then Beowulf came as king this broad
realm to wield; and he ruled it well
fifty winters, a wise old prince,
warding his land, until One began
in the dark of night, a Dragon, to rage.
In the grave on the hill a hoard it guarded,
in the stone-barrow steep. A strait path reached it,
unknown to mortals. Some man, however,
came by chance that cave within
to the heathen hoard. In hand he took
a golden goblet, nor gave he it back,
stole with it away, while the watcher slept,
by thievish wiles: for the warden's wrath
prince and people must pay betimes!

32

. . . When the dragon awoke, new woe was kindled.
O'er the stone he snuffed. The stark-heart found
footprint of foe who so far had gone
in his hidden craft by the creature's head.—

2. Hygelac perished. Hygelac is identified with the historical Chlochilaicus, who was killed in a raid against the Franks and Frisians about 521. After his death, as we learn in a later section of the poem, the throne was offered by his queen Hygd to Beowulf, who, however, refused to interfere with the rightful succession of Hygelac's young son Heardred. The hero served as his cousin's guardian, and, when Heardred was killed in a renewed war with the Swedes, succeeded him. **6. Heatho-Scylfings,** the Swedes. **7. Hereric's nephew,** Heardred, the son of Hereric's sister Hygd. **10. fifty winters,** that is, for a long time. **14. stone barrow,** a prehistoric burial mound, of the type often found in northern Europe, whose stone sides and top were covered with earth. **strait,** narrow.

So may the undoomed easily flee
evils and exile, if only he gain
the grace of The Wielder!—That warden of gold
o'er the ground went seeking, greedy to find
the man who wrought him such wrong in sleep.
Savage and burning, the barrow he circled
all without; nor was any there,
none in the waste. . . . Yet war he desired,
was eager for battle. The barrow he entered,
sought the cup, and discovered soon
that some one of mortals had searched his treasure,
his lordly gold. The guardian waited
ill-enduring till evening came;
boiling with wrath was the barrow's keeper,
and fain with flame the foe to pay
for the dear cup's loss.—Now day was fled
as the worm had wished. By its wall no more
was it glad to bide, but burning flew
folded in flame: a fearful beginning
for sons of the soil; and soon it came,
in the doom of their lord, to a dreadful end.

33

Then the baleful fiend its fire belched out,
and bright homes burned. The blaze stood high
all landsfolk frighting. No living thing
would that loathly one leave as aloft it flew.
Wide was the dragon's warring seen,
its fiendish fury far and near,
as the grim destroyer those Geatish people
hated and hounded. To hidden lair,
to its hoard it hastened at hint of dawn.
Folk of the land it had lapped in flame,
with bale and brand. In its barrow it trusted,
its battling and bulwarks: that boast was vain!

To Beowulf then the bale was told
quickly and truly: the king's own home,
of buildings the best, in brand-waves melted,
that gift-throne of Geats. To the good old man
sad in heart, 'twas heaviest sorrow.
The sage assumed that his sovran God
he had angered, breaking ancient law,
and embittered the Lord. His breast within
with black thoughts welled, as his wont was never.
The folk's own fastness that fiery dragon
with flame had destroyed, and the stronghold all
washed by waves; but the warlike king,
prince of the Weders, plotted vengeance.
Warriors'-bulwark, he bade them work
all of iron—the earl's commander—

7. The Wielder, God. **21. worm.** The word formerly denoted a poisonous serpent.

a war-shield wondrous: well he knew
that forest-wood against fire were worthless,
linden could aid not.—Atheling brave,
he was fated to finish this fleeting life,
his days on earth, and the dragon with him,
though long it had watched o'er the wealth of the hoard!—
Shame he reckoned it, sharer-of-rings,
to follow the flyer-afar with a host,
a broad-flung band; nor the battle feared he,
nor deemed he dreadful the dragon's warring,
its vigor and valor: ventures desperate
he had passed a-plenty, and perils of war,
contest-crash, since, conqueror proud,
Hrothgar's hall he had wholly purged,
and in grapple had killed the kin of Grendel,
loathsome breed! . . .

[Section 33 continues with a recounting of some of Beowulf's earlier adventures. In Section 34 in a long speech the hero recalls the exploits of his youth.]

35

. . . Beowulf spake, and a battle-vow made,
his last of all: "I have lived through many
wars in my youth; now once again,
old folk-defender, feud will I seek,
do doughty deeds, if the dark destroyer
forth from his cavern come to fight me!"
Then hailed he the helmeted heroes all,
for the last time greeting his liegemen dear,
comrades of war: "I should carry no weapon,
no sword to the serpent, if sure I knew
how, with such enemy, else my vows
I could gain as I did in Grendel's day.
But fire in this fight I must fear me now,
and poisonous breath; so I bring with me
breastplate and board. From the barrow's keeper
no footbreadth flee I. One fight shall end
our war by the wall, as Wyrd allots,
all mankind's master. My mood is bold
but forbears to boast o'er this battling-flyer.
—Now abide by the barrow, ye breastplate-mailed,
ye heroes in harness, which of us twain
better from battle-rush bear his wounds.
Wait ye the finish. The fight is not yours,
nor meet for any but me alone
to measure might with this monster here
and play the hero. Hardily I
shall win that wealth, or war shall seize,
cruel killing, your king and lord!"

15. board, shield.

Up stood then with shield the sturdy champion,
stayed by the strength of his single manhood,
and hardy 'neath helmet his harness bore
under cleft of the cliffs: no coward's path!
Soon spied by the wall that warrior chief,
survivor of many a victory-field
where foemen fought with furious clashings,
an arch of stone; and within, a stream
that broke from the barrow. The brooklet's wave
was hot with fire. The hoard that way
he never could hope unharmed to near,
or endure those deeps, for the dragon's flame.
Then let from his breast, for he burst with rage,
the Weder-Geat prince a word outgo;
stormed the stark-heart; stern went ringing
and clear his cry 'neath the cliff-rocks gray.
The hoard-guard heard a human voice;
his rage was enkindled. No respite now
for pact of peace! The poison-breath
of the foul worm first came forth from the cave,
hot reek-of-fight: the rocks resounded.
Stout by the stone-way his shield he raised,
lord of the Geats, against the loathèd-one;
while with courage keen that coilèd foe
came seeking strife. The sturdy king
had drawn his sword, not dull of edge,
heirloom old; and each of the two
felt fear of his foe, though fierce their mood.
Stoutly stood with his shield high-raised
the warrior king, as the worm now coiled
together amain: the mailed-one waited.
Now, spire by spire, fast sped and glided
that blazing serpent. The shield protected
soul and body a shorter while
for the hero-king than his heart desired,
could his will have wielded the welcome respite
but once in his life! But Wyrd denied it,
and victory's honors.—His arm he lifted,
lord of the Geats, the grim foe smote
with atheling's heirloom. Its edge was turned,
brown-blade, on the bone, and bit more feebly
than its noble master had need of then
in his baleful stress.—Then the barrow's keeper
waxed full wild for that weighty blow,
cast deadly flames; wide drove and far
those vicious fires. No victor's glory
the Geats' lord boasted; his brand had failed,
naked in battle, as never it should,
excellent iron!—'Twas no easy path
that Ecgtheow's honored heir must tread
over the plain to the place of the foe;
for against his will he must win a home
elsewhere far, as must all men, leaving
this lapsing life!—Not long it was
ere those champions grimly closed again.
The hoard-guard was heartened; high heaved his breast
once more; and by peril was pressed again,
enfolded in flames, the folk-commander!
Nor yet about him his band of comrades,
sons of athelings, armèd stood
with warlike front: to the woods they bent them,
their lives to save. But the soul of one
with care was cumbered. Kinship true
can never be marred in a noble mind!

36

Wiglaf his name was, Weohstan's son,
linden-thane loved, the lord of Scylfings,
Aelfhere's kinsman. His king he now saw
with heat under helmet hard oppressed.
He minded the prizes his prince had given him,
wealthy seat of the Waegmunding line,
and folk-rights that his father owned.
Not long he lingered. The linden yellow,
his shield, he seized; the old sword he drew:—
as heirloom of Eanmund earth-dwellers knew it,
who was slain by the sword-edge, son of Ohthere,
friendless exile, erst in fray
killed by Weohstan, who won for his kin
brown-bright helmet, breastplate ringed,
old sword of Eotens, Onela's gift,
weeds of war of the warrior-thane,
battle-gear brave: though a brother's child
had been felled, the feud was unfelt by Onela.
For winters this war-gear Weohstan kept,
breastplate and board, till his bairn had grown
earlship to earn as the old sire did:
then he gave him, mid Geats, the gear of battle,
portion huge, when he passed from life,
fared agèd forth. For the first time now
with his leader-lord the liegeman young
was bidden to share the shock of battle.
Neither softened his soul, nor the sire's bequest
weakened in war. So the worm found out
when once in fight the foes had met!
Wiglaf spake,—and his words were sage;

87. Nor yet . . . comrades. It must be remembered that Beowulf had declared (lines 23–28 above) that the fight was his alone. **1. Wiglaf.** Wiglaf's family connections are not clear. His father, Weohstan, seems to have been a Geat in the service of Onela, King of the Swedes, but had later been forced to flee to Geatland. **2. linden-thane,** shield-warrior. **Scylfings,** the reigning family among the Swedes. **6. Waegmunding line,** the family to which Beowulf and his father belonged, and to which Wiglaf was also related. **7. folk-rights,** his shares in the common property of the tribe. **10. Eanmund,** the son of Onela's brother, Ohthere, whom Weohstan had killed on Onela's behalf.

sad in spirit, he said to his comrades:—
"I remember the time, when mead we took,
what promise we made to this prince of ours
in the banquet-hall, to our breaker-of-rings,
for gear of combat to give him requital,
for hard-sword and helmet, if hap should bring
stress of this sort! Himself who chose us
from all his army to aid him now,
urged us to glory, and gave these treasures,
because he counted us keen with the spear
and hardy 'neath helm, though this hero-work
our leader hoped unhelped and alone
to finish for us,—folk-defender
who hath got him glory greater than all men
for daring deeds! Now the day is come
that our noble master has need of the might
of warriors stout. Let us stride along
the hero to help while the heat is about him
glowing and grim! For God is my witness
I am far more fain the fire should seize
along with my lord these limbs of mine!
Unsuiting it seems our shields to bear
homeward hence, save here we essay
to fell the foe and defend the life
of the Weders' lord. I wot 'twere shame
on the law of our land if alone the king
out of Geatish warriors woe endured
and sank in the struggle! My sword and helmet,
breastplate and board, for us both shall serve!"
Through slaughter-reek strode he to succor his chieftain,
his battle-helm bore, and brief words spake:—
"Beowulf dearest, do all bravely,
as in youthful days of yore thou vowedst
that while life should last thou wouldst let no wise
thy glory droop! Now, great in deeds,
atheling steadfast, with all thy strength
shield thy life! I will stand to help thee."
At the words the worm came once again,
murderous monster mad with rage,
with fire-billows flaming, its foes to seek,
the hated men. In heat-waves burned
that board to the boss, and the breastplate failed
to shelter at all the spear-thane young.
Yet quickly under his kinsman's shield
went eager the earl, since his own was now
all burned by the blaze. The bold king again
had mind of his glory: with might his glaive
was driven into the dragon's head,—
blow nerved by hate. But Naegling was shivered,
broken in battle was Beowulf's sword,
old and gray. 'Twas granted him not
that ever the edge of iron at all
could help him at strife: too strong was his hand,
so the tale is told, and he tried too far
with strength of stroke all swords he wielded,
though sturdy their steel: they steaded him nought.
Then for the third time thought on its feud
that folk-destroyer, fire-dread dragon,
and rushed on the hero, where room allowed,
battle-grim, burning; its bitter teeth
closed on his neck, and covered him
with waves of blood from his breast that welled.

50. far more fain, that is, he prefers death to disloyalty. **72. that board,** Wiglaf's wooden shield. **79. Naegling,** Beowulf's sword.

37

'Twas now, men say, in his sovran's need
that the earl made known his noble strain,
craft and keenness and courage enduring.
Heedless of harm, though his hand was burned,
hardy-hearted, he helped his kinsman.
A little lower the loathsome beast
he smote with sword; his steel drove in
bright and burnished; that blaze began
to lose and lessen. At last the king
wielded his wits again, war-knife drew,
a biting blade by his breastplate hanging,
and the Weders'-helm smote that worm asunder,
felled the foe, flung forth its life.
So had they killed it, kinsmen both,
athelings twain: thus an earl should be
in danger's day!—Of deeds of valor
this conqueror's-hour of the king was last,
of his work in the world. The wound began,
which that dragon-of-earth had erst inflicted,
to swell and smart; and soon he found
in his breast was boiling, baleful and deep,
pain of poison. The prince walked on,
wise in his thought, to the wall of rock;
then sat, and stared at the structure of giants,
where arch of stone and steadfast column
upheld forever that hall in earth.
Yet here must the hand of the henchman peerless
lave with water his winsome lord,
the king and conqueror covered with blood,
with struggle spent, and unspan his helmet.
Beowulf spake in spite of his hurt,
his mortal wound; full well he knew
his portion now was past and gone
of earthly bliss, and all had fled
of his file of days, and death was near:
"I would fain bestow on son of mine
this gear of war, were given me now
that any heir should after me come

89. the hero, Beowulf. **2. the earl,** Wiglaf.

of my proper blood. This people I ruled
fifty winters. No folk-king was there,
none at all, of the neighboring clans
who war would wage me with 'warriors'-friends'
and threat me with horrors. At home I bided
what fate might come, and I cared for mine own;
feuds I sought not, nor falsely swore
ever on oath. For all these things,
though fatally wounded, fain am I!
From the Ruler-of-Man no wrath shall seize me,
when life from my frame must flee away,
for killing of kinsmen! Now quickly go
and gaze on that hoard 'neath the hoary rock,
Wiglaf loved, now the worm lies low,
sleeps, heart-sore, of his spoil bereaved.
And fare in haste. I would fain behold
the gorgeous heirlooms, golden store,
have joy in the jewels and gems, lay down
softlier for sight of this splendid hoard
my life and the lordship I long have held."

38

I have heard that swiftly the son of Weohstan
at wish and word of his wounded king,—
war-sick warrior,—woven mail-coat,
battle-sark, bore 'neath the barrow's roof.
Then the clansman keen, of conquest proud,
passing the seat, saw store of jewels
and glistening gold the ground along;
by the wall were marvels, and many a vessel
in the den of the dragon, the dawn-flyer old:
unburnished bowls of bygone men
reft of richness; rusty helms
of the olden age; and arm-rings many
wondrously woven.—Such wealth of gold,
booty from barrow, can burden with pride
each human wight: let him hide it who will!—
His glance too fell on a gold-wove banner
high o'er the hoard, of handiwork noblest,
brilliantly broidered; so bright its gleam,
all the earth-floor he easily saw
and viewed all these vessels. No vestige now
was seen of the serpent: the sword had ta'en him.
Then, I heard, the hill of its hoard was reft,
old work of giants, by one alone;
he burdened his bosom with beakers and plate
at his own good will, and the ensign took,
brightest of beacons.—The blade of his lord
—its edge was iron—had injured deep
one that guarded the golden hoard
many a year and its murder-fire
spread hot round the barrow in horror-billows
at midnight hour, till it met its doom.
Hasted the herald, the hoard so spurred him
his track to retrace; he was troubled by doubt,
high-souled hero, if haply he'd find
alive, where he left him, the lord of Weders,
weakening fast by the wall of the cave.
So he carried the load. His lord and king
he found all bleeding, famous chief,
at the lapse of life. The liegeman again
plashed him with water, till point of word
broke through the breast-hoard. Beowulf spake,
sage and sad, as he stared at the gold:—
"For the gold and treasure, to God my thanks,
to the Wielder-of-Wonders, with words I say,
for what I behold, to Heaven's Lord,
for the grace that I give such gifts to my folk
or ever the day of my death be run!
Now I've bartered here for booty of treasure
the last of my life, so look ye well
to the needs of my land! No longer I tarry.
A barrow bid ye the battle-famed raise
for my ashes. 'Twill shine by the shore of the flood,
to folk of mine memorial fair
on Hronës Headland high uplifted,
that ocean-wanderers oft may hail
Beowulf's Barrow, as back from far
they drive their keels o'er the darkling wave."
From his neck he unclasped the collar of gold,
valorous king, to his vassal gave it
with bright-gold helmet, breastplate, and ring,
to the youthful thane: bade him use them in joy.
"Thou art end and remnant of all our race,
the Waegmunding name. For Wyrd hath swept them,
all my line, to the land of doom,
earls in their glory: I after them go."
This word was the last which the wise old man
harbored in heart ere hot death-waves
of balefire he chose. From his bosom fled
his soul to seek the saints' reward.

39

It was heavy hap for that hero young
on his lord beloved to look and find him
lying on earth with life at end,
sorrowful sight. But the slayer too,
awful earth-dragon, empty of breath,
lay felled in fight, nor, fain of its treasure,
could the writhing monster rule it more.
For edges of iron had ended its days,

42. 'warriors'-friends,' swords. **47. fain,** glad. **23. one alone,** Wiglaf.

54. Hronës Headland, Whale's Headland.

hard and battle-sharp, hammers' leaving;
and that flyer-afar had fallen to ground
hushed by its hurt, its hoard all near,
no longer lusty aloft to whirl
at midnight, making its merriment seen,
proud of its prizes: prone it sank
by the handiwork of the hero-king.
Forsooth among folk but few achieve,
—though sturdy and strong, as stories tell me,
and never so daring in deed of valor,—
the perilous breath of a poison-foe
to brave, and to rush on the ring-hoard hall,
whenever his watch the warden keeps
bold in the barrow. Beowulf paid
the price of death for that precious hoard;
and each of the foes had found the end
of this fleeting life.
Befell erelong
that the laggards in war the wood had left,
trothbreakers, cowards, ten together,
fearing before to flourish a spear
in the sore distress of their sovran lord.
Now in their shame their shields they carried,
armor of fight, where the old man lay;
and they gazed on Wiglaf. Wearied he sat
at his sovran's shoulder, shieldsman good,
to wake him with water. Nowise it availed.
Though well he wished it, in world no more
could he barrier life for that leader-of-battles
nor baffle the will of all-wielding God.
Doom of the Lord was law o'er the deeds
of every man, as it is to-day.
Grim was the answer, easy to get,
from the youth for those that had yielded to fear!
Wiglaf spake, the son of Weohstan,—
mournful he looked on those men unloved:—
"Who sooth will speak, can say indeed
that the ruler who gave you golden rings
and the harness of war in which ye stand
—for he at ale-bench often-times
bestowed on hall-folk helm and breastplate,
lord to liegemen, the likeliest gear
which near or far he could find to give,—
threw away and wasted these weeds of battle,
on men who failed when the foemen came!
Not at all could the king of his comrades-in-arms
venture to vaunt, though the Victory-Wielder,
God, gave him grace that he got revenge
sole with his sword in stress and need.
To rescue his life, 'twas little that I
could serve him in struggle; yet shift I made
(hopeless it seemed) to help my kinsman.
Its strength ever waned, when with weapon I struck
that fatal foe, and the fire less strongly
flowed from its head.—Too few the heroes
in throe of contest that thronged to our king!
Now gift of treasure and girding of sword,
joy of the house and home-delight
shall fail your folk; his freehold-land
every clansman within your kin
shall lose and leave, when lords highborn
hear afar of that flight of yours,
a fameless deed. Yea, death is better
for liegemen all than a life of shame!"

40

That battle-toil bade he at burg to announce,
at the fort on the cliff, where, full of sorrow,
all the morning earls had sat,
daring shieldsmen, in doubt of twain:
would they wail as dead, or welcome home,
their lord belovèd? Little kept back
of the tidings new, but told them all,
the herald that up the headland rode.—
"Now the willing-giver to Weder folk
in death-bed lies, the Lord of Geats
on the slaughter-bed sleeps by the serpent's deed!
And beside him is stretched that slayer-of-men
with knife-wounds sick: no sword availed
on the awesome thing in any wise
to work a wound. There Wiglaf sitteth,
Weohstan's bairn, by Beowulf's side,
the living earl by the other dead,
and heavy of heart a head-watch keeps
o'er friend and foe. . . .

41

. . . "Now haste is best,
that we go to gaze on our Geatish lord,
and bear the bountiful breaker-of-rings
to the funeral pyre. No fragments merely
shall burn with the warrior. Wealth of jewels,
gold untold and gained in terror,
treasure at last with his life obtained,
all of that booty the brands shall take,
fire shall eat it. No earl must carry
memorial jewel. No maiden fair
shall wreathe her neck with noble ring:
nay, sad in spirit and shorn of her gold,
oft shall she pass o'er paths of exile

9. hammers' leaving, what has been left by hammers (a kenning for "swords"). **36. barrier,** guard or protect, as behind a barrier.

Section 41, **9–15. fire . . . revel,** a prophecy that the Geats will be attacked and conquered.

now our lord all laughter has laid aside,
all mirth and revel. Many a spear
morning-cold shall be clasped amain,
lifted aloft; nor shall lilt of harp
those warriors wake; but the wan-hued raven,
fain o'er the fallen, his feast shall praise
and boast to the eagle how bravely he ate
when he and the wolf were wasting the slain."

So he told his sorrowful tidings,
and little he lied, the loyal man
of word or of work. The warriors rose;
sad, they climbed to the Cliff-of-Eagles,
went, welling with tears, the wonder to view.
Found on the sand there, stretched at rest,
their lifeless lord, who had lavished rings
of old upon them. Ending-day
had dawned on the doughty-one; death had seized
in woful slaughter the Weders' king.
There saw they, besides, the strangest being,
loathsome, lying their leader near,
prone on the field. The fiery dragon,
fearful fiend, with flame was scorched.
Reckoned by feet, it was fifty measures
in length as it lay. Aloft erewhile
it had revelled by night, and anon come back,
seeking its den; now in death's sure clutch
it had come to the end of its earth-hall joys.
By it there stood the stoups and jars;
dishes lay there, and dear-decked swords
eaten with rust, as, on earth's lap resting,
a thousand winters they waited there.
For all that heritage huge, that gold
of bygone men, was bound by a spell,
so the treasure-hall could be touched by none
of human kind,—save that Heaven's King,
God himself, might give whom he would,
Helper of Heroes, the hoard to open,—
even such a man as seemed to him meet.

42

. . . Wiglaf spake, the son of Weohstan:—
"At the mandate of one, oft warriors many
sorrow must suffer; and so must we.
The people's-shepherd showed not aught
of care for our counsel, king belovèd!
That guardian of gold he should grapple not, urged we,
but let him lie where he long had been
in his earth-hall waiting the end of the world,
the hest of heaven.—This hoard is ours,
but grievously gotten; too grim the fate
which thither carried our king and lord.
I was within there, and all I viewed,
the chambered treasure, when chance allowed me
(and my path was made in no pleasant wise)
under the earth-wall. Eager, I seized
such heap from the hoard as hands could bear
and hurriedly carried it hither back
to my liege and lord. Alive was he still,
still wielding his wits. The wise old man
spake much in his sorrow, and sent you greetings
and bade that ye build, when he breathed no more,
on the place of his balefire a barrow high,
memorial mighty. Of men was he
worthiest warrior wide earth o'er
the while he had joy of his jewels and burg.
Let us set out in haste now, the second time
to see and search this store of treasure,
these wall-hid wonders,—the way I show you,—
where, gathered near, ye may gaze your fill
at broad-gold and rings. Let the bier, soon made,
be all in order when out we come,
our king and captain to carry thither
—man beloved—where long he shall bide
safe in the shelter of sovran God."
Then the bairn of Weohstan bade command,
hardy chief, to heroes many
that owned their homesteads, hither to bring
firewood from far—o'er the folk they ruled—
for the famed-one's funeral. "Fire shall devour
and wan flames feed on the fearless warrior
who oft stood stout in the iron-shower,
when, sped from the string, a storm of arrows
shot o'er the shield-wall: the shaft held firm,
featly feathered, followed the barb."
And now the sage young son of Weohstan
seven chose of the chieftain's thanes,
the best he found that band within,
and went with these warriors, one of eight,
under hostile roof. In hand one bore
a lighted torch and led the way.
No lots they cast for keeping the hoard
when once the warriors saw it in hall,
altogether without a guardian,
lying there lost. And little they mourned
when they had hastily haled it out,
dear-bought treasure! The dragon they cast,
the worm, o'er the wall for the wave to take,
and surges swallowed that shepherd of gems.
Then the woven gold on a wain was laden—
countless quite!—and the king was borne,
hoary hero, to Hronës-Ness.

51. No lots they cast, that is, they did not stand on ceremony. **59. wain,** wagon. **61. Hronës-Ness,** Whale's Headland.

43

Then fashioned for him the folk of Geats
firm on the earth a funeral-pile,
and hung it with helmets and harness of war
and breastplates bright, as the boon he asked;
and they laid amid it the mighty chieftain,
heroes mourning their master dear.
Then on the hill that hugest of balefires
the warriors wakened. Wood-smoke rose
black over blaze, and blent was the roar,
of flame with weeping (the wind was still),
till the fire had broken the frame of bones,
hot at the heart. In heavy mood
their misery moaned they, their master's death.
Wailing her woe, the widow old,
her hair upbound, for Beowulf's death
sung in her sorrow, and said full oft
she dreaded the doleful days to come,
deaths enow, and doom of battle,
and shame.—The smoke by the sky was devoured.
  The folk of the Weders fashioned there
on the headland a barrow broad and high,
by ocean-farers far descried:
in ten days' time their toil had raised it,
the battle-brave's beacon. Round brands of the pyre
a wall they built, the worthiest ever
that wit could prompt in their wisest men.
They placed in the barrow that precious booty,
the rounds and the rings they had reft erewhile,
hardy heroes, from hoard in cave,—
trusting the ground with treasure of earls,
gold in the earth, where ever it lies
useless to men as of yore it was.
  Then about that barrow the battle-keen rode,
atheling-born, a band of twelve,
lament to make, to mourn their king,
chant their dirge, and their chieftain honor.
They praised his earlship, his acts of prowess
worthily witnessed: and well it is
that men their master-friend mightily laud,
heartily love, when hence he goes
from life in the body forlorn away.

  Thus made their mourning the men of Geatland,
for their hero's passing his hearth-companions:
quoth that of all the kings of earth,
of men he was mildest and most belovèd,
to his kin the kindest, keenest for praise.

14. the widow old. There is no proof that the old woman here referred to is Beowulf's widow, and most scholars do not so identify her. Her wailing may be considered an old woman's counterpart of the dirge chanted by the twelve warriors mentioned in line 36 below.

PART II. THE LATER MIDDLE AGES

The Norman Invasion

DURING the early years of the tenth century, while the heirs of Alfred the Great were consolidating and extending his victories over the Danes in England, a band of Scandinavians had forced the King of France to recognize their ownership of a territory in the northwest of France across the English Channel from Britain. Because the new owners of the territory were Northmen, the territory came to be called Normandy. Its inhabitants, the Normans, mingled freely with the native population, speedily abandoned their own language, and soon became all but indistinguishable from the inhabitants of the neighboring provinces. They retained, however, a fierce, driving energy, and a willingness to take desperate chances. They also kept, or acquired, a passion for order—always provided, however, that the order was of their own choosing. They were, at least nominally, feudal subjects of the French king, but the Norman dukes regarded the feudal bonds between themselves and their subjects with far more veneration than they did those which bound them in allegiance to the king.

How it was possible for Duke William of Normandy in 1066 to conquer with ease a land many times larger and more thickly populated than his own, is hardly indicated in the only contemporary English account of the Norman Conquest in the *Anglo-Saxon Chronicle*. England was disunited, disillusioned, and weary. Canute's empire had fallen to pieces at his death in 1035, and after a period of civil war, a young king, Edward, called the Confessor because of his piety, came to the throne in 1042. But Edward was too much a cleric and too foreign in his sympathies to bring together a stubbornly, even selfishly, individualistic people. There is little reason to doubt that he had encouraged his cousin William of Normandy to consider himself as his favored heir; when Edward died childless in 1066, William, then thirty-nine, was firmly established as ruler of Normandy, influential in the neighboring provinces and regarded with respectful distaste by the King of France. Nevertheless, the members of the Witan (Council of State) who could be brought hastily together did not hesitate to elect Harold Godwinson King of England. Harold's genuine abilities might well have won him the confidence of all England—which held many who remembered all too well his unscrupulous father—had he been free from foreign interference.

While confronted with the threat of Norman invasion in the south, Harold was suddenly called to York to repel a Norwegian attack. His success there was complete, but an unkind sky chose this very moment to give William of Normandy the winds he needed to carry his fleet across the Channel. Without a moment of delay or rest for himself and his men, Harold dashed south to meet this new threat. At the first opportunity he staked his life and his throne on a single battle at Hastings—and lost both. With apparently no more than five thousand men, perhaps two thousand of them mounted knights, of whom many were non-Norman volunteers, William conquered the English people in one pitched battle.

With the perspective of history, the clash of Englishman and Norman at Hastings appears as the last phase of the long struggle between the Norse and the Roman cultures for supremacy in England. Harold, the last of the Saxons, who had conquered the Northmen in battle in Yorkshire, was now slain by the Northmen at Hastings, but by Northmen who had become Europeans, and who invaded England with the blessing of the Pope. Thus, six hundred years after the Romans had left Britain, the island was restored, by the descendants of the Northmen, to the society of European nations.

However liberally or conscientiously William might have been disposed to rule England, the stubbornness of the English drove him to assert his authority in ruthless fashion. In the years after Hastings England was subjected to the most thorough exploitation it had ever known, an exploitation all the more thorough because carried out systematically, legalistically, and by a very few. When William conquered England he took it, literally, as his own. Naturally he could not hold it all in his own hands. He had committed himself to reward his followers, and he did so generously. The entire government of the country was placed in the hands of the Norman nobility, but the Conqueror had no intention of permitting any of his nobles to acquire the independent local authority which he himself possessed in Normandy at the expense of the French king.

The immediate result of the Conquest was the wiping out of the old English ruling class economically, but for some 90 per cent of the population there was merely a change of masters. The overwhelming majority of Englishmen had been serfs, in fact if not in name, and they remained so after the Conquest. There was more exploitation, more resentment, and perhaps less hope, but the basic difference was only in degree.

The most important and far-reaching result socially and governmentally of the Norman Conquest was the establishment on a firm political basis of the feudal system. The feudal relation, that is to say the bond between lord and vassal, by which the lord granted land and protection in return for stipulated services, was the form of social organization throughout Western Europe and Britain during the Middle Ages. The relation existed in England before the coming of the Normans, but under William the system was extended and strengthened and made the agency by which he ruled England. Under this system all the land and all its inhabitants belonged to the king. The king leased the land to individuals among his most prominent nobles, who paid for its use in various ways, chiefly in terms of military service. These noblemen in turn sub-leased their lands to lesser noblemen, from whom they likewise received payment in forms similar to those they rendered the king. To check disintegration and to prevent his vassals and sub-vassals from banding together against him, William forced them individually to swear fealty to himself in person and to be faithful to the king before all other men. Thus was established a great pyramidal structure at the top of which was the king and at the broad base of which was the common people. The whole was cemented together by the sacred obligations of feudal loyalty and homage. And all—king, nobles, and commons together—acknowledged the spiritual overlordship of the Pope as head of western Christendom.

One of William's first steps was to frighten the conquered populace by means of strategically placed and impregnable fortresses, built and maintained by himself or by his trusted lieutenants. Thus the Normans gave England an architectural novelty, the castle. The Anglo-Saxons had learned nothing from the walled Romano-British towns, and their first lessons in artificial defense seem to have been slowly and painfully imparted by the marauding Danes, who had a disconcerting trick of throwing up earthworks to which they could retire in case of temporary defeat. Old English fortifications were singularly shoddy affairs at best, never equaling the great hill forts of the Celtic Iron Age. The typical rectangular Norman keep, built on or around a natural or artificial eminence, with towers at the four corners and one small and well-defended entrance, was something both to surprise the English and to discourage revolt. The Tower of London is one of many such structures that still stand as witnesses to Norman strength. The earlier Norman castles were simple fortresses; it was only gradually that they came to be elaborated by the addition of complicated systems of outworks calculated to permit those within to endure long sieges. Defense kept ahead of offense, and prolonged siege and starvation remained the only effective way to reduce a well-arranged fortress until the use of gunpowder rendered both castles and armor obsolete. Even so, as late as the mid-seventeenth century more than one medieval castle in Royalist hands caused trouble to its Parliamentarian besiegers.

In other than military architecture the Norman Conquest also brought unqualified artistic improvement over what had been before. The rambling nature of the English residence had prevented unity and its wooden materials had prevented permanence. Ecclesiastical architecture had been little better. The Normans were able workers in stone, and the solid structures of their houses and palaces are still standing in many places. Norman cathedrals, with the ornate round arches of the Romanesque style, are still the glory of Durham, Ely, Peterborough, and other English cities.

The Church

The Church was, without exception, the greatest single factor in the medieval world. Every medieval Englishman was a Roman Catholic, since heresy was practically unknown on the island from the time of Pelagius in the fifth century to that of John Wyclif in the fourteenth. The Conquest brought about notable and, for the most part, advantageous changes in the English Church, which was in need of a strong and righteous hand. William found this in Lanfranc, an Italian by birth, whom he named Archbishop of Canterbury. Lanfranc, a man of learning, integrity, and wisdom, was able to adhere firmly to the principles of the Church Universal and still work with William, who was strongly of the belief that he and not the Pope must have practical control of the English Church. The sees of numerous bishops were moved to more populous centers, thus bringing clerical and secular administrators into closer touch. Bishops were excluded from the lay courts, a step which served to strengthen and even extend the authority of the ecclesiastical courts. A comprehensive, if not completely realistic, picture of the duties and functioning of these latter is given by Chaucer in his descriptions of the Summoner on the pilgrimage and the other summoner who is lampooned by the Friar (pages 105 and 108).

The basis of the Church's authority was spiritual in that it and it alone could make clear the path to Heaven, and the Pope was the head of western Christendom. But the Church had more than spiritual power. From the time of Constantine on it had been given great temporal possessions, until the Middle Ages saw the corporate Church infinitely richer and potentially more powerful than any single king or emperor. Under the feudal system, as we have seen, all land belonged to the king and was leased by him to individuals, who paid for its use in various ways. Since church land was no exception to this rule, we find secular authority vested in the persons who administered the lands which the Church held of the king. Consequently the king felt that he had a right, even a duty, to dictate appointments to high church offices, and the lords under the king felt an equal interest in the holders of the lesser ecclesiastical posts. Moreover, because education, or at least literacy, was required in high administrative posts, it was first necessary and later customary for the king to appoint churchmen to fill them, and inevitably many men without true spiritual vocation became bishops or even archbishops because of their practical usefulness to the state.

Under the Normans the monasteries were purged and purified. There was a new emphasis on a knowledge of Latin, and inevitably, of French, and promising Anglo-Norman and English youths were sent to study in Continental schools. The monasteries were enriched, and new monastic orders appeared in England. Notable among these last were the Cistercians, who must be praised for their practical encouragement of sheep-breeding, soon to become the cornerstone of England's economic structure, and for their artistic sense in erecting such abbeys as Tintern, Fountains, and Rievaulx.

The Norman clergy brought with them to England a capacity for organization and the sense of strict discipline which William's contemporary, Pope Gregory VII, had imposed upon the continental Church. Celibacy was enforced among the superior clergy, and strong steps were taken to remove married priests and to prevent those who had not yet wed from embarking upon matrimony. Celibacy, although common among parish priests as early as the third century, was first rigorously applied to those ecclesiastics who were not members of an order by Gregory VII. It is probable that in 1066 most English parish priests were married men, and that there was a marked tendency to treat benefices as hereditary. The inadequacies and imperfections of the parish system were remedied to a great extent by the monasteries, usually rural in location, which cared for many souls otherwise unreached, and for a time after their arrival in the thirteenth century the friars made every effort to minister to the spiritually underprivileged of both city slum and country moor.

The relations between Church and State were on the whole amicable while William the Conqueror and Lanfranc were at their respective helms, but conflicting claims of pope and king arose during the succeeding reigns. Lanfranc's successor, Anselm, was unable in conscience to endure the tyranny of William's son and successor, William Rufus, who deposed him. Henry I, William's youngest son, restored Anselm to his position, but disagreed with him over the lay investiture of clerics. A compromise was reached by which the king technically relinquished all but his purely feudal authority over prelates, although in practice he controlled most clerical elections and customarily received the oath of feudal loyalty before the actual consecration. During the reign of Stephen, the grandson of the Conqueror, despite the political activities of many of the higher ecclesiastics, the Church made notable gains, especially in the establishment of scores of monastic houses. Thousands of men and women in a troubled world sought security and a place to exercise their talents in the peace and useful activity that the cloisters alone could offer.

A desire for restoring order in the land and for curbing a rebellious baronage and a strong Church were the ruling principles of Henry II, grandson of Henry I and great-grandson of the Conqueror. When in 1162 he had the chance to fill the see of Canterbury, he doubtless felt that by promoting his able, congenial, and worldly Chancellor, Thomas Becket, he was giving himself a willing ally in curtailing the powers which the Church had wrung from Stephen. Nothing could have been farther from the truth: Becket acted with the single purpose of defending the rights of the Church and wherever possible, extending them. The result was the drawn-out and undignified feud which ended with Becket's murder in Canterbury Cathedral by some of Henry's knights in 1170. Henry was forced to do penance, but he lost few of the royal powers. The real test of strength between State and Church came in the reign of his son King John, when the Papacy won. Between John's day and the appearance of Wyclif, this general rule held true: a strong king controlled the Church, the Church checked or controlled a weak king.

The Norman Kings

In affairs of state William the Conqueror (1066–1087) consulted his lords at appropriate times and followed their counsel, especially when it coincided with his own judgment. For a century after the Conquest, local justice was administered by means of the traditional hundred (a subdivision of a shire or county) and the shire moot, a deliberative assembly of which all the freemen of a village or town were theoretically members. The feudal system brought with it the lords' (seignorial) courts, which were to be found on every manor, and these gradually took into their own jurisdiction matters previously dealt with by the moots.

William Rufus (1087–1100), son of the Conqueror, suppressed every attempted revolt against his authority. His brother, Henry I (1100–1135), was defied by the great lords, who were still more attached to their Norman estates than to their English ones; but the dogged support of the English and of those lesser lords of Norman blood whose holdings were solely in England enabled him to maintain his prerogative in both England and Normandy. Henry, who desired above all to be on good terms with his English subjects, married a British princess, advanced men of purely English blood, and indeed included them among his councilors. He made use of able clerics to strengthen his administration, and widened the base of his government by consulting not only his official household and the greater lords but also lords of lower degree. The reign of Henry's nephew Stephen (1135–1154) was such a time of anarchy and distress that, as the *Anglo-Saxon Chronicle* laments, "people said commonly that Christ slept, and his saints with him."

The Early Plantagenets

The anarchy of Stephen's reign prepared the people to accept the absolutism of Henry of Anjou, or Henry Plantagenet,[1] who ruled as Henry II from 1154 to 1189. Since Henry was lord of all western France except Brittany, he brought England territorial problems which were to vex her for centuries. Yet his instinct of government and his unflagging energy contrived to give England an efficient and lasting system for the administration of public affairs. He vastly extended the authority and activity of his own court of justice at Westminster, and developed a series of assizes, or sessions of the High Court in each county, to deal with both civil and criminal actions. These assizes were presided over by justices in eyre (traveling justices), who at regular intervals brought royal decisions and royal authority to every part of England. The result was one of incalculable benefit for the social underdog, since it overthrew in large measure the petty tyranny of the manor courts. In many ways Henry diminished the power and importance of the great barons. He destroyed their castles, interfered with their courts of justice, and forbade their coining money. By accepting scutage (shield money) in lieu of service in the field, he lessened their opportunities of training skilled retainers and at the same time acquired funds with which he could hire foreign mercenaries to use as he would. Thus began the destruction of the feudal system which his great-grandfather, the Conqueror, had established in England. But within the administrative system which he established lay the seeds of the forces which were during the next century to limit the absolute power of the kingship which he had built up. Henry's son, Richard I (Cœur-de-Lion), spent only a few months in England during his reign of ten years (1189–1199), but during his absence on the Third Crusade and elsewhere the executive machinery set in motion by his father operated smoothly. There was a steady growth in the principle of election of the men who weighed evidence at the assizes, the forerunners of the jury, and the no less important group whose duty it was to assess, and often to collect, taxes.

Richard's brother John, who has become a byword for viciousness and worthlessness, suffered two humiliating defeats during his reign (1199–1216). His quarrels with his French barons and the French king led to the loss of Normandy. The quarrels between John and his English barons, which had become aggravated as the king's despotic acts became more and more severe, resulted in his enforced signing in 1215 of Magna Carta—the Great Charter. The Great Charter is more important as a symbol than in any other way, but it is the most important symbol in English constitutional history. Though it contains no hint of anything resembling "democracy," its signing was the first step in the long struggle for popular government in England. Most of its provisions merely brought together and expressed in due form and with greater exactness "customs" which had been

[1] Plantagenet was the nickname of Henry's father, Count Geoffrey of Anjou, who had married Matilda, daughter of Henry I. The name, which is applied to all the sovereigns of England from Henry II through Richard II, comes from the sprig of the broom-plant (*planta genista*) which Count Geoffrey used to wear in his hat.

long observed but either not cast into permanent shape or not considered in relation to one another. Its intention was not so much to decrease the king's power as to prevent the king's misuse of that power with respect either to his vassals or to the Church. The king's power to tax was limited, and he was required to summon the lords spiritual and temporal "for the holding of the general council of the kingdom." The importance of some of its articles in the development of the judicial system of England and all English-speaking countries may be seen in such provisions as the following: "No freeman shall be taken or imprisoned, or disseised,[2] or outlawed, or banished . . . unless by the lawful judgment of his peers, or by the law of the land." "We will sell to no man, we will not deny to any man, either justice or right." The Great Charter was repudiated by John, but was later reissued with changes and additions, and succeeding generations by their use and interpretation of it made it in spirit, even if it was not in fact, the guarantee of English liberties.

The Thirteenth Century: The Evolution of Parliament

The civil war which followed John's attempts to evade his commitments in the Great Charter ended in his sudden death in 1216, and his crown, which the outraged barons had offered to the French prince Louis, was eventually settled on the head of his young son, Henry III. The latter was as religious and refined as his father had been vicious. It is to his piety that England owes the erection of Westminster Abbey in its present form. But as a king he was weak and vacillating, and the nation suffered from misgovernment and inefficiency at home and abroad. Foreigners ruled the court and the foreign expenditures of the king increased the burden of taxation. It was in such circumstances that the King's Council began to exert more and more authority and to refuse Henry's requests for subsidies. Attempts, unsuccessful at first, were also made to secure the appointment of administrative officers who should be responsible to the Council. It is this somewhat indefinite group of councilors called the *curia regis*, the King's Court, sitting with his tenants-in-chief and the great barons, both lay and clerical, that in Henry III's reign was first called Parliament. And it is this court or council which through the years and with many changes in form and functions evolved into the Parliament of later English history—the Parliament which has been called the most important institution in the history of modern democracy.

Misgovernment and discontent eventually burst into civil war—the Barons' War (1264)—in which Simon de Montfort, Earl of Leicester, with the support of the lower clergy, the towns, and the universities, defeated the king's forces and took him and his son Edward prisoners. In the following year De Montfort, ruling in the king's name, summoned the Parliament which has made his name famous. To this Parliament he summoned, in addition to the barons, two knights from each shire and two representatives from each chartered borough. At last—and for the first time—all the elements of Parliament were now assembled in a national council. Upon the death of Henry in 1272, his strong son Edward became in name, as he had already become in fact, king of England.

Edward I may be called the first truly national king of England, although it is doubtful whether he could speak a word of English. His greatest service to his country during the thirty-five years of his eventful reign lay in the legislation which he restored, extended, and confirmed. Parliaments were summoned more regularly, and the so-called Model Parliament of 1295, although still not a Parliament in the modern sense of the word, is regarded as having set a precedent for later development and as having marked a turning-point in English constitutional history. Within a generation thereafter, Parliament was to achieve an authority superior to that of the sovereign, as was proved when in 1327 it displaced Edward I's weak son, Edward II, and gave the crown to the latter's son, Edward III. The one useful purpose that Edward III's wars with the French may be said to have served was that, by forcing the king to appeal to Parliament for funds to maintain his armies, they gave Parliament the opportunity to demand concessions from the king in return for grants. Thus gradually the king's powers were shorn away, Parliament assumed the exclusive right of taxation, and more and more the king's ministers became responsible to the representatives of the people. The forty-eight Parliaments which met during the fifty years of Edward III's reign made constitutional progress more speedily than it had ever been made before. In 1399 Edward's son, Richard II, was tried in Parliament and deposed chiefly on the grounds of having asserted absolute sovereignty and thus having transgressed the constitutional rights of the nation.

[2] Dispossessed of land.

Fourteenth-Century England

England in the fourteenth century was profoundly affected by three related series of events: the Hundred Years' War, the Black Death, and the Peasants' Revolt. In 1337 war began between England and France, a war destined to last longer than the hundred years from which it gets its name. We are likely to ascribe its beginning to the claims of Edward III that through his mother, daughter of Philip IV, he was the rightful king of France. The real cause, however, is to be found in the fact that English kings were, as vassals of the French crown, forced to do homage to the French kings for their lands in France. The French cast covetous eyes on the English possessions, made the homage as annoying as possible, and pursued a systematic policy of interfering, legally and otherwise, between the king of England and his French vassals. Edward made war as much to keep what he had, and to regain what he and his predecessors had lost, as to acquire something new.

It was not until 1346 that a decisive engagement was fought at Crécy, where the overwhelming English victory was the result of simple and brilliant strategy. This tactic was to give to a heavy center of well-equipped men at arms two long wings of archers, and when the enemy charged the center, to throw him into confusion with arrows. There was incredible French slaughter at Crécy, and almost incredibly little English loss of life. Ten years later the invincible conservatism of the French permitted the same methods to work again at Poitiers. Between the two great victories, however, England had made little progress.

The inability of the English to take advantage of Crécy was due chiefly to the widespread pestilence which swept Europe in 1348 and 1349. The Black Death, a particularly virulent variety of bubonic plague carried by rats, appeared in Constantinople in 1347 after it had traveled across Asia. Mediterranean traffic picked it up promptly, and by midsummer of 1348 it was raging throughout Western Europe and had broken out in England, where it remained in all its deadly virulence throughout 1349. It is impossible to estimate just how many died, but certainly from one-third to one-half of the population; naturally enough, the heaviest losses were among the poorest classes, who lived in particularly crowded and dirty quarters.

A labor problem immediately arose. One of the most important phenomena of the late thirteenth century and the fourteenth in England had been the gradual and irregular reduction of land-bound serfs and the emergence of a group of landless laborers who worked for wages. With a growing population, as was the case up to 1348, employers were able to get workmen at what seemed to them reasonable rates. In and after 1349 the laborers who survived suddenly found themselves in a position to demand, and they did demand, higher wages. Such subversive action called for remedial steps on the part of the employers (not all nobles by any means), and the Statute of Laborers of 1349 declared it illegal to give and accept wages above the general level of 1346. Valiant efforts were made to enforce the law, but individual employers with work which had to be done did not hesitate to violate it by paying higher wages and even by taking fugitive serfs into their employ as free laborers. Those who were still serfs, and they were many, had their unhappy lot brought even more clearly home to them by the increased prosperity both of their fellows who were free and their more energetic fellows who dared to emancipate themselves by simply fleeing their posts. Then too, despite pious hopes, sometimes expressed in laws, that prices would not rise, a planned economy was by no means feasible, and the standard of living became lower even for those whose wages were increased. By 1381 a very considerable proportion of the lower classes was ripe for mischief, in a state of hopeless misery which made them willing to risk the dangerous and, for England, unprecedented step of a revolt against their betters. The majority of the revolters, however, had no thought of changing the form of government. They considered themselves loyal to the king, though exasperated by his agents, especially those engaged in collecting the highly unpopular poll tax; as it seemed to them, they were merely trying to gain what they saw others possess under the existing order. Nor were they engaged in an antireligious or heretical movement. They hated and attacked certain ecclesiastics, but only as landowners and government officials.

The Peasants' Revolt was one of those rare revolutions born of the desperation of the abjectly poor rather than of the dissatisfaction of a considerable group of the well-to-do. This very flouting of tradition, which made the initial attitude of the gentry one of pained incredulity, was probably largely responsible for the early success of the insurrection. The revolt was ended by a masterly stroke of royal treachery when the young king, Richard II, promised to be the rebels' leader, without specifying the direction in which he would lead them; the violent but rather aimless life of the insurrection was shortly buried under the corpses of a few hundreds of its participants. The uprising had little genuine effect on the gradual process of the freeing of the serfs; if anything, it retarded the movement when it reinforced by fear the natural suspicion which the ruling classes felt for innovation.

A revolt of another nature, perhaps not altogether unconnected with the general upheaval and social unrest caused by the ravages of the Black Death, was that led by John Wyclif, the most radical and controversial religious figure of the century. Wyclif (*c.* 1320–1384), a Yorkshireman and an Oxford scholar, was in his earlier career an eminently successful Scholastic philosopher and theologian, and an orthodox and honored member of the Church. Gradually, however, he came to doubt and then to attack certain features of the ecclesiastical system of his day, from administrative matters to those purely theological. He associated himself with the anticlerical elements in the nation, and by 1374 he was asserting that the lay power as represented by the king should have authority over the Church, as represented by the Pope. His theory that Church property should be subject to civil princes brought him the favor of John of Gaunt, Duke of Lancaster, a son of Edward III, and the most powerful lord in England. This theory caused Wyclif to be tried by the Archbishop of Canterbury and the Bishop of London, but on this occasion his propositions were declared not so much erroneous as ill-sounding. Wyclif also declared that the Church was made corrupt by too many possessions, and that it was wrong for the clergy to meddle in worldly affairs. He attacked the ignorance and laziness of the clergy, both high and low, and of the far too wealthy monks. It was not, however, until he attacked the doctrine of transubstantiation in 1380 that he was condemned as a heretic by the Church. At no time did Wyclif consider himself outside the Church; rather, he conceived it his duty to purge the Church of those elements and teachings which were not validated by a fairly literal interpretation of the Bible. His views (not all expressed at one time or in one book) made Wyclif a marked man. They aroused both anger and fear in bishops and monks, but the friendship of John of Gaunt and the court freed him from several attempted ecclesiastical trials, and permitted him to live out his life personally unmolested at a time when his followers, known as the Lollards, were being brought severely to book.

Wyclif's sermons at Oxford and London and the preaching of the "Poor Priests," an itinerant order that he founded, carried to the people the doctrine that the Scriptures, rather than the Church, are the supreme authority, and are independent of ecclesiastical sacraments and systems. At home Wyclif's followers flourished for only a brief period. Kings as well as bishops came to recognize the danger to their power that the spread of Lollardry would bring, and it was suppressed by Henry V about 1414. Historically, however, the Lollards can be seen as forerunners of the Protestant reformers of the sixteenth century both in England and on the Continent, where Wyclif's teachings influenced John Huss in Bohemia and through him Martin Luther and others.

Most of Wyclif's writings are in Latin, and it is through the English translation of the Bible called after his name that he is connected with English literature. It is certain that Wyclif inspired and probably supervised the first complete rendering into English of the Bible, but there is no evidence that any of the actual translation is his. The so-called Wycliffite or Lollard Bible (page 49) has come down to us in two versions. The first is a fairly literal translation of the Vulgate (St. Jerome's Latin version of the Hebrew Old Testament and the Greek New Testament); the second contains glosses and interpretations, some of which the Church regards as heretical.

The Towns and the Trade Guilds

While these far-reaching changes were occurring in the fabric of the political, ecclesiastical, and social systems, an important economic development—that of the free towns and of the merchant class—was taking place. The emergence of the free townsmen, the middle class, as an influential group is indicated in the provisions of the Great Charter of 1215. The towns were secured by the Charter in their newly bought privileges, and the growing importance of trade is illustrated in the steps taken by the authors of the Charter to protect the interests of the merchants. The two most important factors in the growth of an English town were the freeing of the municipality from any feudal obligation save to the central government, and the close organization of the merchants and craftsmen into fraternities called guilds. We have noticed that Henry I in the twelfth century effectually began the destruction of the feudal system by accepting shield money from his vassals in lieu of service in the field, and further steps toward freedom from feudal obligations were made as men became able to anticipate a demand for services by means of the use of coins. The growth of trade brought money to the traders. Commerce drew together those who benefited from it and taught them first the use and then the power of common action. The towns soon found that they could buy privileges from their lords by taking advantage of inertia, inability, or financial weakness.

The sense of unity in the urban middle class found practical expression in three types of guilds. There was the merchants' guild, in which all the important merchants of a town pooled their resources in order to further their interests as citizens and men of business. Then there were the craft or trade guilds, in which the followers of various occupations—brewers, bakers, hatmakers, watercarriers, goldsmiths—joined to maintain standards of income and good workmanship. Finally, there were those guilds which cut across craft and even class lines to improve the religious and social lives of their members. Every layman of importance in a town was an active member of a guild, with the result that municipal government was guild government.

By all modern standards medieval London was a small city indeed. At the end of Edward III's reign (1377) it is estimated to have held some 45,000 out of the country's total population of 2,500,000. The next largest city, York, had less than 8,000. Norman London was a walled city, but most of the houses were small, mean, and inflammable. The fourteenth century saw buildings of as many as three stories, but seldom more. The streets were narrow, often crooked, and the houses themselves were not always in regular order. Residential sections being unknown, the ground floor of almost every dwelling was a shop or a small manufactory. The noise and the confusion in the crowded shopping sections were overwhelming. Sidewalks were nonexistent, there was no paving, and the open gutters, which also served as sewers, did little more than make mud and mire general.

On holidays, boys and young men, apprentices and all, raced horses, matched cocks, and played football. Songs were sung and stories were told by professional minstrels and amateurs; there was dancing in the open places of the city and in the fields. There were wrestling matches and bouts with quarter-staves, and bears and bulls were baited with dogs. Night life was practically nonexistent, and what little there was caused the authorities and all proper people to be extremely anxious to eliminate it. Lack of lighting made the streets, bad enough by day, totally unsafe at night, and indeed it was the general custom of our ancestors, great and small, to rise before dawn and retire shortly after sunset.

Education

There had been formal education of a sort and for the very few in England ever since the conversion of the island to Christianity. Aelfric's Latin *Colloquy* pictures daily life in a monastic school of the tenth century. The *Colloquy* was intended to teach English boys to speak Latin and had the highly practical purpose of acquainting the boys with the roles which their elders were performing in everyday life. Similar schools were attached to cathedrals, and parish and chantry priests gave elementary instruction in song schools such as that referred to in Chaucer's *Prioress's Tale* (page 121). Grammar schools emphasized reading, writing, and speaking Latin.

The Norman Conquest, as we have seen, brought to England notable scholars such as Lanfranc and his pupil and successor Anselm from the Abbey of Bec, and from European universities came other scholars and ecclesiastics who cultivated the Latin tongue. The monasteries were filled with English youths who devoted themselves to the scholar's life. Higher education was, on the whole, scantily represented in England before the close of the twelfth century, but English scholars went freely to Continental universities, such as Paris and Bologna, since the universality of Latin made education completely international.

Both of the great universities, Oxford and Cambridge, have their origins in the twelfth century in the schools of monks and the groups which were attracted to religious scholars and teachers. Oxford, the oldest institution of higher learning in England, emerged about 1170 as the result of a mass migration of English scholars and students from Paris. At first the organization of the university was loose. Gradually, however, the students came to live together in halls, each with a principal, usually a Master of Arts, and with expenses paid out of a common fund to which all contributed. Although there was nothing which resembled any kind of uniformity, students would seem to have started their university career at fourteen or fifteen. The Bachelor of Arts degree followed upon four years' devotion to the seven liberal arts, divided into the elementary trivium (grammar, rhetoric, and logic), partly anticipated in the grammar schools, and the more advanced quadrivium (arithmetic, geometry, music, and astronomy). The Master of Arts degree required three or four more years and the degree of Doctor of Divinity perhaps another twelve. As early as 1250 every student was obliged to be under one special master from whom he was to receive daily instruction, but discipline was difficult to maintain. The students, lacking the restraint of today, were an unruly lot; their quarrels among themselves and the townsmen often resulted in riots and even murder.

Discipline and order came with the regularly endowed colleges, of which the first was Merton, established after 1263, with a warden and twenty students who received all their expenses and some pocket money. The elaborate rules included silence at meals, save for one student who read edifying works aloud. The first attempt to co-ordinate school and university education was the establishment of a secondary school at Winchester (the first English "public" school), from which students proceeded after the age of fifteen to New College, which had been founded to receive seventy of them at Oxford. Some were to study civil or canon law, a few medicine or astronomy, and the rest arts or divinity. At its height Oxford had perhaps three thousand students, the majority preparing for a place in the Church. They came, for the most part, from the middle class, since the sons of the very poor rarely received even elementary schooling and the sons of the nobility were trained for other things in other ways and were usually no more than barely literate. Chaucer makes clear the difference between the Squire, who was educated in the hall, in the bower, and on the jousting field, and the Clerk of Oxford (page 101).

Few medieval studies have the horrifying fascination for modern times that medicine does. Popular medicine was partly superstition and partly a practical utilization of common herbs, mainly of a purgative effect, an admirable example of which is afforded by Pertelote's advice to her husband (page 126). The surgeon was only an ill-esteemed bloodletter, bone-setter, tooth-puller, and barber. The educated physician was almost too well read in classical, Arabic, and contemporary authorities. Chaucer's Doctor of Physic (page 103) is a prime specimen. Medieval physicians often meant well; some of them showed great heroism in time of pestilence, even though their most portentous utterances have the odor of quackery. But the Middle Ages saw the beginning of experimental science in such figures as the misunderstood, persecuted, and silenced scholar, Roger Bacon (*c.* 1214–1294), who denounced authority and insisted on the validity of observation. And modern chemistry owes its start to the alchemists, who experimented tirelessly in search of the unattainable.

The Fifteenth Century

The fifteenth century saw the prolonged death struggle of the medieval period. On the whole the century was one of retrogression and decay. War and pestilence ravaged the land, and the social, intellectual, and religious energies of the nation suffered a profound eclipse. In the early years of the century Henry V, who had inherited from his father, Henry IV, the first monarch of the House of Lancaster, a firmly established throne, was an able and popular ruler and brilliant warrior. He gave England a brief period of renewed military glory, but his French conquests were wiped out during the reign of his son, Henry VI, who came to the throne as an infant of nine months and whose mind and body broke under the strain of kingship. The ideals of chivalry had languished, and the armor of the knights was not sufficient to withstand the shots from the long-bows of yeomen. Joan of Arc, the Maid of Orleans, who led the French to victory over the English soldiers in 1429, has been called the last of the knights. After the middle of the century, chivalry, where it survived at all, was mere play-acting and literary reminiscence; see the introduction to the selections from Sir Thomas Malory (page 148). The Church, suffering from the devastating effects of the Great Schism, the forty-year struggle between rival popes, was not sufficiently alarmed by the ominous outbursts of heresy in England and Bohemia to amend its ways, and, in the main, it continued in corrupt and contented indolence, ripe for Reformation and Counter-Reformation.

Once more there was a period of virtual anarchy as the royal princes struggled for control of the government. The dynastic feud culminated in the Wars of the Roses (1459–1485), in which the royal House of Lancaster (with its symbol of the red rose) fought a losing battle against the rival claimants of the House of York (the white rose). The civil strife continued intermittently under the Yorkist kings, Edward IV and his brother, Richard III, until the latter was slain in battle in 1485 by Henry Tudor, Earl of Richmond. Henry, the last surviving heir of the House of Lancaster, had been assisted in overthrowing Richard by disaffected Yorkists upon his promise to wed the Princess Elizabeth, daughter of Edward IV. He was proclaimed king as Henry VII, and in the royal marriage the Houses of Lancaster and York were united. The aristocracy was almost completely wiped out during the long period of dynastic struggle, and most of the noble families that survived were impoverished. A few wealthy peers remained to exert power greater even than that of the king until Henry's strong hand suppressed them.

The picture of fifteenth-century England is, however, not one of unrelieved darkness. The machinery of government and justice, although at times interfered with, continued to function. Although elections were often manipulated, Parliaments continued to be summoned and in general controlled the public purse-strings, no matter who was king. The wars, foreign and domestic, interfered with trade and commerce, and pirates infested the seas; nevertheless the burgess class, as a whole, increased in wealth and authority. Throughout the shires, too, many of the country families, well-to-do non-noble landholders like Chaucer's Franklin (page 101) of the previous century, prospered and somehow managed to keep aloof from the bloody wars. Such a family is the Pastons of Norfolk, whose habit of hoarding every scrap of paper with writing on it has left us an invaluable picture of fifteenth-century England. Their sons went to the university, their womenfolk were literate, and members of the family owned books and employed scribes.

Nor did culture and the arts languish entirely. Henry VI founded the grammar school of Eton and built King's College Chapel at Cambridge. The latter is one of the finest examples of Perpendicular Gothic, an exclusively English style, of which the great glory is the fan tracery vaulting. If the art of stone-carving had passed its peak, that of wood-carving reached perhaps its greatest perfection at this time. The impulse that had led to the erection of the great Gothic cathedrals and splendid abbeys had gone, but in spite of the increase in materialism, which characterized the age, the building of churches continued unabated. The beautiful Lady Chapel of Ely and the great central tower of Canterbury Cathedral are among the contributions of the time to ecclesiastical architecture.

In the last quarter of the century events were taking place which were to have tremendous significance for the intellectual life of England. In 1476, in the reign of Edward IV, William Caxton (page 149) set up the first printing press in England at Westminster. During the next two decades the influence of the new classical Renaissance was to reach Oxford from Italy. Thus the great movement called Humanism, which grew out of the new interest in ancient Greek literature, enabled English scholars of the late fifteenth century to discover the intellectual and cultural world of the classical writers at the same time Columbus and Cabot were discovering new areas of the physical world. The earlier English Humanists, men who had studied in Italy and been associated with Italian scholars, were chiefly collectors of manuscripts. They were few in number and their influence was slight because they made no systematic effort to pass their learning on to others. In 1487 the physician Thomas Linacre went to Italy where he stayed twelve years, and with his return English Humanism passed from sterile acquisition to active transmission when it entered the teaching phase. The Humanists in England were all reformers, and the spirit of the movement manifested itself in new educational and religious policies, in the establishment of schools, and in a general quickening of the intellectual and moral life of the nation.

Before the century ended, Greek was being taught at Oxford, the center of humanistic studies. Here gathered an incomparable group of scholars including Linacre, the teacher of Erasmus and the founder of the Royal College of Physicians; John Colet, the founder of St. Paul's School, who introduced studies in the Greek New Testament to Oxford; and the learned and saintly Sir Thomas More. The New Learning, aided and disseminated by the newly established printing press, became an incalculably great influence in the fostering of Elizabethan culture and literature. Just as the Christian introduction of writing into England made possible the preservation of what had hitherto been an oral, and thus ultimately an ephemeral, literature, so the introduction of printing made books—previously few in number, uncertain in quality, and too costly for many to obtain—available to the general run of men. The printing press was to become the most important single factor in the making of the modern world, although unfortunately gunpowder, the use of which first became general in the fifteenth century, claims a close second place.

Middle English Literature

Literary activity in English after the Norman Conquest fell for a time to almost nothing. The change in masters put secular and spiritual rule into the hands of men who, having Norman-French as a native tongue and Latin as an acquired tongue, could have no use for English. The vernacular English educational system was destroyed. The bulk of the people continued to speak English, many of the newcomers acquired a working knowledge of their subjects' tongue, but it was well-nigh a century and a half before English was again taken seriously as a vehicle for literary expression. There is little evidence of composition in Anglo-French during the first years after the Conquest, but gradually we find an increasing number of works in that dialect, none really distinguished. The outstanding works of the twelfth century were produced by Englishmen who wrote in Latin. Among these authors were Geoffrey of Monmouth, the first comprehensive "historian" of Britain and of King Arthur (page 54), and Nigellus Wireker, a poet and humorous satirist.

The second half of the twelfth century, however, saw the shy emergence of original compositions in English, two of which proved not only that English was a fit medium for extensive works of true genius, but that the Old English literary tradition had, in some measure, continued to live underground. A poem of almost uniformly high literary quality, with many exalted and moving passages, is the *Brut* of Lawman (called also Layamon) who took his material from Wace, a Norman poet, who in his turn had put Geoffrey of Monmouth's *Histories of the Kings of Britain* into Norman French verse. Lawman's verse is principally a modification of the Old English alliterative line, but rhyme and assonance are also found. The language is almost purely English, with few traces of French influence. The best pieces of English in the thirteenth century are the secular and religious lyrics (page 51), which show metrical skill and virtuosity, combined with amorous and religious emotion. From a manuscript of this period comes also the oldest known popular ballad, although the bulk of medieval ballads now extant comes from the fourteenth and fifteenth centuries (page 135). Metrical romances, which had begun in the twelfth century, dealing with themes that were to be popular in later romances (page 53) were developed. *King Horn*, one of the earliest of Middle English romances, holds its own with the best of the later ones. The best prose of the century is the *Ancren Riwle* (*The Rule for Anchoresses*), a manual (rule) for the guidance of ladies who have retired from the world.

Middle English literature reached a pinnacle in the fourteenth century, the "Age of Chaucer." To the great poet who dominated his era we shall make only a passing reference here. Of the poetic compositions of Chaucer's day the most important after his own contributions are the romances (page 53). The majority of the Middle English romances that have survived belong to the fourteenth century, and among these perhaps the most noteworthy are a group composed after 1350 in alliterative verse. The meter is considerably less regular than that employed by the Old English poets, and there is a large proportion of words of French origin; still, we have here undeniable evidence that the pre-Conquest poetic tradition had not died, but was preserved by the people in their orally transmitted compositions until a group of gifted literary artists saw fit to adopt it. All the alliterative romances (by unknown authors) are united by a vigorous style, acute observation of nature, realistic description of action, and occasional passages of quiet but genuine humor. By far the best is *Sir Gawain and the Green Knight* (page 54).

The tribulation, disorder, and inequalities of the fourteenth century produced a literature of social complaint and satire. There are many documents of this kind, the greatest of which is *Piers Plowman* (page 86), although *Piers Plowman* contains more than satire. It was with a poem of this nature that the most distinguished of Chaucer's contemporaries, John Gower, began his literary career. In a French poem of nearly thirty thousand lines, the *Mirour de l'Omme* (*Mirror of Man*), written before 1377, Gower describes the genealogy and nature of the Seven Deadly Sins (Pride, Envy, Wrath, Sloth, Avarice, Gluttony, and Lust) and the corresponding Virtues. He then enumerates the various categories and classes of mankind, from the Pope to the peasant, and takes them to task for their wickedness. This last section contains good satire and a vivid, if depressing, picture of contemporary life. The same can be said for portions of his ten-thousand-line Latin poem, *Vox Clamantis* (*The Voice of One Crying*—in the wilderness), although the major interest of that work lies in its revelation of the impression the Peasants' Revolt made on an observant and somewhat judicious man of property and position. He allegorizes the rebels as monstrous and ferocious beasts, can say no good of them or their motives, and ends by counseling repressive measures.

It was as a neat and accomplished story-teller that Gower finally found his proper function as a poet and man of letters. The short story in verse is a literary form which may be said to have reached its highest level in the fourteenth century. The chief practitioner of the form is Chaucer, but we must not fail to pay tribute to Gower and to his *Confessio Amantis* (*The Lover's Confession*). Like Chaucer's *Canterbury Tales* (page 97), the *Confessio Amantis* is a frame-story, but unlike the *Canterbury Tales* it was completed; it runs to more than 33,000 lines of octosyllabic couplets of an almost excessive regularity. Many of the tales are the equal of anything of the sort in Middle English outside of Chaucer. Gower emphasizes the plots of his stories and, generally speaking, omits those details of description and characterization which make Chaucer's narratives particularly alive and real. Gower at times gives evidence of a slight sense of humor, but his general inability to view any situation other than seriously makes specially fitting the epithet "moral Gower" which Chaucer applies to him at the end of *Troilus and Criseyde*, a poem he addressed to Gower. And, finally, although Gower draws his plots from numerous ancient and medieval stories, none of them deals with contemporary England.

We can make the same contrast between Chaucer's *Canterbury Tales* and the anonymous romances, with the exception of *Gamelyn*. However good their stories, the romances almost never give an identifying touch of ordinary contemporary life. Medieval narratives in general, if we except some of the chivalric elements—and medieval chivalry would seem often to have sprung from literature rather than to have inspired it—are almost purely a literature of escape. They are stories of other times and other lands; the characters are almost without exception kings and nobles; little attention is paid to the middle class and none, save for an occasional abusive reference, to the lower class; supernatural creatures and events abound; the way of life, the buildings, the food, and the attire are usually so splendid as to have no relation to reality. There is little or nothing in the bulk of medieval fiction to remind a reader or a listener of that time of the world in which he lived. If his existence was hard, if his surroundings were sordid, if his future was dark, the romances opened the door to a world in which he could find temporary relief from his cares and fears.

In Chaucer, to be sure, we find gods and goddesses, kings and queens, lords and ladies, scenes in Troy and Athens and Tartary, palaces, feasts, magic, and the lure of the unknown. But we find more than that; we find side by side with the customary paraphernalia of romance carefully drawn pictures of the commonplace England about him. We must not expect the exact, often depressing, realism of some present-day writers, although it sometimes appears. Chaucer was an artist. He realized and exploited the emotional appeal of recognizable details. Chaucer makes us say not, "I wish that I could see, or do, something like that," but "Why, of course, that's exactly what must have happened." Chaucer was a middle-class man who spent most of his life in close association with the nobility. He wrote for the upper and middle classes, and it would almost seem that he was the first to understand that the English nobles, unlike their Continental counterparts, were becoming essentially middle-class in thought and reaction. Chaucer won the favor of all Englishmen to whom circumstances gave a right to an opinion by presenting them, among other things, with a series of pictures from the middle- (often the lower-middle) class England of their day. Chaucer was a consummate story-teller, but when we think back on his tales after an interval the passages which are most vivid are likely to be those in which the plot does not progress so much as receive substance from characterization and setting.

The religious drama of the Middle Ages played an important role in bringing about what we may term a sense of national literary unity. Developed by the Church, the miracle plays (often called "mystery plays" or "mysteries"), which altogether gave a roughly consecutive picture of Biblical history from the Fall of Lucifer to the Last Judgment, were taken over by the guilds. Each had its wagon (pageant) which could be moved from place to place. A "pageant" was a box-shaped structure on wheels in the interior of which the actors could remain when not playing. The flat, railed-in roof, which afforded an upper stage, was reached by a trap door; there was another door in one of the sides of the pageant. A number of low platforms were erected in the roomier streets or squares of the town; these were the stations at which the plays were performed. At dawn of the appointed day the first pageant, that of the Fall of Lucifer, would lumber up to the first station, perhaps just inside the west gate. There, using the platform for a lower stage and the roof for an upper one, the play was put on for the benefit of the crowd which packed the street and filled the windows of the surrounding houses. When the performance was over the pageant moved on to the next station and a new audience; the second pageant, that of the Creation, took its place. Soon there was a pageant at each station all the way across the city; by staying in one place all day long a person could see the entire cycle, sometimes consisting of nearly fifty plays.

The actors were at first ordinary members of the guilds, and though in time it was recognized that a certain amount of histrionic ability was advisable for the leading roles, nothing like a caste of professional actors was ever developed. It was a cross section of England which saw the plays; king and nobles, churchmen of all ranks, citizens and countrymen, rich men and poor men, beggarmen and thieves—all were there, and all were on that common level which is an audience.

Just as the miracle plays dramatized the Bible, so the moralities dramatized allegorical literature.

The morality, it is often said, seeks to answer the question "What must I do to be saved?" In the typical morality there is a neutral figure, who represents Man, for whom Vices and Virtues contend with word and action. At the beginning of the play the hero is good, surrounded by and obeying the Virtues. After a few years, however, the Vices appear and make him their all too willing captive while the Virtues look on in helpless sorrow. Often there is a temporary return to proper behavior, but the Vices prevail once more, and it is only when Death approaches that Man finally turns back to good. Sometimes, as a matter of fact, he does not turn back at all, and is carried to Hell. *Everyman*, the best and best known of the genre, gives only the last portion of the typical plot.

In the history of fourteenth-century prose two names stand out—those of Richard Rolle of Hampole (*c.* 1300—*c.* 1349) and John Wyclif, both religious writers and both Yorkshiremen. Rolle ("Richard Hermit," as he was called) was a mystic who composed both in verse and prose some of the most beautiful devotional pieces in the language. His book of *Meditations on the Passion* is as admirable for the conciseness and clarity of its prose as for its spiritual qualities. Rolle also translated and paraphrased the Psalms of the Old Testament, and his rules for translation suggest those which seem to have guided Wyclif and his collaborators a half-century later. The Wycliffite Bible, of which mention has been made, may not be Wyclif's, but the spirit of the work is his. This first complete rendering of the Bible into English is of great importance as being at the fountainhead of the tradition which was to guide most of the later English translators of the Scriptures—that of using simple, direct, and familiar English words. Both Rolle and Wyclif showed, as no prose writer before them had, the effectiveness of simple, everyday English words in expressing the noblest thoughts. The English of Wyclif's Bible is often awkward and chaotic, and the construction is often more Latin than English, but there are many touches of genius and felicity. In reading his translation of St. Luke's account of the birth of Christ, one comes with pleasure upon the "multitude of heavenly knighthood," and "men of good will." The translators of the King James version of the Bible more than two centuries later were to be indebted to Wyclif for many phrases, including his happy rendering of the Vulgate's phrase *profunda Dei*, "the deep things of God" (I Corinthians 2:10). Since the Wycliffite version was widely known and used, it may safely be given credit for having helped greatly in the development of English prose as a serviceable and beautiful means of expression.

With Chaucer's death in 1400 English poetry entered a period of decline from which it was not to emerge for more than a century. Men like Hoccleve and Lydgate wrote voluminously, praised Chaucer, and considered themselves, however unworthy, his disciples; but their works, although often interesting and even significant in subject matter, exhibit no trace of literary taste or skill. While the Scottish followers of Chaucer, such as Henryson, Dunbar, and Gavin Douglas, show much greater ability, their use of the Northern dialect kept them out of the direct stream of English literature; except for Henryson, their best work was done in the sixteenth century.

The fifteenth century is the only period in English literature in which prose excelled the best compositions of the poets. The masterpiece of fifteenth-century prose is the product of a soldier rather than of a man of letters—the *Morte Darthur* of Sir Thomas Malory (page 149). We probably owe our knowledge of it to the fact that it was printed by Caxton, the first English printer and himself a merchant adventurer before he was a literary man. The *Morte Darthur* is the most significant work that had yet been composed in English prose, and more than any other author Malory forms a link between Chaucer and Spenser. The chief contribution of the fifteenth century to English literature is, therefore, its development of English prose, and a contribution perhaps greater than any other century made to that development.

There was at last, despite the continued existence of local dialects, one standard language for all England—the Midland dialect of London and the Thames Valley. This was the dialect in which Chaucer wrote and in which Malory and Caxton composed their works a century later. The speech of the capital would inevitably have become standard even without such writers. It was the printer Caxton who, by the products of his press, effectually sealed the triumph of Midland English as the standard for the future. There was still, however, a long period of evolution ahead. In the preface to his translation of a French romance, the *Eneydos*, Caxton confides to the reader some of the difficulties presented to a writer by the constant changes in the language and the varying dialects. When on one bank of the Thames a hungry man must ask for *egges* and on the other for *eyren*, what is a writer to do? It is largely to Caxton that we owe the fact that English-speaking people throughout the world today have *eggs* rather than *eyers* for breakfast! By the end of the century the English language had rid itself of most of the inflectional endings, and by extensive borrowings from Latin, French, and Scandinavian had become a worthy vehicle for the most elevated literary expression.

Summary

The thousand years that lay between the Anglo-Saxon invasion of England and the accession of Henry VII in 1485 had seen the inhabitants of the island welded into one nation. The scattered and unorganized warrior bands of the mid-fifth century had united to form a people cohesive and rugged enough to absorb many Britons and to assimilate successive waves of Danish and Norman invaders. Under the stimulus of the Norman sense of order, loose and largely personal codes of law and government had been systematized and centralized until there was a firm machinery capable of ruling the land and administering justice. The feudal system had come and gone; slavery had vanished, and most of the former serfs had become copyhold tenants as the older system of personal service to the lord had been commuted into service for money.

For the old folk moot and witenagemot (council of wise men) a Parliament had been substituted which represented the burgesses and the country gentry as well as the nobles and the churchmen. The people, acting as a whole, had known how to curb bad rulers, but it had also learned by sad experience that despotism was preferable to anarchy. England had lost all its Continental holdings and its pride lay now in those things which were distinctively English. The old distaste for town life had vanished, commerce and manufacture had steadily increased, and these things, coupled with the growing feeling that the sea, especially the "narrow sea," was peculiarly an English possession, were starting England along the road which was to make it for a time the richest nation on earth.

England now had one people, one law, and one language; even more than that, it had a strength not yet fully tested, an exuberance almost of youth, a vigor and an ambition that were to carry the people and the language to the four quarters of the globe. Seven years after Henry VII came to the throne a New World was discovered across the ocean, and that discovery was destined to influence and direct English action, thought, and literature until the present day.

Middle English Pronunciation

The student who wishes to get most satisfaction from the Middle English lyrics and the poetry of Chaucer in this section, must be willing to take the trouble to learn to pronounce the language in an approximately correct fashion. Study of the following table and practice in reading aloud should soon give a reasonable facility. The beginner will doubtless be forgiven if, unlike Chaucer, he does not make a careful distinction between open and close ē and ō.

VOWELS AND DIPHTHONGS

SOUND	PRONUNCIATION	SPELLING	EXAMPLES
ā	like *a* in *father*	a, aa	ale, caas
a	like *a* in *lagoon*	a	that, pace (vb.)
ē (close)	like *a* in *date*	e, ee	slepen, sweete
ę̄ (open)	like *e* in *there*	e, ee	ever, heeth
e	like *e* in *set*	e	tendre
e (final unstressed)	like *a* in *China*	e	soote, roote
ī, ȳ	like *i* in *machine*	i, y	shires, tyme
i, y	like *i* in *pit*	i, y	priketh, nyght
ō (close)	like *o* in *note*	o, oo	bote, roote
ǭ (open)	like *oa* in *broad*	o, oo	cold, rood (vb.)
o	like *o* in *lot*	o	holt
ū	like *oo* in *boot*	ou, ow	hous, fowles
u	like *u* in *full*	u, o	but, sonne
iū	like *u* in *mute*	u, ew	vertu, Pruce, trewe
ēi	like ę̄ (open) + i	ai, ay, ei, ey	batailles, sayle, feith, wey

au	like *ou* in *mouse*	au, aw	draughte, sawe
ēu	like ē (close) + u	eu, ew	reule, knew
ę̄u	like ę̄ (open) + u	eu, ew	lewed
oi	like *oy* in *boy*	oi, oy	poison, joye
ōu	like *ow* in *know*	ou, ow	soule, growe

CONSONANTS

The pronunciation of Middle English consonants is much the same as in modern English. Certain points, however, must be kept in mind. Consonants were sounded which have become "silent" in modern English, such as the *k* in *knyght* and *knowe*, the *g* in *gnawe*, the *w* in *wrighte*, the *l* in *folk* and *palmeres* and the like. Double consonants were given their full value; thus *son-ne* (sun) is quite distinct from *so-ne* (son).

SOUND	PRONUNCIATION	EXAMPLES
c before back vowels (a, o, u)	like *k*	caas, corages, curs
c before front vowels (e, i, y)	like *s*	certes, citole
ch	like *tch*	chapman, charge
gg (except in words like "frogges" and "legges")	like *dg* in *bridge*	juggen, brigge
h (medial and final, written gh, after back vowels)	like *ch* in German *doch*	foghtren, though
h (medial and final, written gh, after front vowels)	like *ch* in German *ich*	knyght
ng	like *ng* in *finger*	thing
r	strongly trilled	
s (except as below)	like *s* in *sand*	
s (between two vowels)	like *s* in *those*	
th (except as below)	like *th* in *thin*	
th (between two vowels)	like *th* in *those*	

Middle English Lyrics

The Middle English lyric, as illustrated here, did not spring directly from anything to be found in Old English literature. Certain Old English poems are often called lyrics, but the reference is not to the form, but rather to the elegiac tone, to the prevailingly subjective melancholy of content. Even here we miss the outstanding theme of lyric poetry—romantic love, the love of courtship. Lyrics readily recognizable to us did not appear in England until after the Norman Conquest, and an analysis of style, metrics, and subject matter shows the strong influence of compositions in Latin, Provençal, and French. Although we know that English lyrics, secular as well as religious, were being sung in the twelfth century, only fragments survive from the period before 1200. The great majority of the extant Middle English lyrics are religious, but while many of these are extremely good, the fewer secular, usually amorous, lyrics are of higher artistic quality.

The lyrics make a more immediate appeal to us than do most medieval poems, and that despite the frequent difficulty of the language. Translations spoil the meter or the sense, and frequently both. We respond readily to the lilting melody, the images and figures taken from nature, the prevailing atmosphere of spring and youth. We may feel, perhaps, as we read more widely, that too many of the lovers are unsuccessful, and that they celebrate their misfortunes rather too freely in histrionic lovesick wailing, but here we have part of the conventions of courtly love. One wonders just how effective this approach has ever been to the female heart, and perhaps we can afford to conclude that it is a literary, rather than a practical, device.

The first two lyrics given here are reprinted from Carleton Brown's *English Lyrics of the XIIIth Century*, Oxford Press, 1932, and the last two are from his *Religious Lyrics of the XVth Century*, Oxford, 1939.

THE CUCKOO SONG

"The Cuckoo Song" is the best-known Middle English lyric, and probably familiarity has given it a fame beyond its intrinsic merit. We must admit, however, that it has the freshness of youth, as well as spring, and a realism not always appreciated by its readers. The music to which the words were sung is extant and constitutes one of the oldest secular tunes known.

Sumer is icumen in,
Lhude sing cuccu!
Groweth sed and bloweth med
And springth the wode nu.
Sing cuccu!

Awe bleteth after lomb,
Lhouth after calve cu,
Bulluc sterteth, bucke verteth.
Murie sing cuccu!
Cuccu, cuccu,
Wel singes thu, cuccu.
Ne swik thu naver nu!

Sing cuccu nu, Sing cuccu!
Sing cuccu, Sing cuccu nu!

ALYSOUN

Even if the author of "Alysoun" had not been sleeping well, he wrote a poem whose lilt and swing has seldom been equaled. The refrain displays a happy optimism by no means common in the lyrics.

Bytuene Mersh and Averil
When spray beginneth to springe,
The lutel foul hath hire wyl
On hyre lud to synge.
Ich libbe in lovelonginge
For semlokest of alle thynge;
He may me blisse bringe,
Icham in hire baundoun.
    An hendy hap ichabbe yhent,
    Ichot from hevene it is me sent—
    From alle wymmen mi love is lent,
    And lyht on Alysoun.

On heu hire her is fayr ynoh,
Hire browe broune, hire eye blake,
With lossum chere he on me loh;
With middel smal and wel ymake.
Bote he me wolle to hire take
Forte buen hire owen make,
Longe to lyven ichulle forsake
And feye fallen adoun.
    An hendy hap &c.

Nihtes when y wende and wake—
For-thi myn wonges waxeth won—
Leuedi, al for thine sake,
Longinge is ylent me on.
In world nis non so wyter mon
That al hire bounte telle con;
Hire swyre is whittore then the swon,
And feyrest may in toune.
    An hendy hap &c.

Icham for wowyng al forwake,
Wery so water in wore;
Lest eny reve me my make
Ychabbe y-yyrned yore.
Betere is tholien whyle sore
Then mournen evermore;
Geynest under gore,
Herkne to my roun.
    An hendy hap &c.

BLESS THE TIME THE APPLE WAS TAKEN!

Adam lay y-bowndyn, bowndyn in a bond,
Fowre thowsand wynter thowt he not to long;
And al was for an appil, an appil that he tok,
As clerkis fyndyn wretyn in here book.

The Cuckoo Song. **2. Lhude,** loudly. **3. sed,** seed. **bloweth med,** blossometh (the) meadow. **4. wode,** wood, forest. **nu,** now. **6. Awe,** ewe. **7. Lhouth,** loweth. **cu,** cow. **8. sterteth,** leapeth. **verteth,** breaks wind. **9. Murie,** merrily. **12. swik,** cease. *Alysoun.* **3. lutel foul,** little bird. **4. On hyre lud,** in her language, voice. **5. Ich libbe,** I live. **6. semlokest,** fairest. **7. He,** she. **8. Icham in hire baundoun,** I am in her power. **9. hendy hap,** pleasant fortune. **ichabbe yhent,** I have received. **10. Ichot,** I wot, I know. **11. lent,** taken away. **12. lyht,** alighted, placed.

13. On heu . . . ynoh. In color (hue) her hair is fair enough. **15. lossum chere,** loving looks. **loh,** laughed. **16. ymake,** made. **17. Bote,** unless. **wolle,** be willing. **18. Forte buen,** for to be. **make,** mate. **19. ichulle,** I will. **20. feye,** doomed to die. **22. y wende,** I turn, toss. **23. For-thi,** therefore, for which reason. **wonges,** cheeks. **won,** wan, pallid. **24. Leuedi,** lady. **25. ylent me on,** come upon me. **26. nis,** is not. **so wyter mon,** so wise a man. **27. bounte,** goodness. **28. swyre,** neck. **29. may,** maid. **31. wowyng,** wooing. **forwake,** wearied with wakefulness. **32. Wery . . . wore,** weary as water in a weir (mill-race). **33. reve,** bereave, deprive. **34. Ychabbe y-yyrned yore,** I have yearned for a long time. **35. tholien whyle sore,** suffer a while sorely. **36. Then,** than. **37. Geynest under gore,** fairest in the world (literally, under a dress). **38. roun,** song ("rune"). *Bless the Time.* **1. y-bowndyn,** bound. **2. thowt,** thought. **to,** too. **4. here,** their.

Ne hadde the appil take ben, the appil taken ben,
Ne hadde never our Lady a ben hevene Qwen;
Blyssid be the tyme that appil take was,
Ther-fore we mown syngyn, "Deo gracias!"

THE MATCHLESS MAIDEN

I syng of a myden that is makeles,
Kyng of alle kynges to here sone che ches.

He cam also stylle ther his moder was
As dew in Aprille, that fallyt on the gras.

He cam also stylle to his moderes bowr
As dew in Aprille, that fallyt on the flour.

He cam also stylle ther his moder lay
As dew in Aprille, that fallyt on the spray.

Moder and mayden was never non but che—
Wel may swych a lady Godes moder be.

Romances

In the later Middle Ages there was far more intelligent interest in literature than we are always accustomed to realize. Like most periods, it was a time in which the principal appeal, even to the literate, as opposed to the scholarly, was in narrative, in stories and storytelling. If these stories had the semblance of history, they were all the more appreciated. The stories which interested our ancestors are grouped under the general heading of "Romances." The word "romance" originally meant something written in French, or some other vernacular dialect of Latin descent, rather than in Latin; something, in other words, written for the entertainment of the laity. A romance, as we understand it, is a fictitious narrative, at first always in verse, but later also in prose, dealing with the adventures, often wild and incredible, of a hero or a group of heroes. With such a definition it may seem difficult to differentiate a romance from such heroic poems as the *Beowulf* and the *Song of Roland*. The difference lies in the fact that whereas in heroic poetry the emphasis is on feats of bravery, in the romances the central point is ordinarily love. We do not suggest by this that the romances contain no accounts of brave heroes overcoming enormous odds, human or even superhuman, because the contrary is true. In *Guy of Warwick*, for example, Guy goes throughout Christendom and beyond, fighting Saracens and all other comers up to dragons; in the number and nature of his exploits he puts Beowulf to shame; but we must never forget that Guy left Warwick on his proud career because Felice, the Earl's daughter, declared that she could give him her love only when he had proved himself the first knight in all the world. We shall find the matter summed up neatly in certain remarks made to Sir Gawain by the Green Knight's wife (see page 73).

The love element was introduced partly because, from the twelfth century on, women took an increasingly active interest in literature and, naturally enough, they wished to read or hear or write about love. The rise of the romance was contemporaneous with the rise in religious fervor throughout Europe, and particularly with the intense devotion to the Virgin Mary. In the romances the counterpart of the devotion to the Blessed Virgin was the devotion of the knight to his liege lady. This lady was of noble blood, the wife of a king or lord, and the lover's homage to her was expressed in the elaborate system known as "courtly love," a literary cult which grew up in Provence, in southern France, during the late eleventh and twelfth centuries. This "religion of love," according to the prescribed and elaborate ritual of which a knight obeyed without question the commands of his lady, was celebrated by the Troubadours of Provence in their passionate love lyrics. From the lyrics the cult passed naturally into love stories, and from Continental sources the love stories, now called romances, eventually came to England. It has been conjectured that the metrical romance was brought to England by Eleanor of Aquitaine when she became the wife of Henry II in 1152.

During the earliest period romances in English were intended for the lower classes, who did not understand French, and certain rather fundamental changes were made. The English were obviously little interested in fine points of courtly love or in artistic details of motivation and description. The author of *Ywain and Gawain*, which is drawn from Chrétien de Troyes's *Yvain, ou Le Chevalier au Lion*, gets along with over four thousand fewer lines than

6. a ben, have been. **8. mown,** may. **"Deo gracias!"** thanks be to God! *The Matchless Maiden.* **1. makeles,** matchless. **2. che ches,** she chose.

3. also, as. **ther,** where.

his original, and, while he does not ignore the subject, it is in the sometimes painfully minute dissections of amorous psychology that he makes his most effective condensation. Though the English did not relish the wails and self-analyses of (at least temporarily) frustrated or unfulfilled love, they did want more and better deeds of daring. Where the hero of a French romance may kill four or five hundred of his foes on a single occasion, the carefree exuberance of the English adapter will often take the figure up to ten thousand or even more. Despite this occasional happy lack of realism the English versions gain as stories by the excision of extraneous matter, and are likely to be far more lively, racy, and to a certain extent even more wholesome than their French originals.

We group medieval romances in accordance with their subject matter, following the very serviceable classification of the French poet, Jean Bodel, who died about 1210. Bodel said that the stories which people generally read dealt with three "matters": the matter of France, the matter of Britain, and the matter of Rome the Great. The matter of France contains the stories of Charlemagne and his peers, that of Britain those of Arthur and his knights, and that of Rome the Great the whole mass of stories inherited from classical antiquity, whether the subject be Thebes, Troy, Alexander, or Julius Caesar.

Matter of Britain

Arthur of Britain, his origin shrouded in mystery, caught and held the imagination of the world of story. We need not debate here whether or not there actually was a late fifth-century British or Roman-British leader who had some success against the invading Germans. One may say that if Arthur did not exist in life, it was necessary to invent him for literature. He is apparently first mentioned in the ninth-century work of Nennius, but the first full-length biography of King Arthur was given in Geoffrey of Monmouth's *Historia Regum Britanniæ*, *c.* 1137. Geoffrey has been called the true father of the Arthurian legend, and his "History" is in effect the first Arthurian romance.

Geoffrey's sources are still a matter for furious controversy, but it is probably safe to say that he molded popular Celtic—that is, Welsh and Breton—traditions into historical or pseudo-historical form. Geoffrey's Arthur was a great king, an invincible conqueror, who was finally brought low by treachery in his own household. French writers of romance, notably Chrétien de Troyes, adopted him at once, and almost immediately we find a change in his character and position. The great king remains great in name and royal rank, but in the individual romances the emphasis shifts from him to some one of his knights. Gradually, almost imperceptibly, we see the operation of what is known as "epic degeneration," or the tendency to debase a hero. Instead of majestic, we find him petty and ridiculous, though often pathetic; no longer the great king-conqueror, but a deceived husband, more or less complacent in his shame. Except for the "historical" framework Arthur is in the background, a subsidiary figure from whose court knights set forth on adventures and to which they return, in triumph or disgrace, at the end.

Nowadays we think of Lancelot as Arthur's chief knight, but he is actually a newcomer, an upstart invented by the French writers of romance. It is perhaps chiefly to Chrétien de Troyes that we owe the glorification of Lancelot as the perfect knight and hero. In the earliest forms of the cycle Arthur's closest companion had been Gawain, the king's sister's son. This close uncle-nephew relationship is thought to be a survival from the ancient matriarchal system, and there are other significant examples: Hygelac and Beowulf, Charlemagne and Roland, Conchobar and Cu Chulainn, even Robin Hood and Will Scathlok (Scarlet). Gawain was the darling of the Middle English romancers, and his fame is celebrated in a dozen poems, the greatest of which by far is *Sir Gawain and the Green Knight.*

SIR GAWAIN AND THE GREEN KNIGHT

Sir Gawain and the Green Knight is found in a manuscript of the late fourteenth or early fifteenth century which also contains *The Pearl*, *Patience*, and *Purity*. The four poems are often held to be by one author, called for convenience' sake the Pearl Poet, a theory which, although it cannot be proved absolutely, is attractive. *Sir Gawain*, one of the finest of medieval romances, combines two stories, both of which had been told independently about Gawain and other heroes before they were brought together here—the story of the Challenge or Beheading Game and that of the Temptation of the Knight. The elements of the poem are Celtic, and may have reached the poet without the aid of French intermediaries.

The poet was an idealist who utilized his material in such a way as to stress the best virtues of knighthood exemplified in the person of Gawain: bravery, honor, faith, and chastity. We must also admire his minute attention to detail in such passages as the description of the Green Knight and his steed, the arming of Gawain, and, above all, the accounts of the Green Knight's three hunting expeditions, which are as full as most medieval manuals of the chase and certainly far more picturesque. One of the most striking things about the poem is the attention given to external nature, which the poet handles in a way quite different from most medieval writers. Here is no conventional May-morning mood, no picture of a man-made, carefully tended landscape, but a realistic and varied portrayal of actuality.

Readers for whom Malory, or perhaps Tennyson, has been the authorized version of the Arthurian story will hardly recognize the principal character. This is the old Gawain before he was supplanted by Lancelot and deliberately debased by the writers who advanced the new hero. This Gawain is the one referred to by Chaucer in "The Squire's Tale":

> This straunge knyght, that cam thus sodeynly,
> Al armed, save his heed, ful richely,
> Salueth kyng and queene and lordes alle,
> By ordre, as they seten in the halle,
> With so heigh reverence and obeisaunce,
> As wel in speche as in contenaunce,
> That Gawayn, with his olde curteisye,
> Thogh he were come agayn out of fairye,
> Ne koude hym nat amende with a word.

He is the antithesis of Tennyson's Gawain (in "The Passing of Arthur"), who came in a dream to Arthur before "that last weird battle in the west":

> the ghost of Gawain blown
> Along a wandering wind, and past his ear
> Went shrilling: 'Hollow, hollow all delight!
> Hail, King! to-morrow thou shall pass away.
> Farewell! there is an isle of rest for thee.
> And I am blown along a wandering wind,
> And hollow, hollow, hollow all delight!'

And Bedivere says:

> 'Light was Gawain in life, and light in death
> Is Gawain, for the ghost is as the man.'

It was a long unhappy road which ran from *Sir Gawain and the Green Knight* and "The Squire's Tale" to "The Passing of Arthur."

The poem is written in strophes of varying lengths, a number of long alliterative lines being followed by five short rhyming lines which mark the end of the strophe. The language is very difficult; love of detail, the requirements of alliteration, and an apparent fondness for unusual expressions led the poet to make use of a vocabulary far different from that found in the ordinary run of fourteenth-century verse.

The most comprehensive account of the poem is G. L. Kittredge's *A Study of Gawain and the Green Knight*, Harvard University Press, 1916. A valuable edition of the poem, with a prose translation, is that of J. R. R. Tolkien and E. V. Gordon, Oxford University Press, 1936. The most recent edition is that of the Early English Text Society by Sir Israel Gollancz, with introductory essays by Mabel Day and M. S. Serjeantson, Oxford University Press, 1940. The theory that the poem is derived directly from Celtic sources is propounded by James R. Hulbert in his study, "Syr Gawayn and the Grene Knyght," *Modern Philology*, vol. 13, nos. 8 and 12 (1915–16).

We reprint here the translation of the poem in the original meter by Theodore Howard Banks, copyright 1929, Appleton-Century-Crofts, Inc., New York.

I

When the siege and assault ceased at Troy, and the city
Was broken, and burned all to brands and to ashes,
The warrior who wove there the web of his treachery
Tried was for treason, the truest on earth.
'T was Æneas, who later with lords of his lineage
Provinces quelled, and became the possessors
Of well-nigh the whole of the wealth of the West Isles.
Then swiftly to Rome rich Romulus journeyed,
And soon with great splendor builded that city,
Named with his own name, as now we still know it.
Ticius to Tuscany turns for his dwellings;
In Lombardy Langobard lifts up his homes;
And far o'er the French flood fortunate Brutus
With happiness Britain on hillsides full broad
Doth found.
War, waste, and wonder there
Have dwelt within its bound;
And bliss has changed to care
In quick and shifting round.

And after this famous knight founded his Britain,
Bold lords were bred there, delighting in battle,
Who many times dealt in destruction. More marvels
Befell in those fields since the days of their finding
Than anywhere else upon earth that I know of.
Yet of all kings who came there was Arthur most comely;
My intention is, therefore, to tell an adventure
Strange and surprising, as some men consider,
A strange thing among all the marvels of Arthur.
And if you will list to the lay for a little,
Forthwith I shall tell it, as I in the town

3. **the warrior,** probably Æneas who, in medieval accounts of the Trojan war, was held guilty of treason and tried for treachery. 13. **Brutus,** great-grandson of Æneas, and eponymous founder of Britain (the "land of Brut").

Heard it told
As it doth fast endure
In story brave and bold,
Whose words are fixed and sure,
Known in the land of old.

In Camelot Arthur the King lay at Christmas,
With many a peerless lord princely companioned,
The whole noble number of knights of the Round Table;
Here right royally held his high revels,
Care-free and mirthful. Now much of the company,
Knightly born gentlemen, joyously jousted,
Now came to the court to make caroles; so kept they
For full fifteen days this fashion of feasting,
All meat and all mirth that a man might devise.
Glorious to hear was the glad-hearted gaiety,
Dancing at night, merry din in the daytime;
So found in the courts and the chambers the fortunate
Ladies and lords the delights they best loved.
In greatest well-being abode they together:
The knights whose renown was next to the Saviour's,
The loveliest ladies who ever were living,
And he who held court, the most comely of kings.
For these fine folk were yet in their first flush of youth

Seated there,
The happiest of their kind,
With a king beyond compare.
It would be hard to find
A company so fair.

And now while the New Year was young were the nobles
Doubly served as they sat on the dais,
When Arthur had come to the hall with his court,
In the chapel had ceased the singing of mass;
Loud shouts were there uttered by priests and by others,
Anew praising Noel, naming it often.
Then hastened the lords to give handsel, cried loudly
These gifts of the New Year, and gave them in person;
Debated about them busily, briskly.
Even though they were losers, the ladies laughed loudly,
Nor wroth was the winner, as well ye may know.
All this manner of mirth they made till meat-time,
Then when they had washed, they went to be seated,
Were placed in the way that appeared most proper,
The best men above. And Guinevere, beautiful,
Was in the midst of the merriment seated
Upon the rich dais, adorned all about:
Fine silks on all sides, and spread as a canopy
Tapestries treasured of Tars and Toulouse,
Embroidered and set with stones most splendid—
They'd prove of great price if ye pence gave to buy them

Some day.
The comeliest was the Queen,
With dancing eyes of grey.
That a fairer he had seen
No man might truly say.

But Arthur would eat not till all were attended;
Youthfully mirthful and merry in manner,
He loved well his life, and little it pleased him
Or long to be seated, or long to lie down,
His young blood and wild brain were so busy and brisk.
Moreover, the King was moved by a custom
He once had assumed in a spirit of splendor:
Never to fall to his feast on a festival
Till a strange story of something eventful
Was told him, some marvel that merited credence
Of kings, or of arms, or all kinds of adventures;
Or some one besought him to send a true knight
To join him in proving the perils of jousting,
Life against life, each leaving the other
To have, as fortune would help him, the fairer lot.
This, when the King held his court, was his custom
At every fine feast 'mid his followers, freemen,

In hall.
And so with countenance clear
He stands there strong and tall,
Alert on that New Year,
And makes much mirth with all.

At his place the strong King stands in person, full courtly
Talking of trifles before the high table.
There sat the good Gawain by Guinevere's side,

34–35. words . . . of old. The reference is probably to the alliterative devices familiar since the days of Old English poetry. **36. Camelot.** King Arthur's capital was identified with several different cities, among them Winchester in Hampshire. To this day there hangs on the wall of the hall of Winchester Castle an ancient relic known as King Arthur's Round Table, which is referred to in Caxton's preface to Malory's *Morte Darthur* (page 150). **42. caroles,** dances accompanied by singing. **65. handsel,** New Year's gifts.

68. even . . . losers. Not clear; perhaps the meaning is "even though they had failed to receive particularly good gifts." **77. Tars and Toulouse,** Tharsia (Turkestan) and Toulouse, in southern France. **108. high table.** The chief table, on a dais or platform at the end of the hall, at which the most distinguished persons sat.

And Sir Agravain, he of the Hard Hand, also,
True knights, and sons of the sister of Arthur.
At the top, Bishop Baldwin the table begins,
And Ywain beside him ate, Urien's son.
On the dais these sat, and were served with distinction;
Then many a staunch, trusty man at the side tables.
The first course was served to the sharp sound of trumpets,
With numerous banners beneath hanging brightly.
Then newly the kettledrums sounded and noble pipes;
Wild and loud warbles awakened such echoes
That many a heart leaped on high at their melody.
Came then the choice meats, cates rare and costly,
Of fair and fresh food such profusion of dishes
'T was hard to find place to put by the people
The silver that carried the various stews
On the cloth.
Each to his best loved fare
Himself helps, nothing loth;
Each two, twelve dishes share,
Good beer and bright wine both.

And now I will say nothing more of their service,
For well one may know that naught there was wanted.
Now another new noise drew nigh of a sudden,
To let all the folk take their fill of the feast.
And scarcely the music had ceased for a moment,
The first course been suitably served in the court,
When a being most dreadful burst through the hall-door,
Among the most mighty of men in his measure.
From his throat to his thighs so thick were his sinews,
His loins and his limbs so large and so long,
That I hold him half-giant, the hugest of men,
And the handsomest, too, in his height, upon horseback.
Though stalwart in breast and in back was his body,
His waist and his belly were worthily small;
Fashioned fairly he was in his form, and in features
Cut clean.
Men wondered at the hue
That in his face was seen.
A splendid man to view
He came, entirely green.

All green was the man, and green were his garments:
A coat, straight and close, that clung to his sides,
A bright mantle on top of this, trimmed on the inside
With closely-cut fur, right fair, that showed clearly,
The lining with white fur most lovely, and hood too,
Caught back from his locks, and laid on his shoulders,
Neat stockings that clung to his calves, tightly stretched,
Of the same green, and under them spurs of gold shining
Brightly on bands of fine silk, richly barred;
And under his legs, where he rides, guards of leather.
His vesture was verily color of verdure:
Both bars of his belt and other stones, beautiful,
Richly arranged in his splendid array
On himself and his saddle, on silken designs.
'T would be truly too hard to tell half the trifles
Embroidered about it with birds and with flies
In gay, verdant green with gold in the middle;
The bit-studs, the crupper, the breast-trappings' pendants,
And everything metal enameled in emerald.
The stirrups he stood on the same way were colored,
His saddle-bows too, and the studded nails splendid,
That all with green gems ever glimmered and glinted.
The horse he bestrode was in hue still the same,
Indeed;
Green, thick, and of great height,
And hard to curb, a steed
In broidered bridle bright
That such a man would need.

This hero in green was habited gaily,
And likewise the hair on the head of his good horse;
Fair, flowing tresses enfolded his shoulders,
And big as a bush a beard hung on his breast.
This, and the hair from his head hanging splendid,
Was clipped off evenly over his elbows,
In cut like a king's hood, covering the neck,
So that half of his arms were held underneath it.
The mane of the mighty horse much this resembled,
Well curled and combed, and with many knots covered,
Braided with gold threads about the fair green,
Now a strand made of hair, now a second of gold.
The forelock and tail were twined in this fashion,
And both of them bound with a band of bright green.

111. sister of Arthur. Margawse, Arthur's sister, was married to King Lot of Lothian and Orkney. **115. side tables,** tables which were placed on a lower level along the sides of the hall. **149. entirely green,** to signify the "marvelous" nature of the knight, since green was a fairy color.

For the dock's length the tail was decked with stones dearly,
And then was tied with a thong in a tight knot,
Where many bright bells of burnished gold rang.
In the hall not one single man's seen before this
Such a horse here on earth, such a hero as on him
Goes.
That his look was lightning bright
Right certain were all those
Who saw. It seemed none might
Endure beneath his blows.

Yet the hero carried nor helmet nor hauberk,
But bare was of armor, breastplate or gorget,
Spear-shaft or shield, to thrust or to smite.
But in one hand he bore a bough of bright holly,
That grows most greenly when bare are the groves,
In the other an axe, gigantic, awful,
A terrible weapon, wondrous to tell of.
Large was the head, in length a whole ell-yard,
The blade of green steel and beaten gold both;
The bit had a broad edge, and brightly was burnished,
As suitably shaped as sharp razors for shearing.
This steel by its strong shaft the stern hero gripped:
With iron it was wound to the end of the wood,
And in work green and graceful was everywhere graven.
About it a fair thong was folded, made fast
At the head, and oft looped down the length of the handle.
To this were attached many splendid tassels,
On buttons of bright green richly embroidered.
Thus into the hall came the hero, and hastened
Direct to the dais, fearing no danger.
He gave no one greeting, but haughtily gazed,
And his first words were, "Where can I find him who governs
This goodly assemblage? for gladly that man
I would see and have speech with." So saying, from toe
To crown
On the knights his look he threw,
And rolled it up and down;
He stopped to take note who
Had there the most renown.

There sat all the lords, looking long at the stranger,
Each man of them marveling what it might mean
For a horse and a hero to have such a hue.
It seemed to them green as the grown grass, or greener,
Gleaming more bright than on gold green enamel.

209. ell-yard, i.e., an ell long (about four feet).

The nobles who stood there, astonished, drew nearer,
And deeply they wondered what deed he would do,
Since never a marvel they'd met with like this one,
The folk all felt it was magic or phantasy.
Many great lords then were loth to give answer,
And sat stone-still, at his speaking astounded,
In swooning silence that spread through the hall.
As their speech on a sudden was stilled, fast asleep
They did seem.
They felt not only fright
But courtesy, I deem.
Let him address the knight,
Him whom they all esteem.

This happening the King, ever keen and courageous,
Saw from on high, and saluted the stranger
Suitably, saying, "Sir, you are welcome.
I, the head of this household, am Arthur;
In courtesy light, and linger, I pray you,
And later, my lord, we shall learn your desire."
"Nay, so help me He seated on high," quoth the hero,
"My mission was not to remain here a moment;
But, sir, since thy name is so nobly renowned,
Since thy city the best is considered, thy barons
The stoutest in steel gear that ride upon steeds,
Of all men in the world the most worthy and brave,
Right valiant to play with in other pure pastimes,
Since here, I have heard, is the highest of courtesy—
Truly, all these things have brought me at this time.
Sure ye may be by this branch that I bear
That I pass as in peace, proposing no fight.
If I'd come with comrades, equipped for a quarrel,
I have at my home both hauberk and helmet,
Shield and sharp spear, brightly shining, and other
Weapons to wield, full well I know also.
Yet softer my weeds are, since warfare I wished not;
But art thou as bold as is bruited by all,
Thou wilt graciously grant me the game that I ask for
By right."
Arthur good answer gave,
And said, "Sir courteous knight,
If battle here you crave,
You shall not lack a fight."

"Nay, I ask for no fight; in faith, now I tell thee
But beardless babes are about on this bench.
Were I hasped in my armor, and high on a horse,
Here is no man to match me, your might is so feeble.
So I crave but a Christmas game in this court;

270. weeds, garments. **271. bruited,** rumored.

Yule and New Year are come, and here men have courage;
If one in this house himself holds so hardy,
So bold in his blood, in his brain so unbalanced
To dare stiffly strike one stroke for another,
I give this gisarme, this rich axe, as a gift to him,
Heavy enough, to handle as pleases him;
Bare as I sit, I shall bide the first blow.
If a knight be so tough as to try what I tell,
Let him leap to me lightly; I leave him this weapon,
Quitclaim it forever, to keep as his own;
And his stroke here, firm on this floor, I shall suffer,
This boon if thou grant'st me, the blow with another
To pay;
Yet let his respite be
A twelvemonth and a day.
Come, let us quickly see
If one here aught dare say."

If at first he had startled them, stiller then sat there
The whole of the court, low and high, in the hall.
The knight on his steed turned himself in his saddle,
And fiercely his red eyes he rolled all around,
Bent his bristling brows, with green gleaming brightly,
And waved his beard, waiting for one there to rise.
And when none of the knights spoke, he coughed right noisily,
Straightened up proudly, and started to speak:
"What!" quoth the hero, "Is this Arthur's household,
The fame of whose fellowship fills many kingdoms?
Now where is your vainglory? Where are your victories?
Where is your grimness, your great words, your anger?
For now the Round Table's renown and its revel
Is worsted by one word of one person's speech,
For all shiver with fear before a stroke's shown."
Then so loudly he laughed that the lord was grieved greatly,
And into his fair face his blood shot up fiercely
For shame.
As wroth as wind he grew,
And all there did the same.
The King that no fear knew
Then to that stout man came.

And said, "Sir, by heaven, strange thy request is;
As folly thou soughtest, so shouldest thou find it.
I know that not one of the knights is aghast
Of thy great words. Give me thy weapon, for God's sake,
And gladly the boon thou hast begged I shall grant thee."
He leaped to him quickly, caught at his hand,
And fiercely the other lord lights on his feet.
Now Arthur lays hold of the axe by the handle,
As if he would strike with it, swings it round sternly.
Before him the strong man stood, in stature
A head and more higher than all in the house.
Stroking his beard, he stood with stern bearing,
And with a calm countenance drew down his coat,
No more frightened or stunned by the axe Arthur flourished
Than if on the bench some one brought him a flagon
Of wine.
Gawain by Guinevere
Did to the King incline:
"I pray in accents clear
To let this fray be mine."

"If you now, honored lord," said this knight to King Arthur,
"Would bid me to step from this bench, and to stand there
Beside you—so could I with courtesy quit then
The table, unless my liege lady disliked it—
I'd come to your aid before all your great court.
For truly I think it a thing most unseemly
So boldly to beg such a boon in your hall here,
Though you in person are pleased to fulfill it,
While here on the benches such brave ones are seated,
Than whom under heaven, I think, none are higher
In spirit, none better in body for battle.
I am weakest and feeblest in wit, I know well,
And my life, to say truth, would be least loss of any.
I only since you are my uncle have honor;
Your blood the sole virtue I bear in my body.
Unfit is this foolish affair for you. Give it
To me who soonest have sought it, and let
All this court if my speech is not seemly, decide
Without blame."
The nobles gather round,
And all advise the same:
To free the King that's crowned,
And Gawain give the game.

The King then commanded his kinsman to rise,
And quickly he rose up and came to him courteously,
Kneeled by the King, and caught the weapon,
He left it graciously, lifted his hand,
And gave him God's blessing, and gladly bade him
Be sure that his heart and his hand both were hardy.

"Take care," quoth the King, "how you start, coz, your cutting,
And truly, I think, if rightly you treat him,
That blow you'll endure that he deals you after."
Weapon in hand, Gawain goes to the hero,
Who boldly remains there, dismayed none the more.
Then the knight in the green thus greeted Sir Gawain,
"Let us state our agreement again ere proceeding.
And now first, sir knight, what your name is I beg
That you truly will tell, so in that I may trust."
"In truth," said the good knight, "I'm called Sir Gawain,
Who fetch you this blow, whatsoever befalls,
And another will take in return, this time twelvemonth,
From you, with what weapon you will; with no other I'll go."
The other made reply:
"By my life here below,
Gawain, right glad am I
To have you strike this blow.

"By God," said the Green Knight, "Sir Gawain, it pleases me—
Here, at thy hand, I shall have what I sought.
Thou hast rightly rehearsed to me, truly and readily,
All of the covenant asked of King Arthur;
Except that thou shalt, by thy troth, sir, assure me
Thyself and none other shalt seek me, wherever
Thou thinkest to find me, and fetch thee what wages
Are due for the stroke that to-day thou dost deal me
Before all this splendid assembly." "Where should I,"
Said Gawain, "go look for the land where thou livest?
The realm where thy home is, by Him who hath wrought me,
I know not, nor thee, sir, thy court nor thy name.
Truly tell me thy title, and teach me the road,
And I'll use all my wit to win my way thither.
And so by my sure word truly I swear."
"'T is enough. No more now at New Year is needed,"
The knight in the green said to Gawain the courteous:
"If truly I tell when I've taken your tap
And softly you've struck me, if swiftly I tell you
My name and my house and my home, you may then
Of my conduct make trial, and your covenant keep;
And if no speech I speak, you speed all the better:
No longer need look, but may stay in your land.
But ho!
Take your grim tool with speed,
And let us see your blow."
Stroking his axe, "Indeed,"
Said Gawain, "gladly so."

With speed then the Green Knight took up his stand,
Inclined his head forward, uncovering the flesh,
And laid o'er his crown his locks long and lovely,
And bare left the nape of his neck for the business.
His axe Gawain seized, and swung it on high;
On the floor his left foot he planted before him,
And swiftly the naked flesh smote with his weapon.
The sharp edge severed the bones of the stranger,
Cut through the clear flesh and cleft it in twain,
So the blade of the brown steel bit the ground deeply.
The fair head fell from the neck to the floor,
So that where it rolled forth with their feet many spurned it.
The blood on the green glistened, burst from the body;
And yet neither fell nor faltered the hero,
But stoutly he started forth, strong in his stride;
Fiercely he rushed 'mid the ranks of the Round Table,
Seized and uplifted his lovely head straightway;
Then back to his horse went, laid hold of the bridle,
Stepped into the stirrup and strode up aloft,
His head holding fast in his hand by the hair.
And the man as soberly sat in his saddle
As if he unharmed were, although now headless, Instead.
His trunk around he spun,
That ugly body that bled.
Frightened was many a one
When he his words had said.

For upright he holds the head in his hand,
And confronts with the face the fine folk on the dais.
It lifted its lids, and looked forth directly,
Speaking this much with its mouth, as ye hear:
"Gawain, look that to go as agreed you are ready,
And seek for me faithfully, sir, till you find me,
As, heard by these heroes, you vowed in this hall.
To the Green Chapel go you, I charge you, to get
Such a stroke as you struck. You are surely deserving,
Sir knight, to be promptly repaid at the New Year.
As Knight of the Green Chapel many men know me;
If therefore to find me you try, you will fail not;
Then come, or be recreant called as befits thee."

371. coz, short for "cousin," kinsman.

With furious wrench of the reins he turned round,
And rushed from the hall-door, his head in his hands,
So the fire of the flint flew out from the foal's hoofs.
Not one of the lords knew the land where he went to,
No more than the realm whence he rushed in among them.
What then?
The King and Gawain there
At the Green Knight laughed again;
Yet this the name did bear
Of wonder among men.

Though much in his mind did the courtly King marvel,
He let not a semblance be seen, but said loudly
With courteous speech to the Queen, most comely:
"To-day, my dear lady, be never alarmed;
Such affairs are for Christmas well fitted to sing of
And gaily to laugh at when giving an interlude,
'Mid all the company's caroles, most courtly.
None the less I may go now to get my meat;
For I needs must admit I have met with a marvel."
He glanced at Sir Gawain, and gladsomely said:
"Now sir, hang up thine axe; enough it has hewn."
O'er the dais 't was placed, to hang on the dosser,
That men might remark it there as a marvel,
And truly describing, might tell of the wonder.
Together these two then turned to the table,
The sovereign and good knight, and swiftly men served them
With dainties twofold, as indeed was most fitting,
All manner of meat and of minstrelsy both.
So the whole day in pleasure they passed till night fell
O'er the land.
Now take heed Gawain lest,
Fearing the Green Knight's brand,
Thou shrinkest from the quest
That thou hast ta'en in hand.

II

This sample had Arthur of strange things right early,
When young was the year, for he yearned to hear boasts.
Though such words when they went to be seated were wanting,
Yet stocked are they now with handfuls of stern work.
In the hall glad was Gawain those games to begin,
But not strange it would seem if sad were the ending;
For though men having drunk much are merry in mind,
Full swift flies a year, never yielding the same,
The start and the close very seldom according.
So past went this Yule, and the year followed after,
Each season in turn succeeding the other.
There came after Christmas the crabbed Lenten,
With fish and with plainer food trying the flesh;
But then the world's weather with winter contends;
Down to earth shrinks the cold, the clouds are uplifted;
In showers full warm descends the bright rain,
And falls on the fair fields. Flowers unfold;
The ground and the groves are green in their garments;
Birds hasten to build, blithesomely singing
For soft summer's solace ensuing on slopes
Everywhere.
The blossoms swell and blow,
In hedge-rows rich and rare,
And notes most lovely flow
From out the forest fair.

After this comes the season of soft winds of summer,
When Zephyrus sighs on the seeds and the green plants.
The herb that then grows in the ground is right happy,
When down from the leaves drops the dampening dew
To abide the bright sun that is blissfully shining.
But autumn comes speeding, soon grows severe,
And warns it to wax full ripe for the winter.
With drought then the dust is driven to rise,
From the face of the fields to fly to the heaven.
With the sun the wild wind of the welkin is struggling;
The leaves from the limbs drop, and light on the ground;
And withers the grass that grew once so greenly.
Then all ripens that formerly flourished, and rots;
And thus passes the year in yesterdays many,
And winter, in truth, as the way of the world is,
Draws near,
Till comes the Michaelmas moon
With pledge of winter sere.
Then thinks Sir Gawain soon
Of his dread voyage drear.

Till the tide of Allhallows with Arthur he tarried;

478. **dosser,** the tapestry wall-hanging back of the throne.

532. **Michaelmas,** September 29. 536. **Allhallows,** All Saints' Day, November 1.

The King made ado on that day for his sake
With rich and rare revel of all of the Round Table,
Knights most courteous, comely ladies,
All of them heavy at heart for the hero.
Yet nothing but mirth was uttered, though many
Joyless made jests for that gentleman's sake.
After meat, with sorrow he speaks to his uncle,
And openly talks of his travel, saying:
"Liege lord of my life, now I ask of you leave.
You know my case and condition, nor care I
To tell of its troubles even a trifle.
I must, for the blow I am bound to, to-morrow
Go seek as God guides me the man in the green."
Then came there together the best in the castle:
Ywain, Eric, and others full many,
Sir Dodinel de Sauvage, the Duke of Clarence,
Lancelot, Lyonel, Lucan the good,
Sir Bors and Sir Bedevere, both of them big men,
Mador de la Port, and many more nobles.
All these knights of the court came near to the King
With care in their hearts to counsel the hero;
Heavy and deep was the dole in the hall
That one worthy as Gawain should go on that errand,
To suffer an onerous stroke, and his own sword
To stay.
The knight was of good cheer:
"Why should I shrink away
From a fate stern and drear?
A man can but essay."

He remained there that day; in the morning made ready.
Early he asked for his arms; all were brought him.
And first a fine carpet was laid on the floor,
And much was the gilt gear that glittered upon it.
Thereon stepped the strong man, and handled the steel,
Dressed in a doublet of Tars that cost dearly,
A hood made craftily, closed at the top,
And about on the lining bound with a bright fur.
Then they set on his feet shoes fashioned of steel,
And with fine greaves of steel encircled his legs.
Knee-pieces to these were connected, well polished,
Secured round his knees with knots of gold.
Then came goodly cuisses, with cunning enclosing
His thick, brawny thighs; with thongs they attached them.
Then the man was encased in a coat of fine mail,
With rings of bright steel on a rich stuff woven,
Braces well burnished on both of his arms,
Elbow-pieces gay, good, and gloves of plate,
All the goodliest gear that would give him most succor
That tide:
Coat armor richly made,
His gold spurs fixed with pride,
Girt his unfailing blade
By a silk sash to his side.

When in arms he was clasped, his costume was costly;
The least of the lacings or loops gleamed with gold.
And armed in this manner, the man heard mass,
At the altar adored and made offering, and afterward
Came to the King and all of his courtiers,
Gently took leave of the ladies and lords;
Him they kissed and escorted, to Christ him commending.
Then was Gringolet ready, girt with a saddle
That gaily with many a gold fringe was gleaming,
With nails studded newly, prepared for the nonce.
The bridle was bound about, barred with bright gold;
With the bow of the saddle, the breastplate, the splendid skirts,
Crupper, and cloth in adornment accorded,
With gold nails arrayed on a groundwork of red,
That glittered and glinted like gleams of the sun.
Then he caught up his helm, and hastily kissed it;
It stoutly was stapled and stuffed well within,
High on his head, and hasped well behind,
With a light linen veil laid over the visor,
Embroidered and bound with the brightest of gems
On a silken border; with birds on the seams
Like painted parroquets preening; true love-knots
As thickly with turtle doves tangled as though
Many women had been at the work seven winters
In town.
Great was the circle's price
Encompassing his crown;
Of diamonds its device,
That were both bright and brown.

Then they showed him his shield, sheer gules, whereon shone
The pentangle painted in pure golden hue.
On his baldric he caught, and about his neck cast it;
And fairly the hero's form it befitted.
And why that great prince the pentangle suited
Intend I to tell, in my tale though I tarry.
'T is a sign that Solomon formerly set

597. Gringolet, Gawain's horse. **620. pentangle (pentacle),** a five-pointed star; an ancient symbol of perfection, used by the Pythagoreans. In the Middle Ages it was believed to have magic powers. **625. Solomon.** Solomon's seal is a circle with a pentangle inside it.

As a token, for so it doth symbol, of truth.
A figure it is that with five points is furnished;
Each line overlaps and locks in another,
Nor comes to an end; and Englishmen call it
Everywhere, hear I, the endless knot.
It became then the knight and his noble arms also,
In five ways, and five times each way still faithful.
Sir Gawain was known as the good, refined gold,
Graced with virtues of castle, of villainy void,
Made clean.
So the pentangle new
On shield and coat was seen,
As man of speech most true,
And gentlest knight of mien.

First, in his five wits he faultless was found;
In his five fingers too the man never failed;
And on earth all his faith was fixed on the five wounds
That Christ, as the creed tells, endured on the cross.
Wheresoever this man was midmost in battle,
His thought above everything else was in this,
To draw all his fire from the fivefold joys
That the fair Queen of Heaven felt in her child.
And because of this fitly he carried her image
Displayed on his shield, on its larger part,
That whenever he saw it his spirit should sink not.
The fifth five the hero made use of, I find,
More than all were his liberalness, love of his fellows,
His courtesy, chasteness, unchangeable ever,
And pity, all further traits passing. These five
In this hero more surely were set than in any.
In truth now, fivefold they were fixed in the knight,
Linked each to the other without any end,
And all of them fastened on five points unfailing;
Each side they neither united nor sundered,
Evermore endless at every angle,
Where equally either they ended or started.
And so his fair shield was adorned with this symbol,
Thus richly with red gold wrought on red gules,
So by people the pentangle perfect 't was called,
As it ought.
Gawain in arms is gay;
Right there his lance he caught,
And gave them all good-day
For ever, as he thought.

He set spurs to his steed, and sprang on his way
So swiftly that sparks from the stone flew behind him.
All who saw him, so seemly, sighed, sad at heart;
The same thing, in sooth, each said to the other,
Concerned for that comely man: "Christ, 't is a shame
Thou, sir knight, must be lost whose life is so noble!
To find, faith! his equal on earth is not easy.
'T would wiser have been to have acted more warily,
Dubbed yonder dear one a duke. He seems clearly
To be in the land here a brilliant leader:
So better had been than brought thus to naught,
By an elf-man beheaded for haughty boasting.
Who e'er knew any king such counsel to take,
As foolish as one in a Christmas frolic?"
Much was the warm water welling from eyes
When the seemly hero set out from the city
That day.
Nowhere he abode,
But swiftly went his way;
By devious paths he rode,
As I the book heard say.

Through the realm of Logres now rides this lord,
Sir Gawain, for God's sake, no game though he thought it.
Oft alone, uncompanioned he lodges at night
Where he finds not the fare that he likes set before him.
Save his foal, he'd no fellow by forests and hills;
On the way, no soul but the Saviour to speak to.
At length he drew nigh unto North Wales, and leaving
To left of him all of the islands of Anglesey,
Fared by the forelands and over the fords
Near the Holy Head; hastening hence to the mainland,
In Wyral he went through the wilderness. There,
Lived but few who loved God or their fellows with good heart.
And always he asked of any he met,
As he journeyed, if nearby a giant they knew of,
A green knight, known as the Knight of the Green Chapel.
All denied it with nay, in their lives they had never
Once seen any hero who had such a hue
Of green.
The knight takes roadways strange
In many a wild terrene;
Often his feelings change
Before that chapel's seen.

646. fivefold joys, usually considered to be those of the Annunciation, the Nativity, the Resurrection, the Ascension, and the Assumption of the Blessed Virgin into heaven.

691. Logres. England in general, southern England in particular. Gawain's journey led him from Camelot, in southern England, to North Wales and presumably to Cumberland on the Scottish border. **700. Holy Head,** a small island off the west coast of Anglesey Island, North Wales. **701. Wyral,** in the palatinate of Chester, on the east border of Wales.

Over many cliffs climbed he in foreign countries;
From friends far sundered, he fared as a stranger;
And wondrous it were, at each water or shore
That he passed, if he found not before him a foe,
So foul too and fell that to fight he could fail not.
The marvels he met with amount to so many
Too tedious were it to tell of the tenth part.
For sometimes with serpents he struggled and wolves too,
With wood-trolls sometimes in stony steeps dwelling,
And sometimes with bulls and with bears and with boars;
And giants from high fells hunted and harassed him.
If he'd been not enduring and doughty, and served God,
These doubtless would often have done him to death.
Though warfare was grievous, worse was the winter,
When cold, clear water was shed from the clouds
That froze ere it fell to the earth, all faded.
With sleet nearly slain, he slept in his armor
More nights than enough on the naked rocks,
Where splashing the cold stream sprang from the summit,
And hung in hard icicles high o'er his head.
Thus in peril and pain and desperate plights,
Till Christmas Eve wanders this wight through the country
Alone.
Truly the knight that tide
To Mary made his moan,
That she direct his ride
To where some hearth-fire shone.

By a mount on the morn he merrily rides
To a wood dense and deep that was wondrously wild;
High hills on each hand, with forests of hoar oaks
Beneath them most huge, a hundred together.
Thickly the hazel and hawthorn were tangled,
Everywhere mantled with moss rough and ragged,
With many a bird on the bare twigs, mournful,
That piteously piped for pain of the cold.
Sir Gawain on Gringolet goes underneath them
Through many a marsh and many a mire,
Unfriended, fearing to fail in devotion,
And see not His service, that Sire's, on that very night
Born of a Virgin to vanquish our pain.
And so sighing he said: "Lord, I beseech Thee,
And Mary, the mildest mother so dear,
For some lodging wherein to hear mass full lowly,
And matins, meekly I ask it, to-morrow;
So promptly I pray my pater and ave
And creed."
Thus rode he as he prayed,
Lamenting each misdeed;
Often the sign he made,
And said, "Christ's cross me speed."

He scarcely had signed himself thrice, ere he saw
In the wood on a mound a moated mansion,
Above a fair field, enfolded in branches
Of many a huge tree hard by the ditches:
The comeliest castle that knight ever kept.
In a meadow 't was placed, with a park all about,
And a palisade, spiked and pointed, set stoutly
Round many a tree for more than two miles.
The lord on that one side looked at the stronghold
That shimmered and shone through the shapely oak trees;
Then duly his helm doffed, and gave his thanks humbly
To Jesus and Julian, both of them gentle,
For showing him courtesy, hearing his cry.
"Now good lodging," quoth Gawain, "I beg you to grant me."
Then with spurs in his gilt heels he Gringolet strikes,
Who chooses the chief path by chance that conducted
The man to the bridge-end ere many a minute
Had passed.
The bridge secure was made,
Upraised; the gates shut fast;
The walls were well arrayed.
It feared no tempest's blast.

The hero abode on his horse by the bank
Of the deep, double ditch that surrounded the dwelling.
The wall stood wonderfully deep in the water,
And again to a huge height sprang overhead;
Of hard, hewn rock that reached to the cornices,
Built up with outworks under the battlements
Finely; at intervals, turrets fair fashioned,
With many good loopholes that shut tight; this lord
Had ne'er looked at a barbican better than this one.
Further in he beheld the high hall; here and there
Towers were stationed set thickly with spires,
With finials wondrously long and fair fitting,
Whose points were cunningly carven, and craftily.
There numerous chalk-white chimneys he noticed
That bright from the tops of the towers were gleaming.

774. **Julian,** the saint of hospitality; see *The Canterbury Tales,* "The General Prologue," page 102, line 340.

Such pinnacles painted, so placed about everywhere,
Clustering so thick 'mid the crenels, the castle
Surely appeared to be shaped to cut paper.
The knight on his foal it fair enough fancies
If into the court he may manage to come,
In that lodging to live while the holiday lasts
With delight.
A porter came at call,
His mission learned, and right
Civilly from the wall
Greeted the errant knight.

Quoth Gawain: "Good sir, will you go on my errand,
Harbor to crave of this house's high lord?"
"Yea, by Peter. I know well, sir knight," said the porter,
"You're welcome as long as you list here to tarry."
Then went the man quickly, and with him, to welcome
The knight to the castle, a courteous company.
Down the great drawbridge they dropped, and went eagerly
Forth; on the frozen earth fell on their knees
To welcome this knight in the way they thought worthy;
Threw wide the great gate for Gawain to enter.
He bid them rise promptly, and rode o'er the bridge.
His saddle several seized as he lighted,
And stout men in plenty stabled his steed.
And next there descended knights and esquires
To lead to the hall with delight this hero.
When he raised his helmet, many made haste
From his hand to catch it, to care for the courtly man.
Some of them took then his sword and his shield both.
Then Gawain graciously greeted each knight;
Many proud men pressing to honor that prince,
To the hall they led him, all hasped in his harness,
Where fiercely a fair fire flamed on the hearth.
Then came the lord of this land from his chamber
To fittingly meet the man on the floor,
And said: "You are welcome to do what your will is;
To hold as your own, you have all that is here
In this place."
"Thank you," said Gawain then,
"May Christ reward this grace."
The two like joyful men
Each other then embrace.

Gawain gazed at the man who so graciously greeted him;
Doughty he looked, the lord of that dwelling,
A hero indeed huge, hale, in his prime;
His beard broad and bright, its hue all of beaver;
Stern, and on stalwart shanks steadily standing;
Fell-faced as the fire, in speech fair and free.
In sooth, well suited he seemed, thought Gawain,
To govern as prince of a goodly people.
To his steward the lord turned, and strictly commanded
To send men to Gawain to give him good service;
And prompt at his bidding were people in plenty.
To a bright room they brought him, the bed nobly decked
With hangings of pure silk with clear golden hems.
And curious coverings with comely panels,
Embroidered with bright fur above at the edges;
On cords curtains running with rings of red gold;
From Tars and Toulouse were the tapestries covering
The walls; under foot on the floor more to match.
There he soon, with mirthful speeches, was stripped
Of his coat of linked mail and his armor; and quickly
Men ran, and brought him rich robes, that the best
He might pick out and choose as his change of apparel.
When lapped was the lord in the one he selected,
That fitted him fairly with flowing skirts,
The fur by his face, in faith it seemed made,
To the company there, entirely of colors,
Glowing and lovely; beneath all his limbs were.
That never made Christ a comelier knight
They thought.
On earth, or far or near,
It seemed as if he ought
To be a prince sans peer
In fields where fierce men fought.

A chair by the chimney where charcoal was burning
For Gawain was fitted most finely with cloths,
Both cushions and coverlets, cunningly made.
Then a comely mantle was cast on the man,
Of a brown, silken fabric bravely embroidered,
Within fairly furred with the finest of skins,
Made lovely with ermine, his hood fashioned likewise.
He sat on that settle in clothes rich and seemly;
His mood, when well he was warmed, quickly mended.

801. crenels, small openings or gaps at regular intervals in the parapet of a battlement.

845. beaver, reddish brown. **847. Fell-faced,** fierce of countenance.

Soon was set up a table on trestles most fair;
With a clean cloth that showed a clear white it was covered,
With top-cloth and salt-cellar, spoons too of silver.
When he would the man washed, and went to his meat,
And seemly enough men served him with several
Excellent stews in the best manner seasoned,
Twofold as was fitting, and various fishes;
In bread some were baked, some broiled on the coals,
Some seethed, some in stews that were savored with spices;
And ever such subtly made sauces as pleased him.
He freely and frequently called it a feast,
Most courtly; the company there all acclaimed him
Well-bred.
"But now this penance take,
And soon 't will mend," they said.
That man much mirth did make,
As wine went to his head.

They enquired then and queried in guarded questions
Tactfully put to the prince himself,
Till he courteously owned he came of the court
The lord Arthur, gracious and goodly, alone holds,
Who rich is and royal, the Round Table's King;
And that Gawain himself in that dwelling was seated,
For Christmas come, as the case had befallen.
When he learned that he had that hero, the lord
Laughed loudly thereat so delightful he thought it.
Much merriment made all the men in that castle
By promptly appearing then in his presence;
For all prowess and worth and pure polished manners
Pertain to his person. He ever is praised;
Of all heroes on earth his fame is the highest.
Each knight full softly said to his neighbor,
"We now shall see, happily, knightly behavior,
And faultless terms of talking most noble;
What profit's in speech we may learn without seeking,
For nurture's fine father has found here a welcome;
In truth God has graciously given His grace
Who grants us to have such a guest as Gawain
When men for His birth's sake sit merry and sing.
To each
Of us this hero now
Will noble manners teach;
Who hear him will learn how
To utter loving speech."

When at length the dinner was done, and the lords
Had risen, the night-time nearly was come.
The chaplains went their way to the chapels
And rang right joyfully, just as they should do,
For evensong solemn this festival season.
To this goes the lord, and the lady likewise;
She comes in with grace to the pew closed and comely,
And straightway Gawain goes thither right gaily;
The lord by his robe took him, led to a seat,
Acknowledged him kindly and called him by name,
Saying none in the world was as welcome as he was.
He heartily thanked him; the heroes embraced,
And together they soberly sat through the service.
Then longed the lady to look on the knight.
And emerged from her pew with many fair maidens;
In face she was fairest of all, and in figure,
In skin and in color, all bodily qualities;
Lovelier, Gawain thought, even than Guinevere.
He goes through the chancel to greet her, so gracious.
By the left hand another was leading her, older
Than she, a lady who looked as if agèd,
By heroes around her reverenced highly.
The ladies, however, unlike were to look on:
If fresh was the younger, the other was yellow;
Rich red on the one was rioting everywhere,
Rough wrinkled cheeks hung in rolls on the other;
One's kerchiefs, with clear pearls covered and many,
Displayed both her breast and her bright throat all bare,
Shining fairer than snow on the hillsides falling;
The second her neck in a neck-cloth enswathed,
That enveloped in chalk-white veils her black chin;
Her forehead in silk was wrapped and enfolded
Adorned and tricked with trifles about it
Till nothing was bare but the lady's black brows,
Her two eyes, her nose, and her lips, all naked,
And those were bleared strangely, and ugly to see.
A goodly lady, so men before God
Might decide!
Her body thick and short,
Her hips were round and wide;
One of more pleasant sort
She led there by her side.

When Gawain had gazed on that gay one so gracious
In look, he took leave of the lord and went toward them,
Saluted the elder, bowing full lowly,
The lovelier lapped in his two arms a little,
And knightly and comely greeted and kissed her.
They craved his acquaintance, and quickly he asked

To be truly their servant if so they desired it.
They took him between them, and led him with talk
To the sitting-room's hearth; then straightway for spices
They called, which men sped to unsparingly bring,
And with them as well pleasant wine at each coming.
Up leaped right often the courteous lord,
Urged many a time that the men should make merry,
Snatched off his hood, on a spear gaily hung it,
And waved it, that one for a prize might win it
Who caused the most mirth on that Christmas season.
"I shall try, by my faith, to contend with the finest
Ere hoodless I find myself, helped by my friends."
Thus with laughing speeches the lord makes merry
That night, to gladden Sir Gawain with games.
So they spent
The evening in the hall.
The king for lights then sent,
And taking leave of all
To bed Sir Gawain went.

On the morn when the Lord, as men all remember,
Was born, who would die for our doom, in each dwelling
On earth grows happiness greater for His sake;
So it did on that day there with many a dainty:
With dishes cunningly cooked at meal-times,
With doughty men dressed in their best on the dais.
The old lady was seated the highest; beside her
Politely the lord took his place, I believe;
The gay lady and Gawain together sat, mid-most,
Where fitly the food came, and afterward fairly
Was served through the hall as beseemed them the best,
Of the company each in accord with his station.
There was meat and mirth, there was much joy, too troublous
To tell, though I tried in detail to describe it;
Yet I know both the lovely lady and Gawain
So sweet found each other's society (pleasant
And polished their converse, courtly and private;
Unfailing their courtesy, free from offence)
That surpassing, in truth, any play of a prince was
Their game.
There trumpets, drums and airs
Of piping loudly came.
Each minded his affairs,
And those two did the same.

Much mirth was that day and the day after made,
And the third followed fast, as full of delight.
Sweet was the joy of St. John's day to hear of,
The last, as the folk there believed, of the festival.
Guests were to go in the grey dawn, and therefore
They wondrously late were awake with their wine,
And danced delightful, long lasting caroles.
At length when 't was late they took their leave,
Each strong man among them to start on his way.
Gawain gave him good-day; then the good man laid hold of him,
Led to the hearth in his own room the hero;
There took him aside, and gave suitable thanks
For the gracious distinction that Gawain had given
In honoring his house that holiday season,
And gracing his castle with courteous company.
"I'll truly as long as I live be the better
That Gawain at God's own feast was my guest."
"Gramercy," said Gawain, "by God, sir, not mine
Is the worth, but your own; may the high King reward you.
I am here at your will to work your behest,
As in high and low it behooves me to do
By right."
The lord intently tries
Longer to hold the knight;
Gawain to him replies
That he in no way might.

Then the man with courteous question enquired
What dark deed that feast time had driven him forth,
From the King's court to journey alone with such courage,
Ere fully in homes was the festival finished.
"In sooth," said the knight, "sir, ye say but the truth;
From these hearths a high and a hasty task took me.
Myself, I am summoned to seek such a place
As to find it I know not whither to fare.
I'd not fail to have reached it the first of the New Year,
So help me our Lord, for the whole land of Logres;
And therefore, I beg this boon of you here, sir;
Tell me, in truth, if you ever heard tale
Of the Chapel of Green, of the ground where it stands,
And the knight, green colored, who keeps it. By solemn
Agreement a tryst was established between us,
That man at that landmark to meet if I lived.
And now there lacks of New Year but little;
I'd look at that lord, if God would but let me,

1021. St. John's Day, December 27.

More gladly than own any good thing, by God's Son.
And hence, by your leave, it behooves me to go;
I now have but barely three days to be busy.
As fain would I fall dead as fail of my mission."
Then laughing the lord said: "You longer must stay,
For I'll point out the way to that place ere the time's end,
The ground of the Green Chapel. Grieve no further;
For, sir, you shall be in your bed at your ease
Until late, and fare forth the first of the year,
To your meeting place come by mid-morning, to do there
Your pleasure.
Tarry till New Year's day,
Then rise and go at leisure.
I'll set you on your way;
Not two miles is the measure."

Then was Gawain right glad, and gleefully laughed.
"Now for this more than anything else, sir, I thank you.
I have come to the end of my quest; at your will
I shall bide, and in all things act as you bid me."
The lord then seized him, and set him beside him,
And sent for the ladies to better delight him.
Seemly the pleasure among them in private.
So gay were the speeches he spoke, and so friendly,
The host seemed a man well-nigh mad in behavior.
He called to the knight there, crying aloud:
"Ye have bound you to do the deed that I bid you.
Here, and at once, will you hold to your word, sir?"
"Yes, certainly, sir," the true hero said;
"While I bide in your house I obey your behest."
"You have toiled," said the lord; "from afar have traveled,
And here have caroused, nor are wholly recovered
In sleep or in nourishment, know I for certain.
In your room you shall linger, and lie at your ease
Tomorrow till mass-time, and go to your meat
When you will, and with you my wife to amuse you
With company, till to the court I return.
You stay
And I shall early rise,
And hunting go my way."
Bowing in courteous wise,
Gawain grants all this play.

"And more," said the man, "let us make an agreement:
Whatever I win the wood shall be yours;
And what chance you shall meet shall be mine in exchange.
Sir, let's so strike our bargain and swear to tell truly
Whate'er fortune brings, whether bad, sir, or better."
Quoth Gawain the good: "By God, I do grant it.
What pastime you please appears to me pleasant."
"On the beverage brought us the bargain is made,"
So the lord of the land said. All of them laughed,
And drank, and light-heartedly reveled and dallied,
Those ladies and lords, as long as they liked.
Then they rose with elaborate politeness, and lingered,
With many fair speeches spoke softly together,
Right lovingly kissed, and took leave of each other.
Gay troops of attendants with glimmering torches
In comfort escorted each man to his couch
To rest.
Yet ere they left the board
Their promise they professed
Often. That people's lord
Could well maintain a jest.

III

Betimes rose the folk ere the first of the day;
The guests that were going then summoned their grooms,
Who hastily sprang up to saddle their horses,
Packed their bags and prepared all their gear.
The nobles made ready, to ride all arrayed;
And quickly they leaped and caught up their bridles,
And started, each wight on the way that well pleased him.
The land's beloved lord not last was equipped
For riding, with many a man too. A morsel
He hurriedly ate when mass he had heard,
And promptly with horn to the hunting field hastened.
And ere any daylight had dawned upon earth,
Both he and his knights were high on their horses.
The dog-grooms, accomplished, the hounds then coupled,
The door of the kennel unclosed, called them out,
On the bugle mightily blew three single notes;
Whereupon bayed with a wild noise the brachets,
And some they turned back that went straying, and punished.
The hunters, I heard, were a hundred. To station
They go,
The keepers of the hounds,
And off the leashes throw.
With noise the wood resounds
From the good blasts they blow.

At the first sound of questing, the wild creatures quaked;
The deer fled, foolish from fright, in the dale,
To the high ground hastened, but quickly were halted
By beaters, loud shouting, stationed about
In a circle. The harts were let pass with their high heads,
And also the bucks, broad-antlered and bold;
For the generous lord by law had forbidden
All men with the male deer to meddle in close season.
The hinds were hemmed in with hey! and ware!
The does to the deep valleys driven with great din.
You might see as they loosed them the shafts swiftly soar—
At each turn of the forest their feathers went flying—
That deep into brown hides bit with their broad heads;
Lo! they brayed on the hill-sides, bled there, and died,
And hounds, fleet-footed, followed them headlong.
And hunters after them hastened with horns
So loud in their sharp burst of sound as to sunder
The cliffs. What creatures escaped from the shooters,
Hunted and harried from heights to the waters,
Were pulled down and rent at the places there ready;
Such skill the men showed at these low-lying stations,
So great were the greyhounds that quickly they got them
And dragged them down, fast as the folk there might look
At the sight.
Carried with bliss away,
The lord did oft alight,
Oft gallop; so that day
He passed till the dark night.

Thus frolicked the lord on the fringe of the forest,
And Gawain the good in his gay bed reposed,
Lying snugly, till sunlight shone on the walls,
'Neath a coverlet bright with curtains about it.
As softly he slumbered, a slight sound he heard
At his door, made with caution, and quickly it opened.
The hero heaved up his head from the clothes;
By a corner he caught up the curtain a little,
And glanced out with heed to behold what had happened.
The lady it was, most lovely to look at,
Who shut the door after her stealthily, slyly,
And turned toward the bed. Then the brave man, embarrassed,
Lay down again subtly to seem as if sleeping;
And stilly she stepped, and stole to his bed,
There cast up the curtain, and creeping within it,
Seated herself on the bedside right softly,
And waited a long while to watch when he woke.
And the lord too, lurking, lay there a long while,
Wondering at heart what might come of this happening,
Or what it might mean—a marvel he thought it.
Yet he said to himself, "'T would be surely more seemly
By speaking at once to see what she wishes."
Then roused he from sleep, and stretching turned toward her,
His eyelids unlocked, made believe that he wondered,
And signed himself so by his prayers to be safer
From fall.
Right sweet in chin and cheek,
Both white and red withal,
Full fairly she did speak
With laughing lips and small.

"Good morrow, Sir Gawain," that gay lady said,
"You're a sleeper unwary, since so one may steal in.
In a trice you are ta'en! If we make not a truce,
In your bed, be you certain of this, I shall bind you."
All laughing, the lady delivered those jests.
"Good morrow, fair lady," said Gawain the merry,
"You may do what you will, and well it doth please me,
For quickly I yield me, crying for mercy;
This method to me seems the best—for I must!"
So the lord in turn jested with laughter right joyous.
"But if, lovely lady, you would, give me leave,
Your prisoner release and pray him to rise,
And I'd come from this bed and clothe myself better;
So could I converse with you then with more comfort."
"Indeed no, fair sir," that sweet lady said,
"You'll not move from your bed; I shall manage you better;
For here—and on that side too—I shall hold you,
And next I shall talk with the knight I have taken.
For well do I know that your name is Sir Gawain,
By everyone honored wherever you ride;
Most highly acclaimed is your courtly behavior
With lords and ladies and all who are living.

1149. questing, the baying of the hounds.

And now you're here, truly, and none but we two;
My lord and his followers far off have fared;
Other men remain in their beds, and my maidens;
The door is closed, and secured with a strong hasp;
Since him who delights all I have in my house,
My time, as long as it lasts, I with talking
Shall fill.
My body's gladly yours;
Upon me work your will.
Your servant I, perforce,
Am now, and shall be still."

"In faith," quoth Sir Gawain, "a favor I think it,
Although I am now not the knight you speak of;
To reach to such fame as here you set forth,
I am one, as I well know myself, most unworthy.
By God, should you think it were good, I'd be glad
If I could or in word or action accomplish
Your ladyship's pleasure—a pure joy 't would prove."
"In good faith, Sir Gawain," the gay lady said,
"Ill-bred I should be if I blamed or belittled
The worth and prowess that please all others.
There are ladies enough who'd be now more delighted
To have you in thraldom, as here, sir, I have you,
To trifle gaily in talk most engaging,
To give themselves comfort and quiet their cares,
Than have much of the gold and the goods they command.
But to Him I give praise that ruleth the heavens,
That wholly I have in my hand what all wish."
So she
Gave him good cheer that day,
She who was fair to see.
To what she chanced to say
With pure speech answered he.

Quoth the merry man, "Madam, Mary reward you,
For noble, in faith, I've found you, and generous.
People by others pattern their actions,
But more than I merit to me they give praise;
'T is your courteous self who can show naught but kindness."
"By Mary," said she, "to me it seems other!
Were I worth all the host of women now living,
And had I the wealth of the world in my hands,
Should I chaffer and choose to get me a champion,
Sir, from the signs I've seen in you here
Of courtesy, merry demeanor, and beauty,
From what I have heard, and hold to be true,
Before you no lord now alive would be chosen."
"A better choice, madam, you truly have made;
Yet I'm proud of the value you put now upon me.
Your servant as seemly, I hold you my sovereign,
Become your knight, and Christ give you quittance."
Thus of much they talked till mid-morning was past.
The lady behaved as if greatly she loved him,
But Gawain, on guard, right gracefully acted.
"Though I were the most lovely of ladies," she thought,
"The less would he take with him love." He was seeking,
With speed,
Grief that must be: the stroke
That him should stun indeed.
She then of leaving spoke,
And promptly he agreed.

Then she gave him good-day, and glanced at him, laughing,
And startled him speaking sharp words as she stood:
"He who blesses all words reward this reception!
I doubt if indeed I may dub you Gawain."
"Wherefore?" he queried, quickly enquiring,
Afraid that he'd failed in his fashion of speech.
But the fair lady blessed him, speaking as follows:
"One as good as is Gawain the gracious considered,
(And courtly behavior's found wholly in him)
Not lightly so long could remain with a lady
Without, in courtesy, craving a kiss
At some slight subtle hint at the end of a story."
"Let it be as you like, lovely lady," said Gawain;
"As a knight is so bound, I'll kiss at your bidding,
And lest he displease you, so plead no longer."
Then closer she comes, and catches the knight
In her arms, and salutes him, leaning down affably.
Kindly each other to Christ they commend.
She goes forth at the door without further ado,
And he quickly makes ready to rise, and hastens,
Calls to his chamberlain, chooses his clothes,
And merrily marches, when ready, to mass.
Then he fared to his meat, and fitly he feasted,
Made merry all day with amusements till moonrise.
None knew
A knight to better fare
With dames so worthy, two:
One old, one younger. There
Much mirth did then ensue.

Still was absent the lord of that land on his pleasure,
To hunt barren hinds in wood and in heath.
By the set of the sun he had slain such a number
Of does and different deer that 't was wondrous.
Eagerly flocked in the folk at the finish,

And quickly made of the killed deer a quarry;
To this went the nobles with numerous men;
The game whose flesh was the fattest they gathered;
With care, as the case required, cut them open.
And some the deer searched at the spot of assay,
And two fingers of fat they found in the poorest.
They slit at the base of the throat, seized the stomach,
Scraped it away with a sharp knife and sewed it;
Next slit the four limbs and stripped off the hide;
Then opened the belly and took out the bowels
And flesh of the knot, quickly flinging them out.
They laid hold of the throat, made haste to divide, then,
The windpipe and gullet, and tossed out the guts;
With their sharp knives carved out the shoulders and carried them
Held through a small hole to have the sides perfect.
The breast they sliced, and split it in two;
And then they began once again at the throat,
And quickly as far as its fork they cut it;
Pulled out the pluck, and promptly thereafter
Beside the ribs swiftly severed the fillets,
Cleared them off readily right by the backbone,
Straight down to the haunch, all hanging together.
They heaved it up whole, and hewed it off there,
And the rest by the name of the numbles—and rightly—
They knew.
Then where divide the thighs,
The folds behind they hew,
Hasten to cut the prize
Along the spine in two.

And next both the head and the neck off they hewed;
The sides from the backbone swiftly they sundered;
The fee of the ravens they flung in the branches.
They ran through each thick side a hole by the ribs,
And hung up both by the hocks of the haunches,
Each fellow to have the fee that was fitting.
On the fair beast's hide, they fed their hounds
With the liver and lights and the paunch's lining,
Among which bread steeped in blood was mingled.
They blew boldly the blast for the prize; the hounds barked.
Then the venison took they and turned toward home,
And stoutly many a shrill note they sounded.
Ere close of the daylight, the company came
To the comely castle where Gawain in comfort
Sojourned.
And when he met the knight
As thither he returned,
Joy had they and delight,
Where the fire brightly burned.

In the hall the lord bade all his household to gather,
And both of the dames to come down with their damsels.
In the room there before all the folk he ordered
His followers, truly, to fetch him his venison.
Gawain he called with courteous gaiety,
Asked him to notice the number of nimble beasts,
Showed him the fairness of flesh on the ribs.
"Are you pleased with this play? Have I won your praise?
Have I thoroughly earned your thanks through my cunning?"
"In faith," said Sir Gawain, "this game is the fairest
I've seen in the season of winter these seven years."
"The whole of it, Gawain, I give you," the host said;
"Because of our compact, as yours you may claim it."
"That is true," the knight said, "and I tell you the same:
That this I have worthily won within doors,
And surely to you with as good will I yield it."
With both of his arms his fair neck he embraced,
And the hero as courteously kissed as he could.
"I give you my gains. I got nothing further;
I freely would grant it, although it were greater."
"It is good," said the good man; "I give you my thanks.
Yet things so may be that you'd think it better
To tell where you won this same wealth by your wit."
"'T was no part of our pact," said he; "press me no more;
For trust entirely in this, that you've taken
Your due."
With laughing merriment
And knightly speech and true,
To supper soon they went
With store of dainties new.

In a chamber they sat, by the side of the chimney,
Where men right frequently fetched them mulled wine.
In their jesting, again they agreed on the morrow
To keep the same compact they came to before:
That whatever should chance, they'd exchange at evening,

1323. quarry, the pile of animals killed during the day. **1346. numbles,** entrails used for food. **1354. fee of the ravens,** a regular offering. **1359. lights,** lungs.

When greeting again, the new things they had gotten.
Before all the court they agreed to the covenant;
Then was the beverage brought forth in jest.
At last they politely took leave of each other,
And quickly each hero made haste to his couch.
When the cock but three times had crowed and cackled,
The lord and his men had leaped from their beds.
So that duly their meal was dealt with, and mass,
And ere daylight they'd fared toward the forest, on hunting
Intent.
The huntsmen with loud horns
Through level fields soon went,
Uncoupling 'mid the thorns
The hounds swift on the scent.

Soon they cry for a search by the side of a swamp.
The huntsmen encourage the hounds that first catch there
The scent, and sharp words they shout at them loudly;
And thither the hounds that heard them hastened,
And fast to the trail fell, forty at once.
Then such clamor and din from the dogs that had come there
Arose that the rocks all around them rang.
With horn and with mouth the hunters heartened them;
They gathered together then, all in a group,
'Twixt a pool in that copse and a crag most forbidding.
At a stone-heap, beside the swamp, by a cliff,
Where the rough rock had fallen in rugged confusion,
They fared to the finding, the folk coming after.
Around both the crag and the rubble-heap searched
The hunters, sure that within them was hidden
The beast whose presence was bayed by the bloodhounds.
Then they beat on the bushes, and bade him rise up,
And wildly he made for the men in his way,
Rushing suddenly forth, of swine the most splendid.
Apart from the herd he'd grown hoary with age,
For fierce was the beast, the biggest of boars.
Then many men grieved, full grim when he grunted,
For three at his first thrust he threw to the earth,
And then hurtled forth swiftly, no harm doing further.
They shrilly cried hi! and shouted hey! hey!
Put bugles to mouth, loudly blew the recall.
The men and dogs merry in voice were and many:
With outcry they all hurry after this boar
To slay.
He maims the pack when, fell,
He often stands at bay.
Loudly they howl and yell,
Sore wounded in the fray.

Then to shoot at him came up the company quickly.
Arrows that hit him right often they aimed,
But their sharp points failed that fell on his shoulders'
Tough skin, and the barbs would not bite in his flesh;
But the smooth-shaven shafts were shivered in pieces,
The heads wherever they hit him rebounding.
But when hurt by the strength of the strokes they struck,
Then mad for the fray he falls on the men,
And deeply he wounds them as forward he dashes.
Then many were frightened, and drew back in fear;
But the lord galloped off on a light horse after him,
Blew like a huntsman right bold the recall
On his bugle, and rode through the thick of the bushes,
Pursuing this swine till the sun shone clearly.
Thus the day they passed in doing these deeds,
While bides our gracious knight Gawain in bed,
With bed-clothes in color right rich, at the castle
Behind.
The dame did not forget
To give him greetings kind.
She soon upon him set,
To make him change his mind.

Approaching the curtain, she peeps at the prince.
And at once Sir Gawain welcomes her worthily.
Promptly the lady makes her reply.
By his side she seats herself softly, heartily
Laughs, and with lovely look these words delivers:
"If you, sir, are Gawain, greatly I wonder
That one so given at all times to goodness
Should be not well versed in social conventions,
Or, made once to know, should dismiss them from mind.
You have promptly forgotten what I in the plainest
Of talk that I knew of yesterday taught you."
"What is that?" said the knight. "For truly I know not;
If it be as you say, I am surely to blame."
"Yet I taught you," quoth the fair lady, "of kissing;
When clearly he's favored, quickly to claim one
Becomes each knight who practices courtesy."

"Cease, dear lady, such speech," said the strong man;
"I dare not for fear of refusal do that.
'T would be wrong to proffer and then be repulsed."
"In faith, you may not be refused," said the fair one;
"Sir, if you pleased, you have strength to compel it,
Should one be so rude as to wish to deny you."
"By God, yes," said Gawain, "good is your speech;
But unlucky is force in the land I live in,
And every gift that with good will's not given.
Your word I await to embrace when you wish;
You may start when you please, and stop at your pleasure."
With grace
The lady, bending low,
Most sweetly kissed his face.
Of joy in love and woe
They talked for a long space.

"I should like," said the lady, "from you, sir, to learn,
If I roused not your anger by asking, the reason
Why you, who are now so young and valiant,
So known far and wide as knightly and courteous
(And principally, picked from all knighthood, is praised
The sport of true love and the science of arms;
For to tell of these true knights' toil, it is surely
The title inscribed and the text of their deeds,
How men their lives for their leal love adventured,
Endured for their passion doleful days,
Then themselves with valor avenged, and their sorrow
Cast off, and brought bliss into bowers by their virtues),
Why you, thought the noblest knight of your time,
Whose renown and honor are everywhere noted,
Have so let me sit on two separate occasions
Beside you, and hear proceed from your head
Not one word relating to love, less or more.
You so goodly in vowing your service and gracious
Ought gladly to give to a young thing your guidance,
And show me some sign of the sleights of true love.
What! know you nothing, and have all renown?
Or else do you deem me too dull, for your talking
Unfit?
For shame! Alone I come;
To learn some sport I sit;
My lord is far from home;
Now, teach me by your wit."

"In good faith," said Gawain, "God you reward;
For great is the happiness, huge the gladness
That one so worthy should want to come hither,
And pains for so poor a man take, as in play
With your knight with looks of regard; it delights me.
But to take up the task of telling of true love,
To touch on those themes, and on tales of arms
To you who've more skill in that art, I am certain,
By half than a hundred men have such as I,
Or ever shall have while here upon earth,
By my faith, 't would be, madam, a manifold folly.
Your bidding I'll do, as in duty bound,
To the height of my power, and will hold myself ever
Your ladyship's servant, so save me the Lord."
Thus the fair lady tempted and tested him often
To make the man sin—whate'er more she'd in mind;
But so fair his defence was, no fault was apparent,
Nor evil on either side; each knew but joy
On that day.
At last she kissed him lightly,
After long mirth and play,
And took her leave politely,
And went upon her way.

The man bestirs himself, springs up for mass.
Then made ready and splendidly served was their dinner;
In sport with the ladies he spent all the day.
But the lord through fields oft dashed as he followed
The savage swine, that sped o'er the slopes,
And in two bit the backs of the best of his hounds
Where he stood at bay; till 't was broken by bowmen,
Who made him, despite himself, move to the open,
The shafts flew so thick when the throng had assembled.
Yet sometimes he forced the stoutest to flinch,
Till at last too weary he was to run longer,
But came with such haste as he could to a hole
In a mound, by a rock whence the rivulet runs out.
He started to scrape the soil, backed by the slope,
While froth from his mouth's ugly corners came foaming.
White were the tushes he whetted. The bold men
Who stood round grew tired of trying from far
To annoy him, but dared not for danger draw nearer.
Before,
So many he did pierce
That all were loth a boar
So frenzied and so fierce
Should tear with tusks once more,

1497. **good is your speech,** what you say is true.
1515. **leal,** loyal, true.

1563. **'t was broken,** i.e., the boar's stand.

Till the hero himself came, spurring his horse,
Saw him standing at bay, the hunters beside him.
He leaped down right lordly, leaving his courser,
Unsheathed a bright sword and strode forth stoutly,
Made haste through the ford where that fierce one was waiting.
Aware of the hero with weapon in hand,
So savagely, bristling his back up, he snorted
All feared for the wight lest the worst befall him.
Then rushed out the boar directly upon him,
And man was mingled with beast in the midst
Of the wildest water. The boar had the worse,
For the man aimed a blow at the beast as he met him,
And surely with sharp blade struck o'er his breast bone,
That smote to the hilt, and his heart cleft asunder.
He squealing gave way, and swift through the water
Went back.
By a hundred hounds he's caught,
Who fiercely him attack;
To open ground he's brought,
And killed there by the pack.

The blast for the beast's death was blown on sharp horns,
And the lords there loudly and clearly hallooed.
At the beast bayed the brachets, as bid by their masters,
The chief, in that hard, long chase, of the hunters.
Then one who was wise in woodcraft began
To slice up this swine in the seemliest manner.
First he hews off his head, and sets it on high;
Then along the back roughly rends him apart.
He hales out the bowels, and broils them on hot coals,
With these mixed with bread, rewarding his brachets.
Then slices the flesh in fine, broad slabs,
And pulls out the edible entrails properly.
Whole, though, he gathers the halves together,
And proudly upon a stout pole he places them.
Homeward they now with this very swine hasten,
Bearing in front of the hero the boar's head,
Since him at the ford by the force of his strong hand
He slew.
It seemed long till he met
In hall Sir Gawain, who
Hastened, when called, to get
The payment that was due.

The lord called out loudly, merrily laughed
When Gawain he saw, and gladsomely spoke.
The good ladies were sent for, the household assembled;
He shows them the slices of flesh, and the story
He tells of his largeness and length, and how fierce
Was the war in the woods where the wild swine had fled.
Sir Gawain commended his deeds right graciously,
Praised them as giving a proof of great prowess.
Such brawn on a beast, the bold man declared,
And such sides on a swine he had ne'er before seen.
Then they handled the huge head; the courteous hero
Praised it, horror-struck, honoring his host.
Quoth the good man, "Now, Gawain, yours is this game
By our covenant, fast and firm, you know truly."
"It is so," said the knight; "and as certain and sure
All I get I'll give you again as I pledged you."
He about the neck caught, with courtesy kissed him,
And soon a second time served him the same way.
Said Gawain, "We've fairly fulfilled the agreement
This evening we entered on, each to the other
Most true."
"I, by Saint Giles, have met
None," said the lord, "like you.
Riches you soon will get,
If you such business do."

And then the tables they raised upon trestles,
And laid on them cloths; the light leaped up clearly
Along by the walls, where the waxen torches
Were set by the henchmen who served in the hall.
A great sound of sport and merriment sprang up
Close by the fire, and on frequent occasions
At supper and afterward, many a splendid song,
Conduits of Christmas, new carols, all kinds
Of mannerly mirth that a man may tell of.
Our seemly knight ever sat at the side
Of the lady, who made so agreeable her manner,
With sly, secret glances to glad him, so stalwart,
That greatly astonished was Gawain, and wroth
With himself; he in courtesy could not refuse her,
But acted becomingly, courtly, whatever
The end, good or bad, of his action might be.
When quite
Done was their play at last,
The host called to the knight,
And to his room they passed
To where the fire burned bright.

The men there make merry and drink, and once more

1654. Conduits . . . new carols, part songs and dancing-songs.

The same pact for New Year's Eve is proposed;
But the knight craved permission to mount on the morrow:
The appointment approached where he had to appear.
But the lord him persuaded to stay and linger,
And said, "On my word as a knight I assure you
You'll get to the Green Chapel, Gawain, on New Year's,
And far before prime, to finish your business.
Remain in your room then, and take your rest.
I shall hunt in the wood and exchange with you winnings,
As bound by our bargain, when back I return,
For twice I've found you were faithful when tried:
In the morning 'best be the third time,' remember.
Let's be mindful of mirth while we may, and make merry,
For care when one wants it is quickly encountered."
At once this was granted, and Gawain is stayed;
Drink blithely was brought him; to bed they were lighted.
The guest
In quiet and comfort spent
The night, and took his rest.
On his affairs intent,
The host was early dressed.

After mass a morsel he took with his men.
The morning was merry; his mount he demanded.
The knights who'd ride in his train were in readiness,
Dressed and horsed at the door of the hall.
Wondrous fair were the fields, for the frost was clinging;
Bright red in the cloud-rack rises the sun,
And full clear sails close past the clouds in the sky.
The hunters unleashed all the hounds by a wood-side:
The rocks with the blast of their bugles were ringing.
Some dogs there fall on the scent where the fox is,
And trail oft a traitoress using her tricks.
A hound gives tongue at it; huntsmen call to him;
Hastens the pack to the hound sniffing hard,
And right on his track run off in a rabble,
He scampering before them. They started the fox soon;
When finally they saw him, they followed fast,
Denouncing him clearly with clamorous anger.
Through many a dense grove he dodges and twists,
Doubling back and harkening at hedges right often;
At last by a little ditch leaps o'er a thorn-hedge,
Steals out stealthily, skirting a thicket
In thought from the wood to escape by his wiles
From the hounds; then, unknowing, drew near to a hunting-stand.
There hurled themselves, three at once, on him strong hounds,
All gray.
With quick swerve he doth start
Afresh without dismay.
With great grief in his heart
To the wood he goes away.

Huge was the joy then to hark to the hounds.
When the pack all met him, mingled together,
Such curses they heaped on his head at the sight
That the clustering cliffs seemed to clatter down round them
In heaps. The men, when they met him, hailed him,
And loudly with chiding speeches hallooed him;
Threats were oft thrown at him, thief he was called;
At his tail were the greyhounds, that tarry he might not.
They rushed at him oft when he raced for the open,
And ran to the wood again, Reynard the wily.
Thus he led them, all muddied, the lord and his men,
In this manner along through the hills until mid-day.
At home, the noble knight wholesomely slept
In the cold of the morn within comely curtains.
But the lady, for love, did not let herself sleep,
Or fail in the purpose fixed in her heart;
But quickly she roused herself, came there quickly,
Arrayed in a gay robe that reached to the ground,
The skins of the splendid fur skillfully trimmed close.
On her head no colors save jewels, well-cut,
That were twined in her hair-fret in clusters of twenty.
Her fair face was completely exposed, and her throat;
In front her breast too was bare, and her back.
She comes through the chamber-door, closes it after her,
Swings wide a window, speaks to the wight,
And rallies him soon in speech full of sport
And good cheer.
"Ah! man, how can you sleep?
The morning is so clear."
He was in sorrow deep,
Yet her he then did hear.

In a dream muttered Gawain, deep in its gloom,

1675. prime, about six o'clock in the morning. Prime is the first of the daytime canonical offices or hours.
1680. 'best be the third time,' a proverb.

Like a man by a throng of sad thoughts sorely moved 1751
Of how fate was to deal out his destiny to him
That morn, when he met the man at the Green Chapel,
Bound to abide his blow, unresisting.
But as soon as that comely one came to his senses,
Started from slumber and speedily answered,
The lovely lady came near, sweetly laughing,
Bent down o'er his fair face and daintily kissed him.
And well, in a worthy manner, he welcomed her.
Seeing her glorious, gaily attired, 1760
Without fault in her features, most fine in her color,
Deep joy came welling up, warming his heart.
With sweet, gentle smiling they straightway grew merry;
So passed naught between them but pleasure, joy,
And delight.
Goodly was their debate,
Nor was their gladness slight.
Their peril had been great
Had Mary quit her knight. 1769

For that noble princess pressed him so closely,
Brought him so near the last bound, that her love
He was forced to accept, or, offending, refuse her:
Concerned for his courtesy not to prove caitiff,
And more for his ruin if wrong he committed,
Betraying the hero, the head of that house.
"God forbid," said the knight; "that never shall be";
And lovingly laughing a little, he parried
The words of fondness that fell from her mouth.
She said to him, "Sir, you are surely to blame
If you love not the lady beside whom you're lying,
Of all the world's women most wounded in heart,
Unless you've one dearer, a lover you like more,
Your faith to her plighted, so firmly made fast 1783
You desire not to loosen it—so I believe.
Now tell me truly I pray you; the truth,
By all of the loves that in life are, conceal not
Through guile."
The knight said, "By Saint John,"
And pleasantly to smile
Began, "In faith I've none, 1790
Nor will have for a while."

"Such words," said the lady, "the worst are of all;
But in sooth I am answered, and sad it seems to me.
Kiss me now kindly, and quickly I'll go;
I on earth may but mourn, as a much loving mortal."
Sighing she stoops down, and kisses him seemly;
Then starting away from him, says as she stands,
"Now, my dear, at parting, do me this pleasure:
Give me some gift, thy glove if it might be,
To bring you to mind, sir, my mourning to lessen."
"On my word," quoth the hero, "I would that I had here, 1801
For thy sake, the thing that I think the dearest
I own, for in sooth you've deserved very often
A greater reward than one I could give.
But a pledge of love would profit but little;
'T would help not your honor to have at this time
For a keepsake a glove, as a gift of Gawain.
I've come on a mission to countries most strange;
I've no servants with splendid things filling their sacks:
That displeases me, lady, for love's sake, at present;
Yet each man without murmur must do what he may 1811
Nor repine."
"Nay, lord of honors high,
Though I have naught of thine,"
Quoth the lovely lady, "I
Shall give you gift of mine."

She offered a rich ring, wrought in red gold,
With a blazing stone that stood out above it,
And shot forth brilliant rays bright as the sun;
Wit you well that wealth right huge it was worth.
But promptly the hero replied, refusing it, 1821
"Madam, I care not for gifts now to keep;
I have none to tender and naught will I take."
Thus he ever declined her offer right earnest,
And swore on his word that he would not accept it;
And, sad he declined, she thereupon said,
"If my ring you refuse, since it seems too rich,
If you would not so highly to me be beholden,
My girdle, that profits you less, I'll give you."
She swiftly removed the belt circling her sides, 1830
Round her tunic knotted, beneath her bright mantle;
'T was fashioned of green silk, and fair made with gold,
With gold, too, the borders embellished and beautiful.
To Gawain she gave it, and gaily besought him
To take it, although he thought it but trifling.
He swore by no manner of means he'd accept
Either gold or treasure ere God gave him grace
To attain the adventure he'd there undertaken.
"And, therefore, I pray, let it prove not displeasing,
But give up your suit, for to grant it I'll never 1840
Agree.
I'm deeply in your debt
For your kind ways to me.
In hot and cold I yet
Will your true servant be."

"Refuse ye this silk," the lady then said,
"As slight in itself? Truly it seems so.
Lo! it is little, and less is its worth;
But one knowing the nature knit up within it,
Would give it a value more great, peradventure;
For no man girt with this girdle of green,
And bearing it fairly made fast about him,
Might ever be cut down by any on earth,
For his life in no way in the world could be taken."
Then mused the man, and it came to his mind
In the peril appointed him precious 't would prove,
When he'd found the chapel, to face there his fortune.
The device, might he slaying evade, would be splendid.
Her suit then he suffered, and let her speak;
And the belt she offered him, earnestly urging it
(And Gawain consented), and gave it with good will,
And prayed him for her sake ne'er to display it,
But, true, from her husband to hide it. The hero
Agreed that no one should know of it ever.
Then he
Thanked her with all his might
Of heart and thought; and she
By then to this stout knight
Had given kisses three.

Then the lady departs, there leaving the lord,
For more pleasure she could not procure from that prince.
When she's gone, then quickly Sir Gawain clothes himself,
Rises and dresses in noble array,
Lays by the love-lace the lady had left him,
Faithfully hides it where later he'd find it.
At once then went on his way to the chapel,
Approached in private a priest, and prayed him
To make his life purer, more plainly him teach
How his soul, when he had to go hence, should be saved.
He declared his faults, confessing them fully,
The more and the less, and mercy besought,
And then of the priest implored absolution.
He surely absolved him, and made him as spotless,
Indeed, as if doomsday were due on the morrow.
Then among the fair ladies he made more merry
With lovely caroles, all kinds of delights,
That day than before, until darkness fell.
All there
Were treated courteously,
"And never," they declare,
"Has Gawain shown such glee
Since hither he did fare."

In that nook where his lot may be love let him linger!
The lord's in the meadow still, leading his men.
He has slain this fox that he followed so long;
As he vaulted a hedge to get view of the villain,
Hearing the hounds that hastened hard after him,
Reynard from out a rough thicket came running,
And right at his heels in a rush all the rabble.
He, seeing that wild thing, wary, awaits him,
Unsheaths his bright brand and strikes at the beast.
And he swerved from its sharpness and back would have started;
A hound, ere he could, came hurrying up to him;
All of them fell on him fast by the horse's feet,
Worried that sly one with wrathful sound.
And quickly the lord alights, and catches him,
Takes him in haste from the teeth of the hounds,
And over his head holds him high, loudly shouting,
Where brachets, many and fierce, at him barked.
Thither huntsmen made haste with many a horn,
The recall, till they saw him, sounding right clearly.
As soon as his splendid troop had assembled,
All bearing a bugle blew them together,
The others having no horns all hallooed.
'T was the merriest baying that man ever heard
That was raised for the soul of Reynard with sounding
Din.
They fondle each dog's head
Who his reward did win.
Then take they Reynard dead
And strip him of his skin.

And now, since near was the night, they turned homeward,
Strongly and sturdily sounding their horns.
At last at his loved home the lord alighted,
A fire on the hearth found, the hero beside it,
Sir Gawain the good, who glad was withal,
For he had 'mong the ladies in love much delight.
A blue robe that fell to the floor he was wearing;
His surcoat, that softly was furred, well beseemed him;
A hood of the same hue hung on his shoulders,
And both were bordered with white all about.
He, mid-most, met the good man in the hall,
And greeted him gladly, graciously saying:
"Now shall I first fulfil our agreement
We struck to good purpose, when drink was not spared."
Then Gawain embraced him, gave him three kisses,
The sweetest and soundest a man could bestow.
"By Christ, you'd great happiness," quoth then the host,

"In getting these wares, if good were your bargains."
"Take no care for the cost," the other said quickly,
"Since plainly the debt that is due I have paid."
Said the other, "By Mary, mine's of less worth.
The whole of the day I have hunted, and gotten
The skin of this fox—the fiend take its foulness!—
Right poor to pay for things of such price
As you've pressed on me here so heartily, kisses
So good."
"Say no more," Gawain saith;
"I thank you, by the rood!"
How the fox met his death
He told him as they stood.

With mirth and minstrelsy, meat at their pleasure
They made as merry as any men might
(With ladies' laughter, and launching of jests
Right glad were they both, the good man and Gawain)
Unless they had doted or else had been drunken.
Both the man and the company make many jokes,
Till the time is come when the two must be parted,
When finally the knights are forced to go bedward.
And first of the lord his respectful leave
This goodly man took, and graciously thanked him:
"May God you reward for the welcome you gave me
This high feast, the splendid sojourn I've had here.
I give you myself, if you'd like it, to serve you.
I must, as you know, on the morrow move on;
Give me some one to show me the path, as you said,
To the Green Chapel, there, as God will allow me,
On New Year the fate that is fixed to perform."
"With a good will, indeed," said the good man; "whatever
I promised to do I deem myself ready."
He a servant assigns on his way to set him,
To take him by hills that no trouble he'd have,
And through grove and wood by the way most direct
Might repair.
The lord he thanked again
For the honor done him there.
The knight his farewell then
Took of those ladies fair.

To them with sorrow and kissing he spoke,
And besought them his thanks most sincere to accept;
And they, replying, promptly returned them,
With sighings full sore to the Saviour commended him.
Then he with courtesy quitted the company,
Giving each man that he met his thanks
For kindness, for trouble he'd taken, for care
Whereby each had sought to serve him right eagerly.
Pained was each person to part with him then,
As if long they in honor had lived with that noble.
With people and lights he was led to his chamber,
To bed gaily brought there to be at his rest;
Yet I dare not say whether soundly he slept,
For much, if he would, on the morn to remember
Had he.
Let him lie stilly there
Near what he sought to see.
What happened I'll declare,
If you will silent be.

IV

The New Year draws near, and the nighttime now passes;
The day, as the Lord bids, drives on to darkness.
Outside, there sprang up wild storms in the world;
The clouds cast keenly the cold to the earth
With enough of the north sting to trouble the naked;
Down shivered the snow, nipping sharply the wild beasts;
The wind from the heights, shrilly howling, came rushing,
And heaped up each dale full of drifts right huge.
Full well the man listened who lay in his bed.
Though he shut tight his lids, he slept but a little;
He knew by each cock that crowed 't was the tryst time,
And swiftly ere dawn of the day he arose,
For there shone then the light of a lamp in his room;
To his chamberlain called, who answered him quickly,
And bade him his saddle to bring and his mailshirt.
The other man roused up and fetched him his raiment,
Arrayed then that knight in a fashion right noble.
First he clad him in clothes to ward off the cold,
Then his other equipment, carefully kept:
His pieces of plate armor, polished right cleanly,
The rings of his rich mail burnished from rust.
All was fresh as at first; he was fain to give thanks
To the men.
He had on every piece
Full brightly burnished then.
He, gayest from here to Greece,
Ordered his steed again.

He garbed himself there in the loveliest garments
(His coat had its blazon of beautiful needlework
Stitched upon velvet for show, its rich stones

1949. rood, the Holy Cross.

Set about it and studded, its seams all embroidered,
Its lovely fur in the fairest of linings),
Yet he left not the lace, the gift of the lady:
That, Gawain did not, for his own sake, forget.
When the brand on his rounded thighs he had belted,
He twisted the love-token two times about him.
That lord round his waist with delight quickly wound
The girdle of green silk, that seemed very gay
Upon royal red cloth that was rich to behold.
But Gawain the girdle wore not for its great price,
Or pride in its pendants although they were polished,
Though glittering gold there gleamed on the ends,
But himself to save when he needs must suffer
The death, nor could stroke then of sword or of knife
Him defend.
Then was the bold man dressed;
Quickly his way did wend;
To all the court expressed
His great thanks without end.

Then was Gringolet ready that great was and huge,
Who had safely, as seemed to him pleasant, been stabled;
That proud horse pranced, in the pink of condition.
The lord then comes to him, looks at his coat,
And soberly says, and swears on his word,
"In this castle's a company mindful of courtesy,
Led by this hero. Delight may they have;
And may love the dear lady betide all her lifetime.
If they for charity cherish a guest,
And give so great welcome, may God reward them,
Who rules the heaven on high, and the rest of you.
Might I for long live my life on the earth,
Some repayment with pleasure I'd make, if 't were possible."
He steps in the stirrup, strides into the saddle,
Receives on his shoulder the shield his man brings him,
And spurs into Gringolet strikes with his gilt heels;
Who leaps on the stones and lingers no longer
To prance.
The knight on his horse sits,
Who bears his spear and lance,
The house to Christ commits,
And wishes it good chance.

2032. brand, sword.

Then down the drawbridge they dropped, the broad gates
Unbarred, and on both sides bore them wide open.
He blessed them quickly, and crossed o'er the planks there
(He praises the porter, who knelt by the prince
Begging God to save Gawain, and gave him good-day),
And went on his way with but one man attended
To show him the turns to that sorrowful spot
Where he must to that onerous onset submit.
By hillsides where branches were bare they both journeyed;
They climbed over cliffs where the cold was clinging.
The clouds hung aloft, but 't was lowering beneath them.
On the moor dripped the mist, on the mountains melted;
Each hill had a hat, a mist-cloak right huge.
The brooks foamed and bubbled on hillsides about them,
And brightly broke on their banks as they rushed down.
Full wandering the way was they went through the wood,
Until soon it was time for the sun to be springing.
Then they
Were on a hill full high;
White snow beside them lay.
The servant who rode nigh
Then bade his master stay.

"I have led you hither, my lord, at this time,
And not far are you now from that famous place
You have sought for, and asked so especially after.
Yet, sir, to you surely I'll say, since I know you,
A man in this world whom I love right well,
If you'd follow my judgment, the better you'd fare.
You make haste to a place that is held full of peril;
One dwells, the worst in the world, in that waste,
For he's strong and stern, and takes pleasure in striking.
No man on the earth can equal his might;
He is bigger in body than four of the best men
In Arthur's own household, Hestor or others.
And thus he brings it about at the chapel:
That place no one passes so proud in his arms
That he smites him not dead with a stroke of his hand.

2102. Hestor. Although the manuscript reads "Hestor," the reference is almost certainly to the Trojan hero, Hector, famous for his prowess. See Caxton's catalogue of the "nine worthies," page 149.

He's a man most immoderate, showing no mercy;
Be it chaplain or churl that rides by the chapel,
Monk or priest, any manner of man,
Him to slay seems as sweet as to still live himself.
So I say, as sure as you sit in your saddle
You're killed, should the knight so choose, if you come here;
That take as the truth, though you twenty lives had
To spend.
He's lived in this place long
In battles without end.
Against his strokes right strong
You cannot you defend.

"So let him alone, good Sir Gawain, and leave
By a different road, for God's sake, and ride
To some other country where Christ may reward you.
And homeward again I will hie me, and promise
To swear by the Lord and all his good saints
(So help me the oaths on God's halidom sworn)
That I'll guard well your secret, and give out no story
You hastened to flee any hero I've heard of."
"Thank you," said Gawain, and grudgingly added,
"Good fortune go with you for wishing me well.
And truly I think you'd not tell; yet though never
So surely you hid it, if hence I should hasten,
Fearful, to fly in the fashion you tell of,
A coward I'd prove, and could not be pardoned.
The chapel I'll find whatsoever befalls,
And talk with that wight the way that I want to,
Let weal or woe follow as fate may wish.
Though the knave,
Hard to subdue and fell,
Should stand there with a stave,
Yet still the Lord knows well
His servants how to save."

Quoth the man, "By Mary, you've said now this much:
That you wish to bring down your own doom on your head.
Since you'd lose your life, I will stay you no longer.
Put your helm on your head, take your spear in your hand,
And ride down this road by the side of that rock
Till it brings you down to the dale's rugged bottom;
Then look at the glade on the left hand a little:
You'll see in the valley that self-same chapel,
And near it the great-limbed knight who is guarding it.
Gawain the noble, farewell now, in God's name!

2123. halidom, holiness; also, a holy relic.

I would not go with thee for all the world's wealth,
Nor in fellowship ride one more foot through the forest."
The man in the trees there then turns his bridle,
As hard as he can hits his horse with his heels,
And across the fields gallops, there leaving Sir Gawain
Alone.
"By God," the knight said, "now
I'll neither weep nor groan.
Unto God's will I bow,
And make myself his own."

He strikes spurs into Gringolet, starts on the path;
By a bank at the side of a small wood he pushes in,
Rides down the rugged slope right to the dale.
Then about him he looks, and the land seems wild,
And nowhere he sees any sign of a shelter,
But slopes on each side of him, high and steep,
And rocks, gnarled and rough, and stones right rugged.
The clouds there seemed to him scraped by the crags.
Then he halted and held back his horse at that time,
And spied on all sides in search of the chapel;
Such nowhere he saw, but soon, what seemed strange,
In the midst of a glade a mound, as it might be,
A smooth, swelling knoll by the side of the water,
The falls of a rivulet running close by;
In its banks the brook bubbled as though it were boiling.
The knight urged on Gringolet, came to the glade,
There leaped down lightly and tied to the limb
Of a tree, right rugged, the reins of his noble steed,
Went to the mound, and walked all about it,
Debating what manner of thing it might be:
On the end and on each side an opening; everywhere
Over it grass was growing in patches,
All hollow inside, it seemed an old cave
Or a crag's old cleft: which, he could not decide.
Said the knight,
"Is this the chapel here?
Alas, dear Lord! here might
The fiend, when midnight's near,
His matin prayers recite.

"Of a truth," said Gawain, "the glade here is gloomy;
The Green Chapel's ugly, with herbs overgrown.
It greatly becomes here that hero, green-clad,

2171. a mound, a "fairy mound"; actually, from the description, a prehistoric tumulus.

To perform in the devil's own fashion his worship.
I feel in my five senses this is the fiend
Who has made me come to this meeting to kill me.
Destruction fall on this church of ill-fortune!
The cursedest chapel that ever I came to!"
With helm on his head and lance in his hand
He went right to the rock of that rugged abode.
From that high hill he heard, from a hard rock over
The stream, on the hillside, a sound wondrous loud.
Lo! it clattered on cliffs fit to cleave them, as though
A scythe on a grindstone some one were grinding.
It whirred, lo! and whizzed like a water-mill's wheel;
Lo! it ground and it grated, grievous to hear.
"By God, this thing, as I think," then said Gawain,
"Is done now for me, since my due turn to meet it
Is near.
God's will be done! 'Ah woe!'
No whit doth aid me here.
Though I my life forego
No sound shall make me fear."

And then the man there commenced to call loudly,
"Who here is the master, with me to hold tryst?
For Gawain the good now is going right near.
He who craves aught of me let him come hither quickly;
'T is now or never; he needs to make haste."
Said somebody, "Stop," from the slope up above him,
"And promptly you'll get what I promised to give you."
Yet he kept up the whirring noise quickly a while,
Turned to finish his sharpening before he'd descend.
Then he came by a crag, from a cavern emerging,
Whirled out of a den with a dreadful weapon,
A new Danish axe to answer the blow with:
Its blade right heavy, curved back to the handle,
Sharp filed with the filing tool, four feet in length,
'T was no less, by the reach of that lace gleaming brightly.
The fellow in green was garbed as at first,
Both his face and his legs, his locks and his beard,
Save that fast o'er the earth on his feet he went fairly,
The shaft on the stone set, and stalked on beside it.
On reaching the water, he would not wade it;
On his axe he hopped over, and hastily strode,
Very fierce, through the broad field filled all about him
With snow.
Sir Gawain met the man,
And bowed by no means low,
Who said, "Good sir, men can
Trust you to tryst to go."

Said the green man, "Gawain, may God you guard!
You are welcome indeed, sir knight, at my dwelling.
Your travel you've timed as a true man should,
And you know the compact we came to between us;
A twelvemonth ago you took what chance gave,
And I promptly at New Year was pledged to repay you.
In truth, we are down in this dale all alone;
Though we fight as we please, here there's no one to part us.
Put your helm from your head, and have here your payment;
Debate no further than I did before,
When you slashed off my head with a single stroke."
"Nay," quoth Gawain, "by God who gave me my spirit,
I'll harbor no grudge whatever harm happens.
Exceed not one stroke and still I shall stand;
You may do as you please, I'll in no way oppose
The blow."
He left the flesh all bare,
Bending his neck down low
As if he feared naught there,
For fear he would not show.

Then the man in green raiment quickly made ready,
Uplifted his grim tool Sir Gawain to smite;
With the whole of his strength he heaved it on high,
As threateningly swung it as though he would slay him.
Had it fallen again with the force he intended
That lord, ever-brave, from the blow had been lifeless.
But Gawain a side glance gave at the weapon
As down it came gliding to do him to death;
With his shoulders shrank from the sharp iron a little.
The other with sudden jerk stayed the bright axe,
And reproved then that prince with proud words in plenty:
"Not Gawain thou art who so good is considered,
Ne'er daunted by host in hill or in dale;
Now in fear, ere thou feelest a hurt, thou art flinching;
Such cowardice never I knew of that knight.
When you swung at me, sir, I fled not nor started;

2223. Danish axe, an axe with a long blade; not the same weapon that the Green Knight had brought to Arthur's court. **2226. lace,** the thongs that bound the axe to the handle.

No cavil I offered in King Arthur's castle.
My head at my feet fell, yet never I flinched,
And thy heart is afraid ere a hurt thou feelest,
And therefore thy better I'm bound to be thought
On that score."
"I shrank once," Gawain said,
"And I will shrink no more;
Yet cannot I my head,
If it fall down, restore.

"But make ready, sir, quickly, and come to the point;
My destiny deal me, and do it forthwith;
For a stroke I will suffer, and start no further
Till hit with thy weapon; have here my pledged word."
Quoth the other, heaving it high, "Have at thee!"
As fierce in his manner as if he were mad,
He mightily swung but struck not the man,
Withheld on a sudden his hand ere it hurt him.
And firmly he waited and flinched in no member,
But stood there as still as a stone or a stump
In rocky ground held by a hundred roots.
Then the Green Knight again began to speak gaily:
"It behooves me to hit, now that whole is thy heart.
Thy high hood that Arthur once gave you now hold back,
Take care that your neck at this cut may recover."
And Gawain full fiercely said in a fury,
"Come! lay on, thou dread man; too long thou art threatening.
I think that afraid of your own self you feel."
"In sooth," said the other, "thy speech is so savage
No more will I hinder thy mission nor have it
Delayed."
With puckered lips and brow
He stands with ready blade.
Not strange 't is hateful now
To him past hope of aid.

He lifts his axe lightly, and lets it down deftly,
The blade's edge next to the naked neck.
Though he mightily hammered he hurt him no more
Than to give him a slight nick that severed the skin there.
Through fair skin the keen axe so cut to the flesh
That shining blood shot to the earth o'er his shoulders.
As soon as he saw his blood gleam on the snow
He sprang forth in one leap, for more than a spear length;
His helm fiercely caught up and clapped on his head;
With his shoulders his fair shield shot round in front of him,
Pulled out his bright sword, and said in a passion
(And since he was mortal man born of his mother
The hero was never so happy by half),
"Cease thy violence, man; no more to me offer,
For here I've received, unresisting, a stroke.
If a second thou strikest I soon will requite thee,
And swiftly and fiercely, be certain of that,
Will repay.
One stroke on me might fall
By bargain struck that way,
Arranged in Arthur's hall;
Therefore, sir knight, now stay!"

The man turned away, on his weapon rested,
The shaft on the ground set, leaned on the sharp edge,
And gazed at Sir Gawain there in the glade;
Saw that bold man, unblenching, standing right bravely,
Full-harnessed and gallant; at heart he was glad.
Then gaily the Green Knight spoke in a great voice,
And said to the man in speech that resounded,
"Now be not so savage, bold sir, for towards you
None here has acted unhandsomely, save
In accord with the compact arranged in the King's court.
I promised the stroke you've received, so hold you
Well payed. I free you from all duties further.
If brisk I had been, peradventure a buffet
I'd harshly have dealt that harm would have done you.
In mirth, with a feint I menaced you first,
With no direful wound rent you; right was my deed,
By the bargain that bound us both on the first night,
When, faithful and true, you fulfilled our agreement,
And gave me your gain as a good man ought to.
The second I struck at you, sir, for the morning
You kissed my fair wife and the kisses accorded me.
Two mere feints for both times I made at you, man,
Without woe.
True men restore by right,
One fears no danger so;
You failed the third time, knight,
And therefore took that blow.

"'T is my garment you're wearing, that woven girdle,
Bestowed by my wife, as in truth I know well.
I know also your kisses and all of your acts
And my wife's advances; myself, I devised them.
I sent her to try you, and truly you seem

2347. the first night. Gawain now learns for the first time the identity of the Green Knight.

The most faultless of men that e'er fared on his feet.
As a pearl compared to white peas is more precious,
So next to the other gay knights is Sir Gawain.
But a little you lacked, and loyalty wanted,
Yet truly 't was not for intrigue or for wooing,
But love of your life; the less do I blame you."
Sir Gawain stood in a study a great while,
So sunk in disgrace that in spirit he groaned;
To his face all the blood in his body was flowing;
For shame, as the other was talking, he shrank.
And these were the first words that fell from his lips:
"Be cowardice cursed, and coveting! In you
Are vice and villainy, virtue destroying."
The lace he then seized, and loosened the strands,
And fiercely the girdle flung at the Green Knight.
"Lo! there is faith-breaking! evil befall it.
To coveting came I, for cowardice caused me
From fear of your stroke to forsake in myself
What belongs to a knight: munificence, loyalty.
I'm faulty and false, who've been ever afraid
Of untruth and treachery; sorrow betide both
And care!
Here I confess my sin;
All faulty did I fare.
Your good will let me win,
And then I will beware."

Then the Green Knight laughed, and right graciously said,
"I am sure that the harm is healed that I suffered.
So clean you're confessed, so cleared of your faults,
Having had the point of my weapon's plain penance,
I hold you now purged of offence, and as perfectly
Spotless as though you'd ne'er sinned in your life.
And I give to you, sir, the golden-hemmed girdle,
As green as my gown. Sir Gawain, when going
Forth on your way among famous princes,
Think still of our strife and this token right splendid,
'Mid chivalrous knights, of the chapel's adventure.
This New Year you'll come to my castle again,
And the rest of this feast in revel most pleasant
Will go."
Then pressed him hard the lord:
"My wife and you, I know
We surely will accord,
Who was your bitter foe."

"No indeed," quoth the hero, his helm seized and doffed it
Graciously, thanking the Green Knight; "I've stayed
Long enough. May good fortune befall you; may He
Who all fame doth confer give it fully to you, sir.
To your lady, gracious and lovely, commend me,
To her and that other, my honored ladies,
That so with their sleights deceived their knight subtly.
But no marvel it is for a fool to act madly,
Through woman's wiles to be brought to woe.
So for certain was Adam deceived by some woman,
By several Solomon, Samson besides;
Delilah dealt him his doom; and David
Was duped by Bath-sheba, enduring much sorrow.
Since these were grieved by their guile, 't would be great gain
To love them yet never believe them, if knights could.
For formerly these were most noble and fortunate,
More than all others who lived on the earth;
And these few
By women's wiles were caught
With whom they had to do.
Though I'm beguiled, I ought
To be excused now too.

"But your girdle," said Gawain, "may God you reward!
With a good will I'll use it, yet not for the gold,
The sash or the silk, or the sweeping pendants,
Or fame, or its workmanship wondrous, or cost,
But in sign of my sin I shall see it oft.
When in glory I move, with remorse I'll remember
The frailty and fault of the stubborn flesh,
How soon 't is infected with stains of defilement;
And thus when I'm proud of my prowess in arms,
The sight of this sash shall humble my spirit.
But one thing I pray, if it prove not displeasing;
Because you are lord of the land where I stayed
In your house with great worship (may He now reward you
Who sitteth on high and upholdeth the heavens),
What name do you bear? No more would I know."
And then "That truly I'll tell," said the other;
"Bercilak de Hautdesert here am I called.
Through her might who lives with me, Morgan le Fay,
Well-versed in the crafts and cunning of magic
(Many of Merlin's arts she has mastered,
For long since she dealt in the dalliance of love
With him whom your heroes at home know, that sage

2446. Through her might . . . The sentence is incomplete; perhaps a line is lost which stated that the Green Knight owed his ability as a shape-shifter to Morgan's power. **Morgan le Fay,** a sister of Arthur, was, as Malory tells us, "a great clerk of necromancy." She was a pupil, and in some stories the mistress, of Merlin the magician.

Without blame.
'Morgan the goddess,' so
She's rightly known by name.
No one so proud doth go
That him she cannot tame),

"I was sent in this way to your splendid hall
To make trial of your pride, and to see if the people's
Tales were true of the Table's great glory.
This wonder she sent to unsettle your wits,
And to daunt so the Queen as to cause her to die
From fear at the sight of that phantom speaker
Holding his head in his hand at the high table.
Lives she at home there, that ancient lady;
She's even thine aunt, King Arthur's half-sister,
Tyntagel's duchess's daughter, whom Uther
Made later the mother of mighty Lord Arthur.
I beg thee, sir, therefore, come back to thine aunt;
In my castle make merry. My company love thee,
And I, sir, wish thee as well, on my word,
As any on earth for thy high sense of honor."
He said to him, nay, this he'd never consent to.
The men kiss, embrace, and each other commend
To the Prince of Paradise; there they part
In the cold.
Gawain on his fair horse
To Arthur hastens bold;
The bright Green Knight his course
Doth at his pleasure hold.

Through the wood now goes Sir Gawain by wild ways
On Gringolet, given by God's grace his life.
Oft in houses, and oft in the open he lodged,
Met many adventures, won many a victory:
These I intend not to tell in this tale.
Now whole was the hurt he had in his neck,
And about it the glimmering belt he was bearing,
Bound to his side like a baldric obliquely,
Tied under his left arm, that lace, with a knot
As a sign that with stain of sin he'd been found.
And thus to the court he comes all securely.
Delight in that dwelling arose when its lord knew
That Gawain had come; a good thing he thought it.
The King kissed the lord, and the Queen did likewise,
And next many knights drew near him to greet him
And ask how he'd fared; and he wondrously answered,
Confessed all the hardships that him had befallen,
The happenings at chapel, the hero's behavior,
The lady's love, and lastly the lace.
He showed them the nick in his neck all naked
The blow that the Green Knight gave for deceit
Him to blame.
In torment this he owned;
Blood in his face did flame;
With wrath and grief he groaned,
When showing it with shame.

Laying hold of the lace, quoth the hero, "Lo! lord!
The band of this fault I bear on my neck;
And this is the scathe and damage I've suffered,
For cowardice caught there, and coveting also,
The badge of untruth in which I was taken.
And this for as long as I live I must wear,
For his fault none may hide without meeting misfortune,
For once it is fixed, it can ne'er be unfastened."
To the knight then the King gave comfort; the court too
Laughed greatly, and made this gracious agreement:
That ladies and lords to the Table belonging,
All of the brotherhood, baldrics should bear
Obliquely about them, bands of bright green,
Thus following suit for the sake of the hero.
For the Round Table's glory was granted that lace,
And he held himself honored who had it thereafter,
As told in the book, the best of romances.
In the days of King Arthur this deed was done
Whereof witness is borne by Brutus's book.
Since Brutus, that bold man, first came here to Britain,
When ceased, indeed, had the siege and assault
At Troy's wall,
Full many feats ere now
Like this one did befall.
May He with thorn-crowned brow
To His bliss bring us all. Amen.

HONY SOYT QUI MAL PENCE.*

2460. to daunt so the Queen. Guinevere had interfered in one of Morgan's love affairs. **2465. Uther.** Uther Pendragon, father of Arthur by Ygern (Ygraine), wife of Gorlois, Duke of Tyntagel. After the duke's death, Uther visited Ygern in her husband's shape, which had been given him by Merlin.

2519. Round Table's . . . lace. This passage is sometimes taken to be a connection between *Sir Gawain and the Green Knight* and the founding of the Order of the Garter (*c.* 1344), the oldest and most important order of knighthood in England. But even the presence of the motto of the Garter at the end of the poem does not make this theory very convincing. The passage does, indeed, suggest the founding of an order, but of what nature there is no certain evidence. **2523. Brutus's book.** The term "Brut" came to be applied to any chronicle of Britain, but we know of no chronicle that mentions this story of Gawain. *** Hony soyt qui mal pence.** "Shamed he be who thinks ill of it." (The motto of the Order of the Garter.)

William Langland

c. 1332–c. 1400

Piers Plowman, customarily ranked next to the poems of Chaucer in literary merit, is in many respects the most puzzling of fourteenth-century writings. The authorship of the poem has long been a matter of debate, but the latest scholarly opinion accepts the traditional view that the three main texts of the poem are in substance the work of one man, that the one man is the dreamer of the poem, and that he was William Langland. There are no contemporary records of Langland. Of his life we know almost nothing, and most of what we know is derived from scattered passages of what are assumed to be autobiographical references in the third and latest version of the poem. From such inferences emerge the scanty statistics that Langland was born about 1332 near the Malvern Hills, that he was probably the son of a peasant woman and probably born out of wedlock. He was sent to school by his father and some friends. He took Minor Orders in the Church, and probably remained an acolyte for the rest of his life. He wandered as a shepherd about the Malvern Hills and later made his way to London. He seems to have lived in a house in the Cornhill district of London with his wife Kit and a daughter, and to have earned a pittance by praying for the souls of his benefactors. He died probably about the end of the century.

This almost anonymous poet, who would be entirely unknown except for his poem, is thus an almost exact contemporary of the greatest poet of the age, Geoffrey Chaucer. But this most shadowy of literary figures has one of the strongest personalities in English literature. Professor E. Talbot Donaldson in the most recent study of Langland and his poem remarks "how curiously provocative and attractive is the personality that casts its shadow upon every page of the poem. Indeed, for the modern reader, the strong sense of personality is one of the poem's greatest charms. The poet seems to have been incapable of artistic aloofness. As a result, his personality, immensely verbose, self-consciously picturesque, ironical and realistic, tactless and inquisitive, playful yet savagely severe, becomes, to a very large extent, his poem."

Piers Plowman has come down to us in some fifty-two manuscripts, which vary in text and shape—a circumstance which attests the great popularity of a poem composed a century before William Caxton set up his printing press. The many variants also suggest that some of the different versions were transmitted through recitation. There are three main versions of the poem, conveniently designated A, B, and C, which vary greatly in length and material. Version A, by far the shortest and clearest, dates from about 1362; Version B, which greatly amplifies Version A, dates from about 1376; Version C may have been composed at any time between 1377 and 1399 but is now thought to have been completed about 1386. Version C is a much less drastic revision of B than B is of A.

The poem belongs to a common medieval literary type, the dream-vision, but it is very different from the typical dream-visions of the French poets whom Chaucer followed. The spiritual kinship of *Piers Plowman* is not with the limpid and conventional allegories of love which sprang from the first part of the *Roman de la Rose,* but rather with Dante's *Divine Comedy.* Langland's dream-vision is also a spiritual forerunner of John Bunyan's seventeenth-century Protestant allegory, the *Pilgrim's Progress.* Although different in form and theology from Bunyan's book, Langland's allegory is, like the latter, a series of visions of this world and the next, and its theme, like Bunyan's, is the salvation of the soul of Everyman and the spiritual progress from the world of the flesh to the world of the spirit.

The poem is divided into two main parts, the Vision of Piers Plowman proper and the Lives of Do-Well, Do-Bet, and Do-Best. The internal structure of the poem is too intricate and the story has too many digressions to permit discussion here, but a certain unity of impression is given to the whole by the author's serious concern with one subject only—the means by which man may and must obtain salvation. The hero, Piers the Plowman, appears in various guises throughout the poem—as plowman, as priest, as bishop—but always as a symbol of the sincere follower of Truth. Out of the whole emerges also a detailed picture of England in the second half of the fourteenth century, with its *dramatis personae* of knights, tinkers, tailors, minstrels, preachers, pilgrims, friars, beggars, and thieves. Parts of the picture remind us of what we gather about contemporary life from Chaucer's *Canterbury Tales*, but the differences between the two impressions are greater than the similarities. Chaucer's own feelings may have been deep enough, and there are subtle hints that they were, but he wrote for an audience which did not care to be reminded too directly of painful, shameful events and trends. Many of Chaucer's audience, indeed, must have been uneasily aware of their own complicity in the sorry state of the nation. *Piers Plowman*, on the other hand, shows none of Chaucer's compunction or restraint. Here, only occasionally obscured by the allegory, we see how, as the century dragged out its weary years, England suffered from the effects of a series of catastrophes: the Black Death of 1348–49, with the consequent disruption of the balance and distribution of man power; the Hundred Years' War, at first so glorious and so rich in booty, but always expensive and debilitating, and later conducted in a shamefully inept fashion; the uncertain, uneven, unequal, but inevitable breaking-down of the feudal system; the Peasants' Revolt of 1381; the unblushing rapacity of the various cliques which controlled or sought to control the Government; the corruption, ignorance, and greed of many of the clergy; the conflict within the Church itself, symbolized, perhaps, by the Schism; the bitter dynastic feud which culminated in the overthrow and death of Richard II. All these things and more combined to keep the land from being a "Merry England," and it is no "Merry England" which emerges from the pages of *Piers Plowman*.

The poem reveals an intense awareness of the interrelation of events, of the connection between corruption at the top and misery at the bottom of the social scale, but it is in no way class-conscious. Rather it is a dissection, too passionate to be aloof, of all the classes. *Piers Plowman* has sometimes been considered a Lollard or Wycliffite document; that, however, is not the case. Its basic doctrine is orthodox, conservative Catholicism, however painfully aware it is of abuses in the Church. There is no opposition to the tenets of the Church, but there is a pitiless exposure of the misuse of its forms, and an indignant outcry against the rascals who utilize Holy Church as a screen for their misdeeds.

The meter of the poem is the long alliterative line which was revived with such successful results in the middle of the fourteenth century. The irregular, four-beat line with middle stop can best be illustrated by the following quotation from the opening of the Induction in Version A:

In a somer sesun, whon softe was the sonne,
I schop me in-to a schroud, a scheep as I were;
In habite of an hermite unholy of werkes,
Wende I wydene in this world wondres to here.
Bote in a Mayes morwnynge on Malverne hulles
Me bi-fel a ferly, a feyrie me thouhte;
I was weori of wandringe and wente me to reste
Under a brod banke bi a bourne syde,
And as I lay and leonede and lokede on the watres,
I slumberde in a slepyng, hit sownede so murie.

The standard edition of the poem is that of W. W. Skeat in two volumes, published by the Oxford University Press, 1886. Among valuable recent studies of the author and his work are E. Talbot Donaldson's *Piers Plowman: The C-Text and Its Poet*, Yale University Press, 1949; Allan H. Bright's *New Light on "Piers Plowman,"* with a preface by R. W. Chambers, Oxford University Press, 1928; and Nevill Coghill's *Visions from Piers Plowman*, Oxford University Press, 1950. The latter consists of translations of the most important sections of the poem and two valuable appendices, one on "The Form and Meaning of the Poem" and the other on "Medieval Allegory." The first complete rendering of the poem in modern English verse is by Henry W. Wells in his volume, *William Langland: The Vision of Piers Plowman*, with an introduction by Nevill Coghill and notes by the translator, copyright, 1945, by Sheed and Ward, New York. By special permission of the publishers we reprint selections from Mr. Wells's translation.[1]

from THE VISION OF PIERS PLOWMAN

THE INDUCTION

The Vision of the Field of Folk

In a summer season when the sun was softest,
Shrouded in a smock, in shepherd's clothing,
In the habit of a hermit of unholy living
I went through this world to witness wonders.
On a May morning on a Malvern hillside
I saw strange sights like scenes of Faerie.

[1] In his translation Mr. Wells has attempted to combine the best qualities and passages of all three of the main texts of the poem. **5. Malvern hillside.** The Malvern Hills are on the border of Worcestershire and Herefordshire. **6. Faerie** enchantment.

I was weary of wandering and went to rest
By the bank of a brook in a broad meadow.
As I lay and leaned and looked on the water
I slumbered and slept, so sweetly it murmured.

Then I met with marvellous visions.
I was in a wilderness; where, I knew not.
I looked up at the East at the high sun,
And saw a tower on a toft artfully fashioned.
A deep dale was beneath with a dungeon in it,
And deep ditches and dark, dreadful to see.

A fair field full of folk I found between them,
With all manner of men, the meanest and the richest,
Working and wandering as the world demanded.
Some put them to the plow and practised hardship
In setting and sowing and seldom had leisure;
They won what wasters consumed in gluttony.
Some practised pride and quaint behaviour,
And came disguised in clothes and features.
Prayer and penance prevailed with many.
For the love of our Lord they lived in strictness,
To have bliss hereafter and heavenly riches.
Hermits and anchorites held to their dwellings,
Gave up the course of country roving
And all lusty living that delights the body.
Some turned to trade; they tried barter;
And seemed in our sight to succeed better.
Some men were mirthful, learned minstrelsies,
And got gold as gleemen—a guiltless practice.
Yet jesters and janglers, Judas' children,
Feigned idle fancies and wore fools' clothing,
But had wit as they wished to work as others.
What Paul has preached I proffer without glossing:
Qui loquitur turpiloquium, is Lucifer's servant.

Bidders and beggars ride about the country
With bread to the brim in their bags and bellies;
They feign that they are famished and fight in the ale-house.
God wot, they go in gluttony to their chambers
And rise with ribaldry, like Robert's children.
Sleep and sloth pursue them always.

Pilgrims and palmers were plighted together
To seek Saint James and saints in Rome.
They went on their way with many wise stories,
And had leave to lie for a lifetime after.
I saw some who said that they sought for relics;
In each tale that they told their tongue would always
Speak more than was so, it seemed to my thinking.

A host of hermits with hooked staves
Went to Walsingham with their wenches behind them.
These great lubbers and long, who were loath to labor,
Clothed themselves in copes to be distinguished from others,
And robed themselves as hermits to roam at their leisure.
There I found friars of all the four orders,
Who preached to the people for the profit of their bellies,
And glossed the gospel to their own good pleasure;
They coveted their copes, and construed it to their liking.
Many master-brothers may clothe themselves to their fancy,
For their money and their merchandise multiply together.
Since Charity has turned chapman to shrive lords and ladies,
Strange sights have been seen in a few short years.
Unless they and Holy Church hold closer together
The worst misery of man will mount up quickly.

There a pardoner preached as priest of the parish,
And brought out a bull with a bishop's signet,
Said that he himself might assoil all men
Of all falsehood in fasting and vows that were broken.
Common folk confided in him and liked his preaching,
And crept up on cowed knees and kissed his pardons.
He abused them with brevets and blinded their eyesight;
His devil's devices drew rings and brooches.
They gave their gold to keep gluttons,
And believed in liars and lovers of lechery.
If the bishop were blessed and worth both his ears
His seal would not be sent to deceive the people.
But the power of the bishop is not this preacher's license,

14. toft, hillock. **17. field full of folk,** the world. Cf. Matthew 13:38. **35. janglers,** storytellers. **39.** ***Qui . . . turpiloquium,*** who speaks wickedness. Cf. Ephesians 5:4. **40. Bidders,** beggars. **44. Robert's children,** rogues. The allusion is not known. **47. Saint James,** the shrine of Saint James at Compostella in Galicia.

54. Walsingham, the shrine of Our Lady at Walsingham in Norfolk. **58. the four orders,** Carmelites, Augustinians, Dominicans (Jacobins), and Minorites. **64. chapman,** merchant. **68. pardoner.** Compare Chaucer's Pardoner, pages 106 and 113. **69. bull,** episcopal (or papal) edict. **70. assoil,** absolve. **74. brevets,** letters of indulgence.

For the parish priest and the pardoner share the profits together
Which the poor of the parish would have if these were honest.

Because parishes were poor since the pestilence season,
Parsons and parish priests petitioned the bishops
For a license to leave and live in London
And sing there for simony, for silver is sweet.

Bishops and bachelors, both masters and doctors,
Who have cures under Christ and are crowned with the tonsure,
In sign of their service to shrive the parish,
To pray and preach and give the poor nourishment,
Lodge in London in Lent and the long year after,
Some are counting coins in the king's chamber,
Or in exchequer and chancery challenging his debts
From wards and wardmotes, waifs and strays.
Some serve as servants to lords and ladies
And sit in the seats of steward and butler.
They hear mass and matins and many of their hours
Are done without devotion. There is danger that at last
Christ in his consistory will curse many.

I pondered on the power which Peter was given
To bind and to unbind as the Book tells us.
He left it with love at our Lord's commandment
And in care of four virtues, which are fairest of all virtues,
These are called cardinal, or hinges to the gateway
Where Christ is in his kingdom; they close it to many
And open it to many others and show them heaven's glory.
Yet I dare not deny that the dignity of Peter
Is in cardinals at court who command this title
And presume on its power in the pontiff's election.
The election belongs to love and learning.
I might but I must not speak more of their college.

Then there came a king in the company of knighthood.
The might of the Commune made him a ruler.
Common Wit came after and created advisers,
As a council for the king and for the common safety.
The king and the clergy and the company of knighthood
Decreed that the commons should contrive their welfare.
Common Wit and the Commune made craftsmen and tradesmen,
And put others to the plow for the people's profit,
To till and to toil as true life bade them.
The king and the Commune and Common Wit also
Ordained loyalty and law, and each man knew his own.

Then a fool came forth, a long lean fellow,
And knelt to the king and spoke like a cleric:
"Christ keep you, my king, and all your kingdom also,
So live in your land that loyalty may love you,
And righteous rule be rewarded in heaven!"

Then high in the air an angel from heaven
Spoke loudly in Latin, that laymen might never
Either judge or justify or object to opinions,
But suffer and serve; and thus spoke the angel:
Sum Rex, sum Princeps; neutrum fortasse deinceps;
O qui jura regis Christi specialia regis,
Hoc quod agas melius, justus es, esto pius!
Nudum jus a te vestiri vult pietate;
Qualia vis metere, talia grana sere.
Si jus nudatur, nudo de jure metatur;
Si seritur pietas, de pietate metas!

Then a glutton of language, a scandalous jester,
Answered the angel, who hovered about them:
Dum rex a regere dicatur nomen habere;
Nomen habet sine re, nisi studet jura tenere.

83. the pestilence season, no doubt 1348–49, the years of the Black Death. **87–94. Bishops . . . strays.** There were frequent protests against the number of clerics in public service, protests which came as often from hopeful laymen as from indignant ecclesiastics. **94. wardmotes,** ward meetings. **waifs and strays,** property without an owner, as strayed cattle. **101. the Book.** See Matthew 16:18, 19. **103. four virtues,** the four active or moral virtues: prudence, temperance, justice, and fortitude. **104. cardinal,** from the Latin *cardo*, hinge. **108. cardinals at court,** the College of Cardinals at Rome.

113. the Commune, the community, the commons. This interesting line and the context testify to the growing importance of the commons and to the sympathies of the poet. **114. Common Wit,** common sense, natural intelligence. **123. a fool,** doubtless the dreamer himself. It was a frequent convention in satire for the satirist to pose as a lunatic or simpleton and thus waive responsibility for his words. **129. Spoke loudly in Latin.** The passage satirizes the snobbish attitude of the Church. **132–138. *Sum Rex . . . metas!*** "I am a King, I am a Prince" [thou sayest]; but thou mayest perhaps be neither hereafter. O thou that dost administer the special laws of King Christ, that thou mayest do this the better, be just, be merciful! Naked justice needs to be clothed by thee in mercy. Such harvest as thou wouldst reap, such seeds thou must sow. If justice be stripped naked, mayest thou meet with naked justice. If mercy be sown, mayest thou reap mercy. **141–42. *Dum . . . tenere.*** Since a king may be said to have the name of king from the act of ruling, he has the name without the reality unless he strives to keep the laws.

Then the crowd of the commons cried out in Latin
To the king's council for all to construe it:
Praecepta regis sunt nobis vincula legis.
A rabble of rats ran suddenly hither
With a swarm of small mice sporting among them.
They came to a council for the common profit.
A cat of the court would come at his pleasure,
Sport and spring and seize whom he fancied,
Play with them perilously and push them before him.
"We dread the danger and dare not come forward,
And if we grudge him his game he will grieve us further,
Scratch us or claw us or take us in his clutches,
And make life loathsome before he leave us.
If we had the wit to withstand his pleasure
We might be lords aloft and live at our leisure."

A rat of renown, a ready speaker,
Sought for the sovereign salve for his people:
"I have seen men," he said, "in the city of London
Bearing bright chains about their shoulders,
On cunning collars; they go at random
Through warren and waste as their will inclines them.
And at other times elsewhere, as I hear reported.
If they bore bells, I believe, by heaven,
One might hear where they went and run away!
So," said the speaker, "reason shows clearly
That we should buy a bell of brass, or bright silver,
Clasp it on a collar, and for the common profit
Hang it on the cat's head, and then we may hear him
When he roams or is at rest or runs to frolic.
When his mood is mild we may move at pleasure,
And appear in his presence when he is playfully minded,
And be ware of his wrath and wary of his coming."

The rabble of rats thought his reasons clever;
But when the bell was brought and bound to the collar,
There was no rat in all the rout, for the realm of Louis,
Who dared bind the bell about the cat's shoulders,
Nor hang it on the cat's head to win all England.
They granted themselves cowards and their counsel feeble,
And their labor was lost and all their long sessions.

Then a mouse of importance, and of merit, as I thought him,
Strode forth sternly and stood before the council,
And with the rout of rats reasoned as follows:
"If we killed the cat there would still come another,
To catch us and all our kin, though we crept under benches.
So I counsel the Commune to let the cat wander,
And never be bold to bring him the collar.
For my sire said, seven years past,
Where the cat is a kitten the court is in sorrow.
So Holy Writ witnesses; who will may read it:
Vae terrae ubi puer rex est, etc.
For no one could rest for rats in the night.
While the cat catches rabbits he cares for us little,
But feeds wholly on that venison—never defame him!
A little loss is better than a long sorrow,
And the raids of a robber than ruin for ever.
We mice would demolish the malt of many,
And the rout of rats rend men's clothing,
If that cat of the court could not control you.
For if you rats had your way you could not rule yourselves.
For my part," said the mouse, "I see so much further,
That neither the cat nor the kitten should be grieved at my counsel.
Neither complain I at the collar that cost me nothing.
If it had cost me a crown I should never confess it.
We must suffer our rulers to roam at their pleasure
Uncoupled or coupled, and catch what they will.
And I warn the wise to watch out for themselves."
What this dream may mean, you men who are clever,
Divine, for I dare not, by dear God in heaven!

Hundreds in silk hoods hovered about me,
They seemed to be sergeants who served in the court rooms,
Took pounds or pence, and pled for justice,

145. *Praecepta . . . legis.* The commands of the king are for us the chains of law. **146. A rabble of rats.** This version of the well-known fable of the belling of the cat is apparently the earliest in English. The rats represent certain members of the nobility or the more important burgesses in the House of Commons; the mice are persons of less social importance. The cat is the aged King Edward III, who died in 1377. The kitten is his grandson, Richard II, who came to the throne at the age of eleven. The fable obviously refers to the events following the "Good Parliament" of 1376 when the grievances of the people were voiced by the House of Commons and to the early years of Richard's reign, but it is not certain whether the passage was written before or after the events referred to—whether it constitutes a prophecy of what was likely to happen or a commentary on what had come to pass. **161. bright chains,** the chains of office worn as insignia by officials. **163. warren,** hutch, dwelling.

177. the realm of Louis, France. **192. *Vae . . . est,* etc.** Woe to thee, O land, when thy king is a child, and thy princes eat in the morning! (Ecclesiastes 10:16) **212. sergeants.** Compare Chaucer's Sergeant of the Law, page 101.

Nor for the love of our Lord unlocked their lips ever.
Better measure the mist on Malvern hillsides,
Than hear a mumble from their mouths till money is promised.
I saw in the press, as you shall hear hereafter,
Barons and burgesses and village bondmen,
Bakers and butchers and brewers without number,
Wool-websters and weavers of linen,
Tailors and tinkers and tollmen in markets,
Masons and miners and many other craftsmen.
All lived in labor. But others leapt forward,
Dykemen and diggers who do their work badly,
And drive out the long day with *Dieu vous save, dame Emme!*
Cooks and their knaves cried, "Hot pies, hot!
Good geese and bacon! Come dine, come!"
Taverners too were tossed in the turmoil,
"White wine of Alsace and red wine of Gascony,
Rhine and Rochelle digest the roast!"—
I saw all this sleeping, and seven times more.

PASSUS I*

The Vision of the Holy Church

The meaning of the mountain, of the murky valley
And of the field full of folk, I shall first show you.
A lovely lady in linen garments
Came down from the castle and greeted me softly,
And said, "Son, do you sleep? do you see this people,
How busy they are about the meadow?
Most of the men who move in this meadow
Have their worship in this world and wish no better;
No heaven but here holds their fancy."

I was afraid of her face, for all her beauty,
And said, "Mercy, Madam, what is your meaning?"
"The tower on the toft," she said, "is Truth's dwelling;
Would that you worked as his word teaches!
He is father of faith, and fashioned you wholly,
Blood and bone, and bestowed five wits
To worship him here while you are mortal.
He has willed the world to yield to all men
Woolen, linen, and life's sustenance.
He has measured the mean of a moderate comfort,
And bestowed from his bounty three blessings in common;
None are needful but these. Now I shall name them—
Though I know their natures—and do you name them after.
The first is clothing to keep out the cold;
Meat at meal-time to maintain the body,
And drink to the thirsty; but do not drink always.
You are the worse for that when the work hour calls you. . . .
Moderation is a medicine for men of yearning.
All is not safe for the soul that the stomach calls for,
Nor best for the body, best for the spirit.

Believe not the body, for a liar is his teacher,
The wretched world—he would betray you!
For the fiend and the flesh follow you together,
And seduce the soul with soft whispers.
I warn men to beware and to watch warily."
"Mercy, Madam," I said, "your words delight me;
But the wealth of this world, that men hold so fiercely,
Tell me, Madam, to whom this treasure belongs."
"Go to the Gospel," she said, "where God answered
The people who pressed him with a penny in the temple,
Asking him whether they should worship Caesar.
God asked them whose was the inscription,
And whose the sign that stood within it.
'Caesar's,' they said, 'we see it clearly.'
'*Reddite Caesari,*' said God, 'what belongs to Caesar,
Et quae sunt Dei Deo, or else you do evil.'
For good counsel should govern you always,
Common Wit be warden of wealth's treasure,
And tell when the time to dispense arises;
Counsel and Common Wit are companions of husbandry."

Then I humbly asked by him who made me,
"Madam, may I know what meaning is hidden
In the dismal dungeon of the dale beneath us?"
"That is the castle of Care. Who comes within it
May ban his birth in body and soul.
Wrong is the name of the wretch who lives there:
The Father of Falsehood was first to build it.
He egged Adam and Eve to mischief,
And counseled Cain to kill his brother.

220. Wool-websters. A webster was a female weaver. **224. Dykemen,** ditchers. **225.** ***Dieu . . . Emme!*** evidently a quotation from a lost popular song. **228. Taverners,** innkeepers. **230. Rhine and Rochelle,** i.e., wines from the Rhine and from La Rochelle, France. *** Passus I.** The Latin word *passus* (step, pace) is used to indicate a division of a poem or story. **12. Truth's dwelling.** Truth is used here to signify God. Elsewhere it signifies faith, the true way of life, etc.

53–54. ***Reddite . . . Deo.*** Render therefore unto Caesar the things which are Caesar's; and unto God the things that are God's. (Matthew 22:21) **64. Wrong,** here synonymous with Satan, the "Father of Falsehood."

He jested with Judas for Jewish silver,
And afterwards hung him high on an elder.
He is the leader of liars and love's traitor,
Yet betrays the soonest all who trust in his treasure."

When I heard this I wondered who was this woman,
Whose words were weighed in the wisdom of Scripture,
I hailed her on the high name, and asked that she tell me
What title she bore, who taught me so mildly.

"I am Holy Church," she said, "and you should know me.
I first found you. My faith I taught you.
You brought me pledges to be at my bidding,
And to love me loyally while life lasted."

Then I kissed the ground, and cried her mercy,
And piteously I prayed her to pray for a sinner,
And tenderly teach me to believe in Christ,
That I might work his will who wrought me to man!
"Tell me of no treasure, but teach me only
How I may save my soul, O Sainted Lady!"

"When all treasures are tried," she said, "Truth is the fairest.
It is as dear a dowry as the dear God himself." . . .

"But I have no natural knowledge," said I, "to teach me
How Truth descends and dwells in my body."

"You are a blunt blockhead and a blind pupil,
You learnt too little Latin, lad, in your schooldays.
Heu michi! quia sterilem duxi vitam juvenilem!
By the common gift of Nature hearts acknowledge
The love of the Lord above the love of self,
And dread to do evil though death may follow.
This I trust is true. Who teaches you better,
You must suffer to speak, and pursue his teaching.
God's word is the witness; work in that doctrine.
For Truth tells that love is the treacle of heaven,
No sin may be seen where that spice preserves you.
All his works are wrought with love and freedom;
He taught love in the law of Moses; it is most like heaven,
The plant of peace, the most precious of virtues.

Heaven might not hold it, it was itself so heavy,
Till it had eaten heartily of the earth beneath it.
In the flesh of the fold, in the blood of your body,
No leaf of the linden was lighter on the branches;
It was as piercing and poignant as the point of a needle;
No walls nor armor withheld its passage.

So Love is leader of the Lord's folk in heaven,
And a mean, as the mayor, between the king and the commune.
So love is a leader, and takes law upon him
For the amerciament of men in the mischief they practise.
The Might of the Maker begat it in Nature;
Its head-spring is the heart, where all arises.
The Might that is moving in a man's conscience
Fell from the Father who fashioned all men.
He looked on us with love, and let his son
Die in meekness for our misdeeds, to amend us all.
Yet he wished no evil to the wretches who pained him,
But meekly murmured that Mercy might hear him
And have pity on the people who pained him and slew him. . . .

Love is leach of life, and our Lord is with him,
It is the wicket gate that goes to heaven.
I say now as I said first, with these texts to witness,
When all treasures are tried, Truth is the fairest.
Love it," said the lady, "I may not linger
With my lesson of love,"—and she left me gently.

[The dreamer asks Lady Holy Church how he may know Falsehood, and is shown both Falsehood and Flattery. He sees also Lady Meed (i.e., Reward or Bribery), whose adventures are recounted in Passus III and IV. In Passus V the dreamer awakes only to fall asleep again. Once more he sees the field full of folk and Reason preaching to the people. Many of them confess their sins, which are represented as speaking in their own persons in the Vision of the Seven Deadly Sins. Of the seven confessions, parts of two, those of Gluttony and Sloth, are given below.]

PASSUS V

Gula (*Gluttony*)

Now Gluttony gets him on his way to confession,
And shuffles churchward to show his offenses.
But Breton the brewster bade him good morrow,
And asked him with that whither he was going.
"To holy church," said he, "to hear the service,
And so I will be shriven and sin no longer."
"I have good ale, gossip; Glutton, will you try it?"
"What have you?" he asked,—"any hot spices?"

141. ***Heu michi! . . . juvenilem!*** Woe is me! what a fruitless life I led when I was young!

162. amerciament, penalty, fine. **205. leach,** physician. **422. brewster,** a female brewer. **426. gossip,** neighbor.

"I have pepper and peonies," she said, "and a pound of garlic,
And a farthing worth of fennel seed for fasting seasons."
Then Gluttony goes in with a great crowd after:
Cis the shoemaker sat on the benches,
Watt the warner, and his wife beside him,
Tim the tinker and two of his prentices,
Hick the hackneyman and Hugh the needle-seller,
Clarice of Cockslain and the clerk of the parish,
Daw the ditcher and a dozen others—
Sir Piers of Predie and Pernelle of Flanders,
A rebeck player, a rat-catcher, a raker of Cheapside,
A rope-maker, a rider, and Rose the dish-seller,
Godfrey of Garlickhithe and Griffin the Welshman,
And an whole heap of upholsterers, early in the morning,
Gave Glutton good cheer and good ale a-plenty.

Clement the cobbler cast off his jacket
And played New Fair, and put it to wager.
Hick the hackneyman threw his hood after it,
And bade Bet the butcher be of his party.
Then venders were found to value the wager,
For he who had the hood should have amends for his jacket.
Two were up in a hurry, whispering together,
And appraising these pennyworths apart in a corner.
For conscience' sake they could not agree peaceably
Till Robin the rope-maker arose for justice
And named himself an umpire, so that no one should quarrel,
And the bargain be tried between the three of them.

Hick the hackneyman had the jacket,
In agreement that Clement should cup him nobly,
And have the hackneyman's hood, and hold himself contented;
He who first repented should rise up afterwards,
And greet Sir Glutton with a gallon of ale.

Then there was laughing and lowering and "Let the cup go it,"
And sitting till evensong and singing catches,
Till Glutton had gulped a gallon and a gill. . . .

He could neither step nor stand till a staff held him,
And then began to go like a gleeman's mongrel,
Sometimes aside and sometimes backwards,
Like one who lays lures to lime wild-fowl.

As he drew to the door all dimmed before him,
He stumbled on the threshold and was thrown forwards.
Clement the cobbler caught him by the stomach
To lay him on his lap, but he lifted badly;
Glutton, the great churl, was a grim burden,
And coughed up a caudle in Clement's breeches.
There was no hungry hound in Hertfordshire
Durst lap up the leavings, they stank so loudly.

With all the weeping in the world his wife and his daughter
Bore him home to his bed and brought him in it.
After all this excess he was attacked with slothfulness,
And slept Saturday and Sunday till the sun was setting.
Then he awoke and winked, and wiped his eyelids,
And the first word that he uttered was, "Where's the bowl?"
Wife and Conscience upbraided him for his wicked living.
The shrew was ashamed, and shrived himself earnestly,
And prayed before Repentance: "Have pity on me, a sinner,
Thou living Lord and life of all things!
To thee, God, I, Glutton, yield me guilty
Of more trespass through tongue than I can tell thee ever.
I have sworn 'By thy soul!' and 'By thy sides!' and 'So help me God Almighty!'
When there was no need, and many times falsely.
I have sat too long at supper and sometimes at breakfast,
Till I, Glutton, gulped it up before I had gone a furlong,
And spilt what might have been spared and spent on the hungry.
I have drunk and eaten delicately on days of fasting,
And sat sometimes so long that I have slept and eaten together.
I have sought taverns for love of tales and to drink the longer.
And I have eaten meat before noon on days of fasting."

430. Gluttony goes in. The description of the interior of the alehouse has been compared, for distinctive and realistic details, to a drawing by the eighteenth-century painter Hogarth. **432. warner,** gamekeeper. **434. hackneyman,** one who kept horses for hire. **435. Cockslain,** Cock Lane, an area set aside for prostitutes. **437. Sir Piers,** a priest. **Pernelle,** a name commonly given to a woman of suspect reputation. **438. rebeck,** a kind of fiddle. **raker,** scavenger. **444. New Fair,** a game of barter.

469. gleeman's mongrel. Perhaps the reference is to a blind minstrel led by his dog. **487. shrew,** scoundrel.

"This showing your shrift," said Repentance, "shall be merit for you."
And then Glutton grieved and made a great dolour,
For the loathsome life that he had lived in evil.
He vowed to fast: "Neither thirst nor hunger
Shall make fish on Friday defile my stomach,
Till my aunt Abstinence has given me permission;
And yet I have hated her all my lifetime."

Accidia (*Sloth*)

Then Sloth came all beslobbered, with slime on his eyelids;
"I must sit," he said, "or else I shall slumber.
I cannot stand or stoop, and want a stool for kneeling.
If I were brought to bed, unless my buttocks made me,
No ringing should make me rise till I was ripe for dinner."

He began *Benedicite* with a belch, and beat his forehead,
And roared and raved and snored for a conclusion.
"Awake! awake! wretch," cried Repentance, "make ready for shriving."
"If I should die today I should never do it.
I cannot say *Pater noster* perfectly, as the priest sings it.
I know rhymes of Robin Hood and Randolph, Earl of Chester,
But of our Lord or of our Lady I have learned nothing.
I have made forty vows and forgotten them on the morrow.
I never performed the penance as the priest commanded,
Nor was sorry for my sins as a man should be.
And if I pray at my beads, unless Wrath bids me,
What I tell with my tongue is two miles from my meaning.
I am occupied each day, on holy days and all days,
With idle tales at ale, or at other times in churches.
Rarely do I remember God's pain and passion.
I never visit the feeble nor the fettered men in prison.
I had rather hear ribaldry or a summer game of cobblers,
Or lies to laugh at and belie my neighbour,
Than all that the four evangelists have ever written.
Vigils and fasting days slip unheeded.
I lie abed in Lent with my leman beside me,
And when matins and mass are over I go to my friars.
If I arrive at *Ite, missa est* I have done my duty.
Sometimes I am not shriven, unless sickness force me,
More than twice in two years, and then I do it by guess work.

I have been priest and parson for the past thirty winters,
Yet I know neither the scales nor the singing nor the Saints' Legends.
I can find an hare afield or frighten him from his furrow
Better than read *Beatus vir* or *Beati omnes*,
Construe their clauses and instruct my parishioners.
I can hold love-days and hear a reeve's reckoning,
But I cannot construe a line in the Canons or Decretals.

If I beg or borrow and it be not tallied
I forget it as quickly; men can ask me
Six times or seven and I will swear to the falsehood.
So I trouble true men twenty times over.

The salary of my servants is seldom even.
I answer angrily when the accounts are reckoned,
And my workmen's wages are wrath and cursing.
If any man does me a favor or helps me in trouble,
I answer courtesy with unkindness, and cannot understand it.
I have now and I have ever had a hawk's manners.

518. Robin Hood. This, the earliest known allusion to the famous outlaw, indicates clearly that ballads (which is doubtless what "rhymes" means here) about him were thoroughly familiar by the last quarter of the fourteenth century. **Randolph.** A case can be, and has been, made for either the Randolph who was Earl of Chester between 1128 and 1153 or his grandson, the earl from 1181 to 1232. Whichever may have been the hero, we have here evidence of a lost cycle of ballads dealing with an indisputably historical character. **523. unless Wrath bids me,** that is, as an oath. **526. in churches.** Foolish chatter in church was considered then, as now, especially reprehensible.

529. summer game of cobblers. It was customary to have a festival on Midsummer Day (St. John Baptist's Day), June 24. The reference here is presumably to a celebration performed by the cobblers' guild. **533. leman,** sweetheart. **535. *Ite, missa est.*** The last words of the mass. **541. *Beatus vir,*** Psalm 1 or Psalm 111 ("Blessed is the man"). ***Beati omnes,*** Psalm 127 ("Blessed are all they"). **543. love-days,** fixed days on which common people sought to settle their disputes by arbitration rather than by recourse to the lawcourts. Men of consequence and reputed learning such as Sloth and Chaucer's Friar (see page 101) would serve as arbitrators. **reeve's reckoning.** The reeve, as his lord's immediate representative on an estate, made regular financial reports which the lord, not without reason, would have examined by someone with a knowledge of local conditions; see Chaucer's Reeve, page 105. **544. Canons,** the laws of the Church or, less probably, a part of the mass. **Decretals,** a collection of papal decrees which were part of the canon law. **545. tallied,** marked on a tally stick.

I am not lured with love where nothing lies in the fingers.
Sixty times I, Sloth, have since forgotten
The kindness that fellow Christians have granted to me.
Sometimes I spill—in speech or silence—
Both flesh and fish and many other victuals,
Bread and ale, butter, milk, and cheeses,
All slobbered in my service till they may serve no man.

I was a roamer in my youth and reckless in study,
And ever since have been a beggar from foul slothfulness:
Heu michi! quia sterilem vitam duxi juvenilem!"

"Do you repent?" said Repentance,—but the wretch was swooning,
Till Vigilate, the watcher, threw water on his forehead,
And flung it in his face, and vehemently addressed him,
And cried, "Beware of Desperation, that betrays many!
Say, 'I am sorry for my sins'; say it and believe it.
Beat your breast, and beseech Him to have mercy;
For there is no guilt so great that His goodness is not greater."

Then Sloth sat up and so crossed himself quickly,
And made a vow before God: "For my foul living
Every Sunday this seven years, unless sickness keep me,
I will go down before day break to the dear chapel,
And hear matins and mass, like a monk in his cloister.
No ale after meat shall hold me absent
Till I have heard evensong, I vow by the rood-tree." . . .

555. not lured . . . fingers. Compare the proverb, "With empty hands men may lure no hawks." ***564. Heu . . . juvenilem!*** Woe is me! what a fruitless life I led when I was young! ***566. Vigilate,*** "Watch!" See Mark 13:37.

[Piers the Plowman is not mentioned until after the Vision of the Seven Deadly Sins in Passus V. The repentant sinners set out to seek after Truth, but no one knows the way. Finally, Piers the Plowman, who has followed Truth for forty years, describes the way to Truth. The greater part of the poem is taken up with a series of visions (Passus VIII–XX) dealing with the lives of "Do-Well," "Do-Bet," and "Do-Best." The last vision ends as Conscience arouses himself and vows:

I will become a pilgrim
And walk as wide as all the world endures
To seek Piers the Plowman; by him shall Pride perish,

and the dreamer awakes.]

578. rood tree, the Holy Cross.

Geoffrey Chaucer

c. 1340–1400

Geoffrey Chaucer was born into a turbulent century, one which saw change and decay in almost every institution in Western Europe. Chaucer took an active part in many of the events of his time; he was no stooped, retiring scholar, living in the ageless universe of books and unaware of what was going on about him. The greater part of his life was spent in the public service, and he brought to his literary art much practical experience of the world. Yet there is a paradox in the fact that the great social, political, and economic events of Chaucer's lifetime are hardly reflected in his writings.[1]

Chaucer's family were reasonably well-to-do mercantile folk; both his father and grandfather were in the wine business, which may account for the appreciative description of the fraudulent dilution of wine which Chaucer put into "The Pardoner's Tale." His father held a few positions in the royal service at one time or another and evidently had influence enough to get Geoffrey a berth in the royal household. We first hear of Geoffrey Chaucer as a page to the Countess of Ulster, daughter-in-law of Edward III, and in 1357 he was in the service of Lionel, one of the royal princes. Two years later he was with the English army in France, was captured, and in 1360 was released as a prisoner of war upon the opportune payment of £16 by the king. Then follows a gap of seven years, presumably spent in the service of the king, during which he married a sister of the future wife of John of Gaunt, son of the

[1] See the introduction to *Piers Plowman* (page 86) for a brief and gloomy picture of Chaucer's world.

king. From this period he emerged with a pension given him as the king's "dilectus vallectus noster" —"our dearly beloved attendant."

We know nothing about Chaucer's formal education. He gives us in "The Prioress's Tale" a charming picture of a schoolboy and his school, but we have no real right to take that as a transcript of his personal experience. There is no evidence that Chaucer went to either university, but plenty of evidence that he knew university men. We find among the Canterbury pilgrims the learned, bookish, half-starved Clerk, and in the *Tales* his fellow Jankin, fifth husband of the Wife of Bath, and the reprehensible Nicholas of the Miller's sorry tale— men of Oxford, one and all. Balancing them are the two Cambridge scamps of "The Reeve's Tale." Many of the duties with which Chaucer was entrusted in later life would have required legal training of the sort a man could best obtain in the Inns of Court. The tradition that, as a member of the Inner Temple, Chaucer was once fined two shillings for beating a Franciscan friar in Fleet Street has better backing than many of the anecdotes of literary men. But whatever the facts of his educational career, one thing is certain: he managed to become very well read indeed in Biblical, classical, and medieval writings.

In 1368 began a period of a dozen years or so during which Chaucer was frequently employed as a diplomatic agent of the government, making trips to the Continent to negotiate treaties and to perform other business for the king. In 1374 he was appointed Comptroller of Customs for the Port of London, a position in which he was confirmed by Richard II when he became king in 1377. This was a good and remunerative position, but one which required regular attendance and personal clerical work relating to wool and hides and wines. Chaucer kept the job twelve years, living for the most part in a house above Aldgate in London. He seems to have lost it through a change in administration when the Duke of Gloucester, posing as a strict constitutionalist, seized political control, liquidated the young king's party, and put his own followers in office. Chaucer was lucky, perhaps, to lose no more than his position in the purge, as some of Richard's friends were exiled and others executed. During the time that he was in the customs Chaucer had engaged in intermittent diplomatic activity, including at least one trip to Italy in 1378. After relinquishing the comptrollership, he served for a while as justice of the peace in Kent and as a member of Parliament.

When Richard came of age in 1389 and took the government into his own hands once more, Chaucer was made Clerk of the King's Works, a position which he held for nearly two years. It was his duty to direct and oversee the care, maintenance, and repair of ten scattered royal residences, including the Tower of London and the palace at Westminster. Then, too, for a time he was a member of the Thames Commission. In this post he must have traveled extensively, controlled numerous groups of men, and expended much public money. In September, 1390, he managed to be robbed twice within two or three days, once of £10 and again of £9 and a horse. The money was the king's, but the horse was Chaucer's. The following year he gave up the Thames Commission office, or was removed. He still enjoyed the royal favor—gifts, an annuity, and a butt of wine a year. When Henry IV came to the throne in October, 1399, he renewed Chaucer's annuity and the annual butt of wine. Full of optimism, on December 4, 1399, Chaucer took a fifty-three-year lease of a house in Westminster, but he occupied it less than one year. We place Chaucer's death in 1400, not because we have any contemporary record, but simply because his pension was collected in June of that year and not thereafter. His tomb is in the Poets' Corner of Westminster Abbey.

In coming to a consideration of Chaucer's literary accomplishments, one may at first be tempted to think that a man so busy with the everyday affairs of the world must have regarded the reading and writing of books as a mere avocation. But we have ample evidence from Chaucer's own writings that he delighted in books, and that all his reading was fused and reinforced by the fine sensibility with which he observed human action and human character. Literary historians often divide Chaucer's literary life into three periods, corresponding to the predominating literary influences—French, Italian, and English. This arrangement is convenient and will do very well so long as we bear in mind that the process was progressive, and that each period represents wide reading and great versatility. Furthermore, we cannot always be certain of the exact dates of Chaucer's compositions.

Chaucer's first important work was his translation of part of the French *Roman de la Rose*, the fountain and source of the current French poetic style. The poem is cast in the form of a dream-vision, in which the author relates a series of allegorical adventures which befell him while asleep. The *Roman de la Rose* exerted perhaps a greater influence on Chaucer than any other single work. In 1369 he wrote, also in the form of a dream-allegory, an elegy on the

Duchess of Lancaster, the wife of his patron John of Gaunt. In this poem Chaucer altered the purpose and purport of the type, while retaining the form, and gives us a genuinely moving personal elegy. Echoes of the French period, in which Chaucer was on borrowing terms with two living French authors, Machaut and Froissart, continue to be heard throughout his later work in dreams and visions and waking reflections on April showers and May mornings and the song of birds on spring boughs.

From 1372 and 1373, when he was in Genoa and Florence on the king's business, we ordinarily date the beginning of the Italian influence on Chaucer's work. In Italy he came to know the writings of Dante, Petrarch, and Boccaccio, and to the knowledge of Ovid, his first and longest love among the Latin poets, he added that of the greatest of them, Virgil. These new influences made themselves felt first in *The House of Fame*, an uncompleted dream-vision. The poem is divided into books, adorned with summaries of Virgil's *Aeneid*, embellished with prologues which owe much to Dante, and it scintillates with even more miscellaneous learning. Throughout the work, however, Chaucer's own self is strikingly present, and his characteristic humor enlivens passage after passage.

During his years in the customs house and immediately after, Chaucer did still more important literary work. We may reasonably date between 1380 and 1387 his prose translation of Boethius's *Consolation of Philosophy* and his long poems, *The Parliament of Fowls*, *Troilus and Criseyde*, and *The Legend of Good Women*. *The Parliament of Fowls* is another dream-vision in which the poet is taken to see the birds assemble on St. Valentine's Day to choose their mates for the coming year. The poem is extraordinarily vivacious, and some of the birds are very well characterized, especially the lower-class birds, like the ducks, who have little patience with the doctrines of courtly love which their betters, such as the turtledoves, utter. In *Troilus and Criseyde*, as in the later "Knight's Tale," we find Chaucer dealing with themes taken from classical antiquity, the first connected with Troy and the second with Thebes and Athens. Chaucer's immediate source in each case is a contemporary Italian author, Giovanni Boccaccio. There is no conscientious attempt, however, to recreate the classical setting; Chaucer follows common medieval usage instead, remaking the ancient world in the image of his own time and not allowing anachronisms to disturb him. Chaucer's *Troilus and Criseyde* is nearly three thousand lines longer than Boccaccio's poem. One of the great long poems in English literature, it is his finest work before *The Canterbury Tales*. Chaucer transcends his Italian model in all important respects, most notably in its dramatic interest and searching insight into human character. In *The Legend of Good Women*, which is incomplete, Chaucer returns once again to the dream-vision and to French sources, and tells of the lives of the saints of Cupid, beginning with that of Cleopatra.

The thirteen years (1387–1400) which constitute Chaucer's "English" period were, as we have seen, taken up with many duties. It is a matter of wonder that he should have found time to write at all. At odd moments he composed some minor poems and his prose *Treatise on the Astrolabe*. The latter, his one specimen of scientific writing, is a translation. It was made for a boy not yet able to read Latin, perhaps his own son Lewis, and it deals with the importance of astronomical studies in education. But the great achievement of this latter period is, of course, Chaucer's masterpiece, *The Canterbury Tales*, on which he worked intermittently over the thirteen years, and which, vast, sprawling, unfinished, and disjointed as it is, ranks as one of the great glories of English literature.

The Canterbury Tales is a frame-story; that is, a device is used to make it appear natural that a number of quite unrelated stories should appear together in one book. Chaucer's device is to have a group of pilgrims take part in a story-telling competition on their journey from London to the shrine of St. Thomas Becket in Canterbury. There was nothing new about a frame-story. It had originated centuries before, and we have examples in Sanskrit and the familiar *Arabian Nights* to illustrate its popularity in India and the Near East. The European Middle Ages had their frame-stories, too—*The Seven Sages of Rome*, Boccaccio's *Decameron*, Sercambi's *Novelle*, itself a pilgrimage frame, and John Gower's *Confessio Amantis*. Nor did it die out with the Middle Ages, for we have Longfellow's *Tales of a Wayside Inn* and William Morris's *The Earthly Paradise*. Chaucer's series was no innovation, then, and some of the other practitioners of the genre were story-tellers of rare merit, notably the authors of the *Arabian Nights* and Boccaccio. Yet nowhere is Chaucer's mastery more evident than in his handling of the frame. In almost all the other collections the stories alone matter, but the fictitious tellers of Chaucer's tales are more real than the tales they tell. Most of them stand out in our minds as clearly as the characters in the best of literature, and, indeed, as the real people in our own world. They are distinct individuals one and all, and among them is one of the two greatest and richest comic creations in

English literature. That is the Wife of Bath, and only Shakespeare's Falstaff is her peer.

However real the portraits are in "The General Prologue," Chaucer does not leave his characters there. They continue to live and move along the way, and in the links, prologues, and epilogues, as well as by the interpolations in the tales themselves, we grow to know them better as we observe their actions and reactions. We see their friendships and their feuds, their quarrels and rivalries, their foibles and weaknesses. Their very stories sometimes grow out of their conduct, which can frequently fall short of the ideal and the admirable. The Miller and the Reeve, the Friar and the Summoner, the Host and the Cook, the Pardoner and the Host, and the irrepressible Alice of Bath, all quarrel or fight or both, and tell tales out of school. Three centuries after Chaucer, John Dryden, in his *Preface to the Fables* (see pages 468–477), reviewed with wonder and admiration the human comedy of the fourteenth century and of every century which the genius of Chaucer has provided for us. The twentieth century reader finds himself, another three hundred years later, echoing Dryden's summary of Chaucer's *dramatis personae:* "Here is God's plenty."

The standard edition of Chaucer is W. W. Skeat's *The Complete Works of Geoffrey Chaucer*, 7 volumes, Oxford University Press, 1894–97. The most useful and convenient edition for the student is F. N. Robinson's *The Complete Works of Geoffrey Chaucer*, Houghton Mifflin, 1933. The present text is taken, by the kind permission of the copyright owner, from the monumental *Text of the Canterbury Tales*, edited by J. M. Manly and Edith Rickert, published by the University of Chicago Press, 1940. The present editor has supplied punctuation and standard capitalization, and has followed modern typographical usage in the matter of "i," "j," "u," "v," and the like. The notes, which are intended to explain words and idioms obsolete, strange, or altered in sense, have been kept at a minimum. Certain more or less conventional expurgations are indicated in the line numbering. For a more complete exegesis of the text the student is advised to turn to the notes of the editions already mentioned.

Of the almost innumerable writings on Chaucer and his works the following are listed for their general factual and critical usefulness: G. G. Coulton, *Chaucer and His England*, Putnam, 1908; Emile Legouis, *Geoffrey Chaucer*, translated by Lailavoix, Dutton, 1912; G. L. Kittredge, *Chaucer and His Poetry*, Harvard University Press, 1915; J. L. Lowes, *Geoffrey Chaucer and the Development of His Genius*, Houghton Mifflin, 1934; H. R. Patch, *On Rereading Chaucer*, Harvard University Press, 1939; R. K. Root, *The Poetry of Chaucer* (rev. ed.), Princeton University Press, 1934; R. D. French, *A Chaucer Handbook* (rev. ed.), Crofts, 1947. A lively account of Chaucer's life and times for the general reader is Marchette Chute's *Geoffrey Chaucer of England*, Dutton, 1946.

from THE CANTERBURY TALES

THE GENERAL PROLOGUE [1]

Whan that Aprill with his shoures soote
The droghte of March hath perced to the roote,
And bathed every veyne in swich licour
Of which vertu engendred is the flour;
Whan Zephirus eek with his sweete breeth
Inspired hath in every holt and heeth
The tendre croppes, and the yonge sonne
Hath in the Ram his half cours yronne,
And smale foweles maken melodye,
That slepen al the nyght with open eye
(So priketh hem nature in hir corages):
Than longen folk to goon on pilgrymages,
And palmeres for to seken straunge strondes,
To ferne halwes, kouthe in sondry londes;
And specially from every shires ende
Of Engelond to Caunterbury they wende,
The holy blisful martir for to seke,
That hem hath holpen whan that they were seeke.

[1] In "The General Prologue" and in most of *The Canterbury Tales* Chaucer uses the iambic pentameter rhyming couplet, consisting of two lines of matched verse in immediate succession. It was Chaucer who started the couplet on its long career in English poetry. **1. his,** its. Note the forms of the pronouns: *his* (his, its), *hem* (them), *hir* or *hire* (their, her). **soote,** sweet. **3. swich licour,** such moisture. **4. vertu,** strength, efficacy. **flour,** flower. **5. Zephirus,** the west wind. **eek,** also. **6. holt and heeth,** plantation and heath. **7. tendre croppes,** new shoots. **yonge sonne.** The sun is young because the year in Chaucer's time began at the vernal equinox.

8. in the Ram his half cours. The constellation of the Ram (Aries) is one of the twelve signs of the zodiac which mark the apparent path of the sun in the heavens. The sun has passed about halfway through Aries at the beginning of April. **9. foweles,** birds. **11. (So priketh . . . corages):** Nature so incites them in their hearts (instincts). **13. palmeres,** pilgrims, especially those who had been to the Holy Land. **strondes,** shores. **14. ferne halwes,** distant shrines (hallowed places). **kouthe,** known. **17. martir,** St. Thomas Becket. See page 39. **18. holpen,** helped. **seeke,** sick.

Bifel that, in that sesoun on a day,
In Southwerk at the Tabard as I lay
Redy to wenden on my pilgrymage
To Caunterbury with ful devout corage,
At nyght was come into that hostelrye
Wel nyne and twenty in a compaignye,
Of sondry folk, by aventure yfalle
In felaweshipe, and pilgrymes were they alle,
That toward Caunterbury wolden ryde.
The chambres and the stables weren wyde,
And wel we weren esed atte beste.
And shortly, whan the sonne was to reste,
So hadde I spoken with hem everichon,
That I was of hir felaweshipe anon,
And made forward erly for to ryse,
To take oure wey ther as I yow devyse.

But nathelees, whil I have tyme and space,
Er that I ferther in this tale pace,
Me thynketh it acordant to resoun
To telle yow al the condicioun
Of ech of hem, so as it semed me,
And whiche they weren, and of what degree,
And eek in what array that they were inne:
And at a Knyght than wol I first bigynne.

A KNYGHT ther was, and that a worthy man,
That fro the tyme that he first bigan
To riden out, he loved chivalrye,
Trouthe and honour, fredom and curteisye.
Ful worthy was he in his lordes werre,
And ther-to hadde he riden, no man ferre,
As wel in Cristendom as in hethenesse,
And evere honoured for his worthynesse.
At Alisaundre he was whan it was wonne.
Ful ofte tyme he hadde the bord bigonne
Aboven alle nacions in Pruce.
In Lettow hadde he reysed and in Ruce,
No Cristen man so ofte of his degree.
In Gernade at the seege eek hadde he be
Of Algezir, and riden in Belmarye.
At Lyeys was he and at Satalye,
Whan they were wonne; and in the Grete See
At many a noble armee hadde he be.
At mortal batailles hadde he been fiftene,
And foghten for oure feith at Tramyssene
In lystes thries, and ay slayn his foo.
This ilke worthy knyght hadde been also
Som-tyme with the lord of Palatye,
Agayn another hethen in Turkye.
And evere-moore he hadde a sovereyn prys;
And though that he were worthy, he was wys,
And of his port as meke as is a mayde.
He nevere yet no vileynye ne sayde
In al his lyf un-to no maner wight.
He was a verray, parfit gentil knyght.
But for to tellen yow of his array,
Hise hors were goode, but he was nat gay.
Of fustian he wered a gypoun
Al bismotered with his habergeoun,
For he was late ycome from his viage,
And wente for to doon his pilgrymage.

With hym ther was his sone, a yong SQUYER,
A lovere and a lusty bacheler,
With lokkes crulle, as they were leyd in presse.
Of twenty yeer of age he was, I gesse.
Of his stature he was of evene lengthe,
And wonderly delyvere, and of greet strengthe
And he hadde been som-tyme in chivachye
In Flaundres, in Artoys, and Picardye,
And born hym wel, as of so litel space,
In hope to stonden in his lady grace.
Embrouded was he, as it were a meede
Al ful of fresshe floures, white and reede.
Syngynge he was, or floytynge, al the day;
He was as fressh as is the monthe of May.
Short was his gowne, with sleves longe and wyde.
Wel koude he sitte on hors and faire ryde.
He koude songes make and wel endite,

20. Southwerk. Southwark was a suburb of London. The **Tabard** was an inn which had for its sign a tabard, or sleeveless jacket. **25. aventure,** chance. **yfalle,** befallen. **28. wyde,** spacious. **29. esed atte beste,** entertained in the best manner. **31. everichon,** everyone. **33. forward,** agreement. **34. ther as I yow devyse,** where I shall tell you of. **37. Me thynketh it,** it seems to me. **45. riden out,** go on expeditions. **46. fredom,** generosity. **47. his lordes werre,** his king's war, the Hundred Years' War in France. **48. ferre,** farther. **51–66. At Alisaundre . . . Turkye.** The Knight campaigned in three crusades against the enemies of Christian Europe: (1) the Moors in Spain and North Africa, (2) the Turks and other Mohammedans in Asia Minor and Egypt, (3) the pagan Prussians, Lithuanians, and Russians on the shores of the Baltic. It is unlikely that any one actual knight could have taken part in wars so widely separated in time. **52. the bord bigonne,** taken the head of the table. **54. reysed,** campaigned.

59. Grete See, Mediterranean. **60. armee,** armed expedition. **63. lystes,** lists, enclosed places for a tournament. **64. ilke,** same. **67. sovereyn prys,** very high praise, reputation. **68. wys,** prudent. **69. port,** bearing. **70. vileynye,** discourtesy. **71. wight,** person. **72. verray,** true. **parfit,** perfect. **74. hors,** horses. **he,** the knight. **75. fustian,** thick cotton cloth. **gypoun,** short blouse (worn under armor). **76. bismotered,** stained. **habergeoun,** coat of mail. **79. Squyer,** candidate for knighthood. **80. bacheler,** aspirant to knighthood. **81. crulle,** curly. **presse,** curling iron. **83. evene lengthe,** medium height. **84. wonderly delyvere,** wonderfully agile. **85. chivachye,** cavalry expedition. **88. lady,** lady's. **89. Embrouded,** embroidered; the reference may be either to his costume or to his complexion. **meede,** meadow. **91. floytynge,** whistling, or playing on the flute. **95. songes . . . endite,** compose both music and words.

Juste and eek daunce, and wel purtreye and write.
So hoote he lovede, that by nyghtertale
He slepte namoore than dooth a nyghtyngale.
  Curteys he was, lowely, and servysable,
And carf biforn his fader at the table.

  A Yeman hadde he and servantz namo
At that tyme, for hym liste ryde so;
And he was clad in coote and hood of grene.
A sheef of pecok arwes bright and kene
Under his belt he bar ful thriftily,
(Wel koude he dresse his takel yemanly:
His arwes drouped noght with fetheres lowe),
And in his hand he bar a myghty bowe.
A not heed hadde he, with a broun visage.
Of wodecraft wel koude he al the usage.
Upon his arm he bar a gay bracer,
And by his syde a swerd and a bokeler,
And on that oother syde a gay daggere,
Harneysed wel and sharp as poynt of spere,
A Cristofre on his brest of silver shene.
An horn he bar, the bawdryk was of grene;
A forster was he, soothly, as I gesse.

  Ther was also a nonne, a Prioresse,
That of hir smylyng was ful symple and coy;
Hir gretteste ooth was but by Seint Loy;
And she was cleped Madame Eglentyne.
  Ful wel she soong the servyce dyvyne,
Entuned in hir nose ful semely,
And Frenssh she spak ful faire and fetisly,
After the scole of Stratford-atte-Bowe,
For Frenssh of Parys was to hire unknowe.
  At mete wel ytaught was she with alle:
She leet no morsel from hir lippes falle,
Ne wette hir fyngres in hir sauce depe.
Wel koude she carie a morsel and wel kepe
That no drope ne fille up-on hir brest.
In curteisie was set ful muchel hir lest.
Hir over lippe wyped she so clene
That in hir coppe ther was no ferthyng sene
Of grece, whan she dronken hadde hir draughte.
Ful semely after hir mete she raughte.
And sikerly she was of greet desport,
And ful plesaunt, and amyable of port,
And peyned hire to countrefete cheere
Of court, and to been estatlich of manere,
And to been holden digne of reverence.
  But, for to speken of hir conscience,
She was so charitable and so pitous
She wolde wepe, if that she sawe a mous
Caught in a trappe, if it were deed or bledde.
Of smale houndes hadde she, that she fedde
With rosted flessh, or mylk and wastel breed.
But soore wepte she if oon of hem were deed,
Or if men smoot it with a yerde smerte;
And al was conscience and tendre herte.
  Ful semely hir wympel pynched was;
Hir nose tretys, hir eyen greye as glas,
Hir mouth ful smal, and ther-to softe and reed;
But sikerly she hadde a fair forheed:
It was almoost a spanne brood, I trowe;
For, hardily, she was nat undergrowe.
Ful fetys was hir cloke, as I was war.
Of smal coral aboute hir arm she bar
A peyre of bedes, gauded al with grene,
And ther-on heng a brooch of gold ful shene,
On which ther was first writen a crowned A,
And after *Amor vincit omnia.*

  Another Nonne with hire hadde she,
That was hir chapeleyne, and preestes thre.

  A Monk ther was, a fair for the maistrye,
An outridere, that lovede venerye,
A manly man, to been an abbot able.
Ful many a deyntee hors hadde he in stable,
And whanne he rood, men myghte his brydel heere
Gynglen in a whistlynge wynd as cleere,
And eek as loude, as dooth the chapel belle,
Ther-as this lord was kepere of the celle.

96. Juste, joust, fight in a tournament. **purtreye,** draw. **97. nyghtertale,** nighttime. **99. Curteys,** courteous. **100. carf biforn,** carved the meat for. **101. Yeman,** yeoman. **he,** the Knight. **102. hym liste ryde,** it pleased him to ride. **104. arwes,** arrows. **106. dresse his takel,** prepare his weapons. **109. not heed,** closely clipped head, or one shaped like a nut. **110. koude,** knew. **111. bracer,** archer's arm-protector. **112. bokeler,** buckler. **114. Harneysed,** mounted. **115. Cristofre,** image of St. Christopher, the patron of foresters. **shene,** bright. **116. bawdryk,** baldric, belt to hold the horn. **117. forster,** forester or gamekeeper. **soothly,** truly. **118. nonne,** nun. **Prioresse,** head of a nunnery. **119. symple and coy,** unaffected and quiet. **120. Seint Loy,** St. Eligius, a French saint who was artist and courtier. **121. cleped,** called. **123. semely,** nicely. **124. fetisly,** neatly. **125. Stratford-atte-Bowe,** a nunnery near London. **127. At mete,** at table. **132. ful muchel hir lest,** very much her delight. **134. ferthyng,** particle.

135. grece, grease. **136. raughte,** reached. **137. sikerly,** certainly. **desport,** mirth. **139. peyned . . . cheere,** took pains to imitate the manners. **140. estatlich,** stately. **141. digne,** worthy. **142. conscience,** sensitivity of feeling. **143. pitous,** full of pity. **147. wastel breed,** fine white bread. **149. yerde,** stick. **smerte,** sharply. **151. wympel,** covering for head, neck, and chin. **pynched,** pleated. **152. tretys,** well formed. **155. trowe,** believe. **156. hardily,** certainly. **157. fetys,** well made. **159. peyre,** string, rosary. **gauded . . . grene,** set with green beads to mark each Paternoster. **162. *Amor . . . omnia,*** Love conquers all things. **164. chapeleyne,** secretary. **preestes thre,** probably a slip of some kind, since we hear of but one later, and three would have made the pilgrims' number thirty-one instead of the twenty-nine of l. 24. **165. a fair . . . maistrye,** an extremely good one. **166. outridere,** inspector of monastic estates. **venerye,** hunting. **172. celle,** subordinate monastery.

The reule of Seint Maure or of Seint Beneit,
By cause that it was old and somdel streit,—
This ilke Monk leet olde thynges pace,
And heeld after the newe world the space.
He yaf nat of that text a pulled hen,
That seith that hunters been nat holy men,
Ne that a monk whan he is recchelees,
Is likned til a fissh that is waterlees—
This is to seyn, a monk out of his cloystre;
But thilke text heeld he nat worth an oystre,
And I seyde his opinioun was good.
What sholde he studie and make hym-selven wood,
Upon a book in cloystre alwey to poure,
Or swynken with his handes, and laboure,
As Austyn bit? How shal the world be served?
Lat Austyn have his swynk to hym reserved!
Therfore he was a prikasour aright;
Grehoundes he hadde, as swift as fowel in flight;
Of prikyng and of huntyng for the hare
Was al his lust, for no cost wolde he spare.
I seigh his sleves ypurfiled at the hond
With grys, and that the fyneste of a lond;
And, for to festne his hood under his chyn,
He hadde of gold wroght a ful curious pyn;
A love knotte in the gretter ende ther was.
His heed was balled, that shoon as any glas,
And eek his face, as he hadde been enoynt.
He was a lord ful fat and in good poynt;
Hise eyen stepe, and rollynge in his heed,
That stemed as a forneys of a leed;
His bootes souple, his hors in greet estat.
Now certeynly he was a fair prelat;
He was nat pale as a forpyned goost.
A fat swan loved he best of any roost.
His palfrey was as broun as is a berye.

A FRERE ther was, a wantowne and a merye,
A lymytour, a ful solempne man.
In alle the ordres foure is noon that kan
So muche of daliaunce and fair langage.
He hadde maad ful many a mariage
Of yonge wommen at his owene cost.
Un-to his ordre he was a noble post.
Ful wel biloved and famulier was he
With frankeleyns over al in his contree,
And with worthy wommen of the toun;
For he hadde power of confessioun,
As seyde hym-self, moore than a curat,
For of his ordre he was licenciat.
Ful swetely herde he confessioun,
And plesaunt was his absolucioun;
He was an esy man to yeve penaunce,
Ther-as he wiste to have a good pitaunce.
For un-to a povre ordre for to yive
Is signe that a man is wel yshryve;
For if he yaf, he dorste make avaunt,
He wiste that a man was repentaunt;
For many a man so hard is of his herte,
He may not wepe, al-thogh hym soore smerte.
Ther-fore in stede of wepynge and preyeres,
Men moote yeve silver to the povre freres.
His typet was ay farsed ful of knyves
And pynnes, for to yeven faire wyves.
And certeynly he hadde a murye note;
Wel koude he synge and pleyen on a rote;
Of yeddynges he bar outrely the prys.
His nekke whit was as the flour de lys;
Ther-to he strong was as a champioun.
He knew the tavernes wel in every toun,
And every hostiler and tappestere
Bet than a lazar or a beggestere;
For un-to swich a worthy man as he
Accorded nat, as by his facultee,
To have with sike lazars aqueyntaunce.
It is nat honeste, it may nat avaunce
For to deelen with no swich poraille,
But al with riche and selleres of vitaille.
And over-al, ther as profit sholde arise,
Curteys he was and lowely of servyse.
Ther was no man no wher so vertuous.
He was the beste beggere in his hous,
For thogh a wydwe hadde noght a sho,
So plesaunt was his *In principio*,
Yet wolde he have a ferthyng, er he wente.

173. reule . . . Beneit, rule of St. Maurus or of St. Benedict. **174. somdel streit,** somewhat strict. **176. the space,** in the meantime. **177. pulled,** plucked. **179. recchelees,** careless, negligent. **180. til,** to. **184. What,** why. **make hym-selven wood,** make himself mad. **186. swynken,** work. **187. As Austyn bit,** as St. Augustine commands. **189. prikasour,** hard-riding hunter. **191. prikyng,** tracking (by footprints). **192. lust,** pleasure. **193. seigh,** saw. **ypurfiled,** trimmed. **194. grys,** gray fur. **199. enoynt,** anointed. **200. poynt,** condition. **201. stepe,** protruding, or shining. **202. stemed,** shone. **forneys . . . leed,** furnace under a caldron. **205. forpyned,** wasted away. **208. Frere,** begging friar. **wantowne,** gay. **209. lymytour,** one licensed to beg within a limited territory. **solempne,** important. **210. the ordres foure.** See *Piers Plowman*, page 87. **kan,** knows. **211. daliaunce,** gossip, chit-chat, playfulness.

216. frankeleyns, prosperous country squires. **220. licenciat,** one licensed to hear confessions. **223. yeve,** give. **224. wiste,** knew. **pitaunce,** allowance, gift. **226. yshryve,** shriven. **227. dorste make avaunt,** dared boast. **230. hym . . . smerte,** it pains him sorely. **232. moote,** may. **233. typet,** loose hood. **farsed,** stuffed. **236. rote,** stringed instrument. **237. yeddynges,** ballads. **bar outrely the prys,** decidedly carried off the prize. **241. tappestere,** barmaid. **242. lazar,** leper. **beggestere,** beggar woman. **244. facultee,** position. **246. honeste,** respectable. **avaunce,** be profitable. **247. poraille,** poor folk, trash. **248. vitaille,** provisions. **251. vertuous,** effective. **253. sho,** shoe. **254. *In principio*,** "In the beginning," opening of the Gospel of John, held by the ignorant to be a magic formula, and consequently used by friars as a prelude to begging.

His purchas was wel bettre than his rente.
And rage he koude, as it were right a whelpe.
In lovedayes ther koude he muchel helpe:
For ther he was nat lyk a cloystrer
With a thredbare cope, as is a povre scoler,
But he was lyk a maister or a pope.
Of double worstede was his semycope,
That rounded as a belle out of the presse.
Somwhat he lipsed, for his wantownesse,
To make his Englissh sweete up-on his tonge;
And in his harpyng, whan that he hadde songe,
Hise eyen twynkled in his heed aright,
As doon the sterres in the frosty nyght.
This worthy lymytour was cleped Huberd.

A Marchant was ther with a forked berd,
In motlee, and hye on hors he sat,
Up-on his heed a Flaundryssh bevere hat,
His bootes clasped faire and fetisly.
Hise resons he spak ful solempnely,
Sownynge alwey th' encrees of his wynnyng.
He wolde the see were kept for any thyng
Bitwixe Middelburgh and Orewelle.
Wel koude he in eschaunge sheeldes selle.
This worthy man ful wel his wit bisette:
Ther wiste no wight that he was in dette,
So estatly was he of his governaunce,
With his bargaynes and with his chevysaunce.
For sothe he was a worthy man with alle,
But, sooth to seyn, I noot how men hym calle.

A Clerk ther was of Oxenford also,
That un-to logyk hadde longe ygo.
As leene was his hors as is a rake,
And he was nat right fat, I undertake,
But looked holwe, and ther-to sobrely.
Ful thredbare was his overeste courtepy;
For he hadde geten hym yet no benefice,
Ne was so worldly for to have office.
For hym was levere have at his beddes heed
Twenty bookes, clad in blak or reed,
Of Aristotle and his philosophie,
Than robes riche, or fithele, or gay sautrie.
But al be that he was a philosophre,
Yet hadde he but litel gold in cofre;
But al that he myghte of his frendes hente,
On bookes and on lernynge he it spente,
And bisily gan for the soules preye
Of hem that yaf hym wher-with to scoleye.
Of studie took he moost cure and moost heede.
Noght oo word spak he moore than was neede,
And that was seid in forme and reverence,
And short and quyk and ful of heigh sentence.
Sownynge in moral vertu was his speche,
And gladly wolde he lerne and gladly teche.

A Sergeant of the Lawe, war and wys,
That often hadde been at the Parvys,
Ther was also, ful riche of excellence.
Discreet he was and of greet reverence—
He semed swich, hise wordes weren so wyse
Justice he was ful often in assise,
By patente and by pleyn commissioun.
For his science and for his heigh renoun,
Of fees and robes hadde he many oon.
So greet a purchasour was nowher noon;
Al was fee symple to hym in effect,
His purchasyng myghte nat been infect.
Nowher so bisy a man as he ther nas,
And yet he semed bisier than he was.
In termes hadde he caas and doomes alle,
That from the tyme of Kyng William were falle.
Ther-to he koude endite, and make a thyng,
Ther koude no wight pynchen at his writyng;
And every statut koude he pleyn by roote.
He rood but hoomly in a medlee coote,
Girt with a ceynt of silk, with barres smale;
Of his array telle I no lenger tale.

A Frankeleyn was in his compaignye;
Whit was his berd as is the dayesye;

256. **purchas,** (illegal) gains. **rente,** (legal) income. 257. **rage,** behave wantonly. 258. **lovedayes,** days for settling disputes by arbitration. 262. **semycope,** short cape. 263. **presse,** mould. 264. **lipsed,** lisped. **wantownesse,** affectation. 270. **Marchant,** merchant. 271. **motlee,** figured cloth. 273. **fetisly,** neatly. 274. **resons,** opinions. **solempnely,** pompously. 275. **Sownynge,** proclaiming. 277. **Middelburgh and Orewelle.** Middelburgh was on the island of Walcheren in Holland; Orwell on the English coast opposite Middelburgh. 278. **sheeldes,** French gold coins. 279. **bisette,** employed. 281. **governaunce,** demeanor. 282. **chevysaunce,** business dealings, often with a hint of illegality. 284. **noot,** know not. 285. **Clerk,** ecclesiastical student. 286. **ygo,** begun. 289. **holwe,** hollow. **ther-to,** also. 290. **overeste courtepy,** upper short coat. 292. **office,** secular employment. 293. **hym was levere,** he had rather.

296. **fithele,** fiddle. **sautrie,** psaltery, a stringed instrument. 297. **philosophre,** often used to mean alchemist, one who was supposed to be able to turn base metals into gold. 299. **hente,** obtain. 302. **scoleye,** study. 303. **cure,** care. 304. **oo,** one. 306. **heigh sentence,** elevated meaning. 307. **Sownynge in,** tending towards. 309. **Sergeant of the Lawe,** legal servant of the king; one of the twenty or so leading lawyers of the land. **war,** prudent. 310. **Parvys,** Court of the Exchequer, or, possibly, the porch of St. Paul's, a gathering-place for lawyers. 314. **assise,** county court. 315. **patente,** a special royal letter of appointment. **pleyn,** full. 316. **science,** professional knowledge. 318. **purchasour,** conveyancer (?), buyer of land (?). 319. **fee symple,** absolute possession. 320. **infect,** defective in title. 323. **caas and doomes,** law cases and judgments. 325. **endite . . . thyng,** draw up a legal document. 326. **pynchen at,** find fault with. 327. **koude,** knew. 328. **hoomly,** informally. **medlee,** of mixed color. 329. **ceynt,** girdle.

Of his complexioun he was sangwyn.
Wel loved he by the morwe a sop in wyn.
To lyven in delyt was evere his wone,
For he was Epicurus owene sone,
That heeld opynyoun that pleyn delit
Was verray felicitee parfit.
An housholdere, and that a greet, was he;
Seint Julyan he was in his contree.
His breed, his ale, was alweys after oon;
A bettre envyned man was nevere noon.
Withoute bake mete was nevere his hous,
Of fissh and flessh, and that so plentevous,
It snewed in his hous of mete and drynke.
Of alle deyntees that men koude thynke
After the sondry sesons of the yeer,
So chaunged he his mete and his soper.
Ful many a fat partrich hadde he in muwe,
And many a breem and many a luce in stuwe.
Wo was his cook, but if his sauce were
Poynaunt and sharp, and redy al his geere.
His table dormaunt in his halle alway
Stood redy-covered al the longe day.
At sessions ther he was lord and sire;
Ful ofte tyme he was knyght of the shire.
An anlaas and a gipser al of silk
Heeng at his girdel, whit as morne mylk.
A shirreve hadde he been, and a countour;
Was nowher swich a worthy vavasour.

An Haberdasshere and a Carpenter,
A Webbe, a Dyere, and a Tapycer—
And they were clothed alle in oo lyveree
Of a solempne and a greet fraternytee.
Ful fressh and newe hir geere apiked was;
Hir knyves were chaped noght with bras,
But al with silver; wroght ful clene and wel
Hir girdles and hir pouches everydel.
Wel semed ech of hem a fair burgeys
To sitten in a yeldehalle on a deys.
Everych for the wisdom that he kan,
Was shaply for to been an alderman.
For catel hadde they ynogh and rente,
And eek hir wyves wolde it wel assente;
And elles certeyn they were to blame:
It is ful fair to been ycleped madame,
And goon to vigilies al bifore,
And have a mantel roialliche ybore.

A Cook they hadde with him for the nones,
To boille the chiknes with the marybones,
And poudre marchaunt tart, and galyngale.
Wel koude he knowe a draughte of Londoun ale.
He koude rooste, and sethe, and broille, and frye,
Maken mortreux, and wel bake a pye.
But greet harm was it, as it thoughte me,
That on his shyne a mormal hadde he,
For blankmanger that made he with the beste.

A Shipman was ther, wonyng fer by weste:
For aught I woot, he was of Dertemouthe.
He rood upon a rouncy, as he kouthe,
In a gowne of faldyng to the knee.
A daggere hangynge on a laas hadde he
Aboute his nekke, under his arm adoun.
The hoote somer had maad his hewe al broun.
And certeynly he was a good felawe;
Ful many a draughte of wyn hadde he drawe
Fro Burdeuxward, whil that the chapman sleep.
Of nyce conscience took he no keep.
If that he faught, and had the hyer hond,
By water he sente hem hoom to every lond.
But of his craft to rekene wel his tydes,
His stremes and his daungers hym bisydes,
His herberwe, and his moone, his lodemenage,
Ther nas noon swich from Hulle to Cartage.
Hardy he was, and wys to undertake;
With many a tempest hadde his berd been shake.
He knew alle the havenes, as they were,
Fro Gootland to the cape of Fynystere,

333. **complexioun . . . sangwyn.** By temperament and complexion he was "sanguine," since he was a well-fed man and blood (*sanguis*) predominated in his makeup. 334. **by the morwe,** in the morning. **sop,** piece of bread. 335. **wone,** custom. 340. **Seint Julyan.** See note on page 64. **contree,** district. 341. **after oon,** of uniform goodness. 342. **envyned,** stocked with wine. 345. **snewed,** snowed, abounded. 348. **soper,** supper. 349. **muwe,** pen. 350. **breem . . . luce,** fishes. **stuwe,** fishpond. 352. **geere,** utensils. 353. **dormaunt,** fixed. 355. **sessions,** local court sessions. 356. **knyght of the shire,** member of Parliament. 357. **anlaas,** dagger. **gipser,** purse. 359. **shirreve,** sheriff (administrative officer of the county). **countour,** auditor. 360. **vavasour,** country squire. 361. **Haberdasshere,** dealer in small wares. 362. **Webbe,** weaver. **Tapycer,** tapestry-maker. 365. **apiked,** adorned. 366. **chaped,** mounted. 369. **burgeys,** burgess. 370. **yeldehalle,** gildhall. **deys,** dais, platform. 371. **kan,** knows.

372. **shaply,** suitable. 373. **catel,** property. 377. **vigilies,** gild festivals; religious services on the eves of feasts. 378. **ybore,** carried (by a servant). 379. **for the nones,** for the occasion. 380. **marybones,** marrowbones. 381. **poudre marchaunt,** a sour flavoring powder. **galyngale,** an aromatic East Indian spice. 383. **sethe,** boil. 384. **mortreux,** stew. 385. **it thoughte me,** it seemed to me. 386. **mormal,** sore. 387. **blankmanger,** creamed fowl sweetened and spiced. 388. **Shipman,** ship's captain. **wonyng . . . weste,** living far to the west. 389. **woot,** know. 390. **rouncy . . . kouthe,** nag as well as he knew how to. 391. **faldyng,** coarse wool. 392. **laas,** cord. 395. **felawe,** rascal. 397. **chapman sleep,** merchant slept. 398. **nyce conscience,** tenderheartedness. **keep,** heed. 400. **By water . . . hoom,** he made them walk the plank. 402. **stremes,** currents. **daungers,** general mastery of the science of navigation. **hym bisydes,** at his finger-tips. 403. **herberwe,** harbors, anchorage. **lodemenage,** pilot's craft. 404. **Hulle to Cartage,** from Hull in Yorkshire to Cartagena in Spain. 408. **Gootland to Fynystere,** from the island of Gothland in the Baltic to Cape Finistere in Spain.

And every cryke in Britaigne and in Spayne.
His barge ycleped was the Mawdelayne.

With us ther was a Doctour of Phisik,
In al this world ne was ther noon hym lyk,
To speke of phisik and of surgerye,
For he was grounded in astronomye.
He kepte his pacient a ful greet deel
In houres by his magik natureel.
Wel koude he fortunen the ascendent
Of hise ymages for his pacient.
He knew the cause of every maladye,
Were it of hoot, or coold, or moyste, or drye,
And where engendred, and of what humour.
He was a verray, parfit practisour.
The cause yknowe, and of his harm the roote,
Anon he yaf the sike man his boote.
Ful redy hadde he hise apothecaries,
To sende hym drogges and his letuaries,
For ech of hem made oother for to wynne:
Hir frendshipe nas nat newe to begynne.
Wel knew he the olde Esculapius,
And Deïscorides, and eek Rusus,
Old Ypocras, Haly, and Galyen,
Serapion, Razis, and Avycen,
Averrois, Damascien, and Constantyn,
Bernard, and Gatesden, and Gilbertyn.
Of his diete mesurable was he,
For it was of no superfluitee,
But of greet norissynge and digestible.
His studie was but litel on the Bible.
In sangwyn and in pers he clad was al,
Lyned with taffata and with sendal;
And yet he was but esy of dispence;
He kepte that he wan in pestilence.
For gold in phisik is a cordial,
Therfore he loved gold in special.

A good Wyf was ther of biside Bathe,
But she was som del deef, and that was scathe.
Of clooth makyng she hadde swich an haunt,
She passed hem of Ypres and of Gaunt.
In al the parisshe wyf ne was ther noon
That to the offrynge bifore hire sholde goon;
And if ther dide, certeyn so wrooth was she,
That she was out of alle charitee.
Hir coverchiefs ful fyne were of ground;
I dorste swere they weyeden ten pound
That on a Sonday weren up-on hir heed.
Hir hosen weren of fyn scarlet reed,
Ful streite yteyd, and shoes ful moyste and newe.
Boold was hir face, and fair, and reed of hewe.
She was a worthy womman al hir lyve;
Housbondes at chirche dore she hadde fyve,
With-outen oother compaignye in youthe,—
But ther-of nedeth nat to speke as nouthe.
And thries hadde she been at Jerusalem;
She hadde passed many a straunge strem;
At Rome she hadde been, and at Boloyne,
In Galice at Seint Jame, and at Coloyne.
She koude muche of wandrynge by the weye.
Gat-tothed was she, soothly for to seye.
Upon an amblere esily she sat,
Ywympled wel, and on hir heed an hat
As brood as is a bokeler or a targe;
A foot mantel about hir hipes large,
And on hir feet a peyre of spores sharpe.
In felawship wel koude she laughe and carpe.
Of remedies of love she knew par chaunce,
For she koude of that art the olde daunce.

A good man was ther of religioun,
And was a povre Persoun of a toun,
But riche he was of holy thoght and werk.
He was also a lerned man, a clerk,
That Cristes gospel trewely wolde preche;
His parisshens devoutly wolde he teche.
Benygne he was, and wonder diligent,
And in adversitee ful pacient,
And swich he was preved ofte sithes.

409. Britaigne, Brittany. **411. Doctour of Phisik,** physician and surgeon. **413. phisik,** medicine. **414. astronomye,** astrology. **415–16. kepte . . . houres,** watched for favorable hours for his patient. **magik natureel,** astrology and the like, not witchcraft. **417. fortunen . . . ascendent,** cast the horoscope. **418. ymages,** representations either of the patient or of signs of the zodiac, probably the latter. **421. humour.** The four "humours" of the body were: blood (hot and moist), phlegm (cold and moist), bile or choler (hot and dry), black bile or melancholy (cold and dry). **423. yknowe,** known. **424. boote,** remedy. **426. letuaries,** remedies. **429–34. Esculapius . . . Gilbertyn,** the authors, classical, Arabian, and medieval, of the standard works on medicine consulted in Chaucer's day. **435. mesurable,** temperate. **437. norissynge,** nourishment. **439. sangwyn,** red. **pers,** blue-gray. **440. sendal,** thin silk. **441. esy,** sparing. **442. wan,** won. **443. gold,** gold in solution (*aurum potabile*). **cordial,** stimulant for the heart. **445. good Wyf,** goodwife, matron. **biside,** just outside. **446. scathe,** a pity.

447. haunt, skill. **448. passed,** surpassed. **Ypres . . . Gaunt,** Ypres and Ghent were famous centers of the Flemish wool trade. **450. offrynge,** the offering (at the altar) of something as an act of worship. **452. charitee,** Christian love. **453. coverchiefs,** kerchiefs, head-coverings. **ground,** texture. **454. dorste,** might venture to. **457. streite yteyd,** tightly tied. **461. With-outen,** not to mention. **462. as nouthe,** just now. **463. thries,** thrice. **464. straunge,** foreign. **465. Boloyne,** probably Boulogne-sur-mer in France. **466. Galice,** Galicia (in Spain). Cf. *Piers Plowman*, page 87. **Coloyne,** Cologne, in Germany, where was the shrine of the Three Kings. **468. Gat-tothed,** gap-toothed. **469. amblere,** easy-going horse. **471. targe,** shield. **472. foot mantel,** riding-skirt. **474. carpe,** talk. **478. Persoun,** parson. **485. preved ofte sithes,** proved many times.

Ful looth were hym to cursen for his tithes,
But rather wolde he yeven, out of doute,
Un-to his poure parisshens aboute
Of his offrynge and eek of his substaunce.
He koude in litel thyng have suffisaunce.
Wyd was his parisshe, and houses fer asonder,
But he ne lafte nat, for reyn ne thonder,
In siknesse nor in meschief, to visite
The ferreste in his parisshe, muche and lite,
Up-on his feet, and in his hond a staf.
This noble ensample to his sheep he yaf,
That first he wroghte, and afterward he taughte.
Out of the gospel he tho wordes caughte,
And this figure he added eek ther-to,
That if gold ruste, what sholde iren do?
For if a preest be foule, on whom we truste,
No wonder is a lewed man to ruste;
And shame it is, if a preest take keep,
A shiten shepherde and a clene sheep.
Wel oghte a preest ensample for to yive,
By his clennesse, how that his sheep sholde lyve.
He sette nat his benefice to hyre,
And leet his sheep encombred in the myre,
And ran to Londoun, un-to Seint Poules,
To seken hym a chauntrye for soules,
Or with a bretherhede to been withholde;
But dwelte at hoom, and kepte wel his folde,
So that the wolf ne made it nat myscarye;
He was a shepherde and noght a mercenarye.
And thogh he hooly were and vertuous,
He was noght to synful men despitous,
Ne of his speche daungerous ne digne,
But in his techyng discreet and benigne.
To drawen folk to hevene by fairnesse,
By good ensample, this was his bisynesse,
But it were any persone obstinat,
What so he were, of heigh or lowe estat,
Hym wolde he snybben sharply for the nonys.
A bettre preest I trowe that nowher noon ys.
He wayted after no pompe and reverence,
Ne maked hym a spiced conscience,
But Cristes loore, and his apostles twelve,
He taughte, but first he folwed it hym-selve.

With hym ther was a PLOWMAN, was his brother,
That hadde ylad of donge ful many a fother;
A trewe swynkere and a good was he,
Lyvynge in pees and parfit charitee.
God loved he best with al his hoole herte
At alle tymes, thogh hym gamed or smerte,
And thanne his neighebore right as hym-selve.
He wolde thresshe, and ther-to dyke and delve,
For Cristes sake, for every poure wight,
With-outen hire, if it lay in his myght.
His tithes payde he ful faire and wel,
Bothe of his propre swynk and his catel.
In a tabard he rood upon a mere.
Ther was also a REVE, and a MILLERE,
A SOMNOUR, and a PARDONER also,
A MAUNCIPLE, and my-self: ther were namo.
The MILLER was a stout carl for the nones,
Ful big he was of brawn, and eek of bones;
That proved wel, for over-al ther he cam,
At wrastlynge he wolde have alwey the ram.
He was short sholdred, brood, a thikke knarre;
Ther was no dore that he nolde heve of harre,
Or breke it at a rennyng, with his heed.
His berd as any sowe or fox was reed,
And ther-to brood as though it were a spade.
Upon the cop right of his nose he hade
A werte, and ther-on stood a tuft of herys,
Reed as the bristles of a sowes erys;
His nosethirles blake were and wyde.
A swerd and a bokeler bar he by his syde.
His mouth as greet was as a greet fourneys.
He was a jangler and a goliardeys,
And that was moost of synne and harlotries.
Wel koude he stelen corn and tollen thries;
And yet he hadde a thombe of gold, pardee.
A whit cote and a blew hood wered hee.
A baggepipe wel koude he blowe and sowne,
And therwithal he broghte us out of towne.

A gentil MAUNCIPLE was ther of a temple,
Of which achatours myghte take exemple
For to be wys in byynge of vitaille;

486. looth were hym to cursen, he was loath to excommunicate. **487. yeven,** give. **492. lafte,** neglected. **494. muche and lite,** great and small. **496. yaf,** gave. **498–500. gospel . . . do?** See Matthew 5:19. **502. lewed,** ignorant. **506. clennesse,** purity. **508. leet,** left. **510. chauntrye for soules,** endowment for singing masses for the dead. **511. bretherhede,** guild. **withholde,** engaged as chaplain. **516. despitous,** spiteful. **517. daungerous ne digne,** disdainful nor scornful. **523. snybben,** rebuke. **525. wayted after,** demanded. **526. spiced,** overscrupulous. **530. ylad . . . fother,** drawn very many loads of manure.

531. swynkere, worker. **534. thogh . . . smerte,** though things pleased him or pained him. **536. dyke,** dig ditches. **541. tabard,** laborer's loose coat. **542. Reve,** an administrative officer of a country estate. **543. Somnour,** (summoner) a process-server for an ecclesiastical court. **Pardoner,** seller of papal indulgences (remission of temporal or purgatorial punishments). **544. Maunciple,** purchasing agent for a college or similar organization. **545. carl for the nones,** fellow, exceptionally. **549. knarre,** knotted, thickset churl. **550. nolde . . . harre,** would not heave off its hinges. **551. rennyng,** running. **554. cop,** top. **555. werte,** wart. **herys,** hairs. **556. erys,** ears. **557. nosethirles,** nostrils. **560. jangler,** babbler. **goliardeys,** coarse jester. **562. stelen corn and tollen thries,** steal corn and take triple toll for grinding. **563. he . . . gold,** proverbial: "He was honest for a miller." **564. wered,** wore. **565. sowne,** play upon. **567. of a temple,** law school, perhaps the Inner or Middle Temple. **568. achatours,** buyers.

For wheither that he payde or took by taille,
Algate he wayted so in his achaat,
That he was ay biform and in good staat.
Now is nat that of God a ful fair grace
That swich a lewed mannes wit shal pace
The wisdom of an heep of lerned men?
Of maistres hadde he mo than thries ten,
That weren of lawe expert and curious,
Of whiche ther were a dozeyne in that hous
Worthy to been stywardes of rente and lond
Of any lord that is in Engelond,
To make hym lyve by his propre good,
In honour detteles, but if he were wood
Or lyve as scarsly as hym list desire;
And able for to helpen al a shire
In any caas that myghte falle or happe;
And yet this Maunciple sette hir aller cappe.

The Reve was a sclendre, colerik man.
His berd was shave as neigh as ever he kan;
His heer was by his erys ful round yshorn;
His top was dokked lyk a preest byforn.
Ful longe were his legges and ful lene,
Ylik a staf ther was no calf ysene.
Wel koude he kepe a gerner and a bynne;
Ther was noon auditour koude on hym wynne.
Wel wiste he by the droghte and by the reyn
The yeldynge of his seed and of his greyn.
His lordes sheep, his neet, his dayerye
His swyn, his hors, his stoor, and his pultrye,
Was hoolly in this Reves governynge,
And by his covenant yaf the rekenynge,
Syn that his lord was twenty yeer of age.
Ther koude no man brynge hym in arrerage.
Ther nas baillif, ne hierde, ne oother hyne,
That he ne knew his sleighte and his covyne:
They were adrad of hym as of the deeth.
His wonyng was ful faire upon an heeth,
With grene trees shadwed was his place.
He koude bettre than his lord purchace.
Ful riche he was astored pryvely,
His lord wel koude he plesen subtilly,
To yeve and lene hym of his owene good,
And have a thank, and yet a coote and hood.
In youthe he hadde lerned a good myster:
He was a wel good wrighte, a carpenter.
This Reve sat up-on a ful good stot,
That was al pomely grey and highte Scot.
A long surcote of pers up-on he hade,
And by his syde he baar a rusty blade.
Of Northfolk was this Reve of which I telle,
Biside a toun men clepen Baldeswelle.
Tukked he was as is a frere aboute,
And evere he rood the hyndreste of oure route.

A Somnour was ther with us in that place,
That hadde a fyr-reed cherubynnes face,
For saucefleem he was, with eyen narwe.
As hoot he was and lecherous as a sparwe;
With scaled browes blake, and piled berd;
Of his visage children were aferd.
Ther nas quyk silver, lytarge, ne brymstoon,
Boras, ceruce, ne oille of tartre noon,
Ne oynement that wolde clense and byte,
That hym myghte helpen of his whelkes white,
Nor of the knobbes sittynge on his chekes.
Wel loved he garlek, oynons, and eek lekes,
And for to drynke strong wyn, reed as blood.
Thanne wolde he speke and crye as he were wood;
And whan that he wel dronken hadde the wyn,
Thanne wolde he speke no word but Latyn.
A fewe termes hadde he, two or thre,
That he had lerned out of som decre—
No wonder is: he herde it al the day—
And eek ye knowen wel how that a jay
Kan clepen "Watte" as wel as kan the pope.
But who so koude in oother thyng hym grope,
Thanne hadde he spent al his philosophie;
Ay "*Questio quid juris*" wolde he crie.
He was a gentil harlot and a kynde;
A bettre felawe sholde men noght fynde.
He wolde suffre for a quart of wyn
A good felawe to have his concubyn
A twelf monthe, and excuse hym atte fulle.
Ful pryvely a fynch eek koude he pulle.
And if he foond owher a good felawe,
He wolde techen hym to have noon awe,
In swich caas, of the ercedekenes curs,
But if a mannes soule were in his purs;
For in his purs he sholde ypunysshed be.
"Purs is the ercedekenes helle," seyde he.

570. **by taille,** on credit. 571. **Algate . . . achaat,** in every way he watched so in his buying. 577. **curious,** skillful. 579. **stywardes,** stewards. 582. **wood,** mad. 583. **scarsly as hym list,** economically as it pleases him to. 586. **sette . . . cappe,** made fools of all of them. 593. **gerner,** granary. 597. **neet,** cattle. 598. **stoor,** stock. 601. **Syn,** since. 602. **brynge hym in arrerage,** catch him arrears. 603. **baillif,** bailiff, overseer subordinate to the Reeve. **hierde,** herdsman. **hyne,** farm laborer. 604. **sleighte,** trickery. **covyne,** deceitfulness. 606. **wonyng,** dwelling. 611. **lene,** lend. 613. **myster,** craft.

615. **stot,** stallion. 616. **pomely,** dappled. **highte,** was called. 624. **fyr. . . face,** fire-red face of a cherub. 625. **saucefleem,** afflicted with a disease not unlike leprosy. 627. **scaled,** scabby. **piled berd,** thin beard. 629–30. **quyk silver . . . tartre,** the regular remedies for the Summoner's disease. 632. **whelkes,** pimples. 636. **wood,** mad. 643. **clepen "Watte,"** call "Wat," short for Walter; jays were trained to say "Watte" as parrots are to say "Polly." 644. **grope,** test. 646. **"Questio . . . juris."** "The question is what part of the law is involved." 647. **harlot,** rascal. 652. **fynch . . . pulle,** practice seduction. 653. **owher,** anywhere. 655. **ercedekenes,** archdeacon's.

But wel I woot he lyed right in dede;
Of cursyng oghte ech gilty man hym drede,
For curs wol slee right as assoillyng savith,
And also war hym of a *Significavit!*
In daunger hadde he at his owene gyse
The yonge gerles of the diocise,
And knew hir counseil, and was al hir reed.
A gerland hadde he set up-on his heed
As greet as it were for an ale stake;
A bokeler hadde he maad hym of a cake.

With hym ther rood a gentil PARDONER
Of Rouncival, his freend and his comper,
That streight was comen fro the court of Rome.
Ful loude he soong, "Com hider, love, to me!"
This Somnour bar to hym a stif burdoun,
Was nevere trompe of half so greet a soun.
This Pardoner hadde heer as yelow as wex,
But smothe it heeng as dooth a strike of flex;
By ounces henge his lokkes that he hadde,
And ther-with he his shuldres overspradde;
But thynne it lay, by colpons oon and oon;
But hood, for jolitee, wered he noon,
For it was trussed up in his walet.
Hym thoughte he rood al of the newe jet;
Dischevelee, save his cappe, he rood al bare.
Swiche glarynge eyen hadde he as an hare.
A vernycle hadde he sowed up-on his cappe.
His walet biforn hym in his lappe,
Bret-ful of pardoun, comen from Rome al hoot.
A voys he hadde as smal as hath a goot.
No berd hadde he, ne nevere sholde have,
As smothe it was as it were late yshave:
I trowe he were a geldyng or a mare.
But of his craft, fro Berwyk into Ware,
Ne was ther swich another pardoner.
For in his male he hadde a pilwe beer,
Which that he seyde was Oure Lady veyl;
He seyde he hadde a gobet of the seyl
That Seint Peter hadde, whan that he wente
Up-on the see, til Jesu Crist hym hente.

660. drede, dread. **661. slee,** slay. **assoillyng savith,** absolution saves. **662. war . . . Significavit!** Let him beware of a writ of arrest, so called from its first word. **663. daunger,** control. **gyse,** way. **664. yonge gerles,** young of both sexes. **665. reed,** adviser. **666. gerland,** wreath. **667. ale stake,** sign of an alehouse. **670. comper,** comrade. **672. hider,** hither. **673. bar . . . burdoun,** accompanied him with a strong bass. **674. trompe,** trumpet. **soun,** sound. **675. wex,** wax. **676. strike . . . flex,** bunch of flax. **677. ounces,** thin strands. **679. colpons,** shreds. **682. Hym thoughte,** it seemed to him. **jet,** fashion. **683. Dischevelee,** with hair hanging loosely. **684. eyen,** eyes. **685. vernycle,** reproduction of St. Veronica's handkerchief bearing the likeness of Christ's face. **687. Bret-ful of pardoun,** brimful of pardons. **694. male,** bag. **pilwe beer,** pillowcase. **695. Oure Lady veyl,** The Virgin's veil. **696. gobet,** piece. **698. hente,** caught.

He hadde a croys of latoun ful of stones,
And in a glas he hadde pigges bones.
But with thise relikes, whan that he fond
A poure persoun dwellyng up-on lond,
Up-on a day he gat hym moore moneye
Than that the persoun gat in monthes tweye.
And thus, with feyned flaterye and japes,
He made the persoun and the peple his apes.
But trewely to tellen, atte laste,
He was in chirche a noble ecclesiaste.
Wel koude he rede a lessoun or a storie,
But alderbest he song an offertorie;
For wel he wiste, whan that song was songe,
He moste preche and wel affile his tonge
To wynne silver, as he ful wel koude;
Ther-fore he song the murierly and loude.

Now have I told yow soothly, in a clause,
Th' estaat, th' array, the nombre, and eek the cause
Why that assembled was this compaignye
In Southwerk, at this gentil hostelrye
That highte the Tabard, faste by the Belle.
But now is tyme to yow for to telle
How that we baren us that ilke nyght,
Whan we were in that hostelrie alyght;
And after wol I telle of oure viage,
And al the remenant of oure pilgrymage.
But first I pray yow, of youre curteisye,
That ye n'arette it nat my vileynye,
Thogh that I pleynly speke in this matere,
To telle yow hir wordes and hir cheere,
Ne thogh I speke hir wordes proprely.
For this ye knowen also wel as I,
Who-so shal telle a tale after a man,
He moot reherce as neigh as evere he kan
Everich a word, if it be in his charge,
Al speke he nevere so rudeliche and large,
Or ellis he moot telle his tale untrewe,
Or feyne thyng, or fynde wordes newe.
He may nat spare, al-thogh he were his brother,
He moot as wel seye o word as another.
Crist spak hym-self ful brode in holy writ,
And wel ye woot, no vileynye is it.
Eek Plato seith, who-so kan hym rede,
The wordes mote be cosyn to the dede.

699. croys of latoun, cross of latten, a mixed metal much like brass. **702. up-on lond,** in the country. **705. japes,** tricks. **706. made . . . his apes,** made fools of the parson and the people. **710. alderbest,** best of all. **711. wiste,** knew. **712. affile,** smooth. **719. faste by,** close to. **722. alyght,** alighted. **723. viage,** journey. **726. n'arette . . . vileynye,** blame it not on my lack of good breeding. **727. pleynly,** plainly. **728. hir cheere,** their behavior. **729. proprely,** exactly as they spoke. **733. Everich a,** every single. **734. Al,** although. **rudeliche and large,** rudely and broadly. **736. feyne thyng,** make something up. **739. brode,** plainly. **742. cosyn,** cousin.

Also I pray yow to foryeve it me,
Al have I nat set folk in hir degree
Here in this tale, as that they sholde stonde:
My wit is short, ye may wel understonde.
Greet cheere made oure Hoost us everichon,
And to the soper sette he us anon.
He served us with vitaille at the beste;
Strong was the wyn, and wel to drynke us leste.
A semely man oure Hoost was with-alle
For to been a marchal in an halle.
A large man he was with eyen stepe,
A fairer burgeys was ther noon in Chepe,
Boold of his speche, and wys, and wel ytaught,
And of manhode hym lakked right naught.
Eke ther-to he was right a murye man,
And after soper pleyen he bigan,
And spak of myrthe amonges othere thynges,
Whan that we hadde maad oure rekenynges,
And seyde thus, "Now, lordynges, trewely,
Ye been to me right welcome, hertely;
For by my trouthe, if that I shal not lye,
I saugh nat this yeer so murye a compaignye
At ones in this herberwe as is now.
Fayn wolde I doon yow myrthe, wiste I how.
And of a myrthe I am right now bythoght,
To doon yow ese, and it shal coste noght.
"Ye goon to Caunterbury—God yow spede,
The blisful martir quyte yow youre mede!
And wel I woot, as ye goon by the weye,
Ye shapen yow to talen and to pleye;
For trewely, confort ne myrthe is noon
To ryde by the weye domb as a stoon;
And ther-fore wol I maken yow disport,
As I seyde erst, and doon yow som confort.
And if yow liketh alle, by oon assent,
For to stonden at my juggement,
And for to werken as I shal yow seye,
Tomorwe, whan ye riden by the weye,
Now, by my fader soule that is deed,
But ye be murye, I wol yeve yow myn heed!
Hoold up youre hondes, with-outen moore speche."
Oure conseil was nat longe for to seche;
Us thoughte it was nat worth to make it wys,
And graunted hym with-outen moore avys,
And bad hym seye his voirdit as hym leste.
"Lordynges," quod he, "now herkneth for the beste;
But taketh it not, I pray yow, in desdeyn;
This is the poynt, to speken short and pleyn,
That ech of yow, to shorte with oure weye,
In this viage shal telle tales tweye
To Caunterburyward, I mene it so,
And homward he shal tellen othere two,
Of aventures that whilom have bifalle.
And which of yow that bereth hym best of alle,
That is to seyn, that telleth in this caas
Tales of best sentence and moost solaas,
Shal have a soper at oure aller cost
Here in this place, sittyng by this post,
Whan that we come agayn fro Caunterbury.
And for to make yow the moore mury,
I wol my-self goodly with yow ryde,
Right at myn owene cost, and be your gyde.
And who-so wole my juggement withseye
Shal paye al that we spende by the weye.
And if ye vouche sauf that it be so,
Tel me anoon, with-outen wordes mo,
And I wol erly shape me ther-fore."
This thyng was graunted, and oure othes swore
With ful glad herte, and preyden hym also
That he wolde vouche sauf for to do so,
And that he wolde been oure governour,
And of oure tales juge and reportour,
And sette a soper at a certeyn prys,
And we wol reuled been at his devys
In heigh and lough; and thus by oon assent
We been acorded to his juggement.
And ther-upon the wyn was fet anoon;
We dronken, and to reste wente echon,
With-outen any lenger taryynge.
Amorwe, whan that day bigan to sprynge,
Up roos oure Hoost, and was oure aller cok,
And gadred us togidre in a flok,
And forth we riden, a litel moore than pas,
Unto the wateryng of Seint Thomas;
And there oure Hoost bigan his hors areste,
And seyde, "Lordynges, herkneth, if yow leste:

744. Al have . . . degree, although I have not arranged the tales in the order of the tellers' social ranks. **747. Hoost,** Harry Bailly, the innkeeper. **everichon,** every one. **748. anon,** at once. **750. us leste,** it pleased us. **753. eyen stepe,** protruding, or sparkling, eyes. **754. Chepe,** Cheapside, the business district of London. **762. hertely,** heartily. **764. saugh,** saw. **765. herberwe,** lodging. **770. quyte . . . mede,** repay you your reward. **771. goon,** go. **772. shapen yow to talen,** intend to tell tales. **776. erst,** before. **777. yow . . . alle,** it pleases you all. **778. stonden . . . juggement,** submit to my judgment. **781. by . . . deed,** by the soul of my dead father. **783. Hoold . . . hondes,** vote by show of your hands. **784. seche,** seek. **785. Us . . . wys.** It seemed to us not worth making any difficulty about.

786. graunted hym, we granted his wish. **avys,** deliberation. **787. voirdit,** decision. **788. quod,** said. **791. to shorte . . . weye,** to shorten our way with. **795. whilom,** formerly. **798. sentence,** instruction. **solaas,** entertainment. **799. oure aller cost,** the cost of us all. **805. withseye,** oppose. **807. vouche sauf,** grant. **810. swore,** were sworn. **811. preyden,** we asked. **816. devys,** direction. **817. In . . . lough,** in all respects. **819. fet,** fetched. **823. roos . . . cok,** our Host awakened us all, as by a rooster's crowing. **825. litel moore . . . pas,** a little more than a footpace.

Ye woot youre forward, and it yow recorde.
If evensong and morwesong acorde,
Lat se now who shal telle the firste tale.
As evere moot I drynke wyn or ale,
Who so be rebel to my juggement
Shal paye for al that by the wey is spent.
Now draweth cut, er that we ferrer twynne;
He which that hath the shorteste shal bigynne.
Sire Knyght," quod he, "my mayster and my lord,
Now draweth cut, for that is myn acord.
Cometh neer," quod he, "my lady Prioresse,
And ye, sire Clerk, lat be youre shamefastnesse,
Ne studieth noght; ley hond to, every man!"
  Anoon to drawen every wight began,
And shortly for to tellen as it was,
Were it by aventure, or sort, or cas,
The sothe is this, the cut fil to the Knyght,
Of which ful blithe and glad was every wight,
And telle he moste his tale, as was resoun,
By forward and by composicioun,
As ye han herd; what nedeth wordes mo?
  And whan this goode man saugh that it was so,
As he that wys was and obedient
To kepe his forward by his free assent,
He seyde, "Syn I shal bigynne the game,
What, welcome be the cut, a Goddes name!
Now lat us ryde, and herkneth what I seye."
And with that word we ryden forth oure weye,
And he bigan with right a murye cheere
His tale anoon, and seyde as ye may heere.

[The Knight and several others of the pilgrims have told various tales, all appropriate to the tellers' characters and tastes. Now the Host has interrupted a quarrel between the Friar and the Summoner, which is flaring up for the second time, and requests the Friar to tell his story.]

THE FRIAR'S PROLOGUE

  This worthy lymytour, this noble Frere,
He made alwey a maner louryng cheere
Upon the Somnour, but for honestee
No vileyns word as yet to hym spak he.
But atte laste he seyde unto the Wyf,
"Dame," quod he, "God yeve yow right good lyf!
Ye han heer touched, also mote I thee,
In scole matere greet difficultee.
Ye han seyd muche thyng right wel, I seye;
But, dame, here as we ryden by the weye,
Us nedeth nat to speken but of game,
And lete auctoritees, on Goddes name,
To prechyng and to scole of clergye.
But if it like to this compaignye,
I wol yow of a somnour telle a game.
Pardee, ye may wel knowe by the name,
That of a somnour may no good be sayd—
I praye that noon of yow be yvel apayd.
A somnour is a rennere up and doun
With mandementz for fornicacioun,
And is ybet at every tounes ende."
  Oure Hoost tho spak, "A! sire, ye sholde be hende
And curteys, as a man of youre estaat;
In compaignye we wol no debaat.
Telleth youre tale, and lat the Somnour be."
  "Nay," quod the Somnour, "lat hym seye to me
What so hym list; whan it comth to my lot,
By God! I shal hym quyten every grot.
I shal hym telle which a gret honour
It is to be a flaterynge lymytour;
And of many another manere cryme
Which nedeth nat rehercen at this tyme;
And his office I shal hym telle, ywys."
  Oure Hoost answerde, "Pees! namoore of this!"
And after this he seyde unto the Frere,
"Tel forth youre tale, leeve maister deere."

THE FRIAR'S TALE

  Whilom ther was dwellynge in my contree
An erchedekene, a man of heigh degree,
That boldely dide execucioun
In punysshynge of fornicacioun,
Of wicchecraft, and eek of bawderye,
Of diffamacioun, and avoutrye,
Of chirche reves, and of testamentz,
Of contractes, and of lakke of sacramentz,
Of usure, and of symonye also.
But certes, lecchours dide he grettest wo;

829. **forward,** agreement. **recorde,** recall. 830. **acorde,** agree ("if you feel this morning as you felt last night"). 832. **As . . . moot,** as surely as I hope to. 835. **draweth cut,** draw lots. **ferrer twynne,** set out farther. 838. **acord,** agreement. 840. **shamefastnesse,** shyness. 841. **studieth,** meditate. 844. **aventure, or sort, or cas,** chance. 845. **sothe,** truth. **fil,** fell. 848. **composicioun,** agreement. 854. **a . . . name,** in God's name. 1. **lymytour,** a friar licensed, in return for a rental, to beg within specified limits. 2. **maner . . . cheere,** a sort of frowning expression. 3. **honestee,** good manners. 4. **vileyns,** rude.

6. **yeve,** give. 7. **also . . . thee,** as I hope to prosper. 12. **lete,** leave. 18. **be . . . apayd,** be ill-pleased. 19. **rennere,** runner. 20. **mandementz,** summonses to appear in court. 21. **ybet,** beaten. 22. **hende,** pleasant. 28. **quyten,** repay. **grot,** bit. 36. **leeve . . . deere,"** dearly beloved master. 1. **Whilom,** once upon a time. 2. **erchedekene,** archdeacon. 6. **diffamacioun,** libel. **avoutrye,** adultery. 7. **chirche reves,** church stewards. **testamentz,** wills. 8. **lakke of sacramentz,** failure to take the required sacraments. 9. **usure,** loaning on interest. **symonye,** selling church offices. 10. **lecchours, lewd** people

They sholde syngen if that they were hent;
And smale tytheres were foule yshent,
If any persone wolde upon hem pleyne;
Ther myghte asterte hym no pecunyal peyne.
For smale tithes and smal offrynge,
He made the peple pitously to synge.
For er the bisshop caughte hem with his hook,
They weren in the erchedekenes book;
And thanne hadde he thurgh his jurisdiccioun,
Power to doon on hem correccioun.
He hadde a somnour redy to his hond,
A slyer boy was noon in Engelond;
For subtilly he hadde his espiaille,
That taughte hym wher hym myghte availle.
He koude spare of lecchours oon or two,
To techen hym to foure and twenty mo.
For theigh this somnour wood were as an hare,
To telle his harlotrye I wol nat spare;
For we been out of his correccioun.
They han of us no jurisdiccioun,
Ne nevere shullen terme of alle hir lyves,—
"Peter! so been wommen of the styves,"
Quod the Somnour, "yput out of my cure!"
"Pees! with myschaunce and with mysaventure!"
Thus seyde oure Hoost, "and lat hym telle his tale.
Now telleth forth, thogh that the Somnour gale,
Ne spareth nat, myn owene maister deere."
  This false theef, this somnour—quod the Frere—
Hadde alwey baudes redy to his hond
As any hauk to lure in Engelond,
That tolde hym al the secree that they knewe;
For hir acqueyntance was nat come of newe,
They weren hise approwours pryvely.
He took hym-self a greet profit therby;
His maister knewe nat alwey what he wan.
Withouten mandement a lewed man
He koude somne on peyne of Cristes curs.
And they were glade for to fille his purs
And make hym grete festes atte nale.
And right as Judas hadde purses smale
And was a theef, right swich a theef was he;
His maister hadde but half his duetee.
He was, if I shal yeven hym his laude,
A theef, and eek a somnour, and a baude. . . .
Certeyn, he knew of briberyes mo 67
Than possible is to telle in yeres two;
For in this world nys dogge for the bowe
That kan an hurt deer from an hool knowe
Bet than this somnour knewe a sly lecchour,
Or an avouter, or a paramour.
And for that was the fruyt of al his rente,
Therfore on it he sette al his entente.
  And so bifel that ones on a day
This somnour evere waityng on his pray,
For to somne an old widwe, a ribibe—
Feynynge a cause, for he wolde brybe—
Happed that he say bifore hym ryde
A gay yeman, under a forest syde.
A bowe he bar and arwes brighte and kene;
He hadde upon a courtepy of grene;
An hat upon his heed, with frenges blake.
"Sire," quod this somnour, "hayl, and wel atake!"
"Welcome," quod he, "and every good felawe!
Where ridestow under this grene wode shawe?"
Seyde this yeman. "Wiltow fer today?"
  This somnour hym answerde, and seyde, "Nay.
Here faste by," quod he, "is myn entente,
To ryden for to reysen up a rente
That longeth to my lordes duetee."
  "Artow thanne a bailly?" "Ye," quod he.
He dorste nat, for verray filthe and shame,
Seye that he was a somnour, for the name.
  "*Depardieux*," quod this yeman, "deere brother;
Thou art a bailly, and I am another.
I am unknowen, as in this contree;
Of thyn aqueyntance I wolde praye thee,
And eek of bretherhede if that yow leste.
I have gold and silver in my cheste;
If that thee happe to comen in oure shire,
Al shal be thyn, right as thou wolt desire."
  "*Graunt mercy*," quod this somnour, "by my feith!"
Everych in ootheres hond his trouthe leith,
For to be sworn bretheren til they deye.
In daliaunce they ryden forth and pleye.
  This somnour, which that was as ful of jangles
As ful of venym been thise waryangles,
And evere enqueryng upon every thyng,
"Brother," quod he, "where is now youre dwellyng,

11. syngen, cry. **hent,** caught. **12. smale tytheres,** those who failed to pay the full tithe (church tax). **foule yshent,** foully injured. **13. persone,** parson. **pleyne,** complain. **14. Ther . . . peyne.** The archdeacon never omitted a pecuniary punishment. **17. hook,** an allusion to the bishop's crosier. **20. doon . . . correccioun,** punish them. **22. boy,** knave. **23. espiaille,** crew of spies. **24. hym . . . availle,** he might catch someone. **26. techen hym to,** show him how to find. **27. theigh,** though. **wood,** mad. **28. harlotrye,** rascality. **29. For . . . correccioun,** for we friars are out of his power to punish. **31. terme of,** during. **32. Peter!** oath by St. Peter. **styves,** brothels. **33. cure!** care, custody. **36. gale,** cry out. **43. approwours,** informers. **46. mandement,** summons. **lewed,** ignorant. **47. somne,** summon. **49. atte nale,** at the ale-house. **52. his duetee,** the amount due him.

53. laude, praise. **70. hool,** sound, unwounded. **71. Bet,** better. **72. avouter,** adulterer. **73. rente,** income. **77. ribibe,** a term of contempt for an old woman. **79. say,** saw. **80. yeman,** yeoman. **82. courtepy,** upper short coat. **84. atake!** overtaken. **86. shawe,** wood. **87. Wiltow fer,** wilt thou go far. **91. longeth,** belongs. **92. bailly,** bailiff. **95. "*Depardieux*,"** in God's name! **99. if . . . leste,** if that pleases you. **104. Everych,** each. **106. daliaunce,** conversation. **108. waryangles,** butcher-birds.

Another day if that I sholde yow seche?"
This yeman hym answerde in softe speche;
"Brother," quod he, "fer in the north contree,
Where-as I hope som-tyme I shal thee see.
Er we departe, I shal thee so wel wisse
That of myn hous ne shaltow nevere mysse."
"Now brother," quod this somnour, "I yow preye,
Teche me, whil that we ryden by the weye—
Syn that ye been a baillyf as am I—
Som subtiltee, and tel me feithfully
In myn office how I may moost wynne;
And spareth nat for conscience ne synne,
But as my brother tel me how do ye."
"Now by my trouthe, brother deere," seyde he,
"As I shal tellen thee a feithful tale.
My wages been ful streite and ful smale.
My lord is hard to me, and daungerous;
And myn office is ful laborous;
And therfore by extorcions I lyve.
Forsothe, I take al that men wol me yeve.
Algate, by sleyghte or by violence,
Fro yeer to yeer I wynne al my dispence.
I kan no bettre tellen, feithfully."
"Now certes," quod this somnour, "so fare I;
I spare nat to taken, God it woot,
But-if it be to hevy or to hoot.
What I may gete in conseil pryvely,
No manere conscience of that have I.
Nere myn extorcioun, I myghte nat lyven.
Ne of swiche japes wol I nat be shryven;
Stomak ne conscience ne knowe I noon;
I shrewe thise shrifte-fadres everychon.
Wel be we met, by God and by Seint Jame!
But leeve brother, tel me thanne thy name,"
Quod this somnour, "in this mene while."
This yeman gan a litel for to smyle.
"Brother," quod he, "woltow that I thee telle?
I am a feend; my dwellyng is in helle.
And here I ryde aboute my purchasyng,
To wite wher men wol yeve me anythyng.
My purchas is th' effect of al my rente.
Looke how thou rydest for the same entente—
To wynne good, thou rekkest nevere how;
Right so fare I, for ryde wold I now
Unto the worldes ende for a preye."
"A!" quod this somnour, "*benedicite* what sey ye?
I wende ye were a yeman, trewely;
Ye han a mannes shap as wel as I.
Han ye a figure thanne determynat
In helle, ther ye been in youre estat?"
"Nay, certeinly," quod he; "ther have we noon;
But whan us liketh we kan take us oon,
Or elles make yow seme we ben shape.
Som-tyme lyk a man, or lyk an ape,
Or lyk an aungel, kan I ryde or go.
It is no wonder thyng thogh it be so;
A lousy jogelour kan deceyve thee,
And *pardee*, yet kan I moore craft than he."
"Whi," quod this somnour, "ryde ye thanne or goon
In sondry shap, and nat alwey in oon?"
"For we," quod he, "wol us swiche formes make
As moost able is oure preyes for to take."
"What maketh yow to han al this labour?"
"Ful many a cause, leve sire somnour,"
Seyde this feend. "But alle thyng hath tyme;
The day is short, and it is passed pryme,
And yet ne wan I nothyng in this day.
I wol entende to wynnyng if I may,
And nat entende oure wittes to declare;
For brother myn, thy wit is al to bare
To understonde, althogh I tolde hem thee.
But for thou axest why labouren we—
For som-tyme we been Goddes instrumentz
And meenes, to doon his comandementz,
Whan that hym list upon his creatures,
In divers art and in diverse figures.
With-outen hym we han no myght, certayn,
If that hym lyst to stonden ther agayn.
And som-tyme, at oure preyere, han we leve
Oonly the body and nat the soule greve;
Witnesse on Job, whom that we diden wo.
And som-tyme han we myght of bothe two—
This is to seyn, of soule and body eke.
And som-tyme be we suffred for to seke
Upon a man and doon his soule unreste
And nat his body. And al is for the beste.
Whan he with-standeth oure temptacioun,
It is a cause of his savacioun;
Al be it that it was nat oure entente
He sholde be sauf, but that we wolde hym hente.

115. wisse, instruct. **126. streite,** scanty. **127. daungerous,** niggardly. **131. Algate,** nevertheless. **132. dispence,** expenses. **133. kan,** know. **135. woot,** knows. **136. But-if,** unless. **137. conseil,** secret. **139. Nere,** were it not for. **140. japes,** tricks. **wol . . . shryven,** i.e., I will not confess them. **142. shrewe,** curse. **shrift-fadres,** priests. **149. purchasyng,** business of acquiring. **150. wite,** know. **151. th' effect,** the sum.

156. *benedicite*, bless (the Lord). **157. wende,** imagined. **159. determynat,** fixed, unchangeable. **160. ther,** where. **163. make . . . shape,** make it appear to you that we have a shape. **168. *pardee*,** certainly (by God). **171. swiche,** such. **176. pryme,** the period between 6 and 9 in the morning. **188. hym lyst,** it pleases him. **agayn,** opposite, opposed. **200. sauf,** safe, saved. **hente,** catch.

And som-tyme be we servant unto man;
As to the erchebisshop, Seint Dunstan,
And to the apostles servant eek was I."
"Yet tel me," quod the somnour, "feithfully;
Make ye yow newe bodyes thus alway
Of elementz?" The feend answerde, "Nay.
Som-tyme we feyne; and som-tyme we aryse
With dede bodyes in ful sondry wyse,
And speke as renably and faire and wel
As to the Phitonissa dide Samuel;
And yet wol som men seye it was nat he.
I do no fors of youre dyvynytee;
But o thyng warne I thee, I wol nat jape:
Thou wolt algates wite how we been shape?
Thou shalt her-afterwardes, my brother deere,
Come there thee nedeth nat of me to lere;
For thou shalt, by thyn owene experience,
Konne in a chayer rede of this sentence
Bet than Virgile whil he was on lyve,
Or Dant also. Now lat us ryde blyve,
For I wol holde compaignye with thee
Til it be so that thow forsake me."
"Nay," quod this somnour, "that shal nat bityde.
I am a yeman, knowen is ful wyde;
My trouthe wol I holde, as in this cas;
For though thow were the devel Sathanas,
My trouthe wol I holde to thee my brother
As I am sworn—and ech of us til oother—
For to be trewe brother in this cas.
And bothe we goon abouten oure purchas.
Taak thou thy part, what that men wol thee yeve,
And I shal myn; thus may we bothe lyve.
And if that any of us have moore than oother,
Lat hym be trewe and parte it with his brother."
"I graunte," quod the devel, "by my fey!"
And with that word, they ryden forth hir wey.
And right at the entryng of the tounes ende,
To which this somnour shoop hym for to wende,
They saye a cart that charged was with hey,
Which that a cartere droof forth in his wey.
Deep was the wey; for which the carte stood.

202. Seint Dunstan, Archbishop of Canterbury in the tenth century. The legend is that at Glastonbury, his birthplace, he once seized the devil by the nose with a pair of red-hot pincers and refused to release him until he promised never to tempt him again. **207. feyne,** feign, dissimulate. **209. renably,** fluently. **210. the Phitonissa,** the pythoness. The original pythoness was Apollo's priestess at Delphi; hence, any woman supposed to be able to foretell future events. The reference here is to the witch of Endor, who called up the prophet Samuel from the dead. See I Samuel 28:7–20. **212. do no fors of,** put no faith in. **213. jape,** joke. **214. algates wite,** always know. **216. there,** where. **lere,** learn. **218. Konne,** learn. **chayer,** chair. **219. on lyve,** alive. **220. Dant,** Dante. **blyve,** quickly. **226. Sathanas,** Satan. **238. shoop hym,** intended. **239. saye,** saw.

The cartere smoot, and cryde as he were wood,
"Hayt, Brok! hayt, Scot! what spare ye for the stones?
The feend," quod he, "yow fecche, body and bones!
As ferforthly as evere were ye foled,
So muche wo as I have with yow tholed,
The devel have al, bothe hors and cart and hey!"
This somnour seyde, "Heer shal we have a pley!"
And neer the feend he drough, as noght ne were,
Ful pryvely, and rowned in his ere:
"Herkne, my brother! herkne, by thy feith!
Herestow nat how that the cartere seith?
Hent it anon, for he hath yeve it thee—
Bothe hey and cart, and eek hise caples thre."
"Nay," quod the devel; "God woot, never a del.
It is nat his entente, trust me wel.
Axe hym thyself, it thou nat trowest me;
Or elles stynt a while, and thou shalt se."
This cartere thakketh his hors upon the croupe,
And they bigonne to drawen and to stoupe.
"Heyt now!" quod he, "ther Jesu Crist yow blesse,
And al his handwerk, bothe moore and lesse!
That was wel twight, myn owene lyard boy!
I pray God save thee, and Seint Loy!
Now is my cart out of the slow, *pardee*."
"Lo, brother," quod the feend, "what tolde I thee?
Heer may ye se, myn owene deere brother,
The carl spak o thing, but he thoghte another.
Lat us go forth abouten oure viage;
Heere wynne I no-thyng upon cariage."
Whan that they comen som-what out of toune,
This somnour to his brother gan to roune:
"Brother," quod he, "here woneth an old rebekke,
That hadde almoost as leef to lese hir nekke
As for to yeve a peny of hir good.
I wol han twelf pens, thogh that she be wood,
Or I wol somoune hire unto oure office;
And yet, God wot, of hire knowe I no vice.
But for thou kanst nat as in this contree
Wynne thy cost, taak heer ensample of me."
This somnour clappeth at the wydwes gate.
"Com out," quod he, "thou olde viritrate!

243. Hayt. This was a cry to spur horses on. The carter also calls the horses by name. **245. ferforthly,** completely. **246. tholed,** suffered. **249. drough,** drew. **250. rowned,** whispered. **254. caples,** horses. **257. trowest,** believe. **259. thakketh,** striketh. **hors,** horses. **263. twight,** pulled. **lyard,** gray. **264. Seint Loy!** St. Eligius. This is the saint by whom the Prioress, more gently, swore. **265. slow,** slough. **268. carl,** fellow. **269. viage,** journey. **272. roune,** whisper. **273. woneth,** dwelleth. **rebekke,** dame. **275. good,** goods. **276. wood,** angry. **282. viritrate!** hag.

I trowe thou hast som frere or preest with thee."
"Who clappeth?" seyde this wyf, "*benedicite!*
God save you sire; what is youre swete wille?"
"I have," quod he, "of somonce a bille.
Up peyne of cursyng, looke that thow be
To-morn bifore the erchedeknes knee,
T' answere to the court of certeyn thynges."
"Now, Lord," quod she, "Crist Jesu, kyng of kynges,
So wisly helpe me, as I ne may.
I have been syk, and that ful many a day.
I may nat go so fer," quod she, "ne ryde,
But I be deed, so priketh it in my syde.
May I nat axe a libel, sire somnour,
And answere there by my procuratour
To swich thyng as men wole opposen me?"
"Yis," quod this somnour; "pay anon—lat se—
Twelf pens to me, and I wol thee acquyte.
I shal no profit han ther-by but lite;
My maister hath the profit and nat I.
Com of, and lat me ryden hastily;
Yif me twelf pens; I may no lenger tarye."
"Twelf pens!" quod she, "Now, lady Seinte Marie
So wisly help me out of care and synne,
This wyde world thogh that I sholde wynne,
Ne have I nat twelf pens with-inne myn hoold.
Ye knowen wel that I am povre and oold;
Kythe youre almesse on me, povre wrecche."
"Nay thanne"; quod he, "the foule feend me fecche
If I th' excuse, though thow shul be spilt!"
"Allas!" quod she; "God woot, I have no gilt."
"Pay me," quod he, "or by the swete Seint Anne,
As I wol bere awey thy newe panne
For dette which thou owest me of oold.
Whan that thou madest thyn housbonde cokewold,
I payde at hom for thy correccioun."
"Thou lixt!" quod she; "by my savacioun,
Ne was I nevere er now, wydwe ne wyf,
Somoned unto youre court in al my lyf;
Ne nevere I nas but of my body trewe.
Unto the devel, blak and rough of hewe,
Yeve I thy body and my panne also!"
And whan the devel herde hire cursen so,
Upon hir knees, he seyde in this manere:
"Now, Mabely, myn owene moder dere,
Is this youre wyl in ernest that ye seye?"

286. somonce, summons. **287. Up,** upon. **295. libel,** written statement. **309. Kythe,** show. **almesse,** alms. **313. Seint Anne,** mother of the Blessed Virgin. **318. lixt,** liest.

"The devel," quod she, "so fecche hym er he deye,
And panne and al, but he wol hym repente!"
"Nay, olde stot, that is nat myn entente,"
Quod this somnour, "for to repente me
For anythyng that I have had of thee.
I wolde I hadde thy smok and every clooth."
"Now, brother," quod the devel, "be nat wrooth.
Thy body and this panne been myne by right;
Thou shalt with me to helle yet tonyght,
Where thou shalt knowen of oure privetee
Moore than a maister of dyvynytee."
And with that word this foule feend hym hente;
Body and soule he with the devel wente
Where-as that somnours han hir heritage.
And God, that made after his ymage
Mankynde, save and gyde us alle and some,
And leve thise somnours goode men bycome!
Lordynges, I koude han told yow, quod this Frere,
Hadde I had leyser, for this Somnour heere,
After the text of Crist, Poul, and John,
And of oure othere doctours many oon,
Swiche peynes that youre hertes myghte agryse;
Al be it so no tonge may it devyse,
Thogh that I myghte a thousand wynter telle
The peynes of thilke cursed hous of helle.
But for to kepe us fro that cursed place
Waketh, and preyeth Jesu for his grace
So kepe us fro the temptour, Sathanas.
Herketh this word! beth war, as in this cas:
The leoun sit in his awayt alway
To sle the innocent if that he may.
Disposeth ay youre hertes to withstonde
The feend, that yow wolde make thral and bonde.
He may nat tempte yow over youre myght;
For Crist wol be youre champion and knyght.
And prayeth that this somnour hym repente
Of his mysdedes, er that the feend hym hente!

[Chaucer's Summoner retaliates in telling his tale of a greedy friar, and after a few others of the pilgrims have regaled the company with their stories, the Host calls upon the Pardoner for a "murie tale." He agrees at once to tell one, but must first refresh himself with bread and ale at a nearby tavern. While drinking he hits upon the brilliant idea of describing his tactics in the pulpit, and treats the pilgrims to a remarkable exposé of his art and his unscrupulousness.]

330. stot, heifer. **349. agryse,** shudder. **356. beth war,** be wary. **358. sle,** slay. **363. prayeth,** pray.

THE PARDONER'S PROLOGUE

Radix malorum est Cupiditas. Ad Thimotheum sexto.

"Lordynges," quod he, "in chirches whan I preche,
I peyne me to han an hauteyn speche,
And rynge it out as round as gooth a belle,
For I kan al by rote that I telle.
My theme is alwey oon and evere was:
Radix malorum est cupiditas.
"First I pronounce whennes that I come,
And thanne my bulles shewe I, alle and some.
Oure lige lordes seel on my patente,
That shewe I first, my body to warente,
That no man be so boold, ne preest ne clerk,
Me to destourbe of Cristes holy werk.
And after that thanne telle I forth my tales,
Bulles of popes and of cardynales,
Of patriarkes and bisshopes I shewe,
And in Latyn I speke a wordes fewe,
To saffron with my predicacioun,
And for to stire hem to devocioun.
Thanne shewe I forth my longe cristal stones,
Ycrammed ful of cloutes and of bones,
Relikes been they, as wenen they echon.
Thanne have I in latoun a shulder-bon
Which that was of an holy Jewes sheep.
'Goode men,' I seye, 'tak of my wordes keep:
If that this boon be wasshe in any welle,
If cow, or calf, or sheep, or oxe swelle
That any worm hath ete, or worm ystonge,
Taak water of that welle and wassh his tonge,
And it is hool anoon; and forther-moor,
Of pokkes and of scabbe, and every soor
Shal every sheep be hool, that of this welle
Drynketh a draughte; taak kepe eek what I telle.
" 'If that the goode man, that the bestes oweth,
Wol every wyke, er that the cok hym croweth,
Fastynge, drynken of this welle a draughte,
As thilke holy Jew oure eldres taughte,
Hise bestes and his stoor shal multiplie.
" 'And, sire, also it heeleth jalousie;
For, thogh a man be falle in jalous rage,
Lat maken with this water his potage,
And nevere shal he moore his wyf mystriste,
Thogh he the soothe of hir defaute wiste,
Al hadde she taken preestes two or thre.
" 'Heere is a miteyn eek, that ye may se.
He that his hand wol putte in this mitayn,
He shal have multiplyyng of his grayn,
Whan he hath sowen, be it whete or otes,
So that he offre pens, or ellis grotes.
" 'Goode men and wommen, o thyng warne I yow:
If any wight be in this chirche now
That hath doon synne horrible, that he
Dar nat, for shame, of it yshryven be,
Or any womman, be she yong or old,
That hath ymaked hir housbond cokewold,
Swich folk shal have no power ne no grace
To offren to my relikes in this place.
And who-so fyndeth hym out of swich blame,
They wol come up and offre a Goddes name,
And I assoille hym by the auctoritee
Which that by bulle ygraunted was to me.'
"By this gaude have I wonne, yeer by yeer,
An hundred mark sith I was pardoner.
I stonde lyk a clerk in my pulpet,
And whan the lewed peple is doun yset,
I preche so as ye han herd bifore,
And telle an hundred false japes more.
Thanne peyne I me to strecche forth the nekke,
And est and west up-on the peple I bekke,
As dooth a dowve sittyng on a berne.
Myne handes and my tonge goon so yerne,
That it is joye to se my bisynesse.
Of avarice and of swich cursednesse
Is al my prechyng, for to make hem free
To yeven hir pens, and namely un-to me.
For myn entente is nat but for to wynne,
And no-thyng for correccioun of synne.
I rekke nevere, whan that they been beryed,
Thogh that hir soules goon a blakeberyed!
For certes, many a predicacioun
Comth ofte tyme of yvel entencioun;
Som for plesance of folk and flaterye,
To been avanced by ypocrisye,
And som for veyne glorie, and som for hate.
For whan I dar noon oother weyes debate,
Thanne wol I stynge hym with my tonge smerte

Radix . . . Cupiditas, "The desire of money is the root of all evils" (I Timothy 6:10). **2. hauteyn,** arrogant. **3. round,** melodiously. **4. kan,** know. **8. bulles,** papal warrants. See *Piers Plowman,* page 87, lines 68 ff. **9. Oure . . . seel,** the seal of the pope (or bishop). **patente,** license. **10. warente,** protect. **12. destourbe of,** disturb in. **17. saffron,** spice or color (my preaching). **19. cristal stones,** glass cases. **20. cloutes** rags. **21. wenen they,** his auditors think. **22. latoun,** a case made of a brass-like mixed metal. **24. keep,** heed. **27. That . . . ystonge,** that has eaten any snake, or any snake has stung. **29. hool,** healed. **30. pokkes,** the pustules of any eruptive disease. **33. oweth,** owneth. **34. wyke,** week. **37. stoor,** stock. **38. heeleth,** heals.

40. potage, broth. **41. mystriste,** mistrust. **42. defaute,** fault. **44. miteyn eek,** mitten also. **48. pens,** pennies. **grotes,** small coins. **49. o,** one. **51. that he,** so that he. **61. gaude,** trick. **64. lewed,** uneducated. **68. bekke,** nod. **69. dowve . . . berne,** dove on a barn. **70. yerne,** briskly. **73. free,** generous. **77. rekke,** care. **beryed,** buried. **78. goon . . . blakeberyed?** go blackberrying, that is, any old place. **80. Comth,** comes. **yvel entencioun,** evil intention. **84. debate,** fight. **85. hym,** some man in the congregation.

In prechyng, so that he shal nat asterte
To been defamed falsly, if that he
Hath trespased to my bretheren or to me.
For thogh I telle noght his propre name,
Men shal wel knowe that it is the same
By signes and by othere circumstances.
Thus quyte I folk that doon us displesances;
Thus spitte I out my venym under hewe
Of holynesse, to seme holy and trewe.
"But shortly myn entente I wol devyse:
I preche of no thyng but for coveityse.
Ther-fore my theme is yet, and evere was,
Radix malorum est cupiditas.
Thus kan I preche agayn that same vice
Which that I use, and that is avarice.
But though my-self be gilty in that synne,
Yet kan I maken oother folk to twynne
From avarice, and soore to repente.
But that is nat my principal entente;
I preche no-thyng but for coveitise;
Of this matere it oghte ynow suffise.
"Thanne telle I hem ensamples many oon
Of olde stories, longe tyme agoon.
For lewed peple loven tales olde;
Swiche thynges kan they wel reporte and holde.
What, trowe ye, that whiles I may preche,
And wynne gold and silver for I teche,
That I wol lyve in poverte wilfully?
Nay, nay, I thoghte it nevere, trewely!
For I wol preche and begge in sondry landes;
I wol nat do no labour with myne handes,
Ne make baskettes, and lyve ther-by,
By cause I wol nat beggen ydelly.
I wol noon of the apostles countrefete;
I wol have moneye, wolle, chese, and whete,
Al were it yeven of the povereste page,
Or of the povereste widwe in a village,
Al sholde hir children sterve for famyne.
Nay, I wol drynke licour of the vyne,
And have a joly wenche in every toun.
"But herkneth, lordynges, in conclusioun,
Your likyng is that I shal telle a tale.
Now have I dronke a draghte of corny ale,
By God, I hope I shal yow telle a thyng
That shal, by resoun, been at youre likyng.
For thogh my-self be a ful vicious man,
A moral tale yet I yow telle kan,
Which I am wont to preche, for to wynne.
Now holde youre pees, my tale I wol bigynne."

86. **asterte,** avoid. 88. **bretheren,** other pardoners. 92. **quyte,** requite. 95. **entente,** purpose. **devyse,** explain. 99. **agayn,** against. 102. **twynne,** turn. 103. **soore,** sorely. 106. **ynow,** enough. 107. **ensamples,** examples, illustrative anecdotes. 113. **wilfully,** willingly. 119. **countrefete,** imitate. 120. **wol,** will. **wolle,** wool. 121. **Al,** although.

THE PARDONER'S TALE

The Pardoner's tale of the three young roisterers who go to seek Death and find him in the manner they least expect is one of the "ensamples" or *exempla* of the medieval sermon. The story is an ancient one, of Oriental origin, but Chaucer's immediate source is not known. No other version of the story, surely, could surpass Chaucer's in dramatic effectiveness. The circumstances of the Black Death of 1348–1349 added a touch of realistic horror to the tale. A bit of comic relief and realism is supplied at the conclusion in the exchange of words between the Pardoner and the Host, and the episode adds an effective link to the general narrative of the pilgrimage to Canterbury.

In Flaundres whilom was a compaignye
Of yonge folk that haunteden folye,
As riot, hasard, stewes, and tavernes,
Where-as, with harpes, lutes, and gyternes,
They daunce and pleyen at dees bothe day and nyght,
And ete also and drynke over hir myght,
Thurgh which they doon the devel sacrifise
With-inne that develes temple, in cursed wise,
By superfluytee abhomynable.
Hir othes been so grete and so dampnable,
That it is grisly for to heere hem swere;
Oure blissed Lordes body they to-tere—
Hem thoughte that Jewes rente hym noght ynough—
And ech of hem at otheres synne lough.
And right anon thanne comen tombesteres
Fetys and smale, and yonge frutesteres,
Syngeres with harpes, baudes, wafereres,
Whiche been the verray develes officeres
To kyndle and blowe the fyr of lecherye,
That is annexed un-to glotonye.
The holy writ take I to my witnesse,
That luxurie is in wyn and dronkenesse.
Lo, how that dronken Loth, unkyndely,
Lay by his doghtres two, unwityngly;
So dronke he was, he nyste what he wroghte.
Herodes, who-so wel the stories soghte,
Whan he of wyn was replet at his feste,

1. **whilom,** once upon a time. 2. **haunteden folye,** indulged in folly. 3. **riot, hasard, stewes,** riotous conduct, gambling (specifically a game at dice), brothels. 4. **gyternes,** guitars. 5. **dees,** dice. 11. **grisly,** horrible. 12. **to-tere,** tear in pieces. 14. **lough,** laughed. 15. **tombesteres,** female acrobats. 16. **Fetys,** graceful. **frutesteres,** female fruit-sellers. 17. **baudes,** procurers. **wafereres,** pastry-sellers. 22. **luxurie,** lust. 23. **Loth, unkyndely,** Lot, unnaturally. 25. **nyste . . . wroghte,** knew not what he did. 26. **Herodes . . . soghte,** Herod, as whoever examines the stories well (will discover).

Right at his owene table he yaf his heste
To sleen the Baptist John ful giltelees.
Senec seith a good word doutelees:
He seith he kan no difference fynde
Bitwix a man that is out of his mynde
And a man which that is dronkelewe,
But that woodnesse, yfallen in a shrewe,
Persevereth lenger than dooth dronkenesse.
O glotonye, ful of cursednesse!
O cause first of oure confusioun!
O original of oure dampnacioun,
Til Crist hadde boght us with his blood agayn!
Lo, how deere, shortly for to sayn,
Aboght was thilke cursed vileynye!
Corrupt was al this world for glotonye!
  Adam oure fader, and his wyf also,
Fro Paradys to labour and to wo
Were dryven for that vice, it is no drede;
For whil that Adam fasted, as I rede,
He was in Paradys; and whan that he
Eet of the fruyt defended on the tree,
Anon he was out cast to wo and peyne.
O glotonye, on thee wel oghte us pleyne!
O, wiste a man how manye maladies
Folwen of excesse and of glotonyes,
He wolde been the moore mesurable
Of his diete, sittyng at his table.
Allas! the shorte throte, the tendre mouth,
Maketh that est and west, and north and south,
In erthe, in eyr, in water, men to swynke
To gete a glotoun deyntee mete and drynke!
Of this matere, O Paul, wel kanstow trete:
"Mete un-to wombe, and wombe eek un-to mete,
Shal God destroyen bothe," as Paulus seith.
Allas! a foul thyng is it, by my feith,
To seye this word, and fouler is the dede,
Whan man so drynketh of the white and rede
That of his throte he maketh his pryvee,
Thurgh thilke cursed superfluitee.
  The apostle wepyng seith ful pitously,
"Ther walken manye of whiche yow toold have I,
I seye it now wepyng with pitous voys,
Ther been enemys of Cristes croys,
Of whiche the ende is deth, wombe is hir god!"
O wombe! O bely! O stynkyng cod,
Fulfilled of donge and of corrupcioun!
At either ende of thee foul is the soun.
How greet labour and cost is thee to fynde!
Thise cokes, how they stampe, and streyne, and grynde,
And turnen substaunce in to accident,
To fulfillen al thy likerous talent!
Out of the harde bones knokke they
The mary, for they caste noght awey
That may go thurgh the golet softe and soote.
Of spicerie, of leef, bark, and roote
Shal been his sauce ymaked by delit,
To make hym yet a newer appetit.
But, certes, he that haunteth swiche delices
Is deed, whil that he lyveth in tho vices.
  A lecherous thyng is wyn, and dronkenesse
Is ful of stryvyng and of wrecchednesse.
O dronke man, disfigured is thy face,
Sour is thy breeth, foul artow to embrace,
And thurgh thy dronke nose semeth the soun
As thogh thou seydest ay "Sampsoun, Sampsoun!"
And yet, God woot, Sampsoun drank nevere no wyn.
Thou fallest as it were a stiked swyn;
Thy tonge is lost, and al thyn honeste cure;
For dronkenesse is verray sepulture
Of mannes wit and his discrecioun.
In whom that drynke hath dominacioun,
He kan no conseil kepe, it is no drede.
Now kepe yow fro the white and fro the rede,
And namely fro the white wyn of Lepe,
That is to selle in Fisshstrete or in Chepe.
This wyn of Spaigne crepeth subtilly
In othere wynes, growynge faste by,
Of which ther riseth swich fumositee,
That whan a man hath dronken draghtes thre,
And weneth that he be at hoom in Chepe,
He is in Spaigne, right at the toune of Lepe,
Nat at the Rochel, ne at Burdeux toun;
And thanne wol he seyn "Sampsoun, Sampsoun!"

28. **yaf . . . heste,** gave his command. 29. **sleen,** slay. 33. **dronkelewe,** drunken. 34. **woodnesse . . . shrewe,** madness having come upon an ill-tempered person. 37. **confusioun,** ruin. 39. **boght . . . agayn,** redeemed by with his blood. 40–41. **deere . . . Aboght,** dearly atoned for. **vileynye,** evil deed. 48. **defended,** forbidden. 50. **pleyne!** complain. 51. **wiste a man,** if a man knew. 52. **Folwen of,** follow on. 53. **mesurable,** temperate. 57. **swynke,** labor. 59. **kanstow trete,** can you treat. 60–61. **"Mete . . . bothe."** "Meats for the belly . . ." See I Corinthians 6:13. 64. **white and rede,** white wine and red. 65. **That . . . pryvee,** that is, so that he vomits. 68–71. **"Ther . . . god."** See Philippians 3:18–19. **croys,** cross.

72. **cod,** stomach. 75. **fynde,** provide for. 77. **substaunce,** essence. **accident,** externals. 78. **likerous talent,** greedy appetite. 80. **mary,** marrow. 81. **golet,** gullet. 83. **by delit,** delightfully. 85. **delices,** delights. 91. **semeth the soun,** seems the sound. 92. **"Sampsoun,** the sound a drunkard makes in snoring. 94. **stiked swyn,** stuck pig. 95. **thyn . . . cure,** care for your reputation. 101. **Lepe,** a Spanish wine center. 102. **Fisshstrete . . . Chepe,** in London's market section. 105. **fumositee,** vapors which were supposed to be able to rise from the stomach into the head. 107. **weneth,** thinks. 109. **Rochel . . . Burdeux toun,** La Rochelle, Bordeaux (French wine centers); a reference, apparently, to the practice of adulterating French wines with the cheaper Spanish varieties.

But herkneth, lordynges, o word, I yow preye,
That alle the sovereyn actes, dar I seye,
Of victories in the Olde Testament,
Thurgh verray God, that is omnipotent,
Were doon in abstinence and in prayere;
Looketh the Bible, and ther ye may it leere.
Looke, Attila, the grete conquerour,
Deyde in his sleep, with shame and dishonour,
Bledyng at his nose in dronkenesse.
A capitayn sholde lyve in sobrenesse.
And over al this, avyseth yow right wel,
What was comaunded un-to Lamwel—
Nat Samuel, but Lamwel, seye I—
Redeth the Bible, and fynd it expresly
Of wyn-yevyng to hem that han justise.
Namoore of this, for it may wel suffise.
And now that I have spoken of glotonye,
Now wol I yow defenden hasardrye.
Hasard is verray moder of lesynges,
And of deceite, and cursed forswerynges,
Blaspheme of Crist, manslaughtre, and wast also
Of catel and of tyme; and forther-mo,
It is repreve and contrarie of honour
For to ben holde a commune hasardour
And evere the hyer he is of estaat,
The moore is he holden desolat.
If that a prynce useth hasardrye,
In alle governaunce and policye
He is, as by commune opynyoun,
Yholde the lasse in reputacioun.
Stilbon, that was a wys embassadour,
Was sent to Corynthe, in ful gret honour,
Fro Lacedomye, to make hire alliaunce.
And whan he cam, hym happed, par chaunce,
That alle the gretteste that were of that lond,
Pleiynge atte hasard he hem fond.
For which, as soone as it myghte be,
He stal hym hoom agayn to his contree,
And seyde, "Ther wol I nat lese my name,
N'y wol nat take on me so greet defame,
Yow for to allie un-to none hasardours.
Sendeth othere wise embassadours;
For, by my trouthe, me were levere dye
Than I yow sholde to hasardours allye.
For ye that been so glorious in honours
Shal nat allye yow with hasardours.
As by my wyl, ne as by my tretee."
This wise philosophre, thus seyde he.

116. Looketh, look in. **leere,** learn. **117. Attila,** Hunnish conqueror of much of Europe; died A.D. 453. **120. capitayn,** military leader. **122. Lamwel,** Lemuel. See Proverbs 31:4 ff. **128. defenden hasardrye,** forbid gambling. **129. lesynges,** lies. **131. wast,** waste. **132. catel,** property. **133. repreve,** shame. **136. desolat,** abandoned, evil. **141. Stilbon,** really Chilon. **148. stal hym,** hurried secretly. **149. lese,** lose. **150. N'y wol nat,** nor will I.

Looke eek that, to the kyng Demetrius,
The kyng of Parthes, as the book seith us,
Sente hym a paire of dees of gold in scorn,
For he hadde used hasard ther-biforn;
For which he heeld his glorie or his renoun
At no value or reputacioun.
Lordes may fynden oother manere pley
Honeste ynow to dryve the day awey.
Now wol I speke of oothes false and grete
A word or two, as olde bokes trete.
Greet sweryng is a thyng abhomynable,
And fals sweryng is yet moore reprevable.
The heighe God forbad sweryng at al,
Witnesse on Mathew; but in special
Of sweryng seith the holy Jeremye,
"Thow shalt swere sooth thyne othes, and nat lye,
And swere in doom, and eek in rightwisnesse;"
But ydel sweryng is a cursednesse.
Bihoold and se, that in the firste table
Of heighe Goddes hestes honurable,
How that the seconde heste of hym is this:
"Take nat my name in ydel or amys."
Lo, rather he forbedeth swich sweryng
Than homycide or many a cursed thyng;
I seye that, as by ordre, thus it standeth;
This knowen, that hise hestes understandeth,
How that the seconde heste of God is that.
And forther-over, I wol thee telle al plat,
That vengeance shal nat parten from his hous
That of hise othes is to outrageous
"By Goddes precious herte! and by his nayles!
And by the blood of Crist that is in Hayles!
Sevene is my chaunce, and thyn is *cynk* and *treye!*"
"By Goddes armes, if thow falsly pleye,
This daggere shal thurgh-out thyn herte go!"
This fruyt cometh of the bicched bones two,
Forsweryng, ire, falsnesse, homycide.
Now, for the love of Crist, that for us dyde,
Lete youre othes, bothe grete and smale.
But, sires, now wol I telle forth my tale.
Thise riotours thre of whiche I telle,
Longe erst er pryme rong of any belle,
Were set hem in a taverne to drynke,
And as they sat, they herde a belle clynke
Biforn a cors was caried to his grave.

160. Parthes, Parthians. **175. doom,** judgment. **rightwisnesse,** righteousness. **177–78. firste . . . hestes,** first half of the table (of the Ten Commandments). **181. rather,** earlier. **184. This . . . understandeth,** those who understand his commandments know this. **186. plat,** plainly. **188. to,** too. **189–193. "By . . . go,"** dicers' profane talk. **in Hayles,** at the abbey of Hayles, near Wichcomb in Gloucestershire. **cynk and treye!"** five and three! **194. bicched,** cursed. **197. Lete,** leave off. **200. Longe . . . pryme,** long before 6 A.M. Sometimes prime was the period between 6 and 9, and even the latter hour.

That oon of hem gan callen to his knave,
"Go bet," quod he, "and axe redily,
What cors is this that passeth heer forby;
And looke that thow reporte his name wel."
"Sire," quod this boy, "it nedeth never-a-del.
It was me told er ye cam heer two houres;
He was, pardee, an old felawe of youres;
And sodeynly he was yslayn to-nyght,
Fordronke, as he sat on his bench up-right.
Ther cam a pryvee theef, men clepeth Deeth,
That in this contree al the peple sleeth,
And with his spere he smoot his herte atwo,
And wente his wey with-outen wordes mo.
He hath a thousand slayn this pestilence;
And, maister, er ye come in his presence,
Me thynketh that it were necessarie
For to be war of swich an adversarie.
Beth redy for to meete hym evere-moore;
Thus taughte me my dame; I sey namoore."
"By Seinte Marie," seyde this taverner,
"The child seith sooth, for he hath slayn this yer,
Henne over a myle, with-inne a greet village
Bothe man and womman, child, and hyne, and page.
I trowe his habitacioun be there.
To been avysed greet wisdom it were,
Er that he dide a man a dishonour."
"Ye, Goddes armes!" quod this riotour,
"Is it swich peril with hym for to meete?
I shal hym seke by wey and eek by strete,
I make avow to Goddes digne bones!
Herkneth, felawes, we thre been al ones;
Lat ech of us holde up his hand til oother,
And ech of us bicome otheres brother,
And we wol sleen this false traytour Deeth;
He shal be slayn, he that so manye sleeth,
By Goddes dignytee, er it be nyght!"
Togidres han thise thre hir trouthes plight,
To lyve and dyen ech of hem for oother,
As thogh he were his owene ybore brother.
And up they stirte al dronken, in this rage,
And forth they goon towardes that village
Of which the taverner hadde spoke biforn;
And many a grisly ooth thanne han they sworn,
And Cristes blessed body they to-rente;
Deeth shal be deed if that they may hym hente!

Whan they han goon nat fully half a myle,
Right as they wolde han treden over a stile,
An old man and a poure with hem mette.
This olde man ful mekely hem grette,
And seyde thus, "Now, lordes, God yow se!"
The proudeste of thise riotours thre
Answerde agayn, "What! carl, with sory grace!
Why artow al forwrapped save thy face?
Why lyvestow so longe in so greet age?"
This olde man gan looke in his visage,
And seyde thus, "For I ne kan nat fynde
A man, thogh that I walked in-to Inde,
Neither in citee ne in no village,
That wolde chaunge his youthe for myn age;
And therfore moot I han myn age stille,
As longe tyme as it is Goddes wille.
"Ne Deeth, allas! ne wol nat han my lyf.
Thus walke I, lyk a restelees caytyf,
And on the ground, which is my modres gate,
I knokke with my staf, bothe erly and late,
And seye, 'Leeve moder, leet me in!
Lo, how I vanysshe, flessh, and blood, and skyn!
Allas! whan shul my bones been at reste?
Moder, with yow wolde I chaunge my cheste,
That in my chambre longe tyme hath be,
Ye, for an heyre clowt to wrappe me!'
But yet to me she wol nat do that grace,
For which ful pale and welked is my face.
"But, sires, to yow it is no curteisye
To speken to an old man vileynye,
But he trespase in word, or elles in dede.
In holy writ ye may your self wel rede:
'Agayns an old man, hoor up-on his heed,
Ye sholde arise'; wherfore I yeve yow reed,
Ne dooth un-to an old man noon harm now,
Namoore than that ye wolde men dide to yow
In age, if that ye so longe abyde.
And God be with yow, wher ye go or ryde.
I moot go thider as I have to go."
"Nay, olde cherl, by God, thow shalt nat so!"
Seyde this oother hasardour anon,
"Thow partest nat so lightly, by Seint John!
Thow spak right now of thilke traytour Deeth,
That in this contree alle oure freendes sleeth.
Have here my trouthe, as thow art his espye,

205. **Go bet,** go quickly. 206. **heer forby,** past here. 208. **it . . . never-a-del,** it is not a bit necessary. 211. **to-nyght,** last night. 212. **Fordronke,** very drunken. 213. **pryvee theef,** secret criminal. 214. **sleeth,** slays. 222. **my dame,** my mother. 225. **Henne . . . myle,** over a mile hence. 226. **hyne,** hind, farm laborer. 240. **Togidres,** together. **plight,** plighted. 242. **ybore,** born. 243. **stirte,** jump. 247. **to-rente,** rent in pieces. 248. **hente,** catch.

250. **wolde . . . stile,** would have climbed over a stile. 252. **grette,** greeted. 253. **se!"** see (with favor), protect. 255. **carl . . . grace!** fellow, ill luck to you! 256. **forwrapped,** wrapped about. 266. **caytyf,** wretch. 267. **modres,** mother's. 273. **be,** been. 274. **heyre clowt,** piece of haircloth. 276. **welked,** withered. 278. **vileynye,** rudeness. 279. **But,** unless. 281. **Agayns,** in the presence of. **hoor,** white-haired. 282. **yeve . . . reed,** give you counsel. 286. **wher . . . ryde,** whether you walk or ride; that is, under all circumstances. 287. **thider,** thither. 293. **espye,** spy.

Telle wher he is, or thow shalt it abye,
By God, and by the holy sacrament!
For soothly thow art oon of his assent,
To sleen us yonge folk, thow false theef!"
"Now sires," quod he, "if that yow be so leef
To fynde Deeth, turn up this croked wey,
For in that grove I lafte hym, by my fey,
Under a tree, and ther he wol abyde;
Nat for youre boost he wol hym no thyng hyde.
Se ye that ook? Right ther ye shal hym fynde.
God save yow, that boghte agayn man-kynde,
And yow amende!" Thus seyde this olde man.
And everich of thise riotours ran
Til they came to that tree, and ther they founde
Of floryns fyne of gold ycoyned rounde,
Wel ny an eighte busshels, as hem thoughte.
No lenger thanne after Deeth they soughte,
But ech of hem so glad was of the sighte,
For that the floryns been so faire and brighte,
That doun they sette hem by this precious hoord.
The worste of hem he spak the firste word.
"Bretheren," quod he, "taak kepe what I seye;
My wit is greet, thogh that I bourde and pleye.
This tresor hath fortune un-to us yeven,
In myrthe and jolitee oure lyf to lyven,
And lightly as it cometh, so wol we spende.
By Goddes precious dignytee, who wende
To-day that we sholde han so fair a grace?
But myghte this gold be caried fro this place
Hoom to myn hous, or ellis un-to youres—
For wel ye woot that al this gold is oures—
Thanne were we in heigh felicitee.
But trewely, by daye it may nat be;
Men wolde seyn that we were theves stronge,
And for oure owene tresor doon us honge.
This tresor moste ycaried be by nyghte
As wisly and as slyly as it myghte.
Wher-fore I rede that cut among us alle
Be drawe, and lat se wher the cut wol falle;
And he that hath the cut with herte blithe
Shal renne to toune, and that ful swithe,
And brynge us breed and wyn ful pryvely.
And two of us shul kepen subtilly
This tresor wel; and, if he wol nat tarie,
Whan it is nyght, we wol this tresor carie,
By oon assent, wher as us thynketh best."
That oon of hem the cut broghte in his fest,
And bad hem drawe, and looke wher it wol falle;
And it fil on the yongeste of hem alle,
And forth toward the toun he wente anon.
And also soone as that he was agon,
That oon of hem spak thus un-to that oother:
"Thow knowest wel thow art my sworn brother,
Thy profit wol I telle thee anon.
Thow woost wel that oure felawe is agon,
And heere is gold, and that ful greet plentee,
That shal departed been among us thre.
But nathelees, if I kan shape it so
That it departed were among us two,
Hadde I nat doon a freendes torn to thee?"
That oother answerde, "I noot how that may be.
He woot that the gold is with us tweye;
What shal we doon? What shal we to hym seye?"
"Shal it be conseil?" seyde the firste shrewe,
"And I shal tellen in a wordes fewe
What we shul doon, and brynge it wel aboute."
"I graunte," quod that oother, "out of doute,
That, by my trouthe, I wol thee nat biwreye."
"Now," quod the firste, "thow woost wel we be tweye,
And two of us shul strenger be than oon.
Looke whan that he is set, that right anoon
Arys, as though thow woldest with hym pleye,
And I shal ryve hym thurgh the sydes tweye
Whil that thow strogelest with hym as in game,
And with thy daggere looke thow do the same;
And thanne shal al this gold departed be,
My deere freend, bitwixe me and thee.
Thanne may we bothe oure lustes al fulfille,
And pleye at dees right at oure owene wille."
And thus acorded been thise shrewes tweye
To sleen the thridde, as ye han herd me seye.
This yongeste, which that wente to the toun,
Ful ofte in herte he rolleth up and doun
The beautee of thise floryns newe and brighte.
"O Lord!" quod he, "if so were that I myghte
Have al this tresor to my-self allone,
Ther is no man that lyveth under the trone
Of God, that sholde lyve so myrie as I!"
And atte laste the feend, oure enemy,
Putte in his thoght that he sholde poyson beye,
With which he myghte sleen his felawes tweye;
For-why the feend foond hym in swich lyvynge
That he hadde leve hym to sorwe brynge.
For this was outrely his ful entente
To sleen hem bothe, and nevere to repente.
And forth he goth, no lenger wolde he tarie,
In to the toun, un-to a pothecarie,

294. it abye, suffer for it. **296. assent,** opinion. **298. yow . . . leef,** you desire so. **300. fey,** faith. **308. floryns,** coins. **316. bourde,** jest. **317. tresor,** treasure. **320. wende,** would have thought. **328. doon us honge,** cause us to be hanged. **331. rede,** advise. **334. swithe,** quickly. **340. fest.** fist.

357. conseil, in confidence. **shrewe,** scoundrel. **361. biwreye,** reveal, betray. **362. tweye,** two. **366. ryve,** thrust. **380. trone,** throne. **382. feend,** devil. **383. beye,** buy. **385. For-why . . . lyvynge,** because the fiend found him in such a manner of life. **386. leve,** permission. **387. outrely his,** utterly the youngest rioter's.

And preyed hym that he hym wolde selle
Som poysoun, that he myghte his rattes quelle;
And eek ther was a polcat in his hawe,
That, as he seyde, his capouns hadde yslawe,
And fayn he wolde wreke hym, if he myghte,
On vermyn that destroyed hym by nyghte.
The pothecarie answerde, "And thow shalt have
A thyng that, also God my soule save,
In al this world ther is no creature,
That ete or dronke hath of this confiture
Nat but the montaunce of a corn of whete,
That he ne shal his lyf anoon forlete;
Ye, sterve he shal, and that in lasse while
Than thow wolt goon a paas nat but a myle,
The poysoun is so strong and violent."
This cursed man hath in his hond yhent
This poysoun in a box, and sith he ran
In-to the nexte strete un-to a man,
And borwed hym large botels thre;
And in the two his poyson poured he;
The thridde he kepte clene for his drynke.
For al the nyght he shoop hym for to swynke
In cariyng of the gold out of that place.
And whan this riotour, with sory grace,
Hadde filled with wyn hise grete botels thre,
To hise felawes agayn repaireth he.
What nedeth it to sermone of it moore?
For right as they hadde cast his deeth bifore,
Right so they han hym slayn, and that anon.
And whan that this was doon, thus spak that oon:
"Now lat us sitte and drynke, and make us merye,
And afterward we wol his body berye."
And with that word it happed hym, par cas,
To take the botel ther the poysoun was,
And drank, and yaf his felawe drynke also,
For which anon they storven bothe two.
But, certes, I suppose that Avycen
Wroot nevere in no canon, ne in no fen,
Mo wonder signes of empoysonyng
Than hadde thise wrecches two, er hir endyng.
Thus ended been thise homicides two,
And eek the false empoysonere also.
O cursed synne of alle cursednesse!
O traytours homicide, o wikkednesse!

392. quelle, kill. **393. hawe,** yard. **394. capouns,** capons. **yslawe,** been killed. **395. fayn . . . hym,** he would be glad to avenge himself. **396. destroyed,** disturbed. **398. also,** as may. **400. confiture,** concoction. **401. montaunce,** amount. **corn,** grain. **402. forlete,** give up. **403. sterve,** die. **lasse while,** less time. **404. goon a paas,** walk at a footpace. **409. borwed,** borrowed. **412. shoop hym,** planned. **417. sermone,** speak. **418. cast,** planned. **423. par cas,** by chance. **426. storven,** died. **427. Avycen,** Avicenna (980–1037), Arabian authority on medicine. **428. canon,** rule. **fen,** division of his book. **429. Mo . . . signes,** more wonderful symptoms.

O glotonye, luxurie, and hasardrye!
Thou blasphemour of Crist with vileynye
And othes grete, of usage and of pryde!
Allas! mankynde, how may it bityde,
That to thy Creatour, which that thee wroghte,
And with his precious herte blood the boghte,
Thow art so fals and so unkynde, allas!
Now, goode men, God foryeve yow youre trespas,
And ware yow fro the synne of avarice!
Myn holy pardoun may yow alle warice,
So that ye offre nobles or sterlynges,
Or elles silver broches, spones, rynges.
Boweth youre heed under this holy bulle!
Cometh up, ye wyves, offreth of youre wolle!
Youre name I entre here in my rolle anon;
In-to the blisse of hevene shul ye gon;
I yow assoille, by myn heigh power,
Yow that wol offre, as clene and eek as cler
As ye were born.—And lo, sires, thus I preche.
And Jesu Crist, that is oure soules leche,
So graunte yow his pardoun to receyve,
For that is best; I wol yow nat deceyve.
But, sires, o word forgat I in my tale:
I have relikes and pardon in my male,
As faire as any man in Engelond,
Whiche were me yeven by the Popes hond.
If any of yow wol, of devocioun,
Offren, and han myn absolucioun,
Com forth anon, and kneleth here adoun,
And mekely receyveth my pardoun;
Or ellis, taketh pardoun as ye wende,
Al newe and fressh, at every myles ende,
So that ye offren alwey newe and newe
Nobles or pens, whiche that been goode and trewe.
It is an honour to everich that is heer
That ye mowe have a suffisant pardoner
T'assoille yow, in contree as ye ryde,
For aventures whiche that may bityde.
Peraventure ther may falle oon or two
Doun of his hors, and breke his nekke atwo.
Looke which a seuretee is it to yow alle
That I am in youre felaweship yfalle,
That may assoille yow, bothe moore and lasse,
Whan that the soule shal fro the body passe.

441. unkynde, unnatural. **443. ware,** guard. **444. warice,** cure. **445. nobles . . . sterlynges,** coins of considerable value. **446. spones,** spoons. **452. cler,** clear of sin. **453.** [What follows is the Pardoner's Epilogue. In it he speaks to his fellow pilgrims directly instead of addressing an imaginary congregation.] **454. leche,** physician. **458. male,** bag. **460. Whiche . . . hond,** a lie, of course. **465. wende,** travel. **470. mowe,** may. **suffisant,** able. **471. in . . . ryde,** as you ride in the country. **472. aventures,** accidents. **bityde,** happen. **473. Peraventure,** perhaps. **474. of,** off. **atwo,** in two. **475. seuretee,** insurance. **477. moore . . . lasse,** more and less important—everyone. **478. fro,** from.

I rede that oure Hoost shal bigynne,
For he is moost envoluped in synne.
Com forth, sire Hoost, and offre first anon,
And thow shalt kisse the relikes everychon,
Ye, for a grote! Unbokele anon thy purs."
"Nay, nay!" quod he, "thanne have I Cristes curs!
Lat be," quod he, "it shal nat be, so theech!
Thow woldest make me kisse thyn olde breech,
And swere it were a relyk of a seint!" . . .

This Pardoner answerde nat a word;
So wrooth he was, no word ne wolde he seye.
"Now," quod oure Hoost, "I wol no lenger pleye
With thee, ne with noon oother angry man."
But right anon the worthy Knyght bigan,
Whan that he saugh that al the peple lough,
"Namoore of this, for it is right ynough.
Sire Pardoner, be glad and murye of cheere;
And ye, sire Hoost, that been to me so deere,
I pray yow that ye kisse the Pardoner.
And Pardoner, I pray thee, drawe thee neer,
And, as we diden, lat us laughe and pleye."
Anon they kiste, and ryden forth hir weye.

[The Shipman tells a tale of a worldly monk who borrows money of his friend, a merchant, and with it seduces his friend's wife. Later, when the merchant, in need of some ready money, politely asks for repayment, the monk explains that the money has long since been repaid to the merchant's wife.]

BIHOLD THE MURIE WORDES OF THE HOOST TO THE SHIPMAN AND TO THE LADY PRIORESSE

"Wel seyed, by *corpus dominus*," quod oure Hoost,
"Now longe moote thow saille by the coost,
Sire gentil maister, gentil maryner!
God yeve the monk a thousand last quade yeer!
A ha! felawes, beth war of swich a jape!
The monk putte in the mannes hood an ape,
And in his wyves eek, by Seint Austyn!
Draweth no monkes moore in-to youre in.
"But now passe over, and lat us seke aboute,
Who shal now telle first of al this route
Another tale." And with that word he sayde,
As curteisly as it hadde been a mayde,
"My lady Prioresse, by youre leve,
So that I wiste I sholde yow nat greve,
I wolde demen that ye tellen sholde
A tale next, if so were that ye wolde.
Now wol ye vouche sauf, my lady deere?"
"Gladly," quod she, and seyde as ye shal heere.

THE PROLOGUE OF THE PRIORESS'S TALE

Domine dominus noster

"O Lord, oure Lord, thy name how merveillous
Is in this large worlde ysprad," quod she;
"For nat oonly thy laude precious
Parfourned is by men of dignytee,
But by the mouth of children thy bountee
Parfourned is, for on the brest soukynge
Som tyme shewen they thyn heriynge.

Wher-fore in laude, as I best kan or may,
Of thee and of the white lilye flour
Which that the bar, and is a mayde alway,
To telle a storie I wol do my labour;
Nat that I may encressen hir honour,
For she hir-self is honour and the roote
Of bountee, next hir Sone, and soules boote.

O moder Mayde! o mayde Moder free!
O bussh unbrent, brennyng in Moyses sighte,
That ravysedest doun fro the Deitee,
Thurgh thyn humblesse, the Goost that in th' alighte,
Of whos vertu, whan he thyn herte lighte,
Conceyved was the Fadres sapience,
Help me to telle it in thy reverence!

Lady, thy bountee, thy magnificence,
Thy vertu, and thy grete humylitee,
Ther may no tonge expresse in no science;
For som tyme, Lady, er men praye to thee,
Thow goost biforn of thy benygnytee,
And getest us the light of thy prayere
To gyden us un-to thy Sone so deere.

My konnyng is so wayk, O blisful Queene,
For to declare thy grete worthynesse,

479. rede, advise. **480. envoluped,** enveloped. **484. thanne have I,** when I do, may I have. **485. so theech!** as I hope to prosper! **499. saugh,** saw. **506. ryden . . . weye,** rode forth on their way. **1. *corpus dominus*,** the Host's blundering Latin for "body of the Lord." **4. thousand . . . yeer!** thousand loads of bad years. **5. beth war,** beware. **6. putte . . . ape,** made a fool of the man. **8. in,** dwelling. **12. as it,** as though he.

15. demen, judge. **17. vouche sauf,** consent. ***Domine dominus noster*.** The first words of Psalm 8, the first two verses of which the Prioress paraphrases in the first stanza of her prologue. **2. ysprad,** spread abroad. **3. laude,** honor. **4. Parfourned,** declared. **5. bountee,** kindness. **7. heriynge,** praise. **9. lilye flour,** the symbol of the Blessed Virgin. **10. the,** thee. **14. boote,** salvation. **16. unbrent,** unburnt. **Moyses,** Moses's. (For the story of Moses and the burning bush, see Exodus 3.) **17. ravysedest,** broughtest. **18. the Goost . . . alighte,** the (Holy) Ghost that alighted in thee. **19. lighte,** illuminated. **20. sapience,** wisdom, i.e., Christ. **24. science,** learned language. **26. goost biforn,** goest before, anticipatest. **27. of,** because of. **29. konnyng is so wayk,** ability is so weak.

That I ne may the weighte nat sustene,
But as a child of twelf month old, or lesse,
That kan unnethe any word expresse,
Right so fare I, and ther-fore I yow preye,
Gydeth my song that I shal of yow seye."

THE PRIORESS'S TALE

As a literary type "The Prioress's Tale" is a legend or miracle of the Virgin. As in the case of "The Pardoner's Tale," Chaucer's immediate source of the story is not known although more than a score of analogues have been found. There is every reason to suppose that, as in "The Pardoner's Tale," Chaucer's version is superior in literary skill to that of his original.

Professor Carleton Brown, the chief authority on "The Prioress's Tale," has shown that the legend of the murder of Christian children by Jews had taken shape by the end of the twelfth century, although the tradition is much older. The best known legend of this kind is connected with St. Hugh of Lincoln (to whom the Prioress refers), who, according to a chronicler, was murdered by Jews at Lincoln in the middle of the thirteenth century. Professor Brown has also demonstrated the paucity of the evidence for belief in stories of Jewish ritual murders. As for the Prioress, she could have had, of course, no personal knowledge of and no personal animosity towards the Jews, who had been expelled from England in 1290. It is noteworthy that the scene is laid in a remote place—"in Asye, in a greet citee." The emphasis in the story is on the "bountee" of the heavenly mother, the Blessed Virgin, the distress of the little schoolboy's mother, and the innocence and pathos of the boy himself.

The verse of the tale and of the prologue, as beautiful as any Chaucer ever wrote, is in the seven-line iambic pentameter stanza, which seems to have been first used by Chaucer himself in his "Complaint unto Pity," and is known as the Chaucerian stanza or *rime royal* (see "Poetic Forms and Patterns," page 1343).

THE PRIORESS'S TALE

Ther was in Asye, in a greet citee,
Amonges Cristen folk, a Jewerye,
Sustened by a lord of that contree
For foul usure and lucre of vileynye,
Hateful to Crist and to his compaignye;
And thurgh this strete men myghte ryde and wende,
For it was free, and open at eyther ende.

A litel scole of Cristen folk ther stood
Doun at the ferther ende, in which ther were
Children an heep, ycomen of Cristen blood,
That lerned in that scole yeer by yere
Swich manere doctrine as men used there,
This is to seyn, to syngen and to rede,
As smale children doon in hir childhede.

Among thise children was a wydwes sone,
A litel clergeoun, seven yeer of age,
That day by day to scole was his wone,
And eek also, wher as he say th'ymage
Of Cristes moder, hadde he in usage,
As hym was taught, to knele adoun and seye
His *Ave Marie*, as he goth by the weye.

Thus hath this wydwe hir litel sone ytaught
Oure blisful Lady, Cristes moder deere,
To worshipe ay, and he forgat it naught,
For sely child wol alwey soone lere.
But ay, whan I remembre on this matere,
Seint Nicholas stant evere in my presence,
For he so yong to Crist dide reverence.

This litel child, his litel book lernynge,
As he sat in the scole at his prymer,
He *Alma redemptoris* herde synge,
As children lerned hir Antiphoner;
And, as he dorste, he drow hym ner and ner,
And herkned ay the wordes and the note,
Til he the firste vers koude al by rote.

Noght wiste he what this Latyn was to seye,
For he so yong and tendre was of age.
But on a day his felawe gan he preye
T'expounden hym this song in his langage,
Or telle hym why this song was in usage;
This preyde he hym to construen and declare
Ful ofte tyme up-on his knowes bare.

His felawe, which that elder was than he,
Answerde hym thus: "This song, I have herd seye,
Was maked of oure blisful Lady free,
Hire to salue, and eek hire for to preye
To been oure help and socour whan we deye.
I kan namoore expounde in this matere:
I lerne song, I kan but smal gramere."

"And is this song maked in reverence
Of Cristes moder?" seyde this innocent.
"Now, certes, I wol do my diligence

The Prioress's Tale. **1. Asye,** Asia. **2. Jewerye,** ghetto. **3. Sustened,** maintained. **4. usure,** lending on interest, forbidden by the medieval Church. **lucre of vileynye,** filthy lucre. **6. wende,** walk.

15. wydwes sone, widow's son. **16. clergeoun,** pupil. **17. That . . . wone,** whose habit was to go to school day by day. **18. say,** saw. **25. sely,** innocent. **lere,** learn. **27. stant,** stands. **31.** ***Alma redemptoris*** (mater), "Dear mother of the Redeemer," opening of a hymn to the Virgin. **32. Antiphoner,** anthem book. **33. as he dorste,** as much as he dared. **ner,** nearer. **34. note,** tune. **35. koude,** knew. **36. was to seye,** meant. **42. knowes,** knees. **46. salue,** salute. **47. socour,** succor. **49. kan,** know.

To konne it al er Cristemasse be went;
Thogh that I for my prymer shal be shent,
And shal be beten thries in an houre,
I wol it konne oure Lady for to honoure."

His felawe taughte hym homward pryvely
Fro day to day, til he koude it by rote,
And thanne he song it wel and boldely
Fro word to word, acordyng with the note.
Twyes a day it passed thurgh his throte,
To scoleward and homward whan he wente;
On Cristes moder set was his entente.

As I have seyd, thurgh out the Juerye,
This litel child, as he cam to and fro,
Ful murily wolde he synge, and crye
O Alma redemptoris evere mo.
The swetnesse his herte perced so
Of Cristes moder, that, to hire to preye,
He kan nat stynte of syngyng by the weye.

Oure firste foo, the serpent Sathanas,
That hath in Jewes herte his waspes nest,
Up swal, and seyde, "O Hebrayk peple, allas!
Is this to yow a thyng that is honest,
That swich a boy shal walken as hym lest
In youre despit, and synge of swich sentence
Which is agayns oure lawes reverence?"

Fro thennes forth the Jewes han conspired
This innocent out of the world to chace.
An homycide ther-to han they hired,
That in an aleye hadde a pryvee place;
And as the child gan for-by for to pace,
This cursed Jew hym hente and heeld hym faste,
And kitte his throte, and in a pit hym caste.

I seye that in a wardrobe they hym threwe
Wher as thise Jewes purgen hir entraille.
O cursed folk of Herodes al newe,
What may youre yvel entente yow availle?
Mordre wol out, certeyn, it wol nat faille,
And namely ther as th'onour of God shal sprede,
The blood out crieth on youre cursed dede.

O martir, souded to virginitee,
Now maystow syngen, folwyng evere in oon
The white Lamb celestial—quod she—
Of which the grete evangelist, Seint John,
In Pathmos wroot, which seith that they that gon
Biforn this Lamb, and synge a song al newe,
That nevere, flesshly, wommen they ne knewe.

This povre wydwe awaiteth al that nyght
After hir litel child, but he cam noght;
For which, as soone as it was dayes lyght,
With face pale of drede and bisy thoght,
She hath at scole and elles-where hym soght,
Til fynally she gan so fer espie
That he last seyn was in the Jewerie.

With modres pitee in hir brest enclosed,
She goth, as she were half out of hir mynde,
To every place wher she hath supposed
By liklyhede hir litel child to fynde;
And evere on Cristes moder meke and kynde
She cryde, and at the laste thus she wroghte,
Among the cursed Jewes she hym soghte.

She frayneth and she preyeth pitously
To every Jew that dwelte in thilke place,
To telle hire if hir child wente oght forby.
They seyde, "Nay"; but Jesu, of his grace,
Yaf in hir thought, in-with a litel space,
That in that place after hir sone she cryde,
Wher he was casten in a pit bisyde.

O grete God that parfournest thy laude
By mouth of innocentz, lo, here thy myght!
This gemme of chastitee, this emeraude,
And eek of martirdom the ruby bright,
Ther he with throte ykorven lay upright,
He *Alma redemptoris* gan to synge
So loude, that al the place gan to rynge.

The Cristen folk, that thurgh the strete wente,
In coomen for to wondre up-on this thyng,
And hastily they for the provost sente;
He cam anon with-outen tariyng,
And herieth Crist that is of hevene kyng,
And eek his moder, honour of mankynde,
And after that the Jewes leet he bynde.

53. **konne,** learn. **er,** before. **went,** gone. 54. **shent,** reproached. 57. **homward pryvely,** secretly on the way home. 68–69. **The swetnesse . . . moder,** the sweetness of Christ's mother so pierced his heart. 73. **swal,** swelled. **Hebrayk,** Hebrew. 74. **honest,** honorable. 75. **as . . . lest,** as it pleases him. 76. **In youre despit,** in scorn of you. **sentence,** matter. 83. **hente,** seized. 84. **kitte,** cut. 85. **wardrobe,** privy. 87. **of Herodes al newe,** (composed) of new Herods. 89. **Mordre wol out,** a proverb. 90. **And . . . sprede,** and especially where the honor of God will be spread by its discovery. 92. **souded to,** confirmed in.

93. **evere in oon,** always the same. 96. **Pathmos,** Patmos, where St. John wrote Revelation. 98. **flesshly,** carnally. 104. **espie,** discover. 109. **liklyhede,** likelihood. 113. **frayneth,** asks. 117. **Yaf . . . thought,** put it into her thought. 124. **ykorven,** cut. **upright,** face up. 128. **coomen,** came. 129. **provost,** magistrate. 131. **herieth,** praises. 133. **leet he bynde,** caused to be bound.

This child with pitous lamentacioun
Up-taken was, syngynge his song alway,
And with honour of greet processioun
They carien hym un-to the nexte abbay.
His moder swownyng by his beere lay;
Unnethe myghte the peple that was there
This newe Rachel bryngen fro his beere.

With torment and with shameful deth echon
This provost dooth thise Jewes for to sterve
That of this mordre wiste, and that anon;
He nolde no swich cursednesse observe.
Yvel shal have, that yvel wol deserve;
Ther-fore with wilde hors he dide hem drawe,
And after that he heng hem by the lawe.

Up-on this beere ay lith this innocent
Biforn the chief auter, whil the masse laste,
And after that, the abbot with his covent
Han sped hem for to burien hym ful faste;
And whan they holy water on hym caste,
Yet spak this child, whan spreynd was holy water,
And song *O Alma redemptoris mater!*

This abbot, which that was an holy man
As monkes ben, or elles oghten be,
This yonge child to conjure he bigan,
And seyde, "O deere child, I halsen thee,
In vertu of the holy Trinitee,
Tel me what is thy cause for to synge,
Sith that thy throte is kit, to my semynge?"

"My throte is kit un-to my nekke boon,"
Seyde this child, "and, as by wey of kynde,
I sholde have dyed, ye, longe tyme agoon,
But Jesu Crist, as ye in bokes fynde,
Wol that his glorie laste and be in mynde,
And for the worship of his moder deere
Yet may I synge *O Alma* loude and clere.

"This welle of mercy, Cristes moder swete,
I loved alwey, as after my konnynge;
And whan that I my lyf sholde forlete,
To me she cam, and bad me for to synge

137. **nexte,** nearest. 138. **swownyng,** swooning. **beere,** bier. 141. **torment,** torture. **echon,** each one. 142. **dooth . . . sterve,** causes to die. 144. **observe,** favor. 146. **with . . . drawe,** he had each one tied to the tail of a wild horse and dragged (to the gallows). 147. **heng . . . by,** hanged them according to. 148. **ay lith,** still lies. 149. **auter,** altar. 150. **covent,** monastery; "convent" was not synonymous with "nunnery" in the Middle Ages. 153. **spreynd,** sprinkled. 157. **conjure,** beseech. 158. **halsen,** implore. 163. **as . . . kynde,** according to the law of nature. 170. **as . . . konnynge,** according to my knowledge. 171. **forlete,** give up. 172. **cam,** came.

This anteme verraily in my deiynge,
As ye han herd, and whan that I had songe,
Me thoughte she leyde a greyn up-on my tonge.

"Wher-fore I synge, and synge moot certeyn,
In honour of that blisful Mayden free,
Til fro my tonge of-taken is the greyn;
And after that thus seyde she to me:
'My litel child, now wol I fecche thee,
Whan that the greyn is fro thy tonge ytake;
Be nat agast, I wol thee nat forsake.'"

This holy monk, this abbot, hym mene I,
His tonge out-caughte, and took awey the greyn,
And he yaf up the goost ful softely.
And whan this abbot hadde this wonder seyn,
His salte teerys trikled doun as reyn,
And gruf he fil al plat up-on the grounde,
And stille he lay as he hadde been ybounde.

The covent eek lay on the pavement
Wepynge, and herying Cristes moder deere,
And after that they ryse, and forth been went,
And toke awey this martir from his beere,
And in a tombe of marbilstones cleere
Enclosen they this litel body swete.
Ther he is now, God leve us for to meete!

O yonge Hugh of Lyncoln, slayn also,
With cursed Jewes, as it is notable,
For it is but a litel while ago,
Preye eek for us, we synful folk unstable,
That, of his mercy, God so merciable
On us his grete mercy multiplie,
For reverence of his moder Marie. *Amen.*

THE PROLOGUE OF THE NUN'S PRIEST'S TALE

The Monk has been telling his tale—a collection of short "tragedies," as defined by him in his prologue:

Tragedie is to seyn a certeyn storie,
As olde bookes maken us memorie,
Of hym that stood in greet prosperitee,
And is yfallen out of heigh degree
Into myserie, and endeth wrecchedly.

The seventeen unhappy subjects of the Monk's discourse range from Lucifer and Adam to three contemporaries of Chaucer. The Knight, overcome by such a flood of tales of misfortune (so unlike the story of the Monk's career), finally interrupts the Monk's recital.

173. **anteme,** anthem. 175. **greyn,** perhaps a pearl, symbol of the Virgin. 182. **agast,** frightened. 188. **gruf . . . plat,** face down he fell all flat. 192. **been went,** have gone. 196. **leve,** permit. 197. **Hugh,** victim of a similar crime said to have been perpetrated in Lincoln, England, in 1255. 201. **merciable,** merciful.

"Ho!" quod the Knyght, "good sire, namoore of this!
That ye han seyd is right ynow, ywis,
And muchel moore; for litel hevynesse
Is right ynow to muche folk, I gesse.
I seye for me, it is a greet disese,
Wher-as men han been in greet welthe and ese,
To heeren of hir sodeyn fal, allas!
And the contrarie is joye and greet solas,
As whan a man hath been in povre estaat,
And clymbeth up, and wexeth fortunat,
And ther abideth in prosperitee;
Swich thyng is gladsom, as it thynketh me,
And of swich thyng were goodly for to telle."
"Ye," quod oure Hoost, "by Seint Poules belle!
Ye seye right sooth; this Monk, he clappeth loude.
He spak how Fortune covered with a cloude—
I noot nevere what; and also of a tragedie
Right now ye herde, and, pardee, no remedie
It is for to biwaille ne compleyne
That that is doon, and als it is a peyne,
As ye han seyd, to heere of hevynesse.
"Sir Monk, namoore of this, so God yow blesse!
Youre tale anoyeth al this compaignye.
Swich talkyng is nat worth a boterflye,
For ther-inne is ther no desport ne game.
"Wher-fore, sire Monk, Daun Piers by youre name,
I prey yow hertely telle us som-what elles,
For sikerly, nere clynkyng of youre belles,
That on youre bridel hange on every syde,
By hevene Kyng, that for us alle dyde,
I sholde er this have fallen doun for sleep,
Al-thogh the slough hadde nevere ben so deep;
Thanne hadde youre tale al be toold in veyn:
For certeynly, as that thise clerkes seyn,
Where-as a man may have noon audience,
Noght helpeth it to tellen his sentence.
And wel I woot the substaunce is in me,
If any thyng shal wel reported be.
Sire, sey som-what of huntyng, I yow preye."
"Nay," quod this Monk, "I have no lust to pleye.
Now lat another telle, as I have toold."
Thanne spak oure Hoost with rude speche and boold,
And seyde un-to the Nonnes Preest anon,
"Com neer, thow preest, com hider, thow sire John,
Telle us swich thyng as may oure hertes glade.
Be blithe, though thow ryde up-on a jade.
What though thyn hors be bothe foul and lene,
If he wol serve thee, rekke nat a bene!
Looke that thyn herte be murye evere-mo."
"Yis, sire," quod he, "yis, Hoost, so mote I go,
But I be murye, ywis, I wol be blamed."
And right anon his tale he hath attamed,
And thus he seyde un-to us everichon,
This sweete preest, this goodly man, sire John.

2. right ynow, true enough. **3. muchel moore,** much more than enough. **hevynesse,** sorrow. **4. right ynow,** certainly enough. **5. disese,** unpleasantness. **7. sodeyn,** sudden. **8. solas,** comfort. **10. wexeth,** becomes. **12. thynketh me,** seems to me. **14. Seint Poules,** St. Paul's Cathedral, London. **17. noot,** know not. **20. als,** also. **23. anoyeth,** bores. **28. nere,** were it not for. **30. hevene Kyng,** the king of heaven. **dyde,** died. **32. slough,** mud, mire. **36. sentence,** matter. **37. substaunce,** basis, foundation; that is, only by the Host can any tale be reported and judged.

46. jade, poor nag. **47. foul and lene,** ugly and lean. **48. rekke . . . bene!** care less than the worth of a bean. **50. so . . . go,** as I hope to continue to be able to walk. **52. attamed,** commenced.

THE NUN'S PRIEST'S TALE

Chaucer gives to the Nun's Priest—one of the "preestes three" of line 164 of "The General Prologue"—the wittiest of his Canterbury tales. The good nature of the priest has been indicated in the prologue to his tale, and this kindly and humorous disposition serves him well in his role of parson and preacher. He knows that "many a true word was spoke in jest," and the "moralitee" of his tale is all the more effective because of the delightful story in which it is conveyed. Like the Pardoner's tale, the Nun's Priest's is an *exemplum*—a popular story adapted to moral and didactic purposes.

The story—that of the Cock and the Fox—is one of the most familiar of the beast-fables, and is part of the collection of stories concerning Reynard the Fox. It is told in mock-heroic style, and the characters of the hero and heroine, Chauntecleer and Pertelote, and of the villain, Don Russell, are among the finest things of the sort in our literature. That the Nun's Priest is also a master of satire is evident in his picture of the married life of the hero and heroine. The reader will not fail to note, here and there, the gentle fun that he pokes at his patroness, the Prioress, in his mischievous echoing of certain episodes in the tale she has told. The happy combination of elements in the story and the great artistry displayed in the telling of the tale have never been surpassed even by Chaucer himself.

A povre widwe, somdel stape in age,
Was whilom dwellynge in a narwe cotage,
Biside a grove, stondyng in a dale.
This widwe, of which I telle yow my tale,
Syn thilke day that she was last a wyf,
In pacience ladde a ful symple lyf,
For litel was hire catel and hire rente.
By housbondrye of swich as God hire sente

1. stape, advanced. **2. narwe,** narrow, small. **3. dale,** valley. **7. catel,** property. **rente,** income. **8. housbondrye,** thrift. **of,** out of.

She foond hire-self, and eek hire doghtren two.
Thre large sowes hadde she, and namo,
Thre kyn, and eek a sheep that highte Malle.
Ful sooty was hire bour, and eek hire halle,
In which she eet ful many a sklendre meel.
Of poynaunt sauce hir neded never a deel.
No deyntee morsel passed thurgh hir throte;
Hir diete was acordant to hir cote.
Repleccioun ne made hire nevere syk;
Attempree diete was al hir phisyk,
And excercise, and hertes suffisaunce.
The goute lette hire no-thyng for to daunce,
N'apoplexie shente nat hir heed
No wyn ne drank she, neither whit ne reed;
Hir bord was served moost with whit and blak,
Milk and broun breed, in which she foond no lak,
Seynd bacoun, and som-tyme an ey or tweye,
For she was, as it were, a maner deye.
A yeerd she hadde, enclosed al aboute
With stikkes, and a drye dych with-oute,
In which she hadde a cok, heet Chauntecleer;
In al the land of crowyng nas his peer.
His voys was murier than the myrie orgon
On massedayes that in the chirche gon.
Wel sikerer was his crowyng in his logge
Than is a clokke or any abbey orlogge.
By nature he knew ech ascensioun
Of the equinoxial in thilke toun;
For whan degrees fiftene were ascended,
Thanne krew he, that it myghte nat ben amended.
His comb was redder than the fyn coral,
And batailled as it were a castel wal.
His byle was blak, and as the jeet it shoon;
Lyk asure were hise legges and his toon;
Hise nayles whitter than the lylye flour,
And lyk the burned gold was his colour.
This gentil cok hadde in his governaunce
Sevene hennes for to doon al his plesaunce,
Whiche were hise sustres and his paramours,

9. foond, provided for. **doghtren,** daughters. **11. kyn,** cows. **12. bour,** bower, women's apartments. **halle,** great hall (ironic, since the widow lived in a one-room cottage). **13. sklendre meel,** skimpy meal. **14. poynaunt,** sharp. **hir . . . deel,** she never needed a bit. **16. acordant . . . cote,** suitable to her cottage. **17. Repleccioun,** overeating. **18. Attempree,** temperate. **phisyk,** medicine. **19. hertes suffisaunce,** a satisfied heart. **20. goute lette hire no-thyng,** gout never hindered her. **21. shente,** harmed. **25. Seynd,** broiled. **ey,** egg. **26. maner deye,** kind of dairywoman. **27. yeerd,** yard. **28. stikkes,** paling fence. **with-oute,** surrounding the fence. **29. heet,** called. **30. peer,** equal. **31–32. orgon . . . gon,** organs . . . that are played. **33. sikerer,** more accurate. **34. orlogge,** clock. **35. By nature.** The Middle Ages believed that cocks could tell time by instinct as well as men did by the heavenly bodies. **38. that . . . amended,** so that it might not be improved. **40. batailled . . . wal,** notched like the battlements on a castle wall. **41. byle,** bill. **jeet,** jet. **42. toon,** toes. **47. paramours,** sweethearts.

And wonder lyke to hym as of colours;
Of whiche the faireste hewed on hire throte
Was cleped faire damoysele Pertelote.
Curteys she was, discreet, and debonaire,
And compaignable, and bar hir-self so faire,
Syn thilke day that she was seven nyght oold,
That trewely she hath the herte in hoold
Of Chauntecleer, loken in every lith;
He loved hire so that wel was hym ther-with.
But swich a joye was it to here hem synge,
Whan that the brighte sonne gan to sprynge,
In swete acord, "My leef is faren in londe!"
For thilke tyme, as I have understonde,
Beestes and briddes koude speke and synge.
And so bifel, that in a dawenynge,
As Chauntecleer among hise wyves alle
Sat on his perche, that was in the halle,
And next hym sat this faire Pertelote,
This Chauntecleer gan gronen in his throte,
As man that in his dreem is drecched soore.
And whan that Pertelote thus herde hym rore,
She was agast, and seyde, "Herte deere,
What eyleth yow, to grone in this manere?
Ye ben a verray slepere, fy, for shame!"
And he answerde, and seyde thus, "Madame,
I prey yow that ye take it nat agrief.
By God, me mette I was in swich meschief
Right now, that yet myn herte is soore afright.
Now God," quod he, "my swevene recche aright,
And kepe my body out of foul prisoun!
Me mette how that I romed up and doun
With-inne oure yeerd, where-as I say a beest
Was lyk an hound, and wolde han maad areest
Up-on my body, and han had me deed.
His colour was bitwixe yelow and reed,
And tipped was his tayl and bothe hise erys
With blak, unlik the remenaunt of hise herys,
His snowte smal, with glowyng eyen tweye.
Yet of his look for fere almoost I deye;
This caused me my gronyng, doutelees."
"Avoy!" quod she, "fy on yow, hertelees!
Allas!" quod she, "for by that God above,
Now han ye lost myn herte and al my love!
I kan nat love a coward, by my feith!
For, certes, what so any womman seith,
We alle desiren, if it myghte be,

52. compaignable, companionable. **54. in hoold,** in her hold. **55. loken . . . lith,** locked in every limb. **58. sprynge,** rise. **59. "My . . . londe!"** "My beloved has gone to the country." **64. halle.** The chicken roost was inside the widow's cottage. **67. drecched soore,** sorely troubled. **71. verray,** out-and-out. **74. me mette,** I dreamed. **76. swevene . . . aright,** interpret my dream fortunately. **79. say,** saw. **80–81. maad . . . deed,** seized my body and killed me. **83. erys,** ears. **84. remenaunt,** rest. **88. "Avoy!"** "Fie!" **hertelees!** faint-hearted.

To han housbondes hardy, wise, and fre,
And secree, and no nygard, ne no fool,
Ne hym that is agast of every tool,
Ne noon avauntour, by that God above!
How dorste ye seyn, for shame, un-to youre love
That any thyng myghte make yow aferd?
Have ye no mannes herte, and han a berd?
“Allas! and konne ye ben agast of swevenys?
No thyng, God woot, but vanytee in swevene is.
Swevenes engendren of replexions,
And ofte of fume, and of complexions,
Whan humours ben to habundant in a wight.
“Certes this dreem which ye han met to-nyght,
Comth of the grete superfluytee
Of youre rede colera, pardee,
Which causeth folk to dreden in hir dremes
Of arwes, and of fyr with rede lemes,
Of rede bestes, that they wol hem byte,
Of contek, and of whelpes grete and lyte;
Right as the humour of malencolie
Causeth ful many a man in sleep to crie
For fere of blake beres, or boles blake,
Or elles blake develes wol hem take.
“Of othere humours koude I telle also,
That werken many a man in sleep ful wo;
But I wol passe as lightly as I kan.
“Lo Catoun, which that was so wys a man,
Seyde he nat, thus, ‘Ne do no fors of dremes?’
“Now sire,” quod she, “whan we fle fro the bemes,
For Goddes love, as taak some laxatif;
Up peril of my soule and of my lif,
I conseille yow the beste, I wol nat lye,
That bothe of colere and of malencolye
Ye purge yow; and for ye shal nat tarye,
Thogh in this toun is noon apothecarye,
I shal my-self to herbes techen yow,
That shul ben for youre heele and for youre prow;
And in oure yerd tho herbes shal I fynde
The whiche han of hire propretee, by kynde,
To purge yow bynethe and eek above.
Foryet nat this, for Goddes owene love!
Ye ben ful colerik of complexioun.
Ware the sonne in his ascensioun
Ne fynde yow nat replet of humours hote;
And if it do, I dar wel leye a grote,
That ye shul have a fevere terciane,
Or an agu, that may be youre bane.
A day or two ye shul have digestyves
Of wormes, er ye take youre laxatyves
Of lauriol, centaure, and fumetere,
Or elles of ellebor, that groweth there,
Of katapuce, or of gaitrys beryis,
Of herbe yve, growyng in oure yerd, ther merye is;
Pekke hem up right as they growe and ete hem in.
Be myrie, housbonde, for youre fader kyn!
Dredeth no dreem, I kan sey yow namoore.”
“Madame,” quod he, “graunt mercy of youre loore.
But nathelees, as touchyng Daun Catoun,
That hath of wisdom swich a gret renoun,
Thogh that he bad no dremes for to drede,
By God, men may in olde bokes rede
Of many a man, moore of auctoritee
Than evere Catoun was, so mote I thee,
That al the revers seyn of his sentence,
And han wel founden by experience
That dremes ben significaciouns
As wel of joye as of tribulaciouns
That folk enduren in this lyf present.
Ther nedeth make of this noon argument:
The verray preeve sheweth it in dede.
“Oon of the gretteste auctor that men rede
Seith thus, that whilom two felawes wente
On pilgrymage, in a ful good entente;
And happed so, they coomen in a toun,
Where as ther was swich congregacioun
Of peple, and eek so steit of herbergage,
That they ne founde as muche as a cotage
In which they bothe myghte ylogged be.
Wherfore they mosten of necessitee,
As for that nyght, departen compaignye;
And ech of hem gooth to his hostelrye,
And took his loggyng as it wolde falle.
That oon of hem was logged in a stalle,

94. fre, generous. **95. secree,** opposite of **avauntour,** boaster, l. 97. **nygard,** stingy person. **96. agast . . . tool,** afraid of every weapon. **99. aferd,** afraid. **103. replexions,** overeating. **104. fume.** See note on “fumositee,” page 115. **105. humours.** According to classical and later medical theory, the four humours were four fluids (blood, phlegm, bile, black bile), the relative proportions of which in a person's body determined his “complexion” or temperament as sanguine, phlegmatic, choleric, or melancholy. **to habundant,** too plentiful. **106. Certes,** certainly. **met to-nyght,** dreamed last night. **108. rede colera,** red bile, as opposed to black. **110. lemes,** flames. **111. bestes,** beasts. **112. contek,** strife. **113. malencolie,** black bile. **115. beres,** bears. **boles,** bulls. **120. Lo Catoun,** the so-called Dionysius Cato, supposed author of a collection of wise sayings popular in the Middle Ages and the Renaissance. **121. Ne . . . of,** pay no attention to. **122. fle fro,** fly from. **124. Up,** upon. **126. colere,** bile. **127. for,** in order that. **129. to . . . yow,** to teach you concerning herbs. **132. propretee, by kynde,** function, naturally.

136. Ware, beware lest. **139. fevere terciane,** fever striking every third (alternate) day. **140. agu,** ague. **bane,** death. **142. wormes,** not henyard lore: earthworms mashed up with wine or oil were prescribed for tertian fever from ancient Greek times to Chaucer's day. **144–46. ellebor . . . yve,** common medieval medicinal herbs with purging properties. **150. graunt . . . loore,** thank you very much for your learning. **151. nathelees,** nevertheless. **156. so . . . thee,** as I hope to prosper. **157. revers seyn,** opposites say. **sentence,** opinion. **169. streit,** inadequate. **173. departen,** part.

Fer in a yeerd, with oxen of the plough,
That oother man was logged wel ynough,
As was his aventure or his fortune,
That us governeth alle as in commune.
"And so bifel that, longe er it were day,
This man mette in his bed, ther as he lay,
How that his felawe gan up-on hym calle,
And seyde, 'Allas! for in an oxes stalle
This nyght I shal be mordred ther I lye.
Now help me, deere brother or I dye!
In alle haste com to me!' he sayde.
"This man out of his sleep for feere abrayde;
But whan that he was wakned of his sleep,
He turned hym, and took of this no keep.
Hym thoughte his dreem nas but a vanytee.
Thus twies in his slepyng dremed he.
And atte thridde tyme yet his felawe
Cam, as hym thoughte, and seyde, 'I am now slawe!
Bihoold my blody woundes, depe and wyde!
Arys up erly in the morwe tyde,
And at the west gate of the toun,' quod he,
'A carte ful of donge ther shaltow se,
In which my body is hid ful pryvely;
Do thilke carte aresten boldely.
My gold caused my mordre, sooth to seyn.'
And tolde hym every poynt how he was slayn,
With a ful pitous face, pale of hewe.
And truste wel, his dreem he fond ful trewe,
For on the morwe, as soone as it was day,
To his felawes in he took the way;
And whan that he cam to this oxes stalle,
After his felawe he bigan to calle.
"The hostiler answerde hym anon,
And seyde, 'Sire, youre felawe is agon;
As soone as day he wente out of the toun.'
"This man gan fallen in suspecioun,
Remembrynge on hise dremes that he mette,
And forth he gooth, no lenger wolde he lette,
Unto the west gate of the toun, and fond
A dong-carte, wente as it were to donge lond,
That was arrayed in the same wise
As ye han herd the dede man devyse.
And with an hardy herte he gan to crye
Vengeaunce and justice of this felonye:
'My felawe mordred is this same nyght,
And in this carte heere he lyth gapyng upright.
I crye out on the mynystres,' quod he,
'That sholden kepe and reulen this citee.
Harrow! allas! heere lith my felawe slayn!'
What sholde I moore un-to this tale sayn?
The peple out sterte, and caste the cart to grounde,
And in the myddel of the dong they founde
The dede man, that mordred was al newe.
"O blisful God, that art so just and trewe,
Lo, how that thow biwreyest mordre alway!
Mordre wol out, that se we day by day.
Mordre is so wlatsom and abhomynable
To God, that is so just and resonable,
That he ne wol nat suffre it heled be;
Though it abyde a yeer, or two, or thre,
Mordre wol out, this is my conclusioun.
And right anon ministres of that toun
Han hent the cartere, and so soore hym pyned,
And eek the hostiler so soore engyned,
That they biknewe hir wikkednesse anon,
And were an-hanged by the nekke bon.
"Heere may men seen that dremes ben to drede.
And, certes, in the same book I rede,
Right in the nexte chapitre after this—
I gabbe nat so have I joye or blys—
"Two men that wolde han passed over see,
For certeyn cause, in-to a fer contree,
If that the wynd ne hadde ben contrarie,
That made hem in a citee for to tarie,
That stood ful myrie up-on an haven syde.
But on a day, agayn the even-tyde,
The wynd gan chaunge, and blew right as hem leste.
Jolif and glad they wente un-to reste,
And casten hem ful erly for to saille.
"But herkneth, to that o man fil a greet mervaille:
That oon of hem, in slepyng as he lay,
Hym mette a wonder dreem, agayn the day;
Hym thoughte a man stood by his beddes syde,
And hym comanded that he sholde abyde,
And seyde hym thus, 'If thow tomorwe wende,
Thow shalt be dreynt; my tale is at an ende.'
"He wook, and tolde his felawe what he mette,
And preyde hym his viage to lette;
As for that day, he preyde hym to abyde.
"His felawe, that lay by his beddes syde,

179. **aventure,** chance. 182. **mette,** dreamed. 186. **or,** before. 188. **abrayde,** started up. 190. **took . . . keep,** paid no attention to this. 194. **slawe!** slain. 196. **Arys,** arise. **morwe tyde,** morning. 198. **donge,** manure. 200. **Do . . . boldely,** boldly cause this cart to be stopped. 206. **in,** lodging. 214. **lette,** tarry. 215. **fond,** found. 216. **wente . . . lond,** that was going, as it seemed, to spread manure on a field. 218. **devyse,** describe. 222. **upright,** face up.

223. **mynystres,** administrators of justice. 229. **al newe,** recently. 231. **biwreyest,** expose. 233. **wlatsom,** disgusting. 235. **heled,** hidden. 239. **Han hent,** have seized. **soore hym pyned,** tortured him sorely. 240. **engyned,** tortured on the rack. 241. **biknewe,** made known. 242. **an-hanged . . . bon,** hanged by the neck bone. 246. **gabbe,** speak idly. 252. **agayn . . . even-tyde,** toward the time of evening. 254. **Jolif,** jolly. 255. **casten,** planned. 258. **wonder,** wonderful. 259. **Hym thoughte,** it seemed to him that. 261. **wende,** set forth. 262. **dreynt,** drowned. 264. **viage to lette,** to delay his voyage.

Gan for to laughe, and scorned hym ful faste.
'No dreem,' quod he, 'may so myn herte agaste
That I wol lette for to do my thynges.
I sette nat a straw by thy dremynges,
For swevenes ben but vanytees and japes.
Men dreme alday of owles and of apes,
And of many a maze ther-with-al;
Men dreme of thyng that nevere was ne shal.
But sith I see that thow wolt here abyde,
And thus forslewthen wilfully thy tyde,
God woot, it reweth me; and have good day.'
And thus he took his leve, and wente his way.
But er that he hadde half his cours yseyled,
Noot I nat why, ne what meschaunce it eyled,
But casuelly the shippes botme rente,
And ship and man under the water wente
In sighte of othere shippes it bisyde,
That with hem seyled at the same tyde.
And therfore, faire Pertelote so deere,
By swiche ensamples olde maystow leere
That no man sholde been to recchelees
Of dremes, for I sey thee, doutelees,
That many a dreem ful soore is for to drede.
"Lo, in the lyf of Seint Kenelm I rede,
That was Kenulphus sone, the noble kyng
Of Mercenrike, how Kenelm mette a thyng.
A lite er he was mordred, on a day,
His mordre in his avysioun he say.
His norice hym expowned every del
His swevene, and bad hym for to kepe hym wel
For traisoun, but he nas but sevene yeer old,
And therfore litel tale hath he told
Of any dreem, so holy was his herte.
By God! I hadde levere than my sherte
That ye hadde rad his legende, as have I.
Dame Pertelote, I sey yow trewely,
Macrobeus that writ the avysioun
In Affrike of the worthy Cipioun,
Affermeth dremes, and seith that they ben
Warnynge of thynges that men after sen.
"And forther-moore, I pray yow, looketh wel
In the Olde Testament, of Danyel,
If he heeld dremes any vanytee.

268. agaste, frighten. **273. maze,** bewilderment. **276. forslewthen,** waste in sloth. **tyde,** time. **277. it . . . me,** it makes me sorry. **280. it eyled,** ailed it. **281. casuelly,** by chance. **rente,** burst. **287. recchelees,** unheedful. **289. ful . . . drede,** is very sorely to be dreaded. **291–92. Kenulphus,** king of Mercia (**Mercenrike**) d. 821. **293. lite er,** little before. **294. avysioun,** vision. **say,** saw. **295. norice,** nurse. **expowned,** explained. **296–97. kepe . . . traisoun,** guard himself well against treason. **298. litel . . . told,** he took little heed. **301. legende.** The *Somnium Scipionis* was part of Cicero's *De Republica;* it was edited by Macrobius about A.D. 400, and the latter's commentary became the leading medieval handbook on dreams.

"Rede eek of Joseph, and there shul ye see
Wher dremes be som-tyme—I sey nat alle—
Warnynge of thynges that shul after falle.
"Looke of Egipte the kyng, Daun Pharao,
His bakere and his butiller also,
Wher they ne felte noon effect in dremes.
Who-so wol seke actes of sondry remes
May rede of dremes many a wonder thyng.
"Lo Cresus, which that was of Lyde kyng,
Mette he nat that he sat up-on a tree,
Which signified he sholde an-hanged be?
"Lo heere Andromacha, Ectores wyf,
That day that Ector sholde lese his lyf,
She dremed on the same nyght biforn,
How that the lyf of Ector sholde be lorn,
If thilke day he wente in-to bataille;
She warned hym, but it myghte nat availle;
He wente for to fighte nathelees,
But he was slayn anon of Achilles.
But thilke tale is al to long to telle,
And eek it is ny day, I may nat dwelle.
Shortly I seye, as for conclusioun,
That I shal han of this avysioun
Adversitee; and I seye forther-moor,
That I ne telle of laxatyves no stoor,
For they ben venymes, I woot it wel;
I hem deffye, I love hem never a del!
"Now lat us speke of myrthe, and stynte al this.
Madame Pertelote, so have I blis,
Of o thyng God hath sent me large grace:
For whan I se the beautee of youre face,
Ye ben so scarlet reed aboute youre eyen,
It maketh al my drede for to dyen;
For also siker as *In principio,*
Mulier est hominis confusio—
"Madame, the sentence of this Latyn is,
'Woman is mannes joye and al his blis.'
For whan I feele a nyght youre softe syde,
Al be it that I may nat on you ryde,
For that oure perche is maad so narwe, allas!
I am so ful of joye and of solas,
That I deffye bothe swevene and dreem!"
And with that word he fley doun fro the beem,
For it was day, and eke hise hennes alle,
And with a chuk he gan hem for to calle,
For he hadde founde a corn lay in the yerd.
Real he was, he was namoore aferd;
He fethered Pertelote twenty tyme,

315. Wher . . . dremes, whether they experienced no reality in dreams. **316. remes,** realms. **321. Ectores,** Hector's. **322. lese,** lose. **324. lorn,** lost. **330. ny,** near. **dwelle,** tarry. **334. telle . . . stoor,** take no stock in. **335. venymes,** poisons. **343. siker,** certain. ***In principio.*** See note to line 254 on page 100. **344. *Mulier . . . confusio.*** Woman is man's ruin. **345. sentence,** meaning. **352. fley,** flew. **356. Real,** regal.

And trad as ofte, er it was pryme.
He looketh as it were a grym leoun,
And on hise toos he rometh up and doun,
Hym deyned nat to sette his foot to grounde.
He chukketh, whan he hath a corn yfounde,
And to hym rennen thanne hise wyves alle.
Thus real, as a prince is in his halle,
Leve I this Chauntecleer in his pasture,
And after wol I telle his aventure.
Whan that the monthe in which the world bigan,
That highte March, whan God first maked man,
Was complet, and passed were also,
Syn March bigan, thritty dayes and two,
Bifel that Chauntecler in al his pryde,
Hise sevene wyves walkyng hym bisyde,
Caste up hise eyen to the brighte sonne,
That in the signe of Taurus hadde yronne
Twenty degrees and oon, and som-what moore,
And knew by kynde, and by noon oother loore,
That it was pryme, and krew with blisful stevene.
"The sonne," he seyde, "is clomben up on hevene
Fourty degrees and oon, and moore ywis.
Madame Pertelote, my worldes blis,
Herkneth thise blisful briddes how they synge,
And se the fresshe floures how they sprynge,
Ful is myn herte of revel and solas!"
But sodeynly him fil a sorweful cas;
For evere the latter ende of joye is wo.
God woot that worldly joye is soone ago;
And if a rethor koude faire endite,
He in a cronycle saufly myghte it write,
As for a sovereyn notabilitee.
Now every wys man, lat hym herkne me:
This storie is also trewe, I undertake,
As is the bok of Launcelot de Lake,
That wommen holde in ful gret reverence.
Now wol I torne agayn to my sentence.
A colfox, ful of sly iniquitee,
That in the grove hadde woned yeres three,
By heigh ymaginacioun forncast,
The same nyght thurgh-out the hegges brast
In-to the yerd, ther Chauntecleer the faire
Was wont, and eek hise wyves, to repaire;
And in a bed of wortes stille he lay,
Til it was passed undren of the day,
Waitynge his tyme on Chauntecleer to falle,
As gladly doon thise homycides alle,
That in awayt liggen to mordre men.
O false mordrour, lurkynge in thy den!
O newe Scariot, newe Genyloun!
False dissimilour, O Greek Synoun,
That broghtest Troye al outrely to sorwe!
O Chauntecleer, acursed be that morwe
That thow in-to the yerd flaugh fro the bemes!
Thow were ful wel ywarned by thy dremes,
That thilke day was perilous to thee.
But what that God forwoot moot nedes be,
After the opynyoun of certeyn clerkis.
Witnesse on hym that any parfit clerk is,
That in scole is greet altercacioun
In this matere, and greet disputisoun,
And hath ben of an hundred thousand men.
But I ne kan nat bulte it to the bren,
As kan the holy doctour Augustyn,
Or Boece, or the bisshop Bradwardyn,
Wheither that Goddes worthy forewityng
Streyneth me nedely for to doon a thyng—
"Nedely" clepe I symple necessitee—
Or ellis, if fre choys be graunted me
To do that same thyng, or do it noght,
Though God forwoot it, er that it was wroght;
Or if his wityng streyneth never a del
But by necessitee condicionel.
I wol nat han to do of swich matere;
My tale is of a cok, as ye may heere,
That took his conseil of his wyf, with sorwe,
To walken in the yerd up-on that morwe
That he hadde met the dreem that I yow tolde.
Wommens conseils ben ful ofte colde;
Wommanes conseil broghte us first to wo,
And made Adam fro Paradys to go,

359. leoun, lion. **361. Hym . . . nat,** he did not deign. **362. corn,** grain. **367–68. Whan . . . man.** The Creation was believed to have taken place at the spring equinox (now March 21). **374. Taurus,** sign of the zodiac (the Bull). **376. kynde,** natural ability. **377. pryme,** 6 A.M.; sometimes the period from 6 to 9, and even the latter hour. **stevene,** voice. **378. is clomben,** has climbed. **381. briddes,** birds. **383. revel,** revelry. **384. him fil . . . cas,** a sorry chance befell him. **386. ago,** gone. **387. rethor,** rhetorician. **388. cronycle saufly,** chronicle safely. **389. sovereyn notabilitee,** exceptionally notable event. **391. also,** as. **undertake,** guarantee. **392–93. As . . . reverence,** probably as much a sly dig at female literary taste as an attack on the veracity of the romance of Lancelot. **394. torne,** turn. **sentence,** matter. **395. colfox,** fox with considerable black in its fur. **396. woned,** lived. **397. By . . . forncast,** predestined by divine foreknowledge.

398. thurgh-out . . . brast, broke through. **400. repaire,** resort. **401. wortes,** herbs. **402. undren,** the time indicated by "undren" varies; here, apparently, it is early forenoon. **404. gladly,** habitually. **405. liggen,** lie. **407. Scariot,** Judas Iscariot. **Genyloun,** Ganelon, traitor in *The Song of Roland.* **408. dissimilour,** dissembler. **Synoun,** Sinon, who secured the entry of the Trojan Horse into the city. **409. outrely,** utterly. **411. flaugh,** flew. **415. clerkis,** learned authorities. **420. bulte . . . bren,** sift it to the bran. **421. Augustyn,** St. Augustine of Hippo. **422. Boece,** Boethius (d. 524), whose *Consolations of Philosophy* Chaucer translated and drew upon constantly, and who also wrote on music (see l. 474). **Bradwardyn,** Thomas Bradwardyn, Archbishop of Canterbury (d. 1349). **423. forewityng,** foreknowing. **424. Streyneth,** constrains. **425. clepe,** call. **433. with sorwe,** a mild oath. **436. colde,** fatal; the line is proverbial.

Ther as he was ful myrie and wel at ese.
But for I noot to whom it myghte displese,
If I conseil of wommen wolde blame,
Passe over, for I seyde it in my game.
Rede auctours, where they trete of swich matere,
And what they seyn of wommen ye may heere.
Thise ben the cokkes wordes, and nat myne;
I kan noon harm of no womman devyne.
  Faire in the sond, to bathe hire myrily,
Lith Pertelote, and alle hir sustres by,
Agayn the sonne, and Chauntecleer so free
Song myrier than the mermayde in the see;
For Phisiologus seith sikerly,
How that they syngen wel and myrily.
  And so bifel that, as he caste his eye
Among the wortes, on a boterflye,
He was war of this fox that lay ful lowe.
No-thyng ne liste hym thanne for to crowe,
But cryde anon, "Cok! cok!" and up he sterte,
As man that was affrayed in his herte.
For naturelly a beest desireth flee
Fro his contrarie, if he may it see,
Though he nevere erst hadde seyn it with his eye.
  This Chauntecleer, whan he gan hym espye,
He wolde han fled, but that the fox anon
Seyde, "Gentil sire, allas! wher wol ye gon?
Be ye affrayed of me that am youre freend?
Now, certes, I were worse than a feend,
If I to yow wolde harm or vileynye!
I am nat come youre conseil for t'espye,
But trewely, the cause of my comynge
Was oonly for to herkne how that ye synge.
For trewely, ye han as myrie a stevene
As any aungel hath, that is in hevene.
Ther-with ye han in musyk moore feelynge
Than hadde Boece, or any that kan synge.
My lord youre fader—God his soule blesse!—
And eek youre moder, of hire gentillesse,
Han in myn hous yben, to my greet ese;
And, certes, sire, ful fayn wolde I yow plese.
  "But for men speke of syngynge, I wol seye,
So mote I brouke wel myne eyen tweye,
Save ye, I herde nevere man so synge
As dide youre fader in the morwenynge.
Certes, it was of herte, al that he song.
And for to make his voys the moore strong,
He wolde so peyne hym, that with bothe hise eyen
He moste wynke, so loude he wolde cryen,

447. **sond**, sand. 448. **Lith**, lies. **sustres**, sisters. 449. **Agayn**, exposed to. 451. **Phisiologus**, the Latin bestiary, a medieval treatise on animals, real and imaginary. 459. **naturelly**, by instinct. 460. **contrarie**, a creature instinctively his enemy. 461. **erst**, before. 471. **stevene**, voice. 477. **Han . . . yben**, have been in my house. 480. **brouke**, have the use of. 485–86. **with . . . wynke**, he had to shut both eyes.

And stonden on his tiptoon ther-with-al,
And strecche forth his nekke long and smal.
And eek he was of swich discrecioun,
That ther nas no man in no regioun
That hym in song or wisdom myghte passe.
I have wel rad in Daun Burnel the Asse,
Among his vers, how that ther was a cok,
For a preestes sone yaf hym a knok
Up-on his leg, whil he was yong and nyce,
He made hym for to lese his benefice.
But certeyn, ther nys no comparisoun
Bitwix the wisdom and discrecioun
Of youre fader and of his subtiltee.
Now syngeth, sire, for seinte Charitee!
Lat se, konne ye youre fader countrefete?"
  This Chauntecleer hise wynges gan to bete,
As man that koude his traysoun nat espie,
So was he ravysshed with his flaterie.
  Allas! ye lordes, many a fals flatour
Is in youre court, and many a losengeour,
That plesen yow wel moore, by my feith,
Than he that soothfastnesse un-to yow seith.
Redeth Ecclesiaste of flaterye;
Beth war, ye lordes, of hir trecherye.
This Chauntecler stood hye up-on his toos,
Strecchynge his nekke, and heeld hise eyen cloos,
And gan to crowe loude for the nones.
And Daun Russell the fox stirte up atones,
And by the gargat hente Chauntecleer,
And on his bak toward the wode hym beer,
For yet ne was ther no man that hym sewed.
  O destynee, that mayst nat ben eschewed!
Allas, that Chauntecler fleigh fro the bemes!
Allas, his wif ne roghte nat of dremes!
And on a Friday fil al this meschaunce.
  O Venus, that art goddesse of plesaunce,
Syn that thy servant was this Chauntecleer,
And in thy servyce dide al his power,
Moore for delit, than world to multiplie,
Why woldestow suffre hym on thy day to dye?
  O Gaufred, deere maister soverayn,

487. **tiptoon**, tiptoes. 492. **Daun Burnel**, the hero of a twelfth-century satire by Nigellus Wireker. 495. **nyce**, foolish. 496. **lese his benefice**, lose his benefice, salaried church office. The cock crowed so late that the young man overslept on the crucial day of his ordination. 499. **his**, that of the vengeful cock. 500. **seinte**, blessed. 501. **countrefete**, imitate. 503. **his**, that of the fox. 505. **flatour**, flatterer. 506. **losengeour**, flatterer. 508. **soothfastnesse**, truthfulness. 509. **Ecclesiaste**, Ecclesiasticus, in the Apocrypha. 510. **Beth war**, beware. 513. **for the nones**, especially. 515. **by . . . hente**, seized by the throat. 516. **wode**, wood. **beer**, bore. 517. **sewed**, pursued. 518. **eschewed**, avoided. 519. **fleigh**, flew. 520. **ne . . . of**, cared nothing for. 526. **thy day**. Friday is "the day of the goddess Frigg," a translation of *dies Veneris*, the day of Venus—French *vendredi*. 527. **Gaufred**, Geoffrey de Vinsauf, twelfth-century poet.

That, whan thy worthy kyng, Richard, was slayn
With shot, compleynedest his deth so soore,
Why ne hadde I now thy sentence and thy loore,
The Friday for to chide, as diden ye?
For on a Friday, soothly, slayn was he.
Thanne wolde I shewe yow how that I koude pleyne
For Chauntecleres drede and for his peyne.
Certes, swich cry ne lamentacioun
Was nevere of ladyes maad whan Ylioun
Was wonne, and Pirrus with his streite swerd,
Whanne he hadde hent Kyng Priam by the berd,
And slayn hym, as seith us *Eneydos*,
As maden alle the hennes in the cloos,
Whan they hadde seyn of Chauntecleer the sighte.
But sovereynly Dame Pertelote shrighte,
Ful louder than dide Hasdrubales wyf,
Whan that hire housbonde hadde lost his lyf,
And that the Romayns hadden brend Cartage:
She was so ful of torment and of rage,
That wilfully in-to the fyr she sterte,
And brende hir-selven with a stedefast herte.
O woful hennes, right so cryden ye,
As whan that Nero brende the citee
Of Rome, cryden senatours wyves,
For that hir housbondes losten alle hire lyves;
With-outen gilt this Nero hath hem slayn.
Now wol I turne to my tale agayn.
The sely widwe, and eek hire doghtres two,
Herden thise hennes crye and maken wo,
And out atte dores stirten they anon,
And syen the fox toward the grove gon,
And bar up-on his bak the cok away,
And criden, "Out! harrow! and weilaway!
Ha! ha! the fox!" and after hym they ran,
And eek with staves many another man.
Ran Colle oure dogge, and Talbot, and Gerland,
And Malkyn, with a distaf in hire hand;
Ran cow and calf, and eek the verray hogges,
So fered for berkyng of the dogges
And showtynge of the men and wommen eek,
They ronne so, hem thoughte hir herte breek.
They yelleden as fendes doon in helle;
The dokes cryden as men wolde hem quelle;
The gees for feere flowen over the trees;
Out of the hyve cam the swarm of bees.
So hydous was the noyse, a! *benedicitee!*
Certes, he Jakke Straw, and his meynee,
Ne made nevere shoutes half so shrille,
Whan that they wolden any Flemyng kille,
As thilke day was maad up-on the fox.
Of bras they broghten bemes, and of box,
Of horn, of boon, in whiche they blewe and powped,
And ther-with-al they skryked and they howped:
It semed as that heuene sholde falle!
Now, goode men, I prey yow herkneth alle:
Lo, how Fortune turneth sodeynly
The hope and pryde eek of hire enemy!
This cok, that lay up-on the foxes bak,
In al his drede un-to the fox he spak,
And seyde, "Sire, if that I were as ye,
Yit sholde I seyn, as wys God helpe me,
'Turneth agayn, ye proude cherles alle!
A verray pestilence up-on yow falle!
Now I am come un-to this wodes syde,
Maugree youre heed, the cok shal here abyde.
I wol hym ete, in feith, and that anon!'"
The fox answerde, "In feith, it shal be done."
And as he spak that word, al sodeynly
This cok brak from his mouth delyverly,
And hye up-on a tree he fley anon.
And whan the fox say that he was gon,
"Allas!" quod he, "O Chauntecleer, allas!
I have to yow," quod he, "ydoon trespas,
In as muche as I maked yow aferd,
Whan I yow hente, and broghte out of the yerd.
But, sire, I dide it in no wikke entente.
Com doun, and I shal telle yow what I mente.
I shal seye sooth to yow, God help me so!"
"Nay thanne," quod he, "I shrewe us bothe two!
And first I shrewe my-self, bothe blood and bones,
If thow bigile me any ofter than ones.
Thow shalt namoore, thurgh thy flaterye,
Do me to synge and wynke with myn eye.
For he that wynketh, whan he sholde see,
Al wilfully, God lat hym nevere thee!"
"Nay," quod the fox, "but God yeve hym meschaunce,

528. **Richard,** Richard I, the Lion-hearted. 530. **sentence,** sententiousness. **loore,** poetic skill. 534. **drede,** dread. **peyne,** suffering. 536. **Ylioun,** Troy. 537. **Pirrus,** Pyrrhus, son of Achilles. **streite,** drawn. 539. **as . . . *Eneydos*,** as the *Aeneid* tells us. 540. **cloos,** enclosure. 542. **sovereynly,** above the rest. **shrighte,** shrieked. 543. **Hasdrubales,** of Hasdrubal, Carthaginian ruler. 545. **brend,** burned. 555. **sely,** poor. 558. **syen,** saw. 563. **oure,** "our" from the point of view of the widow; two more dogs are named in the line. 566. **fered for,** frightened by. 568. **ronne,** ran. **hem . . . breek,** it seemed to them that their hearts broke. 570. **dokes,** ducks. **quelle,** kill.

573. **hydous,** hideous. 574. **Jakke Straw,** Jack Straw, one of the leaders of the Peasants' Revolt of 1381. **meynee,** followers. 576. **Flemyng.** The Flemish had annoyed the native English laboring class, not particularly the peasants, by furnishing cheap, but good, foreign labor. Chaucer's only clear reference to the Peasants' Revolt is thus curiously limited. 578. **bemes,** trumpets. **box,** boxwood. 579. **powped,** puffed. 580. **skryked . . . howped,** shrieked . . . whooped. 592. **Maugree,** in spite of. 596. **brak,** broke away. **delyverly,** agilely. 597. **fley,** flew. 598. **say,** saw. 603. **in . . . entente,** with no wicked intention. 606. **shrewe,** curse. 610. **Do me to,** cause me to. 612. **thee,** thrive. 613. **meschaunce,** misfortune.

That is so undiscreet of governaunce,
That jangleth whan he sholde holde his pees."
Lo, swich it is for to be recchelees
And necligent, and truste on flaterye.
But ye that holden this tale a folye,
As of a fox, or of a cok and hen,
Taketh the moralitee, goode men.
For Seint Poul seith, that al that writen is,
To oure doctryne it is ywrite, ywis:
Taketh the fruyt, and lat the chaf be stille.
Now, goode God, if that it be thy wille,
As seith my lord, so make us alle goode men,
And brynge us to his heye blisse! *Amen.*

Chaucer's Retraction

The authenticity of the "Retraction" has been challenged, and each reader, no doubt, must determine for himself the likelihood of such a profound spiritual revulsion on Chaucer's part.

Heere taketh the makere of this book his leve:

Now preye I to hem alle that herkne this litel tretys or rede, that if ther be any thyng in it that liketh hem, that ther-of they thanken oure Lord Jesu Crist, of whom procedeth al wit and al goodnesse. And if ther be any thyng that displese hem, I preye hem also that they arrette it to the defaute of myn unkonnynge, and nat to my wyl, that wolde fayn have seyd bettre if I hadde had konnynge. For oure book seith, "Al that is writen is writen for oure doctrine," and that is myn entente.

Wherfore I biseke yow mekely, for the mercy of God, that ye preye for me that Crist have mercy on me and foryeve me my giltes, and namely, of my translacions and enditynges of worldly vanitees, the whiche I revoke in my retracciouns: As is the book of Troilus; The book also of Fame; The book of the xxv Ladies; The book of the Duchesse; The book of Seint Valentynes day of the parlement of briddes; The Tales of Caunterbury, thilke that sownen in-to synne; The book of the Leoun; and many another book, if they were in my remembrance, and many a song and many a leccherous lay; that Crist for his grete mercy foryeve me the synne.

But of the translacioun of Boece *de consolacione*, and othere bookes of legendes of seints, and omelies, and moralitee, and devocioun, that thanke I oure Lord Jesu Crist and his blisful Moder, and alle the seintes of hevene, bisekynge hem that they from hennes forth un-to my lyves ende, sende me grace to biwayle my giltes, and to studie to the savacioun of my soule, and graunte me grace of verray penitence, confessioun and satisfaccioun to doon in this present lyf; thurgh the benigne grace of hym that is Kyng of kynges and Preest of alle preestes, that boughte us with the precious blood of his herte; so that I may ben oon of hem at the day of doome that shulle be saved. *Qui cum patre & cetera.*

Heere is ended the book of the tales of Caunterbury, compiled by Geffrey Chaucer, of whos soule Jesu Crist have mercy. Amen.

614. **governaunce,** behavior. 615. **jangleth,** chatters. **pees,** peace. 616. **recchelees,** careless. 617. **necligent,** negligent. 621–22. **Seint Poul . . . ywrite,** St. Paul. See II Timothy 3:16. 623. **fruyt,** grain. **lat . . . stille,** leave the chaff alone. 626. **heye,** high. 22. **rede,** read it. 26. **arrette,** ascribe. 26–27. **defaute of myn unkonnynge,** fault of my ignorance. 34. **enditynges,** literary compositions. 36–37. **The book of the xxv Ladies,** *The Legend of Good Women.* 40. **sownen in-to,** tend towards. **The book of the Leoun,** lost, but probably a translation of Machaut's *Dit du Lyon.*

CHAUCERS WORDES UNTO ADAM, HIS OWNE SCRIVEYN

Adam scriveyn, if ever it thee bifalle
Boece or Troilus for to wryten newe,
Under thy lokkes thou most have the scalle,
But after my making thou wryte trewe.
So ofte a daye I mot thy werk renewe,
Hit to correcte and eek to rubbe and scrape;
And al is through thy negligence and rape.

THE COMPLEINT OF CHAUCER TO HIS EMPTY PURSE

To you, my purse, and to non other wight
Compleyne I, for ye be my lady dere!
I am so sory, now that ye be light;
For certes, but ye make me hevy chere,
Me were as leef be leyd up-on my bere;
For whiche un-to your mercy thus I crye:
Beth hevy ageyn, or elles mot I dye!

Now voucheth sauf this day, or hit be night,
That I of you the blisful soun may here,

1. **lay,** poem. 4. **omelies,** homilies. 8. **bisekynge,** beseeching. 11. **satisfaccioun,** performance of penance. *Chaucers Wordes.* 1. **scriveyn,** scribe, professional copyist. 2. **Boece,** A.N.S. Boethius (died 524), whose *De Consolatione Philosophiae* King Alfred and Chaucer both translated. 3. **scalle,** a scaly or scabby skin disease. 5. **renewe,** revise. 7. **rape,** haste. *The Compleint.* 7. **Beth,** be. 8. **voucheth sauf,** vouchsafe, grant. 9. **soun,** sound.

Or see your colour lyk the sonne bright,
That of yelownesse hadde never pere.
Ye be my lyf, ye be myn hertes stere,
Quene of comfort and of good companye:
Beth hevy ageyn, or elles mot I dye!

Now purs, that be to me my lyves light,
And saveour, as doun in this worlde here,
Out of this toune help me through your might,
Sin that ye wole nat been my tresorere;
For I am shave as nye as any frere.
But yit I pray un-to your curtesye:
Beth hevy ageyn, or elles mot I dye!

Lenvoy de Chaucer

O conquerour of Brutes Albioun!
Which that by lyne and free eleccioun
Ben verray king, this song to you I sende;
And ye, that mowen al our harm amende,
Have minde up-on my supplicacioun!

Song from THE PARLIAMENT OF FOWLS

Now welcom somer, with thy sonne softe
That hast this wintres weders over-shake,
And driven awey the longe nightes blake!
Seynt Valentyn, that art ful hy on-lofte;—
Thus singen smale foules for thy sake—
Now welcom somer, with thy sonne softe
That hast this wintres weders over-shake.

Wel han they cause for to gladen ofte,
Sith ech of hem recovered hath his make
Ful blisful may they singen whan they wake;
Now welcom somer, with thy sonne softe,
That hast this wintres weders over-shake,
And driven awey the longe nightes blake!

12. stere, rudder. **17. toune,** presumably London. **18. Sin,** since. **19. For . . . frere,** I have as little money as a friar has hair. **22. conquerour,** Henry IV, who became formally king on September 30, 1399. It is held that *Lenvoy* at least must have been written between that date and October 3, when the new king increased Chaucer's pension. **Brutes Albioun,** the Albion (Britain) of Brutus, for whom see page 55. **23. lyne,** lineage. *Song.* **1. Now.** The song is sung by the birds at the end of *The Parliament of Fowls.* In form it is a *roundel,* a short poem in which the first line or lines are repeated as a refrain in the middle and at the end. **4. Seynt Valentyn.** Birds were supposed to choose their mates on St. Valentine's Day (February 14).

GENTILESSE

The firste stoke, fader of gentilesse—
What man that claymeth gentil for to be,
Must folowe his trace, and alle his wittes dresse
Vertu to sewe, and vyces for to flee.
For unto vertu longeth dignitee,
And noght the revers, saufly dar I deme,
Al were he mytre, croune, or diademe.

This firste stok was ful of rightwisnesse,
Trewe of his word, sobre, pitous, and free,
Clene of his goste, and loved besinesse
Ageinst the vyce of slouthe, in honestee;
And, but his heir love vertu, as dide he,
He is noght gentil, thogh he riche seme,
Al were he mytre, croune, or diademe.

Vyce may wel be heir to old richesse;
But ther may no man, as men may wel see,
Bequethe his heir his vertuous noblesse
That is appropred unto no degree,
But to the firste fader in magestee,
That maketh him his heir, that can him queme,
Al were he mytre, croune, or diademe.

Gentilesse. **1. firste stok,** God or Christ. **gentilesse,** the sum of all the qualities which comprise true nobility of character and behavior. **3. dresse,** set in order. **4. sewe,** follow. **5. longeth,** belongeth. **6. saufly,** safely. **7. Al,** although. **were,** wear. **10. Clene of his goste,** pure of heart. **12. but,** unless. **18. appropred,** appropriated. **20. queme,** please.

The Popular Ballad

Although this brief discussion must deal exclusively with English and Scottish popular ballads, it should not be forgotten that the ballad, despite various and natural differences from country to country, is a distinct and recognizable literary form found all over Europe and wherever European settlers have gone.

The popular, or traditional, ballads have had a universality of appeal granted to almost no other literary type. Created by, or close to, the common people, the folk ballads have been loved and remembered, sung or recited, from the often dateless time of their origin until the present day. But they have not been limited to the cottage fireside or the village green. At least since the sixteenth century critics and creative men of letters have picked them out, often after having borne them in mind from childhood, for praise and for the sincere, if frequently misguided, flattery of imitation. The charm of the ballad is re-proved from day to day: student after student who has previously found poetry difficult discovers that "Chevy Chase" or "Sir Patrick Spens" or "Barbara Allen" can quicken a dormant sense of the beauty of measured syllables and chiming sounds.

What is a popular ballad? A ballad is a narrative poem, usually but not invariably short, originally and ordinarily intended to be sung. The importance of the musical accompaniment, largely unrecognized or ignored by the eighteenth- and nineteenth-century collectors, whose primary interest was in the words, is now clearly recognized. Indeed, some students believe that the association of the words with a short and recurrent melody had much to do with fixing the traditional form and texture of the ballad as a literary type.

A ballad, then, is "a song that tells a story"; but the story is presented in terms of a relatively fixed formula and method. A ballad is severely concentrated on a single theme, indeed on a single episode—the climactic one—of that theme. We find ourselves plunged into the situation in the middle of things; whatever background we are to receive is given to us incidentally as we go along, sometimes given obscurely and often not given at all. Why, for instance, did Sir Patrick Spens put to sea? The version which we print will never tell us, although there are others which say that he was sent to Norway to bring back—or take home—a princess, who is sometimes Scottish, sometimes Norse. Motivation, then, is reduced to a minimum or may even be wanting altogether. Once the situation is before us, the plot develops rapidly and naturally by means of action, simply stated, and dialogue, tersely expressed. The amount of dialogue in the ballads and the effect of drama which it arouses is worthy of notice. Above all else, perhaps, the narrative advances impersonally; at no time are we aware of the individuality of the author. The ballad, indeed, is often said to sing itself. In style we notice a simplicity of language which never lapses into vulgarity; use of only the most transparent figures of speech—"milk-white steed" and "berry-brown sword"; the repetition of set phrases to describe identical or almost identical situations; and a complete lack of differentiation between the speech of king and commoner. All these things are the hallmarks of the ballad and serve to distinguish it sharply from more conscious and formal literary compositions.

Two other and highly important ballad characteristics must be noted, for they lead directly to the troublesome problem of ballad origins. The first is the appearance in many of our ballad texts of a refrain, which suggests choral singing by what is often called in this connection a "dancing throng." Dancing to the accompaniment of the dancers' own singing of songs, lyric or narrative, has been an established custom from the earliest times to the present. Secondly, we find in certain ballads what Professor Gummere in his valuable study, *The Popular Ballad*, designated "incremental repetition," a term which indicates a method of carrying on a story by means of significant variations within an otherwise repeated pattern. This device is effectively employed in "Lord Randal," and another excellent example is "The Maid Freed from the Gallows," the first three stanzas of which are:

"O good Lord Judge, and sweet Lord Judge,
 Peace for a little while!
Methinks I see my own father,
 Come riding by the stile.

"Oh father, oh father, a little of your gold,
And likewise of your fee!
To keep my body from yonder grave,
And my neck from the gallows-tree."

"None of my gold now you shall have,
Nor likewise of my fee;
For I am come to see you hanged,
And hanged you shall be."

The fourth and fifth stanzas are identical with the first and second, except that "mother" is substituted for father, and the sixth repeats the third. Then follow "brother" and "sister," each as heartless as the unnatural parents. But in the thirteenth and fourteenth stanzas we have the "true-love," so that the ballad ends triumphantly:

"Some of my gold now you shall have,
And likewise of my fee;
For I am come to see you saved,
And saved you shall be."

The text as it stands, we must confess, does not depict a very comprehensible situation, but it was certainly easy to compose; that it is equally easy to remember is demonstrated by the fact that, despite its relative lack of interest, the ballad is still sung in England, the West Indies, and the United States.

The problem of ballad origins has become one of the most perplexing in literary history, and is almost too complex and disputed for brief discussion, but we must glance in its direction. Bishop Thomas Percy, in the preface to his famous and influential *Reliques of Ancient English Poetry*, 1765, ascribed the ballads to medieval minstrels. With the Romantic period, however, a new theory appeared: namely, that the popular ballad swelled, full-fledged and lilting, from the massed voices of a homogeneous folk. This "communal theory," as it is called, has been so vigorously attacked and defended, varied and modified now for nearly a century and a half that one may well feel it is better to read ballads than to read about their origin. No sane critic ever contended seriously that a group of people, no matter how small or how large, suddenly with one accord and with one voice, as it were, sang a hitherto unknown song. Furthermore, the origin of the ballad as a literary type, which occurred, we may hazard a venture, not too long after the year 1000, must not be confused with the origin of any one of the ballads that we possess today. But it is not improbable that groups of men and women, all with essentially the same background and outlook, got in the habit of accompanying their simple dances with simple melodies to which, as they danced, they extemporized simple narrative songs, with more than one of the dancers taking part in the composition of the words. Many people today are familiar with the experience, in informal singing groups at college or camp or elsewhere, of hearing some particularly imaginative person with a flair for extemporization compose new stanzas for old songs, or new songs on old themes, with the rest of the group joining in the refrain. The theory that postulates a dancing, singing, extemporizing, homogeneous group would account for most of the characteristics which we associate with the popular ballad. But to suppose that such a ballad as "Sir Patrick Spens" or "Edward" came into existence in any such way is something quite different and obviously absurd.

The people, then, supplied the mold in which individual authors made the ballads we have. The term "individual authors" must perhaps be defined in connection with the ballads. These individuals were scarcely separated from their fellows to whom, and with whom, as the use of the refrain shows, they sang. They composed orally, or even if, late in the period, they put their words first into writing, they delivered them orally and transmitted them orally. That neither the author nor the hearers of a ballad had, or have, any sense of personal ownership is evidenced by the impersonality of the ballad itself. Nor was there anything sacred in the exact words of the text. If we today read a poem and like it well enough to memorize it, and have the fortune to find others with patience to hear our rendition, we feel bound to name the author and not to deviate from his phrasing. If, on the other hand, we hear a good story, we seldom think it necessary to give credit to the person who told it to us, and we certainly alter the phraseology in retelling, either unconsciously or in hope of improvement. So it was with a ballad; once it was sung it became the property of all who heard it, and, as has been said, it may well be affirmed that a ballad is recomposed with every rendition. Although in a volume such as *The College Survey* only one version of a ballad can be given we should note that most of the eighteen ballads printed here have been collected more than once (sometimes, as in the case of "Barbara Allan," literally hundreds of times) and that no two versions are likely to be identical. Every singer makes changes of his own, changes as often due to poetic taste, however unconscious, as to forgetfulness or carelessness. This process of variation plays a marked part in ballad development; it has operated clearly from generation to generation and from century to century, involving many individuals without names or literary personalities.

It is impossible, of course, to date the ballads. Few of them in their present form can be older than the fifteenth century, hence they may fairly be considered as representative of the popular poetry of the time. Most of the ballads in the group given here are, however, of earlier origin, although the language in which we have them is in most cases later than the fifteenth century, and, as will be noticed, is often intermixed with Scots dialect.

There is one last consideration of particular interest to American students. Despite the gloomy prognostications of each new generation of ballad collectors and critics from the late eighteenth century on, the traditional ballad is quite alive today, not only in Great Britain but in many parts of the United States and Canada. The seventeenth- and eighteenth-century settlers of the English-speaking sections of the Western Hemisphere brought their songs with them and, less miraculously than we are at first inclined to think, the songs survived, especially in the more isolated communities. During the past thirty years collectors have done notable work in recording variants of popular ballads, including approximately one-third of the three hundred and five brought together late in the nineteenth century in Francis J. Child's invaluable *English and Scottish Popular Ballads*. Nor is the field worked out. There is scarcely a person who reads these words, especially if he has access to rural communities along the Atlantic seaboard, and in the hills behind it, from Maine to Florida, who cannot with a little patience and ingenuity come upon individuals able to sing or recite the old ballads. In many cases they scarcely know that they know them, but they do know them just the same. Few greater thrills of a literary kind can be experienced than to find for oneself a ballad, say "Lord Randal," treated as a real story in a living song and not as one of the dry bones which clatter dully in anthologies.

Furthermore, the process of ballad-making still continues in certain types of communities and groups in the United States and other English-speaking countries, particularly in the Kentucky and Tennessee mountains, in the lumber camps of the Northwest, and on the great plains of the western states and Australia. Of the more familiar modern American ballads one need only mention "Frankie and Johnny," "Jesse James," "Bold Jack Donahue," and "Casey Jones." From Australia came the wartime favorite, "Waltzing Matilda."

In the late eighteenth and nineteenth centuries the popular ballad was imitated by the romantic poets and some of their successors. Inevitably, however, such conscious and deliberate artists failed to capture the peculiar spirit of the older ballads. Of the "literary ballads," as they are called, the nearest in spirit and form to the popular ballads are those of Sir Walter Scott, himself a collector and connoisseur of old ballads, and a spiritual descendant of the ballad-makers. (See pages 783–788 for his "Lochinvar," "Jock of Hazeldean," and "Proud Maisie.") Other examples of the literary ballad, which may be profitably compared with the popular ballad, are Keats's "La Belle Dame Sans Merci" (page 877) and Rossetti's "Sister Helen" (page 1100).

Our standard collection of traditional ballads is Child's *English and Scottish Popular Ballads* (5 vols., Boston, 1882–1898). Child's numbering of the ballads is followed in our footnotes. An abridged, but in itself complete, edition of this great work was made by H. C. Sargent and G. L. Kittredge (Houghton Mifflin, 1904), and from this the following ballads are taken by permission of the copyright owner. In addition to Kittredge's brief but invaluable introduction to the volume in question, the following studies are commended to the student: Francis B. Gummere, *The Popular Ballad*, Houghton Mifflin, 1907; Louise Pound, *Poetic Origins and the Ballad*, Macmillan, 1921; G. H. Gerould, *The Ballad of Tradition*, Oxford University Press, 1932; and William J. Entwistle, *European Balladry*, Oxford University Press, 1939. Among the many collections from America are the following: Phillips Barry, F. H. Eckstrom, and M. W. Smyth, *British Ballads from Maine*, Yale University Press, 1929; C. J. Sharp and O. D. Campbell, *English Folk-Songs from the Southern Appalachians*, Oxford University Press, 1929; A. K. Davis, Jr., *Traditional Ballads of Virginia*, Harvard University Press, 1929; W. R. Mackenzie, *Ballads and Sea Songs from Nova Scotia*, Harvard University Press, 1928; Reed Smith, *South Carolina Ballads*, Harvard University Press, 1928.

The most recent and one of the most informative and charming studies of the ballad is Evelyn K. Wells's *The Ballad Tree, A Study of British and American Ballads, Their Folklore, Verse, and Music*, Ronald Press, 1950. The book contains introduction, notes, bibliographies, and sixty traditional ballads and their tunes.

THE TWA SISTERS

This ballad is found in Scandinavia as well as Great Britain, and was brought to the United States. By means of repetition of the first line and use of the refrain (which, like most, has no connection with the plot) a single couplet is built up to a seven-line stanza. There is a recording of an American version by Andrew R. Summers in Columbia, Old World Ballads in America (M–408).

There was twa sisters in a bowr,
Edinburgh, Edinburgh
There was twa sisters in a bowr,
Stirling for ay
There was twa sisters in a bowr,
There came a knight to be their wooer.
Bonny Saint Johnston stands upon Tay.

He courted the eldest wi glove an ring,
But he lovd the youngest above a' thing.

He courted the eldest wi brotch an knife,
But lovd the youngest as his life.

The eldest she was vexed sair,
An much envied her sister fair.

Into her bowr she could not rest,
Wi grief an spite she almos brast.

Upon a morning fair an clear,
She cried upon her sister dear:

"O sister, come to yon sea stran,
An see our father's ships come to lan."

She's taen her by the milk-white han
An led her down to yon sea stran.

The youngest stood upon a stane,
The eldest came an threw her in.

She tooke her by the middle sma,
An dashd her bonny back to the jaw.

"O sister, sister, tak my han,
An Ise mack you heir to a' my lan.

"O sister, sister, tak my middle,
An yes get my goud and my gouden girdle.

"O sister, sister, save my life,
An I swear Ise never be nae man's wife."

"Foul fa the han that I should tacke,
It twined me an my wardles make.

"Your cherry cheeks an yallow hair
Gars me gae maiden for evermair."

Sometimes she sank, an sometimes she swam,
Till she came down yon bonny mill-dam.

O out it came the miller's son,
An saw the fair maid swimmin in.

"O father, father, draw your dam,
Here's either a mermaid or a swan."

The miller quickly drew the dam,
An there he found a drownd woman.

You coudna see her yallow hair
For gould and pearle that were so rare.

You coudna see her middle sma
For gouden girdle that was sae braw.

You coudna see her fingers white,
For gouden rings that was sae gryte.

An by there came a harper fine,
That harped to the king at dine.

When he did look that lady upon,
He sighd and made a heavy moan.

He's taen three locks o her yallow hair,
And wi them strung his harp sae fair.

The first tune he did play and sing,
Was, "Farewell to my father the king."

The nextin tune that he playd syne,
Was, "Farewell to my mother the queen."

The lasten tune that he playd then,
Was, "Wae to my sister, fair Ellen."

The Twa Sisters (Child 10). **10. brotch,** brooch. **12. sair,** sorely. **15. brast,** burst. **20. taen,** taken. **24. sma,** small. **25. jaw,** billow. **27. Ise,** I shall. **29. yes,** ye shall. **goud,** gold. **32. fa,** fall. **33. twined,** separated. **wardles make,** world's mate. **35. Gars,** causes. **47. braw,** handsome. **49. gryte,** great. **51. dine,** dinner. **58. syne,** afterward.

LORD RANDAL

Incremental repetition is a significant feature of this ballad as well as of one which follows it. So, too, as in "Edward," we find the common device of the "legacy" of a dying or departing hero. "Lord Randal" was, and is, popular in the United States and has been collected in New England as well as in the South.

"O where ha you been, Lord Randal, my son?
And where ha you been, my handsome young man?"

Lord Randal (Child 12).

"I ha been at the greenwood; mother, mak my bed soon,
For I'm wearied wi hunting, and fain wad lie down."

"An wha met ye there, Lord Randal, my son?
An wha met you there, my handsome young man?"
"O I met wi my true-love; mother, mak my bed soon,
For I'm wearied wi huntin, an fain wad lie down."

"And what did she give you, Lord Randal, my son?
And what did she give you, my handsome young man?"
"Eels fried in a pan; mother, mak my bed soon,
For I'm wearied wi huntin, and fain wad lie down."

"And wha gat your leavins, Lord Randal, my son?
And wha gat your leavins, my handsom young man?"
"My hawks and my hounds; mother, mak my bed soon,
For I'm wearied wi hunting, and fain wad lie down."

"And what becam of them, Lord Randal, my son?
And what becam of them, my handsome young man?"
"They stretched their legs out an died; mother, mak my bed soon,
For I'm wearied wi huntin, and fain wad lie down."

"O I fear you are poisoned, Lord Randal, my son!
I fear you are poisoned, my handsome young man!"
"O yes, I am poisoned; mother, mak my bed soon,
For I'm sick at the heart, and I fain wad lie down."

"What d' ye leave to your mother, Lord Randal, my son?
What d' ye leave to your mother, my handsome young man?"
"Four and twenty milk kye; mother, mak my bed soon,
For I'm sick at the heart, and I fain wad lie down."

"What d' ye leave to your sister, Lord Randal, my son?
What d' ye leave to your sister, my handsome young man?"
"My gold and my silver; mother, mak my bed soon,
For I'm sick at the heart, an I fain wad lie down."

27. kye, cows.

"What d' ye leave to your brother, Lord Randal, my son?
What d' ye leave to your brother, my handsome young man?"
"My houses and my lands; mother, mak my bed soon,
For I'm sick at the heart, and I fain wad lie down."

"What d' ye leave to your true-love, Lord Randal, my son?
What d' ye leave to your true-love, my handsome young man?"
"I leave her hell and fire; mother, mak my bed soon,
For I'm sick at the heart, and I fain wad lie down."

EDWARD

The "surprise ending," though by no means uncommon, is not altogether typical of the popular ballads, but in "Edward" it is used with superb effect. The mother's persistent questioning is given a grim underscoring by the last stanza, which makes clear that she had in some way caused her son to kill his own father. "Edward" is an excellent example of how few details the ballad authors need to give in order to make us feel a complete and even haunting impression of a situation.

"Why dois your brand sae drap wi bluid,
Edward, Edward,
Why dois your brand sae drap wi bluid,
And why sae sad gang yee O?"
"O I hae killed my hauke sae guid,
Mither, mither,
O I hae killed my hauke sae guid,
And I had nae mair bot hee O."

"Your haukis bluid was nevir sae reid,
Edward, Edward,
Your haukis bluid was nevir sae reid,
My deir son I tell thee O."
"O I hae killed my reid-roan steid,
Mither, mither,
O I hae killed my reid-roan steid,
That erst was sae fair and frie O."

"Your steid was auld, and ye hae gat mair,
Edward, Edward,
Your steid was auld, and ye hae gat mair,
Sum other dule ye drie O."
"O I hae killed my fadir deir,
Mither, mither,

Edward (Child 13). **4. gang,** go. **13. reid-roan,** of a prevailingly red color. **16. erst,** once. **frie,** spirited. **20. dule,** grief. **drie,** suffer.

O I hae killed my fadir deir,
  Alas, and wae is mee O!"

"And whatten penance wul ye drie for that,
                    Edward, Edward?
And whatten penance will ye drie for that?
  My deir son, now tell me O."
"Ile set my feit in yonder boat,
                    Mither, mither,
Ile set my feit in yonder boat,
  And Ile fare ovir the sea O."

"And what wul ye doe wi your towirs and your ha,
                    Edward, Edward?
And what wul ye doe wi your towirs and your ha,
  That were sae fair to see O?"
"Ile let thame stand tul they doun fa,
                    Mither, mither,
Ile let thame stand tul they doun fa,
  For here nevir mair maun I bee O."

"And what wul ye leive to your bairns and your wife,
                    Edward, Edward?
And what wul ye leive to your bairns and your wife,
  Whan ye gang ovir the sea O?"
"The warldis room, late them beg thrae life,
                    Mither, mither,
The warldis room, late them beg thrae life,
  For thame nevir mair wul I see O."

"And what wul ye leive to your ain mither deir,
                    Edward, Edward?
And what wul ye leive to your ain mither deir?
  My deir son, now tell me O."
"The curse of hell frae me sall ye beir,
                    Mither, mither,
The curse of hell frae me sall ye beir,
  Sic counseils ye gave to me O."

HIND HORN

If this ballad is compared with its original, the romance of *King Horn*, it will be observed that details of action and motivation have disappeared, and that the ballad really deals with only one episode, though that perhaps the most striking, of the romance. At the end we get more than a hint of the popular ballad scene in which the hero tests the heroine's love by making it appear that he is reduced to poverty. The refrain, to be repeated with each stanza, is merely a series of meaningless syllables to carry the tune.

25. whatten, what kind of. **33. ha,** hall. **37. tul,** till. **fa,** fall. **40. maun,** must. **41. bairns,** children. **45. late,** let. **thrae,** through. **56. Sic,** such. *Hind Horn* (Child 17).

In Scotland there was a babie born,
  Lill lal, etc.
And his name it was called young Hind Horn.
  With a fal lal, etc.

He sent a letter to our king
That he was in love with his daughter Jean.

He's gien to her a silver wand,
With seven living lavrocks sitting thereon.

She's gien to him a diamond ring,
With seven bright diamonds set therein.

"When this ring grows pale and wan,
You may know by it my love is gane."

One day as he looked his ring upon,
He saw the diamonds pale and wan.

He left the sea and came to land,
And the first that he met was an old beggar man.

"What news, what news?" said young Hind Horn;
"No news, no news," said the old beggar man.

"No news," said the beggar, "no news at a',
But there is a wedding in the king's ha.

"But there is a wedding in the king's ha,
That has halden these forty days and twa."

"Will ye lend me your begging coat?
And I'll lend you my scarlet cloak.

"Will you lend me your beggar's rung?
And I'll gie you my steed to ride upon.

"Will you lend me your wig o hair,
To cover mine, because it is fair?"

The auld beggar man was bound for the mill,
But young Hind Horn for the king's hall.

The auld beggar man was bound for to ride,
But young Hind Horn was bound for the bride.

When he came to the king's gate,
He sought a drink for Hind Horn's sake.

The bride came down with a glass of wine,
When he drank out the glass, and dropt in the ring.

3. Hind, Youth. **7. gien,** given. **8. lavrocks,** larks. **25. rung,** staff.

"O got ye this by sea or land?
Or got ye it off a dead man's hand?"

"I got not it by sea, I got it by land,
And I got it, madam, out of your own hand."

"O I'll cast off my gowns of brown,
And beg wi you frae town to town.

"O I'll cast off my gowns of red,
And I'll beg wi' you to win my bread."

"Ye needna cast off your gowns of brown,
For I'll make you lady o many a town.

"Ye needna cast off your gowns of red,
It's only a sham, the begging o my bread."

The bridegroom he had wedded the bride,
But young Hind Horn he took her to bed.

THE TWA CORBIES

The ballad's power of suggestion is made unusually striking here, when we contrast the blandly sinister fashion in which the ravens detail their future conduct with the little they tell us about the way in which the unfortunate knight came to his death.

As I was walking all alane,
I heard twa corbies making a mane;
The tane unto the t'other say,
"Where sall we gang and dine to-day?"

"In behint yon auld fail dyke,
I wot there lies a new slain knight;
And naebody kens that he lies there,
But his hawk, his hound, and lady fair.

"His hound is to the hunting gane,
His hawk to fetch the wild-fowl hame,
His lady's ta'en another mate,
So we may mak our dinner sweet.

"Ye'll sit on his white hause-bane,
And I'll pike out his bonny blue een;
Wi ae lock o his gowden hair
We'll theek our nest when it grows bare.

"Mony a one for him makes mane,
But nane sall ken where he is gane;
Oer his white banes, when they are bare,
The wind sall blaw for evermair."

The Twa Corbies (Child 26). **2. corbies,** ravens. **mane,** lament. **3. tane,** t(he) one. **4. sall,** shall. **5. fail dyke,** turf wall. **7. kens,** knows. **13. hause-bane,** neck bone. **14. een,** eyes. **15. gowden,** golden. **16. theek,** thatch.

THOMAS RYMER

Thomas the Rymer, that is, Thomas of Ercildoune, would appear to have been a historical personage of the thirteenth century who had, or gained soon after his death, a great reputation as poet and prophet. In the former capacity a version of the romance of Tristam was ascribed to him as early as 1330, and in the latter he is probably still remembered in Scotland. According to a late fourteenth-century poem which bears his name (see J. E. Wells, *A Manual of the Writings in Middle English*, Yale University Press, 1916, pp. 224 ff.) his prophecies were given to him by the queen of the elves or fairies. Some progenitor of this poem which did not contain, or at least, stress, the prophecies, is doubtless the ultimate source of the ballad.

One of the best of the numerous tales which deal with the union of a mortal to a fairy—the "otherworld bride" motif—is Marie de France's lay of "Lanval," which was turned into Middle English by Thomas Chester.

True Thomas lay oer yond grassy bank,
  And he beheld a ladie gay,
A ladie that was brisk and bold,
  Come riding oer the fernie brae.

Her skirt was of the grass-green silk,
  Her mantel of the velvet fine,
At ilka tett of her horse's mane
  Hung fifty silver bells and nine.

True Thomas he took off his hat,
  And bowed him low down till his knee:
"All hail, thou mighty Queen of Heaven!
  For your peer on earth I never did see."

"O no, O no, True Thomas," she says,
  "That name does not belong to me;
I am but the queen of fair Elfland,
  And I'm come here for to visit thee.

"But ye maun go wi me now, Thomas,
  True Thomas, ye maun go wi me,
For ye maun serve me seven years,
  Thro weel or wae as may chance to be."

Thomas Rymer (Child 37). **4. brae,** hillside. **7. ilka tett,** each lock. **16. thee.** There is something missing after this line. **17. maun,** must.

She turned about her milk-white steed,
And took True Thomas up behind,
And aye wheneer her bridle rang,
The steed flew swifter than the wind.

For forty days and forty nights
He wade thro red blude to the knee,
And he saw neither sun nor moon,
But heard the roaring of the sea.

O they rade on, and further on,
Until they came to a garden green:
"Light down, light down, ye ladie free,
Some of that fruit let me pull to thee."

"O no, O no, True Thomas," she says,
"That fruit maun not be touched by thee,
For a' the plagues that are in hell
Light on the fruit of this countrie.

"But I have a loaf here in my lap,
Likewise a bottle of claret wine,
And now ere we go farther on,
We'll rest a while, and ye may dine."

When he had eaten and drunk his fill,
"Lay down your head upon my knee,"
The lady sayd, "ere we climb yon hill,
And I will show you fairlies three.

"O see not ye yon narrow road,
So thick beset wi thorns and briers?
That is the path of righteousness,
Tho after it but few enquires.

"And see not ye that braid braid road,
That lies across yon lillie leven?
That is the path of wickedness,
Tho some call it the road to heaven.

"And see not ye that bonny road,
Which winds about the fernie brae?
That is the road to fair Elfland,
Where you and I this night maun gae.

"But Thomas, ye maun hold your tongue,
Whatever you may hear or see,
For gin ae word you should chance to speak,
You will neer get back to your ain countrie."

He has gotten a coat of the even cloth,
And a pair of shoes of velvet green,
And till seven years were past and gone
True Thomas on earth was never seen.

44. fairlies, wonders. **49. braid,** broad. **50. lillie leven,** charming glade. **59. gin ae,** if one. **61. even,** uniform in quality.

THE CHERRY-TREE CAROL

This delightful bit of New Testament apocrypha has been popular among American ballad-singers, and a version was recorded by Andrew R. Summers for Columbia, Old World Ballads in America (M-408).

Joseph was an old man,
And an old man was he,
When he wedded Mary,
In the land of Galilee.

Joseph and Mary walked
Through an orchard good,
Where was cherries and berries,
So red as any blood.

Joseph and Mary walked
Through an orchard green,
Where was berries and cherries,
As thick as might be seen.

O then bespoke Mary,
So meek and so mild:
"Pluck me one cherry, Joseph,
For I am with child."

O then bespoke Joseph,
With words most unkind:
"Let him pluck thee a cherry
That brought thee with child."

O then bespoke the babe,
Within his mother's womb:
"Bow down then the tallest tree,
For my mother to have some."

Then bowed down the highest tree
Unto his mother's hand;
Then she cried, "See, Joseph,
I have cherries at command."

O then bespake Joseph:
"I have done Mary wrong;
But cheer up, my dearest,
And be not cast down."

Then Mary plucked a cherry,
As red as the blood,
Then Mary went home
With her heavy load.

Then Mary took her babe,
And sat him on her knee

The Cherry-Tree Carol (Child 54).

Saying, "My dear son, tell me
What this world will be."

"O I shall be as dead, mother,
As the stones in the wall;
O the stones in the streets, mother,
Shall mourn for me all.

"Upon Easter-day, mother,
My uprising shall be;
O the sun and the moon, mother,
Shall both rise with me."

SIR PATRICK SPENS

It really matters very little whether it is possible to identify Sir Patrick Spens with some Scottish sea dog or other, or whether his death is to be connected in any way with the marriage in 1281 of Margaret, daughter of Alexander III of Scotland, to King Eric of Norway. The ballad, whatever its source, celebrates the acts of men who, without too much regard to their own immediate judgment, carry out the orders of their king. Even with a tear in his eye Sir Patrick is of the breed that brings nobility to human life.

The king sits in Dumferling toune,
Drinking the blude-reid wine:
"O whar will I get guid sailor,
To sail this schip of mine?"

Up and spak an eldern knicht,
Sat at the kings richt kne:
"Sir Patrick Spence is the best sailor
That sails upon the se."

The king has written a braid letter,
And signd it wi his hand,
And sent it to Sir Patrick Spence,
Was walking on the sand.

The first line that Sir Patrick red,
A loud lauch lauched he;
The next line that Sir Patrick red,
The teir blinded his ee.

"O wha is this has don this deid,
This ill deid don to me,
To send me out this time o' the yeir,
To sail upon the se!

"Mak hast, mak haste, my mirry men all,
Our guid schip sails the morne":
"O say na sae, my master deir,
For I feir a deadlie storme.

"Late late yestreen I saw the new moone,
Wi the auld moone in her arme,
And I feir, I feir, my deir master,
That we will cum to harme."

O our Scots nobles wer richt laith
To weet their cork-heild schoone;
Bot lang owre a' the play wer playd,
Thair hats they swam aboone.

O lang, lang may their ladies sit,
Wi thair fans into their hand,
Or eir they se Sir Patrick Spence
Cum sailing to the land.

O lang, lang may the ladies stand,
Wi thair gold kems in their hair,
Waiting for thair ain deir lords,
For they'll se thame na mair.

Haf owre, haf owre to Aberdour,
It's fiftie fadom deip,
And thair lies guid Sir Patrick Spence,
Wi the Scots lords at his feit.

Sir Patrick Spens (Child 58). **9. braid,** broad. **16. ee,** eye.

29. laith, loath. **30. cork-heild schoone,** cork-heeled shoes. **31. owre,** ere, before. **32. aboone,** above. **35. Or eir,** ere ever. **38. kems,** combs. **41. haf owre,** halfway over; i.e., halfway home.

THE WIFE OF USHER'S WELL

In many ballads and tales the dead return, but almost never in the casual fashion of the sons in this version of "The Wife of Usher's Well." Here the returned sons seem anxious only to give momentary consolation to their sorrowing mother. The simplicity of the poem is profoundly moving, and we are especially touched by the quiet enumeration of domestic details in the final stanza. An American version called "Lady Gay" was recorded by Andrew R. Summers for Columbia, Old World Ballads in America (M–408).

There lived a wife at Usher's Well,
And a wealthy wife was she;
She had three stout and stalwart sons,
And sent them oer the sea.

They hadna been a week from her,
A week but barely ane,
Whan word came to the carline wife
That her three sons were gane.

They hadna been a week from her,
A week but barely three,

The Wife of Usher's Well (Child 79). **7. carline,** woman, old woman.

Whan word came to the carline wife
  That her sons she'd never see.

"I wish the wind may never cease,
  Nor fashes in the flood,
Till my three sons come hame to me,
  In earthly flesh and blood."

It fell about the Martinmass,
  When nights are lang and mirk,
The carlin wife's three sons came hame,
  And their hats were o the birk.

It neither grew in syke nor ditch,
  Nor yet in ony sheugh;
But at the gates o Paradise,
  That birk grew fair eneugh.

"Blow up the fire, my maidens,
  Bring water from the well;
For a' my house shall feast this night,
  Since my three sons are well."

And she has made to them a bed,
  She's made it large and wide,
And she's taen her mantle her about,
  Sat down at the bed-side.

Up then crew the red, red cock,
  And up and crew the gray;
The eldest to the youngest said,
  " 'T is time we were away."

The cock he hadna crawd but once,
  And clappd his wings at a',
When the youngest to the eldest said,
  "Brother, we must awa."

"The cock doth craw, the day doth daw,
  The channerin worm doth chide;
Gin we be mist out o our place,
  A sair pain we maun bide.

"Fare ye weel, my mother dear!
  Fareweel to barn and byre!
And fare ye weel, the bonny lass
  That kindles my mother's fire!"

BONNY BARBARA ALLAN

It is probably safe to say that no one of the Child ballads has been collected in America more often than "Barbara Allan." Samuel Pepys heard his favorite Mrs. Knipp sing it in 1666 and we can still hear it today. Of the many American recordings the best is that of John J. Niles for Victor, Early American Ballads (M–604).

14. fashes, troubles. **17. Martinmass,** November 11. **18. mirk,** dark. **20. birk,** birch. **21. syke,** trench. **22. sheugh,** furrow. **36. 'T is time.** At cockcrow the dead must return to their graves. **38. And,** and (had not). **41. daw,** dawn. **42. channerin,** fretting. **46. byre,** cow house. *Bonny Barbara Allan* (Child 84).

It was in and about the Martinmas time,
  When the green leaves were a falling,
That Sir John Graeme, in the West Country,
  Fell in love with Barbara Allan.

He sent his man down through the town,
  To the place where she was dwelling:
"O haste and come to my master dear,
  Gin ye be Barbara Allan."

O hooly, hooly rose she up,
  To the place where he was lying,
And when she drew the curtain by,
  "Young man, I think you 're dying."

"O it's I'm sick, and very, very sick,
  And 't is a' for Barbara Allan":
"O the better for me ye's never be,
  Tho your heart's blood were a spilling.

"O dinna ye mind, young man," said she,
  "When ye was in the tavern a drinking,
That ye made the healths gae round and round,
  And slighted Barbara Allan?"

He turnd his face unto the wall,
  And death was with him dealing:
"Adieu, adieu, my dear friends all,
  And be kind to Barbara Allan."

And slowly, slowly raise she up,
  And slowly, slowly left him,
And sighing said, she coud not stay,
  Since death of life had reft him.

She had not gane a mile but twa,
  When she heard the dead-bell ringing,
And every jow that the dead-bell geid,
  It cry'd, Woe to Barbara Allan!

"O mother, mother, make my bed!
  O make it saft and narrow!
Since my love died for me to-day,
  I'll die for him to-morrow."

JOHNIE ARMSTRONG

Centuries of warfare between England and Scotland inevitably led to the creation of a disputed borderland

1. Martinmas, November 11. **8. Gin,** if. **9. hooly,** softly. **15. ye's,** you shall. **17. dinna ye mind,** don't you remember? **31. jow,** stroke. **geid,** gave. *Johnie Armstrong* (Child 169).

between the two countries; as inevitably the inhabitants of the border became so inured to strife and its convenient confusion between "mine and thine" that they felt free to overlook an occasional truce or peace. The borderers, however, were not only fighters and thieves; they were also composers and singers of ballads, and some of our most stirring poems sprang from their irregular way of life. John Armstrong, like most of his peers, was no respecter of nationality, and, himself a Scot, was executed during James V's efforts to pacify his borders in 1530. Despite the tone of this ballad, doubtless composed and cherished in the Armstrong clan, we need not feel that John's death was necessarily an act of treachery and murder.

There dwelt a man in faire Westmerland,
  Jonne Armestrong men did him call,
He had nither lands nor rents coming in,
  Yet he kept eight score men in his hall.

He had horse and harness for them all,
  Goodly steeds were all milke-white;
O the golden bands an about their necks,
  And their weapons, they were all alike.

Newes then was brought unto the king
  That there was sicke a won as hee,
That lived lyke a bold out-law,
  And robbed all the north country.

The king he writt an a letter then,
  A letter which was large and long;
He signed it with his owne hand,
  And promised to doe him no wrong.

When this letter came Jonne untill,
  His heart it was as blythe as birds on the tree:
"Never was I sent for before any king,
  My father, my grandfather, nor none but mee.

"And if wee goe the king before,
  I would we went most orderly;
Every man of you shall have his scarlet cloak,
  Laced with silver laces three.

"Every won of you shall have his velvett coat,
  Laced with sillver lace so white;
O the golden bands an about your necks,
  Black hatts, white feathers, all alyke."

By the morrow morninge at ten of the clock,
  Towards Edenburough gon was hee,
And with him all his eight score men;
  Good lord, it was a goodly sight for to see!

When Jonne came befower the king,
  He fell downe on his knee;
"O pardon, my soveraine leige," he said,
  "O pardon my eight score men and mee!"

"Thou shalt have no pardon, thou traytor strong,
  For thy eight score men nor thee;
For to-morrow morning by ten of the clock,
  Both thou and them shall hang on the gallow-tree.

But Jonne looke'd over his left shoulder,
  Good Lord, what a grevious look looked hee!
Saying, "Asking grace of a graceles face—
  Why there is none for you nor me."

But Jonne had a bright sword by his side,
  And it was made of the mettle so free,
That had not the king stept his foot aside,
  He had smitten his head from his faire bodde.

Saying, "Fight on, my merry men all,
  And see that none of you be taine;
For rather then men shall say we were hanged,
  Let them report how we were slaine."

Then, God wott, faire Eddenburrough rose,
  And so besett poore Jonne rounde,
That fowerscore and tenn of Jonnes best men
  Lay gasping all upon the ground.

Then like a mad man Jonne laide about,
  And like a mad man then fought hee,
Untill a falce Scot came Jonne behinde,
  And runn him through the faire boddee.

Saying, "Fight on, my merry men all,
  And see that none of you be taine;
And I will stand by and bleed but awhile,
  And then will I come and fight againe."

Newes then was brought to young Jonne Armestrong,
  As he stood by his nurses knee,
Who vowed if ere he lived for to be a man,
  O the treacherous Scots revengd hee'd be.

MARY HAMILTON

The tragic and moving story of Mary Hamilton has been connected with an incident at the Scottish court and with another, involving a Scots girl named Hamilton, at the court of Peter the Great of Russia. In the ballad itself

10. sicke a won, such a one. **17. Jonne untill,** unto Johnie.

46. mettle so free, metal so fine. **50. taine,** taken. **68. O,** on. *Mary Hamilton* (Child 173).

the "hichest Stewart of a' " is Darnley and the "auld queen," who would have taken little pleasure in the adjective, since she was only twenty-five when Darnley was murdered, is Mary Queen of Scots. An American version, which omits the reason for the execution, was recorded by Andrew R. Summers for Columbia, Old World Ballads in America (M–408).

Word's gane to the kitchen,
  And word's gane to the ha,
That Marie Hamilton gangs wi bairn
  To the hichest Stewart of a'.

He's courted her in the kitchen,
  He's courted her in the ha,
He's courted her in the laigh cellar,
  And that was warst of a'.

She's tyed it in her apron
  And she's thrown it in the sea;
Says, "Sink ye, swim ye, bonny wee babe!
  You'l neer get mair o me."

Down then cam the auld queen,
  Goud tassels tying her hair:
"O Marie, where's the bonny wee babe
  That I heard greet sae sair?"

"There was never a babe intill my room,
  As little designs to be;
It was but a touch o my sair side,
  Come oer my fair bodie."

"O Marie, put on your robes o black,
  Or else your robes o brown,
For ye maun gang wi me the night,
  To see fair Edinbro town."

"I winna put on my robes o black,
  Nor yet my robes o brown;
But I'll put on my robes o white,
  To shine through Edinbro town."

When she gaed up the Cannogate,
  She laughed loud laughters three;
But whan she cam down the Cannogate
  The tear blinded her ee.

When she gaed up the Parliament stair,
  The heel cam aff her shee;
And lang or she cam down again
  She was condemnd to dee.

When she cam down the Cannogate,
  The Cannogate sae free,
Many a ladie lookd oer her window,
  Weeping for this ladie.

"Ye need nae weep for me," she says,
  "Ye need nae weep for me;
For had I not slain mine own sweet babe,
  This death I wadna dee.

"Bring me a bottle of wine," she says,
  "The best that eer ye hae,
That I may drink to my weil-wishers,
  And they may drink to me.

"Here's a health to the jolly sailors,
  That sail upon the main;
Let them never let on to my father and mother
  But what I'm coming hame.

"Here's a health to the jolly sailors,
  That sail upon the sea;
Let them never let on to my father and mother
  That I cam here to dee.

"Oh little did my mother think,
  The day she cradled me,
What lands I was to travel through,
  What death I was to dee.

"Oh little did my father think,
  The day he held up me,
What lands I was to travel through,
  What death I was to dee.

"Last night I washd the queen's feet,
  And gently laid her down;
And a' the thanks I've gotten the nicht
  To be hangd in Edinbro town!

"Last nicht there was four Maries,
  The nicht there'l be but three;
There was Marie Seton, and Marie Beton,
  And Marie Carmichael, and me."

2. ha, hall. **4. hichest,** highest. **7. laigh,** low. **14. Goud,** gold. **16. greet,** cry, weep. **23. maun,** must. **29. Cannogate,** Canongate, the street leading to the palace. **34. shee,** shoe.

46. eer ye hae, ever you have.

THE BONNY EARL OF MURRAY

James Stewart, Earl of Murray, was killed in 1592 by his bitter enemy George Gordon, first Marquess of Huntly.

Ye Highlands, and ye Lawlands,
  Oh where have you been?

The Bonny Earl of Murray (Child 181).

They have slain the Earl of Murray,
And they layd him on the green.

"Now wae be to thee, Huntly!
And wherefore did you sae?
I bade you bring him wi you,
But forbade you him to slay."

He was a braw gallant,
And he rid at the ring;
And the bonny Earl of Murray,
Oh he might have been a king!

He was a braw gallant,
And he playd at the ba;
And the bonny Earl of Murray
Was the flower amang them a'.

He was a braw gallant,
And he playd at the glove;
And the bonny Earl of Murray,
Oh he was the Queen's love!

Oh lang will his lady
Look oer the castle Down,
Eer she see the Earl of Murray
Come sounding thro the town!

GET UP AND BAR THE DOOR

"Get Up and Bar the Door" is one of the very few humorous popular ballads. Another, "Our Goodman," is still current in many American versions, most of which are none too seemly.

It fell about the Martinmas time,
And a gay time it was then,
When our good wife got puddings to make,
And she's boild them in the pan.

The wind sae cauld blew south and north,
And blew into the floor;
Quoth our goodman to our goodwife,
"Gae out and bar the door."

9. braw, fine. **10. rid . . . ring,** a riding game, the point of which was to catch on one's spear a ring hanging from a pole. **14. ba,** ball. **22. Down,** Doune in Perthshire. **24. sounding,** blowing a trumpet or bugle. *Get Up and Bar the Door* (Child 275). **3. puddings,** sausages.

"My hand is in my hussyfskap,
Goodman, as ye may see;
An it shoud nae be barrd this hundred year,
It's no be barrd for me."

They made a paction tween them twa,
They made it firm and sure,
That the first word whaeer shoud speak,
Shoud rise and bar the door.

Then by there came two gentlemen,
At twelve oclock at night,
And they could neither see house nor hall,
Nor coal nor candle-light.

"Now whether is this a rich man's house,
Or whether is it a poor?"
But neer a word wad ane o them speak,
For barring of the door.

And first they ate the white puddings,
And then they ate the black;
Tho muckle thought the goodwife to hersel,
Yet neer a word she spake.

Then said the one unto the other,
"Here, man, tak ye my knife;
Do ye tak aff the auld man's beard,
And I'll kiss the goodwife."

"But there's nae water in the house,
And what shall we do than?"
"What ails ye at the pudding-broo,
That boils into the pan?"

O up then started our goodman,
An angry man was he:
"Will ye kiss my wife before my een,
And scad me wi pudding-bree?"

Then up and started our goodwife,
Gied three skips on the floor:
"Goodman, you've spoken the foremost word,
Get up and bar the door."

9. hussyfskap, housewifery. **15. whaeer,** whoever. **27. Tho muckle,** though much. **34. what . . . than?** that is, for shaving water. **35. broo,** broth. **40. scad,** scald.

Sir Thomas Malory
c. 1408–1471

Sir Thomas Malory ranks high in English court records as well as in literary annals if we assume, as most scholars now do, that the author of the *Morte Darthur* was the Sir Thomas Malory of Newbold Revel in Warwickshire about whom some rather startling facts have been discovered in the twentieth century. The knight of Newbold Revel was arrested at least four times between 1451 and 1468 and variously charged with assault, extortion, breaking prison, theft, violently breaking into a monastery and carrying off jewels and money, with rape and robbery and cattle-stealing, and finally with sedition. It is difficult, as Sir Edmund Chambers and others have remarked, to believe such things of the man who introduces in the *Morte Darthur* such verdicts as: "What!" said Sir Launcelot, "is he a thief and a knight and a ravisher of women? He doth shame unto the order of knighthood, and contrary unto his oath; it is pity that he liveth." Indeed, there is a fair chance the crimes in the record were legal rather than real. It is from the lawyers that we get the charges, and in the courts of the fifteenth century evidence was not very scientifically sifted. It was not hard to bring charges against an enemy; medieval authorities seemed to consider the violence of the indictment more than half the court battle. All save one of these offenses were allegedly committed in 1451 and 1452, and Malory seems to have escaped with but brief periods of incarceration. The charge of sedition, however, had put him in prison at least by 1468, and, for all we know, kept him there until his death in 1471.

The family of Sir Thomas Malory of Newbold Revel was good and his early career was distinguished. In his youth he had served under Richard Beauchamp, Earl of Warwick, whose early career resembles that of Chaucer's Knight, and whom the Emperor Sigismund gratefully called "Father of Courtesy." In 1445, some years after he had succeeded his father, Malory sat in Parliament. His difficulties in 1451 seem to have centered in a dispute, probably over lands, with a monastery, and his later trouble may have risen because he was a Lancastrian partisan. If that is the case, it is ironical that Caxton, the printer of his book, enjoyed extensive Yorkist patronage. Malory tells us that he ended his book in the ninth year (1469–1470) of King Edward's reign, and we may safely assume that it had served to while away his dreary hours in prison.

One of the most important literary discoveries of the twentieth century was made in 1934 when Mr. W. F. Oakeshott, the librarian of Winchester College, found in the college library a manuscript of Malory's Arthurian romances. This, the only known manuscript of Malory's great work, is roughly contemporary with Caxton's printed version of the *Morte Darthur* (1485), but independent of it. Since it differs in many respects from Caxton's version, we are now able to see what cuts and alterations Caxton made, and to see for the first time from the fuller text of the manuscript, although it is not an autograph copy, the text of the *Morte Darthur* essentially as it left Malory's hands. The manuscript has been edited, with introductions and invaluable notes, by Professor Eugène Vinaver in three volumes entitled *The Works of Sir Thomas Malory*, Oxford University Press, 1947. In his earlier study, *Malory* (Oxford, 1929), Professor Vinaver had provided the most comprehensive study of the newly discovered biographical material.

The title of Professor Vinaver's edition is significant, for, as he shows, Malory wrote not one long romance but eight short ones. It was Caxton who combined the eight into one, and gave to the whole combination the title of the last one. There is, thus, no point in attempting to establish the unity of what for more than four centuries has been known as the *Morte Darthur*. Professor Vinaver proves clearly that this great prose narrative was not originally composed in the form and order in which Caxton gave it to us, beginning with Arthur's birth and early years, proceeding through his wars and victories, meandering through bypaths of chivalric adventures and searching for the Holy Grail, and finally moving on to the triangular tragedy of Arthur and Launcelot and Guenever, the downfall of the court, and the passing of Arthur. Such unity as the *Morte Darthur* has was imparted by Caxton, who arranged the material chronologically as best he could.

Of Malory's methods in compiling his romances

Professor Vinaver corroborates the traditional opinion, that Malory had drawn on a huge cycle of French prose romances and a few Middle English sources, but he establishes the significant fact, not hitherto suspected, that Malory first became familiar with the Arthurian legend not through "French books," but through an English poem, the fourteenth-century alliterative *Morte Arthure*. "It is a new and helpful sidelight on the continuity of the English tradition," says Professor Vinaver, "that by the time Malory came to 'reduce' his French books into English his attitude to Arthurian knighthood had been fixed in his mind by his reading of native poetry." Malory thus takes his place in the general line of progress of English prose and English literature, and an important place it is. Professor Vinaver shows that Malory is the real ancestor of the writers of modern fiction. His narrative method is strikingly different from that of medieval writers. Whereas a medieval cycle of romances is like a tapestry, with many threads interwoven in an intricate pattern, Malory breaks up the threads and makes a series of individual stories.

However much he may have disliked or misunderstood some of the trappings of chivalry, there can be no doubt of Malory's enthusiasm for knighthood and the ideal knight. He unquestionably felt that here his book would furnish an inspiration and a corrective for his own age, so tarnished by the wholesale proscriptions and abrupt executions of the Wars of the Roses. Sir Ector's eulogy of the dead Launcelot (see page 157) sums up, if with a certain confusion, Malory's conception of the perfect knight. With it we may compare Chaucer's portrait of his Knight (see page 98) and Froissart's remarks on Guichard d'Angle, Earl of Huntington: "And truly this gentyll knyght was well worthy to have honoure, for in his tyme he had all noble vertues that a knyght ought to have; he was mery, true, amorous, sage, secrete, large, prewe, hardy, adventurous and chyvalrous." Malory does not give us nearly so complete a picture of the Middle Ages as Chaucer. But the *Morte Darthur* reflects faithfully certain phases of medieval thought and life, especially the chivalric ideals (in the first half of the book) and the ideals of Christianity as the Middle Ages understood them (in the second half). Malory's lack of humor would doubtless have made him distressed by such modern treatments of his world of knights and ladies as Mark Twain's *A Connecticut Yankee at King Arthur's Court*, John Erskine's *Galahad*, or even by T. H. White's delightful novels, *The Sword in the Stone* and *The Witch in the Wood*.

More than any other factor, Malory's presentation has been responsible for the continued popularity of the Arthurian story in the English-speaking world, and especially for its amazing vitality in the nineteenth and twentieth centuries. The *Morte Darthur*, as Caxton gave it to us, has been the source-book of the legends that have had the greatest influence upon later English writers. Indeed, no other single compilation of material except the Bible has supplied so much of spirit and ideals and substance to so many. Milton and Tennyson and William Morris, and, in America, Edwin Arlington Robinson—to name but a few—have used the *Morte Darthur* with pleasure and profit to themselves and their readers.

Malory's simple, flexible, and lucid style made his narrative the first extensive piece of English prose that has been read with enjoyment and comprehension by succeeding generations. Sir Walter Scott called the *Morte Darthur* "indisputably the best prose romance the language can boast." Malory's "ringing prose," as it has been called, left its mark on the style of the King James Version of the Bible, and is so individual and picturesque as to be unforgettable. The general reading public which has been first introduced to a knowledge of Arthur and his knights in juvenile paraphrases, and then has gone on to Tennyson's perverted if sonorous versions, will always find in Malory a miraculous combination of sense and style. There are phrases of pure magic, as when the young Arthur "lightly and fiercely" draws the sword from the stone, and fine examples of economy in words and temper, as when, after a particularly bombastic challenge from Sir Turquine, Sir Launcelot retorts, "That is overmuch said." There are superb tributes to knightly prowess which no poet could improve upon: "The best of us all had been full cold at the heart-root had not Sir Launcelot often been better than we." And no declaration of love in our literature can compare with the confession of the Fair Maid of Astolat to Gawaine concerning Launcelot: "Nay truly, I know not his name nor from whence he cometh, but to say that I love him, I promise you and God that I love him."

Space permits the reprinting here of only a small portion of what its first printer called a "noble and joyous history." We have chosen from the latter part Malory's idyll of true love and the end of the story, in which the author gives us the tragic result of the conflict of loyalties involved in Launcelot's feudal devotion to his king and his love of the king's wife, Guenever.

from LE MORTE DARTHUR

CAXTON'S PREFACE[1]

William Caxton (*c.* 1424–*c.* 1491), even apart from his own writings unquestionably one of the greatest practical benefactors English literature ever had, was born in Kent. We know little specific about his family, but his parents were well connected enough to be able to apprentice him in 1438 to Robert Large, a prominent member of the wealthy Mercers' Company. When Large died in 1441 Caxton's apprenticeship was still unfinished, and it would appear that he went to complete it at Bruges, one of the great Flemish textile cities. For more than thirty years Bruges was his home, and there he rose to a position of affluence and influence, being at one time governor of the English Nation. We may assume that he had long had an interest in literature and that he gladly agreed to the request of Margaret, Duchess of Burgundy, sister to Edward IV of England, that he should carry to completion a translation of Raoul le Fèvre's *Le recueil des histoires de Troyes*. Caxton was in Cologne in 1471–1472 and there, no doubt, he learned the printer's trade. Returning to Bruges, he took a partner and established a printing office, from which in 1474 came Caxton's *Recuyell of the Historyes of Troye*, the first English book to appear in print.

In 1476 he came back to England, set up a shop in the precincts of Westminster Abbey and, probably after a number of undated pamphlets and books, brought forth Lord Rivers's translation, *The Dictes or Sayengis of the Philosophres*, in 1477. There is romance and high adventure in what Caxton had done. When nearly fifty, an age proportionally far more advanced then than now, he had turned from the mercantile routine of a lifetime to literature and, what is more amazing, to the practice of a new mechanical craft. By the time that he was fifty-three he had printed the first books in English and in England.

From then until his death, probably in 1491, he labored at a prodigious rate as author, translator, editor, and printer. The list of his works testifies amply to his literary taste, piety, patriotism, and, what is sometimes overlooked, sound sense of that which would, as well as should, sell. There is no space here to list the hundred books which are known to have issued from Caxton's shop. Among the English "classics" he printed much of Chaucer, Gower's *Confessio Amantis*, some of John Lydgate, and the *Morte Darthur* of his contemporary, Sir Thomas Malory. His own translations were many and often extensive, ranging from the *Distichs* of Cato to the *Golden Legend*, from the *Game and Playe of the Chesse* to the *Mirrour of the World*, from the *History of Jason* to *Charles the Grete*, and from the *Eneydos* to *Reynard the Fox*. We do not expect great originality or stylistic excellence in translations, especially when the sources are often themselves undistinguished, but Caxton's style was adequate, and on occasion he did not hesitate to amplify his originals. The Prologues and Epilogues to his various books afford the best clue to a sound, stimulating, and often whimsical personality. The debt which the English Renaissance owes to William Caxton can never be adequately expressed.

Two useful and informative books on Caxton are Henry R. Plomer's *William Caxton*, Small, Maynard, 1925, and Nellie S. Aurner, *Caxton, Mirrour of Fifteenth Century Letters*, Houghton Mifflin, 1926.

[1] *Caxton's Preface.* In Caxton's preface and in the selections from the *Morte Darthur* modern typographical usage with respect to spelling, capitalization, and punctuation have, so far as possible, been followed.

AFTER that I had accomplished and finished divers histories, as well of contemplation as of other historical and worldly acts of great conquerors and princes, and also certain books of ensamples and doctrine, many noble and divers gentlemen of this realm of England came and demanded me many and oft times, wherefore that I have not do made and imprinted the noble history of the Saint Grail, and of the most renowned Christian king, first and chief of the three best Christian, and worthy, King Arthur, which ought most to be remembered among us Englishmen tofore all other Christian kings; for it is notoriously known through the universal world, that there be nine worthy and the best that ever were, that is to wit, three Paynims, three Jews, and three Christian men. As for the Paynims, they were tofore the Incarnation of Christ, which were named, the first Hector of Troy, of whom the history is common both in ballad and in prose, the second Alexander the Great, and the third Julius Caesar, Emperor of Rome, of whom the histories be well known and had. And as for the three Jews, which also were tofore the Incarnation of our Lord, of whom the first was duke Joshua which brought the children of Israel into the land of behest, the second David, king of Jerusalem, and the third Judas Maccabeus, of these three the Bible rehearseth all their noble histories and acts. And sith the said Incarnation have been three noble Christian men, stalled and admitted through the universal world into the number of the nine best and worthy. Of whom was first the noble Arthur, whose noble acts I purpose to write in this present book here following. The second was Charlemagne, or Charles the Great, of whom the history is had in many places,

4. **ensamples,** illustrative instances. 7. **do made,** had made. 8. **Saint,** holy. 10. **worthy,** one of the nine worthies. 12. **tofore,** before. 13. **notoriously,** admittedly. 25. **behest,** promise. 28. **sith,** since. 30. **stalled,** placed.

both in French and in English. And the third and last was Godfrey of Bouillon, of whose acts and life I made a book unto the excellent prince and king of noble memory, King Edward the Fourth.

The said noble gentlemen instantly required me to imprint the history of the said noble king and conqueror King Arthur, and of his knights, with the history of the Saint Grail, and of the death and ending of the said Arthur; affirming that I ought rather to imprint his acts and noble feats, than of Godfrey of Bouillon, or any of the other eight, considering that he was a man born within this realm, and king and emperor of the same: and that there be in French divers and many noble volumes of his acts, and also of his knights. To whom I answered that divers men hold opinion that there was no such Arthur, and that all such books as been made of him be feigned and fables, because that some chronicles make of him no mention, nor remember him nothing, nor of his knights. Whereto they answered, and one in special said, that in him that should say or think that there was never such a king called Arthur might well be aretted great folly and blindness. For he said that there were many evidences of the contrary. First ye may see his sepulchre in the monastery of Glastonbury. And also in *Polychronicon*, in the fifth book the sixth chapter, and in the seventh book the twenty-third chapter, where his body was buried, and after found, and translated into the said monastery. Ye shall see also in the history of Boccaccio, in his book *De Casu Principum*, part of his noble acts, and also of his fall. Also Galfridus in his British book recounteth his life: and in divers places of England many remembrances be yet of him, and shall remain perpetually, and also of his knights. First in the Abbey of Westminster, at St. Edward's shrine, remaineth the print of his seal in red wax closed in beryl, in which is written, *Patricius Arthurus Britannie, Gallie, Germanie, Dacie, Imperator.* Item, in the castle of Dover ye may see Gawaine's skull, and Cradok's mantle; at Winchester the Round Table; at other places Launcelot's sword and many other things. Then all these things considered, there can no man reasonably gainsay but there was a king of this land named Arthur. For in all places, Christian and heathen, he is reputed and taken for one of the nine worthy, and the first of the three Christian men. And also, he is more spoken of beyond the sea, more books made of his noble acts than there be in England, as well in Dutch, Italian, Spanish, and Greek, as in French. And yet of record remain in witness of him in Wales, in the town of Camelot, the great stones and marvellous works of iron lying under the ground, and royal vaults, which divers now living hath seen. Wherefore it is a marvel why he is no more renowned in his own country, save only it accordeth to the Word of God, which saith that no man is accepted for a prophet in his own country.

Then all these things aforesaid alleged, I could not well deny but that there was such a noble king named Arthur, and reputed one of the nine worthy, and first and chief of the Christian men. And many noble volumes be made of him and of his noble knights in French, which I have seen and read beyond the sea, which be not had in our maternal tongue. But in Welsh be many and also in French, and some in English but nowhere nigh all. Wherefore, such as have late been drawn out briefly into English I have after the simple conning that God hath sent to me, under the favour and correction of all noble lords and gentlemen, emprised to imprint a book of the noble histories of the said King Arthur, and of certain of his knights, after a copy unto me delivered, which copy Sir Thomas Malory did take out of certain books of French, and reduced it into English. And I, according to my copy, have done set it in imprint, to the intent that noble men may see and learn the noble acts of chivalry, the gentle and virtuous deeds that some knights used in those days, by which they came to honour, and how they

2. Godfrey of Bouillon (*c.* 1060–1100), one of the leaders of the First Crusade. After the capture of Jerusalem in 1099 he was made the first head of the new kingdom. **4–5. Edward the Fourth** (1442–1483), became king of England in 1461. His sons Edward (briefly king) and Richard were murdered in the Tower at the order of their father's brother Richard; see Shakespeare's *Richard the Third*. **23. aretted,** charged with. **26. *Polychronicon*,** a highly popular universal history by Ranulph, or Ralph, Higden (*c.* 1299–1363), was translated from Latin into English by John of Trevisa (d. 1412), in 1387. Trevisa's translation, in "modernized" form, was printed by Caxton in 1482. **29. translated,** moved. **31. *De . . . Principum*,** Boccaccio's *De Casibus Virorum Illustrium* inspired Chaucer's "Monk's Tale" and was translated into English by Lydgate from a French version. **33. British book.** Geoffrey of Monmouth's *Historia Regum Britanniae*, drawn, doubtless, from oral and written sources, contains the first full-length picture of Arthur. **36. St. Edward's,** of Edward the Confessor.

1. beryl, a transparent precious stone. **4. Cradok's mantle,** a reference to an amusing by-product of Arthurian romance. In the ballad of "The Boy and the Mantle" (Child 29) a boy brings to Arthur's Court a mantle which will not fit a wife who has "done amisse." The wife of Cradok (Cradoc) is the only lady who can wear it, and other proof is given that Cradok is no cuckold. **16. Camelot,** not safely identified with any modern locality. **33. conning,** understanding. **35. emprised,** undertaken. **39. reduced,** translated.

that were vicious were punished and oft put to shame and rebuke; humbly beseeching all noble lords and ladies, with all other estates, of what estate or degree they been of, that shall see and read in this said book and work, that they take the good and honest acts in their remembrance, and follow the same. Wherein they shall find many joyous and pleasant histories, and noble and renowned acts of humanity, gentleness, and chivalry. For herein may be seen noble chivalry, courtesy, humanity, friendliness, hardiness, love, friendship, cowardice, murder, hate, virtue, and sin. Do after the good and leave the evil, and it shall bring you to good fame and renown. And for to pass the time this book shall be pleasant to read in, but for to give faith and belief that all is true that is contained herein, ye be at your liberty: but all is written for our doctrine, and for to beware that we fall not to vice nor sin, but to exercise and follow virtue, by which we may come and attain to good fame and renown in this life, and after this short and transitory life to come unto everlasting bliss in heaven; the which He grant us that reigneth in heaven, the blessed Trinity. Amen.

Then to proceed forth in this said book, which I direct unto all noble princes, lords and ladies, gentlemen or gentlewomen, that desire to read or hear read of the noble and joyous history of the great conqueror and excellent king, King Arthur, sometime king of this noble realm, then called Britain; I, William Caxton, simple person, present this book following, which I have emprised to imprint: and treateth of the noble acts, feats of arms of chivalry, prowess, hardiness, humanity, love, courtesy, and very gentleness, with many wonderful histories and adventures. And for to understand briefly the content of this volume, I have divided it into twenty-one books, and every book chaptered, as hereafter shall by God's grace follow. . . .

BOOK XVIII

Chapter 25: *How true love is likened to summer.*

AND thus it passed on from Candlemass until after Easter, that the month of May was come, when every lusty heart beginneth to blossom, and to bring forth fruit; for like as herbs and trees bring forth fruit and flourish in May, in likewise every lusty heart, that is in any manner a lover, springeth and flourisheth in lusty deeds. For it giveth unto all lovers courage, that lusty month of May, in something to constrain him to some manner of thing more in that month than in any other month, for divers causes. For then all herbs and trees renew a man and woman, and in likewise lovers call again to their mind old gentleness and old service, and many kind deeds that were forgotten by negligence. For like as winter rasure doth alway arase and deface green summer, so fareth it by unstable love in man and woman. For in many persons there is no stability; for we may see all day, for a little blast of winter's rasure, anon we shall deface and lay apart true love for little or nought, that cost much thing. This is no wisdom nor stability, but it is feebleness of nature and great disworship, whomsoever useth this.

Therefore, like as May month flowereth and flourisheth in many gardens, so in likewise let every man of worship flourish his heart in this world, first unto God, and next unto the joy of them that he promised his faith unto; for there was never worshipful man nor worshipful woman, but they loved one better than another; and worship in arms may never be foiled, but first reserve the honour to God, and secondly the quarrel must come of thy lady: and such love I call virtuous love.

But nowadays men cannot love seven night but they must have all their desires: that love may not endure by reason; for where they be soon accorded, and hasty heat, soon it cooleth. Right so fareth love nowadays, soon hot soon cold: this is no stability. But the old love was not so; men and women could love together seven years, and no lycours lusts were between them, and then there was love, truth, and faithfulness: and lo, in likewise was used love in King Arthur's days. Wherefore I liken love nowadays unto summer and winter; for like as the one is hot and the other cold, so fareth love nowadays. Therefore all ye that be lovers, call unto your remembrance the month of May, like as did Queen Guenever, for whom I make here a little mention, that while she lived she was a true lover, and therefore she had a good end.

BOOK XXI

Chapter 1: *How Sir Mordred presumed and took on him to be King of England, and would have married the Queen, his father's wife.*

AS Sir Mordred was ruler of all England, he did do make letters as though that they came from

17. doctrine, teaching. See Romans 13:4, and Chaucer's "Nun's Priest's Tale," lines 621–22, page 132.

51. do make, have made.

beyond the sea, and the letters specified that King Arthur was slain in battle with Sir Launcelot. Wherefore Sir Mordred made a parliament, and called the lords together, and there he made them to choose him king; and so was he crowned at Canterbury, and held a feast there fifteen days; and afterward he drew him unto Winchester, and there he took the Queen Guenever, and said plainly that he would wed her which was his uncle's wife and his father's wife. And so he made ready for the feast, and a day prefixed that they should be wedded; wherefore Queen Guenever was passing heavy. But she durst not discover her heart, but spake fair and agreed to Sir Mordred's will. Then she desired of Sir Mordred for to go to London, to buy all manner of things that longed unto the wedding. And because of her fair speech Sir Mordred trusted her well enough and gave her leave to go. And so when she came to London she took the Tower of London, and suddenly in all haste possible she stuffed it with all manner of victual, and well garnished it with men, and so kept it.

Then when Sir Mordred wist and understood how he was beguiled he was passing wroth out of measure. And a short tale for to make, he went and laid a mighty siege about the Tower of London, and made many great assaults thereat, and threw many great engines unto them, and shot great guns. But all might not prevail Sir Mordred, for Queen Guenever would never for fair speech nor for foul trust to come in his hands again.

Then came the Bishop of Canterbury, the which was a noble clerk and an holy man, and thus he said to Sir Mordred: "Sir, what will ye do? Will ye first displease God and sithen shame yourself, and all knighthood? Is not King Arthur your uncle, no farther but your mother's brother, and on her himself King Arthur begat you upon his own sister, therefore how may you wed your father's wife? Sir," said the noble clerk, "leave this opinion or I shall curse you with book and bell and candle." "Do thou thy worst," said Sir Mordred, "wit thou well I shall defy thee." "Sir," said the Bishop, "and wit you well I shall not fear me to do that me ought to do. Also where ye noise where my lord Arthur is slain, and that is not so, and therefore ye will make a foul work in this land." "Peace, thou false priest," said Sir Mordred, "for an thou chafe me any more I shall make strike off thy head." So the Bishop departed and did the cursing in the most orgulist wise that might be done. And then Sir Mordred sought the Bishop of Canterbury, for to have slain him. Then the Bishop fled, and took part of his goods with him, and went nigh unto Glastonbury; and there he was as priest-hermit in a chapel, and lived in poverty and in holy prayers, for well he understood that mischievous war was at hand.

Then Sir Mordred sought on Queen Guenever by letters and sonds, and by fair means and foul means, for to have her to come out of the Tower of London; but all this availed not, for she answered him shortly, openly and privily, that she had liefer slay herself than to be married with him. Then came word to Sir Mordred that King Arthur had araised the siege for Sir Launcelot, and he was coming homeward with a great host to be avenged upon Sir Mordred; wherefore Sir Mordred made write writs to all the barony of this land, and much people drew to him. For then was the common voice among them that with Arthur was none other life but war and strife, and with Sir Mordred was great joy and bliss. Thus was Sir Arthur depraved, and evil said of. And many there were that King Arthur had made up of nought, and given them lands, might not then say him a good word. Lo ye, all Englishmen, see ye not what a mischief here was! For he that was the most king and knight of the world, and most loved the fellowship of noble knights, and by him they were all upholden, now might not these Englishmen hold them content with him. Lo, thus was the old custom and usage of this land; and also men say that we of this land have not yet lost nor forgotten that custom and usage. Alas, this is a great default of us Englishmen, for there may no thing please us no term. And so fared the people at that time, they were better pleased with Sir Mordred than they were with King Arthur; and much people drew unto Sir Mordred, and said they would abide with him for better and for worse. And so Sir Mordred drew with a great host to Dover, for there he heard say that Sir Arthur would arrive, and so he thought to beat his own father from his lands; and the most part of all England held with Sir Mordred, the people were so new-fangle.

1–2. King Arthur . . . Launcelot. Arthur had invaded Launcelot's country of Benwick in France, for "Sir Launcelot and his nephews were lords of all France." **9. uncle's . . . wife.** Mordred was the offspring of an incestuous, though casual, union between Arthur and his own sister. **11. prefixed,** appointed. **12–13. wherefore . . . heavy.** In some of the earlier versions Guenever was Mordred's willing mistress. **16. longed unto,** concerned. **22. garnished,** supplied. **28. engines,** catapults and the like. **guns,** an obvious anachronism. **35. sithen,** afterwards. **41. curse,** excommunicate. **45. noise,** report.

3. an, if. **5. orgulist,** proudest, most ceremonious. **14. sonds,** messages. **19. araised,** lifted. **27. depraved,** defamed. **39–40. Alas . . . term.** The Wars of the Roses had given sufficient examples of this. **50. new-fangle,** fond of novelty.

Chapter 2: *How after that King Arthur had tidings, he returned and came to Dover, where Sir Mordred met him to let his landing; and of the death of Sir Gawaine.*

AND so as Sir Mordred was at Dover with his host, there came King Arthur with a great navy of ships and galleys and carracks. And there was Sir Mordred ready awaiting upon his landing, to let his own father to land upon the land that he was king over. Then there was launching of great boats and small, and full of noble men of arms, and there was much slaughter of gentle knights, and many a full bold baron was laid full low on both parties. But King Arthur was so courageous that there might no manner of knights let him to land, and his knights fiercely followed him; and so they landed maugre Sir Mordred and all his power, and put Sir Mordred aback, that he fled and all his people.

So when this battle was done, King Arthur let bury his people that were dead. And then was noble Sir Gawaine found in a great boat, lying more than half dead. When Sir Arthur wist that Sir Gawaine was laid so low, he went unto him; and there the king made sorrow out of measure, and took Sir Gawaine in his arms, and thrice he there swooned. And then when he awaked, he said: "Alas, Sir Gawaine, my sister's son, here now thou liest, the man in the world that I loved most; and now is my joy gone, for now, my nephew Sir Gawaine, I will discover me unto your person: in Sir Launcelot and you I most had my joy and mine affiance, and now have I lost my joy of you both; wherefore all mine earthly joy is gone from me." "Mine uncle, King Arthur," said Sir Gawaine, "wit you well my death-day is come, and all is through mine own hastiness and wilfulness; for I am smitten upon the old wound the which Sir Launcelot gave me, on the which I feel well I must die; and had Sir Launcelot been with you as he was, this unhappy war had never begun; and of all this am I causer, for Sir Launcelot and his blood, through their prowess, held all your cankered enemies in subjection and daunger. And now," said Sir Gawaine, "ye shall miss Sir Launcelot. But alas, I would not accord with him, and therefore," said Sir Gawaine, "I pray you, fair uncle, that I may have paper, pen, and ink, that I may write to Sir Launcelot a cedle with mine own hands."

And then when paper and ink was brought, then Gawaine was set up weakly by King Arthur, for he was shriven a little tofore; and then he wrote thus, as the French book maketh mention: "Unto Sir Launcelot, flower of all noble knights that ever I heard of or saw by my days, I, Sir Gawaine, King Lot's son of Orkney, sister's son unto the noble King Arthur, send thee greeting, and let thee have knowledge that the tenth day of May I was smitten upon the old wound that thou gavest me afore the city of Benwick, and through the same wound that thou gavest me I am come to my death-day. And I will that all the world wit, that I, Sir Gawaine, knight of the Table Round, sought my death, and not through thy deserving, but it was mine own seeking; wherefore I beseech thee, Sir Launcelot, to return again unto this realm, and see my tomb, and pray some prayer more or less for my soul. And this same day that I wrote this cedle, I was hurt to the death in the same wound, the which I had of thy hand, Sir Launcelot; for of a more nobler man might I not be slain. Also Sir Launcelot, for all the love that ever was betwixt us, make no tarrying, but come over the sea in all haste, that thou mayst with thy noble knights rescue that noble king that made thee knight, that is my lord Arthur; for he is full straitly bestead with a false traitor, that is my half-brother, Sir Mordred; and he hath let crown him king, and would have wedded my lady Queen Guenever, and so had he done had she not put herself in the Tower of London. And so the tenth day of May last past, my lord Arthur and we all landed upon them at Dover; and there we put that false traitor, Sir Mordred, to flight, and there it misfortuned me to be stricken upon thy stroke. And at the date of this letter was written, but two hours and a half afore my death, written with mine own hand, and so subscribed with part of my heart's blood. And I require thee, most famous knight of the world, that thou wilt see my tomb." And then Sir Gawaine wept, and King Arthur wept; and then they swooned both. And when they awaked both, the king made Sir Gawaine to receive his Saviour. And then Sir Gawaine prayed the king for to send for Sir Launcelot, and to cherish him above all other knights.

And so at the hour of noon Sir Gawaine yielded up the spirit; and then the king let inter him in a chapel within Dover Castle; and there yet all men may see the skull of him, and the same wound is seen that Sir Launcelot gave him in battle. Then

8. carracks, large ships. **10. let,** prevent. **18. maugre,** despite. **32. discover me,** make known, speak candidly. **34. affiance,** trust. **43. blood,** relatives. **44. cankered,** malignant. **50. cedle,** schedule, short note.

2. weakly, in weak condition. **27. straitly bestead,** closely harassed. **44. his Saviour,** the bread of the Sacrament.

was it told the king that Sir Mordred had pight a new field upon Barham Down. And upon the morn the king rode thither to him, and there was a great battle betwixt them, and much people was slain on both parties; but at the last Sir Arthur's party stood best, and Sir Mordred and his party fled unto Canterbury.

Chapter 3: *How after, Sir Gawaine's ghost appeared to King Arthur, and warned him that he should not fight that day.*

AND then the king let search all the towns for his knights that were slain, and interred them; and salved them with soft salves that so sore were wounded. Then much people drew unto King Arthur. And then they said that Sir Mordred warred upon King Arthur with wrong. And then King Arthur drew him with his host down by the seaside, westward toward Salisbury; and there was a day assigned betwixt King Arthur and Sir Mordred, that they should meet upon a down beside Salisbury, and not far from the seaside; and this day was assigned on a Monday after Trinity Sunday, whereof King Arthur was passing glad, that he might be avenged upon Sir Mordred. Then Sir Mordred araised much people about London, for they of Kent, Southsex, and Surrey, Essex, and of Suffolk, and of Norfolk, held the most part with Sir Mordred; and many a full noble knight drew unto Sir Mordred and to the king: but they that loved Sir Launcelot drew unto Sir Mordred.

So upon Trinity Sunday at night, King Arthur dreamed a wonderful dream, and that was this: that him seemed he sat upon a chaflet in a chair, and the chair was fast to a wheel, and thereupon sat King Arthur in the richest cloth of gold that might be made; and the king thought there was under him, far from him, an hideous deep black water, and therein were all manner of serpents, and worms, and wild beasts, foul and horrible; and suddenly the king thought the wheel turned up-so-down, and he fell among the serpents, and every beast took him by a limb; and then the king cried as he lay in his bed and slept, "Help!" And then knights, squires, and yeomen awaked the king; and then he was so amazed that he wist not where he was; and then he fell a-slumbering again, not sleeping nor thoroughly waking. So the king seemed verily that there came Sir Gawaine unto him with a number of fair ladies with him. And when King Arthur saw him, then he said: "Welcome, my sister's son; I weened thou hadst been dead, and now I see thee alive, much am I beholden unto almighty Jesu. O fair nephew and my sister's son, what be these ladies that hither be come with you?" "Sir," said Sir Gawaine, "all these be ladies for whom I have foughten when I was man living, and all these are those that I did battle for in righteous quarrel; and God hath given them that grace at their great prayer, because I did battle for them, that they should bring me hither unto you: thus much hath God given me leave, for to warn you of your death; for an ye fight as tomorn with Sir Mordred, as ye both have assigned, doubt ye not ye must be slain, and the most part of your people on both parties. And for the great grace and goodness that almighty Jesu hath unto you, and for pity of you, and many more other good men there shall be slain, God hath sent me to you of his special grace, to give you warning that in no wise ye do battle as tomorn, but that ye take a treaty for a month day; and proffer you largely, so as tomorn to be put in a delay. For within a month shall come Sir Launcelot with all his noble knights, and rescue you worshipfully, and slay Sir Mordred, and all that ever will hold with him." Then Sir Gawaine and all the ladies vanished.

And anon the king called upon his knights, squires, and yeomen, and charged them wightly to fetch his noble lords and wise bishops unto him. And when they were come, the king told them his avision, what Sir Gawaine had told him, and warned him that if he fought on the morn he should be slain. Then the king commanded Sir Lucan the Butler, and his brother Sir Bedivere, with two bishops with them, and charged them in any wise, an they might, "Take a treaty for a month day with Sir Mordred, and spare not, proffer him lands and goods as much as ye think best." So then they departed, and came to Sir Mordred, where he had a grim host of an hundred thousand men. And there they entreated Sir Mordred long time; and at the last Sir Mordred was agreed for to have Cornwall and Kent, by Arthur's days: after, all England, after the days of King Arthur.

Chapter 4: *How by misadventure of an adder the battle began, where Mordred was slain, and Arthur hurt to the death.*

THEN were they condescended that King Arthur and Sir Mordred should meet betwixt both their hosts, and each of them should bring

1–2. pight . . . Down, prepared for battle (in Kent). **23. Trinity Sunday,** the Sunday after Whitsunday. **34. chaflet,** platform (?). **48. seemed, thought.**

21. month day, the space of a month. **largely,** generously. **28. wightly,** valiantly. **43. by,** during. **49. condescended,** agreed.

fourteen persons; and they came with this word unto Arthur. Then said he: "I am glad that this is done"; and so he went into the field. And when Arthur should depart, he warned all his host that an they see any sword drawn: "Look ye come on fiercely, and slay that traitor, Sir Mordred, for I in no wise trust him." In like wise Sir Mordred warned his host that: "An ye see any sword drawn, look that ye come on fiercely, and so slay all that ever before you standeth; for in no wise I will not trust for this treaty, for I know well my father will be avenged on me." And so they met as their appointment was, and so they were agreed and accorded thoroughly; and wine was fetched, and they drank. Right soon came an adder out of a little heath bush, and it stung a knight on the foot. And when the knight felt him stung, he looked down and saw the adder, and then he drew his sword to slay the adder, and thought of none other harm. And when the host on both parties saw that sword drawn, then they blew bemes, trumpets, and horns, and shouted grimly. And so both hosts dressed them together. And King Arthur took his horse, and said: "Alas this unhappy day!" and so rode to his party. And Sir Mordred in like wise. And never was there seen a more dolefuller battle in no Christian land; for there was but rushing and riding, foining and striking, and many a deadly stroke. But ever King Arthur rode throughout the battle of Sir Mordred many times, and did full nobly as a noble king should, and at all times he fainted never; and Sir Mordred that day put him in devoir, and in great peril. And thus they fought all the long day, and never stinted till the noble knights were laid to the cold earth; and ever they fought still till it was near night, and by that time was there an hundred thousand laid dead upon the down. Then was Arthur wood wroth out of measure, when he saw his people so slain from him.

Then the king looked about him, and then was he ware, of all his host and of all his good knights, were left no more alive but two knights; that one was Sir Lucan the Butler, and his brother Sir Bedivere, and they were full sore wounded. "Jesu mercy," said the king, "where are all my noble knights become? Alas that ever I should see this doleful day, for now," said Arthur, "I am come to mine end. But would to God that I wist where were that traitor Sir Mordred, that hath caused all this mischief." Then was King Arthur ware where Sir Mordred leaned upon his sword among a great heap of dead men. "Now give me my spear," said Arthur unto Sir Lucan, "for yonder I have espied the traitor that all this woe hath wrought." "Sir, let him be," said Sir Lucan, "for he is unhappy; and if ye pass this unhappy day ye shall be right well revenged upon him. Good lord, remember ye of your night's dream, and what the spirit of Sir Gawaine told you this night, yet God of his great goodness hath preserved you hitherto. Therefore, for God's sake, my lord, leave off by this, for blessed be God ye have won the field, for here we be three on live, and with Sir Mordred is none on live; and if ye leave off now this wicked day of destiny is past." "Tide me death, betide me life," saith the king, "now I see him yonder alone he shall never escape mine hands, for at a better avail shall I never have him." "God speed you well," said Sir Bedivere.

Then the king gat his spear in both his hands, and ran toward Sir Mordred, crying: "Traitor, now is thy death-day come." And when Sir Mordred heard Sir Arthur, he ran until him with his sword drawn in his hand. And there King Arthur smote Sir Mordred under the shield, with a foin of his spear, throughout the body, more than a fathom. And when Sir Mordred felt that he had his death wound he thrust himself with the might that he had up to the burr of King Arthur's spear. And right so he smote his father Arthur, with his sword held in both his hands, on the side of the head, that the sword pierced the helmet and the brain-pan, and therewithal Sir Mordred fell stark dead to the earth; and the noble Arthur fell in a swoon to the earth, and there he swooned ofttimes. And Sir Lucan the Butler and Sir Bedivere ofttimes heaved him up. And so weakly they led him betwixt them both, to a little chapel not far from the seaside. And when the king was there he thought him well eased.

Then heard they people cry in the field. "Now go thou, Sir Lucan," said the king, "and do me to wit what betokens that noise in the field." So Sir Lucan departed, for he was grievously wounded in many places. And so as he yede, he saw and hearkened by the moonlight, how that pillers and robbers were come into the field, to pill and to rob many a full noble knight of brooches and beads, of many a good ring, and of many a rich jewel; and who that were not dead all out, there they slew them for their harness and their riches. When Sir Lucan understood this work, he came to the king

21. bemes, trumpets. **22. dressed them,** went. **28. foining,** thrusting. **29. battle,** army. **32. put . . . devoir,** did his knightly duty. **38. wood,** mad.

4. unhappy, troublesome. **12. on live,** alive. **16. avail,** advantage. **23. foin,** thrust. **27. burr,** the ring on a spear just behind the place for the hand. **43. yede,** went. **44. pillers,** thieves. **48. all out,** completely.

as soon as he might, and told him all what he had heard and seen. "Therefore by my rede," said Sir Lucan, "it is best that we bring you to some town." "I would it were so," said the king.

Chapter 5: *How King Arthur commanded to cast his sword Excalibur into the water, and how he was delivered to ladies in a barge.*

BUT I may not stand, mine head works so. Ah Sir Launcelot," said King Arthur, "this day have I sore missed thee: alas, that ever I was against thee, for now have I my death, whereof Sir Gawaine me warned in my dream." Then Sir Lucan took up the king the one part, and Sir Bedivere the other part, and in the lifting the king swooned; and Sir Lucan fell in a swoon with the lift, that the part of his guts fell out of his body, and therewith the noble knight's heart brast. And when the king awoke, he beheld Sir Lucan, how he lay foaming at the mouth, and part of his guts lay at his feet. "Alas," said the king, "this is to me a full heavy sight, to see this noble duke so die for my sake, for he would have holpen me, that had more need of help than I. Alas, he would not complain him, his heart was so set to help me: now Jesu have mercy upon his soul!" Then Sir Bedivere wept for the death of his brother. "Leave this mourning and weeping," said the king, "for all this will not avail me, for wit thou well an I might live myself, the death of Sir Lucan would grieve me evermore; but my time hieth fast," said the king. "Therefore," said Arthur unto Sir Bedivere, "take thou Excalibur, my good sword, and go with it to yonder water-side, and when thou comest there I charge thee throw my sword in that water, and come again and tell me what thou there seest." "My lord, said Bedivere, "your commandment shall be done, and lightly bring you word again."

So Sir Bedivere departed, and by the way he beheld that noble sword, that the pommel and the haft was all of precious stones; and then he said to himself: "If I throw this rich sword in the water, thereof shall never come good, but harm and loss." And then Sir Bedivere hid Excalibur under a tree. And so, as soon as he might, he came again unto the king, and said he had been at the water, and had thrown the sword in the water. "What saw thou there?" said the king. "Sir," he said, "I saw nothing but waves and winds." "That is untruly said of thee," said the king, "therefore go thou lightly again, and do my commandment; as thou art to me lief and dear, spare not, but throw it in." Then Sir Bedivere returned again, and took the sword in his hand; and then him thought sin and shame to throw away that noble sword, and so eft he hid the sword, and returned again, and told to the king that he had been at the water, and done his commandment. "What saw thou there?" said the king. "Sir," he said, "I saw nothing but the waters wap and waves wane." "Ah, traitor untrue," said King Arthur, "now hast thou betrayed me twice. Who would have weened that, thou that has been to me so lief and dear? And thou art named a noble knight, and would betray me for the richness of the sword. But now go again lightly, for thy long tarrying putteth me in great jeopardy of my life, for I have taken cold. And but if thou do now as I bid thee, if ever I may see thee, I shall slay thee with mine own hands; for thou wouldst for my rich sword see me dead."

Then Sir Bedivere departed, and went to the sword, and lightly took it up, and went to the water-side; and there he bound the girdle about the hilts, and then he threw the sword as far into the water as he might; and there came an arm and an hand above the water and met it, and caught it, and so shook it thrice and brandished, and then vanished away the hand with the sword in the water. So Sir Bedivere came again to the king, and told him what he saw. "Alas," said the king, "help me hence, for I dread me I have tarried over long." Then Sir Bedivere took the king upon his back, and so went with him to that water-side. And when they were at the water-side, even fast by the bank hoved a little barge with many fair ladies in it, and among them all was a queen, and all they had black hoods, and all they wept and shrieked when they saw King Arthur. "Now put me into the barge," said the king. And so he did softly; and there received him three queens with great mourning; and so they set them down, and in one of their laps King Arthur laid his head. And then that queen said: "Ah, dear brother, why have ye tarried so long from me? Alas, this wound on your head hath caught over-much cold." And so then they rowed from the land, and Sir Bedivere beheld all those ladies go from him. Then Sir Bedivere cried, "Ah my lord Arthur, what shall become of me, now ye go from me and leave me here alone among mine enemies?" "Comfort thyself," said the king, "and do as well as thou mayst, for in me is no trust for to trust in; for I will into the vale of Avilion to heal me of my grievous wound: and if

2. rede, advice. **10. works,** hurts. **19. brast,** burst. **39. lightly,** quickly

5. eft, again. **9. wap,** beat. **16–17. but if,** unless. **52. Avilion,** Avalon, the abode of the blessed.

thou hear never more of me, pray for my soul." But ever the queens and ladies wept and shrieked, that it was pity to hear. And as soon as Sir Bedivere had lost the sight of the barge, he wept and wailed, and so took the forest; and so he went all that night, and in the morning he was ware betwixt two holts hoar, of a chapel and an hermitage.

Chapter 6: *How Sir Bedivere found him on the morrow dead in an hermitage, and how he abode there with the hermit.*

THEN was Sir Bedivere glad, and thither he went; and when he came into the chapel, he saw where lay an hermit grovelling on all four, there fast by a tomb was new graven. When the hermit saw Sir Bedivere he knew him well, for he was but little tofore Bishop of Canterbury, that Sir Mordred flemed. "Sir," said Bedivere, "what man is there interred that ye pray so fast for?" "Fair son," said the hermit, "I wot not verily, but by deeming. But this night, at midnight, here came a number of ladies, and brought hither a dead corpse, and prayed me to bury him; and here they offered an hundred tapers, and they gave me an hundred bezants." "Alas," said Sir Bedivere, "that was my lord King Arthur, that here lieth buried in this chapel." Then Sir Bedivere swooned; and when he awoke he prayed the hermit he might abide with him still there, to live with fasting and prayers. "For from hence will I never go," said Sir Bedivere, "by my will, but all the days of my life here to pray for my lord Arthur." "Ye are welcome to me," said the hermit, "for I know ye better than ye ween that I do. Ye are the bold Bedivere, and the full noble duke, Sir Lucan the Butler, was your brother." Then Sir Bedivere told the hermit all as ye have heard tofore. So there bode Sir Bedivere with the hermit that was tofore Bishop of Canterbury, and there Sir Bedivere put upon him poor clothes, and served the hermit full lowly in fasting and in prayers.

Thus of Arthur I find never more written in books that be authorised, nor more of the very certainty of his death heard I never read, but thus was he led away in a ship wherein were three queens; that one was King Arthur's sister, Queen Morgan le Fay, the other was the Queen of North-galis, the third was the Queen of the Waste Lands. Also there was Nimue, the chief lady of the lake, that had wedded Pelleas the good knight; and this lady had done much for King Arthur, for she would never suffer Sir Pelleas to be in no place where he should be in danger of his life; and so he lived to the uttermost of his days with her in great rest. More of the death of King Arthur could I never find, but that ladies brought him to his burials; and such one was buried there, that the hermit bare witness that sometime was Bishop of Canterbury, but yet the hermit knew not in certain that he was verily the body of King Arthur; for this tale Sir Bedivere, knight of the Table Round, made it to be written.

Chapter 7: *Of the opinion of some men of the death of King Arthur; and how Queen Guenever made her a nun in Almesbury.*

YET some men say in many parts of England that King Arthur is not dead, but had by the will of our Lord Jesu into another place; and men say that he shall come again, and he shall win the holy cross. I will not say it shall be so, but rather I will say: here in this world he changed his life. But many men say that there is written upon his tomb this verse: *Hic jacet Arthurus, Rex quondam, Rexque futurus.* Thus leave I here Sir Bedivere with the hermit, that dwelled that time in a chapel beside Glastonbury, and there was his hermitage. And so they lived in their prayers, and fastings, and great abstinence. And when Queen Guenever understood that King Arthur was slain, and all the noble knights, Sir Mordred and all the remnant, then the queen stole away, and five ladies with her, and so she went to Almesbury; and there she let make herself a nun, and wore white clothes and black, and great penance she took, as ever did sinful lady in this land, and never creature could make her merry; but lived in fasting, prayers, and alms-deeds, that all manner of people marvelled how virtuously she was changed. Now leave we Queen Guenever in Amesbury, a nun in white clothes and black, and there she was abbess and ruler as reason would; and turn we from her; and speak we of Sir Launcelot du Lake.

Chapter 8: *How when Sir Launcelot heard of the death of King Arthur, and of Sir Gawaine, and other matters, he came into England.*

AND when he heard in his country that Sir Mordred was crowned king in England, and made war against King Arthur, his own father, and

5. took, went into. **6–7. holts hoar,** gray woods. **18. flemed,** put to flight. **21. deeming,** surmise. **25. bezants,** gold coins worth a sovereign or less. **37. bode,** remained. **48. Nimue,** the lady who had betrayed Merlin.

17. had, was taken. **23–24.** *Hic jacet . . . futurus.* Here lies Arthur, King that was, and King that is to be. **32. Almesbury,** Amesbury, in Wiltshire.

would let him to land in his own land; also it was told Sir Launcelot how that Sir Mordred had laid siege about the Tower of London, because the queen would not wed him; then was Sir Launcelot wroth out of measure, and said to his kinsmen: "Alas, that double traitor Sir Mordred, now me repenteth that ever he escaped my hands, for much shame hath he done unto my lord Arthur; for all I feel by the doleful letter that my lord Sir Gawaine sent me, on whose soul Jesu have mercy, that my lord Arthur is full hard bestead. Alas," said Sir Launcelot, "that ever I should live to hear that most noble king that made me knight thus to be overset with his subject in his own realm. And this doleful letter that my lord, Sir Gawaine, hath sent me afore his death, praying me to see his tomb, wit you well his doleful words shall never go from mine heart, for he was a full noble knight as ever was born; and in an unhappy hour was I born that ever I should have that unhap to slay first Sir Gawaine, Sir Gaheris the good knight, and mine own friend Sir Gareth, that full noble knight. Alas, I may say I am unhappy," said Sir Launcelot, "that ever I should do thus unhappily, and, alas, yet might I never have hap to slay that traitor, Sir Mordred."

"Leave your complaints," said Sir Bors, "and first revenge you of the death of Sir Gawaine; and it will be well done that ye see Sir Gawaine's tomb, and secondly that ye revenge my lord Arthur, and my lady Queen Guenever." "I thank you," said Sir Launcelot, "for ever ye will my worship."

Then they made them ready in all the haste that might be, with ships and galleys, with Sir Launcelot and his host to pass into England. And so he passed over the sea till he came to Dover, and there he landed with seven kings, and the number was hideous to behold. Then Sir Launcelot speered of men of Dover where was King Arthur become. Then the people told him how that he was slain, and Sir Mordred and an hundred thousand died on a day; and how Sir Mordred gave King Arthur there the first battle at his landing, and there was good Sir Gawaine slain; and on the morn Sir Mordred fought with the king upon Barham Down, and there the king put Sir Mordred to the worse. "Alas," said Sir Launcelot, "this is the heaviest tidings that ever came to me. Now, fair sirs," said Sir Launcelot, "shew me the tomb of Sir Gawaine." And then certain people of the town brought him into the castle of Dover, and shewed him the tomb. Then Sir Launcelot kneeled down and wept, and prayed heartily for his soul. And that night he made a dole, and all they that would come had as much flesh, fish, wine, and ale, and every man and woman had twelve pence, come who would. Thus with his own hand dealt he this money, in a mourning gown; and ever he wept, and prayed them to pray for the soul of Sir Gawaine. And on the morn all the priests and clerks that might be gotten in the country were there, and sang mass of requiem; and there offered first Sir Launcelot, and he offered an hundred pound; and then the seven kings offered forty pound apiece; and also there was a thousand knights, and each of them offered a pound; and the offering dured from morn till night, and Sir Launcelot lay two nights on his tomb in prayers and weeping.

Then on the third day Sir Launcelot called the kings, dukes, earls, barons, and knights, and said thus: "My fair lords, I thank you all of your coming into this country with me, but we came too late, and that shall repent me while I live, but against death may no man rebel. But sithen it is so," said Sir Launcelot, "I will myself ride and seek my lady, Queen Guenever, for as I hear say she hath had great pain and much disease; and I heard say that she is fled into the west. Therefore ye all shall abide me here, and but if I come again within fifteen days, then take your ships and your fellowship, and depart into your country, for I will do as I say to you."

Chapter 9: *How Sir Launcelot departed to seek the Queen Guenever, and how he found her at Almesbury.*

THEN came Sir Bors de Ganis, and said: "My lord Sir Launcelot, what think ye for to do, now to ride in this realm? Wit ye well ye shall find few friends." "Be as be may," said Sir Launcelot, "keep you still here, for I will forth on my journey, and no man nor child shall go with me." So it was no boot to strive, but he departed and rode westerly, and there he sought a seven or eight days; and at the last he came to a nunnery, and then was Queen Guenever ware of Sir Launcelot as he walked in the cloister. And when she saw him there she swooned thrice, that all the ladies and gentlewomen had work enough to hold the queen up. So when she might speak, she called ladies and

1. let, prevent. **20. unhap,** misfortune. **32–33. will . . . worship,** desire my honor. **40. speered,** asked.

11. requiem, for the repose of the souls of the dead. **16. dured,** lasted. **27. disease,** discomfort. **44. boot,** use gentlewomen to her, and said: "Ye marvel, fair ladies, why I make this fare. Truly," she said, "it is for the sight of yonder knight that yonder standeth; wherefore I pray you all call him to me."

When Sir Launcelot was brought to her, then she said to all the ladies: "Through this man and me hath all this war been wrought; for through our love that we have loved together is my most noble lord slain. Therefore, Sir Launcelot, wit thou well I am set in such a plight to get my soul-heal; and yet I trust through God's grace that after my death to have a sight of the blessed face of Christ, and at doomsday to sit on his right side, for as sinful as ever I was are saints in heaven. Therefore, Sir Launcelot, I require thee and beseech thee heartily, for all the love that ever was betwixt us, that thou never see me more in the visage; and I command thee, on God's behalf, that thou forsake my company, and to thy kingdom thou turn again, and keep well thy realm from war and wrack; for as well as I have loved thee, mine heart will not serve me to see thee, for through thee and me is the flower of kings and knights destroyed; therefore, Sir Launcelot, go to thy realm, and there take thee a wife, and live with her with joy and bliss; and I pray thee heartily, pray for me to our Lord that I may amend my misliving." "Now, sweet madam," said Sir Launcelot, "would ye that I should now return again unto my country, and there to wed a lady? Nay, madam, wit you well that shall I never do, for I shall never be so false to you of that I have promised; but the same destiny that ye have taken you to, I will take me unto, for to please Jesu, and ever for you I cast me specially to pray." "If thou wilt do so," said the queen, "hold thy promise, but I may never believe but that thou wilt turn to the world again." "Well, madam," said he, "ye say as pleaseth you, yet wist you me never false of my promise, and God defend but I should forsake the world as ye have done. For in the quest of the Saint Grail I had forsaken the vanities of the world had not your lord been. And if I had done so at that time, with my heart, will, and thought, I had passed all the knights that were in the Saint Grail except Sir Galahad, my son. And therefore, lady, sithen ye have taken you to perfection, I must needs take me to perfection, of right. For I take record of God, in you I have had mine earthly joy; and if I had found you now so disposed, I had cast me to have had you into mine own realm."

2. fare, display. **18. in the visage,** to my face. **21. wrack,** harm. **35. cast me,** intend. **47. sithen,** since.

Chapter 10: *How Sir Launcelot came to the hermitage where the Archbishop of Canterbury was, and how he took the habit on him.*

BUT sithen I find you thus disposed, I ensure you faithfully, I will ever take me to penance, and pray while my life lasteth, if I may find any hermit, either gray or white, that will receive me. Wherefore, madam, I pray you kiss me and never no more." "Nay," said the queen, "that shall I never do, but abstain you from such works"; and they departed. But there was never so hard an hearted man but he would have wept to see the dolour that they made; for there was lamentation as they had been stung with spears; and many times they swooned, and the ladies bare the queen to her chamber.

And Sir Launcelot awoke, and went and took his horse, and rode all that day and all night in a forest, weeping. And at the last he was ware of an hermitage and a chapel stood betwixt two cliffs; and then he heard a little bell ring to mass, and thither he rode and alit, and tied his horse to the gate, and heard mass. And he that sang mass was the Bishop of Canterbury. Both the Bishop and Sir Bedivere knew Sir Launcelot, and they spake together after mass. But when Sir Bedivere had told his tale all whole, Sir Launcelot's heart almost brast for sorrow, and Sir Launcelot threw his arms abroad, and said: "Alas, who may trust this world?" And then he kneeled down on his knee, and prayed the Bishop to shrive him and assoil him. And then he besought the Bishop that he might be his brother. Then the Bishop said: "I will gladly"; and there he put an habit upon Sir Launcelot, and there he served God day and night with prayers and fastings.

Thus the great host abode at Dover. And then Sir Lionel took fifteen lords with him, and rode to London to seek Sir Launcelot; and there Sir Lionel was slain and many of his lords. Then Sir Bors de Ganis made the great host for to go home again; and Sir Bors, Sir Ector de Maris, Sir Blamore, Sir Bleoberis, with more other of Sir Launcelot's kin, took on them to ride all England overthwart and endlong, to seek Sir Launcelot. So Sir Bors by fortune rode so long till he came to the same chapel where Sir Launcelot was; and so Sir Bors heard a little bell knell, that rang to mass; and there he alit and heard mass. And when

6. ensure, assure. **13. departed,** separated. **15. dolour,** sorrow. **34. assoil,** absolve. **46–47. overthwart and endlong,** throughout.

mass was done, the Bishop, Sir Launcelot, and Sir Bedivere came to Sir Bors. And when Sir Bors saw Sir Launcelot in that manner clothing, then he prayed the Bishop that he might be in the same suit. And so there was an habit put upon him, and there he lived in prayers and fasting. And within half a year, there was come Sir Galihud, Sir Galihodin, Sir Blamore, Sir Bleoberis, Sir Villiars, Sir Clarras, and Sir Gahalantine. So all these seven noble knights there abode still. And when they saw Sir Launcelot had taken him to such perfection, they had no lust to depart, but took such an habit as he had.

Thus they endured in great penance six year; and then Sir Launcelot took the habit of priesthood of the Bishop, and a twelvemonth he sang mass. And there was none of these other knights but they read in books, and helped for to sing mass, and rang bells, and did bodily all manner of service. And so their horses went where they would, for they took no regard of no worldly riches. For when they saw Sir Launcelot endure such penance, in prayers and fastings, they took no force what pain they endured, for to see the noblest knight of the world take such abstinence that he waxed full lean. And thus upon a night, there came a vision to Sir Launcelot, and charged him, in remission of his sins, to haste him unto Almesbury: "And by then thou come there, thou shalt find Queen Guenever dead. And therefore take thy fellows with thee, and purvey them of an horse-bier, and fetch thou the corpse of her, and bury her by her husband, the noble King Arthur." So this advision came to Sir Launcelot thrice in one night.

CHAPTER II: *How Sir Launcelot went with his seven fellows to Almesbury, and found there Queen Guenever dead, whom they brought to Glastonbury.*

THEN Sir Launcelot rose up or day, and told the hermit. "It were well done," said the hermit, "that ye made you ready, and that you disobey not the advision." Then Sir Launcelot took his seven fellows with him, and on foot they yede from Glastonbury to Almesbury, the which is little more than thirty mile. And thither they came within two days, for they were weak and feeble to go. And when Sir Launcelot was come to Almesbury within the nunnery, Queen Guenever died but half an hour afore. And the ladies told Sir Launcelot that Queen Guenever told them all or she passed, that Sir Launcelot had been priest near a twelvemonth, "And hither he cometh as fast as he may to fetch my corpse, and beside my lord, King Arthur, he shall bury me." Wherefore the queen said in hearing of them all: "I beseech Almighty God that I may never have power to see Sir Launcelot with my worldly eyen." And thus, said all the ladies, was ever her prayer these two days, till she was dead. Then Sir Launcelot saw her visage, but he wept not greatly, but sighed. And so he did all the observance of the service himself, both the dirge, and on the morn he sang mass. And there was ordained an horse-bier; and so with an hundred torches ever brenning about the corpse of the queen, and ever Sir Launcelot with his seven fellows went about the horse-bier, singing and reading many an holy orison, and frankincense upon the corpse incensed. Thus Sir Launcelot and his seven fellows went on foot from Almesbury unto Glastonbury.

And when they were come to the chapel and the hermitage, there she had a dirge, with great devotion. And on the morn the hermit that sometime was Bishop of Canterbury sang the mass of requiem with great devotion. And Sir Launcelot was the first that offered, and then also his seven fellows. And then she was wrapped in cered cloth of Raines, from the top to the toe, in thirtyfold; and after she was put in a web of lead, and then in a coffin of marble. And when she was put in the earth Sir Launcelot swooned, and lay long still, while the hermit came and awakened him, and said: "Ye be to blame, for ye displease God with such manner of sorrow-making." "Truly," said Sir Launcelot, "I trust I do not displease God, for He knoweth mine intent. For my sorrow was not, nor is not, for any rejoicing of sin, but my sorrow may never have end. For when I remember of her beauty, and of her noblesse, that was both with her king and with her, so when I saw his corpse and her corpse so lie together, truly mine heart would not serve to sustain my careful body. Also when I remember me how by my default, mine orgule and my pride, that they were both laid full low, that were peerless that ever was living of Christian people, wit you well," said Sir Launcelot, "this remembered, of their kindness and mine unkindness, sank so to mine heart, that I might not sustain myself." So the French book maketh mention.

12. lust, desire. **23. took no force,** paid no heed to. **31. purvey them of,** provide them with. **42. or,** before. **46. yede,** went.

16. brenning, burning. **19. orison,** prayer. **29. cered cloth,** cerecloth, a waxed winding-sheet, **31. web,** sheet. **44. careful,** sorrowful. **45. orgule,** pride.

Chapter 12: *How Sir Launcelot began to sicken, and after died, whose body was borne to Joyous Gard for to be buried.*

THEN Sir Launcelot never after ate but little meat, nor drank, till he was dead. For then he sickened more and more, and dried, and dwined away. For the Bishop nor none of his fellows might not make him to eat, and little he drank, that he was waxen by a cubit shorter than he was, that the people could not know him. For evermore, day and night, he prayed, but sometime he slumbered a broken sleep; ever he was lying grovelling on the tomb of King Arthur and Queen Guenever. And there was no comfort that the Bishop, nor Sir Bors, nor none of his fellows, could make him, it availed not. So within six weeks after, Sir Launcelot fell sick, and lay in his bed; and then he sent for the Bishop that there was hermit, and all his true fellows. Then Sir Launcelot said with dreary steven: "Sir Bishop, I pray you give to me all my rites that longeth to a Christian man." "It shall not need you," said the hermit and all his fellows, "it is but heaviness of your blood, ye shall be well mended by the grace of God tomorn." "My fair lords," said Sir Launcelot, "wit you well my careful body will into the earth, I have warning more than now I will say; therefore give me my rites." So when he was houseled and aneled, and had all that a Christian man ought to have, he prayed the Bishop that his fellows might bear his body to Joyous Gard. Some men say it was Alnwick, and some men say it was Bamborough. "Howbeit," said Sir Launcelot, "me repenteth sore, but I made mine avow sometime, that in Joyous Gard I would be buried. And because of breaking of mine avow, I pray you all, lead me thither." Then there was weeping and wringing of hands among his fellows.

So at a season of the night they all went to their beds, for they all lay in one chamber. And so after midnight, against day, the Bishop that was hermit, as he lay in his bed asleep, he fell upon a great laughter. And therewith all the fellowship awoke, and came to the Bishop, and asked him what he ailed. "Ah Jesu mercy," said the Bishop, "why did ye awake me? I was never in all my life so merry and so well at ease." "Wherefore?" said Sir Bors. "Truly," said the Bishop, "here was Sir Launcelot with me with more angels than ever I saw men in one day. And I saw the angels heave up Sir Launcelot unto heaven, and the gates of heaven opened against him." "It is but dretching of swevens," said Sir Bors, "for I doubt not Sir Launcelot aileth nothing but good." "It may well be," said the Bishop, "go ye to his bed, and then shall ye prove the sooth." So when Sir Bors and his fellows came to his bed they found him stark dead, and he lay as he had smiled, and the sweetest savour about him that ever they felt.

7. dwined, wasted. **10. cubit,** a unit of length varying from 18 to 22 inches. **21. steven,** voice. **29. houseled and aneled,** given the sacrament and extreme unction. **32–33. Alnwick . . . Bamborough,** in Northumberland. **50. heave,** lift.

Then was there weeping and wringing of hands, and the greatest dole they made that ever made men. And on the morn the Bishop did his mass of requiem; and after, the Bishop and all the nine knights put Sir Launcelot in the same horse-bier that Queen Guenever was laid in tofore that she was buried. And so the Bishop and they all together went with the body of Sir Launcelot daily, till they came to Joyous Gard; and ever they had an hundred torches brenning about him. And so within fifteen days they came to Joyous Gard. And there they laid his corpse in the body of the choir, and sang and read many psalters and prayers over him and about him. And ever his visage was laid open and naked, that all folks might behold him. For such was the custom in those days, that all men of worship should so lie with open visage till that they were buried. And right thus as they were at their service, there came Sir Ector de Maris, that had seven years sought all England, Scotland, and Wales, seeking his brother, Sir Launcelot.

Chapter 13: *How Sir Ector found Sir Launcelot his brother dead, and how Constantine reigned next after Arthur; and of the end of this book.*

AND when Sir Ector heard such noise and light in the choir of Joyous Gard, he alit and put his horse from him, and came into the choir, and there he saw men sing and weep. And all they knew Sir Ector, but he knew not them. Then went Sir Bors unto Sir Ector, and told him how there lay his brother, Sir Launcelot, dead; and then Sir Ector threw his shield, sword, and helm from him. And when he beheld Sir Launcelot's visage, he fell down in a swoon. And when he waked it were hard any tongue to tell the doleful complaints that he made for his brother. "Ah Launcelot," he said, "thou were head of all Christian knights, and now I dare say," said Sir Ector, "thou Sir Launcelot, there thou liest, that thou were never matched of earthly knight's hand. And thou were the courteoust knight that ever bare shield. And thou were the truest friend to thy lover that ever bestrad horse. And

2. against, before. **dretching of swevens,** torment of dreams.

thou were the truest lover of a sinful man that ever loved woman. And thou were the kindest man that ever struck with sword. And thou were the goodliest person that ever came among press of knights. And thou were the meekest man and the gentlest that ever ate in hall among ladies. And thou were the sternest knight to thy mortal foe that ever put spear in the rest." Then there was weeping and dolour out of measure.

Thus they kept Sir Launcelot's corpse aloft fifteen days, and then they buried it with great devotion. And then at leisure they went all with the Bishop of Canterbury to his hermitage, and there they were together more than a month. Then Sir Constantine, that was Sir Cador's son of Cornwall, was chosen king of England. And he was a full noble knight, and worshipfully he ruled this realm. And then this King Constantine sent for the Bishop of Canterbury, for he heard say where he was. And so he was restored unto his Bishopric, and left that hermitage. And Sir Bedivere was there ever still hermit to his life's end. Then Sir Bors de Ganis, Sir Ector de Maris, Sir Gahalantine, Sir Galihud, Sir Galihodin, Sir Blamore, Sir Bleoberis, Sir Villiars le Valiant, Sir Clarrus of Clermont, all these knights drew them to their countries. Howbeit King Constantine would have had them with him, but they would not abide in this realm. And there they all lived in their countries as holy men. And some English books make mention that they went never out of England after the death of Sir Launcelot, but that was but favour of makers. For the French book maketh mention, and is authorised, that Sir Bors, Sir Ector, Sir Blamore, and Sir Bleoberis, went into the Holy Land there as Jesu Christ was quick and dead, and anon as they had stablished their lands. For the book saith, so Sir Launcelot commanded them for to do, or ever he passed out of this world. And these four knights did many battles upon the miscreants or Turks. And there they died upon a Good Friday for God's sake.

Here is the end of the book of King Arthur, and of his noble knights of the Round Table, that when they were whole together there was ever an hundred and forty. And here is the end of the death of Arthur. I pray you all, gentlemen and gentlewomen that readeth this book of Arthur and his knights, from the beginning to the ending, pray for me while I am alive, that God send me good deliverance, and when I am dead, I pray you all pray for my soul. For this book was ended the ninth year of the reign of King Edward the Fourth, by Sir Thomas Malory, knight, as Jesu help him for his great might, as he is the servant of Jesu both day and night.

Thus endeth this noble and joyous book entitled Le Morte Darthur. Notwithstanding it treateth of the birth, life, and acts of the said King Arthur, of his noble knights of the Round Table, their marvellous enquests and adventures, the achieving of the Saint Grail, and in the end the dolorous death and departing out of this world of them all. Which book was reduced into English by Sir Thomas Malory, knight, as afore is said, and by me divided into twenty-one books, chaptered and enprinted, and finished in the abbey Westminster the last day of July the year of our Lord MCCCCLXXXV.

Caxton me fieri fecit.

10. aloft, unburied. **32. makers,** poets.

4. miscreants, infidels. **26. enquests,** quests. ***35. Caxton . . . fecit.*** Caxton had me made.

SUGGESTIONS FOR FURTHER READING

This list is to be supplemented by the General Bibliography at the beginning of the volume and by the brief lists of books mentioned in the various introductions to specific authors and works.

The Old English Era

HISTORICAL AND POLITICAL BACKGROUND

Collingwood, R. S., and Myres, J. N. L. *Roman Britain and the English Settlements.* Vol. I in the *Oxford History of England,* Oxford University Press, 1937. The most up-to-date and thoroughly readable account of the period from 55 B.C. to about A.D. 560.

Gummere, F. B. *Founders of England,* rev. by F. P. Magoun, Jr., Stechert, 1930. A rich account of the public and private life of the Germanic people, both before and after their coming to England.

Hodgkin, R. H. *A History of the Anglo-Saxons,* 2 vols., Oxford University Press, 1939. A sumptuously printed, richly illustrated, and highly readable work but extending only through Alfred.

Lees, B. A. *Alfred the Great,* Putnam, 1915.

Stenton, F. M. *Anglo-Saxon England.* Vol. II in the *Oxford History of England,* 1943. A lucid and vigorous account of Anglo-Saxon civilization down to the Norman Conquest.

CULTURAL AND SOCIAL BACKGROUND

Hunt, William. *The English Church From Its Foundation to the Norman Conquest*, Macmillan, 1899.

Kendrick, T. D. *Anglo-Saxon Art to A.D. 900*, Methuen, 1938.

—— *Late Saxon and Viking Art*, Methuen, 1950. Both works are profusely illustrated with plates, drawings, maps, etc.

Martin-Clarke, D. Elizabeth. *Culture in Early Anglo-Saxon England*, Johns Hopkins Press, 1947. The most recent study, based on new archeological and literary discoveries, of the Christian culture of oldest England.

Wingfield-Stratford, Esmé. *The History of British Civilization*, Vol. I, Harcourt, Brace, 1928.

THE OLD ENGLISH LANGUAGE

Cook, A. S., *A First Book in Old English*, rev. ed., Ginn, 1921. Grammar, reader, notes, and vocabulary.

Sievers, Eduard. *An Old English Grammar*, rev. ed. Translated and edited by A. S. Cook, Ginn, 1903.

LITERATURE OF THE PERIOD

COLLECTIONS AND TRANSLATIONS

Cook, A. S., and Tinker, C. B., eds. *Select Translations from Old English Poetry*, rev. ed., Harvard University Press, 1926. Renderings in both verse and prose.

—— *Select Translations from Old English Prose*, Harvard University Press, 1908.

Gordon, R. K. *Anglo-Saxon Poetry*, Everyman's Library, Dutton, 1926; reprinted 1949. Prose translation of nearly the whole body of Old English poetry, with a valuable introduction.

Spaeth, J. D. *Old English Poetry*, Princeton University Press, 1922. Another and useful volume of modern translations of the more important Old English poems, with introductions, notes, and a bibliography.

CRITICISM

Kennedy, C. W. *The Earliest English Poetry*, Oxford University Press, 1943. The most recent critical survey of Old English poetry, with illustrative translations.

Malone, Kemp, and Baugh, A. C. *A Literary History of England*. Vol. I, *The Middle Ages*, Appleton-Century-Crofts, 1948. Part I deals with the Old English period in a comprehensive, up-to-date, and readable fashion.

Wardale, E. E. *Chapters on Old English Literature* rev. ed., K. Paul, Trench, Trübner, 1935.

The Middle Ages

HISTORICAL AND POLITICAL BACKGROUND

Cambridge Medieval History, 8 vols., Macmillan, 1911–1936; Vol. I, Chap. 13; II, 15–17; IV, 13–15, 19, 20; V, 15–17; VI, 7, 8, 17, 24, 25; VII, 12, 14–19; VIII, 7, 12–14, 23, 25. Concise and scholarly chapters which integrate English and Continental events; valuable bibliographies.

Davis, H. W. C. *England under the Normans and Angevins*, 1066–1272, Putnam, 1926.

Jacob, E. F. *Henry V and the Invasion of France*, Macmillan, 1950. A sprightly and valuable little volume in the Teach-Yourself-History Library.

Kelly, Amy. *Eleanor of Aquitaine and the Four Kings*, Harvard University Press, 1950. A fascinating historical account of the life and times of the indomitable wife of Louis VII of France and Henry I of England and mother of Richard the Lion-Hearted and King John.

Thompson, Faith. *Magna Carta. Its Role in the Making of the English Constitution, 1300–1629*, University of Minnesota Press, 1948. An invaluable study of the working during four centuries of Magna Carta, the first great constitutional document.

Thompson, J. W. *An Introduction to Medieval Europe*, Norton, 1937.

Vickers, Kenneth. *England in the Later Middle Ages*, Putnam, 1919.

CULTURAL AND SOCIAL BACKGROUND

Bennett, H. S. *Life on the English Manor; A Study of Peasant Conditions, 1150–1400*, Macmillan, 1938. By far the best account of the shift from serfdom to freedom.

—— *The Pastons and Their England*, Macmillan, 1922; see page 46. An admirable digest of the famous letters.

Bird, Ruth. *The Turbulent London of Richard II*, Longmans, 1949. A carefully documented history of the social, economic, and political conflicts of Chaucer's London.

Clapham, A. W. *English Romanesque Architecture after the Conquest*, Oxford University Press, 1930.

Coulton, G. G. *Medieval Panorama: The English Scene from Conquest to Reformation*, Macmillan, 1938. Informative and readable on almost every phase of medieval life.

Hartley, Dorothy, and Elliott, M. M. *The Life and Work of the People of England: A Pictorial Record from Contemporary Sources; the Fourteenth and Fifteenth Centuries*, 2 vols., Putnam, 1926.

Haskins, C. H. *Studies in the History of Medieval Science*, Harvard University Press, 1924.

Jusserand, J. J. *English Wayfaring Life in the Middle Ages*, Putnam, 1950. A new edition of a classic of irresistible charm and interest.

Oman, C. W. C. *A History of the Art of War in the Middle Ages*, Houghton Mifflin, 1924. Sad proof that we have not improved.

Owst, G. R. *Literature and Pulpit in Medieval England*, Macmillan, 1933. Provides invaluable studies of medieval sermon literature as a means of approach to social and literary history. The discussion of the connection between pulpit utterances and religious drama is specially notable.

Power Eileen E. *Medieval People*, Houghton Mifflin, 1932. A standard work.

Rait, R. S. *Life in the Medieval University*, rev. ed., Cambridge University Press, 1931.

Reisman, David. *The Story of Medicine in the Middle Ages*, Hoeber, 1935. Grimly fascinating.

Rickert, Edith (compiler), Olson, C. C., and Crow,

M. M., eds. *Chaucer's World*, Columbia University Press, 1948. A fascinating, expertly arranged collection of excerpts from medieval documents, records, and literature, illustrating and describing the life Chaucer knew in England and France. Most of the material has not been translated or published before.

Saunders, O. E. *History of English Art in the Middle Ages*, Oxford University Press, 1932.

Taylor, H. O. *The Mediaeval Mind*, Harvard University Press, 1950. A new edition of a classic work dealing with the intellectual, emotional, and spiritual attitudes of the Middle Ages.

Trevelyan, G. M. *Chaucer's England and the Early Tudors*, Longmans, 1950. The first volume, illustrated, of the author's *English Social History*.

LITERATURE OF THE PERIOD

COLLECTIONS

Adams, J. Q., ed. *Chief Pre-Shakespearean Dramas*, Houghton Mifflin, 1924. The standard selection of plays illustrating the history of the English drama from its origin down to Shakespeare.

Everyman and Other Interludes, Everyman's Library, Dutton, 1926.

French W. H., and Hale, C. B., eds. *Middle English Metrical Romances*, Prentice-Hall, 1930. The most comprehensive collection of its kind; well-glossed originals.

Jones, C. W., ed. *Medieval Literature in Translation*, Longmans, 1950. An excellent group of selections translated from the Latin, Old Irish, Old French, and other languages. Helpful maps and indexes are appended.

Loomis, R. S., and Willard, Rudolph, eds. *Medieval English Verse and Prose*, Appleton-Century-Crofts, 1948. Selections, in modernized versions, chosen to provide a representative survey of verse and prose between the twelfth and fifteenth centuries.

Ross, J. B., and McLaughlin, Mary M., eds. *The Portable Medieval Reader*, Viking Press, 1949. An attractive and inexpensive anthology of widely varied writings from four centuries.

Sisam, Kenneth, ed. *Fourteenth-Century Prose and Verse*, Oxford University Press, 1921. An edition of the original poems, with introduction, bibliography, and vocabulary.

CRITICISM

Bennett, H. S. *Chaucer and the Fifteenth Century*, Oxford University Press, 1948. This is Part 1 of Vol. II of the *Oxford History of English Literature*. A reassessment of the work of Chaucer and the century that followed him. Readable and sound.

Chambers, E. K. *English Literature at the Close of the Middle Ages*, Oxford University Press, 1945. This is Part 2 of Vol. II of the *Oxford History of English Literature*, and deals with Malory, the ballads, medieval drama, and the medieval lyric.

Chambers, E. K. *The Mediaeval Stage*, 2 vols., Oxford University Press, 1903. The standard, encyclopedic work.

Chaytor, H. J. *From Script to Print, An Introduction to Medieval Literature*, Cambridge University Press, 1945. A learned and very readable study of the circumstances and methods of literary composition in the early Middle Ages.

Ker, W. P. *Epic and Romance*, Macmillan, 1926. One of the best possible introductions to medieval narrative poetry.

Krapp, G. P. *The Rise of English Literary Prose*, Oxford University Press, 1915. The first two chapters contain the best account of the early prose through Wyclif.

Malone, Kemp, and Baugh, A. C. *A Literary History of England*. Vol. I, *The Middle Ages*, Appleton-Century-Crofts, 1948. Part 2 deals with the Middle English period (1100–1500). The most comprehensive, up-to-date, and generally readable and satisfactory history of medieval literature.

Young, Karl. *The Drama of the Mediaeval Church*, 2 vols., Oxford University Press, 1933. The standard work on church drama.

INDIVIDUAL AUTHORS

Ancren Riwle (*Ancrene Wisse*), trans. by J. Morton, ed. by Abbot Gasquet, Oxford University Press, 1924 (Medieval Library). See page 47.

Geoffrey of Monmouth. *Histories of the Kings of Britain*, Everyman's Library, Dutton, 1928. See page 47.

Lawman (Layamon). *The Brut*, in Eugene Mason, *Arthurian Chronicles Represented by Wace and Layamon*, Everyman's Library, Dutton, 1921. See page 47.

Marie de France, in Eugene Mason, *French Medieval Romances from the Lays of Marie de France*, Everyman's Library, Dutton, 1924. Prose translations of some of the best poetic short stories ever written.

Rolle, Richard, in F. M. M. Comper's *The Life of Richard Rolle, together with an Edition of His English Lyrics*, Dutton, 1929. An admirable account of a great fourteenth-century religious mystic, with specimens of his work. See page 49.

The Voiage and Travayle of Syr John Maundeville, Knight, Everyman's Library, Dutton, 1928. A travel book the appeal of which is doubled by the fact that much in it is not true.

ARTHURIAN ROMANCE

Chambers, E. K. *Arthur of Britain*, Sidgwick and Jackson, Ltd., 1927. Notable for its publication of the documents upon which a discussion of the historicity of Arthur depends.

Loomis, R. S. *Celtic Myth and Arthurian Romance*, Columbia University Press, 1927.

Reid, Margaret J. C., *The Arthurian Legend: Comparison of Treatment in Modern and Medieval Literature. A Study in the Literary Value of Myth and Legend*, Oliver and Boyd, 1938. The most inclusive account of modern treatments.

THE SIXTEENTH CENTURY

PLATE V

A MAP OF THE WORLD (*Bettmann Archive*)

A comparison of this map, engraved in 1639, with the Anglo-Saxon map facing page 2 shows the vast progress made in geography and cartography from the medieval period to the Renaissance. Here is a recognizable, modern concept of the world, drawn on the basis of scientific data, its purpose to present scientific information rather than to interpret doctrine. The decorative element which was an essential feature of medieval maps is here secondary, although the decorations themselves are much more elaborate than those on the Anglo-Saxon map. The two small circles contain maps of the heavens based on the observations of the great Danish astronomer, Tycho Brahe.

B AN ATTACK ON THE ARMADA (*Engraving by John Pine from a Flemish tapestry*)

A few years after the defeat of the Spanish Armada, Lord Howard, who was Lord Admiral in 1588, ordered a set of tapestries illustrating the glorious victory. In this formalized representation, the English fleet is on the left. In the foreground is a Spanish ship whose powder magazine has just exploded.

The English experience in attacking Spanish treasure galleons stood them in good stead when they came to grips with the Armada—their seamanship and gunnery far surpassed the Spanish; with their smaller ships they cleverly kept to windward and fought at long range, thus outmaneuvering the larger, clumsier Spanish vessels.

But the defeat of the Armada was more than just a victory of one fleet over another—it established British supremacy on the seas which in turn made possible the great colonizing ventures of later centuries.

PLATE VI

A QUEEN ELIZABETH GOING TO BLACKFRIARS (*Colonel F. J. B. Wingfield Digby, Sherborne Castle, Dorset*)

In this painting by Marcus Gheeraerts the Younger, a Flemish artist, we see Queen Elizabeth attended by her court on the way to witness a wedding. The bride, who follows the litter on foot is Anne Russell, one of her maids of honor. The bridegroom, who is dressed in a white costume and supports the litter at right, is the son of the Earl of Worcester.

Colorful pageants like this were a common occurrence in Elizabeth's reign. They satisfied the Elizabethan love of pageantry, and they served also to keep Elizabeth always in the public eye and heart. To her subjects Elizabeth was indeed Gloriana, the glorious one, to whom Spenser dedicated his *Faerie Queene:*

> To the most high, mightie and magnificent empresse renowmed for pietie, vertue, and all gratious government Elizabeth by the grace of God Queene of England Fraunce and Ireland and of Virginia, defendour of the faith, &c. Her most humble servaunt Edmund Spenser doth in all humilitie dedicate, present and consecrate these his labours to live with the eternitie of her fame.

B HENRY VIII (*A portrait by Hans Holbein the Younger in the Palazzo Corsini Gallery, Rome*)

Hans Holbein the Younger, a German by birth and a Swiss by early residence, was the court painter of Henry VIII's reign, and his portraits are a living gallery of the great figures of the Tudor dynasty. Holbein's home was in Basel, Switzerland, until his unsatisfactory income drove him abroad in 1526. His destination was perhaps suggested by one of his most famous subjects—Erasmus, whose *Praise of Folly* Holbein had illustrated. We know that he took with him to England a letter of introduction from Erasmus to Sir Thomas More and that More, then Chancellor of the Exchequer, gave Holbein commissions and introduced him to many of the English nobility. Among those whom he painted were John Fisher, the Bishop of Rochester, Sir Henry Wyat, Sir Thomas Elyot, and Lady Elyot.

In 1538 the king sent Holbein to Brussels to paint Christina of Denmark, the widowed Duchess of Milan, whom Henry was interested in marrying. The following year Holbein was commissioned to make portraits of the daughters of the Duke of Cleves, on the basis of which Henry picked Anne of Cleves to be his fourth wife.

C HAMPTON COURT PALACE, QUEEN ANNE BOLEYN'S GATEWAY (*British Information*)

The secular spirit of the Elizabethan era and the Elizabethan love of luxury and display found expression in the "great houses" built by the nobles

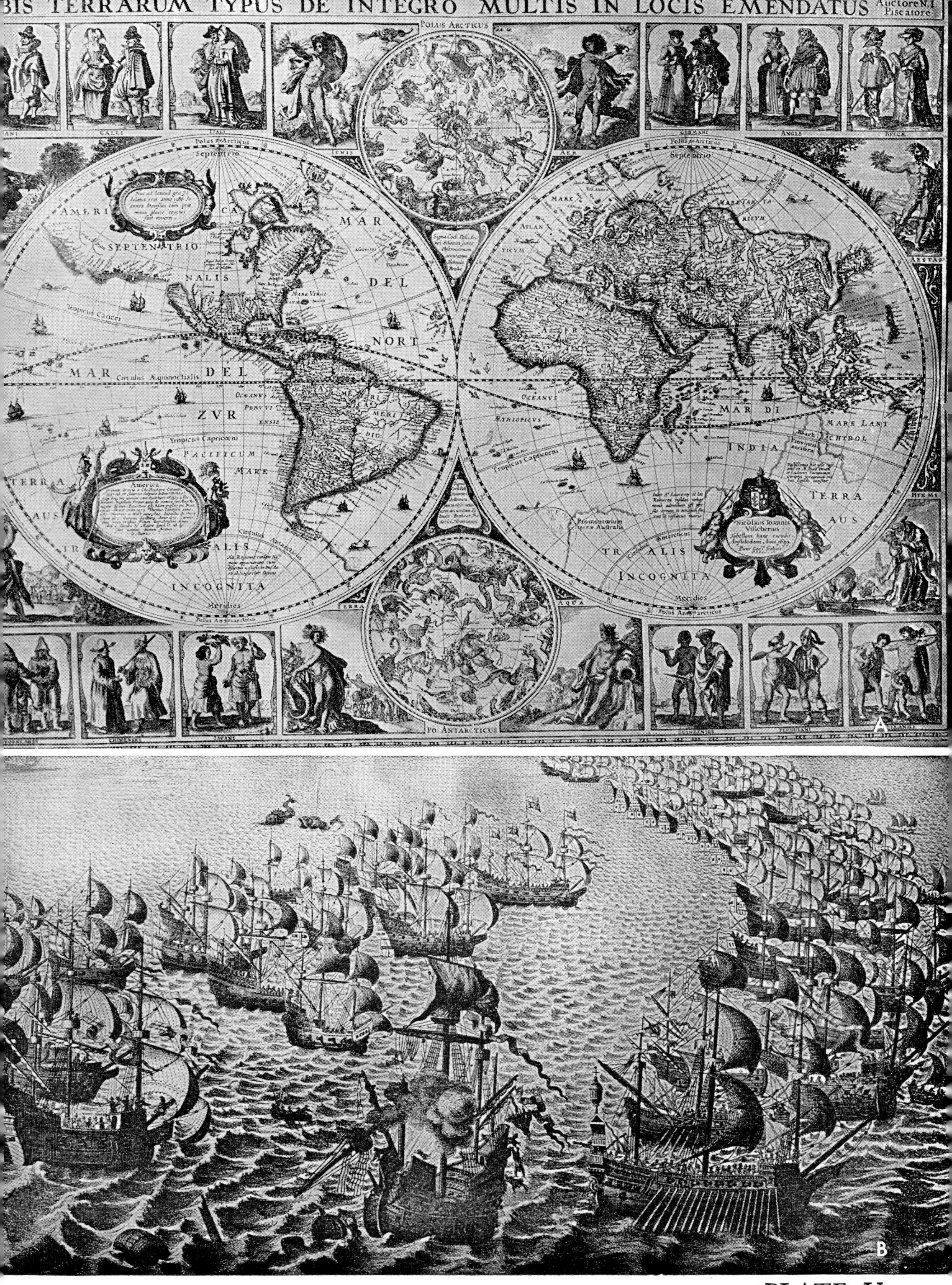
BIS TERRARUM TYPUS DE INTEGRO MULTIS IN LOCIS EMENDATUS
Auctore N. I Piscatore
POLUS ARCTICUS
GALLI
GERMANI
ANGLI
BELGAE
Septentrio
AMERI CA
SEPTENTRIO NALIS
MAR DEL NORT
MAR DEL ZUR
Circulus Æquinoctialis
Tropicus Cancri
Tropicus Capricorni
PACIFICUM MARE
TERRA AUS TRALIS INCOGNITA
Meridies
Polus Antarcticus
ATLAN TICUM
OCEANUS
ÆTHIOPICUS
MAR DI INDIA
Nicolaus Ioannis Visscherius
PO: ANTARCTICUS
CHINENSES
JAVANI
A
B

PLATE V

A

PLATE VI

B

C

MR. WILLIAM
SHAKESPEARES
COMEDIES,
HISTORIES, &
TRAGEDIES.
Publiſhed according to the True Originall Copies.

Martin Droeshout sculpsit London.

LONDON
Printed by Isaac Iagg..d, and Ed. Blount. 1623

D

PLATE VII

A

B

C

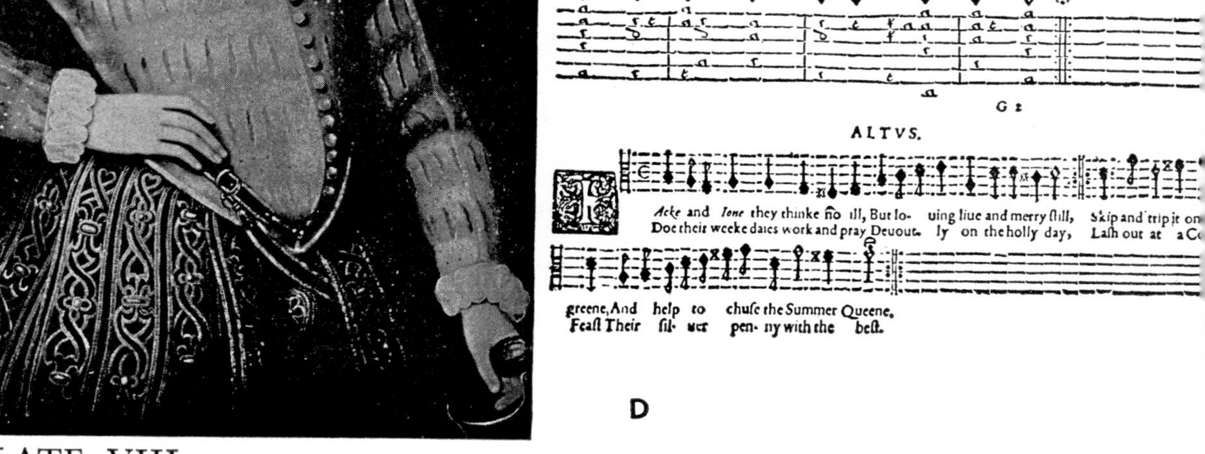

D

PLATE VIII

during the period. These magnificent homes were the dominant type of architecture in the sixteenth century as the cathedrals had been in the preceding era. One of the earliest, and still most magnificent, of these great houses is Hampton Court.

In 1515, Cardinal Wolsey took a ninety-nine-year lease on a tract of land belonging to the Knights Hospitalers, for which he paid £1,000 a year, and thereon built a house to suit his lavish tastes. Henry VIII was often entertained there and evidently found the palace to his liking because, sometime during the 1520's, Wolsey thought it expedient to make a gift of Hampton Court to the King. Both men occupied it off and on until Wolsey fell out of favor in 1529.

After Henry definitely took possession of the palace, he made a number of changes, and subsequent monarchs have further altered it, but some of Wolsey's original design still remains. The gate shown here is one of these portions. Wolsey's coat of arms can be seen over the doorway and above it is an astronomical clock made for Henry by Nicholas Oursian which tells the hour, the month, the day of the month, the number of days since the new year, the phases of the moon, and the time of high tide at London Bridge.

PLATE VII

A SECTION OF THE ENGRAVING *SLOTH*, AFTER PETER BRUEGHEL (*Courtesy of the Metropolitan Museum of Art*)

Peter Brueghel the Elder (1520?–1569) painted in a realistic tradition untouched by the Italian influence that dominated his native Flanders during his lifetime. His canvases and drawings reveal an almost brutal realism and, at the same time, a great sympathy and affection for the common people from whom he sprang. The drawing *Sloth* is part of a series on the seven vices.

The procession of the seven vices, or deadly sins, in the *Faerie Queene* is just one reminder of the great body of tradition that the Elizabethans inherited from the Middle Ages. This background is sometimes almost lost in the blazing light of sixteenth-century discoveries and awakenings, but it was an essential part of Elizabethan thinking. E. M. W. Tillyard sums the matter up in *The Elizabethan World Picture*, "You could revolt against it, but you could not ignore it [i.e., orthodox belief]. Atheism not agnosticism was the rule. It was far easier to be very wicked and think yourself so than to be a little wicked without a sense of sin."

B ANNE HATHAWAY'S COTTAGE (*Armstrong Roberts*)

The Anne Hathaway house in Shottery, just outside Stratford-on-Avon, is a representative sixteenth-century middle-class home.

C MODEL OF THE GLOBE THEATER (*Dr. John C. Adams, Hofstra College*)

The most famous of the Elizabethan playhouses is the Globe, for which the ground was leased in 1599 by a group of actors—among them William Shakespeare. It was an octagonal building, measuring about thirty-six feet on each side, with a capacity of from two to three thousand spectators. Some of these occupied the three-tiered gallery, and the rest, the "groundlings," stood in the open area around the stage. Contact between the players and the audience was much more intimate in the Elizabethan playhouse than it is today. There was no curtain and the stage jutted out into the audience. The absence of scenery made it necessary for the playwright to describe his settings. As Professor Harrison remarks in the Introduction to his edition of Shakespeare's major plays and sonnets, "We owe the poetry of Shakespeare's plays to the barrenness of the Elizabethan stage and to the appreciation of the Elizabethan audience." And the Elizabethan audience *was* appreciative. It included many levels of society, and hence a wide variety of tastes. Because no reservations were made in advance, the early comers got the best places. Unlike present-day audiences, everyone was in his place, ready and waiting, when the actors first walked out on the stage.

D THE FIRST FOLIO OF SHAKESPEARE'S PLAYS (*Albert A. and Henry W. Berg Collection of the New York Public Library*)

Published in 1623 under the supervision of two of Shakespeare's associates in the King's Company, John Heminge and Henry Condell, the First Folio (first collected edition) of Shakespeare's plays made a twofold contribution to the literary world. The Folio is the sole source of twenty of the plays, the only authentic source of two others, and it provides superior readings for seven others. Moreover, it established the right of drama to a dominant place in the world of literature. Before the publication of the First Folio, plays were regarded as ephemeral products, made to last a season and worth printing, if at all, only in cheap paper editions. In 1616 Ben Jonson dared to include nine plays among his collected works and was ridiculed for doing so. But the success of the Shakespeare Folio, which was reprinted three times during the seventeeth century, led publishers to venture upon other editions of plays, and it became recognized that a play was something that could be *read* as well as seen.

PLATE VIII

A SIR THOMAS MORE, BY HANS HOLBEIN THE YOUNGER (*Copyright The Frick Collection*)

Sir Thomas More was Holbein's first patron in England and introduced him to many of the notables who commissioned portraits by him. Holbein's painting of More is one of his best works, revealing fully the dignity, spirituality, and intellect of his subject.

B SIR WALTER RALEGH, FROM A PORTRAIT ATTRIBUTED TO ZUCCARO (*Bettman Archive*)

This portrait is dated 1583 and therefore shows Ralegh at about the age of thirty-one.

As Thomas More represents the scholarly and spiritual aspects of the early sixteenth century, so Ralegh typifies the secular magnificence of the end of the century. The rich ornamentation of his clothing reflects the Elizabethan love of lavishness and color. His keen, self-confident expression is that of a man who was a bold explorer of strange worlds of the intellect and spirit, and who was equally adventurous in penetrating into unknown realms beyond the seas. For his own glory and that of Gloriana, he personally searched for El Dorado in Guiana. It is interesting to note from Edward Bancroft's *Essay on the Natural History of Guiana* that, as late as 1769, memories of Ralegh still persisted among the natives.

C SIR PHILIP SIDNEY, PORTRAIT BY AN UNKNOWN ARTIST (*National Portrait Gallery, London*)

More than any other figure of his time, Sir Philip Sidney epitomizes the Renaissance courtier. Even in his own day he seems to have represented an ideal in the minds of the English people, if one judges from the tributes that were written to him and the great crowd that mourned at his funeral. His friend and first biographer, Sir Fulke Greville, thus describes him as the perfect amateur and man of action:

> But the truth is: his end was not writing, even while he wrote; nor his knowledge moulded for tables, or schools; but both his wit, and understanding bent upon his heart, to make himself and others, not in words or opinion, but in life, and action, good and great.

D "JACK AND JOAN," FROM THOMAS CAMPION'S *TWO BOOKES OF AYRES*, 1610 (*Reproduced by permission of The Huntington Library, San Marino, California*)

No period in English history is so musical as that of the reign of Queen Elizabeth. Ability to play an instrument and to sing part songs was considered an essential of good breeding, and in the life of every Englishman, from the poorest laborer to the monarch herself, music had a daily place.

The time abounded in talented composers, whose work usually took the form either of the *madrigal*, an intricately woven, polyphonic composition for several voices, or the *air*, a strain for a single voice, accompanied by the lute. Thomas Campion (1567–1620) wrote both. Like many of his contemporaries, he was apparently a composer and musician more by avocation than by profession. After studying for a while at Peterhouse, Cambridge, Campion was admitted to Gray's Inn, perhaps at the request of his father who was presumably a law clerk. But Campion never became a practicing barrister. Some years later he seems to have gone on a military expedition to France under Essex, and five years after that, in 1606, we find him with a degree of doctor of physic. Medicine seemed to be his final choice of career, and he practiced until his death. Beginning in 1595, Campion published four *Bookes of Ayres*, for which he wrote all the words and most of the music. He also produced a technical treatise on counterpoint, books of Latin poetry, and *Observations in the Art of English Poesie*, a plea for the use of the Latin quantitative verse system in English poetry. Several masques, too, came from his pen.

The Sixteenth Century

The Course of the Renaissance

THE words "Renaissance" and "Elizabethan" bring before the mind's eye vivid images of the first teachers of Greek at Italian courts and at English universities; the classics exquisitely printed for the first time in the elegant italic font of Aldus; Erasmus' ironical exposé of superstition and pedantry in *The Praise of Folly;* Sir Thomas More's merry wit and saintly martyrdom; Roger Ascham at dinner at Lord Burghley's discussing the Eton boys who had run away to escape flogging; the hapless wives of Henry VIII; the traitors' heads on London Bridge; the first smoking of tobacco in England; Queen Elizabeth knighting Sir Francis Drake on the *Golden Hind* at the conclusion of the first English circumnavigation of the globe, and that same notable queen making magnificent progresses from castle to castle of her ambitious nobles or sending her rebellious favorite, the Earl of Essex, to the scaffold; Shakespeare writing the world's greatest plays in order to establish himself as a wealthy Stratford burgher; patriotic privateers waylaying gold-laden Spanish galleons; and sunburnt seamen bringing back strange tales of new worlds over the seas.

Such tales were heard with avidity by citizens of a London, become a city of nearly 200,000, which was still medieval in appearance though it was swept by innumerable Renaissance air currents. Within its castellated walls and around its fortressed Tower sprawled networks of narrow unpaved streets lined with shops and taverns and houses. The city was afflicted not infrequently with devastating epidemics. By day citizens had to rely upon their own strength to protect themselves from ruffians and criminals, and by night exceedingly ineffective protection was rendered them by such a fumbling volunteer watch as Shakespeare satirized in *Much Ado About Nothing*. Long hours of toil were offset by periods of violent and spontaneous recreation. Outdoor sports and games of skill and strength were extremely popular, and on Sundays cockneys flocked to the fields outside the city walls and over London Bridge to the malodorous suburbs south of the Thames to watch contests of football or archery or bull- and bear-baiting. Services in the scores of churches whose spires rose out of the cluttered masses of timber-and-plaster dwellings and shops were sparsely attended, and St. Paul's Cathedral was less famous for its choir where the liturgy was celebrated than for its transepts, which were the rendezvous of merchants and lawyers bent on professional transactions and of courtiers and dandies bent on displaying their gorgeous raiment.

London served admirably as one of the levers by which the Tudor sovereigns established a strong government and created commercial prosperity. Under the Tudors, from Henry VII, who came to the throne in 1485, to Elizabeth, who died in 1603, Parliament became increasingly subservient, the nobility declined in power and prestige, and the Church submitted to the royal will. The Sovereign had virtual control over Parliament: he dictated the choice of the religious peers in the House of

Lords and gained the support of the temporal peers by granting them profitable sinecures and monopolies. In the House of Commons he maintained the power of veto, and selected the Speaker and the borough representatives. He could summon or dismiss the body at will. After Henry VIII's break with Rome, the Sovereign became the Supreme Head of the Church, and thus the recipient of numerous ecclesiastical taxes, grants, and bequests. He also presided over the Privy Council, which Henry VIII established primarily to determine matters of foreign policy.

English foreign policy fluctuated wildly under the influence of successive monarchs, and reached its most dynamic stage under Elizabeth. Henry VIII's chief concern was peace with Europe; to this end he strengthened national relations with France and Scotland. In 1512 the King was persuaded by his Minister Wolsey and by King Ferdinand of Spain to go to war with France, but the conflict ended with a peace treaty in 1514. In 1543, Henry joined the Emperor Charles V in another attempt to invade France, but Charles gave up the fight and, after the French failed to invade England, Henry made a treaty with the French King, Francis I, by which England gained control of Boulogne. In 1549, France, indignant over the loss of Boulogne, declared war on England, and regained the disputed territory. In 1558, at the close of the reign of Mary Tudor, the loss of Calais ended England's territorial holdings on the Continent.

During the reign of Elizabeth there was a steadily mounting friction between England and Spain. England was Protestant; Spain, zealously Catholic. The countries not only were radically different in creeds and cultures, but were bitter rivals in commerce and colonization. Realizing that an overt conflict was imminent, Elizabeth pretended to be considering a marriage with Philip II, the widower of her half-sister, Mary Tudor, while she sanctioned military and monetary aid to the opponents of Spanish rule in the Netherlands. Philip, angered by this duplicity, became accessory to plots to displace Elizabeth and to put her Catholic cousin, Mary Queen of Scots, on the throne. When this plot was frustrated by the execution of Mary in 1587, Philip laid claim to the English throne, and in 1588 sent the Spanish Armada against England to support his claim. But the courageous English Navy, aided and abetted by terrific storms at sea, brought about the complete destruction of the great fleet, and put an end to Philip's scheming. This epoch-making victory not only ended the Spanish menace but also initiated England in the role of mistress of the seas.

The term "Renaissance" requires close analysis if we are to understand the cultural changes that occurred in England during the sixteenth and seventeenth centuries. The term suggests too readily that the most important movement of the period was the classical revival, the renewed enthusiasm for Greek and Roman life and literature that was to have such far-reaching consequences for the intellectual and esthetic life of the modern world. As a matter of fact, the Renaissance is to be differentiated from the Middle Ages not merely by its eager devotion to the study of classical life and literature but also by movements of equal, if not greater, importance: the secularization of the fine arts, the beginnings of modern capitalism, the birth of modern science, and the rise of Protestantism.[1]

The secularization of the fine arts came about as the direct result of the weakened hold of theological authority and supernaturalism over artists generally. In the Middle Ages, it has been said, art was the handmaid of theology; in the Renaissance it became the mistress of princes. Secularization took place as artists under the influence of classical art and literature rediscovered the world of man and of nature. "No Gothic artist," George Rowley wrote, "is interested in nature for its own sake but rather as a means to a spiritual end. In the Renaissance, the material world for the first time became the sole inspiration for plastic and pictorial invention. For example, Gothic artists attempted portraiture and the nude as incidental parts of their paintings, but only in the Renaissance could Pollaiuolo create a group of nudes as the sole interest of his picture."[2] Renaissance artists celebrated the rediscovered beauties of the human form in magnificent canvases and statues. Such masterpieces as Titian's "Venus and the Lute Player" and Michelangelo's "David" would have been unthinkable in the Middle Ages. More clearly than any literary tradition they make intelligible such sensuous Italianate narratives as Marlowe's *Hero and Leander* and Shakespeare's *Venus and Adonis*. Marlowe and Shakespeare were attempting to achieve in poetry what Titian and Michelangelo had attained in painting and sculpture.

Modern capitalism began in the greatest economic crisis Europe had seen since the fall of Rome. Profound changes were taking place in both the external and the internal economies of European

[1] Since the classical revival must be discussed at considerable length, the discussion of it will be deferred until the other movements characteristic of the Renaissance have been considered briefly. [2] "The Art of the Renaissance" in *The Civilization of the Renaissance*, University of Chicago Press, 1929, pp. 106–107.

politics. The economic decline of Venice and the cities of Southern Germany, the economic expansion of Spain and Portugal, and the rise to preeminence of Antwerp as the center of international finance were paralleled by equally important changes in the internal economy: the substitution of the livery company for the craft guild, the organization of trade on national rather than on local lines, and the application of capital to the mining and textile industries. The importation of great quantities of gold that resulted from the Spanish ravages of Mexico and Central America intensified the monetary problems inherited from the Middle Ages.[3]

From the point of view of the physical sciences, the Renaissance in England was not at first a rebirth. For, although the intellectual curiosity of the early Humanists was wide-ranging, their acceptance of Greek and Latin writers as supreme authorities tended to inhibit rather than to promote advances in scientific studies. To science, sixteenth-century England made no important contributions. For really memorable scientific advances in the sixteenth century we have to turn to such Continental works as Copernicus' *Concerning the Revolutions of the Heavenly Bodies*, 1543, which put the earth in its right place in the solar system, and Vesalius' *Concerning the Structure of the Human Body*, 1543, which overthrew the medieval authority of Galen and prepared the way for anatomical studies based on observation and dissection. In the early seventeenth century, however, as the forces set in motion by Humanism increased and extended and permeated the intellectual life of Europe, England's activity in science became significant. William Gilbert's studies in terrestrial magnetism and Bacon's writings on experimental research come to mind, as well as William Harvey's discovery of the true method of the circulation of the blood.

The classical revival, however, was an indirect cause of important developments in physics and anatomy. Artists under the sway of their passionate admiration for Greek sculpture found themselves forced to study the human figure scientifically before they could represent it with anatomical accuracy, and the sketches and studies of such artists as Pollaiuolo and Leonardo da Vinci have as great scientific as esthetic interest. Furthermore, the quickened interest in the world around the artist, and the incentive to represent its buildings, furniture, and tiled floors precisely rather than symbolically, encouraged studies in mechanics and perspective which resulted in scientific as well as artistic progress.[4]

But neither on the Continent nor in England was the sixteenth century prolific in epoch-making scientific studies; it remained for the seventeenth century to establish modern science and the scientific view of the world which we take for granted.

The Reformation

For England at least, the influence of the movement generally known as the Reformation had results, in the sixteenth century, though more particularly in the seventeenth century, comparable in depth and range to the secular movements of the Renaissance. In England, the Renaissance and the Reformation developed simultaneously. This simultaneity, the vigor of the medieval inheritance in England, and the strongly moralistic bent in the English character gave the Reformation a significance and a weight in England beyond that found in any other European country except Germany. It is the equal strength of the two forces—the Renaissance and the Reformation—that gives Spenser and Milton, for instance, a markedly English character, and that accounts for the relatively slight reaction in England away from otherworldliness to worldliness. Michelet's famous definition of the Renaissance as "the discovery of the world and of man" is broadly applicable to England, but Englishmen in their discovery of man never lost sight of the fact that his most important element was his soul, and that its salvation was of greater moment than anything the world could give.

Of the origins and the causes of the Reformation as a European movement we can do no more here than recall the rise of Lutheranism in Germany after Luther posted his ninety-five theses on the doors of the cathedral at Wittenberg in 1517, the development of Calvinism with its theological headquarters in Geneva, and the rise of Presbyterianism (Scottish Calvinism) under John Knox. Unquestionably, the Reformation would have had its effect on English religious thought and practice through gradual infiltration, but Henry VIII's severance of England's relationship to the Pope, and his assumption of the title of Supreme Head of the Church, hastened immeasurably the progress of Protestantism in England. To the theological and political consequences of his action, Henry was al-

[3] For a fuller treatment of this aspect of the Renaissance, see Richard H. Tawney, *Religion and the Rise of Capitalism*, Harcourt, Brace, 1926, pp. 66–79.

[4] For a fuller discussion of this general topic, see George Sarton, "Science in the Renaissance" in *The Civilization of the Renaissance*, pp. 75–95.

most completely blind. The King himself had already won from the Pope the title of Defender of the Faith as a doughty champion against Lutheranism, and, anti-Protestant as he was, he would have been horrified if he had been able to foresee the consequences of his act.

Of the major religious events of Henry's reign, the most consequential was the severing of relations with Rome. However dubious its motivation, that severance led immediately, not to a reformation of the Church (such a reformation was the least of Henry's intentions) but to a revolution in the relations between Church and State. Henceforth the heads of Church and State were to be not two, the Pope and the King, but one, the English sovereign; and numerous powers and privileges hitherto appertaining to the Pope now fell into the eager hands of Henry. Undoubtedly some of the English monasteries had become lax and corrupt, and might well have been dissolved, but the wholesale dissolution and spoliation of the monasteries by Henry had as primary motivation not reform of abuses but satisfaction of greed. That motive, however, could hardly have resulted in violent action under the previously existing relations between Church and State. Although expediency kept Henry usually on the conservative path so far as dogma was concerned, he could not prevent an increase in the discussion of doctrinal issues or the raising of questions already argued among Protestants abroad.

Of these questions one of the most potentially revolutionary was that of the translation of the Bible into English. The major argument against such a procedure was that if the Bible were accessible in the only language known to the unlettered among the laity, it might encourage novel and dangerous interpretations of the Scriptures. But although many of Henry's counselors, lay and clerical, regarded the procedure with apprehension, Archbishop Cranmer in 1544 gave his sanction to an English translation of the Bible. This act—far more than Henry's break with Rome—prepared the way for the development of the Reformation and ultimately the rise of Puritanism in England. For with the Scriptures accessible, men soon came to feel that the private individual had the right and the duty to decide for himself problems involved in his relation to the Deity. This right of private judgment was the ultimate source not only of the modern liberal-democratic doctrine of freedom of thought and expression but also of all the extravagant heresies possible under Protestantism.

By the Act of Succession (1536), the King secured the throne for his puny son, Edward VI, but on Henry's death in 1547 the real power passed into the hands of the Duke of Somerset, who through the medium of the Privy Council ruled England, and strenuously furthered the cause of the Reformation. England opened her doors to a horde of Protestant teachers exiled from the Continent, and, despite the opposition of such conservative members of the clergy as Bishops Gardiner and Bonner, the Protector encouraged practices and doctrines far more extreme than those permitted under Henry. Orders in Council were issued for the destruction of "abused images," that is to say, statues, stained-glass windows, paintings, and carvings that might be regarded as objects of idolatry; the marriage of the clergy was permitted; church services could be conducted in English; the communion in both kinds was authorized.[5]

Edward VI died in 1553 at the age of sixteen, and was succeeded by his older sister Mary, the Catholic daughter of Queen Catherine of Aragon, whom Henry had put away. Upon Mary's accession, the changes brought about under Henry and his son were promptly wiped out, and the Anglican Church was once more united with the Roman. Church and State were purged of Protestant heretics, college and university were cleansed of unbelievers, and the clerical leaders of the Reformation, Cranmer and Latimer, were burned at the stake. In the main, the bulk of the clergy accepted the reversion to Catholicism without compunction, and popular tradition has probably been unfair in burdening Mary with the epithet "Bloody," since, although the fires of Smithfield were put out, Elizabeth was responsible in one way or another for as many persecutions as Mary.

When Mary died in 1558 and Elizabeth came to the throne at the age of twenty-five, England was faced with the necessity of plotting its course between Catholicism and the Protestantisms stemming from the Continent and Scotland. Within England itself there were not only Romanist and Anglican elements but even indications of the beginnings of Puritanism and Separatism. The problem that confronted Elizabeth and her counselors was weighty and difficult, since it had not merely theological but also national and international political implications. Elizabeth herself was personally sympathetic with the conservative doctrinal views of her father, but her most influential advisers favored the reformed doctrines on theological and political grounds, and Elizabeth saw the wisdom of

[5] Communion in both kinds permits the laity to partake of both bread and wine; wine is not given the laity in the Roman Catholic rite.

following the middle course. The Act of Supremacy and the Act of Uniformity indicated that course by defining the doctrine of the Church narrowly enough to eliminate both determined Romanists and determined Calvinists, but broadly enough to include both conservative and advanced Protestants. During most of the Queen's long reign, the Elizabethan compromise worked admirably. Toward the end of it, as her personal prestige waned, there arose from the Puritan elements within the Church louder and louder protests against various points of Anglican doctrine, in particular, the system of the government of the Church by bishops. With this Puritan movement, Elizabeth's closest counselors, Lord Burghley, Sir Francis Bacon, the Earl of Leicester, and Sir Francis Walsingham, were openly or secretly in sympathy. But Elizabeth's shrewdness and skill were sufficient to keep the Puritan movement in hand and to transmit the knotty problem to her less adroit successor, James I, son of her rival, Mary Queen of Scots, her Catholic cousin whose death warrant for treason Elizabeth signed in 1587.

"It need hardly be said," writes Professor J. B. Black in his volume *The Reign of Queen Elizabeth*, "that a completely objective account of events in Elizabeth's reign, however desirable it may be in theory, cannot in actual fact be written. From time to time one treads on embers of controversies that still flicker with a baleful light as soon as they are disturbed. And there are questions on which historians will probably be divided to the end of time, for the simple reason that their points of view differ so greatly that the gulf between them is unbridgeable." As for Elizabeth herself, she is likely to remain an unsolved enigma for ever. There were many qualities in her character and behavior that were far from attractive: egoism, guile, inordinate ambition, shiftiness, parsimony; and her private life often fitted ill with her public position. Much in her life may be explained, if not excused, by the time and circumstances in which she lived. But even her worst enemies among historians and biographers, however they deplore her conduct as a gentlewoman, admit her greatness as a queen. She was fiercely patriotic, and she called forth, as only a woman could, the love and devotion of her people. She had one quality in abundance—common sense—and it was the triumph of this most English of qualities that saved her and the nation. At the end of her long reign England had achieved a solidity, a strength, and a position in the world that she had never before possessed; and if it was not the Queen who had created the position, it was she who had presided over the creation of it and who, more than any other person, had inspired it. The age which saw the Renaissance in England reach its finest flowering is not inappropriately called after her name, nor is it inappropriate that Shakespeare, the chief glory of English literature, had her for his Queen.

The Influence of the Classics

Although the dawn of Humanism in Italy was truly a lifting of darkness and a spreading of light, the darkness was not so profound or the illumination so sudden as is often supposed. In Bologna and Florence and other cities of northern Italy the first stirrings of Humanism occurred about the beginning of the fourteenth century, not as a reaction or a revival, but rather as "a spontaneous and natural development of classical studies as pursued during the later Middle Ages."[6] It is important for us to remember that most of the great Roman writers were studied throughout the Middle Ages, and that in the later Middle Ages some of the Greeks, especially Plato and Aristotle, were tolerably well known in Latin translations. What the Renaissance brought was chiefly a shift in emphasis—from the Latin language to the Greek, from certain Latin writers to others, and, in the case of the Greeks, from certain works to other works of the same authors. The *Poetics* of Aristotle, for example, greatly increased in prominence with the Renaissance, although it was known only at second hand, in Latin, in the sixteenth century. It is such shifts of emphasis as these that often have more far-reaching consequences than brand-new discoveries.

The revival of interest in classical literature and life was not, as one might think, primarily esthetic but rather moral in its motivation. Renaissance students of the classics were only remotely concerned with the esthetic excellence of the literature of classical antiquity; they were more profoundly stirred by the conviction that the classics would open up to them another way to the good life different from, or in addition to, that laid down by the Church and the Scriptures. But before the new way could be explored, and certainly before it could be imitated, various practical problems had to be solved. Since Latin had for centuries been the language for learned and international communication, its renewed study did not present the acute problem that faced men who wished to penetrate

[6] Dr. Roberto Weiss made these observations in his inaugural address as Professor of Italian in the University of London in 1947.

the enchanted world of Greek literature. Even in Italy in the fifteenth century the number of persons able to teach Greek was almost negligible, but as the century passed, young Englishmen in increasing numbers made their way to Italy as the only place where a knowledge of Greek could be satisfactorily acquired. But not all eager students could travel so far afield, and it soon seemed desirable and became practicable to bring to English universities men capable of teaching Greek.

A further problem that faced the early Humanists was that of acquiring adequate texts. This involved the collating of manuscripts, the establishment and annotation of texts, and the printing and publishing of editions of the classics that could be easily diffused through western Europe. In this particular service, the printing and publishing house of Aldus in Venice played the primary role. The various members of that distinguished family who successively headed this press displayed extraordinary energy and intelligence in their selection of the most capable editors available for the preparation of classical texts, and in their persistence in printing, as the decades passed, most of the important Greek and Latin classics in beautifully designed editions.

Many of the Humanists were remarkable linguists, and, indeed, would have accomplished very little without their linguistic interests and activity. In the fields of textual criticism, translation, and grammatical studies, their accomplishments were equal to those of any age. The major results of the eager and enthusiastic study of the classics were perhaps four: the translating of the classics for readers inexpert in the tongues; the application of classical critical standards to the existent vernacular literatures; the attempt by imitation to create a new literature worthy of comparison with classical literature; and the attempt to evolve out of the ethical elements in classical literature a new conception of the good life. Of the first three of these results, more will be said below; to the fourth—the movement commonly known as Humanism—some consideration must be given here.

Humanism was not primarily an esthetic or literary or antitheological movement, but an ethical and moral one. It was an attempt to sketch in the outlines of the good life and to point the way toward it. It has all too frequently been said that Humanism was one of the Renaissance manifestations of a general reaction from medieval otherworldliness, that it found its values in this world and not in another. Such an interpretation falsifies the position of such major English Humanists as Colet, Linacre, Fisher, and More. These men were all devout and also enlightened Catholics. What these English Humanists aimed at was a redefinition of the good life in the light of religion and the teachings of the classical philosophers and moralists. Their aim was the synthesis of the best in religion and the best in classical secular thought.

The Humanists strove for a fresh conception of the life of the individual and of his relation to society, and for the consequent reform of the state itself. No one of the early Humanists defined his purpose more clearly than did John Milton, over a century later, when, writing his *Tractate on Education* in the full Humanistic spirit, he defined the ideal education as that which fitted "a man to perform justly, skilfully, and magnanimously all the duties, public and private, of peace and war." The Humanists believed in the freedom of the will and in man's perfectibility. They believed man capable of developing public and private virtues through the proper sort of education. They were concerned with the nature of true as distinguished from conventional nobility, and believed that the former was to be found only in association with character, virtue, learning, and the ability to serve the commonweal. They were concerned with the reform, not the destruction, of the Church, and while some of them attacked satirically its current weaknesses, others attempted to purify the concepts of religion much as the Puritans attempted to do a century later. The Humanists were concerned with the ethical aspects of government. Their ideal was Plato's philosopher-king, surrounded by officials similarly trained in virtue and wisdom, and dedicated to the service of the state.

To the great generation of English Humanists belong John Colet (1467?–1519), Thomas Linacre (1460?–1524), John Fisher, Bishop of Rochester (1459–1535), and Sir Thomas (now St. Thomas) More (1478–1535). John Colet, Dean of St. Paul's, is best known as the founder of St. Paul's School, a private school with a secular board of control. The Latin-English grammar devised for this school by Colet, and by its first headmaster William Lyly, was later revised by Erasmus, the great Dutch Humanist and close friend of Colet and More, and was still in use two hundred years later. But equally important was Colet's devotion to the reform of the Church. Like many another devout Catholic, he opposed relics and pilgrimages, and believed that the Bible should be translated for the use of the unlettered laity. More significantly, he insisted in his sermons on the historical interpretation of the Bible as against the medieval allegorical and mystical interpretations, and pleaded for a thoroughgoing reform of the spiritual life of the Church. For these advanced views, he was summoned before Archbishop Warham on charges of heresy, which the broad-minded prelate dismissed. Thomas Linacre's services to Humanism were more secular. After studying Greek at Oxford under Cornelio Vitelli, he continued his classical studies in Italy under the tutors of Lorenzo de' Medici's sons, read Plato in the Vatican library, assisted the printing house of Aldus in its edition of Aristotle, and studied medicine at Padua and Vicenza. After his return to England, he taught Greek to Colet, More, and Erasmus, became Henry VIII's personal physician, founded the Royal College of Physicians, and acted as tutor to the Princess Mary. He translated classical works on medicine, restored the Hippocratic method of treating diseases on the basis of careful observation, and gave a valuable medical library to All Souls College, Oxford. Bishop Fisher's services to Humanism were primarily administrative. As Chancellor of the University of Cambridge, he encouraged preaching in English and was instrumental in persuading Erasmus to teach Greek there between 1511 and 1514. In religion and theology, he was stanchly conservative, and his writings were intensely anti-Protestant. He refused to acknowledge Henry VIII's claim to be head of the Church, and was, in consequence, executed on June 22, 1535. In his heroic devotion to the old faith, he had a close companion in the greatest of the English Humanists, Sir Thomas More.[7]

The Course of Education

The program the Humanists laid down was to be carried out by means of education, and it is natural therefore that their work should have played a considerable part in the rise of Humanistic education in Renaissance England. Public education during the sixteenth century suffered from a number of profoundly disturbing influences, of which the two most important were the dissolution of the monasteries and the conflict between Catholicism and Protestantism. The dissolution of the monasteries had certain immediate unfortunate results: the destruction of precious books and manuscripts; the breaking up of those colleges at Oxford and Cambridge that were sponsored and controlled by the monastic orders and the consequent decline in the number of university students; the cessation of elementary schools maintained by the monasteries; the pre-emption of the public schools by the upper classes; and the severance of cultural intercourse between English monastic houses and the Continental orders. Educationally, the dissolution of the monasteries may be taken as a violent symbol of the process of secularization which is one of the major distinguishing characteristics of the Renaissance. Unhappy as the immediate results were, the dissolution meant, for better or worse, the ultimate secularization of education, the substitution of a Humanistic for a Scholastic educational ideal, and the rapid increase in educational institutions of all ranks as the laity and the state became increasingly aware of their responsibilities in the field of education.

Educational progress in the sixteenth century may be measured in two ways: the founding of new institutions, and the definition and discussion of the ideals and methods of education. The institutions founded in this century ranged from grammar schools to universities. On the whole, the number of foundations increased rapidly under Edward VI, declined under Mary Tudor, and multiplied under Elizabeth.

The ideals and methods of the new education were derived not only from the general reawakening enthusiasm for the study of Greek and Latin, but specifically from three classical works on education: Cicero's *Concerning Invention*, Quintilian's *Oratorical Education*, and Plutarch's *On the Education of Children*. Cicero's youthful and incomplete treatise maintained its prestige from the twelfth century to the seventeenth century because of its author's pre-eminence as an orator. His prose style came to be regarded by many educators of the Renaissance as the ideal to be aimed at, and an important school of writers in both Latin and English attempted to write with the precise rhythms of Cicero. Quintilian's treatise, known imperfectly during the Middle Ages, achieved a wider fame after a complete manuscript of it was discovered at St. Gall in 1416. The book was a guide not only to success in oratory but to life as well, for, according to Quintilian, "No man unless he be good can be an orator." "We are educating," he wrote, "a man who will bring to human affairs a mind eminent in natural endowments and, in particular, embracing the fairest qualities within its folds, a man such as no previous age has known, and perfect on every side, thinking the best thoughts and expressing them in the best language."[8] It was from the particular point of view of the orator that Quintilian considered the utility of various forms of knowledge, but it was his ideas on more general educational topics that achieved the widest currency in the Renais-

[7] For More's relation to Humanism, see page 184.

[8] John W. Adamson, *A Short History of Education*, Macmillan, 1919, pp. 93–94.

sance. To him may be traced the unfortunate emphasis on the training of the child's memory, the importance of play as a mode of educating little children, and the significance of rivalry and rewards in attaining the desired results. On the subject of the imitation of Cicero, Quintilian displayed a balance that the sixteenth-century rhetoricians might well have imitated. For although he said, "Let a man know that he has made progress when he takes great pleasure in Cicero," he also said, "What is the harm in assuming in certain passages the force of Caesar, the roughness of Caelius, the earnestness of Pollio, the discernment of Calvus?" Plutarch's little treatise *On the Education of Children* had a long and complex history of translation and adaptation during the Renaissance.[9] The aim of education, according to Plutarch, is the moral life, since virtue is the best of all earthly goods. To the attainment of this end, education and especially philosophical studies are the major means. But the Renaissance was most attentive to Plutarch's specific observations with regard to the nursing of children by their mothers rather than by hired nurses, the habitual carelessness of parents in the selection of their children's tutors, and the importance of the example set their children by parents. His distribution of emphasis over morals, manners, effective speech, and bodily exercise had a potent influence, especially in England.

Sixteenth-century England produced no first-rate original thinkers on educational theory, but there were a number of men who did valiant service in making the classical doctrines available to English readers. Probably the most important was Roger Ascham, whose *The Schoolmaster*[10] greatly influenced the teaching of the time.

The Ideal Courtier

A special branch of Renaissance educational doctrine was concerned not so much with education generally as with the education of the gentleman, the courtier, or the prince. The source of this special interest was the Humanists' belief that if the right goal for education could be envisioned and the right methods discovered, there could be trained a philosopher-king, who, with similarly trained courtly advisers, might bring about the reformation of the state and of the relations of all classes to the state. To the education of the courtier, or more generally to the doctrine of courtesy, almost a thousand treatises of one or another kind were devoted during the Renaissance.[11] Of these, by all odds the most influential was Count Baldassare Castiglione's *Il Cortegiano* (*The Courtier*), published by Aldus in 1528, and translated into English by Sir Thomas Hoby in 1561.

The courtly ideal was the many-sided but harmonious development of all the gentleman's potentialities; the elaborateness and the complexity of the ideal would make it seem impossible of attainment if the Renaissance had not furnished us numerous examples of men like the young Henry VIII, Sir Philip Sidney, the Earl of Essex, and Sir Walter Ralegh who came close to embodying it. The ideal involved the development of the courtier as a physical, political, religious, social, and esthetic being. The physical program laid down for the neophyte was an arduous one. Its results were to be grace in society, skill in sports, and valor in battle. No military exercise or game of physical skill was denied him except those which might impair his social standing in a rigidly stratified society. Thus, Sir Thomas Elyot in his *Book Named the Governour*, 1531, writes: "Wrestling is a very good exercise . . . so that it be with one that is equal in strength or somewhat under, and that the place be soft so that in falling their bodies be not bruised." But of bowling and quoits, he says: "Verily as for two the last, [they] be to be utterly abjected of all noble men, in like wise football, wherein is nothing but beastly fury and extreme violence, whereof proceedeth hurt, and consequently rancour and malice do remain with them that be wounded; wherefore it is to be put into perpetual silence." In his relation to the philosopher-king, the ideal courtier should be trained to serve as adviser and diplomat in times of peace and as a soldier in times of war.

But it was perhaps to the courtier as a social being and as an amateur artist that the Renaissance gave the freshest and most attractive turn to the chivalric ideal. The doctrine of courtesy assumed an equality between the sexes in social relations that implied for both gentlemen and ladies a high degree of skill in discourse, both light and learned. In Boccaccio's *Decameron*, for example, we have an early Renaissance illustration of the conversational resources of a group of seven ladies and three gentlemen who have fled from the plague to a country refuge at Fiesole, and Castiglione in the *Courtier* thought it appropriate to impart his doctrine through the discussions of a similar courtly group.

[9] For the details of its vogue in the Renaissance, see the introductory note on John Lyly, page 205. [10] For fuller comment on Ascham and a selection from his major work, see pages 197–204.

[11] Most of these are listed, and their doctrines analyzed and systematized, in Ruth Kelso's *The Doctrine of the English Gentleman in the Sixteenth Century*, University of Illinois, 1930.

The courtier's more specific social graces lay in the field of the arts. Not only must he be able to sing and to play an instrument to accompany his singing, but also he must be able to write verses in honor of his lady. In all these activities, however, he must preserve his amateur standing, and allow no financial consideration to enter into his poetic or musical productions. Thence derives the custom persistent in the Renaissance, and illustrated strikingly in the case of Sir Philip Sidney, of circulating one's works in manuscript and persistently refraining from the publication of them.

Not the least important aspect of courtly education was the training of the courtier as a lover, and probably no facet of the complex ideal had so great an influence on Renaissance literature as the code of love developed during the Renaissance. This code was a synthesis of the medieval code of courtly love, the elaboration of this tradition by Dante and Petrarch, and the revival of the Neo-Platonic conception of love that derived ultimately from Plato's *Symposium*. Plato had conceived of love as one of the major modes of experience by means of which man could attain an awareness of ideal and perfect Beauty, as important an element in the Platonic triad as Truth and Goodness. So considered, love became a highly idealized and moral experience, and however short of the ideal men and women of the Renaissance may have fallen, the poets at any rate welcomed this intense ennobling of the universal human experience.

The Program for Literature

Before turning to a discussion of the imaginative literature of the Renaissance, we must give some attention to the critical and esthetic background of that literature, since most of it was produced in a conscious attempt to carry out a well-considered program. Renaissance critical theorists and estheticians faced two major problems, which they attempted to solve with all the intelligence and ingenuity at their disposal. Their first task was the justification of literature, the defense of its value, and the determination of its purpose. The second major task was the laying down of a program which writers should follow in order to create a native literature worthy of comparison with Greek and Latin literature and of evaluation in terms of it.

The defense of literature followed several fairly distinct lines: historical, esthetic, and moral. The historical argument called attention to the exceeding antiquity of poetry, its universality, and its approval by the learned and great. The chief esthetic defense was grounded on Aristotle's theory of imitation as expressive of a fundamental human instinct and as giving what we should nowadays call the pleasure of recognition, even though the object imitated be itself unpleasant. With this esthetic delight in imitation, the Renaissance critics generally linked a didactic or moral value. Horace himself had written:

> "*Aut prodesse volunt, aut delectare poetae*
> *Aut simul et jucunda, et idonea dicere vitae*";

or as Ben Jonson had translated it:

> "Poets would either profit or delight,
> Or, mixing sweet and fit, teach life the right."

The authority of either poet was enough for most budding classicists of the late sixteenth century. This combination of delight and profit is repeated again and again in the critical theory of the period. Thus, Webbe in his *Discourse of English Poetrie*, 1586, wrote, "The perfect perfection of poetry is this, to mingle delight with profit in such wise that a reader might by his reading be partaker of both," although Puttenham was liberal enough to say in his *Arte of English Poetry*, 1589, that poetry, "being used for recreation only, may allowably bear matter not always of the gravest or of any great commodity of profit, but rather in some sort, vain, dissolute, or wanton if it be not very scandalous or of evil purpose."[12]

But the defense of literature against its assailants was only one of the tasks of the critical theorists of the Renaissance. Once literature had been justified, it became necessary for them to lay down a program to the carrying out of which serious-minded writers should devote themselves. The need for such a program was felt because to the critical temper, heightened by close contact with the Greek and Latin classics, the existing vernacular literature seemed faulty in almost every respect. Furthermore, the newborn nationalism of the Renaissance aroused in writers the desire to produce works in their native language that should be comparable with the masterpieces of antiquity. It seemed to most of the Renaissance theorists that the surest means of achieving the desired results was to use the classics as models and to follow them as closely as possible. They were encouraged in this conception of esthetic imitation not only by their misunderstanding of Aristotle's use of the term and Horace's more nar-

[12] For Sir Philip Sidney's treatment of the arguments for and against literature, see the selections from his *Defence of Poesy* on page 212.

row interpretation of it, but by their own abysmal humility before the masterpieces of classical literature. As a result, therefore, the literary types exhibited by ancient literature—epic, drama, lyric, elegy, epistle, epigram, and pastoral—became the sanctioned forms for Renaissance writing, and the stylistic and technical features of these types were carefully worked out and systematized, although it remained for the Frenchman Boileau in the seventeenth century and Pope in the eighteenth century to give them their final Neoclassical delineation.

Broadly speaking, then, the program of Renaissance writers was the classicizing of native literature. This program met with varying success in various countries. During the sixteenth century in England it met with only modified success, since it had to combat the profoundly romantic and undisciplined spirit of most of the major writers of the century. As the period neared its end, the theory and practice of Ben Jonson pointed the way to a complete assimilation of the classical spirit.

Different Types of Prose

In considering the development of sixteenth-century prose, we should do well to distinguish between utilitarian and imaginative prose, that is, between prose the purpose of which is primarily information or didacticism and the prose the purpose of which is primarily "delight" or esthetic pleasure. In both utilitarian and imaginative prose the sixteenth century is rich indeed, but it is possible to maintain that Tudor writers solved the problems of utilitarian prose more satisfactorily than they did those of artistic prose, if general effectiveness and cogency of communication are the criteria of success.

The rise of nationalism during the Tudor period was accompanied and perhaps to a degree re-enforced by a widespread curiosity concerning England's past. This appetite was fed not merely by an astonishing amount of poetry and drama utilizing historical material, but by less widely read works of a more strictly historical sort. Such was the impressive series of chronicles which stud the sixteenth century, from Robert Fabyan's *New Chronicles of England and of France*, 1516, and Edward Hall's *Union of the Noble and Illustrate Families of Lancaster & York*, 1542, to Raphael Holinshed's *Chronicles*, of which the first edition appeared in 1578 and a revised edition in 1587. Holinshed's is the best and most famous of the chronicles. Shakespeare made much use of the second edition of it in writing some of his plays.

The sixteenth century was also richly productive in accounts of voyages, either historical or contemporary. The most avid collector of accounts of discovery and exploration in all the languages of western Europe was Richard Hakluyt, the crown of whose life work was *The Principall Voyages, Traffiques, and Discoveries of the English Nation*, which appeared in three huge volumes between 1598 and 1600. The most interesting examples of travel literature were, of course, produced by the voyagers themselves. In this category fall such memorable accounts as Sir John Hawkins's *True Declaration of the Troublesome Voyage of M. John Hawkins to the Parts of Guiana and the West Indies*, 1569; Sir Humphrey Gilbert's *Discourse of a Discovery for a New Passage to Cataia* (China), 1576; and Sir Walter Ralegh's *Discoverie of the Large, Rich, and Beautiful Empire of Guiana*, 1596.

The religious issues of the century were responsible for the production of more prose writings, perhaps, than any other questions or interests of the day. Although the great bulk of such writings is controversial and polemical in nature, there are a few of them whose fame and influence are as important from the point of view of the student of literature as from that of the theologian. One of these is William Tyndale's translation of the New Testament from the original Greek of Erasmus' edition. This translation, printed abroad in 1525, was the first to be made in English from the Greek and the first printed edition in English of the Bible or part thereof. The translation, revised by Tyndale in 1534 and 1535, is in simple and vigorous English. Its influence upon the King James translation of the Bible in 1611 (see page 310) and through that on succeeding translations and on the development of English prose is very great. Another translation of the Scriptures, this time of the entire Bible, and based in part on Tyndale's text, was that of Miles Coverdale, 1535. This, the first complete printed Bible in English, was dedicated to Henry VIII. It has not the homely vigor of Tyndale, but, especially in the Psalms, which are translated from the Latin Vulgate, has a sweetness and felicity of phrasing and cadence that have caused Coverdale's Psalms to be retained to this day in the Book of Common Prayer of the Church of England. The Book of Common Prayer, 1549, is itself one of the noblest examples of English prose. It is largely the work of Archbishop Cranmer, and has all the beauty and rhythm and power of the best sixteenth-century prose without its verbosity. Hilaire Belloc, who deplores the disruption of the fabric of western Christendom which led to the existence of an English Book of Common

Prayer, and finds little that is admirable in Cranmer, the chief architect of the book, writes in his *Thomas Cranmer* that its author "gave to the Church of England a treasure, by the aesthetic effect of which, more than anything else, her spirit has remained alive, and she has attached herself to the hearts of men."

The translations of the Bible and the Book of Common Prayer are only a few of the great works which were brought into English prose during this golden age of translation. Most of the masterpieces of the classical languages, and many of the French and Italian classics, were naturalized in English during the sixteenth and the early seventeenth centuries, and became part of the English scheme of things. Sir Thomas North's English version of Plutarch's *Lives* provided English dramatists with material for plots and gave to Shakespeare the substance and sometimes the very words of some of his most memorable passages.

The best of these translations, whether of religious or secular works, and whether in prose or verse, have a vigor and robustness which go far to make amends for their frequent lack of faithfulness to their originals. And, for better or worse, the translators have left the impression of their own personalities on the works of the authors they imported into English. To most English-speaking people for three centuries Plutarch has spoken with the accents of Sir Thomas North; Montaigne has been the Montaigne of John Florio's translation (1603); and as for the Bible, though the voice has been the voice of the Hebrew prophets, poets, and apostles, the words have been the words of Tyndale, Coverdale, and King James's translators.

On a wavering line between fact and fiction lies the vast body of Tudor pamphleteering literature, of which the avowed purpose was reformatory, but of which the initial incentive was frequently purely commercial. Perhaps the best-known pamphleteer of the period is Robert Greene, who during the 1590's launched upon a sensation-eager audience his accounts, avowedly autobiographical, of his adventures in the criminal world of London and in the countryside. These "cony-catching" pamphlets—so called, because the criminal's victim was, in the underworld slang of the period, called a cony, that is, a rabbit, and so easily befuddled—give us vivid if not perfectly reliable glimpses into the Tudor underworld.[13] Thomas Dekker was another poverty-stricken hack writer who turned out pamphlets to every taste. Of these the most famous is *The Gull's Hornbook*, 1609, a satirical handbook for the would-be man-about-town. A special type of pamphlet emanated from Puritan sources. Some of these, like Stephen Gosson's *School of Abuse* and Philip Stubbes's *Anatomy of Abuses*, attacked the vices and foibles of the time from a severely moralistic point of view. Others, like the "Martin Marprelate" pamphlets which were printed surreptitiously in the last few years of the century, were virulent attacks on episcopacy by Puritan extremists.

The character of sixteenth-century prose was, in large measure, the result of confused theories as to the border line between prose and verse and the role of the imagination in literature. Writers of prose fiction, that is of prose dealing with imaginative subjects with the aim primarily of delight, felt it incumbent upon them to create a prose which should be comparable in quality with the poetry which was being produced under the impetus of the classical revival. The means by which they solved their problem were conditioned by their conviction that if prose were to be comparable to poetry, it ought to have as many of the characteristics of poetry as possible, with the exception of verse and rhyme. This conviction explains the excessively ornamental character of the two types of imaginative prose (euphuistic and Arcadian) which had a marked influence on minor and imitative writers. The first—euphuistic prose—took its name from the novel of John Lyly, *Euphues, the Anatomy of Wit*, 1578. Lyly used to be regarded as the inventor of euphuistic prose, but English writers before Lyly had used all or most of the devices found in *Euphues*, and it has now been shown that prose of this type originated in the attempt to carry over into English stylistic devices that appear in late Latin writers and that flourish in medieval Latin, particularly in sermons. Aside from the numerous figures of speech from what has been called "unnatural natural history," the basic feature of euphuistic prose is the excessive use of "word schemes," various complicated patterns of sound that take the form of balanced words, phrases, clauses, or sentences, or of simple or complex forms of alliteration. By using these devices more lavishly than any of his English predecessors had done, Lyly initiated a vogue that for a decade had a good deal of intensity. The second major type of imaginative prose—Arcadian—takes its name from the long pastoral romance which Sir Philip Sidney wrote for the amusement of his learned sister, the Countess of Pembroke. Here

[13] A number of Greene's "cony-catching" pamphlets have been reprinted by John Lane in the Bodley Head Quartos series. A convenient collection of Tudor rogue literature is Arthur V. Judges, ed., *The Elizabethan Underworld*, Dutton, 1930.

there is less emphasis on patterns of sound and more on figures of speech. Sidney seems to be aiming to come just as close to the tone, language, and figures of poetry as he could come without writing verse. The result has a complex poetic charm, but the style, like Lyly's, is so weighted with poetic devices that it quite loses the movement essential to narrative. Sidney, like Lyly, had a host of imitators no one of whom, with the possible exception of Thomas Lodge in his *Rosalynde* (the source of Shakespeare's *As You Like It*), caught the overelaborate charm of their master.[14]

Different Types of Poetry

Sixteenth-century poets writing under the influence of the critical theories of the period were well schooled in the types and styles appropriate for poetry that aimed at qualities in English comparable to those of classical poetry. The major classical categories—epic, drama, and lyric—challenged their powers and imaginations, and the minor types—epistle, elegy, epigram, and satire—found fairly frequent adherents.

The Tudor poets had some difficulty in solving two problems of very different degrees of importance, and some of their answers seem to us to have been exceedingly unfortunate. One problem was that of metrics. The question was raised as to whether English poets could produce a poetry really comparable to classical poetry unless they abandoned the traditional accentual metrical system and adopted the classical quantitative system. A part of the controversy involved rhyme, which some writers regarded askance because they did not find it in classical Greek and Latin. Not until the end of the century were both these questions emphatically decided in favor of accentual meter, with or without rhyme, although as late as Dryden's *Essay of Dramatic Poesie*, 1668, the question of rhyme *vs.* no-rhyme was being discussed animatedly.

The other problem which Tudor poets were less successful in solving was that of the subject matter appropriate to poetry. Both dramatic and nondramatic poets utilized a great deal of subject matter—historical or even geographical—which seems to us poetically refractory. Their incentive was the ambition to produce epic poetry as fine as that of Homer and Virgil. This ambition necessitated their utilizing material from English history, and although not all the historical poems of the period are cast in the true epic mold, they all aim at something like epic grandeur and national significance.[15]

The epic impulse manifested itself also in the field of translation toward the close of the century. In 1598 began the appearance of George Chapman's vigorous poetic version of Homer's *Iliad*, which he completed, together with the *Odyssey*, during the next two decades. Although more Elizabethan than Homeric in style and substance, it brought many Elizabethans into closer touch with the Greek epics than they had been before, and was destined two centuries later to open up to John Keats a new world and a new poetic experience (see page 865). Two Italian epics also were put into English verse during the last years of the century—Ariosto's *Orlando Furioso* (*Orlando Mad*), by Sir John Harington, in 1591, and Tasso's *Gerusalemme Liberata* (*Jerusalem Delivered*), by Edward Fairfax, in 1600.

Of epic proportions and spirit, if not of form, is Edmund Spenser's *The Faerie Queene*, 1590–1596, the most monumental, even in its unfinished state, of Elizabethan nondramatic productions in poetry. Like an epic, also, *The Faerie Queene* gathers into itself the habits of thought, the mind and spirit, of the age, and becomes a kind of mirror, at times a museum, of the English Renaissance. Into his great work Spenser put all that he had learned from the ancients and from his contemporaries, at the university and the court and in political service. It is a political poem and a religious poem, ardently Elizabethan and Protestant, and yet abounding in medieval and Catholic substance and imagery.

In the minor classical forms—satire and epistle—the sixteenth century is not very rich. In the vein of the classical satires of Horace are such early poems as Sir Thomas Wyatt's "Of the Mean and Sure Estate" and "Of the Courtier's Life."[16] Toward the end of the century several books of satires appeared in the more virulent veins of Juvenal and Martial; such books are Joseph Hall's *Virgidemiarum*, 1597, and John Marston's *The Scourge of Villainy*, 1598. These were so violent in tone that the Archbishop of Canterbury ordered them burned. To this decade belong also most of the satires of John Donne. In this period, the epistle is a more important form than the satire. It was used frequently by such poets

[14] Certain writers of prose fiction who for one or another reason worked outside the euphuistic and Arcadian modes produced prose that is nowadays decidedly more readable. Thomas Nashe, although he parodied Sidney in certain passages in his picaresque novel *The Unfortunate Traveller*, 1594, was too willing to use any type of prose that seemed momentarily effective, to create a consistent prose style. Thomas Deloney, who wrote tales of bourgeois life for a middle-class audience, produced in his collection of stories, *The Gentle Craft*, 1597(?), a type of prose much closer to that of later English prose fiction. Its diction and sentence-structure are colloquial and earthy.

[15] For an example of literary work utilizing historical materials, see page 364. [16] For text of latter poem, see page 192.

as Samuel Daniel and Michael Drayton, not to mention Ben Jonson and John Donne, whose work is usually associated with the seventeenth century. The type of epistle most popular was that addressed to some noble and cultivated lady or patroness of poets, and devoted to the meditative presentation of a philosophical or moral subject. Other types of epistles are illustrated in John Donne's "The Calm" and "To Sir Henry Wotton" and Ben Jonson's "To Penshurst." Michael Drayton's "To Henry Reynolds" is a particularly attractive epistle, sketching in his poetic education and giving his opinions of other contemporary poets.

The finest poetical product of the sixteenth century—aside, of course, from the drama—was the lyric (see pages 275–288). An astonishing number of writers—from Henry VIII to Robert Greene, Thomas Dekker, and others—wrote lyrics of great beauty and charm. It is in the lyric that the sunny golden spirit of the Elizabethan period expresses itself most directly, most economically, and most beguilingly. Lyrics were omnipresent and inescapable. They reached the public in diversified ways: in miscellanies or anthologies, in songbooks where they were accompanied by music, in the drama from the lips of sweet singers, and in the form of broadside ballads sold at street corners and at the annual fairs in town and country. The lyric attempted many moods, tragic and humorous, impassioned and gallant, decorous and indecorous, and many subjects—amatory, philosophical, didactic, and elegiac. In no other literary form cultivated in this century was perfection so frequently achieved.[17]

A special and intensive manifestation of the lyrical impulse was the writing of sonnets, a vogue which reached its peak in the early 1590's. To a very large extent, the subjects, attitudes, forms, and style of the Elizabethan sonnet were determined by Petrarch and his innumerable imitators in every modern European language, particularly Italian and French. By the time the craze of sonneteering reached England, the poetic game had developed an almost incredible number of rules and conventions. The wonder is that even minor sonneteers occasionally achieved an effect of freshness and sincerity. And even though many of the sonnets of such writers as Spenser, Sidney, Shakespeare, Daniel, and Drayton are little more than literary exercises, all these writers occasionally, and some of them very frequently, stamp the form with what seems to be personal emotion and intensity.[18]

[17] For a collection of lyrics from various sources, see pages 275–288. [18] For further comment on the sonnet conventions, see introductory note on Sidney's sonnets, page 210.

The Drama

The Elizabethan playhouse was modeled on the inn courtyards in which strolling bands of actors presented plays for the delectation of audiences assembled from the neighborhood. The typical theater was a structure, circular or polygonal in shape, built around an open court or "pit" into which projected a rectangular raised platform. In the pit and on three sides of the platform stood the "groundlings." The more well-to-do members of the audiences paid a higher admission fee and sat in the tiers of galleries that surrounded the pit and that were partitioned off into "boxes." Thus, the theaters accommodated audiences with a very wide social and intellectual range, from noblemen to pickpockets, from scholars to fishwives.

The play was acted on the raised platform, which was closed in at the back by a curtained alcove or "inner stage," to be used for scenes that took place indoors. Above this alcove was a balcony, also curtained off, which could serve for scenes on city walls or in bedchambers. At either side of the inner stage were entrances from the actors' "tiring" rooms. On the front or "apron" of the platform, adequately equipped with trapdoors, occurred most of the action, especially of those scenes for which the text indicated no specific location. Over a large portion of this outer stage a slanting roof extended, from above the balcony to two supporting pillars. This covering protected the actors and their splendid costumes from disagreeable weather, and housed mechanisms used for lowering gods and spirits to the level of the stage.

Each theatrical company was required by law to secure a nobleman as its patron. Most of the companies adopted the name of their patron and used it for purposes of identification, not only during their London seasons but also on the frequent tours occasioned by the closing of the city theaters on account of epidemics or disagreements with the Puritanical city fathers. The companies were usually organized on a profit-sharing plan by which the leading actors were joint owners of equipment, repertory, and playhouse. Full membership in the troupe was granted on the basis of ability and years of service. The underlings served as apprentices until they became eligible for promotion. Women's parts were acted by young men or boys. Plays were supplied or revised by dramatists who were likely to keep in mind the talents or the capacities of a particular company.

It is in the drama, particularly in the plays of Shakespeare, that the age achieved transcendent expression, and it is by its drama and by its lyrics—most frequently those from plays—that the literature of the period is now most widely known. The drama of the English Renaissance was the result of the fusion of certain medieval and classical elements. From the medieval drama came the conception of drama as a succession of scenes occurring in a series of places and times, the habit of mingling tragedy and comedy, the use of verse, and the fundamentally moral interpretation of human experience. From the classical tradition came conventions as to subject matter and form. In tragedy, for instance, there was almost universal acceptance of the convention of noble personages as the characters required by tragedy, and of the Aristotelian theory as to the nature of the tragic hero, namely, a person of unusual position or powers who falls to disaster as a result of a flaw of character or an error of judgment. Elizabethan playwrights ransacked the Latin tragedies of Seneca rather than the more subtle and civilized Greek tragedies, not only for elaborate stylistic effects and sententious utterances but also for an imposing array of devices of terror and horror—ghosts, dreams, prophecies, and appallingly gruesome details of bloodshed, suicide, and murder. From the Graeco-Roman comedy came conventions as to the plot structure and tone, and a handy collection of easily adaptable comic character types. The more devout among the Renaissance classicists attempted to impose the three unities on English drama, but it was only in the comedies and tragedies of Ben Jonson that these restrictive conventions played any very important part.

In addition to tragedies and comedies, classical or romantic, and history plays, we can also see the beginnings of a comedy and a tragedy that might be called realistic. Dekker's *The Shoemaker's Holiday*, 1599, is touched with the gaiety and glamour of the period, but, though sentimental, it recreates realistically the lives of the London streets, of prosperous craftsmen and lusty apprentices. In the anonymous *Arden of Feversham*, 1592, and Thomas Heywood's *A Woman Killed with Kindness*, 1603, there are premonitions of modern domestic or bourgeois tragedy.

The drama of the English Renaissance was very slow in coming to maturity, and despite serious though unsuccessful efforts, in such plays as *Gorboduc*, 1561, and *The Misfortunes of Arthur*, 1588, to apply the classical technique to English subject matter, it is not until 1590 that we reach any dramatic work approaching the first-rate in quality. Then Marlowe and Shakespeare, Kyd, Greene, Lyly, and Lodge, appear almost simultaneously on the stage, Of these the greatest, of course, are Marlowe and Shakespeare, but each of the others contributed some important element to the development of the Elizabethan drama.

The conventional classification of Shakespeare's plays as tragedies, comedies, or histories is serviceable for the drama as a whole. It reminds us that in the history or chronicle play the age was conscious of creating a type of drama that does not fit easily into either of the conventional classical dramatic categories. But this threefold classification fails to indicate the rich variety of the drama of the English Renaissance. On the whole, the age found the somewhat dry and satirical vein of classical comedy inadequate for the expression of its comic spirit, and it somewhat fumblingly created a type of romantic comedy difficult to characterize but easy to identify. In romantic comedy the plot, though sometimes intricate, is of little consequence; there is frequent use of mistaken identities; there is a tendency to use exotic settings—the Forest of Arden, Illyria, Venice; the characters are less definitely types than are those of classical comedy, and are more genially contemplated; the happy ending, though frequently contrived, is inevitable, and even villains and knaves usually escape with light punishment. Atmosphere and mood are all-important; the dramatists lure their audience into a world where the characters "fleet the time carelessly as they did in the golden world," where every shepherd has his pipe and plays it "as though he should never be old."

At the very end of the sixteenth century, Ben Jonson began to devote his great talent to a series of valiant attempts to subdue English drama to the classical spirit. But despite a considerable influence in the seventeenth century on the comedies of Thomas Middleton, Philip Massinger, and James Shirley, Jonson failed to overcome the indomitable romanticism of the Elizabethan drama. His failure is rendered the more conspicuous by the fact that the opening years of the new century saw the greatest triumph of that spirit in Shakespeare's dramatic romances, *Twelfth Night*, *The Winter's Tale*, and *The Tempest*, and in his great tragedies, *Hamlet*, *Othello*, *King Lear*, *Macbeth*, and *Antony and Cleopatra*.

Summary

The century which divides the decade in which Columbus discovered the West Indies from that in which the Englishman John Cabot visited the coast of North America and took possession of it in the king's name is one of the great watersheds of history, so effectively does it divide the medieval world from the modern. For England particularly it was a period of transition and transformation in every department of life, an age of expansion in which the people of England, together with those of Europe, had come into possession of a world vastly larger than that of their grandfathers. We have noticed the quickening of the intellectual life of England and the burgeoning of arts and letters as the nation came into the radiance of the Renaissance. The order and peace which came to the country with Henry VII attracted from the Continent persons of varied skills—scholars and artists and craftsmen. If the Tudor rule was despotic, it was not blind to the welfare of the nation and to the development of national wealth. The commercial, industrial, and maritime potentialities of the country were developed as never before. London became the leading trade center of Europe, and ordinary people for the first time could make money by capitalist enterprise. The nation which had scarcely any ships at the beginning of the century arrived, after the defeat of the Spanish Armada, at the beginning of her long career as mistress of the seas. Politically, also, sixteenth-century England belongs to the modern rather than the medieval order. The House of Commons as an active part of the machinery of government was largely the creation of the Tudors, although their aim in magnifying its importance and their attitude toward it was in no sense democratic. The religious dissensions and controversies affected every phase of English life. The dissolution of the monasteries had profound effects on the economic and the intellectual as well as the religious level. The breach between the Church of England and the Church of Rome produced, before the century had closed, a national Church with a printed Bible and liturgy and hymns in the national language.

Together with this great awakening of nationalism in so many phases of English life and thought came a greatly increased internationalism in the world of arts and letters. England was brought into contact with the language and literature of ancient Greece, and the classics of antiquity as well as of modern Europe became available to scholars in their original tongues and to the public in English translations. English literature during the century reflects this greatly expanded world and the varied types of men and women and human experience that went into its making. In prose and verse, in sermon and pamphlet and essay, in the lyric, the sonnet, the allegory, and the drama, English literature moved from medieval thought and expression to the themes and the vehicles of modern life and thought. Both the language and the prose were to undergo further development before they achieved their distinctive modern idioms, but in the best work of More and Tyndale and Cranmer and Ascham they showed what the nature of that idiom was to be and what special capabilities they possessed for the making of the flexible and serviceable medium of modern communication. English poetry, thanks to Shakespeare and his contemporaries, reached heights, especially in the lyric and the drama, which it had never attained before, and which are not likely to be surpassed.

It is customary to think of Marlowe's Dr. Faustus as the most thorough expression of the intellectual curiosity, ambition, and pretensions of the new age, of the triumph of the individual will over the private soul. Of the confusion and unrest and uneasiness of such an age, of the mutilations of the human spirit and human nature inflicted by such a triumph, it is inevitable that one should choose Shakespeare's Hamlet as the symptom and symbol. Both Dr. Faustus and Hamlet are unmistakable children of the sixteenth century, and in no way does their century show itself more certainly the threshold of the world we live in than in its "paradox of lusty confidence and immanent despair."

Sir Thomas More

1478–1535

Thomas More was born in 1478, the son of Sir John More, a judge. He received his elementary education at St. Anthony's School, London, and then became a page in the household of John Morton, Archbishop of Canterbury, Lord Chancellor, and later Cardinal. In this brilliant Humanistic household, he may have witnessed the beginnings of the English secular drama in the performances of Henry Medwall's *Fulgens and Lucrece*, and, according to tradition, showed his own wit in dramatic improvisations. Later, at Canterbury Hall, Oxford, he began the study of Greek under Linacre and Grocyn, who became his lifelong mentors and friends. He read for the law in London, made friends with the great Dutch Humanist Erasmus, and for a time contemplated becoming a monk. He decided, however, on marriage and a career in the world. His rise to a position of great power and responsibility was rapid. He became a Privy Councillor in 1518, was knighted and made Treasurer of the Exchequer in 1521, became Speaker of the House of Commons in 1523, and was made Chancellor of the Duchy of Lancaster in 1525. When Wolsey fell, Henry VIII appointed him Lord Chancellor against his own wishes. He discharged his duties wisely and well, but a conflict between More's principles and the King's lack of principle was bound to come, and when More, though willing to swear to obey the Act of Succession, refused to affirm that Henry's marriage to Catherine of Aragon had been void *ab initio*, he was sent to the Tower, charged with high treason, tried, and condemned. He was beheaded on July 7, 1535. He was beatified by the Roman Catholic Church in 1886, and was canonized in 1935.

Sir Thomas More combined the sternest principles with great intelligence and wit and a compelling personal charm. His friendships with the early Humanists were warm and devoted. Erasmus, who described More's "kind and friendly cheerfulness, with a little air of raillery," wrote at his suggestion *The Praise of Folly*, the Latin title of which, *Encomium Moriae*, contains a pun on his host's name. Though privately devoted to ascetic practices, More was the witty and genial center of a household famous for affection and culture, and through his relationships with the Rastells and the Heywoods was the fountainhead of a strong Catholic tradition which manifested its religious devotion through the persecutions of the sixteenth century. It is not too fanciful, perhaps, to believe that something of John Donne's genius depended on descent from this talented group.

Aside from the *Utopia*, 1516, More's writings in both verse and prose are infinitely less attractive than the man. Of them, one of the most significant is his translation from the Latin in 1510 of a life of Pico della Mirandola, who attracted More by a curious blend of philosophical ideas not unlike his own. Perhaps the most brilliant of the prose works ascribed to him is the *History of Richard the Third*, written probably in 1513. Some scholars believe this to be the work of Cardinal Morton himself; others, that it is a translation by More of a Latin work of Morton's. Certainly, much of the material came from the Cardinal's reminiscences of the royal tyrant. The artful vivid characterization makes it an important contribution to the pre-Shakespearean Richard III saga. Most of More's other works belong to the literature of anti-Protestant controversy. The conflict between More and William Tyndale, "the classic controversy of the Reformation," touches issues which are still vital. More's prose style suffers often from the heat of controversy, but at his best, as R. W. Chambers says in his standard biography of More, he may properly be called the first modern prose stylist in English.

from UTOPIA

More's most famous work, the *Utopia*, gave its name to the literary type to which it belongs. It is only one of many works, from Plato's *Republic* to Aldous Huxley's *Brave New World*, which attempt to depict an ideal society. The *Utopia* is divided into two books. In the first, More represents himself as meeting in Antwerp his friend Peter Giles in company with an old sailor, Raphael Hythloday (Teller-of-Idle-Tales). They retire to More's garden, where they listen to the sailor's tales of his adventures in the New World, and discuss the shocking social wrongs of the Old World. In the second book, Hythloday explains to them the ideal society on the island Utopia, in sharp contrast to the defective society of Europe. In Utopia (Nowhere), social and economic life is elaborately planned and supervised. The work, play, home life, and education of every man, woman, and child are exactly and monotonously prescribed. Every form of religion, including Christianity, is tolerated; atheism alone is prohibited. War and the use of gold as coinage are severely condemned. Ethics is completely rationalistic.

There has been much discussion in recent years as to the agreement of the theories set forth in the *Utopia* with More's personality and beliefs. Views of the question range from that which regards it as a serious expression of More's ideas to that which considers it only a sally of wit. In coming to a conclusion on this subject, one should remember that the work is in the form of a dialogue, and that Utopian society is described not by More but by Hythloday.

Father Edward L. Surtz, S.J., in an article, "Thomas More and Communism,"[1] concludes that "In his heart, More realizes that his Utopian commonwealth, like the republic of Plato, will never exist in the Christian West, unless the perfect sons of the perfect God are born to dwell therein. The ideal Christian Utopia must wait until men become ideal Christians, perhaps only in 'the holy city, New Jerusalem, coming down out of heaven from God.'"

More wrote the *Utopia* in Latin, and it was published in Louvain in 1516. The first English translation, by Ralph Robinson, was published in 1551. The selection below is from Robinson's translation, reprinted with modernized spelling and punctuation.

THE SECOND BOOK

The Second Book of the Communication of Raphael Hythloday, concerning the best state of a commonwealth, containing the description of Utopia, with a large declaration of the politic government, and of all the good laws and orders of the same land.

. . . There be in the island fifty-four large and fair cities, or shire towns, agreeing all together in one tongue, in like manners, institutions, and laws. They be all set and situate alike, and in all points fashioned alike, as far forth as the place or plot suffereth.

Of these cities they that be nighest together be twenty-four miles asunder. Again there is none of them distant from the next above one day's journey afoot. There come yearly to Amaurote out of every city three old men wise and well experienced, there to entreat and debate, of the common matters of the land. For this city (because it standeth just in the midst of the island, and is therefore most meet for the ambassadors of all parts of the realm) is taken for the chief and head city. The precincts and bounds of the shires be so commodiously appointed out, and set forth for the cities, that none of them all hath of any side less than twenty miles of ground, and of some side also much more, as of that part where the cities be of farther distance asunder. None of the cities desire to enlarge the bounds and limits of their shires. For they count themselves rather the good husbands than the owners of their lands. They have in the country in all parts of the shire houses or farms builded, well appointed and furnished with all sorts of instruments and tools belonging to husbandry. These houses be inhabited of the citizens, which come thither to dwell by course. No household or farm in the country hath fewer than forty persons men and women, besides two bondmen, which be all under the rule and order of the good man, and the good wife of the house, being both very sage, discreet and ancient persons. And every thirty farms or families have one head ruler, which is called a philarch, being as it were a head bailiff. Out of every one of these families or farms cometh every year into the city twenty persons which have continued two years before in the country. In their place so many fresh be sent thither out of the city, who, of them that have been there a year already, and be therefore expert and cunning in husbandry, shall be instructed and taught. And they the next year shall teach other. This manner and fashion of yearly changing and renewing the occupiers of husbandry, though it be solemn and customably used, to the intent that no man shall be constrained against his will to continue long in that hard and sharp kind of life, yet many of them have such a pleasure and delight in husbandry, that they obtain a longer space of years. These husbandmen plough and till the ground, and breed up cattle, and provide and make ready wood, which they carry to the city either by land, or by water, as they may most conveniently. They bring up a great multitude of poultry, and that by a marvellous policy. For the hens do not sit upon the eggs; but by keeping them in a certain equal heat they bring life into them, and hatch them. The chickens, as soon as they be come out of the shell, follow men and women instead of the hens. They bring up very few horses; nor none, but very fierce ones; and that for none other use or purpose, but only to exercise their youth in riding and feats of arms. For oxen be put to all the labour of ploughing and drawing. . . . Whatsoever necessary things be lacking in the country, all such stuff they fetch out of the city: where without any exchange they easily obtain it of the magistrates of the city. For every month many of

[1] *Publications of the Modern Language Association*, Vol. 64, pp. 549–64.

8. **husbands,** husbandmen, caretakers, cultivators.

them go into the city on the holy day. When their harvest day draweth near and is at hand, then the philarchs, which be the head officers and bailiffs of husbandry, send word to the magistrates of the city what number of harvest men is needful to be sent to them out of the city. The which company of harvest men being ready at the day appointed, almost in one fair day dispatcheth all the harvest work. . . .

Of their living and mutual conversation together

But now will I declare how the citizens use themselves one towards another: what familiar occupying and entertainment there is among the people, and what fashion they use in the distribution of every thing. First the city consisteth of families; the families most commonly be made of kindreds. For the women, when they be married at a lawful age, they go into their husbands' houses. But the male children with all the whole male offspring continue still in their own family and be governed of the eldest and ancientest father, unless he dote for age: for then the next to him in age is placed in his room. But to the intent the prescript number of the citizens should neither decrease, nor above measure increase, it is ordained that no family which in every city be six thousand in the whole, besides them of the country, shall at once have fewer children of the age of fourteen years or thereabout than ten or more than sixteen, for of children under this age no number can be prescribed or appointed. This measure or number is easily observed and kept, by putting them that in fuller families be above the number into families of smaller increase. But if chance be that in the whole city the store increase above the just number, therewith they fill up the lack of other cities. But if so be that the multitude throughout the whole island pass and exceed the due number, then they choose out of every city certain citizens, and build up a town under their own laws in the next land where the inhabitants have much waste and unoccupied ground, receiving also of the same country people to them, if they will join and dwell with them. They thus joining and dwelling together do easily agree in one fashion of living, and that to the great wealth of both the peoples. For they so bring the matter about by their laws, that the ground which before was neither good nor profitable for the one nor for the other, is now sufficient and fruitful enough for them both. But if the inhabitants of that land will not dwell with them to be ordered by their laws, then they drive them out of those bounds which they have limited and appointed out for themselves. And if they resist and rebel, then they make war against them. For they count this the most just cause of war, when any people holdeth a piece of ground void and vacant to no good nor profitable use, keeping others from the use and possession of it, which notwithstanding by the law of nature ought thereof to be nourished and relieved. If any chance do so much diminish the number of any of their cities that it cannot be filled up again, without the diminishing of the just number of the other cities (which they say chanced but twice since the beginning of the land through a great pestilent plague), then they fulfil and make up the number of citizens fetched out of their own foreign towns, for they had rather suffer their foreign towns to decay and perish than any city of their own island to be diminished. But now again to the conversation of the citizens among themselves. The eldest (as I said) ruleth the family. The wives be ministers to their husbands, the children to their parents, and, to be short, the younger to their elders. Every city is divided into four equal parts or quarters. In the midst of every quarter there is a market-place of all manner of things. Thither the works of every family be brought into certain houses. And every kind of thing is laid up several in barns or storehouses. From hence the father of every family or every householder fetcheth whatsoever he and his have need of, and carrieth it away with him without money, without exchange, without any gage, pawn, or pledge. For why should anything be denied unto him, seeing there is abundance of all things, and that it is not to be feared lest any man will ask more than he needeth? For why should it be thought that that man would ask more than enough, which is sure never to lack? Certainly in all kinds of living creatures either fear of lack doth cause covetousness and ravin, or, in man only, pride, which counteth it a glorious thing to pass and excel other in the superfluous and vain ostentation of things. The which kind of vice among the Utopians can have no place. Next to the market-places that I spoke of, stand meat markets: whither be brought not only all sorts of herbs, and the fruits of trees, with bread, but also fish, and all manner of four-footed beasts, and wild fowl that be man's meat. But first the filthiness and ordure thereof is clean washed away in the running river without the city in places ap-

14–15. occupying and entertainment, business and intercourse. **25. prescript,** prescribed. **42. next land,** the nearest portion of the continent.

30. several, separately. **42. ravin,** ravenousness. **50. meat,** formerly, any kind of food.

pointed meet for the same purpose. From thence the beasts be brought in killed and clean washed by the hands of their bondmen. For they permit not their free citizens to accustom themselves to the killing of beasts, through the use whereof they think clemency, the gentlest affection of our nature, by little and little to decay and perish. Neither they suffer anything that is filthy, loathsome, or uncleanly to be brought into the city, lest the air, by the stench thereof infected and corrupt, should cause pestilent diseases.

Moreover every street hath certain great large halls set in equal distance one from another, every one known by a several name. In these halls dwell the syphogrants. And to every one of the same halls be appointed thirty families, on either side fifteen. The stewards of every hall at a certain hour come into the meat markets, where they receive meat according to the number of their halls. But first and chiefly of all, respect is had to the sick that be cured in the hospitals. For in the circuit of the city, a little without the walls, they have four hospitals, so big and so wide, so ample, and so large, that they may seem four little towns, which were devised of that bigness partly to the intent the sick, be they never so many in number, should not lie too throng or strait, and therefore uneasily and incommodiously: and partly that they which were taken and holden with contagious diseases, such as be wont by infection to creep from one to another, might be laid apart far from the company of the residue. These hospitals be so well appointed, and with all things necessary to health so furnished, and moreover so diligent attendance through the continual presence of cunning physicians is given, that though no man be sent thither against his will, yet notwithstanding there is no sick person in all the city that had not rather lie there than at home in his own house. When the steward of the sick hath received such meats as the physicians have prescribed, then the best is equally divided among the halls, according to the company of every one, saving that there is had a respect to the prince, the bishop, the tranibors, and to ambassadors and all strangers, if there be any, which be very few and seldom. But they also when they be there have certain several houses appointed and prepared for them.

To these halls at the set hours of dinner and supper come all the whole syphogranty or ward, warned by the noise of a brass trumpet, except such as be sick in the hospitals, or else in their own houses. Howbeit no man is prohibited or forbid, after the halls be served, to fetch home meat out of the market to his own house, for they know that no man will do it without a cause reasonable. For though no man be prohibited to dine at home, yet no man doth it willingly, because it is counted a point of small honesty. And also it were a folly to take the pain to dress a bad dinner at home when they may be welcome to good and fine fare so nigh hand at the hall. In this hall all vile service, all slavery and drudgery, with all laboursome toil and base business is done by bondmen. But the women of every family by course have the office and charge of cookery for seething and dressing the meat, and ordering all things thereto belonging. They sit at three tables or more, according to the number of their company. The men sit upon the bench next the wall, and the women against them on the other side of the table, that if any sudden evil should chance to them, as many times happeneth to women with child, they may rise without trouble or disturbance of anybody and go thence into the nursery. The nurses sit several alone with their young sucklings in a certain parlour appointed and deputed to the same purpose, never without fire and clean water, nor yet without cradles, that when they will they may lay down the young infants, and at their pleasure take them out of their swaddling clothes, and hold them to the fire, and refresh them with play. Every mother is nurse to her own child, unless either death or sickness be the let. When that chanceth, the wives of the syphogrants quickly provide a nurse. And that is not hard to be done, for they that can do it proffer themselves to no service so gladly as to that, because that there this kind of pity is much praised, and the child that is nourished ever after taketh his nurse for his own natural mother. Also among the nurses sit all the children that be under the age of five years. All the other children of both kinds, as well boys as girls, that be under the age of marriage, do either serve at the tables, or else if they be too young thereto, yet they stand by with marvellous silence. That which is given to them from the table they eat, and other several dinner time they have none. The syphogrant and his wife sit in the midst of the high table, forasmuch as that is counted the honourablest place, and because from

15. **syphogrants,** a word apparently made from the Greek word for "sty," and possibly punning on "steward," styward. 19. **number of their halls,** number of persons in the thirty families eating in their respective halls. 21. **cured in the hospitals,** cared for in the hospitals. 27. **throng or strait,** crowded or confined. 44. **tranibors,** a word made from Greek roots meaning "bench-eaters" and probably intended to suggest the Benchers of an Inn of Court.

10–11. **of small honesty,** of little credit to one. 17. **by course,** in turn. 18. **seething,** boiling. 22. **against,** opposite. 35. **let,** hindrance.

thence all the whole company is in their sight, for that table stands overthwart the over end of the hall. To them be joined two of the ancientest and eldest, for at every table they sit four at a mess. But if there be a church standing in that syphogranty or ward, then the priest and his wife sit with the syphogrant, as chief in the company. On both sides of them sit young men, and next unto them again old men. And thus throughout all the house equal of age be set together, and yet be mixed and matched with unequal ages. This, they say, was ordained to the intent that the sage gravity and reverence of the elders should keep the youngers from wanton licence of words and behaviour. Forasmuch as nothing can be so secretly spoken or done at the table, but either they that sit on the one side or on the other must needs perceive it. The dishes be not set down in order from the first place, but all the old men (whose places be marked with some special token to be known) be first served of their meat, and then the residue equally. The old men divide their dainties as they think best to the younger on each side of them.

Thus the elders be not defrauded of their due honour, and nevertheless equal commodity cometh to everyone. They begin every dinner and supper of reading something that pertaineth to good manners and virtue. But it is short, because no man shall be grieved therewith. Hereof the elders take occasion of honest communication, but neither sad nor unpleasant. Howbeit they do not spend all the whole dinnertime themselves with long and tedious talks, but they gladly hear also the young men; yea, and purposely provoke them to talk, to the intent that they may have a proof of every man's wit and towardness or disposition to virtue, which commonly in the liberty of feasting doth show and utter itself. Their dinners be very short, but their suppers be somewhat longer, because that after dinner follows labour, after supper sleep and natural rest, which they think to be of more strength and efficacy to wholesome and healthful digestion. No supper is passed without music. Nor their banquets lack no conceits nor junkets. They burn sweet gums and spices or perfumes, and pleasant smells, and sprinkle about sweet ointments and waters; yea, they leave nothing undone that makes for the cheering of the company. For they be much inclined to this opinion: to think no kind of pleasure forbidden, whereof cometh no harm. Thus therefore and after this sort they live together in the city, but in the country they that dwell alone far from any neighbours do dine and sup at home in their own houses. For no family there lacketh any kind of victuals, as from whom cometh all that the citizens eat and live by.

2. overthwart the over end, across the upper end. **13. wanton,** careless, unrestrained. **22. dainties.** After this word Robinson omitted a clause which Burnet translated "if there be not such an abundance of them that the whole company may be served alike."

3. honest communication, creditable conversation. **16. banquets,** desserts. **17. conceits nor junkets,** fancy confectionery and cakes. **27–28. as from whom,** as they are those from whom.

Sir Thomas Wyatt

c. 1503–1542

Sir Thomas Wyatt comes as close as any of the pre-Elizabethan poets to the courtly ideal of the Renaissance. His life, though brief, was many-sided; his manifold gifts, political and esthetic, were utilized to the full. He was born in Kent in the castle of his father, who while Wyatt was a child was joint constable of Norwich Castle along with Sir Thomas, the father of Anne Boleyn. Wyatt served as a page at court, and entered St. John's College, Cambridge, in 1516, the year of its founding. He took his M.A. degree about 1520, and in the following year married Elizabeth, the daughter of Lord Cobham. An extant letter to his son Thomas suggests that his married life was not very happy; at any rate, Wyatt sought consolation elsewhere.

In the service of the King, he made an important journey to Italy in 1526–27, visiting Rome, Venice, and other cities, and from 1528 to 1532 he served as Marshal of Calais. He was knighted in 1536, but was imprisoned in the same year, ostensibly because of a quarrel with the Duke of Suffolk but presumably on the suspicion that he was a lover of Queen Anne. He regained the King's favor, however, became a member of the Privy Council, and served as Ambassador to Spain from 1537 to 1539. In 1541, he was imprisoned on the charge of traitorous behavior during his residence in Spain, but defended himself eloquently and was unconditionally pardoned. In 1542, he was a member of Parliament, and was appointed Commander of the Fleet. In the autumn, on a hurried trip to Falmouth to meet the Spanish Ambassador, he fell ill of a fever, and died at Sherborne, Dorsetshire, on October 11, 1542.

Wyatt's visit to Italy was all-important for his poetic activities. There he became deeply interested in Petrarch and other Italian lyricists, and he later drew heavily on them for themes and verse forms. One of his first works, however, was a translation of a Latin version of Plutarch's *περὶ εὐθυμίας* which he presented under the title of *Quiet of Mind* as a New Year's gift to Queen Catherine in 1528. His *Seven Penitential Psalms* was a very free rendering of a work by Pietro Aretino, the sensualist and satirist. Aside from the sonnets and lyrics, most of Wyatt's work was in the newly revived forms: satires, influenced by Horace and the contemporary Italian Luigi Alamanni, and epigrams, inspired by the *Strambotti* of Serafino dell' Aquila. The sonnets, numbering about thirty, are important, not only as the first to be written in English, but also as evidence of the strong appeal of the Petrarchan love conventions. Many of these Wyatt accepted humbly, but occasionally he rebelled manfully against the traditionally subservient role of the lover. Wyatt's renderings frequently seem rough and awkward, but it has been argued that some of the crudities are due to Tottel's highhanded editing of Wyatt's manuscripts, and others to our failure to understand Wyatt's personal system of stresses and accents. Probably his lyrics—obviously intended for singing with a lute accompaniment—represent the height of his technical skill. But Wyatt was as important as an influence, on Surrey and other courtly makers, as he was as a poet.

A few of Wyatt's poems were first printed about 1542 in a miscellany entitled *The Court of Venus*, of which only a few fragments are extant. Ninety-seven of his poems were included by Tottel in his famous miscellany *Songs and Sonnets*, 1557. Other poems have been recovered in modern times from contemporary manuscripts.

SONNETS

Wyatt and Surrey introduced the sonnet into English on the pattern derived from Petrarch and Sannazaro through Saint-Gelais and other French poets. Wyatt retains the conventional Petrarchan love themes embellished by conceits, but he often departs from the rhyme scheme of his Italian models by ending his sonnets with a final couplet; thus the rhyme scheme of a majority of his sonnets is *a b b a, a b b a, c d d c, e e.*

With the adoption of this form, Wyatt revived lyrical beauty in English poetry. Imitation of Petrarch introduced bold and new images, variety in metaphor, and subtleties of phrasing. The individual quality of Wyatt's verse, however, is its strong, rapid flow combined with simplicity and directness of speech. Since the sonnets describe a lover's emotional state under the trials of court romance, imaginative feeling prevails throughout. Wyatt sang his love tale in spontaneous, virile notes modulated by strains of melancholy and sweetness, but always maintaining its tone of deep earnestness.

THE LOVER COMPARETH HIS STATE TO A SHIP IN PERILOUS STORM TOSSED ON THE SEA

My galley chargèd with forgetfulness
Through sharp seas, in winter nights, doth pass
'Tween rock and rock; and eke my foe, alas,
That is my lord, steereth with cruelness;
And every oar a thought in readiness,
As though that death were light in such a case.
An endless wind doth tear the sail apace,
Of forcèd sighs and trusty fearfulness;
A rain of tears, a cloud of dark disdain,
Have done the wearied cords great hinderance;
Wreathèd with error and with ignorance,
The stars be hid that led me to this pain;
Drownèd is reason, that should be my comfòrt,
And I remain despairing of the port.

DESCRIPTION OF THE CONTRARIOUS PASSIONS IN A LOVER

I find no peace, and all my war is done;
I fear and hope; I burn, and freeze like ice;
I fly aloft, yet can I not arise;
And nought I have, and all the world I season,
That locks nor looseth, holdeth me in prison,
And holds me not, yet can I 'scape no wise;
Nor lets me live, nor die, at my devise,
And yet of death it giveth me occasion.
Without eye, I see; without tongue, I plain;
I wish to perish, yet I ask for health;
I love another, and thus I hate myself;
I feed me in sorrow, and laugh in all my pain.
Lo, thus displeaseth me both death and life,
And my delight is causer of this strife.

THE LOVER FOR SHAMEFASTNESS HIDETH HIS DESIRE WITHIN HIS FAITHFUL HEART

The long love that in my thought I harbour,
And in my heart doth keep his residence,
Into my face presseth with bold pretence
And there campeth, displaying his banner.
She that me learns to love and to suffer
And wills that my trust and lust's negligence
Be reined by reason, shame, and reverence,
With his hardiness takes displeàsure.
Wherewith love to the heart's forest he fleeth,
Leaving his enterprise with pain and cry,
And there him hideth, and not appeareth:
What may I do, when my master feareth,
But in the field with him to live and die?
For good is the life ending faithfully.

WHOSO LIST TO HUNT

Whoso list to hunt, I know where is an hind,
But as for me—alas, I may no more.
The vain travail hath wearied me so sore,
I am of them that farthest come behind.
Yet may I, by no means, my wearied mind
Draw from the deer; but as she fleeth afore
Fainting I follow. I leave off therefore,
Since in a net I seek to hold the wind.
Who list her hunt, I put him out of doubt,
As well as I, may spend his time in vain.
And graven with diamonds in letters plain
There is written, her fair neck round about:
Noli me tangere, for Caesar's I am,
And wild for to hold, though I seem tame.

THE LOVER SHOWETH HOW HE IS FORSAKEN OF SUCH AS HE SOMETIME ENJOYED

They flee from me, that sometime did me seek,
With naked foot stalking within my chamber.
Once have I seen them gentle, tame, and meek,
That now are wild, and do not once remember
That sometime they have put themselves in danger
To take bread at my hand; and now they range,
Busily seeking in continual change.
Thanked be fortune it hath been otherwise,
Twenty times better; but once especïal,
In thin array, after a pleasant guise,
When her loose gown did from her shoulders fall,
And she me caught in her arms long and small,
And therewithal so sweetly did me kiss
And softly said, Dear heart, how like you this?
It was no dream, for I lay broad awaking.
But all is turned now, through my gentleness,
Into a bitter fashion of forsaking;
And I have leave to go, of her goodness,
And she also to use newfangleness.
But since that I unkindly so am served,
How like you this? what hath she now deserved?

The Lover Compareth. **3. my foe,** my love, as is also **my lord** in the next line. *Description.* **4. season,** seize. **9. plain,** complain.

The Lover for Shamefastness. The student should compare this translation of Petrarch's Sonnet 109 with Surrey's translation of it under the title "Complaint of a Lover Rebuked."

Whoso list. **13. Noli me tangere.** Touch me not. This line has led some scholars to believe that this sonnet refers to Anne Boleyn.

FORGET NOT YET

Forget not yet the tried intent
Of such a truth as I have meant,
My great travail, so gladly spent,
Forget not yet.

Forget not yet when first began
The weary life ye know, since whan
The suit, the service none tell can,
Forget not yet.

Forget not yet the great assays,
The cruel wrong, the scornful ways;
The painful patience in denays,
Forget not yet.

Forget not yet, forget not this,
How long ago hath been, and is,
The mind that never meant amiss,—
Forget not yet.

Forget not, then, thine own approved,
The which so long hath thee so loved,
Whose steadfast faith yet never moved,
Forget not this.

AN EARNEST SUIT TO HIS UNKIND MISTRESS NOT TO FORSAKE HIM

And wilt thou leave me thus?
Say nay, say nay, for shame!
To save thee from the blame
Of all my grief and grame.
And wilt thou leave me thus?
Say nay! say nay!

And wilt thou leave me thus,
That hath loved thee so long
In wealth and woe among:
And is thy heart so strong
As for to leave me thus?
Say nay! say nay!

And wilt thou leave me thus,
That hath given thee my heart
Never for to depart
Neither for pain nor smart:
And wilt thou leave me thus?
Say nay! say nay!

And wilt thou leave me thus,
And have no more pity
Of him that loveth thee?
Alas, thy cruelty!
And wilt thou leave me thus?
Say nay! say nay!

THE LOVER COMPLAINETH THE UNKINDNESS OF HIS LOVE

My lute, awake, perform the last
Labor that thou and I shall waste,
And end that I have now begun.
And when this song is sung and past,
My lute, be still, for I have done.

As to be heard where ear is none,
As lead to grave in marble stone,
My song may pierce her heart as soon.
Should we then sigh, or sing, or moan?
No, no, my lute, for I have done.

The rocks do not so cruelly
Repulse the waves continually,
As she my suit and affectiòn;
So that I am past remedy,
Whereby my lute and I have done.

Proud of the spoil that thou hast got
Of simple hearts through Lovës shot,
By whom unkind thou hast them won,
Think not he hath his bow forgot,
Although my lute and I have done.

Vengeance shall fall on thy disdain,
That makest but game of earnest pain;
Trow not alone under the sun
Unquit to cause thy lovers plain,
Although my lute and I have done.

May chance thee lie withered and old
In winter nights, that are so cold,
Plaining in vain unto the moon;
Thy wishes then dare not be told:
Care then who list, for I have done.

And then may chance thee to repent
The time that thou hast lost and spent,
To cause thy lovers sigh and swoon:
Then shalt thou know beauty but lent,
And wish and want, as I have done.

Forget Not Yet. **6. whan,** when **11. denays.** denials.
An Earnest Suit. **4. grame,** sadness.

The Lover Complaineth. **7. grave,** engrave.

Now cease, my lute! This is the last
Labor that thou and I shall waste;
And ended is that we begun:
Now is thy song both sung and past;
My lute, be still, for I have done.

OF THE COURTIER'S LIFE

WRITTEN TO JOHN POINS

This satire sets forth Wyatt's aversion to life at court in a verse epistle to John Poins, explaining the author's reasons for leaving the court to return home. He is unable to tolerate the hypocrisy and dissipation characteristic of the court. Pomp, avarice, deceit, servility, cruelty, and lechery, he ironically observes, are the traits requisite for a courtier. In preference to these, Wyatt chooses to live in liberty within the bounds of his father's estate, where he is free to walk and rhyme as he pleases. He contrasts the life at court with the life in the country, and ends with an invitation to John Poins to join him.

Mine own John Poins, since ye delight to know
The causes why that homeward I me draw,
And flee the press of courts, whereso they go,
Rather than to live thrall under the awe
Of lordly looks, wrappèd within my cloak,
To will and lust learning to set a law;
It is not because I scorn or mock
The power of them, whom fortune here hath lent
Charge over us, of right to strike the stroke.
But true it is that I have always meant
Less to esteem them than the common sort,
Of outward things that judge in their intent
Without regard what inward doth resort.
I grant sometime of glory that the fire
Doth touch my heart. Me list not to report
Blame by honour, and honour to desire.
But how may I this honour now attain,
That cannot dye the colour black a liar?
My Poins, I cannot frame my tune to feign,
To cloak the truth, for praise without desert,
Of them that list all vice for to retain.
I cannot honour them that set their part
With Venus and Bacchus all their life long;
Nor hold my peace of them, although I smart.
I cannot crouch nor kneel to such a wrong,
To worship them like God on earth alone,
That are as wolves these seely lambs among.
I cannot with my words complain and moan
And suffer nought, nor smart without complaint,
Nor turn the word that from my mouth is gone;
I cannot speak and look like as a saint,

27. seely, foolish.

Use wiles for wit, and make deceit a pleasure;
Call craft counsel, for lucre still to paint;
I cannot wrest the law to fill the coffer;
With innocent blood to feed myself fat;
And do most hurt where that most help I offer.
I am not he that can allow the state
Of high Caesar, and damn Cato to die;
That with his death did scape out of the gate
From Caesar's hands, if Livy doth not lie,
And would not live where liberty was lost,
So did his heart the commonwealth apply.
I am not he, such eloquence to boast,
To make the crow in singing as the swan,
Nor call the lion of coward beasts the most,
That cannot take a mouse as the cat can;
And he that dieth for hunger of the gold,
Call him Alexander, and say that Pan
Passeth Apollo in music manifold;
Praise Sir Thopas for a noble tale,
And scorn the story that the Knight told;
Praise him for counsel that is drunk of ale;
Grin when he laughs that beareth all the sway,
Frown when he frowns, and groan when he is pale;
On others' lust to hang both night and day.
None of these points would ever frame in me;
My wit is nought, I cannot learn the way.
And much the less of things that greater be,
That asken help of colours to devise
To join the mean with each extremity;
With nearest virtue aye to cloak the vice.
And as to purpose likewise it shall fall,
To press the virtue that it may not rise;
As drunkenness good fellowship to call;
The friendly foe, with his fair double face,
Say he is gentle and courteous therewithal;
Affirm that favel hath a goodly grace
In eloquence; and cruelty to name
Zeal of justice, and change in time and place;
And he that suff'reth offence without blame,
Call him pitiful, and him true and plain
That raileth reckless unto each man's shame;
Say he is rude that cannot lie and feign;
The lecher a lover, and tyranny
To be the right of a prince's reign.
I cannot, I; no, no, it will not be.
This is the cause that I could never yet
Hang on their sleeves, that weigh, as thou mayst see,
A chip of chance more than a pound of wit.

56. frame in, serve, profit. **67. favel,** cunning, deception by flattery; from the favel, or fallow-colored horse, used as a type of cunning, as in the proverbial expression "to curry favel (favor)." **69. change . . . place.** Cruelty is often excused by the plea that in some times and places custom makes or has made it justifiable. **79. chip of chance . . . wit.** Wyatt's several imprisonments were due to a sudden change in the temper or policy of the King.

This maketh me at home to hunt and hawk,
And in foul weather at my book to sit,
In frost and snow then with my bow to stalk.
No man doth mark whereso I ride or go.
In lusty leas at liberty I walk,
And of these news I feel nor weal nor woe,
Save that a clog doth hang yet at my heel.
No force for that, for it is ordered so
That I may leap both hedge and dike full well;
I am not now in France, to judge the wine,
With sav'ry sauce those delicates to feel.
Nor yet in Spain where one must him incline,
Rather than to be, outwardly to seem.
I meddle not with wits that be so fine,
Nor Flanders' cheer lets not my sight to deem
Of black and white, nor takes my wits away
With beastliness; such do those beasts esteem.
Nor I am not where truth is given in prey
For money, poison, and treason; of some
A common practice, usèd night and day.
But I am here in Kent and Christendom,
Among the Muses, where I read and rhyme;
Where if thou list, mine own John Poins, to come,
Thou shalt be judge how I do spend my time.

Henry Howard, Earl of Surrey

c. 1517–1547

Surrey, Wyatt's most brilliant disciple, had a life that was briefer and more turbulent than his poetic master's, but which, like his, was in many ways a very close approximation of the ideal of Castiglione's *Courtier*. Born about 1517, he was of royal blood, since his father, the Earl of Surrey (afterwards Duke of Norfolk), was descended from Edward the Confessor, and his mother, Elinor Percy, from Edward III. His mother was apparently a patroness of letters. Skelton composed *A Garland of Laurel* under her roof, and represents her as crowning him at the end of the poem.

Surrey was tutored by the learned John Clerk, and was well trained in Latin, Spanish, Italian, and French. At the age of thirteen, he was appointed companion to the Duke of Richmond, the illegitimate son of Henry VIII, and enjoyed princely privileges at Windsor and in 1532 in France, whither the young friends went in the train of the King to the ceremonies at the Field of the Cloth of Gold and where they remained as guests of the young sons of King Francis I. They were recalled to England for the marriage of Richmond to Surrey's sister Mary. Surrey had already been married to Lady Frances Vere in 1532, but because of their youth, the couple did not set up a household until 1535, when he built Mount Surrey, a classical mansion on St. Leonard's Hill, near Norwich.

Surrey is described in a contemporary record as "the most foolish proud boy that is in England," and he seems to have been guilty of an unusual number of violent misdemeanors. In 1537, he struck a courtier who cast aspersions on his devotion to the King, and since the offense occurred in the royal park at Hampton Court, Surrey ran the risk of losing his right hand; but this gruesome penalty was commuted to punishment, and Surrey was imprisoned for a season at Windsor. In 1542 he was imprisoned again as the result of another quarrel, and in 1543 he was consigned to Fleet Prison for rioting in the streets and eating meat in Lent.

But in the service of the King he performed a number of official and martial services. He assisted his father in suppressing a rebellion in Yorkshire, in bringing about the overthrow of Thomas Cromwell, and in repressing the Scots. In 1540 he was a leader of a tournament in honor of the marriage of Henry and Anne of Cleves, and in 1541 served as steward of Cambridge University. Between 1544 and 1546 he engaged in various campaigns against France, and in 1545–46 he was commander at Boulogne. In December, 1546, he was arrested and charged with high treason, possibly through the influence of a brother of Queen Jane Seymour. At the time, Henry VIII was seriously ill, and the problem of the succession was in the minds of all. Surrey was charged with putting forth his father's claim to the throne by quartering his arms with those of Edward the Confessor. He was condemned to death, and was beheaded on January 21, 1547, a week before the death of Henry himself.

Surrey's poems give little evidence of his haughty and violent nature. In them he submitted himself with greater ease than Wyatt to the Petrarchan

86. clog. Wyatt was not at perfect liberty, but was confined to his father's estate on parole.

94–95. Flanders' cheer . . . Of, the strong liquor of Flanders does not prevent my sight's distinguishing between.

love conventions, and the dominant tone of his lyrics is rather sweetly melancholy. He is, moreover, a much more smooth and skillful versifier than his poetic master. Surrey made two important contributions to English poetic forms. The first is the English or Shakespearean sonnet, consisting of three quatrains, rhyming alternately, and a concluding couplet. The second, and more important contribution, was what is loosely called blank verse, namely, unrhymed iambic pentameters.

Probably Surrey's first printed work was his elegy on Sir Thomas Wyatt, which appeared under the title *An Excellent Epitaph* about 1542; his next publication was the translation of Martial's epigram which William Baldwin incorporated in his *Treatise of Moral Philosophy* in 1547. Surrey's blank-verse translation of the fourth book of Virgil's *Aeneid* was probably first printed about 1554. A slightly different version of this and of the second book was printed by Tottel in 1557, about two weeks after he had published forty of Surrey's poems in his *Songs and Sonnets*. Surrey's use of blank verse was probably encouraged by various Italian unrhymed translations of Virgil.

SONNETS

In addition to the new English rhyme scheme, Surrey's sonnets anticipated Elizabethan poetry in their fine musical quality and dramatic strength. They show the influence of a sensitive ear and a mind that sees life vividly in terms of action.

This verse has an easy motion and slow and stately harmonies. Concordant vowel sounds echo through the sonnets and assume the quality of overtones: *flowering*, *to-morrow*, *soote*, *bloom*, *bright*, *hight*, and the alliteration has a similar effect in accentuating the rhythm. Ordinarily the impression is distinctly pleasing, but occasionally Surrey overemploys this device, as in "The soote season that bud and bloom forth brings," where this self-conscious attention to sound has the effect of surfeit. For the most part, fortunately, the melody of these sonnets has a cumulative, sonorous effect.

Surrey's diction is direct and firm, but flexible and euphonious. He employs just enough words of Latin and French origin to give richness and dignity to the homely native element without appearing highly artificial. There is an archaic flavor in his use of certain characteristically Chaucerian words, phrases, and constructions; and quaintness in his tendency to use nouns and adjectives as verbs, or adjectives and verbs as nouns: "With *green* hath clad the hill and eke the vale."

His subject matter is almost exclusively Petrarchan love themes or nature descriptions, which he treats with a gentle, sentimental melancholy. In general the slight trace of insincerity of feeling found in Surrey's sonnets is lost in the beauty of his lyrical expression.

DESCRIPTION OF SPRING, WHEREIN EACH THING RENEWS SAVE ONLY THE LOVER

The soote season that bud and bloom forth brings
With green hath clad the hill and eke the vale,
The nightingale with feathers new she sings,
The turtle to her make hath told her tale.
Summer is come, for every spray now springs,
The hart hath hung his old head on the pale,
The buck in brake his winter coat he flings,
The fishes float with new repairèd scale,
The adder all her slough away she slings,
The swift swallow pursueth the flyès smale,
The busy bee her honey now she mings,—
Winter is worn, that was the flowers' bale:
And thus I see, among these pleasant things
Each care decays—and yet my sorrow springs.

THE FRAILTY AND HURTFULNESS OF BEAUTY

Brittle beauty that nature made so frail,
Whereof the gift is small, and short the season,
Flow'ring to-day, to-morrow apt to fail,
Tickle treasure, abhorrèd of reason,
Dangerous to deal with, vain, of none avail,
Costly in keeping, passed not worth two peason,
Slipper in sliding as is an eelè's tail,
Hard to attain, once gotten not geason,
Jewel of jeopardy that peril doth assail,
False and untrue, enticèd oft to treason,
En'my to youth (that most may I bewail!),
Ah, bitter sweet! infecting as the poison,
Thou farest as fruit that with the frost is taken:
To-day ready ripe, to-morrow all to-shaken.

DESCRIPTION AND PRAISE OF HIS LOVE GERALDINE

This sonnet gave rise to the persistent legend that Surrey was the lover of Elizabeth Fitzgerald, daughter of the Irish Earl of Kildare, and that he addressed all his love poetry to her. Modern scholars consider this poem the only reference to a passing fancy for this young girl.

From Tuscan came my lady's worthy race,
Fair Florence was sometime her ancient seat,

Description of Spring. **1. soote,** sweet, as used by Chaucer. **4. turtle,** turtledove. **make,** mate. **6. pale,** paling, fence; Surrey has in mind the deer kept in enclosures. **10. smale,** small. **11. mings,** mingles, produces by mixing, though "remembers" is a possible meaning. **12. bale,** funeral pyre. *The Frailty.* **4. Tickle,** delicate. **6. peason,** peas. **8. geason,** rare. *Description and Praise.* **1. Tuscan.** The Fitzgeralds were supposed to be descended from the Geraldis of Florence.

The western isle whose pleasant shore doth face
Wild Camber's cliffs did give her lively heat;
Fostered she was with milk of Irish breast,
Her sire an earl, her dame of princes' blood;
From tender years in Britain she doth rest
With king's child, where she tasteth costly food.
Hunsdon did first present her to mine eyne;
Bright is her hue, and Geraldine she hight;
Hampton me taught to wish her first for mine,
And Windsor, alas, doth chase me from her sight.
Her beauty, of kind; her virtues, from above;
Happy is he that can obtain her love.

A COMPLAINT BY NIGHT OF THE LOVER NOT BELOVED

Alas, so all things now do hold their peace,
Heaven and earth disturbèd in nothing;
The beasts, the air, the birds their song do cease,
The nightè's chair the stars about doth bring;
Calm is the sea, the waves work less and less.
So am not I, whom love, alas, doth wring,
Bringing before my face the great increase
Of my desires, whereat I weep and sing
In joy and woe, as in a doubtful ease.
For my sweet thoughts sometime do pleasure bring,
But by and by the cause of my disease
Gives me a pang that inwardly doth sting,
When that I think what grief it is again
To live and lack the thing should rid my pain.

OF THE DEATH OF SIR T. W. THE ELDER

Wyatt resteth here, that quick could never rest;
Whose heavenly gifts increasèd by disdain,
And virtue sank the deeper in his breast,
Such profit he by envy could obtain.
A head where wisdom mysteries did frame,
Whose hammers beat still in that lively brain
As on a stithy, where that some work of fame
Was daily wrought, to turn to Britain's gain.
A visage stern and mild, where both did grow
Vice to contemn, in virtue to rejoice;
Amid great storms whom grace assurèd so
To live upright and smile at fortune's choice.
A hand that taught what might be said in rhyme,
That reft Chaucer the glory of his wit,
A mark the which (unparfited, for time)
Some may approach, but never none shall hit.
A tongue that served in foreign realms his king;
Whose courteous talk to virtue did inflame
Each noble heart; a worthy guide to bring
Our English youth by travail unto fame.
An eye whose judgment none affect could blind,
Friends to allure and foes to reconcile;
Whose piercing look did represent a mind
With virtue fraught, reposèd, void of guile.
A heart where dread was never so impressed,
To hide the thought that might the truth advance;
In neither fortune lost nor yet repressed,
To swell in wealth or yield unto mischance.
A valiant corps where force and beauty met,
Happy—alas, too happy, but for foes!
Lived, and ran the race that nature set,
Of manhood's shape where she the mould did lose.
But to the heavens that simple soul is fled,
Which left with such as covet Christ to know
Witness of faith that never shall be dead;
Sent for our health, but nor receivèd so.
Thus for our guilt this jewel have we lost:
The earth, his bones; the heavens possess his ghost.

THE THINGS THAT CAUSE A QUIET LIFE

WRITTEN BY MARTIAL

My friend, the things that do attain
The happy life be these, I find:
The riches left, not got with pain,
The fruitful ground, the quiet mind.

The equal friend—no grudge, no strife;
No charge of rule, nor governance;
Without disease, the healthy life,
The household of continuance;

The mean diet, no dainty fare;
Wisdom joined with simpleness;
The night dischargèd of all care,
Where wine the wit may not oppress.

The faithful wife, without debate;
Such sleeps as may beguile the night:
Content thyself with thine estate,
Neither wish death, nor fear his might.

3–4. **western isle . . . cliffs.** Elizabeth grew up in a part of Ireland that faces the cliffs of Wales. 6. **princes' blood.** Geraldine's mother was the granddaughter of Edward IV's queen. 8. **With king's child,** in the household of the Princess Mary. 9. **Hunsdon.** The meeting of Surrey and Elizabeth probably took place at Hunsdon in March, 1537. 11. **Hampton.** Princess Mary, and presumably Elizabeth, were at Hampton Court in July, 1537. *Complaint.* 4. **chair,** chariot. *Of the Death.* 1. **quick,** alive. 2. **disdain,** i.e., of vice.

15. **unparfited,** unfinished. 21. **none affect,** no passion. 38. **ghost,** spirit. *The Things That Cause.* 8. **continuance,** permanence, stability.

PRISONED IN WINDSOR, HE RECOUNTETH HIS PLEASURE THERE PASSED

So cruel prison how could betide, alas,
As proud Windsor? Where I in lust and joy
With a king's son my childish years did pass
In greater feast than Priam's sons of Troy;
Where each sweet place returns a taste full sour:
The large green courts where we were wont to hove
With eyes cast up into the maidens' tower,
And easy sighs, such as folk draw in love;
The stately seats, the ladies bright of hue,
The dances short, long tales of great delight;
With words and looks that tigers could but rue,
Where each of us did plead the other's right;
The palm play where, despoilèd for the game,
With dazèd eyes oft we by gleams of love
Have missed the ball and got sight of our dame,
To bait her eyes, which kept the leads above;
The gravel ground, with sleeves tied on the helm,
On foaming horse, with swords and friendly hearts,
With cheer, as though one should another whelm,
Where we have fought, and chasèd oft with darts;
With silver drops the mead yet spread for ruth,
In active games of nimbleness and strength,
Where we did strain, trainèd with swarms of youth,
Our tender limbs that yet shot up in length;
The secret groves which oft we made resound
Of pleasant plaint and of our ladies' praise,
Recording oft what grace each one had found,
What hope of speed, what dread of long delays;
The wild forest, the clothèd holts with green,
With reins avaled, and swift ybreathèd horse,
With cry of hounds and merry blasts between,
Where we did chase the fearful hart of force;
The wide vales eke that harboured us each night,
Wherewith, alas, reviveth in my breast
The sweet accord; such sleeps as yet delight,
The pleasant dreams, the quiet bed of rest;
The secret thoughts imparted with such trust,
The wanton talk, the divers change of play,
The friendship sworn, each promise kept so just,
Wherewith we passed the winter night away.
And with this thought the blood forsakes the face,
The tears berain my cheeks of deadly hue,
The which as soon as sobbing sighs, alas,
Upsuppèd have, thus I my plaint renew:
O place of bliss, renewer of my woes,
Give me account—where is my noble fere?
Whom in thy walls thou dost each night enclose,
To other lief, but unto me most dear!
Echo, alas, that doth my sorrow rue,
Returns thereto a hollow sound of plaint.
Thus I alone, where all my freedom grew,
In prison pine with bondage and restraint;
And with remembrance of the greater grief
To banish the less, I find my chief relief.

Prisoned. **6. hove,** linger. **11. rue,** melt, awaken pity in. **13. palm play,** old form of tennis, resembling modern hand-ball. **despoilèd,** with impeding garments stripped off. **16. leads,** either the leaden window-strips of the maidens' tower or small flat roofs whence the ladies watched the game. **17. sleeves . . . helm,** a lady's favor on the helmet. **21. silver drops,** probably dew, in which case **for ruth** later in the line is figurative. **30. avaled,** slackened, lowered.

46. fere? companion. **48. lief,** pleasing, acceptable.

from VIRGIL'S *AENEID:* BOOK IV

Aeneas, chided by Mercury for his neglect of high duty, resolves to steal from the pleasant company of Dido, Queen of Carthage.

Aeneas with that vision striken down,
Well near distraught, upstart his hair for dread,
Amid his throatal his voice likewise 'gan stick.
For to depart by night he longeth now,
And the sweet land to leave, astoined sore
With this advise and message of the Gods.
What may he do, alas! or by what words
Dare he persuade the raging Queen in love?
Or in what sort may he his tale begin?
Now here, now there his rechless mind 'gan run,
And diversely him draws, discoursing all.
After long doubts this sentence seemèd best:
Mnestheus first, and strong Cloanthus eke
He calls to him, with Sergest; unto whom
He gave in charge his navy secretly
For to prepare, and drive to the sea coast
His people; and their armour to address;
And for the cause of change to feign excuse:
And that he, when good Dido least foreknew,
Or did suspect so great a love could break,
Would wait his time to speak thereof most meet;
The nearest way to hasten his intent.
Gladly his will and biddings they obey.

Roger Ascham
1515–1568

Roger Ascham was the best-known English writer of sixteenth-century treatises on education. His life and experience were an admirable preparation for the composition of his distinguished book, *The Schoolmaster*. Born in 1515 in Yorkshire, he entered St. John's College, Cambridge, about 1530,—shortly after his teacher and master, Sir John Cheke—and became one of the brightest ornaments of this period in the university's Humanistic ascendancy. He became a distinguished classicist, and is said to have been the first lecturer on the Platonic dialogues at Cambridge. In 1545, he published *Toxophilus*, a dialogue (modeled on Plato) on the benefits of archery, as a pastime, a means of defense—for which he prefers it to cannon—and a form of physical training. In this discourse he strongly reprobated gambling, although, as Andrew Lang pointed out, he displayed "a rather unholy knowledge of all the tricks of the dice-board." On many aspects of archery, Ascham is still regarded as authoritative. The *Toxophilus* introduces a charming reminiscence at second hand of Erasmus at Cambridge, to illustrate the point that most scholars do not take enough exercise: "This pastime for the mind only be nothing fit for students, because the body which is the most hurt by study should take away no profit at all thereat. This knew Erasmus very well when he was at Cambridge; which, when he had been sore at his book (as Garret our bookbinder hath oft told me) for lack of better exercise would take his horse and ride about the market hill and come again."

From 1548 to 1550, Ascham and his protégé William Grindal acted as tutors to the Princess Elizabeth, and under their direction she acquired a thorough knowledge of Greek and Latin literature, and the faculty of expressing herself with vigor in Latin, Italian, and French. His admiration for her intellectual parts is expressed enthusiastically in the selection which follows. That she was not unaware of her accomplishments may be gleaned from one of her speeches to Parliament: "I thank God that if I were turned out of the realm in my petticoat, I were able to live in any place in Christendom." Between 1550 and 1553, Ascham served as secretary to Sir Richard Morison, Ambassador at the court of Emperor Charles V. In 1553, Ascham wrote up his impressions of his experience, which were printed in 1570 under the title *The Report and Discourse of the Affairs and State of Germany*. Ascham, like his friend Sir John Cheke, was an ardent Protestant, but when on Mary's accession to the throne Cheke fled into exile, Ascham, by some gift of tact, became Mary's Latin Secretary. Ascham died in 1568, and in the year of his death, Camden, the antiquarian, in his *Annales* records that he lived and died a poor man because of his addiction to dicing and to cockfighting; on the latter subject, at least, he had promised in *The Schoolmaster* to write a treatise.

That Ascham left his family in poor circumstances is apparent from the dedication to *The Schoolmaster* which his wife Margaret addressed to Lord Burghley. In the course of it, she wrote "how much my said husband was many ways bound into you, and how gladly and comfortably he used in his life to recognize and report your goodness toward him, leaving with me then his poor widow and a great sort of orphans a good comfort in the hope of your good continuance, which I have truly found to me and mine." In the preface to the work, Ascham, explaining the occasion for writing it, gives us a vivid impression of an Elizabethan dinner-table conversation. At dinner at Sir William Cecil's, there was talk of some boys who had run away from Eton to escape whipping. In the discussion of educational methods that followed, Sir Richard Sackville asked Ascham to write out his views for the sake of his little grandson Robert. Despite Sir Richard's death, Ascham carried out his request.

from THE SCHOOLMASTER

The Schoolmaster is in two books, and although it is marked by many digressions, it covers rather thoroughly Ascham's views on the reasons for the decay of learning in England, his general theories on education, and his methods for teaching Latin prose. On the latter point, he particularly recommends translating from Latin into English, and then, after an interval, translating the English back into Latin, and comparing the results. In his conception of Latin prose, Ascham was a fairly stanch Ciceronian, but the fact that he decided to write his treatise in English suggests his awareness of the trend of the times. He realizes that writing in Latin would be "more honest" for his name, but writing in English will further "the pleasure or commodity of the gentlemen and yeomen of England," and will also set the example of a good style, since most English prose is composed "in a manner so meanly, both for matter and handling, that no man can do worse." Most interesting to modern readers are Ascham's extended digressions—on the glories of Cambridge during his student days, on his brilliant pupils, from the unfortunate Lady Jane Grey to Queen Elizabeth, and on his pious Puritan hostility to medieval literature and to contemporary Italian life and literature.

The passage from Book I, given below with modern spelling and punctuation, sets forth some of his reasons for the deplorable behavior of the younger generation.

THERE is another discommodity, besides cruelty in schoolmasters in beating away the love of learning from children, which hindereth learning and virtue and good bringing up of youth, and namely young gentlemen, very much in England. This fault is clean contrary to the first. I wished before to have love of learning bred up in children; I wish as much now to have young men brought up in good order of living, and in some more severe discipline than commonly they be. We have lack in England of such good order as the old noble Persians so carefully used; whose children, to the age of twenty-one years, were brought up in learning and exercises of labour; and that in such place where they should neither see that was uncomely nor hear that was unhonest. Yea, a young gentleman was never free to go where he would and do what he list himself; but under the keep and by the counsel of some grave governor, until he was either married or called to bear some office in the commonwealth.

And see the great obedience that was used in old time to fathers and governors. No son, were he never so old of years, never so great of birth, though he were a king's son, might not marry but by his father's and mother's also consent. Cyrus the Great, after he had conquered Babylon and subdued rich king Croesus, with whole Asia Minor, coming triumphantly home, his uncle Cyaxeres offered him his daughter to wife. Cyrus thanked his uncle, and praised the maid; but for marriage, he answered him with these wise and sweet words, as they be uttered by Xenophon: ὦ Κυαξάρη, τό τε γένος ἐπαινῶ, *καὶ τὴν παῖδα, καὶ δῶρα.* Βούλομαι δέ, ἔφη, *σὺν τῇ τοῦ πατρὸς γνώμῃ καὶτῇ τῆς μητρὸς ταῦτά σοι συναινέσαι.* That is to say, "Uncle Cyaxares, I commend the stock, I like the maid, and I allow well the dowry; but"—saith he—"by the counsel and consent of my father and mother, I will determine farther of these matters."

Strong Samson also in Scripture saw a maid that liked him; but he spake not to her, but went home to his father and his mother and desired both father and mother to make the marriage for him. Doth this modesty, doth this obedience, that was in great King Cyrus and stout Samson, remain in our young men at this day? No surely; for we live not longer after them by time than we live far different from them by good order. Our time is so far from that old discipline and obedience as now not only young gentlemen but even very girls dare, without all fear, though not without open shame, where they list, and how they list, marry themselves in spite of father, mother, God, good order, and all. The cause of this evil is that youth is least looked unto when they stand in most need of good keep and regard. It availeth not to see them well taught in young years, and after when they come to lust and youthful days to give them licence to live as they lust themselves. For if ye suffer the eye of a young gentleman once to be entangled with vain sights, and the ear to be corrupted with fond or filthy talk, the mind shall quickly fall sick, and soon vomit and cast up all the wholesome doctrine that he received in childhood, though he were never so well brought up before. And being once inglutted with vanity, he will straightway loathe all learning, and all good counsel to the same; and the parents, for all their great cost and charge, reap only in the end the fruit of grief and care.

This evil is not common to poor men, as God will have it, but proper to rich and great men's children, as they deserve it. Indeed from seven to seventeen, young gentlemen commonly be carefully enough brought up; but from seventeen to seven-and-twenty (the most dangerous time of all a man's life, and most slippery to stay well in) they have commonly the rein of all licence in their own hand, and specially such as do live in the court. And that which is most to be marvelled at, commonly the wisest and also best men be found the fondest fathers in this behalf. And if some good father would seek some remedy herein, yet the mother (if the house hold of our lady) had rather, yea, and will too, have her son cunning and bold, in making him to live trimly when he is young, than by learning and travel to be able to serve his prince and his country, both wisely in peace and stoutly in war, when he is old.

The fault is in yourselves, ye noble men's sons, and therefore ye deserve the greater blame, that

3–6. Samson . . . for him. See Judges 14.

commonly the meaner men's children come to be the wisest counsellors and greatest doers, in the weighty affairs of this realm. And why? For God will have it so of his providence, because ye will have it no otherwise by your negligence.

And God is a good God, and wisest in all his doings, that will place virtue and displace vice in those kingdoms where he doth govern. For he knoweth that nobility without virtue and wisdom is blood indeed, but blood truly without bones and sinews; and so of itself, without the other, very weak to bear the burden of weighty affairs.

The greatest ship indeed commonly carrieth the greatest burden, but yet always with the greatest jeopardy, not only for the persons and goods committed unto it but even for the ship itself, except it be governed with the greatest wisdom.

But nobility, governed by learning and wisdom, is indeed most like a fair ship, having tide and wind at will, under the rule of a skilful master: when contrariwise, a ship carried, yea, with the highest tide and greatest wind, lacking a skilful master, most commonly doth either sink itself upon sands or break itself upon rocks. And even so, how many have been either drowned in vain pleasure or overwhelmed by stout wilfulness, the histories of England be able to afford over-many examples unto us. Therefore, ye great and noble men's children, if ye will have rightfully that praise and enjoy surely that place which your fathers have and elders had and left unto you, ye must keep it as they gat it; and that is by the only way of virtue, wisdom, and worthiness.

For wisdom and virtue, there be many fair examples in this court for young gentlemen to follow; but they be like fair marks in the field, out of a man's reach, too far off to shoot at well. The best and worthiest men indeed be sometimes seen, but seldom talked withal. A young gentleman may sometime kneel to their person, but smally use their company for their better instruction.

But young gentlemen are fain commonly to do in the court as young archers do in the field; that is, take such marks as be nigh them, although they be never so foul to shoot at: I mean, they be driven to keep company with the worst; and what force ill company hath to corrupt good wits, the wisest men know best.

And not ill company only, but the ill opinion also of the most part, doth much harm; and namely of those which should be wise in the true deciphering of the good disposition of nature, of comeliness in courtly manners, and all right doings of men.

But error and fantasy do commonly occupy the place of truth and judgment. For if a young gentleman be demure and still of nature they say he is simple and lacketh wit; if he be bashful, and will soon blush, they call him a babish and ill brought up thing; when Xenophon doth precisely note in Cyrus, that his bashfulness in youth was the very true sign of his virtue and stoutness after. If he be innocent and ignorant of ill, they say he is rude and hath no grace: so ungraciously do some graceless men misuse the fair and godly word "grace."

But if ye would know what grace they mean, go and look, and learn amongst them, and ye shall see that it is:

First, to blush at nothing; and "blushing in youth," saith Aristotle, "is nothing else but fear to do ill"; which fear being once lustily frayed away from youth, then followeth to dare do any mischief, to contemn stoutly any goodness, to be busy in every matter, to be skilful in everything, to acknowledge no ignorance at all. To do thus in court is counted of some the chief and greatest grace of all; and termed by the name of a virtue, called courage and boldness; when Crassus in Cicero teacheth the clean contrary, and that most wittily, saying thus, "Audere, cum bonis etiam rebus conjunctum, per seipsum est magnopere fugiendum:" which is to say, "To be bold, yea in a good matter, is for itself greatly to be eschewed."

Moreover, where the swing goeth, there to follow, fawn, flatter, laugh, and lie lustily at other men's liking; to face, stand foremost, shove back; and to the meaner man, or unknown in the court, to seem somewhat solemn, coy, big, and dangerous of look, talk, and answer; to think well of himself, to be lusty in contemning of others, to have some trim grace in a privy mock; and in greater presence to bear a brave look, to be warlike; though he never looked enemy in the face in war, yet some warlike sign must be used, either a slovenly buskin, or an overstaring frounced head, as though out of every hair's top should suddenly start out a good big oath when need requireth. Yet, praised be God, England hath at this time many worthy captains and good soldiers, which be indeed so honest of behaviour, so comely of conditions, so mild of manners, as they may be examples of good order to a good sort of others, which never came in war.—But to return where I left: in place also to be able to raise talk, and make discourse of every rishe;

40. smally, in small degree. **45. foul,** poor. **50. namely,** especially.

6. babish, babyish. **18. frayed,** frightened. **30. eschewed,** avoided. **31. where the swing goeth,** wherever one's inclination leads. **51. rishe,** rush. that is. a trifle.

to have a very good will to hear himself speak; to be seen in palmistry, whereby to convey to chaste ears some fond and filthy talk.

And if some Smithfield ruffian take up some strange going, some new mowing with the mouth, some wrinching with the shoulder, some brave proverb, some fresh new oath that is not stale, but will run round in the mouth; some new disguised garment, or desperate hat, fond in fashion, or garish in colour, whatsoever it cost, how small soever his living be, by what shift soever it be gotten, gotten must it be, and used with the first, or else the grace of it is stale and gone. Some part of this graceless grace was described by me in a little rude verse long ago.

> To laugh, to lie, to flatter, to face,
> Four ways in court to win men grace.
> If thou be thrall to none of these,
> Away good Peckgoose, hence John Cheese.
> Mark well my word, and mark their deed,
> And think this verse part of thy creed.

Would to God this talk were not true, and that some men's doings were not thus. I write not to hurt any, but to profit some; to accuse none, but to monish such who, allured by ill counsel and following ill example contrary to their good bringing up, and against their own good nature, yield overmuch to these follies and faults. I know many serving-men of good order, and well staid; and again, I hear say there be some serving-men do but ill service to their young masters. Yea, read Terence and Plautus advisedly over, and ye shall find in those two wise writers, almost in every comedy, no unthrifty young man that is not brought thereunto by the subtle enticement of some lewd servant. And even now in our days, Getae, and Davi, Gnathos, and many bold bawdy Phormios too, be pressing in to prattle on every stage, to meddle in every matter; when honest Parmenos shall not be heard, but bear small swing with their masters. Their company, their talk, their over-great experience in mischief, doth easily corrupt the best natures and best brought up wits.

But I marvel the less that these misorders be amongst some in the court; for commonly in the country also every where, innocency is gone, bashfulness is banished; much presumption in youth, small authority in age; reverence is neglected, duties be confounded; and, to be short, disobedience doth overflow the banks of good order almost in every place, almost in every degree of man.

Mean men have eyes to see, and cause to lament and occasion to complain of these miseries; but other have authority to remedy them, and will do so too, when God shall think time fit. For all these misorders be God's just plagues, by his sufferance brought justly upon us for our sins, which be infinite in number and horrible in deed; but namely for the great abominable sin of unkindness; but what unkindness? Even such unkindness as was in the Jews, in contemning God's voice, in shrinking from his word, in wishing back again for Egypt, in committing adultery and whoredom, not with the women, but with the doctrine of Babylon, and did bring all the plagues, destructions, and captivities that fell so oft and horrible upon Israel.

We have cause also in England to beware of unkindness, who have had in so few years the candle of God's word so oft lightened, so oft put out; and yet will venture by our unthankfulness in doctrine and sinful life to leese again light, candle, candlestick and all.

God keep us in his fear; God graft in us the true knowledge of his word, with a forward will to follow it, and so to bring forth the sweet fruits of it; and then shall he preserve us by his grace from all manner of terrible days.

The remedy of this doth not stand only in making good common laws for the whole realm, but also (and perchance chiefly) in observing private discipline, every man carefully in his own house; and namely, if special regard be had to youth; and that not so much in teaching them what is good as in keeping them from that that is ill.

Therefore, if wise fathers be not as well ware in weeding from their children ill things and ill company, as they were before in grafting in them learning and providing for them good schoolmasters, what fruit they shall reap of all their cost and care, common experience doth tell.

Here is the place, in youth is the time when some ignorance is as necessary as much knowledge; and not in matters of our duty towards God, as some wilful wits willingly against their own knowledge, perniciously against their own conscience, have of late openly taught. Indeed St. Chrysostom, that noble and eloquent doctor, in a sermon *contra fatum* and the curious searching of nativities, doth wisely say that ignorance therein is better than knowledge. But to wring this sentence, to wrest thereby out

4. Smithfield, a low section in London. **26. monish,** admonish. **37–40. Getae, . . . Parmenos,** characters in the comedies of Plautus and Terence.

2. Mean, humble, common. **21. leese,** lose. **35. ware,** careful. **46. St. Chrysostom,** St. John Chrysostom (345?–407). **47. contra fatum,** against fate. **48. curious searching of nativities,** overinquisitive casting of horoscopes.

of men's hands the knowledge of God's doctrine, is without all reason, against common sense, contrary to the judgment also of them which be the discreetest men and best learned on their own side. I know Julianus Apostata did so: but I never heard or read that any ancient Father of the primitive church either thought or wrote so.

But this ignorance in youth which I speak on, or rather this simplicity, or most truly this innocency, is that which the noble Persians, as wise Xenophon doth testify, were so careful to breed up their youth in. But Christian fathers commonly do not so. And I will tell you a tale, as much to be misliked as the Persians' example is to be followed.

This last summer I was in a gentleman's house, where a young child, somewhat past four year old, could in no wise frame his tongue to say a little short grace; and yet he could roundly rap out so many ugly oaths, and those of the newest fashion, as some good man of fourscore year old hath never heard named before. And that which was most detestable of all, his father and mother would laugh at it. I much doubt what comfort another day this child shall bring unto them. This child, using much the company of serving-men and giving good ear to their talk, did easily learn which he shall hardly forget all the days of his life hereafter. So likewise in the court, if a young gentleman will venture himself into the company of ruffians, it is over-great a jeopardy lest their fashions, manners, thoughts, talk, and deeds, will very soon be ever like. The confounding of companies breedeth confusion of good manners, both in the court and everywhere else.

And it may be a great wonder, but a greater shame to us Christian men, to understand what a heathen writer, Isocrates, doth leave in memory of writing, concerning the care that the noble city of Athens had to bring up their youth in honest company and virtuous discipline; whose talk in Greek is to this effect in English:

"The city was not more careful to see their children well taught than to see their young men well governed; which they brought to pass not so much by common law as by private discipline. For they had more regard that their youth by good order should not offend than how by law they might be punished; and if offence were committed, there was neither way to hide it, nor hope of pardon for it. Good natures were not so much openly praised as they were secretly marked and watchfully regarded, lest they should leese the goodness they had. Therefore in schools of singing and dancing, and other honest exercises, governors were appointed more diligent to oversee their good manners than their masters were to teach them any learning. It was some shame to a young man to be seen in the open market; and if for business he passed through it, he did it with a marvellous modesty and bashful fashion. To eat or drink in a tavern was not only a shame, but also punishable, in a young man. To contrary, or to stand in terms with an old man, was more heinous than in some place to rebuke and scold with his own father." With many other more good orders and fair disciplines, which I refer to their reading that have lust to look upon the description of such a worthy commonwealth.

And to know what worthy fruit did spring of such worthy seed, I will tell you the most marvel of all, and yet such a truth as no man shall deny it except such as be ignorant in knowledge of the best stories.

Athens, by this discipline and good ordering of youth, did breed up, within the circuit of that one city, within the compass of one hundred year, within the memory of one man's life, so many notable captains in war, for worthiness, wisdom, and learning, as be scarce matchable, no, not in the state of Rome, in the compass of those seven hundred years when it flourished most.

And because I will not only say it, but also prove it, the names of them be these: Miltiades, Themistocles, Xantippus, Pericles, Cimon, Alcibiades, Thrasybulus, Conon, Iphicrates, Xenophon, Timotheus, Theopompus, Demetrius, and divers other more; of which every one may justly be spoken that worthy praise which was given to Scipio Africanus, who Cicero doubteth, whether he were more noble captain in war, or more eloquent and wise counsellor in peace. And if ye believe not me, read diligently Aemilius Probus in Latin, and Plutarch in Greek; which two had no cause either to flatter or lie upon any of those which I have recited.

And beside nobility in war, for excellent and matchless masters in all manner of learning, in that one city, in memory of one age, were more learned men, and that in a manner altogether, than all time doth remember, than all place doth afford, than all other tongues do contain. And I do not mean of those authors which by injury of time, by negligence of men, by cruelty of fire and sword, be lost; but even of those which by God's grace are left yet unto us; of which, I thank God, even my poor study lacketh not one. As, in philosophy, Plato, Aristotle, Xenophon, Euclid, and Theophrast;

5. **Julianus Apostata,** Julian the Apostate (331–363), Roman emperor 361–63. 37. **Isocrates,** Athenian orator and teacher (436–338 B.C.).

in eloquence and civil law, Demosthenes, Aeschines, Lycurgus, Dinarchus, Demades, Isocrates, Isaeus, Lysias, Antisthenes, Andocides; in histories, Herodotus, Thucydides, Xenophon, and, which we lack to our great loss, Theopompus and Ephorus; in poetry, Aeschylus, Sophocles, Euripides, Aristophanes, and somewhat of Menander, Demosthenes' sister son.

Now let Italian, and Latin itself, Spanish, French, Dutch, and English bring forth their learning and recite their authorities; Cicero only excepted, and one or two more in Latin, they be all patched clouts and rags, in comparison of fair woven broadcloths; and truly, if there be any good in them it is either learned, borrowed, or stolen from some of those worthy wits of Athens.

The remembrance of such a commonwealth, using such discipline and order for youth, and thereby bringing forth to their praise, and leaving to us for our example, such captains for war, such counsellors for peace, and matchless masters for all kind of learning, is pleasant for me to recite, and not irksome, I trust, for other to hear, except it be such as make neither account of virtue nor learning.

And whether there be any such or no, I cannot well tell; yet I hear say, some young gentlemen of ours count it their shame to be counted learned; and perchance they count it their shame to be counted honest also; for I hear say they meddle as little with the one as with the other. A marvellous case, that gentlemen should so be ashamed of good learning, and never a whit ashamed of ill manners! Such do say for them that the gentlemen of France do so; which is a lie, as God will have it. Langaeus and Bellaeus, that be dead, and the noble Vidam of Chartres, that is alive, and infinite more in France, which I hear tell of, prove this to be most false. And though some in France, which will needs be gentlemen, whether men will or no, and have more gentleship in their hat than in their head, be at deadly feud with both learning and honesty; yet I believe if that noble prince, King Francis the First, were alive they should have neither place in his court nor pension in his wars, if he had knowledge of them. This opinion is not French, but plain Turkish, from whence some French fetch more faults than this; which I pray God keep out of England, and send also those of ours better minds, which bend themselves against virtue and learning, to the contempt of God, dishonour of their country, to the hurt of many others, and at length to the greatest harm and utter destruction of themselves.

Some other, having better nature but less wit (for ill commonly have over-much wit), do not utterly dispraise learning, but they say that without learning, common experience, knowledge of all fashions, and haunting all companies shall work in youth both wisdom and ability to execute any weighty affair. Surely long experience doth profit much, but most, and almost only, to him (if we mean honest affairs) that is diligently before instructed with precepts of well doing. For good precepts of learning be the eyes of the mind, to look wisely before a man, which way to go right and which not.

Learning teacheth more in one year than experience in twenty; and learning teacheth safely, when experience maketh more miserable than wise. He hazardeth sore that waxeth wise by experience. An unhappy master he is that is made cunning by many shipwrecks; a miserable merchant, that is neither rich nor wise but after some bankrouts. It is costly wisdom that is bought by experience. We know by experience itself that it is a marvellous pain to find out but a short way by long wandering. And, surely, he that would prove wise by experience, he may be witty indeed, but even like a swift runner, that runneth fast out of his way and upon the night, he knoweth not whither. And verily they be fewest of number that be happy or wise by unlearned experience. And look well upon the former life of those few, whether your example be old or young, who without learning have gathered by long experience a little wisdom and some happiness; and when you do consider what mischief they have committed, what dangers they have escaped (and yet twenty for one do perish in the adventure), then think well with yourself whether you would that your own son should come to wisdom and happiness by the way of such experience or no.

It is a notable tale, that old Sir Roger Chamloe sometime chief justice, would tell of himself. When he was ancient in Inn of Court, certain young gentlemen were brought before him to be corrected for certain misorders: and one of the lustiest said "Sir, we be young gentlemen; and wise men before us have proved all fashions, and yet those have done full well." This they said because it was well known that Sir Roger had been a good fellow in his youth. But he answered them very wisely: "Indeed," saith he, "in youth I was as you are now and I had twelve fellows like unto myself, but not one of them came to a good end. And therefore follow not my example in youth, but follow my

19. bankrouts, bankruptcies. **41. ancient,** the designation of the oldest barristers.

counsel in age, if ever ye think to come to this place, or to these years that I am come unto; lest ye meet either with poverty or Tyburn in the way."

This experience of all fashions in youth, being in proof always dangerous, in issue seldom lucky, is a way indeed to over-much knowledge, yet used commonly of such men which be either carried by some curious affection of mind, or driven by some hard necessity of life, to hazard the trial of over-many perilous adventures.

Erasmus, the honour of learning of all our time, said wisely that experience is the common school-house of fools and ill men. Men of wit and honesty be otherwise instructed. For there be, that keep them out of fire, and yet was never burned; that be ware of water, and yet was never nigh drowning; that hate harlots, and was never at the stews; that abhor falsehood, and never brake promise themselves.

But will ye see a fit similitude of this adventured experience? A father that doth let loose his son to all experiences is most like a fond hunter that letteth slip a whelp to the whole herd; twenty to one he shall fall upon a rascal, and let go the fair game. Men that hunt so be either ignorant persons, privy stealers, or night-walkers.

Learning therefore, ye wise fathers, and good bringing up, and not blind and dangerous experience, is the next and readiest way that must lead your children, first to wisdom, and then to worthiness, if ever ye purpose they shall come there.

And to say all in short, though I lack authority to give counsel, yet I lack not good will to wish, that the youth in England, especially gentlemen, and namely nobility, should be by good bringing up so grounded in judgment of learning, so founded in love of honesty, as, when they should be called forth to the execution of great affairs, in service of their prince and country, they might be able to use and to order all experiences, were they good, were they bad, and that according to the square, rule, and line of wisdom, learning, and virtue.

And do I not mean, by all this my talk, that young gentlemen should always be poring on a book, and by using good studies should leese honest pleasure and haunt no good pastime; I mean nothing less. For it is well known that I both like and love, and have always, and do yet still use, all exercises and pastimes that be fit for my nature and ability; and beside natural disposition, in judgment also I was never either stoic in doctrine or anabaptist in religion, to mislike a merry, pleasant, and playful nature, if no outrage be committed against law, measure, and good order.

Therefore I would wish that beside some good time fitly appointed and constantly kept, to increase by reading the knowledge of the tongues and learning, young gentlemen should use and delight in all courtly exercises and gentlemanlike pastimes. And good cause why; for the self-same noble city of Athens, justly commended of me before, did wisely, and upon great consideration, appoint the Muses, Apollo, and Pallas, to be patrons of learning to their youth. For the Muses, besides learning, were also ladies of dancing, mirth, and minstrelsy; Apollo was god of shooting, and author of cunning playing upon instruments; Pallas also was lady mistress in wars. Whereby was nothing else meant but that learning should be always mingled with honest mirth and comely exercises; and that war also should be governed by learning and moderated by wisdom; as did well appear in those captains of Athens named by me before, and also in Scipio and Caesar, the two diamonds of Rome. And Pallas was no more feared in wearing *aegida* than she was praised for choosing *oliva;* whereby shineth the glory of learning, which thus was governor and mistress in the noble city of Athens, both of war and peace.

Therefore to ride comely, to run fair at the tilt or ring; to play at all weapons, to shoot fair in bow, or surely in gun; to vault lustily, to run, to leap, to wrestle, to swim; to dance comely, to sing, and play of instruments cunningly; to hawk, to hunt; to play at tennis, and all pastimes generally, which be joined with labour, used in open place, and on the day-light, containing either some fit exercise for war, or some pleasant pastime for peace, be not only comely and decent, but also very necessary for a courtly gentlemen to use.

But of all kind of pastimes fit for a gentleman, I will, God willing, in fitter place more at large declare fully, in my book of the cockpit; which I do write to satisfy some, I trust with some reason, that be more curious in marking other men's doings than careful in mending their own faults. And some also will needs busy themselves in marvelling, and adding thereunto unfriendly talk, why I, a man of good years, and of no ill place, I thank God and my prince, do make choice to spend such time in writing of trifles, as the School of Shooting, the Cockpit, and this book of the First Principles of Grammar, rather than to take some weighty matter in hand, either of religion or civil discipline.

3. **Tyburn,** the gallows on Tyburn Hill. 22. **fond,** foolish. 24. **rascal,** an inferior deer. 43. **do I not,** I do not. 23–24. **aegida . . . oliva,** shields (for war), olive branches (for peace).

Wise men, I know, will well allow of my choice herein; and as for such who have not wit of themselves but must learn of others to judge right of men's doings, let them read that wise poet Horace in his *Arte Poetica*, who willeth wise men to beware of high and lofty titles. For great ships require costly tackling, and also afterward dangerous government: small boats be neither very chargeable in making, nor very oft in great jeopardy; and yet they carry many times as good and costly ware as greater vessels do. A mean argument may easily bear the light burden of a small fault, and have always at hand a ready excuse for ill handling; and some praise it is, if it so chance to be better indeed than a man dare venture to seem. A high title doth charge a man with the heavy burden of too great a promise; and therefore saith Horace, very wittily, that that poet was a very fool that began his book with a goodly verse indeed but overproud a promise:

"Fortunam Priami cantabo, et nobile bellum."

And after as wisely:

"Quanto rectius hic, qui nil molitur inepte!" etc.;

meaning Homer; who, within the compass of a small argument of one harlot and of one good wife, did utter so much learning in all kind of sciences as, by the judgment of Quintilian, he deserveth so high a praise that no man yet deserved to sit in the second degree beneath him. And thus much out of my way, concerning my purpose in spending pen and paper and time upon trifles; and namely, to answer some that have neither wit nor learning to do anything themselves, neither will nor honesty to say well of other.

To join learning with comely exercises, Conto Baldesar Castiglione, in his book *Cortegiano*, doth trimly teach; which book advisedly read and diligently followed but one year at home in England would do a young gentleman more good, I wiss, than three years' travel abroad spent in Italy. And I marvel this book is no more read in the court than it is, seeing it is so well translated into English by a worthy gentleman, Sir Thomas Hoby, who was many ways well furnished with learning, and very expert in knowledge of divers tongues.

And beside good precepts in books, in all kind of tongues, this court also never lacked many fair examples for young gentlemen to follow; and surely one example is more valuable, both to good and ill than twenty precepts written in books; and so Plato, not in one or two, but divers places, doth plainly teach.

If King Edward had lived a little longer, his only example had bred such a race of worthy learned gentlemen as this realm never yet did afford.

And in the second degree, two noble primroses of nobility, the young Duke of Suffolk and Lord Henry Matrevers, were two such examples to the court for learning as our time may rather wish than look for again. At Cambridge, also, in St. John's College, in my time, I do know that not so much the good statutes as two gentlemen of worthy memory, Sir John Cheke and Dr. Redman, by their only example of excellency in learning, of godliness in living, of diligency in studying. of counsel in exhorting, of good order in all things, did breed up so many learned men in that one college of St. John's at one time as I believe the whole university of Louvain in many years was never able to afford.

Present examples of this present time I list not to touch; yet there is one example for all the gentlemen of this court to follow, that may well satisfy them, or nothing will serve them, nor no example move them to goodness and learning.

It is your shame (I speak to you all, you young gentlemen of England) that one maid should go beyond you all in excellency of learning and knowledge of divers tongues. Point forth six of the best given gentlemen of this court, and all they together show not so much good will, spend not so much time, bestow not so many hours daily, orderly, and constantly, for the increase of learning and knowledge, as doth the Queen's Majesty herself. Yea, I believe that beside her perfect readiness in Latin, Italian, French, and Spanish, she readeth here now at Windsor more Greek every day than some prebendary of this church doth read Latin in a whole week. And that which is most praiseworthy of all, within the walls of her privy chamber she hath obtained that excellency of learning to understand, speak, and write both wittily with head and fair with hand, as scarce one or two rare wits in both the universities have in many years reached unto. Amongst all the benefits that God hath blessed me withal, next the knowledge of Christ's true religion, I count this the greatest, that it pleased God to call me to be one poor minister in setting forward these excellent gifts of learning in this most excellent prince; whose only example if the rest of our nobility would follow, then might England be for learning and wisdom in nobility a spectacle to all the world beside. . . .

8. chargeable, costly. **21. "Fortunam . . . bellum."** "The fortune of Priam I shall sing, and the famous war." **24. "Quanto . . . inepte!"** "How much better this other, who attempted nothing foolishly!" **41. wiss,** know.

John Lyly
c. 1553–1606

John Lyly is commonly known as the author of "the first English novel" and as an influential predecessor of Shakespeare in the writing of comedy. Of the young men who turned from their university studies to engage in literature, he had perhaps the most fortunate career. Born, probably in Kent, in 1553 or 1554, he entered Magdalen College, Oxford, in 1569, and received his bachelor's degree in 1573 and his master's degree in 1575. He was an unsuccessful competitor for a fellowship. In 1579, he achieved literary fame on the publication of his prose narrative *Euphues: The Anatomy of Wit*, and attempted to capitalize on its success by writing and publishing a sequel, *Euphues and His England*, in 1580. His connection with the theater began in 1583, when, after serving as secretary to the Earl of Oxford, he was given the lease of the private theater Blackfriars, and undertook to furnish plays for the company of child-actors assembled from the choirboys of the Chapel Royal and St. Paul's Cathedral. It was for this company and this playhouse that Lyly wrote his first two plays in 1584, *Alexander and Campaspe* and *Sappho and Phao*. In that year the company was forced to vacate Blackfriars, and in 1585 Lyly was made assistant master of St. Paul's Cathedral School, with the duty of providing the choirboys with plays. Between 1585 and 1590, the rest of Lyly's plays were written and performed by this company, among them *Endymion*, 1591; *Midas*, 1592; and *Mother Bombie*, 1594.

Lyly's comedies retell freely various familiar classical legends, the main features of which the dramatist was bent on utilizing. But he felt free to invent subsidiary and comic figures, and his witty page boys engage in charming verbal banter. In certain of his plays, there was for a courtly audience the additional curiosity of an alleged allegorical significance. Thus, *Sappho and Phao* is supposed to allude to the courtship of Queen Elizabeth by the Duke of Alençon, *Endymion* refers to the rivalry between Elizabeth and her cousin Mary Queen of Scots, and *Midas* satirizes the overweening ambition of Philip II of Spain.

Lyly's contribution to the development of English comedy lay in his unity of tone and mood, his elegant and pointed prose dialogue, his deft grouping of characters, and his romanticizing of ancient classical stories. The exquisite lyrics, which appeared for the first time in a collected edition of his plays printed in 1632, may or may not be from his hand.

Lyly's later life is of little literary significance. Toward the end of his connection with St. Paul's School, he may have got into difficulties through the publication of his anti-Puritan pamphlet, *Pap with a Hatchet*, 1589. He did, however, obtain a minor post in the Revels Office in 1588, and he kept it until 1604. His attempts to become Master of the Revels were unsuccessful. He was a Member of Parliament on four occasions between 1589 and 1601. He died in 1606.

from EUPHUES: THE ANATOMY OF WIT

The plot of Lyly's *Euphues* is an extremely simple one. Euphues, a gifted young gentleman from Athens, goes to Naples, and, although warned by an old man, Eubulus, of its dangers, gives himself over to the dissipations of the city. He makes friends with Philautus, and is introduced to the latter's fiancée, Lucilla. Forgetful of his friendship, he tries to win Lucilla for himself, but in the end the fickle heroine leaves both young men in the lurch. They are reconciled, and Euphues retires into seclusion to devote himself to philosophy.

The slight story is augmented with a series of appendices, consisting of Euphues' letters and essays on the fickleness of women and on the theory of education. The selection given below is from the essay entitled "Euphues and his Ephoebus," that is, Euphues and his disciple. It draws its subject matter from Plutarch's classical tractate *On the Education of Children*, which had been ransacked for ideas by various Renaissance writers (including Erasmus) before Lyly undertook to amplify it. The attack on the state of learning at Athens is a thinly disguised satire on Lyly's own university, Oxford.

I WOULD have them first of all to follow philosophy, as most ancient, yea most excellent, for as it is pleasant to pass through many fair cities, but most pleasant to dwell in the fairest, even so to read many histories and arts it is pleasant, but as it were to lodge with philosophy most profitable.

It was prettily said of Bion the philosopher:

even as when the wooers could not have the company of Penelope they run to her handmaids; so they that cannot attain to the knowledge of philosophy, apply their minds to things most vile and contemptible. Wherefore we must prefer philosophy, as the only princess of all sciences, and other arts as waiting maids. For the curing and keeping in temper of the body, man by his industry has found two things, physic and exercise, the one cureth sickness, the other preserveth the body in temper, but there is nothing that may heal diseases or cure the wounds of the mind but only philosophy. By this shall we learn what is honest, what dishonest, what is right, what is wrong, and that I may in one word say what may be said, what is to be known, what is to be avoided, what to be embraced, how we ought to obey our parents, reverence our elders, entertain strangers, honour the magistrates, love our friends, live with our wives, use our servants, how we should worship God, be dutiful to our fathers, stand in awe of our superiors, obey laws, give place to officers, how we may choose friends, nurture our children, and that which is most noble, how we should neither be too proud in prosperity, neither pensive in adversity, neither like beasts overcome with anger. And here I cannot but lament Athens, which having been always the nurse of philosophers, doth now nourish only the name of philosophy. For to speak plainly of the disorder of Athens, who doth not see it, and sorrow at it? Such playing at dice, such quaffing of drink, such dalliance with women, such dancing, that in my opinion there is no quaffer in Flanders so given to tippling, no courtier in Italy so given to riot, no creature in the world so misled as a student in Athens. Such a confusion of degrees, that the Scholar knoweth not his duty to the Bachelor, nor the Bachelor to the Master, nor the Master to the Doctor. Such corruption of manners, contempt of magistrates, such open sins, such privy villainy, such quarrelling in the streets, such subtile practices in chambers, as maketh my heart to melt with sorrow to think of it, and should cause your minds, gentlemen, to be penitent to remember it.

Moreover, who doth know a scholar by his habit? Is there any hat of so unseemly a fashion, any doublet of so long a waist, any hose so short, any attire either so costly or so courtly, either so strange in making or so monstrous in wearing that is not worn of a scholar? Have they not now instead of black cloth black velvet, instead of coarse sackcloth fine silk? Be they not more like courtiers than scholars, more like stage-players than students, more like ruffians of Naples than disputers in Athens? I would to God they did not imitate all other nations in the vice of the mind as they do in the attire of their body, for certainly as there is no nation whose fashion in apparel they do not use, so is there no wickedness published in any place, that they do not practise. I think that in Sodom and Gomorrah there was never more filthiness, never more pride in Rome, more poisoning in Italy, more lying in Crete, more privy spoiling in Spain, more idolatry in Egypt, than is at this day in Athens, never such sects among the heathens, such schisms among the Turks, such misbelief among the infidels, as is now among scholars. Be there not many in Athens which think there is no God? no redemption? no resurrection?

What shame is this, gentlemen, that a place so renowned for good learning should be so shamed for ill lying? that where grace doth abound, sin should so superabound? that where the greatest profession of knowledge is, there should also be the least practising of honesty? I have read of many universities, as of Padua in Italy, Paris in France, Wittenberg in Germany, in England of Oxford and Cambridge, which if they were half so ill as Athens they were too too bad, and as I have heard as they be, they be stark nought.

But I can speak the less against them, for that I was never in them; yet can I not choose but be aggrieved, that by report I am enforced rather to accuse them of vanity than excuse them any way. Ah, gentlemen, what is to be looked for, nay, what is not to be feared, when the temple of Vesta where virgins should live is like the stews, fraught with strumpets, when the altar where nothing but sanctity and holiness should be used is polluted with uncleanness, when the universities of Christendom which should be the eyes, the lights, the leaven, the salt, the seasoning of the world are dimmed with blind concupiscence, put out with pride, and have lost their savour with impiety?

Is it not become a byword amongst the common people that they had rather send their children to the cart than to the university, being induced so to say for the abuse that reigneth in the universities, who, sending their sons to attain knowledge, find them little better learned, but a great deal worse lived than when they went, and not only unthrifty of their money, but also bankrupt of good manners: was not this the cause that caused a simple woman in Greece to exclaim against Athens, saying:

"The master and the scholar, the tutor and the pupil be both agreed, for the one careth not how

43. the cart, the wagon taking prisoners to the gallows.

little pain he taketh for his money, the other how little learning."

I perceive that in Athens there be no changelings: When of old it was said to a Lacedemonian, that all the Grecians knew honesty, but not one practised it. When Panathaenea were celebrated at Athens, an old man going to take a place was mockingly rejected, at the last, coming among the Lacedemonians, all the youth gave him place, which the Athenians liked well of; then one of the Spartans cried out: "Verily the Athenians know what should be done, but they never do it." When one of the Lacedemonians had been for a certain time in Athens seeing nothing but dancing, dicing, banqueting, surfeiting, and licentious behaviour, returning home he was asked how all things stood in Athens, to whom he answered, "All things are honest there," meaning that the Athenians accounted all things good, and nothing bad. How such abuses should or might be redressed in all universities, especially in Athens, if I were of authority to command, it should be seen, or of credit to persuade those that have the dealings with them, it should soon be shown.

And until I see better reformation in Athens, my young Ephoebus shall not be nurtured in Athens. I have spoken all this that you gentlemen might see how the philosophers in Athens practise nothing less than philosophy. What scholar is he that is so zealous at his book as Chrisippus, who, had not his maid Melissa thrust meat into his mouth had perished with famine, being always studying? Who so watchful as Aristotle, who going to bed would have a ball of brass in his hand, that if he should be taken in a slumber it might fall and awaken him? No, no, the times are changed, as Ovid saith, and we are changed in the times; let us endeavour every one to amend one, and we shall all soon be amended; let us give no occasion of reproach, and we shall more easily bear the burden of false reports, and as we see by learning what we should do, so let us do as we learn; then shall Athens flourish, then shall the students be had in great reputation, then shall learning have his hire, and every good scholar his hope. But return we once again to philosophy.

There is among men a threefold kind of life: active, which is about civil function and administration of the common weal; speculative, which is in continual meditation and study; the third, a life led, most commonly a lewd life, an idle and vain life, the life that the Epicures account their whole felicity, a voluptuous life replenished with all kinds of vanity. If this active life be without philosophy, it is an idle life, or at the least a life evil employed, which is worse. If the contemplative life be separated from the active, it is most unprofitable. I would therefore have my youth so to bestow his study as he may both be exercised in the common weal, to common profit, and well employed privately for his own perfection, so as by his study the rule he shall bear may be directed, and by his government his study may be increased: in this manner did Pericles deal in civil affairs, after this sort did Architas the Tarentine, Dion the Syracusian, the Theban Epaminondas govern their cities.

For the exercise of the body it is necessary also somewhat be added, that is, that the child should be at such times permitted to recreate himself, when his mind is overcome with study, lest dulling himself with overmuch industry he become unfit afterward to conceive readily; besides this, it will cause an apt composition and that natural strength that it before retained. A good composition of the body layeth a good foundation of old age, for as in the fair summer we prepare all things necessary for the cold winter, so good manners in youth and lawful exercises be as it were victuals and nourishments for age: yet are their labours and pastimes so to be tempered that they weaken not their bodies more by play than otherwise they should have done by study, and so to be used that they addict not themselves more to the exercise of the limbs than the following of learning; the greatest enemies to discipline, as Plato recounteth, are labours and sleep. It is also requisite that he be expert in martial affairs, in shooting, in darting, that he hawk and hunt, for his honest pastime and recreation, and if after these pastimes he shall seem secure, nothing regarding his books, I would not have him scourged with stripes, but threatened with words, not dulled with blows, like servants the which the more they are beaten the better they bear it, and the less they care for it; for children of good disposition are either incited by praise to go forward, or shamed by dispraise to commit the like offence; those of obstinate and blockish behaviour are neither with words to be persuaded, neither with stripes to be corrected. They must now be taunted with sharp rebukes, straightways admonished with fair words, now threatened a payment, by and by promised a reward, and dealt withal as nurses do with the babes, whom after they have made to cry, they proffer the teat. But diligent heed must be taken that he be not praised above measure, lest standing too much in his own

44. blockish, stupid.

conceit, he become also obstinate in his own opinions. I have known many fathers whose great love towards their sons hath been the cause in time that they loved them not, for when they see a sharp wit in their son to conceive, for the desire they have that he should outrun his fellows, they load him with continual exercise, which is the only cause that he sinketh under his burden, and giveth over in the plain field. Plants are nourished with little rain, yet drowned with much; even so the mind with indifferent labour waxeth more perfect; with much study it is made fruitless. We must consider that all our life is divided into remission and study.

As there is watching, so is there sleep; as there is war, so is there peace; as there is winter, so is there summer; as there be many working days, so is there also many holidays; and if I may speak all in one word, ease is the sauce of labour, which is plainly to be seen not only in living things, but also in things without life. We unbend the bow that we may the better bend him; we unloose the harp that we may the sooner tune him; the body is kept in health as well with fasting as eating, the mind healed with ease as well as with labour. Those parents are in mind to be misliked which commit the whole care of their child to the custody of a hireling, neither asking, neither knowing, how their children profit in learning. For if the father were desirous to examine his son in that which he hath learned, the master would be more careful what he did teach. But seeing the father careless what they learn, he is also secure what he teacheth. That notable saying of the horse-keeper may here be applied, which said, nothing did so fatten the horse as the eye of the king. Moreover, I would have the memory of children continually to be exercised, which is the greatest furtherance to learning that can be. For this cause they fained in their old fables memory to be the mother of perfection. . . .

Descend into your own consciences; consider with your selves the great difference between staring and stark blind, wit and wisdom, love and lust; be merry but with modesty; be sober but not too sullen; be valiant but not too venturous; let your attire be comely but not too costly; your diet wholesome but not excessive; use pastime, as the word importeth, to pass the time in honest recreation. Mistrust no man without cause; neither be you credulous without proof; be not light to follow every man's opinion, neither obstinate to stand in your own conceits; serve God, fear God, love God, and God will bless you, as either your hearts can wish, or your friends desire. This was his grave and godly advice whose counsel I would have you all to follow: frequent lectures, use disputations openly, neglect not your private studies, let not degrees be given for love but for learning, not for money but for knowledge, and because you shall be the better encouraged to follow my counsel, I will be as it were an example myself, desiring you all to imitate me. . . .

SONGS

These songs from plays, and others attributed to Lyly, were printed for the first time in 1632 in a posthumous edition of his plays. Modern scholars have disagreed as to their authorship. But whether or not they come from the hand of Lyly, they exhibit the charm and grace of the songs frequently introduced into the plays of this period. The second and third songs illustrate the happy use of motifs from English country life and folklore. The first two are from *Alexander and Campaspe*, the third from *Endymion*.

CUPID AND MY CAMPASPE

Cupid and my Campaspe played
At cards for kisses; Cupid paid.
He stakes his quiver, bow, and arrows,
His mother's doves and team of sparrows,
Loses them too; then down he throws
The coral of his lip, the rose
Growing on's cheek (but none knows how),
With these the crystal of his brow,
And then the dimple of his chin:
All these did my Campaspe win.
At last he set her both his eyes;
She won, and Cupid blind did rise.
O Love! has she done this to thee?
What shall, alas, become of me?

WHAT BIRD SO SINGS

What bird so sings, yet so does wail?
Oh, 'tis the ravished nightingale.
Jug, jug, jug, jug, tereu, she cries,
And still her woes at midnight rise.
Brave prick-song! who is't now we hear?
None but the lark so shrill and clear;
How at heaven's gates she claps her wings,
The morn not waking till she sings.
Hark, hark, with what a pretty throat
Poor robin redbreast tunes his note;
Hark how the jolly cuckoos sing
Cuckoo, to welcome in the spring,
Cuckoo, to welcome in the spring.

What Bird So Sings? 5. **prick-song,** written music.

SONG BY FAIRIES

Omnes. Pinch him, pinch him, black and blue,
Saucy mortals must not view
What the queen of stars is doing,
Nor pry into our fairy wooing.
1 *Fairy.* Pinch him blue.
2 *Fairy.* And pinch him black.
3 *Fairy.* Let him not lack
Sharp nails to pinch him blue and red,
Till sleep has rocked his addlehead.
4 *Fairy.* For the trespass he hath done,
Spots o'er all his flesh shall run.
Kiss Endymion, kiss his eyes,
Then to our midnight haydegyes.

Sir Philip Sidney
1554–1586

In character and attainments, Sidney was a closer approximation to the ideal of the Renaissance courtier than any other person of his time. He was born on November 30, 1554, at the fine country place of his father, Penshurst, Kent. His father was Sir Henry Sidney, who served three times as Lord Deputy of Ireland; his mother was Lady Mary Dudley, a sister of Elizabeth's favorite, Robert Dudley, first Earl of Leicester. His sister Mary, after her marriage to the second Earl of Pembroke, became the greatest patroness of letters of her time.

Sidney entered Shrewsbury School on the same day as Fulke Greville, who became his lifelong friend and his first biographer. From 1567 to 1571, he was a student at Christ Church, Oxford, and later for a brief time at Cambridge, but he took no degree from either university. In May, 1572, he embarked on a grand tour of Europe which was to last until 1575. First, he went to Paris in the train of the English Ambassador and there he witnessed the Massacre of St. Bartholomew, an experience which deepened his attachment to the Protestant cause. He spent a considerable period at Frankfort in the company of the Humanist Hubert Languet, and traveled with him to Vienna. He penetrated to Hungary, and in Italy visited Venice, Genoa, and Padua. In the first of these cities, he met the great painters Tintoretto and Veronese. He passed the winter of 1574–75 in Vienna, but returned through the Low Countries to England in time to be present at the extravagant series of entertainments which Leicester staged in honor of Elizabeth's visit to Kenilworth, July 9–27, 1575. He followed the court to Chartley Castle, the home seat of the Earl of Essex, and there may be supposed to have met Penelope Devereux, Essex's daughter, then a girl of thirteen. By 1576, he was a serious suitor for her hand, and Essex before his death in 1576 expressed a wish that the marriage should take place. But though Sidney's uncle, Leicester, married Penelope's mother, Lady Essex, in 1577, the young people's marriage did not take place.

In 1577 Sidney was sent abroad by the Queen to serve as Ambassador to the Emperor of Germany and the Elector Palatine. In the following year, he wrote a masque, *The Lady of May*, which was presented before the Queen at Leicester's castle at Wanstead. During the next few years Sidney was a member of an informal group called the Areopagus, interested in literature generally, but more particularly in the movement to adapt classical meters to English usage. He was further inspired to composition by the publication in 1579 of Stephen Gosson's Puritanical attack on poetry and the drama in *The School of Abuse*, dedicated to Sidney without the latter's permission. Sidney's reply, *The Defence of Poesy*, was probably begun shortly after this event.

In 1580, Sidney was afforded a further opportunity for composition when as a result of his open letter to Elizabeth, protesting against her projected marriage to the Duke of Anjou, he was forced into temporary retirement. At the Pembrokes' beautiful country seat, Wilton House, Wiltshire, he began his long pastoral romance, *Arcadia*, for the amusement of his sister, the Countess of Pembroke. In 1581, the marriage of Penelope Devereux to the elderly Lord Rich seems to have rekindled his interest in the young girl, and most of his amatory sonnets were probably written during this period.

Restored to court favor in 1581, Sidney was knighted by Elizabeth in 1583, and in the same

13. **haydegyes**, popular dances. This song occurs in a scene where Corsites is prevented by the fairies from carrying off the sleeping Endymion.

year married Frances, the daughter of Sir Francis Walsingham, one of the Queen's intensely Protestant counselors. In the winter of 1584–85 he sat in Parliament, and was considering an expedition to America with Sir Francis Drake when he was appointed Governor of Flushing, Holland, as a part of the Queen's plans for aiding the Protestants in the Low Countries against her archenemy, Philip II. In September, 1586, he was mortally wounded in an unimportant engagement between the English and the Spanish at Zutphen. Fulke Greville tells how, as Sidney was about to slake his thirst after being wounded, he saw a dying soldier, and took the drink "from his head before he drank, and delivered it to the poor man with these words, 'Thy necessity is greater than mine.' " He lingered for twenty-six days, during which he composed a song about his wound, "*La Cuisse Rompue*," and had it sung to him. He died on October 17, 1586, and was given a magnificent funeral and burial in St. Paul's Cathedral. Elegies upon his death were written by Spenser, James I, Drayton, and other poets.

Sidney complied with the Renaissance courtly code by not allowing his writing to be published. But two of his poems were set to music by William Byrd and printed in songbooks of 1588 and 1589. An incompletely revised version of the *Arcadia* was published in 1590, and a version revised by his sister in 1593. Two printed editions of *Astrophel and Stella* appeared in 1591. His critical treatise was published twice in 1593, first under the title *The Defence of Poesy* and then under the title *An Apology for Poetry*. An authorized edition of his principal works, prepared by the Countess of Pembroke, was published in 1598. By 1724, his works had reached a fourteenth edition.

Sidney served English literature in a number of important ways, as poet, as fictionist, and as critic. Aside from a great deal of interesting though unimpressive poetic experimentation in the lyrical interludes of *Arcadia*, his most notable poetic achievement was *Astrophel and Stella*, the first real sonnet sequence in English and the stimulus to an extraordinary amount of emulation in the decade after its publication. In the *Arcadia*, he wrote the first very extended piece of Renaissance prose fiction, blended the pastoral and the heroic modes, and demonstrated the poetic potentialities of a highly decorated prose style. Probably *The Defence of Poesy* is his most noteworthy contribution, since this critical work is the most important in its kind produced in England during the Renaissance.

from ASTROPHEL AND STELLA

The publication of *Astrophel and Stella* in 1591 was the signal for the production of a large number of sequences of sonnets in the Petrarchan vein. Wyatt and Surrey had introduced Petrarchan themes and stylistic devices into English poetry, but Sidney was the first English poet to tell an orderly story in this exacting form.

Although Sidney asserts his independence of Petrarch and other sonneteers, both his subject and his style are highly conventional. Like the other Petrarchans, he represents his lady as unattainable, and his love as unrequited. Like them, also, he treats the inevitable topics: the lover's instability of emotion, his sleeplessness, his invocation to the moon, his ecstatic hopes and abysmal fears. But Sidney's chaste and modest spirit makes itself felt despite the basic conventionality of the poetic type.

I

Loving in truth, and fain in verse my love to show,
That she, dear she, might take some pleasure of my pain,
Pleasure might cause her read, reading might make her know,
Knowledge might pity win, and pity grace obtain,—
I sought fit words to paint the blackest face of woe;
Studying inventions fine, her wits to entertain,
Oft turning others' leaves to see if thence would flow
Some fresh and fruitful showers upon my sunburned brain.
But words came halting forth, wanting invention's stay;
Invention, nature's child, fled step-dame Study's blows,
And others' feet still seemed but strangers in my way.
Thus, great with child to speak, and helpless in my throes,
Biting my truant pen, beating myself for spite,
Fool, said my muse to me, look in thy heart and write.

5

It is most true that eyes are formed to serve
The inward light, and that the heavenly part
Ought to be king, from whose rules who do swerve,
Rebels to nature, strive for their own smart.
It is most true what we call Cupid's dart
An image is which for ourselves we carve,
And, fools, adore in temple of our heart
Till that good god make church and churchman starve.

True, that true beauty virtue is indeed,
  Whereof this beauty can be but a shade,
  Which elements with mortal mixture breed.
True, that on earth we are but pilgrims made,
  And should in soul up to our country move;
  True, and yet true that I must Stella love.

14

Alas, have I not pain enough, my friend,
  Upon whose breast a fiercer gripe doth tire
  Than did on him who first stole down the fire,
  While Love on me doth all his quiver spend,—
But with your rhubarb words ye must contend,
  To grieve me worse, in saying that desire
  Doth plunge my well-formed soul even in the mire
  Of sinful thoughts which do in ruin end?
If that be sin which doth the manners frame,
  Well stayed with truth in word and faith of deed,
  Ready of wit and fearing nought but shame;
If that be sin which in fixed hearts doth breed
  A loathing of all loose unchastity,
  Then love is sin, and let me sinful be.

31

With how sad steps, O moon, thou climb'st the skies!
  How silently, and with how wan a face!
  What! may it be that even in heavenly place
  That busy archer his sharp arrows tries?
Sure, if that long-with-love-acquainted eyes
  Can judge of love, thou feel'st a lover's case;
  I read it in thy looks,—thy languished grace
  To me, that feel the like, thy state descries.
Then, ev'n of fellowship, O moon, tell me,
  Is constant love deemed there but want of wit?
  Are beauties there as proud as here they be?
Do they above love to be loved, and yet
  Those lovers scorn whom that love doth possess?
  Do they call virtue there ungratefulness?

39

Come sleep! O sleep, the certain knot of peace,
  The baiting place of wit, the balm of woe,
  The poor man's wealth, the prisoner's release,
  Th' indifferent judge between the high and low;
With shield of proof shield me from out the prease
  Of those fierce darts despair at me doth throw;
  O make in me those civil wars to cease;
  I will good tribute pay, if thou do so.

Sec. 14. 5. **rhubarb,** bitter, tart, with the suggestion also of medicinal. *Sec. 39.* 5. **prease,** press.

Take thou of me smooth pillows, sweetest bed,
  A chamber deaf to noise and blind to light,
  A rosy garland and a weary head;
And if these things, as being thine by right,
  Move not thy heavy grace, thou shalt in me,
  Livelier than elsewhere, Stella's image see.

54

Because I breathe not love to every one,
  Nor do not use set colours for to wear,
  Nor nourish special locks of vowèd hair,
  Nor give each speech a full point of a groan,
The courtly nymphs, acquainted with the moan
  Of them who in their lips Love's standard bear,
  What, he! say they of me, Now I dare swear
  He cannot love; no, no, let him alone.
And think so still, so Stella know my mind;
  Profess indeed I do not Cupid's art;
  But you, fair maids, at length this true shall find,
That his right badge is but worn in the heart;
  Dumb swans, not chattering pies, do lovers prove;
  They love indeed who quake to say they love.

MY TRUE-LOVE HATH MY HEART

My true-love hath my heart, and I have his,
By just exchange one for another given:
I hold his dear, and mine he cannot miss,
There never was a better bargain driven:
  My true-love hath my heart, and I have his.

His heart in me keeps him and me in one,
My heart in him his thoughts and senses guides:
He loves my heart, for once it was his own,
I cherish his because in me it bides:
  My true-love hath my heart, and I have his.

from CERTAIN SONNETS

This sonnet is eloquently expressive of the deeply religious side of Sidney's nature.

Leave me, O love which reachest but to dust;
And thou, my mind, aspire to higher things;
Grow rich in that which never taketh rust,
Whatever fades but fading pleasure brings.
Draw in thy beams, and humble all thy might
To that sweet yoke where lasting freedoms be;
Which breaks the clouds and opens forth the light,
That doth both shine and give us sight to see.
O take fast hold; let that light be thy guide
In this small course which birth draws out to death,

And think how evil becometh him to slide,
Who seeketh heaven, and comes of heavenly
breath.
Then farewell, world; thy uttermost I see;
Eternal Love, maintain thy life in me.

from THE DEFENCE OF POESY

Sidney's *Defence of Poesy* is a skillful synthesis of Classical and Renaissance literary-critical theory. It represents wide reading in the Renaissance interpreters of the doctrines of Plato, Aristotle, and Horace, and a willing acceptance of their theories. The essay is carefully organized. The first part is devoted to an affirmative statement of the case for poetry. The second part is an attempt at a rebuttal of the attack on poetry. The final section evaluates the English literature of Sidney's time in accordance with the Neoclassical principles in which he believes. The author's amiability and good humor are apparent throughout the essay. The selection given below consists of the summary of the first part and all the remainder of *The Defence.*

SINCE, then, poetry is of all human learnings the most ancient, and of most fatherly antiquity, as from whence other learnings have taken their beginnings; since it is so universal that no learned nation doth despise it, nor barbarous nation is without it; since both Roman and Greek gave such divine names unto it, the one of prophesying, the other of making, and that indeed that name of making is fit for him, considering that where all other arts retain themselves within their subject, and receive, as it were, their being from it, the poet only, only bringeth his own stuff, and doth not learn a conceit out of a matter, but maketh matter for a conceit; since neither his description nor end containeth any evil, the thing described cannot be evil; since his effects be so good as to teach goodness, and delight the learners of it; since therein (namely in moral doctrine, the chief of all knowledges) he doth not only far pass the historian, but, for instructing, is well nigh comparable to the philosopher, for moving, leaveth him behind him; since the Holy Scripture (wherein there is no uncleanness) hath whole parts in it poetical, and that even our Saviour Christ vouchsafed to use the flowers of it; since all his kinds are not only in their united forms but in their severed dissections fully commendable; I think, and think I think rightly, the laurel crown appointed for triumphant captains doth worthily, of all other learnings, honour the poet's triumph.

But because we have ears as well as tongues, and that the lightest reasons that may be will seem to weigh greatly if nothing be put in the counterbalance, let us hear, and, as well as we can, ponder, what objections be made against this art, which may be worthy either of yielding or answering.

First, truly, I note, not only in these *μισομούσοι*, poet-haters, but in all that kind of people who seek a praise by dispraising others, that they do prodigally spend a great many wandering words in quips and scoffs, carping and taunting at each thing which, by stirring the spleen, may stay the brain from a thorough beholding the worthiness of the subject. Those kind of objections, as they are full of a very idle easiness (since there is nothing of so sacred a majesty but that an itching tongue may rub itself upon it), so deserve they no other answer but, instead of laughing at the jest, to laugh at the jester. We know a playing wit can praise the discretion of an ass, the comfortableness of being in debt, and the jolly commodities of being sick of the plague; so, of the contrary side, if we will turn Ovid's verse,

"*Ut lateat virtus, proximitate mali.*"

"That good lie hid in nearness of the evil," Agrippa will be as merry in showing the vanity of science, as Erasmus was in the commending of folly; neither shall any man or matter escape some touch of these smiling railers. But for Erasmus and Agrippa, they had another foundation than the superficial part would promise. Marry, these other pleasant faultfinders, who will correct the verb before they understand the noun, and confute others' knowledge before they confirm their own; I would have them only remember, that scoffing cometh not of wisdom; so as the best title in true English they get with their merriments is to be called good fools; for so have our grave forefathers ever termed that humorous kind of jesters.

But that which giveth greatest scope to their scorning humour is rhyming and versing. It is already said, and, as I think, truly said, it is not rhyming and versing that maketh poesy; one may be a poet without versing, and a versifier without poetry. But yet, presuppose it were inseparable, as indeed it seemeth Scaliger judgeth, truly it were an inseparable commendation; for if *oratio* next to *ratio*, speech next to reason, be the greatest gift bestowed upon mortality, that can not be praiseless which doth most polish that blessing of speech; which considereth each word, not only as a man may say by his forcible quality, but by his best measured quantity; carrying even in themselves a harmony; without, perchance, number, measure, order, proportion be in our time grown odious.

But lay aside the just praise it hath, by being the only fit speech for music—music, I say, the most divine striker of the senses—thus much is undoubtedly true, that if reading be foolish without remembering, memory being the only treasure of knowledge, those words which are fittest for memory are likewise most convenient for knowledge. Now, that verse far exceedeth prose in the knitting up of the memory, the reason is manifest; the words, besides their delight, which hath a great affinity to memory, being so set as one cannot be lost but the whole work fails; which accusing itself calleth the remembrance back to itself, and so most strongly confirmeth it. Besides, one word so, as it were, begetting another as, be it in rhyme or measured verse, by the former a man shall have a near guess to the follower. Lastly, even they that have taught the art of memory have showed nothing so apt for it as a certain room divided into many places, well and thoroughly known; now that hath the verse in effect perfectly, every word having his natural seat, which seat must needs make the word remembered. But what needs more in a thing so known to all men? Who is it that ever was scholar that doth not carry away some verses of Virgil, Horace, or Cato, which in his youth he learned, and even to his old age serve him for hourly lessons? as,

> "*Percontatorem fugito: nam garrulus idem est.*
> *Dum sibi quisque placet credula turba sumus.*"

But the fitness it hath for memory is notably proved by all delivery of arts, wherein, for the most part, from grammar to logic, mathematics, physic, and the rest, the rules chiefly necessary to be borne away are compiled in verses. So that verse being in itself sweet and orderly, and being best for memory, the only handle of knowledge, it must be in jest that any man can speak against it.

Now then go we to the most important imputations laid to the poor poets; for aught I can yet learn, they are these:

First, that there being many other more fruitful knowledges, a man might better spend his time in them than in this.

Secondly, that it is the mother of lies.

Thirdly, that it is the nurse of abuse, infecting us with many pestilent desires, with a siren's sweetness drawing the mind to the serpent's tail of sinful fancies; and herein, especially, comedies give the largest field to ear, as Chaucer saith; how, both in other nations and ours, before poets did soften us, we were full of courage, given to martial exercises, the pillars of manlike liberty, and not lulled asleep in shady idleness with poets' pastimes.

And lastly and chiefly, they cry out with open mouth, as if they had overshot Robin Hood, that Plato banished them out of his commonwealth. Truly this is much, if there be much truth in it.

First, to the first, that a man might better spend his time is a reason indeed; but it doth, as they say, but *petere principium*. For if it be, as I affirm, that no learning is so good as that which teacheth and moveth to virtue, and that none can both teach and move thereto so much as poesy, then is the conclusion manifest, that ink and paper cannot be to a more profitable purpose employed. And certainly, though a man should grant their first assumption, it should follow, methinks, very unwillingly, that good is not good because better is better. But I still and utterly deny that there is sprung out of earth a more fruitful knowledge.

To the second, therefore, that they should be the principal liars, I answer paradoxically, but truly, I think truly, that of all writers under the sun, the poet is the least liar; and though he would, as a poet can scarcely be a liar. The astronomer, with his cousin the geometrician, can hardly escape when they take upon them to measure the height of the stars. How often, think you, do the physicians lie, when they aver things good for sicknesses which afterwards send Charon a great number of souls drowned in a potion before they come to his ferry? And no less of the rest which take upon them to affirm. Now for the poet, he nothing affirmeth, and therefore never lieth; for, as I take it, to lie is to affirm that to be true which is false; so as the other artists, and especially the historian, affirming many things, can, in the cloudy knowledge of mankind, hardly escape from many lies. But the poet, as I said before, never affirmeth; the poet never maketh any circles about your imagination, to conjure you to believe for true what he writeth; he citeth not authorities of other histories, but even for his entry calleth the sweet Muses to inspire into him a good invention; in truth, not labouring to tell you what is or is not, but what should or should not be. And, therefore, though he recount things not true, yet because he telleth them not for true he lieth not; without we will say that Nathan lied in his speech, before alleged, to David; which, as a wicked man durst scarce say, so think I none so simple would say that Aesop lied in the tales of his beasts; for who

29–30. "Percontatorem . . . sumus." "Fly from the inquisitive man, for he is likewise garrulous. While each one pleases himself we are a credulous crowd." **51. ear,** plow.

11. petere principium, beg the question. **49. Nathan.** See II Samuel 12:1–14. Sidney had referred to this earlier.

thinketh that Aesop wrote it for actually true were well worthy to have his name chronicled among the beasts he writeth of. What child is there that cometh to a play, and seeing Thebes written in great letters upon an old door, doth believe that it is Thebes? If then a man can arrive to the child's age, to know that the poet's persons and doings are but pictures what should be, and not stories what have been, they will never give the lie to things not affirmatively, but allegorically and figuratively written; and therefore, as in history, looking for truth, they may go away full fraught with falsehood, so in poesy, looking but for fiction, they shall use the narration but as an imaginative groundplot of a profitable invention.

But hereto is replied, that the poets give names to men they write of, which argueth a conceit of an actual truth, and so, not being true, proveth a falsehood. And doth the lawyer lie then, when, under the names of John of the Stile, and John of the Nokes, he putteth his case? But that is easily answered. Their naming of men is but to make their picture the more lively, and not to build any history. Painting men, they cannot leave men nameless; we see we cannot play at chess but that we must give names to our chessmen; and yet, methinks, he were a very partial champion of truth that would say we lied for giving a piece of wood the reverend title of a bishop. The poet nameth Cyrus and Aeneas no other way than to show what men of their fames, fortunes, and estates should do.

Their third is, how much it abuseth men's wit, training it to wanton sinfulness and lustful love. For, indeed, that is the principal if not only abuse I can hear alleged. They say the comedies rather teach than reprehend amorous conceits; they say the lyric is larded with passionate sonnets; the elegiac weeps the want of his mistress; and that even to the heroical Cupid hath ambitiously climbed. Alas! Love, I would thou couldst as well defend thyself as thou canst offend others! I would those on whom thou dost attend could either put thee away or yield good reason why they keep thee! But grant love of beauty to be a beastly fault, although it be very hard, since only man, and no beast, hath that gift to discern beauty; grant that lovely name of love to deserve all hateful reproaches, although even some of my masters the philosophers spent a good deal of their lamp-oil in setting forth the excellency of it; grant, I say, what they will have granted, that not only love, but lust, but vanity, but, if they list, scurrility, possess many leaves of the poets' books; yet, think I, when this is granted, they will find their sentence may, with good manners, put the last words foremost; and not say that poetry abuseth man's wit, but that man's wit abuseth poetry. For I will not deny but that man's wit may make poesy, which should be *φραστική*, which some learned have defined, figuring forth good things, to be *φανταστική*, which doth contrariwise infect the fancy with unworthy objects; as the painter that should give to the eye either some excellent perspective, or some fine picture fit for building or fortification, or containing in it some notable example, as Abraham sacrificing his son Isaac, Judith killing Holofernes, David fighting with Goliath, may leave those, and please an ill-pleased eye with wanton shows of better-hidden matters.

But, what! Shall the abuse of a thing make the right use odious? Nay, truly, though I yield that poesy may not only be abused, but that being abused, by the reason of his sweet charming force it can do more hurt than any other army of words, yet shall it be so far from concluding that the abuse shall give reproach to the abused, that, contrariwise, it is a good reason that whatsoever being abused doth most harm, being rightly used (and upon the right use each thing receives his title) doth most good. Do we not see skill of physic, the best rampire to our often-assaulted bodies, being abused, teach poison, the most violent destroyer? Doth not knowledge of law, whose end is to even and right all things, being abused, grow the crooked fosterer of horrible injuries? Doth not (to go to the highest) God's word abused breed heresy, and his name abused become blasphemy? Truly, a needle cannot do much hurt, and as truly (with leave of ladies be it spoken) it cannot do much good. With a sword thou mayst kill thy father, and with a sword thou mayst defend thy prince and country; so that, as in their calling poets fathers of lies they said nothing, so in this their argument of abuse, they prove the commendation.

They allege herewith, that before poets began to be in price, our nation had set their heart's delight upon action, and not imagination; rather doing things worthy to be written than writing things fit to be done. What that before-time was, I think scarcely Sphinx can tell; since no memory is so ancient that gives not the precedence to poetry. And certain it is that, in our plainest homeliness, yet never was the Albion nation without poetry. Marry, this argument, though it be levelled

5–6. **φραστικὴ . . . φανταστικὴ.** In the two adjectives Sidney contrasts poetry that is soundly creative and poetry that is morbidly creative. **19. his,** its—as always at this time. **27. rampire,** rampart.

against poetry, yet it is indeed a chain-shot against all learning—or bookishness, as they commonly term it. Of such mind were certain Goths, of whom it is written that having in the spoil of a famous city taken a fair library, one hangman, belike fit to execute the fruits of their wits, who had murthered a great number of bodies, would have set fire in it. "No," said another, very gravely, "take heed what you do, for while they are busy about those toys we shall with more leisure conquer their countries." This, indeed, is the ordinary doctrine of ignorance, and many words sometimes I have heard spent in it; but because this reason is generally against all learning, as well as poetry, or rather all learning but poetry; because it were too large a digression to handle it, or at least too superfluous, since it is manifest that all government of action is to be gotten by knowledge, and knowledge best by gathering many knowledges, which is reading; I only say with Horace, to him that is of that opinion,

"*Iubeo stultum esse libenter*——"

for as for poetry itself, it is the freest from this objection, for poetry is the companion of camps. I dare undertake, Orlando Furioso or honest King Arthur will never displease a soldier: but the quiddity of *ens* and *prima materia* will hardly agree with a corselet. And, therefore, as I said in the beginning, even Turks and Tartars are delighted with poets. Homer, a Greek, flourished before Greece flourished; and if to a slight conjecture a conjecture may be opposed, truly it may seem, that as by him their learned men took almost their first light of knowledge, so their active men received their first motions of courage. Only Alexander's example may serve, who by Plutarch is accounted of such virtue that fortune was not his guide but his footstool; whose acts speak for him, though Plutarch did not; indeed, the phoenix of warlike princes. This Alexander left his schoolmaster, living Aristotle, behind him, but took dead Homer with him. He put the philosopher Callisthenes to death, for his seeming philosophical, indeed mutinous, stubbornness; but the chief thing he was ever heard to wish for was that Homer had been alive. He well found he received more bravery of mind by the pattern of Achilles than by hearing the definition of fortitude. And, therefore, if Cato misliked Fulvius for carrying Ennius with him to the field, it may be answered that if Cato misliked it the noble Fulvius liked it, or else he had not done it; for it was not the excellent Cato Uticensis, whose authority I would much more have reverenced, but it was the former, in truth a bitter punisher of faults, but else a man that had never sacrificed to the Graces. He misliked and cried out against all Greek learning, and yet, being fourscore years old, began to learn it, belike fearing that Pluto understood not Latin. Indeed, the Roman laws allowed no person to be carried to the wars but he that was in the soldiers' roll. And, therefore, though Cato misliked his unmustered person, he misliked not his work. And if he had, Scipio Nasica (judged by common consent the best Roman) loved him; both the other Scipio brothers, who had by their virtues no less surnames than of Asia and Afric, so loved him that they caused his body to be buried in their sepulture. So as Cato's authority being but against his person, and that answered with so far greater than himself, is herein of no validity.

But now, indeed, my burthen is great, that Plato his name is laid upon me, whom, I must confess, of all philosophers I have ever esteemed most worthy of reverence; and with good reason, since of all philosophers he is the most poetical; yet if he will defile the fountain out of which his flowing streams have proceeded, let us boldly examine with what reasons he did it.

First, truly, a man might maliciously object that Plato, being a philosopher, was a natural enemy of poets. For, indeed, after the philosophers had picked out of the sweet mysteries of poetry the right discerning true points of knowledge, they forthwith, putting it in method, and making a school-art of that which the poets did only teach by a divine delightfulness, beginning to spurn at their guides, like ungrateful apprentices, were not content to set up shop for themselves, but sought by all means to discredit their masters; which, by the force of delight being barred them, the less they could overthrow them, the more they hated them. For, indeed, they found for Homer seven cities strove who should have him for their citizen, where many cities banished philosophers as not fit members to live among them. For only repeating certain of Euripides' verses many Athenians had their lives saved of the Syracusans, where the Athenians themselves thought many philosophers unworthy to live. Certain poets, as Simonides and Pindarus, had so prevailed with Hiero the First, that of a tyrant they made him a just king; where Plato could do so little with Dionysius that he himself of a philosopher was made a slave. But who should do

22. "Iubeo . . . libenter——." "I bid him enjoy his own foolishness." **28. quiddity,** essence; also, fine distinction. **ens . . . prima materia,** being, primary matter—terms of philosophy.

thus, I confess, should requite the objections made against poets with like cavillations against philosophers; as likewise one should do that should bid one read *Phaedrus* or *Symposium* in Plato, or the discourse of Love in Plutarch, and see whether any poet do authorize abominable filthiness as they do.

Again, a man might ask, out of what commonwealth Plato doth banish them. In sooth, thence where he himself alloweth community of women. So as belike this banishment grew not for effeminate wantonness, since little should poetical sonnets be hurtful when a man might have what woman he listed. But I honour philosophical instructions, and bless the wits which bred them, so as they be not abused, which is likewise stretched to poetry. St. Paul himself sets a watchword upon philosophy, indeed upon the abuse. So doth Plato upon the abuse, not upon poetry. Plato found fault that the poets of his time filled the world with wrong opinions of the gods, making light tales of that unspotted essence, and therefore would not have the youth depraved with such opinions. Herein may much be said; let this suffice: the poets did not induce such opinions, but did imitate those opinions already induced. For all the Greek stories can well testify that the very religion of that time stood upon many and many-fashioned gods; not taught so by poets, but followed according to their nature of imitation. Who list may read in Plutarch the discourses of Isis and Osiris, of the cause why oracles ceased, of the divine providence, and see whether the theology of that nation stood not upon such dreams, which the poets indeed superstitiously observed; and truly, since they had not the light of Christ, did much better in it than the philosophers, who, shaking off superstition, brought in atheism.

Plato, therefore, whose authority I had much rather justly construe than unjustly resist, meant not in general of poets, in those words of which Julius Scaliger saith, "*Qua authoritate barbari quidam atque hispidi abuti velint ad poetas e republica exigendos*": but only meant to drive out those wrong opinions of the Deity, whereof now, without farther law, Christianity hath taken away all the hurtful belief, perchance, as he thought, nourished by the then esteemed poets. And a man need go no further than to Plato himself to know his meaning; who, in his dialogue called *Ion*, giveth high and rightly divine commendation unto poetry. So as Plato, banishing the abuse not the thing, not banishing it, but giving due honour to it, shall be our patron and not our adversary. For, indeed, I had much rather, since truly I may do it, show their mistaking of Plato, under whose lion's skin they would make an ass-like braying against poesy, than go about to overthrow his authority; whom, the wiser a man is, the more just cause he shall find to have in admiration; especially since he attributeth unto poesy more than myself do, namely, to be a very inspiring of a divine force, far above man's wit, as in the forenamed dialogue is apparent.

Of the other side, who would show the honours have been by the best sort of judgments granted them, a whole sea of examples would present themselves; Alexanders, Caesars, Scipios, all favourers of poets; Laelius, called the Roman Socrates, himself a poet; so as part of *Heautontimoroumenos*, in Terence, was supposed to be made by him. And even the Greek Socrates, whom Apollo confirmed to be the only wise man, is said to have spent part of his old time in putting Aesop's fables into verse; and, therefore, full evil should it become his scholar Plato to put such words in his master's mouth against poets. But what needs more? Aristotle writes the *Art of Poesy;* and why, if it should not be written? Plutarch teacheth the use to be gathered of them; and how, if they should not be read? And who reads Plutarch's either history or philosophy, shall find he trimmeth both their garments with guards of poesy.

But I list not to defend poesy with the help of his underling historiography. Let it suffice to have showed it is a fit soil for praise to dwell upon; and what dispraise may be set upon it is either easily overcome, or transformed into just commendation. So that since the excellences of it may be so easily and so justly confirmed, and the low creeping objections so soon trodden down; it not being an art of lies, but of true doctrine; not of effeminateness, but of notable stirring of courage; not of abusing man's wit, but of strengthening man's wit; not banished, but honoured by Plato; let us rather plant more laurels for to ingarland the poets' heads (which honour of being laureate, as besides them only triumphant captains were, is a sufficient authority to show the price they ought to be held in) than suffer the ill-savoured breath of such wrong speakers once to blow upon the clear springs of poesy.

But since I have run so long a career in this matter, methinks, before I give my pen a full stop, it shall be but a little more lost time to inquire why England, the mother of excellent minds, should be

40–41. "Qua . . . exigendos." "Which authority certain barbarous and rude writers would wrest into meaning that poets were to be thrust out of a state."

16. Heautontimoroumenos, *The Self-Tormentor*, a comedy adapted from Menander.

grown so hard a step-mother to poets, who certainly in wit ought to pass all others, since all only proceeds from their wit, being, indeed, makers of themselves, not takers of others. How can I but exclaim,

"*Musa, mihi causas memora, quo numine laeso?*"

Sweet poesy! that hath anciently had kings, emperors, senators, great captains, such as, besides a thousand others, David, Adrian, Sophocles, Germanicus, not only to favour poets, but to be poets; and of our nearer times can present for her patrons, a Robert, King of Sicily; the great King Francis of France; King James of Scotland; such cardinals as Bembus and Bibiena; such famous preachers and teachers as Beza and Melancthon; so learned philosophers as Fracastorius and Scaliger; so great orators as Pontanus and Muretus; so piercing wits as George Buchanan; so grave counsellors as, besides many, but before all, that Hospital of France, than whom, I think, that realm never brought forth a more accomplished judgment more firmly builded upon virtue; I say these, with numbers of others, not only to read others' poesies, but to poetize for others' reading; that poesy, thus embraced in all other places, should only find in our time a hard welcome in England, I think the very earth laments it, and therefore decks our soil with fewer laurels than it was accustomed. For heretofore poets have in England also flourished; and, which is to be noted, even in those times when the trumpet of Mars did sound loudest. And now that an over-faint quietness should seem to strew the house for poets, they are almost in as good reputation as the mountebanks at Venice. Truly, even that, as of the one side it giveth great praise to poesy, which, like Venus (but to better purpose), had rather be troubled in the net with Mars than enjoy the homely quiet of Vulcan; so serveth it for a piece of a reason why they are less grateful to idle England, which now can scarce endure the pain of a pen. Upon this necessarily followeth that base men with servile wits undertake it, who think it enough if they can be rewarded of the printer; and so as Epaminondas is said with the honour of his virtue to have made an office, by his exercising it, which before was contemptible, to become highly respected; so these men, no more but setting their names to it, by their own disgracefulness disgrace the most graceful poesy. For now, as if all the Muses were got with child to bring forth bastard poets, without any commission they do post over the banks of Helicon, until they make their readers more weary than post-horses; while, in the meantime, they,

"*Queis meliore luto finxit praecordia Titan,*"

are better content to suppress the outflowings of their wit than by publishing them to be accounted knights of the same order.

But I, that before ever I durst aspire unto the dignity am admitted into the company of the paper-blurrers, do find the very true cause of our wanting estimation is want of desert, taking upon us to be poets in despite of Pallas. Now, wherein we want desert were a thankworthy labour to express. But if I knew, I should have mended myself; but as I never desired the title, so have I neglected the means to come by it; only, overmastered by some thoughts, I yielded an inky tribute unto them. Marry, they that delight in poesy itself should seek to know what they do, and how they do; and especially look themselves in an unflattering glass of reason, if they be inclinable unto it.

For poesy must not be drawn by the ears, it must be gently led, or rather it must lead; which was partly the cause that made the ancient learned affirm it was a divine gift, and no human skill, since all other knowledges lie ready for any that have strength of wit, a poet no industry can make, if his own genius be not carried into it. And therefore is an old proverb, *Orator fit, poeta nascitur.* Yet confess I always, that as the fertilest ground must be manured, so must the highest flying wit have a Daedalus to guide him. That Daedalus, they say, both in this and in other, hath three wings to bear itself up into the air of due commendation; that is art, imitation, and exercise. But these neither artificial rules nor imitative patterns we much cumber ourselves withal. Exercise, indeed, we do, but that very forebackwardly; for where we should exercise to know, we exercise as having known; and so is our brain delivered of much matter which never was begotten by knowledge. For there being two principal parts, matter to be expressed by words, and words to express the matter, in neither we use art or imitation rightly. Our matter is *quodlibet*, indeed, though wrongly performing Ovid's verse,

"*Quicquid conabor dicere, versus erit;*"

never marshalling it into any assured rank, that almost the readers cannot tell where to find themselves.

6. "Musa . . . laeso?" "Muse, bring to my mind the causes of these things: what divinity was injured?"

3. "Queis . . . Titan." "Whose hearts the Titan formed with a better clay." **29. Orator . . . nascitur.** The orator is made, the poet born. **44. quodlibet,** what you will. **46. "Quicquid . . . erit."** "Whatever I shall try to write will be verse."

Chaucer undoubtedly did excellently in his *Troilus and Criseyde;* of whom, truly, I know not whether to marvel more, either that he in that misty time could see so clearly, or that we in this clear age go so stumblingly after him. Yet had he great wants, fit to be forgiven in so reverent an antiquity. I account the *Mirror of Magistrates* meetly furnished of beautiful parts. And in the Earl of Surrey's lyrics, many things tasting of a noble birth, and worthy of a noble mind. The *Shepherds' Calendar* hath much poesy in his eclogues, indeed, worthy the reading, if I be not deceived. That same framing of his style to an old rustic language, I dare not allow; since neither Theocritus in Greek, Virgil in Latin, nor Sannazaro in Italian, did affect it. Besides these, I do not remember to have seen but few (to speak boldly) printed that have poetical sinews in them. For proof whereof, let but most of the verses be put in prose, and then ask the meaning, and it will be found that one verse did but beget another, without ordering at the first what should be at the last; which becomes a confused mass of words, with a tinkling sound of rhyme, barely accompanied with reason.

Our tragedies and comedies, not without cause cried out against, observing rules neither of honest civility nor skilful poetry. Excepting *Gorboduc* (again I say of those that I have seen), which notwithstanding as it is full of stately speeches and well-sounding phrases, climbing to the height of Seneca his style, and as full of notable morality, which it doth most delightfully teach, and so obtain the very end of poesy; yet, in truth, it is very defectious in the circumstances, which grieves me, because it might not remain as an exact model of all tragedies. For it is faulty both in place and time, the two necessary companions of all corporal actions. For where the stage should always represent but one place, and the uttermost time presupposed in it should be, both by Aristotle's precept and common reason, but one day; there is both many days and many places inartificially imagined.

But if it be so in *Gorboduc*, how much more in all the rest? Where you shall have Asia of the one side, and Afric of the other, and so many other underkingdoms, that the player, when he comes in, must ever begin with telling where he is, or else the tale will not be conceived. Now shall you have three ladies walk to gather flowers, and then we must believe the stage to be a garden. By and by, we hear news of shipwreck in the same place, then we are to blame if we accept it not for a rock. Upon the back of that comes out a hideous monster with fire and smoke, and then the miserable beholders are bound to take it for a cave; while, in the meantime, two armies fly in, represented with four swords and bucklers, and then what hard heart will not receive it for a pitched field?

Now of time they are much more liberal; for ordinary it is, that two young princes fall in love; after many traverses she is got with child, delivered of a fair boy, he is lost, groweth a man, falleth in love, and is ready to get another child; and all this in two hours' space; which, how absurd it is in sense, even sense may imagine, and art hath taught, and all ancient examples justified, and at this day the ordinary players in Italy will not err in. Yet will some bring in an example of the *Eunuch*, in Terence, that containeth matter of two days, yet far short of twenty years. True it is, and so was it to be played in two days, and so fitted to the time it set forth. And though Plautus have in one place done amiss, let us hit it with him, and not miss with him. But they will say, how then shall we set forth a story which contains both many places and many times? And do they not know that a tragedy is tied to the laws of poesy, and not of history; not bound to follow the story, but having liberty either to feign a quite new matter or to frame the history to the most tragical conveniency? Again, many things may be told, which cannot be showed—if they know the difference betwixt reporting and representing. As for example, I may speak, though I am here, of Peru, and in speech digress from that to the description of Calicut; but in action I cannot represent it without Pacolet's horse. And so was the manner the ancients took, by some *Nuntius* to recount things done in former time, or other place.

Lastly, if they will represent an history they must not, as Horace saith, begin *ab ovo*, but they must come to the principal point of that one action which they will represent. By example this will be best expressed; I have a story of young Polydorus, delivered, for safety's sake, with great riches, by his father Priamus to Polymnestor, King of Thrace, in the Trojan war time. He, after some years, hearing of the overthrow of Priamus, for to make the treasure his own, murthereth the child; the body of the child is taken up; Hecuba, she, the same day, findeth a sleight to be revenged most cruelly of the tyrant. Where, now, would one of our tragedy-writers begin, but with the delivery of the child? Then should he sail over into Thrace, and so spend I know not how many years, and travel numbers of places. But where doth Euripides? Even with the finding of the body; leaving the rest to be told

33. Nuntius, messenger. 37. ab ovo, from the egg.

by the spirit of Polydorus. This needs no further to be enlarged; the dullest wit may conceive it.

But, besides these gross absurdities, how all their plays be neither right tragedies nor right comedies, mingling kings and clowns, not because the matter so carrieth it, but thrust in the clown by head and shoulders to play a part in majestical matters, with neither decency nor discretion; so as neither the admiration and commiseration, nor the right sportfulness, is by their mongrel tragi-comedy obtained. I know Apuleius did somewhat so, but that is a thing recounted with space of time, not represented in one moment; and I know the ancients have one or two examples of tragi-comedies as Plautus hath *Amphytrio*. But, if we mark them well, we shall find that they never, or very daintily, match hornpipes and funerals. So falleth it out that, having indeed no right comedy in that comical part of our tragedy, we have nothing but scurrility, unworthy of any chaste ears; or some extreme show of doltishness, indeed fit to lift up a loud laughter, and nothing else; where the whole tract of a comedy should be full of delight; as the tragedy should be still maintained in a well-raised admiration.

But our comedians think there is no delight without laughter, which is very wrong; for though laughter may come with delight, yet cometh it not of delight, as though delight should be the cause of laughter; but well may one thing breed both together. Nay, rather in themselves they have, as it were, a kind of contrariety. For delight we scarcely do, but in things that have a conveniency to ourselves, or to the general nature; laughter almost ever cometh of things most disproportioned to ourselves and nature. Delight hath a joy in it either permanent or present; laughter hath only a scornful tickling. For example, we are ravished with delight to see a fair woman, and yet are far from being moved to laughter; we laugh at deformed creatures, wherein certainly we cannot delight. We delight in good chances; we laugh at mischances. We delight to hear the happiness of our friends and country, at which he were worthy to be laughed at that would laugh; we shall, contrarily, sometimes laugh to find a matter quite mistaken, and go down the hill against the bias, in the mouth of some such men as for the respect of them one shall be heartily sorry he cannot choose but laugh, and so is rather pained than delighted with laughter. Yet deny I not but that they may go well together; for as in Alexander's picture well set out we delight without laughter, and in twenty mad antics we laugh without delight: so in Hercules, painted, with his great beard and furious countenance, in a woman's attire, spinning at Omphale's commandment, it breeds both delight and laughter; for the representing of so strange a power in love procures delight, and the scornfulness of the action stirreth laughter.

But I speak to this purpose, that all the end of the comical part be not upon such scornful matters as stir laughter only, but mix with it that delightful teaching which is the end of poesy. And the great fault, even in that point of laughter, and forbidden plainly by Aristotle, is, that they stir laughter in sinful things, which are rather execrable than ridiculous; or in miserable, which are rather to be pitied than scorned. For what is it to make folks gape at a wretched beggar, and a beggarly clown; or against law of hospitality, to jest at strangers because they speak not English so well as we do? What do we learn? Since it is certain,

> "*Nil habet infelix paupertas durius in se,*
> *Quam quod ridiculos homines facit.*"

But rather a busy loving courtier, and a heartless threatening Thraso; a self-wise-seeming schoolmaster; a wry-transformed traveller: these, if we saw walk in stage names, which we play naturally, therein were delightful laughter, and teaching delightfulness; as in the other, the tragedies of Buchanan do justly bring forth a divine admiration.

But I have lavished out too many words of this play matter; I do it because, as they are excelling parts of poesy, so is there none so much used in England, and none can be more pitifully abused; which, like an unmannerly daughter, showing a bad education, causeth her mother Poesy's honesty to be called in question.

Other sorts of poetry almost have we none, but that lyrical kind of songs and sonnets, which, Lord if he gave us so good minds, how well it might be employed, and with how heavenly fruits, both private and public, in singing the praises of the immortal beauty, the immortal goodness of that God who giveth us hands to write and wits to conceive! of which we might well want words, but never matter; of which we could turn our eyes to nothing but we should ever have new-budding occasions.

But, truly, many of such writings as come under the banner of unresistible love, if I were a mistress, would never persuade me they were in love; so coldly they apply fiery speeches, as men that had rather read lovers' writings, and so caught up certain swelling phrases—which hang together like a

19–20. "Nil habet . . . facit." "Unhappy poverty has nothing in it harder than this, that it makes men ridiculous."

man that once told me the wind was at northwest and by south, because he would be sure to name winds enough—than that in truth they feel those passions, which easily, as I think, may be bewrayed by that same forcibleness, or *energia* (as the Greeks call it) of the writer. But let this be a sufficient, though short note, that we miss the right use of the material point of poesy.

Now for the outside of it, which is words, or (as I may term it) diction, it is even well worse; so is it that honey-flowing matron Eloquence, apparelled, or rather disguised, in a courtezan-like painted affectation; one time with so far-fet words that many seem monsters, but must seem strangers, to any poor Englishman; another time with coursing of a letter, as if they were bound to follow the method of a dictionary; another time with figures and flowers, extremely winter-starved.

But I would this fault were only peculiar to versifiers, and had not as large possession among prose-printers; and, which is to be marvelled, among many scholars, and, which is to be pitied, among some preachers. Truly, I could wish (if at least I might be so bold to wish, in a thing beyond the reach of my capacity) the diligent imitators of Tully and Demosthenes (most worthy to be imitated) did not so much keep Nizolian paperbooks of their figures and phrases, as by attentive translation, as it were, devour them whole, and make them wholly theirs. For now they cast sugar and spice upon every dish that is served at the table; like those Indians, not content to wear ear-rings at the fit and natural place of the ears, but they will thrust jewels through their nose and lips, because they will be sure to be fine. Tully, when he was to drive out Catiline, as it were with a thunderbolt of eloquence, often useth the figure of repetition, as "*Vivit et vincit, imo in senatum venit, imo in senatum venit*," &c. Indeed, inflamed with a well-grounded rage, he would have his words, as it were, double out of his mouth; and so do that artificially which we see men in choler do naturally. And we, having noted the grace of those words, hale them in sometimes to a familiar epistle, when it were too much choler to be choleric.

How well store of *similiter* cadences doth sound with the gravity of the pulpit, I would but invoke Demosthenes' soul to tell, who with a rare daintiness useth them. Truly, they have made me think of the sophister, that with too much subtilty would prove two eggs three, and though he may be counted a sophister, had none for his labour. So these men bringing in such a kind of eloquence, well may they obtain an opinion of a seeming fineness, but persuade few, which should be the end of their fineness,

Now for similitudes in certain printed discourses, I think all herbarists, all stories of beasts, fowls, and fishes, are rifled up, that they may come in multitudes to wait upon any of our conceits, which certainly is as absurd a surfeit to the ears as is possible. For the force of a similitude not being to prove anything to a contrary disputer, but only to explain to a willing hearer: when that is done, the rest is a most tedious prattling, rather overswaying the memory from the purpose whereto they were applied, than any whit informing the judgment, already either satisfied, or by similitudes not to be satisfied.

For my part, I do not doubt, when Antonius and Crassus, the great forefathers of Cicero in eloquence, the one (as Cicero testifieth of them) pretended not to know art, the other not to set by it, because with a plain sensibleness they might win credit of popular ears, which credit is the nearest step to persuasion (which persuasion is the chief mark of oratory); I do not doubt, I say, but that they used these knacks very sparingly; which who doth generally use, any man may see doth dance to his own music; and so to be noted by the audience, more carefully to speak curiously than truly. Undoubtedly (at least to my opinion undoubtedly) I have found in divers small-learned courtiers a more sound style than in some professors of learning; of which I can guess no other cause, but that the courtier following that which by practice he findeth fittest to nature, therein (though he know it not) doth according to art, though not by art: where the other, using art to show art, and not hide art (as in these cases he should do), flieth from nature, and indeed abuseth art.

But what! Methinks I deserve to be pounded for straying from poetry to oratory; but both have such an affinity in the wordish consideration, that I think this digression will make my meaning receive the fuller understanding: which is not to take upon me to teach poets how they should do, but only finding myself sick among the rest, to show some one or two spots of the common infection grown among the most part of writers; that, acknowledging ourselves somewhat awry, we may bend to the right use both of matter and manner; whereto our language giveth us great occasion, being, indeed, capable of any excellent exercising of it. I know some will say, it is a mingled language: and why

4. bewrayed, revealed, disclosed. **13. far-fet,** far-fetched. **38–39. "Vivit . . . venit."** "He lives and conquers, nay, comes to the Senate, nay, comes to the Senate." **46. similiter cadences,** cadences produced by groups of words with similar endings.

8. rifled up, ransacked.

not so much the better, taking the best of both the other? Another will say, it wanteth grammar. Nay, truly, it hath that praise, that it wants not grammar; for grammar it might have, but it needs it not; being so easy in itself, and so void of those cumbersome differences of cases, genders, moods, and tenses; which, I think, was a piece of the tower of Babylon's curse, that a man should be put to school to learn his mother tongue. But for the uttering sweetly and properly the conceit of the mind, which is the end of speech, that hath it equally with any other tongue in the world; and is particularly happy in compositions of two or three words together, near the Greek, far beyond the Latin; which is one of the greatest beauties can be in a language.

Now, of versifying there are two sorts, the one ancient, the other modern. The ancient marked the quantity of each syllable, and according to that framed his verse; the modern, observing only number, with some regard of the accent, the chief life of it standeth in that like sounding of the words, which we call rhyme. Whether of these be the more excellent would bear many speeches; the ancient no doubt more fit for music, both words and tune observing quantity; and more fit lively to express divers passions, by the low or lofty sound of the well-weighed syllable. The latter, likewise, with his rhyme striketh a certain music to the ear; and, in fine, since it doth delight, though by another way, it obtaineth the same purpose; there being in either, sweetness, and wanting in neither, majesty. Truly the English, before any vulgar language I know, is fit for both sorts; for, for the ancient, the Italian is so full of vowels that it must ever be cumbered with elisions; the Dutch so, of the other side, with consonants that they cannot yield the sweet sliding fit for a verse. The French, in his whole language, hath not one word that hath his accent in the last syllable saving two, called antepenultima; and little more hath the Spanish; and therefore very gracelessly may they use dactyls. The English is subject to none of these defects.

Now for rhyme, though we do not observe quantity, we observe the accent very precisely, which other languages either cannot do, or will not do so absolutely. That *caesura*, or breathing-place in the midst of the verse, neither Italian nor Spanish have; the French and we never almost fail of. Lastly, even the very rhyme itself the Italian cannot put in the last syllable, by the French named the masculine rhyme, but still in the next to the last, which the French call the female; or the next before that, which the Italians term "sdrucciola." The example of the former is, "buono," "suono"; of the sdrucciola is, "femina," "semina." The French, of the other side, hath both the male, as "bon," "son," and the female, as "plaise," "taise"; but the "sdrucciola" he hath not. Where the English hath all three, as "due," "true," "father," "rather," "motïon," "potïon"; with much more which might be said, but that already I find the trifling of this discourse is much too much enlarged.

So that since the ever praiseworthy poesy is full of virtue, breeding delightfulness, and void of no gift that ought to be in the noble name of learning; since the blames laid against it are either false or feeble; since the cause why it is not esteemed in England is the fault of poet-apes, not poets; since, lastly, our tongue is most fit to honour poesy, and to be honoured by poesy; I conjure you all that have had the evil luck to read this ink-wasting toy of mine, even in the name of the Nine Muses, no more to scorn the sacred mysteries of poesy; no more to laugh at the name of poets, as though they were next inheritors to fools; no more to jest at the reverend title of "a rhymer"; but to believe, with Aristotle, that they were the ancient treasurers of the Grecians' divinity; to believe, with Bembus, that they were the first bringers in of all civility; to believe, with Scaliger, that no philosopher's precepts can sooner make you an honest man than the reading of Virgil; to believe, with Clauserus, the translator of Cornutus, that it pleased the heavenly deity by Hesiod and Homer, under the veil of fables, to give us all knowledge, logic, rhetoric, philosophy natural and moral, and *quid non;* to believe, with me, that there are many mysteries contained in poetry, which of purpose were written darkly, lest by profane wits it should be abused; to believe, with Landin, that they are so beloved of the gods that whatsoever they write proceeds of a divine fury. Lastly, to believe themselves, when they tell you they will make you immortal by their verses.

Thus doing, your name shall flourish in the printers' shops. Thus doing, you shall be of kin to many a poetical preface. Thus doing, you shall be most fair, most rich, most wise, most all; you shall dwell upon superlatives. Thus doing, though you be "*Libertino patre natus*," you shall suddenly grow "*Herculea proles*,"

"*Si quid mea Carmina possunt.*"

Thus doing, your soul shall be placed with Dante's Beatrix, or Virgil's Anchises.

32. quid non, what not. **45. "Libertino . . . natus."** "Born of a freedman." **46. "Herculea proles."** "The offspring of Hercules." **47. "Si quid . . . possunt."** "If my verses are able to accomplish anything."

But if (fie of such a but!) you be born so near the dull-making cataract of Nilus that you cannot hear the planet-like music of poetry; if you have so earth-creeping a mind that it cannot lift itself up to look to the sky of poetry, or rather, by a certain rustical disdain, will become such a mome as to be a Momus of poetry; then, though I will not wish unto you the ass's ears of Midas, nor to be driven by a poet's verses, as Bubonax was, to hang himself, nor to be rhymed to death, as is said to be done in Ireland; yet thus much curse I must send you in the behalf of all poets: that while you live, you live in love, and never get favour for lacking skill of a sonnet; and when you die, your memory die from the earth for want of an epitaph.

6. **mome,** buffoon. used as a pun on Momus, a mocking god.

Christopher Marlowe
1564–1593

Marlowe was born at Canterbury in February, 1564, about two months before the birth of Shakespeare at Stratford. His father was a prosperous shoe-manufacturer, and a citizen of good repute. The boy attended the King's School at Canterbury from 1579 to 1581, and then entered Corpus Christi College, Cambridge, on a scholarship created by the will of the late Archbishop Parker. He received his B.A. in 1584, but the award of his M.A. was delayed by repeated absences and by rumors about his conduct displeasing to the academic authorities. Apparently he was engaged in secret government service, for an entry in the Privy Council Register recommends that the "orderly and discreet" young man "be furthered in the degree he was to take this next Commencement, because it was not Her Majesty's pleasure that any one employed in matters touching the benefit of his country should be defamed by those ignorant in the affairs he went about." His master's degree was awarded in July, 1587, shortly after this recommendation. Before he left the university, Marlowe must have abandoned the plan to take religious orders, possibly because of his growing heterodoxy.

Before the end of 1587, Marlowe made a sensational reputation as a playwright by the production of *Tamburlaine.* This and most of his remaining plays were written for the actor Edward Alleyn, whose towering physical stature and great powers of elocution must have been needed to meet the terrific demands of Marlowe's title roles. His last play, *Edward the Second*, 1593, was probably acted by a company—either Lord Strange's or the Earl of Pembroke's—with which Shakespeare was associated near the beginning of his career, and the two young poets may have collaborated on the plays now known as the second and third parts of *Henry VI.*

There are a number of contemporary indications of Marlowe's quarrelsome temperament, and his death was correspondingly violent. According to the depositions discovered by Leslie Hotson in 1925, Marlowe and three companions had spent most of May 30, 1593, in a tavern at Deptford. In the evening, one of them, Ingram Frizer, and Marlowe quarreled about the payment of the reckoning; Marlowe attacked Frizer, and the latter killed Marlowe in self-defense. These records have been interpreted variously. It has been suggested that since Marlowe and Frizer had both been secret political agents, the quarrel may have been due to some obscure factional rivalry. In any case, the records give only the survivors' story, and they were naturally anxious to clear themselves of blame.

The sudden death of the brilliant young poet and playwright at the age of twenty-nine was followed by a number of attacks upon his character. Puritans regarded his murder as an appropriate judgment on a writer of stage plays. Thomas Kyd, the author of *The Spanish Tragedy*, accused Marlowe of having been an atheist, and certainly there is evidence of his wild and ribald talk about the holy mysteries. Marlowe, it is known, belonged to what was erroneously called "Ralegh's School of Atheism," but what was actually a group of freethinkers interested in the new science and philosophy. Both intellectually and imaginatively, Marlowe was closer to the Italian than to the English Renaissance.

Marlowe's audacious dramas are likely to overshadow his nondramatic writing. Most of the latter was a normal result of the influence of a classical university training on a poetic temperament.

During either his university or his London days, he translated the *Amores* of Ovid, the classical poet to whom he was most devoted, and rendered the first book of Lucan's *Pharsalia* into blank verse. His most substantial poetic achievement, *Hero and Leander*, is an uncompleted elaboration of a Greek poem by Musaeus. The early and feeble drama *Dido, Queen of Carthage*, in which he may have collaborated with Thomas Nashe, was a direct reflection of his intensive classical training.

Marlowe caught the imagination of London theatergoers with his first major play, *Tamburlaine*, which with its sequel was probably performed in 1587. This pair of plays is epic rather than dramatic in conception; they narrate the world-shaking conquests of the fourteenth-century Tatar chief Timur, in monologues and dialogues of untiring imaginative exuberance. More sophisticated audiences soon came to ridicule the extravagant poetic vein of this play, but they could never forget such spectacular scenes as Tamburlaine's victim, Bajazet, beating out his brains on the bars of his cage, or the world hero entering in a chariot drawn by captive kings, whom he hailed as "pampered jades of Asia." In 1589, Marlowe matched the overweening political ambition of Tamburlaine with the unscrupulous intellectual audacity of Dr. Faustus, and soon after exhibited the insatiable hungers for wealth and revenge in *The Jew of Malta*, a most successful play for that time, which may have encouraged Shakespeare in the creation of Shylock a few years later. Marlowe's most subtle and satisfactory drama, *Edward the Second*, a history play, studied the tragedy of a royal weakling with surprising insight, and achieved an impressive dramatic unity and coherence by telescoping the events of many years. Only in the villain, Mortimer, are there echoes of the early exuberance. Shakespeare's *Richard II* seems to be an attempt to invest similar material with an even greater beauty and power.

Marlowe was unquestionably the most gifted of the "university wits" who began to bring their gifts to the English drama in the 1580's. From him Shakespeare and his fellows learned many important lessons in play construction, the focusing of interest on a single overpowering character, and, most significantly, the handling of blank verse. Ben Jonson's commendation of Marlowe's "mighty line" is proverbial, but the poet was capable of other effects than the orotund and the inflated. To him, primarily, is due the demonstration of the extraordinarily various effects of which dramatic blank verse is capable.

THE PASSIONATE SHEPHERD TO HIS LOVE

This delightful pastoral lyric was deservedly popular in the seventeenth century, and inspired a number of imitations or replies. Of these, the best known are Ralegh's "Nymph's Reply," John Donne's "The Bait," and Robert Herrick's "To Phyllis, to Love and Live with Him."

Come live with me and be my love,
And we will all the pleasures prove
That valleys, groves, hills, and fields,
Woods, or steepy mountain yields.

And we will sit upon the rocks,
Seeing the shepherds feed their flocks,
By shallow rivers to whose falls
Melodious birds sing madrigals.

And I will make thee beds of roses
And a thousand fragrant posies,
A cap of flowers, and a kirtle
Embroidered all with leaves of myrtle;

A gown made of the finest wool
Which from our pretty lambs we pull;
Fair linèd slippers for the cold,
With buckles of the purest gold;

A belt of straw and ivy buds,
With coral clasps and amber studs:
And if these pleasures may thee move,
Come live with me, and be my love.

The shepherds' swains shall dance and sing
For thy delight each May morning:
If these delights thy mind may move,
Then live with me and be my love.

from THE TRAGICAL HISTORY OF DOCTOR FAUSTUS

Although *Faustus* is not Marlowe's most completely satisfying play, it is highly characteristic of his energetic and influential contributions to the drama. Like Marlowe's other heroes, Tamburlaine and the Jew of Malta, Faustus is dominated by a ruling passion. In his case, it is the yearning for forbidden knowledge and power that causes him to sell his soul to Satan and brings him to destruction. The play depicts with vigor the essential steps in Faustus's tragic downfall: temptation, fall, power, and penalty. Marlowe's dramatic genius is clearly shown in the imaginative handling of these elements. The portion of the play given below is the last scene, the conclusion of the struggle between the forces of good and evil for possession of the sinner's soul.

[*Enter* WAGNER, *solus*.]

Wag. I think my master means to die shortly,
For he hath given to me all his goods;
And yet, methinks, if that death were near,
He would not banquet and carouse and swill
Amongst the students, as even now he doth,
Who are at supper with such belly-cheer
As Wagner ne'er beheld in all his life.
See where they come! Belike the feast is ended.

[*Enter* FAUSTUS, *with two or three* SCHOLARS *and* MEPHISTOPHILIS.]

1 *Schol*. Master Doctor Faustus, since our conference about fair ladies, which was the beautifullest in all the world, we have determined with ourselves that Helen of Greece was the admirablest lady that ever lived: therefore, Master Doctor, if you will do us that favour, as to let us see that peerless dame of Greece, whom all the world admires for majesty, we should think ourselves much beholding unto you.

Faust. Gentlemen,
For that I know your friendship is unfeigned,
And Faustus' custom is not to deny
The just requests of those that wish him well,
You shall behold that peerless dame of Greece,
No otherways for pomp and majesty
Than when Sir Paris crossed the seas with her,
And brought the spoils to rich Dardania.
Be silent, then, for danger is in words.

[*Music sounds, and* HELEN *passeth over the stage*.]

2 *Schol*. Too simple is my wit to tell her praise,
Whom all the world admires for majesty.

3 *Schol*. No marvel though the angry Greeks pursued
With ten years' war the rape of such a queen,
Whose heavenly beauty passeth all compare.

1 *Schol*. Since we have seen the pride of Nature's works,
And only paragon of exellence,

[*Enter an* OLD MAN.]

Let us depart; and for this glorious deed
Happy and blest be Faustus evermore.

Faustus. Gentlemen, farewell—the same I wish to you. [*Exeunt* SCHOLARS *and* WAGNER.

Old Man. Ah, Doctor Faustus, that I might prevail
To guide thy steps unto the way of life,
By which sweet path thou may'st attain the goal
That shall conduct thee to celestial rest!
Break heart, drop blood, and mingle it with tears,
Tears falling from repentant heaviness
Of thy most vile and loathsome filthiness,
The stench whereof corrupts the inward soul
With such flagitious crimes of heinous sins
As no commiseration may expel,
But mercy, Faustus, of thy Saviour sweet,
Whose blood alone must wash away thy guilt.

Faust. Where art thou, Faustus? Wretch, what hast thou done?
Damned art thou, Faustus, damned; despair and die!
Hell calls for right, and with a roaring voice
Says "Faustus! come! thine hour is almost come!"
And Faustus now will come to do thee right.

[MEPHISTOPHILIS *gives him a dagger*.]

Old Man. Ah stay, good Faustus, stay thy desperate steps!
I see an angel hovers o'er thy head,
And, with a vial full of precious grace,
Offers to pour the same into thy soul:
Then call for mercy, and avoid despair.

Faust. Ah, my sweet friend, I feel
Thy words do comfort my distressèd soul.
Leave me a while to ponder on my sins.

Old Man. I go, sweet Faustus, but with heavy cheer,
Fearing the ruin of thy hopeless soul. [*Exit*.

Faust. Accursèd Faustus, where is mercy now?
I do repent; and yet I do despair;
Hell strives with grace for conquest in my breast:
What shall I do to shun the snares of death?

Meph. Thou traitor, Faustus, I arrest thy soul
For disobedience to my sovereign lord;
Revolt, or I'll in piecemeal tear thy flesh.

Faust. Sweet Mephistophilis, entreat thy lord
To pardon my unjust presumption,
And with my blood again I will confirm
My former vow I made to Lucifer.

Meph. Do it now then quickly, with unfeigned heart,
Lest danger do attend thy drift.

Faust. Torment, sweet friend, that base and crooked age,
That durst dissuade me from my Lucifer,
With greatest torments that our hell affords.

Meph. His faith is great, I cannot touch his soul;

Stage dir. **Wagner**, servant to Faustus. **Mephistophilis**, the personification of the devil. **1312. Dardania**, Troy, from Dardanus, the founder of the Trojan race.

1326–27. goal That shall conduct thee, that is, a happy death. **1329. repentant heaviness**, heavy repentance. **1340. to do thee right**, to pay what he owes. **1363. drift**, purpose. **1364. age**, old man.

But what I may afflict his body with
I will attempt, which is but little worth.
Faust. One thing, good servant, let me crave of thee,
To glut the longing of my heart's desire,—
That I might have unto my paramour
That heavenly Helen, which I saw of late,
Whose sweet embracings may extinguish clean
These thoughts that do dissuade me from my vow,
And keep mine oath I made to Lucifer.
Meph. Faustus, this or what else thou shalt desire
Shall be performed in twinkling of an eye.

[*Re-enter* HELEN.]

Faust. Was this the face that launched a thousand ships,
And burnt the topless towers of Ilium?
Sweet Helen, make me immortal with a kiss.
Her lips suck forth my soul; see where it flies!—
Come, Helen, come, give me my soul again.
Here will I dwell, for Heaven be in these lips,
And all is dross that is not Helena.

[*Enter* OLD MAN.]

I will be Paris, and for love of thee,
Instead of Troy, shall Wittenberg be sacked;
And I will combat with weak Menelaus,
And wear thy colours on my plumèd crest;
Yea, I will wound Achilles in the heel,
And then return to Helen for a kiss.
Oh, thou art fairer than the evening air
Clad in the beauty of a thousand stars;
Brighter art thou than flaming Jupiter
When he appeared to hapless Semele;
More lovely than the monarch of the sky
In wanton Arethusa's azured arms:
And none but thou shalt be my paramour. [*Exeunt.*
Old Man. Accursèd Faustus, miserable man,
That from thy soul exclud'st the grace of Heaven,
And fly'st the throne of his tribunal seat!

[*Enter* DEVILS.]

Satan begins to sift me with his pride:
As in this furnace God shall try my faith,
My faith, vile hell, shall triumph over thee.
Ambitious fiends! see how the heavens smiles
At your repulse, and laughs your state to scorn!
Hence, hell! for hence I fly unto my God. [*Exeunt.*

[*Enter* FAUSTUS *with the* SCHOLARS.]

Faust. Ah, gentlemen!

1 *Schol.* What ails Faustus?

Faust. Ah, my sweet chamber-fellow, had I lived with thee, then had I lived still! but now I die eternally. Look, comes he not, comes he not?

2 *Schol.* What means Faustus?

3 *Schol.* Belike he is grown into some sickness by being over solitary.

1 *Schol.* If it be so, we'll have physicians to cure him. 'T is but a surfeit. Never fear, man.

Faust. A surfeit of deadly sin that hath damned both body and soul.

2 *Schol.* Yet, Faustus, look up to Heaven; remember God's mercies are infinite.

Faust. But Faustus' offences can never be pardoned: the serpent that tempted Eve may be saved, but not Faustus. Ah, gentlemen, hear me with patience, and tremble not at my speeches! Though my heart pants and quivers to remember that I have been a student here these thirty years, oh, would I had never seen Wittenberg, never read book! And what wonders I have done, all Germany can witness, yea, the world; for which Faustus hath lost both Germany and the world, yea Heaven itself, Heaven, the seat of God, the throne of the blessed, the kingdom of joy; and must remain in hell for ever, hell, ah, hell, for ever! Sweet friends! what shall become of Faustus being in hell for ever?

3 *Schol.* Yet, Faustus, call on God.

Faust. On God, whom Faustus hath abjured! on God, whom Faustus hath blasphemed! Ah, my God, I would weep, but the Devil draws in my tears! Gush forth blood instead of tears! Yea, life and soul! Oh, he stays my tongue! I would lift up my hands, but see, they hold them, they hold them!

All. Who, Faustus?

Faust. Lucifer and Mephistophilis. Ah, gentlemen, I gave them my soul for my cunning!

All. God forbid!

Faust. God forbade it indeed; but Faustus hath done it. For vain pleasure of twenty-four years hath Faustus lost eternal joy and felicity. I writ them a bill with mine own blood: the date is expired; the time will come, and he will fetch me.

1 *Schol.* Why did not Faustus tell us of this before, that divines might have prayed for thee?

Faust. Oft have I thought to have done so; but the Devil threatened to tear me in pieces if I named

1380. topless, unsurpassed in height. **1390. wound Achilles,** as Paris did, his arrow being guided by Apollo. **1395. hapless Semele,** who asked Zeus to appear before her in the splendor which he showed Juno but who, when he so appeared, was consumed by lightning. **1396–97. monarch of the sky . . . Arethusa's azured arms.** If this is Apollo, the sun god, there is no record of his connection with the nymph Arethusa. **wanton,** playful. **1402. sift me.** See Luke 22:31—"Satan hath desired to have you, that he may sift you as wheat." **pride,** powerful array.

God; to fetch both body and soul if I once gave ear to divinity: and now 't is too late. Gentlemen, away! lest you perish with me.

2 *Schol.* Oh, what shall we do to save Faustus?

Faust. Talk not of me, but save yourselves, and depart.

3 *Schol.* God will strengthen me. I will stay with Faustus.

1 *Schol.* Tempt not God, sweet friend; but let us into the next room, and there pray for him.

Faust. Ay, pray for me, pray for me! and what noise soever ye hear, come not unto me, for nothing can rescue me.

2 *Schol.* Pray thou, and we will pray that God may have mercy upon thee.

Faust. Gentlemen, farewell! If I live till morning I'll visit you: if not—Faustus is gone to hell.

All. Faustus, farewell!

[*Exeunt* SCHOLARS. *The clock strikes eleven.*

Faust. Ah, Faustus,
Now hast thou but one bare hour to live,
And then thou must be damned perpetually!
Stand still, you ever-moving spheres of Heaven,
That time may cease, and midnight never come;
Fair Nature's eye, rise, rise again and make
Perpetual day; or let this hour be but
A year, a month, a week, a natural day,
That Faustus may repent and save his soul!
O lente, lente, currite noctis equi!
The stars move still, time runs, the clock will strike,
The Devil will come, and Faustus must be damned.
O, I'll leap up to my God! Who pulls me down?
See, see where Christ's blood streams in the firmament!
One drop would save my soul—half a drop: ah, my Christ!
Ah, rend not my heart for naming of my Christ!
Yet will I call on him: O spare me, Lucifer!—
Where is it now? 'T is gone; and see where God
Stretcheth out his arm, and bends his ireful brows!
Mountain and hills come, come and fall on me,
And hide me from the heavy wrath of God!
No! no!
Then will I headlong run into the earth;
Earth gape! O no, it will not harbour me!
You stars that reigned at my nativity,
Whose influence hath allotted death and hell,
Now draw up Faustus like a foggy mist
Into the entrails of yon labouring clouds,
That when they vomit forth into the air,
My limbs may issue from their smoky mouths,
So that my soul may but ascend to Heaven.

[*The watch strikes.*]

Ah, half the hour is past! 'T will all be past anon!
O God!
If thou wilt not have mercy on my soul,
Yet for Christ's sake whose blood hath ransomed me,
Impose some end to my incessant pain;
Let Faustus live in hell a thousand years—
A hundred thousand, and at last be saved!
O, no end is limited to damned souls!
Why wert thou not a creature wanting soul?
Or why is this immortal that thou hast?
Ah, Pythagoras' metempsychosis! were that true,
This soul should fly from me, and I be changed
Unto some brutish beast! All beasts are happy,
For, when they die,
Their souls are soon dissolved in elements;
But mine must live, still to be plagued in hell.
Curst be the parents that engendred me!
No, Faustus: curse thyself: curse Lucifer
That hath deprived thee of the joys of Heaven.

[*The clock striketh twelve.*]

O, it strikes, it strikes! Now, body, turn to air,
Or Lucifer will bear thee quick to hell.

[*Thunder and lightning.*]

O soul, be changed into little water-drops,
And fall into the ocean—ne'er be found.
My God! my God! look not so fierce on me!

[*Enter* DEVILS.]

Adders and serpents, let me breathe awhile!
Ugly hell, gape not! come not, Lucifer!
I'll burn my books!—Ah Mephistophilis!

[*Exeunt* DEVILS *with* FAUSTUS.

[*Enter* CHORUS.]

Cho. Cut is the branch that might have grown full straight,
And burnèd is Apollo's laurel bough,
That sometimes grew within this learned man.
Faustus is gone; regard his hellish fall,
Whose fiendful fortune may exhort the wise
Only to wonder at unlawful things,
Whose deepness doth entice such forward wits
To practise more than heavenly power permits.

[*Exit.*

1485. *O lente . . . equi!* Run slowly, slowly, ye steeds of the night!—from Ovid's *Amores*, Book I, sec. 13, ll. 39–40. **1486. move still,** move without ceasing. **1493. it,** the vision of Lucifer.

1517. Pythagoras' metempsychosis! Pythagoras, Greek philosopher (born *c.* 570 B.C.), taught the doctrine of metempsychosis or transmigration of souls. **1535. Apollo's laurel bough.** Here Apollo is apparently regarded as the patron of learning, an office more commonly assigned to Minerva.

Edmund Spenser

c. 1552–1599

The date of Spenser's birth is uncertain, but from the internal evidence of one of his sonnets he seems to have been born about 1552. Although he claimed kinship with a distinguished family in Northamptonshire, his father was a journeyman clothmaker in London, and the circumstances of his education suggest the family's financial status. He attended the Merchant Taylors' School on a scholarship intended for a poor man's son, but what is more important is that the master of the school was Richard Mulcaster, a distinguished educator with a patriotic enthusiasm for the teaching of English as distinct from the classical languages. In 1569, rough translations young Spenser had made of French poems by Du Bellay and Marot were published in a miscellaneous collection, entitled *A Theatre for Voluptuous Worldlings;* twenty years later he took the trouble to polish them up and to include them in the volume entitled *Complaints*. Spenser entered Pembroke Hall, Cambridge, in 1569, and as a sizar was expected to work his way through college. At Pembroke, he came under the influence of a group of enthusiastic Puritans, and found a lasting friend in Gabriel Harvey, one of its Fellows.

Spenser took his B.A. in 1573 and his M.A. in 1576. In 1578 he acted as secretary to John Young, who had been Master of Pembroke while Spenser was an undergraduate, and was now Bishop of Rochester. In 1579, Spenser was a member of the household of the first Earl of Leicester, and in these circumstances he may have become acquainted with Sidney, Leicester's nephew. In any case, Sidney, Fulke Greville, Harvey, and Spenser were the leading spirits in a loosely organized group calling itself the Areopagus, and devoted to introducing classical meters into English poetry. In 1579, Spenser seems to have married Machabyas Childe, of whose subsequent life and death nothing is known. In this year also Spenser by publishing *The Shepheardes Calender* announced the arrival of the first great poet of the English Renaissance. For the next decade, although he continued writing, he seems to have published nothing. During that time, he was occupied with his duties as secretary to Lord Grey, Lord Deputy of Ireland. He lived in Dublin, and in addition to his duties as secretary, he served as Commissioner of Musters in 1583 and 1584, occupying a variety of minor offices. In or about 1586, he leased Kilcolman Castle in the County of Cork, and undertook the management of a huge estate on which he was supposed to plant English farmers. Here he was visited in 1589 by Ralegh, to whom he read portions of the earlier books of *The Faerie Queene*.

He returned to London in the autumn of that year, to superintend the publication of the first three books of his great poem in 1590, and to attempt to gain favor at Court. Although Elizabeth granted him a pension of fifty pounds, he seems to have been disappointed by his experiences at court. In 1591 he published a miscellaneous collection of poems called *Complaints*, apparently in order to follow up the success of *The Faerie Queene*. The most important poems in this volume were two satires, "Mother Hubbard's Tale" and "Muiopotmos, or, The Fate of the Butterfly." There were besides translations from Petrarch and Du Bellay. During the early nineties, he was probably writing the sonnet sequence *Amoretti*, which was published along with his *Epithalamion* in 1595. Both of these poems are generally supposed to refer to his courtship and marriage in 1594 of his second wife, Elizabeth Boyle, who at the time was probably the widow of one Tristram Pease. In 1595 he also published two elegies on Sidney, "Astrophel" and "The Doleful Lay of Clorinda," and "Colin Clout's Come Home Again," poetic reminiscences of Ralegh's visit to Kilcolman and of Spenser's impressions of London from 1589 to 1591. In this year also, he returned to London to see to the publication of a new edition of *The Faerie Queene*, with three more books, and also his *Four Hymns*, the most explicit statement of Spenser's Christian Platonism.

In 1597, he purchased lands in the County Cork for the benefit of his infant son, Peregrine. Before 1598 he wrote *A View of the Present State of Ireland*, which was not, however, published until 1633. In it he supported enthusiastically the stern repressive policy of his chief, Lord Grey. In 1598 Kilcolman Castle was sacked and burned during Tyrone's rebellion, one of Spenser's infant children lost his life, and Spenser, his wife, and the three other children took refuge in Cork. In December, he was sent to London with important dispatches, and died there, according to tradition, in poverty, on January 16, 1599. The expenses of interment in Westminster Abbey were borne by the Earl of Essex.

Spenser was the most successful of the Renaissance poets in achieving a satisfactory synthesis of the complex and seemingly contradictory creeds of his age. For he was not only a great poet, in the narrowly technical sense, but a poet in whose work were blended the elements of Platonism, Puritanism, and patriotism. His Platonism ennobles his love sonnets and exalts his hymns to Heavenly Love and to Heavenly Beauty. His Puritanism furnishes the most significant moral basis for the sensory mazes of his verse. His patriotism appears in his sense of England's great destiny and his hostility to those forces within and without that seemed to him to threaten her integrity. Spenser has been called the poet's poet, because from him so many have taken lessons in superb artistry. It is easy and tempting to read Spenser on the purely poetic level, but he will not be well read until one weights, as he did, the philosophical, moral, and political elements in his greatest works.

from AMORETTI

The eighty-eight sonnets of Spenser's *Amoretti*, which according to tradition were written during his courtship of Elizabeth Boyle, who became his second wife, constitute one of the finer sonnet sequences of the Elizabethan age. They not only show an adroit use of many familiar Petrarchan conventions but are distinguished by a moral beauty and dignity arising from the poet's view of his beloved as a manifestation of the Platonic Idea of Beauty and Goodness.

1

Happy ye leaves when as those lilly hands,
Which hold my life in their dead doing might,
Shall handle you and hold in loves soft bands,
Lyke captives trembling at the victors sight.
And happy lines, on which with starry light,
Those lamping eyes will deigne sometimes to look
And reade the sorrowes of my dying spright,
Written with teares in harts close bleeding book.
And happy rymes bathed in the sacred brooke,
Of *Helicon* whence she derivèd is,
When ye behold that Angels blessèd looke,
My soules long lackèd foode, my heavens blis.
Leaves, lines, and rymes, seeke her to please alone,
Whom if ye please, I care for other none.

6

Be nought dismayd that her unmovèd mind
Doth still persist in her rebellious pride:
Such love not lyke to lusts of baser kynd,
The harder wonne, the firmer will abide.
The durefull Oake, whose sap is not yet dride,
Is long ere it conceive the kindling fyre:
But when it once doth burne, it doth divide
Great heat, and makes his flames to heaven aspire.
So hard it is to kindle new desire
In gentle brest that shall endure for ever:
Deepe is the wound, that dints the parts entire
With chast affects, that naught but death can sever.
Then thinke not long in taking litle paine,
To knit the knot, that ever shall remaine.

34

Lyke as a ship that through the Ocean wyde,
By conduct of some star doth make her way,
Whenas a storme hath dimd her trusty guyde
Out of her course doth wander far astray;
So I whose star, that wont with her bright ray
Me to direct, with cloudes is overcast,
Doe wander now in darkness and dismay,
Through hidden perils round about me plast.
Yet hope I well that when this storme is past
My Helice the lodestar of my lyfe
Will shine again, and looke on me at last,
With lovely light to cleare my cloudy grief,
Till then I wander carefull comfortlesse
In secret sorrow and sad pensivenesse.

67

Lyke as a huntsman after weary chace,
Seeing the game from him escapt away,
Sits downe to rest him in some shady place,
With panting hounds beguilèd of their pray:
So after long pursuit and vaine assay,
When I all weary had the chace forsooke,
The gentle deare returnd the selfe-same way,
Thinking to quench her thirst at the next brooke.
There she beholding me with mylder looke,
Sought not to fly, but fearelesse still did bide:
Till I in hand her yet halfe trembling tooke,
And with her owne goodwill hir fyrmely tyde.
Strange thing me seemd to see a beast so wyld,
So goodly wonne with her owne will beguyld.

75

One day I wrote her name upon the strand,
But came the waves and washèd it away:
Agayne I wrote it with a second hand,
But came the tyde, and made my paynes his pray.
Vayne man, sayd she, that doest in vaine assay,
A mortall thing so to immortalize,
For I my selve shall lyke to this decay,
And eek my name bee wyped out lykewize.

Not so, (quod I) let baser things devize
To dy in dust, but you shall live by fame:
My verse your vertues rare shall eternize,
And in the hevens wryte your glorious name.
Where whenas death shall all the world subdew,
Our love shall live, and later life renew.

79

Men call you fayre, and you doe credit it,
For that your selfe ye dayly such doe see:
But the trew fayre, that is the gentle wit
And vertuous mind, is much more praysd of me.
For all the rest, how ever fayre it be,
Shall turne to nought and loose that glorious hew:
But onely that is permanent and free
From frayle corruption, that doth flesh ensew.
That is true beautie: that doth argue you
To be divine and borne of heavenly seed:
Derived from that fayre Spirit, from whom al true
And perfect beauty did at first proceed.
He onely fayre, and what he fayre hath made,
All other fayre lyke flowres untymely fade.

EPITHALAMION

The *epithalamion* (*epithalamium*), a bridal song, is a form cultivated by the ancient Greek poets Pindar, Theocritus, and Sappho, and by the Roman poet Catullus. The Song of Songs in the Old Testament is an *epithalamion* or collection of *epithalamia*. Among more modern poets the French Ronsard and the English Spenser are the most celebrated writers of *epithalamia*. Spenser's *Epithalamion*, published with the *Amoretti* in 1595, to celebrate his marriage to Elizabeth Boyle, is generally regarded as the most beautiful nuptial poem in the language and as his highest poetic achievement. In it he not only uses brilliantly the conventions of the classical *epithalamia*, but achieves a highly individual quality through his remarkable fusion of passionate ardor and moral elevation.

Ye learnèd sisters, which have oftentimes
Beene to me ayding, others to adorne:
Whom ye thought worthy of your gracefull rymes,
That even the greatest did not greatly scorne
To heare theyr names sung in your simple layes,
But joyèd in theyr prayse.
And when ye list your owne mishaps to mourne,
Which death, or love, or fortunes wreck did rayse,
Your string could soone to sadder tenour turne,
And teach the woods and waters to lament
Your dolefull dreriment.
Now lay those sorrowfull complaints aside,
And having all your heads with girland crownd,
Helpe me mine owne loves prayses to resound,
Ne let the same of any be envide:
So Orpheus did for his owne bride,
So I unto my selfe alone will sing,
The woods shall to me answer and my Eccho ring.

Early, before the worlds light giving lampe
His golden beame upon the hils doth spred,
Having disperst the nights unchearefull dampe,
Doe ye awake, and with fresh lusty hed,
Go to the bowre of my beloved love,
My truest turtle dove,
Bid her awake; for Hymen is awake,
And long since ready forth his maske to move,
With his bright Tead that flames with many a flake,
And many a bachelor to waite on him,
In theyr fresh gaments trim.
Bid her awake therefore and soone her dight,
For lo the wishèd day is come at last,
That shall for al the paynes and sorrowes past,
Pay to her usury of long delight:
And whylest she doth her dight,
Doe ye to her of joy and solace sing,
That all the woods may answer and your eccho ring.

Bring with you all the Nymphes that you can heare
Both of the rivers and the forrests greene:
And of the sea that neighbours to her neare,
Al with gay girlands goodly wel beseene.
And let them also with them bring in hand,
Another gay girland
For my fayre love of lillyes and of roses,
Bound truelove wize with a blew silke riband.
And let them make great store of bridale poses,
And let them eeke bring store of other flowers
To deck the bridale bowers.
And let the ground whereas her foot shall tread,
For feare the stones her tender foot should wrong
Be strewed with fragrant flowers all along,
And diapred lyke the discoloured mead.
Which done, doe at her chamber dore awayt,
For she will waken strayt,
The whiles doe ye this song unto her sing,
The woods shall to you answer and your Eccho ring.

Ye Nymphes of Mulla which with carefull heed,
The silver scaly trouts doe tend full well,
And greedy pikes which use therein to feed,
(Those trouts and pikes all others doo excell)

1. learnèd sisters, the nine Muses. **8. wreck,** violence. **11. dreriment,** affliction.

25. Hymen, the god of marriage. **26. maske,** court entertainment, pageant. **27. Tead,** a torch, symbol of Hymen, used in Roman bridal processions. **28. bachelor,** candidate for knighthood. **30. dight,** dress. **51. diapred,** diversified. **discoloured,** many-colored. **56. Mulla,** an Irish stream near Kilcolman.

And ye likewise which keepe the rushy lake,
Where none doo fishes take,
Bynd up the locks the which hang scatterd light,
And in his waters which your mirrour make,
Behold your faces as the christall bright,
That when you come whereas my love doth lie,
No blemish she may spie.
And eke ye lightfoot mayds which keepe the deere,
That on the hoary mountayne use to towre,
And the wylde wolves which seek them to devoure,
With your steele darts doo chace from comming neer,
Be also present heere,
To helpe to decke her and to help to sing,
That all the woods may answer and your eccho ring.

Wake, now my love, awake; for it is time,
The Rosy Morne long since left Tithones bed,
All ready to her silver coche to clyme,
And Phoebus gins to shew his glorious hed.
Hark how the cheerefull birds do chaunt theyr laies
And carroll of loves praise.
The merry Larke hir mattins sings aloft,
The thrush replyes, the Mavis descant playes,
The Ouzell shrills, the Ruddock warbles soft,
So goodly all agree with sweet consent,
To this dayes merriment.
Ah my deere love why doe ye sleepe thus long,
When meeter were that ye should now awake,
T' awayt the comming of your joyous make,
And hearken to the birds lovelearnèd song,
The deawy leaves among.
For they of joy and pleasance to you sing,
That all the woods them answer and theyr eccho ring.

My love is now awake out of her dreame,
And her fayre eyes like stars that dimmèd were
With darksome cloud, now shew theyr goodly beams
More bright then Hesperus his head doth rere.
Come now ye damzels, daughters of delight,
Helpe quickly her to dight,
But first come ye fayre houres which were begot
In Joves sweet paradice, of Day and Night,
Which doe the seasons of the yeare allot,
And al that ever in this world is fayre
Doe make and still repayre.
And ye three handmayds of the Cyprian Queene,
The which doe still adorne her beauties pride,
Helpe to addorne my beautifullest bride:

68. towre, climb in a spiral. **80. mattins,** morning songs. **81. descant,** song. **82. Ruddock,** robin redbreast. **87. make,** mate. **95. Hesperus,** the evening star. **103. three handmayds,** the Graces, attendants of Aphrodite, who was born on the island of Cyprus.

And as ye her array, still throw betweene
Some graces to be seene,
And as ye use to Venus, to her sing,
The whiles the woods shal answer and your eccho ring.

Now is my love all ready forth to come,
Let all the virgins therefore well awayt,
And ye fresh boyes that tend upon her groome
Prepare your selves; for he is comming strayt.
Set all your things in seemely good aray
Fit for so joyfull day,
The joyfulst day that ever sunne did see.
Faire Sun, shew forth thy favourable ray,
And let thy lifull heat not fervent be
For feare of burning her sunshyny face,
Her beauty to disgrace.
O fayrest Phoebus, father of the Muse,
If ever I did honour thee aright,
Or sing the thing, that mote thy mind delight,
Doe not thy servants simple boone refuse,
But let this day, let this one day be myne,
Let all the rest be thine.
Then I thy soverayne prayses loud wil sing,
That all the woods shal answer and theyr eccho ring.

Harke how the Minstrels gin to shrill aloud
Their merry Musick that resounds from far,
The pipe, the tabor, and the trembling Croud,
That well agree withouten breach or jar.
But most of all the Damzels doe delite,
When they their tymbrels smyte,
And thereunto doe daunce and carrol sweet,
That all the sences they doe ravish quite,
The whyles the boyes run up and downe the street,
Crying aloud with strong confusèd noyce,
As if it were one voyce.
Hymen io Hymen, Hymen they do shout,
That even to the heavens theyr shouting shrill
Doth reach, and all the firmament doth fill,
To which the people standing all about,
As in approvance doe thereto applaud
And loud advaunce her laud,
And evermore they Hymen Hymen sing,
That al the woods them answer and theyr eccho ring.

Loe where she comes along with portly pace
Lyke Phoebe from her chamber of the East,
Arysing forth to run her mighty race,

118. lifull, lifeful. **123. mote,** might. **124. boone,** prayer. **131. tabor,** a small drum. **Croud,** a stringed instrument. **148. portly,** stately.

Clad all in white, that seemes a virgin best.
So well it her beseemes that ye would weene
Some angell she had beene.
Her long loose yellow locks lyke golden wyre,
Sprinckled with perle, and perling flowres a tweene,
Doe lyke a golden mantle her attyre,
And being crownèd with a girland greene,
Seeme lyke some mayden Queene.
Her modest eyes abashèd to behold
So many gazers, as on her do stare,
Upon the lowly ground affixèd are.
Ne dare lift up her countenance too bold,
But blush to heare her prayses sung so loud,
So farre from being proud.
Nathlesse doe ye still loud her prayses sing.
That all the woods may answer and your eccho ring.

Tell me ye merchants daughters did ye see
So fayre a creature in your towne before,
So sweet, so lovely, and so mild as she,
Adornd with beautyes grace and vertues store,
Her goodly eyes lyke Saphyres shining bright,
Her forehead yvory white,
Her cheekes lyke apples which the sun hath rudded,
Her lips lyke cherryes charming men to byte,
Her brest like to a bowle of creame uncrudded,
Her paps lyke lyllies budded,
Her snowie necke lyke to a marble towre,
And all her body like a pallace fayre,
Ascending uppe with many a stately stayre,
To honours seat and chastities sweet bowre.
Why stand ye still ye virgins in amaze,
Upon her so to gaze,
Whiles ye forget your former lay to sing,
To which the woods did answer and your eccho ring.

But if ye saw that which no eyes can see,
The inward beauty of her lively spright,
Garnisht with heavenly guifts of high degree,
Much more then would ye wonder at that sight,
And stand astonisht lyke to those which red
Medusaes mazeful hed.
There dwels sweet love and constant chastity,
Unspotted fayth and comely womanhood,
Regard of honour and mild modesty,
There vertue raynes as Queene in royal throne,
And giveth lawes alone.

175. uncrudded, uncurdled. **177. marble towre.** The imagery here and elsewhere in this stanza is derived from the Song of Songs, chapter 4. **189. red,** saw. **190. Medusaes mazeful hed,** the head of the Gorgon Medusa, which had serpents for hairs, and turned to stone all who looked at it.

The which the base affections doe obay,
And yeeld theyr services unto her will,
Ne thought of thing uncomely ever may
Thereto approch to tempt her mind to ill.
Had ye once seene these her celestial threasures,
And unrevealèd pleasures,
Then would ye wonder and her prayses sing,
That al the woods should answer and your eccho ring.

Open the temple gates unto my love,
Open them wide that she may enter in,
And all the postes adorne as doth behove,
And all the pillours deck with girlands trim,
For to recyve this Saynt with honour dew,
That commeth in to you.
With trembling steps and humble reverence,
She commeth in, before th'almighties vew,
Of her ye virgins learne obedience,
When so ye come into those holy places,
To humble your proud faces:
Bring her up to th' high altar, that she may
The sacred ceremonies there partake,
The which do endlesse matrimony make,
And let the roring Organs loudly play
The praises of the Lord in lively notes,
The whiles with hollow throates
The Choristers the joyous Antheme sing,
That al the woods may answer and their eccho ring.

Behold whiles she before the altar stands
Hearing the holy priest that to her speakes
And blesseth her with his two happy hands,
How the red roses flush up in her cheekes,
And the pure snow with goodly vermill stayne,
Like crimsin dyde in grayne,
That even th' Angels which continually,
About the sacred Altare doe remaine,
Forget their service and about her fly,
Ofte peeping in her face that seemes more fayre,
The more they on it stare.
But her sad eyes still fastened on the ground,
Are governèd with goodly modesty,
That suffers not one looke to glaunce awry,
Which may let in a little thought unsownd.
Why blush ye love to give to me your hand,
The pledge of all our band?
Sing ye sweet Angels, Alleluya sing,
That all the woods may answer and your eccho ring.

Now al is done; bring home the bride againe,
Bring home the triumph of our victory,
Bring home with you the glory of her gaine,

234. sad, serious. **239. band,** bond, union.

With joyance bring her and with jollity.
Never had man more joyfull day then this,
Whom heaven would heape with blis.
Make feast therefore now all this live long day,
This day for ever to me holy is,
Poure out the wine without restraint or stay,
Poure not by cups, but by the belly full,
Poure out to all that wull,
And sprinkle all the postes and wals with wine,
That they may sweat, and drunken be withall.
Crowne ye God Bacchus with a coronall,
And Hymen also crowne with wreathes of vine,
And let the Graces daunce unto the rest;
For they can doo it best:
The whiles the maydens doe theyr carroll sing,
To which the woods shall answer and theyr eccho ring.

Ring ye the bels, ye yong men of the towne,
And leave your wonted labours for this day:
This day is holy; doe ye write it downe,
That ye for ever it remember may.
This day the sunne is in his chiefest hight,
With Barnaby the bright,
From whence declining daily by degrees,
He somewhat loseth of his heat and light,
When once the Crab behind his back he sees.
But for this time it ill ordainèd was,
To chose the longest day in all the yeare,
And shortest night, when longest fitter weare:
Yet never day so long, but late would passe.
Ring ye the bels, to make it weare away,
And bonefiers make all day,
And daunce about them, and about them sing:
That all the woods may answer, and your eccho ring.

Ah when will this long weary day have end,
And lende me leave to come unto my love?
How slowly do the houres theyr numbers spend?
How slowly does sad Time his feathers move?
Hast thee O fayrest Planet to thy home
Within the Westerne fome:
Thy tyred steedes long since have need of rest.
Long though it be, at last I see it gloome,
And the bright evening star with golden creast
Appeare out of the East.
Fayre childe of beauty, glorious lampe of love
That all the host of heaven in rankes doost lead,
And guydest lovers through the nightès dread,
How chearefully thou lookest from above,
And seemst to laugh atweene thy twinkling light
As joying in the sight
Of these glad many which for joy doe sing,
That all the woods them answer and theyr eccho ring.

Now ceasse ye damsels your delights forepast;
Enough is it, that all the day was youres:
Now day is doen, and night is nighing fast:
Now bring the Bryde into the brydall boures.
Now night is come, now soone her disaray,
And in her bed her lay;
Lay her in lillies and in violets,
And silken courteins over her display,
And odourd sheetes, and Arras coverlets.
Behold how goodly my faire love does ly
In proud humility;
Like unto Maia, when as Jove her tooke,
In Tempe, lying on the flowry gras,
Twixt sleepe and wake, after she weary was,
With bathing in the Acidalian brooke.
Now it is night, ye damsels may be gon,
And leave my love alone,
And leave likewise your former lay to sing:
The woods no more shal answer, nor your eccho ring.

Now welcome night, thou night so long expected,
That long daies labour doest at last defray,
And all my cares, which cruell love collected,
Hast sumd in one, and cancellèd for aye:
Spread thy broad wing over my love and me,
That no man may us see,
And in thy sable mantle us enwrap,
From feare of perrill and foule horror free.
Let no false treason seeke us to entrap,
Nor any dread disquiet once annoy
The safety of our joy:
But let the night be calme and quietsome,
Without tempestuous storms or sad afray:
Lyke as when Jove with fayre Alcmena lay,
When he begot the great Tirynthian groome:
Or lyke as when he with thy selfe did lie,
And begot Majesty.
And let the mayds and yongmen cease to sing:
Ne let the woods them answer, nor theyr eccho ring.

Let no lamenting cryes, nor dolefull teares,
Be heard all night within nor yet without:
Ne let false whispers, breeding hidden feares,
Breake gentle sleepe with misconceivèd dout.
Let no deluding dreames, nor dreadful sights
Make sudden sad affrights;

252. **wull,** will, wish. 266. **Barnaby the bright,** St. Barnabas' Day, the eleventh of June. 269. **Crab,** Cancer, sign of the zodiac.

329. **Tirynthian groome,** Hercules.

Ne let housefyres, nor lightnings helpelesse harmes,
Ne let the Pouke, nor other evill sprights,
Ne let mischivous witches with theyr charmes,
Ne let hob Goblins, names whose sence we see not,
Fray us with things that be not.
Let not the shriech Oule, nor the Storke be heard:
Nor the night Raven that still deadly yels,
Nor damnèd ghosts cald up with mighty spels,
Nor grisly vultures make us once affeard:
Ne let th' unpleasant Quyre of Frogs still croking
Make us to wish theyr choking.
Let none of these theyr drery accents sing;
Ne let the woods them answer, nor theyr eccho ring.

But let stil Silence trew night watches keepe,
That sacred Peace may in assurance rayne,
And tymely Sleep, when it is tyme to sleepe,
May poure his limbs forth on your pleasant playne,
The whiles an hundred little wingèd loves,
Like divers fethered doves,
Shall fly and flutter round about your bed,
And in the secret darke, that none reproves,
Their prety stealthes shal worke, and snares shal spread
To filch away sweet snatches of delight,
Conceald through covert night.
Ye sonnes of Venus, play your sports at will,
For greedy pleasure, carelesse of your toyes,
Thinks more upon her paradise of joyes,
Then what ye do, al be it good or ill.
All night therefore attend your merry play,
For it will soone be day:
Now none doth hinder you, that say or sing,
Ne will the woods now answer, nor your Eccho ring.

Who is the same, which at my window peepes?
Or whose is that faire face, that shines so bright,
Is it not Cinthia, she that never sleepes,
But walkes about high heaven al the night?
O fayrest goddesse, do thou not envy
My love with me to spy:
For thou likewise didst love, though now unthought,
And for a fleece of woll, which privily,
The Latmian shephard once unto thee brought,
His pleasures with thee wrought.
Therefore to us be favourable now;
And sith of wemens labours thou hast charge
And generation goodly dost enlarge,
Encline thy will t' effect our wishfull vow,
And the chast wombe informe with timely seed,
That may our comfort breed:
Till which we cease our hopefull hap to sing,
Ne let the woods us answere, nor our Eccho ring.

And thou great Juno, which with awful might
The lawes of wedlock still dost patronize,
And the religion of the faith first plight
With sacred rites hast taught to solemnize:
And eeke for comfort often callèd art
Of women in their smart,
Eternally bind thou this lovely band,
And all thy blessings unto us impart.
And thou glad Genius, in whose gentle hand,
The bridale bowre and geniall bed remaine,
Without blemish or staine,
And the sweet pleasures of theyr loves delight
With secret ayde doest succour and supply,
Till they bring forth the fruitfull progeny,
Send us the timely fruit of this same night.
And thou fayre Hebe, and thou Hymen free,
Grant that it may so be.
Til which we cease your further prayse to sing,
Ne any woods shal answer, nor your Eccho ring.

And ye high heavens, the temple of the gods,
In which a thousand torches flaming bright
Doe burne, that to us wretched earthly clods,
In dreadful darknesse lend desirèd light;
And all ye powers which in the same remayne,
More then we men can fayne,
Poure out your blessing on us plentiously,
And happy influence upon us raine,
That we may raise a large posterity,
Which from the earth, which they may long possesse,
With lasting happinesse,
Up to your haughty pallaces may mount,
And for the guerdon of theyr glorious merit
May heavenly tabernacles there inherit,
Of blessed Saints for to increase the count.
So let us rest, sweet love, in hope of this,
And cease till then our tymely joyes to sing,
The woods no more us answer, nor our eccho ring.

Song made in lieu of many ornaments,
With which my love should duly have bene dect,
Which cutting off through hasty accidents,
Ye would not stay your dew time to expect,
But promist both to recompens,
Be unto her a goodly ornament,
And for short time an endlesse moniment.

341. the Pouke, the fairy Robin Goodfellow, known also as Puck. **374. Cinthia,** the moon. **380. Latmian shephard,** Endymion, a shepherd boy from Mount Latmos, of whom the moon goddess became enamored as he slept.

388. hap, good fortune. **405. Hebe,** the goddess of youth.

from THE FAERIE QUEENE

Spenser planned *The Faerie Queene* both as a great tribute to his own monarch and as a philosophical and moral allegory setting forth, in Prince Arthur's quest for Gloriana, the ordeals and pitfalls that bestrew the path of a noble-minded character. The purpose of the poem, as Spenser himself expressed it, was "to fashion a gentleman or noble person in vertuous and gentle discipline."

Upon that conception, Spenser built his plot. In his original plan, *The Faerie Queene* was to contain twelve books, corresponding to what he called "the twelve moral virtues as Aristotle hath devised," and each book was to illustrate in allegorical fashion the exercise of a separate virtue. To prevent the poem from falling into twelve disconnected stories, however, Spenser conceived as his main plot and connecting links the adventures that befall Prince Arthur on his quest for the Faerie Queen. Thus, before the opening of the poem, Prince Arthur has seen Gloriana in a vision and, stricken by her beauty, has resolved to seek her in Faeryland. As it happens, each year the Faerie Queen holds in her court a great feast lasting twelve days; and on each day she sends forth a knight embodying a different virtue to aid some suppliant in distress. A separate book was to be devoted chiefly to the adventures of each knight, but in all of them, Prince Arthur, still searching for Gloriana, was to play some part so that in the end he would have gained experience in all that befitted a perfect character. Partly because of classical precedent, and partly because of his desire to make his description of Gloriana's court the climax of his poem, Spenser plunged immediately into the midst of his story, beginning with the adventures of his first knight.

Besides its general moral allegory (wherein the Red Cross Knight signifies Holiness; Una, Truth; Duessa, Falsehood; Archimago, Hypocrisy; and so on), *The Faerie Queene* often has a topical significance in that certain characters and situations suggest parallels in the actual world in which Spenser lived. Thus, Queen Elizabeth is portrayed not only in Gloriana, but also in Belphoebe, Una, and Britomart; Arthur is now Sidney, now Leicester; and Sir Calidore, at one time Sidney, at another Essex. By giving life to abstractions and idealizing real persons, Spenser achieves in *The Faerie Queene* a fusion of the real world and the mythological world of faery.

Book I, the Legend of Holiness, is the most carefully organized narrative in *The Faerie Queene*. As Spenser explained in his prefatory letter to Ralegh, the story began with the appearance at the court of Gloriana of a tall, clownish young man who obtained from the astonished Queen the granting of his request to achieve whatever adventure should befall during her annual feast. Shortly thereafter, when Una appeared with her dwarf—who kept charge of a warlike steed and full knightly regalia—and begged aid of the Queen in the liberation of her parents from a great dragon, the young rustic sprang up demanding this assignment. Notwithstanding doubts cast upon his abilities by both Una and the Queen, the youth gained his point, put on the armor, and after assuming the role of Christian knighthood, set off with Una to achieve his quest.

The actual narrative begins at this point and follows a logical pattern through climax and resolution to its denouement at the end. Upon the separation of hero and heroine in the second canto, two lines of action develop; but these are kept closely related, both through Una's search for the knight and through the evil contrivances practiced in common upon the two by their several enemies, as well as through the close relations maintained between those enemies. Moreover, as the following summary of the omitted cantos will show, Spenser tightens his plot still further by means of various repeated motifs. The theme of pride, for example, symbolized by Lucifera in the fourth canto, reappears climactically and in a more dangerous form in Orgoglio; while sorrow, portrayed by Sansjoy, deepens into the sinister embodiment of Despair.

In Canto II, the knight abandons Una because of a trick played upon him by Archimago and falls in with Duessa, who promptly leads him astray after he has despatched Sansfoy, the first of three evil brothers. Una pursues her way alone in Canto III, charms a ferocious lion, and then sets off with him in search of the knight, the lion performing occasional services in her defense. Presently Archimago, disguised as the knight, reappears on the scene intending to mislead Una; before fully accomplishing his purpose, however, he is mistakenly attacked by the vengeful Sansloy, who also slays the lion and makes Una his prisoner. Cantos IV and V take up again the story of the knight, whom Duessa leads to Lucifera's House of Pride. After seeing there the procession of the Seven Deadly Sins, the knight is challenged to a duel by the third brother, Sansjoy, who, though defeated in a fair field, is saved and resuscitated by the faithless Duessa. Sorely beset meanwhile by lecherous Sansloy, Una finds refuge in Canto VI with Satyrane and his creatures of the forest but there receives—again from Archimago—sad though false tidings of the death of her knight. Canto VII approaches the climax as the knight, on the one hand, falls into the power of the giant Orgoglio, whom Duessa now favors; while Una, on the other, meets Prince Arthur, learns of his quest for Gloriana, and enlists his aid in behalf of the knight. With all principals now massed together, the climax occurs in Canto VIII, when Arthur, at Una's instigation, rescues the knight from Orgoglio and strips the false habiliments from Duessa. Thereafter the resolution of the story proceeds, though delayed complications further stimulate the suspense: first, in Despair's tempting of the knight to suicide in Canto IX, and again in Duessa's letter in Canto XII. Having saved the knight from destroying himself, Una brings him in Canto X to the House of Holiness, where through repentance and self-discipline he gains enough courage and moral strength to defeat the dragon of evil. This task he finally accomplishes, after a prolonged battle, in Canto XI.

The stanzaic form in which *The Faerie Queene* is written, the form commonly called the Spenserian stanza, consists of eight lines of iambic pentameter and a final Alexandrine, rhyming *ababbcbcc*. Some critics have felt that the final Alexandrine produces so definite a pause at the end of each stanza that the form is inappropriate to a narrative poem. But Spenser's narrative is intentionally slow-paced, and the definite break between stanzas gives him ample opportunity for static pictorial and descriptive effects. On many occasions, moreover, he bridges the gap between stanzas by repeating the final line, by using the *c*-rhyme of one stanza as the *a*-rhyme of the next, and by other forms of linkage. The revival of this stanza in the eighteenth century and its superb use later by Keats in "The Eve of St. Agnes" (see pages 872–877) illustrate the interest the Romantics took in great Renaissance writers whom the Neoclassicists had neglected.

BOOK I

Canto I

The Patron of true Holinesse,
Foule Errour doth defeate:
Hypocrisie him to entrappe,
Doth to his home entreate.

I

A Gentle Knight was pricking on the plaine,
Y-cladd in mightie armes and silver shielde,
Wherein old dints of deepe wounds did remaine,
The cruell markes of many a bloudy fielde;
Yet armes till that time did he never wield:
His angry steede did chide his foming bitt,
As much disdayning to the curbe to yield:
Full jolly knight he seemd, and faire did sitt,
As one for knightly giusts and fierce encounters fitt.

2

But on his brest a bloudie Crosse he bore,
The deare remembrance of his dying Lord,
For whose sweete sake that glorious badge he wore,
And dead as living ever him adored:
Upon his shield the like was also scored,
For soveraine hope, which in his helpe he had:
Right faithfull true he was in deede and word,
But of his cheere did seeme too solemne sad;
Yet nothing did he dread, but ever was ydrad.

1. pricking, riding, using spurs. **8. jolly,** handsome. **9. giusts,** jousts, tournaments. **15. soveraine hope,** indicating his great hope. **17. cheere,** countenance. **18. ydrad,** dreaded, the past participle.

3

Upon a great adventure he was bond,
That greatest *Gloriana* to him gave,
That greatest Glorious Queene of *Faerie* lond,
To winne him worship, and her grace to have,
Which of all earthly things he most did crave;
And ever as he rode, his hart did earne
To prove his puissance in battell brave
Upon his foe, and his new force to learne;
Upon his foe, a Dragon horrible and stearne.

4

A lovely Ladie rode him faire beside,
Upon a lowly Asse more white then snow,
Yet she much whiter, but the same did hide
Under a vele, that wimpled was full low,
And over all a blacke stole she did throw,
As one that inly mournd: so was she sad,
And heavie sat upon her palfrey slow:
Seemèd in heart some hidden care she had,
And by her in a line a milke white lambe she lad.

5

So pure and innocent, as that same lambe,
She was in life and every vertuous lore,
And by descent from Royall lynage came
Of ancient Kings and Queenes, that had of yore
Their sceptres stretcht from East to Westerne shore,
And all the world in their subjection held;
Till that infernall feend with foule uprore
Forwasted all their land, and them expeld:
Whom to avenge, she had this Knight from far compeld.

6

Behind her farre away a Dwarfe did lag,
That lasie seemd in being ever last,
Or wearièd with bearing of her bag
Of needments at his backe. Thus as they past,
The day with cloudes was suddeine overcast,
And angry Jove an hideous storme of raine
Did poure into his Lemans lap so fast,
That every wight to shrowd it did constrain,
And this faire couple eke to shroud themselves were fain.

20. Gloriana, Queen Elizabeth. **24. earne,** yearn. **27. Dragon,** Sin. **28. Ladie,** Una or Truth. **31. wimpled,** folded, pleated. **44. Forwasted,** ravished; the prefix "for-" is intensive. **45. compeld,** summoned. **46. Dwarfe,** Prudence. **52. Lemans lap,** beloved's lap; that is, the earth. **53. shrowd,** take cover.

7

Enforst to seeke some covert nigh at hand,
A shadie grove not far away they spide,
That promist ayde the tempest to withstand:
Whose loftie trees yclad with sommers pride,
Did spred so broad, that heavens light did hide,
Not perceable with power of any starre:
And all within were pathes and alleies wide,
With footing worne, and leading inward farre:
Faire harbour that them seemes; so in they entred arre.

8

And foorth they passe, with pleasure forward led,
Joying to heare the birdes sweete harmony,
Which therein shrouded from the tempest dred,
Seemd in their song to scorne the cruell sky.
Much can they prayse the trees so straight and hy,
The sayling Pine, the Cedar proud and tall,
The vine-prop Elme, the Poplar never dry,
The builder Oake, sole king of forests all,
The Aspine good for staves, the Cypresse funerall.

9

The Laurell, meed of mightie Conquerours
And Poets sage, the Firre that weepeth still,
The Willow worne of forlorne Paramours,
The Eugh obedient to the benders will,
The Birch for shaftes, the Sallow for the mill,
The Mirrhe sweete bleeding in the bitter wound,
The warlike Beech, the Ash for nothing ill,
The fruitfull Olive, and the Platane round,
The carver Holme, the Maple seeldom inward sound.

10

Led with delight, they thus beguile the way,
Untill the blustring storme is overblowne;
When weening to returne, whence they did stray,
They cannot finde that path, which first was showne,
But wander too and fro in wayes unknowne,
Furthest from end then, when they neerest weene,
That makes them doubt, their wits be not their owne:
So many pathes, so many turnings seene,
That which of them to take, in diverse doubt they been.

76. **Eugh,** yew. 77. **Sallow,** broad-leaved willow.
80. **Platane,** plane tree. 81. **Holme,** evergreen oak.
84. **weening,** thinking. 88. **doubt,** fear.

11

At last resolving forward still to fare,
Till that some end they finde or in or out,
That path they take, that beaten seemd most bare,
And like to lead the labyrinth about;
Which when by tract they hunted had throughout,
At length it brought them to a hollow cave,
Amid the thickest woods. The Champion stout
Eftsoones dismounted from his courser brave,
And to the Dwarfe a while his needlesse spere he gave.

12

Be well aware, quoth then that Ladie milde,
Least suddaine mischiefe ye too rash provoke:
The danger hid, the place unknowne and wilde,
Breedes dreadfull doubts: Oft fire is without smoke,
And perill without show: therefore your stroke
Sir knight with-hold, till further triall made.
Ah Ladie (said he) shame were to revoke
The forward footing for an hidden shade:
Vertue gives her selfe light, through darkenesse for to wade.

13

Yea but (quoth she) the perill of this place
I better wot then you, though now too late
To wish you backe returne with foule disgrace,
Yet wisedome warnes, whilest foot is in the gate,
To stay the steppe, ere forcèd to retrate.
This is the wandring wood, this *Errours den*,
A monster vile, whom God and man does hate:
Therefore I read beware. Fly fly (quoth then
The fearefull Dwarfe:) this is no place for living men.

14

But full of fire and greedy hardiment,
The youthfull knight could not for ought be staide,
But forth unto the darksome hole he went,
And lookèd in: his glistring armour made
A litle glooming light, much like a shade,
By which he saw the ugly monster plaine,
Halfe like a serpent horribly displaide,
But th'other halfe did womans shape retaine,
Most lothsom, filthie, foule, and full of vile disdaine.

94. **about,** out of. 98. **Eftsoones,** promptly, immediately.
112. **gate,** path. 116. **read,** advise.

15

And as she lay upon the durtie ground,
Her huge long taile her den all overspred,
Yet was in knots and many boughtes upwound,
Pointed with mortall sting. Of her there bred
A thousand yong ones, which she dayly fed,
Sucking upon her poisonous dugs eachone
Of sundry shapes, yet all ill favourèd:
Soone as that uncouth light upon them shone,
Into her mouth they crept, and suddain all were gone.

16

Their dam upstart, out of her den effraide,
And rushèd forth, hurling her hideous taile
About her cursèd head, whose folds displaid
Were stretcht now forth at length without entraile.
She lookt about, and seeing one in mayle
Armèd to point, sought backe to turne againe;
For light she hated as the deadly bale,
Ay wont in desert darknesse to remaine,
Where plaine none might see her, nor she see any plaine.

17

Which when the valiant Elfe perceived, he lept
As Lyon fierce upon the flying pray,
And with his trenchard blade her boldly kept
From turning backe, and forcèd her to stay:
Therewith enraged she loudly gan to bray,
And turning fierce, her speckled taile advaunst,
Threatning her angry sting, him to dismay:
Who nought aghast, his mightie hand enhaunst:
The stroke down from her head unto her shoulder glaunst.

18

Much daunted with that dint, her sence was dazd,
Yet kindling rage, her selfe she gathered round,
And all attonce her beastly body raizd
With doubled forces high above the ground:
Tho wrapping up her wrethèd sterne arownd,
Lept fierce upon his shield, and her huge traine
All suddenly about his body wound,
That hand or foot to stirre he strove in vaine:
God helpe the man so wrapt in *Errours* endlesse traine.

129. boughtes, coils, folds. **133. ill favourèd,** of ugly face. **139. entraile,** coiling. **142. bale,** destruction. **143. Ay wont,** always accustomed. **145. Elfe.** The Red Cross Knight was son of an elf. **152. enhaunst,** raised, lifted up.

19

His Lady sad to see his sore constraint,
Cride out, Now now Sir knight, shew what ye bee,
Add faith unto your force, and be not faint:
Strangle her, else she sure will strangle thee.
That when he heard, in great perplexitie,
His gall did grate for griefe and high disdaine,
And knitting all his force got one hand free,
Wherewith he grypt her gorge with so great paine,
That soone to loose her wicked bands did her constraine.

20

Therewith she spewd out of her filthy maw
A floud of poyson horrible and blacke,
Full of great lumpes of flesh and gobbets raw,
Which stunck so vildly, that it forst him slacke
His grasping hold, and from her turne him backe:
Her vomit full of bookes and papers was,
With loathly frogs and toades, which eyes did lacke,
And creeping sought way in the weedy gras:
Her filthy parbreake all the place defilèd has.

21

As when old father *Nilus* gins to swell
With timely pride above the *Aegyptian* vale,
His fattie waves do fertile slime outwell,
And overflow each plaine and lowly dale:
But when his later spring gins to avale,
Huge heapes of mudd he leaves, wherein there breed
Ten thousand kindes of creatures, partly male
And partly female of his fruitfull seed;
Such ugly monstrous shapes elswhere may no man reed.

22

The same so sore annoyèd has the knight,
That welnigh chokèd with the deadly stinke,
His forces faile, ne can no longer fight.
Whose corage when the feend perceived to shrinke,
She pourèd forth out of her hellish sinke
Her fruitfull cursèd spawne of serpents small,
Deformèd monsters, fowle, and blacke as inke,
Which swarming all about his legs did crall,
And him encombred sore, but could not hurt at all.

168. gall did grate for griefe, anger was stirred through pain. **177. vomit full of bookes and papers,** anti-Protestant writings attacking Queen Elizabeth and the Church of England. **180. parbreake,** vomit. **185. avale,** moderate, abate. **189. reed,** see.

23

As gentle Shepheard in sweete even-tide,
When ruddy *Phoebus* gins to welke in west,
High on an hill, his flocke to vewen wide,
Markes which do byte their hasty supper best;
A cloud of combrous gnattes do him molest,
All striving to infixe their feeble stings,
That from their noyance he no where can rest,
But with his clownish hands their tender wings
He brusheth oft, and oft doth mar their murmurings.

24

Thus ill bestedd, and fearefull more of shame,
Then of the certaine perill he stood in,
Halfe furious unto his foe he came,
Resolved in minde all suddenly to win,
Or soone to lose, before he once would lin;
And strooke at her with more then manly force,
That from her body full of filthie sin
He raft her hatefull head without remorse;
A streame of cole black bloud forth gushèd from her corse.

25

Her scattred brood, soone as their Parent deare
They saw so rudely falling to the ground,
Groning full deadly, all with troublous feare,
Gathred themselves about her body round,
Weening their wonted entrance to have found
At her wide mouth: but being there withstood
They flockèd all about her bleeding wound,
And suckèd up their dying mothers blood,
Making her death their life, and eke her hurt their good.

26

That detestable sight him much amazde,
To see th'unkindly Impes of heaven accurst,
Devoure their dam; on whom while so he gazd,
Having all satisfide their bloudy thurst,
Their bellies swolne he saw with fulnesse burst,
And bowels gushing forth: well worthy end
Of such as drunke her life, the which them nurst;
Now needeth him no lenger labour spend,
His foes have slaine themselves, with whom he should contend.

27

His Ladie seeing all, that chaunst, from farre
Approcht in hast to greet his victorie,
And said, Faire knight, borne under happy starre,
Who see your vanquisht foes before you lye:
Well worthy be you of that Armorie,
Wherein ye have great glory wonne this day,
And prooved your strength on a strong enimie,
Your first adventure: many such I pray,
And henceforth ever wish, that like succeed it may.

28

Then mounted he upon his Steede againe,
And with the Lady backward sought to wend;
That path he kept, which beaten was most plaine,
Ne ever would to any by-way bend,
But still did follow one unto the end,
The which at last out of the wood them brought.
So forward on his way (with God to frend)
He passèd forth, and new adventure sought;
Long way he travellèd, before he heard of ought.

29

At length they chaunst to meet upon the way
An agèd Sire, in long blacke weedes yclad,
His feete all bare, his beard all hoarie gray,
And by his belt his booke he hanging had;
Sober he seemde, and very sagely sad,
And to the ground his eyes were lowly bent,
Simple in shew, and voyde of malice bad,
And all the way he prayèd, as he went,
And often knockt his brest, as one that did repent.

30

He faire the knight saluted, louting low,
Who faire him quited, as that courteous was:
And after askèd him, if he did know
Of straunge adventures, which abroad did pas.
Ah my deare Sonne (quoth he) how should, alas,
Silly old man, that lives in hidden cell,
Bidding his beades all day for his trespas,
Tydings of warre and worldly trouble tell?
With holy father sits not with such things to mell.

31

But if of daunger which hereby doth dwell,
And homebred evil ye desire to heare,
Of a straunge man I can you tidings tell,
That wasteth all this countrey farre and neare.
Of such (said he) I chiefly do inquere,
And shall you well reward to shew the place,
In which that wicked wight his dayes doth weare:

200. welke, wane. **208. bestedd,** placed. **212. lin,** cease, stop. **215. raft,** took away. **227. unkindly,** unnatural.

239. Armorie, a Christian's armor. **254. Sire,** Archimago, playing the part of Hypocrisy. **262. louting,** bending. **267. Silly,** simple. **268. Bidding,** telling. **270. sits not,** is not fitting. **mell,** meddle.

For to all knighthood it is foule disgrace,
That such a cursèd creature lives so long a space.

32

Far hence (quoth he) in wastfull wildernesse
His dwelling is, by which no living wight
May ever passe, but thorough great distresse.
Now (sayd the Lady) draweth toward night,
And well I wote, that of your later fight
Ye all forwearied be: for what so strong,
But wanting rest will also want of might?
The Sunne that measures heaven all day long,
At night doth baite his steedes the *Ocean* waves emong.

33

Then with the Sunne take Sir, your timely rest,
And with new day new worke at once begin:
Untroubled night they say gives counsell best.
Right well Sir knight ye have advisèd bin,
(Quoth then that agèd man;) the way to win
Is wisely to advise: now day is spent;
Therefore with me ye may take up your In
For this same night. The knight was well content:
So with that godly father to his home they went.

34

A little lowly Hermitage it was,
Downe in a dale, hard by a forests side,
Far from resort of people, that did pas
In travell to and froe: a little wyde
There was an holy Chappell edifyde,
Wherein the Hermite dewly wont to say
His holy things each morne and eventyde:
Thereby a Christall streame did gently play,
Which from a sacred fountaine wellèd forth alway.

35

Arrivèd there, the little house they fill,
Ne looke for entertainement, where none was:
Rest is their feast, and all things at their will;
The noblest mind the best contentment has.
With faire discourse the evening so they pas:
For that old man of pleasing wordes had store,
And well could file his tongue as smooth as glas;
He told of Saintes and Popes, and evermore
He strowd an *Ave-Mary* after and before.

36

The drouping Night thus creepeth on them fast,
And the sad humour loading their eye liddes,
As messenger of *Morpheus* on them cast
Sweet slombring deaw, the which to sleepe them biddes.
Unto their lodgings then his guestes he riddes:
Where when all drownd in deadly sleepe he findes,
He to his study goes, and there amiddes
His Magick bookes and artes of sundry kindes,
He seekes out mighty charmes, to trouble sleepy mindes.

37

Then choosing out few wordes most horrible,
(Let none them read) thereof did verses frame,
With which and other spelles like terrible,
He bad awake blacke *Plutoes* griesly Dame,
And cursèd heaven, and spake reprochfull shame
Of highest God, the Lord of life and light;
A bold bad man, that dared to call by name
Great *Gorgon*, Prince of darknesse and dead night,
At which *Cocytus* quakes, and *Styx* is put to flight.

38

And forth he cald out of deepe darknesse dred
Legions of Sprights, the which like little flyes
Fluttring about his ever damnèd hed,
A-waite whereto their service he applyes,
To aide his friends, or fray his enimies:
Of those he chose out two, the falsest twoo,
And fittest for to forge true-seeming lyes;
The one of them he gave a message too,
The other by him selfe staide other worke to doo.

39

He making speedy way through spersèd ayre,
And through the world of waters wide and deepe,
To *Morpheus* house doth hastily repaire.
Amid the bowels of the earth full steepe,
And low, where dawning day doth never peepe,
His dwelling is; there *Tethys* his wet bed
Doth ever wash, and *Cynthia* still doth steepe
In silver deaw his ever-drouping hed,
Whiles sad Night over him her mantle black doth spred.

40

Whose double gates he findeth lockèd fast,
The one faire framed of burnisht Yvory,

288. **baite,** refresh. 295. **In,** lodging. 301. **wyde,** apart, a short distance away. 302. **edifyde,** built. 317. **sad humour,** heavy dampness.

320. **riddes,** dismisses. 328. **Dame,** Proserpine. 332. **Gorgon,** Demogorgon, the demon magician of the underworld, whose name alone was terrifying to all. 333. **Cocytus . . . Styx,** rivers in Hades. 338. **fray,** frighten. 343. **spersèd,** dispersed. 348. **Tethys,** the ocean. 349. **Cynthia,** the moon.

The other all with silver overcast;
And wakefull dogges before them farre do lye,
Watching to banish Care their enimy,
Who oft is wont to trouble gentle Sleepe.
By them the Sprite doth passe in quietly,
And unto *Morpheus* comes, whom drownèd deepe
In drowsie fit he findes: of nothing he takes keepe.

41

And more, to lulle him in his slumber soft,
A trickling streame from high rocke tumbling downe
And ever-drizling raine upon the loft,
Mixt with a murmuring winde, much like the sowne
Of swarming Bees, did cast him in a swowne:
No other noyse, nor peoples troublous cryes,
As still are wont t' annoy the wallèd towne,
Might there be heard: but carelesse Quiet lyes,
Wrapt in eternall silence farre from enemyes.

42

The messenger approching to him spake,
But his wast wordes returnd to him in vaine:
So sound he slept, that nought mought him awake.
Then rudely he him thrust, and pusht with paine,
Whereat he gan to stretch: but he againe
Shooke him so hard, that forcèd him to speake.
As one then in a dreame, whose dryer braine
Is tost with troubled sights and fancies weake,
He mumbled soft, but would not all his silence breake.

43

The Sprite then gan more boldly him to wake,
And threatned unto him the dreaded name
Of *Hecate:* whereat he gan to quake,
And lifting up his lumpish head, with blame
Halfe angry askèd him, for what he came.
Hither (quoth he) me *Archimago* sent,
He that the stubborne Sprites can wisely tame,
He bids thee to him send for his intent
A fit false dreame, that can delude the sleepers sent.

44

The God obayde, and calling forth straight way
A diverse dreame out of his prison darke,
Delivered it to him, and downe did lay
His heavie head, devoide of carefull carke,
Whose sences all were straight benumbd and starke.
He backe returning by the Yvorie dore,
Remounted up as light as chearefull Larke,
And on his litle winges the dreame he bore
In hast unto his Lord, where he him left afore.

360. keepe, heed. **363. loft,** upper floor. **376. dryer braine.** A dry brain was thought to be more active and stronger than a moist one. **381. Hecate,** underworld goddess of witchcraft. **382. lumpish,** heavy. **387. sent,** sense. **389. diverse,** misleading. **391. carke,** worry.

45

Who all this while with charmes and hidden artes,
Had made a Lady of that other Spright,
And framed of liquid ayre her tender partes
So lively, and so like in all mens sight,
That weaker sence it could have ravisht quight:
The maker selfe for all his wondrous witt,
Was nigh beguilèd with so goodly sight:
Her all in white he clad, and over it
Cast a blacke stole, most like to seeme for *Una* fit.

46

Now when that ydle dreame was to him brought,
Unto that Elfin knight he bad him fly,
Where he slept soundly void of evill thought,
And with false shewes abuse his fantasy,
In sort as he him schoolèd privily:
And that new creature borne without her dew,
Full of the makers guile, with usage sly
He taught to imitate that Lady trew,
Whose semblance she did carrie under feignèd hew.

47

Thus well instructed, to their worke they hast,
And comming where the knight in slomber lay,
The one upon his hardy head him plast,
And made him dreame of loves and lustfull play,
That nigh his manly hart did melt away,
Bathèd in wanton blis and wicked joy:
Then seemèd him his Lady by him lay,
And to him playnd, how that false wingèd boy
Her chast hart had subdewd, to learne Dame pleasures toy.

48

And she her selfe of beautie soveraigne Queene,
Faire *Venus* seemde unto his bed to bring
Her, whom he waking evermore did weene
To be the chastest flowre, that ay did spring
On earthly braunch, the daughter of a king,
Now a loose Leman to vile service bound:
And eke the *Graces* seemèd all to sing,
Hymen Iö Hymen, dauncing all around,
Whilst freshest *Flora* her with Ivie girlond crownd.

410. In sort as, in the way that. **411. dew,** due, **that is,** unnaturally. **422. wingèd boy,** Cupid.

49

In this great passion of unwonted lust,
Or wonted feare of doing ought amis,
He started up, as seeming to mistrust
Some secret ill, or hidden foe of his:
Lo there before his face his Lady is,
Under blake stole hyding her bayted hooke,
And as halfe blushing offred him to kis,
With gentle blandishment and lovely looke,
Most like that virgin true, which for her knight him took.

50

All cleane dismayd to see so uncouth sight,
And halfe enragèd at her shamelesse guise,
He thought have slaine her in his fierce despight:
But hasty heat tempring with sufferance wise,
He stayde his hand, and gan himselfe advise
To prove his sense, and tempt her faignèd truth.
Wringing her hands in wemens pitteous wise,
Tho can she weepe, to stirre up gentle ruth,
Both for her noble bloud, and for her tender youth.

51

And said, Ah Sir, my liege Lord and my love,
Shall I accuse the hidden cruell fate,
And mightie causes wrought in heaven above,
Or the blind God, that doth me thus amate,
For hopèd love to winne me certaine hate?
Yet thus perforce he bids me do, or die.
Die is my dew: yet rew my wretched state
You, whom my hard avenging destinie
Hath made judge of my life or death indifferently.

52

Your owne deare sake forst me at first to leave
My Fathers kingdome, There she stopt with teares;
Her swollen hart her speach seemd to bereave,
And then againe begun, My weaker yeares
Captived to fortune and frayle worldly feares,
Fly to your faith for succour and sure ayde:
Let me not dye in languor and long teares.
Why Dame (quoth he) what hath ye thus dismayd?
What frayes ye, that were wont to comfort me affrayd?

53

Love of your selfe, she said, and deare constraint
Lets me not sleepe, but wast the wearie night
In secret anguish and unpittied plaint,
Whiles you in carelesse sleepe are drownèd quight.
Her doubtfull words made that redoubted knight
Suspect her truth: yet since no untruth he knew,
Her fawning love with foule disdainefull spight
He would not shend, but said, Deare dame I rew,
That for my sake unknowne such griefe unto you grew.

54

Assure your selfe, it fell not all to ground;
For all so deare as life is to my hart,
I deeme your love, and hold me to you bound;
Ne let vaine feares procure your needlesse smart,
Where cause is none, but to your rest depart.
Not all content, yet seemd she to appease
Her mournefull plaintes, beguilèd of her art,
And fed with words, that could not chuse but please,
So slyding softly forth, she turnd as to her ease.

55

Long after lay he musing at her mood,
Much grieved to thinke that gentle Dame so light,
For whose defence he was to shed his blood.
At last dull wearinesse of former fight
Having yrockt a sleepe his irkesome spright,
That troublous dreame gan freshly tosse his braine,
With bowres, and beds, and Ladies deare delight:
But when he saw his labour all was vaine,
With that misformèd spright he backe returnd againe.

Canto XI

The knight with that old Dragon fights
two dayes incessantly:
The third him overthrowes, and gayns
most glorious victory.

I

High time now gan it wex for *Una* faire,
To thinke of those her captive Parents deare,
And their forwasted kingdome to repaire:
Whereto whenas they now approchèd neare,
With hartie words her knight she gan to cheare,
And in her modest manner thus bespake;
Deare knight, as deare, as ever knight was deare,

449. Tho can, then did. **ruth,** pity. **454. amate,** discourage. **469. constraint,** necessity.

476. shend, reproach, reject. **483. appease,** cease. **1. wex,** waxed, grew.

That all these sorrowes suffer for my sake,
High heaven behold the tedious toyle, ye for me take.

2

Now are we come unto my native soyle,
And to the place, where all our perils dwell;
Here haunts that feend, and does his dayly spoyle,
Therefore henceforth be at your keeping well,
And ever ready for your foeman fell.
The sparke of noble courage now awake,
And strive your excellent selfe to excell;
That shall ye evermore renowmèd make,
Above all knights on earth, that batteill undertake.

3

And pointing forth, lo yonder is (said she)
The brasen towre in which my parents deare
For dread of that huge feend emprisond be,
Whom I from far see on the walles appeare,
Whose sight my feeble soule doth greatly cheare:
And on the top of all I do espye
The watchman wayting tydings glad to heare,
That O my parents might I happily
Unto you bring, to ease you of your misery.

4

With that they heard a roaring hideous sound,
That all the ayre with terrour fillèd wide,
And seemd uneath to shake the stedfast ground.
Eftsoones that dreadfull Dragon they espide,
Where stretcht he lay upon the sunny side
Of a great hill, himselfe like a great hill.
But all so soone, as he from far descride
Those glistring armes, that heaven with light did fill,
He rousd himselfe full blith, and hastned them untill.

5

Then bad the knight his Lady yede aloofe,
And to an hill her selfe withdraw aside,
From whence she might behold that battailles proof
And eke be safe from daunger far descryde:
She him obayd, and turnd a little wyde.
Now O thou sacred Muse, most learnèd Dame,
Faire ympe of *Phoebus*, and his agèd bride,
The Nourse of time, and everlasting fame,
That warlike hands ennoblest with immortall name;

6

O gently come into my feeble brest,
Come gently, but not with that mighty rage,
Wherewith the martiall troupes thou doest infest,
And harts of great Heroès doest enrage,
That nought their kindled courage may aswage,
Soone as thy dreadfull trompe begins to sownd;
The God of warre with his fiers equipage
Thou doest awake, sleepe never he so sownd,
And scarèd nations doest with horrour sterne astownd.

7

Faire Goddesse lay that furious fit aside,
Till I of warres and bloudy *Mars* do sing,
And Briton fields with Sarazin bloud bedyde,
Twixt that great faery Queene and Paynim king,
That with their horrour heaven and earth did ring,
A worke of labour long, and endlesse prayse:
But now a while let downe that haughtie string,
And to my tunes thy second tenor rayse,
That I this man of God his godly armes may blaze.

8

By this the dreadfull Beast drew nigh to hand,
Halfe flying, and halfe footing in his hast,
That with his largenesse measurèd much land,
And made wide shadow under his huge wast;
As mountaine doth the valley overcast.
Approching nigh, he rearèd high afore
His body monstrous, horrible, and vast,
Which to increase his wondrous greatnesse more,
Was swolne with wrath, and poyson, and with bloudy gore.

9

And over, all with brasen scales was armd,
Like plated coate of steele, so couchèd neare,
That nought mote perce, ne might his corse be harmd
With dint of sword, nor push of pointed speare;
Which as an Eagle, seeing pray appeare,
His aëry plumes doth rouze, full rudely dight,
So shakèd he, that horrour was to heare,
For as the clashing of an Armour bright,
Such noyse his rouzèd scales did send unto the knight.

13. **be . . . keeping well,** be well on your guard. 30. **uneath,** almost. 37. **yede,** go. 42. **Muse,** Clio, the Muse of history. 43. **agèd bride,** Mnemosyne, or Memory.

52. **God of warre,** Mars. 55. **fit,** strain of music. 58. **Twixt . . . king,** a reference to an incident supposed to take place in one of the later (unwritten) books. 63. **blaze,** praise. 74. **so couchèd neare,** so closely interlocked. 78. **rouze,** ruffle.

10

His flaggy wings when forth he did display,
Were like two sayles, in which the hollow wynd
Is gathered full, and worketh speedy way:
And eke the pennes, that did his pineons bynd,
Were like mayne-yards, with flying canvas lynd,
With which whenas him list the ayre to beat,
And there by force unwonted passage find,
The cloudes before him fled for terrour great,
And all the heavens stood still amazèd with his threat.

11

His huge long tayle wound up in hundred foldes,
Does overspred his long bras-scaly backe,
Whose wreathèd boughts when ever he unfoldes,
And thicke entangled knots adown does slacke,
Bespotted as with shields of red and blacke,
It sweepeth all the land behind him farre,
And of three furlongs does but litle lacke;
And at the point two stings in-fixèd arre,
Both deadly sharpe, that sharpest steele exceeden farre.

12

But stings and sharpest steele did far exceed
The sharpnesse of his cruell rending clawes;
Dead was it sure, as sure as death in deed,
What ever thing does touch his ravenous pawes,
Or what within his reach he ever drawes.
But his most hideous head my toung to tell
Does tremble: for his deepe devouring jawes
Wide gapèd, like the griesly mouth of hell,
Through which into his darke abisse all ravin fell.

13

And that more wondrous was, in either jaw
Three ranckes of yron teeth enraungèd were,
In which yet trickling bloud and gobbets raw
Of late devourèd bodies did appeare,
That sight thereof bred cold congealèd feare:
Which to increase, and all atonce to kill,
A cloud of smoothering smoke and sulphur seare
Out of his stinking gorge forth steemèd still,
That all the ayre about with smoke and stench did fill.

14

His blazing eyes, like two bright shining shields,
Did burne with wrath, and sparkled living fyre;
As two broad Beacons, set in open fields,
Send forth their flames farre off to every shyre,
And warning give, that enemies conspyre,
With fire and sword the region to invade;
So flamed his eyne with rage and rancorous yre:
But farre within, as in a hollow glade,
Those glaring lampes were set, that made a dreadfull shade.

15

So dreadfully he towards him did pas,
Forelifting up aloft his speckled brest,
And often bounding on the brusèd gras,
As for great joyance of his newcome guest.
Eftsoones he gan advance his haughtie crest,
As chauffèd Bore his bristles doth upreare,
And shoke his scales to battell readie drest;
That made the *Redcrosse* knight nigh quake for feare,
As bidding bold defiance to his foeman neare.

16

The knight gan fairely couch his steadie speare,
And fiercely ran at him with rigorous might:
The pointed steele arriving rudely theare,
His harder hide would neither perce, nor bight,
But glauncing by forth passèd forward right;
Yet sore amovèd with so puissant push,
The wrathfull beast about him turnèd light,
And him so rudely passing by, did brush
With his long tayle, that horse and man to ground did rush.

17

Both horse and man up lightly rose againe,
And fresh encounter towards him addrest:
But th' idle stroke yet backe recoyld in vaine,
And found no place his deadly point to rest.
Exceeding rage enflamed the furious beast,
To be avengèd of so great despight;
For never felt his imperceable brest
So wondrous force, from hand of living wight;
Yet had he proved the powre of many a puissant knight.

18

Then with his waving wings displayèd wyde,
Himselfe up high he lifted from the ground,
And with strong flight did forcibly divide
The yielding aire, which nigh too feeble found
Her flitting partes, and element unsound,
To beare so great a weight: he cutting way
With his broad sayles, about him soarèd round:
At last low stouping with unweldie sway,
Snatcht up both horse and man, to beare them quite away.

85. pennes, feathers. **93. boughts,** coils.

132. chauffèd, irritated.

19

Long he them bore above the subject plaine,
So farre as Ewghen bow a shaft may send,
Till struggling strong did him at last constraine,
To let them downe before his flightès end:
As hagard hauke presuming to contend
With hardie fowle, above his hable might,
His wearie pounces all in vaine doth spend,
To trusse the pray too heavie for his flight;
Which comming downe to ground, does free it selfe by fight.

20

He so disseizèd of his gryping grosse,
The knight his thrillant speare againe assayd
In his bras-plated body to embosse,
And three mens strength unto the stroke he layd;
Wherewith the stiffe beame quakèd, as affrayd,
And glauncing from his scaly necke, did glyde
Close under his left wing, then broad displayd.
The percing steele there wrought a wound full wyde,
That with the uncouth smart the Monster lowdly cryde.

21

He cryde, as raging seas are wont to rore,
When wintry storme his wrathfull wreck does threat,
The rolling billowes beat the ragged shore,
As they the earth would shoulder from her seat,
And greedie gulfe does gape, as he would eat
His neighbour element in his revenge:
Then gin the blustring brethren boldly threat,
To move the world from off his stedfast henge,
And boystrous battell make, each other to avenge.

22

The steely head stucke fast still in his flesh,
Till with his cruell clawes he snatcht the wood,
And quite a sunder broke. Forth flowèd fresh
A gushing river of blacke goarie blood,
That drownèd all the land, whereon he stood;
The streame thereof would drive a water-mill.
Trebly augmented was his furious mood
With bitter sense of his deepe rooted ill,
That flames of fire he threw forth from his large nosethrill.

163. subject plaine, ground lying below. **164. Ewghen,** yew: pronounce "yewen." **167. hagard,** wild. **168. hable might,** beyond his power. **169. pounces,** claws. **170. trusse,** pierce so as to hold a thing or grip it. **172. disseizèd,** deprived. **gryping grosse,** rough, heavy, or awkward grasp. **173. thrillant,** piercing. **180. uncouth,** unusual. **187. brethren,** the winds.

23

His hideous tayle then hurlèd he about,
And therewith all enwrapt the nimble thyes
Of his froth-fomy steed, whose courage stout
Striving to loose the knot, that fast him tyes,
Himselfe in streighter bandes too rash implyes,
That to the ground he is perforce constraynd
To throw his rider: who can quickly ryse
From off the earth, with durty bloud distaynd,
For that reprochfull fall right fowly he disdaynd.

24

And fiercely tooke his trenchand blade in hand,
With which he stroke so furious and so fell,
That nothing seemd the puissance could withstand:
Upon his crest the hardned yron fell,
But his more hardned crest was armd so well,
That deeper dint therein it would not make;
Yet so extremely did the buffe him quell,
That from thenceforth he shund the like to take,
But when he saw them come, he did them still forsake.

25

The knight was wrath to see his stroke beguyld,
And smote againe with more outrageous might;
But backe againe the sparckling steele recoyld,
And left not any marke, where it did light;
As if in Adamant rocke it had bene pight.
The beast impatient of his smarting wound,
And of so fierce and forcible despight,
Thought with his wings to stye above the ground;
But his late wounded wing unserviceable found.

26

Then full of griefe and anguish vehement,
He lowdly brayd, that like was never heard,
And from his wide devouring oven sent
A flake of fire, that flashing in his beard,
Him all amazd, and almost made affeard:
The scorching flame sore swingèd all his face,
And through his armour all his bodie seard,
That he could not endure so cruell cace,
But thought his armes to leave, and helmet to unlace.

27

Not that great Champion of the antique world,
Whom famous Poetes verse so much doth vaunt,

203. implyes, enfolds. **205. can,** "gan," did. **206. distaynd,** stained. **214. buffe,** blow. **216. still,** ever. **217. beguyld,** foiled. **221. pight,** pitched. **224. stye,** ascend. **231. swingèd,** singed. **235. Champion,** Hercules.

And hath for twelve huge labours high extold,
So many furies and sharpe fits did haunt,
When him the poysoned garment did enchaunt
With *Centaures* bloud, and bloudie verses charmed,
As did this knight twelve thousand dolours daunt,
Whom fyrie steele now burnt, that earst him armed,
That erst him goodly armed, now most of all him harmed.

28

Faint, wearie, sore, emboylèd, grievèd, brent
With heat, toyle, wounds, armes, smart, and inward fire
That never man such mischiefes did torment;
Death better were, death did he oft desire,
But death will never come, when needes require.
Whom so dismayd when that his foe beheld,
He cast to suffer him no more respire,
But gan his sturdie sterne about to weld,
And him so strongly stroke, that to the ground him feld.

29

It fortunèd (as faire it then befell)
Behind his backe unweeting, where he stood,
Of auncient time there was a springing well,
From which fast trickled forth a silver flood,
Full of great vertues, and for med'cine good.
Whylome, before that cursèd Dragon got
That happie land, and all with innocent blood
Defyld those sacred waves, it rightly hot
The well of life, ne yet his vertues had forgot.

30

For unto life the dead it could restore,
And guilt of sinfull crimes cleane wash away,
Those that with sicknesse were infected sore,
It could recure, and agèd long decay
Renew, as one were borne that very day.
Both *Silo* this, and *Jordan* did excell,
And th' English *Bath*, and eke the german *Spau*,
Ne can *Cephise*, nor *Hebrus* match this well:
Into the same the knight backe overthrowen, fell.

31

Now gan the golden *Phoebus* for to steepe
His fierie face in billowes of the west,
And his faint steedes watred in Ocean deepe,
Whiles from their journall labours they did rest,
When that infernall Monster, having kest
His wearie foe into that living well,
Can high advance his broad discoloured brest,
Above his wonted pitch, with countenance fell,
And clapt his yron wings, as victor he did dwell.

32

Which when his pensive Ladie saw from farre,
Great woe and sorrow did her soule assay,
As weening that the sad end of the warre,
And gan to highest God entirely pray,
That fearèd chance from her to turne away;
With folded hands and knees full lowly bent
All night she watcht, ne once adowne would lay
Her daintie limbs in her sad dreriment,
But praying still did wake, and waking did lament.

33

The morrow next gan early to appeare,
That *Titan* rose to runne his daily race;
But early ere the morrow next gan reare
Out of the sea faire *Titans* deawy face,
Up rose the gentle virgin from her place,
And lookèd all about, if she might spy
Her lovèd knight to move his manly pace:
For she had great doubt of his safèty,
Since late she saw him fall before his enemy.

34

At last she saw, where he upstarted brave
Out of the well, wherein he drenchèd lay;
As Eagle fresh out of the Ocean wave,
Where he hath left his plumes all hoary gray,
And deckt himselfe with feathers youthly gay,
Like Eyas hauke up mounts unto the skies,
His newly budded pineons to assay,
And marveiles at himselfe, still as he flies:
So new this new-borne knight to battell new did rise.

35

Whom when the damnèd feend so fresh did spy,
No wonder if he wondred at the sight,
And doubted, whether his late enemy
It were, or other new supplièd knight.
He, now to prove his late renewèd might,
High brandishing his bright deaw-burning blade,
Upon his crested scalpe so sore did smite,
That to the scull a yawning wound it made:
The deadly dint his dullèd senses all dismaid.

250. respire, respite. **251. sterne,** tail. **260. hot,** was named. **261. well of life.** The well symbolizes divine grace. **267. Silo,** Siloam, a healing pool mentioned in the Bible; the others are well-known streams or watering-places.

274. journall, daily. **303. Eyas,** young. **312. deaw-burning,** glistening with dew.

36

I wote not, whether the revenging steele
Were hardned with that holy water dew,
Wherein he fell, or sharper edge did feele,
Or his baptizèd hands now greater grew;
Or other secret vertue did ensew;
Else never could the force of fleshly arme,
Ne molten mettall in his bloud embrew:
For till that stownd could never wight him harme,
By subtilty, nor slight, nor might, nor mighty charme.

37

The cruell wound enragèd him so sore,
That loud he yellèd for exceeding paine;
As hundred ramping Lyons seemed to rore,
Whom ravenous hunger did there to constraine:
Then gan he tosse aloft his stretchèd traine,
And therewith scourge the buxome aire so sore,
That to his force to yeelden it was faine;
Ne ought his sturdie strokes might stand afore,
That high trees overthrew, and rocks in peeces tore.

38

The same advauncing high above his head,
With sharpe intended sting so rude him smot,
That to the earth him drove, as stricken dead,
Ne living wight would have him life behot:
The mortall sting his angry needle shot
Quite through his shield, and in his shoulder seasd,
Where fast it stucke, ne would there out be got:
The griefe thereof him wondrous sore diseasd,
Ne might his ranckling paine with patience be appeasd.

39

But yet more mindfull of his honour deare,
Then of the grievous smart, which him did wring,
From loathèd soile he can him lightly reare,
And strove to loose the farre infixèd sting:
Which when in vaine he tryde with struggeling,
Inflamed with wrath, his raging blade he heft,
And strooke so strongly, that the knotty string
Of his huge taile he quite a sunder cleft,
Five joynts thereof he hewd, and but the stump him left.

322. molten mettall, metal that had been forged. **embrew,** plunge. **330. buxome,** bending, unresisting. **335. intended,** outstretched. **337. behot,** held out hope for. **345. can,** "gan."

40

Hart cannot thinke, what outrage, and what cryes,
With foule enfouldred smoake and flashing fire,
The hell-bred beast threw forth unto the skyes,
That all was coverèd with darknesse dire:
Then fraught with rancour, and engorgèd ire,
He cast at once him to avenge for all,
And gathering up himselfe out of the mire,
With his uneven wings did fiercely fall
Upon his sunne-bright shield, and gript it fast withall.

41

Much was the man encombred with his hold,
In feare to lose his weapon in his paw,
Ne wist yet, how his talants to unfold;
Nor harder was from *Cerberus* greedie jaw
To plucke a bone, then from his cruell claw
To reave by strength the gripèd gage away:
Thrise he assayd it from his foot to draw,
And thrise in vaine to draw it did assay,
It booted nought to thinke, to robbe him of his pray.

42

Tho when he saw no power might prevaile,
His trustie sword he cald to his last aid,
Wherewith he fiercely did his foe assaile,
And double blowes about him stoutly laid,
That glauncing fire out of the yron plaid;
As sparckles from the Andvile use to fly,
When heavie hammers on the wedge are swaid;
Therewith at last he forst him to unty
One of his grasping feete, him to defend thereby.

43

The other foot, fast fixèd on his shield,
Whenas no strength, nor stroks mote him constraine
To loose, ne yet the warlike pledge to yield,
He smot thereat with all his might and maine,
That nought so wondrous puissance might sustaine;
Upon the joynt the lucky steele did light,
And made such way, that hewd it quite in twaine;
The paw yet missèd not his minisht might,
But hong still on the shield, as it at first was pight.

44

For griefe thereof, and divelish despight,
From his infernall fournace forth he threw
Huge flames, that dimmèd all the heavens light,

353. enfouldred, like a thunderstorm. **363. talants,** claws. **366. reave,** take.

Enrold in duskish smoke and brimstone blew;
As burning *Aetna* from his boyling stew
Doth belch out flames, and rockes in peeces broke,
And ragged ribs of mountaines molten new,
Enwrapt in coleblacke clouds and filthy smoke,
That all the land with stench, and heaven with horrour choke.

45

The heate whereof, and harmefull pestilence
So sore him noyd, that forst him to retire
A little backward for his best defence,
To save his bodie from the scorching fire,
Which he from hellish entrailes did expire.
It chaunst (eternall God that chaunce did guide)
As he recoylèd backward, in the mire
His nigh forwearied feeble feet did slide,
And downe he fell, with dread of shame sore terrifide.

46

There grew a goodly tree him faire beside,
Loaden with fruit and apples rosie red,
As they in pure vermilion had beene dide,
Whereof great vertues over all were red:
For happie life to all, which thereon fed,
And life eke everlasting did befall:
Great God it planted in that blessèd sted
With his almightie hand, and did it call
The tree of life, the crime of our first fathers fall.

47

In all the world like was not to be found,
Save in that soile, where all good things did grow,
And freely sprong out of the fruitfull ground,
As incorrupted Nature did them sow,
Till that dread Dragon all did overthrow.
Another like faire tree eke grew thereby,
Whereof who so did eat, eftsoones did know
Both good and ill: O mournefull memory:
That tree through one mans fault hath doen us all to dy.

48

From that first tree forth flowd, as from a well,
A trickling streame of Balme, most soveraine
And daintie deare, which on the ground still fell,
And overflowêd all the fertill plaine,
As it had deawèd bene with timely raine:
Life and long health that gratious ointment gave,
And deadly woundes could heale, and reare againe
The senselesse corse appointed for the grave.
Into that same he fell: which did from death him save.

49

For nigh thereto the ever damnèd beast
Durst not approch, for he was deadly made,
And all that life preservèd, did detest:
Yet he it oft adventured to invade.
By this the drouping day-light gan to fade,
And yeeld his roome to sad succeeding night,
Who with her sable mantle gan to shade
The face of earth, and wayes of living wight;
And high her burning torch set up in heaven bright.

50

When gentle *Una* saw the second fall
Of her deare knight, who wearie of long fight,
And faint through losse of bloud, moved not at all,
But lay as in a dreame of deepe delight,
Besmeard with pretious Balme, whose vertuous might
Did heale his wounds, and scorching heat alay,
Againe she stricken was with sore affright,
And for his safetie gan devoutly pray;
And watch the noyous night, and wait for joyous day.

51

The joyous day gan early to appeare,
And faire *Aurora* from the deawy bed
Of aged *Tithone* gan her selfe to reare,
With rosie cheekes, for shame as blushing red;
Her golden lockes for haste were loosely shed
About her eares, when *Una* her did marke
Clymbe to her charet, all with flowers spred,
From heaven high to chase the chearelesse darke;
With merry note her loud salutes the mounting larke.

52

Then freshly up arose the doughtie knight,
All healèd of his hurts and woundès wide,
And did himselfe to battell readie dight;
Whose early foe awaiting him beside
To have devourd, so soone as day he spyde,
When now he saw himselfe so freshly reare,
As if late fight had nought him damnifyde,
He woxe dismayd, and gan his fate to feare;
Nathlesse with wonted rage he him advauncèd neare.

409. red, perceived. **412. sted,** place. **426. deare, rare,** very costly.

441. torch, the moon. **467. woxe,** waxed, grew.

53

And in his first encounter, gaping wide,
He thought attonce him to have swallowd quight,
And rusht upon him with outragious pride;
Who him r'encountring fierce, as hauke in flight,
Perforce rebutted backe. The weapon bright
Taking advantage of his open jaw,
Ran through his mouth with so importune might,
That deepe emperst his darksome hollow maw,
And back retyrd, his life bloud forth with all did draw.

54

So downe he fell, and forth his life did breath,
That vanisht into smoke and cloudès swift;
So downe he fell, that th' earth him underneath
Did grone, as feeble so great load to lift;
So downe he fell, as an huge rockie clift,
Whose false foundation waves have washt away,
With dreadfull poyse is from the mayneland rift,
And rolling downe, great *Neptune* doth dismay;
So downe he fell, and like an heapèd mountaine lay.

55

The knight himselfe even trembled at his fall,
So huge and horrible a masse it seemed;
And his deare Ladie, that beheld it all,
Durst not approch for dred, which she misdeemed,
But yet at last, when as the direfull feend
She saw not stirre, off-shaking vaine affright,
She nigher drew, and saw that joyous end:
Then God she praysd, and thankt her faithfull knight,
That had atchieved so great a conquest by his might.

Canto XII

Faire Una to the Redcrosse knight
betrouthèd is with joy:
Though false Duessa it to barre
her false sleights doe imploy.

1

Behold I see the haven nigh at hand,
To which I meane my wearie course to bend;
Vere the maine shete, and beare up with the land,
The which afore is fairely to be kend,
And seemeth safe from stormes, that may offend;
There this faire virgin wearie of her way
Must landed be, now at her journeyes end:
There eke my feeble barke a while may stay,
Till merry wind and weather call her thence away.

2

Scarsely had *Phoebus* in the glooming East
Yet harnessèd his firie-footed teeme,
Ne reard above the earth his flaming creast,
When the last deadly smoke aloft did steeme,
That signe of last outbreathèd life did seeme
Unto the watchman on the castle wall;
Who thereby dead that balefull Beast did deeme,
And to his Lord and Ladie lowd gan call,
To tell, how he had seene the Dragons fatall fall.

3

Uprose with hastie joy, and feeble speed
That agèd Sire, the Lord of all that land,
And lookèd forth, to weet, if true indeede
Those tydings were, as he did understand,
Which whenas true by tryall he out fond,
He bad to open wyde his brazen gate,
Which long time had bene shut, and out of hond
Proclaymèd joy and peace through all his state;
For dead now was their foe, which them forrayèd late.

4

Then gan triumphant Trompets sound on hie,
That sent to heaven the ecchoèd report
Of their new joy, and happie victorie
Gainst him, that had them long opprest with tort
And fast imprisonèd in siegèd fort.
Then all the people, as in solemne feast,
To him assembled with one full consort,
Rejoycing at the fall of that great beast,
From whose eternall bondage now they were releast.

5

Forth came that auncient Lord and agèd Queene,
Arayd in antique robes downe to the ground,
And sad habiliments right well beseene;
A noble crew about them waited round
Of sage and sober Peres, all gravely gownd;
Whom farre before did march a goodly band
Of tall young men, all hable armes to sownd,
But now they laurell braunches bore in hand;
Glad signe of victorie and peace in all their land.

6

Unto that doughtie Conquerour they came,
And him before themselves prostrating low,

477. **retyrd,** withdrawn. 484. **poyse,** crash. 490. **misdeemed,** was mistaken about.

31. **tort,** wrong. 39. **sad habiliments right well beseene,** sober clothing, appropriate to their condition. 43. **armes to sownd,** to clash arms, hence to wage battle.

Their Lord and Patrone loud did him proclame,
And at his feet their laurell boughes did throw.
Soone after them all dauncing on a row
The comely virgins came, with girlands dight,
As fresh as flowres in medow greene do grow,
When morning deaw upon their leaves doth light:
And in their hands sweet Timbrels all upheld on hight.

7

And them before, the fry of children young
Their wanton sports and childish mirth did play,
And to the Maydens sounding tymbrels sung
In well attunèd notes, a joyous lay,
And made delightfull musicke all the way,
Untill they came, where that faire virgin stood;
As faire *Diana* in fresh sommers day
Beholds her Nymphes, enraunged in shadie wood,
Some wrestle, some do run, some bathe in christall flood.

8

So she beheld those maydens meriment
With chearefull vew; who when to her they came,
Themselves to ground with gratious humblesse bent,
And her adored by honourable name,
Lifting to heaven her everlasting fame:
Then on her head they set a girland greene,
And crownèd her twixt earnest and twixt game;
Who in her selfe-resemblance well beseene,
Did seeme such, as she was, a goodly maiden Queene.

9

And after, all the raskall many ran,
Heapèd together in rude rablement,
To see the face of that victorious man:
Whom all admirèd, as from heaven sent,
And gazd upon with gaping wonderment.
But when they came, where that dead Dragon lay,
Stretcht on the ground in monstrous large extent,
The sight with idle feare did them dismay,
Ne durst approch him nigh, to touch, or once assay.

10

Some feard, and fled; some feard and well it faynd;
One that would wiser seeme, then all the rest,
Warnd him not touch, for yet perhaps remaynd
Some lingring life within his hollow brest,
Or in his wombe might lurke some hidden nest
Of many Dragonets, his fruitfull seed;
Another said, that in his eyes did rest
Yet sparckling fire, and bad thereof take heed;
Another said, he saw him move his eyes indeed.

11

One mother, when as her foolehardie chyld
Did come too neare, and with his talants play,
Halfe dead through feare, her litle babe revyld,
And to her gossips gan in counsell say;
How can I tell, but that his talants may
Yet scratch my sonne, or rend his tender hand?
So diversly themselves in vaine they fray;
Whiles some more bold, to measure him nigh stand,
To prove how many acres he did spread of land.

12

Thus flockèd all the folke him round about,
The whiles that hoarie king, with all his traine,
Being arrivèd, where that champion stout
After his foes defeasance did remaine,
Him goodly greetes, and faire does entertaine,
With princely gifts of yvorie and gold,
And thousand thankes him yeelds for all his paine.
Then when his daughter deare he does behold,
Her dearely doth imbrace, and kisseth manifold.

13

And after to his Pallace he them brings,
With shaumes, and trompets, and with Clarions sweet;
And all the way the joyous people sings,
And with their garments strowes the pavèd street:
Whence mounting up, they find purveyance meet
Of all, that royall Princes court became,
And all the floore was underneath their feet
Bespred with costly scarlot of great name,
On which they lowly sit, and fitting purpose frame.

14

What needs me tell their feast and goodly guize,
In which was nothing riotous nor vaine?
What needs of daintie dishes to devize,
Of comely services, or courtly trayne?
My narrow leaves cannot in them containe
The large discourse of royall Princes state.

71. **selfe-resemblance well beseene,** that is, being crowned, she now resembled her real self. 73. **raskall many,** the common crowd.

92. **talants,** claws. 110. **shaumes,** wind instruments made of a double reed pipe set in a round mouthpiece. 116. **scarlot of great name,** noted or costly scarlet cloth.

Yet was their manner then but bare and plaine:
For th' antique world excesse and pride did hate;
Such proud luxurious pompe is swollen up but late.

15

Then when with meates and drinkes of every kinde
Their fervent appetites they quenchèd had,
That auncient Lord gan fit occasion finde,
Of straunge adventures, and of perils sad,
Which in his travell him befallen had,
For to demaund of his renowmèd guest:
Who then with utt'rance grave, and count'nance sad,
From point to point, as is before exprest,
Discourst his voyage long, according his request.

16

Great pleasure mixt with pittifull regard,
That godly King and Queene did passionate,
Whiles they his pittifull adventures heard,
That oft they did lament his lucklesse state,
And often blame the too importune fate,
That heapd on him so many wrathfull wreakes:
For never gentle knight, as he of late,
So tossèd was in fortunes cruell freakes;
And all the while salt teares bedeawd the hearers cheaks.

17

Then said that royall Pere in sober wise;
Deare Sonne, great beene the evils, which ye bore
From first to last in your late enterprise,
That I note, whether prayse, or pitty more:
For never living man, I weene, so sore
In sea of deadly daungers was distrest;
But since now safe ye seisèd have the shore,
And well arrivèd are, (high God be blest)
Let us devize of ease and everlasting rest.

18

Ah dearest Lord, said then that doughty knight,
Of ease or rest I may not yet devize;
For by the faith, which I to armes have plight,
I bounden am streight after this emprize,
As that your daughter can ye well advize,
Backe to returne to that great Faerie Queene,
And her to serve six yeares in warlike wize,
Gainst that proud Paynim king, that workes her teene:
Therefore I ought crave pardon, till I there have beene.

137. passionate, express sympathetically. **148. note,** do not know. **151. seisèd,** reached, got possession of. **161. teene,** sorrow.

19

Unhappie falles that hard necessitie,
(Quoth he) the troubler of my happie peace,
And vowèd foe of my felicitie;
Ne I against the same can justly preace:
But since that band ye cannot now release,
Nor doen undo; (for vowes may not be vaine)
Soone as the terme of those six yeares shall cease,
Ye then shall hither backe returne againe,
The marriage to accomplish vowd betwixt you twain.

20

Which for my part I covet to performe,
In sort as through the world I did proclame,
That who so kild that monster most deforme,
And him in hardy battaile overcame,
Should have mine onely daughter to his Dame,
And of my kingdome heire apparaunt bee:
Therefore since now to thee perteines the same,
By dew desert of noble chevalree,
Both daughter and eke kingdome, lo I yield to thee.

21

Then forth he callèd that his daughter faire,
The fairest *Un'* his onely daughter deare,
His onely daughter, and his onely heyre;
Who forth proceeding with sad sober cheare,
As bright as doth the morning starre appeare
Out of the East, with flaming lockes bedight,
To tell that dawning day is drawing neare,
And to the world does bring long wishèd light;
So faire and fresh that Lady shewd her selfe in sight.

22

So faire and fresh, as freshest flowre in May;
For she had layd her mournefull stole aside,
And widow-like sad wimple throwne away,
Wherewith her heavenly beautie she did hide,
Whiles on her wearie journey she did ride;
And on her now a garment she did weare,
All lilly white, withoutten spot, or pride,
That seemd like silke and silver woven neare,
But neither silke nor silver therein did appeare.

23

The blazing brightnesse of her beauties beame,
And glorious light of her sunshyny face
To tell, were as to strive against the streame.
My ragged rimes are all too rude and bace,

173. In sort as, according as. **192. wimple,** the pleated veil (see Canto I, l. 31). **196. pride,** decoration. **197. woven neare,** close-woven.

Her heavenly lineaments for to enchace.
Ne wonder; for her owne deare lovèd knight,
All were she dayly with himselfe in place,
Did wonder much at her celestiall sight:
Oft had he seene her faire, but never so faire dight.

24

So fairely dight, when she in presence came,
She to her Sire made humble reverence,
And bowèd low, that her right well became,
And added grace unto her excellence:
Who with great wisedome, and grave eloquence
Thus gan to say. But eare he thus had said,
With flying speede, and seeming great pretence,
Came running in, much like a man dismaid,
A Messenger with letters, which his message said.

25

All in the open hall amazèd stood,
At suddeinnesse of that unwarie sight,
And wondred at his breathlesse hastie mood.
But he for nought would stay his passage right
Till fast before the king he did alight;
Where falling flat, great humblesse he did make,
And kist the ground, whereon his foot was pight;
Then to his hands that writ he did betake,
Which he disclosing, red thus, as the paper spake.

26

To thee, most mighty king of *Eden* faire,
Her greeting sends in these sad lines addrest,
The wofull daughter, and forsaken heire
Of that great Emperour of all the West;
And bids thee be advizèd for the best,
Ere thou thy daughter linck in holy band
Of wedlocke to that new unknowen guest:
For he already plighted his right hand
Unto another love, and to another land.

27

To me sad mayd, or rather widow sad,
He was affiauncèd long time before,
And sacred pledges he both gave, and had,
False erraunt knight, infamous, and forswore:
Witnesse the burning Altars, which he swore,
And guiltie heavens of his bold perjury,
Which though he hath polluted oft of yore,
Yet I to them for judgement just do fly,
And them conjure t' avenge this shamefull injury.

203. enchace, serve as setting to. **214. pretence,** importance. **218. unwarie,** unexpected. **220. passage right,** going straight on. **221. fast,** close. **225. disclosing,** unfolding. **229. Emperour of all the West,** the Pope. **240. guiltie heavens of,** heavens polluted by.

28

Therefore since mine he is, or free or bond,
Or false or trew, or living or else dead,
Withhold, O soveraine Prince, your hasty hond
From knitting league with him, I you aread;
Ne weene my right with strength adowne to tread,
Through weakenesse of my widowhed, or woe:
For truth is strong, her rightfull cause to plead,
And shall find friends, if need requireth soe,
So bids thee well to fare, Thy neither friend, nor foe, *Fidessa.*

29

When he these bitter byting words had red,
The tydings straunge did him abashèd make,
That still he sate long time astonishèd
As in great muse, ne word to creature spake.
At last his solemne silence thus he brake,
With doubtfull eyes fast fixèd on his guest;
Redoubted knight, that for mine onely sake
Thy life and honour late adventurest,
Let nought be hid from me, that ought to be exprest.

30

What meane these bloudy vowes, and idle threats,
Throwne out from womanish impatient mind?
What heavens? what altars? what enragèd heates
Here heapèd up with termes of love unkind,
My conscience cleare with guilty bands would bind?
High God be witnesse, that I guiltlesse ame.
But if your selfe, Sir knight, ye faultie find,
Or wrappèd be in loves of former Dame,
With crime do not it cover, but disclose the same.

31

To whom the *Redcrosse* knight this answere sent,
My Lord, my King, be nought hereat dismayd,
Till well ye wote by grave intendiment,
What woman, and wherefore doth me upbrayd
With breach of love, and loyalty betrayd.
It was in my mishaps, as hitherward
I lately traveild, that unwares I strayd
Out of my way, through perils straunge and hard;
That day should faile me, ere I had them all declard.

32

There did I find, or rather I was found
Of this false woman, that *Fidessa* hight,

252. well to fare, farewell. **Fidessa,** Duessa, the false enchantress.

Fidessa hight the falsest Dame on ground,
Most false *Duessa*, royall richly dight,
That easie was t' invegle weaker sight:
Who by her wicked arts, and wylie skill,
Too false and strong for earthly skill or might,
Unwares me wrought unto her wicked will,
And to my foe betrayd, when least I fearèd ill.

33

Then steppèd forth the goodly royall Mayd,
And on the ground her selfe prostrating low,
With sober countenaunce thus to him sayd;
O pardon me, my soveraigne Lord, to show
The secret treasons, which of late I know
To have bene wroght by that false sorceresse.
She onely she it is, that earst did throw
This gentle knight into so great distresse,
That death him did awaite in dayly wretchednesse.

34

And now it seemes, that she subornèd hath
This craftie messenger with letters vaine,
To worke new woe and improvided scath,
By breaking of the band betwixt us twaine;
Wherein she usèd hath the practicke paine
Of this false footman, clokt with simplenesse,
Whom if ye please for to discover plaine,
Ye shall him *Archimago* find, I ghesse,
The falsest man alive; who tries shall find no lesse.

35

The king was greatly movèd at her speach,
And all with suddein indignation fraight,
Bad on that Messenger rude hands to reach.
Eftsoones the Gard, which on his state did wait,
Attacht that faitor false, and bound him strait:
Who seeming sorely chauffèd at his band,
As chainèd Beare, whom cruell dogs do bait,
With idle force did faine them to withstand,
And often semblaunce made to scape out of their hand.

36

But they him layd full low in dungeon deepe,
And bound him hand and foote with yron chains.
And with continuall watch did warely keepe;
Who then would thinke, that by his subtile trains
He could escape fowle death or deadly paines?
Thus when that Princes wrath was pacifide,
He gan renew the late forbidden banes,
And to the knight his daughter deare he tyde,
With sacred rites and vowes for ever to abyde.

37

His owne two hands the holy knots did knit,
That none but death for ever can devide;
His owne two hands, for such a turne most fit,
The housling fire did kindle and provide,
And holy water thereon sprinckled wide;
At which the bushy Teade a groome did light,
And sacred lampe in secret chamber hide,
Where it should not be quenchèd day nor night,
For feare of evill fates, but burnen ever bright.

38

Then gan they sprinckle all the posts with wine,
And made great feast to solemnize that day;
They all perfumde with frankencense divine,
And precious odours fetcht from far away,
That all the house did sweat with great aray:
And all the while sweete Musicke did apply
Her curious skill, the warbling notes to play,
To drive away the dull Melancholy;
The whiles one sung a song of love and jollity.

39

During the which there was an heavenly noise
Heard sound through all the Pallace pleasantly,
Like as it had bene many an Angels voice,
Singing before th' eternall majesty,
In their trinall triplicities on hye;
Yet wist no creature, whence that heavenly sweet
Proceeded, yet each one felt secretly
Himselfe thereby reft of his sences meet,
And ravishèd with rare impression in his sprite.

40

Great joy was made that day of young and old,
And solemne feast proclaimd throughout the land,
That their exceeding merth may not be told:
Suffice it heare by signes to understand
The usuall joyes at knitting of loves band.
Thrise happy man the knight himselfe did hold,
Possessèd of his Ladies hart and hand,
And ever, when his eye did her behold,
His heart did seeme to melt in pleasures manifold.

292. pardon me, give me leave. **300. improvided scath,** unexpected harm. **302. practicke paine,** artful pains or clever trick. **311. faitor,** impostor. **322. banes,** banns.

328. housling, purifying. **330. Teade.** See note 27, page 221. **347. trinall triplicities,** the thrice threefold hierarchy of Angels, first systematized by Dionysius the Areopagite.

41

Her joyous presence and sweet company
  In full content he there did long enjoy,
  Ne wicked envie, ne vile gealosy
  His deare delights were able to annoy:
  Yet swimming in that sea of blisfull joy,
  He nought forgot, how he whilome had sworne,
  In case he could that monstrous beast destroy,
  Unto his Farie Queene backe to returne:
The which he shortly did, and *Una* left to mourne.

42

Now strike your sailes ye jolly Mariners,
  For we be come unto a quiet rode,
  Where we must land some of our passengers,
  And light this wearie vessell of her lode.
  Here she a while may make her safe abode,
  Till she repairèd have her tackles spent,
  And wants supplide. And then againe abroad
  On the long voyage whereto she is bent:
Well may she speede and fairely finish her intent.

PROTHALAMION

Spenser wrote *Prothalamion* ("a song sung before a wedding") in honor of the double marriage of the Lady Elizabeth and the Lady Katherine Somerset, daughters of the Earl of Worcester, in 1596. The poem describes their ceremonial visit, in barges up the Thames, to Essex House, where they were joined by their prospective husbands. The ladies are described as two white swans. The stanza-form is suggestive of the elaborate and intricate stanza-form which he invented for his own wedding-hymn, the *Epithalamion*, although it is not so irregular as that of the earlier poem. The two wedding-hymns are unexcelled in English for felicity of rhyme and for beauty and variety of verbal music and imagery.

1

Calme was the day, and through the trembling ayre
Sweete breathing Zephyrus did softly play,
A gentle spirit, that lightly did delay
Hot Titans beames, which then did glyster fayre:
When I, whom sullein care,
Through discontent of my long fruitlesse stay
In princes court, and expectation vayne
Of idle hopes, which still doe fly away,
Like empty shaddowes, did aflict my brayne,
Walkt forth to ease my payne
Along the shoare of silver streaming Themmes;
Whose rutty bancke, the which his river hemmes,
Was paynted all with variable flowers,
And all the meades adornd with daintie gemmes,
Fit to decke maydens bowres,
And crowne their paramours,
Against the brydale day, which is not long:
  Sweete Themmes, runne softly, till I end my song.

2

There, in a meadow, by the rivers side,
A flocke of nymphes I chauncèd to espy,
All lovely daughters of the flood thereby,
With goodly greenish locks all loose untyde,
As each had bene a bryde:
And each one had a little wicker basket,
Made of fine twigs entraylèd curiously,
In which they gathered flowers to fill their flasket;
And with fine fingers cropt full feateously
The tender stalkes on hye.
Of every sort, which in that meadow grew,
They gathered some; the violet pallid blew,
The little dazie, that at evening closes,
The virgin lillie, and the primrose trew,
With store of vermeil roses,
To decke their bridegromes posies
Against the brydale day, which was not long:
  Sweete Themmes, runne softly, till I end my song.

3

With that I saw two swannes of goodly hewe
Come softly swimming downe along the lee;
Two fairer birds I yet did never see:
The snow which doth the top of Pindus strew
Did never whiter shew;
Nor Jove himselfe, when he a swan would be
For love of Leda, whiter did appeare:
Yet Leda was, they say, as white as he,
Yet not so white as these, nor nothing neare;
So purely white they were,
That even the gentle streame, the which them bare,
Seem'd foule to them, and bad his billowes spare
To wet their silken feathers, least they might
Soyle their fayre plumes with water not so fayre,
And marre their beauties bright,
That shone as heavens light,
Against their brydale day, which was not long:
  Sweete Themmes, runne softly, till I end my song.

Stanza 42. **371. rode,** roadway, harbor. **375. spent,** worn out. *Prothalamion.* **2. Zephyrus,** the west wind. **4. Titans,** the sun's. **12. rutty,** rooty.

13. variable, various. **17. long,** far distant. **26. flasket,** a long, shallow basket. **27. feateously,** deftly. **38. lee,** surface of the stream. **40. Pindus,** a mountain in Greece.

4

Eftsoones the nymphes, which now had flowers their fill,
Ran all in haste to see that silver brood,
As they came floating on the christal flood;
Whom when they sawe, they stood amazèd still,
Their wondring eyes to fill.
Them seem'd they never saw a sight so fayre,
Of fowles so lovely, that they sure did deeme
Them heavenly borne, or to be that same payre
Which through the skie draw Venus silver teeme;
For sure they did not seeme
To be begot of any earthly seede,
But rather angels or of angels breede:
Yet were they bred of Somers-heat, they say,
In sweetest season, when each flower and weede
The earth did fresh aray;
So fresh they seem'd as day,
Even as their brydale day, which was not long:
Sweete Themmes, runne softly, till I end my song.

5

Then forth they all out of their baskets drew
Great store of flowers, the honour of the field,
That to the sense did fragrant odours yeild,
All which upon those goodly birds they threw,
And all the waves did strew,
That like old Peneus waters they did seeme,
When downe along by pleasant Tempes shore,
Scattred with flowres, through Thessaly they streeme,
That they appeare, through lillies plenteous store,
Like a brydes chamber flore.
Two of those nymphes, meane while, two garlands bound
Of freshest flowres which in that mead they found,
The which presenting all in trim array,
Their snowie foreheads therewithall they crownd,
Whil'st one did sing this lay,
Prepar'd against that day,
Against their brydale day, which was not long:
Sweete Themmes, runne softly, till I end my song.

6

"Ye gentle birdes, the worlds faire ornament,
And heavens glorie, whom this happie hower
Doth leade unto your lovers blissfull bower,
Joy may you have and gentle hearts content
Of your loves couplement:
And let faire Venus, that is Queene of Love,
With her heart-quelling sonne upon you smile,
Whose smile, they say, hath vertue to remove
All loves dislike, and friendships faultie guile
For ever to assoile.
Let endlesse peace your steadfast hearts accord,
And blessèd plentie wait upon your bord;
And let your bed with pleasures chast abound,
That fruitfull issue may to you afford,
Which may your foes confound,
And make your joyes redound,
Upon your brydale day, which is not long:
Sweete Themmes, run softlie, till I end my song."

7

So ended she; and all the rest around
To her redoubled that her undersong,
Which said, their bridale daye should not be long.
And gentle Eccho from the neighbour ground
Their accents did resound.
So forth those joyous birdes did passe along,
Adowne the lee, that to them murmurde low,
As he would speake, but that he lackt a tong,
Yeat did by signes his glad affection show,
Making his streame run slow.
And all the foule which in his flood did dwell
Gan flock about these twaine, that did excell
The rest so far as Cynthia doth shend
The lesser starres. So they, enrangèd well,
Did on those two attend,
And their best service lend,
Against their wedding day, which was not long:
Sweete Themmes, run softly, til I end my song.

8

At length they all to mery London came,
To mery London, my most kyndly nurse,
That to me gave this lifes first native sourse;
Though from another place I take my name,
An house of auncient fame.
There when they came, whereas those bricky towres,
The which on Themmes brode agèd backe doe ryde,
Where now the studious lawyers have their bowers,
There whylome wont the Templer Knights to byde,
Till they decayd through pride:
Next whereunto there standes a stately place,
Where oft I gaynèd giftes and goodly grace

55. Eftsoones, presently. **67. Somers-heat,** a pun on "Somerset," the family name of the ladies. **78. Peneus,** a river in Thessaly.

110. redoubled, re-echoed. **121. Cynthia,** Diana, the goddess of the moon. **130. another place,** Lancashire. **134. Where . . . lawyers,** the Temple, formerly the abode of the Knights Templars. In Spenser's time, as now, it was the residence of students of the Common Law. **137. a stately place,** the palace of the Earl of Essex (see l. 145), but formerly the residence of Spenser's patron, the Earl of Leicester (see l. 139).

Of that great lord which therein wont to dwell,
Whose want too well now feeles my freendles case:
But ah! here fits not well
Olde woes, but joyes to tell
Against the bridale daye, which is not long:
  Sweet Themmes, runne softly, till I end my song.

9

Yet therein now doth lodge a noble peer,
Great Englands glory and the worlds wide wonder,
Whose dreadfull name late through all Spaine did thunder,
And Hercules two pillors standing neere
Did make to quake and feare.
Faire branch of honor, flower of chevalrie,
That fillest England with thy triumphes fame,
Joy have thou of thy noble victorie,
And endlesse happinesse of thine owne name
That promiseth the same:
That through thy prowesse and victorious armes,
Thy country may be freed from forraine harmes;
And great Elisaes glorious name may ring
Through al the world, fil'd with thy wide alarmes,
Which some brave Muse may sing
To ages following,
Upon the brydale day, which is not long:
  Sweete Themmes, runne softly, till I end my song.

10

From those high towers this noble lord issuing,
Like radiant Hesper when his golden hayre
In th' ocean billowes he hath bathèd fayre,
Descended to the rivers open vewing,
With a great traine ensuing.
Above the rest were goodly to bee seene
Two gentle knights of lovely face and feature,
Beseeming well the bower of anie queene,
With gifts of wit and ornaments of nature,
Fit for so goodly stature:
That like the twins of Jove they seem'd in sight,
Which decke the bauldricke of the heavens bright.
They two, forth pacing to the rivers side,
Received those two faire brides, their loves delight,
Which, at th' appointed tyde,
Each one did make his bryde,
Against their brydale day, which is not long:
  Sweet Themmes, runne softly, till I end my song.

Sir Walter Ralegh

c. 1552–1618

Sir Walter Ralegh, though not so attractive a character as Sir Philip Sidney, is an even more typical Renaissance courtier and adventurer. His life was longer than Sidney's, and it was marked by greater extremities of good and ill fortune. "Most lofty, insolent, and passionate" are the epithets applied to his verse by Puttenham in the *Art of English Poetry*, 1589, and the adjectives fit his personality even better than they describe his poetry. Unscrupulously ambitious, violent of temper, intellectually audacious, Ralegh is perhaps best remembered as the first Englishman to be stirred imaginatively by the New World and by the possibility of colonizing it.

Ralegh was born in Devonshire about 1552 of a well-connected family that was rising in the world. He seems to have attended Oriel College, Oxford, for a brief period. He served as a volunteer with the Huguenot armies in 1569, and in 1578, with Sir Humphrey Gilbert, his half-brother, he fitted out a fleet ostensibly for purposes of discovery but actually for preying on Spanish shipping. His ship's motto was, characteristically, "*Nec mortem peto, nec finem fugio*,"—"I neither seek death nor flee the end." In 1580, he took part in a military expedition to Ireland, and put to death six hundred Spaniards who fell into his hands. He owed his introduction to court to the influence of the Earl of Leicester, an early favorite of Elizabeth's and the uncle of Sir Philip Sidney. Ralegh's person—tall, dark, handsome, vigorous—made a deep impression on the Queen, and she lavished so many honors on him that he

146. Great Englands glory. The Earl of Essex had just returned, in August, 1596, from his brilliant expedition against Cadiz, in Spain. **148. Hercules two pillors,** the rocks at the Straits of Gibraltar. **153–54. thine owne name . . . the same,** apparently a pun on Essex's family name "Devereux" (*heureux* = happy, or *devenir heureux* = to become happy). **157. Elisaes,** Queen Elizabeth's.

159. brave, illustrious. **164. Hesper,** the evening star. **173. the twins of Jove,** Castor and Pollux, the sons of Zeus and Leda (see ll. 42, 43). After their death Zeus placed them among the stars as the constellation Gemini (the Twins). **174. bauldricke,** belt; the Zodiac. **177. tyde,** time.

rapidly became one of the wealthiest of her courtiers. Although the Queen refused to give him permission to lead voyages of discovery in person, he sent out an expedition which took possession of an immense tract on the Atlantic seaboard, to which the Queen, with some self-flattery, gave the name Virginia. Ralegh was knighted in 1585 and was made warden of the mines of Cornwall and Devon and Lord Lieutenant of Cornwall. In 1586, he was made captain of the Queen's guard, and given an estate of forty thousand acres in Ireland. In the late eighties, he invested £40,000 in three expeditions to colonize Virginia. The efforts failed completely; possibly the most important results were the introduction of potatoes and tobacco in England; of tobacco, Ralegh became one of the first enthusiastic smokers.

In the youthful Earl of Essex, Ralegh found an unscrupulous rival for royal favors, and although the Queen was pleased when a Ralegh expedition captured a Spanish carrack with a cargo of gold worth £500,000 sterling, she was infuriated when she discovered that Ralegh, while addressing poems of adulation to her, had been intriguing with a maid of honor named Elizabeth Throgmorton, and imprisoned them both. She released Ralegh only after she had taken unto herself the larger share of the carrack's spoils. After Ralegh's marriage to his mistress and their settlement at his estate at Sherborne, he seems to have entered into a close association with some of the most advanced thinkers of the day, including Thomas Hariot the deist and Christopher Marlowe, who was suspected of atheism. Although Ralegh's religious views were probably orthodox, the heretical reputation of "Ralegh's School of Atheism" led to an official investigation. Ralegh believed that untold wealth was to be gained if he could find the legendary city of Eldorado, and in 1595 he sailed with an expedition which made its way for about four hundred miles up the Orinoco, but brought back only a cargo of rumors and of "false-gold." He wrote and published in 1596 an account of his venture under the title *Discovery of the Empire of Guiana*. For a time he was reconciled with both the Queen and Essex, and took part in a naval foray that ended with the capture of Fayal, in the Azores. In 1600, he was made governor of the island of Jersey.

Rumors of Ralegh's opposition to James's claim to the throne had reached the King before the death of Elizabeth, and upon James's accession Ralegh was deprived of most of his offices, and in 1603 was sent to the Tower on suspicion of his complicity in a plot against the King's life. He received a most unfair trial, and was sentenced to death. The sentence was commuted to imprisonment, and most of the rest of Ralegh's life was spent with his family in the Tower. There, befriended by the brilliant young Prince Henry, he was encouraged to undertake his *History of the World*, the first part of which was published in 1614. Ralegh had not yet given up hopes of finding Eldorado, and he obtained his release from prison on condition that he should lead an expedition and bring back gold to England. The venture failed miserably, and, under the influence of the Spanish Ambassador, furious at the destruction of San Tomas, Trinidad, by one of Ralegh's captains, the King revived the old charge of conspiracy and had Ralegh executed on October 28, 1618.

Ralegh's reputation as a poet has long been obscured because, aside from a number of commendatory verses like "A Vision upon This Conceit of the Faerie Queene," his poems were published anonymously during his lifetime. The process of accumulating and identifying them has been slow and hazardous, and the results are by no means certain. The longest of Ralegh's poems is the fragment of "The Ocean to Cynthia," a long poem of adulation addressed to the Queen. The extant version is probably later than the one read in 1589 by Ralegh to Spenser, who had already bestowed on him the epithet Shepherd of the Ocean. Ralegh appears most attractively in his lyrics. They are not in the conventional style and mood of most Elizabethan lyrics; instead, they are free in form and show a sardonic and embittered spirit which may have resulted from the author's own experience of human capriciousness and ingratitude.

Ralegh's major prose works are his brief narrative of the last epoch-making fight of the *Revenge*, 1591; his *Discovery of Guiana*, 1596; and his *History of the World*, 1614. Ralegh shows little skill in organizing his material, and his digressions are likely to be more interesting than the sweep of his narrative. But his style, although frequently syntactically obscure, is spontaneous and free from the conceits cultivated by Sidney and Lyly, and the apostrophe to Death from the *History* is justly famous:

"O eloquent, just and mighty death, whom none could advise, thou hast persuaded; what none hath presumed, thou hast done; and whom all the world hath flattered, thou hast cast out of the world and despised: thou hast drawn together all the extravagant greatness, all the pride, cruelty and ambition of man, and covered all over with two narrow words: *Hic jacet.*" [1]

[1] **Hic jacet.**" "Here lies—" usual first words on a tombstone.

A VISION UPON THIS CONCEIT OF THE FAERIE QUEENE

This complimentary sonnet was written in honor of Spenser's *Faerie Queene* and first published with it.

Methought I saw the grave where Laura lay,
Within that temple where the vestal flame
Was wont to burn; and passing by that way
To see that buried dust of living fame,
Whose tomb fair Love and fairer Virtue kept,
All suddenly I saw the Fairy Queen;
At whose approach the soul of Petrarch wept,
And from thenceforth those graces were not seen,
For they this Queen attended; in whose stead
Oblivion laid him down on Laura's hearse.
Hereat the hardest stones were seen to bleed,
And groans of buried ghosts the heavens did pierce;
  Where Homer's sprite did tremble all for grief,
  And cursed th' access of that celestial thief.

THE NYMPH'S REPLY TO THE SHEPHERD

This is one of the many poetic answers to Marlowe's "The Passionate Shepherd."

If all the world and love were young,
And truth in every shepherd's tongue,
These pretty pleasures might me move
To live with thee and be thy love.

Time drives the flocks from field to fold
When rivers rage and rocks grow cold,
And Philomel becometh dumb;
The rest complains of cares to come.

The flowers do fade, and wanton fields
To wayward winter reckoning yields;
A honey tongue, a heart of gall,
Is fancy's spring, but sorrow's fall.

Thy gowns, thy shoes, thy beds of roses,
Thy cap, thy kirtle, and thy posies
Soon break, soon wither, soon forgotten,—
In folly ripe, in reason rotten.

Thy belt of straw and ivy buds,
Thy coral clasps and amber studs,
All these in me no means can move
To come to thee and be thy love.

But could youth last and love still breed,
Had joys no date nor age no need,
Then these delights my mind might move
To live with thee and be thy love.

THE LIE

Go, soul, the body's guest,
Upon a thankless arrant.
Fear not to touch the best;
The truth shall be thy warrant.
  Go, since I needs must die,
  And give the world the lie.

Say to the court, it glows
And shines like rotten wood;
Say to the church, it shows
What's good, and doth no good:
  If church and court reply,
  Then give them both the lie.

Tell potentates, they live
Acting by others' action,
Not loved unless they give,
Not strong but by affection:
  If potentates reply,
  Give potentates the lie.

Tell men of high condition
That manage the estate,
Their purpose is ambition,
Their practice only hate:
  And if they once reply,
  Then give them all the lie.

Tell them that brave it most,
They beg for more by spending,
Who, in their greatest cost,
Like nothing but commending:
  And if they make reply,
  Then give them all the lie.

Tell zeal it wants devotion;
Tell love it is but lust;
Tell time it meets but motion;
Tell flesh it is but dust:
  And wish them not reply,
  For thou must give the lie.

Tell age it daily wasteth;
Tell honour how it alters;
Tell beauty how she blasteth;
Tell favour how it falters:
  And as they shall reply,
  Give every one the lie.

2, arrant, errand. **16, affection,** in some MSS. "a faction."

Tell wit how much it wrangles
In tickle points of niceness;
Tell wisdom she entangles
Herself in over-wiseness:
And when they do reply,
Straight give them both the lie.

Tell physic of her boldness;
Tell skill it is prevention;
Tell charity of coldness;
Tell law it is contention:
And as they do reply,
So give them still the lie.

Tell fortune of her blindness;
Tell nature of decay;
Tell friendship of unkindness;
Tell justice of delay:
And if they will reply,
Then give them all the lie.

Tell arts they have no soundness,
But vary by esteeming;
Tell schools they want profoundness,
And stand too much on seeming:
If arts and schools reply,
Give arts and schools the lie.

Tell faith it's fled the city;
Tell how the country erreth;
Tell, manhood shakes off pity,
Tell, virtue least preferrèd:
And if they do reply,
Spare not to give the lie.

So when thou hast, as I
Commanded thee, done blabbing,
Because to give the lie
Deserves no less than stabbing,
Stab at thee he that will—
No stab thy soul can kill.

HIS PILGRIMAGE

Give me my scallop-shell of quiet,
My staff of faith to walk upon,
My scrip of joy, immortal diet,
My bottle of salvatïon,
My gown of glory, hope's true gage,
And thus I'll take my pilgrimage.

1. scallop-shell, worn by pilgrims as a badge. **3. scrip,** wallet.

Blood must be my body's balmer,
No other balm will there be given,
Whilst my soul like a white palmer
Travels to the land of heaven,
Over the silver mountains,
Where spring the nectar fountains;
And there I'll kiss
The bowl of bliss,
And drink my eternal fill
On every milken hill.
My soul will be a-dry before,
But after it will ne'er thirst more;
And by the happy blissful way
More peaceful pilgrims I shall see,
That have shook off their gowns of clay
And go appareled fresh like me.

I'll bring them first
To slake their thirst,
And then to taste those nectar suckets,
At the clear wells
Where sweetness dwells,
Drawn up by saints in crystal buckets.

And when our bottles and all we
Are filled with immortality,
Then the holy paths we'll travel,
Strewed with rubies thick as gravel,
Ceilings of diamonds, sapphire floors,
High walls of coral, and pearl bowers.

From thence to heaven's bribeless hall
Where no corrupted voices brawl,
No conscience molten into gold,
Nor forged accusers bought and sold,
No cause deferred, nor vain-spent journey,
For there Christ is the king's attorney,
Who pleads for all without degrees,
And he hath angels, but no fees.
When the grand twelve million jury
Of our sins and sinful fury,
'Gainst our souls black verdicts give,
Christ pleads his death, and then we live.
Be thou my speaker, taintless pleader,
Unblotted lawyer, true proceeder,
Thou movest salvation even for alms,
Not with a bribèd lawyer's palms.

And this is my eternal plea
To him that made heaven, earth, and sea,

7. balmer, embalmer. **25. suckets,** candied fruits. **35–50. From thence . . . lawyer's palms,** reference to the unjust trial of Ralegh in 1603 and the bitter denunciations of him by Sir Edward Coke, Attorney-General. **42. angels,** a pun on the gold coin, the angel.

Seeing my flesh must die so soon,
And want a head to dine next noon,
Just at the stroke when my veins start and spread,
Set on my soul an everlasting head.
Then am I ready, like a palmer fit,
To tread those blest paths which before I writ.

EVEN SUCH IS TIME

According to legend, this stanza was written by Ralegh on the night before his execution. As a matter of fact, a slightly different version had appeared as the final stanza of an earlier poem of thirty-six lines, describing the creation by Nature of a beautiful but heartless woman and the destruction by Time of her beauty, wit, and wantonness. The first stanza of the poem follows:

Nature, that washed her hands in milk,
And had forgot to dry them,
Instead of earth took snow and silk,
At love's request to try them,
If she a mistress could compose
To please love's fancy out of those.

Even such is time, that takes in trust
Our youth, our joys, our all we have,
And pays us but with earth and dust;
Who, in the dark and silent grave,
When we have wandered all our ways,
Shuts up the story of our days.
But from this earth, this grave, this dust,
My God shall raise me up, I trust!

Thomas Dekker

c. 1570–c. 1632

Though the facts of Thomas Dekker's life are unusually meager, his personality makes itself felt even in his hurried and frequently tasteless collaborations, his pamphleteering and hack writing, and no author of the period excels him in sweetness and fineness of spirit. The dates of both his birth and death are uncertain; 1570 is frequently given as the first, and 1632 or 1641 as the second. He may have been of Dutch stock, but his education was certainly scant, and his life not too fortunate. Like many another hack writer of his time, he seems to have spent various periods of his life in a debtor's prison. One of the earliest records concerning him reveals the shrewd illiterate theatrical manager, Philip Henslow, paying forty shillings to get Dekker out of the "Counter in the Poultry."

Dekker earned his uncertain living by writing plays, by collaborating with other playwrights, good and bad, and by producing miscellaneous prose pamphlets on whatever subject seemed at the moment likely to interest the purchasing public. He is best known as a playwright. Of the plays due to his hand alone, the most important are *Old Fortunatus*, acted in 1599, a dramatization of a German folk tale with many vestigial remains of the medieval drama; *The Shoemaker's Holiday*, acted in 1600, a most genial and sunny comic representation of the London life of citizens and apprentices; and *The Honest Whore*, of which the first part was acted in 1604, and the sequel in 1605. This pair of plays treats with insight and compassion the reformation of a prostitute, although contemporary audiences may have preferred the elementary farce of the subplots which disfigure the plays. Dekker's tenderness and compassion can be discerned in his collaboration with Philip Massinger in *The Virgin Martyr*, and with John Ford in *The Witch of Edmonton*. Dekker's plays are rather carelessly constructed, and his sense of humor is not impeccable, but the plays show a very winning combination of manly robustness and lyrical sweetness. Not the least of their attractions are the singularly pure and lucid and serene lyrics.

Dekker produced most of his prose pamphlets in the first decade of the seventeenth century. *The Wonderful Year*, 1603, is a painfully vivid description of London stricken by an epidemic. To the rogue literature, which Robert Greene had popularized in the nineties, Dekker contributed *The Seven Deadly Sins of London*, 1606; *The Belman of London*, 1608; and *News from Hell Brought by the Devil's Carrier*, 1606. His most famous prose work is *The Gull's Hornbook*, 1609.

from THE GULL'S HORNBOOK

The Gull's Hornbook is a very free adaptation of a sixteenth-century Latin poem by the German poet Frederick Dedekind. But the original Grobianus, a coarse, gross lout, is a very different figure from Dekker's affected, pretentious man about town. The type and the milieu are completely domesticated, and Dekker's little book gives us a vivid though ironical series of pictures of some of the absurder follies of his time.

The "gull" is a numskull, an ignorant, boorish person trying to acquire the manners and habits of a gentleman. A "hornbook" was a printed page containing the alphabet and simple words and protected by a thin sheet of horn. Dekker uses it to mean "primer."

In the portions of *The Gull's Hornbook* not printed here, Dekker dedicates the manual of courtesy to unmannerliness, and recommends it for the study of would-be gallants. He urges the gull not to rise before noon, to dispossess those around the fireplace, and, having toasted himself, to don his extravagant attire. He should then go to St. Paul's, where he can hide from his creditors, show off his clothes, and air his acquaintance with knights and squires. For the midday meal, he should choose the restaurant most frequented by gallants and, attaching himself to a company of them, he should talk loudly of his exploits as soldier, courtier, or poet. After gambling away his money, he may go to the latest play.

Chapter 6: HOW A GALLANT SHOULD BEHAVE HIMSELF IN A PLAY-HOUSE

THE theatre is your poets' Royal Exchange, upon which their muses (that are now turned to merchants) meeting, barter away that light commodity of words for a lighter ware than words, plaudities, and the breath of the great beast; which, like the threatenings of two cowards, vanish all into air. Players are their factors, who put away the stuff, and make the best of it they possibly can (as indeed 'tis their parts so to do). Your gallant, your courtier, and your captain had wont to be the soundest paymasters; and I think are still the surest chapmen; and these, by means that their heads are well stocked, deal upon this comical freight by the gross; when your groundling and gallery-commoner buys his sport by the penny and, like a haggler, is glad to utter it again by retailing.

Sithence then the place is so free in entertainment, allowing a stool as well to the farmer's son as to your templar; that your stinkard has the selfsame liberty to be there in his tobacco fumes, which your sweet courtier hath; and that your carman and tinker claim as strong a voice in their suffrage, and sit to give judgment on the play's life and death, as well as the proudest momus among the tribe of critic; it is fit that he, whom the most tailors' bills do make room for, when he comes, should not be basely (like a viol) cased up in a corner.

Whether therefore the gatherers of the public or private play-house stand to receive the afternoon's rent, let our gallant (having paid it) presently advance himself up to the throne of the stage. I mean not into the lord's room, which is now but the stage's suburbs; no, those boxes, by the iniquity of custom, conspiracy of waiting women and gentlemen ushers, that there sweat together, and the covetousness of sharers, are contemptibly thrust into the rear, and much new satin is there damned by being smothered to death in darkness. But on the very rushes where the comedy is to dance, yea, and under the state of Cambises himself, must our feathered estridge, like a piece of ordnance, be planted, valiantly (because impudently) beating down the mews and hisses of the opposed rascality.

For do but cast up a reckoning, what large comings-in are pursed up by sitting on the stage. First a conspicuous eminence is gotten; by which means the best and most essential parts of a gallant (good clothes, a proportionable leg, white hand, the Persian lock, and a tolerable beard) are perfectly revealed.

By sitting on the stage you have a signed patent to engross the whole commodity of censure; may lawfully presume to be a girder; and stand at the helm to steer the passage of scenes; yet no man shall once offer to hinder you from obtaining the title of an insolent, overweening coxcomb.

By sitting on the stage, you may, without travelling for it, at the very next door ask whose play it is; and, by that quest of inquiry, the law warrants you to avoid much mistaking; if you know not the author, you may rail against him; and peradventure so behave yourself that you may enforce the author to know you.

By sitting on the stage, if you be a knight you may happily get you a mistress; if a mere Fleet-street gentleman, a wife; but assure yourself, by continual residence, you are the first and principal man in election to begin the number of We Three.

By spreading your body on the stage, and by being a justice in examining of plays, you shall put yourself into such true scenical authority that some poet shall not dare to present his muse rudely upon your eyes, without having first unmasked her, rifled her, and discovered all her bare and most mystical parts before you at a tavern, when you most knightly shall, for his pains, pay for both their suppers.

By sitting on the stage, you may (with small cost) purchase the dear acquaintance of the boys; have a good stool for sixpence; at any time know what

27. plaudities, applause. **38. utter it,** put it into circulation. **41. templar,** a member of one of the Inns of Court. **46. momus,** a carping critic.

12. estridge, ostrich. **24. girder,** sneerer. **39. We Three,** an allusion to the picture of two boobies with the inscription, "We three, loggerheads be." The spectator supplies the third!

particular part any of the infants present; get your match lighted, examine the play-suits' lace, and perhaps win wagers upon laying 'tis copper, etc. And to conclude, whether you be a fool or a justice of peace, a cuckold or a captain, a lord-mayor's son or a dawcock, a knave or an under-sheriff; of what stamp soever you be, current or counterfeit, the stage, like time, will bring you to most perfect light and lay you open; neither are you to be hunted from thence, though the scarecrows in the yard hoot at you, hiss at you, spit at you, yea, throw dirt even in your teeth; 'tis most gentlemanlike patience to endure all this and to laugh at the silly animals; but if the rabble, with a full throat, cry, "Away with the fool," you were worse than a madman to tarry by it; for the gentleman and the fool should never sit on the stage together.

Marry, let this observation go hand in hand with the rest; or rather, like a country serving-man, some five yards before them. Present not yourself on the stage (especially at a new play) until the quaking Prologue hath (by rubbing) got colour into his cheeks, and is ready to give the trumpets their cue that he's upon point to enter; for then it is time, as though you were one of the properties or that you dropped out of the hangings, to creep from behind the arras, with your tripos or three-footed stool in one hand and a teston mounted between a fore-finger and a thumb in the other; for if you should bestow your person upon the vulgar when the belly of the house is but half full, your apparel is quite eaten up, the fashion lost, and the proportion of your body in more danger to be devoured than if it were served up in the Counter amongst the poultry; avoid that as you would the bastone. It shall crown you with rich commendation to laugh aloud in the midst of the most serious and saddest scene of the terriblest tragedy; and to let that clapper, your tongue, be tossed so high that all the house may ring of it. Your lords use it; your knights are apes to the lords, and do so too; your Inn-a-Court-man is zany to the knights, and (many, very scurvily) comes likewise limping after it; be thou a beagle to them all, and never lin snuffing, till you have scented them; for by talking and laughing (like a ploughman in a morris) you heap Pelion upon Ossa, glory upon glory; as first, all the eyes in the galleries will leave walking after the players and only follow you; the simplest dolt in the house snatches up your name, and when he meets you in the streets, or that you fall into his hands in the middle of a watch, his word shall be taken for you; he'll cry "He's such a gallant," and you pass. Secondly, you publish your temperance to the world, in that you seem not to resort thither to taste vain pleasures with a hungry appetite; but only as a gentleman to spend a foolish hour or two, because you can do nothing else; thirdly, you mightily disrelish the audience and disgrace the author; marry, you take up (though it be at the worst hand) a strong opinion of your own judgment, and enforce the poet to take pity of your weakness and, by some dedicated sonnet, to bring you into a better paradise only to stop your mouth.

If you can, either for love or money, provide yourself a lodging by the water side; for, above the convenience it brings to shun shoulder-clapping and to ship away your cockatrice betimes in the morning, it adds a kind of state unto you to be carried from thence to the stairs of your play-house; hate a sculler (remember that) worse than to be acquainted with one o' the scullery. No, your oars are your only sea-crabs, board them, and take heed you never go twice together with one pair; often shifting is a great credit to gentlemen; and that dividing of your fare will make the poor watersnakes be ready to pull you in pieces to enjoy your custom; no matter whether upon landing you have money or no; you may swim in twenty of their boats over the river upon ticket; marry, when silver comes in, remember to pay treble their fare, and it will make your flounder-catchers to send more thanks after you when you do not draw than when you do; for they know it will be their own another day.

Before the play begins, fall to cards; you may win or lose (as fencers do in a prize) and beat one another by confederacy, yet share the money when you meet at supper; notwithstanding, to gull the ragamuffins that stand aloof gaping at you, throw the cards (having first torn four or five of them) round about the stage, just upon the third sound, as though you had lost; it skills not if the four knaves lie on their backs, and outface the audience; there's none such fools as dare take exceptions at them, because, ere the play go off, better knaves than they will fall into the company.

Now, sir, if the writer be a fellow that hath either epigrammed you, or hath had a flirt at your mistress, or hath brought either your feather, or your red beard, or your little legs, etc., on the stage, you shall disgrace him worse than by tossing him in a blanket or giving him the bastinado in a tavern, if, in the middle of his play (be it pastoral or comedy,

6. dawcock, silly fellow. **28. teston,** a coin worth sixpence. **34. Counter,** a debtors' prison, where Dekker had been confined. **35. bastone,** a blow with a stick or cudgel. **41. zany,** buffoon. **44. lin,** stop.

17. cockatrice, mistress. **25. watersnakes,** river boatmen. **37. gull,** trick, cheat. **41. skills,** matters.

moral or tragedy) you rise with a screwed and discontented face from your stool to be gone; no matter whether the scenes be good or no; the better they are, the worse do you distaste them; and, being on your feet, sneak not away like a coward, but salute all your gentle acquaintance that are spread either on the rushes or on stools about you, and draw what troop you can from the stage after you. The mimics are beholden to you for allowing them elbow-room; their poet cries, perhaps, "A pox go with you," but care not you for that, there's no music without frets.

Marry, if either the company or indisposition of the weather bind you to sit it out, my counsel is then that you turn plain ape, take up a rush, and tickle the earnest ears of your fellow gallants, to make other fools fall a-laughing; mew at passionate speeches, blare at merry, find fault with the music, whew at the children's action, whistle at the songs; and above all, curse the sharers, that whereas the same day you had bestowed forty shillings on an embroidered felt and feather (Scotch-fashion) for your mistress in the court or your punk in the city, within two hours after you encounter with the very same block on the stage, when the haberdasher swore to you the impression was extant but that morning.

To conclude, hoard up the finest play-scraps you can get, upon which your lean wit may most savourly feed, for want of other stuff, when the Arcadian and Euphuized gentlewomen have their tongues sharpened to set upon you; that quality (next to your shuttlecock) is the only furniture to a courtier that's but a new beginner, and is but in his A B C of compliment. The next places that are filled, after the play-houses be emptied, are (or ought to be) taverns. Into a tavern then let us next march, where the brains of one hogshead must be beaten out to make up another.

ART THOU POOR?

This song, from Dekker's play, *Patient Grissill*, illustrates the playwright's skill in investing even poverty with a romantic aura. The theme was a favorite with poets of the period, but the lightly running music and warmth of tone are Dekker's.

Art thou poor, yet hast thou golden slumbers?
  Oh, sweet content!
 Art thou rich, yet is thy mind perplexed?
  Oh, punishment!
 Dost thou laugh to see how fools are vexed
 To add to golden numbers, golden numbers?
  Oh, sweet content, oh, sweet content.

 Work apace, apace, apace, apace;
 Honest labour bears a lovely face,
 Then hey noney, noney, hey noney, noney.

Canst drink the waters of the crispèd spring?
  Oh, sweet content!
 Swim'st thou in wealth, yet sink'st in thine own
   tears?
  Oh, punishment!
 Then he that patiently want's burden bears,
 No burden bears, but is a king, a king.
  Oh, sweet content, &c.

 Work apace, apace, &c.

Michael Drayton
1563–1631

Michael Drayton was born in Warwickshire in 1563, and was brought up as a page in the household of Sir Henry Goodere at Polesworth Castle on the river Anker on the borders of the Forest of Arden. He seems to have received his education from tutors in the courtly household, and probably did not go on to a university. He developed an early desire to be a poet, and during most of his long life he devoted himself to writing the kinds of poetry most popular at the time, while he subsisted on the favors of a series of noble patrons.

His first published work, *The Harmony of the Church*, 1591, was an unpromising series of Biblical paraphrases in primitive fourteen-line stanzas. For some reason it attracted the displeasure of the Archbishop of Canterbury, and it was ordered burned. A happier reception awaited his *Idea: The Shepherd's Garland*, 1593, nine eclogues inspired by the *Shepheardes Calender* of Spenser, who was to be the

20. sharers, the members of a theatrical company who shared in the risks and profits of the undertaking. **23. punk,** whore.

most important and persistent of poetical influences upon Drayton. In 1594, he contributed *Idea's Mirrour* to the sonnet sequences in vogue at the moment. The *Idea* of the title is derived from a French sequence by Claude de Pontoux; although it suggests the Platonic Idea of Beauty, it also represents Drayton's sublimated feelings for Anne, the younger daughter of his patron, with whom he remained on terms of warm friendship for years after her marriage.

In the late nineties, his relations with his patrons seem to have become strained, and he was forced to the distasteful task of hack writing for the stage. Before 1602, he had collaborated on at least thirty plays. He failed to find favor with King James, and expressed his disappointment in two indifferent satires, but under the patronage of Sir Walter Aston he returned to the writing of poetry. His *Poems Lyrical and Pastoral*, 1606, contained some of his most spirited odes. Drayton had long been meditating a major historical work, and in 1612 the first eighteen "songs" of his *Poly-Olbion* (Having Many Blessings) appeared, to be followed by twelve more in 1622. In this laborious and uncompleted enterprise he undertook a typographical survey of the British Isles, treating his subject allegorically with elaborate historical and legendary interludes. Some of his finest work was done in his old age, when he helped establish the fluent lucid Spenserianism of the period in *The Shepherd's Sirena*, 1627, and *The Muses' Elisium*, 1630. He died in 1631 and was buried in Westminster Abbey.

Francis Meres described Drayton as "a man of virtues of well-governed carriage, which is almost miraculous among good wits of this declining and corrupt time." He seems to have looked for his audience not in the sophisticated court, but among the more solid and serious elements of the minor nobility. His popularity is attested by the large number of editions in which his poems appeared during his lifetime. He was a scrupulous workman, and although on occasions—as in the *Poly-Olbion*—he seems to have been unfortunate in his choice of meter, in general he showed a great sensitivity to metrical forms, and he devoted a great deal of time to reworking his own poems, not always to their advantage. But Drayton was much more than a competent poet; he can be depended on to treat almost any form or type of poem with clarity, elegance, sweetness, and freshness. His poetic powers did not wane with the advance of age, and his latest poems, though diffuse, are more melodious than those of his youth. To the Spenserians of the early seventeenth century, he was a kind of mentor and exemplar. His fondness for the rhymed couplet sustained his reputation into the Restoration. For us, he is perhaps most significant as a representative poet of the period, a writer who reflects with clarity and grace the changing poetic modes of several literary generations.

from IDEA'S MIRROUR

Drayton's sonnets, published under the title *Idea's Mirrour*, differ from most of the sonnet sequences of the time in that they treat of a number of subjects that are not strictly amatory, and do not tell a very coherent story. Despite some Petrarchan elements, Drayton's sonnets are cool rather than impassioned. As the title suggests, they celebrate his beloved, not so much as a woman but as a manifestation of ideal beauty. The most colloquial and dramatic of his sonnets, beginning "Since there's no help, come let us kiss and part," was written long after the earliest of his sonnets was published.

1

Like an adventurous seafarer am I,
Who hath some long and dang'rous voyage been,
And called to tell of his discovery,
How far he sailed, what countries he had seen;
Proceeding from the port whence he put forth,
Shows by his compass how his course he steered,
When east, when west, when south, and when by north,
As how the pole to ev'ry place was reared,
What capes he doubled, of what continent,
The gulfs and straits that strangely he had passed,
Where most becalmed, where with foul weather spent,
And on what rocks in peril to be cast:
Thus in my love, time calls me to relate
My tedious travels and oft-varying fate.

6

How many paltry, foolish, painted things,
That now in coaches trouble ev'ry street,
Shall be forgotten, whom no poet sings,
Ere they be well wrapped in their winding sheet!
Where I to thee eternity shall give,
When nothing else remaineth of these days,
And queens hereafter shall be glad to live
Upon the alms of thy superfluous praise;
Virgins and matrons reading these my rhymes
Shall be so much delighted with thy story
That they shall grieve they lived not in these times,
To have seen thee, their sex's only glory.
So shalt thou fly above the vulgar throng,
Still to survive in my immortal song.

47

In pride of wit, when high desire of fame
Gave life and courage to my lab'ring pen,
And first the sound and virtue of my name
Won grace and credit in the ears of men;
With those the throngèd theatres that press
I in the circuit for the laurel strove,
Where the full praise, I freely must confess,
In heat of blood, a modest mind might move.
With shouts and claps at ev'ry little pause,
When the proud round on ev'ry side hath rung,
Sadly I sit, unmoved with the applause,
As though to me it nothing did belong.
  No public glory vainly I pursue,
  All that I seek is to eternize you.

53

Clear Anker, on whose silver-sanded shore
My soul-shrined saint, my fair Idea lies,
O blessed brook, whose milk-white swans adore
Thy crystal stream, refinèd by her eyes,
Where sweet myrrh-breathing Zephyr in the spring
Gently distils his nectar-dropping showers,
Where nightingales in Arden sit and sing
Amongst the dainty dew-empearlèd flowers;
Say thus, fair brook, when thou shalt see thy queen;
Lo, here thy shepherd spent his wand'ring years,
And in these shades, dear nymph, he oft hath been,
And here to thee he sacrificed his tears.
  Fair Arden, thou my Tempe art alone,
  And thou, sweet Anker, art my Helicon.

61

Since there's no help, come let us kiss and part;
Nay, I have done, you get no more of me,
And I am glad, yea glad with all my heart
That thus so cleanly I myself can free;
Shake hands for ever, cancel all our vows,
And when we meet at any time again,
Be it not seen in either of our brows
That we one jot of former love retain.
Now at the last gasp of love's latest breath,
When, his pulse failing, passion speechless lies,
When faith is kneeling by his bed of death,
And innocence is closing up his eyes,
  Now if thou wouldst, when all have given him over,
  From death to life thou mightst him yet recover.

AGINCOURT

In this poem Drayton sounds a poetic trumpet in honor of the victory won by the greatly outnumbered forces of King Henry V at Agincourt over the French on St. Crispin's Day, October 25, 1415. The invasion of France, undertaken by Henry as claimant to the French throne, supplied Shakespeare with the inspiration and the chief theme of his *King Henry V.* In this vigorous and colorful literary ballad the clash of swords and the cries of battle ring out, and the spirited rhythm of the quick iambic and trochaic accents suggests the resistless march of tramping feet.

Fair stood the wind for France,
When we our sails advance,
Nor now to prove our chance,
  Longer will tarry;
But putting to the main
At Kaux, the mouth of Seine,
With all his martial train,
  Landed King Harry.

And taking many a fort,
Furnished in warlike sort,
Marcheth towards Agincourt,
  In happy hour;
Skirmishing day by day
With those that stopped his way,
Where the French gen'ral lay
  With all his power.

Which in his height of pride,
King Henry to deride,
His ransom to provide
  To the King sending;
Which he neglects the while
As from a nation vile,
Yet with an angry smile
  Their fall portending.

And turning to his men,
Quoth our brave Henry then:
Though they to one be ten,
  Be not amazèd.
Yet have we well begun,
Battles so bravely won
Have ever to the sun
  By fame been raisèd.

And for myself, quoth he,
This my full rest shall be,
England ne'er mourn for me,
  Nor more esteem me;
Victor I will remain,

8. King Harry, Henry V. **17. Which,** the French general, D'Albret, Constable of France. **21. Which,** the demand for the ransom. **he,** the French general. **22. vile,** base, puny. **27. to one be ten.** The French army was actually only four times as large as the English. **34. rest,** resolution.

Or on this earth lie slain,
Never shall she sustain
  Loss to redeem me.

Poitiers and Crécy tell,
 When most their pride did swell,
Under our swords they fell;
  No less our skill is
Than when our grandsire great,
Claiming the regal seat
By many a warlike feat,
  Lopped the French lilies.

The Duke of York so dread
The eager vaward led;
With the main Henry sped
  Amongst his henchmen.
Excester had the rear,
O braver man not there,
O Lord, how hot they were
  On the false Frenchmen!

They now to fight are gone,
Armour on armour shone,
Drum now to drum did groan,
  To hear was wonder,
That with cries they make
The very earth did shake,
Trumpet to trumpet spake,
  Thunder to thunder.

Well it thine age became,
O noble Erpingham,
Which didst the signal aim
  To our hid forces;
When from a meadow by,
Like a storm suddenly,
The English archery
  Stuck the French horses.

With Spanish yew so strong,
Arrows a cloth-yard long,
That like to serpents stung,
  Piercing the weather;
None from his fellow starts,
But playing manly parts,
And like true English hearts,
  Stuck close together.

When down their bows they threw,
And forth their bilboes drew,
And on the French they flew,
  Not one was tardy;
Arms were from shoulders sent,
Scalps to the teeth were rent,
Down the French peasants went;
  Our men were hardy.

This while our noble King,
His broad sword brandishing,
Down the French host did ding,
  As to o'erwhelm it;
And many a deep wound lent,
His arms with blood besprent,
And many a cruel dent
  Bruisèd his helmet.

Gloster, that Duke so good,
Next of the royal blood,
For famous England stood
  With his brave brother;
Clarence, in steel so bright,
Though but a maiden knight,
Yet in that furious fight,
  Scarce such another.

Warwick in blood did wade,
Oxford the foe invade,
And cruel slaughter made,
  Still as they ran up;
Suffolk his axe did ply,
Beaumont and Willoughby
Bare them right doughtily,
  Ferrers and Fanhope.

Upon Saint Crispin's day
Fought was this noble fray,
Which fame did not delay
  To England to carry;
Oh, when shall English men
With such acts fill a pen,
Or England breed again
  Such a King Harry?

41. Poitiers and Crécy, battles in the Hundred Years' War, 1356 and 1346 respectively, won by the English over the French. **45. grandsire,** Edward III, great-grandfather of Henry V. **50. vaward,** van. **51. main,** main body of troops. **53. Excester,** Exeter. **73. Spanish yew,** of which the English long-bows and arrows were made. **76. weather,** atmosphere, air.

82. bilboes, swords (made at Balboa, Spain). **87. peasants,** here used derisively. **91. ding,** throw, beat. **97. Gloster,** Humphrey, Duke of Gloucester, brother to Henry V, but not senior to the Duke of Clarence, as Drayton's lines indicate. **100. brave brother,** Henry V. **102. maiden,** young, inexperienced.

William Shakespeare
1564–1616

Shakespeare was born on or about the twenty-third of April, 1564, at Stratford-on-Avon. His father was John Shakespeare, a fairly prosperous glover and a citizen of prominence in the little community; his mother, Mary Arden, was the daughter of a well-to-do landowner of Wilmcote. By 1577, however, his father's economic status was seriously impaired, and his civic prestige deteriorated. In all probability, the boy attended the grammar school in the village. So far as is known, he had no further formal education, although there is a tradition that he was for a time a schoolmaster in the country.

On November 28, 1582, he was married hurriedly to Anne Hathaway, eight years his senior. Their first child, Susanna, was born in May, 1583, and they became the parents of twins, Judith and Hamnet, in February, 1585. At about this time Shakespeare seems to have left Stratford in search of opportunities larger than the town offered for maintaining his family and restoring its social status. Before 1593, he had apparently attached himself to a London theatrical company, as an actor-apprentice, and then as a refurbisher of old plays. It is in the latter role that he was attacked by Robert Greene in his *Groatsworth of Wit* as "an upstart crow, beautified with our feathers, that with his Tiger's heart wrapt in a player's hide, supposes he is as well able to bombast out a blank verse as the best of you; and being an absolute Johannes Factotum, is in his own conceit the only Shake-scene in a country." Shakespeare's character was defended by Henry Chettle, and his fortunes mended rapidly. He began to compose plays of his own, and as a result of his earnings as actor, playwright, and a sharer in the company and later in the ownership of the Globe and Blackfriars theaters he encouraged his father to apply for the permission to bear a coat of arms in 1596, bought the second largest house in Stratford in 1597, and in the years to follow added considerably to his real-estate holdings in and around Stratford and in London. For almost twenty years, he produced an average of two plays a year for the brilliant company of which he was a part. But he seems to have been eager to live the part of a country gentleman, for which his restored fortunes had prepared him. He withdrew from dramatic activities early in the second decade of the century, and after a few years spent in retirement, died on April 23, 1616, and was buried in the Stratford church in which he had been baptized.

The incongruity between Shakespeare's hard-working existence and his conventional life ideal on the one hand, and the poetic force and imaginative range of his plays on the other, has encouraged some to believe that he was not the author of the plays ascribed to him. The incongruity can be resolved only by the hypothesis of a genius relatively unconscious of his powers, and certainly careless of the fate of his productions beyond their immediate success or failure.

Persons disappointed by the normality of Shakespeare's life have been unanimous as to the uniqueness of his genius. Shakespeare's dramatic poetry is incomparable; the variety and persuasiveness of his characterization are unparalleled in literature. Shakespeare was not an innovator in the sense that he struck out new forms or new ideas. He did what other playwrights were doing, wrote what the public of the time seemed to want. His distinction lies in the extent to which he outdistanced his rivals and exceeded the expectations of audiences of any period.

It is customary to divide Shakespeare's career as a writer into four periods. These were once regarded as reflecting his own emotional and intellectual history, but a wider study of the Elizabethan drama has made it clear that changes in the type and tone of his plays are the results of external conditions rather than inner promptings. The first period, extending from 1590 to 1596, is that during which he experimented with a number of kinds of comedy: classical in *The Comedy of Errors*, romantic in *The Two Gentlemen of Verona*, euphuistic in *Love's Labour's Lost* and with the history play in *Richard III*, and tragedy in *Romeo and Juliet*. This is also the period in which he wrote and published his erotic narratives, *Venus and Adonis*, 1593, and *The Rape of Lucrece*, 1594, and wrote a considerable number of the sonnets, which were not, however, published until 1609. The second period, running from 1596 to 1601, is that of the great history plays, *King Henry IV* (two parts) and *The Life of King Henry V*, and of the matchless trio of comedies, *Much Ado about Nothing*, *As You Like It*, and *Twelfth-Night*.

The third period, from 1601 to 1608, is that of the great tragedies, *Hamlet*, *King Lear*, and *Antony and Cleopatra*, and the "bitter" comedies, *All's Well That Ends Well* and *Measure for Measure*. The final period (1608 to 1610) is that of the romances, *Cymbeline*, *The Winter's Tale*, and *The Tempest*, but as late as 1613 he seems to have collaborated with his successor John Fletcher in *Henry VIII* and *The Two Noble Kinsmen*.

It is impossible to do more than suggest some of the reasons for Shakespeare's pre-eminence. The essential conventionality of his ideas and his unerring grasp of moral values have made his work palatable to even the censorious. The fullness and liveliness of his plots have ensured the effectiveness of his plays when produced before even uncultivated audiences. To more perceptive readers and auditors, he is first among playwrights in richness and range of characterization. Shakespeare's interpretations of the English kings, for example, make a far deeper impression upon the imagination than a dozen histories. His equal facility in the creation of both male and female characters has given enduring life to such manifold creatures of the imagination as Juliet and Cleopatra, Falstaff and Hamlet. Although, to judge by his titles, he seems to have taken the writing of comedy more casually than the creation of tragedy, he is unique among playwrights in being equally gifted in both the dramatic kinds. His depths are psychological rather than philosophical. His reading of the significance of human destiny is, and should be considered, an incidental and not a primary element in his great works.

from SONNETS

Shakespeare's *Sonnets* were first published in 1609, apparently without authorization by the poet. They were probably written at irregular intervals between the early 1590's and the opening years of the seventeenth century. Although they tell a more complicated story than that of any of the other sequences, that story is neither very clear nor conclusive. The characters involved are a poet, a young male friend, a dark lady, with whom the friend falls in love, and a rival poet. Scholars have naturally been interested in the possible autobiographical significance of the sequence, and countless attempts have been made to identify the characters. No identification has been established without question. One is on safe ground if he reads the *Sonnets* as a poetic narrative which, like other works of Shakespeare, may have borne a relationship, now obscure, to events in his own experience.

The *Sonnets* show a wide range of values. Many of the earlier ones seem little more than poetic finger exercises, rather monotonous variations on a single theme. Some of them, like Sonnet 130 given below, are satires on some aspect of the Petrarchan convention. The finer sonnets are superb expressions of the exaltations and agonies of romantic devotion. The greatest of them, like Sonnets 129 and 146, have a psychological realism, honesty, and depth unequaled in English poetry.

18

Shall I compare thee to a summer's day?
Thou art more lovely and more temperate:
Rough winds do shake the darling buds of May,
And summer's lease hath all too short a date:
Sometime too hot the eye of heaven shines,
And often is his gold complexion dimmed;
And every fair from fair sometime declines,
By chance, or nature's changing course untrimmed;
But thy eternal summer shall not fade,
Nor lose possession of that fair thou ow'st,
Nor shall death brag thou wander'st in his shade,
When in eternal lines to time thou grow'st;
So long as men can breathe, or eyes can see,
So long lives this, and this gives life to thee.

27

Weary with toil, I haste me to my bed,
The dear repose for limbs with travel tired;
But then begins a journey in my head
To work my mind, when body's work's expired:
For then my thoughts—from far where I abide—
Intend a zealous pilgrimage to thee,
And keep my drooping eyelids open wide,
Looking on darkness which the blind do see:
Save that my soul's imaginary sight
Presents thy shadow to my sightless view,
Which, like a jewel hung in ghastly night,
Makes black night beauteous and her old face new.
Lo! thus, by day my limbs, by night my mind,
For thee, and for myself no quiet find.

29

When in disgrace with fortune and men's eyes
I all alone beweep my outcast state,
And trouble deaf heaven with my bootless cries,
And look upon myself, and curse my fate,
Wishing me like to one more rich in hope,
Featured like him, like him with friends possessed,
Desiring this man's art, and that man's scope,
With what I most enjoy contented least;
Yet in these thoughts myself almost despising,

No. 18. **7. every fair from fair,** every beauty from its beauty. **8. untrimmed,** despoiled of its charm. **12. to time thou grow'st.** Thy fame will grow with the lapse of time. *No. 27.* **6. Intend,** bend or direct. **10. shadow,** image. *No. 29.* **6. like him, like him,** like a second man, like a third.

Haply I think on thee,—and then my state,
Like to the lark at break of day arising
From sullen earth, sings hymns at heaven's gate;
  For thy sweet love remembered such wealth brings
  That then I scorn to change my state with kings.

30

When to the sessions of sweet silent thought
I summon up remembrance of things past,
I sigh the lack of many a thing I sought,
And with old woes new wail my dear times' waste:
Then can I drown an eye, unused to flow,
For precious friends hid in death's dateless night,
And weep afresh love's long since cancelled woe,
And moan the expense of many a vanished sight:
Then can I grieve at grievances foregone,
And heavily from woe to woe tell o'er
The sad account of fore-bemoanèd moan,
Which I new pay as if not paid before.
  But if the while I think on thee, dear friend,
  All losses are restored and sorrows end.

33

Full many a glorious morning have I seen
Flatter the mountain-tops with sovereign eye,
Kissing with golden face the meadows green,
Gilding pale streams with heavenly alchemy;
Anon permit the basest clouds to ride
With ugly rack on his celestial face,
And from the forlorn world his visage hide,
Stealing unseen to west with this disgrace:
Even so my sun one early morn did shine,
With all-triumphant splendour on my brow;
But, out! alack! he was but one hour mine,
The region cloud hath masked him from me now.
  Yet him for this my love no whit disdaineth;
  Suns of the world may stain when heaven's sun staineth.

50

How heavy do I journey on the way,
When what I seek, my weary travel's end,
Doth teach that ease and that repose to say,
"Thus far the miles are measured from thy friend!"

No. 30. **1–2. sessions . . . summon,** a legal metaphor. **4. new,** anew. **6. dateless,** used in the legal sense of no fixed termination. **8. expense,** the passing away. **vanished sight,** former scene. **9. grievances foregone,** past distresses. *No. 33.* **2. sovereign eye,** eye of a king. **6. rack,** clouds driven by the wind. **8. disgrace,** disfigurement. **12. region cloud,** cloud in the upper air. **14. may stain,** be obscured. *No. 50.* **1. journey.** When a theatrical company was on tour, the leading actors traveled on horseback.

The beast that bears me, tired with my woe,
Plods dully on, to bear that weight in me,
As if by some instinct the wretch did know
His rider loved not speed, being made from thee:
The bloody spur cannot provoke him on
That sometimes anger thrusts into his hide,
Which heavily he answers with a groan
More sharp to me than spurring to his side;
  For that same groan doth put this in my mind:
  My grief lies onward, and my joy behind.

55

Not marble, nor the gilded monuments
Of princes, shall outlive this powerful rime;
But you shall shine more bright in these contents
Than unswept stone, besmeared with sluttish time.
When wasteful war shall statues overturn,
And broils root out the work of masonry,
Nor Mars his sword nor war's quick fire shall burn
The living record of your memory.
'Gainst death and all-oblivious enmity
Shall you pace forth; your praise shall still find room
Even in the eyes of all posterity
That wear this world out to the ending doom.
  So, till the judgment that yourself arise,
  You live in this, and dwell in lovers' eyes.

57

Being your slave, what should I do but tend
Upon the hours and times of your desire?
I have no precious time at all to spend,
Nor services to do, till you require.
Nor dare I chide the world-without-end hour
Whilst I, my sovereign, watch the clock for you,
Nor think the bitterness of absence sour
When you have bid your servant once adieu;
Nor dare I question with my jealous thought
Where you may be, or your affairs suppose,
But, like a sad slave, stay and think of nought,
Save, where you are how happy you make those.
  So true a fool is love that in your will,
  Though you do anything, he thinks no ill.

60

Like as the waves make towards the pebbled shore,
So do our minutes hasten to their end;
Each changing place with that which goes before,
In sequent toil all forwards do contend.

No. 55. **3. these contents,** what is contained in these verses of mine. **13. till the judgment that,** till the Judgment Day when. *No. 57.* **13. will,** possibly a pun, as elsewhere in the *Sonnets,* on Shakespeare's name. *No. 60.* **4. In sequent . . . contend,** toiling and following one after the other, all the waves push forward.

Nativity, once in the main of light,
Crawls to maturity, wherewith being crowned,
Crooked eclipses 'gainst his glory fight,
And Time that gave doth now his gift confound.
Time doth transfix the flourish set on youth
And delves the parallels in beauty's brow,
Feeds on the rarities of nature's truth,
And nothing stands but for his scythe to mow:
  And yet to times in hope my verse shall stand,
  Praising thy worth, despite his cruel hand.

64

When I have seen by Time's fell hand defaced
The rich-proud cost of outworn buried age;
When sometime lofty towers I see down-razed,
And brass eternal slave to mortal rage;
When I have seen the hungry ocean gain
Advantage on the kingdom of the shore,
And the firm soil win of the watery main,
Increasing store with loss, and loss with store;
When I have seen such interchange of state,
Or state itself confounded to decay;
Ruin hath taught me thus to ruminate—
That Time will come and take my love away.
  This thought is as a death, which cannot choose
  But weep to have that which it fears to lose.

66

Tired with all these, for restful death I cry
As to behold desèrt a beggar born,
And needy nothing trimmed in jollity,
And purest faith unhappily forsworn,
And gilded honour shamefully misplaced,
And maiden virtue rudely strumpeted,
And right perfection wrongfully disgraced,
And strength by limping sway disablèd,
And art made tongue-tied by authority,
And folly—doctor-like—controlling skill,
And simple truth miscalled simplicity,
And captive good attending captain ill:
  Tired with all these, from these would I be gone,
  Save that to die, I leave my love alone.

71

No longer mourn for me when I am dead
Than you shall hear the surly sullen bell
Give warning to the world that I am fled
From this vile world, with vilest worms to dwell:
Nay, if you read this line, remember not
The hand that writ it; for I love you so,
That I in your sweet thoughts would be forgot,
If thinking on me then should make you woe.
O! if, I say, you look upon this verse,
When I perhaps compounded am with clay,
Do not so much as my poor name rehearse,
But let your love even with my life decay;
  Lest the wise world should look into your moan,
  And mock you with me after I am gone.

73

That time of year thou may'st in me behold
When yellow leaves, or none, or few, do hang
Upon those boughs which shake against the cold,
Bare ruined choirs, where late the sweet birds sang.
In me thou see'st the twilight of such day
As after sunset fadeth in the west;
Which by and by black night doth take away,
Death's second self, that seals up all in rest.
In me thou see'st the glowing of such fire,
That on the ashes of his youth doth lie,
As the death-bed whereon it must expire
Consumed with that which it was nourished by.
  This thou perceiv'st, which makes thy love more strong,
  To love that well which thou must leave ere long.

87

Farewell! thou art too dear for my possessing,
And like enough thou know'st thy estimate:
The charter of thy worth gives thee releasing;
My bonds in thee are all determinate.
For how do I hold thee but by thy granting?
And for that riches where is my deserving?
The cause of this fair gift in me is wanting,
And so my patent back again is swerving.
Thyself thou gav'st, thy own worth then not knowing,

No. 60. **5. main,** sea. **7. Crooked,** malignant. **9. transfix the flourish,** transfigure (remove) the flowering beauty. **10. parallels,** wrinkles. **13. times in hope,** the hoped-for future. *No. 64.* **3. sometime,** once, formerly. **4. brass eternal slave,** i.e., eternal brass the slave. **8. store,** abundance. **9. state,** condition. **10. state itself,** stately splendor. **13. which,** i.e., the thought which. *No. 66.* **3. needy nothing trimmed in jollity,** empty vanity adorned with finery. **4. unhappily forsworn,** unfortunately deceived. **5. misplaced,** bestowed improperly. **8. disablèd,** made powerless. **11. simplicity,** foolishness.

No. 71. **13. wise,** used ironically as equivalent to "worldly-wise." *No. 73.* **12. Consumed . . . by,** choked by the ashes of the wood that sustained the flame. **14. leave,** renounce. *No. 87.* In this sonnet Shakespeare seems to be attempting the effect of the incessant feminine endings in sonnets written in Italian. **2. estimate,** worth. **3. The charter of thy worth,** the privilege your dignity gave you. **4. determinate,** outdated, one of the many legal terms in this sonnet. **8. my patent . . . swerving.** The love granted to me is now reverting to its original possessor. The phrase suggests a royal patent for a monopoly.

Or me, to whom thou gav'st it, else mistaking;
So thy great gift, upon misprision growing,
Comes home again, on better judgment making.
  Thus have I had thee, as a dream doth flatter,
  In sleep a king, but, waking, no such matter.

97

How like a winter hath my absence been
From thee, the pleasure of the fleeting year!
What freezings have I felt, what dark days seen!
What old December's bareness every where!
And yet this time removed was summer's time;
The teeming autumn, big with rich increase,
Bearing the wanton burden of the prime,
Like widowed wombs after their lords' decease:
Yet this abundant issue seemed to me
But hope of orphans and unfathered fruit;
For summer and his pleasures wait on thee,
And, thou away, the very birds are mute:
  Or, if they sing, 'tis with so dull a cheer,
  That leaves look pale, dreading the winter's near.

104

To me, fair friend, you never can be old,
For as you were when first your eye I eyed,
Such seems your beauty still. Three winters cold
Have from the forests shook three summers' pride,
Three beauteous springs to yellow autumn turned
In process of the seasons have I seen,
Three April perfumes in three hot Junes burned,
Since first I saw you fresh, which yet are green.
Ah! yet doth beauty, like a dial-hand,
Steal from his figure, and no pace perceived;
So your sweet hue, which methinks still doth stand,
Hath motion, and mine eye may be deceived:
  For fear of which, hear this, thou age unbred:
  Ere you were born was beauty's summer dead.

106

When in the chronicle of wasted time
I see descriptions of the fairest wights,
And beauty making beautiful old rime,
In praise of ladies dead and lovely knights,
Then, in the blazon of sweet beauty's best,
Of hand, of foot, of lip, of eye, of brow,
I see their antique pen would have expressed
Even such a beauty as you master now.
So all their praises are but prophecies
Of this our time, all you prefiguring;
And, for they looked but with divining eyes,
They had not skill enough your worth to sing:
  For we, which now behold these present days,
  Have eyes to wonder, but lack tongues to praise.

109

O, never say that I was false of heart,
Though absence seemed my flame to qualify.
As easy might I from myself depart
As from my soul, which in thy breast doth lie:
That is my home of love: if I have ranged,
Like him that travels, I return again;
Just to the time, not with the time exchanged,
So that myself bring water for my stain.
Never believe, though in my nature reigned
All frailties that besiege all kinds of blood,
That it could so preposterously be stained,
To leave for nothing all thy sum of good;
  For nothing this wide universe I call,
  Save thou, my rose; in it thou art my all.

116

Let me not to the marriage of true minds
Admit impediments. Love is not love
Which alters when it alteration finds,
Or bends with the remover to remove:
O, no! it is an ever-fixèd mark,
That looks on tempests and is never shaken;
It is the star to every wandering bark,
Whose worth's unknown, although his height be taken.
Love's not Time's fool, though rosy lips and cheeks
Within his bending sickle's compass come;
Love alters not with his brief hours and weeks,
But bears it out even to the edge of doom.
  If this be error, and upon me proved,
  I never writ, nor no man ever loved.

123

No, Time, thou shalt not boast that I do change:
Thy pyramids built up with newer might
To me are nothing novel, nothing strange;

11. upon misprision growing, arising out of an erroneous estimate. **12. on better judgment making,** as a result of a review of the case in a higher court. *No. 97.* **3. this time removed,** this time in which I was remote from thee. **7. the wanton burden of the prime,** the children of the wanton springtime. *No. 104.* **9. dial-hand,** hand of a watch. *No. 106.* **5. blazon,** description, with the connotation of encomium. **8. master,** are master of.

No. 109. **2. qualify,** moderate, lessen. **7. Just to the time,** punctually. **exchanged,** changed. **8. myself . . . stain,** bring justification of my alleged fault (of absence). **11. preposterously,** unnaturally. *No. 116.* **2. impediments,** a reference to the marriage service of the Church of England. The impediments not admitted by Shakespeare are change of circumstance and inconstancy. **4. bends . . . remove,** changes as the beloved changes, in situation or devotion. **8. Whose worth's unknown,** whose occult influence is not calculable. **height,** elevation. *No. 123.* **2. Thy pyramids,** any man-made creation that seems to defy change.

They are but dressings of a former sight.
Our dates are brief, and therefore we admire
What thou dost foist upon us that is old;
And rather make them born to our desire
Than think that we before have heard them told.
Thy registers and thee I both defy,
Not wondering at the present nor the past,
For thy recòrds and what we see doth lie,
Made more or less by thy continual haste.
  This I do vow, and this shall ever be;
  I will be true, despite thy scythe and thee.

129

The expense of spirit in a waste of shame
Is lust in action; and till action, lust
Is perjured, murderous, bloody, full of blame,
Savage, extreme, rude, cruel, not to trust;
Enjoyed no sooner but despisèd straight;
Past reason hunted; and no sooner had,
Past reason hated, as a swallowed bait,
On purpose laid to make the taker mad:
Mad in pursuit, and in possession so;
Had, having, and in quest to have, extreme;
A bliss in proof,—and proved, a very woe;
Before, a joy proposed; behind, a dream.
  All this the world well knows; yet none knows well
  To shun the heaven that leads men to this hell.

130

My mistress' eyes are nothing like the sun;
Coral is far more red than her lips' red:
If snow be white, why then her breasts are dun;
If hairs be wires, black wires grow on her head.
I have seen roses damasked, red and white,
But no such roses see I in her cheeks;
And in some perfumes is there more delight
Than in the breath that from my mistress reeks.
I love to hear her speak, yet well I know
That music hath a far more pleasing sound:
I grant I never saw a goddess go,—
My mistress, when she walks, treads on the ground:
  And yet, by heaven, I think my love as rare
  As any she belied with false compare.

No. 129. **1. expense,** expenditure. **4. not to trust,** treacherous. **9. Mad . . . so,** irrational in anticipation and after fulfillment. **11. in proof,** in the process of its being experienced. **proved,** experienced. **12. proposed,** in theory. *No. 130.* This sonnet satirizes the conventional blond beauty of the Petrarchan heroine. The deliberately unpleasant realism is an element in the satire. **4. If hairs be wires,** a reference to the trite comparison of golden hair to golden wires.

138

When my love swears that she is made of truth,
I do believe her, though I know she lies,
That she might think me some untutored youth,
Unlearnèd in the world's false subtleties.
Thus vainly thinking that she thinks me young,
Although she knows my days are past the best,
Simply I credit her false-speaking tongue:
On both sides thus is simple truth supprest.
But wherefore says she not she is unjust?
And wherefore say not I that I am old?
O! love's best habit is in seeming trust,
And age in love loves not to have years told:
  Therefore I lie with her, and she with me,
  And in our faults by lies we flattered be.

144

Two loves I have of comfort and despair,
Which like two spirits do suggest me still:
The better angel is a man right fair,
The worser spirit a woman, coloured ill.
To win me soon to hell, my female evil
Tempteth my better angel from my side,
And would corrupt my saint to be a devil,
Wooing his purity with her foul pride.
And whether that my angel be turned fiend
Suspect I may, but not directly tell;
But being both from me, both to each friend,
I guess one angel in another's hell:
  Yet this shall I ne'er know, but live in doubt,
  Till my bad angel fire my good one out.

146

Poor soul, the centre of my sinful earth,
Fooled by these rebel powers that thee array,
Why dost thou pine within and suffer dearth,
Painting thy outward walls so costly gay?
Why so large cost, having so short a lease,
Dost thou upon thy fading mansion spend?
Shall worms, inheritors of this excess,
Eat up thy charge? Is this thy body's end?
Then, soul, live thou upon thy servant's loss,
And let that pine to aggravate thy store;
Buy terms divine in selling hours of dross;
Within be fed, without be rich no more:

No. 138. **7. Simply,** like a simpleton. **9. unjust,** faithless. **11. habit,** deportment. **in seeming trust,** in pretending to be trusting. *No. 144.* The sonnet is built upon the metaphor of man's good and evil angels, represented as dramatis personae in Marlowe's *Faustus.* **2. suggest,** tempt. **11. both from me, both to each friend,** both away from me, each friendly to the other. *No. 146.* **2. these rebel powers,** the rebellious element in the flesh that is the garment of the soul. **10. aggravate,** increase. **11. terms divine,** eternity.

So shalt thou feed on Death, that feeds on men,
And Death once dead, there's no more dying then.

SONGS FROM SHAKESPEARE'S PLAYS

Considerations of space make it impossible to present here the text of a complete Shakespeare play. Well-annotated editions of his plays are, however, readily available. Since the reign of Elizabeth was the golden age of song in the drama, and since in Shakespeare song on the stage reached its greatest perfection, the lyrical genius of the greatest dramatist of the time, as well as the different effects he produced by song, may conveniently be illustrated by a selection of songs from his plays.

The songs serve various purposes in the plays. By combining with lyrical utterance the additional charms of the singing voice and instrumental accompaniment, they usually point up the tone of a scene or emphasize the mood of a character, as in the case of the two songs from *Twelfth Night*, or suggest a view of life akin to that of the play, as in *As You Like It*. More rarely, a song like "Tell Me Where Is Fancy Bred," from *The Merchant of Venice*, or "Full Fathom Five" from *The Tempest*, seems to have a direct bearing on the course of action. But each of Shakespeare's songs, apart from its dramatic context, is an expert evocation of theme, atmosphere, and mood.

For studies of Shakespeare's use of songs in his plays, see E. B. Reed, ed., *Songs from the British Drama*, Yale University Press, 1925, and J. R. Moore, *The Function of the Songs in Shakespeare's Plays*, University of Wisconsin Press, 1916.

WHEN DAISIES PIED

When daisies pied and violets blue
  And lady-smocks all silver-white
And cuckoo-buds of yellow hue
  Do paint the meadows with delight,
The cuckoo then, on every tree,
Mocks married men; for thus sings he,
    "Cuckoo!
Cuckoo, cuckoo!" Oh word of fear,
Unpleasing to a married ear!

When shepherds pipe on oaten straws,
  And merry larks are ploughmen's clocks,
When turtles tread, and rooks, and daws,
  And maidens bleach their summer smocks,
The cuckoo then, on every tree,
Mocks married men; for thus sings he,
    "Cuckoo!
Cuckoo, cuckoo!" Oh word of fear,
Unpleasing to a married ear!

WHEN ICICLES HANG BY THE WALL

When icicles hang by the wall,
  And Dick the shepherd blows his nail,
And Tom bears logs into the hall,
  And milk comes frozen home in pail,
When blood is nipped and ways be foul,
Then nightly sings the staring owl,
"Tu-whit, tu-who!" A merry note,
While greasy Joan doth keel the pot.

When all aloud the wind doth blow,
  And coughing drowns the parson's saw,
And birds sit brooding in the snow,
  And Marian's nose looks red and raw,
When roasted crabs hiss in the bowl,
Then nightly sings the staring owl,
"Tu-whit, tu-who!" A merry note,
While greasy Joan doth keel the pot.

WHO IS SILVIA?

Who is Silvia? What is she,
  That all our swains commend her?
Holy, fair, and wise is she;
  The heaven such grace did lend her.
That she might admirèd be.

Is she kind as she is fair?
  For beauty lives with kindness.
Love doth to her eyes repair,
  To help him of his blindness;
And, being helped, inhabits there.

Then to Silvia let us sing,
  That Silvia is excelling;
She excels each mortal thing
  Upon the dull earth dwelling.
To her let us garlands bring.

13. feed on Death, consume the mortal elements in yourself. **14. Death . . . then,** because the mortal has put on immortality. *When Daisies Pied.* This and the following song conclude Shakespeare's early comedy *Love's Labour's Lost.* They are both built on the same pattern, and in each song the mood is given piquancy by the introduction of an alien element, in one, the cuckoo, and in the other, the owl. **2. lady-smocks,** spring flowers of the cress family, sometimes called cuckoo flowers.

When Icicles Hang by the Wall. The accurate Dutch realism of this song is unusual with Shakespeare, most of whose songs are deliberately romantic in tone. **8. keel,** cool by stirring. **13. roasted crabs,** roasted crab apples, dropped into a bowl of spiced and sweetened ale. *Who Is Silvia?* This song from *Two Gentlemen of Verona* has been frequently set to music. Schubert's setting is probably the best known in modern times.

OVER HILL, OVER DALE

Over hill, over dale,
Thorough bush, thorough brier,
Over park, over pale,
Thorough flood, thorough fire,
I do wander every where,
Swifter than the moon's sphere;
And I serve the fairy queen,
To dew her orbs upon the green.
The cowslips tall her pensioners be;
In their gold coats spots you see,
Those be rubies, fairy favours,
In those freckles live their savours.
I must go seek some dewdrops here,
And hang a pearl in every cowslip's ear.

TELL ME WHERE IS FANCY BRED

Tell me where is fancy bred,
Or in the heart, or in the head?
How begot, how nourishèd?
Reply, reply.
It is engendr'èd in the eyes,
With gazing fed; and fancy dies
In the cradle where it lies.
Let us all ring fancy's knell;
I'll begin it—Ding, dong, bell.
Ding, dong, bell.

BLOW, BLOW, THOU WINTER WIND

Blow, blow, thou winter wind!
Thou art not so unkind
As man's ingratitude;
Thy tooth is not so keen,
Because thou art not seen,
Although thy breath be rude.

Heigh ho! sing, heigh ho! unto the green holly;
Most friendship is feigning, most loving mere folly.
Then, heigh ho, the holly!
This life is most jolly.

Freeze, freeze, thou bitter sky!
That dost not bite so nigh
As benefits forgot;
Though thou the waters warp,
Thy sting is not so sharp
As friend remembered not.

Heigh ho! sing, heigh ho! etc.

UNDER THE GREENWOOD TREE

Under the greenwood tree
Who loves to lie with me,
And turn his merry note
Unto the sweet bird's throat,
Come hither, come hither, come hither!
Here shall he see
No enemy
But winter and rough weather.

Who doth ambition shun,
And loves to live i' the sun,
Seeking the food he eats,
And pleased with what he gets,
Come hither, come hither, come hither!
Here shall he see
No enemy
But winter and rough weather.

COME AWAY, COME AWAY, DEATH

Come away, come away, death,
And in sad cypress let me be laid;
Fly away, fly away, breath;
I am slain by a fair cruel maid.
My shroud of white, stuck all with yew,
Oh, prepare it!
My part of death, no one so true
Did share it.

Not a flower, not a flower sweet,
On my black coffin let there be strown;
Not a friend, not a friend greet
My poor corpse, where my bones shall be thrown.

Over Hill, Over Dale. This song, from *A Midsummer Night's Dream,* is sung to Puck by one of the attendants of Titania, the queen of the fairies. **3. pale,** enclosed ground. **8. orbs,** rings in the greensward made by the dancing fairies. **9. pensioners,** probably a reference to Elizabeth's bodyguard of handsome young nobles. *Tell Me Where Is Fancy Bred.* Sung while Bassanio is making his choice in *The Merchant of Venice,* this song is probably intended to give him a hint as to the lucky casket. The number of words rhyming with lead is significant. **1. fancy,** love aroused by the senses rather than the heart. *Blow, Blow, Thou Winter Wind.* Sung at the request of the exiled Duke in *As You Like It,* this song contrasts the unkindness of man with the less biting unkindness of wintry nature.

Blow, Blow, Thou Winter Wind. **16. As friend remembered not,** as what an unremembered friend feels. *Under the Greenwood Tree.* In contrast to the cynicism of the preceding lyric, this second song from *As You Like It* stresses the carefree and idyllic life of the greenwood where they "fleet the time carelessly as they did in the golden world." The first line is an old ballad refrain. *Come Away, Come Away, Death.* Feste, the clown in *Twelfth-Night,* repeats this song at the request of the love-melancholy Duke, who says it is "old and plain . . . And dallies with the innocence of love, Like the old age." **2. cypress,** a coffin of cypress wood.

A thousand thousand sighs to save,
Lay me, oh, where
Sad true lover never find my grave,
To weep there!

O MISTRESS MINE

O mistress mine, where are you roaming?
O, stay and hear; your true love's coming,
That can sing both high and low.
Trip no further, pretty sweeting,
Journeys end in lovers meeting,
Every wise man's son doth know.

What is love? 'Tis not hereafter;
Present mirth hath present laughter;
What's to come is still unsure.
In delay there lies no plenty;
Then come kiss me, sweet and twenty,
Youth's a stuff will not endure.

SIGH NO MORE

Sigh no more, ladies, sigh no more;
Men were deceivers ever;
One foot in sea, and one on shore,
To one thing constant never.
Then sigh not so, but let them go,
And be you blithe and bonny,
Converting all your sounds of woe
Into "Hey nonny, nonny!"

Sing no more ditties, sing no moe
Of dumps so dull and heavy;
The fraud of men was ever so,
Since summer first was leavy.
Then sigh not so, but let them go,
And be you blithe and bonny,
Converting all your sounds of woe
Into "Hey nonny, nonny!"

TAKE, OH, TAKE THOSE LIPS AWAY

Take, oh, take those lips away,
That so sweetly were forsworn;
And those eyes, the break of day,
Lights that do mislead the morn.
But my kisses bring again,
Bring again;
Seals of love, but sealed in vain,
Sealed in vain.

HARK, HARK! THE LARK

Hark, hark! The lark at heaven's gate sings,
And Phoebus 'gins arise,
His steeds to water at those springs
On chaliced flowers that lies;
And winking Mary-buds begin
To ope their golden eyes.
With every thing that pretty is,
My lady sweet, arise!
Arise, arise!

FEAR NO MORE THE HEAT O' THE SUN

Fear no more the heat o' the sun,
Nor the furious winter's rages;
Thou thy worldly task hast done,
Home art gone, and ta'en thy wages.
Golden lads and girls all must,
As chimney-sweepers, come to dust.

Fear no more the frown o' the great;
Thou art past the tyrant's stroke;
Care no more to clothe and eat;
To thee the reed is as the oak.
The sceptre, learning, physic, must
All follow this, and come to dust.

Fear no more the lightning-flash,
Nor the all-dreaded thunder-stone;
Fear not slander, censure rash;
Thou hast finished joy and moan.
All lovers young, all lovers must
Consign to thee, and come to dust.

No exorciser harm thee!
Nor no witchcraft charm thee!
Ghost unlaid forbear thee!
Nothing ill come near thee!
Quiet consummation have;
And renownèd be thy grave!

O Mistress Mine. This song is sung by Feste in *Twelfth-Night* at the request of the revelers Sir Toby Belch and Sir Andrew Aguecheek, both of whom pride themselves on their own singing. *Sigh No More.* This is from *Much Ado About Nothing.* **9. moe,** more. **10. dumps,** mournful tunes. **12. leavy,** leafy. *Take, Oh, Take Those Lips Away.* Sung by Mariana's page in *Measure for Measure* and accompanied by her, this song expresses her unhappiness at being jilted by her lover, Angelo.

Take, Oh, Take Those Lips Away. **7. Seals of love,** written instruments under seal, a legal figure. *Hark, Hark! The Lark.* This song from *Cymbeline* is sung to Imogen, grieved at the exile of her husband, by a musician attendant on Cloten, who is attempting to woo her. **4. chaliced,** cup-shaped. **5. Mary-buds,** marigolds that open at sunrise and close at sunset. *Fear No More the Heat o' the Sun.* This pathetic rather than tragic song from *Cymbeline* is sung over Fidele (Imogen, disguised as a page) by her half-brothers, who have failed to identify her. **14. thunder-stone,** thunderbolt.

WHEN DAFFODILS BEGIN TO PEER

When daffodils begin to peer,
  With hey! the doxy over the dale,
Why, then comes in the sweet o' the year;
  For the red blood reigns in the winter's pale.

The white sheet bleaching on the hedge,
  With hey! the sweet birds, oh, how they sing!
Doth set my pugging tooth on edge;
  For a quart of ale is a dish for a king.

The lark, that tirra-lirra chants,
  With hey! with hey! the thrush and the jay,
Are summer songs for me and my aunts,
  While we lie tumbling in the hay.

FULL FATHOM FIVE

Full fathom five thy father lies.
    Of his bones are coral made;
Those are pearls that were his eyes;
    Nothing of him that doth fade
But doth suffer a sea-change
Into something rich and strange.
Sea-nymphs hourly ring his knell:
                Ding-dong!
Hark! now I hear them—Ding-dong, bell!

Elizabethan Lyrics

The sixteenth century was pre-eminently a singing era. In no other period in English history was the practice so universal or so esteemed. The incomparable distinction of the lyrics of the time is intimately dependent on the vogue of vocal music. To be able to carry a part was as indispensable a skill of the educated man or woman as the ability to read Latin or to compose verses. An anecdote from Henry Morley's *Plain and Easy Introduction to Practical Music*, 1597, illustrates the universality of this custom. "Supper being ended," he writes, "and music-books (according to the custom) being brought to the tables, the mistress of the house presented me with a part, earnestly requesting me to sing. But when, after many excuses I protested unfainedly that I could not, every one began to wonder. Yea, some whispered to others, demanding how I was brought up." Even the journeyman shoemaker, according to Thomas Deloney's *Gentle Craft*, 1598, had to be able "to sound the trumpet, or play upon the flute, and bear his part in a three man's song, and readily reckon up his tools in rhyme." And as late as 1622 Henry Peacham in *The Compleat Gentleman* could assert that one of the essential accomplishments of the educated man was the ability "to sing your part sure, at first sight, withal to play the same upon your viol or the exercise of your lute."

In the foregoing selections the reader has experienced the richness of Elizabethan lyrical poetry, the variety of which the following poems further illustrate.

The first and most famous of the miscellanies is that edited by Tottel, published in 1557, under the title *Songs and Sonnets*, but commonly known as *Tottel's Miscellany*. This collection is invaluable for its first printings of ninety-seven poems by Sir Thomas Wyatt and forty poems by Surrey. It ran into eight editions in thirty years, and was obviously a favorite of Shakespeare's Slender, who lamented, "I had rather than forty shillings I had my book of *Songs and Sonnets* here." Other famous miscellanies were Richard Edwards's *Paradise of Dainty Devices*, 1577; Thomas Proctor's *Gorgeous Gallery of Gallant Inventions*, 1578; *The Phoenix Nest*, 1593, which contained lyrics by Spenser, Sidney, Lodge, and Breton; and *England's Helicon*, 1600, the greatest of them all, since it not only drew on the earlier miscellanies but included some exquisite songs from plays, works of fiction, and the songbooks.

The lyrics which appear in the songbooks are treated in two distinct ways. The words may be adapted for singing as an air or as a madrigal. In the air, a solo voice sang the words, to the accompaniment of a lute, a lute and a viola da gamba, or a larger group of instruments, or on occasion by accompanying but subordinate voices. The madrigal, as described by John Hebel and H. H. Hudson in their collection *Poetry of the English Renaissance*, Crofts, 1936, was "an unaccompanied song of from three to six voice parts, to be sung by a small group

When Daffodils Begin to Peer. Sung by the rogue Autolycus in *The Winter's Tale*, this song is a fresh and earthy mixture of sensitivity and sensuality. **2. doxy,** thieves' slang for mistress. **4. pale,** a pun on "pallor" and "enclosure." **7. pugging,** thieving.

11. aunts, slang for mistresses. *Full Fathom Five*. This song, sung by Ariel to Ferdinand in the *Tempest*, suggests the supposed fate of Ferdinand's father in the storm with which the play begins. The lyric is a supreme illustration of the power of great poetry to make the unpleasant and abhorrent, in this case, death by drowning, beautiful and consoling.

of friends sitting around a table in a home or in the tavern. It differed from our part-song, for it was polyphonic. No one voice carried the melody with the others subordinated as an accompaniment, but all parts were of equal interest, often of the same melodic material, and the voices entered successively rather than simultaneously. The poem was treated in phrases, each several times repeated, and commonly overlapping in the different voices. With this repetition the true madrigal seldom used more than one stanza of six to ten lines." The finest musicians of England's most brilliant musical period—William Byrd, Thomas Campion, Orlando Gibbons, John Dowland—lavished their talents on song-writing.

Lyrics occur with considerable frequency in works of fiction in the pastoral mode, for the reason that the Continental pastoral literature most influential in England—Sannazaro's *Arcadia* and Montemayor's *Diana*—though in prose, was studded with pastoral lyrics. But it is in the plays of the period that many of the supreme lyrics first found their setting. The prominence of the lyric in the Elizabethan drama is due in very large part not only to the popularity of singing with all classes but also to the facts that the children's companies were made up of boys highly trained in vocal performance, and that the adult companies used for feminine roles and for pages' parts boys who had had identical or similar training. It is not always possible to be certain that the author of a given play is also the author of the songs introduced into that play, but there is a great probability that most of the exquisite songs in Shakespeare's plays are from his hand, and that such playwrights as Fletcher and Dekker wrote almost no lyrics except those incidental to their plays.

A NYMPH'S DISDAIN OF LOVE

Hey down, a down, did Dian sing,
  Amongst her virgins sitting,
Than love there is no vainer thing,
  For maidens most unfitting.
And so think I, with a down, down, derry.

When women knew no woe,
  But lived themselves to please,
Men's feigning guiles they did not know,
  The ground of their disease.
Unborn was false suspect,
  No thought of jealousy;
From wanton toys and fond affect
  The virgin's life was free.
    Hey down, a down, did Dian sing, &c.

At length men usèd charms;
  To which what maids gave ear,
Embracing gladly endless harms,
  Anon enthrallèd were.
Thus women welcomed woe
  Disguised in name of love;
A jealous hell, a painted show,
  So shall they find that prove.

Hey down, a down, did Dian sing,
  Amongst her virgins sitting,
Than love there is no vainer thing,
  For virgins most unfitting.
And so think I, with a down, down, derry.

A Nymph's Disdain. This song, taken from the finest of the Elizabethan anthologies, *England's Helicon*, is there signed "Ignoto," that is, "Anonymous."

BACK AND SIDE GO BARE, GO BARE

Back and side go bare, go bare,
  Both foot and hand go cold;
But, belly, God send thee good ale enough,
  Whether it be new or old.

I cannot eat but little meat,
  My stomach is not good;
But sure I think that I can drink
  With him that wears a hood.
Though I go bare, take ye no care,
  I am nothing a-cold;
I stuff my skin so full within
  Of jolly good ale and old.

Back and side go bare, go bare,
  Both foot and hand go cold;
But, belly, God send thee good ale enough,
  Whether it be new or old.

I love no roast but a nutbrown toast,
  And a crab laid in the fire;
A little bread shall do me stead,
  Much bread I not desire.
No frost nor snow, no wind, I trow,
  Can hurt me if I would,
I am so wrapped, and throughly lapped
  Of jolly good ale and old.

Back and side go bare, &c.

Back and Side Go Bare. This lusty drinking song is from the vigorous farce *Gammer Gurton's Needle*, usually ascribed to William Stevenson. The song, however, is probably much older than the play, and is therefore preferably called anonymous. **17. nutbrown toast,** toasted bread, dipped or floated in the beverage. **18. crab,** crab apple.

And Tib my wife, that as her life
Loveth well good ale to seek,
Full oft drinks she, till ye may see
The tears run down her cheek.
Then doth she troll to me the bowl,
Even as a maltworm should,
And saith, Sweetheart, I took my part
Of this jolly good ale and old.

Back and side go bare, &c.

Now let them drink, till they nod and wink,
Even as good fellows should do;
They shall not miss to have the bliss
Good ale doth bring men to;
And all poor souls that have scoured bowls
Or have them lustily trolled,
God save the lives of them and their wives,
Whether they be young or old.

Back and side go bare, &c.

THE PROMISE OF A CONSTANT LOVER

As laurel leaves that cease not to be green,
From parching sun, nor yet from winter's threat,
As hardened oak that fear'th no sword so keen,
As flint for tool in twain that will not fret,
As fast as rock or pillar surely set,—
Assurèdly whom I cannot forget,
For joy, for pain, for torment, nor for tene,
For loss, for gain, for frowning, nor for threat:
But ever one,—yea, both in calm and blast,
Your faithful friend, and will be to my last.

Richard Barnfield
1574–1627

IF MUSIC AND SWEET POETRY AGREE

If music and sweet poetry agree,
As they must needs (the sister and the brother),
Then must the love be great 'twixt thee and me,
Because thou lov'st the one, and I the other.
Dowland to thee is dear, whose heavenly touch
Upon the lute doth ravish human sense;
Spenser to me, whose deep conceit is such
As, passing all conceit, needs no defence.
Thou lov'st to hear the sweet melodious sound
That Phoebus' lute (the queen of music) makes;
And I in deep delight am chiefly drowned
Whenas himself to singing he betakes.
One god is god of both (as poets feign),
One knight loves both, and both in thee remain.

30. troll, circulate, pass around. **31. maltworm,** toper. *The Promise of a Constant Lover*. This anonymous poem is taken from Tottell's *Songs and Sonnets*, 1557. *If Music and Sweet Poetry Agree*. This sonnet by the minor poet Richard Barnfield first appeared in his *Poems in Divers Humours*, 1598.

Nicholas Breton
1545?–1626?

A PASTORAL OF PHILLIS AND CORYDON

On a hill there grows a flower,
Fair befall the dainty sweet!
By that flower there is a bower
Where the heavenly Muses meet.

In that bower there is a chair
Fringèd all about with gold,
Where doth sit the fairest fair
That did ever eye behold.

It is Phillis fair and bright,
She that is the shepherds' joy,
She that Venus did despite
And did blind her little boy.

This is she, the wise, the rich,
And the world desires to see;
This is *ipsa quae* the which
There is none but only she.

Who would not this face admire?
Who would not this saint adore?
Who would not this sight desire,
Though he thought to see no more?

O fair eyes, yet let me see!
One good look, and I am gone,
Look on me, for I am he—
Thy poor silly Corydon.

Thou that art the shepherds' queen,
Look upon thy silly swain;
By thy comfort have been seen
Dead men brought to life again.

A Pastoral of Phillis and Corydon. This charming lyric, which has in its first two stanzas the tone and manner of the folk song, was first published in *The Arbour of Amorous Devices* in 1597. **15. ipsa quae,** the very she, she herself.

Thomas Campion

1567–1620

NEVER LOVE UNLESS YOU CAN

Never love unless you can
Bear with all the faults of man;
Men sometimes will jealous be,
Though but little cause they see,
  And hang the head, as discontent,
  And speak what straight they will repent.

Men that but one saint adore
Make a show of love to more;
Beauty must be scorned in none,
Though but truly served in one;
  For what is courtship but disguise?
  True hearts may have dissembling eyes.

Men when their affairs require
Must a while themselves retire,
Sometimes hunt, and sometimes hawk,
And not ever sit and talk.
  If these and such like you can bear,
  Then like, and love, and never fear.

JACK AND JOAN

Jack and Joan they think no ill,
But loving live, and merry still;
Do their week-days' work and pray
Devoutly on the holy day;
Skip and trip it on the green,
And help to choose the summer queen;
Lash out, at a country feast,
Their silver penny with the best.
Well can they judge of nappy ale,
And tell at large a winter tale;
Climb up to the apple loft,
And turn the crabs till they be soft.
Tib is all the father's joy,
And little Tom the mother's boy.
All their pleasure is content,
And care, to pay their yearly rent.
Joan can call by name her cows,
And deck her windows with green boughs;
She can wreaths and tutties make,
And trim with plums a bridal cake.
Jack knows what brings gain or loss,
And his long flail can stoutly toss;
Make the hedge, which others break,
And ever thinks what he doth speak.
Now, you courtly dames and knights,
That study only strange delights,
Though you scorn the home-spun gray,
And revel in your rich array;
Though your tongues dissemble deep,
And can your heads from danger keep;
Yet for all your pomp and train,
Securer lives the silly swain.

ROSE-CHEEKED LAURA, COME

  Rose-cheeked Laura, come
Sing thou smoothly with thy beauties
Silent music, either other
    Sweetly gracing.

  Lovely forms do flow
From consent divinely framèd;
Heav'n is music, and thy beauty's
    Birth is heavenly.

  These dull notes we sing
Discords need for helps to grace them;
Only beauty purely loving
    Knows no discord,

  But still moves delight
Like clear springs renewed by flowing,
Ever perfect, ever in them—
    Selves eternal.

TO MUSIC BENT IS MY RETIRÈD MIND

To music bent is my retirèd mind,
  And fain would I some song of pleasure sing,
But in vain joys no comfort now I find;
  From heavenly thoughts all true delight doth spring.
Thy power, O God, thy mercies, to record,
Will sweeten every note and every word.

All earthly pomp or beauty to express,
  Is but to carve in snow, on waves to write.

Never Love Unless You Can. This serene but worldly wise lyric first appeared in the *Third and Fourth Book of Airs.* This and the seven following songs illustrate the range and perfection of the lyrical production of the finest of the poet-musicians of the period. **16. ever,** always. *Jack and Joan.* This song treats the conventional theme of the joys of the simple life in the manner of a folk song. It first appeared in Campion's *Two Books of Airs*, 1613(?). **7. Lash out,** lavish, squander. **9. nappy,** strong, heady.

19. tutties, nosegays, bouquets. *To Music Bent.* This song, which suggests the more spiritual side of Campion's lyricism, first appeared in his *Two Books of Airs.*

Celestial things, though men conceive them less,
Yet fullest are they in themselves of light;
Such beams they yield as know no means to die,
Such heat they cast as lifts the spirit high.

THE MAN OF LIFE UPRIGHT

The man of life upright,
Whose guiltless heart is free
From all dishonest deeds,
Or thought of vanity;

The man whose silent days
In harmless joys are spent,
Whom hopes cannot delude,
Nor sorrow discontent;

That man needs neither towers
Nor armour for defence,
Nor secret vaults to fly
From thunder's violence.

He only can behold
With unaffrighted eyes
The horrors of the deep
And terrors of the skies.

Thus, scorning all the cares
That fate or fortune brings,
He makes the heaven his book,
His wisdom heavenly things,

Good thoughts his only friends,
His wealth a well-spent age,
The earth his sober inn
And quiet pilgrimage.

WHEN TO HER LUTE CORINNA SINGS

When to her lute Corinna sings,
Her voice revives the leaden strings,
And doth in highest notes appear
As any challenged echo clear;
But when she doth of mourning speak,
Ev'n with her sighs the strings do break.

And as her lute doth live or die,
Led by her passion, so must I:
For when of pleasure she doth sing,
My thoughts enjoy a sudden spring,
But if she doth of sorrow speak,
Ev'n from my heart the strings do break.

MY SWEETEST LESBIA

My sweetest Lesbia, let us live and love,
And though the sager sort our deeds reprove,
Let us not weigh them. Heaven's great lamps do dive
Into their west, and straight again revive,
But soon as once set is our little light,
Then must we sleep one ever-during night.

If all would lead their lives in love like me,
Then bloody swords and armour should not be;
No drum nor trumpet peaceful sleeps should move,
Unless alarm came from the camp of love.
But fools do live, and waste their little light,
And seek with pain their ever-during night.

When timely death my life and fortune ends,
Let not my hearse be vexed with mourning friends,
But let all lovers, rich in triumph, come
And with sweet pastimes grace my happy tomb;
And Lesbia, close up thou my little light,
And crown with love my ever-during night.

THERE IS A GARDEN IN HER FACE

There is a garden in her face,
Where roses and white lilies grow;
A heavenly paradise is that place,
Wherein all pleasant fruits do flow.
There cherries grow which none may buy
Till cherry-ripe themselves do cry.

Those cherries fairly do enclose
Of orient pearl a double row,
Which when her lovely laughter shows,
They look like rosebuds filled with snow.
Yet them nor peer nor prince can buy,
Till cherry-ripe themselves do cry.

Her eyes like angels watch them still;
Her brows like bended bows do stand,
Threat'ning with piercing frowns to kill
All that attempt with eye or hand
Those sacred cherries to come nigh,
Till cherry-ripe themselves do cry.

The Man of Life Upright. This song, which is one of the finest of the innumerable English adaptations of Horace's "*Integer Vitae*" ode, appeared in Campion's first *Book of Airs*, 1601. The following song is from the same collection.

My Sweetest Lesbia. This song is one of many adaptations English poets have made of Catullus' famous lyric. *There Is a Garden.* This song first appeared in the *Third and Fourth Book of Airs.* **6. cherry-ripe,** the cry of the London street venders.

Henry Constable
1562–1613

THE SHEPHERD'S SONG OF VENUS AND ADONIS

Venus fair did ride,
Silver doves they drew her
By the pleasant lawns,
Ere the sun did rise;
Vesta's beauty rich
Opened wide to view her,
Philomel records
Pleasing harmonies;
Every bird of spring
Cheerfully did sing,
Paphos' goddess they salute.
Now love's queen so fair
Had of mirth no care,
For her son had made her mute.
In her breast so tender
He a shaft did enter,
When her eyes beheld a boy,
Adonis was he named,
By his mother shamed,
Yet he now is Venus' joy.

Him alone she met,
Ready bound for hunting;
Him she kindly greets,
And his journey stays;
Him she seeks to kiss,
No devices wanting,
Him her eyes still woo,
Him her tongue still prays.
He with blushing red
Hangeth down the head,
Not a kiss can he afford;
His face is turned away,
Silence said her nay,
Still she wooed him for a word.
Speak, she said, thou fairest,
Beauty thou impairest;
See me, I am pale and wan;
Lovers all adore me,
I for love implore thee.
Crystal tears with that ran down.

Him herewith she forced
To come sit down by her;
She his neck embraced,
Gazing in his face;
He, like one transformed,
Stirred no look to eye her.
Every herb did woo him,
Growing in that place;
Each bird with a ditty
Prayèd him for pity
In behalf of beauty's queen;
Waters' gentle murmur
Cravèd him to love her,
Yet no liking could be seen.
Boy, she said, look on me,
Still I gaze upon thee,
Speak, I pray thee, my delight.
Coldly he replied,
And, in brief, denied
To bestow on her a sight.

I am now too young
To be won by beauty;
Tender are my years,
I am yet a bud.
Fair thou art, she said,
Then it is thy duty,
Wert thou but a blossom,
To effect my good.
Every beauteous flower
Boasteth in my power,
Birds and beasts my laws effect.
Myrrha, thy fair mother,
Most of any other
Did my lovely hests respect.
Be with me delighted,
Thou shalt be requited,
Every nymph on thee shall tend;
All the gods shall love thee,
Man shall not reprove thee,
Love himself shall be thy friend.

Wend thee from me, Venus,
I am not disposed;
Thou wring'st me too hard,
Prithee, let me go;
Fie, what a pain it is
Thus to be enclosed;
If love begin with labour,
It will end in woe.
Kiss me, I will leave.
Here a kiss receive.
A short kiss I do it find,

The Shepherd's Song. This pastoral version of the classical myth which Shakespeare had treated in the Italianate fashion in his *Venus and Adonis*, 1593, is taken from *England's Helicon*, 1600. **5. Vesta,** sometimes identified with Terra, the earth.

72. Myrrha. Adonis was the incestuous offspring of Myrrha and her father Cinyras, king of Assyria and Cyprus.

Wilt thou leave me so?
Yet thou shalt not go;
Breathe once more thy balmy wind,
It smelleth of the myrrh tree
That to the world did bring thee,
Never was perfume so sweet.
When she had thus spoken,
She gave him a token,
And their naked bosoms meet.

Now, he said, let's go,
Hark, the hounds are crying,
Grisly boar is up,
Huntsmen follow fast.
At the name of boar
Venus seemèd dying,
Deadly-coloured pale,
Roses overcast.
Speak, said she, no more
Of following the boar;
Thou, unfit for such a chase,
Course the fearful hare,
Venison do not spare,
If thou wilt yield Venus grace.
Shun the boar, I pray thee,
Else I still will stay thee.
Herein he vowed to please her mind;
Then her arms enlarged,
Loath she him discharged,
Forth he went as swift as wind.

Thetis Phoebus' steeds
In the west retained;
Hunting sport was past,
Love her love did seek;
Sight of him too soon,
Gentle queen she gained.
On the ground he lay;
Blood had left his cheek,
For an orpèd swine
Smit him in the groin,
Deadly wound his death did bring.
Which when Venus found
She fell in a swound,
And awaked, her hands did wring.
Nymphs and satyrs skipping
Came together tripping,
Echo every cry expressed.
Venus by her power
Turned him to a flower,
Which she weareth in her crest.

129. orpèd swine, fierce boar. **139. flower,** the anemone, formerly called the adonium.

John Dowland

1563–1626

FINE KNACKS FOR LADIES

Fine knacks for ladies, cheap, choice, brave, and new!
Good pennyworths! but money cannot move.
I keep a fair but for the fair to view;
A beggar may be liberal of love.
Though all my wares be trash, the heart is true.

Great gifts are guiles and look for gifts again;
My trifles come as treasures from my mind.
It is a precious jewel to be plain;
Sometimes in shell th' orient'st pearls we find.
Of others take a sheaf, of me a grain.

Within this pack, pins, points, laces, and gloves,
And divers toys fitting a country fair;
But my heart lives where duty serves and loves,
Turtles and twins, court's brood, a heavenly pair.
Happy the heart that thinks of no removes!

Sir Edward Dyer

1543–1607

MY MIND TO ME A KINGDOM IS

My mind to me a kingdom is;
Such perfect joy therein I find
That it excels all other bliss
Which God or Nature hath assigned.
Though much I want that most would have,
Yet still my mind forbids to crave.

No princely port, nor wealthy store,
No force to win a victory,
No wily wit to salve a sore,
No shape to win a loving eye;
To none of these I yield as thrall,—
For why? my mind despise them all.

I see that plenty surfeit oft,
And hasty climbers soonest fall;
I see that such as are aloft
Mishap doth threaten most of all.

Fine Knacks. This song by one of the finest of Elizabethan composers of airs for the lute first appeared in his *Second Book of Songs and Airs*, 1600. *My Mind to Me a Kingdom Is.* This succinct and telling expression of the stoicism popular in the period is the work of one of the minor courtly poets. It was set to music by perhaps the greatest composer of the time, William Byrd, and appeared in his *Psalms, Sonnets, and Songs*, 1588.

These get with toil and keep with fear;
Such cares my mind can never bear.

I press to bear no haughty sway,
I wish no more than may suffice,
I do no more than well I may,
Look, what I want my mind supplies.
Lo! thus I triumph like a king,
My mind content with anything.

I laugh not at another's loss,
Nor grudge not at another's gain;
No worldly waves my mind can toss;
I brook that is another's bane.
I fear no foe, nor fawn on friend,
I loathe not life, nor dread mine end.

My wealth is health and perfect ease,
And conscience clear my chief defence;
I never seek by bribes to please,
Nor by desert to give offence.
Thus do I live, thus will I die,—
Would all did so as well as I!

John Fletcher

1579–1625

LAY A GARLAND ON MY HEARSE

Lay a garland on my hearse of the dismal yew,
Maidens, willow branches bear, say I dièd true.
My love was false, but I was firm from my hour of birth;
Upon my buried body lay lightly, gently, earth.

MELANCHOLY

Hence, all you vain delights,
As short as are the nights
Wherein you spend your folly,
There's nought in this life sweet,
If man were wise to see't,
But only melancholy,
Oh, sweetest melancholy.
Welcome, folded arms and fixèd eyes,
A sigh that piercing mortifies,
A look that's fastened to the ground,
A tongue chained up without a sound.
Fountain-heads, and pathless groves,
Places which pale passion loves,
Moonlight walks, when all the fowls
Are warmly housed, save bats and owls,
A midnight bell, a parting groan,
These are the sounds we feed upon;
Then stretch our bones in a still gloomy valley,
Nothing's so dainty sweet as lovely melancholy.

SLEEP

Care-charming Sleep, thou easer of all woes,
Brother to Death, sweetly thyself dispose
On this afflicted prince; fall like a cloud
In gentle showers; give nothing that is loud
Or painful to his slumbers; easy, sweet,
And as a purling stream, thou son of Night,
Pass by his troubled senses; sing his pain,
Like hollow murmuring wind or silver rain;
Into this prince gently, oh, gently slide,
And kiss him into slumbers like a bride.

THE DRINKING SONG

Drink to-day, and drown all sorrow,
You shall perhaps not do it to-morrow.
Best, while you have it, use your breath;
There is no drinking after death.

Wine works the heart up, wakes the wit;
There is no cure 'gainst age but it.
It helps the headache, cough, and tisic,
And is for all diseases physic.

Then let us swill, boys, for our health;
Who drinks well, loves the commonwealth.
And he that will to bed go sober,
Falls with the leaf still in October.

LET THE BELLS RING

Let the bells ring, and let the boys sing,
The young lasses skip and play,
Let the cups go round, till round goes the ground,
Our learnèd old vicar will stay.

Let the pig turn merrily, merrily, ah,
And let the fat goose swim,
For verily, verily, verily, ah,
Our vicar this day shall be trim.

Lay a Garland. This exquisite dirge is from the play *The Maid's Tragedy*, written by Fletcher in collaboration with Francis Beaumont. *Melancholy.* This song is from Fletcher's play *Nice Valour.* It is one of the sources of the opening lines of Milton's "Il Penseroso."

Sleep. This song is from Fletcher's tragedy *Valentinian.* *The Drinking Song.* This philosophical defense of potations is from Fletcher's tragedy *The Bloody Brother.* **7. tisic,** phthisic, consumption. *Let the Bells Ring.* This homely, lusty lyric is from Fletcher's comedy of intrigue *The Spanish Curate.*

The stewed cock shall crow, cock-a-loodle-loo,
  A loud cock-a-loodle shall he crow;
The duck and the drake shall swim in a lake
  Of onions and claret below.

Our wives shall be neat, to bring in our meat
  To thee, our most noble adviser;
Our pains shall be great, and bottles shall sweat,
  And we ourselves will be wiser.

We'll labour and swink, we'll kiss and we'll drink,
  And tithes shall come thicker and thicker;
We'll fall to our plough, and get children enow,
  And thou shalt be learnèd old vicar.

WEEP NO MORE

Weep no more, nor sigh, nor groan,
Sorrow calls no time that's gone;
Violets plucked, the sweetest rain
Makes not fresh nor grow again;
Trim thy locks, look cheerfully;
Fate's hid ends eyes cannot see.
Joys as wingèd dreams fly fast,
Why should sadness longer last?
Grief is but a wound to woe;
Gentlest fair, mourn, mourn no mo.

Orlando Gibbons

1583–1625

THE SILVER SWAN

The silver swan, who living had no note,
When death approached, unlocked her silent
  throat;
Leaning her breast against the reedy shore,
Thus sung her first and last, and sung no more.
Farewell, all joys; O death, come close mine eyes;
More geese than swans now live, more fools than
  wise.

Gray of Reading

THE KING'S HUNT IS UP

The hunt is up, the hunt is up,
And it is well nigh day;
And Harry our king is gone hunting,
To bring his deer to bay.

The east is bright with morning light,
And darkness it is fled;
And the merry horn wakes up the morn
To leave his idle bed.

Behold the skies with golden dyes
Are glowing all around;
The grass is green, and so are the treen,
All laughing with the sound.

The horses snort to be at the sport,
The dogs are running free;
The woods rejoice at the merry noise
Of hey tantara tee ree!

The sun is glad to see us clad
All in our lusty green,
And smiles in the sky as he riseth high
To see and to be seen.

Awake all men, I say again,
Be merry as you may;
For Harry our king is gone hunting
To bring his deer to bay.

Let the Bells Ring. **17. swink,** slave. *Weep No More*. This touching consolatory lyric is from Fletcher's *Queen of Corinth*. *The Silver Swan*. This perfect but brief lyric, set to one of the most beautiful of Gibbons's madrigals, becomes more impressive if one recalls the manifold repetitions inevitable in that musical form. It first appeared in his *First Set of Madrigals and Motets*, 1612. *The King's Hunt Is Up*. This lively ballad, although written during the reign of Henry the Eighth, was not printed until some time after 1565. The term "hunt's up" referred originally to the tune played on the hunting horns, to arouse sportsmen in the morning.

Robert Greene

1558?–1592

SEPHESTIA'S SONG TO HER CHILD

Weep not, my wanton, smile upon my knee,
When thou art old there's grief enough for thee.
  Mother's wag, pretty boy,
  Father's sorrow, father's joy,
  When thy father first did see
  Such a boy by him and me,
  He was glad, I was woe;
  Fortune changed made him so,
  When he left his pretty boy,
  Last his sorrow, first his joy.

Weep not, my wanton, smile upon my knee,
When thou art old there's grief enough for thee.
  Streaming tears that never stint,
  Like pearl-drops from a flint,
  Fell by course from his eyes,
  That one another's place supplies.

Sephestia's Song. This lyric is from Robert Greene's prose romance *Menaphon*, 1589. **1. wanton,** pet.

Thus he grieved in every part;
Tears of blood fell from his heart,
When he left his pretty boy,
Father's sorrow, father's joy.

Weep not, my wanton, smile upon my knee,
When thou art old there's grief enough for thee.
The wanton smiled, father wept,
Mother cried, baby leapt;
More he crowed, more we cried,
Nature could not sorrow hide.
He must go, he must kiss
Child and mother, baby bliss,
For he left his pretty boy,
Father's sorrow, father's joy.
Weep not, my wanton, smile upon my knee,
When thou art old there's grief enough for thee.

THE SHEPHERD'S WIFE'S SONG

Ah, what is love? It is a pretty thing,
As sweet unto a shepherd as a king—
And sweeter too,
For kings have cares that wait upon a crown,
And cares can make the sweetest love to frown.
Ah then, ah then,
If country loves such sweet desires do gain,
What lady would not love a shepherd swain?

His flocks once folded, he comes home at night
As merry as a king in his delight—
And merrier too,
For kings bethink them what the state require,
Where shepherds careless carol by the fire.
Ah then, ah then,
If country loves such sweet desires gain,
What lady would not love a shepherd swain?

He kisseth first, then sits as blithe to eat
His cream and curds as doth the king his meat—
And blither too,
For kings have often fears when they do sup,
Where shepherds dread no poison in their cup.
Ah then, ah then,
If country loves such sweet desires gain,
What lady would not love a shepherd swain?

To bed he goes, as wanton then, I ween,
As is a king in dalliance with a queen—
More wanton too,
For kings have many griefs, affects to move,
Where shepherds have no greater grief than love.
Ah then, ah then,
If country loves such sweet desires gain,
What lady would not love a shepherd swain?

Upon his couch of straw he sleeps as sound
As doth the king upon his beds of down—
More sounder too,
For cares cause kings full oft their sleep to spill,
Where weary shepherds lie and snort their fill.
Ah then, ah then,
If country loves such sweet desires gain,
What lady would not love a shepherd swain?

Thus with his wife he spends the year, as blithe
As doth the king, at every tide or sithe—
And blither too,
For kings have wars and broils to take in hand,
Where shepherds laugh and love upon the land.
Ah then, ah then,
If country loves such sweet desires gain,
What lady would not love a shepherd swain?

SWEET ARE THE THOUGHTS

Sweet are the thoughts that savour of content,
The quiet mind is richer than a crown;
Sweet are the nights in careless slumber spent,
The poor estate scorns fortune's angry frown:
Such sweet content, such minds, such sleep, such bliss,
Beggars enjoy, when princes oft do miss.

The homely house that harbours quiet rest,
The cottage that affords no pride nor care,
The mean that grees with country music best,
The sweet consort of mirth and music's fare,
Obscurèd life sets down a type of bliss;
A mind content both crown and kingdom is.

CUPID ABROAD WAS LATED

Cupid abroad was lated in the night,
His wings were wet with ranging in the rain;
Harbour he sought, to me he took his flight
To dry his plumes. I heard the boy complain;
I oped the door and granted his desire,
I rose myself, and made the wag a fire.

Looking more narrow by the fire's flame,
I spied his quiver hanging by his back.
Doubting the boy might my misfortune frame,
I would have gone, for fear of further wrack;

The Shepherd's Wife's Song. This charming treatment of the contrast between the simple and the sophisticated life is from Greene's prose fiction *Greene's Mourning Garment*, 1590. **28. affects,** passions.

The Shepherd's Wife's Song. **42. sithe,** time. *Sweet Are the Thoughts.* This song from *Greene's Farewell to Folly*, 1591, should be compared with the lyrics by Dekker (page 262) and Dyer (page 281), which treat the same stoical theme. *Cupid Abroad.* This song in the Anacreontic vein is from Greene's prose tale *Orpharion*, 1599. Cf. Herrick's treatment of the same theme in "The Cheat of Cupid," p. 352.

But what I drad did me, poor wretch, betide,
For forth he drew an arrow from his side.

He pierced the quick, and I began to start,
A pleasing wound but that it was too high;
His shaft procured a sharp yet sugared smart.
Away he flew, for why his wings were dry;
But left the arrow sticking in my breast,
That sore I grieved I welcomed such a guest.

Tobias Hume
d. 1645

TOBACCO, TOBACCO

Tobacco, tobacco, sing sweetly for tobacco!
Tobacco is like love, oh love it;
For you see, I will prove it.
Love maketh lean the fat men's tumour,
So doth tobacco.
Love still dries up the wanton humour,
So doth tobacco.
Love makes men sail from shore to shore,
So doth tobacco.
'Tis fond love often makes men poor,
So doth tobacco.
Love makes men scorn all coward fears,
So doth tobacco.
Love often sets men by the ears,
So doth tobacco.
Tobacco, tobacco,
Sing sweetly for tobacco.
Tobacco is like love, oh love it;
For you see I have proved it.

Thomas Lodge
1558?–1625

ROSALYNDE'S MADRIGAL

Love in my bosom like a bee
Doth suck his sweet;
Now with his wings he plays with me,
Now with his feet.
Within mine eyes he makes his nest,
His bed amidst my tender breast,
My kisses are his daily feast,
And yet he robs me of my rest—
Ah, wanton, will ye?

And if I sleep, then percheth he
With pretty flight,
And makes his pillow of my knee
The livelong night.
Strike I my lute, he tunes the string,
He music plays if so I sing,
He lends me every lovely thing,
Yet cruel he my heart doth sting—
Whist, wanton, still ye!

Else I with roses every day
Will whip you hence,
And bind you, when you long to play,
For your offence.
I'll shut mine eyes to keep you in,
I'll make you fast it for your sin,
I'll count your power not worth a pin;
Alas! what hereby shall I win
If he gainsay me?

What if I beat the wanton boy
With many a rod?
He will repay me with annoy,
Because a god.
Then sit thou safely on my knee,
And let thy bower my bosom be,
Lurk in mine eyes, I like of thee.
O Cupid, so thou pity me,
Spare not, but play thee!

Anthony Munday
1553–1633

TO COLIN CLOUT

Beauty sat bathing by a spring
Where fairest shades did hide her;
The winds blew calm, the birds did sing,
The cool streams ran beside her.
My wanton thoughts enticed mine eye
To see what was forbidden,
But better memory said fie!
So vain desire was chidden.
Hey nonny, nonny, &c.

Into a slumber then I fell,
When fond imagination
Seemed to see, but could not tell
Her feature or her fashion.
But even as babes in dreams do smile
And sometime fall a-weeping,

Cupid Abroad. **16. for why,** because. *Tobacco.* This song from Hume's *Musical Humours, the First Part of Airs,* 1605, may suggest the rapidity with which smoking became popular after its introduction by Sir Walter Ralegh. *Rosalynde's Madrigal.* This Anacreontic lyric is taken from Lodge's pastoral romance *Rosalynde,* from which Shakespeare took the plot of *As You Like It.*

To Colin Clout. This song is taken from *England's Helicon.*

So I awaked, as wise this while
As when I fell a-sleeping.
Hey nonny, nonny, &c.

Thomas Nashe

1567–1601

SPRING, THE SWEET SPRING

Spring, the sweet spring, is the year's pleasant king;
Then blooms each thing, then maids dance in a ring,
Cold doth not sting, the pretty birds do sing:
Cuckoo, jug-jug, pu-we, to-witta-woo!

The palm and may make country houses gay,
Lambs frisk and play, the shepherds pipe all day,
And we hear aye birds tune this merry lay:
Cuckoo, jug-jug, pu-we, to-witta-woo!

The fields breathe sweet, the daisies kiss our feet,
Young lovers meet, old wives a-sunning sit,
In every street these tunes our ears do greet:
Cuckoo, jug-jug, pu-we, to-witta-woo!
Spring, the sweet spring!

LITANY IN TIME OF PLAGUE

Adieu, farewell earth's bliss,
This world uncertain is;
Fond are life's lustful joys,
Death proves them all but toys,
None from his darts can fly.
I am sick, I must die.
Lord, have mercy on us!

Rich men, trust not in wealth,
Gold cannot buy you health;
Physic himself must fade,
All things to end are made.
The plague full swift goes by;
I am sick, I must die.
Lord, have mercy on us!

Beauty is but a flower
Which wrinkles will devour:
Brightness falls from the air,
Queens have died young and fair,
Dust hath closed Helen's eye.
I am sick, I must die.
Lord, have mercy on us!

Strength stoops unto the grave,
Worms feed on Hector brave,
Swords may not fight with fate.
Earth still holds ope her gate;
Come! come! the bells do cry.
I am sick, I must die.
Lord, have mercy on us!

Wit with his wantonness
Tasteth death's bitterness;
Hell's executioner
Hath no ears for to hear
What vain art can reply.
I am sick, I must die.
Lord, have mercy on us!

Haste, therefore, each degree,
To welcome destiny.
Heaven is our heritage,
Earth but a player's stage;
Mount we unto the sky.
I am sick, I must die.
Lord, have mercy on us!

Spring, the Sweet Spring. This song and the next, expressing two very different moods, are from Nashe's play *Summer's Last Will and Testament*.

George Peele

1558?–1597?

PARIS AND OENONE

Oenone. Fair and fair and twice so fair,
As fair as any may be;
The fairest shepherd on our green,
A love for any lady.

Paris. Fair and fair and twice so fair,
As fair as any may be;
Thy love is fair for thee alone,
And for no other lady.

Oenone. My love is fair, my love is gay,
As fresh as been the flowers in May,
And of my love my roundelay,
My merry, merry, merry roundelay
Concludes with Cupid's curse:
They that do change old love for new,
Pray gods they change for worse.

Ambo simul. They that do change, &c.
Oenone. Fair and fair, &c.
Paris. Fair and fair, &c. Thy love is fair, &c.

Oenone. My love can pipe, my love can sing,
My love can many a pretty thing,
And of his lovely praises ring

Paris and Oenone. This song is from Peele's play *The Arraignment of Paris*, which was acted before Her Majesty by the company of Children of the Chapel Royal.

My merry, merry roundelays.
Amen to Cupid's curse:
They that do change, &c.

Paris. They that do change, &c.
Ambo. Fair and fair, &c.

HIS GOLDEN LOCKS

His golden locks time hath to silver turned;
Oh, time too swift, oh, swiftness never ceasing!
His youth 'gainst time and age hath ever spurned,
But spurned in vain; youth waneth by increasing.
Beauty, strength, youth, are flowers but fading seen;
Duty, faith, love, are roots, and ever green.

His helmet now shall make a hive for bees,
And lover's sonnets turned to holy psalms,
A man-at-arms must now serve on his knees,
And feed on prayers, which are age his alms;
But though from court to cottage he depart,
His saint is sure of his unspotted heart.

And when he saddest sits in homely cell,
He'll teach his swains this carol for a song:
Blest be the hearts that wish my sovereign well,
Cursed be the souls that think her any wrong!
Goddess, allow this agèd man his right,
To be your beadsman now, that was your knight.

Robert Southwell

1561?–1595

THE BURNING BABE

As I in hoary winter's night stood shivering in the snow,
Surprised I was with sudden heat which made my heart to glow;
And lifting up a fearful eye to view what fire was near,
A pretty babe all burning bright did in the air appear;
Who, scorchèd with excessive heat, such floods of tears did shed
As though his floods should quench his flames which with his tears were fed.
Alas, quoth he, but newly born in fiery heats I fry,
Yet none approach to warm their hearts or feel my fire but I!

His Golden Locks. This song was written by Peele at the request of Sir Henry Lee, who, finding himself too old to engage in a tournament in honor of Queen Elizabeth, had this poetic apology rendered instead. *The Burning Babe.* This impassioned lyric, written in old-fashioned "fourteeners," is the best-known poem of the Catholic poet Southwell.

My faultless breast the furnace is, the fuel wounding thorns,
Love is the fire, and sighs the smoke, the ashes shame and scorns;
The fuel justice layeth on, and mercy blows the coals,
The metal in this furnace wrought are men's defilèd souls,
For which, as now on fire I am to work them to their good,
So will I melt into a bath to wash them in my blood.
With this he vanished out of sight and swiftly shrunk away,
And straight I callèd unto mind that it was Christmas day.

John Webster

1580?–1625

DIRGE

Call for the robin redbreast and the wren,
Since o'er shady groves they hover,
And with leaves and flowers do cover
The friendless bodies of unburied men.
Call unto his funeral dole
The ant, the field-mouse, and the mole,
To rear him hillocks that shall keep him warm,
And, when gay tombs are robbed, sustain no harm;
But keep the wolf far thence, that's foe to men,
For with his nails he'll dig them up again.

DEATH–SONG

Hark, now everything is still;
The screech-owl and the whistler shrill
Call upon our dame aloud,
And bid her quickly don her shroud;
Much you had of land and rent,
Your length in clay's now competent.
A long war disturbed your mind;
Here your perfect peace is signed.
Of what is 't fools make such vain keeping?
Sin their conception, their birth weeping,
Their life a general mist of error,
Their death a hideous storm of terror.
Strew your hair with powders sweet,
Don clean linen, bathe your feet,
And, the foul fiend more to check,

Dirge. This macabre dirge is from Webster's tragedy *The White Devil.* *Death-Song.* This song from Webster's tragedy *The Duchess of Malfi* suggests admirably his preoccupation with dissolution and death. **6. competent,** qualified, fit.

A crucifix let bless your neck;
'Tis now full tide, 'tween night and day,
End your groan and come away.

Thomas Weelkes

1577?–1623

THESE THINGS SEEM WONDROUS

Thule, the period of cosmography,
Doth vaunt of Hecla, whose sulphureous fire
Doth melt the frozen clime and thaw the sky;
Trinacrian Etna's flames ascend not higher:
These things seem wondrous, yet more wondrous I,
Whose heart with fear doth freeze, with love doth
fry.

The Andalusian merchant, that returns
Laden with cochineal and china dishes,
Reports in Spain how strangely Fogo burns
Amidst an ocean full of flying fishes:

These Things Seem Wondrous. This lyric first appeared in Weelkes's *Madrigals of Six Parts*, 1600. **1. Thule,** the name given by the ancients to the northernmost country in the world; in this case, Iceland. **2. Hecla,** a volcano. **4. Trinacrian,** Sicilian. **8. cochineal,** dyestuff. **9. Fogo,** a volcano in the Cape Verde Islands.

These things seem wondrous, yet more wondrous I,
Whose heart with fear doth freeze, with love doth
fry.

Samuel Daniel

1562–1619

CARE-CHARMER SLEEP

Care-charmer sleep, son of the sable night,
Brother to death, in silent darkness born,
Relieve my languish and restore the light;
With dark forgetting of my care, return.
And let the day be time enough to mourn
The shipwreck of my ill-adventured youth;
Let waking eyes suffice to wail their scorn
Without the torment of the night's untruth.
Cease, dreams, th' images of day-desires,
To model forth the passions of the morrow;
Never let rising sun approve you liars,
To add more grief to aggravate my sorrow.
Still let me sleep, embracing clouds in vain,
And never wake to feel the day's disdain.

Care-Charmer Sleep. This sonnet, from Daniel's sonnet-sequence *Delia*, 1592, illustrates his purity of diction, tranquillity of rhythm, and perfect mastery of single lines. Its form is that of the English or Shakespearean sonnet.

SUGGESTIONS FOR FURTHER READING

This list is to be supplemented by the brief lists of books given in the general introduction and in the various introductions to specific authors and works.

HISTORICAL AND POLITICAL BACKGROUND

Allen, J. W. *History of Political Thought in the Sixteenth Century*, Dial Press, 1928. An excellent general survey.

Black, J. B. *The Reign of Elizabeth, 1558–1603*, Oxford University Press, 1936. A recent history embodying the latest results of research.

Neale, J. E. *Queen Elizabeth*, Harcourt, Brace, 1937. Probably the best recent study of that enigmatical queen.

—— *The Elizabethan House of Commons*, Yale University Press, 1950. An informative and fascinating account of the politics, politicians, and elections of Elizabethan days.

Payne, E. J., ed. *Voyages of the Elizabethan Seamen to America*, Oxford University Press, 1893. Lively contemporary accounts of adventure and exploration.

Read, Conyers. *The Tudors: Personalities and Practical Politics in Sixteenth-Century England*, Holt, 1936. Brief but meaty studies of the Tudor sovereigns.

Strachey, Lytton. *Elizabeth and Essex: A Tragic History*, Harcourt, Brace, 1928. A brilliant study of the relations of the two.

Williamson, J. A. *Hawkins of Plymouth*, Macmillan, 1950. A brilliant biography of Sir John Hawkins, a key figure in the defeat of the Armada. The whole history of the period is illuminated by the story of one man's part in it.

—— *The Age of Drake*, Macmillan, 1938.

CULTURAL AND SOCIAL BACKGROUND

Baker, C. H. C., and Constable, W. G. *English Painting of the Sixteenth and Seventeenth Centuries*, Harcourt, Brace, 1930.

Boyd, M. C. *Elizabethan Music and Musical Criticism*, University of Pennsylvania Press, 1940.

Burckhardt, J. C. *The Civilization of the Renaissance in Italy*, Boni, 1935. The standard nineteenth-century study of the Renaissance, first published in 1860. This edition contains "The Civilization of the Renaissance in Pictures," selected and arranged by Ludwig Goldscheider.

Byrne, M. St. Clare. *Elizabethan Life in Town and Country*, Houghton Mifflin, 1926. Attractively illustrated.

Castiglione, Baldassare. *The Book of the Courtier*, Everyman's Library, Dutton, 1928. The most famous analysis of the ideals of the Renaissance gentleman and courtier.

Chappell, William. *Popular Music of the Olden Time*, London, 1855. A standard and very readable book on sixteenth-century music.

Craig, Hardin. *The Enchanted Glass: The Elizabethan Mind in Literature*, Oxford University Press, 1936. A difficult but rewarding book.

Davis, W. S. *Life in Elizabethan Days: A Picture of a Typical English Community at the End of the Sixteenth Century*, Harper, 1930.

Dunham, W. H., and Pargellis, S. M., eds. *Complaint and Reform in England, 1436–1714*, Oxford University Press, 1938. Fifty writings of the period on politics, religion, society, economics, architecture, science, and education.

Harrison, G. B. *England in Shakespeare's Day*, Harcourt, Brace, 1928.

—— *The Elizabethan Journals, Being a Record of Those Things Mostly Talked of During the Years 1591–1603*, Macmillan, 1939. A fictitious diary, but based on historical sources.

Harrison, William. *Elizabethan England*, Simmons, 1904. The most famous and full contemporary description of Elizabeth's England.

Haydn, Hiram. *The Counter-Renaissance*, Scribner, 1950. The most recent and stimulating history of the intellectual crosscurrents of the Renaissance and Reformation.

Kastendieck, M. M. *England's Musical Poet, Thomas Campion*, Oxford University Press, 1938. A valuable study of the interrelationship of poetry and music in English literature and in the Elizabethan lyric.

Morse, H. K. *Elizabethan Pageantry, a Pictorial Survey of Costume and Its Commentators from c. 1560–1620*, Studio Publications, 1934.

Onions, C. T., ed. *Shakespeare's England, an Account of the Life and Manners of His Age*, Oxford University Press, 1916. A standard and invaluable co-operative scholarly review of the social life of the age.

Traill, H. D. *Social England*, Vol. III, Putnam, 1902–1904. An excellent study of the period.

Williams, F. B. *Elizabethan England*, Boston Museum of Fine Arts, Illustrative Set No. 1, 1939. An excellent pictorial survey of the period.

Wright, L. B. *Middle-Class Culture in Elizabethan England*, University of North Carolina Press, 1935. What the solid citizen was reading and thinking.

LITERATURE OF THE PERIOD

COLLECTIONS

Ault, Norman, ed., *Elizabethan Lyrics, from the Original Texts*, Longmans, 1925; 3rd ed., William Sloane Associates, 1949. A distinguished collection of familiar and less familiar lyrics.

Brooke, Tucker, and Paradise, N. B., eds. *English Drama, 1580–1642*, Heath, 1933. Contains the text of thirty plays, representing the work of the contemporaries and immediate successors of Shakespeare.

Chambers, E. K., ed. *The Oxford Book of Sixteenth-Century Verse*, Oxford University Press, 1932. A standard and generous collection.

Clements, A. F., ed. *Tudor Translations: An Anthology*, Oxford University Press, 1940.

Hebel, J. W., and Hudson, H. H., eds. *Poetry of the English Renaissance, 1509–1660*, Crofts, 1929. An invaluable collection of lyric and nondramatic poems, with introductions, notes, and bibliographies.

Lamson, Roy, and Smith, Hallett, eds. *The Golden Hind: An Anthology of Elizabethan Prose and Poetry*, Norton, 1942. A generous selection of pieces from the nondramatic literature, with introductions, notes, and bibliographies.

Rollins, H. E., ed. *The Pack of Autolycus*, Harvard University Press, 1927. A fascinating collection of Elizabethan broadside ballads.

Rollins, H. E., ed. *Tottel's Miscellany (1557–1587)*, Harvard University Press, 1928. The pioneer anthology of English poems, in which Wyatt and Surrey were first presented to the public.

CRITICISM

Berdan, J. M. *Early Tudor Poetry*, Macmillan 1920. The standard study of early sixteenth-century poetry and the circumstances in which it was written.

Boas, F. S. *An Introduction to Tudor Drama*, Oxford University Press, 1933.

Chambers, E. K. *The Elizabethan Stage*, 4 vols., Oxford University Press, 1923. The definitive treatment of the subject.

Dunn, Esther C. *The Literature of Shakespeare's England*, Scribner, 1936. One of the most readable of the recent surveys.

John, L. C. *The Elizabethan Sonnet Sequence*, Columbia University Press, 1938. A thorough discussion of this popular literary convention, with particular consideration of the imagery.

Krapp, G. P. *The Rise of English Literary Prose*, Oxford University Press, 1915. The most thorough study of Elizabethan prose.

Linthicum, M. C. *Costume in the Drama of Shakespeare and His Contemporaries*, Oxford University Press, 1936. A fascinating and encyclopedic discussion of the subject.

Matthiessen, F. O. *Translation: An Elizabethan Art*, Harvard University Press, 1931.

Pinto, V. de Sola. *The English Renaissance, 1510–1688*, McBride, 1938. The best single-volume introduction to the literature and bibliography of the period, with a chapter on "Literature and Music" by Bruce Pattison.

Saintsbury, George. *History of Elizabethan Literature*, Macmillan, 1906. A standard and readable survey.

Schelling, F. E. *Elizabethan Playwrights: A Short History of the English Drama from Mediaeval Times to the Closing of the Theatres in 1642*, Harper, 1925.

Stoll, E. E. *Poets and Playwrights: Shakespeare, Jonson, Spenser, Milton*, University of Minnesota Press, 1930. One of the most stimulating books on Elizabethan authors, drama, and stage.

Taylor, H. O. *Thought and Expression in the Sixteenth Century*, Macmillan. The best general survey of the subject.

Wells, H. W. *Elizabethan and Jacobean Playwrights*, Columbia University Press, 1939. An illuminating discussion of the most abundant period in the history of the English theater.

MARLOWE

The Works of Christopher Marlowe, ed. by C. F. T. Brooke. Oxford University Press, 1910. An excellent one-volume edition.

Bakeless, John. *Christopher Marlowe: The Man in His Time*, Morrow, 1937.

—— *The Tragical History of Christopher Marlowe*, Harvard University Press, 1942. The two volumes by Bakeless constitute the fullest and most detailed study of Marlowe's works, their origins, and their influence.

Hotson, J. L. *The Death of Christopher Marlowe*, Nonesuch Press, 1925. Ingenious and exciting detective work in tracking down Marlowe's murderer.

MORE

Selections from the English Works of Sir Thomas More, ed. by P. S. and H. M. Allen. Clarendon Press, Oxford, 1924. A very useful selection, with extracts from the lives of More by Erasmus and Roper.

Chambers, R. W. *Thomas More*, Cape, 1935. The standard biography and the most valuable study of the meaning and importance of More and his work. An indispensable book for the study of the whole period.

Roper, William. *The Life of Sir Thomas More*, ed. by J. M. Cline, Morrow, 1950. The most recent edition of the earliest life of More by his son-in-law, with introduction and notes.

RALEGH

The Poems of Sir Walter Ralegh, ed. by Agnes M. C. Latham, Houghton Mifflin. The standard modern edition, with valuable introduction and notes.

Selections from the Prose Works of Sir Walter Ralegh, ed. by G. E. Hadow, Oxford University Press, 1917.

Thompson, Edward. *Sir Walter Ralegh, Last of the Elizabethans*, Yale University Press, 1936. The most recent study of Ralegh and his age.

SHAKESPEARE

Shakespeare: Major Plays and the Sonnets, ed. by G. B. Harrison, Harcourt, Brace, 1948. An excellent new edition for college students, with introductions, notes, and illustrations dealing with twenty-three plays and the sonnets.

The Complete Works of William Shakespeare, ed. by G. L. Kittredge, Ginn, 1936. A convenient one-volume edition with brief introductions by America's most famous teacher of Shakespeare.

The Shakespeare Songs, ed. by C. F. T. Brooke, Morrow, 1929.

Shakespeare's Sonnets, ed. by C. F. T. Brooke, Oxford University Press, 1936.

Adams, J. Q. *A Life of William Shakespeare*, Houghton Mifflin, 1923. Perhaps the best brief biography.

Bradley, A. C. *Shakespearean Tragedy*, Macmillan, 1949. A reissue of the most distinguished study of Shakespeare's chief tragedies.

Brooke, C. F. T. *Shakespeare of Stratford: A Handbook for Students*, Yale University Press, 1926. A convenient collection of the documents that concern the poet's life.

Chute, Marchette. *Shakespeare of London*, Dutton, 1949. The most recent and one of the best popular lives of Shakespeare written for the general reader.

Granville-Barker, Harley. *Prefaces to Shakespeare*, 2 vols., Princeton University Press, 1948. Brilliant analyses of the major plays and of their staging in Elizabethan and modern times.

Neilson, W. A., and Thorndike, A. H. *The Facts about Shakespeare*, Macmillan, 1913. The most useful general handbook, with information on the author, the plays, and the theaters of Shakespeare's time.

Spencer, Hazelton. *The Art and Life of William Shakespeare*, Harcourt, Brace, 1940. A valuable and stimulating study.

Spurgeon, Caroline F. E. *Shakespeare's Imagery*, Cambridge University Press, 1935. One of the most valuable and influential studies in poetic imagery.

Wilson, J. Dover. *The Essential Shakespeare*, Cambridge University Press, 1932. An illuminating study by one of the most distinguished modern critics.

SIDNEY

The Poems of Sir Philip Sidney, with introduction by John Drinkwater, Dutton, 1922.

Sidney's Defense of Poesy, ed. by A. S. Cook, Ginn, 1890. The most thoroughly annotated modern edition.

Wilson, Mona. *Sir Philip Sidney*, Duckworth, 1931. One of the best modern studies.

SPENSER

The Complete Poetical Works of Edmund Spenser, Dodge, R. E. N., ed., Houghton Mifflin, 1908. The best one-volume edition.

Bradner, Leicester. *Edmund Spenser and the "Faerie Queene,"* University of Chicago Press, 1948. The most recent and, for the general student, the most valuable study of Spenser and his great poem. The book contains a very illuminating discussion of Spenser's allegory.

Jones, H. S. V. *A Spenser Handbook*, Crofts, 1930. An admirable and indispensable volume for the student.

Legouis, Emile. *Spenser*, Dutton, 1926. A brilliant study of the English poet by a distinguished French critic.

Watkins, W. B. C. *Shakespeare and Spenser*, Princeton University Press, 1950. A valuable discussion of the themes and techniques of the two poets.

THE SEVENTEENTH CENTURY

PLATE IX

A THE PTOLEMAIC COSMOLOGY (*Bettmann Archive*)

Although Milton was familiar with the Copernican view of the universe, in *Paradise Lost* he used the older Ptolemaic cosmology, which placed the earth at the center of the universe. It is easy to see that the Ptolemaic arrangement is better adapted to an epic of Heaven, Paradise, and Hell than a conception in which the earth is merely a satellite moving around the central sun. A further reason that influenced Milton to keep to the older concept was the poetic and theological tradition which hallowed it. In Milton's great plan, even earth-shaking scientific discoveries were secondary to the truths of religion. And, while he absorbed the new astronomical knowledge and was affected by it, he was not "scientifically minded" in the professional sense that Bacon was.

B THE GREAT FIRE OF LONDON (*Bettmann Archive*)

Even today it is terrifying to contemplate such an event as the Great Fire of London. We can get some idea of the effect of the blaze on the seventeenth-century inhabitants of the city by reading Samuel Pepys's account of it in his *Diary* and the numerous poetic descriptions of the holocaust. The best of these is undoubtedly that in Dryden's *Annus Mirabilis*. In a letter prefaced to this poem Dryden attempts to express the magnitude of the event.

". . . I have, in the fire, the most deplorable, but withal the greatest, argument that can be imagined: the destruction being so swift, so sudden, so vast, and miserable, as nothing can parallel in story."

PLATE X

A THE TRUE MINISTER; THE SEDUCER AND FALSE PROPHET (*Bettmann Archive*)

This quaint drawing is an illustration for a pamphlet published in 1648 called *A Glasse for the Times, By which According to the Scriptures, you may clearly behold the true Ministers of Christ, how farre differing from false Teachers.*

A Glasse for the Times is an interesting reflection of the turbulent decades in the mid-seventeenth century whose dangers and insecurities led men to question many accepted religious beliefs. The prevailing Puritanism, however, would not tolerate "false Teachers" who deviated from accepted doctrines. These false prophets ranged from extreme Calvinists, who argued that the doctrine of election absolved the elected individual from any responsibility for his behavior, to the liberal Roger Williams whose *Bloody Tenent* advocated freedom for every man to worship as he pleased and urged toleration even of non-Christians.

One section of *A Glasse for the Times* considers those whose doctrines are so heretical as to require no confutation. Among them is Mr. John Milton, whose Doctrine of Divorce is the object of attack: "That unfitnesse or contrariety of minde betwixt man and wife from a naturell cause which hindereth solace and peace are a great reason of divorce."

B CHARLES I, BY ANTHONY VAN DYCK (*Louvre, Paris*)

Like Hans Holbein a hundred years before him, Anthony Van Dyck (1599–1641) came to the English court after establishing himself as a successful painter on the Continent. Charles I was evidently glad to receive Van Dyck, for he shortly conferred upon him the title of Painter in Ordinary to the Court, a pension of £200 per annum, and a knighthood. A vast number of portraits of the English royalty and nobility came from Van Dyck's brush, among them the Pembroke family, Sir George and Sir Francis Villiers, the Earls of Bristol, Bedford, and Derby. In 1639 Van Dyck completed his nationalization by marrying an English noblewoman, Lady Mary Ruthven.

It is interesting to contrast the elegance and grace of the two Van Dyck portraits in this section—Charles I and Sir John Suckling—with the force and vigor of the two Holbeins in the preceding group of illustrations. The differences reflect the great changes in English manners and in the art of painting between the accession of the Tudors and the reign of the Stuarts.

C ST. CLEMENT DANES, LONDON (*Black Star*)

St. Clement Danes is one of the fifty or more London churches designed by Christopher Wren after the Great Fire of 1666 necessitated rebuilding practically the entire city. The most famous of these churches is, of course, St. Paul's Cathedral. In St. Paul's and in all his other buildings, Wren imitated the classic forms of architecture that were revived in

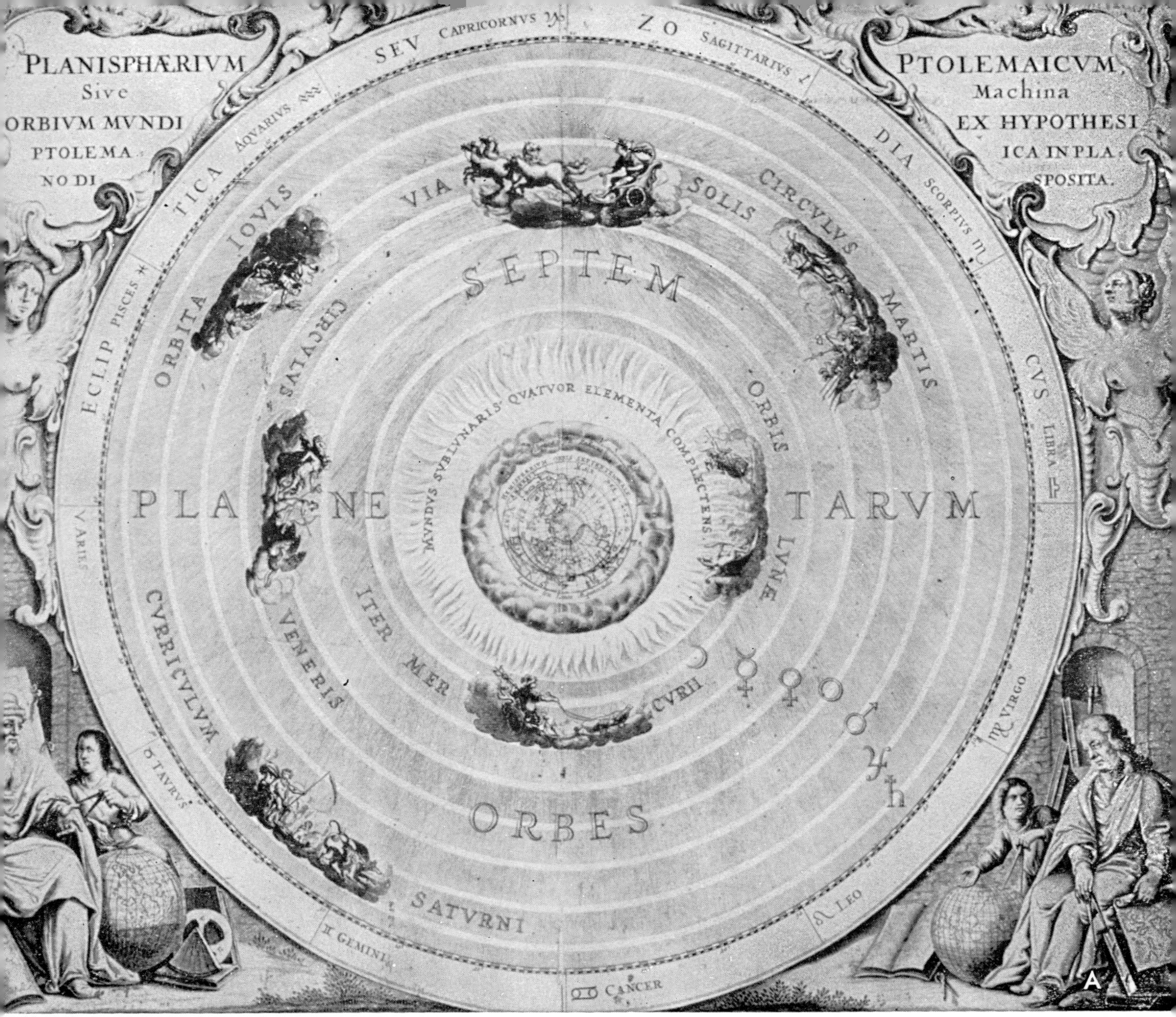

PLANISPHÆRIVM PTOLEMAICVM,
Sive Machina
ORBIVM MVNDI EX HYPOTHESI
PTOLEMA ICA IN PLA
NO DI SPOSITA.

SEV CAPRICORNVS ♑ ZO SAGITTARIVS ♐ DIA SCORPIVS ♏ CVS LIBRA ♎ ♍ VIRGO ♌ LEO ♋ CANCER ♊ GEMINI ♉ TAVRVS ♈ ARIES ECLIP PISCES ♓ TICA AQVARIVS ♒

SEPTEM PLANETARVM ORBES

VIA SOLIS CIRCVLVS
ORBITA IOVIS
CIRCVLVS MARTIS
CIRCVLVS VENERIS
ORBIS LVNÆ
ITER MERCVRII
CVRRICVLVM SATVRNI

MVNDVS SVBLVNARIS QVATVOR ELEMENTA COMPLECTENS

A

B

PLATE IX

Minister,
the Seducer and false Prophet.

B

CAROLVS
II
REGALIS
AVTHOR
PATRONVS
Presented to the R. Society from the Author
by the hands of Dr John Wilkins, Octob.
D

PLATE X

DIT HVYS IS TE HVER
THIS HOVSE IS TO LE
Be gone you rogues
You haue Sate long enough
Cuper
C. Lam
G. O Cromwel.
This is a
A
B 
C 

PLATE XI

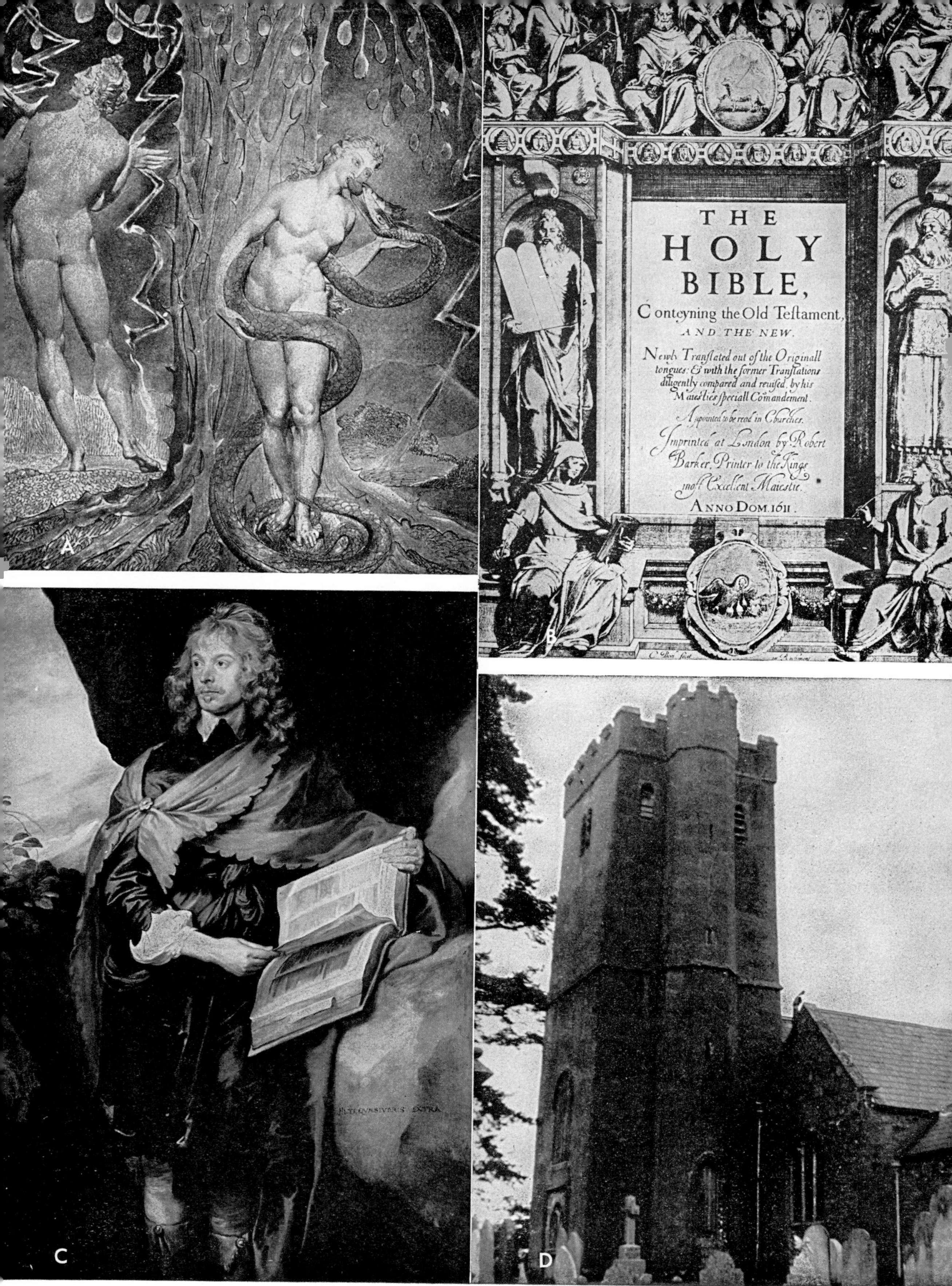
THE
HOLY
BIBLE,
Conteyning the Old Testament,
AND THE NEW.
Newly Translated out of the Originall
tongues: & with the former Translations
diligently compared and reuised, by his
Maiesties speciall Cōmandement.
Appointed to be read in Churches.
Imprinted at London by Robert
Barker, Printer to the Kings
most Excellent Maiestie.
ANNO DOM. 1611.

PLATE XII

the Italian Renaissance. He and his contemporaries considered Gothic architecture a remnant from a barbarous age. Even before the Great Fire, for example, he submitted a plan for renovating old St. Paul's that would have removed practically all its Gothic features.

Like a good number of his contemporaries, Wren was a man of many parts. At Oxford he distinguished himself in geometry and applied mathematics; later he became Savilian professor of astronomy there. He was a founding member of the Royal Society, and in 1681 was elected president of the organization. A member of Parliament for many years, he also held the post of Surveyor of the Royal Works. Others of his buildings that have survived until the present time are the Sheldonian Theatre and Tom Tower at Oxford, the Library of Trinity College and the Chapel of Pembroke College, both at Cambridge. Appropriately, St. Paul's, Wren's greatest achievement, is also his final resting place. He is buried under the choir there.

D A DRAWING COMMEMORATING THE FOUNDING OF THE ROYAL SOCIETY

One of the first secretaries of the Royal Society, Sir John Wilkins, presented this picture to the organization in 1667. It shows Lord Brouncker, the first president of the Society, on the left; Charles II, who, through granting the charter to the Society, considered himself a founder and sponsor, in the center; and Francis Bacon, on the right. Since Bacon's *Novum Organum* and his scientific researches at the beginning of the century were such an impetus to the later growth of scientific thought, it was appropriate that he be recognized as a motivating force in the founding of the Royal Society.

Although its Charter of Incorporation was not granted by Charles II until 1662, the history of the Royal Society of London for Improving Natural Knowledge (to give it its full title) goes back to about 1645. The Society began with a series of weekly meetings in London held by men interested in the new science—the "Invisible College" mentioned by the physicist Robert Boyle in his letters.

In the early years of the Society, experiments were performed at its weekly meetings. Robert Hooke, who was the first to hold the position of curator, was in charge of these experiments. The extensive correspondence with scientists on the Continent, which was another important part of the Society's early activities, formed the beginnings of its famous *Philosophical Transactions*. The Society also published separate treatises, the best known being Newton's *Principia*. Newton was made a fellow of the Society in 1671 and became president in 1703. But the Royal Society attracted not only scientists; among its early members we find men of affairs like Samuel Pepys, the diarist John Evelyn, John Aubrey, the inquisitive biographer of Oxford men, and the poets Dryden, Cowley, and Waller.

PLATE XI

A CROMWELL DISSOLVING PARLIAMENT

The widespread interest of Europeans in the events of the English Civil War is shown by this satirical print from Holland. It depicts Cromwell's dissolution of the Rump Parliament (the purged remnant of the Long Parliament that had sat since 1640) in 1653. This act of Cromwell's inspired the popular ballad:

Brave Oliver came to the House like a sprite,
His fiery face struck the Speaker dumb;
"Begone," said he, "you have sate long enough,
Do you think to sit here till Doomsday come?"

The Dutch attitude toward the English Commonwealth was more than a little influenced by the fact that the two nations were fighting a naval war. One of Cromwell's first acts, when he had been made Protector by the Parliament that succeeded the Rump, was to bring this war to a conclusion.

B MODEL OF THE DORSET GARDEN THEATER (*From Allardyce Nicoll's* The Development of the Theatre)

The stage of this Restoration theater is set for a production of Dryden's heroic tragedy, *All for Love.*

The London theaters of the Restoration were quite different from the open-air stages of Shakespeare's time. Under the influence of the elaborately staged court masques, which were performed up until the Civil War, plays moved permanently indoors. The stage was framed by a proscenium arch before which hung a curtain, and scenery became an integral part of stage production. However, two features of the older theaters were retained in the new buildings. Despite the picture-frame type of stage, much of the action in Restoration plays took place on a large apron that jutted out into the auditorium. And doors opened out onto this apron from either side of the stage, as they had in the Elizabethan theaters.

C FISHING IN THE SEVENTEENTH CENTURY

Over the years, the English love of sport has been variously expressed. It is probably because of Izaak Walton that fishing somehow seems characteristic of seventeenth-century life. *The Compleat Angler* is the work of an amateur enthusiast who took his sport seriously, just as thousands of anglers do today. Indeed, with a few modifications of style, this might be a twentieth-century fisherman speaking to a hesitant beginner at the sport:

O, Sir, doubt not but that angling is an art! Is it not an art to deceive a trout with an artificial fly? a trout! that is more sharp-sighted than any hawk you have named and more watchful and timorous than your high-mettled merlin is bold! And yet I doubt not to catch a brace or two tomorrow for a friend's breakfast. Doubt not therefore, Sir, but that angling is an art and an art worth your learning. The question is rather whether you be capable of learning it! for angling is somewhat like poetry, men are to be born so. I mean, with inclinations to it, though both may be heightened by practice and experience; but he that hopes to be a good angler must not only bring an inquiring, searching, observing wit, but he must bring a large measure of hope and patience and a love and propensity to the art itself; but having once got and practised it, then doubt not but angling will prove to be so pleasant that it will prove, like virtue, a reward to itself.

Walton's book and his long, peaceful life are a reminder that even in time of revolution men must eat and sleep, and take some time for recreation. It is worth remembering that while a Civil War raged and a whole new form of government was taking shape, Walton—and thousands of other Englishmen—went fishing.

PLATE XII

A SATAN WITH ADAM AND EVE, BY WILLIAM BLAKE (*Courtesy of The Museum of Fine Arts, Boston*)

This is one of a series of nine water colors made by Blake in 1808 to illustrate *Paradise Lost.* Milton's early and continuing influence on Blake found expression not only in this series of paintings but also in the prophetic book, *Milton,* in which the Puritan poet enters the body of Blake to correct his mistakes of insight in writing *Paradise Lost.* A nineteenth-century critic has said of the *Paradise Lost* illustrations that "Blake is here king of all his powers of design, draughtsmanship, conception, spiritual meaning, and impression."

B THE TITLE PAGE OF THE KING JAMES VERSION OF THE BIBLE (*Courtesy of The Museum of Fine Arts, Boston*)

C SIR JOHN SUCKLING, BY ANTHONY VAN DYCK (*Copyright The Frick Collection*)

Van Dyck's portrait of the Cavalier poet is perhaps somewhat idealized if we compare it with Aubrey's description, also made at first hand: "He was of middle stature and slight strength, brisque round eie, reddish fac't and red nose (ill liver), his head not very big, his hayre a kind of sand colour; his beard turned-up naturally, so that he had a brisk and gracefull looke." The painter has, however, brilliantly captured the elegant nonchalance and intellectual vigor that characterized Suckling.

D HERRICK'S CHURCH, DEAN PRIOR (*W. A. Borst*)

Herrick was probably buried in his Dean Prior Churchyard, but nothing remains today to mark his burial place. His epitaph for his village neighbors, Sir Edward and Lady Giles, is engraved under their kneeling effigies within the church, but his own epitaph is found only in the poem, "To Robin Red-brest":

Laid out for dead, let thy last kindness be
With leaves and moss-work for to cover me;
And while the wood-nymphs my cold corpse inter,
Sing then my dirge, sweet-warbling chorister!
For epitaph, in foliage next write this:
Here, here the tomb of Robin Herrick is.

THE SEVENTEENTH CENTURY

The Background of the Century

THE "Age of Elizabeth" did not end with the passing of the great Queen. Indeed, some of the greatest "Elizabethans" were as much a part of the England of James I and Charles I as of that of Elizabeth. Sir Walter Ralegh, who is commonly regarded as the very embodiment of Elizabethanism, did his greatest work as both man and writer in the seventeenth century. Shakespeare lived on to write all his greatest plays after 1600. By far the most important part of Ben Jonson's work appeared after the turn of the century. On the other hand, John Donne, who is usually thought of as peculiarly of the seventeenth century, probably wrote most of his better-known poetry before the death of Elizabeth. Again, such definitely seventeenth-century figures as Herrick, Milton, and Marvell exhibit here and there so much spiritual kinship with the great writers of the generations preceding them that each has been by someone or other styled "the last of the Elizabethans."

It is clear that the year 1600 marked no special turning-point in English thought or expression, and was neither the end nor the beginning of an "age." For the sake of convenience, however, we may take 1603, the year in which Queen Elizabeth died, as a vantage point from which to view the scene that she left, and to survey the stirring acts which were to come.

The hundred years which elapsed between the death of Elizabeth (1603) and the death of William of Orange (1702) saw the coming into being of the England and the British Empire and, indeed, the America that we know. During this period the English language as we know it, English prose as we write it, and a large number of the greatest classics of English literature came into existence. It may be questioned whether any single century in British history added so many strands to the fabric into which are woven the fundamental ideals, faiths, philosophies, habits of mind, and principles of action of the English-speaking peoples. Physically, intellectually, politically, and socially, the England of Elizabeth was transformed almost beyond recognition, and in many ways of which Elizabeth perhaps would not have approved. The old Queen would probably have felt more at home in the London of Chaucer than in that of Dryden and Pope.

The seventeenth century constitutes one of the major periods of transition in European history. The most fervent Elizabethan imagination could hardly have dreamed of the expansion that was to take place in both the physical boundaries and the intellectual horizons of the English people. At the beginning of the century, England was only a part of a small island in the North Sea. Great Britain itself had not yet come into being as a political unit, as Scotland was still a separate kingdom. In 1601 England did not own a single possession outside Europe. Under the Stuarts the exodus and the great expansion began, prompted by various causes—love of adventure, desire for power, the influence of commerce, and the seeking of freedom from religious persecutions. Whatever the cause, the result was that within the century Englishmen scattered themselves over the world as settlers, traders, and seekers of liberty of worship—in the Americas from Nova Scotia to Florida, in the West Indies and the East Indies, in the Near East and the Far East, and in the Southern Seas. The insularity of England began to pass away; the household gods of little England were carried over the seas to other countries, and there evolved gradually a New England, a new Thames, a new Boston, and a New York. Sir Walter Ralegh, the first of the great empire-builders, had a vision of such an empire as had not been seen on earth for over a thousand years, embracing a vast region in South America, governed by just laws, and developed honorably by the riches of the soil.

While men were extending their boundaries and acquainting themselves with the planet on which they lived, they were also beginning to increase their knowledge of the universe which lies beyond it. Galileo's telescope in 1609 brought within their ken the satellites of Jupiter, and disclosed to their eyes worlds which had not been dreamed of before. It would be hard to overestimate the effect on the human mind and imagination of the "Tuscan artist's optic glass." It was not until Galileo had thus demonstrated Jupiter's system of satellites that the world began to accept the Copernican hypothesis of the solar system, which had been given to the world in 1543. As the man of the twentieth century looks back at the seventeenth, one of the things which impress him most is the sense of space and spaciousness which developed in the European mind during that period. This enlarged universe is reflected in both the prose and the poetry of seventeenth-century writers. The vast cosmic distances of Milton's *Paradise Lost*, as Miss Marjorie Nicolson has pointed out,[1] would have been unthinkable fifty years before. Meanwhile, man was discovering still another world through the microscope, and acquiring an entirely new realm for observation and research. The telescope and the microscope in a single century added perhaps as much to man's accurate knowledge of physical phenomena as all the previous centuries had made possible.

The seventeenth century was not a peaceful, easy, or happy period. Politically, the first half of the century was overshadowed by the progress of the Thirty Years' War. It was, throughout, an age of strife and conflict, of both minds and armies. There were conflicting ideals of liberty and despotism, of reason and authority, of skepticism and superstition, of the laboratory and the library. And yet, defaced as it was by wars, persecutions, intolerance, superstition, and prejudice, the age has impressed historians on the whole as a period of progress and development. Preserved Smith in his survey[2] sees no decisive victory on either side in the warfare between many conflicting ideas and ideals, but as the century wore on the progressives and the liberals got the advantage of their opponents, and, for better or worse, "made the world safer for the Republican, the Protestant, the heretic, the scientist, and the modern."

The great men of the century were builders rather than destroyers. And the history of the seventeenth century in Europe is not so much a record of things and events as of men. Few equal periods of time can show such a gallery of great characters. The essence of Renaissance thought was its humanism, its belief in man and in the creative power of man's mind. In the seventeenth century "rugged individualism" triumphed as it had seldom triumphed before. Whatever department of endeavor one surveys presents men of heroic qualities to the eye. Philosophy flourished with Bacon, Descartes, Spinoza, Hobbes, Leibnitz, and Locke. Galileo and Kepler helped usher in the century, and Newton, Boyle, and Napier illumined its progress and charted its course. Shakespeare's genius reached its maturity during the first two decades, and Milton raised English poetry to new heights during its span. English music flourished with Henry Purcell. The oratorio and the opera came of age with Monteverde and Alessandro Scarlatti. A single year, 1685, saw the birth of Bach, Handel, and Domenico Scarlatti. To paint its canvases the century had, among many others, El Greco, Rembrandt, Rubens, Vermeer, Velasquez, Van Dyck, and Murillo. The captains and the kings included Louis XIV, Richelieu, Cromwell, and Peter the Great. In Britain alone, and among men of lesser stature, the names that come to mind call up stirring memories: Ralegh, Eliot, Hampden, Pym, Donne, Burton, Bunyan, Penn, Pepys, and Dryden. The century mothered such men as Defoe, Swift, Addison, and Pope. "The imaginative drama had died out," says Thorold Rogers, "since living men were more characteristic than the subtlest pictures of the past. There has been and there will be no period in English history which commands and deserves such attention . . . for memory sees gods ascending out of the earth."[3]

Something of the intellectual and social ferment

[1] "Milton and the Telescope," *Journal of English Literary History*, Vol. II, pp. 1–32.

[2] *A History of Modern Culture*, Holt, 1930, Vol. I.

[3] J. E. Thorold Rogers, *Six Centuries of Work and Wages*, Scribner, 1884, chap. XVI.

of the time has already been indicated. Many old systems of thought and practice were crumbling, and new systems and ideas were slowly and uncertainly, but none the less surely, taking their places. The discoveries were not always pleasant—they included the spots on the sun as well as the moons of Jupiter. The line of progress was not a straight or a steady one. Bacon, through the inductive method of reasoning that he developed in his *Novum Organum* and the great inspiration which he gave to all inquiring minds by his advocacy of experimental research, proved his right to the title Macaulay gave him—"the man that moved the minds that moved the world." And yet Bacon refused to accept Kepler's theories of the density and solidity of the earth, and steadfastly denied its revolution about the sun. If Galileo felt the effects of the bigotry of the Inquisition, he displayed even worse bigotry in his treatment of Kepler, whose completion of the work of Copernicus he rejected. King Charles II was sufficiently interested in scientific experiments to become in 1662 the patron of the "Royal Society of London for Promoting Natural Knowledge," but Pepys tells us that "he mightily laughed at" the members of the society "for spending time only in weighing of air, and doing nothing else since they sat."[4]

The seventeenth century may be truly said to have laid the foundations of modern astronomy, but astrology continued active long after 1700, and has indeed its ardent adherents in the twentieth century. Kepler, who perfected the Copernican hypothesis and discovered and charted the motions of the planets, was not above casting horoscopes for noble families. It has been wittily remarked that Superstition brought up Science until the ungrateful youngster left home. The first Astronomer Royal of England, the Reverend John Flamsteed, believed in and practiced astrology, and it is a significant fact that the foundation stone of the Royal Observatory at Greenwich was laid on August 10, 1675, at the hour and minute determined as most favorable by Flamsteed's astrological reckonings.

The literature of the day affords numerous illustrations of the intellectual interest in the new astronomy mingled with sentimental attachments to older notions, as in John Donne's sonnet beginning

At the round earth's imagined corners, blow
Your trumpets, angels. . . .

Milton seems to have been intellectually convinced of the truth of the Copernican hypothesis, and in Book VIII of *Paradise Lost* the Archangel Raphael speculates interestingly upon "celestial motions." For theological and artistic reasons, however, Milton employs, with adaptations, the Ptolemaic theory for the cosmology of his great poem. Intellectually curious as he was, and as he wished his Adam to be, he represents Raphael as less interested in Adam's acquiring a thorough knowledge of all the heavenly motions than in his pupil's understanding the priority and excellence of spiritual integrity and moral obedience:

This to attain, whether heaven move or earth,
Imports not, if thou reckon right. . . .

The seventeenth century gave chemistry to the world, and yet it produced its full quota of treatises on alchemy. Ben Jonson in his play *The Alchemist* was not describing or satirizing an imaginary situation. Alchemy was the great love of Sir Isaac Newton's life, as his notes testify. Robert Boyle, "the father of chemistry," a believer in the transmutability of metals, confided to Newton and Locke his recipe for "multiplying gold," and a company was formed in London to put the process into operation. "I am half of opinion," Sir Thomas Browne had a habit of saying, and the century as a whole was of a mind with Sir Thomas. Samuel Pepys, though a president of the Royal Society, and keenly interested in every new scientific discovery, nevertheless preserved old charms and spells, and kept his hare's foot in his pocket to be on the safe side. There was no clear distinction between the realms and functions of religion and theology and those of natural science. The Bible was considered the final authority on all matters of which it treats, and sooner or later it treats of most matters in the heavens above and the earth beneath. The Bible declares, "Thou shalt not suffer a witch to live," and in the face of such a categorical statement it was a bold man who would undertake to doubt the existence of witches. Furthermore, to deny the existence of evil spirits, such as witches, seemed to many to imply the denial of the existence of beneficent spiritual forces, and such a denial would have been unthinkable in the seventeenth century. So Sir Thomas Browne, although he undertook in his *Pseudodoxia Epidemica, or Vulgar Errors* to disprove many erroneous opinions "commonly presumed truths," never questioned

[4] *Diary*, Feb. 1, 1663/4. "What they were doing," says G. N. Clark, *The Later Stuarts, 1660–1714*, Oxford Press, 1929, p. 42, "was to investigate atmospheric pressure, and it was a short step to the pressure of steam. The experimenters themselves did not foresee that the motive power which came into practical use as a result of their work, and which before the death of Queen Anne was raising water from a mine in Staffordshire, was to become after two more generations one of the governing forces of the world."

the existence of witches. Among his learned contemporaries who likewise believed in them were Henry More, Sir Isaac Newton, and Joseph Glanvill.[5] Sir Thomas saw clearly that "the mortallest enemy unto knowledge, and that which hath done the greatest execution upon truth, hath been a peremptory adhesion unto authority, and, more especially, the establishing of our belief upon the dictates of antiquity."[6] In this he agrees with Bacon, but, in characteristic fashion, he calls up one authority to lay low another, and too often blasts one dictate of antiquity with another of the same vintage. Sir Thomas was an experimentalist, and produced some results of lasting value by his use of the laboratory method. But there were occasions when he had to regret that there was no time to conduct "those infallible experiments and those assured determinations which the subject sometimes requireth."

The age of specialization had, of course, not yet arrived. Bacon, it will be remembered, took all knowledge for his province. The seventeenth century was the golden age of the amateur, and the world has perhaps never seen such a group of versatile, accomplished, and well-rounded men. Clergymen were authorities on all matters, bishops designed flying boats, lawyers knew the fine points of theology, physicians wrote exquisite lyrics and impassioned prose. The Warden of the Mint, Sir Isaac Newton, discovered the laws of motion and gravity, and also found time for a treatise on the Book of Revelation which he considered the crowning achievement of his life. If such restless and insatiable curiosity about all things, and such wholesale and universal interest in all departments of human life and thought, were bound to lead often to shallowness and irrelevancy, the men of the seventeenth century at any rate avoided the pitfalls of too great specialization of interest and research, which the men of the twentieth century do not always escape.

There was not yet a sufficient recognition of the fact that there are different categories of knowledge and phenomena. In the desire to solve the great puzzle of the world and to discover relations between groups of phenomena, the love of tracing analogy and the temptation to press an analogy once discerned ever farther and farther led many men of the Middle Ages to false conclusions in many matters. The bulk of medieval science has been briefly characterized as a misuse of analogy, and such misuse has continued to be one of the greatest sources of human error. The importance of the proper use of analogy and its indispensable service as a handmaid of scientific thought are, of course, not to be questioned. But by the extensive misuse of analogy, and by often reasoning logically from false premises, men had managed to construct a scheme of the universe that was fairly coherent, but which, when tested by observation and experiment, was bound to crumble.[7] The seventeenth century inherited such schemes, and much of the ancient and medieval misinformation about natural phenomena remained part of the "mental climate" of Europe until well on in the century. The important fact, however, that emerges from a study of the scientific thought and opinion of the century is not that such and such persons believed such and such things, but that a good many persons were beginning to question old beliefs, and to discover that much which had been accepted on the authority of the ancients is not true.

Philosophy tended more and more during the century to concern itself with "reason" and with matters capable of scientific experimentation and mathematical demonstration. The "laws of nature" occupied an increasingly larger share of man's thought, and began to take their place by the side of the "revealed truth" of the Bible. To the more devout scientists these studies in natural philosophy seemed to supplement and re-enforce rather than to supersede the truths of the Bible. Sir Thomas Browne, an ardent believer in the Bible, commended those who magnify God by "judicious inquiry into His acts and deliberate research into His creatures." By the end of the century, thanks to the work of the scientists and the philosophers, a state of mind had been induced in which such phenomena as conflagrations, plagues, and death came to be viewed less as evidences of Divine displeasure than as natural effects and circumstances, and natural methods were undertaken to deal with them. Before the century was over, both fire insurance and life insurance had arrived in England.

The development of education and scholarship, though retarded somewhat by civil unrest, proceeded apace. The opening years of the century found both Oxford and Cambridge largely medieval in methods, aims, and outlook. The medieval

[5] For all its belief in witchcraft, the seventeenth century was also the first in which there was expressed an official disbelief of it, and Sir Matthew Hale, the Lord Chief Justice, has the honor of being the first judge in England to refuse a conviction for witchcraft. [6] *Pseudodoxia Epidemica*, Book I, chap. VI.

[7] One of the most interesting of all analogies, and perhaps the most popular in the seventeenth century, is that between the body and life of man, the "microcosm," on the one hand, and the matter and forces of the universe, the "macrocosm," on the other. For a discussion of the ramifications of this analogy and of many other related matters, see John Read, *Prelude to Chemistry*, Macmillan, 1937.

shells had not been entirely discarded by 1700, but in no comparable period, perhaps, did more new ideas penetrate the ancient institutions, and seldom have they ever been subject to more severe criticism than they received from their bright young men during that time. Milton, though he would still have found much to disapprove of at Cambridge, would not have had so much justification in 1700 as he had in 1644 for contemptuously dismissing the entire curriculum as "an asinine feast of sow-thistles and brambles." The beginnings of modern English scholarship may be traced to the period of the Stuarts. The study of the Old English language and grammar, of old customs, laws, and precedents, was revived, both to re-enforce the arguments against the prevailing theory of the divine right of kings and out of "remembrance of things past." Interest in medieval scholarship flourished in England as never before. Scholars played an active part in the life of the time, and exercised in their writings a lasting influence on national character.

The intellectual resurgence at Cambridge was due chiefly to the group of scholars and philosophers known as the Cambridge Platonists. Most of their leaders, including Benjamin Whichcote, Ralph Cudworth, and John Smith, were trained at Emmanuel College, which was their physical home and the center from which their spiritual influence radiated. Another leader, Henry More, came from Christ's College, which he had entered half a year before Milton left. Their aim was to bring the Christian Church back to "her old loving nurse, the Platonic philosophy." Their Platonism has been described in the Wordsworthian phrase, "Reason in her most exalted mood," and the best summary of their attitude is the dictum of John Smith: "To follow reason is to follow God." They believed, as did Sir Thomas Browne, that there is no conflict between "reason" and "revelation," and that Divine revelation is not confined to the Bible or to the period of history with which it is concerned. More than any other men of their day they reconciled and brought to a focus in their own system of thought the religious, philosophic, and scientific thinking of the day. They were Puritan in origin, but they steered a middle course between Puritan and Royalist controversy as they did between Protestant and Catholic dogmatism. In their lives they united the vision and spiritual sensitiveness of the mystics with a belief in practical and positive goodness. In their desire to reconcile the historic beliefs of the Christian religion with the philosophy of their time, they were as a group drawn to the principles of Descartes, who had shown sufficiently clearly that faith and reason were not antagonists but mutual supports. Dr. Whichcote went so far as to advocate the use of the inductive method of reasoning in the solution of theological problems as well as those of natural science. They were hostile to the materialistic philosophy of Hobbes, and tried valiantly to check its influence. Since they were moderate men and advocates of "sweet reasonableness," the extremists of the day in religion and politics would have none of them. Their influence, if it could have been more widespread, might have helped to avoid the crisis of civil war. In their quiet way they began the renewal of the intellectual life of Cambridge, and from Emmanuel College their influence spread to other sections of the university. It was from Emmanuel College that John Harvard came to Massachusetts to save the little college that was later to bear his name, and thus the intellectual leaven of the Cambridge Platonists was brought across the Atlantic.[8]

The attempts to improve the educational methods of the secondary schools on the Continent and in England were even more numerous and effective. The modern world is indebted to the theories of Comenius, Milton, Cowley, Locke, and their contemporaries for some of its most cherished ideas relating to the education of children. Learning for learning's sake came to be less and less esteemed; the knowledge of foreign languages was beginning to be regarded as a means rather than as an end in itself. The teaching of things rather than words was advocated. The ideal of education came more and more to be the preparation of a man for service in a world of men and affairs, rather than the production of a cloistered polyglot. For comprehensiveness Milton's definition of education in 1644 can hardly be improved upon: "I call, therefore, a complete and generous education, that which fits a man to perform justly, skilfully, and magnanimously, all the offices, both private and public, of peace and war." John Locke, one of the first great champions of the rights of children as rational individuals, announced in his little book *Some Thoughts Concerning Education*, 1693, what has become an essential formula in modern education: "A sound mind in a sound body is a short but full description of a happy state in this world. He that has these two has little more to wish for; and he that wants either of them will be but little better for anything else." Before the century had run its course, Mary Astell and

[8] For a discussion of the Cambridge Platonists and their significance, see F. J. Powicke, *The Cambridge Platonists*, Harvard University Press, 1926, and W. R. Inge, *The Platonic Tradition in English Religious Thought*, Longmans, Green, 1926.

others were turning their attention to the education of girls and young women.[9] These educational advantages were, of course, open only to young gentlemen and ladies. The children of the poor had still to wait two centuries before they began to receive similar consideration.

In spite of social and intellectual cleavages and distinctions, the various classes of society were, nevertheless, in a very real sense members of one another, and all were alike subject to the alarums and excursions of the time. The birth rate and the death rate were high among rich and poor—infant mortality appallingly high. Famines exacted their toll, and conflagrations, of which the Great Fire of London (1666) was the most terrible, wiped out cathedrals and palaces as well as hovels and tenements. And yet population increased in the midst of wars and plagues and poverty and fire. The England of William III had, it is estimated, five and a half million people, an increase of a million over that of Elizabeth, and London had by 1700 become a metropolis of more than a quarter of a million inhabitants. The city that was dominated by Sir Christopher Wren's new St. Paul's had more and finer churches than ever, and, in addition, libraries, museums, banks, coffeehouses, and many other institutions which Elizabethan London had never known.

English History in the Seventeenth Century

The most important factor in the political as in the literary history of the time was the religious revolution which came to a focus in the Puritan revolt. In this matter, as in most others, the era of the Stuarts cannot be dissociated from that of Elizabeth. Puritanism as a religious force had already assumed such proportions before Elizabeth died as to cause alarm or thanksgiving, according to the respective principles of those who viewed its growth. Thomas Fuller gives the following account of the origin of the Puritans:

"The English bishops . . . began to show their authority in urging the clergy of their diocese to subscribe to the liturgy, ceremonies, and discipline of the Church, and such as refused the same were branded with the odious name of Puritans; a name which in this notion first began in this year [1563–64]."[10]

[9] See Mary Astell, *A Serious Proposal to the Ladies for the Advancement of Their True and Greatest Interest*, 1694. [10] *Church History of Britain*, 1655

The Queen expressed by word and deed her displeasure at the motives and methods of the Puritans, and increasingly severe measures were taken to force them to conform. By 1593 Puritanism had been made an offense against the statute law, and as a result many of the more conspicuous Puritans crossed the sea to Holland. The comparatively peaceful period which closed Elizabeth's reign was abruptly ended when her successor, James I, full of a sense of importance as head of Church and State, and obsessed with the idea of the divine right of both kings and bishops, added to the burdens of the Puritans as well as to those of most of his subjects. James's troubles with Parliament began soon after his accession. Elizabeth, thanks to her sex, her age, and her prestige, had taken many liberties and done many things which her successor, a man and a Stuart, was not permitted by Parliament to do with impunity. But the King had his way in the Church. Hundreds of ministers who could not subscribe to the articles of the Church were deprived of their livings, many of them were imprisoned, and the number of exiles constantly increased. By the end of his reign in 1625, James had, through his bigotry, his worldliness, and his general disregard for the convictions of his more sober and decent subjects, as well as for the opinions of the House of Commons, brought the country to almost open insurrection. The breach between the Puritans on one hand, and Church and State on the other had become irreparable. The condition in which his son, Charles I, found England is described by one of his subjects, James Howell:

"He is left engaged in a war with a potent prince, the people by long desuetude unapt for arms, the fleet royal in quarter repair, himself without a queen, his sister without a country, the crown pitifully laden with debts, and the purse of the state lightly ballasted, though it never had better opportunity to be rich than it had these last twenty years."[11]

Of all men in England the new king was the least likely to undo the damage and restore national unity. He was more sincerely devoted to the Church than was his father, and, if not so strongly addicted to the doctrine of the divine right of the King, he nevertheless pressed it farther. His absolutist theories, which were encouraged by the bishops, increased the hostility of Parliament to both King and bishops. His marriage to the Roman Catholic princess, Henrietta Maria of France, seriously disturbed

[11] *Familiar Letters*, Sec. 4, Letter 7.

the country, which was becoming increasingly fearful of the growth of Catholicism. Financial difficulties increased, the Crown jewels were pawned, and forced loans were instituted. Two Parliaments were dissolved by the imperious sovereign when they failed to comply with his demands for money. But the King could not get along without funds, and he could not get funds without Parliament. He called a third Parliament in 1628, and in this assembly he met his match. He was forced to sign the Petition of Right, which, among other things, declared illegal such measures as forced loans, martial law in time of peace, and invasions of the rights of subjects such as the billeting of soldiers in private houses.[12]

The King's character and methods had not changed, however. This Parliament, too, was dissolved, and for eleven years, from 1629 until 1640, the King ruled without Parliament. Conditions grew steadily more intolerable. The King's activities included both petty exactions and restrictions and major offenses against the law of the land. Obsolete laws and customs were revived. Charles felt it necessary to strengthen the fleet against the French and the Dutch, and as there was no Parliament to grant him the necessary funds, he resorted in 1634 to an ancient custom and issued writs to the port towns requiring them to furnish ships. In the following year he included inland counties in the demand. With the money thus obtained the King built up a navy entirely under his own control, and continued the levy of ship money to maintain the fleet. The principle involved, that of raising taxes without parliamentary grant, was so important, and so capable of abuse, that John Hampden, a gentleman of Buckinghamshire, determined to bring the question of the legality of ship money before the courts by refusing to pay his tax. The courts were under the power of the King, and decided the case in the royal favor.

The decision in the ship-money case opened the eyes of the nation as nothing previously had done, and events moved on to a crisis. The Puritans were meanwhile being further alienated and oppressed by Archbishop Laud. The Earl of Strafford and his policy of "Thorough," by which the country was to be made subject to a standing army, embittered and made hostile a still larger group of civilians. The normal rights and privileges of citizens were abrogated by the courts of Star Chamber and High Commission. As if intoxicated by arbitrary power, and increasingly oblivious or careless of the feelings and temper of his people in both England and Scotland, Charles attempted to force a Book of Common Prayer on Scotland. The opposition to the new liturgy gradually grew into open rebellion, and the long-expected crisis came in 1639 when war between the King and the Scottish Covenanters broke out. Without funds, and with a united and determined Scotland opposing him, Charles was reluctantly forced to summon Parliament after its intermission of eleven years. The "Long Parliament," which sat for thirteen years, and the King were soon at open war. The revenge of the Parliament on the King, the bishops, the heads of the King's army, the inquisitorial courts, and the whole system which the King had established and fostered, was swift and sure.

The principles at issue in the conflict between King and Parliament in the seventeenth century concern themselves so much with such terms as despotism, tyranny, freedom, rights, and liberties, that the struggle has come, in the minds of many in later generations of British and Americans, to be regarded as the pattern conflict between a despot and a people striving to gain its freedom. It is true that Hampden, Pym, Cromwell, Milton, and others of their side with sword or pen fought some of our battles for us, and their names have ever since been an inspiration to men who cherish religious and political freedom, and who have fought or who may have to fight for such freedom. But from a historical point of view it is a mistake to think of the English Civil War in terms of modern political and religious ideas. The members of the Long Parliament were no more democrats than Charles. Politically they were fighting to replace the authority of the King with their own authority, to substitute the rule of a capitalistic oligarchy for that of monarchy, and they succeeded in doing so. In religious matters the Puritans, although they differed from Archbishop Laud on certain details of faith and practice, were as convinced as he of the necessity and wholesomeness of uniformity in religion "according to the Word of God." They disagreed with him violently in the interpretation of that Word. Religious freedom in the modern sense of the word did not exist, and by most God-fearing persons was not desired. Toleration of the religious beliefs, or lack of them, of others was not part of the program of most seventeenth-century Christians. "Toleration," declared a seventeenth-century president of Harvard College, "is the first-born of abominations."

Penal laws against minority groups, particularly religious minorities, were characteristic functions of

[12] The principles, and some of the provisions, of the Petition of Right are suggestive of those in the Bill of Rights, set forth in the first ten amendments to the Constitution of the United States.

the legislation of the century. Quakers, Roman Catholics, and Nonconformists in general all felt, at one time or another, the burdens of penal codes inflicted on them. Roger Williams was almost the sole advocate of absolute liberty of conscience. He opposed a national church and all state interference with religion, but his real hope was in America rather than in England, and his difficulties even in America make an interesting page of our history. A few people here and there, among them Sir Thomas Browne, Bishop Jeremy Taylor, Milton, and the Cambridge Platonists, were prepared to tolerate a certain divergence from what was considered the norm, and to recognize a limited variety of religious faiths and practices. But Taylor considered indispensable a belief in the Apostles' Creed, and Milton, in his *Areopagitica*, after an eloquent plea for toleration and freedom of thought and speech, adds "I mean not tolerated popery." The leaders of both sides in the great conflict were sincere in their convictions, religious and political, and proved their sincerity by fighting—but they fought to preserve or to establish the religion and the government which they were convinced were right and good and necessary for all men.

The twentieth century has reversed many of the verdicts of previous generations on both Charles I and the Puritans. Charles and Cromwell and their respective adherents seem to modern students of history to be less villains than victims of the times and circumstances in which they lived and acted. It is conceivable that in happier times Charles might have been a successful and popular monarch; it is doubtful if England has ever produced an essentially greater Englishman than Oliver Cromwell. Though Charles was politically and doctrinally opposed to the Puritans, his own personal character contained many elements which are now commonly called Puritanical. Charles inherited a government of Church and State the corruption of which was patent to most thoughtful Englishmen. The crown which he inherited was barely self-supporting. Taxes were necessary, and the King had to depend on Parliament to levy them. It has been said of Charles that he was a more law-abiding king than most of his predecessors had been, and that it was not altogether his fault if Parliament put upon him so many restrictions that to obey them meant that he would no longer be a king according to the traditional concept of kingship. He had the misfortune to believe in pure monarchy at a time when men like the great lawyer John Selden and the great writer John Milton could think in terms of an impersonal government. He failed partly because he could not see that law, as Dean Pound of Harvard has said, though stable cannot be static.

The momentum of the Puritans carried them farther than in the beginning they had thought of going. Even Milton in 1641 did not dream of any better system than monarchy. He and his fellows were merely bent on improving the existing system. To effect the desired reforms, and particularly to get rid of some of the evils of prelacy, Parliament had to get some of the King's power into its own hands. In return for the financial assistance which it gave the King, the latter was made to sign over some of his authority to Parliament. The zeal of Parliament gradually gathered such impetus that the result was the reformation of the monarchical system out of existence!

The Civil War was marked by gallantry and brave deeds on both sides, and, as always, by the shedding of some of the country's best blood. In the circumstances it could have had only one outcome—the victory of Cromwell's Ironsides. Stronger kings than Charles, and greater armies than those of his Cavaliers, have failed to win against such deadly earnestness and soldierly discipline as that of the Roundheads. In bringing Charles to the block on January 30, 1649, his enemies seemed to have scored a triumph, but though they won the day and the decade, they lost in the century. For the dead King became a martyr, and as a martyr he triumphed as he could never have triumphed in life. By a strange irony he who while still living had come to be more and more the embodiment of royal tyranny came to represent more and more after his death "the sole and sacred repository of the laws and liberties of his people." In the light of history it seems to many an irreparable injury that Cromwell did his cause in 1649, when, as G. M. Young says, "in a volcanic hour of anger, disappointment, ambition, impatience, and perhaps despair, he flung himself against the English tradition at the point where it has always been strongest and most sensitive, its respect for law."[13] As for tyranny, the Puritans in the saddle were to show themselves at times as stern taskmasters as any king or royal court of Star Chamber or High Commission. Those who had themselves suffered from the tyranny of the Church made the adherents of the Church and all others who differed with them feel the weight of their displeasure. The Presbyterians were as ruthless in forbidding the use of the Book of Common Prayer as the King and the bishops had been in enforcing its use. Milton, who had at one time upheld them, had sorrowfully to admit that "New Presbyter is but

[13] *Charles I and Cromwell*, London, 1935, pp. 144–45.

old Priest writ large," and even to many an ardent Parliamentarian the second tyranny seemed worse than the first.

The republic which came into existence after the execution of Charles brought several years of vigorous and able government. The army and navy of Cromwell were in effect the beginning of the modern British army and navy, and under Cromwell England was more feared and respected in Europe than she had been since the fourteenth century. The republic lasted four years, and Cromwell was installed as Lord Protector at Westminster Abbey in December, 1653. It has been said that the tragedy of Cromwell's career was that men united to support him when he destroyed, but when he tried to build he had to work alone in the midst of squabbling factions. With his army he kept control until his death in 1658, but with his passing all the pent-up forces were released, and a complete disintegration of the Commonwealth followed. The anarchy and military despotism that succeeded the Commonwealth oppressed trade by its foreign policy and by the heavy taxation necessary for a standing army. Cromwell's weak son and successor, Richard, abdicated in 1659, and the exiled son of Charles I came into his own again as Charles II in May, 1660. The cause of the Puritans seemed for the time to have failed, but it was to win its real triumphs later, and the principles that found their best expression in the writings of Milton and Bunyan have over the years contributed effectively to the shaping of the Britain and the America of the present day.

With Charles II on the throne, the forces against which Cromwell had fought regained control. The lords temporal and spiritual began again to exercise their former powers. An Act of Amnesty was passed, but it did not benefit most of the dead King's judges. Some of them escaped to America; thirteen of them were put to death. The bodies of such chief offenders as Cromwell and Ireton were disinterred and hanged in chains. Milton, who had been Cromwell's Latin Secretary and the most eloquent defender of the Commonwealth and the regicides, was heavily fined and had to remain in hiding until after the Act of Oblivion was passed. His anti-Royalist books were burned by the common hangman, and he seems to have escaped being put to death only through the influence of Andrew Marvell and other friends. It was now the turn of the Nonconformist ministers to be deprived of their livings and privileges, and many like John Bunyan found themselves in jail. Royalist clergymen, among them Robert Herrick, who had been ejected from their livings by the Puritans, now returned to them.

To Milton and those who shared his feelings, the country had "fallen on evil days," and the "sons of Belial" were abroad in the land. Public morality sank to its lowest ebb. The scandalousness of Charles's court is proverbial, and the King himself was a pensioner of Louis XIV, a master of intrigue, and a shameless appropriator of public funds. Conditions at home and abroad became more and more unsettled. The plague of 1665, the great fire of 1666, and the burning of English shipping in the Thames by the Dutch in 1667, struck terror into the heart of London. The religious disturbances reached a climax with the famous imposture known as the Popish Plot, invented by certain anti-Catholic fanatics, who accused the Roman Catholics of plotting to murder the King and to restore Roman Catholicism. The ready belief that was accorded the alleged design, and the cruel punishment which was inflicted on innocent people, were symptomatic of the uneasy state of mind which prevailed in the country.

In Parliament the fears and excitement resulted in the proposal of the Exclusion Bill, by which the King's brother, the Duke of York, a Roman Catholic, would have been barred from succeeding him. In the country at large the first Earl of Shaftesbury fomented interest in the bill and headed a plot to depose Charles in favor of his illegitimate son, the Duke of Monmouth, who had in his favor both charming manners and a reputation for loyalty to the established faith.[14] The plot and the Exclusion Bill failed, and Charles died King of England. His reign, for all its disturbances, was marked by real constitutional progress. The great Habeas Corpus Act, which prevented illegal imprisonment by securing the imprisoned citizen's right to be tried or to be liberated, was passed by Parliament in 1679. The two political factions called "Petitioners" and "Abhorrers" with respect to their attitude toward the Exclusion Bill were the beginnings of the two great political parties, the Whigs and the Tories, and their establishment was the greatest single step toward parliamentary rule.[15]

[14] For Dryden's satire on the plot, *Absalom and Achitophel*, see p. 454. [15] "It is no mere coincidence," says G. N. Clark, *The Later Stuarts*, p. 97, "that the two party names Whig and Tory became current about this time. Both were originally terms of abuse: whigs were Scots Presbyterian rebels and tories Irish Catholic bandits. The parties to which they were applied were on the one hand the exclusionists, who wanted parliamentary limitation of the Crown and toleration for Protestants only, on the other hand the supporters of hereditary succession and the prerogative. They disagreed about these principles, and they were competitors for office and power, so that their principles were then and always subject to the constant transforming pressure of personal and tactical interests."

The Duke of York, as James II, succeeded his brother on the throne in 1685. In spite of his oath to preserve the established religion, he set to work to restore the Roman Catholic faith to England. The reign began with a rebellion in Scotland and another in England, the latter headed by the Duke of Monmouth, and both rebellions were inspired by Protestant interests. The necessity of suppressing Monmouth's Rebellion gave the King the excuse for increasing his army, and among the officers added were many Roman Catholics. The rebellion brought into prominence, as the chief prosecutor of the cases of treason arising out of it, the infamous Judge Jeffreys, who took such cruel revenge on Monmouth's followers in the western counties that his sessions of court received the name of the "Bloody Assizes." James's troubled reign of three years was brought to an end by a circumstance which in normal times, and to most kings and subjects, would seem the most favorable event possible—the birth of a son and heir. But the knowledge that the heir to the throne would be a Roman Catholic caused the leaders of both parties to invite Prince William of Orange, the husband of James's daughter Mary and the nephew of Charles II, to come to the rescue of England, her laws, and her religion. William landed in November, 1688, and James, deserted by his army, fled to France. The crown was offered in joint sovereignty the following year to William and Mary.

The Revolution of 1688–89, however considered, is one of the most monumental events in English history. It accomplished far more than the securing of a Protestant succession to the throne and the establishment of the Protestant religion in England. For one thing, it transformed the bitter feuds of the two political parties into what was at least an armed truce, to the great benefit of the state. It transferred definitely and finally the ultimate power of the King to the Parliament, and in the Parliament to the House of Commons. The Bill of Rights, which the House of Commons proceeded to pass, limited the powers of the Crown, and expressly provided for the maintenance of the people's liberties. And Parliament has sat every year since 1689.

During the remaining decade of the century, the powers and prerogatives of the Crown were still further curtailed. The first cabinet government was instituted in England when William, acting on advice, selected as his ministers the leading members of the two Houses who had the confidence of the House of Commons. In the year before the King died he gave his assent to the Act of Settlement, which secured the succession of the Crown to the House of Hanover, to the exclusion of Roman Catholic claimants—the act which has determined the occupancy of the throne to the present day.

Within the century England had undergone both a religious and a political revolution. Two other revolutions, the industrial and the social, were forced to wait until the political and religious forces had worked out their destinies. The political events did not, however, leave social conditions entirely unchanged. The civil wars did away with the semi-feudal conditions which governed class relations under Elizabeth and the first two Stuarts. The nobleman at the end of the century had much more in common with the modern English gentleman than with the medieval baron. The country squire and the country parson continued to preside at the top of the hierarchy which had as its broad base the yeomen, the laborers, and the artisans. The progress of these humbler constituents of rural society, the growth and increasing importance of London in the British scheme of things, the rise to wealth and power of the commercial class, the development of agriculture and industry, belong to the history of the century that follows.

English Literature in the Seventeenth Century

The literature of seventeenth-century England was not a thing apart from the social, political, religious, and intellectual movements that have been mentioned in the foregoing pages. The poetry and prose of the period constitute, indeed, the best mirror of the events and forces of the age. The men who wrote the century's literature also helped to fight the century's battles, administer its government, preach its sermons, heal its sick, fish its streams, and carry on the work of the day. Milton, the greatest poet of the century, giving the years of his prime to the service of the state, is symbolic of the close connection between the world of letters and the world of action. Both the poetry and the prose of the time came largely from men who wrote because they had something to say which but for them would go unsaid, not because it was fashionable to write, or to satisfy external demands and requirements. In 1646, when civil strife and pamphlet warfare filled the land, Henry Vaughan, in the preface to his *Poems*, confesses "to all ingenious lovers of poesy": "I know the years, and what coarse entertainment they afford poetry. . . . It is for you only that I have adventured thus far, and invaded the press with verse." Few if any of the writers of the day could be called professional poets or men of letters, and none of them claimed as the privilege of genius the right to retire to an ivory tower. The literature, both religious and secular, was much given to introspection and self-analysis, and the lyrics of the century have been called fragments of autobiographies.

The very conflict between science and religion, and the confusion of mind that resulted from their pitched battles, were responsible for some of the most beautiful poetry and prose of the day. It is not an accident that any anthology of English mystical verse draws more heavily on the poets of the seventeenth century than of any other. Many like the later Donne, and Herbert, Vaughan, and Crashaw, wearied with the conflicting philosophies of the day and with the hoarse noises of dispute, turned from the uncertainties of the world of physical sense and perception to what seemed to them the unchanging truths of the spiritual mysteries that lay beyond the ken of the intellect. In the realm of prose the contemplation of "this great mystery of our religion" raises such writers as Sir Thomas Browne and Jeremy Taylor to heights of eloquence and a magnificence of phrase which have never been surpassed.

In sermons, as well as in lyrics, epics, and allegories, the exposition of religious and theological truths produced literature of beauty and power. The seventeenth century has been called the golden age of the sermon, and it may be said that no literary form is more characteristic of the age.[16] The richly furnished mind of Donne makes of his sermons prose counterparts of his poems, and a study of the eloquent compositions designed for the congregation of St. Paul's will help greatly in the understanding of his verse. The development of English prose across the century can be fairly and interestingly traced in the sermon literature of the time, from Donne and Andrewes to Baxter, Taylor, Barrow, and Tillotson. Dryden has testified to the influence on the style of his own prose of some of the seventeenth-century divines.

It is the chief glory of the first two decades of the century that they gave to English literature the King James Version of the Bible and all the greater plays of Shakespeare. These alone would serve to make the period the golden age of the literature. They are such a large part of the common heritage, and have entered so much into the language and life of English-speaking people during the past three hundred years, that they cannot be properly represented in any single category or period. In every sense they are not of an age but for all time.

The Drama

To the first decade and the very beginning of the second decade of the seventeenth century belong Shakespeare's great tragedies and his late dramatic romances. In this period also come Ben Jonson's satirical comedies dealing with the "humors" of society and his tragedies cast in the classical mold. Contemporary with these were the most notable plays of John Webster, a poet of macabre powers and sinister imagination. With the second decade of the century begins the career of the prolific John Fletcher, who in the course of fifteen years, with a series of collaborators from Francis Beaumont to Philip Massinger, produced a quantity of drama immensely rich in comic verve and tragic variety, if somewhat poetically and morally lax. After Fletcher's death in 1625, Massinger dominated the scene with a series of notable satirical comedies in the Jonsonian tradition and a number of tragedies loftier in tone and style than those written by his less scrupulous contemporaries.

During the time of a generation between the death of Elizabeth and the official closing of the theaters in 1642, English drama was undergoing a general disintegration. The elements which were so mixed in Shakespeare were separated and exploited by lesser persons. What had been a pastime that the public as a whole had enjoyed, an afternoon's entertainment in which both tragedy and comedy had their parts, gave way to a series of plays and entertainments for separate and diverse groups. The masque, a private entertainment in which dance and spectacle were all-important; the "comedy of humors," in which a particular type of man animated by some one predominant trait or "humor" was portrayed; the drama in which poetry gave way to rhetoric, and a perverse passion was exploited beyond measure—these appealed to and were supported by their respective adherents. There are, to be sure, moving scenes and memorable passages of poetry in many of these plays; and even so ephemeral a form as the masque, with its primary appeal to the senses and its dependence on machinery and setting, was made the vehicle for beautiful and enduring poetry by Ben Jonson in a dozen pieces and by Milton in his *Comus*. But there is no better way of demonstrating Shakespeare's superiority as poet or dramatist than by comparing

[16] For an interesting and thorough discussion of the popularity and importance of the sermon in seventeenth-century life and letters, see C. F. Richardson, *English Preachers and Preaching, 1640–1670*, Macmillan, 1928.

his dramas with the best of those that were written in the quarter of a century following his death. No great loss, perhaps, was suffered by either the English theater or English literature when the Puritans decided in 1642 that "stage plays do not suit with times of humiliation," and decreed that public performances of them should cease.

On the whole, the decadence of the early seventeenth-century drama is esthetic rather than moral. That is to say, decadence is apparent in an absence of originality and in the skillful repetition of timeworn situations, characters, and devices, such as one finds in the tragedies of James Shirley. Decadence of a moral sort was unquestionably a preoccupation of John Ford, the best of the later dramatists. But when the Puritans closed the theaters in 1642, numerous gifted playwrights were still active, and in Shirley's comedies of manners and in the Cavalier dramas of love and honor, one can see types and tastes that were to persist surreptitiously until the Restoration.

The official ban on the theaters did not prevent entirely either the writing or the public performance of plays, but civil strife and Puritan domination were not helpful to the already moribund drama. Alfred Harbage, in his study of the drama of the middle years of the century, is of the opinion that if Charles I had stayed on the throne and the playhouses had remained open, the drama would have continued to disintegrate, becoming less and less popular and getting more and more under the control of the court and into the hands of the courtly amateurs.[17] The drama acted in such theaters as might have continued to exist would probably have been very much what was in fashion after the Restoration—heroic tragedy and the comedy of manners. The continuity of the dramatic tradition, such as it was, is illustrated in the work of Sir William Davenant, whose earliest plays came nearly a decade before the official closing of the theaters, and whose drama *The Siege of Rhodes*, 1656, replete with music and elaborate scenery to justify its pretense to being an "opera" and not a play, foreshadowed the heroic drama of the Restoration. Students of the Restoration drama see in Davenant's *Siege of Rhodes* almost all the elements of earlier dramatic compositions—the music and scenery of the masque, the heroic themes of Marlowe and Beaumont and Fletcher, and, as Mr. Harbage has shown, the Cavalier's conception of valor, and even the rhymed heroic couplet. In addition to native elements there were also ingredients of Italian opera and French drama. French influence, "after his Majesty's being so long abroad," is to be noted in much of Restoration drama, especially in the rhymed heroic drama of Dryden and Sir Robert Howard. English tragedy and dramatic theory were greatly influenced by the classical tragedies of Corneille, and Restoration writers of comedy turned to Molière for plots, incidents, and characters. Professor Nettleton reminds us, however, that English influence was still the underlying factor, and that the roots of Restoration drama lie in Elizabethan soil.[18]

The dramatic repertory of the Restoration was diversified also by revivals and adaptations of Shakespeare, Jonson, and Beaumont and Fletcher. Dryden, though most of his plays were written in the fashionable heroic couplet, achieved his greatest dramatic success in blank verse in his *All for Love*, 1678, which took its theme from Shakespeare's *Antony and Cleopatra*. In prose the comedy of manners in the hands of Etherege, Wycherley, and Congreve brought to the English stage and to English literature brilliance if not greatness. In the plays of Congreve, especially, English comedy reached a height which it was not to attain again for nearly a hundred years.

Poetry

When we turn our eyes to nondramatic verse, we find that the fabric of seventeenth-century poetry is of a piece with that of the Elizabethan period. The predominating patterns and colors at its beginning are those of three great artists who began their work before the sixteenth century was over—Spenser, Jonson, and Donne. Spenser did not live to see the new century, but the pastoral and allegorical figures of his poetry were the inspiration and the models of much of the work of William Drummond, George Wither, Giles and Phineas Fletcher, and of many other minor poets of the generation following him, and his influence is to be detected in the early work of his great admirer, Milton. The incomparable lyric felicity and melody of Spenser's verse, best described in Milton's phrase, "linkèd sweetness long drawn out," are echoed and imitated in scores of poems which mourn departed shepherds, sing of faithful loves and ideal beauty, and celebrate the fresh woods and green pastures of an England which had not yet ceased altogether to be a land of faerie.

[17] See Alfred Harbage, *Cavalier Drama*, Modern Language Association, 1936.

[18] For the most thorough discussion of the literary aspects of Restoration drama see G. H. Nettleton, *English Drama of the Restoration and Eighteenth Century, 1642–1780*, Macmillan, 1923.

In sharp contrast to the romantic formlessness and long-drawn-out sweetness, as well as to the moralizing songs, of Spenser and his followers, are the neatness, the precision, and the classic grace and restraint of Ben Jonson's lyrics. No single influence in the poetry of the century is so strongly marked as that of Jonson. It informs more or less the society verse of Carew, the songs of the Cavaliers, and the lyrics of Herrick. It was felt by Milton, as may be seen from his early songs, by the court poets of the Restoration, by Marvell, and by Dryden. With Jonson and the "Sons of Ben" the lyric poem could talk as well as sing, and, whether talking or singing, approached more nearly the sureness of the Latin line than English verse had ever done before.

The most vigorous, and certainly the most unconventional, of the poets of Elizabethan and Jacobean England was John Donne. The poetry of Donne and of those who followed more or less his original and fantastic style has, since Dryden's criticism of it in his *Discourse Concerning Satire* and Dr. Johnson's discussion of it in his *Life of Cowley*, been called "metaphysical," although this term does not adequately or properly describe it.[19] No single word could accurately express the extraordinary figurativeness, the intellectual ingenuity and resourcefulness, of John Donne. He is commonly thought of as a rebel against the conventional sweetness and melody, the overworked themes of spring and larks at heaven's gate, the imaginary shepherds and shepherdesses, and the often meaningless but prettily phrased sentiments of Petrarchan and Spenserian poetry, and such in effect he was. But his work, in both verse and prose, was probably not so much the result of a conscious revolt as of an effort to be himself, and to express himself in his own way, without consideration first of all for artistic beauty or appropriateness. His language is essentially the language of prose, and by his use of homely and colloquial diction he brought back the virtues of prose to English poetry at a time when it needed to be revivified and purged of too poetic and artificial phrases. The harshness and ruggedness of Donne's verse, which are perhaps the first qualities to strike a reader, are due both to impatience with conventional patterns and rhythms and to a desire to shock the reader into attention. The richness of his verse, as of the sermons of his later years, he attains not by the archaic effect of Spenser's pseudo-Chaucerian language, or by languorous conceits made up of learned and philosophic terms, but by remote and striking analogies, daring metaphors, bizarre similes, and an amazing fecundity of figurativeness in general. To his subjects he brought candor, a fierce emotional intensity, and an unprecedented intellectual passion and curiosity. The subjects themselves are as varied as the thoughts and experiences of the age in which he lived.

Such an original genius could not fail to attract attention and imitation. Donne's influence upon his contemporaries was peculiar in that it was an influence exerted by poems still in manuscript circulation. Herbert was the first to follow in his steps. He shows Donne's influence in his curiosity, the luxuriance of his figures, and his habit of going into strange places for his metaphors. Vaughan, Crashaw, Carew, Cowley, Marvell, all of them artists in their own right, were affected for better or for worse by Donne's habit of thought and mannerisms, and adapted and modified them, each in his own way. The Cavaliers, Lovelace and Suckling, after their fashion, likewise give evidence that they have studied Donne. Even Dryden, who was to be in his maturer years the chief opponent of the theory and practice of "metaphysical" poetry, began his poetical career under the spell of Donne, and spun his conceits with the best, and the worst, of the "Metaphysicals." For the greater part of the century, English poetry was different because of Donne, and it is this "metaphysical" quality, more easily discerned and felt than defined, that sets so much of the poetry of the seventeenth century apart from that of other periods.[20]

Of all the poets of the far side of the Restoration, Milton alone escaped the influence of Donne's peculiar style and turn of thought. Milton belongs to no one school, although he acknowledged Spenser as his master. But he transcended Spenser, as he transcended all the poets who came after him. Milton embodied in himself and synthesized in his poetry all the wealth of ancient literature and learning, all the richness of myth and legend and fable, all the spiritual harvest of Hebraic morals and clas-

[19] The ablest discussion of metaphysical poetry and of the significance of Donne is that of Professor H. J. C. Grierson in the introduction to his *Metaphysical Lyrics and Poems of the Seventeenth Century*, Oxford University Press, 1925.

[20] The powerful appeal which Donne, more than any other of the older poets, has had for young poets of all political faiths in the present century is interesting to students of contemporary literature. Many poets of the last quarter of a century, both in Britain and in America, have seen in Donne the reflection of an age of instability and confusion, of mental revolt and reorientation, very like our own. Twentieth-century ears, also, have become weary with the more conventional patterns and rhythms of nineteenth-century verse, and the poetry of Donne is refreshing because it is different. For a discussion of some aspects of this present-day interest in Donne and the "metaphysical" poets, see Elisabeth Tomlinson, "The Metaphysical Tradition in Three Modern Poets," *College English*, December, 1939, pp. 208–22.

sical art and philosophy. Only such a man and such a poet, nourished by all the poets and all the schools, could have given to English literature the body of poetry which unites in itself the moral earnestness of the Hebrew prophets, the classical sense of form, the intellectual vigor of the Renaissance, and the richness and exuberance of the great Elizabethans.

The influence of "metaphysical" poetry waned after the middle of the century, and the inevitable reaction set in against it. The excessive figurativeness and the roughness and angularity of the verse of Donne and of those who followed in his wake came to seem quaintly old-fashioned or downright barbarous and "Gothic" to a younger generation of poets who preferred the smoothness and precision of French verse and the rules and restraints of Latin poets and critics. Waller, Denham, and Dryden developed the closed couplet, and polished it into the perfect medium for commenting brilliantly, sarcastically, and satirically upon public and private topics of the moment, or for generalizations on man's place in the great scheme of things. The labor and the frenzy, the passionate mysticism, of the first half of the century disappeared. It is as if poetry had tired itself out with wonderment and speculation and analysis of the great mysteries of life, and had settled down to a reasoning consideration and a reasonable explanation of the more ordinary phenomena of existence. "Perspicacity, propriety, decency," according to Dryden, are the essential qualities of good poetry, and Dryden dictated to the second half of the century as Donne and Jonson had dictated to the first.[21] The lyric poetry of the Restoration is, therefore, not equal to that of the preceding generations. The sensibility and artistic energy of the period found its best expression in satire, in the comedy of manners, and in heroic tragedy, and, outside literature, in architecture, painting, and scientific experiment. Poetry, especially in the work of Samuel Butler and Dryden, was clever and often brilliant talk, and such it was to remain for half a century more until Gray and Collins and others revived the antiquarian, the archaic, and the picturesque, to be the bases of a new kind of written, not spoken, discourse.

Donne and Dryden have been called the two electrodes of the literature of the seventeenth century. Dryden, although very different from Donne, performed somewhat the same transitional function at the close of the century as Donne performed at its beginning. Dryden is the most versatile of all the literary figures of a very versatile century. He contributed to the drama, to lyrical and philosophical poetry, to satire, and, above all, to criticism. The latter two he raised to an eminence that they had not occupied before in English. He ushered in the classical movement which was to be brought to its highest development in the next generation by Pope. And it is from Pope that we have the happiest description of Dryden's chief merits as a poet as well as the best statement of the chief accomplishment of the classical movement in English literature:

Dryden taught to join
The varying verse, the full-resounding line,
The long majestic march, and energy divine.

Prose

The history of English prose in the seventeenth century discloses tendencies and developments not unlike those that marked the progress of poetry. There was not during the first half of the century any carefully marked distinction between the style and function of poetry and those of prose, and Bacon is one of the few writers of the time who did not use both mediums. Bacon's prose is, however, rich in imagery, and few poets have been more sensitive than he to felicities of cadence and rhythm. Donne's sermons are at times more truly poetic than many of his poems, and even in such works as Ralegh's *History of the World* and Milton's *Areopagitica*, where one might least expect to find poetry, the thought often takes fire, and chronology and statistics give way to genuinely poetic meditations on the deeper meanings of history and human life, the blessings of freedom, and the excellency of truth. The prose of the period, like the poetry, was much given to introspection and intellectual subtlety. Paradoxes and problems, anatomies, discoveries upon men and matter—these furnished the titles, the methods, and the substance of both poetry and prose. And the artist in prose—for prose was in the early seventeenth century more of an art and less of a handicraft than it has ever been since—brought to the discussion of his subject the same well-furnished mind and the same teeming vocabulary that the poet employed in his art.

Of the types of prose, the essay, which has been called a prose lyric, is the most distinctive contribution of the period to the literature. As the years passed the essay took on the duties of a prose maid-of-all-work. From a collection of apothegms and aphoristic conceits, as usually with Bacon, it de-

[21] Milton, like Donne, though in a very different manner, greatly influenced the substance and technique of later poetry. For a thorough discussion of the subject, see R. D. Havens, *The Influence of Milton on English Poetry*, Harvard University Press, 1922.

veloped into such extended, well-knit, and carefully arranged pieces of exposition as the chapters in Hobbes's *Leviathan* and Locke's *Essay Concerning Human Understanding*, or the dialogues of Dryden's *Essay of Dramatic Poesy*. In the interval between Bacon and Locke it served a multitude of men and purposes, and appeared in various forms as "characters," "resolves," meditations, sermons, prefaces, and pamphlets. One of the most interesting uses to which it was put is that of biography, as with Thomas Fuller and Izaak Walton, and it is worth noting that the words "biographer" and "biography" stem from this period of our literature. With the arrival of magazines, such as the *Athenian Gazette* and the *Gentleman's Journal*, came the periodical essay, and before the century had closed the "editorial" of modern journalism had begun to help form the nation's opinions.

The history of the newspaper is not properly part of the story of English literature, but no account of the development of modern literature could fail to mention the genesis in the seventeenth century of this most important institution. The beginnings of the English press are intimately bound up with the events of the time, for it was chiefly out of the desire for news of current happenings, battles and political activities, of the period of the Civil War that the newspaper was born. As early as 1622 there was a *Weekly News*, but it was not until 1642 that the first real English newspaper, a weekly, began under the name, *The Head of Several Proceedings in the Present Parliament, or Diurnal Occurrences*. The honor of being the first daily English newspaper belongs to the *Postbag*, of which four numbers appeared in 1693. It remained for the eighteenth century to produce the first regular daily paper, the *Daily Courant*, but the seventeenth century saw the Fourth Estate through its birth throes, and through the first rounds of the inevitable and unending struggle for the freedom of the press.

To the eighteenth century it was left also to bring English fiction to its maturity in the novel. The seventeenth century's propensity for exposition, as seen in the popularity of the essay, the "anatomy," and the sermon, did not foster the art of narration. Most of the writers of the time were constitutionally unable to get on with the story, and could not resist the temptation to dig in for a bit of analysis. When the author had played with his subject as a cat plays with a mouse, or, as in the words of Burton, when it had been "philosophically, medicinally, historically, opened and cut up," he would move on to the next point, but not till then. To Mrs. Aphra Behn belongs the credit of being the one real novelist of the time, as well as the first professional English authoress. Her most celebrated novel, *Oroonoko, or The Royal Slave*, 1688, presents a picture of the "noble savage" almost a century before Rousseau discoursed upon the virtues of the natural man, and, however one may discount the loftiness of her intentions in writing the romance, or the profundity of her humanitarian sentiments, she contrived, almost two hundred years before *Uncle Tom's Cabin*, to create a sympathetic interest in the victims of human slavery. In other less well-known stories she shows her ability to handle the picaresque, and, what is more remarkable for one who was a successful Restoration dramatist, a knowledge and appreciation of English country life and scenes.

In a work of a very different nature, Bunyan's allegory, *The Pilgrim's Progress*, there is evidence of a genuine gift for storytelling and realistic description, which has made it the most famous prose narrative of the century. The autobiographical and didactic elements of the book prevent its technical classification as fiction, but in the history of the English novel Bunyan's place is assured and unique. The close connection between other forms of biography and autobiography, genuine or fictitious, and the novel is illustrated in the rogue stories of the later seventeenth century. Historians of the novel see in the elements and methods of some of these the germs of the style of Daniel Defoe, "the first great English novelist," who was born the year before the Restoration, and who represents the culmination of the tendencies in fiction during the last decades of the century.

The general trend in prose was toward informality, simplicity, and realism. The progress of scientific thought assisted the process of simplification. Dr. Thomas Sprat in his *History of the Royal Society*, 1667, informs us that that society required of its members reports of the results of their researches in "a close, naked, natural way of speaking; positive expressions; clear senses; a native easiness; bringing all things as near the mathematical plainness as they can: and preferring the language of artisans, countrymen, and merchants before that of wits or scholars." The "poetic prose" of the first half of the century, with its magisterial manner, its purple passages, and its gargantuan sentences, inevitably gave way gradually to the more agile and colloquial style of the memoir, the pamphlet, and the newspaper. The monumental perorations of Donne and Sir Thomas Browne with their sesquipedalian terms and sonorous Latinisms were succeeded by such brief summaries as that which ends

Dryden's discussion of Chaucer—"Here is God's plenty"—and the conclusion of *The Pilgrim's Progress*—"So I awoke, and behold it was a dream."

By 1660 the composition of the language with respect to the relative proportions of native and foreign elements had become largely what it is today. English had shaken itself loose from the excessive Latinism of the earlier days, and had proved itself capable of expressing well and sufficiently all the thoughts that might arise in English minds and hearts. English books had become "citizens of the world," which, according to Bacon, they were not at the beginning of the century. English literature, which could hardly be said to have existed for the learned men of the days before the Civil War, achieved sufficient prestige to merit the critical appraisal of Dryden and his contemporaries. The evolution of a critical temper and the development of literary criticism in England are undoubtedly related to the growth of the scientific spirit and habit of thought which took place during the century. In Dryden's *Essay of Dramatic Poesy* and the prefaces to his various works, English literary criticism may be said to have come of age.

from The Authorized or King James Version of the Holy Bible

The man who more than any other laid the foundation of the English Bible as we have it was William Tyndale, whose translation of the New Testament was published at Worms in Germany in 1525—the first printed edition of the New Testament in English. Tyndale subsequently translated about half of the Old Testament, from Genesis through II Chronicles, and would undoubtedly have translated the whole Bible had he lived. But his enemies triumphed, and he was burned at the stake near Brussels in 1536. The sturdy simplicity of Tyndale's diction and the rhythm of his phrases provided the pattern and much of the substance of the 1611 Bible. The task of completing the English Bible fell to Miles Coverdale, who brought out the first printed English Bible in 1535.

Other revisions and editions followed over the years. The Great Bible of 1540 was prepared by Coverdale to meet Henry VIII's injunctions of 1538, that a copy "of the whole Bible of the largest volume in English be set up in churches," and that every person be "expressly provoked, stirred, and exhorted" to read the same. The Geneva Bible, which Shakespeare used and which came to America in the Mayflower, appeared in 1560. The Bishops' Bible, a revision by the Anglican Bishops of the Great Bible, was brought out in 1568, and later served as the working text of the revision of 1611. One other important translation preceded that of the Authorized Version. The Roman Catholic English version of the New Testament, prepared by members of the English College at Douay, was printed at Rheims in 1582, and their version of the Old Testament was published at Douay in 1609. The Authorized Version of 1611, "translated out of the original tongues, and with the former translations diligently compared and revised," was thus the culmination of the efforts of many men, of different faiths and orders, but all devoted to the task of making accessible to English readers the Word of God.

The masterpiece of 1611 has been called "the only classic ever created by a committee," although its compilers never thought of it in such terms. From a purely literary point of view, it is something of a miracle that the committee of scholars should have produced such a consistently beautiful book, of which the extracts given below are but the merest sample. Some of the circumstances in their favor may be mentioned. There were the simple, pastoral beauty, the spiritual fervor, and the childlike piety of the original Hebrew Scriptures, and the vigorous Greek which carried the Christian message of the New Testament. The translators lived in an age of faith, and had a conviction that they were handling, as Wyclif put it, "the deep things of God." They had the advantage of all the English versions that had come before them. They wrote at a time when the English language was at the highest point of strength and beauty it had yet reached. Poetry was in the air, and English speech had a natural stateliness which it has since lost. However one may account for the excellence of the work, and after all its indebtedness to other sources and versions has been admitted, the King James Bible remains a classic in its own right, a piece of English literature, different from the original Hebrew or Greek, and unlike the Bible in any other language.

All art, it has been said, relies on the existence of a tradition, on a body of knowledge and ideas taken for granted. Thus the Greek tragedians built on Homer, and English-speaking writers of the last three centuries have built largely on the Authorized Version of the Bible and Shakespeare. The effect of the continual reading of the Bible on the character, imagination, and thought of the British and American peoples is greater, as all historians agree, than that of any other book or of any literary movement in English or European history. The great writers have been under the constant impact of its matchless poetry and prose, and its phrases have enriched the everyday speech of ordinary men and women. It cannot be replaced, though it should be supplemented, by modern versions. To be ignorant of it is to be out of touch with the greatest single influence in both the literature and the life of England and America.

THE TWENTY-THIRD PSALM

(Varying Translations)

THE GREAT BIBLE, 1540

Coverdale's version of the Psalms in the Great Bible was later used in the Bishops' Bible. It is still retained in the Book of Common Prayer of the Church of England, and, with a few alterations, in that of the Protestant Episcopal Church in the United States, both because it has endeared itself to the people and because its melody and felicity of phrase make it especially appropriate to liturgical use.

The Lord is my shepherd; therefore can I lack nothing.

He shall feed me in a green pasture, and lead me forth beside the waters of comfort.

He shall convert my soul, and bring me forth in the paths of righteousness for his Name's sake.

Yea, though I walk through the valley of the shadow of death, I will fear no evil; for thou art with me; thy rod and thy staff comfort me.

Thou shalt prepare a table before me against them that trouble me; thou hast anointed my head with oil, and my cup shall be full.

But thy loving-kindness and mercy shall follow me all the days of my life; and I will dwell in the house of the Lord for ever.

THE GENEVA BIBLE, 1560

The Geneva Bible was the most popular and widely used Bible of the sixteenth and early seventeenth centuries, and it was not until about 1640 that the King James Version finally supplanted it in popular favor. By then some two hundred editions of it had been brought out. It was pre-eminently the Puritan Bible, and its notes largely contributed to the Puritan spirit of the time. It is now popularly known as the "Breeches Bible" because of the translation of Genesis 3:7: "They sewed figtree leaves together, and made themselves breeches."

The Lord is my shepherd; I shall not want.

He maketh me to rest in green pasture, and leadeth me by the still waters.

He restoreth my soul, and leadeth me in the paths of righteousness for his Name's sake.

Yea, though I should walk through the valley of the shadow of death, I will fear no evil; for thou art with me; thy rod and thy staff, they comfort me.

Thou dost prepare a table before me in the sight of mine adversaries; thou dost anoint my head with oil, and my cup runneth over.

Doubtless kindness and mercy shall follow me all the days of my life, and I shall remain a long season in the house of the Lord.

THE DOUAY BIBLE, 1609

The Douay version of the Bible was made from the text of the Latin Vulgate, and being a translation of a translation is not so close to the original Hebrew as the other versions here represented. The chief concern of the English translators was fidelity to the text of the Vulgate, hence the unusual number of Latinisms. This psalm appears as Psalm 22 in the Douay Bible.

Our Lord ruleth me, and nothing shall be wanting to me; in place of pasture there he hath placed me.

Upon the water of refection he hath brought me up; he hath converted my soul.

He hath conducted me upon the paths of justice, for his name.

For although I shall walk in the midst of the shadow of death, I will not fear evils; because thou art with me.

Thy rod and thy staff, they have comforted me.

Thou hast prepared in my sight a table against them that trouble me.

Thou hast fatted my head with oil, and my chalice inebriating, how goodly is it!

And thy mercy shall follow me all the days of my life.

And that I may dwell in the house of our Lord in longitude of days.

THE AUTHORIZED VERSION, 1611

The Lord is my shepherd; I shall not want.

He maketh me to lie down in green pastures: he leadeth me beside the still waters.

He restoreth my soul: he leadeth me in the paths of righteousness for his name's sake.

Yea, though I walk through the valley of the shadow of death, I will fear no evil: for thou art with me; thy rod and thy staff they comfort me.

Thou preparest a table before me in the presence of mine enemies: thou anointest my head with oil; my cup runneth over.

Surely goodness and mercy shall follow me all the days of my life: and I will dwell in the house of the Lord for ever.

from THE BOOK OF JOB

The Book of Job is one of the great philosophical books of the world. Carlyle called it "our first, oldest statement of the never-ending Problem,—man's destiny, and God's ways with him here in this earth." The extracts here given are from the latter part of the poetical portion of the book, and follow the heated discussion between Job and his friends. Job's friends have argued that his troubles are the punishments for his wrongdoing. Against them Job has indignantly maintained his innocence, and has accused God of being arbitrary in his dealings with men. The Voice from the Whirlwind, as Professor R. G. Moulton says, is to lift the discussion into a wider sphere. "For the hopeless suffering in which there is nothing of guilt, what treatment can be better than to lose the individual pain in sympathetic wonder over nature in her inexhaustible variety? . . . Job and his friends had fastened their attention upon suffering and evil, and had broken down under the weight of the mystery; but the individual experience now seems a small thing in the range of all nature's ways. Hence we have a Fourth Solution of the Mystery of Suffering: That the whole universe is an unfathomed mystery, and the Evil in it is not more mysterious than the Good and the Great."—"The Book of Job" in *The Modern Reader's Bible*, ed. by R. G. Moulton, Macmillan, 1930, pp. 1492–93. The text here and in the following selections is that of the Authorized Version.

Chapter 38

Then the Lord answered Job out of the whirlwind, and said,

Who is this that darkeneth counsel by words without knowledge?

49. the Lord answered Job. God challenges him to the contest which he has been demanding.

Gird up now thy loins like a man; for I will demand of thee, and answer thou me.

Where wast thou when I laid the foundations of the earth? declare, if thou hast understanding.

Who hath laid the measures thereof, if thou knowest? or who hath stretched the line upon it?

Whereupon are the foundations thereof fastened? or who laid the corner stone thereof;

When the morning stars sang together, and all the sons of God shouted for joy?

Or who shut up the sea with doors, when it brake forth, as if it had issued out of the womb?

When I made the cloud the garment thereof, and thick darkness a swaddling band for it,

And brake up for it my decreed place, and set bars and doors,

And said, Hitherto shalt thou come, but no further: and here shall thy proud waves be stayed?

Hast thou commanded the morning since thy days, and caused the dayspring to know his place;

That it might take hold of the ends of the earth, that the wicked might be shaken out of it?

It is turned as clay to the seal; and they stand as a garment.

And from the wicked their light is withholden, and the high arm shall be broken.

Hast thou entered into the springs of the sea? or hast thou walked in the search of the depth?

Have the gates of death been opened unto thee? or hast thou seen the doors of the shadow of death?

Hast thou perceived the breadth of the earth? declare if thou knowest it all.

Where is the way where light dwelleth? and as for darkness, where is the place thereof,

That thou shouldest take it to the bound thereof, and that thou shouldest know the paths to the house thereof?

Knowest thou it, because thou wast then born? or because the number of thy days is great?

Hast thou entered into the treasures of the snow? or hast thou seen the treasures of the hail,

Which I have reserved against the time of trouble, against the day of battle and war?

By what way is the light parted, which scattereth the east wind upon the earth?

Who hath divided a water-course for the overflowing of waters, or a way for the lightning of thunder;

To cause it to rain on the earth, where no man is; on the wilderness, wherein there is no man;

20. dayspring, dawn. **23–24. they stand as a garment** Professor James Moffatt translates this verse as follows: "earth stands out clear like clay stamped by a seal, in all its colours like a robe."—*The Holy Bible: A New Translation* by James Moffatt, Harper.

To satisfy the desolate and waste ground; and to cause the bud of the tender herb to spring forth?

Hath the rain a father? or who hath begotten the drops of dew?

Out of whose womb came the ice? and the hoary frost of heaven, who hath gendered it?

The waters are hid as with a stone, and the face of the deep is frozen.

Canst thou bind the sweet influences of Pleiades, or loose the bands of Orion?

Canst thou bring forth Mazzaroth in his season? or canst thou guide Arcturus with his sons?

Knowest thou the ordinances of heaven? canst thou set the dominion thereof in the earth?

Canst thou lift up thy voice to the clouds, that abundance of waters may cover thee?

Canst thou send lightnings, that they may go, and say unto thee, Here we are?

Who hath put wisdom in the inward parts? or who hath given understanding to the heart?

Who can number the clouds in wisdom? or who can stay the bottles of heaven,

When the dust groweth into hardness, and the clods cleave fast together?

Wilt thou hunt the prey for the lion? or fill the appetite of the young lions,

When they couch in their dens, and abide in the covert to lie in wait?

Who provideth for the raven his food? when his young ones cry unto God, they wander for lack of meat.

Chapter 42

Then Job answered the Lord, and said,

I know that thou canst do every thing, and that no thought can be withholden from thee.

Who is he that hideth counsel without knowledge? therefore have I uttered that I understood not; things too wonderful for me, which I knew not.

Hear, I beseech thee, and I will speak: I will demand of thee, and declare thou unto me.

I have heard of thee by the hearing of the ear: but now mine eye seeth thee:

Wherefore I abhor myself, and repent in dust and ashes. . . .

9–12. Canst thou bind . . . Arcturus with his sons? Moffatt's translation is:

> "Can you bind up the Pleiades in a cluster,
> or loose the chains of Orion:
> Can you direct the signs of the Zodiac,
> or guide the constellations of the Bear?"

22. stay the bottles of heaven, Moffatt: "tilt the pitchers of the sky."

from THE GOSPEL ACCORDING TO ST. MATTHEW

This extract is taken from the words of Jesus in the passage familiarly called the Sermon on the Mount.

Chapter 6: 19–34

TYNDALE'S VERSION, 1534

Se that ye gaddre you not treasure upon the erth/ where rust and mothes corrupte/ and where theves breake through and steale. But gaddre ye treasure togeder in heven/ where nether rust nor mothes corrupte/ and where theves nether breake up nor yet steale. For where soever youre treasure ys/ there will youre hertes be also.

The light of the body is thyne eye. Wherfore if thyne eye be syngle/ all thy body shalbe full of light. But and if thyne eye be wycked then all thy body shalbe full of derckenes. Wherfore yf the light that is in the/ be darckenes: how greate is that darckenes.

No man can serve two masters. For ether he shall hate the one and love the other: or els he shall lene to the one and despise the other: ye can not serve God and mammon. Therfore I saye unto you/ be not carefull for your lyfe/ what ye shall eate/ or what ye shall drincke/ nor yet for youre body/ what ye shall put on. Ys not the lyfe more worth then meate/ and the body more of value then rayment? Beholde the foules of the ayer: for they sowe not/ nether reepe/ nor yet cary in to the barnes: and yet youre hevenly father fedeth them. Are ye not moche better then they?

Which of you (though he toke thought therfore) coulde put one cubit unto his stature? And why care ye then for rayment? Considre the lylies of the felde/ how they growe. They labour not nether spynne. And yet for all that I saye unto you/ that even Salomon in all his royalte was not arayd lyke unto one of these. Wherfore yf God so clothe the grasse/ which ys to daye in the felde/ and to morowe shalbe caste into the fournace: shall he not moche more do the same unto you/ o ye of lytle fayth?

Therfore take no thought sayinge: what shall we eate/ or what shall we drincke/ or wherwith shall we be clothed? After all these thynges seke the gentyls. For youre hevenly father knoweth that ye have neade of all these thynges. But rather seke ye fyrst the kyngdome of heven and the rightwisnes therof/ and all these thynges shalbe ministred unto you.

Care not then for the morow/ but let the morow care for it selfe: for the daye present hath ever ynough of his awne trouble.

THE AUTHORIZED VERSION, 1611

Lay not up for yourselves treasures upon earth, where moth and rust doth corrupt, and where thieves break through and steal:

But lay up for yourselves treasures in heaven, where neither moth nor rust doth corrupt, and where thieves do not break through nor steal:

For where your treasure is, there will your heart be also.

The light of the body is the eye: if therefore thine eye be single, thy whole body shall be full of light.

But if thine eye be evil, thy whole body shall be full of darkness. If therefore the light that is in thee be darkness, how great is that darkness!

No man can serve two masters: for either he will hate the one, and love the other; or else he will hold to the one, and despise the other. Ye cannot serve God and mammon.

Therefore I say unto you, Take no thought for your life, what ye shall eat, or what ye shall drink; nor yet for your body, what ye shall put on. Is not the life more than meat, and the body than raiment?

Behold the fowls of the air: for they sow not, neither do they reap, nor gather into barns; yet your heavenly Father feedeth them. Are ye not much better than they?

Which of you by taking thought can add one cubit unto his stature?

And why take ye thought for raiment? Consider the lilies of the field, how they grow; they toil not, neither do they spin:

And yet I say unto you, That even Solomon in all his glory was not arrayed like one of these.

Wherefore, if God so clothe the grass of the field, which to day is, and to morrow is cast into the oven, shall he not much more clothe you, O ye of little faith?

Therefore take no thought, saying, What shall we eat? or, What shall we drink? or, Wherewithal shall we be clothed?

(For after all these things do the Gentiles seek:) for your heavenly Father knoweth that ye have need of all these things.

But seek ye first the kingdom of God, and his righteousness; and all these things shall be added unto you.

Take therefore no thought for the morrow: for the morrow shall take thought for the things of itself. Sufficient unto the day is the evil thereof.

from THE FIRST EPISTLE OF ST. PAUL TO THE CORINTHIANS

Chapter 13

Though I speak with the tongues of men and of angels, and have not charity, I am become as sounding brass, or a tinkling cymbal.

And though I have the gift of prophecy, and understand all mysteries, and all knowledge; and though I have all faith, so that I could remove mountains, and have not charity, I am nothing.

And though I bestow all my goods to feed the poor, and though I give my body to be burned, and have not charity, it profiteth me nothing.

Charity suffereth long, and is kind; charity envieth not; charity vaunteth not itself, is not puffed up,

Doth not behave itself unseemly, seeketh not her own, is not easily provoked, thinketh no evil;

Rejoiceth not in iniquity, but rejoiceth in the truth;

Beareth all things, believeth all things, hopeth all things, endureth all things.

Charity never faileth: but whether there be prophecies, they shall fail; whether there be tongues, they shall cease; whether there be knowledge, it shall vanish away.

For we know in part, and we prophesy in part.

But when that which is perfect is come, then that which is in part shall be done away.

When I was a child, I spake as a child, I understood as a child, I thought as a child: but when I became a man, I put away childish things.

For now we see through a glass, darkly; but then face to face: now I know in part; but then shall I know even as also I am known.

And now abideth faith, hope, charity, these three; but the greatest of these is charity.

15. sounding brass, or a tinkling cymbal. Moffatt: "a noisy gong or a clanging cymbal." **24. vaunteth not itself,** Moffatt: "makes no parade." **42. through a glass, darkly,** as in a mirror, imperfectly. The mirrors of St. Paul's days were polished metal, and the reflections were at best imperfect.

Francis Bacon

1561–1626

The story of the first sixty years of Bacon's life is largely that of his rise to offices and dignities in the world of politics and in the realm of philosophic thought. His last five years were spent "in disgrace with fortune and men's eyes." He was the younger son of Sir Nicholas Bacon, Lord Keeper of the Seals, and Ann Cook, sister-in-law of the Lord Treasurer, Burghley. At twelve he went to Trinity College, Cambridge, but left in disgust two years later. He was admitted to the study of law at Gray's Inn in 1576, and for the next three years he was in France. By 1582 he had begun his advancement in the legal profession. He was in Parliament at the age of twenty-two, and soon won the patronage of the Earl of Essex. In 1596 he was made Queen's Counsel. In 1601 he was appointed to investigate the causes of the Earl of Essex's revolt, and was instrumental in convicting the Earl. Bacon has been accused of downright disloyalty to his friend and patron, but there are reasons for believing that he did what he could to save him. The Earl's own foolishness, the state of mind of the Queen, and the calculating hatred of Burghley would have been enough to condemn him.

Bacon, at any rate, continued to advance. He was knighted by James I in 1603, and he had for patron the Duke of Buckingham. He was married in 1606 to Alice Barnham, the daughter of a wealthy alderman. Within a dozen years he became successively Solicitor-General, Privy Councillor, Lord Keeper, and Lord Chancellor. When King James was making his royal progress in Scotland, Bacon ruled England. He was as much a philosopher as a statesman, however, and he found time during these years to write some of his *Essays*, and to produce *The Advancement of Learning*, 1605, in which he affirmed the dignity of knowledge, reviewed the present state of learning, and suggested methods by which it could be further advanced. The *Novum Organum*, 1620, was his *New Instrument* for inquiring into truth, and a description of the methods by which a renovation of knowledge was to be achieved.

For all his abilities and advancements, however, Bacon was chronically in need of funds. His father's death left him at nineteen an impecunious young man, and he had early to resort to moneylenders. He was always extravagant, living beyond his means, and was pursued by creditors most of his life. In 1621 he was arraigned before the House of Lords on the charge of bribery and judicial corruption. He pleaded guilty to "corruption and neglect," but denied that he had allowed the bribes to influence the decisions of his court. In his confession he pleaded that he had acted no worse than other officials, but acknowledged the justice of the verdict, and expressed the hope that his own disgrace would help to bring about a higher standard of morality in the courts of law. He was deprived of his offices, fined £40,000, and condemned to imprisonment during the King's pleasure. The fine was remitted; Bacon was in the Tower only two days, and was then allowed to retire to his own house. A yearly pension was granted him, and the five remaining years of his life were devoted to his literary and philosophical interests.

In his retirement he enlarged and revised his *Essays*, 1625, wrote the *History of Henry VII*, 1622, and composed the fragment of the *New Atlantis*, which was published posthumously in 1627. In this his last work he describes some aspects of his program of scientific investigation under the control of the Government. He found time for experiments of his own, and it was while collecting snow to test its preservative qualities that he caught the chill from which he died.

No figure in English history has been so variously estimated as Bacon, and none has been the subject of more extravagant praise or vituperation. Pope called him "the wisest, brightest, meanest of mankind." Blake described his *Essays* as "good advice for Satan's kingdom." His contemporary, Ben Jonson, said of him, "He seemed to me ever, by his work, one of the greatest men, and most worthy of admiration that had been in many ages." His character was such a curious mixture of the great and the base that such different evaluations are inevitable. He was a public-spirited man who seems to have lacked a private conscience, and who preferred economic to moral values. It has been said that in his *Essays* he shows us man as he is; in his writings on science, man as he ought to be. Bacon at least had knowledge of both states of man. If there was one thing to which he was genuinely devoted, apart from his own success, it was the welfare of humanity, and especially the good and the security of the State. He is often likened to Bunyan's Mr. Worldly Wiseman. It is only fair to remember that he also had many of the qualities of Valiant-for-truth.

from ESSAYS OR COUNSELS, CIVIL AND MORAL

Ten of Bacon's essays, beginning with "Of Studies," were published in 1597. A second edition containing thirty-eight, and including "Of Marriage and Single Life," "Of Death," and "Of Love," appeared in 1612. A third edition was published in 1625. In this, the last edition prepared by Bacon, there were fifty-eight essays, of which the earlier ones had been extensively revised and amplified.

OF TRUTH

WHAT is truth? said jesting Pilate; and would not stay for an answer. Certainly there be that delight in giddiness, and count it a bondage to fix a belief; affecting free-will in thinking, as well as in acting. And though the sects of philosophers of that kind be gone, yet there remain certain discoursing wits, which are of the same veins, though there be not so much blood in them as was in those of the ancients. But it is not only the difficulty and labour which men take in finding out of truth; nor again, that when it is found, it imposeth upon men's thoughts, that doth bring lies in favour; but a natural though corrupt love of the lie itself. One of the later schools of the Grecians examineth the matter, and is at a stand to think what should be in it, that men should love lies; where neither they make for pleasure, as with poets; nor for advantage, as with the merchant, but for the lie's sake. But I cannot tell: this same truth is a naked and open daylight, that doth not show the masks and mummeries and triumphs of the world, half so stately and daintily as candle-lights. Truth may perhaps come to the price of a pearl, that showeth best by day, but it will not rise to the price of a diamond or carbuncle, that showeth best in varied lights. A mixture of a lie doth ever add pleasure. Doth any man doubt, that if there were taken out of men's minds vain opinions, flattering hopes, false valuations, imaginations as one would, and the like, but it would leave the minds of a number of men poor shrunken things, full of melancholy and indisposition, and unpleasing to themselves? One of the fathers, in great severity, called poesy *vinum daemonum*, because it filleth the imagination, and yet it is but with the shadow of a lie. But it is not the lie that passeth through the mind, but the lie that sinketh in, and settleth in it, that doth the hurt, such as we spake of before. But howsoever these things are thus in men's depraved judgments and affections, yet truth, which only doth judge itself, teacheth that the inquiry of truth, which is the love-making, or wooing of it, the knowledge of truth, which is the presence of it, and the belief of truth, which is the enjoying of it, is the sovereign good of human nature. The first creature of God, in the works of the days, was the light of the sense: the last was the light of reason: and his sabbath work ever since, is the illumination of his Spirit. First, he breathed light upon the face of the matter, or chaos; then he breathed light into the face of man; and still he breatheth and inspireth light into the face of his chosen. The poet that beautified the sect that was otherwise inferior to the rest saith yet excellently well: "It is a pleasure to stand upon the shore, and to see ships tossed upon the sea: a pleasure to stand in the window of a castle, and to see a battle, and the adventures thereof below: but no pleasure is comparable to the standing upon the vantage ground of truth" (a hill not to be commanded, and where the air is always clear and serene) "and to see the errors, and wanderings, and mists, and tempests, in the vale below": so always that this prospect be with pity, and not with swelling or pride. Certainly, it is heaven upon earth, to have a man's mind move in charity, rest in providence, and turn upon the poles of truth.

To pass from theological and philosophical truth to the truth of civil business; it will be acknowledged even by those that practise it not, that clear and round dealing is the honour of man's nature, and that mixture of falsehood is like alloy in coin of gold and silver, which may make the metal work the better, but it embaseth it. For these winding and crooked courses are the goings of the serpent; which goeth basely upon the belly, and not upon

23. Pilate. See John 18:38. **25. giddiness,** that is, "a whirl of thoughts." **27–28. philosophers of that kind,** the Greek Skeptics, who taught that absolute certainty in knowledge is impossible. **28–29. discoursing wits,** rambling and talkative minds. **33. imposeth upon,** restrains. **39. as with poets.** Here as elsewhere Bacon's derogatory comments on poets and poetry are to be noted. **44. daintily,** elegantly.

7–8. One of the fathers, perhaps St. Augustine, in his *Confessions*. **8–9. vinum daemonum,** the wine of devils. **27. poet,** the Epicurean Lucretius, of the first century B.C. **34. commanded,** subject to attack. **45. round dealing.** We should say "square dealing."

the feet. There is no vice that doth so cover a man with shame as to be found false and perfidious; and therefore Montaigne saith prettily, when he inquired the reason why the word of the lie should be such a disgrace, and such an odious charge, saith he, "If it be well weighed, to say that a man lieth, is as much as to say that he is brave towards God and a coward towards men. For a lie faces God, and shrinks from man." Surely the wickedness of falsehood and breach of faith cannot possibly be so highly expressed, as in that it shall be the last peal to call the judgments of God upon the generations of men, it being foretold that when "Christ cometh," he shall not "find faith upon the earth."

OF DEATH

MEN fear death as children fear to go in the dark; and as that natural fear in children is increased with tales, so is the other. Certainly, the contemplation of death as the wages of sin, and passage to another world, is holy and religious; but the fear of it, as a tribute due unto nature, is weak. Yet in religious meditations there is sometimes mixture of vanity and of superstition. You shall read in some of the friars' books of mortification that a man should think with himself what the pain is if he have but his finger's end pressed or tortured; and thereby imagine what the pains of death are, when the whole body is corrupted and dissolved; when many times death passeth with less pain than the torture of a limb; for the most vital parts are not the quickest of sense. And by him that spake only as a philosopher, and natural man, it was well said, *Pompa mortis magis terret, quam mors ipsa*. Groans and convulsions, and a discoloured face, and friends weeping, and blacks and obsequies, and the like, show death terrible. It is worthy the observing that there is no passion in the mind of man so weak, but it mates and masters the fear of death; and therefore death is no such terrible enemy when a man hath so many attendants about him that can win the combat of him. Revenge triumphs over death; love slights it; honour aspireth to it; grief flieth to it; fear preoccupateth it; nay, we read, after Otho the emperor had slain himself, pity, which is the tenderest of affections, provoked many to die out of mere compassion to their sovereign, and as the truest sort of followers. Nay, Seneca adds, niceness and satiety: *Cogita quamdiu eadem feceris; mori velle, non tantum fortis, aut miser, sed etiam fastidiosus potest.* A man would die, though he were neither valiant nor miserable, only upon a weariness to do the same thing so oft over and over. It is no less worthy to observe, how little alteration in good spirits the approaches of death make: for they appear to be the same men till the last instant. Augustus Caesar died in a compliment, *Livia, conjugii nostri memor, vive et vale*. Tiberius in dissimulation, as Tacitus saith of him, *Jam Tiberium vires et corpus, non dissimulatio, deserebant;* Vespasian in a jest, sitting upon the stool, *Ut puto Deus fio:* Galba with a sentence, *Feri, si ex re sit populi Romani*, holding forth his neck; Septimus Severus in dispatch, *Adeste, si quid mihi restat agendum*, and the like. Certainly the Stoics bestowed too much cost upon death, and by their great preparations made it appear more fearful. Better, saith he, *qui finem vitae extremum inter munera ponit naturae*. It is as natural to die as to be born; and to a little infant, perhaps, the one is as painful as the other. He that dies in an earnest pursuit, is like one that is wounded in hot blood; who for the time scarce feels the hurt; and therefore a mind fixed and bent upon somewhat that is good, doth avert the dolours of death. But, above all, believe it, the sweetest canticle is *Nunc dimittis*, when a man hath obtained worthy ends and expectations. Death hath this also, that it openeth the gate to good fame, and extinguisheth envy: *Extinctus amabitur idem*.

OF MARRIAGE AND SINGLE LIFE

HE that hath wife and children hath given hostages to fortune; for they are impediments to great enterprises, either of virtue or mischief. Certainly the best works, and of greatest merit for the public, have proceeded from the unmarried or

3. Montaigne, in his *Essays*, Book II, chap. 18. It was from Montaigne (1533–1592) that Bacon took the name, and doubtless some of the ideas, of his essays. **14. "find faith upon the earth."** See Luke 18:8. **34. by him,** Seneca, in his *Epistles*, Book III, Ep. 3, l. 14. **36. Pompa . . . ipsa.** The circumstances connected with death terrify more than death itself. **38. blacks,** black draperies.

2. niceness, fastidiousness. **3–4. Cogita . . . potest.** Consider how long you have done the same things; a man may wish to die not only because he is brave, or miserable, but also because he is simply tired of life. **11–12. Livia . . . vale.** Livia, mindful of our marriage, live on, and fare thee well. **13–14. Jam . . . deserebant.** His physical powers and vitality were deserting Tiberius, but not his duplicity. **15. Ut puto Deus fio.** As I think, I am becoming a God. **16. Feri . . . Romani.** Strike, if it be for the good of the Roman people. **17–18. Adeste . . . agendum.** Make haste, if anything remains for me to do. **21–22. qui . . . naturae,** who considers the close of life one of the blessings of nature.—Juvenal, *Satires*, X, l. 358 **29. Nunc dimittis.** Now lettest thou thy servant depart in peace. See Luke 2:29. **32. Extinctus amabitur idem.** The same man (who was envied while alive) shall be loved when dead.

childless men, which both in affection and means have married and endowed the public. Yet it were great reason that those that have children should have greatest care of future times, unto which they know they must transmit their dearest pledges. Some there are who, though they lead a single life, yet their thoughts do end with themselves, and account future times impertinences. Nay, there are some other that account wife and children but as bills of charges. Nay more, there are some foolish rich covetous men, that take a pride in having no children, because they may be thought so much the richer. For perhaps they have heard some talk, "Such an one is a great rich man," and another except to it, "Yea, but he hath a great charge of children"; as if it were an abatement to his riches. But the most ordinary cause of a single life is liberty, especially in certain self-pleasing and humorous minds, which are so sensible of every restraint, as they will go near to think their girdles and garters to be bonds and shackles. Unmarried men are best friends, best masters, best servants, but not always best subjects, for they are light to run away, and almost all fugitives are of that condition. A single life doth well with churchmen, for charity will hardly water the ground where it must first fill a pool. It is indifferent for judges and magistrates, for if they be facile and corrupt, you shall have a servant five times worse than a wife. For soldiers, I find the generals commonly in their hortatives put men in mind of their wives and children; and I think the despising of marriage amongst the Turks maketh the vulgar soldier more base. Certainly wife and children are a kind of discipline of humanity; and single men, though they be many times more charitable, because their means are less exhaust, yet, on the other side, they are more cruel and hard-hearted (good to make severe inquisitors), because their tenderness is not so oft called upon. Grave natures, led by custom, and therefore constant, are commonly loving husbands, as was said of Ulysses, *Vetulam suam praetulit immortalitati.* Chaste women are often proud and froward, as presuming upon the merit of their chastity. It is one of the best bonds, both of chastity and obedience, in the wife if she think her husband wise, which she will never do if she find him jealous. Wives are young men's mistresses, companions for middle age, and old men's nurses, so as a man may have a quarrel to marry when he will. But yet he was reputed one of the wise men that made answer to the question when a man should marry: "A young man not yet, an elder man not at all." It is often seen that bad husbands have very good wives; whether it be that it raiseth the price of their husbands' kindness when it comes, or that the wives take a pride in their patience. But this never fails, if the bad husbands were of their own choosing, against their friends' consent; for then they will be sure to make good their own folly.

18. **humorous,** eccentric. 42. **Vetulam . . . immortalitati.** He preferred his aged wife (Penelope) to immortality. 50. **quarrel,** pretext.

OF LOVE

THE stage is more beholding to love than the life of man. For as to the stage, love is ever matter of comedies, and now and then of tragedies; but in life it doth much mischief, sometimes like a siren, sometimes like a fury. You may observe, that amongst all the great and worthy persons whereof the memory remaineth, either ancient or recent, there is not one that hath been transported to the mad degree of love; which shows that great spirits and great business do keep out this weak passion. You must except, nevertheless, Marcus Antonius, the half partner of the empire of Rome, and Appius Claudius, the Decemvir and lawgiver; whereof the former was indeed a voluptuous man, and inordinate; but the latter was an austere and wise man. And therefore it seems (though rarely) that love can find entrance, not only into an open heart, but also into a heart well fortified, if watch be not well kept. It is a poor saying of Epicurus, *Satis magnum alter alteri theatrum sumus:* as if man, made for the contemplation of heaven and all noble objects, should do nothing but kneel before a little idol, and make himself subject, though not of the mouth, as beasts are, yet of the eye, which was given him for higher purposes. It is a strange thing to note the excess of this passion, and how it braves the nature and value of things by this, that the speaking in a perpetual hyperbole is comely in nothing but in love. Neither is it merely in the phrase. For whereas it hath been well said, "That the arch flatterer, with whom all the petty flatterers have intelligence, is a man's self," certainly the lover is more. For there was never proud man thought so absurdly well of himself as the lover doth of the person loved; and therefore it was well said, "That it is impossible

14. **beholding to,** beholden to, attached to. 24. **Marcus Antonius,** in love with Cleopatra, queen of Egypt. 26. **Claudius.** Appius Claudius tried basely to get possession of Virginia, daughter of a plebeian, Virginius. The father slew his daughter to prevent her falling into the hands of Appius. 32–33. **Satis . . . sumus.** Each of us is to the other a sufficiently large theater. 39. **braves,** insults.

to love and to be wise." Neither doth this weakness appear to others only, and not to the party loved, but to the loved most of all, except the love be reciprocal. For it is a true rule, that love is ever rewarded, either with the reciprocal, or with an inward and secret contempt; by how much the more men ought to beware of this passion, which loseth not only other things, but itself. As for the other losses, the poet's relation doth well figure them, "That he that preferred Helena, quitted the gifts of Juno and Pallas." For whosoever esteemeth too much of amorous affection, quitteth both riches and wisdom. This passion hath his floods in the very times of weakness, which are great prosperity and great adversity, though this latter hath been less observed. Both which times kindle love, and make it more fervent, and therefore show it to be the child of folly. They do best who, if they cannot but admit love, yet make it keep quarter, and sever it wholly from their serious affairs and actions of life. For if it check once with business, it troubleth men's fortunes, and maketh men that they can nowise be true to their own ends. I know not how, but martial men are given to love. I think it is but as they are given to wine, for perils commonly ask to be paid in pleasures. There is in man's nature a secret inclination and motion towards love of others, which if it be not spent upon some one or a few, doth naturally spread itself towards many, and maketh men become humane and charitable, as it is seen sometimes in friars. Nuptial love maketh mankind, friendly love perfecteth it, but wanton love corrupteth and embaseth it.

OF GREAT PLACE

MEN in great place are thrice servants—servants of the sovereign or state, servants of fame, and servants of business. So as they have no freedom, neither in their persons, nor in their actions, nor in their times. It is a strange desire to seek power and to lose liberty; or to seek power over others, and to lose power over a man's self. The rising unto place is laborious, and by pains men come to greater pains; and it is sometimes base, and by indignities men come to dignities. The standing is slippery, and the regress is either a downfall, or at least an eclipse, which is a melancholy thing: *Cum non sis qui fueris, non esse cur velis vivere.* Nay, retire men cannot when they would, neither will they when it were reason; but are impatient of privateness even in age and sickness, which require the shadow; like old townsmen, that will be still sitting at their street-door, though thereby they offer age to scorn. Certainly great persons had need to borrow other men's opinions to think themselves happy; for if they judge by their own feeling, they cannot find it; but if they think with themselves what other men think of them, and that other men would fain be as they are, then they are happy as it were by report, when, perhaps, they find the contrary within. For they are the first that find their own griefs, though they be the last that find their own faults. Certainly men in great fortunes are strangers to themselves, and while they are in the puzzle of business they have no time to tend their health either of body or mind. *Illi mors gravis incubat, qui notus nimis omnibus, ignotus moritur sibi.* In place there is licence to do good and evil; whereof the latter is a curse: for in evil the best condition is not to will, the second not to can. But power to do good is the true and lawful end of aspiring; for good thoughts, though God accept them, yet towards men are little better than good dreams, except they be put in act; and that cannot be without power and place, as the vantage and commanding ground. Merit and good works is the end of man's motion, and conscience of the same is the accomplishment of man's rest: for if a man can be partaker of God's theatre, he shall likewise be partaker of God's rest. *Et conversus Deus, ut aspiceret opera, quae fecerunt manus suae, vidit quod omnia essent bona nimis;* and then the Sabbath.

In the discharge of thy place set before thee the best examples; for imitation is a globe of precepts. And after a time set before thee thine own example; and examine thyself strictly whether thou didst not best at first. Neglect not also the examples of those that have carried themselves ill in the same place; not to set off thyself by taxing their memory, but to direct thyself what to avoid. Reform, therefore, without bravery or scandal of former times and persons; but yet set it down to thyself, as well to create good precedents as to follow them. Reduce things to the first institution, and observe wherein and how they have degenerated; but yet ask counsel of both times—of the ancient time what is best, and

10. he that preferred, Paris, son of Priam, king of Troy. His abduction of Helen led to the Trojan War. **21. check,** interfere. **50. Cum . . . vivere.** Since you are not what you were, there is no reason why you should wish to live.

18–20. Illi . . . sibi. Death lies heavily upon him who, well known to all others, dies unknown to himself. **22. to can,** to know. **29. conscience,** consciousness. **31. theatre,** spectacle; that is, can see what God saw. **32–34. Et conversus . . . nimis.** Genesis 1:31, quoted from the Vulgate: "And God, having looked upon all the works which his hands had made, saw that all were very good." **41. taxing,** censuring. **43. bravery,** boastfulness, ostentation.

of the latter time what is fittest. Seek to make thy course regular, that men may know beforehand what they may expect; but be not too positive and peremptory; and express thyself well when thou digressest from thy rule. Preserve the right of thy place, but stir not questions of jurisdiction; and rather assume thy right in silence, and *de facto*, than voice it with claims and challenges. Preserve likewise the rights of inferior places; and think it more honour to direct in chief than to be busy in all. Embrace and invite helps and advices touching the execution of thy place; and do not drive away such as bring thee information as meddlers, but accept of them in good part. The vices of authority are chiefly four: delays, corruption, roughness, and facility. For delays give easy access, keep times appointed, go through with that which is in hand, and interlace not business but of necessity. For corruption, do not only bind thine own hands or thy servant's hands from taking, but bind the hands of suitors also from offering. For integrity used doth the one, but integrity professed, and with a manifest detestation of bribery, doth the other. And avoid not only the fault, but the suspicion. Whosoever is found variable, and changeth manifestly without manifest cause, giveth suspicion of corruption. Therefore, always when thou changest thine opinion or course, profess it plainly, and declare it, together with the reasons that move thee to change, and do not think to steal it. A servant or a favourite, if he be inward, and no other apparent cause of esteem, is commonly thought but a by-way to close corruption. For roughness, it is a needless cause of discontent: severity breedeth fear, but roughness breedeth hate. Even reproofs from authority ought to be grave, and not taunting. As for facility, it is worse than bribery; for bribes come but now and then; but if importunity or idle respects lead a man, he shall never be without. As Solomon saith, "To respect persons is not good; for such a man will transgress for a piece of bread."

It is most true that was anciently spoken: "A place showeth the man; and it showeth some to the better and some to the worse." *Omnium consensu capax imperii, nisi imperasset*, saith Tacitus of Galba; but of Vespasian he saith, *Solus imperantium Vespasianus mutatus in melius:* though the one was meant of sufficiency, the other of manners and affection. It is an assured sign of a worthy and generous spirit, whom honour amends; for honour is, or should be, the place of virtue; and as in nature things move violently to their place, and calmly in their place, so virtue in ambition is violent, in authority settled and calm. All rising to great place is by a winding stair; and if there be factions, it is good to side a man's self whilst he is in the rising, and to balance himself when he is placed. Use the memory of thy predecessor fairly and tenderly; for if thou dost not, it is a debt will sure be paid when thou art gone. If thou have colleagues, respect them; and rather call them when they look not for it, than exclude them when they have reason to look to be called. Be not too sensible or too remembering of thy place in conversation and private answers to suitors; but let it rather be said, "When he sits in place he is another man."

OF TRAVEL

TRAVEL, in the younger sort, is a part of education; in the elder, a part of experience. He that travelleth into a country before he hath some entrance into the language, goeth to school, and not to travel. That young men travel under some tutor or grave servant, I allow well; so that he be such a one that hath the language, and hath been in the country before; whereby he may be able to tell them what things are worthy to be seen in the country where they go, what acquaintances they are to seek, what exercises or discipline the place yieldeth; for else young men shall go hooded, and look abroad little. It is a strange thing that in sea voyages, where there is nothing to be seen but sky and sea, men should make diaries; but in land travel, wherein so much is to be observed, for the most part they omit it; as if chance were fitter to be registered than observation. Let diaries, therefore, be brought in use. The things to be seen and observed are: the courts of princes, especially when they give audience to ambassadors; the courts of justice, while they sit and hear causes; and so of consistories ecclesiastic; the churches and monasteries, with the monuments which are therein extant; the walls and fortifications of cities and towns; and so the havens and harbours, antiquities and ruins, libraries, colleges, disputations, and lectures, where any are; shipping and navies; houses and gardens of state and pleasure,

7. de facto, as a matter of course. **15–16. facility,** easiness to be led. **30. steal it,** do it by stealth. **31. inward,** confidential. **39. Solomon.** See Proverbs 28:21. **44–45. Omnium . . . imperasset.** Everyone would have thought him capable of ruling—if he had not ruled. **46–47. Solus . . . melius.** Of the emperors, Vespasian alone changed for the better (when in power). **47–48. sufficiency,** ability. **48. affection,** disposition.

7. side, stand or be on the side of. **28. allow,** approve. **33. discipline,** learning. **48–49. disputations,** formal philosophical debates, which were a regular part of the academic curriculum in Renaissance Europe.

near great cities; armories, arsenals, magazines, exchanges, burses, warehouses, exercises of horsemanship, fencing, training of soldiers, and the like; comedies, such whereunto the better sort of persons do resort; treasuries of jewels and robes; cabinets and rarities; and, to conclude, whatsoever is memorable in the places where they go; after all which the tutors or servants ought to make diligent inquiry. As for triumphs, masks, feasts, weddings, funerals, capital executions, and such shows, men need not to be put in mind of them; yet are they not to be neglected. If you will have a young man to put his travel into a little room, and in short time to gather much, this you must do: first, as was said, he must have some entrance into the language before he goeth; then he must have such a servant, or tutor, as knoweth the country, as was likewise said; let him carry with him also some card, or book, describing the country where he travelleth, which will be a good key to his inquiry; let him keep also a diary; let him not stay long in one city or town, more or less as the place deserveth, but not long; nay, when he stayeth in one city or town, let him change his lodging from one end and part of the town to another, which is a great adamant of acquaintance; let him sequester himself from the company of his countrymen, and diet in such places where there is good company of the nation where he travelleth. Let him, upon his removes from one place to another, procure recommendation to some person of quality residing in the place whither he removeth, that he may use his favour in those things he desireth to see or know. Thus he may abridge his travel with much profit. As for the acquaintance which is to be sought in travel, that which is most of all profitable is acquaintance with the secretaries and employed men of ambassadors; for so in travelling in one country he shall suck the experience of many. Let him also see and visit eminent persons in all kinds, which are of great name abroad, that he may be able to tell how the life agreeth with the fame. For quarrels, they are with care and discretion to be avoided. They are commonly for mistresses, healths, place, and words. And let a man beware how he keepeth company with choleric and quarrelsome persons, for they will engage him into their own quarrels. When a traveller returneth home, let him not leave the countries where he hath travelled altogether behind him, but maintain a correspondence by letters with those of his acquaintance which are of most worth. And let his travel appear rather in his discourse than in his apparel or gesture; and in his discourse let him be rather advised in his answers, than forward to tell stories. And let it appear that he doth not change his country manners for those of foreign parts, but only prick in some flowers of that he hath learned abroad into the customs of his own country.

2. burses, stock exchanges. **18. card,** chart, map. **25. adamant,** loadstone, magnet.

OF STUDIES

STUDIES serve for delight, for ornament, and for ability. Their chief use for delight is in privateness and retiring; for ornament, is in discourse; and for ability, is in the judgment and disposition of business. For expert men can execute, and perhaps judge of particulars, one by one; but the general counsels, and the plots and marshalling of affairs come best from those that are learned. To spend too much time in studies is sloth; to use them too much for ornament is affectation; to make judgment wholly by their rules is the humour of a scholar. They perfect nature, and are perfected by experience: for natural abilities are like natural plants, that need pruning by study; and studies themselves do give forth directions too much at large, except they be bounded in by experience. Crafty men contemn studies, simple men admire them, and wise men use them; for they teach not their own use; but that is a wisdom without them and above them, won by observation. Read not to contradict and confute, nor to believe and take for granted, nor to find talk and discourse, but to weigh and consider. Some books are to be tasted, others to be swallowed, and some few to be chewed and digested; that is, some books are to be read only in parts; others to be read, but not curiously; and some few to be read wholly, and with diligence and attention. Some books also may be read by deputy, and extracts made of them by others; but that would be only in the less important arguments and the meaner sort of books; else distilled books are, like common distilled waters, flashy things. Reading maketh a full man; conference a ready man; and writing an exact man. And, therefore, if a man write little, he had need have a great memory; if he confer little, he had need have a present wit; and if he read little, he had need have much cunning, to seem to know that he doth not. Histories make men wise; poets, witty; the mathematics, subtile; natural philosophy, deep; moral, grave; logic and rhetoric,

3. country manners, those of his own country. **12–13. privateness and retiring,** privacy and retirement. **36. curiously,** carefully. **42. flashy,** flat or showy. **49. poets, witty,** another interesting bit of evidence as to Bacon's view of the function of poets and poetry.

able to contend. *Abeunt studia in mores.* Nay, there is no stond or impediment in the wit but may be wrought out by fit studies, like as diseases of the body may have appropriate exercises. Bowling is good for the stone and reins, shooting for the lungs and breast, gentle walking for the stomach, riding for the head and the like. So if a man's wit be wandering, let him study the mathematics; for in demonstrations, if his wit be called away never so little, he must begin again. If his wit be not apt to distinguish or find difference, let him study the school men; for they are *Cymini sectores.* If he be not apt to beat over matters, and to call up one thing to prove and illustrate another, let him study the lawyers' cases. So every defect of the mind may have a special receipt.

from NEW ATLANTIS

Bacon's *New Atlantis* furnishes an interesting counterpart to Shakespeare's *The Tempest.* One is the supreme presentation of the scientist's idea of an imaginary island, as the other is of the poet's, and consequently the essential differences between the scientist's mind and methods and those of the poet could hardly be better illustrated than in these two pieces. Bacon's island is not the creation of a poet. It has no such delightful creatures of the imagination as Ariel, or such monsters as Caliban. Instead of magical voices we have telephones (means "to convey sounds in trunks and pipes, in strange lines and distances") and loud-speakers ("to represent small sounds as great and deep"). Solomon's House is no palace of magic, but a matter-of-fact laboratory of scientific research. It is the product not of a magician's wand but of hard work and much cerebration. It may be taken as the prototype of the great Royal Society and of all the other institutions and associations which by co-operation and experimentation are engaged in discovering "the knowledge of causes, and secret motions of things; and the enlarging of the bounds of human empire, to the effecting of all things possible."

[SOLOMON'S HOUSE]

AND as we were thus in conference, there came one that seemed to be a messenger, in a rich huke, that spake with the Jew; whereupon he turned to me, and said, "You will pardon me, for I am commanded away in haste." The next morning he came to me again, joyful as it seemed, and said, "There is word come to the Governor of the city, that one of the fathers of Solomon's House will be here this day seven-night; we have seen none of them this dozen years. His coming is in state; but the cause of his coming is secret. I will provide you and your fellows of a good standing to see his entry." I thanked him, and told him I was most glad of the news.

The day being come he made his entry. He was a man of middle stature and age, comely of person, and had an aspect as if he pitied men. He was clothed in a robe of fine black cloth, with wide sleeves, and a cape: his under garment was of excellent white linen down to the foot, girt with a girdle of the same; and a sindon or tippet of the same about his neck. He had gloves that were curious, and set with stone; and shoes of peach-coloured velvet. His neck was bare to the shoulders. His hat was like a helmet, or Spanish montero; and his locks curled below it decently: they were of colour brown. His beard was cut round and of the same colour with his hair, somewhat lighter. He was carried in a rich chariot, without wheels, litter-wise, with two horses at either end, richly trapped in blue velvet embroidered; and two footmen on each side in the like attire. The chariot was all of cedar, gilt, and adorned with crystal; save that the fore-end had panels of sapphires, set in borders of gold, and the hinder-end the like of emeralds of the Peru colour. There was also a sun of gold, radiant upon the top, in the midst; and on the top before, a small cherub of gold, with wings displayed. The chariot was covered with cloth of gold tissued upon blue. He had before him fifty attendants, young men all, in white satin loose coats to the mid-leg; and stockings of white silk, and shoes of blue velvet; and hats of blue velvet, with fine plumes of divers colours, set round like hat-bands. Next before the chariot went two men, bare-headed, in linen garments down to the foot, girt, and shoes of blue velvet, who carried the one a crosier, the other a pastoral staff like a sheephook: neither of them of metal, but the crosier of balm-wood, the pastoral staff of cedar. Horsemen he had none, neither before nor behind his chariot: as it seemeth, to avoid all tumult and trouble. Behind his chariot went all the officers and principals of the companies of the city. He sat alone, upon cushions, of a kind of excellent plush, blue; and under his foot curious carpets of silk of divers colours, like the Persian, but far finer. He held up his bare hand, as he went, as blessing the people, but in silence. The street was wonderfully well kept; so that

1. Abeunt studia in mores. Studies pass into (that is, form) manners. **2. stond,** stand, difficulty. **5. stone,** of the bladder or **reins** (kidneys). **12. Cymini sectores,** dividers of cuminseed; that is, hairsplitters. See Matthew 23:23. **46. huke,** a kind of cape with a hood.

15. curious, of rare workmanship. **18. montero,** hunting cap. **31. displayed,** outspread. **32. tissued,** worked in threads.

there was never any army had their men stand in better battle-array than the people stood. The windows likewise were not crowded, but every one stood in them, as if they had been placed.

When the show was passed, the Jew said to me, "I shall not be able to attend you as I would, in regard of some charge the city hath laid upon me for the entertaining of this great person." Three days after the Jew came to me again, and said, "Ye are happy men; for the father of Solomon's House taketh knowledge of your being here, and commanded me to tell you, that he will admit all your company to his presence, and have private conference with one of you, that ye shall choose; and for this hath appointed the next day after to-morrow. And because he meaneth to give you his blessing, he hath appointed it in the forenoon."

We came at our day and hour, and I was chosen by my fellows for the private access. We found him in a fair chamber, richly hanged, and carpeted under foot, without any degrees to the state. He was set upon a low throne richly adorned, and a rich cloth of state over his head, of blue satin embroidered. He was alone, save that he had two pages of honour, on either hand one, finely attired in white. His under garments were the like that we saw him wear in the chariot; but instead of his gown, he had on him a mantle with a cape, of the same fine black, fastened about him. When we came in, as we were taught, we bowed low at our first entrance; and when we were come near his chair, he stood up, holding forth his hand ungloved, and in posture of blessing; and we every one of us stooped down, and kissed the hem of his tippet. That done, the rest departed, and I remained. Then he warned the pages forth of the room, and caused me to sit down beside him, and spake to me thus in the Spanish tongue:

"God bless thee, my son; I will give thee the greatest jewel I have. For I will impart unto thee, for the love of God and men, a relation of the true state of Solomon's House. Son, to make you know the true state of Solomon's House, I will keep this order. First, I will set forth unto you the end of our foundation. Secondly, the preparations and instruments we have for our works. Thirdly, the several employments and functions whereto our fellows are assigned. And fourthly, the ordinances and rites which we observe.

"The end of our foundation is the knowledge of causes, and secret motions of things; and the enlarging of the bounds of human empire, to the effecting of all things possible.

"The preparations and instruments are these. We have large and deep caves of several depths: the deepest are sunk six hundred fathoms; and some of them are digged and made under great hills and mountains; so that if you reckon together the depth of the hill, and the depth of the cave, they are, some of them, above three miles deep. For we find that the depth of a hill, and the depth of a cave from the flat, is the same thing; both remote alike from the sun and heaven's beams, and from the open air. These caves we call the lower region, and we use them for all coagulations, indurations, refrigerations, and conservations of bodies. We use them likewise for the imitation of natural mines, and the producing also of new artificial metals, by compositions and materials which we use, and lay there for many years. We use them also sometimes (which may seem strange) for curing of some diseases, and for prolongation of life, in some hermits that choose to live there, well accommodated of all things necessary, and indeed live very long; by whom also we learn many things.

"We have burials in several earths, where we put divers cements, as the Chinese do their porcelain. But we have them in greater variety, and some of them more fine. We also have great variety of composts and soils, for the making of the earth fruitful.

"We have high towers, the highest about half a mile in height, and some of them likewise set upon high mountains, so that the vantage of the hill, with the tower, is in the highest of them three miles at least. And these places we call the upper region, accounting the air between the high places and the low as a middle region. We use these towers, according to their several heights and situations, for insolation, refrigeration, conservation, and for the view of divers meteors—as winds, rain, snow, hail; and some of the fiery meteors also. And upon them, in some places, are dwellings of hermits, whom we visit sometimes, and instruct what to observe.

"We have great lakes, both salt and fresh, whereof we have use for the fish and fowl. We use them also for burials of some natural bodies, for we find a difference in things buried in earth, or in air below the earth, and things buried in water. We have also pools, of which some do strain fresh water out of salt, and others by art do turn fresh water into salt. We have also some rocks in the midst of the sea, and some bays upon the shore for some works, wherein is

20. richly hanged, with rich hangings. **21. without any degrees to the state,** without any steps leading to the canopy. **35. warned,** ordered.

14. indurations, experiments of hardening. **28–29. composts,** fertilizers. **38. insolation,** exposure to the action of the sun. **39. meteors,** meteorological phenomena.

required the air and vapour of the sea. We have likewise violent streams and cataracts, which serve us for many motions; and likewise engines for multiplying and enforcing of winds to set also on divers motions.

"We have also a number of artificial wells and fountains, made in imitation of the natural sources and baths, as tincted upon vitriol, sulphur, steel, brass, lead, nitre, and other minerals; and again, we have little wells for infusions of many things, where the waters take the virtue quicker and better than in vessels or basins. And amongst them we have a water, which we call Water of Paradise, being by that we do to it made very sovereign for health and prolongation of life.

"We have also great and spacious houses, where we imitate and demonstrate meteors—as snow, hail, rain, some artificial rains of bodies, and not of water, thunders, lightnings; also generations of bodies in air—as frogs, flies, and divers others.

"We have also certain chambers, which we call chambers of health, where we qualify the air as we think good and proper for the cure of divers diseases, and preservation of health.

"We have also fair and large baths, of several mixtures, for the cure of diseases, and the restoring of man's body from arefaction; and others for the confirming of it in strength of sinews, vital parts, and the very juice and substance of the body.

"We have also large and various orchards and gardens, wherein we do not so much respect beauty as variety of ground and soil, proper for divers trees and herbs, and some very spacious, where trees and berries are set, whereof we make divers kinds of drinks, besides the vineyards. In these we practise likewise all conclusions of grafting and inoculating, as well of wild-trees as fruit-trees, which produceth many effects. And we make by art, in the same orchards and gardens, trees and flowers, to come earlier or later than their seasons, and to come up and bear more speedily than by their natural course they do. We make them also by art greater much than their nature; and their fruit greater and sweeter, and of differing taste, smell, colour, and figure, from their nature. And many of them we so order as they become of medicinal use.

"We have also means to make divers plants rise by mixtures of earths without seeds, and likewise to make divers new plants, differing from the vulgar, and to make one tree or plant turn into another.

4. enforcing, increasing the force. **8. tincted upon,** tinctured with. **11. virtue,** the specific property of the substances. **27. arefaction,** drying up. **36. conclusions,** theories. **49. vulgar,** ordinary.

"We have also parks, and enclosures of all sorts, of beasts and birds; which we use not only for view or rareness, but likewise for dissections and trials, that thereby we may take light what may be wrought upon the body of man. Wherein we find many strange effects: as continuing life in them, though divers parts, which you account vital, be perished and taken forth; resuscitating of some that seem dead in appearance, and the like. We try also all poisons, and other medicines upon them, as well of chirurgery as physic. By art likewise we make them greater or taller than their kind is, and contrariwise dwarf them and stay their growth; we make them more fruitful and bearing than their kind is, and contrariwise barren and not generative. Also we make them differ in colour, shape, activity, many ways. We find means to make commixtures and copulations of divers kinds, which have produced many new kinds, and them not barren, as the general opinion is. We make a number of kinds, of serpents, worms, flies, fishes, of putrefaction, whereof some are advanced (in effect) to be perfect creatures, like beasts or birds, and have sexes, and do propagate. Neither do we this by chance, but we know beforehand of what matter and commixture, what kind of those creatures will arise.

"We have also particular pools where we make trials upon fishes, as we have said before of beasts and birds.

"We have also places for breed and generation of those kinds of worms and flies which are of special use; such as are with you your silkworms and bees.

"I will not hold you long with recounting of our brew-houses, bake-houses, and kitchens, where are made divers drinks, breads, and meats, rare and of special effects. Wines we have of grapes, and drinks of other juice, of fruits, of grains, and of roots, and of mixtures with honey, sugar, manna, and fruits dried and decocted; also of the tears or woundings of trees, and of the pulp of canes. And these drinks are of several ages, some to the age or last of forty years. We have drinks also brewed with several herbs, and roots and spices; yea, with several fleshes and white-meats; whereof some of the drinks are such as they are in effect meat and drink both, so that divers, especially in age, do desire to live with them with little or no meat or bread. And above all we strive to have drinks of extreme thin parts, to insinuate into the body, and yet without all biting, sharpness, or fretting; insomuch as some of them, put upon the back of your hand, will with a little stay pass through to the palm, and taste yet mild to the mouth. We have also waters, which we ripen in that

11. chirurgery, surgery. **41. last,** duration.

fashion, as they become nourishing, so that they are indeed excellent drinks, and many will use no other. Bread we have of several grains, roots, and kernels; yea, and some of flesh, and fish, dried; with divers kinds of leavenings and seasonings; so that some do extremely move appetites, some do nourish so, as divers do live of them, without any other meat, who live very long. So for meats, we have some of them so beaten, and made tender, and mortified, yet without all corrupting, as a weak heat of the stomach will turn them into good chylus, as well as a strong heat would meat otherwise prepared. We have some meats also, and breads, and drinks, which taken by men, enable them to fast long after; and some other, that used make the very flesh of men's bodies sensibly more hard and tough, and their strength far greater than otherwise it would be.

"We have dispensatories or shops of medicines; wherein you may easily think, if we have such variety of plants, and living creatures, more than you have in Europe (for we know what you have), the simples, drugs and ingredients of medicines, must likewise be in so much the greater variety. We have them likewise of divers ages, and long fermentations. And for their preparations, we have not only all manner of exquisite distillations and separations, and especially by gentle heats, and percolations through divers strainers, yea, and substances; but also exact forms of composition, whereby they incorporate almost as they were natural simples.

"We have also divers mechanical arts, which you have not; and stuffs made by them, as papers, linen, silks, tissues, dainty works of feathers of wonderful lustre, excellent dyes, and many others: and shops likewise, as well for such as are not brought into vulgar use amongst us, as for those that are. For you must know, that of the things before recited, many of them are grown into use throughout the kingdom, but yet, if they did flow from our invention, we have of them also for patterns and principals.

"We have also furnaces of great diversities, and that keep great diversity of heats: fierce and quick, strong and constant, soft and mild; blown, quiet, dry, moist, and the like. But above all we have heats, in imitation of the sun's and heavenly bodies' heats, that pass divers inequalities, and (as it were) orbs, progresses, and returns, whereby we produce admirable effects. Besides, we have heats of dungs, and of bellies and maws of living creatures and of their bloods and bodies, and of hays and herbs laid up moist, of lime unquenched, and such like. Instruments also which generate heat only by motion. And farther, places for strong insolations; and again, places under the earth, which by nature or art yield heat. These divers heats we use as the nature of the operation which we intend requireth.

"We have also perspective houses, where we make demonstrations of all lights and radiations, and of all colours; and out of things uncoloured and transparent we can represent unto you all several colours, not in rainbows (as it is in gems and prisms), but of themselves single. We represent also all multiplications of light, which we carry to great distance, and make so sharp, as to discern small points and lines. Also all colourations of light; all delusions and deceits of the sight, in figures, magnitudes, motions, colours; all demonstrations of shadows. We find also divers means yet unknown to you, of producing of light, originally from divers bodies. We procure means of seeing objects afar off, as in the heaven and remote places; and represent things near as afar off, and things afar off as near; making feigned distances. We have also helps for the sight, far above spectacles and glasses in use. We have also glasses and means to see small and minute bodies, perfectly and distinctly; as the shapes and colours of small flies and worms, grains, and flaws in gems which cannot otherwise be seen, observations in urine and blood not otherwise to be seen. We make artificial rainbows, halos, and circles about light. We represent also all manner of reflections, refractions, and multiplications of visual beams of objects.

"We have also precious stones of all kinds, many of them of great beauty and to you unknown; crystals likewise, and glasses of divers kinds; and amongst them some of metals vitrificated, and other materials, besides those of which you make glass. Also a number of fossils and imperfect minerals, which you have not. Likewise loadstones of prodigious virtue: and other rare stones, both natural and artificial.

"We have also sound-houses, where we practise and demonstrate all sounds and their generation. We have harmonies which you have not, of quarter sounds and lesser slides of sounds. Divers instruments of music likewise to you unknown, some sweeter than any you have; together with bells and rings that are dainty and sweet. We represent small sounds as great and deep; likewise great sounds, extenuate and sharp; we make divers tremblings and warblings of sounds, which in their original are en-

11. chylus, chyle. **18. dispensatories,** dispensaries. **22. simples,** herbs. **26. separations,** methods of separating the elements of substances. **29. forms of composition,** compounds. **40. principals,** patterns, models.

37. vitrificated, turned into glass. **50–51. extenuate,** made thin.

tire. We represent and imitate all articulate sounds and letters, and the voices and notes of beasts and birds. We have certain helps, which set to the ear do further the hearing greatly. We have also divers strange and artificial echoes, reflecting the voice many times, and as it were tossing it; and some that give back the voice louder than it came, some shriller and some deeper; yea, some rendering the voice, differing in the letters or articulate sound from that they receive. We have also means to convey sounds in trunks and pipes, in strange lines and distances.

"We have also perfume-houses, wherewith we join also practices of taste. We multiply smells, which may seem strange: we imitate smells, making all smells to breathe out of other mixtures than those that give them. We make divers imitations of taste likewise, so that they will deceive any man's taste. And in this house we contain also a confiture-house, where we make all sweatmeats, dry and moist, and divers pleasant wines, milks, broths, and salads, far in greater variety than you have.

"We have also engine-houses, where are prepared engines and instruments for all sorts of motions. There we imitate and practise to make swifter motions than any you have, either out of your muskets or any engine that you have; and to make them and multiply them more easily and with small force, by wheels and other means, and to make them stronger and more violent than yours are, exceeding your greatest cannons and basilisks. We represent also ordnance and instruments of war and engines of all kinds; and likewise new mixtures and compositions of gunpowder, wild-fires burning in water and unquenchable, also fire-works of all variety, both for pleasure and use. We imitate also flights of birds; we have some degrees of flying in the air. We have ships and boats for going under water and brooking of seas, also swimming-girdles and supporters. We have divers curious clocks, and other like motions of return, and some perpetual motions. We imitate also motions of living creatures by images of men, beasts, birds, fishes, and serpents; we have also a great number of other various motions, strange for equality, fineness, and subtlety.

"We have also a mathematical-house, where are represented all instruments, as well of geometry as astronomy, exquisitely made.

"We have also houses of deceits of the senses, where we represent all manner of feats of juggling, false apparitions, impostures and illusions, and their fallacies. And surely you will easily believe that we, that have so many things truly natural which induce admiration, could in a world of particulars deceive the senses if we would disguise those things, and labour to make them seem more miraculous. But we do hate all impostures and lies, insomuch as we have severely forbidden it to all our fellows, under pain of ignominy and fines, that they do not show any natural work or thing adorned or swelling, but only pure as it is, and without all affectation of strangeness.

"These are, my son, the riches of Solomon's House.

"For the several employments and offices of our fellows, we have twelve that sail into foreign countries under the names of other nations (for our own we conceal), who bring us the books and abstracts, and patterns of experiments of all other parts. These we call Merchants of Light.

"We have three that collect the experiments which are in all books. These we call Depredators.

"We have three that collect the experiments of all mechanical arts, and also of liberal sciences, and also of practices which are not brought into arts. These we call Mystery-men.

"We have three that try new experiments, such as themselves think good. These we call Pioneers or Miners.

"We have three that draw the experiments of the former four into titles and tables, to give the better light for the drawing of observations and axioms out of them. These we call Compilers.

"We have three that bend themselves, looking into the experiments of their fellows, and cast about how to draw out of them things of use and practice for man's life and knowledge, as well for works as for plain demonstration of causes, means of natural divinations, and the easy and clear discovery of the virtues and parts of bodies. These we call dowry-men or Benefactors.

"Then after divers meetings and consults of our whole number, to consider of the former labours and collections, we have three that take care out of them to direct new experiments, of a higher light, more penetrating into Nature than the former. These we call Lamps.

"We have three others that do execute the experiments so directed, and report them. These we call Inoculators.

"Lastly, we have three that raise the former discoveries by experiments into greater observations,

11. trunks, tubes. **31. basilisks,** a particular kind of cannon, named after the legendary basilisk serpent, which killed by a glance of the eye. **37. we have some degrees of flying,** that is, we have made some progress in flying. **39. brooking,** enduring, withstanding. **41. motions of return,** oscillation.

axioms, and aphorisms. These we call Interpreters of Nature.

"We have also, as you must think, novices and apprentices, that the succession of the former employed men do not fail; besides a great number of servants and attendants, men and women. And this we do also: we have consultations, which of the inventions and experiences which we have discovered shall be published, and which not; and take all an oath of secrecy for the concealing of those which we think fit to keep secret; though some of those we do reveal sometimes to the State, and some not.

"For our ordinances and rites, we have two very long and fair galleries: in one of these we place patterns and samples of all manner of the more rare and excellent inventions; in the other we place the statues of all principal inventors. There we have the statue of your Columbus, that discovered the West Indies; also the inventor of ships; your monk that was the inventor of ordnance and of gunpowder; the inventor of music; the inventor of letters; the inventor of printing; the inventor of observations of astronomy; the inventor of works in metal; the inventor of glass; the inventor of silk of the worm; the inventor of wine; the inventor of corn and bread; the inventor of sugars; and all these by more certain tradition than you have. Then we have divers inventors of our own, of excellent works, which since you have not seen, it were too long to make descriptions of them; and besides, in the right understanding of those descriptions you might easily err. For upon every invention of value we erect a statue to the inventor, and give him a liberal and honourable reward. These statues are some of brass, some of marble and touchstone, some of cedar and other special woods gilt and adorned; some of iron, some of silver, some of gold.

"We have certain hymns and services, which we say daily, of laud and thanks to God for His marvellous works. And forms of prayer, imploring His aid and blessing for the illumination of our labours, and the turning of them into good and holy uses.

"Lastly, we have circuits or visits, of divers principal cities of the kingdom; where, as it cometh to pass, we do publish such new profitable inventions as we think good. And we do also declare natural divinations of diseases, plagues, swarms of hurtful creatures, scarcity, tempests, earthquakes, great inundations, comets, temperature of the year, and divers other things; and we give counsel thereupon, what the people shall do for the prevention and remedy of them."

And when he had said this he stood up; and I, as I had been taught, knelt down; and he laid his right hand upon my head, and said, "God bless thee, my son, and God bless this relation which I have made. I give thee leave to publish it, for the good of other nations; for we here are in God's bosom, a land unknown." And so he left me; having assigned a value of about two thousand ducats for a bounty to me and my fellows. For they give great largesses, where they come, upon all occasions.

The rest was not perfected

19. your monk, Roger Bacon (1214?–1294?), one of the most ingenious English philosophers and men of science. The fame of Friar Bacon in popular estimation rests on his mechanical discoveries. He is reputed to have invented a telescope, and to have discovered gunpowder in his experiments on pure niter. His recipe for gunpowder is, at any rate, the earliest extant.

3. touchstone, a fine-grained, dark-colored variety of jasper, used in testing the quality of alloys. **16. divinations,** forecasts or prognostications based on natural facts.

Ben Jonson
1572–1637

Although of Scottish Border descent, Jonson was born at London, and it is as a Londoner that he is known and remembered. His only formal education was at Westminster School, but he amassed enough erudition to supply a university, and he was, indeed, given a degree by both Oxford and Cambridge. After leaving school he began work at his stepfather's trade of bricklaying, from which he ran away to join the English troops in Flanders. When he had had his fill of adventures there, he returned to London and gave up the army for the stage. By 1597 he was connected as player and playwright with Philip Henslowe's company of actors. The thirty years which followed Jonson's entry into the world of the theater were full of excitement for him and his fellows. His incorrigible obstreperousness was continually getting him into quarrels and into prison. He killed a fellow actor, Gabriel Spenser, in a duel, and escaped hanging by claiming the ancient "benefit of clergy," which exempted from the penalty a person who could read. While in prison he became a Roman Catholic, but after twelve years reverted to the Protestant faith.

To a large extent he found his characters and the materials of his plots in the life about him, and the zest with which he portrayed and emphasized the eccentricities of his colleagues and acquaintances led to further quarrels and further plays. In the history of the English drama, Jonson is famous for his development of the "comedy of humors," in which the development of character consists chiefly in presenting in an exaggerated fashion the outstanding trait or "humor" of a person or a class. The first and most sensational of these comedies was his *Every Man in His Humour*, which was performed, with Shakespeare in the cast, in 1598. At about this time and in such circumstances began the "War of the Theaters," one of the most famous of literary quarrels, which involved some of the foremost dramatists of the day, including Shakespeare, whose company, the Lord Chamberlain's Men, Jonson had slandered in *The Poetaster*, 1601. Of the comedies of "humors," in which he conveyed brilliant criticism of contemporary conditions, the two greatest are *Volpone, or the Fox*, 1606, and *The Alchemist*, 1610. His first extant tragedy, *Sejanus*, was produced by Shakespeare's company at the Globe in Southwark in 1603. In 1604 he was again in prison, this time voluntarily, through sympathy with his collaborators in a comedy *Eastward Ho*, which ridiculed the Scots and King James himself.

In 1605 Jonson began to interest himself in the production of masques, beloved of the Elizabethan and Stuart courts for their music and dancing and ornate settings. For many of the plots and lyrics which Jonson devised, Inigo Jones contrived the spectacle. Out of this collaboration grew in 1631 a final quarrel between the two. Jonson upheld the poet's pre-eminence in the production of the masque over the designer of the external trappings of the piece. The architect won the battle, and Jonson lost the patronage of the court, but the exquisite poetry of his *Oberon*, 1610–11, and *The Gipsies Metamorphosed*, 1621, has long outlived the machinery of even an Inigo Jones.

Jonson's high opinion of his compositions is illustrated by his publication in 1616 of a collection of his plays and poems in a folio volume which he called his *Works*, to the amusement of everybody. About this time he was granted a pension by the King, and became in fact, though not in name, poet laureate. In 1618 he went on foot to Scotland, where he visited William Drummond, "the Scottish Petrarch," whom he shocked with the characteristically racy comments on books and authors which Drummond has recorded in the *Conversations*. In Drummond's notes and in Jonson's own compilation of critical observations entitled *Timber, or Discoveries Made upon Men and Matters*, 1641, we have some of the sagest literary criticism in the language, and invaluable comments on some of Jonson's contemporaries.

The overbearing, satirical Jonson is more spectacular, but not more the essential Jonson, than the man who was the center of a group of friends that included Shakespeare, Marlowe, Ralegh, Bacon, and Donne. Younger poets, among them Herrick, Carew, and Suckling, who worshiped him and delighted to call themselves "Sons of Ben," have written lyric accounts of the meetings over which he presided at the Mermaid and the Devil. No poet in English literature has received more testimonies of affection during his life, or such an outpouring of tributes as when he was buried in the Poet's Corner of the Abbey. The diversity of his gifts, the abounding energy and vitality of his character, the flexibility of his genius, ranging from the severely classical to the gently lyrical, and from robust criticism to creations of the most dainty imagination, cannot be properly illustrated in a few selections. His influence on his "sons" and on those who come after him may be traced through the rest of the century.

EPIGRAMS

ON MY FIRST DAUGHTER

Here lies, to each her parents' ruth,
Mary, the daughter of their youth;
Yet all heaven's gifts being heaven's due,
It makes the father less to rue.
At six months' end she parted hence
With safety of her innocence;
Whose soul heaven's queen, whose name she bears,
In comfort of her mother's tears,
Hath placed amongst her virgin-train:
Where while that severed doth remain,
This grave partakes the fleshly birth,
Which cover lightly, gentle earth!

TO JOHN DONNE

Donne, the delight of Phoebus and each Muse.
 Who, to thy one, all other brains refuse;

On My First Daughter. 2. **Mary, the daughter.** From an entry in the parish register of St. Martin's in the Fields in London, it is supposed that Jonson's daughter died of the plague in November, 1593.

Vhose every work of thy most early wit
 Came forth example, and remains so yet;
onger a knowing than most wits do live,
 And which no affection praise enough can give!
o it, thy language, letters, arts, best life,
 Which might with half mankind maintain a strife;
ll which I mean to praise, and yet I would,
 But leave, because I cannot as I should.

So, by error, to his fate
 They all consented;
But viewing him since, alas, too late!
 They have repented,
And have sought, to give new birth,
 In baths to steep him;
But being so much too good for earth,
 Heaven vows to keep him.

ON MY FIRST SON

Jonson's son was born in 1596 and died of the plague 1603. Jonson, who was absent at the time of the boy's eath, had a vision of his son in which, as he described it William Drummond, the lad appeared "of a manly ape," and of that growth "he shall be at the resurrecon."

arewell, thou child of my right hand, and joy;
 My sin was too much hope of thee, loved boy:
even years thou wert lent to me, and I thee pay,
 Exacted by thy fate, on the just day.
 could I lose all father now! for why
 Will man lament the state he should envy—
o have so soon 'scaped world's and flesh's rage,
 And if no other misery, yet age?
est in soft peace, and asked, say, "Here doth lie
 Ben Jonson his best piece of poetry;
or whose sake henceforth all his vows be such
 As what he loves may never like too much."

EPITAPH ON S[ALOMON] P[AVY], A CHILD OF QUEEN ELIZABETH'S CHAPEL

Weep with me, all you that read
 This little story;
And know, for whom a tear you shed
 Death's self is sorry.
'Twas a child that so did thrive
 In grace and feature,
As heaven and nature seemed to strive
 Which owned the creature.
Years he numbered scarce thirteen
 When fates turned cruel,
Yet three filled zodiacs had he been
 The stage's jewel;
And did act, what now we moan,
 Old men so duly,
As, sooth, the Parcae thought him one,
 He played so truly.

Salomon (or *Solomon*) *Pavy*. One of the child actors who had ken part in two of Jonson's plays. **11. three filled zodis.** The boy had acted for three full years. **15. the Parcae,** e three Fates, who determined the duration of human life.

EPITAPH ON ELIZABETH, L. H.

Elizabeth, L. H. has not been identified. It has been suggested that she may have been Elizabeth, Lady Hatton, wife of Sir Edward Coke.

Wouldst thou hear what man can say
In a little? Reader, stay.
Underneath this stone doth lie
As much beauty as could die;
Which in life did harbour give
To more virtue than doth live.
If at all she had a fault,
Leave it buried in this vault.
One name was Elizabeth;
The other, let it sleep with death:
Fitter, where it died, to tell,
Than that it lived at all. Farewell!

SONGS FROM THE PLAYS AND MASQUES

QUEEN AND HUNTRESS

Queen and huntress, chaste and fair,
Now the sun is laid to sleep,
Seated in thy silver chair,
State in wonted manner keep:
 Hesperus entreats thy light,
 Goddess excellently bright.

Earth, let not thy envious shade
Dare itself to interpose;
Cynthia's shining orb was made
Heaven to clear when day did close:
 Bless us, then, with wishèd sight,
 Goddess excellently bright.

22. In baths to steep him, a reference to the story of Aeson, the aged father of Jason, hero of the expedition for the Golden Fleece, who was made young again by a magic bath administered by Medea. *Queen and Huntress.* **1. Queen and huntress,** Cynthia, or Diana. A tribute to Queen Elizabeth, who, in the masques that conclude the play, was represented by Cynthia. **5. Hesperus,** the evening star. **10. clear,** make bright.

Lay thy bow of pearl apart,
And thy crystal-shining quiver;
Give unto the flying hart
Space to breathe, how short soever;
Thou that mak'st a day of night,
Goddess excellently bright.

—*Cynthia's Revels*

COME, MY CELIA, LET US PROVE

This song is, in part, a paraphrase of the fifth ode of Catullus, the Latin lyric poet.

Come, my Celia, let us prove,
While we can, the sports of love;
Time will not be ours for ever,
He, at length, our goods will sever.
Spend not then his gifts in vain:
Suns that set may rise again;
But if once we lose this light,
'Tis with us perpetual night.
Why should we defer our joys?
Fame and rumour are but toys.
Cannot we delude the eyes
Of a few poor household spies?
Or his easier ears beguile,
Thus removèd by our wile?
'Tis no sin love's fruits to steal,
But the sweet thefts to reveal;
To be taken, to be seen,
These have crimes accounted been.

—*Volpone*

STILL TO BE NEAT

This poem is based on an anonymous late Latin poem.

Still to be neat, still to be dressed,
As you were going to a feast;
Still to be powdered, still perfumed:
Lady, it is to be presumed,
Though art's hid causes are not found,
All is not sweet, all is not sound.

Give me a look, give me a face,
That makes simplicity a grace;
Robes loosely flowing, hair as free:
Such sweet neglect more taketh me
Than all the adulteries of art;
They strike mine eyes, but not my heart.

—*Epicoene*

SONG: TO CELIA

This, the best known of Jonson's songs, is, like others of his lyrics, based on Latin originals. It is a series of paraphrases of passages in four letters of Philostratus, a Greek rhetorician of the second and third centuries A.D. It has been conjectured that this and the other songs to Celia were written about the same time, and were addressed to some lady of Jonson's acquaintance.

Drink to me only with thine eyes,
And I will pledge with mine;
Or leave a kiss but in the cup,
And I'll not look for wine.
The thirst that from the soul doth rise
Doth ask a drink divine;
But might I of Jove's nectar sup,
I would not change for thine.

I sent thee late a rosy wreath,
Not so much honouring thee
As giving it a hope, that there
It could not withered be.
But thou thereon didst only breathe,
And sent'st it back to me;
Since when it grows, and smells, I swear,
Not of itself but thee.

from A CELEBRATION OF CHARIS

HIS EXCUSE FOR LOVING

Let it not your wonder move,
Less your laughter, that I love.
Though I now write fifty years,
I have had, and have, my peers;
Poets though divine are men,
Some have loved as old again.
And it is not always face,
Clothes, or fortune, gives the grace,
Or the feature, or the youth;
But the language and the truth,
With the ardour and the passion,
Gives the lover weight and fashion.
If you then will read the story,
First prepare you to be sorry
That you never knew till now
Either whom to love, or how;
But be glad, as soon with me,
When you know that this is she
Of whose beauty it was sung:
She shall make the old man young,
Keep the middle age at stay,
And let nothing high decay;
Till she be the reason why
All the world for love may die.

HER TRIUMPH

See the chariot at hand here of Love,
Wherein my lady rideth!
Each that draws is a swan or a dove,
And well the car Love guideth.
As she goes, all hearts do duty
Unto her beauty;
And, enamoured, do wish, so they might
But enjoy such a sight,
That they still were to run by her side,
Through swords, through seas, whither she would ride.

Do but look on her eyes; they do light
All that Love's world compriseth!
Do but look on her hair; it is bright
As Love's star when it riseth!
Do but mark, her forehead's smoother
Than words that soothe her!
And from her arched brows, such a grace
Sheds itself through the face,
As alone there triumphs to the life
All the gain, all the good, of the elements' strife.

Have you seen but a bright lily grow,
Before rude hands have touched it?
Ha' you marked but the fall of the snow
Before the soil hath smutched it?
Ha' you felt the wool of beaver
Or swan's down ever?
Or have smelt o' the bud o' the brier?
Or the nard in the fire?
Or have tasted the bag of the bee?
O so white, O so soft, O so sweet is she!

from A PINDARIC ODE

TO THE IMMORTAL MEMORY AND FRIENDSHIP OF THAT NOBLE PAIR SIR LUCIUS CARY AND SIR H. MORISON

It is not growing like a tree
In bulk, doth make man better be;
Or standing long an oak, three hundred year,
To fall a log at last, dry, bald, and sear:
A lily of a day
Is fairer far, in May,
Although it fall and die that night;
It was the plant and flower of light.
In small proportions we just beauties see,
And in short measures life may perfect be.

28. nard, an aromatic balsam.

To the Memory of My Beloved the Author, MR. WILLIAM SHAKESPEARE, And What He Hath Left Us

These lines were written for the First Folio of Shakespeare, published in 1623.

To draw no envy, Shakespeare, on thy name,
Am I thus ample to thy book and fame,
While I confess thy writings to be such
As neither man nor Muse can praise too much.
'Tis true, and all men's suffrage. But these ways
Were not the paths I meant unto thy praise:
For seeliest ignorance on these may light,
Which, when it sounds at best, but echoes right;
Or blind affection, which does ne'er advance
The truth, but gropes, and urgeth all by chance;
Or crafty malice might pretend this praise,
And think to ruin where it seemed to raise.
These are as some infamous bawd or whore
Should praise a matron—what could hurt her more?
But thou are proof against them, and, indeed,
Above the ill fortune of them, or the need.
I therefore will begin. Soul of the age,
The applause, delight, the wonder of our stage,
My Shakespeare, rise! I will not lodge thee by
Chaucer or Spenser, or bid Beaumont lie
A little further to make thee a room:
Thou art a monument without a tomb,
And art alive still while thy book doth live,
And we have wits to read and praise to give.
That I not mix thee so, my brain excuses,
I mean with great, but disproportioned Muses;
For, if I thought my judgment were of years,
I should commit thee surely with thy peers,
And tell how far thou didst our Lyly outshine,
Or sporting Kyd, or Marlowe's mighty line.
And though thou hadst small Latin and less Greek,
From thence to honour thee, I would not seek

2. ample, generous. **5. suffrage,** vote, consensus. **7. seeliest,** most foolish. **20. Chaucer . . . Spenser . . . Beaumont.** These three poets were buried in Westminster Abbey. Jonson disagrees with those who would have had Shakespeare buried in the Abbey beside them, instead of at Stratford-on-Avon. **26. disproportioned Muses,** lesser poets. **28. commit,** join. **30. Kyd,** Thomas Kyd, a contemporary dramatist, author of *The Spanish Tragedy.* **31. small Latin and less Greek.** Jonson's famous line has caused Shakespeare's knowledge of Latin and Greek to be unduly disparaged. From what we know of the curriculum of the grammar schools of his day, Shakespeare must have been master of enough Latin, at least, to put the modern college student to shame.

For names, but call forth thundering Aeschylus,
Euripides, and Sophocles to us,
Pacuvius, Accius, him of Cordova dead,
To life again, to hear thy buskin tread
And shake a stage; or when thy socks were on,
Leave thee alone for the comparison
Of all that insolent Greece or haughty Rome
Sent forth, or since did from their ashes come.
Triumph, my Britain; thou hast one to show
To whom all scenes of Europe homage owe.
He was not of an age, but for all time!
And all the Muses still were in their prime
When like Apollo he came forth to warm
Our ears, or like a Mercury to charm.
Nature herself was proud of his designs,
And joyed to wear the dressing of his lines,
Which were so richly spun, and woven so fit,
As, since, she will vouchsafe no other wit:
The merry Greek, tart Aristophanes,
Neat Terence, witty Plautus, now not please,
But antiquated and deserted lie,
As they were not of Nature's family.
Yet must I not give nature all; thy art,
My gentle Shakespeare, must enjoy a part:
For though the poet's matter nature be,
His art doth give the fashion; and that he
Who casts to write a living line must sweat
(Such as thine are) and strike the second heat
Upon the Muses' anvil, turn the same,
And himself with it, that he thinks to frame,
Or for the laurel he may gain a scorn;
For a good poet's made as well as born.
And such wert thou! Look how the father's face
Lives in his issue; even so the race
Of Shakespeare's mind and manners brightly shines
In his well-turnèd and true-filèd lines,
In each of which he seems to shake a lance,
As brandished at the eyes of ignorance.
Sweet swan of Avon, what a sight it were
To see thee in our waters yet appear,
And make those flights upon the banks of Thames
That so did take Eliza and our James!
But stay; I see thee in the hemisphere
Advanced and made a constellation there!
Shine forth, thou star of poets, and with rage
Or influence chide or cheer the drooping stage,
Which, since thy flight from hence, hath mourned like night
And despairs day, but for thy volume's light.

35. **Pacuvius, Accius,** Roman tragic poets of the second century, B.C. **him of Cordova.** Seneca (4 B.C.–A.D. 65), Latin philosopher and dramatist, whose plays greatly influenced Elizabethan drama, was born in Cordova, Spain. 36–37. **buskin . . . socks.** The buskin, a high-heeled boot, worn by Greek tragic actors, is used symbolically for Shakespeare's tragedies; the sock, the low-heeled slipper worn by comic actors, for his comedies. 42. **scenes of Europe,** theaters on the Continent. 45. **warm,** thrill. 46. **Mercury,** the Roman messenger of the gods, who carried a charming-rod, the *caduceus*. 51. **tart Aristophanes,** as famous for the satire as for the humor of his comedies. 52. **Terence . . . Plautus,** the two best-known writers of Latin comedy. 59. **casts,** intends.

ON SHAKESPEARE[1]

I remember the players have often mentioned it as an honour to Shakespeare, that in his writing (whatsoever he penned) he never blotted out a line. My answer hath been, "Would he had blotted a thousand!" which they thought a malevolent speech. I had not told posterity this but for their ignorance who chose that circumstance to commend their friend by wherein he most faulted; and to justify mine own candour, for I loved the man, and do honour his memory on this side idolatry as much as any. He was, indeed, honest, and of an open and free nature; had an excellent phantasy, brave notions, and gentle expressions, wherein he flowed with that facility that sometimes it was necessary he should be stopped. "*Sufflaminandus erat,*" as Augustus said of Haterius. His wit was in his own power; would the rule of it had been so, too! Many times he fell into those things could not escape laughter, as when he said in the person of Caesar, one speaking to him, "Caesar, thou dost me wrong." He replied, "Caesar did never wrong but with just cause"; and such like, which were ridiculous. But he redeemed his vices with his virtues. There was ever more in him to be praised than to be pardoned.

69. **shake a lance,** a pun on "Shakespeare." 74. **Eliza and our James,** Queen Elizabeth and James I. 77. **rage,** poetic enthusiasm or rapture. 78. **influence,** of the stars. Astrological terms, despite the diminishing belief in astrology, continued to be used in poetry throughout the greater part of the century. [1] From *Timber, or Discoveries*, 1641. 15. **Sufflaminandus erat,** he ought to have been clogged. 19. **Caesar,** cf. *Julius Caesar*, Act III, sc. i, l. 47. Jonson is presumably quoting either an early Quarto version which has since disappeared or the acting version current in Shakespeare's lifetime.

John Donne
1571?–1631

Donne's life spans the last third of the sixteenth and the first third of the seventeenth century, and provides a good index to the intellectual, religious, social, and literary movements of the time. He was born and brought up a Roman Catholic, in a distinguished family of which several members had suffered for their faith. He studied at both Oxford and Cambridge, but left the universities without a degree because, on account of his religion, he could not take the required oaths. Later he studied law at Lincoln's Inn, and found time to dip into the Church Fathers and theology, medicine, and the other sciences old and new. As a gay, handsome, wealthy young gentleman of Elizabethan London, Donne could not give himself wholly to the bar or the university or the Church. Nor, as the possessor of one of the most active, curious, and versatile minds of his age, could he give all his time or energy to his pleasures. By the time he was of age he had argued himself out of the Church of Rome, but had not reached any stable or satisfying religious convictions.

There probably never lived a man more eager for knowledge and experience of all sorts and on all the levels of existence, from the lowest and fleshliest to the highest and most spiritual. The devious paths along which Donne's unsatisfied yearnings led him in his young manhood are not exactly known. He ran through his fortune early. He probably traveled on the Continent in his early twenties. He went with the Earl of Essex on his expedition to Cadiz in 1596, and to the Azores with Essex in 1597.

The poems which came out of the emotions and experiences of these years are unlike any that had appeared before, and may still be called unique. Donne took none of his predecessors or contemporaries as models. For the conventional rhythms and subjects of Spenser and the other Elizabethans he showed the most scornful indifference. In his early poems his attitude toward women and love is almost entirely cynical. In terms now harsh, now playful, at times coarsely bitter, at others amusingly disparaging, he records or reflects upon his experiences, attacks inconstancy in women, or defends the variety of his own experiments and experiences.

A new and very different chapter in his life began upon his return to England when he became secretary to Sir Thomas Egerton, Lord Keeper of the Great Seal. The door to worldly success seemed to have opened to him. But the position was lost and the door was very firmly closed when, in 1601, he fell in love with and secretly married Anne More, Sir Thomas's sixteen-year-old niece. If from the worldly point of view it was the worst thing he could have done, it was, from all others, the best thing that could have happened to him. His love for Anne was as spiritual as it was lasting, and it transformed his life and his poems. Their mutual love was the one ray of light in the dark and poverty-stricken years that followed his dismissal by Egerton.

In 1615, after a dozen unhappy years of religious and intellectual uncertainty, and unsuccessful searching for worldly preferment, Donne was persuaded to enter the priesthood of the Church of England. His brilliant sermons brought him to the notice of King James, and his destiny finally led him to the deanship of St. Paul's Cathedral, and to fame as one of the most eloquent and devout preachers of the English Church.

Donne's poems furnish a curious record of his emotional, intellectual, and spiritual progress through life. He brings all the resources of a mind rich in learning to a focus in his poetry. His mind has been likened to that of a chess-player; he tests mentally all moves, and writes them down as he does so. Into the religious verse and prose of his later years he puts the same fierce energy, the same unconventional figures and expressions, that had distinguished the love poems of his youth. He is the first and greatest of the "Metaphysical Poets." His influence on those who came after him in his own century, as well as the fascination he has held for poets in the twentieth century, will be in evidence in the pages that follow.

from SONGS AND SONNETS

SONG

Go and catch a falling star,
    Get with child a mandrake root,

Song. **2. mandrake root.** The forked root of the mandrake (mandragora) suggested the human body.

Tell me where all past years are,
Or who cleft the Devil's foot,
Teach me to hear mermaids singing,
Or to keep off envy's stinging,
And find
What wind
Serves to advance an honest mind.

If thou be'st born to strange sights,
Things invisible to see,
Ride ten thousand days and nights,
Till age snow white hairs on thee,
Thou, when thou return'st, wilt tell me
All strange wonders that befell thee,
And swear
Nowhere
Lives a woman true, and fair.

If thou find'st one, let me know;
Such a pilgrimage were sweet.
Yet do not; I would not go,
Though at next door we might meet.
Though she were true when you met her,
And last till you write your letter,
Yet she
Will be
False, ere I come, to two or three.

THE BAIT

Come live with me, and be my love,
And we will some new pleasures prove,
Of golden sands, and crystal brooks,
With silken lines, and silver hooks.

There will the river whispering run,
Warmed by thy eyes more than the sun,
And there the enamoured fish will stay,
Begging themselves they may betray.

When thou wilt swim in that live bath,
Each fish, which every channel hath,
Will amorously to thee swim,
Gladder to catch thee, than thou him.

If thou, to be so seen, beest loth,
By sun or moon, thou darkenest both;
And if myself have leave to see,
I need not their light, having thee.

Let others freeze with angling reeds,
And cut their legs with shells and weeds,
Or treacherously poor fish beset
With strangling snare, or windowy net.

Let coarse bold hands from slimy nest
The bedded fish in banks out-wrest,
Or curious traitors, sleave-silk flies,
Bewitch poor fishes' wandering eyes.

For thee, thou need'st no such deceit,
For thou thyself art thine own bait;
The fish that is not catched thereby,
Alas, is wiser far than I.

THE INDIFFERENT

I can love both fair and brown;
Her whom abundance melts, and her whom want betrays;
Her who loves loneness best, and her who masks and plays;
Her whom the country formed, and whom the town;
Her who believes, and her who tries;
Her who still weeps with spongy eyes,
And her who is dry cork and never cries.
I can love her, and her, and you, and you;
I can love any, so she be not true.

Will no other vice content you?
Will it not serve your turn to do as did your mothers?
Or have you all old vices spent, and now would find out others?
Or doth a fear that men are true torment you?
Oh, we are not; be not you so;
Let me, and do you, twenty know.
Rob me, but bind me not, and let me go.
Must I, who came to travail thorough you,
Grow your fixed subject because you are true?

Venus heard me sigh this song,
And by love's sweetest part, variety, she swore
She heard not this till now, and that it should be so no more.
She went, examined, and returned ere long,
And said, "Alas! some two or three
Poor heretics in love there be,
Which think to 'stablish dangerous constancy.
But I have told them, 'Since you will be true,
You shall be true to them who are false to you.' "

5. **mermaids,** here identified, as in Spenser and other contemporary authors, with the sirens. *The Bait.* A parody of Marlowe's "The Passionate Shepherd to His Love," p. 223.

The Bait. 23. **sleave-silk,** silk thread which can be separated into smaller filaments. *The Indifferent.* 5. **tries,** tests, examines. 10. **other,** other than constancy. 17. **thorough,** through.

THE CANONIZATION

For God's sake hold your tongue, and let me love;
Or chide my palsy, or my gout,
My five grey hairs, or ruined fortune flout;
With wealth your state, your mind with arts improve,
Take you a course, get you a place,
Observe his Honour, or his Grace,
Or the king's real, or his stamped face
Contemplate; what you will, approve,
So you will let me love.

Alas, alas, who's injured by my love?
What merchant's ships have my sighs drowned?
Who says my tears have overflowed his ground?
When did my colds a forward spring remove?
When did the heats which my veins fill
Add one more to the plaguy bill?
Soldiers find wars, and lawyers find out still
Litigious men, which quarrels move,
Though she and I do love.

Call us what you will, we are made such by love;
Call her one, me another fly,
We're tapers too, and at our own cost die,
And we in us find the Eagle and the Dove.
The Phoenix riddle hath more wit
By us; we two being one, are it.
So, to one neutral thing both sexes fit.
We die and rise the same, and prove
Mysterious by this love.

We can die by it, if not live by love,
And if unfit for tombs and hearse
Our legend be, it will be fit for verse;
And if no piece of chronicle we prove,
We'll build in sonnets pretty rooms;
As well a well-wrought urn becomes
The greatest ashes, as half-acre tombs,
And by these hymns all shall approve
Us canonized for Love;

And thus invoke us: You whom reverend love
Made one another's hermitage;
You, to whom love was peace, that now is rage;
Who did the whole world's soul contract, and drove
Into the glasses of your eyes
(So made such mirrors, and such spies,
That they did all to you epitomize)
Countries, towns, courts: beg from above
A pattern of your love!

The Canonization. **7. stamped face,** on coins. **15. plaguy bill,** the list, published weekly, of the victims of the plague.

THE GOOD-MORROW

I wonder, by my troth, what thou and I
Did till we loved? were we not weaned till then?
But sucked on country pleasures, childishly?
Or snorted we in the seven sleepers' den?
'Twas so; but this, all pleasures fancies be.
If ever any beauty I did see,
Which I desired, and got, 'twas but a dream of thee.

And now good-morrow to our waking souls,
Which watch not one another out of fear;
For love all love of other sights controls,
And makes one little room an everywhere.
Let sea-discoverers to new worlds have gone;
Let maps to other, worlds on worlds have shown;
Let us possess one world; each hath one, and is one.

My face in thine eye, thine in mine appears,
And true plain hearts do in the faces rest;
Where can we find two better hemispheres
Without sharp north, without declining west?
Whatever dies, was not mixed equally;
If our two loves be one, or thou and I
Love so alike that none do slacken, none can die.

THE ANNIVERSARY

All kings, and all their favourites,
All glory of honours, beauties, wits,
The sun itself, which makes times, as they pass,
Is elder by a year now than it was
When thou and I first one another saw.
All other things to their destruction draw,
Only our love hath no decay;
This no to-morrow hath, nor yesterday;
Running, it never runs from us away,
But truly keeps his first, last, everlasting day.

Two graves must hide thine and my corse;
If one might, death were no divorce.
Alas, as well as other princes, we,

4. seven sleepers' den, the cave in which, according to legend, seven Christian youths hid during the persecutions of Decius, and slept on for over two centuries. **5. but this,** except this love of ours. **15–17. thine in mine . . . hemispheres.** The two lovers find their respective worlds, or hemispheres, in each other's eyes. For a similar expression of the idea, see "The Canonization," ll. 39–44. **20–21. If our two loves . . . die.** Professor Grierson's interpretation of the passage is as follows: "If our two loves are *one*, dissolution is impossible; and the same is true if, though *two*, they are always alike. What is simple—as God or the soul—cannot be dissolved; nor compounds, e.g. the Heavenly bodies, between whose elements there is no contrariety." *The Anniversary.* **3. times,** seasons.

Who prince enough in one another be,
Must leave at last in death these eyes and ears,
Oft fed with true oaths, and with sweet salt tears;
But souls where nothing dwells but love,
All other thoughts being inmates, then shall prove
This, or a love increasèd there above,
When bodies to their graves, souls from their graves, remove.

And then we shall be throughly blest,
But we no more than all the rest;
Here upon earth we are kings, and none but we
Can be such kings, nor of such subjects be.
Who is so safe as we? where none can do
Treason to us, except one of us two.
True and false fears let us refrain;
Let us love nobly, and live, and add again
Years and years unto years, till we attain
To write threescore: this is the second of our reign.

A VALEDICTION FORBIDDING MOURNING

Izaak Walton, in his *Life of Donne*, says that Donne wrote this poem to his wife on the occasion of his going to the Continent in 1612 with his patron, Sir Robert Drury, and Lady Drury. Walton explains that Donne was unwilling to go because his wife's "divining soul boded her some ill in his absence." Mrs. Donne's forebodings were justified, for during her husband's absence she gave birth to a dead child.

As virtuous men pass mildly away,
And whisper to their souls to go,
Whilst some of their sad friends do say,
"The breath goes now," and some say, "No";

So let us melt, and make no noise,
No tear-floods nor sigh-tempests move;
'Twere profanation of our joys
To tell the laity our love.

Moving of the earth brings harms and fears;
Men reckon what it did and meant;
But trepidation of the spheres,
Though greater far, is innocent.

Dull sublunary lovers' love
(Whose soul is sense) cannot admit
Absence, because it doth remove
Those things which elemented it.

But we, by a love so much refined
That ourselves know not what it is,
Inter-assurèd of the mind,
Care less eyes, lips, and hands to miss.

Our two souls, therefore, which are one,
Though I must go, endure not yet
A breach, but an expansion,
Like gold to airy thinness beat.

If they be two, they are two so
As stiff twin compasses are two;
Thy soul, the fixed foot, makes no show
To move, but doth if the other do.

And though it in the centre sit,
Yet, when the other far doth roam,
It leans, and hearkens after it,
And grows erect as that comes home.

Such wilt thou be to me, who must
Like the other foot obliquely run:
Thy firmness draws my circle just,
And makes me end where I begun.

The Anniversary. **21. throughly,** thoroughly. *A Valediction Forbidding Mourning*. **11. trepidation of the spheres,** a term from the Ptolemaic astronomy, denoting the motion of the eighth (or ninth) sphere, which was thought to cause the "innocent," or harmless, variation in the date of the equinox. **16. elemented,** constituted.

SONG

This song was probably composed on the same occasion as the foregoing "Valediction."

Sweetest love, I do not go
For weariness of thee,
Nor in hope the world can show
A fitter love for me;
But since that I
Must die at last, 'tis best,
To use myself in jest
Thus by feignèd deaths to die.

Yesternight the sun went hence,
And yet is here to-day;
He hath no desire nor sense,
Nor half so short a way:
Then fear not me,
But believe that I shall make
Speedier journeys, since I take
More wings and spurs than he.

O how feeble is man's power,
That if good fortune fall,
Cannot add another hour,
Nor a lost hour recall!
But come bad chance,

26. stiff twin compasses, a pair of dividers. **35. just,** perfect. *Song*. **7. use,** practice. **21. come bad chance,** if bad chance come.

And we join it to our strength,
And we teach it art and length,
Itself o'er us to advance.

When thou sigh'st thou sigh'st not wind,
But sigh'st my soul away,
When thou weep'st, unkindly kind,
My life's blood doth decay.
It cannot be
That thou lov'st me, as thou say'st,
If in thine my life thou waste,
That art the best of me.

Let not thy divining heart
Forethink me any ill;
Destiny may take thy part,
And may thy tears fulfil;
But think that we
Are but turned aside to sleep;
They who one another keep
Alive, ne'er parted be.

THE ECSTASY

Where, like a pillow on a bed,
A pregnant bank swelled up to rest
The violet's reclining head,
Sat we two, one another's best.
Our hands were firmly cemented
With a fast balm, which thence did spring;
Our eye-beams twisted, and did thread
Our eyes upon one double string.
So to intergraft our hands, as yet
Was all the means to make us one;
And pictures in our eyes to get
Was all our propagation.
As, 'twixt two equal armies, fate
Suspends uncertain victory,
Our souls, which, to advance their state,
Were gone out, hung 'twixt her and me.
And whilst our souls negotiate there,
We like sepulchral statues lay;
All day, the same our postures were,
And we said nothing, all the day.
If any, so by love refined
That he soul's language understood,
And by good love were grown all mind,
Within convenient distance stood,
He, though he knew not which soul spake,
Because both meant, both spake, the same,
Might thence a new concoction take,
And part far purer than he came.
This ecstasy doth unperplex
(We said) and tell us what we love;
We see by this it was not sex;
We see, we saw not what did move;
But as all several souls contain
Mixture of things, they know not what,
Love these mixed souls doth mix again
And makes both one, each this and that.
A single violet transplant,
The strength, the colour, and the size,
All which before was poor and scant,
Redoubles still and multiplies.
When love with one another so
Interinanimates two souls,
That abler soul, which thence doth flow,
Defects of loneliness controls.
We then, who are this new soul, know
Of what we are composed and made,
For the atomies of which we grow
Are souls, whom no change can invade.
But O alas! so long, so far,
Our bodies why do we forbear?
They are ours, though they are not we; we are
The intelligences, they the spheres.
We owe them thanks, because they thus
Did us, to us, at first convey,
Yielded their forces, sense, to us,
Nor are dross to us, but allay.
On man heaven's influence works not so,
But that it first imprints the air;
For soul into the soul may flow,
Though it to body first repair.
As our blood labours to beget
Spirits, as like souls as it can,
Because such fingers need to knit
That subtle knot which makes us man,
So must pure lovers' souls descend
To affections, and to faculties,
Which sense may reach and apprehend;
Else a great prince in prison lies.
To our bodies turn we then, that so
Weak men on love revealed may look;
Love's mysteries in souls do grow,
But yet the body is his book.

The Ecstasy. **27. concoction,** purification or sublimation.

31–36. We see . . . we saw not . . . this and that. Grierson explains the passage thus: "We see now, that we did not see before the true source of our love. What we thought was due to bodily beauty, we perceive now to have its source in the soul." **47. atomies,** atoms. **52. intelligences . . . spheres.** The heavenly bodies (spheres) were, according to the medieval Schoolmen, moved and controlled by angels, or "intelligences." **56. allay,** alloy. **58. first imprints the air.** The influence of the stars, according to astrology, was transmitted to man through the air. Donne thinks of the body as providing a similar medium between two souls.

And if some lover, such as we,
Have heard this dialogue of one,
Let him still mark us; he shall see
Small change when we're to bodies gone.

LOVE'S DEITY

I long to talk with some old lover's ghost,
Who died before the god of love was born.
I cannot think that he, who then loved most,
Sunk so low as to love one which did scorn.
But since this god produced a destiny,
And that vice-nature, custom, lets it be,
I must love her that loves not me.

Sure, they which made him god meant not so much,
Nor he in his young godhead practised it;
But when an even flame two hearts did touch,
His office was indulgently to fit
Actives to passives. Correspondency
Only his subject was; it cannot be
Love till I love her that loves me.

But every modern god will now extend
His vast prerogative as far as Jove.
To rage, to lust, to write to, to commend,
All is the purlieu of the god of love.
Oh, were we wakened by this tyranny
To ungod this child again, it could not be
I should love her who loves not me.

Rebel and atheist too, why murmur I,
As though I felt the worst that love could do?
Love might make me leave loving, or might try
A deeper plague, to make her love me too;
Which, since she loves before, I am loth to see.
Falsehood is worse than hate; and that must be
If she whom I love should love me.

THE FUNERAL

The origins of this poem are uncertain, but it may have been addressed to Mrs. Magdalen Herbert, the mother of George Herbert.

Whoever comes to shroud me, do not harm
Nor question much
That subtle wreath of hair which crowns my arm;
The mystery, the sign you must not touch,
For 'tis my outward soul,
Viceroy to that, which, then to heaven being gone,
Will leave this to control,
And keep these limbs, her provinces, from dissolution.
For if the sinewy thread my brain lets fall
Through every part
Can tie those parts, and make me one of all,
These hairs which upward grew, and strength and art
Have from a better brain,
Can better do it; except she meant that I
By this should know my pain,
As prisoners then are manacled, when they're condemned to die.

Whate'er she meant by it, bury it with me,
For since I am
Love's martyr, it might breed idolatry
If into other hands these relics came;
As 'twas humility
To afford to it all that a soul can do,
So, 'tis some bravery,
That since you would have none of me, I bury some of you.

HIS PICTURE

Here take my picture; though I bid farewell,
Thine, in my heart, where my soul dwells, shall dwell.
'Tis like me now, but I dead, 'twill be more
When we are shadows both, than 'twas before.
When weather-beaten I come back; my hand,
Perhaps with rude oars torn, or sun-beams tanned,
My face and breast of haircloth, and my head
With care's rash sudden storms being o'erspread,
My body a sack of bones, broken within,
And powder's blue stains scattered on my skin;
If rival fools tax thee to have loved a man,
So foul, and coarse, as Oh, I may seem then,
This shall say what I was: and thou shalt say,
Do his hurts reach me? doth my worth decay?
Or do they reach his judging mind, that he
Should now love less, what he did love to see?
That which in him was fair and delicate,
Was but the milk, which in love's childish state
Did nurse it: who now is grown strong enough
To feed on that, which to disusèd tastes seems tough.

from HOLY SONNETS

5

I am a little world made cunningly
Of elements, and an angelic sprite;

The Funeral. 9. **sinewy thread,** the spinal cord. 23. **bravery,** bravado, boldness. *Holy Sonnets.* 2. **sprite,** spirit.

But black sin hath betrayed to endless night
My world's both parts, and, oh, both parts must die.
You which beyond that heaven which was most high
Have found new spheres, and of new lands can write,
Pour new seas in mine eyes, that so I might
Drown my world with my weeping earnestly,
Or wash it if it must be drowned no more:
But oh it must be burnt! alas the fire
Of lust and envy have burnt it heretofore,
And made it fouler; let their flames retire,
And burn me, O Lord, with a fiery zeal
Of Thee and Thy house, which doth in eating heal.

7

At the round earth's imagined corners, blow
Your trumpets, angels, and arise, arise
From death, you numberless infinities
Of souls, and to your scattered bodies go;
All whom the flood did, and fire shall o'erthrow;
All whom war, dearth, age, agues, tyrannies,
Despair, law, chance, hath slain, and you whose eyes
Shall behold God, and never taste death's woe.
But let them sleep, Lord, and me mourn a space,
For, if above all these, my sins abound,
'Tis late to ask abundance of Thy grace,
When we are there; here on this lowly ground,
Teach me how to repent; for that's as good
As if Thou hadst sealed my pardon, with Thy blood.

10

Death be not proud, though some have called thee
Mighty and dreadful, for thou art not so;
For those whom thou think'st thou dost overthrow
Die not, poor Death, nor yet canst thou kill me.
From rest and sleep, which but thy pictures be,
Much pleasure, then from thee much more must flow,
And soonest our best men with thee do go,
Rest of their bones and souls' delivery.
Thou art slave to fate, chance, kings, and desperate men,
And dost with poison, war, and sickness dwell,
And poppy, or charms can make us sleep as well,
And better than thy stroke; why swell'st thou then?
One short sleep past, we wake eternally,
And Death shall be no more; Death, thou shalt die.

14

Batter my heart, three-personed God; for You
As yet but knock, breathe, shine, and seek to mend;
That I may rise, and stand, o'erthrow me, and bend
Your force, to break, blow, burn, and make me new.
I, like an usurped town to another due,
Labour to admit You, but oh! to no end;
Reason, Your viceroy in me, me should defend,
But is captived and proves weak or untrue.
Yet dearly I love You, and would be lovèd fain,
But am betrothed unto Your enemy.
Divorce me, untie, or break that knot again,
Take me to You, imprison me, for I
Except You enthrall me, never shall be free;
Nor ever chaste, except You ravish me.

9. **it must be drowned no more,** a reference to the Divine promise (Genesis 9:11) that the earth will not again be destroyed with a flood. 10. **it must be burnt!** that is, at the Day of Judgment. Compare II Peter 3:5–7. 13. **a fiery zeal.** Compare Psalm 69:9: "For the zeal of thine house hath eaten me up." *Son. 7.* 1. **imagined corners.** Compare Revelation 7:1: "And after these things, I saw four angels standing on the four corners of the earth, holding the four winds of the earth." 8. **never taste death's woe.** Compare Luke 9:27: "I tell you of a truth, there be some standing here which shall not taste of death till they see the kingdom of God." *Son. 10.* 9–14. **Thou art slave to fate . . . die.** See Bacon's essay, "Of Death," page 317, for his treatment of this theme.

A HYMN TO GOD THE FATHER

Wilt thou forgive that sin where I begun,
  Which is my sin, though it were done before?
Wilt Thou forgive that sin through which I run,
  And do run still, though still I do deplore?
    When Thou hast done, Thou hast not done,
      For I have more.

Wilt Thou forgive that sin by which I have won
  Others to sin? and made my sin their door?
Wilt Thou forgive that sin which I did shun
  A year, or two, but wallowed in a score?
    When Thou hast done, Thou hast not done,
      For I have more.

I have a sin of fear, that when I have spun
  My last thread, I shall perish on the shore;
Swear by Thyself, that at my death Thy Son
  Shall shine as He shines now, and heretofore;
    And, having done that, Thou hast done,
      I fear no more.

5. **When Thou hast done.** Here and elsewhere in the poem a pun is undoubtedly intended on the poet's name, which was pronounced as "done."

from DEVOTIONS UPON EMERGENT OCCASIONS

During a serious illness in 1623, Donne, then Dean of St. Paul's, kept careful notes on the symptoms and progress of his disease. In his convalescence he fashioned them into a book of *Devotions,* two meditations from which are given below.

MEDITATION 6

The physician is afraid.

I observe the physician with the same diligence as he the disease; I see he fears, and I fear with him; I overtake him, I overrun him in his fear, and I go the faster because he makes his pace slow; I fear the more because he disguises his fear, and I see it with the more sharpness because he would not have me see it. He knows that his fear shall not disorder the practice and exercise of his art, but he knows that my fear may disorder the effect and working of his practice. As the ill affections of the spleen complicate and mingle themselves with every infirmity of the body, so doth fear insinuate itself in every action or passion of the mind; and as wind in the body will counterfeit any disease and seem the stone and seem the gout, so fear will counterfeit any disease of the mind. It shall seem love, a love of having; and it is but a fear, a jealous and suspicious fear of losing. It shall seem valour in despising and undervaluing danger; and it is but fear in an overvaluing of opinion and estimation and a fear of losing that. A man that is not afraid of a lion is afraid of a cat; not afraid of starving and yet is afraid of some joint of meat at the table presented to feed him; not afraid of the sound of drums and trumpets and shot and those which they seek to drown, the last cries of men, and is afraid of some particular harmonious instrument; so much afraid as that with any of these the enemy might drive this man, otherwise valiant enough, out of the field. I know not what fear is, nor I know not what it is that I fear now; I fear not the hastening of my death, and yet I do fear the increase of the disease; I should belie nature if I should deny that I feared this; and if I should say that I feared death, I should belie God. My weakness is from nature, who hath but her measure; my strength is from God, who possesses and distributes infinitely. As then every cold air is not a damp, every shivering is not a stupefaction; so every fear is not a fearfulness, every declination is not a running away, every debating is not a resolving, every wish that it were not thus is not a murmuring nor a dejection, though it be thus; but as my physician's fear puts not him from his practice, neither doth mine put me from receiving from God and man and myself spiritual and civil and moral assistances and consolations.

MEDITATION 17

Now this bell, tolling softly for another, says to me, "Thou must die."

Perchance he for whom this bell tolls may be so ill as that he knows not it tolls for him; and perchance I may think myself so much better than I am as that they who are about me and see my state may have caused it to toll for me, and I know not that. The church is catholic, universal, so are all her actions; all that she does belongs to all. When she baptizes a child, that action concerns me; for that child is thereby connected to that body which is my head too, and ingrafted into that body whereof I am a member. And when she buries a man, that action concerns me. All mankind is of one author, and is one volume; when one man dies, one chapter is not torn out of the book, but translated into a better language; and every chapter must be so translated. God employs several translators; some pieces are translated by age, some by sickness, some by war, some by justice; but God's hand is in every translation, and his hand shall bind up all our scattered leaves again for that library where every book shall lie open to one another. As therefore the bell that rings to a sermon calls not upon the preacher only but upon the congregation to come, so this bell calls us all; but how much more me who am brought so near the door by this sickness! There was a contention as far as a suit—in which piety and dignity, religion and estimation, were mingled —which of the religious orders should ring to prayers first in the morning; and it was determined that they should ring first that rose earliest. If we understand aright the dignity of this bell that tolls for our evening prayer, we would be glad to make it ours by rising early, in that application, that it might be ours as well as his, whose indeed it is. The bell doth toll for him that thinks it doth; and though it intermit again, yet from that minute that that occasion wrought upon him he is united to God. Who casts not up his eye to the sun when it rises? but who takes off his eye from a comet when that breaks out? Who bends not his ear to any bell which upon any occasion rings? but who can remove it from that bell which is passing a piece of himself out of this world? No man is an island entire of itself; every man is a piece of the continent, a part of the main. If a clod be washed away by the sea, Europe is the less, as well as if a promontory were, as well as if a manor of thy friend's or of thine own were. Any man's death diminishes me, because I am involved in mankind, and therefore never send to know for whom the bell tolls; it tolls for thee. Neither can we call this a begging of misery or a borrowing of misery, as though we were not miserable enough of ourselves but must fetch in more from the next house, in taking upon us the misery of our neighbors. Truly it were an excusable covetousness if we did, for affliction is a treasure, and scarce any man hath enough of it. No man hath affliction enough that is not matured and ripened by it and made fit for God by that affliction. If a man carry treasure in bullion or in a wedge of gold and have none coined into current money, his treasure will not defray him as he travels. Tribulation is treasure in the nature of it, but it is not current money in the use of it, except we get nearer and nearer our home, heaven, by it. Another man may be sick too, and sick to death, and this affliction may lie in his bowels as gold in a mine and be of no use to him; but this bell that tells me of his affliction digs out and applies that gold to me, if by this consideration of another's danger I take mine own into contemplation, and so secure myself by making my recourse to my God, who is our only security.

The Character-Writers

The "character" is one of the most popular and ubiquitous literary forms of the seventeenth century. Almost everyone who wrote anything tried his hand at the character sketch in one form or another, and the character book, with its collection of short and "witty" descriptions of various types of personality, is one of the most distinctive contributions of the century to English literature. The impulse to dissect the character of a fellow human being, whether through admiration or malice, for simple amusement or for information, is doubtless as old as the race itself. In English literature from Chaucer's Prologue to his *Canterbury Tales* on through sermon, allegory, drama, essay, satire, and epigram, one meets with descriptions and characterizations of individuals or types. The student of the literature of the late sixteenth and seventeenth centuries is aware of an increasing tendency toward introspection and analysis of characters and motives of action.

The "character" proper is not a portrait or a description of the character of a particular person, but the analysis, more or less accurate, of a type of person. Seventeenth-century England was profoundly class-conscious, and the character books throw much light on the social order of the time by their analyses and descriptions of the habits, prejudices, and functions of the various members of the social organism.

The oldest known character book is that of Theophrastus, the pupil of Aristotle, and greatest of ancient botanists. His *Characters* represent a sort of botany of human nature, with various types of human beings analyzed like so many specimens in a herbarium. The author of the first character book published in England was Joseph Hall, whose *Characters of Virtues and Vices*, 1608, professedly followed the method of "that ancient master of morality." The two most popular character books in English are those of Sir Thomas Overbury and John Earle, from the latter of which the selections given here are taken.

John Earle

1601?–1665

Earle, whose little book the *Microcosmography* is, next to the Overbury collection, the best known of seventeenth-century character books, provides at every point a contrast with Overbury. He is one of the best-loved men and authors of his century. In a time of civil war and dissension he kept his temper and his friendships without sacrificing his principles, and drew commendation from men of all parties. He was as much a man of the university and the Church as Overbury and his associates were men of the court and the town. He was born in the city of York, and matriculated at Christ Church, Oxford, at the age of eighteen. For the next twenty years he was connected with Oxford, as undergraduate, fellow of Merton College, and proctor of the university. His book of characters was begun probably during his undergraduate days and was completed at the university. It has consequently a generous number of "campus characters." The *Microcosmography* was first published anonymously in 1628 after it had become known in manuscript. There was a steady succession of editions of the book, new characters being added from time to time. By the time of the author's death the number of characters had reached seventy-eight and the number of editions ten.

About two years after the book first appeared Earle was made chaplain to the Earl of Pembroke, son of Sir Philip Sidney's sister, who was Chancellor of Oxford and Lord Chamberlain. From the Earl he received also the living of Bishopston in Wiltshire. The young clergyman was shortly after made chaplain to Charles I and tutor to the Prince of Wales, later Charles II. During the struggle between the King and the Parliament, the Roundheads had sufficient regard for Earle's character and abilities to nominate him, despite his attachment to the royal cause, as one of the Westminster Assembly of Divines, but he declined the honor. He was deprived of his church livings, and after the execution of Charles I he lived abroad as chaplain to Charles II. At Charles's request he translated into Latin the *Eikon Basilike*, the *King's Book* of Charles I. After the Restoration Earle fared much better than most of the other loyalists. He was made Dean of Westminster, Bishop of Worcester, and, two years before his death, Bishop of Salisbury. He was one of the revisers of the Book of Common Prayer in 1662. It is characteristic of Earle that as a bishop he made vigorous efforts to ameliorate the condition of the Nonconformists during the persecutions of the Restoration days. He succumbed to the plague of 1665 while with the King and his court at Oxford, and was buried in Merton College Church.

Earle's *Microcosmography* is as much a mirror of his own kindly and sympathetic nature as its characters are of the types they describe. He is of all the character-writers of the time the most interested in the springs and processes of character and action, and more than any other he adopts what we should call the psychological approach. Like a good novelist, he finds some of his most interesting human materials in types that are commonly unregarded. He is never clever at the expense of his subjects, and is rather the counsel for the defense than the prosecuting attorney. We may apply to Earle Ben Jonson's description of the ideal critic in his character of Crites in *Cynthia's Revels* "He strives rather to be that which men call judicious than to be thought so; and is so truly learned that he affects not to show it. . . . In sum, he hath a most ingenious and sweet spirit, a sharp and seasoned wit, a straight judgment, and a strong mind. Fortune could never break him, nor make him less."

from MICROCOSMOGRAPHY,

OR A PIECE OF THE WORLD DISCOVERED

A CHILD

Is a man in a small letter, yet the best copy of Adam before he tasted of Eve or the apple; and he is happy whose small practice in the world can only write his character. He is nature's fresh picture newly drawn in oil, which time, and much handling, dims and defaces. His soul is yet a white paper unscribbled with observations of the world, wherewith, at length, it becomes a blurred notebook. He is purely happy, because he knows no evil, nor hath made means by sin to be acquainted with misery. He arrives not at the misery of being wise, nor endures evils to come, by foreseeing them. He kisses and loves all, and, when the smart of the rod is past, smiles on his beater. Nature and his parents alike dandle him, and tice him on with a bait of sugar to a draught of wormwood. He plays yet, like a young 'prentice the first day, and is not come to his task of melancholy. All the language he speaks yet is tears, and they serve him well enough to express his necessity. His hardest labour is his tongue, as if he were loth to use so deceitful an organ; and he is best company with it when he can but prattle. We laugh at his foolish sports, but his game is our earnest; and his drums, rattles, and hobby-horses, but the emblems and mocking of man's business. His father hath writ him as his own little story, wherein he reads those days that he cannot remember, and sighs to see what innocence he has out-lived. The older he grows, he is a stair lower from God; and, like his first father, much worse in his breeches. He is the Christian's example, and the old man's relapse; the one imitates his pureness, and the other falls into his simplicity. Could he put off his body with his little coat, he had got eternity without a burden, and exchanged but one heaven for another.

A YOUNG MAN

He is now out of nature's protection, though not yet able to guide himself; but left loose to the world

13. white paper, an interesting anticipation of John Locke's theory of the infant's mind as a tabula rasa, or blank paper. See Locke's *Essay Concerning Human Understanding*, 1690, Book I, sec. 1, par. 15. **22. tice,** old form of "entice." **37. breeches,** a pun on Genesis 3:7, which in the Geneva Bible states that Adam and Eve, after their first disobedience, "made themselves breeches."

and fortune, from which the weakness of his childhood preserved him; and now his strength exposes him. He is, indeed, just of age to be miserable, yet in his own conceit first begins to be happy; and he is happier in this imagination, and his misery not felt is less. He sees yet but the outside of the world and man, and conceives them, according to their appearing, glister, and out of this ignorance believes them. He pursues all vanities for happiness, and enjoys them best in this fancy. His reason serves not to curb but understand his appetite, and prosecute the motions thereof with a more eager earnestness. Himself is his own temptation, and needs not Satan, and the world will come hereafter. He leaves repentance for grey hairs, and performs it in being covetous. He is mingled with the vices of the age as the fashion and custom, with which he longs to be acquainted, and sins to better his understanding. He conceives his youth as the season of his lust, and the hour wherein he ought to be bad; and because he would not lose his time, spends it. He distastes religion as a sad thing, and is six years elder for a thought of heaven. He scorns and fears, and yet hopes for old age, but dare not imagine it with wrinkles. He loves and hates with the same inflammation, and when the heat is over is cool alike to friends and enemies. His friendship is seldom so steadfast but that lust, drink, or anger may overturn it. He offers you his blood to-day in kindness, and is ready to take yours to-morrow. He does seldom anything which he wishes not to do again, and is only wise after a misfortune. He suffers much for his knowledge, and a great deal of folly it is that makes him a wise man. He is free from many vices, by being not grown to the performance, and is only more virtuous out of weakness. Every action is his danger, and every man his ambush. He is a ship without pilot or tackling, and only good fortune may steer him. If he scape this age, he has scaped a tempest, and may live to be a man.

A MERE YOUNG GENTLEMAN OF THE UNIVERSITY

Is one that comes there to wear a gown, and to say hereafter, he has been at the university. His father sent him thither because he heard there were the best fencing and dancing schools; from these he has his education, from his tutor the oversight. The first element of his knowledge is to be shown the colleges, and initiated in a tavern by the way, which hereafter he will learn of himself. The two marks of his seniority is the bare velvet of his gown, and his proficiency at tennis, where when he can once play a set, he is a freshman no more. His study has commonly handsome shelves, his books neat silk strings, which he shows to his father's man, and is loth to untie or take down for fear of misplacing. Upon foul days for recreation he retires thither, and looks over the pretty book his tutor reads to him, which is commonly some short history, or a piece of Euphormio; for which his tutor gives him money to spend next day. His main loitering is at the library, where he studies arms and books of honour, and turns a gentleman critic in pedigrees. Of all things he endures not to be mistaken for a scholar, and hates a black suit though it be made of satin. His companion is ordinarily some stale fellow, that has been notorious for an ingle to gold hatbands, whom he admires at first, afterwards scorns. If he have spirit or wit he may light of better company, and may learn some flashes of wit, which may do him knight's service in the country hereafter. But he is now gone to the inns-a-court, where he studies to forget what he learned before, his acquaintances and the fashion.

20. Euphormio, Euphormio Lusinius, pen name of John Barclay (1582–1621), author of the *Argenis*, a popular romance of the time. **23. books of honour,** books giving pedigrees of noble families. **28. an ingle to gold hatbands,** that is, a crony of noblemen at the university, who wore gold tassels on their caps. **33. inns-a-court,** the Inns of Court, the abode of law students.

George Herbert

1593–1633

In the history of the religious lyric in English, George Herbert occupies a unique and prominent place. There had been religious poems and lyrics before him, but Herbert more than any other poet developed and fashioned the devotional lyric into the literary type with which we have been familiar since his time. He is an author with whose character and personality one must be acquainted if one is to appreciate properly the poems he has left us. The details of his life furnish interesting proof of the fact that the ranks of the saints are not recruited wholly from the poor and the so-called lower classes of the world. He was born into one of the greatest houses in England. His older brother, Edward Lord Herbert of Cherbury, went as ambassador to Paris, and George's own training and natural abilities were such as to fit him to be an ambassador and a companion of princes. His mother, Magdalen Herbert, one of the most beautiful and able women of her day, took personal charge of the education of her sons. She followed Edward to Oxford, set up her household, and engaged tutors for George. Here, presumably, began the friendship between Mrs. Herbert and John Donne, which was to be one of the most helpful influences in Donne's life, and which called forth several poems in tribute to the lady.

The next move was to London, and George was sent to Westminster School. Later he went to Trinity College, Cambridge, where he took his B.A. and M.A. degrees. He began to write religious verse while an undergraduate, and took up the study of divinity after receiving his Master's degree. He was made Public Orator of the university in 1619, when he was twenty-six, and the duties and privileges of the position brought him into close association with the rich and the great and with the King himself.

Herbert had been destined for the Church by his mother since his infancy, and while he perhaps never gave up entirely the idea of entering the priesthood, the associations induced by the oratorship were such as to make him think more of worldly preferment and a career at court. His tender conscience also made him feel unworthy of the priestly calling. A serious illness, and the deaths of his mother, his king, and several of his prominent friends, brought him to a realization of the transitoriness of persons and places, and led him eventually to the service of the Church. He resigned the oratorship in his thirty-fourth year. He married Jane Danvers two years later, and in the following year, 1630, he was ordained and became rector of St. Andrew's Church at Bemerton, near Salisbury, one of the smallest churches in England.

The story of the remaining years of his life is one of unstinted devotion to his church and his poor parishioners. Like the Good Parson of Chaucer's *Canterbury Tales*, he preached the gospel and followed it first himself. The countryside was full of stories of his kindness to the poor. He found time for his favorite recreation with the lute, to which he composed many of his poems; and he made frequent walks to Salisbury Cathedral to hear the music. In his prose work, *A Priest to the Temple*, which he wrote at Bemerton, he has given, after the fashion of the character-books, a picture of the ideal country parson, of whom he was himself unconsciously the model.

Herbert wrote some secular verse in his early days, but he destroyed it after his ordination. From his deathbed he sent the manuscript of his religious poems to his friend the pious Nicholas Ferrar, of the religious community of Little Gidding, near Bemerton, to be burned if they seemed unworthy, or to be printed if he thought they might "turn to the advantage of any dejected poor soul." Ferrar saw fit to have them printed in a volume entitled *The Temple* shortly after Herbert's death. The wisdom of his decision was proved by the many editions the book went into during the century. The influence of the book is to be seen in Crashaw's *Steps to the Temple* and in the poems of Henry Vaughan.

Herbert's poems show in many ways the influence of Donne. They have much of his elaborate figurativeness, the same wedding of the homely and colloquial to the "metaphysical" richness of image and analogy. Herbert's fondness for figures and conceits leads him into acrostics, anagrams, and verses shaped, as in "The Altar" and "Easter Wings," to represent the subject. His verses are more artistically constructed than Donne's, and they sing, as Donne's never could. They lack the fire and the fierceness of Donne, and the struggle which such poems as "The Collar" portray is, fortunately, not such a spiritual tumult as harassed the mind and soul of the older poet. Herbert's lyrics, more than any others, constitute the wood wind in the orchestra of seventeenth-century poetry.

THE ALTAR

Poems in which the lines are arranged to form figures, and emblematic verse in general, were much in favor in the seventeenth century. Altars, crosses, and pyramids were especially popular in religious poetry. See Herrick's poem, "The Pillar of Fame," page 355.

A broken altar, Lord, Thy servant rears,
Made of a heart and cémented with tears;
Whose parts are as Thy hand did frame;
No workman's tool hath touched the same.
A heart alone
Is such a stone
As nothing but
Thy power doth cut.
Wherefore each part
Of my hard heart
Meets in this frame
To praise Thy name;
That if I chance to hold my peace,
These stones to praise Thee may not cease.
Oh, let Thy blessed sacrifice be mine,
And sanctify this altar to be Thine.

EASTER WINGS

In the early editions of *The Temple*, the lines of "Easter Wings" were printed vertically, the first two stanzas on the left-hand page facing the last two on the right-hand page.

Lord, who createdst man in wealth and store,
Though foolishly he lost the same,
Decaying more and more
Till he became
Most poor:
✠
With thee
O let me rise
As larks, harmoniously,
And sing this day thy victories:
Then shall the fall further the flight in me.

Easter Wings. **1. store,** abundance.

My tender age in sorrow did begin:
And still with sicknesses and shame
Thou didst so punish sin
That I became
Most thin.
✠
With thee
Let me combine,
And feel this day thy victory;
For, if I imp my wing on thine,
Affliction shall advance the flight in me.

THE COLLAR

Herbert's titles illustrate his fondness for the "metaphysical" conceit and the emblematic style of writing. The collar is an emblem of the claim which God has on him, and of the restraint which it imposes. The poem is a portrayal of his struggles before he finally surrenders to his Master.

I struck the board, and cried, "No more!
I will abroad!
What? Shall I ever sigh and pine?
My lines and life are free, free as the road,
Loose as the wind, as large as store.
Shall I be still in suit?
Have I no harvest but a thorn
To let me blood, and not restore
What I have lost with cordial fruit?
Sure there was wine
Before my sighs did dry it. There was corn
Before my tears did drown it.
Is the year only lost to me?
Have I no bays to crown it?
No flowers, no garlands gay? All blasted?
All wasted?
Not so, my heart! But there is fruit,
And thou hast hands.
Recover all thy sigh-blown age
On double pleasures. Leave thy cold dispute
Of what is fit and not. Forsake thy cage,
Thy rope of sands,
Which petty thoughts have made, and made to thee

Easter Wings. **12. with sicknesses.** Herbert's naturally frail constitution was weakened by his studies and his devotion to his pastoral duties. He died at the age of forty. **19. imp,** a term from falconry; to mend the damaged wing of a hawk by grafting to it feathers from another bird. *The Collar.* **1. board,** table. **5. as large as store,** as large as abundance itself. **6. in suit,** in attendance, as a suitor, for preferment or award. **9. cordial,** restorative. **14. bays,** the poet's wreaths of bay, or laurel. **22. rope of sands,** the teachings of the Church as they seem to the rebellious young man.

Good cable, to enforce and draw,
And be thy law,
While thou didst wink and wouldst not see.
Away! Take heed!
I will abroad!
Call in thy death's head there! Tie up thy fears!
He that forbears
To suit and serve his need
Deserves his load."
But as I raved, and grew more fierce and wild
At every word,
Methoughts I heard one calling, "Child!"
And I replied, "My Lord!"

THE QUIP

"Quip" is used in the sense of "sharp retort." See ll. 23–24.

The merry World did on a day
With his train-bands and mates agree
To meet together where I lay,
And all in sport to jeer at me.

First Beauty crept into a rose;
Which when I plucked not, "Sir," said she,
"Tell me, I pray, whose hands are those?"
But Thou shalt answer, Lord, for me.

Then Money came, and chinking still,
"What tune is this, poor man?" said he;
"I heard in music you had skill."
But Thou shalt answer, Lord, for me.

Then came brave Glory puffing by
In silks that whistled, who but he?
He scarce allowed me half an eye.
But Thou shalt answer, Lord, for me.

Then came quick Wit and Conversation,
And he would needs a comfort be,
And, to be short, make an oration.
But Thou shalt answer, Lord, for me.

Yet when the hour of Thy design
To answer these fine things shall come,
Speak not at large; say I am Thine;
And then they have their answer home.

2. train-bands, citizen soldiers; here used in the sense of comrades. **4. to jeer at me.** The poem depicts Herbert's qualities and accomplishments as a wealthy and cultured young gentleman, and the corresponding temptations. **7. whose hands are those?** that is, why do they not pluck the rose? **11. in music you had skill.** Herbert was known to his friends as an "excellent master" in music. **13. brave,** finely dressed.

THE PULLEY

The title is an emblem of the restlessness that, when all else fails, may raise man towards God.

When God at first made man,
Having a glass of blessings standing by,
"Let us," said He, "pour on him all we can.
Let the world's riches, which dispersèd lie,
Contract into a span."

So strength first made a way;
Then beauty flowed, then wisdom, honour, pleasure.
When almost all was out, God made a stay,
Perceiving that, alone of all His treasure,
Rest in the bottom lay.

"For if I should," said He,
"Bestow this jewel also on my creature,
He would adore my gifts instead of me
And rest in nature, not the God of nature;
So both should losers be.

"Yet let him keep the rest,
But keep them with repining restlessness.
Let him be rich and weary, that at last,
If goodness lead him not, yet weariness
May toss him to my breast."

THE ELIXIR

The elixir was the preparation sought by the alchemists whereby it was thought baser metals might be transmuted into gold. In the last stanza Herbert identifies it with the philosopher's stone.

Teach me, my God and King,
In all things Thee to see;
And what I do in anything,
To do it as for Thee.

Not rudely, as a beast,
To run into an actiòn;
But still to make Thee prepossessed,
And give it his perfectiòn.

A man that looks on glass
On it may stay his eye,

The Pulley. **10. Rest.** The poet characteristically plays on the word in the last two stanzas. *The Elixir.* **7. still to make Thee prepossessed,** always to make Thee possessed of me in advance. **8. his,** its.

Or, if he pleaseth, through it pass,
And then the heaven espy.

All may of Thee partake;
Nothing can be so mean
Which with his tincture, "for Thy sake,"
Will not grow bright and clean.

A servant with this clause
Makes drudgery divine:
Who sweeps a room as for Thy laws
Makes that and the action fine.

This is the famous stone
That turneth all to gold;
For that which God doth touch and own
Cannot for less be told.

DISCIPLINE

Throw away Thy rod,
Throw away Thy wrath.
O my God,
Take the gentle path.

For my heart's desire
Unto Thine is bent;
I aspire
To a full consent.

Not a word or look
I affect to own,
But by book,
And Thy book alone.

Though I fail, I weep;
Though I halt in pace,
Yet I creep
To the throne of grace.

Then let wrath remove;
Love will do the deed,
For with love
Stony hearts will bleed.

Love is swift of foot.
Love's a man of war,
And can shoot,
And can hit from far.

Who can scape his bow?
That which wrought on thee,
Brought thee low,
Needs must work on me.

Throw away Thy rod;
Though man frailties hath,
Thou art God.
Throw away Thy wrath.

LOVE

Love bade me welcome; yet my soul drew back,
Guilty of dust and sin.
But quick-eyed Love, observing me grow slack
From my first entrance in,
Drew nearer to me, sweetly questioning
If I lacked anything.

"A guest," I answered, "worthy to be here."
Love said, "You shall be he."
"I, the unkind, ungrateful? Ah my dear,
I cannot look on Thee."
Love took my hand, and smiling, did reply,
"Who made the eyes but I?"

"Truth, Lord, but I have marred them; let my shame
Go where it doth deserve."
"And know you not," says Love, "who bore the blame?"
"My dear, then I will serve."
"You must sit down," says Love, "and taste my meat."
So I did sit and eat.

THE FLOWER

How fresh, O Lord, how sweet and clean
Are Thy returns! Even as the flowers in spring,
To which, besides their own demean,
The late-past frosts tributes of pleasure bring.
Grief melts away
Like snow in May,
As if there were no such cold thing.

Who would have thought my shrivelled heart
Could have recovered greenness? It was gone
Quite underground, as flowers depart

The Elixir. **15. his tincture,** its essential quality, used here to mean the philosopher's stone. **24. told,** counted.

Love. **7. "A guest . . . worthy to be here."** "I lack being a worthy guest." —Palmer. **16. serve,"** at table. *The Flower.* **3. demean,** demeanor.

To see their mother-root, when they have blown;
Where they together
All the hard weather,
Dead to the world, keep house unknown.

These are Thy wonders, Lord of power,
Killing and quickening, bringing down to hell
And up to heaven in an hour;
Making a chiming of a passing-bell.
We say amiss
This or that is;
Thy word is all, if we could spell.

Oh, that I once past changing were,
Fast in Thy paradise, where no flower can wither!
Many a spring I shoot up fair,
Offering at heaven, growing and groaning thither;
Nor doth my flower
Want a spring shower,
My sins and I joining together.

But while I grow in a straight line,
Still upwards bent, as if heaven were mine own,
Thy anger comes, and I decline.
What frost to that? What pole is not the zone
Where all things burn,
When Thou dost turn,
And the least frown of Thine is shown?

And now in age I bud again;
After so many deaths I live and write;
I once more smell the dew and rain,

11. blown, bloomed. **18. passing-bell,** the bell rung at the time of a death to obtain prayers for the departing soul. Professor George Herbert Palmer paraphrases the line, "Turning a funeral knell into a bridal peal." **21. spell,** comprehend. **25. Offering,** aiming. **28. joining together,** to produce tears of contrition. **32–35. What pole . . . shown?** The coldness of God's frown is, to a sensitive soul like Herbert, so intense as to make even the poles seem like the torrid zone.

And relish versing. O my only Light,
It cannot be
That I am he
On whom Thy tempests fell all night.

These are Thy wonders, Lord of love,
To make us see we are but flowers that glide;
Which when we once can find and prove,
Thou hast a garden for us where to bide.
Who would be more,
Swelling through store,
Forfeit their paradise by their pride.

VIRTUE

Sweet day, so cool, so calm, so bright,
The bridal of the earth and sky,
The dew shall weep thy fall to-night,
For thou must die.

Sweet rose, whose hue, angry and brave,
Bids the rash gazer wipe his eye,
Thy root is ever in its grave,
And thou must die.

Sweet spring, full of sweet days and roses,
A box where sweets compacted lie,
My music shows ye have your closes,
And all must die.

Only a sweet and virtuous soul,
Like seasoned timber, never gives;
But though the whole world turn to coal
Then chiefly lives.

48. store, abundance. **11. closes.** "Close" is a technical term for the conclusion or resolution of a musical phrase. **15. turn to coal,** be burned to embers at the Day of Judgment. See II Peter 3:10.

Robert Herrick
1591–1674

Herrick's life, although one of the longest in English literature, from the point of view of biography is one of the shortest. Most of the facts are missing, and much of what is known has been gathered from statements and hints in his poetry. These statements are often contradictory, for Herrick was a poet of many moods. Fortunately, however, the particular circumstances of his life, and the events of the fourscore and three years which he spent in this world, need concern us as little as they seem to have concerned him. It is of interest to reflect, and a temptation to point out, that he was born only three years after the Spanish Armada sailed against England, and he lived through the great days of Elizabeth, through the reigns of James I and Charles I, through the time of Cromwell and the Interregnum, on past the Restoration, and died in the same year with Milton. But nothing of the historical significance of all this panorama of men and events is reflected in his lyrics. Nor are the literary trends from Spenser to Dryden to be traced through the nearly thirteen hundred poems in his volume. No poet in any language ever showed more sublime indifference to the things which the world calls great, or set to more charming music the timeless commonplaces of the brevity of youth, the need for making the most of a moment, and the transitoriness of all lovely things.

Herrick was born in London, the son of a goldsmith in Cheapside. He was apprenticed to his uncle, also a goldsmith, for ten years. There is something of the delicacy of the goldsmith's art and the fineness of the lapidary's touch in Herrick's verse, and some of his little poems may indeed have been composed to be inscribed on wedding rings and pieces of jewelry. At a rather late age for that time, twenty-two, he went to St. John's College, Cambridge. (Bacon had gone to Cambridge at twelve.) He transferred to Trinity Hall to study law, and received his B.A. degree in 1617. The facts concerning the next ten years are lost to us, but we know from his book that a great part of them was spent in London with Ben Jonson—of whom he was the greatest admirer and pupil—and the other "Sons of Ben" at the taverns made famous by them. In addition to poets and wits, there were among his associates the musicians William and Henry Lawes, who set his verses to music, some of which were sung in the presence of the King and Queen at Whitehall. In the sixteenth and early seventeenth centuries, verse and music were closely interrelated, and more often than not one was considered the natural complement of the other. Herrick's lyrics can be more fully appreciated if it is remembered that many if not most of them were written to be sung, and some of them he composed probably with a melody in mind. His mastery of rhythmical cadences and his use of words and phrases indicate a knowledge of music as well as skill in versemaking. Unfortunately the musical settings of only a few of Herrick's lyrics have survived.

In 1627 Herrick entered the priesthood of the Church of England, for what reasons it is not known, and two years later this most accomplished of lyric poets became Vicar of Dean Prior in Devonshire. Here he lived for twenty years, preaching to the country people and fulfilling the other duties of his parson's calling. We know little of what happened, except as his poems show him now rebelling against the "warty incivility" of the country and yearning for the conversation and conviviality of London, and now delighting in the country sights and sounds and smells. There can be no doubt that this unwilling exile from London and hater of the country came at last to love the festivals, the hock carts, the wassails, the Maypoles, the fairies, and the folklore of the Devon countryside. For all its Englishness, however, his secular verse is full of classical overtones, just as his religious poems sound the pagan note as prominently as they do the Christian. He was not a countryman like Shakespeare, and his religious experience was a very different thing from that of Donne or Herbert or Crashaw or Vaughan. Herrick never married. Whether Julia and Corinna and the other charming creatures of whom he sings ever existed or were, as has been suggested, "the sirens of a lonely heart" can only be conjectured.

In 1647 he was ejected from his vicarage by the Roundheads, and returned to London and Westminster. He published his two books of poems, *Hesperides* and *Noble Numbers*, in one volume in 1648, the least propitious of years for a book singing "of brooks, of blossoms, birds, and bowers" and similar pleasant things. After a period of twelve years in London, of which again we know nothing, he was restored to Dean Prior by Charles II, and remained there until his death. If he wrote other poems after he returned to the country they have not survived.

from HESPERIDES

THE ARGUMENT OF HIS BOOK

"Argument" is the term formerly used for a brief summary of the contents of a book. See page 379.

I sing of brooks, of blossoms, birds, and bowers:
Of April, May, of June, and July flowers.
I sing of May-poles, hock-carts, wassails, wakes,
Of bridegrooms, brides, and of their bridal cakes.
I write of youth, of love, and have access
By these, to sing of cleanly wantonness.
I sing of dews, of rains, and piece by piece
Of balm, of oil, of spice, and ambergris.
I sing of times trans-shifting; and I write
How roses first came red, and lilies white.
I write of groves, of twilights, and I sing
The court of Mab, and of the Fairy King.
I write of hell; I sing (and ever shall)
Of heaven, and hope to have it after all.

CHERRY-RIPE

Cherry-ripe, ripe, ripe, I cry,
Full and fair ones; come and buy;
If so be you ask me where
They do grow, I answer: There,
Where my Julia's lips do smile;
There's the land, or Cherry-Isle:
Whose plantations fully show
All the year where cherries grow.

DELIGHT IN DISORDER

Compare this poem with Ben Jonson's "Still to Be Neat,"

A sweet disorder in the dress
Kindles in clothes a wantonness;
A lawn about the shoulders thrown
Into a fine distractiòn;
An erring lace, which here and there
Enthralls the crimson stomacher;
A cuff neglectful, and thereby
Ribbands to flow confusèdly;
A winning wave (deserving note)
In the tempestuous petticoat;
A careless shoe-string, in whose tie
I see a wild civility;
Do more bewitch me, than when art
Is too precise in every part.

CORINNA'S GOING A-MAYING

Get up, get up, for shame, the blooming morn
Upon her wings presents the god unshorn.
See how Aurora throws her fair
Fresh-quilted colours through the air!
Get up, sweet slug-a-bed, and see
The dew bespangling herb and tree.
Each flower has wept, and bowed toward the East,
Above an hour since; yet you not dressed,
Nay! not so much as out of bed?
When all the birds have matins said,
And sung their thankful hymns: 'tis sin,
Nay, profanation to keep in;
Whenas a thousand virgins on this day
Spring, sooner than the lark, to fetch in may.

Rise, and put on your foliage, and be seen
To come forth, like the spring-time, fresh and green
And sweet as Flora. Take no care
For jewels for your gown, or hair;
Fear not, the leaves will strew
Gems in abundance upon you;
Besides, the childhood of the day has kept,
Against you come, some orient pearls unwept;
Come, and receive them while the light
Hangs on the dew-locks of the night:
And Titan on the eastern hill
Retires himself, or else stands still
Till you come forth. Wash, dress, be brief in praying:
Few beads are best, when once we go a-maying.

The Argument of His Book. 3. **hock-carts**, carts that brought in the last load of the harvest. The celebration of harvest home followed upon their arrival. **wakes**, times of merrymaking. They were formerly held on the anniversary of the dedication of a church, or on the day of the patron saint of the church. 8. **ambergris**, a substance secreted by the sperm whale, and used in making perfumes. 12. **Mab.** See Shakespeare's *Romeo and Juliet*, Act I, sc. 4, ll. 88 ff. **the Fairy King**, Oberon. See Shakespeare's *Midsummer Night's Dream.* *Delight in Disorder.* 2. **wantonness**, mirthfulness.

Delight in Disorder. 3. **lawn**, a scarf of lawn or linen. 4. **distractiòn**, confusion. 5. **erring**, straying. 6. **stomacher**, a part of the dress forming the lower part of the bodice in front. 12. **civility**, order, good breeding. *Corinna's Going a-Maying.* 2. **god unshorn**, Apollo, god of the sun. 3. **Aurora**, goddess of the dawn. 4. **fresh-quilted**, freshly mingled, like colors in a newly made quilt. 14. **may**, hawthorn blossoms. 17. **Flora**, goddess of flowers. 22. **orient**, shining. 25. **Titan**, the sun. 28. **beads**, prayers.

Come, my Corinna, come; and, coming, mark
How each field turns a street, each street a park
 Made green, and trimmed with trees; see how
 Devotion gives each house a bough,
 Or branch; each porch, each door, ere this,
 An ark, a tabernacle is,
Made up of white-thorn neatly interwove;
As if here were those cooler shades of love.
 Can such delights be in the street,
 And open fields, and we not see't?
 Come, we'll abroad; and let's obey
 The proclamation made for May:
And sin no more, as we have done, by staying;
But, my Corinna, come, let's go a-maying.

There's not a budding boy or girl this day
But is got up, and gone to bring in may.
 A deal of youth, ere this, is come
 Back, and with white-thorn laden home.
 Some have dispatched their cakes and cream,
 Before that we have left to dream;
And some have wept, and wooed, and plighted troth,
And chose their priest, ere we can cast off sloth.
 Many a green-gown has been given;
 Many a kiss, both odd and even:
 Many a glance too has been sent
 From out the eye, love's firmament;
Many a jest told of the keys betraying
This night, and locks picked, yet w'are not a-maying.

Come, let us go, while we are in our prime,
And take the harmless folly of the time.
 We shall grow old apace and die
 Before we know our liberty.
 Our life is short, and our days run
 As fast away as does the sun;
And as a vapour, or a drop of rain,
Once lost, can ne'er be found again
 So when or you or I are made
 A fable, song, or fleeting shade,
 All love, all liking, all delight
 Lies drowned with us in endless night.
Then while time serves, and we are but decaying,
Come, my Corinna, come, let's go a-maying.

34. ark, basket. **48. left,** ceased. **51. Many a green-gown,** that is, many a gown made green by rolling on the grass.

TO THE VIRGINS, TO MAKE MUCH OF TIME

Gather ye rose-buds while ye may,
 Old Time is still a-flying;
And this same flower that smiles to-day,
 To-morrow will be dying.

The glorious lamp of heaven, the sun,
 The higher he's a-getting;
The sooner will his race be run,
 And nearer he's to setting.

That age is best which is the first,
 When youth and blood are warmer;
But being spent, the worse, and worst
 Times, still succeed the former.

Then be not coy, but use your time;
 And while ye may, go marry:
For having lost but once your prime,
 You may for ever tarry.

TO ANTHEA, WHO MAY COMMAND HIM ANYTHING

Bid me to live, and I will live
 Thy protestant to be:
Or bid me love, and I will give
 A loving heart to thee.

A heart as soft, a heart as kind,
 A heart as sound and free,
As in the whole world thou canst find,
 That heart I'll give to thee.

Bid that heart stay, and it will stay,
 To honour thy decree;
Or bid it languish quite away,
 And't shall do so for thee.

Bid me to weep, and I will weep,
 While I have eyes to see;
And having none, yet I will keep
 A heart to weep for thee.

Bid me despair, and I'll despair,
 Under that cypress tree;
Or bid me die, and I will dare
 E'en death, to die for thee.

Thou art my life, my love, my heart,
 The very eyes of me;
And hast command of every part,
 To live and die for thee.

2. protestant, one who protests devotion.

TO DAFFODILS

Fair daffodils, we weep to see
You haste away so soon;
As yet the early-rising sun
Has not attained his noon.
Stay, stay,
Until the hasting day
Has run
But to the even-song;
And, having prayed together, we
Will go with you along.

We have short time to stay, as you;
We have as short a spring;
As quick a growth to meet decay,
As you, or any thing.
We die,
As your hours do, and dry
Away
Like to the summer's rain;
Or, as the pearls of morning dew,
Ne'er to be found again.

THE MAD MAID'S SONG

This poem is reminiscent of the anonymous "Tom o' Bedlam's Song." Herrick's lyric inevitably suggests the mad song of Ophelia, *Hamlet*, Act IV, sc. 5.

Good morrow to the day so fair;
Good morning, sir, to you;
Good morrow to mine own torn hair,
Bedabbled with the dew.

Good morning to this primrose too;
Good morrow to each maid,
That will with flowers the tomb bestrew,
Wherein my love is laid.

Ah woe is me, woe, woe is me,
Alack and welladay!
For pity, sir, find out that bee,
Which bore my love away.

I'll seek him in your bonnet brave;
I'll seek him in your eyes;
Nay, now I think they've made his grave
I'the bed of strawberries.

I'll seek him there; I know, ere this,
The cold, cold earth doth shake him;
But I will go, or send a kiss
By you, sir, to awake him.

Pray hurt him not; though he be dead,
He knows well who do love him,
And who with green turfs rear his head,
And who do rudely move him.

He's soft and tender; pray take heed;
With bands of cowslips bind him,
And bring him home;—but 'tis decreed
That I shall never find him.

The Mad Maid's Song. **13. brave,** beautiful. **18. shake,** chill.

THE CHEAT OF CUPID: OR, THE UNGENTLE GUEST

One silent night of late,
When every creature rested,
Came one unto my gate,
And knocking, me molested.

"Who's that," said I, "beats there,
And troubles thus the sleepy?"
"Cast off," said he, "all fear,
And let not locks thus keep ye.

"For I a boy am, who
By moonless nights have swervèd;
And all with show'rs wet through,
And e'en with cold half starvèd."

I pitiful arose,
And soon a taper lighted;
And did myself disclose
Unto the lad benighted.

I saw he had a bow,
And wings, too, which did shiver;
And looking down below,
I spied he had a quiver.

I to my chimney's shine
Brought him, as love professes,
And chafed his hands with mine,
And dried his dropping tresses:

But when he felt him warm'd,
"Let's try this bow of ours,
And string, if they be harm'd,"
Said he, "with these late show'rs."

Forthwith his bow he bent,
And wedded string and arrow,
And struck me that it went
Quite through my heart and marrow.

The Cheat of Cupid. Cf. Greene's treatment of the same theme in "Cupid Abroad Was Lated," p. 284.

Then laughing loud, he flew
Away, and thus said flying,
"Adieu, mine host, adieu,
I'll leave thy heart a-dying."

MISTRESS SUSANNA SOUTHWELL, UPON HER FEET

Her pretty feet
Like snails did creep
A little out, and then,
As if they started at bo-peep,
Did soon draw in again.

MEAT WITHOUT MIRTH

Eaten I have; and though I had good cheer,
I did not sup, because no friends were there.
Where mirth and friends are absent when we dine
Or sup, there wants the incense and the wine.

HIS PRAYER TO BEN JONSON

This is one of half a dozen poems in which Herrick expresses his affection and admiration for Ben Jonson.

When I a verse shall make,
Know I have prayed thee,
For old religion's sake,
Saint Ben, to aid me.

Make the way smooth for me,
When I, thy Herrick,
Honouring thee, on my knee
Offer my lyric.

Candles I'll give to thee,
And a new altar;
And thou, Saint Ben, shalt be
Writ in my psalter.

AN ODE FOR HIM

This ode was evidently written soon after Jonson's death in 1637, and probably composed at Dean Prior, where Herrick must often have thought of the "lyric feasts" which he had shared with Jonson and his group in London.

Ah, Ben!
Say how or when
Shall we, thy guests,
Meet at those lyric feasts
Made at the Sun,
The Dog, the Triple Tun,
Where we such clusters had
As made us nobly wild, not mad;
And yet each verse of thine
Outdid the meat, outdid the frolic wine.

My Ben!
Or come again,
Or send to us
Thy wit's great overplus;
But teach us yet
Wisely to husband it,
Lest we that talent spend,
And having once brought to an end
That precious stock, the store
Of such a wit the world should have no more.

HIS CONTENT IN THE COUNTRY

Here, here I live with what my board
Can with the smallest cost afford;
Though ne'er so mean the viands be,
They well content my Prue and me.
Or pea, or bean, or wort, or beet,
Whatever comes, content makes sweet.
Here we rejoice because no rent
We pay for our poor tenement,
Wherein we rest, and never fear
The landlord or the usurer.
The quarter-day does ne'er affright
Our peaceful slumbers in the night.
We eat our own, and batten more
Because we feed on no man's score;
But pity those whose flanks grow great
Swelled with the lard of others' meat.
We bless our fortunes when we see
Our own belovèd privacy;
And like our living, where we're known
To very few, or else to none.

THE NIGHT-PIECE, TO JULIA

The stanzaic structure of this poem seems to have been suggested by that of Jonson's "The Faery Beam upon You."

Her eyes the glow-worm lend thee;
The shooting stars attend thee;

Mistress Susanna Southwell, upon Her Feet. **4. bo-peep,** peekaboo. *Meat without Mirth.* **2. no friends were there.** This little poem was written probably in the early days of the poet's sojourn in Devonshire when he was keenly conscious of his separation from his fellows of the Tribe of Ben in London.

An Ode for Him. **7. clusters,** grapes, wine. *His Content in the Country.* **4. Prue,** Prudence Baldwin, the faithful servant of Herrick during his residence at Dean Prior. She is the subject of three other poems by him. See page 355. **5. wort,** a potherb.

And the elves also,
Whose little eyes glow
Like the sparks of fire, befriend thee.

No will-o'-the-wisp mis-light thee;
No snake or slow-worm bite thee;
But on, on thy way,
Not making a stay,
Since ghost there's none to affright thee.

Let not the dark thee cumber;
What though the moon does slumber?
The stars of the night
Will lend thee their light,
Like tapers clear without number.

Then, Julia, let me woo thee,
Thus, thus to come unto me;
And when I shall meet
Thy silv'ry feet,
My soul I'll pour into thee.

THE HAG

The hag is astride
This night for to ride,
The Devil and she together;
Through thick and through thin,
Now out and then in,
Though ne'er so foul be the weather.

A thorn or a burr
She takes for a spur;
With a lash of a bramble she rides now;
Through brakes and through briers,
O'er ditches and mires,
She follows the spirit that guides now.

No beast for his food
Dares now range the wood,
But hushed in his lair he lies lurking;
While mischiefs by these,
On lands and on seas,
At noon of night are a-working.

The storm will arise
And trouble the skies;
This night, and more for the wonder,
The ghost from the tomb
Affrighted shall come,
Called out by the clap of the thunder.

The Night-Piece, to Julia. **7. slow-worm,** a small, snakelike lizard. **11. cumber,** trouble.

HIS GRANGE, OR PRIVATE WEALTH

Though clock,
To tell me how the night draws hence, I've none,
A cock
I have, to sing how day draws on.
I have
A maid, my Prue, by good luck sent
To save
That little Fates me gave or lent.
A hen
I keep, which, creaking day by day,
Tells when
She goes her long white egg to lay.
A goose
I have, which with a jealous ear,
Lets loose
Her tongue to tell what danger's near.
A lamb
I keep, tame, with my morsels fed,
Whose dam
An orphan left him, lately dead.
A cat
I keep, that plays about my house,
Grown fat
With eating many a miching mouse.
To these
A Tracy I do keep, whereby
I please
The more my rural privacy.
Which are
But toys to give my heart some ease:
Where care
None is, slight things do lightly please.

A TERNARY OF LITTLES, UPON A PIPKIN OF JELLY SENT TO A LADY

A little saint best fits a little shrine,
A little prop best fits a little vine,
As my small cruse best fits my little wine.

A little seed best fits a little soil,
A little trade best fits a little toil,
As my small jar best fits my little oil.

A little bin best fits a little bread,
A little garland fits a little head,
As my small stuff best fits my little shed.

10. creaking, clucking. **24. miching,** pilfering. **26. Tracy,** Herrick's spaniel.

A little hearth best fits a little fire,
A little chapel fits a little quire,
As my small bell best fits my little spire.

A little stream best fits a little boat,
A little lead best fits a little float,
As my small pipe best fits my little note.

A little meat best fits a little belly,
As sweetly, lady, give me leave to tell ye,
This little pipkin fits this little jelly.

UPON JULIA'S CLOTHES

Whenas in silks my Julia goes,
Then, then, methinks, how sweetly flows
That liquefaction of her clothes.

Next, when I cast mine eyes and see
That brave vibration each way free,
O how that glittering taketh me!

UPON PRUE, HIS MAID

In this little urn is laid
Prudence Baldwin, once my maid,
From whose happy spark here let
Spring the purple violet.

CEREMONIES FOR CHRISTMAS

Come, bring with a noise,
My merry, merry boys,
The Christmas log to the firing;
While my good dame, she
Bids ye all be free,
And drink to your hearts' desiring.

With the last year's brand
Light the new block, and
For good success in his spending,
On your psaltries play,
That sweet luck may
Come while the log is a-teending.

Drink now the strong beer,
Cut the white loaf here,
The while the meat is a-shredding;
For the rare mince-pie
And the plums stand by
To fill the paste that's a-kneading.

Upon a Pipkin. **18. pipkin,** a small earthenware pot. *Upon Julia's Clothes.* **1. Whenas,** when. **5. brave,** bright. *Ceremonies for Christmas.* **1. noise,** that is, a joyful noise, a melodious sound. **10. psaltries.** The psaltery was a medieval stringed instrument. **12. a-teending,** kindling.

THE PILLAR OF FAME

This is one of the "shaped poems" of the period. See the note on Herbert's "The Altar," page 345.

Fame's pillar here at last we set,
Out-during marble, brass, or jet;
Charmed and enchanted so
As to withstand the blow
Of overthrow;
Nor shall the seas,
Or outrages
Of storms, o'erbear
What we uprear;
Tho' kingdoms fall,
This pillar never shall
Decline or waste at all;
But stand for ever by his own
Firm and well-fixed foundatiòn.

To his book's end this last line he'd have placed:
Jocund his Muse was, but his life was chaste.

from NOBLE NUMBERS

HIS LITANY TO THE HOLY SPIRIT

In the hour of my distress,
When temptations me oppress,
And when I my sins confess,
Sweet Spirit, comfort me!

When I lie within my bed,
Sick in heart and sick in head,
And with doubts discomforted,
Sweet Spirit, comfort me!

When the house doth sigh and weep,
And the world is drowned in sleep,
Yet mine eyes the watch do keep,
Sweet Spirit, comfort me!

When the artless doctor sees
No one hope, but of his fees,
And his skill runs on the lees,
Sweet Spirit, comfort me!

When his potion and his pill
Has or none or little skill,
Meet for nothing but to kill,
Sweet Spirit, comfort me!

13. artless, unskilled.

When the passing-bell doth toll,
And the furies in a shoal
Come to fright a parting soul,
Sweet Spirit, comfort me!

When the tapers now burn blue,
And the comforters are few,
And that number more than true,
Sweet Spirit, comfort me!

When the priest his last hath prayed,
And I nod to what is said,
'Cause my speech is now decayed,
Sweet Spirit, comfort me!

When, God knows, I'm tossed about,
Either with despair or doubt,
Yet, before the glass be out,
Sweet Spirit, comfort me!

When the Tempter me pursu'th
With the sins of all my youth,
And half damns me with untruth,
Sweet Spirit, comfort me!

When the flames and hellish cries
Fright mine ears and fright mine eyes,
And all terrors me surprise,
Sweet Spirit, comfort me!

When the Judgment is revealed,
And that opened which was sealed,
When to Thee I have appealed,
Sweet Spirit, comfort me!

GRACE FOR A CHILD

Here a little child I stand,
Heaving up my either hand;
Cold as paddocks though they be,
Here I lift them up to Thee,
For a benison to fall
On our meat and on us all. Amen.

Thomas Carew

1595?–1639?

Most of the facts of Carew's life have so far escaped the biographers, but it may perhaps be said of him, as has been remarked of another and very different character, that we have enough of his life to explain his reputation. He has achieved fame in English literature as one of the most brilliant of the "Sons of Ben," one of the most accomplished lyrists of the language, and arbiter of the elegants of the court of Charles I. He was born in Kent and was educated at Merton College, Oxford. After receiving his B.A. degree he was, ostensibly at least, engaged in the study of law at the Middle Temple in London, until it became as obvious to his father, Sir Matthew Carew, as it was to young Thomas that the son was not cut out to be a lawyer. He was next exposed to the diplomatic profession, and sent to join the staff of Sir Dudley Carleton, the ambassador to Venice. He seems to have been sufficiently successful to be allowed to continue as the ambassador's secretary when he was transferred in 1616 to The Hague. He did not last out the year in his secretaryship, however, as Sir Dudley found it necessary to get rid of him because of his slanderous remarks about the ambassador and his wife.

Carew returned home, and for the next three years was without employment, and with every prospect of going from bad to worse. His father gave him up as hopeless, and did what he could to hinder him. After his father's death he was fortunate enough to secure a place with the household of Lord Herbert of Cherbury when he went as ambassador to Paris in 1619. Of the events of the next nine years little is known. Whether he accompanied Herbert in his travels, and whether he stayed on with the embassy in Paris until Herbert's return, are not known. Some of his spare moments in France were devoted to writing love lyrics which were to be published later. After his return to England he succeeded in attaching himself to the court of Charles I, where he remained for the rest of his life. He was appointed Gentleman of the Privy Chamber and later was made Server in Ordinary, the official taster and server of the dishes for the royal table. There are anecdotes attesting the success of his wit and courtly manners in the royal household, and proving that, however lacking he may have been in more solid qualities, he was undoubtedly one of the most agreeable personalities of his time.

It is significant that Carew was one of the chief

admirers and justest critics of both Donne and Jonson, for he knew and understood both personally, and the qualities of the two poets meet in his own verse more often than in that of any other poet of the day. He had been a parishioner of Donne's at St. Dunstan's-in-the-West, and probably knew him later in London. As one of the Tribe of Ben, he knew better than most of his contemporaries both the virtues and the failings of Jonson. Carew's poetry has none of the naïveté and spontaneity of Herrick's. He worked harder at his verse than any of his fellows, and had a hearty contempt for casual versifiers and "the abortive offspring of their hasty hours." He had the happy art, however, of being able to conceal his art and his labor, and few of the readers who enjoy the easy flow and exquisite rhythms and cadences of his lyrics are aware of the pains and "the dear expense of oil" that went into the making of them, or of the craftsmanship and structural unity that a careful study of them will reveal.

Carew is one of the greatest masters in the language of the octosyllabic couplet, and Tennyson, himself an artist in that kind, shows the influence of Carew in such verses as the lyrics in *The Princess* and elsewhere. It is not surprising that Carew should have been a discerning critic of poets and poetry. His "Elegy upon the Death of Dr. Donne, Dean of Paul's" contains the best contemporary analysis and description of "metaphysical" poetry and of the "giant fancy" of Donne, which had proved too stout for "the soft melting phrases" of more conventional poets. He was a just appraiser of his own work, also, and knew the capabilities and the limitations of his "lyric feet." If the times in which he lived and the circumstances of his own life could have been different, we might have had in Carew not only one of the most graceful lyrists and accomplished technicians but also one of the greatest poets of the language. Pope was more witty than just when he dismissed Carew contemptuously as one of

the wits of either Charles's days,
The mob of gentlemen who wrote with ease.

THE SPRING

Now that the winter's gone, the earth hath lost
Her snow-white robes; and now no more the frost
Candies the grass, or casts an icy cream
Upon the silver lake or crystal stream:
But the warm sun thaws the benumbèd earth,
And makes it tender; gives a sacred birth
To the dead swallow; wakes in hollow tree
The drowsy cuckoo and the humblebee.
Now do a choir of chirping minstrels bring,
In triumph to the world, the youthful spring.
The valleys, hills, and woods in rich array
Welcome the coming of the longed-for May.
Now all things smile; only my love doth lour;
Nor hath the scalding noonday sun the power
To melt that marble ice, which still doth hold
Her heart congealed, and makes her pity cold.
The ox, which lately did for shelter fly
Into the stall, doth now securely lie
In open fields; and love no more is made
By the fireside; but in the cooler shade
Amyntas now doth with his Chloris sleep
Under a sycamore, and all things keep
Time with the season: only she doth carry
June in her eyes, in her heart January.

UPON A RIBBON

This silken wreath, which circles in mine arm,
Is but an emblem of that mystic charm
Wherewith the magic of your beauties binds
My captive soul, and round about it winds
Fetters of lasting love. This hath entwined
My flesh alone; that hath empaled my mind.
Time may wear out these soft weak bands, but those
Strong chains of brass Fate shall not discompose.
This holy relic may preserve my wrist,
But my whole frame does by that power subsist;
To that my prayers and sacrifice, to this
I only pay a superstitious kiss.
This but the idol, that's the deity;
Religion there is due; here, ceremony;
That I receive by faith, this but in trust;
Here I may tender duty, there I must;
This order as a layman I may bear,
But I become Love's priest when that I wear;
This moves like air; that as the centre stands;
That knot your virtue tied, this but your hands;
That, Nature framed; but this was made by art;
This makes my arm your prisoner; that, my heart.

A SONG

Ask me no more where Jove bestows,
When June is past, the fading rose;

Upon a Ribbon. **1. This silken wreath.** Compare Donne, "The Funeral," page 338, l. 3. **19. the centre,** the earth, the center of the universe in the Ptolemaic cosmology.

For in your beauty's orient deep
These flowers, as in their causes, sleep.

Ask me no more whither do stray
The golden atoms of the day;
For in pure love heaven did prepare
Those powders to enrich your hair.

Ask me no more whither doth haste
The nightingale, when May is past;
For in your sweet dividing throat
She winters, and keeps warm her note.

Ask me no more where those stars light,
That downwards fall in dead of night;
For in your eyes they sit, and there
Fixèd become, as in their sphere.

Ask me no more if east or west
The phoenix builds her spicy nest;
For unto you at last she flies,
And in your fragrant bosom dies.

DISDAIN RETURNED

He that loves a rosy cheek,
Or a coral lip admires,
Or from star-like eyes doth seek
Fuel to maintain his fires;
As old Time makes these decay,
So his flames must waste away.

But a smooth and stedfast mind,
Gentle thoughts and calm desires,
Hearts with equal love combined,
Kindle never-dying fires.
Where those are not, I despise
Lovely cheeks, or lips, or eyes.

No tears, Celia, now shall win
My resolved heart to return;
I have searched thy soul within,
And find nought but pride and scorn;
I have learned thy arts, and now
Can disdain as much as thou.
Some power, in my revenge, convey
That love to her I cast away.

AN EPITAPH

This little vault, this narrow room,
Of love and beauty is the tomb;
The dawning beam, that 'gan to clear
Our clouded sky, lies darkened here,
For ever set to us, by death
Sent to inflame the world beneath.
'Twas but a bud, yet did contain
More sweetness than shall spring again;
A budding star, that might have grown
Into a sun when it had blown.
This hopeful beauty did create
New life in love's declining state;
But now his empire ends, and we
From fire and wounding darts are free;
His brand, his bow, let no man fear:
The flames, the arrows, all lie here.

A Song. 3. **orient deep,** lustrous depth. 4. **causes,** the roots, seeds, or buds. 11. **dividing,** articulating harmoniously, singing. 16. **sphere,** an allusion, as often in seventeenth-century poetry, to the transparent globes or spheres of the Ptolemaic astronomy. The eighth of the concentric spheres was that of the fixed stars. 18. **phoenix,** the fabulous Arabian bird which, at the expiration of every five hundred years, built a funeral pyre of spices and died in its flames. From the ashes arose a new phoenix.

Sir John Suckling
1609–1642

Suckling and Lovelace have long been named together as the two Cavalier poets par excellence, and the tendency to contrast them at almost every point, to consider their most famous lines respectively as the "opposite poles" of Cavalier poetry, has proved irresistible. An examination of the facts of their lives will, indeed, disclose many dissimilarities in their characters and activities. It is inevitable that Suckling's dashing manners, gay flippancy, and devil-may-care attitude toward life should be set over against the sober courtliness and grace, the gentlemanly demeanor, and the more conventional and sentimental attitude of the author of the lines to Lucasta and Althea. One may take the liberty, however, to suspect that in Suckling's "Out upon it!" and "The devil take her!" and similar outbursts, the gentleman may be protesting rather too much, that he was perhaps not quite so inconstant in love or casual in composition as he boasts. Even Suckling had his more serious moments. There is Aubrey's story of his journey to Bath to take the waters, on which "he had a cartload of books carried down, and 'twas there at Bath that he writ the little tract in his book about Socinianism." It is less profitable, however, to catalogue the points and degrees of difference between the two Cavaliers than to consider them as complementary to each other, and to enjoy the verses that each contrived to write in his spare moments.

The thirty-three years of Suckling's life were packed as full of opportunities, adventure, and romance as ever befell a young man. He came of a family rich in land and titles. His father, Sir John, was made Secretary of State when the younger John was thirteen, and in the following year the son entered Trinity College, Cambridge. He was probably, as one of his earlier biographers opined, "a polite rather than a deep scholar," but he became one of the most accomplished linguists of his generation. In 1627 he was admitted to the study of law at Gray's Inn, but, his father dying in the same year, he inherited a fortune, gave up his studies, and made the grand tour. He was abroad for three years and on his return to England received his knighthood. He went as a gentleman soldier under the Marquis of Hamilton to serve in the army of Gustavus Adolphus. In a year or two he was back and at the center of courtly gaiety. He was equally at home in literary circles, and had begun to be known for his skill with his pen.

Suckling was easily the most spectacular young gentleman at court. The cost of the production of his play *Aglaura* in 1637 ran into hundreds of pounds, and the costumes were such as to dazzle even the court. Two years later when the King raised an army to send to Scotland, Suckling presented His Majesty with a troop of a hundred men, fitted out in scarlet and white, on which he spent £12,000. The brilliant company came back from the Scottish Border faster than it went, however, and Suckling was not allowed to forget the episode. He was hardly less spectacular in his private amusements. He became the most famous gambler of his time, and spent a large portion of his fortune on bowling, dice, and cards. Whenever public duty required, however, he could give money and energy to the cause, and leave pleasure and convenience as easily as any. He was one of the group who in 1641 conspired to rescue Strafford from the Tower after his impeachment, and had to escape to France. He died in Paris in 1642, by his own hand, according to the more commonly received account, although there is another story which makes him the victim of a servant. No one questions the likelihood of the splendid trifler's taking his own life rather than drawing out his years in exile and poverty. The volume of his poems, *Fragmenta Aurea*, was published in 1646, four years after his death, "by a friend, to perpetuate his memory."

Suckling never professed to be more than an amateur with the pen. He seems never to have worked over his lines, and he was at the farthest remove from such a finished artist as Carew. No verse in English smells less of the lamp than his. One never thinks of Suckling's poems in terms of schools, although he could not escape entirelv the influence of such personalities and poems as those of Donne and Jonson. The reader of his verse will detect phrases and ideas which he imitated or lifted, more or less consciously, from the two poets. He is at his best and happiest when he is on his own, and not affected by "metaphysical" or other influences. His letters are as delightful as his lyrics, and for vivacity and heartiness they are equaled only by the letters of Byron. Twentieth century readers find him still the same "natural, easy Suckling" that Congreve's Millamant quoted with such relish in *The Way of the World*.

SONG

Why so pale and wan, fond lover?
   Prithee, why so pale?
Will, when looking well can't move her,
   Looking ill prevail?
   Prithee, why so pale?

Why so dull and mute, young sinner?
   Prithee, why so mute?
Will, when speaking well can't win her,
   Saying nothing do't?
   Prithee, why so mute?

Quit, quit, for shame; this will not move,
   This cannot take her.
If of herself she will not love,
   Nothing can make her:
   The devil take her!

SONG

Honest lover whatsoever,
If in all thy love there ever
Was one wavering thought, if thy flame
Were not still even, still the same,
      Know this,
   Thou lov'st amiss;
   And to love true,
Thou must begin again, and love anew.

If, when she appears i' the room,
Thou dost not quake, and art struck dumb,
And in striving this to cover,
Dost not speak thy words twice over,
      Know this,
   Thou lov'st amiss;
   And to love true,
Thou must begin again, and love anew.

If fondly thou dost not mistake,
And all defects for graces take,
Persuad'st thyself that jests are broken
When she hath little or nothing spoken,
      Know this,
   Thou lov'st amiss;
   And to love true,
Thou must begin again, and love anew.

If, when thou appear'st to be within,
Thou let'st men not ask and ask again;
And when thou answer'st, if it be
To what was asked thee, properly,
      Know this,
   Thou lov'st amiss;
   And to love true,
Thou must begin again, and love anew.

If, when thy stomach calls to eat,
Thou cut'st not fingers, 'stead of meat,
And with much gazing on her face
Dost not rise hungry from the place,
      Know this,
   Thou lov'st amiss;
   And to love true,
Thou must begin again, and love anew.

If by this thou dost discover
That thou art no perfect lover,
And, desiring to love true,
Thou dost begin to love anew,
      Know this,
   Thou lov'st amiss;
   And to love true,
Thou must begin again, and love anew.

Song (Honest lover). **10. art struck.** "Not" is understood. **17. fondly,** foolishly. **19. persuad'st.** "Not" is understood. **jests are broken,** jokes are cracked.

CONSTANCY

Out upon it! I have loved
   Three whole days together;
And am like to love three more,
   If it prove fair weather.

Time shall moult away his wings,
   Ere he shall discover
In the whole wide world again
   Such a constant lover.

But the spite on it is, no praise
   Is due at all to me:
Love with me had made no stays
   Had it any been but she.

Had it any been but she,
   And that very face,
There had been at least ere this
   A dozen dozen in her place.

Richard Lovelace
1618–1657

Lovelace is probably the most romantic figure in English literature. All the elements that go to make up the beau ideal seem to have met in him, and legend and tradition have added to and re-enforced them. He is the best known of the "Cavalier Poets," and his own name and that of Cavalier have reflected color and glory on each other. He was born into a wealthy family, was educated at Charterhouse School and Gloucester Hall, now Worcester College, at Oxford, where Royalist traditions cluster thickest. He was described by contemporaries as an eminent "soldier, gentleman, and lover," and as "one of the handsomest men of England." He has the distinction, perhaps, of being the only Oxford undergraduate ever to be granted the M.A. degree in his second year—presumably because of his good looks and gracious manners. The award was made at the request of a great lady attending Queen Henrietta Maria when she and Charles I visited the university in 1636. The young Master of Arts left Oxford and took up his residence at the court.

Lovelace followed the tradition of his family and embarked upon a military career. He took part in the Scottish expeditions of 1639 and 1640. In 1642 he was chosen by the County of Kent to present to the Puritan Parliament a petition praying that the King and the Church might be restored to their rights. The Parliament was in no mood for such a petition, even from the bravest and handsomest man in England, and for his boldness in making the request he was thrown into prison for seven weeks. But stone walls and iron bars, though they kept Lovelace in, could not keep romance out, and he whiled away his time by writing songs, one of which, "To Althea, from Prison," has helped make him immortal. Out of prison, he naturally joined the King's forces, supplying equipment at his own charge, and serving as captain. When Oxford was captured in 1646, he served with the French army in Holland. His expedition thither was the occasion of his other famous verses, the farewells to Lucasta. He was wounded at Dunkirk, and from this circumstance the most romantic of the Lovelace legends takes its source. Anthony à Wood relates that a Miss Lucy Sacheverell, who was betrothed to Lovelace, heard a report that he had been killed at Dunkirk, and that the lady subsequently married another. Lovelace, so the story goes, returned to England to find her married, "became very poor in body and purse, was the object of charity, went in ragged clothes, and mostly lodged in obscure and dirty places," at last dying in an alley near Shoe Lane. How much, if any, of the story is true cannot be ascertained.

It is certain that Lovelace was soon back in England, took part in Royalist uprisings in Kent, and was again imprisoned. He took this occasion to prepare his verses for the press. He was released in 1649, and published a collection of his poems under the title *Lucasta*. Whether "Lucasta" was the Lucy Sacheverell of the legends, or whether she ever existed except as a creature of the poet's imagination, is uncertain. Dr. C. H. Wilkinson of Worcester College, the editor of Lovelace's poems, is inclined to identify her as a member of the family of Sir Charles Lucas. There is good reason to believe that Lovelace had spent his energy and his substance in the King's cause, and the gallant soldier of the King probably knew want in his last years.

To the general public, Lovelace is a two-poem poet, and the poems "To Althea, from Prison" and "To Lucasta, Going to the Wars" are the most perfect of their kind in the language. They are on a plane, however, which he never quite reached with any of his other poems. Much of his verse is uninspired, and some of it is downright slovenly in composition. He was enamored of the "metaphysical" conceit; the results are often far from happy, and betray the lack of the saving sense of humor. When, as in the more famous poems and a few others, he is not trying too hard to be poetical, and is content to express his feelings simply, he achieves a quality of verse which is unique and beautiful. In his life and in the first three of the poems given here, the best aspects of the spirit, the manner, and the way of life of the Cavaliers found their perfect expression.

TO ALTHEA, FROM PRISON

When Love with unconfinèd wings
  Hovers within my gates,
And my divine Althea brings
  To whisper at the grates;

When I lie tangled in her hair
And fettered to her eye,
The gods that wanton in the air
Know no such liberty.

When flowing cups run swiftly round,
With no allaying Thames,
Our careless heads with roses bound,
Our hearts with loyal flames;
When thirsty grief in wine we steep,
When healths and draughts go free,
Fishes that tipple in the deep
Know no such liberty.

When, like committed linnets, I
With shriller throat shall sing
The sweetness, mercy, majesty,
And glories of my king;
When I shall voice aloud how good
He is, how great should be,
Enlargèd winds that curl the flood
Know no such liberty.

Stone walls do not a prison make,
Nor iron bars a cage:
Minds innocent and quiet take
That for an hermitage.
If I have freedom in my love,
And in my soul am free,
Angels alone, that soar above,
Enjoy such liberty.

TO LUCASTA, GOING TO THE WARS

Tell me not, sweet, I am unkind,
That from the nunnery
Of thy chaste breast and quiet mind
To war and arms I fly.

True, a new mistress now I chase,
The first foe in the field;
And with a stronger faith embrace
A sword, a horse, a shield.

Yet this inconstancy is such
As you too shall adore;
I could not love thee, dear, so much,
Loved I not honour more.

7. gods. Most seventeenth-century manuscripts read "birds," which seems to be the meaning of "gods" here. **17. committed,** to prison; caged.

TO LUCASTA, GOING BEYOND THE SEAS

If to be absent were to be
Away from thee;
Or that when I am gone,
You or I were alone,
Then, my Lucasta, might I crave
Pity from blustering wind or swallowing wave.

But I'll not sigh one blast or gale
To swell my sail,
Or pay a tear to 'suage
The foaming blow-god's rage;
For whether he will let me pass
Or no, I'm still as happy as I was.

Though seas and land betwixt us both,
Our faith and troth,
Like separated souls,
All time and space controls:
Above the highest sphere we meet,
Unseen, unknown, and greet as angels greet.

So then we do anticipate
Our after-fate,
And are alive i' the skies,
If thus our lips and eyes
Can speak like spirits unconfined
In heaven, their earthly bodies left behind.

GRATIANA DANCING AND SINGING

See! with what constant motión,
Even and glorious as the sun,
Gratiana steers that noble frame,
Soft as her breast, sweet as her voice,
That gave each winding law and poise,
And swifter than the wings of fame.

She beat the happy pavément,
By such a star made firmament,
Which now no more the roof envies,
But swells up high with Atlas even,
Bearing the brighter, nobler heaven,
And in her all the deities.

Each step trod out a lover's thought
And the ambitious hopes he brought,
Chained to her brave feet with such arts,
Such sweet command, and gentle awe.

To Lucasta, Going Beyond the Seas. **9. 'suage,** assuage. **10. blow-god's,** of Aeolus, god of the winds.

As when she ceased, we sighing saw
 The floor lay paved with broken hearts.

So did she move; so did she sing
Like the harmonious spheres that bring
 Unto their rounds their music's aid;
Which she performèd such a way
As all th' enamoured world will say,
 The Graces danced, and Apollo played.

Richard Crashaw

1613?–1649

Crashaw is the most distinguished Roman Catholic poet of his century. He was born into an Anglican family, but early manifested that interest in the beauty of ritual, the splendor of Catholic art and architecture, and the rapturous expression in literature and music of religious devotion and spiritual exaltation that led him eventually into the Roman Church. He went to school at Charterhouse and was later admitted to Pembroke Hall, Cambridge, where he took his B.A. degree in 1634. At Cambridge Crashaw made several literary acquaintances, chief of whom was Abraham Cowley, who was to remain his friend for life, and to write one of the most beautiful elegies in the language on his death.

Crashaw's first volume of verse, *Epigrammatum Sacrorum Liber*, a collection of Latin religious epigrams, was published in the year in which he took his degree. The following year he became a fellow of Peterhouse College at Cambridge, where he found a congenial religious atmosphere, and where his own devoutness and asceticism became a matter of comment: "Like a primitive saint," says the editor of his volume *Steps to the Temple*, "he offered more prayers in the night than others usually offer in the day: there he penned these poems, steps for happy souls to climb Heaven by." There were literary as well as religious associations and exercises at Peterhouse, and the young poet could have remained happy there had not the Civil War interfered. Cambridge was as sympathetic to the Parliamentary cause as Oxford was to that of the King, and Crashaw, a Royalist, was forced to leave and continue life elsewhere in a more congenial environment.

He seems to have been received into the Roman Catholic Church about 1645, and in 1646 fled to Paris, which had become the center for Royalist refugees. He was found there in distress by his friend Cowley, by whom, probably, he was introduced to Queen Henrietta Maria. The Queen sent him with a recommendation to Cardinal Palotto, Governor of Rome, who received him and gave him a place in his household. The young man had enough of the English Puritan in him to be shocked by the laxity of the conduct of some members of the Cardinal's household, and he considered it his duty to make the conditions known to the Cardinal. The attitude toward Crashaw on the part of the accused was such that the Cardinal had to find him a place elsewhere, and he was sent to the Church of Our Lady of Loretto. He died a few weeks after his arrival, and was buried there.

His volume *Steps to the Temple* was published in 1646, and contains most of his religious verse and a section of secular verse entitled "The Delights of the Muses." A posthumous volume, *Carmen Deo Nostro*, which was published in 1652, contains a few new poems and reprints of some of his earlier religious verses. The first editor of *Steps to the Temple* referred to Crashaw as "Herbert's second, but equal," and it is interesting to note that the young Roman Catholic poet was introduced to the English reading public under the aegis of Herbert's *Temple*. But, though Crashaw sincerely admired Herbert, and may be said to be of the school of Herbert and Donne, there is little of the essential Herbert in his work, and there is nothing in the rapturous devotion and mystical splendor of his poetic cathedral which suggests the chaste simplicity of Herbert's parish church or of Herbert's English countryside.

Crashaw is in some ways the least English poet of seventeenth-century England. His fondness for the Italian poet Marino and his readings in the Spanish mystics led him to introduce elaborate conceits and enthusiasms which at times offend good taste, and at other times startle the reader with their exotic beauty. Such poems as the "Hymn to the Name and Honour of the Admirable Saint Teresa" and the concluding lines of "The Flaming Heart" are alive with wonder and worship, and in reading them one must confess with Crashaw that one has taken an angel by the wing.

The diversity of his gifts and the range of his

poetic themes may be illustrated by a comparison with these ecstatic lyrics of some of his secular verse, particularly the charming "Wishes: To His (Supposed) Mistress." No poet in the language has more glaring faults than Crashaw, and his love of elaborate conceits and lack of restraint resulted in some of the worst lines in the language. For all his faults, however, he belongs at his best with Shelley, and the enthusiasm which he has excited in modern poets and readers of poetry is not difficult to understand.

WISHES:

TO HIS (SUPPOSED) MISTRESS*

Whoe'er she be
That not impossible she
That shall command my heart and me;

Where'er she lie,
Locked up from mortal eye,
In shady leaves of destiny;

Till that ripe birth
Of studied fate stand forth,
And teach her fair steps to our earth;

Till that divine
Idea take a shrine
Of crystal flesh, through which to shine:

Meet you her, my wishes,
Bespeak her to my blisses,
And be ye called, my absent kisses.

I wish her beauty,
That owes not all his duty
To gaudy tire, or glist'ring shoe-tie.

Something more than
Taffeta or tissue can,
Or rampant feather, or rich fan.

More than the spoil
Of shop, or silkworm's toil,
Or a bought blush, or a set smile.

A face that's best
By its own beauty drest,
And can alone command the rest.

A face made up
Out of no other shop
Than what Nature's white hand sets ope.

A cheek where youth
And blood, with pen of truth
Write what the reader sweetly ru'th.

A cheek where grows
More than a morning rose,
Which to no box his being owes.

Lips where all day
A lover's kiss may play,
Yet carry nothing thence away.

Looks that oppress
Their richest tires, but dress
Themselves in simple nakedness.

Eyes that displace
The neighbour diamond, and out-face
That sunshine by their own sweet grace.

Tresses that wear
Jewels, but to declare
How much themselves more precious are.

Whose native ray
Can tame the wanton day
Of gems, that in their bright shades play.

Each ruby there,
Or pearl that dares appear,
Be its own blush, be its own tear.

A well-tamed heart
For whose more noble smart
Love may be long choosing a dart.

Eyes that bestow
Full quivers on Love's bow,
Yet pay less arrows than they owe.

Smiles that can warm
The blood, yet teach a charm,
That chastity shall take no harm.

* From "The Delights of the Muses."
9. teach, guide. **17. his,** its. **18. tire,** attire.

30. ope, open. **33. Write what the reader sweetly ru'th.** Professor Kittredge paraphrases the line, "Depict that beauty which makes the beholder suffer the sweet sorrow of love."—F. E. Schelling, *Seventeenth Century Lyrics*, Ginn, 1899, p. 259. **36. his,** its. **40–42. Looks that . . . nakedness.** . . . "looks that *oppress*, overpower the richest apparel which decks them, which clothe and dress up the barest costume."—Schelling. **50. tame the wanton day,** make dull the gay brilliance.

Blushes that bin
The burnish of no sin,
Nor flames of aught too hot within.

Joys that confess
Virtue their mistress,
And have no other head to dress.

Fears, fond and flight,
As the coy bride's, when night
First does the longing lover right.

Tears, quickly fled
And vain, as those are shed
For a dying maidenhead.

Days that need borrow
No part of their good morrow
From a fore-spent night of sorrow.

Days that, in spite
Of darkness, by the light
Of a clear mind are day all night.

Nights sweet as they,
Made short by lovers' play,
Yet long by the absence of the day.

Life that dares send
A challenge to his end,
And, when it comes, say, "Welcome, friend!"

Sidneian showers,
Of sweet discourse, whose powers
Can crown old Winter's head with flowers.

Soft silken hours,
Open suns, shady bowers;
'Bove all, nothing within that lours.

Whate'er delight
Can make Day's forehead bright,
Or give down to the wings of Night.

In her whole frame
Have Nature all the name,
Art and ornament all the shame.

Her flattery,
Picture and poesy:
Her counsel her own virtue be.

I wish her store
Of worth may leave her poor
Of wishes; and I wish—no more.

Now, if Time knows
That her, whose radiant brows
Weave them a garland of my vows;

Her whose just bays
My future hopes can raise
A trophy to her present praise;

Her that dares be
What these lines wish to see:
I seek no further—it is she.

'Tis she, and here
Lo! I unclothe and clear
My wishes' cloudy character.

May she enjoy it
Whose merit dare apply it,
But modesty dares still deny it.

Such worth as this is
Shall fix my flying wishes,
And determine them to kisses.

Let her full glory,
My fancies, fly before ye!
Be ye my fictions, but her story!

64. bin, are. **70. fond and flight,** foolish and fleeting. **88–90. Sidneian showers . . . flowers,** a reference probably to the elegant conversations of Sir Philip Sidney's prose romance *Arcadia*, which still retained its popularity as a ladies' book in Crashaw's day. **98. name,** repute. **100–02. Her flattery . . . be.** However others may flatter her by painting and poetry, let her take counsel only of her own virtue.

104–05. poor of wishes, that is, without need of wishes. **109. bays,** laurels. **123. determine them to,** terminate, or resolve, them into.

from THE HOLY NATIVITY OF OUR LORD GOD

A HYMN AS SUNG BY THE SHEPHERDS*

Chorus

Come, we shepherds, whose blest sight
  Hath met Love's noon in Nature's night;
Come, lift we up our loftier song,
And wake the sun that lies too long.

  To all our world of well-stol'n joy
He slept; and dreamt of no such thing
  While we found out Heav'n's fairer eye,
And kissed the cradle of our King.
  Tell him he rises now, too late
To show us aught worth looking at.

  Tell him we now can show him more

* From *Carmen Deo Nostro.*

Than he e'er showed to mortal sight;
Than he himself e'er saw before,
Which to be seen needs not his light.
Tell him, Tityrus, where th' hast been;
Tell him, Thyrsis, what th' hast seen.

Tityrus

Gloomy night embraced the place
Where the noble Infant lay.
The Babe looked up and showed His face;
In spite of darkness, it was day.
It was Thy day, Sweet! and did rise,
Not from the east, but from Thine eyes.

Thyrsis

Winter chid aloud, and sent
The angry North to wage his wars.
The North forgot his fierce intent,
And left perfumes instead of scars.
By those sweet eyes' persuasive powers,
Where he meant frost he scattered flowers.

Both

We saw Thee in Thy balmy nest,
Young Dawn of our eternal Day!
We saw Thine eyes break from their east,
And chase the trembling shades away.
We saw Thee; and we blessed the sight,
We saw Thee by Thine own sweet light.

Tityrus

Poor world (said I), what wilt thou do
To entertain this starry Stranger?
Is this the best thou canst bestow?
A cold and not too cleanly manger?
Contend, the powers of heaven and earth,
To fit a bed for this huge birth.

Thyrsis

Proud world (said I), cease your contest,
And let the mighty Babe alone.
The phoenix builds the phoenix' nest,
Love's architecture is his own.
The Babe whose birth embraves this morn
Made His own bed ere He was born.

Tityrus

I saw the curled drops, soft and slow,
Come hovering o'er the place's head;
Offering their whitest sheets of snow
To furnish the fair Infant's bed;

45. embraves, beautifies.

Forbear (said I); be not too bold,
Your fleece is white, but 'tis too cold. . . .

Full Chorus

Welcome, all wonders in one sight!
Eternity shut in a span!
Summer in winter, day in night!
Heaven in earth, and God in man!
Great little One! whose all-embracing birth
Lifts earth to heaven, stoops heaven to earth. . . .

To Thee, meek Majesty! soft King
Of simple graces and sweet loves:
Each of us his lamb will bring,
Each his pair of silver doves;
Till burnt at last in fire of Thy fair eyes,
Ourselves become our own best sacrifice.

from THE FLAMING HEART

The lines here printed are the last twenty-two lines of the poem, whose full title is "The Flaming Heart, upon the Book and Picture of the Seraphical Saint Teresa, as She Is Usually Expressed with a Seraphim beside Her" (from *Carmen Deo Nostro*). St. Teresa, the Spanish mystic, who died in 1582 and was canonized in 1622, exerted great influence on Crashaw, and, as in the lines here given, inspired him to unexcelled lyric rhapsody.

Let all thy scattered shafts of light, that play
Among the leaves of thy large books of day,
Combined against this breast, at once break in
And take away from me myself and sin!
This gracious robbery shall thy bounty be,
And my best fortunes such fair spoils of me.
O thou undaunted daughter of desires!
By all thy dower of lights and fires;
By all the eagle in thee, all the dove;
By all thy lives and deaths of love;
By thy large draughts of intellectual day,
And by thy thirsts of love more large than they;
By all thy brim-filled bowls of fierce desire,
By thy last morning's draught of liquid fire;
By the full kingdom of that final kiss
That seized thy parting soul, and sealed thee His;
By all the heavens thou hast in Him,
Fair sister of the seraphim,
By all of Him we have in thee;
Leave nothing of myself in me!
Let me so read thy life that I
Unto all life of mine may die!

Henry Vaughan
1622–1695

Vaughan was as much the poetic disciple of Herbert as Herbert was of Donne, though both disciples did their best work when they did not attempt to follow too closely the mannerisms of their masters. And none of the three would in his younger days have had reason to suppose that he would be best known three hundred years later as a poet. Vaughan is the first Welshman to find a place in the roster of English poets, and his peculiar contribution to English poetry is due in no small measure to his Welsh heritage. He was born in Brecknockshire, at Newton on the River Usk, in southeast Wales, and so devoted was he to his race and to the place of his nativity that he styled himself "the Silurist," after *Silures*, the old Roman name for the inhabitants of his district. He spoke Welsh as a child, and some of the expressions and locutions of his poems are attributable to his knowledge of his native tongue.

His early education was received in Wales, and from his childhood home he went with his twin brother, Thomas, to Jesus College, the headquarters of Welsh students at Oxford. He seems to have left without a degree, and is next heard of at the Inns of Court in London, studying law. Here he fell in with young poets and literary men, tried his hand at poetry, and continued his studies until the Civil War put an end to such peaceful pursuits. Not much is known of his life for the next few years, and indeed his biography is one of the most fragmentary in English literature. He probably served for a while in the King's army, and either before or after the war he studied medicine. After the war and for the rest of his life he was a country doctor in his native district in Wales.

Vaughan's earliest poems consisted probably of the literary exercises after the fashion of Donne which are addressed to "Amoret." Whether the lady so referred to was his first wife is not known. His greatest inspiration to poetry was to come not from the love of a lady, but from religion, and through sickness, the loss of friends, the execution of the King, the death of his wife, and, above all, the death of his twin brother. His volume *Silex Scintillans* (*The Sparkling Flint*), which was published in 1650, was devoted wholly to religious verse, much of it inspired by his brother's death, and most of it shot through with the mystical beliefs which he and his brother had shared. (The poems given here are all from this volume.) A second volume, *Olor Iscanus* (*The Swan of the Usk*), which was published in 1651, contains religious pieces as well as translations and early verse which, says the publisher's preface, the author had long ago condemned to obscurity.

The influence of Herbert on Vaughan has already been mentioned. Many of Vaughan's titles are taken directly or indirectly from Herbert, and one is constantly reminded in Vaughan's best verse of the rhythms of Herbert. He lacks, however, the artistic sense of Herbert, and is given to mixed metaphors and sudden transitions which never mar the calm flow of Herbert's verse. Vaughan's poetry is curiously uneven. Much of it is not above the level of verse that appears in a parish magazine. On the other hand there are unsurpassed flights of lyrical fancy and expressions of mystical experiences of which Herbert was not capable, and which only Crashaw among his contemporaries has equaled.

The twentieth century takes special note of Vaughan's interest in natural phenomena, and his perception of the presence of God in natural objects. This sense of the Divine immanence he believed to be particularly acute in children, and he strove to recapture for himself the state of mind and soul which would make possible communion with nature and the God of nature. In his best-known poem, "The Retreat," he looks backward to the early days of his "angel infancy," before the "white, celestial thought" of his fancy had become sullied with the wickedness of the world. The poem contains the germ of Wordsworth's thought in his "Ode: Intimations of Immortality from Recollections of Early Childhood," but there is no certainty that Wordsworth ever heard of Vaughan or of "The Retreat."

Vaughan was spiritually farsighted. "The world of light" and the departed friends beyond the veil of physical experience were more real to him than the material things of this world. If his readers are continually reminded of what he drew from Donne and Herbert, they are as constantly impressed by the fact that at his best he transcends both. His is such poetry, says a distinguished critic, as Lazarus might have written after he had risen from the dead.

THE RETREAT

The thought of this poem should be compared with that of Wordsworth's "Ode: Intimations of Immortality," page 727.

Happy those early days, when I
Shined in my angel infancy;
Before I understood this place
Appointed for my second race,
Or taught my soul to fancy aught
But a white, celestial thought;
When yet I had not walked above
A mile or two from my first Love,
And looking back, at that short space,
Could see a glimpse of His bright face;
When on some gilded cloud or flower
My gazing soul would dwell an hour,
And in those weaker glories spy
Some shadows of eternity;
Before I taught my tongue to wound
My conscience with a sinful sound,
Or had the black art to dispense
A several sin to every sense,
But felt through all this fleshly dress
Bright shoots of everlastingness.
Oh, how I long to travel back,
And tread again that ancient track!
That I might once more reach that plain
Where first I left my glorious train,
From whence the enlightened spirit sees
That shady city of palm trees.
But, ah! my soul with too much stay
Is drunk, and staggers in the way.
Some men a forward motion love;
But I by backward steps would move,
And when this dust falls to the urn,
In that state I came, return.

19. **fleshly dress,** earthly being.

PEACE

My soul, there is a country
Far beyond the stars,
Where stands a wingèd sentry
All skilful in the wars.
There, above noise and danger,
Sweet Peace sits crowned with smiles,
And One born in a manger
Commands the beauteous files.
He is thy gracious friend,
And—O my soul, awake!—
Did in pure love descend
To die here for thy sake.
If thou canst get but thither,
There grows the flower of peace,
The rose that cannot wither,
Thy fortress and thy ease.
Leave, then, thy foolish ranges;
For none can thee secure
But One who never changes,
Thy God, thy life, thy cure.

THE WORLD

I saw Eternity the other night
Like a great ring of pure and endless light,
All calm as it was bright;
And round beneath it, Time, in hours, days, years,
Driven by the spheres,
Like a vast shadow moved, in which the world
And all her train were hurled.
The doting lover in his quaintest strain
Did there complain;
Near him, his lute, his fancy, and his flights,
Wit's sour delights,
With gloves and knots, the silly snares of pleasure,
Yet his dear treasure,
All scattered lay, while he his eyes did pour
Upon a flower.

The darksome statesman, hung with weights and woe,
Like a thick midnight fog, moved there so slow
He did not stay nor go;
Condemning thoughts, like mad eclipses, scowl
Upon his soul,
And crowds of crying witnesses without
Pursued him with one shout.
Yet digged the mole, and lest his ways be found,
Worked under ground,
Where he did clutch his prey. But one did see
That policy:

Peace. 17. **ranges,** rovings (in search of peace). *The World.* 5. **spheres.** Vaughan is contrasting the great calm, unchanging ring of light above and the constantly revolving spheres of the Ptolemaic universe below with the feverish and vain activities and ambitions of human life at their center. 8. **quaintest,** decorated with the most elaborate conceits and fancies. 12. **knots,** love knots. 16. **darksome statesman,** possibly, but not certainly, a reference to Oliver Cromwell. It is most likely that Vaughan has in mind the typical unscrupulous politician. 26. **policy,** stratagem.

Churches and altars fed him; perjuries
  Were gnats and flies;
It rained about him blood and tears; but he
  Drank them as free.

The fearful miser on a heap of rust
Sat pining all his life there, did scarce trust
  His own hands with the dust;
Yet would not place one piece above, but lives
  In fear of thieves.
Thousands there were as frantic as himself,
  And hugged each one his pelf:
The downright epicure placed heaven in sense,
  And scorned pretence;
While others, slipped into a wide excess,
  Said little less;
The weaker sort, slight trivial wares enslave,
  Who think them brave;
And poor, despisèd Truth sat counting by
  Their victory.

Yet some, who all this while did weep and sing,
And sing and weep, soared up into the ring;
  But most would use no wing.
"O fools!" said I, "thus to prefer dark night
  Before true light!
To live in grots and caves, and hate the day
  Because it shows the way,
The way which from this dead and dark abode
  Leads up to God,
A way where you might tread the sun and be
  More bright than he!"
But, as I did their madness so discuss,
  One whispered thus:
"This ring the Bridegroom did for none provide,
  But for His bride."

THEY ARE ALL GONE INTO THE WORLD OF LIGHT

This poem was first printed in 1655, by which time, as Sir Edmund Chambers points out, Vaughan had lost his brother Thomas and other friends, and possibly also his first wife.

27. Churches and altars fed him, probably an allusion to the abolition of episcopacy by Parliament in 1642. **28. Were gnats and flies,** were of as little importance as gnats and flies. **30. as free,** as freely and liberally as they rained about him. **34. place one piece,** invest one coin. Compare Matthew 6:20: "Lay up for yourselves treasures in heaven, where . . . thieves do not break through nor steal." **43. brave,** fine, beautiful. **44. counting by,** observing, taking note of. **47. the ring.** See l. 2. **59–60. the Bridegroom . . . His bride,"** Christ and His Church. See Revelation 21:9.

They are all gone into the world of light,
  And I alone sit lingering here!
Their very memory is fair and bright,
  And my sad thoughts doth clear.

It glows and glitters in my cloudy breast,
  Like stars upon some gloomy grove,
Or those faint beams in which this hill is dressed
  After the sun's remove.

I see them walking in an air of glory,
  Whose light doth trample on my days;
My days, which are at best but dull and hoary,
  Mere glimmerings and decays.

O holy hope, and high humility,
  High as the heavens above!
These are your walks, and you have showed them me
  To kindle my cold love.

Dear, beauteous death! the jewel of the just,
  Shining nowhere but in the dark;
What mysteries do lie beyond thy dust,
  Could man outlook that mark!

He that hath found some fledged bird's nest may know
  At first sight if the bird be flown;
But what fair well or grove he sings in now,
  That is to him unknown.

And yet, as angels in some brighter dreams
  Call to the soul when man doth sleep,
So some strange thoughts transcend our wonted themes,
  And into glory peep.

If a star were confined into a tomb,
  Her captive flames must needs burn there;
But when the hand that locked her up gives room,
  She'll shine through all the sphere.

O Father of eternal life, and all
  Created glories under Thee!
Resume Thy spirit from this world of thrall
  Into true liberty!

Either disperse these mists, which blot and fill
  My pèrspective still as they pass;
Or else remove me hence unto that hill
  Where I shall need no glass.

4. clear, brighten. **5. It,** the memory of departed friends. **20. mark!** boundary. **35. Resume Thy spirit,** that is, take back my spirit which Thou hast created. **38. pèrspective,** telescope.

Sir Thomas Browne

1605–1682

Sir Thomas Browne is the best-known example in English literature of the physician as man of letters, the provincial doctor as philosopher and commentator on the universe and the mysteries of life and death. Like Burton, that other auditor of the world's accounts, he is also famous for the eccentricities of his genius, and for the exotic (though very different) quality of the prose in which he embalmed his meditations. Burton was "by his profession a divine, by his inclination a physician." Browne, we may say, though by profession a physician, was by his nature a divine and a metaphysician. Like both Burton and Donne, Browne was concerned with the intellectual and religious problems of the day—the seeming conflict between theology and science, the questions relating to man's place, limitations, and possibilities in the great scheme of the universe.

Sir Thomas, unlike the author of the *Anatomy*, saw a good part of the world before he began to philosophize upon it. He was born in London, went to school at Winchester, took his B.A. degree at Oxford in 1626, and his M.A. there in 1629. He was while at Oxford a member of Broadgates Hall, later Pembroke College, which was to shelter Dr. Johnson in the following century. He traveled in Ireland, France, Italy, and Flanders, and studied medicine at Montpellier, Padua, and Leyden, where he took his degree of Doctor of Medicine. He returned to England, and in 1637 settled in the market town of Norwich, where for nearly half a century he practiced his profession successfully, carried on his researches, and wrote his books. In 1641 he married Dorothy Mileham, a charming young woman of one of the county families of Norfolk. The domestic life of Sir Thomas and Dame Dorothy must have been singularly happy. His solicitude for the education and welfare of his children, especially of his sons, Edward and Thomas, and the tone of the correspondence between father and sons later, contribute to one of the pleasantest pictures of family life of the whole century. In 1665 he was made a fellow of the Royal College of Physicians. In 1671 he was knighted on a royal visit to Norwich by Charles II, who, says Dr. Johnson, writing of the incident, "with many frailties and vices, had yet skill to discover excellence, and virtue to reward it." He died on his seventy-sixth birthday, October 19, 1682.

Browne's first book, and the one which has remained most popular, is his *Religio Medici*, written when he was in his twenties, but not published by him until 1643, after two pirated editions had already appeared. It was written for himself and his friends, and is a young physician's confession of religious principles. The *Religio* is a rare exposition of the beliefs of a young man who combined a devout religious temper with an inquiring, skeptical, and scientific turn of mind. It is perhaps less a statement of faith than the revelation of a state of mind; an experiment in the deliberate suspension of judgment before the mysteries of revealed religion. It has been called the best answer of the age to the negativism and despair which tortured Donne and many another. The nobility and sweetness of Browne's character and the all-embracing tolerance of the man's mind are seen throughout the book.

His *Pseudodoxia Epidemica, or Vulgar Errors*, which he brought out in 1646, is an attempt to supply the "calendar of popular errors" which Bacon hoped would be drawn up in order that they might be convicted and disposed of. In it Browne brings together the most amazing array of "errors"—drawn from all the corners of his reading and research—and with more or less success confutes them. The poet and the scientist in him get in each other's way at times, and there are frequent struggles between his head and his heart in disposing of an error. No book was ever undertaken with more methodical gravity, but the modern reader finds it a constant source of amusement, thanks to the irrelevancies, the digressions, the bizarre fancies, and the whimsical speculations in which the author indulges.

Browne's most beautiful prose is to be found in the two pieces published in 1658, *Hydriotaphia: Urn Burial*, and *The Garden of Cyrus*, in which his antiquarian interests predominate. The discovery of some funerary urns leads Browne to the composition of an essay which, except for its companion piece has not its equal in English for solemnly beautiful diction and rhythmical prose. Two other works, *A Letter to a Friend* and *Christian Morals*, were published posthumously in 1690 and 1716.

In all that he wrote Browne is an exponent of the genteel tradition in English literature, an aristocrat in the truest and best sense of the word. He was incapable of thinking or writing anything vulgar. He is the perfect specimen of the "magnanimous man" whose language, as Cardinal Newman says, "expresses not only his great thought, but his great self."

from RELIGIO MEDICI

THE SECOND PART

NOW for that other virtue of charity, without which faith is a mere notion, and of no existence, I have ever endeavoured to nourish the merciful disposition and humane inclination I borrowed from my parents, and regulate it to the written and prescribed laws of charity. And if I hold the true anatomy of myself, I am delineated and naturally framed to such a piece of virtue; for I am of a constitution so general that it consorts and sympathiseth with all things. I have no antipathy, or rather idiosyncrasy, in diet, humour, air, anything. I wonder not at the French for their dishes of frogs, snails and toadstools, nor at the Jews for locusts and grasshoppers; but being amongst them, make them my common viands, and I find they agree with my stomach as well as theirs. I could digest a salad gathered in a church-yard, as well as in a garden. I cannot start at the presence of a serpent, scorpion, lizard, or salamander: at the sight of a toad or viper, I find in me no desire to take up a stone to destroy them. I feel not in myself those common antipathies that I can discover in others: those national repugnances do not touch me, nor do I behold with prejudice the French, Italian, Spaniard, or Dutch: but where I find their actions in balance with my countrymen's, I honour, love, and embrace them in the same degree. I was born in the eighth climate, but seem for to be framed and constellated unto all. I am no plant that will not prosper out of a garden. All places, all airs, make unto me one country; I am in England everywhere, and under any meridian. I have been shipwrackt, yet am not enemy with the sea or winds; I can study, play, or sleep in a tempest. In brief, I am averse from nothing: my conscience would give me the lie if I should say I absolutely detest or hate any essence but the Devil: or so at least abhor anything, but that we might come to composition. If there be any among those common objects of hatred I do contemn and laugh at, it is that great enemy of reason, virtue and religion, the multitude: that numerous piece of monstrosity, which, taken asunder, seem men, and the reasonable creatures of God; but, confused together, make but one great beast, and a monstrosity more prodigious than Hydra. It is no breach of charity to call these *Fools;* it is the style all holy writers have afforded them, set down by Solomon in canonical Scripture, and a point of our Faith to believe so. Neither in the name of *Multitude* do I only include the base and minor sort of people; there is a rabble even amongst the gentry, a sort of plebeian heads, whose fancy moves with the same wheel as these; men in the same level with mechanics, though their fortunes do somewhat gild their infirmities, and their purses compound for their follies. But as, in casting account, three or four men together come short in account of one man placed by himself below them; so neither are a troop of these ignorant doradoes of that true esteem and value, as many a forlorn person, whose condition doth place him below their feet. Let us speak like politicians: there is a nobility without heraldry, a natural dignity, whereby one man is ranked with another, another filed before him, according to the quality of his desert, and pre-eminence of his good parts. Though the corruption of these times and the bias of present practice wheel another way, thus it was in the first and primitive commonwealths, and is yet in the integrity and cradle of well-ordered polities, till corruption getteth ground; ruder desires labouring after that which wiser considerations contemn, every one having a liberty to amass and heap up riches, and they a licence or faculty to do or purchase any thing. . . .

There are wonders in true affection: it is a body of enigmas, mysteries, and riddles; wherein two so become one, as they both become two. I love my friend before myself, and yet methinks I do not love him enough: some few months hence my multiplied affection will make me believe I have not loved him at all. When I am from him, I am dead till I be with him; when I am with him, I am not satisfied, but would still be nearer him. United souls are not satisfied with embraces, but desire to be truly each other; which being impossible, their desires are infinite, and must proceed without a possibility of satisfaction. Another misery there is in affection, that whom we truly love like our own selves, we forget their looks, nor can our memory retain the idea of their faces; and it is no wonder, for they are ourselves, and our affection makes their looks our own. This noble affection falls not on vul-

37. eighth climate, a zone measured on the earth's surface which included England.

5. Solomon. See Proverbs 1:7 and so on. **9. plebeian heads,** base persons. **17. doradoes,** rich men (literally, goldfish).

gar and common constitutions, but on such as are marked for virtue: he that can love his friend with this noble ardour, will in a competent degree affect all. Now, if we can bring our affections to look beyond the body, and cast an eye upon the soul, we have found out the true object, not only of friendship, but charity; and the greatest happiness that we can bequeath the soul, is that wherein we all do place our last felicity, salvation; which though it be not in our power to bestow, it is in our charity and pious invocations to desire, if not procure and further. I cannot contentedly frame a prayer for myself in particular, without a catalogue for my friends; nor request a happiness, wherein my sociable disposition doth not desire the fellowship of my neighbour. I never hear the toll of a passing bell, though in my mirth, without my prayers and best wishes for the departing spirit; I cannot go to cure the body of my patient, but I forget my profession, and call unto GOD for his soul; I cannot see one say his prayers, but, instead of imitating him, I fall into a supplication for him, who perhaps is no more to me than a common nature: and if GOD hath vouchsafed an ear to my supplications, there are surely many happy that never saw me, and enjoy the blessing of mine unknown devotions. To pray for enemies, that is, for their salvation, is no harsh precept, but the practice of our daily and ordinary devotions. I cannot believe the story of the Italian: our bad wishes and uncharitable desires proceed no further than this life; it is the Devil, and the uncharitable votes of Hell, that desire our misery in the World to come. . . .

For my conversation, it is like the sun's, with all men, and with a friendly aspect to good and bad. Methinks there is no man bad, and the worst, best; that is, while they are kept within the circle of those qualities wherein they are good: there is no man's mind of such discordant and jarring a temper, to which a tunable disposition may not strike a harmony. *Magnae virtutes, nec minora vitia;* it is the posy of the best natures, and may be inverted on the worst; there are in the most depraved and venomous dispositions, certain pieces that remain untoucht, which by an *antiperistasis* become more excellent, or by the excellency of their antipathies are able to preserve themselves from the contagion of their enemy vices, and persist entire beyond the general corruption. For it is also thus in nature: the greatest balsams do lie enveloped in the bodies of most powerful corrosives. I say, moreover, and I ground upon experience, that poisons contain within themselves their own antidote, and that which preserves them from the venom of themselves, without which they were not deleterious to others only, but to themselves also. But it is the corruption that I fear within me, not the contagion of commerce without me. 'Tis that unruly regiment within me, that will destroy me; 'tis I that do infect myself; the man without a navel yet lives in me; I feel that original canker and corrode and devour me; and therefore *Defenda me* DIOS *de me*, "LORD deliver me from my self," is a part of my Litany, and the first voice of my retired imaginations. There is no man alone, because every man is a microcosm, and carries the whole world about him. *Nunquam minus solus quam cum solus*, though it be the apothegm of a wise man, is yet true in the mouth of a fool. Indeed, though in a wilderness, a man is never alone, not only because he is with himself and his own thoughts, but because he is with the Devil, who ever consorts with our solitude, and is that unruly rebel that musters up those disordered motions which accompany our sequestered imaginations. And to speak more narrowly, there is no such thing as solitude, nor any thing that can be said to be alone and by itself, but GOD, Who is His own circle, and can subsist by Himself; all others, besides their dissimilary and heterogeneous parts, which in a manner multiply their natures, cannot subsist without the concourse of GOD, and the society of that hand which doth uphold their natures. In brief, there can be nothing truly alone and by itself, which is not truly one; and such is only GOD: all others do transcend an unity, and so by consequence are many.

Now for my life, it is a miracle of thirty years, which to relate were not a history, but a piece of poetry, and would sound to common ears like a fable. For the world, I count it not an inn, but an hospital; and a place not to live, but to die in. The world that I regard is myself; it is the microcosm of my own frame that I cast mine eye on; for the other, I use it but like my globe, and turn it round sometimes for my recreation. Men that look upon my

29–30. the Italian. Sir Thomas refers more specifically in his *Pseudodoxia*, Book VII, chap. 19, to this Italian, "who, after he had inveigled his enemy to disdain his faith for the redemption of his life, did presently poniard him, to prevent repentance, and assure his eternal death." **35. conversation,** behavior. **42. Magnae . . . vitia.** Great virtues, and no smaller vices. **46. antiperistasis,** an opposition of contrary qualities by which one or both are intensified, or the intensification so produced.

4. balsams, healing agents. **13–14. the man without a navel,** Adam. **20–21. Nunquam . . . solus.** Never less alone than when alone.—Cicero, *De Officiis*, Book III, sec. 1. **46. microcosm.** The "microcosm," or "little world" of man, is contrasted with the "macrocosm," or "great world" of the universe.

outside, perusing only my condition and fortunes, do err in my altitude; for I am above Atlas his shoulders. The earth is a point not only in respect of the heavens above us, but of that heavenly and celestial part within us; that mass of flesh that circumscribes me, limits not my mind: that surface that tells the heavens it hath an end, cannot persuade me I have any: I take my circle to be above three hundred and sixty; though the number of the arc do measure my body, it comprehendeth not my mind: whilst I study to find how I am a microcosm, or little world, I find myself something more than the great. There is surely a piece of Divinity in us, something that was before the elements, and owes no homage unto the sun. Nature tells me I am the image of God, as well as Scripture: he that understands not thus much, hath not his introduction or first lesson, and is yet to begin the alphabet of man. Let me not injure the felicity of others, if I say I am as happy as any: *Ruat coelum, fiat voluntas Tua*, salveth all; so that whatsoever happens, it is but what our daily prayers desire. In brief, I am content; and what should Providence add more? Surely this is it we call happiness, and this do I enjoy; with this I am happy in a dream, and as content to enjoy a happiness in a fancy, as others in a more apparent truth and realty. There is surely a nearer apprehension of anything that delights us in our dreams, than in our waked senses: without this I were unhappy; for my awaked judgment discontents me, ever whispering unto me, that I am from my friend; but my friendly dreams in the night requite me, and make me think I am within his arms. I thank God for my happy dreams, as I do for my good rest; for there is a satisfaction in them unto reasonable desires, and such as can be content with a fit of happiness: and surely it is not a melancholy conceit to think we are all asleep in this world, and that the conceits of this life are as mere dreams to those of the next; as the phantasms of the night to the conceits of the day. There is an equal delusion in both, and the one doth but seem to be the emblem or picture of the other: we are somewhat more than ourselves in our sleeps, and the slumber of the body seems to be but the waking of the soul. It is the ligation of sense, but the liberty of reason; and our waking conceptions do not match the fancies of our sleeps. At my nativity my ascendant was the watery sign of Scorpius; I was born in the planetary hour of Saturn, and I think I have a piece of that leaden planet in me. I am no way facetious, nor disposed for the mirth and galliardise of company; yet in one dream I can compose a whole comedy, behold the action, apprehend the jests, and laugh myself awake at the conceits thereof. Were my memory as faithful as my reason is then fruitful, I would never study but in my dreams; and this time also would I choose for my devotions: but our grosser memories have then so little hold of our abstracted understandings, that they forget the story, and can only relate to our awaked souls a confused and broken tale of that that hath passed. Aristotle, who hath written a singular tract *Of Sleep*, hath not, methinks, throughly defined it; nor yet Galen, though he seem to have corrected it; for those noctambuloes and night-walkers, though in their sleep, do yet enjoy the action of their senses. We must therefore say that there is something in us that is not in the jurisdiction of Morpheus; and that those abstracted and ecstatic souls do walk about in their own corpse as spirits with the bodies they assume, wherein they seem to hear, see, and feel, though indeed the organs are destitute of sense, and their natures of those faculties that should inform them. Thus it is observed, that men sometimes, upon the hour of their departure, do speak and reason above themselves; for then the soul, beginning to be freed from the ligaments of the body, begins to reason like herself, and to discourse in a strain above mortality.

We term sleep a death; and yet it is waking that kills us, and destroys those spirits that are the house of life. 'Tis indeed a part of life that best expresseth death; for every man truly lives, so long as he acts his nature, or some way makes good the faculties of himself. Themistocles, therefore, that slew his soldier in his sleep, was a merciful executioner: 'tis a kind of punishment the mildness of no laws hath invented: I wonder the fancy of Lucan and Seneca did not discover it. It is that death by which we may be literally said to die daily; a death which Adam died before his mortality; a death whereby we live a middle and moderating point between life and death: in fine, so like death, I dare not trust it without my prayers, and an half adieu unto the world, and take my farewell in a colloquy with God. . . . This is the dormitive I take to bedward; I need no other laudanum than this to make me sleep; after which I close mine eyes in security, content to take my leave of the sun, and sleep unto the Resurrection. . . .

2. Atlas, the mythological giant who carried the world on his shoulders. **20.** ***Ruat . . . Tua.*** Though the heavens fall, Thy will be done. **37. conceit,** fancy, opinion. **45–46. ligation,** binding. **48. ascendant,** the sign of the zodiac rising over the horizon.

2. galliardise, excessive gaiety. **14. Galen,** Greek physician and medical writer of the second century A.D. **19. Morpheus,** the god of sleep. **46. dormitive,** a medicine to induce sleep.

from HYDRIOTAPHIA: URN BURIAL

Chapter 5

NOW since these dead bones have already outlasted the living ones of Methuselah, and in a yard under ground, and thin walls of clay, out-worn all the strong and specious buildings above it; and quietly rested under the drums and tramplings of three conquests: what prince can promise such diuturnity unto his relics, or might not gladly say,

Sic ego componi versus in ossa velim?

Time which antiquates antiquities, and hath an art to make dust of all things, hath yet spared these minor monuments.

In vain we hope to be known by open and visible conservatories, when to be unknown was the means of their continuation, and obscurity their protection. If they died by violent hands, and were thrust into their urns, these bones become considerable, and some old philosophers would honour them, whose souls they conceived most pure, which were thus snatched from their bodies, and to retain a stranger propension unto them; whereas they weariedly left a languishing corpse, and with faint desires of reunion. If they fell by long and aged decay, yet wrapt up in the bundle of time, they fall into indistinction, and make but one blot with infants. If we begin to die when we live, and long life be but a prolongation of death, our life is a sad composition. We live with death, and die not in a moment. How many pulses made up the life of Methuselah, were work for Archimedes: common counters sum up the life of Moses his man. Our days become considerable like petty sums by minute accumulations; where numerous fractions make up but small round numbers; and our days of a span long make not one little finger.

If the nearness of our last necessity brought a nearer conformity into it, there were a happiness in hoary hairs, and no calamity in half senses. But the long habit of living indisposeth us for dying; when avarice makes us the sport of death; when even David grew politicly cruel; and Solomon could hardly be said to be the wisest of men. But many are too early old, and before the date of age. Adversity stretcheth our days, misery makes Alcmena's nights, and time hath no wings unto it. But the most tedious being is that which can unwish itself, content to be nothing, or never to have been, which was beyond the malcontent of Job, who cursed not the day of his life, but his nativity; content to have so far been, as to have a title to future being, although he had lived here but in an hidden state of life, and as it were an abortion.

What song the sirens sang, or what name Achilles assumed when he hid himself among women, though puzzling questions, are not beyond all conjecture. What time the persons of these ossuaries entered the famous nations of the dead, and slept with princes and counsellours, might admit a wide solution. But who were the proprietaries of these bones, or what bodies these ashes made up, were a question above antiquarism. Not to be resolved by man, nor easily perhaps by spirits, except we consult the provincial guardians, or tutelary observators. Had they made as good provision for their names as they have done for their relics, they had not so grossly erred in the art of perpetuation. But to subsist in bones, and be but pyramidally extant, is a fallacy in duration. Vain ashes, which in the oblivion of names, persons, times, and sexes, have found unto themselves a fruitless continuation, and only arise unto late posterity, as emblems of mortal vanities; antidotes against pride, vainglory, and madding vices. Pagan vainglories which thought the world might last for ever, had encouragement for ambition, and, finding no Atropos unto the immortality of their names, were never dampt with the necessity of oblivion. Even old ambitions had the advantage of ours, in the attempts of their vainglories, who acting early, and before the probable meridian of time, have by this time found great accomplishment of their designs, whereby the ancient Heroes have already out-lasted their monuments, and mechanical preservations. But in this latter scene of time, we cannot expect such mummies unto our memories, when ambition may fear the prophecy of Elias, and Charles the Fifth can never hope to live within two Methuselahs of Hector.

12. **diuturnity,** long duration. 14. ***Sic . . . velim?*** "Thus, when I am turned to bones, would I be disposed." 36. **the life of Moses his man.** "In the Psalm of Moses [Psalm 90:10]." (Browne) 40. **one little finger.** "According to the ancient arithmetic of the hand, wherein the little finger of the right hand contracted, signified an hundred.—*Pierius in Hieroglyph.*" (Browne)

1–2. **Alcmena's nights.** "One night as long as three." (Browne) 5–6. **Job . . . nativity.** See Job 3. 12. **puzzling questions.** "The puzzling questions of Tiberius unto grammarians.—*Marcel. Donatus in Suet.*" (Browne) 13. **ossuaries,** repositories of bones. 15. **wide,** only roughly approximate. 20–21. **tutelary observators,** guardian spirits. 24. **pyramidally extant,** known by monuments only, like a mummy. 32. **Atropos,** the Fate whose duty it was to cut the thread of life. 33. **dampt,** dispirited. 37. **meridian,** noonday. 43. **prophecy of Elias.** "That the world may last but six thousand years." (Browne) 44. **two Methuselahs of Hector.** "Hector's fame lasting above two lives of Methuselah, before that famous prince was extant." (Browne)

And therefore restless inquietude for the diuturnity of our memories unto present considerations, seems a vanity almost out of date, and superannuated piece of folly. We cannot hope to live so long in our names, as some have done in their persons, one face of Janus holds no proportion unto the other. 'Tis too late to be ambitious. The great mutations of the world are acted, or time may be too short for our designs. To extend our memories by monuments, whose death we daily pray for, and whose duration we cannot hope, without injury to our expectations in the advent of the last day, were a contradiction to our beliefs. We whose generations are ordained in this setting part of time, are providentially taken off from such imaginations; and being necessitated to eye the remaining particle of futurity, are naturally constituted unto thoughts of the next world, and cannot excusably decline the consideration of that duration, which maketh pyramids pillars of snow, and all that's past a moment.

Circles and right lines limit and close all bodies, and the mortal right-lined circle must conclude and shut up all. There is no antidote against the opium of time, which temporally considereth all things. Our fathers find their graves in our short memories, and sadly tell us how we may be buried in our survivors. Grave-stones tell truth scarce forty years. Generations pass while some trees stand, and old families last not three oaks. To be read by bare inscriptions like many in Gruter, to hope for eternity by enigmatical epithets or first letters of our names, to be studied by antiquaries, who we were, and have new names given us like many of the mummies, are cold consolations unto the students of perpetuity, even by everlasting languages.

To be content that times to come should only know there was such a man, not caring whether they knew more of him, was a frigid ambition in Cardan: disparaging his horoscopal inclination and judgment of himself, who cares to subsist like Hippocrates' patients, or Achilles' horses in Homer, under naked nominations, without deserts and noble acts, which are the balsam of our memories, the *entelechia* and soul of our subsistences? To be nameless in worthy deeds exceeds an infamous history. The Canaanitish woman lives more happily without a name, than Herodias with one. And who had not rather have been the good thief, than Pilate?

But the iniquity of oblivion blindly scattereth her poppy, and deals with the memory of men without distinction to merit of perpetuity. Who can but pity the founder of the Pyramids? Herostratus lives that burnt the Temple of Diana, he is almost lost that built it. Time hath spared the epitaph of Adrian's horse, confounded that of himself. In vain we compute our felicities by the advantage of our good names, since bad have equal durations; and Thersites is like to live as long as Agamemnon. Who knows whether the best of men be known? or whether there be not more remarkable persons forgot, than any that stand remembered in the known account of time? Without the favour of the everlasting register, the first man had been as unknown as the last, and Methuselah's long life had been his only chronicle.

Oblivion is not to be hired. The greater part must be content to be as though they had not been, to be found in the register of God, not in the record of man. Twenty-seven names make up the first story before the flood, and the recorded names ever since contain not one living century. The number of the dead long exceedeth all that shall live. The night of time far surpasseth the day, and who knows when was the equinox? Every hour adds unto that current arithmetic which scarce stands one moment. And since death must be the Lucina of life, and even pagans could doubt, whether thus to live, were to die; since our longest sun sets at right descensions, and makes but winter arches, and therefore it cannot be long before we lie down in darkness, and have our light in ashes; since the brother of death daily haunts us with dying mementoes, and time that grows old in itself, bids us hope no long duration: diuturnity is a dream and folly of expectation.

Darkness and light divide the course of time, and oblivion shares with memory a great part even of our living beings; we slightly remember our felicities, and the smartest strokes of affliction leave but short smart upon us. Sense endureth no extremities, and sorrows destroy us or themselves. To weep into

6. Janus, the god of beginnings, who had two opposite faces. **21. right,** straight. **close,** inclose. **22. right-lined circle,** "Θ, the character of death." (Browne) **27. scarce forty years.** "Old ones being taken up, and other bodies laid under them." (Browne) **30. Gruter,** Jan Gruter (1560–1627), Dutch scholar who published a work on Latin inscriptions. **33–34. mummies.** "Which men show in several countries, giving them what names they please; and unto some the names of the old Egyptian kings, out of Herodotus." (Browne) **39. Cardan,** Girolamo (1501–1576), Italian mathematician and astrologer. **44. *entelechia*,** being.

1. Canaanitish woman. See Matthew 15:27–28. **2. Herodias.** See Mark 6:22–25. **3–4. good thief . . . Pilate?** See Luke 23. **13–14. Thersites,** the most scurrilous of the Greeks before Troy. **27. century,** hundred. **30–31. that current arithmetic,** that steadily moving progression. **32. Lucina,** the goddess of childbirth. **33. pagans,** "Euripides." (Browne) **37. ashes.** "According to the custom of the Jews, who place a lighted wax-candle in a pot of ashes by the corpse." (Browne) **brother of death.** Sleep and Death are in Greek mythology the children of Night.

stones are fables. Afflictions induce callosities, miseries are slippery, or fall like snow upon us, which notwithstanding is no unhappy stupidity. To be ignorant of evils to come, and forgetful of evils past, is a merciful provision in nature, whereby we digest the mixture of our few and evil days, and our delivered senses not relapsing into cutting remembrances, our sorrows are not kept raw by the edge of repetitions. A great part of antiquity contented their hopes of subsistency with a transmigration of their souls. A good way to continue their memories, while having the advantage of plural successions, they could not but act something remarkable in such variety of beings, and enjoying the fame of their passed selves, make accumulation of glory unto their last durations. Others, rather than be lost in the uncomfortable night of nothing, were content to recede into the common being, and make one particle of the public soul of all things, which was no more than to return into their unknown and divine Original again. Egyptian ingenuity was more unsatisfied, contriving their bodies in sweet consistencies, to attend the return of their souls. But all was vanity, feeding the wind, and folly. The Egyptian mummies, which Cambyses or time hath spared, avarice now consumeth. Mummy is become merchandise, Mizraim cures wounds, and Pharaoh is sold for balsams.

In vain do individuals hope for immortality, or any patent from oblivion, in preservations below the moon; men have been deceived even in their flatteries above the sun, and studied conceits to perpetuate their names in heaven. The various cosmography of that part hath already varied the names of contrived constellations; Nimrod is lost in Orion, and Osiris in the Dog-star. While we look for incorruption in the heavens, we find they are but like the earth;—durable in their main bodies, alterable in their parts: whereof beside comets and new stars, perspectives begin to tell tales. And the spots that wander about the sun, with Phaeton's favour, would make clear conviction.

There is nothing strictly immortal, but immortality; whatever hath no beginning, may be confident of no end—which is the peculiar of that necessary Essence that cannot destroy itself; and the highest strain of omnipotency, to be so powerfully constituted as not to suffer even from the power of itself: all others have a dependent being, and within the reach of destruction. But the sufficiency of Christian immortality frustrates all earthly glory, and the quality of either state after death makes a folly of posthumous memory. God who can only destroy our souls, and hath assured our resurrection, either of our bodies or names hath directly promised no duration. Wherein there is so much of chance, that the boldest expectants have found unhappy frustration; and to hold long subsistence, seems but a scape in oblivion. But man is a noble animal, splendid in ashes, and pompous in the grave, solemnizing nativities and deaths with equal lustre, nor omitting ceremonies of bravery in the infamy of his nature.

Life is a pure flame, and we live by an invisible sun within us. A small fire sufficeth for life, great flames seemed too little after death, while men vainly affected precious pyres, and to burn like Sardanapalus; but the wisdom of funeral laws found the folly of prodigal blazes, and reduced undoing fires unto the rule of sober obsequies, wherein few could be so mean as not to provide wood, pitch, a mourner, and an urn.

Five languages secured not the epitaph of Gordianus. The man of God lives longer without a tomb than any by one, invisibly interred by angels, and adjudged to obscurity, though not without some marks directing human discovery. Enoch and Elias without either tomb or burial, in an anomalous state of being, are the great examples of perpetuity, in their long and living memory, in strict account being still on this side death, and having a late part yet to act upon this stage of earth. If in the decretory term of the world we shall not all die but be changed, according to received translation, the last day will make but few graves; at least quick resurrections will anticipate lasting sepultures; some graves will be opened before they be quite closed, and Lazarus be no wonder. When many that feared to die shall groan that they can die but once, the dismal state is the second and living death, when life puts despair on the damned; when men shall wish the coverings of mountains, not of monuments, and annihilations shall be courted.

While some have studied monuments, others

1. induce callosities, dull our sensitiveness. **26–27. Mummy . . . merchandise.** In the seventeenth century, mummy powder was used as a specific for certain diseases. **Mizraim,** Egypt. **30. patent,** protection. **40. perspectives,** telescopes. **41. Phaeton's favour.** Phaëthon, in classical mythology, was the son of Helios (the Sun). Here he is identified with the sun. **45. peculiar,** peculiar characteristic.

6. can only, can alone. **12. scape in,** poor evasion of. **15. bravery,** ostentation. **26–27. epitaph of Gordianus.** "In Greek, Latin, Hebrew, Egyptian, Arabic; defaced by Licinius the emperor." (Browne) **man of God,** Moses. See Deuteronomy 34. **30–31. Enoch and Elias.** See Genesis 5:24 and II Kings 2:11. **36. decretory term,** the decreed end. **41. Lazarus be no wonder.** See John 11. **45. coverings of mountains.** See Luke 23:30 and Revelation 6:16.

have studiously declined them: and some have been so vainly boisterous that they durst not acknowledge their graves; wherein Alaricus seems most subtle, who had a river turned to hide his bones at the bottom. Even Sylla, that thought himself safe in his urn, could not prevent revenging tongues, and stones thrown at his monument. Happy are they whom privacy makes innocent, who deal so with men in this world, that they are not afraid to meet them in the next, who when they die, make no commotion among the dead, and are not touched with that poetical taunt of Isaiah.

Pyramids, arches, obelisks, were but the irregularities of vain glory, and wild enormities of ancient magnanimity. But the most magnanimous resolution rests in the Christian religion, which trampleth upon pride, and sits on the neck of ambition, humbly pursuing that infallible perpetuity unto which all others must diminish their diameters, and be poorly seen in angles of contingency.

Pious spirits who passed their days in raptures of futurity made little more of this world than the world that was before it, while they lay obscure in the chaos of preordination, and night of their forebeings. And if any have been so happy as truly to understand Christian annihilation, extasis, exolution, liquefaction, transformation, the kiss of the Spouse, gustation of God, and ingression into the divine shadow, they have already had an handsome anticipation of heaven; the glory of the world is surely over, and the earth in ashes unto them.

To subsist in lasting monuments, to live in their productions, to exist in their names and predicament of chimaeras, was large satisfaction unto old expectations, and made one part of their Elysiums. But all this is nothing in the metaphysics of true belief. To live indeed is to be again ourselves, which being not only an hope but an evidence in noble believers, 'tis all one to lie in St. Innocent's churchyard, as in the sands of Egypt: ready to be anything, in the ecstasy of being ever, and as content with six foot as the *Moles* of Adrianus.

——*Tabesne cadavera solvat*
An rogus haud refert.—LUCAN

John Milton
1608–1674

John Milton was born in London, the son of John and Sarah Milton. His father, a scrivener, who had made a comfortable fortune in drawing up business contracts, was a man of culture, a composer of songs, and one of the most generous and sympathetic fathers a young poet ever had. The mother, of whom little is known, destined her son for the Church, and devoted herself to his religious training. Milton's education was begun at home, and the boy took to his studies with such zeal that, as he said later, "from my twelfth year I scarcely ever went to bed before midnight, which was the first cause of injury to my eyes." He later went to St. Paul's School and to Christ's College, Cambridge. Outside his studies, the most important circumstance in his early life was his friendship with Charles Diodati, a schoolmate at St. Paul's. At the university Milton was too reserved to be altogether at home with his fellows, and had too much a mind of his own to be an entirely docile student. He objected to much in the curriculum, to the routine, and, in particular, to his tutor, who had him disciplined and suspended for a term. He enjoyed his enforced holiday and came back to college, where he eventually won the esteem of the students, as much, perhaps, for his ability at fencing as for his intellectual eminence. He received his B.A. degree in his twenty-first year, in 1629, and in the same year composed his ode, "On the Morning of Christ's Nativity," the most important of his early poems. His remaining years at the university seem to have been happy ones, as there is an air of sociability about the verse he composed at that period. Two of his most charming poems, the famous pair "L'Allegro" and "Il Penseroso," were probably written during the last years of his university career.

12. taunt of Isaiah. See Isaiah 14:9. **20. angles of contingency.** "*Angulus contingentiae,* the least of angles." (Browne)

3–6. Christian annihilation . . . divine shadow, terms used in mystical writings to express the mystical union with the divine. **16–17. St. Innocent's churchyard.** "In Paris, where bodies soon consume." (Browne) **19. the *Moles* of Adrianus.** "A stately mausoleum or sepulchral pile, built by Adrianus in Rome, where now standeth the Castle of St. Angelo." (Browne) **21–22. "*Tabesne . . . refert.*"** "It matters little whether earth or the funeral pyre consumes the corpses."

Milton left the university after taking his M.A. degree in 1632. He had by then given up all plans for entering the Church, doubtless because of his disapproval of what he considered the corrupt practices of the bishops and the clergy. He retired to his father's house at Horton, about twenty miles from London, where for five years he gave himself up to intense study for the poet's calling, which he considered a sacred vocation. The ripening of his poetic genius is shown in his chief compositions of this period—"Comus," 1634, and "Lycidas," 1637. "Comus," a masque written at the request of Henry Lawes, Master of the King's Music, and supplied with musical settings by Lawes, combines, as do few other poems in English, Renaissance grace and artistry and Puritan seriousness. The exquisite songs that it contains show Milton's kinship with the Elizabethan lyrists. Three years later the death of a college classmate, Edward King, furnished the occasion for the composition of "Lycidas," a pastoral elegy of unexcelled beauty, in which Milton reveals himself, as Shelley was to acknowledge in *Adonais*, the "most musical of mourners." Here again, in the midst of the enchanting pastoral music of the piece, are heard the sterner notes of Milton's Puritanism in his attack on the corruption of the clergy. In the last line of "Lycidas," the poet indicates a resolution to move on to "fresh woods and pastures new." In the next year, 1638, he left Horton to make the "grand tour" on the Continent. Perhaps the happiest period of Milton's life was that spent in Italy, where, as a charming and cultivated young Englishman, he was welcomed by men distinguished in letters, politics, and science, among them Galileo, the famous astronomer. After about a year his travels were cut short by news of the impending civil strife in England, and his journey home was further saddened by the news of the death of his friend Diodati. His grief for his lost friend he expressed in a Latin elegy, *Epitaphium Damonis*, 1639, in which he bade farewell to his youth and to his Latin verse as well as to his friend.

Back in London, Milton settled down to teaching his two nephews and, apparently, a few other young gentlemen. There now ensued a period of nearly twenty years during which his poetry had largely to be put aside for prose, and the plans he had cherished for writing a great and noble poem had to give way before what seemed to him the more pressing and immediate demands of his duty as a man and as a citizen to defend the cause of liberty. In later years, in his *Second Defense of the People of England*, 1654, he summed up the prose works of his middle years as efforts on behalf of "three species of liberty which are essential to the happiness of social life—religious, domestic, and civil." In defense of what he considered religious liberty he wrote, in 1641 and 1642, five pamphlets attacking the system of episcopacy and the alliance between Church and State in the Church of England, and arguing for the rule of conscience in spiritual affairs.

In 1642, in his thirty-fourth year, Milton married, rather hastily, Mary Powell, the seventeen-year-old daughter of a Cavalier family, who found the scholarly and sedate household of Milton uncongenial, and left him shortly. The circumstance proved the greatest shock of his life to Milton, than whom no man ever had a higher and more ideal conception of married love. After three years, the two were reconciled, and his wife bore him three daughters and a son before her death in 1652. The circumstances of the separation turned Milton's attention to the divorce laws of the country, and he produced between 1643 and 1645 four treatises on divorce, arguing for dissolution of marriage when husband and wife are spiritually and temperamentally incompatible. The divorce pamphlets were punctuated by two treatises on other phases of "domestic liberty." The first was a little tractate *On Education*, 1644, which contains an outline of an encyclopedic course of study and a noble statement of its ends and aims: "I call therefore a complete and generous education that which fits a man to perform justly, skilfully, and magnanimously all the offices, both private and public, of peace and war." Later in the same year came the most famous of his prose works, *Areopagitica*, his eloquent plea for the freedom of the press. In 1645 appeared his first volume of collected poems, containing verse in three languages—English, Latin, and Italian.

Meanwhile the dissension between the King and the Puritan Parliament was coming to a head, and Milton entered into the struggle on behalf of "civil liberty." The first of his political treatises, *The Tenure of Kings and Magistrates*, appeared within a few weeks of the execution of the King early in 1649. Milton was shortly appointed Latin Secretary to the Commonwealth Council of State, and for the next eleven years he gave to the cause most of his energy, his talents, and his eyesight. With the Restoration of Charles II in 1660, all that Milton had hoped and worked for seemed lost. He was arrested but released on the payment of fees. The preceding ten years had also brought domestic changes and sorrows. Death had taken his infant son, his first wife, Mary Powell, and his second wife, Katherine Woodcock, whom he had married in 1655. In 1663 he married Elizabeth Minshull, who was thirty years younger than he, and retired to a small house, where he again took up his poetry. He had begun the composition of his *Paradise Lost* during the last years of the Commonwealth, and now, in circumstances that would have reduced most men to inactivity, he completed the work to which he had dedicated himself. *Paradise Lost*, 1667, *Paradise Regained*, 1671, and *Samson Agonistes*, 1671, different as they are in plan, structure, and content, constitute a great poetic trilogy in which finally and magnificently Milton, even among the ruins, vindicates Eternal Providence and tries to make apparent the justice of God's ways to men.

Such are briefly the annals of the life and work of the man who, next to Shakespeare, is England's greatest writer, and perhaps her greatest poet. Milton is unique among English poets in many ways. No other poet dedicated himself so early and so thoroughly to his high office. No other poet gave the prime years of his life to the often prosaic duties of a citizen and patriot. And no other poet in English ever produced his greatest work in the closing years of his life, "in darkness and with dangers compassed round." From poets who succeeded Milton have come such tributes to the nobility of his character and the beauty of his verse as have been paid to few men in the long history of English literature. At the present time, when many of the battles in which he engaged are still far from won, not a few have cause to echo Wordsworth's lines,

Milton! thou should'st be living at this hour:
England hath need of thee: she is a fen
Of stagnant waters: altar, sword, and pen,
Fireside, the heroic wealth of hall and bower,
Have forfeited their ancient English dower . . .
Oh! raise us up, return to us again.

ON THE MORNING OF CHRIST'S NATIVITY

This ode was composed in December, 1629, as a "birthday gift to Christ." Milton had come of age in that month, and was in his fourth year at Cambridge. It was first printed in the 1645 edition of Milton's poems. It is the finest production of his early maturity, and the first example of the serious and lofty style of which he was later to be the master. It is still, nevertheless, the poem of a young man who has not outgrown his fondness for the conceits and other literary devices of the Spenserians and the Elizabethan sonneteers in general. The erudition of the youthful author is evident throughout the poem. It is as Protestant in feeling as Crashaw's hymn "The Holy Nativity of Our Lord God" (page 365) is Catholic.

This is the month, and this the happy morn,
Wherein the Son of Heaven's eternal King,
Of wedded Maid and Virgin Mother born,
Our great redemption from above did bring;
For so the holy sages once did sing,
  That he our deadly forfeit should release,
And with his Father work us a perpetual peace.

That glorious form, that light unsufferable,
And that far-beaming blaze of majesty,
Wherewith he wont at Heaven's high council-table
To sit the midst of Trinal Unity,
He laid aside, and, here with us to be,
  Forsook the courts of everlasting day,
And chose with us a darksome house of mortal clay.

Say, Heavenly Muse, shall not thy sacred vein
Afford a present to the Infant God?
Hast thou no verse, no hymn, or solemn strain,
To welcome him to this his new abode,
Now while the heaven, by the sun's team untrod,
  Hath took no print of the approaching light,
And all the spangled host keep watch in squadrons
  bright?

See how from far upon the eastern road
The star-led wizards haste with odours sweet!
Oh! run; prevent them with thy humble ode,
And lay it lowly at his blessèd feet;
Have thou the honour first thy Lord to greet,
  And join thy voice unto the angel quire,
From out his secret altar touched with hallowed
  fire.

THE HYMN

It was the winter wild,
While the Heaven-born Child
  All meanly wrapt in the rude manger lies;

5. the holy sages, the Old Testament prophets. **6. he our deadly forfeit should release,** he should remit the fine or penalty of death which resulted from Adam's sin. **10. wont,** was wont, accustomed. **15. Say, Heavenly Muse.** Compare the invocation of the "Heavenly Muse" in *Paradise Lost*, Book I, ll. 6–7. **23. The star-led wizards,** the "Wise Men from the East." See Matthew 2:1–11. **24. prevent,** anticipate. **28. altar . . . fire.** See Isaiah 6:6. Milton's lips, purified by the hallowed fire, would join the "angel quire" in greeting Christ's birth. See Luke 2:13–14.

Nature in awe to him
Had doffed her gaudy trim,
With her great Master so to sympathize:
It was no season then for her
To wanton with the sun her lusty paramour.

Only with speeches fair
She woos the gentle air
To hide her guilty front with innocent snow,
And on her naked shame,
Pollute with sinful blame,
The saintly veil of maiden white to throw,
Confounded, that her Maker's eyes
Should look so near upon her foul deformities.

But he, her fears to cease,
Sent down the meek-eyed Peace;
She crowned with olive green came softly sliding
Down through the turning sphere,
His ready harbinger,
With turtle wing the amorous clouds dividing,
And waving wide her myrtle wand,
She strikes a universal peace through sea and land.

No war, or battle's sound,
Was heard the world around;
The idle spear and shield were high uphung;
The hookèd chariot stood,
Unstained with hostile blood;
The trumpet spake not to the armèd throng;
And kings sat still with awful eye,
As if they surely knew their sovran Lord was by.

But peaceful was the night
Wherein the Prince of Light
His reign of peace upon the earth began.
The winds, with wonder whist,
Smoothly the waters kissed,
Whispering new joys to the mild oceàn,
Who now hath quite forgot to rave,
While birds of calm sit brooding on the charmèd wave.

The stars, with deep amaze,
Stand fixed in steadfast gaze,
Bending one way their precious influence,
And will not take their flight,
For all the morning light,
Or Lucifer that often warned them thence;
But in their glimmering orbs did glow,
Until their Lord himself bespake, and bid them go.

And, though the shady gloom
Had given day her room,
The sun himself withheld his wonted speed,
And hid his head for shame,
As his inferior flame
The new-enlightened world no more should need:
He saw a greater Sun appear
Than his bright throne or burning axletree could bear.

The shepherds on the lawn,
Or ere the point of dawn,
Sat simply chatting in a rustic row;
Full little thought they than
That the mighty Pan
Was kindly come to live with them below;
Perhaps their loves or else their sheep,
Was all that did their silly thoughts so busy keep.

When such music sweet
Their hearts and ears did greet,
As never was by mortal finger strook,
Divinely warbled voice
Answering the stringèd noise,
As all their souls in blissful rapture took:
The air such pleasure loth to lose,
With thousand echoes still prolongs each heavenly close.

Nature that heard such sound
Beneath the hollow round
Of Cynthia's seat, the airy region thrilling,

39. guilty front. Nature is, like man, thought of as under a curse as the result of the Fall of Man. **46. Sent down the meek-eyed Peace.** Milton doubtless had in mind the representation of Peace in an allegorical masque or painting. **48. the turning sphere,** the whole globe of the stars, which, in the Ptolemaic conception of the universe, revolved daily about the earth. **50. turtle,** turtledove. **53–60. No war . . . by,** an allusion to the (relatively) peaceful interlude throughout the Roman Empire at the time of Christ's birth. **56. hookèd,** having hooks, or scythes, projecting from the axles. **59. awful,** full of awe. **64. whist,** hushed. **68. birds of calm,** an allusion to the halcyons, who, according to classical mythology, bred during a calm period at the winter solstice.

69. amaze, amazement, wonder. **71. influence.** The stars were supposed, in astrology, to affect or "influence" the lives of human beings. Milton represents their influence at the time of the birth of Christ as altogether beneficent. **74. Lucifer,** literally "Light-bearer." Either the morning star or the sun. **76. bespake,** spoke. **85. lawn,** field or pasture. **86. Or ere,** before. **88. than,** then. **89. the mighty Pan,** Christ. The Greek god Pan, the deity of universal nature, was frequently identified in the Renaissance poetry with Christ. **92. silly,** simple, innocent. **95. strook,** struck. **97. noise,** harmonious sound. **98. took,** captivated, bewitched. **100. close,** cadence. **102–03. the hollow round of Cynthia's seat,** the sphere of the moon. **thrilling,** penetrating.

Now was almost won
To think her part was done,
And that her reign had here its last fulfilling;
She knew such harmony alone
Could hold all Heaven and Earth in happier union.

At last surrounds their sight
A globe of circular light,
That with long beams the shame-faced night arrayed;
The helmèd cherubim
And swordèd seraphim
Are seen in glittering ranks with wings displayed,
Harping in loud and solemn quire,
With unexpressive notes to Heaven's new-born Heir.

Such music (as 'tis said)
Before was never made,
But when of old the Sons of Morning sung,
While the Creator great
His constellations set,
And the well-balanced world on hinges hung,
And cast the dark foundations deep,
And bid the weltering waves their oozy channel keep.

Ring out, ye crystal spheres!
Once bless our human ears,
If ye have power to touch our senses so;
And let your silver chime
Move in melodious time;
And let the bass of heaven's deep organ blow;
And with your ninefold harmony
Make up full consort to the angelic symphony.

For, if such holy song
Enwrap our fancy long,
Time will run back and fetch the Age of Gold;
And speckled Vanity
Will sicken soon and die;
And leprous Sin will melt from earthly mould;
And Hell itself will pass away,
And leave her dolorous mansions to the peering day.

Yea, Truth and Justice then
Will down return to men,
Orbed in a rainbow; and, like glories wearing,
Mercy will sit between,
Throned in celestial sheen,
With radiant feet the tissued clouds down steering;
And Heaven, as at some festival,
Will open wide the gates of her high palace-hall.

But wisest Fate says No,
This must not yet be so,
The Babe lies yet in smiling infancy,
That on the bitter cross
Must redeem our loss,
So both himself and us to glorify:
Yet first to those ychained in sleep,
The wakeful trump of doom must thunder through the deep,

With such a horrid clang
As on Mount Sinai rang,
While the red fire and smould'ring clouds outbrake:
The agèd Earth aghast
With terror of that blast
Shall from the surface to the centre shake;
When at the world's last session,
The dreadful Judge in middle air shall spread his throne.

And then at last our bliss
Full and perfect is,
But now begins; for from this happy day
The old Dragon under ground
In straiter limits bound,
Not half so far casts his usurpèd sway,
And, wroth to see his kingdom fail,
Swinges the scaly horror of his folded tail.

The oracles are dumb,
No voice or hideous hum
Runs through the archèd roof in words deceiving.
Apollo from his shrine
Can no more divine,
With hollow shriek the steep of Delphos leaving.

107. alone, of itself, without the aid of "Nature" and her system of spheres and so forth. **116. unexpressive,** inexpressible. **119–24. the Sons of Morning sung . . . keep.** See Job 38, page 312. **125–27. Ring out . . . so.** "Let the music made by the turning of the nine celestial spheres become for once audible to human ears."—Hanford **132. consort to,** union with. **133–48. For, if such holy song . . . palace-hall.** Milton here makes a composite picture of the Christian millennium at the end of the world (Revelation 20–22) and the Golden Age of classical mythology, in which Astraea, goddess of justice, "will down return to man." **136. speckled,** plague-spotted.

143. like, similar. **146. tissued,** as if made of "tissue," a cloth interwoven with silver. **155. ychained,** chained. The "y," as often in Chaucer, is a survival of the Old English past-participial prefix, "ge." **sleep,** death. **156. The wakeful trump of doom.** The awakening trumpet of the Day of Doom. **157. horrid,** terrifying. **158. As on Mount Sinai.** See Exodus 19:16. **168. The old Dragon,** Satan. See Revelation 12:9 **172. Swinges,** lashes. **173–80. The oracles . . . cell.** Milton refers to the legend that at the time of Christ's birth pagan oracles ceased to make prophecies. **178. Delphos,** Delphi, the seat of the famous oracle of Apollo.

No nightly trance or breathèd spell
Inspires the pale-eyed priest from the prophetic cell.

The lonely mountains o'er,
And the resounding shore,
A voice of weeping heard, and loud lament;
From haunted spring and dale,
Edged with poplar pale,
The parting Genius is with sighing sent,
With flower-inwoven tresses torn
The nymphs in twilight shade of tangled thickets mourn.

In consecrated earth,
And on the holy hearth,
The Lars and Lemures moan with midnight plaint;
In urns and altars round,
A drear and dying sound
Affrights the Flamens at their service quaint;
And the chill marble seems to sweat,
While each peculiar power forgoes his wonted seat.

Peor and Baälim
Forsake their temples dim,
With that twice-battered god of Palestine;
And moonèd Ashtaroth,
Heaven's queen and mother both,
Now sits not girt with tapers' holy shine;
The Libyc Hammon shrinks his horn,
In vain the Tyrian maids their wounded Thammuz mourn.

And sullen Moloch fled,
Hath left in shadows dread
His burning idol all of blackest hue;
In vain with cymbals' ring
They call the grisly king,
In dismal dance about the furnace blue;
The brutish gods of Nile as fast,
Isis and Orus, and the dog Anubis, haste.

Nor is Osiris seen
In Memphian grove or green,
Trampling the unshowered grass with lowings loud;
Nor can he be at rest
Within his sacred chest;
Nought but profoundest Hell can be his shroud;
In vain, with timbrelled anthems dark,
The sable-stolèd sorcerers bear his worshipped ark.

He feels from Juda's land
The dreaded Infant's hand;
The rays of Bethlehem blind his dusky eyn;
Nor all the gods beside
Longer dare abide,
Not Typhon huge ending in snaky twine:
Our Babe, to show his Godhead true,
Can in his swaddling bands control the damnèd crew.

So, when the sun in bed,
Curtained with cloudy red,
Pillows his chin upon an orient wave,
The flocking shadows pale
Troop to the infernal jail,
Each fettered ghost slips to his several grave,
And the yellow-skirted fays
Fly after the night-steeds, leaving their moon-loved maze.

But see! the Virgin blest
Hath laid her Babe to rest.
Time is our tedious song should here have ending:

186. Genius, the guardian spirit of a locality. **191. The Lars and Lemures,** in Roman mythology the household gods and spirits of the dead. **194. the Flamens at their service quaint,** the priests at their curious (or elaborate) service. **195. marble seems to sweat,** as a portent of the ill fate about to overtake the gods (**marble,** statue). **197–204. Peor and Baälim . . . mourn.** This and the next two stanzas are specially interesting as anticipating Milton's treatment of the demons in *Paradise Lost.* **Peor** is one of the sun gods, called Baals or **Baälim** (the Hebrew masculine plural), whose shrine was on Mount Peor in Moab. See Numbers 23:28. **199. that twice-battered god,** Dagon, the fish god, whose image was thrown down twice before the Ark of the Covenant. See I Samuel 5:4 and *Paradise Lost,* Book I, ll. 457–66. **200. Ashtaroth,** the Hebrew feminine plural of Ashtoreth, or Astarte, identified with the moon. **203. Libyc Hammon,** or Ammon, the Egyptian deity, a ram god, whose shrine was in the Libyan desert. **204. Thammuz,** a Syrian god identified by the Greeks with Adonis, who was slain by a boar. See *Paradise Lost,* Book I, ll. 446–57. **205. Moloch,** a god of the Ammonites, in whose idol children were said to be burned. See *Paradise Lost,* Book I, l. 392.

212–13. Isis and Orus . . . Osiris. Isis was the sister and wife of Osiris, and mother of Orus (Horus). Isis was represented with cow's horns and the disk of the sun between them; Orus, with a hawk's head; and Osiris, the chief Egyptian deity, whose shrine was at Memphis, as a bull. **215. unshowered,** a reference to the lack of rain in Egypt. **220. his worshipped ark,** a small ark or chest in which a figure of the god was kept and carried in processions. **223. eyn,** the old plural of "eye." **226. Typhon,** the monster of Greek mythology, half man and half serpent, vanquished by Zeus and Hercules. **227–28. Our Babe . . . crew.** "The implication here is that Christ slew, or routed, Typhon, as Hercules strangled serpents in his cradle."—A. S. Cook. **231. orient,** lustrous, pearllike. **236. moon-loved maze,** the forests loved by Diana and the other gods.

Heaven's youngest-teemèd star
Hath fixed her polished car,
  Her sleeping Lord with handmaid lamp attending;
And all about the courtly stable
Bright-harnessed angels sit in order serviceable.

ON SHAKESPEARE

This poem, dated 1630 by Milton, was the first of his compositions to appear in print. It was among the commendatory poems prefixed to the Second Folio of Shakespeare's plays in 1632. It should be compared with Jonson's lines on Shakespeare in the First Folio, page 331, which perhaps suggested the theme to Milton. It is full of echoes from other poets, and the "conceit" in ll. 13–16 is in the best (or worst) manner of the fashionable verse of the time.

What needs my Shakespeare for his honoured bones
The labour of an age in pilèd stones?
Or that his hallowed reliques should be hid
Under a star-ypointing pyramid?
Dear son of memory, great heir of fame,
What need'st thou such weak witness of thy name?
Thou in our wonder and astonishment
Hast built thyself a livelong monument.
For whilst, to the shame of slow-endeavouring art,
Thy easy numbers flow, and that each heart
Hath from the leaves of thy unvalued book
Those Delphic lines with deep impression took,
Then thou, our fancy of itself bereaving,
Dost make us marble with too much conceiving,
And so sepùlchred in such pomp dost lie
That kings for such a tomb would wish to die.

HOW SOON HATH TIME

This sonnet was written either on or shortly after Milton's twenty-third birthday, December 9, 1631, and was first printed in 1645. He took his M.A. degree and left Cambridge about the time of its composition. Like other young men, he was faced with the problem of a future career, and was meeting with some criticism for not having already settled that problem. To a friend who had apparently expostulated with him for dreaming away his years "in the arms of studious retirement," Milton sent this sonnet, together with a letter which is preserved in the Trinity College MS. at Cambridge. "I am something suspicious of myself," he writes, "and do take notice of a certain belatedness in me," but he declares that his chief concern is the consideration of "how *best* to undergo, not taking thought of being *late*, so it give advantage to be more *fit*." For a similar expression of this philosophy of life see his sonnet "When I Consider How My Light Is Spent," page 392.

How soon hath Time, the subtle thief of youth,
  Stolen on his wing my three-and-twentieth year!
  My hasting days fly on with full career,
  But my late spring no bud or blossom shew'th.
Perhaps my semblance might deceive the truth
  That I to manhood am arrived so near;
  And inward ripeness doth much less appear,
  That some more timely-happy spirits endu'th.
Yet, be it less or more, or soon or slow,
  It shall be still in strictest measure even
  To that same lot, however mean or high,
Toward which Time leads me, and the will of Heaven.
  All is, if I have grace to use it so,
  As ever in my great Task-Master's eye.

L'ALLEGRO

The date of the two companion lyrics, "L'Allegro" and "Il Penseroso," is uncertain. Professor E. M. W. Tillyard assigns them to the summer of 1631 (*The Miltonic Setting*, Macmillan, 1938, p. 26), and recent scholarship connects them with Milton's university career rather than with the years of his retirement at Horton. They are the best known and best loved of Milton's poems. It has been estimated that more words, phrases, and expressions from them have entered into ordinary English speech than from any other poems of similar length.

The structure of the two poems follows the same general plan. They represent two contrasting, but not mutually exclusive or incompatible, poetic moods, and their author obviously takes as keen delight in depicting one series of experiences as the other. In them scholars have detected echoes of many poets and poems from Theocritus down to Milton's own contemporaries, but a comparison of Milton's lines and phrases with those of his suggested sources only serves to illustrate his genius

240. youngest-teemèd star, newest-born star (the star of Bethlehem). **243. courtly,** because serving as a king's residence. **244. Bright-harnessed,** in bright armor. *On Shakespeare.* **1, 6. What,** why. **3. reliques,** remains. **4. star-ypointing.** See note 155 on "ychained" on page 381. Milton has here prefixed the "y" to the present participle for the sake of the rhythm. **10. numbers,** verses. Milton contrasts Shakespeare's spontaneous genius with the labor and pain of conscious artists. Compare "L'Allegro," ll. 134–35. **11. unvalued,** invaluable. **12. Delphic,** inspired (as by the oracle of Apollo at Delphi). **14. conceiving,** thinking, imagining. Compare "Il Penseroso," l. 42.

5. semblance, outward appearance. **8. timely-happy,** happy in the early maturity of their powers. **endu'th,** endows, supplies with intellectual vigor. **9. it,** inward ripeness. **10. still,** always. **even,** conformable to. **13. All,** all the affairs of life.

and to emphasize the originality of his mind and art. "L'Allegro" is Italian for "The Cheerful Man."

Hence, loathèd Melancholy,
Of Cerberus and blackest Midnight born
In Stygian cave forlorn,
'Mongst horrid shapes, and shrieks, and sights unholy!
Find out some uncouth cell,
Where brooding Darkness spreads his jealous wings,
And the night-raven sings;
There, under ebon shades and low-browed rocks,
As ragged as thy locks,
In dark Cimmerian desert ever dwell.
But come, thou Goddess fair and free,
In heaven yclept Euphrosyne,
And by men heart-easing Mirth;
Whom lovely Venus, at a birth,
With two sister Graces more,
To ivy-crownèd Bacchus bore:
Or whether (as some sager sing)
The frolic wind that breathes the spring,
Zephyr, with Aurora playing,
As he met her once a-Maying,
There, on beds of violets blue,
And fresh-blown roses washed in dew,
Filled her with thee, a daughter fair,
So buxom, blithe, and debonair.
Haste thee, Nymph, and bring with thee
Jest, and youthful Jollity,
Quips and cranks and wanton wiles,
Nods and becks and wreathèd smiles,
Such as hang on Hebe's cheek,
And love to live in dimple sleek;
Sport that wrinkled Care derides,
And Laughter holding both his sides.
Come, and trip it, as you go,
On the light fantastic toe;
And in thy right hand lead with thee
The mountain-nymph, sweet Liberty;
And, if I give thee honour due,
Mirth, admit me of thy crew,
To live with her, and live with thee,
In unreprovèd pleasures free;
To hear the lark begin his flight,
And, singing, startle the dull night,
From his watch-tower in the skies,
Till the dappled dawn doth rise;
Then to come, in spite of sorrow,
And at my window bid good-morrow,
Through the sweet-briar or the vine,
Or the twisted eglantine;
While the cock, with lively din,
Scatters the rear of darkness thin;
And to the stack or the barn door,
Stoutly struts his dames before:
Oft listening how the hounds and horn
Cheerly rouse the slumbering morn,
From the side of some hoar hill,
Through the high wood echoing shrill:
Sometime walking, not unseen,
By hedgerow elms, on hillocks green,
Right against the eastern gate
Where the great sun begins his state,
Robed in flames and amber light,
The clouds in thousand liveries dight;
While the ploughman, near at hand,
Whistles o'er the furrowed land,
And the milkmaid singeth blithe,
And the mower whets his scythe,
And every shepherd tells his tale
Under the hawthorn in the dale.
Straight mine eye hath caught new pleasures,
Whilst the landskip round it measures:
Russet lawns, and fallows grey,
Where the nibbling flocks do stray;
Mountains on whose barren breast
The labouring clouds do often rest;
Meadows trim with daisies pied;
Shallow brooks, and rivers wide;
Towers and battlements it sees
Bosomed high in tufted trees,
Where perhaps some beauty lies,
The cynosure of neighbouring eyes.

1. Melancholy. The genealogy is invented by the poet. **2. Cerberus,** the three-headed watchdog of Hades. **3. Stygian cave.** The cave of Cerberus was on the Styx, one of the four rivers of Hades. **5. uncouth,** unfamiliar, uncanny. **10. Cimmerian.** The Cimmerians, according to Homer, dwelt in "eternal cloud and darkness" beyond the "ocean-stream." **12. yclept,** called. For the prefix "y" see note 155 on page 381. **19. Zephyr . . . Aurora,** the west wind and the dawn. Milton again invents the genealogy to suit his own purposes. **24. buxom,** gracious, lively. **debonair,** courteous. **27. Quips and cranks,** witty turns of speech. **29. Hebe's.** Hebe was goddess of youth and cupbearer of the gods.

40. unreprovèd, innocent. **45–53. Then to come . . .** This is a much-disputed passage. "To come" would seem to be co-ordinate with "To live" in l. 39, "To hear" in l. 41, and "oft listening" in l. 53. **48. twisted eglantine.** Since eglantine is another name for the sweetbrier, it is commonly assumed that Milton here means the woodbine or honeysuckle. **55. hoar.** "Grey from absence of foliage."—*New English Dictionary* **57. not unseen.** See the contrasting circumstance in "Il Penseroso," l. 65. **59. against,** toward. **60. state,** stately progress. **62. dight,** arrayed. **67. tells his tale,** counts his number (of sheep). **70. landskip,** an old spelling of "landscape." **71. fallows,** plowed fields. **75. pied,** of variegated colors. **80. cynosure,** literally, "dog's tail." The name was given to the Polestar, by which ancient seamen guided their ships; hence, an object of attention by reason of its brilliancy or position.

Hard by a cottage chimney smokes
From betwixt two aged oaks,
Where Corydon and Thyrsis met
Are at their savoury dinner set
Of herbs and other country messes,
Which the neat-handed Phillis dresses;
And then in haste her bower she leaves,
With Thestylis to bind the sheaves;
Or, if the earlier season lead,
To the tanned haycock in the mead.
Sometimes, with secure delight,
The upland hamlets will invite,
When the merry bells ring round,
And the jocund rebecks sound
To many a youth and many a maid
Dancing in the chequered shade,
And young and old come forth to play
On a sunshine holiday,
Till the livelong daylight fail:
Then to the spicy nut-brown ale:
With stories told of many a feat,
How Faery Mab the junkets eat.
She was pinched and pulled, she said;
And he, by friar's lantern led,
Tells how the drudging goblin sweat
To earn his cream-bowl duly set,
When in one night, ere glimpse of morn,
His shadowy flail hath threshed the corn
That ten day-labourers could not end;
Then lies him down, the lubber fiend,
And, stretched out all the chimney's length
Basks at the fire his hairy strength,
And crop-full out of doors he flings,
Ere the first cock his matin rings.
Thus done the tales, to bed they creep,
By whispering winds soon lulled asleep.
Towered cities please us then,
And the busy hum of men,
Where throngs of knights and barons bold,
In weeds of peace, high triumphs hold,
With store of ladies, whose bright eyes
Rain influence, and judge the prize
Of wit or arms, while both contend
To win her grace whom all commend.
There let Hymen oft appear
In saffron robe, with taper clear,
And pomp, and feast, and revelry,
With mask and antique pageantry;
Such sights as youthful poets dream
On summer eves by haunted stream.
Then to the well-trod stage anon,
If Jonson's learnèd sock be on,
Or sweetest Shakespeare, Fancy's child,
Warble his native wood-notes wild.
And ever, against eating cares,
Lap me in soft Lydian airs,
Married to immortal verse,
Such as the meeting soul may pierce,
In notes with many a winding bout
Of linkèd sweetness long drawn out
With wanton heed and giddy cunning,
The melting voice through mazes running,
Untwisting all the chains that tie
The hidden soul of harmony;
That Orpheus' self may heave his head
From golden slumber on a bed
Of heaped Elysian flowers, and hear
Such strains as would have won the ear
Of Pluto to have quite set free
His half-regained Eurydice.
These delights if thou canst give,
Mirth, with thee I mean to live.

83–88. Corydon . . . Thyrsis . . . Phillis . . . Thestylis, type names in pastoral poetry for shepherds and shepherdesses. **87. bower,** cottage. **91. secure,** carefree. **94. rebecks,** primitive fiddles. **102. junkets,** sweet curds. **103–04. She . . . he,** individuals in the company. **friar's lantern,** jack-o'-lantern, will-o'-the-wisp. **105. the drudging goblin,** Robin Goodfellow of the country legends, referred to frequently as Hobgoblin. **110. lubber,** clumsy, drudging. **111. chimney's,** that is, the fireplace's. **113. crop-full,** with a full stomach. **114. matin,** morning song. **117. Towered cities.** The passage which follows shifts the scene to the city, and describes typical experiences there. **120. weeds,** garments. **triumphs,** festivals. **121. store,** abundance. **122. Rain influence,** an astrological term, referring to the power of the stars over human beings.

125. Hymen, the god of marriage, a common figure in masques. **132. sock.** See note 36–37 on page 332. **136. Lydian.** The Lydian "mode" of ancient music was characterized by softness and delicacy, in contrast to the Dorian (stateliness) and the Phrygian (liveliness). **138. meeting,** responsive. **pierce,** then pronounced "perse." **139. bout,** turn, passage. **145–50. Orpheus . . . Eurydice,** the legendary poet and musician of Thrace, who, when his wife **Eurydice** died, descended to the underworld to seek her. He so charmed **Pluto** by his music that he gained her release on condition that he should not look back at her on the return journey through the shades. Unable to restrain himself, he looked behind him, and lost her. **Elysian.** Orpheus is represented as with the shades of the blessed in Elysium.

IL PENSEROSO

Milton very probably received suggestions for his poem from Robert Burton's "The Author's Abstract of Melancholy," prefixed in 1628 to his *Anatomy of Melancholy*. The "melancholy" of "Il Penseroso," however, is not that of the *Anatomy*, with its brood of mental, spiritual, and physical disturbances. "As employed in this poem," says Professor Hanford, "it designates a pensive and contemplative mood favorable to reverie and to the more inward kind of poetic feeling." "Il Penseroso" is seventeenth-century Italian for "The Meditative Man."

Hence, vain deluding Joys,
  The brood of Folly without father bred!
How little you bested,
  Or fill the fixed mind with all your toys;
Dwell in some idle brain,
  And fancies fond with gaudy shapes possess,
As thick and numberless
  As the gay motes that people the sunbeams,
Or likest hovering dreams,
  The fickle pensioners of Morpheus' train.
But, hail! thou Goddess sage and holy,
Hail, divinest Melancholy!
Whose saintly visage is too bright
To hit the sense of human sight,
And therefore to our weaker view
O'erlaid with black, staid Wisdom's hue;
Black, but such as in esteem
Prince Memnon's sister might beseem,
Or that starred Ethiop queen that strove
To set her beauty's praise above
The Sea-Nymphs, and their powers offended.
Yet thou art higher far descended:
Thee bright-haired Vesta long of yore
To solitary Saturn bore;
His daughter she; in Saturn's reign
Such mixture was not held a stain.
Oft in glimmering bowers and glades
He met her, and in secret shades
Of woody Ida's inmost grove,
Whilst yet there was no fear of Jove.
Come, pensive Nun, devout and pure,
Sober, steadfast, and demure,
All in a robe of darkest grain,
Flowing with majestic train,
And sable stole of cypress lawn
Over thy decent shoulders drawn.
Come; but keep thy wonted state,
With even step, and musing gait,
And looks commercing with the skies,
Thy rapt soul sitting in thine eyes:
There, held in holy passion still,
Forget thyself to marble, till
With a sad leaden downward cast
Thou fix them on the earth as fast.
And join with thee calm Peace and Quiet,
Spare Fast, that oft with gods doth diet,
And hears the Muses in a ring
Aye round about Jove's altar sing;
And add to these retirèd Leisure,
That in trim gardens takes his pleasure;
But, first and chiefest, with thee bring
Him that yon soars on golden wing,
Guiding the fiery-wheelèd throne,
The Cherub Contemplation;
And the mute Silence hist along,
'Less Philomel will deign a song,
In her sweetest, saddest plight,
Smoothing the rugged brow of Night,
While Cynthia checks her dragon yoke,
Gently o'er the accustomed oak.
Sweet bird that shunn'st the noise of folly,
Most musical, most melancholy!
Thee, chauntress, oft the woods among
I woo, to hear thy even-song;
And, missing thee, I walk unseen
On the dry smooth-shaven green
To behold the wandering moon,
Riding near her hightest noon,
Like one that had been led astray
Through the heaven's wide pathless way,
And oft, as if her head she bowed,
Stooping through a fleecy cloud.
Oft, on a plat of rising ground,
I hear the far-off curfew sound,
Over some wide-watered shore,
Swinging slow with sullen roar;
Or, if the air will not permit,
Some still removèd place will fit,
Where glowing embers through the room
Teach light to counterfeit a gloom,
Far from all resort of mirth,
Save the cricket on the hearth,
Or the bellman's drowsy charm
To bless the doors from nightly harm.
Or let my lamp, at midnight hour,

1. vain deluding Joys. It is to be noted that these are not exactly identical with the pleasures invoked and described in "L'Allegro," nor is the mood that is the theme of "Il Penseroso" the "loathèd Melancholy" of its companion poem. **3. bested,** bestead, avail. **6. fond,** foolish. **10. pensioners,** retinue. **14. hit,** to be congenial or endurable to. **18. Prince Memnon's sister,** Hemera, sister of the beautiful Ethiopian prince who fought with the Trojans (*Odyssey*, Book XI, l. 552). **19. that starred Ethiop queen,** Cassiopeia, mother of Andromeda, whose boasting about her beauty and that of her daughter led to a feud with the Nereids. After death they were placed in the constellations that bear their names. **23–24. Vesta . . . Saturn.** The genealogy is Milton's own, and represents pensiveness as springing from Vesta, the chaste goddess of the hearth, and Saturn, the solitary god and introducer of civilization. There are implications of the moroseness supposed by the astrologers to be the result of the influence of the planet Saturn, and of the golden age of Saturn's reign, brought to an end by the aggressive Jove (l. 30). **29. Ida's inmost grove,** Mt. Ida on the island of Crete, home of Saturn and birthplace of Jupiter, noted for its forests. **33. grain,** color, in this case probably dark purple. **35. stole,** shawl or veil. **cypress lawn,** black linen or crape. **36. decent,** comely.

37. state, stateliness, dignity. **39. commercing,** communing. **43. sad,** sober, serious. **54. The Cherub Contemplation.** Milton has given the name "Contemplation" to one of the cherubs of Ezekiel's vision. See Ezekiel 10. **55. hist along,** bring along silently. **56. Philomel,** the nightingale. **59. Cynthia,** the moon. **73. plat,** plot.

Be seen in some high lonely tower,
Where I may oft outwatch the Bear,
With thrice great Hermes, or unsphere
The spirit of Plato, to unfold
What worlds or what vast regions hold
The immortal mind that hath forsook
Her mansion in this fleshly nook;
And of those demons that are found
In fire, air, flood, or underground,
Whose power hath a true consent
With planet or with element.
Sometime let gorgeous Tragedy
In sceptred pall come sweeping by,
Presenting Thebes, or Pelops' line,
Or the tale of Troy divine,
Or what (though rare) of later age
Ennobled hath the buskined stage,
  But, O sad Virgin! that thy power
Might raise Musaeus from his bower;
Or bid the soul of Orpheus sing
Such notes as, warbled to the string,
Drew iron tears down Pluto's cheek,
And made Hell grant what love did seek;
Or call up him that left half-told
The story of Cambuscan bold,
Of Camball, and of Algarsife,
And who had Canace to wife,
That owned the virtuous ring and glass,
And of the wondrous horse of brass
On which the Tartar king did ride;
And if aught else great bards beside
In sage and solemn tunes have sung,
Of tourneys, and of trophies hung,
Of forests, and enchantments drear,
Where more is meant than meets the ear.
Thus, Night, oft see me in thy pale career,

87. the Bear, the constellation of the Great Dipper, which in northern latitudes does not set, but disappears only with dawn. **88–89. thrice great Hermes,** Hermes Trismegistus, as the Greeks called the Egyptian Thoth, the god of wisdom. **unsphere The spirit of Plato,** bring down from its sphere the spirit of Plato, greatest of philosophers and exponent of the theory of the immortality of the soul. **95. a true consent,** a complete agreement; another reference to astrology. **98. sceptred pall,** royal robe. Ancient tragedy concerned itself chiefly with the "falls of princes." **99–100. Thebes . . . Pelops' line . . . Troy,** allusions to the chief themes of Greek tragedy and epic poetry. **102. buskined.** See the note on Jonson's "To the Memory of . . . Shakespeare," l. 36 (page 332). **104. Musaeus,** a mythical Greek poet, sometimes referred to as the son of Orpheus. See "L'Allegro," l. 145. **110–15. The story of Cambuscan . . . ride,** Chaucer's unfinished "Squire's Tale." Cambuscan (Ghengis Khan), the Tatar king, is represented as the father of two sons, Camball and Algarsife, and a daughter, Canace. The father and the daughter received from the king of Arabia and India the magic gifts here mentioned. Chaucer left untold the name of him "who had Canace to wife." **116–20. And if aught else . . . ear.** The passage probably refers to such works as Spenser's *Faerie Queene* with its allegories, "where more is meant than meets the ear."

Till civil-suited Morn appear,
Not tricked and frounced, as she was wont
With the Attic boy to hunt,
But kerchieft in a comely cloud,
While rocking winds are piping loud,
Or ushered with a shower still,
When the gust hath blown his fill,
Ending on the rustling leaves,
With minute-drops from off the eaves.
And, when the sun begins to fling
His flaring beams, me, Goddess, bring
To archèd walks of twilight groves,
And shadows brown, that Sylvan loves,
Of pine, or monumental oak,
Where the rude axe with heavèd stroke
Was never heard the nymphs to daunt,
Or fright them from their hallowed haunt.
There, in close covert, by some brook,
Where no profaner eye may look,
Hide me from day's garish eye,
While the bee with honeyed thigh,
That at her flowery work doth sing,
And the waters murmuring,
With such consort as they keep,
Entice the dewy-feathered Sleep.
And let some strange mysterious dream
Wave at his wings, in airy stream
Of lively portraiture displayed,
Softly on my eyelids laid;
And, as I wake, sweet music breathe
Above, about, or underneath,
Sent by some Spirit to mortals good,
Or the unseen Genius of the wood.
But let my due feet never fail
To walk the studious cloister's pale,
And love the high embowèd roof,
With antique pillars massy-proof,
And storied windows richly dight,
Casting a dim religious light.
There let the pealing organ blow,
To the full-voiced quire below,
In service high and anthems clear,

122. civil-suited, quietly dressed, in contrast with the flaming "liveries" of the morning in "L'Allegro," l. 62. **123. tricked and frounced,** adorned and becurled like a fop. **124. the Attic boy,** Cephalus of Attica, of whom Eos, goddess of the dawn, became enamored. **130. minute-drops,** drops falling at intervals of a minute. **134. Sylvan,** the woodland god, Sylvanus. See Spenser's *Faerie Queene*, Book I, Canto 6. **145. consort,** company. **147–50. And let . . . laid.** "Let some dream float with undulating motion (*i.e. wave*) at the wings of Sleep, amid a stream of vivid pictures which rest lightly on the eyelids."—Verity **154. Genius,** guardian spirit. **155. due,** accustomed, expected. **156. pale,** enclosure. **157. embowèd,** vaulted. **158. massy-proof,** proof against mass, strong enough to support the roof. **159. storied,** with stained glass representing episodes from the Bible. **dight,** adorned.

As may with sweetness, through mine ear,
Dissolve me into ecstasies,
And bring all Heaven before mine eyes.
And may at last my weary age
Find out the peaceful hermitage,
The hairy gown and mossy cell,
Where I may sit and rightly spell
Of every star that heaven doth shew,
And every herb that sips the dew,
Till old experience do attain
To something like prophetic strain.
These pleasures, Melancholy, give;
And I with thee will choose to live.

ON TIME

In the Trinity College MS. at Cambridge, where this poem is written in Milton's hand, a subtitle, later crossed out, states that the lines were "to be set on a clock case."

Fly, envious Time, till thou run out thy race:
Call on the lazy leaden-stepping Hours,
Whose speed is but the heavy plummet's pace;
And glut thyself with what thy womb devours,
Which is no more than what is false and vain,
And merely mortal dross;
So little is our loss,
So little is thy gain!
For, when as each thing bad thou hast entombed,
And, last of all, thy greedy self consumed,
Then long Eternity shall greet our bliss
With an individual kiss;
And Joy shall overtake us as a flood,
When every thing that is sincerely good
And perfectly divine,
With Truth, and Peace, and Love, shall ever shine
About the supreme throne
Of him, to whose happy-making sight alone
When once our heavenly-guided soul shall climb,
Then, all this earthly grossness quit,
Attired with stars we shall for ever sit,
Triumphing over Death, and Chance, and thee,
O Time!

AT A SOLEMN MUSIC

The theme of the poem is essentially that of the Platonic doctrine of the music of the spheres sung by the celestial Sirens, which cannot be heard by the gross ears of sinful humanity. With the Platonic elements are mingled, as Professor Tillyard points out, the mythology and mysticism of the Old and New Testaments. Milton's aspiration to hear and "answer that melodious noise," and his contemplation of heaven and immortality, are characteristic of his early thought, and a foreshadowing of the philosophy of his later poetry.

Blest pair of Sirens, pledges of Heaven's joy,
Sphere-born harmonious sisters, Voice and Verse,
Wed your divine sounds, and mixed power employ,
Dead things with inbreathed sense able to pierce;
And to our high-raised phantasy present
That undisturbèd song of pure concent,
Aye sung before the sapphire-coloured throne
To him that sits thereon,
With saintly shout and solemn jubilee;
Where the bright Seraphim in burning row
Their loud uplifted angel-trumpets blow,
And the Cherubic host in thousand quires
Touch their immortal harps of golden wires,
With those just Spirits that wear victorious palms,
Hymns devout and holy psalms
Singing everlastingly:
That we on Earth, with undiscording voice,
May rightly answer that melodious noise;
As once we did, till disproportioned sin
Jarred against nature's chime, and with harsh din
Broke the fair music that all creatures made
To their great Lord, whose love their motion swayed
In perfect diapason, whilst they stood
In first obedience, and their state of good.
O, may we soon again renew that song,
And keep in tune with Heaven, till God ere long
To his celestial consort us unite,
To live with him, and sing in endless morn of light!

170. spell, study, ponder. **3. the heavy plummet's pace.** The allusion is to the weight of lead suspended on a string, which operated the works of the clock. **12. individual,** undividable. "The kiss symbolizes the union of the 'individual soul For ever happy' (*P. L.*, V, 610–11) to God."—M. Y. Hughes **16. Truth, and Peace, and Love.** Compare "On the Morning of Christ's Nativity," ll. 141–44 (page 381). **20. quit,** discarded.

1–2. Blest pair of Sirens . . . Voice and Verse. Milton mentions only two of the eight Sirens described by Plato at the close of his *Republic*, and gives them names of his own devising. **5. phantasy,** imagination. **6. concent,** harmony. **7. the sapphire-coloured throne,** from the vision described in Ezekiel 1:26. **10. burning,** shining. **14. those just Spirits,** a reference to the redeemed souls in heaven as St. John saw them in his vision, Revelation 7:9. **16. Singing everlastingly.** See Revelation 14:3–4. The song is known only to the pure in heart. **18. rightly answer,** sing in complete accord with. **23. perfect diapason,** the "concord of the octave"; the entire compass of harmonious tones. The words are used in both a literal and a spiritual sense. **24. In first obedience . . . good,** an interesting anticipation of the theme of *Paradise Lost*. **27. consort,** company of musicians

LYCIDAS

"Lycidas" appeared first in 1638 in a volume of memorial verses on Edward King, a college mate of Milton's who was drowned off the coast of Wales on August 10, 1637. Milton and King were probably not close friends, but the untimely death of a young poet gave Milton an opportunity to lament the uncertainty of life, to question the value of long and earnest preparation for a career which might be cut short just as it was beginning, and to attack the unworthy members of the clergy of the Church of England. In form the poem shows Milton's familiarity with the pastoral elegies of the Greeks—Theocritus, Bion, and Moschus—and the pastoral poetry of Virgil, but it is in no real sense a slavish imitation of the classic elegy or of any of the Renaissance forms which were based on that type of elegy. "Lycidas" is the happiest illustration in the language of the combination of tradition and individual talent, of passionate feeling kept in check by a highly developed sense of form.

In This Monody the Author Bewails a Learned Friend, Unfortunately Drowned in His Passage from Chester on the Irish Seas, 1637; and, by Occasion, Foretells the Ruin of Our Corrupted Clergy, Then in Their Height.

Yet once more, O ye laurels, and once more,
Ye myrtles brown, with ivy never sere,
I come to pluck your berries harsh and crude,
And with forced fingers rude
Shatter your leaves before the mellowing year.
Bitter constraint, and sad occasion dear
Compels me to disturb your season due;
For Lycidas is dead, dead ere his prime,
Young Lycidas, and hath not left his peer.
Who would not sing for Lycidas? he knew
Himself to sing, and build the lofty rhyme.
He must not float upon his watery bier
Unwept, and welter to the parching wind,
Without the meed of some melodious tear.
Begin, then, Sisters of the sacred well
That from beneath the seat of Jove doth spring;
Begin, and somewhat loudly sweep the string.
Hence with denial vain and coy excuse.
So may some gentle Muse
With lucky words favour my destined urn,
And as he passes turn,
And bid fair peace be to my sable shroud!
For we were nursed upon the self-same hill,
Fed the same flock, by fountain, shade, and rill.
Together both, ere the high lawns appeared
Under the opening eyelids of the Morn,
We drove a-field, and both together heard
What time the gray-fly winds her sultry horn,
Battening our flocks with the fresh dews of night,
Oft till the star that rose, at evening, bright
Toward heaven's descent had sloped his westering wheel.
Meanwhile the rural ditties were not mute;
Tempered to the oaten flute,
Rough Satyrs danced, and Fauns with cloven heel
From the glad sound would not be absent long;
And old Damoetas loved to hear our song.
But, oh! the heavy change, now thou art gone,
Now thou art gone and never must return!
Thee, Shepherd, thee the woods and desert caves,
With wild thyme and the gadding vine o'ergrown,
And all their echoes, mourn.
The willows, and the hazel copses green,
Shall now no more be seen
Fanning their joyous leaves to thy soft lays.
As killing as the canker to the rose,
Or taint-worm to the weanling herds that graze,
Or frost to flowers, that their gay wardrobe wear,
When first the white-thorn blows;
Such, Lycidas, thy loss to shepherd's ear.

1–2. **Yet once more.** An interval of four years separates "Lycidas" from *Comus,* Milton's most ambitious poem before "Lycidas." **laurels . . . myrtles . . . ivy,** evergreens with which poets were traditionally crowned. The lines are interesting as suggestive both of Milton's reluctance to write and of his chief concern in the poem with the poet's calling. **brown,** in the sense of dark. **never sere,** ever green. **3–5. I come . . . year,** before my genius has been matured by time. **6. dear,** keenly felt. **8. Lycidas,** a typical shepherd's name in the pastoral elegies. **9. peer,** equal. **10. knew,** knew how. **13. welter,** toss about. King's body was never recovered. **14. meed,** tribute. **melodious tear,** a conventional figure for elegiac verse. **15–16. Sisters . . . spring,** the Muses, to whom certain springs (wells) were sacred. Compare *Paradise Lost,* Book I, l. 11.

17. somewhat loudly, "allegro ma non troppo," as it were! **18. coy,** modest. **19–22. So may some gentle Muse . . . shroud!** an obscure passage which has been variously interpreted. Mr. G. M. Gathorne-Hardy, writing in the London *Times Literary Supplement,* Jan. 18, 1934, suggests that the poet's meaning is that since Lycidas is denied an ordinary funeral, the poem now being written shall take its place. "My destined urn" would then mean "the memorial I am now, under inspiration of the Muses, preparing for Lycidas. . . . Similarly the shroud, at an earlier stage of the funeral procession, in which Lycidas is metaphorically envisaged as 'passing.' 'He' [l. 21] is Lycidas." A more usual but less satisfactory interpretation is that "Muse" in l. 19 must be read "poet," and that Milton is expressing the wish that after his death some poet will write memorial verses for him as he is now writing them for King. **23–36. the self-same hill . . . song,** conventionally pastoral references to Milton's associations with King at Cambridge. **27–28. heard What time the gray-fly,** heard the gray-fly when. **sultry,** in the heat of noon. **29. Battening,** feeding. **32. rural ditties,** a reference probably to their undergraduate poetical exercises. **33. Tempered,** modulated. **36. Damoetas,** another type name from pastoral poetry. Possibly the reference is to some tutor at the university. **40. gadding,** straggling. **45. canker,** the canker worm. **48. white-thorn,** hawthorn.

Where were ye, Nymphs, when the remorseless deep
Closed o'er the head of your loved Lycidas?
For neither were ye playing on the steep
Where your old bards, the famous Druids, lie,
Nor on the shaggy top of Mona high,
Nor yet where Deva spreads her wizard stream.
Ay me! I fondly dream
"Had ye been there," . . . for what could that have done?
What could the Muse herself that Orpheus bore,
The Muse herself, for her enchanting son,
Whom universal nature did lament,
When, by the rout that made the hideous roar,
His gory visage down the stream was sent,
Down the swift Hebrus to the Lesbian shore?
  Alas! what boots it with uncessant care
To tend the homely, slighted, shepherd's trade,
And strictly meditate the thankless Muse?
Were it not better done, as others use,
To sport with Amaryllis in the shade,
Or with the tangles of Neaera's hair?
Fame is the spur that the clear spirit doth raise
(That last infirmity of noble mind)
To scorn delights, and live laborious days;
But the fair guerdon when we hope to find,
And think to burst out into sudden blaze,
Comes the blind Fury with the abhorrèd shears,
And slits the thin-spun life. "But not the praise,"
Phoebus replied, and touched my trembling ears:
"Fame is no plant that grows on mortal soil,

50. Nymphs. The sea nymphs are here identified, as in other pastoral elegies, with the Muses. **52. steep,** mountain. **53. Druids,** the minstrel-priests of the ancient Celts of Britain. **54. Mona,** the Roman name for the isle of Anglesey, off the Welsh coast. **55. Deva,** the river Dee, which flows between England and Wales into the Irish Sea. The adjective **wizard** indicates the supernatural associations connected with the stream. **56. fondly,** foolishly. **58. the Muse,** Calliope, the Muse of epic poetry. **59. enchanting,** given to use enchantments. **61. the rout,** the band of frenzied women of Thrace who, because of Orpheus' slight to them after the loss of Eurydice, tore him in pieces. The story is found in Ovid's *Metamorphoses*, Book XI, ll. 1–60. **64–84. Alas! what boots it . . . meed."** Milton digresses from his principal theme to consider whether the incessant labor and pain of the poet's preparation are, after all, worth while. **boots,** profits. **65. shepherd's trade,** the writing of verse. **66. meditate the . . . Muse,** to give oneself to the composition of poetry. Milton borrows the phrase from Virgil. **67. use,** are accustomed to do. **68–69. Amaryllis . . . Neaera's,** typical names of maidens in pastoral poetry. **70. clear,** pure, noble. **71. (That last infirmity,** that is, the last to be abandoned. **73. guerdon,** reward. **75. blind Fury.** In classical mythology it is Atropos, one of the three Fates, who cuts the thread of life. Milton has purposely identified the Fates with the Furies here to re-enforce the idea of the blind and senseless working of the forces which carried young King off. **77. Phoebus,** Apollo, god of poetic inspiration. **touched my trembling ears,** a Virgilian figure meaning to recall something to one's mind.

Nor in the glistering foil
Set off to the world, nor in broad rumour lies,
But lives and spreads aloft by those pure eyes,
And perfect witness of all-judging Jove;
As he pronounces lastly on each deed,
Of so much fame in heaven expect thy meed."
  O fountain Arethuse, and thou honoured flood,
Smooth-sliding Mincius, crowned with vocal reeds,
That strain I heard was of a higher mood.
But now my oat proceeds,
And listens to the Herald of the Sea
That came in Neptune's plea.
He asked the waves, and asked the felon winds,
What hard mishap hath doomed this gentle swain?
And questioned every gust of rugged wings
That blows from off each beakèd promontory.
They knew not of his story;
And sage Hippotades their answer brings;
That not a blast was from his dungeon strayed,
The air was calm, and on the level brine
Sleek Panope with all her sisters played.
It was that fatal and perfidious bark,
Built in the eclipse, and rigged with curses dark,
That sunk so low that sacred head of thine.
  Next, Camus, reverend sire, went footing slow,
His mantle hairy, and his bonnet sedge,
Inwrought with figures dim, and on the edge
Like to that sanguine flower inscribed with woe.
"Ah! who hath reft," quoth he, "my dearest pledge?"
Last came, and last did go,
The Pilot of the Galilean Lake;
Two massy keys he bore of metals twain
(The golden opes, the iron shuts amain).

79. glistering foil, glittering gold or silver leaf, placed under transparent gems to enhance their brilliance. **82. perfect witness of all-judging Jove.** Compare 1 Samuel 16:7: "The Lord seeth not as man seeth; for man looketh on the outward appearance, but the Lord looketh on the heart." **85–86. fountain Arethuse . . . Mincius.** Arethusa, a spring in Sicily, the country of Theocritus, represents the Greek tradition of pastoral poetry, as Mincius, the river near which Virgil was born, does the Latin. **88. oat,** the shepherd's pipe of oat straw. **89–90. the Herald of the Sea,** Triton, the herald and agent of Neptune, who comes **in Neptune's plea** of innocence of the guilt of having drowned Lycidas. **96. Hippotades,** Aeolus (son of Hippotes), god of the winds. **99. Panope,** one of the fifty Nereids, or sea nymphs. **101. the eclipse,** the proverbial omen of ill fortune. **103. Camus,** a personification of the river Cam, which flows through Cambridge. **106. sanguine,** literally, "bloody." The flower referred to is the purple hyacinth, named for the youth Hyacinthus, slain by Apollo. The hyacinth was reputed to be marked *ai, ai* (woe! woe!). **107. reft,"** snatched away. **pledge?"** child. **109. The Pilot,** St. Peter, the legendary keeper of the keys of heaven. See Matthew 16:19. He is introduced here as the earthly founder and chief pastor of the Church, of which young King was to have been a pastor (shepherd). **111. amain,** with force.

He shook his mitred locks, and stern bespake:—
"How well could I have spared for thee, young swain,
Enow of such as, for their bellies' sake,
Creep, and intrude, and climb into the fold!
Of other care they little reckoning make
Than how to scramble at the shearers' feast,
And shove away the worthy bidden guest.
Blind mouths! that scarce themselves know how to hold
A sheep-hook, or have learnt aught else the least
That to the faithful herdman's art belongs!
What recks it them? What need they? They are sped;
And, when they list, their lean and flashy songs
Grate on their scrannel pipes of wretched straw;
The hungry sheep look up, and are not fed,
But, swoln with wind and the rank mist they draw,
Rot inwardly, and foul contagion spread;
Besides what the grim wolf with privy paw
Daily devours apace, and nothing said.
But that two-handed engine at the door
Stands ready to smite once, and smite no more."
Return, Alpheus; the dread voice is past
That shrunk thy streams; return, Sicilian Muse,
And call the vales, and bid them hither cast
Their bells and flowerets of a thousand hues.
Ye valleys low, where the mild whispers use
Of shades, and wanton winds, and gushing brooks,
On whose fresh lap the swart star sparely looks,
Throw hither all your quaint enamelled eyes,
That on the green turf suck the honeyed showers,
And purple all the ground with vernal flowers.
Bring the rathe primrose that forsaken dies,
The tufted crow-toe, and pale jessamine,
The white pink, and the pansy freaked with jet,
The glowing violet,
The musk rose, and the well-attired woodbine,
With cowslips wan that hang the pensive head,
And every flower that sad embroidery wears;
Bid amaranthus all his beauty shed,
And daffadillies fill their cups with tears,
To strew the laureate hearse where Lycid lies.
For so, to interpose a little ease,
Let our frail thoughts dally with false surmise.
Ay me! whilst thee the shores and sounding seas
Wash far away, where'er thy bones are hurled;
Whether beyond the stormy Hebrides,
Where thou perhaps under the whelming tide
Visit'st the bottom of the monstrous world;
Or whether thou, to our moist vows denied,
Sleep'st by the fable of Bellerus old,
Where the great Vision of the guarded mount
Looks toward Namancos and Bayona's hold.
Look homeward, Angel, now, and melt with ruth:
And, O ye dolphins, waft the hapless youth.
Weep no more, woeful shepherds, weep no more,
For Lycidas, your sorrow, is not dead,
Sunk though he be beneath the watery floor.
So sinks the day-star in the ocean bed,
And yet anon repairs his drooping head,
And tricks his beams, and with new-spangled ore
Flames in the forehead of the morning sky:
So Lycidas sunk low, but mounted high,
Through the dear might of Him that walked the waves,
Where, other groves and other streams along,
With nectar pure his oozy locks he laves,
And hears the unexpressive nuptial song,
In the blest kingdoms meek of joy and love.
There entertain him all the Saints above,
In solemn troops, and sweet societies,
That sing, and singing in their glory move,
And wipe the tears for ever from his eyes.
Now, Lycidas, the shepherds weep no more;
Henceforth thou art the Genius of the shore,

112. mitred, wearing a miter (as a bishop). **114. Enow,** enough. **115–27. Creep . . . spread.** For an interesting analysis of this passage see Ruskin, *Sesame and Lilies*, Secs. 20–24. **122. What recks it them?** What matters it to them? **They are sped,** they have succeeded in getting what they wanted. **124. scrannel,** thin, harsh. **126. rank,** pestilential. **128. the grim wolf,** the Roman Catholic Church. **privy paw,** secret proselytizing. **130. that two-handed engine,** i.e., requiring two hands to wield. Just what particular "engine" or instrument of reform was referred to by Milton is uncertain. The two Houses of Parliament have been suggested, among others. The figure seems to imply a sword or ax, and may have been suggested by such Biblical passages as Revelation 1:16 and Matthew 3:10. **132. Alpheus,** a river whose god was the lover of Arethusa, referred to in l. 85. The invocation to Alpheus and the **Sicilian Muse** signifies Milton's return to the pastoral strain after the digression on the corruption of the Church. **136. use,** are accustomed to dwell. **138. swart star,** the Dog Star, Sirius, whose baleful influence blasts or makes "swart" the summer's flowers. **sparely,** rarely. **139. quaint enamelled eyes,** pretty varicolored blossoms. **142. rathe,** early.

151. hearse, bier. **153. frail,** unable or unwilling to face the fact that the body of Lycidas is not on a flower-decked bier, but tossing in the sea. **158. monstrous,** teeming with monsters. **159. moist vows,** tearful devotions. **160. fable of Bellerus,** of the abode of the fabulous Bellerus—Land's End, the southwestern extremity of England. **161. the guarded mount,** St. Michael's Mount in Cornwall, under the protection of the sword of St. Michael the Archangel. **162. Namancos and Bayona's hold,** in Spain; **hold,** stronghold. **163. Look homeward,** be on guard against internal enemies and dangers. **168. day-star,** the sun. **170. tricks,** dresses. **ore,** gold, radiance. **176. unexpressive,** inexpressible. Compare "At a Solemn Music," ll. 27–28 (page 388). **nuptial song,** at "the marriage supper of the Lamb." See Revelation 19:9. **183. Genius,** guardian spirit.

In thy large recompense, and shalt be good
To all that wander in that perilous flood.

Thus sang the uncouth swain to the oaks and rills,
While the still morn went out with sandals grey:
He touched the tender stops of various quills,
With eager thought warbling his Doric lay:
And now the sun had stretched out all the hills,
And now was dropt into the western bay;
At last he rose, and twitched his mantle blue:
To-morrow to fresh woods, and pastures new.

SONNETS

WHEN I CONSIDER

This sonnet seems to have been written in the early days of Milton's total blindness, and is therefore assigned by Tillyard to 1652, or a slightly later date.

When I consider how my light is spent
  Ere half my days in this dark world and wide,
  And that one talent which is death to hide
  Lodged with me useless, though my soul more bent
To serve therewith my Maker, and present
  My true account, lest He returning chide,
  "Doth God exact day-labour, light denied?"
  I fondly ask. But Patience, to prevent
That murmur, soon replies, "God doth not need
  Either man's work or his own gifts. Who best
  Bear his mild yoke, they serve him best. His state
Is kingly: thousands at his bidding speed,
  And post o'er land and ocean without rest;
  They also serve who only stand and wait."

ON THE LATE MASSACRE IN PIEMONT

"Piemont" is the French form of "Piedmont," now a part of Italy. In 1655, the Waldensians, a Protestant religious sect living in the Piedmontese Alps, were cruelly persecuted by the Duke of Savoy. A wave of indignation swept over England, which elicited official protests from Cromwell, and called forth this most vigorous of Milton's sonnets.

Avenge, O Lord, thy slaughtered saints, whose bones
  Lie scattered on the Alpine mountains cold;
  Even them who kept thy truth so pure of old,
  When all our fathers worshipped stocks and stones,
Forget not: in thy book record their groans
  Who were thy sheep, and in their ancient fold
  Slain by the bloody Piemontese, that rolled
  Mother with infant down the rocks. Their moans
The vales redoubled to the hills, and they
  To heaven. Their martyred blood and ashes sow
  O'er all the Italian fields, where still doth sway
The triple Tyrant; that from these may grow
  A hundredfold, who, having learnt thy way,
  Early may fly the Babylonian woe.

CYRIACK, THIS THREE YEARS' DAY

This sonnet was probably written in 1655, to Cyriack Skinner, a former pupil of Milton's who had become one of his most intimate friends.

Cyriack, this three years' day these eyes, though clear
  To outward view of blemish or of spot,
  Bereft of light, their seeing have forgot;
  Nor to their idle orbs doth sight appear
Of sun, or moon, or star, throughout the year,
  Or man, or woman. Yet I argue not
  Against Heaven's hand or will, nor bate a jot
  Of heart or hope; but still bear up and steer
Right onward. What supports me, dost thou ask?
  The conscience, friend, to have lost them overplied
  In Liberty's defence, my noble task,
Of which all Europe talks from side to side.
  This thought might lead me through the world's vain mask
  Content, though blind, had I no better guide.

186. uncouth, in the original sense of unknown, or rustic. **189. Doric,** the dialect in which the Sicilian pastoral poets wrote. **3. that one talent.** See Matthew 25:14–30. Compare the determination expressed in his sonnet "How Soon Hath Time," ll. 9–14 (page 383). **8. fondly,** foolishly. **12. thousands . . . speed,** the angelic messengers.

On the Late Massacre in Piemont. **3. them who kept . . . of old.** The Waldensians had from the twelfth century maintained the simple practices of the primitive Christians. **4. all our fathers,** the Englishmen and Europeans of pre-Reformation days. **stocks and stones,** images of wood and stone. **5. thy book,** the Book of Life. See Revelation 20:12. **12. The triple Tyrant,** the Pope, who wears a tiara with three crowns. **14. the Babylonian woe,** the punishment reserved for the Church of Rome. The seventeenth-century Protestants identified the Babylon of the Book of Revelation with the Roman Catholic Church. See Revelation 14:8; 17:5; and 18:2. *Cyriack, This Three Years' Day.* **1. this three years' day,** for the past three years. **8. bear up,** a nautical term, meaning "to put the helm 'up' so as to bring the vessel into the direction of the wind."—*New English Dictionary* **10. conscience,** consciousness. **11. my noble task.** Milton refers to his *Defence of the English People*, 1651, which he had given his days and nights to, despite his physicians' orders and warnings. **14. had I no better guide,** that is, than my faith in God and my consciousness of Divine approval.

METHOUGHT I SAW

This is Milton's last sonnet, written supposedly soon after the death in childbirth of his second wife, Katherine Woodcock, in February, 1658. He had presumably never seen her, as he married her several years after he had lost his sight.

Methought I saw my late espousèd saint
 Brought to me like Alcestis from the grave,
 Whom Jove's great son to her glad husband gave,
 Rescued from Death by force, though pale and faint.
Mine, as whom washed from spot of child-bed taint
 Purification in the Old Law did save,
 And such as yet once more I trust to have
 Full sight of her in Heaven without restraint,
Came vested all in white, pure as her mind.
 Her face was veiled; yet to my fancied sight
 Love, sweetness, goodness, in her person shined
So clear as in no face with more delight.
 But, oh! as to embrace me she inclined,
 I waked, she fled, and day brought back my night.

from PARADISE LOST

From his nineteenth year, at least, Milton had the ambition to write a great poem in his native language, and by the time he returned from Italy in 1639 he had resolved to do for his own nation something of what Virgil had done for ancient Rome, and Tasso and Ariosto for Italy. King Arthur was his first hero, but the more Milton studied the records of the ancient British chieftain, the less he felt drawn to the subject. Other ideas came to him as he read, and in the Trinity MS. at Cambridge there are listed some ninety-nine possible subjects, about two-thirds of which have to do with Biblical themes. It is as material for dramatic treatment that they were jotted down, and there are rather detailed outlines of a projected drama on the subject of the Fall of Man. After years of consideration, Milton finally discarded the dramatic for the epic form, and of all the subjects pondered over he chose that which he made the theme of *Paradise Lost*. "Long choosing, and beginning late," as he says near the beginning of Book IX, he completed the poem probably in 1663, when he was fifty-four years old. It was first published in 1667.

Paradise Lost, however considered, is one of the world's greatest poetical compositions. In theme, in scope, and in the success of its execution, it has no equal in English, nor perhaps in any other language. As an epic poem, it conforms in general to the requirements and conventions of the classical epic, without which, of course, it could not have been fashioned. If it misses something of the formal perfection of Virgil's *Aeneid*, it makes up for the loss in depth of religious thought and feeling. The spiritual horizon of mankind was larger and wider in seventeenth-century England than in Augustan Rome, even if it was a good deal less clear.

The elements of *Paradise Lost* are drawn from all Milton's experience and all his reading and thinking. The Biblical matter is supplemented by illustrations and interpretations from rabbinical writings. The Christian material is a composite of modern and medieval, Protestant and patristic, doctrines and dogmas. The Hebraic and the Christian elements are fused and molded in accordance with a thorough knowledge of the Greek and Latin classics and an artistic sense derived from their study.

Paradise Lost is, more than any other poem ever written perhaps, cosmological in setting and theme. Milton was aware of and accepted the implications of the Copernican theory of the universe, as his spokesman, the Archangel Raphael, indicates on occasion; but for philosophical and poetic reasons he chooses as his mise en scène the old Ptolemaic universe of nine concentric spheres with the earth at its center. He is purposely indefinite in his cosmic spaces and dimensions, and does not attempt to be altogether consistent in such details as he does supply. For all its cosmic scope, however, embracing as it does all time—past, present, and future—and all conceivable space, the poem has, in many respects, a surprisingly local and intimate quality. The whole starry universe of our world, in which Man is the most important creature, hangs suspended by a golden chain from the floor of Heaven. Man is the center of the attention of all the powers of Heaven and of all the devils of Hell.

The purpose of the poem is to "assert Eternal Providence" with respect to man, and to "justify the ways of God to men." All the characters of the poem, from the Almighty Father and the Divine Son to the humblest angels in the heavenly hierarchy, are part of the grand plot which centers in the two human beings in the Garden. In every real sense, therefore, the hero of the piece is Man, created, preserved, counseled, punished, and restored by Divine Power; tempted, betrayed, and banished from Paradise through the machinations of the incomparable and irresistible Satan, the villain of the poem. Like Shakespeare's Iago, Milton's Satan is, from the point of view of dramatic interest, the author's most brilliant creation. "The greatness of Iago," said Professor Raleigh, "is shown in this—that Othello never loses our sympathy." Something of that same sympathy, and for a similar reason, may be claimed for Milton's Adam and Eve. The excerpts from the poem given here

1. saint, in the sense of a soul in heaven. **2. Alcestis,** the wife of Admetus, king of Thessaly, who offered to die for her husband, but was rescued from death by Hercules, son of Zeus. Milton is thought to have in mind the *Alcestis* of Euripides.

6. Purification in the Old Law. See Leviticus 12:2–8

present Milton's account of the supernatural forces which converged on his hero and heroine in their happy garden, their fall, and their expulsion into the workaday world of toil and pain and hope.

*The Verse**

The measure is English heroic verse without rime, as that of Homer in Greek, and of Virgil in Latin—rime being no necessary adjunct or true ornament of poem or good verse, in longer works especially, but the invention of a barbarous age, to set off wretched matter and lame metre; graced indeed since by the use of some famous modern poets, carried away by custom, but much to their own vexation, hindrance, and constraint to express many things otherwise, and for the most part worse, than else they would have expressed them. Not without cause, therefore, some both Italian and Spanish poets of prime note have rejected rime both in longer and shorter works, as have also long since our best English tragedies, as a thing of itself, to all judicious ears, trivial and of no true musical delight; which consists only in apt numbers, fit quantity of syllables, and the sense variously drawn out from one verse into another, not in the jingling sound of like endings—a fault avoided by the learned ancients both in poetry and all good oratory. This neglect then of rime so little is to be taken for a defect, though it may seem so perhaps to vulgar readers, that it rather is to be esteemed an example set, the first in English, of ancient liberty recovered to heroic poem from the troublesome and modern bondage of riming.

BOOK I

The Argument

This First Book proposes, first in brief, the whole subject: Man's disobedience, and the loss thereupon of Paradise, wherein he was placed: then touches the prime cause of his fall—the Serpent, or rather Satan in the Serpent; who, revolting from God, and drawing to his side many legions of Angels, was by the command of God driven out of Heaven with all his crew into the great Deep. Which action passed over, the poem hastens into the midst of things; presenting Satan with his Angels now fallen into Hell—described here, not in the Center (for Heaven and Earth may be supposed as yet not made, certainly not yet accursed), but in a place of utter darkness, fitliest called Chaos: here Satan with his Angels lying on the burning lake, thunder-struck and astonished, after a certain space recovers, as from confusion; calls up him who, next in order and dignity, lay by him; they confer of their miserable fall. Satan awakens all his legions, who lay till then in the same manner confounded. They rise: their numbers, array of battle, their chief leaders named, according to the idols known afterwards in Canaan and the countries adjoining. To these Satan directs his speech; comforts them with hope yet of regaining Heaven; but tells them lastly of a new world and new kind of creature to be created, according to an ancient prophecy or report in Heaven; for that Angels were long before this visible creation was the opinion of many ancient Fathers. To find out the truth of this prophecy, and what to determine thereon, he refers to a full council. What his associates thence attempt. Pandemonium, the palace of Satan, rises, suddenly built out of the Deep: the infernal peers there sit in council.

Of man's first disobedience, and the fruit
Of that forbidden tree, whose mortal taste
Brought death into the world, and all our woe,
With loss of Eden, till one greater Man
Restore us, and regain the blissful seat,
Sing, Heavenly Muse, that, on the secret top
Of Oreb or of Sinai, didst inspire
That shepherd, who first taught the chosen seed
In the beginning how the Heavens and Earth
Rose out of Chaos; or, if Sion hill
Delight thee more, and Siloa's brook that flowed
Fast by the oracle of God, I thence
Invoke thy aid to my adventurous song,
That with no middle flight intends to soar
Above the Aonian mount, while it pursues
Things unattempted yet in prose or rhyme.
And chiefly thou, O Spirit, that dost prefer
Before all temples the upright heart and pure,
Instruct me, for thou know'st; thou from the first
Wast present, and, with mighty wings outspread,

*Milton's forthright statement of why his verse is unrhymed was not in the first edition of 1667, but was added in 1668. It contains obvious hits at Dryden, who was the chief defender of rhyme. Milton's contention that his epic is the first important English poem of a nondramatic type written in blank verse is substantially true, as only a few scattered nondramatic pieces in unrhymed pentameter had appeared before *Paradise Lost*.

***The Argument*, the subject matter of what follows.**

2. mortal, deadly. **5. seat,** abode. **6. Sing, Heavenly Muse.** The invocation, or address to the Muse of poetry, is an epic convention, which Milton borrows from Virgil and the classic authors. Milton identifies the Muse of the classical epics with the Holy Spirit of the Bible and Christian theology. **secret,** remote, and therefore mysterious. **7. Oreb . . . Sinai.** Oreb (Horeb) and Sinai are mountains or mountain ranges on which Moses received communications from God. **8. That shepherd,** Moses. See Exodus 3 and 19–31. **9–10. In the beginning . . . Chaos.** See Genesis 1. The first five books of the Bible were supposed to have been written by Moses. **Sion,** one of the hills on which Jerusalem was built, and thus the abode of David, the "sweet singer of Israel." **12. Fast by,** close by. **the oracle,** Solomon's temple. **15. the Aonian mount,** Helicon, the mountain of the classic Muses. Milton is contrasting his great theme with the more earthly subjects of the classic poets. **16. rhyme.** Milton seems to distinguish between "rhyme" as meaning "verse" and "rime" (see "The Verse," first column of this page), "the jingling sound of like endings." **17. thou, O Spirit, the Holy Spirit of the New Testament.**

Dove-like sat'st brooding on the vast Abyss,
And mad'st it pregnant: what in me is dark,
Illumine; what is low, raise and support;
That to the highth of this great argument
I may assert Eternal Providence,
And justify the ways of God to men.
  Say first—for Heaven hides nothing from Thy view,
Nor the deep tract of Hell—say first what cause
Moved our grand parents, in that happy state,
Favoured of Heaven so highly, to fall off
From their Creator, and transgress his will
For one restraint, lords of the world besides.
Who first seduced them to that foul revolt?
  The infernal Serpent; he it was, whose guile,
Stirred up with envy and revenge, deceived
The Mother of Mankind, what time his pride
Had cast him out from Heaven, with all his host
Of rebel Angels, by whose aid, aspiring
To set himself in glory above his peers,
He trusted to have equalled the Most High,
If he opposed; and with ambitious aim
Against the throne and monarchy of God
Raised impious war in Heaven, and battle proud,
With vain attempt. Him the Almighty Power
Hurled headlong flaming from the ethereal sky,
With hideous ruin and combustion, down
To bottomless perdition; there to dwell
In adamantine chains and penal fire,
Who durst defy the Omnipotent to arms.
  Nine times the space that measures day and night
To mortal men, he with his horrid crew
Lay vanquished, rolling in the fiery gulf,
Confounded, though immortal. But his doom
Reserved him to more wrath; for now the thought
Both of lost happiness and lasting pain
Torments him; round he throws his baleful eyes,
That witnessed huge affliction and dismay,
Mixed with obdúrate pride and stedfast hate.
At once, as far as Angels ken, he views
The dismal situation waste and wild:
A dungeon horrible on all sides round
As one great furnace flamed; yet from those flames
No light; but rather darkness visible
Served only to discover sights of woe,
Regions of sorrow, doleful shades, where peace
And rest can never dwell, hope never comes
That comes to all; but torture without end
Still urges, and a fiery deluge, fed
With ever-burning sulphur unconsumed.
Such place Eternal Justice had prepared
For those rebellious; here their prison ordained
In utter darkness, and their portion set,
As far removed from God and light of Heaven,
As from the center thrice to the utmost pole.
Oh, how unlike the place from whence they fell!
There the companions of his fall, o'erwhelmed
With floods and whirlwinds of tempestuous fire,
He soon discerns, and, weltering by his side,
One next himself in power and next in crime,
Long after known in Palestine and named
Beëlzebub. To whom the Arch-Enemy,—
And thence in Heaven called Satan,—with bold words
Breaking the horrid silence, thus began:
  "If thou beest he,—but O, how fallen! how changed
From him, who, in the happy realms of light,
Clothed with transcendent brightness, didst outshine
Myriads though bright!—if he, whom mutual league,
United thoughts and counsels, equal hope
And hazard in the glorious enterprise,
Joined with me once, now misery hath joined
In equal ruin; into what pit, thou seest,
From what highth fallen! so much the stronger proved
He with his thunder; and till then who knew
The force of those dire arms? Yet not for those,
Nor what the potent Victor in his rage
Can else inflict, do I repent or change,
Though changed in outward lustre, that fixed mind,
And high disdain from sense of injured merit,

21. Dove-like sat'st brooding, a happy combination of the New Testament conception of the Holy Spirit "descending like a dove" (Matthew 3:16) and the statement in Genesis 1:2, "the Spirit of God moved upon the face of the waters." **24. highth,** the older form of the word. **argument,** subject. **25. assert,** vindicate, defend. **29. grand,** first, original. **32. For,** because of. **besides,** in all other respects. **34. The infernal Serpent.** Milton is here anticipating the final condition and appearance of Satan, a very different appearance from that of the great archangel of Books I and II. **36. what time,** at the time when. **39. his peers,** his equals, the other archangels. **50–53. Nine times the space . . . immortal.** Milton in Book VI, l. 871, represents the angels as having fallen for nine days, after which for nine days they **lay vanquished. doom,** judgment. **56. baleful,** woeful, full of pain. **59. as far as Angels ken,** as far as the knowledge and perceptive faculties of angels extend.

68. urges, afflicts, presses on. **72. utter,** outer. Milton represents Hell as being at the farthest remove from Heaven. **74. from the center . . . pole.** Milton seems to imply that the distance from Heaven (or the Empyrean) to the gate of Hell is three times the radius of the starry universe. The vast and indeterminate region called Chaos is represented as extending round and below the universe. Hell, the region "prepared for the devil and his angels," is at the bottom of Chaos. **78. weltering,** rolling about. **82. Satan.** *Satan* in Hebrew means "adversary" or "opposer." **93. He,** God. **thunder,** thunderbolt.

That with the Mightiest raised me to contend,
And to the fierce contention brought along
Innumerable force of spirits armed,
That durst dislike his reign, and, me preferring,
His utmost power with adverse power opposed
In dubious battle on the plains of Heaven,
And shook his throne. What though the field be lost?
All is not lost; the unconquerable will,
And study of revenge, immortal hate,
And courage never to submit or yield:
And what is else not to be overcome?
That glory never shall his wrath or might
Extort from me. To bow and sue for grace
With suppliant knee, and deify his power,
Who, from the terror of this arm, so late
Doubted his empire,—that were low indeed,
That were an ignominy and shame beneath
This downfall; since, by fate, the strength of gods
And this empyreal substance cannot fail;
Since, through experience of this great event,
In arms not worse, in foresight much advanced,
We may with more successful hope resolve
To wage by force or guile eternal war,
Irreconcilable to our grand Foe,
Who now triùmphs, and in the excess of joy
Sole reigning holds the tyranny of Heaven."
 So spake the apostate Angel, though in pain,
Vaunting aloud, but racked with deep despair;
And him thus answered soon his bold compeer:
 "O Prince! O Chief of many thronèd Powers!
That led the embattled Seraphim to war
Under thy conduct, and, in dreadful deeds
Fearless, endangered Heaven's perpetual King,
And put to proof his high supremacy,
Whether upheld by strength, or chance, or fate!
Too well I see and rue the dire event
That with sad overthrow and foul defeat
Hath lost us Heaven, and all this mighty host
In horrible destruction laid thus low,
As far as gods and Heavenly essences
Can perish: for the mind and spirit remains

104. In dubious battle. The description of the war in Heaven occurs in Book VI. **107. study,** pursuit, endeavor. **109. And what . . . overcome?** The line, somewhat obscure, is interpreted by Verity: "To retain one's hate, one's courage, etc., is not that to be still unsubdued: in what else but this lies the test of being not overcome?" **110. That glory,** the glory which would redound to God from Satan's submission. **114. Doubted his empire,** doubted whether his power were still his. **127. compeer,** companion. **129. Seraphim.** Milton throughout the poem uses such terms as "Seraphim," "Cherubim," "archangel," and so on loosely, both to obtain variety and to avoid the limitations that would be imposed by a strict adherence to the angelic hierarchy of the medieval Schoolmen. **134. event,** outcome. **138. essences,** beings.

Invincible, and vigour soon returns,
Though all our glory extinct, and happy state
Here swallowed up in endless misery.
But what if he our Conqueror (whom I now
Of force believe almighty, since no less
Than such could have o'erpowered such force as ours)
Have left us this our spirit and strength entire,
Strongly to suffer and support our pains,
That we may so suffice his vengeful ire;
Or do him mightier service, as his thralls
By right of war, whate'er his business be,
Here in the heart of Hell to work in fire,
Or do his errands in the gloomy Deep?
What can it then avail, though yet we feel
Strength undiminished, or eternal being
To undergo eternal punishment?"
 Whereto with speedy words the Arch-Fiend replied:—
"Fallen Cherub, to be weak is miserable,
Doing or suffering: but of this be sure—
To do aught good never will be our task,
But ever to do ill our sole delight,
As being the contrary to his high will
Whom we resist. If then his providence
Out of our evil seek to bring forth good,
Our labour must be to pervert that end,
And out of good still to find means of evil;
Which ofttimes may succeed, so as perhaps
Shall grieve him, if I fail not, and disturb
His inmost counsels from their destined aim.
But see! the angry Victor hath recalled
His ministers of vengeance and pursuit
Back to the gates of Heaven; the sulphurous hail,
Shot after us in storm, o'erblown hath laid
The fiery surge, that from the precipice
Of Heaven received us falling; and the thunder,
Winged with red lightning and impetuous rage,
Perhaps hath spent his shafts, and ceases now
To bellow through the vast and boundless Deep.
Let us not slip the occasion, whether scorn
Or satiate fury yield it from our foe.
Seest thou yon dreary plain, forlorn and wild,
The seat of desolation, void of light,
Save what the glimmering of these livid flames
Casts pale and dreadful? Thither let us tend
From off the tossing of these fiery waves,
There rest, if any rest can harbour there,

144. Of force, of necessity. **148. suffice,** satisfy. **152. Deep?** Chaos. **156. Arch-Fiend.** The old meaning of "fiend" is "one who hates"—the opposite of "friend." **158. suffering,** enduring. **165. still,** always. **167. fail,** mistake. **176. his,** its. **178. slip,** let slip. **179. satiate,** satiated.

And, reassembling our afflicted powers,
Consult how we may henceforth most offend
Our Enemy, our own loss how repair,
How overcome this dire calamity,
What reinforcement we may gain from hope,
If not what resolution from despair."
  Thus Satan, talking to his nearest mate,
With head uplift above the wave, and eyes
That sparkling blazed; his other parts besides
Prone on the flood, extended long and large,
Lay floating many a rood, in bulk as huge
As whom the fables name of monstrous size,
Titanian, or Earth-born, that warred on Jove,
Briareos or Typhon, whom the den
By ancient Tarsus held, or that sea-beast
Leviathan, which God of all his works
Created hugest that swim the ocean-stream;
Him, haply, slumbering on the Norway foam,
The pilot of some small night-foundered skiff
Deeming some island, oft, as seamen tell,
With fixèd anchor in his scaly rind
Moors by his side under the lee, while night
Invests the sea, and wishèd morn delays:
So stretched out huge in length the Arch-Fiend lay,
Chained on the burning lake; nor ever thence
Had risen, or heaved his head, but that the will
And high permission of all-ruling Heaven
Left him at large to his own dark designs,
That with reiterated crimes he might
Heap on himself damnation, while he sought
Evil to others, and, enraged, might see
How all his malice served but to bring forth
Infinite goodness, grace, and mercy, shewn
On Man by him seduced; but on himself
Treble confusion, wrath, and vengeance poured.
  Forthwith upright he rears from off the pool
His mighty stature; on each hand the flames
Driven backward slope their pointing spires, and rolled
In billows, leave in the midst a horrid vale.
Then with expanded wings he steers his flight
Aloft, incumbent on the dusky air
That felt unusual weight; till on dry land
He lights—if it were land that ever burned
With solid, as the lake with liquid fire,
And such appeared in hue; as when the force
Of subterranean wind transports a hill
Torn from Pelorus, or the shattered side
Of thundering Aetna, whose combustible
And fuelled entrails thence conceiving fire,
Sublimed with mineral fury, aid the winds,
And leave a singèd bottom all involved
With stench and smoke: such resting found the sole
Of unblest feet. Him followed his next mate,
Both glorying to have scaped the Stygian flood
As gods, and by their own recovered strength,
Not by the sufferance of supernal power.
  "Is this the region, this the soil, the clime,"
Said then the lost Archangel, "this the seat
That we must change for Heaven? this mournful gloom
For that celestial light? Be it so, since he
Who now is sovran can dispose and bid
What shall be right: farthest from him is best,
Whom reason hath equalled, force hath made supreme
Above his equals. Farewell, happy fields,
Where joy for ever dwells! Hail, horrors! hail,
Infernal world! and thou, profoundest Hell,
Receive thy new possessor; one who brings
A mind not to be changed by place or time.
The mind is its own place, and in itself
Can make a Heaven of Hell, a Hell of Heaven.
What matter, where, if I be still the same,
And what I should be, all but less than he
Whom thunder hath made greater? Here at least
We shall be free; the Almighty hath not built
Here for his envy, will not drive us hence:
Here we may reign secure; and in my choice
To reign is worth ambition, though in Hell:
Better to reign in Hell than serve in Heaven.
But wherefore let we then our faithful friends,
The associates and copartners of our loss,
Lie thus astonished on the oblivious pool,
And call them not to share with us their part

186. afflicted, overthrown. **powers,** forces (the other angels). **187. offend,** do violence to. **197. As whom,** as those whom. **198–99. Titanian . . . Briareos or Typhon.** The Titans were the older deities of Greek mythology, who waged war on the usurper Zeus (or Jove). The Giants were the offspring of Ge (Earth). Briareos, a hundred-handed Giant, assisted Zeus in his battle with the Titans. Typhon, a fire-breathing giant, with a hundred heads, after a fearful struggle with Zeus was subdued by thunderbolts, and was buried in Tartarus under Mt. Aetna. **201. Leviathan,** a reference to the mysterious sea monster of the Bible, and probably to Isaiah 27:1. Milton, in common with others of his day, doubtless thought of it as a whale. **204. night-foundered,** overtaken by night. **207. lee,** sheltered side. **208. Invests,** clothes, covers. **209. in length.** Notice that it is only in length or bulk, not in appearance, that Satan resembles the sea monster. **217–18. to bring forth . . . mercy.** In Book XII Adam in a vision is shown how the Redemption of man is to be accomplished. **223. spires,** tongues of flame.

226. incumbent, lying upon. **232–33. Pelorus . . . Aetna,** mountains in Sicily, the latter the famous volcano. **235. Sublimed,** a technical term from alchemy, meaning here "turned to flame." **238. next,** nearest. **241. sufferance,** permission. **248. Whom reason hath equalled.** Satan likes to think that in every respect but power he is quite equal to God. **251. profoundest,** lowest. **254. its,** one of the few occasions on which Milton uses this word. **257. all but less than he,** second only to him (God). **266. astonished,** thunderstruck, dazed. **oblivious,** producing forgetfulness.

In this unhappy mansion, or once more,
With rallied arms, to try what may be yet
Regained in Heaven, or what more lost in Hell?"
  So Satan spake, and him Beëlzebub
Thus answered: "Leader of those armies bright
Which but the Omnipotent none could have foiled,
If once they hear that voice, their liveliest pledge
Of hope in fears and dangers—heard so oft
In worst extremes, and on the perilous edge
Of battle when it raged, in all assaults
Their surest signal—they will soon resume
New courage and revive, though now they lie
Grovelling and prostrate on yon lake of fire,
As we erewhile, astounded and amazed;
No wonder, fallen such a pernicious highth!"
  He scarce had ceased when the superior Fiend
Was moving toward the shore; his ponderous shield
Ethereal temper, massy, large, and round,
Behind him cast. The broad circumference
Hung on his shoulders like the moon, whose orb
Through optic glass the Tuscan artist views
At evening from the top of Fesole,
Or in Valdarno, to descry new lands,
Rivers, or mountains, in her spotty globe.
His spear—to equal which the tallest pine
Hewn on Norwegian hills, to be the mast
Of some great ammiral, were but a wand—
He walked with, to support uneasy steps
Over the burning marle, not like those steps
On Heaven's azure; and the torrid clime
Smote on him sore besides, vaulted with fire.
Nathless he so endured, till on the beach
Of that inflamèd sea he stood, and called
His legions, Angel forms, who lay entranced,
Thick as autumnal leaves that strew the brooks
In Vallombrosa, where the Etrurian shades
High over-arched embower; or scattered sedge
Afloat, when with fierce winds Orion armed
Hath vexed the Red-Sea coast, whose waves o'erthrew
Busiris and his Memphian chivalry,
While with perfidious hatred they pursued
The sojourners of Goshen, who beheld
From the safe shore their floating carcasses
And broken chariot wheels: so thick bestrewn,
Abject and lost lay these, covering the flood,
Under amazement of their hideous change.
He called so loud, that all the hollow deep
Of Hell resounded: "Princes, Potentates,
Warriors, the flower of Heaven, once yours, now lost,
If such astonishment as this can seize
Eternal spirits! Or have ye chosen this place
After the toil of battle to repose
Your wearied virtue, for the ease you find
To slumber here as in the vales of Heaven?
Or in this abject posture have ye sworn
To adore the Conqueror—who now beholds
Cherub and Seraph rolling in the flood,
With scattered arms and ensigns, till anon
His swift pursuers from Heaven gates discern
The advantage, and, descending, tread us down
Thus drooping, or with linkèd thunderbolts
Transfix us to the bottom of this gulf?—
Awake, arise, or be for ever fallen!"
  They heard, and were abashed, and up they sprung
Upon the wing, as when men wont to watch,
On duty sleeping found by whom they dread,
Rouse and bestir themselves ere well awake.
Nor did they not perceive the evil plight
In which they were, or the fierce pains not feel;
Yet to their General's voice they soon obeyed,
Innumerable. As when the potent rod
Of Amram's son, in Egypt's evil day,
Waved round the coast, up called a pitchy cloud
Of locusts, warping on the eastern wind,
That o'er the realm of impious Pharaoh hung
Like night, and darkened all the land of Nile:
So numberless were those bad Angels seen
Hovering on wing under the cope of Hell,
'Twixt upper, nether, and surrounding fires;
Till, as a signal given, the uplifted spear
Of their great Sultan waving to direct
Their course, in even balance down they light
On the firm brimstone, and fill all the plain:
A multitude like which the populous North
Poured never from her frozen loins, to pass
Rhene or the Danaw, when her barbarous sons
Came like a deluge on the South, and spread

281. amazed, stupefied, bewildered. **282. pernicious,** harmful, destructive. **285. Ethereal,** heavenly. **288. optic glass,** telescope. **the Tuscan artist,** Galileo, whom Milton had met at Florence. **289. Fesole,** Fiesole, on a hill overlooking Florence, in the valley of the Arno (**Valdarno**). **294. ammiral** (admiral), flagship. Milton preferred, when possible, to use the Italian forms or equivalents of certain English words. **296. marle,** soil. **299. Nathless,** nevertheless. **300. inflamèd,** flaming. **303. Vallombrosa,** "Shady Valley,"—about 18 miles from Florence. **305. Orion,** the constellation Orion, the rising and setting of which were attended often by severe storms. **306. Red-Sea.** The Hebrew original means "Reed Sea" or "Sea of Sedge," hence the **scattered sedge** of l. 304. **307. Busiris,** the name of a legendary Egyptian ruler; used here instead of the official title Pharaoh. **Memphian,** of Memphis, one of the capitals of Egypt. **chivalry,** in the sense of cavalry.

309. sojourners of Goshen, the Israelites. See Exodus 14. **312. Abject,** hurled down. **315–30. "Princes, Potentates . . . fallen!"** The irony of Satan's opening remarks is as clever as it is effective. **320. virtue,** valor. **339. Amram's son,** Moses. See Exodus 10:12–15. **340. pitchy,** black as pitch. **341. warping,** undulating. **345. cope,** covering, dome. **353. Rhene . . . Danaw,** Rhine, Danube. These rivers formed the boundary of the Roman Empire, which was invaded by the northern Teutonic tribes.

Beneath Gibraltar to the Libyan sands.
Forthwith, from every squadron and each band,
The heads and leaders thither haste where stood
Their great Commander; godlike shapes, and forms
Excelling human, princely Dignities,
And Powers that erst in Heaven sat on thrones;
Though of their names in Heavenly records now
Be no memorial, blotted out and rased
By their rebellion from the Books of Life.
Nor had they yet among the sons of Eve
Got them new names, till, wandering o'er the Earth,
Through God's high sufferance for the trial of man,
By falsities and lies the greatest part
Of mànkind they corrupted to forsake
God their Creator; and the invisible
Glory of him that made them, to transform
Oft to the image of a brute, adorned
With gay religions full of pomp and gold,
And devils to adore for deities:
Then were they known to men by various names,
And various idols through the heathen world.
  Say, Muse, their names then known, who first, who last,
Roused from the slumber on that fiery couch,
At their great Emperor's call, as next in worth,
Came singly where he stood on the bare strand,
While the promiscuous crowd stood yet aloof.
  The chief were those, who, from the pit of Hell
Roaming to seek their prey on earth, durst fix
Their seats long after next the seat of God,
Their altars by his altar, gods adored
Among the nations round, and durst abide
Jehovah thundering out of Sion, throned
Between the Cherubim: yea, often placed
Within his sanctuary itself their shrines,
Abominations; and with cursèd things
His holy rites and solemn feasts profaned,
And with their darkness durst affront his light.
  First Moloch, horrid king, besmeared with blood
Of human sacrifice, and parents' tears,
Though, for the noise of drums and timbrels loud,
Their children's cries unheard, that passed through fire
To his grim idol. Him the Ammonite
Worshipped in Rabba and her watery plain,
In Argob, and in Basan, to the stream
Of utmost Arnon. Nor content with such
Audacious neighbourhood, the wisest heart
Of Solomon he led by fraud to build
His temple right against the temple of God
On that opprobrious hill, and made his grove
The pleasant valley of Hinnom, Tophet thence
And black Gehenna called, the type of Hell.
  Next, Chemos, the obscene dread of Moab's sons,
From Aroar to Nebo and the wild
Of southmost Abarim; in Hesebon
And Horonaim, Seon's realm, beyond
The flowery dale of Sibma clad with vines,
And Elealè to the Asphaltic Pool—
Peor his other name, when he enticed
Israel in Sittim, on their march from Nile,
To do him wanton rites, which cost them woe.
Yet thence his lustful orgies he enlarged
Even to that hill of scandal, by the grove
Of Moloch homicide, lust hard by hate;
Till good Josiah drove them thence to Hell.
With these came they who, from the bordering flood
Of old Euphrates to the brook that parts
Egypt from Syrian ground, had general names
Of Baälim and Ashtaroth—those male,
These feminine. For spirits, when they please,
Can either sex assume, or both; so soft
And uncompounded is their essence pure,
Not tied or manacled with joint or limb,
Nor founded on the brittle strength of bones,
Like cumbrous flesh; but, in what shape they choose,
Dilated or condensed, bright or obscure,
Can execute their aery purposes,
And works of love or enmity fulfil.
For those the race of Israel oft forsook
Their living Strength, and unfrequented left
His righteous altar, bowing lowly down
To bestial gods; for which their heads as low
Bowed down in battle, sunk before the spear

362. rased, erased. **364–75. Nor had they yet . . . world.** Milton follows the belief of the Church Fathers that the fallen angels had, in process of time, become pagan deities. **372. religions,** rites. **392. Moloch,** a sun god worshiped in the form of a bull. For Biblical references to his sacrifices, see Psalm 106:36–38; Jeremiah 7:31; and Ezekiel 16:21. **394. for,** because of.

403. opprobrious hill, the Mount of Olives. Because of the pagan shrines upon it, it was called "hill of scandal" (see l. 416). **404. Tophet,** from the Hebrew *toph,* drum. See above, l. 394. **404–05. valley of Hinnom . . . Gehenna.** The Jewish reformers turned the beautiful valley, which had been polluted by pagan rites, into a place for casting rubbish. The fires, kept constantly burning to destroy the rubbish, caused the valley to become **the type of Hell;** hence the modern meanings of "Tophet" and "Gehenna." **406. Chemos,** another form of Moloch as he was worshiped by the Moabites. **dread,** dreaded god. **411. the Asphaltic Pool,** the Dead Sea, on the shores of which are asphaltic or bituminous deposits. The towns and sites mentioned in the preceding lines are in its neighborhood. **413. Israel in Sittim.** See Numbers 25. **417. hard,** near. **418. good Josiah drove them thence.** See II Kings 23:13–14. **422. Baälim and Ashtaroth.** See notes on ll. 197–200 of "On the Morning of Christ's Nativity" (page 382). **423–31. spirits . . . fulfil.** Milton in these lines is preparing for important developments later in the poem. **bright or obscure** (l. 429), visible or invisible.

Of despicable foes. With these in troop
Came Astoreth, whom the Phoenicians called
Astarte, Queen of Heaven, with crescent horns;
To whose bright image nightly by the moon
Sidonian virgins paid their vows and songs;
In Sion also not unsung, where stood
Her temple on the offensive mountain, built
By that uxorious king whose heart, though large,
Beguiled by fair idolatresses, fell
To idols foul. Thammuz came next behind,
Whose annual wound in Lebanon allured
The Syrian damsels to lament his fate
In amorous ditties all a summer's day;
While smooth Adonis from his native rock
Ran purple to the sea, supposed with blood
Of Thammuz yearly wounded. The love-tale
Infected Sion's daughters with like heat,
Whose wanton passions in the sacred porch
Ezekiel saw, when, by the vision led,
His eye surveyed the dark idolatries
Of alienated Judah. Next came one
Who mourned in earnest, when the captive ark
Maimed his brute image, head and hands lopt off
In his own temple, on the grunsel edge,
Where he fell flat, and shamed his worshippers:
Dagon his name, sea monster, upward man
And downward fish; yet had his temple high
Reared in Azotus, dreaded through the coast
Of Palestine, in Gath, and Ascalon,
And Accaron, and Gaza's frontier bounds.
Him followed Rimmon, whose delightful seat
Was fair Damascus, on the fertile banks
Of Abbana, and Pharphar, lucid streams.
He also against the house of God was bold:
A leper once he lost and gained a king,
Ahaz, his sottish conqueror, whom he drew
God's altar to disparage and displace
For one of Syrian mode, whereon to burn
His odious offerings, and adore the gods
Whom he had vanquished. After these appeared
A crew, who, under names of old renown,
Osiris, Isis, Orus, and their train,
With monstrous shapes and sorceries abused
Fanatic Egypt and her priests to seek
Their wandering gods disguised in brutish forms
Rather than human. Nor did Israel scape
The infection, when their borrowed gold composed
The calf in Oreb; and the rebel king
Doubled that sin in Bethel and in Dan,
Likening his Maker to the grazèd ox—
Jehovah, who, in one night, when he passed
From Egypt marching, equalled with one stroke
Both her first-born and all her bleating gods.
Belial came last, than whom a spirit more lewd
Fell not from Heaven, or more gross to love
Vice for itself. To him no temple stood
Or altar smoked; yet who more oft than he
In temples and at altars, when the priest
Turns atheist, as did Eli's sons, who filled
With lust and violence the house of God?
In courts and palaces he also reigns,
And in luxurious cities, where the noise
Of riot ascends above their loftiest towers,
And injury and outrage; and when night
Darkens the streets, then wander forth the sons
Of Belial, flown with insolence and wine.
Witness the streets of Sodom, and that night
In Gibeah, when the hospitable door
Exposed a matron, to avoid worse rape.
These were the prime in order and in might;
The rest were long to tell; though far renowned
The Ionian gods—of Javan's issue held
Gods, yet confessed later than Heaven and Earth,
Their boasted parents—Titan, Heaven's first-born
With his enormous brood, and birthright seized
By younger Saturn; he from mightier Jove,
His own and Rhea's son, like measure found;
So Jove usurping reigned. These, first in Crete
And Ida known, thence on the snowy top
Of cold Olympus ruled the middle air,

438. Astoreth, singular of Ashtaroth. See "On the Morning of Christ's Nativity," l. 200 (page 382). **441. Sidonian.** Tyre and Sidon were the chief coast towns of the Phoenicians. **443. offensive mountain.** See ll. 403 and 416 above. **444. uxorious king,** Solomon. See I Kings 11:1–8. **446. Thammuz,** the Greek Adonis. See "On the Morning of Christ's Nativity," l. 204 (page 382). **450. smooth Adonis,** the Phoenician river, named after the god, the waters of which were in the spring reddened with mud. **455. Ezekiel saw.** See Ezekiel 8:14–15. **456. dark,** secret. **459. his brute image,** Dagon the fish god. See "On the Morning of Christ's Nativity," l. 199 (page 382). **460. grunsel,** groundsel, threshold. **464. dreaded,** worshiped. **471. A leper,** Naaman. See II Kings 5. **474. Syrian mode.** See II Kings 16: II Chronicles 28: 20–24.

478. Osiris, Isis, Orus. See "On the Morning of Christ's Nativity," ll. 210–13 (page 382). **479. monstrous,** that is, of animals. **abused,** deceived. **483. borrowed gold.** See Exodus 12:35–36 and chap. 32. **484–85. rebel king . . . sin.** Jeroboam made *two* golden calves. I Kings 12:28–30. **487. when he passed.** See Exodus 12:12. **489. her first-born.** A reference to the tenth of the Egyptian plagues. See Exodus 12. **490. Belial,** not, strictly speaking, a god, but in the original Hebrew an abstract term signifying worthlessness, baseness, "of no account." **495. Eli's sons.** See I Samuel 2:12, 22. **498. luxurious,** lewd. **501–02. the sons Of Belial.** Milton undoubtedly had in mind the bands of roistering young men who roamed the streets of London at night, committing outrages upon citizens. **flown,** flushed. **Sodom.** See Genesis 19:4–8. **504. Gibeah.** See Judges 19:16–25. **506. prime,** chief **508. Javan's issue,** the Ionians, or Greeks, offspring of Javan, son of Japhet. See Genesis 10:2. **held,** considered. **509. later,** to be later. **513. measure,** treatment. **515. Ida,** Mt. Ida, in Crete.

Their highest Heaven; or on the Delphian cliff,
Or in Dodona, and through all the bounds
Of Doric land; or who with Saturn old
Fled over Adria to the Hesperian fields,
And o'er the Celtic roamed the utmost isles.
  All these and more came flocking; but with looks
Downcast and damp, yet such wherein appeared
Obscure some glimpse of joy to have found their chief
Not in despair, to have found themselves not lost
In loss itself; which on his countenance cast
Like doubtful hue. But he, his wonted pride
Soon recollecting, with high words, that bore
Semblance of worth, not substance, gently raised
Their fainted courage, and dispelled their fears:
Then straight commands, that at the warlike sound
Of trumpets loud and clarions, be upreared
His mighty standard. That proud honour claimed
Azazel as his right, a Cherub tall:
Who forthwith from the glittering staff unfurled
The imperial ensign, which, full high advanced,
Shone like a meteor, streaming to the wind,
With gems and golden lustre rich emblazed,
Seraphic arms and trophies; all the while
Sonorous metal blowing martial sounds:
At which the universal host upsent
A shout that tore Hell's concave, and beyond
Frighted the reign of Chaos and old Night.
All in a moment through the gloom were seen
Ten thousand banners rise into the air,
With orient colours waving: with them rose
A forest huge of spears; and thronging helms
Appeared, and serried shields in thick array
Of depth immeasurable. Anon they move
In perfect phalanx to the Dorian mood
Of flutes and soft recorders; such as raised
To highth of noblest temper heroes old
Arming to battle, and, instead of rage,
Deliberate valour breathed, firm and unmoved
With dread of death to flight or foul retreat;
Nor wanting power to mitigate and suage
With solemn touches troubled thoughts, and chase
Anguish and doubt and fear and sorrow and pain
From mortal or immortal minds. Thus they,
Breathing united force with fixèd thought,
Moved on in silence to soft pipes, that charmed
Their painful steps o'er the burnt soil: and now,
Advanced in view, they stand, a horrid front
Of dreadful length and dazzling arms, in guise
Of warriors old with ordered spear and shield,
Awaiting what command their mighty chief
Had to impose. He through the armèd files
Darts his experienced eye, and soon traverse
The whole battalion views, their order due,
Their visages and stature as of gods;
Their number last he sums. And now his heart
Distends with pride, and hardening in his strength
Glories; for never, since created man,
Met such embodied force as named with these
Could merit more than that small infantry
Warred on by cranes: though all the giant brood
Of Phlegra with the heroic race were joined
That fought at Thebes and Ilium, on each side
Mixed with auxiliar gods; and what resounds
In fable or romance of Uther's son,
Begirt with British and Armoric knights;
And all who since, baptized or infidel,
Jousted in Aspramont, or Montalban,
Damasco, or Marocco, or Trebisond;
Or whom Biserta sent from Afric shore
When Charlemain with all his peerage fell
By Fontarabbia. Thus far these beyond
Compare of mortal prowess, yet observed
Their dread commander. He, above the rest
In shape and gesture proudly eminent,
Stood like a tower; his form had yet not lost
All her original brightness, nor appeared
Less than Archangel ruined, and the excess

517. Delphian. The oracle of Apollo was at Delphi, on Mt. Parnassus. **518. Dodona,** the oracle of Zeus (Jove) in Epirus. **519. Doric,** that is, Greek. **520. Adria,** the Adriatic Sea. **the Hesperian fields,** Italy. According to Latin legends, Saturn, driven out by Jupiter, had established his sovereignty and the "Age of Gold" in Italy and Iberia (Spain). **521. the Celtic,** France and Northwestern Europe. **the utmost isles,** the British Isles. **523. damp,** depressed. **526–27. cast Like doubtful hue,** that is, their discouragement was at first reflected in Satan's countenance. **528. recollecting,** re-collecting. **531. straight,** straightway, immediately. **536. advanced,** uplifted. **538. emblazed,** emblazoned. **542. concave,** vault, dome. **543. reign,** realm. **Chaos and old Night.** Chaos here is a person, ruler of the great Deep, also called Chaos, and, with "grandmother Night," as Spenser calls her, ancestor of all things. An interesting analogue to this classical conception is found in Genesis 1:2; "And the earth was *without form, and void,* and *darkness* was upon the face of the *deep.*" **546. orient,** bright. **548. serried,** interlocked. **550. the Dorian mood.** See note 136 on page 385. **551. recorders,** flageolets.

554. unmoved, immovable. **556–59. power to mitigate . . . minds.** Could there be a happier statement of the function and effect of noble music than is contained in these lines? **suage,** assuage. **561. charmed.** The word has connotations of both song and magic (en*chant*ment). **563. horrid,** bristling. **568. traverse,** across. **573. since created man,** a Latinism; the English form would be "since man was created." **574. embodied,** collected. **named with,** compared with. **575–76. that small infantry . . . cranes,** the Pigmies, whose battles with the cranes form the subject of one of the Homeric poems. **577. Phlegra,** the site, in Macedonia, where the giants were conquered by the gods. **the heroic race,** the heroes who fought at Thebes and in the Trojan War. **580. Uther's son,** Arthur. **581. Begirt with,** surrounded by. **Armoric,** of Brittany. **583–87. Aspramont . . . Fontarabbia,** names from the chivalric romances, and intended, doubtless, to induce a romantic sensation in the reader. **588. observed,** did homage to. **592. her.** *Forma* in Latin is feminine; hence the pronoun "her."

Of glory obscured: as when the sun new risen
Looks through the horizontal misty air
Shorn of his beams, or, from behind the moon,
In dim eclipse disastrous twilight sheds
On half the nations, and with fear of change
Perplexes monarchs: darkened so, yet shone
Above them all the Archangel; but his face
Deep scars of thunder had intrenched, and care
Sat on his faded cheek, but under brows
Of dauntless courage, and considerate pride
Waiting revenge. Cruel his eye, but cast
Signs of remorse and passion to behold
The fellows of his crime, the followers rather
(Far other once beheld in bliss), condemned
For ever now to have their lot in pain;
Millions of spirits for his fault amerced
Of Heaven, and from eternal splendours flung
For his revolt: yet faithful how they stood,
Their glory withered; as when Heaven's fire
Hath scathed the forest oaks or mountain pines,
With singèd top their stately growth, though bare,
Stands on the blasted heath. He now prepared
To speak; whereat their doubled ranks they bend
From wing to wing, and half enclose him round
With all his peers; attention held them mute.
Thrice he assayed, and thrice, in spite of scorn,
Tears, such as angels weep, burst forth: at last
Words, interwove with sighs, found out their way:
"O myriads of immortal Spirits! O Powers
Matchless, but with the Almighty!—and that strife
Was not inglorious, though the event was dire,
As this place testifies, and this dire change,
Hateful to utter. But what power of mind,
Foreseeing or presaging, from the depth
Of knowledge past or present, could have feared
How such united force of gods, how such
As stood like these, could ever know repulse?
For who can yet believe, though after loss,
That all these puissant legions, whose exile
Hath emptied Heaven, shall fail to reascend,
Self-raised, and repossess their native seat?
For me, be witness all the host of Heaven,
If counsels different, or dangers shunned
By me, have lost our hopes. But he who reigns
Monarch in Heaven, till then as one secure
Sat on his throne, upheld by old repute,
Consent or custom, and his regal state
Put forth at full, but still his strength concealed;
Which tempted our attempt, and wrought our fall.
Henceforth his might we know, and know our own,
So as not either to provoke, or dread
New war provoked. Our better part remains
To work in close design, by fraud or guile,
What force effected not; that he no less
At length from us may find, who overcomes
By force hath overcome but half his foe.
Space may produce new worlds; whereof so rife
There went a fame in Heaven that he ere long
Intended to create, and therein plant
A generation whom his choice regard
Should favour equal to the Sons of Heaven.
Thither, if but to pry, shall be perhaps
Our first eruption: thither or elsewhere;
For this infernal pit shall never hold
Celestial spirits in bondage, nor the Abyss
Long under darkness cover. But these thoughts
Full counsel must mature. Peace is despaired;
For who can think submission? War then, war
Open or understood, must be resolved."
He spake; and, to confirm his words, out flew
Millions of flaming swords, drawn from the thighs
Of mighty Cherubim; the sudden blaze
Far round illumined Hell. Highly they raged
Against the Highest, and fierce, with graspèd arms,
Clashed on their sounding shields the din of war,
Hurling defiance toward the vault of Heaven.
There stood a hill not far, whose grisly top
Belched fire and rolling smoke; the rest entire
Shone with a glossy scurf, undoubted sign
That in his womb was hid metallic ore,
The work of sulphur. Thither, winged with speed,
A numerous brigad hastened: as when bands
Of pioneers, with spade and pickaxe armed,
Forerun the royal camp, to trench a field,
Or cast a rampart. Mammon led them on,
Mammon, the least erected spirit that fell
From Heaven; for even in Heaven his looks and thoughts
Were always downward bent, admiring more
The riches of Heaven's pavement, trodden gold,
Than aught divine or holy else enjoyed
In vision beatific. By him first
Men also, and by his suggestion taught,

597. disastrous, portending disaster. **601. intrenched,** cut into. **603. considerate,** thoughtful. **605. passion,** deep feeling. **609. amerced,** punished by loss. **619. assayed,** essayed, attempted. **624. event,** outcome. **633. Hath emptied Heaven,** one of Satan's many vain boasts. **636. different,** differing from yours; selfish.

645. better part, wiser course of action. **646. work,** bring about. **close,** secret. **650. rife,** commonly reported. **651. fame,** rumor. **660. despaired,** despaired of. **662. understood,** among ourselves; secret. **670. grisly,** horrible. **672. scurf,** incrustation. **673. his,** its. **674. The work of sulphur,** a reference to the ancient theory that metals were compounded of sulphur and mercury. **676. pioneers,** miners, sappers. **678. Mammon.** Like Belial, Mammon is not the name of a god, but a Chaldaic abstract term for "riches." See Matthew 6:24. **679. erected,** elevated.

Ransacked the Center, and with impious hands
Rifled the bowels of their mother Earth
For treasures better hid. Soon had his crew
Opened into the hill a spacious wound,
And digged out ribs of gold. Let none admire
That riches grow in Hell; that soil may best
Deserve the precious bane. And here let those
Who boast in mortal things, and wondering tell
Of Babel, and the works of Memphian kings,
Learn how their greatest monuments of fame,
And strength, and art, are easily outdone
By spirits reprobate, and in an hour
What in an age they, with incessant toil
And hands innumerable, scarce perform.
Nigh on the plain, in many cells prepared,
That underneath had veins of liquid fire
Sluiced from the lake, a second multitude
With wondrous art founded the massy ore,
Severing each kind, and scummed the bullion dross.
A third as soon had formed within the ground
A various mould, and from the boiling cells
By strange conveyance filled each hollow nook:
As in an organ, from one blast of wind,
To many a row of pipes the sound-board breathes.
Anon out of the earth a fabric huge
Rose like an exhalation, with the sound
Of dulcet symphonies and voices sweet—
Built like a temple, where pilasters round
Were set, and Doric pillars overlaid
With golden architrave; nor did there want
Cornice or frieze, with bossy sculptures graven:
The roof was fretted gold. Not Babylon,
Nor great Alcairo, such magnificence
Equalled in all their glories, to enshrine
Belus or Serapis their gods, or seat
Their kings, when Egypt with Assyria strove
In wealth and luxury. The ascending pile
Stood fixed her stately highth, and straight the doors,
Opening their brazen folds, discover, wide
Within, her ample spaces o'er the smooth
And level pavement: from the archèd roof,
Pendent by subtle magic, many a row
Of starry lamps and blazing cressets, fed
With naphtha and asphaltus, yielded light
As from a sky. The hasty multitude
Admiring entered, and the work some praise,

686. Center, the earth. **690. admire,** wonder. **692. bane,** evil, blight. **694. works of Memphian kings,** the Pyramids. **703. founded,** melted. **704. bullion dross,** slag. **716. bossy,** in high relief; embossed. **717. fretted,** wrought with designs. **718. Alcairo,** Cairo. **720. Belus,** Bel, or Baal. **Serapis,** the Egyptian god of the underworld. **723. fixed,** completed. **straight,** straightway. **728. cressets,** hanging lamps.

And some the architect. His hand was known
In Heaven by many a towered structure high,
Where sceptred Angels held their residence,
And sat as princes, whom the supreme King
Exalted to such power, and gave to rule,
Each in his hierarchy, the orders bright.
Nor was his name unheard, or unadored,
In ancient Greece, and in Ausonian land
Men called him Mulciber: and how he fell
From Heaven they fabled, thrown by angry Jove
Sheer o'er the crystal battlements; from morn
To noon he fell, from noon to dewy eve,
A summer's day; and with the setting sun
Dropt from the zenith like a falling star,
On Lemnos, the Aegean isle. Thus they relate,
Erring; for he with this rebellious rout
Fell long before; nor aught availed him now
To have built in Heaven high towers; nor did he scape
By all his engines, but was headlong sent
With his industrious crew to build in Hell.
Meanwhile the wingèd haralds, by command
Of sovran power, with awful ceremony
And trumpet's sound, throughout the host proclaim
A solemn council forthwith to be held
At Pandaemonium, the high capitol
Of Satan and his peers. Their summons called
From every band and squarèd regiment
By place or choice the worthiest; they anon
With hundreds and with thousands trooping came
Attended. All access was thronged, the gates
And porches wide, but chief the spacious hall
(Though like a covered field, where champions bold
Wont ride in armed, and at the Soldan's chair
Defied the best of Panim chivalry
To mortal combat, or career with lance)
Thick swarmed, both on the ground and in the air,
Brushed with the hiss of rustling wings. As bees
In spring time, when the Sun with Taurus rides,
Pour forth their populous youth about the hive
In clusters; they among fresh dews and flowers
Fly to and fro, or on the smoothèd plank,

732. the architect. Whether the architect is Mammon, and therefore identical with **Mulciber** (l. 740), is not certain. Since Milton has already sufficiently characterized Mammon (ll. 678 ff.), and since the account of Mulciber's activities which follows is quite dissimilar to that of Mammon's, there seems to be good reason for considering Mulciber, the architect, a distinct person from Mammon. (Mulciber is Vulcan.) **739. Ausonian,** Italian. **747. rout,** crew. **750. engines,** devices. **752. haralds,** heralds. **753. awful,** awe-inspiring. **756. Pandaemonium,** literally, "the place of all the demons." **757. peers.** The word has here the meaning of "nobility," as in modern English. **764. Soldan's,** Sultan's. **765. Panim,** pagan. **769. with Taurus,** in the sign of the Bull, one of the signs of the Zodiac (April 19–May 20).

The suburb of their straw-built citadel,
New rubbed with balm, expatiate and confer
Their state affairs. So thick the aery crowd
Swarmed and were straitened; till, the signal given,
Behold a wonder! they but now who seemed
In bigness to surpass Earth's giant sons,
Now less than smallest dwarfs, in narrow room
Throng numberless, like that Pygmean race
Beyond the Indian mount; or faery elves,
Whose midnight revels, by a forest side
Or fountain, some belated peasant sees,
Or dreams he sees, while overhead the Moon
Sits arbitress, and nearer to the Earth
Wheels her pale course; they, on their mirth and dance
Intent, with jocund music charm his ear;
At once with joy and fear his heart rebounds.
Thus incorporeal spirits to smallest forms
Reduced their shapes immense, and were at large,
Though without number still, amidst the hall
Of that infernal court. But far within,
And in their own dimensions like themselves,
The great Seraphic Lords and Cherubim
In close recess and secret conclave sat,
A thousand demi-gods on golden seats,
Frequent and full. After short silence then,
And summons read, the great consùlt began.

BOOK II

The Argument

The consultation begun, Satan debates whether another battle be to be hazarded for the recovery of Heaven: some advise it, others dissuade. A third proposal is preferred, mentioned before by Satan, to search the truth of that prophecy or tradition in Heaven concerning another world, and another kind of creature, equal or not much inferior to themselves, about this time to be created. Their doubt who shall be sent on this difficult search; Satan, their chief, undertakes alone the voyage; is honoured and applauded. The council thus ended, the rest betake them several ways and to several employments, as their inclinations lead them, to entertain the time till Satan return. He passes on his journey to Hell Gates, finds them shut, and who sat there to guard them; by whom at length they are opened, and discover to him the great gulf between Hell and Heaven; with what difficulty he passes through, directed by Chaos, the Power of that place, to the sight of this new World which he sought.

774. expatiate, spread out. **confer,** discuss. **776. straitened,** crowded. **785. arbitress,** witness. **790. at large,** uncrowded. **793. like themselves.** The angels, though having power to change shape and sex at will, are represented as having each his own special form and nature. **797. Frequent,** crowded. **798. consùlt,** consultation.

High on a throne of royal state, which far
Outshone the wealth of Ormus and of Ind,
Or where the gorgeous East, with richest hand,
Showers on her kings barbaric pearl and gold,
Satan exalted sat, by merit raised
To that bad eminence; and, from despair
Thus high uplifted beyond hope, aspires
Beyond thus high, insatiate to pursue
Vain war with Heaven, and, by success untaught,
His proud imaginations thus displayed:
"Powers and Dominions, Deities of Heaven!
For, since no deep within her gulf can hold
Immortal vigour, though oppressed and fallen,
I give not Heaven for lost. From this descent
Celestial Virtues rising will appear
More glorious and more dread than from no fall,
And trust themselves to fear no second fate.
Me, though just right, and the fixed laws of Heaven,
Did first create your leader, next, free choice,
With what besides, in council or in fight,
Hath been achieved of merit, yet this loss,
Thus far at least recovered, hath much more
Established in a safe unenvied throne,
Yielded with full consent. The happier state
In Heaven, which follows dignity, might draw
Envy from each inferior; but who here
Will envy whom the highest place exposes
Foremost to stand against the Thunderer's aim
Your bulwark, and condemns to greatest share
Of endless pain? Where there is then no good
For which to strive, no strife can grow up there
From faction; for none sure will claim in Hell
Precedence, none whose portion is so small
Of present pain, that with ambitious mind
Will covet more. With this advantage then
To union, and firm faith, and firm accord,
More than can be in Heaven, we now return
To claim our just inheritance of old,
Surer to prosper than prosperity
Could have assured us; and by what best way,
Whether of open war or covert guile,
We now debate; who can advise may speak."
He ceased; and next him Moloch, sceptred king,
Stood up, the strongest and the fiercest spirit
That fought in Heaven, now fiercer by despair.
His trust was with the Eternal to be deemed
Equal in strength, and rather than be less
Cared not to be at all; with that care lost

2. Ormus, a town on an island in the Persian Gulf, famous for its diamond trade. **Ind,** India. **4. barbaric,** barbarously magnificent. **9. success,** issue, result, experience. **11. "Powers and Dominions, . . ."** two of the angelic orders. Milton uses the titles in the general sense of "powers of Heaven." **14. give . . . for lost,** consider as lost. **15. Virtues,** one of the orders of angels; used here in a general sense. **16. dread,** to be dreaded.

Went all his fear: of God, or Hell, or worse,
He recked not, and these words thereafter spake:
"My sentence is for open war. Of wiles,
More unexpert, I boast not: them let those
Contrive who need, or when they need; not now.
For while they sit contriving, shall the rest—
Millions that stand in arms, and longing wait
The signal to ascend—sit lingering here,
Heaven's fugitives, and for their dwelling-place
Accept this dark opprobrious den of shame,
The prison of his tyranny who reigns
By our delay? No! let us rather choose,
Armed with Hell flames and fury, all at once
O'er Heaven's high towers to force resistless way,
Turning our tortures into horrid arms
Against the Torturer; when to meet the noise
Of his almighty engine he shall hear
Infernal thunder, and for lightning see
Black fire and horror shot with equal rage
Among his Angels, and his throne itself
Mixed with Tartarean sulphur and strange fire,
His own invented torments. But perhaps
The way seems difficult and steep to scale
With upright wing against a higher foe.
Let such bethink them, if the sleepy drench
Of that forgetful lake benumb not still,
That in our proper motion we ascend
Up to our native seat; descent and fall
To us is adverse. Who but felt of late,
When the fierce foe hung on our broken rear
Insulting, and pursued us through the deep,
With what compulsion and laborious flight
We sunk thus low? The ascent is easy then.
The event is feared: should we again provoke
Our stronger, some worse way his wrath may find
To our destruction—if there be in Hell
Fear to be worse destroyed! What can be worse
Than to dwell here, driven out from bliss, condemned
In this abhorrèd deep to utter woe;
Where pain of unextinguishable fire
Must exercise us, without hope of end,
The vassals of his anger, when the scourge
Inexorably, and the torturing hour,
Calls us to penance? More destroyed than thus,
We should be quite abolished, and expire.
What fear we then? what doubt we to incense
His utmost ire? which, to the highth enraged,
Will either quite consume us, and reduce
To nothing this essential—happier far
Than miserable to have eternal being!
Or if our substance be indeed divine,
And cannot cease to be, we are at worst
On this side nothing; and by proof we feel
Our power sufficient to disturb his Heaven,
And with perpetual inroads to alarm,
Though inaccessible, his fatal throne;
Which, if not victory, is yet revenge."
He ended frowning, and his look denounced
Desperate revenge, and battle dangerous
To less than gods. On the other side up rose
Belial, in act more graceful and humane;
A fairer person lost not heaven; he seemed
For dignity composed and high exploit.
But all was false and hollow; though his tongue
Dropt manna, and could make the worse appear
The better reason, to perplex and dash
Maturest counsels: for his thoughts were low,
To vice industrious, but to nobler deeds
Timorous and slothful. Yet, he pleased the ear,
And with persuasive accent thus began:
"I should be much for open war, O Peers!
As not behind in hate, if what was urged
Main reason to persuade immediate war
Did not dissuade me most, and seem to cast
Ominous conjecture on the whole success;
When he who most excels in fact of arms,
In what he counsels and in what excels
Mistrustful, grounds his courage on despair
And utter dissolution, as the scope
Of all his aim, after some dire revenge.
First, what revenge? The towers of Heaven are filled
With armèd watch, that render all access
Impregnable; oft on the bordering Deep
Encamp their legions, or with òbscure wing
Scout far and wide into the realm of Night,
Scorning surprise. Or could we break our way
By force, and at our heels all Hell should rise
With blackest insurrection, to confound
Heaven's purest light, yet our great Enemy,
All incorruptible, would on his throne
Sit unpolluted, and the ethereal mould,
Incapable of stain, would soon expel
Her mischief, and purge off the baser fire,
Victorious. Thus repulsed, our final hope

50. recked, cared. **51. sentence,** vote, opinion. **52. More unexpert,** less experienced in **wiles** (l. 51); without skill in speech and theoretical strategy. **65. engine,** the thunderbolt. See Book I, l. 174. **69. Mixed,** convulsed. **73. sleepy drench,** sleep-producing draught. **74. forgetful lake.** Compare "oblivious pool," Book I, l. 26. **75. proper motion,** the motion "proper" or natural to us. **77. adverse,** unnatural. **82. event,** outcome. **89. exercise,** torment. **94. What,** why.

97. esssential, existence, essence. **100–01. at worst . . . nothing,** at the worst possible point short of annihilation. **104. fatal,** ordained by fate. **106. denounced,** proclaimed, threatened. **109. humane,** urbane, polished. **113. manna,** honey. **114. dash,** frustrate. **124. fact,** feat. **132. òbscure,** invisible. **139. mould,** substance.

Is flat despair: we must exasperate
The Almighty Victor to spend all his rage;
And that must end us, that must be our cure—
To be no more. Sad cure! for who would lose,
Though full of pain, this intellectual being,
Those thoughts that wander through eternity,
To perish rather, swallowed up and lost
In the wide womb of uncreated Night,
Devoid of sense and motion? And who knows,
Let this be good, whether our angry Foe
Can give it, or will ever? How he can
Is doubtful; that he never will is sure.
Will he, so wise, let loose at once his ire,
Belike through impotence, or unaware,
To give his enemies their wish, and end
Them in his anger, whom his anger saves
To punish endless? 'Wherefore cease we, then?'
Say they who counsel war; 'we are decreed,
Reserved, and destined to eternal woe;
Whatever doing, what can we suffer more,
What can we suffer worse?' Is this then worst,
Thus sitting, thus consulting, thus in arms?
What when we fled amain, pursued and strook
With Heaven's afflicting thunder, and besought
The Deep to shelter us? This Hell then seemed
A refuge from those wounds. Or when we lay
Chained on the burning lake? That sure was worse.
What if the breath that kindled those grim fires,
Awaked, should blow them into sevenfold rage,
And plunge us in the flames? or, from above,
Should intermitted vengeance arm again
His red right hand to plague us? What if all
Her stores were opened, and this firmament
Of Hell should spout her cataracts of fire,
Impendent horrors, threatening hideous fall
One day upon our heads? while we, perhaps,
Designing or exhorting glorious war,
Caught in a fiery tempest, shall be hurled,
Each on his rock transfixed, the sport and prey
Of racking whirlwinds, or for ever sunk
Under yon boiling ocean, wrapt in chains,
There to converse with everlasting groans,
Unrespited, unpitied, unreprieved,
Ages of hopeless end! This would be worse.
War therefore, open or concealed, alike
My voice dissuades; for what can force or guile
With him, or who deceive his mind, whose eye
Views all things at one view? He from Heaven's highth
All these our motions vain sees and derides;
Not more almighty to resist our might
Than wise to frustrate all our plots and wiles.
Shall we then live thus vile, the race of Heaven
Thus trampled, thus expelled, to suffer here
Chains and these torments? Better these than worse,
By my advice; since fate inevitable
Subdues us, and omnipotent decree,
The Victor's will. To suffer, as to do,
Our strength is equal, nor the law unjust
That so ordains. This was at first resolved,
If we were wise, against so great a foe
Contending, and so doubtful what might fall.
I laugh, when those who at the spear are bold
And venturous, if that fail them, shrink, and fear
What yet they know must follow—to endure
Exile, or ignominy, or bonds, or pain,
The sentence of their conqueror. This is now
Our doom; which if we can sustain and bear,
Our Sùpreme Foe in time may much remit
His anger, and perhaps, thus far removed,
Not mind us not offending, satisfied
With what is punished; whence these raging fires
Will slacken, if his breath stir not their flames.
Our purer essence then will overcome
Their noxious vapour, or, inured, not feel;
Or, changed at length, and to the place conformed
In temper and in nature, will receive
Familiar the fierce heat; and, void of pain,
This horror will grow mild, this darkness light;
Besides what hope the never-ending flight
Of future days may bring, what chance, what change
Worth waiting,—since our present lot appears
For happy though but ill, for ill not worst,
If we procure not to ourselves more woe."
  Thus Belial, with words clothed in reason's garb,
Counselled ignoble ease, and peaceful sloth,
Not peace; and after him thus Mammon spake:
  "Either to disenthrone the King of Heaven
We war, if war be best, or to regain
Our own right lost. Him to unthrone we then
May hope, when everlasting Fate shall yield
To fickle Chance, and Chaos judge the strife.
The former, vain to hope, argues as vain
The latter; for what place can be for us
Within Heaven's bound, unless Heaven's Lord Supreme

152. **Let this be,** grant this to be. 156. **Belike,** used ironically, in the sense of "Doubtless!" **impotence,** inability to restrain himself. **unaware,** in ignorance of his enemies' desires. 165. **amain,** with all speed. **strook,** struck. 173. **intermitted,** temporarily suspended. 175. **Her stores,** those of Hell. 177. **Impendent,** overhanging. 182. **racking,** torturing. 184. **converse,** dwell with. 188. **what can force,** what can force achieve?

191. **motions,** schemes. 199. **suffer,** endure. 203. **fall,** befall, happen. 216. **inured,** accustomed to it. 219. **Familiar,** as familiar, and thus not uncomfortable. 223. **waiting,** waiting for. 234. **argues,** shows.

We overpower? Suppose he should relent,
And publish grace to all, on promise made
Of new subjection; with what eyes could we
Stand in his presence humble, and receive
Strict laws imposed, to celebrate his throne
With warbled hymns, and to his Godhead sing
Forced halleluiahs; while he lordly sits
Our envied sovran, and his altar breathes
Ambrosial odours and ambrosial flowers,
Our servile offerings? This must be our task
In Heaven, this our delight. How wearisome
Eternity so spent, in worship paid
To whom we hate! Let us not then pursue
By force impossible, by leave obtained
Unàcceptable, though in Heaven, our state
Of splendid vassalage; but rather seek
Our own good from ourselves, and from our own
Live to ourselves, though in this vast recess,
Free and to none accountable, preferring
Hard liberty before the easy yoke
Of servile pomp. Our greatness will appear
Then most conspicuous, when great things of small,
Useful of hurtful, prosperous of adverse,
We can create; and in what place soe'er
Thrive under evil, and work ease out of pain
Through labour and endurance. This deep world
Of darkness do we dread? How oft amidst
Thick clouds and dark doth Heaven's all-ruling Sire
Choose to reside, his glory unobscured,
And with the majesty of darkness round
Covers his throne, from whence deep thunders roar
Mustering their rage, and Heaven resembles Hell?
As he our darkness, cannot we his light
Imitate when we please? This desert soil
Wants not her hidden lustre, gems and gold;
Nor want we skill or art, from whence to raise
Magnificence; and what can Heaven show more?
Our torments also may in length of time
Become our elements, these piercing fires
As soft as now severe, our temper changed
Into their temper; which must needs remove
The sensible of pain. All things invite
To peaceful counsels, and the settled state
Of order, how in safety best we may
Compose our present evils, with regard
Of what we are and where, dismissing quite
All thoughts of war. Ye have what I advise."
He scarce had finished, when such murmur filled
The assembly, as when hollow rocks retain
The sound of blustering winds, which all night long
Had roused the sea, now with hoarse cadence lull
Seafaring men o'erwatched, whose bark by chance,
Or pinnace, anchors in a craggy bay
After the tempest: such applause was heard
As Mammon ended, and his sentence pleased,
Advising peace; for such another field
They dreaded worse than Hell; so much the fear
Of thunder and the sword of Michaël
Wrought still within them; and no less desire
To found this nether empire, which might rise
By policy, and long process of time,
In emulation opposite to Heaven.
Which when Beëlzebub perceived, than whom,
Satan except, none higher sat, with grave
Aspèct he rose, and in his rising seemed
A pillar of state; deep on his front engraven
Deliberation sat and public care;
And princely counsel in his face yet shone,
Majestic, though in ruin. Sage he stood,
With Atlantean shoulders fit to bear
The weight of mightiest monarchies; his look
Drew audience and attention still as night
Or summer's noon-tide air, while thus he spake:
"Thrones and Imperial Powers, offspring of Heaven,
Ethereal Virtues! or these titles now
Must we renounce, and, changing style, be called
Princes of Hell? for so the popular vote
Inclines, here to continue, and build up here
A growing empire; doubtless, while we dream,
And know not that the King of Heaven hath doomed
This place our dungeon, not our safe retreat
Beyond his potent arm, to live exempt
From Heaven's high jurisdiction, in new league
Banded against his throne, but to remain
In strictest bondage, though thus far removed
Under the inevitable curb, reserved
His captive multitude. For he, be sure,
In highth or depth, still first and last will reign
Sole King, and of his kingdom lose no part
By our revolt, but over Hell extend
His empire, and with iron sceptre rule
Us here, as with his golden those in Heaven.
What sit we then projecting peace and war?
War hath determined us, and foiled with loss
Irreparable; terms of peace yet none
Vouchsafed or sought; for what peace will be given

249. pursue, strive to regain. **271. Wants,** lacks. **275. elements,** congenial surroundings. **278. sensible,** sensibility.

288. o'erwatched, weary with watching. **291. sentence,** opinion, advice. **294. Michaël,** the leader of the heavenly army. "Michael" means "the sword of God." **296. nether,** lower. **302. front,** countenance. **306. Atlantean.** Atlas, one of the Titans, was condemned to bear heaven upon his shoulders. **312. style,** title. **329. What,** why. **330. determined,** put an end to.

To us enslaved, but custody severe,
And stripes, and arbitrary punishment
Inflicted? and what peace can we return,
But, to our power, hostility and hate,
Untamed reluctance, and revenge, though slow,
Yet ever plotting how the Conqueror least
May reap his conquest, and may least rejoice
In doing what we most in suffering feel?
Nor will occasion want, nor shall we need
With dangerous expedition to invade
Heaven, whose high walls fear no assault or siege,
Or ambush from the Deep. What if we find
Some easier enterprise? There is a place
(If ancient and prophetic fame in Heaven
Err not), another World, the happy seat
Of some new race called Man, about this time
To be created like to us, though less
In power and excellence, but favoured more
Of him who rules above; so was his will
Pronounced among the gods, and by an oath,
That shook Heaven's whole circumference, confirmed.
Thither let us bend all our thoughts, to learn
What creatures there inhabit, of what mould
Or substance, how endued, and what their power,
And where their weakness, how attempted best,
By force or subtlety. Though Heaven be shut,
And Heaven's high Arbitrator sit secure
In his own strength, this place may lie exposed,
The utmost border of his kingdom, left
To their defence who hold it. Here perhaps
Some advantageous act may be achieved
By sudden onset: either with Hell fire
To waste his whole creation, or possess
All as our own, and drive, as we were driven,
The puny habitants; or, if not drive,
Seduce them to our party, that their God
May prove their foe, and with repenting hand
Abolish his own works. This would surpass
Common revenge, and interrupt his joy
In our confusion, and our joy upraise
In his disturbance; when his darling sons,
Hurled headlong to partake with us, shall curse
Their frail original, and faded bliss,
Faded so soon. Advise, if this be worth
Attempting, or to sit in darkness here
Hatching vain empires." Thus Beëlzebub
Pleaded his devilish counsel, first devised
By Satan, and in part proposed; for whence,
But from the author of all ill, could spring
So deep a malice, to confound the race
Of mankind in one root, and Earth with Hell
To mingle and involve, done all to spite
The great Creator? But their spite still serves
His glory to augment. The bold design
Pleased highly those infernal States, and joy
Sparkled in all their eyes: with full assent
They vote; whereat his speech he thus renews:
"Well have ye judged, well ended long debate,
Synod of gods! and, like to what ye are,
Great things resolved; which from the lowest deep
Will once more lift us up, in spite of fate,
Nearer our ancient seat—perhaps in view
Of those bright confines, whence, with neighbouring arms
And opportune excursion, we may chance
Re-enter Heaven; or else in some mild zone
Dwell not unvisited of Heaven's fair light,
Secure, and at the brightening orient beam
Purge off this gloom; the soft delicious air,
To heal the scar of these corrosive fires,
Shall breathe her balm. But first, whom shall we send
In search of this new World? whom shall we find
Sufficient? who shall tempt with wandering feet
The dark, unbottomed, infinite Abyss,
And through the palpable obscure find out
His uncouth way, or spread his aery flight,
Upborne with indefatigable wings
Over the vast abrupt, ere he arrive
The happy isle? What strength, what art, can then
Suffice, or what evasion bear him safe
Through the strict senteries and stations thick
Of Angels watching round? Here he had need
All circumspection: and we now no less
Choice in our suffrage; for on whom we send,
The weight of all, and our last hope, relies."
This said, he sat; and expectation held
His look suspense, awaiting who appeared
To second, or oppose, or undertake
The perilous attempt; but all sat mute,
Pondering the danger with deep thoughts; and each
In other's countenance read his own dismay,
Astonished. None among the choice and prime
Of those Heaven-warring champions could be found

336. to, according to. **337. reluctance,** resistance. **341. want,** be lacking. **346. fame,** report, rumor. **357. attempted,** attacked. **365. waste,** lay waste. **367. puny,** younger, and therefore weaker. **375. original,** him who was their origin, Adam. **376. Advise,** consider.

382. confound, ruin utterly. **404. tempt,** attempt, essay. **406. palpable obscure,** "darkness which may be felt," as in the Egyptian plague. See Exodus 10:21. **407. uncouth,** unknown. **409. abrupt,** the abyss of Chaos. **arrive,** arrive at. **410. The happy isle?** The reference is, of course, not to the earth but to the universe, of the structure of which the fallen angels have as yet no knowledge. **412. senteries,** old spelling of "sentries." **414. we now,** we now need. **415. Choice in our suffrage,** care in our voting. **418. suspense,** fixed in suspense.

So hardy as to proffer or accept,
Alone, the dreadful voyage; till at last
Satan, whom now transcendent glory raised
Above his fellows, with monarchal pride
Conscious of highest worth, unmoved thus spake:
"O Progeny of Heaven! Empyreal Thrones!
With reason hath deep silence and demur
Seized us, though undismayed. Long is the way
And hard, that out of Hell leads up to light;
Our prison strong, this huge convex of fire,
Outrageous to devour, immures us round
Ninefold; and gates of burning adamant,
Barred over us, prohibit all egress.
These passed, if any pass, the void profound
Of unessential Night receives him next,
Wide-gaping, and with utter loss of being
Threatens him, plunged in that abortive gulf.
If thence he scape into whatever world,
Or unknown region, what remains him less
Than unknown dangers and as hard escape?
But I should ill become this throne, O Peers,
And this imperial sovranty, adorned
With splendour, armed with power, if aught proposed
And judged of public moment, in the shape
Of difficulty or danger, could deter
Me from attempting. Wherefore do I assume
These royalties, and not refuse to reign,
Refusing to accept as great a share
Of hazard as of honour, due alike
To him who reigns, and so much to him due
Of hazard more, as he above the rest
High honoured sits? Go, therefore, mighty Powers,
Terror of Heaven, though fallen! intend at home,
While here shall be our home, what best may ease
The present misery, and render Hell
More tolerable; if there be cure or charm
To respite, or deceive, or slack the pain
Of this ill mansion. Intermit no watch
Against a wakeful foe, while I abroad
Through all the coasts of dark destruction seek
Deliverance for us all. This enterprise
None shall partake with me." Thus saying, rose
The Monarch, and prevented all reply;
Prudent, lest, from his resolution raised,
Others among the chief might offer now
(Certain to be refused) what erst they feared;
And, so refused, might in opinion stand
His rivals, winning cheap the high repute,
Which he, through hazard huge, must earn. But they
Dreaded not more the adventure than his voice
Forbidding; and at once with him they rose.
Their rising all at once was as the sound
Of thunder heard remote. Towards him they bend
With awful reverence prone; and as a god
Extol him equal to the Highest in Heaven:
Nor failed they to express how much they praised
That for the general safety he despised
His own; for neither do the spirits damned
Lose all their virtue; lest bad men should boast
Their specious deeds on Earth, which glory excites,
Or close ambition varnished o'er with zeal.
Thus they their doubtful consultations dark
Ended, rejoicing in their matchless Chief;
As when from the mountain-tops the dusky clouds
Ascending, while the North wind sleeps, o'erspread
Heaven's cheerful face, the louring element
Scowls o'er the darkened landskip snow or shower;
If chance the radiant sun with farewell sweet
Extend his evening beam, the fields revive,
The birds their notes renew, and bleating herds
Attest their joy, that hill and valley rings.
O shame to men! Devil with devil damned
Firm concord holds; men only disagree
Of creatures rational, though under hope
Of heavenly grace; and, God proclaiming peace,
Yet live in hatred, enmity, and strife
Among themselves, and levy cruel wars,
Wasting the Earth, each other to destroy:
As if (which might induce us to accord)
Man had not hellish foes enow besides,
That day and night for his destruction wait!
The Stygian council thus dissolved; and forth
In order came the grand Infernal Peers;
Midst came their mighty Paramount, and seemed
Alone the antagonist of Heaven, nor less
Than Hell's dread Emperor, with pomp supreme,
And god-like imitated state; him round
A globe of fiery Seraphim enclosed
With bright emblazonry, and horrent arms.
Then of their session ended they bid cry
With trumpet's regal sound the great result:
Toward the four winds four speedy Cherubim
Put to their mouths the sounding alchymy,
By harald's voice explained; the hollow Abyss
Heard far and wide, and all the host of Hell
With deafening shout returned them loud acclaim.

431. demur, delay. **439. unessential,** without substance. **443. remains,** awaits. **457. intend,** consider. **461. deceive,** beguile. **467. prevented,** forestalled. **468. Prudent,** watchful. **from his resolution raised,** encouraged by his fortitude. **470. erst,** at first. **471. opinion,** public opinion.

478. awful, full of awe. **484. specious,** seemingly virtuous. **glory,** love of glory. **485. close,** secret. **490. element,** sky. **504. enow,** enough. **508–09. Paramount,** supreme lord. **seemed Alone the antagonist,** seemed in himself alone to be a sufficient antagonist. **513. horrent,** bristling. **517. sounding alchymy,** brass trumpets.

Thence more at ease their minds, and somewhat raised
By false presumptuous hope, the rangèd Powers
Disband, and, wandering, each his several way
Pursues, as inclination or sad choice
Leads him perplexed, where he may likeliest find
Truce to his restless thoughts, and entertain
The irksome hours, till his great Chief return.
Part on the plain, or in the air sublime,
Upon the wing or in swift race contend,
As at the Olympian games or Pythian fields;
Part curb their fiery steeds, or shun the goal
With rapid wheels, or fronted brigads form:
As when, to warn proud cities, war appears
Waged in the troubled sky, and armies rush
To battle in the clouds; before each van
Prick forth the aery knights, and couch their spears,
Till thickest legions close; with feats of arms
From either end of heaven the welkin burns.
Others, with vast Typhoean rage, more fell,
Rend up both rocks and hills, and ride the air
In whirlwind; Hell scarce holds the wild uproar:—
As when Alcides, from Oechalia crowned
With conquest, felt the envenomed robe, and tore
Through pain up by the roots Thessalian pines,
And Lichas from the top of Oeta threw
Into the Euboic sea. Others, more mild,
Retreated in a silent valley, sing
With notes angelical to many a harp
Their own heroic deeds, and hapless fall
By doom of battle, and complain that Fate
Free Virtue should enthrall to Force or Chance.
Their song was partial; but the harmony
(What could it less when Spirits immortal sing?)
Suspended Hell, and took with ravishment
The thronging audience. In discourse more sweet
(For eloquence the soul, song charms the sense)
Others apart sat on a hill retired,
In thoughts more elevate, and reasoned high
Of providence, foreknowledge, will, and fate—
Fixed fate, free will, foreknowledge absolute,
And found no end, in wandering mazes lost.
Of good and evil much they argued then,
Of happiness and final misery,
Passion and apathy, and glory and shame:
Vain wisdom all, and false philosophy!—
Yet, with a pleasing sorcery, could charm
Pain for a while or anguish, and excite
Fallacious hope, or arm the obdurèd breast
With stubborn patience as with triple steel.
Another part, in squadrons and gross bands,
On bold adventure to discover wide
That dismal world, if any clime perhaps
Might yield them easier habitation, bend
Four ways their flying march, along the banks
Of four infernal rivers, that disgorge
Into the burning lake their baleful streams—
Abhorrèd Styx, the flood of deadly hate;
Sad Acheron of sorrow, black and deep;
Cocytus, named of lamentation loud
Heard on the rueful stream; fierce Phlegeton,
Whose waves of torrent fire inflame with rage.
Far off from these, a slow and silent stream,
Lethe, the river of oblivion, rolls
Her watery labyrinth, whereof who drinks
Forthwith his former state and being forgets—
Forgets both joy and grief, pleasure and pain.
Beyond this flood a frozen continent
Lies dark and wild, beat with perpetual storms
Of whirlwind and dire hail, which on firm land
Thaws not, but gathers heap, and ruin seems
Of ancient pile; all else deep snow and ice,
A gulf profound as that Serbonian bog
Betwixt Damiata and Mount Casius old,
Where armies whole have sunk: the parching air
Burns frore, and cold performs the effect of fire.
Thither, by harpy-footed Furies haled,

522. Powers, armies. **524. inclination or sad choice.** The recreations of the fallen angels are as diverse as those of men, and equally expressive of different temperaments. **526. entertain,** beguile. **528. sublime,** aloft, uplifted. **530. Olympian games . . . Pythian fields.** The Olympic games of ancient Greece were held every fifth year at Olympia in honor of Zeus; the Pythian games, at Delphi in honor of Apollo. **531–2. curb . . . wheels,** engage in horse racing or chariot racing. **goal,** the turning-post in the arena. **532. fronted brigads form,** engage in mock-combats or tournaments. **536. Prick,** ride. **538. welkin,** sky. **539. Typhoean.** Cf. note on Book I, l. 199. **542. Alcides,** Hercules, grandson of Alcaeus. His death was caused by a poisoned robe, brought to him innocently by his friend Lichas, when he was on his way from Oechalia. In his agony he threw Lichas into the sea. **546. Others, more mild,** the poetically and philosophically minded among the fallen angels. **547. Retreated,** withdrawn. **552. partial,** prejudiced; they presented only their own views of the struggle with God. **554. Suspended,** held in suspense, thrilled. **took,** charmed, captivated.

561. found . . . lost, the result of the impairment of their reasoning faculties. **564. Passion and apathy.** Probably a reference to the Stoic philosophy with its ideal of insensibility to suffering, hence freedom from "passion" or feeling. **568. obdurèd,** hardened. **570. gross,** large. **571. wide,** far and wide. **572. clime,** region. **576. baleful,** woeful. **587. frozen continent.** Hell includes both extremes of temperature. **590–1. ruin . . . pile,** i. e., looks like the ruin of some ancient building. **592. Serbonian bog,** the ancient Lake Serbonis in Lower Egypt. **593. Damiata,** a city (now Damietta) on the easternmost mouth of the Nile. **Mount Casius,** between Lower Egypt and Arabia. **595. frore,** frozen, freezing. **596. harpy-footed Furies.** The Furies, the avenging goddesses of classical mythology, are here represented as having the fierce talons of the Harpies, monstrous birds with women's faces. **haled,** hauled, dragged.

At certain revolutions all the damned
Are brought; and feel by turns the bitter change
Of fierce extremes, extremes by change more fierce,
From beds of raging fire to starve in ice
Their soft ethereal warmth, and there to pine
Immovable, infixed, and frozen round
Periods of time,—thence hurried back to fire.
They ferry over this Lethean sound
Both to and fro, their sorrow to augment,
And wish and struggle, as they pass, to reach
The tempting stream, with one small drop to lose
In sweet forgetfulness all pain and woe,
All in one moment, and so near the brink;
But Fate withstands, and, to oppose the attempt,
Medusa with Gorgonian terror guards
The ford, and of itself the water flies
All taste of living wight, as once it fled
The lip of Tantalus. Thus roving on
In cónfused march forlorn, the adventurous bands,
With shuddering horror pale, and eyes aghast,
Viewed first their lamentable lot, and found
No rest. Through many a dark and dreary vale
They passed, and many a region dolorous,
O'er many a frozen, many a fiery Alp,
Rocks, caves, lakes, fens, bogs, dens, and shades of death—
A universe of death, which God by curse
Created evil, for evil only good;
Where all life dies, death lives, and Nature breeds,
Perverse, all monstrous, all prodigious things,
Abominable, unutterable, and worse
Than fables yet have feigned or fear conceived,
Gorgons, and Hydras, and Chimaeras dire.
  Meanwhile the Adversary of God and Man,
Satan, with thoughts inflamed of highest design,
Puts on swift wings, and toward the gates of Hell
Explores his solitary flight: sometimes
He scours the right-hand coast, sometimes the left;
Now shaves with level wing the deep, then soars
Up to the fiery concave towering high.
As when far off at sea a fleet descried
Hangs in the clouds, by equinoctial winds
Close sailing from Bengala, or the isles
Of Ternate and Tidore, whence merchants bring
Their spicy drugs; they on the trading flood,
Through the wide Ethiopian to the Cape,
Ply stemming nightly toward the pole: so seemed
Far off the flying Fiend. At last appear
Hell-bounds, high reaching to the horrid roof,
And thrice threefold the gates; three folds were brass,
Three iron, three of adamantine rock,
Impenetrable, impaled with circling fire
Yet unconsumed. Before the gates there sat
On either side a formidable Shape.
The one seemed woman to the waist, and fair,
But ended foul in many a scaly fold,
Voluminous and vast, a serpent armed
With mortal sting. About her middle round
A cry of Hell-hounds never-ceasing barked
With wide Cerberean mouths full loud, and rung
A hideous peal; yet, when they list, would creep,
If aught disturbed their noise, into her womb,
And kennel there; yet there still barked and howled
Within unseen. Far less abhorred than these
Vexed Scylla, bathing in the sea that parts
Calabria from the hoarse Trinacrian shore;
Nor uglier follow the night-hag, when, called
In secret, riding through the air she comes,
Lured with the smell of infant blood, to dance
With Lapland witches, while the labouring moon
Eclipses at their charms. The other Shape—
If shape it might be called that shape had none
Distinguishable in member, joint, or limb;
Or substance might be called that shadow seemed,
For each seemed either—black it stood as Night,
Fierce as ten Furies, terrible as Hell,
And shook a dreadful dart: what seemed his head
The likeness of a kingly crown had on.

597. revolutions, vicissitudes. **600. starve,** afflict with cold. **604. sound,** strait. **609. brink,** surface. **611. Medusa,** one of the three Gorgons. Her appearance turned all who beheld it to stone. **613. wight,** person. **614. Tantalus,** who was punished for divulging the secrets of Zeus by being afflicted with a raging thirst, and placed in the midst of a lake, the waters of which always receded as soon as he attempted to drink them. **617. first,** for the first time. **620. Alp,** mountain. **621. Rocks . . . death.** The line entirely made up of monosyllables suggests the "sad variety" of Hell, and produces also the effect of hopelessness and dreariness. Edmund Burke, in *The Sublime and Beautiful,* says of this line: "Here is displayed the force of union, . . . which yet would lose the greatest part of the effect if they were not the 'Rocks, caves, lakes, fens, bogs, dens, and shades—of *Death.*' This raises a very great degree of the sublime; and this sublime is raised yet higher by what follows, a 'universe of death.' " **625. prodigious,** unnatural. **628. Hydras, and Chimaeras.** The Hydra was a nine-headed serpent, slain by Hercules; the Chimaera, a fire-breathing monster, part lion, part dragon, part goat. **632. Explores,** pursues in doubt.

635. concave, roof. Cf. Book I, l. 298. **638. Close,** probably in the sense of "close together," but perhaps "close to the wind," i.e., with the wind dead ahead. **Bengala,** in northeast India. **639. Ternate and Tidore,** two of the Moluccas, or Spice Islands. **641. the wide Ethiopian,** the Indian Ocean. Note Milton's interest in the adventurous trade with the East Indies. **649. formidable Shape.** Cf. Spenser's description of the monster Error, *The Faerie Queene,* Book I, Canto i, Stanzas 14, 15, pages 236–7. **655. Cerberean mouths,** like those of Cerberus, the three-headed watchdog of Hades. **660. Scylla,** in classic myth the female sea monster whose dwelling place, between Calabria (in Italy) and Trinacria (Sicily), was destructive to mariners. **665. Lapland,** notorious as the haunt of witches.

Satan was now at hand, and from his seat
The monster moving onward came as fast
With horrid strides; Hell trembled as he strode.
Th' undaunted Fiend what this might be admired—
Admired, not feared; God and his Son except,
Created thing naught valued he nor shunned;
And with disdainful look thus first began:—
"Whence and what art thou, execrable Shape,
That dar'st, though grim and terrible, advance
Thy miscreated front athwart my way
To yonder gates? Through them I mean to pass,
That be assured, without leave asked of thee.
Retire; or taste thy folly, and learn by proof,
Hell-born, not to contend with Spirits of Heaven."
To whom the Goblin, full of wrath, replied:—
"Art thou that Traitor-Angel, art thou he,
Who first broke peace in Heaven and faith, till then
Unbroken, and in proud rebellious arms
Drew after him the third part of Heaven's sons,
Conjured against the Highest—for which both thou
And they, outcast from God, are here condemned
To waste eternal days in woe and pain?
And reck'n'st thou thyself with Spirits of Heaven,
Hell-doomed, and breath'st defiance here and scorn
Where I reign king, and, to enrage thee more,
Thy king and lord? Back to thy punishment,
False fugitive; and to thy speed add wings,
Lest with a whip of scorpions I pursue
Thy ling'ring, or with one stroke of this dart
Strange horror seize thee, and pangs unfelt before."
So spake the grisly Terror, and in shape,
So speaking and so threat'ning, grew tenfold
More dreadful and deform. On th' other side,
Incensed with indignation, Satan stood
Unterrified, and like a comet burned,
That fires the length of Ophiuchus huge
In th' arctic sky, and from his horrid hair
Shakes pestilence and war. Each at the head
Levelled his deadly aim; their fatal hands
No second stroke intend; and such a frown
Each cast at th' other as when two black clouds,
With Heaven's artillery fraught, come rattling on
Over the Caspian, then stand front to front
Hovering a space, till winds the signal blow
To join their dark encounter in mid-air:
So frowned the mighty combatants, that Hell
Grew darker at their frown; so matched they stood;
For never but once more was either like
To meet so great a foe: and now great deeds
Had been achieved, whereof all Hell had rung,
Had not the snaky Sorceress that sat
Fast by Hell-gate and kept the fatal key
Risen, and with hideous outcry rushed between.
"O father, what intends thy hand," she cried,
"Against thy only son? What fury, O son,
Possesses thee to bend that mortal dart
Against thy father's head? and know'st for whom?
For him who sits above, and laughs the while
At thee, ordained his drudge to execute
Whate'er his wrath, which he calls justice, bids—
His wrath, which one day will destroy ye both!"
She spake, and at her words the hellish Pest
Forbore: then these to her Satan returned:—
"So strange thy outcry, and thy words so strange
Thou interposest, that my sudden hand,
Prevented, spares to tell thee yet by deeds
What it intends, till first I know of thee
What thing thou art, thus double-formed, and why,
In this infernal vale first met, thou call'st
Me father, and that phantasm call'st my son.
I know thee not, nor ever saw till now
Sight more detestable than him and thee."
To whom thus the Portress of Hell-gate replied:—
"Hast thou forgot me, then, and do I seem
Now in thine eye so foul?—once deemed so fair
In Heaven, when at th' assembly, and in sight
Of all the Seraphim with thee combined
In bold conspiracy against Heaven's King,
All on a sudden miserable pain
Surprised thee, dim thine eyes, and dizzy swum
In darkness, while thy head flames thick and fast
Threw forth, till on the left side opening wide,
Likest to thee in shape and count'nance bright,
Then shining heavenly fair, a goddess armed,
Out of thy head I sprung. Amazement seized
All th' host of Heaven; back they recoiled afraid
At first, and called me *Sin*, and for a sign
Portentous held me; but, familiar grown,
I pleased, and with attractive graces won
The most averse—thee chiefly, who, full oft
Thyself in me thy perfect image viewing,
Becam'st enamoured; and such joy thou took'st
With me in secret that my womb conceived
A growing burden. Meanwhile war arose
And fields were fought in Heaven: wherein remained

678. Admired, wondered. **709. Ophiuchus,** the constellation "the Serpent-Bearer." **722. so great a foe,** Christ.

727–8. father . . . son. Note that Satan, Sin, and Death constitute an Infernal Trinity of Father, Daughter, and Evil Spirit (proceeding from the Father and the Daughter) in contrast to the Holy Trinity of Father, Son, and Holy Spirit (proceeding from the Father and the Son.) **758. Out of thy head.** Milton ingeniously adapts the classical myth of the birth of Pallas Athene (Minerva) from the head of Zeus (Jupiter), and combines it with the account of the genesis of sin and death in St. James's epistle (1:15): "when lust hath conceived, it bringeth forth sin; and sin, when it is finished, bringeth forth death." Cf. also Romans 6:23, "the wages of sin is death." **768. fields,** battles.

(For what could else?) to our Almighty Foe
Clear victory; to our part loss and rout
Through all the Empyrean. Down they fell,
Driven headlong from the pitch of Heaven, down
Into this deep; and in the general fall
I also: at which time this powerful key
Into my hand was given, with charge to keep
These gates for ever shut, which none can pass
Without my opening. Pensive here I sat
Alone; but long I sat not, till my womb,
Pregnant by thee, and now excessive grown,
Prodigious motion felt and rueful throes.
At last this odious offspring whom thou seest,
Thine own begotten, breaking violent way,
Tore through my entrails, that, with fear and pain
Distorted, all my nether shape thus grew
Transformed: but he my inbred enemy
Forth issued, brandishing his fatal dart,
Made to destroy. I fled, and cried out *Death!*
Hell trembled at the hideous name, and sighed
From all her caves, and back resounded *Death!*
I fled; but he pursued (though more, it seems,
Inflamed with lust than rage), and, swifter far,
Me overtook, his mother, all dismayed,
And, in embraces forcible and foul
Engend'ring with me, of that rape begot
These yelling monsters, that with ceaseless cry
Surround me, as thou saw'st, hourly conceived
And hourly born, with sorrow infinite
To me: for, when they list, into the womb
That bred them they return, and howl, and gnaw
My bowels, their repast; then, bursting forth
Afresh, with conscious terrors vex me round,
That rest or intermission none I find.
Before mine eyes in opposition sits
Grim Death, my son and foe, who sets them on,
And me, his parent, would full soon devour
For want of other prey, but that he knows
His end with mine involved, and knows that I
Should prove a bitter morsel, and his bane,
Whenever that shall be: so Fate pronounced.
But thou, O father, I forewarn thee, shun
His deadly arrow; neither vainly hope
To be invulnerable in those bright arms,
Though tempered heavenly; for that mortal dint,
Save he who reigns above, none can resist."
She finished; and the subtle Fiend his lore
Soon learned, now milder, and thus answered smooth:—
"Dear daughter—since thou claim'st me for thy sire,
And my fair son here show'st me, the dear pledge
Of dalliance had with thee in Heaven, and joys
Then sweet, now sad to mention, through dire change
Befall'n us unforeseen, unthought-of, know
I come no enemy, but to set free
From out this dark and dismal house of pain
Both him and thee, and all the heavenly host
Of Spirits that, in our just pretences armed,
Fell with us from on high. From them I go
This uncouth errand sole, and one for all
Myself expose, with lonely steps to tread
Th' unfounded Deep, and through the void immense
To search, with wand'ring quest, a place foretold
Should be—and, by concurring signs, ere now
Created vast and round—a place of bliss
In the purlieus of Heaven; and therein placed
A race of upstart creatures, to supply
Perhaps our vacant room, though more removed,
Lest Heaven, surcharged with potent multitude,
Might hap to move new broils. Be this, or aught
Than this more secret, now designed, I haste
To know; and, this once known, shall soon return,
And bring ye to the place where thou and Death
Shall dwell at ease, and up and down unseen
Wing silently the buxom air, embalmed
With odours. There ye shall be fed and filled
Immeasurably; all things shall be your prey."
He ceased; for both seemed highly pleased, and Death
Grinned horrible a ghastly smile, to hear
His famine should be filled, and blessed his maw
Destined to that good hour. No less rejoiced
His mother bad, and thus bespake her sire:—
"The key of this infernal Pit, by due
And by command of Heaven's all-powerful King
I keep, by him forbidden to unlock
These adamantine gates; against all force
Death ready stands to interpose his dart,
Fearless to be o'ermatched by living might.
But what owe I to his commands above,
Who hates me, and hath hither thrust me down
Into this gloom of Tartarus profound,
To sit in hateful office here confined,
Inhabitant of Heaven and heavenly-born,
Here in perpetual agony and pain,
With terrors and with clamours compassed round
Of mine own brood, that on my bowels feed?
Thou art my father, thou my author, thou
My being gav'st me; whom should I obey
But thee? whom follow? thou wilt bring me soon

818. pledge, offspring, child.

825. pretences, claims. **827. uncouth,** unknown. **829. unfounded,** without foundations. **Deep,** Chaos. **842. buxom,** unresisting. **849. bespake,** addressed. **850. due,** right.

To that new world of light and bliss, among
The gods who live at ease, where I shall reign
At thy right hand voluptuous, as beseems
Thy daughter and thy darling, without end."
Thus saying, from her side the fatal key,
Sad instrument of all our woe, she took;
And, towards the gate rolling her bestial train,
Forthwith the huge portcullis high up drew,
Which, but herself, not all the Stygian Powers
Could once have moved; then in the key-hole turns
Th' intricate wards, and every bolt and bar
Of massy iron or solid rock with ease
Unfastens. On a sudden open fly,
With impetuous recoil and jarring sound,
Th' infernal doors, and on their hinges grate
Harsh thunder, that the lowest bottom shook
Of Erebus. She opened; but to shut
Excelled her power: the gates wide open stood,
That with extended wings a bannered host,
Under spread ensigns marching, might pass through
With horse and chariots ranked in loose array;
So wide they stood, and like a furnace-mouth
Cast forth redounding smoke and ruddy flame.
Before their eyes in sudden view appear
The secrets of the hoary deep, a dark
Illimitable ocean, without bound,
Without dimension; where length, breadth, and highth,
And time, and place, are lost; where eldest Night
And Chaos, ancestors of Nature, hold
Eternal anarchy, amidst the noise
Of endless wars, and by confusion stand.
For Hot, Cold, Moist, and Dry, four champions fierce,
Strive here for mastery, and to battle bring
Their embryon atoms: they around the flag
Of each his faction, in their several clans,
Light-armed or heavy, sharp, smooth, swift, or slow,
Swarm populous, unnumbered as the sands
Of Barca or Cyrene's torrid soil,
Levied to side with warring winds, and poise
Their lighter wings. To whom these most adhere
He rules a moment: Chaos umpire sits,
And by decision more embroils the fray
By which he reigns: next him, high arbiter,
Chance governs all. Into this wild Abyss,
The womb of Nature, and perhaps her grave,
Of neither sea, nor shore, nor air, nor fire,
But all these in their pregnant causes mixed
Confusedly, and which thus must ever fight,
Unless th' Almighty Maker them ordain
His dark materials to create more worlds—
Into this wild Abyss the wary Fiend
Stood on the brink of Hell and looked a while,
Pondering his voyage; for no narrow frith
He had to cross. Nor was his ear less pealed
With noises loud and ruinous (to compare
Great things with small) than when Bellona storms
With all her battering engines bent to rase
Some capital city; or less than if this frame
Of Heaven were falling, and these elements
In mutiny had from her axle torn
The steadfast Earth. At last his sail-broad vans
He spreads for flight, and, in the surging smoke
Uplifted, spurns the ground; thence many a league,
As in a cloudy chair, ascending rides
Audacious; but, that seat soon failing, meets
A vast vacuity. All unawares,
Fluttering his pennons vain, plumb-down he drops
Ten thousand fathom deep, and to this hour
Down had been falling, had not, by ill chance,
The strong rebuff of some tumultuous cloud,
Instinct with fire and nitre, hurried him
As many miles aloft: that fury stayed,
Quenched in a boggy Syrtis, neither sea,
Nor good dry land: nigh foundered, on he fares,
Treading the crude consistence, half on foot,
Half flying; behoves him now both oar and sail.
As when a gryphon through the wilderness
With winged course, o'er hill or moory dale,
Pursues the Arimaspian, who by stealth
Had from his wakeful custody purloined
The guarded gold; so eagerly the Fiend
O'er bog or steep, through strait, rough, dense, or rare,
With head, hands, wings, or feet, pursues his way,
And swims, or sinks, or wades, or creeps, or flies.
At length a universal hubbub wild
Of stunning sounds, and voices all confused,
Borne through the hollow dark, assaults his ear
With loudest vehemence: thither he plies,
Undaunted, to meet there whatever Power
Or Spirit of the nethermost Abyss
Might in that noise reside, of whom to ask
Which way the nearest coast of darkness lies
Bordering on light; when straight behold the throne
Of Chaos, and his dark pavilion spread

869. At thy right hand, as the Son of God sits at the right hand of his Father. **883. Erebus,** an underground region of darkness; used here as a synonym of Hell. **904. Barca . . . Cyrene's.** These were ancient cities of Libya, in North Africa.

919. frith, firth; arm of the sea. **920. pealed,** struck. **922. Bellona,** Roman goddess of war. **927. vans,** wings. **937. Instinct,** filled. **939. Syrtis,** quicksands off the coast of northern Africa. **943. gryphon,** griffon; in Greek mythology a monster, half lion and half eagle. **945. Arimaspian,** one-eyed people who, according to Greek legend, lived in the north of Europe.

Wide on the wasteful deep; with him enthroned
Sat sable-vested Night, eldest of things,
The consort of his reign; and by them stood
Orcus and Ades, and the dreaded name
Of Demogorgon; Rumour next, and Chance,
And Tumult, and Confusion, all embroiled,
And Discord with a thousand various mouths.
T' whom Satan, turning boldly, thus:—"Ye Powers
And Spirits of this nethermost Abyss,
Chaos and ancient Night, I come no spy
With purpose to explore or to disturb
The secrets of your realm; but, by constraint
Wandering this darksome desert, as my way
Lies through your spacious empire up to light,
Alone and without guide, half lost, I seek
What readiest path leads where your gloomy bounds
Confine with Heaven; or, if some other place,
From your dominion won, th' Ethereal King
Possesses lately, thither to arrive
I travel this profound. Direct my course:
Directed, no mean recompense it brings
To your behoof, if I that region lost,
All usurpation thence expelled, reduce
To her original darkness and your sway
(Which is my present journey), and once more
Erect the standard there of ancient Night;
Yours be th' advantage all, mine the revenge!"
Thus Satan; and him thus the Anarch old,
With falt'ring speech and visage incomposed,
Answered:—"I know thee, stranger, who thou art—
That mighty leading Angel, who of late
Made head against Heaven's King, though overthrown.
I saw and heard; for such a numerous host
Fled not in silence through the frighted Deep,
With ruin upon ruin, rout on rout,
Confusion worse confounded; and Heaven-gates
Poured out by millions her victorious bands,
Pursuing. I upon my frontiers here
Keep residence; if all I can will serve
That little which is left so to defend,
Encroached on still through our intestine broils
Weakening the sceptre of old Night: first, Hell,
Your dungeon, stretching far and wide beneath;
Now lately Heaven and Earth, another world
Hung o'er my realm, linked in a golden chain
To that side Heaven from whence your legions fell!
If that way be your walk, you have not far;
So much the nearer danger. Go, and speed;
Havoc, and spoil, and ruin, are my gain."
He ceased; and Satan stayed not to reply,
But, glad that now his sea should find a shore,
With fresh alacrity and force renewed
Springs upward, like a pyramid of fire,
Into the wild expanse, and through the shock
Of fighting elements, on all sides round
Environed, wins his way; harder beset
And more endangered than when Argo passed
Through Bosporus betwixt the justling rocks,
Or when Ulysses on the larboard shunned
Charybdis, and by th' other whirlpool steered.
So he with difficulty and labour hard
Moved on, with difficulty and labour he;
But, he once passed, soon after, when Man fell,
Strange alteration! Sin and Death amain,
Following his track (such was the will of Heaven),
Paved after him a broad and beaten way
Over the dark Abyss, whose boiling gulf
Tamely endured a bridge of wondrous length,
From Hell continued, reaching th' utmost orb
Of this frail World; by which the Spirits perverse
With easy intercourse pass to and fro
To tempt or punish mortals, except whom
God and good Angels guard by special grace.
But now at last the sacred influence
Of light appears, and from the walls of Heaven
Shoots far into the bosom of dim Night
A glimmering dawn. Here Nature first begins
Her farthest verge, and Chaos to retire,
As from her outmost works, a broken foe,
With tumult less and with less hostile din,
That Satan with less toil, and now with ease.
Wafts on the calmer wave by dubious light,
And, like a weather-beaten vessel, holds
Gladly the port, though shrouds and tackle torn;
Or in the emptier waste, resembling air,
Weighs his spread wings, at leisure to behold
Far off th' empyreal Heaven, extended wide
In circuit, undetermined square or round,
With opal towers and battlements adorned
Of living sapphire, once his native seat;
And, fast by, hanging in a golden chain,
This pendent World, in bigness as a star
Of smallest magnitude close by the moon.
Thither, full fraught with mischievous revenge
Accursed, and in a cursèd hour, he hies.

964. **Orcus,** personification of Hell. **Ades,** Hades, or Pluto. 965. **Demogorgon,** one of the most mysterious, evil, and powerful of the infernal divinities, represented as controlling the fates of both men and gods. 977. **Confine with,** border upon. 980. **profound,** lower depth.

1017. **Argo,** the ship in which Jason and his men went in search of the Golden Fleece. 1020. **Charybdis,** the Sicilian whirlpool opposite Scylla on the Italian side of the Straits of Messina. 1024. **amain,** speedily. 1029. **orb,** the outermost of the ten concentric spheres which, according to Ptolemaic astronomy, surrounded the earth.

BOOK III

The Argument

God, sitting on his throne, sees Satan flying towards this World, then newly created; shows him to the Son, who sat at his right hand; foretells the success of Satan in perverting mankind; clears his own justice and wisdom from all imputation, having created Man free, and able enough to have withstood his Tempter; yet declares his purpose of grace towards him, in regard he fell not of his own malice, as did Satan, but by him seduced. The Son of God renders praises to his Father for the manifestation of his gracious purpose towards Man: but God again declares that Grace cannot be extended towards Man without the satisfaction of Divine Justice; Man hath offended the majesty of God by aspiring to Godhead, and therefore, with all his progeny, devoted to death, must die, unless some one can be found sufficient to answer for his offence, and undergo his punishment. The Son of God freely offers himself a ransom for man: the Father accepts him, ordains his incarnation, pronounces his exaltation above all Names in Heaven and Earth; commands all the Angels to adore him. They obey, and, hymning to their harps in full choir, celebrate the Father and the Son. Meanwhile Satan alights upon the bare convex of this World's outermost orb; where wandering he first finds a place since called the Limbo of Vanity; what persons and things fly up thither: thence comes to the gate of Heaven, described ascending by stairs, and the waters above the firmament that flow about it. His passage thence to the orb of the Sun: he finds there Uriel, the regent of that orb, but first changes himself into the shape of a meaner Angel, and, pretending a zealous desire to behold the new Creation, and Man whom God had placed here, inquires of him the place of his habitation, and is directed: alights first on Mount Niphates.

BOOK IV

The Argument

Satan, now in prospect of Eden, and nigh the place where he must now attempt the bold enterprise which he undertook alone against God and Man, falls into many doubts with himself, and many passions—fear, envy, and despair; but at length confirms himself in evil; journeys on to Paradise, whose outward prospect and situation is described; overleaps the bounds; sits, in the shape of a cormorant, on the Tree of Life, as highest in the Garden, to look about him. The Garden described; Satan's first sight of Adam and Eve; his wonder at their excellent form and happy state, but with resolution to work their fall; overhears their discourse: thence gathers that the Tree of Knowledge was forbidden them to eat of under penalty of death, and thereon intends to found his temptation by seducing them to transgress; then leaves them a while, to know further of their state by some other means. Meanwhile Uriel, descending on a sun-beam, warns Gabriel, who had in charge the gate of Paradise, that some evil spirit had escaped the Deep, and passed at noon by his sphere, in the shape of a good Angel, down to Paradise, discovered after by his furious gestures in the mount. Gabriel promises to find him ere morning. Night coming on, Adam and Eve discourse of going to their rest: their bower described; their evening worship. Gabriel, drawing forth his band of night-watch to walk the round of Paradise, appoints two strong Angels to Adam's bower, lest the evil Spirit should be there doing some harm to Adam or Eve sleeping: there they find him at the ear of Eve, tempting her in a dream, and bring him, though unwilling, to Gabriel; by whom questioned, he scornfully answers; prepares resistance; but, hindered by a sign from Heaven, flies out of Paradise.

BOOK V

The Argument

Morning approached, Eve relates to Adam her troublesome dream; he likes it not, yet comforts her: they come forth to their day labours: their morning hymn at the door of their bower. God, to render Man inexcusable, sends Raphael to admonish him of his obedience, of his free estate, of his enemy near at hand, who he is, and why his enemy, and whatever else may avail Adam to know. Raphael comes down to Paradise; his appearance described; his coming discerned by Adam afar off, sitting at the door of his bower; he goes out to meet him, brings him to his lodge, entertains him with the choicest fruits of Paradise, got together by Eve; their discourse at table. Raphael performs his message, minds Adam of his state and of his enemy; relates, at Adam's request, who that enemy is, and how he came to be so, beginning from his first revolt in Heaven, and the occasion thereof; how he drew his legions after him to the parts of the North, and there incited them to rebel with him, persuading all but Abdiel, a Seraph, who in argument dissuades and opposes him, then forsakes him.

BOOK VI

The Argument

Raphael continues to relate how Michael and Gabriel were sent forth to battle against Satan and his Angels. The first fight described: Satan and his Powers retire under night. He calls a council; invents devilish engines, which, in the second day's fight, put Michael and his Angels to some disorder; but they at length, pulling up mountains, overwhelmed both the force and machines of Satan. Yet, the tumult not so ending, God, on the third day, sends Messiah his Son, for whom he had reserved the glory of that victory. He, in the power of his Father, coming to the place, and causing all his legions to stand still on either side, with his chariot and thunder driving into the midst of his enemies, pursues them, unable to resist, towards the wall of Heaven; which opening, they leap down with horror and confusion into the place of punishment prepared for them in the Deep. Messiah returns with triumph to his Father.

BOOK VII

The Argument

Raphael, at the request of Adam, relates how and wherefore this World was first created: that God, after the expelling of Satan and his Angels out of Heaven, declared his pleasure to create another World, and other creatures to dwell therein; sends his Son with glory, and attendance of Angels, to perform the work of Creation in six days: the Angels celebrate with hymns the performance thereof, and his reascension into Heaven.

BOOK VIII

The Argument

Adam inquires concerning celestial motions; is doubtfully answered, and exhorted to search rather things more worthy of knowledge. Adam assents, and, still desirous to detain Raphael, relates to him what he remembered since his own creation—his placing in Paradise; his talk with God concerning solitude and fit society; his first meeting and nuptials with Eve. His discourse with the Angel thereupon; who, after admonitions repeated, departs.

BOOK IX

The Argument

Satan, having compassed the Earth, with meditated guile returns as a mist by night into Paradise; enters into the Serpent sleeping. Adam and Eve in the morning go forth to their labours, which Eve proposes to divide in several places, each labouring apart: Adam consents not, alleging the danger lest that enemy of whom they were forewarned should attempt her found alone. Eve, loth to be thought not circumspect or firm enough, urges her going apart, the rather desirous to make trial of her strength; Adam at last yields. The Serpent finds her alone: his subtle approach, first gazing, then speaking, with much flattery extolling Eve above all other creatures. Eve, wondering to hear the Serpent speak, asks how he attained to human speech and such understanding not till now; the Serpent answers that by tasting of a certain tree in the Garden he attained both to speech and reason, till then void of both. Eve requires him to bring her to that tree, and finds it to be the Tree of Knowledge forbidden: the Serpent, now grown bolder, with many wiles and arguments induces her at length to eat. She, pleased with the taste, deliberates a while whether to impart thereof to Adam or not; at last brings him of the fruit; relates what persuaded her to eat thereof. Adam, at first amazed, but perceiving her lost, resolves, through vehemence of love, to perish with her, and, extenuating the trespass, eats also of the fruit. The effects thereof in them both; they seek to cover their nakedness; then fall to variance and accusation of one another.

. . . To whom thus Adam fervently replied:
"O Woman, best are all things as the will
Of God ordained them; his creating hand
Nothing imperfect or deficient left
Of all that he created—much less Man,
Or aught that might his happy state secure,
Secure from outward force. Within himself
The danger lies, yet lies within his power;
Against his will he can receive no harm.
But God left free the Will; for what obeys
Reason is free; and Reason he made right,
But bid her well be ware, and still erect,
Lest, by some fair appearing good surprised,
She dictate false, and misinform the Will
To do what God expressly hath forbid.
Not then mistrust, but tender love, enjoins
That I should mind thee oft; and mind thou me.
Firm we subsist, yet possible to swerve,
Since Reason not impossibly may meet
Some specious object by the foe suborned,
And fall into deception unaware,
Not keeping strictest watch, as she was warned.
Seek not temptation, then, which to avoid
Were better, and most likely if from me
Thou sever not: trial will come unsought.
Wouldst thou approve thy constancy, approve
First thy obedience; the other who can know,
Not seeing thee attempted, who attest?
But if thou think trial unsought may find
Us both securer than thus warned thou seem'st,
Go; for thy stay, not free, absents thee more.
Go in thy native innocence; rely

353. **and still erect,** and be always alert. 358. **mind,** remind. 361. **suborned,** literally, "secretly equipped," tricked out. 367. **approve,** prove. 369. **attempted,** tempted. 371. **securer,** less careful, less watchful.

On what thou hast of virtue; summon all;
For God towards thee hath done his part: do thine."
 So spake the Patriarch of Mankind; but Eve
Persisted; yet submiss, though last, replied:
 "With thy permission, then, and thus forewarned,
Chiefly by what thy own last reasoning words
Touched only, that our trial, when least sought,
May find us both perhaps far less prepared,
The willinger I go, nor much expect
A foe so proud will first the weaker seek;
So bent, the more shall shame him his repulse."
 Thus saying, from her husband's hand her hand
Soft she withdrew, and, like a wood-nymph light,
Oread or Dryad, or of Delia's train,
Betook her to the groves, but Delia's self
In gait surpassed and goddess-like deport,
Though not as she with bow and quiver armed,
But with such gardening tools as art, yet rude,
Guiltless of fire had formed, or Angels brought.
To Pales, or Pomona, thus adorned,
Likest she seemed—Pomona when she fled
Vertumnus—or to Ceres in her prime,
Yet virgin of Proserpina from Jove.
Her long with ardent look his eye pursued
Delighted, but desiring more her stay.
Oft he to her his charge of quick return
Repeated; she to him as oft engaged
To be returned by noon amid the bower,
And all things in best order to invite
Noontide repast, or afternoon's repose.
O much deceived, much failing, hapless Eve,
Of thy presumed return! event perverse!
Thou never from that hour in Paradise
Found'st either sweet repast or sound repose;
Such ambush, hid among sweet flowers and shades,
Waited, with hellish rancour imminent,
To intercept thy way, or send thee back
Despoiled of innocence, of faith, of bliss.
For now, and since first break of dawn, the Fiend,
Mere serpent in appearance, forth was come,
And on his quest where likeliest he might find
The only two of mankind, but in them
The whole included race, his purposed prey.
In bower and field he sought, where any tuft
Of grove or garden-plot more pleasant lay,
Their tendance or plantation for delight;
By fountain or by shady rivulet
He sought them both, but wished his hap might find
Eve separate; he wished, but not with hope
Of what so seldom chanced, when to his wish,
Beyond his hope, Eve separate he spies,
Veiled in a cloud of fragrance, where she stood,
Half-spied, so thick the roses bushing round
About her glowed, oft stooping to support
Each flower of slender stalk, whose head, though gay
Carnation, purple, azure, or specked with gold,
Hung drooping unsustained. Them she upstays
Gently with myrtle band, mindless the while
Herself, though fairest unsupported flower,
From her best prop so far, and storm so nigh.
Nearer he drew, and many a walk traversed
Of stateliest covert, cedar, pine, or palm;
Then voluble and bold, now hid, now seen
Among thick-woven arborets, and flowers
Imbordered on each bank, the hand of Eve:
Spot more delicious than those gardens feigned
Or of revived Adonis, or renowned
Alcinous, host of old Laertes' son,
Or that, not mystic, where the sapient king
Held dalliance with his fair Egyptian spouse.
Much he the place admired, the person more.
As one who, long in populous city pent,
Where houses thick and sewers annoy the air,
Forth issuing on a summer's morn, to breathe
Among the pleasant villages and farms
Adjoined, from each thing met conceives delight—
The smell of grain, or tedded grass, or kine,
Or dairy, each rural sight, each rural sound—
If chance with nymph-like step fair virgin pass,
What pleasing seemed, for her now pleases more,
She most, and in her look sums all delight:
Such pleasure took the Serpent to behold
This flowery plat, the sweet recess of Eve
Thus early, thus alone. Her heavenly form
Angelic, but more soft and feminine,
Her graceful innocence, her every air
Of gesture or least action, overawed

377. **submiss,** submissively. 384. **So bent,** on seeking the weaker first. 387. **Oread or Dryad,** mountain nymph or wood nymph. **Delia's train,** the nymphs who attended the huntress Diana, called Delia from her birthplace, the isle of Delos. 389. **deport,** deportment, manner. 393. **Pales,** a Roman goddess of flocks and shepherds. **Pomona,** the Roman goddess of fruit. 395. **Ceres,** goddess of the earth and protectress of agriculture. 396. **Yet virgin of,** not yet mother of. 397. **Her . . . his,** Eve . . . Adam's. 405. **event,** outcome. 413. **Mere,** pure. 418. **more pleasant,** most pleasant.

419. **Their tendance,** the object of their attention or care. 431. **mindless,** heedless, unmindful. 436. **voluble,** rolling, turning. 437. **arborets,** small trees, shrubs. 438. **hand,** handiwork. 440. **revived Adonis.** See Book I, l. 450. For Spenser's description of the Garden of Adonis, see *The Faerie Queene*, Book III, Canto 6. 441. **Laertes' son,** Ulysses. See *Odyssey*, Book VII, ll. 25 ff. 442. **not mystic,** not a mystical, and therefore fanciful, garden of pagan allegory, but the real garden referred to in the history of Solomon in the Bible. See I Kings 3 and the Song of Solomon. 446. **annoy,** make noisome, pollute. 450. **tedded,** spread out to dry for hay. **kine,** cattle. 453. **for her,** because of her. 454. **sums,** comprises, completes. 456. **plat,** plot.

His malice, and with rapine sweet bereaved
His fierceness of the fierce intent it brought.
That space the Evil One abstracted stood
From his own evil, and for the time remained
Stupidly good, of enmity disarmed,
Of guile, of hate, of envy, of revenge.
But the hot Hell that always in him burns,
Though in mid Heaven, soon ended his delight
And tortures him now more, the more he sees
Of pleasure not for him ordained. Then soon
Fierce hate he recollects, and all his thoughts
Of mischief, gratulating, thus excites:
"Thoughts, whither have ye led me? with what sweet
Compulsion thus transported to forget
What hither brought us? hate, not love, nor hope
Of Paradise for Hell, hope here to taste
Of pleasure, but all pleasure to destroy,
Save what is in destroying; other joy
To me is lost. Then let me not let pass
Occasion which now smiles: behold alone
The Woman, opportune to all attempts;
Her husband, for I view far round, not nigh,
Whose higher intellectual more I shun,
And strength, of courage haughty, and of limb
Heroic built, though of terrestrial mould;
Foe not informidable, exempt from wound,
I not; so much hath Hell debased, and pain
Enfeebled me, to what I was in Heaven.
She fair, divinely fair, fit love for gods,
Not terrible, though terror be in love,
And beauty, not approached by stronger hate,
Hate stronger under show of love well feigned,
The way which to her ruin now I tend."
So spake the Enemy of Mankind, enclosed
In serpent, inmate bad, and toward Eve
Addressed his way: not with indented wave,
Prone on the ground, as since, but on his rear,
Circular base of rising folds, that towered
Fold above fold, a surging maze; his head
Crested aloft, and carbuncle his eyes;
With burnished neck of verdant gold, erect
Amidst his circling spires, that on the grass
Floated redundant. Pleasing was his shape
And lovely; never since of serpent kind
Lovelier—not those that in Illyria changed
Hermione and Cadmus, or the god
In Epidaurus; nor to which transformed
Ammonian Jove, or Capitoline, was seen,
He with Olympias, this with her who bore
Scipio, the highth of Rome. With tract oblique
At first, as one who sought access but feared
To interrupt, sidelong he works his way.
As when a ship, by skilful steersman wrought
Nigh river's mouth or foreland, where the wind
Veers oft, as oft so steers, and shifts her sail,
So varied he, and of his tortuous train
Curled many a wanton wreath in sight of Eve,
To lure her eye; she, busied, heard the sound
Of rustling leaves, but minded not, as used
To such disport before her through the field
From every beast, more duteous at her call
Than at Circean call the herd disguised.
He, bolder now, uncalled before her stood,
But as in gaze admiring. Oft he bowed
His turret crest and sleek enamelled neck,
Fawning, and licked the ground whereon she trod.
His gentle dumb expression turned at length
The eye of Eve to mark his play; he, glad
Of her attention gained, with serpent tongue
Organic, or impulse of vocal air,
His fraudulent temptation thus began:
"Wonder not, sovran mistress (if perhaps
Thou canst who art sole wonder), much less arm
Thy looks, the heaven of mildness, with disdain,
Displeased that I approach thee thus, and gaze
Insatiate, I thus single, nor have feared
Thy awful brow, more awful thus retired.
Fairest resemblance of thy Maker fair,
Thee all things living gaze on, all things thine
By gift, and thy celestial beauty adore,
With ravishment beheld—there best beheld
Where universally admired. But here,
In this enclosure wild, these beasts among,
Beholders rude, and shallow to discern
Half what in thee is fair, one man except,
Who sees thee (and what is one!) who shouldst be seen
A Goddess among Gods, adored and served
By Angels numberless, thy daily train?"

461. rapine, robbery. **472. gratulating,** rejoicing. **491. not,** when not. **500. carbuncle,** deep red. **502. spires,** coils. Compare the modern "spiral." **505–06. changed . . . Cadmus,** took the place of. Cadmus and his wife Harmonia **(Hermione),** were, at their own request, transformed into serpents. Milton has in mind Ovid's account in *Metamorphoses*, Book IV, ll. 563 ff. **506. the god,** Aesculapius, the god of healing, who took a serpent's form on occasion. See Ovid, *Metamorphoses*, Book XV, ll. 670 ff.

507. to which transformed, into which was transformed. **508. Ammonian Jove.** Jove (Jupiter Ammon), according to the legend, appeared to Olympias, the mother of Alexander the Great, in the form of a serpent. **Capitoline,** Jupiter, called Capitoline from his temple, the Capitol. **510. Scipio.** Scipio Africanus was said to have been the son of Jupiter by Sempronia. **517. wanton,** playful. **522. Circean.** The enchantress Circe had at her call the herd of men whom she had disguised as beasts. See *Odyssey*, Book X, ll. 214 ff. **525. turret,** towerlike. **530. Organic . . . air,** by direct motion of the serpent's speech organs, or by making the air **vocal** with some other impulse or vibration. **532–33. "Wonder not . . . sole wonder).** Satan begins by appealing to Eve's vanity

So glozed the Tempter, and his proem tuned.
Into the heart of Eve his words made way,
Though at the voice much marvelling; at length,
Not unamazed, she thus in answer spake:
"What may this mean? Language of Man pronounced
By tongue of brute, and human sense expressed!
The first at least of these I thought denied
To beasts, whom God on their creation-day
Created mute to all articulate sound;
The latter I demur, for in their looks
Much reason, and in their actions, oft appears.
Thee, Serpent, subtlest beast of all the field
I knew, but not with human voice endued;
Redouble, then, this miracle, and say,
How cam'st thou speakable of mute, and how
To me so friendly grown above the rest
Of brutal kind that daily are in sight:
Say, for such wonder claims attention due."
To whom the guileful Tempter thus replied:
"Empress of this fair World, resplendent Eve!
Easy to me it is to tell thee all
What thou command'st, and right thou shouldst be obeyed.
I was at first as other beasts that graze
The trodden herb, of abject thoughts and low,
As was my food, nor aught but food discerned
Or sex, and apprehended nothing high:
'Till on a day, roving the field, I chanced
A goodly tree far distant to behold,
Loaden with fruit of fairest colours mixed,
Ruddy and gold: I nearer drew to gaze;
When from the boughs a savoury odour blown,
Grateful to appetite, more pleased my sense
Than smell of sweetest fennel, or the teats
Of ewe or goat dropping with milk at even,
Unsucked of lamb or kid, that tend their play.
To satisfy the sharp desire I had
Of tasting those fair apples, I resolved
Not to defer; hunger and thirst at once,
Powerful persuaders, quickened at the scent
Of that alluring fruit, urged me so keen.
About the mossy trunk I wound me soon;
For, high from ground, the branches would require
Thy utmost reach, or Adam's: round the tree
All other beasts that saw, with like desire
Longing and envying stood, but could not reach.
Amid the tree now got, where plenty hung
Tempting so nigh, to pluck and eat my fill
I spared not; for such pleasure till that hour
At feed or fountain never had I found.
Sated at length, ere long I might perceive
Strange alteration in me, to degree
Of reason in my inward powers, and speech
Wanted not long, though to this shape retained.
Thenceforth to speculations high or deep
I turned my thoughts, and with capacious mind
Considered all things visible in Heaven,
Or Earth, or Middle, all things fair and good.
But all that fair and good in thy divine
Semblance and in thy beauty's heavenly ray,
United I beheld—no fair to thine
Equivalent or second; which compelled
Me thus, though importune perhaps, to come
And gaze, and worship thee of right declared
Sovran of creatures, universal Dame!"
So talked the spirited sly Snake; and Eve,
Yet more amazed, unwary thus replied:
"Serpent, thy overpraising leaves in doubt
The virtue of that fruit, in thee first proved.
But say, where grows the tree? from hence how far?
For many are the trees of God that grow
In Paradise, and various, yet unknown
To us; in such abundance lies our choice
As leaves a greater store of fruit untouched,
Still hanging incorruptible, till men
Grow up to their provision, and more hands
Help to disburden Nature of her bearth."
To whom the wily Adder, blithe and glad:—
"Empress, the way is ready, and not long—
Beyond a row of myrtles, on a flat,
Fast by a fountain, one small thicket past
Of blowing myrrh and balm. If thou accept
My conduct, I can bring thee thither soon."
"Lead, then," said Eve. He, leading, swiftly rolled
In tangles, and made intricate seem straight,
To mischief swift. Hope elevates, and joy
Brightens his crest. As when a wandering fire,
Compact of unctuous vapour, which the night
Condenses, and the cold environs round,
Kindled through agitation to a flame
(Which oft, they say, some evil spirit attends),
Hovering and blazing with delusive light,
Misleads the amazed night-wanderer from his way
To bogs and mires, and oft through pond or pool,
There swallowed up and lost, from succour far:

549. **glozed,** flattered. **proem,** preamble. 558. **demur,** have doubts about (whether reason is denied to brutes). 563. **of mute,** from being mute. 581. **fennel . . . teats.** Popular belief had it that fennel was a favorite food of serpents, and that they sucked the teats of sheep.

599–600. **to degree Of reason,** to the extent of inducing in me some degree of reason. 605. **Middle,** the air. 608. **fair,** fairness, beauty. 612. **Dame!"** mistress (of the universe). 613. **spirited,** inspired (by Satan). 624. **bearth,"** that which she bears; fruit. 629. **blowing,** blossoming. 634. **wandering fire,** will-o'-the-wisp, jack-o'-lantern. Compare "L'Allegro," l. 104. 635. **Compact,** composed. **unctuous,** oily.

So glistered the dire Snake, and into fraud
Led Eve, our credulous mother, to the Tree
Of Prohibition, root of all our woe;
Which when she saw, thus to her guide she spake:
"Serpent, we might have spared our coming hither,
Fruitless to me, though fruit be here to excess,
The credit of whose virtue rest with thee—
Wondrous, indeed, if cause of such effects!
But of this tree we may not taste nor touch;
God so commanded, and left that command
Sole daughter of his voice: the rest, we live
Law to ourselves; our reason is our law."
To whom the Tempter guilefully replied:
"Indeed! Hath God then said that of the fruit
Of all these garden-trees ye shall not eat,
Yet lords declared of all in earth or air?"
To whom thus Eve, yet sinless: "Of the fruit
Of each tree in the garden we may eat;
But of the fruit of this fair tree, amidst
The garden, God hath said, 'Ye shall not eat
Thereof, nor shall ye touch it, lest ye die.' "
She scarce had said, though brief, when now more bold
The Tempter, but with show of zeal and love
To Man, and indignation at his wrong,
New part puts on, and, as to passion moved,
Fluctuates disturbed, yet comely, and in act
Raised, as of some great matter to begin.
As when of old some orator renowned
In Athens or free Rome, where eloquence
Flourished, since mute, to some great cause addressed,
Stood in himself collected, while each part,
Motion, each act, won audience ere the tongue
Sometimes in highth began, as no delay
Of preface brooking through his zeal of right:
So standing, moving, or to highth upgrown,
The Tempter, all impassioned, thus began:
"O sacred, wise, and wisdom-giving Plant,
Mother of science! now I feel thy power
Within me clear, not only to discern
Things in their causes, but to trace the ways
Of highest agents, deemed however wise.
Queen of this Universe! do not believe
Those rigid threats of death; ye shall not die.
How should ye? by the fruit? it gives you life
To knowledge. By the Threatener? look on me,
Me who have touched and tasted, yet both live,
And life more perfect have attained than Fate
Meant me, by venturing higher than my lot.
Shall that be shut to Man which to the Beast
Is open? or will God incense his ire
For such a petty trespass, and not praise
Rather your dauntless virtue, whom the pain
Of death denounced, whatever thing Death be,
Deterred not from achieving what might lead
To happier life, knowledge of Good and Evil?
Of good, how just! of evil—if what is evil
Be real, why not known, since easier shunned?
God therefore cannot hurt ye, and be just;
Not just, not God; not feared then, nor obeyed;
Your fear itself of death removes the fear.
Why, then, was this forbid? Why but to awe,
Why but to keep ye low and ignorant,
His worshippers? He knows that in the day
Ye eat thereof your eyes, that seem so clear,
Yet are but dim, shall perfectly be then
Opened and cleared, and ye shall be as Gods,
Knowing both good and evil, as they know.
That ye should be as Gods, since I as Man,
Internal Man, is but proportion meet—
I, of brute, human; ye, of human, Gods.
So ye shall die perhaps, by putting off
Human, to put on Gods—death to be wished,
Though threatened, which no worse than this can bring!
And what are Gods, that Man may not become
As they, participating god-like food?
The Gods are first, and that advantage use
On our belief, that all from them proceeds.
I question it; for this fair Earth I see,
Warmed by the Sun, producing every kind;
Them nothing. If they all things, who enclosed
Knowledge of good and evil in this tree,
That whoso eats thereof forthwith attains
Wisdom without their leave? and wherein lies
The offence, that Man should thus attain to know?
What can your knowledge hurt him, or this tree
Impart against his will, if all be his?
Or is it envy? and can envy dwell

643. **glistered,** glittered. **fraud,** harm, evil-doing. 644–45. **Tree Of Prohibition,** the Forbidden Tree. 649. **The credit . . . thee.** The proof of whose wonder-working powers may be retained by thee alone. 653. **daughter of his voice,** one of the many Hebraisms of the poem. Compare Wordsworth's "Ode to Duty," page 726. **the rest,** as for the rest (of the trees). 667. **New part puts on,** assumes a new role. 668. **Fluctuates,** moves his body to and fro. 673. **part,** of his body. 674. **audience,** hearing. 675. **highth,** of feeling. 676. **brooking,** enduring, "putting up with." 679 ff. **"O sacred, wise ff.** The shrewdness and persuasiveness of the serpent's speech might well have deceived a person of far greater experience and knowledge than Eve. 680. **science!** knowledge.

687. **To knowledge,** in addition to knowledge. 692. **incense,** kindle. 695. **denounced,** proclaimed, threatened. 710. **Gods.** "Satan speaks like a polytheist, and Eve later falls into the same idolatrous and pagan way of thought."—Hanford 711. **Internal Man,** internally, with manlike faculties, though externally a serpent. 714. **to put on,** to assume the nature of. 722. **If they,** if they produced.

In heavenly breasts? These, these and many more
Causes import your need of this fair fruit.
Goddess humane, reach, then, and freely taste!"
He ended; and his words, replete with guile,
Into her heart too easy entrance won:
Fixed on the fruit she gazed, which to behold
Might tempt alone; and in her ears the sound
Yet rung of his persuasive words, impregned
With reason, to her seeming, and with truth.
Meanwhile the hour of noon drew on, and waked
An eager appetite, raised by the smell
So savoury of that fruit, which with desire,
Inclinable now grown to touch or taste,
Solicited her longing eye; yet first,
Pausing a while, thus to herself she mused:
"Great are thy virtues, doubtless, best of fruits,
Though kept from Man, and worthy to be admired,
Whose taste, too long forborne, at first assay
Gave elocution to the mute, and taught
The tongue not made for speech to speak thy praise.
Thy praise he also who forbids thy use
Conceals not from us, naming thee the Tree
Of Knowledge, knowledge both of good and evil;
Forbids us then to taste; but his forbidding
Commends thee more, while it infers the good
By thee communicated, and our want;
For good unknown sure is not had, or, had
And yet unknown, is as not had at all.
In plain, then, what forbids he but to know,
Forbids us good, forbids us to be wise?
Such prohibitions bind not. But, if Death
Bind us with after-bands, what profits then
Our inward freedom? In the day we eat
Of this fair fruit, our doom is we shall die!
How dies the Serpent? He hath eaten, and lives,
And knows, and speaks, and reasons, and discerns,
Irrational till then. For us alone
Was death invented? or to us denied
This intellectual food, for beasts reserved?
For beasts it seems; yet that one beast which first
Hath tasted envies not, but brings with joy
The good befallen him, author unsuspect,
Friendly to Man, far from deceit or guile.
What fear I, then? rather, what know to fear
Under this ignorance of good and evil,
Of God or Death, of law or penalty?
Here grows the cure of all, this fruit divine,
Fair to the eye, inviting to the taste,
Of virtue to make wise. What hinders, then,
To reach, and feed at once both body and mind?"
So saying, her rash hand in evil hour
Forth reaching to the fruit, she plucked, she eat.
Earth felt the wound, and Nature from her seat,
Sighing through all her works, gave signs of woe
That all was lost. Back to the thicket slunk
The guilty Serpent, and well might, for Eve,
Intent now only on her taste, naught else
Regarded; such delight till then, as seemed,
In fruit she never tasted, whether true,
Or fancied so through expectation high
Of knowledge; nor was Godhead from her thought.
Greedily she ingorged without restraint,
And knew not eating death. Satiate at length,
And heightened as with wine, jocund and boon,
Thus to herself she pleasingly began:
"O sovran, virtuous, precious of all trees
In Paradise! of operation blest
To sapience, hitherto obscured, infamed,
And thy fair fruit let hang, as to no end
Created! but henceforth my early care,
Not without song, each morning, and due praise,
Shall tend thee, and the fertile burden ease
Of thy full branches, offered free to all;
Till, dieted by thee, I grow mature
In knowledge, as the Gods who all things know.
Though others envy what they cannot give—
For, had the gift been theirs, it had not here
Thus grown! Experience, next to thee I owe,
Best guide: not following thee, I had remained
In ignorance; thou open'st Wisdom's way,
And giv'st access, though secret she retire.
And I perhaps am secret: Heaven is high—
High, and remote to see from thence distinct
Each thing on Earth; and other care perhaps
May have diverted from continual watch
Our great Forbidder, safe with all his spies
About him. But to Adam in what sort
Shall I appear? Shall I to him make known
As yet my change, and give him to partake
Full happiness with me, or rather not,

731. import, indicate. **732. humane,** gentle, gracious. **737. impregned,** impregnated. **742. Inclinable,** easily inclined. **754. infers,** implies. **758. In plain,** in plain terms. **771. author unsuspect,** the authority for which information (that is, the serpent), not to be suspected.

778. virtue, power. **781. eat,** past tense (pronounced ĕt). **782–84. Earth . . . lost.** Milton's musicianship, in having **Nature** provide a solemn orchestral punctuation of the fatal climaxes in the poem (the moments when Adam and Eve taste the forbidden fruit) has been likened to that of Wagner in his music dramas, especially in the potion scene in *Tristan und Isolde*. **792. knew not eating,** knew not that she was eating. **793. boon,** gay. **795. sovran,** most sovereign. **796–97. blest To sapience,** blest with the power of conferring wisdom. **infamed,** not known (or, perhaps, falsely reputed). **805 ff. Though others envy ff.** The Devil's first earthly disciple has learned her lesson well! **811. I perhaps . . . high.** Eve's words betray the dawn of a guilty conscience. **815. safe,** not dangerous. **817 ff. Shall I to him ff.** Envy and jealousy are among the chief results of the forbidden fruit.

But keep the odds of knowledge in my power
Without copartner? so to add what wants
In female sex, the more to draw his love,
And render me more equal, and perhaps—
A thing not undesirable—sometime
Superior; for, inferior, who is free?
This may be well; but what if God have seen,
And death ensue? Then I shall be no more;
And Adam, wedded to another Eve,
Shall live with her enjoying, I extinct!
A death to think! Confirmed, then, I resolve
Adam shall share with me in bliss or woe.
So dear I love him that with him all deaths
I could endure, without him live no life."
  So saying, from the tree her step she turned,
But first low reverence done, as to the power
That dwelt within, whose presence had infused
Into the plant sciential sap, derived
From nectar, drink of Gods. Adam the while,
Waiting desirous her return, had wove
Of choicest flowers a garland, to adorn
Her tresses, and her rural labours crown,
As reapers oft are wont their harvest queen.
Great joy he promised to his thoughts, and new
Solace in her return, so long delayed;
Yet oft his heart, divine of something ill,
Misgave him. He the faltering measure felt,
And forth to meet her went, the way she took
That morn when first they parted; by the Tree
Of Knowledge he must pass; there he her met,
Scarce from the tree returning; in her hand
A bough of fairest fruit, that downy smiled,
New gathered, and ambrosial smell diffused.
To him she hasted; in her face excuse
Came prologue, and apology to prompt,
Which, with bland words at will, she thus addressed:
  "Hast thou not wondered, Adam, at my stay?
Thee I have missed, and thought it long, deprived
Thy presence—agony of love till now
Not felt, nor shall be twice; for never more
Mean I to try, what rash untried I sought,
The pain of absence from thy sight. But strange
Hath been the cause, and wonderful to hear.
This tree is not, as we are told, a tree
Of danger tasted, nor to evil unknown
Opening the way, but of divine effect
To open eyes, and make them Gods who taste;
And hath been tasted such. The Serpent wise,
Or not restrained as we, or not obeying,
Hath eaten of the fruit, and is become
Not dead, as we are threatened, but thenceforth
Endued with human voice and human sense,
Reasoning to admiration, and with me
Persuasively hath so prevailed that I
Have also tasted, and have also found
The effects to correspond—opener mine eyes,
Dim erst, dilated spirits, ampler heart,
And growing up to Godhead; which for thee
Chiefly I sought, without thee can despise.
For bliss, as thou hast part, to me is bliss;
Tedious, unshared with thee, and odious soon.
Thou, therefore, also taste, that equal lot
May join us, equal joy, as equal love;
Lest, thou not tasting, different degree
Disjoin us, and I then too late renounce
Deity for thee, when fate will not permit."
  Thus Eve with countenance blithe her story told;
But in her cheek distemper flushing glowed.
On the other side, Adam, soon as he heard
The fatal trespass done by Eve, amazed,
Astonied stood and blank, while horror chill
Ran through his veins, and all his joints relaxed.
From his slack hand the garland wreathed for Eve
Down dropt, and all the faded roses shed.
Speechless he stood and pale, till thus at length
First to himself he inward silence broke:
  "O fairest of Creation, last and best
Of all God's works, creature in whom excelled
Whatever can to sight or thought be formed,
Holy, divine, good, amiable, or sweet!
How art thou lost! how on a sudden lost,
Defaced, deflowered, and now to death devote!
Rather, how hast thou yielded to transgress
The strict forbiddance, how to violate
The sacred fruit forbidden? Some cursèd fraud
Of enemy hath beguiled thee, yet unknown,
And me with thee hath ruined; for with thee
Certain my resolution is to die.
How can I live without thee? how forgo
Thy sweet converse and love so dearly joined,
To live again in these wild woods forlorn?
Should God create another Eve, and I
Another rib afford, yet loss of thee
Would never from my heart. No, no! I feel

835. low reverence . . . to the power, the first manifestation of idolatry. **837. sciential,** conferring knowledge. **845. divine of,** divining, foreboding. **846. faltering measure,** irregular beat. **853–54. excuse Came prologue.** The expression on her face was a suitable prologue to the apology and the hypocritical scene she was about to rehearse. **860. what rash . . . sought,** what I rashly sought after because it was untried and therefore not experienced. **864. tasted,** when tasted.

867. tasted such, found by tasting to be such. **872. to admiration,** in a manner to be wondered at. **876. erst,** formerly. **877 ff. which for thee ff.** Eve now adds a palpable falsehood to her sins. **884. renounce,** try to renounce. **901. devote!** doomed.

The link of nature draw me: flesh of flesh,
Bone of my bone thou art, and from thy state
Mine never shall be parted, bliss or woe."
So having said, as one from sad dismay
Recomforted, and, after thoughts disturbed,
Submitting to what seemed remediless,
Thus in calm mood his words to Eve he turned:
"Bold deed thou hast presumed, adventurous Eve,
And peril great provoked, who thus hast dared,
Had it been only coveting to eye
That sacred fruit, sacred to abstinence,
Much more to taste it, under ban to touch.
But past who can recall, or done undo?
Not God Omnipotent, nor Fate! Yet so
Perhaps thou shalt not die; perhaps the fact
Is not so heinous now—foretasted fruit,
Profaned first by the Serpent, by him first
Made common and unhallowed ere our taste,
Nor yet on him found deadly; he yet lives—
Lives, as thou saidst, and gains to live, as Man,
Higher degree of life: inducement strong
To us, as likely, tasting, to attain
Proportional ascent; which cannot be
But to be Gods, or Angels, demi-gods.
Nor can I think that God, Creator wise,
Though threatening, will in earnest so destroy
Us, his prime creatures, dignified so high,
Set over all his works; which, in our fall,
For us created, needs with us must fail,
Dependent made. So God shall uncreate,
Be frustrate, do, undo, and labour lose—
Not well conceived of God; who, though his power
Creation could repeat, yet would be loth
Us to abolish, lest the Adversary
Triumph and say: 'Fickle their state whom God
Most favours; who can please him long? Me first
He ruined, now Mankind; whom will he next?'
Matter of scorn not to be given the Foe.
However, I with thee have fixed my lot,
Certain to undergo like doom. If death
Consort with thee, death is to me as life;
So forcible within my heart I feel
The bond of Nature draw me to my own—
My own in thee; for what thou art is mine.
Our state cannot be severed; we are one,
One flesh; to lose thee were to lose myself."
So Adam; and thus Eve to him replied:
"O glorious trial of exceeding love,
Illustrious evidence, example high!
Engaging me to emulate; but, short
Of thy perfection, how shall I attain,
Adam? from whose dear side I boast me sprung,
And gladly of our union hear thee speak,
One heart, one soul in both; whereof good proof
This day affords, declaring thee resolved,
Rather than death, or aught than death more dread,
Shall separate us, linked in love so dear,
To undergo with me one guilt, one crime,
If any be, of tasting this fair fruit;
Whose virtue (for of good still good proceeds,
Direct, or by occasion) hath presented
This happy trial of thy love, which else
So eminently never had been known.
Were it I thought death menaced would ensue
This my attempt, I would sustain alone
The worst, and not persuade thee—rather die
Deserted than oblige thee with a fact
Pernicious to thy peace, chiefly assured
Remarkably so late of thy so true,
So faithful, love unequalled. But I feel
Far otherwise the event—not death, but life
Augmented, opened eyes, new hopes, new joys,
Taste so divine that what of sweet before
Hath touched my sense, flat seems to this and harsh.
On my experience, Adam, freely taste,
And fear of death deliver to the winds."
So saying, she embraced him, and for joy
Tenderly wept, much won that he his love
Had so ennobled as of choice to incur
Divine displeasure for her sake, or death.
In recompense (for such compliance bad
Such recompense best merits), from the bough
She gave him of that fair enticing fruit
With liberal hand. He scrupled not to eat,
Against his better knowledge, not deceived,
But fondly overcome with female charm.
Earth trembled from her entrails, as again
In pangs, and Nature gave a second groan;
Sky loured, and, muttering thunder, some sad drops
Wept at completing of the mortal sin
Original; . . .

BOOK X

The Argument

Man's transgression known, the guardian Angels forsake Paradise, and return up to Heaven to approve their vigilance, and are approved; God declaring that the entrance of Satan could not be by them prevented. He sends his Son to judge the transgressors; who descends, and gives sentence accordingly; then, in pity, clothes them both, and reascends. Sin and Death, sitting till then at the gates of Hell, by wondrous sympathy feeling the success of Satan in this new World, and the sin by Man there committed, resolve to sit

914–15. **flesh . . . bone.** See Genesis 2:23. **928. fact,** deed. **945. Not well conceived of God.** That is, it is not easily conceivable that God should undo and lose his work. **953. Certain,** resolved.

980. oblige, involve. **fact,** deed **984. event,** outcome.

no longer confined in Hell, but to follow Satan, their sire, up to the place of Man. To make the way easier from Hell to this World to and fro, they pave a broad highway or bridge over Chaos, according to the track that Satan first made; then, preparing for Earth, they meet him, proud of his success, returning to Hell; their mutual gratulation. Satan arrives at Pandemonium; in full assembly relates, with boasting, his success against Man; instead of applause is entertained with a general hiss by all his audience, transformed, with himself also, suddenly into Serpents, according to his doom given in Paradise; then, deluded with a show of the Forbidden Tree springing up before them, they, greedily reaching to take of the fruit, chew dust and bitter ashes. The proceedings of Sin and Death: God foretells the final victory of his Son over them, and the renewing of all things; but, for the present, commands his Angels to make several alterations in the Heavens and elements. Adam, more and more perceiving his fallen condition, heavily bewails, rejects the condolement of Eve; she persists, and at length appeases him: then, to evade the curse likely to fall on their offspring, proposes to Adam violent ways; which he approves not, but, conceiving better hope, puts her in mind of the late promise made them, that her seed should be revenged on the Serpent, and exhorts her, with him, to seek peace of the offended Deity, by repentance and supplication.

BOOK XI

The Argument

The Son of God presents to his Father the prayers of our first parents now repenting, and intercedes for them. God accepts them, but declares that they must no longer abide in Paradise; sends Michael with a band of Cherubim to dispossess them, but first to reveal to Adam future things: Michael's coming down. Adam shows to Eve certain ominous signs: he discerns Michael's approach; goes out to meet him: the Angel denounces their departure. Eve's lamentation. Adam pleads, but submits: The Angel leads him up to a high hill; sets before him in vision what shall happen till the Flood.

BOOK XII

The Argument

The Angel Michael continues, from the Flood, to relate what shall succeed; then, in the mention of Abraham, comes by degrees to explain who that Seed of the Woman shall be which was promised Adam and Eve in the Fall: his Incarnation, Death, Resurrection, and Ascension; the state of the Church till his second coming. Adam, greatly satisfied and recomforted by these relations and promises, descends the hill with Michael; wakens Eve, who all this while had slept, but with gentle dreams composed to quietness of mind and submission. Michael in either hand leads them out of Paradise, the fiery sword waving behind them, and the Cherubim taking their stations to guard the place.

. . . He ended; and thus Adam last replied:
"How soon hath thy prediction, Seer blest,
Measured this transient World, the race of Time,
Till Time stand fixed! Beyond is all abyss—
Eternity, whose end no eye can reach.
Greatly instructed I shall hence depart,
Greatly in peace of thought, and have my fill
Of knowledge, what this vessel can contain;
Beyond which was my folly to aspire.
Henceforth I learn that to obey is best,
And love with fear the only God, to walk
As in his presence, ever to observe
His providence, and on him sole depend,
Merciful over all his works, with good
Still overcoming evil, and by small
Accomplishing great things—by things deemed weak
Subverting worldly strong, and worldly wise
By simply meek; that suffering for Truth's sake
Is fortitude to highest victory,
And to the faithful death the gate of life—
Taught this by his example whom I now
Acknowledge my Redeemer ever blest."
To whom thus also the Angel last replied:
"This having learned, thou hast attained the sum
Of wisdom; hope no higher, though all the stars
Thou knew'st by name, and all the ethereal powers,
All secrets of the Deep, all Nature's works,
Or works of God in heaven, air, earth, or sea.
And all the riches of this world enjoy'dst,
And all the rule, one empire. Only add
Deeds to thy knowledge answerable; add faith;
Add virtue, patience, temperance; add love,
By name to come called Charity, the soul
Of all the rest: then wilt thou not be loth
To leave this Paradise, but shalt possess
A Paradise within thee, happier far.
Let us descend now, therefore, from this top
Of speculation; for the hour precise
Exacts our parting hence; and, see! the guards,
By me encamped on yonder hill, expect
Their motion, at whose front a flaming sword,
In signal of remove, waves fiercely round.
We may no longer stay. Go, waken Eve;
Her also I with gentle dreams have calmed,
Portending good, and all her spirits composed
To meek submission: thou, at season fit,

33. denounces, announces, proclaims.

552. He, the Angel Michael. **last,** for the last time. **554. Measured,** surveyed. **559. this vessel,** this mind. **584. Charity.** See I Corinthians 13. **588–89. top Of speculation.** "Top" is used in a double sense. "Speculation" means observation (from the Latin *specula*, "watchtower").

Let her with thee partake what thou hast heard—
Chiefly what may concern her faith to know,
The great deliverance by her seed to come
(For by the Woman's Seed) on all mankind—
That ye may live, which will be many days,
Both in one faith unanimous; though sad
With cause for evils past, yet much more cheered
With meditation on the happy end."
  He ended, and they both descend the hill.
Descended, Adam to the bower where Eve
Lay sleeping ran before, but found her waked;
And thus with words not sad she him received:
  "Whence thou return'st and whither went'st I know;
For God is also in sleep, and dreams advise,
Which he hath sent propitious, some great good
Presaging, since, with sorrow and heart's distress
Wearied, I fell asleep: but now lead on;
In me is no delay; with thee to go
Is to stay here; without thee here to stay
Is to go hence unwilling; thou to me
Art all things under Heaven, all places thou,
Who for my wilful crime art banished hence.
This further consolation yet secure
I carry hence: though all by me is lost,
Such favour I unworthy am vouchsafed,
By me the Promised Seed shall all restore."
  So spake our mother Eve; and Adam heard
Well pleased, but answered not; for now too nigh
The Archangel stood, and from the other hill
To their fixed station, all in bright array
The Cherubim descended, on the ground
Gliding meteorous, as evening mist,
Risen from a river, o'er the marish glides,
And gathers ground fast at the labourer's heel
Homeward returning. High in front advanced,
The brandished sword of God before them blazed
Fierce as a comet, which with torrid heat,
And vapour as the Libyan air adust,
Began to parch that temperate clime; whereat
In either hand the hast'ning Angel caught
Our lingering parents, and to the eastern gate
Led them direct, and down the cliff as fast
To the subjected plain; then disappeared.
They, looking back, all the eastern side beheld
Of Paradise, so late their happy seat,
Waved over by that flaming brand, the gate
With dreadful faces thronged and fiery arms:
Some natural tears they dropped, but wiped them soon;
The world was all before them, where to choose
Their place of rest, and Providence their guide:
They, hand in hand, with wandering steps and slow,
Through Eden took their solitary way.

The End.

602. **many days,** an allusion to Adam's long life of 930 years. See Genesis 5: 5.

629. **meteorous,** like meteors. 630. **marish,** marsh. 635. **adust,** scorched. 640. **subjected,** lying below.

from AREOPAGITICA

A SPEECH OF MR. JOHN MILTON FOR THE LIBERTY OF UNLICENSED PRINTING TO THE PARLIAMENT OF ENGLAND

On June 14, 1643, Parliament passed an act requiring all books and pamphlets to be licensed by an official censor before publication. Milton saw in this act and in its implications a denial of liberty disastrous to the nation as a whole and unworthy of those who had fought to overthrow the Stuart tyranny. He had also a very personal interest in the matter, since his divorce pamphlets were being published without official license, and were scandalizing many both in and out of Parliament. In the summer of 1644 Parliament ordered a search for the author of the divorce pamphlets. In November, 1644, Milton published this most famous plea on behalf of free speech and the freedom of the press. His own account of the circumstances in which the *Areopagitica* was written is to be found in his *Second Defence of the People of England*, 1654.

The title is taken from the speech addressed by Isocrates, a contemporary of Plato, to the Areopagus, or Great Council, of Athens. Like Milton's, the Areopagitic Oration of Isocrates appeals to the highest instincts of the Athenian Council, and urges its members to reconsider certain of their acts.

THEY who to states and governors of the Commonwealth direct their speech, High Court of Parliament, or wanting such access in a private condition, write that which they foresee may advance the public good; I suppose them as at the beginning of no mean endeavour, not a little altered and moved inwardly in their minds: some with doubt of what will be the success, others with fear of what will be the censure; some with hope, others with confidence of what they have to speak. And

1. **states,** heads of states, statesmen. 3. **wanting,** lacking. 6. **altered,** disturbed. 8. **success.** outcome. 9. **censure.** judgment.

me perhaps each of these dispositions, as the subject was whereon I entered, may have at other times variously affected; and likely might in these foremost expressions now also disclose which of them swayed most, but that the very attempt of this address thus made, and the thought of whom it hath recourse to, hath got the power within me to a passion, far more welcome than incidental to a preface. Which though I stay not to confess ere any ask, I shall be blameless, if it be no other than the joy and gratulation which it brings to all who wish and promote their country's liberty; whereof this whole discourse proposed will be a certain testimony, if not a trophy. For this is not the liberty which we can hope, that no grievance ever should arise in the Commonwealth, that let no man in this world expect; but when complaints are freely heard, deeply considered, and speedily reformed, then is the utmost bound of civil liberty attained that wise men look for. To which if I now manifest by the very sound of this which I shall utter, that we are already in good part arrived, and yet from such a steep disadvantage of tyranny and superstition grounded into our principles as was beyond the manhood of a Roman recovery, it will be attributed first, as is most due, to the strong assistance of God our deliverer, next to your faithful guidance and undaunted wisdom, Lords and Commons of England. Neither is it in God's esteem the diminution of his glory, when honourable things are spoken of good men and worthy magistrates; which if I now first should begin to do, after so fair a progress of your laudable deeds, and such a long obligement upon the whole realm to your indefatigable virtues, I might be justly reckoned among the tardiest, and the unwillingest of them that praise ye. . . .

If ye be thus resolved, as it were injury to think ye were not, I know not what should withhold me from presenting ye with a fit instance wherein to show both that love of truth which ye eminently profess, and that uprightness of your judgment which is not wont to be partial to yourselves; by judging over again that Order which ye have ordained *to regulate printing. That no book, pamphlet, or paper shall be henceforth printed, unless the same be first approved and licensed by such*, or at least one of such as shall be thereto appointed. For that part which preserves justly every man's copy to himself, or provides for the poor, I touch not, only wish they be not made pretences to abuse and persecute honest and painful men, who offend not in either of these particulars. But that other clause of licensing books, which we thought had died with his brother quadragesimal and matrimonial when the prelates expired, I shall now attend with such a homily, as shall lay before ye, first the inventors of it to be those whom ye will be loth to own; next what is to be thought in general of reading, whatever sort the books be; and that this Order avails nothing to the suppressing of scandalous, seditious, and libellous books, which were mainly intended to be suppressed. Last, that it will be primely to the discouragement of all learning, and the stop of truth, not only by disexercising and blunting our abilities in what we know already, but by hindering and cropping the discovery that might be yet further made both in religious and civil wisdom.

I deny not, but that it is of greatest concernment in the Church and Commonwealth, to have a vigilant eye how books demean themselves, as well as men; and thereafter to confine, imprison, and do sharpest justice on them as malefactors. For books are not absolutely dead things, but do contain a potency of life in them to be as active as that soul was whose progeny they are; nay, they do preserve as in a vial the purest efficacy and extraction of that living intellect that bred them. I know they are as lively, and as vigorously productive, as those fabulous dragon's teeth; and being sown up and down, may chance to spring up armed men. And yet, on the other hand, unless wariness be used, as good almost kill a man as kill a good book; who kills a man kills a reasonable creature, God's image; but he who destroys a good book, kills reason itself, kills the image of God, as it were in the eye. Many a man lives a burden to the earth; but a good book is the precious life-blood of a master-spirit, embalmed and treasured up on purpose to a life beyond life. 'Tis true, no age can restore a life,

1–2. dispositions . . . entered. Milton's five pamphlets on church reform, his treatise on education, and two of his pamphlets on divorce had preceded the *Areopagitica*. **14. if not a trophy,** that is, he may perhaps not win the trophy of victory in his argument for the freedom of the press, but he will have put his own feelings on record. **25. a Roman recovery.** England's recovery from her low estate under the Stuart tyranny had surpassed Rome's recovery from her numerous misfortunes.

3. copy, copyright. **6. painful,** painstaking. **9. quadragesimal,** Lenten license regulating the observance of fast days. **matrimonial.** Milton upheld the theory that marriage was wholly a civil ceremony and contract, in which the Church had properly no part. **10. expired.** The bishops had been deprived of their power by the bill which excluded them from Parliament in 1642. **35. dragon's teeth.** Jason, according to the story in Ovid's *Metamorphoses*, by Medea's direction sowed the teeth of the Colchian dragon, whence armed men sprang up. **41. in the eye.** Reason seems to be referred to as the image of God within the pupil of the eye.

whereof perhaps there is no great loss; and revolutions of ages do not oft recover the loss of a rejected truth, for the want of which whole nations fare the worse. We should be wary therefore what persecution we raise against the living labours of public men, how we spill that seasoned life of man preserved and stored up in books; since we see a kind of homicide may be thus committed, sometimes a martyrdom, and if it extend to the whole impression, a kind of massacre, whereof the execution ends not in the slaying of an elemental life, but strikes at that ethereal and fifth essence, the breath of reason itself, slays an immortality rather than a life. . . .

Good and evil we know in the field of this world grow up together almost inseparably; and the knowledge of good is so involved and interwoven with the knowledge of evil, and in so many cunning resemblances hardly to be discerned, that those confused seeds which were imposed on Psyche as an incessant labour to cull out, and sort asunder, were not more intermixed. It was from out the rind of one apple tasted, that the knowledge of good and evil as two twins cleaving together leaped forth into the world. And perhaps this is that doom which Adam fell into of knowing good and evil, that is to say of knowing good by evil.

As therefore the state of man now is, what wisdom can there be to choose, what continence to forbear without the knowledge of evil? He that can apprehend and consider vice with all her baits and seeming pleasures, and yet abstain, and yet distinguish, and yet prefer that which is truly better, he is the true wayfaring Christian. I cannot praise a fugitive and cloistered virtue, unexercised and unbreathed, that never sallies out and sees her adversary, but slinks out of the race, where that immortal garland is to be run for, not without dust and heat. Assuredly we bring not innocence into the world, we bring impurity much rather: that which purifies us is trial, and trial is by what is contrary. That virtue therefore which is but a youngling in the contemplation of evil, and knows not the utmost that vice promises to her followers, and rejects it, is but a blank virtue, not a pure; her whiteness is but an excremental whiteness. Which was the reason why our sage and serious poet Spenser, whom I dare be known to think a better teacher than Scotus or Aquinas, describing true temperance under the person of Guion, brings him in with his palmer through the cave of Mammon, and the bower of earthly bliss that he might see and know, and yet abstain. Since therefore the knowledge and survey of vice is in this world so necessary to the constituting of human virtue, and the scanning of error to the confirmation of truth, how can we more safely and with less danger scout into the regions of sin and falsity than by reading all manner of tractates, and hearing all manner of reason? And this is the benefit which may be had of books promiscuously read. . . .

Seeing therefore that those books, and those in great abundance which are likeliest to taint both life and doctrine, cannot be suppressed without the fall of learning, and of all ability in disputation, and that these books of either sort are most and soonest catching to the learned, from whom to the common people whatever is heretical or dissolute may quickly be conveyed, and that evil manners are as perfectly learnt without books a thousand other ways which cannot be stopped, and evil doctrine not with books can propagate, except a teacher guide, which he might also do without writing, and so beyond prohibiting, I am not able to unfold, how this cautelous enterprise of licensing can be exempted from the number of vain and impossible attempts. And he who were pleasantly disposed could not well avoid to liken it to the exploit of that gallant man who thought to pound up the crows by shutting his park gate.

Besides another inconvenience, if learned men be the first receivers out of books, and dispreaders both of vice and error, how shall the licensers themselves be confided in, unless we can confer upon them, or they assume to themselves above all others in the land, the grace of infallibility, and uncorruptedness? And again if it be true that a wise man like a good refiner can gather gold out of the drossiest volume, and that a fool will be a fool with the best book, yea or without book, there is no reason that we should deprive a wise man of any advantage to his wisdom, while we seek to restrain

1–2. revolutions, cycles. **9–10. the whole impression,** the total number of copies printed. **11–12. elemental life . . . fifth essence.** An "elemental" life is an earthly, material existence, depending on the four elements; the fifth essence (*quinta essentia*) is not material, but spiritual. **21–23. Psyche . . . intermixed.** The famous story of Cupid and Psyche is an incidental tale in *The Golden Ass* of Apuleius, Books IV–VI. Walter Pater's translation of the story is the best known. **38–39. that immortal garland.** See I Corinthians 9:24.

1. excremental, superficial. **4. Scotus or Aquinas.** Duns Scotus (1265–1308), the great British Franciscan Schoolman, was the chief opponent of St. Thomas Aquinas (1225?–1274), "the Seraphic Doctor" and greatest of medieval metaphysicians. **6–7. the cave of Mammon.** See *The Faerie Queene,* Book II, Canto VII. **the bower of earthly bliss.** See *ibid.,* Canto XII. **31. cautelous,** crafty.

from a fool that which being restrained will be no hindrance to his folly. For if there should be so much exactness always used to keep that from him which is unfit for his reading, we should in the judgment of Aristotle not only, but of Solomon, and of our Saviour, not vouchsafe him good precepts, and by consequence not willingly admit him to good books; as being certain that a wise man will make better use of an idle pamphlet than a fool will do of sacred Scripture.

'Tis next alleged we must not expose ourselves to temptations without necessity, and next to that, not employ our time in vain things. To both these objections one answer will serve, out of the grounds already laid, that to all men such books are not temptations, nor vanities; but useful drugs and materials wherewith to temper and compose effective and strong medicines, which man's life cannot want. The rest, as children and childish men, who have not the art to qualify and prepare these working minerals, well may be exhorted to forbear, but hindered forcibly they cannot be by all the licensing that sainted Inquisition could ever yet contrive; which is what I promised to deliver next, that this order of licensing conduces nothing to the end for which it was framed; and hath almost prevented me by being clear already while thus much hath been explaining. See the ingenuity of Truth, who when she gets a free and willing hand, opens herself faster than the pace of method and discourse can overtake her. It was the task which I began with, to shew that no Nation, or well-instituted State, if they valued books at all, did ever use this way of licensing. . . .

If we think to regulate printing, thereby to rectify manners, we must regulate all recreations and pastimes, all that is delightful to man. No music must be heard, no song be set or sung, but what is grave and Doric. There must be licensing dancers, that no gesture, motion, or deportment be taught our youth but what by their allowance shall be thought honest; for such Plato was provided of. It will ask more than the work of twenty licensers to examine all the lutes, the violins, and the guitars in every house; they must not be suffered to prattle as they do, but must be licensed what they may say. And who shall silence all the airs and madrigals, that whisper softness in chambers? The windows also, and the balconies must be thought on, there are shrewd books, with dangerous frontispieces set to sale; who shall prohibit them, shall twenty licensers? The villages also must have their visitors to inquire what lectures the bagpipe and the rebeck reads even to the ballatry, and the gamut of every municipal fiddler, for these are the countryman's Arcadias, and his Monte Mayors. Next, what more national corruption, for which England hears ill abroad, than household gluttony; who shall be the rectors of our daily rioting? and what shall be done to inhibit the multitudes that frequent those houses where drunkenness is sold and harboured? Our garments also should be referred to the licensing of some more sober work-masters to see them cut into a less wanton garb. Who shall regulate all the mixed conversation of our youth, male and female together, as is the fashion of this country, who shall still appoint what shall be discoursed, what presumed, and no further? Lastly, who shall forbid and separate all idle resort, all evil company? These things will be, and must be; but how they shall be least hurtful, how least enticing, herein consists the grave and governing wisdom of a State. . . .

If every action which is good or evil in man at ripe years were to be under pittance, and prescription, and compulsion, what were virtue but a name, what praise could be then due to well-doing, what gramercy to be sober, just or continent? Many there be that complain of divine Providence for suffering Adam to transgress; foolish tongues! When God gave him reason, he gave him freedom to choose, for reason is but choosing; he had been else a mere artificial Adam, such an Adam as he is in the motions. We ourselves esteem not of that obedience, or love, or gift, which is of force: God therefore left him free, set before him a provoking object, ever almost in his eyes herein consisted his merit, herein the right of his reward, the praise of his abstinence. Wherefore did he create passions within us, pleasures round about us, but that these rightly tempered are the very ingredients of virtue?

They are not skilful considerers of human things, who imagine to remove sin by removing the matter of sin; for, besides that it is a huge heap increasing under the very act of diminishing, though some part of it may for a time be withdrawn from some persons, it cannot from all, in such a universal thing as books are; and when this is done, yet the sin remains entire. Though ye take from a covetous

5. Solomon. See Proverbs 26:5. **6. our Saviour.** See Matthew 7:6. **19. want,** dispense with. **26–27. prevented me,** anticipated my proofs. **39. Doric.** See note 136 on page 385. **50. shrewd,** mischievous.

3. rebeck, a stringed instrument. **6. Monte Mayors.** Jorge de Montemayor (1520?–1561), Portuguese poet, was author of the prose pastoral *Diana Enamorada*, which influenced Sidney's pastoral romance *Arcadia* (1590). **7. hears ill,** is ill spoken of. **28. gramercy,** thanks. **34. motions,** puppet shows. **36. provoking,** enticing.

man all his treasure, he has yet one jewel left, ye cannot bereave him of his covetousness. Banish all objects of lust, shut up all youth into the severest discipline that can be exercised in any hermitage, ye cannot make them chaste that came not thither so: such great care and wisdom is required to the right managing of this point. Suppose we could expel sin by this means; look how much we thus expel of sin, so much we expel of virtue: for the matter of them both is the same; remove that, and ye remove them both alike.

This justifies the high providence of God, who though he commands us temperance, justice, continence, yet pours out before us even to a profuseness all desirable things, and gives us minds that can wander beyond all limit and satiety. Why should we then affect a rigour contrary to the manner of God and of nature, by abridging or scanting those means, which books freely permitted are, both to the trial of virtue, and the exercise of truth. It would be better done to learn that the law must needs be frivolous which goes to restrain things, uncertainly and yet equally working to good, and to evil. And were I the chooser, a dram of well-doing should be preferred before many times as much the forcible hindrance of evil-doing. For God sure esteems the growth and completing of one virtuous person, more than the restraint of ten vicious. . . .

Lords and Commons of England, consider what nation it is whereof ye are, and whereof ye are the governors: a nation not slow and dull, but of a quick, ingenious, and piercing spirit, acute to invent, subtle and sinewy to discourse, not beneath the reach of any point the highest that human capacity can soar to. Therefore the studies of learning in her deepest sciences have been so ancient, and so eminent among us, that writers of good antiquity, and ablest judgment, have been persuaded that even the school of Pythagoras, and the Persian wisdom, took beginning from the old philosophy of this island. And that wise and civil Roman, Julius Agricola, who governed once here for Caesar, preferred the natural wits of Britain before the laboured studies of the French. Nor is it for nothing that the grave and frugal Transylvanian sends out yearly from as far as the mountainous borders of Russia, and beyond the Hercynian wilderness, not their youth, but their staid men, to learn our language, and our theologic arts. . . .

Where there is much desire to learn, there of necessity will be much arguing, much writing, many opinions; for opinion in good men is but knowledge in the making. Under these fantastic terrors of sect and schism, we wrong the earnest and zealous thirst after knowledge and understanding which God hath stirred up in this city. What some lament of, we rather should rejoice at, should rather praise this pious forwardness among men, to reassume the ill-deputed care of their religion into their own hands again. A little generous prudence, a little forbearance of one another, and some grain of charity might win all these diligences to join, and unite into one general and brotherly search after Truth; could we but forego this prelatical tradition of crowding free consciences and Christian liberties into canons and precepts of men. I doubt not, if some great and worthy stranger should come among us, wise to discern the mould and temper of a people, and how to govern it, observing the high hopes and aims, the diligent alacrity of our extended thoughts and reasonings in the pursuance of truth and freedom, but that he would cry out as Pyrrhus did, admiring the Roman docility and courage, "If such were my Epirots, I would not despair the greatest design that could be attempted to make a Church or Kingdom happy."

Yet these are the men cried out against for schismatics and sectaries; as if, while the temple of the Lord was building, some cutting, some squaring the marble, others hewing the cedars, there should be a sort of irrational men who could not consider there must be many schisms and many dissections made in the quarry and in the timber, ere the house of God can be built. And when every stone is laid artfully together, it cannot be united into a continuity, it can but be contiguous in this world; neither can every piece of the building be of one form; nay, rather the perfection consists in this, that out of many moderate varieties and brotherly dissimilitudes that are not vastly disproportional arises the goodly and the graceful symmetry that commends the whole pile and structure.

Let us therefore be more considerate builders, more wise in spiritual architecture, when great reformation is expected. For now the time seems come, wherein Moses the great prophet may sit in heaven rejoicing to see that memorable and glorious wish of his fulfilled, when not only our seventy elders, but all the Lord's people are become prophets. No marvel then though some men, and some

17. affect a rigour, adopt a strictness. **43. civil,** cultured. **49. Hercynian wilderness,** the Roman term for the forests and hills of southern and central Germany.

13. diligences, exertions. **24. Pyrrhus,** the king of Epirus who defeated the Romans at Heraclea in 280 B.C. **32. sort,** set. **50–51. prophets.** See Numbers 11:27–29.

good men too perhaps, but young in goodness, as Joshua then was, envy them. They fret, and out of their own weakness are in agony, lest these divisions and subdivisions will undo us. The adversary again applauds, and waits the hour, when they have branched themselves out, saith he, small enough into parties and partitions, then will be our time. Fool! he sees not the firm root, out of which we all grow, though into branches: nor will beware until he see our small divided maniples cutting through at every angle of his ill-united and unwieldy brigade. And that we are to hope better of all these supposed sects and schisms, and that we shall not need that solicitude, honest, perhaps, though overtimorous, of them that vex in this behalf, but shall laugh in the end at those malicious applauders of our differences, I have these reasons to persuade me.

First, when a city shall be as it were besieged and blocked about, her navigable river infested, inroads and incursions round, defiance and battle oft rumoured to be marching up even to her walls, and suburb trenches, that then the people, or the greater part, more than at other times, wholly taken up with the study of highest and most important matters to be reformed, should be disputing, reasoning, reading, inventing, discoursing, even to a rarity, and admiration, things not before discoursed or written of, argues first a singular good will, contentedness, and confidence in your prudent foresight, and safe government, Lords and Commons; and from thence derives itself to a gallant bravery and well-grounded contempt of their enemies, as if there were no small number of as great spirits among us, as his was, who when Rome was nigh besieged by Hannibal, being in the city, bought that piece of ground at no cheap rate whereon Hannibal himself encamped his own regiment.

Next it is a lively and cheerful presage of our happy success and victory. For as in a body, when the blood is fresh, the spirits pure and vigorous, not only to vital, but to rational faculties, and those in the acutest, and the pertest operations of wit and subtlety, it argues in what good plight and constitution the body is, so when the cheerfulness of the people is so sprightly up, as that it has, not only wherewith to guard well its own freedom and safety, but to spare, and to bestow upon the solidest and sublimest points of controversy, and new invention, it betokens us not degenerated, nor drooping to a fatal decay, but casting off the old and wrinkled skin of corruption to outlive these pangs and wax young again, entering the glorious ways of Truth and prosperous virtue destined to become great and honourable in these latter ages. Methinks I see in my mind a noble and puissant nation rousing herself like a strong man after sleep, and shaking her invincible locks. Methinks I see her as an eagle mewing her mighty youth, and kindling her undazzled eyes at the full mid-day beam; purging and unscaling her long-abused sight at the fountain itself of heavenly radiance; while the whole noise of timorous and flocking birds, with those also that love the twilight, flutter about, amazed at what she means, and in their envious gabble would prognosticate a year of sects and schisms.

What should ye do then, should ye suppress all this flowery crop of knowledge and new light sprung up and yet springing daily in this city, should ye set an oligarchy of twenty engrossers over it, to bring a famine upon our minds again, when we shall know nothing but what is measured to us by their bushel? Believe it, Lords and Commons, they who counsel ye to such a suppressing do as good as bid ye suppress yourselves; and I will soon show how. If it be desired to know the immediate cause of all this free writing and free speaking, there cannot be assigned a truer than your own mild, and free, and humane government. It is the liberty, Lords and Commons, which your own valorous and happy counsels have purchased us, liberty which is the nurse of all great wits; this is that which hath rarefied and enlightened our spirits like the influence of heaven; this is that which hath enfranchised, enlarged and lifted up our apprehensions degrees above themselves.

Ye cannot make us now less capable, less knowing, less eagerly pursuing of the truth, unless ye first make yourselves, that made us so, less the lovers, less the founders of our true liberty. We can grow ignorant again, brutish, formal, and slavish, as ye found us; but you then must first become that which ye cannot be, oppressive, arbitrary, and tyrannous, as they were from whom ye have freed us. That our hearts are now more capacious, our thoughts more erected to the search and expectation of greatest and exactest things, is the issue of your own virtue propagated in us; ye cannot suppress that unless ye reinforce an abrogated and merciless law, that fathers may dispatch at will their own children. And who shall then stick closest to ye, and excite others? Not he who takes up arms for coat and conduct, and his four nobles of Danegelt. Al-

10. maniples, small companies. **42. pertest,** sprightliest.

5. mewing, renewing. **16. engrossers,** those who get a monopoly by buying up large quantities and thus command the market. **48. Danegelt,** probably an allusion to John Hampden's refusal to pay ship money. Danegelt was the old land tax levied in order to protect the country from the Danes. Charles I appealed to the precedent of Danegelt in his attempts to impose ship money. A noble was a coin worth 6*s.* 8*d.*

though I dispraise not the defence of just immunities, yet love my peace better, if that were all. Give me the liberty to know, to utter, and to argue freely according to conscience, above all liberties. . . .

Yet when the new light which we beg for shines in upon us, there be who envy, and oppose, if it come not first in at their casements. What a collusion is this, whenas we are exhorted by the wise man to use diligence, to seek for wisdom as for hidden treasures early and late, that another order shall enjoin us to know nothing but by statute. When a man hath been labouring the hardest labour in the deep mines of knowledge, hath furnished out his findings in all their equipage, drawn forth his reasons as it were a battle ranged, scattered and defeated all objections in his way, calls out his adversary into the plain, offers him the advantage of wind and sun, if he please, only that he may try the matter by dint of argument, for his opponents then to skulk, to lay ambushments, to keep a narrow bridge of licensing where the challenger should pass, though it be valour enough in soldiership, is but weakness and cowardice in the wars of Truth. For who knows not that Truth is strong next to the Almighty; she needs no policies, nor stratagems, nor licensings to make her victorious, those are the shifts and the defences that error uses against her power. Give her but room, and do not bind her when she sleeps, for then she speaks not true, as the old Proteus did, who spake oracles only when he was caught and bound, but then rather she turns herself into all shapes, except her own, and perhaps tunes her voice according to the time, as Micaiah did before Ahab, until she be adjured into her own likeness.

Yet is it not impossible that she may have more shapes than one. What else is all that rank of things indifferent, wherein Truth may be on this side, or on the other, without being unlike herself? What but a vain shadow else is the abolition of those ordinances, that hand-writing nailed to the cross, what great purchase is this Christian liberty which Paul so often boasts of? His doctrine is, that he who eats or eats not, regards a day, or regards it not, may do either to the Lord. How many other things might be tolerated in peace, and left to conscience, had we but charity, and were it not the chief stronghold of our hypocrisy to be ever judging one another. I fear yet this iron yoke of outward conformity hath left a slavish print upon our necks; the ghost of a linen decency yet haunts us. We stumble and are impatient at the least dividing of one visible congregation from another, though it be not in fundamentals; and through our forwardness to suppress, and our backwardness to recover any enthralled piece of truth out of the gripe of custom, we care not to keep truth separated from truth, which is the fiercest rent and disunion of all. We do not see that while we still affect by all means a rigid external formality, we may as soon fall again into a gross conforming stupidity, a stark and dead congealment of wood and hay and stubble forced and frozen together, which is more to the sudden degenerating of a Church than many subdichotomies of petty schisms. . . .

But of these sophisms and elenchs of merchandise I skill not. This I know, that errors in a good government and in a bad are equally almost incident; for what magistrate may not be misinformed, and much the sooner, if liberty of printing be reduced into the power of a few. But to redress willingly and speedily what hath been erred, and in highest authority to esteem a plain advertisement more than others have done a sumptuous bribe, is a virtue (honoured Lords and Commons) answerable to your highest actions, and whereof none can participate but greatest and wisest men.

2. if that were all, if it were merely a question of being immune from paying a tax. **22. bridge of licensing.** The allusion is to the tales of chivalry, in which knights often held a bridge in the manner described. **31. Proteus,** the old man of the sea in Greek mythology, who, to avoid having to prophesy, assumed many different shapes until he was finally caught and bound. **34–35. Micaiah . . . Ahab.** See I Kings 22.

13–14. linen decency, a sarcastic reference to the controversies over ecclesiastical vestments, ceremonies, and so forth. **27. subdichotomies,** subdivisions. **29. sophisms and elenchs,** fallacious arguments. **36–37. advertisement,** notification.

Andrew Marvell
1621–1678

On the statue of Marvell which stands in the city of Hull, an inscription pays tribute to him as "an incorruptible patriot, a wise statesman, and a zealous and energetic representative of this his native town." The writer of the tribute seems not to have known that Marvell was also a poet, and he forgot, or did not know, that he was born not at Hull but at Winestead, thirteen miles away, where his father was rector of the parish. It was as a politician and a public servant that Marvell was known during his lifetime, for his poems were not published until three years after his death. Few if any of his contemporaries knew that he was one of the most gifted lyric poets of England. Marvell is one of the most extraordinary combinations of opposites in English literature. That the homespun original, M.P. for Hull, author of the businesslike letters to his constituents, should be the same person who wrote the charming lyrics on the garden, and the remote Bermudas, the nymph and the fawn, seems impossible. That the author of the lyrics was the author of the savage satires of his later years; that the writer of the lines "To His Coy Mistress" was a Puritan; that the Puritan Marvell was a friend of Royalists and paid one of the finest tributes to Charles I—these are but a few of the paradoxes that meet one everywhere in his life and works.

Marvell had probably learned a good deal about life in the busy shipping town of Hull and in the local grammar school before he entered Trinity College, Cambridge, at the age of twelve. At the university he became proficient in half a dozen ancient languages. He also learned a good deal about poetry, and his verses on the birth of the Princess Anne were published with similar tributes by other undergraduates before he left. While at Cambridge he became for a short period a Roman Catholic, but returned to his father's faith soon afterwards. In 1641, two years after his graduation, his father died, and he began to make his own living as a clerk in a business house in Hull. A period of four years was spent on the Continent, where he may have been a tutor, and where he acquired the principal modern languages. In 1651, in his thirtieth year, happily for him and for English poetry, he was made tutor to the twelve-year-old daughter of Cromwell's Lord General Fairfax at his beautiful estate, Nun Appleton, in Yorkshire. For two years, while Cromwell was making the country safe for Puritanism, Marvell, "easy philosopher," was reading in Nature's book and conferring among the birds and trees. It was not cowardice, or a lack of interest in what was going on, that led Marvell to serve as tutor and write verses while his contemporaries were fighting. He is on record as having said that "the cause was too good to have been fought for," and the twentieth century is inclined to agree with him. The garden at Nun Appleton was the inspiration for Marvell's happiest and best-known lyrics. In 1653 he removed to Eton to become the tutor of William Dutton, a ward of Cromwell's in the home of the Rev. John Oxenbridge. The latter had served as a minister in the Bermudas, and there is no doubt that it was from him that Marvell got the inspiration for his poem on Bermuda.

Four years later Marvell entered public life as assistant to Milton, who was Cromwell's Latin Secretary. It is interesting to think of the two Puritan poets of the century, both of them having laid aside their singing robes, working together over state papers. In 1659 he was elected to Richard Cromwell's Parliament, and remained in Parliament to represent Hull for the rest of his life. It was due partly to his influence that Milton escaped imprisonment and perhaps even death after the Restoration. As a statesman he was a far more flexible and more practical man than Milton. Unlike Milton, Marvell could distinguish between the system and those who served the system. What he asked of public government was that it should deal justly and efficiently with the practical side of living, and so leave men free to pursue the life of sensibility and contemplation and culture. His verse after the Restoration consists of political satires, which were published in 1689.

It is only in the twentieth century that Marvell has come to be appreciated as the remarkable poet he is. It is hardly too much to say that today he is more often than any other poet chosen as the best representative of the peculiar qualities of seventeenth-century poetry. He combined in his verse the best the "metaphysical" tradition had to offer, the Cavalier richness of image and rhythm, and the smoothness and classical precision of Waller and Dryden. He "discovered nature" a century and a half before Wordsworth and the Romantic poets, though his reactions to natural phenomena were not the same as theirs. It has been said of him that he sees nature with the eye of Walton rather than with the eye of Wordsworth. He enjoyed nature as a present good, without regrets or retrospection. More than anyone before him he possessed the power to describe his own moods at the same time and in the same words as he described the external natural conditions that conduced the moods. Thus he portrays not only a scene but a state of mind, as in the famous lines of "The Garden"—a scene as it is envisaged by a selective poetic fancy, and by a fancy that has the rare gift of selecting essence rather than detail. He looked at life at times with the surprise of a schoolboy returning to the country on a holiday, at times with the detachment of a god, and from both points of view he saw that it was good.

THE GARDEN

This poem in particular, and Marvell's other poems in which he celebrates the "happy garden-state," have won for him the title "Poet Laureate of the Garden."

How vainly men themselves amaze
To win the palm, the oak, or bays,
And their incessant labours see
Crowned from some single herb, or tree,
Whose short and narrow-vergèd shade
Does prudently their toils upbraid;
While all flowers and all trees do close
To weave the garlands of repose!

Fair Quiet, have I found thee here,
And Innocence, thy sister dear?
Mistaken long, I sought you then
In busy companies of men.
Your sacred plants, if here below,
Only among the plants will grow;
Society is all but rude
To this delicious solitude.

No white nor red was ever seen
So amorous as this lovely green.
Fond lovers, cruel as their flame,
Cut in these trees their mistress' name:
Little, alas, they know or heed
How far these beauties hers exceed!
Fair trees, wheresoe'er your barks I wound,
No name shall but your own be found.

When we have run our passion's heat,
Love hither makes his best retreat.
The gods, that mortal beauty chase,
Still in a tree did end their race:
Apollo hunted Daphne so,
Only that she might laurel grow;
And Pan did after Syrinx speed,
Not as a nymph, but for a reed.

What wondrous life is this I lead!
Ripe apples drop about my head;
The luscious clusters of the vine
Upon my mouth do crush their wine;
The nectarine and curious peach
Into my hands themselves do reach;
Stumbling on melons, as I pass,
Insnared with flowers, I fall on grass.

Meanwhile the mind, from pleasure less
Withdraws into its happiness;
The mind, that ocean where each kind
Does straight its own resemblance find;
Yet it creates, transcending these,
Far other worlds and other seas,
Annihilating all that's made
To a green thought in a green shade.

Here at the fountain's sliding foot,
Or at some fruit-tree's mossy root,
Casting the body's vest aside,
My soul into the boughs does glide:
There, like a bird, it sits and sings,
Then whets and combs its silver wings,
And, till prepared for longer flight,
Waves in its plumes the various light.

Such was that happy garden-state,
While man there walked without a mate:
After a place so pure and sweet,
What other help could yet be meet!
But 'twas beyond a mortal's share
To wander solitary there:

1. amaze, perplex. **6. prudently,** by its wisdom. **7. close,** unite. **16. To,** in comparison to. **17. white . . . red,** of a lady's complexion. **18. amorous,** lovable, beautiful.

27–32. The gods . . . reed. The stories of the pursuit and transformation of Daphne and Syrinx are told in Book I of Ovid's *Metamorphoses*. **37. curious,** rare, exquisite. **41. from pleasure less.** The meaning is, apparently, "from lesser pleasure." For a careful analysis and interpretation of this stanza, as well as of the poem, see "Marvell's Garden," in William Empson's *English Pastoral Poetry*, Norton, 1938. **51. the body's vest,** the body's garment of flesh. **54. whets,** preens.

Two paradises 'twere in one
To live in paradise alone.

How well the skilful gardener drew,
Of flowers and herbs, this dial new;
Where, from above, the milder sun
Does through a fragrant zodiac run;
And, as it works, the industrious bee
Computes its time as well as we!
How could such sweet and wholesome hours
Be reckoned but with herbs and flowers?

TO HIS COY MISTRESS

Had we but world enough, and time,
This coyness, lady, were no crime.
We would sit down, and think which way
To walk, and pass our long love's day.
Thou by the Indian Ganges' side
Shouldst rubies find; I by the tide
Of Humber would complain. I would
Love you ten years before the flood,
And you should, if you please, refuse
Till the conversion of the Jews.
My vegetable love should grow
Vaster than empires and more slow;
An hundred years should go to praise
Thine eyes, and on thy forehead gaze;
Two hundred to adore each breast,
But thirty thousand to the rest;
An age at least to every part,
And the last age should show your heart.
For, lady, you deserve this state,
Nor would I love at lower rate.
But at my back I always hear
Time's wingèd chariot hurrying near;
And yonder all before us lie
Deserts of vast eternity.
Thy beauty shall no more be found,
Nor, in thy marble vault, shall sound
My echoing song; then worms shall try
That long-preserved virginity,
And your quaint honour turn to dust,
And into ashes all my lust:
The grave's a fine and private place,
But none, I think, do there embrace.
Now therefore, while the youthful hue
Sits on thy skin like morning lew,
And while thy willing soul transpires
At every pore with instant fires,
Now let us sport us while we may,
And now, like amorous birds of prey,
Rather at once our time devour
Than languish in his slow-chapped power.
Let us roll all our strength and all
Our sweetness up into one ball,
And tear our pleasures with rough strife
Thorough the iron gates of life;
Thus, though we cannot make our sun
Stand still, yet we will make him run.

BERMUDAS

The Bermudas, discovered by Juan Bermudez in 1522, were settled in the early seventeenth century by religious exiles from England, who are represented as singing the poem.

Where the remote Bermudas ride,
In the ocean's bosom unespied,
From a small boat that rowed along,
The listening winds received this song:

"What should we do but sing His praise,
That led us through the watery maze
Unto an isle so long unknown,
And yet far kinder than our own?
Where He the huge sea-monsters wracks,
That lift the deep upon their backs;
He lands us on a grassy stage,
Safe from the storms' and prelates' rage.
He gave us this eternal spring
Which here enamels every thing,
And sends the fowls to us in care,
On daily visits through the air;
He hangs in shades the orange bright,
Like golden lamps in a green night,
And does in the pomegranates close
Jewels more rich than Ormus shows;
He makes the figs our mouths to meet,
And throws the melons at our feet;
But apples plants of such a price,
No tree could ever bear them twice;
With cedars, chosen by His hand,
From Lebanon, He stores the land;
And makes the hollow seas, that roar,

The Garden. **66. this dial new,** this garden plot designed in the form of a sundial. *To His Coy Mistress.* **7. Humber,** the river on which is situated Marvell's town of Hull. **complain,** sing plaintively of love, in the fashion of the medieval courtly lover. **11. vegetable,** growing in the manner of plants. **19. state,** dignified treatment. **29. quaint,** fastidious; perhaps there is, also, a suggestion of "old-fashioned." **34. lew,** "warmth."—Margoliouth

To His Coy Mistress. **35. transpires,** comes forth. **36. instant,** eager. **40. slow-chapped,** slow-jawed; that is, slowly devouring. **44. Thorough,** through. *Bermudas.* **9. wracks,** wrecks. **15. fowls,** birds. **20. Ormus.** See *Paradise Lost*, Book II, 1–2 (page 403). **23. apples,** pineapples. **25–26. cedars . . . Lebanon,** with cedars like those of the Lebanon Mountains in Palestine; see Psalm 92:12.

Proclaim the ambergris on shore;
He cast (of which we rather boast)
The Gospel's pearl upon our coast,
And in these rocks for us did frame
A temple, where to sound His name.
Oh! let our voice His praise exalt,
Till it arrive at heaven's vault,
Which, thence (perhaps) rebounding, may
Echo beyond the Mexique Bay."

Thus sung they in the English boat,
An holy and a cheerful note;
And all the way, to guide their chime,
With falling oars they kept the time.

John Bunyan
1628–1688

The annals of Bunyan's life, it will be noted, are very different from those of most of his contemporaries who are represented in this volume. There was no cultured home for him to be born into, no private tutor to guide him, no great public school or university to provide him with a formal—or informal—education. He went through life without the "rights and privileges" of academic degrees. He was the son of a tinsmith, and after learning to read and write at the village school of Elstow in Bedfordshire, where he was born, he began work at his father's trade.

From his earliest years he was possessed of an extraordinary power of imagination and of an acute sense of sinfulness, and the two, acting together, made his boyhood and young manhood miserable almost to insanity. He seemed to himself to be the chief of sinners in his village, and as he was familiar with the Bible, and particularly with the portions of it which describe the punishments reserved for the wicked, his imagination was constantly creating images of fear and apprehensions of danger. The accounts of signs and portents in the Bible led him to look for them in even the most commonplace events of daily life. He served, from sixteen to nineteen, in the Parliamentary army, and was much affected on one occasion when another soldier, who had taken his place during a siege, was shot and killed. His marriage to a poor woman, whose name he does not give us, was an important event, because, although they married "without so much household stuff as a dish or a spoon," she did bring him two religious books, one of which, *The Plain Man's Pathway to Heaven*, was to influence greatly his life and writing. The story of his life up to his conversion, as he tells it in his autobiography, *Grace Abounding to the Chief of Sinners*, is largely one of mental and spiritual torture. Happily, at the age of twenty-seven he heard comfortable words from Heaven, and the struggle was over.

After his conversion he joined the congregation of Baptists in Bedford, and was soon taking a prominent part among them as a preacher. At the Restoration he was arrested for preaching at Nonconformist meetings. He was kept in prison in Bedford for the greater part of twelve years, until the Declaration of Indulgence was issued by Charles II. During his imprisonment he supported himself by making laces, and his vigorous mind found employment in preaching to the other prisoners and in writing. His *Grace Abounding*, 1666, was the chief product of this period. In 1672 he was released and granted a license to preach, and became the pastor of the Baptists at Bedford. In 1675 he was again imprisoned for a short period, during which he wrote the first part of *The Pilgrim's Progress*. This, his twenty-fourth book, was published in 1678. Part II of the book was brought out in 1684. Between those two dates he had published two other important works, *The Life and Death of Mr. Badman*, 1680, which portrays the opposite of the picture in *Grace Abounding*, and *The Holy War*, 1682, an allegory of the "losing and taking again of the town of Mansoul."

Bunyan's writings are based on his own vivid and varied experiences, physical and spiritual. The faculty of imagination which had caused him such anguish in his youth he employed in his *Pilgrim's Progress* so effectively that it long ago took its place among the greatest imaginative works of the world. In the eighteenth century he could, perhaps, with such powers, have competed with such novelists as Fielding and Smollett. As it was, he looked with distrust upon what the world calls

28. ambergris. See note 8 on page 350.

art, and yet he achieved, in spite of himself, a permanent and unique place among literary artists.

The simple, homely style of his book, deriving as it does from the speech of the common people and the vocabulary of the King James Bible, has made *The Pilgrim's Progress* accessible to men, women, and children of all classes. It was one of the first books printed in America, and has gone into more editions and translations than any other English book except the Bible. It is the best proof in literature that the secret of success in writing lies not so much in a conscious striving after artistic effect as in having something to say and saying it simply and directly.

from THE PILGRIM'S PROGRESS

FROM THIS WORLD TO THAT WHICH IS TO COME, DELIVERED UNDER THE SIMILITUDE OF A DREAM

from THE FIRST PART

[*Christian Escapes from the City of Destruction*]

As I walked through the wilderness of this world, I lighted on a certain place where was a den, and I laid me down in that place to sleep: and, as I slept, I dreamed a dream. I dreamed, and behold I saw a man clothed with rags, standing in a certain place, with his face from his own house, a book in his hand, and a great burden upon his back. I looked, and saw him open the book and read therein; and, as he read, he wept, and trembled; and not being able longer to contain, he brake out with a lamentable cry, saying, "What shall I do?"

In this plight, therefore, he went home and refrained himself as long as he could, that his wife and children should not perceive his distress; but he could not be silent long, because that his trouble increased. Wherefore at length he brake his mind to his wife and children; and thus he began to talk to them. "O my dear wife," said he, "and you the children of my bowels, I, your dear friend, am in myself undone by reason of a burden that lieth hard upon me; moreover, I am for certain informed that this our city will be burned with fire from heaven, in which fearful overthrow both myself, with thee, my wife, and you my sweet babes, shall miserably come to ruin, except (the which yet I see not) some way of escape can be found, whereby we may be delivered." At this his relations were sore amazed; not for that they believed that what he had said to them was true, but because they thought that some frenzy distemper had got into his head; therefore, it drawing towards night, and they hoping that sleep might settle his brains, with all haste they got him to bed. But the night was as troublesome to him as the day; wherefore, instead of sleeping, he spent it in sighs and tears. So, when the morning was come, they would know how he did. He told them, "Worse and worse." He also set to talking to them again: but they began to be hardened. They also thought to drive away his distemper by harsh and surly carriages to him; sometimes they would deride, sometimes they would chide, and sometimes they would quite neglect him. Wherefore he began to retire himself to his chamber, to pray for and pity them, and also to condole his own misery; he would also walk solitarily in the fields, sometimes reading, and sometimes praying: and thus for some days he spent his time.

Now, I saw, upon a time, when he was walking in the fields, that he was, as he was wont, reading in his book, and greatly distressed in his mind; and as he read, he burst out, as he had done before, crying, "What shall I do to be saved?"

I saw also that he looked this way and that way, as if he would run; yet he stood still, because, as I perceived, he could not tell which way to go. I looked then, and saw a man named Evangelist coming to him, who asked, "Wherefore dost thou cry?"

He answered, "Sir, I perceive by the book in my hand that I am condemned to die, and after that to come to judgment, and I find that I am not willing to do the first, nor able to do the second."

Then said Evangelist, "Why not willing to die, since this life is attended with so many evils?" The man answered, "Because I fear that this burden that is upon my back will sink me lower than the grave, and I shall fall into Tophet. And, sir, if I be not fit to go to prison, I am not fit to go to judg-

7. I dreamed a dream. From the first sentence of *The Pilgrim's Progress* to the last, almost every line of the book, as, indeed, of all Bunyan's work, shows the influence of the King James Bible. Bunyan knew the Bible by heart, and both consciously and unconsciously used its language. In the original editions, as in all complete modern editions, the quotations from the Bible are indicated in the notes. These are generally omitted here, to simplify the reading. **34. frenzy,** a rare and colloquial use of the noun as adjective.

10–11. surly carriages, surly behavior. **38. Tophet,** Hell.

ment, and from thence to execution; and the thoughts of these things make me cry."

Then said Evangelist, "If this be thy condition, why standest thou still?" He answered, "Because I know not whither to go." Then he gave him a parchment roll, and there was written within, "Fly from the wrath to come."

The man therefore read it, and looking upon Evangelist very carefully, said, "Whither must I fly?" Then said Evangelist, pointing with his finger over a very wide field, "Do you see yonder wicket-gate?" The man said, "No." Then said the other, "Do you see yonder shining light?" He said, "I think I do." Then said Evangelist, "Keep that light in your eye, and go up directly thereto: so shalt thou see the gate; at which when thou knockest it shall be told thee what thou shalt do." So I saw in my dream that the man began to run. Now, he had not run far from his own door, but his wife and children perceiving it, began to cry after him to return; but the man put his fingers in his ears, and ran on, crying, "Life! life! eternal life!" So he looked not behind him, but fled towards the middle of the plain.

The neighbours also came out to see him run; and as he ran, some mocked, others threatened, and some cried after him to return; and, among those that did so, there were two that resolved to fetch him back by force. The name of the one was Obstinate, and the name of the other Pliable. Now by this time, the man was got a good distance from them; but, however, they were resolved to pursue him, which they did, and in a little time they overtook him. Then said the man, "Neighbours, wherefore are ye come?" They said, "To persuade you to go back with us." But he said, "That can by no means be; you dwell," said he, "in the City of Destruction, the place also where I was born. I see it to be so; and dying there, sooner or later, you will sink lower than the grave, into a place that burns with fire and brimstone: be content, good neighbours, and go along with me."

Obst. What! said Obstinate, and leave our friends and our comforts behind us?

Chr. Yes, said Christian (for that was his name), because that all which you shall forsake is not worthy to be compared with a little of that which I am seeking to enjoy; . . .

[*Christian and Apollyon*]

But now in this Valley of Humiliation poor Christian was hard put to it; for he had gone but a little way, before he espied a foul fiend coming over the field to meet him; his name is Apollyon. Then did Christian begin to be afraid, and to cast in his mind whether to go back or to stand his ground. But he considered again that he had no armour for his back; and therefore thought that to turn the back to him might give him the greater advantage with ease to pierce him with his darts. Therefore he resolved to venture and stand his ground; for, thought he, had I no more in mine eye than the saving of my life, it would be the best way to stand.

So he went on, and Apollyon met him. Now the monster was hideous to behold; he was clothed with scales, like a fish (and they are his pride), he had wings like a dragon, feet like a bear, and out of his belly came fire and smoke, and his mouth was as the mouth of a lion. When he was come up to Christian, he beheld him with a disdainful countenance, and thus began to question with him.

Apol. Whence come you? and whither are you bound?

Chr. I am come from the City of Destruction, which is the place of all evil, and am going to the City of Zion.

Apol. By this I perceive thou art one of my subjects, for all that country is mine, and I am the prince and god of it. How is it, then, that thou hast run away from thy king? Were it not that I hope thou mayest do me more service, I would strike thee now, at one blow, to the ground.

Chr. I was born, indeed, in your dominions, but your service was hard, and your wages such as a man could not live on, "for the wages of sin is death"; therefore, when I was come to years, I did as other considerate persons do, look out, if, perhaps, I might mend myself.

Apol. There is no prince that will thus lightly lose his subjects, neither will I as yet lose thee: but since thou complainest of thy service and wages, be content to go back: what our country will afford, I do here promise to give thee.

Chr. But I have let myself to another, even to the King of princes; and how can I, with fairness, go back with thee?

Apol. Thou hast done in this, according to the proverb, "Changed a bad for a worse"; but it is ordinary for those that have professed themselves his servants, after a while to give him the slip, and return again to me. Do thou so too, and all shall be well.

Chr. I have given him my faith, and sworn my

12. wicket-gate, a small gate, often one set into a larger gate.

2. Apollyon, destroyer (Greek). See Revelation 9:11 and 12:2.

allegiance to him; how, then, can I go back from this, and not be hanged as a traitor?

Apol. Thou didst the same to me, and yet I am willing to pass by all, if now thou wilt yet turn again and go back.

Chr. What I promised thee was in my nonage; and, besides, I count the Prince under whose banner now I stand is able to absolve me; yea, and to pardon also what I did as to my compliance with thee; and besides, O thou destroying Apollyon! to speak truth, I like his service, his wages, his servants, his government, his company, and country better than thine; and therefore leave off to persuade me further; I am his servant, and I will follow him.

Apol. Consider, again, when thou art in cool blood, what thou art like to meet with in the way that thou goest. Thou knowest that, for the most part, his servants come to an ill end, because they are transgressors against me and my ways. How many of them have been put to shameful deaths; and, besides, thou countest his service better than mine, whereas he never came yet from the place where he is to deliver any that served him out of their hands; but as for me, how many times, as all the world very well knows, have I delivered, either by power or fraud, those that have faithfully served me, from him and his, though taken by them; and so I will deliver thee.

Chr. His forbearing at present to deliver them is on purpose to try their love, whether they will cleave to him to the end; and as for the ill end thou sayest they come to, that is most glorious in their account; for, for present deliverance, they do not much expect it, for they stay for their glory, and then they shall have it, when their Prince comes in his, and the glory of the angels.

Apol. Thou hast already been unfaithful in thy service to him; and how dost thou think to receive wages of him?

Chr. Wherein, O Apollyon! have I been unfaithful to him?

Apol. Thou didst faint at first setting out, when thou wast almost choked in the Gulf of Despond; thou didst attempt wrong ways to be rid of thy burden, whereas thou shouldest have stayed till thy Prince had taken it off; thou didst sinfully sleep and lose thy choice thing; thou wast, also, almost persuaded to go back, at the sight of the lions; and when thou talkest of thy journey, and of what thou hast heard and seen, thou art inwardly desirous of vain-glory in all that thou sayest or doest.

Chr. All this is true, and much more which thou hast left out; but the Prince whom I serve and honour is merciful, and ready to forgive; but, besides, these infirmities possessed me in thy country, for there I sucked them in; and I have groaned under them, been sorry for them, and have obtained pardon of my Prince.

Apol. Then Apollyon broke out into a grievous rage, saying, I am an enemy to this Prince; I hate his person, his laws, and people; I am come out on purpose to withstand thee.

Chr. Apollyon, beware what you do; for I am in the King's highway, the way of holiness; therefore take heed to yourself.

Apol. Then Apollyon straddled quite over the whole breadth of the way, and said, I am void of fear in this matter: prepare thyself to die; for I swear by my infernal den, that thou shalt go no further; here will I spill thy soul.

And with that he threw a flaming dart at his breast; but Christian had a shield in his hand, with which he caught it, and so prevented the danger of that.

Then did Christian draw, for he saw it was time to bestir him: and Apollyon as fast made at him, throwing darts as thick as hail; by the which, notwithstanding all that Christian could do to avoid it, Apollyon wounded him in his head, his hand, and foot. This made Christian give a little back; Apollyon, therefore, followed his work amain, and Christian again took courage, and resisted as manfully as he could. This sore combat lasted for above half a day, even till Christian was almost quite spent; for you must know that Christian, by reason of his wounds, must needs grow weaker and weaker.

Then Apollyon, espying his opportunity, began to gather up close to Christian, and wrestling with him, gave him a dreadful fall; and with that Christian's sword flew out of his hand. Then said Apollyon, "I am sure of thee now." And with that he had almost pressed him to death, so that Christian began to despair of life: but as God would have it, while Apollyon was fetching of his last blow, thereby to make a full end of this good man, Christian nimbly stretched out his hand for his sword, and caught it, saying, "Rejoice not against me, O mine enemy: when I fall I shall arise"; and with that gave him a deadly thrust, which made him give back, as one that had received his mortal wound. Christian perceiving that, made at him again, saying, "Nay, in all these things we are more

6. nonage, minority; the time of life before legal maturity, during which no contracts binding at law can be made. **48. thy choice thing,** the parchment roll with a seal, which had been given to Christian by one of the Shining Ones, and which was to admit him to the Celestial City. Christian had already recovered it.

than conquerors through him that loved us." And with that Apollyon spread forth his dragon's wings, and sped him away, that Christian for a season saw him no more. . . .

[*Christian and Faithful at Vanity Fair*]

Then I saw in my dream, that when they were got out of the wilderness, they presently saw a town before them, and the name of that town is Vanity; and at the town there is a fair kept, called Vanity Fair: it is kept all the year long; it beareth the name of Vanity Fair, because the town where it is kept is lighter than vanity; and also because all that is there sold, or that cometh thither, is vanity. As is the saying of the wise, "all that cometh is vanity."

This fair is no new-erected business, but a thing of ancient standing; I will show you the original of it.

Almost five thousand years agone, there were pilgrims walking to the Celestial City, as these two honest persons are: and Beelzebub, Apollyon, and Legion, with their companions, perceiving by the path that the pilgrims made, that their way to the city lay through this town of Vanity, they contrived here to set up a fair; a fair wherein should be sold all sorts of vanity, and that it should last all the year long: therefore at this fair are all such merchandise sold, as houses, lands, trades, places, honours, preferments, titles, countries, kingdoms, lusts, pleasures, and delights of all sorts, as whores, bawds, wives, husbands, children, masters, servants, lives, blood, bodies, souls, silver, gold, pearls, precious stones, and what not.

And, moreover, at this fair there is at all times to be seen juggling, cheats, games, plays, fools, apes, knaves, and rogues, and that of every kind.

Here are to be seen, too, and that for nothing, thefts, murders, adulteries, false swearers, and that of a blood-red colour.

And as in other fairs of less moment, there are the several rows and streets, under their proper names, where such and such wares are vended; so here likewise you have the proper places, rows, streets (viz. countries and kingdoms), where the wares of this fair are soonest to be found. Here is the Britain Row, the French Row, the Italian Row, the Spanish Row, the German Row, where several sorts of vanities are to be sold. But, as in other fairs, some one commodity is as the chief of all the fair, so the ware of Rome and her merchandise is greatly promoted in this fair; only our English nation, with some others, have taken a dislike thereat.

Now, as I said, the way to the Celestial City lies just through this town where this lusty fair is kept; and he that will go to the City, and yet not go through this town, must needs "go out of the world." The Prince of princes himself, when here, went through this town to his own country, and that upon a fair day too; yea, and as I think, it was Beelzebub, the chief lord of this fair, that invited him to buy of his vanities; yea, would have made him lord of the fair, would he but have done him reverence as he went through the town. Yea, because he was such a person of honour, Beelzebub had him from street to street, and showed him all the kingdoms of the world in a little time, that he might, if possible, allure the Blessed One to cheapen and buy some of his vanities; but he had no mind to the merchandise, and therefore left the town without laying out so much as one farthing upon these vanities. This fair, therefore, is an ancient thing, of long standing, and a very great fair. Now these pilgrims, as I said, must needs go through this fair. Well, so they did: but, behold, even as they entered into the fair, all the people in the fair were moved, and the town itself as it were in a hubbub about them; and that for several reasons: for—

First, The pilgrims were clothed with such kind of raiment as was diverse from the raiment of any that traded in that fair. The people, therefore, of the fair, made a great gazing upon them: some said they were fools, some they were bedlams, and some they are outlandish men.

Secondly, And as they wondered at their apparel, so they did likewise at their speech; for few could understand what they said; they naturally spoke the language of Canaan, but they that kept the fair were the men of this world; so that, from one end of the fair to the other, they seemed barbarians each to the other.

Thirdly, But that which did not a little amuse the merchandisers was, that these pilgrims set very light by all their wares; they cared not so much as

12. Vanity Fair. Bunyan here coins one of the most famous phrases in the language. In the description of the fair he provides us with an unrivaled and realistic picture of the ancient fairs of England, with all their hubbub, riot, and noise, and, from a moralist's point of view, their thousand and one opportunities to waste time and money on "vanities." Bunyan probably has in mind the largest of all the fairs of his day, that of Stourbridge, which was held for weeks at a time in a large field near Cambridge. Ben Jonson has immortalized its chief rival, Bartholomew Fair, in his play of that name. **24. Legion.** See Mark 5: 9.

11. lusty, joyous. **24. cheapen,** bargain for. **40. outlandish men,** foreigners. **44. the language of Canaan,** that is, the language of the chosen people. **46–47. barbarians,** used in the classical and Biblical sense of "those who speak foreign tongues."

to look upon them; and if they called upon them to buy, they would put their fingers in their ears, and cry, "Turn away mine eyes from beholding vanity," and look upwards, signifying that their trade and traffic was in heaven.

One chanced mockingly, beholding the carriage of the men, to say unto them, "What will ye buy?" But they, looking gravely upon him, answered, "We buy the truth." At that there was an occasion taken to despise the men the more; some mocking, some taunting, some speaking reproachfully, and some calling upon others to smite them. At last things came to a hubbub and great stir in the fair, insomuch that all order was confounded. Now was word presently brought to the great one of the fair, who quickly came down, and deputed some of his most trusty friends to take these men into examination, about whom the fair was almost overturned. So the men were brought to examination; and they that sat upon them asked them whence they came, whither they went, and what they did there, in such an unusual garb? The men told them that they were pilgrims and strangers in the world, and that they were going to their own country, which was the heavenly Jerusalem; and that they had given no occasion to the men of the town, nor yet to the merchandisers, thus to abuse them, and to let them in their journey, except it was for that, when one asked them what they would buy, they said they would buy the truth. But they that were appointed to examine them did not believe them to be any other than bedlams and mad, or else such as came to put all things into a confusion in the fair. Therefore they took them and beat them, and besmeared them with dirt, and then put them into the cage, that they might be made a spectacle to all the men of the fair.

There, therefore, they lay for some time, and were made the objects of any man's sport, or malice, or revenge, the great one of the fair laughing still at all that befell them. But the men being patient, and not rendering railing for railing, but contrariwise, blessing, and giving good words for bad, and kindness for injuries done, some men in the fair that were more observing, and less prejudiced than the rest, began to check and blame the baser sort for their continual abuses done by them to the men; they, therefore, in angry manner, let fly at them again, counting them as bad as the men in the cage, and telling them that they seemed confederates, and should be made partakers of their misfortunes. The other replied, that for aught they could see, the men were quiet, and sober, and intended nobody any harm; and that there were many that traded in their fair that were more worthy to be put into the cage, yea, and pillory too, than were the men they had abused. Thus, after divers words had passed on both sides, the men behaving themselves all the while very wisely and soberly before them, they fell to some blows among themselves, and did harm one to another. Then were these two poor men brought before their examiners again, and there charged as being guilty of the late hubbub that had been in the fair. So they beat them pitifully, and hanged irons upon them, and led them in chains up and down the fair, for an example and a terror to others, lest any should speak in their behalf, or join themselves unto them. But Christian and Faithful behaved themselves yet more wisely, and received the ignominy and shame that was cast upon them, with so much meekness and patience, that it won to their side, though but few in comparison of the rest, several of the men in the fair. This put the other party yet into greater rage, insomuch that they concluded the death of these two men. Wherefore they threatened, that neither cage nor irons should serve their turn, but that they should die, for the abuse they had done, and for deluding the men of the fair.

Then were they remanded to the cage again, until further order should be taken with them. So they put them in, and made their feet fast in the stocks.

Here, therefore, they called again to mind what they had heard from their faithful friend Evangelist, and were the more confirmed in their way and sufferings, by what he told them would happen to them. They also now comforted each other, that whose lot it was to suffer, even he should have the best of it; therefore each man secretly wished that he might have that preferment: but committing themselves to the all-wise disposal of him that ruleth all things, with much content, they abode in the condition in which they were, until they should be otherwise disposed of.

Then a convenient time being appointed, they brought them forth to their trial, in order to their condemnation. When the time was come, they were brought before their enemies and arraigned. The Judge's name was Lord Hate-good. Their indictment was one and the same in substance,

6. carriage, behavior. **28. let,** hinder.

23. concluded, determined upon. **45. to their trial.** The scene which follows is a vivid and realistic portrayal of a Restoration courtroom. Bunyan's mastery of the art of satire, as well as his ability to describe experiences with which he was familiar, is illustrated in his account of the jury, the witnesses, and the judge.

though somewhat varying in form, the contents whereof were this:—

"That they were enemies to and disturbers of their trade; that they had made commotions and divisions in the town, and had won a party to their own most dangerous opinions, in contempt of the law of their prince."

Then Faithful began to answer, that he had only set himself against that which hath set itself against him that is higher than the highest. "And," said he, "as for disturbance, I make none, being myself a man of peace; the parties that were won to us, were won by beholding our truth and innocence, and they are only turned from the worse to the better. And as to the king you talk of, since he is Beelzebub, the enemy of our Lord, I defy him and all his angels."

Then proclamation was made, that they that had aught to say for their lord the king against the prisoner at the bar, should forthwith appear and give in their evidence. So there came in three witnesses, to wit, Envy, Superstition, and Pickthank. They were then asked if they knew the prisoner at the bar; and what they had to say for their lord the king against him.

Then stood forth Envy, and said to this effect: "My Lord, I have known this man a long time, and will attest upon my oath before this honourable bench that he is——"

Judge. Hold! Give him his oath. So they sware him. Then he said:

Envy. My lord, this man, notwithstanding his plausible name, is one of the vilest men in our country. He neither regardeth prince nor people, law nor custom; but doth all that he can to possess all men with certain of his disloyal notions, which he in the general calls principles of faith and holiness. And, in particular, I heard him once myself affirm that Christianity and the customs of our town of Vanity were diametrically opposite, and could not be reconciled. By which saying, my lord, he doth at once not only condemn all our laudable doings, but us in the doing of them.

Judge. Then did the judge say to him, Hast thou any more to say?

Envy. My lord, I could say much more, only I would not be tedious to the court. Yet, if need be, when the other gentlemen have given in their evidence, rather than anything shall be wanting that will despatch him, I will enlarge my testimony against him. So he was bid to stand by.

Then they called Superstition, and bid him look upon the prisoner. They also asked, what he could say for their lord the king against him. Then they sware him; so he began.

Super. My lord, I have no great acquaintance with this man, nor do I desire to have further knowledge of him; however, this I know, that he is a very pestilent fellow, from some discourse that, the other day, I had with him in this town; for then, talking with him, I heard him say, that our religion was naught, and such by which a man could by no means please God. Which sayings of his, my Lord, your Lordship very well knows, what necessarily thence will follow, to wit, that we do still worship in vain, are yet in our sins, and finally shall be damned; and this is that which I have to say.

Then was Pickthank sworn, and bid say what he knew, in behalf of their lord the king, against the prisoner at the bar.

Pick. My Lord, and you gentlemen all, This fellow I have known of a long time, and have heard him speak things that ought not to be spoke; for he hath railed on our noble prince Beelzebub, and hath spoken contemptibly of his honourable friends, whose names are the Lord Old Man, the Lord Carnal Delight, the Lord Luxurious, the Lord Desire-of-Vain-Glory, my old Lord Lechery, Sir Having Greedy, with all the rest of our nobility; and he hath said, moreover, That if all men were of his mind, if possible, there is not one of these noblemen should have any longer a being in this town. Besides, he hath not been afraid to rail on you, my Lord, who are now appointed to be his judge, calling you an ungodly villain, with many other such like vilifying terms, with which he hath bespattered most of the gentry of our town.

When this Pickthank had told his tale, the Judge directed his speech to the prisoner at the bar, saying, "Thou runagate, heretic, and traitor, hast thou heard what these honest gentlemen have witnessed against thee?"

Faith. May I speak a few words in my own defence?

Judge. Sirrah! Sirrah! thou deservest to live no longer, but to be slain immediately upon the place; yet, that all men may see our gentleness towards thee, let us hear what thou, vile runagate, hast to say.

Faith. 1. I say, then, in answer to what Mr. Envy hath spoken, I never said aught but this, That what rule, or laws, or customs, or people, were flat against the Word of God, are diametrically opposite to Christianity. If I have said amiss in this, convince me of my error, and I am ready here before you to make my recantation.

2. As to the second, to wit, Mr. Superstition, and his charge against me, I said only this, That in the worship of God there is required a divine faith; but

there can be no divine faith without a divine revelation of the will of God. Therefore, whatever is thrust into the worship of God that is not agreeable to divine revelation, cannot be done but by a human faith, which faith will not be profitable to eternal life.

3. As to what Mr. Pickthank hath said, I say (avoiding terms, as that I am said to rail, and the like), That the prince of this town, with all the rabblement, his attendants, by this gentleman named, are more fit for a being in hell, than in this town and country: and so, the Lord have mercy upon me!

Then the Judge called to the jury (who all this while stood by, to hear and observe): "Gentlemen of the jury, you see this man about whom so great an uproar hath been made in this town. You have also heard what these worthy gentlemen have witnessed against him. Also you have heard his reply and confession. It lieth now in your breasts to hang him or save his life; but yet I think meet to instruct you into our law.

"There was an act made in the days of Pharaoh the Great, servant to our prince, that lest those of a contrary religion should multiply and grow too strong for him, their males should be thrown into the river. There was also an act made in the days of Nebuchadnezzar the Great, another of his servants, that whosoever would not fall down and worship his golden image, should be thrown into a fiery furnace. There was also an act made in the days of Darius, that whoso, for some time, called upon any god but him, should be cast into the lions' den. Now the substance of these laws this rebel has broken, not only in thought (which is not to be borne), but also in word and deed; which must therefore needs be intolerable.

"For that of Pharaoh, his law was made upon a supposition, to prevent mischief, no crime being yet apparent; but here is a crime apparent. For the second and third, you see he disputeth against our religion; and for the treason he hath confessed, he deserveth to die the death."

Then went the jury out, whose names were, Mr. Blind-man, Mr. No-good, Mr. Malice, Mr. Love-lust, Mr. Live-loose, Mr. Heady, Mr. High-mind, Mr. Enmity, Mr. Liar, Mr. Cruelty, Mr. Hate-light, and Mr. Implacable; who every one gave in his private verdict against him among themselves, and afterwards unanimously concluded to bring him in guilty before the Judge. And first, among themselves, Mr. Blind-man, the foreman, said, "I see clearly that this man is a heretic." Then said Mr. No-good, "Away with such a fellow from the earth." "Ay," said Mr. Malice, "for I hate the very looks of him." Then said Mr. Love-lust, "I could never endure him." "Nor I," said Mr. Live-loose, "for he would always be condemning my way." "Hang him, hang him," said Mr. Heady. "A sorry scrub," said Mr. High-mind. "My heart riseth against him," said Mr. Enmity. "He is a rogue," said Mr. Liar. "Hanging is too good for him," said Mr. Cruelty. "Let us despatch him out of the way," said Mr. Hate-light. Then said Mr. Implacable, "Might I have all the world given me, I could not be reconciled to him; therefore, let us forthwith bring him in guilty of death." And so they did; therefore he was presently condemned to be had from the place where he was, to the place from whence he came, and there to be put to the most cruel death that could be invented.

They, therefore, brought him out, to do with him according to their law; and, first, they scourged him, then they buffeted him, then they lanced his flesh with knives; after that, they stoned him with stones, then pricked him with their swords; and, last of all, they burned him to ashes at the stake. Thus came Faithful to his end.

Now I saw that there stood behind the multitude a chariot and a couple of horses, waiting for Faithful, who (so soon as his adversaries had despatched him) was taken up into it, and straightway was carried up through the clouds, with sound of trumpet, the nearest way to the celestial gate.

But as for Christian, he had some respite, and was remanded back to prison. So he there remained for a space; but he that overrules all things, having the power of their rage in his own hand, so wrought it about, that Christian for that time escaped them, and went his way. . . .

[*Christian and Hopeful in Doubting Castle*]

Now there was, not far from the place where they lay, a castle called Doubting Castle, the owner whereof was Giant Despair; and it was in his grounds they now were sleeping. Wherefore he, getting up in the morning early, and walking up and down in his fields, caught Christian and Hopeful asleep in his grounds. Then, with a grim and surly voice, he bid them awake; and asked them whence they were, and what they did in his

26–27. males should be thrown into the river. See the story of the oppression of the children of Israel in Egypt, Exodus I. **30–31. into a fiery furnace.** See the story of the three Hebrew children, Daniel 3. **33. the lions' den.** See the story of Daniel, Daniel 6.

30. a chariot and . . . horses. See the story of Elijah, II Kings 2:11.

grounds. They told him they were pilgrims, and that they had lost their way. Then said the Giant, "You have this night trespassed on me, by trampling in and lying on my grounds, and therefore you must go along with me." So they were forced to go, because he was stronger than they. They also had but little to say, for they knew themselves in a fault. The Giant, therefore, drove them before him, and put them into his castle, into a very dark dungeon, nasty and stinking to the spirits of these two men. Here, then, they lay from Wednesday morning till Saturday night, without one bit of bread, or drop of drink, or light, or any to ask how they did; they were, therefore, here in evil case, and were far from friends and acquaintance. Now in this place Christian had double sorrow, because it was through his unadvised counsel that they were brought into this distress.

Now, Giant Despair had a wife, and her name was Diffidence. So when he was gone to bed, he told his wife what he had done; to wit, that he had taken a couple of prisoners and cast them into his dungeon, for trespassing on his grounds. Then he asked her also what he had best to do further to them. So she asked him what they were, whence they came, and whither they were bound; and he told her. Then she counselled him that when he arose in the morning he should beat them without any mercy. So, when he arose, he getteth him a grievous crab-tree cudgel, and goes down into the dungeon to them, and there first falls to rating of them as if they were dogs, although they never gave him a word of distaste. Then he falls upon them, and beats them fearfully, in such sort, that they were not able to help themselves, or to turn them upon the floor. This done, he withdraws and leaves them, there to condole their misery, and to mourn under their distress. So all that day they spent the time in nothing but sighs and bitter lamentations. The next night, she, talking with her husband about them further, and understanding they were yet alive, did advise him to counsel them to make away themselves. So when morning was come, he goes to them in a surly manner as before, and perceiving them to be very sore with the stripes that he had given them the day before, he told them, that since they were never like to come out of that place, their only way would be forthwith to make an end of themselves, either with knife, halter, or poison, "for why," said he, "should you choose life, seeing it is attended with so much bitterness?" But they desired him to let them go. With that he looked ugly upon them, and, rushing to them, had doubtless made an end of them himself, but that he fell into one of his fits (for he sometimes, in sunshiny weather, fell into fits), and lost for a time the use of his hand; wherefore he withdrew, and left them as before, to consider what to do. Then did the prisoners consult between themselves, whether 'twas best to take his counsel or no; and thus they began to discourse:—

Chr. Brother, said Christian, what shall we do? The life that we now live is miserable. For my part I know not whether is best, to live thus, or to die out of hand. "My soul chooseth strangling rather than life," and the grave is more easy for me than this dungeon. Shall we be ruled by the Giant?

Hope. Indeed, our present condition is dreadful, and death would be far more welcome to me than thus for ever to abide; but yet, let us consider, the Lord of the country to which we are going hath said, Thou shalt do no murder: no, not to another man's person; much more, then, are we forbidden to take his counsel to kill ourselves. Besides, he that kills another, can but commit murder upon his body; but for one to kill himself is to kill body and soul at once. And, moreover, my brother, thou talkest of ease in the grave; but hast thou forgotten the hell, whither for certain the murderers go? For "no murderer hath eternal life," &c. And let us consider, again, that all the law is not in the hand of Giant Despair. Others, so far as I can understand, have been taken by him, as well as we; and yet have escaped out of his hand. Who knows, but that God that made the world may cause that Giant Despair may die? or that, at some time or other, he may forget to lock us in? or that he may, in a short time, have another of his fits before us, and may lose the use of his limbs? and if ever that should come to pass again, for my part, I am resolved to pluck up the heart of a man, and to try my utmost to get from under his hand. I was a fool that I did not try to do it before; but, however, my brother, let us be patient, and endure a while. The time may come that may give us a happy release; but let us not be our own murderers. With these words, Hopeful at present did moderate the mind of his brother; so they continued together (in the dark) that day, in their sad and doleful condition.

9. dark dungeon. Bunyan wrote *The Pilgrim's Progress* in Bedford jail, and his description of the dungeon was undoubtedly based in part upon his own experience. The adventures of Christian and Hopeful with Giant Despair may have been suggested in part by those of Spenser's Red Cross Knight in the Cave of Despair (see *The Faerie Queene*, Book I, Canto IX). **20. Diffidence.** The word in Bunyan's day meant "distrust, want of confidence in others," rather than "bashfulness."

17. whether. In the seventeenth century the word meant "which" (of two).

Well, towards evening, the Giant goes down into the dungeon again, to see if his prisoners had taken his counsel; but when he came there he found them alive; and truly, alive was all; for now, what for want of bread and water, and by reason of the wounds they received when he beat them, they could do little but breathe. But, I say, he found them alive; at which he fell into a grievous rage, and told them that, seeing they had disobeyed his counsel, it should be worse with them than if they had never been born.

At this they trembled greatly, and I think that Christian fell into a swoon; but, coming a little to himself again, they renewed their discourse about the Giant's counsel; and whether yet they had best to take it or no. Now Christian again seemed to be for doing it, but Hopeful made his second reply as followeth:—

Hope. My brother, said he, rememberest thou not how valiant thou hast been heretofore? Apollyon could not crush thee, nor could all that thou didst hear, or see, or feel, in the Valley of the Shadow of Death. What hardship, terror, and amazement hast thou already gone through, and art thou now nothing but fear! Thou seest that I am in the dungeon with thee, a far weaker man by nature than thou art; also, this Giant has wounded me as well as thee, and hath also cut off the bread and water from my mouth; and with thee I mourn without the light. But let us exercise a little more patience; remember how thou playedst the man at Vanity Fair, and wast neither afraid of the chain, nor cage, nor yet of bloody death. Wherefore let us (at least to avoid the shame, that becomes not a Christian to be found in) bear up with patience as well as we can.

Now, night being come again, and the Giant and his wife being in bed, she asked him concerning the prisoners, and if they had taken his counsel. To which he replied, "They are sturdy rogues, they choose rather to bear all hardship, than to make away themselves." Then said she, "Take them into the castle-yard to-morrow, and show them the bones and skulls of those that thou hast already despatched, and make them believe, ere a week comes to an end, thou also wilt tear them in pieces, as thou hast done their fellows before them."

So when the morning was come, the Giant goes to them again, and takes them into the castle-yard, and shows them, as his wife had bidden him. "These," said he, "were pilgrims as you are, once, and they trespassed in my grounds, as you have done; and when I thought fit, I tore them in pieces, and so, within ten days, I will do you. Go, get you down to your den again"; and with that he beat them all the way thither. They lay, therefore, all day on Saturday in a lamentable case, as before. Now, when night was come, and when Mrs. Diffidence and her husband, the Giant, were got to bed, they began to renew their discourse of their prisoners; and withal the old Giant wondered, that he could neither by his blows nor his counsel bring them to an end. And with that his wife replied, "I fear," said she, "that they live in hope that some will come to relieve them, or that they have picklocks about them, by the means of which they hope to escape." "And sayest thou so, my dear?" said the Giant; "I will, therefore, search them in the morning."

Well, on Saturday, about midnight, they began to pray, and continued in prayer till almost break of day.

Now, a little before it was day, good Christian, as one half amazed, brake out in this passionate speech: "What a fool," quoth he, "am I, thus to lie in a stinking dungeon, when I may as well walk at liberty! I have a key in my bosom, called Promise, that will, I am persuaded, open any lock in Doubting Castle." Then said Hopeful, "That is good news, good brother; pluck it out of thy bosom, and try."

Then Christian pulled it out of his bosom, and began to try at the dungeon door, whose bolt (as he turned the key) gave back, and the door flew open with ease, and Christian and Hopeful both came out. Then he went to the outward door that leads into the castle-yard, and, with his key, opened that door also. After, he went to the iron gate, for that must be opened too; but that lock went damnable hard, yet the key did open it. Then they thrust open the gate to make their escape with speed, but that gate, as it opened, made such a creaking that it waked Giant Despair, who, hastily rising to pursue his prisoners, felt his limbs to fail, for his fits took him again, so that he could by no means go after them. Then they went on, and came to the King's highway, and so were safe, because they were out of his jurisdiction. . . .

[*The Pilgrims Welcomed to the Celestial City*]

Now while they were thus drawing towards the gate, behold a company of the heavenly host came out to meet them; to whom it was said, by the other two Shining Ones, "These are the men that have

1. Well, towards evening. Note the conversational style of Bunyan's narrative.

6. Mrs., pronounced "Mistress" in Bunyan's day.

loved our Lord when they were in the world, and that have left all for his holy name; and he hath sent us to fetch them, and we have brought them thus far on their desired journey, that they may go in and look their Redeemer in the face with joy." Then the heavenly host gave a great shout, saying, "Blessed are they which are called unto the marriage supper of the Lamb." There came out also at this time to meet them, several of the King's trumpeters, clothed in white and shining raiment, who, with melodious noises, and loud, made even the heavens to echo with their sound. These trumpeters saluted Christian and his fellow with ten thousand welcomes from the world; and this they did with shouting, and sound of trumpet.

This done, they compassed them round on every side; some went before, some behind, and some on the right hand, some on the left (as it were to guard them through the upper regions), continually sounding as they went, with melodious noise, in notes on high: so that the very sight was to them that could behold it, as if heaven itself was come down to meet them. Thus, therefore, they walked on together; and as they walked, ever and anon these trumpeters, even with joyful sound, would, by mixing their music with looks and gestures, still signify to Christian and his brother, how welcome they were into their company, and with what gladness they came to meet them; and now were these two men, as it were, in heaven, before they came at it, being swallowed up with the sight of angels, and with hearing of their melodious notes. Here also they had the city itself in view, and they thought they heard all the bells therein to ring, to welcome them thereto. But above all, the warm and joyful thoughts that they had about their own dwelling there, with such company, and that for ever and ever. Oh, by what tongue or pen can their glorious joy be expressed! And thus they came up to the gate.

Now, when they were come up to the gate, there was written over it in letters of gold, "Blessed are they that do his commandments, that they may have right to the tree of life, and may enter in through the gates into the city."

Then I saw in my dream, that the Shining Men bid them call at the gate; the which, when they did, some looked from above over the gate, to wit, Enoch, Moses, and Elijah, &c., to whom it was said, "These pilgrims are come from the City of Destruction, for the love that they bear to the King of this place." And then the pilgrims gave in unto them each man his certificate, which they had received in the beginning; those, therefore, were carried in to the King, who, when he had read them, said, "Where are the men?" To whom it was answered, "They are standing without the gate." The King then commanded to open the gate, "That the righteous nation," said he, "which keepeth the truth may enter in."

Now I saw in my dream that these two men went in at the gate: and lo, as they entered, they were transfigured, and they had raiment put on that shone like gold. There were also that met them with harps and crowns, and gave them to them—the harps to praise withal, and the crowns in token of honour. Then I heard in my dream that all the bells in the city rang again for joy, and that it was said unto them, "ENTER YE INTO THE JOY OF YOUR LORD." I also heard the men themselves, that they sang with a loud voice, saying, "BLESSING AND HONOUR, AND GLORY, AND POWER, BE UNTO HIM THAT SITTETH UPON THE THRONE, AND UNTO THE LAMB, FOR EVER AND EVER."

Now, just as the gates were opened to let in the men, I looked in after them, and, behold, the City shone like the sun; the streets also were paved with gold, and in them walked many men, with crowns on their heads, palms in their hands, and golden harps to sing praises withal.

There were also of them that had wings, and they answered one another without intermission, saying, "Holy, holy, holy is the Lord." And after that they shut up the gates; which, when I had seen, I wished myself among them. . . .

from THE SECOND PART

[*Mr. Great-heart and Mr. Valiant-for-truth*]

Great-heart. Then this was your victory, even your faith.

Valiant. It was so. I believed, and therefore came out, got into the way, fought all that set themselves against me, and, by believing, am come to this place.

Who would true valour see,
 Let him come hither;
One here will constant be,
 Come wind, come weather.
There's no discouragement
Shall make him once relent,
His first avowed intent
 To be a pilgrim.

42. Who would true valour see. Bunyan seems here to be parodying the song "Under the Greenwood Tree," in Shakespeare's *As You Like It*, Act II, sc. 5, with which it should be compared. If he has Shakespeare's song in mind, it is one of the very few instances in which literary influence other than that of the Bible and the religious chapbooks of the day can be detected in his works.

Who so beset him round
　With dismal stories,
Do but themselves confound,—
　His strength the more is;
No lion can him fright,
He'll with a giant fight,
But he will have a right
　To be a pilgrim.

Hobgoblin nor foul fiend
　Can daunt his spirit;
He knows he at the end
　Shall life inherit.
Then fancies fly away,
He'll fear not what men say;
He'll labour night and day
　To be a pilgrim.

By this time they were got to the Enchanted Ground, where the air naturally tended to make one drowsy; and that place was all grown over with briars and thorns, excepting here and there, where was an Enchanted Arbour, upon which, if a man sits, or in which, if a man sleeps, it is a question, say some, whether ever he shall rise or wake again in this world. Over this forest, therefore, they went, both one and the other, and Mr. Great-heart went before, for that he was the guide; and Mr. Valiant-for-truth, he came behind, being there a guard, for fear, lest peradventure some fiend, or dragon, or giant, or thief, should fall upon their rear, and so do mischief. . . .

After this it was noised abroad, that Mr. Valiant-for-truth was taken with a summons by the same post as the other; and had this for a token that the summons was true, "That his pitcher was broken at the fountain." When he understood it, he called for his friends, and told them of it. "Then," said he, "I am going to my Father's; and though with great difficulty I am got hither, yet now I do not repent me of all the trouble I have been at to arrive where I am. My sword I give to him that shall succeed me in my pilgrimage, and my courage and skill to him that can get it. My marks and scars I carry with me, to be a witness for me, that I have fought his battles who now will be my rewarder." When the day that he must go hence was come, many accompanied him to the river side, into which as he went he said, "Death, where is thy sting?" And as he went down deeper, he said, "Grave, where is thy victory?" So he passed over, and all the trumpets sounded for him on the other side. . . .

Samuel Pepys

1633–1703

Mr. Pepys came late to his unique place in English literature. At the beginning of the nineteenth century he was hardly known at all outside British naval circles, but in them he was held in the highest esteem. In 1805, when England was in greater danger of invasion than she had been since 1066, a commission for the investigation of naval affairs reported that the general methods of defense instituted in the time of Samuel Pepys's Secretaryship to the Admiralty were still in force, and highly satisfactory. Twenty years later an entirely different Samuel Pepys burst upon the world in the pages of his diary. Successive editions of the diary gave more and more of its contents to an increasingly delighted world. By the twentieth century Pepys's place in the literature and in the affections of English-speaking people was as secure as Shakespeare's, although, strictly speaking, he was not a man of letters, and only in its very artlessness can his record of daily events be called a work of art.

He was born in London, the son of John Pepys, a tailor—this may account somewhat for his unceasing interest in clothes. He went to Westminster School and Magdalene College, Cambridge. The most significant event of his early years was his marriage, at twenty-two, to Elizabeth le Marchant de St. Michel, aged fifteen, the daughter of a French Huguenot refugee. He was fortunate to have as a first cousin of his father's Sir Edward Montagu, later Earl of Sandwich, and his rise in the world began with his secretaryship to Montagu. Through his influence Pepys became, after the Restoration, Clerk of the Acts in the Navy Office, and subsequently Clerk of the Privy Seal and Secretary to the Admiralty. No public servant was ever more assiduous in his duties than Mr. Pepys. He found the navy in a bad way and put it on a sound financial basis, introducing efficiency and strict

10–11. broken at the fountain." For the context see Ecclesiastes 12.

economy in the victualing of seamen and in the building and equipping of ships. It cannot be denied that he did well by himself also in the management of naval affairs, but the "honest graft" he got out of it was as nothing compared to the money he saved for the nation. There were other activities and honors outside the Navy Office. His interest in natural science led him in 1664 to join the Royal Society, of which he was later president, and in 1679 he was chosen M.P. for Harwich.

The years which saw Pepys's steady rise were not smooth or peaceful, and his own life was not unaffected by the alarms and disturbances. After the Dutch war he was called before the House of Commons to give an accounting, but came off with his own prestige increased. After the "Popish Plot," he was put into the Tower on charges of popery and treason, but was acquitted. He was reappointed in 1684, and threw himself into his tasks with his old vigor. His career in the Navy Office ended in 1688 when his lifelong friend, King James II, went into exile. Once again, in 1690, he was in prison for a brief while on an unproved charge of Jacobite intrigue. His remaining thirteen years were spent in retirement with his friends and his books and his music. He published several volumes dealing with the history and affairs of the navy.

The diary was begun on January 1, 1660, and was written mostly in a system of shorthand devised thirty years before by Thomas Shelton. Passages for which Mr. Pepys wished special secrecy he inscribed in foreign words or in signs of his own invention. His principal desire in all this seems to have been to prevent his wife and servants from reading the contents of his journal. He brought the diary sadly to an end on May 31, 1669, when his failing eyesight forced him to give it up. Mrs. Pepys died later in the same year. Pepys seems to have intended the diary for no eye but his own, but it was so much a part of him that he could not bring himself to destroy it in later years, and at his death he bequeathed it, in six manuscript volumes, containing three thousand and twelve pages and over eight hundred thousand words, with his other books to Magdalene College. Here it lay, all but forgotten, until 1819, when an undergraduate, John Smith, later a clergyman, began the work of transcription, which he finished in 1822. Parts of it were edited and published for the first time, in two volumes, by Lord Braybrooke, in 1825.

The Diary has become so well known that it needs no lengthy description. It should be remembered that it is the diary of a young man (he began it when he was twenty-six), and that it was not intended for publication. It reveals, as everybody knows, the Pepys who was a bon vivant, a mixture of good and bad, a lover of trifles, a philanderer, an insatiably curious man who was interested in every phase of life in a decade full to overflowing with exciting persons and events. But it also reveals, as many seem to forget, a young man who was as enthusiastic about his work as about his play, and who enjoyed his leisure moments all the more because he had earned them with hours of labor. It is as much the diary of Pepys the bee as of Pepys the butterfly. But he speaks for himself in its pages, and his case may be left in his own hands.

from THE DIARY

The text of *The Diary* from which these extracts are taken is, by permission, that of the standard edition of Henry B. Wheatley, published by G. Bell and Sons, Ltd., London, and Harcourt, Brace and Company, New York.

September 1st. [1666] Up and at the office all morning, and then dined at home. Got my new closet made mighty clean against tomorrow. Sir W. Penn and my wife and Mercer and I to "Polichinelly," but were there horribly frighted to see young Killigrew come in with a great many more young sparks; but we hid ourselves, so as we think they did not see us. By and by they went away, and then we were at rest again; and so, the play being done, we to Islington, and there eat and drink and mighty merry; and so home singing, and, after a letter or two at the office, to bed.

2nd (Lord's day). Some of our maids sitting up late last night to get things ready against our feast to-day, Jane called us up about three in the morn-

3–5. **Sir W. Penn,** Sir William Penn, father of William Penn, founder of Pennsylvania. Sir William, with whom Pepys was very intimate, had had a distinguished career. He was Vice-Admiral of England and a general in the first Dutch war at the age of thirty-two. His son, who turned Quaker and was to have so prominent a part in American history, is often alluded to in *The Diary.* **Mercer,** Mary Mercer, Mrs. Pepys's woman, whom, just about a month before, Mr. Pepys had taught to sing. He writes on July 30, 1666: "Thence home; and coming in I find my wife plainly dissatisfied with me that I can spend so much time with Mercer, teaching her to sing, and could never take the pains with her. Which I acknowledge; but it is because that the girl do take music mighty readily, and she do not, and music is the thing of the world that I love most, and all the pleasure almost that I can now take." **"Polichinelly,"** Polichinello (the Italian Punch), the most popular of the puppet shows of the day. Pepys mentions it nine times in his *Diary.* 6. **young Killigrew,** Thomas Killigrew, "the King's Fool or Jester," the author of a scandalous play, a notorious scapegrace, and young man about town.

ing, to tell us of a great fire they saw in the City. So I rose and slipped on my night-gown, and went to her window, and thought it to be on the back-side of Mark-lane at the farthest; but, being unused to such fires as followed, I thought it far enough off; and so went to bed again and to sleep. About seven rose again to dress myself, and there looked out at the window, and saw the fire not so much as it was and further off. So to my closet to set things to rights after yesterday's cleaning. By and by Jane comes and tells me that she hears that above 300 houses have been burned down to-night by the fire we saw, and that it is now burning down all Fish-street, by London Bridge. So I made myself ready presently, and walked to the Tower, and there got up upon one of the high places, Sir J. Robinson's little son going up with me; and there I did see the houses at that end of the bridge all on fire, and an infinite great fire on this and the other side the end of the bridge; which, among other people, did trouble me for poor little Michell and our Sarah on the bridge. So down, with my heart full of trouble, to the Lieutenant of the Tower, who tells me that it begun this morning in the King's baker's house in Pudding-lane, and that it hath burned St. Magnus's Church and most part of Fish-street already. So I down to the water-side, and there got a boat and through bridge, and there saw a lamentable fire. Poor Michell's house, as far as the Old Swan, already burned that way, and the fire running further, that in a very little time it got as far as the Steel-yard, while I was there. Everybody endeavouring to remove their goods, and flinging into the river or bringing them into lighters that lay off; poor people staying in their houses as long as till the very fire touched them, and then running into boats, or clambering from one pair of stairs by the water-side to another. And among other things, the poor pigeons, I perceive, were loth to leave their houses, but hovered about the windows and balconies till they were, some of them, burned, their wings, and fell down. Having stayed, and in an hour's time seen the fire rage every way, and nobody, to my sight, endeavouring to quench it, but to remove their goods, and leave all to the fire, and having seen it get as far as the Steel-yard, and the wind mighty high and driving it into the City; and every thing, after so long a drought, proving combustible, even the very stones of churches, and among other things the poor steeple by which pretty Mrs. —— lives, and whereof my old school-fellow Elborough is parson, taken fire in the very top, and there burned till it fell down: I to Whitehall (with a gentleman with me who desired to go off from the Tower, to see the fire, in my boat); to Whitehall, and there up to the King's closet in the Chapel, where people come about me, and I did give them an account dismayed them all, and word was carried in to the King. So I was called for, and did tell the King and Duke of York what I saw, and that unless His Majesty did command houses to be pulled down nothing could stop the fire. They seemed much troubled, and the King commanded me to go to my Lord Mayor from him, and command him to spare no houses, but to pull down before the fire every way. The Duke of York bid me tell him that if he would have any more soldiers he shall; and so did my Lord Arlington afterwards, as a great secret. Here meeting with Captain Cocke, I in his coach, which he lent me, and Creed with me to Paul's, and there walked along Watling-street, as well as I could, every creature coming away loaden with goods to save, and here and there sick people carried away in beds. Extraordinary good goods carried in carts and on backs. At last met my Lord Mayor in Canning-street, like a man spent, with a handkerchief about his neck. To the King's message he cried, like a fainting woman, "Lord! what can I do? I am spent: people will not obey me. I have been pulling down houses; but the fire overtakes us faster than we can do it." That he needed no more soldiers; and that, for himself, he must go and refresh himself, having been up all night. So he left me, and I him, and walked home, seeing people all almost distracted, and no manner of means used to quench the fire. The houses, too, so very thick thereabouts, and full of matter for burning, as pitch and tar, in Thames-street; and warehouses of oil, and wines, and brandy, and other things. Here I saw Mr. Isaac Houblon, the handsome man, prettily dressed and dirty, at his door at Dowgate, receiving some of his brothers' things, whose houses were on fire; and, as he says, have been removed twice already; and he doubts (as it soon proved) that they must be in a little time removed from his house also, which was a sad consideration. And to see the churches all filling with goods by people who themselves should have been quietly there at this time. By this time it was about twelve o'clock; and so home, and there find my guests, which was Mr. Wood and his wife Barbary

37. **pair**, set. Compare the expression, "pair of virginals," l. 44 on page 450, and the "peyre of bedes" of Chaucer's Prioress, page 99.

3. **Whitehall**, the royal palace. 10. **Duke of York**, Pepys's patron, the brother of Charles II, afterwards King James II. 21. **Paul's**, St. Paul's Cathedral.

Sheldon, and also Mr. Moone: she mighty fine, and her husband, for aught I see, a likely man. But Mr. Moone's design and mine, which was to look over my closet and please him with the sight thereof, which he hath long desired, was wholly disappointed; for we were in great trouble and disturbance at this fire, not knowing what to think of it. However, we had an extraordinary good dinner, and as merry as at this time we could be. While at dinner Mrs. Batelier come to enquire after Mr. Woolfe and Stanes (who, it seems, are related to them), whose houses in Fish-street are all burned, and they in a sad condition. She would not stay in the fright. Soon as dined, I and Moone away, and walked through the City, the streets full of nothing but people and horses and carts loaden with goods, ready to run over one another, and removing goods from one burned house to another. They now removing out of Canning-street (which received goods in the morning) into Lombard-street, and further; and among others I now saw my little goldsmith, Stokes, receiving some friend's goods, whose house itself was burned the day after. We parted at Paul's; he home, and I to Paul's Wharf, where I had appointed a boat to attend me, and took in Mr. Carcasse and his brother, whom I met in the street, and carried them below and above bridge too. And again to see the fire, which was now got further, both below and above, and no likelihood of stopping it. Met with the King and Duke of York in their barge, and with them to Queenhithe, and there called Sir Richard Browne to them. Their order was only to pull down houses apace, and so below bridge at the water-side; but little was or could be done, the fire coming upon them so fast. Good hopes there was of stopping it at the Three Cranes above, and at Buttolph's Wharf below bridge, if care be used; but the wind carries it into the City, so as we know not by the water-side what it do there. River full of lighters and boats taking in goods, and good goods swimming in the water, and only I observed that hardly one lighter or boat in three that had the goods of a house in, but there was a pair of virginals in it. Having seen as much as I could now, I away to Whitehall by appointment, and there walked to St. James's Park, and there met my wife and Creed and Wood and his wife, and walked to my boat; and there upon the water again, and to the fire up and down, it still increasing, and the wind great. So near the fire as we could for smoke; and all over the Thames, with one's face in the wind, you were almost burned with a shower of fire-drops. This is very true: so as houses were burned by these drops and flakes of fire, three or four, nay, five or six houses, one from another. When we could endure no more upon the water, we to a little ale-house on the Bankside, over against the Three Cranes, and there stayed till it was dark almost, and saw the fire grow; and, as it grew darker, appeared more and more, and in corners and upon steeples, and between churches and houses, as far as we could see up the hill of the City, in a most horrid malicious bloody flame, not like the flame of an ordinary fire. Barbary and her husband away before us. We stayed till, it being darkish, we saw the fire as only one entire arch of fire from this to the other side the bridge, and in a bow up the hill for an arch of above a mile long: it made me weep to see it. The churches, houses, and all on fire and flaming at once; and a horrid noise the flames made, and the cracking of houses at their ruin. So home with a sad heart, and there find everybody discoursing and lamenting the fire; and poor Tom Hater come with some few of his goods saved out of his house, which is burned upon Fish-street Hill. I invited him to lie at my house, and did receive his goods, but was deceived in his lying there, the news coming every moment of the growth of the fire; so as we were forced to begin to pack up our own goods, and prepare for their removal; and did by moonshine (it being brave dry and moonshine and warm weather) carry much of my goods into the garden, and Mr. Hater and I did remove my money and iron chests into my cellar, as thinking that the safest place. And got my bags of gold into my office, ready to carry away, and my chief papers of accounts also there, and my tallies into a box by themselves. So great was our fear, as Sir W. Batten hath carts come out of the country to fetch away his goods this night. We did put Mr. Hater, poor man, to bed a little; but he got but very little rest, so much noise being in my house, taking down of goods.

3rd. About four o'clock in the morning, my Lady Batten sent me a cart to carry away all my money, and plate, and best things, to Sir W. Rider's at Bednall-green. Which I did, riding myself in my

4. closet, a small private chamber for valuables or rarities. **40. lighters,** barges. **44. pair of virginals.** See note to "pair of stairs," page 449. The virginal was a small square legless spinet. The spinet proper was triangular in form. The instrument may have received its name from the circumstance that young women usually played on it.

39. tallies. A tally was a strip of wood notched to indicate the amount of a debt. The tally was then split lengthwise through the notches, so that the parts exactly corresponded, and each party to the transaction retained one half. When payment was to be made, the creditor presented his half as evidence of the amount due.

night-gown in the cart; and, Lord! to see how the streets and the highways are crowded with people running and riding, and getting of carts at any rate to fetch away things. I find Sir W. Rider tired with being called up all night, and receiving things from several friends. His house full of goods, and much of Sir W. Batten's and Sir W. Penn's. I am eased at my heart to have my treasure so well secured. Then home, with much ado to find a way, nor any sleep all this night to me nor my poor wife. But then and all this day she and I, and all my people labouring to get away the rest of our things, and did get Mr. Tooker to get me a lighter to take them in, and we did carry them (myself some) over Tower Hill, which was by this time full of people's goods, bringing their goods thither; and down to the lighter, which lay at the next quay, above the Tower Dock. And here was my neighbour's wife, Mrs. ——, with her pretty child, and some few of her things, which I did willingly give way to be saved with mine; but there was no passing with anything through the postern, the crowd was so great. The Duke of York come this day by the office, and spoke to us, and did ride with his guard up and down the City to keep all quiet (he being now General, and having the care of all). This day, Mercer being not at home, but against her mistress's order gone to her mother's, and my wife going thither to speak with W. Hewer, met her there, and was angry; and her mother saying that she was not a 'prentice girl, to ask leave every time she goes abroad, my wife with good reason was angry, and, when she came home, bid her be gone again. And so she went away, which troubled me, but yet less than it would, because of the condition we are in, fear of coming into a little time of being less able to keep one in her quality. At night lay down a little upon a quilt of W. Hewer's in the office, all my own things being packed up or gone; and after me my poor wife did the like, we having fed upon the remains of yesterday's dinner, having no fire nor dishes, nor any opportunity of dressing anything.

4th. Up by break of day to get away the remainder of my things; which I did by a lighter at the Iron gate: and my hands so full, that it was the afternoon before we could get them all away. Sir W. Penn and I to Tower-street, and there met the fire burning three or four doors beyond Mr. Howell's, whose goods, poor man, his trays, and dishes, shovels, etc., were flung all along Tower-street in the kennels, and people working therewith from one end to the other; the fire coming on in that narrow street, on both sides, with infinite fury. Sir W. Batten not knowing how to remove his wine, did dig a pit in the garden, and laid it in there; and I took the opportunity of laying all the papers of my office that I could not otherwise dispose of. And in the evening Sir W. Penn and I did dig another, and put our wine in it; and I my Parmazan cheese, as well as my wine and some other things. The Duke of York was at the office this day, at Sir W. Penn's; but I happened not to be within. This afternoon, sitting melancholy with Sir W. Penn in our garden, and thinking of the certain burning of this office, without extraordinary means, I did propose for the sending up of all our workmen from Woolwich and Deptford yards (none whereof yet appeared), and to write to Sir W. Coventry to have the Duke of York's permission to pull down houses, rather than lose this office, which would much hinder the King's business. So Sir W. Penn he went down this night, in order to the sending them up to-morrow morning; and I wrote to Sir W. Coventry about the business, but received no answer. This night Mrs. Turner (who, poor woman, was removing her goods all this day, good goods into the garden, and knows not how to dispose of them), and her husband supped with my wife and I at night, in the office, upon a shoulder of mutton from the cook's, without napkin or any thing, in a sad manner, but were merry. Only now and then walking into the garden, and saw how horridly the sky looks, all on a fire in the night, was enough to put us out of our wits; and, indeed, it was extremely dreadful, for it looks just as if it was at us, and the whole heaven on fire. I after supper walked in the dark down to Tower-street, and there saw it all on fire, at the Trinity House on that side, and the Dolphin Tavern on this side, which was very near us; and the fire with extraordinary vehemence. Now begins the practice of blowing up of houses in Tower-street, those next the Tower, which at first did frighten people more than anything; but it stopped the fire where it was done, it bringing down the houses to the ground in the same places they stood, and then it was easy to quench what little fire was in it, though it kindled nothing almost. W. Hewer this day went to see how his mother did, and comes late home, telling us how he hath been forced to remove her to Islington, her house in Pie-corner being burned; so the fire is got so far that way, and all the Old Bailey, and was run-

52. kennels, gutters.

8. Parmazan cheese, made in Parma, Italy; now spelled "Parmesan." **50. the Old Bailey,** the London Central Criminal Court, so called because it stood within the ancient bailey (inner circuit of the city wall).

ning down to Fleet-street; and Paul's is burned, and all Cheapside. I wrote to my father this night, but the post-house being burned, the letter could not go.

5th. I lay down in the office again upon W. Hewer's quilt, being mighty weary, and sore in my feet with going till I was hardly able to stand. About two in the morning my wife calls me up and tells me of new cries of fire, it being come to Barking Church, which is the bottom of our lane. I up, and finding it so, resolved presently to take her away, and did, and took my gold, which was about £2,350, W. Hewer, and Jane, down by Proundy's boat to Woolwich; but, Lord! what a sad sight it was by moonlight to see the whole City almost on fire, that you might see it plain at Woolwich, as if you were by it. There, when I come, I find the gates shut, but no guard kept at all, which troubled me, because of discourse now begun, that there is plot in it, and that the French had done it. I got the gates open, and to Mr. Sheldon's, where I locked up my gold, and charged my wife and W. Hewer never to leave the room without one of them in it, night or day. So back again, by the way seeing my goods well in the lighters at Deptford, and watched well by people. Home, and whereas I expected to have seen our house on fire, it being now about seven o'clock, it was not. But to the fire, and there find greater hopes than I expected; for my confidence of finding our office on fire was such, that I durst not ask anybody how it was with us, till I come and saw it not burned. But going to the fire, I find by the blowing up of houses, and the great help given by the workmen out of the King's yards, sent up by Sir W. Penn, there is a good stop given to it, as well at Mark-lane end as at ours; it having only burned the dial of Barking Church, and part of the porch, and was there quenched. I up to the top of Barking steeple, and there saw the saddest sight of desolation that I ever saw; everywhere great fires, oil-cellars, and brimstone, and other things burning. I became afeared to stay there long, and therefore down again as fast as I could, the fire being spread as far as I could see it; and to Sir W. Penn's, and there eat a piece of cold meat, having eaten nothing since Sunday, but the remains of Sunday's dinner. Here I met with Mr. Young and Whistler; and having removed all my things, and received good hopes that the fire at our end is stopped, they and I walked into the town, and find Fanchurch-street, Gracious-street, and Lombard-street all in dust. The Exchange a sad sight, nothing standing there, of all the statues or pillars, but Sir Thomas Gresham's picture in the corner. Walked into Moore fields (our feet ready to burn, walking through the town among the hot coals), and find that full of people, and poor wretches carrying their goods there, and everybody keeping his goods together by themselves (and a great blessing it is to them that it is fair weather for them to keep abroad night and day); drank there, and paid twopence for a plain penny loaf. Thence homeward, having passed through Cheapside and Newgate Market, all burned, and seen Anthony Joyce's house in fire. And took up (which I keep by me) a piece of glass of Mercers' Chapel in the street, where much more was, so melted and buckled by the heat of the fire like parchment. I also did see a poor cat taken out of a hole in the chimney, joining to the wall of the Exchange, with the hair all burned off the body, and yet alive. So home at night, and find there good hopes of saving our office; but great endeavours of watching all night, and having men ready; and so we lodged them in the office, and had drink and bread and cheese for them. And I lay down and slept a good night about midnight, though when I rose I heard that there had been a great alarm of French and Dutch being risen, which proved nothing. But it is a strange thing to see how long this time of life did look since Sunday, having been always full of variety of actions, and little sleep, that it looked like a week or more, and I had forgot almost the day of the week.

12. **about £2,350.** For its approximate value in present-day money, this figure should be multiplied by four. There were, of course, no banks in which Mr. Pepys might deposit his gold.

3. **having eaten nothing.** Mr. Pepys has forgotten, as his editors delight to point out, the shoulder of mutton from the cook's the day before. 12. **picture,** statute.

John Dryden
1631–1700

There are greater poets than Dryden, but certainly none more versatile. Pope remarked that he could select from Dryden's works better specimens of every mode of poetry than any other English writer could supply. He was equally at home in dramatic, satiric, narrative, and didactic poetry, was one of the greatest of English translators, and one of the most accomplished writers of English prose. Dr. Johnson called him the father of English criticism. He was the undisputed king of English letters at his death. And yet, in spite of his prominence, we have surprisingly few facts about him outside of his own writings, and if he had died before he was fifty he would probably not be just now the subject of our consideration.

He was born at Aldwinkle, Northamptonshire, of a Puritan family, and was educated at Westminster School and at Trinity College, Cambridge. He began to try his hand at verse while at school, and produced some exercises in the "metaphysical" style. Shortly after his graduation he came to London to seek his fortune, and became secretary to his cousin, Sir Gilbert Pickering, Cromwell's chamberlain. He began his literary career in 1659 with his *Heroic Stanzas* on the death of Cromwell. It is interesting that the restoration of Charles II in the following year gave him his next occasion for a poem, *Astraea Redux*, in which he celebrated the return of peace and the King. He now settled down to writing plays for a living, and may fairly be called our first professional man of letters. His first play, *The Wild Gallant*, 1663, was a complete failure, but in 1665 he gained fame with *The Indian Emperor*, in which Nell Gwyn made her first appearance at the age of fifteen. He had meanwhile married Lady Elizabeth Howard, the sister of his friend and patron Sir Robert Howard, the "Crites" of his later *Essay of Dramatic Poesy*. A combination of important events furnished the occasion of his first long poem, *Annus Mirabilis*, 1667, in which he describes the war with the Dutch and the Great Fire of London. The next year he achieved fame as a critic in his *Essay of Dramatic Poesy*, said to have been written during his absences from London on account of the plague.

The need of money kept Dryden's pen busy, and his life from now on has been described as "one long literary labor." He produced plays at the rate of three a year for an annual salary of about £300. In 1668 he was appointed poet laureate, and no holder of the laureateship ever did more to earn his salary. With it came also his appointment as Historiographer Royal. The stipends did not relieve him from the necessity of continuing his hack writing. In addition to new plays, he rewrote, or helped in revamping, several of Shakespeare's. He turned *Paradise Lost* into a rhymed opera, *The State of Innocence*, which, however, was never produced. Most of Dryden's plays are of the type known as heroic drama, in which the themes of beauty, love, and honor, and the struggles between them in the breasts of noble warrior-heroes and angelic heroines, are presented against a background of foreign battlefields, and with the rhetorical declamation of exaggerated emotions. The literary medium was the rhymed couplet, and careful attention was paid to the dramatic unities. In 1678, as if he were weary of heroics and rhymes, he produced in blank verse his greatest drama, *All for Love*, on the theme of Antony and Cleopatra.

It was in 1681, and in the midst of another national crisis, that his greatest satire was produced. Feeling was running strong against the Roman Catholic Duke of York, brother of the King and heir presumptive to the throne. The Earl of Shaftesbury became the leader of a plot to depose Charles in favor of his illegitimate son, the Duke of Monmouth. Dryden ingeniously adapted the Biblical story of David and his son Absalom to the circumstances, and published his first and greatest satire, the first part of *Absalom and Achitophel*, a few days before the trial of Shaftesbury for high treason. Other satires arose out of this, culminating in Dryden's *Mac Flecknoe*, 1682.

From political controversy Dryden turned in 1682 to religious and theological debate. His *Religio Laici*, published that year, is an exposition in verse of the reasons in favor of the Church of England. In 1687 he published *The Hind and the Panther*, in defense of the Roman Catholic faith, to which he had meanwhile become converted. Of the sincerity of his conversion, which took place about the time the Roman Catholic James II became king, there has naturally been some doubt. It must be said in his favor that he did not revert to Protestantism when William and Mary came in, although by doing so he could have retained both his laureateship and his pension. In his last years, out of pocket and out of favor, he busied himself with translations of the classics. At sixty-six, and in a single sitting, he wrote his ode "Alexander's Feast." His last poem, the *Secular Masque*, published in the year of his death, contains some of his most vigorous verse. He was, although a Roman Catholic, given burial by the side of Chaucer in Westminster Abbey, where his bust is among the most conspicuous in the Poets' Corner.

from ABSALOM AND ACHITOPHEL

Dryden, with great ingenuity, applies the Biblical story of the revolt of Absalom against his father, King David (II Samuel 13–18), to the plot of the young Duke of Monmouth against his father, Charles II. (See above, page 453.) The Earl of Shaftesbury, the leader of the Whigs, who instigated the plot, is Achitophel; Charles II is David; England is Israel; the English, the Jews; and so on. Dryden in his satire defends the King, at whose request he wrote the poem, and the Tories.

. . . The Jews, a headstrong, moody, murmuring race,
As ever tried the extent and stretch of grace;
God's pampered people, whom, debauched with ease,
No king could govern, nor no God could please
(Gods they had tried of every shape and size
That god-smiths could produce, or priests devise);
These Adam-wits, too fortunately free,
Began to dream they wanted liberty;
And when no rule, no precedent was found,
Of men by laws less circumscribed and bound,
They led their wild desires to woods and caves,
And thought that all but savages were slaves.
They too, when Saul was dead, without a blow,
Made foolish Ishbosheth the crown forego;
Who banished David did from Hebron bring,
And with a general shout proclaimed him King:
Those very Jews, who, at their very best,
Their humour more than loyalty expressed,
Now wondered why so long they had obeyed
An idol monarch, which their hands had made;
Thought they might ruin him they could create,
Or melt him to that golden calf, a State.
But these were random bolts; no formed design,
Nor interest made the factious crowd to join:
The sober part of Israel, free from stain,
Well knew the value of a peaceful reign;
And, looking backward with a wise affright,
Saw seams of wounds, dishonest to the sight:
In contemplation of whose ugly scars
They cursed the memory of civil wars.
The moderate sort of men, thus qualified,
Inclined the balance to the better side;
And David's mildness managed it so well,
The bad found no occasion to rebel.
But when to sin our biassed nature leans,
The careful Devil is still at hand with means;
And providently pimps for ill desires:
The Good Old Cause revived, a plot requires.
Plots, true or false, are necessary things,
To raise up commonwealths and ruin kings. . . .

This plot, which failed for want of common sense,
Had yet a deep and dangerous consequence:
For, as when raging fevers boil the blood,
The standing lake soon floats into a flood,
And every hostile humour, which before
Slept quiet in its channels, bubbles o'er;
So several factions from this first ferment
Work up to foam, and threat the government.
Some by their friends, more by themselves thought wise,
Opposed the power to which they could not rise.
Some had in courts been great, and thrown from thence,
Like fiends were hardened in impenitence;
Some, by their Monarch's fatal mercy, grown
From pardoned rebel kinsmen to the throne,
Were raised in power and public office high;
Strong bands, if bands ungrateful men could tie.
Of these the false Achitophel was first;
A name to all succeeding ages curst:
For close designs and crooked counsels fit;
Sagacious, bold, and turbulent of wit;
Restless, unfixed in principles and place;
In power unpleased, impatient of disgrace:
A fiery soul, which, working out its way,
Fretted the pigmy body to decay,
And o'er-informed the tenement of clay.
A daring pilot in extremity;
Pleased with the danger, when the waves went high,
He sought the storms; but, for a calm unfit,
Would steer too near the sands, to boast his wit.
Great wits are sure to madness near allied,
And thin partitions do their bounds divide;
Else why should he, with wealth and honour blest,
Refuse his age the needful hours of rest?
Punish a body which he could not please;
Bankrupt of life, yet prodigal of ease?

51. Adam-wits, persons who, like Adam in the Garden of Eden, were not contented with their fortunate lot. **57. Saul,** Oliver Cromwell. **58. Ishbosheth,** Richard Cromwell, who succeeded Oliver. **59. Hebron,** probably Scotland, where Charles was crowned king before his coronation in London (Jerusalem). **66. golden calf.** See Exodus 32:1–6. **75. thus qualified,** of such a disposition.

82. The Good Old Cause, that of the Commonwealth. **134. This plot,** the alleged Popish Plot of 1678, about which the Whigs were, or pretended to be, so concerned. See page 303. **150. the false Achitophel.** The Earl of Shaftesbury (Anthony Ashley Cooper), who was leading the plot against Charles, had once been a trusted adviser of the King.

And all to leave what with his toil he won,
To that unfeathered two-legged thing, a son;
Got, while his soul did huddled notions try,
And born a shapeless lump, like anarchy.
In friendship false, implacable in hate;
Resolved to ruin or to rule the State.
To compass this the triple bond he broke,
The pillars of the public safety shook,
And fitted Israel for a foreign yoke;
Then seized with fear, yet still affecting fame,
Usurped a patriot's all-atoning name.
So easy still it proves in factious times,
With public zeal to cancel private crimes.
How safe is treason, and how sacred ill,
Where none can sin against the people's will!
Where crowds can wink, and no offence be known,
Since in another's guilt they find their own!
Yet fame deserved no enemy can grudge;
The statesman we abhor, but praise the judge.
In Israel's courts ne'er sat an Abbethdin
With more discerning eyes, or hands more clean;
Unbribed, unsought, the wretched to redress;
Swift of despatch, and easy of access.
Oh, had he been content to serve the crown,
With virtues proper only to the gown;
Or had the rankness of the soil been freed
From cockle, that oppressed the noble seed;
David for him his tuneful harp had strung,
And Heaven had wanted one immortal song.
But wild Ambition loves to slide, not stand,
And Fortune's ice prefers to Virtue's land.
Achitophel, grown weary to possess
A lawful fame, and lazy happiness,
Disdained the golden fruit to gather free,
And lent the crowd his arm to shake the tree.
Now, manifest of crimes contrived long since,
He stood at bold defiance with his Prince;
Held up the buckler of the people's cause
Against the crown, and skulked behind the laws.
The wished occasion of the Plot he takes;
Some circumstances finds, but more he makes.
By buzzing emissaries fills the ears
Of listening crowds with jealousies and fears
Of arbitrary counsels brought to light,
And proves the King himself a Jebusite.
Weak arguments! which yet he knew full well
Were strong with people easy to rebel.
For, governed by the moon, the giddy Jews
Tread the same track when she the prime renews;
And once in twenty years, their scribes record,
By natural instinct they change their lord.
Achitophel still wants a chief, and none
Was found so fit as warlike Absalom:
Not that he wished his greatness to create
(For politicians neither love nor hate),
But, for he knew his title not allowed,
Would keep him still depending on the crowd,
That kingly power, thus ebbing out, might be
Drawn to the dregs of a democracy.
Him he attempts with studied arts to please,
And sheds his venom with such words as these:
"Auspicious prince, at whose nativity
Some royal planet ruled the southern sky;
Thy longing country's darling and desire;
Their cloudly pillar and their guardian fire,
Their second Moses, whose extended wand
Divides the seas and shows the promised land;
Whose dawning day in every distant age
Has exercised the sacred prophet's rage:
The people's prayer, the glad diviners' theme,
The young men's vision, and the old men's dream!
Thee, Saviour, thee, the nation's vows confess,
And, never satisfied with seeing, bless:
Swift unbespoken pomps thy steps proclaim,
And stammering babes are taught to lisp thy name.
How long wilt thou the general joy detain,
Starve and defraud the people of thy reign?
Content ingloriously to pass thy days
Like one of virtue's fools that feeds on praise;
Till thy fresh glories, which now shine so bright,
Grow stale and tarnish with our daily sight.
Believe me, royal youth, thy fruit must be
Or gathered ripe, or rot upon the tree.
Heaven has to all allotted, soon or late,
Some lucky revolution of their fate;
Whose motions if we watch and guide with skill
(For human good depends on human will),
Our fortune rolls as from a smooth descent,
And from the first impression takes the bent;
But if unseized she glides away like wind,
And leaves repenting folly far behind.
Now, now she meets you with a glorious prize,
And spreads her locks before her as she flies.
Had thus old David, from whose loins you spring,
Not dared, when Fortune called him, to be King,
At Gath an exile he might still remain,
And Heaven's anointing oil had been in vain.
Let his successful youth your hopes engage;
But shun the example of declining age:
Behold him setting in his western skies,
The shadows lengthening as the vapours rise.

171. Got, begot. **huddled,** confused. **175. triple bond,** the alliance, formed in 1667, which bound England, Sweden, and the Dutch Republic against France. It was broken in 1670 by Charles, when England allied herself with France against Holland. Dryden's accusation of Shaftesbury is, in this instance, unjust. **188. Abbethdin,** chief justice of the Jewish court. Shaftesbury had been Lord Chancellor.

264. Gath, Brussels.

He is not now, as when on Jordan's sand
The joyful people thronged to see him land,
Covering the beach, and blackening all the strand;
But, like the Prince of Angels, from his height
Comes tumbling downward with diminished light;
Betrayed by one poor Plot to public scorn
(Our only blessing since his curst return),
Those heaps of people which one sheaf did bind,
Blown off and scattered by a puff of wind.
What strength can he to your designs oppose,
Naked of friends, and round beset with foes?
If Pharaoh's doubtful succour he should use,
A foreign aid would more incense the Jews;
Proud Egypt would dissembled friendship bring,
Foment the war, but not support the King:
Nor would the royal party e'er unite
With Pharaoh's arms to assist the Jebusite;
Or if they should, their interest soon would break,
And with such odious aid make David weak.
All sorts of men by my successful arts,
Abhorring kings, estrange their altered hearts
From David's rule: and 'tis the general cry,
'Religion, commonwealth, and liberty.'
If you, as champion of the public good,
Add to their arms a chief of royal blood,
What may not Israel hope, and what applause
Might such a general gain by such a cause?
Not barren praise alone, that gaudy flower
Fair only to the sight, but solid power;
And nobler is a limited command,
Given by the love of all your native land,
Than a successive title, long and dark,
Drawn from the mouldy rolls of Noah's ark."
  What cannot praise effect in mighty minds,
When flattery soothes, and when ambition blinds!
Desire of power, on earth a vicious weed,
Yet, sprung from high, is of celestial seed;
In God 'tis glory; and when men aspire,
'Tis but a spark too much of heavenly fire.
The ambitious youth, too covetous of fame,
Too full of angels' metal in his frame,
Unwarily was led from virtues ways,
Made drunk with honour, and debauched with praise.
Half loth and half consenting to the ill
(For loyal blood within him struggled still),
He thus replied: "And what pretence have I
To take up arms for public liberty?
My father governs with unquestioned right;
The faith's defender, and mankind's delight;
Good, gracious, just, observant of the laws:
And Heaven by wonders has espoused his cause.
Whom has he wronged in all his peaceful reign?
Who sues for justice to his throne in vain?
What millions has he pardoned of his foes
Whom just revenge did to his wrath expose?
Mild, easy, humble, studious of our good,
Inclined to mercy, and averse from blood;
If mildness ill with stubborn Israel suit,
His crime is God's belovèd attribute.
What could he gain, his people to betray
Or change his right for arbitrary sway?
Let haughty Pharaoh curse with such a reign
His fruitful Nile, and yoke a servile train.
If David's rule Jerusalem displease,
The dog-star heats their brains to this disease.
Why then should I, encouraging the bad,
Turn rebel and run popularly mad?
Were he a tyrant, who by lawless might
Oppressed the Jews and raised the Jebusite,
Well might I mourn; but nature's holy bands
Would curb my spirits and restrain my hands:
The people might assert their liberty,
But what was right in them were crime in me.
His favour leaves me nothing to require,
Prevents my wishes, and outruns desire.
What more can I expect while David lives?
All but his kingly diadem he gives:
And that"—but there he paused; then sighing said—
"Is justly destined for a worthier head.
For when my father from his toils shall rest
And late augment the number of the blest,
His lawful issue shall the throne ascend,
Or the collateral line, where that shall end.
His brother, though oppressed with vulgar spite,
Yet dauntless, and secure of native right,
Of every royal virtue stands possessed;
Still dear to all the bravest and the best.
His courage foes, his friends his truth proclaim;
His loyalty the King, the world his fame.
His mercy even the offending crowd will find,
For sure he comes of a forgiving kind.
Why should I then repine at Heaven's decree,
Which gives me no pretence to royalty?
Yet oh that fate, propitiously inclined,
Had raised my birth, or had debased my mind;
To my large soul not all her treasure lent,
And then betrayed it to a mean descent!
I find, I find my mounting spirits bold,
And David's part disdains my mother's mould.
Why am I scanted by a niggard birth?
My soul disclaims the kindred of her earth
And, made for empire, whispers me within,

270. on Jordan's sand, a reference to the landing of Charles at Dover on May 1, 1660. **281. Pharaoh's doubtful succour.** Charles was a pensioner of Louis XIV (Pharaoh), whose financial aid helped to make him independent of Parliament.

'Desire of greatness is a god-like sin.' "
  Him staggering so when Hell's dire agent found,
While fainting Virtue scarce maintained her ground,
He pours fresh forces in, and thus replies:
  "The eternal God, supremely good and wise,
Imparts not these prodigious gifts in vain:
What wonders are reserved to bless your reign!
Against your will, your arguments have shown,
Such virtue's only given to guide a throne.
Not that your father's mildness I contemn;
But manly force becomes the diadem.
'Tis true he grants the people all they crave
And more, perhaps, than subjects ought to have:
For lavish grants suppose a monarch tame,
And more his goodness than his wit proclaim.
But when should people strive their bonds to break,
If not when kings are negligent or weak?
Let him give on till he can give no more,
The thrifty Sanhedrin shall keep him poor;
And every shekel which he can receive,
Shall cost a limb of his prerogative.
To ply him with new plots shall be my care;
Or plunge him deep in some expensive war;
Which when his treasury can no more supply,
He must, with the remains of kingship, buy.
His faithful friends, our jealousies and fears
Call Jebusites, and Pharaoh's pensioners;
Whom when our fury from his aid has torn,
He shall be naked left to public scorn.
The next successor, whom I fear and hate,
My arts have made obnoxious to the state;
Turned all his virtues to his overthrow,
And gained our elders to pronounce a foe.
His right, for sums of necessary gold,
Shall first be pawned, and afterward be sold;
Till time shall ever-wanting David draw,
To pass your doubtful title into law:
If not, the people have a right supreme
To make their kings; for kings are made for them.
All empire is no more than power in trust,
Which, when resumed, can be no longer just.
Succession, for the general good designed,
In its own wrong a nation cannot bind;
If altering that the people can relieve,
Better one suffer than a nation grieve.
The Jews well know their power: ere Saul they chose,
God was their King, and God they durst depose.
Urge now your piety, your filial name,
A father's right, and fear of future fame;
The public good, that universal call,
To which even Heaven submitted, answers all.
Nor let his love enchant your generous mind;
'Tis Nature's trick to propagate her kind.
Our fond begetters, who would never die,
Love but themselves in their posterity.
Or let his kindness by the effects be tried,
Or let him lay his vain pretence aside.
God said he loved your father; could he bring
A better proof, than to anoint him King?
It surely showed he loved the shepherd well,
Who gave so fair a flock as Israel.
Would David have you thought his darling son?
What means he, then, to alienate the crown?
The name of godly he may blush to bear:
'Tis after God's own heart to cheat his heir.
He to his brother gives supreme command;
To you a legacy of barren land,
Perhaps the old harp, on which he thrums his lays,
Or some dull Hebrew ballad in your praise.
Then the next heir, a prince severe and wise,
Already looks on you with jealous eyes;
Sees through the thin disguises of your arts,
And marks your progress in the people's hearts.
Though now his mighty soul its grief contains,
He meditates revenge who least complains;
And, like a lion, slumbering in the way,
Or sleep dissembling, while he waits his prey,
His fearless foes within his distance draws,
Constrains his roaring, and contracts his paws;
Till at the last, his time for fury found,
He shoots with sudden vengeance from the ground;
The prostrate vulgar passes o'er and spares,
But with a lordly rage his hunter tears.
Your case no tame expedients will afford:
Resolve on death, or conquest by the sword,
Which for no less a stake than life you draw;
And self-defence is Nature's eldest law.
Leave the warm people no considering time;
For then rebellion may be thought a crime.
Prevail yourself of what occasion gives,
But try your title while your father lives;
And that your arms may have a fair pretence,
Proclaim you take them in the King's defence;
Whose sacred life each minute would expose
To plots, from seeming friends, and secret foes.
And who can sound the depth of David's soul?
Perhaps his fear his kindness may control.
He fears his brother, though he loves his son,
For plighted vows too late to be undone.
If so, by force he wishes to be gained,
Like women's lechery, to seem constrained:
Doubt not; but when he most affects the frown,
Commit a pleasing rape upon the crown.

390. Sanhedrin, the supreme council in ancient Jerusalem. Here, of course, it signifies the British Parliament.

Secure his person to secure your cause:
They who possess the Prince, possess the laws."
 He said, and this advice above the rest,
With Absalom's mild nature suited best:
Unblamed of life (ambition set aside),
Not stained with cruelty, nor puffed with pride,
How happy had he been, if destiny
Had higher placed his birth, or not so high!
His kingly virtues could have claimed a throne,
And blest all other countries but his own.
But charming greatness since so few refuse,
'Tis juster to lament him than accuse.
Strong were his hopes a rival to remove,
With blandishments to gain the public love;
To head the faction while their zeal was hot,
And popularly prosecute the plot.
To further this, Achitophel unites
The malcontents of all the Israelites;
Whose differing parties he could wisely join,
For several ends, to serve the same design:
The best (and of the princes some were such),
Who thought the power of monarchy too much;
Mistaken men, and patriots in their hearts;
Not wicked, but seduced by impious arts.
By these the springs of property were bent,
And wound so high, they cracked the government. . . .

Some of their chiefs were princes of the land:
In the first rank of these did Zimri stand;
A man so various, that he seemed to be
Not one, but all mankind's epitome:
Stiff in opinions, always in the wrong;
Was everything by starts, and nothing long;
But, in the course of one revolving moon,
Was chemist, fiddler, statesman, and buffoon:
Then all for women, painting, rhyming, drinking,
Besides ten thousand freaks that died in thinking.
Blest madman, who could every hour employ,
With something new to wish, or to enjoy!
Railing and praising were his usual themes;
And both (to show his judgment) in extremes:
So over-violent, or over-civil,
That every man, with him, was God or Devil.
In squandering wealth was his peculiar art:
Nothing went unrewarded but desert.
Beggared by fools, whom still he found too late,
He had his jest, and they had his estate.
He laughed himself from court; then sought relief
By forming parties, but could ne'er be chief;
For, spite of him, the weight of business fell
On Absalom and wise Achitophel:
Thus, wicked but in will, of means bereft,
He left not faction, but of that was left. . . .

544. Zimri, George Villiers, Duke of Buckingham, whose political and literary philosophies were equally disliked by Dryden. The author thought his character of Zimri "worth the whole poem."

MAC FLECKNOE

OR, A SATIRE UPON THE TRUE-BLUE PROTESTANT POET, T. S.

The Earl of Shaftesbury, the leader of the Whigs, whom Dryden made the villain of his *Absalom and Achitophel*, was acquitted of the charge of high treason and released from the Tower in November, 1681. To celebrate the event, the Whigs issued a medal in his honor. Dryden thereupon wrote a bitter satire, *The Medal, A Satire Against Sedition*, which was published anonymously early in 1682. That year saw also the publication of Dryden's *Mac Flecknoe*, a satirical poem whose exact origins are uncertain but whose intentions are altogether clear.

Whatever the particular occasion of *Mac Flecknoe*, there is no doubt of Dryden's attitude towards Thomas Shadwell, a rival poet and dramatist. The two authors had once been on good terms, but as Dryden was a Tory who eventually became a Roman Catholic and Shadwell was a Whig and a Protestant, it is not surprising that hostility developed between them. The title of the poem, *Mac Flecknoe* (Son of Flecknoe) is due chiefly to a satire by Andrew Marvell, "Fleckno an English Priest at Rome," written about 1645. Richard Flecknoe was actually an Irish priest and the author of what Marvell called "hideous verse." Dryden in his poem, which may have been written shortly after Flecknoe's death in 1678, represents Flecknoe as prince of the realm of Nonsense, who in age yields his throne to his son Shadwell, "who most resembles me."

Of Shadwell, who succeeded Dryden as poet laureate, it is only fair to say that, although by no means a first-rate poet or dramatist, he deserved a much better fate than to be known for ever through Dryden's most devastating couplet:

> The rest to some faint meaning make pretence,
> But Sh——— never deviates into sense.

The brilliance of Dryden's mock-heroic satire is obvious to every reader, and is equaled only by that of Dryden's great successor in the art of personal satire, Alexander Pope, who acknowledged the indebtedness of his *Dunciad* to *Mac Flecknoe*.

All human things are subject to decay,
And when fate summons, monarchs must obey.
This Flecknoe found, who, like Augustus, young

3. Augustus. Augustus Caesar, first Emperor of Rome, was only thirty-two when he came to power.

Was called to empire, and had governed long;
In prose and verse, was owned, without dispute,
Through all the realms of *Nonsense*, absolute.
This aged prince, now flourishing in peace,
And blest with issue of a large increase;
Worn out with business, did at length debate
To settle the succession of the State;
And, pondering which of all his sons was fit
To reign, and wage immortal war with wit,
Cried: "'T is resolved; for nature pleads, that he
Should only rule, who most resembles me.
Sh—— alone my perfect image bears,
Mature in dulness from his tender years:
Sh—— alone, of all my sons, is he
Who stands confirmed in full stupidity.
The rest to some faint meaning make pretence,
But Sh—— never deviates into sense.
Some beams of wit on other souls may fall,
Strike through, and make a lucid interval;
But Sh——'s genuine night admits no ray,
His rising fogs prevail upon the day.
Besides, his goodly fabric fills the eye,
And seems designed for thoughtless majesty;
Thoughtless as monarch oaks that shade the plain,
And, spread in solemn state, supinely reign,
Heywood and Shirley were but types of thee,
Thou last great prophet of tautology.
Even I, a dunce of more renown than they,
Was sent before but to prepare thy way;
And, coarsely clad in Norwich drugget, came
To teach the nations in thy greater name.
My warbling lute, the lute I whilom strung,
When to King John of Portugal I sung,
Was but the prelude of that glorious day,
When thou on silver Thames didst cut thy way,
With well-timed oars before the royal barge,
Swelled with the pride of thy celestial charge;
And big with hymn, commander of a host,
The like was ne'er in Epsom blankets tossed.
Methinks I see the new Arion sail,
The lute still trembling underneath thy nail.
At thy well-sharpened thumb from shore to shore
The treble squeaks for fear, the basses roar;
Echoes from Pissing Alley Sh—— call,
And Sh—— they resound from Aston Hall.
About thy boat the little fishes throng,
As at the morning toast that floats along.
Sometimes, as prince of thy harmonious band,
Thou wield'st thy papers in thy threshing hand.
St. André's feet ne'er kept more equal time,
Not ev'n the feet of thy own *Psyche's* rhyme;
Though they in number as in sense excel:
So just, so like tautology, they fell,
That, pale with envy, Singleton forswore
The lute and sword, which he in triumph bore,
And vowed he ne'er would act Villerius more."
Here stopped the good old sire, and wept for joy
In silent raptures of the hopeful boy.
All arguments, but most his plays, persuade,
That for anointed dulness he was made.

Close to the walls which fair Augusta bind,
(The fair Augusta much to fears inclined)
An ancient fabric raised t' inform the sight,
There stood of yore, and Barbican it hight:
A watchtower once; but now, so fate ordains,
Of all the pile an empty name remains.
From its old ruins brothel-houses rise,
Scenes of lewd loves, and of polluted joys,
Where their vast courts the mother-strumpets keep,
And, undisturbed by watch, in silence sleep.
Near these a Nursery erects its head,
Where queens are formed, and future heroes bred;
Where unfledged actors learn to laugh and cry,
Where infant punks their tender voices try,
And little Maximins the gods defy.
Great Fletcher never treads in buskins here,
Nor greater Jonson dares in socks appear;
But gentle Simkin just reception finds
Amidst this monument of vanished minds;
Pure clinches the suburban Muse affords,
And Panton waging harmless war with words.
Here Flecknoe, as a place to fame well known,
Ambitiously designed his Sh——'s throne;

29. **Heywood and Shirley.** Thomas Heywood and James Shirley, dramatists of the first half of the seventeenth century, do not merit Dryden's contemptuous criticism. 33. **Norwich drugget,** a coarse cloth. 36. **King John of Portugal.** Flecknoe claimed to have had King John as a patron when he was in Portugal. 42. **Epsom blankets.** Shadwell was the author of a lively comedy of manners, *Epsom Wells* and of a comedy of humours, *The Virtuoso*, in which a character is tossed in a blanket. 43. **Arion.** Shadwell, who was a musician as well as an author, is sarcastically likened to Arion, the celebrated Greek lyric poet and musician of the seventh century B.C. Arion's music is said to have charmed fishes, and he is reputed to have been saved from drowning on one occasion when a song-loving dolphin carried him to land.

53. **St. André's feet.** St. André was a well-known French dancing-master of the day. 54. ***Psyche's* rhyme,** a reference to Shadwell's opera *Psyche.* 57. **Singleton,** a contemporary actor and opera singer. 59. **Villerius,** a character in Davenant's *The Siege of Rhodes*, 1656, the first English opera. 65. **Augusta,** London. 67. **hight,** was called. 74. **Nursery,** a training school for young actors. 78. **Maximins.** Maximin, Tyrant of Rome, is a character in Dryden's early heroic drama *Tyrannic Love*, 1669. 79–80. **Fletcher . . . Jonson,** allusions to the Elizabethan tragedies of John Fletcher, the collaborator of Francis Beaumont, and to the comedies of Ben Jonson. Buskins and socks are the symbolic footwear of tragic and comic actors respectively. 81. **Simkin,** a clown of the day. 83. **clinches,** puns. 84. **Panton,** Thomas Panton, a contemporary wit and punster.

For ancient Dekker prophesied long since,
That in this pile should reign a mighty prince,
Born for a scourge of wit, and flail of sense;
To whom true dulness should some *Psyches* owe,
But worlds of *Misers* from his pen should flow;
Humorists and hypocrites it should produce,
Whole Raymond families, and tribes of Bruce.
  Now Empress Fame had published the renown
Of Sh——'s coronation through the town.
Roused by report of Fame, the nations meet,
From near Bunhill, and distant Watling Street.
No Persian carpets spread th' imperial way,
But scattered limbs of mangled poets lay;
From dusty shops neglected authors come,
Martyrs of pies, and relics of the bum.
Much Heywood, Shirley, Ogleby there lay,
But loads of Sh—— almost choked the way.
Bilked stationers for yeomen stood prepared,
And Herringman was captain of the guard.
The hoary prince in majesty appeared,
High on a throne of his own labours reared.
At his right hand our young Ascanius sate,
Rome's other hope, and pillar of the State.
His brows thick fogs, instead of glories, grace,
And lambent dulness played around his face.
As Hannibal did to the altars come,
Sworn by his sire a mortal foe to Rome;
So Sh—— swore, nor should his vow be vain,
That he till death true dulness would maintain;
And, in his father's right, and realm's defence,
Ne'er to have peace with wit, nor truce with sense.
The king himself the sacred unction made,
As king by office, and as priest by trade.
In his sinister hand, instead of ball,
He placed a mighty mug of potent ale;
Love's Kingdom to his right he did convey,
At once his scepter, and his rule of sway;
Whose righteous lore the prince had practised young,
And from whose loins recorded *Psyche* sprung.
His temples, last, with poppies were o'erspread,
That nodding seemed to consecrate his head.
Just at that point of time, if fame not lie,
On his left hand twelve reverend owls did fly.
So Romulus, 'tis sung, by Tiber's brook,
Presage of sway from twice six vultures took.
Th' admiring throng loud acclamations make,
And omens of his future empire take.
The sire then shook the honours of his head,
And from his brows damps of oblivion shed
Full on the filial dulness: long he stood,
Repelling from his breast the raging god;
At length burst out in this prophetic mood:
  "Heavens bless my son, from Ireland let him reign
To far Barbadoes on the western main;
Of his dominion may no end be known,
And greater than his father's be his throne;
Beyond *Love's Kingdom* let him stretch his pen!"
He paused, and all the people cried, "Amen."
Then thus continued he: "My son, advance
Still in new impudence, new ignorance.
Success let others teach, learn thou from me
Pangs without birth, and fruitless industry.
Let *Virtuosos* in five years be writ;
Yet not one thought accuse thy toil of wit.
Let gentle George in triumph tread the stage,
Make Dorimant betray, and Loveit rage;
Let Cully, Cockwood, Fopling, charm the pit,
And in their folly show the writer's wit.
Yet still thy fools shall stand in thy defence,
And justify their author's want of sense.
Let 'em be all by thy own model made
Of dulness, and desire no foreign aid;
That they to future ages may be known,
Not copies drawn, but issue of thy own.
Nay, let thy men of wit too be the same,
All full of thee, and differing but in name.
But let no alien S—dl—y interpose,
To lard with wit thy hungry *Epsom* prose.
And when false flowers of rhetoric thou wouldst cull,
Trust nature, do not labour to be dull;
But write thy best, and top; and, in each line,
Sir Formal's oratory will be thine:

87. Dekker, Thomas Dekker, the Elizabethan poet, dramatist, and pamphleteer. **91–93. *Misers* . . . Bruce.** Shadwell's comedy *The Miser* is an adaptation from Molière. Raymond is a character in his play *The Humorists.* Bruce is a character in his *The Virtuoso,* referred to above. **97. distant Watling Street.** "Distant" is used sarcastically, as both places are in the same small neighborhood. **101. pies . . . bum.** Leaves from books of poetry which were placed under pies or used for toilet paper. **102. Ogleby,** John Ogleby, a third-rate poet and translator of the day. **104. Bilked stationers,** booksellers who had been cheated out of sales. **105. Herringman,** Dryden's former publisher. **108. Ascanius,** the son of Aeneas, hero of Virgil's *Aeneid,* to whom Shadwell is satirically compared. **112. Hannibal,** the Carthaginian general who as a boy was forced to swear eternal hatred to Rome. **120. sinister** (accented on the second syllable), left. **ball,** the orb; a small globe surmounted with a cross which is held in the king's left hand at his coronation as a symbol of sovereignty. **122. *Love's Kingdom*,** a drama by Flecknoe.

130–31. Romulus . . . vultures. Romulus, the legendary founder of Rome, was said to have had the future site of the city revealed to him by the flight of twelve vultures. **149. five years.** Shadwell was reputed to have spent five years writing *The Virtuoso.* **151. gentle George,** Sir George Etherege, one of the most prominent Restoration comic dramatists. The characters mentioned in the next two lines are from his plays. **163. S—dl—y,** Sir Charles Sedley, the famous Restoration dramatist and wit, who had written a prologue to Shadwell's *Epsom Wells.* **168. Sir Formal's oratory,** a reference to the speeches of a character in Shadwell's *The Virtuoso.*

Sir Formal, though unsought, attends thy quill,
And does thy northern dedications fill.
Nor let false friends seduce thy mind to fame,
By arrogating Jonson's hostile name.
Let father Flecknoe fire thy mind with praise,
And uncle Ogleby thy envy raise.
Thou art my blood, where Jonson has no part:
What share have we in nature, or in art?
Where did his wit on learning fix a brand,
And rail at arts he did not understand?
Where made he love in Prince Nicander's vein,
Or swept the dust in *Psyche's* humble strain?
Where sold he bargains, 'whip-stitch, kiss my arse,'
Promised a play and dwindled to a farce?
When did his Muse from Fletcher scenes purloin,
As thou whole Etherege dost transfuse to thine?
But so transfused, as oil on water's flow,
His always floats above, thine sinks below.
This is thy province, this thy wondrous way,
New humours to invent for each new play:
This is that boasted bias of thy mind,
By which one way, to dulness, 'tis inclined;
Which makes thy writings lean on one side still,
And, in all changes, that way bends thy will.
Nor let thy mountain-belly make pretence
Of likeness; thine's a tympany of sense.
A tun of man in thy large bulk is writ,
But sure thou'rt but a kilderkin of wit.
Like mine, thy gentle numbers feebly creep;
Thy tragic Muse gives smiles, thy comic sleep.
With whate'er gall thou sett'st thyself to write,
Thy inoffensive satires never bite;
In thy felonious heart though venom lies,
It does but touch thy Irish pen, and dies.
Thy genius calls thee not to purchase fame
In keen iambics, but mild anagram.
Leave writing plays, and choose for thy command
Some peaceful province in Acrostic land.
There thou may'st wings display and altars raise,
And torture one poor word ten thousand ways;
Or, if thou wouldst thy different talents suit,

170. northern dedications. Shadwell had dedicated several of his works to the Duke of Newcastle and his family, whose seat was in the north of England. **172. Jonson's . . . name.** In the preface to his first comedy, *The Sullen Lovers*, Shadwell called Jonson "the man of all the world I most passionately admire for his excellency in his dramatic poetry." **179. Nicander,** a character in Shadwell's *Psyche.* **181. 'whip-stitch,'** a tailor. **182. dwindled to a farce?** Jonson, that is to say, never allowed vulgar terms, such as Dryden has quoted in l. 181 from Shadwell's *Virtuoso,* to turn his comedies into farces. **185. flow.** The word is a noun here. **194. tympany.** Dr. Johnson, in quoting this passage in his *Dictionary,* defines *tympany* as follows: "A kind of obstructed flatulence that swells the body like a drum." **196. kilderkin,** a small barrel. **207. wings display,** an allusion to the fancifully shaped poems of some of the Metaphysical Poets. See Herbert's "Easter Wings," page 345.

Set thy own songs, and sing them to thy lute."
He said:—but his last words were scarcely heard;
For Bruce and Longvil had a trap prepared,
And down they sent the yet declaiming bard.
Sinking he left his drugget robe behind,
Borne upwards by a subterranean wind.
The mantle fell to the young prophet's part,
With double portion of his father's art.

from THRENODIA AUGUSTALIS

A FUNERAL PINDARIC POEM TO THE HAPPY MEMORY OF KING CHARLES II

15

A warlike Prince ascends the regal state,
A Prince long exercised by Fate:
Long may he keep, though he obtains it late.
Heroes in Heaven's peculiar mould are cast,
They and their poets are not formed in haste;
Man was the first in God's design, and man was made the last.
False heroes, made by flattery so,
Heaven can strike out, like sparkles, at a blow;
But ere a Prince is to perfection brought,
He costs Omnipotence a second thought.
With toil and sweat,
With hardening cold and forming heat
The Cyclops did their strokes repeat,
Before the impenetrable shield was wrought.
It looks as if the Maker would not own
The noble work for his,
Before 'twas tried and found a masterpiece.

from THE HIND AND THE PANTHER

Dryden became a Roman Catholic in 1686, during the first year of the reign of James II, and *The Hind and the Panther*, his most famous religious poem, is a defense of his new faith. It was published in April, 1687, one week after James had issued his Declaration of Indulgence

212. Bruce . . . trap. In Shadwell's *Virtuoso* these two characters remove Sir Formal from the scene in similar fashion. **216–17. mantle . . . double portion.** An irreverent allusion to the prophet Elisha's receiving the mantle and a double portion of the spirit of his master Elijah when the latter was taken up into heaven by a whirlwind. Cf. II Kings 2. **429. A warlike Prince,** James II, who succeeded his brother, Charles II, in 1685. James's reign, in spite of Dryden's prayer, was one of the shortest in English history. He was deposed in 1688 and fled to France. **441. The Cyclops,** the giants or Titans of Greek mythology who had only one eye, in their foreheads. They are represented in various legends as assistants of Hephaestus (Vulcan) and makers of the metal armor and ornaments of gods and heroes.

for all dissenters from the Church of England, which suspended all penal laws and abrogated all acts which imposed a religious test for any secular office. In his preface to the poem, which is more conciliatory to the Protestant dissenters than is the body of the poem itself, Dryden indicates that James's Declaration had taken him by surprise, and that he would have treated the Protestant dissenters with less severity if he had at first known of James's intention.

In the poem the Hind represents the Roman Catholic Church, persecuted by the Panther (the Church of England), the Wolf (the Presbyterians), and other animals symbolizing various sects. The poem is in three parts, of the first of which Dryden says "I have endeavoured to raise and give it the majestic turn of heroic poesy."

PART I

[*The Hind*]

A milk-white Hind, immortal and unchanged,
Fed on the lawns, and in the forest ranged;
Without unspotted, innocent within,
She feared no danger, for she knew no sin.
Yet had she oft been chased with horns and hounds
And Scythian shafts, and many wingèd wounds
Aimed at her heart; was often forced to fly,
And doomed to death, though fated not to die.
Not so her young; for their unequal line
Was hero's make, half human, half divine.
Their earthly mould obnoxious was to fate,
The immortal part assumed immortal state.
Of these a slaughtered army lay in blood,
Extended o'er the Caledonian wood,
Their native walk; whose vocal blood arose
And cried for pardon on their perjured foes.
Their fate was fruitful, and the sanguine seed,
Endued with souls, increased the sacred breed.
So captive Israel multiplied in chains,
A numerous exile, and enjoyed her pains.
With grief and gladness mixed, their mother viewed
Her martyred offspring and their race renewed;
Their corps to perish, but their kind to last,
So much the deathless plant the dying fruit surpassed.
Panting and pensive now she ranged alone,
And wandered in the kingdoms once her own.
The common hunt, though from their rage restrained
By sovereign power, her company disdained,
Grinned as they passed, and with a glaring eye
Gave gloomy signs of secret enmity.
'Tis true she bounded by and tripped so light,
They had not time to take a steady sight;
For truth has such a face and such a mien
As to be loved needs only to be seen. . . .

[*Faith and Reason*]

What weight of ancient witness can prevail,
If private reason hold the public scale?
But, gracious God, how well dost thou provide
For erring judgments an unerring guide!
Thy throne is darkness in the abyss of light,
A blaze of glory that forbids the sight.
O teach me to believe Thee thus concealed,
And search no farther than Thyself revealed;
But her alone for my director take,
Whom Thou hast promised never to forsake!
My thoughtless youth was winged with vain desires;
My manhood, long misled by wandering fires,
Followed false lights; and when their glimpse was gone
My pride struck out new sparkles of her own.
Such was I, such by nature still I am;
Be Thine the glory and be mine the shame!
Good life be now my task; my doubts are done;
(What more could fright my faith, than Three in One?)
Can I believe eternal God could lie
Disguised in mortal mould and infancy,
That the great Maker of the world could die?
And, after that, trust my imperfect sense
Which calls in question His omnipotence?
Can I my reason to my faith compel,
And shall my sight and touch and taste rebel?
Superior faculties are set aside;
Shall their subservient organs be my guide?
Then let the moon usurp the rule of day,
And winking tapers show the sun his way;
For what my senses can themselves perceive
I need no revelation to believe. . . .
Let Reason then at her own quarry fly,
But how can finite grasp infinity?
'Tis urged again, that faith did first commence
By miracles which are appeals to sense,
And thence concluded, that our sense must be
The motive still of credibility.
For latter ages must on former wait,
And what began belief must propagate.

6. Scythian shafts. The ancient Scythians were famous archers and used poisoned arrows. **13. a slaughtered army.** This is commonly interpreted to mean the Roman Catholic priests executed in Britain since the Reformation. **14. Caledonian wood.** Perhaps a reference to the Caledonian wood of ancient Britain, but possibly a reference to the Calydonian forest of classical mythology, in which the famous boar was killed by Meleager. **23. corps,** corpses, bodies.

33–34. For truth . . . seen. Cf. ll. 217–18 of Epistle II of Pope's *Essay on Man*, p. 562. **70. her alone,** the Roman Catholic Church.

But winnow well this thought, and you shall find
'Tis light as chaff that flies before the wind.
Were all those wonders wrought by power divine
As means or ends of some more deep design?
Most sure as means, whose end was this alone,
To prove the Godhead of the Eternal Son.
God thus asserted: man is to believe
Beyond what Sense and Reason can conceive,
And for mysterious things of faith rely
On the proponent Heaven's authority.
If then our faith we for our guide admit,
Vain is the farther search of human wit;
As when the building gains a surer stay,
We take the unuseful scaffolding away.
Reason by sense no more can understand;
The game is played into another hand.
Why choose we then like bilanders to creep
Along the coast, and land in view to keep,
When safely we may launch into the deep? . . .
To take up half on trust and half to try,
Name it not faith, but bungling bigotry.
Both knave and fool the merchant we may call
To pay great sums and to compound the small,
For who would break with Heaven, and would not break for all?
Rest then, my soul, from endless anguish freed:
Nor sciences thy guide, nor sense thy creed.
Faith is the best insurer of thy bliss;
The bank above must fail before the venture miss. . . .

[*Religious Persecution*]

Of all the tyrannies on human kind
The worst is that which persecutes the mind.
Let us but weigh at what offence we strike;
'Tis but because we cannot think alike.
In punishing of this, we overthrow
The laws of nations and of nature too.
Beasts are the subjects of tyrannic sway,
Where still the stronger on the weaker prey;
Man only of a softer mould is made,
Not for his fellows' ruin, but their aid:
Created kind, beneficent, and free,
The noble image of the Deity.
One portion of informing fire was given
To brutes, the inferior family of Heaven:
The Smith Divine, as with a careless beat,
Struck out the mute creation at a heat;
But when arrived at last to human race,
The Godhead took a deep considering space,
And, to distinguish man from all the rest,
Unlocked the sacred treasures of his breast,
And mercy mixed with reason did impart,
One to his head, the other to his heart;
Reason to rule, but mercy to forgive,
The first is law, the last prerogative.
And like his mind his outward form appeared,
When issuing naked to the wondering herd
He charmed their eyes, and for they loved they feared.
Not armed with horns of arbitrary might,
Or claws to seize their furry spoils in fight,
Or with increase of feet to o'ertake them in their flight:
Of easy shape, and pliant every way,
Confessing still the softness of his clay,
And kind as kings upon their coronation day;
With open hands, and with extended space
Of arms to satisfy a large embrace.
Thus kneaded up with milk, the new-made man
His kingdom o'er his kindred world began;
Till knowledge misapplied, misunderstood,
And pride of empire soured his balmy blood.
Then, first rebelling, his own stamp he coins;
The murderer Cain was latent in his loins;
And blood began its first and loudest cry
For differing worship of the Deity.
Thus persecution rose, and farther space
Produced the mighty hunter of his race.
Not so the blessed Pan his flock increased,
Content to fold them from the famished beast:
Mild were his laws; the Sheep and harmless Hind
Were never of the persecuting kind.
Such pity now the pious pastor shows,
Such mercy from the British Lion flows
That both provide protection for their foes. . . .

[*The Panther*]

The Panther, sure the noblest next the Hind,
And fairest creature of the spotted kind;
Oh, could her inborn stains be washed away,
She were too good to be a beast of prey!
How can I praise or blame, and not offend,
Or how divide the frailty from the friend?
Her faults and virtues lie so mixed, that she
Nor wholly stands condemned nor wholly free.
Then, like her injured Lion, let me speak;
He cannot bend her and he would not break.
Unkind already, and estranged in part,

279. Cain. See Genesis 4:1–16. **283. the mighty hunter,** Nimrod. See Genesis 10:8, 9. **284. the blessed Pan,** Jesus Christ. See note on l. 89 of Milton's "On the Morning of Christ's Nativity," p. 380. **288–90. Such pity . . . foes.** These lines were probably added after the Declaration of Indulgence, and were intended as a compliment to James II. **327. The Panther,** the Church of England. **335. injured Lion,** James II.

The Wolf begins to share her wandering heart.
Though unpolluted yet with actual ill,
She half commits, who sins but in her will.
If, as our dreaming Platonists report,
There could be spirits of a middle sort,
Too black for heaven and yet too white for hell,
Who just dropped half-way down, nor lower fell;
So poised, so gently she descends from high,
It seems a soft dismission from the sky.
Her house not ancient, whatsoe'er pretence
Her clergy heralds make in her defence;
A second century not half-way run,
Since the new honours of her blood begun. . . .

PART II

[*The Roman Catholic Church*]

"One in herself, not rent by schism, but sound,
Entire, one solid shining diamond,
Not sparkles shattered into sects like you:
One is the Church, and must be to be true,
One central principle of unity.
As undivided, so from errors free;
As one in faith, so one in sanctity.
Thus she, and none but she, the insulting rage
Of heretics opposed from age to age;
Still when the giant-brood invades her throne,
She stoops from Heaven and meets them half way down,
And with paternal thunder vindicates her crown. . . .
"Thus one, thus pure, behold her largely spread,
Like the fair ocean from her mother-bed;
From east to west triumphantly she rides,
All shores are watered by her wealthy tides.
The gospel-sound, diffused from pole to pole,
Where winds can carry and where waves can roll,
The self-same doctrine of the sacred page
Conveyed to every clime, in every age." . . .

LINES ON MILTON

These lines were engraved, without the author's name, under the portrait of Milton in the frontispiece of Tonson's folio edition (the fourth edition) of *Paradise Lost* in 1688. The poets referred to are Homer, Virgil, and Milton.

Three poets, in three distant ages born,
Greece, Italy, and England did adorn.
The first in loftiness of thought surpassed,
The next in majesty, in both the last:
The force of Nature could no farther go;
To make a third she joined the former two.

525–55. "One in herself . . . in every age." This passage is part of the Hind's speech to the Panther.

SONGS FROM THE PLAYS

AH, FADING JOY

Ah, fading joy, how quickly art thou past!
Yet we thy ruin haste.
As if the cares of human life were few,
We seek out new;
And follow fate, that does too fast pursue.

See how on every bough the birds express
In their sweet notes their happiness.
They all enjoy and nothing spare,
But on their Mother Nature lay their care:
Why then should man, the lord of all below,
Such troubles choose to know
As none of all his subjects undergo?

Hark, hark, the waters fall, fall, fall,
And with a murmuring sound
Dash, dash, upon the ground,
To gentle slumbers call.

—*The Indian Emperor*

YOU PLEASING DREAMS

You pleasing dreams of love and sweet delight,
Appear before this slumbering virgin's sight;
Soft visions, set her free
From mournful piety.
Let her sad thoughts from Heaven retire;
And let the melancholy love
Of those remoter joys above
Give place to your more sprightly fire.
Let purling streams be in her fancy seen,
And flowery meads, and vales of cheerful green;
And in the midst of deathless groves
Soft sighing wishes lie,
And smiling hopes fast by,
And just beyond 'em ever-laughing loves.

—*Tyrannic Love*

MERCURY'S SONG TO PHAEDRA

Fair Iris I love, and hourly I die,
But not for a lip, nor a languishing eye:
She's fickle and false, and there we agree;
But I am as false and as fickle as she.
We neither believe what either can say;
And, neither believing, we neither betray.

'Tis civil to swear, and say things of course;
We mean not the taking for better or worse.
When present, we love; when absent, agree;
I think not of Iris, nor Iris of me.
The legend of love no couple can find,
So easy to part, or so equally joined.

—*Amphitryon*

ALEXANDER'S FEAST;

OR, THE POWER OF MUSIC

An Ode in Honour of St. Cecilia's Day

This ode was composed in 1697 at the request of a London society which had been organized in 1683 to celebrate annually the day of St. Cecilia (November 22), patron saint of music. Dryden had already composed an earlier ode for the society in 1687.

1

'Twas at the royal feast, for Persia won
By Philip's warlike son:
Aloft in awful state,
The godlike hero sate
On his imperial throne;
His valiant peers were placed around,
Their brows with roses and with myrtles bound
(So should desert in arms be crowned).
The lovely Thais, by his side,
Sate like a blooming Eastern bride,
In flower of youth and beauty's pride.
Happy, happy, happy pair!
None but the brave,
None but the brave,
None but the brave deserves the fair.

Chorus

Happy, happy, happy pair!
None but the brave,
None but the brave,
None but the brave deserves the fair.

2

Timotheus, placed on high
Amid the tuneful quire,
With flying fingers touched the lyre:
The trembling notes ascend the sky,
And heavenly joys inspire.
The song began from Jove,
Who left his blissful seats above,
(Such is the power of mighty love).
A dragon's fiery form belied the god:
Sublime on radiant spires he rode,
When he to fair Olympia pressed;
And while he sought her snowy breast,
Then round her slender waist he curled,
And stamped an image of himself, a sovereign of the world.
The listening crowd admire the lofty sound:
"A present deity!" they shout around;
"A present deity!" the vaulted roofs rebound.
With ravished ears
The monarch hears;
Assumes the god,
Affects to nod,
And seems to shake the spheres.

Chorus

With ravished ears
The monarch hears;
Assumes the god,
Affects to nod,
And seems to shake the spheres.

3

The praise of Bacchus then the sweet musician sung,
Of Bacchus ever fair and ever young.
The jolly god in triumph comes:
Sound the trumpets, beat the drums!
Flushed with a purple grace,
He shows his honest face:
Now give the hautboys breath! he comes, he comes!
Bacchus, ever fair and young,
Drinking joys did first ordain:
Bacchus' blessings are a treasure;
Drinking is the soldier's pleasure;
Rich the treasure,
Sweet the pleasure,
Sweet is pleasure after pain.

Chorus

Bacchus' blessings are a treasure;
Drinking is the soldier's pleasure;
Rich the treasure,
Sweet the pleasure;
Sweet is pleasure after pain.

4

Soothed with the sound, the king grew vain,
Fought all his battles o'er again,
And thrice he routed all his foes, and thrice he slew the slain.
The master saw the madness rise,
His glowing cheeks, his ardent eyes;
And while he heaven and earth defied,
Changed his hand and checked his pride.
He chose a mournful Muse,
Soft pity to infuse:

1. royal feast, in celebration of Alexander's victory at Arbela, 331 B.C. **9. Thais,** the Greek courtesan who accompanied Alexander back to Asia. **20. Timotheus,** Alexander's favorite musician. **25. began from Jove,** proceeded from the story about Jove which immediately follows. **28. belied,** disguised, concealed. **29. Sublime on radiant spires,** aloft on radiant spirals, or coils. **30. Olympia,** Olympias, the mother of Alexander.

41. seems to shake the spheres, seems, like Jove, to shake the heavens with his nod. **52. honest,** handsome. **53. hautboys,** oboes. **72. his pride,** Alexander's pride.

He sung Darius great and good,
By too severe a fate,
Fallen, fallen, fallen, fallen,
Fallen from his high estate,
And weltering in his blood;
Deserted at his utmost need
By those his former bounty fed,
On the bare earth exposed he lies,
With not a friend to close his eyes.
With downcast looks the joyless victor sate,
Revolving in his altered soul
The various turns of chance below;
And now and then a sigh he stole,
And tears began to flow.

Chorus

Revolving in his altered soul
The various turns of chance below;
And now and then a sigh he stole,
And tears began to flow.

5

The mighty master smiled to see
That love was in the next degree;
'Twas but a kindred sound to move,
For pity melts the mind to love.
Softly sweet, in Lydian measures,
Soon he soothed his soul to pleasures.
"War," he sung, "is toil and trouble;
Honour, but an empty bubble;
Never ending, still beginning,
Fighting still, and still destroying:
If the world be worth thy winning,
Think, O think it worth enjoying.
Lovely Thais sits beside thee,
Take the good the gods provide thee."
The many rend the skies with loud applause;
So Love was crowned, but Music won the cause.
The prince, unable to conceal his pain,
Gazed on the fair,
Who caused his care,
And sighed and looked, sighed and looked,
Sighed and looked, and sighed again;
At length, with love and wine at once oppressed,
The vanquished victor sunk upon her breast.

Chorus

The prince, unable to conceal his pain,
Gazed on the fair
Who caused his care,
And sighed and looked, sighed and looked,
Sighed and looked, and sighed again;
At length, with love and wine at once oppressed,
The vanquished victor sunk upon her breast.

6

Now strike the golden lyre again:
A louder yet, and yet a louder strain.
Break his bands of sleep asunder,
And rouse him, like a rattling peal of thunder.
Hark, hark! the horrid sound
Has raised up his head;
As awaked from the dead,
And amazed, he stares around.
"Revenge, revenge!" Timotheus cries;
"See the Furies arise!
See the snakes that they rear,
How they hiss in their hair,
And the sparkles that flash from their eyes!
Behold a ghastly band,
Each a torch in his hand!
Those are Grecian ghosts, that in battle were slain,
And unburied remain
Inglorious on the plain:
Give the vengeance due
To the valiant crew!
Behold how they toss their torches on high,
How they point to the Persian abodes,
And glittering temples of their hostile gods!"
The princes applaud with a furious joy,
And the king seized a flambeau with zeal to destroy;
Thais led the way,
To light him to his prey,
And, like another Helen, fired another Troy.

Chorus

And the king seized a flambeau with zeal to destroy;
Thais led the way,
To light him to his prey,
And, like another Helen, fired another Troy.

7

Thus, long ago,
Ere heaving bellows learned to blow,
While organs yet were mute,
Timotheus, to his breathing flute
And sounding lyre,
Could swell the soul to rage or kindle soft desire.
At last divine Cecilia came,
Inventress of the vocal frame:

75. Darius, king of Persia, conquered by Alexander. The unfortunate king was stabbed by one of his companions as Alexander was on the point of capturing him. **97. Lydian measures.** See note 136 on page 385.

148. Thais led the way. After the capture of Persepolis Alexander set fire to the palace of the city. There is little authority for the legend that it was in the revelry of a banquet and at the instigation of Thais. **162. Inventress of the vocal frame.** Although St. Cecilia had long been associated with the organ in art and legend, no one before Dryden seems to have credited her with its invention.

The sweet enthusiast, from her sacred store,
  Enlarged the former narrow bounds,
  And added length to solemn sounds,
With Nature's mother-wit, and arts unknown before.
  Let old Timotheus yield the prize,
    Or both divide the crown:
  He raised a mortal to the skies;
    She drew an angel down.

Grand Chorus

    At last divine Cecilia came,
    Inventress of the vocal frame:
The sweet enthusiast, from her sacred store,
    Enlarged the former narrow bounds,
    And added length to solemn sounds,
With Nature's mother-wit, and arts unknown before.
    Let old Timotheus yield the prize,
      Or both divide the crown:
    He raised a mortal to the skies;
      She drew an angel down.

from AN ESSAY OF DRAMATIC POESY

The essay takes the form of a conversation among four friends: Eugenius (Sir Charles Sackville, later Earl of Dorset); Crites (Sir Robert Howard, Dryden's brother-in-law); Lisideius (Sir Charles Sedley); and Neander (Dryden). They are represented as boating on the Thames on the day that the English and the Dutch fleets were fighting in the mouth of the river (June 3, 1665). As they leave the sound of the guns behind, the conversation turns on the respective merits of the French and the English drama and of the earlier and later English drama. This extract, in which Neander is speaking, is taken from the last third of the essay.

TO begin, then, with Shakespeare. He was the man who of all modern, and perhaps ancient poets, had the largest and most comprehensive soul. All the images of Nature were still present to him, and he drew them, not laboriously, but luckily; when he describes anything, you more than see it, you feel it too. Those who accuse him to have wanted learning give him the greater commendation: he was naturally learned. He needed not the spectacles of books to read Nature; he looked inwards, and found her there. I cannot say he is everywhere alike; were he so, I should do him injury to compare him with the greatest of mankind. He is many times flat, insipid; his comic wit degenerating into clenches, his serious swelling into bombast. But he is always great when some great occasion is presented to him; no man can say he ever had a fit subject for his wit and did not raise himself as high above the rest of poets,

Quantum lenta solent inter viburna cupressi.

The consideration of this made Mr. Hales of Eton say, that there is no subject of which any poet ever writ, but he would produce it much better done in Shakespeare; and however others are now more generally preferred before him, yet the age wherein he lived, which had contemporaries with him Fletcher and Jonson, never equalled them to him in their esteem: and in the last King's court, when Ben's reputation was at highest, Sir John Suckling, and with him the greater part of the courtiers, set our Shakespeare far above him.

"Beaumont and Fletcher, of whom I am next to speak, had, with the advantage of Shakespeare's wit, which was their precedent, great natural gifts, improved by study: Beaumont especially being so accurate a judge of plays, that Ben Jonson, while he lived, submitted all his writings to his censure, and, 'tis thought, used his judgment in correcting, if not contriving, all his plots. What value he had for him, appears by the verses he writ to him; and therefore I need speak no farther of it. The first play that brought Fletcher and him in esteem was their *Philaster:* for, before that, they had written two or three very unsuccessfully, as the like is reported of Ben Jonson, before he writ *Every Man in His Humour.* Their plots were generally more regular than Shakespeare's, especially those that were made before Beaumont's death; and they understood and imitated the conversation of gentlemen much better; whose wild debaucheries, and quickness of wit in repartees, no poet before them could paint as they have done. Humour, which Ben Jonson derived from particular persons, they made it their business not to describe: they represented all the passions very lively, but above all, love. I am apt to believe the English language in them arrived to its highest perfection: what words have since been taken in are rather superfluous than ornamental. Their plays are now the most pleasant and frequent entertainments of the stage; two of theirs being acted through

170. She drew an angel down. No authority has been found for Dryden's representation of St. Cecilia as having the power to draw an angel to her by her music. **42. still,** always.

4. clenches, puns. **9. Quantum . . . cupressi.** As cypresses tower among the humbler trees of the wayside. **10. Mr. Hales,** John Hales, fellow of Eton, and author of *The Golden Remains,* 1659. **41. Humour,** the portrayal of eccentricities of character.

the year for one of Shakespeare's or Jonson's: the reason is, because there is a certain gaiety in their comedies, and pathos in their more serious plays, which suit generally with all men's humours. Shakespeare's language is likewise a little obsolete, and Ben Jonson's wit comes short of theirs.

"As for Jonson, to whose character I am now arrived, if we look upon him while he was himself (for his last plays were but his dotages), I think him the most learned and judicious writer which any theatre ever had. He was a most severe judge of himself, as well as others. One cannot say he wanted wit, but rather that he was frugal of it. In his works you find little to retrench or alter. Wit, and language, and humour also in some measure we had before him; but something of art was wanting to the drama till he came. He managed his strength to more advantage than any who preceded him. You seldom find him making love in any of his scenes, or endeavouring to move the passions; his genius was too sullen and saturnine to do it gracefully, especially when he knew he came after those who had performed both to such an height. Humour was his proper sphere; and in that he delighted most to represent mechanic people. He was deeply conversant in the ancients, both Greek and Latin, and he borrowed boldly from them: there is scarcely a poet or historian among the Roman authors of those times whom he has not translated in *Sejanus* and *Catiline*. But he has done his robberies so openly, that one may see he fears not to be taxed by any law. He invades authors like a monarch; and what would be theft in other poets is only victory in him. With the spoils of these writers he so represents old Rome to us, in its rites, ceremonies, and customs, that if one of their poets had written either of his tragedies, we had seen less of it than in him. If there was any fault in his language, 'twas that he weaved it too closely and laboriously, in his comedies especially: perhaps, too, he did a little too much to Romanize our tongue, leaving the words which he translated almost as much Latin as when he found them: wherein, though he learnedly followed their language, he did not enough comply with the idiom of ours. If I would compare him with Shakespeare, I must acknowledge him the more correct poet, but Shakespeare the greater wit. Shakespeare was the Homer, or father of our dramatic poets; Jonson was the Virgil, the pattern of elaborate writing; I admire him, but I love Shakespeare. To conclude of him; as he has given us the most correct plays, so in the precepts which he has laid down in his *Discoveries*, we have as many and profitable rules for perfecting the stage, as any wherewith the French can furnish us. . . ."

25. mechanic people, working people, tradesmen.

from PREFACE TO THE FABLES

I PROCEED to Ovid and Chaucer, considering the former only in relation to the latter. With Ovid ended the Golden Age of the Roman tongue; from Chaucer the purity of the English tongue began. The manners of the poets were not unlike. Both of them were well-bred, well-natured, amorous, and libertine, at least in their writings; it may be also in their lives. Their studies were the same, philosophy and philology. Both of them were knowing in astronomy; of which Ovid's books of the *Roman Feasts* and Chaucer's *Treatise of the Astrolabe* are sufficient witnesses. But Chaucer was likewise an astrologer, as were Virgil, Horace, Persius, and Manilius. Both writ with wonderful facility and clearness; neither were great inventors: for Ovid only copied the Grecian fables, and most of Chaucer's stories were taken from his Italian contemporaries, or their predecessors. Boccace his *Decameron* was first published, and from thence our Englishman has borrowed many of his *Canterbury Tales;* yet that of Palamon and Arcite was written, in all probability, by some Italian wit, in a former age, as I shall prove hereafter. The tale of Griselda was the invention of Petrarch; by him sent to Boccace, from whom it came to Chaucer. *Troilus and Criseyde* was also written by a Lombard author, but much amplified by our English translator, as well as beautified; the genius of our countrymen, in general, rather being to improve an invention than to invent themselves, as is evident not only in our poetry but in many of our manufactures. I find I have anticipated already, and taken up from Boccace before I come to him; but there is so much less behind; and I am of the temper of most kings, who love to be in debt, are all for present money, no matter how they pay it afterwards; besides, the nature of a preface is rambling, never wholly out of the way, nor in it.

6. Ovid . . . Chaucer. The discussion of Ovid and Chaucer follows that of Homer. **14. philology.** Philology here has not its present meaning, but connotes the study of literature and polite learning in general. **24–25. from thence . . . borrowed.** Modern scholarship has shown that Chaucer probably did not know the *Decameron*, although he was acquainted with other works of Boccaccio. **29. the invention of Petrarch.** Dryden is also in error here. Petrarch, as is now well known, took the story of Griselda from the last novella of the *Decameron*, and Chaucer's version is based on Petrarch's Latin version, or possibly some French translation of it. **30–31. Troilus and Criseyde.** The main elements of Chaucer's poem came from Boccaccio's *Filostrato*. Dryden is misled by Chaucer's statement that he is following "myn auctor called Lollius," who remains unidentified. It has been suggested that Chaucer did not know who the author of *Filostrato* was.

This I have learned from the practice of honest Montaigne, and return at my pleasure to Ovid and Chaucer, of whom I have little more to say.

Both of them built on the inventions of other men; yet since Chaucer had something of his own, as *The Wife of Bath's Tale, The Cock and the Fox,* which I have translated, and some others, I may justly give our countryman the precedence in that part; since I can remember nothing of Ovid which was wholly his. Both of them understood the manners, under which name I comprehend the passions, and, in a larger sense the descriptions of persons, and their very habits. For an example, I see Baucis and Philemon as perfectly before me, as if some ancient painter had drawn them; and all the pilgrims in the *Canterbury Tales,* their humours, their features, and the very dress, as distinctly as if I had supped with them at the Tabard in Southwark. Yet even there, too, the figures of Chaucer are much more lively, and set in a better light; which though I have not time to prove, yet I appeal to the reader, and am sure he will clear me from partiality. The thoughts and words remain to be considered in the comparison of the two poets, and I have saved myself one half of that labour, by owning that Ovid lived when the Roman tongue was in its meridian; Chaucer, in the dawning of our language; therefore that part of the comparison stands not on an equal foot, any more than the diction of Ennius and Ovid, or of Chaucer and our present English. The words are given up, as a post not to be defended in our poet, because he wanted the modern art of fortifying. The thoughts remain to be considered; and they are to be measured only by their propriety; that is, as they flow more or less naturally from the persons described, on such and such occasions. The vulgar judges, which are nine parts in ten of all nations, who call conceits and jingles wit, who see Ovid full of them, and Chaucer altogether without them, will think me little less than mad for preferring the Englishman to the Roman. Yet, with their leave, I must presume to say, that the things they admire are only glittering trifles, and so far from being witty, that in a serious poem they are nauseous, because they are unnatural. Would any man who is ready to die for love describe his passion like Narcissus? Would he think of *inopem me copia fecit,* and a dozen more of such expressions, poured on the neck of one another, and signifying all the same thing? If this were wit, was this a time to be witty, when the poor wretch was in the agony of death? This is just John Littlewit, in *Bartholomew Fair,* who had a conceit (as he tells you) left him in his misery; a miserable conceit. On these occasions the poet should endeavour to raise pity; but, instead of this, Ovid is tickling you to laugh. Virgil never made use of such machines when he was moving you to commiserate the death of Dido: he would not destroy what he was building. Chaucer makes Arcite violent in his love, and unjust in the pursuit of it; yet when he came to die, he made him think more reasonably; he repents not of his love, for that had altered his character; but acknowledges the injustice of his proceedings, and resigns Emilia to Palamon. What would Ovid have done on this occasion? He would certainly have made Arcite witty on his death-bed; he had complained he was further off from possession, by being so near, and a thousand such boyisms, which Chaucer rejected as below the dignity of the subject. They who think otherwise, would, by the same reason, prefer Lucan and Ovid to Homer and Virgil, and Martial to all four of them. As for the turn of words, in which Ovid particularly excels all poets, they are sometimes a fault, and sometimes a beauty, as they are used properly or improperly; but in strong passions always to be shunned, because passions are serious, and will admit no playing. The French have a high value for them; and, I confess, they are often what they call delicate, when they are introduced with judgment; but Chaucer writ with more simplicity, and followed nature more closely than to use them. I have thus far, to the best of my knowledge, been an upright judge betwixt the parties in competition, not meddling with the design nor the disposition of it; because the design was not their own; and in the disposing of it they were equal. It remains that I say somewhat of Chaucer in particular.

In the first place, as he is the father of English poetry, so I hold him in the same degree of veneration as the Grecians held Homer, or the Romans Virgil. He is a perpetual fountain of good sense; learned in all sciences; and, therefore, speaks properly on all subjects. As he knew what to say, so he knows also when to leave off; a continence, which is practised by few writers, and scarcely by any of the ancients, excepting Virgil and Horace. One of our

6. *The Cock and the Fox,* *The Nun's Priest's Tale.* Neither of the tales mentioned was invented by Chaucer. **13–14. Baucis and Philemon,** characters in a story in Ovid's *Metamorphoses.* **27. the dawning of our language.** Dryden mistakenly considers Middle English immature and inferior in all respects to Modern English. **29. Ennius,** Latin epic poet (239–169 B.C.), regarded by the Romans as the father of Latin poetry. **47. *inopem me copia fecit,*** my abundance has made me poor (*Metamorphoses,* III, 466).

5. *Bartholomew Fair,* by Ben Jonson. **11. Dido,** Queen of Carthage, who, when Aeneas is compelled to leave her, burns herself to death on a funeral pile (*Aeneid,* Book IV). **12. Arcite,** in Chaucer's *Knight's Tale.* **50 ff. One of . . . poets,** Abraham Cowley, 1618–1667.

late great poets is sunk in his reputation, because he could never forgive any conceit which came in his way; but swept, like a drag-net, great and small. There was plenty enough, but the dishes were ill-sorted; whole pyramids of sweet-meats for boys and women, but little of solid meat for men. All this proceeded not from any want of knowledge, but of judgment. Neither did he want that in discerning the beauties and faults of other poets, but only indulged himself in the luxury of writing; and perhaps knew it was a fault, but hoped the reader would not find it. For this reason, though he must always be thought a great poet, he is no longer esteemed a good writer; and for ten impressions which his works have had in so many successive years, yet at present a hundred books are scarcely purchased once a twelve-month; for, as my last Lord Rochester said, though somewhat profanely, "Not being of God, he could not stand."

Chaucer followed Nature everywhere, but was never so bold to go beyond her; and there is a great difference of being *poeta* and *nimis poeta*, if we may believe Catullus, as much as betwixt a modest behaviour and affectation. The verse of Chaucer, I confess, is not harmonious to us; but 'tis like the eloquence of one whom Tacitus commends, it was *auribus istius temporis accommodata:* they who lived with him, and some time after him, thought it musical; and it continues so, even in our judgment, if compared with the numbers of Lidgate and Gower, his contemporaries; there is the rude sweetness of a Scotch tune in it, which is natural and pleasing, though not perfect. 'Tis true, I cannot go so far as he who published the last edition of him; for he would make us believe the fault is in our ears, and that there were really ten syllables in a verse where we find but nine; but this opinion is not worth confuting; 'tis so gross and obvious an error, that common sense (which is a rule in everything but matters of faith and revelation) must convince the reader, that equality of numbers, in every verse which we call heroic, was either not known, or not always practised, in Chaucer's age. It were an easy matter to produce some thousands of his verses, which are lame for want of half a foot, and sometimes a whole one, and which no pronunciation can make otherwise. We can only say, that he lived in the infancy of our poetry, and that nothing is brought to perfection at the first. We must be children before we grow men. There was an Ennius, and in process of time a Lucilius, and a Lucretius, before Virgil and Horace; even after Chaucer there was a Spenser, a Harington, a Fairfax, before Waller and Denham were in being; and our numbers were in their nonage till these last appeared. I need say little of his parentage, life, and fortunes; they are to be found at large in all the editions of his works. He was employed abroad, and favoured, by Edward the Third, Richard the Second, and Henry the Fourth, and was poet, as I suppose, to all three of them. In Richard's time, I doubt, he was a little dipped in the rebellion of the Commons; and being brother-in-law to John of Gaunt, it was no wonder if he followed the fortunes of that family; and was well with Henry the Fourth when he had deposed his predecessor. Neither is it to be admired, that Henry, who was a wise as well as a valiant prince, who claimed by succession, and was sensible that his title was not sound, but was rightfully in Mortimer, who had married the heir of York; it was not to be admired, I say, if that great politician should be pleased to have the greatest wit of those times in his interests, and to be the trumpet of his praises. Augustus had given him the example, by the advice of Maecenas, who recommended Virgil and Horace to him; whose praises helped to make him popular while he was alive, and after his death have made him precious to posterity. As for the religion of our poet, he seems to have some little bias towards the opinions of Wycliffe, after John of Gaunt his patron; somewhat of which appears in the tale of Piers Plowman; yet I cannot blame him for inveighing so sharply against the vices of the clergy in his age; their pride, their ambition, their pomp, their avarice, their worldly interest, deserved the lashes which he gave them, both in that, and in most of his *Canterbury Tales*. Neither has his contemporary Boccace spared them: yet both those poets lived in much esteem with good and holy men in orders; for the scandal which is given by particular priests reflects not on the sacred function. Chaucer's Monk, his Canon, and his Friar, took not from the character of his Good Parson. A satirical poet is the check of the laymen on bad priests. We are only to take care that we involve not the innocent with the guilty in

22. ***poeta*** **and** ***nimis poeta*****,** a poet and too much a poet. Dryden is nodding here. He has in mind a line from Martial. 27. ***auribus . . . accommodata*****,** adapted to the ears of that time. 34. **he who published the last edition.** Dryden refers to the edition of Thomas Speght, reprinted in 1687. The proper pronunciation of Chaucer's Middle English was not understood in Dryden's time. Furthermore, in Speght's edition the final "e" in many words was omitted, and Dryden can hardly be blamed for failing to appreciate the melodious quality of Chaucer's lines as he wrote them.

7. **Harington,** Sir John Harington, whose translation of Ariosto's *Orlando Furioso* was published in 1591. **Fairfax,** Edward Fairfax, translator of Tasso's *Gerusalemme Liberata*, 1604. 15. **doubt,** suspect. 20. **admired,** wondered at. 35. **Piers Plowman,** not the fourteenth-century poem, but "The Plowman's Tale," formerly thought to be Chaucer's.

the same condemnation. The good cannot be too much honoured, nor the bad too coarsely used; for the corruption of the best becomes the worst. When a clergyman is whipped, his gown is first taken off, by which the dignity of his order is secured. If he be wrongfully accused, he has his action of slander; and 'tis at the poet's peril if he transgress the law. But they will tell us that all kind of satire, though never so well deserved by particular priests, yet brings the whole order into contempt. Is then the peerage of England anything dishonoured when a peer suffers for his treason? If he be libelled, or any way defamed, he has his *scandalum magnatum* to punish the offender. They who use this kind of argument seem to be conscious to themselves of somewhat which has deserved the poet's lash, and are less concerned for their public capacity than for their private; at least there is pride at the bottom of their reasoning. If the faults of men in orders are only to be judged among themselves, they are all in some sort parties; for, since they say the honour of their order is concerned in every member of it, how can we be sure that they will be impartial judges? How far I may be allowed to speak my opinion in this case I know not; but I am sure a dispute of this nature caused mischief in abundance betwixt a King of England and an Archbishop of Canterbury; one standing up for the laws of his land, and the other for the honour (as he called it) of God's Church; which ended in the murder of the prelate, and in the whipping of his Majesty from post to pillar for his penance. The learned and ingenious Dr. Drake has saved me the labour of inquiring into the esteem and reverence which the priests have had of old; and I would rather extend than diminish any part of it; yet I must needs say, that when a priest provokes me without occasion given him, I have no reason, unless it be the charity of a Christian, to forgive him: *prior laesit* is justification sufficient in the civil law. If I answer him in his own language, self-defence I am sure must be allowed me; and if I carry it further, even to a sharp recrimination, somewhat may be indulged to human frailty. Yet my resentment has not wrought so far but that I have followed Chaucer in his character of a holy man, and have enlarged on that subject with some pleasure; reserving to myself the right, if I shall think fit hereafter, to describe another sort of priests, such as are more easily to be found than the Good Parson; such as have given the last blow to Christianity in this age, by a practice so contrary to their doctrine. But this will keep cold till another time. In the meanwhile, I take up Chaucer where I left him.

He must have been a man of a most wonderful comprehensive nature, because, as it has been truly observed of him, he has taken into the compass of his *Canterbury Tales* the various manners and humours (as we now call them) of the whole English nation, in his age. Not a single character has escaped him. All his pilgrims are severally distinguished from each other; and not only in their inclinations but in their very physiognomies and persons. Baptista Porta could not have described their natures better, than by the marks which the poet gives them. The matter and manner of their tales, and of their telling, are so suited to their different educations, humours, and callings, that each of them would be improper in any other mouth. Even the grave and serious characters are distinguished by their several sorts of gravity: their discourses are such as belong to their age, their calling, and their breeding; such as are becoming of them, and of them only. Some of his persons are vicious, and some virtuous; some are unlearned, or (as Chaucer calls them) lewd, and some are learned. Even the ribaldry of the low characters is different: the Reeve, the Miller, and the Cook, are several men, and distinguished from each other as much as the mincing Lady-Prioress and the broad-speaking, gap-toothed Wife of Bath. But enough of this; there is such a variety of game springing up before me, that I am distracted in my choice, and know not which to follow. 'Tis sufficient to say, according to the proverb, that here is God's plenty. We have our forefathers and great-grand-dames all before us, as they were in Chaucer's days: their general characters are still remaining in mankind, and even in England, though they are called by other names than those of monks, and friars, and canons, and lady-abbesses, and nuns; for mankind is ever the same, and nothing lost out of nature, though everything is altered. . . .

13. ***scandalum magnatum***, the offense of slandering those in power. **26–27. a King . . . and an Archbishop,** Henry II and Thomas Becket. **32. Dr. Drake,** James Drake, whose reply to Jeremy Collier's *Short View of the English Stage*, 1698, was published in 1699. **39.** ***prior laesit***, "he hit me first."

19. Baptista Porta, the famous Italian physiognomist (1538–1615).

SUGGESTIONS FOR FURTHER READING

This list is to be supplemented by the brief lists of books given in the General Bibliography and in the various introductions to authors and works of the period.

HISTORICAL AND POLITICAL BACKGROUND

Adams, G. B. *Constitutional History of England*, Holt, 1924; revised by R. L. Schuyler, 1934. A standard study of seventeenth-century political theory and practice.

Buchan, John. *Oliver Cromwell*, Houghton Mifflin, 1934. The best biography for the general reader.

Clark, G. N. *The Later Stuarts, 1660–1714*, Clarendon Press, Oxford, 1934. A volume in the *Oxford History of England*.

Davies, Godfrey. *The Early Stuarts, 1603–1660*, Clarendon Press, Oxford, 1935. Another volume in the same series.

Trevelyan, G. M. *England under the Stuarts*, Longmans, 1933. One of the most valuable single-volume histories of the period.

CULTURAL AND SOCIAL BACKGROUND

Baker, C. H. C., and Constable, W. G. *English Painting of the Sixteenth and Seventeenth Centuries*, Harcourt, Brace, 1930.

Brooke, Iris. *English Costume of the Seventeenth Century*, London, A. and C. Black, 1934. A charmingly illustrated little volume.

Clark, G. N. *The Seventeenth Century*, Clarendon Press, Oxford, 1929. The most useful one-volume survey of seventeenth-century life, thought, religion, politics, and art.

Jordan, W. K. *The Development of Religious Toleration in England, 1640–1660*, Harvard University Press, 1938. The most authoritative study of the subject.

Mathew, David. *The Social Structure in Caroline England*, Clarendon Press, Oxford, 1948. A helpful study, full of humor and tolerance, which can be enjoyed equally by the general reader and the student of the period.

Parry, Sir Hubert. *The Music of the Seventeenth Century*, revised by E. J. Dent, Oxford University Press, 1938. Vol. III in the *Oxford History of Music*.

Randall, J. H. *The Making of the Modern Mind*, Houghton Mifflin, 1926. An excellent treatment of the history of thought during the period.

Willey, Basil. *The Seventeenth-Century Background*, London, Chatto and Windus, 1934. An excellent survey of philosophic crosscurrents of the period.

LITERATURE OF THE PERIOD

COLLECTIONS

Coffin, R. P. T., and Witherspoon, A. M., eds. *Seventeenth-Century Prose and Poetry*, Harcourt, Brace, 1946. Selections from the more important prose writers and poets, with introductions and notes.

Grierson, H. J. C., ed. *Metaphysical Lyrics and Poems*, Oxford University Press, 1936. The introduction is one of the most illuminating essays on metaphysical poetry.

Hebel, J. W., and Hudson, H. H., eds. *Poetry of the English Renaissance, 1509–1660*, Crofts, 1929. One of the most distinguished anthologies, with introductions, notes, and bibliographies.

The Mermaid Series of English Dramatists, newly issued by A. A. Wyn, New York. A famous series of Elizabethan and Restoration dramatists in single volumes, edited with introduction and notes. Contains the best plays of Jonson, Webster, Tourneur, Shirley, Massinger, Shadwell, Ford, Congreve, Vanbrugh, Farquhar, Wycherley, and Dryden.

CRITICISM

Bush, Douglas. *English Literature in the Earlier Seventeenth Century, 1600–1660*, Oxford University Press, 1945. The first volume to appear in the *Oxford History of English Literature*, and the most thorough and scholarly treatment of the subject. Contains exhaustive bibliographies, chronological tables, etc.

Pinto, V. de Sola. *The English Renaissance, 1510–1688*, McBride, 1938. An invaluable one-volume introduction to all phases of Elizabethan and seventeenth-century literature, with a chapter on "Literature and Music" by Bruce Pattison. Contains helpful bibliographies.

Wedgwood, C. V. *Seventeenth-Century English Literature*, Oxford University Press, 1950. An invaluable brief study.

Bush, Douglas. *Mythology and the Renaissance Tradition in English Poetry*, University of Minnesota Press, 1932.

Eliot, T. S. "The Metaphysical Poets," in *Selected Essays*, Harcourt, Brace, 1932, 1950. One of the most valuable discussions of metaphysical poets and poetry, by the twentieth-century "leader of the return to the Metaphysicals."

Mahood, M. M. *Poetry and Humanism*, Yale University Press, 1950. The most recent study of the devotional poets of the seventeenth century.

Tuve, Rosemond. *Elizabethan and Metaphysical Imagery: Renaissance Poetic and Twentieth-Century Critics*, University of Chicago Press, 1947. A stimulating and provocative study of seventeenth-century imagery.

Ellis-Fermor, Una M. *The Jacobean Drama, An Interpretation*, London, Methuen, 1936. A discerning study of early seventeenth-century drama.

Nicoll, Allardyce. *A History of Restoration Drama*, Cambridge University Press, 1923. The standard work on the subject.

Stauffer, Donald A. *English Biography before 1700*, Harvard University Press, 1930. The standard work on early English biography.

THE AUTHORIZED VERSION OF THE BIBLE

Daiches, David. *The King James Version of the English Bible*, University of Chicago Press, 1941. A succinct, scholarly, and interesting history of English Bible translation from 1523 to 1611.

Robinson, H. W., ed. *The Bible in Its Ancient and English Versions*, Oxford University Press, 1940. Probably the best short account of the history and character of the Bible.

Watts, H. H. *The Modern Reader's Guide to the Bible*, Harper, 1949. One of the most useful of recent handbooks on the Bible as literature.

BACON

Essays, Advancement of Learning, New Atlantis, and Other Pieces, ed. by R. F. Jones, Doubleday, Doran, 1937; Odyssey Press, 1950. An inexpensive and well-annotated edition.

Sturt, Mary. *Francis Bacon*, Morrow, 1932. An interpretation of Bacon the man.

BROWNE

Religio Medici and Other Writings (*Hydriotaphia, Brampton Urns, Letter to a Friend, The Garden of Cyrus, Christian Morals*), Everyman's Library, Dutton, 1906.

Merton, E. S. *Science and Imagination in Sir Thomas Browne*, Columbia University Press, 1949. The most recent and one of the most valuable studies of Browne as scientist and artist.

BUNYAN

Grace Abounding to the Chief of Sinners, The Life and Death of Mr. Badman, Everyman's Library, Dutton.

Pilgrim's Progress, Everyman's Library, Dutton.

Brittain, Vera. *Valiant Pilgrim: The Story of John Bunyan and Puritan England*, Macmillan, 1950. The most recent study of Bunyan, based on newly discovered material, and illustrated with 55 photographs.

Harrison, G. B. *John Bunyan, A Study in Personality*, London, Dent, 1928. The best brief biography.

CAREW

Howarth, R. G., ed. *Minor Poets of the Seventeenth Century*, Everyman's Library, Dutton, 1931. Contains the complete poems of Carew.

Leavis, F. R. *Revaluations*, London, Chatto and Windus, 1936. Contains one of the most recent and discriminating discussions of Carew's verse.

THE CHARACTER-WRITERS

Aldington, Richard, ed. *A Book of Characters*, Dutton, 1924. Contains a valuable introduction, the characters of Overbury, Earle, and other English character-writers, and characters from foreign authors such as Theophrastus and La Bruyère.

Boyce, Benjamin. *The Theophrastan Character in England to 1642*, Harvard University Press, 1947. The most thorough treatment of the development of character writing in England.

CRASHAW

The Verse in English of Richard Crashaw, New York, Grove Press, 1950. An inexpensive edition of Crashaw's English poems, together with a selection of critical commentaries from Abraham Cowley in the seventeenth century to William Empson in the twentieth.

Crashaw's Poetical Works, ed. by L. C. Martin, Oxford University Press, 1927. The standard edition, with full critical apparatus.

Warren, Austin. *Richard Crashaw, A Study in Baroque Sensibility*, Louisiana State University Press, 1939. The fullest and best discussion of the poet and his work.

DONNE

The Complete Poems of John Donne, ed. by R. B. Bennett, Farrar, Straus, 1942. A scholarly and inexpensive edition.

The Poems of John Donne, 2 vols., ed. by H. J. C. Grierson, Oxford University Press, 1912, 1929. The standard edition, with valuable notes and commentary.

Coffin, C. M. *John Donne and the New Philosophy*, Columbia University Press, 1937. A study of the impact on Donne's thought of the new sciences of the time.

Spencer, Theodore, ed. *A Garland for John Donne*, Harvard University Press, 1931. A valuable collection of essays by Spencer, T. S. Eliot, and others.

Walton, Izaak. *The Lives of Dr. John Donne and Others*, 1670. Reprinted in the World's Classics, Oxford University Press. Walton's *Life*, a classic in its own right, is still the foundation of Donne's biography.

DRYDEN

The Poetical Works of John Dryden, ed. by G. R. Noyes, New Cambridge Edition, Houghton Mifflin, 1950. The best one-volume edition of the nondramatic poems, with introduction and notes.

Smith, D. Nichol. *John Dryden*, Cambridge University Press, 1950. The most recent study, and a judicious analysis of Dryden's achievement as a writer.

HERBERT

The Poems of George Herbert, with an introduction by Arthur Waugh, the World's Classics, Oxford University Press, 1907. A convenient and inexpensive edition.

The Works of George Herbert, ed. by F. E. Hutchinson, Oxford University Press, 1941. The standard edition of both the poetry and prose.

Walton, Izaak. "The Life of Mr. George Herbert," in his *Lives*, 1670. Published in the World's Classics, Oxford University Press. Walton's account of "holy Mr. Herbert" is still an invaluable biographical study.

Warren, Austin. "George Herbert," in the *American Review*, vii, pp. 249–271 (1936). One of the most penetrating of recent critical studies of Herbert.

HERRICK

The Poetical Works of Robert Herrick, ed. by F. W. Moorman, Oxford University Press, 1915. The standard edition, with critical apparatus. The text, with most of the epigrams omitted, was reprinted in the series of Oxford Poets in 1921, and in the World's Classics in 1933.

Macaulay, Rose. *The Shadow Flies*, Harper, 1932. An absorbing study of the life and times of Herrick in the form of a novel.

Moorman, F. W. *Robert Herrick: A Biographical and Critical Study*, London, John Lane, 1910. The standard biography and critique.

JONSON

Selected Works of Ben Jonson, ed. by Harry Levin, Random House, 1938. The editor provides a clear, readable text of his own and a brilliant introduction.

The Poems of Ben Jonson, ed. by B. H. Newdigate, Oxford, Blackwell, 1936. The most convenient edition of the nondramatic poetry.

Selected Plays of Ben Jonson, 2 vols., ed. by F. E. Schelling, Everyman's Library, Dutton, 1910. An inexpensive edition of the plays with a valuable introduction.

Bentley, G. E. *Shakespeare and Jonson*, 2 vols., University of Chicago Press, 1945. A thorough discussion of Jonson's accomplishments and reputation in the seventeenth century.

Palmer, John. *Ben Jonson*, Viking Press, 1934. An excellent introduction to Jonson.

LOVELACE

The Poems of Richard Lovelace, ed. by C. H. Wilkinson, Oxford University Press, 1930. The standard edition.

Hartmann, C. H. *The Cavalier Spirit and Its Influence on the Life and Work of Richard Lovelace*, Dutton, 1925. The fullest discussion of the poet.

MARVELL

The Poems and Satires of Andrew Marvell, 2 vols., The Muses' Library, Dutton, 1892, 1901. The most convenient edition.

Birrell, Augustine. *Andrew Marvell*, Macmillan, 1905. An excellent brief biography in the English Men of Letters Series.

Bradbrook, M. C., and Lloyd Thomas, M. G. *Andrew Marvell*, Cambridge University Press, 1940. A very readable and rewarding study of Marvell's poetry.

MILTON

Paradise Lost, ed. by M. Y. Hughes, Odyssey Press, 1937. Contains excellent introductions and notes.

Paradise Regained, The Minor Poems, and Samson Agonistes, ed. by M. Y. Hughes, Odyssey Press, 1937. A companion volume, fully annotated.

The Portable Milton, ed. by Douglas Bush, Viking Press, 1949. A generous selection of the best poetry and prose, with a valuable introduction and glossary.

Banks, T. H. *Milton's Imagery*, Columbia University Press, 1950. The most recent and thorough study of Milton's images and their significance.

Bowra, C. M. *From Virgil to Milton*, Macmillan, 1945. A brilliant study of the epic and of Milton's contributions to the form.

Bush, Douglas. *"Paradise Lost" in Our Time*, Cornell University Press, 1945.

Hanford, J. H. *John Milton, Englishman*, Crown Publishers, 1949. The most recent and one of the most valuable biographical and critical studies.

—— *A Milton Handbook*, 4th ed., Appleton-Century-Crofts, 1946. The best general guide to the study of Milton, with extensive bibliographies.

Hutchinson, F. E. *Milton and the English Mind*, Macmillan, 1947. An up-to-date and valuable brief biography.

Lewis, C. S. *A Preface to "Paradise Lost,"* Oxford University Press, 1942. A brilliant and stimulating little book on the great poem.

Saurat, Denis. *Milton: Man and Thinker*, rev. ed., London, Dent, 1944. One of the most valuable and influential studies of Milton's philosophical ideas.

Tillyard, E. M. W. *Milton*, Dial Press, 1930. A solid and stimulating study of the life and work of Milton.

PEPYS

The Diary of Samuel Pepys, 8 vols. in 3, ed. by H. B. Wheatley, Harcourt, Brace, 1926. The only full edition of the diary; from the transcription by the Rev. Mynors Bright.

The Diary of Samuel Pepys, 2 vols., Everyman's Library, Dutton. A convenient edition of the first transcription by the Rev. John Smith.

Bryant, Arthur. *Samuel Pepys*, 3 vols., Macmillan, 1933–1938. The standard life of Pepys, and a thoroughly readable biography.

SUCKLING

The Works of Sir John Suckling, ed. by A. H. Thompson, Dutton, 1910. The standard edition of both the poetry and the prose.

Lynch, Katherine. *The Social Mode of Restoration Comedy*, Macmillan, 1926. Contains an interesting discussion of Suckling.

VAUGHAN

The Works of Henry Vaughan, 2 vols., ed. by L. C. Martin, Oxford University Press, 1914. The standard edition.

Hutchinson, F. E. *Henry Vaughan, A Life and Interpretation*, Oxford University Press, 1947. The latest and fullest treatment of Vaughan's life and thought. Contains a valuable chapter on the influence on Vaughan's style of the Welsh language and Welsh poetry.

THE EIGHTEENTH CENTURY

PLATE XIII

A THE COWPER AND GORE FAMILIES, BY JOHN ZOFFANY (*Collection of Lady Desborough, Panshanger House, England*)

English painting may be said to have been in its infancy at the beginning of the eighteenth century. In domestic architecture and the applied arts English artists had developed an exquisite sense of propriety and taste, but there was little to correspond with this in painting. During the eighteenth century the great increase in wealth in England provided the necessary economic basis for the establishment of stately homes, and an enlightened and active patronage demanded paintings and other works of art to embellish them. The art of portrait painting flourished in England as never before. The aristocracy and the well-to-do commercial classes commissioned artists like Zoffany to provide portraits and representations of themselves, their society, and their surroundings. This "conversation piece" of the Cowper and Gore families illustrates the manner in which the arts of music and painting were woven into the texture of elegant and gracious everyday life. The painting on the wall provides an appropriately classical note for the Augustan drawing room, and a representation of English mountain scenery supplies a "picturesque" background for the cultivated group.

B GIN LANE, BY WILLIAM HOGARTH

At the other end of the social scale from the aristocratic ladies and gentlemen painted by Zoffany and Gainsborough and described by Pope were the uncared-for poor who have been immortalized in the engravings of Hogarth. Squalor and crime and mortality were greatly increased in the early eighteenth century by the new taste for gin, which was taking the place of the old-fashioned ale and beer. Professor Trevelyan states that the yearly average of British spirits distilled rose from about half a million gallons in 1684 to nearly five and a half million gallons in 1735. Gin was as cheap as it was deadly for the poor who could get "drunk for a penny and dead drunk for twopence." It was conditions of this sort that the evangelists John Wesley and George Whitefield attempted, not without success, to ameliorate. Hogarth's savage indignation at the plight of the poor in the crowded slums of London is evident. The pity that he displays has been pointed out by Charles Lamb in his essay on Hogarth: "Take the mild, supplicating posture of patient Poverty in the poor woman that is persuading the pawnbroker to accept her clothes in pledge, in the plate of 'Gin Lane,' for instance. A little does it, a little of the *good* nature overpowers a world of *bad*."

C THE EAST INDIA WHARF (*Bettmann Archive, from a painting by Monarny in the Victoria and Albert Museum*)

The eighteenth century saw a phenomenal growth in England's foreign trade and commerce, and to London's docks and wharves came ships from the East Indies and the Orient bringing wealth which made possible the great houses and gardens and the magnificent art collections. It was these ships that brought the luxuries with which the poet Pope, in *The Rape of the Lock*, surrounds his heroine Belinda, on whose dressing table "The various offerings of the world appear":

This casket India's glowing gems unlocks,
And all Arabia breathes from yonder box.
The tortoise here and elephant unite,
Transformed to combs, the speckled and the white.

Pope supplies a poetic inventory of treasures from the far corners of the earth—a "frail China jar," a "new brocade," a "charming Indian screen," fans, and gums, and pomatums, Japanese lacquer ware, teacups and tea, chocolate, and, perhaps most important of all, coffee. Such were the outward and visible signs at home in England of the young and growing British Empire.

PLATE XIV

A BLENHEIM PALACE (*Combine*)

This magnificent palace, not far from Oxford, was built by the first Duke of Marlborough, the great British general and ancestor of Winston Churchill. It was paid for by a grateful Parliament, which voted him a sum of half a million pounds in recognition of his numerous victories, the chief of these being the Battle of Blenheim. The park in which the palace stands, about twelve miles in circumference, was also a gift of Parliament. The architect was Sir John Vanbrugh, who is also remembered as a Restoration dramatist. Vanbrugh's predilection for the massive and grandiose is nowhere better illustrated than in Blenheim Palace, with its great Corinthian portico in the center and two projecting wings. The length of the

A

B

C

PLATE XIII

A

Martin Folkes *Addison*

B

C

D

PLATE XIV

A

COMMON— WEALTH

The COLOSSUS

Tell to me, if you are vitty
Whose wooden Leg is in de City
Eh biene drole, tis de great Pity
Doodle do
De broad brim Hat he thrust his Nob in
De vhile St Stephens throng are throbbing
One Crutch in America is Bobbing
Doodle do
But who be yonder Odd man there sir
Building de Castle in de Air sir
O' tis de Temple one may swear Sir
Doodle do
Stamp Act La Diable. dats de Jobb sir
Dat Stamp't it in de Stiltmans Nob sir
To be America's Nabob sir
Doodle do
De English dream vid leetel vit sir
For de French day make de pit sir
Tis a pit for them, who now are bit sir
Doodle Noodle do

Sedition

Pension

Popularity

Royal Exchange

Loyalty

Publick Spirit

Money

York

St Stephens Chapel

Patriot

Pension

Connections

War

Peace

Gold Boxes

Minority

Majority

Sing Tantarera Puff all Puff all Sing Tantarerare all Puff

B

PLATE XV

LONDON

I wander thro' each charterd street,
Near where the charterd Thames does flow
And mark in every face I meet
Marks of weakness, marks of woe.

In every cry of every Man,
In every Infants cry of fear,
In every voice: in every ban,
The mind-forg'd manacles I hear

How the Chimney-sweepers cry
Every blackning Church appalls,
And the hapless Soldiers sigh
Runs in blood down Palace walls

But most thro' midnight streets I hear
How the youthful Harlots curse
Blasts the new born Infants tear
And blights with plagues the Marriage hearse

PLATE XVI

façade is nearly 400 feet. A wit of the time proposed the following epitaph for Vanbrugh:

> Lie heavy on him, Earth! for he
> Laid many heavy loads on thee!

B SCENE IN A COFFEE-HOUSE (*S. Ireland after Hogarth*)

The coffee-house was at the height of its glory in Queen Anne's London. There were many varieties of this kind of public house, catering to many levels of taste, where anybody who could pay the price of a cup of coffee, usually a penny, was welcome. The coffee-house was the center of the social, political, and literary life of an age in which social intercourse was considered the supreme achievement of civilization. Prominent literary and political personages came to be associated with particular coffee-houses. Dryden, in the late seventeenth century, presided over the conversation at Will's, and Addison was the undisputed master at Button's. St. James's was the center of the Whig politicians, and the Chocolate House and the Cocoa Tree were the gathering places of the Tories. Other groups favored other houses.

It is difficult to imagine such periodicals as *The Tatler* and *The Spectator* without the coffee-house as their origin and as the rendezvous of their readers. In the accompanying print Addison is seen in conversation with the scientist and antiquarian Martin Folkes, later president of the Royal Society.

C STOKE POGES CHURCH (*British Information*)

Stoke Poges Churchyard in Buckinghamshire is commonly considered to have inspired Gray's famous *Elegy*. Over 100,000 persons visit the little churchyard each year, most of them armed with a copy of the *Elegy* and eager to identify such landmarks as "those rugged elms, that yew-tree's shade." Gray's own grave is near the church amid "many a mouldering heap," under which lie "the rude forefathers of the hamlet." The church, with its "ivy-mantled tower," whence "The moping owl does to the moon complain," is an emblem of the late eighteenth century's romantic interest in melancholy.

D THE HONORABLE FRANCES DUNCOMBE, BY THOMAS GAINSBOROUGH (*Copyright The Frick Collection*)

Gainsborough's portrait of the Honorable Frances Duncombe, like Pope's poem *The Rape of the Lock*, reminds us of the enormous amount of time, energy, silks, brocade, jewelry, and feathers that went into preparing a fashionable lady of the eighteenth century for her appearance in public.

Much of the best artistic effort of the century went into portraits like this one of fashionable ladies and gentlemen. Professor C. B. Tinker, in his *Painter and Poet*, refers to Gainsborough's skill in representing his subjects out of doors, particularly in his later work, thus uniting portraiture with landscape, and adding greatly to the decorative quality of the painting as a whole.

PLATE XV

A PRIOR PARK, BATH (*British Information*)

"If we want to realize what manner of folk were those who set the standard of taste and governed eighteenth-century England," says Esmé Wingfield-Stratford in his *History of British Civilization*, "we should do well to visit the town in which the ideal of life is recorded for all time in fair, white stone." The modern Bath is on the site of the fashionable watering place of Roman Britain. Its modern career began with Queen Anne, and it remained the center of fashion throughout the century. Eighteenth-century Bath was largely the product of two architects of genius, the elder and younger John Wood, who had as their patron Ralph Allen. The latter, says Wingfield-Stratford, was "one of the best type of eighteenth-century gentlemen, a man of business and a philanthropist, gifted in both capacities with something of the old Greek virtue of magnificence. Allen's beautifully placed mansion of Prior Park, the masterpiece of the elder Wood, with its conscious yet refined dignity of aspect, forms a fitting crown to the pride, pomp, and circumstance that is Bath."

B WILLIAM PITT THE ELDER AS THE COLOSSUS (*Courtesy of the Pierpont Morgan Library*)

The political cartoon of today's newspaper is a direct descendant of such eighteenth-century drawings as this of William Pitt the Elder. Pitt was the strongest English opponent of the policy of taxing the English colonies in America. This drawing was inspired by Pitt's desire for the repeal of the Stamp Act, which was passed in 1765, and which required the affixing of stamps to legal documents in the colonies to help provide funds for the upkeep of royal forces in America. Pitt's warnings to Parliament and King George III were in vain, and for his pains he was called a "trumpet of sedition."

This cartoon comes from a collection of 3300 political caricatures, portraits, and lampoons, ranging from the time of Cromwell to the reign of George IV. The collection belonged originally to Sir Robert Peel, the nineteenth-century statesman, remembered today as the founder of the London police force whose members are still called "bobbies," in his honor.

PLATE XVI

A JONATHAN SWIFT (*Bettmann Archive, from a painting in the National Portrait Gallery, London*)

Of the physical appearance of the author of *Gulliver's Travels* we have the following account by the Earl of Orrery in 1752: "Dr. Swift had a natural severity of face, which even his smiles could never soften, or his utmost gaiety render placid and serene; but when that sternness of visage was increased by rage, it is scarcely possible to imagine looks or features that carried in them more terror and austerity." His contemporary Daniel Defoe described him as "a walking index of books, who has all the libraries of Europe in his head, . . . but he is cynic in behavior, a fury in temper, impolite in conversation, abusive in language, and ungovernable in passion." Swift's friend Joseph Addison, who knew him better than either the Earl of Orrery or Defoe, inscribed a copy of his *Travels in Italy* to Swift in these words: "To Jonathan Swift, the most agreeable companion, the truest friend, the greatest genius of his age, this work is presented by his most humble servant, the author."

B A PAGE FROM WILLIAM BLAKE'S SONGS OF EXPERIENCE (*Courtesy of The Metropolitan Museum of Art*)

Some idea of the unique combination of poet and painter in Blake's work may be gained from the accompanying reproduction of "London," one of the poems in the first edition of his *Songs of Experience*. Both the text of the poem and the decorative designs were engraved by the poet on copper, and tinted by his own hand after printing.

C THE KING OF CLUBS FROM THE GAME OF OMBRE (*From Catherine P. Hargrave's* A History of Playing Cards, *courtesy of the United States Playing Card Company*)

Ombre, a game of Spanish origin, was the most popular card game of the eighteenth century. Pope's mock-heroic description of a fashionable game of ombre in *The Rape of the Lock* is an interesting proof of this fact. In the eighteenth century, as in earlier days, the figures of the Kings, Queens, and Knaves in the four suits were portrayed in full length. Pope describes the King of Clubs and his fate at the hands of Belinda as follows:

> The Club's black tyrant first her victim died,
> Spite of his haughty mien and barbarous pride:
> What boots the regal circle on his head,
> His giant limbs, in state unwieldy spread;
> That long behind he trails his pompous robe,
> And of all monarchs only grasps the globe?

It is an interesting circumstance that in modern playing cards the King of Clubs is still the only one of the four Kings who "grasps the globe," that is, holds in his left hand the orb, the symbol of sovereignty.

D SAMUEL JOHNSON, BY SIR JOSHUA REYNOLDS

The portrait of Dr. Johnson is the best known of the many representations of the Great Cham of English Letters. It is appropriate that the portrait should be the work of a man who was not only one of the greatest portrait painters of his day but who won fame for his remarkable contributions to the theory of art embodied in his *Discourses*. In the portrait of Johnson, Reynolds displays his great power of interpreting character while he produces a physical likeness. Of Johnson's appearance Boswell tells us in his *Life*: "His figure was large and well formed, and his countenance of the cast of an ancient statue; yet his appearance was rendered strange and somewhat uncouth by convulsive cramps, by the scars of that distemper which it was once imagined the royal touch could cure, and by a slovenly mode of dress. . . . That with his constitution and habits of life he should have lived seventy-five years is a proof that an inherent *vivida vis* is a powerful preservative of the human frame."

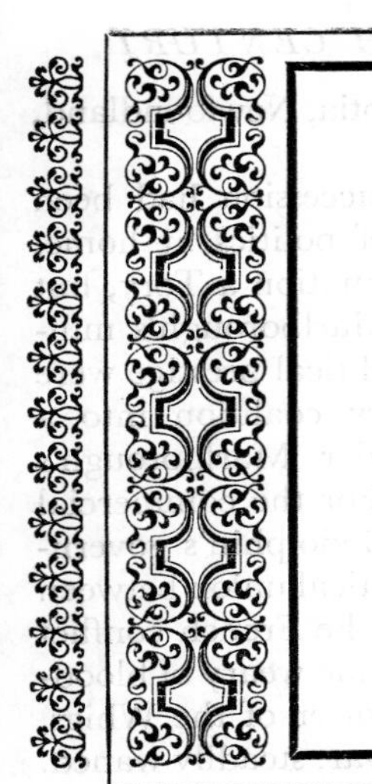

The Eighteenth Century

The Historical and Political Background

THE eighteenth century has been called the "indispensable" century in preparing the way for the modern world.[1] It saw the establishment of English parliamentary government; it witnessed the spread of the British Empire to Canada and India and the beginning of British settlement in Australia. This was the age in which English inventors—Watt, the perfecter of the steam engine, the Darbys who discovered how to smelt iron with coal, and others—laid the foundations of the Industrial Revolution. Even England's great setback in the eighteenth century, her loss of the American colonies, can in a sense be looked upon as another triumph in the spread of England's free institutions. It was so regarded on the continent of Europe at the time, and by such English friends of the colonists as Edmund Burke; in seeking to avert war with the colonies, Burke declared in Parliament: "I do not choose to consume its [America's] strength along with our own, because in all parts it is the British strength that I consume." In America, furthermore, the authors of the Declaration of Independence and the Constitution felt that in framing these great documents they were simply putting into practice the reasonable laws for human society which were current among enlightened Englishmen everywhere.

More definitive than any dates the calendar provides for the beginning and end of the eighteenth century in England were a bloodless English revolution at one extremity and an earth-shaking French revolution at the other. Between the "Glorious Revolution" of 1688, which established William and Mary on the English throne, and the storming of the Bastille in 1789, English politics and English society evolved into much the same forms we know today. At the opening of the period most continental Europeans considered England as "free" to the point of anarchy, a "giddy" nation (in Dryden's phrase) whose people assumed the unheard-of right to change their rulers "every twenty years." By the last quarter of the century, after a long period of prosperity and comparative quiet at home, and of empire building abroad, England had become the leading conservative nation of Europe; Englishmen in the 1790's could look with horror across the channel at France, aflame with a bloody passion for liberty and engaged in open warfare "against all kings in behalf of all peoples."

No Englishman in 1688 was sure that the gains of the Glorious Revolution would prove permanent. True, Parliament had asserted its right to choose a Protestant king by offering James II's crown to his Dutch son-in-law, William of Orange. But James had fled to France where his "divine right" to the English throne—and that of his son after him—was still recognized by his powerful patron, Louis XIV. And at home many Tories supported his claim.

The reigns of William and Mary (1688–1694), of William alone (1694–1702), and of Anne, Mary's younger sister and last of the Stuarts (1702–1714), formed a period of confused but inevitable transition. Though William, a better European than

[1] Basil Willey, *The Eighteenth Century Background*, Chatto and Windus, 1940.

Englishman, made vigorous efforts to hold his own, Parliament was clearly becoming the dominant force in English government. The Revolution of 1688 had in effect transferred power from an aristocratic monarchy to a group of politically minded aristocratic families who wrestled among themselves for the fruits of office. Finding the Whigs in a majority during the early part of his reign, William sought to ease the strain upon him by choosing all ministers from the dominant party. When, however, the Tories later gained a majority and compelled the King to give them similar preferential treatment, the monarch could not stave off party control much longer. War with France occupied William until 1697, and at the time of his death five years later—a fall from his horse at Hampton Court proved fatal—he was about to lead English troops abroad in an effort to prevent Spanish dominions from falling into the eager hands of Louis XIV.

When Anne became queen, England had a population of some six millions—fewer than the city of London alone boasts today—and that small England was at war with the twenty millions of France. Anne brought determination but no real abilities to the throne. It was extremely fortunate that in the mighty Duke of Marlborough she had, however, a man far more than a match for the generals of Louis XIV. In military and foreign affairs—and their importance in the reign of Queen Anne can hardly be overemphasized—it was Marlborough rather than the Queen who truly succeeded William III.

Before his death William had placed John Churchill (Duke of Marlborough, and Winston Churchill's great ancestor) in command of the allied forces on the Continent, and Anne quickly confirmed Marlborough in his role as commander-in-chief of the English and Dutch armies. There followed, under Marlborough's magnificent leadership, one of the boldest and most skillful series of victories in military history. Through a decade, battles in this War of the Spanish Succession were fought on land and sea, in Europe, Asia, and America. Of these, Marlborough's four brilliant victories—Blenheim in Bavaria (1704), Ramillies (1706) and Oudenarde (1708) in Belgium, and Malplaquet in France (1709)—were the most destructive to French power. When the Peace of Utrecht was signed in 1713 England emerged with the strongest fleet in the world, with control of the Mediterranean by virtue of her possession of Gibraltar and Minorca, and with an extended colonial empire in the New World through recognition of her claims to Nova Scotia, Newfoundland, and the Hudson Bay territory.

The War of the Spanish Succession had been determining also the course of politics at home. Anne was by training and inclination a Tory, but by the middle of the decade Marlborough's military successes and enhanced political prestige were transforming a moderate Tory coalition into a Whig party government, under Marlborough's friend the Earl of Godolphin. For the commercial advantage of both countries, Godolphin's government had effected in 1707 a political union between England and Scotland. But as the French conflict dragged on and the nation became weary of bloodshed and swelling taxes, the power of the Whigs, who were in effect waging the war, steadily waned. Nor had the government's bold-faced attempt to prosecute the extremist Tory preacher, Henry Sacheverell, helped matters. When, therefore, the Queen dismissed the Whig ministers in 1710, there was a resounding Tory victory at the polls and the reins of government had passed into the hands of the Earl of Oxford and Viscount Bolingbroke. The Tories now enjoyed their few years in the saddle, but they had barely had time to negotiate the Peace of Utrecht when in 1714 Queen Anne died; the Tory ministers were speedily indicted, and their party went into decline for nearly half a century.

The briefest note on domestic politics must contain the reminder that continuity in English government resided, then as now, in the person of the sovereign. Parliament did not yet represent more than a minority of the citizens, and the ministers who were responsible to Parliament were also responsible to, and were appointed by, the monarch. Whigs and Tories fought out their political battles, but to the man in the street the difference between a Whig duke and a Tory duke was difficult to discern, and whatever changes in high affairs of state might follow from the fall of a ministry, the effect on the lives of the poor was generally negligible. Not until the nineteenth century did the full implications of a democratic system dawn on the minds even of the political reformers. The bloodless Revolution of 1688 had in effect transferred power from an autocratic monarchy to a group of aristocratic families who, however much they might have wrestled among themselves for the fruits of office, seldom thought of passing their privileges to the mass of society. Not until the Reform Bill of 1832 was the demand of all Englishmen for a voice in their own government strong enough to force concessions from their mildly liberal rulers.

The new king, George I, was a descendant of James I on his mother's side, but that was the extent of his Englishness. First and last, he was the Elector of Hanover, a German prince who knew no English and had slight interest in his new realm. Yet the great majority of Englishmen preferred this uninspiring foreigner, with all his faults, to James II's Catholic son, in whose behalf an unsuccessful revolt broke out in Scotland shortly after the Hanoverian accession. We now see the British throne occupied for thirteen years by this first of the Hanoverians, the only constitutional monarch in Europe, who ruled not by divine right but ostensibly by the will of the people expressed through Parliament.

During the reigns of the first two Georges the prestige of the crown sank to a low level from which it never completely recovered until the nineteenth century. George I wasted no time in turning active leadership over to the eager but somewhat disorganized Whigs. A really responsible ministry was not forthcoming, however, until wildly speculative investment in the government-sponsored South Sea Company (which at one point was ready to assume the national debt) burst this famous "South Sea Bubble" in 1720 and brought Robert Walpole to the head of the government. Walpole became "the great man of the early eighteenth century, the steadying influence that kept England on the path of peace and freedom." [2] It was his great merit for the times that he saw things as they were, not as imagination would paint them. By exercise of consummate practical sagacity Walpole first put the national economy back on a sound footing; he then initiated and brilliantly carried through a long-term program to maintain those most dearly sought commodities, peace and prosperity. He did not accomplish his ends without recourse to political methods that outraged his enemies, who included the chief literary figures of the period, and also those friends whose consciences were tidier than his own. But, serving in fact if not in name as England's first prime minister, he dexterously kept his country from entanglements abroad and thus provided British commerce with the opportunity to grow by leaps and bounds.

Walpole proved as invaluable to the second George—who succeeded his father in 1727—as he had been to the first. But once he had made the economic foundations secure, he could not forever withstand the mounting tide of militant imperialism. The War of Jenkins' Ear—an English sea captain insisted that his ear had been cut off by the ruthlessly colonizing Spanish—was more picturesque in name than in fact, and its failure precipitated the resignation of Walpole in 1742.

Up to the date of his resignation, Walpole had sought to keep his country free from foreign wars and entanglements; his caution and discretion infuriated his political opponents, but certainly helped to secure that growing stability in English life which was reflected not imperfectly in the arts and sciences. If turmoil would have upset this habit of mind, credit must be given to the man who from 1715 to 1742 labored to keep turmoil at bay. The War of the Austrian Succession absorbed the smaller conflict, lasting on until 1748, and was more a Hanoverian than an English affair; during the battle of Dettingen (1743) an English king took part in actual warfare for the last time. In his journal for January 17, 1763, James Boswell recorded a conversation (among Scotsmen, it is true) in which the company agreed "that by the Revolution we got a shabby family to reign over us, and that the German war, a consequence of having a German sovereign, was the most destructive thing this nation ever saw." They were not far wrong.

Through the later years of Walpole's ministry there had been growing dissatisfaction with corruption and with the cynically low level on which the activities of government were proceeding. Walpole found he had enemies even within his own party. The most conspicuous of these, a stirring speaker and an ardent patriot, was William Pitt, who spent twenty years in Parliament before he at length gained the opportunity to rise toweringly above the succession of mediocre prime ministers who succeeded Walpole. When in the continuing struggle for colonies between Great Britain and France the tide looked to be turning against his country, Pitt was ready to provide the vigorous and high-minded leadership the times demanded. The Seven Years' War (1756–1763) eventually gained for England the eastern part of North America and supremacy in India and reaffirmed her command of the seas; it was also William Pitt's great triumph. Utilizing to the full the financial resources that had been strengthened by Walpole, Pitt pursued a policy of keeping France busy and exhausting her energies on the Continent while he maintained and extended the Empire against the French in India and America.

Robert Clive's victory at Plassey (1757) avenged the crime of the Black Hole of Calcutta and at the same time immeasurably strengthened the British hold on India. Successes on the Continent and

[2] James A. Williamson, *The Evolution of England*, Oxford University Press, 1931.

crushing victories over the French fleet were climaxed in 1759 by the intoxicating news that General Wolfe had captured Quebec. Well might Horace Walpole, prosaic Sir Robert's remarkably literary son, observe during that year that "We are forced to ask every morning what victory there is for fear of missing one." British colonial power had attained new and somewhat dizzying proportions, and Pitt was a national hero. When George II died in 1760 the Seven Years' War still had several years to run, but the foundations of British power in the nineteenth century were already firmly laid.

Under the first two Georges, graceless boors who thought of Hanover before they thought of England, the country had been governed by the Whigs. But when George III came to the throne as a young man of twenty-two, he could convincingly say that "Born and educated in this country, I glory in the name of Briton." Moreover, the third George revealed himself to be an astute and stubborn man who from the first determined he would be king in more than name. To accomplish this end, it was first necessary to destroy the long-standing Whig supremacy and provide for the appointment of ministers and a Parliament that would do his bidding. The concept of a strong "patriot king" ruling for his people's good was thoroughly in accord with Tory principles, which, however, had for many decades found no expression in practice. Now George III secured for his support a parliamentary majority, soon known as "The King's Friends," that, while not wholly Tory in label, was Tory in action. George managed first to rid himself of the powerful Pitt and brought to as speedy an end as possible (1763) the war which Pitt had waged so successfully and on which much of his reputation depended. Then, placing subservient ministers beneath him, George became virtually his own prime minister for over a decade.

Such highhanded and wide-awake tactics on the part of a royal house that had been slumbering for nearly a half century could hardly fail to arouse violent reaction. The political crisis that followed was dramatized by the case of John Wilkes, who in his journal, *The North Briton*, attacked George III only to find himself expelled from the House of Commons by the King's influence. Wilkes's re-election in defiance of King and Commons was a triumph for the will of the people. But the King's most insistent challenge now came from across the Atlantic Ocean.

With the danger of French attacks removed, the American colonies were becoming less dependent on their mother country. Moreover, as commercial opportunities for the colonies expanded, the Navigation Acts had long been working increased hardship on American merchants. The situation was already tense when the Tory ministry precipitated a crisis with America in 1765 by passing the Stamp Act. To be sure, the hue and cry over "taxation without representation" forced the repeal of this measure, but hard upon it came the series of harsh restrictive measures on American commerce that received their first dramatic answer in the Boston Tea Party of 1773. Resentment against arbitrary interference had grown into a wholehearted American desire for independence when the guns were heard at Lexington in the spring of 1775, and the Declaration of Independence was but a step away. Despite the protests of men of the stature of Pitt, Burke, and Charles James Fox, the King insisted on riding the revolt down. The resulting American War of Independence (1775–1783) proved to be more than British forces could cope with, especially when France and Holland eventually joined forces with the colonists, and at the end George III looked out to find his colonial empire in the west fallen away. A brilliant English historian has pointed the moral: "England had no doubt ordered her relations with the colonies on a reasonable, and probably a sound business footing, but it was the fatal weakness of the system that it placed the Empire on a business footing alone." [3]

When the Versailles Treaty of 1783 restored peace, it became apparent that George III's personal experiment in reasserting the royal power had also failed. With his Tory supporters discredited and out of office, it was the Whigs who made the peace treaty. The King had for consolation the fact that at the other extreme of the Empire the skill of Clive and later Warren Hastings had maintained and consolidated British influence in India. And at home it did not displease him that Whig factions experienced difficulty in hanging together until another William Pitt—his great father had died in 1778—accepted appointment as prime minister at the age of twenty-five. The younger Pitt put himself in the Tory camp by accepting personal appointment from the King, and the result was a new type of Tory regime under Pitt that lasted well into the next century. Pitt made repeated efforts at political and economic reform during the long period of his ascendancy, but he met party opposition sufficient to delay any effectual measures until the nineteenth century. Impeachment proceedings against Warren Hastings—

[3] Esmé Wingfield-Stratford, *The History of British Civilization*, Harcourt, Brace, 1930.

who was rightfully acquitted—moved Burke, Fox, and Sheridan to some of their most inspired oratory, in the wrong cause, on the very eve of the French Revolution. That volcanic eruption on the Continent, and the bitter struggles against post-revolutionary France and Napoleon that were to wear out Pitt's brilliant life too early, are, by every other criterion than strict chronology, part of the story of the nineteenth century.

The Social Setting

When we turn from the chronicle of outward events to observe the less dramatic but equally absorbing social scene in eighteenth-century England, we need not look far to find reflections of the national destiny. In the light of the crown's diminished prestige, it is small wonder the social importance of the court declined under the early Hanoverian monarchs. More and more the country houses of the great landowners and the fashionable drawing rooms of London came to occupy the dominant position in English society. London's coffee-houses and clubs—already a noteworthy feature of life in the Restoration period, but now opening their doors not in hundreds but in thousands—became the gathering places of various groups, particularly the writers, actors, and professional men of the day. Will's Coffee House had been the favorite resort of Dryden. Whigs like Addison and Steele now patronized Button's. When Steele conceived the idea of the *Tatler*, he advised his potential readers that "All accounts of gallantry, pleasure, and entertainment shall be under the article of White's Chocolate-house; poetry under that of Will's Coffee-house; learning, under the title of Grecian; foreign and domestic news you will have from St. James's Coffee-house." Later in the century Doctor Johnson's famous "Club" met at the Turk's Head in Gerrard Street. Businessmen resorted to Lloyd's Coffee-house to hear the latest shipping news, and eventually a group of them formed the great insurance company which goes by the name of Lloyds today. Free exchange of ideas was the very life of the coffee-houses, but it is significant of the eighteenth century's distrust of religious argument that religion was the one topic which was taboo.

The eighteenth century that first meets and delights the eye—and this can be true in a literal sense, for we still see much of the period around us—is a reflection of the elegant way of life enjoyed by the wealthy landowners who for the most part controlled the affairs of the realm, and also by the fashionable folk of London, among whom were now families that the largess bestowed by foreign trade had raised to a level of living comparable to that of the established aristocracy. The balanced dignity and clear lines of Georgian architecture, isolated museumlike in Colonial Williamsburg but also to be seen throughout contemporary America in buildings old and new, are perhaps our most readily visible link with eighteenth-century England. But admiration and imitation in our time of the artistic contours of an aristocratic eighteenth-century society have not stopped with architecture; in the smaller arts of furniture and ceramics the Chippendale cabinet and Sheraton chairs, Lowestoft and Wedgwood china, are graceful reminders of indebtedness to the eighteenth century in the surroundings of our daily lives.

English painting, which flowered in the time of Sir Joshua Reynolds, Gainsborough, Romney, and Hogarth as it had never flowered before, mirrors and often takes as its very subject matter the leisurely, refined existence of the privileged classes, in whose country houses and London mansions hung many of these splendid portraits—more often than not celebrating the owners themselves—and the idealized landscapes. In paintings that continue to command our admiration, we can still see these highly polished men and women, posing for the artist before Arcadian backgrounds, listening to the delicious, precise measures of Handel's music, promenading on the Mall in St. James's Park, or relaxing in the gardens of their spacious country estates. And we meet members of this same fashionable society in the pages of Pope's *Rape of the Lock*. Sometimes the refinement was skin-deep and it was often complacent.[4] But it is, nevertheless, easy to forget, amidst the artificial splendor and elegant demeanor of the eighteenth-century world of fashion, that by encouraging the arts and things of the mind, this English aristocracy contributed more to the culture and intellectual life of the period than did, to choose a shocking example, the languid universities.

If the landed aristocracy was in virtual control of political affairs and by its patronage did much

[4] "The age of Queen Anne was, on the whole, one of boundless self-complacency. The English navy ruled the seas unchallenged, the army was a partaker in victories the like of which had never been heard of since Agincourt, money was accumulating in almost unhealthy profusion. And it seemed as if a new age of right and reason had already dawned to which every other age was, by comparison, barbarous. Literature was honoured as never before. Statesmen did not disdain to solicit the friendship of noblemen." Esmé Wingfield-Stratford, *The History of British Civilization*.

to foster the arts and learning, a great deal of the creative energy of the age managed to find its expression in other ranks of society. The emergence of a prosperous middle class, made wealthy by the boom in foreign and colonial trade, was a striking phenomenon as the century grew older; this development was of immense significance for the future. Yet there smoldered in England nothing even resembling a class struggle. Indeed, the rise of a substantial merchant class hastened rather than hindered the process of consolidation that was an important part of the work of the eighteenth century. Alexander Pope, who came to mingle in the highest society, was the son of a linen merchant; William Collins, the son of a "respectable hatter." The painter Hogarth, a devastatingly effective critic of the affectations and cruelties of the age, stemmed from the sturdy North Country yeomanry. England's first genuine novelist, Samuel Richardson, was the son of a Derbyshire joiner. Swift and Johnson grew up in poverty, Gray was the son of a scrivener, Cowper and Thomson of ministers. Addison's father, to be sure, held the more exalted post of Dean of Lichfield Cathedral, and indeed it would be a mistake to labor too far the humble origins of many of the dominating and sensitive spirits of the age. Art and affluence, for one thing, have always proved rather uncomfortable bedfellows; and a truly democratic spirit was by no means characteristic of this age of rank and privilege. Yet, stratified though the eighteenth-century social structure was, it afforded a good deal of opportunity for individual talent and enterprise, commercial, intellectual, or whatever.

The life of the lower classes is less attractive to contemplate. An age of unprecedented material prosperity showed little concern for the poverty, disease, and brutality that attended the lives of the great mass of humanity. Reforms achieved under Walpole were more often political and legal than social and humanitarian, and even those acts left the propertyless poor with no voice in political affairs. Through the first half of the century in London, prodigious consumption of bad gin carried further the degradation of the common people. Crime, especially in the city, was rampant. The continued indifference of all but a few responsible citizens, among whom Hogarth, the unflinching painter, and Henry Fielding, the clear-eyed novelist and magistrate, were conspicuous, left the simple annals of the poor bleak and far from hopeful. When toward the end of the century an emphatic humanitarian movement sprang up, it was long overdue. But by then the Industrial Revolution was already so transforming the economic structure that the crying need for social reforms would have to be met in new and more insistent terms during the century to come.

It was not until the early years of George III's reign that the transforming process we know as the Industrial Revolution began really to get under way. Yet the principal ingredients for a new industrial age had for some time been there: scientific knowledge and curiosity, freedom for individual enterprise, foreign markets, and the necessary capital. Now, with an improved canal system and a series of remarkable inventions (Hargreaves's spinning jenny, 1764; Arkwright's water frame, 1769; Watt's double-action steam engine, 1785), the factory system and the development of England's great cotton, woolen, and iron centers were closer at hand than many Englishmen would have wanted to realize. In the words of Professor Trevelyan, "Throughout his [George III's] long reign, new forces of machinery and capitalized industry worked their blind will upon a loosely organized, aristocratic society that did not even perceive that its fate had come upon it."

The Intellectual and Religious Background

A large share of the philosophical and scientific activity of the eighteenth century was concerned with developing and turning to practical uses the stupendous philosophical and scientific ideas of the preceding century. As Newton's law of gravitation encouraged men to seek for reason and order in every aspect of their world, the full force of John Locke's observations on the human mind began also to be felt in the new age. With the exception of the Bible itself, no one book had so great an influence on the eighteenth century as Locke's great *Essay concerning Human Understanding* (1690).

Locke's rejection of innate ideas and his stress on the evidence of the senses permitted men to believe they could with comparative ease bring their ideas and conduct in harmony with a universal natural order. By and large the chief thinkers of the time now concerned themselves with finding that benevolent "natural law" which could apply to all branches of human activity. "Steam bubbling from the spout of a kettle, smoke whisking up a chimney, morning mist lifting from the meadows—here was nature all about, moving in ways not mysterious her wonders to perform; and revealing, to the eyes of common men no less than to the learned, those laws that imposed on all things their reasonable and beneficent, even if curious and intricate, commands." [5]

In the early years of the century this "natural law" was held to be identical with the proper use of the human reason. The truth about all things, including the very nature and existence of God, must be inferred from the observable behavior of the world. In such an intellectual climate it is hardly surprising that many Englishmen found in Deism, a philosophical doctrine first elaborated in England by Lord Herbert of Cherbury in the seventeenth century, an attitude which was perfectly "reasonable" while at the same time it allowed them to enjoy the comforts of religion. This God of the Deists was Himself a thoroughly benevolent and enlightened Being, no friend of inquisitions and hairsplitting theology. The Deists have been described as "rationalists with a nostalgia for religion"—and that indicates the proportion pretty fairly. Dogmatic Christianity was in disfavor; enthusiasm was suspect; men had seen only too recently to what unseemly and inhuman lengths religious controversy could go, and they wanted no more of it. Belief in God was "reasonable" from the evidence of Nature; to complicate the matter further by reference to Holy Writ and ecclesiastical dogma seemed unnecessary, and dangerous. With the Deists the old-fashioned "fear of God" and the "sense of sin" yielded to a more "rational" view of the universe and to a firm belief in the operation of "natural law."

The third Earl of Shaftesbury's *Characteristics* (1711) is in many respects the prime text of the complacent Deism of the early part of the century. His points were elegant and all-sufficient: Nature is divine; "orthodox" and codified religion is the enemy of true, natural, religion; man is good by nature and his moral sense can be trusted, just as his native good sense in other matters requires no special emphasis; above all, the educated man is at liberty to think what he likes, and if he disagrees with others it is only necessary for him to laugh, not to groan or persecute. Now, although the official apologists of the Church of England spoke temperately for the retention of rather more in the way of mystic faith than a Shaftesbury would allow, they did nevertheless conduct their arguments—and, indeed, their parish duties—much more in the manner of Deists. When they came to defend the supernatural, it was as rational men that they did so, claiming that too great a degree of incredulity was no less unreasonable than too great a degree of credulity.

Yet it was a bishop—the great Berkeley—who, himself well-experienced as politician, ecclesiast, economist, and man of letters, set out rationally and coolly to shake men's faith in the evidence of their own senses. As Mr. Desmond MacCarthy has written: "To Leibnitz his own nose was a congregation of spiritual beings; to a modern physicist his own nose is a wild dance of electrons; for Bishop Berkeley his own nose only existed from time to time when he blew it." Berkeley's *Principles of Human Knowledge* (1710) is the work of a polite and moderate skeptic who went further than Locke. The only realities, he proclaims, are ideas; and appearances themselves are realities only because they too are ideas. Berkeley's prose was a model of clear exposition, a gentlemanly treatise written for educated nonspecialists, who would read it without calling for excommunication or girding on a crusader's sword. Argue as they might among themselves, the philosophers were agreed on one point: superstition and enthusiasm must alike be banished. With them, they seem for a time to have banished the sense of sin and the consciousness of guilt. But later in the century, other thinkers had to discover anew (as we in our turn have had to discover it) that the irrational and dark aspects of man's nature may be driven out the door, but only to re-enter through the window.

Meanwhile in other fields the doctrine of natural law held sway. In politics the law of nature found its most effective formulation in Locke's theory of the "rights of man." Locke, the intellectual architect of the Revolution of 1688, had had no love for the Tory principle of the divine right of kings. Governments, he declared, do not rule by divine right; instead (to use the language of the American Declaration of Independence which owes much to Locke) they "derive their just powers from the consent of the governed." It is the people, then, who have certain "natural rights," given them at birth. Only in order to attain the benefits of an organized society do the people voluntarily curtail these rights by entering into a "compact" with rulers of their own choosing. Edmund Burke held fast to a belief in the natural goodness of man, but in 1790 one could no longer be so complacent about it as in 1710. Pure reason might well lead men to desperate revolutionary remedies, but "Nature is without Reason and above it," and "Politics ought to be adapted not to Human Reasoning but to Human Nature."

In the year that the Declaration of Independence

[5] Carl Becker, *The Heavenly City of the Eighteenth-Century Philosophers*, Yale University Press, 1932.

was written, Adam Smith published *An Inquiry into the Nature and Causes of the Wealth of Nations*, wherein he developed the classical theory of free trade known as *laissez faire*. Trade, too, Smith insisted, had its natural law, the law of supply and demand. The less governments interfere with this law, the more trade will flourish. Smith's theories provided the handbook for capitalism during its great expansive period in the nineteenth century and *laissez faire* remains the dominant economic philosophy in the United States today.

There is perhaps the temptation to assume that as the decades passed, eighteenth-century religion dwindled away into a polite social morality. But Samuel Johnson, the outstanding literary figure of his age, was a solid embodiment of orthodox piety. And it is well to consider also the tremendous achievements of John Wesley. It was in 1738 that Wesley experienced the change of heart which he described in words which are still uttered from a thousand pulpits on both sides of the Atlantic: "I felt my heart strangely warmed. I felt that I did trust in Christ, Christ alone for salvation; and an assurance was given me that He had taken *my* sins, even *mine*, and saved me from the law of sin and death." We shall gravely err in our estimate of the century if we forget the power and influence of Wesley and his Methodists. The fervor of Methodism spread like fire among many to whom the thin-lipped platitudes of polite religion offered little help or hope. The insistence on religious revelation as a matter of personal experience rather than of dogma and theory, the direct simplicity and appeal to personal feelings in the hymns of John and Charles Wesley, helped to bring about the obvious break in style that marked the beginnings of the Romantic Movement. The poetry of William Cowper would have been very different but for his contact with fervid evangelists of the new order. Bishops might dally with atheistic sciences, but congregations elsewhere were singing of the Blood of the Lamb. Praise for believers rejoicing, wrestling with God for sinners backsliding: these were preoccupations of men and women—and, in time, of writers too—who never stopped to read skeptical philosophy. And it may well be that by turning the attention of many workers to the state of their souls and hence away from their social and economic distresses, John Wesley helped, unconsciously, to weaken the strength of revolutionary movements which all the cunning of the politicians would have been helpless to avert.

As the century advanced there was, then, a growing tendency to replace the cult of Reason with a cult of Feeling. It was still assumed that men could arrive at an understanding of the Truth by the use of their own faculties, unaided by supernatural revelation. But the faculty to be relied on was emotional, not rational. In mid-century David Hume (1711–1776) carried the attack on Reason into all branches of human knowledge. In his *Treatise on Human Nature* Hume declares that the difference between the truth and falsity of all ideas is a matter of subjective feeling. We recognize the "true" ideas because we feel them with "superior force or vivacity." If men were dependent on reason alone to ascertain the truth they would be in a sorry fix since the judgments of reason are wholly fallible. But fortunately (and here Hume is the comfortable eighteenth-century optimist) they have "feeling" to guide them.

Yet this theoretical optimism was accompanied by an increasing sense of dissatisfaction with the world as it actually existed. Human beings might be born with all sorts of "natural" virtues, but somehow the world they lived in was full of gross inequalities and flagrant injustice. Traditional Christian theology had explained this unhappy state of affairs by reference to the doctrine of original sin: ever since the fall of Adam, man has been tainted with evil and his works are bound to be imperfect. But this age of enlightenment was not inclined to respect such theological "myths." Instead it tended to substitute a myth of its own: man had been "good" as long as he remained in a "state of nature" but civilization had debauched him.

It was this most civilized of periods that developed the cult of the "Noble Savage." With one ear to Jean Jacques Rousseau in France, men of the later eighteenth century liked to believe that beyond the boundaries of civilization, in the backwoods of America or on the islands of the South Seas, lived races of men who were freer, happier, and more "good" than Europeans simply because they had never been civilized. Benjamin Franklin himself was cherished by the court of Versailles as a sort of embodiment of the Noble Savage, an example of that wisdom and sober virtue which, supposedly, could flourish in comparatively uncivilized places like America!

It is easy to make fun of the eighteenth century's cult of the primitive. We who know a great deal more about anthropology know that South Sea Island natives are subject to as many taboos as any eighteenth-century gentleman ever was. But the excesses of this revolt against civilization should not blind us to what it achieved on the positive side.

The first part of the century had been too content with the status quo. The latter half was increasingly occupied with practical measures of reform.

The age of the arch-primitivist, Rousseau (who, in Voltaire's phrase, wanted men "to walk on all fours"), was also the time when Jeremy Bentham began to spend his life in an effort to correct legal abuses in England and to humanize the treatment of criminals. The growing criticism of reason was not always a way of escaping into sentimental irresponsibility; more often it was an effort to arrive at a deeper, more humane version of the truth. No one better illustrates this than Burke. To the harsh "metaphysical politics" of the French Revolution, bent on turning out a new world according to a rational blueprint, Burke could oppose his masterly definition: "A disposition to preserve, taken together with an ability to improve, would be my standard of a statesman."

Eighteenth-Century Prose

The eighteenth century opened in circumstances which favored the development of a great age of prose. The Augustan Age [6] followed Dryden in his emphasis on a clear style which would avoid the ornamentations of language for their own sake. But Dryden had written chiefly for the court, and in a time of religious and political crises. The writers of the eighteenth century enjoyed a wider public and a calmer atmosphere. With the Whig revolution, the upper middle class had come into its own, and it set the standards of the time. In the court of Charles II writers like Congreve had been content to leave "work to the idle, wisdom to fools," and to make "wit their faculty." The new age had little patience with such flippant standards, and small admiraton for that "noble laziness of mind" which had distinguished the Merry Monarch himself. Extremes were out of fashion, whether of courtly license or of puritanical virtue. Prose had a practical work to do in exploring man and in making both his morals and his manners "reasonable."

The Restoration court of Charles II had encouraged the view, pardonable enough after the Puritan excesses of the Commonwealth, that culture and seriousness were incompatible. The Augustans desired to instruct without pedantry, to please without loss of dignity; in short, to observe in their writing those same standards of politeness and good breeding that they valued in social life. It became the delicate task of Steele and Addison, as the diviners and formulators of a new social conscience, to reconcile good breeding, good taste, and the "good life"; to moralize refinement and to refine morality. Lord Chesterfield continually exhorted his son to "cultivate the graces," but it is apparent that he regarded the graces as amounting to a kind of virtue. And Burke could praise the society of pre-revolutionary France as one in which "vice lost half its evil by losing all its grossness."

The age's confidence in literature as an instrument for reforming society is well illustrated in Pope's remark that if he and Swift and Bolingbroke might only live and write together for three years, the combined effect of their satiric output could "accomplish some good even upon this age." The prose which could best achieve this work of enlightenment and reform should be easily readable and at the same time elegant; such prose as that of Addison. "Whoever wishes to attain an English style," wrote Dr. Johnson, "familiar but not coarse, and elegant but not ostentatious, must give his days and nights to the volumes of Addison." The young Boswell, seeking to enter high society in the 1760's, modeled himself cunningly on Addison's *Spectator*. The social virtues informing *The Spectator* (1711–12, 1714) were still held in high esteem at the end of the eighteenth century, and, indeed, beyond; for Addison has been called the first Victorian.

Ladies and gentlemen of the Augustan Age found it agreeable to be assured that virtue was not a matter of fervid emotion, but of breeding and simple good sense. It is a far cry from the inspired utterances of Milton, writing with a sublime disregard for the interests and opinions of his readers, to Pope with his genial doctrine, "Self-love and Social are the same," or to the lay sermons of Addison, preached in a clubman's prose to the newly dominant middle class. To present that sober, comfortable view of life which the middle class approved, Addison and Steele developed a new literary form, the journalistic essay. In the tenth number of *The Spectator* Addison remarked: "It was said of Socrates that he brought philosophy down from heaven to inhabit among men; and I shall be ambitious to have it said of me that I have brought philosophy out of closets and libraries, schools and colleges, to dwell in clubs and assemblies, at tea-

[6] So named from a fancied cultural resemblance between the Rome of the Emperor Augustus (27 B.C.–14 A.D.) and the London of Queen Anne. Eighteenth-century writers turned with reverence to the great authors of classical antiquity as the unfailing authorities on literary art and surest models for imitation. Even a robust writer like Henry Fielding, whose greatest novel, *Tom Jones*, seems as English as roast beef, felt called upon to cite Horace to prove his theory of what a novelist should be.

tables and in coffee-houses." In the character of Sir Roger de Coverley these essays presented the middle classes with a man after their own hearts, one whom they could approve of while still smiling indulgently at his absurdities. Sir Roger is well-born, but by no means a great nobleman. He is goodhearted and innocently snobbish. "He is eccentric, unpractical, untidy, but glories in it and implies superiority over the foreigner; he prefers home-grown vegetables to exotic fruits." [7]

"The proper study of Mankind is Man," said Pope. *The Spectator* studied social man—or perhaps "studied" is too deliberate and excessive a verb: "surveyed" might be more gentlemanly and therefore more appropriate. We are, it has been suggested, less inclined nowadays than people once were to be irritated by the firm social code implied by the writings of an Addison or a Pope. On one point there can now be general agreement: that the existence of generally recognized standards of conduct in life and art was of great benefit to all but the greatest writers; minor writers, when they could not attain the heights, were at least prevented by "general principles" from plumbing the depths. If post-Addisonian prose was rarely inspired, it was rarely unreadable. If Pope's successors failed to stir, they usually managed to avoid offense to the reader.

They were, these Augustans, cheerful pessimists. Life was untidy and in many ways disappointing, but a decent social discipline could render it tolerable and even enjoyable. Man was brutish by nature but could be a reasonable companion if he paid attention to his behavior. And if rules and regulations were useful in society, then rules and regulations were useful to the writers who, in their own chosen field, served society. Such was their view.

To show what happened when a writer of passion and genius based himself on these same assumptions, it is necessary to turn to the work of the greatest satirist of the age, Dean Swift—that fervid moralist who devoted a demoniac energy to the defense of the normal, that master of sensuality who lashed out, from within the cool temperate zone of the Anglican church, at the irrational appetites and impulses of men.

But for his genius, Jonathan Swift would serve as an admirable example of Augustan virtues in a prose writer and also of the social circumstances guiding and controlling the output of an author during the first half of the century. Raised and nurtured a Whig, he became the most brilliant pamphleteer and controversialist of the Tory faction. Social historian, man of affairs, ecclesiastical dignitary and exponent, he was well fitted to supply for later generations a clever "inside" commentary on the public affairs of his time. And, indeed, his works can still be read in such a sense: all these things he did to perfection. But to read *Gulliver's Travels*, 1726, and the blistering pity-turned-to-scorn of *A Modest Proposal*, 1729, is to gain contact with a mind and sensibility far too passionate, far too vulnerably human, to serve only as a social reflector.

"Satire is a glass wherein beholders do generally discover anybody's face but their own," he wrote (*The Battle of the Books*). So much for the limitations of "social" satire. And where does Swift stand? "I hate and detest that animal man," he wrote in a letter to Pope, "although I heartily love John, Peter, Thomas, and so forth." The love he bore was for ever disappointed. There is so little charity in the world that men are only tolerable in the mass when they are hedged in by the minimum rules of decent conduct: to the extent of this belief, Swift was a true Augustan. But men are also, to Swift's too sensitive apprehension, nasty animals who pay more regard to gross bodily functions than to the free play of intellect or the blossoming of individual souls. At this level of compassionate misanthropy, social assumptions mean nothing. That is why the reader cannot sit complacently at Swift's side, sharing (or guessing) his viewpoint and then, secure in unanimity, laughing *at* other people. Swift's attacks come from all sides; no sooner do you range yourself by his side for greater safety, than he changes direction and lashes out unmercifully at himself and *you*.

Throughout all his works there is evidence of a loathing for and obsession with the physical facts of life, a morbid fury that men should use their reason to gratify rather than control their baser passions, should degrade speech into lying and in every way pervert the mind's guidance. This inexhaustible fund of energy—be it love or hate—translates itself into a vigor of style which, under stern control, takes the form of irony: One devastating sentence of his begins with the words: "Last week I saw a woman flayed." Now, how would a simple social reformer complete that sentence? By some such phrase as "and it was a disgrace to the community." And how would a witty satirist amuse his audience? Perhaps by saying "and I must say she looked the better for it." How does Swift proceed? Physical disgust, restrained and doubled irony, and yet direct statement too hopeless and disillusioned for remedial comment: all these char-

[7] Cyril Connolly, *Enemies of Promise*, Macmillan, 1948.

acteristics are present in *his* savage and shaming observation: "Last week I saw a woman flayed, and you will hardly believe how much it altered her person for the worse."

It was inevitable that the eighteenth century should be a great age of satire. The tone of the age, particularly in its early half, was set by "the Town," that comparatively small group of educated and well-bred people who lived in and near London. They were able to polish their wit and refine their opinions by almost daily contact with one another. Everyone knew that when Pope penned his brilliant character sketch of Atticus in the *Epistle to Dr. Arbuthnot,* he was referring to Addison, and that the vicious portrait of Sporus in the *Dunciad* could be none other than the fatuous Lord Hervey.

Dr. Johnson defined Addison's style as being of the "middle" type, by which he meant midway between ordinary speech and a more elevated style. Johnson's own prose moved somewhat above the middle level of Addison's. Where Addison's style owed much to the genteel conversation of the time, Johnson's was more influenced by Cicero in its use of antithesis and sonorous periods. In this it is like the style of Chesterfield, Gibbon, and Burke. This Ciceronian style the century regarded as most appropriate for lofty subjects. It was also the style of the "great gentleman."

It is unfortunate that in the popular opinion Dr. Johnson's style consists of sentences puffed up with magisterial generalizations and phrases of ponderous rebuke. True indeed it is that Samuel Johnson, by dint of great erudition and a triumphant confidence of personality, attained the rank and sway of literary dictator to an extent not shared by any Englishman before or since. True, too, that the man's piety, sense of proportion, and orthodox regard for the existing order of things all combined to make him a devastating critic of eccentricities and affectations. But turn to *Rasselas,* on page 585 below, and read the chapter describing the invention of a glider (two hundred years in advance of our modern invention), and you will be agreeably surprised by Johnson's powers of imagination, amused by his sense of the ludicrous, and forcibly struck by the validity of his moral reasoning. To see the snuff-stained and shambling Johnson of legend grappling two centuries in advance with the moral implications of aerial warfare is one simple way of achieving a new respect for Johnson the man, and a chastening readiness to search his pronouncements for truth as well as weight, for wisdom as well as rhetoric.

When Boswell met him in 1763, Johnson had already made his name and fame. His great *Dictionary* was completed in 1755; his satirical poems *London* and *The Vanity of Human Wishes* appeared respectively in 1738 and 1749; his edition of Shakespeare was almost ready for printing; *Rasselas* had been out for four years; the essay written for the periodical *The Rambler,* and other essays contributed to a weekly paper under the general title *The Idler,* had already reappeared in collected form. It was, then, of a man already famous that James Boswell wrote: "I shall mark what I remember of his conversation." What Boswell remembered of Johnson's conversation has been known to successive generations as the liveliest and best-loved record of the acts and words of any English man of letters.

The Preface to his edition of Shakespeare exhibits Johnson's critical soundness in all its strength and solidity and humanity. Wherever we turn in Johnson's critical writings, we shall stumble upon instances of the breadth of his sympathy triumphing over the narrow bounds he set himself. To turn no farther afield, the *Life of Cowley* itself provides ample testimony to Johnson's steady critical criteria. Does it give real pleasure to the reader? Is it true? Is it reasonable? Has it any practical value? Does it show genuine originality of mind? Does it move; does it express real feeling? These are the questions he always asks of the work under discussion; if the answer to these searching questions is negative, then no amount of pretty trifling and fancy phrasing will compensate for the loss of high seriousness. These are the criteria by which he judges a genre of poetry so foreign to his own personal taste as that of Cowley and the "metaphysical poets." He misses much, it must be admitted, by so limiting his judgment. (He missed much, for similar reasons, in the poetry of Milton.) But it may be doubted if any succeeding "romantic" critic, addressing himself to the appraisal of the literature of a period equally unsympathetic to his personal prejudices, ever attained the measure of Johnson's fairness and the remarkable breadth of his toleration, when he was faced with a similar critical problem.

The strength of Johnson's criticism resides in the sureness with which he speaks, not only for himself, but as the enunciator of the moods and methods of judgment most characteristic of his day and age. Many good things slipped through his critical net, and he was harsh to the claims of any non-Augustan logic. But when all is said, he was right nine times out of ten, and stuck firmly to a dogma so sensible as to be overlooked by less stable observers: "Great thoughts are always general, and consist in positions not limited by exceptions."

The poems of Oliver Goldsmith were not included in the collection of *The English Poets* to which Dr. Johnson, a few years after his friend's death, contributed biographical prefaces. Thus was Goldsmith, so often the butt of Johnson's none too sensitive jests, denied the considered appraisal which his friend would surely have afforded him—and for a reason only too familiar during his lifetime: the wretched subservience of a hack writer. Johnson and other members of his circle had known poverty too, but in Goldsmith's case improvidence, whether in the material realm or the regions of sensibility, was somehow always a matter for amusement. "Poor old Goldsmith," they all said at one time or another. He, more than most, needed the stabilizing generalities of Johnson's appreciation.

But if Goldsmith's reputation has suffered from the bantering attitude of his contemporaries, *The Vicar of Wakefield*, 1766, has given more genuine pleasure than most eighteenth-century novels, and *She Stoops to Conquer* has probably been revived more often than any other play of the period. As for his prose (of which the essays of *The Citizen of the World* are the best examples), it is idle to pretend that Goldsmith's pages glow with marked originality of thought, but it is possible to browse with the assurance that if fireworks are few and far between, there will be sound sense in most of Goldsmith's observations and a fluent onward motion. When we ask impatiently for instances and examples, Goldsmith—like Johnson—too often replies with a rounded observation, graced with a kind of generalized particularity. But the novel form, even in Goldsmith's day, could not be sustained wholly by general statements. That is one reason why the lay sermons in *The Vicar of Wakefield* are still tolerable—we see beyond and around them to the fond foolish tenderness of the Vicar himself. "Good-natured" is justly the automatic adjective for Goldsmith's writing. *The Citizen of the World* gently ridicules the English social scene, but it is possible to read it without that insecure fear—which makes *Gulliver's Travels* at once so exhilarating and damaging a book—that the author, when you are laughing with him at somebody else, will suddenly turn and rend *you*.

A note on Edward Gibbon must serve here to exemplify many prose writers of the latter half of the century. For Gibbon's strength, like Johnson's, is to speak at one with his time, to embody the assumptions and prejudices of his contemporaries; his "genius" is truly in step with the "genius" of his cultural heritage. The first volume of his great work *The Decline and Fall of the Roman Empire* was published in 1776; but long before that date the young Gibbon had written with a self-conscious measure of proportion and balance. The superb confidence with which he set out to master, and then narrate, the full story of the Roman Empire, is matched and illustrated in his own brand of superior irony. The heavy Latin elegance of his paragraphs is for ever enlivened by the scorn of a "rational" man amused by the antics of a former age to which he feels his own age is immensely superior in every way. To enjoy the famous Chapter XV, for example, one must sit for the moment, unflinchingly, beside the historian as he surveys with Olympian detachment the excesses of religious belief and the irrational behavior of Jews and Christians alike. It is not for nothing, indeed, that Gibbon was himself a Member of Parliament, and his every sentence asks to be read aloud.

This social, gossipy century was probably the greatest age of English letter writers. By 1700 the post was well established and yet there were no such modern "advantages" as the telephone. Since it was not necessary to maintain a measured, rational tone in personal correspondence, the letters of the time give us a perfect picture of the age in "undress." We can read Thomas Gray's chatty description of Horace Walpole's "gothic" bedroom at Strawberry Hill, learn what Lady Mary Wortley Montagu thought of the harems in Constantinople, and get William Cowper's exasperated reaction to Johnson's unsympathetic treatment of Milton in the *Lives of the Poets*. The outstanding letter writer of the period is perhaps Horace Walpole. Because Walpole's interests were broad his letters give us an extraordinarily comprehensive view of the life of the educated classes in his time. He can discuss the American Revolution with Sir Horace Mann (he considered Britain's policy hopelessly stupid), exchange notes on poetry and the fine arts with his friend Thomas Gray, or describe the latest London ball to one of his adoring lady friends. In his later life Walpole is said to have refused invitations to the houses of friends so that he would have the pleasure of writing them his news in a letter!

The Development of the Novel

The year 1719 saw the appearance of the first part of Daniel Defoe's *Robinson Crusoe*. The date may be taken as the beginning of the modern English novel. There had been prose fiction in English before this, but nothing so persuasively realistic as *Crusoe.* Defoe, whose long experience in journalism served him well when it came to writing his most famous book, had already been accused of being a master "of the little art . . . of forging a story, and imposing it on the world for truth," yet that statement might well be considered the very definition of a good novelist.

In our time, the novel has taken over much of the territory formerly occupied by poetry, and many phrases originally invented with poetry in mind ("pure realization," "the sensuous awareness of the moment") can rightly be applied to the work of favored craftsmen in fiction. But the eighteenth-century novel in England was at once a less subtle and more robust form. To Richardson and Fielding, Smollett and even Sterne, the narrative (whatever may be the differences of narrative technique) is all-important; the effect on the reader is cumulative. We may justly turn to these and other writers in their time for a picture of the *age*, but not until the turn of the century did the novelists think it fitting to use the storytelling technique as a medium for unveiling *themselves.* To place even the most whimsical page of Sterne's *Tristram Shandy* beside a page from a modern novelist—say, Virginia Woolf—is to see at once how the quirks and quiddities of Sterne were subdued to the generally accepted pattern of narrative, and in all their oddity still impelled the reader to "see what happens on the next page" rather than linger over more static excellences along the way. The difference is fundamental.

At the same time, the narrative skill of eighteenth-century novelists can often be used to sweep the reader onward through long passages of philosophical speculation, sermons, exhortations, and other semi-fictional matter. Just as *The Spectator* had entertained its readers and at the same time instructed them, so the novelists of the latter half of the century, by extending the scope and magnifying the figures of *their* Sir Roger de Coverleys, could experiment in character drawing and find a more lively vehicle for the presentation of their own opinions. From the eighteenth century onward, the English novel has been a rag bag into which writers have thrown whatever interested them at the moment of writing. Some recent writers have so overloaded their novels in this fashion that they are no longer readable. It was the prime virtue of the writers whose names follow that they always remembered to tell a story.

In 1740 Samuel Richardson published the first part of *Pamela.* If only to arouse astonishment that such a work caused so great a flutter, it is worth recording the original description of the book: "*Pamela, or Virtue Rewarded. In a Series of Familiar Letters from a beautiful young Damsel to her Parents. Now first published in order to cultivate the Principles of Virtue and Religion in the Minds of the Youth of both Sexes. Narrative which has its Foundation in Truth and Nature; and at the same time that it agreeably entertains by a Variety of curious and affecting Incidents, is intirely divested of all those Images, which, in too many Pieces calculated for Amusement only, tend to inflame the Minds they should instruct.*" A fair summary! Yet those with patience to explore these apparently prim pages will be struck by the psychological realism of Richardson's portraits, and will see in *Pamela,* and in the succeeding novels *Clarissa Harlowe* (1747–1748) and *Sir Charles Grandison* (1753–1754), an unexpected similarity to the works of many modern novelists who have imagined psychology to be a twentieth-century invention.

If the meticulous Richardson may be termed the first great introvert of English fiction, then Henry Fielding and Tobias Smollett may at once be named the most talented extroverts. Fielding's first publication, indeed, was a farcical skit on *Pamela,* entitled *Shamela.* This was followed the next year (1742) by *Joseph Andrews,* which began also as a parody of *Pamela* but developed into a vigorous, humorous, very readable novel in its own right. Fielding's masterpiece and one of the very great novels of English literature, *The History of Tom Jones* (1746–1749), has plenty of moral observation, but it is packed full of incident, adventure, improbable coincidences, and highly dramatic reversals of fortune. In his novels, and in those of Smollett (*Humphry Clinker* is the best), we are transported back into the less polite company of the eighteenth century; we hear strange oaths and meet shady gangsters; we sit at the inn fireside and listen to terrifying stories; we go to sea with the tough rascals to whom naval warfare was but an organized piracy; we meet the bawds and hucksters of London and the eccentric teachers and parsons of the country; we rumble along in coaches and start at the crack of a highwayman's pistol. The old epic has become alive again, in prose, for a new class of reader. No caviar and snuffboxes, but cakes and ale in plenty. Fielding could be sentimental when his good-natured humorous sense mellowed into an affection for his own characters; Smollett's robustness was for ever overstepping the mark toward brutality and gross vulgarity of word and sentiment. Yet both Fielding and Smollett remind us that there was strength as well as delicacy in this age of industrial crisis and imperial expansion, and they brought into the new literary form that exuberance which has characterized much of the main stream of English literature since Chaucer's day.

Laurence Sterne fits no category. *Tristram Shandy* (1760–1767) is erudite, irreverent, mischievously perplexing to the reader, full of high spirits and literary jokes and wise eccentricities. *The Sentimental Journey*, 1768, a collection of short travel sketches and semi-fictional observations, created an intellectual furore both in England and abroad. Sterne is sly where Richardson is moral, he insinuates where Fielding states, he hints where Smollett swears. He was perhaps the first Englishman to proclaim, in a popular prose work, the value of tender sentiment. His hero can weep at the sight of a dead donkey or philander delicately with women who would doubtless have accepted the embraces of Smollett's more vigorous rascals with little ceremony. After Sterne, floods of tears invaded English (and Continental) fiction. Henry Mackenzie's *Man of Feeling* is but one of the many novels of unadulterated sentiment stemming from his works. It is strange, but true, that the great flowering of English fiction during the sixty years from 1740 pointed the way not only to the roistering adventure and comedy of Scott and later of Dickens, but also to the whimsical horror of "Gothic" romances and the inward anguish of Goethe's *Werther* and the Byronic poet-heroes of the next century.

From mid-century onward, there were innumerable examples of what we now call the "novel of escape." Horace Walpole's *Castle of Otranto*, 1764, mingles medieval horror with romantic sighs and something of the interest of detective fiction; William Beckford's *Vathek*, 1786, seeks to thrill and awe the reader with oriental extravagance; the circulating libraries offered long novels by female writers which were "calculated to touch the springs of tender sympathy." Within a period of fifty years the English novel, as we know it, was launched on its course.

Poetry

The modern reader, who can readily appreciate the prose of the eighteenth century, may find that its poetry at first comes less easily to him. The poetic taste of many of us is conditioned—and in most respects this is our great good fortune—by the rich and abundant energy of Elizabethan poetry, the imaginative splendor of Milton, and the "fine excess" (Keats's phrase) of the nineteenth-century Romantics. But the poets of the Augustan Age sought for something quite different. They valued clarity of language and precision of thought. Their poetry might be "elevated" but it remained "sensible." Moreover, because man in his social relations occupied the center of their thought, these poets were often concerned with pointing an explicit moral. Dr. Johnson, too late and too towering a figure in his own right to be labeled an Augustan, yet reflects the didactic preoccupation which persisted beyond the mid-century when he criticizes Shakespeare on the ground that he "is so much more careful to please than to instruct that he seems to write without any moral purpose."

Pope, Johnson, Goldsmith, George Crabbe, and lesser men found the poetic form ideally suited for their purposes in the heroic couplet, whose descriptive, narrative, and satirical possibilities Chaucer and Dryden before them had so brilliantly illustrated. It must be admitted at once that the rhymed couplet, in the hands of an indifferent versifier, can be as maddening as the trilling of an unanswered telephone. Similarly, the conventional epithets and inflated language of many eighteenth-century poems can be only too easily ridiculed; often we do not feel the poet is succeeding in his intention of avoiding language which is mean and low and giving to poetry a proper nobility. "Piscatorial swain" (Sir John Squire's twentieth-century parody) for "fisherman" is not more farfetched than Pope's "smoking tide" for "tea." Pope himself was indeed the most devastating critic of the stereotyped phrases of lesser poets:

Where'er you find "the cooling western breeze,"
In the next line, it "whispers thro' the trees."
If "crystal streams with pleasing murmurs creep,"
The reader's threatened (not in vain) with "sleep."

Yet falsely rhetorical though this poetry may sound at its worst, at its best it possesses solid virtues. Abstract nouns, for example, can have splendor and communicate that carved, timeless quality we associate with classic art.

If the heroic couplet is to be used with effect, the content must be as close-packed and taut with meaning as the form itself is severe. Pope's astonishing skill in saying "what oft was thought, but ne'er so well expressed" can frequently be related to the Augustan habit of selection—and hence compression. This power of concentration in Pope's best poetry is fully apparent in the portrait of the Duke of Buckingham in *Of the Use of Riches* (1732):

In the worst inn's worst room, with mat half-hung,
The floors of plaister, and the walls of dung,
On once a flockbed, but repair'd with straw,
With tape-ty'd curtains, never meant to draw,
The George and Garter dangling from that bed
Where tawdry yellow strove with dirty red,
Great *Villiers* lies—alas! how chang'd from him,
That life of pleasure, and that soul of whim! . . .
There, Victor of his health, of fortune, friends,
And fame, this lord of useless thousands ends.
Such is the room which one rude beam divides,
And naked rafters from the sloping sides;
Where the vile bands that bind the thatch are seen,
And lath and mud are all that lie between. . . .

There is very little imagery here, but the "floors of plaister and the wall of dung" where Great Villiers lies are presented with a concentrated imaginative vigor. Imagination has welded, in Pope's lines, every dingy detail into a living re-creation of squalor, made doubly effective by contrast with Buckingham's past glories. "All this," says Pope, "was inherent in the man's career from the beginning: there is nothing surprising about it. This is how a 'lord of useless fortune' ends; his fortune was indeed useless even while he had it. All this is part and parcel of the man: the 'tawdry yellow' of the room and the emblem of the highest Order of Chivalry, the 'George and Garter dangling from *that* bed,' unite to form one quintessential picture of Buckingham."

In *The Rape of the Lock*, 1714, the most famous mock epic in the language, Pope matches a highly inflated style with an essentially trivial content; the effect is, as he intended, to make the subject matter ridiculous. The heroine's dressing table, for example, is described with all the awe proper to a description of an altar. The implication is that to Belinda her toilet table *is* an altar: she worships artificial beauty. For her, the world exists only to supply her with fashionable articles, and to admire her when she has made use of them. Her sense of proportion is woeful.

How does Pope express his own attitude? By indignation? No. By an overt social commentary? No. By a statistical survey of income groups in contemporary London? No. It is all done by his handling of the couplet, by his sardonic juxtaposition of great and small, the wealth of the world and the use to which it is put, the sacred and the profane:

This casket *India's* glowing gems unlocks,
And all *Arabia* breathes from yonder box.
The Tortoise here and Elephant unite,
Transform'd to Combs, the speckled and the white.
Here files of Pins extend their shining rows,
Puffs, Powders, Patches, Bibles, Billet-doux.

From Belinda's point of view, tortoise shell and ivory are merely the materials of her combs. From Belinda's point of view, too, we are led to suppose, the Bible and a beauty patch are of equal importance. It is certainly a measure of the strength of the Augustan system of manners and morals, and the implied identity of view between the author and the reader, that a satirist could make his points with such concentrated venom, and yet with never a hint of posturing or preaching. In Pope's hands, the heroic couplet could be more than a clever way of saying things; it could serve, by imprisoning within one unforgettable rhyme two contrasting subjects—the ideal and the actual, the illusion and the reality, the shadow and the substance—to express his own assumptions, his own judgment of life. And in achieving just such remarkable effects as these Pope carried his favorite verse form to a final pitch of virtuosity.

Yet the heroic couplet was by no means universally employed as a verse form even in Pope's time. James Thomson, Thomas Gray, William Collins, and William Cowper found their more natural expression in the ode, blank verse, and other forms. Cowper, speaking of Pope, wisely observed that "unless we could imitate him in the closeness and compactness of his expression, as well as the smoothness of his numbers, we had better drop the imitation which serves no other purpose than to emasculate all we write."

Contemptuous of the past, patronizing in their attitude toward those who, like Shakespeare, warbled their native wood-notes wild, the Augustan writers had set up a general code of conduct for those whose place in a well-ordered society was to provide the gentleman-of-letters with his reading: exact verse, balanced prose; a diet for meditation, melancholy, hope, and whatever other passion might inhabit, for a due season, the temperate breast. It was all very splendid while it lasted; or, rather, while the social and intellectual conditions fitted the manner. But the manner was so comfortable that it outlasted the conditions of life and thought in relation to which it alone had meaning. Well before the middle of the century, poets and other creative writers who had non-Augustan matter to impart and non-Augustan feelings to express, found themselves waxing "romantic" in "classic" form, or measuring out balanced periods of prose the content of which cried aloud for freedom and experiment. Much of the "cold" writing of the eighteenth century reveals, on a close examination, a passion beneath the surface.

The strain was great, and something had to snap. It is astonishing that the principles of good taste laid down by Addison and Pope and their followers could for so long contain the expression of a rapidly expanding society. It is this curious cultural situation that caused the signs of frustration and maladjustment apparent in some mid-eighteenth century poetry.

A shift toward more predominantly "romantic" attitudes was under way, but it did not happen overnight. To read some histories of literature, one would suppose that Thomson and the other "pre-Romantics" were already half aware of the figures of Wordsworth and Coleridge ready to loom over the horizon; that they were, indeed, conscious of being "pre-Romantic" and were yearning to become "Romantic," to leap foreward toward the onrushing *Lyrical Ballads*, to jump into the next chapter. But we cannot assume a whole literary generation to have been gifted with such prophetic insight.

The poetry of Oliver Goldsmith provides one admirable example of the process described by T. S. Eliot, who wrote, in an essay [8] on eighteenth-century poetry: "What really happened is that after Pope there was no one who thought and felt nearly enough like Pope to be able to use his language quite successfully; but a good many second-rate writers tried to write something like it, unaware of the fact that the change of sensibility demanded a change of idiom." Goldsmith's neat couplets at times betray a sentimentality far from Augustan, but he was also capable of combining the old form and the new spirit in a just proportion: there are couplets in *The Deserted Village*, 1770, where gentle comedy is as well pointed as Pope's moral indignation:

The broken soldier, kindly bade to stay,
Sate by his fire, and talked the night away;
Wept o'er his wounds, or tales of sorrow done,
Shouldered his crutch, and shewed how fields were won.

But wit is one thing and humor is another. Goldsmith's humor had no hard glitter; it no longer based itself on the kind of talk suited to the familiar superiority of intellectuals in a coffee-house. The lines from *The Deserted Village:*

Ill fares the land, to hastening ills a prey,
Where wealth accumulates, and men decay . . .

almost invite Hilaire Belloc's counter-platitude:

But how much more unfortunate are those
Where wealth decays, and population grows.

It is significant that the poets who, unlike Goldsmith, struggled to break away from the Augustan practice and precepts, and who shook timid fists at "authority," sought everywhere to find some *other* precedent or authority for their change of heart. They found it (as a century later the Pre-Raphaelites, reacting in their turn against the fashions of their time, were to find it) in the Middle Ages. Not, indeed, in a strict scholarly appraisal of medieval life and literature, but rather in those aspects of medieval expression, whether real or imaginary, which best suited their needs. After the middle of the century, writers were reaching out in all directions for models and for inspiration. Gothic, Gaelic, Icelandic, Teutonic, old ballads and the Old Testament—all was grist to their busy mills. The scholar-poet Thomas Gray undertook translations from the Icelandic; James Macpherson's strange forgery *Ossian* (1760–1765) and young Thomas Chatterton's *Rowley Poems*, 1778, concocted a new synthetic spice from old Scots and English ingredients; the learned Bishop Percy's *Reliques*, 1765, rescued and revived the almost dying art of ballad poetry; barbaric Highland songs and the exquisitely civilized Provençal lyrics alike became popular again—and it was not long before eighteenth-century prose fiction was filling the heads of less learned and self-conscious readers with Gothic "horrours" and the machinations of medieval monks.

Many critical essays set forth these bold new claims to originality. Edward Young's *Conjectures on Original Composition* (1759), was the most effective, and had as its main argument that literature, like science, must be liberated from the rules of bygone authorities. No imitation can ever be so good as an original, since "illustrious examples engross, prejudice, and intimidate." One telling phrase indicates the new point of view: "The less we copy the renowned Antients, we shall resemble them the more." And again: "For rules, like crutches, are a needful aid to the lame, tho' an impediment to the strong."

How all these various experiments affected the sensibility of a genuine poet may be seen in the works of William Collins. A perceptive critic has called attention to the very significant change made by Collins in one stanza of the *Ode to Evening*. The first (1747) version had read:

[8] An introduction to Johnson's *Verse Satires*, 1930.

Then let me rove some wild and heathy scene,
Or find some ruin midst its dreary dells,
Whose walls more awful nod
By thy religious gleams.

The accumulation of ready-made evocative words, and the self-induced atmosphere of literary horror, were signs of the need to simulate emotions the poet did not genuinely feel. Striking out this verse, Collins replaced it in the second version, the following year, with these lovely lines:

Then lead, calm votaress, where some sheety lake
Cheers the lone heath, or some time-hallow'd pile,
Or upland fallows grey
Reflect its last cool gleam.

Still aided and reinforced by conventional literary associations ("calm votaress," "lone heath," "time-hallow'd pile"), Collins now allows his own felt and observed emotions to fill out the stanza with a personal sensibility not released in the earlier version.

Two other poets, James Thomson and William Cowper, achieved an individual expression well worth careful study in their poems. Both had sought to learn from Milton the secret of a verse form "nobler" and less chilly than that bequeathed by Pope. Neither fully succeeded; but Thomson found in natural beauty, and Cowper in the quiet domestic virtues of friendship and a hard-won religious calm, subjects lending themselves to an individual, "personal," expression.

Toward the close of the century Robert Burns and William Blake struck out for themselves and produced poetry which is strikingly different from anything else the eighteenth century has to offer. Burns, a Scottish peasant, enriched the literature by verse which was not indebted to rules and schools but owed its inspiration and its accents to the dialect of his native land and the common folk by whom it was spoken. There is nothing narrowly Scottish about his poetry, however, for his theme is "nature's social union," which embraces every "earth-born creature and fellow mortal"—mountain daisy and field mouse, Highland lass and Lowland plowboy. Burns's lyrics are among the best and most popular love songs in the literature, and in his concern with the joys and sorrows of common humanity he links his own songs with the "Lyrical Ballads" of Wordsworth and Coleridge.

Blake, a child of the city, also sang in accents unlike those of his fellow Englishmen. Although his home was in London, he lived most of the time, as his wife said of him, in Paradise, and much of his mystical verse, therefore, does not readily yield its meaning to the casual reader. His own eyes discerned strange spiritual forces and motions in physical forms, and in the engravings with which he illustrated his own poems and those of Dante, Milton, Gray, and others, he made as rich and beautiful a contribution to English pictorial art as his verse made to English literature. Unlike Burns as he is, he nevertheless shares with him something of his warm humanitarian sympathy and his sense of the community of interests inherent in all created things.

The highly individual verse of Burns and Blake completes the progress of English poetry across the century from the Augustan code of correctness and precision to the threshold of that revolution in English literature which we know as the Romantic Movement.

The Dramatists

The emergence of the English novel coincided with a comparatively dreary period in the history of the theater. Between Restoration comedy and Sheridan there is much to interest the student of dramatic history, but little to excite a modern playgoer. When the century opened, "Restoration" comedy had become in a way less immoral than "Restoration" heroic tragedy, for while the one, shamelessly coarse and gracefully licentious, was the mirror of a cynical coterie, the other was more insidious, providing as it did a false virtue for admiration. Exalted on the stage was an impossible code of nobility altogether unknown to the audience in its daily life. Added to this desire of an artificial and corrupt court to see artificial and impossible virtue, there had come the influence of the French stage to harden and codify these attitudes into an exaggerated convention of heroism, plus an exaggerated set of classical rules for playwriting. For the most part, such rules were adopted with natural sympathy by Augustan critics, and Addison's *Cato* (1713) contains fair examples of the chilly high sentiments thought proper for the Neoclassical stage.

The first two decades saw the rise of a curious new genre, the sentimental comedy. In these plays, of which Richard Steele was the best-known practitioner, preaching and tears took the place of the wit and bawdry of the Restoration stage. The audiences who flocked to the new "comedies" wept copiously with the actors when the virtuous heroines forgave the erring heroes. For a time the theater became so starchy with morality that the actor-producer, David Garrick, suggested it would be appropriate to build church steeples over all the playhouses in London.

The sentimental dramatists did not, however, have everything their own way. There were still robust playwrights like Henry Fielding, whose farces had the same vigorous satire he was to display later in his more famous novels. The success of Gay's *Beggar's Opera* in 1727 was further proof that Londoners had not forgotten how to laugh. The *Beggar's Opera* was the great "smash hit" of the century. Following Swift's suggestion that he write a "Newgate pastoral," Gay made his piece a burlesque of current fads and attitudes and filled it with characters whom his audience could easily identify (such as the gallant highwayman who was obviously Sir Robert Walpole, the prime minister). Walpole was sufficiently stung by Gay's portrait to refuse him a license for his next play. But Gay's fortune was made.

The change from all this to the mid-century *bourgeois drama* was nevertheless no sudden surprise. Social changes were prompting the playwrights to flatter the middle classes by introducing them into their plays no longer as buffoons but as sober, honest, and praiseworthy citizens. At the same time, changes in political thought deflected attention from the "Love and Honor" conventions to the new feeling for liberty which began to animate British breasts. "My Lord," says a character in a play of 1714, "the English are by nature, what the ancient Romans were by discipline—courageous, bold, hardy, and in love with liberty."

These were but minor steps. The real father of domestic drama is Lillo's prose play *The London Merchant, or, George Barnwell* (1731). Its didactic moral sentiments are indeed uttered in a prose so artificial, by modern standards, as to bear unacknowledged many of the rhythms of blank verse; but this play, and Edward Moore's *The Gamester* (1753) had a great effect on theatrical development not only in England but also in France and Germany.

During the third quarter of the century, high comedy was displaced by sentimental exercises in polite love-making and a heavy-handed delicacy. A new spirit of benevolence was driving wit from the stage, and the poorer examples were themselves to be driven off not by critical opposition but by better exercises in the same mode. In Goldsmith's *She Stoops to Conquer*, as Professor Allardyce Nicoll has succinctly phrased it, "for once in the century the spirit of *Twelfth Night* was revived."

Richard Brinsley Sheridan alone could free the comedy of manners from coarseness and unpleasant frivolity without at the same time depriving it of its saving wit. He is a social satirist whose touch is so light that his attacks on the follies of his age are more entertaining than the follies themselves. The dialogue of *The Rivals* (1775) is in places stilted and the exposition clumsy, but the famous character Mrs. Malaprop added a new word to the English language (for malapropisms like "She's as headstrong as an allegory on the banks of the Nile") and the author's sense of social accuracy marked him out as a potential master of the comedy of manners. *The School for Scandal*, two years later, redeemed the promise. Here, the necessary mechanics of exposition are themselves effected with comedy, and sharpened by a wit too long absent from the English stage. Sheridan's social satire, too, is not so closely related to minor affairs of the moment as to be inapplicable today. The brilliance of Sheridan's *The Critic*, an extended piece of dramatic criticism in dramatic form, also deserves mention. Sheridan obviously enjoyed writing his plays: that is why they are still enjoyable to the modern reader or theatergoer.

Summary

In seeking for one distinguishing clue to the unifying mode of perception during the eighteenth century, we can hardly fail to note the broad enveloping movements on every front of civilized life, of argument and expression as conveyed by the *written word*. Eighteenth-century politics were more closely entangled with literature (both in personalities and principles) than ever, before or since, in English history; scientists prided themselves on the clarity of their expository prose style; religion was removed from the sphere of warfare into the cooler and more rational field of the written or (as in the case of Wesley and the revivalists) the spoken word; and in every branch of the human science we now call "sociology," practical measures came almost as an afterthought in the train of philosophical disquisition.

With respect to the political background, one direct contact between politics and letters—that involved in the institution of patronage—may be referred to at this point. A writer with the genius of Pope or the moral integrity of Johnson could "take it or leave it," as we now say of more dangerous matters, when tempted to accept literary patronage from political sources. Smaller men tried with varying success to sell their talents to the highest bidder. Condemn as we may the waste of time and talent involved in these and similar transactions of the age, it must be admitted that until a large reading public was able and willing to support its purveyors of reading matter, the patron—"a wretch," as Johnson defined him, "who supports with insolence and is paid with flattery"—did serve some useful purpose in freeing many a writer from drudgery and easing his leisure hours. In the latter half of the century writers could at last stand up to the booksellers and exact reasonable, and even handsome, terms. Patronage was still welcome (nor, indeed, is it dead today, if we remember the aids to culture granted by states and philanthropic foundations), but it was no longer a necessity. It is tempting to think that a more firmly entrenched institution even than eighteenth-century patronage might well have shriveled under the blistering contempt of Johnson's great *Letter to Lord Chesterfield*, that unmatched exercise in polite vituperation.

Once the aims and achievements of this pre-eminently "literary" century have been apprehended, however imperfectly, then other aspects of this teeming age of economic and social development fall into some sort of pattern. We have only to consider for one moment how little the affairs of our present day and age can be interpreted through the medium of contemporary literature, to note how singular and distinctive was this characteristic of the literary art in eighteenth-century England. It touched at every point the public life of the age, and as the century wore on it was changed, not without effort and awkward strains, in line with new possibilities of personal life. From the time of Pope to the time of Wordsworth, men of letters—by accident or design—truly mirrored their age rather than *themselves* as individuals. If we understand them, we are more likely to grasp some of the essential features of the world—now settled and now in ferment, now complacent and now stricken—in which they lived.

We all seem to throw a shadow over our immediate past, so that what was drab to our grandfathers has become bright again for us. So it has been with respect to the eighteenth century. Our nineteenth-century forebears tended to find it cold, bleak, uninviting. We, casting our shadow over the post-Romantic scene, have discovered with enthusiastic surprise the neglected merits of the Augustans and their sober successors. Perhaps, indeed, we have discovered, in the brightness exaggerated by the lifting of the shadow of disapproval and neglect, qualities that are not really there at all. At any rate, the eighteenth century has become fashionable again; we admire its poise, we strive to recover its sense of Reason, Truth, and Nature; we think back wistfully to its intellectual cohesion, and we climb to our grandfathers' lumber rooms to fetch down *objets d'art* for our most favored pedestals.

The pressing claims of the twentieth-century foreground make the rediscovery of eighteenth-century writers at once a painful and a refreshing exercise. Painful, because in all their conflicting theories about the nature of Reason and the reasonableness of Nature, there is evidence of a belief not only in infallible and liberating laws which our world can now hold only in the face of contrary evidence, but also a sense of indefinite time ahead in which these necessary but unpressing disquisitions could be carried on. If there was a general anxiety, among eighteenth-century moralists, to interpret fundamental law, there was also a certainty that given patience and an ability to correct the erroneous readings of others, this work could surely be done. It is just because we ourselves do not enjoy a pleasurable feeling of "ample room and verge enough" that the apparent leisure of those days is so attractive.

At the beginning of the eighteenth century, says Basil Willey, "biology had as yet revealed no disturbing ancestries, and man was still unassailed by anthropology and psycho-analysis. Materialism itself could scarcely dispense with a divine hypothesis (though this soon followed): the Great Machine presupposed the Divine Mechanic."[9] The spangled heavens were still judged competent to proclaim their great Original, and a genial mixture of revealed Christianity and Neo-Platonism satisfied those who were prepared to agree with Locke that "the works of Nature everywhere sufficiently evidence a Deity." Against this background of "Cosmic Toryism" it is not surprising that the literature of the English Augustans should have been confident to the point of complacency. Now that the last shreds of our own complacency have been torn away, it is possible to look back from the vantage point of "Whatever is, is wrong," to that of "Whatever is, is right," with a strange sympathy and understanding. "Augustan" poetry of classification and social security is a relief from that unwritten poetry of speculation which, but for want of energy, our present age would be producing.

Indeed, as has been hinted, our present tendency is to over-estimate certain selected qualities of the English eighteenth century. Lord David Cecil, who has played his part in the general refurbishment, has put the matter, and voiced the warning, with an agreeable sense of historical irony:

"To-day the eighteenth century is the fashion; we print eighteenth-century memoirs; we reprint eighteenth-century novels; we anthologize eighteenth-century poems; we translate eighteenth-century romances. . . . And, like earlier ages, we

[9] *The Eighteenth-Century Background.*

imitate as well as admire. Modern architects design in a severely classical style, all pilaster and pediment. Modern story-tellers emulate the grammatical nakedness of Defoe. . . . People like the eighteenth century because they see it as possessing these qualities and no others. They like its sensibility because they dislike emotion, and it seems to express itself in emotions so deliberate as hardly to deserve the name at all. They profess to like pure form, whatever that may mean; and the eighteenth century had a talent for form. So they represent its music as all form and no matter, its novels all form and no morals, and its religion all form and no faith. . . . The eighteenth century of their imagination is a series of salons, where people with snuff-boxes and a worldly-wise outlook make *mots* in a mood of urbane scepticism born of an extensive experience of the brighter side of life in the capitals of Europe."[10]

It is only too easy, in a word, to remember the culture of coffee-houses and forget the degradation of the gin-soaked rabble who people the drawings of Hogarth and Rowlandson. The classic beauty of Bath crescents and Palladian country houses expressed, and helped to perpetuate, an aesthetic sense never so well developed in England; but in British affairs it has often been found that the aesthetic and moral nerves are closely connected, and a perfunctory examination of the servants' quarters in those elegant crescents and rural palaces will serve to twitch that other nerve.

While Blake sang his angry songs and a new breed of poets and novelists competed for the favors of an entirely new and enlarged reading public the consequences of agrarian and industrial changes were working themselves out in the daily island life of England. But there were hard struggles ahead, and much blood was to flow before an exhausted nation, too desperate to pay much attention to its brilliant new writers, could in 1815 meditate in a distracted hope the consequences of the Battle of Waterloo.

Jonathan Swift
1667–1745

Swift was born and bred of English parents in Ireland, a country for which he had great compassion but little liking. It is significant that the childhood and youth of the sensitive, proud, and precocious lad were spent in poverty and dependence. Through the assistance of relatives he went to the Kilkenny Grammar School and later to Trinity College, Dublin. Although he was endowed with keen intelligence, his performance as a student was so desultory that he received his degree only by special favor. Out of college, he found employment at the age of twenty-one as secretary to a distant relative, Sir William Temple, a distinguished politician and patron of letters. His years in Temple's household at Moor Park in Surrey, although they seemed to Swift years of subserviency, brought him a fruitful leisure and influential acquaintances. Here he wrote some verse and his first major prose pieces. One of these was *The Battle of the Books*, a mock-epic satire in which the books on the shelves of a library fight the battle of the relative merits of the ancients and the moderns. The other, *A Tale of a Tub*, is a brilliant and cutting satire on the divisions of Christianity.

[10] *The Stricken Deer*, World's Classics, Oxford University Press.

It was also at Moor Park that Swift met a young lady, Esther Johnson (Stella), the daughter of the companion to Temple's sister. The friendship between the two ripened into the deepest and most passionate love of Swift's life.

After Temple's death in 1699, Swift, who had taken holy orders in the Church of England, was given a parish at Laracor, near Dublin. He attracted public notice after the anonymous publication in 1704 of his first two great satires, and as author of *A Tale of a Tub* he was recognized as a genius and as the ablest pamphleteer of the day. The brilliant young man of letters won the friendship of such authors as Pope, Addison, Steele, Prior, and Gay. His pamphlets on political subjects won him the support of the Whig leaders, but by 1710 he had gone over to the Tory side. No literary man, perhaps, has ever been such a power in public life as was Swift during the next three years. While engaged with his political satires he had found time for other and different kinds of writing. In 1708 he published a whimsical and ironical pamphlet, *An Argument to Prove that the Abolishing of Christianity in England May, as Things now Stand, be Attended with some Inconveniences, and Perhaps Not Produce those Many Good Effects Proposed Thereby*. About the same time some lighter and gayer pieces came from his pen—*The Bickerstaff Papers, A Meditation upon a Broomstick*, and the *Journal to Stella*, an account of the events of his days in London, written for the pleasure of Esther Johnson.

Swift's chances for advancement in the Church had been seriously damaged by *A Tale of a Tub*, but he did secure appointment as Dean of St. Patrick's Cathedral (Church of England) in Dublin in 1713. Most of the following year he spent in London, but in 1714, when Queen Anne died and the Tories lost out in the struggle for place and power, Swift returned to Ireland to spend the greater part of the embittered remainder of his days. There the presence of his beloved Stella helped to cheer his loneliness until her death in 1728. There also his life was further complicated by the presence and persistent affection of another lady, Hester Vanhomrigh (Vanessa), whom he had met in London. The unhappy situation was ended only by the death of Vanessa in 1723.

During the first fifteen years after his return to Ireland Swift employed his pen in various ways. On behalf of the Irish people, whom the Whig government in England was exploiting, he wrote his *Drapier's Letters*, 1724, which purported to come from a Dublin tradesman, "M. B. Drapier," and which forced the English government to relinquish its scheme for debasing Irish coinage. Five years later came his devastating satire, *A Modest Proposal*, the result of his deep concern for the wretched condition of the Irish peasants. Meanwhile, in 1726, had appeared his greatest work, *Gulliver's Travels*, on the composition of which he had spent five harassed years. It became at once the literary sensation of the day and its place as one of the world's literary masterpieces has never met serious challenge since.

The last fifteen years of his life saw Swift sink under the ills of body and mind, without friends and without hope for himself or mankind. During his last five years his mental condition was such that his affairs had to be administered by guardians. His will directed that his estate should be given to the poor. He was buried in October, 1745, beside Stella in his Cathedral of St. Patrick.

In clarity and directness Swift's prose style has never been surpassed. It was an instrument admirably suited to his particular needs and occasions, whether he was satirizing the politicians of Lilliput-England, lashing the English people for their harsh, tyrannical behavior toward their Irish neighbors, or relating with superb irony how the three sons in *A Tale of a Tub*—each representing a division of Christianity—wilfully altered and distorted their inherited coats to fit their personal desires. Swift made his simple, powerful prose the vehicle for what George Orwell, perhaps Swift's most direct descendant in our time, has called his "terrible intensity of vision, capable of picking out a single hidden truth and then magnifying and distorting it." [1]

It has been justly said that Jonathan Swift was the only English writer of his time who might have been the hero of a Shakespearean tragedy, and this is a way of reminding us that his faults and failures as a man were closely related to magnificence. He reached nearer to greatness than any of his contemporaries. The mystery of his life and of his mind has fascinated thousands. In the epitaph he wrote for himself he reminds the passer-by that his body has at last found a place where savage indignation can no longer tear his heart. If he could know how his imaginings and indignations have worked upon the thought of the last two hundred years, even his fierce pride might find some satisfaction.

A MEDITATION UPON A BROOMSTICK

Swift, according to Thomas Sheridan, while acting as secretary and adviser to Lady Berkeley was often required to read to her out of the *Meditations* of Robert Boyle (1627–1691), the famous scientist. He found them so insufferably tedious and platitudinous that he wrote the following parody, and gravely read it aloud from his own manuscript which he had slipped into the volume.

THIS single stick, which you now behold ingloriously lying in that neglected corner, I once knew in a flourishing state in a forest: it was full of sap, full of leaves, and full of boughs; but now, in vain does the busy art of man pretend to vie with nature, by tying that withered bundle of twigs to its sapless trunk; 'tis now, at best, but the reverse of what it was, a tree turned upside down, the branches on the earth, and the root in the air; 'tis now handled by every dirty wench, condemned to do her drudgery, and by a capricious kind of fate, destined to make other things clean, and be nasty itself; at length, worn to the stumps in the service of the maids, it is either thrown out of doors, or condemned to the last use, of kindling a fire. When I beheld this, I sighed, and said within myself, *Surely Man is a Broomstick!* Nature sent him into the world strong, and lusty, in a thriving condition, wearing his own hair on his head, the proper

[1] *Shooting an Elephant*, Harcourt, Brace, 1950.

branches of this reasoning vegetable, until the ax of intemperance has lopped off his green boughs, and left him a withered trunk; he then flies to art, and puts on a periwig, valuing himself upon an unnatural bundle of hairs (all covered with powder) that never grew on his head; but now, should this our broomstick pretend to enter the scene, proud of those birchen spoils it never bore, and all covered with dust, though the sweepings of the finest lady's chamber, we should be apt to ridicule and despise its vanity. Partial judges that we are of our own excellencies, and other men's defaults!

But a broomstick, perhaps you will say, is an emblem of a tree standing on its head; and pray what is man, but a topsy-turvy creature, his animal faculties perpetually mounted on his rational, his head where his heels should be, grovelling on the earth! And yet, with all his faults, he sets up to be a universal reformer and corrector of abuses, a remover of grievances, rakes into every slut's corner of nature, bringing hidden corruption to the light, and raises a mighty dust where there was none before; sharing deeply all the while in the very same pollutions he pretends to sweep away; his last days are spent in slavery to women, and generally the least deserving; till worn out to the stumps, like his brother's besom, he is either kicked out of doors, or made use of to kindle flames for others to warm themselves by.

THOUGHTS ON VARIOUS SUBJECTS

The following epigrams are selected from a considerably larger number of detached "thoughts" set down by Swift about the year 1706. They are related in style to the *pensées* in which many French writers have excelled, and in their emphasis upon the theme of self-love they resemble the *Maximes* of La Rochefoucauld.

We have just enough religion to make us hate, but not enough to make us love one another.

Positiveness is a good quality for preachers and orators, because he that would obtrude his thoughts and reasons upon a multitude, will convince others the more, as he appears convinced himself.

How is it possible to expect that mankind will take advice, when they will not so much as take warning?

27. besom, broom.

No preacher is listened to but time, which gives us the same train and turn of thought that elder people have tried in vain to put into our heads before.

Religion seems to have grown an infant with age, and requires miracles to nurse it, as it had in its infancy.

Would a writer know how to behave himself with relation to posterity, let him consider in old books what he finds that he is glad to know, and what omissions he most laments.

When a true genius appears in the world, you may know him by this sign, that the dunces are in confederacy against him.

I am apt to think that in the day of judgment there will be small allowance given to the wise for their want of morals, and to the ignorant for their want of faith, because both are without excuse. This renders the advantages equal of ignorance and knowledge. But some scruples in the wise, and some vices in the ignorant, will perhaps be forgiven, upon the strength of temptation to each.

The chameleon, who is said to feed upon nothing but air, has of all animals the nimblest tongue.

There are but three ways for a man to revenge himself of the censure of the world: to despise it, to return the like, or to endeavour to live so as to avoid it: the first of these is usually pretended, the last is almost impossible, the universal practice is for the second.

What they do in Heaven we are ignorant of; what they do not we are told expressly, that they neither marry, nor are given in marriage.

The stoical scheme of supplying our wants, by lopping off our desires, is like cutting off our feet when we want shoes.

The reason why so few marriages are happy, is, because young ladies spend their time in making nets, not in making cages.

If a man will observe as he walks the streets, I believe he will find the merriest countenances in mourning coaches.

No wise man ever wished to be younger.

Complaint is the largest tribute heaven receives, and the sincerest part of our devotion.

Apollo was held the god of physic, and sender of diseases. Both were originally the same trade, and still continue.

Most sorts of diversion in men, children, and other animals, are in imitation of fighting.

That was excellently observed, say I, when I read a passage in an author, where his opinion agrees with mine. When we differ, there I pronounce him to be mistaken.

Very few men, properly speaking, live at present, but are providing to live another time.

As universal a practice as lying is, and as easy a one as it seems, I do not remember to have heard three good lies in all my conversation, even from those who were most celebrated in that faculty.

A man seeing a wasp creeping into a vial filled with honey, that was hung on a fruit tree, said thus: "Why, thou sottish animal, art thou mad to go into the vial, where you see many hundred of your kind dying before you?"—"The reproach is just," answered the wasp, "but not from you men, who are so far from taking example by other people's follies, that you will not take warning by your own. If after falling several times into this vial, and escaping by chance, I should fall in again, I should then but resemble you."

from GULLIVER'S TRAVELS

Gulliver's Travels has been called a "universal satire." "I have ever hated all nations, professions, and communities," Swift once wrote to Pope, "and all my love is toward individuals. . . . I hate and detest that animal called man, although I heartily love John, Peter, Thomas, and so forth." If, as Swift said, he wrote *Gulliver's Travels* "to vex the world rather than to divert it," he failed in his purpose, for millions of readers, including great numbers of children, have been diverted by the adventures and observations of his imaginary traveler. Few, it seems likely, have ever been seriously vexed, at least by the first two parts of the book. The ageless charm of *Gulliver's Travels* lies in its boldness of conception and its ingenuity of execution.

The first of Lemuel Gulliver's voyages—the one that takes him to Lilliput, the land of little people—is the most interesting and the most familiar. In Part II he visits Brobdingnag, a land of giants. In Part III he discovers Laputa, a realm of learned fools. In Part IV he comes to the country of the Houyhnhnms, noble horses, who are served by a debased race of human beings called Yahoos. As the satire proceeds, the playfulness of the first two parts gives way to bitter sarcasm, and Part IV resolves itself into a morbid and savage denunciation of the whole human race. The first voyage is given here entire.

PART I: A VOYAGE TO LILLIPUT

Chapter I

The Author gives some account of himself and family, his first inducements to travel. He is shipwrecked, and swims for his life, gets safe on shore in the country of Lilliput, *is made a prisoner, and is carried up country.*

MY father had a small estate in Nottinghamshire; I was the third of five sons. He sent me to Emanuel College in Cambridge, at fourteen years old, where I resided three years, and applied myself close to my studies; but the charge of maintaining me (although I had a very scanty allowance) being too great for a narrow fortune, I was bound apprentice to Mr. James Bates, an eminent surgeon in London, with whom I continued four years; and my father now and then sending me small sums of money, I laid them out in learning navigation, and other parts of the mathematics, useful to those who intend to travel, as I always believed it would be some time or other my fortune to do. When I left Mr. Bates, I went down to my father; where, by the assistance of him and my uncle John, and some other relations, I got forty pounds, and a promise of thirty pounds a year to maintain me at Leyden: there I studied physic two years and seven months, knowing it would be useful in long voyages.

Soon after my return from Leyden, I was recommended by my good master, Mr. Bates, to be surgeon to the *Swallow*, Captain Abraham Pannell, commander; with whom I continued three years and a half, making a voyage or two into the Levant, and some other parts. When I came back I resolved to settle in London, to which Mr. Bates, my master, encouraged me, and by him I was recommended to several patients. I took part of a small house in the Old Jury; and being advised to alter my condition, I married Mrs. Mary Burton, second daughter to Mr. Edmund Burton, hosier, in Newgate-street, with whom I received four hundred pounds for a portion.

But, my good master Bates dying in two years after, and I having few friends, my business began to fail; for my conscience would not suffer me to imitate the bad practice of too many among my brethren. Having therefore consulted with my wife, and some of my acquaintance, I determined to go again to sea. I was surgeon successively in two ships, and made several voyages, for six years, to the East and West-Indies, by which I got some addition to my fortune. My hours of leisure I spent in reading the best authors, ancient and modern, being always provided with a good number of books; and when I was ashore, in observing the manners and dispositions of the people, as well as learning their language, wherein I had a great facility by the strength of my memory.

The last of these voyages not proving very fortunate, I grew weary of the sea, and intended to stay at home with my wife and family. I removed from the Old Jury to Fetter-Lane, and from thence to Wapping, hoping to get business among the sailors; but it would not turn to account. After three years expectation that things would mend, I accepted an advantageous offer from Captain William Prichard, master of the *Antelope*, who was making a voyage to the South-Sea. We set sail from Bristol, May 4, 1699, and our voyage at first was very prosperous.

It would not be proper, for some reasons, to trouble the reader with the particulars of our adventures in those seas: let it suffice to inform him, that in our passage from thence to the East-Indies, we were driven by a violent storm to the north-west of Van Diemen's Land. By an observation, we found ourselves in the latitude of 30 degrees 2 minutes south. Twelve of our crew were dead by immoderate labour, and ill food; the rest were in a very weak condition. On the fifth of November, which was the beginning of summer in those parts, the weather being very hazy, the seamen spied a rock, within half a cable's length of the ship; but the wind was so strong, that we were driven directly upon it, and immediately split. Six of the crew, of whom I was one, having let down the boat into the sea, made a shift to get clear of the ship, and the rock. We rowed, by my computation, about three leagues, till we were able to work no longer, being already spent with labour while we were in the ship. We therefore trusted ourselves to the mercy of the waves, and in about half an hour the boat was overset by a sudden flurry from the north. What became of my companions in the boat, as well as of those who escaped on the rock, or were left in the vessel, I cannot tell; but conclude they were all lost. For my own part, I swam as fortune directed me, and was pushed forward by wind and tide. I often let my legs drop, and could feel no bottom: but when I was almost gone, and able to struggle no longer, I found myself within my depth; and by this time the storm was much abated. The declivity was so small, that I walked near a mile before I got to the shore, which I conjectured was about eight a clock in the evening. I then advanced forward near half a mile, but could not discover any sign of houses or inhabitants; at least I was in so weak a condition, that I did not observe them. I was extremely tired, and with that, and the heat of the weather, and about half a pint of brandy that I drank as I left the ship, I found myself much inclined to sleep. I lay down on the grass, which was very short and soft, where I slept sounder than ever I remember to have done in my life, and, as I reckoned, about nine hours; for when I awaked, it was just day-light. I attempted to rise, but was not able to stir: for as I happened to lie on my back, I found my arms and legs were strongly fastened on each side to the ground; and my hair, which was long and thick, tied down in the same manner. I likewise felt several slender ligatures across my body, from my arm-pits to my thighs. I could only look upwards, the sun began to grow hot, and the light offended my eyes. I heard a confused noise about me, but in the posture I lay, could see nothing except the sky. In a little time I felt something alive moving on my left leg, which advancing gently forward over my breast, came almost up to my chin; when bending my eyes downwards as much as I could, I perceived it to be a human creature not six inches high, with a bow and arrow in his hands, and a quiver at his back. In the mean time, I felt at least forty more of the same kind (as I conjectured) following the first. I was in the utmost astonishment, and roared so loud, that they all ran back in a fright; and some of them, as I was afterwards told, were hurt with the falls they got by leaping from my sides upon the ground. However, they soon returned, and one of them, who ventured so far as to get a full sight of my face, lifting up his hands and eyes by way of admiration, cried out in a shrill, but

4. Mrs., again for an unmarried woman. **43. south.** This would be in the region of Tasmania.

17. a clock, old form.

distinct voice, *Hekinah degul:* the others repeated the same words several times, but then I knew not what they meant. I lay all this while, as the reader may believe, in great uneasiness: at length, struggling to get loose, I had the fortune to break the strings, and wrench out the pegs that fastened my left arm to the ground: for, by lifting it up to my face, I discovered the methods they had taken to bind me, and at the same time with a violent pull, which gave me excessive pain, I a little loosened the strings that tied down my hair on the left side, so that I was just able to turn my head about two inches. But the creatures ran off a second time, before I could seize them; whereupon there was a great shout in a very shrill accent, and after it ceased, I heard one of them cry aloud *Tolgo phonac;* when in an instant I felt above an hundred arrows discharged on my left hand, which pricked me like so many needles; and besides, they shot another flight into the air, as we do bombs in Europe, whereof many, I suppose, fell on my body, (though I felt them not) and some on my face, which I immediately covered with my left hand. When this shower of arrows was over, I fell a groaning with grief and pain, and then striving again to get loose, they discharged another volley larger than the first, and some of them attempted with spears to stick me in the sides; but, by good luck, I had on a buff jerkin, which they could not pierce. I thought it the most prudent method to lie still, and my design was to continue so till night, when, my left hand being already loose, I could easily free myself: and as for the inhabitants, I had reason to believe I might be a match for the greatest armies they could bring against me, if they were all of the same size with him that I saw. But fortune disposed otherwise of me. When the people observed I was quiet, they discharged no more arrows; but, by the noise I heard, I knew their numbers increased; and about four yards from me, over-against my right ear, I heard a knocking for above an hour, like that of people at work; when turning my head that way, as well as the pegs and strings would permit me, I saw a stage erected, about a foot and a half from the ground, capable of holding four of the inhabitants, with two or three ladders to mount it: from whence one of them, who seemed to be a person of quality, made me a long speech, whereof I understood not one syllable. But I should have mentioned, that before the principal person began his oration, he cried out three times, *Langro dehul san:* (these words and the former were afterwards repeated and explained to me). Whereupon immediately about fifty of the inhabitants came and cut the strings that fastened the left side of my head, which gave me the liberty of turning it to the right, and of observing the person and gesture of him that was to speak. He appeared to be of a middle age, and taller than any of the other three who attended him, whereof one was a page that held up his train, and seemed to be somewhat longer than my middle finger; the other two stood one on each side to support him. He acted every part of an orator, and I could observe many periods of threatenings, and others of promises, pity, and kindness. I answered in a few words, but in the most submissive manner, lifting up my left hand, and both my eyes to the sun, as calling him for a witness; and being almost famished with hunger, having not eaten a morsel for some hours before I left the ship, I found the demands of nature so strong upon me, that I could not forbear showing my impatience (perhaps against the strict rules of decency) by putting my finger frequently on my mouth, to signify that I wanted food. The *Hurgo* (for so they call a great lord, as I afterwards learnt) understood me very well. He descended from the stage, and commanded that several ladders should be applied to my sides, on which above an hundred of the inhabitants mounted and walked towards my mouth, laden with baskets full of meat, which had been provided and sent thither by the King's orders, upon the first intelligence he received of me. I observed there was the flesh of several animals, but could not distinguish them by the taste. There were shoulders, legs, and loins, shaped like those of mutton, and very well dressed, but smaller than the wings of a lark. I eat them by two or three at a mouthful, and took three loaves at a time, about the bigness of musket bullets. They supplied me as fast as they could, showing a thousand marks of wonder and astonishment at my bulk and appetite. I then made another sign that I wanted drink. They found by my eating, that a small quantity would not suffice me; and being a most ingenious people, they slung up with great dexterity one of their largest hogsheads, then rolled it towards my hand, and beat out the top; I drank it off at a draught, which I might well do, for it did not hold half a pint, and tasted like a small wine of Burgundy, but much more delicious. They brought me a second hogshead, which I drank in the same manner, and made signs for more, but they had none to give me. When I had performed these wonders, they shouted for joy, and danced upon my breast, repeating several times as they did at first, *Hekinah degul.* They made me a sign that I should throw down the two hogsheads, but first warning the people below to stand out of the way, crying aloud, *Borach mivola,* and when they saw the vessels in the air, there was an universal shout of *Hekinah degul.* I confess I was often tempted, while they were passing backwards and forwards on my body, to seize forty or fifty of the first that came in my reach, and dash them against the ground. But the remembrance of what I had felt, which probably might not be the worst they could do, and the promise of honour I made them, for so I interpreted my submissive behaviour, soon drove out these imaginations. Besides, I now considered myself as bound by the laws of hospitality to a people who had treated me with so much expense and magnificence. However, in my thoughts, I could not sufficiently wonder at the intrepidity of these diminutive mortals, who durst venture to mount and walk upon my body, while one of my hands was at liberty, without trembling at the very sight of so prodigious a creature as I must appear to them. After some time, when they observed that I made no more demands for meat, there appeared before me a person of high rank from his Imperial Majesty. His Excellency, having mounted on the small of my right leg, advanced forwards up to my face, with about a dozen of his retinue. And producing his credentials under the Signet Royal, which he applied close to my eyes, spoke about ten minutes, without any signs of anger, but with a kind of determinate resolution; often pointing forwards, which, as I afterwards found, was toward the capital city, about half a mile distant, whither it was agreed by his Majesty in council that I must be conveyed. I answered in few words, but to no purpose, and made a sign with my hand that was loose, putting it to the other (but over his Excellency's head for fear of hurting him or his train) and then to my own head and body, to signify that I desired my liberty. It appeared that he understood me well enough, for he shook his head by way of disapprobation, and held his hand in a posture to show that I must be carried as a prisoner. However, he made other signs to let me understand that I should have meat and drink enough, and very good treatment. Whereupon I once more thought of attempting to break my bonds; but again, when I felt the smart of their arrows, upon my face and hands, which were all in blisters, and many of the darts still sticking in them, and observing likewise that the number of my enemies increased, I gave tokens to let them know that they might do with me what they pleased. Upon this, the *Hurgo* and his train withdrew, with much civility and cheerful countenances. Soon after I heard a general shout, with frequent repetitions of the words, *Peplom selan,* and I felt great numbers of people on my left side relaxing the cords to such a degree, that I was able to turn upon my right, and to ease myself with making water; which I very plentifully did, to the great astonishment of the people, who conjecturing by my motions what I was going to do, immediately opened to the right and left on that side, to avoid the torrent which fell with such noise and violence from me. But before this, they had daubed my face and both my hands with a sort of ointment very pleasant to the smell, which in a few minutes removed all the smart of their arrows. These circumstances, added to the refreshment I had received by their victuals and drink, which were very nourishing, disposed me to sleep. I slept about eight hours, as I was afterwards assured; and it was no wonder, for the physicians, by the Emperor's order, had mingled a sleepy potion in the hogshead of wine.

It seems that upon the first moment I was discovered sleeping on the ground after my landing, the Emperor had early notice of it by an express; and determined in council that I should be tied in the manner I have related, (which was done in the night while I slept) that plenty of meat and drink should be sent to me, and a machine prepared to carry me to the capital city.

This resolution perhaps may appear very bold and dangerous, and I am confident would not be imitated by any prince in Europe on the like occasion; however, in my opinion, it was extremely prudent, as well as generous: for supposing these people had endeavoured to kill me with their spears and arrows while I was asleep, I should certainly have awaked with the first sense of smart, which might so far have roused my rage and strength, as to have enabled me to break the strings wherewith I was tied; after which, as they were not able to make resistance, so they could expect no mercy.

These people are most excellent mathematicians, and arrived to a great perfection in mechanics, by the countenance and encouragement of the Emperor, who is a renowned patron of learning. This prince hath several machines fixed on wheels, for the carriage of trees and other great weights. He often builds his largest men of war, whereof some are nine foot long, in the woods where the timber grows, and has them carried on these engines three or four hundred yards to the sea. Five hundred carpenters and engineers were immediately set at work to prepare the greatest engine they had. It was a frame of wood raised three inches from the ground, about seven foot long and four wide, moving upon twenty-two wheels. The shout I heard was upon the arrival of this engine, which it seems set out in four hours after my landing. It was brought parallel to me as I lay. But the principal difficulty was to raise and place me in this vehicle. Eighty poles, each of one foot high, were erected for this purpose, and very strong cords of the bigness of packthread were fastened by hooks to many bandages, which the workmen had girt round my neck, my hands, my body, and my legs. Nine hundred of the strongest men were employed to draw up these cords by many pulleys fastened on the poles, and thus, in less than three hours, I was raised and slung into the engine, and there tied fast. All this I was told, for, while the whole operation was performing, I lay in a profound sleep, by the force of that soporiferous medicine infused into my liquor. Fifteen hundred of the Emperor's largest horses, each about four inches and a half high, were employed to draw me towards the metropolis, which, as I said, was half a mile distant.

About four hours after we began our journey, I awaked by a very ridiculous accident; for the carriage being stopped a while to adjust something that was out of order, two or three of the young natives had the curiosity to see how I looked when I was asleep; they climbed up into the engine, and advancing very softly to my face, one of them, an officer in the guards, put the sharp end of his half-pike a good way up into my left nostril, which tickled my nose like a straw, and made me sneeze violently: whereupon they stole off unperceived, and it was three weeks before I knew the cause of my awaking so suddenly. We made a long march the remaining part of that day, and rested at night with five hundred guards on each side of me, half with torches, and half with bows and arrows, ready to shoot me if I should offer to stir. The next morning at sunrise we continued our march, and arrived within two hundred yards of the city gates about noon. The Emperor, and all his court, came out to meet us; but his great officers would by no means suffer his Majesty to endanger his person by mounting on my body.

At the place where the carriage stopped, there stood an ancient temple, esteemed to be the largest in the whole kingdom; which having been polluted some years before by an unnatural murder, was, according to the zeal of those people, looked upon as profane, and therefore had been applied to common uses, and all the ornaments and furniture carried away. In this edifice it was determined I should lodge. The great gate fronting to the north was about four foot high, and almost two foot wide, through which I could easily creep. On each side of the gate was a small window not above six inches from the ground: into that on the left side, the King's smiths conveyed fourscore and eleven chains, like those that hang to a lady's watch in Europe, and almost as large, which were locked to my left leg with six and thirty padlocks. Over against this temple, on the other side of the great highway, at twenty foot distance, there was a turret at least five foot high. Here the Emperor ascended, with many principal lords of his court, to have an opportunity of viewing me, as I was told, for I could not see them. It was reckoned that above an hundred thousand inhabitants came out of the town upon the same errand; and, in spite of my guards, I believe there could not be fewer than ten thousand at several times, who mounted my body by the help of ladders. But a proclamation was soon issued to forbid it upon pain of death. When the workmen found it was impossible for me to break loose, they cut all the strings that bound me; whereupon I rose up, with as melancholy a disposition as ever I had in my life. But the noise and astonishment of the people at seeing me rise and walk, are not to be expressed. The chains that held my left leg were about two yards long, and gave me not only the liberty of walking backwards and forwards in a semicircle; but, being fixed within four inches of the gate, allowed me to creep in, and lie at my full length in the temple.

Chapter 2

The Emperor of Lilliput, *attended by several of the nobility, comes to see the Author in his confinement. The Emperor's person and habit described. Learned men appointed to teach the Author their language. He gains favour by his mild disposition. His pockets are searched, and his sword and pistols taken from him.*

WHEN I found myself on my feet, I looked about me, and must confess I never beheld a more entertaining prospect. The country round appeared like a continued garden, and the inclosed fields, which were generally forty foot square, resembled so many beds of flowers. These fields were intermingled with woods of half a stang, and the tallest trees, as I could judge, appeared to be seven foot high. I viewed the town on my left hand, which looked like the painted scene of a city in a theatre.

I had been for some hours extremely pressed by the necessities of nature; which was no wonder, it being almost two days since I had last disburthened myself. I was under great difficulties between urgency and shame. The best expedient I could think on, was to creep into my house, which I accordingly did; and shutting the gate after me, I went as far as

43. stang, a pole or perch, $16\frac{1}{2}$ feet.

the length of my chain would suffer, and discharged my body of that uneasy load. But this was the only time I was ever guilty of so uncleanly an action; for which I cannot but hope the candid reader will give some allowance, after he hath maturely and impartially considered my case, and the distress I was in. From this time my constant practice was, as soon as I rose, to perform that business in open air, at the full extent of my chain, and due care was taken every morning before company came, that the offensive matter should be carried off in wheelbarrows, by two servants appointed for that purpose. I would not have dwelt so long upon a circumstance, that perhaps at first sight may appear not very momentous, if I had not thought it necessary to justify my character in point of cleanliness to the world; which I am told some of my maligners have been pleased, upon this and other occasions, to call in question.

When this adventure was at an end, I came back out of my house, having occasion for fresh air. The Emperor was already descended from the tower, and advancing on horseback towards me, which had like to have cost him dear; for the beast, though very well trained, yet wholly unused to such a sight, which appeared as if a mountain moved before him, reared up on his hinder feet: but that prince, who is an excellent horseman, kept his seat, till his attendants ran in, and held the bridle, while his Majesty had time to dismount. When he alighted, he surveyed me round with great admiration, but kept beyond the length of my chain. He ordered his cooks and butlers, who were already prepared, to give me victuals and drink, which they pushed forward in a sort of vehicles upon wheels, till I could reach them. I took these vehicles, and soon emptied them all; twenty of them were filled with meat, and ten with liquor; each of the former afforded me two or three good mouthfuls, and I emptied the liquor of ten vessels, which was contained in earthen vials, into one vehicle, drinking it off at a draught; and so I did with the rest. The Empress, and young Princes of the blood of both sexes, attended by many ladies, sat at some distance in their chairs; but upon the accident that happened to the Emperor's horse, they alighted, and came near his person, which I am now going to describe. He is taller by almost the breadth of my nail, than any of his court; which alone is enough to strike an awe into the beholders. His features are strong and masculine, with an Austrian lip and arched nose, his complexion olive, his countenance erect, his body and limbs well proportioned, all his motions graceful, and his deportment majestic. He was then past his prime, being twenty-eight years and three quarters old, of which he had reigned about seven, in great felicity, and generally victorious. For the better convenience of beholding him, I lay on my side, so that my face was parallel to his, and he stood but three yards off: however, I have had him since many times in my hand, and therefore cannot be deceived in the description. His dress was very plain and simple, and the fashion of it between the Asiatic and the European: but he had on his head a light helmet of gold, adorned with jewels, and a plume on the crest. He held his sword drawn in his hand, to defend himself, if I should happen to break loose; it was almost three inches long, the hilt and scabbard were gold enriched with diamonds. His voice was shrill, but very clear and articulate, and I could distinctly hear it when I stood up. The ladies and courtiers were all most magnificently clad, so that the spot they stood upon seemed to resemble a petticoat spread on the ground, embroidered with figures of gold and silver. His Imperial Majesty spoke often to me, and I returned answers, but neither of us could understand a syllable. There were several of his priests and lawyers present (as I conjectured by their habits) who were commanded to address themselves to me, and I spoke to them in as many languages as I had the least smattering of, which were High and Low Dutch, Latin, French, Spanish, Italian, and Lingua Franca; but all to no purpose. After about two hours the court retired, and I was left with a strong guard, to prevent the impertinence, and probably the malice of the rabble, who were very impatient to crowd about me as near as they durst, and some of them had the impudence to shoot their arrows at me as I sat on the ground by the door of my house, whereof one very narrowly missed my left eye. But the colonel ordered six of the ringleaders to be seized, and thought no punishment so proper as to deliver them bound into my hands, which some of his soldiers accordingly did, pushing them forwards with the butt-ends of their pikes into my reach; I took them all in my right hand, put five of them into my coat-pocket, and as to the sixth, I made a countenance as if I would eat him alive. The poor man squalled terribly, and the colonel and his officers were in much pain, especially when they saw me take out my penknife: but I soon put them out of fear: for, looking mildly, and immediately cutting the strings he was bound with, I set him gently on the ground, and away he ran. I treated the rest in the same manner, taking them one by one out of my pocket, and I ob-

31–32. admiration, wonder.

served both the soldiers and people were highly obliged at this mark of my clemency, which was represented very much to my advantage at court.

Towards night I got with some difficulty into my house, where I lay on the ground, and continued to do so about a fortnight; during which time the Emperor gave orders to have a bed prepared for me. Six hundred beds of the common measure were brought in carriages, and worked up in my house; an hundred and fifty of their beds sewn together made up the breadth and length, and these were four double, which however kept me but very indifferently from the hardness of the floor, that was of smooth stone. By the same computation they provided me with sheets, blankets, and coverlets, tolerable enough for one who had been so long inured to hardships as I.

As the news of my arrival spread through the kingdom, it brought prodigious numbers of rich, idle, and curious people to see me; so that the villages were almost emptied, and great neglect of tillage and household affairs must have ensued, if his Imperial Majesty had not provided, by several proclamations and orders of state, against this inconveniency. He directed that those who had already beheld me should return home, and not presume to come within fifty yards of my house without licence from court; whereby the secretaries of state got considerable fees.

In the meantime, the Emperor held frequent councils to debate what course should be taken with me; and I was afterwards assured by a particular friend, a person of great quality, who was looked upon to be as much in the secret as any, that the court was under many difficulties concerning me. They apprehended my breaking loose, that my diet would be very expensive, and might cause a famine. Sometimes they determined to starve me, or at least to shoot me in the face and hands with poisoned arrows, which would soon dispatch me; but again they considered, that the stench of so large a carcass might produce a plague in the metropolis, and probably spread through the whole kingdom. In the midst of these consultations, several officers of the army went to the door of the great council-chamber; and two of them being admitted, gave an account of my behaviour to the six criminals above-mentioned, which made so favourable an impression in the breast of his Majesty and the whole board, in my behalf, that an Imperial Commission was issued out, obliging all the villages nine hundred yards around the city, to deliver in every morning six beeves, forty sheep, and other victuals for my sustenance; together with a proportionable quantity of bread, and wine, and other liquors; for the due payment of which his Majesty gave assignments upon his treasury. For this prince lives chiefly upon his own demesnes, seldom, except upon great occasions, raising any subsidies upon his subjects, who are bound to attend him in his wars at their own expense. An establishment was also made of six hundred persons to be my domestics, who had board-wages allowed for their maintenance, and tents built for them very conveniently on each side of my door. It was likewise ordered, that three hundred tailors should make me a suit of clothes after the fashion of the country: that six of his Majesty's greatest scholars should be employed to instruct me in their language: and, lastly, that the Emperor's horses, and those of the nobility, and troops of guards, should be frequently exercised in my sight, to accustom themselves to me. All these orders were duly put in execution, and in about three weeks I made a great progress in learning their language; during which time, the Emperor frequently honoured me with his visits, and was pleased to assist my masters in teaching me. We began already to converse together in some sort; and the first words I learnt were to express my desire that he would please to give me my liberty, which I every day repeated on my knees. His answer, as I could comprehend it, was, that this must be a work of time, not to be thought on without the advice of his council, and that first I must *Lumos kelmin pesso desmar lon Emposo;* that is, swear a peace with him and his kingdom. However, that I should be used with all kindness; and he advised me to acquire, by my patience and discreet behaviour, the good opinion of himself and his subjects. He desired I would not take it ill, if he gave orders to certain proper officers to search me; for probably I might carry about me several weapons, which must needs be dangerous things, if they answered the bulk of so prodigious a person. I said, his Majesty should be satisfied, for I was ready to strip myself, and turn up my pockets before him. This I delivered part in words, and part in signs. He replied, that by the laws of the kingdom I must be searched by two of his officers; that he knew this could not be done without my consent and assistance; that he had so good an opinion of my generosity and justice, as to trust their persons in my hands: that whatever they took from me should be returned when I left the country, or paid for at the rate which I would set upon them. I took up the two officers in my hands, put them first into my coat-pockets, and then into every other pocket about me, except my two fobs, and another secret pocket which I had no mind should be searched, wherein I had some little necessaries that were of no consequence to any but myself. In one of my fobs there was a silver watch, and in the other a small quantity of gold in a purse. These gentlemen, having pen, ink, and paper about them, made an exact inventory of every thing they saw; and when they had done, desired I would set them down, that they might deliver it to the Emperor. This inventory I afterwards translated into English, and is word for word as follows:

Imprimis, In the right coat-pocket of the Great Man-Mountain (for so I interpret the words *Quinbus Flestrin*) after the strictest search, we found only one great piece of coarse cloth, large enough to be a foot-cloth for your Majesty's chief room of state. In the left pocket we saw a huge silver chest, with a cover of the same metal, which we, the searchers, were not able to lift. We desired it should be opened, and one of us stepping into it, found himself up to the mid leg in a sort of dust, some part whereof flying up to our faces, set us both a sneezing for several times together. In his right waistcoat-pocket we found a prodigious bundle of white thin substances, folded one over another, about the bigness of three men, tied with a strong cable, and marked with black figures; which we humbly conceive to be writings, every letter almost half as large as the palm of our hands. In the left there was a sort of engine, from the back of which were extended twenty long poles, resembling the pallisadoes before your Majesty's court; wherewith we conjecture the Man-Mountain combs his head; for we did not always trouble him with questions, because we found it a great difficulty to make him understand us. In the large pocket on the right side of his middle cover (so I translate the word *ranfu-lo*, by which they meant my breeches) we saw a hollow pillar of iron, about the length of a man, fastened to a strong piece of timber, larger than the pillar; and upon one side of the pillar were huge pieces of iron sticking out, cut into strange figures, which we know not what to make of. In the left pocket, another engine of the same kind. In the smaller pocket on the right side, were several round flat pieces of white and red metal, of different bulk; some of the white, which seemed to be silver, were so large and heavy, that my comrade and I could hardly lift them. In the left pocket were two black pillars irregularly shaped: we could not, without difficulty, reach the top of them as we stood at the bottom of his pocket. One of them was covered, and seemed all of a piece: but at the upper end of the other, there appeared a white round substance, about twice the bigness of our heads. Within each of these was enclosed a prodigious plate of steel; which, by our orders, we obliged him to show us, because we apprehended they might be dangerous engines. He took them out of their cases, and told us, that in his own country his practice was to shave his beard with one of these, and cut his meat with the other. There were two pockets which we could not enter: these he called his fobs; they were two large slits cut into the top of his middle cover, but squeezed close by the pressure of his belly. Out of the right fob hung a great silver chain, with a wonderful kind of engine at the bottom. We directed him to draw out whatever was fastened to that chain; which appeared to be a globe, half silver, and half of some transparent metal; for, on the transparent side, we saw certain strange figures circularly drawn, and thought we could touch them, till we found our fingers stopped by that lucid substance. He put this engine to our ears, which made an incessant noise like that of a water-mill. And we conjecture it is either some unknown animal, or the god that he worships; but we are more inclined to the latter opinion, because he assured us, (if we understood him right, for he expressed himself very imperfectly) that he seldom did any thing without consulting it. He called it his oracle, and said it pointed out the time for every action of his life. From the left fob he took out a net almost large enough for a fisherman, but contrived to open and shut like a purse, and served him for the same use: we found therein several massy pieces of yellow metal, which, if they be real gold, must be of immense value.

Having thus, in obedience to your Majesty's commands, diligently searched all his pockets, we observed a girdle about his waist made of the hide of some prodigious animal; from which, on the left side, hung a sword of the length of five men; and on the right, a bag or pouch divided into two cells, each capable of holding three of your Majesty's subjects. In one of these cells were several globes or balls of a most ponderous metal, about the bigness of our heads, and requiring a strong hand to lift them: the other cell contained a heap of certain black grains, but of no great bulk or weight, for we could hold about fifty of them in the palms of our hands.

This is an exact inventory of what we found about the body of the Man-Mountain, who used us with great civility, and due respect to your Majesty's Commission. Signed and sealed on the fourth day of the eighty-ninth moon of your Majesty's auspicious reign.

CLEFRIN FRELOCK, MARSI FRELOCK.

When this inventory was read over to the Emperor, he directed me, although in very gentle terms, to deliver up the several particulars. He first called for my scimitar, which I took out, scabbard and all. In the mean time he ordered three thousand of his choicest troops (who then attended him) to surround me at a distance, with their bows and arrows just ready to discharge: but I did not observe it, for my eyes were wholly fixed upon his Majesty. He then desired me to draw my scimitar, which, although it had got some rust by the sea-water, was in most parts exceeding bright. I did so, and immediately all the troops gave a shout between terror and surprise; for the sun shone clear, and the reflection dazzled their eyes, as I waved the scimitar to and fro in my hand. His Majesty, who is a most magnanimous prince, was less daunted than I could expect; he ordered me to return it into the scabbard, and cast it on the ground as gently as I could, about six foot from the end of my chain. The next thing he demanded, was one of the hollow iron pillars, by which he meant my pocket-pistols. I drew it out, and at his desire, as well as I could, expressed to him the use of it; and charging it only with powder, which, by the closeness of my pouch, happened to escape wetting in the sea (an inconvenience against which all prudent mariners take special care to provide,) I first cautioned the Emperor not to be afraid, and then I let it off in the air. The astonishment here was much greater than at the sight of my scimitar. Hundreds fell down as if they had been struck dead; and even the Emperor, although he stood his ground, could not recover himself in some time. I delivered up both my pistols in the same manner as I had done my scimitar, and then my pouch of powder and bullets; begging him that the former might be kept from fire, for it would kindle with the smallest spark, and blow up his imperial palace into the air. I likewise delivered up my watch, which the Emperor was very curious to see, and commanded two of his tallest yeomen of the guards to bear it on a pole upon their shoulders, as draymen in England do a barrel of ale. He was amazed at the continual noise it made, and the motion of the minute-hand, which he could easily discern; for their sight is much more acute than ours: and asked the opinions of his learned men about him, which were various and remote, as the reader may well imagine without my repeating; although indeed I could not very perfectly understand them. I then gave up my silver and copper money, my purse, with nine large pieces of gold, and some smaller ones; my knife and razor, my comb and silver snuff-box, my handkerchief and journal-book. My scimitar, pistols, and pouch, were conveyed in carriages to his Majesty's stores; but the rest of my goods were returned to me.

I had, as I before observed, one private pocket which escaped their search, wherein there was a pair of spectacles, (which I sometimes use for the weakness of my eyes) a pocket perspective, and several other little conveniences; which being of no consequence to the Emperor, I did not think myself bound in honour to discover, and I apprehended they might be lost or spoiled if I ventured them out of my possession.

Chapter 3

The Author diverts the Emperor, and his nobility of both sexes, in a very uncommon manner. The diversions of the court of Lilliput *described. The Author has his liberty granted him upon certain conditions.*

MY gentleness and good behaviour had gained so far on the Emperor and his court, and indeed upon the army and people in general, that I began to conceive hopes of getting my liberty in a short time. I took all possible methods to cultivate this favourable disposition. The natives came by degrees to be less apprehensive of any danger from me. I would sometimes lie down, and let five or six of them dance on my hand. And at last the boys and girls would venture to come and play at hide and seek in my hair. I had now made a good progress in understanding and speaking their language. The Emperor had a mind one day to entertain me with several of the country shows, wherein they exceed all nations I have known, both for dexterity and magnificence. I was diverted with none so much as that of the rope-dancers, performed upon a slender white thread, extended about two foot and twelve inches from the ground. Upon which I shall desire liberty, with the reader's patience, to enlarge a little.

This diversion is only practised by those persons who are candidates for great employments, and high favour, at court. They are trained in this art from their youth, and are not always of noble birth, or liberal education. When a great office is vacant, either by death or disgrace, (which often happens) five or six of those candidates petition the Emperor to entertain his Majesty and the court with a dance on the rope, and whoever jumps the highest without falling, succeeds in the office. Very often the chief ministers themselves are commanded to show their

44. court. The following passage is a satire upon the court of England.

skill, and to convince the Emperor that they have not lost their faculty. Flimnap, the Treasurer, is allowed to cut a caper on the straight rope, at least an inch higher than any other lord in the whole empire. I have seen him do the summerset several times together upon a trencher fixed on the rope, which is no thicker than a common packthread in England. My friend Reldresal, principal Secretary for Private Affairs, is, in my opinion, if I am not partial, the second after the Treasurer; the rest of the great officers are much upon a par.

These diversions are often attended with fatal accidents, whereof great numbers are on record. I myself have seen two or three candidates break a limb. But the danger is much greater when the ministers themselves are commanded to show their dexterity; for, by contending to excel themselves and their fellows, they strain so far, that there is hardly one of them who hath not received a fall, and some of them two or three. I was assured that a year or two before my arrival, Flimnap would have infallibly broke his neck, if one of the King's cushions, that accidentally lay on the ground, had not weakened the force of his fall.

There is likewise another diversion, which is only shown before the Emperor and Empress, and first minister, upon particular occasions. The Emperor lays on the table three fine silken threads of six inches long. One is blue, the other red, and the third green. These threads are proposed as prizes for those persons whom the Emperor hath a mind to distinguish by a peculiar mark of his favour. The ceremony is performed in his Majesty's great chamber of state, where the candidates are to undergo a trial of dexterity very different from the former, and such as I have not observed the least resemblance of in any other country of the old or the new world. The Emperor holds a stick in his hands, both ends parallel to the horizon, while the candidates advancing one by one, sometimes leap over the stick, sometimes creep under it backwards and forwards several times, according as the stick is advanced or depressed. Sometimes the Emperor holds one end of the stick, and his first minister the other; sometimes the minister has it entirely to himself. Whoever performs his part with most agility, and holds out the longest in leaping and creeping, is rewarded with the blue-coloured silk; the red is given to the next, and the green to the third, which they all wear girt twice round about the middle; and you see few great persons about this court, who are not adorned with one of these girdles.

The horses of the army, and those of the royal stables, having been daily led before me, were no longer shy, but would come up to my very feet without starting. The riders would leap them over my hand as I held it on the ground, and one of the Emperor's huntsmen, upon a larger courser, took my foot, shoe and all; which was indeed a prodigious leap. I had the good fortune to divert the Emperor one day after a very extraordinary manner. I desired he would order several sticks of two foot high, and the thickness of an ordinary cane, to be brought me; whereupon his Majesty commanded the master of his woods to give directions accordingly; and the next morning six woodmen arrived with as many carriages, drawn by eight horses to each. I took nine of these sticks, fixing them firmly in the ground in a quadrangular figure, two foot and a half square. I took four other sticks, and tied them parallel at each corner, about two foot from the ground; then I fastened my handkerchief to the nine sticks that stood erect, and extended it on all sides, till it was tight as the top of a drum; and the four parallel sticks rising about five inches higher than the handkerchief, served as ledges on each side. When I had finished my work, I desired the Emperor to let a troop of his best horse, twenty-four in number, come and exercise upon this plain. His Majesty approved of the proposal, and I took them up, one by one, in my hands, ready mounted and armed, with the proper officers to exercise them. As soon as they got into order, they divided into two parties, performed mock skirmishes, discharged blunt arrows, drew their swords, fled and pursued, attacked and retired, and in short discovered the best military discipline I ever beheld. The parallel sticks secured them and their horses from falling over the stage; and the Emperor was so much delighted that he ordered this entertainment to be repeated several days, and once was pleased to be lifted up and give the word of command; and, with great difficulty, persuaded even the Empress herself to let me hold her in her close chair within two yards of the stage, from whence she was able to take a full view of the whole performance. It was my good fortune that no ill accident happened in these entertainments, only once a fiery horse, that belonged to one of the captains, pawing with his hoof, struck a hole in my handkerchief, and his foot slipping, he overthrew his rider and himself; but I immediately relieved them both, and covering the hole with one hand, I set down the troop with the other, in the same manner as I took

2. Flimnap, probably meant for Sir Robert Walpole.
28. threads, corresponding to the English orders of the Garter, the Bath, and the Thistle.

them up. The horse that fell was strained in the left shoulder, but the rider got no hurt, and I repaired my handkerchief as well as I could: however, I would not trust to the strength of it any more in such dangerous enterprises.

About two or three days before I was set at liberty, as I was entertaining the court with these kind of feats, there arrived an express to inform his Majesty, that some of his subjects riding near the place where I was first taken up, had seen a great black substance lying on the ground, very oddly shaped, extending its edges round as wide as his Majesty's bedchamber, and rising up in the middle as high as a man; that it was no living creature, as they at first apprehended, for it lay on the grass without motion, and some of them had walked round it several times: that by mounting upon each other's shoulders, they had got to the top, which was flat and even, and stamping upon it they found it was hollow within; that they humbly conceived it might be something belonging to the Man-Mountain; and if his Majesty pleased, they would undertake to bring it with only five horses. I presently knew what they meant, and was glad at heart to receive this intelligence. It seems upon my first reaching the shore after our shipwreck, I was in such confusion, that before I came to the place where I went to sleep, my hat, which I had fastened with a string to my head while I was rowing, and had stuck on all the time I was swimming, fell off after I came to land; the string, as I conjecture, breaking by some accident which I never observed, but thought my hat had been lost at sea. I intreated his Imperial Majesty to give orders it might be brought to me as soon as possible, describing to him the use and the nature of it: and the next day the waggoners arrived with it, but not in a very good condition; they had bored two holes in the brim, within an inch and half of the edge, and fastened two hooks in the holes; these hooks were tied by a long cord to the harness, and thus my hat was dragged along for above half an English mile; but the ground in that country being extremely smooth and level, it received less damage than I expected.

Two days after this adventure, the Emperor having ordered that part of his army which quarters in and about his metropolis to be in readiness, took a fancy of diverting himself in a very singular manner. He desired I would stand like a Colossus, with my legs as far asunder as I conveniently could. He then commanded his General (who was an old experienced leader, and a great patron of mine) to draw up the troops in close order, and march them under me; the foot by twenty-four in a breast, and the horse by sixteen, with drums beating, colours flying, and pikes advanced. This body consisted of three thousand foot, and a thousand horse. His Majesty gave orders, upon pain of death, that every soldier in his march should observe the strictest decency with regard to my person; which, however, could not prevent some of the younger officers from turning up their eyes as they passed under me. And, to confess the truth, my breeches were at that time in so ill a condition, that they afforded some opportunities for laughter and admiration.

I had sent so many memorials and petitions for my liberty, that his Majesty at length mentioned the matter, first in his cabinet, and then in a full council; where it was opposed by none, except Skyresh Bolgolam, who was pleased, without any provocation, to be my mortal enemy. But it was carried against him by the whole board, and confirmed by the Emperor. That minister was *Galbet*, or Admiral of the Realm, very much in his master's confidence, and a person well versed in affairs, but of a morose and sour complexion. However, he was at length persuaded to comply; but prevailed that the articles and conditions upon which I should be set free, and to which I must swear, should be drawn up by himself. These articles were brought to me by Skyresh Bolgolam in person, attended by two under-secretaries, and several persons of distinction. After they were read, I was demanded to swear to the performance of them; first in the manner of my own country, and afterwards in the method prescribed by their laws; which was to hold my right foot in my left hand, to place the middle finger of my right hand on the crown of my head, and my thumb on the tip of my right ear. But because the reader may be curious to have some idea of the style and manner of expression peculiar to that people, as well as to know the articles upon which I recovered my liberty, I have made a translation of the whole instrument word for word, as near as I was able, which I here offer to the public.

Golbasto Momarem Evlame Gurdilo Shefin Mully Ully Gue, most mighty Emperor of Lilliput, delight and terror of the universe, whose dominions extend five thousand *blustrugs* (about twelve miles in circumference) to the extremities of the globe; monarch of all monarchs, taller than the sons of men; whose feet press down to the centre, and whose head strikes against the sun; at whose nod the princes of the earth shake their knees; pleasant as the spring, comfortable as the summer, fruitful as autumn, dreadful as winter. His most sublime Majesty proposeth to the Man-Mountain, lately arrived to our celestial dominions, the following articles, which by a solemn oath he shall be obliged to perform.

First, The Man-Mountain shall not depart from our dominions, without our licence under our great seal.

2d, He shall not presume to come into our metropolis, without our express order; at which time, the inhabitants shall have two hours warning to keep within their doors.

3rd, The said Man-Mountain shall confine his walks to our principal high roads, and not offer to walk or lie down in a meadow or field of corn.

4th, As he walks the said roads, he shall take the utmost care not to trample upon the bodies of any of our loving subjects, their horses, or carriages, nor take any of our subjects into his hands, without their own consent.

5th, If an express requires extraordinary dispatch, the Man-Mountain shall be obliged to carry in his pocket the messenger and horse a six days journey once in every moon, and return the said messenger back (if so required) safe to our Imperial Presence.

6th, He shall be our ally against our enemies in the Island of Blefuscu and do his utmost to destroy their fleet, which is now preparing to invade us.

7th, That the said Man-Mountain shall, at his times of leisure, be aiding and assisting to our workmen, in helping to raise certain great stones, towards covering the wall of the principal park, and other our royal buildings.

8th, That the said Man-Mountain shall, in two moons' time, deliver in an exact survey of the circumference of our dominions by a computation of his own paces round the coast.

Lastly, That upon his solemn oath to observe all the above articles, the said Man-Mountain shall have a daily allowance of meat and drink sufficient for the support of 1728 of our subjects, with free access to our Royal Person, and other marks of our favour. Given at our Palace at Belfaborac the twelfth day of the ninety-first moon of our reign.

I swore and subscribed to these articles with great cheerfulness and content, although some of them were not so honourable as I could have wished; which proceeded wholly from the malice of Skyresh Bolgolam, the High-Admiral: whereupon my chains were immediately unlocked, and I was at full liberty; the Emperor himself in person did me the honour to be by at the whole ceremony. I made my acknowledgements by prostrating myself at his Majesty's feet: but he commanded me to rise; and after many gracious expressions, which, to avoid the censure of vanity, I shall not repeat, he added, that he hoped I should prove a useful servant, and well deserve all the favours he had already conferred upon me, or might do for the future.

The reader may please to observe, that in the last article for the recovery of my liberty, the Emperor stipulates to allow me a quantity of meat and drink sufficient for the support of 1728 Lilliputians. Some time after, asking a friend at court how they came to fix on that determinate number, he told me that his Majesty's mathematicians, having taken the height of my body by the help of a quadrant, and finding it to exceed theirs in the proportion of twelve to one they concluded from the similarity of their bodies, that mine must contain at least 1728 of theirs, and consequently would require as much food as was necessary to support that number of Lilliputians. By which, the reader may conceive an idea of the ingenuity of that people, as well as the prudent and exact economy of so great a prince.

Chapter 4

Mildendo, *the metropolis of* Lilliput, *described, together with the Emperor's palace. A conversation between the Author and a principal Secretary, concerning the affairs of that empire. The Author's offer to serve the Emperor in his wars.*

THE first request I made after I had obtained my liberty, was, that I might have licence to see Mildendo, the metropolis; which the Emperor easily granted me, but with a special charge to do no hurt either to the inhabitants or their houses. The people had notice by proclamation of my design to visit the town. The wall which encompassed it, is two foot and a half high, and at least eleven inches broad, so that a coach and horses may be driven very safely round it; and it is flanked with strong towers at ten foot distance. I stepped over the great Western Gate, and passed very gently, and sideling through the two principal streets, only in my short waistcoat, for fear of damaging the roofs and eaves of the houses with the skirts of my coat. I walked with the utmost circumspection, to avoid treading on any stragglers, that might remain in the streets, although the orders were very strict, that all people should keep in their houses, at their own peril. The garret windows and tops of houses were so crowded with spectators, that I thought in

27. Blefuscu, France.

45. sideling, old form.

all my travels I had not seen a more populous place. The city is an exact square, each side of the wall being five hundred foot long. The two great streets, which run cross and divide it into four quarters, are five foot wide. The lanes and alleys, which I could not enter, but only viewed them as I passed, are from twelve to eighteen inches. The town is capable of holding five hundred thousand souls. The houses are from three to five stories. The shops and markets well provided.

The Emperor's palace is in the centre of the city, where the two great streets meet. It is inclosed by a wall of two foot high, and twenty foot distant from the buildings. I had his Majesty's permission to step over this wall; and the space being so wide between that and the palace, I could easily view it on every side. The outward court is a square of forty foot, and includes two other courts: in the inmost are the royal apartments, which I was very desirous to see, but found it extremely difficult; for the great gates, from one square into another, were but eighteen inches high, and seven inches wide. Now the buildings of the outer court were at least five foot high, and it was impossible for me to stride over them without infinite damage to the pile, though the walls were strongly built of hewn stone, and four inches thick. At the same time the Emperor had a great desire that I should see the magnificence of his palace; but this I was not able to do till three days after, which I spent in cutting down with my knife some of the largest trees in the royal park, about an hundred yards distant from the city. Of these trees I made two stools, each about three foot high, and strong enough to bear my weight. The people having received notice a second time, I went again through the city to the palace, with my two stools in my hands. When I came to the side of the outer court, I stood upon one stool, and took the other in my hand: this I lifted over the roof, and gently set it down on the space between the first and second court, which was eight foot wide. I then stept over the buildings very conveniently from one stool to the other, and drew up the first after me with a hooked stick. By this contrivance I got into the inmost court; and lying down upon my side, I applied my face to the windows of the middle stories, which were left open on purpose, and discovered the most splendid apartments that can be imagined. There I saw the Empress and the young Princes, in their several lodgings, with their chief attendants about them. Her Imperial Majesty was pleased to smile very graciously upon me, and gave me out of the window her hand to kiss.

But I shall not anticipate the reader with farther descriptions of this kind, because I reserve them for a greater work, which is now almost ready for the press, containing a general description of this empire, from its first erection, through a long series of princes, with a particular account of their wars and politics, laws, learning, and religion: their plants and animals, their peculiar manners and customs, with other matters very curious and useful; my chief design at present being only to relate such events and transactions as happened to the public, or to myself, during a residence of about nine months in that empire.

One morning, about a fortnight after I had obtained my liberty, Reldresal, principal Secretary (as they style him) of Private Affairs, came to my house attended only by one servant. He ordered his coach to wait at a distance, and desired I would give him an hour's audience; which I readily consented to, on account of his quality and personal merits, as well as the many good offices he had done me during my solicitations at court. I offered to lie down, that he might the more conveniently reach my ear; but he chose rather to let me hold him in my hand during our conversation. He began with compliments on my liberty; said he might pretend to some merit in it: but, however, added, that if it had not been for the present situation of things at court, perhaps I might not have obtained it so soon. "For," said he, "as flourishing a condition as we may appear to be in to foreigners, we labour under two mighty evils; a violent faction at home, and the danger of an invasion by a most potent enemy from abroad. As to the first, you are to understand, that for about seventy moons past there have been two struggling parties in this empire, under the names of *Tramecksan* and *Slamecksan*, from the high and low heels on their shoes, by which they distinguish themselves. It is alleged indeed, that the high heels are most agreeable to our ancient constitution: but however this be, his Majesty hath determined to make use of only low heels in the administration of the government, and all offices in the gift of the Crown, as you cannot but observe; and particularly, that his Majesty's Imperial heels are lower at least by a *drurr* than any of his court; (*drurr* is a measure about the fourteenth part of an inch). The animosities between these two parties run so high, that they will neither eat nor drink, nor talk with each other. We compute the *Tramecksan*, or High-Heels, to exceed us in number; but the power is wholly on our side. We apprehend

39. themselves, the English Tories and Whigs. **42. low heels,** the Whigs, whom King George I of England favored.

his Imperial Highness, the Heir to the Crown, to have some tendency towards the High-Heels; at least we can plainly discover one of his heels higher than the other, which gives him a hobble in his gait. Now, in the midst of these intestine disquiets, we are threatened with an invasion from the Island of Blefuscu, which is the other great empire of the universe, almost as large and powerful as this of his Majesty. For as to what we have heard you affirm, that there are other kingdoms and states in the world inhabited by human creatures as large as yourself, our philosophers are in much doubt, and would rather conjecture that you dropped from the moon, or one of the stars; because it is certain, that an hundred mortals of your bulk would, in a short time, destroy all the fruits and cattle of his Majesty's dominions. Besides, our histories of six thousand moons make no mention of any other regions, than the two great empires of Lilliput and Blefuscu. Which two mighty powers have, as I was going to tell you, been engaged in a most obstinate war for six and thirty moons past. It began upon the following occasion. It is allowed on all hands, that the primitive way of breaking eggs, before we eat them, was upon the larger end: but his present Majesty's grandfather, while he was a boy, going to eat an egg, and breaking it according to the ancient practice, happened to cut one of his fingers. Whereupon the Emperor his father published an edict, commanding all his subjects, upon great penalties, to break the smaller end of their eggs. The people so highly resented this law, that our histories tell us there have been six rebellions raised on that account; wherein one Emperor lost his life, and another his crown. These civil commotions were constantly fomented by the monarchs of Blefuscu; and when they were quelled, the exiles always fled for refuge to that empire. It is computed, that eleven thousand persons have, at several times, suffered death, rather than submit to break their eggs at the smaller end. Many hundred large volumes have been published upon this controversy: but the books of the Big-Endians have been long forbidden, and the whole party rendered incapable by law of holding employments. During the course of these troubles, the Emperors of Blefuscu did frequently expostulate by their ambassadors, accusing us of making a schism of religion, by offending against a fundamental doctrine of our great prophet Lustrog, in the fifty-fourth chapter of the Blundecral (which is their Alcoran). This, however, is thought to be a mere strain upon the text: for the words are these: *That all true believers break their eggs at the convenient end:* and which is the convenient end, seems, in my humble opinion, to be left to every man's conscience, or at least in the power of the chief magistrate to determine. Now the Big-Endian exiles have found so much credit in the Emperor of Blefuscu's court, and so much private assistance and encouragement from their party here at home, that a bloody war has been carried on between the two empires for six and thirty moons with various success; during which time we have lost forty capital ships, and a much greater number of smaller vessels, together with thirty thousand of our best seamen and soldiers; and the damage received by the enemy is reckoned to be somewhat greater than ours. However, they have now equipped a numerous fleet, and are just preparing to make a descent upon us; and his Imperial Majesty, placing great confidence in your valour and strength, has commanded me to lay this account of his affairs before you."

I desired the Secretary to present my humble duty to the Emperor, and to let him know, that I thought it would not become me, who was a foreigner, to interfere with parties; but I was ready, with the hazard of my life, to defend his person and state against all invaders.

26. grandfather, Henry VIII. **34–35. one Emperor . . . another,** Charles I and James II. **43. Big-Endians,** Roman Catholics; Little Endians, Protestants.

Chapter 5

The Author, by an extraordinary stratagem, prevents an invasion. A high title of honour is conferred upon him. Ambassadors arrive from the Emperor of Blefuscu, *and sue for peace. The Empress's apartment on fire by an accident; the Author instrumental in saving the rest of the palace.*

THE Empire of Blefuscu is an island situated to the north north-east side of Lilliput, from whence it is parted only by a channel of eight hundred yards wide. I had not yet seen it, and upon this notice of an intended invasion, I avoided appearing on that side of the coast, for fear of being discovered by some of the enemy's ships, who had received no intelligence of me, all intercourse between the two empires having been strictly forbidden during the war, upon pain of death, and an embargo laid by our Emperor upon all vessels whatsoever. I communicated to his Majesty a project I had formed of seizing the enemy's whole fleet: which, as our scouts assured us, lay at anchor in the harbour ready to sail with the first fair wind. I consulted the most experienced seamen, upon the depth of the channel, which they had often plumbed, who told me, that in the middle at high-water it was seventy *glumgluffs* deep, which is about six foot of European measure; and the rest of it fifty *glumgluffs* at most. I walked towards the north-east coast over against Blefuscu; and lying down behind a hillock, took out my small pocket perspective-glass, and viewed the enemy's fleet at anchor, consisting of about fifty men of war, and a great number of transports: I then came back to my house, and gave order (for which I had a warrant) for a great quantity of the strongest cable and bars of iron. The cable was about as thick as packthread, and the bars of the length and size of a knitting-needle. I trebled the cable to make it stronger, and for the same reason I twisted three of the iron bars together, binding the extremities into a hook. Having thus fixed fifty hooks to as many cables, I went back to the north-east coast, and putting off my coat, shoes, and stockings, walked into the sea in my leathern jerkin, about half an hour before high water. I waded with what haste I could, and swam in the middle about thirty yards till I felt ground; I arrived at the fleet in less than half an hour. The enemy was so frighted when they saw me, that they leaped out of their ships, and swam to shore, where there could not be fewer than thirty thousand souls. I then took my tackling, and fastening a hook to the hole at the prow of each, I tied all the cords together at the end. While I was thus employed, the enemy discharged several thousand arrows, many of which stuck in my hands and face; and besides the excessive smart, gave me much disturbance in my work. My greatest apprehension was for my eyes, which I should have infallibly lost, if I had not suddenly thought of an expedient. I kept among other little necessaries a pair of spectacles in a private pocket, which, as I observed before, had scaped the Emperor's searchers. These I took out and fastened as strongly as I could upon my nose, and thus armed went on boldly with my work in spite of the enemy's arrows, many of which struck against the glasses of my spectacles, but without any other effect, further than a little to discompose them. I had now fastened all the hooks, and taking the knot in my hand, began to pull; but not a ship would stir, for they were all too fast held by their anchors, so that the boldest part of my enterprise remained. I therefore let go the cord, and leaving the hooks fixed to the ships, I resolutely cut with my knife the cables that fastened the anchors, receiving about two hundred shots in my face and hands; then I took up the knotted end of the cables, to which my hooks were tied, and with great ease drew fifty of the enemy's largest men of war after me.

The Blefuscudians, who had not the least imagination of what I intended, were at first confounded with astonishment. They had seen me cut the cables, and thought my design was only to let the ships run a-drift, or fall foul on each other: but when they perceived the whole fleet moving in order, and saw me pulling at the end, they set up such a scream of grief and despair, that it is almost impossible to describe or conceive. When I had got out of danger, I stopped awhile to pick out the arrows that stuck in my hands and face; and rubbed on some of the same ointment that was given me at my first arrival, as I have formerly mentioned. I then took off my spectacles, and waiting about an hour, till the tide was a little fallen, I waded through the middle with my cargo, and arrived safe at the royal port of Lilliput.

The Emperor and his whole court stood on the shore, expecting the issue of this great adventure. They saw the ships move forward in a large half-moon, but could not discern me, who was up to my breast in water. When I advanced in the middle of the channel, they were yet in more pain, because I was under water to my neck. The Emperor concluded me to be drowned, and that the enemy's fleet was approaching in a hostile manner: but he was soon eased of his fears, for the channel growing shallower every step I made, I came in a short time within hearing, and holding up the end of the cable by which the fleet was fastened, I cried in a loud voice, *Long live the most puissant Emperor of Lilliput!* This great prince received me at my landing with all possible encomiums, and created me a *Nardac* upon the spot, which is the highest title of honour among them.

His Majesty desired I would take some other opportunity of bringing all the rest of his enemy's ships into his ports. And so unmeasureable is the ambition of princes, that he seemed to think of nothing less than reducing the whole empire of Blefuscu into a province and governing it by a viceroy; of destroying the Big-Endian exiles, and compelling the people to break the smaller end of their eggs, by which he would remain the sole monarch of the whole world. But I endeavoured to divert him from this design, by many arguments drawn from the topics of policy as well as justice; and I plainly protested, that I would never be an instrument of bringing a free and brave people into slavery. And when the matter was debated in council, the wisest part of the ministry were of my opinion.

38. **scaped,** escaped.

This open bold declaration of mine was so opposite to the schemes and politics of his Imperial Majesty, that he could never forgive it; he mentioned it in a very artful manner at council, where I was told that some of the wisest appeared, at least by their silence, to be of my opinion; but others, who were my secret enemies, could not forbear some expressions, which by a side-wind reflected on me. And from this time began an intrigue between his Majesty and a junto of ministers maliciously bent against me, which broke out in less than two months, and had like to have ended in my utter destruction. Of so little weight are the greatest services to princes, when put into the balance with a refusal to gratify their passions.

About three weeks after this exploit, there arrived a solemn embassy from Blefuscu, with humble offers of a peace; which was soon concluded upon conditions very advantageous to our Emperor, wherewith I shall not trouble the reader. There were six ambassadors, with a train of about five hundred persons, and their entry was very magnificent, suitable to the grandeur of their master, and the importance of their business. When their treaty was finished, wherein I did them several good offices by the credit I now had, or at least appeared to have at court, their Excellencies, who were privately told how much I had been their friend, made me a visit in form. They began with many compliments upon my valour and generosity, invited me to that kingdom in the Emperor their master's name, and desired me to show them some proofs of my prodigious strength, of which they had heard so many wonders; wherein I readily obliged them, but shall not trouble the reader with the particulars.

When I had for some time entertained their Excellencies, to their infinite satisfaction and surprise, I desired they would do me the honour to present my most humble respects to the Emperor their master, the renown of whose virtues had so justly filled the whole world with admiration, and whose royal person I resolved to attend before I returned to my own country: accordingly, the next time I had the honour to see our Emperor, I desired his general licence to wait on the Blefuscudian monarch, which he was pleased to grant me, as I could perceive, in a very cold manner; but could not guess the reason, till I had a whisper from a certain person, that Flimnap and Bolgolam had represented my intercourse with those ambassadors as a mark of disaffection, from which I am sure my heart was wholly free. And this was the first time I began to conceive some imperfect idea of courts and ministers.

It is to be observed, that these ambassadors spoke to me by an interpreter, the languages of both empires differing as much from each other as any two in Europe, and each nation priding itself upon the antiquity, beauty, and energy of their own tongues, with an avowed contempt for that of their neighbour; yet our Emperor, standing upon the advantage he had got by seizure of their fleet, obliged them to deliver their credentials, and make their speech in the Lilliputian tongue. And it must be confessed, that from the great intercourse of trade and commerce between both realms, from the continual reception of exiles, which is mutual among them, and from the custom in each empire to send their young nobility and richer gentry to the other, in order to polish themselves by seeing the world, and understanding men and manners; there are few persons of distinction, or merchants, or seamen, who dwell in the maritime parts, but what can hold conversation in both tongues; as I found some weeks after, when I went to pay my respects to the Emperor of Blefuscu, which in the midst of great misfortunes, through the malice of my enemies, proved a very happy adventure to me, as I shall relate in its proper place.

The reader may remember, that when I signed those articles upon which I recovered my liberty, there were some which I disliked upon account of their being too servile, neither could anything but an extreme necessity have forced me to submit. But being now a *Nardac* of the highest rank in that empire, such offices were looked upon as below my dignity, and the Emperor (to do him justice) never once mentioned them to me. However, it was not long before I had an opportunity of doing his Majesty, at least, as I then thought, a most signal service. I was alarmed at midnight with the cries of many hundred people at my door; by which being suddenly awaked, I was in some kind of terror. I heard the word *burglum* repeated incessantly: several of the Emperor's court, making their way through the crowd, entreated me to come immediately to the palace, where her Imperial Majesty's apartment was on fire, by the carelessness of a maid of honour, who fell asleep while she was reading a romance. I got up in an instant; and orders being given to clear the way before me, and it being likewise a moonshine night, I made a shift to get to the Palace without trampling on any of the people. I found they had already applied ladders to the walls of the apartment, and were well provided with buckets, but the water was at some distance. These buckets were about the size of a large thimble, and the poor people supplied me with them as fast as they could; but the flame was so violent that they did little good. I might easily have stifled it with my coat, which I unfortunately left behind me for haste, and came away only in my leathern jerkin. The case seemed wholly desperate and deplorable; and this magnificent palace would have infallibly been burnt down to the ground, if, by a presence of mind, unusual to me, I had not suddenly thought of an expedient. I had the evening before drunk plentifully of a most delicious wine, called *glimigrim*, (the Blefuscudians call it *flunec*, but ours is esteemed the better sort) which is very diuretic. By the luckiest chance in the world, I had not discharged myself of any part of it. The heat I had contracted by coming very near the flames, and by labouring to quench them, made the wine begin to operate by urine; which I voided in such a quantity, and applied so well to the proper places, that in three minutes the fire was wholly extinguished, and the rest of that noble pile, which had cost so many ages in erecting, preserved from destruction.

It was now day-light, and I returned to my house without waiting to congratulate with the Emperor: because, although I had done a very eminent piece of service, yet I could not tell how his Majesty might resent the manner by which I had performed it: for, by the fundamental laws of the realm, it is capital in any person, of what quality soever, to make water within the precincts of the palace. But I was a little comforted by a message from his Majesty, that he would give orders to the Grand Justiciary for passing my pardon in form; which, however, I could not obtain. And I was privately assured, that the Empress, conceiving the greatest abhorrence of what I had done, removed to the most distant side of the court, firmly resolved that those buildings should never be repaired for her use; and, in the presence of her chief confidents could not forbear vowing revenge.

Chapter 6

Of the inhabitants of Lilliput; *their learning, laws, and customs, the manner of educating their children. The Author's way of living in that country. His vindication of a great lady.*

ALTHOUGH I intend to leave the description of this empire to a particular treatise, yet in the mean time I am content to gratify the curious reader with some general ideas. As the common size of the natives is somewhat under six inches high, so there is an exact proportion in all other animals, as well as plants and trees: for instance, the tallest horses and oxen are between four and five inches in height, the sheep an inch and a half, more or less: their geese about the bigness of a sparrow, and so the several gradations downwards till you come to the smallest, which, to my sight, were almost invisible; but nature hath adapted the eyes of the Lilliputians to all objects proper for their view: they see with great exactness, but at no great distance. And to show the sharpness of their sight towards objects that are near, I have been much pleased with observing a cook pulling a lark, which was not so large as a common fly; and a young girl threading an invisible needle with invisible silk. Their tallest trees are about seven foot high: I mean some of those in the great royal park, the tops whereof I could but just reach with my fist clinched. The other vegetables are in the same proportion; but this I leave to the reader's imagination.

I shall say but little at present of their learning, which for many ages hath flourished in all its branches among them: but their manner of writing is very peculiar, being neither from the left to the right, like the Europeans; nor from the right to the left, like the Arabians; nor from up to down, like the Chinese; nor from down to up, like the Cascagians; but aslant from one corner of the paper to the other, like ladies in England.

They bury their dead with their heads directly downwards, because they hold an opinion, that in eleven thousand moons they are all to rise again, in which period the earth (which they conceive to be flat) will turn upside down, and by this means they shall, at their resurrection, be found ready standing on their feet. The learned among them confess the absurdity of this doctrine, but the practice still continues, in compliance to the vulgar.

There are some laws and customs in this empire very peculiar; and if they were not so directly contrary to those of my own dear country, I should be tempted to say a little in their justification. It is only to be wished, that they were as well executed. The first I shall mention, relates to informers. All crimes against the state are punished here with the utmost severity; but if the person accused maketh his innocence plainly to appear upon his trial, the accuser is immediately put to an ignominious death; and out of his goods or lands, the innocent person is quadruply recompensed for the loss of his time, for the danger he underwent, for the hardship of his imprisonment, and for all the charges he hath been at in making his defence. Or, if that fund be deficient, it is largely supplied by the Crown. The Emperor does also confer on him some public mark of his favour, and proclamation is made of his innocence through the whole city.

They look upon fraud as a greater crime than theft, and therefore seldom fail to punish it with death; for they allege, that care and vigilance, with a very common understanding, may preserve a man's goods from thieves, but honesty has no fence against superior cunning; and since it is necessary that there should be a perpetual intercourse of buying and selling, and dealing upon credit, where fraud is permitted and connived at, or hath no law to punish it, the honest dealer is always undone, and the knave gets the advantage. I remember when I was once interceding with the Emperor for a criminal who had wronged his master of a great sum of money, which he had received by order, and ran away with; and happening to tell his Majesty, by way of extenuation, that it was only a breach of trust; the Emperor thought it monstrous in me to offer, as a defence, the greatest aggravation of the crime: and truly I had little to say in return, farther than the common answer, that different nations had different customs; for, I confess, I was heartily ashamed.

Although we usually call reward and punishment the two hinges upon which all government turns, yet I could never observe this maxim to be put in practice by any nation except that of Lilliput. Whoever can there bring sufficient proof that he hath strictly observed the laws of his country for seventy-three moons, hath a claim to certain privileges, according to his quality and condition of life, with a proportionable sum of money out of a fund appropriated for that use: he likewise acquires the title of *Snilpall*, or Legal, which is added to his name, but does not descend to his posterity. And these people thought it a prodigious defect of policy among us, when I told them that our laws were enforced only by penalties, without any mention of reward. It is upon this account that the image of Justice, in their courts of judicature, is formed with six eyes, two before, as many behind, and on each side one, to signify circumspection; with a bag of gold open in her right hand, and a sword sheathed in her left, to show she is more disposed to reward than to punish.

In choosing persons for all employments, they have more regard to good morals than to great abilities; for, since government is necessary to mankind, they believe that the common size of human understandings is fitted to some station or other, and that Providence never intended to make the management of public affairs a mystery, to be comprehended only by a few persons of sublime genius, of which there seldom are three born in an age: but they suppose truth, justice, temperance, and the like, to be in every man's power; the practice of which virtues, assisted by experience and a good intention, would qualify any man for the service of his country, except where a course of study is required. But they thought the want of moral virtues was so far from being supplied by superior endowments of the mind, that employments could never be put into such dangerous hands as those of persons so qualified; and at least, that the mistakes committed by ignorance in a virtuous disposition, would never be of such fatal consequence to the public weal, as the practices of a man whose inclinations led him to be corrupt, and had great abilities to manage, and multiply, and defend his corruptions.

In like manner, the disbelief of a Divine Providence renders a man uncapable of holding any public station; for, since kings avow themselves to be the deputies of Providence, the Lilliputians think nothing can be more absurd than for a prince to employ such men as disown the authority under which he acts.

In relating these and the following laws, I would only be understood to mean the original institutions, and not the most scandalous corruptions into which these people are fallen by the degenerate nature of man. For as to that infamous practice of acquiring great employments by dancing on the ropes, or badges of favour and distinction by leaping over sticks and creeping under them, the reader is to observe, that they were first introduced by the grandfather of the Emperor now reigning, and grew to the present height, by the gradual increase of party and faction.

Ingratitude is among them a capital crime, as we read it to have been in some other countries: for they reason thus, that whoever makes ill returns to his benefactor, must needs be a common enemy to the rest of mankind, from whom he hath received no obligation, and therefore such a man is not fit to live.

Their notions relating to the duties of parents and children differ extremely from ours. For, since the conjunction of male and female is founded upon the great law of nature, in order to propagate and continue the species, the Lilliputians will needs have it, that men and women are joined together like other animals, by the motives of concupiscence; and that their tenderness towards their young proceeds from the like natural principle: for which reason they will never allow, that a child is under any obligation to his father for begetting him, or to his mother for bringing him into the world, which, considering the

33. grandfather, James I.

miseries of human life, was neither a benefit in itself, nor intended so by his parents, whose thoughts in their love-encounters were otherwise employed. Upon these, and the like reasonings, their opinion is, that parents are the last of all others to be trusted with the education of their own children; and therefore they have in every town public nurseries, where all parents, except cottagers and labourers, are obliged to send their infants of both sexes to be reared and educated when they come to the age of twenty moons, at which time they are supposed to have some rudiments of docility. These schools are of several kinds, suited to different qualities, and to both sexes. They have certain professors well skilled in preparing children for such a condition of life as befits the rank of their parents, and their own capacities as well as inclinations. I shall first say something of the male nurseries, and then of the female.

The nurseries for males of noble or eminent birth, are provided with grave and learned professors, and their several deputies. The clothes and food of the children are plain and simple. They are bred up in the principles of honour, justice, courage, modesty, clemency, religion, and love of their country; they are always employed in some business, except in the times of eating and sleeping, which are very short, and two hours for diversions, consisting of bodily exercises. They are dressed by men till four years of age, and then are obliged to dress themselves, although their quality be ever so great; and the women attendants, who are aged proportionably to ours at fifty, perform only the most menial offices. They are never suffered to converse with servants, but go together in small or greater numbers to take their diversions, and always in the presence of a professor, or one of his deputies; whereby they avoid those early bad impressions of folly and vice to which our children are subject. Their parents are suffered to see them only twice a year; the visit is to last but an hour. They are allowed to kiss the child at meeting and parting; but a professor, who always stands by on those occasions, will not suffer them to whisper, or use any fondling expressions, or bring any presents of toys, sweetmeats, and the like.

The pension from each family for the education and entertainment of a child, upon failure of due payment, is levied by the Emperor's officers.

The nurseries for children of ordinary gentlemen, merchants, traders, and handicrafts, are managed proportionably after the same manner; only those designed for trades, are put out apprentices at eleven years old, whereas those of persons of quality continue in their exercises till fifteen, which answers to one and twenty with us: but the confinement is gradually lessened for the last three years.

In the female nurseries, the young girls of quality are educated much like the males, only they are dressed by orderly servants of their own sex; but always in the presence of a professor or deputy, till they come to dress themselves, which is at five years old. And if it be found that these nurses ever presume to entertain the girl with frightful or foolish stories, or the common follies practised by chambermaids among us, they are publicly whipped thrice about the city, imprisoned for a year, and banished for life to the most desolate part of the country. Thus the young ladies there are as much ashamed of being cowards and fools, as the men, and despise all personal ornaments beyond decency and cleanliness: neither did I perceive any difference in their education, made by their difference of sex, only that the exercises of the females were not altogether so robust; and that some rules were given them relating to domestic life, and a smaller compass of learning was enjoined them: for their maxim is, that among people of quality, a wife should be always a reasonable and agreeable companion, because she cannot always be young. When the girls are twelve years old, which among them is the marriageable age, their parents or guardians take them home, with great expressions of gratitude to the professors, and seldom without tears of the young lady and her companions.

In the nurseries of females of the meaner sort, the children are instructed in all kinds of works proper for their sex, and their several degrees: those intended for apprentices, are dismissed at seven years old, the rest are kept to eleven.

The meaner families who have children at these nurseries, are obliged, besides their annual pension, which is as low as possible, to return to the steward of the nursery a small monthly share of their gettings, to be a portion for the child; and therefore all parents are limited in their expenses by the law. For the Lilliputians think nothing can be more unjust, than for people, in subservience to their own appetites, to bring children into the world, and leave the burthen of supporting them on the public. As to persons of quality, they give security to appropriate a certain sum for each child, suitable to their condition; and these funds are always managed with good husbandry, and the most exact justice.

The cottagers and labourers keep their children at home, their business being only to till and cultivate the earth, and therefore their education is of little consequence to the public; but the old and dis-

12. docility, teachableness. **46. pension,** tuition.

eased among them are supported by hospitals: for begging is a trade unknown in this empire.

And here it may perhaps divert the curious reader, to give some account of my domestic, and my manner of living in this country, during a residence of nine months and thirteen days. Having a head mechanically turned, and being likewise forced by necessity, I had made for myself a table and chair convenient enough, out of the largest trees in the royal park. Two hundred sempstresses were employed to make me shirts, and linen for my bed and table, all of the strongest and coarsest kind they could get; which, however, they were forced to quilt together in several folds, for the thickest was some degrees finer than lawn. Their linen was usually three inches wide, and three foot make a piece. The sempstresses took my measure as I lay on the ground, one standing at my neck, and another at my mid-leg, with a strong cord extended, that each held by the end, while the third measured the length of the cord with a rule an inch long. Then they measured my right thumb, and desired no more; for by a mathematical computation, that twice round the thumb is once round the wrist, and so on to the neck and the waist, and by the help of my old shirt, which I displayed on the ground before them for a pattern, they fitted me exactly. Three hundred tailors were employed in the same manner to make me clothes; but they had another contrivance for taking my measure. I kneeled down, and they raised a ladder from the ground to my neck; upon this ladder one of them mounted, and let fall a plumb-line from my collar to the floor, which just answered the length of my coat: but my waist and arms I measured myself. When my clothes were finished, which was done in my house, (for the largest of theirs would not have been able to hold them) they looked like the patch-work made by the ladies in England, only that mine were all of a color.

I had three hundred cooks to dress my victuals, in little convenient huts built about my house, where they and their families lived, and prepared me two dishes a-piece. I took up twenty waiters in my hand, and placed them on the table: an hundred more attended below on the ground, some with dishes of meat, and some with barrels of wine, and other liquors, slung on their shoulders; all which the waiters above drew up as I wanted, in a very ingenious manner, by certain cords, as we draw the bucket up a well in Europe. A dish of their meat was a good mouthful, and a barrel of their liquor a reasonable draught. Their mutton yields to ours, but their beef is excellent. I have had a sirloin so large, that I have been forced to make three bits of it; but this is rare. My servants were astonished to see me eat it bones and all, as in our country we do the leg of a lark. Their geese and turkeys I usually eat at a mouthful, and I must confess they far exceed ours. Of their smaller fowl I could take up twenty or thirty at the end of my knife.

One day his Imperial Majesty, being informed of my way of living, desired that himself and his Royal Consort, with the young Princes of the blood of both sexes, might have the happiness (as he was pleased to call it) of dining with me. They came accordingly, and I placed them in chairs of state on my table, just over against me, with their guards about them. Flimnap, the Lord High Treasurer, attended there likewise with his white staff; and I observed he often looked on me with a sour countenance, which I would not seem to regard, but eat more than usual, in honour to my dear country, as well as to fill the court with admiration. I have some private reasons to believe, that this visit from his Majesty gave Flimnap an opportunity of doing me ill offices to his master. That minister had always been my secret enemy, though he outwardly caressed me more than was usual to the moroseness of his nature. He represented to the Emperor the low condition of his treasury; that he was forced to take up money at great discount; that exchequer bills would not circulate under nine per cent. below par; that in short I had cost his Majesty above a million and a half of *sprugs* (their greatest gold coin, about the bigness of a spangle); and upon the whole, that it would be advisable in the Emperor to take the first fair occasion of dismissing me.

I am here obliged to vindicate the reputation of an excellent lady, who was an innocent sufferer upon my account. The Treasurer took a fancy to be jealous of his wife, from the malice of some evil tongues, who informed him that her Grace had taken a violent affection for my person; and the court-scandal ran for some time, that she once came privately to my lodging. This I solemnly declare to be a most infamous falsehood, without any grounds, farther than that her Grace was pleased to treat me with all innocent marks of freedom and friendship. I own she came often to my house, but always publicly, nor ever without three more in the coach, who were usually her sister and young daughter, and some particular acquaintance; but this was common to many other ladies of the court. And I still appeal to my servants round, whether they at any time saw a coach at my door without knowing what persons were in it. On those occasions, when a servant had given me notice, my custom was to go immediately to the door; and, after paying my respects, to take up the coach and two horses very carefully in my hands, (for, if there were six horses, the postillion always unharnessed four) and place them on a table, where I had fixed a moveable rim quite round, of five inches high, to prevent accidents. And I have often had four coaches and horses at once on my table full of company, while I sat in my chair leaning my face towards them; and when I was engaged with one set, the coachmen would gently drive the others round my table. I have passed many an afternoon very agreeably in these conversations. But I defy the Treasurer, or his two informers (I will name them, and let them make their best of it) Clustril and Drunlo, to prove that any person ever came to me *incognito*, except the secretary Reldresal, who was sent by express command of his Imperial Majesty, as I have before related. I should not have dwelt so long upon this particular, if it had not been a point wherein the reputation of a great lady is so nearly concerned, to say nothing of my own; though I then had the honour to be a *Nardac*, which the Treasurer himself is not; for all the world knows he is only a *Glumglum*, a title inferior by one degree, as that of a Marquis is to a Duke in England, although I allow he preceded me in right of his post. These false informations, which I afterwards came to the knowledge of, by an accident not proper to mention, made Flimnap, the Treasurer, show his lady for some time an ill countenance, and me a worse; and although he were at last undeceived and reconciled to her, yet I lost all credit with him, and found my interest decline very fast with the Emperor himself, who was indeed too much governed by that favourite.

Chapter 7

The Author, being informed of a design to accuse him of high-treason, makes his escape to Blefuscu. *His reception there.*

BEFORE I proceed to give an account of my leaving this kingdom, it may be proper to inform the reader of a private intrigue which had been for two months forming against me.

I had been hitherto all my life a stranger to courts, for which I was unqualified by the meanness of my condition. I had indeed heard and read enough of the dispositions of great princes and ministers; but never expected to have found such terrible effects of them in so remote a country, governed, as I thought, by very different maxims from those in Europe.

When I was just preparing to pay my attendance on the Emperor of Blefuscu, a considerable person at court (to whom I had been very serviceable at a time when he lay under the highest displeasure of his Imperial Majesty) came to my house very privately at night in a close chair, and without sending his name, desired admittance. The chair-men were dismissed; I put the chair, with his Lordship in it, into my coat-pocket: and giving orders to a trusty servant to say I was indisposed and gone to sleep, I fastened the door of my house, placed the chair on the table, according to my usual custom, and sat down by it. After the common salutations were over, observing his Lordship's countenance full of concern, and enquiring into the reason, he desired I would hear him with patience in a matter that highly concerned my honour and my life. His speech was to the following effect, for I took notes of it as soon as he left me:

"You are to know," said he, "that several Committees of Council have been lately called in the most private manner on your account; and it is but two days since his Majesty came to a full resolution.

"You are very sensible that Skyresh Bolgolam (*Galbet*, or High-Admiral) hath been your mortal enemy almost ever since your arrival. His original reasons I know not; but his hatred is much increased since your great success against Blefuscu, by which his glory, as Admiral, is obscured. This Lord, in conjunction with Flimnap the High-Treasurer, whose enmity against you is notorious on account of his lady, Limtoc the General, Lalcon the Chamberlain, and Balmuff the Grand Justiciary, have prepared articles of impeachment against you, for treason, and other capital crimes."

This preface made me so impatient, being conscious of my own merits and innocence, that I was going to interrupt; when he entreated me to be silent, and thus proceeded:

"Out of gratitude for the favours you have done me, I procured information of the whole proceedings, and a copy of the articles, wherein I venture my head for your service.

Articles of Impeachment against Quinbus Flestrin (*the* Man-Mountain.)

ARTICLE I

"'Whereas, by a statute made in the reign of his Imperial Majesty Calin Deffar Plune, it is enacted, that whoever shall make water within the precincts of the royal palace, shall be liable to the pains and penalties of high treason; notwithstanding, the said Quinbus Flestrin, in open breach of the said law, under colour of extinguishing the fire kindled in the apartment of his Majesty's most dear Imperial Consort, did maliciously, traitorously, and devilishly, by discharge of his urine, put out the said fire kindled in the said apartment, lying and being within the precincts of the said royal palace, against the statute in that case provided, *etc.* against the duty, *etc.*

ARTICLE II

"'That the said Quinbus Flestrin having brought the imperial fleet of Blefuscu into the royal port, and being afterwards commanded by his Imperial Majesty to seize all the other ships of the said empire of Blefuscu, and reduce that empire to a province, to be governed by a viceroy from hence, and to destroy and put to death not only all the Big-Endian exiles, but likewise all the people of that empire, who would not immediately forsake the Big-Endian heresy: He, the said Flestrin, like a false traitor against his most Auspicious, Serene, Imperial Majesty, did petition to be excused from the said service, upon pretence of unwillingness to force the consciences, or destroy the liberties and lives of an innocent people.

ARTICLE III

"'That, whereas certain ambassadors arrived from the court of Blefuscu, to sue for peace in his Majesty's court: He, the said Flestrin, did, like a false traitor, aid, abet, comfort, and divert the said ambassadors, although he knew them to be servants to a Prince who was lately an open enemy to his Imperial Majesty, and in open war against his said Majesty.

ARTICLE IV

"'That the said Quinbus Flestrin, contrary to the duty of a faithful subject, is now preparing to make a voyage to the court and empire of Blefuscu, for which he hath received only verbal licence from his Imperial Majesty; and under colour of the said licence, doth falsely and traitorously intend to take the said voyage, and thereby to aid, comfort, and abet the Emperor of Blefuscu, so late an enemy, and in open war with his Imperial Majesty aforesaid.'

"There are some other articles, but these are the most important, of which I have read you an abstract.

"In the several debates upon this impeachment, it must be confessed that his Majesty gave many marks of his great lenity, often urging the services you had done him, and endeavouring to extenuate your crimes. The Treasurer and Admiral insisted that you should be put to the most painful and ignominious death, by setting fire on your house at night, and the General was to attend with twenty thousand men armed with poisoned arrows to shoot you on the face and hands. Some of your servants were to have private orders to strew a poisonous juice on your shirts, which would soon make you tear your own flesh, and die in the utmost torture. The General came into the same opinion; so that for a long time there was a majority against you. But his Majesty resolving, if possible, to spare your life, at last brought off the Chamberlain.

"Upon this incident, Reldresal, principal Secretary for Private Affairs, who always approved himself your true friend, was commanded by the Emperor to deliver his opinion, which he accordingly did; and therein justified the good thoughts you have of him. He allowed your crimes to be great, but that still there was room for mercy, the most commendable virtue in a prince, and for which his Majesty was so justly celebrated. He said, the friendship between you and him was so well known to the world, that perhaps the most honourable board might think him partial: however, in obedience to the command he had received, he would freely offer his sentiments. That if his Majesty, in consideration of your services, and pursuant to his own merciful disposition, would please to spare your life, and only give orders to put out both your eyes, he humbly conceived, that by this expedient, justice might in some measure be satisfied, and all the world would applaud the lenity of the Emperor, as well as the fair and generous proceedings of those who have the honour to be his counsellors. That the loss of your eyes would be no impediment to your bodily strength, by which you might still be useful to his Majesty. That blindness is an addition to courage, by concealing dangers from us; that the fear you had for your eyes, was the greatest difficulty in bringing over the enemy's fleet, and it would be sufficient for you to see by the eyes of the ministers, since the greatest princes do no more.

"This proposal was received with the utmost disapprobation by the whole board. Bolgolam, the Admiral, could not preserve his temper; but rising up in fury, said, he wondered how the Secretary durst presume to give his opinion for preserving the life of a traitor: that the services you had performed, were, by all true reasons of state, the great aggravation of your crimes; that you, who were able to extinguish the fire, by discharge of urine in her Majesty's apartment (which he mentioned with horror), might, at another time, raise an inundation by the same means, to drown the whole palace; and the same strength which enabled you to bring over the enemy's fleet, might serve, upon the first discontent, to carry it back: that he had good reasons to think you were a Big-Endian in your heart; and as treason begins in the heart, before it appears in overt acts, so he accused you as a traitor on that account, and therefore insisted you should be put to death.

"The Treasurer was of the same opinion; he showed to what straits his Majesty's revenue was reduced by the charge of maintaining you, which would soon grow insupportable: that the Secretary's expedient of putting out your eyes was so far from being a remedy against this evil, that it would probably increase it, as it is manifest from the common practice of blinding some kind of fowl, after which they fed the faster, and grew sooner fat: that his sacred Majesty and the Council, who are your judges, were in their own consciences fully convinced of your guilt, which was a sufficient argument to condemn you to death, without the formal proofs required by the strict letter of the law.

"But his Imperial Majesty, fully determined against capital punishment, was graciously pleased to say, that since the Council thought the loss of your eyes too easy a censure, some other may be inflicted hereafter. And your friend the Secretary humbly desiring to be heard again, in answer to what the Treasurer had objected concerning the great charge his Majesty was at in maintaining you, said, that his Excellency, who had the sole disposal of the Emperor's revenue, might easily provide against that evil, by gradually lessening your establishment; by which, for want of sufficient food, you would grow weak and faint, and lose your appetite, and consequently decay and consume in a few months; neither would the stench of your carcass be then so dangerous, when it should become more than half diminished; and immediately upon your death, five or six thousand of his Majesty's subjects might, in two or three days, cut your flesh from your bones, take it away by cart-loads, and bury it in distant parts to prevent infection, leaving the skeleton as a monument of admiration to posterity.

"Thus by the great friendship of the Secretary, the whole affair was compromised. It was strictly enjoined, that the project of starving you by degrees should be kept a secret, but the sentence of putting out your eyes was entered on the books; none dissenting except Bolgolam the Admiral, who, being a creature of the Empress, was perpetually instigated by her Majesty to insist upon your death, she having borne perpetual malice against you, on account of that infamous and illegal method you took to extinguish the fire in her apartment.

"In three days your friend the Secretary will be directed to come to your house, and read before you the articles of impeachment; and then to signify the great lenity and favour of his Majesty and Council, whereby you are only condemned to the loss of your eyes, which his Majesty doth not question you will gratefully and humbly submit to; and twenty of his Majesty's surgeons will attend, in order to see the operation well performed, by discharging very sharp-pointed arrows into the balls of your eyes, as you lie on the ground.

"I leave to your prudence what measures you will take; and to avoid suspicion, I must immediately return in as private a manner as I came."

His Lordship did so, and I remained alone, under many doubts and perplexities of mind.

It was a custom introduced by this prince and his ministry (very different, as I have been assured, from the practices of former times,) that after the court had decreed any cruel execution, either to gratify the monarch's resentment, or the malice of a favourite, the Emperor always made a speech to his whole Council, expressing his great lenity and tenderness, as qualities known and confessed by all the world. This speech was immediately published through the kingdom; nor did any thing terrify the people so much as those encomiums on his Majesty's mercy; because it was observed, that the more these praises were enlarged and insisted on, the more inhuman was the punishment, and the sufferer more innocent. And as to myself, I must confess, having never been designed for a courtier either by my birth or education, I was so ill a judge of things, that I could not discover the lenity and favour of his sentence, but conceived it (perhaps erroneously) rather to be rigorous than gentle. I sometimes thought of standing my trial, for although I could not deny the facts alleged in the several articles, yet I hoped they would admit of some extenuations. But having in my life perused many state-trials, which I ever observed to terminate as the judges thought fit to direct, I durst not rely on so dangerous a decision, in so critical a juncture, and against such powerful enemies. Once I was strongly bent upon resistance, for while I had liberty, the whole strength of that empire could hardly subdue me, and I might easily with stones pelt the metropolis to pieces; but I soon rejected that project with horror, by remembering the oath I had made to the Emperor, the favours I received from him, and the high title of *Nardac* he conferred upon me. Neither had I so soon learned the gratitude of courtiers, to persuade myself that his Majesty's present severities acquitted me of all past obligations.

At last I fixed upon a resolution, for which it is probable I may incur some censure, and not unjustly; for I confess I owe the preserving my eyes, and consequently my liberty, to my own great rashness and want of experience: because if I had then known the nature of princes and ministers, which I have since observed in many other courts, and their methods of treating criminals less obnoxious than myself, I should with great alacrity and readiness have submitted to so easy a punishment. But hurried on by the precipitancy of youth, and having his Imperial Majesty's licence to pay my attendance upon the Emperor of Blefuscu, I took this opportunity, before the three days were elapsed, to send a letter to my friend the Secretary, signifying my resolution of setting out that morning for Blefuscu pursuant to the leave I had got; and without waiting for an answer, I went to that side of the island where our fleet lay. I seized a large man of war, tied a cable to the prow, and, lifting up the anchors, I stripped myself, put my clothes (together with my coverlet, which I brought under my arm) into the vessel, and drawing it after me between wading and swimming, arrived at the royal port of Blefuscu, where the people had long expected me: they lent me two guides to direct me to the capital city, which is of the same name. I held them in my hands till I came within two hundred yards of the gate, and desired them to signify my arrival to one of the secretaries, and let him know, I there waited his Majesty's command. I had an answer in about an hour, that his Majesty, attended by the Royal Family, and great officers of the court, was coming out to receive me. I advanced a hundred yards. The Emperor and his train alighted from their horses, the Empress and ladies from their coaches, and I did not perceive they were in any fright or concern. I lay on the ground to kiss his Majesty's and the Empress's hands. I told his Majesty, that I was come according to my promise, and with the licence of the Emperor my master, to have the honour of seeing so mighty a monarch, and to offer him any service in my power, consistent with my duty to my own prince; not mentioning a word of my disgrace, because I had hitherto no regular information of it, and might suppose myself wholly ignorant of any such design; neither could I reasonably conceive that the Emperor would discover the secret while I was out of his power; wherein, however, it soon appeared I was deceived.

I shall not trouble the reader with the particular account of my reception at this court, which was suitable to the generosity of so great a prince; nor of the difficulties I was in for want of a house and bed, being forced to lie on the ground, wrapped up in my coverlet.

Chapter 8

The Author, by a lucky accident, finds means to leave Blefuscu; *and, after some difficulties, returns safe to his native country.*

THREE days after my arrival, walking out of curiosity to the north-east coast of the island, I observed, about half a league off, in the sea, somewhat that looked like a boat overturned. I pulled off my shoes and stockings, and wading two or three hundred yards, I found the object to approach nearer by force of the tide; and then plainly saw it to be a real boat, which I supposed might, by some tempest, have been driven from a ship; whereupon I returned immediately towards the city, and desired his Imperial Majesty to lend me twenty of the tallest vessels he had left after the loss of his fleet, and three thousand seamen under the command of his Vice-Admiral. This fleet sailed round, while I went back the shortest way to the coast where I first discovered the boat; I found the tide had driven it still nearer. The seamen were all provided with cordage, which I had beforehand twisted to a sufficient strength. When the ships came up, I stripped myself, and waded till I came within an hundred yards of the boat, after which I was forced to swim till I got up to it. The seamen threw me the end of the cord, which I fastened to a hole in the fore-part of the boat, and the other end to a man of war; but I found all my labour to little purpose; for being out of my depth, I was not able to work. In this necessity, I was forced to swim behind, and push the boat forwards as often as I could, with one of my hands; and the tide favouring me, I advanced so far, that I could just hold up my chin and feel the ground. I rested two or three minutes, and then gave the boat another shove, and so on till the sea was no higher than my arm-pits; and now the most laborious part being over, I took out my other cables, which were stowed in one of the ships, and fastening them first to the boat, and then to nine of the vessels which attended me; the wind being favourable, the seamen towed, and I shoved till we arrived within forty yards of the shore; and waiting till the tide was out, I got dry to the boat, and by the assistance of two thousand men, with ropes and engines, I made a shift to turn it on its bottom, and found it was but little damaged.

I shall not trouble the reader with the difficulties I was under by the help of certain paddles, which cost me ten days making, to get my boat to the royal port of Blefuscu, where a mighty concourse of people appeared upon my arrival, full of wonder at the sight of so prodigious a vessel. I told the Emperor that my good fortune had thrown this boat in my way, to carry me to some place from whence I might return into my native country, and begged his Majesty's orders for getting materials to fit it up, together with his licence to depart; which, after some kind expostulations, he was pleased to grant.

I did very much wonder, in all this time, not to have heard of any express relating to me from our Emperor to the court of Blefuscu. But I was afterwards given privately to understand, that his Imperial Majesty, never imagining I had the least notice of his designs, believed I was only gone to Blefuscu in performance of my promise, according to the licence he had given me, which was well known at our court, and would return in a few days when that ceremony was ended. But he was at last in pain at my long absence; and after consulting with the Treasurer, and the rest of that cabal, a person of quality was dispatched with the copy of the articles against me. This envoy had instructions to represent to the monarch of Blefuscu, the great lenity of his master, who was content to punish me no farther than with the loss of my eyes; that I had fled from justice, and if I did not return in two hours, I should be deprived of my title of *Nardac*, and declared a traitor. The envoy further added, that in order to maintain the peace and amity between both empires, his master expected, that his brother of Blefuscu would give orders to have me sent back to Lilliput, bound hand and foot, to be punished as a traitor.

The Emperor of Blefuscu having taken three days to consult, returned an answer consisting of many civilities and excuses. He said, that as for sending me bound, his brother knew it was impossible; that although I had deprived him of his fleet, yet he owed great obligations to me for many good offices I had done him in making the peace. That however both their Majesties would soon be made easy; for I had found a prodigious vessel on the shore, able to carry me on the sea, which he had given order to fit up with my own assistance and direction; and he hoped in a few weeks both empires would be freed from so insupportable an incumbrance.

With this answer the envoy returned to Lilliput, and the monarch of Blefuscu related to me all that had passed; offering me at the same time (but under the strictest confidence) his gracious protection, if I would continue in his service; wherein although I believed him sincere, yet I resolved never more to put any confidence in princes or ministers, where I could possibly avoid it; and therefore, with all due acknowledgements for his favourable intentions, I humbly begged to be excused. I told him, that since fortune, whether good or evil, had thrown a vessel in my way, I was resolved to venture myself in the ocean, rather than be an occasion of difference between two such mighty monarchs. Neither did I find the Emperor at all displeased; and I discovered by a certain accident, that he was very glad of my resolution, and so were most of his ministers.

These considerations moved me to hasten my departure somewhat sooner than I intended; to which the court, impatient to have me gone, very readily contributed. Five hundred workmen were employed to make two sails to my boat, according to my directions, by quilting thirteen fold of their strongest linen together. I was at the pains of making ropes and cables, by twisting ten, twenty or thirty of the thickest and strongest of theirs. A great stone that I happened to find, after a long search, by the sea-shore, served me for an anchor. I had the tallow of three hundred cows for greasing my boat, and other uses. I was at incredible pains in cutting down some of the largest timber-trees for oars and masts, wherein I was, however, much assisted by his Majesty's ship-carpenters, who helped me in smoothing them, after I had done the rough work.

In about a month, when all was prepared, I sent to receive his Majesty's commands, and take my leave. The Emperor and Royal Family came out of the palace; I lay down on my face to kiss his hand, which he very graciously gave me: so did the Empress and young Princes of the blood. His Majesty presented me with fifty purses of two hundred *sprugs* a-piece, together with his picture at full length, which I put immediately into one of my gloves, to keep it from being hurt. The ceremonies at my departure were too many to trouble the reader with at this time.

I stored the boat with the carcasses of an hundred oxen, and three hundred sheep, with bread and drink proportionable, and as much meat ready dressed as four hundred cooks could provide. I took with me six cows and two bulls alive, with as many ewes and rams, intending to carry them into my own country, and propagate the breed. And to feed them on board, I had a good bundle of hay, and a bag of corn. I would gladly have taken a dozen of the natives, but this was a thing the Emperor would by no means permit; and besides a diligent search into my pockets, his Majesty engaged my honour not to carry away any of his subjects, although with their own consent and desire.

Having thus prepared all things as well as I was able, I set sail on the twenty-fourth day of September 1701, at six in the morning; and when I had gone about four leagues to the northward, the wind being at south-east, at six in the evening I descried a small island about half a league to the north-west. I advanced forward, and cast anchor on the lee-side of the island, which seemed to be uninhabited. I then took some refreshment, and went to my rest. I slept well, and as I conjecture at least six hours, for I found the day broke in two hours after I awaked. It was a clear night. I eat my breakfast before the sun was up; and heaving anchor, the wind being favourable, I steered the same course that I had done the day before, wherein I was directed by my pocket-compass. My intention was to reach, if possible, one of those islands, which I had reason to believe lay to the north-east of Van Diemen's Land. I discovered nothing all that day; but upon the next, about three in the afternoon, when I had by my computation made twenty-four leagues from Blefuscu, I descried a sail steering to the south-east; my course was due east. I hailed her, but could get no answer; yet I found I gained upon her, for the wind slackened. I made all the sail I could, and in half an hour she spied me, then hung out her ancient, and discharged a gun. It is not easy to express the joy I was in upon the unexpected hope of once more seeing my beloved country, and the dear pledges I had left in it. The ship slackened her sails, and I came up with her between five and six in the evening, September 26; but my heart leaped within me to see her English colours. I put my cows and sheep into my coat-pockets, and got on board with all my little cargo of provisions. The vessel was an English merchantman, returning from Japan by the North and South Seas; the Captain, Mr. John Biddel of Deptford, a very civil man, and an excellent sailor. We were now in the latitude of 30 degrees south; there were about fifty men in the ship; and here I met an old comrade of mine, one Peter Williams, who gave me a good character to the Captain. This gentleman treated me with kindness, and desired I would let him know what place I came from last, and whither I was bound; which I did in a few words, but he thought I was raving, and that the dangers I underwent had disturbed my head; whereupon I took my black cattle and sheep out of my pocket, which, after great astonishment, clearly convinced him of my veracity. I then showed him the gold given me by the Emperor of Blefuscu, together with his Majesty's picture at full length, and some other rarities of that country. I gave him two purses of two hundred *sprugs* each, and promised, when we arrived in England, to make him a present of a cow and a sheep big with young.

I shall not trouble the reader with a particular account of this voyage, which was very prosperous for the most part. We arrived in the Downs on the 13th of April, 1702. I had only one misfortune, that the rats on board carried away one of my sheep; I found her bones in a hole, picked clean from the flesh. The rest of my cattle I got safe on shore, and set them a grazing in a bowling-green at Greenwich, where the fineness of the grass made them feed very heartily, though I had always feared the contrary: neither could I possibly have preserved them in so long a voyage, if the Captain had not allowed me some of his best biscuit, which, rubbed to powder, and mingled with water, was their constant food. The short time I continued in England, I made a considerable profit by showing my cattle to many persons of quality, and others: and before I began my second voyage, I sold them for six hundred pounds. Since my last return, I find the breed is considerably increased, especially the sheep; which I hope will prove much to the advantage of the woollen manufacture, by the fineness of the fleeces.

I stayed but two months with my wife and family; for my insatiable desire of seeing foreign countries would suffer me to continue no longer. I left fifteen hundred pounds with my wife, and fixed her in a good house at Redriff. My remaining stock I carried with me, part in money, and part in goods, in hopes to improve my fortunes. My eldest uncle John had left me an estate in land, near Epping, of about thirty pounds a year; and I had a long lease of the Black Bull in Fetter-Lane, which yielded me as much more; so that I was not in any danger of leaving my family upon the parish. My son Johnny, named so after his uncle, was at the Grammar School, and a towardly child. My daughter Betty (who is now well married, and has children) was then at her needle-work. I took leave of my wife, and boy and girl, with tears on both sides, and went on board the *Adventure*, a merchant-ship of three hundred tons, bound for Surat, Captain John Nicholas, of Liverpool, Commander. But my account of this voyage must be referred to the second part of my Travels.

23. ancient, flag, or ensign.

40. towardly, docile. **45. Surat,** north of Bombay, India.

A MODEST PROPOSAL

FOR PREVENTING THE CHILDREN OF POOR PEOPLE IN IRELAND FROM BEING A BURTHEN TO THEIR PARENTS OR COUNTRY, AND FOR MAKING THEM BENEFICIAL TO THE PUBLIC

1729

Swift's hatred of all cruelty is shown in this bitterly ironical pamphlet where he attacks the English for their brutal treatment of the Irish, whom he despised.

IT is a melancholy object to those who walk through this great town or travel in the country, when they see the streets, the roads, and cabin-doors, crowded with beggars of the female sex, followed by three, four, or six children, *all in rags*, and importuning every passenger for an alms. These mothers, instead of being able to work for their honest livelihood, are forced to employ all their time in strolling, to beg sustenance for their helpless infants, who, as they grow up, either turn thieves for want of work, or leave their dear native country to fight for the Pretender in Spain, or sell themselves to the Barbadoes.

I think it is agreed by all parties that this prodigious number of children, in the arms, or on the backs, or at the heels of their mothers, and frequently of their fathers, is in the present deplorable state of the kingdom a very great additional grievance; and therefore whoever could find out a fair, cheap, and easy method of making these children sound, useful members of the commonwealth, would deserve so well of the public as to have his statue set up for a preserver of the nation.

But my intention is very far from being confined to provide only for the children of professed beggars; it is of a much greater extent, and shall take in the whole number of infants at a certain age, who are born of parents in effect as little able to support them as those who demand our charity in the streets.

As to my own part, having turned my thoughts for many years upon this important subject, and maturely weighed the several schemes of other projectors, I have always found them grossly mistaken in their computation. It is true, a child, just dropped from its dam, may be supported by her milk for a solar year with little other nourishment, at most not above the value of two shillings, which the mother may certainly get, or the value in scraps, by her lawful occupation of begging; and it is exactly at one year old that I propose to provide for them in such a manner as instead of being a charge upon their parents or the parish, or wanting food and raiment for the rest of their lives, they shall, on the contrary, contribute to the feeding and partly to the clothing of many thousands.

There is likewise another great advantage in my scheme, that it will prevent those voluntary abortions, and that horrid practice of women murdering their bastard children, alas, too frequent among us, sacrificing the poor innocent babes, I doubt, more to avoid the expense than the shame, which would move tears and pity in the most savage and inhuman breast.

The number of souls in this kingdom being usually reckoned one million and a half, of these I calculate there may be about two hundred thousand couple whose wives are breeders; from which number I subtract thirty thousand couple who are able to maintain their own children, although I apprehend there cannot be so many under the present distresses of the kingdom; but this being granted, there will remain an hundred and seventy thousand breeders. I again subtract fifty thousand for those women who miscarry, or whose children die by accident or disease within the year. There only remain an hundred and twenty thousand children of poor parents annually born. The question therefore is, how this number shall be reared and provided for, which, as I have already said, under the present situation of affairs, is utterly impossible by all the methods hitherto proposed, for we can neither employ them in handicraft or agriculture; we neither build houses (I mean in the country) nor cultivate land; they can very seldom pick up a livelihood by stealing till they arrive at six years old, except where they are of towardly parts, although I confess they learn the rudiments much earlier, during which time, they can however be properly looked upon only as *probationers;* as I have been informed by a principal gentleman in the County of Cavan, who protested to me, that he never knew above one or two instances under the age of six, even in a part of the kingdom so renowned for the quickest proficiency in that art.

I am assured by our merchants that a boy or a girl before twelve years old is no saleable commodity, and even when they come to this age, they will not yield above three pounds, or three pounds and half-a-crown at most on the Exchange, which cannot turn to account either to the parents or kingdom, the charge of nutriment and rags having been at least four times that value.

15. this . . . town, Dublin. **25. the Pretender,** James Stuart, son of the deposed King James II, who was attempting to secure the British throne.

I shall now therefore humbly propose my own thoughts, which I hope will not be liable to the least objection.

I have been assured by a very knowing American of my acquaintance in London, that a young healthy child well nursed is at a year old a most delicious, nourishing, and wholesome food, whether stewed, roasted, baked, or boiled, and I make no doubt that it will equally serve in a fricassee or a ragout.

I do therefore humbly offer it to public consideration that of the hundred and twenty thousand children already computed, twenty thousand may be reserved for breed, whereof only one fourth part to be males, which is more than we allow to sheep, black cattle, or swine; and my reason is that these children are seldom the fruits of marriage, a circumstance not much regarded by our savages. Therefore one male will be sufficient to serve four females. That the remaining hundred thousand may at a year old be offered in sale to the persons of quality and fortune through the kingdom, always advising the mother to let them suck plentifully in the last month, so as to render them plump and fat for a good table. A child will make two dishes at an entertainment for friends, and when the family dines alone, the fore or hind quarter will make a reasonable dish, and seasoned with a little pepper or salt will be very good boiled on the fourth day, especially in winter.

I have reckoned, upon a medium, that a child just born will weigh 12 pounds, and in a solar year if tolerably nursed will increase to 28 pounds.

I grant this food will be somewhat dear, and therefore very proper for landlords, who, as they have already devoured most of the parents, seem to have the best title to the children.

Infants' flesh will be in season throughout the year, but more plentiful in March, and a little before and after, for we are told by a grave author, an eminent French physician, that fish being a prolific diet, there are more children born in Roman Catholic countries about nine months after Lent, than at any other season; therefore reckoning a year after Lent, the markets will be more glutted than usual, because the number of Popish infants is at least three to one in this kingdom, and therefore it will have one other collateral advantage, by lessening the number of Papists among us.

I have already computed the charge of nursing a beggar's child (in which list I reckon all cottagers, labourers, and four-fifths of the farmers) to be about two shillings *per annum*, rags included, and I believe no gentleman would repine to give ten shillings for the carcass of a good fat child, which, as I have said, will make four dishes of excellent nutritive meat, when he has only some particular friend or his own family to dine with him. Thus the squire will learn to be a good landlord, and grow popular among his tenants, the mother will have eight shillings net profit, and be fit for work till she produces another child.

Those who are more thrifty (as I must confess the times require) may flay the carcass; the skin of which, artificially dressed, will make admirable gloves for ladies, and summer boots for fine gentlemen.

As to our city of Dublin, shambles may be appointed for this purpose in the most convenient parts of it, and butchers we may be assured will not be wanting, although I rather recommend buying the children alive, and dressing them hot from the knife, as we do roasting pigs.

A very worthy person, a true lover of his country, and whose virtues I highly esteem, was lately pleased, in discoursing on this matter, to offer a refinement upon my scheme. He said, that many gentlemen of this kingdom having of late destroyed their deer, he conceived that the want of venison might be well supplied by the bodies of young lads and maidens, not exceeding fourteen years of age, nor under twelve, so great a number of both sexes in every country being now ready to starve, for want of work and service, and these to be disposed of by their parents if alive, or otherwise by their nearest relations. But with due deference to so excellent a friend, and so deserving a patriot, I cannot be altogether in his sentiments; for as to the males, my American acquaintance assured me from frequent experience, that their flesh was generally tough and lean, like that of our schoolboys, by continual exercise, and their taste disagreeable, and to fatten them would not answer the charge. Then as to the females, it would, I think with humble submission, be a loss to the public, because they soon would become breeders themselves. And besides, it is not improbable that some scrupulous people might be apt to censure such a practice (although indeed very unjustly), as a little bordering upon cruelty, which, I confess, has always been with me the strongest objection against any project, however so well intended.

But in order to justify my friend, he confessed that this expedient was put into his head by the famous Psalmanazar, a native of the island Formosa, who came from thence to London, above twenty years ago, and in conversation told my friend, that in his country when any young person

49. **Psalmanazar,** really a Frenchman, who published in 1704 a fictitious description of Formosa.

happened to be put to death, the executioner sold the carcass to persons of quality, as a prime dainty, and that, in his time, the body of a plump girl of fifteen, who was crucified for an attempt to poison the emperor, was sold to his Imperial Majesty's Prime Minister of State, and other great Mandarins of the Court, in joints from the gibbet, at four hundred crowns. Neither indeed can I deny, that if the same use were made of several plump young girls in this town, who, without one single groat to their fortunes, cannot stir abroad without a chair, and appear at the playhouse and assemblies in foreign fineries, which they never will pay for, the kingdom would not be the worse.

Some persons of a desponding spirit are in great concern about that vast number of poor people who are aged, diseased, or maimed, and I have been desired to employ my thoughts what course may be taken, to ease the nation of so grievous an encumbrance. But I am not in the least pain upon that matter, because it is very well known that they are every day dying and rotting, by cold, and famine, and filth, and vermin, as fast as can be reasonably expected. And as to the young labourers, they are now in as hopeful a condition. They cannot get work, and consequently pine away for want of nourishment, to a degree that if at any time they are accidentally hired to common labour, they have not strength to perform it; and thus the country and themselves are happily delivered from the evils to come.

I have too long digressed, and therefore shall return to my subject. I think the advantages by the proposal which I have made are obvious and many, as well as of the highest importance.

For first, as I have already observed, it would greatly lessen the number of Papists, with whom we are yearly over-run, being the principal breeders of the nation, as well as our most dangerous enemies, and who stay at home on purpose to deliver the kingdom to the Pretender, hoping to take their advantage by the absence of so many good Protestants, who have chosen rather to leave their country, than stay at home, and pay tithes against their conscience, to an Episcopal curate.

Secondly, The poorer tenants will have something valuable of their own, which by law may be made liable to distress, and help to pay their landlord's rent, their corn and cattle being already seized, and *money a thing unknown*.

Thirdly, Whereas the maintenance of an hundred thousand children, from two years old and upward, cannot be computed at less than ten shillings a piece per annum, the nation's stock will be thereby increased fifty thousand pounds *per annum*, besides the profit of a new dish, introduced to the tables of all gentlemen of fortune in the kingdom who have any refinement in taste, and the money will circulate among ourselves, the goods being entirely of our own growth and manufacture.

Fourthly, The constant breeders, beside the gain of eight shillings sterling *per annum*, by the sale of their children, will be rid of the charge of maintaining them after the first year.

Fifthly, This food would likewise bring great custom to taverns, where the vintners will certainly be so prudent as to procure the best receipts for dressing it to perfection, and consequently have their houses frequented by all the fine gentlemen who justly value themselves upon their knowledge in good eating; and a skilful cook, who understands how to oblige his guests, will contrive to make it as expensive as they please.

Sixthly, This would be a great inducement to marriage, which all wise nations have either encouraged by rewards, or enforced by laws and penalties. It would increase the care and tenderness of mothers toward their children, when they were sure of a settlement for life, to the poor babes, provided in some sort by the public, to their annual profit instead of expense. We should see an honest emulation among the married women, which of them could bring the fattest child to the market. Men would become as fond of their wives, during the time of their pregnancy, as they are now of their mares in foal, their cows in calf, their sows when they are ready to farrow, nor offer to beat or kick them (as is too frequent a practice) for fear of a miscarriage.

Many other advantages might be enumerated. For instance, the addition of some thousand carcasses in our exportation of barrelled beef, the propagation of swine's flesh, and improvement in the art of making good bacon, so much wanted among us by the great destruction of pigs, too frequent at our table, which are no way comparable in taste, or magnificence, to a well-grown, fat yearling child, which roasted whole will make a considerable figure at a Lord Mayor's feast, or any other public entertainment. But this and many others I omit, being studious of brevity.

Supposing that one thousand families in this city would be constant customers for infants' flesh, beside others who might have it at merry-meetings, particularly at weddings and christenings, I compute that Dublin would take off annually about twenty thousand carcasses; and the rest of the kingdom (where probably they will be sold somewhat cheaper) the remaining eighty thousand.

I can think of no one objection, that will possibly be raised against this proposal, unless it should be urged that the number of people will be thereby much lessened in the kingdom. This I freely own, and it was indeed one principal design in offering it to the world. I desire the reader will observe, that I calculate my remedy *for this one individual kingdom of Ireland, and for no other that ever was, is, or, I think, ever can be upon earth.* Therefore let no man talk to me of other expedients: *Of taxing our absentees at five shillings a pound: Of using neither clothes, nor household furniture, except what is of our own growth and manufacture: Of utterly rejecting the materials and instruments that promote foreign luxury: Of curing the expensiveness of pride, vanity, idleness, and gaming in our women: Of introducing a vein of parsimony, prudence and temperance: Of learning to love our Country, wherein we differ even from* Laplanders, *and the inhabitants of* Topinamboo: *Of quitting our animosities and factions, nor act any longer like the Jews, who were murdering one another at the very moment their city was taken: Of being a little cautious not to sell our country and conscience for nothing: Of teaching landlords to have at least one degree of mercy toward their tenants. Lastly of putting a spirit of honesty, industry, and skill into our shopkeepers, who, if a resolution could now be taken to buy only our native goods, would immediately unite to cheat and exact upon us in the price, the measure, and the goodness, nor could ever yet be brought to make one fair proposal of just dealing, though often and earnestly invited to it.*

Therefore I repeat, let no man talk to me of these and the like expedients till he hath at least some glimpse of hope that there will ever be some hearty and sincere attempt to put them in practice.

But as to myself, having been wearied out for many years with offering vain, idle, visionary thoughts, and at length utterly despairing of success, I fortunately fell upon this proposal, which as it is wholly new, so it hath something solid and real, of no expense and little trouble, full in our own power, and whereby we can incur no danger in *disobliging* ENGLAND. For this kind of commodity will not bear exportation, the flesh being of too tender a consistence to admit a long continuance in salt, *although perhaps I could name a country which would be glad to eat up our whole nation without it.*

After all, I am not so violently bent upon my own opinion as to reject any offer, proposed by wise men, which shall be found equally innocent, cheap, easy and effectual. But before something of that kind shall be advanced in contradiction to my scheme, and offering a better, I desire the author or authors will be pleased maturely to consider two points. First, as things now stand, how they will be able to find food and raiment for an hundred thousand useless mouths and backs. And secondly, there being a round million of creatures in human figure throughout this kingdom, whose whole subsistence put into a common stock would leave them in debt two million pounds sterling, adding those who are beggars by profession to the bulk of farmers, cottagers and labourers, with their wives and children, who are beggars in effect, I desire those politicians, who dislike my overture, and may perhaps be so bold as to attempt an answer, that they will first ask the parents of these mortals, whether they would not at this day think it a great happiness to have been sold for food at a year old, in the manner I prescribe, and thereby have avoided such a perpetual scene of misfortunes as they have since gone through by the oppression of landlords, the impossibility of paying rent without money or trade, the want of common sustenance, with neither house nor clothes to cover them from the inclemencies of the weather, and the most inevitable prospect of entailing the like or greater miseries upon their breed for ever.

I profess, in the sincerity of my heart, that I have not the least personal interest in endeavouring to promote this necessary work, having no other motive than the *public good of my country, by advancing our trade, providing for infants, relieving the poor, and giving some pleasure to the rich.* I have no children by which I can propose to get a single penny; the youngest being nine years old, and my wife past child-bearing.

18. Topinamboo, a district of Brazil supposedly inhabited by savages.

1. not bear exportation. "So that there would be no danger of an objection from England that the English were suffering from Irish competition."—Temple Scott.

Joseph Addison and Richard Steele

1672–1719 1672–1729

The lives of Addison and Steele were so closely interrelated, aside from the fact that the two were born within a few weeks of each other, that we can now scarcely think of either man without some thought of his companion. Steele was born in Dublin and Addison in a Wiltshire village, but both attended the Charterhouse School in London and went from there to Oxford. Each had a career of his own before their famous literary partnership began.

It was characteristic of Addison that after taking his degree he secured a fellowship at Magdalen College and lingered on there in the not very laborious life of a college Fellow—reading widely, conversing shyly, strolling every day along the path still known as Addison's Walk, drinking expensive wines, and writing unexceptionable verses in Latin and English. This, so far as his ambitions were concerned, might have gone on indefinitely, but the young man's somewhat uncommon ability as a versifier attracted the attention of a few leading Whigs when he was about twenty-seven, with the result that he was granted a comfortable pension in order that the Whig party might retain his literary services.

On the funds thus provided Addison spent some four years in European travel and study, thus making himself, according to the easy standards of his age, a rather learned and certainly a very cultivated man. Upon his return to England he repaid the generosity of the Whigs by writing for them a poem called "The Campaign" in celebration of the Duke of Marlborough's recent victory in the Battle of Blenheim. This poem, to our taste a cold and stilted performance, made his political and literary fortune. In 1713 he followed it with a classical tragedy, *Cato*, equally lifeless, and equally successful because of the sound political doctrines it was thought to uphold. In 1708 he had entered Parliament, of which he remained a member until his death. Other political offices came to him, the greatest of which was a Secretaryship of State in 1717, a year after his marriage to the Dowager Countess of Warwick.

Richard Steele, meanwhile, taking the very different path through life of a gay and companionable man, left Oxford without a degree to enter the army. Instead of an academic fellowship he won, before he was thirty, a captaincy. A little after the turn of the century he began to write for the London stage, where his *Lying Lover* and *Tender Husband*, both of them decent yet blithe and gay-hearted comedies, were well received. He held some minor offices of state during the later years of Queen Anne, but shortly after the accession of George I he was elected a member of Parliament, was dubbed a knight, and was granted several sinecures in the gift of the ruling Whig party. Perhaps the greatest honor of his life came in 1715, when he was made manager of Drury Lane Theatre. This prosperity, however, only increased his temptations to the reckless and spendthrift living which had always been his natural tendency. Financial and other troubles obliged him to leave London in 1723, and the last six years of his life were spent rather dismally in various provincial towns.

Addison and Steele came together in their fruitful partnership, lasting from April, 1709, to December, 1712, in their work on two periodicals, *The Tatler* and *The Spectator*. Their joint achievement in the familiar essay gained for them their unique place in literary history and in Sir Roger de Coverley gave to English literature one of its most attractive characters. One need not discuss here the relative merits of their work. Certainly Steele brought to the papers spontaneity, warmth, and initiative, and Addison's prose has hardly its equal for poise, grace, and subtlety. It was Steele who thought out the plan for the two papers—he who had always shown in his writing, if not in his conduct, a deep concern for the morals of London and England. He and Addison agreed—and so, no doubt, did the fifty or more miscellaneous persons who occasionally contributed essays or letters—that the main purpose of *The Tatler* and *The Spectator* was to improve, to mollify, to reform, the manners if not the morals of the English people. These two periodicals, although concerned only to a slight extent with what we should now call news, have an important place in the history of English journalism. Their influence on later periodicals, as on English social behavior, was considerable, and it was exerted not by the harsh methods of satire but by a gentle, good-humored raillery, a steady application of friendly laughter and common sense.

THE SPACIOUS FIRMAMENT ON HIGH

Addison's majestic hymn, based on the opening of the Nineteenth Psalm, is still frequently sung in churches to the familiar tune adapted from Haydn's oratorio *Creation.*

The spacious firmament on high,
With all the blue ethereal sky,
And spangled heavens, a shining frame,
Their great Original proclaim.
Th' unwearied Sun from day to day
Does his Creator's power display;
And publishes to every land
The work of an Almighty hand.

Soon as the evening shades prevail,
The Moon takes up the wondrous tale;
And nightly to the listening Earth
Repeats the story of her birth:
Whilst all the stars that round her burn,
And all the planets in their turn,
Confirm the tidings as they roll,
And spread the truth from pole to pole.

What though in solemn silence all
Move round the dark terrestrial ball;
What though no real voice nor sound
Amidst their radiant orbs be found?
In Reason's ear they all rejoice,
And utter forth a glorious voice;
Forever singing as they shine,
"The Hand that made us is divine."

from THE TATLER

NO. 181. JUNE 6, 1710 (Steele)

—Dies, ni fallor, adest, quem semper acerbum,
Semper honoratum, sic Dii voluistis, habebo.

THERE are those among mankind, who can enjoy no relish of their being, except the world is made acquainted with all that relates to them, and think every thing lost that passes unobserved; but others find a solid delight in stealing by the crowd, and modelling their life after such a manner as is as much above the approbation as the practice of the vulgar. Life being too short to give instances great enough of true friendship or good-will, some sages have thought it pious to preserve a certain reverence for the manes of their deceased friends, and have withdrawn themselves from the rest of the world at certain seasons to commemorate in their own thoughts such of their acquaintance who have gone before them out of this life: and indeed, when we are advanced in years, there is not a more pleasing entertainment, than to recollect in a gloomy moment the many we have parted with that have been dear and agreeable to us, and to cast a melancholy thought or two after those, with whom, perhaps, we have indulged our selves in whole nights of mirth and jollity. With such inclinations in my heart I went to my closet yesterday in the evening, and resolved to be sorrowful; upon which occasion I could not but look with disdain upon myself, that though all the reasons which I had to lament the loss of many of my friends are now as forcible as at the moment of their departure, yet did not my heart swell with the same sorrow which I felt at that time; but I could, without tears, reflect upon many pleasing adventures I have had with some, who have long been blended with common earth. Though it is by the benefit of nature that length of time thus blots out the violence of afflictions, yet with tempers too much given to pleasure, it is almost necessary to revive the old places of grief in our memory, and ponder step by step on past life, to lead the mind into that sobriety of thought which poises the heart, and makes it beat with due time, without being quickened with desire, or retarded with despair, from its proper and equal motion. When we wind up a clock that is out of order, to make it go well for the future, we do not immediately set the hand to the present instant, but we make it strike the round of all its hours, before it can recover the regularity of its time. Such, thought I, shall be my method this evening; and since it is that day of the year which I dedicate to the memory of such in another life as I much delighted in when living, an hour or two shall be sacred to sorrow and their memory, while I run over all the melancholy circumstances of this kind which have occurred to me in my whole life.

The first sense of sorrow I ever knew was upon the death of my father, at which time I was not quite five years of age; but was rather amazed at what all the house meant, than possessed with a real understanding why no body was willing to play with me. I remember I went into the room where his body lay, and my mother sate weeping alone by it. I had my battledore in my hand, and fell a-beating the coffin, and calling "Papa"; for, I know not how, I had some slight idea that he was locked up there. My mother catched me in her arms, and transported

40–41. *Dies . . . . habebo.* And now the rising day renews the year; A day for ever sad, for ever dear.—Dryden's trans. of Virgil's *Aeneid*, Book V, ll. 49–50.

1. manes, spirits. **13. closet,** small room for retirement.

beyond all patience of the silent grief she was before in, she almost smothered me in her embraces; and told me in a flood of tears, Papa could not hear me, and would play with me no more, for they were going to put him under ground whence he could never come to us again. She was a very beautiful woman, of a noble spirit, and there was a dignity in her grief amidst all the wildness of her transport, which, methought, struck me with an instinct of sorrow, which, before I was sensible of what it was to grieve, seized my very soul, and has made pity the weakness of my heart ever since. The mind in infancy is, methinks, like the body in embryo, and receives impressions so forcible that they are as hard to be removed by reason, as any mark with which a child is born is to be taken away by any future application. Hence it is that good nature in me is no merit; but, having been so frequently overwhelmed with her tears before I knew the cause of any affliction, or could draw defences from my own judgment, I imbibed commiseration, remorse, and an unmanly gentleness of mind, which has since insnared me into ten thousand calamities; and from whence I can reap no advantage, except it be that, in such a humour as I am now in, I can the better indulge my self in the softnesses of humanity, and enjoy that sweet anxiety which arises from the memory of past afflictions. . .

from THE SPECTATOR

NO. 2. FRIDAY, MARCH 2, 1711 (Steele)

——*Haec alii sex*
Vel plures uno conclamant ore.
Juv., Sat. VII, 167–8.

THE first of our society is a gentleman of Worcestershire, of ancient descent, a baronet, his name is Sir ROGER DE COVERLEY. His great grandfather was inventor of that famous country-dance which is called after him. All who know that shire are very well acquainted with the parts and merits of Sir ROGER. He is a gentleman that is very singular in his behaviour, but his singularities proceed from his good sense, and are contradictions to the manners of the world only as he thinks the world is in the wrong. However, this humour creates him no enemies, for he does nothing with sourness or obstinacy; and his being unconfined to modes and forms, makes him but the readier and more capable to please and oblige all who know him. When he is in town, he lives in Soho Square: It is said, he keeps himself a batchelour by reason he was crossed in love by a perverse beautiful widow of the next county to him. Before this disappointment, Sir ROGER was what you call a fine gentleman, had often supped with my Lord *Rochester* and *Sir George Etherege*, fought a duel upon his first coming to town, and kicked *Bully Dawson* in a public coffee-house for calling him youngster. But, being ill used by the abovementioned widow, he was very serious for a year and a half; and though, his temper being naturally jovial, he at last got over it, he grew careless of himself, and never dressed afterwards. He continues to wear a coat and doublet of the same cut that were in fashion at the time of his repulse, which, in his merry humours, he tells us, has been in and out twelve times since he first wore it. . . . He is now in his fifty-sixth year, cheerful, gay, and hearty; keeps a good house in both town and country; a great lover of mankind: but there is such a mirthful cast in his behaviour, that he is rather beloved than esteemed. His tenants grow rich, his servants look satisfied, all the young women profess love to him, and the young men are glad of his company. When he comes into a house he calls the servants by their names, and talks all the way up stairs to a visit. I must not omit, that Sir ROGER is a justice of the *quorum;* that he fills the chair at a quarter-session with great abilities, and three months ago, gained universal applause by explaining a passage in the game-act.

The gentleman next in esteem and authority among us is another batchelour, who is a member of the Inner Temple; a man of great probity, wit, and understanding; but he has chosen his place of residence rather to obey the direction of an old humoursome father, than in pursuit of his own inclinations. He was placed there to study the laws of the land, and is the most learned of any of the house in those of the stage. *Aristotle* and *Longinus* are much better understood by him than *Littleton* or *Cooke*. The father sends up every post questions relating to marriage-articles, leases, and tenures, in the neighbourhood; all which questions he agrees with an attorney to answer and take care of in the lump. He is studying the passions themselves, when he should be inquiring into the debates among men which arise from them. He knows the argument of each of the orations of *Demosthenes* and *Tully;* but not one case in the reports of our own courts. No one ever took him for a fool, but none, except his intimate

33–34. Haec . . . ore. Six others or more cry out with one voice. **52. Soho Square,** at the time, a fashionable district.

5. Rochester . . . Etherege, wits and men of letters of the Restoration period. **7. Dawson,** a notorious gambler. **33. Inner Temple,** one of the Inns of Court, a haunt of lawyers. **40. Littleton . . . Cooke** (Coke), authorities on matters of law. **48. Tully,** Cicero.

friends, know he has a great deal of wit. This turn makes him at once both disinterested and agreeable. As few of his thoughts are drawn from business, they are most of them fit for conversation. His taste of books is a little too just for the age he lives in; he has read all, but approves of very few. His familiarity with the customs, manners, actions, and writings of the ancients, makes him a very delicate observer of what occurs to him in the present world. He is an excellent critick, and the time of the play is his hour of business; exactly at five he passes through New Inn, crosses through Russell Court, and takes a turn at Will's till the play begins; he has his shoes rubbed, and his periwig powdered at the barber's as you go into the Rose. It is for the good of the audience when he is at a play; for the actors have an ambition to please him.

The person of next consideration is Sir Andrew Freeport, a merchant of great eminence in the city of London: a person of indefatigable industry, strong reason, and great experience. His notions of trade are noble and generous, and (as every rich man has usually some sly way of jesting, which would make no great figure were he not a rich man) he calls the sea the *British Common.* He is acquainted with commerce in all its parts, and will tell you that it is a stupid and barbarous way to extend dominion by arms, for true power is to be got by arts and industry. He will often argue, that if this part of our trade were well cultivated, we should gain from one nation; and if another, from another. I have heard him prove that diligence makes more lasting acquisitions than valour, and that sloth has ruined more nations than the sword. He abounds in several frugal maxims, amongst which the greatest favourite is, "A penny saved is a penny got." A general trader of good sense is pleasanter company than a general scholar; and Sir Andrew having a natural unaffected eloquence, the perspicuity of his discourse gives the same pleasure that wit would in another man. He has made his fortunes himself; and says that England may be richer than other kingdoms, by as plain methods as he himself is richer than other men; though at the same time I can say this of him, that there is not a point in the compass, but blows home a ship in which he is an owner.

Next to Sir Andrew in the club-room sits Captain Sentry, a gentleman of great courage, good understanding, but invincible modesty. He is one of those that deserve very well, but are very awkward at putting their talents within the observation of such as should take notice of them. He was some years a captain, and behaved himself with great gallantry in several engagements and at several sieges; but having a small estate of his own, and being next heir to Sir Roger, he has quitted a way of life in which no man can rise suitably to his merit who is not something of a courtier as well as a soldier. I have heard him often lament, that in a profession where merit is placed in so conspicuous a view, impudence should get the better of modesty. When he has talked to this purpose, I never heard him make a sour expression, but frankly confess that he left the world, because he was not fit for it. A strict honesty and an even regular behaviour are in themselves obstacles to him that must press through crowds who endeavour at the same end with himself, the favour of a commander. He will, however, in this way of talk, excuse generals, for not disposing according to men's desert, or enquiring into it: for, says he, that great man who has a mind to help me, has as many to break through to come at me as I have to come at him: therefore, he will conclude, that the man who would make a figure, especially in a military way, must get over all false modesty, and assist his patron against the importunity of other pretenders, by a proper assurance in his own vindication. He says it is a civil cowardice to be backward in asserting what you ought to expect, as it is a military fear to be slow in attacking when it is your duty. With this candour does the gentleman speak of himself and others. The same frankness runs through all his conversation. The military part of his life has furnished him with many adventures, in the relation of which he is very agreeable to the company; for he is never overbearing, though accustomed to command men in the utmost degree below him; nor ever too obsequious, from an habit of obeying men highly above him.

But that our society may not appear a set of humourists unacquainted with the gallantries and pleasures of the age, we have among us the gallant Will. Honeycomb, a gentleman who, according to his years, should be in the decline of his life, but having ever been very careful of his person, and always had a very easy fortune, time has made but very little impression, either by wrinkles on his forehead, or traces on his brain. His person is well turned, of a good height. He is very ready at that sort of discourse with which men usually entertain women. He has all his life dressed very well, and remembers habits as others do men. He can smile when one speaks to him, and laughs easily. He knows the history of every mode, and can inform you from which of the French king's wenches our wives and daughters had this manner of curling

13. Will's, a coffeehouse.

their hair, that way of placing their hoods . . . and whose vanity to shew her foot made that part of the dress so short in such a year. In a word, all his conversation and knowledge has been in the female world: as other men of his age will take notice to you what such a minister said upon such and such an occasion, he will tell you when the Duke of *Monmouth* danced at court, such a woman was then smitten, another was taken with him at the head of his troop in the Park. In all these important relations, he has ever about the same time received a kind glance, or a blow of a fan, from some celebrated beauty, mother of the present Lord Such-a-one. . . . This way of talking of his, very much enlivens the conversation among us of a more sedate turn; and I find there is not one of the company but myself, who rarely speak at all, but speaks of him as of that sort of man who is usually called a well-bred fine gentleman. To conclude his character, where women are not concerned, he is an honest worthy man.

I cannot tell whether I am to account him whom I am next to speak of, as one of our company; for he visits us but seldom, but when he does, it adds to every man else a new enjoyment of himself. He is a clergyman, a very philosophick man, of general learning, great sanctity of life, and the most exact good breeding. He has the misfortune to be of a very weak constitution; and consequently cannot accept of such cares and business as preferments in his function would oblige him to. He is therefore among divines what a chamber-counsellor is among lawyers. The probity of his mind, and the integrity of his life, create him followers, as being eloquent or loud advances others. He seldom introduces the subject he speaks upon; but we are so far gone in years, that he observes when he is among us an earnestness to have him fall on some divine topick, which he always treats with much authority, as one who has no interests in this world, as one who is hastening to the object of all his wishes, and conceives hope from his decays and infirmities. These are my ordinary companions. R.

NO. 10. MONDAY, MARCH 12, 1711 (Addison)

Non aliter quàm qui adverso vix flumine lembum
Remigiis subigit; si brachia fortè remisit,
Atque illum in praeceps prono rapit alveus amni.

It is with much satisfaction that I hear this great city inquiring day by day after these my papers, and receiving my morning lectures with a becoming seriousness and attention. My publisher tells me, that there are already three thousand of them distributed every day: so that if I allow twenty readers to every paper, which I look upon as a modest computation, I may reckon about threescore thousand disciples in *London* and *Westminster*, who I hope will take care to distinguish themselves from the thoughtless herd of their ignorant and inattentive brethren. Since I have raised to myself so great an audience, I shall spare no pains to make their instruction agreeable, and their diversion useful. For which reasons I shall endeavour to enliven morality with wit, and to temper wit with morality, that my readers may, if possible, both ways find their account in the speculation of the day. And to the end that their virtue and discretion may not be short, transient, intermitting starts of thought, I have resolved to refresh their memories from day to day, till I have recovered them out of that desperate state of vice and folly, into which the age is fallen. The mind that lies fallow for a single day, sprouts up in follies that are only to be killed by a constant and assiduous culture. It was said of *Socrates*, that he brought philosophy down from heaven, to inhabit among men; and I shall be ambitious to have it said of me, that I have brought philosophy out of closets and libraries, schools and colleges, to dwell in clubs and assemblies, at tea-tables, and in coffee-houses.

I would therefore in a very particular manner recommend these my speculations to all well-regulated families, that set apart an hour in every morning for tea and bread and butter; and would earnestly advise them for their good to order this paper to be served up, and to be looked upon as a part of the tea equipage.

Sir *Francis Bacon* observes, that a well-written book, compared with its rivals and antagonists, is like *Moses's* serpent, that immediately swallowed up and devoured those of the *Aegyptians*. I shall not be so vain as to think, that where the SPECTATOR appears, the other publick prints will vanish; but shall leave it to my reader's consideration, whether it is not much better to be let into the knowledge of one's-self, than to hear what passes in *Muscovy* or *Poland;* and to amuse our selves with such writings as tend to the wearing out of ignorance, passion, and prejudice, than such as naturally conduce to inflame hatreds, and make enmities irreconcilable.

In the next place, I would recommend this paper to the daily perusal of those gentlemen whom I cannot but consider as my good brothers and allies, I

47–49. Non . . . amni.
So the boat's brawny crew the current stem,
And, slow advancing, struggle with the stream;
But if they slack their hands, or cease to strive,
Then down the flood with headlong haste they drive.
—Dryden's translation of Virgil, *Georgics*, I, 201–203.

mean the fraternity of Spectators, who live in the world without having any thing to do in it; and either by the affluence of their fortunes, or laziness of their dispositions, have no other business with the rest of mankind but to look upon them. Under this class of men are comprehended all contemplative tradesmen, titular physicians, fellows of the Royal Society, Templars that are not given to be contentious, and statesmen that are out of business. In short, every one that considers the world as a theatre, and desires to form a right judgment of those who are the actors on it.

There is another set of men that I must likewise lay a claim to, whom I have lately called the blanks of society, as being altogether unfurnished with ideas, till the business and conversation of the day has supplied them. I have often considered these poor souls with an eye of great commiseration, when I have heard them asking the first man they have met with, whether there was any news stirring, and by that means gathering together materials for thinking. These needy persons do not know what to talk of, till about twelve a'clock in the morning; for by that time they are pretty good judges of the weather, know which way the wind sits, and whether the Dutch mail be come in. As they lie at the mercy of the first man they meet, and are grave or impertinent all the day long, according to the notions which they have imbibed in the morning, I would earnestly entreat them not to stir out of their chambers till they have read this paper, and do promise them that I will daily instil into them such sound and wholesome sentiments, as shall have a good effect upon their conversation for the ensuing twelve hours.

But there are none to whom this paper will be more useful than to the female world. I have often thought there has not been sufficient pains taken in finding out proper employment and diversions for the fair ones. Their amusements seem contrived for them rather as they are women, than as they are reasonable creatures; and are more adapted to the sex than to the species. The toilet is their great scene of business, and the right adjusting of their hair the principal employment of their lives. The sorting of a suit of ribbons is reckoned a very good morning's work; and if they make an excursion to a mercer's or a toy-shop, so great a fatigue makes them unfit for any thing else all the day after. Their more serious occupations are sewing and embroidery, and their greatest drudgery the preparation of jellies and sweet-meats. This, I say, is the state of ordinary women; though I know there are multitudes of those of a more elevated life and conversation, that move in an exalted sphere of knowledge and virtue, that join all the beauties of the mind to the ornaments of dress, and inspire a kind of awe and respect, as well as love, into their male-beholders. I hope to increase the number of these by publishing this daily paper, which I shall always endeavour to make an innocent if not an improving entertainment, and by that means at least divert the minds of my female readers from greater trifles. At the same time, as I would fain give some finishing touches to those which are already the most beautiful pieces in humane nature, I shall endeavour to point out all those imperfections that are the blemishes, as well as those virtues which are the embellishments, of the sex. In the mean while I hope these my gentle readers, who have so much time on their hands, will not grudge throwing away a quarter of an hour in a day upon this paper, since they may do it without any hindrance to business.

I know several of my friends and well-wishers are in great pain for me, lest I should not be able to keep up the spirit of a paper which I oblige myself to furnish every day: but to make them easy in this particular, I will promise them faithfully to give it over as soon as I grow dull. This I know will be a matter of great raillery to the small wits; who will frequently put me in mind of my promise, desire me to keep my word, assure me that it is high time to give over, with many other little pleasantries of the like nature, which men of a little smart genius cannot forbear throwing out against their best friends when they have such a handle given them of being witty. But let them remember, that I do hereby enter my caveat against this piece of raillery.

NO. 109. THURSDAY, JULY 5, 1711 (Steele)

Abnormis sapiens—Hor., 2 Sat. ii, 3.

I WAS this morning walking in the gallery, when Sir ROGER entered at the end opposite to me, and, advancing towards me, said he was glad to meet me among his relations the DE COVERLEYS, and hoped I liked the conversation of so much good company, who were as silent as myself. I knew he alluded to the pictures, and as he is a gentleman who does not a little value himself upon his ancient descent, I expected he would give me some ac-

8. Templars, students of law, or lawyers, so called because of living in the Temple in London.

37. caveat, warning—"let him beware." **41. Abnormis sapiens.** Of plain good sense, untutored in the schools. **43. gallery,** at Sir Roger's country house.

count of them. We were now arrived at the upper end of the gallery, when the Knight faced towards one of the pictures, and as we stood before it, he entered into the matter, after his blunt way of saying things, as they occur to his imagination, without regular introduction, or care to preserve the appearance of chain of thought.

"It is," said he, "worth while to consider the force of dress; and how the persons of one age differ from those of another, merely by that only. One may observe also, that the general fashion of one age has been followed by one particular set of people in another, and by them preserved from one generation to another. Thus the vast jetting coat and small bonnet, which was the habit in Harry the Seventh's time, is kept on the Yeomen of the Guard; not without a good and politick view, because they look a foot taller, and a foot and a half broader: besides that the cap leaves the face expanded, and consequently more terrible, and fitter to stand at the entrance of palaces.

"This predecessor of ours, you see, is dressed after this manner, and his cheeks would be no larger than mine, were he in a hat as I am. He was the last man that won a prize in the Tilt-yard (which is now a common street before Whitehall). You see the broken lance that lies there by his right foot. He shivered that lance of his adversary all to pieces; and bearing himself, look you, Sir, in this manner, at the same time he came within the target of the gentleman who rode against him, and taking him with incredible force before him on the pommel of his saddle, he in that manner rid the tournament over, with an air that showed he did it rather to perform the rule of the lists, than expose his enemy; however, it appeared he knew how to make use of a victory, and with a gentle trot he marched up to a gallery where their mistress sat (for they were rivals) and let him down with laudable courtesy and pardonable insolence. I do not know but it might be exactly where the coffee-house is now.

"You are to know this my ancestor was not only of a military genius, but fit also for the arts of peace, for he played on the bass-viol as well as any gentleman at court; you see where his viol hangs by his basket-hilt sword. The action at the Tilt-yard you may be sure won the fair lady, who was a maid of honour and the greatest beauty of her time; here she stands, the next picture. You see, Sir, my great-great-great-grandmother has on the new-fashioned petticoat, except that the modern is gathered at the waist; my grandmother appears as if she stood in a large drum, whereas the ladies now walk as if they were in a go-cart. For all this lady was bred at court, she made an excellent country-wife; she brought ten children, and when I shew you the library, you shall see in her own hand (allowing for the difference of the language) the best receipt now in England for a hasty-pudding and a white-pot.

"If you please to fall back a little, because 'tis necessary to look at the three next pictures at one view; these are three sisters. She on the right hand, who is so very beautiful, died a maid; the next to her, still handsomer, had the same fate, against her will; this homely thing in the middle had both their portions added to her own, and was stolen by a neighbouring gentleman, a man of stratagem and resolution; for he poisoned three mastiffs to come at her, and knocked down two deer-stealers in carrying her off. Misfortunes happen in all families. The theft of this romp and so much money, was no great matter to our estate. But the next heir that possessed it was this soft gentleman, whom you see there. Observe the small buttons, the little boots, the laces, the slashes about his clothes, and above all the posture he is drawn in (which to be sure was his own choosing); you see he sits with one hand on a desk, writing, and looking as it were another way, like an easy writer, or a sonneteer. He was one of those that had too much wit to know how to live in the world. He was a man of no justice, but great good manners; he ruined every body that had any thing to do with him, but never said a rude thing in his life; the most indolent person in the world, he would sign a deed that passed away half his estate with his gloves on, but would not put on his hat before a lady if it were to save his country. He is said to be the first that made love by squeezing the hand. He left the estate with ten thousand pounds' debt upon it, but, however, by all hands I have been informed, that he was every way the finest gentleman in the world. That debt lay heavy on our house for one generation, but it was retrieved by a gift from that honest man you see there, a citizen of our name, but nothing at all akin to us. I know Sir ANDREW FREEPORT has said behind my back, that this man was descended from one of the ten children of the maid of honour I shewed you above; but it was never made out. We winked at the thing indeed, because money was wanting at that time."

Here I saw my friend a little embarrassed, and turned my face to the next portraiture.

Sir ROGER went on with his account of the gallery in the following manner. "This man" (pointing to him I looked at) "I take to be the honour of our

17. Guard, the bodyguard of the English sovereign.
33. rid, rode.

7. white-pot, a dish somewhat like a bread pudding

house, Sir HUMPHREY DE COVERLEY. He was in his dealings as punctual as a tradesman, and as generous as a gentleman. He would have thought himself as much undone by breaking his word, as if it were to be followed by bankruptcy. He served his country as a knight of the shire to his dying day. He found it no easy matter to maintain an integrity in his words and actions, even in things that regarded the offices which were incumbent upon him, in the care of his own affairs and relations of life; and therefore dreaded (though he had great talents) to go into employments of state, where he must be exposed to the snares of ambition. Innocence of life and great ability were the distinguishing parts of his character; the latter, he had often observed, had led to the destruction of the former, and he used frequently to lament that great and good had not the same signification. He was an excellent husbandman, but had resolved not to exceed such a degree of wealth; all above it he bestowed in secret bounties many years after the sum he aimed at for his own use was attained. Yet he did not slacken his industry, but to a decent old age spent the life and fortune which were superfluous to himself, in the service of his friends and neighbours."

Here we were called to dinner, and Sir ROGER ended the discourse of this gentleman, by telling me, as we followed the servant, that this his ancestor was a brave man, and narrowly escaped being killed in the civil wars; "for," said he, "he was sent out of the field with a private message, the day before the battle of Worcester." The whim of narrowly escaping by having been within a day of danger, with other matters above-mentioned, mixed with good sense, left me at a loss whether I was more delighted with my friend's wisdom or simplicity.

NO. 112. MONDAY, JULY 9, 1711 (Addison)

'Αθανάτους μὲν πρῶτα θεοὺς, νόμῳ ὡς διάκειται,
Τίμα. —Pyth.

I AM always very well pleased with a country Sunday, and think, if keeping holy the seventh day were only a human institution, it would be the best method that could have been thought of for the polishing and civilizing of mankind. It is certain the country-people would soon degenerate into a kind of savages and barbarians, were there not such frequent returns of a stated time, in which the whole village meet together with their best faces, and in their cleanliest habits, to converse with one another upon indifferent subjects, hear their duties explained to them, and join together in adoration of the Supreme Being. Sunday clears away the rust of the whole week, not only as it refreshes in their minds the notions of religion, but as it puts both the sexes upon appearing in their most agreeable forms, and exerting all such qualities as are apt to give them a figure in the eye of the village. A country-fellow distinguishes himself as much in the church-yard, as a citizen does upon the 'Change, the whole parish-politicks being generally discussed in that place either after sermon or before the bell rings.

My friend Sir ROGER, being a good churchman, has beautified the inside of his church with several texts of his own chusing: he has likewise given a handsome pulpit-cloth, and railed in the communion-table at his own expence. He has often told me that at his coming to his estate he found his parishioners very irregular; and that in order to make them kneel and join in the responses, he gave every one of them a hassock and a common-prayer book: and at the same time employed an itinerant singing-master, who goes about the country for that purpose, to instruct them rightly in the tunes of the psalms; upon which they now very much value themselves, and indeed out-do most of the country churches that I have ever heard.

As Sir ROGER is landlord to the whole congregation, he keeps them in very good order, and will suffer no body to sleep in it besides himself; for if by chance he has been surprised into a short nap at sermon, upon recovering out of it he stands up and looks about him, and if he sees any body else nodding, either wakes them himself, or sends his servant to them. Several other of the old Knight's particularities break out upon these occasions: sometimes he will be lengthening out a verse in the singing-psalms, half a minute after the rest of the congregation have done with it; sometimes, when he is pleased with the matter of his devotion, he pronounces *Amen* three or four times to the same prayer; and sometimes stands up when every body else is upon their knees, to count the congregation, or see if any of his tenants are missing.

I was yesterday very much surprised to hear my old friend, in the midst of the service, calling out to one *John Matthews* to mind what he was about, and not disturb the congregation. This *John Matthews* it seems is remarkable for being an idle fellow, and at that time was kicking his heels for his diversion. This authority of the Knight, though exerted in that odd manner which accompanies him in all circumstances of life, has a very good effect upon the par-

41–2. 'Αθανάτους . . . Τίμα. "First, in obedience to thy country's rites, worship the immortal gods."—Pythagoras ish, who are not polite enough to see any thing ridiculous in his behaviour; besides that the general good sense and worthiness of his character makes his friends observe these little singularities as foils that rather set off than blemish his good qualities.

As soon as the sermon is finished, no body presumes to stir till Sir ROGER is gone out of the church. The Knight walks down from his seat in the chancel between a double row of his tenants, that stand bowing to him on each side; and every now and then enquires how such an one's wife, or mother, or son, or father do, whom he does not see at church; which is understood as a secret reprimand to the person that is absent.

The chaplain has often told me, that upon a catechising-day, when Sir ROGER has been pleased with a boy that answers well, he has ordered a Bible to be given him next day for his encouragement; and sometimes accompanies it with a flitch of bacon to his mother. Sir ROGER has likewise added five pounds a year to the clerk's place; and that he may encourage the young fellows to make themselves perfect in the church-service, has promised, upon the death of the present incumbent, who is very old, to bestow it according to merit.

The fair understanding between Sir ROGER and his chaplain, and their mutual concurrence in doing good, is the more remarkable, because the very next village is famous for the differences and contentions that rise between the parson and the 'squire, who live in a perpetual state of war. The parson is always preaching at the 'squire, and the 'squire to be revenged on the parson never comes to church. The 'squire has made all his tenants atheists, and tithe-stealers; while the parson instructs them every Sunday in the dignity of his order, and insinuates to them in almost every sermon, that he is a better man than his patron. In short matters have come to such an extremity, that the 'squire has not said his prayers either in publick or private this half year; and that the parson threatens him, if he does not mend his manners, to pray for him in the face of the whole congregation.

Feuds of this nature, though too frequent in the country, are very fatal to the ordinary people; who are so used to be dazzled with riches, that they pay as much deference to the understanding of a man of an estate, as of a man of learning; and are very hardly brought to regard any truth, how important soever it may be, that is preached to them, when they know there are several men of five hundred a year who do not believe it.

1. polite, polished, sophisticated.

NO. 122. FRIDAY, JULY 20, 1711 (Addison)

Comes jucundus in via pro vehiculo est.—PUBLILIUS SYRUS.

A MAN'S first care should be to avoid the reproaches of his own heart; his next, to escape the censures of the world. If the last interferes with the former, it ought to be entirely neglected; but otherwise, there cannot be a greater satisfaction to an honest mind, than to see those approbations which it gives itself seconded by the applauses of the publick: a man is more sure of his conduct, when the verdict which he passes upon his own behaviour is thus warranted and confirmed by the opinion of all that know him.

My worthy friend Sir ROGER is one of those who is not only at peace within himself, but beloved and esteemed by all about him. He receives a suitable tribute for his universal benevolence to mankind, in the returns of affection and good-will, which are paid him by every one that lives within his neighbourhood. I lately met with two or three odd instances of that general respect which is shewn to the good old Knight. He would needs carry *Will. Wimble* and myself with him to the county assizes. As we were upon the road *Will. Wimble* joined a couple of plain men who rid before us, and conversed with them for some time; during which my friend Sir ROGER acquainted me with their characters.

"The first of them," says he, "that has a spaniel by his side, is a yeoman of about an hundred pounds a year, an honest man: he is just within the game-act, and qualified to kill an hare or a pheasant: he knocks down a dinner with his gun twice or thrice a week: and by that means lives much cheaper than those who have not so good an estate as himself. He would be a good neighbour if he did not destroy so many partridges: in short he is a very sensible man, shoots flying; and has been several times foreman of the petty-jury.

"The other that rides along with him is *Tom Touchy*, a fellow famous for taking the law of every body. There is not one in the town where he lives that he has not sued at a quarter-sessions. The rogue had once the impudence to go to law with the widow. His head is full of costs, damages, and ejectments: he plagued a couple of honest gentlemen so

3. Comes . . . est. A merry companion is as good on the road as a coach. **26. assizes,** periodical sessions of a local court. **33. yeoman,** small landowner. **46. quarter-sessions,** a court of limited jurisdiction held in English counties every three months. **48. widow,** a woman with whom Sir Roger had once been in love.

long for a trespass in breaking one of his hedges, till he was forced to sell the ground it enclosed to defray the charges of the prosecution: his father left him fourscore pounds a year; but he has cast and been cast so often, that he is not now worth thirty. I suppose he is going upon the old business of the willow-tree."

As Sir Roger was giving me this account of *Tom Touchy*, *Will. Wimble* and his two companions stopped short till we came up to them. After having paid their respects to Sir Roger, *Will.* told him that Mr. *Touchy* and he must appeal to him upon a dispute that arose between them. *Will.* it seems had been giving his fellow-traveller an account of his angling one day in such a hole; when *Tom Touchy*, instead of hearing out his story, told him that Mr. Such-an-one, if he pleased, might take the law of him for fishing in that part of the river. My friend Sir Roger heard them both upon a round trot; and after having paused some time told them, with the air of a man who would not give his judgment rashly, that *much might be said on both sides.* They were neither of them dissatisfied with the Knight's determination, because neither of them found himself in the wrong by it; upon which we made the best of our way to the assizes.

The court was sat before Sir Roger came; but, notwithstanding all the justices had taken their places upon the bench, they made room for the old Knight at the head of them; who for his reputation in the country took occasion to whisper in the judge's ear that he was glad his lordship had met with so much good weather in his circuit. I was listening to the proceedings of the court with much attention, and infinitely pleased with that great appearance and solemnity which so properly accompanies such a publick administration of our laws; when, after about an hour's sitting, I observed to my great surprize, in the midst of a trial, that my friend Sir Roger was getting up to speak. I was in some pain for him, till I found he had acquitted himself of two or three sentences with a look of much business and great intrepidity.

Upon his first rising the court was hushed, and a general whisper ran among the country people that Sir Roger *was up.* The speech he made was so little to the purpose, that I shall not trouble my readers with an account of it; and I believe was not so much designed by the Knight himself to inform the court as to give him a figure in my eye, and keep up his credit in the country.

I was highly delighted, when the court rose, to see the gentlemen of the country gathering about my old friend, and striving who should compliment him most; at the same time that the ordinary people gazed upon him at a distance, not a little admiring his courage, that was not afraid to speak to the judge.

In our return home we met with a very odd accident; which I cannot forbear relating, because it shews how desirous all who know Sir Roger are of giving him marks of their esteem. When we were arrived upon the verge of his estate, we stopped at a little inn to rest our selves and our horses. The man of the house had it seems been formerly a servant in the Knight's family; and to do honour to his old master, had some time since, unknown to Sir Roger, put him up in a sign-post before the door; so that the *Knight's Head* had hung out upon the road about a week before he himself knew anything of the matter. As soon as Sir Roger was acquainted with it, finding that his servant's indiscretion proceeded wholly from affection and good-will, he only told him that he had made him too high a compliment, and when the fellow seemed to think that could hardly be, added with a more decisive look, that it was too great an honour for any man under a duke; but told him at the same time, that it might be altered with a very few touches, and that he himself would be at the charge of it. Accordingly they got a painter by the Knight's directions to add a pair of whiskers to the face, and by a little aggravation to the features to change it into the *Saracen's Head.* I should not have known this story had not the innkeeper, upon Sir Roger's alighting, told him in my hearing, that his honour's head was brought back last night with the alterations that he had ordered to be made in it. Upon this my friend with his usual cheerfulness related the particulars above-mentioned, and ordered the head to be brought into the room. I could not forbear discovering greater expressions of mirth than ordinary upon the appearance of this monstrous face, under which, notwithstanding it was made to frown and stare in a most extraordinary manner, I could still discover a distant resemblance of my old friend. Sir Roger, upon seeing me laugh, desired me to tell him truly if I thought it possible for people to know him in that disguise. I at first kept my usual silence; but upon the Knight's conjuring me to tell him whether it was not still more like himself than a Saracen, I composed my countenance in the best manner I could, and replied that *much might be said on both sides.*

These several adventures, with the Knight's behaviour in them, gave me as pleasant a day as ever I met with in any of my travels.

4. **cast,** to defeat in a lawsuit.

NO. 159. SATURDAY, SEPTEMBER 1, 1711
(Addison)

. . . omnem, quae nunc obducta tuenti
Mortales hebetat visus tibi, et humida circum
Caligat, nubem eripiam. . . .
—Virg. *Æneid.*

When I was at *Grand Cairo,* I picked up several Oriental manuscripts, which I have still by me. Among others I met with one, entitled *The Visions of Mirzah,* which I have read over with great pleasure. I intend to give it to the publick when I have no other entertainment for them; and shall begin with the first vision, which I have translated word for word as follows:

"On the fifth day of the moon, which according to the custom of my forefathers I always keep holy, after having washed myself, and offered up my morning devotions, I ascended the high hills of *Bagdat,* in order to pass the rest of the day in meditation and prayer. As I was here airing myself on the tops of the mountains, I fell into a profound contemplation on the vanity of human life; and passing from one thought to another, Surely, said I, man is but a shadow and life a dream. Whilst I was thus musing, I cast my eyes towards the summit of a rock that was not far from me, where I discovered one in the habit of a shepherd, with a little musical instrument in his hand. As I looked upon him he applied it to his lips, and began to play upon it. The sound of it was exceeding sweet, and wrought into a variety of tunes that were inexpressibly melodious, and altogether different from any thing I had ever heard. They put me in mind of those heavenly airs that are played to the departed souls of good men upon their first arrival in Paradise, to wear out the impressions of the last agonies, and qualify them for the pleasures of that happy place. My heart melted away in secret raptures.

"I had been often told that the rock before me was the haunt of a Genius; and that several had been entertained with musick who had passed by it, but never heard that the musician had before made himself visible. When he had raised my thoughts, by those transporting airs which he played, to taste the pleasures of his conversation, as I looked upon him like one astonished, he beckoned to me, and by the waving of his hand directed me to approach the place where he sat. I drew near with that reverence which is due to a superior nature; and as my heart was entirely subdued by the captivating strains I had heard, I fell down at his feet and wept. The Genius smiled upon me with a look of compassion and affability that familiarized him to my imagination, and at once dispelled all the fears and apprehensions with which I approached him. He lifted me from the ground, and taking me by the hand, *Mirzah,* said he, I have heard thee in thy soliloquies; follow me.

"He then led me to the highest pinnacle of the rock, and placing me on the top of it, Cast thy eyes eastward, said he, and tell me what thou seest. I see, said I, a huge valley and a prodigious tide of water rolling through it. The valley that thou seest, said he, is the vale of misery, and the tide of water that thou seest is part of the great tide of eternity. What is the reason, said I, that the tide I see rises out of a thick mist at one end, and again loses itself in a thick mist at the other? What thou seest, said he, is that portion of eternity which is called time, measured out by the sun, and reaching from the beginning of the world to its consummation. Examine now, said he, this sea that is bounded with darkness at both ends, and tell me what thou discoverest in it. I see a bridge, said I, standing in the midst of the tide. The bridge thou seest, said he, is human life: consider it attentively. Upon a more leisurely survey of it, I found that it consisted of threescore and ten entire arches, with several broken arches, which, added to those that were entire, made up the number about an hundred. As I was counting the arches, the Genius told me that this bridge consisted at first of a thousand arches; but that a great flood swept away the rest, and left the bridge in the ruinous condition I now beheld it. But tell me further, said he, what thou discoverest on it. I see multitudes of people passing over it, said I, and a black cloud hanging on each end of it. As I looked more attentively, I saw several of the passengers dropping through the bridge, into the great tide that flowed underneath it; and upon farther examination, perceived there were innumerable trap-doors that lay concealed in the bridge, which the passengers no sooner trod upon, but they fell through them into the tide and immediately disappeared. These hidden pit-falls were set very thick at the entrance of the bridge, so that throngs of people no sooner broke through the cloud, but many of them fell into them. They grew thinner towards the middle, but multiplied and lay closer together towards the end of the arches that were entire.

"There were indeed some persons, but their number was very small, that continued a kind of hobbling march on the broken arches, but fell through one after another, being quite tired and spent with so long a walk.

3–5. omnem . . . eripiam. I shall snatch away all the cloud which, now drawn across your eyes, obscures your mortal vision. *Aeneid,* Book II, ll. 604–06.

"I passed some time in the contemplation of this wonderful structure, and the great variety of objects which it presented. My heart was filled with a deep melancholy to see several dropping unexpectedly in the midst of mirth and jollity, and catching at every thing that stood by them to save themselves. Some were looking up towards the heavens in a thoughtful posture, and, in the midst of a speculation, stumbled and fell out of sight. Multitudes were very busy in the pursuit of bubbles that glittered in their eyes and danced before them; but often when they thought themselves within the reach of them their footing failed and down they sunk. In this confusion of objects, I observed some with scimitars in their hands, and others with urinals, who ran to and fro upon the bridge, thrusting several persons on trap-doors which did not seem to lie in their way, and which they might have escaped had they not been thus forced upon them.

"The Genius seeing me indulge my self in this melancholy prospect, told me I had dwelt long enough upon it. Take thine eyes off the bridge, said he, and tell me if thou yet seest any thing thou dost not comprehend. Upon looking up, What mean, said I, those great flights of birds that are perpetually hovering about the bridge, and settling upon it from time to time? I see vultures, harpies, ravens, cormorants; and among many other feathered creatures several little winged boys, that perch in great numbers upon the middle arches. These, said the Genius, are envy, avarice, superstition, despair, love, with the like cares and passions that infest human life.

"I here fetched a deep sigh. Alas, said I, man was made in vain! How is he given away to misery and mortality, tortured in life, and swallowed up in death! The Genius, being moved with compassion towards me, bid me quit so uncomfortable a prospect. Look no more, said he, on man in the first stage of his existence, in his setting out for eternity; but cast thine eye on that thick mist into which the tide bears the several generations of mortals that fall into it. I directed my sight as I was ordered, and (whether or no the good Genius strengthened it with any supernatural force, or dissipated part of the mist that was before too thick for the eye to penetrate) I saw the valley opening at the farther end, and spreading forth into an immense ocean, that had a huge rock of adamant running through the midst of it, and dividing it into two equal parts. The clouds still rested on one half of it, insomuch that I could discover nothing in it; but the other appeared to me a vast ocean planted with innumerable islands, that were covered with fruits and flowers, and interwoven with a thousand little shining seas that ran among them. I could see persons dressed in glorious habits, with garlands upon their heads, passing among the trees, lying down by the side of fountains, or resting on beds of flowers; and could hear a confused harmony of singing birds, falling waters, human voices, and musical instruments. Gladness grew in me upon the discovery of so delightful a scene. I wished for the wings of an eagle, that I might fly away to those happy seats; but the Genius told me there was no passage to them, except through the gates of death that I saw opening every moment upon the bridge. The islands, said he, that lie so fresh and green before thee, and with which the whole face of the ocean appears spotted as far as thou canst see, are more in number than the sands on the sea-shore; there are myriads of islands behind those which thou here discoverest, reaching further than thine eye or even thine imagination can extend itself. These are the mansions of good men after death, who according to the degree and kinds of virtue in which they excelled, are distributed among these several islands, which abound with pleasures of different kinds and degrees, suitable to the relishes and perfections of those who are settled in them; every island is a paradise accommodated to its respective inhabitants. Are not these, O *Mirzah*, habitations worth contending for? Does life appear miserable, that gives thee opportunities of earning such a reward? Is death to be feared, that will convey thee to so happy an existence? Think not man was made in vain, who has such an eternity reserved for him. I gazed with inexpressible pleasure on these happy islands. At length, said I, shew me now, I beseech thee, the secrets that lie hid under those dark clouds which cover the ocean on the other side of the rock of adamant. The Genius making me no answer, I turned about to address myself to him a second time, but I found that he had left me; I then turned again to the vision which I had been so long contemplating; but instead of the rolling tide, the arched bridge, and the happy islands, I saw nothing but the long hollow valley of Bagdat, with oxen, sheep, and camels grazing upon the sides of it."

14–15. scimitars . . . urinals, representing warriors and physicians. **43. it,** that is, the beholder's "sight."

from NO. 291. SATURDAY, FEB. 2, 1712
(Addison)

——*Ubi plura nitent in carmine, non ego paucis*
Offendar maculis, quas aut incuria fudit,
Aut humana parum cavit natura.—Hor.

49–51. *Ubi . . . natura.* But in a poem elegantly writ, I will not quarrel with a slight mistake, Such as our nature's frailty may excuse.—Roscommon's trans. of Horace's *Ars Poetica*, 351–353.

I HAVE now considered Milton's *Paradise Lost* under those four great heads of the fable, the characters, the sentiments, and the language; and have shewn that he excels, in general, under each of these heads. I hope that I have made several discoveries which may appear new, even to those who are versed in critical learning. Were I indeed to chuse my readers, by whose judgment I would stand or fall, they should not be such as are acquainted only with the French and Italian criticks, but also with the ancient and moderns who have written in either of the learned languages. Above all, I would have them well versed in the Greek and Latin poets, without which a man very often fancies that he understands a critick, when in reality he does not comprehend his meaning.

It is in criticism, as in all other sciences and speculations; one who brings with him any implicit notions and observations which he has made in his reading of the poets, will find his own reflections methodized and explained, and perhaps several little hints that have passed in his mind, perfected and improved in the works of a good critick; whereas one who has not these previous lights is often an utter stranger to what he reads, and apt to put a wrong interpretation upon it.

Nor is it sufficient, that a man who sets up for a judge in criticism should have perused the authors above mentioned, unless he has also a clear and logical head. Without this talent he is perpetually puzzled and perplexed amidst his own blunders, mistakes the sense of those he would confute, or if he chances to think right, does not know how to convey his thoughts to another with clearness and perspicuity. *Aristotle*, who was the best critick, was also one of the best logicians that ever appeared in the world. . . .

A true critick ought to dwell rather upon excellencies than imperfections, to discover the concealed beauties of a writer, and communicate to the world such things as are worth their observation. The most exquisite words and finest strokes of an author are those which very often appear the most doubtful and exceptionable to a man who wants a relish for polite learning; and they are these, which a sour undistinguishing critick generally attacks with the greatest violence. *Tully* observes, that it is very easy to brand or fix a mark upon what he calls *verbum ardens*, or, as it may be rendered into English, *a glowing, bold expression*, and to turn it into ridicule by a cold ill-natured criticism. A little wit is equally capable of exposing a beauty, and of aggravating a fault; and though such a treatment of an author naturally produces indignation in the mind of an understanding reader, it has however its effect among the generality of those whose hands it falls into, the rabble of mankind being very apt to think that anything which is laughed at with any mixture of wit is ridiculous in itself.

Such a mirth as this is always unseasonable in a critick, as it rather prejudices the reader than convinces him, and is capable of making a beauty, as well as a blemish, the subject of derision. A man who cannot write with wit on a proper subject is dull and stupid, but one who shews it in an improper place, is as impertinent and absurd. Besides, a man who has the gift of ridicule is apt to find fault with any thing that gives him an opportunity of exerting his beloved talent, and very often censures a passage, not because there is any fault in it, but because he can be merry upon it. Such kinds of pleasantry are very unfair and disingenuous in works of criticism, in which the greatest masters, both ancient and modern, have always appeared with a serious and instructive air.

As I intend in my next paper to show the defects in Milton's *Paradise Lost*, I thought fit to premise these few particulars, to the end that the reader may know I enter upon it, as on a very ungrateful work, and that I shall just point at the imperfections, without endeavouring to enflame them with ridicule. I must also observe, with *Longinus*, that the productions of a great genius, with many lapses and inadvertences, are infinitely preferable to the works of an inferior kind of author which are scrupulously exact, and conformable to all the rules of correct writing.

I shall conclude my paper with a story out of *Boccalini*, which sufficiently shews us the opinion that judicious author entertained of the sort of criticks I have been here mentioning. A famous critick, says he, having gathered together all the faults of an eminent poet, made a present of them to *Apollo*, who received them very graciously, and resolved to make the author a suitable return for the trouble he had been at in collecting them. In order to this, he set before him a sack of wheat, as it had been just threshed out of the sheaf. He then bid him pick out the chaff from among the corn, and lay it aside by itself. The critick applied himself to the task with great industry and pleasure, and, after having made the due separation, was presented by *Apollo* with the chaff for his pains.

29. Longinus. The famous treatise *On the Sublime*, to which Addison refers, formerly attributed to Longinus, a Greek critic of the third century A.D., is now ascribed to an unidentified author of the first century A.D. **35–36. Boccalini,** Trajan Boccalini (1556–1613), an Italian critic and satirist.

Alexander Pope
1688–1744

Alexander Pope, the greatest English poet of his century, and one of the few authors after whom an "age" of literary history has been called, was born in London, the son of a linen-draper. His family were Roman Catholics, and this meant in his time that he could not attend an English public school or university, nor hold public office. Even without this religious disability, however, the boy would probably have been unable to secure a regular education, since he was a semi-invalid from his early years. From early boyhood he read voraciously, rapidly gaining a sufficient command of Latin, Greek, French, and Italian. He was greatly assisted during his youth by members of the cultivated Roman Catholic families near his father's home at Binfield in Windsor Forest. His determination to be a great and famous poet began almost in his childhood. "About fifteen," he once said, "I got acquainted with Mr. Walsh.[1] He used to encourage me much, and used to tell me that there was one way left of excelling; for, though we had several great poets, we never had any one great poet that was correct, and he desired me to make that my study and aim."

Pope won his fame and influence by his single-minded devotion and in spite of many difficulties. His whole life, as he remarked toward the end of it, was "one long disease." By fifteen he had written an epic poem, which he later destroyed, and before he was twenty he had composed his *Pastorals*, which were published in 1709. It was the eager study of "correctness," no doubt, that enabled Pope to write the better part of his brilliant *Essay on Criticism* before he was twenty-one, thereby making a connection with the circle of Addison, who lauded the *Essay* in *The Spectator*. Pope later abandoned Addison and his friends in favor of Swift and the Scriblerus Club. In the *Essay on Criticism* Pope showed proficiency in the use of the closed "heroic couplet," of which he was ever after the master. It was characteristic of him, and of his age as well, that his study of critical theory preceded his more creative writing. Always he wished to know the law before he tried his liberty. It was ever his intention and effort to have the weight of authority on his side. Correctness, orthodoxy, tradition, and the consensus of the past were what he sought from his youth up, so that he gives the impression of never having been really young. At most he had an old head on young shoulders. We do not look to him for boyish rebellion or for youthful enthusiasm. While still a boy in years he spoke in the language of age.

In 1712, when he had turned twenty-four, appeared *The Rape of the Lock*, his gayest and lightest composition, and a masterpiece in the mock-epic vein. From then on Pope was easily first among the poets of his generation. His translation of the *Iliad*, 1720, and of the *Odyssey*, 1725, reinforced his reputation and won him extravagant praise later from Dr. Johnson. Pope's more mature years were spent chiefly in the writing of satires in which he attacked his numerous literary enemies in brilliantly polished couplets. The most elaborate of these is *The Dunciad*, a mock-epic of dunces inspired by Dryden's *Mac Flecknoe* (page 458), on which he was engaged intermittently from 1728 to 1743. In the meantime he wrote his philosophic treatise, *An Essay on Man*, 1732–34, and his *apologia pro vita sua*, the *Epistle to Dr. Arbuthnot*, 1735.

Pope, through his indomitable will, triumphantly achieved in his writing what others aspired to. Other writers of his time, dominated as many of them were by the current notion of the gentleman as one who never worked hard at anything, gave most of their energies to politics, journalism, society, or amiable trifling. Pope was a professional writer, and, though he usually tried to give the impression that his most polished productions were tossed off in his idle hours, it is demonstrable that he worked hard at his profession. He worked at nothing else. He made a good living by poetry because he lived for it. On the proceeds of his verse translation of Homer's *Iliad* he was able to buy himself a small estate near Richmond and to live there during the rest of his life, courted and feared, in security and ease. Thus he needed no patron, and he had none. His independence, because it was recognized by everyone, did much for the dignity of the profession of letters.

The reputation of Alexander Pope is probably higher at present than it has been at any time during the last hundred and fifty years. We do not

[1] William Walsh (1663–1708), a fashionable poet and critic of the day.

think of him as a great or a magnanimous man. Neither do we regard him as profound or in any high degree original. But he was supreme within his own domain. No writer in our literature has produced satirical poetry of such sharp, concentrated brilliance, or employed the heroic couplet with such varied skill.

from AN ESSAY ON CRITICISM

Pope's effort in this brilliant though somewhat discursive poem is not to contribute his own opinions upon an old and much-debated theme but to bring together the tried and accepted doctrines of Aristotle, Horace, and others among the ancients, and of Boileau, chiefly, among critics of more recent times. Although his assertions may seem to a twentieth-century reader highly dogmatic, he is in fact decidedly liberal in his attitude toward the "rules," and it will be seen that he leaves much room for what we call "inspiration." The word "essay" in his title is intended, of course, to suggest an informal and somewhat tentative handling of his theme.

PART I

'Tis hard to say, if greater want of skill
Appear in writing or in judging ill;
But, of the two, less dangerous is the offence
To tire our patience, than mislead our sense.
Some few in that, but numbers err in this,
Ten censure wrong for one who writes amiss;
A fool might once himself alone expose,
Now one in verse makes many more in prose.
'Tis with our judgments as our watches, none
Go just alike, yet each believes his own.
In Poets as true genius is but rare,
True Taste as seldom is the Critic's share;
Both must alike from Heaven derive their light,
These born to judge, as well as those to write.
Let such teach others who themselves excel,
And censure freely who have written well.
Authors are partial to their wit, 'tis true,
But are not Critics to their judgment too?
Yet if we look more closely, we shall find
Most have the seeds of judgment in their mind:
Nature affords at least a glimmering light;
The lines, though touched but faintly, are drawn right.
But as the slightest sketch, if justly traced,
Is by ill-colouring but the more disgraced,
So by false learning is good sense defaced:
Some are bewildered in the maze of schools,
And some made coxcombs Nature meant but fools.
In search of wit these lose their common sense,
And then turn Critics in their own defence:
Each burns alike, who can, or cannot write,
Or with a Rival's, or an Eunuch's spite.
All fools have still an itching to deride,
And fain would be upon the laughing side.
If Maevius scribble in Apollo's spite,
There are who judge still worse than he can write.
Some have at first for Wits, then Poets passed,
Turned Critics next, and proved plain fools at last.
Some neither can for Wits nor Critics pass,
As heavy mules are neither horse nor ass.
Those half-learned witlings, numerous in our isle,
As half-formed insects on the banks of Nile;
Unfinished things, one knows not what to call,
Their generation's so equivocal;
To tell 'em, would a hundred tongues require,
Or one vain wit's, that might a hundred tire.
But you who seek to give and merit fame,
And justly bear a Critic's noble name,
Be sure yourself and your own reach to know,
How far your genius, taste, and learning go;
Launch not beyond your depth, but be discreet,
And mark that point where sense and dulness meet.
Nature to all things fixed the limits fit,
And wisely curbed proud man's pretending wit.
As on the land while here the ocean gains,
In other parts it leaves wide sandy plains;
Thus in the soul while memory prevails,
The solid power of understanding fails;
Where beams of warm imagination play,
The memory's soft figures melt away.
One science only will one genius fit;
So vast is art, so narrow human wit:
Not only bounded to peculiar arts,
But oft in those confined to single parts.
Like kings we lose the conquests gained before,
By vain ambition still to make them more;
Each might his several province well command,
Would all but stoop to what they understand.
First follow Nature, and your judgment frame
By her just standard, which is still the same:
Unerring Nature, still divinely bright,
One clear, unchanged, and universal light,
Life, force, and beauty, must to all impart,
At once the source, and end, and test of Art.
Art from that fund each just supply provides,
Works without show, and without pomp presides:

6. censure, judge.

34. Maevius, a poet contemporary with Virgil, a classic example of the bad poet. **44. tell,** count. **53. wit,** intelligence. In later lines the word is used in several slightly differing senses. **68. Nature.** Pope's varying use of this difficult word should be carefully studied. Usually, as here, he intends it to mean universal, representative, and normal—though not average—human nature, as shown in feeling, thought, taste, and conduct.

In some fair body thus the informing soul
With spirits feeds, with vigour fills the whole,
Each motion guides, and every nerve sustains;
Itself unseen, but in the effects, remains.
Some, to whom Heaven in wit has been profuse,
Want as much more, to turn it to its use;
For wit and judgment often are at strife,
Though meant each other's aid, like man and wife.
'Tis more to guide, than spur the Muse's steed,
Restrain his fury, than provoke his speed;
The wingèd courser, like a generous horse,
Shows most true mettle when you check his course.
  Those Rules of old discovered, not devised,
Are Nature still, but Nature methodized;
Nature, like liberty, is but restrained
By the same laws which first herself ordained.
  Hear how learned Greece her useful rules indites,
When to repress, and when indulge our flights:
High on Parnassus' top her sons she showed,
And pointed out those arduous paths they trod;
Held from afar, aloft, the immortal prize,
And urged the rest by equal steps to rise.
Just precepts thus from great examples given,
She drew from them what they derived from Heaven.
The generous Critic fanned the Poet's fire,
And taught the world with reason to admire.
Then Criticism the Muses' handmaid proved,
To dress her charms, and make her more beloved:
But following wits from that intention strayed;
Who could not win the mistress, wooed the maid;
Against the Poets their own arms they turned,
Sure to hate most the men from whom they learned.
So modern 'Pothecaries, taught the art
By Doctor's bills to play the Doctor's part,
Bold in the practice of mistaken rules,
Prescribe, apply, and call their masters fools.
Some on the leaves of ancient authors prey,
Nor time nor moths e'er spoiled so much as they.
Some drily plain, without invention's aid,
Write dull receipts how poems may be made.
These leave the sense, their learning to display,
And those explain the meaning quite away.
  You then whose judgment the right course would steer,
Know well each Ancient's proper character;
His fable, subject, scope in every page;
Religion, Country, genius of his Age:
Without all these at once before your eyes,
Cavil you may, but never criticize.
Be Homer's works your study and delight,
Read them by day, and meditate by night;
Thence form your judgment, thence your maxims bring,
And trace the Muses upward to their spring.
Still with itself compared, his text peruse,
And let your comment be the Mantuan Muse.
  When first young Maro in his boundless mind
A work to outlast immortal Rome designed,
Perhaps he seemed above the critic's law,
And but from Nature's fountains scorned to draw;
But when to examine every part he came,
Nature and Homer were, he found, the same.
Convinced, amazed, he checks the bold design;
And rules as strict his laboured work confine,
As if the Stagirite o'erlooked each line.
Learn hence for ancient rules a just esteem;
To copy nature is to copy them.
  Some beauties yet no Precepts can declare,
For there's a happiness as well as care.
Music resembles Poetry, in each
Are nameless graces which no methods teach,
And which a master-hand alone can reach.
If, where the rules not far enough extend,
(Since rules were made but to promote their end)
Some lucky Licence answer to the full
The intent proposed, that Licence is a rule.
Thus Pegasus, a nearer way to take,
May boldly deviate from the common track;
From vulgar bounds with brave disorder part,
And snatch a grace beyond the reach of art,
Which without passing through the judgment, gains
The heart, and all its end at once attains.
In prospects thus, some objects please our eyes,
Which out of nature's common order rise,
The shapeless rock, or hanging precipice.
Great wits sometimes may gloriously offend,
And rise to faults true Critics dare not mend.
But though the Ancients thus their rules invade,
(As Kings dispense with laws themselves have made)
Moderns, beware! or if you must offend
Against the precept, ne'er transgress its End;
Let it be seldom, and compelled by need;
And have, at least, their precedent to plead.
The Critic else proceeds without remorse,
Seizes your fame, and puts his laws in force.
  I know there are, to whose presumptuous thoughts
Those freer beauties, even in them, seem faults.
Some figures monstrous and mis-shaped appear,

88. discovered, by Aristotle. **120. fable,** story or plot.

129. Mantuan, Virgil, whose surname was **Maro,** was born in Mantua. **138. Stagirite,** Aristotle, born in Stagira, Macedonia. His *Art of Poetry* has been the most influential of all critical documents, for upon it, rightly and wrongly interpreted, the so-called rules of which Neoclassicism made so much were based. **142. happiness,** good fortune in writing, inspiration. **150. Pegasus,** the winged horse of Greek myth, emblem of poetic inspiration and power. **164. End,** purpose or intention.

Considered singly, or beheld too near,
Which, but proportioned to their light, or place,
Due distance reconciles to form and grace.
A prudent chief not always must display
His powers in equal ranks, and fair array,
But with the occasion and the place comply,
Conceal his force, nay seem sometimes to fly.
Those oft are stratagems which error seem,
Nor is it Homer nods, but we that dream.
  Still green with bays each ancient Altar stands,
Above the reach of sacrilegious hands,
Secure from Flames, from Envy's fiercer rage,
Destructive War, and all-involving Age.
See, from each clime the learned their incense bring!
Hear, in all tongues consenting Paeans ring!
In praise so just let every voice be joined,
And fill the general chorus of mankind.
Hail, Bards triumphant! born in happier days;
Immortal heirs of universal praise!
Whose honours with increase of ages grow,
As streams roll down, enlarging as they flow;
Nations unborn your mighty names shall sound,
And worlds applaud that must not yet be found!
Oh may some spark of your celestial fire,
The last, the meanest of your sons inspire,
(That on weak wings, from far, pursues your flights;
Glows while he reads, but trembles as he writes)
To teach vain Wits a science little known,
To admire superior sense, and doubt their own!

PART II

  Of all the Causes which conspire to blind
Man's erring judgment, and misguide the mind,
What the weak head with strongest bias rules,
Is *Pride*, the never-failing vice of fools.
Whatever nature has in worth denied,
She gives in large recruits of needful pride;
For as in bodies, thus in souls, we find
What wants in blood and spirits, swelled with wind:
Pride, where wit fails, steps in to our defence,
And fills up all the mighty Void of sense.
If once right reason drives that cloud away,
Truth breaks upon us with resistless day.
Trust not yourself; but your defects to know,
Make use of every friend—and every foe.
  A *little learning* is a dangerous thing;
Drink deep, or taste not the Pierian spring.
There shallow draughts intoxicate the brain,
And drinking largely sobers us again.
Fired at first sight with what the Muse imparts,
In fearless youth we tempt the heights of Arts,
While from the bounded level of our mind
Short views we take, nor see the lengths behind;
But more advanced, behold with strange surprise
New distant scenes of endless science rise!
So pleased at first the towering Alps we try,
Mount o'er the vales, and seem to tread the sky,
The eternal snows appear already past,
And the first clouds and mountains seem the last;
But, those attained, we tremble to survey
The growing labours of the lengthened way,
The increasing prospect tires our wandering eyes,
Hills peep o'er hills, and Alps on Alps arise!
  A perfect Judge will read each work of Wit
With the same spirit that its author writ:
Survey the Whole, nor seek slight faults to find
Where nature moves, and rapture warms the mind;
Nor lose, for that malignant dull delight,
The generous pleasure to be charmed with Wit.
But in such lays as neither ebb, nor flow,
Correctly cold, and regularly low,
That, shunning faults, one quiet tenour keep,
We cannot blame indeed—but we may sleep.
In wit, as nature, what affects our hearts
Is not the exactness of peculiar parts;
'Tis not a lip, or eye, we beauty call,
But the joint force and full result of all.
Thus when we view some well-proportioned dome,
(The world's just wonder, and even thine, O Rome!)
No single parts unequally surprise,
All comes united to the admiring eyes;
No monstrous height, or breadth, or length appear;
The Whole at once is bold, and regular.
  Whoever thinks a faultless piece to see,
Thinks what ne'er was, nor is, nor e'er shall be.
In every work regard the writer's End,
Since none can compass more than they intend;
And if the means be just, the conduct true,
Applause, in spite of trivial faults, is due;
As men of breeding, sometimes men of wit,
To avoid great errors, must the less commit:
Neglect the rules each verbal Critic lays,
For not to know some trifles, is a praise.
Most Critics, fond of some subservient art,
Still make the Whole depend upon a Part;
They talk of principles, but notions prize,
And all to one loved Folly sacrifice. . . .
  Some to *Conceit* alone their taste confine,

187. joined. In the pronunciation of Pope's time this word rhymed exactly with "kind," as the word "faults," in l. 170 above, did with "thoughts." **216. Pierian spring,** Hippocrene, at Pieria in Thessaly, birthplace of the Muses. **247. dome,** building. **248. thine, O Rome:** St. Peter's Church in Rome. **289. *Conceit*,** a farfetched metaphor or simile of the kind favored especially by English poets of the seventeenth century.

And glittering thoughts struck out at every line;
Pleased with a work where nothing's just or fit,
One glaring Chaos and wild heap of wit.
Poets like painters, thus, unskilled to trace
The naked nature and the living grace,
With gold and jewels cover every part,
And hide with ornaments their want of art.
True Wit is Nature to advantage dressed,
What oft was thought, but ne'er so well expressed;
Something, whose truth convinced at sight we find,
That gives us back the image of our mind.
As shades more sweetly recommend the light,
So modest plainness sets off sprightly wit.
For works may have more wit than does 'em good,
As bodies perish through excess of blood.
  Others for *Language* all their care express,
And value books, as women men, for Dress:
Their praise is still,—the Style is excellent:
The Sense, they humbly take upon content.
Words are like leaves; and where they most abound,
Much fruit of sense beneath is rarely found.
False Eloquence, like the prismatic glass,
Its gaudy colors spreads on every place;
The face of Nature we no more survey,
All glares alike, without distinction gay:
But true expression, like the unchanging Sun,
Clears and improves whate'er it shines upon,
It gilds all objects, but it alters none.
Expression is the dress of thought, and still
Appears more decent, as more suitable;
A vile conceit in pompous words expressed,
Is like a clown in regal purple dressed:
For different styles with different subjects sort,
As several garbs with country, town, and court.
Some by old words to fame have made pretence,
Ancients in phrase, mere moderns in their sense;
Such laboured nothings, in so strange a style,
Amaze the unlearned, and make the learnèd smile.
Unlucky, as Fungoso in the play,
These sparks with awkward vanity display
What the fine gentleman wore yesterday;
And but so mimic ancient wits at best,
As apes our grandsires, in their doublets drest.
In words, as fashions, the same rule will hold;
Alike fantastic, if too new, or old:
Be not the first by whom the new are tried,
Nor yet the last to lay the old aside.
  But most by Numbers judge a Poet's song;
And smooth or rough, with them is right or wrong:
In the bright Muse though thousand charms conspire,
Her voice is all these tuneful fools admire,
Who haunt Parnassus but to please their ear,
Not mend their minds; as some to Church repair,
Not for the doctrine, but the music there.
These equal syllables alone require,
Though oft the ear the open vowels tire;
While expletives their feeble aid do join,
And ten low words oft creep in one dull line:
While they ring round the same unvaried chimes,
With sure returns of still expected rhymes;
Wher-e'er you find "the cooling western breeze,"
In the next line, it "whispers through the trees":
If crystal streams "with pleasing murmurs creep,"
The reader's threatened (not in vain) with "sleep";
Then, at the last and only couplet fraught
With some unmeaning thing they call a thought,
A needless Alexandrine ends the song
That, like a wounded snake, drags its slow length along.
Leave such to tune their own dull rhymes, and know
What's roundly smooth or languishingly slow;
And praise the easy vigour of a line,
Where Denham's strength, and Waller's sweetness join.
True ease in writing comes from art, not chance,
As those move easiest who have learned to dance.
'Tis not enough no harshness gives offence;
The sound must seem an Echo to the sense:
Soft is the strain when Zephyr gently blows,
And the smooth stream in smoother numbers flows;
But when loud surges lash the sounding shore,
The hoarse, rough verse should like the torrent roar:
When Ajax strives some rock's vast weight to throw,
The line too labours, and the words move slow;
Not so, when swift Camilla scours the plain,
Flies o'er the unbending corn, and skims along the main.
Hear how Timotheus' varied lays surprise,
And bid alternate passions fall and rise!
While, at each change, the son of Libyan Jove
Now burns with glory, and then melts with love,
Now his fierce eyes with sparkling fury glow,
Now sighs steal out, and tears begin to flow:
Persians and Greeks like turns of nature found,
And the world's victor stood subdued by Sound!
The power of Music all our hearts allow,
And what Timotheus was, is DRYDEN now.
  Avoid Extremes, and shun the fault of such,
Who still are pleased too little or too much.

328. Fungoso, in Ben Jonson's *Every Man out of His Humour*.

344. require. In this and in several following lines Pope illustrates the effects of versification that he is discussing. **361. Denham . . . Waller,** poets of the seventeenth century admired by Pope's contemporaries for the vigor, ease, and correctness of their versification. **374. Timotheus.** See Dryden's "Alexander's Feast," page 465. **380. turns,** tropes, or figures of speech.

At every trifle scorn to take offence;
That always shows great pride, or little sense;
Those heads, as stomachs, are not sure the best,
Which nauseate all, and nothing can digest.
Yet let not each gay turn thy rapture move;
For fools admire, but men of sense approve:
As things seem large which we through mists descry,
Dulness is ever apt to magnify.
  Some foreign writers, some our own despise;
The Ancients only, or the Moderns prize.
Thus wit, like Faith, by each man is applied
To one small sect, and all are damned beside.
Meanly they seek the blessing to confine,
And force that sun but on a part to shine,
Which not alone the southern wit sublimes,
But ripens spirits in cold northern climes;
Which from the first has shone on ages past,
Enlights the present, and shall warm the last;
Though each may feel increases and decays,
And see now clearer and now darker days.
Regard not then if Wit be old or new,
But blame the false, and value still the true. . . .
  Be thou the first true merit to befriend;
His praise is lost, who stays till all commend.
Short is the date, alas, of modern rhymes,
And 'tis but just to let them live betimes.
No longer now that golden age appears,
When Patriarch-wits survived a thousand years:
Now length of Fame (our second life) is lost,
And bare threescore is all even that can boast;
Our sons their fathers' failing language see,
And such as Chaucer is, shall Dryden be.
So when the faithful pencil has designed
Some bright Idea of the master's mind,
Where a new world leaps out at his command,
And ready Nature waits upon his hand;
When the ripe colours soften and unite,
And sweetly melt into just shade and light;
When mellowing years their full perfection give,
And each bold figure just begins to live,
The treacherous colours the fair art betray,
And all the bright creation fades away!
  Unhappy Wit, like most mistaken things,
Atones not for that envy which it brings.
In youth alone its empty praise we boast,
But soon the short-lived vanity is lost:
Like some fair flower the early spring supplies,
That gaily blooms, but even in blooming dies.
What is this Wit, which must our cares employ?
The owner's wife, that other men enjoy;
Then most our trouble still when most admired,
And still the more we give, the more required;
Whose fame with pains we guard, but lose with ease,
Sure some to vex, but never all to please;
'Tis what the vicious fear, the virtuous shun,
By fools 'tis hated, and by knaves undone!
  If Wit so much from Ignorance undergo,
Ah, let not Learning too commence its foe!
Of old, those met rewards who could excel,
And such were praised who but endeavoured well:
Though triumphs were to generals only due,
Crowns were reserved to grace the soldiers too.
Now they who reach Parnassus' lofty crown
Employ their pains to spurn some others down;
And while self-love each jealous writer rules,
Contending wits become the sport of fools:
But still the worst with most regret commend,
For each ill Author is as bad a Friend.
To what base ends, and by what abject ways,
Are mortals urged through sacred lust of praise!
Ah, ne'er so dire a thirst of glory boast,
Nor in the Critic let the Man be lost.
Good-nature and good-sense must ever join;
To err is human, to forgive, divine. . . .

391. admire, wonder at.

THE RAPE OF THE LOCK

AN HEROIC-COMICAL POEM

Published at first in two parts and then, two years later, reissued in its present enlarged form, *The Rape of the Lock* has always been by far the most popular of Pope's writings. It is based upon an actual event in which an acquaintance of Pope's, Lord Petre, cut a lock of hair from the head of a Miss Arabella Fermor. Much more was made of this by the families of the two young people than the incident warranted, and this fact may have suggested to Pope the "mock heroic" style of his poem, in which "the little is made great and the great little."

Pope's letter of dedication to "Mrs. Arabella Fermor," the original of "Belinda," was intended not chiefly to placate her wrath at the freedom with which he had treated the incident but to give necessary information to his readers. *Madam,* he says, *It will be in vain to deny that I have some regard for this piece, since I dedicate it to You. Yet you may bear me witness, it was intended only to divert a few young Ladies, who have good sense and good humour enough to laugh not only at their sex's little unguarded follies, but at their own. But as it was communicated with the air of a Secret, it soon found its way into the world. An imperfect copy having been offered to a Bookseller, you had the good-nature for my sake to consent to the publication of one more correct: This I was forced to before I had executed half my design, for the Machinery was entirely wanting to complete it.*

The Machinery, Madam, is a term invented by the Critics to signify that part which the Deities, Angels, or Daemons are made to act in a Poem; For the ancient Poets are in one respect like modern Ladies: let an action be never so trivial in itself, they always make it appear of the utmost importance. These Machines I determined to raise on a very new and odd foundation, the Rosicrucian doctrine of Spirits.

I know how disagreeable it is to make use of hard words before a Lady, but 't is so much the concern of a Poet to have his works understood, and particularly by your Sex, that you must give me leave to explain two or three difficult terms.

The Rosicrucians are a people I must bring you acquainted with. The best account I know of them is in a French book called Le Comte de Gabalis, *which both by its title and size is so like a Novel, that many of the Fair Sex have read it for one by mistake. According to these Gentlemen, the four Elements are inhabited by Spirits, which they call Sylphs, Gnomes, Nymphs, and Salamanders. The Gnomes or Daemons of Earth delight in mischief; but the Sylphs, whose habitation is in the Air, are the best-conditioned creatures imaginable. For they say, any mortals may enjoy the most intimate familiarities with these gentle Spirits, upon a condition very easy to all true Adepts, an inviolate preservation of Chastity.*

As to the following Cantos, all the passages of them are as fabulous, as the Vision at the beginning, or the Transformation at the end (except the loss of your Hair, which I always mention with reverence). The Human persons are as fictitious as the airy ones, and the character of Belinda, as it is now managed, resembles you in nothing but in Beauty.

If this Poem had as many Graces as there are in your Person, or in your Mind, yet I could never hope it should pass through the world half so Uncensured as You have done. But let its fortune be what it will, mine is happy enough to have given me this occasion of assuring you that I am, with the truest esteem, Madam,

Your most obedient, Humble Servant,

A. Pope.

CANTO I

What dire offence from amorous causes springs,
What mighty contests rise from trivial things,
I sing—This verse to CARYL, Muse! is due:
This, even Belinda may vouchsafe to view:
Slight is the subject, but not so the praise,
If She inspire, and He approve my lays.
Say what strange motive, Goddess! could compel
A well-bred Lord to assault a gentle Belle?
O say what stranger cause, yet unexplored,
Could make a gentle Belle reject a Lord?
In tasks so bold, can little men engage,
And in soft bosoms dwells such mighty Rage?
Sol through white curtains shot a timorous ray,
And oped those eyes that must eclipse the day:
Now lap-dogs give themselves the rousing shake,
And sleepless lovers, just at twelve, awake:
Thrice rung the bell, the slipper knocked the ground,
And the pressed watch returned a silver sound.
Belinda still her downy pillow prest,
Her guardian SYLPH prolonged the balmy rest:
'Twas He had summoned to her silent bed
The morning-dream that hovered o'er her head;
A Youth more glittering than a Birth-night Beau,
(That even in slumber caused her cheek to glow)
Seemed to her ear his winning lips to lay,
And thus in whispers said, or seemed to say:
"Fairest of mortals, thou distinguished care
Of thousand bright Inhabitants of Air!
If e'er one vision touched thy infant thought,
Of all the Nurse and all the Priest have taught;
Of airy Elves by moonlight shadows seen,
The silver token, and the circled green,
Or virgins visited by Angel-powers,
With golden crowns and wreaths of heavenly flowers;
Hear and believe! thy own importance know,
Nor bound thy narrow views to things below.
Some secret truths, from learnèd pride concealed,
To Maids alone and Children are revealed:
What though no credit doubting Wits may give?
The Fair and Innocent shall still believe.
Know, then, unnumbered Spirits round thee fly,
The light Militia of the lower sky:
These, though unseen, are ever on the wing,
Hang o'er the Box, and hover round the Ring.
Think what an equipage thou hast in Air,
And view with scorn two Pages and a Chair.
As now your own, our beings were of old,
And once inclosed in Woman's beauteous mould;
Thence, by a soft transition, we repair
From earthly Vehicles to these of air.
Think not, when Woman's transient breath is fled,
That all her vanities at once are dead;
Succeeding vanities she still regards,
And though she plays no more, o'erlooks the cards,
Her joy in gilded Chariots, when alive,
And love of Ombre, after death survive.
For when the Fair in all their pride expire,
To their first Elements their Souls retire:
The Sprites of fiery Termagants in Flame
Mount up, and take a Salamander's name.
Soft yielding minds to Water glide away,
And sip, with Nymphs, their elemental Tea.
The graver Prude sinks downward to a Gnome,
In search of mischief still on Earth to roam.

3. **Caryl,** John Caryll, a common friend of Pope, Lord Petre (the "Baron"), and Arabella Fermor (Belinda). He suggested the present poem to Pope. 12. **Rage,** compare the *Aeneid*, Book I, l. 11. 17. **knocked the ground,** to call the maid.

18. **pressed watch,** the "repeater," a watch that strikes again the hours and parts of the hours when the stem is pressed. 30. **Priest.** Miss Fermor, like the other members of the group here presented, was a Roman Catholic. 32. **silver token,** a sixpence left by the elves as evidence of their visit. 44. **Box,** at the theater. **Ring,** the circular promenade in Hyde Park, London. 46. **Chair,** sedan chair. 56. **Ombre,** a card game fashionable in Pope's day. See Canto III.

The light Coquettes in Sylphs aloft repair,
And sport and flutter in the fields of Air.
"Know further yet: whoever fair and chaste
Rejects mankind, is by some Sylph embraced:
For Spirits, freed from mortal laws, with ease
Assume what sexes and what shapes they please.
What guards the purity of melting Maids,
In courtly balls, and midnight masquerades,
Safe from the treacherous friend, the daring spark,
The glance by day, the whisper in the dark,
When kind occasion prompts their warm desires,
When music softens, and when dancing fires?
'Tis but their Sylph, the wise Celestials know,
Though Honour is the word with Men below.
"Some nymphs there are, too conscious of their face,
For life predestined to the Gnomes' embrace.
These swell their prospects and exalt their pride,
When offers are disdained, and love denied:
Then gay Ideas crowd the vacant brain,
While Peers, and Dukes, and all their sweeping train,
And Garters, Stars, and Coronets appear,
And in soft sounds, Your Grace salutes their ear.
'Tis these that early taint the female soul,
Instruct the eyes of young Coquettes to roll,
Teach Infant-cheeks a bidden blush to know,
And little hearts to flutter at a Beau.
"Oft, when the world imagine women stray,
The Sylphs through mystic mazes guide their way;
Through all the giddy circle they pursue,
And old impertinence expel by new.
What tender maid but must a victim fall
To one man's treat, but for another's ball?
When Florio speaks what virgin could withstand,
If gentle Damon did not squeeze her hand?
With varying vanities, from every part,
They shift the moving Toyshop of their heart;
Where wigs with wigs, with sword-knots sword-knots strive,
Beaux banish beaux, and coaches coaches drive.
This erring mortals Levity may call;
Oh blind to truth! the Sylphs contrive it all.
"Of these am I, who thy protection claim,
A watchful sprite, and Ariel is my name.
Late, as I ranged the crystal wilds of air,
In the clear Mirror of thy ruling Star
I saw, alas! some dread event impend,
Ere to the main this morning sun descend,
But heaven reveals not what, or how, or where:
Warned by the Sylph, oh pious maid, beware!
This to disclose is all thy guardian can:
Beware of all, but most beware of man!"
He said; when Shock, who thought she slept too long,
Leaped up, and waked his mistress with his tongue.
'Twas then, Belinda, if report say true,
Thy eyes first opened on a Billet-doux;
Wounds, Charms, and Ardours were no sooner read,
But all the vision vanished from thy head.
And now, unveiled, the Toilet stands displayed.
Each silver Vase in mystic order laid.
First, robed in white, the Nymph intent adores,
With head uncovered, the Cosmetic powers.
A heavenly image in the glass appears,
To that she bends, to that her eyes she rears;
Th' inferior Priestess, at her altar's side,
Trembling begins the sacred rites of Pride.
Unnumbered treasures ope at once, and here
The various offerings of the world appear;
From each she nicely culls with curious toil,
And decks the Goddess with the glittering spoil.
This casket India's glowing gems unlocks,
And all Arabia breathes from yonder box.
The Tortoise here and Elephant unite,
Transformed to combs, the speckled, and the white.
Here files of pins extend their shining rows,
Puffs, Powders, Patches, Bibles, Billet-doux.
Now awful Beauty puts on all its arms;
The fair each moment rises in her charms,
Repairs her smiles, awakens every grace,
And calls forth all the wonders of her face;
Sees by degrees a purer blush arise,
And keener lightnings quicken in her eyes.
The busy Sylphs surround their darling care,
These set the head, and those divide the hair,
Some fold the sleeve, whilst others plait the gown;
And Betty's praised for labours not her own.

CANTO II

Not with more glories, in th' ethereal plain,
The Sun first rises o'er the purpled main,
Than, issuing forth, the rival of his beams
Launched on the bosom of the silver Thames.
Fair Nymphs and well-drest Youths around her shone,
But every eye was fixed on her alone.
On her white breast a sparkling Cross she wore,
Which Jews might kiss, and Infidels adore.
Her lively looks a sprightly mind disclose,
Quick as her eyes, and as unfixed as those:
Favours to none, to all she smiles extends;
Oft she rejects, but never once offends.
Bright as the sun, her eyes the gazers strike,
And, like the sun, they shine on all alike.

115. Shock, Belinda's lap dog. **127. Th' inferior Priestess,** that is, Belinda's maid, Betty.

Yet graceful ease, and sweetness void of pride,
Might hide her faults, if Belles had faults to hide:
If to her share some female errors fall,
Look on her face, and you'll forget 'em all.
This Nymph, to the destruction of mankind,
Nourished two Locks, which graceful hung behind
In equal curls, and well conspired to deck
With shining ringlets the smooth ivory neck.
Love in these labyrinths his slaves detains,
And mighty hearts are held in slender chains.
With hairy springes we the birds betray,
Slight lines of hair surprise the finny prey,
Fair tresses man's imperial race ensnare,
And beauty draws us with a single hair.
Th' adventurous Baron the bright locks admired;
He saw, he wished, and to the prize aspired.
Resolved to win, he meditates the way,
By force to ravish, or by fraud betray;
For when success a Lover's toil attends,
Few ask, if fraud or force attained his ends.
For this, ere Phoebus rose, he had implored
Propitious heaven, and every power adored,
But chiefly Love—to Love an Altar built,
Of twelve vast French Romances, neatly gilt.
There lay three garters, half a pair of gloves;
And all the trophies of his former loves;
With tender Billet-doux he lights the pyre,
And breathes three amorous sighs to raise the fire.
Then prostrate falls, and begs with ardent eyes
Soon to obtain, and long possess the prize;
The powers gave ear, and granted half his prayer,
The rest, the winds dispersed in empty air.
But now secure the painted vessel glides,
The sun-beams trembling on the floating tides:
While melting music steals upon the sky,
And softened sounds along the waters die;
Smooth flow the waves, the Zephyrs gently play,
Belinda smiled, and all the world was gay.
All but the Sylph—with careful thoughts opprest,
Th' impending woe sat heavy on his breast.
He summons straight his Denizens of air;
The lucid squadrons round the sails repair;
Soft o'er the shrouds aërial whispers breathe,
That seemed but Zephyrs to the train beneath.
Some to the sun their insect-wings unfold,
Waft on the breeze, or sink in clouds of gold;
Transparent forms, too fine for mortal sight,
Their fluid bodies half dissolved in light,
Loose to the wind their airy garments flew,
Thin glittering textures of the filmy dew,
Dipt in the richest tincture of the skies,
Where light disports in ever-mingling dyes,
While every beam new transient colours flings,

35. Phoebus, the sun. **56. repair,** gather.

Colours that change whene'er they wave their wings.
Amid the circle, on the gilded mast,
Superior by the head, was Ariel placed;
His purple pinions opening to the sun,
He raised his azure wand, and thus begun.
"Ye Sylphs and Sylphids, to your chief give ear!
Fays, Fairies, Genii, Elves, and Daemons, hear!
Ye know the spheres and various tasks assigned
By laws eternal to the aërial kind.
Some in the fields of purest Aether play,
And bask and whiten in the blaze of day.
Some guide the course of wandering orbs on high,
Or roll the planets through the boundless sky.
Some less refined, beneath the moon's pale light
Pursue the stars that shoot athwart the night,
Or suck the mists in grosser air below,
Or dip their pinions in the painted bow,
Or brew fierce tempests on the wintry main,
Or o'er the glebe distil the kindly rain.
Others on earth o'er human race preside,
Watch all their ways, and all their actions guide:
Of these the chief the care of Nations own,
And guard with Arms divine the British throne.
"Our humbler province is to tend the Fair,
Not a less pleasing, though less glorious care;
To save the powder from too rude a gale,
Nor let the imprisoned essences exhale;
To draw fresh colours from the vernal flowers;
To steal from rainbows e'er they drop in showers
A brighter wash; to curl their waving hairs,
Assist their blushes, and inspire their airs;
Nay oft, in dreams, invention we bestow,
To change a Flounce, or add a Furbelow.
"This day, black Omens threat the brightest Fair
That e'er deserved a watchful spirit's care;
Some dire disaster, or by force, or slight;
But what, or where, the fates have wrapt in night.
Whether the nymph shall break Diana's law,
Or some frail China jar receive a flaw;
Or stain her honour or her new brocade;
Forget her prayers, or miss a masquerade;
Or lose her heart, or necklace, at a ball;
Or whether Heaven has doomed that Shock must fall.
Haste, then, ye spirits! to your charge repair:
The fluttering fan be Zephyretta's care;
The drops to thee, Brillante, we consign;
And, Momentilla, let the watch be thine;
Do thou, Crispissa, tend her favourite Lock;
Ariel himself shall be the guard of Shock.
"To fifty chosen Sylphs, of special note,
We trust the important charge, the Petticoat:
Oft have we known that seven-fold fence to fail,

105. Diana's law, the law of chastity.

Though stiff with hoops, and armed with ribs of whale;
Form a strong line about the silver bound,
And guard the wide circumference around.
"Whatever spirit, careless of his charge,
His post neglects, or leaves the fair at large,
Shall feel sharp vengeance soon o'ertake his sins,
Be stopped in vials, or transfixed with pins;
Or plunged in lakes of bitter washes lie,
Or wedged whole ages in a bodkin's eye:
Gums and Pomatums shall his flight restrain,
While clogged he beats his silken wings in vain;
Or Alum styptics with contracting power
Shrink his thin essence like a rivelled flower:
Or, as Ixion fixed, the wretch shall feel
The giddy motion of the whirling Mill,
In fumes of burning Chocolate shall glow,
And tremble at the sea that froths below!"
He spoke; the spirits from the sails descend;
Some, orb in orb, around the nymph extend;
Some thrid the mazy ringlets of her hair;
Some hang upon the pendants of her ear;
With beating hearts the dire event they wait,
Anxious, and trembling for the birth of Fate.

CANTO III

Close by those meads, for ever crowned with flowers,
Where Thames with pride surveys his rising towers,
There stands a structure of majestic frame,
Which from the neighbouring Hampton takes its name.
Here Britain's statesmen oft the fall foredoom
Of foreign Tyrants and of Nymphs at home;
Here thou, great ANNA! whom three realms obey,
Dost sometimes counsel take—and sometimes Tea.
Hither the heroes and the nymphs resort,
To taste awhile the pleasures of a Court;
In various talk th' instructive hours they passed,
Who gave the ball, or paid the visit last;
One speaks the glory of the British Queen,
And one describes a charming Indian screen;
A third interprets motions, looks, and eyes;
At every word a reputation dies.
Snuff, or the fan, supply each pause of chat,
With singing, laughing, ogling, *and all that.*
Mean while, declining from the noon of day,
The sun obliquely shoots his burning ray;
The hungry Judges soon the Sentence sign,
And wretches hang that jury-men may dine;
The merchant from th' Exchange returns in peace,
And the long labours of the Toilet cease.
Belinda now, whom thirst of fame invites,
Burns to encounter two adventurous Knights,
At Ombre singly to decide their doom;
And swells her breast with conquests yet to come.
Straight the three bands prepare in arms to join,
Each band the number of the sacred nine.
Soon as she spreads her hand, the aërial guard
Descend, and sit on each important card:
First Ariel perched upon a Matadore,
Then each, according to the rank they bore;
For Sylphs, yet mindful of their ancient race,
Are, as when women, wondrous fond of place.
Behold, four Kings in majesty revered,
With hoary whiskers and a forky beard;
And four fair Queens whose hands sustain a flower,
The expressive emblem of their softer power;
Four Knaves in garbs succinct, a trusty band,
Caps on their heads, and halberts in their hand;
And particoloured troops, a shining train,
Draw forth to combat on the velvet plain.
The skilful nymph reviews her force with care:
"Let Spades be trumps!" she said, and trumps they were.
Now move to war her sable Matadores,
In show like leaders of the swarthy Moors.
Spadillio first, unconquerable Lord!
Led off two captive trumps, and swept the board.
As many more Manillio forced to yield,
And marched a victor from the verdant field.
Him Basto followed, but his fate more hard
Gained but one trump and one Plebeian card.
With his broad sabre next, a chief in years,
The hoary Majesty of Spades appears,
Puts forth one manly leg, to sight revealed;
The rest, his many-coloured robe concealed.
The rebel Knave, who dares his prince engage,
Proves the just victim of his royal rage.
Even mighty Pam, that Kings and Queens o'erthrew
And mowed down armies in the fights of Lu,
Sad chance of war! now destitute of aid,
Falls undistinguished by the victor spade!
Thus far both armies to Belinda yield;
Now to the Baron fate inclines the field.
His warlike Amazon her host invades,
The imperial consort of the crown of Spades.
The Club's black Tyrant first her victim died,

129. Gums and Pomatums, perfumed ointments. **132. rivelled,** shriveled, faded. **3. structure,** the royal palace of Hampton Court. **7. Anna,** "Anne, by the Grace of God, Queen of Great Britain, France, and Ireland." **8. Tea,** pronounced so as to rhyme exactly with "obey."

27. Ombre, a three-handed game in which each player held nine cards. The three principal trumps, called "Matadores," were, first, the ace of spades ("Spadillio"), the deuce of trumps when black or the seven of trumps when red ("Manillio"), and the ace of clubs ("Basto"). **62. Lu,** the game in which **Pam** is the highest card (the knave of clubs).

Spite of his haughty mien, and barbarous pride:
What boots the regal circle on his head,
His giant limbs, in state unwieldy spread;
That long behind he trails his pompous robe,
And, of all monarchs, only grasps the globe?
  The Baron now his Diamonds pours apace;
The embroidered King who shows but half his face,
And his refulgent Queen, with powers combined
Of broken troops an easy conquest find.
Clubs, Diamonds, Hearts, in wild disorder seen,
With throngs promiscuous strow the level green.
Thus when dispersed a routed army runs,
Of Asia's troops, and Afric's sable sons,
With like confusion different nations fly,
Of various habit, and of various dye;
The pierced battalions dis-united fall,
In heaps on heaps; one fate o'erwhelms them all.
  The Knave of Diamonds tries his wily arts,
And wins (oh shameful chance!) the Queen of Hearts.
At this, the blood the virgin's cheek forsook,
A livid paleness spreads o'er all her look;
She sees, and trembles at the approaching ill,
Just in the jaws of ruin, and Codille.
And now (as oft in some distempered State)
On one nice Trick depends the general fate.
An Ace of Hearts steps forth: The King unseen
Lurked in her hand, and mourned his captive Queen:
He springs to Vengeance with an eager pace,
And falls like thunder on the prostrate Ace.
The nymph exulting fills with shouts the sky;
The walls, the woods, and long canals reply.
  Oh thoughtless mortals! ever blind to fate,
Too soon dejected, and too soon elate.
Sudden, these honours shall be snatched away,
And cursed forever this victorious day.
  For lo! the board with cups and spoons is crowned,
The berries crackle, and the mill turns round;
On shining Altars of Japan they raise
The silver lamp; the fiery spirits blaze:
From silver spouts the grateful liquors glide,
While China's earth receives the smoking tide:
At once they gratify their scent and taste,
And frequent cups prolong the rich repast.
Straight hover round the Fair her airy band;
Some, as she sipped, the fuming liquor fanned,
Some o'er her lap their careful plumes displayed,
Trembling, and conscious of the rich brocade.
Coffee, (which makes the politician wise,
And see through all things with his half-shut eyes)
Sent up in vapours to the Baron's brain
New Stratagems, the radiant Lock to gain.
Ah cease, rash youth! desist ere 'tis too late,
Fear the just Gods, and think of Scylla's Fate!
Changed to a bird, and sent to flit in air,
She dearly pays for Nisus' injured hair!
  But when to mischief mortals bend their will,
How soon they find fit instruments of ill!
Just then, Clarissa drew with tempting grace
A two-edged weapon from her shining case:
So Ladies in Romance assist their Knight,
Present the spear, and arm him for the fight.
He takes the gift with reverence, and extends
The little engine on his fingers' ends;
This just behind Belinda's neck he spread,
As o'er the fragrant steams she bends her head.
Swift to the Lock a thousand Sprites repair,
A thousand wings, by turns, blow back the hair;
And thrice they twitched the diamond in her ear;
Thrice she looked back, and thrice the foe drew near.
Just in that instant, anxious Ariel sought
The close recesses of the Virgin's thought;
As on the nosegay in her breast reclined,
He watched the Ideas rising in her mind.
Sudden he viewed, in spite of all her art,
An earthly Lover lurking at her heart.
Amazed, confused, he found his power expired,
Resigned to fate, and with a sigh retired.
  The Peer now spreads the glittering Forfex wide,
To inclose the Lock; now joins it, to divide.
Even then, before the fatal engine closed,
A wretched Sylph too fondly interposed;
Fate urged the shears, and cut the Sylph in twain
(But airy substance soon unites again).
The meeting points the sacred hair dissever
From the fair head, for ever, and for ever!
  Then flashed the living lightning from her eyes,
And screams of horror rend the affrighted skies.
Not louder shrieks to pitying Heaven are cast,
When husbands, or when lap-dogs breathe their last;
Or when rich China vessels fallen from high,
In glittering dust and painted fragments lie!
  "Let wreaths of triumph now my temples twine,"
The victor cried; "the glorious Prize is mine!
While fish in streams, or birds delight in air,
Or in a coach and six the British Fair,

92. Codille, the term used at Ombre when the challenger loses the game. **106. berries,** coffee beans. **107. Altars of Japan,** japanned tables.

122. Scylla's Fate! Scylla here is not the sea monster associated with Charybdis in the Straits of Messina, but the daughter of King Nisus of Megara. She gave to an enemy of her father's a lock of his hair on which his life depended, and for this unnatural act was changed into a bird. **127. Clarissa,** apparently a rival of Belinda's. **147. Forfex,** scissors.

As long as Atalantis shall be read,
Or the small pillow grace a Lady's bed,
While visits shall be paid on solemn days,
When numerous wax-lights in bright order blaze,
While nymphs take treats, or assignations give,
So long my honour, name, and praise shall live!
What Time would spare, from Steel receives its date,
And monuments, like men, submit to fate!
Steel could the labour of the Gods destroy,
And strike to dust th' imperial towers of Troy;
Steel could the works of mortal pride confound,
And hew triumphal arches to the ground.
What wonder then, fair nymph! thy hairs should feel
The conquering force of unresisted steel?"

CANTO IV

But anxious cares the pensive nymph oppressed,
And secret passions laboured in her breast.
Not youthful kings in battle seized alive,
Not scornful virgins who their charms survive,
Not ardent lovers robbed of all their bliss,
Not ancient ladies when refused a kiss,
Not tyrants fierce that unrepenting die,
Not Cynthia when her manteau's pinned awry,
E'er felt such rage, resentment, and despair,
As thou, sad Virgin! for thy ravished Hair.
For, that sad moment, when the Sylphs withdrew
And Ariel weeping from Belinda flew,
Umbriel, a dusky, melancholy sprite,
As ever sullied the fair face of light,
Down to the central earth, his proper scene,
Repaired to search the gloomy Cave of Spleen.
Swift on his sooty pinions flits the Gnome,
And in a vapour reached the dismal dome.
No cheerful breeze this sullen region knows,
The dreaded East is all the wind that blows.
Here in a grotto, sheltered close from air,
And screened in shades from day's detested glare,
She sighs for ever on her pensive bed,
Pain at her side, and Megrim at her head.
Two handmaids wait the throne: alike in place,
But differing far in figure and in face.
Here stood Ill-nature like an ancient maid,
Her wrinkled form in black and white arrayed;
With store of prayers, for mornings, nights, and noons,
Her hand is filled; her bosom with lampoons.
There Affectation, with a sickly mien,
Shows in her cheek the roses of eighteen,
Practised to lisp, and hang the head aside,
Faints into airs, and languishes with pride,
On the rich quilt sinks with becoming woe,
Wrapt in a gown, for sickness, and for show.
The fair ones feel such maladies as these,
When each new night-dress gives a new disease.
A constant Vapour o'er the palace flies;
Strange phantoms rising as the mists arise;
Dreadful, as hermit's dreams in haunted shades,
Or bright, as visions of expiring maids.
Now glaring fiends, and snakes on rolling spires,
Pale spectres, gaping tombs, and purple fires:
Now lakes of liquid gold, Elysian scenes,
And crystal domes, and angels in machines.
Unnumbered throngs on every side are seen,
Of bodies changed to various forms by Spleen.
Here living Tea-pots stand, one arm held out,
One bent; the handle this, and that the spout:
A Pipkin there, like Homer's Tripod walks;
Here sighs a Jar, and there a Goose-pie talks;
Men prove with child, as powerful fancy works,
And maids turned bottles, call aloud for corks.
Safe passed the Gnome through this fantastic band,
A branch of healing Spleenwort in his hand,
Then thus addressed the Power: "Hail, wayward Queen!
Who rule the sex to fifty from fifteen:
Parent of vapours and of female wit,
Who give the hysteric or poetic fit,
On various tempers act by various ways,
Make some take physic, others scribble plays;
Who cause the proud their visits to delay,
And send the godly in a pet to pray.
A nymph there is, that all thy power disdains,
And thousands more in equal mirth maintains.
But oh! if e'er thy Gnome could spoil a grace,
Or raise a pimple on a beauteous face,
Like Citron-waters matrons cheeks inflame,
Or change complexions at a losing game;
If e'er with airy horns I planted heads,
Or rumpled petticoats, or tumbled beds,
Or caused suspicion when no soul was rude,
Or discomposed the head-dress of a Prude,
Or e'er to costive lap-dog gave disease,
Which not the tears of brightest eyes could ease:
Hear me, and touch Belinda with chagrin;
That single act gives half the world the spleen."

165. Atalantis, *The New Atalantis,* 1709, by Mrs. Manley, a book dealing in contemporary scandal. **8. Cynthia,** Diana, goddess of chastity. **16. Spleen,** bad temper. The Cave represents the lower world or hell of classical epic. **24. Megrim,** migraine, melancholy.

39. Vapour. A fashionable disease of Pope's time was the "vapours," or hypochondria, closely related to the "blues" of later generations and to the "melancholy" of the Elizabethans. It induced morbid fancies like those listed below.

The Goddess with a discontented air
Seems to reject him, though she grants his prayer.
A wondrous Bag with both her hands she binds,
Like that where once Ulysses held the winds;
There she collects the force of female lungs,
Sighs, sobs, and passions, and the war of tongues.
A Vial next she fills with fainting fears,
Soft sorrows, melting griefs, and flowing tears.
The Gnome rejoicing bears her gifts away,
Spreads his black wings, and slowly mounts to day.
Sunk in Thalestris' arms the nymph he found,
Her eyes dejected and her hair unbound.
Full o'er their heads the swelling bag he rent,
And all the Furies issued at the vent.
Belinda burns with more than mortal ire,
And fierce Thalestris fans the rising fire.
"O wretched maid!" she spread her hands, and cried,
(While Hampton's echoes, "Wretched maid!" replied)
"Was it for this you took such constant care
The bodkin, comb, and essence to prepare?
For this your locks in paper durance bound,
For this with torturing irons wreathed around?
For this with fillets strained your tender head,
And bravely bore the double loads of lead?
Gods! shall the ravisher display your hair,
While the Fops envy, and the Ladies stare!
Honour forbid! at whose unrivalled shrine
Ease, pleasure, virtue, all our sex resign.
Methinks already I your tears survey,
Already hear the horrid things they say,
Already see you a degraded toast,
And all your honour in a whisper lost!
How shall I, then, your helpless fame defend?
'Twill then be infamy to seem your friend!
And shall this prize, the inestimable prize,
Exposed through crystal to the gazing eyes,
And heightened by the diamond's circling rays,
On that rapacious hand for ever blaze?
Sooner shall grass in Hyde-park Circus grow,
And wits take lodgings in the sound of Bow;
Sooner let earth, air, sea, to Chaos fall,
Men, monkeys, lap-dogs, parrots, perish all!"
She said; then raging to Sir Plume repairs,
And bids her Beau demand the precious hairs:
(Sir Plume of amber snuff-box justly vain,
And the nice conduct of a clouded cane)
With earnest eyes, and round unthinking face,
He first the snuff-box opened, then the case,
And thus broke out—"My Lord, why, what the devil?
Z—ds! damn the lock! 'fore Gad, you must be civil!
Plague on't! 'tis past a jest—nay prithee, pox!
Give her the hair"—he spoke, and rapped his box.
"It grieves me much" (replied the Peer again)
"Who speaks so well should ever speak in vain.
But by this Lock, this sacred Lock, I swear,
(Which never more shall join its parted hair;
Which never more its honours shall renew,
Clipped from the lovely head where late it grew)
That while my nostrils draw the vital air,
This hand, which won it, shall for ever wear."
He spoke, and speaking, in proud triumph spread
The long-contended honours of her head.
But Umbriel, hateful Gnome! forbears not so;
He breaks the Vial whence the sorrows flow.
Then see! the nymph in beauteous grief appears,
Her eyes half-languishing, half-drowned in tears;
On her heaved bosom hung her drooping head,
Which, with a sigh, she raised; and thus she said:
"For ever curst be this detested day,
Which snatched my best, my favourite curl away!
Happy! ah ten times happy had I been,
If Hampton-Court these eyes had never seen!
Yet am not I the first mistaken maid,
By love of Courts to numerous ills betrayed.
Oh had I rather unadmired remained
In some lone isle, or distant Northern land;
Where the gilt Chariot never marks the way,
Where none learn Ombre, none e'er taste Bohea!
There kept my charms concealed from mortal eye,
Like roses, that in deserts bloom and die.
What moved my mind with youthful Lords to roam?
Oh had I stayed, and said my prayers at home!
'Twas this, the morning omens seemed to tell,
Thrice from my trembling hand the patch-box fell;
The tottering China shook without a wind,
Nay, Poll sat mute, and Shock was most unkind!
A Sylph too warned me of the threats of fate,
In mystic visions, now believed too late!
See the poor remnants of these slighted hairs!
My hands shall rend what e'en thy rapine spares:
These in two sable ringlets taught to break,
Once gave new beauties to the snowy neck;
The sister-lock now sits uncouth, alone,
And in its fellow's fate foresees its own;
Uncurled it hangs, the fatal shears demands,
And tempts once more, thy sacrilegious hands.
Oh hadst thou, cruel! been content to seize
Hairs less in sight, or any hairs but these!"

109. toast, a woman whose health was drunk in celebration of her beauty. **118. Bow.** The church of St. Mary le Bow, which had a famous peal of bells, was in an unfashionable part of London. **121. Sir Plume,** Sir George Brown, brother of Mrs. Morley, or "Thalestris."

156. Bohea! an expensive kind of black tea. **162. patch-box,** a box containing small pieces of black or brown plaster worn by women on the face.

CANTO V

She said: the pitying audience melt in tears;
But Fate and Jove had stopped the Baron's ears.
In vain Thalestris with reproach assails,
For who can move when fair Belinda fails?
Not half so fixed the Trojan could remain,
While Anna begged and Dido raged in vain.
Then grave Clarissa graceful waved her fan;
Silence ensued, and thus the nymph began:
"Say why are Beauties praised and honoured most,
The wise man's passion, and the vain man's toast?
Why decked with all that land and sea afford,
Why Angels called, and Angel-like adored?
Why round our coaches crowd the white-gloved Beaux,
Why bows the side-box from its inmost rows;
How vain are all these glories, all our pains,
Unless good sense preserve what beauty gains:
That men may say, when we the front-box grace:
'Behold the first in virtue as in face!'
Oh! if to dance all night, and dress all day,
Charmed the small-pox, or chased old-age away;
Who would not scorn what housewife's cares produce,
Or who would learn one earthly thing of use?
To patch, nay ogle, might become a saint,
Nor could it sure be such a sin to paint.
But since, alas! frail beauty must decay,
Curled or uncurled, since locks will turn to grey;
Since painted, or not painted, all shall fade,
And she who scorns a man, must die a maid;
What then remains but well our power to use,
And keep good-humour still whate'er we lose?
And trust me, dear! good-humour can prevail,
When airs, and flights, and screams, and scolding fail.
Beauties in vain their pretty eyes may roll;
Charms strike the sight, but merit wins the soul."
So spoke the Dame, but no applause ensued;
Belinda frowned, Thalestris called her Prude.
"To arms, to arms!" the fierce Virago cries,
And swift as lightning to the combat flies.
All side in parties, and begin th' attack;
Fans clap, silks rustle, and tough whalebones crack;
Heroes' and Heroines' shouts confusedly rise,
And bass, and treble voices strike the skies.
No common weapons in their hands are found,
Like Gods they fight, nor dread a mortal wound.
So when bold Homer makes the Gods engage,
And heavenly breasts with human passions rage;
'Gainst Pallas, Mars; Latona, Hermes arms;
And all Olympus rings with loud alarms:
Jove's thunder roars, heaven trembles all around,
Blue Neptune storms, the bellowing deeps resound:
Earth shakes her nodding towers, the ground gives way,
And the pale ghosts start at the flash of day!
Triumphant Umbriel on a sconce's height
Clapped his glad wings, and sate to view the fight:
Propped on their bodkin spears, the Sprites survey
The growing combat, or assist the fray.
While through the press enraged Thalestris flies,
And scatters death around from both her eyes,
A Beau and Witling perished in the throng,
One died in metaphor, and one in song.
"O cruel nymph! a living death I bear,"
Cried Dapperwit, and sunk beside his chair.
A mournful glance Sir Fopling upwards cast,
"Those eyes are made so killing"—was his last.
Thus on Maeander's flowery margin lies
The expiring Swan, and as he sings he dies.
When bold Sir Plume had drawn Clarissa down,
Chloe stepped in, and killed him with a frown;
She smiled to see the doughty hero slain,
But, at her smile, the Beau revived again.
Now Jove suspends his golden scales in air,
Weighs the Men's wits against the Lady's hair;
The doubtful beam long nods from side to side;
At length the wits mount up, the hairs subside.
See, fierce Belinda on the Baron flies,
With more than usual lightning in her eyes:
Nor feared the Chief the unequal fight to try,
Who sought no more than on his foe to die.
But this bold Lord with manly strength endued,
She with one finger and a thumb subdued:
Just where the breath of life his nostrils drew,
A charge of snuff the wily virgin threw;
The Gnomes direct, to every atom just,
The pungent grains of titillating dust.
Sudden, with starting tears each eye o'erflows,
And the high dome re-echoes to his nose.
"Now meet thy fate," incensed Belinda cried,
And drew a deadly bodkin from her side.
(The same, his ancient personage to deck,

5. Trojan, Aeneas. For the story of Aeneas's departure from Dido and her sister Anna see the *Aeneid*, Book IV.

53. sconce, a candleholder attached to the wall. **62. Dapperwit,** a fop in Wycherley's comedy *Love in a Wood.* **63. Sir Fopling,** Sir Fopling Flutter, a character in Etherege's comedy *The Man of Mode.* **65. Maeander's . . . margin.** Ovid's "Epistle of Dido to Aeneas" (*Heroides VII*) is the chief source of the concept of the "swan-song" of the dying swan on the banks of the river Maeander in Asia Minor. **71. golden scales.** For Homer's use of the golden scales see the *Iliad*, Book VIII. **88–96. deadly bodkin . . . wears.** A bodkin is a long pin for fastening the hair. The passage, Pope notes, is in imitation of the progress of Agamemnon's sceptre in Book II of the *Iliad.*

Her great great grandsire wore about his neck,
In three seal-rings; which after, melted down,
Formed a vast buckle for his widow's gown:
Her infant grandame's whistle next it grew,
The bells she jingled, and the whistle blew;
Then in a bodkin graced her mother's hairs,
Which long she wore, and now Belinda wears.)
"Boast not my fall," (he cried) "insulting foe!
Thou by some other shalt be laid as low,
Nor think, to die dejects my lofty mind:
All that I dread is leaving you behind!
Rather than so, ah let me still survive,
And burn in Cupid's flames—but burn alive."
"Restore the Lock!" she cries; and all around
"Restore the Lock!" the vaulted roofs rebound.
Not fierce Othello in so loud a strain
Roared for the handkerchief that caused his pain.
But see how oft ambitious aims are crossed,
And chiefs contend till all the prize is lost!
The Lock, obtained with guilt, and kept with pain,
In every place is sought, but sought in vain:
With such a prize no mortal must be blest,
So heaven decrees! With heaven who can contest?
Some thought it mounted to the Lunar sphere,
Since all things lost on earth are treasured there.
There Hero's wits are kept in ponderous vases,
And beaux' in snuff-boxes and tweezer-cases.
There broken vows and death-bed alms are found,
And lovers' hearts with ends of riband bound,
The courtier's promises, and sick man's prayers,
The smiles of harlots, and the tears of heirs,
Cages for gnats, and chains to yoke a flea,
Dried butterflies, and tomes of casuistry.
But trust the Muse—she saw it upward rise,
Though marked by none but quick, poetic eyes
(So Rome's great founder to the heavens withdrew,
To Proculus alone confessed in view);
A sudden Star, it shot through liquid air,
And drew behind a radiant trail of hair.
Not Berenice's Locks first rose so bright,
The heavens bespangling with dishevelled light.
The Sylphs behold it kindling as it flies,
And pleased pursue its progress through the skies.
This the beau monde shall from the Mall survey,
And hail with music its propitious ray.
This the blest Lover shall for Venus take,
And send up vows from Rosamonda's lake.
This Partridge soon shall view in cloudless skies,
When next he looks through Galileo's eyes;
And hence the egregious wizard shall foredoom
The fate of Louis, and the fall of Rome.
Then cease, bright Nymph! to mourn thy ravished hair,
Which adds new glory to the shining sphere!
Not all the tresses that fair head can boast,
Shall draw such envy as the Lock you lost.
For, after all the murders of your eye,
When, after millions slain, yourself shall die:
When those fair suns shall set, as set they must,
And all those tresses shall be laid in dust,
This Lock, the Muse shall consecrate to fame,
And 'midst the stars inscribe Belinda's name.

125. Rome's great founder, Romulus, who, after his translation to the heavens, appeared only to Proculus, to whom he gave a message to the Roman people. **129. Berenice's Locks.** The Egyptian queen pledged a lock of her hair for her husband's safe return. The gods transported it to heaven, where it now shines in the constellation "Berenice's Locks." **133. Mall,** a fashionable walk in St. James's Park. **136. lake,** in St. James's Park.

137. Partridge, a London astrologer. **138. Galileo's eyes,** the telescope.

from AN ESSAY ON MAN

Although it is in some respects the most ambitious of his undertakings, Pope's *Essay on Man* does not represent an original philosophical effort on the poet's part. Many if not most of the ideas it contains were derived, probably in conversation, from the remarkable politician, philosopher, and writer whom we now know as Lord Bolingbroke. These ideas are "Deistic" in tendency. That is to say, they find the evidence for their "natural religion" rather in the study of nature and in human reason than in direct revelation.

The poem in its entirety comprises four epistles, of which only the first and part of the second are printed here. It is more remarkable for its brilliant passages than for strict coherence of thought.

EPISTLE I

Awake, my St. John! leave all meaner things
To low ambition, and the pride of Kings.
Let us (since Life can little more supply
Than just to look about us and to die)
Expatiate free o'er all this scene of Man;
A mighty maze! but not without a plan;
A Wild, where weeds and flowers promiscuous shoot;
Or Garden, tempting with forbidden fruit.
Together let us beat this ample field,
Try what the open, what the covert yield;
The latent tracts, the giddy heights, explore
Of all who blindly creep, or sightless soar;
Eye Nature's walks, shoot Folly as it flies,
And catch the Manners living as they rise;

1. St. John (pronounced "Sinjun") Henry St. John, Viscount Bolingbroke (1678–1751). Lord Chesterfield himself considered him the personification of intelligence, eloquence, and charm. **5. Expatiate,** roam.

Laugh where we must, be candid where we can,
But vindicate the ways of God to Man.
1. Say first, of God above, or Man below,
What can we reason, but from what we know?
Of Man, what see we but his station here,
From which to reason, or to which refer?
Through worlds unnumbered though the God be known,
'Tis ours to trace him only in our own.
He, who through vast immensity can pierce,
See worlds on worlds compose one universe,
Observe how system into system runs,
What other planets circle other suns,
What varied Being peoples every star,
May tell why Heaven has made us as we are.
But of this frame the bearings, and the ties,
The strong connexions, nice dependencies,
Gradations just, has thy pervading soul
Looked through? or can a part contain the whole?
Is the great chain, that draws all to agree,
And drawn supports, upheld by God, or thee?
2. Presumptuous Man! the reason wouldst thou find,
Why formed so weak, so little, and so blind?
First, if thou canst, the harder reason guess,
Why formed no weaker, blinder, and no less?
Ask of thy mother earth, why oaks are made
Taller or stronger than the weeds they shade!
Or ask of yonder argent fields above,
Why Jove's satellites are less than Jove!
Of Systems possible, if 'tis confessed
That Wisdom infinite must form the best,
Where all must full or not coherent be,
And all that rises, rise in due degree;
Then, in the scale of reasoning life, 'tis plain,
There must be, somewhere, such a rank as Man:
And all the question (wrangle e'er so long)
Is only this, if God has placed him wrong?
Respecting Man, whatever wrong we call,
May, must be right, as relative to all.
In human works, though laboured on with pain,
A thousand movements scarce one purpose gain;
In God's, one single can its end produce;
Yet serves to second too some other use.
So Man, who here seems principal alone,
Perhaps acts second to some sphere unknown,
Touches some wheel, or verges to some goal.
'Tis but a part we see, and not a whole.
When the proud steed shall know why Man restrains
His fiery course, or drives him o'er the plains:
When the dull Ox, why now he breaks the clod,
Is now a victim, and now Aegypt's god:
Then shall Man's pride and dulness comprehend
His actions', passions', being's, use and end;
Why doing, suffering, checked, impelled; and why
This hour a slave, the next a deity.
Then say not Man's imperfect, Heaven in fault;
Say rather, Man's as perfect as he ought:
His knowledge measured to his state and place;
His time a moment, and a point his space.
If to be perfect in a certain sphere,
What matter, soon or late, or here or there?
The blest to-day is as completely so,
As who began a thousand years ago.
3. Heaven from all creatures hides the book of Fate,
All but the page prescribed, their present state:
From brutes what men, from men what spirits know,
Or who could suffer being here below?
The lamb thy riot dooms to bleed to-day,
Had he thy Reason, would he skip and play?
Pleased to the last, he crops the flowery food,
And licks the hand just raised to shed his blood.
Oh blindness to the future! kindly given,
That each may fill the circle marked by Heaven,
Who sees with equal eye, as God of all,
A hero perish, or a sparrow fall,
Atoms or systems into ruin hurled,
And now a bubble burst, and now a world.
Hope humbly then; with trembling pinions soar;
Wait the great teacher Death; and God adore.
What future bliss, he gives not thee to know,
But gives that Hope to be thy blessing now.
Hope springs eternal in the human breast:
Man never Is, but always To be blessed;
The soul, uneasy and confined from home,
Rests and expatiates in a life to come.
Lo, the poor Indian! whose untutored mind
Sees God in clouds, or hears him in the wind;
His soul, proud Science never taught to stray
Far as the solar walk, or Milky Way;
Yet simple Nature to his hope has given,
Behind the cloud-topped hill, an humbler heaven;
Some safer world in depth of woods embraced,
Some happier island in the watery waste,
Where slaves once more their native land behold,
No fiends torment, no Christians thirst for gold.
To Be, contents his natural desire;
He asks no Angel's wing, no Seraph's fire;
But thinks, admitted to that equal sky,
His faithful dog shall bear him company.

16. vindicate . . . Man. Cf. Milton's purpose as expressed in *Paradise Lost*, Book I, ll. 25–26, page 395. **41. argent,** silvery. **42. satellites,** pronounced "să-tĕl'-ĭ-tēz."

102. solar walk, the path of the sun through the sky,

4. Go, wiser thou! and, in thy scale of sense,
Weigh thy Opinion against Providence;
Call imperfection what thou fanciest such;
Say, here he gives too little, there too much:
Destroy all Creatures for thy sport or gust,
Yet cry, If Man's unhappy, God's unjust;
If Man alone engross not Heaven's high care,
Alone made perfect here, immortal there:
Snatch from his hand the balance and the rod,
Re-judge his justice, be the God of God.
In Pride, in reasoning Pride, our error lies;
All quit their sphere, and rush into the skies.
Pride still is aiming at the blest abodes,
Men would be Angels, Angels would be Gods.
Aspiring to be Gods, if Angels fell,
Aspiring to be Angels, Men rebel:
And who but wishes to invert the laws
Of Order, sins against the Eternal Cause.
5. Ask for what end the heavenly bodies shine,
Earth for whose use? Pride answers, "'Tis for mine:
For me kind Nature wakes her genial Power,
Suckles each herb, and spreads out every flower;
Annual for me, the grape, the rose renew
The juice nectareous, and the balmy dew;
For me, the mine a thousand treasures brings;
For me, health gushes from a thousand springs;
Seas roll to waft me, suns to light me rise;
My foot-stool earth, my canopy the skies."
But errs not Nature from this gracious end,
From burning suns when livid deaths descend,
When earthquakes swallow, or when tempests sweep
Towns to one grave, whole nations to the deep?
"No," ('tis replied), "the first Almighty Cause
Acts not by partial, but by general laws;
The exceptions few; some change since all began:
And what created perfect?"—Why then Man?
If the great end be human Happiness,
Then Nature deviates; and can Man do less?
As much that end a constant course requires
Of showers and sunshine, as of Man's desires;
As much eternal springs and cloudless skies,
As Men forever temperate, calm, and wise.
If plagues or earthquakes break not Heaven's design,
Why then a Borgia, or a Catiline?
Who knows but He, whose hand the lightning forms,
Who heaves old Ocean, and who wings the storms;
Pours fierce ambition in a Caesar's mind,
Or turns young Ammon loose to scourge mankind?
From pride, from pride, our very reasoning springs;
Account for moral, as for natural things:
Why charge we Heaven in those, in these acquit?
In both, to reason right is to submit.
Better for us, perhaps, it might appear,
Were there all harmony, all virtue here;
That never air or ocean felt the wind;
That never passion discomposed the mind.
But All subsists by elemental strife,
And passions are the elements of life.
The general Order, since the whole began,
Is kept in Nature, and is kept in Man.
6. What would this Man? Now upward will he soar,
And little less than Angel, would be more;
Now looking downwards, just as grieved appears
To want the strength of bulls, the fur of bears.
Made for his use all creatures if he call,
Say what their use, had he the powers of all?
Nature to these, without profusion, kind,
The proper organs, proper powers assigned;
Each seeming want compénsated of course,
Here with degrees of swiftness, there of force;
All in exact proportion to the state;
Nothing to add, and nothing to abate.
Each beast, each insect, happy in its own:
Is Heaven unkind to Man, and Man alone?
Shall he alone, whom rational we call,
Be pleased with nothing, if not blessed with all?
The bliss of Man (could Pride that blessing find)
Is not to act or think beyond mankind;
No powers of body or of soul to share,
But what his nature and his state can bear.
Why has not Man a microscopic eye?
For this plain reason, Man is not a Fly.
Say what the use, were finer optics given,
To inspect a mite, not comprehend the heaven?
Or touch, if tremblingly alive all o'er,
To smart and agonize at every pore?
Or quick effluvia darting through the brain,
Die of a rose in aromatic pain?
If nature thundered in his opening ears,
And stunned him with the music of the spheres,
How would he wish that Heaven had left him still
The whispering Zephyr, and the purling rill?
Who finds not Providence all good and wise,
Alike in what it gives, and what denies?
7. Far as Creation's ample range extends,
The scale of sensual, mental powers ascends:
Mark how it mounts, to Man's imperial race,
From the green myriads in the peopled grass:

117. gust, pleasure. **133. genial,** life-giving. **156. Borgia,** Cesare Borgia (1476–1507), illegitimate son of Pope Alexander VI, notorious for the brilliance, lust, and cruelty typical of his family. **Catiline,** Roman conspirator of the first century B.C., noted for his cruelty and wickedness.

160. Ammon, Alexander the Great, King of Macedon from 336 to 323 B.C., called the son of Zeus Ammon. **176. want,** lack. **208. sensual,** sensory.

What modes of sight betwixt each wide extreme,
The mole's dim curtain and the lynx's beam:
Of smell, the headlong lioness between,
And hound sagacious on the tainted green:
Of hearing, from the life that fills the flood,
To that which warbles through the vernal wood:
The spider's touch, how exquisitely fine!
Feels at each thread, and lives along the line:
In the nice bee, what sense so subtly true
From poisonous herbs extracts the healing dew?
How Instinct varies in the grovelling swine,
Compared, half-reasoning elephant, with thine!
'Twixt that, and Reason, what a nice barrier,
Forever separate, yet forever near!
Remembrance and Reflection how allied;
What thin partitions Sense from Thought divide:
And middle natures, how they long to join,
Yet never pass the insuperable line!
Without this just gradation, could they be
Subjected, these to those, or all to thee?
The powers of all subdued by thee alone,
Is not thy reason all these powers in one?

8. See, through this air, this ocean, and this earth,
All matter quick, and bursting into birth.
Above, how high progressive life may go!
Around, how wide! how deep extend below!
Vast chain of Being! which from God began,
Natures ethereal, human, angel, man,
Beast, bird, fish, insect, what no eye can see,
No glass can reach; from Infinite to thee,
From thee to Nothing.—On superior powers
Were we to press, inferior might on ours:
Or in the full creation leave a void,
Where, one step broken, the great scale's destroyed:
From Nature's chain whatever link you strike,
Tenth or ten thousandth, breaks the chain alike.

And, if each system in gradation roll
Alike essential to the amazing Whole,
The least confusion but in one, not all
That system only, but the Whole must fall.
Let Earth unbalanced from her orbit fly,
Planets and Suns run lawless through the sky;
Let ruling angels from their spheres be hurled,
Being on Being wrecked, and world on world;
Heaven's whole foundations to their centre nod,
And Nature tremble to the throne of God.
All this dread Order break—for whom? for thee?
Vile worm!—Oh Madness! Pride! Impiety!

9. What if the foot, ordained the dust to tread,
Or hand, to toil, aspired to be the head?
What if the head, the eye, or ear repined
To serve mere engines to the ruling Mind?
Just as absurd for any part to claim
To be another, in this general frame:
Just as absurd, to mourn the tasks or pains
The great directing Mind of All ordains.

All are but parts of one stupendous whole,
Whose body Nature is, and God the soul;
That, changed through all, and yet in all the same,
Great in the earth, as in the ethereal frame,
Warms in the sun, refreshes in the breeze,
Glows in the stars, and blossoms in the trees,
Lives through all life, extends through all extent,
Spreads undivided, operates unspent;
Breathes in our soul, informs our mortal part,
As full, as perfect, in a hair as heart:
As full, as perfect, in vile Man that mourns,
As the rapt Seraph that adores and burns:
To him no high, no low, no great, no small;
He fills, he bounds, connects, and equals all.

10. Cease then, nor Order imperfection name;
Our proper bliss depends on what we blame.
Know thy own point: this kind, this due degree
Of blindness, weakness, Heaven bestows on thee.
Submit.—In this, or any other sphere,
Secure to be as blessed as thou canst bear:
Safe in the hand of one disposing Power,
Or in the natal or the mortal hour.
All Nature is but Art, unknown to thee;
All Chance, Direction, which thou canst not see;
All Discord, Harmony not understood;
All partial Evil, universal Good:
And, spite of Pride, in erring Reason's spite,
One truth is clear, WHATEVER IS, IS RIGHT.

219. nice, discriminating, delicate. **223. barrier,** pronounced in two syllables, with the accent on the second. **234. quick,** alive.

EPISTLE II

1. Know then thyself, presume not God to scan;
The proper study of Mankind is Man.
Placed on this isthmus of a middle state,
A Being darkly wise, and rudely great:
With too much knowledge for the Sceptic side,
With too much weakness for the Stoic's pride,
He hangs between; in doubt to act, or rest;
In doubt to deem himself a God, or Beast;
In doubt his Mind or Body to prefer;
Born but to die, and reasoning but to err;
Alike in ignorance, his reason such,
Whether he thinks too little, or too much:
Chaos of Thought and Passion, all confused;

5. Sceptic, philosophically, one whose attitude is characterized by doubt or suspended judgment, and who believes in the necessity of critical inquiry into every belief. **6. Stoic's pride.** Stoicism teaches that men should be free from passion and unmoved by joy or grief.

Still by himself abused, or disabused;
Created half to rise, and half to fall;
Great lord of all things, yet a prey to all;
Sole judge of Truth, in endless Error hurled:
The glory, jest, and riddle of the world!
Go, wondrous creature! mount where Science guides;
Go, measure earth, weigh air, and state the tides;
Instruct the planets in what orbs to run,
Correct old Time, and regulate the Sun;
Go, soar with Plato to the empyreal sphere,
To the first good, first perfect, and first fair;
Or tread the mazy round his followers trod,
And quitting sense call imitating God;
As Eastern priests in giddy circles run,
And turn their heads to imitate the Sun.
Go, teach Eternal Wisdom how to rule—
Then drop into thyself, and be a fool!
Superior beings, when of late they saw
A mortal Man unfold all Nature's law,
Admired such wisdom in an earthly shape,
And showed a Newton as we show an Ape.
Could he, whose rules the rapid Comet bind,
Describe or fix one movement of his Mind?
Who saw its fires here rise, and there descend,
Explain his own beginning, or his end?
Alas, what wonder! Man's superior part
Unchecked may rise, and climb from art to art;
But when his own great work is but begun,
What Reason weaves, by Passion is undone.
Trace Science then, with Modesty thy guide,
First strip off all her equipage of Pride;
Deduct what is but Vanity, or Dress,
Or Learning's Luxury, or Idleness;
Or tricks to show the stretch of human brain,
Mere curious pleasure, or ingenious pain;
Expunge the whole, or lop the excrescent parts
Of all our Vices have created Arts;
Then see how little the remaining sum,
Which served the past, and must the times to come! . . .
5. Vice is a monster of so frightful mien,
As, to be hated, needs but to be seen;
Yet seen too oft, familiar with her face,
We first endure, then pity, then embrace.
But where the Extreme of Vice, was ne'er agreed:
Ask where's the North? at York, 'tis on the Tweed;
In Scotland, at the Orcades; and there,
At Greenland, Zembla, or the Lord knows where.
No creature owns it in the first degree,
But thinks his neighbour further gone than he;
Even those who dwell beneath its very zone,
Or never feel the rage, or never own;
What happier natures shrink at with affright,
The hard inhabitant contends is right.
6. Virtuous and vicious every Man must be,
Few in the extreme, but all in the degree;
The rogue and fool by fits is fair and wise;
And even the best, by fits, what they despise.
'Tis but by parts we follow good or ill,
For, Vice or Virtue, Self directs it still;
Each individual seeks a several goal,
But Heaven's great view is One, and that the Whole.
That counter-works each folly and caprice;
That disappoints the effect of every vice;
That, happy frailties to all ranks applied,
Shame to the virgin, to the matron pride,
Fear to the statesman, rashness to the chief,
To kings presumption, and to crowds belief:
That, Virtue's ends from Vanity can raise,
Which seeks no interest, no reward but praise;
And builds on wants, and on defects of mind,
The joy, the peace, the glory of Mankind.
Heaven forming each on other to depend,
A master, or a servant, or a friend,
Bids each on other for assistance call,
Till one man's weakness grows the strength of all.
Wants, frailties, passions, closer still ally
The common interest, or endear the tie.
To these we owe true friendship, love sincere,
Each home-felt joy that life inherits here;
Yet from the same we learn, in its decline,
Those joys, those loves, those interests to resign;
Taught half by Reason, half by mere decay,
To welcome death, and calmly pass away.
Whate'er the Passion, knowledge, fame, or pelf,
Not one will change his neighbour with himself.
The learned is happy nature to explore.
The fool is happy that he knows no more,
The rich is happy in the plenty given,
The poor contents him with the care of Heaven.
See the blind beggar dance, the cripple sing,
The sot a hero, lunatic a king;
The starving chemist in his golden views
Supremely blest, the poet in his Muse.
See some strange comfort every state attend,
And Pride bestowed on all, a common friend;
See some fit Passion every age supply.
Hope travels through, nor quits us when we die.
Behold the child, by Nature's kindly law,

23–24. Plato . . . fair. A reference to the Platonic belief that beyond this transitory and illusive world there is the serene and immutable eternity of truth, beauty, and goodness. **34. Newton,** Sir Isaac Newton (1642–1727), discoverer of the laws of gravitation and one of the great minds of history.

227. zone, track of the sun. **269. chemist,** alchemist, with his hope of making gold out of the baser metals.

Pleased with a rattle, tickled with a straw;
Some livelier play-thing gives his youth delight,
A little louder, but as empty quite:
Scarfs, garters, gold, amuse his riper stage,
And beads and prayer-books are the toys of age:
Pleased with this bauble still, as that before;
Till tired he sleeps, and Life's poor play is o'er.
  Mean-while Opinion gilds with varying rays
Those painted clouds that beautify our days;
Each want of happiness by hope supplied,
And each vacuity of sense by Pride.
These build as fast as knowledge can destroy;
In Folly's cup still laughs the bubble, joy;
One prospect lost, another still we gain,
And not a vanity is given in vain;
Even mean Self-love becomes, by force divine,
The scale to measure others' wants by thine.
See! and confess, one comfort still must rise.
'Tis this, Though Man's a fool, yet God is wise.

EPISTLE TO DR. ARBUTHNOT

Dr. John Arbuthnot (1667–1735) was the lifelong friend of Pope and Swift, and a distinguished physician and man of letters in his own right. Born in Scotland, he made his reputation in London, and was physician to Queen Anne from 1709 to 1714. He was the author of *The History of John Bull*, 1712, in which he described the essential Englishman and named him "John Bull." He helped to form the Scriblerus Club, a Tory organization of both political and literary fame. Among the important literary works which had their inception in the deliberations of the club was Swift's *Gulliver's Travels*. *The Memoirs of Martinus Scriblerus*, a brilliant satirical work, was largely the work of Arbuthnot.

The *Epistle to Dr. Arbuthnot* is in form a dialogue between Pope and Arbuthnot, and was occasioned, as Pope tells us in his "Advertisement," by the publication of some verses which attacked "in a very extraordinary manner, not only my writings . . . but my person, morals, and family, whereof, to those who know me not, a truer information may be requisite." The poem contains many passages of biographical and critical interest, and, in the sketch of "Atticus," Pope gives us a brilliant, if not altogether complete, portrait of his contemporary Addison.

P. Shut, shut the door, good John! fatigued, I said,
Tie up the knocker, say I'm sick, I'm dead.
The Dog-star rages! nay 'tis past a doubt,
All Bedlam, or Parnassus, is let out:
Fire in each eye, and papers in each hand,
They rave, recite, and madden round the land.
  What walls can guard me, or what shades can hide?
They pierce my thickets, through my grot they glide;
By land, by water, they renew the charge,
They stop the chariot, and they board the barge.
No place is sacred, not the church is free;
E'en Sunday shines no Sabbath day to me:
Then from the Mint walks forth the man of rhyme,
Happy to catch me just at dinner-time.
  Is there a parson, much bemused in beer,
A maudlin poetess, a rhyming peer,
A clerk, foredoomed his father's soul to cross,
Who pens a stanza, when he should engross?
Is there, who, locked from ink and paper, scrawls
With desperate charcoal round his darkened walls?
All fly to Twit'nam, and in humble strain
Apply to me, to keep them mad or vain.
Arthur, whose giddy son neglects the laws,
Imputes to me and my damned works the cause:
Poor Cornus sees his frantic wife elope,
And curses wit, and poetry, and Pope.
  Friend to my life! (which did not you prolong,
The world had wanted many an idle song)
What drop or nostrum can this plague remove?
Or which must end me, a fool's wrath or love?
A dire dilemma! either way I'm sped,
If foes, they write, if friends, they read me dead.
Seized and tied down to judge, how wretched I!
Who can't be silent, and who will not lie.
To laugh, were want of goodness and of grace.
And to be grave, exceeds all power of face.
I sit with sad civility, I read
With honest anguish, and an aching head;
And drop at last, but in unwilling ears,
This saving counsel, "Keep your piece nine years."
  "Nine years!" cries he, who high in Drury Lane,

1. good John, John Searl, Pope's household servant at Twickenham. **3. Dog-star.** Sirius, the dog-star, rises with the sun in late July and early August, and to the combination the ancients attributed the hottest days of the summer (the "dog days"). Pope implies that human beings, like dogs, have gone mad and turned to scribbling verses.

4. Bedlam, Bethlehem Hospital, the notorious London asylum for the insane. **8. grot,** an artificial grotto on Pope's estate at Twickenham near London. **13. Mint,** a district in Southwark, London, where debtors were free from arrest. On Sundays no man could be taken into custody for debt, and the refugees might safely leave the district. **18. engross,** to write out a legal document. **21. Twit'nam,** the popular pronunciation of Twickenham. **23. Arthur,** Arthur Moore, member of Parliament and well-known economist, the father of James Moore-Smythe (see note to l. 98). **25. Cornus,** Sir Robert Walpole, the Whig prime minister. The appellation "cornus" (Latin *cornu*, horn) refers to the ancient jest that husbands of unfaithful wives wear horns on their foreheads. **40. "Keep . . . years,"** Horace's advice in his *Ars Poetica*, l. 338. **41. Drury Lane.** Like Grub Street (see l. 111), Drury Lane was a resort of poverty-stricken writers.

Lulled by soft zephyrs through the broken pane,
Rhymes ere he wakes, and prints before term ends,
Obliged by hunger, and request of friends:
"The piece, you think, is incorrect? why, take it,
I'm all submission, what you'd have it, make it."
  Three things another's modest wishes bound,
My friendship, and a prologue, and ten pound.
  Pitholeon sends to me: "You know his Grace,
I want a patron; ask him for a place."
Pitholeon libeled me—"but here's a letter
Informs you, sir, 'twas when he knew no better.
Dare you refuse him? Curll invites to dine,
He'll write a *Journal*, or he'll turn divine."
  Bless me! a packet.—"'Tis a stranger sues,
A Virgin Tragedy, an orphan Muse."
If I dislike it, "Furies, death and rage!"
If I approve, "Commend it to the stage."
There (thank my stars) my whole commission ends,
The players and I are, luckily, no friends.
Fired that the house reject him, "'Sdeath, I'll print it,
And shame the fools——Your interest, sir, with Lintot!"
Lintot, dull rogue! will think your price too much:
"Not, sir, if you revise it, and retouch."
All my demurs but double his attacks;
At last he whispers, "Do; and we go snacks."
Glad of a quarrel, straight I clap the door,
"Sir, let me see your works and you no more."
  'Tis sung, when Midas' ears began to spring
(Midas, a sacred person and a king),
His very minister sho spied them first,
(Some say his queen) was forced to speak, or burst.
And is not mine, my friend, a sorer case,
When every coxcomb perks them in my face?
A. Good friend, forbear! you deal in dangerous things.
I'd never name queens, ministers, or kings;
Keep close to ears, and those let asses prick;
'Tis nothing—*P.* Nothing? if they bite and kick?
Out with it, *Dunciad!* let the secret pass,
That secret to each fool, that he's an ass:
The truth once told (and wherefore should we lie?)
The queen of Midas slept, and so may I.
  You think this cruel? take it for a rule,
No creature smarts so little as a fool.
Let peals of laughter, Codrus! round thee break,
Thou unconcerned canst hear the mighty crack:
Pit, box, and gallery in convulsions hurled,
Thou stand'st unshook amidst a bursting world.
Who shames a scribbler? break one cobweb through,
He spins the slight, self-pleasing thread anew:
Destroy his fib or sophistry, in vain;
The creature's at his dirty work again,
Throned in the center of his thin designs,
Proud of a vast extent of flimsy lines!
Whom have I hurt? has poet yet, or peer,
Lost the arched eye-brow, or Parnassian sneer?
And has not Colley still his lord and whore?
His butchers Henley? his freemasons Moore?
Does not one table Bavius still admit?
Still to one bishop, Philips seem a wit?
Still Sappho— *A.* Hold! for God's sake—you'll offend,
No names!—be calm!—learn prudence of a friend!
I too could write, and I am twice as tall;
But foes like these— *P.* One flatterer's worse than all.
Of all mad creatures, if the learned are right,
It is the slaver kills, and not the bite.
A fool quite angry is quite innocent:
Alas! 'tis ten times worse when they *repent.*
  One dedicates in high heroic prose,
And ridicules beyond a hundred foes:
One from all Grub Street will my fame defend,

43. **term ends.** The London "term" or session of the law courts ended three weeks after Trinity Sunday. 49. **Pitholeon,** a poetaster of Rhodes who pretended to a knowledge of Greek. Pope is referring to Leonard Welsted, a minor poet, who had accused him of occasioning a lady's death. He is referred to again in l. 375. 53. **Curll,** Edmund Curll, a piratical bookseller who incurred Pope's enduring enmity by publishing some of his poems without permission. 56. **A Virgin Tragedy,** an allusion to *The Virgin Queen*, by Richard Barford, who had displeased Pope by adapting in one of his poems Pope's "machinery" of the Sylphs in *The Rape of the Lock.* **an orphan Muse,** probably a slap at Pope's enemy Lewis Theobald (pronounced "Tibbald"), who had published a play which he alleged to have been written by Shakespeare and which he therefore referred to in his dedication as "an orphan play." 61. **'Sdeath,** a contraction of the oath "God's death!" 62. **Lintot,** Bernard Lintot, a publisher who had brought out volumes by Pope, Gay, Steele, and other prominent writers.

79. ***Dunciad*,** Pope's most elaborate satire, the "epic of the dunces," in which he lashes all his enemies. 85. **Codrus,** a weak poet mentioned by Juvenal, hence a conventional name for any poetaster. 97. **Colley,** Colley Cibber, actor, manager, playwright, and poet laureate. Pope's early friendship with him changed to enmity, which culminated in Cibber's being made the hero of the *Dunciad.* 98. **Henley,** John Henley, the "Orator," who practiced his oratory on London butchers. He also appears in the *Dunciad.* **Moore,** James Moore-Smythe, a dandified poetaster, son of Arthur Moore (see l. 23). 99. **Bavius,** a minor Roman poet and another conventional name for any versemonger. 100. **Philips,** Ambrose Philips, a poet whose *Pastorals* had been adjudged superior to Pope's by Addison and others. The bishop referred to was Bishop Boulter, Primate of Ireland, who had collaborated with Philips in some periodical essays. 101. **Sappho,** the most famous of Greek poetesses. Pope refers here to Lady Mary Wortley Montagu, one of the most brilliant women of the century, whom he had once greatly admired, but with whom he had quarreled. She was probably author of some of the verses which occasioned the writing of the *Epistle to Dr. Arbuthnot.* 106. **slaver,** slobber.

And, more abusive, calls himself my friend.
This prints my *letters*, that expects a bribe,
And others roar aloud, "Subscribe, subscribe."
There are, who to my person pay their court:
I cough like Horace, and, though lean, am short,
Ammon's great son one shoulder had too high,
Such Ovid's nose, and "Sir! you have an eye"—
Go on, obliging creatures, make me see
All that disgraced my betters, met in me.
Say for my comfort, languishing in bed,
"Just so immortal Maro held his head":
And when I die, be sure you let me know
Great Homer died three thousand years ago.
Why did I write? what sin to me unknown
Dipped me in ink, my parents', or my own?
As yet a child, nor yet a fool to fame,
I lisped in numbers, for the numbers came.
I left no calling for this idle trade,
No duty broke, no father disobeyed.
The Muse but served to ease some friend, not wife,
To help me through this long disease, my life,
To second, Arbuthnot! thy art and care,
And teach the being you preserved, to bear.
But why then publish? Granville the polite,
And knowing Walsh, would tell me I could write;
Well-natured Garth inflamed with early praise;
And Congreve loved, and Swift endured my lays;
The courtly Talbot, Somers, Sheffield, read;
E'en mitered Rochester would nod the head,
And St. John's self (great Dryden's friends before)
With open arms received one poet more.
Happy my studies, when by these approved!
Happier their author, when by these beloved!
From these the world will judge of men and books,
Not from the Burnets, Oldmixons, and Cookes.
Soft were my numbers; who could take offence,
While pure description held the place of sense?
Like gentle Fanny's was my flowery theme,
A painted mistress, or a purling stream.
Yet then did Gildon draw his venal quill;—
I wished the man a dinner, and sat still.
Yet then did Dennis rave in furious fret;
I never answered—I was not in debt.
If want provoked, or madness made them print,
I waged no war with Bedlam or the Mint.
Did some more sober critic come abroad;
If wrong, I smiled; if right, I kissed the rod.
Pains, reading, study, are their just pretence,
And all they want is spirit, taste, and sense.
Commas and points they set exactly right,
And 'twere a sin to rob them of their mite.
Yet ne'er one sprig of laurel graced these ribalds,
From slashing Bentley down to piddling Tibbalds;
Each wight, who reads not, and but scans and spells,
Each word-catcher, that lives on syllables,
Ev'n such small critics some regard may claim,
Preserved in Milton's or in Shakespeare's name.
Pretty! in amber to observe the forms
Of hairs, or straws, or dirt, or grubs, or worms!
The things, we know, are neither rich nor rare,
But wonder how the devil they got there.
Were others angry: I excused them too;
Well might they rage, I gave them but their due.
A man's true merit 'tis not hard to find;
But each man's secret standard in his mind,—
That casting-weight pride adds to emptiness,—
This, who can gratify? for who can guess?
The bard whom pilfered Pastorals renown,
Who turns a Persian tale for half a crown,
Just writes to make his barrenness appear,
And strains from hard-bound brains, eight lines a year;

117. Ammon's great son, Alexander the Great, reputed to be the son of Zeus Ammon. **122. Maro,** Virgil (Publius Virgilius Maro). **135. Granville,** George Granville, Lord Lansdowne, politician, versifier, and dramatist, who was one of the first to commend Pope's verse. **136. Walsh,** William Walsh, poet and critic, who advised Pope to aim at "correctness" in composing his verse. **137. Garth,** Samuel Garth, a physician and man of letters. **138. Congreve,** William Congreve, the most brilliant of Restoration dramatists, to whom Pope dedicated his *Iliad*. **139. Talbot, Somers, Sheffield.** Charles Talbot, Duke of Shrewsbury, was a prominent statesman. John, Baron Somers, was Lord Chancellor and a friend and patron of Addison, Steele, Swift, and others. John Sheffield, Duke of Buckingham, was a Tory statesman, a patron of Dryden, and author of an *Essay on Poetry*. **140. Rochester,** Francis Atterbury, Bishop of Rochester. **141. St. John's self,** Henry St. John, Viscount Bolingbroke. See note to the first line of Epistle I of the *Essay on Man*, p. 558. **146. Burnets, Oldmixons, and Cookes.** Gilbert Burnet, Bishop of Salisbury, had antagonized the Tories with his *History of My Own Time*. John Oldmixon was a contemporary historian and pamphleteer who is satirized in the *Dunciad*. Thomas Cooke, a Whig pamphleteer, had attacked Pope in a pamphlet.

149. Fanny's, a contemptuous reference to Lord John Hervey, a statesman, whom Pope satirizes as "Sporus" in ll. 305–332 below. **151. Gildon,** Charles Gildon, a critic and dramatist who had attacked Pope. The latter believed Gildon had been hired to do so by Addison, hence the adjective "venal." **153. Dennis,** John Dennis, a prominent critic of the day. **164. slashing Bentley,** Richard Bentley, Master of Trinity College, Cambridge, one of the greatest classical scholars of his time, who had criticized Pope's *Iliad*. The epithet "slashing" refers particularly to Bentley's method in his edition of Milton's *Paradise Lost* in which he had printed many of the finest passages in square brackets on the ground that they were not Milton's but had been inserted by the printer. **piddling Tibbalds.** Lewis Theobald (see note to l. 56) was an author and a Shakespearean scholar. He had criticized unfavorably Pope's edition of Shakespeare. Pope made him hero of the *Dunciad* in its original form. **179–180. pilfered Pastorals . . . Persian tale.** Ambrose Philips (see l. 100) had published some pastoral verses which Pope here alleges unfairly to have been "pilfered" from the classics. Philips was also the translator of a collection of "Persian Tales" from the French.

He, who still wanting, though he lives on theft,
Steals much, spends little, yet has nothing left;
And he, who now to sense, now nonsense leaning,
Means not, but blunders round about a meaning;
And he, whose fustian's so sublimely bad,
It is not poetry, but prose run mad:
All these, my modest satire bade translate,
And owned that nine such poets made a Tate.
How did they fume, and stamp, and roar, and chafe!
And swear, not Addison himself was safe.
Peace to all such! but were there one whose fires
True genius kindles, and fair fame inspires;
Blessed with each talent and each art to please,
And born to write, converse, and live with ease:
Should such a man, too fond to rule alone,
Bear, like the Turk, no brother near the throne,
View him with scornful, yet with jealous eyes,
And hate for arts that caused himself to rise;
Damn with faint praise, assent with civil leer,
And without sneering, teach the rest to sneer;
Willing to wound, and yet afraid to strike,
Just hint a fault, and hesitate dislike;
Alike reserved to blame, or to commend,
A timorous foe, and a suspicious friend;
Dreading e'en fools, by flatterers besieged,
And so obliging, that he ne'er obliged;
Like Cato, give his little senate laws,
And sit attentive to his own applause;
While wits and Templars every sentence raise,
And wonder with a foolish face of praise—
Who but must laugh, if such a man there be?
Who would not weep, if Atticus were he?
What though my name stood rubric on the walls,
Or plastered posts, with claps, in capitals?
Or smoking forth, a hundred hawkers load,
On wings of winds came flying all abroad?
I sought no homage from the race that write;
I kept, like Asian monarchs, from their sight:
Poems I heeded (now be-rhymed so long)
No more than thou, great George! a birthday song.
I ne'er with wits or witlings passed my days,
To spread about the itch of verse and praise;
Nor like a puppy, daggled through the town,
To fetch and carry sing-song up and down;
Nor at rehearsals sweat, and mouthed, and cried,
With handkerchief and orange at my side;
But sick of fops, and poetry, and prate,
To Bufo left the whole Castalian state.
Proud as Apollo on his forked hill,
Sat full-blown Bufo, puffed by every quill;
Fed with soft dedication all day long,
Horace and he went hand in hand in song.
His library (where busts of poets dead
And a true Pindar stood without a head)
Received of wits an undistinguished race,
Who first his judgment asked, and then a place:
Much they extolled his pictures, much his seat,
And flattered every day, and some days eat:
Till grown more frugal in his riper days,
He paid some bards with port, and some with praise,
To some a dry rehearsal was assigned,
And others (harder still) he paid in kind.
Dryden alone (what wonder?) came not nigh,
Dryden alone escaped this judging eye:
But still the great have kindness in reserve,
He helped to bury whom he helped to starve.
May some choice patron bless each grey goose quill!
May every Bavius have his Bufo still!
So, when a statesman wants a day's defence,
Or envy holds a whole week's war with sense,
Or simple pride for flattery makes demands,
May dunce by dunce be whistled off my hands!
Blest be the great! for those they take away,
And those they left me; for they left me Gay;
Left me to see neglected genius bloom,
Neglected die, and tell it on his tomb:
Of all thy blameless life the sole return

190. Tate, Nahum Tate, dramatist and poet laureate, now best known for his paraphrases of the Psalms. **193–214. were there one . . . if Atticus were he?** This passage, directed at Addison, contains one of the most celebrated satiric portraits in literature. Pope wrote the lines during Addison's lifetime, and said that he had sent them to Addison. They were first printed, perhaps without Pope's consent, several years after Addison's death, in a magazine. **208. obliged,** pronounced "obleeged." **209. Cato,** the hero of Addison's tragedy of that name, which dealt with the famous Roman statesman, general, and writer of the third and second centuries B.C. Line 209 is quoted from the prologue which Pope wrote for the play. The "little senate" refers to the group of minor writers who regarded Addison as a literary dictator. **211. Templars,** law students resident in the Inner Temple. **raise,** applaud. **214. Atticus,** a Roman author of the first century B.C. and friend of Cicero, noted for his urbanity and culture. **215. rubric,** in red. The title pages of new books were printed in red letters and pasted on booksellers' walls.

222. great George! George II, king of England at the time. Pope refers more particularly to the king's indifference to English literature in his *Epistle to Augustus.* **230. Bufo,** probably the Earl of Halifax (Charles Montagu), the Whig leader. **Castalian state,** the realm of poetry. The fountain of Castalia was supposed to give poetic inspiration. **236. Pindar,** a lyric poet of Greece in the fifth century B.C. Pope informs us that the passage "ridicules the affectation of antiquaries, who frequently exhibit the headless trunks and terms of statues for Plato, Homer, Pindar, etc." **248. helped to bury.** Halifax offered to pay the expenses of Dryden's funeral, but the offer was refused by Dryden's friends. **250. Bavius,** a conventional name for a hack poet. **256. Gay,** John Gay, author of the *Beggar's Opera.*

My verse, and Queensb'ry weeping o'er thy urn!
Oh let me live my own, and die so too!
(To live and die is all I have to do)
Maintain a poet's dignity and ease,
And see what friends, and read what books I please;
Above a patron, though I condescend
Sometimes to call a minister my friend.
I was not born for courts or great affairs;
I pay my debts, believe, and say my prayers;
Can sleep without a poem in my head,
Nor know if Dennis be alive or dead.
Why am I asked what next shall see the light?
Heavens! was I born for nothing but to write?
Has life no joys for me? or (to be grave)
Have I no friend to serve, no soul to save?
"I found him close with Swift"—"Indeed? no doubt
(Cries prating Balbus) something will come out."
'Tis all in vain, deny it as I will;
"No, such a genius never can lie still":
And then for mine obligingly mistakes
The first lampoon Sir Will or Bubo makes.
Poor guiltless I! and can I choose but smile,
When every coxcomb knows me by my style?
Curst be the verse, how well soe'er it flow,
That tends to make one worthy man my foe,
Give virtue scandal, innocence a fear,
Or from the soft-eyed virgin steal a tear!
But he who hurts a harmless neighbour's peace,
Insults fallen worth, or beauty in distress,
Who loves a lie, lame slander helps about,
Who writes a libel, or who copies out:
That fop, whose pride affects a patron's name,
Yet absent, wounds an author's honest fame:
Who can your merit selfishly approve,
And show the sense of it without the love;
Who has the vanity to call you friend,
Yet wants the honour, injured, to defend;
Who tells whate'er you think, whate'er you say,
And, if he lie not, must at least betray:
Who to the Dean, and silver bell can swear,
And sees at Canons what was never there;
Who reads, but with a lust to misapply,
Make satire a lampoon, and fiction, lie.
A lash like mine no honest man shall dread,
But all such babbling blockheads in his stead.
Let Sporus tremble—*A.* What? that thing of silk,
Sporus, that mere white curd of ass's milk!
Satire or sense, alas! can Sporus feel?
Who breaks a butterfly upon a wheel?
P. Yet let me flap this bug with gilded wings,
This painted child of dirt, that stinks and stings;
Whose buzz the witty and the fair annoys,
Yet wit ne'er tastes, and beauty ne'er enjoys:
So well-bred spaniels civilly delight
In mumbling of the game they dare not bite.
Eternal smiles his emptiness betray,
As shallow streams run dimpling all the way.
Whether in florid impotence he speaks,
And, as the prompter breathes, the puppet squeaks;
Or at the ear of Eve, familiar toad,
Half froth, half venom, spits himself abroad,
In puns, or politics, or tales, or lies,
Or spite, or smut, or rhymes, or blasphemies.
His wit all see-saw, between that and this,
Now high, now low, now master up, now miss,
And he himself, one vile antithesis.
Amphibious thing! that acting either part,
The trifling head or the corrupted heart,
Fop at the toilet, flatterer at the board,
Now trips a lady, and now struts a lord.
Eve's tempter thus the rabbins have expressed,
A cherub's face, a reptile all the rest;
Beauty that shocks you, parts that none will trust;
Wit that can creep, and pride that licks the dust.
Not fortune's worshiper, nor fashion's fool,
Not lucre's madman, nor ambition's tool,
Not proud, nor servile;—be one poet's praise,
That, if he pleased, he pleased by manly ways:
That flattery, e'en to kings, he held a shame,
And thought a lie in verse or prose the same.
That not in fancy's maze he wandered long,
But stooped to truth, and moralized his song:

260. Queensb'ry. Gay died in the home of Charles Douglas, Duke of Queensberry, and his wife Catherine, who erected a monument to him in Westminster Abbey. **276. Balbus,** probably a reference to the Earl of Kinnoul, ambassador to Turkey and Spain. **280. Sir Will,** Sir William Yonge, a Whig politician and writer of verses. **Bubo,** George Bubb Dodington, Lord Melcombe, a politician and literary dabbler. **299–300. the Dean . . . Canons.** In his *Moral Essays,* Pope had satirized an unnamed nobleman for the vulgar ostentation displayed at his country estate, the private chapel of which had a "soft Dean" and silver bells. The passage was interpreted by many as an attack on the Duke of Chandos and his country estate, "Canons."

305. Sporus, an effeminate favorite of the emperor Nero. Pope applies the name to Lord John Hervey, a member of Walpole's government and a favorite counselor of Queen Caroline. Pope believed Hervey to be the joint author of a satirical pamphlet asserting that the poet had been assaulted by two gentlemen whom he had offended and had been beaten until he shed tears. The description of "Sporus" is another of Pope's famous satirical portraits. **306. curd . . . milk.** Hervey's delicate health had caused him to be placed on a diet of ass's milk. **319. Eve,** Queen Caroline. Cf. *Paradise Lost,* IV, 800. **329. trips a lady,** i.e., trips like a lady. **330. rabbins,** Jewish rabbis. It was not the rabbis, however, but European painters who depicted Satan in such wise. **334. Not fortune's worshiper.** In the passage beginning here Pope is referring to himself. **341. stooped to truth,** a term from falconry, alluding to the bird's circling in air before "stooping to" its prey.

That not for fame, but virtue's better end,
He stood the furious foe, the timid friend,
The damning critic, half-approving wit,
The coxcomb hit, or fearing to be hit;
Laughed at the loss of friends he never had,
The dull, the proud, the wicked, and the mad;
The distant threats of vengeance on his head,
The blow unfelt, the tear he never shed;
The tale revived, the lie so oft o'erthrown,
Th' imputed trash, and dullness not his own;
The morals blackened when the writings 'scape,
The libeled person, and the pictured shape;
Abuse, on all he loved, or loved him, spread,
A friend in exile, or a father dead;
The whisper, that to greatness still too near,
Perhaps, yet vibrates on his Sovereign's ear:—
Welcome for thee, fair virtue! all the past;
For thee, fair virtue! welcome e'en the last!
  A. But why insult the poor, affront the great?
P. A knave's a knave, to me, in every state:
Alike my scorn, if he succeed or fail.
Sporus at court, or Japhet in a jail,
A hireling scribbler, or a hireling peer,
Knight of the post corrupt, or of the shire;
If on a pillory, or near a throne,
He gain his prince's ear, or lose his own.
  Yet soft by nature, more a dupe than wit,
Sappho can tell you how this man was bit;
This dreaded satirist Dennis will confess
Foe to his pride, but friend to his distress:
So humble, he has knocked at Tibbald's door,
Has drunk with Cibber, nay has rhymed for Moore.
Full ten years slandered, did he once reply?
Three thousand suns went down on Welsted's lie.
To please a mistress one aspersed his life;
He lashed him not, but let her be his wife.
Let Budgell charge low Grub Street on his quill,
And write whate'er he pleased, except his will;
Let the two Curlls of town and court, abuse
His father, mother, body, soul, and muse.
Yet why? that father held it for a rule,
It was a sin to call our neighbour fool;
That harmless mother thought no wife a whore:
Hear this, and spare his family, James Moore!
Unspotted names, and memorable long!

349. The blow unfelt. See note on l. 305. **363. Japhet,** Japhet Crooke, a notorious forger, who had been punished by having his nose and ears cut off. **365. Knight of the post,** a reference to unscrupulous bondsmen who stood near the pillars of the sheriff's court to be hired to testify to anything desired. **369. Sappho.** See note on l. 101. **373. James Moore.** See note on l. 98. **375. Welsted's lie.** See note on l. 49. **378. Budgell,** Eustace Budgell, a minor poet and author of some of the *Spectator* papers. He had charged Pope with attacking him in *The Grub Street Journal.* **380. the two Curlls,** Edmund Curll (see note on l. 53) and his son Henry, also an unscrupulous publisher.

If there be force in virtue, or in song.
  Of gentle blood (part shed in honour's cause,
While yet in Britain honour had applause)
Each parent sprung—*A.* What fortune, pray?—
  P. Their own,
And better got, than Bestia's from the throne.
Born to no pride, inheriting no strife,
Nor marrying discord in a noble wife,
Stranger to civil and religious rage,
The good man walked innoxious through his age.
Nor courts he saw, no suits would ever try,
Nor dared an oath, nor hazarded a lie.
Unlearned, he knew no schoolman's subtle art,
No language, but the language of the heart.
By nature honest, by experience wise,
Healthy by temperance, and by exercise;
His life, though long to sickness past unknown,
His death was instant, and without a groan.
O grant me, thus to live, and thus to die!
Who sprung from kings shall know less joy than I.
  O friend! may each domestic bliss be thine!
Be no unpleasing melancholy mine:
Me, let the tender office long engage,
To rock the cradle of reposing age,
With lenient arts extend a mother's breath,
Make languor smile, and smooth the bed of death,
Explore the thought, explain the asking eye,
And keep a while one parent from the sky!
On cares like these if length of days attend,
May Heaven, to bless those days, preserve my
  friend,
Preserve him social, cheerful, and serene,
And just as rich as when he served a queen.
A. Whether that blessing be denied or given,
Thus far was right, the rest belongs to Heaven.

from THE DUNCIAD, BOOK IV

The first three books of *The Dunciad*, Pope's longest satire, were published anonymously in 1728, and constituted a general indictment of all his critics. The mock-epic poem followed the pattern of Dryden's *Mac Flecknoe* (see p. 458). The fourth book is in effect an independent poem, and the satire in it is of a general nature rather than, as in the earlier books, directed against specific and often unimportant writers. It contains some of Pope's most vigorous and brilliant verse, and the noble lines of its conclusion, here reprinted, were aptly de-

388. Of gentle blood. Pope claimed to be descended from the Earls of Downe. **391. Bestia's.** Probably a reference to the Duke of Marlborough, whose numerous public offices brought him a large income. Bestia was a Roman proconsul of the second century B.C. who was bribed into making a dishonorable peace with Jugurtha, King of Numidia. **417. served a queen.** Arbuthnot was physician to Queen Anne.

scribed by Thackeray as a "silver trumpet ringing defiance to falsehood and tyranny, deceit, dulness, and superstition."

In vain, in vain—the all-composing hour
Resistless falls: the Muse obeys the power.
She comes! she comes! the sable throne behold
Of Night primeval and of Chaos old!
Before her, Fancy's gilded clouds decay,
And all its varying rainbows die away.
Wit shoots in vain its momentary fires,
The meteor drops, and in a flash expires.
As one by one, at dread Medea's strain,
The sickening stars fade off th' ethereal plain;
As Argus' eyes, by Hermes' wand oppressed,
Closed one by one to everlasting rest;
Thus at her felt approach, and secret might,
Art after art goes out, and all is night.
See skulking Truth to her old cavern fled,
Mountains of casuistry heaped o'er her head!
Philosophy, that leaned on Heaven before,
Shrinks to her second cause, and is no more.
Physic of Metaphysic begs defence,
And Metaphysic calls for aid on Sense!
See Mystery to Mathematics fly!
In vain! they gaze, turn giddy, rave, and die.
Religion blushing veils her sacred fires,
And unawares Morality expires.
Nor public flame, nor private, dares to shine;
Nor human spark is left, nor glimpse divine!
Lo! thy dread empire, Chaos! is restored;
Light dies before thy uncreating word:
Thy hand, great Anarch! lets the curtain fall;
And universal darkness buries all.

James Thomson

1700–1748

Thomson, the son of a Scottish clergyman, was born at Ednam, Roxburyshire, in 1700, the year of Dryden's death. After being graduated at Edinburgh University he went to London in 1725 planning to make his career as a clergyman, but fortunately carried along in his pocket the manuscript of a poem called "Winter." This poem was one of four which, when the series was completed in 1730, he called *The Seasons*, and which made him famous at thirty. Meanwhile in 1727 he had produced his poem "To the Memory of Sir Isaac Newton," in which he voiced the eighteenth century's pride in the intellectual implications of Newton's discoveries. *The Castle of Indolence*, his most important production after *The Seasons*, was finished in the year in which he died. In an ode which he wrote for the last scene of a dramatic piece called *Alfred: A Masque* (1740), in which he was a collaborator, appeared his most widely known lines:

Rule, Britannia, rule the waves;
Britons never will be slaves.

Thomson was the chief writer of blank verse during the eighteenth century, and so discerning a critic as George Saintsbury considered that Thomson's blank verse ranked as one of the chief original models of that meter. He was also the first poet to revive the use of the Spenserian stanza. No one since Spenser has achieved more of the true Spenserian music and flavor than Thomson in the best stanzas of *The Castle of Indolence*. He was a friend of Pope's, and found several patrons, so it is not surprising that he allowed his natural gift for sharp delineation to be blurred frequently by that "grandeur of generality" for which all fashionable poets were in his time trying. Nevertheless his gift for realistic description of details of natural scenery is equaled only by that of Wordsworth and his nineteenth-century contemporaries. In a spring garden he notes

The yellow wall-flower stained with iron brown,

and on a snow-swept moor in winter marks how

In his own loose-revolving fields the swain
Disastered stands.

Thomson had a wider range of emotion than most of the famous men among whom he lived. The contrast is sharp and clear, for example, between the enthusiastic vision of his ode "To the

635. Medea's strain. The vengeance and violence of the sorceress Medea are celebrated in Greek legend and drama as well as in later literature. **637. Argus' eyes.** Argus, the hundred-eyed creature of Greek legend, was charmed to sleep and slain by Hermes, the messenger of the gods. **641. Truth to her old cavern fled.** "Alluding to the saying of Democritus, that Truth lay at the bottom of a deep well, from whence he had drawn her." (Pope) **653. Lo! thy dread empire.** This and the following lines allude to Milton's description of Chaos, *Paradise Lost*, II, 988–1006.

Memory of Sir Isaac Newton" and Jonathan Swift's contempt for natural science. And the man who was moved by scientific discoveries had also a gift of song which was denied to most of his contemporaries. He employs the accents of Tennyson a hundred years before him:

> On utmost Kilda's shore, whose lonely race
> Resign the setting sun to Indian worlds,

and weaves the harmonies of Keats into a "Hymn on the Seasons":

> ye harvests, wave to Him—
> Breathe your still song into the reaper's heart
> As home he goes beneath the joyous moon.

Thomson, in fact, helped to shape the modern mind and temper. He has his honorable place in the tradition of the Western world. He had a sense of the vast spatial backgrounds and the huge natural panorama against which our lives are led. Most of his contemporaries thought and fancied in terms of a single city as though it were the universe, but he in terms of land and sea and the cloud-laden air.

from THE SEASONS

Thomson held that "there is no subject more elevating, more amusing, more ready to awake poetical enthusiasm, philosophic reflection, and moral sentiment, than the works of Nature." The four poems in *The Seasons* contain some of the most felicitous descriptions of natural phenomena and country life in the language.

from SPRING

The North-east spends his rage, and, now shut up
Within his iron caves, the effusive South
Warms the wide air, and o'er the void of heaven
Breathes the big clouds with vernal showers distent.
At first a dusky wreath they seem to rise,
Scarce staining ether; but by fast degrees,
In heaps on heaps the doubling vapour sails
Along the loaded sky, and mingling deep
Sits on the horizon round a settled gloom;
Not such as wintry storms on mortals shed,
Oppressing life; but lovely, gentle, kind,
And full of every hope and every joy,
The wish of Nature. Gradual sinks the breeze
Into a perfect calm; that not a breath
Is heard to quiver through the closing woods,
Or rustling turn the many-twinkling leaves
Of aspen tall. The uncurling floods, diffused
In glassy breadth, seem through delusive lapse
Forgetful of their course. 'Tis silence all,
And pleasing expectation. Herds and flocks
Drop the dry sprig, and, mute-imploring, eye
The falling verdure. Hushed in short suspense,
The plumy people streak their wings with oil
To throw the lucid moisture trickling off,
And wait the approaching sign to strike at once
Into the general choir. Even mountains, vales,
And forests seem, impatient, to demand
The promised sweetness. Man superior walks
Amid the glad creation, musing praise
And looking lively gratitude. At last
The clouds consign their treasures to the fields,
And, softly shaking on the dimpled pool
Prelusive drops, let all their moisture flow
In large effusion o'er the freshened world.
The stealing shower is scarce to patter heard
By such as wander through the forest-walks,
Beneath the umbrageous multitude of leaves.
But who can hold the shade while Heaven descends
In universal bounty, shedding herbs
And fruits and flowers on Nature's ample lap?
Swift fancy fired anticipates their growth;
And, while the milky nutriment distills,
Beholds the kindling country colour round.
Thus all day long the full-distended clouds
Indulge their genial stores, and well-showered earth
Is deep enriched with vegetable life;
Till, in the western sky, the downward sun
Looks out effulgent from amid the flush
Of broken clouds, gay-shifting to his beam.
The rapid radiance instantaneous strikes
The illumined mountain, through the forest streams,
Shakes on the floods, and in a yellow mist,
Far smoking o'er the interminable plain,
In twinkling myriads lights the dewy gems.
Moist, bright, and green, the landscape laughs around.
Full swell the woods; their every music wakes,
Mixed in wild concert, with the warbling brooks
Increased, the distant bleatings of the hills,
The hollow lows responsive from the vales,
Whence, blending all, the sweetened zephyr springs.
Meantime, refracted from yon eastern cloud,
Bestriding earth, the grand ethereal bow
Shoots up immense; and every hue unfolds,
In fair proportion running from the red
To where the violet fades into the sky.
Here, awful Newton, the dissolving clouds
Form, fronting on the sun, thy showery prism;
And to the sage-instructed eye unfold
The various twine of light, by thee disclosed

146. distent, distended, spread.

165. plumy people, poetic diction for "birds."

From the white mingling maze. Not so the swain;
He wondering views the bright enchantment bend
Delightful o'er the radiant fields, and runs
To catch the falling glory; but amazed
Beholds the amusive arch before him fly,
Then vanish quite away. Still night succeeds,
A softened shade, and saturated earth
Awaits the morning beam, to give to light,
Raised through ten thousand different plastic tubes,
The balmy treasures of the former day. . . .

from SUMMER

Now swarms the village o'er the jovial mead—
The rustic youth, brown with meridian toil,
Healthful and strong; full as the summer rose
Blown by prevailing suns, the ruddy maid,
Half naked, swelling on the sight, and all
Her kindled graces burning o'er her cheek.
Even stooping age is here; and infant hands
Trail the long rake, or, with the fragrant load
O'ercharged, amid the kind oppression roll.
Wide flies the tedded grain; all in a row
Advancing broad, or wheeling round the field,
They spread the breathing harvest to the sun,
That throws refreshful round a rural smell;
Or, as they rake the green-appearing ground,
And drive the dusky wave along the mead,
The russet haycock rises thick behind
In order gay: while heard from dale to dale,
Waking the breeze, resounds the blended voice
Of happy labour, love, and social glee.
Or, rushing thence, in one diffusive band
They drive the troubled flocks, by many a dog
Compelled, to where the mazy-running brook
Forms a deep pool, this bank abrupt and high,
And that fair-spreading in a pebbled shore.
Urged to the giddy brink, much is the toil,
The clamour much of men and boys and dogs
Ere the soft, fearful people to the flood
Commit their woolly sides. And oft the swain,
On some impatient seizing, hurls them in:
Emboldened then, nor hesitating more,
Fast, fast they plunge amid the flashing wave,
And, panting, labour to the farther shore.
Repeated this, till deep the well-washed fleece
Has drunk the flood, and from his lively haunt
The trout is banished by the sordid stream.
Heavy and dripping, to the breezy brow
Slow move the harmless race; where, as they spread
Their swelling treasures to the sunny ray,
Inly disturbed, and wondering what this wild
Outrageous tumult means, their loud complaints
The country fill; and, tossed from rock to rock,
Incessant bleatings run around the hills.
At last, of snowy white the gathered flocks
Are in the wattled pen innumerous pressed,
Head above head; and, ranged in lusty rows,
The shepherds sit, and whet the sounding shears.
The housewife waits to roll her fleecy stores,
With all her gay-drest maids attending round.
One, chief, in gracious dignity enthroned,
Shines o'er the rest, the pastoral queen, and rays
Her smiles sweet-beaming on her shepherd-king;
While the glad circle round them yield their souls
To festive mirth, and wit that knows no gall.
Meantime, their joyous task goes on apace:
Some mingling stir the melted tar, and some,
Deep on the new-shorn vagrant's heaving side
To stamp the master's cipher ready stand;
Others the unwilling wether drag along;
And, glorying in his might, the sturdy boy
Holds by the twisted horns the indignant ram.
Behold where bound, and of its robe bereft
By needy man, that all-depending lord,
How meek, how patient, the mild creature lies!
What softness in its melancholy face,
What dumb complaining innocence appears!
Fear not, ye gentle tribes! 'tis not the knife
Of horrid slaughter that is o'er you waved;
No, 'tis the tender swain's well-guided shears,
Who having now, to pay his annual care,
Borrowed your fleece, to you a cumbrous load,
Will send you bounding to your hills again. . . .

from AUTUMN

When Autumn scatters his departing gleams,
Warned of approaching Winter, gathered, play
The swallow-people; and, tossed wide around,
O'er the calm sky in convolution swift
The feathered eddy floats, rejoicing once
Ere to their wintry slumbers they retire,
In clusters clung beneath the mouldering bank,
And where, unpierced by frost, the cavern sweats;
Or rather, into warmer climes conveyed,
With other kindred birds of season, there
They twitter cheerful, till the vernal months
Invite them welcome back—for thronging now
Innumerous wings are in commotion all.
Where the Rhine loses his majestic force
In Belgian plains, won from the raging deep
By diligence amazing and the strong

220. **plastic,** capable of shaping or creating. **tubes,** i.e., the stems of plants. 353. **meridian,** midday. 361. **tedded,** spread out for drying. *378.* **soft, fearful people,** poetic diction for "sheep."

Unconquerable hand of liberty,
The stork-assembly meets, for many a day
Consulting deep and various ere they take
Their arduous voyage through the liquid sky.
And now, their route designed, their leaders chose,
Their tribes adjusted, cleaned their vigorous wings,
And many a circle, many a short essay,
Wheeled round and round, in congregation full
The figured flight ascends, and, riding high
The aerial billows, mixes with the clouds.
Or, where the Northern Ocean in vast whirls
Boils round the naked melancholy isles
Of farthest Thulè, and the Atlantic surge
Pours in among the stormy Hebrides,
Who can recount what transmigrations there
Are annual made? what nations come and go?
And how the living clouds on clouds arise,
Infinite wings! till all the plume-dark air
And rude resounding shore are one wild cry?
Here the plain harmless native his small flock
And herd diminutive of many hues
Tends on the little island's verdant swell,
The shepherd's sea-girt reign; or, to the rocks
Dire-clinging, gathers his ovarious food;
Or sweeps the fishy shore; or treasures up
The plumage, rising full, to form the bed
Of luxury. And here a while the Muse,
High hovering o'er the broad cerulean scene,
Sees Caledonia in romantic view—
Her airy mountains from the waving main
Invested with a keen diffusive sky,
Breathing the soul acute; her forests huge,
Incult, robust, and tall, by Nature's hand
Planted of old; her azure lakes between,
Poured out extensive, and of watery wealth
Full; winding deep and green, her fertile vales,
With many a cool translucent brimming flood
Washed lovely, from the Tweed (pure parent stream),
Whose pastoral banks first heard my Doric reed, . . .

from WINTER

The keener tempests rise: and, fuming dun
From all the livid east or piercing north,
Thick clouds ascend, in whose capacious womb
A vapoury deluge lies, to snow congealed.
Heavy they roll their fleecy world along,
And the sky saddens with the gathered storm.
Through the hushed air the whitening shower descends,
At first thin-wavering; till at last the flakes
Fall broad and wide and fast, dimming the day
With a continual flow. The cherished fields
Put on their winter robe of purest white.
'Tis brightness all; save where the new snow melts
Along the mazy current. Low the woods
Bow their hoar head; and, ere the languid sun
Faint from the west emits his evening ray,
Earth's universal face, deep-hid and chill,
Is one wild dazzling waste, that buries wide
The works of man. Drooping, the labourer-ox
Stands covered o'er with snow, and then demands
The fruit of all his toil. The fowls of heaven,
Tamed by the cruel season, crowd around
The winnowing store, and claim the little boon
Which Providence assigns them. One alone,
The redbreast, sacred to the household gods,
Wisely regardful of the embroiling sky,
In joyless fields and thorny thickets leaves
His shivering mates, and pays to trusted man
His annual visit. Half-afraid, he first
Against the window beats; then brisk alights
On the warm hearth; then, hopping o'er the floor,
Eyes all the smiling family askance,
And pecks, and starts, and wonders where he is—
Till, more familiar grown, the table-crumbs
Attract his slender feet. The foodless wilds
Pour forth their brown inhabitants. The hare,
Though timorous of heart, and hard beset
By death in various forms, dark snares, and dogs,
And more unpitying men, the garden seeks,
Urged on by fearless want. The bleating kind
Eye the bleak heaven, and next the glistening earth,
With looks of dumb despair; then, sad-dispersed,
Dig for the withered herb through heaps of snow.
Now, shepherds, to your helpless charge be kind:
Baffle the raging year, and fill their pens
With food at will; lodge them below the storm,
And watch them strict: for, from the bellowing east,
In this dire season, oft the whirlwind's wing
Sweeps up the burden of whole wintry plains
In one wide waft, and o'er the hapless flocks,
Hid in the hollow of two neighbouring hills,
The billowy tempest whelms; till, upward urged,
The valley to a shining mountain swells,
Tipped with a wreath high-curling in the sky. . . .

852. hand of liberty, an allusion to the old superstition that storks are to be found and will live only in republics or free states. Cf. Sir Thomas Browne, *Vulgar Errors*, Book III, chap. 27. **864. Thulè,** the name given by the ancients to the extreme northern limit of the world; here applied to the Shetland Islands, the northernmost of the British Isles. **875. ovarious food,** poetic diction for "eggs." **880. Caledonia,** Scotland. **884. Incult,** uncultivated.

from A HYMN ON THE SEASONS

English Deism, a body of religious and philosophical doctrine prominent in Thomson's time, asserted that there is to be found in the natural world a sufficient revelation not only of God but also of moral truth. From this doctrine it followed that the human mind may proceed "through nature to nature's God," and the opinion was sometimes advanced that in the contemplation or study of nature one is really engaged in divine worship. Although James Thomson was not himself an avowed Deist, one sees in the present poem, written to complete his series of poems on the four seasons, that he was affected by Deistic thought. The same influence is to be discerned in Joseph Addison's hymn "The Spacious Firmament on High," and also in Coleridge's "Hymn before Sunrise in the Vale of Chamouni."

Nature, attend! join, every living soul
Beneath the spacious temple of the sky,
In adoration join; and ardent raise
One general song! To Him, ye vocal gales,
Breathe soft, whose spirit in your freshness breathes:
Oh! talk of Him in solitary glooms,
Where, o'er the rock, the scarcely-waving pine
Fills the brown shade with a religious awe.
And ye, whose bolder note is heard afar,
Who shake the astonished world, lift high to Heaven
The impetuous song, and say from whom you rage.
His praise, ye brooks, attune, ye trembling rills;
And let me catch it as I muse along.
Ye headlong torrents, rapid and profound;
Ye softer floods, that lead the humid maze
Along the vale; and thou, majestic main,
A secret world of wonders in thyself,
Sound His stupendous praise, whose greater voice
Or bids you roar or bids your roarings fall.
Soft roll your incense, herbs, and fruits, and flowers,
In mingled clouds to Him, whose sun exalts,
Whose breath perfumes you, and whose pencil paints.
Ye forests, bend; ye harvests wave to Him—
Breathe your still song into the reaper's heart
As home he goes beneath the joyous moon.
Ye that keep watch in heaven, as earth asleep
Unconscious lies, effuse your mildest beams,
Ye constellations! while your angels strike
Amid the spangled sky the silver lyre.
Great source of day! best image here below
Of thy Creator, ever pouring wide
From world to world the vital ocean round!
On nature write with every beam His praise.
The thunder rolls: be hushed the prostrate world,
While cloud to cloud returns the solemn hymn.
Bleat out afresh, ye hills; ye mossy rocks,
Retain the sound; the broad responsive low,
Ye valleys, raise; for the Great Shepherd reigns,
And His unsuffering kingdom yet will come.
Ye woodlands all, awake: a boundless song
Burst from the groves; and, when the restless day,
Expiring, lays the warbling world asleep,
Sweetest of birds, sweet Philomela! charm
The listening shades, and teach the night His praise!
Ye, chief, for whom the whole creation smiles,
At once the head, the heart, the tongue of all,
Crown the great hymn! In swarming cities vast,
Assembled men, to the deep organ join
The long-resounding voice, oft breaking clear
At solemn pauses through the swelling bass;
And, as each mingling flame increases each,
In one united ardour rise to heaven.
Or, if you rather choose the rural shade,
And find a fane in every sacred grove,
There let the shepherd's flute, the virgin's lay,
The prompting seraph, and the poet's lyre
Still sing the God of Seasons as they roll.
For me, when I forget the darling theme,
Whether the blossom blows, the summer-ray
Russets the plain, inspiring autumn gleams,
Or winter rises in the blackening east,
Be my tongue mute, may fancy paint no more,
And, dead to joy, forget my heart to beat! . . .

Thomas Gray
1716–1771

Thomas Gray was born in London on December 26, 1716, the only one of a family of twelve children to reach maturity. The temperament of the man and many of the circumstances of his life are to be explained, partly at least, by his unhappy childhood. If, to use a line from his famous *Elegy*, "Melancholy marked him for her own," his melancholy and his shyness were caused to some extent by what Lord David Cecil calls "that fundamental suspicion of life engendered in him by too early an acquaintance with its power to hurt." His father, a scrivener, neglected him, but his mother gave him affection and sheltered him as much as possible from parental quarrels. Later she kept a millinery shop to provide the money for his schooling at Eton, where her brother was an assistant master. At school he found security, peace, and, above all, friendship. Young Gray and three other Eton lads—Horace Walpole, Richard West, and Thomas Ashton—formed a "Quadruple Alliance." The most prominent of the four was the lively-witted Walpole, son of the Prime Minister, and the friendship between him and Gray was to endure, with ups and downs, for the remaining forty years of the poet's lifetime. The death at twenty-six of his dearest friend, Richard West, produced the greatest emotional crisis of Gray's life.

From Eton Gray went to Cambridge, his mother providing the means, and at Cambridge he was to remain for most of his life, although he hated the place for its dullness and provinciality. His days there were spent in academic seclusion and quiet, chiefly reading and writing. This routine was broken when, in 1739, he set out with his friend Walpole, at the latter's invitation and expense, on the "grand tour" of France, Switzerland, and Italy. The letters of the two friends are among the most delightful of the century's records of travel and descriptions of natural phenomena. The friendship suffered a rupture toward the close of the journey, but it was resumed in later years.

Gray returned from the Continent in 1741 and the next year went to Cambridge where he remained until his death except for excursions to London and the country. During his holidays he got as far afield as the Lake District, Scotland, and Wales, and discovered the "picturesque" landscapes of those regions. The chief product of his retired and studious life at Cambridge was a small amount of carefully wrought verse. In 1742 he composed "Ode to Spring," "Hymn to Adversity," and "Ode on a Distant Prospect of Eton College."

Five years passed before another poem came from Gray's pen, this time a piece in an entirely different vein, "Ode on the Death of a Favourite Cat," a charming bit of light "society verse." Three years then elapsed before he completed his next and most famous poem, "Elegy Written in a Country Churchyard." He was as reluctant to publish his verses as he had been to write them. His friend Walpole was the first to recognize his genius and it was probably he who had encouraged Gray to bring out the "Ode on a Distant Prospect of Eton College" in 1747. In 1748 Walpole sponsored the publication of Gray's first three poems, anonymously, in Dodsley's *Collection of Poems.* It was only because Gray had heard that his *Elegy* was about to be printed in an imperfect version in a magazine and without his consent that he permitted it to be published in 1751, but without his name. In this episode also Walpole played a leading part. And because Gray felt it beneath the dignity of a gentleman to accept money for the composition of poetry, he permitted his publisher, Dodsley, to take the entire profits.

In 1753, appeared a little volume entitled *Six Poems*, including his "Hymn to Adversity," which has been facetiously called his "Collected Works." In 1757 a small volume containing two of Gray's most important poems, "The Progress of Poesy" and "The Bard," was published at his friend Walpole's Strawberry Hill Press. "The Bard" and "The Fatal Sisters" and "The Descent of Odin" which followed in 1761, were the products of his studies in Norse and Celtic legends. He lived on for fifteen years but added no more poems of importance to his scanty stock. In 1757, on the death of Colley Cibber, he was offered the post of poet laureate, but declined the honor. His academic studies received some tangible reward four years before his death when he was appointed Regius Professor of Modern History at Cambridge. Like some other professors of the day, however, he did not deliver a single lecture.

The retired and outwardly uneventful life of Gray is at the farthest remove from the busy lives of Chaucer, Shakespeare, Milton, and Browning. He is the poet of the library *par excellence*. It is in his letters—and he is among the half-dozen best letter writers in English—that we discover the affectionate nature of Gray and the spirit of good comradeship, the intellectual vigor, and the other qualities that attracted to him and held so discerning and worldly-wise a man as Horace Walpole. Despite the small volume of his verse, his place in eighteenth-century literature is distinctive and assured. Only Pope among his contemporaries wrote more felicitous and polished verse in the Neoclassical style, and more than Thomson or any other poet of his time Gray prepared the way for the Romantic poets. Not until Wordsworth do we find more exactness of description and greater feeling in the treatment of natural scenes. In those poems of Gray's which were inspired by Norse and Celtic themes "Romantic" poetry may be said to announce itself. The literary criticism in his letters is marked by a soundness and perspicuity not found elsewhere in his day. This most academic of poets produced in his "Elegy in a Country Churchyard" what was, until the twentieth century at least, the most popular and beloved poem in the language—a poem which could supply equally well an epigram for a British general dying at Quebec or a platitude for the man of business in Manchester or New York.

ODE ON A DISTANT PROSPECT OF ETON COLLEGE

The spires of Eton and Windsor Castle were visible in Gray's time from the village of Stoke Poges, where, in the summer of 1742, this poem was written. Gray's recollection of the brief happiness he had enjoyed in his school days at Eton was darkened at this time by the fact that he had recently lost the dearest of his boyhood companions, Richard West, and that he was temporarily estranged from two other friends, Thomas Ashton and Horace Walpole, who were also fellow Etonians.

Ye distant spires, ye antique towers,
That crown the watery glade,
Where grateful Science still adores
Her Henry's holy Shade;
And ye, that from the stately brow
Of Windsor's heights the expanse below
Of grove, of lawn, of mead survey,
Whose turf, whose shade, whose flowers among
Wanders the hoary Thames along
His silver-winding way:

Ah happy hills, ah, pleasing shade,
Ah fields beloved in vain,
Where once my careless childhood strayed,
A stranger yet to pain!
I feel the gales that from ye blow
A momentary bliss bestow,
As, waving fresh their gladsome wing,
My weary soul they seem to soothe
And, redolent of joy and youth,
To breathe a second spring.

Say, Father Thames, for thou hast seen
Full many a sprightly race
Disporting on thy margent green
The paths of pleasure trace,
Who foremost now delight to cleave
With pliant arm thy glassy wave?
The captive linnet which enthrall?
What idle progeny succeed
To chase the rolling circle's speed,
Or urge the flying ball?

While some on earnest business bent
Their murmuring labours ply
'Gainst graver hours, that bring constraint
To sweeten liberty:
Some bold adventurers disdain
The limits of their little reign,
And unknown regions dare descry:
Still as they run they look behind,
They hear a voice in every wind,
And snatch a fearful joy.

Gay hope is theirs, by fancy fed,
Less pleasing when possest;
The tear forgot as soon as shed,
The sunshine of the breast;
Theirs buxom health of rosy hue,
Wild wit, invention ever new,
And lively cheer of vigour born;
The thoughtless day, the easy night,
The spirits pure, the slumbers light,
That fly the approach of morn.

Alas, regardless of their doom,
The little victims play!
No sense have they of ills to come,
Nor care beyond to-day:
Yet see how all around 'em wait
The ministers of human fate,
And black Misfortune's baleful train!
Ah, shew them where in ambush stand

4. Henry, Henry VI, founder of Eton College.

29. circle's, hoop's.

To seize their prey the murtherous band!
Ah, tell them, they are men!

These shall the fury Passions tear,
The vultures of the mind,
Disdainful Anger, pallid Fear,
And Shame that skulks behind;
Or pining Love shall waste their youth,
Or Jealousy with rankling tooth,
That inly gnaws the secret heart,
And Envy wan, and faded Care,
Grim-visaged comfortless Despair,
And Sorrow's piercing dart.

Ambition this shall tempt to rise,
Then whirl the wretch from high,
To bitter Scorn a sacrifice,
And grinning Infamy.
The stings of Falsehood those shall try,
And hard Unkindness' altered eye,
That mocks the tear it forced to flow;
And keen Remorse with blood defiled,
And moody Madness laughing wild
Amid severest woe.

Lo, in the vale of years beneath
A grisly troop are seen,
The painful family of Death,
More hideous than their queen:
This racks the joints, this fires the veins,
That every labouring sinew strains,
Those in the deeper vitals rage:
Lo, Poverty, to fill the band,
That numbs the soul with icy hand,
And slow-consuming Age.

To each his sufferings: all are men,
Condemned alike to groan,
The tender for another's pain;
The unfeeling for his own.
Yet ah! why should they know their fate?
Since sorrow never comes too late,
And happiness too swiftly flies.
Thought would destroy their paradise.
No more; where ignorance is bliss,
'Tis folly to be wise.

ODE ON THE DEATH OF A FAVOURITE CAT

DROWNED IN A TUB OF GOLDFISHES

"The pensive Selima," whose death inspired these playfully solemn verses, was a pet of Gray's friend Horace Walpole.

'Twas on a lofty vase's side,
Where China's gayest art had dyed
The azure flowers, that blow;
Demurest of the tabby kind,
The pensive Selima reclined,
Gazed on the lake below.

Her conscious tail her joy declared;
The fair round face, the snowy beard,
The velvet of her paws,
Her coat, that with the tortoise vies,
Her ears of jet, and emerald eyes,
She saw; and purred applause.

Still had she gazed; but 'midst the tide
Two angel forms were seen to glide,
The genii of the stream;
Their scaly armour's Tyrian hue
Through richest purple to the view
Betrayed a golden gleam.

The hapless nymph with wonder saw:
A whisker first and then a claw,
With many an ardent wish,
She stretched in vain to reach the prize.
What female heart can gold despise?
What cat's averse to fish?

Presumptuous maid! with looks intent
Again she stretched, again she bent,
Nor knew the gulf between.
(Malignant Fate sat by, and smiled)
The slippery verge her feet beguiled,
She tumbled headlong in.

Eight times emerging from the flood
She mewed to every watery god,
Some speedy aid to send.
No dolphin came, no nereid stirred:
Nor cruel Tom, nor Susan heard.
A favourite has no friend!

From hence, ye beauties, undeceived,
Know, one false step is ne'er retrieved,
And be with caution bold.
Not all that tempts your wandering eyes
And heedless hearts, is lawful prize;
Nor all that glisters, gold.

34. **dolphin.** In Greek legend the poet Arion, who had been cast adrift by pirates, was brought safely to shore by a dolphin. **nereid,** a sea nymph; one of the fifty daughters of Nereus, the wise old man of the sea.

ELEGY WRITTEN IN A COUNTRY CHURCH-YARD

Gray began the best and most famous of his poems at Stoke Poges, near Windsor, in the summer of 1742, shortly after the death of his dearest friend, Richard West. The scene of the poem is probably the Stoke Poges churchyard, although Thanington churchyard, about a mile from Canterbury, and the Bell Harry Tower of Canterbury Cathedral also lay claim to having furnished the setting. The poem as a whole is in the Neoclassical tradition, and is replete with "poetic diction," but more than any other poem of the century it anticipates the work of the Romantic poets in its feeling for natural scenes and the humble folk associated with them, as well as in the gentle tone of melancholy which pervades the piece. There is more of the early nineteenth century than of the eighteenth in such lines as

> Oft have we seen him at the peep of dawn
> Brushing with hasty steps the dews away,
> To meet the sun upon the upland lawn.

Matthew Arnold declared that in admiring the *Elegy* the public showed a true feeling for poetry. In any case its readers were responding to the best illustration in the language of Pope's epigram, "What oft was thought, but ne'er so well expressed."

The curfew tolls the knell of parting day,
The lowing herd wind slowly o'er the lea,
The plowman homeward plods his weary way,
And leaves the world to darkness and to me.

Now fades the glimmering landscape on the sight,
And all the air a solemn stillness holds,
Save where the beetle wheels his droning flight,
And drowsy tinklings lull the distant folds;

Save that from yonder ivy-mantled tower
The moping owl does to the moon complain
Of such as, wandering near her secret bower,
Molest her ancient solitary reign.

Beneath those rugged elms, that yew-tree's shade,
Where heaves the turf in many a mouldering heap,
Each in his narrow cell for ever laid,
The rude forefathers of the hamlet sleep.

The breezy call of incense-breathing Morn,
The swallow twittering from the straw-built shed,
The cock's shrill clarion, or the echoing horn,
No more shall rouse them from their lowly bed.

For them no more the blazing hearth shall burn,
Or busy housewife ply her evening care:

19. horn, of the hunters.

No children run to lisp their sire's return,
Or climb his knees the envied kiss to share.

Oft did the harvest to their sickle yield,
Their furrow oft the stubborn glebe has broke;
How jocund did they drive their team afield!
How bowed the woods beneath their sturdy stroke!

Let not Ambition mock their useful toil,
Their homely joys, and destiny obscure;
Nor Grandeur hear with a disdainful smile
The short and simple annals of the poor.

The boast of heraldry, the pomp of power,
And all that beauty, all that wealth e'er gave,
Awaits alike the inevitable hour.
The paths of glory lead but to the grave.

Nor you, ye Proud, impute to these the fault,
If Memory o'er their tomb no trophies raise,
Where through the long-drawn aisle and fretted vault
The pealing anthem swells the note of praise.

Can storied urn or animated bust
Back to its mansion call the fleeting breath?
Can Honour's voice provoke the silent dust,
Or Flattery soothe the dull cold ear of Death?

Perhaps in this neglected spot is laid
Some heart once pregnant with celestial fire;
Hands, that the rod of empire might have swayed,
Or waked to ecstasy the living lyre.

But Knowledge to their eyes her ample page
Rich with the spoils of time did ne'er unroll;
Chill Penury repressed their noble rage,
And froze the genial current of the soul.

Full many a gem of purest ray serene,
The dark unfathomed caves of ocean bear:
Full many a flower is born to blush unseen,
And waste its sweetness on the desert air.

Some village Hampden, that with dauntless breast
The little tyrant of his fields withstood;
Some mute, inglorious Milton here may rest,
Some Cromwell guiltless of his country's blood.

The applause of listening senates to command,
The threats of pain and ruin to despise,
To scatter plenty o'er a smiling land,
And read their history in a nation's eyes,

26. glebe, soil. **33. heraldry,** noble lineage. **39. fretted,** decorated. **41. storied urn,** funeral urn with an inscription. **animated,** lifelike. **43. provoke,** call forth. **51. rage,** enthusiasm. **52. genial,** life-giving. **57. Hampden,** John Hampden, English patriot (1595–1643.)

Their lot forbade; nor circumscribed alone
Their growing virtues, but their crimes confined;
Forbade to wade through slaughter to a throne,
And shut the gates of mercy on mankind;

The struggling pangs of conscious truth to hide,
To quench the blushes of ingenuous shame,
Or heap the shrine of Luxury and Pride
With incense kindled at the Muse's flame.

Far from the madding crowd's ignoble strife,
Their sober wishes never learned to stray;
Along the cool sequestered vale of life
They kept the noiseless tenor of their way.

Yet ev'n these bones from insult to protect,
Some frail memorial still erected nigh,
With uncouth rimes and shapeless sculpture decked,
Implores the passing tribute of a sigh.

Their name, their years, spelt by the unlettered Muse,
The place of fame and elegy supply;
And many a holy text around she strews,
That teach the rustic moralist to die.

For who, to dumb Forgetfulness a prey,
This pleasing anxious being e'er resigned,
Let the warm precincts of the cheerful day,
Nor cast one longing, lingering look behind?

On some fond breast the parting soul relies,
Some pious drops the closing eye requires;
Ev'n from the tomb the voice of Nature cries,
Ev'n in our ashes live their wonted fires.

For thee who, mindful of the unhonoured dead,
Dost in these lines their artless tale relate;
If chance, by lonely contemplation led,
Some kindred spirit shall inquire thy fate,

Haply some hoary-headed swain may say,
"Oft have we seen him at the peep of dawn
Brushing with hasty steps the dews away,
To meet the sun upon the upland lawn.

"There at the foot of yonder nodding beech
That wreathes its old fantastic roots so high,
His listless length at noontide would he stretch,
And pore upon the brook that babbles by.

"Hard by yon wood, now smiling as in scorn,
Muttering his wayward fancies he would rove;

79. uncouth, strange, odd. **82. elegy,** versified praise. **93. thee,** the poet Gray himself. **98. him,** probably another reference to Gray himself.

Now drooping, woeful wan, like one forlorn,
Or crazed with care, or crossed in hopeless love.

"One morn I missed him on the customed hill,
Along the heath, and near his favourite tree;
Another came; nor yet beside the rill,
Nor up the lawn, nor at the wood was he;

"The next with dirges due in sad array,
Slow through the church-way path we saw him borne.
Approach and read (for thou canst read) the lay,
Graved on the stone beneath yon agèd thorn."

THE EPITAPH

Here rests his head upon the lap of Earth,
A Youth to Fortune and to Fame unknown.
Fair Science frowned not on his humble birth,
And Melancholy marked him for her own.

Large was his bounty, and his soul sincere,
Heaven did a recompence as largely send:
He gave to Misery all he had, a tear,
He gained from Heaven ('twas all he wished) a friend.

No farther seek his merits to disclose,
Or draw his frailties from their dread abode,
(There they alike in trembling hope repose,)
The bosom of his Father and his God.

SONNET

ON THE DEATH OF MR. RICHARD WEST

In vain to me the smiling mornings shine,
And reddening Phoebus lifts his golden fire:
The birds in vain their amorous descant join,
Or cheerful fields resume their green attire:
These ears, alas! for other notes repine,
A different object do these eyes require.
My lonely anguish melts no heart but mine;
And in my breast the imperfect joys expire.
Yet morning smiles the busy race to cheer, 9
And new-born pleasure brings to happier men:
The fields to all their wonted tribute bear:
To warm their little loves the birds complain:
I fruitless mourn to him that cannot hear,
And weep the more because I weep in vain.

116. thorn, hawthorn tree. *Sonnet.* See Wordsworth's comments on this sonnet, pages 703–704.

THE BARD

A PINDARIC ODE

"The Bard" is based upon a legend that King Edward I of England, when he overran Wales in 1276–84, ordered that all the Welsh bards should be put to death.

Gray gives the following plan:

The army of Edward I, as they march through a deep valley and approach Mount Snowdon, are suddenly stopped by the appearance of a venerable figure seated on the summit of an inaccessible rock, who, with a voice more than human, reproaches the king with all the desolation and misery which he had brought upon his country, foretells the misfortunes of the Norman race, and with prophetic spirit declares that all his cruelty shall never extinguish the noble ardour of poetic genius in this island, and that men shall never be wanting to celebrate true virtue and valour in immortal strains, to expose vice and infamous pleasure, and boldly censure tyranny and oppression. His song ended, he precipitates himself from the mountain and is swallowed up in the river that rolls at its foot.

I. 1.

"Ruin seize thee, ruthless King!
Confusion on thy banners wait,
Though fanned by Conquest's crimson wing
They mock the air with idle state.
Helm, nor Hauberk's twisted mail,
Nor e'en thy virtues, Tyrant, shall avail
To save thy secret soul from nightly fears,
From Cambria's curse, from Cambria's tears!"
Such were the sounds, that o'er the crested pride
Of the first Edward scattered wild dismay,
As down the steep of Snowdon's shaggy side
He wound with toilsome march his long array.
Stout Glo'ster stood aghast in speechless trance:
To arms! cried Mortimer, and couched his quivering lance.

I. 2.

On a rock, whose haughty brow
Frowns o'er old Conway's foaming flood,
Robed in the sable garb of woe,
With haggard eyes the Poet stood
(Loose his beard, and hoary hair
Streamed, like a meteor, to the troubled air)
And with a Master's hand and Prophet's fire
Struck the deep sorrows of his lyre.
"Hark, how each giant-oak, and desert cave
Sighs to the torrent's aweful voice beneath!
O'er thee, oh King! their hundred arms they wave,
Revenge on thee in hoarser murmurs breathe;
Vocal no more, since Cambria's fatal day,
To high-born Hoel's harp, or soft Llewellyn's lay.

I. 3.

"Cold is Cadwallo's tongue,
That hushed the stormy main;
Brave Urien sleeps upon his craggy bed:
Mountains, ye mourn in vain
Modred, whose magic song
Made huge Plinlimmon bow his cloud-topped head.
On dreary Arvon's shore they lie,
Smeared with gore, and ghastly pale:
Far, far aloof the affrighted ravens sail;
The famished Eagle screams, and passes by.
Dear lost companions of my tuneful art,
Dear as the light that visits these sad eyes,
Dear as the ruddy drops that warm my heart,
Ye died amidst your dying country's cries—
No more I weep. They do not sleep.
On yonder cliffs, a griesly band,
I see them sit; they linger yet,
Avengers of their native land:
With me in dreadful harmony they join,
And weave with bloody hands the tissue of thy line.

II. 1.

" 'Weave the warp, and weave the woof,
The winding-sheet of Edward's race.
Give ample room, and verge enough
The characters of hell to trace.
Mark the year, and mark the night,
When Severn shall re-echo with affright
The shrieks of death, through Berkley's roofs that ring,
Shrieks of an agonizing King!
She-Wolf of France, with unrelenting fangs,
That tear'st the bowels of thy mangled Mate,
From thee be born, who o'er thy country hangs
The scourge of Heaven. What Terrors round him wait!
Amazement in his van, with Flight combined,
And Sorrow's faded form, and Solitude behind.

II. 2.

" 'Mighty Victor, mighty Lord,
Low on his funeral couch he lies!
No pitying heart, no eye, afford
A tear to grace his obsequies.
Is the sable Warriour fled?

8. Cambria, Wales. **13. Glo'ster,** The Earl of Gloucester and Hereford, King Edward's son-in-law.

28. Hoel, a royal poet of the twelfth century. **lay,** poem. **34. Plinlimmon,** a mountain in Wales. **35. shore,** opposite Anglesea. **56. King!** Edward II, murdered at Berkeley Castle. **57. She-Wolf,** Isabel of France, wife of Edward II. **60. him,** Edward III. **67. sable Warriour,** Edward the Black Prince.

Thy son is gone. He rests among the Dead.
The Swarm that in thy noon-tide beam were born?
Gone to salute the rising Morn.
Fair laughs the Morn, and soft the Zephyr blows,
While proudly riding o'er the azure realm
In gallant trim the gilded Vessel goes;
Youth on the prow, and Pleasure at the helm;
Regardless of the sweeping Whirlwind's sway,
That, hushed in grim repose, expects his evening-prey.

II. 3.

" 'Fill high the sparkling bowl,
The rich repast prepare,
Reft of a crown, he yet may share the feast:
Close by the regal chair
Fell Thirst and Famine scowl
A baleful smile upon their baffled Guest.
Heard ye the din of battle bray,
Lance to lance, and horse to horse?
Long Years of havock urge their destined course,
And through the kindred squadrons mow their way.
Ye Towers of Julius, London's lasting shame,
With many a foul and midnight murther fed,
Revere his Consort's faith, his Father's fame,
And spare the meek Usurper's holy head.
Above, below, the rose of snow,
Twined with her blushing foe, we spread:
The bristled Boar in infant-gore
Wallows beneath the thorny shade.
Now, Brothers, bending o'er the accursèd loom,
Stamp we our vengeance deep, and ratify his doom.

III. 1.

" 'Edward, lo! to sudden fate
(Weave we the woof. The thread is spun.)
Half of thy heart we consecrate.
(The web is wove. The work is done.)' "
"Stay, oh stay! nor thus forlorn
Leave me unblessed, unpitied, here to mourn:
In yon bright track, that fires the western skies,
They melt, they vanish from my eyes.
But oh! what solemn scenes on Snowdon's height
Descending slow their glittering skirts unroll?
Visions of glory, spare my aching sight,
Ye unborn Ages, crowd not on my soul!

85. havock, the Wars of the Roses. **89. Consort,** Margaret of Anjou, wife of Henry VI. **Father,** Henry V. **90. Usurper,** Henry VI. **92. foe,** the red rose of Lancaster, foe to the white rose of York. **93. Boar,** emblem of Richard III. **101. Stay.** From this point the Bard speaks only for himself.

No more our long-lost Arthur we bewail.
All-hail, ye genuine Kings, Britannia's Issue, hail!

III. 2.

"Girt with many a baron bold
Sublime their starry fronts they rear;
And gorgeous Dames, and Statesmen old
In bearded majesty, appear.
In the midst a Form divine!
Her eye proclaims her of the Briton-Line;
Her lyon-port, her awe-commanding face,
Attempered sweet to virgin-grace.
What strings symphonious tremble in the air,
What strains of vocal transport round her play!
Hear from the grave, great Taliessin, hear;
They breathe a soul to animate thy clay.
Bright Rapture calls, and soaring, as she sings,
Waves in the eye of Heaven her many-coloured wings.

III. 3.

"The verse adorn again
Fierce War, and faithful Love,
And Truth severe, by fairy Fiction drest.
In buskined measures move
Pale Grief, and pleasing Pain,
With Horrour, tyrant of the throbbing breast.
A Voice, as of the Cherub-Choir,
Gales from blooming Eden bear;
And distant warblings lessen on my ear,
That lost in long futurity expire.
Fond impious Man, think'st thou, yon sanguine cloud,
Raised by thy breath, has quenched the Orb of day?
To-morrow he repairs the golden flood,
And warms the nations with redoubled ray.
Enough for me: with joy I see
The different doom our Fates assign.
Be thine Despair, and sceptered Care;
To triumph, and to die, are mine."
He spoke, and headlong from the mountain's height
Deep in the roaring tide he plunged to endless night.

109. Arthur, regarded by the Welsh as still living. **110. Kings,** of the House of Tudor, which was of Welsh origin. **115. Form divine!** Queen Elizabeth. **120. strains,** Elizabethan poetry. **121. Taliessin,** a Welsh bard. **127. drest,** in Spenser's *Faerie Queene*. **128. measures,** of Shakespeare's tragedies. **131. Voice,** Milton. **133. warblings,** of poets following Milton. **135. Man,** Edward I.

William Collins

1721–1759

The short and rather pitiful life of William Collins began in the cathedral city of Chichester, near the southern coast of England. He began to write verse while yet a schoolboy at Winchester College and continued to do so during his years at Oxford. After taking his degree he spent some time in the literary circles of London, apparently with a vague intention of trying to make a living by his pen. Several ambitious literary plans were brought to nothing by his indolence, intemperance, and fits of despondency. His *Persian Eclogues*, 1742, and his *Odes on Several Descriptive and Allegoric Subjects*, 1746, failed so dismally that when, at the age of twenty-eight, he inherited a small fortune from an uncle, he was glad to return to his native town. A main reason for his retirement from London, probably, was the gradual increase of a nervous and mental disorder which darkened the last decade of his life.

Collins won his modest but secure position in English literature by some five or six poems, most of them short and all of them written before he was twenty-nine. He did indeed turn out a number of frigid, awkward, and scarcely readable verses that were quite as bad as his friend Dr. Johnson thought them, but the world has wisely chosen to remember the exquisite beauty of the few things he did surpassingly well. Those odes and songs are an unfailing source of delight.

ODE TO SIMPLICITY

O thou by Nature taught
To breathe her genuine thought,
In numbers warmly pure, and sweetly strong;
Who first on mountains wild,
In Fancy, loveliest child,
Thy babe, or Pleasure's, nursed the powers of song!

Thou, who with hermit heart
Disdain'st the wealth of art,
And gauds, and pageant weeds, and trailing pall;
But com'st a decent maid,
In Attic robe arrayed,
O chaste unboastful nymph, to thee I call!

By all the honeyed store
On Hybla's thymy shore,
By all her blooms and mingled murmurs dear,
By her, whose lovelorn woe
In evening musings slow,
Soothed sweetly sad *Electra's* poet's ear:

By old Cephisus deep,
Who spread his wavy sweep
In warbled wanderings round thy green retreat,
On whose enamelled side,
When holy Freedom died,
No equal haunt allured thy future feet:

O sister meek of Truth,
To my admiring youth,
Thy sober aid and native charms infuse!
The flowers that sweetest breathe,
Though beauty culled the wreath,
Still ask thy hand to range their ordered hues.

While Rome could none esteem
But virtue's patriot theme,
You loved her hills, and led her laureate band;
But staid to sing alone
To one distinguished throne,
And turned thy face, and fled her altered land.

No more, in hall or bower,
The passions own thy power;
Love, only love her forceless numbers mean:
For thou hast left her shrine;
Nor olive more, nor vine,
Shall gain thy feet to bless the servile scene.

Though taste, though genius bless,
To some divine excess,
Faints the cold work till thou inspire the whole;
What each, what all supply,
May court, may charm, our eye;
Thou, only thou, canst raise the meeting soul!

Of these let others ask,
To aid some mighty task;
I only seek to find thy temperate vale,

Ode to Simplicity. **9. gauds,** ornaments. **weeds,** garments. **pall,** a long cloak. **10. decent,** decorous. **14. Hybla's . . . shore.** Mt. Hybla in Sicily was famous for its honey. **16. her,** the nightingale, praised by Electra in Sophocles' tragedy of that name. **18. poet's ear,** from Milton's sonnet "When the Assault Was Intended to the City." **19. Cephisus,** a river in Attica. **21. retreat,** Athens. **33. band,** of poets. **35. throne,** of Augustus, patron of poets. **37. bower,** the private apartment of a castle. **39. her,** Rome's, or Italy's. **42. servile scene,** the typical British attitude of the time toward Italian poetry and drama. **49. these,** taste and genius.

Where oft my reed might sound
To maids and shepherds round,
And all thy sons, O Nature, learn my tale.

ODE TO EVENING

If aught of oaten stop, or pastoral song,
May hope, chaste Eve, to soothe thy modest ear,
Like thy own solemn springs,
Thy springs, and dying gales,
O nymph reserved, while now the bright-haired sun
Sits in yon western tent, whose cloudy skirts,
With brede ethereal wove,
O'erhang his wavy bed:
Now air is hushed, save where the weak-eyed bat,
With short shrill shriek flits by on leathern wing,
Or where the beetle winds
His small but sullen horn,
As oft he rises 'midst the twilight path,
Against the pilgrim borne in heedless hum:
Now teach me, maid composed,
To breathe some softened strain,
Whose numbers stealing through thy darkening vale,
May not unseemly with its stillness suit,
As musing slow, I hail
Thy genial loved return!
For when thy folding star arising shews
His paly circlet, at his warning lamp
The fragrant Hours, and elves
Who slept in flowers the day,
And many a nymph who wreaths her brows with sedge,
And sheds the freshening dew, and lovelier still,
The pensive Pleasures sweet
Prepare thy shadowy car.
Then lead, calm votaress, where some sheety lake
Cheers the lone heath, or some time-hallowed pile,
Or up-land fallows grey
Reflect its last cool gleam.
But when chill blustering winds, or driving rain,
Forbid my willing feet, be mine the hut,
That from the mountain's side
Views wilds, and swelling floods,
And hamlets brown, and dim-discovered spires,
And hears their simple bell, and marks o'er all
Thy dewy fingers draw
The gradual dusky veil.
While spring shall pour his showers, as oft he wont,
And bathe thy breathing tresses, meekest Eve!
While Summer loves to sport,
Beneath thy lingering light;
While sallow Autumn fills thy lap with leaves;
Or Winter, yelling thro' the troublous air,
Affrights thy shrinking train,
And rudely rends thy robes;
So long, sure-found beneath the sylvan shed,
Shall Fancy, Friendship, Science, rose-lipped Health,
Thy gentlest influence own,
And hymn thy favourite name!

1. If aught . . . song. If any music from a shepherd's flute. **7. brede,** embroidery. **9. Now.** Supply "while." **21. folding star,** at the rising of which shepherds fold their sheep. **28. car,** triumphal chariot. **32. gleam,** reflection from the lake. **41. wont,** is accustomed to.

THE PASSIONS: AN ODE FOR MUSIC

When Music, heavenly maid, was young,
While yet in early Greece she sung,
The passions oft, to hear her shell,
Thronged around her magic cell,
Exulting, trembling, raging, fainting,
Possessed beyond the Muse's painting;
By turns they felt the glowing mind,
Disturbed, delighted, raised, refined,
Till once, 'tis said, when all were fired,
Filled with fury, rapt, inspired,
From the supporting myrtles round
They snatched her instruments of sound,
And as they oft had heard apart
Sweet lessons of her forceful art,
Each, for madness ruled the hour,
Would prove his own expressive power.

First Fear his hand, its skill to try,
Amid the chords bewildered laid,
And back recoiled, he knew not why,
Ev'n at the sound himself had made.

Next Anger rushed; his eyes on fire
In lightnings owned his secret stings:
In one rude clash he struck the lyre,
And swept with hurried hand the strings.

With woeful measures wan Despair
Low sullen sounds his grief beguiled,
A solemn, strange, and mingled air,
'Twas sad by fits, by starts 'twas wild.

But thou, O Hope, with eyes so fair,
What was thy delightful measure?
Still it whispered promised pleasure,
And bade the lovely scenes at distance hail!
Still would her touch the strain prolong,

3. passions, emotions. **shell,** lyre.

And from the rocks, the woods, the vale,
She called on Echo still through all the song;
And, where her sweetest theme she chose,
A soft responsive voice was heard at every close,
And Hope enchanted smiled, and waved her golden hair.

And longer had she sung,—but with a frown
Revenge impatient rose,
He threw his blood-stained sword in thunder down,
And with a withering look,
The war-denouncing trumpet took,
And blew a blast so loud and dread,
Were ne'er prophetic sounds so full of woe.
And ever and anon he beat
The doubling drum with furious heat;
And though sometimes, each dreary pause between,
Dejected Pity at his side
Her soul-subduing voice applied,
Yet still he kept his wild unaltered mien,
While each strained ball of sight seemed bursting from his head.

Thy numbers, Jealousy, to nought were fixed,
Sad proof of thy distressful state;
Of differing themes the veering song was mixed,
And now it courted Love, now raving called on Hate.

With eyes upraised, as one inspired,
Pale Melancholy sate retired,
And from her wild sequestered seat,
In notes by distance made more sweet,
Poured through the mellow horn her pensive soul:
And dashing soft from rocks around,
Bubbling runnels joined the sound;
Through glades and glooms the mingled measure stole,
Or o'er some haunted stream with fond delay,
Round an holy calm diffusing,
Love of peace and lonely musing,
In hollow murmurs died away.
But O how altered was its sprightlier tone!
When Cheerfulness, a nymph of healthiest hue,
Her bow across her shoulder flung,
Her buskins gemmed with morning dew,
Blew an inspiring air, that dale and thicket rung,
The hunger's call to Faun and Dryad known!
The oak-crowned sisters, and their chaste-eyed queen,
Satyrs and sylvan boys were seen,
Peeping from forth their alleys green;
Brown Exercise rejoiced to hear,
And Sport leaped up, and seized his beechen spear.

Last came Joy's ecstatic trial,
He, with viny crown advancing,
First to the lively pipe his hand addrest,
But soon he saw the brisk awakening viol,
Whose sweet entrancing voice he loved the best.
They would have thought who heard the strain,
They saw in Tempe's vale her native maids,
Amidst the festal sounding shades,
To some unwearied minstrel dancing,
While, as his flying fingers kissed the strings,
Love framed with Mirth a gay fantastic round.
Loose were her tresses seen, her zone unbound,
And he amidst his frolic play,
As if he would the charming air repay,
Shook thousand odours from his dewey wings.

O Music, sphere-descended maid,
Friend of Pleasure, Wisdom's aid,
Why, goddess, why to us denied,
Lay'st thou thy ancient lyre aside?
As in that loved Athenian bower,
You learned an all-commanding power,
Thy mimic soul, O nymph endeared,
Can well recall what then it heard.
Where is thy native simple heart,
Devote to virtue, fancy, art?
Arise as in that elder Time,
Warm, energic, chaste, sublime!
Thy wonders, in that god-like age,
Fill thy recording sister's page—
'Tis said, and I believe the tale,
Thy humblest reed could more prevail,
Had more of strength, diviner rage,
Than all which charms this laggard age,
Ev'n all at once together found,
Caecilia's mingled world of sound—
O bid our vain endeavours cease,
Revive the just designs of Greece,
Return in all thy simple state!
Confirm the tales her sons relate!

ODE

WRITTEN IN THE BEGINNING OF THE YEAR 1746

How sleep the brave, who sink to rest,
By all their country's wishes blest!

36. theme, that of love. **43. war-denouncing,** war-announcing. **75. sisters,** wood nymphs. **queen,** Diana.

81. viny, suggesting that Joy is the same as Bacchus. **86. vale,** in Thessaly. **108. sister,** poetry. **110. reed,** flute. **114. world of sound,** the pipe organ. **115. endeavours,** in Italian opera.

When Spring, with dewy fingers cold,
Returns to deck their hallowed mold,
She there shall dress a sweeter sod,
Than Fancy's feet have ever trod.

By fairy hands their knell is rung,
By forms unseen their dirge is sung;
There Honour comes, a pilgrim grey,
To bless the turf that wraps their clay,
And Freedom shall awhile repair,
To dwell a weeping hermit there!

A SONG FROM SHAKESPEARE'S CYMBELINE

SUNG BY GUIDERUS AND ARVIRAGUS OVER FIDELE, SUPPOSED TO BE DEAD

To fair Fidele's grassy tomb
Soft maids and village hinds shall bring
Each opening sweet, of earliest bloom,
And rifle all the breathing spring.

No wailing ghost shall dare appear
To vex with shrieks this quiet grove:
But shepherd lads assemble here,
And melting virgins own their love.

No withered witch shall here be seen,
No goblins lead their nightly crew:
The female fays shall haunt the green,
And dress thy grave with pearly dew!

The red-breast oft at evening hours
Shall kindly lend his little aid:
With hoary moss, and gathered flowers,
To deck the ground where thou art laid.

When howling winds, and beating rain,
In tempests shake the sylvan cell:
Or midst the chase on every plain,
The tender thought on thee shall dwell.

Each lonely scene shall thee restore,
For thee the tear be duly shed:
Beloved till life can charm no more,
And mourned, till Pity's self be dead.

Samuel Johnson
1709–1784

The literary dictator of late eighteenth-century England was born during the reign of Queen Anne in the northern cathedral city of Lichfield, where his father, an aging man, kept a not very prosperous bookshop. From the excellent school of his native town Johnson went to Oxford; but there, on account of his poverty, he took no degree. At the age of twenty-six he married a widow some fifteen years his senior. After certain abortive attempts at schoolteaching he went up to London in 1737, accompanied by David Garrick, who had been one of his pupils, and settled down to the obscure and ill-paid toil of a hack writer. He wrote hundreds of essays for such periodicals as would take them, and for two, the *Rambler* and the *Idler*, which he conducted himself. His didactic poem *London*, an imitation of Juvenal, appeared in 1738 without his name, and eleven years later he published his more important poem of the same sort called *The Vanity of Human Wishes*. His tragedy entitled *Irene* had slight success.

Fame and money first came to Johnson in 1755 with the publication of his *Dictionary of the English Language*, upon which he had been working for many years. By that time, however, he had lost his beloved wife and success meant far less to him than it would previously have done. His *History of Rasselas, Prince of Abissinia*, appearing in 1759, extended his reputation. In 1762 the King gave him a pension of £300 a year, a sum amounting to at least $6,000 in present buying power.

In the following year Johnson first met James Boswell, and almost immediately realized what the devotion of this intelligent young Scot, so exact and enthusiastic in the taking of notes upon everyday events and conversations, might mean in the way of posthumous fame. Johnson's habitual gloom and despondency were still further alleviated in 1764 by his meeting with the wealthy brewer Mr. Thrale and with his wife—"a bright papilionaceous creature," as Carlyle calls her, "whom the elephant loved to play with, and wave to and fro upon his trunk." His closing years, though saddened by the loss of friends, were lived in a growing light of fame. His edition of Shakespeare was published in 1765, and his *Lives of the Poets* appeared, in ten volumes, in 1779–81. Three years later he died and was buried in Westminster Abbey.

Dr. Johnson—so-called because of the honorary degrees of LL.D. conferred upon him by Oxford and Dublin—owes his huge and still continuing fame and influence as much to qualities of character as to his learning, his wit, his writing, and his massive common sense. James Boswell did not create, and he did not exaggerate, the flawed and whimsical human grandeur that looms above Johnson's prejudices and his sometimes stubborn stupidities. He only uncovered what was there, and what he revealed was—in the full tragic and pathetic sense of the word—a man. Largely by Boswell's help, Dr. Johnson is the most amply recorded writer in the total range of English literature. We know him not only in the many moods of his own writing—much of it cumbered by theory and rule-ridden, but much of it, too, with the accent of his own discursive, dogmatic, and always friendly talk—but we see him also in his hours of ease, away from the writing-desk, at the literary club, in the tavern, in the greenroom of Garrick's theater, on the roads reaching north through Scotland, in his Christian love for helpless and lost people. We hear him talking, always talking for triumph, at the Turk's Head tavern with Reynolds, Burke, Goldsmith, Garrick, Langton, Beauclerk, Fox, and Boswell round him. His resounding voice, his rolling gait and ungainly form, his nearsighted eyes that always saw much more than others suspected, his gruff and bearish demeanor with strangers, his queer and meaningless gestures—all these were part of a genuine, warm-hearted, brotherly man.

Dr. Johnson's literary production, that of a man who had to live by his pen, was miscellaneous. As good an introduction as any, before the reader encounters Johnson at first hand in Boswell's pages, is probably to be gained from *Rasselas* and the later essays in which he revealed himself as a conservative critic who usually mingled conservatism with common sense.

from RASSELAS

The History of Rasselas, Prince of Abissinia was written within ten days in January, 1759, while Johnson was under the shadow of the last illness and death of his mother and in dire need of funds. However distraught he may have been, he has given us in *Rasselas* some of his clearest and most vigorous prose, and, as Hilaire Belloc has said, "never was wisdom better put or more enduringly." *Rasselas* is a philosophical romance, an entertaining narrative illustration of one of Johnson's favorite themes, the vanity of human wishes.

Space permits the printing here of only one of the forty-nine chapters of the history of the princely inhabitants who escape from their happy valley to observe the various conditions of men's lives.

Chapter 6

A DISSERTATION ON THE ART OF FLYING

Among the artists that had been allured into the happy valley, to labour for the accommodation and pleasure of its inhabitants, was a man eminent for his knowledge of the mechanic powers, who had contrived many engines both of use and recreation. By a wheel which the stream turned, he forced the water into a tower, whence it was distributed to all the apartments of the palace. He erected a pavilion in the garden, around which he kept the air always cool by artificial showers. One of the groves, appropriated to the ladies, was ventilated by fans, to which the rivulet that ran through it gave a constant motion; and instruments of soft music were placed at proper distances, of which some played by the impulse of the wind, and some by the power of the stream.

This artist was sometimes visited by Rasselas, who was pleased with every kind of knowledge, imagining that the time would come when all his acquisitions should be of use to him in the open world. He came one day to amuse himself in his usual manner, and found the master busy in building a sailing chariot: he saw that the design was practicable upon a level surface, and with expressions of great esteem solicited its completion. The workman was pleased to find himself so much regarded by the prince, and resolved to gain yet higher honours. "Sir," said he, "you have seen but a small part of what the mechanic sciences can perform. I have been long of opinion, that instead of the tardy conveyance of ships and chariots, man might use the swifter migration of wings; that the fields of air are open to knowledge, and that only ignorance and idleness need crawl upon the ground."

This hint rekindled the prince's desire of passing the mountains; having seen what the mechanist had already performed, he was willing to fancy that he could do more; yet resolved to inquire further, before he suffered hope to afflict him by disappointment. "I am afraid," said he to the artist, "that your imagination prevails over your skill, and that you now tell me rather what you wish, than what

1. **artists,** craftsmen or mechanics.

you know. Every animal has his element assigned him; the birds have the air, and man and beasts the earth." "So," replied the mechanist, "fishes have the water, in which yet beasts can swim by nature, and men by art. He that can swim needs not despair to fly: to swim is to fly in a grosser fluid, and to fly is to swim in a subtler. We are only to proportion our power of resistance to the different density of matter through which we are to pass. You will be necessarily upborne by the air, if you can renew any impulse upon it, faster than the air can recede from the pressure."

"But the exercise of swimming," said the prince, "is very laborious; the strongest limbs are soon wearied; I am afraid the act of flying will be yet more violent, and wings will be of no great use, unless we can fly further than we can swim."

"The labour of rising from the ground," said the artist, "will be great, as we see it in the heavier domestic fowls; but as we mount higher, the earth's attraction, and the body's gravity, will be gradually diminished, till we shall arrive at a region where the man will float in the air without any tendency to fall: no care will then be necessary but to move forwards, which the gentlest impulse will effect. You, Sir, whose curiosity is so extensive, will easily conceive with what pleasure a philosopher, furnished with wings, and hovering in the sky, would see the earth, and all its inhabitants, rolling beneath him, and presenting to him successively, by its diurnal motion, all the countries within the same parallel. How must it amuse the pendent spectator to see the moving scene of land and ocean, cities and deserts! To survey with equal security the marts of trade, and the fields of battle; mountains infested by barbarians, and fruitful regions gladdened by plenty, and lulled by peace! How easily shall we then trace the Nile through all his passage; pass over to distant regions, and examine the face of nature from one extremity of the earth to the other!"

"All this," said the prince, "is much to be desired; but I am afraid that no man will be able to breathe in these regions of speculation and tranquillity. I have been told, that respiration is difficult upon lofty mountains, yet from these precipices, though so high as to produce great tenuity of the air, it is very easy to fall: therefore I suspect, that from any height where life can be supported, there may be danger of too quick descent."

"Nothing," replied the artist, "will ever be attempted, if all possible objections must be first overcome. If you will favour my project, I will try the first flight at my own hazard. I have considered the structure of all volant animals, and find the folding continuity of the bat's wings most easily accommodated to the human form. Upon this model I shall begin my task to-morrow, and in a year expect to tower into the air beyond the malice or pursuit of man. But I will work only on this condition, that the art shall not be divulged, and that you shall not require me to make wings for any but ourselves."

"Why," said Rasselas, "should you envy others so great an advantage? All skill ought to be exerted for universal good; every man has owed much to others, and ought to repay the kindness that he has received."

"If men were all virtuous," returned the artist, "I should with great alacrity teach them all to fly. But what would be the security of the good, if the bad could at pleasure invade them from the sky? Against an army sailing through the clouds, neither walls, nor mountains, nor seas, could afford any security. A flight of northern savages might hover in the wind, and light at once with irresistible violence upon the capital of a fruitful region that was rolling under them. Even this valley, the retreat of princes, the abode of happiness, might be violated by the sudden descent of some of the naked nations that swarm on the coasts of the southern sea."

The prince promised secrecy, and waited for the performance, not wholly hopeless of success. He visited the work from time to time, observed its progress, and remarked many ingenious contrivances to facilitate motion, and unite levity with strength. The artist was every day more certain that he should leave vultures and eagles behind him, and the contagion of his confidence seized upon the prince.

In a year the wings were finished, and, on a morning appointed, the maker appeared furnished for flight on a little promontory: he waved his pinions a while to gather air, then leaped from his stand, and in an instant dropped into the lake. His wings, which were of no use in the air, sustained him in the water, and the prince drew him to land, half dead with terror and vexation.

27. philosopher, what we should now call a scientist.
38. trace the Nile. The sources of this river were in Johnson's time unknown.

38. levity, lightness.

from THE PREFACE TO SHAKESPEARE

Johnson's *Shakespeare* is not one of the greater and more influential editions, although it contains many valuable notes and clarifications of difficult passages. It is remembered today chiefly on account of the editor's thoughtful and elaborate Preface, in which his good sense triumphs over his Neoclassical predilection for the ancients, authority, tradition, and the "rules." About half of this Preface is here presented.

THE poet of whose works I have undertaken the revision may now begin to assume the dignity of an ancient, and claim the privilege of established fame and prescriptive veneration. He has long outlived his century, the term commonly fixed as the test of literary merit. Whatever advantages he might once derive from personal allusions, local customs, or temporary opinions have for many years been lost; and every topic of merriment or motive of sorrow which the modes of artificial life afforded him now only obscure the scenes which they once illuminated. The effects of favour and competition are at an end; the tradition of his friendships and his enmities has perished; his works support no opinion with arguments, nor supply any faction with invectives; they can neither indulge vanity, nor gratify malignity; but are read without any other reason than the desire of pleasure, and are therefore praised only as pleasure is obtained; yet, thus unassisted by interest or passion, they have passed through variations of taste and changes of manners, and, as they devolved from one generation to another, have received new honours at every transmission.

But because human judgment, though it be gradually gaining upon certainty, never becomes infallible; and approbation, though long continued, may yet be only the approbation of prejudice or fashion; it is proper to inquire, by what peculiarities of excellence Shakespeare has gained and kept the favour of his countrymen.

Nothing can please many, and please long, but just representations of general nature. Particular manners can be known to few, and therefore few only can judge how nearly they are copied. The irregular combinations of fanciful invention may delight awhile, by that novelty of which the common satiety of life sends us all in quest; but the pleasures of sudden wonder are soon exhausted, and the mind can only repose on the stability of truth.

Shakespeare is, above all writers, at least above all modern writers, the poet of nature; the poet that holds up to his readers a faithful mirror of manners and of life. His characters are not modified by the customs of particular places, unpractised by the rest of the world; by the peculiarities of studies or professions, which can operate but upon small numbers; or by the accidents of transient fashions or temporary opinions: they are the genuine progeny of common humanity, such as the world will always supply, and observation will always find. His persons act and speak by the influence of those general passions and principles by which all minds are agitated, and the whole system of life is continued in motion. In the writings of other poets a character is too often an individual; in those of Shakespeare it is commonly a species.

It is from this wide extension of design that so much instruction is derived. It is this which fills the plays of Shakespeare with practical axioms and domestic wisdom. It was said of Euripides, that every verse was a precept; and it may be said of Shakespeare, that from his works may be collected a system of civil and economical prudence. Yet his real power is not shewn in the splendour of particular passages, but by the progress of his fable, and the tenor of his dialogue; and he that tries to recommend him by select quotations, will succeed like the pedant in Hierocles, who, when he offered his house to sale, carried a brick in his pocket as a specimen.

It will not easily be imagined how much Shakespeare excels in accommodating his sentiments to real life, but by comparing him with other authors. It was observed of the ancient schools of declamation, that the more diligently they were frequented, the more was the student disqualified for the world, because he found nothing there which he should ever meet in any other place. The same remark may be applied to every stage but that of Shakespeare. The theatre, when it is under any other direction, is peopled by such characters as were never seen, conversing in a language which was never heard, upon topics which will never arise in the commerce of mankind. But the dialogue of this author is often so evidently determined by the incident which produces it, and is pursued with so much ease and simplicity, that it seems scarcely to claim the merit of fiction, but to have been gleaned by diligent selection out of common conversation and common occurrences.

Upon every other stage the universal agent is love, by whose power all good and evil is dis-

29. Hierocles, an ancient compiler of jokes.

tributed, and every action quickened or retarded. To bring a lover, a lady, and a rival into the fable; to entangle them in contradictory obligations, perplex them with oppositions of interest, and harass them with violence of desires inconsistent with each other; to make them meet in rapture, and part in agony; to fill their mouths with hyperbolical joy and outrageous sorrow; to distress them as nothing human ever was distressed; to deliver them as nothing human ever was delivered, is the business of a modern dramatist. For this, probability is violated, life is misrepresented, and language is depraved. But love is only one of many passions, and as it has no great influence upon the sum of life, it has little operation in the dramas of a poet, who caught his ideas from the living world, and exhibited only what he saw before him. He knew, that any other passion, as it was regular or exorbitant, was a cause of happiness or calamity.

Characters thus ample and general were not easily discriminated and preserved, yet perhaps no poet ever kept his personages more distinct from each other. I will not say, with Pope, that every speech may be assigned to the proper speaker, because many speeches there are which have nothing characteristical; but, perhaps, though some may be equally adapted to every person, it will be difficult to find that any can be properly transferred from the present possessor to another claimant. The choice is right, when there is reason for choice.

Other dramatists can only gain attention by hyperbolical or aggravated characters, by fabulous and unexampled excellence or depravity, as the writers of barbarous romances invigorated the reader by a giant and a dwarf; and he that should form his expectations of human affairs from the play, or from the tale, would be equally deceived. Shakespeare has no heroes; his scenes are occupied only by men who act and speak as the reader thinks that he should himself have spoken or acted on the same occasion: even where the agency is supernatural, the dialogue is level with life. Other writers disguise the most natural passions and most frequent incidents; so that he who contemplates them in the book will not know them in the world. Shakespeare approximates the remote, and familiarizes the wonderful; the event which he represents will not happen, but if it were possible, its effects would probably be such as he has assigned; and it may be said, that he has not only shewn human nature as it acts in real exigencies, but as it would be found in trials, to which it cannot be exposed.

This, therefore, is the praise of Shakespeare, that his drama is the mirror of life; that he who has mazed his imagination in following the phantoms which other writers raise up before him may here be cured of his delirious ecstasies, by reading human sentiments in human language; by scenes from which a hermit may estimate the transactions of the world, and a confessor predict the progress of the passions.

His adherence to general nature has exposed him to the censure of critics, who form their judgments on narrower principles. Dennis and Rhymer think his Romans not sufficiently Roman, and Voltaire censures his kings as not completely royal. Dennis is offended that Menenius, a senator of Rome, should play the buffoon; and Voltaire perhaps thinks decency violated when the Danish usurper is represented as a drunkard. But Shakespeare always makes nature predominate over accident; and, if he preserves the essential character, is not very careful of distinctions superinduced and adventitious. His story requires Romans or kings, but he thinks only on men. He knew that Rome, like every other city, had men of all dispositions; and wanting a buffoon, he went into the senate-house for that which the senate-house would certainly have afforded him. He was inclined to show an usurper and a murderer not only odious, but despicable; he therefore added drunkenness to his other qualities, knowing that kings love wine like other men, and that wine exerts its natural power upon kings. These are the petty cavils of petty minds; a poet overlooks the casual distinction of country and conditions, as a painter, satisfied with the figure, neglects the drapery.

The censure which he has incurred by mixing comic and tragic scenes, as it extends to all his works, deserves more consideration. Let the fact be first stated, and then examined.

Shakespeare's plays are not in the rigorous and critical sense either tragedies or comedies, but compositions of a distinct kind; exhibiting the real state of sublunary nature, which partakes of good and evil, joy and sorrow, mingled with endless variety of proportion and innumerable modes of combination; and expressing the course of the world, in which the loss of one is the gain of another; in which, at the same time, the reveller is hasting to his wine, and the mourner burying his friend; in which the malignity of one is sometimes defeated by the frolic of another; and many

12. Dennis, John Dennis, in his *Essay on the Genius and Writings of Shakespeare*, 1711. **13. Rhymer.** Thomas Rymer in his *Short View of Tragedy*, 1693.

mischiefs and many benefits are done and hindered without design.

Out of this chaos of mingled purposes and casualties the ancient poets, according to the laws which custom had prescribed, selected some the crimes of men, and some their absurdities; some the momentous vicissitudes of life, and some the lighter occurrences; some the terrors of distress, and some the gaieties of prosperity. Thus rose the two modes of imitation, known by the names of *tragedy* and *comedy*, compositions intended to promote different ends by contrary means, and considered as so little allied, that I do not recollect among the *Greeks* or *Romans* a single writer who attempted both.

Shakespeare has united the powers of exciting laughter and sorrow not only in one mind, but in one composition. Almost all his plays are divided between serious and ludicrous characters, and, in the successive evolutions of the design, sometimes produce seriousness and sorrow, and sometimes levity and laughter.

That this is a practice contrary to the rules of criticism will be readily allowed; but there is always an appeal open from criticism to nature. The end of writing is to instruct; the end of poetry is to instruct by pleasing. That the mingled drama may convey all the instruction of tragedy or comedy cannot be denied, because it includes both in its alternation of exhibition and approaches nearer than either to the appearance of life, by shewing how great machinations and slender designs may promote or obviate one another, and the high and the low co-operate in the general system by unavoidable concatenation.

It is objected, that by this change of scenes the passions are interrupted in their progression, and that the principal event, being not advanced by a due gradation of preparatory incidents, wants at last the power to move, which constitutes the perfection of dramatic poetry. This reasoning is so specious, that it is received as true even by those who in daily experience feel it to be false. The interchanges of mingled scenes seldom fail to produce the intended vicissitudes of passion. Fiction cannot move so much, but that the attention may be easily transferred; and though it must be allowed that pleasing melancholy be sometimes interrupted by unwelcome levity, yet let it be considered likewise, that melancholy is often not pleasing, and that the disturbance of one man may be the relief of another; that different auditors have different habitudes; and that upon the whole, all pleasure consists in variety.

The players, who in their edition divided our author's works into comedies, histories, and tragedies, seem not to have distinguished the three kinds by any very exact or definite ideas.

An action which ended happily to the principal persons, however serious or distressful through its intermediate incidents, in their opinion, constituted a comedy. This idea of a comedy continued long amongst us; and plays were written, which, by changing the catastrophe, were tragedies to-day, and comedies to-morrow.

Tragedy was not in those times a poem of more general dignity or elevation than comedy; it required only a calamitous conclusion, with which the common criticism of that age was satisfied, whatever lighter pleasure it afforded in its progress.

History was a series of actions with no other than chronological succession, independent on each other, and without any tendency to introduce or regulate the conclusion. It is not always very nicely distinguished from tragedy. There is not much nearer approach to unity of action in the tragedy of *Antony and Cleopatra*, than in the history of *Richard the Second*. But a history might be continued through many plays; as it had no plan, it has no limits.

Through all these denominations of the drama, Shakespeare's mode of composition is the same; an interchange of seriousness and merriment, by which the mind is softened at one time, and exhilarated at another. But whatever be his purpose, whether to gladden or depress, or to conduct the story, without vehemence or emotion, through tracts of easy and familiar dialogue, he never fails to attain his purpose; as he commands us, we laugh or mourn, or sit silent with quiet expectation, in tranquillity without indifference.

When Shakespeare's plan is understood, most of the criticisms of Rhymer and Voltaire vanish away. The play of *Hamlet* is opened, without impropriety, by two sentinels; Iago bellows at Brabantio's window, without injury to the scheme of the play, though in terms which a modern audience would not easily endure; the character of Polonius is seasonable and useful; and the Grave-diggers themselves may be heard with applause.

Shakespeare engaged in dramatic poetry with the world open before him; the rules of the ancients were yet known to few; the public judgment was unformed; he had no example of such fame as might force him upon imitation, nor critics of such authority as might restrain his extravagance. He therefore indulged his natural disposition, and his disposition, as Rhymer has remarked, led him to comedy. In tragedy he often writes, with great appearance of toil and study, what is written at last with little felicity; but in his comic scenes, he seems to produce without labour, what no labour can improve. In tragedy he is always struggling after some occasion to be comic; but in comedy he seems to repose, or to luxuriate, as in a mode of thinking congenial to his nature. In his tragic scenes there is always something wanting, but his comedy often surpasses expectation or desire. His comedy pleases by the thoughts and the language, and his tragedy for the greater part by incident and action. His tragedy seems to be skill, his comedy to be instinct.

The force of his comic scenes has suffered little diminution from the changes made by a century and a half, in manners or in words. As his personages act upon principles arising from genuine passion, very little modified by particular forms, their pleasures and vexations are communicable to all times and to all places; they are natural, and therefore durable; the adventitious peculiarities of personal habits are only superficial dyes, bright and pleasing for a little while, yet soon fading to a dim tinct, without any remains of former lustre; but the discriminations of true passion are the colours of nature; they pervade the whole mass, and can only perish with the body that exhibits them. The accidental compositions of heterogeneous modes are dissolved by the chance which combined them; but the uniform simplicity of primitive qualities neither admits increase, nor suffers decay. The sand heaped by one flood is scattered by another, but the rock always continues in its place. The stream of time, which is continually washing the dissoluble fabrics of other poets, passes without injury by the adamant of Shakespeare.

If there be, what I believe there is, in every nation, a style which never becomes obsolete, a certain mode of phraseology so consonant and congenial to the analogy and principles of its respective language as to remain settled and unaltered; this style is probably to be sought in the common intercourse of life, among those who speak only to be understood, without ambition of elegance. The polite are always catching modish innovations, and the learned depart from established forms of speech, in hope of finding or making better; those who wish for distinction forsake the vulgar, when the vulgar is right; but there is a conversation above grossness and below refinement, where propriety resides, and where this poet seems to have gathered his comic dialogue. He is therefore more agreeable to the ears of the present age than any other author equally remote, and among his other excellencies deserves to be studied as one of the original masters of our language.

These observations are to be considered not as unexceptionably constant, but as containing general and predominant truth. Shakespeare's familiar dialogue is affirmed to be smooth and clear, yet not wholly without ruggedness or difficulty; as a country may be eminently fruitful, though it has spots unfit for cultivation. His characters are praised as natural, though their sentiments are sometimes forced, and their actions improbable; as the earth upon the whole is spherical, though its surface is varied with protuberances and cavities.

Shakespeare with his excellencies has likewise faults, and faults sufficient to obscure and overwhelm any other merit. I shall shew them in the proportion in which they appear to me, without envious malignity or superstitious veneration. No question can be more innocently discussed than a dead poet's pretensions to renown; and little regard is due to that bigotry which sets candour higher than truth.

His first defect is that to which may be imputed most of the evil in books or in men. He sacrifices virtue to convenience, and is so much more careful to please than to instruct, that he seems to write without any moral purpose. From his writings indeed a system of social duty may be selected, for he that thinks reasonably must think morally; but his precepts and axioms drop casually from him; he makes no just distribution of good or evil, nor is always careful to shew in the virtuous a disapprobation of the wicked; he carries his persons indifferently through right and wrong, and at the close dismisses them without further care, and leaves their examples to operate by chance. This fault the barbarity of his age cannot extenuate, for it is always a writer's duty to make the world better, and justice is a virtue independent on time or place.

The plots are often so loosely formed, that a very slight consideration may improve them, and so carelessly pursued, that he seems not always fully to comprehend his own design. He omits opportunities of instructing or delighting, which the train of his story seems to force upon him, and apparently rejects those exhibitions which would be more affecting, for the sake of those which are more easy.

It may be observed, that in many of his plays the latter part is evidently neglected. When he found himself near the end of his work, and in view of his reward, he shortened the labour to snatch the profit. He therefore remits his efforts where he should most vigorously exert them, and his catastrophe is improbably produced or imperfectly represented.

He had no regard to distinction of time or place, but gives to one age or nation, without scruple, the customs, institutions, and opinions of another, at the expense not only of likelihood but of possibility. These faults Pope has endeavoured, with more zeal than judgment, to transfer to his imagined interpolators. We need not wonder to find Hector quoting Aristotle, when we see the loves of Theseus and Hippolyta combined with the Gothic mythology of fairies. Shakespeare, indeed, was not the only violator of chronology, for in the same age Sidney, who wanted not the advantages of learning, has, in his *Arcadia*, confounded the pastoral with the feudal times, the days of innocence, quiet, and security with those of turbulence, violence, and adventure.

In his comic scenes he is seldom very successful when he engages his characters in reciprocations of smartness and contests of sarcasm; their jests are commonly gross, and their pleasantry licentious; neither his gentlemen nor his ladies have much delicacy, nor are sufficiently distinguished from his clowns by any appearance of refined manners. Whether he represented the real conversation of his time is not easy to determine; the reign of Elizabeth is commonly supposed to have been a time of stateliness, formality, and reserve, yet perhaps the relaxations of that severity were not very elegant. There must, however, have been always some modes of gaiety preferable to others, and a writer ought to choose the best.

In tragedy his performance seems constantly to be worse as his labour is more. The effusions of passion, which exigence forces out, are for the most part striking and energetic; but whenever he solicits his invention, or strains his faculties, the offspring of his throes is tumour, meanness, tediousness, and obscurity.

In narration he affects a disproportionate pomp of diction, and a wearisome train of circumlocution, and tells the incident imperfectly in many words, which might have been more plainly delivered in few. Narration in dramatic poetry is naturally tedious, as it is unanimated and inactive, and obstructs the progress of the action; it should therefore always be rapid, and enlivened by frequent interruption. Shakespeare found it an encumbrance, and instead of lightening it by brevity, endeavoured to recommend it by dignity and splendour.

His declamations or set speeches are commonly cold and weak, for his power was the power of nature. When he endeavoured, like other tragic writers, to catch opportunities of amplification, and instead of inquiring what the occasion demanded, to shew how much his stores of knowledge could supply, he seldom escapes without the pity or resentment of his reader.

It is incident to him to be now and then entangled with an unwieldy sentiment, which he cannot well express, and will not reject; he struggles with it a while, and if it continues stubborn, comprises it in words such as occur, and leaves it to be disentangled and evolved by those who have more leisure to bestow upon it.

Not that always where the language is intricate the thought is subtle, or the image always great where the line is bulky. The equality of words to things is very often neglected, and trivial sentiments and vulgar ideas disappoint the attention, to which they are recommended by sonorous epithets and swelling figures.

But the admirers of this great poet have most reason to complain when he approaches nearest to his highest excellence, and seems fully resolved to sink them in dejection, and mollify them with tender emotions by the fall of greatness, the danger of innocence, or the crosses of love. What he does best, he soon ceases to do. He is not long soft and pathetic without some idle conceit, or contemptible equivocation. He no sooner begins to move, than he counteracts himself; and terror and pity, as they are rising in the mind, are checked and blasted by sudden frigidity.

A quibble is to Shakespeare what luminous vapours are to the traveller: he follows it at all adventures; it is sure to lead him out of his way, and sure to engulf him in the mire. It has some malignant power over his mind, and its fascinations are irresistible. Whatever be the dignity or profundity of his disquisition, whether he be enlarging knowledge or exalting affection, whether he be amusing attention with incidents or enchaining it in suspense, let but a quibble spring up before him, and he leaves his work unfinished. A quibble is the golden apple for which he will always turn aside from his career, or stoop from his elevation. A quibble, poor and barren as it is, gave him such delight, that he was content to purchase it by the sacrifice of reason, propriety, and truth. A quibble was to him the fatal Cleopatra for which he lost the world, and was content to lose it.

It will be thought strange, that, in enumerating the defects of this writer, I have not yet mentioned his neglect of the unities; his violation of those laws

9–10. quoting Aristotle, in *Troilus and Cressida,* Act II, sc. 2, l. 166. **12. fairies,** in *A Midsummer Night's Dream.* **38. tumour,** bombast.

which have been instituted and established by the joint authority of poets and critics.

For his other deviations from the art of writing I resign him to critical justice, without making any other demand in his favour than that which must be indulged to all human excellence; that his virtues be rated with his failings: but, from the censure which this irregularity may bring upon him I shall, with due reverence to that learning which I must oppose, adventure to try how I can defend him.

His histories, being neither tragedies nor comedies, are not subject to any of their laws. Nothing more is necessary to all the praise which they expect, than that the changes of action be so prepared as to be understood, that the incidents be various and affecting, and the characters consistent, natural, and distinct. No other unity is intended, and therefore none is to be sought.

In his other works he has well enough preserved the unity of action. He has not, indeed, an intrigue regularly perplexed and regularly unravelled; he does not endeavour to hide his design only to discover it, for this is seldom the order of real events, and Shakespeare is the poet of nature: but his plan has commonly what Aristotle requires, a beginning, a middle, and an end; one event is concatenated with another, and the conclusion follows by easy consequence. There are perhaps some incidents that might be spared, as in other poets there is much talk that only fills up time upon the stage; but the general system makes gradual advances, and the end of the play is the end of expectation.

To the unities of time and place he has shewn no regard; and perhaps a nearer view of the principles on which they stand will diminish their value, and withdraw from them the veneration which, from the time of Corneille, they have very generally received, by discovering that they have given more trouble to the poet than pleasure to the auditor.

The necessity of observing the unities of time and place arises from the supposed necessity of making the drama credible. The critics hold it impossible that an action of months or years can be possibly believed to pass in three hours; or that the spectator can suppose himself to sit in the theatre, while ambassadors go and return between distant kings, while armies are levied and towns besieged, while an exile wanders and returns, or till he whom they saw courting his mistress shall lament the untimely fall of his son. The mind revolts from evident falsehood, and fiction loses its force when it departs from the resemblance of reality.

37. Corneille, Pierre (1606–1684), a French dramatist of the first rank.

From the narrow limitation of time necessarily arises the contraction of place. The spectator who knows that he saw the first act at Alexandria, cannot suppose that he sees the next at Rome, at a distance to which not the dragons of Medea could, in so short a time, have transported him; he knows with certainty that he has not changed his place, and he knows that place cannot change itself: that what was a house cannot become a plain; that what was Thebes can never be Persepolis.

Such is the triumphant language with which a critic exults over the misery of an irregular poet, and exults commonly without resistance or reply. It is time therefore to tell him, by the authority of Shakespeare, that he assumes as an unquestionable principle a position which, while his breath is forming it into words, his understanding pronounces to be false. It is false, that any representation is mistaken for reality; that any dramatic fable in its materiality was ever credible, or, for a single moment, was ever credited.

The objection arising from the impossibility of passing the first hour at Alexandria, and the next at Rome, supposes that when the play opens the spectator really imagines himself at Alexandria, and believes that his walk to the theatre has been a voyage to Egypt, and that he lives in the days of Antony and Cleopatra. Surely he that imagines this may imagine more. He that can take the stage at one time for the palace of the Ptolemies, may take it in half an hour for the promontory of Actium. Delusion, if delusion be admitted, has no certain limitation; if the spectator can be once persuaded that his old acquaintance are Alexander and Caesar, that a room illuminated with candles is the plain of Pharsalia or the bank of Granicus, he is in a state of elevation above the reach of reason or of truth, and from the heights of empyrean poetry may despise the circumscriptions of terrestrial nature. There is no reason why a mind thus wandering in ecstasy should count the clock, or why an hour should not be a century in that calenture of the brains that can make the stage a field.

The truth is, that the spectators are always in their senses, and know, from the first act to the last, that the stage is only a stage, and that the players are only players. They come to hear a certain number of lines recited with just gesture and elegant modulation. The lines relate to some action, and an action must be in some place; but the different actions that complete a story may be in places very remote from each other; and where is the absurdity of allowing that space to represent first Athens, and then Sicily, which was always known to be neither

Sicily nor Athens, but a modern theatre?

By supposition, as place is introduced, time may be extended. The time required by the fable elapses for the most part between the acts; for, of so much of the action as is represented, the real and poetical duration is the same. If, in the first act, preparations for war against Mithridates are represented to be made in Rome, the event of the war may, without absurdity, be represented, in the catastrophe, as happening in Pontus; we know that there is neither war, nor preparation for war; we know that we are neither in Rome nor Pontus; that neither Mithridates nor Lucullus are before us. The drama exhibits successive imitations of successive actions, and why may not the second imitation represent an action that happened years after the first, if it be so connected with it that nothing but time can be supposed to intervene? Time is, of all modes of existence, most obsequious to the imagination; a lapse of years is as easily conceived as a passage of hours. In contemplation we easily contract the time of real actions, and therefore willingly permit it to be contracted when we only see their imitation.

It will be asked how the drama moves, if it is not credited. It is credited with all the credit due to a drama. It is credited, whenever it moves, as a just picture of a real original; as representing to the auditor what he would himself feel, if he were to do or suffer what is there feigned to be suffered or to be done. The reflection that strikes the heart is not that the evils before us are real evils, but that they are evils to which we ourselves may be exposed. If there be any fallacy, it is not that we fancy the players, but that we fancy ourselves, unhappy for a moment; but we rather lament the possibility than suppose the presence of misery, as a mother weeps over her babe when she remembers that death may take it from her. The delight of tragedy proceeds from our consciousness of fiction; if we thought murders and treasons real, they would please no more.

Imitations produce pain or pleasure, not because they are mistaken for realities, but because they bring realities to mind. When the imagination is recreated by a painted landscape, the trees are not supposed capable to give us shade, or the fountains coolness; but we consider how we should be pleased with such fountains playing beside us, and such woods waving over us. We are agitated in reading the history of Henry the Fifth, yet no man takes his book for the field of Agincourt. A dramatic exhibition is a book recited with concomitants that increase or diminish its effect. Familiar comedy is often more powerful on the theatre, than in the page; imperial tragedy is always less. The humour of Petruchio may be heightened by grimace; but what voice or what gesture can hope to add dignity or force to the soliloquy of Cato.

A play read affects the mind like a play acted. It is therefore evident that the action is not supposed to be real; and it follows that between the acts a longer or shorter time may be allowed to pass, and that no more account of space or duration is to be taken by the auditor of a drama than by the reader of a narrative, before whom may pass in an hour the life of a hero, or the revolutions of an empire. . . .

from THE LIVES OF THE POETS: COWLEY

It is to Johnson in his life of Abraham Cowley (1618–1667) that we owe the term "Metaphysical Poets," which is today commonly applied to the group of seventeenth-century poets consisting chiefly of John Donne, George Herbert, Henry Vaughan, Richard Crashaw, Thomas Traherne, and Cowley. The term had in all probability been suggested to Johnson by Dryden's comment on Donne in his *Essay on Satire:* "He affects the metaphysics, not only in his satires but in his amorous verses, where nature only should reign; and perplexes the minds of the fair sex with nice speculations of philosophy, when he should engage their hearts, and entertain them with the softnesses of love." Professor Grierson, in the introduction to his edition of Donne's poems, points out that in Dryden's application the word "metaphysical" means correctly "philosophical," whereas in Johnson's it means no more than "learned." Johnson was particularly objecting to the peculiar subtlety of fancy in the work of the poets in question.

Twentieth-century readers and critics of poetry have found more of themselves and their ideas expressed by Donne and the other "Metaphysical Poets" than by the poets of Johnson's century, and they are therefore more sympathetic to the substance and methods of those seventeenth-century poets than was Johnson. But Johnson's criticism, reprinted below, is still the most famous and provocative discussion of them, and serves admirably as a point of departure in the study of their verse.

[*The Metaphysical Poets*]

Wit, like all other things subject by their nature to the choice of man, has its changes and fashions, and at different times takes different forms. About the beginning of the seventeenth century appeared a race of writers that may be termed the meta-

2. Petruchio, the hero of Shakespeare's comedy *The Taming of the Shrew.* **4. Cato,** in Addison's tragedy of that name.

physical poets; of whom, in a criticism on the works of Cowley, it is not improper to give some account.

The metaphysical poets were men of learning, and to show their learning was their whole endeavour; but, unluckily resolving to shew it in rhyme, instead of writing poetry, they only wrote verses, and very often such verses as stood the trial of the finger better than of the ear; for the modulation was so imperfect, that they were only found to be verses by counting the syllables.

If the father of criticism has rightly denominated poetry τέχνη μιμητική, *an imitative art*, these writers will, without great wrong, lose their right to the name of poets; for they cannot be said to have imitated anything; they neither copied nature nor life; neither painted the forms of matter, nor represented the operations of intellect.

Those, however, who deny them to be poets allow them to be wits. Dryden confesses of himself and his contemporaries, that they fall below Donne in wit, but maintains that they surpass him in poetry.

If Wit be well described by Pope, as being "that which has been often thought, but was never before so well expressed," they certainly never attained, nor ever sought it; for they endeavoured to be singular in their thoughts, and were careless of their diction. But Pope's account of wit is undoubtedly erroneous: he depresses it below its natural dignity, and reduces it from strength of thought to happiness of language.

If by a more noble and more adequate conception that be considered as Wit, which is at once natural and new, that which, though not obvious, is, upon its first production, acknowledged to be just; if it be that, which he that never found it, wonders how he missed; to wit of this kind the metaphysical poets have seldom risen. Their thoughts are often new, but seldom natural; they are not obvious, but neither are they just; and the reader, far from wondering that he missed them, wonders more frequently by what perverseness of industry they were ever found.

But Wit, abstracted from its effects upon the hearer, may be more rigorously and philosophically considered as a kind of *discordia concors;* a combination of dissimilar images, or discovery of occult resemblances in things apparently unlike. Of wit, thus defined, they have more than enough. The most heterogeneous ideas are yoked by violence together; nature and art are ransacked for illustrations, comparisons, and allusions; their learning instructs, and their subtlety surprises; but the reader commonly thinks his improvement dearly bought, and, though he sometimes admires, is seldom pleased.

From this account of their compositions it will be readily inferred, that they were not successful in representing or moving the affections. As they were wholly employed on something unexpected and surprising, they had no regard to that uniformity of sentiment which enables us to conceive and to excite the pains and the pleasure of other minds: they never enquired what, on any occasion, they should have said or done; but wrote rather as beholders than partakers of human nature; as Beings looking upon good and evil, impassive and at leisure; as Epicurean deities making remarks on the actions of men, and the vicissitudes of life, without interest and without emotion. Their courtship was void of fondness, and their lamentation of sorrow. Their wish was only to say what they hoped had been never said before.

Nor was the sublime more within their reach than the pathetic; for they never attempted that comprehension and expanse of thought which at once fills the whole mind, and of which the first effect is sudden astonishment, and the second rational admiration. Sublimity is produced by aggregation, and littleness by dispersion. Great thoughts are always general, and consist in positions not limited by exceptions, and in descriptions not descending to minuteness. It is with great propriety that Subtlety, which in its original import means exility of particles, is taken in its metaphorical meaning for nicety of distinction. Those writers who lay on the watch for novelty could have little hope of greatness; for great things cannot have escaped former observation. Their attempts were always analytic; they broke every image into fragments: and could no more represent, by their slender conceits and laboured particularities, the prospects of nature, or the scenes of life, than he, who dissects a sun-beam with a prism, can exhibit the wide effulgence of a summer noon.

What they wanted however of the sublime, they endeavoured to supply by hyperbole; their amplification had no limits; they left not only reason but fancy behind them; and produced combinations of confused magnificence, that not only could not be credited but could not be imagined.

Yet great labour, directed by great abilities, is

12. the father of criticism, Aristotle. **20. wits.** In his *Dictionary* Johnson defines "wit" as "a man of genius." **24–26. "that . . . expressed."** Johnson is quoting incorrectly ll. 297–298 of Part II of Pope's *Essay on Criticism*, p. 548. **47. *discordia concors*,** harmonious discord.

36. exility, smallness.

never wholly lost: if they frequently threw away their wit upon false conceits, they likewise sometimes struck out unexpected truth: if their conceits were far-fetched, they were often worth the carriage. To write on their plan, it was at least necessary to read and think. No man could be born a metaphysical poet, nor assume the dignity of a writer, by descriptions copied from descriptions, by imitations borrowed from imitations, by traditional imagery, and hereditary similes, by readiness of rhyme, and volubility of syllables.

In perusing the works of this race of authors, the mind is exercised either by recollection or inquiry; either something already learned is to be retrieved, or something new is to be examined. If their greatness seldom elevates, their acuteness often surprises; if the imagination is not always gratified, at least the powers of reflection and comparison are employed; and in the mass of materials which ingenious absurdity has thrown together, genuine wit and useful knowledge may be sometimes found, buried perhaps in grossness of expression, but useful to those who know their value; and such as, when they are expanded to perspicuity, and polished to elegance, may give lustre to works which have more propriety though less copiousness of sentiment.

LETTERS

To the Right Honourable the Earl of Chesterfield

February 7, 1755.

My Lord: I have lately been informed by the proprietor of *The World*, that two papers, in which my *Dictionary* is recommended to the public, were written by your Lordship. To be so distinguished is an honour which, being very little accustomed to favours from the great, I know not well how to receive, or in what terms to acknowledge.

When, upon some slight encouragement, I first visited your Lordship, I was overpowered, like the rest of mankind, by the enchantment of your address; and I could not forbear to wish that I might boast myself "*Le vainqueur du vainqueur de la terre*"; that I might obtain that regard for which I saw the world contending; but I found my attendance so little encouraged, that neither pride nor modesty would suffer me to continue it. When I had once addressed your Lordship in public, I had exhausted all the art of pleasing which a retired and uncourtly scholar can possess. I had done all that I could; and no man is well pleased to have his all neglected, be it ever so little.

Seven years, my Lord, have now passed, since I waited in your outward rooms, or was repulsed from your door; during which time I have been pushing on my work through difficulties, of which it is useless to complain, and have brought it at last to the verge of publication, without one act of assistance, one word of encouragement, or one smile of favour. Such treatment I did not expect, for I never had a patron before.

The shepherd in Virgil grew at last acquainted with Love, and found him a native of the rocks.

Is not a patron, my Lord, one who looks with unconcern on a man struggling for life in the water, and, when he has reached ground, encumbers him with help? The notice which you have been pleased to take of my labours, had it been early, had been kind; but it has been delayed till I am indifferent, and cannot enjoy it; till I am solitary, and cannot impart it; till I am known, and do not want it. I hope it is no very cynical asperity not to confess obligations where no benefit has been received, or to be unwilling that the public should consider me as owing that to a patron, which Providence has enabled me to do for myself.

Having carried on my work thus far with so little obligation to any favourer of learning, I shall not be disappointed though I should conclude it, if less be possible, with less; for I have been long wakened from that dream of hope, in which I once boasted myself with so much exaltation,

My Lord,
Your Lordship's most humble,
Most obedient servant,

SAM. JOHNSON.

To James Macpherson

Mr. James Macpherson: I received your foolish and impudent letter. Any violence offered me I shall do my best to repel; and what I cannot do for myself the law shall do for me. I hope I shall never be deterred from detecting what I think a cheat, by

31. Chesterfield. In 1747 Johnson had addressed the *Prospectus* of his *Dictionary* to Lord Chesterfield, at that time an important Secretary of State, and had gained Chesterfield's approval of its design. When Chesterfield tried to win back Johnson's favor after seven years of neglect, Johnson wrote this famous letter to his would-be patron. **35. proprietor,** Edward Moore, whom Johnson knew well. **45. *Le vainqueur . . . terre*,** the conqueror of the conqueror of the earth.

17. shepherd, Virgil's *Eclogues*, 8, 43 ff. **44. Macpherson** (1736–96), promulgator of the works (*Finegal*, 1761, etc.) which he claimed were translations of the ancient poems of Ossian. Johnson had publicly called the poems a hoax. Macpherson challenged Johnson to a duel, and this letter is Johnson's reply.

the menaces of a ruffian.

What would you have me retract? I thought your book an imposture; I think it an imposture still. For this opinion I have given my reasons to the public, which I here dare you to refute. Your rage I defy. Your abilities, since your *Homer*, are not so formidable; and what I hear of your morals inclines me to pay regard not to what you shall say, but to what you shall prove. You may print this if you will.

(1775) SAM. JOHNSON.

James Boswell

1740–1795

James Boswell is the prime example in English literature of a writer who, by insuring the immortality of another man of letters, has achieved immortality for himself. We should today perhaps not know Boswell at all if he had not written his *Life of Johnson*, and but for that incomparable biography Samuel Johnson would probably not today be ranked as one of the great personalities of English literature. The same assiduity, patience, energy, and devotion that went into Boswell's compilation of the *Life of Johnson* have, by a strange chain of circumstances, succeeded two centuries later in making the personality of James Boswell even better known than Johnson's. Perhaps no man will ever have had his private life so exposed to the public view for both censure and admiration as will James Boswell when all the mass of his private journals and correspondence has been published.

Boswell was born in Edinburgh, the eldest son of the Laird of Auchinleck in Ayrshire. After his elementary education in a private school he went to the University of Edinburgh and thence to the University of Glasgow to study law. In 1760, at the age of twenty, he escaped from paternal restrictions to London, and for three months tasted the life of the town. Two years more were spent in Scotland where he studied law and succeeded in passing the examination in civil law. In 1762 he managed again to get away to London hoping to obtain a commission in the Footguards. In London he lived the life of a young adventurer, and his greatest adventure came a few months after his arrival when he met Dr. Johnson in May, 1763. Famous persons he met included also the great actor David Garrick and the poet Oliver Goldsmith. After this period of adventures in London, carefully recorded in his journal, he set out for the Continent on the Grand Tour. Here he met still other great men—Rousseau, Voltaire, John Wilkes, and the Corsican patriot General Paoli. Out of his friendship with the latter came, in 1768, his *Account of Corsica, The Journal of a Tour to That Island: and Memoirs of Pascal Paoli*. He had meanwhile been admitted to the Scottish bar.

By 1773 Boswell was again in London and Johnson had succeeded in having him elected to his literary club. From then on until Johnson's death in 1784 Boswell was with Johnson as much as possible, although his legal practice and domestic affairs kept him in Scotland much of the time. In 1773 he and Johnson traveled to Edinburgh and on through Scotland to the Highlands and the Hebrides Islands. The events of the trip Boswell described in his *Journal of a Tour to the Hebrides with Samuel Johnson, LL.D.*, which he published a year after Johnson's death. Among many other things which he found time to write during these years were monthly essays, from 1777 to 1783, for the *London Magazine*, under the heading of "The Hypochondriack." And all this time he was taking notes for what was to be the major work of his life, the biography of Johnson. After Johnson's death in 1784 Boswell applied himself with renewed zeal to the task of checking, amplifying, and, where the purposes of art dictated, reshaping the copious entries he had been making in his journal over a period of 20 years. As Boswell himself wrote, "The labour and anxious attention with which I have collected and arranged the materials of which these volumes are composed will hardly be conceived by those who read them with careless facility." The great work was finally completed, amidst the greatest personal difficulties, and was published in 1791, eight years after Johnson's death and only four years before Boswell's own.

The rehabilitation of Boswell's genius has been one of the most extraordinary events of the literary history of the twentieth century. The nineteenth and early twentieth centuries knew Boswell chiefly through Macaulay's brilliant essay on him which

1. *Homer*, Macpherson's weak prose translation of Homer's *Iliad*.

declared contemptuously that "if he had not been a great fool he would never have been a great writer." That Boswell was something more than a ludicrously vain, bustling, inquisitive fool, prone to drink too much and to thrust himself upon the notice of famous persons, might have been suspected by the fact that Johnson admitted him to intimacy and by the record of his friendships with other discerning men. The "restoration" of Boswell may be said to have begun in 1922 with the publication of Professor C. B. Tinker's *Young Boswell*, which was followed by his edition of the *Letters of James Boswell* in 1924. At about the same time Professor Tinker learned of the existence at Malahide Castle in Ireland of a body of manuscript material left by Boswell, and thus began the romantic story of the recovery, substantially intact, of what has been described as the most complete documentation of an important literary figure of any age or country. The mass of papers first discovered at Malahide was acquired by Lieut. Col. Ralph H. Isham in 1928, and by 1936 had been privately printed in nineteen volumes under the editorship of Geoffrey Scott and Frederick A. Pottle. In 1930 further manuscripts were discovered in a neglected croquet box at Malahide which contained several key journals, more letters, a diary by Johnson, and miscellaneous manuscripts by other well-known persons. In 1931, at Fettercairn House in Kincardineshire, still more Boswell papers came to light. In 1946, in a disused cowbarn at Malahide, another cache of papers was found which revealed such treasures as 1300 pages of the original manuscript of the *Life of Johnson*, a mass of correspondence between Boswell and some of his distinguished contemporaries, and manuscripts by Sir Joshua Reynolds and others. By 1948 the whole mass of the Malahide and Fettercairn Papers was in the possession of Colonel Isham, and a year later the material came to a permanent resting-place in the library of Yale University. Since then the discovery of other manuscripts at Malahide has been announced.

The first volume of the new series of Boswell's private papers, *Boswell's London Journal, 1762–1763*, edited by Frederick A. Pottle, was published in November, 1950, by the McGraw-Hill Book Company. In it the youthful Boswell paints a portrait of himself replete with folly and frailty, but also full of kindness, friendship, and companionability, and with a unique genius for understanding and presenting human personality. Thanks to the recovered manuscripts the present-day reader of Boswell will be inclined to agree with Thomas Carlyle, who wrote in his indignant reply to Macaulay that: "Boswell wrote a good book because he had a heart and an eye to discern wisdom and an utterance to render it forth; because of his free insight, his lively talent, and, above all, of his love and childlike open-mindedness."

from BOSWELL'S LONDON JOURNAL, 1762–1763 [1]

WEDNESDAY 1 DECEMBER [1762]. The Duke of Queensberry was now come to town. I had called once or twice, but had never found him. Mrs. Douglas told me that Old Quant the porter would do nothing without the silver key. I therefore called today, and chatting a little with the surly dog, "Mr. Quant," said I, "I give you a great deal of trouble"; bowed and smiled, and put half a crown into his hand. He told me the Duke would be glad to see me next morning at nine.

On Tuesday I wanted to have a silver-hilted sword, but upon examining my pockets as I walked up the Strand, I found that I had left the most of my guineas at home and had not enough to pay for it with me. I determined to make a trial of the civility of my fellow-creatures, and what effect my external appearance and address would have. I accordingly went to the shop of Mr. Jefferys, sword-cutter to his Majesty, looked at a number of his swords, and at last picked out a very handsome one at five guineas. "Mr. Jefferys," said I, "I have not money here to pay for it. Will you trust me?" "Upon my word, Sir," said he, "you must excuse me. It is a thing we never do to a stranger." I bowed genteelly and said, "Indeed, Sir, I believe it is not right." However, I stood and looked at him, and he looked at me. "Come, Sir," cried he, "I will trust you." "Sir," said I, "if you had not trusted me, I should not have bought it from you." He asked my name and place of abode, which I told him. I then chose a belt, put the sword on, told him I would call and pay it tomorrow, and walked off. I called this day and paid him. "Mr. Jefferys," said I, "there is your money. You paid me a very great compliment. I am much obliged to you. But pray don't do such a thing again. It is dangerous." "Sir," said he, "we know our men. I would have trusted you with the value of a hundred pounds."

[1] Reprinted by special permission of the publishers, the McGraw-Hill Book Company, Inc. **1–2. The Duke of Queensberry.** Boswell had come to London with a letter of introduction to the Duke of Queensberry, a friend of King George III and the Prime Minister.

This I think was a good adventure and much to my honour. . . .

After my wild expedition to London in the year 1760, after I got rid of the load of serious reflection which then burthened me, by being always in Lord Eglinton's company, very fond of him, and much caressed by him, I became dissipated and thoughtless. When my father forced me down to Scotland, I was at first very low-spirited, although to appearance very high. I afterwards from my natural vivacity endeavoured to make myself easy; and like a man who takes to drinking to banish care, I threw myself loose as a heedless, dissipated, rattling fellow who might say or do every ridiculous thing. This made me sought after by everybody for the present hour, but I found myself a very inferior being; and I found many people presuming to treat me as such, which notwithstanding of my appearance of undiscerning gaiety, gave me much pain. I was, in short, a character very different from what God intended me and I myself chose. I remember my friend Johnston told me one day after my return from London that I had turned out different from what he imagined, as he thought I would resemble Mr. Addison. I laughed and threw out some loud sally of humour, but the observation struck deep. Indeed, I must do myself the justice to say that I always resolved to be such a man whenever my affairs were made easy and I got upon my own footing. For as I despaired of that, I endeavoured to lower my views and just to be a good-humoured comical being, well liked either as a waiter, a common soldier, a clerk in Jamaica, or some other odd out-of-the-way sphere. Now, when my father at last put me into an independent situation, I felt my mind regain its native dignity. I felt strong dispositions to be a Mr. Addison. Indeed, I had accustomed myself so much to laugh at everything that it required time to render my imagination solid and give me just notions of real life and of religion. But I hoped by degrees to attain to some degree of propriety. Mr. Addison's character in sentiment, mixed with a little of the gaiety of Sir Richard Steele and the manners of Mr. Digges, were the ideas which I aimed to realize. . . .

WEDNESDAY 15 DECEMBER. The enemies of the people of England who would have them considered in the worst light represent them as selfish, beef-eaters, and cruel. In this view I resolved today to be a true-born Old Englishman. I went into the City to Dolly's Steak-house in Paternoster Row and swallowed my dinner by myself to fulfill the charge of selfishness; I had a large fat beefsteak to fulfill the charge of beef-eating; and I went at five o'clock to the Royal Cockpit in St. James's Park and saw cock-fighting for about five hours to fulfill the charge of cruelty.

A beefsteak-house is a most excellent place to dine at. You come in there to a warm, comfortable, large room, where a number of people are sitting at table. You take whatever place you find empty; call for what you like, which you get well and cleverly dressed. You may either chat or not as you like. Nobody minds you, and you pay very reasonably. My dinner (beef, bread and beer and waiter) was only a shilling. The waiters make a great deal of money by these pennies. Indeed, I admire the English for attending to small sums, as many smalls make a great, according to the proverb.

At five I filled my pockets with gingerbread and apples (quite the method), put on my old clothes and laced hat, laid by my watch, purse, and pocket-book, and with oaken stick in my hand sallied to the pit. I was too soon there. So I went into a low inn, sat down amongst a parcel of arrant blackguards, and drank some beer. The sentry near the house had been very civil in showing me the way. It was very cold. I bethought myself of the poor fellow, so I carried out a pint of beer myself to him. He was very thankful and drank my health cordially. He told me his name was Hobard, that he was a watch-maker but in distress for debt, and enlisted that his creditors might not touch him.

I then went to the Cockpit, which is a circular room in the middle of which the cocks fight. It is seated round with rows gradually rising. The pit and the seats are all covered with mat. The cocks, nicely cut and dressed and armed with silver heels, are set down and fight with amazing bitterness and resolution. Some of them were quickly dispatched. One pair fought three quarters of an hour. The uproar and noise of betting is prodigious. A great deal of money made a very quick circulation from hand to hand. There was a number of professed gamblers there. An old cunning dog whose face I had seen at Newmarket sat by me a while. I told him I knew nothing of the matter. "Sir," said he, "you have as good a chance as anybody." He thought I would be a good subject for him. I was young-like. But he found himself balked. I was

5–6. Lord Eglinton's company. Alexander Montgomerie, Earl of Eglinton, was an able, pleasure-loving Scotsman, and a close friend of the King's brother, the Duke of York. **22. my friend Johnston.** John Johnston, a young Scotsman about Boswell's age (twenty-two), was a struggling attorney in Edinburgh and perhaps Boswell's most intimate friend. **44–45. Mr. Digges.** West Digges, the leading man in the theatrical company in Edinburgh, was Boswell's ideal of manly bearing and social elegance.

18. and waiter, i.e., a penny for the waiter.

shocked to see the distraction and anxiety of the betters. I was sorry for the poor cocks. I looked round to see if any of the spectators pitied them when mangled and torn in a most cruel manner, but I could not observe the smallest relenting sign in any countenance. I was therefore not ill pleased to see them endure mental torment. Thus did I complete my true English day, and came home pretty much fatigued and pretty much confounded at the strange turn of this people.

SATURDAY 25 DECEMBER. . . . This day I was in a better frame, being Christmas day, which has always inspired me with most agreeable feelings. I went to St. Paul's church and in that magnificent temple fervently adored the GOD of goodness and mercy, and heard a sermon by the Bishop of Oxford on the publishing of glad tidings of great joy. I then went to Child's, where little was passing. However, here goes the form of a

DIALOGUE AT CHILD'S.

I CITIZEN. Why, here is the bill of mortality. Is it right, Doctor?

PHYSICIAN. Why, I don't know.

I CITIZEN. I'm sure it is not. Sixteen only died of cholics! I dare say you have killed as many yourself.

2 CITIZEN. Ay, and hanged but three! O Lord, ha! ha! ha!

I then sat a while at Coutts's, and then at Macfarlane's, and then went to Davies's. Johnson was gone to Oxford. I was introduced to Mr. Dodsley, a good, jolly, decent, conversable man, and Mr. Goldsmith, a curious, old, pedantic fellow with some genius. It was quite a literary dinner. I had seen no warm victuals for four days, and therefore played a very bold knife and fork. It is inconceivable how hearty I eat and how comfortable I felt myself after it. We talked entirely in the way of Geniuses.

We talked of poetry. Said Goldsmith, "The miscellaneous poetry of this age is nothing like that of the last; it is very poor. Why there, now, Mr. Dodsley, is your *Collection*." DODSLEY. "I think that equal to those made by Dryden and Pope." GOLDSMITH. "To consider them, Sir, as villages, yours may be as good; but let us compare house with house, you can produce me no edifices equal to the *Ode on St. Cecilia's Day*, *Absalom and Achitophel*, or *The Rape of the Lock*." DODSLEY. "We have poems in a different way. There is nothing of the kind in the last age superior to *The Spleen*." BOSWELL. "And what do you think of Gray's odes? Are not they noble?" GOLDSMITH. "Ah, the rumbling thunder! I remember a friend of mine was very fond of Gray. 'Yes,' said I, 'he is very fine indeed; as thus—

> Mark the white and mark the red,
> Mark the blue and mark the green;
> Mark the colours ere they fade,
> Darting thro' the welkin sheen.'

'O, yes,' said he, 'great, great!' 'True, Sir,' said I, 'but I have made the lines this moment.'" BOSWELL. "Well, I admire Gray prodigiously. I have read his odes till I was almost mad." GOLDSMITH. "They are terribly obscure. We must be historians and learned men before we can understand them." DAVIES. "And why not? He is not writing to porters or carmen. He is writing to men of knowledge." GOLDSMITH. "Have you seen *Love in a Village?*" BOSWELL. "I have. I think it a good, pleasing thing." GOLDSMITH. "I am afraid we will have no good plays now. The taste of the audience is spoiled by the pantomime of Shakespeare. The wonderful changes and shiftings." DAVIES. "Nay, but you will allow that Shakespeare has great merit?" GOLDSMITH. "No, I know Shakespeare very well." (Here I said nothing, but thought him a most impudent puppy.) BOSWELL. "What do you think of Johnson?" GOLDSMITH. "He has exceeding great merit. His *Rambler* is a noble work." BOSWELL. "His *Idler* too is very pretty. It is a lighter performance; and he has thrown off the classical fetters very much." DAVIES. "He is a most entertaining companion. And how can it be otherwise, when he has so much imagination, has read so much, and digested it so well?" . . .

THURSDAY 12 MAY [1763]. I went to Drury Lane and saw Mr. Garrick play *King Lear*. So very high is his reputation, even after playing so long, that the pit was full in ten minutes after four, although the play did not begin till half an hour after six. I kept myself at a distance from all acquaintances, and got into a proper frame. Mr. Garrick gave me the most perfect satisfaction. I was fully moved,

20. Child's, Child's Coffee-house, in St. Paul's Churchyard. **29. Coutts's** a prominent Scots banker in London. **29–30. Macfarlane's.** Lady Elizabeth Macfarlane, a Scottish friend of Boswell's, was then living in London. **30. Davies's.** Thomas Davies, an actor and bookseller, had invited Boswell to Christmas dinner to meet Dr. Johnson. **31. Mr. Dodsley,** Robert Dodsley, of the well-known firm of booksellers, R. and J. Dodsley. **32–33. Mr. Goldsmith.** This is Boswell's first meeting with Goldsmith. Professor Pottle notes that it is hard to tell from the tone of the entry whether Boswell knew any of his writings. **37. eat,** i.e., ate. **43. *Collection,*** famous anthology of eighteenth-century verse (1748).

8. *The Spleen,* by Matthew Green (1737). **27. *Love in a Village,*** by the Irish playwright, Isaac Bickerstaff (1762).

and I shed abundance of tears. The farce was *Polly Honeycomb*, at which I laughed a good deal. It gave me great consolation after my late fit of melancholy to find that I was again capable of receiving such high enjoyment.

FRIDAY 13 MAY. I breakfasted with Mr. Garrick. I was proud at being admitted to the society of so great an actor. . . . He said he would undoubtedly go to Scotland some one summer and play a night for each of the charities at Edinburgh. I told him that he would be adored as something above humanity.

I parted with him, and then dined at Clifton's with Temple. We then went to his chambers, where he introduced me to a particular friend of his, a Mr. Nicholls who had been with him at Cambridge. I never saw anybody who engaged me more at the very first than this gentleman. He discovered an amiable disposition, a sweetness of manners, and an easy politeness that pleased me much. We went to Tom's and had a pot of coffee, and sat there for two hours. Our conversation took a literary turn. We talked of Helvétius, Voltaire, Rousseau, Hume. Mr. Nicholls I found to be sensible and elegantly learned; with an agreeable moderation of sentiment intermixed, his character was finely completed. I talked really very well. I have not passed so much rational time I don't know when. The degree of distance due to a stranger restrained me from my effusions of ludicrous nonsense and intemperate mirth. I was rational and composed, yet lively and entertaining. I had a good opinion of myself, and I could perceive my friend Temple much satisfied with me. Could I but fix myself in such a character and preserve it uniformly, I should be exceedingly happy. I hope to do so and to attain a constancy and dignity without which I can never be satisfied, as I have these ideas strong and pride myself in thinking that my natural character is that of dignity. My friend Temple is very good in consoling me by saying that I may be such a man, and that people will say, "Mr. Boswell is quite altered from the dissipated, inconstant fellow that he was. He is now a reserved, grave sort of a man. But indeed that was his real character; and he only deviated into these eccentric paths for a while." Well, then, let me see if I have resolution enough to bring that about. . . .

MONDAY 16 MAY. Temple and his brother breakfasted with me. I went to Love's to try to recover some of the money which he owes me. But, alas, a single guinea was all I could get. He was just going to dinner, so I stayed and eat a bit, though I was angry at myself afterwards. I drank tea at Davies's in Russell Street, and about seven came in the great Mr. Samuel Johnson, whom I have so long wished to see. Mr. Davies introduced me to him. As I knew his mortal antipathy at the Scotch, I cried to Davies, "Don't tell where I come from." However, he said, "From Scotland." "Mr. Johnson," said I, "indeed I come from Scotland, but I cannot help it." "Sir," replied he, "that, I find, is what a very great many of your countrymen cannot help." Mr. Johnson is a man of a most dreadful appearance. He is a very big man, is troubled with sore eyes, the palsy, and the king's evil. He is very slovenly in his dress and speaks with a most uncouth voice. Yet his great knowledge and strength of expression command vast respect and render him very excellent company. He has great humour and is a worthy man. But his dogmatical roughness of manners is disagreeable. I shall mark what I remember of his conversation.

He said that people might be taken in once in imagining that an author is greater than other people in private life. "Uncommon parts require uncommon opportunities for their exertion.

"In barbarous society superiority of parts is of real consequence. Great strength or wisdom is of value to an individual. But in more polished times you have people to do everything for money. And then there are a number of other superiorities, such as those of birth and fortune and rank, that dissipate men's attention and leave superiority of parts no extraordinary share of respect. And this is wisely ordered by Providence, to preserve a mediocrity.

"Lord Kames's *Elements* is a pretty essay and deserves to be held in some estimation, though it is chimerical.

"Wilkes is safe in the eye of the law. But he is an abusive scoundrel; and instead of sending my

2. ***Polly Honeycomb,*** by George Colman the Elder (1760). **13. Clifton's,** a chop-house in Butcher Row. **14. Temple,** William Johnson Temple, an intimate friend of Boswell's. **16. Mr. Nicholls,** Norton Nicholls, who was also a friend of Thomas Gray. **21. Tom's,** a coffee-house in Russell Street.

2. Love's. James Love was the professional name of James Dance, an actor. **8. the great Mr. Samuel Johnson.** With this account of his meeting Johnson, compare Boswell's later description of the event in his *Life of Johnson*, p. 601. **18. the palsy,** rather, convulsive tics. **the king's evil,** i.e., the scars of scrofula, called "king's evil" because it was supposed to be cured by the touch of a king. **40. Lord Kames's** ***Elements,*** a long-famous work on theory of criticism which had appeared the previous year. **43. Wilkes.** John Wilkes was editor of an anti-administration paper, *The North Briton*. He had been served with a subpoena, but had failed to put in an appearance on the grounds that the subpoena was a violation of his privilege.

Lord Chief Justice to him, I would send a parcel of footmen and have him well ducked.

"The notion of liberty amuses the people of England and helps to keep off the *taedium vitae.* When a butcher says that he is in distress for his country, he has no uneasy feeling.

"Sheridan will not succeed at Bath, for ridicule has gone down before him, and I doubt Derrick is his enemy."

I was sorry to leave him there at ten, when I had engaged to be at Dr. Pringle's, with whom I had a serious conversation much to my mind.

I stayed this night at Lord Eglinton's.

from THE LIFE OF SAMUEL JOHNSON

Boswell was occupied with his *Life of Samuel Johnson* for no less than twenty-seven years. Into its making went boldness, imagination, incredible diligence, accuracy, and a sense of humor—also deep human sympathy and a faculty for clear-eyed hero worship.

The life and character of Dr. Johnson, taken together with the set of brilliant persons who made up Johnson's circle—Burke, Garrick, Goldsmith, Reynolds, Gibbon, and others—gave Boswell an almost unparalleled opportunity to which he did ample justice. He had a great subject. In the *Life* he produced the greatest of English biographies and, as Boswell himself quite correctly called it, "one of the most interesting books in the world."

A.D. 1763: AETAT. 54.

This is to me a memorable year; for in it I had the happiness to obtain the acquaintance of that extraordinary man whose memoirs I am now writing; an acquaintance which I shall ever esteem as one of the most fortunate circumstances in my life. Though then but two-and-twenty, I had for several years read his works with delight and instruction, and had the highest reverence for their author, which had grown up in my fancy into a kind of mysterious veneration, by figuring to myself a state of solemn elevated abstraction, in which I supposed him to live in the immense metropolis of London. . . .

Mr. Thomas Davies the actor, who then kept a bookseller's shop in Russel-street, Covent-garden, told me that Johnson was very much his friend, and came frequently to his house, where he more than once invited me to meet him; but by some unlucky accident or other he was prevented from coming to us. . . .

At last, on Monday the 16th of May, when I was sitting in Mr. Davies's back-parlour, after having drunk tea with him and Mrs. Davies, Johnson unexpectedly came into the shop; and Mr. Davies having perceived him through the glass-door in the room in which we were sitting, advancing towards us,—he announced his aweful approach to me, somewhat in the manner of an actor in the part of Horatio, when he addresses Hamlet on the appearance of his father's ghost, "Look, my Lord, it comes." I found that I had a very perfect idea of Johnson's figure, from the portrait of him painted by Sir Joshua Reynolds soon after he had published his *Dictionary*, in the attitude of sitting in his easy chair in deep meditation, which was the first picture his friend did for him, which Sir Joshua very kindly presented to me, and from which an engraving has been made for this work. Mr. Davies mentioned my name, and respectfully introduced me to him. I was much agitated; and recollecting his prejudice against the Scotch, of which I had heard much, I said to Davies, "Don't tell where I come from."—"From Scotland," cried Davies roguishly. "Mr. Johnson, (said I) I do indeed come from Scotland, but I cannot help it." I am willing to flatter myself that I meant this as light pleasantry to soothe and conciliate him, and not as an humiliating abasement at the expense of my country. But however that might be, this speech was somewhat unlucky; for with that quickness of wit for which he was so remarkable, he seized the expression "come from Scotland," which I used in the sense of being of that country; and, as if I had said that I had come away from it, or left it, retorted, "That, Sir, I find, is what a very great many of your countrymen cannot help." This stroke stunned me a good deal; and when we had sat down, I felt myself not a little embarrassed, and apprehensive of what might come next. He then addressed himself to Davies: "What do you think of Garrick? He has refused me an order for the play for Miss Williams, because he knows the house will be full and that an order

4. ***taedium vitae,*** weariness or loathing of life. **7. Sheridan.** Thomas Sheridan, an Irish actor and teacher of elocution; father of Richard Brinsley Sheridan, the famous playwright, who was then a boy of eleven. **8. Derrick,** Samuel Derrick, a Scotsman and "a wretched writer," who had helped to introduce Boswell to the shabbier side of London life in 1760. **11. Dr. Pringle,** Dr. John Pringle, called by Boswell "sour . . . although a sensible learned man, a good philosopher, and an excellent physician." *Aetat. 54*, the fifty-fourth year of Johnson's age.

48. Garrick, David Garrick (1717–1779), Johnson's former pupil, and the most famous actor of the age. **49. Miss Williams,** Anna Williams, one of the several persons whom Johnson supported and lodged in his own house.

would be worth three shillings." Eager to take any opening to get into conversation with him, I ventured to say, "O, Sir, I cannot think Mr. Garrick would grudge such a trifle to you." "Sir, (said he, with a stern look,) I have known David Garrick longer than you have done: and I know no right you have to talk to me on the subject." Perhaps I deserved this check; for it was rather presumptuous in me, an entire stranger, to express any doubt of the justice of his animadversion upon his old acquaintance and pupil. I now felt myself much mortified, and began to think that the hope which I had long indulged of obtaining his acquaintance was blasted. And, in truth, had not my ardour been uncommonly strong, and my resolution uncommonly persevering, so rough a reception might have deterred me for ever from making any further attempts. Fortunately, however, I remained upon the field not wholly discomfited; and was soon rewarded by hearing some of his conversation, of which I preserved the following short minute, without marking the questions and observations by which it was produced.

"People (he remarked) may be taken in once, who imagine that an author is greater in private life than other men. Uncommon parts require uncommon opportunities for their exertion."

"In barbarous society, superiority of parts is of real consequence. Great strength or great wisdom is of much value to an individual. But in more polished times there are people to do every thing for money; and then there are a number of other superiorities, such as those of birth and fortune, and rank, that dissipate men's attention, and leave no extraordinary share of respect for personal and intellectual superiority. This is wisely ordered by Providence, to preserve some equality among mankind."

"Sir, this book (*The Elements of Criticism*, which he had taken up,) is a pretty essay, and deserves to be held in some estimation, though much of it is chimerical."

Speaking of one who with more than ordinary boldness attacked publick measures and the royal family, he said,

"I think he is safe from the law, but he is an abusive scoundrel; and instead of applying to my Lord Chief Justice to punish him, I would send half a dozen footmen and have him well ducked."

"The notion of liberty amuses the people of England, and helps to keep off the *taedium vitae*. When a butcher tells you that *his heart bleeds for his country*, he has, in fact, no uneasy feeling."

"Sheridan will not succeed at Bath with his oratory. Ridicule has gone down before him, and, I doubt, Derrick is his enemy."

"Derrick may do very well, as long as he can outrun his character; but the moment his character gets up with him, it is all over."

It is, however, but just to record, that some years afterwards, when I reminded him of this sarcasm, he said, "Well, but Derrick has now got a character that he need not run away from."

I was highly pleased with the extraordinary vigour of his conversation, and regretted that I was drawn away from it by an engagement at another place. I had, for a part of the evening, been left alone with him, and had ventured to make an observation now and then, which he received very civilly; so that I was satisfied that though there was a roughness in his manner, there was no ill-nature in his disposition. Davies followed me to the door, and when I complained to him a little of the hard blows which the great man had given me, he kindly took upon him to console me by saying, "Don't be uneasy. I can see he likes you very well."

A few days afterwards I called on Davies, and asked him if he thought I might take the liberty of waiting on Mr. Johnson at his Chambers in the Temple. He said I certainly might, and that Mr. Johnson would take it as a compliment. So upon Tuesday the 24th of May, after having been enlivened by the witty sallies of Messieurs Thornton, Wilkes, Churchill and Lloyd, with whom I had passed the morning, I boldly repaired to Johnson. His Chambers were on the first floor of No. 1, Inner-Temple-lane, and I entered them with an impression given me by the Reverend Dr. Blair, of Edinburgh, who had been introduced to him not long before, and described his having "found the Giant in his den"; an expression, which, when I came to be pretty well acquainted with Johnson, I repeated to him, and he was diverted at this picturesque account of himself. Dr. Blair had been presented to him by Dr. James Fordyce. At this time the controversy concerning the pieces published by Mr. James Macpherson, as translations of *Ossian*, was at its height. Johnson had all along denied their authenticity; and, what was still more provoking to their admirers, maintained that they had no merit. The subject having been introduced by Dr. For-

38. The Elements of Criticism, by Henry Horne, Lord **Kames,** a Scottish judge.

5. character, reputation. **30–31. Thornton . . . Lloyd,** all men of letters and persons whom Johnson would have thought disreputable. For John **Wilkes** (1727–1797) at this time Johnson had a special disapprobation partly because of his opinions and partly because of his profligate life. **35. Blair,** the Rev. Hugh Blair, Scottish clergyman and rhetorician. **44. Macpherson,** author of the "Ossianic Poems."

dyce, Dr. Blair, relying on the internal evidence of their antiquity, asked Dr. Johnson whether he thought any man of a modern age could have written such poems? Johnson replied, "Yes, Sir, many men, many women, and many children." Johnson, at this time, did not know that Dr. Blair had just published a *Dissertation*, not only defending their authenticity, but seriously ranking them with the poems of *Homer* and *Virgil;* and when he was afterwards informed of this circumstance, he expressed some displeasure at Dr. Fordyce's having suggested the topic, and said, "I am not sorry that they got thus much for their pains. Sir, it was like leading one to talk of a book when the authour is concealed behind the door."

He received me very courteously; but, it must be confessed, that his apartment, and furniture, and morning dress, were sufficiently uncouth. His brown suit of cloaths looked very rusty; he had on a little old shrivelled unpowdered wig, which was too small for his head; his shirt-neck and knees of his breeches were loose; his black worsted stockings ill drawn up; and he had a pair of unbuckled shoes by way of slippers. But all these slovenly particularities were forgotten the moment that he began to talk. Some gentlemen, whom I do not recollect, were sitting with him; and when they went away, I also rose; but he said to me, "Nay, don't go." "Sir, (said I,) I am afraid that I intrude upon you. It is benevolent to allow me to sit and hear you." He seemed pleased with this compliment, which I sincerely paid him, and answered, "Sir, I am obliged to any man who visits me." I have preserved the following short minute of what passed this day:—

"Madness frequently discovers itself merely by unnecessary deviation from the usual modes of the world. My poor friend Smart shewed the disturbance of his mind, by falling upon his knees, and saying his prayers in the street, or in any other unusual place. Now although, rationally speaking, it is greater madness not to pray at all, than to pray as Smart did, I am afraid there are so many who do not pray, that their understanding is not called in question."

Concerning this unfortunate poet, Christopher Smart, who was confined in a mad-house, he had, at another time, the following conversation with Dr. Burney:—Burney. "How does poor Smart do, Sir; is he likely to recover?" Johnson. "It seems as if his mind had ceased to struggle with the disease; for he grows fat upon it." Burney. "Perhaps, Sir, that may be from want of exercise." Johnson. "No, Sir; he has partly as much exercise as he used to have, for he digs in the garden. Indeed, before his confinement, he used for exercise to walk to the alehouse; but he was *carried* back again. I did not think he ought to be shut up. His infirmities were not noxious to society. He insisted on people praying with him; and I'd as lief pray with Kit Smart as any one else. Another charge was, that he did not love clean linen; and I have no passion for it."—Johnson continued: "Mankind have a great aversion to intellectual labour; but even supposing knowledge to be easily attainable, more people would be content to be ignorant than would take even a little trouble to acquire it."

"The morality of an action depends on the motive from which we act. If I fling half a crown to a beggar with intention to break his head, and he picks it up and buys victuals with it, the physical effect is good; but, with respect to me, the action is very wrong. So, religious exercises, if not performed with an intention to please God, avail us nothing. As our Saviour says of those who perform them from other motives, 'Verily they have their reward.'

"The Christian religion has very strong evidences. It, indeed, appears in some degree strange to reason; but in History we have undoubted facts, against which, reasoning *à priori*, we have more arguments than we have for them; but then, testimony has great weight, and casts the balance. I would recommend to every man whose faith is yet unsettled, Grotius,—Dr. Pearson,—and Dr. Clarke."

Talking of Garrick, he said, "He is the first man in the world for sprightly conversation."

When I rose a second time he again pressed me to stay, which I did.

He told me, that he generally went abroad at four in the afternoon, and seldom came home till two in the morning. I took the liberty to ask if he did not think it wrong to live thus, and not make more use of his great talents. He owned it was a bad habit. On reviewing, at the distance of many years, my journal of this period, I wonder how, at my first visit, I ventured to talk to him so freely, and that he bore it with so much indulgence.

Before we parted, he was so good as to promise to favour me with his company one evening at my lodgings; and, as I took my leave, shook me cordially by the hand. It is almost needless to add, that I felt no little elation at having now so happily established an acquaintance of which I had been so long ambitious.

My readers will, I trust, excuse me for being thus minutely circumstantial, when it is considered that

48. Burney, Charles Burney (1726–1814), a teacher and historian of music, father of Fanny Burney, Madame d'Arblay, the novelist.

the acquaintance of Dr. Johnson was to me a most valuable acquisition, and laid the foundation of whatever instruction and entertainment they may receive from my collections concerning the great subject of the work which they are now perusing. . . .

My next meeting with Johnson was on Friday the 1st of July, when he and I and Dr. Goldsmith supped together at the Mitre. I was before this time pretty well acquainted with Goldsmith, who was one of the brightest ornaments of the Johnsonian school. Goldsmith's respectful attachment to Johnson was then at its height; for his own literary reputation had not yet distinguished him so much as to excite a vain desire of competition with his great Master. He had increased my admiration of the goodness of Johnson's heart, by incidental remarks in the course of conversation, such as, when I mentioned Mr. Levet, whom he entertained under his roof, "He is poor and honest, which is recommendation enough to Johnson"; and when I wondered that he was very kind to a man of whom I had heard a very bad character, "He is now become miserable, and that insures the protection of Johnson."

Goldsmith attempted this evening to maintain, I suppose from an affectation of paradox, "that knowledge was not desirable on its own account, for it often was a source of unhappiness." JOHNSON. "Why, Sir, that knowledge may in some cases produce unhappiness, I allow. But, upon the whole, knowledge, *per se*, is certainly an object which every man would wish to attain, although, perhaps, he may not take the trouble necessary for attaining it."

Dr. John Campbell, the celebrated political and biographical writer, being mentioned, Johnson said, "Campbell is a man of much knowledge, and has a good share of imagination. His *Hermippus Redivivus* is very entertaining, as an account of the Hermetick philosophy, and as furnishing a curious history of the extravagancies of the human mind. If it were merely imaginary it would be nothing at all. Campbell is not always rigidly careful of truth in his conversation; but I do not believe there is any thing of this carelessness in his books. Campbell is a good man, a pious man. I am afraid he has not been in the inside of a church for many years; but he never passes a church without pulling off his hat. This shews that he has good principles. I used to go pretty often to Campbell's on a Sunday evening till I began to consider that the shoals of Scotchmen who flocked about him might probably say, when anything of mine was well done, "Ay, ay, he has learnt this of CAWMELL!"

He talked very contemptuously of Churchill's poetry, observing, that "it had a temporary currency, only from its audacity of abuse, and being filled with living names, and that it would sink into oblivion." I ventured to hint that he was not quite a fair judge, as Churchill had attacked him violently. JOHNSON. "Nay, Sir, I am a very fair judge. He did not attack me violently till he found I did not like his poetry; and his attack on me shall not prevent me from continuing to say what I think of him, from an apprehension that it may be ascribed to resentment. No, Sir, I called the fellow a blockhead at first, and I will call him a blockhead still. However, I will acknowledge that I have a better opinion of him now, than I once had; for he has shewn more fertility than I expected. To be sure, he is a tree that cannot produce good fruit: he only bears crabs. But, Sir, a tree that produces a great many crabs is better than a tree which produces only a few." . . .

On Tuesday the 5th of July, I again visited Johnson. He told me he had looked into the poems of a pretty voluminous writer, Mr. (now Dr.) John Ogilvie, one of the Presbyterian ministers of Scotland, which had lately come out, but could find no thinking in them. BOSWELL. "Is there not imagination in them, Sir?" JOHNSON. "Why, Sir, there is in them what *was* imagination, but it is no more imagination in *him*, than sound is sound in the echo. And his diction too is not his own. We have long ago seen *white-robed innocence*, and *flower-bespangled meads*."

Talking of London, he observed, "Sir, if you wish to have a just notion of the magnitude of this city, you must not be satisfied with seeing its great streets and squares, but must survey the innumerable little lanes and courts. It is not in the showy evolutions of buildings, but in the multiplicity of human habitations which are crouded together, that the wonderful immensity of London consists."—I have often amused myself with thinking how different a place London is to different people. They, whose narrow minds are contracted to the consideration of some one particular pursuit, view it only through that medium. A politician thinks of it merely as the seat of government in its different departments; a grazier, as a vast market for cattle; a mercantile man, as a place where a prodigious deal of business is done upon 'Change; a dramatick enthusiast, as the grand scene of theatrical entertainments; a man of

7. next meeting. There had been several after the last one given here. **9. Mitre,** a tavern in Fleet Street. **19. Levet,** a physician who, having failed in his practice, lived for many years in Johnson's house.

4. Churchill, Charles Churchill (1731–1764), a satiric poet.

pleasure, as an assemblage of taverns, and the great emporium for ladies of easy virtue. But the intellectual man is struck with it, as comprehending the whole of human life in all its variety, the contemplation of which is inexhaustible.

On Wednesday, July 6, he was engaged to sup with me at my lodgings in Downing-street, Westminster. But on the preceding night my landlord having behaved very rudely to me and some company who were with me, I had resolved not to remain another night in his house. I was exceedingly uneasy at the awkward appearance I supposed I should make to Johnson and the other gentlemen whom I had invited, not being able to receive them at home, and being obliged to order supper at the Mitre. I went to Johnson in the morning, and talked of it as a serious distress. He laughed, and said, "Consider, Sir, how insignificant this will appear a twelvemonth hence."—Were this consideration to be applied to most of the little vexatious incidents of life, by which our quiet is too often disturbed, it would prevent many painful sensations. I have tried it frequently, with good effect. "There is nothing (continued he) in this mighty misfortune; nay, we shall be better at the Mitre." I told him that I had been at Sir John Fielding's office, complaining of my landlord, and had been informed, that though I had taken my lodgings for a year, I might, upon proof of his bad behaviour, quit them when I pleased, without being under an obligation to pay rent for any longer time than while I possessed them. The fertility of Johnson's mind could shew itself even upon so small a matter as this. "Why, Sir, (said he,) I suppose this must be the law, since you have been told so in Bow-street. But, if your landlord could hold you to your bargain, and the lodgings should be yours for a year, you may certainly use them as you think fit. So, Sir, you may quarter two life-guardsmen upon him; or you may send the greatest scoundrel you can find into your apartments; or you may say that you want to make some experiments in natural philosophy, and may burn a large quantity of assafoetida in his house."

I had as my guests this evening at the Mitre tavern, Dr. Johnson, Dr. Goldsmith, Mr. Thomas Davies, Mr. Eccles, an Irish gentleman, for whose agreeable company I was obliged to Mr. Davies, and the Reverend Mr. John Ogilvie, who was desirous of being in company with my illustrious friend, while I, in my turn, was proud to have the honour of shewing one of my countrymen upon what easy terms Johnson permitted me to live with him.

Goldsmith, as usual, endeavoured, with too much eagerness, to *shine*, and disputed very warmly with Johnson against the well-known maxim of the British constitution, "the King can do no wrong"; affirming, that "what was morally false could not be politically true; and as the King might, in the exercise of his regal power, command and cause the doing of what was wrong, it certainly might be said, in sense and in reason, that he could do wrong." JOHNSON. "Sir, you are to consider, that in our constitution, according to its true principles, the King is the head; he is supreme; he is above everything, and there is no power by which he can be tried. Therefore, it is, Sir, that we hold the King can do no wrong; that whatever may happen to be wrong in government may not be above our reach, by being ascribed to Majesty. Redress is always to be had against oppression, by punishing the immediate agents. The King, though he should command, cannot force a Judge to condemn a man unjustly; therefore it is the Judge whom we prosecute and punish. Political institutions are formed upon the consideration of what will most frequently tend to the good of the whole, although now and then exceptions may occur. Thus it is better in general that a nation should have a supreme legislative power, although it may at times be abused. And then, Sir, there is this consideration, that *if the abuse be enormous, Nature will rise up, and claiming her original rights, overturn a corrupt political system*." I mark this animated sentence with peculiar pleasure, as a noble instance of that truly dignified spirit of freedom which ever glowed in his heart, though he was charged with slavish tenets by superficial observers; because he was at all times indignant against that false patriotism, that pretended love of freedom, that unruly restlessness, which is inconsistent with the stable authority of any good government.

This generous sentiment, which he uttered with great fervour, struck me exceedingly, and stirred my blood to that pitch of fancied resistance, the possibility of which I am glad to keep in mind, but to which I trust I never shall be forced.

"Great abilities (said he) are not requisite for an Historian; for in historical composition, all the greatest powers of the human mind are quiescent. He has facts ready to his hand; so there is no exercise of invention. Imagination is not required in any high degree; only about as much as is used in the lower kinds of poetry. Some penetration, accuracy, and colouring will fit a man for the task, if he can give the application which is necessary."

26. Sir John Fielding, a justice of the peace, and half-brother of Henry Fielding, author of *Tom Jones*.

"Bayle's *Dictionary* is a very useful work for those to consult who love the biographical part of literature, which is what I love most."

Talking of the eminent writers in Queen Anne's reign, he observed, "I think Dr. Arbuthnot the first man among them. He was the most universal genius, being an excellent physician, a man of deep learning, and a man of much humour. Mr. Addison was, to be sure, a great man; his learning was not profound; but his morality, his humour, and his elegance of writing, set him very high."

Mr. Ogilvie was unlucky enough to choose for the topick of his conversation the praises of his native country. He began with saying, that there was very rich land round Edinburgh. Goldsmith, who had studied physick there, contradicted this, very untruly, with a sneering laugh. Disconcerted a little by this, Mr. Ogilvie then took new ground, where, I suppose, he thought himself perfectly safe; for he observed, that Scotland had a great many noble wild prospects. Johnson. "I believe, Sir, you have a great many. Norway, too, has noble wild prospects; and Lapland is remarkable for prodigious noble wild prospects. But, Sir, let me tell you, the noblest prospect which a Scotchman ever sees, is the high road that leads him to England!" This unexpected and pointed sally produced a roar of applause. After all, however, those, who admire the rude grandeur of Nature, cannot deny it to Caledonia.

On Saturday, July 9, I found Johnson surrounded with a numerous levee, but have not preserved any part of his conversation. On the 14th we had another evening by ourselves at the Mitre. It happening to be a very rainy night, I made some common-place observations on the relaxation of nerves and depression of spirits which such weather occasioned; adding, however, that it was good for the vegetable creation. Johnson, who, as we have already seen, denied that the temperature of the air had any influence on the human frame, answered, with a smile of ridicule, "Why yes, Sir, it is good for vegetables, and for the animals who eat those vegetables, and for the animals who eat those animals." This observation of his aptly enough introduced a good supper; and I soon forgot, in Johnson's company, the influence of a moist atmosphere.

Feeling myself now quite at ease as his companion, though I had all possible reverence for him, I expressed a regret that I could not be so easy with my father, though he was not much older than Johnson, and certainly however respectable had not more learning and greater abilities to depress me. I asked him the reason of this. Johnson. "Why, Sir, I am a man of the world. I live in the world, and I take, in some degree, the colour of the world as it moves along. Your father is a Judge in a remote part of the island, and all his notions are taken from the old world. Besides, Sir, there must always be a struggle between a father and son, while one aims at power and the other at independence." I said, I was afraid my father would force me to be a lawyer. Johnson. "Sir, you need not be afraid of his forcing you to be a laborious practising lawyer; that is not in his power. For as the proverb says, 'One man may lead a horse to the water, but twenty cannot make him drink.' He may be displeased that you are not what he wishes you to be; but that displeasure will not go far. If he insists only on your having as much law as is necessary for a man of property, and then endeavours to get you into Parliament, he is quite in the right."

He enlarged very convincingly upon the excellence of rhyme over blank verse in English poetry. I mentioned to him that Dr. Adam Smith, in his lectures upon composition, when I studied under him in the College of Glasgow, had maintained the same opinion strenuously, and I repeated some of his arguments. Johnson. "Sir, I was once in company with Smith, and we did not take to each other; but had I known that he loved rhyme as much as you tell me he does, I should have hugged him."

Talking of those who denied the truth of Christianity, he said, "It is always easy to be on the negative side. If a man were now to deny that there is salt upon the table, you could not reduce him to an absurdity. Come, let us try this a little further. I deny that Canada is taken, and I can support my denial by pretty good arguments. The French are a much more numerous people than we; and it is not likely that they would allow us to take it. 'But the ministry have assured us, in all the formality of *The Gazette*, that it is taken.'—Very true. But the ministry have put us to an enormous expense by the war in America, and it is their interest to persuade us that we have got something for our money.—'But the fact is confirmed by thousands of men who were at the taking of it.'—Ay, but these men have still more interest in deceiving us. They don't want that you should think the French have beat them, but that they have beat the French. Now suppose you should go over and find that it is really taken, that would only satisfy yourself; for when you come home we will not believe you. We will say, you have been bribed.—Yet, Sir, notwithstanding all these plausi-

1. Dictionary, Pierre Bayle's *Dictionnaire historique et critique,* 1697.

22. Adam Smith, Scottish economist (1723–1790), author of *The Wealth of Nations.*

ble objections, we have no doubt that Canada is really ours. Such is the weight of common testimony. How much stronger are the evidences of the Christian religion!"

"Idleness is a disease which must be combated; but I would not advise a rigid adherence to a particular plan of study. I myself have never persisted in any plan for two days together. A man ought to read just as inclination leads him; for what he reads as a task will do him little good. A young man should read five hours in a day, and so may acquire a great deal of knowledge."

To a man of vigorous intellect and arduous curiosity like his own, reading without a regular plan may be beneficial; though even such a man must submit to it, if he would attain a full understanding of any of the sciences.

To such a degree of unrestrained frankness had he now accustomed me, that in the course of this evening I talked of the numerous reflections which had been thrown out against him on account of his having accepted a pension from his present Majesty. "Why, Sir, (said he, with a hearty laugh,) it is a mighty foolish noise that they make. I have accepted of a pension as a reward which has been thought due to my literary merit; and now that I have this pension, I am the same man in every respect that I have ever been; I retain the same principles. It is true, that I cannot now curse (smiling) the House of Hanover; nor would it be decent for me to drink King James's health in the wine that King George gives me money to pay for. But, Sir, I think that the pleasure of cursing the House of Hanover, and drinking King James's health, are amply overbalanced by three hundred pounds a year."

There was here, most certainly, an affectation of more Jacobitism than he really had; and indeed an intention of admitting, for the moment, in a much greater extent than it really existed, the charge of disaffection imputed to him by the world, merely for the purpose of shewing how dexterously he could repel an attack, even though he were placed in the most disadvantageous position; for I have heard him declare, that if holding up his right hand would have secured victory at Culloden to Prince Charles's army, he was not sure he would have held it up; so little confidence had he in the right claimed by the House of Stuart, and so fearful was he of the consequences of another revolution on the throne of Great-Britain; and Mr. Topham Beauclerk assured me he had heard him say this before he had his pension. At another time he said to Mr. Langton, "Nothing has ever offered, that has made it worth my while to consider the question fully." He, however, also said to the same gentleman, talking of King James the Second, "It was become impossible for him to reign any longer in this country." He no doubt had an early attachment to the House of Stuart; but his zeal had cooled as his reason strengthened. Indeed I heard him once say, that "after the death of a violent Whig, with whom he used to contend with great eagerness, he felt his Toryism much abated." I suppose he meant Mr. Walmsley.

Yet there is no doubt that at earlier periods he was wont often to exercise both his pleasantry and ingenuity in talking Jacobitism. My much respected friend, Dr. Douglas, now Bishop of Salisbury, has favoured me with the following admirable instance from his Lordship's own recollection. One day when dining at old Mr. Langton's where Miss Roberts, his niece, was one of the company, Johnson, with his usual complacent attention to the fair sex, took her by the hand and said, "My dear, I hope you are a Jacobite." Old Mr. Langton, who, though a high and steady Tory, was attached to the present Royal Family, seemed offended, and asked Johnson, with great warmth, what he could mean by putting such a question to his niece? "Why, Sir, (said Johnson) I meant no offence to your niece, I meant her a great compliment. A Jacobite, Sir, believes in the divine right of Kings. He that believes in the divine right of Kings believes in a Divinity. A Jacobite believes in the divine right of Bishops. He that believes in the divine right of Bishops believes in the divine authority of the Christian religion. Therefore, Sir, a Jacobite is neither an Atheist nor a Deist. That cannot be said of a Whig; for *Whiggism is a negation of all principle*."

He advised me, when abroad, to be as much as I could with the Professors in the universities, and with the Clergy; for from their conversation I might expect the best accounts of every thing in whatever country I should be, with the additional advantage of keeping my learning alive.

It will be observed, that when giving me advice as to my travels, Dr. Johnson did not dwell upon cities, and palaces, and pictures, and shows, and Arcadian scenes. He was of Lord Essex's opinion, who advises his kinsman Roger Earl of Rutland, "rather to go an hundred miles to speak with one wise man, than five miles to see a fair town."

31. **King James,** the "Old Pretender," son of James II, who claimed the throne of England and so was an enemy of the Hanoverian King George III. 37. **Jacobitism,** adherence to James II after his abdication, or to his son the "Pretender." The Latin for "James" is *Jacobus*. 45. **Culloden,** the battle, fought in 1746, in which the "Young Pretender," Bonny Prince Charlie, was defeated.

I described to him an impudent fellow from Scotland, who affected to be a savage, and railed at all established systems. JOHNSON. "There is nothing surprising in this, Sir. He wants to make himself conspicuous. He would tumble in a hogstye, as long as you looked at him and called to him to come out. But let him alone, never mind him, and he'll soon give it over."

I added, that the same person maintained that there was no distinction between virtue and vice. JOHNSON. "Why, Sir, if the fellow does not think as he speaks, he is lying; and I see not what honour he can propose to himself from having the character of a liar. But if he does really think that there is no distinction between virtue and vice, why, Sir, when he leaves our houses let us count our spoons. . . ."

He [Johnson] recommended to me to keep a journal of my life, full and unreserved. He said it would be a very good exercise, and would yield me great satisfaction when the particulars were faded from my remembrance. I was uncommonly fortunate in having had a previous coincidence of opinion with him upon this subject, for I had kept such a journal for some time; and it was no small pleasure to me to have this to tell him, and to receive his approbation. He counselled me to keep it private, and said I might surely have a friend who would burn it in case of my death. From this habit I have been enabled to give the world so many anecdotes, which would otherwise have been lost to posterity. I mentioned that I was afraid I put into my journal too many little incidents. JOHNSON. "There is nothing, Sir, too little for so little a creature as man. It is by studying little things that we attain the great art of having as little misery and as much happiness as possible."

Next morning Mr. Dempster happened to call on me, and was so much struck even with the imperfect account which I gave him of Dr. Johnson's conversation, that to his honour be it recorded, when I complained that drinking port and sitting up late with him affected my nerves for some time after, he said, "One had better be palsied at eighteen than not keep company with such a man."

On Tuesday, July 18, I found tall Sir Thomas Robinson sitting with Johnson. Sir Thomas said, that the King of Prussia valued himself upon three things;—upon being a hero, a musician, and an authour. JOHNSON. "Pretty well, Sir, for one man. As to his being an authour, I have not looked at his poetry; but his prose is poor stuff. He writes just as you might suppose Voltaire's footboy to do, who has been his amanuensis. He has such parts as the valet might have, and about as much of the colouring of the style as might be got by transcribing his works." When I was at Ferney, I repeated this to Voltaire, in order to reconcile him somewhat to Johnson, whom he, in affecting the English mode of expression, had previously characterized as "a superstitious dog"; but after hearing such a criticism on Frederick the Great, with whom he was then on bad terms, he exclaimed, "An honest fellow!"

But I think the criticism much too severe; for the *Memoirs of the House of Brandenburgh* are written as well as many works of that kind. His poetry, for the style of which he himself makes a frank apology, "*Jargonnant un François barbare*," though fraught with pernicious ravings of infidelity, has, in many places, great animation, and in some a pathetick tenderness.

Upon this contemptuous animadversion on the King of Prussia, I observed to Johnson, "It would seem then, Sir, that much less parts are necessary to make a King, than to make an Authour; for the King of Prussia is confessedly the greatest King now in Europe, yet you think he makes a very poor figure as an Authour."

Mr. Levet this day showed me Dr. Johnson's library, which was contained in two garrets over his Chambers, where Lintot, son of the celebrated bookseller of that name, had formerly his warehouse. I found a number of good books, but very dusty and in great confusion. The floor was strewed with manuscript leaves, in Johnson's own handwriting, which I beheld with a degree of veneration, supposing they perhaps might contain portions of *The Rambler* or of *Rasselas*. I observed an apparatus for chymical experiments, of which Johnson was all his life very fond. The place seemed to be very favourable for retirement and meditation. Johnson told me, that he went up thither without mentioning it to his servant, when he wanted to study, secure from interruption; for he would not allow his servant to say he was not at home when he really was. "A servant's strict regard for truth, (said he) must be weakened by such a practice. A philosopher may know that it is merely a form of denial; but few servants are such nice distinguishers. If I accustom a servant to tell a lie for *me*, have I not reason to apprehend that he will tell many lies for *himself*." I am, however, satisfied that every servant, of any degree of intelligence, understands saying his master is not at home, not at all as the affirmation of a fact, but as customary words, intimating that his master wishes not to be seen; so that there can be no bad effect from it.

Mr. Temple, now vicar of St. Gluvias, Cornwall,

who had been my intimate friend for many years, had at this time chambers in Farrar's-buildings, at the bottom of Inner-Temple-lane, which he kindly lent me upon my quitting my lodgings, he being to return to Trinity Hall, Cambridge. I found them particularly convenient for me, as they were so near Dr. Johnson's.

On Wednesday, July 20, Dr. Johnson, Mr. Dempster, and my uncle Dr. Boswell, who happened to be now in London, supped with me at these Chambers. JOHNSON. "Pity is not natural to man. Children are always cruel. Savages are always cruel. Pity is acquired and improved by the cultivation of reason. We may have uneasy sensations from seeing a creature in distress, without pity; for we have not pity unless we wish to relieve them. When I am on my way to dine with a friend, and finding it late, have bid the coachman make haste, if I happen to attend when he whips his horses, I may feel unpleasantly that the animals are put to pain, but I do not wish him to desist. No, Sir, I wish him to drive on."

Mr. Alexander Donaldson, bookseller of Edinburgh, had for some time opened a shop in London, and sold his cheap editions, of the most popular English books, in defiance of the supposed common-law right of *Literary Property*. Johnson, though he concurred in the opinion which was afterwards sanctioned by a judgement of the House of Lords, that there was no such right, was at this time very angry that the Booksellers of London, for whom he uniformly professed much regard, should suffer from an invasion of what they had ever considered to be secure: and he was loud and violent against Mr. Donaldson. "He is a fellow who takes advantage of the law to injure his brethren; for, notwithstanding that the statute secures only fourteen years of exclusive right, it has always been understood by *the trade*, that he, who buys the copyright of a book from the authour, obtains a perpetual property; and upon that belief, numberless bargains are made to transfer that property after the expiration of the statutory term. Now Donaldson, I say, takes advantage here, of people who have really an equitable title from usage; and if we consider how few of the books, of which they buy the property, succeed so well as to bring profit, we should be of opinion that the term of fourteen years is too short; it should be sixty years." DEMPSTER. "Donaldson, Sir, is anxious for the encouragement of literature. He reduces the price of books, so that poor students may buy them." JOHNSON, (laughing). "Well, Sir, allowing that to be his motive, he is no better than Robin Hood, who robbed the rich in order to give to the poor."

It is remarkable, that when the great question concerning Literary Property came to be ultimately tried before the supreme tribunal of this country, in consequence of the very spirited exertions of Mr. Donaldson, Dr. Johnson was zealous against a perpetuity; but he thought that the term of the exclusive right of authours should be considerably enlarged. He was then for granting a hundred years.

The conversation now turned upon Mr. David Hume's style. JOHNSON. "Why, Sir, his style is not English; the structure of his sentences is French. Now the French structure and the English structure may, in the nature of things, be equally good. But if you allow that the English language is established, he is wrong. My name might originally have been Nicholson, as well as Johnson; but were you to call me Nicholson now, you would call me very absurdly."

Rousseau's treatise on the inequality of mankind was at this time a fashionable topick. It gave rise to an observation by Mr. Dempster, that the advantages of fortune and rank were nothing to a wise man, who ought to value only merit. JOHNSON. "If man were a savage, living in the woods by himself, this might be true; but in civilized society we all depend upon each other, and our happiness is very much owing to the good opinion of mankind. Now, Sir, in civilized society, external advantages make us more respected. A man with a good coat upon his back meets with a better reception than he who has a bad one. Sir, you may analyse this, and say what is there in it? But that will avail you nothing, for it is a part of a general system. Pound St. Paul's Church into atoms, and consider any single atom; it is, to be sure, good for nothing: but, put all these atoms together, and you have St. Paul's Church. So it is with human felicity, which is made up of many ingredients, each of which may be shown to be very insignificant. In civilized society, personal merit will not serve you so much as money will. Sir, you may make the experiment. Go into the street, and give one man a lecture on morality, and another a shilling, and see which will respect you most. If you wish only to support nature, Sir William Petty fixes your allowance at three pounds a year; but as times are much altered, let us call it six pounds. This sum will fill your belly, shelter you from the weather, and even get you a strong and lasting coat, supposing it to be made of good bull's hide.

10–11. David Hume (1711–1776), a philosopher and historian who was disliked by Dr. Johnson because of his skepticism. **45. Sir William Petty** (1623–1687), an important early statistician and political economist.

Now, Sir, all beyond this is artificial, and is desired in order to obtain a greater degree of respect from our fellow-creatures. And, Sir, if six hundred pounds a year procure a man more consequence, and, of course, more happiness than six pounds a year, the same proportion will hold as to six thousand, and so on as far as opulence can be carried. Perhaps he who has a large fortune may not be so happy as he who has a small one; but that must proceed from other causes than from his having the large fortune: for, *caeteris paribus*, he who is rich in a civilized society, must be happier than he who is poor; as riches, if properly used, (and it is a man's own fault if they are not,) must be productive of the highest advantages. Money, to be sure, of itself is of no use; for its only use is to part with it. Rousseau, and all those who deal in paradoxes, are led away by a childish desire of novelty. When I was a boy, I used always to choose the wrong side of a debate, because most ingenious things, that is to say, most new things, could be said upon it. Sir, there is nothing for which you may not muster up more plausible arguments, than those which are urged against wealth and other external advantages. Why, now, there is stealing; why should it be thought a crime? When we consider by what unjust methods property has been often acquired, and that what was unjustly got it must be unjust to keep, where is the harm in one man's taking the property of another from him? Besides, Sir, when we consider the bad use that many people make of their property, and how much better use the thief may make of it, it may be defended as a very allowable practice. Yet, Sir, the experience of mankind has discovered stealing to be so very bad a thing, that they make no scruple to hang a man for it. When I was running about this town a very poor fellow, I was a great arguer for the advantages of poverty; but I was, at the same time, very sorry to be poor. Sir, all the arguments which are brought to represent poverty as no evil, shew it to be evidently a great evil. You never find people labouring to convince you that you may live very happily upon a plentiful fortune.—So you hear people talking how miserable a King must be; and yet they all wish to be in his place."

It was suggested that Kings must be unhappy, because they are deprived of the greatest of all satisfactions, easy and unreserved society. Johnson. "That is an ill-founded notion. Being a King does not exclude a man from such society. Great Kings have always been social. The King of Prussia, the only great King at present, is very social. Charles the Second, the last King of England who was a man of parts, was social; and our Henrys and Edwards were all social."

Mr. Dempster having endeavoured to maintain that intrinsick merit *ought* to make the only distinction amongst mankind. Johnson. "Why, Sir, mankind have found that this cannot be. How shall we determine the proportion of intrinsick merit? Were that to be the only distinction amongst mankind, we should soon quarrel about the degrees of it. Were all distinctions abolished, the strongest would not long acquiesce, but would endeavour to obtain a superiority by their bodily strength. But, Sir, as subordination is very necessary for society, and contentions for superiority very dangerous, mankind, that is to say, all civilized nations, have settled it upon a plain invariable principle. A man is born to hereditary rank; or his being appointed to certain offices, gives him a certain rank. Subordination tends greatly to human happiness. Were we all upon an equality, we should have no other enjoyment than mere animal pleasure."

I said, I considered distinction of rank to be of so much importance in civilized society, that if I were asked on the same day to dine with the first Duke in England, and with the first man in Britain for genius, I should hesitate which to prefer. Johnson. "To be sure, Sir, if you were to dine only once, and it were never to be known where you dined, you would choose rather to dine with the first man for genius; but to gain most respect, you should dine with the first Duke in England. For nine people in ten that you meet with, would have a higher opinion of you for having dined with a Duke; and the great genius himself would receive you better, because you had been with the great Duke."

He took care to guard himself against any possible suspicion that his settled principles of reverence for rank and respect for wealth were at all owing to mean or interested motives; for he asserted his own independence as a literary man. "No man (said he) who ever lived by literature, has lived more independently than I have done." He said he had taken longer time than he needed to have done in composing his *Dictionary*. He received our compliments upon that great work with complacency, and told us that the Academy *della Crusca* could scarcely believe that it was done by one man.

Next morning I found him alone, and have preserved the following fragments of his conversation. Of a gentleman who was mentioned, he said, "I have not met with any man for a long time who

11. caeteris paribus, other things being equal.

47. Crusca, Accademia della Crusca, a learned society founded at Florence in 1582.

has given me such general displeasure. He is totally unfixed in his principles, and wants to puzzle other people." I said his principles had been poisoned by a noted infidel writer, but that he was, nevertheless, a benevolent good man. JOHNSON. "We can have no dependance upon that instinctive, that constitutional goodness which is not founded upon principle. I grant you that such a man may be a very amiable member of society. I can conceive him placed in such a situation that he is not much tempted to deviate from what is right; and as every man prefers virtue, when there is not some strong incitement to transgress its precepts, I can conceive him doing nothing wrong. But if such a man stood in need of money, I should not like to trust him; and I should certainly not trust him with young ladies, for *there* there is always temptation. Hume, and other sceptical innovators, are vain men, and will gratify themselves at any expense. Truth will not afford sufficient food to their vanity; so they have betaken themselves to error. Truth, Sir, is a cow which will yield such people no more milk, and so they are gone to milk the bull. If I could have allowed myself to gratify my vanity at the expense of truth, what fame might I have acquired. Every thing which Hume has advanced against Christianity had passed through my mind long before he wrote. Always remember this, that after a system is well settled upon positive evidence, a few partial objections ought not to shake it. The human mind is so limited, that it cannot take in all the parts of a subject, so that there may be objections raised against any thing. There are objections against a *plenum*, and objections against a *vacuum;* yet one of them must certainly be true."

I mentioned Hume's argument against the belief of miracles, that it is more probable that the witnesses to the truth of them are mistaken, or speak falsely, than that the miracles should be true. JOHNSON. "Why, Sir, the great difficulty of proving miracles should make us very cautious in believing them. But let us consider; although GOD has made Nature to operate by certain fixed laws, yet it is not unreasonable to think that he may suspend those laws, in order to establish a system highly advantageous to mankind. Now the Christian religion is a most beneficial system, as it gives us light and certainty where we were before in darkness and doubt. The miracles which prove it are attested by men who had no interest in deceiving us; but who, on the contrary, were told that they should suffer persecution, and did actually lay down their lives in confirmation of the truth of the facts which they asserted. Indeed, for some centuries the heathens did not pretend to deny the miracles; but said they were performed by the aid of evil spirits. This is a circumstance of great weight. Then, Sir, when we take the proofs derived from prophecies which have been so exactly fulfilled, we have most satisfactory evidence. Supposing a miracle possible, as to which, in my opinion, there can be no doubt, we have as strong evidence for the miracles in support of Christianity, as the nature of the thing admits."

At night Mr. Johnson and I supped in a private room at the Turk's Head coffee-house, in the Strand. "I encourage this house (said he;) for the mistress of it is a good civil woman, and has not much business."

"Sir, I love the acquaintance of young people; because, in the first place, I don't like to think myself growing old. In the next place, young acquaintances must last longest, if they do last; and then, Sir, young men have more virtue than old men; they have more generous sentiments in every respect. I love the young dogs of this age: they have more wit and humour and knowledge of life than we had; but then the dogs are not so good scholars. Sir, in my early years I read very hard. It is a sad reflection, but a true one, that I knew almost as much at eighteen as I do now. My judgement, to be sure, was not so good; but I had all the facts. I remember very well, when I was at Oxford, an old gentleman said to me, 'Young man, ply your book diligently now, and acquire a stock of knowledge; for when years come upon you, you will find that poring upon books will be but an irksome task.' "

This account of his reading, given by himself in plain words, sufficiently confirms what I have already advanced upon the disputed question as to his application. It reconciles any seeming inconsistency in his way of talking upon it at different times; and shows that idleness and reading hard were with him relative terms, the import of which, as used by him, must be gathered from a comparison with what scholars of different degrees of ardour and assiduity have been known to do. And let it be remembered, that he was now talking spontaneously, and expressing his genuine sentiments; whereas at other times he might be induced from his spirit of contradiction, or more properly from his love of argumentative contest, to speak lightly of his own application to study. It is pleasing to consider that the old gentleman's gloomy prophecy as to the irksomeness of books to men of an advanced age, which is too often fulfilled, was so far from be-

34. plenum . . . vacuum, space entirely filled with matter, space entirely empty of matter.

ing verified in Johnson, that his ardour for literature never failed, and his last writings had more ease and vivacity than any of his earlier productions.

He mentioned to me now, for the first time, that he had been distrest by melancholy, and for that reason had been obliged to fly from study and meditation, to the dissipating variety of life. Against melancholy he recommended constant occupation of mind, a great deal of exercise, moderation in eating and drinking, and especially to shun drinking at night. He said melancholy people were apt to fly to intemperance for relief, but that it sunk them much deeper in misery. He observed, that labouring men who work hard, and live sparingly, are seldom or never troubled with low spirits.

He again insisted on the duty of maintaining subordination of rank. "Sir, I would no more deprive a nobleman of his respect, than of his money. I consider myself as acting a part in the great system of society, and I do to others as I would have them to do to me. I would behave to a nobleman as I should expect he would behave to me, were I a nobleman and he Sam. Johnson. Sir, there is one Mrs. Macaulay in this town, a great republican. One day when I was at her house, I put on a very grave countenance, and said to her, 'Madam, I am now become a convert to your way of thinking. I am convinced that all mankind are upon an equal footing; and to give you an unquestionable proof, Madam, that I am in earnest, here is a very sensible, civil, well-behaved fellow-citizen, your footman; I desire that he may be allowed to sit down and dine with us.' I thus, Sir, showed her the absurdity of the levelling doctrine. She has never liked me since. Sir, your levellers wish to level *down* as far as themselves; but they cannot bear levelling *up* to themselves. They would all have some people under them; why not then have some people above them?" I mentioned a certain authour who disgusted me by his forwardness, and by shewing no deference to noblemen into whose company he was admitted. JOHNSON. "Suppose a shoemaker should claim an equality with him, as he does with a Lord; how he would stare. 'Why, Sir, do you stare? (says the shoemaker,) I do great service to society. 'Tis true I am paid for doing it; but so are you, Sir: and I am sorry to say it, paid better than I am, for doing something not so necessary. For mankind could do better without your books, than without my shoes.' Thus, Sir, there would be a perpetual struggle for precedence, were there no fixed invariable rules for the distinction of rank, which creates no jealousy, as it is allowed to be accidental."

He said, Dr. Joseph Warton was a very agreeable man, and his *Essay on the Genius and Writings of Pope*, a very pleasing book. I wondered that he delayed so long to give us the continuation of it. JOHNSON. "Why, Sir, I suppose he finds himself a little disappointed, in not having been able to persuade the world to be of his opinion as to Pope."

We have now been favoured with the concluding volume, in which, to use a parliamentary expression, he has *explained*, so as not to appear quite so adverse to the opinion of the world, concerning Pope, as was at first thought; and we must all agree that his work is a most valuable accession to English literature.

A writer of deserved eminence being mentioned, Johnson said, "Why, Sir, he is a man of good parts, but being originally poor, he has got a love of mean company and low jocularity; a very bad thing, Sir. To laugh is good, as to talk is good. But you ought no more to think it enough if you laugh, than you are to think it enough if you talk. You may laugh in as many ways as you talk; and surely *every* way of talking that is practised cannot be esteemed."

I spoke of Sir James Macdonald as a young man of most distinguished merit, who united the highest reputation at Eton and Oxford, with the patriarchal spirit of a great Highland Chieftain. I mentioned that Sir James had said to me, that he had never seen Mr. Johnson, but he had a great respect for him, though at the same time it was mixed with some degree of terrour. JOHNSON. "Sir, if he were to be acquainted with me, it might lessen both."

The mention of this gentleman led us to talk of the Western Islands of Scotland, to visit which he expressed a wish that then appeared to me a very romantick fancy, which I little thought would be afterwards realised. He told me, that his father had put Martin's account of those islands into his hands when he was very young, and that he was highly pleased with it; that he was particularly struck with the St. Kilda man's notion that the high church of Glasgow had been hollowed out of a rock; a circumstance to which old Mr. Johnson had directed his attention. He said he would go to the Hebrides with me, when I returned from my travels, unless some very good companion should offer when I was absent, which he did not think probable; adding, "There are few people to whom I take so much to

24. Mrs. Macaulay, a learned lady and "bluestocking" who was known as "the celebrated female historian" (1731–1791).

3. Joseph Warton, a teacher, poet, and scholar of romantic tendency (1722–1800). His account of Pope was not wholly favorable. **46. Hebrides.** Johnson and Boswell did take this journey in 1773, and both men wrote the story of their adventure.

as you." And when I talked of my leaving England, he said with a very affectionate air, "My dear Boswell, I should be very unhappy at parting, did I think we were not to meet again." I cannot too often remind my readers, that although such instances of his kindness are doubtless very flattering to me, yet I hope my recording them will be ascribed to a better motive than to vanity; for they afford unquestionable evidence of his tenderness and complacency, which some, while they were forced to acknowledge his great powers, have been so strenuous to deny.

He maintained that a boy at school was the happiest of human beings. I supported a different opinion, from which I have never yet varied, that a man is happier; and I enlarged upon the anxiety and sufferings which are endured at school. JOHNSON. "Ah! Sir, a boy's being flogged is not so severe as a man's having the hiss of the world against him. Men have a solicitude about fame; and the greater share they have of it, the more afraid they are of losing it." I silently asked myself, "Is it possible that the great SAMUEL JOHNSON really entertains any such apprehension, and is not confident that his exalted fame is established upon a foundation never to be shaken?"

He this evening drank a bumper to Sir David Dalrymple, "as a man of worth, a scholar, and a wit." "I have (said he) never heard of him except from you; but let him know my opinion of him: for as he does not shew himself much in the world, he should have the praise of the few who hear of him."

On Tuesday, July 26, I found Mr. Johnson alone. It was a very wet day, and I again complained of the disagreeable effects of such weather. JOHNSON. "Sir, this is all imagination, which physicians encourage; for man lives in air, as a fish lives in water; so that if the atmosphere press heavy from above, there is an equal resistance from below. To be sure, bad weather is hard upon people who are obliged to be abroad; and men cannot labour so well in the open air in bad weather, as in good; but, Sir, a smith or a taylor, whose work is within doors, will surely do as much in rainy weather, as in fair. Some very delicate frames, indeed, may be affected by wet weather; but not common constitutions."

We talked of the education of children; and I asked him what he thought was best to teach them first. JOHNSON. "Sir, it is no matter what you teach them first, any more than what leg you shall put into your breeches first. Sir, you may stand disputing which is best to put in first, but in the meantime your breech is bare. Sir, while you are considering which of two things you should teach your child first, another boy has learnt them both."

On Thursday, July 28, we again supped in private at the Turk's Head coffee-house. JOHNSON. "Swift has a higher reputation than he deserves. His excellence is strong sense; for his humour, though very well, is not remarkably good. I doubt whether *The Tale of a Tub* be his; for he never owned it, and it is much above his usual manner.

"Thompson, I think, had as much of the poet about him as most writers. Every thing appeared to him through the medium of his favourite pursuit. He could not have viewed those two candles burning but with a poetical eye."

"Has not —— a great deal of wit, Sir?" JOHNSON. "I do not think so, Sir. He is, indeed, continually attempting wit, but he fails. And I have no more pleasure in hearing a man attempting wit and failing, than in seeing a man trying to leap over a ditch and tumbling into it." . . .

I again begged his advice as to my method of study at Utrecht. "Come, (said he) let us make a day of it. Let us go down to Greenwich and dine, and talk of it there." The following Saturday was fixed for this excursion.

As we walked along the Strand to-night arm in arm, a woman of the town accosted us, in the usual enticing manner. "No, no, my girl, (said Johnson) it won't do." He, however, did not treat her with harshness, and we talked of the wretched life of such women; and agreed, that much more misery than happiness, upon the whole, is produced by illicit commerce between the sexes.

On Saturday, July 30, Dr. Johnson and I took a sculler at the Temple-stairs, and set out for Greenwich. I asked him if he really thought a knowledge of the Greek and Latin languages an essential requisite to a good education. JOHNSON. "Most certainly, Sir; for those who know them have a very great advantage over those who do not. Nay, Sir, it is wonderful what a difference learning makes upon people even in the common intercourse of life, which does not appear to be much connected with it." "And yet, (said I) people go through the world very well, and carry on the business of life to good advantage, without learning." JOHNSON. "Why, Sir, that may be true in cases where learning cannot possibly be of any use; for instance, this boy rows us as well without learning, as if he could sing the song of Orpheus to the Argonauts, who were the first sailors." He then called to the boy, "What would

10. Thompson, James Thomson, author of *The Seasons*. See page 570.

you give, my lad, to know about the Argonauts?" "Sir, (said the boy,) I would give what I have." Johnson was much pleased with his answer, and we gave him a double fare. Dr. Johnson then turning to me, "Sir, (said he,) a desire of knowledge is the natural feeling of mankind; and every human being, whose mind is not debauched, will be willing to give all that he has to get knowledge."

We landed at the Old Swan, and walked to Billingsgate, where we took oars, and moved smoothly along the silver Thames. It was a very fine day. We were entertained with the immense number and variety of ships that were lying at anchor, and with the beautiful country on each side of the river.

I talked of preaching, and of the great success which those called Methodists have. JOHNSON. "Sir, it is owing to their expressing themselves in a plain and familiar manner, which is the only way to do good to the common people, and which clergymen of genius and learning ought to do from a principle of duty, when it is suited to their congregations; a practice, for which they will be praised by men of sense. To insist against drunkenness as a crime, because it debases reason, the noblest faculty of man, would be of no service to the common people: but to tell them that they may die in a fit of drunkenness, and shew them how dreadful that would be, cannot fail to make a deep impression. Sir, when your Scotch clergy give up their homely manner, religion will soon decay in that country." Let this observation, as Johnson meant it, be ever remembered.

I was much pleased to find myself with Johnson at Greenwich, which he celebrates in his *London* as a favourite scene. I had the poem in my pocket, and read the lines aloud with enthusiasm:

"On Thames's banks in silent thought we stood:
Where Greenwich smiles upon the silver flood:
Pleased with the seat which gave ELIZA birth,
We kneel, and kiss the consecrated earth."

He remarked that the structure of Greenwich hospital was too magnificent for a place of charity, and that its parts were too much detached to make one great whole. . . .

Afterwards he entered upon the business of the day, which was to give me his advice as to a course of study. And here I am to mention with much regret, that my record of what he said is miserably scanty. I recollect with admiration an animating blaze of eloquence, which roused every intellectual power in me to the highest pitch, but must have dazzled me so much, that my memory could not preserve the substance of his discourse; for the note which I find of it is no more than this:—"He ran over the grand scale of human knowledge; advised me to select some particular branch to excel in, but to acquire a little of every kind." The defect of my minutes will be fully supplied by a long letter upon the subject which he favoured me with, after I had been some time at Utrecht, and which my readers will have the pleasure to peruse in its proper place.

We walked in the evening in Greenwich Park. He asked me, I suppose, by way of trying my disposition, "Is not this very fine?" Having no exquisite relish of the beauties of Nature, and being more delighted with "the busy hum of men," I answered, "Yes, Sir; but not equal to Fleet-street," JOHNSON. "You are right, Sir."

I am aware that many of my readers may censure my want of taste. Let me, however, shelter myself under the authority of a very fashionable Baronet in the brilliant world, who, on his attention being called to the fragrance of a May evening in the country, observed, "This may be very well; but, for my part, I prefer the smell of a flambeau at the playhouse."

We staid so long at Greenwich, that our sail up the river, in our return to London, was by no means so pleasant as in the morning; for the night air was so cold that it made me shiver. I was the more sensible of it from having sat up all the night before, recollecting and writing in my journal what I thought worthy of preservation; an exertion, which, during the first part of my acquaintance with Johnson, I frequently made. I remember having sat up four nights in one week, without being much incommoded in the day time.

Johnson, whose robust frame was not in the least affected by the cold, scolded me, as if my shivering had been a paltry effeminacy, saying, "Why do you shiver?" Sir William Scott, of the Commons, told me, that when he complained of a head-ache in the post-chaise, as they were travelling together to Scotland, Johnson treated him in the same manner: "At your age, Sir, I had no head-ache." It is not easy to make allowance for sensations in others, which we ourselves have not at the time. We must all have experienced how very differently we are affected by the complaints of our neighbours, when we are well and when we are ill. In full health, we can scarcely believe that they suffer much; so faint is the image of pain upon our imagination: when softened by sickness, we readily sympathize with the sufferings of others.

We concluded the day at the Turk's Head coffee-

13. "the busy hum of men," from Milton's "L'Allegro," l. 118.

house very socially. He was pleased to listen to a particular account which I gave him of my family, and of its hereditary estate, as to the extent and population of which he asked questions, and made calculations; recommending, at the same time, a liberal kindness to the tenantry, as people over whom the proprietor was placed by Providence. He took delight in hearing my description of the romantick seat of my ancestors. "I must be there, Sir, (said he) and we will live in the old castle; and if there is not a room in it remaining, we will build one." I was highly flattered, but could scarcely indulge a hope that Auchinleck would indeed be honoured by his presence, and celebrated by a description, as it afterwards was, in his *Journey to the Western Islands.*

After we had again talked of my setting out for Holland, he said, "I must see thee out of England; I will accompany you to Harwich." I could not find words to express what I felt upon this unexpected and very great mark of his affectionate regard.

Next day, Sunday, July 31, I told him I had been that morning at a meeting of the people called Quakers, where I had heard a woman preach. Johnson. "Sir, a woman's preaching is like a dog's walking on his hinder legs. It is not done well; but you are surprized to find it done at all."

On Tuesday, August 2, (the day of my departure from London having been fixed for the 5th,) Dr. Johnson did me the honour to pass a part of the morning with me at my Chambers. He said, that "he always felt an inclination to do nothing." I observed, that it was strange to think that the most indolent man in Britain had written the most laborious work, *The English Dictionary.*

I mentioned an imprudent publication, by a certain friend of his, at an early period of life, and asked him if he thought it would hurt him. Johnson. "No, Sir; not much. It may, perhaps, be mentioned at an election."

I had now made good my title to be a privileged man, and was carried by him in the evening to drink tea with Miss Williams, whom, though under the misfortune of having lost her sight, I found to be agreeable in conversation; for she had a variety of literature, and expressed herself well; but her peculiar value was the intimacy in which she had long lived with Johnson, by which she was well acquainted with his habits, and knew how to lead him on to talk.

After tea he carried me to what he called his walk, which was a long narrow paved court in the neighbourhood, overshadowed by some trees. There we sauntered a considerable time; and I complained to him that my love of London and of his company was such, that I shrunk almost from the thought of going away, even to travel, which is generally so much desired by young men. He roused me by manly and spirited conversation. He advised me, when settled in any place abroad, to study with an eagerness after knowledge, and to apply to Greek an hour every day; and when I was moving about, to read diligently the great book of mankind.

On Wednesday, August 3, we had our last social evening at the Turk's Head coffee-house, before my setting out for foreign parts. I had the misfortune, before we parted, to irritate him unintentionally. I mentioned to him how common it was in the world to tell absurd stories of him, and to ascribe to him very strange sayings. Johnson. "What do they make me say, Sir?" Boswell. "Why, Sir, as an instance very strange indeed, (laughing heartily as I spoke,) David Hume told me, you said that you would stand before a battery of cannon, to restore the Convocation to its full powers." Little did I apprehend that he had actually said this: but I was soon convinced of my errour; for, with a determined look, he thundered out "And would I not, Sir? Shall the Presbyterian *Kirk* of Scotland have its General Assembly, and the Church of England be denied its Convocation?" He was walking up and down the room while I told him the anecdote; but when he uttered this explosion of high-church zeal, he had come close to my chair, and his eyes flashed with indignation. I bowed to the storm, and diverted the force of it, by leading him to expatiate on the influence which religion derived from maintaining the church with great external respectability. . . .

On Friday, August 5, we set out early in the morning in the Harwich stage coach. A fat elderly gentlewoman, and a young Dutchman, seemed the most inclined among us to conversation. At the inn where we dined, the gentlewoman said that she had done her best to educate her children; and particularly, that she had never suffered them to be a moment idle. Johnson. "I wish, madam, you would educate me too; for I have been an idle fellow all my life." "I am sure, Sir, (said she) you have not been idle." Johnson. "Nay, madam, it is very true; and that gentleman there (pointing to me,) has been idle. He was idle at Edinburgh. His father sent him to Glasgow, where he continued to be idle. He then came to London, where he has been very idle; and now he is going to Utrecht, where he will be as idle as ever." I asked him privately how he could expose me so. Johnson. "Poh, poh! (said he) they knew

20. Convocation, an assembly of clergy during the meeting of Parliament. From 1717 to 1861 it was discontinued.

nothing about you, and will think of it no more." In the afternoon the gentlewoman talked violently against the Roman Catholics, and of the horrours of the Inquisition. To the utter astonishment of all the passengers but myself, who knew that he could talk upon any side of a question, he defended the Inquisition, and maintained, that "false doctrine should be checked on its first appearance; that the civil power should unite with the church in punishing those who dared to attack the established religion, and that such only were punished by the Inquisition." He had in his pocket *Pomponius Mela de situ Orbis*, in which he read occasionally, and seemed very intent upon ancient geography. Though by no means niggardly, his attention to what was generally right was so minute, that having observed at one of the stages that I ostentatiously gave a shilling to the coachman, when the custom was for each passenger to give only six-pence, he took me aside and scolded me, saying that what I had done would make the coachman dissatisfied with all the rest of the passengers, who gave him no more than his due. This was a just reprimand; for in whatever way a man may indulge his generosity or his vanity in spending his money, for the sake of others he ought not to raise the price of any article for which there is a constant demand.

He talked of Mr. Blacklock's poetry, so far as it was descriptive of visible objects; and observed, that "as its authour had the misfortune to be blind, we may be absolutely sure that such passages are combinations of what he has remembered of the works of other writers who could see. That foolish fellow, Spence, has laboured to explain philosophically how Blacklock may have done, by means of his own faculties, what it is impossible he should do. The solution, as I have given it, is plain. Suppose, I know a man to be so lame that he is absolutely incapable to move himself, and I find him in a different room from that in which I left him; shall I puzzle myself with idle conjectures, that, perhaps, his nerves have by some unknown change all at once become effective? No, Sir; it is clear how he got into a different room: he was *carried*."

Having stopped a night at Colchester, Johnson talked of that town with veneration, for having stood a siege for Charles the First. The Dutchman alone now remained with us. He spoke English tolerably well; and thinking to recommend himself to us by expatiating on the superiority of the criminal jurisprudence of this country over that of Holland, he inveighed against the barbarity of putting an accused person to the torture, in order to force a confession. But Johnson was as ready for this, as for the Inquisition. "Why, Sir, you do not, I find, understand the law of your own country. The torture in Holland is considered as a favour to an accused person; for no man is put to the torture there, unless there is as much evidence against him as would amount to conviction in England. An accused person among you, therefore, has one chance more to escape punishment, than those who are tried among us."

At supper this night he talked of good eating with uncommon satisfaction. "Some people (said he), have a foolish way of not minding, or pretending not to mind, what they eat. For my part, I mind my belly very studiously, and very carefully; for I look upon it, that he who does not mind his belly will hardly mind anything else." He now appeared to me *Jean Bull philosophe*, and he was, for the moment, not only serious but vehement. Yet I have heard him, upon other occasions, talk with great contempt of people who were anxious to gratify their palates; and the 206th number of his *Rambler* is a masterly essay against gulosity. His practice, indeed, I must acknowledge, may be considered as casting the balance of his different opinions upon this subject; for I never knew any man who relished good eating more than he did. When at table, he was totally absorbed in the business of the moment; his looks seemed rivetted to his plate; nor would he, unless when in very high company, say one word, or even pay the least attention to what was said by others, till he had satisfied his appetite, which was so fierce, and indulged with such intenseness, that while in the act of eating, the veins of his forehead swelled, and generally a strong perspiration was visible. To those whose sensations were delicate, this could not but be disgusting; and it was doubtless not very suitable to the character of a philosopher, who should be distinguished by self-command. But it must be owned, that Johnson, though he could be rigidly *abstemious*, was not a *temperate* man either in eating or drinking. He could refrain, but he could not use moderately. He told me, that he had fasted two days without inconvenience, and that he had never been hungry but once. They who beheld with wonder how much he eat upon all occasions when his dinner was to his taste, could not easily conceive what he must have meant by hunger; and not only was he remarkable for the extraordinary quantity which he eat, but he was, or affected to be, a man of

12. Pomponius Mela, the earliest Roman geographer, born in the first century, A.D. **28. Mr. Blacklock,** Thomas Blacklock (1721–1791), a blind Scottish poet. **34. Spence,** Joseph Spence (1699–1788), author of a valuable collection of anecdotes about his literary contemporaries.

26. gulosity, greediness.

very nice discernment in the science of cookery. He used to descant critically on the dishes which had been at table where he had dined or supped, and to recollect very minutely what he had liked. I remember, when he was in Scotland, his praising "*Gordon's palates*," (a dish of palates at the Honourable Alexander Gordon's) with a warmth of expression which might have done honour to more important subjects. "As for Maclaurin's imitation of a *made dish*, it was a wretched attempt." He about the same time was so much displeased with the performances of a nobleman's French cook, that he exclaimed with vehemence, "I'd throw such a rascal into the river"; and he then proceeded to alarm a lady at whose house he was to sup, by the following manifesto of his skill: "I, Madam, who live at a variety of good tables, am a much better judge of cookery, than any person who has a very tolerable cook, but lives much at home; for his palate is gradually adapted to the taste of his cook; whereas, Madam, in trying by a wider range, I can more exquisitely judge." When invited to dine, even with an intimate friend, he was not pleased if something better than a plain dinner was not prepared for him. I have heard him say on such an occasion, "This was a good dinner enough, to be sure; but it was not a dinner to *ask* a man to." On the other hand, he was wont to express, with great glee, his satisfaction when he had been entertained quite to his mind. One day when we had dined with his neighbour and landlord in Bolt-court, Mr. Allen, the printer, whose old housekeeper had studied his taste in every thing, he pronounced this eulogy: "Sir, we could not have had a better dinner had there been a *Synod of Cooks*."

While we were left by ourselves, after the Dutchman had gone to bed, Dr. Johnson talked of that studied behaviour which many have recommended and practised. He disapproved of it; and said, "I never considered whether I should be a grave man, or a merry man, but just let inclination, for the time, have its course."

He flattered me with some hopes that he would, in the course of the following summer, come over to Holland, and accompany me in a tour through the Netherlands.

I teased him with fanciful apprehensions of unhappiness. A moth having fluttered round the candle, and burnt itself, he laid hold of this little incident to admonish me; saying, with a sly look, and in a solemn but quiet tone, "That creature was its own tormentor, and I believe its name was Boswell."

Next day we got to Harwich to dinner; and my passage in the packet-boat to Helvoetsluys being secured, and my baggage put on board, we dined at our inn by ourselves. I happened to say it would be terrible if he should not find a speedy opportunity of returning to London, and be confined to so dull a place. Johnson. "Don't, Sir, accustom yourself to use big words for little matters. It would *not* be *terrible*, though I *were* to be detained some time here." The practice of using words of disproportionate magnitude, is, no doubt, too frequent everywhere; but, I think, most remarkable among the French, of which, all who have travelled in France must have been struck with innumerable instances.

We went and looked at the church, and having gone into it and walked up to the altar, Johnson, whose piety was constant and fervent, sent me to my knees, saying "Now that you are going to leave your native country, recommend yourself to the protection of your Creator and Redeemer."

After we came out of the church, we stood talking for some time together of Bishop Berkeley's ingenious sophistry to prove the non-existence of matter, and that every thing in the universe is merely ideal. I observed, that though we are satisfied his doctrine is not true, it is impossible to refute it. I shall never forget the alacrity with which Johnson answered, striking his foot with mighty force against a large stone, till he rebounded from it, "I refute it *thus*." This was a stout exemplification of the *first truths* of Père Bouffier, or the *original principles* of Reid and of Beattie; without admitting which, we can no more argue in metaphysicks, than we can argue in mathematicks without axioms. To me it is not conceivable how Berkeley can be answered by pure reasoning; but I know that the nice and difficult task was to have been undertaken by one of the most luminous minds of the present age, had not politics "turned him from calm philosophy aside." What an admirable display of subtilty, united with brilliance, might his contending with Berkeley have afforded us! How must we, when we reflect on the loss of such an intellectual feast, regret that he should be characterized as the man,

"Who born for the universe narrowed his mind,
And to party gave up what was meant for mankind?"

My revered friend walked down with me to the beach, where we embraced and parted with tenderness, and engaged to correspond by letters. I said, "I hope, Sir, you will not forget me in my absence."

28. Bouffier, Claude Buffier (1661–1737), author of a treatise on the source of our judgments. **43–45. "Who . . . mankind?"** from Goldsmith's poem "Retaliation," with reference to Edmund Burke.

JOHNSON. "Nay, Sir, it is more likely you should forget me, than that I should forget you." As the vessel put out to sea, I kept my eyes upon him for a considerable time, while he remained rolling his majestick frame in his usual manner: and at last I perceived him walk back into the town, and he disappeared. . . .

Oliver Goldsmith
1728–1774

Goldsmith was born in the Athlone district of central Ireland, the son of a poor Protestant vicar whose character the poet has portrayed in *The Deserted Village*. He spent his childhood in the village of Lissoy. After graduating in 1749, with great difficulty, at Trinity College, Dublin, where he had been sent by an uncle, he thought at first of taking holy orders. He failed in this, tradition tells us, because the scarlet breeches in which he presented himself before the bishop who was to examine him were not thought to indicate a seriously religious turn of mind. A year or so later he abandoned the tutorial position he had somehow gained, in order to spend the small sum of money that was burning in his pocket. Next, with funds provided by his uncle, he started off for London with the intention of studying law, but got only as far as Dublin, where gamblers relieved him of his money and thus turned him away from a legal career. In 1753 he went to Edinburgh with some thought of studying medicine, and in the following year proceeded to Leyden with the same vague purpose. From there, playing his flute and debating in the universities for a livelihood, he drifted through Flanders, France, Germany, Switzerland, and Italy, making the "grand tour" on foot. At some time and place during these wandering years he seems to have acquired a medical degree. The year 1756 found him in London, working now as an apothecary's assistant, now as an usher in a school, and occasionally as a physician among the poor.

Goldsmith as late as 1759 was still thinking of going out as a doctor to the Coast of Coromandel, but in that year, he began to do steady work as a writer. His first important publication was a brisk and good-humored attack upon the strongholds of scholarship entitled *An Enquiry into the Present State of Polite Learning in Europe*, 1759. In 1762 his series of essays entitled *The Citizen of the World* appeared, and he began to achieve a reputation and a degree of freedom from penury. During the next year he became one of the nine charter members of Dr. Johnson's famous literary club. In 1764 he published his poem *The Traveller*, which was followed two years later by a novel, *The Vicar of Wakefield*. At further two-year intervals came the first of his two plays, *The Good-Natured Man*, 1768, and his poem *The Deserted Village*, 1770. In 1773 his comedy *She Stoops to Conquer* was produced successfully, and in 1774, the year of his death, came his last important work, the poem *Retaliation*, one of the most brilliant of eighteenth-century satires.

It is evident that Goldsmith had remarkable powers of concentrated application, for in the fourteen years of life that were left to him when he settled down in London he not only wrote, translated, and compiled a surprising number of "potboilers" such as his eight-volume *History of the Earth and Animated Nature*, but he attained almost the highest rank among the writers of his time in the widely sundered fields of the essay, the novel, comedy, and poetry. Few writers in the whole stretch of English literature have shown a versatility comparable with his, and yet the assertion of his friend Dr. Johnson that he touched nothing which he did not adorn is certainly true.

This record is the more remarkable because Goldsmith wrote always for money. His improvident habits kept him continually in debt to the booksellers for whom he wrote, and although he earned considerable sums, he never escaped from the laborious slavery of the hack writer in "Grub Street." Yet, during all the years in which he held starvation at bay with the point of his quill, Goldsmith somehow preserved the good-natured ease of a man who writes chiefly for his own pleasure, and consequently for the pleasure of others. He continued to be a "rolling stone" throughout his writing career, turning easily from verse to prose, from biography to criticism, from science to travel, and from sentiment to comedy. Thus in the midst of highly professional labors he maintained all the advantages of the cool and detached amateur. The miscellaneous information that he scraped together on a thousand topics never amounted to learning and so was never a burden. No cloud of weariness or anxiety ever dimmed the sunshine of his mind. It was by means of his warm humanity, his gifts of the heart, his embracing sympathy or fellow feeling, that he won the friendship of Bishop Percy, Dr. Johnson, Edmund Burke, and Sir Joshua Reynolds. This it was, also, that endeared him to hundreds of forgotten people to whom he was kind. His simple, clear, gracious, and always musical prose style mirrors his generous nature. If he is seldom profound, he is never tedious; and if he adds little to our knowledge and wisdom, at any rate he takes nothing from our sense of the goodness of life.

from THE CITIZEN OF THE WORLD

The essays in the series entitled *The Citizen of the World* were published during 1760 and 1761 in a newspaper, *The Public Ledger*. They purported to be letters written by a Chinese philosopher visiting in London, describing to friends in the Orient the strange customs of the English. They took their place in the tradition of the periodical essay begun by Addison and Steele in *The Spectator*, and established Goldsmith's fame as one of the most genial and charming of English essayists.

LETTER XXI

[*The Chinese Goes to See a Play*]

The English are as fond of seeing plays acted as the Chinese; but there is a vast difference in the manner of conducting them. We play our pieces in the open air, the English theirs under cover; we act by daylight, they by the blaze of torches. One of our plays continues eight or ten days successively, an English piece seldom takes up above four hours in the representation.

My companion in black, with whom I am now beginning to contract an intimacy, introduced me a few nights ago to the play-house, where we placed ourselves conveniently at the foot of the stage. As the curtain was not drawn before my arrival, I had an opportunity of observing the behaviour of the spectators, and indulging those reflections which novelty generally inspires.

The rich in general were placed in the lowest seats, and the poor rose above them in degrees proportioned to their poverty. The order of precedence seemed here inverted; those who were undermost all the day, now enjoyed a temporary eminence, and became masters of the ceremonies. It was they who called for the music, indulging every noisy freedom, and testifying all the insolence of beggary in exaltation.

They who held the middle region seemed not so riotous as those above them, nor yet so tame as those below; to judge by their looks, many of them seemed strangers there as well as myself. They were chiefly employed during this period of expectation in eating oranges, reading the story of the play, or making assignations.

Those who sat in the lowest rows, which are called the pit, seemed to consider themselves as judges of the merit of the poet and the performers; they were assembled partly to be amused, and partly to show their taste; appearing to labour under that restraint which an affectation of superior discernment generally produces. My companion, however, informed me, that not one in an hundred of them knew even the first principles of criticism; that they assumed the right of being censors because there was none to contradict their pretensions; and that every man who now called himself a connoisseur, became such to all intents and purposes.

Those who sat in the boxes appeared in the most unhappy situation of all. The rest of the audience came merely for their own amusement; these rather to furnish out a part of the entertainment themselves. I could not avoid considering them as acting parts in dumb show, not a curtsy or nod, that was not the result of art; not a look nor a smile that was not designed for murder. Gentlemen and ladies ogled each other through spectacles; for my companion observed, that blindness was of late become fashionable: all affected indifference and ease, while their hearts at the same time burned for conquest. Upon the whole, the lights, the music, the ladies in their gayest dresses, the men with cheerfulness and expectation in their looks, all conspired to make a most agreeable picture, and to fill an heart that sympathises at human happiness with an expressible serenity.

The expected time for the play to begin at last arrived, the curtain was drawn, and the actors came on. A woman, who personated a queen, came in curtsying to the audience, who clapped their hands upon her appearance. Clapping of hands is, it seems, the manner of applauding in England: the manner is absurd; but every country, you know, has its peculiar absurdities. I was equally

43. companion in black, an English gentleman whom the Chinese had met while visiting Westminster Abbey.

surprised, however, at the submission of the actress, who should have considered herself as a queen, as at the little discernment of the audience who gave her such marks of applause before she attempted to deserve them. Preliminaries between her and the audience being thus adjusted, the dialogue was supported between her and a most hopeful youth, who acted the part of her confidant. They both appeared in extreme distress, for it seems the queen had lost a child some fifteen years before, and still keeps its dear resemblance next her heart, while her kind companion bore a part in her sorrows.

Her lamentations grew loud. Comfort is offered, but she detests the very sound. She bids them preach comfort to the winds. Upon this her husband comes in, who seeing the queen so much afflicted, can himself hardly refrain from tears or avoid partaking in the soft distress. After thus grieving through three scenes, the curtain dropped for the first act.

Truly, said I to my companion, these kings and queens are very much disturbed at no very great misfortune; certain I am were people of humbler stations to act in this manner, they would be thought divested of common sense. I had scarce finished this observation, when the curtain rose, and the king came on in a violent passion. His wife had, it seems, refused his proffered tenderness, had spurned his royal embrace; and he seemed resolved not to survive her fierce disdain. After he had thus fretted, and the queen had fretted through the second act, the curtain was let down once more.

Now, says my companion, you perceive the king to be a man of spirit, he feels at every pore; one of your phlegmatic sons of clay would have given the queen her own way, and let her come to herself by degrees; but the king is for immediate tenderness, or instant death: death and tenderness are leading passions of every modern buskined hero; this moment they embrace, and the next stab, mixing daggers and kisses in every period.

I was going to second his remarks, when my attention was engrossed by a new object; a man came in balancing a straw upon his nose, and the audience were clapping their hands in all the raptures of applause. To what purpose, cried I, does this unmeaning figure make his appearance; is he a part of the plot? Unmeaning do you call him, replied my friend in black; this is one of the most important characters of the whole play; nothing pleases the people more than the seeing a straw balanced; there is a great deal of meaning in the straw; there is something suited to every apprehension in the sight; and a fellow possessed of talents like these is sure of making his fortune.

The third act now began with an actor, who came to inform us that he was the villain of the play, and intended to show strange things before all was over. He was joined by another, who seemed as much disposed for mischief as he; their intrigues continued through this whole division. If that be a villain, said I, he must be a very stupid one, to tell his secrets without being asked; such soliloquies of late are never admitted in China.

The noise of clapping interrupted me once more; a child of six years old was learning to dance on the stage, which gave the ladies and mandarines infinite satisfaction. I am sorry, said I, to see the pretty creature so early learning so very bad a trade. Dancing being, I presume, as contemptible here as in China. Quite the reverse, interrupted my companion; dancing is a very reputable and genteel employment here; men have a greater chance for encouragement from the merit of their heels than their heads. One who jumps up and flourishes his toes three times before he comes to the ground, may have three hundred a year; he who flourishes them four times, gets four hundred; but he who arrives at five is inestimable, and may demand what salary he thinks proper. The female dancers too are valued for this sort of jumping and crossing; and 'tis a cant word among them, that she deserves most who shews highest. But the fourth act is begun, let us be attentive.

In the fourth act the queen finds her long-lost child, now grown up into a youth of smart parts, and great qualifications; wherefore she wisely considers that the crown will fit his head better than that of her husband, whom she knows to be a driveler. The king discovers her design, and here comes on the deep distress; he loves the queen, and he loves the kingdom; he resolves therefore, in order to possess both, that her son must die. The queen exclaims at his barbarity; is frantic with rage, and at length overcome with sorrow, falls into a fit; upon which the curtain drops, and the act is concluded.

Observe the art of the poet, cries my companion; when the queen can say no more, she falls into a fit. While thus her eyes are shut, while she is supported in the arms of Abigail, what horrors do we not fancy. We feel it in every nerve; take my word for it, that fits are the true aposiopesis of modern tragedy.

48. Abigail, a generic name for a lady's maid. **50. aposiopesis,** an abrupt halt in a discourse, generally for rhetorical effect.

The fifth act began, and a busy piece it was. Scenes shifting, trumpets sounding, mobs hallooing, carpets spreading, guards bustling from one door to another; gods, daemons, daggers, racks and ratsbane. But whether the king was killed, or the queen was drowned, or the son was poisoned, I have absolutely forgotten.

When the play was over, I could not avoid observing, that the persons of the drama appeared in as much distress in the first act as the last: how is it possible, said I, to sympathise with them through five long acts; pity is but a short-lived passion; I hate to hear an actor mouthing trifles, neither startings, strainings, nor attitudes affect me unless there be cause: after I have been once or twice deceived by those unmeaning alarms, my heart sleeps in peace, probably unaffected by the principal distress. There should be one great passion aimed at by the actor as well as the poet, all the rest should be subordinate, and only contribute to make that the greater; if the actor therefore exclaims upon every occasion in the tones of despair, he attempts to move us too soon; he anticipates the blow, he ceases to affect though he gains our applause.

I scarce perceived that the audience were almost all departed; wherefore mixing with the crowd, my companion and I got into the street; where essaying an hundred obstacles from coach wheels and palanquin poles, like birds in their flight through the branches of a forest, after various turnings, we both at length got home in safety.

Adieu.

LETTER CXVII

[*City Night Piece*]

The clock just struck two, the expiring taper rises and sinks in the socket, the watchman forgets the hour in slumber, the laborious and the happy, are at rest, and nothing wakes but meditation, guilt, revelry, and despair. The drunkard once more fills the destroying bowl, the robber walks his midnight round, and the suicide lifts his guilty arm against his own sacred person. . . .

What a gloom hangs all around; the dying lamp feebly emits a yellow gleam, no sound is heard but of the chiming clock, or the distant watch-dog. All the bustle of human pride is forgotten, an hour like this may well display the emptiness of human vanity. . . .

What cities, as great as this, have once triumphed in existence, had their victories as great, joy as just, and as unbounded, and with short sighted presumption, promised themselves immortality. Posterity can hardly trace the situation of some. The sorrowful traveller wanders over the awful ruins of others; and as he beholds, he learns wisdom, and feels the transience of every sublunary possession.

Here, he cries, stood their citadel, now grown over with weeds; there their senate-house, but now the haunt of every noxious reptile; temples and theatres stood here, now only an undistinguished heap of ruin. They are fallen, for luxury and avarice first made them feeble. The rewards of state were conferred on amusing, and not on useful, members of society. Their riches and opulence invited the invaders, who though at first repulsed, returned again, conquered by perseverance, and at last swept the defendants into undistinguished destruction. . . .

But who are those who make the streets their couch, and find a short repose from wretchedness at the doors of the opulent? These are strangers, wanderers, and orphans, whose circumstances are too humble to expect redress, and whose distresses are too great even for pity. Their wretchedness excites rather horror than pity. Some are without the covering even of rags, and others emaciated with disease; the world has disclaimed them; society turns its back upon their distress, and has given them up to nakedness and hunger. These poor shivering females have once seen happier days, and been flattered into beauty. They have been prostituted to the gay luxurious villain, and are now turned out to meet the severity of winter. Perhaps, now lying at the doors of their betrayers, they sue to wretches whose hearts are insensible, or debauchees who may curse, but will not relieve them.

Why, why was I born a man, and yet see the suffering of wretches I cannot relieve! Poor houseless creatures! the world will give you reproaches, but will not give you relief. The slightest misfortunes of the great, the most imaginary uneasiness of the rich, are aggravated with all the power of eloquence, and held up to engage our attention and sympathetic sorrow. The poor weep unheeded, persecuted by every subordinate species of tyranny; and every law, which gives others security, becomes an enemy to them.

Why was this heart of mine formed with so much sensibility! or why was not my fortune adapted to its impulse! Tenderness, without a capacity of relieving, only makes the man who feels it more wretched than the object which sues for assistance.

Adieu.

THE DESERTED VILLAGE

This didactic poem—published in 1770, the year of Wordsworth's birth—went through five editions in its first twelvemonth. Evidently, therefore, it expressed a mood in which many shared, as its great companion piece, Gray's *Elegy*, had done nineteen years before.

In some degree *The Deserted Village* is autobiographical, resting back upon Goldsmith's recollections of his childhood in the village of Lissoy in Ireland. The "Auburn" of the poem is, however, more of an English than an Irish village. Far more important in it, however, is the poet's firsthand knowledge of contemporary conditions in the ancient villages of England, where the Enclosure Acts and the Industrial Revolution were in his time swiftly destroying a pattern of life which had endured for more than a thousand years.

In his dedication of the poem to Sir Joshua Reynolds, Goldsmith declares: "I have taken all possible pains in my country excursions, for these four or five years past, to be certain of what I allege." These "country excursions" are reflected in the poem in the pictures of rural life and scenery and in the poet's generous sympathy with the village folk.

Sweet AUBURN! loveliest village of the plain,
Where health and plenty cheered the labouring swain,
Where smiling spring its earliest visit paid,
And parting summer's lingering blooms delayed:
Dear lovely bowers of innocence and ease,
Seats of my youth, when every sport could please,
How often have I loitered o'er thy green,
Where humble happiness endeared each scene;
How often have I paused on every charm,
The sheltered cot, the cultivated farm,
The never-failing brook, the busy mill,
The decent church that topped the neighbouring hill,
The hawthorn bush, with seats beneath the shade,
For talking age and whispering lovers made;
How often have I blessed the coming day,
When toil remitting lent its turn to play,
And all the village train, from labour free,
Led up their sports beneath the spreading tree;
While many a pastime circled in the shade,
The young contending as the old surveyed;
And many a gambol frolicked o'er the ground,
And sleights of art and feats of strength went round;
And still, as each repeated pleasure tired,
Succeeding sports the mirthful band inspired;
The dancing pair that simply sought renown,
By holding out to tire each other down;
The swain mistrustless of his smutted face,
While secret laughter tittered round the place;
The bashful virgin's side-long looks of love,
The matron's glance that would those looks reprove:
These were thy charms, sweet village; sports like these,
With sweet succession taught even toil to please;
These round thy bowers their cheerful influence shed,
These were thy charms—but all these charms are fled.

Sweet smiling village, loveliest of the lawn,
Thy sports are fled, and all thy charms withdrawn;
Amidst thy bowers the tyrant's hand is seen,
And desolation saddens all thy green:
One only master grasps the whole domain,
And half a tillage stints thy smiling plain.
No more thy glassy brook reflects the day,
But choked with sedges, works its weedy way.
Along thy glades, a solitary guest,
The hollow-sounding bittern guards its nest;
Amidst thy desert walks the lapwing flies,
And tires their echoes with unvaried cries.
Sunk are thy bowers in shapeless ruin all,
And the long grass o'ertops the mouldering wall;
And, trembling, shrinking from the spoiler's hand,
Far, far away, thy children leave the land.

Ill fares the land, to hastening ills a prey,
Where wealth accumulates and men decay;
Princes and lords may flourish, or may fade;
A breath can make them, as a breath has made;
But a bold peasantry, their country's pride,
When once destroyed, can never be supplied.

A time there was, ere England's griefs began,
When every rood of ground maintained its man;
For him light labour spread her wholesome store,
Just gave what life required, but gave no more:
His best companions, innocence and health;
And his best riches, ignorance of wealth.

But times are altered; trade's unfeeling train
Usurp the land, and dispossess the swain;
Along the lawn, where scattered hamlets rose,
Unwieldy wealth and cumbrous pomp repose;
And every want to opulence allied,
And every pang that folly pays to pride.
Those gentle hours that plenty bade to bloom,

Those calm desires that asked but little room,
Those healthful sports that graced the peaceful scene,
Lived in each look, and brightened all the green;
These, far departing, seek a kinder shore,
And rural mirth and manners are no more.

Sweet AUBURN! parent of the blissful hour,
Thy glades forlorn confess the tyrant's power.
Here, as I take my solitary rounds,
Amidst thy tangling walks, and ruined grounds,
And, many a year elapsed, return to view
Where once the cottage stood, the hawthorn grew,
Remembrance wakes with all her busy train,
Swells at my breast, and turns the past to pain.

In all my wanderings round this world of care,
In all my griefs—and GOD has given my share—
I still had hopes my latest hours to crown,
Amidst these humble bowers to lay me down;
To husband out life's taper at the close,
And keep the flame from wasting by repose.
I still had hopes, for pride attends us still,
Amidst the swains to show my book-learned skill,
Around my fire an evening group to draw,
And tell of all I felt, and all I saw;
And, as a hare, whom hounds and horns pursue,
Pants to the place from whence at first she flew,
I still had hopes, my long vexations passed,
Here to return—and die at home at last.

O blest retirement, friend to life's decline,
Retreats from care, that never must be mine,
How happy he who crowns in shades like these
A youth of labour with an age of ease;
Who quits a world where strong temptations try,
And, since 'tis hard to combat, learns to fly!
For him no wretches, born to work and weep,
Explore the mine, or tempt the dangerous deep;
No surly porter stands in guilty state
To spurn imploring famine from the gate;
But on he moves to meet his latter end,
Angels around befriending virtue's friend;
Bends to the grave with unperceived decay,
While resignation gently slopes the way;
And, all his prospects brightening to the last,
His Heaven commences ere the world be past!

Sweet was the sound, when oft at evening's close
Up yonder hill the village murmur rose;
There, as I passed with careless steps and slow,
The mingling notes came softened from below;
The swain responsive as the milk-maid sung,
The sober herd that lowed to meet their young;
The noisy geese that gabbled o'er the pool,
The playful children just let loose from school;
The watchdog's voice that bayed the whispering wind,
And the loud laugh that spoke the vacant mind;
These all in sweet confusion sought the shade,
And filled each pause the nightingale had made.
But now the sounds of population fail,
No cheerful murmurs fluctuate in the gale,
No busy steps the grass-grown foot-way tread,
For all the bloomy flush of life is fled.
All but yon widowed, solitary thing
That feebly bends beside the plashy spring;
She, wretched matron, forced, in age, for bread,
To strip the brook with mantling cresses spread,
To pick her wintry faggot from the thorn,
To seek her nightly shed, and weep till morn;
She only left of all the harmless train,
The sad historian of the pensive plain.

Near yonder copse, where once the garden smiled,
And still where many a garden flower grows wild;
There, where a few torn shrubs the place disclose,
The village preacher's modest mansion rose.
A man he was to all the country dear,
And passing rich with forty pounds a year;
Remote from towns he ran his godly race,
Nor e'er had changed, nor wished to change his place;
Unpractised he to fawn, or seek for power,
By doctrines fashioned to the varying hour;
Far other aims his heart had learned to prize,
More skilled to raise the wretched than to rise.
His house was known to all the vagrant train,
He chid their wanderings, but relieved their pain;
The long-remembered beggar was his guest,
Whose beard descending swept his aged breast;
The ruined spendthrift, now no longer proud,
Claimed kindred there, and had his claims allowed;
The broken soldier, kindly bade to stay,
Sat by his fire and talked the night away;
Wept o'er his wounds, or tales of sorrow done,
Shouldered his crutch, and showed how fields were won.
Pleased with his guests, the good man learned to glow,
And quite forgot their vices in their woe;
Careless their merits, or their faults to scan,
His pity gave ere charity began.

122. vacant, carefree.

Thus to relieve the wretched was his pride,
And even his failings leaned to Virtue's side;
But in his duty prompt at every call,
He watched and wept, he prayed and felt, for all.
And, as a bird each fond endearment tries
To tempt its new-fledged offspring to the skies,
He tried each art, reproved each dull delay,
Allured to brighter worlds, and led the way.

Beside the bed where parting life was laid,
And sorrow, guilt, and pain, by turns dismayed,
The reverend champion stood. At his control
Despair and anguish fled the struggling soul;
Comfort came down the trembling wretch to raise,
And his last faltering accents whispered praise.

At church, with meek and unaffected grace,
His looks adorned the venerable place;
Truth from his lips prevailed with double sway,
And fools, who came to scoff, remained to pray.
The service passed, around the pious man,
With steady zeal, each honest rustic ran;
Even children followed, with endearing wile,
And plucked his gown, to share the good man's smile.
His ready smile a parent's warmth expressed,
Their welfare pleased him and their cares distressed;
To them his heart, his love, his griefs were given,
But all his serious thoughts had rest in Heaven.
As some tall cliff that lifts its awful form,
Swells from the vale, and midway leaves the storm,
Though round its breast the rolling clouds are spread,
Eternal sunshine settles on its head.

Beside yon straggling fence that skirts the way,
With blossomed furze unprofitably gay,
There, in his noisy mansion, skilled to rule,
The village master taught his little school;
A man severe he was, and stern to view;
I knew him well, and every truant knew;
Well had the boding tremblers learned to trace
The day's disasters in his morning face;
Full well they laughed, with counterfeited glee,
At all his jokes, for many a joke had he;
Full well the busy whisper, circling round,
Conveyed the dismal tidings when he frowned;
Yet he was kind; or, if severe in aught,
The love he bore to learning was in fault;
The village all declared how much he knew;
'Twas certain he could write, and cypher too;
Lands he could measure, terms and tides presage,
And even the story ran that he could gauge.
In arguing too, the parson owned his skill,
For even though vanquished, he could argue still;
While words of learned length and thundering sound
Amazed the gazing rustics ranged around;
And still they gazed, and still the wonder grew,
That one small head could carry all he knew.

But past is all his fame. The very spot
Where many a time he triumphed, is forgot.
Near yonder thorn, that lifts its head on high,
Where once the sign-post caught the passing eye,
Low lies that house where nut-brown draughts inspired,
Where grey-beard mirth and smiling toil retired,
Where village statesmen talked with looks profound,
And news much older than their ale went round.
Imagination fondly stoops to trace
The parlour splendours of that festive place;
The white-washed wall, the nicely sanded floor,
The varnished clock that clicked behind the door;
The chest contrived a double debt to pay,
A bed by night, a chest of drawers by day;
The pictures placed for ornament and use,
The twelve good rules, the royal game of goose;
The hearth, except when winter chilled the day,
With aspen boughs, and flowers, and fennel gay;
While broken tea-cups, wisely kept for shew,
Ranged o'er the chimney, glistened in a row.

Vain transitory splendours! Could not all
Reprieve the tottering mansion from its fall?
Obscure it sinks, nor shall it more impart
An hour's importance to the poor man's heart;
Thither no more the peasant shall repair
To sweet oblivion of his daily care;
No more the farmer's news, the barber's tale,
No more the wood-man's ballad shall prevail;
No more the smith his dusky brow shall clear,
Relax his ponderous strength, and lean to hear;
The host himself no longer shall be found
Careful to see the mantling bliss go round;
Nor the coy maid, half willing to be pressed,
Shall kiss the cup to pass it to the rest.

Yes! let the rich deride, the proud disdain,
These simple blessings of the lowly train;
To me more dear, congenial to my heart,
One native charm, than all the gloss of art;

209. **terms,** periods in which courts of justice held daily sessions.

210. **gauge,** calculate the capacity of vessels. 232. **rules,** of conduct, often hung up in taverns. They were attributed to Charles I. **goose,** a game somewhat like pachisi.

Spontaneous joys, where Nature has its play,
The soul adopts, and owns their first-born sway;
Lightly they frolic o'er the vacant mind,
Unenvied, unmolested, unconfined.
But the long pomp, the midnight masquerade,
With all the freaks of wanton wealth arrayed,
In these, ere triflers half their wish obtain,
The toiling pleasure sickens into pain;
And even while fashion's brightest arts decoy,
The heart distrusting asks, if this be joy.

Ye friends to truth, ye statesmen, who survey
The rich man's joys increase, the poor's decay,
'Tis yours to judge how wide the limits stand
Between a splendid and a happy land.
Proud swells the tide with loads of freighted ore,
And shouting Folly hails them from her shore;
Hoards, even beyond the miser's wish abound,
And rich men flock from all the world around.
Yet count our gains. This wealth is but a name
That leaves our useful products still the same.
Not so the loss. The man of wealth and pride
Takes up a space that many poor supplied;
Space for his lake, his park's extended bounds,
Space for his horses, equipage, and hounds;
The robe that wraps his limbs in silken sloth
Has robbed the neighbouring fields of half their growth;
His seat, where solitary sports are seen,
Indignant spurns the cottage from the green;
Around the world each needful product flies,
For all the luxuries the world supplies:
While thus the land adorned for pleasure, all
In barren splendour feebly waits the fall.

As some fair female unadorned and plain,
Secure to please while youth confirms her reign,
Slights every borrowed charm that dress supplies,
Nor shares with art the triumph of her eyes;
But when those charms are passed, for charms are frail,
When time advances, and when lovers fail,
She then shines forth, solicitous to bless,
In all the glaring impotence of dress:
Thus fares the land, by luxury betrayed,
In nature's simplest charms at first arrayed;
But verging to decline, its splendours rise,
Its vistas strike, its palaces surprise;
While scourged by famine from the smiling land,
The mournful peasant leads his humble band;
And while he sinks, without one arm to save,
The country blooms—a garden, and a grave.

Where then, ah! where, shall poverty reside,
To 'scape the pressure of contiguous pride?
If to some common's fenceless limits strayed,
He drives his flock to pick the scanty blade,
Those fenceless fields the sons of wealth divide,
And even the bare-worn common is denied.

If to the city sped—what waits him there?
To see profusion that he must not share;
To see ten thousand baneful arts combined
To pamper luxury, and thin mankind;
To see those joys the sons of pleasure know
Extorted from his fellow-creature's woe.
Here while the courtier glitters in brocade,
There the pale artist plies the sickly trade;
Here while the proud their long-drawn pomps display,
There the black gibbet glooms beside the way;
The dome where Pleasure holds her midnight reign,
Here, richly decked, admits the gorgeous train;
Tumultuous grandeur crowds the blazing square,
The rattling chariots clash, the torches glare.
Sure scenes like these no troubles e'er annoy!
Sure these denote one universal joy!
Are these thy serious thoughts?—Ah, turn thine eyes
Where the poor houseless shivering female lies.
She once, perhaps, in village plenty blessed,
Has wept at tales of innocence distressed;
Her modest looks the cottage might adorn,
Sweet as the primrose peeps beneath the thorn;
Now lost to all; her friends, her virtue fled,
Near her betrayer's door she lays her head,
And, pinched with cold, and shrinking from the shower,
With heavy heart deplores that luckless hour,
When idly first, ambitious of the town,
She left her wheel and robes of country brown.

Do thine, sweet AUBURN, thine, the loveliest train,
Do thy fair tribes participate her pain?
Even now, perhaps, by cold and hunger led,
At proud men's doors they ask a little bread!

Ah, no. To distant climes, a dreary scene,
Where half the convex world intrudes between,
Through torrid tracts with fainting steps they go,
Where wild Altama murmurs to their woe.
Far different there from all that charmed before,
The various terrors of that horrid shore;
Those blazing suns that dart a downward ray,
And fiercely shed intolerable day;

316. artist, artisan, craftsman. **344. Altama,** the Altamaha river, in Georgia. Details of the following passage were probably drawn from the talk of General Oglethorpe, founder of Georgia, with whom Goldsmith was acquainted.

Those matted woods where birds forget to sing,
But silent bats in drowsy clusters cling;
Those poisonous fields with rank luxuriance crowned,
Where the dark scorpion gathers death around;
Where at each step the stranger fears to wake
The rattling terrors of the vengeful snake;
Where crouching tigers wait their hapless prey,
And savage men more murderous still than they;
While oft in whirls the mad tornado flies,
Mingling the ravaged landscape with the skies.
Far different these from every former scene,
The cooling brook, the grassy-vested green,
The breezy covert of the warbling grove,
That only sheltered thefts of harmless love.

Good Heaven! what sorrows gloomed that parting day
That called them from their native walks away;
When the poor exiles, every pleasure past,
Hung round their bowers, and fondly looked their last,
And took a long farewell, and wished in vain
For seats like these beyond the western main;
And shuddering still to face the distant deep,
Returned and wept, and still returned to weep.
The good old sire the first prepared to go
To new-found worlds, and wept for others' woe;
But for himself, in conscious virtue brave,
He only wished for worlds beyond the grave.
His lovely daughter, lovelier in her tears,
The fond companion of his helpless years,
Silent went next, neglectful of her charms,
And left a lover's for a father's arms.
With louder plaints the mother spoke her woes,
And blessed the cot where every pleasure rose,
And kissed her thoughtless babes with many a tear,
And clasped them close, in sorrow doubly dear;
Whilst her fond husband strove to lend relief
In all the silent manliness of grief.

O Luxury! thou cursed by Heaven's decree,
How ill exchanged are things like these for thee!
How do thy potions, with insidious joy,
Diffuse their pleasures only to destroy!
Kingdoms by thee, to sickly greatness grown,
Boast of a florid vigour not their own;
At every draught more large and large they grow,
A bloated mass of rank, unwieldy woe;
Till sapped their strength, and every part unsound,
Down, down they sink, and spread a ruin round.

Even now the devastation is begun,
And half the business of destruction done;
Even now, methinks, as pondering here I stand,
I see the rural virtues leave the land:
Down where yon anchoring vessel spreads the sail,
That idly waiting flaps with every gale,
Downward they move, a melancholy band,
Pass from the shore, and darken all the strand.
Contented toil, and hospitable care,
And kind connubial tenderness are there;
And piety with wishes placed above,
And steady loyalty, and faithful love.
And thou, sweet Poetry, thou loveliest maid,
Still first to fly where sensual joys invade,
Unfit, in these degenerate times of shame,
To catch the heart, or strike for honest fame;
Dear charming nymph, neglected and decried,
My shame in crowds, my solitary pride;
Thou source of all my bliss, and all my woe,
That found'st me poor at first, and keep'st me so;
Thou guide by which the nobler arts excel,
Thou nurse of every virtue, fare thee well!
Farewell! and oh! where'er thy voice be tried,
On Torno's cliffs, or Pambamarca's side,
Whether where equinoctial fervours glow,
Or winter wraps the polar world in snow,
Still let thy voice, prevailing over time,
Redress the rigours of the inclement clime;
Aid slighted truth; with thy persuasive strain
Teach erring man to spurn the rage of gain;
Teach him, that states of native strength possessed,
Though very poor, may still be very blest;
That trade's proud empire hastes to swift decay,
As ocean sweeps the laboured mole away;
While self-dependent power can time defy,
As rocks resist the billows and the sky.

355. tigers, catamounts.

418. Torno's cliffs . . . Pambamarca, places near the North Pole and near the Equator, respectively, at which scientific expeditions studied, in Goldsmith's time, the curvature of the earth. **427–30. That trade's . . . sky.** These last four lines were written by Dr. Johnson.

Edmund Burke

1729–1797

The most powerful political writer and one of the most devoted patriots in English history was born in Dublin on January 12, 1729, and educated there at Trinity College. He studied law in London, but, partly because he was drawn aside by strong philosophic and literary interests, never entered the legal profession. His career in the House of Commons, lasting from 1765 to 1794, was less brilliant than it might have been but for the fact that he was steadily in opposition to the "personal government" of George III. This opposition was shown in the first of his three chief political efforts, that which led up to his great speech *On Conciliation with America*, delivered in 1775. His next decade was given primarily to questions of British rule in India and to the impeachment and trial of Warren Hastings. From the year 1789 until his death he gave the greater part of his strength to the problems outlined in his noblest production, the *Reflections on the Revolution in France*, 1790.

Edmund Burke did not possess all the qualities that make for immediate oratorical success, but no one has ever surpassed him, in any language, as a political thinker and writer. His answers to the basic questions of statecraft and statesmanship are grounded in philosophy and enlivened by a poetic imagination of high order. In his own thought and writing, at any rate, he lifted politics to the high levels which they attained now and then in the ancient world, showing once more that the tasks of the true statesman call for the loftiest and most disinterested endeavor of the most gifted minds.

To use terms familiar in our day, Burke was both liberal and conservative. He was at the same time an exponent of idealism and a champion of common sense. Although it was the ingrained habit of his mind to carry every question back to first principles, he was also, upon what seemed to him the right occasions, an advocate of expediency. Superficially considered, his career may seem inconsistent, and many have asked how it happened that he who was so favorably inclined toward the revolution in the American colonies could be so bitterly opposed to the revolution in France. But there is in fact no contradiction here. Throughout his life Burke fought for an ordered and regular liberty such as he believed the American colonies were seeking. He passionately believed, like Tennyson, in "freedom slowly broadening down from precedent to precedent." But a wild freedom, on the other hand, expressing itself in defiance of all tradition, he feared and hated. He brought over into political and social philosophy that delight in order—a delight at once intellectual and esthetic and religious—which, since the time of Sir Isaac Newton, had been a prime characteristic of thoughtful Englishmen. To this he added the fire of an Irish fancy, an amazing amplitude of utterance, vast knowledge of literature and history and contemporary affairs, and a dignity of mind and character to match the splendor of all that he wrote and spoke.

Burke's prose may err at times on the side of amplitude. Occasionally it may be too highly colored. Its frequently amazing vividness of pictorial effect dazzles the eyes of a generation brought up to distrust all rhetorical display. It has a wide emotional gamut ranging from tenderness to fiery indignation, and this too we tend to distrust. Yet it should be apparent to anyone—or, if it is not, then the effort to write a logical brief of the speech *On Conciliation* should make it so—that Burke's prose has an admirable solidity of structure. It shows "fundamental brainwork" to a degree in which it is seldom found even in the most restrained and purely intellectual writers. If Burke's mural decorations seem to us too garish, we do well to remember that he built the walls he painted.

The speeches and writings of Edmund Burke have been strangely neglected in recent years, as though we had come to feel, even here in America, that they have nothing more to teach us. Yet the time may come, and not long hence, when we shall feel the need of a political and social wisdom drawn, as Burke's was, not from the passing hour and day but from the ages. We too may have to consider in some time of supreme national crisis, as Burke did, the history and precise nature of that liberty within the law which is perhaps the most precious gift handed down to us out of the English past. In such a time, if it comes, we may well return to the pages of Edmund Burke not only for the glory of their eloquence but for that light of the mind and warmth of the heart which our fathers found in them.

from REFLECTIONS ON THE REVOLUTION IN FRANCE

AND

ON THE PROCEEDINGS IN CERTAIN SOCIETIES IN LONDON RELATIVE TO THAT EVENT

IN A LETTER

INTENDED TO HAVE BEEN SENT TO A GENTLEMAN IN PARIS

YOU will observe, that, from Magna Charta to the Declaration of Right, it has been the uniform policy of our Constitution to claim and assert our liberties, as an *entailed inheritance* derived to us from our forefathers, and to be transmitted to our posterity; as an estate specially belonging to the people of this kingdom, without any reference whatever to any other more general or prior right. By this means our Constitution preserves an unity in so great a diversity of its parts. We have an inheritable crown; an inheritable peerage; and a House of Commons and a people inheriting privileges, franchises, and liberties, from a long line of ancestors.

This policy appears to me to be the result of profound reflection; or rather the happy effect of following nature, which is wisdom without reflection, and above it. A spirit of innovation is generally the result of a selfish temper and confined views. People will not look forward to posterity, who never look backward to their ancestors. Besides, the people of England well know, that the idea of inheritance furnishes a sure principle of conservation, and a sure principle of transmission; without at all excluding a principle of improvement. It leaves acquisition free; but it secures what it acquires. Whatever advantages are obtained by a state proceeding on these maxims, are locked fast as in a sort of family settlement; grasped as in a kind of mortmain for ever. By a constitutional policy, working after the pattern of nature, we receive, we hold, we transmit our government and our privileges, in the same manner in which we enjoy and transmit our property and our lives. The institutions of policy, the goods of fortune, the gifts of Providence, are handed down to us, and from us, in the same course and order. Our political system is placed in a just correspondence and symmetry with the order of the world, and with the mode of existence decreed to a permanent body composed of transitory parts; wherein, by the disposition of a stupendous wisdom, moulding together the great mysterious incorporation of the human race, the whole, at one time, is never old, or middle-aged, or young, but, in a condition of unchangeable constancy, moves on through the varied tenour of perpetual decay, fall, renovation, and progression. Thus, by preserving the method of nature in the conduct of the state, in what we improve we are never wholly new; in what we retain we are never wholly obsolete. By adhering in this manner and on those principles to our forefathers, we are guided not by the superstition of antiquarians, but by the spirit of philosophic analogy. In this choice of inheritance we have given to our frame of polity the image of a relation in blood; binding up the Constitution of our country with our dearest domestic ties; adopting our fundamental laws into the bosom of our family affections; keeping inseparable, and cherishing with the warmth of all their combined and mutually reflected charities, our state, our hearths, our sepulchres, and our altars. . . .

You had all these advantages in your ancient states; but you chose to act as if you had never been moulded into civil society, and had everything to begin anew. You began ill, because you began by despising everything that belonged to you. You set up your trade without a capital. If the last generations of your country appeared without much lustre in your eyes, you might have passed them by, and derived your claims from a more early race of ancestors. Under a pious predilection for those ancestors, your imaginations would have realized in them a standard of virtue and wisdom, beyond the vulgar practice of the hour: and you would have risen with the example to whose imitation you aspired. Respecting your forefathers, you would have been taught to respect yourselves. You would not have chosen to consider the French as a people of yesterday, as a nation of low-born servile wretches until the emancipating year of 1789. In order to furnish, at the expense of your honour, an excuse to your apologists here for several enormities of yours, you would not have been content to be represented as a gang of Maroon slaves, suddenly broke loose from the house of bondage, and therefore to be pardoned for your abuse of the liberty to which you were not accustomed, and were ill fitted. . . .

10–11. Gentleman in Paris, a young Frenchman by the name of T. M. Dupont who had asked Burke's opinion on the events of the French Revolution. **14. Declaration of Right,** presented to William and Mary on February 13, 1689. Burke elsewhere calls it "the corner-stone of our Constitution."

49. Maroon slaves, fugitive slaves living as savages in the West Indies and Guiana.

Were all these dreadful things necessary? Were they the inevitable results of the desperate struggle of determined patriots, compelled to wade through blood and tumult, to the quiet shore of a tranquil and prosperous liberty? No! nothing like it. The fresh ruins of France, which shock our feelings wherever we can turn our eyes, are not the devastation of civil war; they are the sad but instructive monuments of rash and ignorant counsel in time of profound peace. They are the display of inconsiderate and presumptuous, because unresisted and irresistible authority. The persons who have thus squandered away the precious treasure of their crimes, the persons who have made this prodigal and wild waste of public evils (the last stake reserved for the ultimate ransom of the state) have met in their progress with little, or rather with no opposition at all. Their whole march was more like a triumphal procession than the progress of a war. Their pioneers have gone before them, and demolished and laid everything level at their feet. . . .

This unforced choice, this fond election of evil, would appear perfectly unaccountable, if we did not consider the composition of the National Assembly; I do not mean its formal constitution, which, as it now stands, is exceptionable enough, but the materials of which, in a great measure, it is composed, which is of ten thousand times greater consequence than all the formalities in the world. If we were to know nothing of this assembly but by its title and function, no colours could paint to the imagination anything more venerable. In that light the mind of an inquirer, subdued by such an awful image as that of the virtue and wisdom of a whole people collected into one focus, would pause and hesitate in condemning things even of the very worst aspect. Instead of blamable, they would appear only mysterious. But no name, no power, no function, no artificial institution whatsoever, can make the men of whom any system of authority is composed, any other than God, and nature, and education, and their habits of life have made them. Capacities beyond these the people have not to give. Virtue and wisdom may be the objects of their choice; but their choice confers neither the one nor the other on those upon whom they lay their ordaining hands. They have not the engagement of nature, they have not the promise of revelation for any such powers. . . .

It is now sixteen or seventeen years since I saw the Queen of France, then the dauphiness, at Versailles; and surely never lighted on this orb, which she hardly seemed to touch, a more delightful vision. I saw her just above the horizon, decorating and cheering the elevated sphere she just began to move in—glittering like the morning-star, full of life, and splendour, and joy. Oh! what a revolution! and what a heart must I have, to contemplate without emotion that elevation and that fall! Little did I dream when she added titles of veneration to those of enthusiastic, distant, respectful love, that she should ever be obliged to carry the sharp antidote against disgrace concealed in that bosom; little did I dream that I should have lived to see such disasters fallen upon her in a nation of gallant men, in a nation of men of honour, and of cavaliers. I thought ten thousand swords must have leaped from their scabbards to avenge even a look that threatened her with insult. But the age of chivalry is gone. That of sophisters, economists, and calculators, has succeeded; and the glory of Europe is extinguished for ever. Never, never more, shall we behold that generous loyalty to rank and sex, that proud submission, that dignified obedience, that subordination of the heart, which kept alive, even in servitude itself, the spirit of an exalted freedom. The unbought grace of life, the cheap defence of nations, the nurse of manly sentiment and heroic enterprise is gone! It is gone, that sensibility of principle, that chastity of honour, which felt a stain like a wound, which inspired courage whilst it mitigated ferocity, which ennobled whatever it touched, and under which vice itself lost half its evil, by losing all its grossness.

This mixed system of opinion and sentiment had its origin in the ancient chivalry; and the principle, though varied in its appearance by the varying state of human affairs, subsisted and influenced through a long succession of generations, even to the time we live in. If it should ever be totally extinguished, the loss I fear will be great. It is this which has given its character to modern Europe. It is this which has distinguished it under all its forms of government, and distinguished it to its advantage, from the states of Asia, and possibly from those states which flourished in the most brilliant periods of the antique world. It was this which, without confounding ranks, had produced a noble equality, and handed it down through all the gradations of social life. It was this opinion which mitigated kings into companions, and raised private men to be fellows with kings. Without force, or opposition, it subdued the fierceness of pride and power; it obliged sovereigns to submit to the soft collar of social esteem, compelled stern authority to submit

19. pioneers, pick-and-shovel men who prepare the way for an army.

to elegance, and gave a domination, vanquisher of laws, to be subdued by manners.

But now all is to be changed. All the pleasing illusions, which made power gentle, and obedience liberal, which harmonized the different shades of life, and which, by a bland assimilation, incorporated into politics the sentiments which beautify and soften private society, are to be dissolved by this new conquering empire of light and reason. All the decent drapery of life is to be rudely torn off. All the superadded ideas, furnished from the wardrobe of a moral imagination, which the heart owns and the understanding ratifies, as necessary to cover the defects of our naked, shivering nature, and to raise it to dignity in our own estimation, are to be exploded as a ridiculous, absurd, and antiquated fashion.

On this scheme of things, a king is but a man, a queen is but a woman; a woman is but an animal; and an animal not of the highest order. All homage paid to the sex in general as such, and without distinct views, is to be regarded as romance and folly. Regicide, and parricide, and sacrilege, are but fictions of superstition, corrupting jurisprudence by destroying its simplicity. The murder of a king, or a queen, or a bishop, or a father, are only common homicide; and if the people are by any chance or in any way gainers by it, a sort of homicide much the most pardonable, and into which we ought not to make too severe a scrutiny.

On the scheme of this barbarous philosophy, which is the offspring of cold hearts and muddy understandings, and which is as void of solid wisdom, as it is destitute of all taste and elegance, laws are to be supported only by their own terrors, and by the concern, which each individual may find in them, from his own private speculations, or can spare to them from his own private interests. In the groves of *their* academy, at the end of every vista, you see nothing but the gallows. Nothing is left which engages the affections on the part of the commonwealth. On the principles of this mechanic philosophy, our institutions can never be embodied, if I may use the expression, in persons; so as to create in us love, veneration, admiration, or attachment. But that sort of reason which banishes the affections is incapable of filling their place. These public affections, combined with manners, are required sometimes as supplements, sometimes as correctives, always as aids to law. The precept given by a wise man, as well as a great critic, for the construction of poems, is equally true as to states:—*Non satis est pulchra esse poemata, dulcia sunto.* There ought to be a system of manners in every nation, which a well-formed mind would be disposed to relish. To make us love our country, our country ought to be lovely.

But power, of some kind or other, will survive the shock in which manners and opinions perish; and it will find other and worse means for its support. The usurpation which, in order to subvert ancient institutions, has destroyed ancient principles, will hold power by arts similar to those by which it has acquired it. When the old feudal and chivalrous spirit of *fealty*, which, by freeing kings from fear, freed both kings and subjects from the precautions of tyranny, shall be extinct in the minds of men, plots and assassinations will be anticipated by preventive murder and preventive confiscation, and that long roll of grim and bloody maxims, which form the political code of all power, not standing on its own honour, and the honour of those who are to obey it. Kings will be tyrants from policy, when subjects are rebels from principle.

When ancient opinions and rules of life are taken away, the loss cannot possibly be estimated. From that moment we have no compass to govern us; nor can we know distinctly to what port we steer. Europe, undoubtedly, taken in a mass, was in a flourishing condition the day on which your Revolution was completed. How much of that prosperous state was owing to the spirit of our old manners and opinions is not easy to say; but as such causes cannot be indifferent in their operation, we must presume, that, on the whole, their operation was beneficial.

We are but too apt to consider things in the state in which we find them, without sufficiently adverting to the causes by which they have been produced, and possibly may be upheld. Nothing is more certain, than that our manners, our civilization, and all the good things which are connected with manners, and with civilization, have, in this European world of ours, depended for ages upon two principles; and were indeed the result of both combined; I mean the spirit of a gentleman, and the spirit of religion. The nobility and the clergy, the one by profession, the other by patronage, kept learning in existence, even in the midst of arms and confusions, and whilst governments were rather in their causes, than formed. Learning paid back what it received to nobility and to priesthood; and paid it with usury, by enlarging their ideas, and by furnishing their minds. Happy if they had all continued to know their indissoluble union, and their

53. Non . . . sunto. It is not enough for poems to be beautiful. They must be affecting as well. The quotation is from Horace, *Ars Poetica*, l. 99.

proper place! Happy if learning, not debauched by ambition, had been satisfied to continue the instructor, and not aspired to be the master! Along with its natural protectors and guardians, learning will be cast into the mire, and trodden down under the hoofs of a swinish multitude.

If, as I suspect, modern letters owe more than they are always willing to own to ancient manners, so do other interests which we value full as much as they are worth. Even commerce, and trade, and manufacture, the gods of our economical politicians, are themselves perhaps but creatures; are themselves but effects, which, as first causes, we choose to worship. They certainly grew under the same shade in which learning flourished. They too may decay with their natural protecting principles. With you, for the present at least, they all threaten to disappear together. Where trade and manufactures are wanting to a people, and the spirit of nobility and religion remains, sentiment supplies, and not always ill supplies, their place; but if commerce and the arts should be lost in an experiment to try how well a state may stand without these old fundamental principles, what sort of a thing must be a nation of gross, stupid, ferocious, and, at the same time, poor and sordid barbarians, destitute of religion, honour, or manly pride, possessing nothing at present, and hoping for nothing hereafter?

I wish you may not be going fast, and by the shortest cut, to that horrible and disgustful situation. Already there appears a poverty of conception, a coarseness and vulgarity in all the proceedings of the assembly and of all their instructors. Their liberty is not liberal. Their science is presumptuous ignorance. Their humanity is savage and brutal.

It is not clear, whether in England we learned those grand and decorous principles, and manners, of which considerable traces yet remain, from you, or whether you took them from us. But to you, I think, we trace them best. You seem to me to be—*gentis incunabula nostrae*. France has always more or less influenced manners in England: and when your fountain is choked up and polluted, the stream will not run long, or not run clear, with us, or perhaps with any nation. This gives all Europe, in my opinion, but too close and connected a concern in what is done in France. Excuse me, therefore, if I have dwelt too long on the atrocious spectacle of the 6th of October, 1789, or have given too much scope to the reflections which have arisen in my mind on occasion of the most important of all revolutions, which may be dated from that day, I mean a revolution in sentiments, manners, and moral opinions. As things now stand, with everything respectable destroyed without us, and an attempt to destroy within us every principle of respect, one is almost forced to apologize for harbouring the common feelings of men.

41. gentis . . . nostrae, the cradle of our race. From Virgil's *Aeneid*, Book III, l. 105.

We know, and what is better, we feel inwardly, that religion is the basis of civil society, and the source of all good, and of all comfort. In England we are so convinced of this, that there is no rust of superstititon, with which the accumulated absurdity of the human mind might have crusted it over in the course of ages, that ninety-nine in a hundred of the people of England would not prefer to impiety. We shall never be such fools as to call in an enemy to the substance of any system to remove its corruptions, to supply its defects, or to perfect its construction. If our religious tenets should ever want a further elucidation, we shall not call on atheism to explain them. We shall not light up our temple from that unhallowed fire. It will be illuminated with other lights. It will be perfumed with other incense, than the infectious stuff which is imported by the smugglers of adulterated metaphysics. If our ecclesiastical establishment should want a revision, it is not avarice or rapacity, public or private, that we shall employ for the audit, or receipt, or application of its consecrated revenue. Violently condemning neither the Greek nor the Armenian, nor, since heats are subsided, the Roman system of religion, we prefer the Protestant: not because we think it has less of the Christian religion in it, but because, in our judgment, it has more. We are Protestants, not from indifference, but from zeal.

We know, and it is our pride to know, that man is by his constitution a religious animal; that atheism is against, not only our reason, but our instincts; and that it cannot prevail long. But if, in the moment of riot, and in a drunken delirium from the hot spirit drawn out of the alembic of hell, which in France is now so furiously boiling, we should uncover our nakedness, by throwing off that Christian religion which has hitherto been our boast and comfort, and one great source of civilization amongst us, and amongst many other nations, we are apprehensive (being well aware that the mind will not endure a void) that some uncouth, pernicious, and degrading superstition might take place of it.

For that reason, before we take from our establishment the natural, human means of estimation, and give it up to contempt, as you have done, and in doing it have incurred the penalties you well deserve to suffer, we desire that some other may be presented to us in the place of it. We shall then form our judgment.

On these ideas, instead of quarrelling with establishments, as some do, who have made a philosophy and a religion of their hostility to such institutions, we cleave closely to them. We are resolved to keep an established church, an established monarchy, an established aristocracy, and an established democracy, each in the degree it exists, and in no greater. I shall show you presently how much of each of these we possess.

It has been the misfortune (not, as these gentlemen think it, the glory) of this age, that everything is to be discussed, as if the Constitution of our country were to be always a subject rather of altercation than enjoyment. For this reason, as well as for the satisfaction of those among you (if any such you have among you) who may wish to profit of examples, I venture to trouble you with a few thoughts upon each of these establishments. I do not think they were unwise in ancient Rome, who, when they wished to new-model their laws, set commissioners to examine the best constituted republics within their reach.

First, I beg leave to speak of our church establishment, which is the first of our prejudices; not a prejudice destitute of reason, but involving in it profound and extensive wisdom. I speak of it first. It is first, and last, and midst in our minds. For, taking ground on that religious system, of which we are now in possession, we continue to act on the early received, and uniformly continued sense of mankind. That sense not only, like a wise architect, hath built up the august fabric of states, but like a provident proprietor, to preserve the structure from profanation and ruin, as a sacred temple, purged from all the impurities of fraud, and violence, and injustice, and tyranny, hath solemnly and for ever consecrated the commonwealth, and all that officiate in it. This consecration is made, that all who administer in the government of men, in which they stand in the person of God Himself, should have high and worthy notions of their function and destination; that their hope should be full of immortality; that they should not look to the paltry pelf of the moment, nor to the temporary and transient praise of the vulgar, but to a solid, permanent existence, in the permanent part of their nature, and to a permanent fame and glory, in the example they leave as a rich inheritance to the world.

Such sublime principles ought to be infused into persons of exalted situations; and religious establishments provided, that may continually revive and enforce them. Every sort of moral, every sort of civil, every sort of politic institution, aiding the rational and natural ties that connect the human understanding and affections to the divine, are not more than necessary, in order to build up that wonderful structure, Man; whose prerogative it is, to be in a great degree a creature of his own making; and who, when made as he ought to be made, is destined to hold no trivial place in the creation. But whenever man is put over men, as the better nature ought ever to preside, in that case more particularly he should as nearly as possible be approximated to his perfection.

The consecration of the state by a state religious establishment is necessary also to operate with a wholesome awe upon free citizens; because, in order to secure their freedom, they must enjoy some determinate portion of power. To them therefore a religion connected with the state, and with their duty towards it, becomes even more necessary than in such societies, where the people, by the terms of their subjection, are confined to private sentiments, and the management of their own family concerns. All persons possessing any portion of power ought to be strongly and awfully impressed with an idea that they act in trust; and that they are to account for their conduct in that trust to the one great Master, Author and Founder of society.

This principle ought even to be more strongly impressed upon the minds of those who compose the collective sovereignty, than upon those of single princes. Without instruments, these princes can do nothing. Whoever uses instruments, in finding helps, finds also impediments. Their power is therefore by no means complete; nor are they safe in extreme abuse. Such persons, however elevated by flattery, arrogance, and self-opinion, must be sensible, that, whether covered or not by positive law, in some way or other they are accountable even here for the abuse of their trust. If they are not cut off by a rebellion of their people, they may be strangled by the very janissaries kept for their security against all other rebellion. Thus we have seen the King of France sold by his soldiers for an increase of pay. But where popular authority is absolute and unrestrained, the people have an infinitely greater, because a far better founded, confidence in their own power. They are themselves in a great measure their own instruments. They are nearer to their objects. Besides, they are

34. continued sense, enduring consensus.

less under responsibility to one of the greatest controlling powers on earth, the sense of fame and estimation. The share of infamy, that is likely to fall to the lot of each individual in public acts, is small indeed; the operation of opinion being in the inverse ratio to the number of those who abuse power. Their own approbation of their own acts has to them the appearance of a public judgment in their favour. A perfect democracy is therefore the most shameless thing in the world. As it is the most shameless, it is also the most fearless. No man apprehends in his person that he can be made subject to punishment. Certainly the people at large never ought: for, as all punishments are for example towards the conservation of the people at large, the people at large can never become the subject of punishments by any human hand. It is therefore of infinite importance that they should not be suffered to imagine that their will, any more than that of kings, is the standard of right and wrong. They ought to be persuaded that they are full as little entitled, and far less qualified, with safety to themselves, to use any arbitrary power whatsoever; that therefore they are not, under a false show of liberty, but, in truth, to exercise an unnatural, inverted domination, tyrannically to exact, from those who officiate in the state, not an entire devotion to their interest, which is their right, but an abject submission to their occasional will; extinguishing thereby, in all those who serve them, all moral principle, all sense of dignity, all use of judgment, and all consistency of character; whilst by the very same process they give themselves up a proper, a suitable, but a most contemptible prey to the servile ambition of popular sycophants, or courtly flatterers.

When the people have emptied themselves of all the lust of selfish will, which without religion it is utterly impossible they ever should,—when they are conscious that they exercise, and exercise perhaps in a higher link of the order of delegation, the power, which to be legitimate must be according to that eternal, immutable law, in which will and reason are the same,—they will be more careful how they place power in base and incapable hands. In their nomination to office, they will not appoint to the exercise of authority, as to a pitiful job, but as to a holy function; not according to their sordid, selfish interest, nor to their wanton caprice, nor to their arbitrary will; but they will confer that power (which any man may well tremble to give or to receive) on those only, in whom they may discern that predominant proportion of active virtue and wisdom, taken together and fitted to the charge, such as, in the great and inevitable mixed mass of human imperfections and infirmities, is to be found.

When they are habitually convinced that no evil can be acceptable, either in the act or the permission, to Him whose essence is good, they will be better able to extirpate out of the minds of all magistrates, civil, ecclesiastical, or military, anything that bears the least resemblance to a proud and lawless domination.

But one of the first and most leading principles on which the commonwealth and the laws are consecrated is, lest the temporary possessors and life-renters in it, unmindful of what they have received from their ancestors, or of what is due to their posterity, should act as if they were the entire masters; that they should not think it among their rights to cut off the entail, or commit waste on the inheritance, by destroying at their pleasure the whole original fabric of their society: hazarding to leave to those who come after them a ruin instead of an habitation—and teaching these successors as little to respect their contrivances, as they had themselves respected the institutions of their forefathers. By this unprincipled facility of changing the state as often, and as much, and in as many ways, as there are floating fancies or fashions, the whole chain and continuity of the commonwealth would be broken. No one generation could link with the other. Men would become little better than the flies of a summer.

And first of all, the science of jurisprudence, the pride of the human intellect, which, with all its defects, redundancies, and errors, is the collected reason of ages, combining the principles of original justice with the infinite variety of human concerns, as a heap of old exploded errors, would be no longer studied. Personal self-sufficiency and arrogance (the certain attendants upon all those who have never experienced a wisdom greater than their own) would usurp the tribunal. Of course no certain laws, establishing invariable grounds of hope and fear, would keep the actions of men in a certain course, or direct them to a certain end. Nothing stable in the modes of holding property, or exercising function, could form a solid ground on which any parent could speculate in the education of his offspring, or in a choice for their future establishment in the world. No principles would be early worked into the habits. As soon as the most able instructor had completed his laborious course of institution, instead of sending forth his pupil, accomplished in a virtuous discipline, fitted to procure him attention and respect, in his place in society, he would find everything altered; and that he had turned out a poor creature to the contempt and derision of the world, ignorant of the true grounds of estimation. Who would insure a tender and delicate sense of honour to beat almost with the first pulses of the heart, when no man could know what would be the test of honour in a nation, continually varying the standard of its coin? No part of life would retain its acquisitions. Barbarism with regard to science and literature, unskilfulness with regard to arts and manufactures, would infallibly succeed to the want of a steady education and settled principle; and thus the commonwealth itself would, in a few generations, crumble away, be disconnected into the dust and powder of individuality, and at length dispersed to all the winds of heaven.

To avoid, therefore, the evils of inconstancy and versatility, ten thousand times worse than those of obstinacy and the blindest prejudice, we have consecrated the state, that no man should approach to look into its defects or corruptions but with due caution; that he should never dream of beginning its reformation by its subversion; that he should approach to the faults of the state as to the wounds of a father, with pious awe and trembling solicitude. By this wise prejudice we are taught to look with horror on those children of their country, who are prompt rashly to hack that aged parent in pieces, and put him into the kettle of magicians, in hopes that by their poisonous weeds, and wild incantations, they may regenerate the paternal constitution, and renovate their father's life.

Society is, indeed, a contract. Subordinate contracts for objects of mere occasional interest may be dissolved at pleasure—but the state ought not to be considered as nothing better than a partnership agreement in a trade of pepper and coffee, calico or tobacco, or some other such low concern, to be taken up for a little temporary interest, and to be dissolved by the fancy of the parties. It is to be looked on with other reverence; because it is not a partnership in things subservient only to the gross animal existence of a temporary and perishable nature. It is a partnership in all science; a partnership in all art; a partnership in every virtue, and in all perfection. As the ends of such a partnership cannot be obtained in many generations, it becomes a partnership not only between those who are living, but between those who are living, those who are dead, and those who are to be born. Each contract of each particular state is but a clause in the great primaeval contract of eternal society, linking the lower with the higher natures, connecting the visible and invisible world, according to a fixed compact sanctioned by the inviolable oath which holds all physical and all moral natures, each in their appointed place. This law is not subject to the will of those who, by an obligation above them, and infinitely superior, are bound to submit their will to that law. The municipal corporations of that universal kingdom are not morally at liberty, at their pleasure, and on their speculations of a contingent improvement, wholly to separate and tear asunder the bands of their subordinate community, and to dissolve it into an unsocial, uncivil, unconnected chaos of elementary principles. It is the first and supreme necessity only, a necessity that is not chosen, but chooses, a necessity paramount to deliberation, that admits no discussion, and demands no evidence, which alone can justify a resort to anarchy. This necessity is no exception to the rule; because this necessity itself is a part too of that moral and physical disposition of things, to which man must be obedient by consent or force: but if that which is only submission to necessity should be made the object of choice, the law is broken, Nature is disobeyed, and the rebellious are outlawed, cast forth, and exiled, from this world of reason, and order, and peace, and virtue, and fruitful penitence, into the antagonist world of madness, discord, vice, confusion, and unavailing sorrow.

30. kettle of magicians. Burke has in mind the myth of the sorceress Medea.

William Cowper

1731–1800

The pitiful life-story of William Cowper is soon told. Born the son of a country rector who was chaplain to George II, he lost his mother when he was six years old. At school he was browbeaten and miserable. His study of law and his brief period of service in governmental offices did little to relieve his tendency toward gloom, and before reaching the age of thirty-five he suffered the first of several lapses into insanity. After recovering from this attack he retired to the village of Olney, in central England, and there spent the quiet remainder of his life in the company of various friends, of whom the chief was Mrs. Mary Unwin.

Although he came of a distinguished ancestry long prominent in the law and including the poet John Donne, Cowper had no heart for the struggles and rewards of the world. Sensitive to a morbid degree, he suffered during most of his life with a religious melancholia based upon the conviction that he was irretrievably damned. For distraction he turned to his friends, to the solaces of nature, to gardening and carpentry and the care of animals, and finally, at fifty years of age, to poetic composition.

If Cowper's hymns, poems, and letters seem to us at first almost intolerably mild, the reason may be that we do not read them, as he believed they were written, in the red light of hell. Like his great kinsman John Donne, he had that tragic sense of life and its destiny which we of the twentieth century are only beginning to recover. Yet every moment that he spent with his flowers, his pet hares, with ax and saw, or with pen and paper, was to him a moment of transient happiness snatched from endless woe. He made so much of the frail creatures of time because he could not always bear to think of eternity.

Hence came those innovations in the writing of Cowper which give him a greater importance in the history of literature than his actual accomplishment would at first seem to warrant. His feeling of fellowship with all things doomed to death leads on into an affection for mankind in general, for birds and animals, for trees and plants and flowers, which relates him rather to Burns and Wordsworth and Shelley than to the poets of the school of Pope.

And yet Cowper's work has high value of its own. While recognizing that he wins our love rather than our admiration, we should not forget that he wrote several of the best hymns and many of the most delightful letters that have come down to us from his time, together with a few poems that will always have devoted readers. His pervasive humor, his delicacy of thought and feeling, and the wisdom that he showed in making much of little, soon endear him to those who once make his acquaintance. That same tenderness and humility which unfitted him for active life render him an ideal fireside companion for those who have fully learned that our lives are brief, tragic, beautiful, and surrounded by mystery.

from THE TASK

Accepting from his friend Lady Austen "the task" of writing about a sofa, Cowper produced, in 1785, a blank-verse poem running to six books in which he discussed many diverse themes. The tendency of the entire poem, he said, was "to discountenance the modern enthusiasm after a London life, and to recommend rural ease and leisure as friendly to the cause of piety and virtue."

It is in the fourth book of the poem, a masterpiece of unobtrusive art, that this purpose is most fully achieved.

Book IV

THE WINTER EVENING

Hark! 'tis the twanging horn! O'er yonder bridge,
That with its wearisome but needful length
Bestrides the wintry flood, in which the moon
Sees her unwrinkled face reflected bright;—
He comes, the herald of a noisy world,
With spattered boots, strapped waist, and frozen locks;
News from all nations lumbering at his back.
True to his charge, the close-packed load behind,
Yet careless what he brings, his one concern
Is to conduct it to the destined inn,
And, having dropped the expected bag, pass on.
He whistles as he goes, light-hearted wretch,
Cold and yet cheerful: messenger of grief

10. inn, from which the mail was distributed.

Perhaps to thousands, and of joy to some;
To him indifferent whether grief or joy.
Houses in ashes, and the fall of stocks,
Births, deaths, and marriages, epistles wet
With tears that trickled down the writer's cheeks
Fast as the periods from his fluent quill,
Or charged with amorous sighs of absent swains
Or nymphs responsive, equally affect
His horse and him, unconscious of them all.
But oh the important budget! ushered in
With such heart-shaking music, who can say
What are its tidings? Have our troops awaked?
Or do they still, as if with opium drugged,
Snore to the murmurs of the Atlantic wave?
Is India free, and does she wear her plumed
And jewelled turban with a smile of peace,
Or do we grind her still? The grand debate,
The popular harangue, the tart reply,
The logic, and the wisdom, and the wit,
And the loud laugh—I long to know them all;
I burn to set the imprisoned wranglers free,
And give them voice and utterance once again.
  Now stir the fire, and close the shutters fast,
Let fall the curtains, wheel the sofa round,
And, while the bubbling and loud-hissing urn
Throws up a steamy column, and the cups
That cheer but not inebriate, wait on each,
So let us welcome peaceful evening in.
Not such his evening, who with shining face
Sweats in the crowded theatre, and, squeezed
And bored with elbow-points through both his sides,
Out-scolds the ranting actor on the stage:
Nor his, who patient stands till his feet throb,
And his head thumps, to feed upon the breath
Of patriots, bursting with heroic rage,
Or placemen, all tranquillity and smiles.
This folio of four pages, happy work!
Which not even critics criticise; that holds
Inquisitive attention, while I read,
Fast bound in chains of silence, which the fair,
Though eloquent themselves, yet fear to break;
What is it, but a map of busy life,
Its fluctuations, and its vast concerns?
Here runs the mountainous and craggy ridge
That tempts ambition. On the summit see
The seals of office glitter in his eyes;
He climbs, he pants, he grasps them! At his heels,
Close at his heels, a demagogue ascends,
And with a dexterous jerk soon twists him down,
And wins them, but to lose them in his turn.
Here rills of oily eloquence in soft
Meanders lubricate the course they take;
The modest speaker is ashamed and grieved
To engross a moment's notice, and yet begs,
Begs a propitious ear for his poor thoughts,
However trivial all that he conceives.
Sweet bashfulness! It claims at least this praise,
The dearth of information and good sense
That it foretells us always comes to pass.
Cataracts of declamation thunder here;
There forests of no meaning spread the page,
In which all comprehension wanders, lost;
While fields of pleasantry amuse us there
With merry descants on a nation's woes.
The rest appears a wilderness of strange
But gay confusion; roses for the cheeks,
And lilies for the brows of faded age,
Teeth for the toothless, ringlets for the bald,
Heaven, earth, and ocean, plundered of their sweets,
Nectareous essences, Olympian dews,
Sermons, and city feasts, and favourite airs,
Aethereal journeys, submarine exploits,
And Katterfelto, with his hair on end
At his own wonders, wondering for his bread.
  'Tis pleasant through the loop-holes of retreat
To peep at such a world; to see the stir
Of the great Babel, and not feel the crowd;
To hear the roar she sends through all her gates
At a safe distance, where the dying sound
Falls a soft murmur on the uninjured ear.
Thus sitting, and surveying thus at ease
The globe and its concerns, I seem advanced
To some secure and more than mortal height,
That liberates and exempts me from them all.
It turns submitted to my view, turns round
With all its generations; I behold
The tumult, and am still. The sound of war
Has lost its terrors ere it reaches me;
Grieves, but alarms me not. I mourn the pride
And avarice that make man a wolf to man;
Hear the faint echo of those brazen throats
By which he speaks the language of his heart,
And sigh, but never tremble at the sound.
He travels and expatiates, as the bee
From flower to flower, so he from land to land;
The manners, customs, policy of all
Pay contribution to the store he gleans;
He sucks intelligence in every clime,
And spreads the honey of his deep research

27. snore, referring to the supposed inaction of British troops in America. **28. India,** referring to the first Mahratta war, 1782. **49. placemen,** officeholders. **50. folio,** the newspaper.

85. Aethereal journeys. The first ascents in a balloon were made in 1783. **86. Katterfelto,** a quack doctor. **107. expatiates.** wanders.

At his return—a rich repast for me.
He travels, and I too. I tread his deck,
Ascend his topmast, through his peering eyes
Discover countries, with a kindred heart
Suffer his woes, and share in his escapes;
While fancy, like the finger of a clock,
Runs the great circuit, and is still at home.
  O Winter, ruler of the inverted year,
Thy scattered hair with sleet like ashes filled,
Thy breath congealed upon thy lips, thy cheeks
Fringed with a beard made white with other snows
Than those of age, thy forehead wrapt in clouds,
A leafless branch thy sceptre, and thy throne
A sliding car, indebted to no wheels,
But urged by storms along its slippery way,
I love thee, all unlovely as thou seem'st,
And dreaded as thou art! Thou hold'st the sun
A prisoner in the yet undawning east,
Shortening his journey between morn and noon,
And hurrying him, impatient of his stay,
Down to the rosy west; but kindly still
Compensating his loss with added hours
Of social converse and instructive ease,
And gathering, at short notice, in one group
The family dispersed, and fixing thought,
Not less dispersed by day-light and its cares.
I crown thee king of intimate delights,
Fire-side enjoyments, home-born happiness,
And all the comforts that the lowly roof
Of undisturbed retirement, and the hours
Of long uninterrupted evening, know.
No rattling wheels stop short before these gates;
No powdered pert, proficient in the art
Of sounding an alarm, assaults these doors
Till the street rings; no stationary steeds
Cough their own knell, while, heedless of the sound,
The silent circle fan themselves, and quake:
But here the needle plies its busy task,
The pattern grows, the well-depicted flower,
Wrought patiently into the snowy lawn,
Unfolds its bosom; buds, and leaves, and sprigs,
And curling tendrils, gracefully disposed,
Follow the nimble finger of the fair;
A wreath that cannot fade, of flowers that blow
With most success when all besides decay.
The poet's or historian's page, by one
Made vocal for the amusement of the rest;
The sprightly lyre, whose treasure of sweet sounds
The touch from many a trembling chord shakes out;
And the clear voice symphonious, yet distinct,
And in the charming strife triumphant still,
Beguile the night, and set a keener edge
On female industry: the threaded steel
Flies swiftly, and unfelt the task proceeds.
The volume closed, the customary rites
Of the last meal commence. A Roman meal,
Such as the mistress of the world once found
Delicious, when her patriots of high note,
Perhaps by moonlight, at their humble doors,
And under an old oak's domestic shade,
Enjoyed—spare feast!—a radish and an egg!
Discourse ensues, not trivial, yet not dull,
Nor such as with a frown forbids the play
Of fancy, or proscribes the sound of mirth:
Nor do we madly, like an impious world,
Who deem religion frenzy, and the God
That made them an intruder on their joys,
Start at his awful name, or deem his praise
A jarring note—themes of a graver tone
Exciting oft our gratitude and love,
While we retrace with memory's pointing wand,
That calls the past to our exact review,
The dangers we have 'scaped, the broken snare,
The disappointed foe, deliverance found
Unlooked for, life preserved and peace restored—
Fruits of omnipotent eternal love.
"Oh evenings worthy of the gods!" exclaimed
The Sabine bard. "Oh evenings," I reply,
"More to be prized and coveted than yours,
As more illumined, and with nobler truths,
That I, and mine, and those we love, enjoy."
  Is winter hideous in a garb like this?
Needs he the tragic fur, the smoke of lamps
The pent-up breath of an unsavoury throng,
To thaw him into feeling; or the smart
And snappish dialogue, that flippant wits
Call comedy, to prompt him with a smile?
The self-compacent actor, when he views
(Stealing a side-long glance at a full house)
The slope of faces, from the floor to the roof,
(As if one master-spring controlled them all)
Relaxed into an universal grin,
Sees not a countenance there that speaks of joy
Half so refined or so sincere as our's.
Cards were superfluous here, with all the tricks
That idleness has ever yet contrived
To fill the void of an unfurnished brain,
To palliate dullness, and give time a shove.
Time, as he passes us, has a dove's wing,
Unsoiled, and swift, and of a silken sound;
But the world's time is time in masquerade!
Their's, should I paint him, has his pinions fledged
With motley plumes; and, where the peacock shows
His azure eyes, is tinctured black and red
With spots quadrangular of diamond form,
Ensanguined hearts, clubs typical of strife,

190. Sabine bard, Horace, in *Satires*, Book II, Satire 2, l. 65. **195. tragic,** because secured by the deaths of animals.

And spades, the emblem of untimely graves.
What should be and what was an hour-glass once,
Becomes a dice-box, and a billiard mast
Well does the work of his destructive scythe.
Thus decked, he charms a world whom fashion blinds
To his true worth, most pleased when idle most;
Whose only happy are their wasted hours.
Even misses, at whose age their mothers wore
The back-string and the bib, assume the dress
Of womanhood, sit pupils in the school
Of card-devoted time, and, night by night,
Placed at some vacant corner of the board,
Learn every trick, and soon play all the game.
But truce with censure. Roving as I rove,
Where shall I find an end, or how proceed?
As he that travels far oft turns aside
To view some rugged rock or mouldering tower,
Which, seen, delights him not; then, coming home,
Describes and prints it, that the world may know
How far he went for what was nothing worth;
So I, with brush in hand and pallet spread,
With colours mixed for a far different use,
Paint cards and dolls and every idle thing
That fancy finds in her excursive flights.
  Come, Evening, once again, season of peace;
Return, sweet Evening, and continue long!
Methinks I see thee in the streaky west,
With matron step slow-moving, while the night
Treads on thy sweeping train; one hand employed
In letting fall the curtain of repose
On bird and beast, the other charged for man
With sweet oblivion of the cares of day:
Not sumptuously adorned, nor needing aid,
Like homely featured night, of clustering gems;
A star or two, just twinkling on thy brow,
Suffices thee, save that the moon is thine
No less than her's, not worn indeed on high
With ostentatious pageantry, but set
With modest grandeur in thy purple zone,
Resplendent less, but of an ampler round.
Come then, and thou shalt find thy votary calm,
Or make me so. Composure is thy gift:
And, whether I devote thy gentle hours
To books, to music, or the poet's toil;
To weaving nets for bird-alluring fruit;
Or twining silken threads round ivory reels,
When they command whom man was born to please,
I slight thee not, but make thee welcome still.
  Just when our drawing-rooms begin to blaze
With lights, by clear reflection multiplied
From many a mirror, in which he of Gath,
Goliath, might have seen his giant bulk
Whole, without stooping, towering crest and all,
My pleasures, too, begin. But me, perhaps,
The glowing hearth may satisfy awhile
With faint illumination, that uplifts
The shadow to the ceiling, there by fits
Dancing uncouthly to the quivering flame.
Not undelightful is an hour to me
So spent in parlour twilight: such a gloom
Suits well the thoughtful or unthinking mind,
The mind contemplative, with some new theme
Pregnant, or indisposed alike to all.
Laugh ye, who boast your more mercurial powers,
That never feel a stupor, know no pause,
Nor need one; I am conscious, and confess,
Fearless, a soul that does not always think.
Me oft has fancy, ludicrous and wild,
Soothed with a waking dream of houses, towers,
Trees, churches, and strange visages, expressed
In the red cinders, while with poring eye
I gazed, myself creating what I saw.
Nor less amused have I quiescent watched
The sooty films that play upon the bars,
Pendulous, and foreboding in the view
Of superstition, prophesying still,
Though still deceived, some stranger's near approach.
'Tis thus the understanding takes repose
In indolent vacuity of thought,
And sleeps and is refreshed. Meanwhile the face
Conceals the mood lethargic with a mask
Of deep deliberation, as the man
Were tasked to his full strength, absorbed and lost.
Thus oft, reclined at ease, I lose an hour
At evening, till at length the freezing blast,
That sweeps the bolted shutter, summons home
The recollected powers; and, snapping short
The glassy threads with which the fancy weaves
Her brittle toys, restores me to myself.
How calm is my recess; and how the frost,
Raging abroad, and the rough wind, endear
The silence and the warmth enjoyed within!
I saw the woods and fields, at close of day,
A variegated show; the meadows green,
Though faded; and the lands, where lately waved
The golden harvest, of a mellow brown,
Upturned so lately by the forceful share.
I saw far off the weedy fallows smile
With verdure not unprofitable, grazed
By flocks, fast feeding, and selecting each
His favourite herb; while all the leafless groves
That skirt the horizon wore a sable hue,
Scarce noticed in the kindred dusk of eve.

221. mast, cue. **227. back-string,** leading string.

To-morrow brings a change, a total change!
Which even now, though silently performed,
And slowly, and by most unfelt, the face
Of universal nature undergoes.
Fast falls a fleecy shower: the downy flakes,
Descending, and with never-ceasing lapse,
Softly alighting upon all below,
Assimilate all objects. Earth receives
Gladly the thickening mantle, and the green
And tender blade, that feared the chilling blast,
Escapes unhurt beneath so warm a veil.
In such a world, so thorny, and where none
Finds happiness unblighted, or, if found,
Without some thistly sorrow at its side,
It seems the part of wisdom, and no sin
Against the law of love, to measure lots
With less distinguished than ourselves; that thus
We may with patience bear our moderate ills,
And sympathise with others, suffering more.
Ill fares the traveller now, and he that stalks
In ponderous boots beside his reeking team.
The wain goes heavily, impeded sore
By congregated loads adhering close
To the clogged wheels; and in its sluggish pace,
Noiseless, appears a moving hill of snow.
The toiling steeds expand the nostril wide,
While every breath, by respiration strong
Forced downward, is consolidated soon
Upon their jutting chests. He, formed to bear
The pelting brunt of the tempestuous night,
With half-shut eyes, and puckered cheeks, and teeth
Presented bare against the storm, plods on.
One hand secures his hat, save when with both
He brandishes his pliant length of whip,
Resounding oft, and never heard in vain.
Oh happy; and, in my account, denied
That sensibility of pain with which
Refinement is endued, thrice happy thou!
Thy frame, robust and hardy, feels indeed
The piercing cold, but feels it unimpaired.
The learnèd finger never need explore
Thy vigorous pulse; and the unhealthful east,
That breathes the spleen, and searches every bone
Of the infirm, is wholesome air to thee.
Thy days roll on, exempt from household care;
The waggon is thy wife; and the poor beasts
That drag the dull companion to and fro,
Thine helpless charge, dependent on thy care.
Ah, treat them kindly! rude as thou appear'st,
Yet show that thou hast mercy! which the great,
With needless hurry whirled from place to place,
Humane as they would seem, not always show.

329. Assimilate, make similar in appearance.

Poor, yet industrious, modest, quiet, neat;
Such claim compassion in a night like this,
And have a friend in every feeling heart.
Warmed, while it lasts, by labour, all day long
They brave the season, and yet find at eve,
Ill clad and fed but sparely, time to cool.
The frugal housewife trembles when she lights
Her scanty stock of brush-wood, blazing clear,
But dying soon, like all terrestrial joys.
The few small embers left she nurses well;
And, while her infant race, with outspread hands
And crowded knees, sit cowering o'er the sparks,
Retires, content to quake, so they be warmed.
The man feels least, as more inured than she
To winter, and the current in his veins
More briskly moved by his severer toil;
Yet he, too, finds his own distress in their's.
The taper soon extinguished, which I saw
Dangled along at the cold finger's end
Just when the day declined, and the brown loaf
Lodged on the shelf, half eaten, without sauce
Of savoury cheese, or butter, costlier still;
Sleep seems their only refuge: for, alas,
Where penury is felt the thought is chained,
And sweet colloquial pleasures are but few!
With all this thrift they thrive not. All the care
Ingenious parsimony takes but just
Saves the small inventory, bed and stool,
Skillet, and old carved chest, from public sale.
They live, and live without extorted alms
From grudging hands; but other boast have none
To soothe their honest pride, that scorns to beg,
Nor comfort else, but in their mutual love.
I praise you much, ye meek and patient pair,
For ye are worthy; choosing rather far
A dry but independent crust, hard earned,
And eaten with a sigh, than to endure
The rugged frowns and insolent rebuffs
Of knaves in office, partial in the work
Of distribution: liberal of their aid
To clamorous importunity in rags,
But oft-times deaf to suppliants who would blush
To wear a tattered garb however coarse,
Whom famine cannot reconcile to filth:
These ask with painful shyness, and, refused
Because deserving, silently retire!
But be ye of good courage! Time itself
Shall much befriend you. Time shall give increase;
And all your numerous progeny, well-trained,
But helpless, in few years shall find their hands,
And labour too. Meanwhile ye shall not want
What, concious of your virtues, we can spare,
Nor what a wealthier than ourselves may send.

I mean the man, who, when the distant poor
Need help, denies them nothing but his name.
  But poverty, with most who whimper forth
Their long complaints, is self-inflicted woe;
The effect of laziness or sottish waste.
Now goes the nightly thief prowling abroad
For plunder; much solicitous how best
He may compensate for a day of sloth
By works of darkness and nocturnal wrong.
Woe to the gardener's pale, the farmer's hedge,
Plashed neatly, and secured with driven stakes
Deep in the loamy bank. Uptorn by strength,
Resistless in so bad a cause, but lame
To better deeds, he bundles up the spoil—
An ass's burden—and, when laden most
And heaviest, light of foot, steals fast away.
Nor does the boarded hovel better guard
The well-stacked pile of riven logs and roots
From his pernicious force. Nor will he leave
Unwrenched the door, however well secured,
Where Chanticleer amidst his harem sleeps
In unsuspecting pomp. Twitched from the perch,
He gives the princely bird, with all his wives,
To his voracious bag, struggling in vain,
And loudly wondering at the sudden change.—
Nor this to feed his own! 'Twere some excuse
Did pity of their sufferings warp aside
His principle, and tempt him into sin
For their support, so destitute.—But they
Neglected pine at home; themselves, as more
Exposed than others, with less scruple made
His victims, robbed of their defenceless all.
Cruel is all he does. 'Tis quenchless thirst
Of ruinous ebriety that prompts
His every action, and imbrutes the man.
Oh for a law to noose the villain's neck
Who starves his own; who persecutes the blood
He gave them in his children's veins, and hates
And wrongs the woman he has sworn to love!
  Pass where we may, through city or through town,
Village or hamlet of this merry land,
Though lean and beggared, every twentieth pace
Conducts the unguarded nose to such a whiff
Of stale debauch, forth-issuing from the sties
That law has licensed, as makes temperance reel.
There sit, involved and lost in curling clouds
Of Indian fume, and guzzling deep, the boor,
The lackey, and the groom: the craftsman there
Takes a Lethean leave of all his toil;
Smith, cobbler, joiner, he that plies the shears,
And he that kneads the dough; all loud alike,
All learnèd, and all drunk! The fiddle screams
Plaintive and piteous, as it wept and wailed
Its wasted tones and harmony unheard:
Fierce the dispute, whate'er the theme; while she,
Fell Discord, arbitress of such debate,
Perched on the sign-post, holds with even hand
Her undecisive scales. In this she lays
A weight of ignorance; in that, of pride;
And smiles, delighted with the eternal poise.
Dire is the frequent curse, and its twin sound
The cheek-distending oath, not to be praised
As ornamental, musical, polite,
Like those which modern senators employ,
Whose oath is rhetoric, and who swear for fame!
Behold the schools in which plebeian minds,
Once simple, are initiated in arts
Which some may practise with politer grace,
But none with readier skill!—'tis here they learn
The road that leads, from competence and peace,
To indigence and rapine; till at last
Society, grown weary of the load,
Shakes her encumbered lap, and casts them out.
But censure profits little: vain the attempt
To advertise in verse a public pest,
That, like the filth with which the peasant feeds
His hungry acres, stinks, and is of use.
The excise is fattened with the rich result
Of all this riot; and ten thousand casks,
For ever dribbling out their base contents,
Touched by the Midas finger of the state,
Bleed gold for ministers to sport away.
Drink, and be mad, then; 'tis your country bids!
Gloriously drunk, obey the important call!
Her cause demands the assistance of your throats;—
Ye all can swallow, and she asks no more.
  Would I had fallen upon those happier days
That poets celebrate; those golden times
And those Arcadian scenes that Maro sings,
And Sidney, warbler of poetic prose.
Nymphs were Dianas then, and swains had hearts
That felt their virtues: innocence, it seems,
From courts dismissed, found shelter in the groves;
The footsteps of simplicity, impressed
Upon the yielding herbage, (so they sing)
Then were not all effaced: then speech profane,
And manners profligate, were rarely found;
Observed as prodigies, and soon reclaimed.
Vain wish! those days were never: airy dreams
Sat for the picture; and the poet's hand,
Imparting substance to an empty shade,
Imposed a gay delirium for a truth.
Grant it:—I still must envy them an age

428. name. See, below, Cowper's letter of October 10, 1784. **437. Plashed,** with interwoven branches. **460. ebriety,** drunkenness. **473. Indian fume,** tobacco.

504. excise, a tax on liquor. **515. Maro,** Virgil.

That favoured such a dream; in days like these
Impossible, when virtue is so scarce,
That to suppose a scene where she presides,
Is tramontane, and stumbles all belief.
No: we are polished now! the rural lass,
Whom once her virgin modesty and grace,
Her artless manners, and her neat attire,
So dignified that she was hardly less
Than the fair shepherdess of old romance,
Is seen no more. The character is lost!
Her head, adorned with lappets pinned aloft,
And ribbands streaming gay, superbly raised,
And magnified beyond all human size,
Indebted to some smart wig-weaver's hand
For more than half the tresses it sustains;
Her elbows ruffled, and her tottering form
Ill propped upon French heels, she might be deemed
(But that the basket dangling on her arm
Interprets her more truly) of a rank
Too proud for dairy work, or sale of eggs.
Expect her soon with foot-boy at her heels,
No longer blushing for her awkward load,
Her train and her umbrella all her care!
  The town has tinged the country; and the stain
Appears a spot upon a vestal's robe,
The worse for what it soils. The fashion runs
Down into scenes still rural; but, alas,
Scenes rarely graced with rural manners now!
Time was when, in the pastoral retreat,
The unguarded door was safe; men did not watch
To invade another's right, or guard their own.
Then sleep was undisturbed by fear, unscared
By drunken howlings; and the chilling tale
Of midnight murder was a wonder heard
With doubtful credit, told to frighten babes.
But farewell now to unsuspicious nights,
And slumbers unalarmed! Now, ere you sleep,
See that your polished arms be primed with care,
And drop the night-bolt;—ruffians are abroad;
And the first larum of the cock's shrill throat
May prove a trumpet, summoning your ear
To horrid sounds of hostile feet within.
Even day-light has its dangers; and the walk
Through pathless wastes and woods, unconscious once
Of other tenants than melodious birds,
Or harmless flocks, is hazardous and bold.
Lamented change! to which full many a cause
Inveterate, hopeless of a cure, conspires.
The course of human things from good to ill,
From ill to worse, is fatal, never fails.
Increase of power begets increase of wealth;
Wealth luxury, and luxury excess;
Excess, the scrofulous and itchy plague
That seizes first the opulent, descends
To the next rank contagious, and in time
Taints downward all the graduated scale
Of order, from the chariot to the plough.
The rich, and they that have an arm to check
The licence of the lowest in degree,
Desert their office; and themselves, intent
On pleasure, haunt the capital, and thus
To all the violence of lawless hands
Resign the scenes their presence might protect.
Authority herself not seldom sleeps,
Though resident, and witness of the wrong.
The plump convivial parson often bears
The magisterial sword in vain, and lays
His reverence and his worship both to rest
On the same cushion of habitual sloth.
Perhaps timidity restrains his arm;
When he should strike he trembles, and sets free,
Himself enslaved by terror of the band,
The audacious convict, whom he dares not bind.
Perhaps, though by profession ghostly pure,
He too may have his vice, and sometimes prove
Less dainty than becomes his grave outside
In lucrative concerns. Examine well
His milk-white hand; the palm is hardly clean—
But here and there an ugly smutch appears.
Foh! 'twas a bribe that left it: he has touched
Corruption! Whoso seeks an audit here
Propitious, pays his tribute, game or fish,
Wild-fowl or venison; and his errand speeds.
  But faster far, and more than all the rest,
A noble cause, which none who bears a spark
Of public virtue ever wished removed,
Works the deplored and mischievous effect.
'Tis universal soldiership has stabbed
The heart of merit in the meaner class.
Arms, through the vanity and brainless rage
Of those that bear them, in whatever cause,
Seem most at variance with all moral good,
And incompatible with serious thought.
The clown, the child of nature, without guile,
Blessed with an infant's ignorance of all
But his own simple pleasures—now and then
A wrestling-match, a foot-race, or a fair—
Is ballotted, and trembles at the news:
Sheepish he doffs his hat, and, mumbling, swears
A bible-oath to be whate'er they please,

533. tramontane, barbarous or naïve; literally, "lying beyond the mountains." **540. lappets,** flaps on a head-dress.

579. fatal, determined by fate. **596. sword,** symbol of his office as a magistrate. **603. ghostly,** spiritually. **627. ballotted,** drafted.

To do he knows not what! The task performed,
That instant he becomes the serjeant's care,
His pupil, and his torment, and his jest.
His awkward gait, his introverted toes,
Bent knees, round shoulders, and dejected looks,
Procure him many a curse. By slow degrees,
Unapt to learn, and formed of stubborn stuff,
He yet by slow degrees puts off himself,
Grows conscious of a change, and likes it well:
He stands erect; his slouch becomes a walk;
He steps right onward, martial in his air,
His form and movement; is as smart above
As meal and larded locks can make him; wears
His hat, or his plumed helmet, with a grace;
And, his three years of heroship expired,
Returns indignant to the slighted plough.
He hates the field, in which no fife or drum
Attends him; drives his cattle to a march;
And sighs for the smart comrades he has left.
'Twere well if his exterior change were all—
But with his clumsy port the wretch has lost
His ignorance and harmless manners too!
To swear, to game, to drink; to show at home
By lewdness, idleness, and sabbath-breach,
The great proficiency he made abroad;
To astonish and to grieve his gazing friends,
To break some maiden's and his mother's heart;
To be a pest where he was useful once;
Are his sole aim, and all his glory, now!
  Man in society is like a flower
Blown in its native bed: 'tis there alone
His faculties, expanded in full bloom,
Shine out; there only reach their proper use.
But man, associated and leagued with man
By regal warrant, or self-joined by bond
For interest's sake, or swarming into clans
Beneath one head for purposes of war,
Like flowers selected from the rest, and bound
And bundled close to fill some crowded vase,
Fades rapidly, and, by compression marred,
Contracts defilement not to be endured.
Hence chartered boroughs are such public plagues;
And burghers, men immaculate perhaps
In all their private functions, once combined,
Become a loathsome body, only fit
For dissolution, hurtful to the main.
Hence merchants, unimpeachable of sin
Against the charities of domestic life,
Incorporated, seem at once to lose
Their nature; and, disclaiming all regard
For mercy and the common rights of man,
Build factories with blood, conducting trade
At the sword's point, and dyeing the white robe
Of innocent commercial justice red.
Hence, too, the field of glory, as the world
Misdeems it, dazzled by its bright array,
With all its majesty of thundering pomp,
Enchanting music, and immortal wreaths,
Is but a school where thoughtlessness is taught
On principle, where foppery atones
For folly, gallantry for every vice.
  But, slighted as it is, and by the great
Abandoned, and, which still I more regret,
Infected with the manners and the modes
It knew not once, the country wins me still.
I never framed a wish, or formed a plan,
That flattered me with hopes of earthly bliss,
But there I laid the scene. There early strayed
My fancy, ere yet liberty of choice
Had found me, or the hope of being free:
My very dreams were rural; rural, too,
The first-born efforts of my youthful muse,
Sportive, and jingling her poetic bells
Ere yet her ear was mistress of their powers.
No bard could please me but whose lyre was tuned
To Nature's praises. Heroes and their feats
Fatigued me, never weary of the pipe
Of Tityrus, assembling, as he sang,
The rustic throng beneath his favourite beech.
Then Milton had indeed a poet's charms:
New to my taste, his Paradise surpassed
The struggling efforts of my boyish tongue
To speak its excellence. I danced for joy.
I marvelled much that, at so ripe an age
As twice seven years, his beauties had then first
Engaged my wonder; and, admiring still,
And still admiring, with regret supposed
The joy half lost because not sooner found.
Thee too, enamoured of the life I loved,
Pathetic in its praise, in its pursuit
Determined, and possessing it at last
With transports such as favoured lovers feel,
I studied, prized, and wished that I had known,
Ingenious Cowley! and, though now reclaimed
By modern lights from an erroneous taste,
I cannot but lament thy splendid wit
Entangled in the cobwebs of the schools.
I still revere thee, courtly though retired;
Though stretched at ease in Chertsey's silent bowers,
Not unemployed; and finding rich amends
For a lost world in solitude and verse.

681. build factories, at the beginning of the Industrial Revolution.

707. Tityrus, the chief speaker in Virgil's first Eclogue, and so a representative of pastoral poetry. **723. Cowley!** Abraham Cowley, whose delight in the rural life was not unlike Cowper's own. **728. Chertsey,** a village on the Thames to which Cowley retired.

'Tis born with all: the love of nature's works
Is an ingredient in the compound man,
Infused at the creation of the kind.
And, though the Almighty Maker has throughout
Discriminated each from each, by strokes
And touches of his hand, with so much art
Diversified, that two were never found
Twins at all points—yet this obtains in all,
That all discern a beauty in his works,
And all can taste them: minds that have been formed
And tutored, with a relish more exact,
But none without some relish, none unmoved.
It is a flame that dies not even there,
Where nothing feeds it: neither business, crowds,
Nor habits of luxurious city-life,
Whatever else they smother of true worth
In human bosoms, quench it, or abate.
The villas with which London stands begirt,
Like a swarth Indian with his belt of beads,
Prove it. A breath of unadulterate air,
The glimpse of a green pasture, how they cheer
The citizen, and brace his languid frame!
Even in the stifling bosom of the town,
A garden, in which nothing thrives, has charms
That soothe the rich possessor; much consoled,
That here and there some sprigs of mournful mint,
Of nightshade, or valerian, grace the well
He cultivates. These serve him with a hint
That nature lives; that sight-refreshing green
Is still the livery she delights to wear,
Though sickly samples of the exuberant whole.
What are the casements lined with creeping herbs,
The prouder sashes fronted with a range
Of orange, myrtle, or the fragrant weed,
The Frenchman's darling? are they not all proofs
That man, immured in cities, still retains
His inborn inextinguishable thirst
Of rural scenes, compensating his loss
By supplemental shifts, the best he may?
The most unfurnished with the means of life,
And they that never pass their brick-wall bounds
To range the fields and treat their lungs with air,
Yet feel the burning instinct; over head
Suspend their crazy boxes, planted thick,
And watered duly. There the pitcher stands
A fragment, and the spoutless tea-pot there;
Sad witnesses how close-pent man regrets
The country, with what ardour he contrives
A peep at nature, when he can no more.
  Hail, therefore, patroness of health, and ease,
And contemplation, heart-consoling joys

738. obtains, holds true. **748. villas,** country homes. **765. Frenchman's darling,** mignonette.

And harmless pleasures, in the thronged abode
Of multitudes unknown! hail, rural life!
Address himself who will to the pursuit
Of honours, or emolument, or fame;
I shall not add myself to such a chase,
Thwart his attempts, or envy his success.
Some must be great. Great offices will have
Great talents. And God gives to every man
The virtue, temper, understanding, taste,
That lifts him into life; and lets him fall
Just in the niche he was ordained to fill.
To the deliverer of an injured land
He gives a tongue to enlarge upon, an heart
To feel, and courage to redress her wrongs;
To monarchs dignity; to judges sense;
To artists ingenuity and skill;
To me an unambitious mind, content
In the low vale of life, that early felt
A wish for ease and leisure, and ere long
Found here that leisure and that ease I wished.

THE POPLAR-FIELD

The poplars are felled, farewell to the shade
And the whispering sound of the cool colonnade,
The winds play no longer, and sing in the leaves,
Nor Ouse on his bosom their image receives.

Twelve years have elapsed since I first took a view
Of my favourite field and the bank where they grew,
And now in the grass behold they are laid,
And the tree is my seat that once lent me a shade.

The blackbird has fled to another retreat
Where the hazels afford him a screen from the heat,
And the scene where his melody charmed me before,
Resounds with his sweet-flowing ditty no more.

My fugitive years are all hasting away,
And I must ere long lie as lowly as they,
With a turf on my breast, and a stone at my head,
Ere another such grove shall arise in its stead.

'Tis a sight to engage me, if any thing can,
To muse on the perishing pleasures of man;
Though his life be a dream, his enjoyments, I see,
Have a being less durable even than he.

THE CASTAWAY

Written in the last year of the poet's life, this poem shows more affectingly than any other the obsession against which Cowper had struggled since his youth.

The incident here narrated is drawn from **George, Lord** Anson's *Voyage round the World*, 1748.

Obscurest night involved the sky,
The Atlantic billows roared,
When such a destined wretch as I,
Washed headlong from on board,
Of friends, of hope, of all bereft,
His floating home for ever left.

No braver chief could Albion boast
Than he with whom he went,
Nor ever ship left Albion's coast,
With warmer wishes sent.
He loved them both, but both in vain,
Nor him beheld, nor her again.

Not long beneath the whelming brine,
Expert to swim, he lay;
Nor soon he felt his strength decline,
Or courage die away;
But waged with death a lasting strife,
Supported by despair of life.

He shouted: nor his friends had failed
To check the vessel's course,
But so the furious blast prevailed,
That, pitiless perforce,
They left their outcast mate behind,
And scudded still before the wind.

Some succour yet they could afford;
And, such as storms allow,
The cask, the coop, the floated cord,
Delayed not to bestow.
But he (they knew) nor ship, nor shore,
Whate'er they gave, should visit more.

Nor, cruel as it seemed, could he
Their haste himself condemn,
Aware that flight, in such a sea,
Alone could rescue them;
Yet bitter felt it still to die
Deserted, and his friends so nigh.

He long survives, who lives an hour
In ocean, self-upheld;
And so long he, with unspent power,
His destiny repelled;
And ever, as the minutes flew,
Entreated help, or cried—Adieu!

At length, his transient respite past,
His comrades, who before
Had heard his voice in every blast,
Could catch the sound no more.
For then, by toil subdued, he drank
The stifling wave, and then he sank.

No poet wept him; but the page
Of narrative sincere,
That tells his name, his worth, his age,
Is wet with Anson's tear.
And tears by bards or heroes shed
Alike immortalize the dead.

I therefore purpose not, or dream,
Descanting on his fate,
To give the melancholy theme
A more enduring date;
But misery still delights to trace
Its semblance in another's case.

No voice divine the storm allayed,
No light propitious shone,
When, snatched from all effectual aid,
We perished, each alone;
But I beneath a rougher sea,
And whelmed in deeper gulphs than he.

LETTERS

In an age that made an art of correspondence the letters of William Cowper were unsurpassed. They reveal the man as he was known to his closest friends. They show the delicacy, verve, and quiet humor that usually lay concealed beneath his diffidence. Here his earnest thought and his whimsicality melt into each other and set each other off. Cowper's letters provide the best comment upon his poetry. Indeed, they bid fair to outlive all but a slender sheaf of his poems and to become the mainstay of his literary reputation.

TO THE REV. WILLIAM UNWIN

October 10, 1784.

My Dear William,

I send you four quires of verse, which having sent, I shall dismiss from my thoughts, and think no more of, till I see them in print. I have not after all found time or industry enough to give the last hand to the points. I believe, however, they are not very erroneous, though in so long a work, and in a work that requires nicety in their particular, some inaccuracies will escape. Where you find any, you will oblige me by correcting them.

1. Rev. William Unwin, only son of Cowper's closest friend, Mrs. Mary Unwin. **4. quires.** Twenty-four sheets of writing paper make a quire. This was the manuscript of *The Task*. **8. points,** punctuation marks.

In some passages, especially in the second book, you will observe me very satirical. Writing on such subjects I could not be otherwise. I can write nothing without aiming at least at usefulness: it were beneath my years to do it, and still more dishonourable to my religion. I know that a reformation of such abuses as I have censured is not to be expected from the efforts of a poet; but to contemplate the world, its follies, its vices, its indifference to duty, and its strenuous attachment to what is evil, and not to reprehend were to approve it. From this charge at least I shall be clear, for I have neither tacitly nor expressly flattered either its characters or its customs. I have paid one, and only one compliment, which was so justly due, that I did not know how to withhold it, especially having so fair an occasion;—I forget myself, there is another in the first book to Mr. Throckmorton,—but the compliment I mean is to Mr. Smith. It is however so managed, that nobody but himself can make the application, and you, to whom I disclose the secret; a delicacy on my part, which so much delicacy on his obliged me to the observance of.

What there is of a religious cast in the volume I have thrown towards the end of it, for two reasons; first, that I might not revolt the reader at his entrance,—and secondly, that my best impressions might be made last. Were I to write as many volumes as Lope de Vega, or Voltaire, not one of them would be without this tincture. If the world like it not, so much the worse for them. I make all the concessions I can, that I may please them, but I will not please them at the expense of conscience.

My descriptions are all from nature: not one of them second-handed. My delineations of the heart are from my own experience: not one of them borrowed from books, or in the least degree conjectural. In my numbers, which I have varied as much as I could, (for blank verse without variety of numbers is no better than bladder and string,) I have imitated nobody, though sometimes perhaps there may be an apparent resemblance; because at the same time that I would not imitate, I have not affectedly differed.

If the work cannot boast a regular plan, (in which respect however I do not think it altogether indefensible,) it may yet boast, that the reflections are naturally suggested always by the preceding passage, and that except the fifth book, which is rather of a political aspect, the whole has one tendency: to discountenance the modern enthusiasm after a London life, and to recommend rural ease and leisure, as friendly to the cause of piety and virtue.

If it please you I shall be happy, and collect from your pleasure in it an omen of its general acceptance.

Yours, my dear friend,

W. C.

Your mother's love. She wishes that you would buy her a second-hand cream-pot, small, either kit, jug, or ewer of silver.

I shall be glad of an immediate line to apprise me of its safe arrival.

TO THE REV. JOHN NEWTON

December 13, 1784.

My Dear Friend,

Having imitated no man, I may reasonably hope that I shall not incur the disadvantage of a comparison with my betters. Milton's manner was peculiar. So is Thomson's. He that should write like either of them, would, in my judgment, deserve the name of a copyist, but not of a poet. A judicious and sensible reader therefore, like yourself, will not say that my manner is not good, because it does not resemble theirs, but will rather consider what it is in itself. Blank verse is susceptible of a much greater diversification of manner, than verse in rhyme: and why the modern writers of it have all thought proper to cast their numbers alike, I know not. Certainly it was not necessity that compelled them to it. I flatter myself however that I have avoided that sameness with others, which would entitle me to nothing but a share in one common oblivion with them all. It is possible that, as the reviewer of my former volume found cause to say that he knew not to what class of writers to refer me, the reviewer of this, whosoever he shall be, may see occasion to remark the same singularity. At any rate, though as little apt to be sanguine as most men, and more prone to fear and despond, than to overrate my own productions, I am persuaded that I shall not forfeit any thing by this volume that I gained by the last.

As to the title, I take it to be the best that is to be had. It is not possible that a book, including such a variety of subjects, and in which no particular one is predominant, should find a title adapted to them all. In such a case, it seemed almost necessary to accommodate the name to the incident that gave birth to the poem; nor does it appear to me, that because I

15. **compliment.** See, above, *The Task*, Book IV, ll. 427–28. 18. **Throckmorton.** See *The Task*, Book I, l. 262. 19. **Mr. Smith,** an anonymous benefactor of the poor in Olney.

14. **Rev. John Newton,** an evangelical clergyman of whom Cowper stood usually in awe. He had recently criticized *The Task* adversely. 36. **volume.** that of 1782.

performed more than my task, therefore the Task is not a suitable title. A house would still be a house, though the builder of it should make it ten times as big as he at first intended. I might indeed, following the example of the Sunday newsmonger, call it the Olio. But I should do myself wrong; for though it have much variety, it has, I trust, no confusion.

For the same reason none of the interior titles apply themselves to the contents at large of that book to which they belong. They are, every one of them, taken either from the leading (I should say the introductory) passage of that particular book, or from that which makes the most conspicuous figure in it. Had I set off with a design to write upon a gridiron, and had I actually written near two hundred lines upon that utensil, as I have upon the Sofa, the Gridiron should have been my title. But the Sofa being, as I may say, the starting-post from which I addressed myself to the long race that I soon conceived a design to run, it acquired a just pre-eminence in my account, and was very worthily advanced to the titular honour it enjoys, its right being at least so far a good one, that no word in the language could pretend a better. . . .

We do not often see, or rather feel, so severe a frost before Christmas. Unexpected, at least by me, it had like to have been too much for my greenhouse, my myrtles having found themselves yesterday morning in an atmosphere so cold that the mercury was fallen eight degrees below the freezing point.

Be pleased to remember us to the young ladies, and to all under your roof and elsewhere, who are mindful of us.—And believe me,

Your affectionate
Wm. Cowper.

Your letters are gone to their address. The oysters were very good.

6. Olio, miscellany.

TO SAMUEL ROSE

Weston, July 24, 1787.

Dear Sir,

This is the first time I have written these six months, and nothing but the constraint of obligation could induce me to write now. I cannot be so wanting to myself as not to endeavour at least to thank you both for the visits with which you have favoured me, and the poems that you sent me; in my present state of mind I taste nothing, nevertheless I read, partly from habit, and partly because it is the only thing that I am capable of.

I have therefore read Burns's poems, and have read them twice; and though they be written in a language that is new to me, and many of them on subjects much inferior to the author's ability, I think them on the whole a very extraordinary production. He is, I believe, the only poet these kingdoms have produced in the lower rank of life since Shakespeare (I should rather say since Prior), who need not be indebted for any part of his praise to a charitable consideration of his origin, and the disadvantages under which he has laboured. It will be pity if he should not hereafter divest himself of barbarism, and content himself with writing pure English, in which he appears perfectly qualified to excel. He who can command admiration, dishonours himself if he aims no higher than to raise a laugh.

I am, dear sir, with my best wishes for your prosperity, and with Mrs. Unwin's respects,

Your obliged and affectionate humble servant,
W. C.

1. Samuel Rose, an old friend and assistant of Cowper. **5–6. these six months,** during which Cowper had suffered a return of insanity. **14. Burns's poems.** Burns's *Poems, Chiefly in the Scottish Dialect* was first published in 1786. A second edition was brought out in 1787. **21. Prior,** Matthew Prior (1664–1721), author of epigrams, satires, and society verse.

Robert Burns

1759–1796

Scotland's foremost poet was born in a two-room cottage at Alloway, a village in Ayrshire, Scotland. He was the eldest of the seven children of poor, hard-working, and intelligent parents. The boy had some three years of schooling at Kirkoswald, near Ayr, and such instruction as his earnest and ambitious father could give him. His education included the elements of mathematics, English grammar, and some Latin and French. From his mother, a sensitive and high-spirited country woman, he learned old Scottish songs and tales. Burns's youth was spent chiefly in the hard labor of a plowboy on several unproductive farms, and there is no doubt that his health, particularly his heart, was permanently injured by the strenuous exertions of his early years. As in many a poor Scottish home, all the members of Burns's family were readers, and the lad fortunately found some time for eager reading of Scottish and English literature. Time also was found for the composition of verses in which he used the dialect and the stories of his country neighbors. At twenty-two he became a flax-dresser in the town of Irvine, and began to make the acquaintance of the young men and women of the town and of the pleasures it afforded.

Upon the death of his father, "a specimen of industry and integrity never rewarded in this life," Burns, now in his twenty-fifth year, found himself the head of a family of eight. He moved the family to Mossgiel Farm near Mauchline, where he and his brother Gilbert tried to make a living. The difficulties inherent in operating a poor eighteen-acre farm were aggravated by the young farmer's becoming involved with several young women of the neighborhood, among them Mary Campbell, Elizabeth Paton, and the one he was eventually to marry, Jean Armour, the "Bonnie Jean" of his poems. So entangled were Burns's love affairs becoming that, in order to escape the complications, he thought of leaving Scotland, and accepted a clerkship in Jamaica. During this period he wrote some of his most characteristic poems—"The Jolly Beggars," "The Cotter's Saturday Night," "Holy Willie's Prayer," and many of his best lyrics. To obtain funds for the voyage across the Atlantic he published his first volume, *Poems, Chiefly in the Scottish Dialect*, at Kilmarnock in July, 1786. The success of the book, which he had intended for a restricted audience, brought a change in his plans, and his fame, which had started locally, soon spread through Scotland. Instead of journeying to Jamaica he went to the Scottish capital, Edinburgh, and the visit of the plowboy poet to that Athens of the North caused a sensation in literary circles. A second and enlarged edition of his *Poems*, Edinburgh, 1787, brought the poet more than £500. With the proceeds he managed to take two tours, one through the Highlands of Scotland and the other through northern England. In 1788 he left Edinburgh and returned to the country, married Jean Armour, bought the farm of Ellisland near Dumfries, and settled down again to farming and writing poetry. To supplement his scanty income he became an exciseman for the district. With the inevitable failure of the farm in 1791 he moved to Dumfries, where his political sympathies with the French Revolutionists cost him many friends and almost lost him his position as excise officer.

Burns's literary activity continued through 1792 and produced original songs by the score for such collections as Johnson's *Scots Musical Museum* and Thomson's *Scottish Airs.* He retained his enthusiasm for old Scots songs and ballads, many of which he collected and edited with their melodies. Overborne by poverty, toil, misfortune, and eventual despair, Burns's health failed rapidly in Dumfries, and he died in July, 1796. All the indications go to show that he died of endocarditis, an ailment stemming from the exertions of his early years on the farm.

Burns's life and work present the reader with rather more than the usual budget of paradoxes that one encounters in a genius. He was a poet and a man of many moods and roles. By choosing some of the verses he wrote for raffish friends, one may prove him to have been a sot and a seducer. Such songs as "Mary Morison," "Of A' the Airts," and "A Red, Red Rose" exhibit him as a tender, sincere, and romantic lover. His "Holy Willie's Prayer," which has been called "the most terrific satirical poem in all literature," has been cited to prove his anti-religious sentiment, but "The Cotter's Saturday Night" will prove exactly the opposite. His poems in the Scottish dialect have caused him to be labeled parochial, and "Scots Wha Hae" has been called patriotic rant, but no poem ever written breathes a more genuine spirit of international brotherhood than "A Man's a Man for A' That," and all the world sings his songs.

Turning from the welter of contradictory opinions, one may venture a few conclusions. So far as his character is concerned, Burns was his own severest critic and he catalogued all, or almost all, his faults. On the credit side of the ledger, he must be reckoned first among the poets of human relationships. In the oldest and truest sense of the word Burns is "convivial." An Englishman, Aldous Huxley, has written of him: "After Chaucer, he is the least pretentious and portentous; the most completely and harmoniously human of all the English poets." More than all, he had the transcendent gift of song. And it was Burns more than any other poet who brought back nature into English poetry. His short life spanned the transition from Neoclassical to Romantic domination; he died two years before the appearance of the *Lyrical Ballads* of Wordsworth and Coleridge. It is certain that he helped to hasten the transition by his exquisite perception and descriptive power, and by showing, as Wordsworth said,

How Verse may build a princely throne
On humble truth.

THE COTTER'S SATURDAY NIGHT

Inscribed to R. Aiken, Esq.

This poem is based upon experiences of Burns's boyhood and youth, and is valuable for its picture of the home life of the Scottish peasantry of the eighteenth century. It indicates Burns's acquaintance with such practitioners of the Spenserian stanza as James Thomson, James Beattie, and William Shenstone. There are also echoes of Gray's *Elegy in a Country Churchyard,*

Let not Ambition mock their useful toil,
Their homely joys, and destiny obscure;
Nor Grandeur hear with a disdainful smile
The short and simple annals of the poor.
—Gray

My loved, my honoured, much respected friend!
No mercenary bard his homage pays:
With honest pride I scorn each selfish end,
My dearest meed a friend's esteem and praise:
To you I sing, in simple Scottish lays,
The lowly train in life's sequestered scene;
The native feelings strong, the guileless ways;
What Aiken in a cottage would have been—
Ah! though his worth unknown, far happier there, I ween!

November chill blaws loud wi' angry sugh;
The shortening winter-day is near a close;
The miry beasts retreating frae the pleugh;
The blackening trains o' craws to their repose:
The toil-worn Cotter frae his labour goes,
This night his weekly moil is at an end,
Collects his spades, his mattocks, and his hoes,
Hoping the morn in ease and rest to spend,
And weary, o'er the moor, his course does hameward bend.

At length his lonely cot appears in view,
Beneath the shelter of an agèd tree;
The expectant wee things, toddlin', stacher through
To meet their Dad, wi' flichterin' noise an' glee.
His wee bit ingle, blinkin bonnilie,
His clean hearth-stane, his thrifty wifie's smile,
The lisping infant prattling on his knee,
Does a' his weary kiaugh and care beguile,
An' makes him quite forget his labour an' his toil.

Belyve the elder bairns come drapping in,
At service out, amang the farmers roun';
Some ca' the pleugh, some herd, some tentie rin
A cannie errand to a neibor town:
Their eldest hope, their Jenny, woman-grown,
In youthfu' bloom, love sparkling in her e'e,
Comes hame, perhaps, to shew a braw new gown,
Or deposite her sair-won penny-fee,
To help her parents dear, if they in hardship be.

With joy unfeigned brothers and sisters meet,
An' each for other's weelfare kindly spiers:

1. friend! Robert Aiken, a lawyer of Ayr. **10. sugh,** sough, the sound of the wind. **12. pleugh,** plow. **21. stacher,** stagger. **22. flichterin',** fluttering. **23. ingle,** fireplace. **26. kiaugh,** anxiety. **28. Belyve,** soon. **30. tentie rin,** watchfully run. **34. braw,** fine (brave). **35. deposite,** accent first syllable. **38. spiers,** asks.

The social hours, swift-winged, unnoticed fleet;
Each tells the uncos that he sees or hears;
The parents, partial, eye their hopeful years;
Anticipation forward points the view.
The mother, wi' her needle an' her sheers,
Gars auld claes look amaist as weel's the new;
The father mixes a' wi' admonition due.

Their master's an' their mistress's command,
The younkers a' are warnèd to obey;
An' mind their labours wi' an eydent hand,
An' ne'er, though out o' sight, to jauk or play;
"And O! be sure to fear the Lord alway,
An' mind your duty, duly, morn an' night!
Lest in temptation's path ye gang astray,
Implore His counsel and assisting might:
They never sought in vain that sought the Lord aright!"

But hark! a rap comes gently to the door;
Jenny, wha kens the meaning o' the same,
Tells how a neibor lad cam o'er the moor,
To do some errands, and convoy her hame.
The wily mother sees the conscious flame
Sparkle in Jenny's e'e, and flush her cheek;
Wi' heart-struck anxious care, inquires his name,
While Jenny hafflins is afraid to speak;
Weel pleased the mother hears, it's nae wild, worthless rake.

Wi' kindly welcome, Jenny brings him ben;
A strappin' youth, he takes the mother's eye;
Blythe Jenny sees the visit's no ill ta'en;
The father cracks of horses, pleughs, and kye.
The youngster's artless heart o'erflows wi' joy,
But blate and laithfu', scarce can weel behave;
The mother, wi' a woman's wiles, can spy
What makes the youth sae bashfu' an' sae grave;
Weel-pleased to think her bairn's respected like the lave.

O happy love! where love like this is found;
O heart-felt raptures! bliss beyond compare!
I've pacèd much this weary, mortal round,
And sage experience bids me this declare—
"If Heaven a draught of heavenly pleasure spare,
One cordial in this melancholy vale,
'Tis when a youthful, loving, modest pair
In other's arms breathe out the tender tale,
Beneath the milk-white thorn that scents the evening gale."

Is there, in human form, that bears a heart—
A wretch, a villain, lost to love and truth—
That can, with studied, sly, ensnaring art,
Betray sweet Jenny's unsuspecting youth?
Curse on his perjured arts! dissembling smooth!
Are honour, virtue, conscience, all exiled?
Is there no pity, no relenting ruth,
Points to the parents fondling o'er their child?
Then paints the ruined maid, and their distraction wild?

But now the supper crowns their simple board,
The halesome parritch, chief of Scotia's food:
The sowpe their only hawkie does afford,
That 'yont the hallan snugly chows her cood;
The dame brings forth in complimental mood,
To grace the lad, her weel-hained kebbuck, fell;
An' aft he's prest, and aft he ca's it guid;
The frugal wifie, garrulous, will tell
How 'twas a towmond auld sin' lint was i' the bell.

The cheerfu' supper done, wi' serious face,
They round the ingle form a circle wide;
The sire turns o'er, wi' patriarchal grace,
The big ha'-bible, ance his father's pride:
His bonnet reverently is laid aside,
His lyart haffets wearing thin an' bare;
Those strains that once did sweet in Zion glide—
He wales a portion with judicious care;
And "Let us worship God!" he says with solemn air.

They chant their artless notes in simple guise;
They tune their hearts, by far the noblest aim:
Perhaps Dundee's wild warbling measures rise,
Or plaintive Martyrs, worthy of the name;
Or noble Elgin beets the heavenward flame,
The sweetest far of Scotia's holy lays:
Compared with these, Italian trills are tame;
The tickled ears no heartfelt raptures raise;
Nae unison hae they with our Creator's praise.

40. uncos, uncommon things. **44. Gars,** makes. **48. eydent,** diligent. **49. jauk,** dally. **62. hafflins,** half. **64. ben,** into the room. **67. cracks,** chats. **69. blate and laithfu',** bashful and sheepish. **72. lave,** rest.

92. halesome parritch, wholesome porridge. **93. sowpe . . . hawkie,** sup . . . cow. **94. hallan,** partition wall. **96. weel-hained kebbuck,** well-saved cheese. **fell,** pungent. **99. towmond . . . bell,** twelvemonth-old since flax was in blossom. **105. lyart haffets,** gray locks. **107. wales,** chooses. **113. beets,** enkindles.

The priest-like father reads the sacred page,
How Abram was the friend of God on high;
Or Moses bade eternal warfare wage
With Amalek's ungracious progeny;
Or how the royal bard did groaning lie
Beneath the stroke of Heaven's avenging ire;
Or Job's pathetic plaint, and wailing cry;
Or rapt Isaiah's wild seraphic fire;
Or other holy seers that tune the sacred lyre.

Perhaps the Christian volume is the theme,
How guiltless blood for guilty man was shed;
How He who bore in Heaven the second name
Had not on earth whereon to lay His head;
How His first followers and servants sped;
The precepts sage they wrote to many a land:
How he who lone in Patmos banishèd,
Saw in the sun a mighty angel stand
And heard great Babylon's doom pronounced by Heaven's command.

Then kneeling down, to Heaven's Eternal King,
The saint, the father, and the husband prays:
Hope "springs exulting on triumphant wing"
That thus they all shall meet in future days:
There ever bask in uncreated rays,
No more to sigh, or shed the bitter tear,
Together hymning their Creator's praise,
In such society, yet still more dear;
While circling Time moves round in an eternal sphere.

Compared with this, how poor Religion's pride,
In all the pomp of method and of art,
When men display to congregations wide
Devotion's every grace, except the heart!
The Power, incensed, the pageant will desert,
The pompous strain, the sacerdotal stole;
But haply, in some cottage far apart,
May hear, well pleased, the language of the soul;
And in His Book of Life the inmates poor enrol.

Then homeward all take off their several way;
The youngling cottagers retire to rest:
The parent-pair their secret homage pay,
And proffer up to Heaven the warm request,
That He who stills the raven's clamorous nest,
And decks the lily fair in flowery pride,
Would, in the way His wisdom sees the best,
For them and for their little ones provide;
But chiefly in their hearts with grace divine preside.

138. "springs . . . wing," rewording of Pope's *Windsor-Forest*, l. 112.

From scenes like these old Scotia's grandeur springs,
That makes her loved at home, revered abroad:
Princes and lords are but the breath of kings,
"An honest man's the noblest work of God";
And certes, in fair virtue's heavenly road,
The cottage leaves the palace far behind;
What is a lordling's pomp? a cumbrous load,
Disguising oft the wretch of human kind,
Studied in arts of hell, in wickedness refined!

O Scotia! my dear, my native soil!
For whom my warmest wish to Heaven is sent!
Long may thy hardy sons of rustic toil
Be blest with health, and peace, and sweet content!
And, O may Heaven their simple lives prevent
From luxury's contagion, weak and vile;
Then, howe'er crowns and coronets be rent,
A virtuous populace may rise the while,
And stand a wall of fire around their much-loved isle.

O Thou! who poured the patriotic tide
That streamed through Wallace's undaunted heart;
Who dared to nobly stem tyrannic pride,
Or nobly die, the second glorious part,
(The patriot's God, peculiarly thou art,
His friend, inspirer, guardian, and reward!)
O never, never, Scotia's realm desert;
But still the patriot, and the patriot-bard,
In bright succession raise, her ornament and guard!

TO A MOUSE

ON TURNING HER UP IN HER NEST WITH THE PLOUGH

Wee, sleekit, cow'rin', tim'rous beastie,
O what a panic's in thy breastie!
Thou need na start awa sae hasty,
Wi' bickering brattle!
I wad be laith to rin an' chase thee,
Wi' murdering pattle!

I'm truly sorry man's dominion
Has broken Nature's social union,

166. "An honest man's . . . God," from Pope's *Essay on Man*, Ep. IV, l. 248. **1. sleekit,** smooth-coated. **4. bickering brattle,** scampering haste. **6. pattle,** plow staff.

An' justifies that ill opinion
Which makes thee startle
At me, thy poor earth-born companion,
An' fellow-mortal!

I doubt na, whiles, but thou may thieve;
What then? poor beastie, thou maun live!
A daimen-icker in a thrave
'S a sma' request:
I'll get a blessin wi' the lave,
And never miss 't!

Thy wee bit housie, too, in ruin!
Its silly wa's the win's are strewin'!
An' naething, now, to big a new ane,
O' foggage green!
An' bleak December's winds ensuin',
Baith snell an' keen!

Thou saw the fields laid bare and waste,
An' weary winter comin' fast,
An' cozie here, beneath the blast,
Thou thought to dwell,
Till crash! the cruel coulter past
Out-through thy cell.

That wee bit heap o' leaves an' stibble
Has cost thee mony a weary nibble!
Now thou's turned out, for a' thy trouble,
But house or hald,
To thole the winter's sleety dribble,
An' cranreuch cauld!

But, Mousie, thou art no thy lane,
In proving foresight may be vain:
The best laid schemes o' mice an' men
Gang aft a-gley,
An' lea'e us nought but grief an' pain
For promised joy.

Still thou art blest compared wi' me!
The present only toucheth thee:
But oh! I backward cast my e'e
On prospects drear!
An' forward tho' I canna see,
I guess an' fear!

13. whiles, at times. **15. daimen-icker . . . thrave,** an occasional ear in twenty-four sheaves. **17. lave,** rest. **20. silly,** weak, helpless. **21. big,** build. **22. foggage,** coarse grass. **24. snell,** biting. **34. But . . . hald,** without house or property. **35. thole,** endure. **36. cranreuch,** frost. **37. no thy lane,** not alone. **40. Gang aft a-gley,** go oft astray.

TO A MOUNTAIN DAISY

ON TURNING ONE DOWN WITH THE PLOUGH

Wee modest crimson-tippèd flower,
Thou'st met me in an evil hour;
For I maun crush amang the stoure
Thy slender stem:
To spare thee now is past my power,
Thou bonie gem.

Alas! it's no thy neibor sweet,
The bonnie lark, companion meet,
Bending thee 'mang the dewy weet
Wi's sprecklèd breast,
When upward springing, blythe to greet
The purpling east.

Cauld blew the bitter-biting north
Upon thy early humble birth;
Yet cheerfully thou glinted forth
Amid the storm,
Scarce reared above the parent-earth
Thy tender form.

The flaunting flowers our gardens yield
High sheltering woods and wa's maun shield,
But thou, beneath the random bield
O' clod or stane,
Adorns the histie stibble-field,
Unseen, alane.

There, in thy scanty mantle clad,
Thy snawy bosom sun-ward spread,
Thou lifts thy unassuming head
In humble guise;
But now the share uptears thy bed,
And low thou lies!

Such is the fate of artless maid,
Sweet floweret of the rural shade,
By love's simplicity betrayed,
And guileless trust,
Till she like thee, all soiled, is laid
Low i' the dust.

Such is the fate of simple bard,
On life's rough ocean luckless starred:
Unskilful he to note the card
Of prudent lore,
Till billows rage, and gales blow hard,
And whelm him o'er!

3. stoure, dust. **6. gem,** bud. **21. bield,** shelter. **23. histie,** barren. **39. card,** compass card.

Such fate to suffering worth is given,
Who long with wants and woes has striven,
By human pride or cunning driven
To misery's brink,
Till wrenched of every stay but Heaven,
He, ruined, sink!

Ev'n thou who mourn'st the Daisy's fate,
That fate is thine—no distant date;
Stern Ruin's ploughshare drives elate
Full on thy bloom,
Till crushed beneath the furrow's weight
Shall be thy doom!

GREEN GROW THE RASHES

Green grow the rashes O,
Green grow the rashes O;
The sweetest hours that e'er I spend,
Are spent amang the lasses O!

There's nought but care on every han',
In every hour that passes O;
What signifies the life o' man,
An' 'twere na for the lasses O.

The warly race may riches chase,
An' riches still may fly them O;
An' though at last they catch them fast,
Their hearts can ne'er enjoy them O.

But gie me a canny hour at e'en,
My arms about my dearie O;
An' warly cares, an' warly men,
May a' gae tapsalteerie O!

For you sae douce, ye sneer at this,
Ye're nought but senseless asses O:
The wisest man the warl' saw,
He dearly loved the lasses O.

Auld nature swears, the lovely dears
Her noblest work she classes O;
Her prentice han' she tried on man,
An' then she made the lasses O.

WILLIE BREWED A PECK O' MAUT

O Willie brewed a peck o' maut,
And Rob and Allan cam to see;
Three blyther hearts, that lee-lang night,
Ye wad na found in Christendie.

Chorus

We are na fou, we're no that fou,
But just a drappie in our ee;
The cock may craw, the day may daw,
And aye we'll taste the barley bree!

Here are we met, three merry boys,
Three merry boys, I trow, are we;
And monie a night we've merry been,
And monie mae we hope to be!

It is the moon, I ken her horn,
That's blinkin' in the lift saw hie;
She shines sae bright to wyle us hame,
But, by my sooth, she'll wait a wee!

Wha first shall rise to gang awa,
A cuckold, coward loun is he!
Wha first beside his chair shall fa',
He is the King among us three!

ADDRESS TO THE UNCO GUID, OR THE RIGIDLY RIGHTEOUS

My son, these maxims make a rule,
An' lump them aye thegither:
The rigid righteous is a fool,
The rigid wise anither:
The cleanest corn that e'er was dight,
May hae some pyles o' caff in;
So ne'er a fellow-creature slight
For random fits o' daffin.

Solomon (Eccles. vii. 16).

O ye wha are sae guid yoursel,
Sae pious and sae holy,
Ye've nought to do but mark and tell
Your neibour's fauts and folly!
Whase life is like a weel-gaun mill,
Supplied wi' store o' water,
The heapèd happer's ebbing still,
And still the clap plays clatter:

1. **rashes,** rushes, reeds. 8. **An',** if. 9. **warly,** worldly. 16. **tapsalteerie,** topsy-turvy. 17. **douce,** sober. 19. **wisest man,** Solomon. *Willie Brewed a Peck o' Maut.* 1. **maut,** malt. 3. **lee-lang,** livelong. 5. **fou,** full, drunk. 6. **drappie,** small drop. 8. **barley bree!** barley brew. 12. **mae,** more. 14. **lift,** sky. 15. **wyle,** entice. 18. **loun,** rascal. *Address to the Unco Guid. Introduction.* **aye thegither,** always together. **dight,** winnowed. **pyles o' caff,** grains of chaff. **daffin,** larking. 5. **weel-gaun,** smoothly running. 7. **happer,** hopper. 8. **clap,** clapper.

Hear me, ye venerable core,
As counsel for poor mortals,
That frequent pass douce Wisdom's door,
For glaikit Folly's portals;
I, for their thoughtless, careless sakes,
Would here propone defences,—
Their donsie tricks, their black mistakes,
Their failings and mischances.

Ye see your state wi' their's compared,
And shudder at the niffer;
But cast a moment's fair regard—
What makes the mighty differ?
Discount what scant occasion gave,
That purity ye pride in,
And (what's aft mair than a' the lave)
Your better art o' hidin'.

Think, when your castigated pulse
Gies now and then a wallop,
What ragings must his veins convulse,
That still eternal gallop!
Wi' wind and tide fair i' your tail,
Right on ye scud your sea-way;
But in the teeth o' baith to sail,
It maks an unco leeway.

See Social life and Glee sit down,
All joyous and unthinking,
Till, quite transmogrified, they're grown
Debauchery and Drinking:
O would they stay to calculate
The eternal consequences;
Or your more dreaded hell to state,
Damnation of expenses!

Ye high, exalted, virtuous Dames,
Tied up in godly laces,
Before ye gie poor Frailty names,
Suppose a change o' cases;
A dear loved lad, convenience snug,
A treacherous inclination—
But, let me whisper i' your lug,
Ye're aiblins nae temptation.

Then gently scan your brother man,
Still gentler sister woman;
Though they may gang a kennin wrang,
To step aside is human.
One point must still be greatly dark,
The moving *why* they do it;
And just as lamely can ye mark
How far perhaps they rue it.

Who made the heart, 'tis He alone
Decidedly can try us;
He knows each chord, its various tone,
Each spring, its various bias.
Then at the balance let's be mute,
We never can adjust it;
What's done we partly may compute,
But know not what's resisted.

9. **core,** company. 12. **glaikit,** giddy. 15. **donsie,** unfortunate. 18. **niffer,** difference. 47. **lug,** ear. 48. **aiblins,** perhaps. 51. **kennin,** trifle.

ADDRESS TO THE DEIL

O Prince, O chief of many thronèd powers,
That led the embattled Seraphim to war.

—MILTON

O thou! whatever title suit thee,
Auld Hornie, Satan, Nick, or Clootie,
Wha in yon cavern grim an' sootie,
Closed under hatches,
Spairges about the brunstane cootie,
To scaud poor wretches!

Hear me, auld Hangie, for a wee,
An' let poor damnèd bodies be;
I'm sure sma' pleasure it can gie,
Ev'n to a deil,
To skelp an' scaud poor dogs like me,
An' hear us squeal!

Great is thy power, an' great thy fame;
Far kenned an' noted is thy name;
An' though yon lowin heugh's thy hame,
Thou travels far;
An' faith! thou's neither lag nor lame,
Nor blate nor scaur.

Whyles rangin' like a roarin' lion
For prey, a' holes an' corners tryin';
Whyles on the strong-winged tempest flyin',
Tirlin' the kirks;
Whyles, in the human bosom pryin',
Unseen thou lurks.

Address to the Deil. The poem is a jolly tongue-in-the-cheek chat with the Devil, who is here something of a burlesque of Milton's Infernal Prince. The opening lines are a parody of Pope's address to Swift in *The Dunciad*, Part I, ll. 19-20:

O Thou! whatever title please thine ear,
Dean, Drapier, Bickerstaff, or Gulliver!

5. **Spairges,** splashes. **cootie,** dish. 6. **scaud,** scald. 11. **skelp,** strike. 15. **lowin heugh,** flaming pit. 17. **lag,** slow. 18. **blate nor scaur,** bashful nor timid. 22. **Tirlin',** unroofing.

I've heard my reverend graunie say,
In lanely glens ye like to stray;
Or, where auld ruined castles gray
Nod to the moon,
Ye fright the nightly wanderer's way,
Wi' eldritch croon.

When twilight did my graunie summon
To say her prayers, douce, honest woman!
Aft yont the dyke she's heard you bummin',
Wi' eerie drone;
Or, rustlin', through the boortrees comin',
Wi' heavy groan.

Ae dreary windy winter night
The stars shot down wi' sklentin' light,
Wi' you mysel I gat a fright
Ayont the lough;
Ye like a rash-buss stood in sight
Wi' waving sough.

The cudgel in my nieve did shake,
Each bristled hair stood like a stake,
When, wi' an eldritch stoor "quaick, quaick,"
Amang the springs,
Awa ye squattered like a drake,
On whistlin' wings.

Let warlocks grim an' withered hags
Tell how wi' you on ragweed nags
They skim the muirs, an' dizzy crags,
Wi' wicked speed;
And in kirk-yards renew their leagues
Owre howkit dead.

Thence country wives, wi' toil an' pain,
May plunge an' plunge the kirn in vain;
For oh! the yellow treasure's taen
By witchin' skill;
An' dawtit twal-pint Hawkie's gane
As yell 's the bill.

Thence mystic knots mak great abuse
On young guidmen, fond, keen, an' crouse;
When the best wark-lume i' the house,
By cantrip wit,
Is instant made no worth a louse,
Just at the bit.

When thowes dissolve the snawy hoord,
An' float the jinglin' icy boord,
Then water-kelpies haunt the foord,
By your direction,
An' 'nighted travellers are allured
To their destruction.

An' aft your moss-traversing spunkies
Decoy the wight that late an' drunk is:
The bleezin, curst, mischievous monkies
Delude his eyes,
Till in some miry slough he sunk is,
Ne'er mair to rise.

When masons' mystic word an' grip
In storms an' tempests raise you up,
Some cock or cat your rage maun stop,
Or, strange to tell!
The youngest brither ye wad whip
Aff straught to hell.

Lang syne, in Eden's bonie yard,
When youthfu' lovers first were paired,
And all the soul of love they shared,
The raptured hour,
Sweet on the fragrant flowery swaird,
In shady bower;

Then you, ye auld, snick-drawing dog!
Ye cam to Paradise incog,
An' played on man a cursèd brogue,
(Black be you fa!)
An' gied the infant warld a shog,
'Maist ruined a'.

D'ye mind that day, when in a bizz,
Wi' reekit duds, an' reestit gizz,
Ye did present your smoutie phiz
'Mang better folk,
An' sklented on the man of Uz
Your spitefu' joke?

An' how ye gat him i' your thrall,
An' brak him out o' house an' hal',
While scabs an' blotches did him gall
Wi' bitter claw,
An' lowsed his ill-tongued, wicked scawl,
Was warst ava?

33. bummin', humming. **35. boortrees,** elder bushes. **38. sklentin',** slanting. **40. lough,** lake. **41. rash-buss,** clump of rushes. **43. nieve,** fist. **45. eldritch stoor,** unearthly hoarse. **50. ragweed nags,** brooms. **54. howkit,** dug-up. **56. kirn,** churn. **59–60. dawtit . . . bill,** the favorite twelve-pint cow has gone as dry as the bull. **62. crouse,** self-assured. **64. cantrip,** supernatural. **66. bit,** critical moment.

67. thowes, thaws. **73. spunkies,** will-o'-the-wisps. **75. bleezin,** blazing. **81. maun,** must. **85. Lang syne,** long since. **bonie yard,** beautiful enclosure. **91. snick-drawing,** cheating. **93. brogue,** trick. **94. fa!** lot, destiny. **95. shog,** shake. **97. bizz,** flurry. **98. reekit . . . gizz,** smoking clothes and singed wig. **99. smoutie,** smutty. **107. lowsed . . . scawl,** loosed his scold, that is, Job's wife. **108. ava?** of all.

But a' your doings to rehearse,
Your wily snares an' fechtin fierce,
Sin' that day Michael did you pierce,
Down to this time,
Wad ding a' Lallan tongue, or Erse,
In prose or rhyme.

An' now, auld Cloots, I ken ye're thinkin',
A certain Bardie's rantin', drinkin',
Some luckless hour will send him linkin',
To your black pit;
But faith! he'll turn a corner jinkin',
An' cheat you yet.

But fare you weel, auld Nickie-ben!
O wad ye tak a thought an' men'!
Ye aiblins might—I dinna ken—
Still hae a stake:
I'm wae to think upo' yon den,
Ev'n for your sake!

TAM O' SHANTER

The scene and story of this highly popular poem had been familiar to Burns from his childhood. It was published in *Antiquities of Scotland* (1789–91) by Francis Grose, an antiquarian friend of Burns, who supplied an engraving and description of Alloway Kirk to accompany the poem. Shanter is a farm in southern Ayrshire, and its tenant, Douglas Graham, is supposed to have been the protagonist of Tam. Composed, according to tradition, in a single day, it has the speed and ease of oral narration, as though it had been made less for the library than for the tavern and fireside, and not for the world in general but for a group of old cronies. Burns considered "Tam o' Shanter" his best poem, and Sir Walter Scott shared his opinion.

A TALE

Of Brownyis and of Bogillis full is this Buke.
—Gawin Douglas

When chapman billies leave the street,
And drouthy neibors neibors meet,
As market-days are wearing late,
An' folk begin to tak the gate;
While we sit bousing at the nappy,
An' getting fou and unco happy,
We think na on the lang Scots miles,
The mosses, waters, slaps, and styles,
That lie between us and our hame,
Where sits our sulky sullen dame,
Gathering her brows like gathering storm,
Nursing her wrath to keep it warm.
This truth fand honest Tam o' Shanter,
As he frae Ayr ae night did canter—
(Auld Ayr, wham ne'er a town surpasses
For honest men and bonie lasses).
O Tam! hadst thou but been sae wise,
As ta'en thy ain wife Kate's advice!
She tauld thee weel thou was a skellum,
A bletherin', blusterin', drunken blellum;
That frae November till October,
Ae market-day thou was na sober;
That ilka melder wi' the miller
Thou sat as lang as thou had siller;
That every naig was ca'd a shoe on,
The smith and thee gat roarin' fou on;
That at the Lord's house, even on Sunday,
Thou drank wi' Kirkton Jean till Monday.
She prophesied that, late or soon,
Thou would be found deep drowned in Doon;
Or catched wi' warlocks in the mirk
By Alloway's auld haunted kirk.
Ah, gentle dames! it gars me greet
To think how mony counsels sweet,
How mony lengthened sage advices,
The husband frae the wife despises!
But to our tale: Ae market night,
Tam had got planted unco right,
Fast by an ingle, bleezing finely,
Wi' reaming swats, that drank divinely;
And at his elbow, Souter Johnny,
His ancient, trusty, drouthy crony;
Tam lo'ed him like a very brither;
They had been fou for weeks thegither.
The night drave on wi' sangs and clatter;
And aye the ale was growing better:
The landlady and Tam grew gracious,
Wi' favours secret, sweet, and precious:
The souter tauld his queerest stories;
The landlord's laugh was ready chorus:
The storm without might rair and rustle,
Tam did na mind the storm a whistle.
Care, mad to see a man sae happy,
E'en drowned himsel amang the nappy:
As bees flee hame wi' lades o' treasure,
The minutes winged their way wi' pleasure;

113. ding . . . Erse, beat any Lowland tongue, or any Gaelic one. **117. linkin',** tripping. **119. jinkin',** dodging. **124. stake,** gambler's chance. **125. wae,** sorry. **1. chapman billies,** peddlers. **2. drouthy,** thirsty. **4. tak the gate,** start on the way home. **5. nappy,** ale. **7. Scots miles,** longer than the English.

8. slaps, gates. **19. skellum,** good-for-nothing. **20. blellum,** babbler. **23. melder,** grinding of grain. **24. siller,** silver. **25. every . . . on,** every time a horse was shod. **31. warlocks in the mirk,** wizards in the dark. **33. gars me greet,** makes me weep. **40. reaming swats,** foaming new ale. **41. Souter,** cobbler.

Kings may be blest, but Tam was glorious,
O'er a' the ills o' life victorious!
But pleasures are like poppies spread,
You seize the flower, its bloom is shed;
Or like the snow falls in the river—
A moment white, then melts for ever;
Or like the borealis race,
That flit ere you can point their place;
Or like the rainbow's lovely form
Evanishing amid the storm.
Nae man can tether time nor tide;
The hour approaches Tam maun ride;
That hour, o' night's black arch the key-stane,
That dreary hour, he mounts his beast in;
And sic a night he taks the road in,
As ne'er poor sinner was abroad in.
The wind blew as 'twad blawn its last;
The rattling showers rose on the blast;
The speedy gleams the darkness swallowed;
Loud, deep, and lang, the thunder bellowed:
That night, a child might understand,
The Deil had business on his hand.
Weel mounted on his gray mare, Meg—
A better never lifted leg—
Tam skelpit on through dub and mire,
Despising wind, and rain, and fire;
Whiles holding fast his guid blue bonnet;
Whiles crooning o'er some auld Scots sonnet;
Whiles glowering round wi' prudent cares,
Lest bogles catch him unawares.
Kirk-Alloway was drawing nigh,
Whare ghaists and houlets nightly cry.
By this time he was cross the ford,
Where in the snaw the chapman smoored;
And past the birks and meikle stane,
Where drunken Charlie brak's neck-bane;
And through the whins, and by the cairn,
Where hunters fand the murdered bairn;
And near the thorn, aboon the well,
Where Mungo's mither hanged hersel.
Before him Doon pours all his floods;
The doubling storm roars through the woods;
The lightnings flash from pole to pole;
Near and more near the thunders roll:
When, glimmering through the groaning trees,
Kirk-Alloway seemed in a bleeze;
Through ilka bore the beams were glancing;
And loud resounded mirth and dancing.
Inspiring bold John Barleycorn!
What dangers thou canst make us scorn!

81. skelpit, hurried. **dub,** puddle. **84. sonnet,** song. **86. bogles,** goblins. **88. ghaists,** ghosts. **houlets,** owls. **90. smoored,** smothered. **91. birks,** birches. **93. whins,** furze bushes. **103. ilka bore,** every chink.

Wi' tippenny, we fear nae evil;
Wi' usquebae we'll face the devil!
The swats sae reamed in Tammie's noddle,
Fair play, he cared na deils a boddle!
But Maggie stood right sair astonished,
Till, by the heel and hand admonished,
She ventured forward on the light;
And, vow! Tam saw an unco sight!
Warlocks and witches in a dance!
Nae cotillon brent new frae France,
But hornpipes, jigs, strathspeys, and reels,
Put life and mettle in their heels.
A winnock-bunker in the east,
There sat auld Nick, in shape o' beast—
A touzie tyke, black, grim, and large!
To gie them music was his charge:
He screwed the pipes and gart them skirl,
Till roof and rafters a' did dirl.
Coffins stood round like open presses,
That shawed the dead in their last dresses;
And by some devilish cantraip sleight
Each in its cauld hand held a light,
By which heroic Tam was able
To note upon the haly table
A murderer's banes in gibbet-airns;
Twa span-lang, wee, unchristened bairns;
A thief new-cutted frae a rape,
Wi' his last gasp his gab did gape;
Five tomahawks, wi' blude red-rusted;
Five scymitars, wi' murder crusted;
A garter, which a babe had strangled;
A knife, a father's throat had mangled,
Whom his ain son o' life bereft,
The gray hairs yet stack to the heft;
Wi' mair of horrible and awfu',
Which even to name wad be unlawfu'.
As Tammie glowred, amazed, and curious,
The mirth and fun grew fast and furious:
The piper loud and louder blew;
The dancers quick and quicker flew;
They reeled, they set, they crossed, they cleekit,
Till ilka carlin swat and reekit,
And coost her duddies to the wark,
And linkit at it in her sark!
Now Tam, O Tam! had thae been queans,
A' plump and strapping in their teens;

107. tippenny, twopenny ale. **108. usquebae,** whisky. **109. swats . . . reamed,** new ale so creamed. **110. boddle,** farthing. **116. brent,** brand. **119. winnock-bunker.** window seat. **121. touzie tyke,** shaggy cur. **123. gart them skirl,** made them scream. **124. dirl,** ring. **127. cantraip sleight,** magic trick. **130. haly,** holy. **131. airns,** irons (iron chains). **134. gab,** mouth. **147. cleekit,** clutched. **148. carlin,** hag. **149. coost . . . wark,** threw her clothes off for the work. **150. linkit . . . sark,** went at it in her shift (chemise). **151. queans,** young wenches.

Their sarks, instead o' creeshie flannen,
Been snaw-white seventeen hunder linen!
Thir breeks o' mine, my only pair,
That ance were plush, o' gude blue hair,
I wad hae gi'en them off my hurdies,
For ae blink o' the bonie burdies!
But withered beldams, auld and droll,
Rigwoodie hags wad spean a foal,
Louping and flinging on a crummock,
I wonder didna turn thy stomach.
But Tam kend what was what fu' brawlie.
There was ae winsome wench and walie
That night enlisted in the core,
Lang after kent on Carrick shore!
(For mony a beast to dead she shot,
And perished mony a bonnie boat,
And shook baith meikle corn and bear,
And kept the country-side in fear.)
Her cutty sark, o' Paisley harn,
That while a lassie she had worn,
In longitude though sorely scanty,
It was her best, and she was vauntie.
Ah! little kent thy reverend grannie
That sark she coft for her wee Nannie
Wi' twa pund Scots ('twas a' her riches)
Wad ever graced a dance of witches!
But here my Muse her wing maun cour;
Sic flights are far beyond her power—
To sing how Nannie lap and flang,
(A souple jade she was, and strang),
And how Tam stood, like ane bewitched,
And thought his very een enriched;
Even Satan glowred, and fidged fu' fain,
And hotched and blew wi' might and main:
Till first ae caper, syne anither,
Tam tint his reason a' thegither,
And roars out "Weel done, Cutty-sark!"
And in an instant all was dark!
And scarcely had he Maggie rallied,
When out the hellish legion sallied.
As bees bizz out wi' angry fyke
When plundering herds assail their byke;
As open pussie's mortal foes,
When pop! she starts before their nose,
As eager runs the market-crowd,
When "Catch the thief!" resounds aloud;
So Maggie runs; the witches follow,
Wi' mony an eldritch skriech and hollow.
Ah, Tam! ah, Tam! thou'll get thy fairin'!
In hell they'll roast thee like a herrin'!
In vain thy Kate awaits thy comin'!
Kate soon will be a woefu' woman!
Now do thy speedy utmost, Meg,
And win the key-stane o' the brig;
There at them thou thy tail may toss,
A running stream they darena cross.
But ere the key-stane she could make,
The fient a tail she had to shake!
For Nannie, far before the rest,
Hard upon noble Maggie prest,
And flew at Tam wi' furious ettle;
But little wist she Maggie's mettle!
Ae spring brought off her master hale,
But left behind her ain gray tail:
The carlin claught her by the rump,
And left poor Maggie scarce a stump.
Now, wha this tale o' truth shall read,
Each man and mother's son, take heed;
Whene'er to drink you are inclined,
Or cutty-sarks rin in your mind,
Think! ye may buy the joys o'er dear;
Remember Tam o' Shanter's mare.

153. creeshie flannen, greasy flannel. **155. Thir breeks,** these breeches. **157. hurdies,** haunches. **158. ae blink,** one glimpse. **160. Rigwoodie . . . foal,** ancient hags that would wean a foal, with disgust. **161. crummock,** crooked staff. **163. kend,** knew. **brawlie,** well. **164. walie,** buxom. **166. Carrick,** southeast Ayrshire. **169. corn and bear,** wheat and barley. **171. cutty sark,** short shift (chemise). **harn,** coarse linen. **174. vauntie,** proud of it. **176. coft,** bought. **179. cour,** lower, modern "cower." **185. fidged fu' fain,** fidgeted with pleasure. **186. hotched,** hitched, fidgeted. **188. tint,** lost. **193. fyke,** fuss. **194. herds,** shepherds. **byke,** hive. **195. pussie's,** hare's.

201. fairin'! reward. **206. brig,** bridge. **210. fient,** devil. **213. ettle,** intent. **214. wist,** knew. **217. claught,** seized. **5. weet,** wet. **7. draigl't,** bedraggled. **9. Gin,** if.

COMIN' THRO' THE RYE

Comin' thro' the rye, poor body,
Comin' thro' the rye,
She draigl't a' her petticoatie
Comin' thro' the rye.
Oh Jenny's a' weet, poor body,
Jenny's seldom dry;
She draigl't a' her petticoatie
Comin' thro' the rye.

Gin a body meet a body
Comin' thro' the rye,
Gin a body kiss a body,
Need a body cry?
Oh Jenny's a' weet, poor body,
Jenny's seldom dry;
She draigl't a' her petticoatie
Comin' thro' the rye.

Gin a body meet a body
  Comin' thro' the glen;
Gin a body kiss a body,
  Need the warld ken?
    Oh Jenny's a' weet, poor body,
      Jenny's seldom dry;
    She draigl't a' her petticoatie
      Comin' thro' the rye.

OF A' THE AIRTS

Of a' the airts the wind can blaw,
  I dearly like the west,
For there the bonie lassie lives,
  The lassie I lo'e best:
There's wild woods grow, and rivers row,
  And mony a hill between;
But day and night my fancy's flight
  Is ever wi' my Jean.

I see her in the dewy flowers,
  I see her sweet and fair:
I hear her in the tunefu' birds,
  I hear her charm the air:
There's not a bonie flower that springs
  By fountain, shaw, or green,
There's not a bonie bird that sings,
  But minds me o' my Jean.

JOHN ANDERSON MY JO

John Anderson my jo, John,
  When we were first acquent,
Your locks were like the raven,
  Your bonie brow was brent;
But now your brow is beld, John,
  Your locks are like the snow;
But blessings on your frosty pow,
  John Anderson, my jo.

John Anderson my jo, John,
  We clamb the hill thegither;
And mony a canty day, John,
  We've had wi' ane anither:
Now we maun totter down, John,
  And hand in hand we'll go,
And sleep thegither at the foot,
  John Anderson, my jo.

20. ken, know. *Of A' the Airts.* **1. airts,** directions. **5. row,** roll **8. Jean,** Burns's wife. **14. shaw,** woodland. *John Anderson My Jo.* **1. jo,** darling. **4. brent,** smooth. **5. beld,** bald. **7. pow,** head. **11. canty,** happy.

SCOTS, WHA HAE

In this ringing battle-song Burns takes his theme, for once, from history. He would have us imagine that the words were spoken by Robert Bruce just before the Battle of Bannockburn (1314), in which the Scots defeated an English army under Edward II. Clearly, however, the patriotic intensity of the poem, written in 1793, owes something to Burns's enthusiasm for the French Revolution.

"I have rarely met with anything in history," Burns wrote with this poem in mind, "which interests my feelings as a man equal with the story of Bannockburn. On the one hand a cruel but able usurper, leading on the finest army in Europe, to extinguish the last spark of freedom among a greatly daring and greatly injured people; on the other, the desperate relics of a gallant nation devoting themselves to rescue their bleeding country or perish with her. Liberty, thou art a prize truly and indeed invaluable, for never canst thou be too dearly bought!"

Scots, wha hae wi' Wallace bled,
Scots, wham Bruce has aften led,
Welcome to your gory bed,
    Or to victorie.

Now's the day, and now's the hour;
See the front o' battle lour!
See approach proud Edward's power—
    Chains and slaverie!

Wha will be a traitor knave?
Wha can fill a coward's grave?
Wha sae base as be a slave?
    Let him turn and flee!

Wha for Scotland's King and law
Freedom's sword will strongly draw,
Freeman stand, or freeman fa'?
    Let him follow me!

By oppression's woes and pains!
By your sons in servile chains!
We will drain our dearest veins,
    But they shall be free!

Lay the proud usurpers low!
Tyrants fall in every foe!
Liberty's in every blow!
    Let us do, or die!

AULD LANG SYNE

Should auld acquaintance be forgot,
  And never brought to min'?
Should auld acquaintance be forgot,
  And auld lang syne!

  For auld lang syne, my jo,
    For auld lang syne,
  We'll tak a cup o' kindness yet,
    For auld lang syne.

And surely ye'll be your pint-stowp,
  And surely I'll be mine;
And we'll tak a cup o' kindness yet
  For auld lang syne.

We twa hae run about the braes,
  And pu'd the gowans fine;
But we've wander'd mony a weary foot
  Sin' auld lang syne.

We twa hae paidled i' the burn,
  From morning sun till dine;
But seas between us braid hae roared,
  Sin' auld lang syne.

And there's a hand, my trusty fiere,
  And gie's a hand o' thine!
And we'll tak a right guid-willie-waught,
  For auld lang syne.

DUNCAN GRAY

Duncan Gray came here to woo,
    Ha, ha, the wooing o't,
On blythe Yule night when we were fou,
    Ha, ha, the wooing o't,
Maggie coost her head fu' high,
Looked asklent and unco skeigh,
Gart poor Duncan stand abeigh;
    Ha, ha, the wooing o't.

Duncan fleeched, and Duncan prayed,
    Ha, ha, the wooing o't,
Meg was deaf as Ailsa Craig,
    Ha, ha, the wooing o't.
Duncan sighed baith out and in,
Grat his een baith bleer't and blin',
Spak o' lowpin o'er a linn;
    Ha, ha, the wooing o't.

Time and chance are but a tide,
    Ha, ha, the wooing o't,
Slighted love is sair to bide,
    Ha, ha, the wooing o't.
Shall I, like a fool, quoth he,
For a haughty hizzie die?
She may gae to—France for me!
    Ha, ha, the wooing o't.

How it comes let doctors tell,
    Ha, ha, the wooing o't,
Meg grew sick as he grew haill,
    Ha, ha, the wooing o't.
Something in her bosom wrings,
For relief a sigh she brings;
And O, her een they spak sic things!
    Ha, ha, the wooing o't.

Duncan was a lad o' grace,
    Ha, ha, the wooing o't,
Maggie's was a piteous case,
    Ha, ha, the wooing o't.
Duncan couldna be her death,
Swelling pity smoored his wrath;
Now they're crouse and cantie baith!
    Ha, ha, the wooing o't.

FOR A' THAT AND A' THAT

Is there, for honest poverty,
  That hings his head, and a' that?
The coward-slave, we pass him by,
  We dare be poor for a' that!
    For a' that, and a' that,
      Our toils obscure, and a' that,
    The rank is but the guinea's stamp;
      The man's the gowd for a' that.

Auld Lang Syne. 4. **auld lang syne!** old long ago (since). 9. **ye'll . . . pint-stowp,** you will pay for your pint cup of drink. 13. **braes,** hillsides. 14. **pu'd . . . gowans,** plucked the daisies. 17. **paidled . . . burn,** paddled in the brook. 19. **braid,** broad. 21. **fiere,** comrade. 23. **guid-willie-waught,** a deep and hearty drink. *Duncan Gray*. 5. **coost,** tossed. 6. **skeigh,** haughty. 7. **Gart,** made. **abeigh,** aside. 9. **fleeched,** pleaded or flattered. 11. **Ailsa Craig,** a rocky island. 14. **Grat,** wept. 15. **lowpin . . . linn,** leaping over a waterfall. 19. **sair to bide,** hard to endure. 22. **hizzie,** pert young woman, hussy. 31. **sic,** such. 39. **crouse . . . baith,** bright and cheerful both. *For A' That and A' That*. 8. **gowd,** gold.

What though on hamely fare we dine,
  Wear hodden-gray, and a' that;
Gie fools their silks, and knaves their wine,
  A man's a man for a' that.
    For a' that, and a' that,
      Their tinsel show, and a' that,
    The honest man, though e'er sae poor,
      Is King o' men for a' that.

Ye see yon birkie, ca'd a lord,
  Wha struts, and stares, and a' that;
Though hundreds worship at his word,
  He's but a coof for a' that:
    For a' that, and a' that,
      His riband, star, and a' that,
    The man of independent mind,
      He looks and laughs at a' that.

A prince can mak a belted knight,
  A marquis, duke, and a' that;
But an honest man's aboon his might,
  Guid faith, he mauna fa' that!
    For a' that, and a' that,
      Their dignities, and a' that,
    The pith o' sense, and pride o' worth,
      Are higher rank than a' that.

Then let us pray that come it may,
  As come it will, for a' that,
That sense and worth o'er a' the earth
  Shall bear the gree, and a' that!
    For a' that and a' that,
      It's comin yet, for a' that,
    That man to man the warld o'er,
      Shall brothers be for a' that.

A RED, RED ROSE

My love is like a red, red rose,
  That's newly sprung in June:
My love is like the melodie
  That's sweetly play'd in tune.

So fair art thou, my bonie lass,
  So deep in love am I;
And I will love thee still, my dear,
  Till a' the seas gang dry.

Till a' the seas gang dry, my dear,
  And the rocks melt wi' the sun:
And I will love thee still, my dear,
  While the sands o' life shall run.

And fare thee weel, my only love!
  And fare thee weel awhile!
And I will come again, my love,
  Tho' it were ten thousand mile!

10. hodden-gray, coarse undyed woolen cloth. **17. birkie,** young fellow. **20. coof,** fool. **27. aboon,** above. **28. mauna fa',** must not claim. **36. bear the gree,** win the prize.

AE FOND KISS

Ae fond kiss, and then we sever!
Ae fareweel, alas, for ever!
Deep in heart-wrung tears I'll pledge thee,
Warring sighs and groans I'll wage thee.
Who shall say that fortune grieves him
While the star of hope she leaves him?
Me, nae cheerfu' twinkle lights me,
Dark despair around benights me.

I'll ne'er blame my partial fancy,
Naething could resist my Nancy;
But to see her was to love her,
Love but her, and love for ever.
Had we never loved sae kindly,
Had we never loved sae blindly,
Never met—or never parted,
We had ne'er been broken-hearted.

Fare thee weel, thou first and fairest!
Fare thee weel, thou best and dearest!
Thine be ilka joy and treasure,
Peace, enjoyment, love, and pleasure!
Ae fond kiss, and then we sever;
Ae fareweel, alas, for ever!
Deep in heart-wrung tears I'll pledge thee,
Warring sighs and groans I'll wage thee.

MARY MORISON

O Mary, at thy window be,
  It is the wished, the trysted hour!
Those smiles and glances let me see,
  That make the miser's treasure poor:
How blythely wad I bide the stoure,
  A weary slave frae sun to sun,
Could I the rich reward secure,
  The lovely Mary Morison.

Yestreen, when to the trembling string
  The dance gaed through the lighted ha',
To thee my fancy took its wing,
  I sat, but neither heard nor saw:
Though this was fair, and that was braw,

Ae Fond Kiss. **4. wage,** pledge. **19. ilka,** every. *Mary Morison.* **5. bide the stoure,** endure the strife. **13. braw,** handsome.

And yon the toast of a' the town,
I sighed, and said amang them a',
"Ye are na Mary Morison."

O Mary, canst thou wreck his peace,
Wha for thy sake wad gladly die?
Or canst thou break that heart of his,
Whase only faut is loving thee?
If love for love thou wilt na gie,
At least be pity to me shown!
A thought ungentle canna be
The thought o' Mary Morison.

YE FLOWERY BANKS

Ye flowery banks o' bonie Doon,
How can ye blume sae fair?
How can ye chant, ye little birds,
And I sae fu' o' care?

Thou 'll break my heart, thou bonie bird,
That sings upon the bough;
Thou minds me o' the happy days
When my fause luve was true.

Thou 'll break my heart, thou bonie bird,
That sings beside thy mate;
For sae I sat, and sae I sang,
And wist na o' my fate.

Aft hae I roved by bonie Doon
To see the woodbine twine,
And ilka bird sang o' its luve,
And sae did I o' mine.

Wi' lightsome heart I pu'd a rose
Frae aff its thorny tree,
And my fause luver staw my rose,
But left the thorn wi' me.

O, WERT THOU IN THE CAULD BLAST

O, wert thou in the cauld blast,
On yonder lea, on yonder lea,
My plaidie to the angry airt,
I'd shelter thee, I'd shelter thee.
Or did misfortune's bitter storms
Around thee blaw, around thee blaw,
Thy bield should be my bosom,
To share it a', to share it a'.

Or were I in the wildest waste,
Sae black and bare, sae black and bare,
The desert were a paradise,
If thou wert there, if thou wert there.
Or were I monarch o' the globe,
Wi' thee to reign, wi' thee to reign,
The brightest jewel in my crown
Wad be my queen, wad be my queen.

William Blake

1757–1827

Born in London, the son of a small tradesman, William Blake early absorbed from the talk he heard in his father's house the mystical ideas of Swedenborg and Jacob Boehme. That awareness of Divine Presence which illumined and emboldened his whole life came to him in early childhood, and at the age of twelve he began to compose verses in which the long-lost grace of the Elizabethan lyrists was mingled with mystical ecstasy. He had no schooling other than that given him by his drawing masters, by the engraver to whom he was apprenticed, and at the Royal Academy where he studied for a short time. Otherwise he taught himself, beating out the lonely path of an "original genius." He learned to see form, color, and motion with the eye of a plastic artist, but also, looking beyond these externalities, he learned to see into their spiritual significances. Thus he came to regard the world of the senses as a tapestry woven full of symbols, a mine of metaphors, in which every object and event points beyond itself to a transcendental meaning. To use his own vivid words, he learned

To see a world in a Grain of Sand,
And a Heaven in a Wild flower;
Hold Infinity in the palm of [his] hand,
And Eternity in an hour.

Blake's *Poetical Sketches*, 1783, *Songs of Innocence*, 1789, and *Songs of Experience*, 1794, contain most of

1. Doon, a river not far from the birthplace of Burns.

Ye Flowery Banks. **15. ilka,** every. **19. staw,** stole. *O, Wert Thou.* **3. airt,** direction of the wind. **7. bield,** shelter.

the poems from his pen that are now widely known. Usually simple at least in theme, prevailingly lyrical in tone, all lighted up from inside and charged with a strange new music, these poems yield much of their value to that slow brooding contemplation which all pure poetry demands. They were hardly more than the start, however, in Blake's long mental journey. In the same year as the *Songs of Innocence* appeared *The Book of Thel*, the first of a series of "Prophetic Books," which include *The Marriage of Heaven and Hell* (1790), *The Gates of Paradise* (1793), *The Vision of the Daughters of Albion* (1793), *Jerusalem* (1804), *The Emanation of the Giant Albion* (1804), and *Milton* (1804). In these books Blake's ever-deepening reflections about God and the Soul were phrased with an ever more clouded grandeur.

During the last twenty years of his life he wrote nothing to equal his earlier poetry, but his genius as an artist never shone more clearly than in his illustrations for an edition of Robert Blair's poem, *The Grave* (1804–1805), in his painting of Chaucer's Canterbury Pilgrims (1809), and above all in his illustrations of the Book of Job (*c.* 1825). It is often asserted that Blake's work as a pictorial artist improved, during his last decades, at the expense of his work as poet. He himself made no distinction between the two modes of expression, feeling that he could worship God as well with the burin and paintbrush as with the quill. In both mediums, equally, he was concerned with the representation of eternal things in terms of their earthly symbols. All his publications except the first, the *Poetical Sketches*, were designed, illustrated, engraved, and colored by his own hand. The same startling energy of conception and execution bristles forth from his illustrations, made late in life, of Dante's *Divine Comedy*, Gray's poems, and the Book of Job, as that which all discern in his much earlier poem on the tiger. He wrote like a painter and painted like a poet.

Like other mystics, Blake failed to find a language that could convey his intuitions to others, so that the effect of his later works is often that of a majestic soliloquy. Blake's earlier critics were inclined to think them works of insanity, but in recent years many students have come to feel that the later poetical works are superior to those upon which the poet's fame has hitherto been founded. However this may be, the easy opinion that Blake must have been mad because he often soars beyond our comprehension is no longer tenable. The fact appears to be that he saw things in heaven and earth which are not dreamt of in our philosophy. He was caught up into levels of being to which few of us penetrate, and if he spoke somewhat darkly of these visions it may have been for St. Paul's reason, that he had seen things "not lawful for a man to utter." His wife once said: "I have very little of Mr. Blake's company. He is always in Paradise." Blake lived nearly all his life in the dull and ugly streets of London, working like a craftsman with a craftsman's worldly rewards. After seventy years of obscure, toilsome, impoverished, solitary, and greatly joyous life he died almost unknown, uttering cheerful songs to his Maker.

One cannot relate William Blake to the eighteenth century in any but a negative way—showing how he denied and derided its rules and respectabilities at every turn. He stands alone, unclassified, defying our critical categories, independent of time and place. There is in him the mystery called "genius," for which no critic can be expected to account.

from POETICAL SKETCHES

In these early lyrics, each globed and limpid as a drop of dew, Blake bids farewell, before setting out on his own lonely path, to the old worn roads. As though wishing to prove that he might easily have continued the traditions of English verse, he moves at once, in the still perfection of the first three or four poems given below, beyond the attainment in this kind even of William Collins. Elsewhere in his first book he meets the Elizabethan and Jacobean song-writers on their own ground, showing himself at least their equal. Thus he makes it clear that he has served his apprenticeship to the past, and that he is ready now for his journeyman days. And there is nothing regretful in his backward look. "To the Muses"—one of the most nearly perfect things in English poetry, a marvel of classical restraint and proportion—is no more an epitaph than it is a prophecy.

TO THE MUSES

Whether on Ida's shady brow,
Or in the chambers of the East,
The chambers of the sun, that now
From ancient melody have ceased;

Whether in Heaven ye wander fair,
Or the green corners of the earth,

Or the blue regions of the air
Where the melodious winds have birth;

Whether on chrystal rocks ye rove,
Beneath the bosom of the sea
Wandering in many a coral grove,
Fair Nine, forsaking Poetry!

How have you left the antient love
That bards of old enjoyed in you!
The languid strings do scarcely move!
The sound is forced, the notes are few!

TO SPRING

O thou with dewy locks, who lookest down
Through the clear windows of the morning, turn
Thine angel eyes upon our western isle,
Which in full choir hails thy approach, O Spring!

The hills tell each other, and the listening
Valleys hear; all our longing eyes are turned
Up to thy bright pavillions: issue forth,
And let thy holy feet visit our clime.

Come o'er the eastern hills, and let our winds
Kiss thy perfumèd garments; let us taste
Thy morn and evening breath; scatter thy pearls
Upon our love-sick land that mourns for thee.

O deck her forth with thy fair fingers; pour
Thy soft kisses on her bosom; and put
Thy golden crown upon her languished head,
Whose modest tresses were bound up for thee!

TO THE EVENING STAR

Thou fair-haired angel of the evening,
Now, whilst the sun rests on the mountains, light
Thy bright torch of love; thy radiant crown
Put on, and smile upon our evening bed!
Smile on our loves, and, while thou drawest the
Blue curtains of the sky, scatter thy silver dew
On every flower that shuts its sweet eyes
In timely sleep. Let thy west wind sleep on
The lake; speak silence with thy glimmering eyes,
And wash the dusk with silver. Soon, full soon,
Dost thou withdraw; then the wolf rages wide,
And the lion glares through the dun forest:
The fleeces of our flocks are covered with
Thy sacred dew: protect them with thine influence.

SONG

Fresh from the dewy hill, the merry year
Smiles on my head and mounts his flaming car;
Round my young brows the laurel wreathes a shade,
And rising glories beam around my head.

My feet are winged, while o'er the dewy lawn,
I meet my maiden, risen like the morn:
Oh bless those holy feet, likc angels' feet;
Oh bless those limbs, beaming with heavenly light.

Like as an angel glittering in the sky
In times of innocence and holy joy,
The joyful shepherd stops his grateful song
To hear the music of an angel's tongue.

So when she speaks, the voice of Heaven I hear:
So when we walk, nothing impure comes near;
Each field seems Eden, and each calm retreat;
Each village seems the haunt of holy feet.

But that sweet village where my black-eyed maid
Closes her eyes in sleep beneath night's shade,
Whene'er I enter, more than mortal fire
Burns in my soul, and does my song inspire.

SONG

How sweet I roamed from field to field
And tasted all the summer's pride,
Till I the Prince of Love beheld
Who in the sunny beams did glide!

He shewed me lilies for my hair,
And blushing roses for my brow;
He led me through his gardens fair
Where all his golden pleasures grow.

With sweet May dews my wings were wet,
And Phoebus fired my vocal rage;
He caught me in his silken net,
And shut me in his golden cage.

He loves to sit and hear me sing,
Then, laughing, sports and plays with me;
Then stretches out my golden wing,
And mocks my loss of liberty.

SONG

My silks and fine array,
My smiles and languished air,
By love are driven away;
And mournful lean Despair
Brings me yew to deck my grave:
Such end true lovers have.

His face is fair as heaven
When springing buds unfold;
O why to him was 't given
Whose heart is wintry cold?
His breast is love's all-worshipped tomb,
Where all love's pilgrims come.

Bring me an axe and spade.
Bring me a winding sheet;
When I my grave have made
Let winds and tempests beat:
Then down I'll lie as cold as clay.
True love doth pass away!

SONG

Memory, hither come,
And tune your merry notes:
And, while upon the wind
Your music floats,
I'll pore upon the stream
Where sighing lovers dream,
And fish for fancies as they pass
Within the watery glass.

I'll drink of the clear stream
And hear the linnet's song;
And there I'll lie and dream
The day along:
And when night comes, I'll go
To places fit for woe,
Walking along the darkened valley
With silent Melancholy.

MAD SONG

The wild winds weep,
And the night is a-cold;
Come hither, Sleep,
And my griefs unfold:
But lo! the morning peeps
Over the eastern steeps,
And the rustling birds of dawn
The earth do scorn.

Lo! to the vault
Of pavèd heaven,
With sorrow fraught
My notes are driven:
They strike the ear of night,
Make weep the eyes of day;
They make mad the roaring winds,
And with tempests play.

Like a fiend in a cloud,
With howling woe,
After night I do crowd,
And with night will go;
I turn my back to the east
From whence comforts have increased;
For light doth seize my brain
With frantic pain.

Song, My silks, written perhaps, as the second line particularly indicates, after a reading of Shakespeare's *As You Like It. Mad Song,* somehow related to the *Tom o' Bedlam's Song* of the seventeenth century.

from SONGS OF INNOCENCE, 1789

The *Songs of Innocence* are the first of Blake's books to be illustrated, engraved, and printed on copper plates by a process of his own. The printed pages were then hand-colored by Blake and his wife. The poems in the collection have escaped entirely from Neoclassic tradition, and are, indeed, unique in English literature.

INTRODUCTION

Piping down the valleys wild,
Piping songs of pleasant glee,
On a cloud I saw a child,
And he laughing said to me:

"Pipe a song about a Lamb!"
So I piped with merry cheer.
"Piper, pipe that song again";
So I piped: he wept to hear.

"Drop thy pipe, thy happy pipe;
Sing thy songs of happy cheer":
So I sung the same again,
While he wept with joy to hear.

"Piper, sit thee down and write
In a book, that all may read."
So he vanished from my sight,
And I plucked a hollow reed,

And I made a rural pen,
And I stained the water clear,
And I wrote my happy songs
Every child may joy to hear.

THE ECHOING GREEN

The Sun does arise,
And make happy the skies;
The merry bells ring
To welcome the Spring;
The skylark and thrush,
The birds of the bush,
Sing louder around
To the bells' cheerful sound,
While our sports shall be seen
On the Echoing Green.

Old John, with white hair,
Does laugh away care,
Sitting under the oak,
Among the old folk.
They laugh at our play,
And soon they all say:
"Such, such were the joys
When we all, girls and boys,
In our youth time were seen
On the Echoing Green."

Till the little ones, weary,
No more can be merry;
The sun does descend,
And our sports have an end.
Round the laps of their mothers
Many sisters and brothers,
Like birds in their nest,
Are ready for rest,
And sport no more seen
On the darkening Green.

THE LAMB

Little Lamb, who made thee?
Dost thou know who made thee?
Gave thee life, and bid thee feed
By the stream and o'er the mead;
Gave thee clothing of delight,
Softest clothing, wooly, bright;
Gave thee such a tender voice,
Making all the vales rejoice?
Little Lamb, who made thee?
Dost thou know who made thee?

Little Lamb, I'll tell thee,
Little Lamb, I'll tell thee:
He is callèd by thy name,
For he calls himself a Lamb.
He is meek, and he is mild;
He became a little child.
I a child, and thou a lamb,
We are callèd by his name.
Little Lamb, God bless thee!
Little Lamb, God bless thee!

THE LITTLE BLACK BOY

My mother bore me in the southern wild,
And I am black, but O! my soul is white;
White as an angel is the English child,
But I am black, as if bereaved of light.

My mother taught me underneath a tree,
And, sitting down before the heat of day,
She took me on her lap and kissèd me,
And, pointing to the east, began to say:

"Look on the rising sun: there God does live,
And gives His light, and gives His heat away;
And flowers and trees and beasts and men receive
Comfort in morning, joy in the noonday.

"And we are put on earth a little space,
That we may learn to bear the beams of love;
And these black bodies and this sunburnt face
Is but a cloud, and like a shady grove.

"For when our souls have learned the heat to bear,
The cloud will vanish; we shall hear His voice,
Saying: 'Come out from the grove, My love and care,
And round My golden tent like lambs rejoice.'"

Thus did my mother say, and kissèd me;
And thus I say to little English boy:
When I from black, and he from white cloud free,
And round the tent of God like lambs we joy,

I'll shade him from the heat, till he can bear
To lean in joy upon our Father's knee;
And then I'll stand and stroke his silver hair,
And be like him, and he will then love me.

THE CHIMNEY SWEEPER

When my mother died I was very young,
And my father sold me while yet my tongue
Could scarcely cry "'weep! 'weep! 'weep! 'weep!"
So your chimneys I sweep, and in soot I sleep.

There's little Tom Dacre, who cried when his head,
That curled like a lamb's back, was shaved: so I said
"Hush, Tom! never mind it, for when your head's bare
You know that the soot cannot spoil your white hair."

And so he was quiet, and that very night,
As Tom was a-sleeping, he had such a sight!
That thousands of sweepers, Dick, Joe, Ned, and Jack,
Were all of them locked up in coffins of black.

And by came an Angel who had a bright key,
And he opened the coffins and set them all free;
Then down a green plain leaping, laughing, they run,
And wash in a river, and shine in the sun.

Then naked and white, all their bags left behind,
They rise upon clouds and sport in the wind;
And the Angel told Tom, if he'd be a good boy,
He'd have God for his father, and never want joy.

And so Tom awoke; and we rose in the dark,
And got with our bags and our brushes to work.
Though the morning was cold, Tom was happy and warm:
So if all do their duty they need not fear harm.

LAUGHING SONG

When the green woods laugh with the voice of joy,
And the dimpling stream runs laughing by;
When the air does laugh with our merry wit,
And the green hill laughs with the noise of it;

When the meadows laugh with lively green,
And the grasshopper laughs in the merry scene,
When Mary and Susan and Emily
With their sweet round mouths sing "Ha, Ha, He!"

When the painted birds laugh in the shade,
Where our table with cherries and nuts is spread,
Come live, and be merry, and join with me,
To sing the sweet chorus of "Ha, Ha, He!"

A CRADLE SONG

Sweet dreams, form a shade
O'er my lovely infant's head;
Sweet dreams of pleasant streams
By happy, silent, moony beams.

Sweet sleep, with soft down
Weave thy brows an infant crown.
Sweet sleep, Angel mild,
Hover o'er my happy child.

Sweet smiles, in the night
Hover over my delight;
Sweet smiles, Mother's smiles,
All the livelong night beguiles.

Sweet moans, dovelike sighs,
Chase not slumber from thy eyes.
Sweet moans, sweeter smiles,
All the dovelike moans beguiles.

Sleep, sleep, happy child,
All creation slept and smiled;
Sleep, sleep, happy sleep,
While o'er thee thy mother weep.

Sweet babe, in thy face
Holy image I can trace.
Sweet babe, once like thee,
Thy Maker lay and wept for me.

Wept for me, for thee, for all,
When He was an infant small.
Thou His image ever see,
Heavenly face that smiles on thee.

Smiles on thee, on me, on all;
Who became an infant small.
Infant smiles are His own smiles:
Heaven and earth to peace beguiles.

NURSE'S SONG

When the voices of children are heard on the green,
And laughing is heard on the hill,
My heart is at rest within my breast,
And everything else is still.

"Then come home, my children, the sun is gone down,
And the dews of night arise;
Come, come, leave off play, and let us away
Till the morning appears in the skies."

"No, no, let us play, for it is yet day,
And we cannot go to sleep;
Besides, in the sky the little birds fly,
And the hills are all covered with sheep."

"Well, well, go and play till the light fades away,
And then go home to bed."
The little ones leapèd and shouted and laughed
And all the hills echoèd.

INFANT JOY

"I have no name:
I am but two days old."
What shall I call thee?

"I happy am,
Joy is my name."
Sweet joy befall thee!

Pretty Joy!
Sweet Joy, but two days old,
Sweet Joy I call thee:
Thou dost smile,
I sing the while,
Sweet joy befall thee!

from SONGS OF EXPERIENCE

The exact relationship between this collection of lyrics and the *Songs of Innocence*, although it is a relationship both close and important, is not easy to state. Clearly, however, Blake does not mean to imply that childhood is superior to maturity. Having made his own peace with the Principle of Evil and found it good, he does not believe that the experience of mature life, because it takes on the tarnish of the world, marks a retrogression from childhood's inborn wisdom. He feels, rather, that even though this experience brings pain, disillusionment, and a darkening of the soul's sky, it is a necessary stage of our progress toward the eternal light.

This opinion of Blake's should be thoughtfully compared with the quite different one expressed in Henry Vaughan's "The Retreat" and in Wordsworth's "Intimations of Immortality."

THE CHIMNEY-SWEEPER

A little black thing among the snow,
Crying "'weep! 'weep!" in notes of woe!
"Where are thy father and mother, say?"—
"They are both gone up to the church to pray.

"Because I was happy upon the heath,
And smiled among the winter's snow,
They clothèd me in the clothes of death,
And taught me to sing the notes of woe.

"And because I am happy and dance and sing,
They think they have done me no injury,
And are gone to praise God and His Priest and King,
Who make up a heaven of our misery."

THE TIGER

Tiger! tiger! burning bright
In the forests of the night,
What immortal hand or eye
Could frame thy fearful symmetry?

In what distant deeps or skies
Burnt the fire of thine eyes?
On what wings dare he aspire?
What the hand dare seize the fire?

And what shoulder, and what art,
Could twist the sinews of thy heart?
And when thy heart began to beat,
What dread hand? and what dread feet?

What the hammer? what the chain?
In what furnace was thy brain?
What the anvil? what dread grasp
Dare its deadly terrors clasp?

When the stars threw down their spears,
And watered heaven with their tears,
Did he smile his work to see?
Did he who made the Lamb make thee?

Tiger! Tiger! burning bright
In the forests of the night,
What immortal hand or eye,
Dare frame thy fearful symmetry?

AH! SUN-FLOWER

Ah, Sun-flower! weary of time,
Who countest the steps of the sun;
Seeking after that sweet golden clime
Where the traveller's journey is done;

Where the youth pined away with desire,
And the pale virgin shrouded in snow,
Arise from their graves, and aspire
Where my Sun-flower wishes to go.

LONDON

I wander through each chartered street,
Near where the chartered Thames does flow,
And mark in every face I meet
Marks of weakness, marks of woe.

In every cry of every Man,
In every Infant's cry of fear,
In every voice, in every ban,
The mind-forged manacles I hear.

How the chimney sweeper's cry
Every blackening church appals;
And the hapless soldier's sigh
Runs in blood down palace walls.

But most through midnight streets I hear
How the youthful harlot's curse

Blasts the new-born infant's tear,
And blights with plagues the marriage hearse.

THE HUMAN ABSTRACT

Pity would be no more
If we did not make somebody poor;
And Mercy no more could be
If all were as happy as we.

And mutual fear brings peace,
Till the selfish loves increase;
Then Cruelty knits a snare,
And spreads his baits with care.

He sits down with holy fears,
And waters the ground with tears;
Then Humility takes its root
Underneath his foot.

Soon spreads the dismal shade
Of Mystery over his head;
And the caterpillar and fly
Feed on the Mystery.

And it bears the fruit of Deceit,
Ruddy and sweet to eat;
And the raven his nest has made
In its thickest shade.

The gods of the earth and sea
Sought through Nature to find this tree;
But their search was all in vain:
There grows one in the human brain.

AUGURIES OF INNOCENCE

To see a World in a grain of sand
And a Heaven in a wild flower,
Hold Infinity in the palm of your hand,
And Eternity in an hour.
A robin redbreast in a cage
Puts all Heaven in a rage.
A dove-house filled with doves and pigeons
Shudders Hell through all its regions.
A dog starved at his master's gate
Predicts the ruin of the State.
A horse misused upon the road
Calls to Heaven for human blood.
Each outcry of the hunted hare
A fibre from the brain does tear.
A skylark wounded in the wing,
A cherubim does cease to sing;
The game-cock clipped and armed for fight
Does the rising sun affright.
Every wolf's and lion's howl
Raises from Hell a Human soul.
The wild deer, wandering here and there,
Keeps the Human soul from care.
The lamb misused breeds public strife
And yet forgives the butcher's knife.
The bat that flits at close of eve
Has left the brain that won't believe.
The owl that calls upon the night
Speaks the unbeliever's fright.
He who shall hurt the little wren
Shall never be beloved by men.
He who the ox to wrath has moved
Shall never be by woman loved.
The wanton boy that kills the fly
Shall feel the spider's enmity.
He who torments the chafer's sprite
Weaves a bower in endless night.
The caterpillar on the leaf
Repeats to thee thy mother's grief.
Kill not the moth nor butterfly,
For the Last Judgment draweth nigh.
He who shall train the horse to war
Shall never pass the polar bar.
The beggar's dog and widow's cat,
Feed them and thou wilt grow fat.
The gnat that sings his summer's song
Poison gets from Slander's tongue.
The poison of the snake and newt
Is the sweat of Envy's foot.
The poison of the honey-bee
Is the artist's jealousy.
The prince's robes and beggar's rags
Are toadstools on the miser's bags.
A truth that's told with bad intent
Beats all the lies you can invent.
It is right it should be so;
Man was made for joy and woe;
And when this we rightly know,
Through the world we safely go.
Joy and woe are woven fine,
A clothing for the soul divine.
Under every grief and pine
Runs a joy with silken twine.
The babe is more than swaddling-bands;
Throughout all these human lands
Tools were made, and born were hands,
Every farmer understands.
Every tear from every eye
Becomes a babe in Eternity;
This is caught by Females bright,
And returned to its own delight.

The bleat, the bark, bellow, and roar
Are waves that beat on Heaven's shore.
The babe that weeps the rod beneath
Writes revenge in realms of death.
The beggar's rags, fluttering in air,
Does to rags the heavens tear.
The soldier, armed with sword and gun,
Palsied strikes the summer's sun.
The poor man's farthing is worth more
Than all the gold on Afric's shore.
One mite wrung from the labourer's hands
Shall buy and sell the miser's lands;
Or, if protected from on high,
Does that whole nation sell and buy.
He who mocks the infant's faith
Shall be mocked in Age and Death.
He who shall teach the child to doubt
The rotting grave shall ne'er get out.
He who respects the infant's faith
Triumphs over Hell and Death.
The child's toys and the old man's reasons
Are the fruits of the two seasons.
The questioner, who sits so sly,
Shall never know how to reply.
He who replies to words of Doubt
Doth put the light of knowledge out.
The strongest poison ever known
Came from Caesar's laurel crown.
Naught can deform the human race
Like to the armour's iron brace.
When gold and gems adorn the plow
To peaceful arts shall Envy bow.
A riddle, or the cricket's cry,
Is to Doubt a fit reply.
The emmet's inch and eagle's mile
Make lame Philosophy to smile.
He who doubts from what he sees
Will ne'er believe, do what you please.
If the Sun and Moon should doubt,
They'd immediately go out.
To be in a passion you good may do,
But no good if a passion is in you.
The whore and gambler by the state
Licensed, build that nation's fate.
The harlot's cry from street to street
Shall weave Old England's winding-sheet.
The winner's shout, the loser's curse,
Dance before dead England's hearse.
Every night and every morn
Some to misery are born.
Every morn and every night
Some are born to sweet delight.
Some are born to sweet delight,
Some are born to endless night.
We are led to believe a lie
When we see not through the eye,
Which was born in a night, to perish in a night,
When the Soul slept in beams of light.
God appears, and God is Light,
To those poor souls who dwell in Night,
But does a Human Form display
To those who dwell in realms of Day.

from MILTON

And did those feet in ancient time
Walk upon England's mountains green?
And was the holy Lamb of God
On England's pleasant pastures seen?

And did the Countenance Divine
Shine forth upon our clouded hills?
And was Jerusalem builded here
Among these dark Satanic mills?

Bring me my bow of burning gold!
Bring me my arrows of desire!
Bring me my spear! O clouds, unfold!
Bring me my chariot of fire!

I will not cease from mental fight,
Nor shall my sword sleep in my hand,
Till we have built Jerusalem
In England's green and pleasant land.

SUGGESTIONS FOR FURTHER READING

This list is to be supplemented by the brief lists of books mentioned in the General Bibliography and in the introductions and notes to authors and works of the period.

HISTORICAL AND POLITICAL BACKGROUND

Laski, H. J. *Political Thought in England from Locke to Bentham*, Holt, 1920.

Mantoux, P. J. *The Industrial Revolution in the Eighteenth Century*, Harcourt, Brace, 1935.

Plumb, J. H. *England in the Eighteenth Century*, Pelican Books, 1950. Inexpensive and invaluable.

Trevelyan, G. M. *England under Queen Anne*, 3 vols., Longmans, 1932–1934. The standard history.

CULTURAL AND SOCIAL BACKGROUND

Becker, Carl L. *The Heavenly City of the Eighteenth-Century Philosophers*, Yale University Press, 1932.

Botsford, J. B. *English Society in the Eighteenth Century*, Macmillan, 1924.

Creed, J. M. and Smith, J. S. B. *Religious Thought in the Eighteenth Century Illustrated from Writers of the Period*, Cambridge University Press, 1934.

James, D. G. *The Life of Reason*, Longmans, 1949. The first of a projected four-volume study of "the state of affairs with which the literary men had to come to terms."

Lovejoy, A. O. *The Great Chain of Being*. Harvard University Press, 1936. An invaluable study of Renaissance ideas of religious, social, and cosmic order.

Smith, Preserved. *History of Modern Culture*, 2 vols., Holt, 1934. Vol. II is the most thorough account of the eighteenth century's culture.

Thackeray, W. M. *The English Humourists of the Eighteenth Century*, 1853, and *The Four Georges*, 1861, Everyman's Library, Dutton. A perennially delightful introduction to eighteenth-century men and manners.

Turberville, A. S., ed. *English Men and Manners in the Eighteenth Century*, 2nd ed., Oxford University Press, 1929. This and the two volumes of the next title offer an admirable survey of the whole century.

—— ed. *Johnson's England*, 2 vols., Oxford University Press, 1933.

LITERATURE OF THE PERIOD

COLLECTIONS

Bredvold, L. I., McKillop, A. D., and Whitney, Lois, eds. *Eighteenth-Century Poetry and Prose*, Ronald Press, 1939. A generous selection of the best works of the major authors, with notes and bibliographies.

Hampden, J., ed. *Eighteenth-Century Plays*, Everyman's Library, Dutton. A representative selection.

Sypher, Wylie. *Enlightened England: An Anthology of Eighteenth-Century Literature*, Norton, 1947. Representative selections of poetry and prose considered with respect to music, architecture, sculpture, painting, etc.

CRITICISM

Allen, B. S. *Tides in English Taste, 1619–1800*, 2 vols., Harvard University Press, 1937.

Bate, W. J. *From Classic to Romantic*, Harvard University Press, 1946.

Butt, John. *The Augustan Age*, Longmans, 1950. A stimulating study of Swift, Pope, Johnson, and others.

Dyson, H. V. D. and Butt, John. *Augustans and Romantics*, The Cresset Press, 1940.

Fairchild, H. N. *The Noble Savage*, Columbia University Press, 1928. An invaluable study of an important figure in eighteenth-century and later literature.

McCutcheon, R. P. *Eighteenth-Century English Literature*, Oxford University Press, 1949. An inexpensive and very readable brief introduction.

Railo, Eino. *The Haunted Castle: A Study of the Elements of English Romanticism*, Dutton, 1927.

Sherburn, George. *The Restoration and Eighteenth Century*, Appleton-Century-Crofts, 1948. Vol. III of *A Literary History of England*, and a very valuable work.

Stauffer, D. A. *The Art of Biography in Eighteenth-Century England*, Princeton University Press, 1941. The standard work on the subject.

Willey, Basil. *The Eighteenth-Century Background*, Chatto and Windus, 1940. A valuable study of the intellectual and social milieu of eighteenth-century writers.

Bush, Douglas. *Mythology and the Romantic Tradition in English Poetry*, Harvard University Press, 1937.

Fairchild, H. N. *Religious Trends in English Poetry*, 3 vols., Columbia University Press, 1939–1949. Vol. I discusses "Protestantism and the Cult of Sentiment," 1700–1740; Vol. II, "Religious Sentimentalism in the Age of Johnson," 1740–1780; Vol. III, "Romantic Faith," 1780–1830.

Leavis, F. R. *Revaluations*, Chatto and Windus, 1936. Provocative essays on Pope and the Augustans.

Quayle, Thomas. *Poetic Diction: A Study of Eighteenth-Century Verse*, Methuen, 1924.

Sutherland, James. *A Preface to Eighteenth-Century Poetry*, Oxford University Press, 1948. A study of the function of eighteenth-century poets with respect to matters of taste, manners, morality, and religion.

Nettleton, G. H. *English Drama of the Restoration and Eighteenth Century*, Macmillan, 1923.

Nicoll, Allardyce. *A History of Early Eighteenth-Century Drama, 1700–1740*, Cambridge University Press, 1929.

—— *A History of Late Eighteenth-Century Drama*, Cambridge University Press, 1927.

Thaler, Alwin. *Shakespeare to Sheridan*, Harvard University Press, 1922. Contains illustrations from the Harvard Theater Collection.

Barker, E. A. *The History of the English Novel*, Witherby 1936–1942. Vols. III–V of this standard history of the English novel deal with eighteenth-century fiction.

Foster, J. R. *History of the Pre-Romantic Novel in England*, Oxford University Press, 1949. A fresh and very full treatment of various types of fiction and fiction writers.

ADDISON AND STEELE

The Spectator, 4 vols., Everyman's Library, Dutton.

Selections from the Tatler, Spectator, and Their Successors, ed. by Walter Graham, Nelson, 1928. An excellent selection of eighteenth-century periodical essays.

Courthope, W. J. *The Life of Joseph Addison*, English Men of Letters Series, Macmillan, 1903. The best brief biography.

Connely, Willard. *Sir Richard Steele*, Scribner, 1934. A recent and very readable study.

BLAKE

Poems, ed. by Max Plowman, Everyman's Library, Dutton.

The Portable Blake, ed. by Alfred Kazin, Viking Press, 1947. A handsome collection, including most of the verse and prose and the illustrations for the Book of Job.

Margoliouth, H. M. *William Blake*, Oxford University Press, 1951. The most recent and valuable short study of Blake's life and work, with equal attention to Blake's text and pictures, and new information on his family.

BOSWELL

Boswell's London Journal, 1762–1763, ed. by F. A. Pottle, in The Yale Editions of the Private Papers of James Boswell, McGraw-Hill, 1950. The vivacious journal of Boswell's early days in London, published for the first time from the original manuscript.

Journal of a Tour to the Hebrides, ed. by A. Glover, Everyman's Library, Dutton.

Pottle, F. A. *The Literary Career of James Boswell*, Oxford University Press, 1929.

Tinker, C. B. *Young Boswell*, Atlantic Monthly Press, 1922.

—— ed., *Letters of James Boswell*, Oxford University Press, 1924.

Vulliamy, C. E. *James Boswell*, G. Bles, 1932.

BURKE

Speeches and Letters on American Affairs, with introduction by Hugh Law, Everyman's Library, Dutton.

Reflections on the French Revolution, etc., with introduction by A. J. Grieve, Everyman's Library, Dutton.

Selected Writings of Edmund Burke, ed. by Sir Philip Magnus, Falcon Press, 1948.

Copeland, T. W. *Our Eminent Friend, Edmund Burke*, Yale University Press, 1949. The most recent study of Burke's life and his relations with his contemporaries.

BURNS

Poetical Works, ed. by J. L. Robertson, Oxford University Press, 1926. The best edition, with notes, glossary, etc.

Selected Poems, ed. by L. Brander, World's Classics, Oxford University Press. With introduction and glossary.

Barke, James. *The Wind That Shakes the Barley*, 1947; *The Song in the Green Thorn Tree*, 1948; *The Wonder of All the Gay World*, 1950, Macmillan. Three novels dealing with the life and loves of Burns.

Daiches, David. *Robert Burns*, Rinehart, 1951. The most complete presentation of Burns the poet, with a careful study of the technical aspects of his poetry, and a fresh account of his Scottish literary background.

Ferguson, J. D. *Pride and Passion: Robert Burns*, Oxford University Press, 1939. A penetrating study of Burns.

COLLINS

Poems, with the poems of Thomas Gray, Oxford Standard Authors, Oxford University Press.

Ainsworth, E. G. *Poor Collins, His Life, His Art, and His Influence*, Cornell University Press, 1937. The most recent and thorough study of the poet.

COWPER

Poems, ed. by H. I'A. Fausset, Everyman's Library, Dutton. A convenient and inexpensive edition.

Selected Letters, ed. by W. Hadley, Everyman's Library, Dutton.

Cecil, Lord David. *The Stricken Deer*, World's Classics, Oxford University Press. A sympathetic and beautifully written study of Cowper and his background.

Thomas, Gilbert. *William Cowper in the Eighteenth Century*, rev. ed., Macmillan, 1949. Cowper in his relationship to the Evangelical movement of the eighteenth century.

GOLDSMITH

Poems and Plays, ed. by Austin Dobson, Everyman's Library, Dutton.

The Citizen of the World and *The Bee*, with introd. by Richard Church, Everyman's Library, Dutton.

Selected Works, ed. by Richard Garnett, R. Hart-Davis, 1950. The first new edition of Goldsmith's works in a half century. Contains *The Vicar of Wakefield*, both the plays, almost all the poems, some sixty essays, etc.

Collected Letters, ed. by Katherine C. Balderston, Cambridge University Press, 1928.

Gwynn, Stephen. *Oliver Goldsmith*, Holt, 1935. The standard biography.

GRAY

Poems, with the poems of William Collins, Oxford Standard Authors, Oxford University Press.

Poems, with a Selection of Letters and Essays, with introd. by John Drinkwater, Everyman's Library, Dutton.

Cecil, Lord David. *Two Quiet Lives: Dorothy Osborne and Thomas Gray*, Bobbs-Merrill, 1948. One of the most charming and sympathetic studies of Gray.

Jones, W. P. *Thomas Gray, Scholar*, Harvard University Press, 1937.

JOHNSON

The Lives of the Poets, ed. by G. B. Hill, 3 vols., Oxford University Press, 1905. The standard edition.

Rasselas, ed. by R. W. Chapman, Oxford University Press, 1927. The most thoroughly annotated edition.

Journey to the Western Isles of Scotland and Boswell's *Journal of a Tour to the Hebrides*, ed. by R. W. Chapman, Oxford University Press, 1924.

The Portable Johnson and Boswell, ed. by Louis Kronenberger, Viking Press, 1948. A selection of the writings of the two men.

The Poems of Dr. Johnson, ed. by D. N. Smith and E. L. McAdam, 2 vols., Oxford University Press, 1941.

Boswell, James, *The Life of Samuel Johnson, LL.D.*, ed. by G. B. Hill, 1905, rev. ed., L. F. Powell, 6 vols., Oxford University Press, 1934–1940. The standard edition. A convenient single-volume edition of the *Life* is also published by the Oxford University Press. A new edition of the *Life* is that of S. C. Roberts in Everyman's Library, Dutton. An abridged edition by C. G. Osgood is published by Scribner.

Cairns, W. T. *The Religion of Dr. Johnson*, Oxford University Press, 1946.

Krutch, J. W. *Samuel Johnson*, Holt, 1944. The most valuable full-length biography since Boswell's.

POPE

Complete Poetical Works, ed. by H. W. Boynton, Houghton Mifflin, 1903. The best single-volume edition.

The Best of Pope, ed. by George Sherburn, Nelson, 1931. Contains a valuable introduction.

Selected Poems, ed. by L. I. Bredvold, Crofts, 1926. An excellent selection, with an essay on "The Element of Art in Eighteenth-Century Poetry."

The Pleasures of Pope, ed. by Peter Quennell, Pantheon Books, 1950. A representative selection with an illuminating critical introduction.

Root, R. K. *The Poetical Career of Alexander Pope*, Princeton University Press, 1938. One of the most useful studies.

Sitwell, Edith. *Alexander Pope*, Cosmopolitan Book Corp., 1930. A discerning and close scrutiny of Pope by a twentieth-century poet and critic.

Tillotson, Geoffrey. *On the Poetry of Pope*, Oxford University Press, 1938. An admirable study of the poet.

SWIFT

The Portable Swift, ed. by Carl Van Doren, Viking Press, 1948. A generous collection of Swift's most important writings, with a valuable introduction.

Gulliver's Travels, Tale of a Tub, and *Battle of the Books*, in one volume, ed. by W. A. Eddy, Oxford University Press, 1929.

Satires and Personal Writings, ed. by W. A. Eddy, Oxford University Press, 1932.

Selected Prose Works, ed. with introd. by John Hayward, Chanticleer Press, 1950. An excellent selection.

Gulliver's Travels, ed. by A. E. Case, Nelson, 1938. The most thoroughly annotated edition of the work.

Quintana, Ricardo. *The Mind and Art of Jonathan Swift*, Oxford University Press, 1936. One of the most discerning studies of Swift's artistry.

Van Doren, Carl. *Swift*, Viking Press, 1930. A standard work on Swift.

Watkins, W. B. C. *Perilous Balance*, Princeton University Press, 1939. Essays on Swift and his contemporaries.

THOMSON

Poetical Works, ed. by J. Logie Robertson, Oxford University Press, 1908. The standard edition.

The Seasons, ed. by H. D. Roberts and Sir Edmund Gosse, 2 vols., Dutton, 1906. A complete edition of Thomson's poems, with a biographical note and critical study.

Sherwood, Margaret. *Undercurrents of Influence in English Romantic Poetry*, Harvard University Press, 1934. Contains a valuable discussion of Thomson's influence.

NOVELS

Following is a list of representative English novels of the eighteenth century, all but one of which—Walpole's *The Castle of Otranto*—are published in Everyman's Library, Dutton; most of them are also available in other inexpensive editions.

Burney, Fanny. *Evelina*, 1778. A tale—beloved by Dr. Johnson, Burke, and Reynolds—of London society as seen by a girl from the country.

Defoe, Daniel. *Moll Flanders*, 1722. The slums of London linked with the plantations of Virginia in a fictional autobiography of a female adventurer.

Fielding, Henry. *Tom Jones*, 1749. An ample and intricate story, crowded with vivacious characters and told with masculine vigor.

Goldsmith, Oliver. *The Vicar of Wakefield*, 1766. Relating the misfortunes and final triumph of a simple-minded and warm-hearted clergyman.

Richardson, Samuel. *Clarissa Harlowe*, 1747–1748. A love story in epistolary form concerning a young lady "of great delicacy, mistress of all the accomplishments, natural and acquired, that adorn the Sex."

Smollett, Tobias. *Roderick Random*, 1748. A coarsely vigorous personal narrative which includes vivid scenes from the life of a sailor in the British Navy.

Sterne, Laurence. *Tristram Shandy*, 1760–1767. A humorous, libidinous, and sentimental work of a creative genius running wild.

Walpole, Horace. *The Castle of Otranto*, 1765, ed. with an introduction and notes by Oswald Doughty, Scholartis Press, 1929. The most famous of the "Gothic romances," the "thrillers" of the eighteenth century.

LETTERS

Hardly less interesting than the fiction is the private correspondence that we inherit from the eighteenth century. Everyman's Library contains adequate selections from the letters of Burns (Lockhart's *Life of Burns*, with some of Burns's letters, journals, and diaries); Cowper (*Selected Letters*); Lord Chesterfield (*Letters to His Son, and Others*); Gray (*Poems, with a Selection of Letters and Essays*); Swift (*Journal to Stella*); Lady Mary Wortley Montagu (*Letters*); Horace Walpole (*Selected Letters*). The Oxford World's Classics also contain valuable volumes.

OTHER PROSE

(All in Everyman's Library, Dutton)

Gibbon, Edward. *The Decline and Fall of the Roman Empire*, 1776–1778. A magnificent work of patient scholarship, bold thought, and blazing imagination.

Hume, David. *A Treatise on Human Nature*, 1739–1740. Difficult reading, but well worth the effort it costs.

Paine, Thomas. *The Rights of Man*, 1791–1792. An influential treatise, directed against the detractors of the French Revolution, by a chief figure in the American Revolution.

Reynolds, Sir Joshua. *Fifteen Discourses Delivered in the Royal Academy*, 1769–1790 (*Discourses on Art* in Everyman's Library). A clear statement of Neoclassical doctrine, applied to the art of painting.

Smith, Adam. *The Wealth of Nations*, 1776. The foundation stone of modern political economy.

Wesley, John. *Journal*, 1771–1774. The day-to-day record of a devoted, laborious, and greatly influential life.

White, Gilbert. *The Natural History and Antiquities of Selborne*, 1789. One of the most charming books on natural history, and a pioneer in its field.

THE ROMANTIC PERIOD

PLATE XVII

A DERWENTWATER, THE LAKE COUNTRY (*British Information*)

Much of the literature of the earlier Romantic Movement, especially the poetry of Wordsworth, is inseparable from the beautiful lake and mountain country in northwestern England where it was written. Derwentwater, a Cumberland lake whose charm is enhanced by its richly wooded islands and the surrounding mountains, is close by the town of Keswick, where Coleridge and Southey had homes; this was one of the favorite scenes of Wordsworth, most of whose life was lived within a few miles of the shores of Derwentwater.

B CAPTURE OF THE BASTILLE, FROM A CONTEMPORARY ENGRAVING BY DUPLESSIS-BERTAUX (*Bettmann Archive*)

"The Bastille was a great oblong castle, consisting of eight prison towers, high and round, joined together by equally high walls; it was protected by a moat with drawbridges and by many outer courts and walls. It dominated the Faubourg Saint Antoine, a turbulent workmen's quarter; the cannon on its battlements could sweep all approaches, and it contained powder enough to blow the quarter to pieces. It stood, not only to Paris and to France, but to Europe as well, as a symbol of oppression and injustice." (E. D. Bradby, *A Short History of the French Revolution.*) When the Parisian mob destroyed the Bastille on July 14, 1789, lovers of liberty everywhere rejoiced. But the mood of exultation that animated many Englishmen—among them Wordsworth, Coleridge, Southey, and Hazlitt—in the early years of the Revolution, turned to dismay when violence and cruelty gained the ascendance. Yet the first revolutionary fervor was born again in Shelley and Byron, and inspired champions of liberty through the century. When Carlyle came to write his vast, panoramic *French Revolution*, he admitted that to describe the siege of the Bastille "perhaps transcends the talent of mortals."

C INTERIOR OF TINTERN ABBEY, MONMOUTHSHIRE (*Ewing Galloway*)

The setting of Wordsworth's poem is related to Tintern Abbey only by geographical propinquity. However, apart from the beauty of its situation in a hollow of the Monmouth hills on the west bank of the River Wye, this ruined thirteenth-century Cistercian abbey is in itself a symbol of many aspects of Romanticism: love of the medieval past, aspiring Gothic magnificence, the fascination of decay. The abbey buildings fell into ruin after Henry VIII dissolved the monastery in 1537. Since the late nineteenth century Tintern has been perhaps the best preserved of the ruined abbeys of England.

PLATE XVIII

A ARTHUR WELLESLEY, DUKE OF WELLINGTON, BY GOYA (*Collection of the Duke of Leeds, Hornby Castle*)

Wellington entered Madrid in August, 1812, with his victorious army. During the British commander's stay in the capital, Goya did several paintings of him; this half-length portrait is perhaps the most striking of them. As Antonina Vallentin, Goya's most recent biographer observes: "The Spaniard has painted the typical Englishman, in all the impassivity of his race, reinforced by that personal feature of self-mastery."

B PISA (*Drawing from Miss Elizabeth Batty's* Italian Scenery, *1820*)

The warm sun and attractive landscape of Italy, as well as its glorious past, attracted each of the younger generation of Romantic poets—Shelley, Byron, and Keats. An Italian town whose beauty especially delighted Englishmen was Pisa. The Shelleys first visited Pisa in the spring of 1818. After stays in Rome and with Byron in Venice, Shelley lived in or near Pisa from late January, 1820, until his tragic death, writing *Epipsychidion*, *Hellas*, and *Adonais*. Byron went there from Ravenna in the early fall of 1821, leasing the Lanfranchi Palace on the north bank of the Arno; at Pisa he saw much of the Shelleys, Leigh Hunt, Trelawny, Medwin, and his Italian friends, the Gambas; worked on the later cantos of *Don Juan;* and involved himself in revolutionary political activity. When, after some months in Pisa, Byron still preferred the charms of Venice, Shelley urged him: "Stand on the marble bridge, cast your eye if you are not dazzled on its river glowing as with fire, then follow the graceful curve of the palaces of the Lung' Arno until the arch is naved by the massy dungeon-tower, forming in dark relief, and tell me if anything can surpass a sunset at Pisa."

A

B

C

PLATE XVII

A

B

C

PLATE XVIII

PLATE XIX

Endymion Book 1st

A thing of beauty is a joy for ever:
Its loveliness increases; it will never
Pass into nothingness; but still will keep
A Bower quiet for us, and a sleep
Full of sweet dreams, and health, and quiet breathing.
Therefore, on every morrow, are we wreathing
A flowery band to bind us to the earth,
Spite of Despondence, & of the inhuman dearth
Of noble natures, of the gloomy days,
Of all the unhealthy and o'er-darkened ways
Made for our searching: yes, in spite of all
Some shape of beauty moves away the Pall
From our dark Spirits. ~~and before us dances~~
~~Like glitter on the points of Arthur's lances~~.
~~Of these bright powers are~~ Such the Sun, ~~and~~ the Moon
Trees old, and young sprouting a shady boon
For simple sheep; ~~of these~~ and such are daffodils
~~And~~ With the green world they live in; and clear rills
That for themselves a cooling covert make

C

LYRICAL BALLADS,

WITH

A FEW OTHER POEMS.

BRISTOL:

PRINTED BY BIGGS AND COTTLE,

FOR T. N. LONGMAN, PATERNOSTER-ROW, LONDON.

1798.

D

PLATE XX

C THE COMBAT BETWEEN THE GIAOUR AND THE PASHA, BY DELACROIX (*Courtesy of the Art Institute of Chicago*)

The paintings of Eugène Delacroix (1798–1863) show unmistakably that the triumphs of Romanticism were not limited to literature alone. This great French painter not only knew and loved French literature, but he also read enthusiastically, in English, Shakespeare, Scott, and Byron. Byron, with whom he felt a temperamental affinity, was his special favorite. Delacroix's veneration illustrates the enormous influence Byron exerted on the Continent throughout the nineteenth century both as a Romantic poet and as a symbol of liberty. Like the early Byron, Delacroix became fascinated with Eastern subject matter, and like the later Byron, he was stirred by the Greek war for independence. Scenes from Byron's Oriental Tales (*The Giaour*, *The Bride of Abydos*, *The Corsair*, *Lara*) filled Delacroix's imagination and were but a few of the specifically Byronic subjects (*The Shipwreck of Don Juan*, *The Prisoner of Chillon*, etc.) he painted during his long career. Less than a month after Byron's death, on the very day he began painting *The Combat between the Giaour and the Pasha*, Delacroix expressed the close relationship between poetry and painting in his journal: "How I should like to be a poet! But at least, create in painting! The poet is very rich: remember eternally certain passages from Byron to inflame your imagination for all time."

PLATE XIX

A ABBOTSFORD (*Gendreau*)

In the same year that Scott, with *The Lay of the Last Minstrel*, *Marmion*, and *The Lady of the Lake* behind him, was turning his attention from poetry to the novel, he began building his famous home, Abbotsford, high on the banks of the Tweed a few miles from the ruins of Melrose Abbey. This was 1812, the year of Napoleon's disastrous retreat from Moscow, and the year in which *Childe Harold's Pilgrimage* made Byron famous. Though Scott and his family moved to the Abbotsford estate in 1812, a dozen years were to pass before the large architectural project—much of it initiated and carried forward under Scott's personal direction—was fully realized. The building and adornment of Abbotsford, a stately red-sandstone mansion in the Scottish Baronial style, afforded Scott some of his chief pleasures during the last two decades of his life. There he entertained his friends with splendid hospitality, while the great series of novels that followed *Waverley* raised him to the height of his fame.

B THESEUS (*Elgin Marbles, British Museum*)

A dispute that raged through the early years of the nineteenth century, and that is not without artistic and political consequence even to this day, centered about the removal to England of many of the masterpieces of ancient Greek sculpture, among them the "Fates," the "Illisos," the Parthenon friezes, and the famous "Theseus." Because the older buildings in Athens were rapidly deteriorating and their artistic treasures in danger of being lost to the world forever, Thomas Bruce, Lord Elgin, gained permission from the Turkish government (then in control of Greece) to remove some of the statues and friezes and ship them to England for safer keeping.

At first, opinion was divided with regard both to the value of the marbles and to the code of international ethics reflected in Elgin's activities. English taste, conditioned to the more graceful and familiar Greco-Roman art, was slow to recognize the rougher, more realistic beauties of ancient Greek sculpture. And many Englishmen agreed with Byron, who visited Greece in 1810 and ever after scorchingly opposed "the robbery of ruins from Athens, to instruct the English in sculpture (who are as capable of sculpture as the Egyptians are of skating)." A few artistically perceptive individuals like Keats's friend, Benjamin Robert Haydon, did, however, sense the merits of the Athenian marbles, and as time went on, more and more men of distinction in the world of art proclaimed their tremendous value. Wordsworth and Keats were enraptured at their first sight of the marbles. Moreover, despite the continued charge of artistic imperialism, responsible opinion has since agreed that, in the light of conditions at Athens, Elgin had good justification for removing the sculptures for preservation, and that not merely England but the world in general has benefited from his efforts.

C AN EIGHTEENTH-CENTURY LONDON SHOP FRONT (*Reece Winstone*)

Charles Lamb had a lifelong affection for the city of London—for its crowded streets, its little shops, its hurrying life. Here he speaks of the fascination of the city:

O! her lamps of a night! her rich goldsmiths, printshops, toyshops, mercers, hardware men, pastrycooks, St. Paul's Churchyard, the Strand, Exeter Change, Charing Cross. . . . All the streets and pavements are pure gold, I warrant you. At least I know an alchemy that turns her mud into that metal—a mind that loves to be at home in crowds.

D "THE LAND OF ICE," FROM FREDERICK MARTENS' "VOYAGE INTO SPITZBERGEN AND GREENLAND," 1675. (*From the Reserve Division, New York Public Library*)

In *The Road to Xanadu*, a monument of twentieth-century literary scholarship, John Livingston Lowes has traced in fascinating detail the genesis of Coleridge's "Rime of the Ancient Mariner" and "Kubla Khan." Recognizing that no mere "sources" could ever have been fused into works of poetic art without the shaping power of genius, Professor Lowes nevertheless points to many of the materials in Coleridge's reading and experience that eventually became enriched and transformed into poetry. One book which must have influenced Coleridge's creative imagination was an old German text, Frederick Martens' *The Voyage into Spitzbergen and Greenland*, from the 1675 Hamburg edition of which this scene is reproduced. In connection with the latter stanzas of Part I of "The Ancient Mariner" such passages as the following, translated from Martens' book, are of interest, if only to show how the poet, often unconsciously, builds from countless details, impressions, and suggestions his own essentially original creation:

"On the 2d of June . . . in the night we saw the Moon very pale, as it used to look in the day time in our Country, with clear sun-shine, whereupon followed mist and snow." Six pages later Martens wrote, "the Ice came a floating down apace . . . and it was very cold." In a later passage he described "a Rain-bow, figured by the Sun, which Bow are the Drops that by the Heat of the Sun are changed into a Vapour or Fog, and this Vapour shews like smoak in the Air."

PLATE XX

A PORTRAIT OF KEATS, BY SEVERN (*Bettmann Archive*)

Joseph Severn (1793–1879) lived more than a half-century after Keats, but as he himself predicted, he is best remembered as the devoted friend—and painter—of the young poet. Keats first mentioned Severn casually in a letter dated December 17, 1816. Severn wrote more emotionally of his first acquaintance with Keats: "A new world was opened to me, and I was raised from the mechanical drudgery of my art to the hope of brighter and more elevated courses." The friendship grew during the remaining five years of Keats's short life. In 1821 Severn accompanied Keats to Italy and attended him unselfishly to the very end, when Keats died in his arms. Severn painted a number of portraits of Keats, and his letters and reminiscences provide invaluable material concerning the poet's last days. After Keats's death Severn went on to a very respectable, if not distinguished, career as a painter. He was buried beside Keats in the Protestant Cemetery in Rome.

B WILLIAM WORDSWORTH, 1805

This portrait of Wordsworth at the age of thirty-five, when he was finishing his first version of *The Prelude*, is from a tinted drawing by Henry Edridge, an associate of the Royal Academy.

C THE OPENING PAGE OF ENDYMION (*Courtesy of the Pierpont Morgan Library*)

Keats's manuscripts have been the subject of much investigation by scholars who are interested in the nature of the creative process. Even this small section of *Endymion* shows the care with which Keats revised and corrected his work.

D TITLE PAGE OF "LYRICAL BALLADS," BRISTOL EDITION (*Albert A. and Henry W. Berg Collection, New York Public Library*)

The unpretentiousness of this small volume contrasts strikingly with its great importance in the history of English literature.

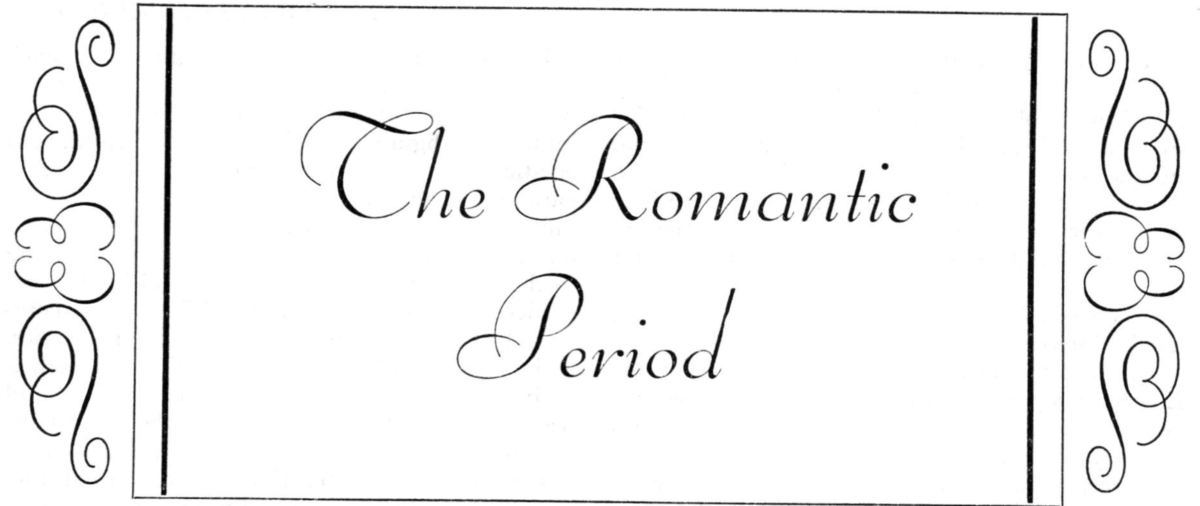

The Romantic Period

The Elements of Romanticism

NO term in the vocabulary of criticism has defied precise limitation more stoutly through the years than has Romanticism. A recent writer playfully estimated there were in existence 11,396 books on Romanticism; he then went on to add his own, a sprightly 11,397th. And others have appeared since.

The adjective "romantic" first appeared in English in the seventeenth century. It was then used in a somewhat unfavorable sense, meaning "of a fabulous or fictitious character, having no foundation in fact." Early in the eighteenth century, well before the term gave its name to a whole literary age, "romantic" came to be associated with three moods or attitudes—love of nature, "melancholy," and "enthusiasm"; persons given to such attitudes were described by the influential philosopher, the first Earl of Shaftesbury, as "plainly out of their wits."

The noun "romanticism" made its first appearance early in the nineteenth century, and since that time it has been subjected to many attempts at definition.[1] None of the resulting descriptions is entirely satisfactory, but all are useful as illustrating various aspects of the life, thought, and literature of what has come to be called "the Romantic Period." To some, Romanticism has meant the revival of the life and thought of the Middle Ages. Others have hailed it as "the addition of strangeness to beauty," as "the renascence of wonder."[2] While the label has been applied to the attitude of those who urge the fullest development of the unique potentialities of every man, a twentieth-century critic has taken a darker view of Romanticism as "fundamentally the struggle to retain an illusioned view of life in the face of the obstacles presented by the rise of science." Many still think of it as the essence of rebellion against any and all arbitrary restraints and shackles, and the expression of man's longing for freedom.

It is clear from such diversity of opinion and definition that, as Bacon said of the essay, "The word is late, but the thing is ancient." Romanticism represents an attitude toward life and experience older than Christianity, as permanent as love, and as many-sided as truth. In early English literature it shows itself in glimpses of the eerie moors and goblin-haunted meres of *Beowulf*, in the homeless and Fate-hunted melancholy of *The Wanderer*, in the homely poignancy of the old ballads and the bright chivalry of *Sir Gawain and*

[1] For interesting discussions of the terms "romantic" and "romanticism" see the following: Irving Babbitt, *Rousseau and Romanticism*, Houghton Mifflin, 1919; Lascelles Abercrombie, *Romanticism*, Viking Press, 1927; F. L. Lucas, *The Decline and Fall of the Romantic Ideal*, Macmillan, 1936; J. H. Randall, *The Making of the Modern Mind*, 1926; H. N. Fairchild, *The Romantic Quest*, Columbia University Press, 1931; Jacques Barzun, *Romanticism and the Modern Ego*, Little, Brown, 1944.

[2] "A thing is romantic," we are told, "when it is strange, unexpected, intense, superlative, extreme, unique, etc. A thing is classical, on the other hand, when it is not unique, but representative of a class."

the Green Knight; in later literature we see Romantic elements in the mazy enchantments and shining idealizations of *The Faerie Queene*, in the imaginative freedom and splendor of Elizabethan drama, and in the grandeur and pathos of *Paradise Lost.* These qualities dominated English literature long before the words "romantic" and "romanticism" appeared, and will continue to enrich it, for romanticism is inherent in the English character. But between Milton and Pope a set of attitudes, ideals, interests, and conventions, in many ways alien to the prevailingly romantic spirit of the English people and their literature, gained ascendancy (see the introduction to "The Eighteenth Century"). Even before these reached their height, however, men began to sense, consciously or unconsciously, how much of the older views of an infinite world and boundless human possibilities this new literature was forcing them to surrender. Protest arose. Hence, much of what has been called the beginning of the Romantic Movement is really a return to an older habit of thought and manner of expression, for Romanticism itself never died.

The Philosophical and Political Background

To many men of the time, the middle years of the eighteenth century seemed a period that represented the ultimate in philosophical security and political stability. Pope proclaimed in his *Essay on Man* (1733) that "Whatever is, is right." To Edward Gibbon, author of the great *Decline and Fall of the Roman Empire* (1776–1788), the political, economic, and social systems in which he lived seemed as stable as they seemed sensible. But before the century had run its course, almost every institution and habit of thought in England and France had been questioned or attacked or overthrown. There began a series of revolutions—religious, philosophical, political, social, industrial, literary, artistic—in which we still find ourselves involved.

The Methodist movement, begun at Oxford by Charles Wesley in the 1730's, developed from an internal schism to a revolution against the Church of England. It helped to make religion a vital personal experience for many persons, and to reveal its social responsibilities. The evangelical movement, led later on by John Newton and William Wilberforce, was also aimed at reform and regeneration within the Established Church.

In the realm of secular thought the French philosopher Jean Jacques Rousseau (1712–1778) was to become one of the most revolutionary and influential figures of the modern world. An erratic and emotional writer of tracts and novels, gathering many of his ideas from the writings of philosophers, economists, natural scientists, and mathematicians, Rousseau succeeded in appealing to the masses as his more erudite and intellectual predecessors could not do. His philosophy, a compound of religious, political, and social theories, had as its central principle the belief that man is at bottom essentially good, and is happiest and best in a state of nature, free from the institutions and the artificial restraints of organized society. His God was not the Deity of organized and established religion, but a beneficent force that worked in and through man and nature, and was most nearly approached and most clearly perceived through contemplation of and communion with nature. By such contemplation and contact, and by divesting himself of the fetters which the church and the state had through the centuries put upon him, man could attain to perfection in this world. The books in which Rousseau expressed the theories that opened up the possibilities of a new and better world were written in a style in which emotion and eloquence played a larger part than logic and cold facts. But such a philosophy and such a style inevitably appealed powerfully to human beings who were not unwilling to excuse and justify their alleged imperfections. Rousseau's influence was widespread among those who wished to evade responsibilities to social systems and institutions, under which many had suffered acutely. More than any other writer of his day Rousseau became the chief prophet of Revolution and Romanticism.[3]

The high tide of Romanticism in English literature came during the latter part of the reign of George III (1760–1820) and the reign of George IV (1820–1830). Developments in literature paralleled four great historical movements: (1) the French Revolution; (2) the Napoleonic Wars; (3) the waves of reaction, suppression, and continental secondary revolution; and (4) British reform after the defeat of Napoleon. Much Romantic literature is concerned with the two Georges, the political and military leaders, and the events and ideas of the times.

In 1775, as a result of the growing protests against the colonial policy of Great Britain, the

[3] See Byron's tributes to him in *Childe Harold, III*, stanzas 76–83; for a skeptical view of the literary value of Rousseau's influence see Babbitt's *Rousseau and Romanticism.*

American Revolution began, furnishing to many in France what seemed to be a practical example of the success of Rousseau's doctrines. Washington was inaugurated first President of the United States on April 30, 1789. On the next day the Estates General began to assemble at Versailles. Within the month a revolution was under way that was to stir profoundly human thought, emotion, and action, to shake every throne in Europe, and to transform the life of every country in the Western world.

The French Revolution began as a protest against the outworn social order based on feudalism, against the privileges of caste, against bureaucracy and despotism. An assertion of the equal value of every human personality, it attempted to reconstruct human society in accordance with theories of the Rights of Man that had been developing, both in France and in England, since the Renaissance. Rousseau, as we have seen, was its chief prophet; from him came, in Byron's words, "Those oracles which set the world in flames, Nor ceased to burn till kingdoms were no more." The revolution began in France, not so much because the French common people were more oppressed than any other European people, but because they had leaders who were better educated in political theory. For a while the cause of the French people seemed to be the cause of all mankind. The early phases stirred hope of a brighter, better future for the human race. But the growing violence of the mob and the spread of anarchy in France undermined such constructive acts as the framing of a constitution, the Declaration of the Rights of Man, and the reorganization of government. The final phase of the Revolution began in 1792 with the proclamation of France as a republic and the declaration of war "against all kings in behalf of all peoples"; the trial and execution of the King followed in January, 1793. Soon the period known as the Reign of Terror gripped France, and it lasted for sixteen dreadful months, to be terminated only by the death of the extremist Robespierre in July, 1794. Finally, after the defeat of the European coalitions against France, the Revolution proper ended with the establishment of the Directory in 1795.

At the outset, a majority of young and well-educated Englishmen hailed the French Revolution with joy. The first generation of the Romanticists, Wordsworth, Coleridge, Southey, Hazlitt, Landor, and Scott, were in their late teens when it started. All of them except Scott saw in it the salvation of mankind. "Bliss was it in that dawn to be alive," wrote Wordsworth in his thirties, looking back on his twenties when he had known love and revolution on the soil of France. At the very climax of the Terror, Wordsworth wrote a letter justifying the execution of Louis XVI, repudiating caste and privilege, and affirming his faith in the French cause as the cause of humanity. Neither he nor his contemporaries ever forgot the exaltation of those years. And the brave hopes of that early phase were to be revived by the generation of Byron and Shelley, born on the eve or just at the beginning of the Revolution and growing up to rejoice that "Mankind hath felt their strength, and made it felt."

The course of events gradually disillusioned all but the most inveterate die-hards, such as Hazlitt. War between England and France began in 1793. During the early campaigns, so great was the dismay of many young Englishmen like Wordsworth that they would not join in church prayers for the success of English arms. But the excesses and the blind fury of the French revolutionists in their dealings with such basic institutions as religion and the family, and their early invasions of Venice and Switzerland, reputed to be free and democratic countries, were enough to destroy the revolutionary faith of many; Coleridge wrote his recantation, "France, An Ode," in 1798. England was constantly threatened with invasion, especially in 1796 and 1797, until English victory in the Battle of the Nile removed the threat of immediate danger. The war dragged on until 1802, when the Peace of Amiens gave a short breathing-spell for the more deadly struggle to follow.

Since 1795 or thereabouts Napoleon Bonaparte had been in control of affairs in France. The second war, which was to overthrow him, lasted intermittently from 1803 until the Battle of Waterloo in June, 1815. During this war England was making a desperate fight not only for the preservation of her empire but for survival itself. For a time she was alone against Napoleon; again (1803–1805) she lived in hourly dread of invasion. The election of Napoleon as Consul for life in 1802, his coronation as Emperor in 1804, the crash of great nations across the water—all these events re-echo in English Romantic poetry. No better record of the fears, disillusionments, despair, and spiritual anguish of these years can be found than that which Wordsworth wrote in *The Prelude* and in "Poems Dedicated to National Independence and Liberty."

In England, from the beginning of the French Revolution, growing pressure had encouraged dictatorial methods of government. Menaced by invasion from without, the country was torn by dissension within. Agitators for the independence of the Spanish colonies in South America embarrassed foreign relations. Many radical associations sprang up to proclaim sympathy with France and even to urge overthrow of the British monarchy. Edmund Burke had taken issue with these radical associations in his vigorous and eloquent *Reflections on the Revolution* (1790), and agitators like Tom Paine answered him. William Godwin preached philosophical anarchy (*Political Justice*, 1793). To meet this rising tide of dissent, the government, controlled by Pitt and the Tory party, adopted severe measures to repress freedom of speech, of assembly, and of the press. Intellectual radicals were tried for high treason, among them Coleridge's friend John Thelwall, who was, however, acquitted by a sensible English jury. In Birmingham a government-provoked mob wrecked the chemical laboratory of Coleridge's friend Joseph Priestley, who had expressed himself imprudently on issues of the day. The conservatism of the English people tolerated a strong government in the interest of national defense. By pointing out the dire effects of the revolution in France and the menace of French armies, the Tory party was able to maintain itself against what was becoming known as the "liberal wing" of both the Whig and Tory parties.

Under Tory leadership in the sphere of foreign relations, the policy of forming coalitions with absolute monarchies in order to contain the French was continued. In 1811, when George III became blind and permanently insane, young George, the Prince of Wales, was appointed Regent. No greater or more intolerant enemy of the liberal minority could have come to the fore. When Leigh Hunt, a poet and journalist, made an offensive personal allusion to the Regent in print, the result was a two-year jail sentence. Hunt's release from prison later inspired one of Keats's earliest sonnets. After the defeat of Napoleon, England joined Russia, Prussia, and Austria in a Quadruple Alliance, the avowed purpose of which was "to preserve monarchical governments and stamp out the spirit of revolution." At this discouraging stage, the cause of liberalism and reform seemed hopeless to such persons as Byron and Shelley.

But agitation for reform, particularly of representation in Parliament, did not die. The example of the American people, who had won their independence and then, in the War of 1812, successfully defended it, helped to keep the democratic spirit alive. The frightful economic distress under wartime conditions and after-war adjustments steadily increased the pressure for reform. From 1815 to 1822, however, the reactionary Tory party, led by firm, narrow-minded men like Viscount Castlereagh and Lord Eldon, coped with the spirit of reform by riding it down, as Shelley pictures them doing in *The Masque of Anarchy*. It was to the two "Bobs"—Castlereagh (Robert Stewart) and the "turncoat" poet laureate Robert Southey—that Byron mockingly dedicated the first and second cantos of *Don Juan*. It was Lord Eldon who refused Shelley the custody of his own children, in part because of the poet's moral and political views as expressed in *Queen Mab*. During this post-Waterloo period the government enacted even more severe laws against sedition, and employed a host of spies to ferret out disturbers. Severe outbreaks of mob spirit occurred. One of the most spectacular was the "Peterloo Massacre" in 1819 at Manchester, where soldiers broke up a mass meeting and killed several workers. Shelley heard of this act of violence in Italy and denounced it in his "Song to the Men of England" and "England in 1819."

The death of George III in 1820—though it occasioned first the heavy laureate hexameters of Southey, then Byron's brilliant retaliatory *The Vision of Judgment*—brought little improvement in the political sphere. The new King was the old Regent. The Tories, however, realizing that they were losing ground, tried to save themselves by adopting occasional conciliatory and liberal measures. In 1822 the new Foreign Secretary, George Canning, who had succeeded Castlereagh (a suicide), disregarded the Holy Alliance in acknowledging the independence of the revolting South American countries; the following year he supported the Monroe Doctrine with the British navy; in 1825–1827 he shielded the Greeks from Turkish conquest. In 1829 the Catholic Emancipation Bill finally passed through Parliament. (Byron had spoken in favor of it nearly twenty years earlier.) Also, the accession of William IV in 1830 and successful revolutions against the Bourbons in France and Belgium greatly encouraged the liberal cause. Finally, in the great Reform Bill of 1832, a long step was taken toward guaranteeing government by free and equitable representation in Parliament.

Social, Economic, and Scientific Forces

Another revolution, not less catastrophic and far-reaching than the philosophical and political revolutions discussed above, was brought about in the closing years of the eighteenth century by the great number of mechanical inventions and the application of steam power to manufacture and then to transportation. The Industrial Revolution, as it is called, transformed economic and social life, and remade an England that had been predominantly agricultural into the chief industrial nation of the world. The early nineteenth century witnessed some of the most painful effects of this transformation. As the individual worker and his hand labor gave way to more powerful and productive machines, thousands of home craftsmen were forced by large-scale factory competition to go to the cities for employment or to give up their trades. The problem of unemployment, precipitated by the Industrial Revolution, was aggravated by the long war's dislocation of markets, as Wordsworth's story of Margaret, for example, shows with moving pathos (*The Excursion*, Book I). In the mushrooming industrial towns of the Midlands there were no housing regulations, few sanitary provisions, no labor laws. With inadequate representation in Parliament, laborers could find no relief through governmental regulation. The right to strike was not recognized. Only a few generous spirits like Byron had now and then lifted their voices in defense of workers' rights. Meanwhile the Corn Laws, constituting a protective tariff on grain, kept the price of foodstuffs beyond reach of the poorest. In the country districts the landlords pocketed the benefits of government protection of agriculture. Tenants, as Shelley declared, starved or were stabbed to death in the fields. The suffering in the cities of the underprivileged sweatshop worker and the streetwalker found utterance only in a lesser poet, Thomas Hood.

During these troubled years the aristocracy and the upper middle class remained on the whole ignorant of or indifferent to the condition of the poor. But on sensitive souls among the intellectuals, government oppression and the misery of the working classes weighed heavily, and it is small wonder that many half-baked social schemes were devised. The most interesting of these was Pantisocracy, conceived in 1794 by Southey, just out of Oxford, Coleridge, who had recently withdrawn from Cambridge, and Robert Lovell, a young Quaker. Twelve young gentlemen and twelve young ladies were "to sail to America, and, on the banks of the Susquehannah [in Pennsylvania] to form a Social Colony, in which there was to be a community of property, and where all that was selfish was to be proscribed." The only result of the Pantisocratic dream, aside from its literary reflections, was the providing of wives for Southey and Coleridge—for the latter an incompatible one.

The growth of humanitarian feeling is also noticeable through this period. The penal laws were reformed. The British slave trade in the colonies was abolished in the first decade of the nineteenth century. And in 1833 the movement, led by William Wilberforce, to abolish slavery in all lands under British control came to a successful consummation in the passage of the Emancipation Bill.

While skepticism and atheism found expression through such publicists as Thomas Paine and William Godwin, and were flaunted by youngsters like Wordsworth in the 1790's and by Shelley twenty years later, a great religious movement was perhaps saving England at the turn of the century from the violence of revolution by arms and bloodshed. Methodism had become one of the most deeply formative influences in modern English social history. It had brought the Gospel to the poor, and together with the evangelical movement, led by Newton and Wilberforce, it was quietly transforming the spiritual life of the English people. The poetry of Coleridge and of the later Wordsworth carries on the deep current of religious feeling that had been set in motion during the preceding century by such poets as William Cowper.

Religion was soon, however, to face a formidable challenge as knowledge of the natural sciences increased. For this was a period of brilliant scientific achievement. In astronomy Sir William Herschel had been calculating the depths of space and the distances of the stars, and with his new telescope had discovered the planet Uranus in 1781. Lagrange had explained why the moon shows only one side of itself, and Laplace in 1796 elaborated the nebular hypothesis. James Hutton laid the foundations of modern geology in his *Theory of the Earth*, which was published in 1798; the following year William Smith began the valuable geological investigations that were to earn for him the good-humored nickname of "Strata" Smith. Meanwhile in chemistry and physics Sir Humphry Davy, Joseph Priestley, Henry Cavendish, and John Dalton were discovering new elements, gases, and properties of electricity.

The poets of the Romantic period showed awareness of these varied activities and in several instances they even shared in them. As a student at Eton and Oxford, Shelley was addicted to scientific dabbling; from early youth he read scientific works with avidity and embodied their theories in his poetry. Wordsworth became a close friend of the great astronomer Sir William Rowan Hamilton, who furnished him with subjects for several poems. Both Wordsworth and Shelley refer to the geological theories of the day. Wordsworth and Coleridge were friends of the famous chemist Sir Humphry Davy, and received from him directions for study; Coleridge was one of those who assisted Davy in experiments with nitrous oxide, better known as laughing gas.

Yet the Romanticists in general vacillated between lively admiration for science and fear that it would destroy a spiritual interpretation of the universe. The early nineteenth century was seeing the beginnings of the conflict between science and religion that raged for over fifty years. In a moment of optimism Wordsworth wrote that "poetry is the breath and finer spirit of all knowledge; it is the impassioned expression which is in the countenance of all Science." The poet, he said, "will be ready to follow the steps of the man of science . . . carrying sensation into the midst of the objects of science itself." Yet the spiritual histories of most of the Romanticists are records of inner conflicts between the claims of materialism and idealism. Some of their greatest poems, like *The Prelude* and *Prometheus Unbound*, testify to the reconciliation of those ancient antagonists, the World and the Soul. Great systems meet in such statements as Wordsworth's

> the light of sense
> Goes out, but with a flash that has revealed
> The invisible world.

The Drift toward Romanticism in Eighteenth-Century Literature

In describing the origins and varying interpretations of Romanticism, we have already suggested that the literary "new direction" called the Romantic Movement did not spring up suddenly and full-blown at the end of the eighteenth century. Behind these exciting new conceptions and new events and these great new personalities there had existed in England since the early 1700's a group of attitudes and ideas that anticipated certain aspects of the fully developed Romantic Movement. These new interests, while running counter to some of the dominant tendencies of the times, nevertheless found increasing expression in literature as the eighteenth century grew older.

Among these early undercurrents was a reaction against one of the forces that most powerfully affected the literature of the late seventeenth and the eighteenth centuries. We noted earlier the predominating influence of Rationalism, a system of scientific, religious, and philosophical thought based upon reason rather than upon the evidence of the senses, the revelations of the Scriptures, or the authority of the wise and the good. But it would be a mistake to assume that even so controlling a "spirit of the times" as Rationalism enjoyed a sway over the minds of men that was universal and unquestioned. Shortly after the beginning of the eighteenth century, the teachings of Anthony Ashley Cooper, third Earl of Shaftesbury, began to confirm a tendency, that was already present in drama, to emphasize the emotional rather than the rational elements of human nature and experience. Man, Shaftesbury held, is naturally good, born with an instinct for righteous conduct called the moral sense. Nature is good. Between it and man there is moral and spiritual harmony, and the closer man lives to nature, in a moral as well as physical sense, the closer he is to the fountain of goodness. Nature is a manifestation of God, benevolent like Him. When man lives close to nature and to God, he feels and acts benevolently. Hence men find in their spontaneous emotions, especially their social sympathies, the strongest motives to good conduct.

The similarity of such ideas to those preached in France by Rousseau is quickly recognized. We have already seen their literary manifestations in the "sensibility" observable in a variety of eighteenth-century literary forms. Addison and Steele in *The Spectator*, Richardson in his novel, *Pamela*, and among poets Thomson in *The Seasons*, Collins in his odes and songs, and Cowper in *The Task*, treated situations, scenes, characters, and human conduct and motives with "sensibility."[4] Collins and Cowper had already begun to endow it with a "confessional strain," which was carried on in the poetry of Wordsworth,

[4] See Ernest Bernbaum, *The Drama of Sensibility*, Ginn, 1915.

Byron, and Shelley, and in the essays of Lamb, Hazlitt, and De Quincey. Based as "sensibility" was on belief in the goodness of human nature and the essential nobility of the ordinary man in his everyday surroundings, it was to become an important element in Romantic literature.

It will be profitable to review several other aspects of eighteenth-century literature in the new perspective of their relation to the Romantic Movement. Beginning as a reaction against too exclusive preoccupation with urban subjects, the movement known as "the return to nature" was also sanctioned by Shaftesbury's teachings. At the same time Swift was busy with his *Gulliver's Travels*, the countryman Thomson was writing minute and loving descriptions of natural scenery; in *The Seasons* we find expression of simple pleasure in woods and fields and quiet country life, and the infusion of a strain of moral and religious meditation evoked by natural surroundings. These traits were fully developed in the poetry of Cowper, especially *The Task*. Thus the eighteenth century left a legacy of ideas about nature that are basic in Romantic poetry: nature gives calmness and peace to the human mind; it induces a religious feeling; it offers sensible evidence of the beauty and goodness of God; it is the dwelling place of God; it may be God manifest in us; it quickens social sympathies. But fully as important as their ideas is the fact that such eighteenth-century poets as Collins, Gray, and Cowper learned to subordinate a landscape to a human mood. That is the essential feature of all great nature poetry.

Meanwhile the scientific writers mentioned earlier—and others—were storing up in the eighteenth century a great fund of materials which the Romanticists were to find full of imaginative and emotional potentialities. The increasing interest in natural science produced more accurate studies of flora and fauna of different sections of the country and the world. The last years of the century brought forth a shelf of books rich with the findings of explorers in various unfamiliar regions ranging from the Highlands of Scotland to darkest Africa and the South Atlantic seaboard. These books were read by most of the Romanticists, and the uses to which this exciting new material was put by such a poet as Coleridge, for example, have been shown in our own time by John Livingston Lowes in *The Road to Xanadu*.

Other undercurrents, growing in power through the eighteenth century, invite attention. Parallel to the reviving interest in nature and natural phenomena was the increasing concern with the common man and folk life. This, too, was a protest against the prevailing absorption in city people, and against the social stratification of England. In Thomson, Gray, and Cowper we have found evidence of sympathetic interest in country people's homes and everyday lives, in their welfare, rights, and natural nobility. In fact, much Romantic literature was from the first primitivistic: that is, expressive of the belief that crude, simple folk, even savages, exhibit virtues that put civilized people to shame.[5] This attitude was enormously encouraged by the writings of Rousseau, with his view of the arts and sciences as inimical to human happiness and his advocacy of a back-to-nature movement. The savage, the peasant, the mountaineer, the fisherman, the shepherd, were glorified. Their folklore became a noble source of literary inspiration and material. Hence the ballad collections, to be noted later, and hence William Collins's poetic program in his *Ode on the Superstitions of the Highlands of Scotland* (written 1749, published 1788); here was "the whole Romantic School in its germ," later to be fully exemplified by Walter Scott. And before the end of the century Robert Burns, himself a peasant, in his *Poems, Chiefly in the Scottish Dialect* had given the sturdiest, most genuine, most poetic expression to these ideas about the common man and lowly life. He "showed my youth," says Wordsworth, "How verse may build a princely throne On humble truth."

The increasing interest in the common man as a type led naturally to a concern with the individual man and with his personal experiences. This concern was first manifested clearly in the Methodist movement of the Wesleys in the 1730's. The humanitarian aspects of the interest in the common man, the submerged and oppressed individual, appeared in the fiction of the century and particularly in the novels of Henry Fielding, who was profoundly impressed by the social injustices of the day. They were conspicuous also in such poems as Goldsmith's *Deserted Village* (1770) and George Crabbe's *The Village* (1783) and *The Borough* (1810), with their realistic descriptions of the inhabitants.

It was inevitable that the interest in what a city-minded civilization had found unfamiliar should take on antiquarian aspects and involve the rediscovery and the reinterpretation of the past. The study of Old Norse, Old English, and the Celtic languages and literatures soon embraced

[5] See H. N. Fairchild, *The Noble Savage: A Study in Romantic Naturalism*, Columbia University Press, 1928.

everything belonging to the Middle Ages and the centuries of British history preceding the "Enlightenment" of the eighteenth century, in which the rediscoverers lived. Of particular importance to the growing number of writers with such "Romantic" inclinations was the revival of interest in Scottish ballads, folk songs, and other dialect poetry. Bishop Percy's *Reliques of Ancient English Poetry* (1765), the most famous and influential of the collections of ballads published during the century, has been called "the Bible of the Romantic Movement," so fertile was it in suggestions of themes, diction, style, and—to Coleridge, and Wordsworth—even of critical theory. In the Ossianic poems of James Macpherson, with their world of shadowy landscapes, dim legendary figures, and musical prose, Coleridge, Wordsworth, Scott, and Byron later found another storehouse of poetic imagery and phrases.[6]

During the decade of the *Reliques* and *Ossian*, Bishop Richard Hurd in his *Letters on Chivalry and Romance* advocated "the Gothic chivalry" and "the spirit of romance" as superior for poetic purposes to the customs and religion of "Homer's age." And in 1764 Horace Walpole published *The Castle of Otranto*, a whimsical, half-cynical horror tale of a medieval Italian nobleman and his family living in an ancient castle. Hurd's *Letters* and Walpole's novel did most to encourage the "Gothic" vogue in English fiction and poetry, which produced the "Gothic romance" with its sensational terrors and picturesque superstitions, and which came to flower in such works of the full-blown Romantic Movement as Coleridge's *Christabel*, Keats's "The Eve of St. Agnes," and some of the Waverley novels of Scott.

By the middle of the eighteenth century, contemplation of the past, of ancient glories real or imagined, and reflection on the transitoriness of man's life, were combining with moods of sensibility to produce a poetry of melancholy. Edward Young's *Night Thoughts* (1742), Robert Blair's *The Grave* (1743), and Thomas Gray's famous *Elegy Written in a Country Churchyard* (1751) treated the themes of life, death, and immortality. The lugubriousness of these poems, and the preoccupation of some of them with the physical aspects of death, won for their authors the designation "Graveyard School." Besides establishing a conventional atmosphere of meditation (ruins, ivy, tombs, moping owls, moonlight), the Graveyard Poets suggested one of the greatest themes of Romantic lyric poetry—the debate between Joy and Melancholy, later treated in Coleridge's "Dejection," Wordsworth's "Ode: Intimations of Immortality," Shelley's "Lines Written Among the Euganean Hills," Byron's *Childe Harold*, and Keats's odes.

While a fair share of eighteenth century imaginative literature was moving in the directions that have been described, there existed, side by side with the more orthodox neo-classical principles of the time, a corresponding development of critical ideas and theories. Many of the precepts and points of view that later became fundamental in Romantic criticism were expressed or implied by eighteenth-century critics. Good taste, many of them asserted, is innate, not acquired or dictated by authority. Others felt the need for a change, a fresh start, in poetry. Originality was declared to be superior to imitation and perfect technique. Poetry, it was maintained, appeals to feeling and imagination rather than to intellect and reason. Shakespeare, Spenser, and Milton began to take precedence over Homer, Virgil, and Horace. The medieval Christian tradition came to be considered superior for literary material to the pagan classical tradition. And as the eighteenth century grew older, more writers looked upon the greatest of English dramatists, Shakespeare, not as a lawless barbarian beyond the pale of critical jurisdiction, but as a great creative artist expressing his own age and obeying the laws of his own genius. Through the century such critics as we have mentioned remained in the minority, but they were ever growing in strength.

The chief literary forms of Romantic expression had meanwhile been taking shape. There was a notable revival of older verse forms. Abandoning the dominant form of the heroic couplet, James Thomson brought out the first of *The Seasons* in 1726 in blank verse reminiscent of Milton. By the end of the century blank verse had become a favorite medium for reflective poetry, notably with Cowper and Blake. The Spenserian stanza, revived in William Shenstone's *The Schoolmistress* (1737), was used in poems as different as Thomson's *The Castle of Indolence* and Burns's *The Cotter's Saturday Night*, and went on to new glories in the work of Scott, Byron, Shelley, and Keats. The revival of the sonnet by Gray, Cowper, and others was one of the most fruitful developments in lyric poetry, for in the hands of Wordsworth and Keats and their contemporaries it proved one of the happiest instruments of Romantic expression.

[6] See E. D. Snyder, *The Celtic Revival in English Literature, 1760–1800*, Harvard University Press, 1923.

Original poems by Chatterton, Cowper, and Burns, in stanzas patterned after those of the old ballads, established a precedent for *Lyrical Ballads* and the early poems of Scott. The ode, though it had not been abandoned by poets of the late seventeenth and early eighteenth centuries was revivified by Collins and Gray for the treatment of fresh themes. And the hymn which, as written by the Wesleys and Cowper, represented the popular flowering of the new poetic movement was to maintain its hold throughout the nineteenth century.

In the *Spectator* papers and in Goldsmith's contributions to magazines we have seen eighteenth-century ancestors of the familiar essays of Lamb, Hazlitt, De Quincey, and Hunt. The variety and the scope of prose fiction were greatly enlarged. In addition to the Gothic novel, attempts were made at the historical novel, which was later to achieve its greatest success with Sir Walter Scott. The novel with a serious social or religious purpose was initiated in 1794 in *Caleb Williams*, by William Godwin, the radical philosopher, whose daughter Mary later married Shelley.

The latter years of the eighteenth century saw an increasing acceleration of the literary tendencies that have been described. Most of the important themes, ideas, and attitudes that were to move the Romantic writers were first suggested during these years. The works of two poets especially, Burns and Blake, who appeared after the middle of the century, show in different ways but with equal originality the reassertion of feeling and awakening of imagination that were to characterize the poets of the Romantic period. Burns and Blake were the truest forerunners of the Romantic poets.

Flood Tides and Main Currents of Romanticism

English literature of the period 1798–1832, when Romanticism was dominant, has been likened to a flood tide. The first great rise came with the *Lyrical Ballads* of Wordsworth and Coleridge. It was followed by "currents" of verse and fiction from Scott; of criticism and the familiar essay from Lamb, Hazlitt, and De Quincey; of biography and prose fiction, as well as lyric and narrative poetry, from Southey and Landor. The wave of this, the first generation of the Romanticists, was at the crest about 1817.

In their original collaborative program Wordsworth and Coleridge endeavored to enrich poetic experience by two complementary methods. One, Wordsworth's, was to look intently at common things and familiar life, to rub from them the film that custom had deposited on them, and by directing attention to essential qualities in them to arouse in the beholder a sense of their beauty and mystery. The other method, Coleridge's, beginning at the opposite end of human experience with the far-away, the mysterious, even the supernatural, was to make such experience real by truthful description of human reactions to it. These poets adopted for purposes of expression direct and living language: Wordsworth, the words really used by men in a state of excitement; Coleridge, the forthright diction of the old ballads, romances, and other forms of popular literature.

Wordsworth's share of the program involved in the main a reinterpretation of nature, of man's relation to it, and of the relation of both to God; a vindication of the beauty and dignity of common men as he knew them or imagined them to be; and a search for human happiness

> in the very world, which is the world
> Of all of us,—the place where, in the end,
> We find our happiness, or not at all.

His themes and choice of material illustrate the Romantic preoccupation with sensibility and self-confession, with the return to nature and the glorification of man in his natural, primitive surroundings; by reviving older poetic forms and styles he equally showed himself the true Romantic. More than any other poet, Wordsworth completed what had begun during the eighteenth century, adding the accent of his own personality and the emphasis of his age. And, more than any other poet, he determined the character of nineteenth-century poetry. Wordsworth is the key to understanding many aspects of the poetry of Byron, Shelley, Keats, Tennyson, Arnold, and Meredith.

As a poet, Coleridge made his greatest contribution in about fifty pages of living poetry, including *The Rime of the Ancient Mariner*, *Christabel*, "Kubla Khan," "France, An Ode," and "Dejection: An Ode." The first was published in *Lyrical Ballads; Christabel* was designed for the second edition, but was never completed, and was not published until 1816. These two poems and "Kubla Khan" are the greatest triumphs of "the renascence of wonder"; they illustrate perfectly Coleridge's role in the collaborative effort with Wordsworth. "France" is perhaps the best short political poem of the age; it is the most eloquent condemnation of the French Revolution. "Dejection" is at once a confession of poetic failure, transcendentally explained, and a triumph of the poetic power which the poet says he has lost. Besides these, Coleridge's comparatively small poetic output included some delicate and lovely nature poems.

But Coleridge's significance is as great in the field of criticism as in that of original poetry. His criticism of Wordsworth's theory and practice of poetry, his profoundly philosophical exposition of his own theory, his reinterpretation of Shakespeare, and his vindication of ideal values against the growing materialistic philosophy of his own age are more than compensations for his atrophy as poet.

Coleridge's interest in earlier literature and Wordsworth's preoccupation with natural scenery and peasants found original and splendid parallels in the work of Walter Scott. Scott's verse has been overshadowed by his prose fiction, but he was one of the true singers among the Romanticists, ranking as a lyrist with Robert Burns. Scott excelled also in the field of narrative verse, where of his contemporaries only Byron surpassed him. As an editor and composer of ballads, as a romancer in the manner suggested by medieval romances and *Christabel*, Scott stands alone—also as a walking and exceedingly articulate encyclopedia of Scottish folklore and history. Early in his verse romances and later in the Waverley novels, he painted a living gallery of Scottish common folk. Scott knew his native countryside as well and lovingly as Wordsworth knew the mountains and dales of Cumberland; his descriptions of natural scenery are clear and firm.

The chief Romantic essayists were friends of Wordsworth and Coleridge and familiar with their poetic endeavors. Charles Lamb in letters to Wordsworth, Hazlitt in "My First Acquaintance with Poets," and De Quincey in his memoirs, have left a vivid record of a great literary period in the making. In his own sphere Lamb showed that a vast city can be as beautiful and strange, and as lovable, as the Lake Country; that the old dramatists and prose writers are as interesting as the romancers; that the essay is sometimes as effective as poetry for purposes of self-revelation—and rather more intimate and amusing. Hazlitt, besides appraising the poetry of Wordsworth, Coleridge, and their contemporaries, enlarged his art on the subjects of painting and acting. He is one of the most discerning critics in the whole range of English literature from the Elizabethans down to his own age. And in such essays as "The Fight" and "On Going a Journey" he is a lively and incisive commentator on everyday life. De Quincey, younger than the other two, was among the first youthful readers to applaud the *Lyrical Ballads*. He made himself a disciple and friend of Coleridge, gained acquaintance with Wordsworth, and settled in the Lake District. In *Confessions of an English Opium-Eater* De Quincey extended the scope and sharpened the psychology of confessional writing. His "On the Knocking at the Gate in Macbeth" treats problems of Shakespearean dramaturgy in the refreshing spirit of Coleridge. His imaginative essays, such as *Suspiria de Profundis* and *The English Mail-Coach*, are prose analogues of Romantic lyrical poems and musical fugues.

Robert Southey and Walter Savage Landor were friends and were acquainted with most of the other Romanticists. The French Revolution excited them as undergraduates, but while Landor remained steadfast in his conception of liberal principles, Southey gradually turned conservative. In different ways they exploited the past—Southey, in homely ballads reminiscent of Coleridge's, later in long narrative poems on Oriental and Welsh themes, then in histories and admirable short biographies; Landor, in his epics *Gebir* and *Chrysaor*, in hundreds of exquisite epigrams and idyls on Greek, Roman, and Italian subjects, and on a larger scale, in the stately portrait galleries of *Imaginary Conversations*. Southey and Landor share the fate of being neglected today—remembered, as much as they are remembered at all, for their short poems and their prose rather than for their ambitious poetic efforts.

With Byron, Shelley, and Keats, a change comes not only in Romantic poetry but also in the spirit of English literature—a change determined largely by the transformation that was taking place in the social and political conditions of Europe. Their birth-dates—1788, 1792, and 1795, respectively—place these poets about a generation later than Wordsworth (b. 1770) and Coleridge (b. 1772), the early leaders of revolt against the eighteenth-century order. As a result there was an unfortunate lack of understanding of the two older poets on the part of the younger men. The older generation, particularly Wordsworth and Coleridge, had, in the critic Legouis' phrase, been "nourished by the faiths and regenerative principles brought into being by the French Revolution." Napoleon's blood-stained career and the European reaction against liberty and toward absolutism spread over the interval between the heyday of Wordsworth and Coleridge and the period in which the three younger poets did their most characteristic work. Byron, Shelley, and Keats flourished as poets in an age of shattered faiths, of cynical political dictatorships, and of profound disillusionment.

Between the two generations there were also differences in critical theory and in literary practice. The older generation, confounding the eighteenth century's imitation of classical standards of art with the genuinely classical, had rebelled against the literature current in its own age and gone back to the ballad, to medieval romance, and to Spenser, Milton, and a romantic interpretation of Shakespeare. But Byron in his *English Bards and Scotch Reviewers* and in later poems reacted against the theory of poetry displayed in *Lyrical Ballads*, idolized Pope, and adhered to the humanistic view of Shakespeare. Keats and Shelley, while showing the influence of Wordsworth and Coleridge in ideas and style, "revived the cold ashes of Hellenism." Keats especially drew inspiration from the Renaissance, largely through the medium of sixteenth- and seventeenth-century English poetry. All three were more affected by Italian literature than their predecessors had been.

Intimate friends from 1816 until Shelley's death in 1822, Byron and Shelley shared certain ruling passions, but differed, sometimes as widely as the poles, in their philosophical and religious beliefs and social theories. They were both fascinated by the past of Greece, Rome, Italy, and the East. But whereas to Byron history with its pageantry and splendor sometimes lighted up the sorry present and consoled his wounded spirit, to Shelley, when it interested him at all, history was a dark record of man's inhumanity to man, shot through now and then with gleams of heroic self-sacrifice kindling hope for the future. Both are apostles of liberty, but Byron's thought scarcely goes beyond hatred of tyranny, derision of its ministers, and exultation over its destruction. His poetry is often a volcanic eruption devastating the whole social order. Shelley hates tyranny as passionately as Byron, but he has a more constructive gospel. He envisages a world liberated and transformed by the spirit of intellectual freedom and love. For a time (1816) the two were influenced by Wordsworth's idealistic interpretation of nature. From Byron's pen came the splendid speculations, in the third canto of *Childe Harold* and the Augusta poems, on the relationship of his own soul to the cosmos. Shelley went even beyond Wordsworth in the dizzy raptures of "Euganean Hills" and *Prometheus Unbound*, and in his "Hymn to Intellectual Beauty," soaring above the ever-changing world of sense and matter into the ideal world of Plato, he found true reality in abstract reason. Byron was indeed less comfortable with abstractions than was Shelley. Already the leading literary personality of his age, in the last years of his short life Byron combined his vigorous eloquence with superb wit and worldly perception to become one of the world's great satirical poets.

John Keats sailed his own course; never close personally to his fellow Romantic poets, he however shared many of their attitudes and enthusiasms. Like Coleridge, he is the poet of "witchery by daylight" ("La Belle Dame sans Merci" and *Lamia*) as well as by moonlight (*Endymion* and "The Eve of St. Agnes"). Like Shelley, he is fascinated by the ancient beauty of Greece and Italy; like Wordsworth, by the old pagan religion of nature. But more than any of his contemporaries Keats was preoccupied with every aspect of beauty. Whether Beauty embodied herself in physical nature, in ancient sculpture, myth and tale, or in philosophic thought, she was his religion, he was her priest, and poetry was his liturgy. Yet these themes are not the whole of Keats's poetry. His central and controlling faith, the essence of what he tried to say, is that life, however cruel and ugly in the human aspects of his day, can be justified by faith in beauty and truth (aspects of the same ultimate reality), and that poetry is the chief minister of this faith. Much of Keats's poetry is about poetry—its origin, its sources, its themes, its ministrations to human life, its relation to truth. Beginning with the Wordsworthian ethics that make poetry a balm to humanity through its power to inspire sympathy and helpfulness, he resolved this into a faith more noble and austere in its efficacy for enabling us "to bear all naked truths, And to envisage circumstance, all calm . . ."

Thomas Moore and Leigh Hunt invite attention both for themselves and as friends of greater poets. Moore, long an intimate of Byron, and his official biographer, managed to sing movingly about the ancient glories and wrongs of his native Ireland without offending his English friends. In his own way he did for his country a service comparable to that done for Scotland by Scott. Moore understood the technical relations of lyric poetry to music better than did most of the Romanticists;

many of his songs are still parlor favorites. His Oriental romance *Lalla Rookh* lacks the dark, throbbing passion and wildness of Byron's Turkish tales, but is more readable than Southey's long poems about Arabian devil-worshipers and Indian Brahmins. Leigh Hunt, leader of the so-called Cockney School derided by Byron, Moore, and the reviewers, introduced the young Keats to Italian themes, encouraged his early poetic efforts, and gave him two stylistic models—an adaptation of the heroic couplet (as in Hunt's *Rimini*), which was partly to the good, and a prettified, capersome poetic diction, which was altogether to the bad. But Hunt's steady exposition and defense of Romantic poetry, his felicity in criticizing it by sampling it, and his graceful essays are more solid claims to remembrance.

The genius of the writers of the Romantic Period, as we have seen, expressed itself most spontaneously and effectively in poetry, and particularly in lyric poetry. The fortunes of English drama were at the lowest ebb. It is a mark of the versatility of the greatest poets of the time that they also wrote plays in verse, but the results must be considered on the whole as dramatic poetry rather than true poetic drama. The poetry in them far outstrips the drama in excellence. The one really successful poetic drama of the group is Shelley's tragedy, *The Cenci* (1820), which recalls some of the great qualities of Elizabethan drama, and has been effectively presented on the twentieth-century stage. Less successful as drama, but well above the average level of the time, are Byron's *Manfred* and *Cain*.

The prose fiction of the period, like the other literary forms, had roots in the eighteenth century. As the nineteenth century began, the vogue of the Gothic romance,[7] inaugurated by Walpole's *Castle of Otranto*, increased with the spread of circulating libraries and six-penny editions. The wild romances of the "black writers" were the thrillers and the "literature of escape" of the early 1800's, and were read with much eagerness by persons in all walks of life, including Byron and Shelley when they were schoolboys. Of the scores of novels that belong in this category two only need be mentioned here: *Frankenstein* (1816) by Mary Godwin Shelley, the poet's wife, which gave to the world Frankenstein's notorious monster, devoid of all human feeling; and Charles Robert Maturin's *Melmoth the Wanderer* (1820), which has been called the masterpiece of this type of fiction. The Gothic tradition in sensational romance extended on through the Victorian era to include Bulwer-Lytton, Wilkie Collins, and Sheridan Le Fanu, the terror-novelist par excellence of the later years. That the Age of Reason had not sunk without trace, however, is proved by the amusing burlesque of the Gothic romance in Jane Austen's *Northanger Abbey*, which appeared in 1818.

Jane Austen (1775–1817) is the one notable literary figure of her time who was not affected by the Romantic influences of either the eighteenth or the nineteenth century, except in so far as she was led to disapprove of them. She was *in* the Romantic period rather than *of* it. Her line of descent from such literary forebears as Fielding, Fanny Burney, Addison, and Goldsmith is unmistakably clear. Neither her life nor her works have anything to do with revolutions, philosophical, political, or industrial, and her half-dozen novels reflect none of the industrial problems or social tension of the day. *Sense and Sensibility* (1811), *Pride and Prejudice* (1813), *Emma* (1816), and others are novels of manners, not of propaganda, and they have no more serious purpose than to amuse her well-bred readers. Her gentle satire of the sentimentality of much of the fiction of the day and of the foibles of human nature in general remains as effective and amusing as ever. Her innate good sense, with respect to both her capabilities and her limitations, and her lightness of touch have assured Jane Austen a place among the greatest artists of English fiction and have won for her a constant group of admirers in the twentieth century.

Two other women novelists should be mentioned. Maria Edgeworth (1767–1849) introduced into the novel of manners a more serious moral purpose. She is known today chiefly for her pictures of her native Ireland with its absentee landlords and their poor tenants. Her best-known novels, *Castle Rackrent* (1800) and *The Absentee* (1809), vivaciously written and masterpieces of their kind, gave Walter Scott some suggestions for treatment of his native country and its people. Still nearer Scott is Jane Porter (1776–1850), whose historical novels *Thaddeus of Warsaw* (1803) and *The Scottish Chiefs* (1810) were very popular in the last century and represent perhaps the highest achievement in the historical novel before Scott took control of the field.

Sir Walter Scott did not cease altogether to be a poet when he began to write his novels, and his prose has much of the quality of his narrative

[7] See Edith Birkhead, *The Tale of Terror: A Study of the Gothic Romance*, Dutton, 1921, and Eino Railo, *The Haunted Castle: A Study of the Elements in English Romanticism*, Dutton, 1927.

verse and ballads. Almost all the characteristic qualities of Romantic literature come to a focus in Scott's verse and in his nearly thirty novels. He is one of the world's great tellers of stories, which in his case range in time from the twelfth century to his own day and in setting from his native Scotland to continental Europe and the Holy Land. Scott's antiquarianism, his wide reading in history and romance, his incomparable knowledge of ballads and folklore, his vivid imagination, and his close observation of men and manners and scenes—all these brought together abundant materials for his use. The number and variety of characters in his novels are surpassed perhaps only in those of Dickens. Scott's faults and limitations are easily seen. His characters do not always come to life as human beings. He wrote too rapidly and too much to produce work of uniform excellence. Indeed, he himself admitted his lack of the delicate and subtle craftsmanship of Jane Austen, and characterized his own as a "bow-wow strain." But the genius and the extraordinary nobility of Scott shine through all his artistic faults, and the gusto and sweep of his best narratives are without equal in English fiction. His Scottish novels have held their ground better than any of the others, and of them all *The Heart of Midlothian* with its heroine, Jeanie Deans, has been most highly regarded in recent years.

Strong though Romantic literature had grown as a creative force, the early years of the nineteenth century saw it constantly on the defensive. Three great periodicals—the *Edinburgh Review* (founded 1802), the *Quarterly Review* (1809), and *Blackwood's Magazine* (1817)—lifted the discussion of books from the plane of trade advertising to that of literary criticism. In their attitudes toward writers and in their political views these journals differed. The *Edinburgh*, edited by Francis Jeffrey, was Whig in politics, and in the main it opposed the tendencies of Romantic literature on grounds of established taste and principles belonging to the earlier age. Lord Brougham's sarcastic review of Byron's *Hours of Idleness*, which appeared in the *Edinburgh*, provoked Byron's *English Bards and Scotch Reviewers*. Ignoring Shelley, the *Edinburgh* eventually modified its early opinions of Scott and Byron; but its adverse criticism of Wordsworth never changed in Jeffrey's lifetime. The Tory *Quarterly*, edited by Scott's son-in-law and biographer, J. G. Lockhart, published the infamous review of Keats's *Endymion*, and abused Hunt, Hazlitt, Lamb, and Shelley, but treated Wordsworth and the Lake School respectfully and fairly. The third of these influential journals, *Blackwood's*, edited by "Christopher North" (John Wilson), was kind to Wordsworth, appreciative of Shelley's poetic genius but hard on his morals and judgment, harsh to Leigh Hunt and Hazlitt and their Cockney School. In these three periodicals were published articles and reviews by Scott, Southey, Hazlitt, and De Quincey. The *London Magazine* (founded in 1820) was a late but brilliant entry into the field. Its career was distinguished but brief. In those days of savage reviews the editing of a magazine was a perilous occupation, and the *London Magazine's* editor, John Scott, was killed in a duel. But while he and the magazine lived, he had the honor of publishing in it Lamb's *Essays of Elia*, Hazlitt's *Table Talk*, and De Quincey's *Confessions of an English Opium-Eater*.

The Romantic Period, which began with the publication of *Lyrical Ballads* in 1798, may be considered to end in 1832, the year of Scott's death. Two years before, in 1830, a young poet, Alfred Tennyson, aged twenty-one, had brought out his first volume of poems under his own name. A new era in English literature was beginning.

William Wordsworth 1770–1850

"Fair seed-time had my soul," says Wordsworth of his childhood, and adds that he grew up "Fostered alike by beauty and by fear." He was born on April 7, 1770, at Cockermouth, Cumberland, on the edge of the Lake District, in an old brick house near the "bright blue river" Derwent. His father, John Wordsworth, was an attorney, and the law agent and manor steward for Sir James Lowther; his mother, Anne Cookson Wordsworth, the daughter of a dry-goods merchant of the town of Penrith. There were five children, of whom Dorothy (born December 25, 1771) and John (born December 4, 1772) were his favorites. For about a year he attended an infant school at Penrith with Mary Hutchinson, who was to become his wife. Perhaps his first experience of pain and loss came with the death of his mother, when he was eight years old. The death of his father, five years later, completed the breakup of his home life. The children were scattered, William returning to Hawkshead School, which he had entered in 1778. Here, under the motherly care of old Anne Tyson, who boarded him, and under the excellent tutelage of William Taylor, he received a good classical preparation for college. Equally as important, if not more important, was the informal education he received from his natural surroundings in this beautiful region of lakes and mountains and from his rough-and-tumble fellowship with the other middle-class boys of the school (*The Prelude*, Books First and Second). Trapping among the hills (sometimes taking the other boys' catches and feeling uneasy and fearful for the deed), skating on the lake, "borrowing" a boat that was not his own (and taking fright from "the huge and mighty forms" that drove him from the water and troubled his dreams long thereafter), hanging on the giddy edge of cliffs while bird-nesting (and hearing in the wind "strange utterance") —these are some of the Presences of Nature that wrought upon him the impressive discipline of pain and fear, of beauty and joy.

At seventeen, he entered St. John's College, Cambridge University (*The Prelude*, Books Third, Fourth, Sixth). Here his excellent preparation encouraged him to be "an idler among academic bowers." Here he took more interest in his independent reading and in his imaginative life based on communion with natural surroundings than in the curriculum. But here he felt the sacredness of ground which Spenser and Milton and Newton and the other great Cambridge alumni had trod, and he "ran a boisterous course" with the other undergraduates. The two most memorable events of his college years occurred during summer vacations. The first was a half-mystical experience of self-dedication to poetry that came to him one morning after a night spent at a country dance (*The Prelude*, Book Fourth, ll. 309 ff.). The other occurred during his third summer vacation. Instead of staying at Cambridge and preparing for his "senior comprehensive" examinations, due the following January, he set off with a friend, Robert Jones, for the Alps, walking, "hitchhiking," and floating on canalboats across France, then aflame with early ardors of the Revolution (*The Prelude*, Book Sixth).

The years 1791 to 1796 constitute Wordsworth's period of storm and stress. Graduating from Cambridge in January, 1791, he refused to settle down to a vocation. After loafing in London and in Wales, he went to France with the idea of learning French well enough to qualify himself as a traveling companion and tutor to some young gentleman. At Orleans he met two people who profoundly influenced the course of his life, Captain Michel Beaupuy and Annette Vallon. Captain Beaupuy converted him to the cause of the French Revolution, an experience which constituted the second crisis of his life. At Orleans and later at Blois his association with Annette Vallon, a young Frenchwoman, developed into a *liaison* that resulted in her becoming the mother of a child (Carolyn) by him. Torn by the claims of the revolution and of love, he was on the point of casting his lot with the French people, but financial exhaustion that in part prevented marriage or longer residence in France forced him back home. His probable plan to recoup, return, and marry Annette was prevented by the outbreak of war between France and England in 1793. Unless he smuggled himself across the channel in 1793 to visit her, he did not see her again until the short peace of 1802, during which time they met, agreed upon the inadvisability of marriage, and settled the relationship in a manner honorable to him. His agitation over this passion and its frustration, the shock he received when England went to war with France in 1793, his gradual disillusionment in the revolution as it ceased to be a struggle for human liberation and became a bloody and heartless game of power politics, his fruitless search for congenial employment, his homeless wanderings, and the failure of Godwin's rationalism to offer a philosophic stay, all brought him to a spiritual catastrophe in which he "Yielded up moral questions in despair" (*The Prelude*, Book Eleventh).

In the meantime, an event had occurred to make possible the visitation of three good angels. In 1795 a wealthy young gentleman, Raisley Calvert, whom Wordsworth had served as nurse and companion, died leaving him the income from a legacy of about $4500. This enabled him to take a cottage with his beloved sister Dorothy at Racedown, on the southern coast. About the same time he met Samuel Taylor Coleridge. Dorothy and Coleridge brought him back to those sweet counsels between head and heart and to that consolation of nature which he had lost during his period of despair. The growing intimacy of the three young people induced William and Dorothy to move to Alfoxden, in Somerset, to be neighbors to Coleridge, who lived at Nether Stowey, three miles away. From July, 1797, to June, 1798, they were "three persons and one soul," visiting almost daily and writing most of the poems that were to go into *Lyrical Ballads*.

Shortly before this little volume appeared (in September, 1798), the three set out for Germany, to study its language, literature, science, and philosophy. Instead of seriously pursuing any of these, Wordsworth became homesick, wrote the Lucy poems (possibly about some English girl he had known in his boyhood), recorded scenes and incidents of his early life which he was to incorporate later in *The Prelude*, and felt the glow of reviving love for his country. By May, 1799, he and Dorothy had returned and were visiting Mary Hutchinson, whom William was too poor to marry. Late that year he and Dorothy settled in Dove Cottage, Grasmere, within thirty miles of his birthplace. In this neighborhood, the heart of the Lake Country, the poet was to spend the rest of his life.

Compared with the first twenty-nine years, the next fifty-one were "unenriched by strange event." Steady devotion to poetic composition, the results of which appeared in successive editions of *Lyrical Ballads*, *Poems in Two Volumes* (1807), and *The Excursion* (1814) and a collective edition of his poems (1815); his settlement with Annette in 1802 and his marriage with Mary Hutchinson; grief and distress over Coleridge's physical and moral degradation (see "Dejection: An Ode" and "Resolution and Independence"); indignation at Napoleon's bloody rise to power, and a corresponding growth of patriotic fervor (sonnets of 1802); a steady drift toward political conservatism; a tour of Scotland; the death by drowning of his sailor brother John in February, 1805; the growth of a family; the gradual waning of his power to react vividly to natural beauty, a sense of "the unimaginable touch of time"—these are some of the events and experiences of the middle years recorded in Wordsworth's poetry. He published much verse after 1815, most of it fine in workmanship, some of it recapturing his early freshness and power; but except for *The Prelude* (finished in its first form in 1805, constantly revised thereafter for thirty years, and published posthumously), little of Wordsworth's poetry after 1815 is of interest to any but scholars. Popularity came late to him, but when he died in 1850 he was generally recognized as the greatest and noblest poet of his generation, and Tennyson was proud to receive the laureateship from him, greener because of the head of him that had worn it.

In the phrase "On man, on nature, and on human life, Musing in solitude," Wordsworth names the three great themes of his poetry; he also describes the mood in which his poetry was composed, and suggests the dominant emotional chord that it strikes in the heart of a receptive reader. Whatever vitality of meaning and appeal his poetry may have today derives from the freshness with which he described objects and scenes suggesting these themes, and the power and insight with which he treated their interrelationships.

More than any other poet Wordsworth is concerned with the relation between the inner life of man and the outward life of the world of nature. It was his fundamental conviction that the individual mind is fitted to the external world, and the external world is fitted to the mind. Human happiness was to be found only when "the discerning intellect of Man" was "wedded to this goodly universe In love and holy passion." His own experience and the associational psychology which he learned in his late twenties taught him that the mind of man, with all its ideas, its feelings, its pains and pleasures, was built up from sensations by some mysterious spiritual power in man and in the universe. The ultimate source of all sensations was nature. Nature operated upon his nervous organism in two reciprocal ways, producing emotion and calmness, excitation and peace. Since it was the fount of all his feelings and ideas, he should expose himself to its purest and most beautiful forms. The best attitude toward this source of goodness and truth was not pride in intellect and reason, not hot and selfish striving, but a wise passiveness, an opening of the windows of the soul. The universe itself was spirit. Truth pulsed through it, and the soul must be energized and attuned. Human life was a progressive development of power to respond to the beauty and truth of the universe revealed through nature. In childhood, this response was merely physical stimulation, increased animal activity. In youth, it was feeling and passion, but not reflective thought or deep social sympathy. In manhood, however, it was sensitiveness to "the still sad music of humanity," and "a sense sublime of something far more deeply interfused"; that is, a living knowledge of the spirit of the universe and an ability to unite ecstatically with it in the ultimate of religious experience. Such a votary of nature was Wordsworth at the height of his optimistic faith (as in "Tintern Abbey" and *The Prelude*):

> well pleased to recognize
> In nature and the language of the sense
> The anchor of my purest thoughts, the nurse,
> The guide, the guardian of my heart, and soul
> Of all my moral being.

The story of Wordsworth's career as a poet after about 1805 is the story of growing doubts of that religion of nature, of brave but not often convincing reassertions of it, of a gradual modification of it in the direction of increasing reliance upon the powers and virtues of man as man, not as a creature of nature, and upon orthodox Christianity. "Resolution and Independence," "Ode to Duty," "Elegiac Stanzas (Peele Castle)," "Ode: Intimations of Immortality," "Composed upon an Evening of Extraordinary Splendour and Beauty"—these most plainly tell the story. Side by side with them and closely connected with them are other poems, such as "My Heart Leaps Up," "To the Cuckoo," and "To a Butterfly," which on smaller scales than "Tintern Abbey" and *The Prelude* show the poet trying to bind his days together, to view human life as an integral, organic, unfolding experience, having its origin and its continuation in eternity.

Through his development of his second great theme, man in this world and in society, Wordsworth made perhaps his most permanent impression upon modern thought and life. If in his poetry of nature he pointed out sources of beauty to which we are no longer so responsive as men once were, and if in his interpretation of its significance he affirms a faith that many good men and women cannot share with him, the same can hardly be said about his treatment of the human figures near the soil whom he painted against his backgrounds of austere mountains and lonely moors and Highland glens. His faith in the dignity and nobility of simple men and women—in his Old Cumberland Beggar, his Simon Lee, his Margaret of the ruined cottage, his Highland women, his Michael, his Leech-gatherer—has hardly been subjected to the same discount. With the sanction of such poets as Walt Whitman, lonely roads continue to be open schools in which we daily read with delight the passions of mankind.

The hundredth anniversary of Wordsworth's death in 1950 was the occasion for renewed critical acclaim and reissues of his works. Today the poetry of William Wordsworth is the inspiration and rallying ground of many cultivated people who believe that the physical universe is a spiritually habitable home for man. Wordsworth is the champion of those who affirm the worth, the dignity, and the nobility of our common humanity. He is on the side of primal human instincts, elemental affections, simple human decency, plain living and high thinking, freedom of the spirit, and a conception of life not as a huddled confusion, a thing of shreds and patches, but as a unified, progressive, infinite experience.

> Our destiny, our being's heart and home
> Is with infinitude, and only there.
>
> *The Prelude*, Book VI, ll. 604–605

from THE PRELUDE

OR, GROWTH OF A POET'S MIND

An Autobiographical Poem

"Several years ago," wrote Wordsworth in the preface to the 1814 edition of *The Excursion*, "when the Author retired to his native mountains, with the hope of being able to construct a literary work that might live, it was a reasonable thing that he should take a review of his own mind, and examine how far Nature and Education had qualified him for such employment. As subsidiary to this preparation, he undertook to record, in verse, the origin and progress of his own powers, as far as he was acquainted with them. That Work [*The Prelude*], addressed to a dear Friend [Coleridge], most distinguished for his knowledge and genius, and to whom the Author's Intellect is deeply indebted, has been long finished; and the result of the investigation which gave rise to it was a determination to compose a philosophical poem, containing views of Man, Nature, and Society."

Of this larger project, *The Recluse*, Wordsworth completed only two sections: *The Prelude* ("the preparatory poem") and *The Excursion*, which was to have been the second section of the poem proper. *The Prelude* was completed, in the first version, in 1805; read to Coleridge in 1807 (see pages 731–32 below); revised constantly between that date and 1839; and published, after the author's death, in 1850. Mrs. Wordsworth supplied the title, and Bishop Wordsworth, the poet's youngest brother, the subtitle. In 1928 the 1805 version was published by Professor Ernest de Selincourt, on pages facing the 1850 version, from which our selections are taken.

"*The Prelude*," says Professor de Selincourt, "is the essential living document for the interpretation of Wordsworth's life and poetry." The following selections include the major crises in Wordsworth's life (pointed out in the footnotes). In reading these selections, the student will do well to refer frequently to the preceding biographical-critical sketch of Wordsworth.

BOOK FIRST—CHILDHOOD AND SCHOOL-TIME

When he had left the mountains and received
On his smooth breast the shadow of those towers
That yet survive, a shattered monument
Of feudal sway, the bright blue river passed
Along the margin of our terrace walk;
A tempting playmate whom we dearly loved.
Oh, many a time have I, a five years' child,
In a small mill-race severed from his stream,
Made one long bathing of a summer's day;
Basked in the sun, and plunged and basked again
Alternate, all a summer's day, or scoured
The sandy fields, leaping through flowery groves
Of yellow ragwort; or when rock and hill,
The woods, and distant Skiddaw's lofty height,
Were bronzed with deepest radiance, stood alone
Beneath the sky, as if I had been born
On Indian plains, and from my mother's hut
Had run abroad in wantonness, to sport,
A naked savage, in the thunder shower.

Fair seed-time had my soul, and I grew up
Fostered alike by beauty and by fear:
Much favoured in my birth-place, and no less
In that belovèd Vale to which erelong
We were transplanted;—there were we let loose
For sports of wider range. Ere I had told
Ten birth-days, when among the mountain slopes
Frost, and the breath of frosty wind, had snapped
The last autumnal crocus, 'twas my joy
With store of springes o'er my shoulder hung
To range the open heights where woodcocks run
Among the smooth green turf. Through half the night,
Scudding away from snare to snare, I plied
That anxious visitation;—moon and stars
Were shining o'er my head. I was alone,
And seemed to be a trouble to the peace
That dwelt among them. Sometimes it befell
In these night wanderings, that a strong desire
O'erpowered my better reason, and the bird
Which was the captive of another's toil
Became my prey; and when the deed was done
I heard among the solitary hills
Low breathings coming after me, and sounds
Of undistinguishable motion, steps
Almost as silent as the turf they trod.

Nor less, when spring had warmed the cultured vale,
Moved we as plunderers where the mother-bird
Had in high places built her lodge; though mean
Our object and inglorious, yet the end
Was not ignoble. Oh! when I have hung
Above the raven's nest, by knots of grass
And half-inch fissures in the slippery rock
But ill sustained, and almost (so it seemed)
Suspended by the blast that blew amain,
Shouldering the naked crag, oh, at that time
While on the perilous ridge I hung alone,
With what strange utterance did the loud dry wind

283. those towers, Cockermouth Castle. **285. river,** the Derwent.

295. Skiddaw, a mountain in Cumberland. **304. Vale,** Esthwaite, where Hawkshead School was. **310. springes,** snares or nooses.

Blow through my ear! the sky seemed not a sky
Of earth—and with what motion moved the clouds!

Dust as we are, the immortal spirit grows
Like harmony in music; there is a dark
Inscrutable workmanship that reconciles
Discordant elements, makes them cling together
In one society. How strange, that all
The terrors, pains, and early miseries,
Regrets, vexations, lassitudes interfused
Within my mind, should e'er have borne a part,
And that a needful part, in making up
The calm existence that is mine when I
Am worthy of myself! Praise to the end!
Thanks to the means which Nature deigned to employ;
Whether her fearless visitings, or those
That came with soft alarm, like hurtless light
Opening the peaceful clouds; or she would use
Severer interventions, ministry
More palpable, as best might suit her aim.

One summer evening (led by her) I found
A little boat tied to a willow tree
Within a rocky cave, its usual home.
Straight I unloosed her chain, and stepping in
Pushed from the shore. It was an act of stealth
And troubled pleasure, nor without the voice
Of mountain-echoes did my boat move on;
Leaving behind her still, on either side,
Small circles glittering idly in the moon,
Until they melted all into one track
Of sparkling light. But now, like one who rows,
Proud of his skill, to reach a chosen point
With an unswerving line, I fixed my view
Upon the summit of a craggy ridge,
The horizon's utmost boundary; far above
Was nothing but the stars and the grey sky.
She was an elfin pinnace; lustily
I dipped my oars into the silent lake,
And, as I rose upon the stroke, my boat
Went heaving through the water like a swan;
When, from behind that craggy steep till then
The horizon's bound, a huge peak, black and huge,
As if with voluntary power instinct,
Upreared its head. I struck and struck again,
And growing still in stature the grim shape
Towered up between me and the stars, and still,
For so it seemed, with purpose of its own
And measured motion like a living thing,
Strode after me. With trembling oars I turned,
And through the silent water stole my way
Back to the covert of the willow tree;
There in her mooring-place I left my bark,—
And through the meadows homeward went, in grave
And serious mood; but after I had seen
That spectacle, for many days, my brain
Worked with a dim and undetermined sense
Of unknown modes of being; o'er my thoughts
There hung a darkness, call it solitude
Or blank desertion. No familiar shapes
Remained, no pleasant images of trees,
Of sea or sky, no colours of green fields;
But huge and mighty forms, that do not live
Like living men, moved slowly through the mind
By day, and were a trouble to my dreams.

Wisdom and Spirit of the universe!
Thou Soul that art the eternity of thought,
That givest to forms and images a breath
And everlasting motion, not in vain
By day or star-light thus from my first dawn
Of childhood didst thou intertwine for me
The passions that build up our human soul;
Not with the mean and vulgar works of man,
But with high objects, with enduring things—
With life and nature—purifying thus
The elements of feeling and of thought,
And sanctifying, by such discipline,
Both pain and fear, until we recognise
A grandeur in the beatings of the heart.
Nor was this fellowship vouchsafed to me
With stinted kindness. In November days,
When vapours rolling down the valley made
A lonely scene more lonesome, among woods,
At noon and 'mid the calm of summer nights,
When, by the margin of the trembling lake,
Beneath the gloomy hills homeward I went
In solitude, such intercourse was mine;
Mine was it in the fields both day and night,
And by the waters, all the summer long.

And in the frosty season, when the sun
Was set, and visible for many a mile
The cottage windows blazed through twilight gloom,
I heeded not their summons: happy time
It was indeed for all of us—for me
It was a time of rapture! Clear and loud
The village clock tolled six,—I wheeled about,
Proud and exulting like an untired horse
That cares not for his home. All shod with steel,
We hissed along the polished ice in games
Confederate, imitative of the chase

340. Dust as we are. One of several statements of the principle in accordance with which the poet's mind and soul developed. **357. her,** Nature.

And woodland pleasures,—the resounding horn,
The pack loud chiming, and the hunted hare.
So through the darkness and the cold we flew,
And not a voice was idle; with the din
Smitten, the precipices rang aloud;
The leafless trees and every icy crag
Tinkled like iron; while far distant hills
Into the tumult sent an alien sound
Of melancholy not unnoticed, while the stars
Eastward were sparkling clear, and in the west
The orange sky of evening died away.
Not seldom from the uproar I retired
Into a silent bay, or sportively
Glanced sideway, leaving the tumultuous throng,
To cut across the reflex of a star
That fled, and, flying still before me, gleamed
Upon the glassy plain; and oftentimes,
When we had given our bodies to the wind,
And all the shadowy banks on either side
Came sweeping through the darkness, spinning still
The rapid line of motion, then at once
Have I, reclining back upon my heels,
Stopped short; yet still the solitary cliffs
Wheeled by me—even as if the earth had rolled
With visible motion her diurnal round!
Behind me did they stretch in solemn train,
Feebler and feebler, and I stood and watched
Till all was tranquil as a dreamless sleep.

Ye Presences of Nature in the sky
And on the earth! Ye Visions of the hills!
And Souls of lonely places! can I think
A vulgar hope was yours when we employed
Such ministry, when ye, through many a year
Haunting me thus among my boyish sports,
On caves and trees, upon the woods and hills,
Impressed, upon all forms, the characters
Of danger or desire; and thus did make
The surface of the universal earth,
With triumph and delight, with hope and fear,
Work like a sea?
Not uselessly employed,
Might I pursue this theme through every change
Of exercise and play, to which the year
Did summon us in his delightful round.

We were a noisy crew; the sun in heaven
Beheld not vales more beautiful than ours;
Nor saw a band in happiness and joy
Richer, or worthier of the ground they trod.
I could record with no reluctant voice
The woods of autumn, and their hazel bowers
With milk-white clusters hung; the rod and line,
True symbol of hope's foolishness, whose strong
And unreproved enchantment led us on
By rocks and pools shut out from every star,
All the green summer, to forlorn cascades
Among the windings hid of mountain brooks.
—Unfading recollections! at this hour
The heart is almost mine with which I felt,
From some hill-top on sunny afternoons,
The paper kite high among fleecy clouds
Pull at her rein like an impetuous courser;
Or, from the meadows sent on gusty days,
Beheld her breast the wind, then suddenly
Dashed headlong, and rejected by the storm.

Ye lowly cottages wherein we dwelt,
A ministration of your own was yours;
Can I forget you, being as you were
So beautiful among the pleasant fields
In which ye stood? or can I here forget
The plain and seemly countenance with which
Ye dealt out your plain comforts? Yet had ye
Delights and exultations of your own.
Eager and never weary we pursued
Our home-amusements by the warm peat-fire
At evening, when with pencil, and smooth slate
In square divisions parceled out and all
With crosses and with ciphers scribbled o'er,
We schemed and puzzled, head opposed to head
In strife too humble to be named in verse;
Or round the naked table, snow-white deal,
Cherry or maple, sate in close array,
And to the combat, Loo or Whist, led on
A thick-ribbed army; not, as in the world,
Neglected and ungratefully thrown by
Even for the very service they had wrought,
But husbanded through many a long compaign.
Uncouth assemblage was it, where no few
Had changed their functions; some, plebeian cards
Which Fate, beyond the promise of their birth,
Had dignified, and called to represent
The persons of departed potentates.
Oh, with what echoes on the board they fell!
Ironic diamonds—clubs, hearts, diamonds, spades,
A congregation piteously akin!
Cheap matter offered they to boyish wit,
Those sooty knaves, precipitated down
With scoffs and taunts, like Vulcan out of heaven:

439. with the din, the beginning of a passage notable for its onomatopoeia (choice of words imitative of natural sounds).

499. cottages. The cottage of Anne Tyson, in which Wordsworth lodged, is still standing at Hawkshead. **514. deal,** fir or pine wood. **516. Loo,** a card game, with penalties paid to the pool. Cf. Pope's *Rape of the Lock*, Canto III, ll. 37 ff. (p. 553). **531. Vulcan,** the Roman god of fire, hurled from heaven by Jupiter.

The paramount ace, a moon in her eclipse,
Queens gleaming through their splendour's last decay,
And monarchs surly at the wrongs sustained
By royal visages. Meanwhile abroad
Incessant rain was falling, or the frost
Raged bitterly, with keen and silent tooth;
And, interrupting oft that eager game,
From under Esthwaite's splitting fields of ice
The pent-up air, struggling to free itself,
Gave out to meadow-grounds and hills a loud
Protracted yelling, like the noise of wolves
Howling in troops along the Bothnic Main.

Nor, sedulous as I have been to trace
How Nature by extrinsic passion first
Peopled the mind with forms sublime or fair,
And made me love them, may I here omit
How other pleasures have been mine, and joys
Of subtler origin; how I have felt,
Not seldom even in that tempestuous time,
Those hallowed and pure emotions of the sense
Which seem, in their simplicity, to own
An intellectual charm; that calm delight
Which, if I err not, surely must belong
To those first-born affinities that fit
Our new existence to existing things,
And, in our dawn of being, constitute
The bond of union between life and joy.

BOOK FOURTH—SUMMER VACATION

'Mid a throng
Of maids and youths, old men, and matrons staid,
A medley of all tempers, I had passed
The night in dancing, gaiety, and mirth.
With din of instruments and shuffling feet,
And glancing forms, and tapers glittering,
And unaimed prattle flying up and down;
Spirits upon the stretch, and here and there
Slight shocks of young love-liking interspersed,
Whose transient pleasure mounted to the head,
And tingled through the veins. Ere we retired,
The cock had crowed, and now the eastern sky
Was kindling, not unseen, from humble copse
And open field, through which the pathway wound,

543. Bothnic Main, the Gulf of Bothnia, part of the Baltic Sea, between Sweden and Finland. **555. first-born affinities.** With these lines compare the theme of *Ode: Intimations of Immortality*, pp. 727 ff.

And homeward led my steps. Magnificent
The morning rose, in memorable pomp,
Glorious as e'er I had beheld—in front,
The sea lay laughing at a distance; near,
The solid mountains shone, bright as the clouds,
Grain-tinctured, drenched in empyrean light;
And in the meadows and the lower grounds
Was all the sweetness of a common dawn—
Dews, vapours, and the melody of birds,
And labourers going forth to till the fields.
Ah! need I say, dear Friend! that to the brim
My heart was full; I made no vows, but vows
Were then made for me; bond unknown to me
Was given, that I should be, else sinning greatly,
A dedicated Spirit. On I walked
In thankful blessedness, which yet survives. . . .

BOOK NINTH—RESIDENCE IN FRANCE

France lured me forth; the realm that I had crossed
So lately, journeying toward the snow-clad Alps.
But now, relinquishing the scrip and staff,
And all enjoyment which the summer sun
Sheds round the steps of those who meet the day
With motion constant as his own, I went
Prepared to sojourn in a pleasant town,
Washed by the current of the stately Loire.

Through Paris lay my readiest course, and there
Sojourning a few days, I visited
In haste, each spot of old or recent fame,
The latter chiefly; from the field of Mars
Down to the suburbs of St. Antony,
And from the Mont Martre southward to the Dome
Of Geneviève. In both her clamorous Halls,
The National Synod and the Jacobins,
I saw the Revolutionary Power
Toss like a ship at anchor, rocked by storms;
The Arcades I traversed, in the Palace huge
Of Orleans; coasted round and round the line
Of Tavern, Brothel, Gaming-house, and Shop,
Great rendezvous of worst and best, the walk
Of all who had a purpose, or had not;
I stared and listened, with a stranger's ears,
To Hawkers and Haranguers, hubbub wild!
And hissing Factionists with ardent eyes,

328. Grain-tinctured, dyed scarlet or purple. **337. dedicated Spirit.** The passage ending here marks Wordsworth's first personal crisis.

In knots, or pairs, or single. Not a look
Hope takes, or Doubt or Fear is forced to wear,
But seemed there present; and I scanned them all,
Watched every gesture uncontrollable,
Of anger, and vexation, and despite,
All side by side, and struggling face to face,
With gaiety and dissolute idleness.

Where silent zephyrs sported with the dust
Of the Bastille, I sate in the open sun,
And from the rubbish gathered up a stone,
And pocketed the relic, in the guise
Of an enthusiast: yet, in honest truth,
I looked for something that I could not find,
Affecting more emotion than I felt;
For 'tis most certain, that these various sights,
However potent their first shock, with me
Appeared to recompense the traveller's pains
Less than the painted Magdalene of Le Brun,
A beauty exquisitely wrought, with hair
Dishevelled, gleaming eyes, and rueful cheek
Pale and bedropped with overflowing tears.

But hence to my more permanent abode
I hasten; there, by novelties in speech,
Domestic manners, customs, gestures, looks,
And all the attire of ordinary life,
Attention was engrossed; and, thus amused,
I stood, 'mid those concussions, unconcerned,
Tranquil almost, and careless as a flower
Glassed in a greenhouse, or a parlour shrub
That spreads its leaves in unmolested peace,
While every bush and tree, the country through,
Is shaking to the roots: indifference this
Which may seem strange: but I was unprepared
With needful knowledge, had abruptly passed
Into a theatre, whose stage was filled
And busy with an action far advanced.
Like others, I had skimmed, and sometimes read
With care, the master-pamphlets of the day;
Nor wanted such half-insight as grew wild
Upon that meagre soil, helped out by talk
And public news; but having never seen
A chronicle that might suffice to show
Whence the main organs of the public power
Had sprung, their transmigrations, when and how
Accomplished, giving thus unto events
A form and body; all things were to me
Loose and disjointed, and the affections left
Without a vital interest. At that time,
Moreover, the first storm was overblown,
And the strong hand of outward violence
Locked up in quiet. For myself, I fear
Now in connection with so great a theme,
To speak (as I must be compelled to do)
Of one so unimportant; night by night
Did I frequent the formal haunts of men,
Whom, in the city, privilege of birth
Sequestered from the rest, societies
Polished in arts, and in punctilio versed;
Whence, and from deeper causes, all discourse
Of good and evil of the time was shunned
With scrupulous care; but these restrictions soon
Proved tedious, and I gradually withdrew
Into a noisier world, and thus ere long
Became a patriot; and my heart was all
Given to the people, and my love was theirs. . . .

Among that band of Officers was one,
Already hinted at, of other mould—
A patriot, thence rejected by the rest,
And with oriental loathing spurned,
As of a different caste. A meeker man
Than this lived never, nor a more benign,
Meek though enthusiastic. Injuries
Made *him* more gracious, and his nature then
Did breathe its sweetness out most sensibly,
As aromatic flowers on Alpine turf,
When foot hath crushed them. He through the events
Of that great change wandered in perfect faith,
As through a book, an old romance, or tale
Of Fairy, or some dream of actions wrought
Behind the summer clouds. By birth he ranked
With the most noble, but unto the poor
Among mankind he was in service bound,
As by some tie invisible, oaths professed
To a religious order. Man he loved
As man; and, to the mean and the obscure,
And all the homely in their homely works,
Transferred a courtesy which had no air
Of condescension; but did rather seem
A passion and a gallantry, like that
Which he, a soldier, in his idler day
Had paid to woman: somewhat vain he was,
Or seemed so, yet it was not vanity,
But fondness, and a kind of radiant joy

77. Le Brun, Charles Le Brun (1619–1690), French historical painter. **81. abode.** Wordsworth apparently refers either to Orleans or Blois.

122. noisier world, Blois. **290. A patriot,** Captain Michel Beaupuy.

Diffused around him, while he was intent
On works of love or freedom, or revolved
Complacently the progress of a cause,
Whereof he was a part: yet this was meek
And placid, and took nothing from the man
That was delightful. Oft in solitude
With him did I discourse about the end
Of civil government, and its wisest forms;
Of ancient loyalty, and chartered rights,
Custom and habit, novelty and change. . . .

And when we chanced
One day to meet a hunger-bitten girl,
Who crept along fitting her languid gait
Unto a heifer's motion, by a cord
Tied to her arm, and picking thus from the lane
Its sustenance, while the girl with pallid hands
Was busy knitting in a heartless mood
Of solitude, and at the sight my friend
In agitation said, " 'Tis against *that*
That we are fighting," I with him believed
That a benignant spirit was abroad
Which might not be withstood, that poverty
Abject as this would in a little time
Be found no more, that we should see the earth
Unthwarted in her wish to recompense
The meek, the lowly, patient child of toil,
All institutes for ever blotted out
That legalised exclusion, empty pomp
Abolished, sensual state and cruel power,
Whether by edict of the one or few;
And finally, as sum and crown of all,
Should see the people having a strong hand
In framing their own laws; whence better days
To all mankind. . . .

BOOK ELEVENTH—FRANCE (*concluded*)

Bliss was it in that dawn to be alive,
But to be young was very Heaven! O times,
In which the meagre, stale, forbidding ways
Of custom, law, and statute, took at once
The attraction of a country in romance!
When Reason seemed the most to assert her rights,
When most intent on making of herself
A prime enchantress—to assist the work,
Which then was going forward in her name!
Not favoured spots alone, but the whole Earth,
The beauty wore of promise—that which sets
(As at some moments might not be unfelt
Among the bowers of Paradise itself)
The budding rose above the rose full blown.
What temper at the prospect did not wake
To happiness unthought of? The inert
Were roused, and lively natures rapt away! . . .

Were called upon to exercise their skill,
Not in Utopia,—subterranean fields,—
Or some secreted island, Heaven knows where!
But in the very world, which is the world
Of all of us,—the place where, in the end,
We find our happiness, or not at all! . . .

But now, become oppressors in their turn,
Frenchmen had changed a war of self-defence
For one of conquest, losing sight of all
Which they had struggled for: up mounted now,
Openly in the eye of earth and heaven,
The scale of liberty. I read her doom. . . .

I summoned my best skill, and toiled, intent
To anatomize the frame of social life;
Yea, the whole body of society
Searched to its heart. . . .

So I fared,
Dragging all precepts, judgments, maxims, creeds,
Like culprits to the bar; calling the mind,
Suspiciously, to establish in plain day
Her titles and her honours; now believing,
Now disbelieving; endlessly perplexed
With impulse, motive, right and wrong, the ground
Of obligation, what the rule and whence
The sanction; till, demanding formal *proof*,
And seeking in every thing, I lost
All feeling of conviction, and, in fine,
Sick, wearied out with contrarieties,
Yielded up moral questions in despair.

This was the crisis of that strong disease,
This the soul's last and lowest ebb; I drooped. . . .

Then it was— 333
Thanks to the bounteous Giver of all good!—
That the beloved Sister in whose sight
Those days were passed, now speaking in a voice
Of sudden admonition—like a brook

518. I with him believed, Wordsworth's second crisis—conversion to the revolution, love of man. **108. Bliss was it,** the apex of Wordsworth's hopes for the French Revolution, and with it for mankind.

121. The budding rose. The idea is characteristically Romantic. **306. This was the crisis.** The preceding passage marks the catastrophe of *The Prelude*—the destruction of Wordsworth's hopes for mankind through the French Revolution. **333. Then it was.** Here Wordsworth's account of his recovery begins. Note that he mentions two of his good angels—Dorothy and Nature. The third, Coleridge, was thanked in the 1805 version. Omission of him for 1850 was perhaps due to the estrangement between the two poets.

That did but *cross* a lonely road, and now
Is seen, heard, felt, and caught at every turn,
Companion never lost through many a league—
Maintained for me a saving intercourse
With my true self; for, though bedimmed and changed
Much, as it seemed, I was no further changed
Than as a clouded and a waning moon:
She whispered still that brightness would return;
She, in the midst of all, preserved me still
A Poet, made me seek beneath that name,
And that alone, my office upon earth;
And, lastly, as hereafter will be shown,
If willing audience fail not, Nature's self,
By all varieties of human love
Assisted, let me back through opening day
To those sweet counsels between head and heart
Whence grew that genuine knowledge, fraught with peace,
Which, through the later sinkings of this cause,
Hath still upheld me, and upholds me now. . . .

BOOK TWELFTH—IMAGINATION AND TASTE, HOW IMPAIRED AND RESTORED

There are in our existence spots of time,
That which distinct pre-eminence retain
A renovating virtue, whence—depressed
By false opinion and contentious thought,
Or aught of heavier or more deadly weight,
In trivial occupations, and the round
Of ordinary intercourse—our minds
Are nourished and invisibly repaired;
A virtue, by which pleasure is enhanced,
That penetrates, enables us to mount,
When high, more high, and lifts us up when fallen.
This efficacious spirit chiefly lurks
Among those passages of life that give
Profoundest knowledge to what point, and how,
The mind is lord and master—outward sense
The obedient servant of her will. Such moments
Are scattered everywhere, taking their date
From our first childhood. . . .

BOOK THIRTEENTH—IMAGINATION AND TASTE, HOW IMPAIRED AND RESTORED (*concluded*)

From Nature doth emotion come, and moods
Of calmness equally are Nature's gift:
This is her glory; these two attributes
Are sister horns that constitute her strength.
Hence Genius, born to thrive by interchange
Of peace and excitation, finds in her
His best and purest friend; from her receives
That energy by which he seeks the truth,
From her that happy stillness of the mind
Which fits him to receive it when unsought.

Such benefit the humblest intellects
Partake of, each in their degree; 'tis mine
To speak, what I myself have known and felt;
Smooth task! for words find easy way, inspired
By gratitude, and confidence in truth.
Long time in search of knowledge did I range
The field of human life, in heart and mind
Benighted; but, the dawn beginning now
To re-appear, 'twas proved that not in vain
I had been taught to reverence a Power
That is the visible quality and shape
And image of right reason; that matures
Her processes by steadfast laws; gives birth
To no impatient or fallacious hopes,
No heat of passion or excessive zeal,
No vain conceits; provokes to no quick turns
Of self-applauding intellect; but trains
To meekness, and exalts by humble faith;
Holds up before the mind intoxicate
With present objects, and the busy dance
Of things that pass away, a temperate show
Of objects that endure; and by this course
Disposes her, when over-fondly set
On throwing off incumbrances, to seek
In man, and in the frame of social life,
Whate'er there is desirable and good
Of kindred permanence, unchanged in form
And function, or, through strict vicissitude
Of life and death, revolving. Above all
Were re-established now those watchful thoughts
Which, seeing little worthy or sublime
In what the Historian's pen so much delights
To blazon—power and energy detached
From moral purpose—early tutored me
To look with feelings of fraternal love
Upon the unassuming things that hold
A silent station in this beauteous world. . . .

Who doth not love to follow with his eye 142
The windings of a public way? the sight,
Familiar object as it is, hath wrought
On my imagination since the morn
Of childhood, when a disappearing line,
One daily present to my eyes, that crossed

225. From our first childhood. See "Ode: Intimations of Immortality." **1. From Nature.** Here begins the poet's statement of one of the cardinal points in his faith. See the discussion in the biographical-critical sketch.

142. Who doth not love. This is the second point in Wordsworth's faith.

The naked summit of a far-off hill
Beyond the limits that my feet had trod,
Was like an invitation into space
Boundless, or guide into eternity.
Yes, something of the grandeur which invests
The mariner, who sails the roaring sea
Through storm and darkness, early in my mind
Surrounded, too, the wanderers of the earth;
Grandeur as much, and loveliness far more.
Awed have I been by strolling Bedlamites;
From many other uncouth vagrants (passed
In fear) have walked with quicker step; but why
Take note of this? When I began to inquire,
To watch and question those I met, and speak
Without reserve to them, the lonely roads
Were open schools in which I daily read
With most delight the passions of mankind,
Whether by words, looks, sighs, or tears, revealed;
There saw into the depth of human souls,
Souls that appear to have no depth at all
To careless eyes. . . .

Also, about this time did I receive
Convictions still more strong than heretofore,
Not only that the inner frame is good,
And graciously composed, but that, no less,
Nature for all conditions wants not power
To consecrate, if we have eyes to see,
The outside of her creatures, and to breathe
Grandeur upon the very humblest face
Of human life. I felt that the array
Of act and circumstance, and visible form,
Is mainly to the pleasure of the mind
What passion makes them; that meanwhile the forms
Of Nature have a passion in themselves,
That intermingles with those works of man
To which she summons him; although the works
Be mean, have nothing lofty of their own;
And that the Genius of the Poet hence
May boldly take his way among mankind
Wherever Nature leads; that he hath stood
By Natures' side among the men of old,
And so shall stand for ever. . . .

BOOK FOURTEENTH—CONCLUSION

To fear and love,
To love as prime and chief, for there fear ends,
Be this ascribed; to early intercourse,
In presence of sublime or beautiful forms,
With the adverse principles of pain and joy—
Evil as one is rashly named by men
Who know not what they speak. By love subsists
All lasting grandeur, by pervading love;
That gone, we are as dust. . . .

This spiritual Love acts not nor can exist
Without Imagination, which, in truth,
Is but another name for absolute power
And clearest insight, amplitude of mind,
And Reason in her most exalted mood.
This faculty hath been the feeding source
Of our long labour: we have traced the stream
From the blind cavern whence is faintly heard
Its natal murmur; followed it to light
And open day; accompanied its course
Among the ways of Nature, for a time
Lost sight of it bewildered and engulphed;
Then given it greeting as it rose once more
In strength, reflecting from its placid breast
The works of man and face of human life;
And lastly, from its progress have we drawn
Faith in life endless, the sustaining thought
Of human Being, Eternity, and God. . . .

from PREFACE

TO THE SECOND EDITION OF "LYRICAL BALLADS"

Until the student is ready to take up the "Preface" in some detail, especially in comparison with Coleridge's *Biographia Literaria*, it is well to confine attention to the passage beginning with the fifth paragraph ("The principal object") and ending with the ninth. This states the main points of Wordsworth's program—object (including subjects, language, effect sought), differences from contemporary poetry ("having a purpose," feeling giving importance to action and situation), and style (negative and positive features).

THE first Volume of these Poems has already been submitted to general perusal. It was published as an experiment, which, I hoped, might be of some use to ascertain, how far, by fitting to metrical arrangement a selection of the real language of men in a state of vivid sensation, that sort of pleasure and that quantity of pleasure may be imparted, which a Poet may rationally endeavour to impart.

I had formed no very inaccurate estimate of the probable effect of those Poems: I flattered myself that they who should be pleased with them would

157. Bedlamites, madmen. **280. Convictions,** one of Wordsworth's great assertions of the worth and dignity of human life and of the vitality and beneficence of the universe. The poet is the minister of this faith.

Preface. The preface as it now stands contains many alterations of and additions to the original preface which first appeared in the second edition, 1800.

read them with more than common pleasure: and, on the other hand, I was well aware, that by those who should dislike them they would be read with more than common dislike. The result has differed from my expectation in this only, that a greater number have been pleased than I ventured to hope I should please. . . .

Several of my Friends are anxious for the success of these Poems, from a belief that, if the views with which they were composed were indeed realised, a class of Poetry would be produced, well adapted to interest mankind permanently, and not unimportant in the quality and in the multiplicity of its moral relations: and on this account they have advised me to prefix a systematic defence of the theory upon which the Poems were written. But I was unwilling to undertake the task, knowing that on this occasion the Reader would look coldly upon my arguments, since I might be suspected of having been principally influenced by the selfish and foolish hope of *reasoning* him into an approbation of these particular Poems: and I was still more unwilling to undertake the task, because adequately to display the opinions, and fully to enforce the arguments, would require a space wholly disproportionate to a preface. For, to treat the subject with the clearness and coherence of which it is susceptible, it would be necessary to give a full account of the present state of the public taste in this country, and to determine how far this taste is healthy or depraved; which, again, could not be determined without pointing out in what manner language and the human mind act and re-act on each other, and without retracing the revolutions, not of literature alone, but likewise of society itself. I have therefore altogether declined to enter regularly upon this defence; yet I am sensible that there would be something like impropriety in abruptly obtruding upon the Public, without a few words of introduction, Poems so materially different from those upon which general approbation is at present bestowed.

It is supposed that by the act of writing in verse an Author makes a formal engagement that he will gratify certain known habits of association; that he not only thus apprises the Reader that certain classes of ideas and expressions will be found in his book, but that others will be carefully excluded. This exponent or symbol held forth by metrical language must in different eras of literature have excited very different expectations: for example, in the age of Catullus, Terence, and Lucretius, and that of Statius or Claudian; and in our own country, in the age of Shakespeare and Beaumont and Fletcher, and that of Donne and Cowley, or Dryden, or Pope. I will not take upon me to determine the exact import of the promise which, by the act of writing in verse, an Author in the present day makes to his reader; but it will undoubtedly appear to many persons that I have not fulfilled the terms of an engagement thus voluntarily contracted. They who have been accustomed to the gaudiness and inane phraseology of many modern writers, if they persist in reading this book to its conclusion, will, no doubt, frequently have to struggle with feelings of strangeness and awkwardness: they will look round for poetry, and will be induced to inquire by what species of courtesy these attempts can be permitted to assume that title. I hope, therefore, the reader will not censure me for attempting to state what I have proposed to myself to perform; and also (as far as the limits of a preface will permit) to explain some of the chief reasons which have determined me in the choice of my purpose: that at least he may be spared any unpleasant feeling of disappointment, and that I myself may be protected from one of the most dishonourable accusations which can be brought against an Author; namely, that of an indolence which prevents him from endeavouring to ascertain what is his duty, or, when his duty is ascertained, prevents him from performing it.

The principal object, then, proposed in these Poems was to chose incidents and situations from common life, and to relate or describe them throughout, as far as was possible, in a selection of language really used by men, and, at the same time, to throw over them a certain colouring of imagination, whereby ordinary things should be presented to the mind in an unusual aspect; and further, and above all, to make these incidents and situations interesting by tracing in them, truly though not ostentatiously, the primary laws of our nature: chiefly, as far as regards the manner in which we associate ideas in a state of excitement. Humble and rustic life was generally chosen, because, in that condition, the essential passions of the heart find a better soil in which they can attain their maturity, are less under restraint, and speak a plainer and more emphatic language; because in that condition of life our elementary feelings co-exist in a state of greater simplicity, and, consequently, may be more accurately contemplated, and more forcibly communicated; because the manners of rural life germinate from those elementary feelings, and, from the necessary character of rural occupations, are more easily comprehended, and are more durable; and, lastly, because in that condition the passions of men are incorporated with the beautiful and permanent forms of nature. The language, too, of these men has been adopted (purified indeed from what appear to be its real defects, from all lasting and rational causes of dislike or disgust), because such men hourly communicate with the best objects from which the best part of language is originally derived; and because, from their rank in society and the sameness and narrow circle of their intercourse, being less under the influence of social vanity, they convey their feelings and notions in simple and unelaborated expressions. Accordingly, such a language, arising out of repeated experience and regular feelings, is a more permanent, and a far more philosophical language, than that which is frequently substituted for it by Poets, who think that they are conferring honour upon themselves and their art in proportion as they separate themselves from the sympathies of men, and indulge in arbitrary and capricious habits of expression, in order to furnish food for fickle tastes, and fickle appetites, of their own creation.

I cannot, however, be insensible to the present outcry against the triviality and meanness, both of thought and language, which some of my contemporaries have occasionally introduced into their metrical compositions; and I acknowledge that this defect, where it exists, is more dishonourable to the Writer's own character than false refinement or arbitrary innovation, though I should contend at the same time that it is far less pernicious in the sum of its consequences. From such verses the Poems in these volumes will be found distinguished at least by one mark of difference, that each of them has a worthy *purpose*. Not that I always began to write with a distinct purpose formally conceived; but habits of meditation have, I trust, so prompted and regulated my feelings, that my descriptions of such objects as strongly excite those feelings will be found to carry along with them a *purpose*. If this opinion be erroneous, I can have little right to the name of a Poet. For all good poetry is the spontaneous overflow of powerful feelings: and though this be true, Poems to which any value can be attached were never produced on any variety of subjects but by a man who, being possessed of more than usual organic sensibility, had also thought long and deeply. For our continued influxes of feeling are modified and directed by our thoughts, which are indeed the representatives of all our past feelings; and as, by contemplating the relation of these general representatives to each other, we discover what is really important to men, so, by the repetition and continuance of this act, our feelings will be connected with important subjects, till at length, if we be originally possessed of much sensibility, such habits of mind will be produced that, by obeying blindly and mechanically the impulses of those habits, we shall describe objects, and utter sentiments, of such a nature, and in such connection with each other, that the understanding of the Reader must necessarily be in some degree enlightened, and his affections strengthened and purified.

It has been said that each of these Poems has a purpose. Another circumstance must be mentioned which distinguishes these Poems from the popular Poetry of the day; it is this, that the feeling therein developed gives importance to the action and situation, and not the action and situation to the feeling.

A sense of false modesty shall not prevent me from asserting that the Reader's attention is pointed to this mark of distinction, far less for the sake of these particular Poems than from the general importance of the subject. The subject is indeed important! For the human mind is capable of being excited without the application of gross and violent stimulants; and he must have a very faint perception of its beauty and dignity who does not know this, and who does not further know, that one being is elevated above another in proportion as he possesses this capability. It has therefore appeared to me, that to endeavour to produce or enlarge this capability is one of the best services in which, at any period, a Writer can be engaged; but this service, excellent at all times, is especially so at the present day. For a multitude of causes, unknown to former times, are now acting with a combined force to blunt the discriminating powers of the mind, and, unfitting it for all voluntary exertion, to reduce it to a state of almost savage torpor. The most effective of these causes are the great national events which are daily taking place, and the increasing accumulation of men in cities, where the uniformity of their occupations produces a craving for extraordinary incident, which the rapid communication of intelligence hourly gratifies. To this tendency of life and manners the literature and theatrical exhibitions of the country have conformed themselves. The invaluable works of our elder writers, I had almost said the works of Shakespeare and Milton, are driven into neglect by frantic novels, sickly and stupid German Tragedies, and deluges of idle and extravagant stories in verse.—When I think upon this degrading thirst after outrageous stimulation,

15–21. Poets . . . creation. "It is worth while here to observe that the affecting parts of Chaucer are almost always expressed in language pure and universally intelligible even to this day." (Wordsworth)

I am almost ashamed to have spoken of the feeble endeavour made in these volumes to counteract it; and, reflecting upon the magnitude of the general evil, I should be oppressed with no dishonourable melancholy, had I not a deep impression of certain inherent and indestructible qualities of the human mind, and likewise of certain powers in the great and permanent objects that act upon it, which are equally inherent and indestructible; and were there not added to this impression a belief, that the time is approaching when the evil will be systematically opposed by men of greater powers, and with far more distinguished success.

Having dwelt thus long on the subjects and aim of these Poems, I shall request the Reader's permission to apprise him of a few circumstances relating to their *style*, in order, among other reasons, that he may not censure me for not having performed what I never attempted. The Reader will find that personifications of abstract ideas rarely occur in these volumes; and are utterly rejected as an ordinary device to elevate the style and raise it above prose. My purpose was to imitate, and, as far as possible, to adopt the very language of men; and assuredly such personifications do not make any natural or regular part of that language. They are, indeed, a figure of speech occasionally prompted by passion, and I have made use of them as such; but have endeavoured utterly to reject them as a mechanical device of style, or as a family language which Writers in metre seem to lay claim to by prescription. I have wished to keep the Reader in the company of flesh and blood, persuaded that by so doing I shall interest him. Others who pursue a different track will interest him likewise; I do not interfere with their claim, but wish to prefer a claim of my own. There will also be found in these volumes little of what is usually called poetic diction; as much pains has been taken to avoid it as is ordinarily taken to produce it; this has been done for the reason already alleged, to bring my language near to the language of men; and further, because the pleasure which I have proposed to myself to impart is of a kind very different from that which is supposed by many persons to be the proper object of poetry. Without being culpably particular, I do not know how to give my Reader a more exact notion of the style in which it was my wish and intention to write, than by informing him that I have at all times endeavoured to look steadily at my subject; consequently there is, I hope, in these Poems little falsehood of description, and my ideas are expressed in language fitted to their respective importance. Something must have been gained by this practice, as it is friendly to one property of all good poetry, namely, good sense: but it has necessarily cut me off from a large portion of phrases and figures of speech which from father to son have long been regarded as the common inheritance of Poets. I have also thought it expedient to restrict myself still further, having abstained from the use of many expressions, in themselves proper and beautiful, but which have been foolishly repeated by bad Poets, till such feelings of disgust are connected with them as it is scarcely possible by any art of association to overpower.

If in a poem there should be found a series of lines, or even a single line, in which the language, though naturally arranged, and according to the strict laws of metre, does not differ from that of prose, there is a numerous class of critics, who, when they stumble upon these prosaisms, as they call them, imagine that they have made a notable discovery, and exult over the Poet as over a man ignorant of his own profession. Now these men would establish a canon of criticism which the Reader will conclude he must utterly reject, if he wishes to be pleased with these volumes. And it would be a most easy task to prove to him that not only the language of a large portion of every good poem, even of the most elevated character, must necessarily, except with reference to the metre, in no respect differ from that of good prose, but likewise that some of the most interesting parts of the best poems will be found to be strictly the language of prose when prose is well written. The truth of this assertion might be demonstrated by innumerable passages from almost all the poetical writings, even of Milton himself. To illustrate the subject in a general manner, I will here adduce a short composition of Gray, who was at the head of those who, by their reasonings, have attempted to widen the space of separation betwixt Prose and Metrical composition, and was more than any other man curiously elaborate in the structure of his own poetic diction.

In vain to me the smiling mornings shine,
And reddening Phoebus lifts his golden fire;
The birds in vain their amorous descant join,
Or cheerful fields resume their green attire.
These ears, alas! for other notes repine;
A different object do these eyes require;
My lonely anguish melts no heart but mine,
And in my breast the imperfect joys expire;
Yet morning smiles the busy race to cheer,
And new-born pleasure brings to happier men;
The fields to all their wonted tribute bear;
To warm their little loves the birds complain.

35. composition. *Sonnet on the Death of Richard West.*

I fruitless mourn to him that cannot hear,
And weep the more because I weep in vain.

It will easily be perceived, that the only part of this Sonnet which is of any value is the lines printed in Italics; it is equally obvious that, except in the rhyme and in the use of the single word "fruitless" for fruitlessly, which is so far a defect, the language of these lines does in no respect differ from that of prose.

By the foregoing quotation it has been shown that the language of Prose may yet be well adapted to Poetry; and it was previously asserted that a large portion of the language of every good poem can in no respect differ from that of good Prose. We will go further. It may be safely affirmed that there neither is, nor can be, any *essential* difference between the language of prose and metrical composition. We are fond of tracing the resemblance between Poetry and Painting, and, accordingly, we call them Sisters: but where shall we find bonds of connection sufficiently strict to typify the affinity betwixt metrical and prose composition? They both speak by and to the same organs; the bodies in which both of them are clothed may be said to be of the same substance, their affections are kindred, and almost identical, not necessarily differing even in degree; Poetry sheds no tears "such as Angels weep," but natural and human tears; she can boast of no celestial ichor that distinguishes her vital juices from those of Prose; the same human blood circulates through the veins of them both.

If it be affirmed that rhyme and metrical arrangement of themselves constitute a distinction which overturns what has just been said on the strict affinity of metrical language with that of Prose, and paves the way for other artificial distinctions which the mind voluntarily admits, I answer that the language of such Poetry as is here recommended is, as far as is possible, a selection of the language really spoken by men; that this selection, wherever it is made with true taste and feeling, will of itself form a distinction far greater than would at first be imagined, and will entirely separate the composition from the vulgarity and meanness of ordinary life; and, if metre be superadded thereto, I believe that a dissimilitude will be produced altogether sufficient for the gratification of a rational mind. What other distinction would we have? Whence is it to come? And where is it to exist? Not, surely, where the Poet speaks through the mouths of his characters: it cannot be necessary here, either for elevation of style, or any of its supposed ornaments: for, if the Poet's subject be judiciously chosen, it will naturally, and upon fit occasion, lead him to passions, the language of which, if selected truly and judiciously, must necessarily be dignified and variegated, and alive with metaphors and figures. I forbear to speak of an incongruity which would shock the intelligent Reader, should the Poet interweave any foreign splendour of his own with that which the passion naturally suggests: it is sufficient to say that such addition is unnecessary. And, surely, it is more probable that those passages, which with propriety abound with metaphors and figures, will have their due effect if, upon other occasions where the passions are of a milder character, the style also be subdued and temperate.

But, as the pleasure which I hope to give by the Poems now presented to the Reader must depend entirely on just notions upon this subject, and as it is in itself of high importance to our taste and moral feelings, I cannot content myself with these detached remarks. And if, in what I am about to say, it shall appear to some that my labour is unnecessary, and that I am like a man fighting a battle without enemies, such persons may be reminded that, whatever be the language outwardly holden by men, a practical faith in the opinions which I am wishing to establish is almost unknown. If my conclusions are admitted, and carried as far as they must be carried if admitted at all, our judgments concerning the works of the greatest Poets both ancient and modern will be far different from what they are at present, both when we praise, and when we censure: and our moral feelings influencing and influenced by these judgments will, I believe, be corrected and purified.

Taking up the subject, then, upon general grounds, let me ask, what is meant by the word Poet? What is a Poet? To whom does he address himself? And what language is to be expected from him?—He is a man speaking to men: a man, it is true, endowed with more lively sensibility, more enthusiasm and tenderness, who has a greater knowledge of human nature, and a more comprehensive soul, than are supposed to be common among mankind; a man pleased with his own passions and volitions, and who rejoices more than other men in the spirit of life that is in him; de-

28. "I here use the word 'Poetry' (though against my own judgment) as opposed to the word Prose, and synonymous with metrical composition. But much confusion has been introduced into criticism by this contradistinction of Poetry and Prose, instead of the more philosophical one of Poetry and Matter of Fact, or Science. The only strict antithesis to Prose is Metre; nor is this, in truth, a *strict* antithesis, because lines and passages of metre so naturally occur in writing prose, that it would be scarcely possible to avoid them, even were it desirable." (Wordsworth) lighting to contemplate similar volitions and passions as manifested in the goings-on of the Universe, and habitually impelled to create them where he does not find them. To these qualities he has added a disposition to be affected more than other men by absent things as if they were present; an ability of conjuring up in himself passions, which are indeed far from being the same as those produced by real events, yet (especially in those parts of the general sympathy which are pleasing and delightful) do more nearly resemble the passions produced by real events than anything which, from the motions of their own minds merely, other men are accustomed to feel in themselves:—whence, and from practice, he has acquired a greater readiness and power in expressing what he thinks and feels, and especially those thoughts and feelings which, by his own choice, or from the structure of his own mind, arise in him without immediate external excitement.

But whatever portion of this faculty we may suppose even the greatest Poet to possess, there cannot be a doubt that the language which it will suggest to him must often, in liveliness and truth, fall short of that which is uttered by men in real life, under the actual pressure of those passions, certain shadows of which the Poet thus produces, or feels to be produced, in himself.

However exalted a notion we would wish to cherish of the character of a Poet, it is obvious that, while he describes and imitates passions, his employment is in some degree mechanical compared with the freedom and power of real and substantial action and suffering. So that it will be the wish of the Poet to bring his feelings near to those of the persons whose feelings he describes, nay, for short spaces of time, perhaps, to let himself slip into an entire delusion, and even confound and identify his own feelings with theirs; modifying only the language which is thus suggested to him by a consideration that he describes for a particular purpose, that of giving pleasure. Here, then, he will apply the principle of selection which has been already insisted upon. He will depend upon this for removing what would otherwise be painful or disgusting in the passion; he will feel that there is no necessity to trick out or to elevate nature: and, the more industriously he applies this principle the deeper will be his faith that no words, which *his* fancy or imagination can suggest, will be to be compared with those which are the emanations of reality and truth.

But it may be said by those who do not object to the general spirit of these remarks, that, as it is impossible for the Poet to produce upon all occasions language as exquisitely fitted for the passion as that which the real passion itself suggests, it is proper that he should consider himself as in the situation of a translator, who does not scruple to substitute excellencies of another kind for those which are unattainable by him; and endeavours occasionally to surpass his original, in order to make some amends for the general inferiority to which he feels that he must submit. But this would be to encourage idleness and unmanly despair. Further, it is the language of men who speak of what they do not understand; who talk of Poetry, as of a matter of amusement and idle pleasure; who will converse with us as gravely about a *taste* for Poetry, as they express it, as if it were a thing as indifferent as a taste for rope-dancing, or Frontiniac or Sherry. Aristotle, I have been told, has said, that Poetry is the most philosophic of all writing: it is so: its object is truth, not individual and local, but general and operative; not standing upon external testimony, but carried alive into the heart by passion; truth which is its own testimony, which gives competence and confidence to the tribunal to which it appeals, and receives them from the same tribunal. Poetry is the image of man and nature. The obstacles which stand in the way of the fidelity of the Biographer and Historian, and of their consequent utility, are incalculably greater than those which are to be encountered by the Poet who comprehends the dignity of his art. The Poet writes under one restriction only, namely, the necessity of giving immediate pleasure to a human Being possessed of that information which may be expected from him, not as a lawyer, a physician, a mariner, an astronomer, or a natural philosopher, but as a Man. Except this one restriction, there is no object standing between the Poet and the image of things; between this, and the Biographer and Historian, there are a thousand.

Nor let this necessity of producing immediate pleasure be considered as a degradation of the Poet's art. It is far otherwise. It is an acknowledgment of the beauty of the universe, an acknowledgment the more sincere because not formal, but indirect; it is a task light and easy to him who looks at the world in the spirit of love: further, it is a homage paid to the native and naked dignity of man, to the grand elementary principle of pleasure, by which he knows, and feels, and lives, and moves. We have no sympathy but what is propagated by pleasure: I would not be misunderstood; but wherever we sympathise with pain, it will be found that the sympathy is produced and carried on by subtle combinations with pleasure. We have no knowledge, that is, no general principles drawn from the contemplation of particular facts, but what has been built up by pleasure, and exists in us by pleasure alone. The Man of science, the Chemist and Mathematician, whatever difficulties and disgusts they may have had to struggle with, know and feel this. However painful may be the objects with which the Anatomist's knowledge is connected, he feels that his knowledge is pleasure; and where he has no pleasure he has no knowledge. What then does the Poet? He considers man and the objects that surround him as acting and re-acting upon each other, so as to produce an infinite complexity of pain and pleasure; he considers man in his own nature and in his ordinary life as contemplating this with a certain quantity of immediate knowledge, with certain convictions, intuitions, and deductions, which from habit acquire the quality of intuitions; he considers him as looking upon this complex scene of ideas and sensations, and finding everywhere objects that immediately excite in him sympathies which, from the necessities of his nature, are accompanied by an overbalance of enjoyment.

To this knowledge which all men carry about with them, and to these sympathies in which, without any other discipline than that of our daily life, we are fitted to take delight, the Poet principally directs his attention. He considers man and nature as essentially adapted to each other, and the mind of man as naturally the mirror of the fairest and most interesting properties of nature. And thus the Poet, prompted by this feeling of pleasure, which accompanies him through the whole course of his studies, converses with general nature, with affections akin to those which, through labour and length of time, the Man of science has raised up in himself, by conversing with those particular parts of nature which are the objects of his studies. The knowledge both of the Poet and the Man of science is pleasure; but the knowledge of the one cleaves to us as a necessary part of our existence, our natural and unalienable inheritance; the other is a personal and individual acquisition, slow to come to us, and by no habitual and direct sympathy connecting us with our fellow-beings. The Man of science seeks truth as a remote and unknown benefactor; he cherishes and loves it in his solitude: the Poet, singing a song in which all human beings join with him, rejoices in the presence of truth as our visible friend and hourly companion. Poetry is the breath and finer spirit of all knowledge; it is the impassioned expression which is in the countenance of all Science. Emphatically may it be said of the Poet, as Shakespeare hath said of man, "that he looks before and after." He is the rock of defence for human nature; an upholder and preserver, carrying everywhere with him relationship and love. In spite of difference of soil and climate, of language and manners, of laws and customs: in spite of things silently gone out of mind, and things violently destroyed; the Poet binds together by passion and knowledge the vast empire of human society, as it is spread over the whole earth, and over all time. The objects of the Poet's thoughts are everywhere; though the eyes and senses of man are, it is true, his favourite guides, yet he will follow wheresoever he can find an atmosphere of sensation in which to move his wings. Poetry is the first and last of all knowledge—it is as immortal as the heart of man. If the labours of Men of science should ever create any material revolution, direct or indirect, in our condition, and in the impressions which we habitually receive, the Poet will sleep then no more than at present; he will be ready to follow the steps of the Man of science, not only in those general indirect effects, but he will be at his side, carrying sensation into the midst of the objects of the science itself. The remotest discoveries of the Chemist, the Botanist, or Mineralogist, will be as proper objects of the Poet's art as any upon which it can be employed, if the time should ever come when these things shall be familiar to us, and the relations under which they are contemplated by the followers of these respective sciences shall be manifestly and palpably material to us as enjoying and suffering beings. If the time should ever come when what is now called science, thus familiarised to men, shall be ready to put on, as it were, a form of flesh and blood, the Poet will lend his divine spirit to aid the transfiguration, and will welcome the Being thus produced as a dear and genuine inmate of the household of man.—It is not, then, to be supposed that any one, who holds that sublime notion of Poetry which I have attempted to convey, will break in upon the sanctity and truth of his pictures by transitory and accidental ornaments, and endeavour to excite admiration of himself by arts, the necessity of which must manifestly depend upon the assumed meanness of his subject.

What has been thus far said applies to Poetry in general; but especially to those parts of composition where the Poet speaks through the mouths of his characters; and upon this point it appears to authorise the conclusion that there are few persons of good sense who would not allow that the dramatic parts of composition are defective in proportion as they deviate from the real language of nature, and are coloured by a diction of the Poet's own, either peculiar to him as an individual Poet or belonging simply to Poets in general; to a body of men who, from the circumstance of their compositions being in metre, it is expected will employ a particular language.

It is not, then, in the dramatic parts of composition that we look for this distinction of language; but still it may be proper and necessary where the Poet speaks to us in his own person and character. To this I answer by referring the Reader to the description before given of a Poet. Among the qualities there enumerated as principally conducing to form a Poet, is implied nothing differing in kind from other men, but only in degree. The sum of what was said is, that the Poet is chiefly distinguished from other men by a greater promptness to think and feel without immediate external excitement, and a greater power in expressing such thoughts and feelings as are produced in him in that manner. But these passions and thoughts and feelings are the general passions and thoughts and feelings of men. And with what are they connected? Undoubtedly with our moral sentiments and animal sensations, and with the causes which excite these; with the operations of the elements, and the appearances of the visible universe; with storm and sunshine, with the revolutions of the seasons, with cold and heat, with loss of friends and kindred, with injuries and resentments, gratitude and hope, with fear and sorrow. These, and the like, are the sensations and objects which the Poet describes, as they are the sensations of other men and the objects which interest them. The Poet thinks and feels in the spirit of human passions. How, then, can his language differ in any material degree from that of all other men who feel vividly and see clearly? It might be *proved* that it is impossible. But supposing that this were not the case, the Poet might then be allowed to use a peculiar language when expressing his feelings for his own gratification, or that of men like himself. But Poets do not write for Poets alone, but for men. Unless, therefore, we are advocates for that admiration which subsists upon ignorance, and that pleasure which arises from hearing what we do not understand, the Poet must descend from this supposed height; and, in order to excite rational sympathy, he must express himself as other men express themselves. To this it may be added, that while he is only selecting from the real language of men, or, which amounts to the same thing, composing accurately in the spirit of such selection, he is treading upon safe ground, and we know what we are to expect from him. Our feelings are the same with respect to metre; for, as it may be proper to remind the Reader, the distinction of metre is regular and uniform, and not, like that which is produced by what is usually called POETIC DICTION, arbitrary, and subject to infinite caprices, upon which no calculation whatever can be made. In the one case, the Reader is utterly at the mercy of the Poet, respecting what imagery or diction he may choose to connect with the passion; whereas, in the other, the metre obeys certain laws, to which the Poet and Reader both willingly submit because they are certain, and because no interference is made by them with the passion but such as the concurring testimony of ages has shown to heighten and improve the pleasure which co-exists with it.

It will now be proper to answer an obvious question, namely, Why, professing these opinions, have I written in verse? To this, in addition to such answer as is included in what has been already said, I reply, in the first place, Because, however I may have restricted myself, there is still left open to me what confessedly constitutes the most valuable object of all writing, whether in prose or verse; the great and universal passions of men, the most general and interesting of their occupations, and the entire world of nature before me—to supply endless combinations of forms and imagery. Now, supposing for a moment that whatever is interesting in these objects may be as vividly described in prose, why should I be condemned for attempting to superadd to such description the charm which, by the consent of all nations, is acknowledged to exist in metrical language? To this, by such as are yet unconvinced, it may be answered that a very small part of the pleasure given by Poetry depends upon the metre, and that it is injudicious to write in metre, unless it be accompanied with the other artificial distinctions of style with which metre is usually accompanied, and that, by such deviation, more will be lost from the shock which will thereby be given to the Reader's associations than will be counterbalanced by any pleasure which he can derive from the general power of numbers. In answer to those who still contend for the necessity of accompanying metre with certain appropriate colours of style in order to the accomplishment of its appropriate end, and who also, in my opinion, greatly under-rate the power of metre in itself, it might, perhaps, as far as relates to these Volumes, have been almost sufficient to observe, that poems are extant, written upon more humble subjects, and in a still more naked and simple style, which have continued to give pleasure from generation to generation. Now, if nakedness and simplicity be a defect, the fact here mentioned affords a strong presumption that poems somewhat less naked and simple are capable of affording pleasure at the present day; and, what I wished *chiefly* to attempt, at present, was to justify myself for having written under the impression of this belief.

But various causes might be pointed out why, when the style is manly, and the subject of some importance, words metrically arranged will long continue to impart such a pleasure to mankind as he who proves the extent of that pleasure will be desirous to impart. The end of Poetry is to produce excitement in co-existence with an overbalance of pleasure; but, by the supposition, excitement is an unusual and irregular state of the mind; ideas and feelings do not, in that state, succeed each other in accustomed order. If the words, however, by which this excitement is produced be in themselves powerful, or the images and feelings have an undue proportion of pain connected with them, there is some danger that the excitement may be carried beyond its proper bounds. Now the co-presence of something regular, something to which the mind has been accustomed in various moods and in a less excited state, cannot but have great efficacy in tempering and restraining the passion by an intertexture of ordinary feeling, and of feeling not strictly and necessarily connected with the passion. This is unquestionably true; and hence, though the opinion will at first appear paradoxical, from the tendency of metre to divest language, in a certain degree, of its reality, and thus to throw a sort of half-consciousness of unsubstantial existence over the whole composition, there can be little doubt but that more pathetic situations and sentiments, that is, those which have a greater proportion of pain connected with them, may be endured in metrical composition, especially in rhyme, than in prose. The metre of the old ballads is very artless, yet they contain many passages which would illustrate this opinion; and, I hope, if the following poems be attentively perused, similar instances will be found in them. This opinion may be further illustrated by appealing to the Reader's own experience of the reluctance with which he comes to the reperusal of the distressful parts of "Clarissa Harlowe," or the "Gamester"; while Shakespeare's writings, in the most pathetic scenes, never act upon us, as pathetic, beyond the bounds of pleasure—an effect which, in a much greater degree than might at first be imagined, is to be ascribed to small, but continual and regular impulses of pleasurable surprise from the metrical arrangement.—On the other hand (what it must be allowed will much more frequently happen), if the Poet's words should be incommensurate with the passion, and inadequate to raise the Reader to a height of desirable excitement, then (unless the Poet's choice of his metre has been grossly injudicious) in the feelings of pleasure which the Reader has been accustomed to connect with metre in general, and in the feeling, whether cheerful or melancholy, which he has been accustomed to connect with that particular movement of metre, there will be found something which will greatly contribute to impart passion to the words, and to effect the complex end which the Poet proposes to himself.

If I had undertaken a SYSTEMATIC defence of the theory here maintained, it would have been my duty to develop the various causes upon which the pleasure received from metrical language depends. Among the chief of these causes is to be reckoned a principle which must be well known to those who have made any of the Arts the object of accurate reflection; namely, the pleasure which the mind derives from the perception of similitude in dissimilitude. This principle is the great spring of the activity of our minds, and their chief feeder. From this principle the direction of the sexual appetite, and all the passions connected with it, take their origin: it is the life of our ordinary conversation; and upon the accuracy with which similitude in dissimilitude, and dissimilitude in similitude, are perceived, depend our taste and our moral feelings. It would not be a useless employment to apply this principle to the consideration of metre, and to show that metre is hence enabled to afford much pleasure, and to point out in what manner that pleasure is produced. But my limits will not permit me to enter upon this subject, and I must content myself with a general summary.

I have said that poetry is the spontaneous overflow of powerful feelings: it takes its origin from emotion recollected in tranquillity; the emotion is contemplated till, by a species of re-action, the tranquillity gradually disappears, and an emotion, kindred to that which was before the subject of contemplation, is gradually produced, and does itself actually exist in the mind. In this mood successful composition generally begins, and in a mood similar to this it is carried on; but the emotion, of whatever kind, and in whatever degree, from various causes, is qualified by various pleasures, so that in describing any passions whatsoever, which are voluntarily described, the mind will, upon the whole, be in a state of enjoyment. If Nature be thus cautious to preserve in a state of enjoyment a being so employed, the Poet ought to profit by the lesson held forth to him, and ought especially to take care that, whatever passions he communicates to his Reader, those passions, if his Reader's mind be sound and vigorous, should always be accompanied with an overbalance of pleasure. Now the music of harmonious metrical language, the sense of difficulty overcome, and the blind association of pleasure which has been previously received from works of rhyme or metre of the same or similar construction, an indistinct perception perpetually renewed of language closely resembling that of real life, and yet, in the circumstance of metre, differing from it so widely—all these imperceptibly make up a complex feeling of delight, which is of the most important use in tempering the painful feeling always found intermingled with powerful descriptions of the deeper passions. This effect is always produced in pathetic and impassioned poetry; while, in lighter compositions, the ease and gracefulness with which the Poet manages his numbers are themselves confessedly a principal source of the gratification of the Reader. All that it is *necessary* to say, however, upon this subject, may be effected by affirming, what few persons will deny, that, of two descriptions, either of passions, manners, or characters, each of them equally well executed, the one in prose and the other in verse, the verse will be read a hundred times where the prose is read once. . . .

LUCY GRAY

OR, SOLITUDE

"Written at Goslar in Germany. It was founded on a circumstance told me by my Sister, of a little girl who, not far from Halifax in Yorkshire, was bewildered in a snow-storm. Her footsteps were traced by her parents to the middle of the lock of a canal, and no other vestige of her, backward or forward, could be traced." —Wordsworth.

Oft I had heard of Lucy Gray:
And, when I crossed the wild,
I chanced to see at break of day
The solitary child.

No mate, no comrade Lucy knew;
She dwelt on a wide moor,
—The sweetest thing that ever grew
Beside a human door!

You yet may spy the fawn at play,
The hare upon the green;
But the sweet face of Lucy Gray
Will never more be seen.

"To-night will be a stormy night—
You to the town must go;
And take a lantern, Child, to light
Your mother through the snow."

"That, Father! will I gladly do:
'Tis scarcely afternoon—
The minster-clock has just struck two,
And yonder is the moon!"

At this the Father raised his hook,
And snapped a faggot-band;
He plied his work;—and Lucy took
The lantern in her hand.

Not blither is the mountain roe:
With many a wanton stroke
Her feet disperse the powdery snow,
That rises up like smoke.

The storm came on before its time:
She wandered up and down;
And many a hill did Lucy climb:
But never reached the town.

The wretched parents all that night
Went shouting far and wide;
But there was neither sound nor sight
To serve them for a guide.

At day-break on the hill they stood
That overlooked the moor;
And thence they saw the bridge of wood,
A furlong from their door.

They wept—and, turning homeward, cried,
"In heaven we all shall meet";
—When in the snow the mother spied
The print of Lucy's feet.

Then downwards from the steep hill's edge
They tracked the footmarks small;
And through the broken hawthorn hedge,
And by the long stone-wall;

And then an open field they crossed:
The marks were still the same;
They tracked them on, nor ever lost;
And to the bridge they came.

They followed from the snowy bank
Those footmarks, one by one,
Into the middle of the plank;
And further there were none!

—Yet some maintain that to this day
She is a living child;

57. Yet some maintain. Note how this quiet addition throws back over the entire matter-of-fact story a coloring of the supernatural. The effect is somewhat like that achieved by Coleridge in *The Rime of the Ancient Mariner*

That you may see sweet Lucy Gray
Upon the lonesome wild.

O'er rough and smooth she trips along,
And never looks behind;
And sings a solitary song
That whistles in the wind.

THERE WAS A BOY

Sometimes known as "The Boy of Winander," the poem was written in 1798, published in the 1800 *Lyrical Ballads*, and afterwards incorporated in *The Prelude* (Book Five, ll. 364–97). In *The Prelude* the lines follow a passage in which Wordsworth comments unfavorably upon formal systems of education current in his time. "There Was a Boy," then, would seem to exemplify the best way in which the human soul is evolved. In the moment of tense expectancy, while he is listening for the owls' answer to his hootings, the Boy unconsciously receives a revelation of the beauty of his surroundings. In the Library of Congress murals representing the great poets, a picture of The Boy of Winander represents Wordsworth.

There was a Boy; ye knew him well, ye cliffs
And islands of Winander!—many a time,
At evening, when the earliest stars began
To move along the edges of the hills,
Rising or setting, would he stand alone,
Beneath the trees, or by the glimmering lake;
And there, with fingers interwoven, both hands
Pressed closely palm to palm and to his mouth
Uplifted, he, as through an instrument,
Blew mimic hootings to the owls,
That they might answer him.—And they would shout
Across the watery vale, and shout again,
Responsive to his call,—with quivering peals,
And long halloos, and screams, and echoes loud
Redoubled and redoubled; concourse wild
Of jocund din! And, when there came a pause
Of silence such as baffled his best skill:
Then sometimes, in that silence, while he hung
Listening, a gentle shock of mild surprise
Has carried far into his heart the voice
Of mountain-torrents; or the visible scene
Would enter unawares into his mind
With all its solemn imagery, its rocks,
Its woods, and that uncertain heaven received
Into the bosom of the steady lake.

This boy was taken from his mates, and died
In childhood, ere he was full twelve years old.
Pre-eminent in beauty is the vale
Where he was born and bred: the churchyard hangs
Upon a slope above the village-school;
And through that churchyard when my way has led
On summer-evenings, I believe that there
A long half-hour together I have stood
Mute—looking at the grave in which he lies!

MICHAEL

A PASTORAL POEM

"Written at Town-end, Grasmere, about the same time as 'The Brothers.' The Sheepfold, on which so much of the poem turns, remains, or rather the ruins of it. The character and circumstances of Luke were taken from a family to whom had belonged, many years before, the house we lived in at Town-end, along with some fields and woodlands on the eastern shore of Grasmere. The name of the Evening Star was not in fact given to this house, but to another on the same side of the valley, more to the north."—Wordsworth.

Compare *The Prelude*, Book Eight, and the "Preface," which was written for the edition of *Lyrical Ballads* in which "Michael" was first published. Note the significance of the subtitle, "A Pastoral Poem," the poet's account of why and how he became interested in Michael, the emphasis upon Michael's love for his land, the tragic conflict which Michael tries to resolve (love for his land and love for his boy), and the quiet pathos of the conclusion ("And never lifted up a single stone"—said to be Wordsworth's most characteristic line). Note, too, the verse form and the diction.

If from the public way you turn your steps
Up the tumultuous brook of Green-head Ghyll,
You will suppose that with an upright path
Your feet must struggle; in such bold ascent
The pastoral mountains front you, face to face.
But, courage! for around that boisterous brook
The mountains have all opened out themselves,
And made a hidden valley of their own.
No habitation can be seen; but they
Who journey thither find themselves alone
With a few sheep, with rocks and stones, and kites
That overhead are sailing in the sky.
It is in truth an utter solitude;
Nor should I have made mention of this Dell
But for one object which you might pass by,
Might see and notice not. Beside the brook
Appears a straggling heap of unhewn stones!
And to that simple object appertains
A story—unenriched with strange events,
Yet not unfit, I deem, for the fireside,

2. Ghyll, northern dialect word for gulley or ravine.
11. kites, hawklike birds.

Or for the summer shade. It was the first
Of those domestic tales that spake to me
Of shepherds, dwellers in the valleys, men
Whom I already loved;—not verily
For their own sakes, but for the fields and hills
Where was their occupation and abode.
And hence this Tale, while I was yet a Boy
Careless of books, yet having felt the power
Of Nature, by the gentle agency
Of natural objects, led me on to feel
For passions that were not my own, and think
(At random and imperfectly indeed)
On man, the heart of man, and human life.
Therefore, although it be a history
Homely and rude, I will relate the same
For the delight of a few natural hearts;
And, with yet fonder feeling, for the sake
Of youthful Poets, who among these hills
Will be my second self when I am gone.

Upon the forest-side in Grasmere Vale
There dwelt a Shepherd, Michael was his name;
An old man, stout of heart, and strong of limb.
His bodily frame had been from youth to age
Of an unusual strength: his mind was keen,
Intense, and frugal, apt for all affairs,
And in his shepherd's calling he was prompt
And watchful more than ordinary men.
Hence had he learned the meaning of all winds,
Of blasts of every tone; and, oftentimes,
When others heeded not, he heard the South
Make subterraneous music, like the noise
Of bagpipers on distant Highland hills.
The Shepherd, at such warning, of his flock
Bethought him, and he to himself would say,
"The winds are now devising work for me!"
And, truly, at all times, the storm, that drives
The traveller to a shelter, summoned him
Up to the mountains: he had been alone
Amid the heart of many thousand mists,
That came to him, and left him, on the heights.
So lived he till his eightieth year was past.
And grossly that man errs, who should suppose
That the green valleys, and the streams and rocks,
Were things indifferent to the Shepherd's thoughts.
Fields, where with cheerful spirits he had breathed
The common air; hills, which with vigorous step
He had so often climbed; which had impressed
So many incidents upon his mind
Of hardship, skill or courage, joy or fear;
Which, like a book, preserved the memory
Of the dumb animals, whom he had saved,
Had fed or sheltered, linking to such acts
The certainty of honourable gain;
Those fields, those hills—what could they less? had laid
Strong hold on his affections, were to him
A pleasurable feeling of blind love,
The pleasure which there is in life itself.

His days had not been passed in singleness.
His Helpmate was a comely matron, old—
Though younger than himself full twenty years.
She was a woman of a stirring life,
Whose heart was in her house: two wheels she had
Of antique form; this large, for spinning wool;
That small, for flax; and if one wheel had rest,
It was because the other was at work.
The Pair had but one inmate in their house,
An only Child, who had been born to them
When Michael, telling o'er his years, began
To deem that he was old,—in shepherd's phrase,
With one foot in the grave. This only Son,
With two brave sheep-dogs tried in many a storm,
The one of an inestimable worth,
Made all their household. I may truly say,
That they were as a proverb in the vale
For endless industry. When day was gone,
And from their occupations out of doors
The Son and Father were come home, even then,
Their labour did not cease; unless when all
Turned to the cleanly supper-board, and there,
Each with a mess of pottage and skimmed milk,
Sat round the basket piled with oaten cakes,
And their plain home-made cheese. Yet when the meal
Was ended, Luke (for so the Son was named)
And his old Father both betook themselves
To such convenient work as might employ
Their hands by the fireside; perhaps to card
Wool for the Housewife's spindle, or repair
Some injury done to sickle, flail, or scythe,
Or other implement of house or field.

Down from the ceiling, by the chimney's edge,
That in our ancient uncouth country style
With huge and black projection overbrowed
Large space beneath, as duly as the light
Of day grew dim, the Housewife hung a lamp;
An aged utensil, which had performed
Service beyond all others of its kind.
Early at evening did it burn—and late,
Surviving comrade of uncounted hours,
Which, going by from year to year, had found,
And left, the couple neither gay perhaps
Nor cheerful, yet with objects and with hopes,
Living a life of eager industry.

And now, when Luke had reached his eighteenth year,
There by the light of this old lamp they sate,
Father and Son, while far into the night
The Housewife plied her own peculiar work,
Making the cottage through the silent hours
Murmur as with the sound of summer flies.
This light was famous in its neighbourhood,
And was a public symbol of the life
That thrifty Pair had lived. For, as it chanced,
Their cottage on a plot of rising ground
Stood single, with large prospect, north and south,
High into Easedale, up to Dunmail-Raise,
And westward to the village near the lake;
And from this constant light, so regular
And so far seen, the House itself, by all
Who dwelt within the limits of the vale,
Both old and young, was named THE EVENING STAR.

Thus living on through such a length of years,
The Shepherd, if he loved himself, must needs
Have loved his Helpmate; but to Michael's heart
This son of his old age was yet more dear—
Less from instinctive tenderness, the same
Fond spirit that blindly works in the blood of all—
Than that a child, more than all other gifts
That earth can offer to declining man,
Brings hope with it, and forward-looking thoughts,
And stirrings of inquietude, when they
By tendency of nature needs must fail.
Exceeding was the love he bare to him,
His heart and his heart's joy! For oftentimes
Old Michael, while he was a babe in arms,
Had done him female service, not alone
For pastime and delight, as is the use
Of fathers, but with patient mind enforced
To acts of tenderness; and he had rocked
His cradle, as with a woman's gentle hand.

And, in a later time, ere yet the Boy
Had put on boy's attire, did Michael love,
Albeit of a stern unbending mind,
To have the Young-one in his sight, when he
Wrought in the field, or on his shepherd's stool
Sat with a fettered sheep before him stretched
Under the large old oak, that near his door
Stood single, and, from matchless depth of shade,
Chosen for the Shearer's covert from the sun,
Thence in our rustic dialect was called
The CLIPPING TREE, a name which yet it bears.
There, while they two were sitting in the shade,
With others round them, earnest all and blithe,
Would Michael exercise his heart with looks
Of fond correction and reproof bestowed
Upon the Child, if he disturbed the sheep
By catching at their legs, or with his shouts
Scared them, while they lay still beneath the shears.

And when by Heaven's good grace the boy grew up
A healthy Lad, and carried in his cheek
Two steady roses that were five years old,
Then Michael from a winter coppice cut
With his own hand a sapling, which he hooped
With iron, making it throughout in all
Due requisites a perfect shepherd's staff,
And gave it to the Boy; wherewith equipt
He as a watchman oftentimes was placed
At gate or gap, to stem or turn the flock;
And, to his office prematurely called,
There stood the urchin, as you will divine,
Something between a hindrance and a help;
And for this cause not always, I believe,
Receiving from his Father hire of praise;
Though nought was left undone with staff, or voice,
Or looks, or threatening gestures, could perform.

But soon as Luke, full ten years old, could stand
Against the mountain blasts; and to the heights,
Not fearing toil, nor length of weary ways,
He with his Father daily went, and they
Were as companions, why should I relate
That objects which the Shepherd loved before
Were dearer now? that from the Boy there came
Feelings and emanations—things which were
Light to the sun and music to the wind;
And that the old Man's heart seemed born again?

Thus in his Father's sight the Boy grew up:
And now, when he had reached his eighteenth year,
He was his comfort and his daily hope.

While in this sort the simple household lived
From day to day, to Michael's ear there came
Distressful tidings. Long before the time
Of which I speak, the Shepherd had been bound
In surety for his brother's son, a man
Of an industrious life, and ample means;
But unforeseen misfortunes suddenly
Had prest upon him; and old Michael now
Was summoned to discharge the forfeiture,
A grievous penalty, but little less
Than half his substance. This unlooked-for claim,
At the first hearing, for a moment took

169. Clipping Tree. "Clipping is the word used in the North of England for shearing." (Wordsworth) Still so used in the southern United States.

More hope out of his life than he supposed
That any old man ever could have lost.
As soon as he had armed himself with strength
To look his trouble in the face, it seemed
The Shepherd's sole resource to sell at once
A portion of his patrimonial fields.
Such was his first resolve; he thought again,
And his heart failed him. "Isabel," said he,
Two evenings after he had heard the news,
"I have been toiling more than seventy years,
And in the open sunshine of God's love
Have we all lived; yet if these fields of ours
Should pass into a stranger's hand, I think
That I could not lie quiet in my grave.
Our lot is a hard lot; the sun himself
Has scarcely been more diligent than I;
And I have lived to be a fool at last
To my own family. An evil man
That was, and made an evil choice, if he
Were false to us; and if he were not false,
There are ten thousand to whom loss like this
Had been no sorrow. I forgive him;—but
'Twere better to be dumb than to talk thus.

"When I began, my purpose was to speak
Of remedies and of a cheerful hope.
Our Luke shall leave us, Isabel; the land
Shall not go from us, and it shall be free;
He shall possess it, free as is the wind
That passes over it. We have, thou know'st,
Another kinsman—he will be our friend
In this distress. He is a prosperous man,
Thriving in trade—and Luke to him shall go,
And with his kinsman's help and his own thrift
He quickly will repair this loss, and then
He may return to us. If here he stay,
What can be done? Where every one is poor,
What can be gained?"
At this the old Man paused,
And Isabel sat silent, for her mind
Was busy, looking back into past times.
There's Richard Bateman, thought she to herself,
He was a parish-boy—at the church-door
They made a gathering for him, shillings, pence
And halfpennies, wherewith the neighbours bought
A basket, which they filled with pedlar's wares;
And, with this basket on his arm, the lad
Went up to London, found a master there,
Who, out of many, chose the trusty boy
To go and overlook his merchandise
Beyond the seas; where he grew wondrous rich,
And left estates and monies to the poor,
And, at his birth-place, built a chapel, floored
With marble which he sent from foreign lands.
These thoughts, and many others of like sort,
Passed quickly through the mind of Isabel,
And her face brightened. The old Man was glad,
And thus resumed:—"Well, Isabel! this scheme
These two days, has been meat and drink to me.
Far more than we have lost is left us yet.
—We have enough—I wish indeed that I
Were younger;—but this hope is a good hope.
—Make ready Luke's best garments, of the best
Buy for him more, and let us send him forth
To-morrow, or the next day, or to-night:
—If he *could* go, the Boy should go to-night."

Here Michael ceased, and to the fields went forth
With a light heart. The Housewife for five days
Was restless morn and night, and all day long
Wrought on with her best fingers to prepare
Things needful for the journey of her son.
But Isabel was glad when Sunday came
To stop her in her work: for, when she lay
By Michael's side, she through the last two nights
Heard him, how he was troubled in his sleep:
And when they rose at morning she could see
That all his hopes were gone. That day at noon
She said to Luke, while they two by themselves
Were sitting at the door, "Thou must not go:
We have no other Child but thee to lose—
None to remember—do not go away,
For if thou leave thy Father he will die."
The Youth made answer with a jocund voice;
And Isabel, when she had told her fears,
Recovered heart. That evening her best fare
Did she bring forth, and all together sat
Like happy people round a Christmas fire.

With daylight Isabel resumed her work;
And all the ensuing week the house appeared
As cheerful as a grove in Spring: at length
The expected letter from their kinsman came,
With kind assurances that he would do
His utmost for the welfare of the Boy;
To which, requests were added, that forthwith
He might be sent to him. Ten times or more
The letter was read over; Isabel
Went forth to show it to the neighbours round;
Nor was there at that time on English land
A prouder heart than Luke's. When Isabel
Had to her house returned, the old Man said,
"He shall depart to-morrow." To this word
The Housewife answered, talking much of things
Which, if at such short notice he should go,
Would surely be forgotten. But at length
She gave consent, and Michael was at ease.

Near the tumultuous brook of Green-head Ghyll,
In that deep valley, Michael had designed
To build a Sheep-fold; and, before he heard
The tidings of his melancholy loss,
For this same purpose he had gathered up
A heap of stones, which by the streamlet's edge
Lay thrown together, ready for the work.
With Luke that evening thitherward he walked:
And soon as they had reached the place he stopped,
And thus the old Man spake to him:—"My Son,
To-morrow thou wilt leave me: with full heart
I look upon thee, for thou art the same
That wert a promise to me ere thy birth,
And all thy life has been my daily joy.
I will relate to thee some little part
Of our two histories; 'twill do thee good
When thou art from me, even if I should touch
On things thou canst not know of.—After thou
First cam'st into the world—as oft befalls
To new-born infants—thou didst sleep away
Two days, and blessings from thy Father's tongue
Then fell upon thee. Day by day passed on,
And still I loved thee with increasing love.
Never to living ear came sweeter sounds
Than when I heard thee by our own fireside
First uttering, without words, a natural tune;
While thou, a feeding babe, didst in thy joy
Sing at thy Mother's breast. Month followed month,
And in the open fields my life was passed
And on the mountains; else I think that thou
Hadst been brought up upon thy Father's knees.
But we were playmates, Luke: among these hills,
As well thou knowest, in us the old and young
Have played together, nor with me didst thou
Lack any pleasure which a boy can know."
Luke had a manly heart; but at these words
He sobbed aloud. The old Man grasped his hand,
And said, "Nay, do not take it so—I see
That these are things of which I need not speak.
—Even to the utmost I have been to thee
A kind and a good Father: and herein
I but repay a gift which I myself
Received at others' hands; for, though now old
Beyond the common life of man, I still
Remember them who loved me in my youth.
Both of them sleep together: here they lived,
As all their Forefathers had done; and when
At length their time was come, they were not loth
To give their bodies to the family mould.
I wished that thou should'st live the life they lived:
But, 'tis a long time to look back, my Son,
And see so little gain from three score years.
These fields were burthened when they came to me;
Till I was forty years of age, not more
Than half of my inheritance was mine.
I toiled and toiled; God blessed me in my work,
And till these three weeks past the land was free.
—It looks as if it never could endure
Another Master. Heaven forgive me, Luke,
If I judge ill for thee, but it seems good
That thou should'st go."
At this the old Man paused;
Then, pointing to the stones near which they stood,
Thus, after a short silence, he resumed:
"This was a work for us; and now, my Son,
It is a work for me. But, lay one stone—
Here, lay it for me, Luke, with thine own hands.
Nay, Boy, be of good hope;—we both may live
To see a better day. At eighty-four
I still am strong and hale;—do thou thy part;
I will do mine.—I will begin again
With many tasks that were resigned to thee:
Up to the heights, and in among the storms,
Will I without thee go again, and do
All works which I was wont to do alone,
Before I knew thy face.—Heaven bless thee, Boy!
Thy heart these two weeks has been beating fast
With many hopes; it should be so—yes—yes—
I knew that thou could'st never have a wish
To leave me, Luke; thou has been bound to me
Only by links of love: when thou art gone,
What will be left to us!—But, I forget
My purposes. Lay now the corner-stone,
As I requested; and hereafter, Luke,
When thou art gone away, should evil men
Be thy companions, think of me, my Son,
And of this moment; hither turn thy thoughts,
And God will strengthen thee: amid all fear
And all temptation, Luke, I pray that thou
May'st bear in mind the life thy Fathers lived,
Who, being innocent, did for that cause
Bestir them in good deeds. Now, fare thee well—
When thou return'st, thou in this place wilt see
A work which is not here: a covenant
'Twill be between us; but, whatever fate
Befall thee, I shall love thee to the last,
And bear thy memory with me to the grave."

The Shepherd ended here; and Luke stooped down,
And, as his Father had requested, laid
The first stone of the Sheep-fold. At the sight
The old Man's grief broke from him; to his heart
He pressed his Son, he kissèd him and wept;
And to the house together they returned.
—Hushed was that House in peace, or seeming peace,

Ere the night fell:—with morrow's dawn the Boy
Began his journey, and when he had reached
The public way, he put on a bold face;
And all the neighbours, as he passed their doors,
Came forth with wishes and with farewell prayers,
That followed him till he was out of sight.

A good report did from their Kinsman come,
Of Luke and his well-doing: and the Boy
Wrote loving letters, full of wondrous news,
Which, as the Housewife phrased it, were throughout
"The prettiest letters that were ever seen."
Both parents read them with rejoicing hearts.
So, many months passed on: and once again
The Shepherd went about his daily work
With confident and cheerful thoughts; and now
Sometimes when he could find a leisure hour
He to that valley took his way, and there
Wrought at the Sheep-fold. Meantime Luke began
To slacken in his duty; and, at length,
He in the dissolute city gave himself
To evil courses: ignominy and shame
Fell on him, so that he was driven at last
To seek a hiding-place beyond the seas.

There is a comfort in the strength of love;
'Twill make a thing endurable, which else
Would overset the brain, or break the heart:
I have conversed with more than one who well
Remember the old Man, and what he was
Years after he had heard this heavy news.
His bodily frame had been from youth to age
Of an unusual strength. Among the rocks
He went, and still looked up to sun and cloud,
And listened to the wind; and, as before,
Performed all kinds of labour for his sheep,
And for the land, his small inheritance.
And to that hollow dell from time to time
Did he repair, to build the Fold of which
His flock had need. 'Tis not forgotten yet
The pity which was then in every heart
For the old Man—and 'tis believed by all
That many and many a day he thither went,
And never lifted up a single stone.

There, by the Sheep-fold, sometimes was he seen
Sitting alone, or with his faithful Dog,
Then old, beside him, lying at his feet.
The length of full seven years, from time to time,
He at the building of this Sheep-fold wrought,
And left the work unfinished when he died.
Three years, or little more, did Isabel
Survive her Husband: at her death the estate
Was sold, and went into a stranger's hand.
The Cottage which was named the Evening Star
Is gone—the ploughshare has been through the ground
On which it stood; great changes have been wrought
In all the neighborhood:—yet the oak is left
That grew beside their door; and the remains
Of the unfinished Sheep-fold may be seen
Beside the boisterous brook of Green-head Ghyll.

LINES WRITTEN IN EARLY SPRING

The following group of poems, ending with "Tintern Abbey," illustrates certain cardinal points in Wordsworth's faith: "Lines": 1. Nature and man akin in spirit. 2. Nature alive and consciously sentient. 3. Nature's plan perfect and holy; and Nature therefore happy; man's out of harmony, and man consequently miserable. "To My Sister": 1. Love the law of the world. 2. The receptive soul of man may be attuned to the Universe. "Expostulation and Reply": 1. The moral sense innate. 2. Nature a source of truth and wisdom. 3. "Wise passiveness" the best way to receive truth. "The Tables Turned": 1. Anti-intellectualism. 2. Opposition to rationalism and scientific analysis. This group of poems has been the chief basis of attacks made on Wordsworth's philosophy. It must be remembered that he was in high spirits when he wrote them, perhaps inclined to be paradoxical; and that in his later poetry he shows high regard for science, for learning, and for Reason in her exalted forms; but that even after due allowance has been made for his mood and the circumstances, they do express his fundamental faith in the natural order and in the intuitive, instinctive elements of the human mind and spirit.

I heard a thousand blended notes
While in a grove I sate reclined,
In that sweet mood when pleasant thoughts
Bring sad thoughts to the mind.

To her fair works did Nature link
The human soul that through me ran;
And much it grieved my heart to think
What man has made of man.

Through primrose tufts, in that green bower,
The periwinkle trailed its wreaths;
And 'tis my faith that every flower
Enjoys the air it breathes.

The birds around me hopped and played,
Their thoughts I cannot measure:—
But the least motion which they made,
It seemed a thrill of pleasure.

The budding twigs spread out their fan,
To catch the breezy air;
And I must think, do all I can,
That there was pleasure there.

If this belief from heaven be sent,
If such be Nature's holy plan,
Have I not reason to lament
What man has made of man?

TO MY SISTER

It is the first mild day of March:
Each minute sweeter than before;
The redbreast sings from the tall larch
That stands beside our door.

There is a blessing in the air,
Which seems a sense of joy to yield
To the bare trees, and mountains bare,
And grass in the green field.

My sister! ('tis a wish of mine)
Now that our morning meal is done,
Make haste, your morning task resign;
Come forth and feel the sun.

Edward will come with you;—and, pray,
Put on with speed your woodland dress;
And bring no book: for this one day
We'll give to idleness.

No joyless forms shall regulate
Our living calendar:
We from to-day, my Friend, will date
The opening of the year.

Love, now a universal birth,
From heart to heart is stealing,
From earth to man, from man to earth:
—It is the hour of feeling.

One moment now may give us more
Than years of toiling reason:
Our minds shall drink at every pore
The spirit of the season.

Some silent laws our hearts will make,
Which they shall long obey:
We for the year to come may take
Our temper from to-day.

And from the blessed power that rolls
About, below, above,
We'll frame the measure of our souls:
They shall be tuned to love.

Then come, my Sister! come, I pray,
With speed put on your woodland dress;
And bring no book: for this one day
We'll give to idleness.

EXPOSTULATION AND REPLY

"Why, William, on that old grey stone,
Thus for the length of half a day,
Why, William, sit you thus alone,
And dream your time away?

"Where are your books?—that light bequeathed
To Beings else forlorn and blind!
Up! up! and drink the spirit breathed
From dead men to their kind.

"You look round on your Mother Earth,
As if she for no purpose bore you;
As if you were her first-born birth,
And none had lived before you!"

One morning thus, by Esthwaite lake,
When life was sweet, I knew not why,
To me my good friend Matthew spake,
And thus I made reply:

"The eye—it cannot choose but see;
We cannot bid the ear be still;
Our bodies feel, where'er they be,
Against or with our will.

"Nor less I deem that there are Powers
Which of themselves our minds impress;
That we can feed this mind of ours
In a wise passiveness.

"Think you, 'mid all this mighty sum
Of things for ever speaking,
That nothing of itself will come,
But we must still be seeking?

"—Then ask not wherefore, here, alone,
Conversing as I may,
I sit upon this old grey stone,
And dream my time away."

THE TABLES TURNED

AN EVENING SCENE ON THE SAME SUBJECT

Up! up! my Friend, and quit your books;
Or surely you'll grow double:
Up! up! my Friend, and clear your looks;
Why all this toil and trouble?

The sun, above the mountain's head,
A freshening lustre mellow
Through all the long green fields has spread,
His first sweet evening yellow.

Books! 'tis a dull and endless strife:
Come, hear the woodland linnet,
How sweet his music! on my life,
There's more of wisdom in it.

And hark! how blithe the throstle sings!
He, too, is no mean preacher:
Come forth into the light of things,
Let Nature be your teacher.

She has a world of ready wealth,
Our minds and hearts to bless—
Spontaneous wisdom breathed by health,
Truth breathed by cheerfulness.

One impulse from a vernal wood
May teach you more of man,
Of moral evil and of good,
Than all the sages can.

Sweet is the lore which Nature brings;
Our meddling intellect
Mis-shapes the beauteous forms of things:—
We murder to dissect.

Enough of Science and of Art;
Close up those barren leaves;
Come forth, and bring with you a heart
That watches and receives.

LINES

COMPOSED A FEW MILES ABOVE TINTERN ABBEY ON REVISITING THE BANKS OF THE WYE DURING A TOUR. JULY 13, 1798

"Tintern Abbey" is a "key" poem. It is *The Prelude* in miniature, completed just before the trip to Germany and in time to get it into *Lyrical Ballads*. Wordsworth composed it in his head, on a trip from Bristol to the Wye country and back, and wrote it down in a hotel at Bristol. "I have not ventured to call this Poem an Ode," he wrote; "but it was written with a hope that in the transitions and the impassioned music of the versification, would be found the principal requisites of that species of composition." The following summary may be helpful to the student in mastering the main ideas and transitions. It should be noted that the three main topics of the theme are restated in the last two lines of the poem—"landscape" (its meaning), "to me," and "thy sake" (Dorothy's).

Looking at a landscape near Tintern Abbey which he saw five years before (ll. 1–22) and which now serves as a frame and as material for his reflections, the poet: (1) *recalls* (l. 22) that in the interim his memory of the scene has brought him three "gifts"—(a) sensations sweet that restored him mentally and physically (ll. 22–30), (b) promptings to acts of kindness and love to his fellows (ll. 30–35), and (c) the sublime gift of mystical ecstasy by which he was united with the spirit of the universe and through which he saw into the life of things (ll. 35–49); (2) *reaffirms* frequent consolatory recourse of his spirit to the scene (ll. 49–57); (3) *expresses* the hope that in this present pleasure of seeing the landscape again there is food and thought for future years, though he is changed from what he once was (ll. 58–67); (4) consequently *reviews* his experience of nature—(a) from *boyhood* (parenthetical ll. 73–74), when it gave only sensations and animal pleasures, and (b) from *youth* (ll. 67–85, except 73–74), when it gave only a thoughtless, sensuous rapture, (c) to his present *maturity* (ll. 88–111), when it makes him hear the still, sad music of humanity and brings him into the presence of the divine spirit; and (5), turning to his sister (l. 111), who shares the joy of the present moment with him, *prays* (ll. 119 ff.) that she too will pass from a sensuous enjoyment like that of his own youth to a mature communion, like his, with Nature, which never did betray the heart that loved her, but leads on from joy to joy, to love of man, and to communion with the divine spirit.

Five years have past; five summers, with the length
Of five long winters! and again I hear
These waters, rolling from their mountain-springs
With a soft inland murmur.—Once again
Do I behold these steep and lofty cliffs,
That on a wild secluded scene impress
Thoughts of more deep seclusion; and connect
The landscape with the quiet of the sky.
The day is come when I again repose
Here, under this dark sycamore, and view
These plots of cottage-ground, these orchard-tufts,
Which at this season, with their unripe fruits,
Are clad in one green hue, and lose themselves
'Mid groves and copses. Once again I see
These hedge-rows, hardly hedge-rows, little lines
Of sportive wood run wild: these pastoral farms,

Green to the very door; and wreaths of smoke
Sent up, in silence, from among the trees!
With some uncertain notice, as might seem
Of vagrant dwellers in the houseless woods,
Or of some Hermit's cave, where by his fire
The Hermit sits alone.
These beauteous forms,
Through a long absence, have not been to me
As is a landscape to a blind man's eye:
But oft, in lonely rooms, and 'mid the din
Of towns and cities, I have owed to them,
In hours of weariness, sensations sweet,
Felt in the blood, and felt along the heart;
And passing even into my purer mind,
With tranquil restoration:—feelings too
Of unremembered pleasure: such, perhaps,
As have no slight or trivial influence
On that best portion of a good man's life,
His little, nameless, unremembered, acts
Of kindness and of love. Nor less, I trust,
To them I may have owed another gift,
Of aspect more sublime; that blessed mood,
In which the burthen of the mystery,
In which the heavy and the weary weight
Of all this unintelligible world,
Is lightened:—that serene and blessed mood,
In which the affections gently lead us on,—
Until, the breath of this corporeal frame
And even the motion of our human blood
Almost suspended, we are laid asleep
In body, and become a living soul:
While with an eye made quiet by the power
Of harmony, and the deep power of joy,
We see into the life of things.
If this
Be but a vain belief, yet, oh! how oft—
In darkness and amid the many shapes
Of joyless daylight; when the fretful stir
Unprofitable, and the fever of the world,
Have hung upon the beatings of my heart—
How oft, in spirit, have I turned to thee,
O sylvan Wye! thou wanderer through the woods,
How often has my spirit turned to thee!

And now, with gleams of half-extinguished thought,
With many recognitions dim and faint,
And somewhat of a sad perplexity,
The picture of the mind revives again:
While here I stand, not only with the sense
Of present pleasure, but with pleasing thoughts
That in this moment there is life and food
For future years. And so I dare to hope,
Though changed, no doubt, from what I was when first
I came among these hills; when like a roe
I bounded o'er the mountains, by the sides
Of the deep rivers, and the lonely streams,
Wherever nature led: more like a man
Flying from something that he dreads than one
Who sought the thing he loved. For nature then
(The coarser pleasures of my boyish days,
And their glad animal movements all gone by)
To me was all in all.—I cannot paint
What then I was. The sounding cataract
Haunted me like a passion: the tall rock,
The mountain, and the deep and gloomy wood,
Their colours and their forms, were then to me
An appetite; a feeling and a love,
That had no need of a remoter charm,
By thought supplied, nor any interest
Unborrowed from the eye.—That time is past,
And all its aching joys are now no more,
And all its dizzy raptures. Not for this
Faint I, nor mourn nor murmur; other gifts
Have followed; for such loss, I would believe,
Abundant recompense. For I have learned
To look on nature, not as in the hour
Of thoughtless youth; but hearing oftentimes
The still, sad music of humanity,
Nor harsh nor grating, though of ample power
To chasten and subdue. And I have felt
A presence that disturbs me with the joy
Of elevated thoughts; a sense sublime
Of something far more deeply interfused,
Whose dwelling is the light of setting suns,
And the round ocean and the living air,
And the blue sky, and in the mind of man:
A motion and a spirit, that impels
All thinking things, all objects of all thought,
And rolls through all things. Therefore am I still
A lover of the meadows and the woods,
And mountains; and of all that we behold
From this green earth; of all the mighty world
Of eye, and ear,—both what they half create,
And what perceive; well pleased to recognise
In nature and the language of the sense
The anchor of my purest thoughts, the nurse,
The guide, the guardian of my heart, and soul
Of all my moral being.
Nor perchance,
If I were not thus taught, should I the more
Suffer my genial spirits to decay:
For thou art with me here upon the banks
Of this fair river; thou my dearest Friend,
My dear, dear Friend; and in thy voice I catch
The language of my former heart, and read

My former pleasures in the shooting lights
Of thy wild eyes. Oh! yet a little while
May I behold in thee what I was once,
My dear, dear Sister! and this prayer I make,
Knowing that Nature never did betray
The heart that loved her; 'tis her privilege,
Through all the years of this our life, to lead
From joy to joy: for she can so inform
The mind that is within us, so impress
With quietness and beauty, and so feed
With lofty thoughts, that neither evil tongues,
Rash judgments, nor the sneers of selfish men,
Nor greetings where no kindness is, nor all
The dreary intercourse of daily life,
Shall e'er prevail against us, or disturb
Our cheerful faith, that all which we behold
Is full of blessings. Therefore let the moon
Shine on thee in thy solitary walk;
And let the misty mountain-winds be free
To blow against thee: and, in after years,
When these wild esctasies shall be matured
Into a sober pleasure; when thy mind
Shall be a mansion for all lovely forms,
Thy memory be as a dwelling-place
For all sweet sounds and harmonies; oh! then,
If solitude, or fear, or pain, or grief,
Should be thy portion, with what healing thoughts
Of tender joy wilt thou remember me,
And these my exhortations! Nor, perchance—
If I should be where I no more can hear
Thy voice, nor catch from thy wild eyes these gleams
Of past existence—wilt thou then forget
That on the banks of this delightful stream
We stood together; and that I, so long
A worshipper of Nature, hither came
Unwearied in that service: rather say
With warmer love—oh! with far deeper zeal
Of holier love. Nor wilt thou then forget
That after many wanderings, many years
Of absence, these steep woods and lofty cliffs,
And this green pastoral landscape, were to me
More dear, both for themselves and for thy sake!

THE LUCY POEMS

For mention of the circumstances and possible autobiographical implications of the "Lucy Poems," see page 691. All five poems are elegiac in theme and tone. The first is a "lover's fancy." The second expresses the poet's homesickness experienced while he was in Germany. The third describes at some length the process of growing into nature; it is a little poetic essay on the education of nature. The fifth describes dying into nature. The fourth contains two of the most delicate and beautiful nature similes in English poetry, and illustrates the power of expression inherent in reticence ("And, oh, The difference to me!").

1

Strange fits of passion have I known:
And I will dare to tell,
But in the Lover's ear alone,
What once to me befell.

When she I loved looked every day
Fresh as a rose in June,
I to her cottage bent my way,
Beneath an evening-moon.

Upon the moon I fixed my eye,
All over the wide lea;
With quickening pace my horse drew nigh
Those paths so dear to me.

And now we reached the orchard-plot;
And, as we climbed the hill,
The sinking moon to Lucy's cot
Came near, and nearer still.

In one of those sweet dreams I slept,
Kind Nature's gentlest boon!
And all the while my eyes I kept
On the descending moon.

My horse moved on; hoof after hoof
He raised, and never stopped:
When down behind the cottage roof,
At once, the bright moon dropped.

What fond and wayward thoughts will slide
Into a Lover's head!
"O mercy!" to myself I cried,
"If Lucy should be dead!"

2

I travelled among unknown men,
In lands beyond the sea;
Nor, England! did I know till then
What love I bore to thee.

'Tis past, that melancholy dream!
Nor will I quit thy shore
A second time; for still I seem
To love thee more and more.

Among thy mountains did I feel
The joy of my desire;
And she I cherished turned her wheel
Beside an English fire.

Thy mornings showed, thy nights concealed
The bowers where Lucy played;
And thine too is the last green field
That Lucy's eyes surveyed.

3

Three years she grew in sun and shower;
Then Nature said, "A lovelier flower
On earth was never sown;
This Child I to myself will take;
She shall be mine, and I will make
A Lady of my own.

"Myself will to my darling be
Both law and impulse: and with me
The Girl, in rock and plain,
In earth and heaven, in glade and bower,
Shall feel an overseeing power
To kindle or restrain.

"She shall be sportive as the fawn
That wild with glee across the lawn,
Or up the mountain springs;
And hers shall be the breathing balm,
And hers the silence and the calm
Of mute insensate things.

"The floating clouds their state shall lend
To her; for her the willow bend;
Nor shall she fail to see
Even in the motions of the Storm
Grace that shall mould the Maiden's form
By silent sympathy.

"The stars of midnight shall be dear
To her; and she shall lean her ear
In many a secret place
Where rivulets dance their wayward round,
And beauty born of murmuring sound
Shall pass into her face.

"And vital feelings of delight
Shall rear her form to stately height,
Her virgin bosom swell;
Such thoughts to Lucy I will give
While she and I together live
Here in this happy dell."

Thus Nature spake—The work was done—
How soon my Lucy's race was run!
She died, and left to me
This heath, this calm and quiet scene;
The memory of what has been,
And never more will be.

4

She dwelt among the untrodden ways
Beside the springs of Dove,
A Maid whom there were none to praise
And very few to love:

A violet by a mossy stone
Half-hidden from the eye!
—Fair as a star, when only one
Is shining in the sky.

She lived unknown, and few could know
When Lucy ceased to be;
But she is in her grave, and, oh,
The difference to me!

5

A slumber did my spirit seal;
I had no human fears:
She seemed a thing that could not feel
The touch of earthly years.

No motion has she now, no force;
She neither hears nor sees;
Rolled round in earth's diurnal course,
With rocks, and stones, and trees.

MATTHEW

The original of Matthew was probably William Taylor, Wordsworth's master at Hawkshead. The poet mentions "a tablet, on which are inscribed, in gilt letters, the Names of the several persons who have been Schoolmasters [at Hawkshead] since the foundation of the School, with the time at which they entered upon and quitted their office" and tells us that opposite one of the names he wrote the following lines.

If Nature, for a favourite child,
In thee hath tempered so her clay,
That every hour thy heart runs wild,
Yet never once doth go astray,

Read o'er these lines; and then review
This tablet, that thus humbly rears

In such diversity of hue
Its history of two hundred years.

—When through this little wreck of fame,
Cipher and syllable! thine eye
Has travelled down to Matthew's name,
Pause with no common sympathy.

And, if a sleeping tear should wake,
Then be it neither checked nor stayed:
For Matthew a request I make
Which for himself he had not made.

Poor Matthew, all his frolics o'er,
Is silent as a standing pool;
Far from the chimney's merry roar,
And murmur of the village school.

The sighs which Matthew heaved were sighs
Of one tired out with fun and madness;
The tears which came to Matthew's eyes
Were tears of light, the dew of gladness.

Yet sometimes, when the secret cup
Of still and serious thought went round,
It seemed as if he drank it up—
He felt with spirit so profound.

—Thou soul of God's best earthly mould!
Thou happy Soul! and can it be
That these two words of glittering gold
Are all that must remain of thee?

MY HEART LEAPS UP

The briefest treatment of one of Wordsworth's greatest themes—the endeavor to bind his days together. (See "Tintern Abbey," "Ode: Intimations," and *The Prelude*, in the ascending scale of attempts.) The poet rejoices that his heart leaps up now as it did when he was a boy, because his present response proves the man to be the same personality as the boy. "Poetry requires a strong persuasion of self-integrity. It is impossible to people who have forfeited their identity. The imaginative act unifies the world. Unity is created rather than observed."—W. L. Sperry, *Wordsworth's Anti-climax*, Harvard University Press, 1935, pp. 165–66.

My heart leaps up when I behold
A rainbow in the sky:
So was it when my life began;
So is it now I am a man;
So be it when I shall grow old,
Or let me die!
The Child is father of the Man;
And I could wish my days to be
Bound each to each by natural piety.

RESOLUTION AND INDEPENDENCE

This poem, also known as "The Leech-Gatherer," is important as pointing to a modification of Wordsworth's faith, and indicating a realization on his part of some of the less kindly aspects of nature. The change it suggests can best be understood by comparing it with the passage in "Tintern Abbey" beginning with lines 107–08.

To understand the significance of the poem, the student must (1) appreciate fully what happened to the poet *before* he met the leech-gatherer—the early-morning high spirits and optimism the sudden depression of spirits, the accompanying fears: "Solitude, pain of heart, distress, and poverty"; and (2) estimate rightly the *character* of the old man, who is *in* nature but not *of* nature, who draws his strength not from the natural order but from religion and the inner resources of the human spirit. Note that in the conclusion Wordsworth is not merely using the language of prayer; he is really praying in the orthodox sense ("God . . . be my help and stay secure").

1

There was a roaring in the wind all night;
The rain came heavily and fell in floods;
But now the sun is rising calm and bright;
The birds are singing in the distant woods:
Over his own sweet voice the Stock-dove broods;
The Jay makes answer as the Magpie chatters;
And all the air is filled with pleasant noise of waters.

2

All things that love the sun are out of doors;
The sky rejoices in the morning's birth;
The grass is bright with rain-drops;—on the moors
The hare is running races in her mirth;
And with her feet she from the plashy earth
Raises a mist, that, glittering in the sun,
Runs with her all the way, wherever she doth run.

3

I was a Traveller then upon the moor;
I saw the hare that raced about with joy;
I heard the woods and distant waters roar;

My Heart Leaps Up. **9. natural piety,** instinctive love and reverence for the things of nature. One of the chief points in Wordsworth's teaching was the duty of cherishing the child's instincts and intuitions.

Or heard them not, as happy as a boy:
The pleasant season did my heart employ:
My old remembrances went from me wholly;
And all the ways of men, so vain and melancholy.

4

But, as it sometimes chanceth, from the might
Of joy in minds that can no further go,
As high as we have mounted in delight
In our dejection do we sink as low;
To me that morning did it happen so;
And fears and fancies thick upon me came;
Dim sadness—and blind thoughts, I knew not, nor could name.

5

I heard the sky-lark warbling in the sky;
And I bethought me of the playful hare:
Even such a happy Child of earth am I;
Even as these blissful creatures do I fare;
Far from the world I walk, and from all care;
But there may come another day to me—
Solitude, pain of heart, distress, and poverty.

6

My whole life I have lived in pleasant thought,
As if life's business were a summer mood;
As if all needful things would come unsought
To genial faith, still rich in genial good;
But how can he expect that others should
Build for him, sow for him, and at his call
Love him, who for himself will take no heed at all?

7

I thought of Chatterton, the marvellous Boy,
The sleepless Soul that perished in his pride;
Of him who walked in glory and in joy
Following his plough, along the mountain-side:
By our own spirits are we deified:
We Poets in our youth begin in gladness;
But thereof come in the end despondency and madness.

8

Now, whether it were by peculiar grace,
A leading from above, a something given,
Yet it befell that, in this lonely place,
When I with these untoward thoughts had striven,
Beside a pool bare to the eye of heaven
I saw a Man before me unawares:
The oldest man he seemed that ever wore grey hairs.

43. Chatterton. Thomas Chatterton (1752–1770), the boy poet of Bristol, who took his own life. **45. him,** Robert Burns.

9

As a huge stone is sometimes seen to lie
Couched on the bald top of an eminence;
Wonder to all who do the same espy,
By what means it could thither come, and whence;
So that it seems a thing endued with sense:
Like a sea-beast crawled forth, that on a shelf
Of rock or sand reposeth, there to sun itself;

10

Such seemed this Man, not all alive nor dead,
Nor all asleep—in his extreme old age:
His body was bent double, feet and head
Coming together in life's pilgrimage;
As if some dire contraint of pain, or rage
Of sickness felt by him in times long past,
A more than human weight upon his frame had cast.

11

Himself he propped, limbs, body, and pale face,
Upon a long grey staff of shaven wood:
And, still as I drew near with gentle pace,
Upon the margin of that moorish flood
Motionless as a cloud the old Man stood,
That heareth not the loud winds when they call,
And moveth all together, if it move at all.

12

At length, himself unsettling, he the pond
Stirred with his staff, and fixedly did look
Upon the muddy water, which he conned,
As if he had been reading in a book:
And now a stranger's privilege I took;
And, drawing to his side, to him did say,
"This morning gives us promise of a glorious day."

13

A gentle answer did the old Man make,
In courteous speech which forth he slowly drew;
And him with further words I thus bespake:
"What occupation do you there pursue?
This is a lonesome place for one like you."
Ere he replied, a flash of mild surprise
Broke from the sable orbs of his yet-vivid eyes.

14

His words came feebly, from a feeble chest,
But each in solemn order followed each,
With something of a lofty utterance drest—
Choice word and measured phrase, above the reach
Of ordinary men; a stately speech;

Such as Grave Livers do in Scotland use,
Religious men, who give to God and man their dues.

15

He told, that to these waters he had come
To gather leeches, being old and poor:
Employment hazardous and wearisome!
And he had many hardships to endure:
From pond to pond he roamed, from moor to moor;
Housing, with God's good help, by choice or chance;
And in this way he gained an honest maintenance.

16

The old Man still stood talking by my side;
But now his voice to me was like a stream
Scarce heard; nor word from word could I divide;
And the whole body of the Man did seem
Like one whom I had met with in a dream;
Or like a man from some far region sent,
To give me human strength, by apt admonishment.

17

My former thoughts returned: the fear that kills;
And hope that is unwilling to be fed;
Cold, pain, and labour, and all fleshly ills;
And mighty Poets in their misery dead.
—Perplexed, and longing to be comforted,
My question eagerly did I renew,
"How is it that you live, and what is it you do?"

18

He with a smile did then his words repeat;
And said that, gathering leeches, far and wide
He travelled; stirring thus about his feet
The waters of the pools where they abide.
"Once I could meet with them on every side;
But they have dwindled long by slow decay;
Yet still I persevere, and find them where I may."

19

While he was talking thus, the lonely place,
The old Man's shape, and speech—all troubled me:
In my mind's eye I seemed to see him pace
About the weary moors continually,
Wandering about alone and silently.
While I these thoughts within myself pursued,
He, having made a pause, the same discourse renewed.

97. Grave Livers, a strict religious sect. **100. leeches,** aquatic worms, formerly used for bleeding the sick.

20

And soon with this he other matter blended,
Cheerfully uttered, with demeanour kind,
But stately in the main; and, when he ended,
I could have laughed myself to scorn to find
In that decrepit Man so firm a mind.
"God," said I, "be my help and stay secure;
I'll think of the Leech-gatherer on the lonely moor!"

SONNETS

For the autobiographical (experiential and philosophical) significance of the 1802 sonnets, see the biographical-critical sketch of Wordsworth. A few sonnets which were written later than 1802 have been added.

COMPOSED UPON WESTMINSTER BRIDGE, SEPTEMBER 3, 1802

Earth has not anything to show more fair:
Dull would he be of soul who could pass by
A sight so touching in its majesty:
This City now doth like a garment, wear
The beauty of the morning; silent, bare,
Ships, towers, domes, theatres, and temples lie
Open unto the fields, and to the sky;
All bright and glittering in the smokeless air.
Never did sun more beautifully steep
In his first splendour, valley, rock, or hill;
Ne'er saw I, never felt, a calm so deep!
The river glideth at his own sweet will:
Dear God! the very houses seem asleep;
And all that mighty heart is lying still!

COMPOSED BY THE SEA-SIDE NEAR CALAIS, AUGUST 1802

Fair Star of evening, Splendour of the west,
Star of my Country!—on the horizon's brink
Thou hangest, stooping, as might seem, to sink
On England's bosom; yet well pleased to rest,
Meanwhile, and be to her a glorious crest
Conspicuous to the Nations. Thou, I think,
Should'st be my Country's emblem; and should'st wink,
Bright Star! with laughter on her banners, drest
In thy fresh beauty. There! that dusky spot
Beneath thee, that is England; there she lies.
Blessings be on you both! one hope, one lot,
One life, one glory!—I, with many a fear
For my dear Country, many heartfelt sighs,
Among men who do not love her, linger here.

IT IS A BEAUTEOUS EVENING, CALM AND FREE

It is a beauteous evening, calm and free,
The holy time is quiet as a Nun
Breathless with adoration; the broad sun
Is sinking down in its tranquillity;
The gentleness of heaven broods o'er the Sea:
Listen! the mighty Being is awake,
And doth with his eternal motion make
A sound like thunder—everlastingly.
Dear Child! dear Girl! that walkest with me here,
If thou appear untouched by solemn thought,
Thy nature is not therefore less divine:
Thou liest in Abraham's bosom all the year;
And worship'st at the Temple's inner shrine,
God being with thee when we know it not.

THE WORLD IS TOO MUCH WITH US

The world is too much with us; late and soon,
Getting and spending, we lay waste our powers:
Little we see in Nature that is ours;
We have given our hearts away, a sordid boon!
The Sea that bares her bosom to the moon;
The winds that will be howling at all hours,
And are up-gathered now like sleeping flowers;
For this, for everything, we are out of tune;
It moves us not.—Great God! I'd rather be
A Pagan suckled in a creed outworn;
So might I, standing on this pleasant lea,
Have glimpses that would make me less forlorn;
Have sight of Proteus rising from the sea;
Or hear old Triton blow his wreathèd horn.

LONDON, 1802

Milton! thou should'st be living at this hour:
England hath need of thee: she is a fen
Of stagnant waters: altar, sword, and pen,
Fireside, the heroic wealth of hall and bower,
Have forfeited their ancient English dower
Of inward happiness. We are selfish men;
Oh! raise us up, return to us again;
And give us manners, virtue, freedom, power.
Thy soul was like a Star, and dwelt apart;
Thou hadst a voice whose sound was like the sea:
Pure as the naked heavens, majestic, free,
So didst thou travel on life's common way,
In cheerful godliness; and yet thy heart
The lowliest duties on herself did lay.

It Is a Beauteous Evening. **9. Dear Child,** the poet's and Annette's natural daughter, Carolyn. *The World Is Too Much with Us.* **13. Proteus,** a sea god who could assume any shape he chose. **14. Triton,** son of Neptune the sea god. He controlled the waves by blowing a conch shell.

MUTABILITY

From low to high doth dissolution climb,
And sink from high to low, along a scale
Of awful notes, whose concord shall not fail;
A musical but melancholy chime,
Which they can hear who meddle not with crime,
Nor avarice, nor over-anxious care.
Truth fails not; but her outward forms that bear
The longest date do melt like frosty rime,
That in the morning whitened hill and plain
And is no more; drop like the tower sublime
Of yesterday, which royally did wear
His crown of weeds, but could not even sustain
Some casual shout that broke the silent air,
Or the unimaginable touch of Time.

NUNS FRET NOT

Nuns fret not at their convent's narrow room;
And hermits are contented with their cells;
And students with their pensive citadels;
Maids at the wheel, the weaver at his loom,
Sit blithe and happy; bees that soar for bloom,
High as the highest Peak of Furness-fells,
Will murmur by the hour in foxglove bells:
In truth the prison, unto which we doom
Ourselves, no prison is: and hence for me,
In sundry moods, 'twas pastime to be bound
Within the Sonnet's scanty plot of ground;
Pleased if some Souls (for such there needs must be)
Who have felt the weight of too much liberty,
Should find brief solace there, as I have found.

INSIDE OF KING'S COLLEGE CHAPEL, CAMBRIDGE

Tax not the royal Saint with vain expense,
With ill-matched aims the Architect who planned
(Albeit labouring for a scanty band
Of white-robed Scholars only) this immense
And glorious Work of fine intelligence!
Give all thou canst; high Heaven rejects the lore
Of nicely-calculated less or more:—
So deemed the man who fashioned for the sense
These lofty pillars, spread that branching roof
Self-poised, and scooped into ten thousand cells,
Where light and shade repose, where music dwells
Lingering—and wandering on as loth to die;
Like thoughts whose very sweetness yieldeth proof
That they were born for immortality.

THE SOLITARY REAPER

Behold her, single in the field,
Yon solitary Highland Lass!
Reaping and singing by herself;
Stop here, or gently pass!
Alone she cuts and binds the grain,
And sings a melancholy strain;
O listen! for the Vale profound
Is overflowing with the sound.

No Nightingale did ever chaunt
More welcome notes to weary bands
Of travellers in some shady haunt,
Among Arabian sands:
A voice so thrilling ne'er was heard
In spring-time from the Cuckoo-bird,
Breaking the silence of the seas
Among the farthest Hebrides.

Will no one tell me what she sings?—
Perhaps the plaintive numbers flow
For old, unhappy, far-off things,
And battles long ago:
Or is it some more humble lay,
Familiar matter of to-day?
Some natural sorrow, loss, or pain,
That has been, and may be again?

Whate'er the theme, the Maiden sang
As if her song could have no ending;
I saw her singing at her work,
And o'er the sickle bending;—
I listened, motionless and still;
And, as I mounted up the hill,
The music in my heart I bore,
Long after it was heard no more.

TO THE CUCKOO

O blithe New-comer! I have heard,
I hear thee and rejoice.
O Cuckoo! shall I call thee Bird,
Or but a wandering Voice?

While I am lying on the grass
Thy twofold shout I hear;
From hill to hill it seems to pass,
At once far off, and near.

Though babbling only to the Vale,
Of sunshine and of flowers,
Thou bringest unto me a tale
Of visionary hours.

Thrice welcome, darling of the Spring!
Even yet thou art to me
No bird, but an invisible thing,
A voice, a mystery;

The same whom in my schoolboy days
I listened to; that Cry
Which made me look a thousand ways
In bush, and tree, and sky.

To seek thee did I often rove
Through woods and on the green;
And thou wert still a hope, a love;
Still longed for, never seen.

And I can listen to thee yet;
Can lie upon the plain
And listen, till I do beget
That golden time again.

O blessèd Bird! the earth we pace
Again appears to be
An unsubstantial, faery place;
That is fit home for Thee!

I WANDERED LONELY AS A CLOUD

I wandered lonely as a cloud
That floats on high o'er vales and hills,
When all at once I saw a crowd,
A host, of golden daffodils;
Beside the lake, beneath the trees,
Fluttering and dancing in the breeze.

Continuous as the stars that shine
And twinkle on the milky way,
They stretched in never-ending line
Along the margin of a bay:
Ten thousand saw I at a glance,
Tossing their heads in sprightly dance.

16. Hebrides, islands off the west coast of Scotland. Wordsworth wrote this poem during a tour of Scotland, in 1803, with Dorothy. **32. Long after it was heard no more.** Note the importance of memory in many of Wordsworth's lyrics (this; "To the Cuckoo"; "I Wandered Lonely as a Cloud"; and others).

17. The same. See "My Heart Leaps Up" and the notes thereon.

The waves beside them danced; but they
Out-did the sparkling waves in glee:
A poet could not but be gay,
In such a jocund company:
I gazed—and gazed—but little thought
What wealth the show to me had brought:

For oft, when on my couch I lie
In vacant or in pensive mood,
They flash upon that inward eye
Which is the bliss of solitude;
And then my heart with pleasure fills,
And dances with the daffodils.

SHE WAS A PHANTOM OF DELIGHT

"Written at Town-end, Grasmere. The germ of this poem was four lines composed as a part of the verses on the Highland Girl. Though beginning in this way, it was written from my heart, as is sufficiently obvious."
—Wordsworth.

She was a Phantom of delight
When first she gleamed upon my sight;
A lovely Apparition, sent
To be a moment's ornament;
Her eyes as stars of Twilight fair;
Like Twilight's, too, her dusky hair;
But all things else about her drawn
From May-time and the cheerful Dawn·
A dancing Shape, an Image gay,
To haunt, to startle, and way-lay.

I saw her upon nearer view,
A Spirit, yet a Woman too!
Her household motions light and free,
And steps of virgin-liberty;
A countenance in which did meet
Sweet records, promises as sweet;
A Creature not too bright or good
For human nature's daily food;
For transient sorrows, simple wiles,
Praise, blame, love, kisses, tears, and smiles.

And now I see with eye serene
The very pulse of the machine;
A Being breathing thoughtful breath,
A Traveller between life and death;
The reason firm, the temperate will,
Endurance, foresight, strength, and skill;
A perfect Woman, nobly planned,
To warn, to comfort, and command;
And yet a Spirit still, and bright
With something of angelic light.

1. She, the poet's wife, Mary Hutchinson.

ODE TO DUTY

"This ode is on the model of Gray's Ode to Adversity, which is copied from Horace's Ode to Fortune. Many and many a time have I been twitted by my wife and sister for having forgotten this dedication of myself to the stern lawgiver. Transgressor indeed I have been, from hour to hour, from day to day: I would fain hope, however, not more flagrantly or in a worse way than most of my tuneful brethren. But these last words are in a wrong strain. We should be rigorous to ourselves and forbearing, if not indulgent, to others, and, if we make comparisons at all, it ought to be with those who have morally excelled us.

"Jam non consilio bonus, sed more eò perductus, ut non tantum rectè facere possim, sed nisi rectè facere non possim."—Wordsworth

Professor G. M. Harper translated the Latin: "No longer good from taking thought, but led by habit, so that I am not merely able to do right, but cannot help doing right."

The poem marks an important development in the change which began with "Resolution and Independence." Note that here, in order to balance and simplify life, Wordsworth conditionally gives up "the genial sense of youth" (natural impulse, or instinct) for a transcendental, religious guide giving "a repose that ever is the same." With this "genial sense of youth" compare the "something that doth live" of "Intimations."

Stern Daughter of the Voice of God!
O Duty! if that name thou love
Who art a light to guide, a rod
To check the erring, and reprove;
Thou, who art victory and law
When empty terrors overawe;
From vain temptations dost set free;
And calm'st the weary strife of frail humanity!

There are who ask not if thine eye
Be on them; who, in love and truth,
Where no misgiving is, rely
Upon the genial sense of youth:
Glad Hearts! without reproach or blot;
Who do thy work, and know it not:
Oh! if through confidence misplaced
They fail, thy saving arms, dread Power! around
 them cast.

Serene will be our days and bright,
And happy will our nature be,
When love is an unerring light,
And joy its own security

And they a blissful course may hold
Even now, who, not unwisely bold,
Live in the spirit of this creed;
Yet seek thy firm support, according to their need.

I, loving freedom, and untried,
No sport of every random gust,
Yet being to myself a guide,
Too blindly have reposed my trust:
And oft, when in my heart was heard
Thy timely mandate, I deferred
The task, in smoother walks to stray;
But thee I now would serve more strictly, if I may.

Through no disturbance of my soul,
Or strong compunction in me wrought,
I supplicate for thy control;
But in the quietness of thought:
Me this unchartered freedom tires;
I feel the weight of chance-desires:
My hopes no more must change their name,
I long for a repose that ever is the same.

Stern Lawgiver! yet thou dost wear
The Godhead's most benignant grace;
Nor know we anything so fair
As is the smile upon thy face:
Flowers laugh before thee on their beds
And fragrance in thy footing treads;
Thou dost preserve the stars from wrong;
And the most ancient heavens, through Thee, are fresh and strong.

To humbler functions, awful Power!
I call thee: I myself commend
Unto thy guidance from this hour;
Oh, let my weakness have an end!
Give unto me, made lowly wise,
The spirit of self-sacrifice;
The confidence of reason give;
And in the light of truth thy Bondman let me live!

THE REVERIE OF POOR SUSAN

Wordsworth once cited this poem as an illustration of what he meant by his statement, in the "Preface" to *Lyrical Ballads*, "that the feeling therein developed gives importance to the action and situation, and not the action and situation to the feeling." Not the London street scene, not the nostalgic vision evoked by the thrush's song, but Susan's homesickness, is the point of the poem. Wordsworth never describes scenery or tells stories merely for their own sake; human feeling is always the important thing.

At the corner of Wood Street, when daylight appears,
Hangs a Thrush that sings loud, it has sung for three years:
Poor Susan has passed by the spot, and has heard
In the silence of morning the song of the Bird.

'Tis a note of enchantment; what ails her? She sees
A mountain ascending, a vision of trees;
Bright volumes of vapour through Lothbury glide,
And a river flows on through the vale of Cheapside.

Green pastures she views in the midst of the dale,
Down which she so often has tripped with her pail;
And a single small cottage, a nest like a dove's,
The one only dwelling on earth that she loves.

She looks, and her heart is in heaven: but they fade,
The mist and the river, the hill and the shade:
The stream will not flow, and the hill will not rise,
And the colours have all passed away from her eyes!

ODE

INTIMATIONS OF IMMORTALITY FROM RECOLLECTIONS OF EARLY CHILDHOOD

The Child is father of the Man;
And I could wish my days to be
Bound each to each by natural piety.

As the motto suggests, the "Ode" is one of several poems in which Wordsworth tries to bind his days together. For discussion of the general theme, see page 692. Clear recognition of the following main topics may lead to a comprehension of the poem as a whole. 1. Looking back at his childhood (stanzas 1–4), the poet misses something transcendent ("celestial light," "glory," and so on) which he remembers as resting upon all the scenes of his childhood, which he is convinced was not the beauty of nature—for nature in itself is still as beautiful as ever—but which has passed away. "Whither is fled the visionary gleam?" 2. The answer (stanzas 5–8) takes him into a Neo-Platonic account of the descent and forgetfulness of the soul—the soul came from afar, trailing clouds of glory, still conscious of God and its Heavenly home; Nature and the ways of this earth which it had to learn made it forget its divine origin and lose the sense of divine presences. From this point of view, life on this earth is a progressive despiritualization. 3. If life on this earth is a progressive disillusionment, how justify it? The answer (stanzas 9–11) points out, as consolations for what has been lost ("the celestial light"): first, "That nature yet remembers" it; second, that this recollection and the soul's obstinate questionings of sense and outward things are the surest evidence of the soul's immortality, the fountain of our purest wisdom; third, that living and suffering on this earth in primal sympathy with other creatures give us a tenderness, a wisdom, and a faith to be acquired in no other way. Therefore, though the poet has lost the vivid sense of celestial nearness and presence, he can still view nature and live among men with faith and imaginative sympathy.

1

There was a time when meadow, grove, and stream,
The earth, and every common sight,
To me did seem
Apparelled in celestial light,
The glory and the freshness of a dream.
It is not now as it hath been of yore;—
Turn wheresoe'er I may,
By night or day,
The things which I have seen I now can see no more.

2

The Rainbow comes and goes,
And lovely is the Rose;
The Moon doth with delight
Look round her when the heavens are bare;
Waters on a starry night
Are beautiful and fair;
The sunshine is a glorious birth;
But yet I know, where'er I go,
That there hath past away a glory from the earth.

3

Now, while the birds thus sing a joyous song,
And while the young lambs bound
As to the tabor's sound,
To me alone there came a thought of grief:
A timely utterance gave that thought relief,
And I again am strong:
The cataracts blow their trumpets from the steep;
No more shall grief of mine the season wrong;
I hear the Echoes through the mountains throng,
The Winds come to me from the fields of sleep,
And all the earth is gay;
Land and sea
Give themselves up to jollity,
And with the heart of May
Doth every Beast keep holiday;—
Thou Child of Joy,
Shout round me, let me hear thy shouts, thou happy Shepherd-boy!

23. A timely utterance, "My Heart Leaps Up."

4

Ye blessèd Creatures, I have heard the call
Ye to each other make; I see
The heavens laugh with you in your jubilee;
My heart is at your festival,
My head hath its coronal,
The fulness of your bliss, I feel—I feel it all.
Oh evil day! if I were sullen
While Earth herself is adorning,
This sweet May-morning,
And the Children are culling
On every side,
In a thousand valleys far and wide,
Fresh flowers; while the sun shines warm,
And the Babe leaps up on his Mother's arm:—
I hear, I hear, with joy I hear!
—But there's a Tree, of many, one,
A single Field which I have looked upon,
Both of them speak of something that is gone:
The Pansy at my feet
Doth the same tale repeat:
Whither is fled the visionary gleam?
Where is it now, the glory and the dream?

5

Our birth is but a sleep and a forgetting:
The Soul that rises with us, our life's Star,
Hath had elsewhere its setting,
And cometh from afar:
Not in entire forgetfulness,
And not in utter nakedness,
But trailing clouds of glory do we come
From God, who is our home:
Heaven lies about us in our infancy!
Shades of the prison-house begin to close
Upon the growing Boy,
But he beholds the light, and whence it flows,
He sees it in his joy;
The Youth, who daily farther from the east
Must travel, still is Nature's Priest,
And by the vision splendid
Is on his way attended;
At length the Man perceives it die away,
And fade into the light of common day.

6

Earth fills her lap with pleasures of her own;
Yearnings she hath in her own natural kind,
And, even with something of a Mother's mind,
And no unworthy aim,
The homely Nurse doth all she can
To make her Foster-child, her Inmate Man,
Forget the glories he hath known,
And that imperial palace whence he came.

7

Behold the Child among his new-born blisses,
A six years' Darling of a pigmy size!
See, where 'mid work of his own hand he lies,
Fretted by sallies of his mother's kisses,
With light upon him from his father's eyes!
See, at his feet, some little plan or chart,
Some fragment from his dream of human life,
Shaped by himself with newly-learnèd art;
A wedding or a festival,
A mourning or a funeral;
And this hath now his heart,
And unto this he frames his song:
Then will he fit his tongue
To dialogues of business, love, or strife;
But it will not be long
Ere this be thrown aside,
And with new joy and pride
The little Actor cons another part;
Filling from time to time his "humorous stage"
With all the Persons, down to palsied Age,
That Life brings with her in her equipage;
As if his whole vocation
Were endless imitation.

8

Thou, whose exterior semblance doth belie
Thy Soul's immensity;
Thou best Philosopher, who yet dost keep
Thy heritage, thou Eye among the blind,
That, deaf and silent, read'st the eternal deep,
Haunted for ever by the eternal mind,—
Mighty Prophet! Seer blest!
On whom those truths do rest,
Which we are toiling all our lives to find,
In darkness lost, the darkness of the grave;
Thou, over whom thy Immortality
Broods like the Day, a Master o'er a Slave,
A Presence which is not to be put by;
Thou little Child, yet glorious in the might
Of heaven-born freedom on thy being's height,
Why with such earnest pains dost thou provoke
The years to bring the inevitable yoke,
Thus blindly with thy blessedness at strife?
Full soon thy Soul shall have her earthly freight,
And custom lie upon thee with a weight,
Heavy as frost, and deep almost as life!

9

O joy! that in our embers
Is something that doth live,
That nature yet remembers
What was so fugitive!
The thought of our past years in me doth breed
Perpetual benediction: not indeed
For that which is most worthy to be blest;
Delight and liberty, the simple creed
Of Childhood, whether busy or at rest,
With new-fledged hope still fluttering in his breast:—
Not for these I raise
The song of thanks and praise;
But for those obstinate questionings
Of sense and outward things,
Fallings from us, vanishings;
Blank misgivings of a Creature
Moving about in worlds not realised,
High instincts before which our mortal Nature
Did tremble like a guilty Thing surprised:
But for those first affections,
Those shadowy recollections,
Which, be they what they may,
Are yet the fountain light of all our day,
Are yet a master light of all our seeing;
Uphold us, cherish, and have power to make
Our noisy years seem moments in the being
Of the eternal Silence: truths that wake,
To perish never:
Which neither listlessness, nor mad endeavour,
Nor Man nor Boy,
Nor all that is at enmity with joy,
Can utterly abolish or destroy!
Hence in a season of calm weather
Though inland far we be,
Our Souls have sight of that immortal sea
Which brought us hither,
Can in a moment travel thither,
And see the Children sport upon the shore,
And hear the mighty waters rolling evermore.

10

Then sing, ye Birds, sing, sing a joyous song!
And let the young Lambs bound
As to the tabor's sound!
We in thought will join your throng,
Ye that pipe and ye that play,
Ye that through your hearts to-day
Feel the gladness of the May!
What though the radiance which was once bright
Be now for ever taken from my sight,
Though nothing can bring back the hour
Of splendour in the grass, of glory in the flower;
We will grieve not, rather find
Strength in what remains behind;
In the primal sympathy
Which having been must ever be;

In the soothing thoughts that spring
Out of human suffering;
In the faith that looks through death,
In years that bring the philosophic mind.

11

And O, ye Fountains, Meadows, Hills, and Groves,
Forebode not any severing of our loves!
Yet in my heart of hearts I feel your might;
I only have relinquished one delight
To live beneath your more habitual sway.
I love the Brooks which down their channels fret,
Even more than when I tripped lightly as they;
The innocent brightness of a new-born Day
Is lovely yet;
The Clouds that gather round the setting sun
Do take a sober colouring from an eye
That hath kept watch o'er man's mortality;
Another race hath been, and other palms are won.
Thanks to the human heart by which we live,
Thanks to its tenderness, its joys, and fears,
To me the meanest flower that blows can give
Thoughts that do often lie too deep for tears.

Samuel Taylor Coleridge

1772–1834

Samuel Taylor Coleridge was born on October 20, 1772, in the vicarage at Ottery St. Mary, Devonshire. His father, the Reverend John Coleridge, besides being vicar of the parish, was master of the grammar school, and by all accounts was learned, absent-minded, and lovable. The last-born in a family of fourteen, young Samuel was indulged by his parents and alternately petted and bullied by his eight older brothers. Hence he was a precocious boy, thrown upon the resources of reading and dreaming. At the age of six he had read such tales as "Jack the Giant-Killer," *Robinson Crusoe*, and the *Arabian Nights*. "One tale," he wrote, years later, "of a man who was compelled to seek for a pure virgin made so deep an impression on me (I had read it in the evening while my Mother was mending stockings), that I was haunted by spectres, whenever I was in the dark." In the old churchyard of St. Mary's, he loved to read and dream and mope; sometimes he dramatized stories among the gravestones, "cutting down weeds and nettles, as one of the seven champions of Christendom." After a fight in which he used a knife on one of his brothers, he ran away from home with a prayer book in his pocket, fell asleep on the bank of the Otter, and in the night caught a fever that was to afflict him the rest of his life. The old man who was his father once explained "how Jupiter was a thousand times larger than our world and that the other twinkling stars were suns that had worlds rolling round them; and when I came home he shewed me how they rolled round." Thus early, he says, "I regulated my creeds by my conceptions, not by my sight." The death of his father in 1781 broke up this companionship.

In 1782, at the age of nine, he entered Christ's Hospital School in London. His loneliness, his dreamy way of life, and his extraordinary precocity as "the inspired charity boy" are vividly described by his schoolmate Charles Lamb and are recalled in Coleridge's "Frost at Midnight" and *Biographia Literaria.* One day, walking the Strand, in London, and imagining that he was Leander swimming the Hellespont, he unintentionally brushed the pocket of a crusty old gentleman. Challenged as a pickpocket, the boy explained his conduct so eloquently that the old gentleman invited him home and gave him a ticket to a circulating library. As early as 1787 he wrote the first draft of his "Monody on the Death of Chatterton." Before he left Christ's he had walked the London hospitals with his brother Luke and had begun to read and expound the Neo-Platonists.

In October, 1791, Coleridge entered Jesus College, Cambridge, as a sizar (self-help scholar). Here he read widely and deeply, talked brilliantly about David Hartley, Godwin, the French Revolution, the sonnets of William Lisle Bowles (which he copied and distributed among his friends), Plotinus, and the Cambridge Platonists. He also fell in love with Mary Evans and ran up debts. In despair, he left college and enlisted in His Majesty's Fifteenth Light Dragoons, under the name of Silas Tomkyn Comberbacke. Unable to curry, saddle, or ride a horse, he was transferred to hospital service and became a favorite among the soldiers because he wrote fine love letters for them. His friends begged him out of the army, in time to save him, perhaps, from being killed in France, got him reinstated in college, and arranged about his debts. But he did not remain long at Jesus College.

In June, 1794, on a walking tour he stopped at Oxford and had that momentous meeting with Southey which resulted in the Pantisocracy scheme (to form a Utopian Colony in America) and Coleridge's unhappy marriage with Sarah Fricker. By October, 1795, he was married, settled at Clevedon, in Somersetshire, and writing honeymoon poetry. He and his wife were living precariously, partly on the income from his lecturing and writing but chiefly on the charity of friends like Joseph Cottle and Thomas Poole. Since Clevedon was too far from a good library, he moved temporarily to Bristol and then, at Poole's invitation, to Nether Stowey. In the notebook of this Bristol library reading he was accumulating the "Chaos" out of which the cosmic order and beauty of "The Rime of the Ancient Mariner" were to be evoked. Editing a short-lived journal, *The Watchman*, lecturing, and preaching in Unitarian chapels occupied his attention until Josiah Wedgwood, the pottery manufacturer, gave him an allowance of £150 per annum. This, says Hazlitt ("My First Acquaintance with Poets"), Coleridge decided to accept while tying his shoe in the parsonage at Wem.

In the meantime the fateful meeting with Wordsworth had occurred. The two young poets exchanged poems and criticisms. At Racedown, where Coleridge visited William and Dorothy, he "leapt over a gate and bounded down the pathless field" into the most fruitful friendship of his and their lives. Dorothy described him thus:

"He is a wonderful man. His conversation teems with soul, mind, and spirit. . . . I thought him very plain . . . for about three minutes: he is pale and thin, has a wide mouth, thick lips, and not very good teeth, longish, loose-growing half-curling rough black hair. But if you hear him speak for five minutes you think no more of them. His eye is large and full, not dark but grey . . . it has more of the 'poet's eye in a fine frenzy rolling' than I ever witnessed."

Of William, Coleridge wrote, "I feel myself *a little man by his side;* and yet do not think myself the less man than I formerly thought myself." By 1797 the "three persons and one soul" were living at Nether Stowey and Alfoxden, three miles apart, in the Quantock hills. From this point of time until after their return from Germany, the stories of the three are practically one story, and that story has been told. The chief events are the writing and the publication of *Lyrical Ballads*, containing "The Rime of the Ancient Mariner" and "Tintern Abbey," the first and the last poem, respectively, included in that epoch-making little volume; the visit to Germany; and Coleridge's suggestion of *The Recluse* and *The Prelude* to Wordsworth. By 1798, however, Coleridge's political thought had outrun Wordsworth's; in "France: An Ode" he abandoned hope for the French Revolution as a means of achieving liberty and fell back on faith in the *spirit* that informs woods, waves, clouds, and the soul of man.

By 1802 Coleridge's life came to be more and more separated from Wordsworth's, though the two remained close friends for five more years and even after a quarrel became partly reconciled for the remainder of Coleridge's life. Coleridge had settled at Keswick, twelve miles from Dove Cottage, in the Lake Country. Here he wrote the second part of "Christabel," begun at Stowey. Here, too, he contracted an unhappy love for Sarah Hutchinson (see his poem "Love"), sister of the Mary who in October, 1802, became the wife of Wordsworth, and felt all the more poignantly the misery of his ill-matched marriage. In desperation he resumed the opium habit which had produced "Kubla Khan," lost "the deep power of Joy," and wrote "Dejection: An Ode," 1802, which, in its earliest form, drains all these springs of grief. Unable to control his personality, he sank into slothfulness, neglected his wife and children, often leaving them to the charity of his brother-in-law Southey, wandered about talking and lecturing, held a government position in Malta, and returned home in time to hear Wordsworth read *The Prelude* to him in 1806. The next year he began a series of public lectures on the English poets, including Shakespeare, that did much to establish his fame as a critic. Placing himself in the hands of a physician friend, James Gillman, and making London his home, he spent the remainder of his life writing and talking as a critic and philosopher. Among his publications in criticism and philosophy are *Biographia Literaria*, 1817; *The Friend*, 1818; *Aids to Reflection*, 1825; and his Shakespearean criticism, brought out posthumously, a large part of it not until the 1930's. He died in 1834.

Coleridge was the most versatile of the Romanticists—poet, critic, philosopher, theologian. His was the most fertile and stimulating mind of his generation. I. A. Richards (*The Portable Coleridge*, 1950) says he showed Wordsworth "how to become his own poetic self." His chief poems were published in *Lyrical Ballads*, 1798 and 1800; *Christabel, Kubla Khan, and the Pains of Sleep*, 1816; *Sibylline Leaves*, 1817; and the collected *Poetical Works*, 1828, 1829,

1834. A score of these poems (some fifty pages) can be read today with pleasure by a cultivated person who has no special scholarly training in the literature of the period. They are among the most transcendently original poems in our language.

One group of them Coleridge himself called "conversation poems." Most of these are in blank verse and treat subjects intimately personal to the poet. "The Eolian Harp," anticipating his honeymoon with "pensive Sara," describes their jasmine-scented cottage and its surroundings at Clevedon, speculates on "the one Life within us and abroad," and identifies this "Life" with God. "The Lime-Tree Bower My Prison" commemorates happy fellowship with Dorothy and William Wordsworth and Charles Lamb during Lamb's visit to Nether Stowey and Alfoxden in 1797. In "Frost at Midnight," the poet, sitting by the cradle of his baby, recalls his own lonely childhood in London, contrasts its bleak surroundings with the "lovely shapes and sounds" the growing child will know, and asserts a faith in the "Great universal Teacher" who shall mold the child's spirit. "The Nightingale," belonging also to the Nether Stowey period, modulates the outpouring of the poet's affection for William, Dorothy, and little Hartley to the music of the bird's song on an April night. "To William Wordsworth," 1806, is a superb poetical review of *The Prelude.* The whole group expresses ideas about nature and human life which anticipate, parallel, or summarize important doctrines of Wordsworth's poetry. For example, both "Frost at Midnight" and "Tintern Abbey" assert the educational influence of nature on the human spirit.

A second group of Coleridge's living poems is composed of pieces marking "The Renascence of Wonder." In these the author goes back to the age of the old ballads and romances for forms, atmosphere, and narrative technique, and sweeps the horizons of the earth and of history for his matter; but he introduces a new ethic and a new psychology in the treatment of his themes, and achieves original and unprecedented effects. Both "The Rime of the Ancient Mariner" and "Christabel" spring out of medieval literary forms; both dramatize or allegorize the conflict between Good and Evil; both make use of hypnotism, "the power of the eye," in their characterization and narrative development; both cast a spell upon the reader, suggesting the interpenetration of the natural and the supernatural worlds. But whereas "The Rime of the Ancient Mariner," in its treatment of offense, expiation, hope, release, and the return of the evil dream, is the complete execution of a deliberate design, "Christabel" snaps at the height of its "witchery by daylight." "Kubla Khan" is "directionless melody" hovering over a dream landscape combining the extremes of beauty and terror. "The Knight's Tomb" is a sigh for the glamour of a long-vanished age.

Coleridge's other poems of unfaded greatness include two odes, "France" and "Dejection," the themes and autobiographical implications of which have already been noted. "Dejection" shows clearly Coleridge's shift to transcendentalism, most succinctly expressed in the line "And in our life alone does Nature live." With these odes the "Hymn before Sun-Rise, in the Vale of Chamouni" is associated because of its exalted style and the intensity of its religious feeling.

The significance of Coleridge's literary criticism has been partly suggested already. The *Biographia Literaria* account of the origin and purpose of *Lyrical Ballads* and of the defects and excellences of Wordsworth constitutes one of the three or four master expositions of the Romantic theory of poetry. In this work and in his lectures on Shakespeare, Coleridge became the leader of Romantic criticism. To him criticism was something more than the application of a set of external rules. Previous notions of an opposition between genius and artistic law, he declared, were based on a false notion of the critic's business. Great geniuses are not lawless. They work in accordance with laws that the critic should discover by studying their writings. Since art is vital and organic, it takes different shapes under different conditions of human culture. The critic should take these differences of circumstances into consideration in interpreting and judging works of art. The spirit of poetry persists through the ages, though its form may vary from age to age. It is just as unreasonable to judge Shakespeare's plays by the standards of Greek drama as it would be to judge sculpture by the rules of painting. As a Shakespearean critic Coleridge inaugurated points of view, methods, and interpretations which persist today.

from BIOGRAPHIA LITERARIA

CHAPTER 14

Occasion of the *Lyrical Ballads*, and the objects originally proposed . . . definitions of a Poem and Poetry with scholia.

DURING the first year that Mr. Wordsworth and I were neighbours, our conversations turned frequently on the two cardinal points of poetry, the power of exciting the sympathy of the reader by a faithful adherence to the truth of nature, and the power of giving the interest of novelty by the modifying colours of imagination. The sudden charm, which accidents of light and shade, which moonlight or sunset, diffused over a known and familiar landscape, appeared to represent the practicability of combining both. These are the poetry of nature. The thought suggested itself (to which of us I do not recollect) that a series of poems might be composed of *two sorts*. In the one, the incidents and agents were to be, in part at least, supernatural; and the excellence aimed at was to consist in the interesting of the affections by the dramatic truth of such emotions, as would naturally accompany such situations, supposing them real. And real in this sense they have been to every human being who, from whatever source of delusion, has at any time believed himself under supernatural agency. For the second class, subjects were to be chosen from ordinary life; the characters and incidents were to be such as will be found in every village and its vicinity where there is a meditative and feeling mind to seek after them, or to notice them when they present themselves.

In this idea originated the plan of the "Lyrical Ballads"; in which it was agreed that my endeavours should be directed to persons and characters supernatural, or at least romantic; yet so as to transfer from our inward nature a human interest and semblance of truth sufficient to procure for these shadows of imagination that willing suspension of disbelief for the moment, which constitutes poetic faith. Mr. Wordsworth, on the other hand, was to propose to himself as his object, to give the charm of novelty to things of every day, and to excite a feeling analogous to the supernatural, by awakening the mind's attention to the lethargy of custom, and directing it to the loveliness and the wonders of the world before us; an inexhaustible treasure, but for which, in consequence of the film of familiarity and selfish solicitude, we have eyes, yet see not, ears that hear not, and hearts that neither feel nor understand.

With this view I wrote the "Ancient Mariner," and was preparing, among other poems, the "Dark Ladie," and the "Christabel," in which I should have more nearly realized my ideal, than I had done in my first attempt. But Mr. Wordsworth's industry had proved so much more successful, and the number of his poems so much greater, that my compositions, instead of forming a balance, appeared rather an interpolation of heterogeneous matter. Mr. Wordsworth added two or three poems written in his own character, in the impassioned, lofty, and sustained diction which is characteristic of his genius. In this form the "Lyrical Ballads" were published; and were presented by him, as an experiment, whether subjects, which from their nature rejected the usual ornaments and extra-colloquial style of poems in general, might not be so managed in the language of ordinary life as to produce the pleasurable interest, which it is the peculiar business of poetry to impart. . . . [*To be continued*]

THE RIME OF THE ANCIENT MARINER

In Seven Parts

The poem was begun—in collaboration with Wordsworth, who soon dropped out—on November 13, 1797, when the two poets and Dorothy set out on a walking excursion to Linton and the Valley of the Stones; completed, in the first version, March 23, 1798, when Coleridge read it to Dorothy and William; first published in *Lyrical Ballads*, 1798, the first poem in the volume; republished in 1800 with some reduction of the many archaisms; revised between 1800 and 1817; published in its final form, with the addition of the marginal gloss, in *Sibylline Leaves*, 1817. In form it is a ballad, modeled on those of Percy's *Reliques:* one hundred and seven of its one hundred and forty-two stanzas are in regular ballad stanza, 4a3b4c3b, the rest in stanzas ranging from five to nine lines; it follows ballad-narrative technique in the sudden confrontation of characters and unassigned speeches (stanza 1) and in the trick of incremental repetition (see especially ll. 30, 113, 383; and note ll. 59–60, 119–22, 232–35); and it is full of pictures that might have come right out of the old ballads (nodding minstrelsy, bride, and so on). Its theme, stated by Coleridge in the "Argument," has been shown by J. L. Lowes, in *The Road to Xanadu* (Houghton Mifflin, 1930), to have been executed as a "moral and rhythmical harmony": note the conclusion of each of the seven parts, emphasizing the significance of the shooting of the albatross: offense (violating the law of love by the shooting of the albatross—"I shot the Albatross"); penance (appropriately, isolation and loneliness, because the Mariner had broken the law of love—"the Albatross about my neck was hung"); expiation ("Like the whizz of my cross-bow"); release (only after the Mariner had been restored to fellowship by blessing the water snakes—"The Albatross fell off my neck," at the climax or dramatic center of the poem); absolution ("The Albatross's blood"); return of the evil dream (inescapable consequence of a wrong action—"Since then . . . I pass like night"). Lowes further shows that the fabric of the narrative includes three intertwisted threads—the *ship's voyage*, the ground plan, factual as an Admiralty report or a captain's log, making a great poem of "Earth, Air, Fire, and Water in their multiform balefulness and beauty"; what Wordsworth called the *spectral persecution* (that is, the revenge by the guardian spirits of the Antarctic); and the *moral idea* of the inescapable consequences of a moral act. This latter, Professor Lowes asserts, includes far more than the so-called moral at the end ("He prayeth best . . ."); it relates the poem fundamentally to human experience, and is thus one of the principal means by which Coleridge attains reality.

ARGUMENT

How a Ship having first sailed to the Equator, was driven by Storms to the cold Country towards the South Pole; how the Ancient Mariner cruelly and in contempt of the laws of hospitality killed a Sea-bird and how he was followed by many and strange Judgments: and in what manner he came back to his own Country.

Part I

An ancient Mariner meeteth three Gallants bidden to a wedding-feast, and detaineth one.

It is an ancient Mariner,
And he stoppeth one of three.
"By thy long grey beard and glittering eye,
Now wherefore stopp'st thou me?

The Bridegroom's doors are opened wide,
And I am next of kin;
The guests are met, the feast is set:
May'st hear the merry din."

He holds him with his skinny hand,
"There was a ship," quoth he.
"Hold off! unhand me, grey-beard loon!"
Eftsoons his hand dropt he.

The Wedding-Guest is spell-bound by the eye of the old seafaring man, and constrained to hear his tale.

He holds him with his glittering eye—
The Wedding-Guest stood still,
And listens like a three years' child:
The Mariner hath his will.

The Wedding-Guest sat on a stone:
He cannot choose but hear;
And thus spake on that ancient man,
The bright-eyed Mariner.

"The ship was cheered, the harbour cleared,
Merrily did we drop

The Mariner tells how the ship sailed southward with a good wind and fair weather, till it reached the Line.

Below the kirk, below the hill,
Below the lighthouse top.

The Sun came up upon the left,
Out of the sea came he!
And he shone bright, and on the right
Went down into the sea.

Higher and higher every day,
Till over the mast at noon—"
The Wedding-Guest here beat his breast,
For he heard the loud bassoon.

The Wedding-Guest heareth the bridal music; but the Mariner continueth his tale.

The bride hath paced into the hall,
Red as a rose is she;
Nodding their heads before her goes
The merry minstrelsy.

The Wedding-Guest he beat his breast,
Yet he cannot choose but hear;
And thus spake on that ancient man,
The bright-eyed Mariner.

The ship driven by a storm toward the south pole.

"And now the Storm-blast came, and he
Was tyrannous and strong:
He struck with his o'ertaking wings,
And chased us south along.

With sloping masts and dipping prow,
As who pursued with yell and blow
Still treads the shadow of his foe,
And forward bends his head,
The ship drove fast, loud roared the blast,
And southward aye we fled.

And now there came both mist and snow,
And it grew wondrous cold:
And ice, mast-high, came floating by,
As green as emerald.

The land of ice, and of fearful sounds where no living thing was to be seen.

And through the drifts the snowy clifts
Did send a dismal sheen:
Nor shapes of men nor beasts we ken—
The ice was all between.

The ice was here, the ice was there,
The ice was all around:
It cracked and growled, and roared and howled,
Like noises in a swound!

30. over . . . noon. The ship has reached the equator.

Till a great sea-bird, called the Albatross, came through the snow-fog, and was received with great joy and hospitality.

At length did cross an Albatross,
Thorough the fog it came;
As if it had been a Christian soul,
We hailed it in God's name.

It ate the food it ne'er had eat,
And round and round it flew.
The ice did split with a thunder-fit;
The helmsman steered us through!

And lo! the Albatross proveth a bird of good omen, and followeth the ship as it returned northward through fog and floating ice.

And a good south wind sprung up
behind;
The Albatross did follow,
And every day, for food or play,
Came to the mariner's hollo!

In mist or cloud, on mast or shroud,
It perched for vespers nine;
Whiles all the night, through fog-smoke
white,
Glimmered the white Moon-shine."

The ancient Mariner inhospitably killeth the pious bird of good omen.

"God save thee, ancient Mariner!
From the fiends, that plague thee
thus!—
Why look'st thou so?"—"With my cross-
bow
I shot the ALBATROSS.

PART II

The Sun now rose upon the right:
Out of the sea came he,
Still hid in mist, and on the left
Went down into the sea.

And the good south wind still blew
behind,
But no sweet bird did follow,
Nor any day for food or play
Came to the mariners' hollo!

His shipmates cry out against the ancient Mariner, for killing the bird of good luck.

And I had done a hellish thing,
And it would work 'em woe:
For all averred, I had killed the bird
That made the breeze to blow.
Ah wretch! said they, the bird to slay,
That made the breeze to blow!

But when the fog cleared off, they justify the same, and thus make themselves accomplices in the crime.

Nor dim nor red, like God's own head,
The glorious Sun uprist:
Then all averred, I had killed the bird
That brought the fog and mist.
'Twas right, said they, such birds to slay,
That bring the fog and mist.

The fair breeze continues; the ship enters the Pacific Ocean, and sails northward, even till it reaches the Line.

The fair breeze blew, the white foam
flew,
The furrow followed free;
We were the first that ever burst
Into that silent sea.

The ship hath been suddenly becalmed.

Down dropt the breeze, the sails dropt
down,
'Twas sad as sad could be;
And we did speak only to break
The silence of the sea!

All in a hot and copper sky,
The bloody Sun, at noon,
Right up above the mast did stand,
No bigger than the Moon.

Day after day, day after day,
We stuck, nor breath nor motion;
As idle as a painted ship
Upon a painted ocean.

And the Albatross begins to be avenged.

Water, water, every where,
And all the boards did shrink;
Water, water, every where,
Nor any drop to drink.

The very deep did rot: O Christ!
That ever this should be!
Yea, slimy things did crawl with legs
Upon the slimy sea.

A Spirit had followed them; one of the invisible inhabitants of this planet, neither departed souls nor angels; concerning whom the learned Jew, Josephus, and the Platonic Constantinopolitan, Michael Psellus, may be consulted. They are very numerous, and there is no climate or element without one or more.

About, about, in reel and rout
The death-fires danced at night;
The water, like a witch's oils,
Burnt green, and blue and white.

And some in dreams assurèd were
Of the Spirit that plagued us so;
Nine fathom deep he had followed us
From the land of mist and snow.

And every tongue, through utter
drought,
Was withered at the root;
We could not speak, no more than if
We had been choked with soot.

The shipmates, in their sore distress, would fain throw the whole guilt on the ancient Mariner: in sign whereof they hang the dead sea-bird round his neck.

Ah! well a-day! what evil looks
Had I from old and young!
Instead of the cross, the Albatross
About my neck was hung.

105. We were the first, one of several hints about the *time* of the voyage—crossbow, Catholic prayers of the crew (pre-Reformation touch). Note others.

Part III

There passed a weary time. Each throat
Was parched, and glazed each eye.
A weary time! a weary time!
How glazed each weary eye,
When looking westward, I beheld
A something in the sky.

The ancient Mariner beholdeth a sign in the element afar off.

At first it seemed a little speck,
And then it seemed a mist;
It moved and moved, and took at last
A certain shape, I wist.

A speck, a mist, a shape, I wist!
And still it neared and neared:
As if it dodged a water-sprite,
It plunged and tacked and veered.

At its nearer approach, it seemeth him to be a ship; and at a dear ransom he freeth his speech from the bonds of thirst.

With throats unslaked, with black lips baked,
We could nor laugh nor wail;
Through utter drought all dumb we stood!
I bit my arm, I sucked the blood,
And cried, A sail! a sail!

With throats unslaked, with black lips baked,
Agape they heard me call:

A flash of joy;

Grammercy! they for joy did grin,
And all at one their breath drew in,
As they were drinking all.

And horror follows. For can it be a ship that comes onward without wind or tide?

See! see! (I cried) she tacks no more!
Hither to work us weal;
Without a breeze, without a tide,
She steadies with upright keel!

The western wave was all a-flame.
The day was well nigh done!
Almost upon the western wave
Rested the broad bright Sun;
When that strange shape drove suddenly
Betwixt us and the Sun.

It seemeth him but the skeleton of a ship.

And straight the Sun was flecked with bars,
(Heaven's Mother send us grace!)
As if through a dungeon-grate he peered
With broad and burning face.

Alas! (thought I, and my heart beat loud)
How fast she nears and nears!
Are those her sails that glance in the Sun,
Like restless gossameres?

And its ribs are seen as bars on the face of the setting Sun.

Are those her ribs through which the Sun
Did peer, as through a grate?
And is that Woman all her crew?

The Spectre-Woman and her Death-mate, and no other on board the skeleton ship.

Is that a Death? and are there two?
Is Death that woman's mate?

Like vessel, like crew!

Her lips were red, her looks were free,
Her locks were yellow as gold:
Her skin was as white as leprosy,
The Night-mare Life-in-Death was she,
Who thicks man's blood with cold.

Death and Life-in-Death have diced for the ship's crew, and she (the latter) winneth the ancient Mariner.

The naked hulk alongside came,
And the twain were casting dice;
'The game is done! I've won! I've won!'
Quoth she, and whistles thrice.

No twilight within the courts of the Sun.

The Sun's rim dips; the stars rush out:
At one stride comes the dark;
With far-heard whisper, o'er the sea,
Off shot the spectre-bark.

At the rising of the Moon,

We listened and looked sideways up!
Fear at my heart, as at a cup,
My life-blood seemed to sip!
The stars were dim, and thick the night,
The steersman's face by his lamp gleamed white;

From the sails the dew did drip—
Till clomb above the eastern bar
The hornèd Moon, with one bright star
Within the nether tip.

One after another,

One after one, by the star-dogged Moon,
Too quick for groan or sigh,
Each turned his face with a ghastly pang,
And cursed me with his eye.

His shipmates drop down dead.

Four times fifty living men,
(And I heard nor sigh nor groan)
With heavy thump, a lifeless lump,
They dropped down one by one.

But Life-in-Death begins her work on the ancient Mariner.

The souls did from their bodies fly,—
They fled to bliss or woe!
And every soul, it passed me by,
Like the whizz of my cross-bow!"

Part IV

The Wedding-Guest feareth that a Spirit is talking to him;

"I fear thee, ancient Mariner!
I fear thy skinny hand!
And thou art long, and lank, and brown,
As is the ribbed sea-sand.

I fear thee and thy glittering eye,
And thy skinny hand, so brown."—

But the ancient Mariner assureth him of his bodily life, and proceedeth to relate his horrible penance.

"Fear not, fear not, thou Wedding-Guest!
This body dropt not down.

Alone, alone, all, all alone,
Alone on a wide wide sea!
And never a saint took pity on
My soul in agony.

He despiseth the creatures of the calm,

The many men, so beautiful!
And they all dead did lie:
And a thousand thousand slimy things
Lived on; and so did I.

And envieth that they should live, and so many lie dead.

I looked upon the rotting sea,
And drew my eyes away;
I looked upon the rotting deck,
And there the dead men lay.

I looked to heaven, and tried to pray;
But or ever a prayer had gusht,
A wicked whisper came, and made
My heart as dry as dust.

I closed my lids, and kept them close,
And the balls like pulses beat;
For the sky and the sea, and the sea and the sky
Lay like a load on my weary eye,
And the dead were at my feet.

But the curse liveth for him in the eye of the dead men.

The cold sweat melted from their limbs,
Nor rot nor reek did they:
The look with which they looked on me
Had never passed away.

An orphan's curse would drag to hell

In his loneliness and fixedness he yearneth towards the journeying Moon, and the stars that still sojourn, yet still move onward; and every where the blue sky belongs to them, and is their appointed rest, and their native country and their own natural homes, which they enter unannounced, as lords that are certainly expected and yet there is a silent joy at their arrival.

A spirit from on high;
But oh! more horrible than that
Is the curse in a dead man's eye!
Seven days, seven nights, I saw that curse,
And yet I could not die.

The moving Moon went up the sky,
And no where did abide:
Softly she was going up,
And a star or two beside—

Her beams bemocked the sultry main,
Like April hoar-frost spread;
But where the ship's huge shadow lay,
The charmèd water burnt alway
A still and awful red.

By the light of the Moon he beholdeth God's creatures of the great calm.

Beyond the shadow of the ship,
I watched the water-snakes:
They moved in tracks of shining white,
And when they reared, the elfish light
Fell off in hoary flakes.

Within the shadow of the ship
I watched their rich attire:
Blue, glossy green, and velvet black,
They coiled and swam; and every track
Was a flash of golden fire.

Their beauty and their happiness.

O happy living things! no tongue
Their beauty might declare:

He blesseth them in his heart.

A spring of love gushed from my heart,
And I blessed them unaware:
Sure my kind saint took pity on me,
And I blessed them unaware.

The spell begins to break.

The selfsame moment I could pray;
And from my neck so free
The Albatross fell off, and sank
Like lead into the sea.

Part V

Oh sleep! it is a gentle thing,
Beloved from pole to pole!
To Mary Queen the praise be given!
She sent the gentle sleep from Heaven,
That slid into my soul.

By grace of the holy Mother, the ancient Mariner is refreshed with rain.

The silly buckets on the deck,
That had so long remained,
I dreamt that they were filled with dew;
And when I awoke, it rained.

My lips were wet, my throat was cold,
My garments all were dank;
Sure I had drunken in my dreams,
And still my body drank.

I moved, and could not feel my limbs:
I was so light—almost
I thought that I had died in sleep,
And was a blessèd ghost.

He heareth sounds and seeth strange sights and commotions in the sky and the element.

And soon I heard a roaring wind:
It did not come anear;
But with its sound it shook the sails,
That were so thin and sere.

The upper air burst into life!
And a hundred fire-flags sheen,

To and fro they were hurried about!
And to and fro, and in and out,
The wan stars danced between.

And the coming wind did roar more loud,
And the sails did sigh like sedge;
And the rain poured down from one black cloud;
The Moon was at its edge.

The thick black cloud was cleft, and still
The Moon was at its side:
Like waters shot from some high crag,
The lightning fell with never a jag,
A river steep and wide.

The bodies of the ship's crew are inspired, and the ship moves on;

The loud wind never reached the ship,
Yet now the ship moved on!
Beneath the lightning and the Moon
The dead men gave a groan.

They groaned, they stirred, they all uprose,
Nor spake, nor moved their eyes;
It has been strange, even in a dream,
To have seen those dead men rise.

The helmsman steered, the ship moved on;
Yet never a breeze up blew;
The mariners all 'gan work the ropes,
Where they were wont to do;
They raised their limbs like lifeless tools—
We were a ghastly crew.

The body of my brother's son
Stood by me, knee to knee:
The body and I pulled at one rope
But he said nought to me."

But not by the souls of the men, nor by daemons of earth or middle air, but by a blessed troop of angelic spirits, sent down by the invocation of the guardian saint.

"I fear thee, ancient Mariner!"
"Be calm, thou Wedding-Guest!
'Twas not those souls that fled in pain,
Which to their corses came again,
But a troop of spirits blest:

For when it dawned—they dropped their arms,
And clustered round the mast;
Sweet sounds rose slowly through their mouths,
And from their bodies passed.

Around, around, flew each sweet sound,
Then darted to the Sun;
Slowly the sounds came back again,
Now mixed, now one by one.

Sometimes a-dropping from the sky
I heard the sky-lark sing;
Sometimes all little birds that are,
How they seemed to fill the sea and air
With their sweet jargoning!

And now 'twas like all instruments,
Now like a lonely flute;
And now it is an angel's song,
That makes the heavens be mute.

It ceased; yet still the sails made on
A pleasant noise till noon,
A noise like of a hidden brook
In the leafy month of June,
That to the sleeping woods all night
Singeth a quiet tune.

Till noon we quietly sailed on,
Yet never a breeze did breathe:
Slowly and smoothly went the ship,
Moved onward from beneath.

The lonesome Spirit from the south-pole carries on the ship as far as the Line, in obediance to the angelic troop, but still requireth vengeance.

Under the keel nine fathom deep,
From the land of mist and snow,
The spirit slid: and it was he
That made the ship to go.
The sails at noon left off their tune,
And the ship stood still also.

The Sun, right up above the mast,
Had fixed her to the ocean:
But in a minute she 'gan stir,
With a short uneasy motion—
Backwards and forwards half her length
With a short uneasy motion.

Then like a pawing horse let go,
She made a sudden bound:
It flung the blood into my head,
And I fell down in a swound.

The Polar Spirit's fellow-daemons, the invisible inhabitants of the element, take part in his wrong; and two of them relate, one to the other, that penance long and heavy for the ancient Mariner hath been accorded to the Polar Spirit, who returneth southward.

How long in that same fit I lay,
I have not to declare;
But ere my living life returned,
I heard and in my soul discerned
Two voices in the air.

'Is it he?' quoth one, 'Is this the man?
By Him who died on cross,
With his cruel bow he laid full low
The harmless Albatross.

'The spirit who bideth by himself
In the land of mist and snow,
He loved the bird that loved the man
Who shot him with his bow.'

The other was a softer voice,
As soft as honey-dew:
Quoth he, 'The man hath penance done,
And penance more will do.'

Part VI

FIRST VOICE

'But tell me, tell me! speak again,
Thy soft response renewing—
What makes that ship drive on so fast?
What is the ocean doing?'

SECOND VOICE

'Still as a slave before his lord,
The ocean hath no blast;
His great bright eye most silently
Up to the Moon is cast—

If he may know which way to go;
For she guides him smooth or grim.
See, brother, see! how graciously
She looketh down on him.'

FIRST VOICE

The Mariner hath been cast into a trance; for the angelic power causeth the vessel to drive northward faster than human life could endure.

'But why drives on that ship so fast,
Without or wave or wind?'

SECOND VOICE

'The air is cut away before,
And closes from behind.

Fly, brother, fly! more high, more high!
Or we shall be belated:
For slow and slow that ship will go,
When the Mariner's trance is abated.'

The supernatural motion is retarded; the Mariner awakes, and his penance begins anew.

I woke, and we were sailing on
As in a gentle weather:
'Twas night, calm night, the moon was high;
The dead men stood together.

All stood together on the deck,
For a charnel-dungeon fitter:
All fixed on me their stony eyes,
That in the Moon did glitter.

The pang, the curse, with which they died,
Had never passed away:
I could not draw my eyes from theirs,
Nor turn them up to pray.

The curse is finally expiated.

And now this spell was snapt: once more
I viewed the ocean green,
And looked far forth, yet little saw
Of what had else been seen—

Like one, that on a lonesome road
Doth walk in fear and dread,
And having once turned round walks on,
And turns no more his head;
Because he knows, a frightful fiend
Doth close behind him tread.

But soon there breathed a wind on me,
Nor sound nor motion made:
Its path was not upon the sea,
In ripple or in shade.

It raised my hair, it fanned my cheek
Like a meadow-gale of spring—
It mingled strangely with my fears,
Yet it felt like a welcoming.

Swiftly, swiftly flew the ship,
Yet she sailed softly too:
Sweetly, sweetly blew the breeze—
On me alone it blew.

And the ancient Mariner beholdeth his native country.

Oh! dream of joy! is this indeed
The light-house top I see?
Is this the hill? is this the kirk?
Is this mine own countree?

We drifted o'er the harbour-bar,
And I with sobs did pray—
O let me be awake, my God!
Or let me sleep alway.

The harbour-bay was clear as glass,
So smoothly it was strewn!
And on the bay the moonlight lay,
And the shadow of the Moon.

The rock shone bright, the kirk no less,
That stands above the rock:
The moonlight steeped in silentness
The steady weathercock.

The angelic spirits leave the dead bodies,

And the bay was white with silent light,
Till rising from the same,
Full many shapes, that shadows were,
In crimson colours came.

And appear in their own forms of light.

A little distance from the prow
Those crimson shadows were:
I turned my eyes upon the deck—
Oh, Christ! what saw I there!

Each corse lay flat, lifeless and flat,
And, by the holy rood!
A man all light, a seraph-man,
On every corse there stood.

This seraph-band, each waved his hand:
It was a heavenly sight!
They stood as signals to the land,
Each one a lovely light;

This seraph-band, each waved his hand,
No voice did they impart—
No voice; but oh! the silence sank
Like music on my heart.

But soon I heard the dash of oars,
I heard the Pilot's cheer;
My head was turned perforce away
And I saw a boat appear.

The Pilot and the Pilot's boy,
I heard them coming fast:
Dear Lord in Heaven! it was a joy
The dead men could not blast.

I saw a third—I heard his voice:
It is the Hermit good!
He singeth loud his godly hymns
That he makes in the wood.
He'll shrieve my soul, he'll wash away
The Albatross's blood.

Part VII

The Hermit of the Wood,

This Hermit good lives in that wood
Which slopes down to the sea.
How loudly his sweet voice he rears!
He loves to talk with marineres
That come from a far countree.

He kneels at morn, and noon, and eve—
He hath a cushion plump:
It is the moss that wholly hides
The rotted old oak-stump.

The skiff-boat neared: I heard them talk,
'Why, this is strange, I trow!
Where are those lights so many and fair,
That signal made but now?'

Approacheth the ship with wonder.

'Strange, by my faith!' the Hermit said—
'And they answered not our cheer!
The planks looked warped! and see those sails,
How thin they are and sere!
I never saw aught like to them,
Unless perchance it were

Brown skeletons of leaves that lag
My forest-brook along;
When the ivy-tod is heavy with snow,
And the owlet whoops to the wolf below,
That eats the she-wolf's young.'

'Dear Lord! it hath a fiendish look—
(The Pilot made reply)
I am a-feared'—'Push on, push on!'
Said the Hermit cheerily.

The boat came closer to the ship,
But I nor spake nor stirred;
The boat came close beneath the ship,
And straight a sound was heard.

The ship suddenly sinketh.

Under the water it rumbled on,
Still louder and more dread:
It reached the ship, it split the bay;
The ship went down like lead.

The ancient Mariner is saved in the Pilot's boat.

Stunned by that loud and dreadful sound,
Which sky and ocean smote,
Like one that hath been seven days drowned
My body lay afloat;
But swift as dreams, myself I found
Within the Pilot's boat.

Upon the whirl, where sank the ship,
The boat spun round and round;
And all was still, save that the hill
Was telling of the sound.

I moved my lips—the Pilot shrieked
And fell down in a fit;
The holy Hermit raised his eyes,
And prayed where he did sit.

I took the oars: the Pilot's boy,
Who now doth crazy go,
Laughed loud and long, and all the while
His eyes went to and fro.
'Ha! ha!' quoth he, 'full plain I see,
The Devil knows how to row.'

And now, all in my own countree,
I stood on the firm land!
The Hermit stepped forth from the boat,
And scarcely he could stand.

The ancient Mariner earnestly entreateth the Hermit to shrieve him; and the penance of life falls on him.

'O shrieve me, shrieve me, holy man!'
The Hermit crossed his brow.
'Say quick,' quoth he, 'I bid thee say—
What manner of man art thou?'

Forthwith this frame of mine was wrenched
With a woful agony,
Which forced me to begin my tale;
And then it left me free.

And ever and anon throughout his future life an agony constraineth him to travel from land to land,

Since then, at an uncertain hour,
That agony returns:
And till my ghastly tale is told,
This heart within me burns.

I pass, like night, from land to land;
I have strange power of speech;
That moment that his face I see,
I know the man that must hear me:
To him my tale I teach."

"What loud uproar bursts from that door!
The wedding-guests are there:
But in the garden-bower the bride
And bride-maids singing are:
And hark the little vesper bell,
Which biddeth me to prayer!"

"O Wedding-Guest! this soul hath been
Alone on a wide wide sea:
So lonely 'twas, that God himself
Scarce seemèd there to be.

O sweeter than the marriage-feast,
'Tis sweeter far to me,
To walk together to the kirk
With a goodly company!—

To walk together to the kirk,
And all together pray,
While each to his great Father bends,
Old men, and babes, and loving friends,
And youths and maidens gay!

And to teach, by his own example, love and reverence to all things that God made and loveth.

Farewell, farewell! but this I tell
To thee, thou Wedding-Guest!
He prayeth well, who loveth well
Both man and bird and beast.

He prayeth best, who loveth best
All things both great and small,
For the dear God who loveth us,
He made and loveth all."

The Mariner, whose eye is bright,
Whose beard with age is hoar,
Is gone: and now the Wedding-Guest
Turned from the bridegroom's door.

He went like one that hath been stunned,
And is of sense forlorn:
A sadder and a wiser man,
He rose the morrow morn.

from CHRISTABEL

"Christabel" is a fragment composed in bits at various times and places, changes of place having much to do with the scenery of the poem. In form, it is a metrical romance, versified in accordance with the system described in the "Preface" (which is not really new, as Coleridge says; Old English verse and the ballads used it). Its theme is "witchery by daylight." This is developed largely through the suggestion of atmosphere (the Gothic castle with its midnight clock, hooting owl, and crowing cock, its hint of "my lady's shroud," its surroundings of eerie moonlight and fairy wood), and through the character of Geraldine as a witch, or, as has been latterly suggested, a vampire (her strange and wild beauty, her fantastic story, her fainting at the threshold, and her inability to join in praise of the Virgin, her evocation of the mastiff bitch's growl and the flame's flare and the gleam on the shield, her curse on Christabel's mother when Christabel wishes for her, and so on). Geraldine's character is thrown into relief by contrast with the white purity and innocence of Christabel. The bewitchment of Christabel by the power of the eye (reminiscent of the hypnotism of the Ancient Mariner), taking the form of a spell upon her utterance which prevents her from expressing her sense of evil and denouncing her guest, throws into dramatic form the struggle between the powers of Evil and of Good. The conclusion to the poem, never written, would doubtless have shown "That saints will aid if men will call" (l. 330). In Part II, which is not included in this edition, Geraldine seems in a fair way to succeed after having literally "vamped" Sir Leoline and momentarily turned the tongue-tied Christabel into a hissing monster; and saints are clearly needed. Bracy the Bard, with his story of the dove and the bright green snake, is the readiest help. He is dispatched, like one of Sir Walter Scott's knights, to the castle of Sir Roland de Vaux of Tryermaine, the alleged father of Geraldine. Here the narrative proper stops short. In the sequel, as Coleridge is reported to have planned it, Bracy's quest is vain. Meanwhile, Geraldine assumes the form of Christabel's absent lover. The return of the true lover puts Geraldine to flight, and the wedding bells ring according to the prophecy in ll. 200–01. (For further details of the proposed completion, see B. R. McElderry's article in *Studies in Philology*, Vol. 33, and A. H. Nethercot's *The Road to Tryermaine*, University of Chicago Press, 1939.) In the absence of Coleridge's own handling of the conclusion in an artistic manner according with the part written, confident interpretation of the poem is perhaps impossible. That it remains a bafflingly beautiful fragment hardly detracts from it.

PREFACE

The first part of the following poem was written in the year one thousand seven hundred and ninety-seven, at Stowey, in the county of Somerset. The second part, after my return from Germany, in the year one thousand eight hundred, at Keswick, Cumberland. . . . It is probable, that if the poem had been finished at either of the former periods, or if even the first and second part had been published in the year 1800, the impression of its originality would have been much greater than I dare at present expect. But for this, I have only my own indolence to blame. The dates are mentioned for the exclusive purpose of precluding charges of plagiarism or servile imitation from myself. For there is amongst us a set of critics, who seem to hold, that every possible thought and image is traditional; who have no notion that there are such things as fountains in the world, small as well as great; and who would therefore charitably derive every rill they behold flowing, from a perforation made in some other man's tank. I am confident, however, that as far as the present poem is concerned, the celebrated poets[1] whose writings I might be suspected of having imitated, either in particular passages, or in the tone and the spirit of the whole, would be among the first to vindicate me from the charge, and who, on any striking coincidence, would permit me to address them in this doggerel version of two monkish Latin hexameters.

"'Tis mine and it is likewise yours;
But an if this will not do;
Let it be mine, good friend! for I
Am the poorer of the two."

I have only to add that the metre of Christabel is not, properly speaking, irregular, though it may seem so from its being founded on a new principle: namely, that of counting in each line the accents, not the syllables. Though the latter may vary from seven to twelve, yet in each line the accents will be found to be only four. Nevertheless this occasional variation in number of syllables is not introduced wantonly, or for the mere ends of convenience, but in correspondence with some transition, in the nature of the imagery or passion.

PART THE FIRST

'Tis the middle of night by the castle clock,
And the owls have awakened the crowing cock;
Tu—whit!——Tu—whoo!
And hark, again! the crowing cock,
How drowsily it crew.

Sir Leoline, the Baron rich,
Hath a toothless mastiff, which
From her kennel beneath the rock
Maketh answer to the clock,
Four for the quarters, and twelve for the hour;
Ever and aye, by shine and shower,
Sixteen short howls, not over loud;
Some say, she sees my lady's shroud.

Is the night chilly and dark?
The night is chilly, but not dark.
The thin gray cloud is spread on high,
It covers but not hides the sky.
The moon is behind, and at the full;
And yet she looks both small and dull.
The night is chill, the cloud is gray:
'Tis a month before the month of May,
And the Spring comes slowly up this way.

The lovely lady, Christabel,
Whom her father loves so well,
What makes her in the wood so late,
A furlong from the castle gate?
She had dreams all yesternight
Of her own betrothèd knight;
And she in the midnight wood will pray
For the weal of her lover that's far away.

She stole along, she nothing spoke,
The sighs she heaved were soft and low,
And naught was green upon the oak
But moss and rarest mistletoe:
She kneels beneath the huge oak tree,
And in silence prayeth she.

The lady sprang up suddenly,
The lovely lady, Christabel!
It moaned as near, as near can be,
But what it is she cannot tell.—
On the other side it seems to be,
Of the huge, broad-breasted, old oak tree.

The night is chill; the forest bare;
Is it the wind that moaneth bleak?
There is not wind enough in the air
To move away the ringlet curl
From the lovely lady's cheek—
There is not wind enough to twirl
The one red leaf, the last of its clan,
That dances as often as dance it can,
Hanging so light, and hanging so high,
On the topmost twig that looks up at the sky.

[1] **celebrated poets,** Sir Walter Scott and Lord Byron.

Hush, beating heart of Christabel!
Jesu, Maria, shield her well!
She folded her arms beneath her cloak,
And stole to the other side of the oak.
  What sees she there?

There she sees a damsel bright,
Drest in a silken robe of white,
That shadowy in the moonlight shone:
The neck that made that white robe wan,
Her stately neck, and arms were bare;
Her blue-veined feet unsandaled were,
And wildly glittered here and there
The gems entangled in her hair.
I guess, 'twas frightful there to see
A lady so richly clad as she—
Beautiful exceedingly!

Mary mother, save me now!
(Said Christabel,) And who art thou?

The lady strange made answer meet,
And her voice was faint and sweet:—
Have pity on my sore distress,
I scarce can speak for weariness:
Stretch forth thy hand, and have no fear!
Said Christabel, How camest thou here?
And the lady, whose voice was faint and sweet,
Did thus pursue her answer meet:—

My sire is of a noble line,
And my name is Geraldine:
Five warriors seized me yestermorn,
Me, even me, a maid forlorn:
They choked my cries with force and fright,
And tied me on a palfrey white.
The palfrey was as fleet as wind,
And they rode furiously behind.
They spurred amain, their steeds were white:
And once we crossed the shade of night.
As sure as Heaven shall rescue me,
I have no thought what men they be;
Nor do I know how long it is
(For I have laid entranced I wis)
Since one, the tallest of the five,
Took me from the palfrey's back,
A weary woman, scarce alive.
Some muttered words his comrades spoke:
He placed me underneath this oak;
He swore they would return with haste;
Whither they went I cannot tell—
I thought I heard, some minutes past,
Sounds as of a castle bell.
Stretch forth thy hand (thus ended she),
And help a wretched maid to flee.

Then Christabel stretched forth her hand,
And comforted fair Geraldine:
O well, bright dame! may you command
The service of Sir Leoline;
And gladly our stout chivalry
Will he send forth and friends withal
To guide and guard you safe and free
Home to your noble father's hall.

She rose: and forth with steps they passed
That strove to be, and were not, fast.
Her gracious stars the lady blest,
And thus spake on sweet Christabel:
All our household are at rest,
The hall as silent as the cell;
Sir Leoline is weak in health,
And may not well awakened be,
But we will move as if in stealth,
And I beseech your courtesy,
This night, to share your couch with me.

They crossed the moat, and Christabel
Took the key that fitted well;
A little door she opened straight,
All in the middle of the gate;
The gate that was ironed within and without,
Where an army in battle array had marched out.
The lady sank, belike through pain,
And Christabel with might and main
Lifted her up, a weary weight,
Over the threshold of the gate:
Then the lady rose again,
And moved, as she were not in pain.

So free from danger, free from fear,
They crossed the court: right glad they were.
And Christabel devoutedly cried
To the lady by her side,
Praise we the Virgin all divine
Who hath rescued thee from thy distress!
Alas, alas! said Geraldine,
I cannot speak for weariness.
So free from danger, free from fear,
They crossed the court: right glad they were.

Outside her kennel, the mastiff old
Lay fast asleep, in moonshine cold.
The mastiff old did not awake,
Yet she an angry moan did make!
And what can ail the mastiff bitch?
Never till now she uttered yell
Beneath the eye of Christabel.
Perhaps it is the owlet's scritch:
For what can ail the mastiff bitch?

They passed the hall, that echoes still,
Pass as lightly as you will!
The brands were flat, the brands were dying,
Amid their own white ashes lying;
But when the lady passed, there came
A tongue of light, a fit of flame;
And Christabel saw the lady's eye,
And nothing else saw she thereby,
Save the boss of the shield of Sir Leoline tall,
Which hung in a murky old niche in the wall.
O softly tread, said Christabel,
My father seldom sleepeth well.

Sweet Christabel her feet doth bare,
And jealous of the listening air
They steal their way from stair to stair,
Now in glimmer, and now in gloom,
And now they pass the Baron's room,
As still as death, with stifled breath!
And now have reached her chamber door;
And now doth Geraldine press down
The rushes of the chamber floor.

The moon shines dim in the open air,
And not a moonbeam enters here.
But they without its light can see
The chamber carved so curiously,
Carved with figures strange and sweet,
All made out of the carver's brain,
For a lady's chamber meet:
The lamp with twofold silver chain
Is fastened to an angel's feet.

The silver lamp burns dead and dim;
But Christabel the lamp will trim.
She trimmed the lamp, and made it bright,
And left it swinging to and fro,
While Geraldine, in wretched plight,
Sank down upon the floor below.

O weary lady, Geraldine,
I pray you, drink this cordial wine!
It is a wine of virtuous powers;
My mother made it of wild flowers.

And will your mother pity me,
Who am a maiden most forlorn?
Christabel answered—Woe is me!
She died the hour that I was born.
I have heard the grey-haired friar tell
How on her death-bed she did say,
That she should hear the castle-bell
Strike twelve upon my wedding-day.
O mother dear! that thou wert here!
I would, said Geraldine, she were!

But soon with altered voice, said she—
"Off, wandering mother! Peak and pine!
I have power to bid thee flee."
Alas! what ails poor Geraldine?
Why stares she with unsettled eye?
Can she the bodiless dead espy?
And why with hollow voice cries she,
"Off, woman, off! this hour is mine—
Though thou her guardian spirit be,
Off, woman, off! 'tis given to me."

Then Christabel knelt by the lady's side,
And raised to heaven her eyes so blue—
Alas! said she, this ghastly ride—
Dear lady! it hath wildered you!
The lady wiped her moist cold brow,
And faintly said, "'tis over now!'

Again the wild-flower wine she drank:
Her fair large eyes 'gan glitter bright,
And from the floor whereon she sank,
The lofty lady stood upright:
She was most beautiful to see,
Like a lady of a far countrée.

And thus the lofty lady spake—
"All they who live in the upper sky,
Do love you, holy Christabel!
And you love them, and for their sake
And for the good which me befel,
Even I in my degree will try,
Fair maiden, to requite you well.
But now unrobe yourself; for I
Must pray, ere yet in bed I lie."

Quoth Christabel, So let it be!
And as the lady bade, did she.
Her gentle limbs did she undress,
And lay down in her loveliness.

But through her brain of weal and woe
So many thoughts moved to and fro,
That vain it were her lids to close;
So half-way from the bed she rose,
And on her elbow did recline
To look at the lady Geraldine.

Beneath the lamp the lady bowed,
And slowly rolled her eyes around;
Then drawing in her breath aloud,
Like one that shuddered, she unbound
The cincture from beneath her breast:
Her silken robe, and inner vest,
Dropt to her feet, and full in view,
Behold! her bosom and half her side—

A sight to dream of, not to tell!
O shield her! shield sweet Christabel!

Yet Geraldine nor speaks nor stirs;
Ah! what a stricken look was hers!
Deep from within she seems half-way
To lift some weight with sick assay,
And eyes the maid and seeks delay;
Then suddenly, as one defied,
Collects herself in scorn and pride,
And lay down by the Maiden's side!—
And in her arms the maid she took,
Ah wel-a-day!
And with low voice and doleful look
These words did say:
"In the touch of this bosom there worketh a spell,
Which is lord of thy utterance, Christabel!
Thou knowest to-night, and wilt know to-morrow,
This mark of my shame, this seal of my sorrow;
But vainly thou warrest,
For this is alone in
Thy power to declare,
That in the dim forest,
Thou heard'st a low moaning,
And found'st a bright lady, surpassingly fair;
And didst bring her home with thee in love and in charity,
To shield her and shelter her from the damp air."

THE CONCLUSION TO PART THE FIRST

It was a lovely sight to see
The lady Christabel, when she
Was praying at the old oak tree.
Amid the jagged shadows
Of mossy leafless boughs,
Kneeling in the moonlight,
To make her gentle vows;
Her slender palms together prest,
Heaving sometimes on her breast;
Her face resigned to bliss or bale—
Her face, oh call it fair not pale,
And both blue eyes more bright than clear,
Each about to have a tear.

With open eyes (ah woe is me!)
Asleep, and dreaming fearfully,
Fearfully dreaming, yet, I wis,
Dreaming that alone, which is—
O sorrow and shame! Can this be she,
The lady, who knelt at the old oak tree?
And lo! the worker of these harms,
That holds the maiden in her arms,
Seems to slumber still and mild,
As a mother with her child.

A star hath set, a star hath risen,
O Geraldine! since arms of thine
Have been the lovely lady's prison.
O Geraldine! one hour was thine—
Thou'st had thy will! By tairn and rill,
The night-birds all that hour were still.
But now they are jubilant anew.
From cliff and tower, tu—whoo! tu—whoo!
Tu—whoo! tu—whoo! from wood and fell!

And see! the lady Christabel
Gathers herself from out her trance;
Her limbs relax, her countenance
Grows sad and soft; the smooth thin lids
Close o'er her eyes; and tears she sheds—
Large tears that leave the lashes bright!
And oft the while she seems to smile
As infants at a sudden light!

Yea, she doth smile, and she doth weep,
Like a youthful hermitess,
Beauteous in a wilderness,
Who, praying always, prays in sleep.
And, if she move unquietly,
Perchance, 'tis but the blood so free
Comes back and tingles in her feet.
No doubt, she hath a vision sweet.
What if her guardian spirit 'twere,
What if she knew her mother near?
But this she knows, in joys and woes,
That saints will aid if men will call:
For the blue sky bends over all!

THE KNIGHT'S TOMB

Written probably in 1817, but included here with the other poems of "wonder." Sir Arthur lived in the North Country.

Where is the grave of Sir Arthur O'Kellyn?
Where may the grave of that good man be?—
By the side of a spring, on the breast of Helvellyn,
Under the twigs of a young birch tree!
The oak that in summer was sweet to hear,
And rustled its leaves in the fall of the year,
And whistled and roared in the winter alone,
Is gone,—and the birch in its stead is grown.—
The Knight's bones are dust,
And his good sword rust;—
His soul is with the saints, I trust.

306. tairn, a small mountain lake or pond, tarn.

KUBLA KHAN; OR, A VISION IN A DREAM

A FRAGMENT

Coleridge gives this account of the writing of "Kubla Khan": "The following fragment is here published at the request of a poet of great and deserved celebrity [presumably Byron], and, as far as the Author's own opinions are concerned rather as a psychological curiosity, than on the ground of any supposed *poetic* merits.

"In the summer of the year 1797 [probably 1798], the Author, then in ill health, had retired to a lonely farm-house between Porlock and Linton, on the Exmoor confines of Somerset and Devonshire. In consequence of a slight indisposition, an anodyne had been prescribed, from the effects of which he fell asleep in his chair at the moment he was reading the following sentence, or words of the same substance, in 'Purchas's Pilgrimage': 'Here the Khan Kubla commanded a palace to be built, and a stately garden thereunto. And thus ten miles of fertile ground were inclosed with a wall.' The Author continued for about three hours in a profound sleep, at least of the external senses, during which time he has the most vivid confidence, that he could not have composed less than from two to three hundred lines; if that indeed can be called composition in which all the images rose up before him as *things*, with a parallel production of the correspondent expressions, without any sensation or consciousness of effort. On awaking he appeared to himself to have a distinct recollection of the whole, and taking his pen, ink, and paper, instantly and eagerly wrote down the lines that are here preserved. At this moment he was unfortunately called out by a person on business from Porlock, and detained by him above an hour, and on his return to his room, found, to his no small surprise and mortification, that though he still retained some vague and dim recollection of the general purport of the vision, yet, with the exception of some eight or ten scattered lines and images, all the rest had passed away like the images on the surface of a stream into which a stone had been cast, but, alas! without the after restoration of the latter!

Then all the charm
Is broken—all that phantom-world so fair
Vanishes, and a thousand circlets spread,
And each mis-shape[s] the other. Stay awhile,
Poor youth! who scarcely dar'st lift up thine eyes—
The stream will soon renew its smoothness, soon
The visions will return! And lo, he stays,
And soon the fragments dim of lovely forms
Come trembling back, unite, and now once more
The pool becomes a mirror.[1]

"Yet from the still surviving recollections in his mind, the Author has frequently purposed to finish for himself what had been originally, as it were, given to him. Αὔριον ἄδιον ᾄσω[2]: but the tomorrow is yet to come."

[1] From Coleridge's "The Picture; or, The Lover's Resolution." [2] Αὔριον . . . ᾄσω. To sing a sweeter song tomorrow.

In Xanadu did Kubla Khan
A stately pleasure-dome decree:
Where Alph, the sacred river, ran
Through caverns measureless to man
  Down to a sunless sea.
So twice five miles of fertile ground
With walls and towers were girdled round:
And there were gardens bright with sinuous rills,
Where blossomed many an incense-bearing tree;
And here were forests ancient as the hills,
Enfolding sunny spots of greenery.

But oh! that deep romantic chasm which slanted
Down the green hill athwart a cedarn cover!
A savage place! as holy and enchanted
As e'er beneath a waning moon was haunted
By woman wailing for her demon-lover!
And from this chasm, with ceaseless turmoil seething,
As if this earth in fast thick pants were breathing,
A mighty fountain momently was forced:
Amid whose swift half-intermitted burst
Huge fragments vaulted like rebounding hail,
Or chaffy grain beneath the thresher's flail:
And 'mid these dancing rocks at once and ever
It flung up momently the sacred river.
Five miles meandering with a mazy motion
Through wood and dale the sacred river ran,
Then reached the caverns measureless to man,
And sank in tumult to a lifeless ocean:
And 'mid this tumult Kubla heard from far
Ancestral voices prophesying war!

  The shadow of the dome of pleasure
  Floated midway on the waves;
  Where was heard the mingled measure
  From the fountain and the caves.
It was a miracle of rare device,
A sunny pleasure-dome with caves of ice!

  A damsel with a dulcimer
  In a vision once I saw:
  It was an Abyssinian maid,
  And on her dulcimer she played,
  Singing of Mount Abora.
  Could I revive within me
  Her symphony and song,

1. Xanadu, a region in Tartary. **Kubla Khan,** the Cham (Emperor) Kublai (1214–1294), the Mongol conqueror of China. **14–16. A savage place . . . demon-lover!** "In all the millions permitted there are no more than five—five little lines—of which one can say, 'These are the magic. These are the vision. The rest is only poetry.' "—Kipling. The other two are Keats' "Ode to a Nightingale," ll. 69–70. **17–24. And from this chasm . . . sacred river,** suggested by the description of the Florida alligator hole in William Bartram's *Travels*, 1791.

To such a deep delight 'twould win me,
That with music loud and long,
I would build that dome in air,
That sunny dome! those caves of ice!
And all who heard should see them there,
And all should cry, Beware! Beware!
His flashing eyes, his floating hair!
Weave a circle round him thrice,
And close your eyes with holy dread,
For he on honey-dew hath fed,
And drunk the milk of Paradise.

FROST AT MIDNIGHT

The Frost performs its secret ministry,
Unhelped by any wind. The owlet's cry
Came loud—and hark, again! loud as before.
The inmates of my cottage, all at rest,
Have left me to that solitude, which suits
Abstruser musings: save that at my side
My cradled infant slumbers peacefully.
'Tis calm indeed! so calm, that it disturbs
And vexes meditation with its strange
And extreme silentness. Sea, hill, and wood,
This populous village! Sea, and hill, and wood,
With all the numberless goings-on of life,
Inaudible as dreams! the thin blue flame
Lies on my low-burnt fire, and quivers not;
Only that film, which fluttered on the grate,
Still flutters there, the sole unquiet thing.
Methinks, its motion in this hush of nature
Gives it dim sympathies with me who live,
Making it a companionable form,
Whose puny flaps and freaks the idling Spirit
By its own moods interprets, everywhere
Echo or mirror seeking of itself,
And makes a toy of Thought.

But O! how oft,
How oft, at school, with most believing mind,
Presageful, have I gazed upon the bars,
To watch that fluttering *stranger!* and as oft
With unclosed lids, already had I dreamt
Of my sweet birth-place, and the old church-tower,
Whose bells, the poor man's only music, rang
From morn to evening, all the hot Fair-day,
So sweetly, that they stirred and haunted me
With a wild pleasure, falling on mine ear
Most like articulate sounds of things to come!
So gazed I, till the soothing things, I dreamt,
Lulled me to sleep, and sleep prolonged my dreams!
And so I brooded all the following morn,
Awed by the stern preceptor's face, mine eye
Fixed with mock study on my swimming book:
Save if the door half opened, and I snatched
A hasty glance, and still my heart leaped up,
For still I hoped to see the *stranger's* face,
Townsman, or aunt, or sister more beloved,
My play-mate when we both were clothed alike!

Dear Babe, that sleepest cradled by my side,
Whose gentle breathings, heard in this deep calm,
Fill up the interspersèd vacancies
And momentary pauses of the thought!
My babe so beautiful! it thrills my heart
With tender gladness, thus to look at thee,
And think that thou shalt learn far other lore,
And in far other scenes! For I was reared
In the great city, pent 'mid cloisters dim,
And saw nought lovely but the sky and stars.
But *thou*, my babe! shalt wander like a breeze
By lakes and sandy shores, beneath the crags
Of ancient mountain, and beneath the clouds,
Which image in their bulk both lakes and shores
And mountain crags: so shalt thou see and hear
The lovely shapes and sounds intelligible
Of that eternal language, which thy God
Utters, who from eternity doth teach
Himself in all, and all things in himself.
Great universal Teacher! he shall mould
Thy spirit, and by giving make it ask.

Therefore all seasons shall be sweet to thee,
Whether the summer clothe the general earth
With greenness, or the redbreast sit and sing
Betwixt the tufts of snow on the bare branch
Of mossy apple-tree, while the nigh thatch
Smokes in the sun-thaw; whether the eve-drops fall
Heard only in the trances of the blast,
Or if the secret ministry of frost
Shall hang them up in silent icicles,
Quietly shining to the quiet Moon.

26. stranger! "These [soot] films are called *strangers* and are supposed to portend the arrival of some absent friend." —*Poetical Register*

FRANCE: AN ODE

This poem, inspired by the French invasion of Switzerland in 1798, was first printed in the London *Morning Post* in April of that year. It was reprinted in the *Morning Post* in 1802 with a preface giving the purport of the poem.

Ye Clouds! that far above me float and pause,
Whose pathless march no mortal may control!
Ye Ocean-Waves! that, wheresoe'er ye roll,
Yield homage only to eternal laws!
Ye Woods! that listen to the night-birds singing,
Midway the smooth and perilous slope reclined,
Save when your own imperious branches swinging,
Have made a solemn music of the wind!
Where, like a man beloved of God,
Through glooms, which never woodman trod,
How oft, pursuing fancies holy,
My moonlight way o'er flowering weeds I wound,
Inspired, beyond the guess of folly,
By each rude shape and wild unconquerable sound!
O ye loud Waves! and O ye Forests high!
And O ye Clouds that far above me soared!
Thou rising Sun! thou blue rejoicing Sky!
Yea, every thing that is and will be free!
Bear witness for me, wheresoe'er ye be,
With what deep worship I have still adored
The spirit of divinest Liberty.

When France in wrath her giant-limbs upreared,
And with that oath, which smote air, earth, and sea,
Stamped her strong foot and said she would be free,
Bear witness for me, how I hoped and feared!
With what a joy my lofty gratulation
Unawed I sang, amid a slavish band:
And when to whelm the disenchanted nation,
Like fiends embattled by a wizard's wand,
The Monarchs marched in evil day,
And Britain joined the dire array;
Though dear her shores and circling ocean,
Though many friendships, many youthful loves
Had swoln the patriot emotion
And flung a magic light o'er all her hills and groves;
Yet still my voice, unaltered, sang defeat
To all that braved the tyrant-quelling lance,
And shame too long delayed and vain retreat!
For ne'er, O Liberty! with partial aim
I dimmed thy light or damped thy holy flame;
But blessed the paeans of delivered France,
And hung my head and wept at Britain's name.

"And what," I said, "though Blasphemy's loud scream
With that sweet music of deliverance strove!
Though all the fierce and drunken passions wove
A dance more wild than e'er was maniac's dream!
Ye storms, that round the dawning east assembled,
The Sun was rising, though ye hid his light!"
And when, to soothe my soul, that hoped and trembled,
The dissonance ceased, and all seemed calm and bright;
When France her front deep-scarred and gory
Concealed with clustering wreaths of glory;
When, insupportably advancing,
Her arm made mockery of the warrior's ramp;
While timid looks of fury glancing,
Domestic treason, crushed beneath her fatal stamp,
Writhed like a wounded dragon in his gore;
Then I reproached my fears that would not flee;
"And soon," I said, "shall Wisdom teach her lore
In the low huts of them that toil and groan!
And, conquering by her happiness alone,
Shall France compel the nations to be free,
Till Love and Joy look round, and call the Earth their own."

Forgive me, Freedom! O forgive those dreams!
I hear thy voice, I hear thy loud lament,
From bleak Helvetia's icy caverns sent—
I hear thy groans upon her blood-stained streams!
Heroes, that for your peaceful country perished,
And ye that, fleeing, spot your mountain-snows
With bleeding wounds; forgive me, that I cherished
One thought that ever blessed your cruel foes!
To scatter rage, and traitorous guilt,
Where Peace her jealous home had built;
A patriot-race to disinherit
Of all that made their stormy wilds so dear;
And with inexpiable spirit
To taint the bloodless freedom of the mountaineer—
O France, that mockest Heaven, adulterous, blind,
And patriot only in pernicious toils!
Are these thy boasts, Champion of human kind?
To mix with Kings in the low lust of sway,
Yell in the hunt, and share the murderous prey;
To insult the shrine of Liberty with spoils
From freemen torn; to tempt and to betray?

The Sensual and the Dark rebel in vain,
Slaves by their own compulsion! In mad game
They burst their manacles and wear the name
Of Freedom, graven on a heavier chain!
O Liberty! with profitless endeavour

43. Blasphemy's loud scream. In November, 1793, the "Goddess of Reason" had been enthroned in Notre Dame Cathedral in Paris.

54. ramp, threatening posture.

Have I pursued thee, many a weary hour;
But thou nor swell'st the victor's strain, nor ever
Didst breathe thy soul in forms of human power.
Alike from all, howe'er they praise thee,
(Nor prayer, nor boastful name delays thee)
Alike from Priestcraft's harpy minions,
And factious Blasphemy's obscener slaves,
Thou speedest on thy subtle pinions,
The guide of homeless winds, and play-mate of the waves!
And there I felt thee!—on that sea-cliff's verge,
Whose pines, scarce travelled by the breeze above,
Had made one murmur with the distant surge!
Yes, while I stood and gazed, my temples bare,
And shot my being through earth, sea, and air,
Possessing all things with intensest love,
O Liberty! my spirit felt thee there.

DEJECTION: AN ODE

See what is said about the critical importance of this poem in the biographical-critical sketch of Coleridge. The poem was originally addressed to Sarah Hutchinson (see "Love"), then to Wordsworth, finally to "Lady." Wordsworth's "Resolution and Independence" and "Ode: Intimations of Immortality" are in part answers to "Dejection." They treat the same problem: What can the poet do when feeling loses its vividness (and imagination consequently fades)?

Late, late yestreen I saw the new Moon,
With the old Moon in her arms;
And I fear, I fear, my Master dear!
We shall have a deadly storm.
—*Ballad of Sir Patrick Spence*

1

Well! If the Bard was weather-wise, who made
The grand old ballad of Sir Patrick Spence,
This night, so tranquil now, will not go hence
Unroused by winds, that ply a busier trade
Than those which mould yon cloud in lazy flakes,
Or the dull sobbing draft, that moans and rakes
Upon the strings of this Aeolian lute,
Which better far were mute.
For lo! the New-moon winter-bright!
And overspread with phantom light,
(With swimming phantom light o'erspread
But rimmed and circled by a silver thread)
I see the old Moon in her lap, foretelling
The coming-on of rain and squally blast.
And oh! that even now the gust were swelling,
And the slant night-shower driving loud and fast!
Those sounds which oft have raised me, whilst they awed,
And sent my soul abroad,
Might now perhaps their wonted impulse give,
Might startle this dull pain, and make it move and live!

2

A grief without a pang, void, dark, and drear,
A stifled, drowsy, unimpassioned grief,
Which finds no natural outlet, no relief,
In word, or sigh, or tear—
O Lady! in this wan and heartless mood,
To other thoughts by yonder throstle wooed,
All this long eve, so balmy and serene,
Have I been gazing on the western sky,
And its peculiar tint of yellow green:
And still I gaze—and with how blank an eye!
And those thin clouds above, in flakes and bars,
That give away their motion to the stars;
Those stars, that glide behind them or between,
Now sparkling, now bedimmed, but always seen:
Yon crescent Moon, as fixed as if it grew
In its own cloudless, starless lake of blue;
I see them all so excellently fair,
I see, not feel, how beautiful they are!

3

My genial spirits fail;
And what can these avail
To lift the smothering weight from off my breast?
It were a vain endeavour,
Though I should gaze for ever
On that green light that lingers in the west:
I may not hope from outward forms to win
The passion and the life, whose fountains are within.

4

O Lady! we receive but what we give,
And in our life alone does Nature live:
Ours is her wedding garment, ours her shroud!
And would we aught behold, of higher worth,
Than that inanimate cold world allowed
To the poor loveless ever-anxious crowd,
Ah! from the soul itself must issue forth
A light, a glory, a fair luminous cloud
Enveloping the Earth—
And from the soul itself must there be sent
A sweet and potent voice, of its own birth,
Of all sweet sounds the life and element!

7. Aeolian, from Aeolus, god of the winds. An aeolian lute is a stringed instrument producing sounds when exposed to the wind.

39. genial spirits. Compare Wordsworth's phrase, "genial sense of youth," in the "Ode to Duty," written nearly three years later.

5

O pure of heart! thou need'st not ask of me
What this strong music in the soul may be!
What, and wherein it doth exist,
This light, this glory, this fair luminous mist,
This beautiful and beauty-making power.
Joy, virtuous Lady! Joy that ne'er was given,
Save to the pure, and in their purest hour,
Life, and Life's effluence, cloud at once and shower,
Joy, Lady! is the spirit and the power,
Which wedding Nature to us gives in dower
A new Earth and new Heaven,
Undreamt of by the sensual and the proud—
Joy is the sweet voice, Joy the luminous cloud—
We in ourselves rejoice!
And thence flows all that charms or ear or sight,
All melodies the echoes of that voice,
All colours a suffusion from that light.

6

There was a time when, though my path was rough,
This joy within me dallied with distress,
And all misfortunes were but as the stuff
Whence Fancy made me dreams of happiness:
For hope grew round me, like the twining vine,
And fruits, and foliage, not my own, seemed mine.
But now afflictions bow me down to earth:
Nor care I that they rob me of my mirth;
But oh! each visitation
Suspends what nature gave me at my birth,
My shaping spirit of Imagination.
For not to think of what I needs must feel,
But to be still and patient, all I can;
And haply by abstruse research to steal
From my own nature all the natural man—
This was my sole resource, my only plan:
Till that which suits a part infects the whole,
And now is almost grown the habit of my soul.

7

Hence, viper thoughts, that coil around my mind,
Reality's dark dream!
I turn from you, and listen to the wind,
Which long has raved unnoticed. What a scream
Of agony by torture lengthened out
That lute sent forth! Thou Wind, that rav'st without,
Bare crag, or mountain-tairn, or blasted tree,
Or pine-grove whither woodman never clomb,
Or lonely house, long held the witches' home,
Methinks were fitter instruments for thee,
Mad Lutanist! who in this month of showers,
Of dark-brown gardens, and of peeping flowers,
Mak'st Devils' yule, with worse than wintry song,
The blossoms, buds, and timorous leaves among.
Thou Actor, perfect in all tragic sounds!
Thou mighty Poet, e'en to frenzy bold!
What tell'st thou now about?
'Tis of the rushing of an host in rout,
With groans, of trampled men, with smarting wounds—
At once they groan with pain, and shudder with the cold!
But hush! there is a pause of deepest silence!
And all that noise, as of a rushing crowd,
With groans, and tremulous shudderings—all is over—
It tells another tale, with sounds less deep and loud!
A tale of less affright,
And tempered with delight,
As Otway's self had framed the tender lay,—
'Tis of a little child
Upon a lonesome wild,
Not far from home, but she hath lost her way:
And now moans low in bitter grief and fear,
And now screams loud, and hopes to make her mother hear.

8

'Tis midnight, but small thoughts have I of sleep:
Full seldom may my friend such vigils keep!
Visit her, gentle Sleep! with wings of healing,
And may this storm be but a mountain-birth,
May all the stars hang bright above her dwelling,
Silent as though they watched the sleeping Earth!
With light heart may she rise,
Gay fancy, cheerful eyes,
Joy lift her spirit, joy attune her voice;
To her may all things live, from pole to pole,
Their life the eddying of her living soul!
O simple spirit, guided from above,
Dear Lady! friend devoutest of my choice,
Thus mayest thou ever, evermore rejoice.

EPITAPH

Stop, Christian passer-by!—Stop, child of God,
And read with gentle breast. Beneath this sod
A poet lies, or that which once seemed he.
O, lift one thought in prayer for S. T. C.;
That he who many a year with toil of breath
Found death in life, may here find life in death!

120. Otway's self. Thomas Otway was a seventeenth-century dramatist. The allusion is to his tragedy *The Orphan*.
121. 'Tis of a little child. Compare Wordsworth's "Lucy Gray."

Mercy for praise—to be forgiven for fame
He asked, and hoped, through Christ. Do thou the
same!

from BIOGRAPHIA LITERARIA

Several times Coleridge indicated that the original critical ideas in the Preface to *Lyrical Ballads*, 1800, were indistinguishably his own and Wordsworth's. When, in 1815–16, he wrote his *Biographia Literaria*, however, separation from Wordsworth and imperfectly reconciled estrangement between the two gave him a detached point of view toward the "Preface." His object, in the following selections from *Biographia Literaria*, is to explain points of agreement and difference. But first he must explain, as fundamental to his critical ideas, what a poem is and what a poet is. In the paragraph on "The poet, described in ideal perfection" (Chapter 14) is to be found the heart of his critical theory. In Chapter 17 he agrees with Wordsworth in the latter's attack on "poetic diction" (meaning stereotyped "figures and metaphors" from the older poetry that had become well-worn coins of poetic currency), but disagrees with Wordsworth's theory "that the proper diction for poetry in general consists altogether in a language taken, with due exceptions, from the mouths of men in real life." This basic disagreement also involves disagreement with Wordsworth's choice of low and rustic life for his subjects—Wordsworth's own best poems are inconsistent with his theory—and his reasons therefor. Following Chapter 17, Coleridge adversely criticizes Wordsworth's assertion that "there neither is, nor can be, any *essential difference*" between the language of prose and metrical composition. These chapters from *Biographia Literaria* and the "Preface" to which they refer are among the noblest expositions in our language of the nature, the purpose, and the stuff of poetry, and of the spirit and method of true literary criticism.

CHAPTER 14 (*continued*)*

. . . Preface to the second edition [of *Lyrical Ballads*]—The ensuing controversy, its causes and acrimony—Philosophic definitions of a Poem and Poetry with scholia. . . .

TO the second edition he [Wordsworth] added a preface of considerable length; in which, notwithstanding some passages of apparently a contrary import, he was understood to contend for the extension of this style to poetry of all kinds, and to reject as vicious and indefensible all phrases and forms of speech that were not included in what he (unfortunately, I think, adopting an equivocal expression) called the language of real life. From this preface, prefixed to poems in which it was impossible to deny the presence of original genius, however mistaken its direction might be deemed, arose the whole long-continued controversy. For from the conjunction of perceived power with supposed heresy I explain the inveteracy and in some instances, I grieve to say, the acrimonious passions, with which the controversy has been conducted by the assailants.

Had Mr. Wordsworth's poems been the silly, the childish things, which they were for a long time described as being: had they been really distinguished from the compositions of other poets merely by meanness of language and inanity of thought; had they indeed contained nothing more than what is found in the parodies and pretended imitations of them; they must have sunk at once, a dead weight, into the slough of oblivion, and have dragged the preface along with them. But year after year increased the number of Mr. Wordsworth's admirers. They were found too not in the lower classes of the reading public, but chiefly among young men of strong sensibility and meditative minds; and their admiration (inflamed perhaps in some degree by opposition) was distinguished by its intensity, I might almost say, by its religious fervour. These facts, and the intellectual energy of the author, which was more or less consciously felt, where it was outwardly and even boisterously denied, meeting with sentiments of aversion to his opinions, and of alarm at their consequences, produced an eddy of criticism, which would of itself have borne up the poems by the violence with which it whirled them round and round. With many parts of this preface in the sense attributed to them and which the words undoubtedly seem to authorize, I never concurred; but on the contrary objected to them as erroneous in principle, and as contradictory (in appearance at least) both to other parts of the same preface, and to the author's own practice in the greater part of the poems themselves. Mr. Wordsworth in his recent collection has, I find, degraded this prefatory disquisition to the end of his second volume, to be read or not at the reader's choice. But he has not, as far as I can discover, announced any change in his poetic creed. At all events, considering it as the source of a controversy, in which I have been honoured more than I deserve by the frequent conjunction of my name with his, I think it expedient to declare once for all, in what points I coincide with the opinions supported in that preface, and in what points I altogether differ. But in order to render myself intelligible I must previously, in as

* Continued from page 733, where the beginning was printed before Coleridge's "Renascence of Wonder" poems as a statement of his aim in writing them.

few words as possible, explain my views, first, of a Poem; and secondly, of Poetry itself, in kind, and in essence.

The office of philosophical disquisition consists in just distinction; while it is the privilege of the philosopher to preserve himself constantly aware, that distinction is not division. In order to obtain adequate notions of any truth, we must intellectually separate its distinguishable parts; and this is the technical process of philosophy. But having so done, we must then restore them in our conceptions to the unity, in which they actually co-exist; and this is the result of philosophy. A poem contains the same elements as a prose composition; the difference therefore must consist in a different combination of them, in consequence of a different object being proposed. According to the difference of the object will be the difference of the combination. It is possible, that the object may be merely to facilitate the recollection of any given facts or observations by artificial arrangement; and the composition will be a poem, merely because it is distinguished from prose by metre, or by rhyme, or by both conjointly. In this, the lowest sense, a man might attribute the name of a poem to the well-known enumeration of the days in the several months:

> "Thirty days hath September,
> April, June, and November," &c.

and others of the same class and purpose. And as a particular pleasure is found in anticipating the recurrence of sounds and quantities, all compositions that have this charm superadded, whatever be their contents, *may* be entitled poems.

So much for the superficial form. A difference of object and contents supplies an additional ground of distinction. The immediate purpose may be the communication of truths; either of truth absolute and demonstrable, as in works of science; or of facts experienced and recorded, as in history. Pleasure, and that of the highest and most permanent kind, may result from the attainment of the end; but it is not itself the immediate end. In other works the communication of pleasure may be the immediate purpose; and though truth, either moral or intellectual, ought to be the ultimate end, yet this will distinguish the character of the author, not the class to which the work belongs. Blest indeed is that state of society, in which the immediate purpose would be baffled by the perversion of the proper ultimate end; in which no charm of diction or imagery could exempt the BATHYLLUS even of an Anacreon, or the ALEXIS of Virgil, from disgust and aversion!

But the communication of pleasure may be the immediate object of a work not metrically composed; and that object may have been in a high degree attained, as in novels and romances. Would then the mere superaddition of metre, with or without rhyme, entitle these to the name of poems? The answer is, that nothing can permanently please, which does not contain in itself the reason why it is so, and not otherwise. If metre be superadded, all other parts must be made consonant with it. They must be such, as to justify the perpetual and distinct attention to each part, which an exact correspondent recurrence of accent and sound are calculated to excite. The final definition then, so deduced, may be thus worded. A poem is that species of composition, which is opposed to works of science, by proposing for its *immediate* object pleasure, not truth; and from all other species—(having *this* object in common with it)—it is discriminated by proposing to itself such delight from the *whole*, as is compatible with a distinct gratification from each component *part*.

Controversy is not seldom excited in consequence of the disputants attaching each a different meaning to the same word; and in few instances has this been more striking, than in disputes concerning the present subject. If a man chooses to call every composition a poem, which is rhyme, or measure, or both, I must leave his opinion uncontroverted. The distinction is at least competent to characterize the writer's intention. If it were subjoined, that the whole is likewise entertaining or affecting, as a tale, or as a series of interesting reflections, I of course admit this as another fit ingredient of a poem, and an additional merit. But if the definition sought for be that of a *legitimate* poem, I answer, it must be one, the parts of which mutually support and explain each other; all in their proportion harmonizing with, and supporting the purpose and known influences of metrical arrangement. The philosophic critics of all ages coincide with the ultimate judgment of all countries, in equally denying the praises of a just poem, on the one hand, to a series of striking lines or distiches, each of which, absorbing the whole attention of the reader to itself, becomes disjoined from its context, and forms a separate whole, instead of a harmonizing part; and on the other hand, to an unsustained composition, from which the reader collects rapidly the general result unattracted by the component parts. The reader should be carried forward, not merely or chiefly by the mechanical impulse of curiosity, or by a restless desire to arrive at the final solution; but by the pleasurable activity of mind excited by the attractions of the journey itself. Like the motion of a serpent, which the Egyptians made the emblem of intellectual power; or like the path of sound through the air;—at every step he pauses and half recedes, and from the retrogressive movement collects the force which again carries him onward. *Praecipitandus est liber spiritus*, says Petronius most happily. The epithet, *liber*, here balances the preceding verb; and it is not easy to conceive more meaning condensed in fewer words.

But if this should be admitted as a satisfactory character of a poem, we have still to seek for a definition of poetry. The writings of Plato, and Jeremy Taylor, and Burnet's Theory of the Earth, furnish undeniable proofs that poetry of the highest kind may exist without metre, and even without the contradistinguishing objects of a poem. The first chapter of Isaiah—(indeed a very large portion of the whole book)—is poetry in the most emphatic sense; yet it would be not less irrational than strange to assert, that pleasure, and not truth was the immediate object of the prophet. In short, whatever specific import we attach to the word, Poetry, there will be found involved in it, as a necessary consequence, that a poem of any length neither can be, nor ought to be, all poetry. Yet if an harmonious whole is to be produced, the remaining parts must be preserved in keeping with the poetry; and this can be no otherwise effected than by such a studied selection and artificial arrangement, as will partake of one, though not a peculiar property of poetry. And this again can be no other than the property of exciting a more continuous and equal attention than the language of prose aims at, whether colloquial or written.

My own conclusions on the nature of poetry, in the strictest use of the word, have been in part anticipated in some of the remarks on the Fancy and Imagination in the early part of this work. What is poetry?—is so nearly the same question with, what is a poet?—that the answer to the one is involved in the solution of the other. For it is a distinction resulting from the poetic genius itself, which sustains and modifies the images, thoughts, and emotions of the poet's own mind.

The poet, described in ideal perfection, brings the whole soul of man into activity, with the subordination of its faculties to each other according to their relative worth and dignity. He diffuses a tone and spirit of unity, that blends, and (as it were) *fuses*, each into each, by that synthetic and magical power, to which I would exclusively appropriate the name of Imagination. This power, first put in action by the will and understanding, and retained under their irremissive, though gentle and unnoticed, control, *laxis effertur habenis*, reveals itself in the balance or reconcilement of opposite or discordant qualities: of sameness, with difference; of the general with the concrete; the idea with the image; the individual with the representative; the sense of novelty and freshness with old and familiar objects; a more than usual state of emotion with more than usual order; judgment ever awake and steady self-possession with enthusiasm and feeling profound or vehement; and while it blends and harmonizes the natural and the artificial, still subordinates art to nature; the manner to the matter; and our admiration of the poet to our sympathy with the poetry. Doubtless, as Sir John Davies observes of the soul—(and his words may with slight alteration be applied, and even more appropriately, to the poetic Imagination)—

"Doubtless this could not be, but that she turns
  Bodies to *spirit* by sublimation strange,
As fire converts to fire the things it burns,
  As we our food into our nature change.

"From their gross matter she abstracts *their* forms,
  And draws a kind of quintessence from things;
Which to her proper nature she transforms
  To bear them light on her celestial wings.

"*Thus* does she, when from *individual states*
  She doth abstract the universal kinds;
Which then re-clothed in divers names and fates
  Steal access through the senses to our minds."

Finally, Good Sense is the Body of poetic genius, Fancy its Drapery, Motion its Life, and Imagination the Soul that is everywhere, and in each; and forms all into one graceful and intelligent whole.

5–6. Praecipitandus . . . spiritus. "The free spirit must be impelled forward." **45–46. The poet, described in ideal perfection . . . whole.** The paragraph contains the following ideas basic to Coleridge's theory of criticism: 1. The Aristotelian principle that "literature should give us a vision of life, not as it appeared to the understanding, but as it was revealed to reason." 2. The distinction between Fancy and Imagination, Understanding and Reason: (a) Fancy collects and combines particulars—corresponds to Understanding; (b) Imagination discovers the general and permanent—corresponds to Reason. 3. Imagination reveals itself in the balance or reconciliation of opposite or discordant qualities. 4. "Imagination, so far from rejecting the actual, keeps in contact with it, but dissevers from its representation the accidental, the temporary, the contingent, and irregular, retaining only what disclosed its permanent nature and its essential relations to the universe." (See Ernest Bernbaum's *Guide through the Romantic Movement*, Thomas Nelson, 1933, pp. 104–05.) **9. laxis . . . habenis,** "carried along with loose reins."

CHAPTER 17

Examination of the tenets peculiar to Mr. Wordsworth—Rustic life (above all, low and rustic life) especially unfavourable to the formation of a human diction—The best parts of language the product of philosophers, not of clowns or shepherds—Poetry essentially ideal and generic—The language of Milton as much the language of real life, yea, incomparably more so than that of the cottager.

As far then as Mr. Wordsworth in his preface contended, and most ably contended, for a reformation in our poetic diction, as far as he has evinced the truth of passion, and the dramatic propriety of those figures and metaphors in the original poets, which, stripped of their justifying reasons, and converted into mere artifices of connection or ornament, constitute the characteristic falsity in the poetic style of the moderns; and as far as he has, with equal acuteness and clearness, pointed out the process by which this change was effected, and the resemblances between that state into which the reader's mind is thrown by the pleasurable confusion of thought from an unaccustomed train of words and images; and that state which is induced by the natural language of impassioned feeling; he undertook a useful task, and deserves all praise, both for the attempt and for the execution. The provocations to this remonstrance in behalf of truth and nature were still of perpetual recurrence before and after the publication of this preface. I cannot likewise but add, that the comparison of such poems of merit, as have been given to the public within the last ten or twelve years, with the majority of those produced previously to the appearance of that preface, leave[s] no doubt on my mind, that Mr. Wordsworth is fully justified in believing his efforts to have been by no means ineffectual. Not only in the verses of those who have professed their admiration of his genius, but even of those who have distinguished themselves by hostility to his theory, and depreciation of his writings, are the impressions of his principles plainly visible. It is possible, that with these principles others may have been blended, which are not equally evident; and some which are unsteady and subvertible from the narrowness or imperfection of their basis. But it is more than possible, that these errors of defect or exaggeration, by kindling and feeding the controversy, may have conduced not only to the wider propagation of the accompanying truths, but that, by their frequent presentation to the mind in an excited state, they may have won for them a more permanent and practical result. A man will borrow a part from his opponent the more easily, if he feels himself justified in continuing to reject a part. While there remain important points in which he can still feel himself in the right, in which he still finds firm footing for continued resistance, he will gradually adopt those opinions, which were the least remote from his own convictions, as not less congruous with his own theory than with that which he reprobates. In like manner with a kind of instinctive prudence, he will abandon by little and little his weakest posts, till at length he seems to forget that they had ever belonged to him, or affects to consider them at most as accidental and "petty annexments," the removal of which leaves the citadel unhurt and unendangered.

My own differences from certain supposed parts of Mr. Wordsworth's theory ground themselves on the assumption, that his words had been rightly interpreted, as purporting that the proper diction for poetry in general consists altogether in a language taken, with due exceptions, from the mouths of men in real life, a language which actually constitutes the natural conversation of men under the influence of natural feelings. My objection is, first, that in any sense this rule is applicable only to certain classes of poetry; secondly, that even to these classes it is not applicable, except in such a sense, as hath never by any one (as far as I know or have read,) been denied or doubted; and lastly, that as far as, and in that degree in which, it is practicable, it is yet as a rule useless, if not injurious, and therefore either need not, or ought not to be practised. The poet informs his reader, that he had generally chosen low and rustic life; but not as low and rustic, or in order to repeat that pleasure of doubtful moral effect, which persons of elevated rank and of superior refinement oftentimes derive from a happy imitation of the rude unpolished manners and discourse of their inferiors. For the pleasure so derived may be traced to three exciting causes. The first is the naturalness, in fact, of the things represented. The second is the apparent naturalness of the representation, as raised and qualified by an imperceptible infusion of the author's own knowledge and talent, which infusion does, indeed, constitute it an imitation as distinguished from a mere copy. The third cause may be found in the reader's conscious feeling of his superiority awakened by the contrast presented to him; even as for the same purpose the kings and great barons of yore retained, sometimes actual clowns

11. Mr. Wordsworth ff. Here, according to J. H. Shawcross, editor of *Biographia Literaria,* Coleridge is "indicating Wordsworth's true position; but he has not made it the basis of his criticism."

and fools, but more frequently shrewd and witty fellows in that character. These, however, were not Mr. Wordsworth's objects. *He* chose low and rustic life, "because in that condition the essential passions of the heart find a better soil, in which they can attain their maturity, are less under restraint, and speak a plainer and more emphatic language; because in that condition of life our elementary feelings co-exist in a state of greater simplicity, and consequently may be more accurately contemplated, and more forcibly communicated; because the manners of rural life germinate from those elementary feelings; and from the necessary character of rural occupations are more easily comprehended, and are more durable; and lastly, because in that condition the passions of men are incorporated with the beautiful and permanent forms of nature."

Now it is clear to me, that in the most interesting of the poems, in which the author is more or less dramatic, as THE BROTHERS, MICHAEL, RUTH, THE MAD MOTHER, and others, the persons introduced are by no means taken from low or rustic life in the common acceptation of those words! and it is not less clear, that the sentiments and language, as far as they can be conceived to have been really transferred from the minds and conversation of such persons, are attributable to causes and circumstances not necessarily connected with "their occupations and abode." The thoughts, feelings, language, and manners of the shepherd-farmers in the vales of Cumberland and Westmoreland, as far as they are actually adopted in those poems, may be accounted for from causes, which will and do produce the same results in every state of life, whether in town or country. As the two principal I rank that independence, which raises a man above servitude, or daily toil for the profit of others, yet not above the necessity of industry and a frugal simplicity of domestic life; and the accompanying unambitious, but solid and religious, education, which has rendered few books familiar, but the Bible, and the Liturgy or Hymn book. To this latter cause, indeed, which is so far accidental, that it is the blessing of particular countries and a particular age, not the product of particular places or employments, the poet owes the show of probability, that his personages might really feel, think, and talk with any tolerable resemblance to his representation. It is an excellent remark of Dr. Henry More's, that "a man of confined education, but of good parts, by constant reading of the Bible will naturally form a more winning and commanding rhetoric than those that are learned: the intermixture of tongues and of artificial phrases debasing *their* style.'

It is, moreover, to be considered that to the formation of healthy feelings, and a reflecting mind, negations involve impediments not less formidable than sophistication and vicious intermixture. I am convinced, that for the human soul to prosper in rustic life a certain vantage-ground is prerequisite. It is not every man that is likely to be improved by a country life or by country labours. Education, or original sensibility, or both, must pre-exist, if the changes, forms, and incidents of nature are to prove a sufficient stimulant. And where these are not sufficient, the mind contracts and hardens by want of stimulants: and the man becomes selfish, sensual, gross, and hard-hearted. Let the management of the Poor Laws in Liverpool, Manchester, or Bristol be compared with the ordinary dispensation of the poor rates in agricultural villages, where the farmers are the overseers and guardians of the poor. If my own experience have not been particularly unfortunate, as well as that of the many respectable country clergymen with whom I have conversed on the subject, the result would engender more than scepticism concerning the desirable influences of low and rustic life in and for itself. Whatever may be concluded on the other side, from the stronger local attachments and enterprising spirit of the Swiss, and other mountaineers, applies to a particular mode of pastoral life, under forms of property that permit and beget manners truly republican, not to rustic life in general, or to the absence of artificial cultivation. On the contrary the mountaineers, whose manners have been so often eulogized, are in general better educated and greater readers than men of equal rank elsewhere. But where this is not the case, as among the peasantry of North Wales, the ancient mountains, with all their terrors and all their glories, are pictures to the blind, and music to the deaf.

I should not have entered so much into detail upon this passage, but here seems to be the point, to which all the lines of difference converge as to their source and centre;—I mean, as far as, and in whatever respect, my poetic creed *does* differ from the doctrines promulgated in this preface. I adopt with full faith the principle of Aristotle, that poetry, as poetry, is essentially ideal, that it avoids and excludes all accident; that its apparent individualities of rank, character, or occupation must be representative of a class; and that the persons of poetry must be clothed with generic attributes, with the common attributes of the class: not with such as one gifted individual might possibly possess, but such as from his situation it is most probable before-hand that he would possess. If my premises are right and my deductions legitimate, it follows that there can be no poetic medium between the swains of Theocritus and those of an imaginary golden age.

The characters of the vicar and the shepherd-mariner in the poem of THE BROTHERS, and that of the shepherd of Green-head Ghyll in the MICHAEL, have all the verisimilitude and representative quality, that the purposes of poetry can require. They are persons of a known and abiding class, and their manners and sentiments the natural product of circumstances common to the class. Take Michael for instance:

"An old man stout of heart, and strong of limb.
His bodily frame had been from youth to age
Of an unusual strength: his mind was keen,
Intense, and frugal, apt for all affairs,
And in his shepherd's calling he was prompt
And watchful more than ordinary men.
Hence he had learned the meaning of all winds,
Of blasts of every tone; and oftentimes
When others heeded not, He heard the South
Make subterraneous music, like the noise
Of bagpipers on distant Highland hills.
The Shepherd, at such warning, of his flock
Bethought him, and he to himself would say,
'The winds are now devising work for me!'
And truly, at all times, the storm, that drives
The traveller to a shelter, summoned him
Up to the mountains: he had been alone
Amid the heart of many thousand mists,
That came to him and left him on the heights.
So lived he, until his eightieth year was past.
And grossly that man errs, who should suppose
That the green valleys, and the streams and rocks,
Were things indifferent to the Shepherd's thoughts.
Fields, where with cheerful spirits he had breathed
The common air; the hills which he so oft
Had climbed with vigorous steps; which had impressed
So many incidents upon his mind
Of hardship, skill or courage, joy or fear;
Which, like a book, preserved the memory
Of the dumb animals, whom he had saved,
Had fed or sheltered, linking to such acts,
So grateful in themselves, the certainty
Of honourable gain; these fields, these hills
Which were his living Being, even more
Than his own blood—what could they less? had laid
Strong hold on his affections, were to him
A pleasurable feeling of blind love,
The pleasure which there is in life itself."

On the other hand, in the poems which are pitched in a lower key, as the HARRY GILL, and THE IDIOT BOY, the feelings are those of human nature in general; though the poet has judiciously laid the scene in the country, in order to place himself in the vicinity of interesting images, without the necessity of ascribing a sentimental perception of their beauty to the persons of his drama. In THE IDIOT BOY, indeed, the mother's character is not so much the real and native product of a "situation where the essential passions of the heart find a better soil, in which they can attain their maturity and speak a plainer and more emphatic language," as it is an impersonation of an instinct abandoned by judgment. Hence the two following charges seem to me not wholly groundless: at least, they are the only plausible objections, which I have heard to that fine poem. The one is, that the author has not, in the poem itself, taken sufficient care to preclude from the reader's fancy the disgusting images of ordinary morbid idiocy, which yet it was by no means his intention to represent. He has even by the "burr, burr, burr," uncounteracted by any preceding description of the boy's beauty, assisted in recalling them. The other is, that the idiocy of the boy is so evenly balanced by the folly of the mother, as to present to the general reader rather a laughable burlesque on the blindness of anile dotage, than an analytic display of maternal affection in its ordinary workings.

In THE THORN, the poet himself acknowledges in a note the necessity of an introductory poem, in which he should have portrayed the character of the person from whom the words of the poem are supposed to proceed: a superstitious man moderately imaginative, of slow faculties and deep feelings, "a captain of a small trading vessel, for example, who, being past the middle age of life, had retired upon an annuity, or small independent income, to some village or country town of which he was not a native, or in which he had not been accustomed to live. Such men having nothing to do become credulous and talkative from indolence." But in a poem, still more in a lyric poem—and the Nurse in ROMEO AND JULIET alone prevents me from extending the remark even to dramatic poetry, if indeed even the Nurse can be deemed altogether a case in point—it is not possible to imitate truly a dull and garrulous discourser, without repeating the effects of dullness and garrulity. However this may be, I dare assert, that the parts—(and these form the far larger portion of the whole)—which might as well or still better have proceeded from the poet's own imagination, and have been spoken in his own character, are those which have given, and which will continue to give, universal delight; and that the passages exclusively appropriate to the supposed narrator, such as the last couplet of the third stanza; the seven last lines of the tenth; and the five following stanzas, with the exception of the four admirable lines at the commencement of the fourteenth, are felt by many unprejudiced and unsophisticated hearts, as sudden and unpleasant sinkings from the height to which the poet had previously lifted them, and to which he again re-elevates both himself and his reader.

If then I am compelled to doubt the theory, by which the choice of characters was to be directed, not only *a priori*, from grounds of reason, but both from the few instances in which the poet himself need be supposed to have been governed by it, and from the comparative inferiority of those instances; still more must I hesitate in my assent to the sentence which immediately follows the former citation; and which I can neither admit as particular fact, nor as general rule. "The language, too, of these men has been adopted (purified indeed from what appear to be its real defects, from all lasting and rational causes of dislike or disgust) because such men hourly communicate with the best objects from which the best part of language is originally derived; and because, from their rank in society and the sameness and narrow circle of their intercourse, being less under the action of social vanity, they convey their feelings and notions in simple and unelaborated expressions." To this I reply; that a rustic's language, purified from all provincialism and grossness, and so far reconstructed as to be made consistent with the rules of grammar—(which are in essence no other than the laws of universal logic, applied to psychological materials)—will not differ from the language of any other man of common sense, however learned or refined he may be, except as far as the notions, which the rustic has to convey, are fewer and more indiscriminate. This will become still clearer, if we add the consideration—(equally important though less obvious)—that the rustic, from the more imperfect development of his faculties, and from the lower state of their cultivation, aims almost solely to convey insulated facts, either those of his scanty experience or his traditional belief; while the educated man chiefly seeks to discover and express those connections of things, or those relative bearings of fact to fact, from which some more or less general law is deducible. For facts are valuable to a wise man, chiefly as they lead to the discovery of the indwelling law, which is the true being of things, the sole solution of their modes of existence, and in the knowledge of which consists our dignity and our power.

As little can I agree with the assertion, that from the objects with which the rustic hourly communicates the best part of language is formed. For first, if to communicate with an object implies such an acquaintance with it, as renders it capable of being discriminately reflected on, the distinct knowledge of an uneducated rustic would furnish a very scanty vocabulary. The few things and modes of action requisite for his bodily conveniences would alone be individualized; while all the rest of nature would be expressed by a small number of confused general terms. Secondly, I deny that the words and combinations of words derived from the objects, with which the rustic is familiar, whether with distinct or confused knowledge, can be justly said to form the best part of language. It is more than probable, that many classes of the brute creation possess discriminating sounds, by which they can convey to each other notices of such objects as concern their food, shelter, or safety. Yet we hesitate to call the aggregate of such sounds a language, otherwise than metaphorically. The best part of human language, properly so called, is derived from reflection on the acts of the mind itself. It is formed by a voluntary appropriation of fixed symbols to internal acts, to processes and results of imagination, the greater part of which have no place in the consciousness of uneducated man; though in civilized society, by imitation and passive remembrance of what they hear from their religious instructors and other superiors, the most uneducated share in the harvest which they neither sowed, nor reaped. If the history of the phrases in hourly currency among our peasants were traced, a person not previously aware of the fact would be surprised at finding so large a number, which three or four centuries ago were the exclusive property of the universities and the schools; and, at the commencement of the Reformation, had been transferred from the school to the pulpit, and thus gradually passed into common life. The extreme difficulty, and often the impossibility, of finding words for the simplest moral and intellectual processes in the languages of uncivilized tribes has proved perhaps the weightiest obstacle to the progress of our most zealous and adroit mission-

15. a priori, from principles or definitions assumed to be true. **22. "The language" ff.** Miss Marjorie Barstow, in *Wordsworth's Theory of Poetic Diction*, Yale University Press, 1917, thinks that Wordsworth and Coleridge use the word differently: To Coleridge "language" meant words considered in themselves, and especially in their syntactical relations; to Wordsworth, the whole imaginative expression of thought—in most cases, figures of speech.

aries. Yet these tribes are surrounded by the same nature as our peasants are; but in still more impressive forms; and they are, moreover, obliged to particularize many more of them. When, therefore, Mr. Wordsworth adds, "accordingly, such a language"—(meaning, as before, the language of rustic life purified from provincialism)—"arising out of repeated experience and regular feelings, is a more permanent, and a far more philosophical language, than that which is frequently substituted for it by Poets, who think that they are conferring honour upon themselves and their art in proportion as they indulge in arbitrary and capricious habits of expression"; it may be answered, that the language, which he has in view, can be attributed to rustics with no greater right, than the style of Hooker or Bacon to Tom Brown or Sir Roger L'Estrange. Doubtless, if what is peculiar to each were omitted in each, the result must needs be the same. Further, that the poet, who uses an illogical diction, or a style fitted to excite only the low and changeable pleasure of wonder by means of groundless novelty, substitutes a language of folly and vanity, not for that of the rustic, but for that of good sense and natural feeling.

Here let me be permitted to remind the reader, that the positions, which I controvert, are contained in the sentences—"a selection of the real language of men;"—"the language of these men" (that is, men in low and rustic life) "has been adopted; I have proposed to myself to imitate, and, as far as is possible, to adopt the very language of men."

"Between the language of prose and that of metrical composition, there neither is, nor can be, any *essential difference*": it is against these exclusively that my opposition is directed.

I object, in the very first instance, to an equivocation in the use of the word "real." Every man's language varies, according to the extent of his knowledge, the activity of his faculties, and the depth or quickness of his feelings. Every man's language has, first, its individualities; secondly, the common properties of the class to which he belongs; and thirdly, words and phrases of universal use. The language of Hooker, Bacon, Bishop Taylor, and Burke differs from the common language of the learned class only by the superior number and novelty of the thoughts and relations which they had to convey. The language of Algernon Sidney differs not at all from that, which every well-educated gentleman would wish to write, and (with due allowances for the undeliberateness, and less connected train, of thinking natural and proper to conversation) such as he would wish to talk. Neither one nor the other differs half as much from the general language of cultivated society, as the language of Mr. Wordsworth's homeliest composition differs from that of a common peasant. For "real" therefore, we must substitute ordinary, or *lingua communis*. And this, we have proved, is no more to be found in the phraseology of low and rustic life than in that of any other class. Omit the peculiarities of each and the result of course must be common to all. And assuredly the omissions and changes to be made in the language of rustics, before it could be transferred to any species of poem, except the drama or other professed imitation, are at least as numerous and weighty, as would be required in adapting to the same purpose the ordinary language of tradesmen and manufacturers. Not to mention, that the language so highly extolled by Mr. Wordsworth varies in every county, nay in every village, according to the accidental character of the clergyman, the existence or non-existence of schools; or even, perhaps, as the exciseman, publican, and barber happen to be, or not to be, zealous politicians, and readers of the weekly newspaper *pro bono publico*. Anterior to cultivation the *lingua communis* of every country, as Dante has well observed, exists every where in parts, and no where as a whole.

Neither is the case rendered at all more tenable by the addition of the words, "in a state of excitement." For the nature of a man's words, where he is strongly affected by joy, grief, or anger, must necessarily depend on the number and quality of the general truths, conceptions and images, and of the words expressing them, with which his mind had been previously stored. For the property of passion is not to create; but to set in increased activity. At least, whatever new connections of thoughts or images, or—(which is equally, if not more than equally, the appropriate effect of strong excitement)—whatever generalizations of truth or experience the heat of passion may produce; yet the terms of their conveyance must have pre-existed in his former conversations, and are only collected and crowded together by the unusual stimulation. It is indeed very possible to adopt in a poem the unmeaning repetitions, habitual phrases, and other blank counters, which an unfurnished or confused understanding interposes at short intervals, in order to keep hold of his subject, which is still slipping

22. pro bono publico, for the public good. **28–33. For the nature . . . previously stored.** "This is very true," comments Walter Raleigh in *Wordsworth*, Dutton, 1909, "and quite irrelevant. Wordsworth's allusion to the manner in which we associate words in a state of excitement was no part of his theory of diction. Men and women . . . were chosen . . . not as teachers of language but as unusually favorable subjects for the exhibition of the primary laws of our nature."

from him, and to give him time for recollection; or, in mere aid of vacancy, as in the scanty companies of a country stage the same player pops backwards and forwards, in order to prevent the appearance of empty spaces, in the procession of Macbeth, or Henry VIII. But what assistance to the poet, or ornament to the poem, these can supply, I am at a loss to conjecture. Nothing assuredly can differ either in origin or in mode more widely from the apparent tautologies of intense and turbulent feeling, in which the passion is greater and of longer endurance than to be exhausted or satisfied by a single representation of the image or incident exciting it. Such repetitions I admit to be a beauty of the highest kind; as illustrated by Mr. Wordsworth himself from the song of Deborah. *At her feet he bowed, he fell, he lay down: at her feet he bowed, he fell: where he bowed, there he fell down dead.* Judges v. 27.

Charles Lamb

1775–1834

In the quiet seclusion of the Temple, a medieval quarter of the old city of London used by lawyers for their clubs and offices, Charles Lamb was born on February 10, 1775. His father was clerk to a lawyer named Samuel Salt, and possessed considerable literary cultivation. His mother was Elizabeth Field, of Blakesmore, Hertfordshire. One of Lamb's most memorable childhood experiences was a visit to his grandmother in Hertfordshire (see "Mackery End"). Two of the other children of the family lived to maturity—John, twelve years Charles's senior, and Mary, ten years older. Charles was educated at the neighboring Christ's Hospital school, where he was a schoolmate of Coleridge (see "Christ's Hospital"). Unable because of an impediment in speech to win a university scholarship, he went to work as a bookkeeper, first in the South Sea House, where John had a place, and then in the India House. In the latter he remained thirty-three years. An early love affair with Ann Simmons, whom he had met in Hertfordshire, was frustrated by family disaster. In 1796 his sister Mary suddenly became insane and killed their mother. Mary regained her sanity and in mental health retained her social charm, but remained subject to recurrent derangement. The care of her became Charles's labor of love.

As boy and man he had cultivated his literary tastes, and he and Mary made their home a gathering-place for many of the distinguished literati and artists about town. They numbered among their friends Southey, Coleridge, Wordsworth, Hazlitt, Leigh Hunt, and Haydon. Charles's letters to these and others are among the best of a period of fine letter-writers, and contain much brilliant informal literary criticism (for example "Letter to Wordsworth"). "I am a dab at prose; poetry I leave to my betters." After brief but moving poetic efforts of his own (for example, "The Old Familiar Faces"), Lamb began his major critical work by collaborating with Mary on *Tales from Shakespere*, 1807, one of the landmarks of nineteenth-century popular Shakespearean appreciation. After this he edited *Specimens of the Dramatic Poets Who Lived about the Time of Shakespere*, 1808, drawing attention to the merits of dramatists like Heywood and Ford. In 1820, at the age of forty-five, he really found himself when he published in the *London Magazine* the first of his *Essays of Elia*. A few years later he was retired on a pension (see "The Superannuated Man"). He and Mary adopted an orphan girl, Emma Isola, who cheered their home until her marriage. More frequent recurrences of Mary's attacks darkened their last years together. Coleridge's death in July, 1834, shocked Lamb deeply. He followed on December 29, leaving behind him adequate provision for Mary.

Lamb was the prose poet of his native London, a stimulating and sympathetic friend of great writers of his age, an informal literary critic with swift and illuminating insight, but above all one of the greatest masters of the familiar essay. It is chiefly by his *Essays of Elia*, collected in 1833, that he lives and bids fair to live indefinitely. Like Wordsworth, he discovered that his greatest treasure was his memory of the past—of a past spent, however, not in country solitudes but in the teeming heart of a great city. Many of his best essays, such as "The South Sea House," "Christ's Hospital," and "Old China," are at the same time intimately autobiographical and descriptive of the old city that was passing away. "Old China" mentions most of his favorite themes—old books, old plays, old pictures, the theater, the society of Bridget (Mary). Most deeply personal, perhaps, are "Mackery End" and "Dream-Children," with their moods of faraway and long ago, their pathos of the past and the might-have-been. Character types whom Lamb knew are sketched in "Mrs. Battle's Opinions on Whist," "The South Sea House," and "Poor Relations." Lamb's criticism of everyday life and the art of living is well exemplified by "The Two Races of Men" and "Imperfect Sympathies." His best art and literary criticism outside his letters is found in such essays as "The Genius of Hogarth," "The Sanity of True Genius," and "On the Tragedies of Shakespere, Considered with Reference to Their Fitness for Stage Representation." The last-named is a witticism, like the more famous "Dissertation on Roast Pig." It was provoked by the epitaph on the actor David Garrick in Westminster Abbey:

SHAKESPEARE and GARRICK like twin stars shall shine
And earth irradiate with a beam divine.

Irritated by what he considered the impudence of this linking of names, Lamb maintained that Shakespeare's plays are more often than not spoiled by bad acting and, more seriously, that there is in them a flavor to be extracted only in quiet reading.

The charm of Lamb is a personal emanation from his writing. It is the result of a blend of humor and seriousness (never solemnity), willful whimsicality and sound sense, harmless malice (see "Imperfect Sympathies"), and tenderness, and a score more of the nuances of reconciled opposites, all conveyed by one of the most flexible and sensitive of prose styles. Of his writing, as Hazlitt said of his talk, it is true that "His jests scald like tears; and he probes a question with a play upon words." His charm exerts itself upon anyone who opens at leisure and reads an essay here and there in a volume or collection of Elia. And Lamb wears extraordinarily well. No literary source of pleasure will flow more satisfyingly from youth to old age. None can be less disappointing at any stage of the journey.

THE OLD FAMILIAR FACES

Where are they gone, the old familiar faces?

I had a mother, but she died, and left me,
Died prematurely in a day of horrors—
All, all are gone, the old familiar faces.

I have had playmates, I have had companions,
In my days of childhood, in my joyful school-days,
All, all are gone, the old familiar faces.

I have been laughing, I have been carousing,
Drinking late, sitting late, with my bosom cronies,
All, all are gone, the old familiar faces.

I loved a love once, fairest among women.
Closed are her doors on me, I must not see her—
All, all are gone, the old familiar faces.

I have a friend, a kinder friend has no man.
Like an ingrate, I left my friend abruptly;
Left him, to muse on the old familiar faces.

Ghost-like, I paced round the haunts of my childhood.
Earth seemed a desert I was bound to traverse,
Seeking to find the old familiar faces—

Friend of my bosom, thou more than a brother,
Why wert not thou born in my father's dwelling?
So might we talk of the old familiar faces—

For some they have died, and some they have left me,
And some are taken from me; all are departed;
All, all are gone, the old familiar faces.

3. Died prematurely, in 1796, slain by Mary in a fit of insanity. **6. school-days,** at Christ's Hospital. **11. fairest among women,** Ann Simmons, "Alice W." (see "Dream-Children"). **14. friend,** Charles Lloyd. **17. haunts,** the Temple and perhaps Mackery End. **20. Friend of my bosom,** Coleridge. **24. taken from me,** Mary, sent to an asylum.

LETTER TO WORDSWORTH

January 30, 1801

THANKS for your Letter and Present. I had already borrowed your second volume. What most please me are, the Song of Lucy. . . . *Simon's sickly daughter* in the Sexton made me *cry.* Next to these are the description of the continuous Echoes in the story of Joanna's laugh, where the mountains and all the scenery absolutely seem alive—and that fine Shakesperian character of the Happy Man, in the Brothers,

"—that creeps about the fields,
Following his fancies by the hour, to bring
Tears down his cheek, or solitary smiles
Into his face, *until the Setting Sun*
Write Fool upon his forehead."

I will mention one more: the delicate and curious feeling in the wish for the Cumberland Beggar, that he may have about him the melody of Birds, altho' he hear them not. Here the mind knowingly passes

2. second volume, *Lyrical Ballads,* 2nd ed., 1800. **3. Song of Lucy,** "Lucy Gray." **6. Joanna,** "To Joanna," in *Poems on the Naming of Places,* 1800.

a fiction upon herself, first substituting her own feelings for the Beggar's, and, in the same breath detecting the fallacy, will not part with the wish. —The Poet's Epitaph is disfigured, to my taste by the vulgar satire upon parsons and lawyers in the beginning, and the coarse epithet of pin point in the 6th stanza. All the rest is eminently good, and your own. I will just add that it appears to me a fault in the Beggar, that the instructions conveyed in it are too direct and like a lecture: they don't slide into the mind of the reader, while he is imagining no such matter. An intelligent reader finds a sort of insult in being told, I will teach you how to think upon this subject. This fault, if I am right, is in a ten-thousandth worse degree to be found in Sterne and many many novelists & modern poets, who continually put a sign post up to show where you are to feel. They set out with assuming their readers to be stupid. Very different from Robinson Crusoe, The Vicar of Wakefield, Roderick Random, and other beautiful bare narratives. There is implied an unwritten compact between Author and reader; I will tell you a story, and I suppose you will understand it. Modern novels "St. Leon's" and the like are full of such flowers as these "Let not my reader suppose," "Imagine, *if you can*"—modest!—&c.—I will here have done with praise and blame. I have written so much, only that you may not think I have passed over your book without observation.—I am sorry that Coleridge christened his Ancient Marinere "a poet's Reverie"—it is as bad as Bottom the Weaver's declaration that he is not a Lion but only the scenical representation of a Lion. What new idea is gained by this Title, but one subversive of all credit, which the tale should force upon us, of its truth? For me, I was never so affected with any human Tale. After first reading it, I was totally possessed with it for many days—I dislike all the miraculous part of it, but the feelings of the man dragged me along like Tom Piper's magic whistle. I totally differ from your idea that the Marinere should have had a character and profession. This is a Beauty in Gulliver's Travels, where the mind is kept in a placid state of little wonderments; but the Ancient Marinere undergoes such Trials, as overwhelm and bury all individuality or memory of what he was, like the state of a man in a Bad dream, one terrible peculiarity of which is: that all consciousness of personality is gone. Your other observation is I think as well a little unfounded: the Marinere from being conversant in supernatural events *has* acquired a supernatural and strange cast of *phrase*, eye, appearance, &c. which frighten the wedding guest. You will excuse my remarks, because I am hurt and vexed that you should think it necessary, with a prose apology, to open the eyes of dead men that cannot see. To sum up a general opinion of the second vol.—I do not feel any one poem in it so forcibly as the Ancient Marinere, the Mad Mother, and the Lines at Tintern Abbey, in the first.—I could, too, have wished the Critical preface had appeared in a separate treatise. All its dogmas are true and just, and most of them new, *as* criticism. But they associate a *diminishing* idea with the Poems which follow, as having been written for *Experiment* on the public taste, more than having sprung (as they must have done) from living and daily circumstances.—I am prolix, because I am gratifyed in the opportunity of writing to you, and I don't well know when to leave off. I ought before this to have reply'd to your very kind invitation into Cumberland. With you and your Sister I could gang any where. But I am afraid whether I shall ever be able to afford so desperate a Journey. Separate from the pleasure of your company, I don't much care if I never see a mountain in my life. I have passed all my days in London, until I have formed as many and intense local attachments, as any of you mountaineers can have done with dead nature. The Lighted shops of the Strand and Fleet Street, the innumerable trades, tradesmen and customers, coaches, waggons, playhouses, all the bustle and wickedness round about Covent Garden, the very women of the Town, the Watchmen, drunken scenes, rattles,—life awake, if you awake, at all hours of the night, the impossibility of being dull in Fleet Street, the crowds, the very dirt & mud, the Sun shining upon houses and pavements, the print shops, the old book stalls, parsons cheap'ning books, coffee houses, steams of soups from kitchens, the pantomimes, London itself a pantomime and a masquerade,—all these things work themselves in to my mind and feed me, without a power of satiating me. The wonder of these sights impels me into night-walks about her crowded streets, and I often shed tears in the motley Strand from fulness of joy at so much Life.—All these emotions must be strange to you. So are your rural emotions to me. But consider, what must I have been doing all my life, not to have lent great portions of my heart with usury to such scenes?——

24. St. Leon. *St. Leon* was a novel by William Godwin. **31. "a poet's Reverie."** The subtitle was omitted after the 1800 edition. **32–33. Bottom . . . Lion,** in *A Midsummer Night's Dream.*

23. gang, go, used playfully, in reference to Wordsworth's Northern speech.

My attachments are all local, purely local. I have no passion (or have had none since I was in love, and then it was the spurious engendering of poetry & books) to groves and vallies. The rooms where I was born, the furniture which has been before my eyes all my life, a book case which has followed me about (like a faithful dog, only exceeding him in knowledge) wherever I have moved—old chairs, old tables, streets, squares, where I have sunned myself, my old school,—these are my mistresses. Have I not enough, without your mountains? I do not envy you. I should pity you, did I not know, that the Mind will make friends of any thing. Your sun & moon and skys and hills & lakes affect me no more, or scarcely come to me in more venerable characters, than as a gilded room with tapestry and tapers, where I might live with handsome visible objects. I consider the clouds above me but as a roof, beautifully painted but unable to satisfy my mind, and at last, like the pictures of the apartment of a connoisseur, unable to afford him any longer a pleasure. So fading upon me, from disuse, have been the Beauties of Nature, as they have been confinedly called; so ever fresh & green and warm are all the inventions of men, and assemblies of men in this great city. I should certainly have laughed with dear Joanna.

Give my kindest love, *and my sister's*, to D. & yourself and a kiss from me to little Barbara Lewthwaite.

Thank you for Liking my Play!!

C. Lamb

OLD CHINA

I HAVE an almost feminine partiality for old china. When I go to see any great house, I inquire for the china-closet, and next for the picture gallery. I cannot defend the order of preference, but by saying, that we have all some taste or other, of too ancient a date to admit of our remembering distinctly that it was an acquired one. I can call to mind the first play, and the first exhibition, that I was taken to; but I am not conscious of a time when china jars and saucers were introduced into my imagination.

I had no repugnance then—why should I now have?—to those little, lawless, azure-tinctured grotesques, that under the notion of men and women, float about, uncircumscribed by any element, in that world before perspective—a china tea-cup.

I like to see my old friends—whom distance cannot diminish—figuring up in the air (so they appear to our optics), yet on *terra firma* still—for so we must in courtesy interpret that speck of deeper blue, which the decorous artist, to prevent absurdity, had made to spring up beneath their sandals.

I love the men with women's faces, and the women, if possible, with still more womanish expressions.

Here is a young and courtly Mandarin, handing tea to a lady from a salver—two miles off. See how distance seems to set off respect! And here the same lady, or another—for likeness is identity on tea-cups—is stepping into a little fairy boat, moored on the hither side of this calm garden river, with a dainty mincing foot, which in a right angle of incidence (as angles go in our world) must infallibly land her in the midst of a flowery mead—a furlong off on the other side of the same strange stream!

Farther on—if far or near can be predicated of their world—see horses, trees, pagodas, dancing the hays.

Here—a cow and rabbit couchant, and co-extensive—so objects show, seen through the lucid atmosphere of fine Cathay.

I was pointing out to my cousin last evening, over our Hyson (which we are old fashioned enough to drink unmixed still of an afternoon), some of these *speciosa miracula* upon a set of extraordinary old blue china (a recent purchase) which we were now for the first time using; and could not help remarking, how favourable circumstances had been to us of late years, that we could afford to please the eye sometimes with trifles of this sort—when a passing sentiment seemed to over-shade the brows of my companion. I am quick at detecting these summer clouds in Bridget.

"I wish the good old times would come again," she said, "when we were not quite so rich. I do not mean, that I want to be poor; but there was a middle state"—so she was pleased to ramble on,—"in which I am sure we were a great deal happier. A purchase is but a purchase, now that you have money enough and to spare. Formerly it used to be a triumph. When we coveted a cheap luxury (and, O! how much ado I had to get you to consent in those times!) we were used to have a debate two or three days before, and to weigh the *for* and *against*, and think what we might spare it out of, and what saving we could hit upon, that should be an equivalent. A thing was worth buying then, when we felt the money that we paid for it.

29–30. Barbara Lewthwaite, the little girl in Wordsworth's poem "The Pet Lamb." **31. Play,** *John Woodvil, a Tragedy.* Wordsworth was only "politely interested" in it.

22. hays, country dances. **29.** ***speciosa miracula,*** shining wonders. **37. Bridget,** Mary Lamb.

"Do you remember the brown suit, which you made to hang upon you, till all your friends cried shame upon you, it grew so threadbare—and all because of that folio Beaumont and Fletcher, which you dragged home late at night from Barker's in Covent Garden? Do you remember how we eyed it for weeks before we could make up our minds to the purchase, and had not come to a determination till it was near ten o'clock of the Saturday night, when you set off from Islington, fearing you should be too late—and when the old bookseller with some grumbling opened his shop, and by the twinkling taper (for he was setting bedwards) lighted out the relic from his dusty treasures—and when you lugged it home, wishing it were twice as cumbersome—and when you presented it to me—and when we were exploring the perfectness of it (*collating*, you called it)—and while I was repairing some of the loose leaves with paste, which your impatience would not suffer to be left till day-break—was there no pleasure in being a poor man? or can those neat black clothes which you wear now, and are so careful to keep brushed, since we have become rich and finical—give you half the honest vanity with which you flaunted it about in that over-worn suit—your old corbeau—for four or five weeks longer than you should have done, to pacify your conscience for the mighty sum of fifteen—or sixteen shillings was it?—a great affair we thought it then—which you had lavished on the old folio. Now you can afford to buy any book that pleases you, but I do not see that you ever bring me home any nice old purchases now.

"When you came home with twenty apologies for laying out a less number of shillings upon that print after Lionardo, which we christened the 'Lady Blanch'; when you looked at the purchase, and thought of the money—and thought of the money, and looked again at the picture—was there no pleasure in being a poor man? Now, you have nothing to do but to walk into Colnaghi's, and buy a wilderness of Lionardos. Yet do you?

"Then, do you remember our pleasant walks to Enfield, and Potter's Bar, and Waltham, when we had a holyday—holydays and all other fun are gone now we are rich—and the little hand-basket in which I used to deposit our day's fare of savory cold lamb and salad—and how you would pry about at noon-tide for some decent house, where we might go in, and produce our store—only paying for the ale that you must call for—and speculate upon the looks of the landlady, and whether she was likely to allow us a table-cloth—and wish for such another honest hostess, as Izaak Walton has described many a one on the pleasant banks of the Lea, when he went a-fishing—and sometimes they would prove obliging enough, and sometimes they would look grudgingly upon us—but we had cheerful looks still for one another, and would eat our plain food savorily, scarcely grudging Piscator his Trout Hall? Now—when we go out a day's pleasuring, which is seldom moreover, we *ride* part of the way—and go into a fine inn, and order the best of dinners, never debating the expense—which, after all, never has half the relish of those chance country snaps, when we were at the mercy of uncertain usage, and a precarious welcome.

"You are too proud to see a play anywhere now but in the pit. Do you remember where it was we used to sit, when we saw the battle of Hexham, and the Surrender of Calais, and Bannister and Mrs. Bland in the Children in the Wood—when we squeezed out our shillings a-piece to sit three or four times in a season in the one-shilling gallery—where you felt all the time that you ought not to have brought me—and more strongly I felt obligation to you for having brought me—and the pleasure was the better for a little shame—and when the curtain drew up, what cared we for our place in the house, or what mattered it where we were sitting, when our thoughts were with Rosalind in Arden, or with Viola at the Court of Illyria? You used to say, that the gallery was the best place of all for enjoying a play socially—that the relish of such exhibitions must be in proportion to the infrequency of going—that the company we met there, not being in general readers of plays, were obliged to attend the more, and did attend to what was going on, on the stage—because a word lost would have been a chasm, which it was impossible for them to fill up. With such reflections we consoled our pride then—and I appeal to you whether, as a woman, I met generally with less attention and accommodation than I have done since in more expensive situations in the house? The getting in indeed, and the crowding up those inconvenient staircases, was bad enough—but there was still a law of civility to woman recognised to quite as great an extent as we ever found in the other passages—and how a little difficulty overcome heightened the snug seat and the play, afterwards! Now we can only pay our money and walk in. You cannot see, you say, in the galleries now. I am sure we saw, and heard too, well enough then—but sight, and all, I think, is gone with our poverty.

4. Beaumont and Fletcher, Francis Beaumont and John Fletcher were dramatists of Shakespeare's time. **26. corbeau,** greenish, almost black, color.

8. Piscator, a character in *Compleat Angler*. **29. Rosalind,** in *As You Like It*. **29–30. Viola,** in *Twelfth Night*.

"There was pleasure in eating strawberries, before they became quite common—in the first dish of peas, while they were yet dear—to have them for a nice supper, a treat. What treat can we have now? If we were to treat ourselves now—that is, to have dainties a little above our means, it would be selfish and wicked. It is the very little more that we allow ourselves beyond what the actual poor can get at, that makes what I call a treat—when two people, living together, as we have done, now and then indulge themselves in a cheap luxury, which both like; while each apologises, and is willing to take both halves of the blame to his single share. I see no harm in people making much of themselves in that sense of the word. It may give them a hint how to make much of others. But now—what I mean by the word—we never do make much of ourselves. None but the poor can do it. I do not mean the veriest poor of all, but persons as we were, just above poverty.

"I know what you were going to say, that it is mighty pleasant at the end of the year to make all meet,—and much ado we used to have every Thirty-first Night of December to account for our exceedings—many a long face did you make over your puzzled accounts, and in contriving to make it out how we had spent so much—or that we had not spent so much—or that it was impossible we should spend so much next year—and still we found our slender capital decreasing—but then, betwixt ways, and projects, and compromises of one sort or another, and talk of curtailing this charge, and doing without that for the future—and the hope that youth brings, and laughing spirits (in which you were never poor till now) we pocketed up our loss, and in conclusion, with 'lusty brimmers' (as you used to quote it out of *hearty cheerful Mr. Cotton*, as you called him), we used to welcome in the 'coming guest.' Now we have no reckoning at all at the end of the old year—no flattering promises about the new year doing better for us."

Bridget is so sparing of her speech on most occasions, that when she gets into a rhetorical vein, I am careful how I interrupt it. I could not help, however, smiling at the phantom of wealth which her dear imagination had conjured up out of a clear income of poor——hundred pounds a year. "It is true we were happier when we were poorer, but we were also younger, my cousin. I am afraid we must put up with the excess, for if we were to shake the superflux into the sea, we should not much mend ourselves. That we had much to struggle with, as we grew up together, we have reason to be most thankful. It strengthened, and knit our compact closer. We could never have been what we have been to each other, if we had always had the sufficiency which you now complain of. The resisting power—those natural dilations of the youthful spirit, which circumstances cannot straiten—with us are long since passed away. Competence to age is supplementary youth, a sorry supplement indeed, but I fear the best that is to be had. We must ride where we formerly walked: live better, and lie softer—and shall be wise to do so—than we had means to do in those good old days you speak of. Yet could those days return—could you and I once more walk our thirty miles a day—could Bannister and Mrs. Bland again be young, and you and I be young to see them—could the good old one shilling gallery days return—they are dreams, my cousin, now—but could you and I at this moment, instead of this quiet argument, by our well-carpeted fireside, sitting on this luxurious sofa—be once more struggling up those inconvenient stair-cases, pushed about, and squeezed, and elbowed by the poorest rabble of poor gallery scramblers—could I once more hear those anxious shrieks of yours—and the delicious *Thank God, we are safe*, which always followed when the topmost stair, conquered, let in the first light of the whole cheerful theatre down beneath us—I know not the fathom line that ever touched a descent so deep as I would be willing to bury more wealth in than Croesus had, or the great Jew R—— is supposed to have, to purchase it. And now do just look at that merry little Chinese waiter holding an umbrella, big enough for a bed-tester, over the head of that pretty insipid half-Madonna-ish chit of a lady in that very blue summer-house."

DREAM-CHILDREN; A REVERIE

CHILDREN love to listen to stories about their elders, when *they* were children; to stretch their imagination to the conception of a traditionary great-uncle, or grandame, whom they never saw. It was in this spirit that my little ones crept about me the other evening to hear about their great-grandmother Field, who lived in a great house in Norfolk (a hundred times bigger than that in which they and papa lived) which had been the scene—so at least it was generally believed in that part of the country—of the tragic incidents which they had lately become familiar with from the ballad of the

30. R——, Nathan Meyer Rothschild (1777–1836), founder of the great firm of international financiers. **32. bed-tester**, canopy. **44–45. great-grandmother Field.** Mary Field was for fifty years housekeeper at Blakesware, Hertfordshire.

Children in the Wood. Certain it is that the whole story of the children and their cruel uncle was to be seen fairly carved out in wood upon the chimney-piece of the great hall, the whole story down to the Robin Redbreasts, till a foolish rich person pulled it down to set up a marble one of modern invention in its stead, with no story upon it. Here Alice put out one of her dear mother's looks, too tender to be called upbraiding. Then I went on to say, how religious and how good their great-grandmother Field was, how beloved and respected by every body, though she was not indeed the mistress of this great house, but had only the charge of it (and yet in some respects she might be said to be the mistress of it too) committed to her by the owner, who preferred living in a newer and more fashionable mansion which he had purchased somewhere in the adjoining county; but still she lived in it in a manner as if it had been her own, and kept up the dignity of the great house in a sort while she lived, which afterwards came to decay, and was nearly pulled down, and all its old ornaments stripped and carried away to the owner's other house, where they were set up, and looked as awkward as if some one were to carry away the old tombs they had seen lately at the Abbey, and stick them up in Lady C.'s tawdry gilt drawing-room. Here John smiled, as much as to say, "that would be foolish indeed." And then I told how, when she came to die, her funeral was attended by a concourse of all the poor, and some of the gentry too, of the neighbourhood for many miles round, to show their respect for her memory, because she had been such a good and religious woman; so good indeed that she knew all the Psaltery by heart, ay, and a great part of the Testament besides. Here little Alice spread her hands. Then I told what a tall, upright, graceful person their great-grandmother Field once was; and how in her youth she was esteemed the best dancer—here Alice's little right foot played an involuntary movement, till upon my looking grave, it desisted—the best dancer, I was saying, in the county, till a cruel disease, called a cancer, came, and bowed her down with pain; but it could never bend her good spirits, or make them stoop, but they were still upright, because she was so good and religious. Then I told how she was used to sleep by herself in a lone chamber of the great lone house; and how she believed that an apparition of two infants was to be seen at midnight gliding up and down the great staircase near where she slept, but she said "those innocents would do her no harm"; and how frightened I used to be, though in those days I had my maid to sleep with me, because I was never half so good or religious as she—and yet I never saw the infants. Here John expanded all his eye-brows and tried to look courageous. Then I told how good she was to all her grand-children, having us to the great house in the holydays, where I in particular used to spend many hours by myself, in gazing upon the old busts of the Twelve Caesars, that had been Emperors of Rome, till the old marble heads would seem to live again, or I be turned into marble with them; how I never could be tired with roaming about that huge mansion, with its vast empty rooms, with their worn-out hangings, fluttering tapestry, and carved oaken panels, with the gilding almost rubbed out—sometimes in the spacious old-fashioned gardens, which I had almost to myself, unless when now and then a solitary gardening man would cross me—and how the nectarines and peaches hung upon the walls, without my ever offering to pluck them, because they were forbidden fruit, unless now and then,—and because I had more pleasure in strolling about among the old melancholy-looking yew trees, or the firs, and picking up the red berries, and the fir apples, which were good for nothing but to look at—or in lying about upon the fresh grass, with all the fine garden smells around me—or basking in the orangery, till I could almost fancy myself ripening too along with the oranges and the limes in that grateful warmth—or in watching the dace that darted to and fro in the fish-pond, at the bottom of the garden, with here and there a great sulky pike hanging midway down the water in silent state, as if it mocked at their impertinent friskings,—I had more pleasure in these busy-idle diversions than in all the sweet flavours of peaches, nectarines, oranges, and such like common baits of children. Here John slyly deposited back upon the plate a bunch of grapes, which, not unobserved by Alice, he had meditated dividing with her, and both seemed willing to relinquish them for the present as irrelevant. Then in somewhat a more heightened tone, I told how, though their great-grandmother Field loved all her grand-children, yet in an especial manner she might be said to love their uncle, John L——, because he was so handsome and spirited a youth, and a king to the rest of us; and, instead of moping about in solitary corners, like some of us, he would mount the most mettlesome horse he could get, when but an imp no bigger than themselves, and make it carry him half over the county in a morning, and join the hunters when there were any out—and yet he loved the old great

36. Here . . . John slyly deposited. Note the responses of the children, here and elsewhere, to the unfolding of the story. **44. John L——,** John Lamb.

house and gardens too, but had too much spirit to be always pent up within their boundaries—and how their uncle grew up to man's estate as brave as he was handsome, to the admiration of everybody, but of their great-grandmother Field most especially; and how he used to carry me upon his back when I was a lame-footed boy—for he was a good bit older than me—many a mile when I could not walk for pain;—and how in after life he became lame-footed too, and I did not always (I fear) make allowances enough for him when he was impatient, and in pain, nor remember sufficiently how considerate he had been to me when I was lame-footed; and how when he died, though he had not been dead an hour, it seemed as if he had died a great while ago, such a distance there is betwixt life and death; and how I bore his death as I thought pretty well at first, but afterwards it haunted and haunted me; and though I did not cry or take it to heart as some do, and as I think he would have done if I had died, yet I missed him all day long, and knew not till then how much I had loved him. I missed his kindness, and I missed his crossness, and wished him to be alive again, to be quarrelling with him (for we quarrelled sometimes), rather than not have him again, and was as uneasy without him, as he their poor uncle must have been when the doctor took off his limb. Here the children fell a crying, and asked if their little mourning which they had on was not for uncle John, and they looked up, and prayed me not to go on about their uncle, but to tell them some stories about their pretty dead mother. Then I told how for seven long years, in hope sometimes, sometimes in despair, yet persisting ever, I courted the fair Alice W——n; and, as much as children could understand, I explained to them what coyness, and difficulty, and denial meant in maidens—when suddenly, turning to Alice, the soul of the first Alice looked out at her eyes with such a reality of representment, that I became in doubt which of them stood there before me, or whose that bright hair was; and while I stood gazing, both the children gradually grew fainter to my view, receding, and still receding till nothing at last but two mournful features were seen in the uttermost distance, which, without speech, strangely impressed upon me the effects of speech; "We are not of Alice, nor of thee, nor are we children at all. The children of Alice call Bartrum father. We are nothing: less than nothing, and dreams. We are only what might have been, and must wait upon the tedious shores of Lethe millions of ages before we have existence, and a name"—and immediately awaking, I found myself quietly seated in my bachelor arm-chair, where I had fallen asleep, with the faithful Bridget unchanged by my side—but John L. (or James Elia) was gone for ever.

35. Alice W——n, Ann Simmons.

A CHARACTER OF THE LATE ELIA

This playful and discerning self-portrait appeared in the *London Magazine* for January, 1823. An abbreviated version served ten years later as preface to *Last Essays of Elia.*

This gentleman, who for some months past had been in a declining way, hath at length paid his final tribute to nature. He just lived long enough (it was what he wished) to see his papers collected into a volume. The pages of the *London Magazine* will henceforth know him no more.

Exactly at twelve last night, his queer spirit departed; and the bells of Saint Bride's rang him out with the old year. The mournful vibrations were caught in the dining-room of his friends T. and H., and the company, assembled there to welcome in another First of January, checked their carousals in mid-mirth, and were silent. Janus wept. The gentle P———r, in a whisper, signified his intention of devoting an elegy; and Allan C., nobly forgetful of his countrymen's wrongs, vowed a memoir to his *manes* full and friendly as a *Tale of Lyddalcross.*

To say truth, it is time he were gone. The humor of the thing, if there was ever much in it, was pretty well exhausted; and a two years' and a half existence has been a tolerable duration for a phantom.

I am now at liberty to confess, that much which I have heard objected to my late friend's writings was well-founded. Crude they are, I grant you—a sort of unlicked, incondite things—villainously pranked in an affected array of antique modes and phrases. They had not been *his*, if they had been other than such; and better it is, that a writer should be natural in a self-pleasing quaintness, than to affect a naturalness (so called) that should be strange to him. Egotistical they have been pronounced by some who did not know, that what he tells us, as of himself, was often true only (historically) of another; as in a former Essay (to save many instances)—where under the *first person* (his favorite figure) he shadows forth the forlorn estate of a country-boy placed at a London school, far from his friends and connexions—in direct opposition to his own early history. If it be egotism to imply and twine with his own identity the griefs

26. Allan C[unningham] (1784–1842), Scotch poet.

and affections of another—making himself many, or reducing many unto himself—then is the skilful novelist, who all along brings in his hero, or heroine, speaking of themselves, the greatest egotist of all; who yet has never, therefore, been accused of that narrowness. And how shall the intenser dramatist escape being faulty, who doubtless, under cover of passion uttered by another, oftentimes gives blameless vent to his most inward feelings, and expresses his own story modestly?

My late friend was in many respects a singular character. Those who did not like him, hated him; and some, who once liked him, afterwards became his bitterest haters. The truth is, he gave himself too little concern what he uttered, and in whose presence. He observed neither time nor place, and would e'en out with what came uppermost. With the severe religionist he would pass for a free-thinker; while the other faction set him down for a bigot, or persuaded themselves that he belied his sentiments. Few understood him; and I am not certain that at all times he quite understood himself. He too much affected that dangerous figure—irony. He sowed doubtful speeches, and reaped plain, unequivocal hatred.—He would interrupt the gravest discussion with some light jest; and yet, perhaps, not quite irrelevant in ears that could understand it. Your long and much talkers hated him. The informal habit of his mind, joined to an inveterate impediment of speech, forbade him to be an orator; and he seemed determined that no one else should play that part when he was present. He was *petit* and ordinary in his person and appearance. I have seen him sometimes in what is called good company, but where he has been a stranger, sit silent, and be suspected for an odd fellow; till some unlucky occasion provoking it, he would stutter out some senseless pun (not altogether senseless perhaps, if rightly taken) which has stamped his character for the evening. It was hit or miss with him; but nine times out of ten, he contrived by this device to send away a whole company his enemies. His conceptions rose kindlier than his utterance, and his happiest *impromptus* had the appearance of effort. He has been accused of trying to be witty, when in truth he was but struggling to give his poor thoughts articulation. He chose his companions for some individuality of character which they manifested.—Hence, not many persons of science, and few professed *literati*, were of his councils. They were, for the most part, persons of an uncertain fortune; and, as to such people commonly nothing is more obnoxious than a gentleman of settled (though moderate) income, he passed with most of them for a great miser. To my knowledge this was a mistake. His *intimados*, to confess a truth, were in the world's eye a ragged regiment. He found them floating on the surface of society; and the color, or something else, in the weed pleased him. The burrs stuck to him—but they were good and loving burrs for all that. He never greatly cared for the society of what are called good people. If any of these were scandalized (and offences were sure to arise), he could not help it. When he has been remonstrated with for not making more concessions to the feelings of good people, he would retort by asking, what one point did these good people ever concede to him? He was temperate in his meals and diversions, but always kept a little on this side of abstemiousness. Only in the use of the Indian weed he might be thought a little excessive. He took it, he would say, as a solvent of speech. Marry—as the friendly vapor ascended, how his prattle would curl up sometimes with it! the ligaments, which tongue-tied him, were loosened, and the stammerer proceeded a statist!

I do not know whether I ought to bemoan or rejoice that my old friend is departed. His jests were beginning to grow obsolete, and his stories to be found out. He felt the approaches of age; and while he pretended to cling to life, you saw how slender were the ties left to bind him. Discoursing with him latterly on this subject, he expressed himself with a pettishness, which I thought unworthy of him. In our walks about his suburban retreat (as he called it) at Shacklewell, some children belonging to a school of industry had met us, and bowed and curtseyed, as he thought, in an especial manner to *him*. "They take me for a visiting governor," he muttered earnestly. He had a horror, which he carried to a foible, of looking like anything important and parochial. He thought that he approached nearer to that stamp daily. He had a general aversion from being treated like a grave or respectable character, and kept a wary eye upon the advances of age that should so entitle him. He herded always, while it was possible, with people younger than himself. He did not conform to the march of time, but was dragged along in the procession. His manners lagged behind his years. He was too much of the boy-man. The *toga virilis* never sate gracefully on his shoulders. The impressions of infancy had burnt into him, and he resented the impertinence of manhood. These were weaknesses; but such as they were, they are a key to explicate some of his writings.

He left little property behind him. Of course, the little that is left (chiefly in India bonds) devolves upon his cousin Bridget. A few critical dissertations were found in his *escritoire*, which have been handed over to the editor of this magazine, in which it is to be hoped they will shortly appear, retaining his accustomed signature.

He has himself not obscurely hinted that his employment lay in a public office. The gentlemen in the export department of the East India House will forgive me if I acknowledge the readiness with which they assisted me in the retrieval of his few manuscripts. They pointed out in a most obliging manner the desk at which he had been planted for forty years; showed me ponderous tomes of figures, in his own remarkably neat hand, which, more properly than his few printed tracts, might be called his "Works." They seemed affectionate to his memory, and universally commended his expertness in book-keeping. It seems he was the inventor of some ledger which should combine the precision and certainty of the Italian double entry (I think they called it) with the brevity and facility of some newer German system; but I am not able to appreciate the worth of the discovery. I have often heard him express a warm regard for his associates in office, and how fortunate he considered himself in having his lot thrown in amongst them. "There is more sense, more discourse, more shrewdness, and even talent, among these clerks," he would say, "than in twice the number of authors by profession that I have conversed with." He would brighten up sometimes upon the "old days of the India House," when he consorted with Woodroffe and Wissett, and Peter Corbet (a descendant and worthy representative, bating the point of sanctity, of old facetious Bishop Corbet); and Hoole, who translated Tasso; and Bartlemy Brown, whose father (God assoil him therefor!) modernized Walton; and sly, warm-hearted old Jack Cole (King Cole they called him in those days) and Campe and Fombelle, and a world of choice spirits, more than I can remember to name, who associated in those days with Jack Burrell (the *bon-vivant* of the South-Sea House); and little Eyton (said to be a facsimile of Pope—he was a miniature of a gentleman), that was cashier under him; and Dan Voight of the Custom-house, that left the famous library.

Well, Elia is gone—for aught I know, to be reunited with them—and these poor traces of his pen are all we have to show for it. How little survives of the wordiest authors! Of all they said or did in their lifetime, a few glittering words only! His Essays found some favorers, as they appeared separately; they shuffled their way in the crowd well enough singly; how they will *read*, now they are brought together, is a question for the publishers, who have thus ventured to draw out into one piece his "weaved-up follies."

William Hazlitt
1778–1830

William Hazlitt was born April 10, 1778, at Maidstone, Kent, where his father was a Unitarian minister. The Reverend William Hazlitt was a believer in the republican form of government and a friend of Benjamin Franklin. In 1783, in order to enjoy the freedom of the new American republic, he took his family to America. Here he preached to the New Jersey Assembly, lectured in the college that was to become the University of Pennsylvania, and founded the first Unitarian church in Boston. Since the younger William was only four years old at the time of the emigration, and the family did not remain long in America, this sojourn left few memories, the chief one being the taste of barberries that had hung all winter in the New England snow. At Wem, in Shropshire, his education began under his father, who destined him for the ministry. At fifteen he was sent to Hackney College, a Unitarian seminary. Between the ages of sixteen and twenty-one, Hazlitt tells us, he read novels by Fielding and Smollett; Burke's *Letter to a Noble Lord* and *Reflections on the French Revolution*, which impressed him as superb prose; Milton's *Paradise Lost;* and Rousseau's *La nouvelle Héloïse*, which touched the springs of emotion and imagination. He also saw the pictures at Burleigh House. But the greatest single event of his life was his "First Acquaintance with Poets" (the meeting with Coleridge and Wordsworth) in 1798. Of the walk with Coleridge toward Shrewsbury, Hazlitt wrote, twenty-five years later: "The light of his genius shone into my soul, like the sun's rays glittering in the puddles of the road. . . . That my understanding . . . did not remain dull and brutish, or at length found a language to express itself, I owe to Coleridge." His entrance into literature, however, was not immediate. Between 1799 and 1805 he undertook to master the art of painting, beginning under his brother John, who was a successful miniaturist, and studying at the Louvre in Paris. While in France he developed that loyalty to the cause of the French Revolution and that admiration for Napoleon which he never lost and which impelled him to undertake his *Life of Napoleon* as his last great enterprise. In 1805, as a result of matchmaking by Charles and Mary Lamb, he married Sarah Stoddart, who had a cottage at Winterslow and a small income. Convinced by now that he would never make a great painter, he occupied himself by writing various essays on morals, philosophy, and economics.

The year 1812, when Hazlitt made his appearance as a public lecturer on the history of English philosophy, is regarded as a turning-point. Soon he was launched upon the journalistic, lecturing, and literary free-lancing career that was to engage him the rest of his life. He began to write dramatic criticism for the *Morning Chronicle*, at a time when Edmund Kean was the leading actor in a notable Shakespearean revival, and essays for Leigh Hunt's *Examiner*. He had rounded out his acquaintance with most of the literary lights of the period—Coleridge, Wordsworth, Lamb, Leigh Hunt, Keats, and Shelley. These friendships and the enmities he acquired, his journalistic connections, and his steadfast adherence to the principles of the French Revolution lined him up in the literary wars of the time. During 1818–20 he delivered a series of lectures, on *The English Poets*, on *English Comic Writers*, and on the *Dramatic Literature of the Age of Elizabeth*, which established him as a literary critic of the first rank. He was violently attacked by *Blackwood's* and the *Quarterly*, and got himself embroiled in the affair that resulted in the death in a duel of John Scott, editor of the *London Magazine*. About this time, his marriage was drifting toward the rocks because of an infatuation with Sarah Walker, young daughter of his London landlady. At his request Sarah Stoddart Hazlitt divorced him; whereupon the other Sarah refused to marry him. Hazlitt reveals the whole story without reserve in his most imprudent book, *Liber Amoris*. Despite these fevered personal experiences, his writing went serenely on. In 1824 he again married, this time a widow who had an income sufficient for foreign travel for the two. Travel and his *Life of Napoleon* engaged his interest until his death in 1830.

This brief account of the life of Hazlitt suggests the salient features of his personality and character. He was moody, sensitive, and often difficult, even with his friends. Lacking the breeding and the formal education that most of his literary associates had, he suffered at times from an inferiority complex. He lived, loved, hated, talked, and wrote intensely. He quarreled, often to the point of final estrangement or enmity, with nearly every one of his friends except Lamb and Keats. The chief impression he gives of himself is that of an embittered, disillusioned man. Perhaps he was too uncompromising, made too many emotional demands on his friends. Yet his best and perhaps only lifelong friend, Charles Lamb, said of him, "I think William Hazlitt to be, in his natural and healthy state, one of the wisest and finest spirits breathing." Some of Hazlitt's observations of life and of human nature are among the noblest and most winning in English essay-writing.

Hazlitt was a fighting literary critic, an art connoisseur with few rivals except Ruskin and Walter Pater, a master of the familiar essay, and the most comprehensive prose interpreter of the spirit of his age. His chief titles are *The Round Table*, 1817; *The Characters of Shakespear's Plays*, 1817; *Lectures on the English Poets*, 1818; *Lectures on the English Comic Writers*, 1819; *Lectures on the Dramatic Literature of the Age of Elizabeth*, 1820; *Liber Amoris*, 1823; *The Spirit of the Age*, 1825; *The Plain Speaker*, 1826; and *Life of Napoleon*, 1828–30. Except for the last, the twelve stout volumes in the Waller and Glover edition of his *Collected Works* are made up almost entirely of essays.

MY FIRST ACQUAINTANCE WITH POETS

MY father was a Dissenting Minister at W——m in Shropshire; and in the year 1798 (the figures that compose that date are to me like the "dreaded name of Demogorgon") Mr. Coleridge came to Shrewsbury, to succeed Mr. Rowe in the spiritual charge of a Unitarian Congregation there. He did not come till late on the Saturday afternoon before he was to preach; and Mr. Rowe, who himself went down to the coach in a state of anxiety and expectation, to look for the arrival of his successor, could find no one at all answering the description but a round-faced man in a short black coat (like a shooting jacket) which hardly seemed to have been made for him, but who seemed to be talking at a great rate to his fellow-passengers. Mr. Rowe had scarce returned to give an account of his disappointment, when the round-faced man in black entered, and dissipated all doubts on the subject, by beginning to talk. He did not cease while he staid; nor has he since, that I know of. He held the good town of Shrewsbury in delightful suspense for three weeks that he remained there, "fluttering the *proud Salopians* like an eagle in a dove-cote"; and the Welch mountains that skirt the horizon with their tempestuous confusion, agree to have heard no such mystic sounds since the days of

"High-born Hoel's harp or soft Llewellyn's lay!"

As we passed along between W——m and Shrewsbury, and I eyed their blue tops seen through the wintry branches, or the red rustling leaves of the sturdy oak-trees by the road-side, a sound was in my ears as of a Siren's song; I was stunned, startled with it, as from deep sleep; but I had no notion then that I should ever be able to express my admiration to others in motley imagery or quaint allusion, till the light of his genius shone into my soul, like the sun's rays glittering in the puddles of the road. I was at that time dumb, inarticulate, helpless, like a worm by the way-side, crushed, bleeding, lifeless; but now, bursting from the deadly bands that "bound them,

"With Styx nine times round them,"

my ideas float on winged words, and as they expand their plumes, catch the golden light of other years. My soul has indeed remained in its original bondage, dark, obscure, with longings infinite and unsatisfied; my heart, shut up in the prison-house of this rude clay, has never found, nor will it ever find, a heart to speak to; but that my understanding also did not remain dumb and brutish, or at length found a language to express itself, I owe to Coleridge. But this is not to my purpose.

My father lived ten miles from Shrewsbury, and was in the habit of exchanging visits with Mr. Rowe, and with Mr. Jenkins of Whitchurch (nine miles farther on) according to the custom of Dissenting Ministers in each other's neighbourhood. A line of communication is thus established, by which the flame of civil and religious liberty is kept alive, and nourishes its smouldering fire unquenchable, like the fires in the *Agamemnon* of Aeschylus, placed at different stations, that waited for ten long years to announce with their blazing pyramids the destruction of Troy. Coleridge had agreed to come over to see my father, according to the courtesy of the country, as Mr. Rowe's probable successor; but in the meantime I had gone to hear him preach the Sun-

33. W——m, Wem. **36. "dreaded . . . Demogorgon."** See *Paradise Lost*, Book II, l. 964.

2–3. "fluttering . . . dove-cote." See *Coriolanus*, Act V, sc. 6, l. 115. **Salopians** is from Latin *Salopia* **(Shropshire). 8. "High-born . . . lay."** Thomas Gray's "The Bard," l. 28. **23. "With Styx . . . them."** Pope's "Ode on St. Cecilia's Day," l. 90.

day after his arrival. A poet and a philosopher getting up into a Unitarian pulpit to preach the Gospel, was a romance in these degenerate days, a sort of revival of the primitive spirit of Christianity, which was not to be resisted.

It was in January, 1798, that I rose one morning before daylight, to walk ten miles in the mud, and went to hear this celebrated person preach. Never, the longest day I have to live, shall I have such another walk as this cold, raw, comfortless one, in the winter of the year 1798. *Il y a des impressions que ni le tems ni les circonstances peuvent effacer. Dusse-je vivre des siècles entiers, le doux tems de ma jeunesse ne peut renaître pour moi, ni s'effacer jamais dans ma mémoire.* When I got there, the organ was playing the 100th psalm, and, when it was done, Mr. Coleridge rose and gave out his text, "And he went up into the mountain to pray, HIMSELF, ALONE." As he gave out this text, his voice "rose like a steam of rich distilled perfumes," and when he came to the two last words, which he pronounced loud, deep, and distinct, it seemed to me, who was then young, as if the sounds had echoed from the bottom of the human heart, and as if that prayer might have floated in solemn silence through the universe. The idea of St. John came into mind, "of one crying in the wilderness, who had his loins girt about, and whose food was locusts and wild honey." The preacher then launched into his subject, like an eagle dallying with the wind. The sermon was upon peace and war; upon church and state—not their alliance, but their separation—on the spirit of the world and the spirit of Christianity, not as the same, but as opposed to one another. He talked of those who had "inscribed the cross of Christ on banners dripping with human gore." He made a poetical and pastoral excursion,—and to shew the fatal effects of war, drew a striking contrast between the simple shepherd boy, driving his team afield, or sitting under the hawthorn, piping to his flock, "as though he should never be old," and the same poor country-lad, crimped, kidnapped, brought into town, made drunk at an alehouse, turned into a wretched drummer-boy, with his hair sticking on end with powder and pomatum, a long cue at his back, and tricked out in the loathsome finery of the profession of blood.

"Such were the notes our once-loved poet sung."

And for myself, I could not have been more delighted if I had heard the music of the spheres. Poetry and Philosophy had met together. Truth and Genius had embraced, under the eye and with the sanction of Religion. This was even beyond my hopes. I returned home well satisfied. The sun that was still labouring pale and wan through the sky, obscured by thick mists, seemed an emblem of the *good cause;* and the cold dank drops of dew that hung half melted on the beard of the thistle, had something genial and refreshing in them; for there was a spirit of hope and youth in all nature, that turned every thing into good. The face of nature had not then the brand of JUS DIVINUM on it:

"Like to that sanguine flower inscribed with woe."

On the Tuesday following, the half-inspired speaker came. I was called down into the room where he was, and went half-hoping, half-afraid. He received me very graciously, and I listened for a long time without uttering a word. I did not suffer in his opinion by my silence. "For those two hours," he afterwards was pleased to say, "he was conversing with W. H.'s forehead!" His appearance was different from what I had anticipated from seeing him before. At a distance, and in the dim light of the chapel, there was to me a strange wildness in his aspect, a dusky obscurity, and I thought him pitted with the small-pox. His complexion was at that time clear, and even bright—

"As are the children of yon azure sheen."

His forehead was broad and high, light as if built of ivory, with large projecting eyebrows, and his eyes rolling beneath them like a sea with darkened lustre. "A certain tender bloom his face o'erspread," a purple tinge as we see it in the pale thoughtful complexions of the Spanish portrait-painters, Murillo and Velasquez. His mouth was gross, voluptuous, open, eloquent; his chin good-humoured and round; but his nose, the rudder of the face, the index of the will, was small, feeble, nothing—like what he has done. It might seem that the genius of his face as from a height surveyed and projected him (with sufficient capacity and huge aspiration) into the world unknown of thought and imagination, with nothing to support or guide his veering purpose, as if Columbus had launched his adventurous course for the New World in a scallop, without oars or compass. So at least I comment on it after the event.

11–14. *Il y a . . . mémoire.* There are impressions which neither time nor circumstances can efface. If I should live entire centuries, the sweet time of youth cannot return or efface itself from my memory.—Rousseau, *Confessions*, Part II, Book 7. **19. rose . . . perfumes.** See Milton's *Comus*, l. 556. **25. St. John.** See Matthew 3:3, 4. **47. Such . . . sung.** See Pope's *Epistle to Robert, Earl of Oxford.*

9. good cause, the French Revolution. **14. Jus Divinum,** divine right (of kings). **15. Like . . . woe.** See Milton's *Lycidas*, l. 106. **31. As . . . sheen.** James Thomson's *The Castle of Indolence*, Book II, l. 295. **36. A certain . . . o'erspread.** *Ibid.*, I, 507.

Coleridge in his person was rather above the common size, inclining to the corpulent, or like Lord Hamlet, "somewhat fat and pursy." His hair (now, alas! grey) was then black and glossy as the raven's, and fell in smooth masses over his forehead. This long pendulous hair is peculiar to enthusiasts, to those whose minds tend heavenward; and is traditionally inseparable (though of a different colour) from the pictures of Christ. It ought to belong, as a character, to all who preach *Christ crucified*, and Coleridge was at that time one of those!

It was curious to observe the contrast between him and my father, who was a veteran in the cause, and then declining into the vale of years. He had been a poor Irish lad, carefully brought up by his parents, and sent to the University of Glasgow (where he studied under Adam Smith) to prepare him for his future destination. It was his mother's proudest wish to see her son a Dissenting Minister. So if we look back to past generations (as far as eye can reach) we see the same hopes, fears, wishes, followed by the same disappointments, throbbing in the human heart; and so we may see them (if we look forward) rising up for ever, and disappearing, like vapourish bubbles, in the human breast! After being tossed about from congregation to congregation in the heats of the Unitarian controversy, and squabbles about the American war, he had been relegated to an obscure village, where he was to spend the last thirty years of his life, far from the only converse that he loved, the talk about disputed texts of Scripture and the cause of civil and religious liberty. Here he passed his days, repining but resigned, in the study of the Bible, and the perusal of the Commentators,—huge folios, not easily got through, one of which would outlast a winter! Why did he pore on these from morn to night (with the exception of a walk in the fields or a turn in the garden to gather broccoli-plants or kidney-beans of his own rearing, with no small degree of pride and pleasure)? Here were "no figures nor no fantasies"—neither poetry nor philosophy—nothing to dazzle, nothing to excite modern curiosity; but to his lack-lustre eyes there appeared, within the pages of the ponderous, unwieldy, neglected tomes, the sacred name of JEHOVAH in Hebrew capitals: pressed down by the weight of the style, worn to the last fading thinness of the understanding, there were glimpses, glimmering notions of the patriarchal wanderings, with palm-trees hovering in the horizon, and processions of camels at the distance of three thousand years; there was Moses with the Burning Bush, the number of the Twelve Tribes, types, shadows, glosses on the law and the prophets; there were discussions (dull enough) on the age of Methuselah, a mighty speculation! there were outlines, rude guesses at the shape of Noah's Ark and of the riches of Solomon's Temple; questions as to the date of the creation, predictions of the end of all things; the great lapses of time, the strange mutations of the globe were unfolded with the voluminous leaf, as it turned over; and though the soul might slumber with an hieroglyphic veil of inscrutable mysteries drawn over it, yet it was in a slumber ill-exchanged for all the sharpened realities of sense, wit, fancy, or reason. My father's life was comparatively a dream; but it was a dream of infinity and eternity, of death, the resurrection, and a judgment to come!

No two individuals were ever more unlike than were the host and his guest. A poet was to my father a sort of nondescript: yet whatever added grace to the Unitarian cause was to him welcome. He could hardly have been more surprised or pleased, if our visitor had worn wings. Indeed, his thoughts had wings; and as the silken sounds rustled round our little wainscoted parlour, my father threw back his spectacles over his forehead, his white hairs mixing with its sanguine hue; and a smile of delight beamed across his rugged cordial face, to think that Truth had found a new ally in Fancy! Besides, Coleridge seemed to take considerable notice of me, and that of itself was enough. He talked very familiarly, but agreeably, and glanced over a variety of subjects. At dinner-time he grew more animated, and dilated in a very edifying manner on Mary Wolstonecraft and Mackintosh. The last, he said, he considered (on my father's speaking of his *Vindiciae Galliciae* as a capital performance) as a clever scholastic man—a master of the topics,—or as the ready warehouseman of letters, who knew exactly where to lay his hand on what he wanted, though the goods were not his own. He thought him no match for Burke, either in style or matter. Burke was a metaphysician, Mackintosh a mere logician. Burke was an orator (almost a poet) who reasoned in figures, because he had an eye for nature: Mackintosh, on the other hand, was a rhetorician, who had only an eye to common-places. On this I ventured to say that I had always entertained a great opinion of Burke, and that (as far as I could find) the speaking of him with contempt might be made the test of a vulgar democratical mind. This was the first observation I

17. Adam Smith, author of *The Wealth of Nations.*

33. Mary Wollstonecraft, the author of *The Rights of Woman,* 1792, wife of William Godwin, and mother of Shelley's second wife. **Mackintosh,** Sir James Mackintosh, at the time also a sympathizer with the French Revolution.

ever made to Coleridge, and he said it was a very just and striking one. I remember the leg of Welsh mutton and the turnips on the table that day had the finest flavour imaginable. Coleridge added that Mackintosh and Tom Wedgwood (of whom, however, he spoke highly) had expressed a very indifferent opinion of his friend Mr. Wordsworth, on which he remarked to them—"He strides on so far before you, that he dwindles in the distance!" Godwin had once boasted to him of having carried on an argument with Mackintosh for three hours with dubious success; Coleridge told him—"If there had been a man of genius in the room, he would have settled the question in five minutes." He asked me if I had ever seen Mary Wolstonecraft, and I said, I had once for a few moments, and that she seemed to me to turn off Godwin's objections to something she advanced with quite a playful, easy air. He replied, that "this was only one instance of the ascendancy which people of imagination exercised over those of mere intellect." He did not rate Godwin very high (this was caprice or prejudice, real or affected) but he had a great idea of Mrs. Wolstonecraft's powers of conversation, none at all of her talent for book-making. We talked a little about Holcroft. He had been asked if he was not much struck *with* him, and he said, he thought himself in more danger of being struck *by* him. I complained that he would not let me get on at all, for he required a definition of every commonest word, exclaiming, "What do you mean by a *sensation*, Sir? What do you mean by an *idea?*" This, Coleridge said, was barricadoing the road to truth:—it was setting up a turnpike-gate at every step we took. I forget a great number of things, many more than I remember; but the day passed off pleasantly, and the next morning Mr. Coleridge was to return to Shrewsbury. When I came down to breakfast, I found that he had just received a letter from his friend T. Wedgwood, making him an offer of 150*l.* a-year if he chose to waive his present pursuit, and devote himself entirely to the study of poetry and philosophy. Coleridge seemed to make up his mind to close with this proposal in the act of tying on one of his shoes. It threw an additional damp on his departure. It took the wayward enthusiast quite from us to cast him into Deva's winding vales, or by the shores of old romance. Instead of living at ten miles' distance, of being the pastor of a Dissenting congregation at Shrewsbury, he was henceforth to inhabit the Hill of Parnassus, to be a Shepherd on the Delectable Mountains. Alas! I knew not the way thither, and felt very little gratitude for Mr. Wedgwood's bounty. I was presently relieved from the dilemma; for Mr. Coleridge, asking for a pen and ink, and going to a table to write something on a bit of card, advanced towards me with undulating step, and giving me the precious document, said that that was his address, *Mr. Coleridge, Nether Stowey, Somersetshire;* and that he should be glad to see me there in a few weeks' time, and, if I chose, would come half-way to meet me. I was not less surprised than the shepherd-boy (this simile is to be found in *Cassandra*) when he sees a thunderbolt fall close at his feet. I stammered out my acknowledgments and acceptance of this offer (I thought Mr. Wedgwood's annuity a trifle to it) as well as I could; and this mighty business being settled, the poet-preacher took leave, and I accompanied him six miles on the road. It was a fine morning in the middle of winter, and he talked the whole way. The scholar in Chaucer is described as going

——"Sounding on his way."

So Coleridge went on his. In digressing, in dilating, in passing from subject to subject, he appeared to me to float in air, to slide on ice. He told me in confidence (going along) that he should have preached two sermons before he accepted the situation at Shrewsbury, one on Infant Baptism, the other on the Lord's Supper, shewing that he could not administer either, which would have effectually disqualified him for the object in view. I observed that he continually crossed me on the way by shifting from one side of the foot-path to the other. This struck me as an odd movement; but I did not at that time connect it with any instability of purpose or involuntary change of principle, as I have done since. He seemed unable to keep on in a straight line. He spoke slightingly of Hume (whose Essay on Miracles he said was stolen from an objection started in one of South's sermons—*Credat Judaeus Apella!*). I was not very much pleased at this account of Hume, for I had just been reading, with infinite relish, that completest of all metaphysical *choke-pears*, his *Treatise on Human Nature*, to which the *Essays*, in point of scholastic subtlety and close reasoning, are mere elegant trifling, light summer-reading. Coleridge even denied the excellence of Hume's general style, which I think betrayed a want of taste or candour. He however made me amends by the manner in

9–10. Godwin, William Godwin, *Political Justice*, 1793. **25. Holcroft.** Thomas Holcroft was a dramatist and novelist, also a radical. **46. Deva,** the River Dee in North Wales.

22. "Sounding on his way," a slight garbling of Chaucer's *Prologue to the Canterbury Tales*, l. 307, describing the Clerk of Oxford. **41. *Credat . . . Apella!*** Let the Jew Apella believe it! (Horace's *Satires*, Book I, 5, 101.)

which he spoke of Berkeley. He dwelt particularly on his *Essay on Vision* as a masterpiece of analytical reasoning. So it undoubtedly is. He was exceedingly angry with Dr. Johnson for striking the stone with his foot, in allusion to this author's Theory of Matter and Spirit, and saying, "Thus I confute him, Sir." Coleridge drew a parallel (I don't know how he brought about the connection) between Bishop Berkeley and Tom Paine. He said the one was an instance of a subtle, the other of an acute mind, than which no two things could be more distinct. The one was a shop-boy's quality, the other the characteristic of a philosopher. He considered Bishop Butler as a true philosopher, a profound and conscientious thinker, a genuine reader of nature and of his own mind. He did not speak of his *Analogy*, but of his *Sermons at the Rolls' Chapel*, of which I had never heard. Coleridge somehow always contrived to prefer the *unknown* to the *known*. In this instance he was right. The *Analogy* is a tissue of sophistry, of wire-drawn, theological special-pleading; the *Sermons* (with the Preface to them) are in a fine vein of deep, matured reflection, a candid appeal to our observation of human nature, without pedantry and without bias. I told Coleridge I had written a few remarks, and was sometimes foolish enough to believe that I had made a discovery on the same subject (the *Natural Disinterestedness of the Human Mind*)—and I tried to explain my view of it to Coleridge, who listened with great willingness, but I did not succeed in making myself understood. I sat down to the task shortly afterwards for the twentieth time, got new pens and paper, determined to make clear work of it, wrote a few meagre sentences in the skeleton-style of a mathematical demonstration, stopped half-way down the second page; and, after trying in vain to pump up any words, images, notions, apprehensions, facts, or observations, from that gulph of abstraction in which I had plunged myself for four or five years preceding, gave up the attempt as labour in vain, and shed tears of helpless despondency on the blank unfinished paper. I can write fast enough now. Am I better than I was then? Oh no! One truth discovered, one pang of regret at not being able to express it, is better than all the fluency and flippancy in the world. Would that I could go back to what I then was! Why can we not revive past times as we can revisit old places? If I had the quaint Muse of Sir Philip Sidney to assist me, I would write a *Sonnett to the Road between W——m and Shrewsbury*, and immortalise every step of it by some fond enigmatical conceit. I would swear that the very milestones had ears, and that Harmer-hill stooped with all its pines, to listen to a poet, as he passed! I remember but one other topic of discourse in this walk. He mentioned Paley, praised the naturalness and clearness of his style, but condemned his sentiments, thought him a mere time-serving casuist, and said that "the fact of his work on *Moral and Political Philosophy* being made a text-book in our Universities was a disgrace to the national character." We parted at the six-mile stone; and I returned homeward pensive but much pleased. I had met with unexpected notice from a person, whom I believed to have been prejudiced against me. "Kind and affable to me had been his condescension, and should be honoured ever with suitable regard." He was the first poet I had known, and he certainly answered to that inspired name. I had heard a great deal of his powers of conversation, and was not disappointed. In fact, I never met with any thing at all like them, either before or since. I could easily credit the accounts which were circulated of his holding forth to a large party of ladies and gentlemen, an evening or two before, on the Berkeleian Theory, when he made the whole material universe look like a transparency of fine words; and another story (which I believe he has somewhere told himself) of his being asked to a party at Birmingham, of his smoking tobacco and going to sleep after dinner on a sofa, where the company found him to their no small surprise, which was increased to wonder when he started up of a sudden, and rubbing his eyes, looked about him, and launched into a three-hours' description of the third heaven, of which he had had a dream, very different from Mr. Southey's Vision of Judgment, and also from that other Vision of Judgment, which Mr. Murray, the Secretary of the Bridge-street Junto, has taken into his especial keeping!

On my way back, I had a sound in my ears, it was the voice of Fancy: I had a light before me, it was the face of Poetry. The one still lingers there, the other had not quitted my side! Coleridge in truth met me half-way on the ground of philosophy, or I should not have been won over to his imaginative creed. I had an uneasy, pleasurable sensation all the time, till I was to visit him. During those months the chill breath of winter gave me a welcoming; the vernal air was balm and inspiration to me. The golden sun-sets, the silver star of evening, lighted me on my way to new hopes and prospects. *I was to visit Coleridge in the spring*. This circumstance was never absent from my thoughts, and mingled with all my

32–33. **Southey's . . . other Vision,** allusions to Southey's poem on the death of George III and Byron's parody. John Murray, Byron's regular publisher, had his office on Bridge Street.

feelings. I wrote to him at the time proposed, and received an answer postponing my intended visit for a week or two, but very cordially urging me to complete my promise then. This delay did not damp, but rather increased my ardour. In the meantime I went to Llangollen Vale, by way of initiating myself in the mysteries of natural scenery; and I must say I was enchanted with it. I had been reading Coleridge's description of England, in his fine *Ode on the Departing Year*, and I applied it, *con amore*, to the objects before me. That valley was to me (in a manner) the cradle of a new existence: in the river that winds through it, my spirit was baptized in the waters of Helicon!

I returned home, and soon after set out on my journey with unworn heart and untired feet. My way lay through Worcester and Gloucester, and by Upton, where I thought of Tom Jones and the adventure of the muff. I remember getting completely wet through one day, and stopping at an inn (I think it was at Tewkesbury) where I sat up all night to real *Paul and Virginia*. Sweet were the showers in early youth that drenched my body, and sweet the drops of pity that fell upon the books I read! I recollect a remark of Coleridge's upon this very book, that nothing could shew the gross indelicacy of French manners and the entire corruption of their imagination more strongly than the behaviour of the heroine in the last fatal scene, who turns away from a person on board the sinking vessel, that offers to save her life, because he has thrown off his clothes to assist him in swimming. Was this a time to think of such a circumstance? I once hinted to Wordsworth, as we were sailing in his boat on Grasmere lake, that I thought he had borrowed the idea of his *Poems on the Naming of Places* from the local inscriptions of the same kind in *Paul and Virginia*. He did not own the obligation, and stated some distinction without a difference, in defence of his claim to originality. Even the slightest variation would be sufficient for this purpose in his mind; for whatever *he* added or omitted would inevitably be worth all that any one else had done, and contain the marrow of the sentiment. I was still two days before the time fixed for my arrival, for I had taken care to set out early enough. I stopped these two days at Bridgewater, and when I was tired of sauntering on the banks of its muddy river, returned to the inn, and read *Camilla*. So have I loitered my life away, reading books, looking at pictures, going to plays, hearing, thinking, writing on what pleased me best. I have wanting only one thing to make me happy; but wanting that, have wanted everything!

I arrived, and was well received. The country about Nether Stowey is beautiful, green and hilly, and near the sea-shore. I saw it but the other day, after an interval of twenty years, from a hill near Taunton. How was the map of my life spread out before me, as the map of the country lay at my feet! In the afternoon Coleridge took me over to All-Foxden, a romantic old family-mansion of the St. Aubins, where Wordsworth lived. It was then in the possession of a friend of the poet's, who gave him the free use of it. Somehow that period (the time just after the French Revolution) was not a time when *nothing was given for nothing*. The mind opened, and a softness might be perceived coming over the heart of individuals, beneath "the scales that fence" our self-interest. Wordsworth himself was from home, but his sister kept house, and set before us a frugal repast; and we had free access to her brother's poems, the *Lyrical Ballads*, which were still in manuscript, or in the form of *Sibylline Leaves*. I dipped into a few of these with great satisfaction, and with the faith of a novice. I slept that night in an old room with blue hangings, and covered with the round-faced family-portraits of the age of George I. and II. and from the wooded declivity of the adjoining park that overlooked my window, at the dawn of day, could

"——hear the loud stag speak."

In the outset of life (and particularly at this time I felt it so) our imagination has a body to it. We are in a state between sleeping and waking, and have indistinct but glorious glimpses of strange shapes, and there is always something to come better than what we see. As in our dreams the fulness of the blood gives warmth and reality to the coinage of the brain, so in youth our ideas are clothed, and fed, and pampered with our good spirits; we breathe thick with thoughtless happiness, the weight of future years presses on the strong pulses of the heart, and we repose with undisturbed faith in truth and good. As we advance, we exhaust our fund of enjoyment and of hope. We are no longer wrapped in *lamb's-wool*, lulled in Elysium. As we taste the pleasures of life, their spirit evaporates, the sense palls; and nothing is left but the phantoms, the lifeless shadows of what *has been!*

That morning, as soon as breakfast was over, we strolled out into the park, and seating ourselves on the trunk of an old ash-tree that stretched along the

22. ***Paul and Virginia.*** *Paul et Virginie*, 1789, was a sentimental novel by Jacques Henri Bernardin de Saint-Pierre. 49. ***Camilla,*** a novel by Frances Burney, 1796.

13. **free use of it.** Hazlitt was mistaken. Wordsworth paid £23 rent. 22. ***Sibylline Leaves,*** Coleridge's 1817 volume of poems.

ground, Coleridge read aloud with a sonorous and musical voice the ballad of *Betty Foy*. I was not critically or sceptically inclined. I saw touches of truth and nature, and took the rest for granted. But in the *Thorn*, the *Mad Mother*, and the *Complaint of a Poor Indian Woman*, I felt that deeper power and pathos which have been since acknowledged,

> "In spite of pride, in erring reason's spite,"

as the characteristics of this author; and the sense of a new style and a new spirit in poetry came over me. It had to me something of the effect that arises from the turning up of the fresh soil, or of the first welcome breath of Spring:

> "While yet the trembling year is unconfirmed."

Coleridge and myself walked back to Stowey that evening, and his voice sounded high

> "Of Providence, foreknowledge, will, and fate,
> Fixed fate, free-will, foreknowledge absolute,"

as we passed through echoing grove, by fairy stream or waterfall, gleaming in the summer moonlight! He lamented that Wordsworth was not prone enough to believe in the traditional superstitions of the place, and that there was a something corporeal, a *matter-of-fact-ness*, a clinging to the palpable, or often to the petty, in his poetry, in consequence. His genius was not a spirit that descended to him through the air; it sprung out of the ground like a flower, or unfolded itself from a green spray, on which the gold-finch sang. He said, however (if I remember right), that this objection must be confined to his descriptive pieces, that his philosophic poetry had a grand and comprehensive spirit in it, so that his soul seemed to inhabit the universe like a palace, and to discover truth by intuition, rather than by deduction. The next day Wordsworth arrived from Bristol at Coleridge's cottage. I think I see him now. He answered in some degree to his friend's description of him, but was more gaunt and Don Quixote-like. He was quaintly dressed (according to the costume of that unconstrained period) in a brown fustian jacket and striped pantaloons. There was something of a roll, a lounge in his gait, not unlike his own Peter Bell. There was a severe, worn pressure of thought about his temples, a fire in his eye (as if he saw something in objects more than the outward appearance), an intense high narrow forehead, a Roman nose, cheeks furrowed by strong purpose and feeling, and a convulsive inclination to laughter about the mouth, a good deal at variance with the solemn, stately expression of the rest of his face. Chantry's bust wants the marking traits; but he was teased into making it regular and heavy: Haydon's head of him, introduced into the *Entrance of Christ into Jerusalem*, is the most like his drooping weight of thought and expression. He sat down and talked very naturally and freely, with a mixture of clear gushing accents in his voice, a deep gutteral intonation, and a strong tincture of the northern *burr*, like the crust on wine. He instantly began to make havoc of the half of a Cheshire cheese on the table, and said triumphantly that "his marriage with experience had not been so unproductive as Mr. Southey's in teaching him a knowledge of the good things of this life." He had been to see the *Castle Spectre*, by Monk Lewis, while at Bristol, and described it very well. He said "it fitted the taste of the audience like a glove." This *ad captandum* merit was however by no means a recommendation of it, according to the severe principles of the new school, which reject rather than court popular effect. Wordsworth, looking out of the low, latticed window, said, "How beautifully the sun sets on that yellow bank!" I thought within myself, "With what eyes these poets see nature!" and ever after, when I saw the sun-set stream upon the objects facing it, conceived I had made a discovery, or thanked Mr. Wordsworth for having made one for me! We went over to All-Foxden again the day following, and Wordsworth read us the story of Peter Bell in the open air; and the comment made upon it by his face and voice was very different from that of some later critics! Whatever might be thought of the poem, "his face was a book where men might read strange matters," and he announced the fate of his hero in prophetic tones. There is a *chaunt* in the recitation both of Coleridge and Wordsworth, which acts as a spell upon the hearer, and disarms the judgment. Perhaps they have deceived themselves by making habitual use of this ambiguous accompaniment. Coleridge's manner is more full, animated, and varied; Wordsworth's more equable, sustained, and internal. The one might be termed more *dramatic*, the other more *lyrical*. Coleridge has told me that he himself liked to compose in walking over uneven ground, or breaking through the straggling branches of a copse-wood; whereas Wordsworth always wrote (if he could) walking up and down a straight gravel-walk, or in some spot where the continuity of his verse met with no collateral in-

2. **Betty Foy,** in Wordsworth's "The Idiot Boy," published, with the other poems mentioned, in *Lyrical Ballads.*

4. **Haydon's head,** B. R. Haydon, 1786–1846. **15–16. Castle Spectre,** a Gothic drama. Compare the allusion to the spirit of Christabel's mother in Coleridge's "Christabel." **18. ad captandum,** designed to captivate.

terruption. Returning that same evening, I got into a metaphysical argument with Wordsworth, while Coleridge was explaining the different notes of the nightingale to his sister, in which we neither of us succeeded in making ourselves perfectly clear and intelligible. Thus I passed three weeks at Nether Stowey and in the neighbourhood, generally devoting the afternoons to a delightful chat in an arbour made of bark by the poet's friend Tom Poole, sitting under two fine elm-trees, and listening to the bees humming round us, while we quaffed our *flip*. It was agreed, among other things, that we should make a jaunt down the Bristol-Channel, as far as Linton. We set off together on foot, Coleridge, John Chester, and I. This Chester was a native of Nether Stowey, one of those who were attracted to Coleridge's discourse as flies are to honey, or bees in swarming-time to the sound of a brass pan. He "followed in the chace like a dog who hunts, not like one that made up the cry." He had on a brown cloth coat, boots, and corduroy breeches, was low in stature, bow-legged, had a drag in his walk like a drover, which he assisted by a hazel switch, and kept on a sort of trot by the side of Coleridge, like a running footman by a state coach, that he might not lose a syllable or sound that fell from Coleridge's lips. He told me his private opinion, that Coleridge was a wonderful man. He scarcely opened his lips, much less offered an opinion the whole way: yet of the three, had I to chuse during that journey, I would be John Chester. He afterwards followed Coleridge into Germany, where the Kantean philosophers were puzzled how to bring him under any of their categories. When he sat down at table with his idol, John's felicity was complete; Sir Walter Scott's, or Mr. Blackwood's, when they sat down at the same table with the King, was not more so. We passed Dunster on our right, a small town between the brow of a hill and the sea. I remember eying it wistfully as it lay below us: contrasted with the woody scene around, it looked as clear, as pure, as *embrowned* and ideal as any landscape I have seen since, of Gaspar Poussin's or Domenichino's. We had a long day's march—(our feet kept time to the echoes of Coleridge's tongue)—through Minehead and by the Blue Anchor, and on to Linton, which we did not reach till near midnight, and where we had some difficulty in making a lodgment. We however knocked the people of the house up at last, and we were repaid for our apprehensions and fatigue by some excellent rashers of fried bacon and eggs. The view in coming along had been splendid. We walked for miles and miles on dark brown heaths overlooking the Channel, with the Welsh hills beyond, and at times descended into little sheltered valleys close by the sea-side, with a smuggler's face scowling by us, and then had to ascend conical hills with a path winding up through a coppice to a barren top, like a monk's shaven crown, from one of which I pointed out to Coleridge's notice the bare masts of a vessel on the very edge of the horizon and within the red-orbed disk of the setting sun, like his own spectre-ship in the *Ancient Mariner*. At Linton the character of the sea-coast becomes more marked and rugged. There is a place called the *Valley of Rocks* (I suspect this was only the poetical name for it) bedded among precipices overhanging the sea, with rocky caverns beneath, into which the waves dash, and where the sea-gull for ever wheels its screaming flight. On the tops of these are huge stones thrown transverse, as if an earthquake had tossed them there, and behind these is a fretwork of perpendicular rocks, something like the *Giant's Causeway*. A thunder-storm came on while we were at the inn, and Coleridge was running out bareheaded to enjoy the commotion of the elements in the *Valley of Rocks*, but as if in spite, the clouds only muttered a few angry sounds, and let fall a few refreshing drops. Coleridge told me that he and Wordsworth were to have made this place the scene of a prose-tale, which was to have been in the manner of, but far superior to, the *Death of Abel*, but they had relinquished the design. In the morning of the second day, we breakfasted luxuriously in an old-fashioned parlour, on tea, toast, eggs, and honey, in the very sight of the bee-hives from which it had been taken, and a garden full of thyme and wild flowers that had produced it. On this occasion Coleridge spoke of Virgil's Georgics, but not well. I do not think he had much feeling for the classical or elegant. It was in this room that we found a little worn-out copy of the *Seasons*, lying in a window-seat, on which Coleridge exclaimed, "*That* is true fame!" He said Thomson was a great poet, rather than a good one; his style was as meretricious as his thoughts were natural. He spoke of Cowper as the best modern poet. He said the *Lyrical Ballads* were an experiment about to be tried by him and Wordsworth, to see how far the public taste would endure poetry written in a more natural and simple style than had hitherto been attempted; totally discarding the artifices of poetical diction, and making use only of such words as had probably been common in the most ordinary language since the days of Henry II. Some comparison was introduced between Shakespear and Milton. He said "he hardly

9. **Tom Poole,** who invited Coleridge to Nether Stowey.

29. **Death of Abel,** by Solomon Gessner, a Swiss poet.

knew which to prefer. Shakespear appeared to him a mere stripling in the art; he was as tall and as strong, with infinitely more activity than Milton, but he never appeared to have come to man's estate; or if he had, he would not have been a man, but a monster." He spoke with contempt of Gray, and with intolerance of Pope. He did not like the versification of the latter. He observed that "the ears of these couplet-writers might be charged with having short memories, that could not retain the harmony of whole passages." He thought little of Junius as a writer; he had a dislike of Dr. Johnson; and a much higher opinion of Burke as an orator and politician, than of Fox or Pitt. He however thought him very inferior in richness of style and imagery to some of our elder prose-writers, particularly Jeremy Taylor. He liked Richardson, but not Fielding; nor could I get him to enter into the merits of *Caleb Williams*. In short, he was profound and discriminating with respect to those authors whom he liked, and where he gave his judgment fair play; capricious, perverse, and prejudiced in his antipathies and distastes. We loitered on the "ribbed sea-sands," in such talk as this, a whole morning, and, I recollect, met with a curious sea-weed, of which John Chester told us the country name! A fisherman gave Coleridge an account of a boy that had been drowned the day before, and that they had tried to save him at the risk of their own lives. He said "he did not know how it was that they ventured, but, Sir, we have a *nature* towards one another." This expression, Coleridge remarked to me, was a fine illustration of that theory of disinterestedness which I (in common with Butler) had adopted. I broached to him an argument of mine to prove that *likeness* was not mere association of ideas. I said that the mark in the sand put one in mind of a man's foot, not because it was part of a former impression of a man's foot (for it was quite new) but because it was like the shape of a man's foot. He assented to the justness of this distinction (which I have explained at length elsewhere, for the benefit of the curious) and John Chester listened; not from any interest in the subject, but because he was astonished that I should be able to suggest any thing to Coleridge that he did not already know. We returned on the third morning, and Coleridge remarked the silent cottage-smoke curling up the valleys where, a few evenings before, we had seen the lights gleaming through the dark.

In a day or two after we arrived at Stowey, we set out, I on my return home, and he for Germany. It was a Sunday morning, and he was to preach that day for Dr. Toulmin of Taunton. I asked him if he had prepared anything for the occasion? He said he had not even thought of the text, but should as soon as we parted. I did not go to hear him,—this was a fault,—but we met in the evening at Bridgewater. The next day we had a long day's walk to Bristol, and sat down, I recollect, by a well-side on the road, to cool ourselves and satisfy our thirst, when Coleridge repeated to me some descriptive lines from his tragedy of *Remorse;* which I must say became his mouth and that occasion better than they, some years after, did Mr. Elliston's and the Drury-lane boards,—

"Oh memory! shield me from the world's poor
strife,
And give those scenes thine everlasting life."

I saw no more of him for a year or two, during which period he had been wandering in the Hartz Forest in Germany; and his return was cometary, meteorous, unlike his setting out. It was not till some time after that I knew his friends Lamb and Southey. The last always appears to me (as I first saw him) with a common-place book under his arm, and the first with a *bon-mot* in his mouth. It was at Godwin's that I met him with Holcroft and Coleridge, where they were disputing fiercely which was the best—*Man as he was, or man as he is to be*. "Give me," says Lamb, "man as he is *not* to be." This saying was the beginning of a friendship between us, which I believe still continues.—Enough of this for the present.

"But there is matter for another rhyme,
And I to this may add a second tale."

CHARACTERS OF SHAKESPEAR'S PLAYS

HAMLET

THIS is that Hamlet the Dane, whom we read of in our youth, and whom we may be said almost to remember in our after-years; he who made that famous soliloquy on life, who gave the advice to the players, who thought "this goodly frame, the earth, a steril promontory, and this brave o'er-hanging firmament, the air, this majestical roof fretted with golden fire, a foul and pestilent congregation of va-

19. Caleb Williams, a novel by William Godwin expounding in fictional form many of the ideas in *Political Justice.*

35–36. "But . . . second tale." See Wordsworth's "Hart-Leap Well," ll. 95–96.

pours"; whom "man delighted not, nor woman neither"; he who talked with the grave-diggers, and moralised on Yorick's skull; the school-fellow of Rosencrans and Guildenstern at Wittenberg; the friend of Horatio; the lover of Ophelia; he that was mad and sent to England; the slow avenger of his father's death; who lived at the court of Horwendillus five hundred years before we were born, but all those thoughts we seem to know as well as we do our own, because we have read them in Shakespear.

Hamlet is a name; his speeches and sayings but the idle coinage of the poet's brain. What then, are they not real? They are as real as our own thoughts. Their reality is in the reader's mind. It is *we* who are Hamlet. This play has a prophetic truth, which is above that of history. Whoever has become thoughtful and melancholy through his own mishaps or those of others; whoever has borne about with him the clouded brow of reflection, and thought himself "too much i' th' sun"; whoever has seen the golden lamp of day dimmed by envious mists rising in his own breast, and could find in the world before him only a dull blank with nothing left remarkable in it; whoever has known "the pangs of despised love, the insolence of office, or the spurns which patient merit of the unworthy takes"; he who has felt his mind sink within him, and sadness cling to his heart like a malady, who has had his hopes blighted and his youth staggered by the apparitions of strange things; who cannot be well at ease, while he sees evil hovering near him like a spectre; whose powers of action have been eaten up by thought, he to whom the universe seems infinite, and himself nothing; whose bitterness of soul makes him careless of consequences, and who goes to a play as his best resource to shove off, to a second remove, the evils of life by a mock representation of them—this is the true Hamlet.

We have been so used to this tragedy that we hardly know how to criticise it any more than we should know how to describe our own faces. But we must make such observations as we can. It is the one of Shakespear's plays that we think of the oftenest, because it abounds most in striking reflections on human life, and because the distresses of Hamlet are transferred, by the turn of his mind, to the general account of humanity. Whatever happens to him we apply to ourselves, because he applies it so himself as a means of general reasoning. He is a great moraliser; and what makes him worth attending to is that he moralises on his own feelings and experience. He is not a common-place pedant. If *Lear* shows the greatest depth of passion, HAMLET is the most remarkable for the ingenuity, originality, and unstudied development of character. Shakespear had more magnanimity than any other poet, and he has shewn more of it in this play than in any other. There is no attempt to force an interest: every thing is left for time and circumstances to unfold. The attention is excited without effort, the incidents succeed each other as matters of course, the characters think and speak and act just as they might do, if left entirely to themselves. There is no set purpose, no straining at a point. The observations are suggested by the passing scene—the gusts of passion come and go like sounds of music borne on the wind. The whole play is an exact transcript of what might be supposed to have taken place at the court of Denmark, at the remote period of time fixed upon, before the modern refinements in morals and manners were heard of. It would have been interesting enough to have been admitted as a bystander in such a scene, at such a time, to have heard and seen something of what was going on. But here we are more than spectators. We have not only "the outward pageants and the signs of grief"; but "we have that within which passes shew." We read the thoughts of the heart, we catch the passions living as they rise. Other dramatic writers give us very fine versions and paraphrases of nature: but Shakespear, together with his own comments, gives us the original text, that we may judge for ourselves. This is a very great advantage.

The character of Hamlet stands quite by itself. It is not a character marked by strength of will or even of passion, but by refinement of thought and sentiment. Hamlet is as little of the hero as a man can well be: but he is a young and princely novice, full of high enthusiasm and quick sensibility—the sport of circumstances, questioning with fortune and refining on his own feelings, and forced from the natural bias of his disposition by the strangeness of his situation. He seems incapable of deliberate action, and is only hurried into extremities on the spur of the occasion, when he has no time to reflect, as in the scene where he kills Polonius, and again, where he alters the letters which Rosencrans and Guildenstern are taking with them to England, purporting his death. At other times, when he is most bound to act, he remains puzzled, undecided, and sceptical, dallies with his purposes, till the occasion is lost, and always finds some pretence to relapse into indolence and thoughtfulness again. For this reason he refuses to kill the King when he is at his

7–8. who lived . . . born, an allusion to the earliest form of the story, told by the Danish historian Saxo-Grammaticus c. 1200.

prayers, and by a refinement in malice, which is in truth only an excuse for his own want of resolution, defers his revenge to some more fatal opportunity, when he shall be engaged in some act "that has no relish of salvation in it."

"He kneels and prays
And now I'll do 't, and so he goes to heaven,
And so am I revenged; *that would be scanned:*
He killed my father, and for that,
I, his sole son, send him to heaven.
Why this is reward, not revenge.
Up sword and know thou a more horrid time,
When he is drunk, asleep, or in a rage."

He is the prince of philosophical speculators, and because he cannot have his revenge perfect, according to the most refined idea his wish can form, he declines it altogether. So he scruples to trust the suggestions of the ghost, contrives the scene of the play to have surer proof of his uncle's guilt, and then rests satisfied with this confirmation of his suspicions, and the success of his experiment, instead of acting upon it. Yet he is sensible of his own weakness, taxes himself with it, and tries to reason himself out of it.

"How all occasions do inform against me,
And spur my dull revenge! What is a man,
If his chief good and market of his time
Be but to sleep and feed? A beast; no more.
Sure he that made us with such large discourse,
Looking before and after, gave us not
That capability and god-like reason
To rust in us unused: now whether it be
Bestial oblivion, or some craven scruple
Of thinking too precisely on th' event,—
A thought which quartered, hath but one part wisdom,
And ever three parts coward;—I do not know
Why yet I live to say, this thing's to do;
Sith I have cause, and will, and strength, and means
To do it. Examples gross as earth exhort me:
Witness this army of such mass and charge,
Led by a delicate and tender prince,
Whose spirit with divine ambition puffed,
Makes mouths at the invisible event,
Exposing what is mortal and unsure
To all that fortune, death and danger dare,
Even for an egg-shell. 'Tis not to be great
Never to stir without great argument;
But greatly to find quarrel in a straw,
When honour's at the stake. How stand I then,
That have a father killed, a mother stained,
Excitements of my reason and my blood,
And let all sleep, while to my shame I see
The imminent death of twenty thousand men,
That for a fantasy and trick of fame,
Go to their graves like beds, fight for a plot
Whereon the numbers cannot try the cause,
Which is not tomb enough, and continent
To hide the slain?—O, from this time forth,
My thoughts be bloody or be nothing worth."

Still he does nothing; and this very speculation on his own infirmity only affords him another occasion for indulging it. It is not for any want of attachment to his father or abhorrence of his murder that Hamlet is thus dilatory, but it is more to his taste to indulge his imagination in reflecting upon the enormity of the crime and refining on his schemes of vengeance, than to put them into immediate practice. His ruling passion is to think, not to act: and any vague pretext that flatters this propensity instantly diverts him from his previous purposes.

The moral perfection of this character has been called in question, we think, by those who did not understand it. It is more interesting than according to rules; amiable, though not faultless. The ethical delineations of "that noble and liberal casuist" (as Shakespear has been called) do not exhibit the drab-coloured quakerism of morality. His plays are not copied either from the Whole Duty of Man or from The Academy of Compliments! We confess we are a little shocked at the want of refinement in those who are shocked at the want of refinement in Hamlet. The neglect of punctilious exactness in his behaviour either partakes of the "licence of the time," or else belongs to the very excess of intellectual refinement in the character, which makes the common rules of life, as well as his own purposes, sit loose upon him. He may be said to be amenable only to the tribunal of his own thoughts, and is too much taken up with the airy world of contemplation to lay as much stress as he ought on the practical consequences of things. His habitual principles of action are unhinged and out of joint with the time. His conduct to Ophelia is quite natural in his circumstances. It is that of assumed severity only. It is the effect of disappointed hope, of bitter regrets, of affection suspended, not obliterated, by the distractions of the scene around him! Amidst the natural and preternatural horrors of his situation, he

30. Whole Duty of Man, an ethical treatise of the seventeenth century, author unknown. **31. The Academy of Compliments,** another seventeenth-century treatise, on courtship and manners.

might be excused in delicacy from carrying on a regular courtship. When "his father's spirit was in arms," it was not a time for the son to make love in. He could neither marry Ophelia, nor wound her mind by explaining the cause of his alienation, which he durst hardly trust himself to think of. It would have taken him years to have come to a direct explanation on the point. In the harassed state of his mind, he could not have done otherwise than he did. His conduct does not contradict what he says when he sees her funeral,

> "I loved Ophelia: forty thousand brothers
> Could not with all their quantity of love
> Make up my sum."

Nothing can be more affecting or beautiful than the Queen's apostrophe to Ophelia on throwing the flowers into the grave.

> —"Sweets to the sweet, farewell.
> I hoped thou should'st have been my Hamlet's wife:
> I thought thy bride-bed to have decked, sweet maid,
> And not have strewed thy grave."

Shakespear was thoroughly a master of the mixed motives of human character, and he here shews us the Queen, who was so criminal in some respects, not without sensibility and affection in other relations of life.—Ophelia is a character almost too exquisitely touching to be dwelt upon. Oh rose of May, oh flower too soon faded! Her love, her madness, her death, are described with the truest touches of tenderness and pathos. It is a character which nobody but Shakespear could have drawn in the way that he has done, and to the conception of which there is not even the smallest approach, except in some of the old romantic ballads. Her brother, Laertes, is a character we do not like so well: he is too hot and choleric, and somewhat rhodomontade. Polonius is a perfect character in its kind; nor is there any foundation for the objections which have been made to the consistency of this part. It is said that he acts very foolishly and talks very sensibly. There is no inconsistency in that. Again, that he talks wisely at one time and foolishly at another; that his advice to Laertes is very excellent, and his advice to the King and Queen on the subject of Hamlet's madness very ridiculous. But he gives the one as a father, and is sincere in it; he gives the other as a mere courtier, a busy-body, and is accordingly officious, garrulous, and impertinent. In short, Shakespear has been accused of inconsistency in this and other characters, only because he has kept up the distinction which there is in nature, between the understandings and moral habits of men, between the absurdity of their ideas and the absurdity of their motives. Polonius is not a fool, but he makes himself so. His folly, whether in his actions or speeches, comes under the head of impropriety of intention.

We do not like to see our author's plays acted, and least of all, HAMLET. There is no play that suffers so much in being transferred to the stage. Hamlet himself seems hardly capable of being acted. Mr. Kemble unavoidably fails in this character from a want of ease and variety. The character of Hamlet is made up of undulating lines; it has the yielding flexibility of "a wave o' th' sea." Mr. Kemble plays it like a man in armour, with a determined inveteracy of purpose, in one undeviating straight line, which is as remote from the natural grace and refined susceptibility of the character, as the sharp angles and abrupt starts which Mr. Kean introduces into the part. Mr. Kean's Hamlet is as much too splenetic and rash as Mr. Kemble's is too deliberate and formal. His manner is too strong and pointed. He throws a severity, approaching to virulence, into the common observations and answers. There is nothing of this in Hamlet. He is, as it were, wrapped up in his reflections, and only *thinks aloud*. There should therefore be no attempt to impress what he says upon others by a studied exaggeration of emphasis or manner; no *talking at* his hearers. There should be as much of the gentleman and scholar as possible infused into the part, and as little of the actor. A pensive air of sadness should sit reluctantly upon his brow, but no appearance of fixed and sullen gloom. He is full of weakness and melancholy, but there is no harshness in his nature. He is the most amiable of misanthropes.

41. Polonius. With these remarks on Polonius compare those by Coleridge in "Characteristics of Shakspere's Dramas."

16–17. We do not like . . . Hamlet. Lamb had argued similarly in "On the Tragedies of Shakspeare, Considered with Reference to Their Fitness for Stage Representation," 1811.

Sir Walter Scott

1771–1832

Walter Scott was descended from a long line of swashbuckling freebooters with such picturesque nicknames as Auld Wat of Harden and Beardie. His father was the first of the family to settle down to town life, as a Writer to the Signet (attorney) in Edinburgh. Scott was born August 15, 1771, in a house at the head of the College Wynd (lane). His mother was the daughter of a professor in the University of Edinburgh. At the age of eighteen months he was stricken with infantile paralysis, which left his right leg withered. This physical misfortune probably determined his career as a writer, for otherwise he might have been a great man of action. In the belief that country life would be beneficial to him, his parents sent him to live with his grandparents at Sandy-Knowe, a farm with the old ruined tower of Smailholme standing on it. There, in the company of his grandmother, an aunt, an old shepherd, and the farm hands, who taught him the folklore of the countryside, the child became "healthy, high-spirited, and, lameness apart, sturdy." At the age of eight he resumed life with his family in Edinburgh and began attending the High School. More memorable to him than the classics which he studied or the schoolboy gang wars in which he fought was his discovery, at the age of thirteen, of Percy's *Reliques*. "To read and to remember," he wrote, "was in this instance the same thing, and henceforth I overwhelmed my school fellows and all who would listen to me, with tragical recitations from the ballads of Bishop Percy." At the University of Edinburgh a serious illness interrupted his study. Withdrawing, he apprenticed himself to his father for the study of law. (Many of his experiences as a law student are related in his novel *Redgauntlet*.) His passing the examination for license to practice law, in 1792, completed his formal education. Thus the chief components of his training were folklore, romance, and the law, with an intimate knowledge of the scenic and historic Scottish countryside—excellent preparation for the literary career awaiting him.

Already, while in the service of his father, he had started his ballad "raids" (expeditions to collect old ballads). In 1795 this interest was stimulated by his reading of German ballads. In the meantime, after an unhappy love-affair with Williamina Stuart, he fell in love with Charlotte Carpenter, daughter of a French royalist. Having joined the Edinburgh Light Dragoons, a cavalry company organized to resist French invasion, he courted Charlotte in uniform. His marriage to her followed shortly after the publication in 1796 of his first little volume of poetry, containing "William and Helen," a translation of Gottfried August Bürger's "*Lenore*." After making further translations of the sort and composing some original ballads for Monk Lewis's *Tales of Wonder*, he began work on his *Minstrelsy of the Scottish Border*. This magnificent collection of ballads and songs, most of them traditional, some of Scott's own composition, and some by other known authors, with its extensive introductions and notes, is the germinal work of Scott's literary career.

This career is a straightforward, expanding development. The phase of ballad collecting, editing, and imitation flowered in the *Minstrelsy*, 1802–03. From the *Minstrelsy* to metrical romances was the second step. This Scott took in *The Lay of the Last Minstrel*, 1805, a story in verse reminiscent of Coleridge's *Christabel*. *Marmion*, 1808, "a Tale of Flodden," relates the adventures of an English knight, culminating in the famous battle in which Scottish heroism shone in defeat. *The Lady of the Lake*, 1810, purest and sweetest of all Scott's romances, has its setting in the Trossachs country and tells the romantic tale of James IV of Scotland, trying to pacify the Highland clans. *Rokeby*, 1813, about the English civil wars of Charles I's time, and *The Lord of the Isles*, 1815, about Robert Bruce, complete the metrical romances. These made Scott the most popular British poet of the decade 1800–10.

For a while Scott maintained an active law practice. Two years after his marriage he became sheriff of Selkirkshire. He drilled and roistered with his cavalry company, built an estate at Ashestiel and later at Abbotsford, and became a silent partner in the publishing firm of John Ballantyne and Company.

The final and widest phase of Scott's romancing began in 1814. Rummaging in a closet for fishing tackle, he turned up the manuscript of a novel that he had begun some years before. It seemed so promising that he finished it and published it anonymously as *Waverley*. This was the first of the great series of historical novels bearing the collective name Waverley. Taking Scotland of the seventeenth and eighteenth centuries for his settings, Scott wrote and published *Guy Mannering*, 1815; *Old Mortality* and *The Antiquary*, 1816; *The Heart of Midlothian* and *Rob Roy*, 1818; and *The Bride of Lammermoor*, 1819. Then he extended his field in space and time by writing *Ivanhoe*, 1820, treating England in the age of Richard Cœur-de-Lion; *The Abbot*, of the period of Mary Queen of Scots; *Kenilworth*, 1821, with its great scenes in the Age of Elizabeth; and *The Fortunes of Nigel*, 1822, concerned with Elizabeth's successor, James I. *Quentin Durward*, 1823, added France of the age of Louis XI, and *The Talisman*, 1825, added the Holy Land at the time of the Crusades to Scott's empire of romance. *Redgauntlet*, 1824, was a return to the native heath.

These literary conquests brought Scott world fame and wealth such as no writer before him had ever enjoyed from the products of his pen. He accepted the one modestly and shared the other generously. He built a beautiful estate at Abbotsford on the Tweed, established his family there in lordly splendor, and dispensed hospitality to visitors from all parts of the Western world (for example, Wordsworth and Washington Irving). In 1820 he was made a baronet. In 1825 Abbotsford celebrated brilliantly the engagement of his oldest son to a niece of one of the great families of Scotland. The following year brought financial ruin. The panic of the time and the bankruptcy of an English firm with which Ballantyne and Company had become involved broke the Scottish firm. As a silent partner, Scott could have escaped without utter loss. But he held himself to a gentleman's view of the business and accepted ultimate responsibility. He spent his fortune and the labors of his last years, often in pain and sickness, clearing up the obligation. He died peacefully in 1832, admired and lamented by the world.

No brief sketch can fully suggest the amazing vitality and diversity of Scott as a human figure. Of all the Romanticists, he is perhaps the most admirable and attractive personally—the one we should most enjoy as friend and neighbor. His very faults—easy optimism, reckless generosity, overworldliness—are the excesses of his virtues. His open-handedness, his kindliness, his delight in men, women, and children of all walks of life, disarm those who would condemn him as a political Tory, an opponent of the French Revolution, a defender of the feudal status quo that he knew and revered. The scores of great character creations in his poems and novels flock to his defense.

As a literary figure, Scott was the prince of romancers. He revived the past on a scale of unparalleled magnificence and with an aspect of reality scarcely equaled by any writer after him. He reclaimed old ballads, composed new ones almost as good, and got everybody to reading them. He made best-sellers out of metrical romances telling stories centuries old. He created the historical novel and conquered the reading world with it. By his own profound knowledge of past times and by the universality of his understanding heart, he was able to enter imaginatively into the scenes and the lives of bygone ages. Compelled by the tastes of his own day and the conditions that he depicted to plot most of his novels about the figures and movements of aristocrats, he was really most interested in plain or humble folk like Meg Merrilies, Old Elspeth, Cuddie Headrigg, Wandering Willie, Edie Ochiltree, Dandie Dinmont, and Jeanie Deans. In the variety and the number of his authentic character creations he is of the glorious company of Shakespeare and Dickens. He is one of the sweetest singing poets. The numerous ballads and songs scattered through the lays and the novels treat the themes and situations associated with a primitive or feudal order of society. They are breath of his breath, blood of his blood.

from MARMION

LOCHINVAR

O, young Lochinvar is come out of the west,
Through all the wide Border his steed was the best;
And save his good broadsword, he weapons had none,
He rode all unarmed, and he rode all alone.
So faithful in love, and so dauntless in war,
There never was knight like the young Lochinvar.
He staid not for brake, and he stopped not for stone,
He swam the Eske river where ford there was none;
But ere he alighted at Netherby gate,
The bride had consented, the gallant came late:
For a laggard in love, and a dastard in war,
Was to wed the fair Ellen of brave Lochinvar.

So boldly he entered the Netherby Hall,
Among bride's-men, and kinsmen, and brothers, and all:
Then spoke the bride's father, his hand on his sword,
(For the poor craven bridegroom said never a word,)

"O come ye in peace here, or come ye in war,
Or to dance at our bridal, young Lord Lochinvar?"

"I long wooed your daughter, my suit you denied;—
Love swells like the Solway, but ebbs like its tide—
And now am I come, with this lost love of mine,
To lead but one measure, drink one cup of wine.
There are maidens in Scotland more lovely by far,
That would gladly be bride to the young Lochinvar."

The bride kissed the goblet; the knight took it up,
He quaffed off the wine, and he threw down the cup.
She looked down to blush, and she looked up to sigh,
With a smile on her lips, and a tear in her eye.
He took her soft hand, ere her mother could bar,—
"Now tread we a measure!" said young Lochinvar.

So stately his form, and so lovely her face,
That never a hall such a galliard did grace:
While her mother did fret, and her father did fume,
And the bridegroom stood dangling his bonnet and plume;
And the bride-maidens whispered, "'Twere better by far
To have matched our fair cousin with young Lochinvar."

One touch to her hand, and one word in her ear,
When they reached the hall-door, and the charger stood near;
So light to the croupe the fair lady he swung,
So light to the saddle before her he sprung!
"She is won! we are gone, over bank, bush, and scaur;
They'll have fleet steeds that follow," quoth young Lochinvar.

There was mounting 'mong Graemes of the Netherby clan;
Forsters, Fenwicks, and Musgraves, they rode and they ran;
There was racing and chasing, on Cannobie Lee,
But the lost bride of Netherby ne'er did they see.
So daring in love, and so dauntless in war.
Have ye e'er heard of gallant like young Lochinvar?

32. galliard, brisk dance.

from THE LADY OF THE LAKE

CANTO I: THE CHASE

Harp of the North! that mouldering long hast hung
On the witch-elm that shades Saint Fillan's spring,
And down the fitful breeze thy numbers flung,
Till envious ivy did around thee cling,
Muffling with verdant ringlet every string,—
O minstrel Harp! still must thine accents sleep?
'Mid rustling leaves and fountains murmuring,
Still must thy sweeter sounds their silence keep,
Nor bid a warrior smile, nor teach a maid to weep?

Not thus, in ancient days of Caledon,
Was thy voice mute amid the festal crowd,
When lay of hopeless love, or glory won,
Aroused the fearful, or subdued the proud.
At each according pause, was heard aloud
Thine ardent symphony sublime and high!
Fair dames and crested chiefs attention bowed;
For still the burden of thy minstrelsy
Was Knighthood's dauntless deed, and Beauty's matchless eye.

O wake once more! how rude soe'er the hand
That ventures o'er thy magic maze to stray;
O wake once more! though scarce my skill command
Some feeble echoing of thine earlier lay:
Though harsh and faint, and soon to die away,
And all unworthy of thy nobler strain,
Yet if one heart throb higher at its sway,
The wizard note has not been touched in vain.
Then silent be no more! Enchantress, wake again!

I

The stag at eve had drunk his fill,
Where danced the moon on Monan's rill,
And deep his midnight lair had made
In lone Glenartney's hazel shade;
But, when the sun his beacon red
Had kindled on Benvoirlich's head,
The deep-mouthed bloodhound's heavy bay
Resounded up the rocky way,
And faint, from farther distance borne,
Were heard the clanging hoof and horn.

1. Harp of the North, symbolical of the minstrelsy of Scotland. The first twenty-seven lines are the invocation, in Spenserian stanzas. The body of the poem is prevailingly in four-beat couplets, like Coleridge's "Christabel." **29. Monan's rill.** The scene is the Highlands of Scotland, around Loch Lomond and the Trossachs.

2

As Chief, who hears his warder call,
"To arms! the foemen storm the wall,"
The antlered monarch of the waste
Sprung from his heathery couch in haste.
But, ere his fleet career he took,
The dew-drops from his flanks he shook;
Like crested leader proud and high,
Tossed his beamed frontlet to the sky;
A moment gazed adown the dale,
A moment snuffed the tainted gale,
A moment listened to the cry,
That thickened as the chase drew nigh;
Then, as the headmost foes appeared,
With one brave bound the copse he cleared,
And, stretching forward free and far,
Sought the wild heaths of Uam-Var.

3

Yelled on the view the opening pack;
Rock, glen, and cavern, paid them back;
To many a mingled sound at once
The awakened mountain gave response.
A hundred dogs bayed deep and strong,
Clattered a hundred steeds along,
Their peal the merry horns rung out,
A hundred voices joined the shout;
With hark and whoop and wild halloo,
No rest Benvoirlich's echoes knew.
Far from the tumult fled the roe,
Close in her covert cowered the doe;
The falcon, from her cairn on high,
Cast on the rout a wondering eye,
Till far beyond her piercing ken
The hurricane had swept the glen.
Faint and more faint, its failing din
Returned from cavern, cliff, and linn,
And silence settled, wide and still,
On the lone wood and mighty hill.

4

Less loud the sounds of silvan war
Disturbed the heights of Uam-Var,
And roused the cavern, where, 'tis told,
A giant made his den of old;
For ere that steep ascent was won,
High in his pathway hung the sun,
And many a gallant, stayed perforce,
Was fain to breathe his faltering horse,
And of the trackers of the deer,
Scarce half the lessening pack was near;
So shrewdly on the mountain side
Had the bold burst their mettle tried.

71. linn, ravine.

5

The noble stag was pausing now,
Upon the mountain's southern brow,
Where broad extended, far beneath,
The varied realms of fair Menteith.
With anxious eye he wandered o'er
Mountain and meadow, moss and moor,
And pondered refuge from his toil,
By far Lochard or Aberfoyle.
But nearer was the copsewood grey,
That waved and wept on Loch-Achray,
And mingled with the pine-trees blue
On the bold cliffs of Benvenue.
Fresh vigour with the hope returned;
With flying foot the heath he spurned,
Held westward with unwearied race,
And left behind the panting chase.

6

'Twere long to tell what steeds gave o'er,
As swept the hunt through Cambus-more;
What reins were tightened in despair,
When rose Benledi's ridge in air;
Who flagged upon Bochastle's heath,
Who shunned to stem the flooded Teith,—
For twice that day, from shore to shore,
The gallant stag swam stoutly o'er.
Few were the stragglers, following far,
That reached the lake of Vennachar;
And when the Brigg of Turk was won,
The headmost horseman rode alone.

7

Alone, but with unbated zeal,
That horseman plied the scourge and steel;
For jaded now, and spent with toil,
Embossed with foam, and dark with soil,
While every gasp with sobs he drew,
The labouring stag strained full in view.
Two dogs of black Saint Hubert's breed,
Unmatched for courage, breath, and speed,
Fast on his flying traces came,
And all but won that desperate game;
For, scarce a spear's length from his haunch,
Vindictive toiled the bloodhounds stanch;
Nor nearer might the dogs attain,
Nor farther might the quarry strain.
Thus up the margin of the lake,
Between the precipice and brake,
O'er stock and rock their race they take.

8

The Hunter marked that mountain high,
The lone lake's western boundary,

And deemed the stag must turn to bay,
Where that huge rampart barred the way;
Already glorying in the prize,
Measured his antlers with his eyes;
For the death-wound and death-halloo,
Mustered his breath, his whinyard drew;—
But thundering as he came prepared,
With ready arm and weapon bared,
The wily quarry shunned the shock,
And turned him from the opposing rock;
Then, dashing down a darksome glen,
Soon lost to hound and hunter's ken,
In the deep Trossachs' wildest nook
His solitary refuge took.
There, while close couched, the thicket shed
Cold dews and wild-flowers on his head,
He heard the baffled dogs in vain
Rave through the hollow pass amain,
Chiding the rocks that yelled again.

9

Close on the hounds the hunter came,
To cheer them on the vanished game;
But, stumbling in the rugged dell,
The gallant horse exhausted fell.
The impatient rider strove in vain
To rouse him with the spur and rein,
For the good steed, his labours o'er,
Stretched his stiff limbs, to rise no more;
Then touched with pity and remorse,
He sorrowed o'er the expiring horse.
"I little thought, when first thy rein
I slacked upon the banks of Seine,
That Highland eagle e'er should feed
On thy fleet limbs, my matchless steed!
Woe worth the chase, woe worth the day,
That costs thy life, my gallant grey!"

10

Then through the dell his horn resounds,
From vain pursuit to call the hounds.
Back limped, with slow and crippled pace,
The sulky leaders of the chase;
Close to their master's side they pressed,
With drooping tail and humbled crest;
But still the dingle's hollow throat
Prolonged the swelling bugle-note.
The owlets started from their dream,
The eagles answered with their scream,
Round and around the sounds were cast,
Till echo seemed an answering blast;
And on the hunter hied his way,
To join some comrades of the day;
Yet often paused, so strange the road,
So wondrous were the scenes it showed. . . .

138. whinyard, a short sword. **166. worth,** be, become.

from ROKEBY: Canto III

BRIGNALL BANKS

O, Brignall banks are wild and fair,
  And Greta woods are green,
And you may gather garlands there,
  Would grace a summer queen.
And as I rode by Dalton-hall,
  Beneath the turrets high,
A Maiden on the castle wall
  Was singing merrily,—
"O, Brignall banks are fresh and fair,
  And Greta woods are green;
I'd rather rove with Edmund there,
  Than reign our English queen."—

"If, Maiden, thou wouldst wend with me,
  To leave both tower and town,
Thou first must guess what life lead we,
  That dwell by dale and down?
And if thou canst that riddle read,
  As read full well you may,
Then to the greenwood shalt thou speed,
  As blithe as Queen of May."—
Yet sung she, "Brignall banks are fair,
  And Greta woods are green;
I'd rather rove with Edmund there,
  Than reign our English queen.

"I read you, by your bugle-horn,
  And by your palfrey good,
I read you for a ranger sworn,
  To keep the king's greenwood."—
"A Ranger, lady, winds his horn,
  And 'tis at peep of light;
His blast is heard at merry morn,
  And mine at dead of night."
Yet sung she, "Brignall banks are fair,
  And Greta woods are gay;
I would I were with Edmund there,
  To reign his Queen of May!

"With burnished brand and musketoon,
  So gallantly you come,
I read you for a bold Dragoon,
  That lists the tuck of drum."—
"I list no more the tuck of drum,
  No more the trumpet hear;

But when the beetle sounds his hum,
My comrades take the spear.
And O! though Brignall banks be fair,
And Greta woods be gay,
Yet mickle must the maiden dare,
Would reign my Queen of May!

"Maiden! a nameless life I lead,
A nameless death I'll die!
The fiend, whose lantern lights the mead,
Were better mate than I!
And when I'm with my comrades met
Beneath the greenwood bough,
What once we were we all forget,
Nor think what we are now.
Yet Brignall banks are fresh and fair,
And Greta woods are green,
And you may gather garlands there
Would grace a summer queen."

JOCK OF HAZELDEAN

"Why weep ye by the tide, ladie?
Why weep ye by the tide?
I'll wed ye to my youngest son,
And ye sall be his bride;
And ye sall be his bride, ladie,
Sae comely to be seen"—
But aye she loot the tears down fa'
For Jock of Hazeldean.

"Now let this wilfu' grief be done,
And dry that cheek so pale;
Young Frank is chief of Errington,
And Lord of Langley-dale;
His step is first in peaceful ha',
His sword in battle keen"—
But aye she loot the tears down fa'
For Jock of Hazeldean.

"A chain of gold ye sall not lack,
Nor braid to bind your hair;
Nor mettled hound, nor managed hawk,
Nor palfrey fresh and fair;
And you, the foremost o' them a',
Shall ride our forest queen"—
But aye she loot the tears down fa'
For Jock of Hazeldean.

The kirk was decked at morning-tide,
The tapers glimmered fair;
The priest and bridegroom wait the bride,
And dame and knight are there.
They sought her baith by bower and ha';
The ladie was not seen!
She's o'er the Border, and awa'
Wi' Jock of Hazeldean.

47. **mickle,** much.

from THE ANTIQUARY

TIME

"Why sit'st thou by that ruined hall,
Thou aged carle so stern and grey?
Dost thou its former pride recall,
Or ponder how it passed away?"—

"Know'st thou not me?" the Deep Voice cried;
"So long enjoyed, so oft misused—
Alternate, in thy fickle pride,
Desired, neglected, and accused!

"Before my breath, like blazing flax,
Man and his marvels pass away!
And changing empires wane and wax,
Are founded, flourish, and decay.

"Redeem mine hours—the space is brief—
While in my glass the sand-grains shiver,
And measureless thy joy or grief,
When TIME and thou shalt part for ever!"

THE SUN UPON THE WEIRDLAW HILL

The sun upon the Weirdlaw Hill,
In Ettrick's vale, is sinking sweet;
The westland wind is hush and still,
The lake lies sleeping at my feet.
Yet not the landscape to mine eye
Bears those bright hues that once it bore.
Though evening, with her richest dye,
Flames o'er the hills of Ettrick's shore.

With listless look along the plain,
I see Tweed's silver current glide,
And coldly mark the holy fane
Of Melrose rise in ruined pride.
The quiet lake, the balmy air,
The hill, the stream, the tower, the tree,—
Are they still such as once they were?
Or is the dreary change in me?

Time. 2. **carle,** churl, peasant.

Alas, the warped and broken board,
How can it bear the painter's dye!
The harp of strained and tuneless chord,
How to the minstrel's skill reply!
To aching eyes each landscape lowers,
To feverish pulse each gale blows chill;
And Araby's or Eden's bowers
Were barren as this moorland hill.

from THE HEART OF MIDLOTHIAN

PROUD MAISIE

Sung by Madge Wildfire, the insane woman, as she lies dying; one of the most exquisite literary ballads in English. It "gives in its sixteen lines the essence of all that needs to be said about the dying of a young girl."
—Oliver Elton

Proud Maisie is in the wood,
Walking so early;
Sweet Robin sits on the bush,
Singing so rarely.

"Tell me, thou bonny bird,
When shall I marry me?"—
"When six braw gentlemen
Kirkward shall carry ye."

"Who makes the bridal bed,
Birdie, say truly?"—
"The grey-headed sexton
That delves the grave duly.

"The glow-worm o'er grave and stone
Shall light thee steady;
The owl from the steeple sing,
'Welcome, proud lady.'"

FAREWELL TO THE MUSE

Enchantress, farewell, who so oft hast decoyed me,
At the close of the evening through woodlands to roam,
Where the forester, lated, with wonder espied me
Explore the wild scenes he was quitting for home.
Farewell, and take with thee thy numbers wild speaking
The language alternate of rapture and woe:
Oh! none but some lover, whose heart-strings are breaking,
The pang that I feel at our parting can know.

Each joy thou couldst double,—and when there came sorrow,
Or pale disappointment, to darken my way,
What voice was like thine, that could sing of to-morrow,
Till forgot in the strain was the grief of to-day!
But when friends drop around us in life's weary waning,
The grief, Queen of Numbers, thou canst not assuage;
Nor the gradual estrangement of those yet remaining,
The languor of pain, and the chillness of age.

'Twas thou that once taught me, in accents bewailing,
To sing how a warrior lay stretched on the plain,
And a maiden hung o'er him with aid unavailing,
And held to his lips the cold goblet in vain;
As vain thy enchantment, O Queen of wild Numbers,
To a bard when the reign of his fancy is o'er
And the quick pulse of feeling in apathy slumbers—
Farewell, then, Enchantress! I meet thee no more!

from QUENTIN DURWARD

COUNTY GUY

Ah! County Guy, the hour is nigh,
The sun has left the lea,
The orange flower perfumes the bower,
The breeze is on the sea.
The lark, his lay who thrilled all day,
Sits hushed his partner nigh;
Breeze, bird, and flower, confess the hour,
But where is County Guy?

The village maid steals through the shade,
Her shepherd's suit to hear;
To beauty shy, by lattice high,
Sings high-born Cavalier.
The star of Love, all stars above,
Now reigns o'er earth and sky;
And high and low the influence know—
But where is County Guy?

Proud Maisie. 7. **braw,** fine. *Farewell.* 3. **lated,** belated.

22. **when the reign of his fancy is o'er.** Compare Coleridge's "Dejection" and Wordsworth's "Resolution and Independence." 1. **County,** Earl or Count. The song is sung by a little veiled maid in a tower. The music rather than the sense is significant.

George Gordon, Lord Byron

1788–1824

"Wildfire leaped about his cradle." [1] Byron was descended from high-strung, passionate men and women, many of whom led violent and reckless lives and came to sudden ends. His paternal grandfather, Admiral John Byron, was known by his mates as "Foulweather Jack." "He had no rest at sea, nor I on shore," Byron wrote of him. The great-uncle from whom Byron inherited his title killed a man in a duel across a candle-lighted table in an inn. Byron's father, Captain John Byron, a handsome and dissipated guardsman, known as "Mad Jack," eloped with the wife of the Marquis of Carmarthen, later married her, and spent her money before her early death. From this union was born Augusta, who was to be fateful for the poet. Captain Byron's second marriage was to Miss Catherine Gordon of Gight, an heiress descended from the royal house of Scotland, "a hot-headed, hasty-handed race." George Gordon, their only child, was born on January 22, 1788, in London. Important circumstances of his childhood were the natal affliction of a twisted foot, the uncongeniality of his parents before his father died in 1791, the poverty of his early years, his mother's violence of affection and abuse (she taunted him with the epithet "lame brat"), and the scenery of Scotland, where he lived from the age of two to ten. In 1798 the death of the "wicked" Lord Byron gave him title to the barony of Newstead, and his mother took him to the family seat, Newstead Abbey, an ancient Gothic priory in the Robin Hood country which Henry VIII had granted to a Sir John Byron in 1540.

After three years of torture from unsuccessful remedies for his lameness, Byron was sent to Harrow. Under the sympathetic headmastership of Dr. Drury, he was a brilliant but irregular pupil, led in boyish sports, and formed numerous friendships. Quarrels with Dr. Drury and the succeeding master clouded his last months there. A love affair with his cousin, Mary Chaworth, broken off by her marriage to a country squire, left him with memories that were to embitter much of his poetry (for example, "The Dream"). At Cambridge, which he entered when seventeen, he took the college curriculum lightly but read widely, dissipated freely, became proficient as a boxer and a fencer, and versified. His little volume of college verse, *Hours of Idleness*, 1807, was pounced upon by the *Edinburgh Review* and mercilessly ridiculed. Following his boxing master Captain Jackson's advice for a free-for-all, Byron did not take time to pick out his friends but struck out right and left in *English Bards and Scotch Reviewers*, 1809, a brilliant satire modeled on Pope's *Dunciad* and other poems written in the Popean manner. He had received his M.A. degree in July, 1808. In March, 1809, he took his seat in the House of Lords.

In June, Byron and his college friend John Cam Hobhouse set out on a tour of the Mediterranean and the Near East. Landing at Lisbon, they rode horseback nearly five hundred miles across Portugal and Spain while those countries were still in dangerous disorder from the Peninsular Wars with Napoleon. Scenery, battlefields, bullfights, banditti, and memories of the historic past excited them all the way to Seville and Cadiz. At Gibraltar they embarked and proceeded across the Mediterranean, enjoying its moonlit beauty and romance, to Albania, Greece, and Constantinople, visiting historical and scenic spots and encountering numerous adventures, especially in the wild mountain country of the Albanian Ali Pasha. These observations and experiences Byron wrote up in the Spenserian stanzas of *Childe Harold I and II.* The poem was published in 1812, two years after Byron's return to England. "I awoke one morning and found myself famous," he says of the effect of the poem. His Turkish Tales (*The Giaour*, *The Bride of Abydos*, *The Corsair*, and others) drew from the same sources as *Childe Harold* and confirmed his popularity. For nearly four years he was the social lion of London, the most famous young man in Europe.

Intrigues with women, some of them great ladies, a brief political career in the House of Lords, and poetry imperfectly absorbed his energies for a while. He began to think of settling down. In 1815 he was married to Anna Isabella Milbanke, an intellectual and highly proper young lady who thought she might reform him, even as he thought marriage might stabilize him. Both were wrong in their calculations. They were temperamentally ill-adapted

[1] Ethel Colburn Mayne, *Byron*, 2 vols., Scribner, 1912.

to each other. As a husband, Byron was from the first brutal and unreasonable. Lady Byron insisted on an examination to determine his sanity. But there was a more serious cause of alienation growing out of Byron's incestuous relations with his half-sister, Augusta, then the wife of a Colonel Leigh. Shortly after the birth of their daughter, Ada, Lord and Lady Byron agreed to a formal separation. The scandal of the separation, stirred by such imprudences as Byron's "Fare Thee Well," was enormous. From having been its spoiled darling, Byron became the scapegoat of Regency society. On April 25, 1816, he left England for what proved to be forever, a morally banished man. The separation and the exile were the crux of his life.

In Matthew Arnold's phrase, "Making a public show of a very genuine misery, he swept across Europe the pageant of his bleeding heart." His travel itinerary was to give the occasion, the material, and the plan for the third canto of *Childe Harold.* Crossing the English Channel, he passed through the Low Countries, pausing at Waterloo, where the battle burial mound was still fresh and the red rain had made the harvest grow; ascended the Rhine (Drachenfels, Coblenz, Ehrenbreitstein); and on May 25 arrived at Geneva, Switzerland (Lake Leman, Clarens, Lausanne, Ferney), where he rented the Villa Diodati. Shelley, Mary Godwin, and Mary's stepsister Clara Jane Clairmont were neighbors. With Miss Clairmont he half-cynically accepted the status of an affair begun in London; she bore to Byron a daughter, Allegra, the following January. With Shelley and such visitors as Monk Lewis he heard readings from Wordsworth and Goethe, talked about history, literature, and philosophy, and made boating and sight-seeing excursions in the neighborhood. "Half mad during the time . . . between metaphysics, mountains, lakes, love unextinguishable, thoughts unutterable, and the nightmare of my own deliquencies," he composed *Childe Harold*, Canto the Third, *The Prisoner of Chillon*, "Stanzas to Augusta" (two poems with that title), and "The Epistle to Augusta," and began *Manfred: A Dramatic Poem.* Miss Clairmont copied the *Childe Harold* canto, and Shelley took it and the poems for *The Prisoner of Chillon* volume back to England in August for publication there.

By January, 1817, Byron was living in Venice, sunk in its dissipations, but finishing *Manfred* and writing other poems. Poetry had now become his greatest reality and occupation (see *Childe Harold*, Canto the Third, stanzas 4–7). He composed the fourth canto of *Childe Harold*, then made a new departure in the light, mocking vein of *Beppo*, 1818, bubbling up out of his Venetian dissipations. A visit from the Shelleys, trouble with Miss Clairmont and her baby, wilder profligacy, and the beginning of *Don Juan* (I and II completed and published in 1819) occupied him in 1818. From his "devilish deal of wear and tear of mind and body" he was rescued by a meeting with Teresa, the young wife of old Count Guiccioli. The ensuing liaison, regularized so far as it could be by custom, after a Papal decree had separated the Guicciolis, proved to be the most stabilizing single influence in Byron's life. He followed the Countess Guiccioli to Ravenna and lived there with her for nearly two years. During this time he composed poems (for example, *The Prophecy of Dante*) and dramas (for example, *Marino Faliero*) on Italian subjects, wrote and published the third to fifth cantos of *Don Juan*, resumed relations with the Shelley circle, now at Pisa, and interested himself in the Carbonari activities of Pietro Gamba, brother of the Countess. Trouble resulting from his political affiliations caused Byron's removal to Genoa in 1822.

In the meantime, Byron and Shelley had invited Leigh Hunt to Italy, to found and edit the *Liberal.* E. J. Trelawny, a fantastic adventurer who later became one of Byron's and Shelley's biographers, joined the group. These associations were broken up in July by the drowning of Shelley. Byron participated in the burning of Shelley's body on the beach near Via Reggio. At Genoa, where he took up residence in September, 1822, Byron wrote *The Vision of Judgment* (published in the *Liberal*), the sixth to eighth cantos of *Don Juan*, and other poems.

In January, 1823, Byron actively interested himself in the cause of Greek independence. By August he was in Greece with Trelawny and other friends. Before the end of the year he had published the ninth to fourteenth cantos of *Don Juan*, had given his financial support and his personal leadership to a company of Greek soldiers, and had suffered a decline of health. "On This Day I Complete My Thirty-sixth Year," he wrote, January 22, 1824, as a record of fact and as title of a characteristic poem. On April 19, at Missolonghi, in "The land of honorable death," he died of epilepsy or meningitis. The Greeks wished to give him "A soldier's grave" in the country for which he had spent his money and his life; but other wishes prevailed, and he was buried in Hucknall Torkard Church, near Newstead, on July 16.

From this brief story of his career, Byron's personality and character can be inferred only in part. He was far more than a literary man, far more than a celebrity who happened to be a great artist. In the old Goethe's view, he was "a personality in eminence such as never had been and is not likely to come again; a fiery mass of living valor hurling itself on life." A creature of extremes, of contradictions and paradoxes, Byron was a nobleman and (in most of his relations with women) a thorough cad, a sentimentalist and a cynic, a revolutionist and a conservative, a dandified lady-killer and a man's man, an aristocrat and a republican, a frank sensualist and a conventionalist. But certain traits are admirably constant—his downright sincerity, his hatred of hypocrisy, his rugged intellectual honesty, his fidelity to the truth about himself as well as about others. Perhaps the chief quality that sets him apart as a man and as a poet is his power of dramatizing himself, of making himself vivid in an image, striking in a posture, memorable in a phrase. He is a wanderer o'er eternity, a weed flung from the rock but also one whom the waves know as a rider. He embodies and unbosoms that which was most within him—lightning. He stands in the ruined Colosseum and apostrophizes the Eternal City without appearing absurd. He is Manfred eating his heart out in remorse for a nameless and fearful crime but fearlessly rejecting the offices of religion and defying the powers of darkness and evil. He is Juan, passing in tears and scornful laughter along the highways of a world essentially like the world we know today. He is the greatest satirical poet since Pope. His field of satire embraces nearly every aspect of modern life—the rottenness and decadence of high society, injustice and oppression in government and commerce, hypocrisy in religion, conventional morality, venality and weakness in literature, power politics, and war.

Another side of Byron, often at war with his comic spirit, sometimes the ultimate motive of it (as when he laughs to keep from weeping), is his melancholy. Early satiety, disillusionment from having anticipated life, and the resulting bitter despondency, expressed in the first two cantos of *Childe Harold* and the personal lyrics (such as "There's Not a Joy the World Can Give"), deepen into the *Weltschmerz* of the third canto of *Childe Harold* and *Manfred*. He often suggests or expresses a predestinarian or fatalistic explanation: "Thyself to be thy proper hell," "a power upon me . . . which . . . makes it my fatality to live," "Fatal and fated in thy sufferings" (*Manfred*). This melancholy colors the poet's view of historical places and natural scenery. It shapes the unifying theme of such poems as the third canto of *Childe Harold* and those addressed to Augusta, namely, that a sick and alienated soul can find refuge and solace in nature. Hence, Byron's nature poetry differs from Wordsworth's in the point of view and spirit of approach, even when (as in the poems just named and in *The Prisoner of Chillon*) it is under Wordsworthian influence. "The secret of Wordsworth," said Coleridge, "is acquiescence; Byron is in revolt. To him Nature and humanity are antagonists, and he cleaves to Nature, yea, he would take her by violence to mark his alienation and severance from man." It was Byron's very capacity to take with tragic seriousness not only his own fate but the plight of a world out of joint that explains the bitterness of his poetry. If he took the world despairingly, he also knew how to face it with laughing courage or mocking gaiety, and to live and die gallantly. "My pangs shall find a voice," he asserted. This prophecy and a kindred one have been fulfilled—

"There is that within me which shall tire
Torture and Time, and breathe when I expire."

WHEN WE TWO PARTED

When we two parted
  In silence and tears,
Half broken-hearted
  To sever for years,
Pale grew thy cheek and cold,
  Colder thy kiss;
Truly that hour foretold
  Sorrow to this.

The dew of the morning
  Sunk chill on my brow—
It felt like the warning
  Of what I feel now.
Thy vows are all broken,
  And light is thy fame:
I hear thy name spoken,
  And share in its shame.

They name thee before me,
  A knell to mine ear;
A shudder comes o'er me—
  Why wert thou so dear?
They know not I knew thee,
  Who knew thee too well:—
Long, long shall I rue thee,
  Too deeply to tell.

In secret we met—
  In silence I grieve
That thy heart could forget,
  Thy spirit deceive.
If I should meet thee
  After long years,
How should I greet thee?—
  With silence and tears.

MAID OF ATHENS

Ζώη μοῦ, σᾶς ἀγαπῶ.*

Maid of Athens, ere we part,
Give, oh give me back my heart!
Or, since that has left my breast,
Keep it now, and take the rest!
Hear my vow before I go,
Ζώη μοῦ, σᾶς ἀγαπῶ.

By those tresses unconfined,
Woo'd by each Aegean wind;
By those lids whose jetty fringe
Kiss thy soft cheeks' blooming tinge;
By those wild eyes like the roe,
Ζώη μοῦ, σᾶς ἀγαπῶ.

By that lip I long to taste;
By that zone-encircled waist;
By all the token-flowers that tell
What words can never speak so well;
By love's alternate joy and woe,
Ζώη μοῦ, σᾶς ἀγαπῶ.

Maid of Athens! I am gone:
Think of me, sweet! when alone.
Though I fly to Istambol,
Athens holds my heart and soul:
Can I cease to love thee? No!
Ζώη μοῦ, σᾶς ἀγαπῶ.

When We Two Parted. This poem has been thought by many to refer to Byron's early love affair with Mary Chaworth. Byron told Lady Hardy that it was addressed to Lady Frances Wedderburn Webster. *Maid of Athens.* *Ζώη . . . ἀγαπῶ, My life I love you.

SHE WALKS IN BEAUTY

1

She walks in beauty, like the night
  Of cloudless climes and starry skies;
And all that's best of dark and bright
  Meet in her aspect and her eyes:
Thus mellowed to that tender light
  Which heaven to gaudy day denies.

2

One shade the more, one ray the less,
  Had half impaired the nameless grace
Which waves in every raven tress,
  Or softly lightens o'er her face;
Where thoughts serenely sweet express
  How pure, how dear their dwelling-place.

She Walks in Beauty. **1. She,** Byron's cousin, Lady Wilmot Horton, whom he met in June, 1814, at a ball. She was in mourning, with silver spangles on her dress.

3

And on that cheek, and o'er that brow,
So soft, so calm, yet eloquent,
The smiles that win, the tints that glow,
But tell of days in goodness spent,
A mind at peace with all below,
A heart whose love is innocent!

THE DESTRUCTION OF SENNACHERIB

"And it came to pass that night, that the angel of the Lord went out, and smote in the camp of the Assyrians an hundred and fourscore and five thousand: and when they arose early in the morning, behold, they were all dead corpses."—II Kings 19:35. Byron wrote the poem for *Hebrew Melodies*, a songbook by a young Jewish musician named Nathan. The verse is anapestic tetrameter.

1

The Assyrian came down like the wolf on the fold,
And his cohorts were gleaming in purple and gold;
And the sheen of their spears was like stars on the sea,
When the blue wave rolls nightly on deep Galilee.

2

Like the leaves of the forest when Summer is green,
That host with their banners at sunset were seen:
Like the leaves of the forest when Autumn hath blown,
That host on the morrow lay withered and strown.

3

For the Angel of Death spread his wings on the blast,
And breathed in the face of the foe as he passed;
And the eyes of the sleepers waxed deadly and chill,
And their hearts but once heaved, and for ever grew still!

4

And there lay the steed with his nostril all wide,
But through it there rolled not the breath of his pride;
And the foam of his gasping lay white on the turf,
And cold as the spray of the rock-beating surf.

5

And there lay the rider distorted and pale,
With the dew on his brow, and the rust on his mail:
And the tents were all silent—the banners alone—
The lances unlifted—the trumpet unblown.

6

And the widows of Ashur are loud in their wail,
And the idols are broke in the temple of Baal;
And the might of the Gentile, unsmote by the sword,
Hath melted like snow in the glance of the Lord!

STANZAS FOR MUSIC

(There's Not a Joy)

There's not a joy the world can give like that it takes away,
When the glow of early thought declines in feeling's dull decay;
'Tis not on youth's smooth cheek the blush alone, which fades so fast,
But the tender bloom of heart is gone, ere youth itself be past.

Then the few whose spirits float above the wreck of happiness
Are driven o'er the shoals of guilt or ocean of excess:
The magnet of their course is gone, or only points in vain
The shore to which their shivered sail shall never stretch again.

Then the mortal coldness of the soul like death itself comes down;
It cannot feel for others' woes, it dare not dream its own;
That heavy chill has frozen o'er the fountain of our tears,
And though the eye may sparkle still, 'tis where the ice appears.

Though wit may flash from fluent lips, and mirth distract the breast,
Through midnight hours that yield no more their former hope of rest;
'Tis but as ivy-leaves around the ruined turret wreath,
All green and wildly fresh without, but worn and grey beneath.

Oh could I feel as I have felt,—or be what I have been,
Or weep as I could once have wept, o'er many a vanished scene;

2. **feeling's dull decay.** "My passions," wrote Byron, "were developed very early. . . . Perhaps this was one of the reasons which caused the anticipated melancholy of my thoughts,—having anticipated life." The poem was written in March, 1815, shortly after the death of a friend, the Earl of Dorset.

As springs, in deserts found, seem sweet, all brackish though they be,
So, midst the withered waste of life, those tears would flow to me.

FARE THEE WELL

Fare thee well! and if for ever,
  Still for ever, fare *thee well:*
Even though unforgiving, never
  'Gainst thee shall my heart rebel.

Would that breast were bared before thee
  Where thy head so oft hath lain,
While that placid sleep came o'er thee
  Which thou ne'er canst know again:

Would that breast, by thee glanced over,
  Every inmost thought could show!
Then thou wouldst at last discover
  'Twas not well to spurn it so.

Though the world for this commend thee—
  Though it smile upon the blow,
Even its praises must offend thee,
  Founded on another's woe:

Though my many faults defaced me,
  Could no other arm be found,
Than the one which once embraced me,
  To inflict a cureless wound?

Yet, oh yet, thyself deceive not;
  Love may sink by slow decay,
But by sudden wrench, believe not
  Hearts can thus be torn away:

Still thine own its life retaineth—
  Still must mine, though bleeding, beat;
And the undying thought which paineth
  Is—that we no more may meet.

These are words of deeper sorrow
  Than the wail above the dead;
Both shall live—but every morrow
  Wake us from a widowed bed.

And when thou wouldst solace gather,
  When our child's first accents flow,
Wilt thou teach her to say "Father!"
  Though his care she must forego?

When her little hands shall press thee,
  When her lip to thine is pressed,
Think of him whose prayer shall bless thee,
  Think of him thy love *had* blessed!

Should her lineaments resemble
  Those thou never more may'st see,
Then thy heart will softly tremble
  With a pulse yet true to me.

All my faults perchance thou knowest,
  All my madness—none can know;
All my hopes—where'er thou goest—
  Wither—yet with *thee* they go.

Every feeling hath been shaken;
  Pride—which not a world could bow—
Bows to thee—by thee forsaken,
  Even my soul forsakes me now:

But 'tis done—all words are idle—
  Words from me are vainer still;
But the thoughts we cannot bridle
  Force their way without the will.

Fare thee well! thus disunited,
  Torn from every nearer tie,
Seared in heart, and lone, and blighted,
  More than this I scarce can die.

1. thee, Lady Byron. The poem was written during the scandal of the separation, in 1816, with ll. 408–13 and 419–26 of "Christabel" as a motto. As originally published, there was no division into stanzas.

STANZAS FOR MUSIC

(There Be None of Beauty's Daughters)

There be none of Beauty's daughters
  With a magic like thee;
And like music on the waters
  Is thy sweet voice to me:
When, as if its sound were causing
The charmèd Ocean's pausing
The waves lie still and gleaming,
And the lulled winds seem dreaming:

And the Midnight Moon is weaving
  Her bright chain o'er the deep;
Whose breast is gently heaving,
  As an infant's asleep:
So the spirit bows before thee,
To listen and adore thee;
With a full but soft emotion,
Like the swell of Summer's ocean.

THE PRISONER OF CHILLON

A FABLE

The two following poems were written during the first summer of Byron's exile, after a boating tour of Lake Geneva with Shelley. The Castle of Chillon is situated at the eastern end of the lake. The two poems express one of Byron's greatest themes—human emancipation—the "Sonnet" states this theme explicitly, "The Prisoner" presents it dramatically. The subject, François de Bonnivard (1496–1570), was a Swiss patriot who twice suffered imprisonment for his political and religious opinions, under Charles III of Savoy. At the time he wrote the poems Byron "was not sufficiently aware of the history of Bonnivard." Actually no brothers shared Bonnivard's fate; he was imprisoned twice, for two and six years; the dungeon was not below the level of the lake; imprisonment did not break his spirit, for he lived to a ripe old age, endowing a college in Geneva and marrying four times. The changes in the story, however, greatly enhance the pathos of the Prisoner's fate, Byron's artistic theme (see lines 8–10 and 134–37, which state that the Prisoner's fate was typical of all the martyrs of political and religious opinion). The student should note especially the circumstances of imprisonment, the dramatic use made of the other two brothers (the death of the younger being the emotional climax of the poem at line 210); the powerful description of the Prisoner's insensibility (ll. 231–50); the Wordsworthian and Coleridgean treatment of the restorative influences of free nature (ll. 251–365); and the subdued, diminuendo account of the Prisoner's liberation, with its Wordsworthian and Coleridgean idea of the inculcation of sympathy through suffering (ll. 366–92). The Bonnivard of the poem is really an idealized Byron, but Byron in one of his most attractive moods, open to the influences of his fellow Romanticists (Coleridge and Wordsworth, as indicated; Shelley, through personal association; Scott, in the form and spirit of much of the poem).

SONNET ON CHILLON

Eternal Spirit of the chainless Mind!
Brightest in dungeons, Liberty! thou art,
For there thy habitation is the heart—
The heart which love of thee alone can bind;
And when thy sons to fetters are consigned—
To fetters, and the damp vault's dayless gloom,
Their country conquers with their martyrdom,
And Freedom's fame finds wings on every wind.
Chillon! thy prison is a holy place,
And thy sad floor an altar—for 'twas trod,
Until his very steps have left a trace
Worn, as if thy cold pavement were a sod,
By Bonnivard!—May none those marks efface!
For they appeal from tyranny to God.

THE PRISONER OF CHILLON

I

My hair is grey, but not with years,
Nor grew it white
In a single night,
As men's have grown from sudden fears:
My limbs are bowed, though not with toil,
But rusted with a vile repose,
For they have been a dungeon's spoil,
And mine has been the fate of those
To whom the goodly earth and air
Are banned, and barred—forbidden fare;
But this was for my father's faith
I suffered chains and courted death;
That father perished at the stake
For tenets he would not forsake;
And for the same his lineal race
In darkness found a dwelling-place;
We were seven—who now are one,
Six in youth, and one in age,
Finished as they had begun,
Proud of Persecution's rage;
One in fire, and two in field,
Their belief with blood have sealed,
Dying as their father died,
For the God their foes denied;
Three were in a dungeon cast,
Of whom this wreck is left the last.

2

There are seven pillars of Gothic mould,
In Chillon's dungeons deep and old,
There are seven columns, massy and grey,
Dim with a dull imprisoned ray,
A sunbeam which hath lost its way,
And through the crevice and the cleft
Of the thick wall is fallen and left;
Creeping o'er the floor so damp,
Like a marsh's meteor lamp:
And in each pillar there is a ring,
And in each ring there is a chain;
That iron is a cankering thing,
For in these limbs its teeth remain,
With marks that will not wear away,
Till I have done with this new day,
Which now is painful to these eyes,
Which have not seen the sun so rise
For years—I cannot count them o'er,
I lost their long and heavy score,
When my last brother drooped and died,
And I lay living by his side.

3

They chained us each to a column stone,
And we were three—yet, each alone;
We could not move a single pace,
We could not see each other's face,
But with that pale and livid light
That made us strangers in our sight:
And thus together—yet apart,
Fettered in hand, but joined in heart,
'Twas still some solace, in the dearth
Of the pure elements of earth,
To hearken to each other's speech,
And each turn comforter to each
With some new hope, or legend old,
Or song heroically bold;
But even these at length grew cold.
Our voices took a dreary tone,
An echo of the dungeon stone,
  A grating sound, not full and free,
  As they of yore were wont to be:
  It might be fancy—but to me
They never sounded like our own.

4

I was the eldest of the three,
  And to uphold and cheer the rest
  I ought to do—and did my best—
And each did well in his degree.
  The youngest, whom my father loved,
Because our mother's brow was given
To him, with eyes as blue as heaven—
  For him my soul was sorely moved:
And truly might it be distressed
To see such bird in such a nest;
For he was beautiful as day—
  (When day was beautiful to me
  As to young eagles, being free)—
  A polar day, which will not see
A sunset till its summer's gone,
  Its sleepless summer of long light,
The snow-clad offspring of the sun:
  And thus he was as pure and bright,
And in his natural spirit gay,
With tears for naught but others' ills;
And then they flowed like mountain rills,
Unless he could assuage the woe
Which he abhorred to view below.

5

The other was as pure of mind,
But formed to combat with his kind;
Strong in his frame, and of a mood
Which 'gainst the world in war had stood,
And perished in the foremost rank
  With joy:—but not in chains to pine:
His spirit withered with their clank,
  I saw it silently decline—
  And so perchance in sooth did mine:
But yet I forced it on to cheer
Those relics of a home so dear.
He was a hunter of the hills,
  Had followed there the deer and wolf;
  To him his dungeon was a gulf,
And fettered feet the worst of ills.

6

  Lake Leman lies by Chillon's walls:
A thousand feet in depth below
Its massy waters meet and flow;
Thus much the fathom-line was sent
From Chillon's snow-white battlement,
  Which round about the wave inthralls:
A double dungeon wall and wave
Have made—and like a living grave.
Below the surface of the lake
The dark vault lies wherein we lay:
We heard it ripple night and day;
  Sounding o'er our heads it knocked;
And I have felt the winter's spray
Wash through the bars when winds were high
And wanton in the happy sky;
  And then the very rock hath rocked,
  And I have felt it shake, unshocked,
Because I could have smiled to see
The death that would have set me free.

7

I said my nearer brother pined,
I said his mighty heart declined,
He loathed and put away his food;
It was not that 'twas coarse and rude,
For we were used to hunter's fare,
And for the like had little care:
The milk drawn from the mountain goat
Was changed for water from the moat,
Our bread was such as captives' tears
Have moistened many a thousand years,
Since man first pent his fellow men
Like brutes within an iron den;
But what were these to us or him?
These wasted not his heart or limb;
My brother's soul was of that mould
Which in a palace had grown cold,
Had his free breathing been denied
The range of the steep mountain's side;
But why delay the truth?—he died.
I saw, and could not hold his head,

Nor reach his dying hand—nor dead,—
Though hard I strove, but strove in vain,
To rend and gnash my bonds in twain.
He died—and they unlocked his chain,
And scooped for him a shallow grave
Even from the cold earth of our cave.
I begged them, as a boon, to lay
His corse in dust whereon the day
Might shine—it was a foolish thought,
But then within my brain it wrought,
That even in death his freeborn breast
In such a dungeon could not rest.
I might have spared my idle prayer—
They coldly laughed—and laid him there:
The flat and turfless earth above
The being we so much did love;
His empty chain above it leant,
Such Murder's fitting monument!

8

But he, the favourite and the flower,
Most cherished since his natal hour
His mother's image in fair face,
The infant love of all his race,
His martyred father's dearest thought,
My latest care, for whom I sought
To hoard my life, that his might be
Less wretched now, and one day free;
He, too, who yet had held untired
A spirit natural or inspired—
He, too, was struck, and day by day
Was withered on the stalk away.
Oh, God! it is a fearful thing
To see the human soul take wing
In any shape, in any mood:
I've seen it rushing forth in blood,
I've seen it on the breaking ocean
Strive with a swoln convulsive motion,
I've seen the sick and ghastly bed
Of Sin delirious with its dread:
But these were horrors—this was woe
Unmixed with such—but sure and slow:
He faded, and so calm and meek,
So softly worn, so sweetly weak,
So tearless, yet so tender—kind,
And grieved for those he left behind;
With all the while a cheek whose bloom
Was as a mockery of the tomb,
Whose tints as gently sunk away
As a departing rainbow's ray;
An eye of most transparent light
That almost made the dungeon bright;
And not a word of murmur—not
A groan o'er his untimely lot,—
A little talk of better days,
A little hope my own to raise,
For I was sunk in silence—lost
In this last loss, of all the most;
And then the sighs he would suppress
Of fainting Nature's feebleness,
More slowly drawn, grew less and less:
I listened, but I could not hear;
I called, for I was wild with fear;
I knew 'twas hopeless, but my dread
Would not be thus admonishèd;
I called, and thought I heard a sound—
I burst my chain with one strong bound,
And rushed to him:—I found him not,
I only stirred in this black spot,
I only lived, *I* only drew
The accursèd breath of dungeon-dew;
The last, the sole, the dearest link
Between me and the eternal brink,
Which bound me to my failing race,
Was broken in this fatal place.
One on the earth, and one beneath—
My brothers—both had ceased to breathe!
I took that hand which lay so still,
Alas! my own was full as chill;
I had not strength to stir, or strive,
But felt that I was still alive—
A frantic feeling, when we know
That what we love shall ne'er be so.
  I know not why
  I could not die,
I had no earthly hope—but faith,
And that forbade a selfish death.

9

What next befell me then and there
  I know not well—I never knew—
First came the loss of light, and air,
  And then of darkness too:
I had no thought, no feeling—none—
Among the stones I stood a stone,
And was, scarce conscious what I wist,
As shrubless crags within the mist;
For all was blank, and bleak, and grey;
It was not night—it was not day;
It was not even the dungeon-light,
So hateful to my heavy sight,
But vacancy absorbing space,
And fixedness—without a place;
There were no stars—no earth—no time—
No check—no change—no good—no crime—
But silence, and a stirless breath
Which neither was of life nor death;

A sea of stagnant idleness,
Blind, boundless, mute, and motionless!

10

A light broke in upon my brain,—
It was the carol of a bird;
It ceased, and then it came again,
The sweetest song ear ever heard,
And mine was thankful till my eyes
Ran over with the glad surprise,
And they that moment could not see
I was the mate of misery;
But then by dull degrees came back
My senses to their wonted track;
I saw the dungeon walls and floor
Close slowly round me as before,
I saw the glimmer of the sun
Creeping as it before had done,
But through the crevice where it came
That bird was perched, as fond and tame,
And tamer than upon the tree;
A lovely bird, with azure wings,
And song that said a thousand things,
And seemed to say them all for me!
I never saw its like before,
I ne'er shall see its likeness more:
It seemed like me to want a mate,
But was not half so desolate,
And it was come to love me when
None lived to love me so again,
And cheering from my dungeon's brink,
Had brought me back to feel and think.
I know not if it late were free,
Or broke its cage to perch on mine,
But knowing well captivity,
Sweet bird! I could not wish for thine!
Or if it were, in wingèd guise,
A visitant from Paradise;
For—Heaven forgive that thought! the while
Which made me both to weep and smile—
I sometimes deemed that it might be
My brother's soul come down to me;
But when at last away it flew,
And then 'twas mortal well I knew,
For he would never thus have flown—
And left me twice so doubly lone,—
Lone—as the corse within its shroud,
Lone—as a solitary cloud,
A single cloud on a sunny day,
While all the rest of heaven is clear,
A frown upon the atmosphere,
That hath no business to appear
When skies are blue, and earth is gay.

11

A kind of change came in my fate,
My keepers grew compassionate;
I know not what had made them so,
They were inured to sights of woe,
But so it was:—my broken chain
With links unfastened did remain,
And it was liberty to stride
Along my cell from side to side,
And up and down, and then athwart,
And tread it over every part;
And round the pillars one by one
Returning where my walk begun,
Avoiding only, as I trod,
My brothers' graves without a sod;
For if I thought with heedless tread
My step profaned their lowly bed,
My breath came gaspingly and thick,
And my crushed heart fell blind and sick.

12

I made a footing in the wall,
It was not therefrom to escape,
For I had buried one and all
Who loved me in a human shape;
And the whole earth would henceforth be
A wider prison unto me:
No child—no sire—no kin had I,
No partner in my misery;
I thought of this, and I was glad,
For thought of them had made me mad;
But I was curious to ascend
To my barred windows, and to bend
Once more, upon the mountains high,
The quiet of a loving eye.

13

I saw them—and they were the same,
They were not changed like me in frame;
I saw their thousand years of snow
On high—their wide long lake below,
And the blue Rhone in fullest flow;
I heard the torrents leap and gush
O'er channelled rock and broken bush;

268. A lovely bird. Compare "The Ancient Mariner": the Mariner's mental state (ll. 244 ff.) and his redemption through the influence of the water-snakes (272 ff.) and the skylark's song (359 ff.). **292. twice so doubly lone,** because (1) he had lost the bird's companionship, and (2) this desertion proved that the bird was not his brother's spirit, thus depriving him of his comforting illusion.

294. Lone—as a solitary cloud. Compare Wordsworth's "I Wandered Lonely as a Cloud." **331. The quiet of a loving eye.** Here again Byron echoes Wordsworth.

I saw the white-walled distant town,
And whiter sails go skimming down.
And then there was a little isle,
Which in my very face did smile,
The only one in view;
A small green isle, it seemed no more,
Scarce broader than my dungeon floor,
But in it there were three tall trees,
And o'er it blew the mountain breeze,
And by it there were waters flowing,
And on it there were young flowers growing,
Of gentle breath and hue.
The fish swam by the castle wall,
And they seemed joyous each and all;
The eagle rode the rising blast,
Methought he never flew so fast
As then to me he seemed to fly;
And then new tears came in my eye,
And I felt troubled—and would fain
I had not left my recent chain;
And when I did descend again,
The darkness of my dim abode
Fell on me as a heavy load;
It was as is a new-dug grave,
Closing o'er one we sought to save,—
And yet my glance, too much oppressed,
Had almost need of such a rest.

14

It might be months, or years, or days—
I kept no count, I took no note—
I had no hope my eyes to raise,
And clear them of their dreary mote;
At last men came to set me free;
I asked not why, and recked not where:
It was at length the same to me,
Fettered or fetterless to be,
I learned to love despair.
And thus when they appeared at last,
And all my bonds aside were cast,
These heavy walls to me had grown
A hermitage—and all my own!
And half I felt as they were come
To tear me from a second home:
With spiders I had friendship made,
And watched them in their sullen trade,
Had seen the mice by moonlight play,
And why should I feel less than they?
We were all inmates of one place,
And I, the monarch of each race,
Had power to kill—yet, strange to tell!
In quiet we had learned to dwell;
My very chains and I grew friends,
So much a long communion tends
To make us what we are:—even I
Regained my freedom with a sigh.

from CHILDE HAROLD'S PILGRIMAGE

from CANTO THE THIRD

"Afin que cette application vous forçât de penser à autre chose; il n'y a en vérité de remède que celui-là et le temps." *

Lettre du Roi de Prusse à D'Alembert, Sept. 7, 1776.

The student should review what has been said about the autobiographical implications of the poem, about its form, and about its plan, on pages 789–91 of the preceding biographical-critical sketch. (A rough sketch map or a line showing Byron's itinerary on any accessible map of Europe will be helpful in following Byron's movements and the topics treated.) The main topics are the poet's own personal history, nature, European history and politics relating to man's struggle for freedom: really one theme—the poet himself; everything is viewed through the medium of his own personality, profoundly stirred by his recent experiences. The dominant sentiment is "the recourse of a socially alienated mind to an all-tolerant, all-seeing nature" (see especially stanzas 12–13, 68, 72, 75, 88–90, 93, 96–97).

1

Is thy face like thy mother's, my fair child!
Ada! sole daughter of my house and heart?
When last I saw thy young blue eyes they smiled,
And then we parted,—not as now we part,
But with a hope.—
Awaking with a start,
The waters heave around me; and on high
The winds lift up their voices: I depart,
Whither I know not; but the hour's gone by,
When Albion's lessening shores could grieve or glad
mine eye.

2

Once more upon the waters! yet once more!
And the waves bound beneath me as a steed
That knows his rider. Welcome to their roar!

* **"Afin que . . . le temps."** In order that this employment may force you to think of something else; there is indeed no remedy but that and time. **5. Awaking with a start.** Note the dramatic opening—the poet, aboard ship in mid-channel, dreaming about his child, is suddenly awakened by the waves to the reality of his exile. The break in the stanza and the line is called "rhetorical shock," a favorite device of Byron's (see stanzas 17 and 110). **11–16. steed . . . rider . . . weed.** Note the two superb similes of self-characterization.

Swift be their guidance, whereso'er it lead!
Though the strained mast should quiver as a reed,
And the rent canvas fluttering strew the gale,
Still must I on; for I am as a weed,
Flung from the rock, on Ocean's foam to sail
Where'er the surge may sweep, the tempest's breath prevail.

3

In my youth's summer I did sing of One,
The wandering outlaw of his own dark mind;
Again I seize the theme, then but begun,
And bear it with me, as the rushing wind
Bears the cloud onwards: in that Tale I find
The furrows of long thought, and dried-up tears,
Which, ebbing, leave a sterile track behind,
O'er which all heavily the journeying years
Plod the last sands of life,—where not a flower appears.

4

Since my young days of passion—joy or pain—
Perchance my heart and harp have lost a string,
And both may jar: it may be that in vain
I would essay, as I have sung, to sing:
Yet, though a dreary strain, to this I cling;
So that it wean me from the weary dream
Of selfish grief or gladness—so it fling
Forgetfulness around me—it shall seem
To me, though to none else, a not ungrateful theme.

5

He, who grown agèd in this world of woe,
In deeds, not years, piercing the depths of life,
So that no wonder waits him—nor below
Can Love or Sorrow, Fame, Ambition, Strife,
Cut to his heart again with the keen knife
Of silent, sharp endurance—he can tell
Why Thought seeks refuge in lone caves, yet rife
With airy images, and shapes which dwell
Still unimpaired, though old, in the soul's haunted cell.

6

'Tis to create, and in creating live
A being more intense, that we endow
With form our fancy, gaining as we give
The life we image, even as I do now—
What am I? Nothing: but not so art thou,
Soul of my thought! with whom I traverse earth,
Invisible but gazing, as I glow
Mixed with thy spirit, blended with thy birth,
And feeling still with thee in my crushed feelings' dearth.

7

Yet must I think less wildly:—I *have* thought
Too long and darkly, till my brain became,
In its own eddy boiling and o'erwrought,
A whirling gulf of phantasy and flame:
And thus, untaught in youth my heart to tame,
My springs of life were poisoned. 'Tis too late!
Yet am I changed; though still enough the same
In strength to bear what Time can not abate,
And feed on bitter fruits without accusing Fate.

8

Something too much of this:—but now 'tis past,
And the spell closes with its silent seal.
Long absent HAROLD re-appears at last—
He of the breast which fain no more would feel,
Wrung with the wounds which kill not, but ne'er heal;
Yet Time, who changes all, had altered him
In soul and aspect as in age: years steal
Fire from the mind as vigour from the limb;
And Life's enchanted cup but sparkles near the brim.

9

His had been quaffed too quickly, and he found
The dregs were wormwood; but he filled again,
And from a purer fount, on holier ground,
And deemed its spring perpetual!—but in vain!
Still round him clung invisibly a chain
Which galled for ever, fettering though unseen,
And heavy though it clanked not; worn with pain,
Which pined although it spoke not, and grew keen,
Entering with every step he took through many a scene.

10

Secure in guarded coldness, he had mixed
Again in fancied safety with his kind,
And deemed his spirit now so firmly fixed
And sheathed with an invulnerable mind,
That, if no joy, no sorrow lurked behind;

19. One. Childe Harold (in the first and second cantos). ("Childe" means a young gentleman, usually the elder son of a nobleman.) Here begins a review of Byron's life between the end of the first tour and the beginning of his present exile (stanzas 3–15). Note the idea of satiety and disillusionment. Stanza 5 contains the germ of *Manfred, a Dramatic Poem,* written later. **46. 'Tis to create.** Here follows a poetic essay on poetry—why Byron writes it.

66. Long absent Harold re-appears. Note that in this Canto Byron identifies himself with his hero; he had not done so in the first and second.

And he, as one, might 'midst the many stand
Unheeded, searching through the crowd to find
Fit speculation—such as in strange land
He found in wonder-works of God and Nature's hand.

11

But who can view the ripened rose, nor seek
To wear it? who can curiously behold
The smoothness and the sheen of Beauty's cheek,
Nor feel the heart can never all grow old?
Who can contemplate Fame through clouds unfold
The star which rises o'er her steep, nor climb?
Harold, once more within the vortex, rolled
On with the giddy circle, chasing Time,
Yet with a nobler aim than in his Youth's fond prime.

12

But soon he knew himself the most unfit
Of men to herd with Man; with whom he held
Little in common; untaught to submit
His thoughts to others, though his soul was quelled
In youth by his own thoughts; still uncompelled,
He would not yield dominion of his mind
To Spirits against whom his own rebelled,
Proud though in desolation—which could find
A life within itself, to breathe without mankind.

13

Where rose the mountains, there to him were friends;
Where rolled the Ocean, thereon was his home;
Where a blue sky, and glowing clime, extends,
He had the passion and the power to roam;
The desert, forest, cavern, breaker's foam,
Were unto him companionship; they spake
A mutual language, clearer than the tome
Of his land's tongue, which he would oft forsake
For Nature's pages glassed by sunbeams on the lake.

14

Like the Chaldean, he could watch the stars,
Till he had peopled them with beings bright
As their own beams; and earth, and earth-born jars,
And human frailties, were forgotten quite:
Could he have kept his spirit to that flight
He had been happy; but this clay will sink
Its spark immortal, envying it the light
To which it mounts, as if to break the link
That keeps us from yon heaven which woos us to its brink.

15

But in Man's dwellings he became a thing
Restless and worn, and stern and wearisome,
Drooped as a wild-born falcon with clipt wing,
To whom the boundless air alone were home:
Then came his fit again, which to o'er-come,
As eagerly the barred-up bird will beat
His breast and beak against his wiry dome
Till the blood tinge his plumage—so the heat
Of his impeded Soul would through his bosom eat.

16

Self-exiled Harold wanders forth again,
With nought of Hope left, but with less of gloom;
The very knowledge that he lived in vain,
That all was over on this side the tomb,
Had made Despair a smilingness assume,
Which, though 'twere wild,—as on the plundered wreck
When mariners would madly meet their doom
With draughts intemperate on the sinking deck,—
Did yet inspire a cheer, which he forbore to check.

17

Stop!—for thy tread is on an Empire's dust!
An Earthquake's spoil is sepulchred below!
Is the spot marked with no colossal bust?
Nor column trophied for triumphal show?
None; but *the moral's truth* tells simpler so,
As the ground was before, thus let it be;—
How that red rain hath made the harvest grow!
And is this all the world has gained by thee,
Thou first and last of Fields! king-making Victory?

18

And Harold stands upon this place of skulls,
The grave of France, the deadly Waterloo!
How in an hour the Power which gave annuls
Its gifts, transferring fame as fleeting too!—
In "pride of place" here last the Eagle flew,
Then tore with bloody talon the rent plain,
Pierced by the shaft of banded nations through;
Ambition's life and labours all were vain—
He wears the shattered links of the World's broken chain.

145. Empire's dust, Napoleon's empire (and France's). Byron visited Waterloo almost exactly a year after the battle.

19

Fit retribution! Gaul may champ the bit
And foam in fetters;—but is Earth more free?
Did nations combat to make *One* submit;
Or league to teach all Kings true Sovereignty?
What! shall reviving Thraldom again be
The patched-up Idol of enlightened days?
Shall we, who struck the Lion down, shall we
Pay the Wolf homage? proffering lowly gaze
And servile knees to Thrones? No; *prove* before ye praise!

20

If not, o'er one fallen Despot boast no more!
In vain fair cheeks were furrowed with hot tears
For Europe's flowers long rooted up before
The trampler of her vineyards; in vain, years
Of death, depopulation, bondage, fears,
Have all been borne, and broken by the accord
Of roused-up millions; all that most endears
Glory, is when the myrtle wreathes a Sword
Such as Harmodius drew on Athens' tyrant Lord.

21

There was a sound of revelry by night,
And Belgium's Capital had gathered then
Her Beauty and her Chivalry, and bright
The lamps shone o'er fair women and brave men;
A thousand hearts beat happily; and when
Music arose with its voluptuous swell,
Soft eyes looked love to eyes which spake again,
And all went merry as a marriage bell;
But hush! hark! a deep sound strikes like a rising knell!

22

Did ye not hear it?—No—'twas but the Wind,
Or the car rattling o'er the stony street;
On with the dance! let joy be unconfined;
No sleep till morn, when Youth and Pleasure meet
To chase the glowing Hours with flying feet—
But hark!—that heavy sound breaks in once more,
As if the clouds its echo would repeat;
And nearer, clearer, deadlier than before!
Arm! Arm! it is—it is—the cannon's opening roar!

23

Within a windowed niche of that high hall
Sate Brunswick's fated Chieftain; he did hear
That sound the first amidst the festival,
And caught its tone with Death's prophetic ear;
And when they smiled because he deemed it near,
His heart more truly knew that peal too well
Which stretched his father on a bloody bier,
And roused the vengeance blood alone could quell;
He rushed into the field, and, foremost fighting fell.

24

Ah! then and there was hurrying to and fro—
And gathering tears, and tremblings of distress,
And cheeks all pale, which but an hour ago
Blushed at the praise of their own loveliness—
And there were sudden partings, such as press
The life from out young hearts, and choking sighs
Which ne'er might be repeated; who could guess
If ever more should meet those mutual eyes,
Since upon night so sweet such awful morn could rise!

25

And there was mounting in hot haste—the steed,
The mustering squadron, and the clattering car,
Went pouring forward with impetuous speed,
And swiftly forming in the ranks of war—
And deep the thunder peal on peal afar;
And near, the beat of the alarming drum
Roused up the soldier ere the Morning Star;
While thronged the citizens with terror dumb,
Or whispering, with white lips—"The foe! They come! they come!"

26

And wild and high the "Cameron's gathering" rose!
The war-note of Lochiel, which Albyn's hills
Have heard, and heard, too, have her Saxon foes:—
How in the noon of night that pibroch thrills,
Savage and shrill! But with the breath which fills
Their mountain pipe, so fill the mountaineers
With the fierce native daring which instils
The stirring memory of a thousand years,
And Evan's—Donald's—fame rings in each clansman's ears!

27

And Ardennes waves above them her green leaves,
Dewy with Nature's tear-drops, as they pass—
Grieving, if aught inanimate e'er grieves,

181 ff. There was a sound of revelry . . . With this famous account of the Duchess of Richmond's ball, and of Waterloo, compare Thackeray's in *Vanity Fair*, Chaps. 29–32.

227. Albyn's, Scotland's. **234. Evan's—Donald's.** Sir Evan Cameron and Donald Cameron were Scottish chieftains of the seventeenth and eighteenth centuries respectively.

Over the unreturning brave,—alas!
Ere evening to be trodden like the grass
Which *now* beneath them, but *above* shall grow
In its next verdure, when this fiery mass
Of living Valour, rolling on the foe
And burning with high Hope, shall moulder cold and low.

28

Last noon beheld them full of lusty life;—
Last eve in Beauty's circle proudly gay,
The Midnight brought the signal-sound of strife,
The Morn the marshalling in arms,—the Day
Battle's magnificently-stern array!
The thunder-clouds close o'er it, which when rent
The earth is covered thick with other clay,
Which her own clay shall cover, heaped and pent,
Rider and horse,—friend, foe,—in one red burial blent!

50

But Thou, exulting and abounding river!
Making thy waves a blessing as they flow
Through banks whose beauty would endure for ever
Could man but leave thy bright creation so,
Nor its fair promise from the surface mow
With the sharp scythe of conflict,—then to see
Thy valley of sweet waters, were to know
Earth paved like Heaven—and to seem such to me,
Even now what wants thy stream?—that it should Lethe be.

51

A thousand battles have assailed thy banks,
But these and half their fame have passed away,
And Slaughter heaped on high his weltering ranks;
Their very graves are gone, and what are they?
Thy tide washed down the blood of yesterday,
And all was stainless, and on thy clear stream
Glassed, with its dancing light, the sunny ray;
But o'er the blackened Memory's blighting dream
Thy waves would vainly roll, all sweeping as they seem.

52

Thus Harold inly said, and passed along,
Yet not insensible to all which here
Awoke the jocund birds to early song
In glens which might have made even exile dear:

442. But Thou, the Rhine River.

Though on his brow were graven lines austere,
And tranquil sternness, which had ta'en the place
Of feelings fierier far but less severe—
Joy was not always absent from his face
But o'er it in such scenes would steal with transient trace.

53

Nor was all Love shut from him, though his days
Of Passion had consumed themselves to dust.
It is in vain that we would coldly gaze
On such as smile upon us; the heart must
Leap kindly back to kindness, though Disgust
Hath weaned it from all worldings: thus he felt,
For there was soft Remembrance, and sweet Trust
In one fond breast, to which his own would melt,
And in its tenderer hour on that his bosom dwelt.

54

And he had learned to love,—I know not why,
For this in such as him seems strange of mood,—
The helpless looks of blooming Infancy,
Even in its earliest nurture; what subdued,
To change like this, a mind so far imbued
With scorn of man, it little boots to know;
But thus it was; and though in solitude
Small power the nipped affections have to grow,
In him this glowed when all beside had ceased to glow.

55

And there was one soft breast, as hath been said,
Which unto his was bound by stronger ties
Than the church links withal; and,—though unwed,
That love was pure—and, far above disguise,
Had stood the test of mortal enmities,
Still undivided, and cemented more
By peril, dreaded most in female eyes;
But this was firm, and from a foreign shore
Well to that heart might his these absent greetings pour!

I

The castled crag of Drachenfels
Frowns o'er the wide and winding Rhine,
Whose breast of waters broadly swells
Between the banks which bear the vine;
And hills all rich with blossomed trees,
And fields which promise corn and wine,
And scattered cities crowning these,
Whose far white walls along them shine,

476. one fond breast, Augusta's.

Have strewed a scene, which I should see
With double joy wert *thou* with me.

2

And peasant girls, with deep blue eyes,
And hands which offer early flowers,
Walk smiling o'er this Paradise;
Above, the frequent feudal towers
Through green leaves lift their walls of gray;
And many a rock which steeply lowers,
And noble arch in proud decay,
Look o'er this vale of vintage-bowers;
But one thing want these banks of Rhine,—
Thy gentle hand to clasp in mine!

3

I send the lilies given to me—
Though long before thy hand they touch,
I know that they must withered be,
But yet reject them not as such;
For I have cherished them as dear,
Because they yet may meet thine eye,
And guide thy soul to mine even here,—
When thou behold'st them drooping nigh,
And know'st them gathered by the Rhine,
And offered from my heart to thine!

4

The river nobly foams and flows—
The charm of this enchanted ground,
And all its thousand turns disclose
Some fresher beauty's varying round:
The haughtiest breast its wish might bound
Through life to dwell delighted here;
Nor could on earth a spot be found
To nature and to me so dear—
Could thy dear eyes in following mine
Still sweeten more these banks of Rhine!

56

By Coblentz, on a rise of gentle ground,
There is a small and simple Pyramid,
Crowning the summit of the verdant mound;
Beneath its base are Heroes' ashes hid,
Our enemy's—but let not that forbid
Honour to Marceau! o'er whose early tomb
Tears, big tears, gushed from the rough soldier's lid,
Lamenting and yet envying such a doom,
Falling for France, whose rights he battled to resume.

516. I send the lilies. When the poem appeared in 1816, while the scandal was still fresh, Augusta wished the lilies and the poem at the bottom of the Red Sea.

57

Brief, brave, and glorious was his young career,—
His mourners were two hosts, his friends and foes;
And fitly may the stranger lingering here
Pray for his gallant Spirit's bright repose;
For he was Freedom's Champion, one of those,
The few in number, who had not o'erstept
The charter to chastise which she bestows
On such as wield her weapons; he had kept
The whiteness of his soul—and thus men o'er him wept.

58

Here Ehrenbreitstein, with her shattered wall
Black with the miner's blast, upon her height
Yet shows of what she was, when shell and ball
Rebounding idly on her strength did light:—
A Tower of Victory! from whence the flight
Of baffled foes was watched along the plain:
But Peace destroyed what War could never blight,
And laid those proud roofs bare to Summer's rain—
On which the iron shower for years had poured in vain.

59

Adieu to thee, fair Rhine! How long delighted
The stranger fain would linger on his way!
Thine is a scene alike where souls united,
Or lonely Contemplation thus might stray;
And could the ceaseless vultures cease to prey
On self-condemning bosoms, it were here,
Where Nature, nor too sombre nor too gay,
Wild but not rude, awful yet not austere,
Is to the mellow Earth as Autumn to the year.

68

Lake Leman woos me with its crystal face,
The mirror where the stars and mountains view
The stillness of their aspect in each trace
Its clear depth yields of their far height and hue:
There is too much of Man here, to look through
With a fit mind the might which I behold;
But soon in me shall Loneliness renew
Thoughts hid, but not less cherished than of old,
Ere mingling with the herd had penned me in their fold.

69

To fly from, need not be to hate, mankind:
All are not fit with them to stir and toil,
Nor is it discontent to keep the mind
Deep in its fountain, lest it overboil
In the hot throng, where we become the spoil

644. Lake Leman, Lake Geneva.

Of our infection, till too late and long
We may deplore and struggle with the coil,
In wretched interchange of wrong for wrong
Midst a contentious world, striving where none are strong.

70

There, in a moment we may plunge our years
In fatal penitence, and in the blight
Of our own Soul turn all our blood to tears,
And colour things to come with hues of Night;
The race of life becomes a hopeless flight
To those that walk in darkness: on the sea
The boldest steer but where their ports invite—
But there are wanderers o'er Eternity
Whose bark drives on and on, and anchored ne'er shall be.

71

Is it not better, then, to be alone,
And love Earth only for its earthly sake?
By the blue rushing of the arrowy Rhone,
Or the pure bosom of its nursing Lake,
Which feeds it as a mother who doth make
A fair but froward infant her own care,
Kissing its cries away as these awake;—
Is it not better thus our lives to wear,
Than join the crushing crowd, doomed to inflict or bear?

72

I live not in myself, but I become
Portion of that around me; and to me
High mountains are a feeling, but the hum
Of human cities torture: I can see
Nothing to loathe in Nature, save to be
A link reluctant in a fleshly chain,
Classed among creatures, when the soul can flee,
And with the sky—the peak—the heaving plain
Of ocean, or the stars, mingle—and not in vain.

73

And thus I am absorbed, and this is life:—
I look upon the peopled desert past,
As on a place of agony and strife,
Where, for some sin, to Sorrow I was cast,
To act and suffer, but remount at last
With a fresh pinion; which I feel to spring,
Though young, yet waxing vigorous as the Blast
Which it would cope with, on delighted wing,
Spurning the clay-cold bonds which round our being cling.

669. wanderers o'er Eternity. See Shelley's *Adonais*, stanza 30, l. 264, p. 855. **680. I live not in myself.** Compare Wordsworth's ideas about nature, especially in "Tintern Abbey."

74

And when, at length, the mind shall be all free
From what it hates in this degraded form,
Reft of its carnal life, save what shall be
Existent happier in the fly and worm,—
When Elements to Elements conform,
And dust is as it should be, shall I not
Feel all I see less dazzling but more warm?
The bodiless thought? the Spirit of each spot?
Of which, even now, I share at times the immortal lot?

75

Are not the mountains, waves, and skies, a part
Of me and of my Soul, as I of them?
Is not the love of these deep in my heart
With a pure passion? should I not contemn
All objects, if compared with these? and stem
A tide of suffering, rather than forego
Such feelings for the hard and worldly phlegm
Of those whose eyes are only turned below,
Gazing upon the ground, with thoughts which dare not glow?

85

Clear, placid Leman! thy contrasted lake,
With the wild world I dwelt in, is a thing
Which warns me, with its stillness, to forsake
Earth's troubled waters for a purer spring.
This quiet sail is as a noiseless wing
To waft me from distraction; once I loved
Torn Ocean's roar, but thy soft murmuring
Sounds sweet as if a sister's voice reproved,
That I with stern delights should e'er have been so moved.

86

It is the hush of night, and all between
Thy margin and the mountains, dusk, yet clear,
Mellowed and mingling, yet distinctly seen,
Save darkened Jura, whose capt heights appear
Precipitously steep; and drawing near,
There breathes a living fragrance from the shore,
Of flowers yet fresh with childhood; on the ear
Drops the light drip of the suspended oar,
Or chirps the grasshopper one good-night carol more.

698. And when, at length. Study this pantheistic conception of immortality. **797. Clear, placid Leman!** Note that the famous description of Lake Geneva, the summit of the poem, is in three scenes: (1) evening (idyllic peace), (2) night (storm, the climax—in the poet's breast), and (3) morning (the earth fresh and joyous). **809. Jura,** a mountain range between Switzerland and France.

87

He is an evening reveller, who makes
His life an infancy, and sings his fill;
At intervals, some bird from out the brakes
Starts into voice a moment, then is still.
There seems a floating whisper on the hill,
But that is fancy, for the starlight dews
All silently their tears of Love instil,
Weeping themselves away, till they infuse
Deep into Nature's breast the spirit of her hues.

88

Ye Stars! which are the poetry of Heaven!
If in your bright leaves we would read the fate
Of men and empires,—'tis to be forgiven,
That in our aspirations to be great,
Our destinies o'erleap their mortal state,
And claim a kindred with you; for ye are
A Beauty and a Mystery, and create
In us such love and reverence from afar,
That Fortune,—Fame,—Power,—Life, have named themselves a Star.

89

All Heaven and Earth are still—though not in sleep,
But breathless, as we grow when feeling most;
And silent, as we stand in thoughts too deep:—
All Heaven and Earth are still: From the high host
Of stars to the lulled lake and mountain-coast,
All is concentered in a life intense,
Where not a beam, nor air, nor leaf is lost,
But hath a part of Being, and a sense
Of that which is of all Creator and Defence.

90

Then stirs the feeling infinite, so felt
In solitude, where we are *least* alone;
A truth, which through our being then doth melt,
And purifies from self: it is a tone,
The soul and source of Music, which makes known
Eternal harmony, and sheds a charm
Like to the fabled Cytherea's zone,
Binding all things with beauty;—'twould disarm
The spectre Death, had he substantial power to harm.

91

Not vainly did the early Persian make
His altar the high places, and the peak
Of earth-o'ergazing mountains, and thus take
A fit and unwalled temple, there to seek
The Spirit, in whose honour shrines are weak,
Upreared of human hands. Come and compare
Columns and idol-dwellings—Goth or Greek—
With Nature's realms of worship, earth and air—
Nor fix on fond abodes to circumscribe thy prayer!

92

The sky is changed!—and such a change! Oh Night,
And Storm, and Darkness, ye are wondrous strong,
Yet lovely in your strength, as is the light
Of a dark eye in Woman! Far along,
From peak to peak, the rattling crags among
Leaps the live thunder! Not from one lone cloud,
But every mountain now hath found a tongue,
And Jura answers, through her misty shroud,
Back to the joyous Alps, who call to her aloud!

93

And this is in the Night:—Most glorious Night!
Thou wert not sent for slumber! let me be
A sharer in thy fierce and far delight,—
A portion of the tempest and of thee!
How the lit lake shines, a phosphoric sea,
And the big rain comes dancing to the earth!
And now again 'tis black,—and now, the glee
Of the loud hills shakes with its mountain-mirth,
As if they did rejoice o'er a young Earthquake's birth.

94

Now, where the swift Rhone cleaves his way between
Heights which appear as lovers who have parted
In hate, whose mining depths so intervene,
That they can meet no more, though broken-hearted;
Though in their souls, which thus each other thwarted,
Love was the very root of the fond rage
Which blighted their life's bloom, and then departed:—
Itself expired, but leaving them an age
Of years all winters,—war within themselves to wage:

95

Now, where the quick Rhone thus hath cleft his way,
The mightiest of the storms hath taken his stand:
For here, not one, but many, make their play,

848. Cytherea's zone, the girdle of Venus, goddess of love and beauty.

879. Heights which appear. Compare Coleridge's "Christabel," ll. 419–26.

And fling their thunder-bolts from hand to hand,
Flashing and cast around: of all the band,
The brightest through these parted hills hath forked
His lightnings,—as if he did understand,
That in such gaps as Desolation worked,
There the hot shaft should blast whatever therein lurked.

96

Sky—Mountains—River—Winds—Lake—lightnings! he!
With night, and clouds, and thunder, and a Soul
To make these felt and feeling, well may be
Things that have made me watchful; the far roll
Of your departing voices, is the knoll
Of what in me is sleepless,—if I rest.
But where of ye, O Tempests! is the goal?
Are ye like those within the human breast?
Or do ye find, at length, like eagles, some high nest?

97

Could I embody and unbosom now
That which is most within me,—could I wreak
My thoughts upon expression, and thus throw
Soul—heart—mind—passions—feelings—strong or weak—
All that I would have sought, and all I seek,
Bear, know, feel—and yet breathe—into *one* word,
And that one word were Lightning, I would speak;
But as it is, I live and die unheard,
With a most voiceless thought, sheathing it as a sword.

98

The Morn is up again, the dewy Morn,
With breath all incense, and with cheek all bloom—
Laughing the clouds away with playful scorn,
And living as if earth contained no tomb,—
And glowing into day: we may resume
The march of our existence: and thus I,
Still on thy shores, fair Leman! may find room
And food for meditation, nor pass by
Much, that may give us pause, if pondered fittingly.

110

Italia! too, Italia! looking on thee,
Full flashes on the Soul the light of ages,
Since the fierce Carthaginian almost won thee,
To the last halo of the Chiefs and Sages
Who glorify thy consecrated pages;
Thou wert the throne and grave of empires—still,
The fount at which the panting Mind assuages
Her thirst of knowledge, quaffing there her fill,
Flows from the eternal source of Rome's imperial hill.

111

Thus far have I proceeded in a theme
Renewed with no kind auspices:—to feel
We are not what we have been, and to deem
We are not what we should be,—and to steel
The heart against itself; and to conceal,
With a proud caution, love, or hate, or aught,—
Passion or feeling, purpose, grief or zeal,—
Which is the tyrant Spirit of our thought,—
Is a stern task of soul:—No matter,—it is taught.

112

And for these words, thus woven into song,
It may be that they are a harmless wile,—
The colouring of the scenes which fleet along,
Which I would seize, in passing, to beguile
My breast, or that of others, for a while.
Fame is the thirst of youth,—but I am not
So young as to regard men's frown or smile,
As loss or guerdon of a glorious lot;
I stood and stand alone,—remembered or forgot.

113

I have not loved the World, nor the World me;
I have not flattered its rank breath, nor bowed
To its idolatries a patient knee,
Nor coined my cheek to smiles,—nor cried aloud
In worship of an echo; in the crowd
They could not deem me one of such—I stood
Among them, but not of them—in a shroud
Of thoughts which were not their thoughts, and still could,
Had I not filed my mind, which thus itself subdued.

114

I have not loved the World, nor the World me,—
But let us part fair foes; I do believe,
Though I have found them not, that there may be
Words which are things,—hopes which will not deceive,
And Virtues which are merciful, nor weave

900. knoll, knell (archaic). **905. Could I embody,** etc. This stanza has been called "the most essentially Byronic thing in all Byron."

1057. filed, defiled.

Snares for the failing: I would also deem
O'er others' griefs that some sincerely grieve—
That two, or one, are almost what they seem,—
That Goodness is no name—and Happiness no dream.

115

My daughter! with thy name this song begun;
My daughter! with thy name thus much shall end!—
I see thee not—I hear thee not—but none
Can be so wrapt in thee; Thou art the Friend
To whom the shadows of far years extend:
Albeit my brow thou never should'st behold,
My voice shall with thy future visions blend,
And reach into thy heart,—when mine is cold,—
A token and a tone, even from thy father's mould.

116

To aid thy mind's development,—to watch
Thy dawn of little joys,—to sit and see
Almost thy very growth,—to view thee catch
Knowledge of objects,—wonders yet to thee!
To hold thee lightly on a gentle knee,
And print on thy soft cheek a parent's kiss,—
This, it should seem, was not reserved for me—
Yet this was in my nature:—as it is,
I know not what is there, yet something like to this.

117

Yet, though dull Hate as duty should be taught,
I know that thou wilt love me,—though my name
Should be shut from thee, as a spell still fraught
With desolation, and a broken claim;
Though the grave closed between us,—'twere the same—
I know that thou wilt love me—though to drain
My blood from out thy being were an aim,
And an attainment,—all would be in vain,—
Still thou would'st love me, still that more than life retain.

118

The child of Love, though born in bitterness,
And nurtured in Convulsion! Of thy sire
These were the elements,—and thine no less.
As yet such are around thee,—but thy fire
Shall be more tempered, and thy hope far higher.
Sweet be thy cradled slumbers! O'er the sea
And from the mountains where I now respire,
Fain would I waft such blessing upon thee,
As—with a sigh—I deem thou might'st have been to me!

1094. child of Love. The poem ends on the same theme and note on which it began.

from CANTO THE FOURTH

"Visto ho Toscana Lombardia Romagna,
Quel monte che divide, e quel che serra
*Italia, e un mare e l'altro che la bagna."**

Ariosto, Satira iv, ll. 58–60.

Byron's early impressions of Italy furnish the material for the fourth canto of *Childe Harold's Pilgrimage*, which was published in April, 1818. In the final canto the shadowy figure of Childe Harold disappears and the poet expresses in his own person the thoughts evoked by Italy's historic places, notably Venice, Florence, and Rome.

I

I stood in Venice on the Bridge of Sighs,
A palace and a prison on each hand:
I saw from out the wave her structures rise
As from the stroke of the enchanter's wand:
A thousand years their cloudy wings expand
Around me, and a dying Glory smiles
O'er the far times, when many a subject land
Looked to the wingèd Lion's marble piles,
Where Venice sate in state, throned on her hundred isles!

2

She looks a sea Cybéle, fresh from ocean,
Rising with her tiara of proud towers
At airy distance, with majestic motion,
A ruler of the waters and their powers:
And such she was;—her daughters had their dowers
From spoils of nations, and the exhaustless East
Poured in her lap all gems in sparkling showers:
In purple was she robed, and of her feast
Monarchs partook, and deemed their dignity increased.

3

In Venice Tasso's echoes are no more,
And silent rows the songless gondolier;
Her palaces are crumbling to the shore,
And music meets not always now the ear:
Those days are gone,—but Beauty still is here;
States fall, arts fade,—but Nature doth not die,
Nor yet forget how Venice once was dear,
The pleasant place of all festivity,
The revel of the earth, the masque of Italy! . . .

***"Visto ho . . . la bagna."** I have seen Tuscany, Lombardy, the Romagna; that mountain which divides, and that which shuts in Italy; and one sea and the other which bathes it (Italy). **8. wingèd Lion's.** The winged lion is the symbol of St. Mark, patron of Venice. **10. Cybéle,** mother of the gods, represented with a tiara of towers. **19. Tasso's echoes.** Stanzas of Torquato Tasso's epic, *Jerusalem Delivered*, formerly chanted by the gondoliers.

78

O Rome! my country! city of the soul!
The orphans of the heart must turn to thee,
Lone mother of dead empires! and control
In their shut breasts their petty misery.
What are our woes and sufferance? Come and see
The cypress, hear the owl, and plod your way
O'er steps of broken thrones and temples—Ye!
Whose agonies are evils of a day—
A world is at our feet as fragile as our clay.

79

The Niobe of nations! there she stands,
—Childless and crownless, in her voiceless woe;
An empty urn within her withered hands,
Whose holy dust was scattered long ago:
The Scipios' tomb contains no ashes now;
The very sepulchres lie tenantless
Of their heroic dwellers;—dost thou flow,
Old Tiber, through a marble wilderness?
Rise, with thy yellow waves, and mantle her distress!

80

The Goth, the Christian, Time, War, Flood, and Fire,
Have dealt upon the seven-hilled city's pride;
She saw her glories star by star expire,
And up the steep barbarian monarchs ride
Where the car climbed the capitol; far and wide
Temple and tower went down, nor left a site:—
Chaos of ruins! who shall trace the void,
O'er the dim fragments cast a lunar light,
And say, "Here was, or is," where all is doubly night? . . .

139

And here the buzz of eager nations ran,
In murmured pity or loud-roared applause,
As man was slaughtered by his fellow man.
And wherefore slaughtered? wherefore, but because
Such were the bloody Circus' genial laws,
And the imperial pleasure.—Wherefore not?
What matters where we fall to fill the maws
Of worms—on battle-plains or listed spot?
Both are but theatres where the chief actors rot.

140

I see before me the Gladiator lie:
He leans upon his hand—his manly brow
Consents to death, but conquers agony,
And his drooped head sinks gradually low—
And through his side the last drops, ebbing slow
From the red gash, fall heavy, one by one,
Like the first of a thunder-shower; and now
The arena swims around him—he is gone,
Ere ceased the inhuman shout which hailed the wretch who won.

141

He heard it, but he heeded not—his eyes
Were with his heart, and that was far away;
He reck'd not of the life he lost nor prize,
But where his rude hut by the Danube lay,
There were his young barbarians all at play,
There was their Dacian mother—he, their sire,
Butchered to make a Roman holiday—
All this rushed with his blood.—Shall he expire
And unavenged?—Arise! ye Goths, and glut your ire!

142

But here, where Murder breathed her bloody steam;
And here, where buzzing nations choked the ways,
And roared or murmured like a mountain stream
Dashing or winding as its torrent strays;
Here, where the Roman millions' blame or praise
Was death or life, the playthings of a crowd,
My voice sounds much, and fall the stars' faint rays
On the arena void—seats crushed—walls bowed—
And galleries, where my steps seem echoes strangely loud.

143

A ruin—yet what a ruin! From its mass
Walls, palaces, half-cities, have been reared;
Yet oft the enormous skeleton ye pass,
And marvel where the spoil could have appeared.
Hath it indeed been plundered, or but cleared?
Alas! developed, opens the decay,
When the colossal fabric's form is neared:
It will not bear the brightness of the day,
Which streams too much on all years—man—have reft away.

703. Niobe. The queen of Thebes, all of whose children were slain by the jealous Apollo and Artemis, became a symbol of grief. **716. car,** chariot. **718. Chaos of ruins!** The ruins of Byron's Rome had not yet been cleaned and ticketed by archaeologists, nor had any of the modern thoroughfares been constructed. **1247. Circus,** the rounded inclosure in which the gladiatorial combats were held.

1252. Gladiator. The statue which Byron thought to be that of a dying gladiator is now commonly known as "The Dying Gaul." **1266. Dacian.** Thousands of natives were transported from Dacia, now part of Rumania, to be exhibited in martial games in Rome.

144

But when the rising moon begins to climb
Its topmost arch, and gently pauses there;
When the stars twinkle through the loops of time,
And the low night-breeze waves along the air
The garland forest, which the gray walls wear
Like laurels on the bald first Caesar's head;
When the light shines serene but doth not glare,
Then in this magic circle raise the dead:
Heroes have trod this spot—'tis on their dust ye tread.

145

"While stands the Coliseum, Rome shall stand;
When falls the Coliseum, Rome shall fall;
And when Rome falls—the World." From our own land
Thus spake the pilgrims o'er this mighty wall
In Saxon times, which we are wont to call
Ancient; and these three mortal things are still
On their foundations, and unaltered all:
Rome and her Ruin past Redemption's skill,
The World, the same wide den—of thieves, or what ye will. . . .

178

There is a pleasure in the pathless woods,
There is a rapture on the lonely shore,
There is society where none intrudes,
By the deep Sea, and music in its roar:
I love not Man the less, but Nature more,
From these our interviews, in which I steal
From all I may be, or have been before,
To mingle with the Universe, and feel
What I can ne'er express, yet can not all conceal.

179

Roll on, thou deep and dark blue Ocean—roll!
Ten thousand fleets sweep over thee in vain;
Man marks the earth with ruin—his control
Stops with the shore;—upon the watery plain
The wrecks are all thy deed, nor doth remain
A shadow of man's ravage, save his own,
When, for a moment, like a drop of rain,
He sinks into thy depths with bubbling groan,
Without a grave, unknelled, uncoffined, and unknown.

180

His steps are not upon thy paths—thy fields
Are not a spoil for him—thou dost arise
And shake him from thee; the vile strength he wields
For earth's destruction thou dost all despise,
Spurning him from thy bosom to the skies,
And send'st him, shivering in thy playful spray
And howling, to his gods, where haply lies
His petty hope in some near port or bay,
And dashest him again to earth—there let him lay.

181

The armaments which thunderstrike the walls
Of rock-built cities, bidding nations quake,
And monarchs tremble in their capitals,
The oak leviathans, whose huge ribs make
Their clay creator the vain title take
Of lord of thee, and arbiter of war—
These are thy toys, and, as the snowy flake,
They melt into thy yeast of waves, which mar
Alike the Armada's pride or spoils of Trafalgar.

1292. garland forest. The garlands of shrubs and vines were scraped off, to the distress of all naturalists, by later archaeologists.

SO, WE'LL GO NO MORE A-ROVING

So, we'll go no more a-roving
So late into the night,
Though the heart be still as loving,
And the moon be still as bright.

For the sword outwears its sheath,
And the soul wears out the breast,
And the heart must pause to breathe,
And Love itself have rest.

Though the night was made for loving,
And the day returns too soon,
Yet we'll go no more a-roving
By the light of the moon.

MY BOAT IS ON THE SHORE

My boat is on the shore,
And my bark is on the sea;
But, before I go, Tom Moore,
Here's a double health to thee!

Here's a sigh to those who love me,
And a smile to those who hate;
And, whatever sky's above me,
Here's a heart for every fate.

Though the Ocean roar around me,
Yet it still shall bear me on;
Though a desert should surround me,
It hath springs that may be won.

Were't the last drop in the well,
As I gasped upon the brink,
Ere my fainting spirit fell,
'Tis to thee that I would drink.

With that water, as this wine,
The libation I would pour
Should be—peace with thine and mine,
And a health to thee, Tom Moore.

from DON JUAN

"*Difficile est propriè communia dicere.*" *
—Horace

"*Dost thou think, because thou art virtuous, there shall be no more cakes and ale? Yes, by Saint Anne, and ginger shall be hot i' the mouth, too!*"—Shakespeare, *Twelfth Night, or What You Will.*

Don Juan was begun in the summer of 1818 and occupied Byron intermittently the remainder of his life. The first and second cantos were published in 1819, the third to the fifth in 1821, the other completed cantos in 1823 and 1824, a fragment of the seventeenth in 1903. *Don Juan* is Byron's masterpiece and includes about one-fourth of all the poetry he wrote. In form, it is a romance of roguery (not high adventure but low), written in ottava rima (an eight-line stanza in iambic pentameter rhyming abababcc, humorous passages often having double or even triple rhymes, as "laureate . . . Tory at." Because of its jocular references to epic conventions, its mocking tone, its exaltation of low things and its irreverent treatment of high things, it is sometimes called a mock epic, the greatest of its class. A favorite mock-epic device is anticlimax (for example, the lament in Canto the First, stanzas 214–17; the scene in Canto the Second, stanzas 17–20, in which Juan reads Julia's letter.) "I *have* no plan; I *had* no plan; but I have materials," Byron wrote to his friend and publisher Murray. He also said that he "meant to be a little quietly facetious upon everything." The poem, then, is "a satire on the abuses of society, not an eulogy of vice," taking its topics from the wanderings of its disreputable hero, Don Juan, who touches aspects of experience in a world not essentially different from the one we live in today. "It is," wrote Paul Elmer More, "the epic of modern life." In a sense, it is an immature poem. "Byron did not reach manhood in this world, but he was drawing toward it when he wrote *Don Juan*." He got rid of sentimentalism, changing it for mockery; but this is only a halfway position. Byron's evolution was toward "a stoical acceptance of life and the attainment of the comic vision." (On this point, see Professor G. R. Elliott's article in *Publications of the Modern Language Association*, Vol. XXXIX, and Professor C. J. Fuess's *Lord Byron as a Satirist in Verse*, Columbia University Press, 1912.)

Important and interesting recent works dealing with *Don Juan* and Byron's satire are: Elizabeth French Boyd's *Byron's Don Juan: A Critical Study*, Rutgers University Press, 1945; Paul Graham Trueblood's *The Flowering of Byron's Genius*, Stanford University Press, 1945; and *John Bull's Letter to Lord Byron* [by J. G. Lockhart] edited by Alan Lang Strout, University of Oklahoma Press, 1947.

***"Difficile est . . . dicere."** It is difficult to speak properly about common things.

from CANTO THE FIRST

I

I want a hero: an uncommon want,
When every year and month sends forth a new one,
Till, after cloying the gazettes with cant,
The age discovers he is not the true one:
Of such as these I should not care to vaunt,
I'll therefore take our ancient friend Don Juan—
We all have seen him, in the pantomime,
Sent to the Devil somewhat ere his time. . . .

5

Brave men were living before Agamemnon
And since, exceeding valorous and sage,
A good deal like him too, though quite the same none;
But then they shone not on the poet's page,
And so have been forgotten:—I condemn none,
But can't find any in the present age
Fit for my poem (that is, for my new one);
So, as I said, I'll take my friend Don Juan.

6

Most epic poets plunge "*in medias res*"
(Horace makes this the heroic turnpike road),
And then your hero tells, whene'er you please,
What went before—by way of episode,
While seated after dinner at his ease,
Beside his mistress in some soft abode,
Palace, or garden, paradise, or cavern,
Which serves the happy couple for a tavern.

7

That is the usual method, but not mine—
My way is to begin with the beginning;
The regularity of my design
Forbids all wandering as the worst of sinning,
And therefore I shall open with a line
(Although it cost me half an hour in spinning)

41. "*in medias res*," into the middle of the action. An epic convention (compare *Paradise Lost*).

Narrating somewhat of Don Juan's father,
And also of his mother, if you'd rather.

8

In Seville was he born, a pleasant city,
Famous for oranges and women—he
Who has not seen it will be much to pity,
So says the proverb—and I quite agree;
Of all the Spanish towns is none more pretty,
Cadiz perhaps—but that you soon may see;—
Don Juan's parents lived beside the river,
A noble stream, and called the Guadalquivir.

9

His father's name was Jóse—*Don*, of course,
A true Hidalgo, free from every stain
Of Moor or Hebrew blood, he traced his source
Through the most Gothic gentlemen of Spain;
A better cavalier ne'er mounted horse,
Or being mounted, e'er got down again,
Than Jóse, who begot our hero, who
Begot—but that's to come—Well, to renew:

10

His mother was a learnèd lady, famed
For every branch of every science known—
In every Christian language ever named,
With virtues equalled by her wit alone:
She made the cleverest people quite ashamed,
And even the good with inward envy groan,
Finding themselves so very much exceeded,
In their own way, by all the things that she did. . . .

26

Don Jóse and the Donna Inez led
For some time an unhappy sort of life,
Wishing each other, not divorced, but dead;
They lived respectably as man and wife,
Their conduct was exceedingly well-bred,
And gave no outward signs of inward strife,
Until at length the smothered fire broke out,
And put the business past all kind of doubt.

27

For Inez called some druggists and physicians,
And tried to prove her loving lord was *mad*,
But as he had some lucid intermissions,
She next decided he was only *bad;*

65. Jóse. The name is of course properly José; Byron changes the accent for the sake of the meter. **73. His mother.** The following stanza (with twelve more, omitted here) is a satirical portrait of Lady Byron. **209. called some druggists and physicians,** an allusion to Lady Byron's action with reference to Byron.

Yet when they asked her for her depositions,
No sort of explanation could be had,
Save that her duty both to man and God
Required this conduct—which seemed very odd. . . .

32

Their friends had tried at reconciliation,
Then their relations, who made matters worse,
('Twere hard to tell upon a like occasion
To whom it may be best to have recourse—
I can't say much for friend or yet relation):
The lawyers did their utmost for divorce,
But scarce a fee was paid on either side
Before, unluckily, Don Jóse died. . . .

38

Sagest of women, even of widows, she
Resolved that Juan should be quite a paragon
And worthy of the noblest pedigree:
(His Sire was of Castile, his Dam from Aragon):
Then for accomplishments of chivalry,
In case our Lord the King should go to war again,
He learned the arts of riding, fencing, gunnery,
And how to scale a fortress—or a nunnery.

39

But that which Donna Inez most desired,
And saw into herself each day before all
The learnèd tutors whom for him she hired,
Was, that his breeding should be strictly moral:
Much into all his studies she inquired,
And so they were submitted first to her, all,
Arts, sciences—no branch was made a mystery
To Juan's eyes, excepting natural history.

40

The languages, especially the dead,
The sciences, and most of all the abstruse,
The arts, at least all such as could be said
To be the most remote from common use,
In all these he was much and deeply read:
But not a page of anything that's loose,
Or hints continuation of the species,
Was ever suffered, lest he should grow vicious. . . .

44

Juan was taught from out the best edition,
Expurgated by learnèd men, who place,
Judiciously, from out the schoolboy's vision,
The grosser parts; but, fearful to deface

Too much their modest bard by this omission,
And pitying sore this mutilated case,
They only add them all in an appendix,
Which saves, in fact, the trouble of an index. . . .

50

At six, I said, he was a charming child,
At twelve he was a fine, but quiet boy;
Although in infancy a little wild,
They tamed him down amongst them: to destroy
His natural spirit not in vain they toiled,
At least it seemed so; and his mother's joy
Was to declare how sage, and still, and steady,
Her young philosopher was grown already. . . .

52

For my part I say nothing—nothing—but
This I will say—my reasons are my own—
That if I had an only son to put
To school (as God be praised that I have none),
'Tis not with Donna Inez I would shut
Him up to learn his catechism alone,
No—no—I'd send him out betimes to college,
For there it was I picked up my own knowledge.

53

For there one learns—'tis not for me to boast,
Though I acquired—but I pass over *that*,
As well as all the Greek I since have lost:—
I say that there's the place—but "*Verbum sat*,"
I think I picked up too, as well as most,
Knowledge of matters—but no matter *what*—
I never married—but, I think, I know
That sons should not be educated so.

54

Young Juan now was sixteen years of age,
Tall, handsome, slender, but well knit: he seemed
Active, though not so sprightly, as a page;
And everybody but his mother deemed
Him almost man; but she flew in a rage
And bit her lips (for else she might have screamed)
If any said so, for to be precocious
Was in her eyes a thing the most atrocious.

55

Amongst her numerous acquaintance, all
Selected for discretion and devotion,
There was the Donna Julia, whom to call
Pretty were but to give a feeble notion
Of many charms in her as natural
As sweetness to the flower, or salt to ocean,
Her zone to Venus, or his bow to Cupid,
(But this last simile is trite and stupid).

420. "Verbum sat," A word to the wise is sufficient.

56

The darkness of her Oriental eye
Accorded with her Moorish origin;
(Her blood was not all Spanish, by the by;
In Spain, you know, this is a sort of sin;)
When proud Granada fell, and, forced to fly,
Boabdil wept: of Donna Julia's kin
Some went to Africa, some stayed in Spain—
Her great great grandmamma chose to remain.

57

She married (I forget the pedigree)
With an Hidalgo, who transmitted down
His blood less noble than such blood should be;
At such alliances his sires would frown,
In that point so precise in each degree
That they bred *in and in*, as might be shown,
Marrying their cousins—nay, their aunts, and nieces,
Which always spoils the breed, if it increases. . . .

62

Wedded she was some years, and to a man
Of fifty, and such husbands are in plenty;
And yet, I think, instead of such a ONE
'Twere better to have TWO of five-and-twenty,
Especially in countries near the sun:
And now I think on't, "*mi vien in mente*,"
Ladies even of the most uneasy virtue
Prefer a spouse whose age is short of thirty.

63

'Tis a sad thing, I cannot choose but say,
And all the fault of that indecent sun,
Who cannot leave alone our helpless clay,
But will keep baking, broiling, burning on,
That howsoever people fast and pray,
The flesh is frail, and so the soul undone:
What men call gallantry, and gods adultery,
Is much more common where the climate's sultry. . . .

65

Alfonso was the name of Julia's lord,
A man well looking for his years, and who
Was neither much beloved nor yet abhorred:
They lived together as most people do,
Suffering each other's foibles by accord,
And not exactly either *one* or *two;*
Yet he was jealous, though he did not show it,
For Jealousy dislikes the world to know it. . . .

494. "mi vien in mente," it comes into my mind.

69

Juan she saw, and, as a pretty child,
  Caressed him often—such a thing might be
Quite innocently done, and harmless styled,
  When she had twenty years, and thirteen he;
But I am not so sure I should have smiled
  When he was sixteen, Julia twenty-three;
These few short years make wondrous alterations,
Particularly amongst sun-burnt nations.

70

Whate'er the cause might be, they had become
  Changed; for the dame grew distant, the youth shy,
Their looks cast down, their greetings almost dumb,
  And much embarrassment in either eye;
There surely will be little doubt with some
  That Donna Julia knew the reason why,
But as for Juan, he had no more notion
Than he who never saw the sea of Ocean. . . .

136

'Twas midnight—Donna Julia was in bed,
  Sleeping, most probably,—when at her door
Arose a clatter might awake the dead,
  If they had never been awoke before,
And that they have been so we all have read,
  And are to be so, at the least, once more;—
The door was fastened, but with voice and fist
First knocks were heard, then "Madam—Madam —hist! . . .

144

Under the bed they searched, and there they found—
  No matter what—it was not that they sought;
They opened windows, gazing if the ground
  Had signs or footmarks, but the earth said nought;
And then they stared each other's faces round:
  'Tis odd, not one of all these seekers thought,
And seems to me almost a sort of blunder,
Of looking *in* the bed as well as under.

145

During this inquisition Julia's tongue
  Was not asleep—"Yes, search and search," she cried,
"Insult on insult heap, and wrong on wrong!
  It was for this that I became a bride!
For this in silence I have suffered long
  A husband like Alfonso at my side;
But now I'll bear no more, nor here remain,
If there be law or lawyers in all Spain.

146

"Yes, Don Alfonso! husband now no more,
  If ever you indeed deserved the name,
Is't worthy of your years?—you have three score—
  Fifty, or sixty, it is all the same—
Is't wise or fitting, causeless to explore
  For facts against a virtuous woman's fame?
Ungrateful, perjured, barbarous Don Alfonso,
How dare you think your lady would go on so?" . . .

164

With him retired his "*posse comitatus*,"
  The attorney last, who lingered near the door
Reluctantly, still tarrying there as late as
  Antonia let him—not a little sore
At this most strange and unexplained "*hiatus*"
  In Don Alfonso's facts, which just now wore
An awkward look; as he revolved the case,
The door was fastened in his legal face.

165

No sooner was it bolted, than—Oh Shame!
  Oh Sin! Oh Sorrow! and Oh Womankind!
How can you do such things and keep your fame,
  Unless this world, and t'other too, be blind?
Nothing so dear as an unfilched good name!
  But to proceed—for there is more behind:
With much heartfelt reluctance be it said,
Young Juan slipped, half-smothered, from the bed.

166

He had been hid—I don't pretend to say
  How, nor can I indeed describe the where—
Young, slender, and packed easily, he lay,
  No doubt, in little compass, round or square;
But pity him I neither must nor may
  His suffocation by that pretty pair;
'Twere better, sure, to die so, than be shut
With maudlin Clarence in his Malmsey butt. . . .

173

Now, Don Alfonso entering, but alone,
  Closed the oration of the trusty maid:
She loitered, and he told her to be gone,
  An order somewhat sullenly obeyed;
However, present remedy was none,
  And no great good seemed answered if she staid;

1305. "posse comitatus," an armed force made up by a sheriff or other peace officer to quell a riot or catch a criminal. **1328. Clarence . . . Malmsey.** In *Richard III* Clarence is drowned in a cask of wine.

Regarding both with slow and sidelong view,
She snuffed the candle, curtsied, and withdrew. . . .

180

Alfonso closed his speech, and begged her pardon,
Which Julia half withheld, and then half granted,
And laid conditions, he thought very hard on,
Denying several little things he wanted:
He stood like Adam lingering near his garden,
With useless penitence perplexed and haunted,
Beseeching she no further would refuse,
When, lo! he stumbled o'er a pair of shoes.

181

A pair of shoes!—what then? not much, if they
Are such as fit with ladies' feet, but these
(No one can tell how much I grieve to say)
Were masculine; to see them, and to seize,
Was but a moment's act.—Ah! well-a-day!
My teeth begin to chatter, my veins freeze—
Alfonso first examined well their fashion,
And then flew out into another passion.

182

He left the room for his relinquished sword,
And Julia instant to the closet flew.
"Fly, Juan, fly! for heaven's sake—not a word—
The door is open—you may yet slip through
The passage you so often have explored—
Here is the garden-key—Fly—fly—Adieu!
Haste—haste! I hear Alfonso's hurrying feet—
Day has not broke—there's no one in the street."

207

If any person should presume to assert
This story is not moral, first, I pray
That they will not cry out before they're hurt,
Then that they'll read it o'er again, and say
(But, doubtless, nobody will be so pert),
That this is not a moral tale, though gay;
Besides, in Canto Twelfth, I mean to show
The very place where wicked people go. . . .

214

No more—no more—Oh! never more on me
The freshness of the heart can fall like dew,
Which out of all the lovely things we see
Extracts emotions beautiful and new;
Hived in our bosoms like the bag o' the bee.
Think'st thou the honey with those objects grew?
Alas! 'twas not in them, but in thy power
To double even the sweetness of a flower.

215

No more—no more—Oh! never more, my heart,
Canst thou be my sole world, my universe!
Once all in all, but now a thing apart,
Thou canst not be my blessing or my curse:
The illusion's gone for ever, and thou art
Insensible, I trust, but none the worse,
And in thy stead I've got a deal of judgment,
Though Heaven knows how it ever found a lodgment.

216

My days of love are over; me no more
The charms of maid, wife, and still less of widow,
Can make the fool of which they made before,—
In short, I must not lead the life I did do;
The credulous hope of mutual minds is o'er,
The copious use of claret is forbid too,
So for a good old-gentlemanly vice,
I think I must take up with avarice.

217

Ambition was my idol, which was broken
Before the shrines of Sorrow, and of Pleasure;
And the two last have left me many a token
O'er which reflection may be made at leisure;
Now, like Friar Bacon's Brazen Head, I've spoken,
"Time is, Time was, Time's past":—a chymic treasure
Is glittering Youth, which I have spent betimes—
My heart in passion, and my head on rhymes. . . .

221

But for the present, gentle reader! and
Still gentler purchaser! the Bard—that's I—
Must, with permission, shake you by the hand,
And so—your humble servant, and Good-bye!
We meet again, if we should understand
Each other; and if not, I shall not try
Your patience further than by this short sample—
'Twere well if others followed my example.

222

"Go, little Book, from this my solitude!
I cast thee on the waters—go thy ways!
And if—as I believe, thy vein be good,
The World will find thee after many days."
When Southey's read, and Wordsworth understood,
I can't help putting in my claim to praise—

1769 ff. "Go, little Book, . . ." a parody of Southey's "The Lay of the Laureate. L'Envoy."

The four first rhymes are Southey's, every line:
For God's sake, reader! take them not for mine.

from CANTO THE SECOND

8

But to our tale: the Donna Inez sent
Her son to Cadiz only to embark;
To stay there had not answered her intent,
But why?—we leave the reader in the dark—
'Twas for a voyage the young man was meant,
As if a Spanish ship were Noah's ark,
To wean him from the wickedness of earth,
And send him like a Dove of Promise forth.

9

Don Juan bade his valet pack his things
According to direction, then received
A lecture and some money: for four springs
He was to travel; and though Inez grieved
(As every kind of parting has its stings),
She hoped he would improve—perhaps believed:
A letter, too, she gave (he never read it)
Of good advice—and two or three of credit. . . .

11

Juan embarked—the ship got under way,
The wind was fair, the water passing rough;
A devil of a sea rolls in that bay,
As I, who've crossed it oft, know well enough;
And, standing upon deck, the dashing spray
Flies in one's face, and makes it weather-tough:
And there he stood to take, and take again,
His first—perhaps his last—farewell of Spain.

12

I can't but say it is an awkward sight
To see one's native land receding through
The growing waters; it unmans one quite,
Especially when life is rather new:
I recollect Great Britain's coast looks white,
But almost every other country's blue,
When gazing on them, mystified by distance,
We enter on our nautical existence. . . .

17

And Juan wept, and much he sighed and thought,
While his salt tears dropped into the salt sea,
"Sweets to the sweet"; (I like so much to quote;
You must excuse this extract,—'tis where she,
The Queen of Denmark, for Ophelia brought
Flowers to the grave;) and, sobbing often, he
Reflected on his present situation,
And seriously resolved on reformation.

18

"Farewell, my Spain! a long farewell!" he cried,
"Perhaps I may revisit thee no more,
But die, as many an exiled heart hath died,
Of its own thirst to see again thy shore:
Farewell, where Guadalquivir's waters glide!
Farewell, my mother! and, since all is o'er,
Farewell, too, dearest Julia!—(here he drew
Her letter out again, and read it through.)

19

"And oh! if e'er I should forget, I swear—
But that's impossible, and cannot be—
Sooner shall this blue Ocean melt to air,
Sooner shall Earth resolve itself to sea,
Than I resign thine image, oh, my fair!
Or think of anything, excepting thee;
A mind diseased no remedy can physic—
(Here the ship gave a lurch, and he grew sea-sick.)

20

"Sooner shall Heaven kiss earth—(here he fell sicker)
Oh, Julia! what is every other woe?—
(For God's sake let me have a glass of liquor;
Pedro, Battista, help me down below.)
Julia, my love—(you rascal, Pedro, quicker)—
Oh, Julia!—(this curst vessel pitches so)—
Belovèd Julia, hear me still beseeching!"
(Here he grew inarticulate with retching.) . . .

24

The ship, called the most holy "Trinidada,"
Was steering duly for the port Leghorn;
For there the Spanish family Moncada
Were settled long ere Juan's sire was born:
They were relations, and for them he had a
Letter of introduction, which the morn
Of his departure had been sent him by
His Spanish friends for those in Italy.

25

His suite consisted of three servants and
A tutor, the licentiate Pedrillo,
Who several languages did understand,
But now lay sick and speechless on his pillow,
And, rocking in his hammock, longed for land,
His headache being increased by every billow;
And the waves oozing through the port-hole made
His berth a little damp, and him afraid. . . .

49

'Twas twilight, and the sunless day went down
  Over the waste of waters; like a veil,
Which, if withdrawn, would but disclose the frown
  Of one whose hate is masked but to assail.
Thus to their hopeless eyes the night was shown,
  And grimly darkled o'er the faces pale,
And the dim desolate deep: twelve days had Fear
Been their familiar, and now Death was here.

50

Some trial had been making at a raft,
  With little hope in such a rolling sea,
A sort of thing at which one would have laughed,
  If any laughter at such times could be,
Unless with people who too much have quaffed,
  And have a kind of wild and horrid glee,
Half epileptical, and half hysterical:—
Their preservation would have been a miracle.

51

At half-past eight o'clock, booms, hencoops, spars,
  And all things, for a chance, had been cast loose,
That still could keep afloat the struggling tars,
  For yet they strove, although of no great use:
There was no light in heaven but a few stars,
  The boats put off o'ercrowded with their crews;
She gave a heel, and then a lurch to port,
And, going down head foremost—sunk, in short.

52

Then rose from sea to sky the wild farewell—
  Then shrieked the timid, and stood still the brave,—
Then some leaped overboard with dreadful yell,
  As eager to anticipate their grave;
And the sea yawned around her like a hell,
  And down she sucked with her the whirling wave,
Like one who grapples with his enemy,
And strives to strangle him before he die.

53

And first one universal shriek there rushed,
  Louder than the loud Ocean, like a crash
Of echoing thunder; and then all was hushed,
  Save the wild wind and the remorseless dash
Of billows; but at intervals there gushed,
  Accompanied by a convulsive splash,
A solitary shriek, the bubbling cry
Of some strong swimmer in his agony. . . .

56

Juan got into the long-boat, and there
  Contrived to help Pedrillo to a place;
It seemed as if they had exchanged their care,
  For Juan wore the magisterial face
Which courage gives, while poor Pedrillo's pair
  Of eyes were crying for their owner's case:
Battista, though (a name called shortly Tita),
Was lost by getting at some aqua-vita.

57

Pedro, his valet, too, he tried to save,
  But the same cause, conducive to his loss,
Left him so drunk, he jumped into the wave,
  As o'er the cutter's edge he tried to cross,
And so he found a wine-and-watery grave;
  They could not rescue him although so close,
Because the sea ran higher every minute,
And for the boat—the crew kept crowding in it.

111

How long in his damp trance young Juan lay
  He knew not, for the earth was gone for him,
And Time had nothing more of night nor day
  For his congealing blood, and senses dim;
And how this heavy faintness passed away
  He knew not, till each painful pulse and limb,
And tingling vein, seemed throbbing back to life,
For Death, though vanquished, still retired with strife.

112

His eyes he opened, shut, again unclosed,
  For all was doubt and dizziness; he thought
He still was in the boat, and had but dozed,
  And felt again with his despair o'erwrought,
And wished it Death in which he had reposed,
  And then once more his feelings back were brought,
And slowly by his swimming eyes was seen
A lovely female face of seventeen.

113

'Twas bending close o'er his, and the small mouth
  Seemed almost prying into his for breath;
And chafing him, the soft warm hand of youth
  Recalled his answering spirits back from Death;
And, bathing his chill temples, tried to soothe
  Each pulse to animation, till beneath

881. How long . . . trance. Juan has been washed ashore on one of the Cyclades.

Its gentle touch and trembling care, a sigh
To these kind efforts made a low reply.

114

Then was the cordial poured, and mantle flung
Around his scarce-clad limbs; and the fair arm
Raised higher the faint head which o'er it hung;
And her transparent cheek, all pure and warm,
Pillowed his death-like forehead; then she wrung
His dewy curls, long drenched by every storm;
And watched with eagerness each throb that drew
A sigh from his heaved bosom—and hers, too.

115

And lifting him with care into the cave,
The gentle girl, and her attendant,—one
Young, yet her elder, and of brow less grave,
And more robust of figure—then begun
To kindle fire, and as the new flames gave
Light to the rocks that roofed them, which the sun
Had never seen, the maid, or whatsoe'er
She was, appeared distinct, and tall, and fair.

116

Her brow was overhung with coins of gold,
That sparkled o'er the auburn of her hair—
Her clustering hair, whose longer locks were rolled
In braids behind; and though her stature were
Even of the highest for a female mould,
They nearly reached her heel; and in her air
There was a something which bespoke command,
As one who was a Lady in the land.

117

Her hair, I said, was auburn; but her eyes
Were black as Death, their lashes the same hue,
Of downcast length, in whose silk shadow lies
Deepest attraction; for when to the view
Forth from its raven fringe the full glance flies,
Ne'er with such force the swiftest arrow flew;
'Tis as the snake late coiled, who pours his length,
And hurls at once his venom and his strength.

118

Her brow was white and low, her cheek's pure dye
Like twilight rosy still with the set sun;
Short upper lip—sweet lips! that make us sigh
Ever to have seen such; for she was one
Fit for the model of a statuary
(A race of mere impostors, when all's done—
I've seen much finer women, ripe and real,
Than all the nonsense of their stone ideal). . . .

124

I'll tell you who they were, this female pair,
Lest they should seem Princesses in disguise;
Besides, I hate all mystery, and that air
Of clap-trap, which your recent poets prize;
And so, in short, the girls they really were
They shall appear before your curious eyes,
Mistress and maid; the first was only daughter
Of an old man, who lived upon the water.

125

A fisherman he had been in his youth,
And still a sort of fisherman was he;
But other speculations were, in sooth,
Added to his connexion with the sea,
Perhaps not so respectable, in truth:
A little smuggling, and some piracy,
Left him, at last, the sole of many masters
Of an ill-gotten million of piastres.

126

A fisher, therefore, was he,—though of men,
Like Peter the Apostle, and he fished
For wandering merchant-vessels, now and then,
And sometimes caught as many as he wished;
The cargoes he confiscated, and gain
He sought in the slave-market too, and dished
Full many a morsel for that Turkish trade,
By which, no doubt, a good deal may be made.

127

He was a Greek, and on his isle had built
(One of the wild and smaller Cyclades)
A very handsome house from out his guilt,
And there he lived exceedingly at ease;
Heaven knows what cash he got, or blood he spilt,
A sad old fellow was he, if you please;
But this I know, it was a spacious building,
Full of barbaric carving, paint, and gilding.

128

He had an only daughter, called Haidée,
The greatest heiress of the Eastern Isles;
Besides, so very beautiful was she,
Her dowry was as nothing to her smiles:
Still in her teens, and like a lovely tree
She grew to womanhood, and between whiles
Rejected several suitors, just to learn
How to accept a better in his turn. . . .

1000. piastres, Turkish money. **1010. Cyclades,** a great cluster of islands in the Aegean, east of Greece.

188

They were alone, but not alone as they
  Who shut in chambers think it loneliness;
The silent Ocean, and the starlight bay,
  The twilight glow, which momently grew less,
The voiceless sands, and dropping caves, that lay
  Around them, made them to each other press,
As if there were no life beneath the sky
Save theirs, and that their life could never die.

189

They feared no eyes nor ears on that lone beach,
  They felt no terrors from the night; they were
All in all to each other; though their speech
  Was broken words, they *thought* a language there,—
And all the burning tongues the Passions teach
  Found in one sigh the best interpreter
Of Nature's oracle—first love,—that all
Which Eve has left her daughters since her fall.

190

Haidée spoke not of scruples, asked no vows,
  Nor offered any; she had never heard
Of plight and promises to be a spouse,
  Or perils by a loving maid incurred;
She was all which pure Ignorance allows,
  And flew to her young mate like a young bird;
And, never having dreamt of falsehood, she
Had not one word to say of constancy.

191

She loved, and was belovèd—she adored,
  And she was worshipped; after Nature's fashion,
Their intense souls, into each other poured,
  If souls could die, had perished in that passion,—
But by degrees their senses were restored,
  Again to be o'ercome, again to dash on;
And, beating 'gainst *his* bosom, Haidée's heart
Felt as if never more to beat apart.

192

Alas! they were so young, so beautiful,
  So lonely, loving, helpless, and the hour
Was that in which the Heart is always full,
  And, having o'er itself no further power,
Prompts deeds Eternity can not annul,
  But pays off moments in an endless shower
Of hell-fire—all prepared for people giving
Pleasure or pain to one another living.

1497. They were alone. Haidée has resuscitated Juan. They have fallen in love. Lambro has departed. **1521. She loved, and was belovèd.** In its Romantic aspects the love story of Juan and Haidée is a good example of primitivism. But note that Byron flouts his own sentimentality.

193

Alas! for Juan and Haidée! they were
  So loving and so lovely—till then never,
Excepting our first parents, such a pair
  Had run the risk of being damned for ever;
And Haidée, being devout as well as fair,
  Had, doubtless, heard about the Stygian river,
And Hell and Purgatory—but forgot
Just in the very crisis she should not.

194

They look upon each other, and their eyes
  Gleam in the moonlight; and her white arm clasps
Round Juan's head, and his around her lies
  Half buried in the tresses which it grasps;
She sits upon his knee, and drinks his sighs,
  He hers, until they end in broken gasps;
And thus they form a group that's quite antique,
Half naked, loving, natural, and Greek. . . .

199

Alas! the love of Women! it is known
  To be a lovely and a fearful thing;
For all of theirs upon that die is thrown,
  And if 'tis lost, Life hath no more to bring
To them but mockeries of the past alone,
  And their revenge is as the tiger's spring,
Deadly, and quick, and crushing; yet, as real
Torture is theirs—what they inflict they feel.

200

They are right; for man, to Man so oft unjust,
  Is always so to Women; one sole bond
Awaits them, treachery is all their trust;
  Taught to conceal, their bursting hearts despond
Over their idol, till some wealthier lust
  Buys them in marriage—and what rests beyond?
A thankless husband—next a faithless lover—
Then dressing, nursing, praying—and all's over.

201

Some take a lover, some take drams or prayers,
  Some mind their household, others dissipation
Some run away, and but exchange their cares,
  Losing the advantage of a virtuous station;
Few changes e'er can better their affairs,
  Theirs being an unnatural situation,
From the dull palace to the dirty hovel:
Some play the devil, and then write a novel.

202

Haidée was Nature's bride, and knew not this:
Haidée was Passion's child, born where the sun
Showers triple light, and scorches even the kiss
Of his gazelle-eyed daughters; she was one
Made but to love, to feel that she was his
Who was her chosen: what was said or done
Elsewhere was nothing. She had nought to fear,
Hope, care, nor love beyond,—her heart beat *here*.

203

And oh! that quickening of the heart, that beat!
How much it costs us! yet each rising throb
Is in its cause as its effect so sweet,
That Wisdom, ever on the watch to rob
Joy of its alchemy, and to repeat
Fine truths; even Conscience, too, has a tough job
To make us understand each good old maxim,
So good—I wonder Castlereagh don't tax 'em.

204

And now 'twas done—on the lone shore were plighted
Their hearts; the stars, their nuptial torches, shed
Beauty upon the beautiful they lighted:
Ocean their witness, and the cave their bed,
By their own feelings hallowed and united,
Their priest was Solitude, and they were wed:
And they were happy, for to their young eyes
Each was an angel, and earth paradise. . . .

from CANTO THE THIRD

12

Haidée and Juan were not married, but
The fault was theirs, not mine; it is not fair,
Chaste reader, then, in any way to put
The blame on me, unless you wish they were;
Then if you'd have them wedded, please to shut
The book which treats of this erroneous pair,
Before the consequences grow too awful;
'Tis dangerous to read of loves unlawful.

13

Yet they were happy,—happy in the illicit
Indulgence of their innocent desires;
But more imprudent grown with every visit,
Haidée forgot the island was her Sire's;
When we have what we like 'tis hard to miss it,
At least in the beginning, ere one tires;
Thus she came often, not a moment losing,
Whilst her piratical papa was cruising.

14

Let not his mode of raising cash seem strange,
Although he fleeced the flags of every nation,
For into a Prime Minister but change
His title, and 'tis nothing but taxation;
But he, more modest, took an humbler range
Of Life, and in an honester vocation
Pursued o'er the high seas his watery journey,
And merely practised as a sea-attorney.

15

The good old gentleman had been detained
By winds and waves, and some important captures;
And, in the hope of more, at sea remained,
Although a squall or two had damped his raptures,
By swamping one of the prizes; he had chained
His prisoners, dividing them like chapters
In numbered lots; they all had cuffs and collars,
And averaged each from ten to a hundred dollars. . . .

19

Then having settled his marine affairs,
Despatching single cruisers here and there,
His vessel having need of some repairs,
He shaped his course to where his daughter fair
Continued still her hospitable cares;
But that part of the coast being shoal and bare,
And rough with reefs which ran out many a mile,
His port lay on the other side o' the isle. . . .

27

He saw his white walls shining in the sun,
His garden trees all shadowy and green;
He heard his rivulet's light bubbling run,
The distant dog-bark; and perceived between
The umbrage of the wood so cool and dun,
The moving figures, and the sparkling sheen
Of arms (in the East all arm)—and various dyes
Of coloured garbs, as bright as butterflies. . . .

40

Perhaps you think in stumbling on this feast
He flew into a passion, and in fact
There was no mighty reason to be pleased;
Perhaps you prophesy some sudden act,
The whip, the rack, or dungeon at the least,
To teach his people to be more exact,
And that, proceeding at a very high rate,
He showed the royal *penchants* of a pirate. . . .

44

You're wrong.—He was the mildest mannered man
That ever scuttled ship or cut a throat:
With such true breeding of a gentleman,
You never could divine his real thought;
No courtier could, and scarcely woman can
Gird more deceit within a petticoat;
Pity he loved adventurous life's variety,
He was so great a loss to good society. . . .

51

He entered in the house no more his home,
A thing to human feelings the most trying,
And harder for the heart to overcome,
Perhaps, than even the mental pangs of dying;
To find our hearthstone turned into a tomb,
And round its once warm precincts palely lying
The ashes of our hopes, is a deep grief,
Beyond a *single gentleman's* belief. . . .

78

And now they were diverted by their suite,
Dwarfs, dancing girls, black eunuchs, and a poet,
Which made their new establishment complete;
The last was of great fame, and liked to show it:
His verses rarely wanted their due feet—
And for his theme—he seldom sung below it,
He being paid to satirise or flatter,
As the Psalm says, "inditing a good matter." . . .

84

He had travelled 'mongst the Arabs, Turks, and Franks,
And knew the self-loves of the different nations;
And having lived with people of all ranks,
Had something ready upon most occasions—
Which got him a few presents and some thanks.
He varied with some skill his adulations;
To "do at Rome as Romans do," a piece
Of conduct was which *he* observed in Greece.

85

Thus, usually, when *he* was asked to sing,
He gave the different nations something national;
'Twas all the same to him—"God save the king,"
Or "Ça Ira," according to the fashion all:
His Muse made increment of anything,
From the high lyric down to the low rational;
If Pindar sang horse-races, what should hinder
Himself from being as pliable as Pindar?

676. "Ça Ira," "It will succeed," a song of the French Revolution.

86

In France, for instance, he would write a chanson;
In England, a six canto quarto tale;
In Spain he'd make a ballad or romance on
The last war—much the same in Portugal;
In Germany, the Pegasus he'd prance on
Would be old Goethe's—(see what says De Staël);
In Italy, he'd ape the "Trecentisti";
In Greece, he'd sing some sort of hymn like this t'ye:

1

The isles of Greece, the isles of Greece!
Where burning Sappho loved and sung,
Where grew the arts of War and Peace,—
Where Delos rose, and Phoebus sprung!
Eternal summer gilds them yet,
But all, except their sun, is set.

2

The Scian and the Teian muse,
The hero's harp, the lover's lute,
Have found the fame your shores refuse:
Their place of birth alone is mute
To sounds which echo further west
Than your Sires' "Islands of the Blest."

3

The mountains look on Marathon—
And Marathon looks on the sea;
And musing there an hour alone,
I dreamed that Greece might still be free;
For standing on the Persians' grave,
I could not deem myself a slave.

4

A King sate on the rocky brow
Which looks o'er sea-born Salamis;
And ships, by thousands, lay below,
And men in nations;—all were his!
He counted them at break of day—
And when the sun set, where were they?

5

And where are they? and where art thou,
My country? On thy voiceless shore
The heroic lay is tuneless now—
The heroic bosom beats no more!

686. what says De Staël, that Goethe represented all German literature. **687. "Trecentisti,"** imitators of fourteenth-century Italian literature. **695. Scian and . . . Teian,** Homer and Anacreon. **700. "Islands of the Blest,"** islands in the Atlantic where heroes were said to dwell after death. **707. A King,** Xerxes, king of Persia, 486–465 B.C.

And must thy Lyre, so long divine,
Degenerate into hands like mine?

6

'Tis something, in the dearth of Fame,
Though linked among a fettered race,
To feel at least a patriot's shame,
Even as I sing, suffuse my face;
For what is left the poet here?
For Greeks a blush—for Greece a tear.

7

Must *we* but weep o'er days more blest?
Must *we* but blush?—Our fathers bled.
Earth! render back from out thy breast
A remnant of our Spartan dead!
Of the three hundred grant but three,
To make a new Thermopylae!

8

What, silent still? and silent all?
Ah! no;—the voices of the dead
Sound like a distant torrent's fall,
And answer, "Let one living head,
But one arise,—we come, we come!"
'Tis but the living who are dumb.

9

In vain—in vain: strike other chords:
Fill high the cup with Samian wine!
Leave battles to the Turkish hordes,
And shed the blood of Scio's vine!
Hark! rising to the ignoble call—
How answers each bold Bacchanal!

10

You have the Pyrrhic dance as yet:
Where is the Pyrrhic phalanx gone?
Of two such lessons, why forget
The nobler and the manlier one?
You have the letters Cadmus gave—
Think ye he meant them for a slave?

11

Fill high the bowl with Samian wine!
We will not think of themes like these!
It made Anacreon's song divine:
He served—but served Polycrates—
A Tyrant; but our masters then
Were still, at least, our countrymen.

743–44. Pyrrhic dance . . . Pyrrhic phalanx. The Greeks kept the sensuous dance but forgot the world-conquering military formation that Philip and Alexander of Macedon had taught them. These facts and the "Samian wine" help explain their present enslavement.

12

The Tyrant of the Chersonese
Was Freedom's best and bravest friend;
That tyrant was Miltiades!
Oh! that the present hour would lend
Another despot of the kind!
Such chains as his were sure to bind.

13

Fill high the bowl with Samian wine!
On Suli's rock, and Parga's shore,
Exists the remnant of a line
Such as the Doric mothers bore;
And there, perhaps, some seed is sown,
The Heracleidan blood might own.

14

Trust not for freedom to the Franks—
They have a king who buys and sells;
In native swords and native ranks,
The only hope of courage dwells;
But Turkish force, and Latin fraud,
Would break your shield, however broad.

15

Fill high the bowl with Samian wine!
Our virgins dance beneath the shade—
I see their glorious black eyes shine;
But gazing on each glowing maid,
My own the burning tear-drop laves,
To think such breasts must suckle slaves.

16

Place me on Sunium's marbled steep,
Where nothing, save the waves and I,
May hear our mutual murmurs sweep;
There, swan-like, let me sing and die:
A land of slaves shall ne'er be mine—
Dash down yon cup of Samian wine!

87

Thus sung, or would, or could, or should have sung,
The modern Greek, in tolerable verse:
If not like Orpheus quite, when Greece was young,
Yet in these times he might have done much worse:
His strain displayed some feeling—right or wrong;
And feeling, in a poet is the source
Of others' feelings; but they are such liars,
And take all colours—like the hands of dyers. . .

101

T' our tale.—The feast was over, the slaves gone,
The dwarfs and dancing girls had all retired;

The Arab lore and Poet's song were done,
And every sound of revelry expired;
The lady and her lover, left alone,
The rosy flood of Twilight's sky admired;—
Ave Maria! o'er the earth and sea,
That heavenliest hour of Heaven is worthiest thee!

102

Ave Maria! blessèd be the hour!
The time, the clime, the spot, where I so oft
Have felt that moment in its fullest power
Sink o'er the earth—so beautiful and soft—
While swung the deep bell in the distant tower,
Or the faint dying day-hymn stole aloft,
And not a breath crept through the rosy air,
And yet the forest leaves seemed stirred with prayer.

103

Ave Maria! 'tis the hour of prayer!
Ave Maria! 'tis the hour of Love!
Ave Maria! may our spirits dare
Look up to thine and to thy Son's above!
Ave Maria! oh that face so fair!
Those downcast eyes beneath the Almighty Dove—
What though 'tis but a pictured image?—strike—
That painting is no idol,—'tis too like.

104

Some kinder casuists are pleased to say,
In nameless print—that I have no devotion;
But set those persons down with me to pray,
And you shall see who has the properest notion
Of getting into Heaven the shortest way;
My altars are the mountains and the Ocean,
Earth, air, stars,—all that springs from the great Whole,
Who hath produced, and will receive the Soul.

105

Sweet Hour of Twilight!—in the solitude
Of the pine forest, and the silent shore
Which bounds Ravenna's immemorial wood,
Rooted where once the Adrian wave flowed o'er,
To where the last Caesarean fortress stood,
Evergreen forest! which Boccaccio's lore
And Dryden's lay made haunted ground to me,
How have I loved the twilight hour and thee!

106

The shrill cicalas, people of the pine,
Making their summer lives one ceaseless song,
Were the sole echoes, save my steed's and mine,
And Vesper bell's that rose the boughs along;
The spectre huntsman of Onesti's line,
His hell-dogs, and their chase, and the fair throng
Which learned from this example not to fly
From a true lover,—shadowed my mind's eye.

107

Oh, Hesperus! thou bringest all good things—
Home to the weary, to the hungry cheer,
To the young bird the parent's brooding wings,
The welcome stall to the o'erlaboured steer;
Whate'er of peace about our hearth stone clings,
Whate'er our household gods protect of dear,
Are gathered round us by thy look of rest;
Thou bring'st the child, too, to the mother's breast.

108

Soft Hour! which wakes the wish and melts the heart
Of those who sail the seas, on the first day
When they from their sweet friends are torn apart;
Or fills with love the pilgrim on his way
As the far bell of Vesper makes him start,
Seeming to weep the dying day's decay;
Is this a fancy which our reason scorns?
Ah! surely nothing dies but something mourns! . . .

from CANTO THE FOURTH

29

Now pillowed cheek to cheek, in loving sleep,
Haidée and Juan their siesta took,
A gentle slumber, but it was not deep,
For ever and anon a something shook
Juan, and shuddering o'er his frame would creep;
And Haidée's sweet lips murmured like a brook
A wordless music, and her face so fair
Stirred with her dream, as rose-leaves with the air. . . .

31

She dreamed of being alone on the sea-shore,
Chained to a rock; she knew not how, but stir
She could not from the spot, and the loud roar
Grew, and each wave rose roughly, threatening her;
And o'er her upper lip they seemed to pour,
Until she sobbed for breath, and soon they were
Foaming o'er her lone head, so fierce and high—
Each broke to drown her, yet she could not die.

32

Anon—she was released, and then she strayed
O'er the sharp shingles with her bleeding feet,

935. Dryden's lay, Dryden's *Theodore and Honoria*, an adaptation of a tale by Boccaccio.

941. Onesti's. Boccaccio's Onesti is Dryden's Theodore.

And stumbled almost every step she made:
And something rolled before her in a sheet,
Which she must still pursue howe'er afraid:
'Twas white and indistinct, nor stopped to meet
Her glance nor grasp, for still she gazed and grasped,
And ran, but it escaped her as she clasped.

33

The dream changed:—in a cave she stood,—its walls
Were hung with marble icicles; the work
Of ages on its water-fretted halls,
Where waves might wash, and seals might breed and lurk;
Her hair was dripping, and the very balls
Of her black eyes seemed turned to tears, and mirk
The sharp rocks looked below each drop they caught,
Which froze to marble as it fell,—she thought.

34

And wet, and cold, and lifeless at her feet,
Pale as the foam that frothed on his dead brow,
Which she essayed in vain to clear, (how sweet
Were once her cares, how idle seemed they now!)
Lay Juan, nor could aught renew the beat
Of his quenched heart: and the sea dirges low
Rang in her sad ears like a Mermaid's song,
And that brief dream appeared a life too long.

35

And gazing on the dead, she thought his face
Faded, or altered into something new—
Like to her Father's features, till each trace
More like and like to Lambro's aspect grew—
With all his keen worn look and Grecian grace;
And starting, she awoke, and what to view?
Oh! Powers of Heaven! what dark eye meets she there?
'Tis—'tis her Father's—fixed upon the pair!

36

Then shrieking, she arose, and shrieking fell,
With joy and sorrow, hope and fear, to see
Him whom she deemed a habitant where dwell
The ocean-buried, risen from death, to be
Perchance the death of one she loved too well:
Dear as her father had been to Haidée
It was a moment of that awful kind—
I have seen such—but must not call to mind.

37

Up Juan sprung to Haidée's bitter shriek,
And caught her falling, and from off the wall
Snatched down his sabre, in hot haste to wreak
Vengeance on him who was the cause of all:
Then Lambro, who till now forbore to speak,
Smiled scornfully, and said, "Within my call,
A thousand scimitars await the word;
Put up, young man, put up your silly sword."

38

And Haidée clung around him; "Juan, 'tis—
'Tis Lambro—'tis my father! Kneel with me—
He will forgive us—yes—it must be—yes.
Oh! dearest father, in this agony
Of pleasure and of pain—even while I kiss
Thy garment's hem with transport, can it be
That doubt should mingle with my filial joy?
Deal with me as thou wilt, but spare this boy."

39

High and inscrutable the old man stood,
Calm in his voice, and calm within his eye—
Not always signs with him of calmest mood:
He looked upon her, but gave no reply;
Then turned to Juan, in whose cheek the blood
Oft came and went, as there resolved to die;
In arms, at least, he stood, in act to spring
On the first foe whom Lambro's call might bring.

40

"Young man, your sword"; so Lambro once more said:
Juan replied, "Not while this arm is free."
The old man's cheek grew pale, but not with dread,
And drawing from his belt a pistol, he
Replied, "Your blood be then on your own head."
Then looked close at the flint, as if to see
'Twas fresh—for he had lately used the lock—
And next proceeded quietly to cock.

41

It has a strange quick jar upon the ear,
That cocking of a pistol, when you know
A moment more will bring the sight to bear
Upon your person, twelve yards off or so;
A gentlemanly distance, not too near,
If you have got a former friend for foe;
But after being fired at once or twice,
The ear becomes more Irish, and less nice.

42

Lambro presented, and one instant more
Had stopped this Canto, and Don Juan's breath,

When Haidée threw herself her boy before;
Stern as her sire: "On me," she cried, "let Death
Descend—the fault is mine; this fatal shore
He found—but sought not. I have pledged my faith;
I love him—I will die with him; I knew
Your nature's firmness—know your daughter's too." . . .

47

"Let him disarm; or, by my father's head,
His own shall roll before you like a ball!"
He raised his whistle, as the word he said,
And blew; another answered to the call,
And rushing in disorderly, though led,
And armed from boot to turban, one and all,
Some twenty of his train came, rank on rank;
He gave the word,—"Arrest or slay the Frank."

48

Then, with a sudden movement, he withdrew
His daughter; while compressed within his clasp,
'Twixt her and Juan interposed the crew;
In vain she struggled in her father's grasp—
His arms were like a serpent's coil: then flew
Upon their prey, as darts an angry asp,
The file of pirates; save the foremost, who
Had fallen, with his right shoulder half cut through.

49

The second had his cheek laid open; but
The third, a wary, cool old sworder, took
The blows upon his cutlass, and then put
His own well in; so well, ere you could look,
His man was floored, and helpless at his foot,
With the blood running like a little brook
From two smart sabre gashes, deep and red—
One on the arm, the other on the head.

50

And then they bound him where he fell, and bore
Juan from the apartment: with a sign
Old Lambro bade them take him to the shore,
Where lay some ships which were to sail at nine.
They laid him in a boat, and plied the oar
Until they reached some galliots, placed in line;
On board of one of these, and under hatches,
They stowed him, with strict orders to the watches. . . .

376. Frank, Greek or Turkish term for any Western European. **398. galliots,** small boats propelled by sails and oars.

58

The last sight which she saw was Juan's gore,
And he himself o'ermastered and cut down;
His blood was running on the very floor
Where late he trod, her beautiful, her own;
Thus much she viewed an instant and no more,—
Her struggles ceased with one convulsive groan;
On her Sire's arm, which until now scarce held
Her writhing, fell she like a cedar felled.

59

A vein had burst, and her sweet lips' pure dyes
Were dabbled with the deep blood which ran o'er;
And her head drooped as when the lily lies
O'ercharged with rain: her summoned hand-maids bore
Their lady to her couch with gushing eyes;
Of herbs and cordials they produced their store,
But she defied all means they could employ,
Like one life could not hold, nor death destroy.

60

Days lay she in that state unchanged, though chill—
With nothing livid, still her lips were red;
She had no pulse, but death seemed absent still;
No hideous sign proclaimed her surely dead;
Corruption came not in each mind to kill
All hope; to look upon her sweet face bred
New thoughts of life, for it seemed full of soul—
She had so much, earth could not claim the whole.

61

The ruling passion, such as marble shows
When exquisitely chiselled, still lay there,
But fixed as marble's unchanged aspect throws
O'er the fair Venus, but for ever fair;
O'er the Laocoön's all eternal throes,
And ever-dying Gladiator's air,
Their energy like life forms all their fame,
Yet looks not life, for they are still the same. . . .

69

Twelve days and nights she withered thus; at last,
Without a groan, or sigh, or glance, to show
A parting pang, the spirit from her passed:
And they who watched her nearest could not know

484. but for ever fair. Note the effect of "but." Compare Keats's "Ode on a Grecian Urn," stanza 5, p. 878.

The very instant, till the change that cast
  Her sweet face into shadow, dull and slow,
Glazed o'er her eyes—the beautiful, the black—
Oh! to possess such lustre—and then lack! . . .

71

Thus lived—thus died she; never more on her
  Shall Sorrow light, or Shame. She was not made
Through years or moons the inner weight to bear,
  Which colder hearts endure till they are laid
By age in earth: her days and pleasures were
  Brief, but delightful—such as had not staid
Long with her destiny; but she sleeps well
By the sea-shore, whereon she loved to dwell.

72

That isle is now all desolate and bare,
  Its dwellings down, its tenant passed away;
None but her own and Father's grave is there,
  And nothing outward tells of human clay;
Ye could not know where lies a thing so fair,
  No stone is there to show, no tongue to say
What was; no dirge, except the hollow sea's,
Mourns o'er the Beauty of the Cyclades. . . .

STANZAS WRITTEN ON THE ROAD BETWEEN FLORENCE AND PISA

Oh talk not to me of a name great in story—
The days of our Youth are the days of our glory;
And the myrtle and ivy of sweet two-and-twenty
Are worth all your laurels, though ever so plenty.

What are garlands and crowns to the brow that is wrinkled?
'Tis but as a dead flower with May-dew besprinkled:
Then away with all such from the head that is hoary,
What care I for the wreaths that can *only* give glory?

Oh, FAME!—if I e'er took delight in thy praises,
'Twas less for the sake of thy high-sounding phrases,
Than to see the bright eyes of the dear One discover,
She thought that I was not unworthy to love her.

There chiefly I sought thee, *there* only I found thee;
Her Glance was the best of the rays that surround thee;
When it sparkled o'er aught that was bright in my story,
I knew it was Love, and I felt it was Glory.

EPIGRAMS

THE WORLD IS A BUNDLE OF HAY

The world is a bundle of hay,
  Mankind are the asses who pull,
Each tugs it a different way,—
  And the greatest of all is John Bull!

WHO KILLED JOHN KEATS?

"Who killed John Keats?"
  "I," says the *Quarterly*,
  So savage and Tartarly;
"'Twas one of my feats."

"Who shot the arrow?"
  "The poet-priest Milman
  (So ready to kill man),
Or Southey or Barrow."

ON THIS DAY I COMPLETE MY THIRTY-SIXTH YEAR

1

'Tis time this heart should be unmoved,
  Since others it hath ceased to move:
Yet, though I cannot be beloved,
  Still let me love!

2

My days are in the yellow leaf;
  The flowers and fruits of Love are gone;
The worm, the canker, and the grief
  Are mine alone!

3

The fire that on my bosom preys
  Is lone as some volcanic isle;
No torch is kindled at its blaze—
  A funeral pile.

4

The hope, the fear, the zealous care,
  The exalted portion of the pain
And power of love, I cannot share,
  But wear the chain.

5

But 'tis not *thus*—and 'tis not *here*—
  Such thoughts should shake my soul, nor *now*,
Where glory decks the hero's bier,
  Or binds his brow.

6

The sword, the banner, and the field,
Glory and Greece, around me see!
The Spartan, borne upon his shield,
Was not more free.

7

Awake! (not Greece—she *is* awake!)
Awake, my spirit! Think through *whom*
Thy life-blood tracks its parent lake,
And then strike home!

8

Tread those reviving passions down,
Unworthy manhood!—unto thee
Indifferent should the smile or frown
Of beauty be.

9

If thou regret'st thy youth, *why live?*
The land of honourable death
Is here:—up to the field, and give
Away thy breath!

10

Seek out—less often sought than found—
A soldier's grave, for thee the best;
Then look around, and choose thy ground,
And take thy rest.

Missolonghi, Jan. 22, 1824.

LETTERS

As the writer of letters that combine easy vigor of expression with remarkable vividness and wit, Byron is unequalled among English poets. In many respects his letters, surprisingly free from conscious art, afford the surest key to his personality. The two included here grow out of the years in Venice. The first is a high-spirited, spontaneous product of that period of exuberance and intrigue when Byron's attentions were centered on the attractive young Marianna Segati. The second, much more serious in tone, is a forceful statement of artistic independence.

TO THOMAS MOORE

January 28, 1817

Your letter of the 8th is before me. The remedy for your plethora is simple—abstinence. I was obliged to have recourse to the like some years ago, I mean in point of *diet*, and, with the exception of some convivial weeks and days, (it might be months, now and then), have kept to Pythagoras ever since. You must not *indulge in* "filthy beer," nor in porter, nor eat *suppers*—the last are the devil to those who swallow dinner . . .

I think of being in England in the spring. If there is a row, by the sceptre of King Ludd, but I'll be one; and if there is none, and only a continuance of "this meek, piping time of peace," I will take a cottage a hundred yards to the south of your abode, and become your neighbour; and we will compose such canticles, and hold such dialogues, as shall be the terror of the *Times* (including the newspaper of that name), and the wonder, and honour, and praise, of the *Morning Chronicle* and posterity.

I rejoice to hear of your forthcoming in February—though I tremble for the "magnificence," which you attribute to the new *Childe Harold*. I am glad you like it; it is a fine indistinct piece of poetical desolation, and my favourite. I was half mad during the time of its composition, between metaphysics, mountains, lakes, love unextinguishable, thoughts unutterable, and the nightmare of my own delinquencies. I should, many a good day, have blown my brains out, but for the recollection that it would have given pleasure to my mother-in-law; and, even *then*, if I could have been certain to haunt her—but I won't dwell upon these trifling family matters.

Venice is in the *estro* of her carnival, and I have been up these last two nights at the ridotto and the opera, and all that kind of thing. Now for an adventure. A few days ago a gondolier brought me a billet without a subscription, intimating a wish on the part of the writer to meet me either in gondola or at the island of San Lazaro, or at the third rendezvous, indicated in the note. "I know the country's disposition well"—in Venice "they do let Heaven see those tricks they dare not show," etc., etc.; so, for all response, I said that neither of the three places suited me; but that I would either be at home at ten at night *alone*, or be at the ridotto at midnight, where the writer might meet me masked. At ten o'clock I was at home and alone (Marianna was gone with her husband to a conversazione), when the door of my apartment opened, and in walked a well-looking and (for an Italian) *bionda* girl of about nineteen, who informed me that she was married to the brother of

52. **Pythagoras.** Followers of the Greek philosopher practiced asceticism, particularly in the matter of food.

5. **King Ludd.** Byron intentionally confuses a mythical king of Britain and one Ned Ludd, a village "frame-breaker" whose name was given to the Luddites, a band of workmen who had recently been attempting to prevent the use of labor-saving machinery by engaging in sabotage. 28. **estro,** inspiration. 29. **ridotto,** masquerade. 35. **"I know . . . dare not show."** Byron's epistolary style is characterized by frequent allusiveness; here, as often, the lines echoed are from Shakespeare: *Othello,* Act III, sc. iii.

my *amorosa*, and wished to have some conversation with me. I made a decent reply, and we had some talk in Italian and Romaic (her mother being a Greek of Corfu), when lo! in a very few minutes, in marches, to my very great astonishment, Marianna Segati, in *propriâ personâ*, and after making a most polite courtesy to her sister-in-law and to me, without a single word seizes her said sister-in-law by the hair, and bestows upon her some sixteen slaps, which would have made your ear ache only to hear their echo. I need not describe the screaming which ensued. The luckless visitor took flight. I seized Marianna, who, after several vain efforts to get away in pursuit of the enemy, fairly went into fits in my arms; and, in spite of reasoning, eau de Cologne, vinegar, half a pint of water, and God knows what other waters besides, continued so till past midnight.

After damning my servants for letting people in without apprizing me, I found that Marianna in the morning had seen her sister-in-law's gondolier on the stairs, and, suspecting that his apparition boded her no good, had either returned of her own accord, or been followed by her maids or some other spy of her people to the conversazione, from whence she returned to perpetrate this piece of pugilism. I had seen fits before, and also some small scenery of the same genus in and out of our island: but this was not all. After about an hour, in comes—who? why, Signor Segati, her lord and husband, and finds me with his wife fainting upon the sofa, and all the apparatus of confusion, dishevelled hair, hats, handkerchiefs, salts, smelling-bottles—and the lady as pale as ashes, without sense or motion. His first question was, "What is all this?" The lady could not reply—so I did. I told him the explanation was the easiest thing in the world; but in the mean time it would be as well to recover his wife—at least, her senses. This came about in due time of suspiration and respiration.

You need not be alarmed—jealousy is not the order of the day in Venice, and daggers are out of fashion; while duels, on love matters, are unknown —at least, with the husbands. But, for all this, it was an awkward affair; and though he must have known that I made love to Marianna, yet I believe he was not, till that evening, aware of the extent to which it had gone. It is very well known that almost all the married women have a lover; but it is usual to keep up the forms, as in other nations. I did not, therefore, know what the devil to say. I could not out with the truth, out of regard to her, and I did not choose to lie for my sake;—besides, the thing told itself. I thought the best way would be to let her explain it as she chose (a woman being never at a loss—the devil always sticks by them)—only determining to protect and carry her off, in case of any ferocity on the part of the Signor. I saw that he was quite calm. She went to bed, and next day—how they settled it, I know not, but settle it they did. Well—then I had to explain to Marianna about this never-to-be-sufficiently-confounded sister-in-law; which I did by swearing innocence, eternal constancy, etc., etc. . . . But the sister-in-law, very much discomposed with being treated in such wise, has (not having her own shame before her eyes) told the affair to half Venice, and the servants (who were summoned by the fight and the fainting) to the other half. But, here, nobody minds such trifles, except to be amused by them. I don't know whether you will be so, but I have scrawled a long letter out of these follies.

Believe me ever, etc.

B.

TO JOHN MURRAY

April 6, 1819

Dear Sir,—The Second Canto of *Don Juan* was sent, on Saturday last, by post, in 4 packets, two of 4, and two of three sheets each, containing in all two hundred and seventeen stanzas, octave measure. But I will permit no curtailments, except those mentioned about Castlereagh and the two *Bobs* in the Introduction. You sha'n't make *Canticles* of my Cantos. The poem will please, if it is lively; if it is stupid, it will fail; but I will have none of your damned cutting and slashing. If you please, you may publish *anonymously;* it will perhaps be better; but I will battle my way against them all, like a Porcupine.

So you and Mr. Foscolo, etc., want me to undertake what you call a "great work?" an Epic poem, I suppose, or some such pyramid. I'll try no such thing; I hate tasks. And then "seven or eight years!" God send us all well this day three months, let alone years. If one's years can't be better employed than in sweating poesy, a man had better be a ditcher. And works, too!—is *Childe Harold* nothing? You have so many "*divine*" poems, is it nothing to have written a *Human* one? without any of your worn-out machinery. Why, man, I could have spun the thoughts of the four cantos of that poem into twenty, had I wanted to book-make, and its passion into as many modern tragedies. Since

39. Mr. Foscolo. Niccolo Foscolo (1778–1827) was an Italian writer, professor, and patriot.

you want *length*, you shall have enough of *Juan*, for I'll make 50 cantos.

And Foscolo, too! Why does *he* not do something more than the *Letters of Ortis*, and a tragedy, and pamphlets? He has good fifteen years more at his command than I have: what has he done all that time?—proved his Genius, doubtless, but not fixed its fame, nor done his utmost.

Besides, I mean to write my best work in *Italian*, and it will take me nine years more thoroughly to master the language; and then if my fancy exist, and I exist too, I will try what I *can* do *really*. As to the Estimation of the English which you talk of, let them calculate what it is worth, before they insult me with their insolent condescension.

I have not written for their pleasure. If they are pleased, it is that they chose to be so; I have never flattered their opinions, nor their pride; nor will I. Neither will I make "Ladies books" *al dilettar le femine e la plebe*. I have written from the fulness of my mind, from passion, from impulse, from many motives, but not for their "sweet voices."

I know the precise worth of popular applause for few Scribblers have had more of it; and if I chose to swerve into their paths, I could retain it, or resume it, or increase it. But I neither love ye, nor fear ye; and though I buy with ye and sell with ye, and talk with ye, I will neither eat with ye, drink with ye, nor pray with ye. They made me, without my search, a species of popular Idol; they, without reason or judgement, beyond the caprice of their good pleasure, threw down the Image from its pedestal; it was not broken with the fall, and they would, it seems, again replace it—but they shall not.

You ask about my health: about the beginning of the year I was in a state of great exhaustion, attended by such debility of Stomach that nothing remained upon it; and I was obliged to reform my "way of life," which was conducting me from the "yellow leaf" to the Ground, with all deliberate speed. I am better in health and morals, and very much yours ever,

Bn

Percy Bysshe Shelley
1792–1822

Born August 4, 1792, at Field Place, near Horsham, Sussex, Percy Bysshe Shelley was the first child of Timothy and Elizabeth Pilfold Shelley. The family was an old one, of country squires, and Field Place was a charming eighteenth-century mansion overlooking the lovely Sussex countryside.

At Sion House Academy, which he attended for two years with his cousin Thomas Medwin, and later at Eton, where he was a pupil to the age of eighteen, his interest in science and in Gothic tales developed. In both schools the boy ran afoul of the school disciplines and was rebellious and miserable much of the time. At Eton, besides solacing himself with Gothic thrillers and scientific fooling, he began reading such radical literature as Godwin's *Political Justice*. The resulting unorthodox political and religious opinions that he formed brought about the termination by parental authority of a love affair with his cousin Harriet Grove. At the end of his schooling, he was the published author of a book of verse and a Gothic romance, *Zastrozzi*.

Shelley's Oxford sojourn was of a piece with his schooling, only briefer. With his friends, among them Thomas Jefferson Hogg, he read such skeptics as Locke, Hume, and Voltaire. Exhilarated by his skepticism, he amused himself by writing prominent bishops that he was an honest doubter, a soul seeking the light, then demolishing their evidences of Christianity by arguments cribbed from his books. In March of his freshman year he was expelled, and with him his friend Hogg, for "contumaciously refusing to answer [official] questions" about a pamphlet, *The Necessity of Atheism*, which he had written and published at his own expense.

Going to London, where his sisters, then in school, were able to help him, he refused to conciliate his father or seek reinstatement at Oxford. There he met Harriet Westbrook, a schoolmate of his sisters, impressed her with his political and religious views, and assumed the responsibility of enlightening her. He may also have recommended himself as a very eligible prospective husband for Harriet. When, some months later, he learned that Harriet was in disgrace with her parents for having associated with

19–20. ***al dilettar . . . la plebe,*** to please the women and the people.

5–7. **though I buy . . . pray with ye.** Here Byron paraphrases Shylock's famous speech in *The Merchant of Venice*, Act I, sc. 3, ll. 36–8.

an atheist and a rebel, he rescued her, like one of his Gothic knights, by running away with her to Edinburgh and marrying her, she being sixteen, he nineteen. Harriet's father and (later) Shelley's made some allowance for the support of the young couple. An apostle of Godwin and the new freedom, Shelley took his bride to Ireland on a honeymoon crusade of writing and speechmaking for the reform of government in that oppressed and miserable country. Returning to England, they wandered about in that country and in Wales, Shelley engaging in a Platonic friendship with Elizabeth Hitchener, a schoolmistress, experimenting in vegetarianism, and engaging in humanitarian activities. Early in 1813 Shelley published his first important poem, *Queen Mab*, expressing his Necessitarian ideas on the ruling principle of the universe, his denunciation of religion, his socialistic criticism of human society past and present, and his idealistic hopes for the future. Shortly afterward, he became personally acquainted with William Godwin, fell into financial distress, and began to feel that he and Harriet were not intellectually compatible. Meanwhile, he read incessantly, mostly in materialistic philosophy. In 1814, he met seventeen-year-old Mary Wollstonecraft Godwin. Their mutual attraction was electric. In July they eloped to Switzerland. The will of Shelley's grandfather, who died early in 1815, left him with an income of about $5,000. This he divided fairly with Harriet, who was now the mother of two children. The summer of 1816 Shelley, Mary, and her stepsister Clara Jane Clairmont spent in Switzerland, on intimate terms with Byron. Soon after their return to England Harriet drowned herself in the Serpentine River. When Shelley petitioned the Lord Chancellor Eldon for the custody of his children by Harriet, he was denied, on evidence, partly contained in *Queen Mab*, that he was not morally fit to rear them. Shelley regarded the verdict as a stigma and a virtual sentence of exile. For this reason, and also on account of his poor health, in March, 1818, he and his family left England for Italy. Like Byron, Shelley had come under "the Genius of Pain." His career as an intellectual playboy was at an end.

During this period of unsuccessful efforts for social reform and of domestic tragedy, Shelley was steadily acquiring intellectual and poetical power. *Alastor*, 1816, a blank-verse spiritual autobiography in its story of a young poet's quest for ideal beauty, shows new strength of thought and poetic style. "Hymn to Intellectual Beauty," 1817, inspired by Alpine scenery and the philosophy of Plato, realizes a truth that the young poet in *Alastor* had disregarded: ideal beauty, which "Gives grace and truth to life's unquiet dream," cannot be fully incorporated in earthly form or clasped in human shape. *The Revolt of Islam*, 1818, a long narrative poem in Spenserian stanzas about Laon and Cythna, lovers and leaders of a revolution, shows the revival of Shelley's hopes for mankind. Its "Dedication" is one of his most pleasing and revealing autobiographical poems. "Lines Written among the Euganean Hills," 1818, describes the state of mind in which he first came to Italy. The same year that saw the composition of this poem saw the beginning of his masterpiece, *Prometheus Unbound*. His attainment of large poetic stature had been swift.

Coming to Italy in 1818, the Shelleys spent part of the autumn at Byron's villa near Venice. Shelley's sense of humiliation, his remorse perhaps, his spiritual loneliness, and his grief over the death of his little daughter Clara are poignantly expressed in "Lines Written among the Euganean Hills." They are the personal undertone of *Prometheus Unbound*, begun at Byron's villa and completed in Rome and Florence. By this time, however, Shelley had begun to transcend personal sorrow and pain in his contemplation of the wrongs of the world and of mankind's happy deliverance. At Rome he became interested in a Roman murder story of the sixteenth century and dramatized it in *The Cenci*, the tragedy of Beatrice, a young girl violated by her own father and convicted and executed for killing him in revenge. At Florence, where *Prometheus Unbound* was finished and a son, Percy Florence, was born, he felt in the seasonal phenomena the symbol of that ultimate cosmic redemption which he suggests in the last stanza of "Ode to the West Wind." In 1819 he was grieved and angered by news of economic misery and political oppression coming out of England. His "Masque of Anarchy," "Song to the Men of England," and "England in 1819" voice his anger and pity and come nearest of all his poems to advocacy of direct action.

Shelley's last three years were spent in or near Pisa. His and Mary's capacity for making friends is one of the pleasing features of this last phase. They were the center of a circle that included John and Maria Gisborne, Sophia Stacey, Thomas Medwin, and Edward and Jane Williams. Toward the last, Edward Trelawny joined them, and Byron exchanged visits with them. All of these people are significant in one way or another to Shelley's poetry, as in the charming "Letter to Maria Gisborne" and "To Jane, with a Guitar." Acquaintance with the Greek Prince Mavrocordato deepened Shelley's interest in the cause of Greek independence, and he wrote his last long completed poem on the theme, *Hellas, a Lyrical Drama*, published in 1822. A short but intense infatuation with Emilia Viviani produced one of Shelley's greatest love poems. Emilia, a beautiful young Italian girl, was destined by her family to be the bride of an old nobleman, and when she objected to the match was immured in a convent. Shelley's championship of her cause and of love itself is proclaimed in *Epipsychidion*. News of the death of John Keats at Rome in February, 1821, moved Shelley to compose *Adonais*, one of the three greatest pastoral elegies in English poetry. Occasioned by a slight friendship with Keats and by Shelley's feeling that he himself "in another's fate now wept his own," *Adonais* is really a vindication of all poets and a triumphant assertion of their immortality. In the same year with *Epipsychidion*, vindication of love, and with *Adonais*, vindication of the poet, Shelley wrote his noble prose *Defence of Poetry*, in reply to an attack made by his friend Peacock.

Shelley's *Alastor* (ll. 304 ff.), his "Stanzas Written in Dejection near Naples," and *Adonais* contain passages descriptive of death by drowning. Their prophetic import was confirmed by events of the spring and early summer of 1822. In May the Shelleys moved to Casa Magni, near Lerici, on the Gulf of Spezia. In June Leigh Hunt arrived at Leghorn, ready to begin editing the *Liberal*, sponsored by Byron and Shelley. On July 8, after a meeting with Byron to make arrangements for settling the Hunts, Shelley and Williams sailed from Leghorn for home in the *Ariel* (or, as Byron had insisted, the *Don Juan*). Somewhere off Via Reggio a sudden and violent squall arose. The young Englishmen did not arrive at their destination. Nearly two weeks later their bodies were found washed ashore, Shelley's with a volume of Keats in one pocket and a volume of Sophocles in another. Italian sanitary laws required cremation; and Byron, Hunt, Trelawny, and others burned the bodies on the beach. At the last moment Trelawny snatched Shelley's heart from the flames. Mary received the heart. Shelley's ashes were buried in the Protestant cemetery at Rome, which he had described in *Adonais* (stanzas 49–50) as the last resting-place of Keats.

To some of his critics, Shelley seems a political dreamer whose idealism consisted in falling into sheer unreality, a romantic moralist "with a taint of sophistry or sham wisdom." But there is stronger reason for viewing him as a great lyric poet who is also a perceptive social and political thinker, whose natural material of expression is poetry and whose central vision is that of the poet. Shelley is the poet of protest against man's inhumanity to man, of assault against tyranny entrenched in the Church, the State, formalized education, the political and economic order, custom and convention. He is the greatest English prophet of human perfectibility, the poet of ideal love and beauty informing all things, binding all things together, and offering in their fullness the satisfaction of man's physical needs, his moral desires, and his spiritual aspirations. "The essential thought of Shelley's creed," declares Symonds, "was that the universe is penetrated, vitalized, made real by a spirit, which he sometimes calls the Spirit of Nature [as in *Queen Mab*], but which is always conceived as more than Life, as that which gives its actuality to Life, and lastly Love and Beauty [as in *Adonais*]. To adore this spirit, to clasp it with affection, and to blend with it, is, he thought, the true object of man." [1] Thus Shelley's idealism motivates his attack on the world as he knew it and inspires his program and his hopes for the world as it was to be. In its broad principles, Shelley's is as practical as any other system which seeks causes and remedies in the heart of man. His poetic materials are symbols of a spirit of liberation and regeneration that he is convinced must ultimately triumph.

HYMN TO INTELLECTUAL BEAUTY

The awful shadow of some unseen Power
  Floats though unseen among us; visiting
  This various world with as inconstant wing
As summer winds that creep from flower to flower;
Like moonbeams that behind some piny mountain
    shower,
  It visits with inconstant glance
  Each human heart and countenance;
Like hues and harmonies of evening,
  Like clouds in starlight widely spread,
  Like memory of music fled,
  Like aught that for its grace may be
Dear, and yet dearer for its mystery.

Spirit of Beauty, that dost consecrate
  With thine own hues all thou dost shine upon
  Of human thought or form, where art thou gone?
Why dost thou pass away and leave our state,
This dim vast vale of tears, vacant and desolate?
  Ask why the sunlight not for ever

[1] John Addington Symonds, *Shelley*, English Men of Letters Series, Macmillan, 1909, p. 123.

Weaves rainbows o'er yon mountain river,
Why aught should fail and fade that once is shown;
Why fear and dream and death and birth
Cast on the daylight of this earth
Such gloom, why man has such a scope
For love and hate, despondency and hope?

No voice from some sublimer world hath ever
To sage or poet these responses given:
Therefore the names of Demon, Ghost, and Heaven,
Remain the records of their vain endeavour:
Frail spells, whose uttered charm might not avail to sever,
From all we hear and all we see,
Doubt, chance, and mutability.
Thy light alone—like mist o'er mountains driven,
Or music by the night wind sent
Through strings of some still instrument,
Or moonlight on a midnight stream,
Gives grace and truth to life's unquiet dream.

Love, Hope, and Self-esteem, like clouds depart
And come, for some uncertain moments lent.
Man were immortal, and omnipotent,
Didst thou, unknown and awful as thou art,
Keep with thy glorious train firm state within his heart.
Thou messenger of sympathies,
That wax and wane in lovers' eyes;
Thou, that to human thought art nourishment,
Like darkness to a dying flame!
Depart not as thy shadow came:
Depart not, lest the grave should be,
Like life and fear, a dark reality.

While yet a boy I sought for ghosts, and sped
Through many a listening chamber, cave, and ruin,
And starlight wood, with fearful steps pursuing
Hopes of high talk with the departed dead.
I called on poisonous names with which our youth is fed;
I was not heard—I saw them not—
When musing deeply on the lot
Of life, at that sweet time when winds are wooing
All vital things that wake to bring
News of birds and blossoming,—
Sudden, thy shadow fell on me;
I shrieked, and clasped my hands in ecstasy!

I vowed that I would dedicate my powers
To thee and thine: have I not kept the vow?
With beating heart and streaming eyes, even now
I call the phantoms of a thousand hours
Each from his voiceless grave: they have in visioned bowers
Of studious zeal or love's delight
Outwatched with me the envious night:
They know that never joy illumed my brow
Unlinked with hope that thou wouldst free
This world from its dark slavery,
That thou, O awful LOVELINESS,
Wouldst give whate'er these words cannot express.

The day becomes more solemn and serene
When noon is past: there is a harmony
In autumn, and a lustre in its sky,
Which through the summer is not heard or seen,
As if it could not be, as if it had not been!
Thus let thy power, which like the truth
Of nature on my passive youth
Descended,—to my onward life supply
Its calm, to one who worships thee,
And every form containing thee,
Whom, SPIRIT fair, thy spells did bind
To fear himself, and love all human kind.

61. I vowed. See the last paragraph of the biographical-critical sketch of Shelley.

from THE REVOLT OF ISLAM

DEDICATION

There is no danger to a Man, that knows
What life and death is: there's not any law
Exceeds his knowledge: neither is it lawful
That he should stoop to any other law.—Chapman

TO MARY *

I

So now my summer task is ended, Mary,
And I return to thee, mine own heart's home;
As to his Queen some victor Knight of Faëry,
Earning bright spoils for her enchanted dome;
Nor thou disdain, that ere my fame become
A star among the stars of mortal night,
If it indeed may cleave its natal gloom,
Its doubtful promise thus I would unite
With thy belovèd name, thou Child of love and light.

2

The toil which stole from thee so many an hour
Is ended,—and the fruit is at thy feet!

* "Mary" is Mary Godwin. For comment on *The Revolt of Islam*, see the biographical-critical sketch of Shelley.
3. Queen . . . Knight. Shelley and Mary read Spenser's *The Faërie Queene* together at Marlow. Note the Spenserian stanza.

No longer where the woods to frame a bower
With interlacèd branches mix and meet,
Or where, with sounds like many voices sweet,
Waterfalls leap among wild islands green,
Which framed for my lone boat a lone retreat
Of moss-grown trees and weeds, shall I be seen:
But beside thee, where still my heart has ever been.

3

Thoughts of great deeds were mine, dear Friend, when first
The clouds which wrap this world from youth did pass.
I do remember well the hour which burst
My spirit's sleep; a fresh May-dawn it was,
When I walked forth upon the glittering grass,
And wept, I knew not why; until there rose
From the near school-room voices that, alas!
Were but one echo from a world of woes—
The harsh and grating strife of tyrants and of foes.

4

And then I clasped my hands, and looked around,—
But none was near to mock my streaming eyes,
Which poured their warm drops on the sunny ground—
So without shame, I spake:—"I will be wise,
And just, and free, and mild, if in me lies
Such power, for I grow weary to behold
The selfish and the strong still tyrannise
Without reproach or check." I then controlled
My tears, my heart grew calm, and I was meek and bold.

5

And from that hour did I with earnest thought
Heap knowledge from forbidden mines of lore,
Yet nothing that my tyrants knew or taught
I cared to learn, but from that secret store
Wrought linkèd armour for my soul, before
It might walk forth to war among mankind;
Thus power and hope were strengthened more and more
Within me, till there came upon my mind
A sense of loneliness, a thirst with which I pined.

6

Alas that love should be a blight and snare
To those who seek all sympathies in one!—
Such once I sought in vain; then black despair,
The shadow of a starless night, was thrown
Over the world in which I moved alone:—
Yet never found I one not false to me,
Hard hearts, and cold, like weights of icy stone
Which crushed and withered mine, that could not be
Aught but a lifeless clog, until revived by thee.

7

Thou Friend, whose presence on my wintry heart
Fell, like bright Spring upon some herbless plain,
How beautiful and calm and free thou wert
In thy young wisdom, when the mortal chain
Of Custom thou didst burst and rend in twain,
And walk as free as light the clouds among,
Which many an envious slave then breathed in vain
From his dim dungeon, and my spirit sprung
To meet thee from the woes which had begirt it long!

8

No more alone through the world's wilderness,
Although I trod the paths of high intent,
I journeyed now: no more companionless,
Where solitude is like despair, I went.—
There is the wisdom of a stern content
When Poverty can blight the just and good,
When Infamy dares mock the innocent,
And cherished friends turn with the multitude
To trample: this was ours, and we unshaken stood!

9

Now has descended a serener hour,
And with inconstant fortune, friends return;
Though suffering leaves the knowledge and the power
Which says:—Let scorn be not repaid with scorn.
And from thy side two gentle babes are born
To fill our home with smiles, and thus are we
Most fortunate beneath life's beaming morn:
And these delights, and thou, have been to me
The parents of the Song I consecrate to thee.

10

Is it, that now my inexperienced fingers
But strike the prelude of a loftier strain?
Or must the lyre on which my spirit lingers
Soon pause in silence, ne'er to sound again,

21. I do remember well the hour. Compare "Hymn to Intellectual Beauty," ll. 61 ff. The experience is supposed to have occurred at Eton. Compare Wordsworth's similar experience, *Prelude*, Book IV, ll. 309 ff.

48. then black despair, over the ruin of his life with Harriet. **59. Of custom . . . burst.** Shelley and Mary eloped on July 28, 1814.

Though it might shake the Anarch Custom's reign,
And charm the minds of men to Truth's own sway,
Holier than was Amphion's? I would fain
Reply in hope—but I am worn away,
And Death and Love are yet contending for their prey.

11

And what art thou? I know, but dare not speak:
Time may interpret to his silent years.
Yet in the paleness of thy thoughtful cheek,
And in the light thine ample forehead wears,
And in thy sweetest smiles, and in thy tears,
And in thy gentle speech, a prophecy
Is whispered, to subdue my fondest fears:
And through thine eyes, even in thy soul I see
A lamp of vestal fire burning internally.

12

They say that thou wert lovely from thy birth,
Of glorious parents, thou aspiring Child!
I wonder not—for One then left this earth
Whose life was like a setting planet mild,
Which clothed thee in the radiance undefiled
Of its departing glory; still her fame
Shines on thee, through the tempests dark and wild
Which shake these latter days; and thou canst claim
The shelter, from thy Sire, of an immortal name.

13

One voice came forth from many a mighty spirit,
Which was the echo of three thousand years;
And the tumultuous world stood mute to hear it,
As some lone man who in a desert hears
The music of his home:—unwonted fears
Fell on the pale oppressors of our race,
And Faith, and Custom, and low-thoughted cares,
Like thunder-stricken dragons, for a space
Left the torn human heart, their food and dwelling-place.

14

Truth's deathless voice pauses among mankind!
If there must be no response to my cry—
If men must rise and stamp with fury blind
On his pure name who loves them,—thou and I,
Sweet friend! can look from our tranquillity
Like lamps into the world's tempestuous night,—
Two tranquil stars, while clouds are passing by
Which wrap them from the foundering seaman's sight,
That burn from year to year with unextinguished light.

102. for One, Mary Wollstonecraft. **108. Sire,** William Godwin. **109. voice,** that of Truth.

OZYMANDIAS

I met a traveller from an antique land
Who said: Two vast and trunkless legs of stone
Stand in the desert. Near them, on the sand,
Half sunk, a shattered visage lies, whose frown,
And wrinkled lip, and sneer of cold command,
Tell that its sculptor well those passions read
Which yet survive, stamped on these lifeless things,
The hand that mocked them, and the heart that fed;
And on the pedestal these words appear:
"My name is Ozymandias, king of kings;
Look on my works, ye Mighty, and despair!"
Nothing beside remains. Round the decay
Of that colossal wreck, boundless and bare
The lone and level sands stretch far away.

HYMN OF PAN

1

From the forests and highlands
We come, we come;
From the river-girt islands,
Where loud waves are dumb
Listening to my sweet pipings.
The wind in the reeds and the rushes,
The bees on the bells of thyme,
The birds on the myrtle bushes,
The cicale above in the lime,
And the lizards below in the grass,
Were as silent as ever old Tmolus was,
Listening to my sweet pipings.

2

Liquid Peneus was flowing,
And all dark Tempe lay
In Pelion's shadow, outgrowing
The light of the dying day,
Speeded by my sweet pipings.
The Sileni, and Sylvans, and Fauns,
And the Nymphs of the woods and the waves,

Ozymandias. **8. hand . . . heart,** the sculptor's . . . the king's. **10. Ozymandias,** Rameses II, the Epyptian pharaoh who oppressed the children of Israel. The statue of him was at Thebes. *Hymn of Pan.* **9. lime,** lime tree.

To the edge of the moist river-lawns,
  And the brink of the dewy caves,
And all that did then attend and follow,
Were silent with love, as you now, Apollo,
  With envy of my sweet pipings.

3

I sang of the dancing stars,
  I sang of the daedal Earth,
And of Heaven—and the giant wars,
  And Love, and Death, and Birth,—
    And then I changed my pipings,—
Singing how down the vale of Maenalus
  I pursued a maiden and clasped a reed.
Gods and men, we are all deluded thus!
  It breaks in our bosom and then we bleed:
All wept, as I think both ye now would,
If envy or age had not frozen your blood,
    At the sorrow of my sweet pipings.

STANZAS

WRITTEN IN DEJECTION, NEAR NAPLES

I

The sun is warm, the sky is clear,
  The waves are dancing fast and bright;
Blue isles and snowy mountains wear
  The purple noon's transparent might:
The breath of the moist air is light
  Around its unexpanded buds;
Like many a voice of one delight,
  The winds, the birds, the ocean floods,
The City's voice itself is soft like Solitude's.

2

I see the Deep's untrampled floor
  With green and purple sea-weeds strown;
I see the waves upon the shore,
  Like light dissolved in star-showers, thrown:
I sit upon the sands alone,—
  The lightning of the noon-tide ocean
Is flashing round me, and a tone
  Arises from its measured motion,
How sweet! did any heart now share in my emotion.

3

Alas! I have nor hope nor health,
  Nor peace within nor calm around,
Nor that content surpassing wealth
  The sage in meditation found,
And walked with inward glory crowned—
  Nor fame, nor power, nor love, nor leisure.
Others I see whom these surround—
  Smiling they live, and call life pleasure;
To me that cup has been dealt in another measure.

4

Yet now despair itself is mild,
  Even as the winds and waters are;
I could lie down like a tired child,
  And weep away the life of care
Which I have borne and yet must bear,
  Till death like sleep might steal on me,
And I might feel in the warm air
  My cheek grow cold, and hear the sea
Breathe o'er my dying brain its last monotony.

5

Some might lament that I were cold,
  As I, when this sweet day is gone,
Which my lost heart, too soon grown old,
  Insults with this untimely moan;
They might lament—for I am one
  Whom men love not,—and yet regret,
Unlike this day, which, when the sun
  Shall on its stainless glory set,
Will linger, though enjoyed, like joy in memory yet.

SONG TO THE MEN OF ENGLAND

I

Men of England, wherefore plough
For the lords who lay ye low?
Wherefore weave with toil and care
The rich robes your tyrants wear?

2

Wherefore feed, and clothe, and save,
From the cradle to the grave,
Those ungrateful drones who would
Drain your sweat—nay, drink your blood?

26. daedal, curiously made. One of Shelley's favorite words. **19. Alas!** Note Shelley's characteristic self-pity.

27. To me that cup. The irregular "measure" of the line (probably intentional) emphasizes the different "measure" of the cup. **30–36. I could lie down . . . monotony.** With this picture of death by drowning, compare *Adonais,* stanza 55, l. 5. There is a similar one in *Alastor,* ll. 304 ff. **37. Some might lament.** When I am dead, some people may lament me as I lament this day (thus insulting its beauty). But the regrets will be different: Because I am unpopular, when people grieve for my death they will also regret mistakes in my life; whereas my memory of the passing of this day of perfect beauty will be untinged with regret for any defect.

3

Wherefore, Bees of England, forge
Many a weapon, chain, and scourge,
That these stingless drones may spoil
The forced produce of your toil?

4

Have ye leisure, comfort, calm,
Shelter, food, love's gentle balm?
Or what is it ye buy so dear
With your pain and with your fear?

5

The seed ye sow, another reaps;
The wealth ye find, another keeps;
The robes ye weave, another wears;
The arms ye forge, another bears.

6

Sow seed,—but let no tyrant reap;
Find wealth,—let no imposter heap;
Weave robes,—let not the idle wear;
Forge arms,—in your defence to bear.

7

Shrink to your cellars, holes, and cells;
In halls ye deck, another dwells.
Why shake the chains ye wrought? Ye see
The steel ye tempered glance on ye.

8

With plough and spade, and hoe and loom,
Trace your grave, and build your tomb,
And weave your winding-sheet, till fair
England be your sepulchre.

ENGLAND IN 1819

An old, mad, blind, despised, and dying king,—
Princes, the dregs of their dull race, who flow
Through public scorn—mud from a muddy spring;
Rulers, who neither see, nor feel, nor know,
But leech-like to their fainting country cling,
Till they drop, blind in blood, without a blow;
A people starved and stabbed in the untilled field,—
An army, which liberticide and prey
Makes as a two-edged sword to all who wield—
Golden and sanguine laws which tempt and slay,—
Religion Christless, Godless—a book sealed;
A Senate,—Time's worst statute unrepealed,—
Are graves, from which a glorious Phantom may
Burst, to illumine our tempestuous day.

1. **king,** George III.

ODE TO THE WEST WIND

The poem is a superb example of Shelley's mythmaking power in the treatment of natural phenomena, of the controlling moods and emotions of his lyrical poetry, and of his command of poetic structure when he was at his best. It is a modification of terza rima (interlinked iambic pentameter tercets riming aba, bcb, cdc, ded) followed by a couplet, ee, the modification, to round out a strophe. Note the perfect structure: (1) the power and freedom of the wind manifested upon the leaves (stanza 1), the clouds (stanza 2), and the waves (stanza 3); (2) these manifestations summed up in "leaf," "cloud," and "wave" (stanza 4, ll. 43–45), in contrast with the poet's weakness and bondage (stanza 4, ll. 46–56); (3) the poet's prayer for such freedom and power to "Drive his dead thoughts over the universe" for the awakening of mankind (stanza 5, ll. 57–68), and his faith in the wind as a symbol of universal regeneration (stanza 5, ll. 69–70). Note the management of long, sustained sentences and clauses, and the pauses, to suggest the streaming, volleying, and relative lulling of the wind.

1

O wild West Wind, thou breath of Autumn's being,
Thou, from whose unseen presence the leaves dead
Are driven, like ghosts from an enchanter fleeing,

Yellow, and black, and pale, and hectic red,
Pestilence-stricken multitudes: O thou,
Who chariotest to their dark wintry bed

The wingèd seeds, where they lie cold and low,
Each like a corpse within its grave, until
Thine azure sister of the spring shall blow

Her clarion o'er the dreaming earth, and fill
(Driving sweet buds like flocks to feed in air)
With living hues and odours plain and hill:

Wild Spirit, which art moving everywhere;
Destroyer and preserver; hear, oh, hear!

2

Thou on whose stream, 'mid the steep sky's commotion,
Loose clouds like earth's decaying leaves are shed,
Shook from the tangled boughs of Heaven and Ocean,

Angels of rain and lightning: there are spread
On the blue surface of thine aëry surge,
Like the bright hair uplifted from the head

Of some fierce Maenad, even from the dim verge
Of the horizon to the zenith's height,
The locks of the approaching storm. Thou dirge

Of the dying year, to which this closing night
Will be the dome of a vast sepulchre,
Vaulted with all thy congregated might

Of vapours, from whose solid atmosphere
Black rain, and fire, and hail will burst: O, hear!

3

Thou who didst waken from his summer dreams
The blue Mediterranean, where he lay,
Lulled by the coil of his crystalline streams,

Beside a pumice isle in Baiae's bay,
And saw in sleep old palaces and towers
Quivering within the wave's intenser day,

All overgrown with azure moss and flowers
So sweet, the sense faints picturing them! Thou
For whose path the Atlantic's level powers

Cleave themselves into chasms, while far below
The sea-blooms and the oozy woods which wear
The sapless foliage of the ocean, know

Thy voice, and suddenly grow grey with fear,
And tremble and despoil themselves: O, hear!

4

If I were a dead leaf thou mightest bear;
If I were a swift cloud to fly with thee;
A wave to pant beneath thy power, and share

The impulse of thy strength, only less free
Than thou, O uncontrollable! If even
I were as in my boyhood, and could be

The comrade of thy wanderings over heaven,
As then, when to outstrip thy skiey speed
Scarce seemed a vision; I would ne'er have striven

As thus with thee in prayer in my sore need.
Oh! lift me as a wave, a leaf, a cloud!
I fall upon the thorns of life! I bleed!

A heavy weight of hours has chained and bowed
One too like thee: tameless, and swift, and proud.

5

Make me thy lyre, even as the forest is:
What if my leaves are falling like its own!
The tumult of thy mighty harmonies

Will take from both a deep, autumnal tone,
Sweet though in sadness. Be thou, spirit fierce,
My spirit! Be thou me, impetuous one!

Drive my dead thoughts over the universe
Like withered leaves to quicken a new birth!
And, by the incantation of this verse,

Scatter, as from an unextinguished hearth
Ashes and sparks, my words among mankind!
Be through my lips to unawakened earth

The trumpet of a prophecy! O, Wind,
If Winter comes, can Spring be far behind?

43–45. Note that the ideas of the first three stanzas are first summed up in one line each (43–45) and finally in one word each (l. 53).

THE INDIAN SERENADE

I

I arise from dreams of thee
In the first sweet sleep of night,
When the winds are breathing low,
And the stars are shining bright:
I arise from dreams of thee,
And a spirit in my feet
Hath led me—who knows how?
To thy chamber window, Sweet!

2

The wandering airs they faint
On the dark, the silent stream—
The Champak odours fail
Like sweet thoughts in a dream;
The Nightingale's complaint—
It dies upon her heart
As I must die on thine,
Oh, belovèd as thou art!

3

Oh! lift me from the grass!
I die! I faint! I fail!
Let thy love in kisses rain
On my lips and eyelids pale.
My cheek is cold and white, alas!
My heart beats loud and fast,
Oh! press it close to thine again,
Where it will break at last.

LOVE'S PHILOSOPHY

I

The fountains mingle with the river,
And the rivers with the ocean,

11. Champak, a sacred tree of India. The scene and the sentiments are supposed to be Oriental.

The winds of Heaven mix for ever
With a sweet emotion;
Nothing in the world is single;
All things by a law divine
In one another's being mingle—
Why not I with thine?

2

See the mountains kiss high Heaven,
And the waves clasp one another;
No sister flower would be forgiven
If it disdained its brother;
And the sunlight clasps the earth,
And the moonbeams kiss the sea:
What are all these kissings worth,
If thou kiss not me?

POLITICAL GREATNESS*

Nor happiness, nor majesty, nor fame,
Nor peace, nor strength, nor skill in arms or arts,
Shepherd those herds whom tyranny makes tame;
Verse echoes not one beating of their hearts,
History is but the shadow of their shame;
Art veils her glass, or from the pageant starts
As to oblivion their blind millions fleet,
Staining that Heaven with obscene imagery
Of their own likeness. What are numbers knit
By force of custom? Man who man would be,
Must rule the empire of himself; in it
Must be supreme, establishing his throne
On vanquished will, quelling the anarchy
Of hopes and fears, being himself alone.

from PROMETHEUS UNBOUND

A LYRICAL DRAMA IN FOUR ACTS

The poem was begun at Este (Byron's villa) in September, 1818; the first act finished in October; Acts II and III composed near Rome (in the ruins of the Baths of Caracalla) in the spring of 1819; Act IV, an afterthought, written at Florence by December 15; the whole published by Ollier, in a volume including, besides the title poem, "Ode to the West Wind," "The Cloud," "To a Skylark," and "The Sensitive Plant." "*Prometheus Unbound*, I must tell you, is my favorite poem," Shelley wrote in a letter to Ollier, although, since the poem was not, like his drama *The Cenci*, written for the public, he says in the same letter, "I think, if I can judge by its merits, the *Prometheus* cannot sell beyond twenty copies." Only a few magazines (for example, the *London*) reviewed the poem favorably; most (for example, the *Quarterly*) condemned it on the ground that is was immoral, blasphemous, and obscure. One reviewer remarked, "It was well that the author specified *Unbound;* it will never be bound."

The subject of *Prometheus Unbound* is: what was wrong with the world in Shelley's post-Revolutionary time, what sort of miracle was needed to redeem mankind, and what mankind and the world would be like if such a miracle took place (as Shelley believed it would). It is, then, like Dante's *Divine Comedy*, Milton's *Paradise Lost*, Goethe's *Faust*, and Thomas Hardy's *The Dynasts*, a great cosmic poem, in the universality of its theme, in the grandeur of its characters, in the vastness of its setting and action, in the sublimity of its philosophy (a Platonic conception of life and a faith in the perfectibility of man), and in the beauty of its form.

The fable of the poem combines two world-wide myths, that of the Fire-Bringer (Civilizer) and that of the Defier of the Gods or Savior of Mankind. Shelley's treatment of it was in part suggested by the *Prometheus Bound* of Aeschylus but he characteristically rejected Aeschylus' reconciliation of Prometheus and Jupiter. This fable is but a frame for objectifying *a drama within the soul of man.* The characters are all projections of elements in Prometheus' nature; the actions are really all internal—what takes place in the soul of Prometheus (Mankind). In writing the poem Shelley's purpose was "to familiarize the highly refined imagination of the more select classes of poetical readers with beautiful idealisms of moral excellence."

Most critics (Professor N. I. White in the *Publications of the Modern Language Association*, Vol. XL, is the most notable exception) have regarded the poem as allegorical. Whether it is an allegory or not, the characters and the action have symbolical, representative significance. The following are at least working identifications: *Prometheus*—Humanity, the Genius of Man, Spirit of Mankind, Man's deathless aspiration and unconquerable will; *Jupiter*—the Principle of Evil, especially evil formed and fortified by man's religious, political, and social institutions, which have lost their original power for good and have hardened into the tyranny of custom and law; *Demogorgon*—Fate, the Eternal Principle of Change and Progress, Nemesis, Unalterable Law; *Asia*—Nature, the Creative Spirit, Intellectual Beauty, the Divine Principle of Sex; *Ione*—Hope, the Seer; *Panthea*—Faith, the Understander and Believer (the last two are Oceanides, sisters of Asia); *Hercules*—Strength.

Action: Prometheus speaks in agony from the icy rock to which he has been chained for three thousand years. Watching and waiting with him are Panthea and Ione. Purified by suffering, he calls on the Phantasm (subconscious self) of Jupiter to repeat the curse which he has pronounced on Jupiter; he would recall it. His doing so is the first step in self-regeneration and self-redemption.

* *Political Greatness*. Also titled "Sonnet: To the Republic of Benevento."

Mercury arrives and asks him to reveal a secret important to Jupiter and to submit to Jupiter—the price of peace. He refuses. The Furies torture him (with internal agonies and fears); the Spirits comfort him with accounts of human unselfishness and hope of good to be; Panthea reminds him of Asia's love. Act II in the Indian Caucasus shows Asia, lover of Prometheus, and her sisters, Panthea and Ione, mourning for Prometheus. Panthea tells Asia of two dreams, one of Prometheus redeemed and the other of a voice that cries "Follow!" The three follow to the Cave of Demogorgon. Here Demogorgon describes Jupiter, prophesies his overthrow, and gives veiled answers to questions about evil, fate, free will, and the like. The Spirit of the Hour (of Jupiter's overthrow) appears and drives off in her car. Another Hour transports the sisters to Jupiter's court in Heaven. A voice in the Air sings "Life of Life" (Act II, sc. 5, l. 48) and Asia sings "My soul is an enchanted boat" (*ibid.*, l. 72)—the emotional climax. In Act III Jupiter exults on his throne, he and his queen, Thetis, expecting news of the incarnation of their child. When the Car of the Hour arrives, Jupiter hails it with joy. Ironically, the "child," Demogorgon, descends, describes himself as the son of Jupiter and as Eternity, and commands Jupiter to follow him to the abyss. Jupiter at first defies him, then begs for mercy, and follows. This is the objective climax of the poem (Act III, sc. 1, ll. 52 ff.). In Scene 2 Apollo describes to Ocean the fall of Jupiter, and Ocean says she will never again be vexed by tempests (Prometheus' liberation liberates the physical universe). In Scene 3 Hercules unbinds Prometheus in the presence of Asia, Panthea, Ione, the Earth, and the other Spirits. Prometheus, identifying Asia with "Life of Life," tells her how he will be happy with her, orders the Spirit of the Hour to drive her car round the world with the glad tidings of deliverance, and repairs with Asia to a cave. In Scene 4, the Spirit of the Hour returns and tells of the change that has come over the world. Act IV, an afterthought, is a great symphony expressing the rapture of the delivered universe and faith in the human virtues that will redeem it ("This is the day").

For valuable notes and commentaries on *Prometheus Unbound* see W. J. Alexander's *Select Poems by Shelley* (Ginn and Company) and Carlos Baker, *Shelley's Major Poetry*, Princeton University Press, 1948.

DRAMATIS PERSONAE

PROMETHEUS	MERCURY	
DEMOGORGON	HERCULES	
JUPITER	ASIA	Oceanides
THE EARTH	PANTHEA	Oceanides
OCEAN	IONE	Oceanides

APOLLO
THE PHANTASM OF JUPITER
THE SPIRIT OF THE EARTH
THE SPIRIT OF THE MOON
SPIRITS OF THE HOURS
SPIRITS. ECHOES. FAUNS. FURIES

from ACT I

SCENE. *A Ravine of Icy Rocks in the Indian Caucasus.* PROMETHEUS *is discovered bound to the Precipice.* PANTHEA *and* IONE *are seated at his feet. Time, Night. During the Scene, Morning slowly breaks.*

Prometheus. Monarch of Gods and Daemons, and all Spirits
But One, who throng those bright and rolling worlds
Which Thou and I alone of living things
Behold with sleepless eyes! regard this Earth
Made multitudinous with thy slaves, whom thou
Requitest for knee-worship, prayer, and praise,
And toil, and hecatombs of broken hearts,
With fear and self-contempt and barren hope.
Whilst me, who am thy foe, eyeless in hate,
Hast thou made reign and triumph, to thy scorn,
O'er mine own misery and thy vain revenge.
Three thousand years of sleep-unsheltered hours,
And moments aye divided by keen pangs
Till they seemed years, torture and solitude,
Scorn and despair,—these are mine empire.
More glorious far than that which thou surveyest
From thine unenvied throne, O, Mighty God!
Almighty, had I deigned to share the shame
Of thine ill tyranny, and hung not here
Nailed to this wall of eagle-baffling mountain,
Black, wintry, dead, unmeasured; without herb,
Insect, or beast, or shape or sound of life.
Ah me! alas, pain, pain ever, for ever!

No change, no pause, no hope! Yet I endure.
I ask the Earth, have not the mountains felt?
I ask yon Heaven, the all-beholding Sun,
Has it not seen? The Sea, in storm or calm,
Heaven's ever-changing Shadow, spread below,
Have its deaf waves not heard my agony?
Ah me! alas, pain, pain ever, for ever!

The crawling glaciers pierce me with the spears
Of their moon-freezing crystals, the bright chains
Eat with their burning cold into my bones.
Heaven's wingèd hound, polluting from thy lips
His beak in poison not his own, tears up
My heart; and shapeless sights come wandering by,
The ghastly people of the realm of dream,
Mocking me: and the Earthquake-fiends are charged
To wrench the rivets from my quivering wounds
When the rocks split and close again behind:
While from their loud abysses howling throng
The genii of the storm, urging the rage
Of whirlwind, and afflict me with keen hail.
And yet to me welcome is day and night,

Whether one breaks the hoar frost of the morn,
Or starry, dim, and slow, the other climbs
The leaden-coloured east; for then they lead
The wingless, crawling hours, one among whom
—As some dark Priest hales the reluctant victim—
Shall drag thee, cruel King, to kiss the blood
From these pale feet, which then might trample thee
If they disdained not such a prostrate slave.
Disdain! Ah no! I pity thee. What ruin
Will hunt thee undefended through wide Heaven!
How will thy soul, cloven to its depth with terror,
Gape like a hell within! I speak in grief,
Not exultation, for I hate no more,
As then ere misery made me wise. The curse
Once breathed on thee I would recall. Ye Mountains,
Whose many-voicèd Echoes, through the mist
Of cataracts, flung the thunder of that spell!
Ye icy Springs, stagnant with wrinkling frost,
Which vibrated to hear me, and then crept
Shuddering through India! Thou serenest Air,
Through which the Sun walks burning without beams!
And ye swift Whirlwinds, who on poisèd wings
Hung mute and moveless o'er yon hushed abyss,
As thunder, louder than your own, made rock
The orbèd world! If then my words had power,
Though I am changed so that aught evil wish
Is dead within; although no memory be
Of what is hate, let them not lose it now!
What was that curse? for ye all heard me speak. . . .

The Earth. I am the Earth,
Thy mother; she within whose stony veins,
To the last fiber of the loftiest tree
Whose thin leaves trembled in the frozen air,
Joy ran, as blood within a living frame,
When thou didst from her bosom, like a cloud
Of glory, arise, a spirit of keen joy!
And, at thy voice, her pining sons uplifted
Their prostrate brows from the polluting dust,
And our almighty Tyrant with fierce dread
Grew pale, until his thunder chained thee here.
Then, see those million worlds which burn and roll
Around us: their inhabitants beheld
My spherèd light wane in wide Heaven; the sea
Was lifted by strange tempest, and new fire
From earthquake-rifted mountains of bright snow
Shook its portentous hair beneath Heaven's frown;
Lightning and Inundation vexed the plains;
Blue thistles bloomed in cities; foodless toads
Within voluptuous chambers panting crawled:
When Plague had fallen on man, and beast, and worm,
And Famine; and black blight on herb and tree;
And in the corn, and vines, and meadow-grass,
Teemed ineradicable poisonous weeds
Draining their growth, for my wan breast was dry
With grief; and the thin air, my breath, was stained
With the contagion of a mother's hate
Breathed on her child's destroyer; aye, I heard
Thy curse, the which, if thou rememberest not,
Yet my innumerable seas and streams,
Mountains, and caves, and winds, and yon wide air,
And the inarticulate people of the dead,
Preserve, a treasured spell. We meditate
In secret joy and hope those dreadful words,
But dare not speak them.

Prometheus.
Venerable mother!
All else who live and suffer take from thee
Some comfort; flowers, and fruits, and happy sounds,
And love, though fleeting; these may not be mine.
But mine own words, I pray, deny me not.

The Earth. They shall be told. Ere Babylon was dust,
The Magus Zoroaster, my dead child,
Met his own image walking in the garden.
That apparition, sole of men, he saw.
For know, there are two worlds of life and death:
One that which thou beholdest; but the other
Is underneath the grave, where do inhabit
The shadows of all forms that think and live
Till death unite them and they part no more;
Dreams and the light imaginings of men
And all that faith creates or love desires,
Terrible, strange, sublime and beauteous shapes.
There thou art, and dost hang, a writhing shade,
'Mid whirlwind-peopled mountains; all the gods
Are there, and all the powers of nameless worlds,
Vast, sceptred phantoms; heroes, men, and beasts;
And Demogorgon, a tremendous gloom;
And he, the supreme Tyrant, on his throne
Of burning gold. Son, one of these shall utter
The curse which all remember. Call at will
Thine own ghost, or the ghost of Jupiter,
Hades or Typhon, or what mightier Gods
From all-prolific Evil, since thy ruin
Have sprung, and trampled on thy prostrate sons.
Ask, and they must reply: so the revenge
Of the Supreme may sweep through vacant shades,
As rainy wind through the abandoned gate
Of a fallen palace.

192. The Magus Zoroaster, the prophet of ancient Iran in the seventh century B.C., and founder of the national religion. He spiritualized many elements in the older religion, and conceived of the universe as the battleground of the principles of good and evil.

Prometheus. Mother, let not aught
Of that which may be evil, pass again
My lips, or those of aught resembling me.
Phantasm of Jupiter, arise, appear! . . .
Phantasm of Jupiter. Why have the secret powers of this strange world
Driven me, a frail and empty phantom, hither
On direst storms? What unaccustomed sounds
Are hovering on my lips, unlike the voice
With which our pallid race hold ghastly talk
In darkness? And, proud sufferer, who art thou?
Prometheus. Tremendous Image, as thou art must be
He whom thou shadowest forth. I am his foe,
The Titan. Speak the words which I would hear,
Although no thought inform thine empty voice.
The Earth. Listen! And though your echoes must be mute,
Grey mountains, and old woods, and haunted springs,
Prophetic caves, and isle-surrounding streams,
Rejoice to hear what yet ye cannot speak.
Phantasm. A spirit seizes me and speaks within:
It tears me as fire tears a thunder-cloud.
Panthea. See, how he lifts his mighty looks, the Heaven
Darkens above.
Ione.
He speaks! O shelter me!
Prometheus. I see the curse on gestures proud and cold,
And looks of firm defiance, and calm hate,
And such despair as mocks itself with smiles,
Written as on a scroll: yet speak: Oh, speak!

Phantasm [of Jupiter]

Fiend, I defy thee! with a calm, fixed mind,
All that thou canst inflict I bid thee do;
Foul Tyrant both of Gods and Human-kind,
Only one being shalt thou not subdue.
Rain then thy plagues upon me here,
Ghastly disease, and frenzying fear;
And let alternate frost and fire
Eat into me, and be thine ire
Lightning, and cutting hail, and legioned forms
Of furies, driving by upon the wounding storms.

Aye, do thy worst. Thou art omnipotent.
O'er all things but thyself I give thee power,
And my own will. Be thy swift mischiefs sent
To blast mankind, from yon ethereal tower.
Let thy malignant spirit move
In darkness over those I love:

262. Fiend, I defy thee. The Phantasm of Jupiter here repeats the curse Prometheus had pronounced upon Jupiter.

On me and mine I imprecate
The utmost torture of thy hate;
And thus devote to sleepless agony,
This undeclining head while thou must reign on high.
But thou, who art the God and Lord: O, thou
Who fillest with thy soul this world of woe,
To whom all things of Earth and Heaven do bow
In fear and worship: all-prevailing foe!
I curse thee! let a sufferer's curse
Clasp thee, his torturer, like remorse!
Till thine Infinity shall be
A robe of envenomed agony;
And thine Omnipotence a crown of pain,
To cling like burning gold round thy dissolving brain!

Heap on thy soul, by virtue of this Curse,
Ill deeds, then be thou damned, beholding good;
Both infinite as is the universe,
And thou, and thy self-torturing solitude.
An awful image of calm power
Though now thou sittest, let the hour
Come, when thou must appear to be
That which thou art internally.
And after many a false and fruitless crime
Scorn track thy lagging fall through boundless space and time.

Prometheus. Were these my words, O Parent?
The Earth. They were thine.
Prometheus. It doth repent me: words are quick and vain;
Grief for a while is blind, and so was mine.
I wish no living thing to suffer pain. . . .

Mercury. . . . Awful Sufferer!
To thee unwilling, most unwillingly
I come, by the great Father's will driven down,
To execute a doom of new revenge.
Alas! I pity thee, and hate myself
That I can do no more: aye from thy sight
Returning, for a season, heaven seems hell,
So thy worn form pursues me night and day,
Smiling reproach. Wise art thou, firm and good,
But vainly wouldst stand forth alone in strife
Against the Omnipotent; as yon clear lamps
That measure and divide the weary years
From which there is no refuge, long have taught
And long must teach. Even now thy Torturer arms
With the strange might of unimagined pains
The powers who scheme slow agonies in Hell,
And my commission is to lead them here,

Or what more subtle, foul, or savage fiends
People the abyss, and leave them to their task.
Be it not so! there is a secret known
To thee, and to none else of living things,
Which may transfer the sceptre of wide Heaven,
The fear of which perplexes the Supreme:
Clothe it in words, and bid it clasp his throne
In intercession; bend thy soul in prayer,
And like a suppliant in some gorgeous fane,
Let the will kneel within thy haughty heart:
For benefits and meek submission tame
The fiercest and the mightiest.
Prometheus. Evil minds
Change good to their own nature. I gave all
He has; and in return he chains me here
Years, ages, night and day: whether the Sun
Split my parched skin, or in the moony night
The crystal-wingèd snow cling round my hair:
Whilst my belovèd race is trampled down
By his thought-executing ministers.
Such is the tyrant's recompense: 'tis just:
He who is evil can receive no good;
And for a world bestowed, or a friend lost,
He can feel hate, fear, shame; not gratitude:
He but requites me for his own misdeed.
Kindness to such is keen reproach, which breaks
With bitter stings the light sleep of Revenge.
Submission, thou dost know I cannot try;
For what submission but that fatal word,
The death-seal of mankind's captivity,
Like the Sicilian's hair-suspended sword,
Which tremmles o'er his crown, would he accept,
Or could I yield? Which yet I will not yield.
Let others flatter Crime, where it sits throned
In brief Omnipotence: secure are they:
For Justice, when triumphant, will weep down
Pity, not punishment, on her own wrongs,
Too much avenged by those who err. I wait,
Enduring thus, the retributive hour
Which since we spake is even nearer now.
But hark, the hell-hounds clamour: fear delay:
Behold! Heaven lowers under thy Father's frown.
Mercury. Oh, that we might be spared: I to inflict
And thou to suffer! Once more answer me:
Thou knowest not the period of Jove's power?
Prometheus. I know but this, that it must come.
Mercury. Alas!
Thou canst not count thy years to come of pain?
Prometheus. They last while Jove must reign: nor more, nor less
Do I desire or fear.
Mercury. Yet pause, and plunge
Into Eternity, where recorded time,
Even all that we imagine, age on age,
Seems but a point, and the reluctant mind
Flags wearily in its unending flight,
Till it sink, dizzy, blind, lost, shelterless;
Perchance it has not numbered the slow years
Which thou must spend in torture, unreprieved?
Prometheus. Perchance no thought can count them, yet they pass.
Mercury. If thou might'st dwell among the Gods the while,
Lapped in voluptuous joy?
Prometheus. I would not quit
This bleak ravine, these unrepentant pains.
Mercury. Alas! I wonder at, yet pity thee.
Prometheus. Pity the self-despising slaves of Heaven,
Not me, within whose mind sits peace serene,
As light in the sun, throned: how vain is talk!
Call up the fiends. . . .

from ACT II

from SCENE 3. *A Pinnacle of Rock among Mountains.* ASIA *and* PANTHEA.

Panthea. Hither the sound has borne us—to the realm
Of Demogorgon, and the mighty portal,
Like a volcano's meteor-breathing chasm,
Whence the oracular vapour is hurled up
Which lonely men drink wandering in their youth,
And call truth, virtue, love, genius, or joy,
That maddening wine of life, whose dregs they drain
To deep intoxication; and uplift,
Like Mænads who cry loud, Evoe! Evoe!
The voice which is contagion to the world. . . .

from SCENE 4. *The Cave of* DEMOGORGON.

ASIA *and* PANTHEA.

Panthea. What veilèd form sits on that ebon throne?
Asia. The veil has fallen.
Panthea. I see a mighty darkness
Filling the seat of power, and rays of gloom
Dart round, as light from the meridian sun.
Ungazed upon and shapeless; neither limb,
Nor form, nor outline; yet we feel it is
A living Spirit.
Demogorgon. Ask what thou wouldst know.
Asia. What canst thou tell?
Demogorgon. All things thou dar'st demand.
Asia. Who made the living world?
Demogorgon. God.
Asia. Who made all

That it contains? thought, passion, reason, will,
Imagination?
Demogorgon. God: Almighty God.
Asia. Who made that sense which, when the winds of spring
In rarest visitation, or the voice
Of one belovèd heard in youth alone,
Fills the faint eyes with falling tears which dim
The radiant looks of unbewailing flowers,
And leaves this peopled earth a solitude
When it returns no more?
Demogorgon. Merciful God.
Asia. And who made terror, madness, crime, remorse,
Which from the links of the great chain of things,
To every thought within the mind of man
Sway and drag heavily, and each one reels
Under the load towards the pit of death;
Abandoned hope, and love that turns to hate;
And self-contempt, bitterer to drink than blood;
Pain, whose unheeded and familiar speech
Is howling, and keen shrieks, day after day;
And Hell, or the sharp fear of Hell?
Demogorgon. He reigns.
Asia. Utter his name: a world pining in pain
Asks but his name: curses shall drag him down.
Demogorgon. He reigns.
Asia. I feel, I know it: who?
Demogorgon He reigns.
Asia. Who reigns? There was the Heaven and Earth at first,
And Light and Love; then Saturn, from whose throne
Time fell, an envious shadow: such the state
Of the earth's primal spirits beneath his sway,
As the calm joy of flowers and living leaves
Before the wind or sun has withered them
And semivital worms; but he refused
The birthright of their being, knowledge, power,
The skill which wields the elements, the thought
Which pierces this dim universe like light,
Self-empire, and the majesty of love;
For thirst of which they fainted. Then Prometheus
Gave wisdom, which is strength, to Jupiter,
And with this law alone, "Let man be free,"
Clothed him with the dominion of wide Heaven.
To know nor faith, nor love, nor law; to be
Omnipotent but friendless is to reign;
And Jove now reigned; for on the race of man
First famine, and then toil, and then disease,
Strife, wounds, and ghastly death unseen before,
Fell; and the unseasonable seasons drove
With alternating shafts of frost and fire,
Their shelterless, pale tribes to mountain caves:
And in their desert hearts fierce wants he sent,
And mad disquietudes, and shadows idle
Of unreal good, which levied mutual war,
So ruining the lair wherein they raged.
Prometheus saw, and waked the legioned hopes
Which sleep within folded Elysian flowers,
Nepenthe, Moly, Amaranth, fadeless blooms,
That they might hide with thin and rainbow wings
The shape of Death; and Love he sent to bind
The disunited tendrils of that vine
Which bears the wine of life, the human heart;
And he tamed fire which, like some beast of prey,
Most terrible, but lovely, played beneath
The frown of man; and tortured to his will
Iron and gold, the slaves and signs of power,
And gems and poisons, and all subtlest forms
Hidden beneath the mountains and the waves.
He gave man speech, and speech created thought,
Which is the measure of the universe;
And Science struck the thrones of earth and heaven,
Which shook, but fell not; and the harmonious mind
Poured itself forth in all-prophetic song;
And music lifted up the listening spirit
Until it walked, exempt from mortal care,
Godlike, o'er the clear billows of sweet sound;
And human hands first mimicked and then mocked,
With moulded limbs more lovely than its own,
The human form, till marble grew divine,
And mothers, gazing, drank the love men see
Reflected in their race, behold, and perish.
He told the hidden power of herbs and springs,
And Disease drank and slept. Death grew like sleep.
He taught the implicated orbits woven
Of the wide-wandering stars; and how the sun
Changes his lair, and by what secret spell
The pale moon is transformed, when her broad eye
Gazes not on the interlunar sea:
He taught to rule, as life directs the limbs,
The tempest-wingèd chariots of the Ocean,
And the Celt knew the Indian. Cities then
Were built, and through their snow-like columns flowed
The warm winds, and the azure aether shone,
And the blue sea and shadowy hills were seen.
Such, the alleviations of his state,
Prometheus gave to man, for which he hangs
Withering in destined pain: but who rains down
Evil, the immedicable plague, which, while
Man looks on his creation like a God
And sees that it is glorious, drives him on
The wreck of his own will, the scorn of earth,

The outcast, the abandoned, the alone?
Not Jove: while yet his frown shook heaven, aye when
His adversary from adamantine chains
Cursed him, he trembled like a slave. Declare
Who is his master? Is he too a slave?
Demogorgon. All spirits are enslaved which serve things evil:
Thou knowest if Jupiter be such or no.
Asia. Whom called'st thou God?
Demogorgon. I spoke but as ye speak,
For Jove is the supreme of living things.
Asia. Who is the master of the slave?
Demogorgon. If the abysm
Could vomit forth its secrets. . . . But a voice
Is wanting, the deep truth is imageless;
For what would it avail to bid thee gaze
On the revolving world? What to bid speak
Fate, Time, Occasion, Chance and Change? To these
All things are subject but eternal Love.
Asia. So much I asked before, and my heart gave
The response thou hast given; and of such truths
Each to itself must be the oracle.
One more demand; and do thou answer me
As mine own soul would answer, did it know
That which I ask. Prometheus shall arise
Henceforth the sun of this rejoicing world:
When shall the destined hour arrive?
Demogorgon. Behold!
Asia. The rocks are cloven, and through the purple night
I see cars drawn by rainbow-wingèd steeds
Which trample the dim winds: in each there stands
A wild-eyed charioteer urging their flight.
Some look behind, as fiends pursued them there,
And yet I see no shapes but the keen stars:
Others, with burning eyes, lean forth, and drink
With eager lips the wind of their own speed,
As if the thing they loved fled on before,
And now, even now, they clasped it. Their bright locks
Stream like a comet's flashing hair: they all sweep onward.
Demogorgon. These are the immortal Hours,
Of whom thou didst demand. One waits for thee.
Asia. A spirit with a dreadful countenance
Checks its dark chariot by the craggy gulf.
Unlike thy brethren, ghastly charioteer,
Who art thou? Whither wouldst thou bear me? Speak!
Spirit. I am the shadow of a destiny
More dread than is my aspect: ere yon planet
Has set, the darkness which ascends with me
Shall wrap in lasting night heaven's kingless throne.
Asia. What meanest thou?
Panthea. That terrible shadow floats
Up from its throne, as may the lurid smoke
Of earthquake-ruined cities o'er the sea.
Lo! it ascends the car; the coursers fly
Terrified: watch its path among the stars
Blackening the night!
Asia. Thus I am answered: strange!
Panthea. See, near the verge, another chariot stays;
An ivory shell inlaid with crimson fire,
Which comes and goes within its sculptured rim
Of delicate strange tracery; the young spirit
That guides it has the dove-like eyes of hope;
How its soft smiles attract the soul! as light
Lures wingèd insects through the lampless air.

Spirit

My coursers are fed with the lightning,
They drink of the whirlwind's stream,
And when the red morning is bright'ning
They bathe in the fresh sunbeam;
They have strength for their swiftness I deem,
Then ascend with me, daughter of Ocean.

I desire: and their speed makes night kindle;
I fear: they outstrip the Typhoon;
Ere the cloud piled on Atlas can dwindle
We encircle the earth and the moon:
We shall rest from long labours at noon:
Then ascend with me, daughter of Ocean. . . .

from SCENE 5. *The Car pauses within a Cloud on the Top of a snowy Mountain.* ASIA, PANTHEA, *and the* SPIRIT OF THE HOUR.

*Voice (in the air, singing)**

Life of Life! thy lips enkindle
With their love the breath between them;
And thy smiles before they dwindle
Make the cold air fire; then screen them
In those looks, where whoso gazes
Faints, entangled in their mazes.

Child of Light! thy limbs are burning
Through the vest which seems to hide them;
As the radiant lines of morning
Through the clouds ere they divide them;
And this atmosphere divinest
Shrouds thee wheresoe'er thou shinest.

Fair are others; none beholds thee,
But thy voice sounds low and tender
Like the fairest, for it folds thee

* **Voice (in the air, singing).** Presumably that of Prometheus.

From the sight, that liquid splendour,
And all feel, yet see thee never,
As I feel now, lost for ever!

Lamp of Earth! where'er thou movest
Its dim shapes are clad with brightness,
And the souls of whom thou lovest
Walk upon the winds with lightness,
Till they fail, as I am failing,
Dizzy, lost, yet unbewailing!

Asia

My soul is an enchanted boat,
Which, like a sleeping swan, doth float
Upon the silver waves of thy sweet singing;
And thine doth like an angel sit
Beside a helm conducting it,
Whilst all the winds with melody are ringing.
It seems to float ever, for ever,
Upon that many-winding river,
Between mountains, woods, abysses,
A paradise of wildernesses!
Till, like one in slumber bound,
Borne to the ocean, I float down, around,
Into a sea profound, of ever-spreading sound:

Meanwhile thy spirit lifts its pinions
In music's most serene dominions;
Catching the winds that fan that happy heaven.
And we sail on, away, afar,
Without a course, without a star,
But, by the instinct of sweet music driven;
Till through Elysian garden islets
By thee, most beautiful of pilots,
Where never mortal pinnace glided,
The boat of my desire is guided:
Realms where the air we breathe is love,
Which in the winds and on the waves doth move,
Harmonizing this earth with what we feel above.

We have passed Age's icy caves,
And Manhood's dark and tossing waves,
And Youth's smooth ocean, smiling to betray:
Beyond the glassy gulphs we flee
Of shadow-peopled Infancy,
Through Death and Birth, to a diviner day;
A paradise of vaulted bowers,
Lit by downward-gazing flowers,
And watery paths that wind between
Wildernesses calm and green,
Peopled by shapes too bright to see,
And rest, having beheld: somewhat like thee;
Which walk upon the sea, and chant melodiously!

from ACT III

SCENE I. *Heaven.* JUPITER *on his Throne;* THETIS *and the other Deities assembled.*

Jupiter. Ye congregated powers of heaven, who share
The glory and the strength of him ye serve,
Rejoice! henceforth I am omnipotent,
All else had been subdued to me; alone
The soul of man, like unextinguished fire,
Yet burns towards heaven with fierce reproach, and doubt,
And lamentation, and reluctant prayer,
Hurling up insurrection, which might make
Our antique empire insecure, though built
On eldest faith, and hell's coeval, fear;
And though my curses through the pendulous air,
Like snow on herbless peaks, fall flake by flake,
And cling to it; though under my wrath's night
It climb the crags of life, step after step,
Which wound it, as ice wounds unsandalled feet,
It yet remains supreme o'er misery,
Aspiring, unrepressed, yet soon to fall:
Even now have I begotten a strange wonder,
That fatal child, the terror of the earth,
Who waits but till the destined hour arrive,
Bearing from Demogorgon's vacant throne
The dreadful might of ever-living limbs
Which clothed that awful spirit unbeheld,
To redescend, and trample out the spark.

Pour forth heaven's wine, Idæan Ganymede,
And let it fill the Dædal cups like fire,
And from the flower-inwoven soil divine
Ye all-triumphant harmonies arise,
As dew from earth under the twilight stars:
Drink! be the nectar circling through your veins
The soul of joy, ye ever-living Gods,
Till exultation burst in one wide voice
Like music from Elysian winds.
And thou
Ascend beside me, veilèd in the light
Of the desire which makes thee one with me,
Thetis, bright image of eternity!
When thou didst cry, "Insufferable might!
God! Spare me! I sustain not the quick flames,
The penetrating presence; all my being,
Like him whom the Numidian seps did thaw
Into a dew with poison, is dissolved,
Sinking through its foundations": even then
Two mighty spirits, mingling, made a third
Mighter than either, which, unbodied now,
Between us floats, felt, although unbeheld,

40. seps, venomous serpent.

Waiting the incarnation, which ascends,
(Hear ye the thunder of the fiery wheels
Griding the winds?) from Demogorgon's throne.
Victory! victory! Feel'st thou not, O world!
The earthquake of his chariot thundering up
Olympus?
[*The Car of the* HOUR *arrives.* DEMOGORGON *descends, and moves toward the Throne of* JUPITER.]
Awful shape, what art thou? Speak!
Demogorgon. Eternity. Demand no direr name.
Descend, and follow me down the abyss.
I am thy child, as thou wert Saturn's child;
Mightier than thee: and we must dwell together
Henceforth in darkness. Lift thy lightnings not.
The tyranny of heaven none may retain,
Or reassume, or hold, succeeding thee:
Yet if thou wilt, as 'tis the destiny
Of trodden worms to writhe till they are dead,
Put forth thy might.
Jupiter. Detested prodigy!
Even thus beneath the deep Titanian prisons
I trample thee! thou lingerest?
Mercy! mercy!
No pity, no release, no respite! Oh,
That thou wouldst make mine enemy my judge,
Even where he hangs, seared by my long revenge,
On Caucasus! he would not doom me thus.
Gentle, and just, and dreadless, is he not
The monarch of the world? What then art thou?
No refuge! no appeal!
Sink with me then,
We two will sink on the wide waves of ruin,
Even as a vulture and a snake outspent
Drop, twisted in inextricable fight,
Into a shoreless sea. Let hell unlock
Its mounded oceans of tempestuous fire,
And whelm on them into the bottomless void
This desolated world, and thee, and me,
The conqueror and the conquered, and the wreck
Of that for which they combated.
Ai! Ai!
The elements obey me not. I sink
Dizzily down, ever, for ever, down.
And, like a cloud, mine enemy above
Darkens my fall with victory! Ai, Ai!

from SCENE 3. *Caucasus.* PROMETHEUS, HERCULES, IONE, *the* EARTH, SPIRITS, ASIA, *and* PANTHEA, *borne in the Car with the* SPIRIT OF THE HOUR. HERCULES *unbinds* PROMETHEUS, *who descends.*

Hercules. Most glorious among spirits, thus doth strength
To wisdom, courage, and long-suffering love,
And thee, who art the form they animate,
Minister like a slave.
Prometheus. Thy gentle words
Are sweeter even than freedom long desired
And long delayed.
Asia, thou light of life,
Shadow of beauty unbeheld: and ye,
Fair sister nymphs, who made long years of pain
Sweet to remember, through your love and care:
Henceforth we will not part. There is a cave,
All overgrown with trailing odorous plants,
Which curtain out the day with leaves and flowers,
And paved with veinèd emerald, and a fountain
Leaps in the midst with an awakening sound.
From its curved roof the mountain's frozen tears,
Like snow, or silver, or long diamond spires,
Hang downward, raining forth a doubtful light:
And there is heard the ever-moving air,
Whispering without from tree to tree, and birds,
And bees; and all around are mossy seats,
And the rough walls are clothed with long soft grass;
A simple dwelling, which shall be our own;
Where we will sit and talk of time and change,
As the world ebbs and flows, ourselves unchanged.
What can hide man from mutability?
And if ye sigh, then I will smile; and thou,
Ione, shalt chaunt fragments of sea-music,
Until I weep, when ye shall smile away
The tears she brought, which yet were sweet to shed.
We will entangle buds and flowers and beams
Which twinkle on the fountain's brim, and make
Strange combinations out of common things,
Like human babes in their brief innocence;
And we will search, with looks and words of love,
For hidden thoughts, each lovelier than the last,
Our unexhausted spirits; and like lutes
Touched by the skill of the enamoured wind,
Weave harmonies divine, yet ever new,
From difference sweet where discord cannot be;
And hither come, sped on the charmèd winds,
Which meet from all the points of heaven, as bees
From every flower aëreal Enna feeds,
At their known island-homes in Himera,
The echoes of the human world, which tell
Of the low voice of love, almost unheard,
And dove-eyed pity's murmured pain, and music,
Itself the echo of the heart, and all
That tempers or improves man's life, now free;
And lovely apparitions, dim at first,
Then radiant, as the mind, arising bright
From the embrace of beauty, whence the forms
Of which these are the phantoms, casts on them

48. Griding, piercing with a harsh sound.

The gathered rays which are reality,
Shall visit us, the progeny immortal
Of Painting, Sculpture, and rapt Poesy,
And arts, though unimagined, yet to be.
The wandering voices and the shadows these
Of all that man becomes, the mediators
Of that best worship love, by him and us
Given and returned; swift shapes and sounds, which grow
More fair and soft as man grows wise and kind,
And, veil by veil, evil and error fall.
Such virtue has the cave and place around. . . .

from SCENE 4. *A Forest. In the Back-ground a Cave.* PROMETHEUS, ASIA, PANTHEA, IONE, *and the* SPIRIT OF THE EARTH.

The SPIRIT OF THE HOUR *enters.*

Spirit of the Hour. Soon as the sound had ceased whose thunder filled
The abysses of the sky and the wide earth,
There was a change: the impalpable thin air
And the all-circling sunlight were transformed,
As if the sense of love dissolved in them
Had folded itself round the sphered world.
My vision then grew clear, and I could see
Into the mysteries of the universe: . . .

As I have said, I floated to the earth:
It was, as it is still, the pain of bliss
To move, to breathe, to be; I wandering went
Among the haunts and dwellings of mankind,
And first was disappointed not to see
Such mighty change as I had felt within
Expressed in outward things; but soon I looked,
And behold, thrones were kingless, and men walked
One with the other even as spirits do,
None fawned, none trampled; hate, disdain, or fear,
Self-love or self-contempt, on human brows
No more inscribed, as o'er the gate of hell,
"All hope abandon ye who enter here";
None frowned, none trembled, none with eager fear
Gazed on another's eye of cold command,
Until the subject of a tyrant's will
Became, worse fate, the abject of his own,
Which spurred him, like an outspent horse, to death.
None wrought his lips in truth-entangling lines
Which smiled the lie his tongue disdained to speak;
None, with firm sneer, trod out in his own heart
The sparks of love and hope till these remained
Those bitter ashes, a soul self-consumed,
And the wretch crept a vampire among men,
Infecting all with his own hideous ill;
None talked that common, false, cold, hollow talk
Which makes the heart deny the *yes* it breathes,
Yet question that unmeant hypocrisy
With such a self-mistrust as has no name.
And women, too, frank, beautiful, and kind
As the free heaven which rains fresh light and dew
On the wide earth, past; gentle radiant forms,
From custom's evil taint exempt and pure;
Speaking the wisdom once they could not think,
Looking emotions once they feared to feel,
And changed to all which once they dared not be,
Yet being now, made earth like heaven; nor pride,
Nor jealousy, nor envy, nor ill-shame,
The bitterest of those drops of treasured gall,
Spoilt the sweet taste of the nepenthe, love.

Thrones, altars, judgment-seats, and prisons; wherein,
And beside which, by wretched men were borne
Sceptres, tiaras, swords, and chains, and tomes
Of reasoned wrong, glozed on by ignorance,
Were like those monstrous and barbaric shapes,
The ghosts of a no more remembered fame,
Which, from their unworn obelisks, look forth
In triumph o'er the palaces and tombs
Of those who were their conquerors: mouldering round,
Those imaged to the pride of kings and priests,
A dark yet mighty faith, a power as wide
As is the world it wasted, and are now
But an astonishment; even so the tools
And emblems of its last captivity,
Amid the dwellings of the peopled earth,
Stand, not o'erthrown, but unregarded now.
And those foul shapes, abhorred by god and man,
Which, under many a name and many a form
Strange, savage, ghastly, dark, and execrable,
Were Jupiter, the tyrant of the world;
And which the nations, panic-stricken, served
With blood, and hearts broken by long hope, and love
Dragged to his altars soiled and garlandless,
And slain amid men's unreclaiming tears,
Flattering the thing they feared, which fear was hate,
Frown, mouldering fast, o'er their abandoned shrines:
The painted veil, by those who were, called life,
Which mimicked, as with colours idly spread,
All men believed or hoped, is torn aside;
The loathsome mask has fallen, the man remains,—
Sceptreless, free, uncircumscribed,—but man:
Equal, unclassed, tribeless, and nationless,
Exempt from awe, worship, degree, the king
Over himself; just, gentle, wise,—but man:

Passionless? no; yet free from guilt or pain,
Which were, for his will made, or suffered them;
Nor yet exempt, though ruling them like slaves,
From chance, and death, and mutability,
The clogs of that which else might oversoar
The loftiest star of unascended heaven,
Pinnacled dim in the intense inane.

from ACT IV

Demogorgon

This is the day, which down the void abysm
At the Earth-born's spell yawns for Heaven's despotism,
And Conquest is dragged captive through the deep:
Love, from its awful throne of patient power
In the wise heart, from the last giddy hour
Of dread endurance, from the slippery, steep,
And narrow verge of crag-like agony, springs
And folds over the world its healing wings.

Gentleness, Virtue, Wisdom, and Endurance,
These are the seals of that most firm assurance
Which bars the pit over Destruction's strength;
And if, with infirm hand, Eternity,
Mother of many acts and hours, should free
The serpent that would clasp her with his length;
These are the spells by which to re-assume
An empire o'er the disentangled doom.

To suffer woes which Hope thinks infinite;
To forgive wrongs darker than death or night;
To defy Power, which seems omnipotent;
To love, and bear; to hope till Hope creates
From its own wreck the thing it contemplates:
Neither to change, nor falter, nor repent;
This, like thy glory, Titan! is to be
Good, great and joyous, beautiful and free;
This is alone Life, Joy, Empire, and Victory!

THE CLOUD

1

I bring fresh showers for the thirsting flowers,
From the seas and the streams;
I bear light shade for the leaves when laid
In their noon-day dreams.
From my wings are shaken the dews that waken
The sweet buds every one,
When rocked to rest on their mother's breast,
As she dances about the sun.
I wield the flail of the lashing hail,
And whiten the green plains under,
And then again I dissolve it in rain,
And laugh as I pass in thunder.

2

I sift the snow on the mountains below,
And their great pines groan aghast;
And all the night 'tis my pillow white,
While I sleep in the arms of the blast.
Sublime on the towers of my skiey bowers,
Lightning my pilot sits;
In a cavern under is fettered the thunder,
It struggles and howls at fits;
Over earth and ocean, with gentle motion,
This pilot is guiding me,
Lured by the love of the genii that move
In the depths of the purple sea;
Over the rills, and the crags, and the hills,
Over the lakes and the plains,
Wherever he dream, under mountain or stream,
The Spirit he loves remains;
And I all the while bask in heaven's blue smile,
Whilst he is dissolving in rains.

3

The sanguine sunrise, with his meteor eyes,
And his burning plumes outspread,
Leaps on the back of my sailing rack,
When the morning star shines dead;
As on the jag of a mountain crag,
Which an earthquake rocks and swings,
An eagle alit one moment may sit
In the light of its golden wings.
And when sunset may breathe, from the lit sea beneath,
Its ardours of rest and of love,
And the crimson pall of eve may fall
From the depth of heaven above,
With wings folded I rest, on mine airy nest,
As still as a brooding dove.

4

That orbèd maiden with white fire laden,
Whom mortals call the moon,
Glides glimmering o'er my fleece-like floor,
By the midnight breezes strewn;
And wherever the beat of her unseen feet,
Which only the angels hear,
May have broken the woof of my tent's thin roof,
The stars peep behind her and peer;
And I laugh to see them whirl and flee,
Like a swarm of golden bees,
When I widen the rent in my wind-built tent,
Till the calm rivers, lakes, and seas,
Like strips of the sky fallen through me on high,
Are each paved with the moon and these.

5

I bind the sun's throne with a burning zone,
  And the moon's with a girdle of pearl;
The volcanoes are dim, and the stars reel and swim,
  When the whirlwinds my banner unfurl.
From cape to cape, with a bridge-like shape,
  Over a torrent sea,
Sunbeam-proof, I hang like a roof,
  The mountains its columns be.
The triumphal arch through which I march
  With hurricane, fire, and snow,
When the powers of the air are chained to my chair,
  Is the million-coloured bow;
The sphere-fire above its soft colours wove,
  While the moist earth was laughing below.

6

I am the daughter of earth and water,
  And the nursling of the sky;
I pass through the pores of the ocean and shores;
  I change, but I cannot die.
For after the rain when with never a stain
  The pavilion of heaven is bare,
And the winds and sunbeams with their convex gleams
  Build up the blue dome of air,
I silently laugh at my own cenotaph,
  And out of the caverns of rain,
Like a child from the womb, like a ghost from the tomb,
I arise and unbuild it again.

TO A SKYLARK

"It was on a beautiful summer evening while wandering [near Leghorn, Italy] among the lanes, whose myrtle hedges were the bowers of the fireflies, that we heard the caroling of the skylark, which inspired one of the most beautiful of his poems."—Mrs. Shelley.

1

Hail to thee, blithe Spirit!
  Bird thou never wert,
That from Heaven, or near it,
  Pourest thy full heart
In profuse strains of unpremeditated art.

2

Higher still and higher
  From the earth thou springest
Like a cloud of fire;
  The blue deep thou wingest,
And singing still dost soar, and soaring ever singest.

3

In the golden lightning
  Of the sunken Sun,
O'er which clouds are bright'ning,
  Thou dost float and run;
Like an unbodied joy whose race is just begun.

4

The pale purple even
  Melts around thy flight;
Like a star of Heaven,
  In the broad daylight
Thou art unseen, but yet I hear thy shrill delight,

5

Keen as are the arrows
  Of that silver sphere,
Whose intense lamp narrows
  In the white dawn clear,
Until we hardly see, we feel that it is there.

6

All the earth and air
  With thy voice is loud,
As, when Night is bare,
  From one lonely cloud
The moon rains out her beams, and Heaven is overflowed.

7

What thou art we know not;
  What is most like thee?
From rainbow clouds there flow not
  Drops so bright to see,
As from thy presence showers a rain of melody.

8

Like a poet hidden
  In the light of thought,
Singing hymns unbidden,
  Till the world is wrought
To sympathy with hopes and fears it heeded not:

9

Like a high-born maiden
  In a palace-tower,
Soothing her love-laden
  Soul in secret hour
With music sweet as love, which overflows her bower:

6-35. Higher . . . melody, direct description of qualities of the lark's songs (aspiration, in visibility, poignancy, compass, mystery).

36-60. Like a Poet . . . surpass, further description by a series of radiant comparisons and analogies (note that all the similes have one idea in common with the bird's song—"hidden").

10

Like a glowworm golden
 In a dell of dew,
Scattering unbeholden
 Its aërial hue
Among the flowers and grass, which screen it from the view!

11

Like a rose embowered
 In its own green leaves,
By warm winds deflowered,
 Till the scent it gives
Makes faint with too much sweet those heavy-wingèd thieves:

12

Sound of vernal showers
 On the twinkling grass,
Rain-awakened flowers,
 All that ever was
Joyous, and clear, and fresh, thy music doth surpass.

13

Teach us, Sprite or Bird,
 What sweet thoughts are thine:
I have never heard
 Praise of love or wine
That panted forth a flood of rapture so divine.

14

Chorus Hymeneal,
 Or triumphant chaunt,
Matched with thine, would be all
 But an empty vaunt,
A thing wherein we feel there is some hidden want.

15

What objects are the fountains
 Of thy happy strain?
What fields, or waves, or mountains?
 What shapes of sky or plain?
What love of thine own kind? what ignorance of pain?

16

With thy clear keen joyance
 Languor cannot be:
Shadow of annoyance
 Never came near thee:
Thou lovest—but ne'er knew love's sad satiety.

61–85. Teach us . . . stream? What thoughts can provoke such music, such happiness? Compare l. 80, "Thou lovest—but ne'er knew love's sad satiety," with ll. 11–30 of **Keats**'s "Ode on a Grecian Urn."

17

Waking or asleep,
 Thou of death must deem
Things more true and deep
 Than we mortals dream,
Or how could thy notes flow in such a crystal stream?

18

We look before and after,
 And pine for what is not:
Our sincerest laughter
 With some pain is fraught;
Our sweetest songs are those that tell of saddest thought.

19

Yet if we could scorn
 Hate, and pride, and fear;
If we were things born
 Not to shed a tear,
I know not how thy joy we ever should come near.

20

Better than all measures
 Of delightful sound,
Better than all treasures
 That in books are found,
Thy skill to poet were, thou scorner of the ground!

21

Teach me half the gladness
 That thy brain must know,
Such harmonious madness
 From my lips would flow
The world should listen then, as I am listening now.

TO ——

1

I fear thy kisses, gentle maiden,
 Thou needest not fear mine;
My spirit is too deeply laden
 Ever to burthen thine.

86–100. We look before and after . . . ground, contrast between the bird's song and the desires, highest music, and poetry of man. Note "Yet if we could scorn Hate" . . . the condition in Shelley's formula for happiness. Compare Prometheus' recalling the curse, and the last song of *Prometheus Unbound*. **101–05. Teach me . . . now.** The prayer to the bird is the consequence from, the climax to, the preceding. Compare the last stanza of "Ode to the West Wind." On what note does the poem end—hope or despair? Compare the ending of "The Indian Serenade."

2

I fear thy mien, thy tones, thy motion,
  Thou needest not fear mine;
Innocent is the heart's devotion
  With which I worship thine.

THE WORLD'S WANDERERS

This was left unfinished. The MS. adds two lines and the beginning of a third.

1

Tell me, thou Star, whose wings of light
Speed thee in thy fiery flight,
In what cavern of the night
  Will thy pinions close now?

2

Tell me, moon, thou pale and grey
Pilgrim of heaven's homeless way,
In what depth of night or day
  Seekest thou repose now?

3

Weary Wind, who wanderest
Like the world's rejected guest,
Hast thou still some secret nest
  On the tree or billow?

ADONAIS

Adonais was written in June, 1821, at Pisa, and printed there in July. In the three months that had elapsed after the death of Keats at Rome, Shelley seems not to have made inquiries about the causes and circumstances of Keats's death (in his preface to the poem, he even leaves blank the date of death). He was under the impression that the harsh treatment accorded Keats by the reviewers hastened, if it did not actually cause, that untimely end. His motives were therefore three: (1) regret that Keats should thus early have been "hooted off the stage of life"; (2) indignation at the reviewers—from his view Keats was a victim of oppression, the Romantic symbol of the poet hounded by the world's brutality; (3) identification of his own fate with the fate of Keats. The last was undoubtedly the strongest motive. The poem, then, combines two persistent and dominant elements in Shelley's life and thought—his warfare against the oppressors of mankind, and his worship of the ideal over the actual. Shelley's so-called sources had a great deal to do with his treatment of the theme. The poem is a pastoral elegy, in Spenserian stanzas, modeled on two Greek pastoral elegies of the third century B.C.—Bion's *Lament for Adonis* and Moschus's *Lament for Bion*. The first suggested the title, the general idea, the lament refrain, the machinery of the echoes and emotions, the grief of nature, the picture of corruption and physical death, the reabsorption into nature, horror at the brutality of the slaughter. Moschus's *Lament* suggested the added feature of the grief of brother poets, "the mountain shepherds," Byron, Moore, Shelley himself, and Leigh Hunt. Besides these Greek models, Shelley drew upon Keats's poetry, and from his own ideas about the nature of reality and immortality. In its structure the poem, like Milton's "Lycidas," follows the old traditional machinery of the pastoral elegy: invocation, inquiry into causes of death, sympathy of nature, procession of mourners, personal digression, lament, climax, change of mood, and final consolation; but Shelley etherealizes the old framework. The two main movements are these: (1) grief over the death of the poet, indignation at the reviewers, sorrowful questioning of the meaning of life; turn (stanza 38) and (2) rejoicing over the immortality of the poet, triumphant assertion of the superiority of the ideal over the actual (stanzas 39–55).

1

I weep for ADONAIS—he is dead!
Oh, weep for Adonais! though our tears
Thaw not the frost which binds so dear a head!
And thou, sad Hour, selected from all years
To mourn our loss, rouse thy obscure compeers,
And teach them thine own sorrow, say: "With me
Died Adonais; till the Future dares
Forget the Past, his fate and fame shall be
An echo and a light unto eternity!"

2

Where wert thou, mighty Mother, when he
  lay,
When thy Son lay, pierced by the shaft which flies
In darkness? where was lorn Urania
When Adonais died? With veilèd eyes,
'Mid listening Echoes, in her Paradise
She sate, while one, with soft enamoured breath,
Rekindled all the fading melodies,
With which, like flowers that mock the corse be-
  neath,
He had adorned and hid the coming bulk of Death.

3

Oh, weep for Adonais—he is dead!
Wake, melancholy Mother, wake and weep!
Yet wherefore? Quench within their burning bed
Thy fiery tears, and let thy loud heart keep

1. I weep, keynote of stanzas 1–37. **10. mighty Mother.** Mythologically, Urania is goddess of Heavenly Love and Poetry; philosophically, she is the Single Absolute Energy or, in the Platonic sense, the parent of all goodness, truth, and love. Note that the first lament issues from her lips.

Like his, a mute and uncomplaining sleep;
For he is gone, where all things wise and fair
Descend:—oh, dream not that the amorous Deep
Will yet restore him to the vital air;
Death feeds on his mute voice, and laughs at our despair.

4

Most musical of mourners, weep again!
Lament anew, Urania!—He died,
Who was the Sire of an immortal strain,
Blind, old, and lonely, when his country's pride,
The priest, the slave, and the liberticide,
Trampled and mocked with many a loathèd rite
Of lust and blood; he went, unterrified,
Into the gulf of death; but his clear Sprite
Yet reigns o'er earth; the third among the sons of light.

5

Most musical of mourners, weep anew!
Not all to that bright station dared to climb;
And happier they their happiness who knew,
Whose tapers yet burn through that night of time
In which suns perished; others more sublime,
Struck by the envious wrath of man or god,
Have sunk, extinct in their refulgent prime;
And some yet live, treading the thorny road,
Which leads, through toil and hate, to Fame's serene abode.

6

But now, thy youngest, dearest one, has perished,
The nursling of thy widowhood, who grew,
Like a pale flower by some sad maiden cherished,
And fed with true-love tears, instead of dew;
Most musical of mourners, weep anew!
Thy extreme hope, the loveliest and the last,
The bloom, whose petals nipped before they blew
Died on the promise of the fruit, is waste;
The broken lily lies—the storm is overpast.

7

To that high Capital, where kingly Death
Keeps his pale court in beauty and decay,
He came; and bought, with price of purest breath,
A grave among the eternal.—Come away!
Haste, while the vault of blue Italian day
Is yet his fitting charnel-roof! while still
He lies, as if in dewy sleep he lay;
Awake him not! surely he takes his fill
Of deep and liquid rest, forgetful of all ill.

29. He, Milton. **36. the third,** with Homer and Dante. **55. Capital,** Rome, where Keats died and was buried.

8

He will awake no more, oh, never more!—
Within the twilight chamber spreads apace
The shadow of white Death, and at the door
Invisible Corruption waits to trace
His extreme way to her dim dwelling-place;
The eternal Hunger sits, but pity and awe
Soothe her pale rage, nor dares she to deface
So fair a prey, till darkness and the law
Of change, shall o'er his sleep the mortal curtain draw.

9

Oh, weep for Adonais!—The quick Dreams,
The passion-wingèd Ministers of thought,
Who were his flocks, whom near the living streams
Of his young spirit he fed, and whom he taught
The love which was its music, wander not,—
Wander no more, from kindling brain to brain,
But droop there, whence they sprung; and mourn their lot
Round the cold heart, where, after their sweet pain,
They ne'er will gather strength, or find a home again.

10

And one with trembling hands clasps his cold head,
And fans him with her moonlight wings, and cries:
"Our love, our hope, our sorrow, is not dead;
See, on the silken fringe of his faint eyes,
Like dew upon a sleeping flower, there lies
A tear some Dream has loosened from his brain."
Lost Angel of a ruined Paradise!
She knew not 'twas her own; as with no stain
She faded, like a cloud which had outwept its rain.

11

One from a lucid urn of starry dew
Washed his light limbs as if embalming them;
Another clipped her profuse locks, and threw
The wreath upon him, like an anadem,
Which frozen tears instead of pearls begem;
Another in her wilful grief would break
Her bow and wingèd reeds, as if to stem
A greater loss with one which was more weak;
And dull the barbèd fire against his frozen cheek.

73–117. The quick Dreams, . . . stream. The personified abstractions are of Shelley's own imagining. They are preparing the body for burial.

12

Another Splendour on his mouth alit,
That mouth, whence it was wont to draw the breath
Which gave it strength to pierce the guarded wit,
And pass into the panting heart beneath
With lightning and with music: the damp death
Quenched its caress upon his icy lips;
And, as a dying meteor stains a wreath
Of moonlight vapour, which the cold night clips,
It flushed through his pale limbs, and passed to its eclipse.

13

And others came . . . Desires and Adorations,
Wingèd Persuasions and veiled Destinies,
Splendours, and Glooms, and glimmering Incarnations
Of hopes and fears, and twilight Phantasies;
And Sorrow, with her family of Sighs,
And Pleasure, blind with tears, led by the gleam
Of her own dying smile instead of eyes,
Came in slow pomp;—the moving pomp might seem
Like pageantry of mist on an autumnal stream.

14

All he had loved, and moulded into thought,
From shape, and hue, and odour, and sweet sound,
Lamented Adonais. Morning sought
Her eastern watch-tower, and her hair unbound,
Wet with the tears which should adorn the ground,
Dimmed the aërial eyes that kindle day;
Afar the melancholy thunder moaned,
Pale Ocean in unquiet slumber lay,
And the wild Winds flew round, sobbing in their dismay.

15

Lost Echo sits amid the voiceless mountains,
And feeds her grief with his remembered lay,
And will no more reply to winds or fountains,
Or amorous birds perched on the young green spray,
Or herdsman's horn, or bell at closing day;
Since she can mimic not his lips, more dear
Than those for whose disdain she pined away
Into a shadow of all sounds:—a drear
Murmur, between their songs, is all the woodmen hear.

16

Grief made the young Spring wild, and she threw down
Her kindling buds, as if she Autumn were,
Or they dead leaves; since her delight is flown,
For whom should she have waked the sullen year?
To Phoebus was not Hyacinth so dear
Nor to himself Narcissus, as to both
Thou Adonais; wan they stand and sere
Amid the faint companions of their youth,
With dew all turned to tears; odour, to sighing ruth.

17

Thy spirit's sister, the lorn nightingale,
Mourns not her mate with such melodious pain;
Not so the eagle, who like thee could scale
Heaven, and could nourish in the sun's domain
Her mighty youth with morning, doth complain,
Soaring and screaming round her empty nest,
As Albion wails for thee: the curse of Cain
Light on his head who pierced thy innocent breast,
And scared the angel soul that was its earthly guest!

18

Ah, woe is me! Winter is come and gone,
But grief returns with the revolving year;
The airs and streams renew their joyous tone;
The ants, the bees, the swallows reappear;
Fresh leaves and flowers deck the dead Seasons' bier;
The amorous birds now pair in every brake,
And build their mossy homes in field and brere;
And the green lizard, and the golden snake,
Like unimprisoned flames, out of their trance awake.

19

Through wood and stream and field and hill and Ocean
A quickening life from the Earth's heart has burst
As it has ever done, with change and motion,
From the great morning of the world when first
God dawned on Chaos; in its stream immersed,
The lamps of Heaven flash with a softer light;
All baser things pant with life's sacred thirst;
Diffuse themselves; and spend in love's delight,
The beauty and the joy of their renewèd might.

118–50. All he had loved, . . . nest, the grief of Nature, personified in myths, some of which (for example, **the lorn nightingale,** l. 145) Keats himself had created or used.

152. his head, the reviewer's. **154–89. Winter is come and gone . . . sorrow.** The return of physical life in spring makes the fact of human death all the more unbearable and mysterious. **160. brere,** brier.

20

The leprous corpse, touched by this spirit tender,
Exhales itself in flowers of gentle breath;
Like incarnations of the stars, when splendour
Is changed to fragrance, they illumine death
And mock the merry worm that wakes beneath;
Nought we know, dies. Shall that alone which knows
Be as a sword consumed before the sheath
By sightless lightning?—th'intense atom glows
A moment, then is quenched in a most cold repose.

21

Alas! that all we loved of him should be,
But for our grief, as if it had not been,
And grief itself be mortal! Woe is me!
Whence are we, and why are we? of what scene
The actors or spectators? Great and mean
Meet massed in death, who lends what life must borrow.
As long as skies are blue, and fields are green,
Evening must usher night, night urge the morrow,
Month follow month with woe, and year wake year to sorrow.

22

He will awake no more, oh, never more!
"Wake thou," cried Misery, "childless Mother, rise
Out of thy sleep, and slake, in thy heart's core,
A wound more fierce than his, with tears and sighs."
And all the Dreams that watched Urania's eyes,
And all the Echoes whom their sister's song
Had held in holy silence, cried, "Arise!"
Swift as a Thought by the snake Memory stung,
From her ambrosial rest the fading Splendour sprung.

23

She rose like an autumnal Night, that springs
Out of the East, and follows wild and drear
The golden Day, which, on eternal wings,
Even as a ghost abandoning a bier,
Had left the Earth a corpse. Sorrow and fear
So struck, so roused, so rapt Urania;
So saddened round her like an atmosphere
Of stormy mist; so swept her on her way
Even to the mournful place where Adonais lay.

24

Out of her secret Paradise she sped,
Through camps and cities rough with stone, and steel,
And human hearts, which to her aery tread
Yielding not, wounded the invisible
Palms of her tender feet where'er they fell:
And barbèd tongues, and thoughts more sharp than they,
Rent the soft Form they never could repel,
Whose sacred blood, like the young tears of May,
Paved with eternal flowers that undeserving way.

25

In the death-chamber for a moment Death,
Shamed by the presence of that living Might,
Blushed to annihilation, and the breath
Revisited those lips, and Life's pale light
Flashed through those limbs, so late her dear delight.
"Leave me not wild and drear and comfortless,
As silent lightning leaves the starless night!
Leave me not!" cried Urania: her distress
Roused Death: Death rose and smiled, and met her vain caress.

26

"Stay yet awhile! speak to me once again;
Kiss me, so long but as a kiss may live;
And in my heartless breast and burning brain
That word, that kiss, shall all thoughts else survive,
With food of saddest memory kept alive,
Now thou art dead, as if it were a part
Of thee, my Adonais! I would give
All that I am to be as thou now art!
But I am chained to Time, and cannot thence depart!

27

"O gentle child, beautiful as thou wert,
Why didst thou leave the trodden paths of men
Too soon, and with weak hands though mighty heart
Dare the unpastured dragon in his den?
Defenceless as thou wert, oh! where was then

177. Nought we know, dies, that is, matter: Shelley's statement of the theory of the conservation of energy: energy can neither be created nor destroyed. Is it not strange that the mind, "that alone which knows," seems to go out, while what is known, matter, is imperishable? It is as strange as if a bolt of lightning should burn out the blade of the sword (mind) and leave the sheath (the body) unconsumed. The lowest depth of grief and despair in the poem. **179. sightless,** invisible. **186. lends what life must borrow,** that is, plant and animal life feed on dead things.

209 ff. Through camps and cities . . . the world as it was in Shelley's time, and as it is today.

Wisdom the mirrored shield, or scorn the spear?
Or hadst thou waited the full cycle, when
Thy spirit should have filled its crescent sphere,
The monsters of life's waste had fled from thee like deer.

28

"The herded wolves, bold only to pursue;
The obscene ravens, clamorous o'er the dead;
The vultures, to the conqueror's banner true,
Who feed where Desolation first has fed,
And whose wings rain contagion;—how they fled,
When, like Apollo, from his golden bow
The Pythian of the age one arrow sped
And smiled!—The spoilers tempt no second blow,
They fawn on the proud feet that spurn them lying low.

29

"The sun comes forth, and many reptiles spawn;
He sets, and each ephemeral insect then
Is gathered into death without a dawn,
And the immortal stars awake again;
So is it in the world of living men:
A godlike mind soars forth, in its delight
Making earth bare and veiling heaven, and when
It sinks, the swarms that dimmed or shared its light
Leave to its kindred lamps the spirit's awful night."

30

Thus ceased she: and the mountain shepherds came,
Their garlands sere, their magic mantles rent;
The Pilgrim of Eternity, whose fame
Over his living head like Heaven is bent,
An early but enduring monument,
Came, veiling all the lightnings of his song
In sorrow; from her wilds Ierne sent
The sweetest lyrist of her saddest wrong,
And Love taught Grief to fall like music from his tongue.

250. The Pythian of the age . . . sped. Apollo slew the snakes. Similarly, Lord Byron, in *English Bards and Scotch Reviewers,* had castigated the reviewers. A pity that Keats could not have attained the maturity to cope with them! **264. The Pilgrim of Eternity,** Byron. Compare *Childe Harold's Pilgrimage,* Canto the Third, ll. 669–70. This is the beginning of another "procession" of mourners—brother poets—"mountain shepherds"—another specific "pastoral" feature. **268. Ierne,** Ireland. **269. The sweetest lyrist,** Moore.

31

Midst others of less note, came one frail Form,
A phantom among men; companionless
As the last cloud of an expiring storm
Whose thunder is its knell; he, as I guess,
Had gazed on Nature's naked loveliness,
Actaeon-like, and now he fled astray
With feeble steps o'er the world's wilderness,
And his own thoughts, along that rugged way,
Pursued, like raging hounds, their father and their prey.

32

A pardlike Spirit beautiful and swift—
A Love in desolation masked;—a Power
Girt round with weakness;—it can scarce uplift
The weight of the superincumbent hour;
It is a dying lamp, a falling shower,
A breaking billow;—even whilst we speak
Is it not broken? On the withering flower
The killing sun smiles brightly: on a cheek
The life can burn in blood, even while the heart may break.

33

His head was bound with pansies overblown,
And faded violets, white, and pied, and blue;
And a light spear topped with a cypress cone,
Round whose rude shaft dark ivy-tresses grew
Yet dripping with the forest's noon-day dew,
Vibrated, as the ever-beating heart
Shook the weak hand that grasped it; of that crew
He came the last, neglected and apart;
A herd-abandoned deer struck by the hunter's dart.

34

All stood aloof, and at his partial moan
Smiled through their tears; well knew that gentle band
Who in another's fate now wept his own;
As in the accents of an unknown land,
He sung new sorrow; sad Urania scanned
The Stranger's mien, and murmured: "Who art thou?"
He answered not, but with a sudden hand
Made bare his branded and ensanguined brow,
Which was like Cain's or Christ's.—Oh! that it should be so!

271. one frail Form, Shelley's. Note the disproportion between this characterization and those accorded to the other poets (four stanzas to part of 30 and all of 35 for the others). Note, too, l. 300, "Who in another's fate now wept his own," and the characteristic self-pity of the whole passage. **276. Actaeon-like.** Actaeon surprised Diana in her bath and was torn to pieces by her hounds. Thus the glimpse of Immortal Beauty forever haunts the beholder.

35

What softer voice is hushed over the dead?
Athwart what brow is that dark mantle thrown?
What form leans sadly o'er the white death-bed,
In mockery of monumental stone,
The heavy heart heaving without a moan?
If it be He, who, gentlest of the wise,
Taught, soothed, loved, honoured the departed one,
Let me not vex, with inharmonious sighs,
The silence of that heart's accepted sacrifice.

36

Our Adonais has drunk poison—oh!
What deaf and viperous murderer could crown
Life's early cup with such a draught of woe?
The nameless worm would now itself disown:
If felt, yet could escape, the magic tone
Whose prelude held all envy, hate, and wrong,
But what was howling in one breast alone,
Silent with expectation of the song,
Whose master's hand is cold, whose silver lyre unstrung.

37

Live thou, whose infamy is not thy fame!
Live! fear no heavier chastisement from me,
Thou noteless blot on a remembered name!
But be thyself, and know thyself to be!
And ever at thy season be thou free
To spill the venom when thy fangs o'erflow;
Remorse and Self-contempt shall cling to thee;
Hot Shame shall burn upon thy secret brow,
And like a beaten hound tremble thou shalt—as now.

38

Nor let us weep that our delight is fled
Far from these carrion kites that scream below;
He wakes or sleeps with the enduring dead;
Thou canst not soar where he is sitting now.—
Dust to the dust! but the pure spirit shall flow
Back to the burning fountain whence it came,
A portion of the Eternal, which must glow
Through time and change, unquenchably the same,
Whilst thy cold embers choke the sordid hearth of shame.

39

Peace, peace! he is not dead, he doth not sleep—
He hath awakened from the dream of life—
'Tis we, who lost in stormy visions, keep
With phantoms an unprofitable strife,
And in mad trance strike with our spirit's knife
Invulnerable nothings. *We* decay
Like corpses in a charnel; fear and grief
Convulse us and consume us day by day,
And cold hopes swarm like worms within our living clay.

40

He has outsoared the shadow of our night;
Envy and calumny and hate and pain,
And that unrest which men miscall delight,
Can touch him not and torture not again;
From the contagion of the world's slow stain
He is secure, and now can never mourn
A heart grown cold, a head grown grey in vain;
Nor, when the spirit's self has ceased to burn,
With sparkless ashes load an unlamented urn.

41

He lives, he wakes—'tis Death is dead, not he;
Mourn not for Adonais.—Thou young Dawn,
Turn all thy dew to splendour, for from thee
The spirit thou lamentest is not gone;
Ye caverns and ye forests, cease to moan!
Cease, ye faint flowers and fountains, and thou Air,
Which like a morning veil thy scarf hadst thrown
O'er the abandoned Earth, now leave it bare
Even to the joyous stars which smile on its despair!

42

He is made one with Nature: there is heard
His voice in all her music, from the moan
Of thunder, to the song of night's sweet bird;
He is a presence to be felt and known
In darkness and in light, from herb and stone,

307. softer voice, Leigh Hunt's. If Shelley had known more about the circumstances of Keats's death, he might have included Joseph Severn, the young artist who came to Italy with Keats and nursed the poet. **334–42. Nor let us weep . . . shame.** This is the turn. In his indignation at the reviewer, Shelley soars so high that he seems suddenly to realize that the reviewer had not hurt that which was permanent in Keats; hence the following view of immortality and the consequent change from mourning to rejoicing.

343–96. Peace, peace! he is not dead . . . stormy air. In the following passage Shelley, as usual, reverses the ordinary conceptions of life and death. "Death is the veil which those who live call life; They sleep, and it is lifted." (*Prometheus Unbound*, Act III, sc. 3, l. 113.) **370–414. He is made one . . . our throng.** The conception of immortality involves several ideas, not always entirely consistent with one another: (1) The spirit of Adonais is pantheistically reabsorbed into the cycle of nature and continues to manifest itself in all that is lovely in nature; (2) it is similarly reabsorbed into the Platonic essence of creative power ("Spirit's plastic stress") and is to be felt by the young and generous for all time; (3) it is invited by the other "inheritors of unfulfilled renown" (poets who had died untimely and tragically) to ascend the seat reserved for it on another star—the closest the poem comes to the Christian notion of individual and conscious survival.

Spreading itself where'er that Power may move
Which has withdrawn his being to its own;
Which wields the world with never-wearied love,
Sustains it from beneath, and kindles it above.

43

He is a portion of the loveliness
Which once he made more lovely: he doth bear
His part, while the one Spirit's plastic stress
Sweeps through the dull dense world, compelling there,
All new successions to the forms they wear;
Torturing th' unwilling dross that checks its flight
To its own likeness, as each mass may bear;
And bursting in its beauty and its might
From trees and beasts and men into the Heaven's light.

44

The splendours of the firmament of time
May be eclipsed, but are extinguished not;
Like stars to their appointed height they climb,
And death is a low mist which cannot blot
The brightness it may veil. When lofty thought
Lifts a young heart above its mortal lair,
And love and life contend in it, for what
Shall be its earthly doom, the dead live there
And move like winds of light on dark and stormy air.

45

The inheritors of unfulfilled renown
Rose from their thrones, built beyond mortal thought,
Far in the Unapparent. Chatterton
Rose pale,—his solemn agony had not
Yet faded from him; Sidney, as he fought
And as he fell and as he lived and loved
Sublimely mild, a Spirit without spot,
Arose; and Lucan, by his death approved:
Oblivion as they rose shrank like a thing reproved.

46

And many more, whose names on Earth are dark,
But whose transmitted effluence cannot die
So long as fire outlives the parent spark,
Rose, robed in dazzling immortality.
"Thou art become as one of us," they cry;
"It was for thee yon kingless sphere has long
Swung blind in unascended majesty;
Silent alone amid an Heaven of Song.
Assume thy wingèd throne, thou Vesper of our throng!"

47

Who mourns for Adonais? oh come forth,
Fond wretch! and know thyself and him aright.
Clasp with thy panting soul the pendulous Earth;
As from a centre, dart thy spirit's light
Beyond all worlds, until its spacious might
Satiate the void circumference: then shrink
Even to a point within our day and night;
And keep thy heart light lest it make thee sink
When hope has kindled hope, and lured thee to the brink.

48

Or go to Rome, which is the sepulchre,
Oh, not of him, but of our joy: 'tis nought
That ages, empires, and religions there
Lie buried in the ravage they have wrought;
For such as he can lend,—they borrow not
Glory from those who made the world their prey;
And he is gathered to the kings of thought
Who waged contention with their time's decay,
And of the past are all that cannot pass away.

49

Go thou to Rome,—at once the Paradise,
The grave, the city, and the wilderness;
And where its wrecks like shattered mountains rise,
And flowering weeds, and fragrant copses dress
The bones of Desolation's nakedness
Pass, till the Spirit of the spot shall lead
Thy footsteps to a slope of green access
Where, like an infant's smile, over the dead
A light of laughing flowers along the grass is spread;

50

And grey walls moulder round, on which dull Time
Feeds, like slow fire upon a hoary brand,
And one keen pyramid with wedge sublime,
Pavilioning the dust of him who planned
This refuge for his memory, doth stand
Like flame transformed to marble; and beneath,

415–23. come forth . . . the brink. Let him who still doubts the immortality of Adonais imagine he is at the center of the universe and take a universal view; then, so far from mourning Adonais, he will have to restrain himself from leaping into eternity. **424–69. Or go to Rome . . . Heart.** Or, if he is still a doubting Thomas, let him go to Rome and see that, unlike others, who are distinguished by being buried in Rome, Adonais *confers distinction* on the Eternal City for being his last resting-place. The following description is of the Protestant cemetery in Rome, where, in the shadow of the marble tomb of the ancient Roman Emperor Cestius, Keats was buried, and where Shelley's own ashes were to rest in a little more than a year.

A field is spread, on which a newer band
Have pitched in Heaven's smile their camp of death,
Welcoming him we lose with scarce extinguished breath.

51

Here pause: these graves are all too young as yet
To have outgrown the sorrow which consigned
Its charge to each; and if the seal is set,
Here, on one fountain of a mourning mind,
Break it not thou! too surely shalt thou find
Thine own well full, if thou returnest home,
Of tears and gall. From the world's bitter wind
Seek shelter in the shadow of the tomb.
What Adonais is, why fear we to become?

52

The One remains, the many change and pass;
Heaven's light forever shines, Earth's shadows fly;
Life, like a dome of many-coloured glass,
Stains the white radiance of Eternity,
Until Death tramples it to fragments.—Die,
If thou wouldst be with that which thou dost seek!
Follow where all is fled!—Rome's azure sky,
Flowers, ruins, statues, music, words, are weak
The glory they transfuse with fitting truth to speak.

53

Why linger, why turn back, why shrink, my Heart?
Thy hopes are gone before: from all things here
They have departed; thou shouldst now depart!
A light is passed from the revolving year,
And man, and woman; and what still is dear
Attracts to crush, repels to make thee wither.
The soft sky smiles,—the low wind whispers near:
'Tis Adonais calls! oh, hasten thither,
No more let life divide what Death can join together.

54

That Light whose smile kindles the Universe,
That Beauty in which all things work and move,
That Benediction which the eclipsing Curse
Of birth can quench not, that sustaining Love
Which through the web of being blindly wove
By man and beast and earth and air and sea,
Burns bright or dim, as each are mirrors of
The fire for which all thirst; now beams on me,
Consuming the last clouds of cold mortality.

55

The breath whose might I have invoked in song
Descends on me; my spirit's bark is driven,
Far from the shore, far from the trembling throng
Whose sails were never to the tempest given;
The massy earth and spherèd skies are riven!
I am borne darkly, fearfully, afar;
Whilst, burning through the inmost veil of Heaven,
The soul of Adonais, like a star,
Beacons from the abode where the Eternal are.

MUSIC, WHEN SOFT VOICES DIE

TO ——

Music, when soft voices die,
Vibrates in the memory—
Odours, when sweet violets sicken,
Live within the sense they quicken.

Rose leaves, when the rose is dead,
Are heaped for the belovèd's bed;
And so thy thoughts, when thou art gone,
Love itself shall slumber on.

TO NIGHT

I

Swiftly walk o'er the western wave,
Spirit of Night!

460–86. The One . . . mortality. Shelley's most beautiful statement of the nature of Ultimate Reality. "The One" is the Platonic Idea or Essence. In three figures "The One" is contrasted with the individual and temporal ("One" and "many," "Heaven's light" and "Earth's shadows," "dome of many-coloured glass" and the white sunlight of "Eternity"). Just as, under a dome of colored glass, which breaks up light into its primary colors, we should never see white sunlight until the dome was broken, so we, covered by the refracting dome of life, shall never know Ultimate Reality until Death shatters the dome.

478. That Light. Note the climax of ideas about the nature of Ultimate Reality. It runs the gamut from *Queen Mab* through *Prometheus*. This is a higher conception than that the Universe is Thought alone. Shelley transfers his conception from the realm of intellect to the realm of emotion. Love, and Love only, is the Universe. "Shelley's God was the Universe, conceived as conscious and active love, and the worship he gave it was love."—Stopford Brooke, *Naturalism in English Poetry*, Dutton, 1920, p. 207. **487–95. The breath . . . Eternal are.** Perhaps the passage tells as much as any poet ever told about the way he felt when he had completed a great poem. Compare the conclusion to Robert Browning's "Saul." The stanza is also a final assertion of the deathlessness of the poet and of poetry—the larger theme of *Adonais*. *To Night.* **2. Spirit of Night!** Another original and vivid myth. Compare "Ode to the West Wind," "The Cloud," and other poems.

Out of the misty eastern cave,
Where, all the long and lone daylight,
Thou wovest dreams of joy and fear,
Which make thee terrible and dear,—
Swift be thy flight!

2

Wrap thy form in a mantle grey,
Star-inwrought!
Blind with thine hair the eyes of Day;
Kiss her until she be wearied out,
Then wander o'er city, and sea, and land,
Touching all with thine opiate wand—
Come, long-sought!

3

When I arose and saw the dawn,
I sighed for thee;
When Light rode high, and the dew was gone,
And noon lay heavy on flower and tree,
And the weary Day turned to his rest,
Lingering like an unloved guest,
I sighed for thee.

4

Thy brother Death came, and cried,
Wouldst thou me?
Thy sweet child Sleep, the filmy-eyed,
Murmured like a noon-tide bee,
Shall I nestle near thy side?
Wouldst thou me?—and I replied,
No, not thee!

5

Death will come when thou art dead,
Soon, too soon—
Sleep will come when thou art fled;
Of neither would I ask the boon
I ask of thee, belovèd Night—
Swift be thine approaching flight,
Come soon, soon!

A LAMENT

I

O world! O life! O time!
On whose last steps I climb,
Trembling at that where I had stood before;
When will return the glory of your prime?
No more—Oh, never more!

32. boon, perhaps release from the distractions of the day, so that imagination will have free play.

2

Out of the day and night
A joy has taken flight:
Fresh spring, and summer, and winter hoar,
Move my faint heart with grief, but with delight
No more—Oh, never more!

LINES: WHEN THE LAMP IS SHATTERED

I

When the lamp is shattered,
The light in the dust lies dead—
When the cloud is scattered,
The rainbow's glory is shed.
When the lute is broken,
Sweet tones are remembered not;
When the lips have spoken,
Loved accents are soon forgot.

2

As music and splendour
Survive not the lamp and the lute,
The heart's echoes render
No song when the spirit is mute:—
No song but sad dirges,
Like the wind through a ruined cell,
Or the mournful surges
That ring the dead seaman's knell.

3

When hearts have once mingled,
Love first leaves the well-built nest;
The weak one is singled
To endure what it once possest.
O Love! who bewailest
The frailty of all things here,
Why choose you the frailest
For your cradle, your home, and your bier?

4

Its passions will rock thee,
As the storms rock the ravens on high:
Bright reason will mock thee,
Like the sun from a wintry sky.
From thy nest every rafter
Will rot, and thine eagle home
Leave thee naked to laughter,
When leaves fall and cold winds come.

MUTABILITY

We are as clouds that veil the midnight moon;
How restlessly they speed, and gleam, and quiver,
Streaking the darkness radiantly!—yet soon
Night closes round, and they are lost for ever:

Or like forgotten lyres, whose dissonant strings
Give various response to each varying blast,
To whose frail frame no second motion brings
One mood or modulation like the last.

We rest—a dream has power to poison sleep;
We rise—one wandering thought pollutes the day;
We feel, conceive or reason, laugh or weep;
Embrace fond woe, or cast our cares away:

It is the same!—For, be it joy or sorrow,
The path of its departure still is free;
Man's yesterday may ne'er be like his morrow;
Naught may endure but Mutability.

from HELLAS

For an account of *Hellas*, see the biographical-critical sketch. The "Semichoruses" express the main theme of this dramatic poem. The "Chorus" sets forth a theory of the great historical religions of the world.

Semichorus I

Life may change, but it may fly not;
Hope may vanish, but can die not;
Truth be veiled, but still it burneth;
Love repulsed,—but it returneth!

Semichorus II

Yet were life a charnel where
Hope lay coffined with Despair;
Yet were truth a sacred lie,
Love were lust—

Semichorus I

If Liberty
Lent not life its soul of light,
Hope its iris of delight,
Truth its prophet's robe to wear,
Love its power to give and bear. . . .

Chorus

Worlds on worlds are rolling ever
From creation to decay,
Like the bubbles on a river,
Sparkling, bursting, borne away.
But they are still immortal
Who, through birth's orient portal
And death's dark chasm hurrying to and fro,
Clothe their unceasing flight
In the brief dust and light
Gathered around their chariots as they go;
New shapes they still may weave,
New gods, new laws receive,
Bright or dim are they, as the robes they last
On Death's bare ribs had cast.

A power from the unknown God,
A Promethean conqueror, came;
Like a triumphal path he trod
The thorns of death and shame.
A mortal shape to him
Was like the vapour dim
Which the orient planet animates with light;
Hell, Sin, and Slavery came,
Like bloodhounds mild and tame,
Nor preyed until their lord had taken flight;
The moon of Máhomet
Arose, and it shall set:
While blazoned as on Heaven's immortal noon
The cross leads generations on.

Swift as the radiant shapes of sleep
From one, whose dreams are Paradise,
Fly, when the fond wretch wakes to weep,
And Day peers forth with her blank eyes;
So fleet, so faint, so fair,
The Powers of earth and air
Fled from the folding-star of Bethlehem;
Apollo, Pan, and Love,
And even Olympian Jove,
Grew weak, for killing Truth had glared on them;
Our hills and seas and streams,
Dispeopled of their dreams,
Their waters turned to blood, their dew to tears,
Wailed for the golden years.

from A DEFENCE OF POETRY

In spirit and thought, *A Defence of Poetry* is close to the idealism of *Adonais* and *Epipsychidion*, written the same year. It is a "defence" against the attack made by Shelley's friend Thomas Love Peacock, in *The Four Ages of Poetry*, 1820, on Romantic poetry. It was never completed. The two main topics of the part written are stated by Shelley in his transitional tenth paragraph: (1) "what is poetry, and who are poets"; and (2) "its effects on society." The most original and significant portion of the essay belongs to the second topic, though understanding of Shelley's ideas on the first topic is an indispensable preliminary. The main points to be mastered are these: 1. Poetry, a product of the imagination set to metrical language, reveals the order and beauty of the universe; it is the direct expression of perfection ("the very image of life expressed in its eternal truth"). 2. If, then, poetry expresses ideal perfection, should the poet embody in his poems his beliefs about perfection and the way to it? The answer is no. As poetry is directly due to imaginative inspiration, not to reasoning, its true moral effect is produced through imagination, not through doctrine. The student should master Shelley's explanation of all these terms, reasons, and so on. Shelley's account of the moral efficacy of poetry, with his reasons, goes further than that of any of the other Romantics, with the possible exception of Keats. In his discussion of these topics Shelley makes some of the noblest claims ever put forth for poetry: "Poetry is the record of the best and happiest moments of the happiest and best minds." "Poetry redeems from decay the visitations of the divinity in man." "Poets are the unacknowledged legislators of the world," and so forth. (A. S. Cook's edition, *A Defence of Poetry*, Ginn, 1891, including Peacock's essay, and M. T. Solve's *Shelley, His Theory of Poetry*, University of Chicago Press, 1927, are valuable aids to study.)

from PART I [1]

HAVING determined what is poetry, and who are poets, let us proceed to estimate its effects upon society.

Poetry is ever accompanied with pleasure: all spirits on which it falls open themselves to receive the wisdom which is mingled with its delight. In the infancy of the world, neither poets themselves nor their auditors are fully aware of the excellence of poetry: for it acts in a divine and unapprehended manner, beyond and above consciousness; and it is reserved for future generations to contemplate and measure the mighty cause and effect in all the strength and splendour of their union. Even in modern times, no living poet ever arrived at the fulness of his fame; the jury which sits in judgment upon a poet, belonging as he does to all time, must be composed of his peers: it must be impaneled by Time from the selectest of the wise of many generations. A Poet is a nightingale, who sits in darkness and sings to cheer its own solitude with sweet sounds; his auditors are as men entranced by the melody of an unseen musician, who feel that they are moved and softened, yet know not whence or why. The poems of Homer and his contemporaries were the delight of infant Greece; they were the elements of that social system which is the column upon which all succeeding civilization has reposed. Homer embodied the ideal perfection of his age in human character; nor can we doubt that those who read his verses were awakened to an ambition of becoming like to Achilles, Hector, and Ulysses: the truth and beauty of friendship, patriotism, and persevering devotion to an object, were unveiled to the depths in these immortal creations: the sentiments of the auditors must have been refined and enlarged by a sympathy with such great and lovely impersonations, until from admiring they imitated, and from imitation they identified themselves with the objects of their admiration. Nor let it be objected, that these characters are remote from moral perfection, and that they can by no means be considered as edifying patterns for general imitation. Every epoch, under names more or less specious, has deified its peculiar errors; Revenge is the naked Idol of the worship of a semi-barbarous age; and Self-deceit is the veiled Image of unknown evil, before which luxury and satiety lie prostrate. But a poet considers the vices of his contemporaries as the temporary dress in which his creations must be arrayed, and which cover without concealing the eternal proportions of their beauty. An epic or dramatic personage is understood to wear them around his soul, as he may the antient armour or the modern uniform around his body; whilst it is easy to conceive a dress more graceful than either. The beauty of the internal nature cannot be so far concealed by its accidental vesture, but that the spirit of its form shall communicate itself to the very disguise, and indicate the shape it hides from the manner in which it is worn. A majestic form and graceful motions will express themselves through the most barbarous and tasteless costume. Few poets of the highest class have chosen to exhibit the beauty of their conceptions in its naked truth and splendour; and it is doubtful whether the alloy of costume, habit, &c., be not necessary to temper this planetary music for mortal ears.

The whole objection, however, of the immorality of poetry rests upon a misconception of the manner in which poetry acts to produce the moral improvement of man. Ethical science arranges the elements which poetry has created, and propounds schemes and proposes examples of civil and domestic life: nor is it for want of admirable doctrines that men hate, and despise, and censure, and deceive, and subjugate one another. But Poetry acts in another and diviner manner. It awakens and enlarges the mind itself by rendering it the recep-

[1] The projected second and third parts were never written.

tacle of a thousand unapprehended combinations of thought. Poetry lifts the veil from the hidden beauty of the world, and makes familiar objects be as if they were not familiar; it reproduces all that it represents, and the impersonations clothed in its Elysian light stand thenceforward in the minds of those who have once contemplated them, as memorials of that gentle and exalted content which extends itself over all thoughts and actions with which it coexists. The great secret of morals is love; or a going out of our own nature, and an identification of ourselves with the beautiful which exists in thought, action, or person, not our own. A man, to be greatly good, must imagine intensely and comprehensively; he must put himself in the place of another and of many others; the pains and pleasures of his species must become his own. The great instrument of moral good is the imagination; and poetry administers to the effect by acting upon the cause. Poetry enlarges the circumference of the imagination by replenishing it with thoughts of ever new delight, which have the power of attracting and assimilating to their own nature all other thoughts, and which form new intervals and interstices whose void for ever craves fresh food. Poetry strengthens the faculty which is the organ of the moral nature of man, in the same manner as exercise strengthens a limb. A Poet therefore would do ill to embody his own conceptions of right and wrong, which are usually those of his place and time, in his poetical creations, which participate in neither. By this assumption of the inferior office of interpreting the effect, in which perhaps after all he might acquit himself but imperfectly, he would resign a glory in a participation in the cause. There was little danger that Homer, or any of the eternal Poets, should have so far misunderstood themselves as to have abdicated this throne of their widest dominion. Those in whom the poetical faculty, though great, is less intense, as Euripides, Lucan, Tasso, Spenser, have frequently affected a moral aim, and the effect of their poetry is diminished in exact proportion to the degree in which they compel us to advert to this purpose. . . .

The functions of the poetical faculty are twofold; by one it creates new materials for knowledge, and power and pleasure; by the other it engenders in the mind a desire to reproduce and arrange them according to a certain rhythm and order which may be called the beautiful and the good. The cultivation of poetry is never more to be desired than at periods when, from an excess of the selfish and calculating principle, the accumulation of the materials of external life exceed[s] the quantity of the power of assimilating them to the internal laws of human nature. The body has then become too unwieldy for that which animates it.

Poetry is indeed something divine. It is at once the centre and circumference of knowledge; it is that which comprehends all science, and that to which all science must be referred. It is at the same time the root and blossom of all other systems of thought; it is that from which all spring, and that which adorns all; and that which, if blighted, denies the fruit and the seed, and withholds from the barren world the nourishment and the succession of the scions of the tree of life. It is the perfect and consummate surface and bloom of all things; it is as the odour and the colour of the rose to the texture of the elements which compose it, as the form and splendour of unfaded beauty to the secrets of anatomy and corruption. What were Virtue, Love, Patriotism, Friendship—what were the scenery of this beautiful Universe which we inhabit; what were our consolations on this side of the grave, and what were our aspirations beyond it, if Poetry did not ascend to bring light and fire from those eternal regions where the owl-winged faculty of calculation dare not ever soar? . . .

John Keats
1795–1821

The facts about John Keats's early life illustrate the truism that Fortune often lavishes the gift of genius without regard for social circumstances. His father, Thomas Keats, had come from the Land's End country of Cornwall to London, got a job in the livery stable of the Swan and Hoop Inn, and married the daughter of the innkeeper, Frances Jennings. John, the first child, was born on October 29 (or 30), 1795. Three other children—George, Thomas, and Frances (Fanny)—were to be happily associated with him and to be affectionately recorded in his poems and letters, as was Georgiana, George's wife. At the age of eight John was sent to school at Enfield, a suburb ten miles north of London. About a year later, his father, while returning from a visit to the school, was killed by a fall from his horse. The death of the mother, from tuberculosis, terminated the boy's schooling when he was fifteen.

The school at Enfield, though obscure, was sound and thorough. The master, the Reverend John Clarke, and his son and assistant, Charles Cowden Clarke, were competent and sympathetic. The latter, only eight years Keats's senior, was young enough to become a stimulating and affectionate friend as well as teacher. Charles Cowden Clarke's *Autobiography* gives a charming account of their relations and of the boy's mind and character. Keats was, says Clarke, a favorite in the school. He was bright and studious, fond of history, music, and literature, and fascinated by classical mythology, which he read in such books as Tooke's *Pantheon* and Lemprière's *Classical Dictionary*. "Not the less beloved was he," adds Clarke, "for having a highly pugnacious spirit. . . . His passions at times were almost ungovernable . . . not merely [was he] the 'favourite of all,' like a pet prize-fighter, for his terrier courage; but his high-mindedness, his utter unconsciousness of a mean motive, his placability, his generosity, wrought so general a feeling in his behalf, that I never heard a word of disapproval from anyone who had known him." Clarke and others describe Keats as small in stature (even when grown he was little more than five feet in height), but well-knit, agile, and vigorous. His sister-in-law, Georgiana, wrote: "His eyes were dark brown, large, soft, and expressive, and his hair a golden red." As boy and man, he had a keen sense of humor.

Soon after his mother's death, Keats was taken out of school by his guardian, Mr. Richard Abbey, and apprenticed to the apothecary-surgeon, Mr. Thomas Hammond, who lived at Edmonton, two miles from Enfield. Keats continued his medical studies at Guy's and St. Thomas's hospitals in London and passed his examinations for license to practice.

Both while at Edmonton and in London, he kept up his friendship with Charles Cowden Clarke, and began to explore those realms of gold which he had skirted in school. He had learned to love Virgil. When he was fifteen, Clarke read Spenser's *Epithalamion* to him one day in an old arbor. "That night," says Clarke, "he took away with him the *Faery Queen* and went through it . . . as a young horse would through a spring meadow—ramping . . . singled out epithets . . . hoisted himself up and looked burly and dominant, as he said—'What an image that is—"Sea-shouldering whales." ' " His first known poem was "Imitation of Spenser." In 1816 he published his first sonnet, on Leigh Hunt's release from prison. Not long afterward, he visited Hunt and there met Shelley and another young man who was to be one of his best friends, John Hamilton Reynolds, poet and lawyer. During the same period he formed literary acquaintanceships with Hazlitt and Lamb. Early one morning, after he and Clarke had sat up all night reading the Elizabethan poet Chapman's translation of Homer, he left on Clarke's breakfast table the great sonnet recording that adventure. Under Hunt's influence he composed two fairly long poems, "I Stood Tip-Toe" and "Sleep and Poetry," expressing his ideas on the nature of poetry, its themes, its aim, and its function in human life. In 1817, with Shelley's help, he published these and others in a little volume entitled *Poems*.

In 1817, too, his artist friends Joseph Severn and B. R. Haydon showed him the Elgin Marbles, fragments of ancient Greek sculpture, and he wrote two sonnets expressing the sensations of that experience. Plastic art and his study of Wordsworth, Shakespeare, and Milton and other seventeenth-century poets were working upon his imagination. Going down to the Isle of Wight in the spring, he began *Endymion*, a long metrical romance in the free-running couplets he had learned from Hunt, treating the love of a shepherd prince for Diana, the moon goddess, as a type of the soul's search for ideal beauty. Unlike Shelley, who had treated a similar theme in *Alastor*, Keats showed that in order to succeed the hero must sympathize with others along his way and approach ideal beauty through love of a human being. While *Endymion* was still in progress, he wrote *Isabella*, another romance, relating in ottava rima a Boccaccian story of the death of love and beauty. Late in December he met Wordsworth, to whom he had owed much for the ethics of *Endymion*, and was with him frequently for a while thereafter. In April, 1818, he published *Endymion*. Continuing his study of the poets, with the addition of Dante, he began a summer walking tour of northern England, Scotland, and Ireland. A severe cold forced him to return sooner than he had expected. In August *Endymion* and its author were brutally attacked by *Blackwood's Magazine;* in September, they were ridiculed by the *Quarterly Review*. Contrary to popular belief, Keats was not snuffed out by an article. He took the attacks sensibly and bravely, and set about writing a greater poem, *Hyperion*. Toward the end of the year he underwent two profound emotional experiences—watching his brother Tom die of tuberculosis, and falling desperately in love with Fanny Brawne.

Though he was harassed by symptoms of tuberculosis, by poverty, and by despair in his love, the first nine months of 1819 were the period of Keats's noblest work. Besides his great odes, he composed his most beautiful verse romances. These were published, with the romance of 1818, in *Lamia, Isabella, The Eve of St. Agnes and Other Poems*, 1820, his third and last volume. Throughout the remainder of 1819 and the spring and summer of 1820, Keats was steadily losing his fight with disease. In September, with his faithful friend Severn, he began a sorrowful search for health in Italy. They stopped at Rome. There, in the house by the Old Spanish Stairs, he died on February 23, 1821, aged twenty-five years, three months, and twenty-six days. He was buried in the Protestant cemetery near the pyramidal tomb of the ancient Roman emperor Cestius. For his epitaph he had dictated: "Here lies one whose name was writ in water." But he had also said, simply and proudly, that he would be "among the English poets."

Keats's poetical development is like the unrolling of one of those pageants of the seasons—pictures and music—that he and his master Spenser loved to describe. "I Stood Tip-Toe" shyly pipes the coming year, "Sleep and Poetry" paints the tender immaturity of April, and *Endymion* revels in the luxuries of late spring. *Isabella* is "languid June." "The Eve of St. Agnes," for all the bone-piercing cold of its chapel scene and fairy storm, is the ripe midsummer of the poet's art. "La Belle Dame sans Merci" and "Lamia" are fevered August, bright and hard and searing. Last is "Autumn," mellow Autumn, an untroubled recording of a moment of serene and perfect beauty, a complete surrender to Nature's mood, an acquiescent sigh in answer to the whisper of death. "Music wrung from the transience of lovely things runs like a monotone through the 1820 volume, but in different keys." [1] It runs through the great odes—"Psyche," "Indolence," "Grecian Urn," "To a Nightingale," "Melancholy," and "Autumn." It is present in many of the sixty-one sonnets, as in "Bright Star." It is dominant in the three romances written between April, 1818, and September, 1819. Behind these story-poems lies the great tradition of romantic storytelling, from Boccaccio, Spenser, and Shakespeare to Coleridge, Scott, and Byron. Each poem is in a different verse form, mood, and musical key. Each is the essence of romance in its peculiar kind. *Isabella*, 1818, in ottava rima, moans syllables of woe over frustrated love. "The Eve of St. Agnes," January, 1819, in Spenserian stanzas, sings a paean of youthful love triumphant in a world of heartless pomp, hate, cruelty, and death. The ballad "La Belle Dame sans Merci," treating the "wasting power of love" and the bareness of life after Romance has fled, introduces the mood and the theme of "Lamia" (July–August, 1819). In the bright, nervous couplets suggested by a rereading of Dryden, "Lamia" is a sorrowful, disillusioned questioning of passion and romance, a troubled searching after truth.

[1] Ernest de Selincourt, Introduction to *The Poems of John Keats*, London, 1926.

Several of Keats's best poems and letters, scattered through his writing career, are mainly about poetry itself. In "I Stood Tip-Toe," "Sleep and Poetry," *Endymion* (I, ll. 777 ff.), incidentally in the odes, and, finally, in *The Vision of Hyperion* (a reworking of *Hyperion*), he gives a progressively maturing account of the themes of poetry and of its part in human life. First is nature, maker of poets, "the realm of Flora and old Pan," the inexhaustible source of sensations. The poet is one "whose strenuous tongue can burst Joy's grape against his palate fine." Closely related to the delights of nature that he may experience are ancient myths and lovely tales, "a flowery band to bind us to the earth." These are among the earliest forms of man's poetic response to the beauty of nature. Higher than these are "the agonies, the strife Of human hearts"—passion, heroic endeavor, tragedy, "the fierce dispute Betwixt damnation and impassioned clay." But beyond these there is an "ever-fleeting music." The "crown of life" is love and friendship; yet human love and friendship, like the beauty of nature, are but types of a higher reality. For the apprehension and enjoyment of these delights not merely fine senses are requisite, but imagination is indispensable. Imagination works upon the harvest of the senses and transmutes it. The imaginative vision, though based on realities sensuously experienced, is superior to material actuality. "What the imagination seizes as beauty must be truth—whether it existed before or not." Poetry, a blend of sensuous enjoyments transmuted by imagination, should "soothe the cares, and lift the thoughts of man." The true poet "pours out a balm upon the world."

Thus, often concealed by its rich and easily perceived sensuousness, there is a serious intellectual content in Keats's best poetry. "I Stood Tip-Toe" is more than a "posy," "Sleep and Poetry" more than a "Silent entangler of a beauty's tresses," *Endymion* more than a lovely tale, "The Eve of St. Agnes" more than an opulent romance of young love. The "Ode to Psyche" makes us feel that in the beauty of an old myth there is a refuge, "a rosy sanctuary" of the soul from a troubled world. The "Ode on a Grecian Urn" leads us to a perception of the truth, represented by the antique scenes depicted, that the eternal miracle of great art lies in its power to capture beauty and fix it in forms that will forever stir the beholder's or the hearer's imagination in the way the original experience stirred the artist's. In the half-sorrowful, half-glad words of consolation to the youth who will never kiss the girl, to the trees that will never come to fruit, to the piper whose melody will never be sounded, the poet suggests the superiority of art to life because of its changeless record of life's lovely moments. Yet in his recognition of the coldness of this changeless perfection, of the everlasting desolation of that little Greek town whose inhabitants will never return home from the sacrifice, he honestly admits a limitation in response to art that we all feel. Similarly, in "Ode to a Nightingale," though the bird's song, type of all poetry, may lift us for a little while out of this sad and transitory life, may bring us for a moment under the spell of beauty that was not born for death, yet it sinks at last to the word "Forlorn," which sorrowfully tolls us back to our sole selves. It is this search among transient human joys and fading earthly beauties for something that endures, even though we do not, this thrill of triumph in finding it in ideal beauty, this honest admission of our incompleteness in accepting the consolations of ideal beauty, but this dauntless faith in ideal beauty as the greatest good men can know—it is these that make Keats's thought as great as the superb music and imagery that convey it.

EARLY SONNETS

Like this and the following three, Keats's early sonnets (1817 volume) were written in the Petrarchan (Italian) form; most of the later, beginning with "When I Have Fears," coming some pages after this group, in the Shakespearean (English) form.

WRITTEN ON THE DAY THAT MR. LEIGH HUNT LEFT PRISON

What though, for showing truth to flattered state,
Kind Hunt was shut in prison, yet has he,
In his immortal spirit, been as free
As the sky-searching lark, and as elate.
Minion of grandeur! think you he did wait?
Think you he naught but prison walls did see,
Till, so unwilling, thou unturn'dst the key?
Ah, no! far happier, nobler was his fate!
In Spenser's halls he strayed, and bowers fair,
Culling enchanted flowers; and he flew
With daring Milton through the fields of air:
To regions of his own his genius true
Took happy flights. Who shall his fame impair
When thou art dead, and all thy wretched crew?

KEEN, FITFUL GUSTS ARE WHISP'RING HERE AND THERE

Keen, fitful gusts are whisp'ring here and there
Among the bushes half leafless, and dry;
The stars look very cold about the sky,
And I have many miles on foot to fare.
Yet feel I little of the cool bleak air,
Or of the dead leaves rustling drearily,
Or of those silver lamps that burn on high,
Or of the distance from home's pleasant lair:
For I am brimful of the friendliness
That in a little cottage I have found;
Of fair-haired Milton's eloquent distress,
And all his love for gentle Lycid drowned;
Of lovely Laura in her light green dress,
And faithful Petrarch gloriously crowned.

TO ONE WHO HAS BEEN LONG IN CITY PENT

To one who has been long in city pent,
'Tis very sweet to look into the fair
And open face of heaven,—to breathe a prayer
Full in the smile of the blue firmament.
Who is more happy, when, with heart's content,
Fatigued he sinks into some pleasant lair
Of wavy grass, and reads a debonair
And gentle tale of love and languishment?
Returning home at evening, with an ear
Catching the notes of Philomel,—an eye
Watching the sailing cloudlet's bright career,
He mourns that day so soon has glided by:
E'en like the passage of an angel's tear
That falls through the clear ether silently.

ON FIRST LOOKING INTO CHAPMAN'S HOMER

Much have I travelled in the realms of gold,
And many goodly states and kingdoms seen;
Round many western islands have I been
Which bards in fealty to Apollo hold.

Keen, Fitful . . . **4. many miles.** Keats was living in London at the time, frequently visiting Hunt in the Vale of Health, Hampstead. **11–14. Milton . . . Petrarch,** other adventures in reading. *To One Who* . . . **10. Philomel,** the nightingale. *On First* . . . **1. realms of gold,** classical literature. **3. western islands,** European literature of a later date than the classical age.

Oft of one wide expanse had I been told
That deep-browed Homer ruled as his demesne;
Yet did I never breathe its pure serene
Till I heard Chapman speak out loud and bold:
Then felt I like some watcher of the skies
When a new planet swims into his ken;
Or like stout Cortez when with eagle eyes
He stared at the Pacific—and all his men
Looked at each other with a wild surmise—
Silent, upon a peak in Darien.

from ENDYMION

A POETIC ROMANCE

The general theme of *Endymion*, with its modifying ideas, has been stated in the biographical-critical sketch of Keats, page 863. The story opens with a description of the annual sacrificial feast of Pan in Latmos ("Hymn to Pan"). Endymion, young prince of Latmos, comes to the feast melancholy and distraught. Withdrawing with his sister Peona to a little island in a river near by, he tells her of his love for Diana and of three meetings he has already had with the goddess. Peona reproaches him for his madness and for his dreamy, inactive life. Several days later (Book II), wandering brainsick in the forest, Endymion sees a golden butterfly, follows it, and loses it. A wood nymph bids him wander on. From a cavern an airy voice bids him descend into "The silent mysteries of the earth" (in part, a symbol of poetry). He wanders among the enchantments of the subterranean world, encountering many wonders. There he meets two lovers, Alpheus and Arethusa, learns of the curse that had been put upon them, feels sympathy for them, and prays Diana to assist him in releasing them. Then he goes under the sea. In the depths of the sea (Book III), he recognizes other claims upon his benevolence and humanitarianism—another pair of lovers, the sea god Glaucus and the nymph Scylla, enchanted by the jealous Circe (queen of the senses). His sympathetic intercession for these and for Alpheus and Arethusa takes him a further step in his pursuit of divine essence. With the Indian Maiden (Book IV), he passes through the fourth and final stage of his ascent to fellowship with divine essence. He falls in love with her, first because he pities her (see her "Roundelay to Sorrow"). At the end of a voyage through the air with her, he decides to abandon the quest of Diana for her, a human lover, but at this point loses her. At the end, the Indian Maiden reveals herself as Diana, tells him that through sympathy for others and love for a human being he has passed his probation, and gives herself to him.

6. demesne, possession. **8. Chapman.** George Chapman's *Iliad* was published in 1611, his *Odyssey* in 1614. **11. Cortez,** a mistake for Balboa. Keats had seen Titian's picture of Cortez "with eagle eyes."

from BOOK I

[Credo]

A thing of beauty is a joy for ever:
Its loveliness increases; it will never
Pass into nothingness; but still will keep
A bower quiet for us, and a sleep
Full of sweet dreams, and health, and quiet breathing.
Therefore, on every morrow, are we wreathing
A flowery band to bind us to the earth,
Spite of despondence, of the inhuman dearth
Of noble natures, of the gloomy days,
Of all the unhealthy and o'er-darkened ways
Made for our searching: yes, in spite of all,
Some shape of beauty moves away the pall
From our dark spirits. Such the sun, the moon,
Trees old, and young, sprouting a shady boon
For simple sheep; and such are daffodils
With the green world they live in; and clear rills
That for themselves a cooling covert make
'Gainst the hot season; the mid forest brake,
Rich with a sprinkling of fair musk-rose blooms:
And such too is the grandeur of the dooms
We have imagined for the mighty dead;
All lovely tales that we have heard or read:
An endless fountain of immortal drink,
Pouring unto us from the heaven's brink.

Nor do we merely feel these essences
For one short hour; no, even as the trees
That whisper round a temple become soon
Dear as the temple's self, so does the moon,
The passion poesy, glories infinite,
Haunt us till they become a cheering light
Unto our souls, and bound to us so fast,
That, whether there be shine, or gloom o'ercast,
They always must be with us, or we die.

[Schedule]

Therefore, 'tis with full happiness that I
Will trace the story of Endymion.
The very music of the name has gone
Into my being, and each pleasant scene
Is growing fresh before me as the green
Of our own vallies: so I will begin
Now while I cannot hear the city's din;
Now while the early budders are just new,
And run in mazes of the youngest hue

34. Therefore. Believing as he does, he traces the story of Endymion, one of the "lovely tales," a "flowery band to bind us to the earth." **39. so I will begin.** What follows is the poet's calendar of his present work. Note that every month and season is presented sensuously.

About old forests; while the willow trails
Its delicate amber; and the dairy pails
Bring home increase of milk. And, as the year
Grows lush in juicy stalks, I'll smoothly steer
My little boat, for many quiet hours,
With streams that deepen freshly into bowers.
Many and many a verse I hope to write,
Before the daisies, vermeil-rimmed and white,
Hide in deep herbage; and ere yet the bees
Hum about globes of clover and sweet peas,
I must be near the middle of my story.
O may no wintry season, bare and hoary,
See it half finished: but let Autumn bold,
With universal tinge of sober gold,
Be all about me when I make an end.
And now at once, adventuresome, I send
My herald thought into a wilderness:
There let its trumpet blow, and quickly dress
My uncertain path with green, that I may speed
Easily onward, thorough flowers and weed. . . .

[Hymn to Pan]

"O thou, whose mighty palace roof doth hang
From jagged trunks, and overshadoweth
Eternal whispers, glooms, the birth, life, death
Of unseen flowers in heavy peacefulness;
Who lov'st to see the hamadryads dress
Their ruffled locks where meeting hazels darken;
And through whole solemn hours dost sit, and hearken
The dreary melody of bedded reeds—
In desolate places, where dank moisture breeds
The pipy hemlock to strange overgrowth;
Bethinking thee, how melancholy loth
Thou wast to lose fair Syrinx—do thou now,
By thy love's milky brow!
By all the trembling mazes that she ran,
Hear us, great Pan!

"O thou, for whose soul-soothing quiet, turtles
Passion their voices cooingly 'mong myrtles,
What time thou wanderest at eventide
Through sunny meadows, that outskirt the side
Of thine enmossèd realms: O thou, to whom
Broad-leavèd fig trees even now foredoom
Their ripened fruitage; yellow-girted bees
Their golden honeycombs; our village leas
Their fairest blossomed beans and poppied corn;
The chuckling linnet its five young unborn,
To sing for thee; low-creeping strawberries
Their summer coolness; pent-up butterflies
Their freckled wings; yea, the fresh-budding year
All its completions—be quickly near,
By every wind that nods the mountain pine,
O forester divine!

"Thou, to whom every faun and satyr flies
For willing service; whether to surprise
The squatted hare while in half-sleeping fit;
Or upward ragged precipices flit
To save poor lambkins from the eagle's maw;
Or by mysterious enticement draw
Bewildered shepherds to their path again;
Or to tread breathless round the frothy main,
And gather up all fancifullest shells
For thee to tumble into Naiads' cells,
And, being hidden, laugh at their out-peeping;
Or to delight thee with fantastic leaping,
The while they pelt each other on the crown
With silvery oak-apples, and fir-cones brown—
By all the echoes that about thee ring,
Hear us, O satyr king!

"O Hearkener to the loud-clapping shears,
While ever and anon to his shorn peers
A ram goes bleating: Winder of the horn,
When snouted wild-boars routing tender corn
Anger our huntsmen: Breather round our farms,
To keep off mildews, and all weather harms:
Strange ministrant of undescribèd sounds,
That come a-swooning over hollow grounds,
And winter drearily on barren moors:
Dread opener of the mysterious doors
Leading to universal knowledge—see,
Great son of Dryope,
The many that are come to pay their vows
With leaves about their brows!

"Be still the unimaginable lodge
For solitary thinkings; such as dodge
Conception to the very bourne of heaven,
Then leave the naked brain: be still the leaven,
That spreading in this dull and clodded earth
Gives it a touch ethereal—a new birth:
Be still a symbol of immensity;
A firmament reflected in a sea;
An element filling the space between;
An unknown—but no more: we humbly screen
With uplift hands our foreheads, lowly bending,
And giving out a shout most heaven-rending,
Conjure thee to receive our humble Paean,
Upon thy Mount Lycean!" . . .

293. the unimaginable lodge. Note the Neo-Platonic interpretation of nature beginning here. Compare Shelley's "Adonais," stanza 43.

[Pleasure Thermometer]

"Wherein lies happiness? In that which becks
Our ready minds to fellowship divine,
A fellowship with essence; till we shine,
Full alchemized, and free of space. Behold
The clear religion of heaven! Fold
A rose leaf round thy finger's taperness,
And soothe thy lips: hist, when the airy stress
Of music's kiss impregnates the free winds,
And with sympathetic touch unbinds
Aeolian magic from their lucid wombs:
Then old songs waken from enclouded tombs;
Old ditties sigh above their father's grave;
Ghosts of melodious prophesyings rave
Round every spot where trod Apollo's foot;
Bronze clarions awake, and faintly bruit,
Where long ago a giant battle was;
And, from the turf, a lullaby doth pass
In every place where infant Orpheus slept.
Feel we these things?—that moment have we stept
Into a sort of oneness, and our state
Is like a floating spirit's. But there are
Richer entanglements, enthralments far
More self-destroying, leading, by degrees,
To the chief intensity: the crown of these
Is made of love and friendship, and sits high
Upon the forehead of humanity.
All its more ponderous and bulky worth
Is friendship, whence there ever issues forth
A steady splendour; but at the tip-top,
There hangs by unseen film, an orbèd drop
Of light, and that is love: its influence,
Thrown in our eyes, genders a novel sense,
At which we start and fret; till in the end,
Melting into its radiance, we blend,
Mingle, and so become a part of it,—
Nor with aught else can our souls interknit
So wingedly: when we combine therewith,
Life's self is nourished by its proper pith,
And we are nurtured like a pelican brood.
Aye, so delicious is the unsating food,
That men, who might have towered in the van
Of all the congregated world, to fan
And winnow from the coming step of time
All chaff of custom, wipe away all slime
Left by men-slugs and human serpentry,
Have been content to let occasion die,
Whilst they did sleep in love's elysium.
And, truly, I would rather be struck dumb,
Than speak against this ardent listlessness:
For I have ever thought that it might bless
The world with benefits unknowingly;
As does the nightingale, up-perchèd high,
And cloistered among cool and bunchèd leaves—
She sings but to her love, nor e'er conceives
How tiptoe Night holds back her dark-grey hood.
Just so may love, although 'tis understood
The mere commingling of passionate breath,
Produce more than our searching witnesseth:
What I know not: but who, of men, can tell
That flowers would bloom, or that green fruit would swell
To melting pulp, that fish would have bright mail,
The earth its dower of river, wood, and vale,
The meadows runnels, runnels pebble-stones,
The seed its harvest, or the lute its tones,
Tones ravishment, or ravishment its sweet,
If human souls did never kiss and greet?

"Now, if this earthly love has power to make
Men's being mortal, immortal; to shake
Ambition from their memories, and brim
Their measure of content; what merest whim,
Seems all this poor endeavour after fame,
To one, who keeps within his stedfast aim
A love immortal, an immortal too." . . .

777. Wherein lies happiness? These lines (part of Endymion's defense of himself for dreaming and loving) were inserted while the poem was in press. Keats called them his "pleasure thermometer," that is, a graduated arrangement of the themes of poetry. The lines are also, of course, a justification of his telling the story of Endymion, and a suggestion of his Neo-Platonic theme.

from BOOK IV

[Roundelay to Sorrow]

[Sung by the Indian Maiden to Endymion. It wins his pity, which leads to love.]

"O Sorrow,
Why dost borrow
The natural hue of health, from vermeil lips?—
To give maiden blushes
To the white rose bushes?
Or is't thy dewy hand the daisy tips?

"O Sorrow,
Why dost borrow
The lustrous passion from a falcon-eye?—
To give the glow-worm light?
Or, on a moonless night,
To tinge, on syren shores, the salt sea-spry?

"O Sorrow,
Why dost borrow

The mellow ditties from a mourning tongue?
To give at evening pale
Unto the nightingale,
That thou mayst listen the cold dews among?

"O Sorrow,
Why dost borrow
Heart's lightness from the merriment of May?—
A lover would not tread
A cowslip on the head,
Though he should dance from eve till peep of day—
Nor any drooping flower
Held sacred for thy bower,
Wherever he may sport himself and play.

"To Sorrow,
I bade good-morrow,
And thought to leave her far away behind;
But cheerly, cheerly,
She loves me dearly;
She is so constant to me, and so kind:
I would deceive her,
And so leave her,
But ah! she is so constant and so kind." . . .

SONNETS

ON THE SEA

It keeps eternal whisperings around
Desolate shores, and with its mighty swell
Gluts twice ten thousand caverns, till the spell
Of Hecate leaves them their old shadowy sound.
Often 'tis in such gentle temper found,
That scarcely will the very smallest shell
Be moved for days from where it sometime fell,
When last the winds of Heaven were unbound.
Oh ye! who have your eye-balls vexed and tired,
Feast them upon the wideness of the Sea;
Oh ye! whose ears are dinned with uproar rude,
Or fed too much with cloying melody—
Sit ye near some old cavern's mouth, and brood
Until ye start, as if the sea-nymphs quired!

ON SEEING THE ELGIN MARBLES

My spirit is too weak—mortality
Weighs heavily on me like unwilling sleep,
And each imagined pinnacle and steep
Of godlike hardship, tells me I must die
Like a sick eagle looking at the sky.
Yet 'tis a gentle luxury to weep
That I have not the cloudy winds to keep,
Fresh for the opening of the morning's eye.
Such dim-conceivèd glories of the brain
Bring round the heart an indescribable feud;
So do these wonders a most dizzy pain,
That mingles Grecian grandeur with the rude
Wasting of old Time—with a billowy main—
A sun—a shadow of a magnitude.

ON SITTING DOWN TO READ "KING LEAR" ONCE AGAIN

O golden-tongued romance, with sérene lute!
Fair plumèd Syren, Queen of far-away!
Leave melodizing on this wintry day,
Shut up thine olden pages, and be mute:
Adieu! for, once again, the fierce dispute
Betwixt damnation and impassioned clay
Must I burn through; once more humbly assay
The bitter-sweet of this Shakespearian fruit:
Chief Poet! and ye clouds of Albion,
Begetters of our deep eternal theme!
When through the old oak forest I am gone,
Let me not wander in a barren dream,
But when I am consumèd in the fire,
Give me new Phoenix-wings to fly at my desire.

WHEN I HAVE FEARS THAT I MAY CEASE TO BE

This sonnet tells how the poet feels under the shadow of *two* fears of death—that he may die before he writes himself out, and also before he may consummate his love.

Note that this and the next two sonnets here reprinted are in the Shakespearean form.

When I have fears that I may cease to be
Before my pen has gleaned my teeming brain,
Before high-pilèd books, in charact'ry,
Hold like rich garners the full ripened grain;
When I behold, upon the night's starred face,
Huge cloudy symbols of a high romance,
And think that I may never live to trace
Their shadows, with the magic hand of chance;
And when I feel, fair creature of an hour,
That I shall never look upon thee more,

173–81. "To Sorrow . . . so kind." These nine lines are the motto of Thomas Hardy's great novel *The Return of the Native*. **4. Hecate,** the dark goddess of magic and witchcraft, usually associated with the underworld.

On Sitting . . . **6. Betwixt damnation and impassioned clay,** between Fate and human desires and aspirations. *King Lear* is a fate drama of sorts. Compare "As flies to wanton boys, are we to the gods," Act IV, sc. 1, l. 38.

Never have relish in the faery power
  Of unreflecting love;—then on the shore
Of the wide world I stand alone, and think
Till love and fame to nothingness do sink.

THE HUMAN SEASONS

Four seasons fill the measure of the year;
  There are four seasons in the mind of man:
He has his lusty Spring, when fancy clear
  Takes in all beauty with an easy span:
He has his Summer, when luxuriously
  Spring's honied cud of youthful thought he loves
To ruminate, and by such dreaming high
  Is nearest unto heaven: quiet coves
His soul has in its Autumn, when his wings
  He furleth close; contented so to look
On mists in idleness—to let fair things
  Pass by unheeded as a threshold brook.
He has his Winter too of pale misfeature,
Or else he would forego his mortal nature.

TO FANNY

I cry your mercy—pity—love!—aye, love!
  Merciful love that tantalizes not,
One-thoughted, never-wandering, guileless love,
  Unmasked, and being seen—without a blot!
O! let me have thee whole,—all—all—be mine!
  That shape, that fairness, that sweet minor zest
Of love, your kiss—those hands, those eyes divine,
  That warm, white, lucent, million-pleasured
    breast,—
Yourself—your soul—in pity give me all,
  Withhold no atom's atom or I die,
Or living on perhaps, your wretched thrall,
  Forget, in the midst of idle misery,
Life's purposes,—the palate of my mind
Losing its gust, and my ambition blind!

ON THE GRASSHOPPER AND CRICKET

This sonnet was written as the result of a challenge from Leigh Hunt. It is anticipative of "Ode to a Nightingale" (compare stanza 7).

The poetry of earth is never dead:
  When all the birds are faint with the hot sun,
  And hide in cooling trees, a voice will run
From hedge to hedge about the new-mown mead;
That is the Grasshopper's—he takes the lead
  In summer luxury,—he has never done
  With his delights; for when tired out with fun
He rests at ease beneath some pleasant weed.
The poetry of earth is ceasing never:

To Fanny. **14. gust,** taste.

  On a lone winter evening, when the frost
    Has wrought a silence, from the stove there
      shrills
The Cricket's song, in warmth increasing ever,
  And seems to one in drowsiness half lost,
    The Grasshopper's among some grassy hills.

TO SLEEP

O soft embalmer of the still midnight,
  Shutting, with careful fingers and benign,
Our gloom-pleas'd eyes, embower'd from the light,
  Enshaded in forgetfulness divine:
O soothest Sleep! if so it please thee, close
  In midst of this thine hymn my willing eyes,
Or wait the "Amen," ere thy poppy throws
  Around my bed its lulling charities.
Then save me, or the passèd day will shine
Upon my pillow, breeding many woes,—
  Save me from curious Conscience, that still
    lords
Its strength for darkness, burrowing like a mole;
  Turn the key deftly in the oilèd wards,
And seal the hushèd Casket of my Soul.

STANZAS

IN A DREAR-NIGHTED DECEMBER

An early (1818) statement of one of Keats's chief lyrical themes—the transiency of joy and beauty. Happiness belongs only to childhood and early youth, the unreflective period of life; "to think is to be full of sorrow" ("Ode to a Nightingale," l. 27).

I

In a drear-nighted December,
    Too happy, happy tree,
Thy branches ne'er remember
    Their green felicity:
  The north cannot undo them,
  With a sleety whistle through them;
  Nor frozen thawings glue them
    From budding at the prime.

2

In a drear-nighted December,
    Too happy, happy brook,
Thy bubblings ne'er remember
    Apollo's summer look;
  But with a sweet forgetting,
  They stay their crystal fretting,
  Never, never petting
    About the frozen time.

Stanzas. **15. petting,** fretting.

3

Ah! would 'twere so with many
A gentle girl and boy!
But were there ever any
Writhed not at passèd joy?
To know the change and feel it,
When there is none to heal it,
Nor numbèd sense to steal it,
Was never said in rhyme.

ODE

WRITTEN ON THE BLANK PAGE BEFORE BEAUMONT AND FLETCHER'S TRAGI-COMEDY, *THE FAIR MAID OF THE INN.*

Bards of Passion and of Mirth,
Ye have left your souls on earth!
Have ye souls in heaven too,
Double-lived in regions new?
Yes, and those of heaven commune
With the spheres of sun and moon;
With the noise of fountains wond'rous
And the parle of voices thund'rous;
With the whisper of heaven's trees
And one another, in soft ease
Seated on Elysian lawns
Browsed by none but Dian's fawns;
Underneath large blue-bells tented,
Where the daisies are rose-scented,
And the rose herself has got
Perfume which on earth is not;
Where the nightingale doth sing
Not a senseless, trancèd thing,
But divine melodious truth;
Philosophic numbers smooth;
Tales and golden histories
Of heaven and its mysteries.

Thus ye live on high, and then
On the earth ye live again;
And the souls ye left behind you
Teach us, here, the way to find you,
Where your other souls are joying,
Never slumbered, never cloying.
Here, your earth-born souls still speak
To mortals, of their little week;
Of their sorrows and delights;
Of their passions and their spites;
Of their glory and their shame;
What doth strengthen and what maim.
Thus ye teach us, every day,
Wisdom, though fled far away.

Bards of Passion and of Mirth,
Ye have left your souls on earth!
Ye have souls in heaven too,
Double-lived in regions new!

FRAGMENT OF AN ODE TO MAIA

WRITTEN ON MAY DAY, 1818

Mother of Hermes! and still youthful Maia!
May I sing to thee
As thou wast hymned on the shores of Baiae?
Or may I woo thee
In earlier Sicilian? or thy smiles
Seek as they once were sought, in Grecian isles,
By bards who died content on pleasant sward,
Leaving great verse unto a little clan?
O, give me their old vigour, and unheard
Save of the quiet Primrose, and the span
Of heaven and few ears,
Rounded by thee, my song should die away
Content as theirs,
Rich in the simple worship of a day.

LINES ON THE MERMAID TAVERN

Souls of Poets dead and gone,
What Elysium have ye known,
Happy field or mossy cavern,
Choicer than the Mermaid Tavern?
Have ye tippled drink more fine
Than mine host's Canary wine?
Or are fruits of Paradise
Sweeter than those dainty pies
Of venison? O generous food!
Drest as though bold Robin Hood
Would, with his Maid Marian,
Sup and bowse from horn and can.

I have heard that on a day
Mine host's sign-board flew away,
Nobody knew whither, till
An astrologer's old quill
To a sheepskin gave the story,
Said he saw you in your glory,

Stanzas. **21. To know the change and feel it.** Professor J. M. Murry and other scholars prefer a variant reading, "The feel of *not* to feel it." *Ode.* **4. Double-lived.** With the following half-playful notion of poetic immortality, compare Shelley's in *Adonais,* stanzas 42–46.

Lines on the Mermaid Tavern. **4. Mermaid Tavern.** Here, according to tradition, Ben Jonson and Shakespeare and their cronies had their combats of wit. Keats is notable for his return to the Elizabethans. **12. bowse,** variant of "booze."

Underneath a new old sign
Sipping beverage divine,
And pledging with contented smack
The Mermaid in the Zodiac.

Souls of Poets dead and gone,
What Elysium have ye known,
Happy field or mossy cavern,
Choicer than the Mermaid Tavern?

THE EVE OF ST. AGNES

In January, 1819, after his meeting with Fanny Brawne, Keats visited old Mr. Dilke at Chichester and a Mr. Snook at Bedhampton. He wrote his brother and sister: "Nothing worth speaking of happened at either place. I took down some thin paper and wrote on it a little poem called St. Agnes' Eve."

To what has already been said (page 864) about the poem, the following general suggestions for studying it are added. Note carefully the chief elements: (1) The *framework*—setting (including cultural age, Gothic castle, the ascetic devotion of the Beadsman contrasted with the "argent revelry" of the ball in the great castle hall, the superstition about St. Agnes' Eve which makes the action possible, the weather, and so on); (2) the *central picture* of Madeline (stanzas 24 ff.); (3) the *story proper*—a rather slight one of elopement, made possible by Madeline's belief in the superstition and the old nurse's complicity, the confusion of the ball and its aftermath, and the state of the weather. Observe closely the details and the significance of contrasts; for example, the difference between the spectral old age of the Beadsman and Angela and the blooming youth of Madeline and Porphyro, between the ball-room and Madeline's room, between the music of the ball and the music of Porphyro's lute, between the interior of Madeline's room and the outside storm. Contrasted also are the love of Madeline and Porphyro and the hatred of their two families, and, in the last stanza, life and death. Note the suggested meaning of the last scene at the castle gate (and what lies behind it) and in the storm the lovers face.

1

St. Agnes' Eve—Ah, bitter chill it was!
The owl, for all his feathers, was a-cold;
The hare limped trembling through the frozen grass,
And silent was the flock in woolly fold:
Numb were the Beadsman's fingers, while he told
His rosary, and while his frosted breath,
Like pious incense from a censer old,
Seemed taking flight for heaven, without a death,
Past the sweet Virgin's picture, while his prayer he saith.

1. St. Agnes' Eve, January 20, supposed to be the coldest day of the year. **5. Beadsman's.** A beadsman was, literally, a *praying* man. **told,** numbered the beads on, during prayer.

2

His prayer he saith, this patient, holy man;
Then takes his lamp, and riseth from his knees,
And back returneth, meagre, barefoot, wan,
Along the chapel aisle by slow degrees:
The sculptured dead, on each side, seem to freeze,
Emprisoned in black, purgatorial rails:
Knights, ladies, praying in dumb orat'ries,
He passeth by; and his weak spirit fails
To think how they may ache in icy hoods and mails.

3

Northward he turneth through a little door,
And scarce three steps, ere Music's golden tongue
Flattered to tears this aged man and poor;
But no—already had his deathbell rung;
The joys of all his life were said and sung:
His was harsh penance on St. Agnes' Eve:
Another way he went, and soon among
Rough ashes sat he for his soul's reprieve,
And all night kept awake, for sinners' sake to grieve.

4

That ancient Beadsman heard the prelude soft;
And so it chanced, for many a door was wide,
From hurry to and fro. Soon, up aloft,
The silver, snarling trumpets 'gan to chide:
The level chambers, ready with their pride,
Were glowing to receive a thousand guests:
The carvèd angels, ever eager-eyed,
Stared, where upon their heads the cornice rests,
With hair blown back, and wings put cross-wise on their breasts.

5

At length burst in the argent revelry,
With plume, tiara, and all rich array,
Numerous as shadows haunting faerily
The brain, new stuffed, in youth, with triumphs gay
Of old romance. These let us wish away,
And turn, sole-thoughted, to one Lady there,
Whose heart had brooded, all that wintry day,
On Love, and winged St. Agnes' saintly care,
As she had heard old dames full many times declare.

15. black, purgatorial rails. Most editors assume that "rails" means *railings*—"black, purgatorial" because the sculptured dead are in Purgatory. But "rails" may mean *robes* (from O. E. *hrægl*). If so, the dead are sculptured in garments appropriate for Purgatory. **16. dumb orat'ries.** An oratory is a small chapel for prayer; **dumb** because occupied by the sculptured figures of the knights and ladies buried there. **37. argent,** shining.

6

They told her how, upon St. Agnes' Eve,
Young virgins might have visions of delight,
And soft adorings from their loves receive
Upon the honeyed middle of the night,
If ceremonies due they did aright;
As, supperless to bed they must retire,
And couch supine their beauties, lilly white;
Nor look behind, nor sideways, but require
Of Heaven with upward eyes for all that they desire.

7

Full of this whim was thoughtful Madeline:
The music, yearning like a God in pain,
She scarcely heard: her maiden eyes divine,
Fixed on the floor, saw many a sweeping train
Pass by—she heeded not at all: in vain
Came many a tiptoe, amorous cavalier,
And back retired; not cooled by high disdain,
But she saw not: her heart was otherwhere:
She sighed for Agnes' dreams, the sweetest of the year.

8

She danced along with vague, regardless eyes,
Anxious her lips, her breathing quick and short:
The hallowed hour was near at hand: she sighs
Amid the timbrels, and the thronged resort
Of whisperers in anger, or in sport;
'Mid looks of love, defiance, hate, and scorn,
Hoodwinked with faery fancy; all amort,
Save to St. Agnes and her lambs unshorn,
And all the bliss to be before to-morrow morn.

9

So, purposing each moment to retire,
She lingered still. Meantime, across the moors,
Had come young Porphyro, with heart on fire
For Madeline. Beside the portal doors,
Buttressed from moonlight, stands he, and implores
All saints to give him sight of Madeline,
But for one moment in the tedious hours,
That he might gaze and worship all unseen;
Perchance speak, kneel, touch, kiss—in sooth such things have been.

60. tiptoe, amorous cavalier. Note how this characterization sets off Porphyro when he enters. **70. amort,** as if lifeless. **71. lambs.** Unshorn lambs offered on St. Agnes' day were later shorn, and the nuns wove the wool into cloth. (Compare ll. 115–17.) **77. Buttressed from moonlight.** Note the evocative power of the image—suggesting the loom of the Gothic castle. Compare Scott's "Lochinvar."

10

He ventures in: let no buzzed whisper tell:
All eyes be muffled, or a hundred swords
Will storm his heart, Love's fev'rous citadel:
For him, those chambers held barbarian hordes,
Hyena foemen, and hot-blooded lords,
Whose very dogs would execrations howl
Against his lineage: not one breast affords
Him any mercy, in that mansion foul,
Save one old beldame, weak in body and in soul.

11

Ah, happy chance! the agèd creature came,
Shuffling along with ivory-headed wand,
To where he stood, hid from the torch's flame,
Behind a broad hall-pillar, far beyond
The sound of merriment and chorus bland:
He startled her; but soon she knew his face,
And grasped his fingers in her palsied hand,
Saying, "Mercy, Porphyro! hie thee from this place!
They are all here to-night, the whole blood-thirsty race!

12

"Get hence! get hence! there's dwarfish Hildebrand;
He had a fever late, and in the fit
He cursèd thee and thine, both house and land:
Then there's that old Lord Maurice, not a whit
More tame for his gray hairs—Alas me! flit!
Flit like a ghost away."—"Ah, Gossip dear,
We're safe enough; here in this arm-chair sit,
And tell me how"—"Good Saints! not here, not here;
Follow me, child, or else these stones will be thy bier."

13

He followed through a lowly archèd way,
Brushing the cobwebs with his lofty plume;
And as she muttered "Well-a—well-a-day!"
He found him in a little moonlight room,
Pale, latticed, chill, and silent as a tomb.
"Now tell me where is Madeline," said he,
"O tell me, Angela, by the holy loom
Which none but secret sisterhood may see,
When they St. Agnes' wool are weaving, piously."

14

"St. Agnes! Ah! it is St. Agnes' Eve—
Yet men will murder upon holy days:

99. the whole blood-thirsty race. Compare the situation in *Romeo and Juliet.* **105. Gossip,** godmother—**no disrespect.**

Thou must hold water in a witch's sieve,
And be liege-lord of all the Elves and Fays,
To venture so: it fills me with amaze
To see thee, Porphyro!—St. Agnes' Eve!
God's help! my lady fair the conjuror plays
This very night: good angels her deceive!
But let me laugh awhile, I've mickle time to grieve."

15

Feebly she laugheth in the languid moon,
While Porphyro upon her face doth look,
Like puzzled urchin on an aged crone
Who keepeth closed a wond'rous riddle-book,
As spectacled she sits in chimney nook.
But soon his eyes grew brilliant, when she told
His lady's purpose; and he scarce could brook
Tears, at the thought of those enchantments cold,
And Madeline asleep in lap of legends old.

16

Sudden a thought came like a full-blown rose,
Flushing his brow, and in his painèd heart
Made purple riot: then doth he propose
A stratagem, that makes the beldame start:
"A cruel man and impious thou art:
Sweet lady, let her pray, and sleep, and dream
Alone with her good angels, far apart
From wicked men like thee. Go, go! I deem
Thou canst not surely be the same that thou didst seem."

17

"I will not harm her, by all saints I swear,"
Quoth Porphyro: "O may I ne'er find grace
When my weak voice shall whisper its last prayer,
If one of her soft ringlets I displace,
Or look with ruffian passion in her face:
Good Angela, believe me by these tears;
Or I will, even in a moment's space,
Awake, with horrid shout, my foemen's ears,
And beard them, though they be more fanged than wolves and bears."

18

"Ah! why wilt thou affright a feeble soul?
A poor, weak, palsy-stricken, churchyard thing,
Whose passing-bell may ere the midnight toll;
Whose prayers for thee, each morn and evening,
Were never missed."—Thus plaining, doth she bring
A gentler speech from burning Porphyro;
So woful, and of such deep sorrowing,
That Angela gives promise she will do
Whatever he shall wish, betide her weal or woe.

19

Which was, to lead him, in close secrecy,
Even to Madeline's chamber, and there hide
Him in a closet, of such privacy
That he might see her beauty unespied,
And win perhaps that night a peerless bride,
While legioned faeries paced the coverlet,
And pale enchantment held her sleepy-eyed.
Never on such a night have lovers met,
Since Merlin paid his Demon all the monstrous debt.

20

"It shall be as thou wishest," said the Dame:
"All cates and dainties shall be storèd there
Quickly on this feast-night: by the tambour frame
Her own lute thou wilt see: no time to spare,
For I am slow and feeble, and scarce dare
On such a catering trust my dizzy head.
Wait here, my child, with patience; kneel in prayer
The while: Ah! thou must needs the lady wed,
Or may I never leave my grave among the dead."

21

So saying, she hobbled off with busy fear.
The lover's endless minutes slowly passed;
The dame returned, and whispered in his ear
To follow her; with agèd eyes aghast
From fright of dim espial. Safe at last,
Through many a dusky gallery, they gain
The maiden's chamber, silken, hushed, and chaste;
Where Porphyro took covert, pleased amain.
His poor guide hurried back with agues in her brain.

22

Her falt'ring hand upon the balustrade,
Old Angela was feeling for the stair,
When Madeline, St. Agnes' charmèd maid,
Rose, like a missioned spirit, unaware:
With silver taper's light, and pious care,

126. mickle, much. **133. brook,** restrain. **135. And Madeline asleep in lap of legends old,** one of the notably beautiful one-line pictures in the Alexandrine (the hexameter line of a Spenserian stanza). Note others.

171. Demon, his legendary father. **173. cates,** dainty viands. The old Nurse realizes that Madeline, who has gone to bed supperless (l. 51), will need refreshment for the hard journey before her. **174. tambour frame,** drum-shaped embroidery frame. **188. amain,** exceedingly.

She turned, and down the aged gossip led
To a safe level matting. Now prepare,
Young Porphyro, for gazing on that bed;
She comes, she comes again, like ring-dove frayed
and fled.

23

Out went the taper as she hurried in;
Its little smoke, in pallid moonshine, died:
She closed the door, she panted, all akin
To spirits of the air, and visions wide:
No uttered syllable, or, woe betide!
But to her heart, her heart was voluble,
Paining with eloquence her balmy side;
As though a tongueless nightingale should swell
Her throat in vain, and die, heart-stifled, in her
dell.

24

A casement high and triple-arched there was,
All garlanded with carven imag'ries
Of fruits, and flowers, and bunches of knot-grass,
And diamonded with panes of quaint device,
Innumerable of stains and splendid dyes,
As are the tiger-moth's deep-damasked wings;
And in the midst, 'mong thousand heraldries,
And twilight saints, and dim emblazonings,
A shielded scutcheon blushed with blood of queens
and kings.

25

Full on this casement shone the wintry moon,
And threw warm gules on Madeline's fair breast,
As down she knelt for heaven's grace and boon;
Rose-bloom fell on her hands, together prest,
And on her silver cross soft amethyst,
And on her hair a glory, like a saint:
She seemed a splendid angel, newly drest,
Save wings, for heaven:—Porphyro grew faint:
She knelt, so pure a thing, so free from mortal taint.

26

Anon his heart revives: her vespers done,
Of all its wreathèd pearls her hair she frees;
Unclasps her warmèd jewels one by one;
Loosens her fragrant boddice; by degrees
Her rich attire creeps rustling to her knees:
Half-hidden, like a mermaid in sea-weed,
Pensive awhile she dreams awake, and sees,
In fancy, fair St. Agnes in her bed,
But dares not look behind, or all the charm is fled.

27

Soon, trembling in her soft and chilly nest,
In sort of wakeful swoon, perplexed she lay,
Until the poppied warmth of sleep oppressed
Her soothèd limbs, and soul fatigued away;
Flown, like a thought, until the morrow-day;
Blissfully havened both from joy and pain;
Clasped like a missal where swart Paynims pray;
Blinded alike from sunshine and from rain,
As though a rose should shut, and be a bud again.

28

Stol'n to this paradise, and so entranced,
Porphyro gazed upon her empty dress,
And listened to her breathing, if it chanced
To wake into a slumberous tenderness;
Which when he heard, that minute did he bless,
And breathed himself: then from the closet crept,
Noiseless as fear in a wide wilderness,
And over the hushed carpet, silent, stept,
And 'tween the curtains peeped, where, lo!—how
fast she slept.

29

Then by the bed-side, where the faded moon
Made a dim, silver twilight, soft he set
A table, and, half anguished, threw thereon
A cloth of woven crimson, gold, and jet:—
O for some drowsy Morphean amulet!
The boisterous, midnight, festive clarion,
The kettle-drum, and far-heard clarinet,
Affray his ears, though but in dying tone:—
The hall-door shuts again, and all the noise is gone.

30

And still she slept an azure-lidded sleep,
In blanchèd linen, smooth, and lavendered,
While he from forth the closet brought a heap
Of candied apple, quince, and plum, and gourd;
With jellies soother than the creamy curd,
And lucent syrops, tinct with cinnamon;
Manna and dates, in argosy transferred
From Fez; and spicèd dainties, every one,
From silken Samarcand to cedared Lebanon.

198. frayed, frightened. **208. A casement high, ff.** A glance at photographic reproductions of the original MS. of the poem (in Amy Lowell's *John Keats*, 2 vols., Houghton Mifflin, 1925, Vol. II, between pp. 168–69) will show that such poetry is the result of revision after revision until the right images and words are found. Compare, also, the similar reproduction of stanzas 30–38 in M. R. Ridley's *Keats' Craftsmanship*, Oxford Press, 1933, pp. 162–63. **218. gules,** heraldic term for red—the exactly right word for the *center* of the central picture.

241. clasped . . . pray, shut (as with clasps) like a prayer book where pagans (heathen) pray—hence secreted. **257. Morphean amulet,** sleep-producing charm (Morpheus was god of sleep). **266. soother.** smoother.

31

These delicates he heaped with glowing hand
On golden dishes and in baskets bright
Of wreathèd silver: sumptuous they stand
In the retired quiet of the night,
Filling the chilly room with perfume light.—
"And now, my love, my seraph fair, awake!
Thou art my heaven, and I thine eremite:
Open thine eyes, for meek St. Agnes' sake,
Or I shall drowse beside thee, so my soul doth ache."

32

Thus whispering, his warm, unnervèd arm
Sank in her pillow. Shaded was her dream
By the dusk curtains:—'twas a midnight charm
Impossible to melt as icèd stream:
The lustrous salvers in the moonlight gleam;
Broad golden fringe upon the carpet lies:
It seemed he never, never could redeem
From such a stedfast spell his lady's eyes;
So mused awhile, entoiled in woofèd phantasies.

33

Awakening up, he took her hollow lute,—
Tumultuous,—and, in chords that tenderest be,
He played an ancient ditty, long since mute,
In Provence called "La belle dame sans mercy":
Close to her ear touching the melody;—
Wherewith disturbed, she uttered a soft moan:
He ceased—she panted quick—and suddenly
Her blue affrayèd eyes wide open shone:
Upon his knees he sank, pale as smooth-sculptured stone.

34

Her eyes were open, but she still beheld,
Now wide awake, the vision of her sleep:
There was a painful change, that nigh expelled
The blisses of her dream so pure and deep
At which fair Madeline began to weep,
And moan forth witless words with many a sigh;
While still her gaze on Porphyro would keep;
Who knelt, with joinèd hands and piteous eye,
Fearing to move or speak, she looked so dreamingly.

35

"Ah, Porphyro!" said she, "but even now
Thy voice was at sweet tremble in mine ear,

277. eremite, hermit; here, devoted follower. **292. In Provence called . . . mercy."** Alain Chartier, a medieval French poet of Provence (one of the old kingdoms of France), wrote a poem with this title. Keats got no more from it than the title. Compare his ballad of the same title. The phrase means "The beautiful lady without pity."

Made tunable with every sweetest vow;
And those sad eyes were spiritual and clear:
How changed thou art! how pallid, chill, and drear!
Give me that voice again, my Porphyro,
Those looks immortal, those complainings dear!
Oh leave me not in this eternal woe,
For if thou diest, my Love, I know not where to go."

36

Beyond a mortal man impassioned far
At these voluptuous accents, he arose,
Ethereal, flushed, and like a throbbing star
Seen mid the sapphire heaven's deep repose;
Into her dream he melted, as the rose
Blendeth its odour with the violet,—
Solution sweet: meantime the frost-wind blows
Like Love's alarum pattering the sharp sleet
Against the window-panes; St. Agnes' moon hath set.

37

'Tis dark: quick pattereth the flaw-blown sleet:
"This is no dream, my bride, my Madeline!"
'Tis dark: the icèd gusts still rave and beat:
"No dream, alas! alas! and woe is mine!
Porphyro will leave me here to fade and pine.—
Cruel! what traitor could thee hither bring?
I curse not, for my heart is lost in thine,
Though thou forsakest a deceivèd thing;—
A dove forlorn and lost with sick unprunèd wing."

38

"My Madeline! sweet dreamer! lovely bride!
Say, may I be for aye thy vassal blest?
Thy beauty's shield, heart-shaped and vermeil dyed?
Ah, silver shrine, here will I take my rest
After so many hours of toil and quest,
A famished pilgrim,—saved by miracle.
Though I have found, I will not rob thy nest
Saving of thy sweet self; if thou think'st well
To trust, fair Madeline, to no rude infidel.

39

"Hark! 'tis an elfin-storm from faery land,
Of haggard seeming, but a boon indeed:
Arise—arise! the morning is at hand;—
The bloated wassaillers will never heed:—
Let us away, my love, with happy speed;
There are no ears to hear, or eyes to see,—
Drowned all in Rhenish and the sleepy mead:

325. flaw-blown, wind-blown. **344. seeming,** appearance. Compare "haggard" in "La Belle Dame sans Merci."

Awake! arise! my love, and fearless be,
For o'er the southern moors I have a home for thee."

40

She hurried at his words, beset with fears,
For there were sleeping dragons all around,
At glaring watch, perhaps, with ready spears—
Down the wide stairs a darkling way they found.—
In all the house was heard no human sound.
A chain-drooped lamp was flickering by each door;
The arras, rich with horseman, hawk, and hound,
Fluttered in the besieging wind's uproar;
And the long carpets rose along the gusty floor.

41

They glide, like phantoms, into the wide hall;
Like phantoms, to the iron porch, they glide;
Where lay the Porter, in uneasy sprawl,
With a huge empty flagon by his side:
The wakeful bloodhound rose, and shook his hide,
But his sagacious eye an inmate owns:
By one, and one, the bolts full easy slide:—
The chains lie silent on the footworn stones;—
The key turns, and the door upon its hinges groans.

42

And they are gone: aye, ages long ago
These lovers fled away into the storm.
That night the Baron dreamt of many a woe,
And all his warrior-guests, with shade and form
Of witch, and demon, and large coffin-worm,
Were long be-nightmared. Angela the old
Died palsy-twitched, with meagre face deform;
The Beadsman, after thousand aves told,
For aye unsought-for slept among his ashes cold.

358. arras, a fabric (usually for hangings) with interwoven figures.

LA BELLE DAME SANS MERCI

O what can ail thee Knight at arms
Alone and palely loitering?
The sedge has withered from the Lake
And no birds sing!

O what can ail thee Knight at arms
So haggard and so woe begone?
The Squirrel's granary is full
And the harvest's done.

I see a lilly on thy brow
With anguish moist and fever dew
And on thy cheek a fading rose
Fast withereth too.

I met a Lady in the Meads
Full beautiful, a faery's child
Her hair was long, her foot was light
And her eyes were wild—

I made a garland for her head,
And bracelets too, and fragrant zone
She looked at me as she did love
And made sweet moan—

I set her on my pacing steed—
And nothing else saw all day long
For sidelong would she bend and sing
A faerys song—

She found me roots of relish sweet
And honey wild and manna dew
And sure in language strange she said
I love thee true.

She took me to her elfin grot
And there she wept and sighed full sore,
And there I shut her wild wild eyes
With Kisses four.

And there she lullèd me asleep
And there I dreamed. Ah Woe betide!
The latest dream I ever dreamt
On the cold hill side

I saw pale Kings, and Princes too
Pale warriors death pale were they all
They cried La belle dame sans merci
Thee hath in thrall.

I saw their starved lips in the gloam
With horrid warning gapèd wide
And I awoke, and found me here
On the cold hill's side.

And this is why I sojourn here
Alone and palely loitering;
Though the sedge is withered from the Lake
And no birds sing— . . .

13. Lady, as in the old ballad of "Thomas Rymer and Queen of Elfland" (Child, No. 37). **29. elfin grot,** fairy cave. **32. Kisses four.** "Why four Kisses—you will say—why four because . . . I was obliged to choose an even number that both eyes might have fair play. . . . I think two a piece quite sufficient. Suppose I had seven; there would have been three and a half a piece—a very awkward affair." (Keats, in the jesting letter to George and Georgiana enclosing the poem)

ODE ON A GRECIAN URN

For this and the following odes, the student is referred to the general discussion of them on page 865. Perhaps the first step toward understanding and enjoyment of this ode is visual recognition of the little picture groups connected with the "flowery tale" and "leaf-fringed legend" sculptured on the urn: (1) a marriage ceremony or procession ("pursuit" of the bride is a common feature of primitive ceremonies); (2) a piper under the trees; (3) a youth making love to a maiden under the trees; (4) a religious procession led by a priest with a heifer. The first conclusion suggested by these pictures is in stanzas 2–3: "the supremacy of ideal art over nature, because of its unchanging perfection" (Bridges). Stanza 4, with its tone of sadness, suggests another aspect of this conclusion: such art arrests the villagers and cuts them off from the rest of life as if they had been enchanted into eternal immobility. The last stanza expresses a generalization ("Beauty is truth, truth beauty") of which the urn itself and the poem about it are examples: Beauty and truth are aspects of the same ultimate reality. "These two are reached, apprehended, and expressed in different ways; beauty in or through sense or imagination, truth in or by 'thought,' 'knowledge,' or 'philosophy.' But the two are none the less one and the same; so that whatever is felt, perceived, imagined as beautiful, would, if adequately expressed in an intellectual form, be found a reality truly conceived; and truth, adequately transformed into the shape of 'sensation' or imagination, would have turned into beauty."—A. C. Bradley, "Keats and 'Philosophy,'" *The John Keats Memorial Volume,* Lane, 1924, p. 45. (See also Keats's letter to Bailey, November 22, 1817, below.)

1

Thou still unravished bride of quietness,
  Thou foster-child of Silence and slow Time,
Sylvan historian, who canst thus express
  A flowery tale more sweetly than our rhyme:
What leaf-fringed legend haunts about thy shape
  Of deities or mortals, or of both,
    In Tempe or the dales of Arcady?
  What men or gods are these? What maidens loth?
What mad pursuit? What struggle to escape?
    What pipes and timbrels? What wild ecstasy?

2

Heard melodies are sweet, but those unheard
  Are sweeter; therefore, ye soft pipes, play on;
Not to the sensual ear, but, more endeared,
  Pipe to the spirit ditties of no tone:
Fair youth, beneath the trees, thou canst not leave
  Thy song, nor ever can those trees be bare;
    Bold Lover, never, never canst thou kiss,

13. sensual, sensuous.

Though winning near the goal—yet, do not grieve;
  She cannot fade, though thou hast not thy bliss,
    For ever wilt thou love, and she be fair!

3

Ah, happy, happy boughs! that cannot shed
  Your leaves, nor ever bid the Spring adieu;
And, happy melodist, unwearièd,
  For ever piping songs for ever new;
More happy love! more happy, happy love!
  For ever warm and still to be enjoyed,
    For ever panting, and for ever young;
All breathing human passion far above,
  That leaves a heart high-sorrowful and cloyed,
    A burning forehead, and a parching tongue.

4

Who are these coming to the sacrifice?
  To what green altar, O mysterious priest,
Lead'st thou that heifer lowing at the skies,
  And all her silken flanks with garlands drest?
What little town by river or sea shore,
  Or mountain-built with peaceful citadel,
    Is emptied of this folk, this pious morn?
And, little town, thy streets for evermore
  Will silent be; and not a soul to tell
    Why thou art desolate, can e'er return.

5

O Attic shape! Fair attitude! with brede
  Of marble men and maidens overwrought,
With forest branches and the trodden weed;
  Thou, silent form, dost tease us out of thought
As doth eternity: Cold Pastoral!
  When old age shall this generation waste,
    Thou shalt remain, in midst of other woe
Than ours, a friend to man, to whom thou say'st,
  "Beauty is truth, truth beauty,"—that is all
    Ye know on earth, and all ye need to know.

41. brede, embroidery. The word has been read as an unintentional and awkward pun—"brede [breed] of marble men and maidens"! **45. Cold Pastoral,** "Pastoral" because the pictures pertain to country life; "Cold" because the urn is of marble and, perhaps, also because its unchanging perfection makes us sad. Compare Byron's *Don Juan,* Canto IV, stanza 61.

ODE TO A NIGHTINGALE

As in the "Ode on a Grecian Urn," the fundamental idea is the superiority of beauty and joy expressed in great art to beauty and joy as we know them in actual life, because in art they are eternal and unfading, in nature and life, transitory. In "Grecian Urn," plastic art is the subject; in "Nightingale," poetry (the bird's *song,* not the song *bird*). Moreover, "Nightingale" is tragically personal (see biographical facts). The poem is developed in two scenes: (1) the poet sitting in his garden (Brown's Wentworth Place, Hampstead), in the *morning* (l. 9), listening to the nightingale's song, brooding over the difference between life as the bird knows it and life as he knows it, wishing for an escape (wine at first, then poetry, which he takes); and (2) the poet in the imagined world, at *night*, to which the nightingale's song has transported him, glimpsing the immortality which the song suggests, and being brought back at last forlornly to his "sole self."

1

My heart aches, and a drowsy numbness pains
  My sense, as though of hemlock I had drunk,
Or emptied some dull opiate to the drains
  One minute past, and Lethe-wards had sunk:
'Tis not through envy of thy happy lot,
  But being too happy in thine happiness,—
    That thou, light wingèd Dryad of the trees,
      In some melodious plot
  Of beechen green, and shadows numberless,
    Singest of summer in full-throated ease.

2

O, for a draught of vintage! that hath been
  Cooled a long age in the deep-delved earth,
Tasting of Flora and the country green,
  Dance, and Provençal song, and sunburnt mirth!
O for a beaker full of the warm South,
  Full of the true, the blushful Hippocrene,
    With beaded bubbles winking at the brim,
      And purple-stainèd mouth;
  That I might drink, and leave the world unseen,
    And with thee fade away into the forest dim:

3

Fade far away, dissolve, and quite forget
  What thou among the leaves hast never known,
The weariness, the fever, and the fret
  Here, where men sit and hear each other groan;
Where palsy shakes a few, sad, last gray hairs,
  Where youth grows pale, and spectre-thin, and dies;
    Where but to think is to be full of sorrow
      And leaden-eyed despairs,
  Where Beauty cannot keep her lustrous eyes,
    Or new Love pine at them beyond to-morrow.

2. hemlock, poison (Socrates died of it). **4. Lethe-wards.** Lethe was the river of forgetfulness. **13. Flora,** goddess of flowers. **14. Provençal.** Provence was the kingdom of medieval France from which the troubadours and modern lyric poetry came. **16. Hippocrene,** the Muses' fountain in Helicon.

4

Away! away! for I will fly to thee,
  Not charioted by Bacchus and his pards,
But on the viewless wings of Poesy,
  Though the dull brain perplexes and retards:
Already with thee! tender is the night,
  And haply the Queen-Moon is on her throne,
    Clustered around by all her starry Fays;
      But here there is no light,
  Save what from heaven is with the breezes blown
    Through verdurous glooms and winding mossy ways.

5

I cannot see what flowers are at my feet,
  Nor what soft incense hangs upon the boughs,
But, in embalmèd darkness, guess each sweet
  Wherewith the seasonable month endows
The grass, the thicket, and the fruit-tree wild;
  White hawthorn, and the pastoral eglantine;
    Fast fading violets covered up in leaves;
      And mid-May's eldest child,
  The coming musk-rose, full of dewy wine,
    The murmurous haunt of flies on summer eves.

6

Darkling I listen; and, for many a time
  I have been half in love with easeful Death,
Called him soft names in many a musèd rhyme,
  To take into the air my quiet breath;
Now more than ever seems it rich to die,
  To cease upon the midnight with no pain,
    While thou art pouring forth thy soul abroad
      In such an ecstasy!
  Still wouldst thou sing, and I have ears in vain—
    To thy high requiem become a sod.

7

Thou wast not born for death, immortal Bird!
  No hungry generations tread thee down;
The voice I hear this passing night was heard
  In ancient days by emperor and clown:
Perhaps the self-same song that found a path
  Through the sad heart of Ruth, when, sick for home,
    She stood in tears amid the alien corn;
      The same that oft-times hath
  Charmed magic casements, opening on the foam
    Of perilous seas, in faery lands forlorn.

32. pards, leopards. They were supposed to accompany Bacchus, god of wine. **33. viewless,** invisible. **43. embalmèd,** sweet-smelling. **66. Ruth.** See Ruth 2. **69. Charmed magic casements.** Compare the note on Coleridge's "Kubla Khan," ll. 14–16.

8

Forlorn! the very word is like a bell
  To toll me back from thee to my sole self!
Adieu! the fancy cannot cheat so well
  As she is famed to do, deceiving elf.
Adieu! adieu! thy plaintive anthem fades
  Past the near meadows, over the still stream,
    Up the hill-side; and now 'tis buried deep
      In the next valley-glades:
  Was it a vision, or a waking dream?
    Fled is that music:—Do I wake or sleep?

ODE ON MELANCHOLY

In this most poetic treatment of Melancholy, the reader is counseled not to seek death when the melancholy fit shall fall, but to feast his eyes on Beauty. And yet Melancholy is so pervasive that it is closely allied with Beauty and Joy and Pleasure. The conclusion is that the experiencing soul itself will be among the trophies of "Veiled Melancholy."

I

No, no, go not to Lethe, neither twist
  Wolf's-bane, tight-rooted, for its poisonous wine;
Nor suffer thy pale forehead to be kissed
  By nightshade, ruby grape of Proserpine;
Make not your rosary of yew-berries,
  Nor let the beetle, nor the death-moth be
    Your mournful Psyche, nor the downy owl
A partner in your sorrow's mysteries;
  For shade to shade will come too drowsily,
    And drown the wakeful anguish of the soul.

2

But when the melancholy fit shall fall
  Sudden from heaven like a weeping cloud,
That fosters the droop-headed flowers all,
  And hides the green hill in an April shroud;
Then glut thy sorrow on a morning rose,
  Or on the rainbow of the salt sand-wave,
    Or on the wealth of globèd peonies;
Or if thy mistress some rich anger shows,
  Emprison her soft hand, and let her rave,
    And feed deep, deep upon her peerless eyes.

3

She dwells with Beauty—Beauty that must die;
  And Joy, whose hand is ever at his lips
Bidding adieu; and aching Pleasure nigh,
  Turning to Poison while the bee-mouth sips:
Ay, in the very temple of Delight
  Veiled Melancholy has her sovran shrine,
    Though seen of none save him whose strenuous tongue
  Can burst Joy's grape against his palate fine;
His soul shall taste the sadness of her might,
    And be among her cloudy trophies hung.

1–10. Lethe . . . Wolf's-bane . . . nightshade . . . The first stanza lists some of the traditional means of inducing death and some of the conventional "partners" of sorrow. The poem is the distillation of a century's Romantic musings on Melancholy. See Amy Reed's *The Background of Gray's Elegy*, Columbia University Press, 1924. **13. droop-headed flowers all,** "all the flowers only sacred to sorrow."—Bridges.

TO AUTUMN

The last of the 1819 odes; written at Winchester in September, after the poet had seen the harvest fields. The poem is purely objective; the poet surrenders himself to nature's mood; there is no melancholy brooding. The method is purely delineative. "Every line is like a bough . . . weighed down with fruit to the breaking-point"—Oliver Elton, *A Survey of English Literature, 1780–1830*, London, 1912. First is "the scented landscape" (stanza 1); then the season is humanized by the pictures of universal human occupations (these should be clearly recognized and visualized); finally, there is the symphony of natural autumnal sounds. "Nature has never spoken more truly in the human tongue."—H. I'A. Fausset, *Keats*, London, 1922.

I

Season of mists and mellow fruitfulness,
  Close bosom-friend of the maturing sun;
Conspiring with him how to load and bless
  With fruit the vines that round the thatch-eaves run;
To bend with apples the mossed cottage-trees,
  And fill all fruit with ripeness to the core;
    To swell the gourd, and plump the hazel shells
  With a sweet kernel; to set budding more,
And still more, later flowers for the bees,
Until they think warm days will never cease,
    For Summer has o'er-brimmed their clammy cells.

2

Who hath not seen thee oft amid thy store?
  Sometimes whoever seeks abroad may find
Thee sitting careless on a granary floor,
  Thy hair soft-lifted by the winnowing wind;
Or on a half-reaped furrow sound asleep,
  Drowsed with the fume of poppies, while thy hook
    Spares the next swath and all its twinèd flowers:
And sometimes like a gleaner thou dost keep
  Steady thy laden head across a brook;
  Or by a cider-press, with patient look,
    Thou watchest the last oozings hours by hours.

3

Where are the songs of Spring? Ay, where are they?
  Think not of them, thou hast thy music too,—
While barred clouds bloom the soft-dying day,
  And touch the stubble-plains with rosy hue;
Then in a wailful choir the small gnats mourn
  Among the river sallows, borne aloft
    Or sinking as the light wind lives or dies;
And full-grown lambs loud bleat from hilly bourn;
  Hedge-crickets sing; and now with treble soft
  The red-breast whistles from a garden-croft;
    And gathering swallows twitter in the skies.

BRIGHT STAR! WOULD I WERE STEDFAST AS THOU ART

Often called Keats's "last sonnet." When the ship that was taking him to Italy in September, 1820, encountered storms in the Channel and had to turn back for repairs, Keats went ashore and wrote the sonnet in a volume of Shakespeare's poems, facing "The Lover's Complaint." For an excellent critical article taking its title from the first line, see Leonard Bacon's "A Poet Steadfast as His Star," *Saturday Review of Literature*, Sept. 1, 1934.

Bright star! would I were stedfast as thou art—
  Not in lone splendour hung aloft the night
And watching, with eternal lids apart,
  Like Nature's patient, sleepless Eremite,
The moving waters at their priestlike task
  Of pure ablution round earth's human shores,
Or gazing on the new soft-fallen mask
  Of snow upon the mountains and the moors—
No—yet still stedfast, still unchangeable,
  Pillowed upon my fair love's ripening breast,
To feel for ever its soft fall and swell,
  Awake for ever in a sweet unrest,
Still, still to hear her tender-taken breath,
And so live ever—or else swoon to death.

LETTERS

In a period of great letter-writers, Keats's letters are remarkable. Their spontaneity, naturalness, and complete sincerity, the wide range of interests they express, and the experiences they record make them fascinating for themselves and indispensable for an understanding of his personality and art. The first of those which follow sets forth his idea of happiness and of the attitude of mind and mood necessary to attain it; it is also (in the statement about the sparrow) an excellent description of what he meant by Shakespeare's "negative capability," one of the secrets of highest poetic power. The one to Reynolds is an eloquent interpretation of a passage in Wordsworth's "Tintern Abbey" and a tribute to the philosophic vision and understanding of the older poet; it also touches lightly Keats's friendships and his grief. The famous "Vale of Soul-making" passage from his letter to George and Georgiana is one of his noblest utterances on human life.

Keats's letters, in three volumes, have been edited by H. B. Forman (London, 1895) and M. B. Forman (2d ed., Oxford University Press, 1935). In 1933 Mr. Earle V. Weller published *Autobiography of John Keats* (Stanford University Press), an arrangement of Keats's letters and essays, prefaced by Charles Cowden Clarke's account of the poet's boyhood; here, in effect, Keats tells the story of his own life. A useful one-volume edition is Lionel Trilling's *Collected Letters of John Keats*, Farrar, Straus and Young, 1951.

28. sallows, willows. **30. bourn,** domain. Keats uses the word somewhat erroneously.

from "O FOR A LIFE OF SENSATIONS!"

To Benjamin Bailey

[Burford Bridge, November 22, 1817]

My dear Bailey,

. . . What the Imagination seizes as Beauty must be truth—whether it existed before or not,—for I have the same idea of all our passions as of Love: they are all, in their sublime, creative of essential Beauty. In a Word, you may know my favourite speculation by my first Book, and the little Song I sent in my last, which is a representation from the fancy of the probable mode of operating in these Matters.

The Imagination may be compared to Adam's dream,—he awoke and found it truth:—I am more zealous in this affair, because I have never yet been able to perceive how anything can be known for truth by consecutive reasoning—and yet it must be. Can it be that even the greatest Philosopher ever arrived at his Goal without putting aside numerous objections?

However it may be, O for a life of Sensations rather than of Thoughts! It is "a Vision in the form of Youth," a shadow of reality to come—and this consideration has further convinced me,—for it has come as auxiliary to another favourite speculation of mine,—that we shall enjoy ourselves hereafter by having what we called happiness on Earth repeated in a finer tone. And yet such a fate can only befall those who delight in Sensation, rather than hunger as you do after Truth. Adam's dream will do here, and seems to be a Conviction that Imagination and its empyreal reflexion, is the same as human life and its spiritual repetition. But, as I was saying, the simple imaginative Mind may have its rewards in the repetition of its own silent Working coming continually on the Spirit with a fine Suddenness.

To compare great things with small, have you never by being surprised with an old Melody, in a delicious place by a delicious voice, *felt* over again your very speculations and surmises at the time it first operated on your soul? do you not remember forming to yourself the Singer's face—more beautiful than it was possible, and yet, with the elevation of the Moment, you did not think so? Even then you were mounted on the Wings of Imagination, so high that the prototype must be hereafter—that delicious face you will see. What a time! I am continually running away from the subject. Sure this cannot be exactly the Case with a complex mind—one that is imaginative, and at the same time careful of its fruits,—who would exist partly on Sensation, partly on thought—to whom it is necessary that "years should bring the philosophic Mind"? Such a one I consider yours, and therefore it is necessary to your eternal happiness that you not only drink this old Wine of Heaven, which I shall call the redigestion of our most ethereal Musings upon Earth, but also increase in knowledge and know all things. I am glad to hear that you are in a fair way for Easter. You will soon get through your unpleasant reading, and then!—but the world is full of troubles, and I have not much reason to think myself pestered with many.

I think Jane or Marianne has a better opinion of me than I deserve: for, really and truly, I do not think my Brother's illness connected with mine—you know more of the real Cause than they do; nor have I any chance of being rack'd as you have been. You perhaps at one time thought there was such a thing as worldly happiness to be arrived at, at certain periods of time marked out,—you have of necessity from your disposition been thus led away—I scarcely remember counting upon any happiness—I look not for it if it be not in the present hour,—nothing startles me beyond the moment. The Setting Sun will always set me to rights, or if a Sparrow come before my Window, I take part in its existence and pick about the gravel. The first thing that strikes me on hearing a misfortune having befallen another is this—"Well, it cannot be helped: he will have the pleasure of trying the resources of his Spirit"—and I beg now, my dear Bailey, that hereafter should you observe anything cold in me not to put it to the account of heartlessness, but abstraction—for I assure you I sometimes feel not the influence of a passion or affection during a whole Week—and so long this sometimes continues, I begin to suspect myself, and the genuineness of my feelings at other times—thinking them a few barren Tragedy Tears.

My brother Tom is much improved—he is going to Devonshire—whither I shall follow him. At present, I am just arrived at Dorking—to change the Scene—change the Air, and give me a spur to wind up my Poem, of which there are wanting 500 lines. I should have been here a day sooner, but the Reynoldses persuaded me to stop in Town to meet your friend Christie. There were Rice and Martin—we talked about Ghosts. I will have some Talk with Taylor and let you know,—when please God I come down at Christmas. I will find that Examiner if possible. My best regards to Gleig, my Brothers' to you and Mrs. Bentley.

Your affectionate Friend

John Keats.

I want to say much more to you—a few hints will set me going. Direct Burford Bridge near Dorking.

from "A MANSION OF MANY APARTMENTS"

To John Hamilton Reynolds

Teignmouth, 3 May [1818]

My dear Reynolds,

. . . With your patience, I will return to Wordsworth—whether or no he has an extended vision or a circumscribed grandeur—whether he is an eagle in his nest or on the wing. And to be more explicit and to show you how tall I stand by the giant, I will put down a simile of human life as far as I now perceive it; that is, to the point to which I say we both have arrived at—

Well—I compare human life to a large Mansion of Many apartments, two of which I can only describe, the doors of the rest being as yet shut upon me—The first we step into we call the Infant or Thoughtless Chamber, in which we remain as long as we do not think. We remain there a long while, and notwithstanding the doors of the second Chamber remain wide open, showing a bright appearance, we care not to hasten to it; but are at length imperceptibly impelled by the awakening of the thinking principle within us—we no sooner get into the second Chamber, which I shall call the Chamber of Maiden-Thought, than we become intoxicated with the light and the atmosphere, we see nothing but pleasant wonders, and think of delaying there for ever in delight. However among the effects this breathing is father of is that tremendous one of sharpening one's vision into the heart and

7. **Poem,** *Endymion.*

nature of Man—of convincing one's nerves that the world is full of Misery and Heartbreak, Pain, Sickness, and oppression—whereby this Chamber of Maiden-Thought becomes gradually darkened, and at the same time, on all sides of it, many doors are set open—but all dark—all leading to dark passages. We see not the balance of good and evil; we are in a mist, *we* are now in that state—We feel the "burden of the Mystery."

To this point was Wordsworth come, as far as I can conceive, when he wrote "Tintern Abbey," and it seems to me that his Genius is explorative of those dark Passages. Now if we live, and go on thinking, we too shall explore them. . . . He is a genius and superior to us, in so far as he can, more than we, make discoveries, and shed a light in them. Here I must think Wordsworth is deeper than Milton, though I think it has depended more upon the general and gregarious advance of intellect, than individual greatness of Mind. From the Paradise Lost and the other Works of Milton, I hope it is not too presuming, even between ourselves, to say, that his Philosophy, human and divine, may be tolerably understood by one not much advanced in years. In his time Englishmen were just emancipated from a great superstition, and Men had got hold of certain points and resting-places in reasoning which were too newly born to be doubted, and too much opposed by the Mass of Europe not to be thought ethereal and authentically divine—Who could gainsay his ideas on virtue, vice, and Chastity in Comus just at the time of the dismissal of Cod-pieces and a hundred other disgraces? who would not rest satisfied with his hintings at good and evil in the Paradise Lost, when just free from the Inquisition and burning in Smithfield? The Reformation produced such immediate and great benefits, that Protestantism was considered under the immediate eye of heaven, and its own remaining dogmas and superstitions then, as it were, regenerated, constituted those resting-places and seeming sure points of Reasoning—from that I have mentioned, Milton, whatever he may have thought in the sequel, appears to have been content with these of his writings. He did not think into the human heart as Wordsworth has done. Yet Milton as a Philosopher had sure as great Powers as Wordsworth.

What is then to be inferred? O many things. It proves there is a really grand march of intellect; it proves that a mighty Providence subdues the mightiest minds to the service of the time being, whether it be in human Knowledge or Religion. I have often pitied a tutor who has to hear "Nom: Musa" so often dinn'd into his ears—I hope you may not have the same pain in this scribbling—I may have read these things before, but I never had even a thus dim perception of them; and moreover I like to say my lesson to one who will endure my tediousness, for my own sake.

After all there is certainly something real in the world—Moore's present to Hazlitt is real—I like that Moore, and am glad I saw him at the Theatre just before I left Town. Tom has spit a *leetle* blood this afternoon, and that is rather a damper—but I know—the truth is, there is something real in the World. Your third Chamber of Life shall be a lucky and a gentle one—stored with the wine of Love—and the Bread of Friendship.

When you see George, if he should not have received a letter from me tell him he will find one at home most likely—tell Bailey I hope soon to see him. Remember me to all. The leaves have been out here for many a day. I have written to George for the first stanzas of my "Isabel,"—I shall have them soon, and will copy the whole out for you.

Your affectionate friend
John Keats

from "VALE OF SOUL-MAKING"

To George and Georgiana Keats
[April 15, 1819]

My Dear Brother and Sister:

. . . The common cognomen of this world among the misguided and superstitious is "a vale of tears" from which we are to be redeemed by a certain arbitrary interposition of God and taken to Heaven—What a little circumscribed straightened notion! Call the world if you please "The vale of Soul-making." Then you will find out the use of the world (I am speaking now in the highest terms for human nature admitting it to be immortal which I will here take for granted for the purpose of showing a thought which has struck me concerning it) I say "*Soul-making*"—Soul as distinguished from an Intelligence. There may be intelligences or sparks of the divinity in millions—but they are not Souls till they acquire identities, till each one is personally itself. Intelligences are atoms of perception—they know and they see and they are pure, in short they are God.—How then are the Souls to be made? How then are these sparks which are God to have identity given them—so as ever to possess a bliss peculiar to each one's individual existence? How but by the medium of a world like this? . . .

Do you not see how necessary a World of Pains

and troubles is to school an Intelligence and make it a Soul? . . . Seriously I think it probable that this system of Soul-making may have been the Parent of all the more palpable and personal schemes of Redemption among the Zoroastrians, the Christians and the Hindoos. For as one part of the human species must have their carved Jupiter; so another part must have the palpable and named Mediator and Saviour, their Christ, their Oromanes, and their Vishnu.

If what I have said should not be plain enough, as I fear it may not be, I will put you in the place where I began in this series of thoughts—I mean I began by seeing how man was formed by circumstances—and what are circumstances but touchstones of his heart? and what are touchstones but provings of his heart, but fortifiers or alterers of his nature? and what is his altered nature but his Soul?—and what was his Soul before it came into the world and had these provings and alterations and perfectionings?—An intelligence without Identity—and how is this Identity to be made? Through the medium of the Heart? and how is the heart to become this Medium but in a world of Circumstances?

There now I think what with Poetry and Theology you may thank your stars that my pen is not very long winded. Yesterday I received two Letters from your Mother and Henry, which I shall send by young Birkbeck with this.

Friday, April 30

Brown has been here rummaging up some of my old sins—that is to say sonnets. I do not think you remember them, so I will copy them out as well as two or three lately written. I have just written one on Fame—which Brown is transcribing and he has his book and mine. I must employ myself perhaps in a sonnet on the same subject.— . . .

[Here are given the two sonnets on "Fame," and the one "To Sleep."]

The following Poem—the last I have written—is the first and the only one with which I have taken even moderate pains. I have for the most part dash'd off my lines in a hurry. This I have done leisurely—I think it reads the more richly for it, and will I hope encourage me to write other things in even a more peaceable and healthy spirit. You must recollect that Psyche was not embodied as a goddess before the time of Apuleius the Platonist who lived after the Augustan age, and consequently the Goddess was never worshipped or sacrificed to with any of the ancient fervour—and perhaps never thought of in the old religion—I am more orthodox than to let a heathen Goddess be so neglected— . . .

[The "Ode to Psyche" follows here.]

I have been endeavouring to discover a better Sonnet Stanza than we have. The legitimate does not suit the language over well from the pouncing rhymes—the other kind appears too elegiac—and the couplet at the end of it has seldom a pleasing effect—I do not pretend to have succeeded—it will explain itself.

[Sonnet, "If by Dull Rhymes."]

[May 3]

This is the third of May, and everything is in delightful forwardness; the violets are not withered before the peeping of the first rose. You must let me know everything—how parcels go and come, what papers you have, and what newspapers you want, and other things. God bless you, my dear brother and sister,

Your ever affectionate Brother

John Keats.

Thomas De Quincey
1785–1859

Thomas De Quincey was born August 15, 1785, at Manchester. His father was a successful merchant who had some literary taste and cultivation. His mother was a righteous, humorless woman with a vigorous intellect. The children of the family were precocious and high-strung. Two of them died of brain fever, one lived for years in a fantastic world of his own creation, and another, Pink, ran away to sea and encountered adventures rivaling those of one of Stevenson's heroes. A sickly, petted child, too soon acquainted with grief, an omnivorous reader, Thomas spent his early years at The Farm and at Greenhay, near Manchester. He attended schools at Bath, Winkfield, and Manchester. Before he was eleven, he was a skillful Latinist; at thirteen, he wrote Greek with ease and conversed in it. Mr. Morgan, his teacher, said of him, "That boy could harangue an Athenian mob better than you or I could address an English one." In 1802, while he was at Manchester Grammar School, he "was quoting from Wordsworth." Unhappy in his school life, he ran away, in the amusing manner related in his *Confessions of an English Opium-Eater*. Imperfectly reconciled with his family, he embarked upon travels in Wales. There he cut himself loose from the family and wandered at will until his money gave out and winter overtook him. In London, he lived precariously, companion of waif children and vagrants. After a second family reconciliation, he lived for a while at Everton, reading novels, projecting literary works, and keeping a diary.

Partly on Wordsworth's advice, in 1803 he entered Oxford. Here he lived a lonely life, "immersed in metaphysics, psychology, and moral Philosophy," reading Greek daily. His real passion, however, was for the new Romantic literature of Coleridge, Wordsworth, Southey, Lamb, and Landor. At Oxford he formed the opium habit, at first as a palliative for neuralgia brought on by the exposure of his travel years, and had some of the dreams that he was to describe in *Suspiria de Profundis*. He left Oxford in May, 1808, in the midst of his final examinations and therefore without his degree.

By 1807 De Quincey had formed an acquaintance with Lamb, and in that year he met Coleridge "in a muse beneath a gateway at Bridgewater." As the result of an exchange of confidences, De Quincey arranged to give Coleridge the sum of £300. The vividly remembered meeting with Wordsworth followed soon after, and an intimate friendship developed. In 1809 De Quincey succeeded Wordsworth as the tenant of Dove Cottage, Grasmere. He lived there for twenty-one years, in 1816 marrying Margaret Simpson, a farmer's daughter, and enjoying a happy domestic life, in spite of the snobbish attitude of the Wordsworths and others toward his wife. Opium, German philosophy, and writing made up his larger world. His last years he spent in Edinburgh, whither he went in 1830 because of his literary connections. He died peacefully there December 8, 1859.

De Quincey possessed extraordinary gifts—a marvelous memory, power of subtle analysis, sensitiveness to beauty, and sympathy for the weak and suffering. Next to Coleridge's, his conversation seems to have been the most brilliant of the period; his manners were exquisite; his bearing was graceful. His will, when he chose to exercise it, was strong. But he was impractical, a dreamer, an introvert. It is said that while he was in Edinburgh writing an essay on the theory of money he walked the streets one day trying to negotiate a loan of £1 on the security of a £10 Bank of England note! His opium habit seems to have been both a boon, in freeing and heightening his imaginative processes, and a bane, in cutting him off from reality and often defeating his practical purposes.

Very few of De Quincey's writings were originally planned or published as books. Most of them first appeared in such periodicals as the *London Magazine*, *Blackwood's*, and *Tait's Magazine*, from which they were collected into book form. Like Hazlitt's, most of them are in essay form. The chief titles as they are known today are: *Confessions of an English Opium-Eater*, 1821; *On the Knocking at the Gate in Macbeth*, 1823; *Essays on Kant*, 1824–33; *Murder as One of the Fine Arts*, 1827; *Autobiography*, 1834–53; *Revolt of the Tartars*, 1837; *Suspiria de Profundis*, 1845; *Joan of Arc*, 1847; *The Literature of Knowledge and the Literature of Power*, 1848; and *The English Mail-Coach*, 1849. This list falls into three groups—reminiscences; literary, historical, and social criticism; and imaginative or fantastic creations.

De Quincey has been called "the psychologist of style." The term was perhaps meant to describe his extraordinary subtlety in adjusting connotations of words, and sentence patterns and rhythms, to ideas and emotions, as well as in discovering the nuances of ideas and emotions. His polyphonic prose, exemplified by passages in the *Confessions*, *Suspiria*, *Joan of Arc*, and *The English Mail-Coach*, is as famous for its own distinctive organ splendor as Sir Thomas Browne's and Ruskin's are for theirs. Judged, however, by the present-day test of economy of the reader's attention, it has been shown to have serious faults—lack of conciseness, a tendency to digress, unseasonable levity, willfulness in handling quotations. But in his best writings, as Samuel Butler said of Homer, De Quincey struck oil, even though he succeeds only in boring us elsewhere. So long as there are lovers of grand and poetic prose, of sensitive and highly imaginative treatments of strange themes, of the splendid stuffs and dyes of dreams, De Quincey will be read.

from ON THE KNOCKING AT THE GATE IN *MACBETH*

FROM my boyish days I had always felt a great perplexity on one point in *Macbeth*. It was this:—the knocking at the gate which succeeds to the murder of Duncan produced to my feelings an effect for which I never could account. The effect was that it reflected back upon the murderer a peculiar awfulness and a depth of solemnity; yet, however obstinately I endeavoured with my understanding to comprehend this, for many years I never could see *why* it should produce such an effect. . . .

In fact, my understanding said positively that it could *not* produce any effect. But I knew better; I felt that it did; and I waited and clung to the problem until further knowledge should enable me to solve it. At length, in 1812, Mr. Williams made his *début* on the stage of Ratcliffe Highway, and executed those unparalleled murders which have procured for him such a brilliant and undying reputation. On which murders, by the way, I must observe that in one respect they have had an ill effect, by making the connoisseur in murder very fastidious in his taste, and dissatisfied with anything that has been since done in that line. All other murders look pale by the deep crimson of his; and, as an amateur once said to me in a querulous tone, "There has been absolutely nothing *doing* since his time, or nothing that's worth speaking of." But this is wrong, for it is unreasonable to expect all men to be great artists, and born with the genius of Mr. Williams. Now it will be remembered that in the first of these murders (that of the Marrs) the same incident (of a knocking at the door soon after the work of extermination was complete) did actually occur which the genius of Shakespeare has invented; and all good judges, and the most eminent dilettanti, acknowledged the felicity of Shakespeare's suggestion as soon as it was actually realized. Here, then, was a fresh proof that I was right in relying on my own feeling in opposition to my understanding; and again I set myself to study the problem. At length I solved it to my own satisfaction; and my solution is this:—Murder, in ordinary cases, where the sympathy is wholly directed to the case of the murdered person, is an incident of coarse and vulgar horror; and for this reason—that it flings the interest exclusively upon the natural but ignoble instinct by which we cleave to life: an instance which, as being indispensable to the primal law of self-preservation, is the same in kind (though different in degree) amongst all living creatures. This instinct, therefore, because it annihilates all distinctions, and degrades the greatest of men to the level of "the poor beetle that we tread on," exhibits human nature in its most abject and humiliating attitude. Such an attitude would little suit the purposes of the poet. What then must he do? He must throw the interest on the murderer. Our sympathy must be with *him* (of course I mean a sympathy of comprehension, a sympathy by which we enter into his feelings, and are made to understand them—not a sympathy of pity or approbation). In the murdered person, all strife of thought, all flux and reflux of passion and of purpose, are crushed by one overwhelming panic; the fear of instant death smites him "with its petrific mace." But in the murderer, such a murderer as a poet will condescend to, there must be raging some great storm of passion—jealousy, ambition, vengeance, hatred—which will create a hell within him; and into this hell we are to look.

In *Macbeth*, for the sake of gratifying his own enormous and teeming faculty of creation, Shakespeare has introduced two murderers: and, as usual in his hands, they are remarkably discriminated: but—though in Macbeth the strife of mind is greater than in his wife, the tiger spirit not so awake, and his feelings caught chiefly by contagion from her—yet, as both were finally involved in the guilt of murder, the murderous mind of necessity is finally

50. in that line. De Quincey later wrote his extravaganza *Murder Considered as One of the Fine Arts* on the subject.

to be presumed in both. This was to be expressed; and, on its own account, as well as to make it a more proportionable antagonist to the unoffending nature of their victim, "the gracious Duncan," and adequately to expound "the deep damnation of his taking off," this was to be expressed with peculiar energy. We were to be made to feel that the human nature,—*i.e.* the divine nature of love and mercy, spread through the hearts of all creatures, and seldom utterly withdrawn from man,—was gone, vanished, extinct, and that the fiendish nature had taken its place. And, as this effect is marvellously accomplished in the *dialogues* and *soliloquies* themselves, so it is finally consummated by the expedient under consideration; and it is to this that I now solicit the reader's attention. If the reader has ever witnessed a wife, daughter, or sister in a fainting fit, he may chance to have observed that the most affecting moment in such a spectacle is *that* in which a sigh and a stirring announce the recommencement of suspended life. Or, if the reader has ever been present in a vast metropolis on the day when some great national idol was carried in funeral pomp to his grave, and, chancing to walk near the course through which it passed, has felt powerfully, in the silence and desertion of the streets and in the stagnation of ordinary business, the deep interest which at that moment was possessing the heart of man,—if all at once he should hear the death-like stillness broken up by the sound of wheels rattling away from the scene, and making known that the transitory vision was dissolved, he will be aware that at no moment was his sense of the complete suspension and pause in ordinary human concerns so full and affecting as at that moment when the suspension ceases, and the goings-on of human life are suddenly resumed. All action in any direction is best expounded, measured, and made apprehensible, by reaction. Now, apply this to the case in *Macbeth*. Here, as I have said, the retiring of the human heart and the entrance of the fiendish heart was to be expressed and made sensible. Another world has stept in; and the murderers are taken out of the region of human things, human purposes, human desires. They are transfigured: Lady Macbeth is "unsexed"; Macbeth has forgot that he was born of woman; both are conformed to the image of devils; and the world of devils is suddenly revealed. But how shall this be conveyed and made palpable? In order that a new world may step in, this world must for a time disappear. The murderers and the murder must be insulated—cut off by an immeasurable gulf from the ordinary tide and succession of human affairs—locked up and sequestered in some deep recess; we must be made sensible that the world of ordinary life is suddenly arrested, laid asleep, tranced, racked into a dread armistice; time must be annihilated, relation to things without abolished; and all must pass self-withdrawn into a deep syncope and suspension of earthly passion. Hence it is that, when the deed is done, when the work of darkness is perfect, then the world of darkness passes away like a pageantry in the clouds: the knocking at the gate is heard, and it makes known audibly that the reaction has commenced; the human has made its reflux upon the fiendish: the pulses of life are beginning to beat again; and the re-establishment of the goings-on of the world in which we live first makes us profoundly sensible of the awful parenthesis that has suspended them.

O mighty poet! Thy works are not as those of other men, simply and merely great works of art, but are also like the phenomena of nature, like the sun and the sea, the stars and the flowers, like frost and snow, rain and dew, hail-storm and thunder, which are to be studied with entire submission of our own faculties, and in the perfect faith that in them there can be no too much or too little, nothing useless or inert, but that, the farther we press in our discoveries, the more we shall see proofs of design and self-supporting arrangement where the careless eye had seen nothing but accident!

from THE ENGLISH MAIL-COACH

In the October 1849 number of *Blackwood's Magazine* De Quincey published anonymously an article entitled "The Glory of Motion," relating his coaching experiences, especially one ride in which the coach bore to various parts of England the news of the Battle of Waterloo. This article and two more he gave the title "The English Mail-Coach." His original intention was to make the series a part of his *Suspiria de Profundis*, but misunderstanding of its connection with *Suspiria* caused him to detach it.

"Thirty-seven years ago," he wrote, "accident made me, in the dead of night, and of a night memorably solemn, the solitary witness of an appalling scene, which threatened instant death . . . to two young people" riding along the coach road in a light gig. Out of this incident as his motif, as in a musical fugue, he weaves the prose-poetry of his "Dream-Fugue." (In the July, 1938, *Musical Quarterly* Calvin S. Brown, III, has shown that De Quincey knew the fugue form and made it the pattern of this and several of his other essays.)

"*Whence the sound*
Of instruments, that made melodious chime,
Was heard, of harp and organ; and who moved
Their stops and chords was seen; his volant touch

Instinct through all proportions, low and high,
Fled and pursued transverse the resonant fugue."
Paradise Lost, Bk. XI.

SECTION 3—DREAM-FUGUE

FOUNDED ON THE PRECEDING THEME OF SUDDEN DEATH

Tumultuosissimamente

PASSION of sudden death! that once in youth I read and interpreted by the shadows of thy averted signs!—rapture of panic taking the shape (which amongst tombs in churches I have seen) of woman bursting her sepulchral bonds—of woman's Ionic form bending forward from the ruins of her grave with arching foot, with eyes upraised, with clasped adoring hands—waiting, watching, trembling, praying for the trumpet's call to rise from dust for ever! Ah, vision too fearful of shuddering humanity on the brink of almighty abysses!—vision that didst start back, that didst reel away, like a shrivelling scroll from before the wrath of fire racing on the wings of the wind! Epilepsy so brief of horror, wherefore is it that thou canst not die? Passing so suddenly into darkness, wherefore is it that still thou sheddest thy sad funeral blights upon the gorgeous mosaics of dreams? Fragment of music too passionate, heard once, and heard no more, what aileth thee, that thy deep rolling chords come up at intervals through all the worlds of sleep, and after forty years have lost no element of horror?

I

Lo, it is summer—almighty summer! The everlasting gates of life and summer are thrown open wide; and on the ocean, tranquil and verdant as a savannah, the unknown lady from the dreadful vision and I myself are floating—she upon a fairy pinnace, and I upon an English three-decker. Both of us are wooing gales of festal happiness within the domain of our common country, within that ancient watery park, within the pathless chase of ocean, where England takes her pleasure as a huntress through winter and summer, from the rising to the setting sun. Ah, what a wilderness of floral beauty was hidden, or was suddenly revealed, upon the tropic islands through which the pinnace moved! And upon her deck what a bevy of human flowers: young women how lovely, young men how noble, that were dancing together, and slowly drifting towards *us* amidst music and incense, amidst blossoms from forests and gorgeous corymbi from vintages, amidst natural carolling, and the echoes of sweet girlish laughter. Slowly the pinnace nears us, gaily she hails us, and silently she disappears beneath the shadow of our mighty bows. But then, as at some signal from heaven, the music, and the carols, and the sweet echoing of girlish laughter—all are hushed. What evil has smitten the pinnace, meeting or overtaking her? Did ruin to our friends couch within our own dreadful shadow? Was our shadow the shadow of death? I looked over the bow for an answer, and, behold! the pinnace was dismantled; the revel and the revellers were found no more; the glory of the vintage was dust; and the forests with their beauty were left without a witness upon the seas. "But where," and I turned to our crew—"where are the lovely women that danced beneath the awning of flowers and clustering corymbi? Whither have fled the noble young men that danced with *them?*" Answer there was none. But suddenly the man at the mast-head, whose countenance darkened with alarm, cried out, "Sail on the weather beam! Down she comes upon us: in seventy seconds she also will founder."

2

I looked to the weather side, and the summer had departed. The sea was rocking, and shaken with gathering wrath. Upon its surface sat mighty mists, which grouped themselves into arches and long cathedral aisles. Down one of these, with the fiery pace of a quarrel from a cross-bow, ran a frigate right athwart our course. "Are they mad?" some voice exclaimed from our deck. "Do they woo their ruin?" But in a moment, as she was close upon us, some impulse of a heady current or local vortex gave a wheeling bias to her course, and off she forged without a shock. As she ran past us, high aloft amongst the shrouds stood the lady of the pinnace. The deeps opened ahead in malice to receive her, towering surges of foam ran after her, the billows were fierce to catch her. But far away she was borne into desert spaces of the sea: whilst still by sight I followed her, as she ran before the howling gale, chased by angry sea-birds and by maddening billows; still I saw her, at the moment when she ran past us, standing amongst the shrouds, with her white draperies streaming before the wind. There she stood, with hair dishevelled, one hand clutched amongst the tackling—rising, sinking, fluttering,

13. averted signs. "I read the course and changes of the lady's agony in the succession of her involuntary gestures; but it must be remembered that I read all this from the rear, never once catching the lady's full face, and even her profile imperfectly." (De Quincey)

3. corymbi, clusters of fruit or flowers. **34. quarrel,** bolt, of a crossbow.

trembling, praying; there for leagues I saw her as she stood, raising at intervals one hand to heaven, amidst the fiery crests of the pursuing waves and the raving of the storm; until at last, upon a sound from afar of malicious laughter and mockery, all was hidden for ever in driving showers; and afterwards, but when I knew not, nor how.

3

Sweet funeral bells from some incalculable distance, wailing over the dead that die before the dawn, awakened me as I slept in a boat moored to some familiar shore. The morning twilight even then was breaking; and, by the dusky revelations which it spread, I saw a girl, adorned with a garland of white roses about her head for some great festival, running along the solitary strand in extremity of haste. Her running was the running of panic; and often she looked back as to some dreadful enemy in the rear. But, when I leaped ashore, and followed on her steps to warn her of a peril in front, alas! from me she fled as from another peril, and vainly I shouted to her of quicksands that lay ahead. Faster and faster she ran; round a promontory of rocks she wheeled out of sight; in an instant I also wheeled round it, but only to see the treacherous sands gathering above her head. Already her person was buried; only the fair young head and the diadem of white roses around it were still visible to the pitying heavens; and, last of all, was visible one white marble arm. I saw by the early twilight this fair young head, as it was sinking down to darkness—saw this marble arm, as it rose above her head and her treacherous grave, tossing, faltering, rising, clutching, as at some false deceiving hand stretched out from the clouds—saw this marble arm uttering her dying hope, and then uttering her dying despair. The head, the diadem, the arm—these all had sunk; at last over these also the cruel quicksand had closed; and no memorial of the fair young girl remained on earth, except my own solitary tears, and the funeral bells from the desert seas, that, rising again more softly, sang a requiem over the grave of the buried child, and over her blighted dawn.

I sat, and wept in secret the tears that men have ever given to the memory of those that died before the dawn, and by the treachery of earth, our mother. But suddenly the tears and funeral bells were hushed by a shout as of many nations, and by a roar as from some great king's artillery, advancing rapidly along the valleys, and heard afar by echoes from the mountains. "Hush!" I said, as I bent my ear earthwards to listen—"hush!—this either is the very anarchy of strife, or else"—and then I listened more profoundly, and whispered as I raised my head—"or else, oh heavens! it is *victory* that is final, victory that swallows up all strife."

4

Immediately, in trance, I was carried over land and sea to some distant kingdom, and placed upon a triumphal car, amongst companions crowned with laurel. The darkness of gathering midnight, brooding over all the land, hid from us the mighty crowds that were weaving restlessly about ourselves as a centre: we heard them, but saw them not. Tidings had arrived, within an hour, of a grandeur that measured itself against centuries; too full of pathos they were, too full of joy, to utter themselves by other language than by tears, by restless anthems, and *Te Deums* reverberated from the choirs and orchestras of earth. These tidings we that sat upon the laurelled car had it for our privilege to publish amongst all nations. And already, by signs audible through the darkness, by snortings and tramplings, our angry horses, that knew no fear of fleshly weariness, upbraided us with delay. Wherefore *was* it that we delayed? We waited for a secret word, that should bear witness to the hope of nations as now accomplished for ever. At midnight the secret word arrived; which word was—*Waterloo and Recovered Christendom!* The dreadful word shone by its own light; before us it went; high above our leader's heads it rode, and spread a golden light over the paths which we traversed. Every city, at the presence of the secret word, threw open its gates. The rivers were conscious as we crossed. All the forests, as we ran along their margins, shivered in homage to the secret word. And the darkness comprehended it.

Two hours after midnight we approached a mighty Minster. Its gates, which rose to the clouds, were closed. But, when the dreadful word that rode before us reached them with its golden light, silently they moved back upon their hinges; and at a flying gallop our equipage entered the grand aisle of the cathedral. Headlong was our pace; and at every altar, in the little chapels and oratories to the right hand and left of our course, the lamps, dying or sickening, kindled anew in sympathy with the secret word that was flying past. Forty leagues we might have run in the cathedral, and as yet no strength of morning light had reached us, when before us we saw the aerial galleries of organ and choir. Every pinnacle of fretwork, every station of advantage amongst the traceries, was crested by white-robed choristers that sang deliverance; that wept no more tears, as once their fathers had wept; but at intervals that sang together to the generations, saying,

"Chant the deliverer's praise in every tongue,"

and receiving answers from afar,

"Such as once in heaven and earth were sung."

And of their chanting was no end; of our headlong pace was neither pause nor slackening.

Thus as we ran like torrents—thus as we swept with bridal rapture over the Campo Santo of the cathedral graves—suddenly we became aware of a vast necropolis rising upon the far-off horizon—a city of sepulchres, built within the saintly cathedral for the warrior dead that rested from their feuds on earth. Of purple granite was the necropolis; yet, in the first minute, it lay like a purple stain upon the horizon, so mighty was the distance. In the second minute it trembled through many changes, growing into terraces and towers of wondrous altitude, so mighty was the pace. In the third minute already, with our dreadful gallop, we were entering its suburbs. Vast sarcophagi rose on every side, having towers and turrets that, upon the limits of the central aisle, strode forward with haughty intrusion, that ran back with mighty shadows into answering recesses. Every sarcophagus showed many bas-reliefs—bas-reliefs of battles and of battle-fields; battles from forgotten ages, battles from yesterday; battle-fields, that long since, nature had healed and reconciled to herself with the sweet oblivion of flowers; battle-fields that were yet angry and crimson with carnage. Where the terraces ran, there did *we* run; where the towers curved, there did *we* curve. With the flight of swallows our horses swept round every angle. Like rivers in flood wheeling round headlands, like hurricanes that ride into the secrets of forests, faster than ever light unwove the mazes of darkness, our flying equipage carried earthly passions, kindled warrior instincts, amongst the dust that lay around us—dust oftentimes of our noble fathers that had slept in God from Créci to Trafalgar. And now had we reached the last sarcophagus, now were we abreast of the last bas-relief, already had we recovered the arrow-like flight of the illimitable central aisle, when coming up this aisle to meet us we beheld afar off a female child, that rode in a carriage as frail as flowers. The mists which went before her hid the fawns that drew her, but could not hide the shells and tropic flowers with which she played—but could not hide the lovely smiles by which she uttered her trust in the mighty cathedral, and in the cherubim that looked down upon her from the mighty shafts of its pillars. Face to face she was meeting us; face to face she rode, as if danger there were none. "Oh, baby!" I exclaimed, "shalt thou be the ransom for Waterloo? Must we, that carry tidings of great joy to every people, be messengers of ruin to thee!" In horror I rose at the thought; but then also, in horror at the thought, rose one that was sculptured on a bas-relief—a Dying Trumpeter. Solemnly from the field of battle he rose to his feet; and, unslinging his stony trumpet, carried it, in his dying anguish, to his stony lips—sounding once, and yet once again; proclamation that, in *thy* ears, oh baby! spoke from the battlements of death. Immediately deep shadows fell between us, and aboriginal silence. The choir had ceased to sing. The hoofs of our horses, the dreadful rattle of our harness, the groaning of our wheels, alarmed the graves no more. By horror the bas-relief had been unlocked unto life. By horror we, that were so full of life, we men and our horses, with their fiery fore-legs rising in mid air to their everlasting gallop, were frozen to a bas-relief. Then a third time the trumpet sounded; the seals were taken off all pulses; life, and the frenzy of life, tore into their channels again; again the choir burst forth in sunny grandeur, as from the muffling of storms and darkness; again the thunderings of our horses carried temptation into the graves. One cry burst from our lips, as the clouds, drawing off from the aisle, showed it empty before us.—"Whither has the infant fled?—is the young child caught up to God?" Lo! afar off, in a vast recess, rose three mighty windows to the clouds; and on a level with their summits, at height insuperable to man, rose an altar of purest alabaster. On its eastern face was trembling a crimson glory. A glory was it from the reddening dawn that now streamed *through* the windows? Was it from the crimson robes of the martyrs painted *on* the windows? Was it from the bloody bas-reliefs of earth? There, suddenly, within that crimson radiance, rose the apparition of a woman's head, and then of a woman's figure. The child it was—grown up to woman's height. Clinging to the horns of the altar, voiceless she stood—sinking, rising, raving, despairing; and behind the volume of incense that, night and day, streamed upwards from the altar, dimly was seen the fiery font, and the shadow of that dreadful being who should have baptized her with the baptism of death. But by her side was kneeling her better angel, that hid his face with wings; that wept and pleaded for *her;* that

11. Campo Santo, "(or cemetery) at Pisa, composed of earth brought from Jerusalem from a bed of sanctity as the highest prize which the noble piety of crusaders could ask or imagine." (De Quincey)

prayed when *she* could *not;* that fought with Heaven by tears for *her* deliverance; which also, as he raised his immortal countenance from his wings, I saw, by the glory in his eye, that from Heaven he had won at last.

5

Then was completed the passion of the mighty fugue. The golden tubes of the organ, which as yet had but muttered at intervals—gleaming amongst clouds and surges of incense—threw up, as from fountains unfathomable, columns of heart-shattering music. Choir and anti-choir were filling fast with unknown voices. Thou also, Dying Trumpeter, with thy love that was victorious, and thy anguish that was finishing, didst enter the tumult; trumpet and echo—farewell love, and farewell anguish—rang through the dreadful *sanctus.* Oh, darkness of the grave! that from the crimson altar and from the fiery font wert visited and searched by the effulgence in the angel's eye—were these indeed thy children? Pomps of life, that, from the burials of centuries, rose again to the voice of perfect joy, did ye indeed mingle with the festivals of Death? Lo! as I looked back for seventy leagues through the mighty cathedral, I saw the quick and the dead that sang together to God, together that sang to the generations of man. All the hosts of jubilation, like armies that ride in pursuit, moved with one step. Us, that, with laurelled heads, were passing from the cathedral, they overtook, and, as with a garment, they wrapped us round with thunders greater than our own. As brothers we moved together; to the dawn that advanced, to the stars that fled; rendering thanks to God in the highest—that, having hid His face through one generation behind thick clouds of War, once again was ascending, from the Campo Santo of Waterloo was ascending, in the visions of Peace; rendering thanks for thee, young girl! whom having overshadowed with His ineffable passion of death, suddenly did God relent, suffered thy angel to turn aside His arm, and even in thee, sister unknown! shown to me for a moment only to be hidden for ever, found an occasion to glorify His goodness. A thousand times, amongst the phantoms of sleep, have I seen thee entering the gates of the golden dawn, with the secret word riding before thee, with the armies of the grave behind thee,—seen thee sinking, rising, raving, despairing; a thousand times in the worlds of sleep have seen thee followed by God's angel through storms, through desert seas, through the darkness of quicksands, through dreams and the dreadful revelations that are in dreams; only that at the last, with one sling of His victorious arm, He might snatch thee back from ruin, and might emblazon in thy deliverance the endless resurrections of His love!

SUGGESTIONS FOR FURTHER READING

This list is to be supplemented by the brief lists of books given in the General Bibliography and in the various introductions to specific authors and works.

HISTORICAL AND POLITICAL BACKGROUND

Brinton, Crane. *The Political Ideas of the English Romanticists,* Oxford University Press, 1926.

Brown, P. A. *The French Revolution in English History,* Lockwood, 1918.

Bryant, Arthur. *The Years of Endurance, 1793–1802,* Collins, 1942.

——— *The Years of Victory, 1802–1812,* Collins, 1944.

Bushnell, N. S. *The Historical Background of English Literature,* Holt, 1930, Chaps, XI–XIII. Perhaps the best brief treatment of the period.

Cunningham, William. *Growth of English Industry and Commerce,* rev. ed., Cambridge University Press, 1925–29. Vol. V contains the best treatment of the mercantile system in Great Britain.

Dowden, Edward. *The French Revolution and English Literature,* Scribner, 1914. A classic work.

Mowat, R. B. *The Romantic Age: Europe in the Nineteenth Century,* Harrap, 1937.

Nicolson, Harold. *The Congress of Vienna,* Constable, 1946.

Thompson, J. M. *The French Revolution,* Blackwell, 1943.

Trevelyan, G. M. *British History in the Nineteenth Century,* Longmans, 1938. A standard and very readable work.

CULTURAL AND SOCIAL BACKGROUND

Bradbury, Ronald. *The Romantic Theories of Architecture of the Nineteenth Century in Germany, England, and France,* Dorothy Press, 1934.

Dannreather, Edward. *The Romantic Period, Oxford History of Music,* Vol. VI, Oxford University Press, 1937.

Einstein, Alfred. *Music in the Romantic Era,* Norton, 1947.

Gill, Frederick C. *The Romantic Movement and Methodism,* Epworth Press, 1937.

McKinney, H. D., and Anderson, W. R. *Music in History, the Evolution of an Art,* American Book Company, 1940. Illustrated. The chapter, "Music Becomes More Personal" describes "The Romantic Ideal in Art."

MacLean, Kenneth. *Agrarian Age: A Background for Wordsworth,* Yale University Press, 1950. A study of "romantic ruralism" and its economic, social, and intellectual milieu.

Morison, Stanley. *The English Newspaper*, Harvard University Press, 1932. An enlightening account of the development of English journalism during a critical period.

Randall, J. H. *The Making of the Modern Mind*, Houghton Mifflin, 1926.

Somervell, D. C. *English Thought in the Nineteenth Century*, Longmans, 1936. Chap. I, especially "IV: Five Poets," is excellent.

Whitley, W. T. *Art in England, 1800–1820*, Macmillan, 1928.

——— *Art in England, 1821–1837*, Cambridge University Press, 1930. Both volumes are richly illustrated.

LITERATURE OF THE PERIOD

COLLECTIONS

Bernbaum, Ernest, ed. *Anthology of Romanticism*, Ronald Press, 1948. The most inclusive anthology of Romantic poetry.

Campbell, Oscar J., and Pyre, J. F. A., eds. *Poetry and Criticism of the Romantic Movement*, Crofts, 1932.

Sampson, George, ed. *Nineteenth Century Essays*, Columbia University Press, 1934.

Stephens, James, Beck, Edwin L., and Snow, Royall H., eds. *English Romantic Poets*, American Book Company, 1933.

Woods, George B., ed. *English Poetry and Prose of the Romantic Movement*, rev. ed., Scott, Foresman, 1950.

CRITICISM

Babbitt, Irving. *Rousseau and Romanticism*, rev. ed., Houghton Mifflin, 1930. Valuable for the background of European thought and feeling, but essentially an indictment of Romanticism for its idealization of emotionalism, irrationality, and egotism.

Beach, J. W. *The Concept of Nature in Nineteenth Century English Poetry*, Macmillan, 1936.

Bernbaum, Ernest. *Guide through the Romantic Movement*, Ronald Press, 1949.

Bowra, C. M. *The Romantic Imagination*, Harvard University Press, 1949. An illuminating study of the English Romantic poets.

Bush, Douglas. *Mythology and the Romantic Tradition*, Harvard University Press, 1937. A standard work.

Dobrée, Bonamy. *English Essayists*, Collins, 1946.

Dodds, A. E. *The Romantic Theory of Poetry*, Longmans, 1926.

Elwin, Malcolm. *The First Romantics*, Longmans, 1948. A solid and lively study of Wordsworth, Southey, and Coleridge.

James, D. G. *The Romantic Comedy*, Oxford University Press, 1948.

Knight, G. Wilson. *The Starlit Dome: Studies in the Poetry of Vision*, Oxford University Press, 1941.

Lovett, R. M., and Hughes, H. S. *The History of the Novel in England*, Houghton Mifflin, 1932. Chaps. VI–VIII are the best brief treatment of the period.

Raleigh, Sir W. A. *Romance: Two Lectures*, Princeton University Press, 1916. Excellent criticism.

Symons, Arthur. *The Romantic Movement in English Poetry*, Dutton, 1909. An admirable volume of criticism by a poet-critic of taste and discrimination.

BYRON

Complete Poetical Works, ed. by Paul Elmer More, Cambridge Edition, Houghton Mifflin. The best 1-vol. edition.

Childe Harold's Pilgrimage and Other Romantic Poems, ed. by S. C. Chew, Odyssey Press, Excellent introduction and notes.

Don Juan and Other Satirical Poems, ed. by Louis L. Bredvold, Odyssey Press. The most thoroughly annotated edition, with an excellent introduction.

Letters, Everyman's Library, Dutton.

Calvert, William J. *Byron: Romantic Paradox*, University of North Carolina Press, 1935.

Maurois, André. *Byron*, tr. by Hamish Miles, Cape, 1930.

Nicolson, Harold. *Byron, the Last Journey*, rev. ed., Houghton Mifflin, 1947.

Quennell, Peter. *Byron in Italy*, Viking, 1941.

COLERIDGE

Complete Poems, ed. by E. H. Coleridge, Oxford Standard Authors, Oxford University Press. The best inexpensive edition.

Biographia Literaria, Everyman's Library, Dutton.

The Portable Coleridge, ed. by I. A. Richards, Viking, 1951.

Armour, Richard W., and Howes, Raymond F., eds. *Coleridge the Talker: A Series of Contemporary Descriptions and Comments*, Cornell University Press, 1940.

Chambers, E. K. *Samuel Taylor Coleridge, A Biographical Study*, Oxford University Press, 1938.

Lowes, John Livingston. *The Road to Xanadu*, Houghton Mifflin, new ed., 1930. A fascinating piece of criticism and literary detective work.

McKenzie, Gordon. *Organic Unity in Coleridge*, University of California Press, 1939.

Richards, I. A. *Coleridge on the Imagination*, Harcourt, Brace, 1935.

Willey, Basil. *Coleridge on Imagination and Fancy*, London, G. Cumberlege, 1947.

DE QUINCEY

Selected Writings, introd. by Philip Van Doren Stern, Modern Library.

Confessions of an English Opium Eater, World's Classics, Oxford University Press.

Selections, with Essays by Leslie Stephen and Francis Thompson, ed. by M. R. Ridley, Clarendon English Series, Oxford University Press.

Eaton, Horace A. *Thomas de Quincey: A Biographical Narrative*, Oxford University Press, 1936. Sound and interesting.

HAZLITT

Characters of Shakespeare's Plays, World's Classics, Oxford University Press.

Lectures on English Comic Writers, and Miscellaneous Essays, Everyman's Library, Dutton.

Lectures on the English Poets, World's Classics, Oxford University Press.

Sketches and Essays, World's Classics, Oxford University Press.

MacLean, Catherine M. *Born under Saturn, a Biography of William Hazlitt*, London, Collins, 1943.

——— *Hazlitt Painted by Himself*, Macmillan, 1948. Delightful dissertations by Hazlitt on many subjects, arranged chronologically.

KEATS

Complete Poetical Works and Letters, ed. by H. E. Scudder, Cambridge Edition, Houghton Mifflin. Perhaps the best inexpensive edition of the scope indicated. (Compare the Shelley list.)

Complete Poems and Selected Letters, ed. by C. D. Thorpe, Odyssey Press. Very satisfactory introduction and notes; 58 of the most important and interesting letters.

Finney, C. L. *The Evolution of Keats's Poetry*, Harvard University Press, 1937.

Ford, G. H. *Keats and the Victorians*, Yale University Press, 1944.

Garrod, H. W. *Keats*, Oxford University Press, 1939. Excellent criticism.

Hewlett, Dorothy. *A Life of John Keats (Adonais)*, Hurst and Blackett, London, 1949. A new edition revised and enlarged. A fuller account of Keats than in any other single study.

Murry, J. M. *Keats and Shakespeare: A Study of Keats's Poetic Life from 1816 to 1820*, Oxford University Press, 1935.

Rollins, H. E., ed. *The Keats Circle: Letters and Papers 1816–1878*, Harvard University Press, 1948.

Thorpe, C. D. *The Mind of John Keats*, Oxford University Press, 1926. Thoroughly useful.

LAMB

Complete Works and Letters, Modern Library. The only inexpensive complete 1-vol. edition.

The Portable Lamb, ed. by John Mason Brown, Viking. A generous selection of essays, poems, and letters.

Ainger, Alfred. *Charles Lamb*, English Men of Letters Series, Macmillan.

SCOTT

Poetical Works, Oxford Standard Authors, Oxford University Press. The least expensive of the standard editions.

Novels. See below.

Lockhart, J. G. *Memoirs of Sir Walter Scott*, 5 vols., Houghton Mifflin, 1901. The classic biography by Scott's son-in-law in a modern edition. Also available in shortened 1-vol. edition, Everyman's Library, Dutton.

Pope-Hennessy, Dame Una B. *Sir Walter Scott*, London, Home and Van Thal, 1948.

SHELLEY

Complete Poetical Works, ed. by Thomas Hutchinson, Oxford Standard Authors. Little except difference of cost to choose between this and the Student's Cambridge Edition, Houghton Mifflin. The Modern Library offers the complete poems of Keats and Shelley in one inexpensive volume.

Literary and Philosophical Criticism, ed. by John Shawcross, Oxford Miscellany Series, Oxford University Press.

Baker, Carlos. *Shelley's Major Poetry*, Princeton University Press, 1948. A critical survey of his developing thought.

Blunden, Edmund. *Shelley, A Life Story*, Viking, 1946.

Trelawny, E. J. *Recollections of the Last Days of Shelley and Byron*, 1858, with Introduction by Edward Dowden, Oxford University Press, 1923.

White, Newman Ivey. *Shelley*, 2 vols., Knopf, 1940. Will be recognized, perhaps, as the definitive biography.

——— *Portrait of Shelley*, Knopf, 1945. Based upon the larger work, but more convenient and less expensive.

WORDSWORTH

Complete Poetical Works, ed. by Thomas Hutchinson and with introduction and notes by G. M. Harper, Oxford Standard Authors. Lacks a few features found in the Student's Cambridge edition, Houghton Mifflin, but less expensive.

The Prelude . . . (Text of 1805) ed. by Ernest de Selincourt, Oxford Standard Authors. The poem as Wordsworth the young man wrote it.

Garrod, H. W. *Wordsworth: Lectures and Essays*, new ed., Oxford, 1927.

Harper, G. M. *William Wordsworth: His Life, Works, and Influences*, 2 vols., Scribner's, 1929. The standard biography.

Selincourt, Ernest de. *Wordsworthian and Other Studies*, Oxford, 1947.

Wordsworth, Dorothy. *Journals*, ed. by Ernest de Selincourt, Macmillan, 1934. Interesting for their own sake and for the light they cast on Wordsworth's poetry.

NOVELS

These and the other principal works of three chief novelists of the period are obtainable in Everyman's Library, Dutton; Pocket Classics, Macmillan; World's Classics, Oxford; and similar inexpensive editions.

Austen, Jane. *Sense and Sensibility*, 1811; *Pride and Prejudice*, 1813; *Mansfield Park*, 1814; *Emma*, 1816; *Northanger Abbey*, 1818; *Persuasion*, 1818.

Edgeworth, Maria. *Castle Rackrent*, 1800.

Scott, Sir Walter. *Waverley*, 1814; *Guy Mannering*, 1815; *The Antiquary*, 1816; *Rob Roy*, 1817; *The Heart of Midlothian*, 1818; *The Bride of Lammermoor*, 1819; *Kenilworth*, 1821.

THE VICTORIAN PERIOD

PLATE XXI

A QUEEN VICTORIA (*From a contemporary engraving*)

This engraving shows the Queen as she appeared shortly after the death of Prince Albert. The remarkable devotion of Victoria to her husband persisted to the end of her life despite the fact that Albert died forty years before her. "How one *loves* to cling to one's grief," she once wrote, and she cherished the loss of Albert with great tenacity. After his death, her entire life was devoted to carrying out his desires and plans, both public and private. But, even though she rarely went to London and hardly ever appeared in public after 1861, she worked steadily on the problems of governing, always following the principles laid down by Albert. The great change wrought in her by the Prince's death is described by E. F. Benson in his biography of the Queen: "Straight from the exuberant noonday of her life, and the vivid vitality of her early middle-age, she passed without pause into a long-drawn and melancholy evening."

B A CONTEMPORARY REACTION TO DARWIN'S THEORY OF EVOLUTION (*Bettmann Archive*)

Violent and dismaying as was the impact of the doctrine of evolution on most Victorian minds, it was still possible for some people to consider its less solemn implications. The humorists, in reacting to Darwin's revolutionary theory, usually took the monkey's part. The obvious twist on the affront to human dignity was, of course, to have the monkey insulted by being shown his relation to mankind. Or, as in this cartoon, there was always the possibility of the monkey's asserting the rights of his relationship.

C AN IMPERIAL DURBAR AT DELHI, INDIA (*Bettmann Archive*)

A durbar was a formal reception held by the Governor General of India for the princes of the native states.

By 1860, the British Empire had attained the considerable area of two and a half million square miles, and embraced one hundred and forty-five million people. But by 1900 it had become a colossus thirteen million square miles on which lived three hundred and seventy million people. The problems of administering a vast portion of the world on which "the sun never set" occupied much of the energy of the British government, and Kipling could write feelingly of "the white man's burden."

D THE CRYSTAL PALACE (*British Information*)

The Crystal Palace was the great architectural triumph of Victoria's era. It came into being through the desire of the Society of Arts (of which Prince Albert was president) to house fittingly a projected international exposition of arts and crafts. A Royal Commission was appointed to select a plan for the new exhibition building. After studying two hundred and forty-five proposals and rejecting all of them, it proceeded to draw up its own scheme, which was greeted with universal disapprobation. Just when it seemed too late to do anything but follow the design of the Commission, Joseph Paxton came along with a daring suggestion for a building of glass—something unheard of in the history of architecture.

Paxton's life is a success story in the best rags-to-riches Victorian tradition. He began as a gardener on the estate of the Duke of Devonshire; by his energy and genius for organization he became manager of the Duke's affairs, a builder of villages and public works, a director of railways, and even, for a time, a newspaper owner. The idea for the Crystal Palace came from his success in designing magnificent hothouses for the Duke's estates.

Not without warnings of disaster (for who had ever heard of a building of glass, especially one of this size?), Paxton's design was accepted and the building began. It quickly caught the public fancy and thousands of people came to observe its progress, among them the Duke of Wellington, the Prince Consort, and Victoria herself. In twenty-two months it was finished and proved impervious to wind and hail; on May 1, 1851, the exhibit opened with a magnificent spectacle in which Victoria and Albert took the leading roles.

To the Victorians the Palace was a wonder of wonders, more beautiful and romantic than the Arabian Nights. Its end was as spectacular as its beginning: on the evening of the thirtieth of November, 1936, a fire broke out which was visible even to a pilot in the middle of the English Channel and which, by morning, had turned Paxton's triumph into a heap of twisted steel and molten glass.

PLATE XXI

PLATE XXII

PLATE XXIII

A

HEREBEGINNETH THE TALES OF CANTERBURY AND FIRST THE PROLOGUE THEREOF

WHAN THAT Aprille with his shoures soote
The droghte of March hath perced to the roote,
And bathed every veyne in swich licour,
Of which vertu engendred is the flour;
Whan Zephirus eek with his swete breeth
Inspired hath in every holt and heeth
The tendre croppes, and the yonge sonne
Hath in the Ram his halfe cours yronne,
And smale foweles maken melodye,
That slepen al the nyght with open eye,
So priketh hem nature in hir corages;
Thanne longen folk to goon on pilgrimages,
And palmeres for to seken straunge strondes,
To ferne halwes, kowthe in sondry londes;
And specially, from every shires ende
Of Engelond, to Caunterbury they wende,
The hooly blisful martir for to seke,
That hem hath holpen whan that they were seeke.

BIFIL that in that seson on a day,
In Southwerk at the Tabard as I lay,
Redy to wenden on my pilgrymage
To Caunterbury with ful devout corage,
At nyght were come into that hostelrye
Wel nyne and twenty in a compaignye,
Of sondry folk, by aventure yfalle
In felaweshipe, and pilgrimes were they alle,
That toward Caunterbury wolden ryde.

B

C

D

PLATE XXIV

PLATE XXII

A THE HOUSES OF PARLIAMENT (*Gendreau*)

In 1834 a disastrous fire destroyed the Houses of Parliament. The buildings that were erected to replace the old structure were in the style of perpendicular Gothic. Gothic architecture, which had been out of favor with the classicists of the seventeenth and eighteenth centuries, regained its popularity with the Romantic revival of medievalism and remained a favorite form of architecture throughout the Victorian era.

B A WINE TABLE OF IRISH BOG OAK, BY JONES OF DUBLIN (*From Peter Quennell's* Victorian Panorama *by kind permission of B. T. Batsford, Ltd., London*)

Victorian taste was highly eclectic. All styles and all periods were acceptable, especially if they were mixed in ornate profusion. Functionalism disappeared completely in a mass of carving, statuary, and gilt. And, if a fitting sentiment could somehow be attached to the resulting conglomeration, so much the better. "The Victorian artist," remarks Peter Quennell in the *Victorian Panorama*, "triumphed in the defeat of his material and was proud to show that no mere practical consideration had hampered the high-minded romantic élan with which he addressed himself to the undertaking."

C A VIEW OF OXFORD (*From Ingram's* Memorials)

Oxford occupied a peculiarly important place in the history of nineteenth-century thought, for it was the university of Newman, Ruskin, Arnold, Pater, Morris, Clough, and Swinburne. England's oldest university also gave its name to the great religious revival of the century. Matthew Arnold expressed the deep attachment of many nineteenth-century Oxonians to their university when he wrote:

. . . Adorable dreamer, whose heart has been so romantic! who hast given thyself so prodigally, given thyself to sides and to heroes not mine, only never to the Philistines! home of lost causes, and forsaken beliefs and unpopular names, and impossible loyalties.

D VIEW OF BOLOGNA THROUGH TREES, BY JOHN RUSKIN

During his travels in Italy, Ruskin made many sketches in the process of formulating his theories. These drawings were not intended to be works of art but precise studies for future reference. They were made with meticulous attention to detail and often served as illustrations in Ruskin's theoretical works.

E A SCENE IN THE LONDON SLUMS, BY GUSTAVE DORÉ (*Bettmann Archive*)

The utter misery of the English industrial worker's life, so forcefully depicted in this drawing by Gustave Doré, the French painter and illustrator, evoked such poems as Elizabeth Barrett Browning's "The Cry of the Children" and "The Cry of the Human," and Thomas Hood's "Song of the Shirt." Indeed, much of the social thought and activity of the century was devoted to the amelioration of the appalling conditions of the working classes.

PLATE XXIII

A BROWNING TAKING TEA WITH THE BROWNING SOCIETY, BY MAX BEERBOHM (*From* The Poet's Corner)

In his later years, Browning was the center of a circle of admirers whose adulation he gracefully accepted while he tried to answer their questions about obscure portions of his poetry. It is reported that on one occasion some earnest young ladies at Newnham College, Cambridge, invited him to tea and placed a crown of roses (without thorns, of course) on his head.

B ILLUSTRATIONS FROM THE "BAB BALLADS," BY WILLIAM SCHWENCK GILBERT (*Macmillan and Co., Ltd., London*)

If we are inclined to think of the Victorian era as all high seriousness, William S. Gilbert, Lewis Carroll, Edward Lear, and many of their contemporaries serve to remind us that the century had a sense of humor. Gilbert is remembered particularly for his contribution to the most original light operas ever produced in England. In them he satirized such sacred English institutions as Parliament, the navy, the army, the police force, the judicial system. And in *Patience* he ridiculed unmercifully Oscar Wilde and "art for art's sake." The *Bab Ballads*, for which Gilbert drew his own illustrations, are in a similar vein of light, bantering humor which often conceals a satirical dart. From left to right, the sketches illustrate "Captain Reece," "The Rival Curates," and "The Reverend Micah Sowls."

C DISRAELI IN 1852

This drawing shows Disraeli just after he had been made Chancellor of the Exchequer. Although Disraeli, at the time this sketch was made, had not yet achieved many political triumphs, he had already made a reputation as a novelist. Disraeli the statesman has somewhat obscured Disraeli the novelist today, but in the eighteen thirties he was well known as the author of fashionable romances like *Vivian Grey* and *Venetia* (a romance about Byron and Shelley) which were popular despite the fact that they attracted little notice from the critics. In the eighteen forties, he wrote political novels—*Coningsby*, which sets forth the ideals of the Young Englander party; *Sybil*, an exposé of the deplorable conditions in the coal mines; *Tancred*, a highly romantic vision of the world to come. In a final period of writing during the eighteen sixties he produced *Lothair*, which Edmund Gosse called "an ironic romance" and his finest novel. In his novels, Disraeli revealed a real gift for wit and satire, despite the occasional extravagances of his language, and a "buoyant and radiant temperament."

D THE BRONTË SISTERS, BY PATRICK BRANWELL BRONTË (*British Information*)

Anne, the youngest is on the left; Emily is in the middle; Charlotte, on the right.

Not the least talented member of the strange Brontë family was Patrick Branwell, the only brother of Charlotte, Emily, and Anne. Like his sisters, he wrote brilliantly from the time he was eleven or twelve years old; he was a good amateur musician; and he might have been a successful portrait painter. This picture of his sisters does not reveal any remarkable talent, but it suggests admirably the moody, introspective character of the three girls.

PLATE XXIV

A THE BLESSED DAMOZEL, BY DANTE GABRIEL ROSSETTI

Few poets are so fortunate as to be able to illustrate their own works. Rossetti was one of these happy few, and his painting of the Blessed Damozel is the best possible visualization one could imagine for the poem. Its elaborate detail is characteristic of the style of the Pre-Raphaelite Brotherhood. Like other products of this school, the Blessed Damozel was painted with great care, and with a deep regard for the "truth" of the subject.

B THE FIRST PAGE OF THE KELMSCOTT PRESS EDITION OF CHAUCER (*Courtesy, the Spencer Collection of the New York Public Library*)

Among William Morris's many activities was the founding and operation of the Kelmscott Press, devoted to the making of fine books. One of the most ambitious works to come from the Press was a complete edition of Chaucer, edited by F. S. Ellis, with eighty-seven illustrations by Edward Burne-Jones, a Pre-Raphaelite painter. The title page, decorative initials, and type face were designed by Morris himself. Only four hundred and thirty-eight copies of the Chaucer were printed, but it took twenty-one months to produce them. When the book was finally issued in June, 1896, it was hailed by contemporary reviewers as "the noblest book as yet achieved by any English printer" and "the greatest triumph of English typography." It seems appropriate that Morris's most distinguished achievement in printing was an edition of a great medieval poet who represented the era Morris loved best.

C ALFRED, LORD TENNYSON (*Bettmann Archive*)

D MATTHEW ARNOLD (*Elliott and Fry*)

Here is Matthew Arnold as the camera saw him. The art of photography was in its infancy during the nineteenth century, but, fortunately, many of the leading figures of the time submitted to the ordeal of having their pictures taken. The somewhat fixed and strained expression observable in most early camera studies resulted from the length of time required to expose the plate properly.

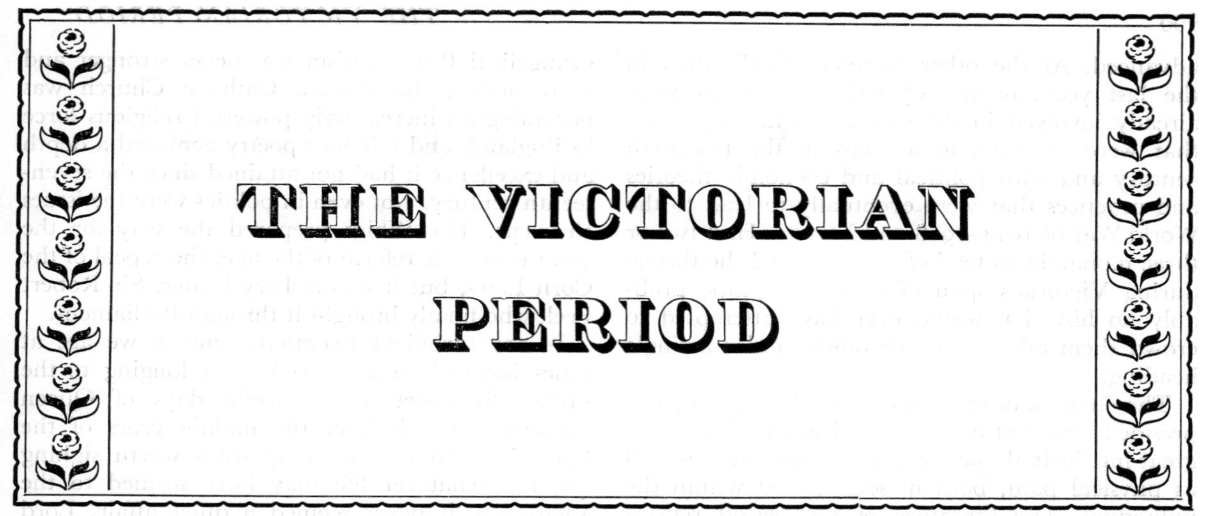

The General Character of the Period

NO British sovereign since Queen Elizabeth has exerted such a profound influence on an age as that other great Queen, Victoria. But Victoria did not, like Elizabeth or Louis XIV, decide by her personal choice the trend and policy of the age that bears her name. She presided over the period rather than shaped it, and in many respects she was the moderator of the great meeting of men and forces in nineteenth-century England and Europe. In an age of continual change and unparalleled expansion in almost every field of activity, she was a symbol of steadiness. Governments and governmental policies came and went, but Victoria remained the head of the government, and her throne was far more firmly established when she quitted it than it had been when she ascended it. If, as one of her biographers has said, "she never seemed to doubt that the country was *hers*, that the Ministers were *her* Ministers, and that the people were *her* people," it may be said with equal truth that the country, the Ministers, and the people never seemed to doubt that the little woman of German descent was *their* Queen. While the territory over which she reigned was expanding into the vastest empire the world had ever seen, her crown became more and more the symbol that held the great agglomeration of peoples and lands together. She who had begun as Queen of England became the Empress of India and Sovereign Lady of the isles beyond the seas. And yet it was Victoria the woman, the wife, the mother, the widow, even more than Victoria the Queen and Empress, who appealed most strongly to the people of the island and the empire and who exerted the greatest influence upon them. In her Journal on the day of her accession she wrote: "Since it has pleased Providence to place me in this station, I shall do my utmost to fulfill my duty towards my country." Her industry, constancy, and devotion in carrying this resolution into effect throughout her long reign won her a place in the hearts of her people and in history which cleverness and intellectual genius could never have achieved unaided. It is largely because the British monarch has since followed the example of domestic decorum and public probity which she established that it continues to enjoy such loyalty, respect, and affection as were demonstrated—half a century after Victoria's own Diamond Jubilee—at the wedding in 1947 of her great-great-granddaughter, Princess Elizabeth.

The reign of Queen Victoria extended from 1837 to 1901, but the limits of the "Age of Victoria" are not so neatly defined. The "Age of Elizabeth" had a degree of unity that we do not discover in the last two-thirds of the nineteenth century in England. At one extreme, the Victorians inherited the problems and carried forward many of the attitudes and policies of the post-Napoleonic years. The Romantic period had been one of revolutions —in industry, in society, in intellectual and religious spheres, in literature—and these revolutions were accelerated as the nineteenth century advanced. At the other extreme, Englishmen in the last years of the Queen's long reign were already involved in the social and literary issues that were to come to a focus in the twentieth century and with political and economic theories and practices that were eventually to lead to the World War of 1914–1918 and beyond. Had two or three monarchs instead of one occupied the throne during Victoria's span of sixty-four years, probably no historian would ever have attempted to crowd them all into the chronicle under a single heading.

The changes in the scene over which the Queen presided were not accomplished easily. There was great intellectual and spiritual disturbance, as well as physical pain, both in society and within the individual. The literature of the period reflects the conflict between advocates of the triumphant material prosperity of the country and those others who felt it had been achieved by the exploitation of human beings and at the expense of spiritual and esthetic values. Carlyle, Ruskin, and Arnold protested against the decline in spiritual life and the sense of beauty that were observable in a generation too much given to the process of getting and spending. William Morris deplored the ugliness that industrialism brought with it in the growth of cities and factories and in the system of mass production.

The Victorians, even the greatest of them, were often badly puzzled men, and their literature bears ample testimony of their bewilderment. It has been fashionable to berate them for their tendency to compromise, to patch things up, to "muddle through," instead of going to the root of their difficulties. But one reason for their compromising may be that life had grown too complex for the out-and-out solutions sometimes found in earlier days. If Victorian horizons were much wider than those of an earlier England, they were also much less clear. This is partly why the Victorians were among the most paradoxical of men. In theory they committed themselves on the whole to a hard-headed utilitarianism, yet most of their literature is idealistic and decorously romantic. Despite the imperialism of the age, never was literature more distinctly English than during the great period of empire-building. The Victorians were cosmopolitan and they were insular. They were respectable even when they were not moral, pious even when they were not religious. The prophets of the time deplored the inroads of science upon religious faith; but the Church of England was revivified by the Oxford Movement, evangelical Protestantism was never stronger and more active, the Roman Catholic Church was becoming an increasingly powerful religious force in England, and religious poetry achieved a depth and excellence it had not attained since the seventeenth century. Not even in politics were the issues clear-cut. The Whigs prepared the way for the great economic reform of the age, the repeal of the Corn Laws, but it was a Tory leader, Sir Robert Peel, who finally brought it through Parliament.

In the turbulent twentieth century we are at times inclined to look back with longing to the supposedly quiet and peaceful days of Queen Victoria. And, indeed, the middle years of the Queen's reign are in many ways worth sighing for. But whatever life may have seemed to the Victorians, it never seemed a quiet affair. Lord David Cecil, writing in our own day, correctly speaks of "the tumultuous energy" of the time. The Victorians thought of themselves as moving with breakneck speed, in Tennyson's words, "down the ringing grooves of change." And they were right about it, for in many ways 1901 was farther away from 1837 than 1837 had been from 1066.

An Age of Political and Economic Reform

The first great "Victorian" reform actually antedated Victoria by five years. Until 1832 the old Tudor list of boroughs was still in use. As a result, large towns of recent growth were unrepresented in Parliament, while some of the localities which sent "representatives" were unpopulated. The lords who controlled the "rotten boroughs," as the unpopulated sections were called, sold seats to the highest bidders. This corrupt political pattern was broken when the Reform Bill of 1832 abolished all boroughs having less than two thousand inhabitants, and decreased by 50 per cent the number of representatives admitted from towns with a population between two thousand and four thousand. In urban districts the vote was given to all adult males who paid an annual rental of £10 or more for their houses; in the country a comparable property qualification was set up. Fear alone put the Reform Bill through. The first time the Commons passed it, the House of Lords rejected it. Rioting broke out, and civil war seemed imminent. King William IV cast the deciding vote when he told Lord Grey, the Prime Minister, that if necessary he would create enough new Whig peers to outvote the Tory enemies of the measure in the upper house.

Yet the Reform Bill was less revolutionary than it seemed. It was not a genuinely democratic measure; it gave the vote neither to factory workers nor to agricultural laborers. Furthermore the conservatism of the new voters made its effects less sensational than its enemies had feared. It was the thriving middle classes—the merchants and the bankers and the manufacturers—who had worked for it, and it was their interests that were served. A new commercial aristocracy was remaking England and preparing to take control of the government. New party names as well as a new principle of representation came at this time. The Whigs, who were identified with the progressive middle class, now called themselves Liberals. The Tories, committed to the preservation of time-honored institutions and customs, chose the name Conservatives.

With the first Parliament elected on the new basis came several important reforms. In 1833 the Emancipation Bill ended slavery in British colonies, with heavy compensation to the owners. The Poor Law of 1834, which attempted to check the growth of pauperism by substituting workhouse relief for the system of the dole, was, although well-intentioned, bitterly resented by the poorer classes. Indigent persons had been accustomed to live where they pleased and to supplement government aid in any way they wished. Now they must live in the workhouse, "the Bastille of the Poor," and permit creatures like Oliver Twist's Mr. Bumble to rule them body and soul, or else starve.

Chattel slavery was abolished in 1833, but industrial slavery continued. The seventh Earl of Shaftesbury was the great hero of factory-reform legislation. The first important Factory Law, in 1833, prohibited the employment in factories of children under nine years old. Children between nine and thirteen might be employed not more than nine hours a day. Night work was prohibited for persons under twenty-one and for all women. Schooling for factory children on alternate days or half-days was provided by subsequent legislation. Reforms in municipal government, providing for a system of elected councils, were meanwhile forced upon a reluctant House of Commons in 1835.

But there was room for further improvement. The undemocratic character of the Reform Bill of 1832, the unpopularity of the Poor Law, and the generally unhappy condition of the laborers led to the Chartist Movement of the 1840's. The working classes, convinced that conditions would be no better until they were themselves better represented in Parliament, organized a campaign to bring about some desired changes. In 1838 a program for the campaign was agreed upon. It embodied six demands: (1) the abolition of property qualifications for members of Parliament; (2) salaries for members of Parliament; (3) annual election of Parliament; (4) equal electoral districts; (5) equal manhood suffrage; (6) voting by secret ballot. To the Conservatives all this seemed very dangerous indeed.

The Chartists circulated monster petitions and secured thousands of signatures; in 1848 they undertook an abortive march on London. Yet Chartism, the most formidable working-class movement England had ever seen, failed—chiefly because, unlike the advocates of the Reform Bill, and unlike those who brought about the repeal of the Corn Laws, the Chartists found no way to identify their cause with the special interests of any influential class. Ultimately most of the ends they sought were achieved by less violent and more characteristically English methods of free discussion and legislative action, which resulted in the Reform Bills of 1867 and 1884–1885. The violent methods of the Chartists, however, drew the attention of the government and the community to the misery of the working classes, and showed that the people of those classes were beginning to think and to seek legislative solutions of their problems.

The Corn[1] Laws had added greatly to the distress of the poor. These were protective tariffs passed in 1815 in the interests of landlords and farmers to prevent the importation of cheap foreign grain, which would depress the market. The failure of the potato crop in Ireland in 1845 and the resulting famine that threatened several million people with starvation brought matters to a crisis. In 1846 the Prime Minister, Sir Robert Peel, proposed and brought about the passage of a bill repealing the Corn Laws. Within a dozen years all other protective tariffs were removed, and England entered upon a period of free trade, with a subsequently rapid increase in manufacture and commerce.

The political life of the Victorian period, in its domestic aspects at least, is intimately tied up with its economic theories. The doctrine of *laissez faire* ("let alone," "hands off") derives in part from Adam Smith's *Wealth of Nations*, 1776, but was elaborated by Jeremy Bentham, T. R. Malthus, and other economic theorists of the nineteenth century. Bentham is famous as the exponent of

[1] Corn, in England, means grain, specifically wheat.

the philosophical doctrine of Utility, the principle of which he defined as "the greatest happiness for the greatest number." In the economic sphere this principle meant to him that the government should let things alone and allow the economic situation to adjust itself automatically and naturally. Wages and profits, according to this doctrine, are fixed by the automatic laws of supply and demand, by which at one extreme a man makes a million pounds, or at the other he starves to death in the gutter. But to assist the beggar is to upset the sacred laws of economics. Malthus, a clergyman, made his special contribution to the political economy of the time in 1798 by calculating that, whereas the population of a country increases in geometric proportion (2, 4, 16, 256, 65,536, and so on), the food supply can increase only in arithmetical proportion (2, 4, 8, 16, 32, and so on). Although Malthus was quick to add that "moral restraint" could hold the population in check, popular faith in moral restraint was not sufficient to prevent the specter of coming starvation from haunting men's minds.

Such economic principles constituted the "dismal science," as Carlyle called it. Dickens, who derived many of his ideas from Carlyle, castigated it again and again, never more effectively than in *The Chimes*, where Mr. Filer and Alderman Cute break Toby's faith in life by proving conclusively that, being long past the average age, he has no right to exist at all, and whenever he eats tripe—notoriously the most extravagant food a man can eat—he takes every bite he swallows out of the mouths of widows and orphans. If it be objected that Dickens was a caricaturist, it may be remembered that the *Westminster Review*, the organ of the Utilitarians, found Scrooge's presentation of a turkey to Bob Cratchit, in Dickens's *Christmas Carol*, quite incompatible with the principles of political economy.

Yet the Utilitarians were not monsters. On one side of him, indeed, Bentham (himself enough of an eccentric to qualify for any novel of Dickens) was an apostle of human liberty. He believed in free speech and free assembly; he accepted most of the ideas of the Chartists; he championed labor's right to organize; he would educate poor children, and abolish cruel punishments. The Utilitarians helped to bring about the repeal of the Corn Laws. Such a reform was wholly in line with laissez-faire principles, for customs duties interfere with trade between nations quite as definitely as, say, factory legislation or child labor laws represent an intrusion of government into the business of money-making or into the home. When the farmers argued that the repeal of protective tariffs would make it impossible to raise crops in England, the free traders replied that England would simply have to buy her food beyond the seas, and pay for it with manufactured articles that she could produce better and more cheaply than other nations. As it turned out, English agriculture was not destroyed, though its importance declined. The time was close at hand when neither free trade nor protection could make it possible for the little island to feed her expanding population without supplies from overseas. Then she would have to sell enough goods abroad to buy the food she needed, and keep the sea lanes open to bring it in.

As the country awoke to the degradation of the working classes, industrial reform proceeded gradually but inevitably, in spite of the advocates of laissez faire and industrial freedom. In 1842 the employment of women and children in the coal mines was ended. In 1847 the Ten Hours Bill reduced to ten the number of hours in the working day for women and young persons in factories and as a practical result brought a similar reduction for all factory employees. In 1850 the textile industry accepted a Saturday half-holiday. These reforms were brought about by the labors of many persons—philanthropists, statesmen, clergymen, poets, and novelists. The press also had its share in them. In 1843 *Blackwood's Magazine* opened its columns to Mrs. Browning's passionate poem "The Cry of the Children," and in the same year Thomas Hood's indictment of sweated labor, "The Song of the Shirt," appeared in the great magazine of British humor, *Punch*, which was often surprisingly valiant in championing the cause of the underprivileged.

But the masses were no longer depending helplessly on the aid they might receive from fair-minded individuals among the upper classes. Gradually they were winning the right to help themselves. Trade-unionism was legalized in 1864; twenty years later the Cooperative Societies were successfully established, to the immeasurable benefit of working-class families. In 1859 the right to strike had been won.

Karl Marx founded the first International Workingmen's Association in London in 1864; three years later he published *Das Kapital*, the Bible of modern communism. But there was no real interest in communism (or socialism, for that matter) in England before the 1880's. William Morris's socialism was less revolutionary than it appeared. It rested on his love of beauty; he simply could not endure the ugliness that modern capitalism and mass production had created. But he never found a party that satisfied him, and was himself one of the most uncompromising individualists who ever lived. In 1884 the Fabian Society appeared, headed by Beatrice and Sidney Webb, George Bernard Shaw, and other upper-middle-class intellectuals. The Fabians, as their name indicates, believed that socialism could come only gradually, through a steady widening of the functions of the state, and they set themselves steadily against violent revolution.

In fairness to nineteenth-century Britain we cannot permit ourselves to be shocked by the economic and social evils that the Industrial Revolution brought in its wake, unless we remember also that Britain led in the legislation designed to secure the laborer fair living and working conditions. Trade-unionism, also, is a product of Victorian England. If we are shocked, as well we may be, by the amount of suffering the Victorians tolerated, it is only fair to remember how much suffering they put an end to, or alleviated. In the 1840's, for the first time in human history, the use of anesthetics in America and Britain relieved the pain of the operating table and made surgical progress possible. In the legal sphere the Victorians did away with an enormous number of ancient cruelties. When Victoria ascended the throne, four hundred and thirty-eight offenses were still punishable by death in England. During her reign the death penalty was limited to two offenses only—murder and treason. Executions, which had always been conducted in public to discourage offenders, finally came to be performed in the privacy of prisons. And, with the softening of penalties and the stressing of prevention and correction rather than punishment, came a decrease in crime. The unarmed police force of our day came into being with Sir Robert Peel's "bobbies" in 1829, and the swift, sure, efficient administration of justice that characterizes contemporary Britain was in process of development.

Once the rights of women and children had been recognized in industry, it was inevitable that they should be recognized elsewhere as well. There was the right to an education, for example. In 1870, for the first time in English history, the Elementary Education Bill was designed to provide sufficient schools for everybody. In 1891 a common-school education, free to all, became compulsory. After 1867 women were admitted to examinations in the University of London. Girton College, for the higher education of women, was incorporated at Cambridge in 1872. Such women as Frances Power Cobbe, Octavia Hill, Emma Cons, and Barbara Leigh-Smith, names not often recalled today, worked hard to win for women the privileges they now enjoy. So, also, directly or indirectly, did the great women novelists; and so did Florence Nightingale, "the Lady of the Lamp," out of whose hospital experiences during the Crimean War grew the modern profession of nursing. There were also men, like the novelist and poet George Meredith and the philosopher and economist John Stuart Mill, who worked as hard as any woman for "female emancipation."

Foreign affairs during the Victorian period are of less importance to the student of literature than the changing scenes on the domestic stage, and they were of less interest to the Victorians, who were not on the whole politically minded. For about forty years—from Waterloo, 1815, until the Crimean War, 1854–1856—England managed to keep out of European wars, thanks partly to her preoccupation with matters at home and partly to good luck. The great improvement in economic and social conditions in England, and the subsequent lessening of discontent and tension, combined with the increase in the prosperity of the middle class and the innate conservatism of the English to spare the country from such convulsions and upheavals as the continent was subjected to in 1830 and 1848. The Crimean War, which resulted from Britain's policy of protecting Turkey as a buffer against Russia, was badly mismanaged. The charge of the Light Brigade, which Tennyson celebrated with bitter, unconscious irony, might well symbolize the conflict as a whole.

Relations with the United States thrice approached the breaking-point: first in 1844, when James K. Polk was elected President on a platform which demanded that Latitude 54° 40′ N. be established as the northern boundary of the United States; next during the War Between the States, when the Union blockade of Confederate ports cut off England's supply of cotton; finally in Cleveland's administration, when the Venezuela boundary dispute threatened the Monroe Doctrine. These crises were fortunately resolved by the exercise of wisdom and patience on both sides of the Atlantic. The last of the three, which was settled by arbitration, resulted in greatly improved relations between Britain and the United States, and provided a triumph for the new method of arbitration in cases of disputes among nations.

The closing years of the old Queen's reign saw the British involved in a war which was the outcome of the clashing interests of their colonists and the Boers, the descendants of the Dutch settlers in South Africa. Of more significance than the South African War, however, was the speedy reconciliation between the British and the Boers. In a few years after the conflict the Boer states became self-governing provinces of the Union of South Africa, a British dominion, with rights equal to those of the British. Half a century after the war, in 1948, General Smuts, who as commander in chief of the Boer forces in Cape Colony had held out to the last against the British armies, was installed as Chancellor of Cambridge University.

The second half of Victoria's reign constituted a period of great prosperity, such as the impoverished nation of the 1830's could hardly have dreamed of. The first world's fair, the Great Exhibition of 1851, organized by the Queen's consort, Prince Albert, drew the attention of the world to the commercial and industrial possibilities of the British Empire. The center of this festival of international good will was the Crystal Palace, one of the most remarkable of nineteenth-century structures, consisting entirely of glass and iron. Scientific inventions had mechanized, modified, reshaped, and enriched life in many ways during the century. The steam engine, first successfully used in land and ocean transportation in the 1830's, had drawn the country and the world together as never before. The process of communication was greatly simplified and extended by the introduction of the first adhesive postage stamp by Sir Rowland Hill and the advent of the "penny post" in 1840. The telegraph and the telephone still further accelerated the process, and in the year before the Queen celebrated her Diamond Jubilee Marconi gave his first demonstration of wireless telegraphy. It is hard to realize that Queen Victoria was the first British sovereign to speak through the telephone, to hear her voice as recorded on wax cylinders, to be photographed by each new process in turn, and, before her reign was over, to be photographed in motion.

The steady growth of the democratic spirit throughout the century is evident in this brief chronicle of the main political and social reforms of the Victorian period. The middle class steadily assumed more and more of the responsibility and honor of governing the country. The two greatest statesmen of the Queen's later years, the Conservative Benjamin Disraeli and the Liberal William Ewart Gladstone, were both from the middle class. Disraeli, however, was never a democrat in the sense in which his great rival was a democrat. He sought at all costs to avoid breaking the line of historic continuity. To him the state was not a mechanism but an organism. In his earlier years his "Young England" party planned to save the country by restoring feudal ideals. In later years when he became Prime Minister, Disraeli did not restore feudalism. But his mysticism and Hebrew romanticism contributed to the building of the empire, and they survive today in the half-mystical ideal that pervades the group of democratic countries comprising the British Commonwealth of Nations. For Gladstone, on the other hand, the people's voice was the voice of God. The people, through Parliament, were the rulers of England, and he, as their agent and Prime Minister, was prepared to carry out their mandates.

Religion, Theology, and Science

But politics and economics do not make up the whole of a nation's life, and in the nineteenth century both religion and science touched human experience and affected the thought and literature of the time quite as closely as political and economic circumstances. The spirit of reform was not confined to government and industry. In 1833, the year after the first Reform Bill, a group of Oxford men, as dissatisfied with conditions in the Church of England as others were with those in Parliament, began a movement to bring about a reformation in the Church, to increase its spiritual power, and to restore and emphasize Catholic doctrine and ritual. This Oxford Movement, as it is called, was begun by John Keble, a disciple of Wordsworth and author of a volume of religious poems, *The Christian Year*. The movement, coming as it did toward the close of the Romantic period, was related, though probably unconsciously, to the Romantic revival of interest in the Middle Ages, especially the beliefs and ceremonies of those times. The most influential of the reformers was John Henry Newman, vicar of St. Mary's, the university church. A bitter struggle ensued for a decade between the different parties within the Church of England. The reformers carried on their campaign chiefly in a series of papers called *Tracts for the Times*, which gave the name Tractarian to the movement. Its chief results were the conversion of Newman to the Roman Catholic Church in 1845, the formation of the High Church group within the Church of England, and a general quickening of the spiritual life of the Church.

The Broad Church Movement, of which Charles Kingsley, clergyman and novelist, was one of the initiators, provided a middle ground between the High Church, with its Catholic principles and practices, and the evangelical Low Church, which had more in common with the Dissenters, the followers of the Wesleys, and other Protestants. The reinvigoration of the Church was manifested in social as well as spiritual matters. A group known as the Christian Socialists, of whom Kingsley was the most active, perceived the necessity of applying Christianity to social and economic problems. Kingsley advocated Christian Socialism in a series of tracts and in his novels, *Yeast*, 1848, and *Alton Locke*, 1850.

The rapid expansion of industry, which was the result of the application of new scientific processes to the age-old methods of getting a living, was disturbing to such prophets as Carlyle and Ruskin, who saw material prosperity being attained at the expense of spiritual values. New scientific and philosophical researches in the fields of geology and biology were profoundly influencing and disquieting the religious mind of England. A series of discoveries with respect to the origin and nature of men and matter was challenging accepted opinions of the universe and man's place in it. One of the most important works of the century, Sir Charles Lyell's *Principles of Geology*, 1830–1833, established a continuous history for life on this planet. Michael Faraday's discoveries, which grew out of his study of the transformation of mechanical energy to electrical energy, attracted attention. Sir Francis Galton, a cousin of Charles Darwin, did pioneer work in the field of heredity, coining the word "eugenics." Perhaps the most important and profoundly influential scientific work of the century was Charles Darwin's *Origin of Species*, 1859, which gave to the world the theory of evolution known as Darwinism—the theory that living forms originate by development from earlier forms, not by special creation. Darwin's theory had in certain aspects been anticipated by others.[2] In 1844 Robert Chambers, the indefatigable proprietor of *Chambers's Journal*, had startled the English public with the suggestion that man had descended from a monkey, or both monkey and man from some common ancestor. Although scientists did not take Chambers's *Vestiges of the Natural History of Creation* seriously, it had a considerable influence on the popular mind, and Disraeli burlesqued it in his novel *Tancred*. But it was Darwin's book that made the real impact. *The Origin of Species* was based on a wealth of data and organized in a superb fashion. Moreover, Darwin had a gifted writer and lecturer to support it and explain it to the public in Thomas Henry Huxley, his self-appointed "bulldog."

The Origin of Species maintained that all living creatures had developed through infinite differentiations from a single source. Darwin's special emphasis on the idea of the survival of the fittest through "natural selection" caught the popular imagination. *Punch*, in 1861, referred familiarly and facetiously to the work and to the earlier *Vestiges* of Chambers. But it was no laughing matter to the serious thinkers of the day and to most orthodox Christians. To many people it seemed obvious that, if the evolutionists were right, the Church could no longer maintain the historicity of the Book of Genesis, nor could she continue to believe, in terms of Archbishop Ussher's chronology, that God had created the world in the year 4004 B.C. Darwinism divided the religious world into three groups: (1) There were those who regarded the evolutionary hypothesis as an unconfirmed theory. They did not believe that Darwin's evidence justified the conclusions he had drawn. The great majority of religious persons of all denominations was in this group. (2) There were those who, regretfully or enthusiastically, felt not only that Darwin had established his hypothesis, but that, having done so, he had left no room for God in the universe. They, therefore, were compelled to reorient all their thinking on a naturalistic basis. (3) There were those, finally, who felt that evolution was simply "God's way of doing things." They embraced the new hypothesis eagerly; it seemed to them that they had a greater God to worship than they had ever known before.

The conflict between the theologians and the scientists raged throughout the rest of the century, and, indeed, continues into our own day. Huxley expounded Darwin's theories to the layman in such able works as *Man's Place in Nature*, 1863, and *Lay Sermons*, 1870. Herbert Spencer applied the theory of evolution to particular sciences. In 1870 appeared *Contributions to the Theory of Natural Selection* by Alfred Russel Wallace, who worked out his theories of evolution independently of Darwin. A

[2] Aristotle and other ancient philosophers had considered the possibility of a succession of simpler organisms leading to the human. St. Augustine had propounded the belief that it is not per se improbable that God should have made use of natural, evolutionary, original causes in the production of man's body. The work of Lamarck, the French naturalist, was important as a forerunner to that of Darwin, as were Lyell's *Principles* and *The Development Hypothesis* by Herbert Spencer, 1852.

year later Darwin published his *Descent of Man*. The claims of theology were supported by the clergymen generally, led by Bishop Samuel Wilberforce, son of the philanthropist, who debated publicly on the subject with Huxley at Oxford in 1860. Charles Kingsley arrayed himself against the new biology in his novel *Water Babies*, 1863.

Not all the problems that disturbed the religious mind were posed by natural science. The Church was invaded by the "higher criticism," largely a German importation, which insisted on applying to the literary study of the Bible the same criteria that were being applied to Homer and Shakespeare. George Eliot translated David Strauss's rationalistic, but by no means atheistic, *Life of Jesus* in 1846, and found herself obliged to give up the Christian religion as she had understood it. Bishop Colenso of Natal created a tremendous sensation in 1862 when he denied not only the Mosaic authorship of the Pentateuch but the historical character of much of it. His fellow bishops in South Africa excommunicated him; in England only one bishop took his part.

All these battles were but skirmishes, however; they did not touch the real problem. The fundamental question was not whether Moses wrote the Pentateuch, nor even whether men had descended from monkeys, but whether man was a machine or a spiritual entity. Could the spirit of religion survive in a mechanized world? Such churchmen and scholars as Joseph Barber Lightfoot and Fenton J. A. Hort, men of God with a blazing passion for social righteousness, answered triumphantly in the affirmative. But they were not all England. Others like Harriet Martineau and Charles Bradlaugh did not hesitate to propagandize on behalf of out-and-out atheism. Even more dangerous to established religion were those who did recognize spiritual values but who felt that the time had come to transfer values from heaven to earth. For some, the evolutionary process itself had taken on religious significance, and this was all the religion they felt they needed or could accept. "Progress," said Herbert Spencer, "is not an accident but a necessity. What we call evil and immorality must disappear. It is certain that man must become perfect." One cannot entertain such an idea without having all his other beliefs affected. One reason why David Strauss found it impossible to accept the Jesus of the New Testament was that as an evolutionist he could not believe that the perfect man had appeared so early in human history.

There were bigotry and narrow-mindedness on both sides. Many theologians as well as humbler believers were too conservative to be able to accept new ideas. Thus and so had religion always been conceived. One must continue to conceive it thus and so; otherwise one must scrap religion altogether. Many of the scientists, although theoretically taking their stand wholly on the principle of pure reason and free experimentation, were quite as dogmatic as the narrowest of the theologians.

The importance for Victorian literature of religion and the struggle between the new science and the old faith appears clearly in the fact that one can classify most of the poets of the time largely in terms of their religious attitudes. Tennyson and Browning are, of course, the great poets of faith. Tennyson, the greatest exponent in poetry of Victorian life and thought, faced at one period or another all the problems of his time. The questions posed by the theory of evolution—for instance, the view of "Nature, red in tooth and claw," caring neither for the individual nor the type—find utterance in his poems. But he can still "trust the larger hope"—"behind the veil." Tennyson helped his contemporaries because he made it possible for them to think his thoughts after him. Browning doubted and struggled only in the early and uncharacteristic *Pauline*. If he had any doubts thereafter, he kept them to himself. His published work is one vigorous, unceasing affirmation. Matthew Arnold and Arthur Hugh Clough, however, stand opposite Tennyson and Browning as the poets of doubt. They were quite as deeply interested in religion, and, though they failed to find the same certainty, they were quite as religious in spirit. Also poets of faith are those in the Roman Catholic group—Coventry Patmore, Gerard Manley Hopkins, Francis Thompson, and Alice Meynell. Christina Rossetti was not a Roman Catholic, but she has much of the Catholic devotional spirit.

With the later Victorians, however, the attitude toward religion changed. The reaction was perhaps as inevitable as it was unfortunate. Tennyson's *In Memoriam*, for all its greatness, is no doubt a painfully introspective work, and a series of weak imitations of *In Memoriam* would doubtless have been intolerable. The change appears not so much in Swinburne, whose very hostility to Christianity had much of evangelical fervor about it; nor in Hardy, for all his devastating irony. Whatever may be said of his head, Hardy's heart, like George Eliot's, clung passionately to the God of the old religion. It is rather in men like Meredith, Rossetti, and Morris that one most clearly sees the change. Meredith was not irreligious, but no trace of otherworldliness ever appears in him. Rossetti was a mystic of sorts, but his mysticism concerned itself with man and woman rather than with man and God. Morris began as a Tractarian but ended without allegiance to any religious dogma.

Victorian Literature

Victorian literature reflects the extraordinary richness, variety, and complexity of the period that produced it. One cannot characterize it by a single word or phrase. Unlike the literature of the two periods that preceded the Victorian, it has no one dominant mood or quality. The writers of the age excelled in all modern forms except the drama. The variety of the poetry and prose they produced is matched only by its bulk, which testifies to the prodigious industry of Victorian authors.

The greatness of the literature is all the more impressive when we consider the comparatively slight achievements of the Victorians in the other arts. Their painting was not impressive. English music had been negligible since the seventeenth century, although there were signs of hope toward the end of the Victorian era—for example, in Sir Edward Elgar's setting for John Henry Newman's poem *The Dream of Gerontius*, the operas and orchestral compositions of Frederick Delius, and, in lighter vein, the enchanting comic operas of Gilbert and Sullivan.

Like Elizabethan literature, that of the Victorian is remarkable as having touched a high level in many different fields. It is curious, therefore, that the Victorians should have been weakest just where the Elizabethans were so wonderfully strong—in the drama. They had, to be sure, their great actors—Macready, Irving, Ellen Terry—but when these great artists wished to appear in great plays, they were obliged to choose plays of the past. The "star system" and the "long run" are often blamed for this condition. It is true that for many years the "legitimate" drama in London was legally confined to three theaters, Covent Garden, Drury Lane, and the Haymarket. As the population of the city increased, the three auditoriums were so greatly enlarged that at last only spectacular effects could hope for any success. It is not correct to say that the great writers of the period were not interested in the drama; they were, but they had not mastered the technique of playwriting. Tennyson and Browning wrote poetic dramas which are not without dramatically effective scenes, but their appeal is to the reader rather than to the audience in the theater. Such lesser writers as Bulwer-Lytton, Tom Taylor, and Dion Boucicault turned out many interesting plays. But when all is said and done, one can hardly take these writers very seriously as dramatists. *Society*, *Caste*, and other plays by T. W. Robertson performed an important pioneering service. In their own time they were daring experiments in the direction of naturalism, yet as we read them today they seem curiously old-fashioned. The real dramatic revival did not begin until the 1890's, when Oscar Wilde, Henry Arthur Jones, and Arthur Wing Pinero set to work. These "society" playwrights were soon followed by the exponents of the drama of purpose, which had its fountainhead in Ibsen and whose most distinguished representative in England was George Bernard Shaw.

But if the Victorians failed with the drama, they more than made up for it in their remarkable development of a type of literature that was only modestly beginning in Queen Elizabeth's time and that has now become the outstanding modern type—the novel. Unfortunately the novel cannot be illustrated in such a book as this, but some Victorian contributions to the history of the English novel may at least be noted.

The marvelous creative fertility of Charles Dickens is surpassed in England only by that of Shakespeare himself. Dickens did not idealize the past as his great predecessor Sir Walter Scott had done. He was a romanticist, but it was the romance of the here and now that enthralled him. He is the only modern novelist, perhaps, whose contact with his audience is as intimate as that of the primitive folk bard. Yet on one side he leaned toward naturalism; if we allow for the picturesque exaggeration of George Bernard Shaw, his statement that Dickens's *Little Dorrit* is a more seditious book than *Das Kapital* is not without point.

Dickens's sensationalism and his didacticism were taken up by Wilkie Collins and Charles Reade. Mrs. Gaskell and Charles Kingsley belong to the "school" of Dickens by an extension of the term on the didactic side. Mrs. Gaskell's best work was done, however, not in sociological novels like *Mary Barton* and *North and South*, where she actually anticipated Dickens and Reade in applying the novel to the study of labor problems, but in *Cranford* and *Wives and Daughters*, which concern themselves with more personal, more feminine interests. Kingsley was always in the thick of the fight for human betterment. *Yeast* and *Alton Locke* reflect the Chartist movement directly, and even when he wrote historical novels—*Hypatia* or *Westward Ho!*—he carried all the problems of the present along with him.

Opposite the school of Dickens stands William Makepeace Thackeray. Yet the differences between Dickens and Thackeray can easily be exaggerated. Both men inherited the eighteenth-century tradition, Dickens from Smollett, Thackeray from Fielding. Both evoked rather than constructed their characters. But never until he reached the beautiful novel he did not live to finish, *Denis Duval*, did Thackeray surrender to romance. He was an upper-class man, a snob and a cynic at the same time that he was a sentimentalist and an innocent. Dickens's strenuous idealism was beyond him. It has often been pointed out that *Vanity Fair* is the most comprehensive picture and the most serious criticism of English society that fiction had thus far achieved.

Anthony Trollope, the most prolific of all the great Victorian novelists, was, like Thackeray, a realist. The six Barsetshire novels, which describe life in and about a cathedral city, are his most popular books, but equally good work went into the political novels and into many others unconnected with any series. Trollope is frequently reproached for his lack of subtlety, but he was sufficiently subtle to deceive most of the people who have written about him. As Michael Sadleir has remarked, he honored all the conventions of his time, yet he made it clear to the really discerning reader that there was not much about men and women that he did not know.

Charlotte Brontë greatly admired Thackeray, but neither she nor her sister Emily belongs to any literary school. They were outstanding individualists in a great age of individualism. In them romanticism and subjectivity took full possession of the English novel. Charlotte's *Jane Eyre* is a unique and interesting combination of realism and Gothic romance. Emily's *Wuthering Heights* was in its own time generally considered a strange, chaotic book. We know now that it was as deliberately constructed as a symphony of Mozart's, and Lord David Cecil is by no means alone in considering it the greatest of all Victorian novels.

The apparent outward similarities between the novels of George Eliot (the pen name of Mary Ann Evans) and those of her predecessors may easily blind us to the revolutionary character of her work. She turned away from the novel of Dickens and Thackeray toward what we understand as the novel today. George Eliot brought mature intellectuality and a carefully formulated philosophy of life to her fiction. Of creative power in the manner of Scott and Dickens she had little. She was not so much interested in telling a story as in expounding a theme; her books are not entertainment but serious criticism of life. Herbert Spencer wanted no novels admitted to the London Library "except, of course, those of George Eliot." The Victorians gave her a place among the great writers of all time; she is certainly among the greatest of the Victorians.

George Meredith may be compared and contrasted with both George Eliot and Thomas Hardy. Like George Eliot, he is a moralist; like her, he finds selfishness the cause of all human ills. But unlike George Eliot, he works through comedy, not tragedy, and he attempts in his novels no actual reconstruction of society. In the mirror that he holds up to his times we get a reflection not of human life as it is but of what it might have been in a world of his own making. His style is willful, highly elliptical, and deliberately difficult. He asks more of his reader than any English novelist had asked since Laurence Sterne.

Thomas Hardy's methods were old-fashioned compared with Meredith's, but his ideas were devastating, revolutionary. Like Meredith, he accepted the teachings of modern science, but Meredith was an optimist, Hardy a pessimist. Nature in Meredith is friendly to man; in Hardy it crushes him, not malevolently but through sheer indifference. His characters inhabit that world of shrinking values which was all that science had left the unhappy intellectuals of Victoria's last years.

George Eliot, Meredith, and Hardy brought modern thought into the English novel; it remained for Robert Louis Stevenson and Henry James (who, though an American by birth, did much of his best work in England, and died a British subject) to establish it as an art form. Different as they were in temperament and in subject matter, Stevenson and James stand together in their intense preoccupation with their medium as well as in their tendency to reject the old Fielding convention of the omniscient author and to tell their story from the point of view of, preferably, some semi-detached participant. Stevenson asserted a neo-Christian, neo-Stoic optimism against the pessimism of Schopenhauer, the *Rubáiyát*, and Thomas Hardy, and against the delicate esthetic despair of Walter Pater and the "decadents" of the end of the century. Stevenson rejected realism because he considered it unreal; his frankly subjective romanticism dedicated itself to the task of describing life as it appears to the man who lives it. Henry James is the novelist par excellence of the inner life. Nothing much happens in his books, yet he could declare: "Of course, for myself I live, live intensely and am fed by life, and my value, whatever it be, lies in my own kind of expression of that." James traced processes of development as no one else since Richardson had cared to trace them in English fiction. His influence on twentieth-century fiction has been great.

The non-fictional prose of the latter two-thirds of the nineteenth century represents a more distinct break with the Romantic period than do the other literary forms of the Victorians. Macaulay, Newman, and Ruskin, born though they were during the flood tide of Romanticism, displayed few of the characteristic literary qualities of their immediate predecessors. It is hard to believe that Carlyle and Keats were born in the same year. The Victorian prose writers inherited, to be sure, some of the prophetic spirit of the great Romantics, and the earliest work of Carlyle and Ruskin, like much of theirs, had to do with criticism of literature or art. But a sense of the urgency of the social problems of the day drove the Victorians on to become critics of men and manners, of politics and economics. Arnold, whose early verse shows traces of Romantic influence, likewise gave the greater part of his time and energy to attacks on the materialism and vulgarity of the time. Macaulay had something of the Romantic interest in the past, the people and events of which he brought to life in the vigorous and brilliant pages of his *History*.

Victorian prose on the whole lacks the autobiographical element, which adds much to the charm of the Romantic essayists. Instead of the personal likes and dislikes of the authors, and the events great or small of their everyday lives, Victorian prose reflects the great movements of the age, the reforms and need of reforms in church and state and society, and passes judgment, favorable or unfavorable, upon them. Most of it is not light reading, but it offers a great variety of subjects and styles from authors as different in matter and manner as Macaulay and Carlyle, Newman and Huxley, Ruskin and Pater, John Stuart Mill and Stevenson. As with the poets and novelists of the time, there are few problems that are not broached by the prose writers, whether they have to do with esthetics or the business of making a living or the salvation of one's soul. One may not agree with all the answers they gave, but it must be admitted that they asked many of the right questions.

The poetry of the Victorian period will be allowed to speak for itself, and the poetry of no period in English literature is more capable of doing so. The progress of poetry across the century follows the general pattern of the history of the time. There was, as we have noted, no definite break between the Romantic period and the later nineteenth century. The poetry of the late 1830's carried on the traditions dominant in the beginning of the decade. Tennyson's first volume in 1830 was influenced by Keats, and his early enthusiasm for Byron is well known. Browning first came under the spell of Byron and then under that of Shelley. Arnold chose Wordsworth for a master. Nor did the later verse of these poets and their contemporaries lose all traces of qualities that might be called Romantic. The past continued to exert its spell over poets as it did over many of the prose writers. The antiquarianism of the earlier years disappeared pretty largely, but the interest in the Middle Ages persisted. To the poets whose horizons were darkened by the smoke of industrial centers, medieval landscapes took on a brightness and freshness that they never had before. The knights and ladies with whom the poets peopled these landscapes often bore little resemblance to either the real men and women of the Middle Ages or to the legendary characters by whose names they were called. Indeed, medieval characters in Victorian poetry are at times, to use Keats's phrase, "symbols of a high romance," and at times mere figures that exist to point a moral lesson.

The poets of the mid-nineteenth century could no more escape the pressure of the forces that were transforming English life and thought than could the novelists and the essayists of the time. Nor, for better or worse, did they try to. Poetry was for most of them what Arnold said it should be, a criticism of life. In no period of English literature, perhaps, have poets shown so keen a social consciousness. The economic problems, the conditions under which men and women lived, the various reform movements and the excitement and discussions they engendered, are reflected in contemporary verse. The intellectual conflicts and tensions, the warfare between the old faith and the new science, inspire some of the best verse of the century. The personal problems that arise in the relationship of men and women are often the themes of the two chief poets, Tennyson and Browning. One may choose more or less at random half a dozen poems of Tennyson, among poets the chief exponent of his age, to illustrate his interest in the life about him. In "Dora" he treats with homely realism problems of human relationship. In *The Princess* he deals with the question of higher education for women. In "The Poet" and "The Palace of Art" he expresses views on the function of poetry and art. In "Locksley Hall" he rejoices in the scientific achievements of his "wondrous Mother-Age," anticipates in a remarkable fashion some events and circumstances of our own time, and dips farther into the future to see "the Parliament of Man, the Federation of the World." It is not surprising that he has a poem "By an Evolutionist," or that in *In Memoriam* and elsewhere he wrestles with the question of the seeming strife between God and Nature. Indeed, *In Memoriam* is in itself and in its implications a conspectus of Victorian England.

It is not, however, merely or chiefly the social consciousness of Victorian poets, or their morality, or the purposefulness of their work, or their fidelity in recording and interpreting the problems, the strain, and the stress of their times that makes their poetry great. All these qualities and faculties they might have had and yet failed to produce poems which belong among the greatest in English literature if they had not also brought to the treatment of their themes superb technical skill, varied and supple versification, and almost unequaled inventiveness and dexterity in the use of a variety of verse forms. At the century's end, some of that mastery persisted in the vigorous poetry of Kipling, who won acclaim as the "uncrowned laureate of the Empire."

The poetry of this complex period cannot be adequately characterized in such general terms as we have been using. "The Victorians," says a recent writer, "are too easily portrayed as solemn, pernickety, self-analytical; in fact, they were gay, spirited, rumbustious." That at least some of them were is attested by the novels of Dickens and Thackeray, by the light verse of C. S. Calverley, Edward Lear, Lewis Carroll, and W. S. Gilbert. Victorian poetry, like Tennyson's "Ulysses," was a part of all that it met, and in two-thirds of a century it met most of the problems and aspirations, the foibles and the follies that flesh is heir to, and expressed them with unexcelled variety and felicity.

Thomas Babington Macaulay 1800–1859

Macaulay was born at Rothley in Leicestershire, the eldest of nine children, on October 25, 1800. His father, Zachary Macaulay, an Evangelical philanthropist and religious editor, saw no contradiction between risking his fortune for his anti-slavery principles and urging the Government to take a strong line against restive English workmen. Tom was an amazing but unpretentious infant prodigy. During his residence at Trinity College, Cambridge, where he distinguished himself as a classicist but ignored mathematics, and became a Fellow in 1824, he abandoned his inherited Tory standards and took side with the Whigs.

The future historian was no writer merely; he was a man of large affairs. In 1826 he was called to the bar; in 1829 he was appointed Commissioner of Bankruptcy. In 1830 he was elected to Parliament, and he made his maiden speech in the House of Commons on the Reform Bill of 1832. In 1832 he became a member of the Board of Control concerned with Indian affairs; for several years he was stationed in India, where he earned a large fortune, and made an enviably humane and able record as administrator. In 1839 he became Secretary-at-War in Lord Melbourne's Cabinet; in 1846 he was Paymaster General.

When Macaulay practically retired from public life in 1847 to devote himself to literature, he had already been writing for many years. His first essay, "Milton," was published in 1825 in the *Edinburgh Review*, and for twenty years thereafter Macaulay had been the mainstay of the *Review*. Most of his famous "brief lives in the manner of Plutarch" were "book reviews" in the *Edinburgh* or articles for the *Encyclopædia Britannica*, in which his life of Samuel Johnson was published. The *Lays of Ancient Rome*, heroic narrative poetry, once known to "every schoolboy" (to use a favorite phrase of Macaulay's own) were published in 1842, the first two volumes of his *History of England*, in 1849. Macaulay had hoped to continue the history down to the Reform Bill, but it took him twenty years to write the five volumes which covered the years 1688–1702, and the last of these did not appear until after his own death, December 28, 1859. Meanwhile, among many other honors, he had been raised to the peerage (in 1857) as Baron Macaulay of Rothley.

"The history of our country during the past hundred and sixty years," he wrote, "is eminently the history of physical, of moral, and of intellectual improvement." It was from this point of view that he approached the problem when he came to write his great history, and the definitely Whiggish interpretation he presented was to rule the public mind without serious challenge at least until the war of 1914–1918. Macaulay was the first writer to "popularize" history, which he caused to displace the latest novel in the fashionable lady's boudoir and to take its place beside Shakespeare and the Bible on the pioneer's narrow bookshelf, and this he was able to accomplish without resort to any of the cheap and feeble tricks in which so many later popularizers have indulged. His superb narrative skill held the attention of countless readers for whom the pages of history had previously offered little attraction. The force and clarity of Macaulay's prose, whether in the *History* or in his essays, must always command respect. And if his full rhetorical style, dependent as it is upon balance and contrast, abundance of illustration, the devices of epigram and paradox, dazzles us less than it did his contemporaries, it has been without rival in its kind until the prose of Mr. Winston Churchill. Macaulay's very sureness and ease of expression mirrored those habits of mind and attitude which a later generation has chosen to label "Victorian complacency." It must be granted that his world *was*, in many ways, a deceptively simple, assured, and prosperous one. Whatever his subject, Macaulay's tone reflects that world. First and last, he was an enormously learned, eloquent spokesman—and panegyrist—of his own times.

from THE HISTORY OF ENGLAND FROM THE ACCESSION OF JAMES II

from Chapter 3

[England in 1685]

A great many notes, particularly of a geographical character, which might have been added to this selection have been omitted on the ground that they are not necessary to the understanding of an allusive but very clear piece of writing. Macaulay's own notes, mainly of a documentary character, have been omitted also.

In the seventeenth century the City was the merchant's residence. Those mansions of the great old burghers which still exist have been turned into counting houses and warehouses: but it is evident that they were originally not inferior in magnificence to the dwellings which were then inhabited by the nobility. They sometimes stand in retired and gloomy courts, and are accessible only by inconvenient passages: but their dimensions are ample, and their aspect stately. The entrances are decorated with richly carved pillars and canopies. The staircases and landing places are not wanting in grandeur. The floors are sometimes of wood, tessellated after the fashion of France. The palace of Sir Robert Clayton, in the Old Jewry, contained a superb banqueting room wainscoted with cedar, and adorned with battles of gods and giants in fresco. Sir Dudley North expended four thousand pounds, a sum which would then have been important to a Duke, on the rich furniture of his reception rooms in Basinghall Street. In such abodes, under the last Stuarts, the heads of the great firms lived splendidly and hospitably. To their dwelling place they were bound by the strongest ties of interest and affection. There they had passed their youth, had made their friendships, had courted their wives, had seen their children grow up, had laid the remains of their parents in the earth, and expected that their own remains would be laid. That intense patriotism which is peculiar to the members of societies congregated within a narrow space was, in such circumstances, strongly developed. London was, to the Londoner, what Athens was to the Athenian of the age of Pericles, what Florence was to the Florentine of the fifteenth century. The citizen was proud of the grandeur of his city, punctilious about her claims to respect, ambitious of her offices, and zealous for her franchises. . . .

We should greatly err if we were to suppose that any of the streets and squares then bore the same aspect as at present. The great majority of the houses, indeed, have, since that time, been wholly, or in great part, rebuilt. If the most fashionable parts of the capital could be placed before us such as they then were, we should be disgusted by their squalid appearance, and poisoned by their noisome atmosphere. In Covent Garden a filthy and noisy market was held close to the dwellings of the great. Fruit women screamed, carters fought, cabbage stalks and rotten apples accumulated in heaps at the thresholds of the Countess of Berkshire and of the Bishop of Durham.

The centre of Lincoln's Inn Fields was an open space where the rabble congregated every evening, within a few yards of Cardigan House and Winchester House, to hear mountebanks harangue, to see bears dance, and to set dogs at oxen. Rubbish was shot in every part of the area. Horses were ex-

7. **Old Jewry,** a street near Mercer's Hall, so called from the fact that the Jews lived there in medieval times.

ercised there. The beggars were as noisy and importunate as in the worst governed cities of the Continent. A Lincoln's Inn mumper was a proverb. The whole fraternity knew the arms and liveries of every charitably disposed grandee in the neighbourhood, and, as soon as his lordship's coach and six appeared, came hopping and crawling in crowds to persecute him. These disorders lasted, in spite of many accidents, and of some legal proceedings, till, in the reign of George the Second, Sir Joseph Jekyll, Master of the Rolls, was knocked down and nearly killed in the middle of the square. Then at length palisades were set up, and a pleasant garden laid out.

Saint James's Square was a receptacle for all the offal and cinders, for all the dead cats and dead dogs of Westminster. At one time a cudgel player kept the ring there. At another time an impudent squatter settled himself there, and built a shed for rubbish under the windows of the gilded saloons in which the first magnates of the realm, Norfolk, Ormond, Kent, and Pembroke, gave banquets and balls. It was not till these nuisances had lasted through a whole generation, and till much had been written about them, that the inhabitants applied to Parliament for permission to put up rails, and to plant trees.

When such was the state of the region inhabited by the most luxurious portion of society, we may easily believe that the great body of the population suffered what would now be considered as insupportable grievances. The pavement was detestable; all foreigners cried shame upon it. The drainage was so bad that in rainy weather the gutters soon became torrents. Several facetious poets have commemorated the fury with which these black rivulets roared down Snow Hill and Ludgate Hill, bearing to Fleet Ditch a vast tribute of animal and vegetable filth from the stalls of butchers and greengrocers. This flood was profusely thrown to right and left by coaches and carts. To keep as far from the carriage road as possible was therefore the wish of every pedestrian. The mild and timid gave the wall. The bold and athletic took it. If two roisterers met, they cocked their hats in each other's faces, and pushed each other about till the weaker was shoved towards the kennel. If he was a mere bully he sneaked off, muttering that he should find a time. If he was pugnacious, the encounter probably ended in a duel behind Montague House.

The houses were not numbered. There would indeed have been little advantage in numbering them; for of the coachmen, chairmen, porters, and errand boys of London, a very small proportion could read. It was necessary to use marks which the most ignorant could understand. The shops were therefore distinguished by painted or sculptured signs, which gave a gay and grotesque aspect to the streets. The walk from Charing Cross to Whitechapel lay through an endless succession of Saracens' Heads, Royal Oaks, Blue Bears, and Golden Lambs, which disappeared when they were no longer required for the direction of the common people.

When the evening closed in, the difficulty and danger of walking about London became serious indeed. The garret windows were opened, and pails were emptied, with little regard to those who were passing below. Falls, bruises, and broken bones were of constant occurrence. For, till the last year of the reign of Charles the Second, most of the streets were left in profound darkness. Thieves and robbers plied their trade with impunity: yet they were hardly so terrible to peaceable citizens as another class of ruffians. It was a favourite amusement of dissolute young gentlemen to swagger by night about the town, breaking windows, upsetting sedans, beating quiet men, and offering rude caresses to pretty women. Several dynasties of these tyrants had, since the Restoration, domineered over the streets. The Muns and Tityre Tus had given place to the Hectors, and the Hectors had been recently succeeded by the Scourers. At a later period arose the Nicker, the Hawcubite, and the yet more dreaded name of Mohawk. The machinery for keeping the peace was utterly contemptible. There was an Act of Common Council which provided that more than a thousand watchmen should be constantly on the alert in the city, from sunset to sunrise, and that every inhabitant should take his turn of duty. But this Act was negligently executed. Few of those who were summoned left their homes; and those few generally found it more agreeable to tipple in alehouses than to pace the streets.

It ought to be noticed that, in the last year of the reign of Charles the Second, began a great change in the police of London, a change which has perhaps added as much to the happiness of the body of the people as revolutions of much greater fame. An ingenious projector, named Edward Heming, obtained letters patent conveying to him, for a term of years, the exclusive right of lighting up London. He undertook, for a moderate consideration, to place a light before every tenth door, on moonless

3. mumper, beggar. **10. the reign of George the Second,** 1727–60. **47. kennel,** gutter.

19. the reign of Charles the Second, 1660–85.

nights, from Michaelmas to Lady Day, and from six to twelve of the clock. Those who now see the capital all the year round, from dusk to dawn, blazing with a splendour beside which the illuminations for La Hogue and Blenheim would have looked pale, may perhaps smile to think of Heming's lanterns, which glimmered feebly before one house in ten during a small part of one night in three. But such was not the feeling of his contemporaries. His scheme was enthusiastically applauded, and furiously attacked. The friends of improvement extolled him as the greatest of all the benefactors of his city. What, they asked, were the boasted inventions of Archimedes, when compared with the achievement of the man who had turned the nocturnal shades into noon day? In spite of these eloquent eulogies the cause of darkness was not left undefended. There were fools in that age who opposed the introduction of what was called the new light as strenuously as fools in our age have opposed the introduction of vaccination and railroads, as strenuously as the fools of an age anterior to the dawn of history doubtless opposed the introduction of the plough and of alphabetical writing. Many years after the date of Heming's patent there were extensive districts in which no lamp was seen.

We may easily imagine what, in such times, must have been the state of the quarters of London which were peopled by the outcasts of society. Among those quarters one had attained a scandalous preeminence. On the confines of the City and the Temple had been founded, in the thirteenth century, a House of Carmelite Friars, distinguished by their white hoods. The precinct of this house had, before the Reformation, been a sanctuary for criminals, and still retained the privilege of protecting debtors from arrest. Insolvents consequently were to be found in every dwelling, from cellar to garret. Of these a large proportion were knaves and libertines, and were followed to their asylum by women more abandoned than themselves. The civil power was unable to keep order in a district swarming with such inhabitants; and thus Whitefriars became the favourite resort of all who wished to be emancipated from the restraints of the law. Though the immunities legally belonging to the place extended only to cases of debt, cheats, false witnesses, forgers, and highwaymen found refuge there. For amidst a rabble so desperate no peace officer's life was in safety. At the cry of "Rescue," bullies with swords and cudgels, and termagant hags with spits and broomsticks, poured forth by hundreds; and the intruder was fortunate if he escaped back into Fleet Street, hustled, stripped, and pumped upon. Even the warrant of the Chief Justice of England could not be executed without the help of a company of musketeers. Such relics of the barbarism of the darkest ages were to be found within a short walk of the chambers where Somers was studying history and law, of the chapel where Tillotson was preaching, of the coffee house where Dryden was passing judgment on poems and plays, and of the hall where the Royal Society was examining the astronomical system of Isaac Newton.

Each of the two cities which made up the capital of England had its own centre of attraction. In the metropolis of commerce the point of convergence was the Exchange; in the metropolis of fashion the Palace. But the Palace did not retain its influence so long as the Exchange. The Revolution completely altered the relations between the Court and the higher classes of society. It was by degrees discovered that the King, in his individual capacity, had very little to give; that coronets and garters, bishoprics and embassies, lordships of the Treasury and tellerships of the Exchequer, nay, even charges in the royal stud and bedchamber, were really bestowed, not by him, but by his advisers. Every ambitious and covetous man perceived that he would consult his own interest far better by acquiring the dominion of a Cornish borough, and by rendering good service to the ministry during a critical session, than by becoming the companion, or even the minion, of his prince. It was therefore in the antechambers, not of George the First and of George the Second, but of Walpole and of Pelham, that the daily crowd of courtiers was to be found. It is also to be remarked that the same Revolution, which made it impossible that our Kings should use the patronage of the state, merely for the purpose of gratifying their personal predilections, gave us several Kings unfitted by their education and habits to

1. from Michaelmas to Lady Day, from September 29 (the feast of the Archangel Michael) to March 25 (the feast of the Annunciation of the Virgin Mary). **5. La Hogue,** a roadstead in Normandy, off which Admiral Russell defeated the French fleet, 1692. **Blenheim,** a village in Bavaria, near which Marlborough defeated the French, 1704. **14. Archimedes,** Greek mathematician (*c.* 287–212 B.C.). **35–36. a sanctuary for criminals,** because civil law was inoperative within sacred precincts.

12. Somers, John, Baron Somers (1651–1716), Lord Chancellor. **13. Tillotson,** John Tillotson (1630–1694), Archbishop of Canterbury. **17. Isaac Newton,** mathematician and philosopher (1642–1727), who discovered the law of universal gravitation. **38. George the First,** reigned 1714–27. **39. Walpole,** Sir Robert Walpole (1676–1745), Prime Minister and Chancellor of the Exchequer. **Pelham,** Sir Thomas Pelham-Hobbes (1693–1768), who opposed Walpole. **41ff. the same Revolution . . . hosts.** The kings who followed James II, banished from England by the "Bloodless Revolution" of 1688, were unable to speak English.

be gracious and affable hosts. They had been born and bred on the Continent. They never felt themselves at home in our island. If they spoke our language, they spoke it inelegantly and with effort. Our national character they never fully understood. Our national manners they hardly attempted to acquire. The most important part of their duty they performed better than any ruler who had preceded them: for they governed strictly according to law: but they could not be the first gentlemen of the realm, the heads of polite society. If ever they unbent, it was in a very small circle where hardly an English face was to be seen; and they were never so happy as when they could escape for a summer to their native land. They had indeed their days of reception for our nobility and gentry; but the reception was mere matter of form, and became at last as solemn a ceremony as a funeral.

Not such was the court of Charles the Second. Whitehall, when he dwelt there, was the focus of political intrigue and of fashionable gaiety. Half the jobbing and half the flirting of the metropolis went on under his roof. Whoever could make himself agreeable to the prince, or could secure the good offices of the mistress, might hope to rise in the world without rendering any service to the government, without being even known by sight to any minister of state. This courtier got a frigate, and that a company; a third, the pardon of a rich offender; a fourth, a lease of crown land on easy terms. If the King notified his pleasure that a briefless lawyer should be made a judge, or that a libertine baronet should be made a peer, the gravest counsellors, after a little murmuring, submitted. Interest, therefore, drew a constant press of suitors to the gates of the palace; and those gates always stood wide. The King kept open house every day, and all day long, for the good society of London, the extreme Whigs only excepted. Hardly any gentleman had any difficulty in making his way to the royal presence. The levee was exactly what the word imports. Some men of quality came every morning to stand round their master, to chat with him while his wig was combed and his cravat tied, and to accompany him on his early walk through the Park. All persons who had been properly introduced might, without any special invitation, go to see him dine, sup, dance, and play at hazard, and might have the pleasure of hearing him tell stories, which indeed he told remarkably well, about his flight from Worcester, and about the misery which he had endured when he was a state prisoner in the hands of the canting meddling preachers of Scotland. Bystanders whom His Majesty recognised often came in for a courteous word. This proved a far more successful kingcraft than any that his father or grandfather had practised. It was not easy for the most austere republican of the school of Marvel to resist the fascination of so much good humour and affability: and many a veteran Cavalier, in whose heart the remembrance of unrequited sacrifices and services had been festering during twenty years, was compensated in one moment for wounds and sequestrations by his sovereign's kind nod, and "God bless you, my old friend!"

People, in the time of Charles the Second, travelled with six horses, because with a smaller number there was great danger of sticking fast in the mire. Nor were even six horses always sufficient. Vanbrugh, in the succeeding generation, described with great humour the way in which a country gentleman, newly chosen a member of Parliament, went up to London. On that occasion all the exertions of six beasts, two of which had been taken from the plough, could not save the family coach from being imbedded in a quagmire.

Public carriages had recently been much improved. During the years which immediately followed the Restoration, a diligence ran between London and Oxford in two days. The passengers slept at Beaconsfield. At length, in the spring of 1669, a great and daring innovation was attempted. It was announced that a vehicle, described as the Flying Coach, would perform the whole journey between sunrise and sunset. This spirited undertaking was solemnly considered and sanctioned by the Heads of the University, and appears to have excited the same sort of interest which is excited in our own time by the opening of a new railway. The Vicechancellor, by a notice affixed in all public places, prescribed the hour and place of departure. The success of the experiment was complete. At six in the morning the carriage began to move from before the ancient front of All Souls College: and at seven in the evening the adventurous gentlemen who had run the first risk were safely deposited at their inn in London. The emulation of the sister University was moved; and soon a diligence was set up which in one day carried passengers from Cambridge to the capital. At the close of the reign of Charles the Second, flying carriages ran thrice a

51. Worcester, where Cromwell defeated the royalist Scotch army, September 3, 1651.

7. Marvel, Andrew Marvell (1621–1678), poet and friend of Milton. **18–20. Vanbrugh . . . described with great humour,** in his unfinished play *A Journey to London*, completed by Colley Cibber as *The Provoked Husband*, 1728.

week from London to the chief towns. But no stage coach, indeed no stage waggon, appears to have proceeded further north than York, or further west than Exeter. The ordinary day's journey of a flying coach was about fifty miles in the summer; but in winter, when the ways were bad and the nights long, little more than thirty. The Chester coach, the York coach, and the Exeter coach generally reached London in four days during the fine season, but at Christmas not till the sixth day. The passengers, six in number, were all seated in the carriage. For accidents were so frequent that it would have been most perilous to mount the roof. The ordinary fare was about twopence halfpenny a mile in summer, and somewhat more in winter.

This mode of travelling, which by Englishmen of the present day would be regarded as insufferably slow, seemed to our ancestors wonderfully and indeed alarmingly rapid. In a work published a few months before the death of Charles the Second, the flying coaches are extolled as far superior to any similar vehicles ever known in the world. . . .

In spite of the attractions of the flying coaches, it was still usual for men who enjoyed health and vigour, and who were not encumbered by much baggage, to perform long journeys on horseback. If the traveller wished to move expeditiously he rode post. Fresh saddle horses and guides were to be procured at convenient distances along all the great lines of road. The charge was threepence a mile for each horse, and fourpence a stage for the guide. In this manner, when the ways were good, it was possible to travel, for a considerable time, as rapidly as by any conveyance known in England, till vehicles were propelled by steam. . . .

Literature which could be carried by the post bag then formed the greater part of the intellectual nutriment ruminated by the country divines and country justices. The difficulty and expense of conveying large packets from place to place was so great, that an extensive work was longer in making its way from Paternoster Row to Devonshire or Lancashire than it now is in reaching Kentucky. How scantily a rural parsonage was then furnished, even with books the most necessary to a theologian, has already been remarked. The houses of the gentry were not more plentifully supplied. Few knights of the shire had libraries so good as may now perpetually be found in a servants' hall, or in the back parlour of a small shopkeeper. An esquire passed among his neighbours for a great scholar, if Hudibras and Baker's Chronicle, Tarlton's Jests and The Seven Champions of Christendom, lay in his hall window among the fishing rods and fowling pieces. . . .

Thomas Carlyle

1795–1881

Carlyle was the Hebrew prophet among Victorian writers; if both Ruskin and Matthew Arnold understood the social malady as well as he did (and prescribed for it more clearly), none other attained his apocalyptic splendor. Like all great writers, he owed at least as much to his style as to his ideas.

That style is like no other. In a sense Carlyle has created a vital, insistent language all his own. As one critic observes, "He will not consent to use the current verbal coinage; every phrase (and many actual words) must come molten from the forge. For Carlyle writes almost exclusively from the heart or the solar-plexus, not from the head. He sees by flashes and does not think connectedly; summer-lightning, not sunshine, is the light that guides him."[1]

[1] Basil Willey, *Nineteenth Century Studies*, Columbia University Press, 1949.

Carlyle was born, of peasant stock, in Ecclefechan, Dumfriesshire, Scotland, December 4, 1795. He rejected the dogmas of his inherited Calvinism, but he never escaped its integrity, its harshness, its respect for authority, its indifference to the fine arts and the spirit of good nature, its worship of work. Though he attended Edinburgh University from 1809 to 1814, he left without taking a degree; he rejected the ministry, he rejected, after brief experiments, both schoolteaching and the law.

15. Paternoster Row, the center of English publishing activity. **24–26. Hudibras,** by Samuel Butler, 1663, 1664, 1678, a savage satire on the Puritans, said to have been Charles II's favorite poem. **Baker's Chronicle,** of the kings of England from the Roman period to Charles II, written by Sir Richard Baker in 1643. **Tarlton's Jests,** attributed to Richard Tarlton, the Charlie Chaplin of Shakespeare's time and one of the most famous clowns of all time. **The Seven Champions of Christendom,** a famous romance by Richard Johnson, published about 1597.

Four years, from 1818 to 1822, he spent in an agonized self-searching of one of the most turbulent souls God ever gave a man; he studied mathematics, chemistry, physics, and mineralogy, but he found himself at last through the German Transcendentalists, and to make them known in England was his first self-appointed task. In 1826 he married Jane Welsh, who was quite as thin-skinned and high-spirited as he was himself, and who made him one of the most fascinating, one of the most fiercely loyal, but by no means one of the most comfortable, wives a man of letters ever had. "Mr. and Mrs. Carlyle on the whole enjoyed life together," said Tennyson, "else they would not have chaffed one another so heartily."

From 1828 to 1834 the Carlyles lived on Jane's farm at Craigenputtock, where sometimes, for three months running, not so much as a beggar came to the door. Here, among other things, Carlyle wrote his greatest book, *Sartor Resartus* (see below), and hence he removed to 24, Cheyne Row, Chelsea, London, where he continued to reside until his death, February 5, 1881.

The first great work Carlyle produced in London was *The French Revolution*, 1837, a vivid but not impartial history which established his fame as *Sartor Resartus* had failed to do. *Heroes and Hero-Worship* was the text of a series of lectures delivered in 1840. Later Carlyle studied two heroes at greater length. Mrs. Carlyle lived for years "in the valley of the shadow of Cromwell," and when her husband's book about him came out in 1845, it turned out to be *Oliver Cromwell's Letters and Speeches: with Elucidations*, rather than a complete biography. It established a favorable view of the great dictator, however, against the judgments of earlier historians, a view which has only recently been seriously questioned. *The History of Friedrich II of Prussia, called Frederick the Great*, published in six volumes between 1858 and 1865, dealt with an even more dubious hero; today it is the most neglected of all Carlyle's books. *The Life of John Sterling*, 1851—to complete the record on its biographical side—was a gracious tribute to a personal friend.

Meanwhile Carlyle had continued his direct discussion of contemporary problems, notably in *Chartism*, 1840; *Past and Present*, 1843 (see page 928); and *Latter-Day Pamphlets*, 1850.

In 1866 Carlyle experienced his greatest triumph and his greatest sorrow; while he was in Edinburgh to deliver his inaugural address as Lord Rector of the university, Mrs. Carlyle died. With her, Carlyle himself largely died; despite the homage of many great men, he lived his last years in bleak loneliness. His *Reminiscences* were posthumously published in 1881.

Carlyle's hatred of democracy, his praise of "the beneficent whip," his adoration of the man on horseback, do not help his fame today in English-speaking countries. But later world-conditions must not be permitted to prejudice us against the vital elements in Carlyle's work or let us forget his heroes included the prophets and poets. Prescriptions were never his forte; like Emerson, who was so closely connected with him, he had essentially a seminal mind, if not a completely consistent one. He forgot, as Matthew Arnold never forgot, that the value of a man's doing is wholly dependent on what he does. But when all allowances are made, Carlyle is still the archenemy of Victorian materialism—"Nature is no longer dead hostile Matter, but the veil and mysterious garment of the unseen"—and in this aspect many a great Victorian marches under his banner.

from SARTOR RESARTUS

Sartor Resartus (*The Tailor Retailored*) takes its point of departure from an extended metaphor in Section 3 of Swift's *Tale of a Tub*, where God is conceived of as a tailor and the universe as a huge suit of clothes. Not only is the material world clothing, but man's body is clothing, social institutions are clothing, Time and Space themselves are clothing. This idea is developed in Books I and III. Carlyle's purpose was not to advocate either a physical or a spiritual nudism, but to teach men the necessity of differentiating between the essential and the nonessential, to establish the fundamentally spiritual character of Reality, and to bring men face to face with this Reality.

The method of development is fantastic. In Part II he purports to be the editor of autobiographical fragments from the writings of Diogenes Teufelsdröckh, Professor of Things in General at the University of Weissnichtwo (Don't-Know-Where). "Teufelsdreck," as Carlyle originally spelled the word, means "Devil's dung," and is the popular German word for the drug asafetida. To his brother John he wrote, "I sometimes think the book will prove a kind of medicinal asafoetida for the pudding stomach of England, and produce new secretions there." In *Sartor Resartus*, Carlyle is telling his readers, says Professor John J. Parry, "that England is bloated with wealth that she has not digested and that his divinely inspired message, although it may prove unpleasant, will perhaps prove salutary for her."

The present reprint presents the portions of the three

chapters from Book II in which the great spiritual crisis of Teufelsdröckh's life is set forth.

The editor of *Fraser's Magazine* was bold enough to serialize *Sartor* in 1833–34, with almost disastrous results for the magazine. Emerson got the book published in America in 1836, but it did not appear in England until two years later.

BOOK II: Chapter 7

The Everlasting No

UNDER the strange nebulous envelopment, wherein our Professor has now shrouded himself, no doubt but his spiritual nature is nevertheless progressive, and growing: for how can the "Son of Time," in any case, stand still? We behold him, through those dim years, in a state of crisis, of transition: his mad Pilgrimings, and general solution into aimless Discontinuity, what is all this but a mad Fermentation; wherefrom, the fiercer it is, the clearer product will one day evolve itself?

Such transitions are ever full of pain; thus the Eagle when he moults is sickly; and, to attain his new beak, must harshly dash-off the old one upon rocks. What Stoicism soever our Wanderer, in his individual acts and motions, may affect, it is clear that there is a hot fever of anarchy and misery raging within; coruscations of which flash out: as, indeed, how could there be other? Have we not seen him disappointed, bemocked of Destiny, through long years? All that the young heart might desire and pray for has been denied; nay, as in the last worst instance, offered and then snatched away. Ever an "excellent Passivity"; but of useful, reasonable Activity, essential to the former as Food to Hunger, nothing granted: till at length, in this wild Pilgrimage, he must forcibly seize for himself an Activity, though useless, unreasonable. Alas, his cup of bitterness, which had been filling drop by drop, ever since that first "ruddy morning" in the Hinterschlag Gymnasium, was at the very lip; and then with that poison-drop, of the Towgood-and-Blumine business, it runs over, and even hisses over in a deluge of foam.

He himself says once, with more justice than originality: "Man is, properly speaking, based upon Hope, he has no other possession but Hope; this world of his is emphatically the 'Place of Hope.'"

What, then, was our Professor's possession? We see him, for the present, quite shut-out from Hope; looking not into the golden orient, but vaguely all round into a dim copper firmament, pregnant with earthquake and tornado.

Alas, shut-out from Hope, in a deeper sense than we yet dream of! For, as he wanders wearisomely through this world, he has now lost all tidings of another and higher. Full of religion, or at least of religiosity, as our Friend has since exhibited himself, he hides not that, in those days, he was wholly irreligious: "Doubt had darkened into Unbelief," says he; "shade after shade goes grimly over your soul, till you have the fixed, starless, Tartarean black." To such readers as have reflected, what can be called reflecting, on man's life, and happily discovered, in contradiction to much Profit-and-Loss Philosophy, speculative and practical, that Soul is *not* synonymous with Stomach; who understand, therefore, in our Friend's words, "that, for man's well-being, Faith is properly the one thing needful; how, with it, Martyrs, otherwise weak, can cheerfully endure the shame and the cross; and without it, Worldlings puke-up their sick existence, by suicide, in the midst of luxury": to such it will be clear that, for a pure moral nature, the loss of his religious Belief was the loss of everything. Unhappy young man! All wounds, the crush of long-continued Destitution, the stab of false Friendship and of false Love, all wounds in thy so genial heart, would have healed again, had not its life-warmth been withdrawn. Well might he exclaim, in his wild way: "Is there no God, then; but at best an absentee God, sitting idle, ever since the first Sabbath, at the outside of his Universe, and *see*ing it go? Has the word Duty no meaning; is what we call Duty no divine Messenger and Guide, but a false earthly Fantasm, made-up of Desire and Fear, of emanations from the Gallows and from Dr. Graham's Celestial-Bed? Happiness of an approving Conscience! Did not Paul of Tarsus, whom admiring men have since named Saint, feel that *he* was 'the chief of sinners'; and Nero of Rome, jocund in spirit (*wohlgemuth*), spend much of his time in fiddling?

15–16. Son of Time, a phrase from Goethe's poem *"Gott, Gemüth, und Welt."* **40–41. Hinterschlag,** Smite-Behind. **Gymnasium,** the German high school. Carlyle is thinking of an experience of his own at Annan Academy. **42–43. Towgood . . . business.** Teufelsdröckh's lady-love, Blumine, had rejected him, after having seemed to love him, and had married his most intimate friend, Towgood.

14. Tartarean, infernal. **17–18. Profit-and-Loss Philosophy,** Utilitarianism; see pages 901–902. **21. the one thing needful.** See Luke 10:42. **23. endure the shame and the cross.** See Hebrews 12:2. **33–35. Is there . . . go.** Eighteenth-century Deists thought of God as transcendent rather than immanent; He made the world and then went off and left it. **39–40. Dr. Graham's Celestial-Bed,** an elaborate contraption, supposed to cure sterility in married persons, invented by a quack named James Graham (1745–1794). **42–43. the chief of sinners.** See I Timothy 1:15. **43–44. Nero . . . fiddling,** according to Tacitus and Suetonius. He is popularly believed to have "fiddled" while Rome burned.

Foolish Word-monger and Motive-grinder, who in thy Logic-mill hast an earthly mechanism for the Godlike itself, and wouldst fain grind me out Virtue from the husks of Pleasure,—I tell thee, Nay! To the unregenerate Prometheus Vinctus of a man, it is ever the bitterest aggravation of his wretchedness that he is conscious of Virtue, that he feels himself the victim not of suffering only, but of injustice. What then? Is the heroic inspiration we name Virtue but some Passion; some bubble of the blood, bubbling in the direction others *profit* by? I know not: only this I know, If what thou namest Happiness be our true aim, then are we all astray. With Stupidity and sound Digestion man may front much. But what, in these dull unimaginative days, are the terrors of Conscience to the diseases of the Liver! Not on Morality, but on Cookery, let us build our stronghold: there brandishing our frying-pan, as censer, let us offer sweet incense to the Devil, and live at ease on the fat things *he* has provided for his Elect!"

Thus has the bewildered Wanderer to stand, as so many have done, shouting question after question into the Sibyl-cave of Destiny, and receive no Answer but an Echo. It is all a grim Desert, this once-fair world of his; wherein is heard only the howling of wild-beasts, or the shrieks of despairing, hate-filled men; and no Pillar of Cloud by day, and no Pillar of Fire by night, any longer guides the Pilgrim. To such length has the spirit of Inquiry carried him. "But what boots it (*was thut's*)?" cries he: "it is but the common lot in this era. Not having come to spiritual majority prior to the *Siècle de Louis Quinze*, and not being born purely a Loghead (*Dummkopf*), thou hast no other outlook. The whole world is, like thee, sold to Unbelief; their old Temples of the Godhead, which for long have not been rainproof, crumble down; and men ask now: Where is the Godhead; our eyes never saw him?"

Pitiful enough were it, for all these wild utterances, to call our Diogenes wicked. Unprofitable servants as we all are, perhaps at no era of his life was he more decisively the Servant of Goodness, the Servant of God, than even now when doubting God's existence. "One circumstance I note," says he: "after all the nameless woe that Inquiry, which for me, what it is not always, was genuine Love of Truth, had wrought me, I nevertheless still loved Truth, and would bate no jot of my allegiance to her. 'Truth!' I cried, 'though the Heavens crush me for following her: no Falsehood! though a whole celestial Lubberland were the price of Apostasy.' In conduct it was the same. Had a divine Messenger from the clouds, or miraculous Handwriting on the wall, convincingly proclaimed to me *This thou shalt do*, with what passionate readiness, as I often thought, would I have done it, had it been leaping into the infernal Fire. Thus, in spite of all Motive-grinders, and Mechanical Profit-and-Loss Philosophies, with the sick ophthalmia and hallucination they had brought on, was the Infinite nature of Duty still dimly present to me: living without God in the world, of God's light I was not utterly bereft; if my as yet sealed eyes, with their unspeakable longing, could nowhere see Him, nevertheless in my heart He was present, and His heaven-written Law still stood legible and sacred there."

Meanwhile, under all these tribulations, and temporal and spiritual destitutions, what must the Wanderer, in his silent soul, have endured! "The painfullest feeling," writes he, "is that of your own Feebleness (*Unkraft*); ever, as the English Milton says, to be weak is the true misery. And yet of your Strength there is and can be no clear feeling, save by what you have prospered in, by what you have done. Between vague wavering Capability and fixed indubitable Performance, what a difference! A certain inarticulate Self-consciousness dwells dimly in us; which only our Works can render articulate and decisively discernible. Our Works are the mirror wherein the spirit first sees its natural lineaments. Hence, too, the folly of that impossible Precept, *Know thyself*; till it be translated into this partially possible one, *Know what thou canst work-at*.

"But for me, so strangely unprosperous had I been, the net-result of my Workings amounted as yet simply to—Nothing. How then could I believe in my Strength, when there was as yet no mirror to see it in? Ever did this agitating, yet, as I now perceive, quite frivolous question, remain to me insoluble: Hast thou a certain Faculty, a certain Worth, such even as the most have not; or art thou the completest Dullard of these modern times? Alas! the fearful Unbelief is unbelief in yourself; and how could I believe? Had not my first, last Faith in

5. Prometheus Vinctus, a drama by Aeschylus. Because he stole fire from heaven for men, Prometheus was chained to a rock in the Caucasus, with a vulture gnawing his vitals. **21. his Elect,** who, according to the Calvinistic theology by which Carlyle was deeply influenced, and against which he rebelled, have been foreordained to salvation. **23–24. shouting . . . Destiny.** See *Aeneid*, Book VI, ll. 36 ff. **28–29. Pillar of Cloud . . . by night.** See Exodus 13:21–22. **33–34. Siècle de Louis Quinze,** Voltaire's *Précis du siècle de Louis XV* (*The Age of Louis XV*), which Carlyle disliked. **41–42. Unprofitable servants . . . are.** See Luke 17:10.

7. Lubberland, land of sluggards. **9–10. miraculous . . . wall,** as in Daniel 5:5–28. **17–18. living . . . world.** See Ephesians 2:12. **27–28. as the English . . . misery.** See *Paradise Lost*, Book I, ll. 157 ff. **38. Know thyself,** the motto on the temple at Delphi.

myself, when even to me the Heavens seemed laid open, and I dared to love, been all-too cruelly belied? The speculative Mystery of Life grew ever more mysterious to me: neither in the practical Mystery had I made the slightest progress, but been everywhere buffeted, foiled, and contemptuously cast-out. A feeble unit in the middle of a threatening Infinitude, I seemed to have nothing given me but eyes, whereby to discern my own wretchedness. Invisible yet impenetrable walls, as of Enchantment, divided me from all living: was there, in the wide world, any true bosom I could press trustfully to mine? O Heaven, No, there was none! I kept a lock upon my lips: why should I speak much with that shifting variety of so-called Friends, in whose withered, vain and too-hungry souls Friendship was but an incredible tradition? In such cases, your resource is to talk little, and that little mostly from the Newspapers. Now when I look back, it was a strange isolation I then lived in. The men and women around me, even speaking with me, were but Figures; I had, practically, forgotten that they were alive, that they were not merely automatic. In the midst of their crowded streets and assemblages, I walked solitary; and (except as it was my own heart, not another's, that I kept devouring) savage also, as the tiger in his jungle. Some comfort it would have been, could I, like a Faust, have fancied myself tempted and tormented of the Devil; for a Hell, as I imagine, without Life, though only diabolic Life, were more frightful: but in our age of Downpulling and Disbelief, the very Devil has been pulled down, you cannot so much as believe in a Devil. To me the Universe was all void of Life, of Purpose, of Volition, even of Hostility: it was one huge, dead, immeasurable Steam-engine, rolling on, in its dead indifference, to grind me limb from limb. O, the vast, gloomy, solitary Golgotha, and Mill of Death! Why was the Living banished thither companionless, conscious? Why, if there is no Devil; nay, unless the Devil is your God?"

A prey incessantly to such corrosions, might not, moreover, as the worst aggravation to them, the iron constitution even of a Teufelsdröckh threaten to fail? We conjecture that he has known sickness; and, in spite of his locomotive habits, perhaps sickness of the chronic sort. Hear this, for example: "How beautiful to die of broken-heart, on Paper! Quite another thing in practice; every window of your Feeling, even of your Intellect, as it were, begrimed and mud-bespattered, so that no pure ray can enter; a whole Drugshop in your inwards; the fordone soul drowning slowly in quagmires of Disgust?"

Putting all which external and internal miseries together, may we not find in the following sentences, quite in our Professor's still vein, significance enough? "From Suicide a certain aftershine (*Nachschein*) of Christianity withheld me: perhaps also a certain indolence of character; for, was not that a remedy I had at any time within reach? Often, however, was there a question present to me: Should some one now, at the turning of that corner, blow thee suddenly out of Space, into the other World, or other No-World, by pistol-shot,—how were it? On which ground, too, I have often, in sea-storms and sieged cities and other death-scenes, exhibited an imperturbability, which passed, falsely enough, for courage."

"So had it lasted," concludes the Wanderer, "so had it lasted, as in bitter protracted Death-agony, through long years. The heart within me, unvisited by any heavenly dewdrop, was smouldering in sulphurous, slow-consuming fire. Almost since earliest memory I had shed no tear; or once only when I, murmuring half-audibly, recited Faust's Deathsong, that wild *Selig der den er im Siegesglanze findet* (Happy whom *he* finds in Battle's splendour), and thought that of this last Friend even I was not forsaken, that Destiny itself could not doom me not to die. Having no hope, neither had I any definite fear, were it of Man or of Devil: nay, I often felt as if it might be solacing, could the Arch-Devil himself, though in Tartarean terrors, but rise to me, that I might tell him a little of my mind. And yet, strangely enough, I lived in a continual, indefinite, pining fear; tremulous, pusillanimous, apprehensive of I knew not what: it seemed as if all things in the Heavens above and the Earth beneath would hurt me; as if the Heavens and the Earth were but boundless jaws of a devouring monster, wherein I, palpitating, waited to be devoured.

"Full of such humour, and perhaps the miserablest man in the whole French Capital or Suburbs, was I, one sultry Dogday, after much perambulation, toiling along the dirty little *Rue Saint-Thomas de l'Enfer*, among civic rubbish enough, in a close

5. Mystery, occupation. **28–29. like a Faust . . . Devil.** In the old German legend, which reached its apogee in Goethe's *Faust* (1808, 1832), Faust sold his soul to the Devil for a life of pleasure of the senses. **38. Golgotha,** the Place of a Skull, where Jesus was crucified. **46–47. perhaps . . . sort,** an autobiographical reference to Carlyle's own dyspepsia. **48. How beautiful . . . Paper!** Like the romantic poets—Byron, or Goethe in *Wilhelm Meister*.

10. Suicide. Carlyle had contemplated suicide during an unhappy period of his life. **29–30. Selig . . . findet,** inaccurately quoted from Goethe's *Faust*, Part I, sc. 4, ll. 1572–1576. **48–49. Rue Saint-Thomas de l'Enfer,** St.-Thomas-of-Hell Street. Carlyle had the experience described in Leith Walk, Edinburgh, in June, 1821.

atmosphere, and over pavements hot as Nebuchadnezzar's Furnace; whereby doubtless my spirits were little cheered; when, all at once, there rose a Thought in me, and I asked myself: 'What *art* thou afraid of? Wherefore, like a coward, dost thou forever pip and whimper, and go cowering and trembling? Despicable biped! what is the sum-total of the worst that lies before thee? Death? Well, Death; and say the pangs of Tophet too, and all that the Devil and Man may, will or can do against thee! Hast thou not a heart; canst thou not suffer whatsoever it be; and, as a Child of Freedom, though outcast, trample Tophet itself under thy feet, while it consumes thee? Let it come, then; I will meet it and defy it!' And as I so thought, there rushed like a stream of fire over my whole soul; and I shook base Fear away from me forever. I was strong, of unknown strength; a spirit, almost a god. Ever from that time, the temper of my misery was changed: not Fear or whining Sorrow was it, but Indignation and grim fire-eyed Defiance.

"Thus had the EVERLASTING No (*das ewige Nein*) pealed authoritatively through all the recesses of my Being, of my ME; and then was it that my whole ME stood up, in native God-created majesty, and with emphasis recorded its Protest. Such a Protest, the most important transaction in Life, may that same Indignation and Defiance, in a psychological point of view, be fitly called. The Everlasting No had said: 'Behold, thou art fatherless, outcast, and the Universe is mine (the Devil's)'; to which my whole Me now made answer: '*I* am not thine, but Free, and forever hate thee!'

"It is from this hour that I incline to date my Spiritual New-birth, or Baphometic Fire-baptism; perhaps I directly thereupon began to be a Man."

from Chapter 8

Centre of Indifference

Though, after this "Baphometic Fire-baptism" of his, our Wanderer signifies that his Unrest was but increased; as, indeed, "Indignation and Defiance," especially against things in general, are not the most peaceable inmates; yet can the Psychologist surmise that it was no longer a quite hopeless Unrest; that henceforth it had at least a fixed centre to revolve round. For the fire-baptised soul, long so scathed and thunder-riven, here feels its own Freedom, which feeling is its Baphometic Baptism: the citadel of its whole kingdom it has thus gained by assault, and will keep inexpugnable; outwards from which the remaining dominions, not indeed without hard battling, will doubtless by degrees be conquered and pacificated. Under another figure, we might say, if in that great moment, in the *Rue Saint-Thomas de l'Enfer*, the old inward Satanic School was not yet thrown out of doors, it received peremptory judicial notice to quit;—whereby, for the rest, its howl-chantings, Ernulphus-cursings, and rebellious gnashings of teeth, might, in the meanwhile, become only the more tumultuous, and difficult to keep secret.

Accordingly, if we scrutinise these Pilgrimings well, there is perhaps discernible henceforth a certain incipient method in their madness. Not wholly as a Spectre does Teufelsdröckh now storm through the world; at worst as a spectre-fighting Man, nay who will one day be a Spectre-queller. If pilgriming restlessly to so many "Saints' Wells," and ever without quenching of his thirst, he nevertheless finds little secular wells, whereby from time to time some alleviation is ministered. In a word, he is now, if not ceasing, yet intermitting to "eat his own heart"; and clutches round him outwardly on the NOT-ME for wholesomer food. Does not the following glimpse exhibit him in a much more natural state?

"Towns also and Cities, especially the ancient, I failed not to look upon with interest. How beautiful to see thereby, as through a long vista, into the remote Time; to have, as it were, an actual section of almost the earliest Past brought safe into the Present, and set before your eyes! There, in that old City, was a live ember of Culinary Fire put down, say only two thousand years ago; and there, burning more or less triumphantly, with such fuel as the region yielded, it has burnt, and still burns, and thou thyself seest the very smoke thereof. Ah! and the far more mysterious live ember of Vital Fire was then also put down there; and still miraculously burns and spreads; and the smoke and ashes thereof (in these Judgment-Halls and Churchyards), and its bellows-engines (in these Churches), thou still seest; and its flame, looking out from

1–2. Nebuchadnezzar's Furnace. See Daniel 3. **9. Tophet,** a furnace near Jerusalem where human sacrifices were performed; later used loosely, as here, to signify hell. See II Kings 23:10. **35. Baphometic Fire-baptism.** In Zacharias Werner's drama *The Sons of the Valley*, a character reads the story of how Baffometus, the Master of the Templars, was, for his sin of avarice, subjected by God to a baptism by molten gold.

14. Ernulphus-cursings. The curse of Ernulphus (1040–1124), Bishop of Rochester, is one of the most elaborate on record. It may be read in Sterne's *Tristram Shandy*, Vol. 3, chap. 11. **18–19. a certain . . . madness.** See *Hamlet*, Act II, sc. 2, ll. 211–12. **28–29. the Not-Me,** a philosophical term for the objective world, existing outside one's own personality.

every kind countenance, and every hateful one, still warms thee or scorches thee.

"Of Man's Activity and Attainment the chief results are aeriform, mystic, and preserved in Tradition only: such are his Forms of Government, with the Authority they rest on; his Customs, or Fashions both of Cloth-habits and of Soul-habits; much more his collective stock of Handicrafts, the whole Faculty he has acquired of manipulating Nature: all these things, as indispensable and priceless as they are, cannot in any way be fixed under lock and key, but must flit, spirit-like, on impalpable vehicles, from Father to Son; if you demand sight of them, they are nowhere to be met with. Visible Ploughmen and Hammermen there have been, ever from Cain and Tubalcain downwards: but where does your accumulated Agricultural, Metallurgic, and other Manufacturing Skill lie warehoused? It transmits itself on the atmospheric air, on the sun's rays (by Hearing and by Vision); it is a thing aeriform, impalpable, of quite spiritual sort. In like manner, ask me not, Where are the Laws; where is the Government? In vain wilt thou go to Schönbrunn, to Downing Street, to the Palais Bourbon: thou findest nothing there but brick or stone houses, and some bundles of Papers tied with tape. Where, then, is that same cunningly-devised almighty Government of theirs to be laid hands on? Everywhere, yet nowhere: seen only in its works, this too is a thing aeriform, invisible; or if you will, mystic and miraculous. So spiritual (*geistig*) is our whole daily Life: all that we do springs out of Mystery, Spirit, invisible Force; only like a little Cloud-image, or Armida's Palace, air-built, does the Actual body itself forth from the great mystic Deep.

"Visible and tangible products of the Past, again, I reckon-up to the extent of three: Cities, with their Cabinets and Arsenals; then tilled Fields, to either or to both of which divisions Roads with their Bridges may belong; and thirdly—Books. In which third truly, the last invented, lies a worth far surpassing that of the two others. Wondrous indeed is the virtue of a true Book. Not like a dead city of stones, yearly crumbling, yearly needing repair; more like a tilled field, but then a spiritual field: like a spiritual tree, let me rather say, it stands from year to year, and from age to age (we have Books that already number some hundred-and-fifty human ages); and yearly comes its new produce of leaves (Commentaries, Deductions, Philosophical, Political Systems; or were it only Sermons, Pamphlets, Journalistic Essays), every one of which is talismanic and thaumaturgic, for it can persuade men. O thou who art able to write a Book, which once in the two centuries or oftener there is a man gifted to do, envy not him whom they name City-builder, and inexpressibly pity him whom they name Conqueror or City-burner! Thou too art a Conqueror and Victor: but of the true sort, namely over the Devil: thou too hast built what will outlast all marble and metal, and be a wonder-bringing City of the Mind, a Temple and Seminary and Prophetic Mount, whereto all kindreds of the Earth will pilgrim.—Fool! why journeyest thou wearisomely, in thy antiquarian fervour, to gaze on the stone pyramids of Geeza, or the clay ones of Sacchara? These stand there, as I can tell thee, idle and inert, looking over the Desert, foolishly enough, for the last three-thousand years: but canst thou not open thy Hebrew Bible, then, or even Luther's Version thereof?"

No less satisfactory is his sudden appearance not in Battle, yet on some Battle-field; which, we soon gather, must be that of Wagram; so that here, for once, is a certain approximation to distinctness of date. Omitting much, let us impart what follows:

"Horrible enough! A whole Marchfeld strewed with shell-splinters, cannon-shot, ruined tumbrils, and dead men and horses; stragglers still remaining not so much as buried. And those red mould heaps: ay, there lie the Shells of Men, out of which all the Life and Virtue has been blown; and now are they swept together, and crammed-down out of sight, like blown Egg-shells!—Did Nature, when she bade the Donau bring down his mould-cargoes from the Carinthian and Carpathian Heights, and spread them out here into the softest, richest level,—intend thee, O Marchfeld, for a corn-bearing Nursery, whereon her children might be nursed; or for a Cockpit, wherein they might the more commodiously be throttled and tattered? Were thy three broad Highways, meeting here from the ends of Europe, made for Ammunition-wagons, then? Were thy Wagrams and Stillfrieds but so many ready-

16. Cain and Tubalcain. See Genesis 4:2, 22. **24–25. Schönbrunn . . . Downing Street . . . Palais Bourbon,** centers of government in Vienna, London, Paris. **34. Armida's Palace,** in Tasso's *Jerusalem Delivered*, to which the sorceress Armida lured the Christian knights.

17–18. Geeza . . . Sacchara, Gizeh, Sakkara, near Cairo. **21–22. Luther's Version,** a famous and influential translation of the Bible into German (1534–35) by Martin Luther. **25. Wagram,** a village near Vienna where Napoleon defeated the Austrians, July 5–6, 1809. **28. Marchfeld,** the plain in the midst of which Wagram lies; here, at Stillfried, Ottokar II, King of Bohemia, defeated the Hungarians in 1260, and was himself defeated and slain by Rodolf of Hapsburg in 1278; here Napoleon won the victory alluded to in the last note. **36. Donau,** Danube.

built Casemates, wherein the house of Hapsburg might batter with artillery, and with artillery be battered? König Ottokar, amid yonder hillocks, dies under Rodolf's truncheon; here Kaiser Franz falls a-swoon under Napoleon's: within which five centuries, to omit the others, how has thy breast, fair Plain, been defaced and defiled! The greensward is torn-up and trampled-down; man's fond care of it, his fruit-trees, hedge-rows, and pleasant dwellings, blown-away with gunpowder; and the kind seedfield lies a desolate, hideous Place of Skulls.—Nevertheless, Nature is at work; neither shall these Powder-Devilkins with their utmost devilry gainsay her: but all that gore and carnage will be shrouded-in, absorbed into manure; and next year the Marchfeld will be green, nay greener. Thrifty unwearied Nature, ever out of our great waste educing some little profit of thy own,—how dost thou, from the very carcass of the Killer, bring Life for the Living!

"What, speaking in quite unofficial language, is the net-purport and upshot of war? To my own knowledge, for example, there dwell and toil, in the British village of Dumdrudge, usually some five-hundred souls. From these, by certain 'Natural Enemies' of the French, there are successively selected, during the French war, say thirty able-bodied men: Dumdrudge, at her own expense, has suckled and nursed them: she has, not without difficulty and sorrow, fed them up to manhood, and even trained them to crafts, so that one can weave, another build, another hammer, and the weakest can stand under thirty stone avoirdupois. Nevertheless, amid much weeping and swearing, they are selected; all dressed in red; and shipped away, at the public charges, some two-thousand miles, or say only to the south of Spain; and fed there till wanted. And now to that same spot, in the south of Spain, are thirty similar French artisans, from a French Dumdrudge, in like manner wending: till at length, after infinite effort, the two parties come into actual juxtaposition; and Thirty stands fronting Thirty, each with a gun in his hand. Straightway the word 'Fire!' is given: and they blow the souls out of one another; and in place of sixty brisk useful craftsmen, the world has sixty dead carcasses, which it must bury, and anew shed tears for. Had these men any quarrel? Busy as the Devil is, not the smallest! They lived far enough apart; were the entirest strangers; nay, in so wide a Universe, there was even, unconsciously, by Commerce, some mutual helpfulness between them. How then? Simpleton! their Governors had fallen-out; and, instead of shooting one another, had the cunning to make these poor blockheads shoot.—Alas, so is it in Deutschland, and hitherto in all other lands; still as of old, 'what devilry soever Kings do, the Greeks must pay the piper!'—In that fiction of the English Smollett, it is true, the final Cessation of War is perhaps prophetically shadowed forth; where the two Natural Enemies, in person, take each a Tobacco-pipe, filled with Brimstone; light the same, and smoke in one another's faces, till the weaker gives in: but from such predicted Peace-Era, what blood-filled trenches, and contentious centuries, may still divide us!"

Thus can the Professor, at least in lucid intervals, look away from his own sorrows, over the many-coloured world, and pertinently enough note what is passing there. . . .

But amid these specialties, let us not forget the great generality, which is our chief quest here: How prospered the inner man of Teufelsdröckh under so much outward shifting? Does Legion still lurk in him, though repressed; or has he exorcised that Devil's Brood? We can answer that the symptoms continue promising. Experience is the grand spiritual Doctor; and with him Teufelsdröckh has now been long a patient, swallowing many a bitter bolus. Unless our poor Friend belong to the numerous class of Incurables, which seems not likely, some cure will doubtless be effected. We should rather say that Legion, or the Satanic School, was now pretty well extirpated and cast out, but next to nothing introduced in its room; whereby the heart remains, for the while, in a quiet but no comfortable state.

"At length, after so much roasting," thus writes our Autobiographer, "I was what you might name calcined. Pray only that it be not rather, as is the more frequent issue, reduced to a *caput-mortuum!* But in any case, by mere dint of practice, I had grown familiar with many things. Wretchedness was still wretched; but I could now partly see

1. house of Hapsburg, one of the great royal families of Europe, embracing many Holy Roman Emperors, rulers of Spain from 1516 to 1700, rulers of Austria from 1276 to 1918. **4. Kaiser Franz,** Francis I of Austria, who ruled from 1792 to 1835. **11–12. Place of Skulls,** Calvary, or Golgotha; see John 19:17. **19–20. from the very . . . Living.** Carlyle was thinking of Samson's experience, Judges 14. **24. Dumdrudge,** a coined name intended to suggest "dumb drudgery." **25–26. 'Natural Enemies,'** a term applied to the French by the English during the Napoleonic Wars.

11–12. devilry . . . piper. See Horace, *Epistles,* I, 2, 14. **13. Smollett.** Tobias Smollett (1721–1771), in his *Adventures of Ferdinand Count Fathom.* **28. Legion.** See Mark 5:9. **34. bolus,** large pill. **37. Satanic School.** Southey had given this epithet to Byron, Shelley, and other romantic poets. **45. *caput-mortuum*** death's-head, worthless residue.

through it, and despise it. Which highest mortal, in this inane Existence, had I not found a Shadow-hunter, or Shadow-hunted; and, when I looked through his brave garnitures, miserable enough? Thy wishes have all been sniffed aside, thought I: but what, had they even been all granted! Did not the Boy Alexander weep because he had not two Planets to conquer; or a whole Solar System; or after that, a whole Universe? *Ach Gott*, when I gazed into these Stars, have they not looked down on me as if with pity, from their serene spaces; like Eyes glistening with heavenly tears over the little lot of man! Thousands of human generations, all as noisy as our own, have been swallowed-up of Time, and there remains no wreck of them any more; and Arcturus and Orion and Sirius and the Pleiades are still shining in their courses, clear and young, as when the Shepherd first noted them in the plain of Shinar. Pshaw! what is this paltry little Dog-cage of an Earth; what art thou that sittest whining there? Thou art still Nothing, Nobody: true; but who, then, is Something, Somebody? For thee the Family of Man has no use; it rejects thee; thou art wholly as a dissevered limb: so be it; perhaps it is better so!"

Too-heavy-laden Teufelsdröckh! Yet surely his bands are loosening; one day he will hurl the burden far from him, and bound forth free and with a second youth.

"This," says our Professor, "was the CENTRE OF INDIFFERENCE I had now reached; through which whoso travels from the Negative Pole to the Positive must necessarily pass."

Chapter 9

The Everlasting Yea

"Temptations in the Wilderness!" exclaims Teufelsdröckh: "Have we not all to be tried with such? Not so easily can the old Adam, lodged in us by birth, be dispossessed. Our Life is compassed round with Necessity; yet is the meaning of Life itself no other than Freedom, than Voluntary Force: thus have we a warfare; in the beginning, especially, a hard-fought battle. For the God-given mandate, *Work thou in Welldoing*, lies mysteriously written, in Promethean Prophetic Characters, in our hearts; and leaves us no rest, night or day, till it be deciphered and obeyed; till it burn forth, in our conduct, a visible, acted Gospel of Freedom. And as the clay-given mandate, *Eat thou and be filled*, at the same time persuasively proclaims itself through every nerve,—must not there be a confusion, a contest, before the better Influence can become the upper?

"To me nothing seems more natural than that the Son of Man, when such God-given mandate first prophetically stirs within him, and the Clay must now be vanquished, or vanquish,—should be carried of the spirit into grim Solitudes, and there fronting the Tempter do grimmest battle with him; defiantly setting him at naught, till he yield and fly. Name it as we choose: with or without visible Devil, whether in the natural Desert of rocks and sands, or in the populous moral Desert of selfishness and baseness,—to such Temptation are we all called. Unhappy if we are not! Unhappy if we are but Half-men, in whom that divine handwriting has never blazed forth, all-subduing, in true sun-splendour; but quivers dubiously amid meaner lights: or smoulders, in dull pain, in darkness, under earthly vapours!—Our Wilderness is the wide World in an Atheistic Century; our Forty Days are long years of suffering and fasting: nevertheless, to these also comes an end. Yes, to me also was given, if not Victory, yet the consciousness of Battle, and the resolve to persevere therein while life or faculty is left. To me also, entangled in the enchanted forests, demon-peopled, doleful of sight and of sound, it was given, after weariest wanderings, to work out my way into the higher sunlit slopes—of that Mountain which has no summit, or whose summit is in Heaven only!"

He says elsewhere, under a less ambitious figure; as figures are, once for all, natural to him: "Has not thy Life been that of most sufficient men (*tüchtigen Männer*) thou hast known in this generation? An outflush of foolish young Enthusiasm, like the first fallow-crop, wherein are as many weeds as valuable herbs: this all parched away, under the Droughts of practical and spiritual Unbelief, as Disappointment, in thought and act, often-repeated gave rise to Doubt, and Doubt gradually settled into Denial! If I have had a second-crop, and now see the perennial greensward, and sit under umbrageous cedars, which defy all Drought (and Doubt); herein too, be the Heavens praised, I am not without examples, and even exemplars."

So that, for Teufelsdröckh also, there has been a "glorious revolution": these mad shadow-hunting and shadow-hunted Pilgrimings of his were but

6–8. Did not . . . conquer, Alexander the Great (356–323 B.C.). **19. Shinar,** where Abraham ("the Shepherd") was bidden by God to observe the innumerable stars as a symbol of his descendants. See Genesis 15:5. **39. Temptations in the Wilderness.** For Jesus' temptation in the wilderness, see Matthew 4 and Luke 4. **41. the old Adam,** man's sinful nature; see Colossians 3:9. **47. Work thou in Welldoing.** See 2 Thessalonians 3:13.

some purifying "Temptation in the Wilderness," before his Apostolic work (such as it was) could begin; which Temptation is now happily over, and the Devil once more worsted! Was "that high moment in the *Rue de l'Enfer*," then, properly the turning-point of the battle; when the Fiend said, *Worship me, or be torn in shreds;* and was answered valiantly with an *Apage Satana?*—Singular Teufelsdröckh, would thou hadst told thy singular story in plain words! But it is fruitless to look there, in those Paper-bags, for such. Nothing but innuendoes, figurative crotchets: a typical Shadow, fitfully wavering, prophetico-satiric; no clear logical Picture. "How paint to the sensual eye," asks he once, "what passes in the Holy-of-Holies of Man's Soul; in what words, known to these profane times, speak even afar-off of the unspeakable?" We ask in turn: Why perplex these times, profane as they are, with needless obscurity, by omission and by commission? Not mystical only is our Professor, but whimsical; and involves himself, now more than ever, in eye-bewildering *chiaroscuro*. Successive glimpses, here faithfully imparted, our more gifted readers must endeavour to combine for their own behoof.

He says: "The hot Harmattan wind had raged itself out; its howl went silent within me; and the long-deafened soul could now hear. I paused in my wild wanderings; and sat me down to wait, and consider; for it was as if the hour of change drew nigh. I seemed to surrender, to renounce utterly, and say: Fly, then, false shadows of Hope; I will chase you no more, I will believe you no more. And ye too, haggard spectres of Fear, I care not for you; ye too are all shadows and a lie. Let me rest here: for I am way-weary and life-weary; I will rest here, were it but to die: to die or to live is alike to me; alike insignificant."—And again: "Here, then, as I lay in that Center of Indifference; cast, doubtless by benignant upper Influence, into a healing sleep, the heavy dreams rolled gradually away, and I awoke to a new Heaven and a new Earth. The first preliminary moral Act, Annihilation of Self (*Selbsttödtung*), had been happily accomplished; and my mind's eyes were now unsealed, and its hands ungyved."

Might we not also conjecture that the following passage refers to his Locality, during this same "healing sleep"; that his Pilgrim-staff lies cast aside here, on "the high table-land"; and indeed that the repose is already taking wholesome effect on him? If it were not that the tone, in some parts, has more of riancy, even of levity, than we could have expected! However, in Teufelsdröckh, there is always the strangest Dualism: light dancing, with guitar-music, will be going on in the fore-court, while by fits from within comes the faint whimpering of woe and wail. We transcribe the piece entire:

"Beautiful it was to sit there, as in my skyey Tent, musing and meditating; on the high table-land, in front of the Mountains; over me, as roof, the azure Dome, and around me, for walls, four azure-flowing curtains,—namely, of the Four azure Winds, on whose bottom-fringes also I have seen gilding. And then to fancy the fair Castles that stood sheltered in these Mountain hollows; with their green flower-lawns, and white dames and damosels, lovely enough: or better still, the straw-roofed Cottages, wherein stood many a Mother baking bread, with her children round her:—all hidden and protectingly folded-up in the valley-folds; yet there and alive, as sure as if I beheld them. Or to see, as well as fancy, the nine Towns and Villages, that lay round my mountain-seat, which, in still weather, were wont to speak to me (by their steeple-bells) with metal tongue; and, in almost all weather, proclaimed their vitality by repeated Smoke-clouds; whereon, as on a culinary horologe, I might read the hour of the day. For it was the smoke of cookery, as kind housewives at morning, midday, eventide, were boiling their husbands' kettles; and ever a blue pillar rose up into the air, successively or simultaneously, from each of the nine, saying, as plainly as smoke could say: Such and such a meal is getting ready here. Not uninteresting! For you have the whole Borough, with all its love-makings and scandal-mongeries, contentions and contentments, as in miniature, and could cover it all with your hat.—If, in my wide Wayfarings, I had learned to look into the business of the World in its details, here perhaps was the place for combining it into general propositions, and deducing inferences therefrom.

"Often also could I see the black Tempest marching in anger through the Distance: round some Schreckhorn, as yet grim-blue, would the eddying vapour gather, and there tumultuously eddy, and flow down like a mad witch's hair; till, after a space, it vanished, and, in the clear sunbeam, your Schreckhorn stood smiling grim-white, for the vapour had held snow. How thou fermentest and elaboratest, in thy great fermenting-vat and laboratory of an Atmosphere, of a World, O Nature!—Or what is Nature? Ha! why do I not name thee

8. *Apage Satana,* Get thee hence, Satan: See Matthew 4:10; Luke 4:8. **11. Paper-bags,** into which Teufelsdröckh's manuscripts were alleged to have been thrust. **22. *chiaroscuro,*** pictorial art employing only light and shade. **25. Harmattan,** a wind which blows from the interior of Africa to the Atlantic coast.

44. Schreckhorn, Peak of Terror. Several in the Bernese Alps are so named.

God? Art not thou the 'Living Garment of God'? O Heavens, is it, in very deed, He, then, that ever speaks through thee; that lives and loves in thee, that lives and loves in me?

"Fore-shadows, call them rather fore-splendours, of that Truth, and Beginning of Truths, fell mysteriously over my soul. Sweeter than Dayspring to the Shipwrecked in Nova Zembla; ah, like the mother's voice to her little child that strays bewildered, weeping, in unknown tumults; like soft streamings of celestial music to my too-exasperated heart, came that Evangel. The Universe is not dead and demoniacal, a charnel-house with spectres; but godlike, and my Father's!

"With other eyes, too, could I now look upon my fellow man; with an infinite Love, an infinite Pity. Poor, wandering, wayward man! Art thou not tired, and beaten with stripes, even as I am? Ever, whether thou bear the royal mantle or the beggar's gabardine, art thou not so weary, so heavy-laden; and thy Bed of Rest is but a Grave. O my Brother, my Brother, why cannot I shelter thee in my bosom, and wipe away all tears from thy eyes! Truly, the din of many-voiced Life, which, in this solitude, with the mind's organ, I could hear, was no longer a maddening discord, but a melting one; like inarticulate cries, and sobbings of a dumb creature, which in the ear of Heaven are prayers. The poor Earth, with her poor joys, was now my needy Mother, not my cruel Stepdame; man, with his so mad Wants and so mean Endeavours, had become the dearer to me; and even for his sufferings and his sins, I now first named him Brother. Thus I was standing in the porch of that '*Sanctuary of Sorrow*'; by strange, steep ways had I too been guided thither; and ere long its sacred gates would open, and the '*Divine Depth of Sorrow*' lie disclosed to me."

The Professor says, he here first got eye on the Knot that had been strangling him, and straightway could unfasten it, and was free. "A vain interminable controversy," writes he, "touching what is at present called Origin of Evil, or some such thing, arises in every soul, since the beginning of the world; and in every soul, that would pass from idle Suffering into actual Endeavouring, must first be put an end to. The most, in our time, have to go content with a simple, incomplete enough Suppression of this controversy; to a few some Solution of it is indispensable. In every new era, too, such Solution comes-out in different terms; and ever the Solution of the last era has become obsolete, and is found unserviceable. For it is man's nature to change his Dialect from century to century; he cannot help it though he would. The authentic *Church-Catechism* of our present century has not yet fallen into my hands: meanwhile, for my own private behoof, I attempt to elucidate the matter so. Man's Unhappiness, as I construe, comes of his Greatness; it is because there is an Infinite in him, which with all his cunning he cannot quite bury under the Finite. Will the whole Finance Ministers and Upholsterers and Confectioners of modern Europe undertake, in joint-stock company, to make one Shoeblack happy? They cannot accomplish it, above an hour or two; for the Shoeblack also has a Soul quite other than his Stomach; and would require, if you consider it, for his permanent satisfaction and saturation, simply this allotment, no more, and no less: *God's infinite Universe altogether to himself*, therein to enjoy infinitely, and fill every wish as fast as it rose. Oceans of Hochheimer, a Throat like that of Ophiuchus: speak not of them; to the infinite Shoeblack they are as nothing. No sooner is your ocean filled, than he grumbles that it might have been of better vintage. Try him with half of a Universe, of an Omnipotence, he sets to quarrelling with the proprietor of the other half, and declares himself the most maltreated of men.—Always there is a black spot in our sunshine: it is even, as I said, the *Shadow of Ourselves*.

"But the whim we have of Happiness is somewhat thus. By certain valuations, and averages, of our own striking, we come upon some sort of average terrestrial lot; this we fancy belongs to us by nature, and of indefeasible right. It is simple payment of our wages, of our deserts; requires neither thanks nor complaint; only such *overplus* as there may be do we account Happiness; any *deficit* again is Misery. Now consider that we have the valuation of our own deserts ourselves, and what a fund of Self-conceit there is in each of us,—do you wonder that the balance should so often dip the wrong way, and many a Blockhead cry: See there, what a payment; was ever worthy gentleman so used!—I tell thee, Blockhead, it all comes of thy Vanity; of what thou *fanciest* those same deserts of thine to be. Fancy that thou deservest to be hanged (as is most likely), thou wilt feel it happiness to be only shot: fancy that thou deservest to be hanged in a hair-halter, it will be a luxury to die in hemp.

1. 'Living Garment of God.' See Goethe's *Faust*, Part I, sc. 1, ll. 501–09. **8. Nova Zembla,** an arctic archipelago, separating the Kara and Barents seas. Carlyle refers to an ill-starred Dutch expedition thither in May, 1596. **23. and wipe . . . eyes.** See Revelation 21:4. **34–37. 'Sanctuary of Sorrow' . . . 'Divine Depth of Sorrow,'** Goethean phrases from *Wilhelm Meister*.

23. Hochheimer, a German wine. **24. Ophiuchus,** the constellation Serpentarius; see *Paradise Lost*, Book II, l. 708.

"So true is it, what I then said, that *the Fraction of Life can be increased in value not so much by increasing your Numerator as by lessening your Denominator*. Nay, unless my Algebra deceive me, *Unity* itself divided by *Zero* will give *Infinity*. Make thy claim of wages a zero, then; thou hast the world under thy feet. Well did the Wisest of our time write: 'It is only with Renunciation (*Entsagen*) that Life, properly speaking, can be said to begin.'

"I asked myself: What is this that, ever since earliest years, thou hast been fretting and fuming, and lamenting and self-tormenting, on account of? Say it in a word: is it not because thou art not HAPPY? Because the THOU (sweet gentleman) is not sufficiently honoured, nourished, soft-bedded, and lovingly cared for? Foolish soul! What Act of Legislature was there that *thou* shouldst be Happy? A little while ago thou hadst no right to *be* at all. What if thou wert born and predestined not to be Happy, but to be Unhappy! Art thou nothing other than a Vulture, then, that fliest through the Universe seeking after somewhat to *eat;* and shrieking dolefully because carrion enough is not given thee? Close thy *Byron;* open thy *Goethe*."

"*Es leuchtet mir ein*, I see a glimpse of it!" cries he elsewhere: "there is in man a HIGHER than Love of Happiness: he can do without Happiness, and instead thereof find Blessedness! Was it not to preach-forth this same HIGHER that sages and martyrs, the Poet and the Priest, in all times, have spoken and suffered; bearing testimony, through life and through death, of the Godlike that is in Man, and how in the Godlike only has he Strength and Freedom? Which God-inspired Doctrine art thou also honoured to be taught; O Heavens! and broken with manifold merciful afflictions, even till thou become contrite, and learn it! O, thank thy Destiny for these; thankfully bear what yet remain: thou hadst need of them; the Self in thee needed to be annihilated. By benignant fever-paroxysms in Life rooting out the deep-seated chronic Disease, and triumphs over Death. On the roaring billows of Time, thou art not engulfed, but borne aloft into the azure of Eternity. Love not Pleasure; love God. This is the EVERLASTING YEA, wherein all contradiction is solved: wherein whoso walks and works, it is well with him."

And again: "Small is it that thou canst trample the Earth with its injuries under thy feet, as old Greek Zeno trained thee: thou canst love the Earth while it injures thee, and even because it injures thee; for this a Greater than Zeno was needed, and he too was sent. Knowest thou that '*Worship of Sorrow*'? The Temple thereof, founded some eighteen centuries ago, now lies in ruins, overgrown with jungle, the habitation of doleful creatures: nevertheless, venture forward; in a low crypt, arched out of falling fragments, thou findest the Altar still there, and its sacred Lamp perennially burning."

Without pretending to comment on which strange utterances, the Editor will only remark, that there lies beside them much of a still more questionable character; unsuited to the general apprehension; nay wherein he himself does not see his way. Nebulous disquisitions on Religion, yet not without bursts of splendour; on the "perennial continuance of Inspiration"; on Prophecy; that there are "true Priests, as well as Baal-Priests, in our own day": with more of the like sort. We select some fractions, by way of finish to this farrago.

"Cease, my much-respected Herr von Voltaire," thus apostrophises the Professor: "shut thy sweet voice; for the task appointed thee seems finished. Sufficiently hast thou demonstrated this proposition, considerable or otherwise: That the Mythus of the Christian Religion looks not in the eighteenth century as it did in the eighth. Alas, were thy six-and-thirty quartos, and the six-and-thirty thousand other quartos and folios, and flying sheets or reams, printed before and since on the same subject, all needed to convince us of so little! But what next? Wilt thou help us to embody the divine Spirit of that Religion in a new Mythus, in a new vehicle and vesture, that our Souls, otherwise too like perishing, may live? What! thou hast no faculty in that kind? Only a torch for burning, no hammer for building? Take our thanks, then, and——thyself away.

"Meanwhile what are antiquated Mythuses to me? Or is the God present, felt in my own heart, a thing which Herr von Voltaire will dispute out of me; or dispute into me? To the '*Worship of Sorrow*' ascribe what origin and genesis thou pleasest, *has* not that Worship originated, and been generated; is it not *here?* Feel it in thy heart, and then say whether it is of God! This is Belief; all else is Opinion,—for which latter whoso will, let him worry and be worried."

"Neither," observes he elsewhere, "shall ye tear-

7. the Wisest of our time, Goethe. **19–20. What if thou . . . Unhappy,** an interesting survival of Carlyle's Calvinistic background. **27. he,** Wilhelm Meister. **44. Love . . . God.** See 2 Timothy 3:4. **49. Zeno,** Greek Stoic philosopher of the third century B.C., who taught that virtue, not pleasure, is the end of life.

2. Greater than Zeno, Christ. **6. the habitation . . . creatures.** See Isaiah 13:21. **19. Baal-Priests,** the priests who, in Israel in Elijah's time, served not Jehovah but Baal of Canaan; see, especially, 1 Kings 18.

out one another's eyes, struggling over 'Plenary Inspiration,' and suchlike: try rather to get a little even Partial Inspiration, each of you for himself. One BIBLE I know, of whose Plenary Inspiration doubt is not so much as possible; nay with my own eyes I saw the God's-Hand writing it: thereof all other Bibles are but leaves,—say, in Picture-Writing to assist the weaker faculty."

Or, to give the wearied reader relief, and bring it to an end, let him take the following perhaps more intelligible passage:

"To me, in this our life," says the Professor, "which is an internecine warfare with the Time-spirit, other warfare seems questionable. Hast thou in any way a Contention with thy brother, I advise thee, think well what the meaning thereof is. If thou gauge it to the bottom, it is simply this: 'Fellow, see! thou art taking more than thy share of Happiness in the world, something from *my* share: which, by the Heavens, thou shalt not; nay I will fight thee rather.'—Alas, and the whole lot to be divided is such a beggarly matter, truly a 'feast of shells,' for the substance has been spilled out: not enough to quench one Appetite; and the collective human species clutching at them!—Can we not, in all such cases, rather say: 'Take it, thou too-ravenous individual; take that pitiful additional fraction of a share, which I reckoned mine, but which thou so wantest; take it with a blessing: would to Heaven I had enough for thee!'—If Fichte's *Wissenschaftslehre* be, 'to a certain extent, Applied Christianity,' surely to a still greater extent, so is this. We have here not a Whole Duty of Man, yet a Half Duty, namely the Passive half: could we but do it, as we can demonstrate it!

"But indeed Conviction, were it never so excellent, is worthless till it convert itself into Conduct. Nay properly Conviction is not possible till then; inasmuch as all Speculation is by nature endless, formless, a vortex amid vortices: only by a felt indubitable certainty of Experience does it find any centre to revolve round, and so fashion itself into a system. Most true is it, as a wise man teaches us, that 'Doubt of any sort cannot be removed except by Action.' On which ground, too, let him who gropes painfully in darkness or uncertain light, and prays vehemently that the dawn may ripen into day, lay this other precept well to heart, which to me was of invaluable service: '*Do the Duty which lies nearest thee*,' which thou knowest to be a Duty! Thy second Duty will already have become clearer.

"May we not say, however, that the hour of Spiritual Enfranchisement is even this: When your Ideal World, wherein the whole man has been dimly struggling and inexpressibly languishing to work, becomes revealed, and thrown open; and you discover, with amazement enough, like the Lothario in *Wilhelm Meister*, that your 'America is here or nowhere'? The Situation that has not its Duty, its Ideal, was never yet occupied by man. Yes here, in this poor, miserable, hampered, despicable Actual, wherein thou even now standest, here or nowhere is thy Ideal: work it out therefrom; and working, believe, live, be free. Fool! the Ideal is in thyself, the impediment too is in thyself: thy Condition is but the stuff thou art to shape that same Ideal out of: what matters whether such stuff be of this sort or that, so the Form thou give it be heroic, be poetic? O thou that pinest in the imprisonment of the Actual, and criest bitterly to the gods for a kingdom wherein to rule and create, know this of a truth: the thing thou seekest is already with thee, 'here or nowhere,' couldst thou only see!

"But it is with man's Soul as it was with Nature: the beginning of Creation is—Light. Till the eye have vision, the whole members are in bonds. Divine moment, when over the tempest-tost Soul, as once over the wild-weltering Chaos, it is spoken: Let there be Light! Ever to the greatest that has felt such moment, is it not miraculous and God-announcing; even as, under simpler figures, to the simplest and least. The mad primeval Discord is hushed; the rudely-jumbled conflicting elements bind themselves into separate Firmaments: deep silent rock-foundations are built beneath; and the skyey vault with its everlasting Luminaries above: instead of a dark wasteful Chaos, we have a blooming, fertile, heaven-encompassed World.

"I too could now say to myself: Be no longer a Chaos, but a World, or even Worldkin. Produce! Produce! Were it but the pitifullest infinitesimal fraction of a Product, produce it, in God's name! 'Tis the utmost thou hast in thee: out with it, then. Up, up! Whatsoever thy hand findeth to do, do it with thy whole might. Work while it is called Today; for the Night cometh, wherein no man can work."

1–2. 'Plenary Inspiration,' the doctrine that the Bible is completely inspired. **30–31. Fichte's . . . Christianity.** *Wissenschaftslehre* (*The Doctrine of Knowledge*) was published in 1794 by Johann Gottlieb Fichte, an eminent philosopher of the school of Kant. The quotation in this passage is from Novalis. **33. Whole Duty of Man,** the title of a famous devotional book, of unknown authorship, published in 1659. See also Ecclesiastes 12:13. **44–45. Doubt . . . Action,** from *Wilhelm Meister*.

28. the beginning . . . Light. See Genesis 1:3. **28–29. Till the eye . . . bonds.** See Matthew 6:22–23. **47–50. Whatsoever . . . work.** See Ecclesiastes 9:10; John 9:4.

from PAST AND PRESENT

Past and Present was described by its author as "a somewhat fiery and questionable 'Tract for the Times,' *not* by a Puseyite, which the terrible aspect of things here has forced from me." Breaking in upon his work on Oliver Cromwell, it got itself written during the first two months of 1843, and was published in the same year. It constitutes probably Carlyle's most important public service.

It is divided into four books: Proem, The Ancient Monk, The Modern Worker, and Horoscope. The second part is based on *The Chronica Jocelini de Brakelonda*, which had just been published by the Camden Society, and describes, by way of contrast to modern conditions, the life of a twelfth-century abbey under Abbot Samson, "a man worth looking at," in a day when reverence for God, respect for authority and authorized leaders, and unselfish devotion to work created a stable world. Carlyle did not believe in the possibility of organizing life in nineteenth-century England on the feudal plan, but he did maintain the necessity of reviving the ideals to which Abbot Samson and his contemporaries gave their allegiance; especially did he insist upon modern "Captains of Industry" assuming the responsibilities which rulers under the feudal system had once assumed. Strangely combining bitter hatred of the democratic system with a burning sympathy for the poor, *Past and Present* became one of the strong Victorian influences in the direction of social amelioration.

from BOOK III: Chapter 5

The English

AND yet, with all thy theoretic platitudes, what a depth of practical sense in thee, great England! A depth of sense, of justice, and courage; in which, under all emergencies and world-bewilderments, and under this most complex of emergencies we now live in, there is still hope, there is still assurance!

The English are a dumb people. They can do great acts, but not describe them. Like the old Romans, and some few others, *their* Epic Poem is written on the Earth's surface: England her Mark! It is complained that they have no artists: one Shakespeare indeed; but for Raphael only a Reynolds; for Mozart nothing but a Mr. Bishop: not a picture, not a song. And yet they did produce one Shakespeare: consider how the element of Shakespearean melody does lie imprisoned in their nature; reduce to unfold itself in mere Cotton-mills, Constitutional Governments, and such like;—all the more interesting when it does become visible, as even in such unexpected shapes it succeeds in doing! Goethe spoke of the Horse, how impressive, almost affecting it was that an animal of such qualities should stand obstructed so; its speech nothing but an inarticulate neighing, its handiness mere *hoof*iness, the fingers all constricted, tied together, the finger-nails coagulated into a mere hoof, shod with iron. The more significant, thinks he, are those eye-flashings of the generous noble quadruped; those prancings, curvings of the neck clothed with thunder. . . .

The spoken Word, the written Poem, is said to be an epitome of the man; how much more the done Work. Whatsoever of morality and of intelligence; what of patience, perseverance, faithfulness, of method, insight, ingenuity, energy; in a word, whatsoever of Strength the man had in him will lie written in the Work he does. To work: why, it is to try himself against Nature, and her everlasting unerring Laws; these will tell a true verdict as to the man. So much of virtue and of faculty did *we* find in him; so much and no more! He had such capacity of harmonising himself with *me* and my unalterable ever-veracious Laws; of coöperating and working as *I* bade him;—and has prospered, and has not prospered, as you see! . . .

How one loves to see the burly figure of him, this thick-skinned, seemingly opaque, perhaps sulky, almost stupid Man of Practice, pitted against some light adroit Man of Theory, all equipped with clear logic, and able anywhere to give you Why for Wherefore! The adroit Man of Theory, so light of movement, clear of utterance, with his bow full-bent and quiver full of arrow-arguments,—surely he will strike down the game, transfix everywhere the heart of the matter; triumph everywhere, as he proves that he shall and must do? To your astonishment, it turns out oftenest No. The cloudy-browed, thick-soled, opaque Practicality, with no logic utterance, in silence mainly, with here and there a low grunt or growl, has in him what transcends all logic-utterance: a Congruity with the Unuttered. The Speakable, which lies atop, as a superficial film, or outer skin, is his or is not his: but the Doable, which reaches down to the World's centre, you find him there! . . .

Of all the Nations in the world at present the English are the stupidest in speech, the wisest in

42–43. but for Raphael . . . Mr. Bishop. Raphael, one of the most famous of all Italian painters (1483–1520). **Reynolds,** Sir Joshua Reynolds (1723–1792), English portrait-painter. **Mozart,** Wolfgang Amadeus Mozart (1756–1791), Austrian composer, one of the greatest. **Bishop,** Sir Henry R. Bishop (1786–1855), English composer, teacher, and musical director action. As good as a "dumb" Nation, I say, who cannot speak, and have never yet spoken,—spite of the Shakespeares and Miltons who show us what possibilities there are!—O Mr. Bull, I look in that surly face of thine with a mixture of pity and laughter, yet also with wonder and veneration. Thou complainest not, my illustrious friend; and yet I believe the heart of thee is full of sorrow, of unspoken sadness, seriousness,—profound melancholy (as some have said) the basis of thy being. Unconsciously, for thou speakest of nothing, this great Universe is great to thee. Not by levity of floating, but by stubborn force of swimming, shalt thou make thy way. The Fates sing of thee that thou shalt many times be thought an ass and a dull ox, and shalt with a godlike indifference believe it. My friend,—and it is all untrue, nothing ever falser in point of fact! Thou art of those great ones whose greatness the small passer-by does not discern. Thy very stupidity is wiser than their wisdom. A grand *vis inertiae* is in thee; how many grand qualities unknown to small men! Nature alone knows thee, acknowledges the bulk and strength of thee: thy Epic, unsung in words, is written in huge characters on the face of this Planet,—sea-moles, cotton-trades, railways, fleets and cities, Indian Empires, Americas, New-Hollands; legible throughout the Solar System! . . .

Ask Bull his spoken opinion of any matter,—oftentimes the force of dullness can no farther go. You stand silent, incredulous, as over a platitude that borders on the Infinite. The man's Churchisms, Dissenterisms, Puseyisms, Benthamisms, College Philosophies, Fashionable Literatures, are unexampled in this world. Fate's prophecy is fulfilled; you call the man an ox and an ass. But set him once to work,—respectable man! His spoken sense is next to nothing, nine-tenths of it palpable *non*sense: but his unspoken sense, his inner silent feeling of what is true, what does agree with fact, what is doable and what is not doable,—this seeks its fellow in the world. A terrible worker; irresistible against marshes, mountains, impediments, disorder, incivilization; everywhere vanquishing disorder, leaving it behind him as method and order. . . .

Nay withal, stupid as he is, our dear John,—ever, after infinite tumblings, and spoken platitudes innumerable from barrel-heads and parliament-benches, he does settle down somewhere about the just conclusion; you are certain that his jumblings and tumblings will end, after years or centuries, in the stable equilibrium. Stable equilibrium, I say; centre-of-gravity lowest;—not the unstable, with centre-of-gravity highest, as I have known it done by quicker people! For indeed, do but jumble and tumble sufficiently, you avoid that worse fault, of settling with your centre-of-gravity highest; your centre-of-gravity is certain to come lowest, and to stay there. If slowness, what we in our impatience call "stupidity," be the price of stable equilibrium over unstable, shall we grudge a little slowness? Not the least admirable quality of Bull is, after all, that of remaining insensible to logic; holding out for considerable periods, ten years or more, as in this of the Corn-Laws, after all arguments and shadow of arguments have faded away from him, till the very urchins on the street titter at the arguments he brings. Logic,—Λογική, the "Art of Speech,"—does indeed speak so and so; clear enough; nevertheless Bull still shakes his head; will see whether nothing else *illogical*, not yet "spoken," not yet able to be "spoken," do not lie in the business, as there so often does!—My firm belief is, that, finding himself now enchanted, hand-shackled, foot-shackled, in Poor-Law Bastilles and elsewhere, he will retire three days to his bed, and *arrive* at a conclusion or two! His three-years' "total stagnation of trade," alas, is not that a painful enough "lying in bed to consider himself"? Poor Bull!

Bull is a born Conservative; for this too I inexpressibly honour him. All great Peoples are conservative; slow to believe in novelties; patient of much error in actualities; deeply and for ever certain of the greatness that is in LAW, in Custom once solemnly established, and now long recognised as just and final.—True, O Radical Reformer, there is no Custom that can, properly speaking, be final; none. And yet thou seest *Customs* which, in all civilised countries, are accounted final; nay, under the Old-Roman name of *Mores*, are accounted *Morality*, Virtue, Laws of God Himself. Such, I assure thee, not a few of them are; such almost all of them once were. And greatly do I respect the solid character,—a blockhead, thou wilt say; yes, but a well-conditioned blockhead, and the best-

4. Mr. Bull, John Bull, who typifies England, as Uncle Sam typifies America. **21. vis inertiae,** force of inertia. **33–34. Churchisms,** referring to the Established Church and possibly to the Oxford Movement. **Dissenterisms** refers to Methodists, Congregationalists, Quakers, and so on. **Puseyisms** refers to the Oxford Movement; see introduction to Cardinal Newman. **Benthamisms** refers to Utilitarianism; see pages 901–902 and introduction to selections from John Stuart Mill.

19. Corn-Laws. See page 901. **29. Poor-Law Bastilles,** workhouses; see page 901. **30–31. he will retire . . . or two,** as was the custom of the famous but illiterate engineer James Brindley (1716–1772), to whom Carlyle paid his tribute in a portion of this essay not included in the present reprint.

conditioned,—who esteems all "Customs once solemnly acknowledged" to be ultimate, divine, and the rule for a man to walk by, nothing doubting, not inquiring farther. What a time of it had we, were all men's life and trade still, in all parts of it, a problem, a hypothetic seeking, to be settled by painful Logics and Baconian Inductions! The Clerk in Eastcheap cannot spend the day in verifying his Ready-Reckoner; he must take it as verified, true and indisputable; or his Bookkeeping by Double Entry will stand still. "Where is your Posted Ledger?" asks the Master at night.—"Sir," answers the other, "I was verifying my Ready-Reckoner, and find some errors. The Ledger is—!"—Fancy such a thing! . . .

O my Conservative friends, who still specially name and struggle to approve yourselves "Conservative," would to Heaven I could persuade you of this world-old fact, than which Fate is not surer, That Truth and Justice alone are *capable* of being "conserved" and preserved! The thing which is unjust, which is *not* according to God's Law, will you, in a God's Universe, try to conserve that? It is so old, say you? Yes, and the hotter haste ought *you*, of all others, to be in to let it grow no older! If but the faintest whisper in your hearts intimate to you that it is not fair,—hasten, for the sake of Conservatism itself, to probe it rigorously, to cast it forth at once and forever if guilty. How will or can you preserve *it*, the thing that is not fair? "Impossibility" a thousandfold is marked on that. And ye call yourselves Conservatives, Aristocracies:—ought not honour and nobleness of mind, if they had departed from all the Earth elsewhere, to find their last refuge with you? Ye unfortunate!

The bough that is dead shall be cut away, for the sake of the tree itself. Old? Yes, it is too old. Many a weary winter has it swung and creaked there, and gnawed and fretted, with its dead wood, the organic substance and still living fibre of this good tree; many a long summer has its ugly naked brown defaced the fair green umbrage; every day it has done mischief, and that only: off with it, for the tree's sake, if for nothing more; let the Conservatism that would preserve cut *it* away. Did no wood-forester apprise you that a dead bough with its dead root left sticking there is extraneous, poisonous; is as a dead iron spike, some horrid rusty ploughshare driven into the living substance;—nay is far worse; for in every windstorm ("commercial crisis" or the like), it frets and creaks, jolts itself to and fro, and cannot lie quiet as your dead iron spike would.

If I were the Conservative Party of England (which is another bold figure of speech), I would not for a hundred thousand pounds an hour allow those Corn-Laws to continue! Potosi and Golconda put together would not purchase my assent to them. Do you count what treasuries of bitter indignation they are laying up for you in every just English heart? Do you know what questions, not as to Corn-prices and Sliding-scales alone, they are *forcing* every reflective Englishman to ask himself? Questions insoluble, or hitherto unsolved; deeper than any of our Logic-plummets hitherto will sound: questions deep enough,—which it were better that we did not name even in thought! You are forcing us to think of them, to begin uttering them. The utterance of them is begun; and where will it be ended, think you? When two millions of one's brother-men sit in Workhouses, and five millions, as is insolently said, "rejoice in potatoes," there are various things that must be begun, let them end where they can.

from Chapter 11

Labour

For there is a perennial nobleness, and even sacredness, in Work. Were he never so benighted, forgetful of his high calling, there is always hope in a man that actually and earnestly works: in Idleness alone is there perpetual despair. Work, never so Mammonish, mean, *is* in communication with Nature; the real desire to get Work done will itself lead one more and more to truth, to Nature's appointments and regulations, which are truth.

The latest Gospel in this world is, Know thy work and do it. "Know thyself": long enough has that poor "self" of thine tormented thee; thou wilt never get to "know" it, I believe! Think it not thy business, this of knowing thyself; thou art an unknowable individual: know what thou canst work at; and work at it, like a Hercules! That will be thy better plan.

It has been written, "an endless significance lies in Work"; a man perfects himself by working. Foul jungles are cleared away, fair seed-fields rise

7. Baconian Inductions. Sir Francis Bacon set forth the inductive method of reasoning (as opposed to the deductive method employed by the Scholastic philosophers) in his *Novum Organum*, 1620. **8. Eastcheap,** a street in London's financial district.

7. Potosi, a department of Bolivia, rich in ore. **Golconda,** a fortress and ruined city in India, known for its diamonds. **34. Mammonish.** In the New Testament, mammon is either riches (Luke 16:9–11) or the god of riches (Matthew 6:24; Luke 16:13). See *Paradise Lost*, Book II, ll. 226 ff. **39. "Know thyself."** See note 38, page 918—a favorite quotation with Carlyle.

instead, and stately cities; and withal the man himself first ceases to be a jungle and foul unwholesome desert thereby. Consider how, even in the meanest sorts of Labour, the whole soul of a man is composed into a kind of real harmony, the instant he sets himself to work! Doubt, Desire, Sorrow, Remorse, Indignation, Despair itself, all these like helldogs lie beleaguering the soul of the poor dayworker, as of every man: but he bends himself with free valour against his task, and all these are stilled, all these shrink murmuring far off into their caves. The man is now a man. The blessed glow of Labour in him, is it not as purifying fire, where in all poison is burnt up, and of sour smoke itself there is made bright blessed flame!

Destiny, on the whole, has no other way of cultivating us. A formless Chaos, once set it *revolving*, grows round and ever rounder; ranges itself, by mere force of gravity, into strata, spherical courses; is no longer a Chaos, but a round compacted World. What would become of the Earth, did she cease to revolve? In the poor old Earth, so long as she revolves, all inequalities, irregularities disperse themselves; all irregularities are incessantly becoming regular. Hast thou looked on the Potter's wheel, one of the venerablest objects; old as the Prophet Ezekiel and far older? Rude lumps of clay, how they spin themselves up, by mere quick whirling, into beautiful circular dishes. And fancy the most assiduous Potter, but without his wheel; reduced to make dishes, or rather amorphous botches, by mere kneading and baking! Even such a Potter were Destiny, with a human soul that would rest and lie at ease, that would not work and spin! Of an idle unrevolving man the kindest Destiny, like the most assiduous Potter without wheel, can bake and knead nothing other than a botch; let her spend on him what expensive colouring, what gilding and enamelling she will, he is but a botch. Not a dish; no, a bulging, kneaded, crooked, shambling, squint-cornered, amorphous botch,—a mere enamelled vessel of dishonour! Let the idle think of this.

Blessed is he who has found his work; let him ask no other blessedness. He has a work, a life-purpose; he has found it, and will follow it! How, as a free-flowing channel, dug and torn by noble force through the sour mud-swamp of one's existence, like an ever-deepening river there, it runs and flows;—draining-off the sour festering water, gradually from the root of the remotest grass-blade; making, instead of pestilential swamp, a green fruitful meadow with its clear-flowing stream. How blessed for the meadow itself, let the stream and *its* value be great or small! Labour is Life: from the inmost heart of the Worker rises his god-given Force, the sacred celestial Life-essence breathed into him by Almighty God; from his inmost heart awakens him to all nobleness,—to all knowledge, "self-knowledge" and much else, so soon as Work fitly begins. Knowledge? The knowledge that will hold good in working, cleave thou to that; for Nature herself accredits that, says Yea to that. Properly thou hast no other knowledge but what thou hast got by working: the rest is yet all a hypothesis of knowledge; a thing to be argued of in schools, a thing floating in the clouds, in endless logic-vortices, till we try it and fix it. "Doubt, of whatever kind, can be ended by Action alone." . . .

Brave Sea-captain, Norse Sea-king,—Columbus, my hero, royallest Sea-king of all! it is no friendly environment this of thine, in the waste deep waters; around thee mutinous discouraged souls, behind thee disgrace and ruin, before thee the unpenetrated veil of Night. Brother, these wild water-mountains, bounding from their deep bases (ten miles deep, I am told), are not entirely there on thy behalf! Meseems *they* have other work than floating thee forward:—and the huge Winds, that sweep from Ursa Major to the Tropics and Equators, dancing their giant-waltz through the kingdoms of Chaos and Immensity, they care little about filling rightly or filling wrongly the small shoulder-of-mutton sails in this cockle-skiff of thine! Thou art not among articulate-speaking friends, my brother; thou art among immeasurable dumb monsters, tumbling, howling wide as the world here. Secret, far off, invisible to all hearts but thine, there lies a help in them: see how thou wilt get at that. Patiently thou wilt wait till the mad South-wester spend itself, saving thyself by dextrous science of defence, the while: valiantly, with swift decision, wilt thou strike in, when the favouring East, the Possible, springs up. Mutiny of men thou wilt sternly repress; weakness, despondency, thou wilt cheerily encourage: thou wilt swallow down complaint, unreason, weariness, weakness of others and thyself;—how much wilt thou swallow down! There shall be a depth of Silence in thee, deeper than this Sea, which is but ten miles deep: a Silence unsoundable; known to God only. Thou shalt be a Great Man. Yes, my World-Soldier, thou of the World Marine-service,—thou wilt have to be *greater* than this tumultuous unmeasured World here round thee is: thou, in thy strong soul, as with wrestler's arms, shalt embrace it, harness it down, and make it bear thee on,—to new Americas, or whither God wills!

John Henry Newman
1801–1890

John Henry Newman was born in London, February 21, 1801. His father was a banker; his mother had French Huguenot blood. Even as a child he manifested an imaginative, spiritual nature; it seemed natural to him to think of the world as filled with angels. He expressed this view later in one of his sermons:

"And yet in spite of the universal world which we see, there is another world, quite as far-spreading, quite as close to us, and more wonderful; another world all around us, though we see it not, and more wonderful than the world we see, for this reason if for no other, that we do not see it. All around us are numberless objects, coming and going, watching, working, or waiting, which we see not: this is that other world, which the eyes reach not unto, but faith only."

In 1816 Newman experienced an inner conversion and dedicated himself to the religious life, his conception of which already included celibacy. In 1822 he became a fellow of Oriel College, Oxford; in 1824 he was ordained a deacon in the Anglican Church, in 1825 a priest; in 1826 he became a tutor at Oriel. In 1828 he was appointed vicar of St. Mary's Church at Oxford. In 1832 he toured southern Europe and made up his mind that it was his mission to redeem the English Church.

The Oxford Movement, sometimes called by its contemporaries Tractarianism or Puseyism, gave Newman his opportunity. This movement began July 14, 1833, with a sermon on "National Apostasy" in which John Keble protested against the abolition by Parliament of a number of Anglican bishoprics in Ireland. The bishoprics themselves were, in a Roman Catholic country, of no particular importance; the real issue was the old, old problem of the relationship between Church and State. The Oxford Movement was romantic in its feeling for the past, its desire to restore something of the fervor and color of medievalism to the modern Church—Newman's love for Scott's novels was no accident—but it had no truck with the revolutionary spirit of Romanticism. Its conception of religion was the sacramentarian conception; it took its stand on the basis of authority. The Church was God's representative on earth; to her the truth had been entrusted. On the whole the movement was more classic than romantic. Newman reasoned his position closely every step of the way; if he used intuition also, this was because he was always reasonable enough to understand that reason is not all of human life.

Newman and his associates wished to appeal to the authority of the undivided Church. They recognized the need of reform, but they hoped to bring this about not through introducing new elements but by re-emphasizing the neglected Catholic elements already present. For Protestantism, liberalism, rationalism—"the doctrine that there is no positive truth in religion, but that one creed is as good as another"—Newman had no sympathy.

Newman, Keble, Froude, Pusey, and their associates carried on their propaganda through many sermons and through a series of ninety *Tracts for the Times*, 1833–41. Tract 90, in which Newman himself argued for a Catholic interpretation of the Thirty-nine Articles (the authoritative statement of Anglican faith, adopted in 1562), marked the end of the first stage of the movement and an important crisis in his own career. The storm of protest awakened proved clearly that the Anglican Church rejected the Catholic view; unless Newman were either to surrender his logic or betray his principles, he must, therefore, set his feet on the road to Rome. In 1842 he resigned from St. Mary's, and went with a few close followers into a semimonastic retreat at Littlemore; in 1845 he became a Roman Catholic; in 1846 he was ordained a priest.

The last half of Newman's life was, in general, much quieter than the first. He lived near Birmingham at the head of the Oratory at Egbaston, and his efforts were now necessarily largely confined to his own coreligionists. In his Catholic faith he found perfect peace and confidence, but his relations with the hierarchy were not always happy. The thwarting of his attempt to establish a Catholic University in Dublin (see page 881) was typical of many sad experiences; there were times when he asked himself whether his years as a Catholic had been wasted. In 1864, however, his *Apologia pro Vita Sua* brought him once more before the public as prominently as ever in his Oxford days; his saintly character came at last to be appreciated; Englishmen of all shades of belief began to realize that here was a great man whose apprehension of life, though importantly different from their own, might still possess validity. In 1877 the aging man became an honorary fellow of Trinity College, Oxford; in 1879 Pope Leo XIII made him a cardinal; he died August 11, 1890.

Newman was always the churchman; except for his poems—*Lyra Apostolica*, 1836; *The Dream of Gerontius*, 1865, and others—and two novels mediocre as fiction but extremely interesting on the ideational side—*Loss and Gain*, 1848, and *Callista*, 1856—his mode and method were never "literary." Yet he belongs to English literature by virtue of the classical purity and elevation of his style; and surely few men have been more importantly concerned with English civilization. Through his Tractarian years he lived in the eyes of the nation; the fate of religion itself seemed to hang on his decisions. As a Catholic, though a less representative figure, he was no less challenging and revealing.

The Oxford Movement touched literature at many points: we see it in such poets as Coventry Patmore and Christina Rossetti; the early William Morris shows traces of it; so does Tennyson. Joseph Ellis Baker has devoted a whole book to *The Novel and the Oxford Movement* (Princeton University Press, 1932). Charlotte M. Yonge (*The Heir of Redclyffe*, 1853) was the great Church of England novelist, but the finest monument of the movement in fiction is that glorious novel by Joseph Henry Shorthouse, *John Inglesant*, 1880.

THE SIGN OF THE CROSS

Whene'er across this sinful flesh of mine
  I draw the Holy Sign,
All good thoughts stir within me, and renew
  Their slumbering strength divine;
Till there springs up a courage high and true
  To suffer and to do.

And who shall say, but hateful spirits around,
  For their brief hour unbound,
Shudder to see, and wail their overthrow?
  While on far heathen ground
Some lonely Saint hails the fresh odour, though
  Its source he cannot know.

THE PILLAR OF THE CLOUD

Set to music by J. W. Dykes, these lines, universally known as "Lead, Kindly Light," have become one of the great hymns of the Christian Church. For the circumstances of Newman's composition of this poem, see his own account on page 888 of this volume. For the origin of the title, see Exodus 13.

Lead, Kindly Light, amid the encircling gloom,
  Lead Thou me on!
The night is dark, and I am far from home—
  Lead Thou me on!
Keep Thou my feet; I do not ask to see
The distant scene,—one step enough for me.

I was not ever thus, nor prayed that Thou
  Shouldst lead me on.
I loved to choose and see my path; but now
  Lead Thou me on!
I loved the garish day, and, spite of fears,
Pride ruled my will: remember not past years.

So long Thy power hath blest me, sure it still
  Will lead me on,
O'er moor and fen, o'er crag and torrent, till
  The night is gone;
And with the morn those angel faces smile
Which I have loved long since, and lost awhile.

from THE IDEA OF A UNIVERSITY

The series of lectures looking toward the establishment of a Catholic university which Newman, the rector elect, delivered in Dublin in 1852 as "The Scope and Nature of University Education" still remains one of our best statements of the liberal ideal. In practice Newman was to find that the Irish bishops did not share his views; his tenure of office was brief. The lectures, published as *The Idea of a University* in 1873, are now conveniently available, together with other papers on kindred themes, in "Everyman's Library" under the title *Essays on University Subjects*. Newman's views on education should be compared and contrasted with those of Arnold and Huxley, as given elsewhere in this volume.

from Discourse V

Knowledge Its Own End

I

I HAVE said that all branches of knowledge are connected together, because the subject-matter of knowledge is intimately united in itself, as being the acts and the work of the Creator. Hence it is that the Sciences, into which our knowledge may be said to be cast, have multiplied bearings one on another, and an internal sympathy, and admit, or rather demand, comparison and adjustment. They complete, correct, balance each other. This consideration, if well-founded, must be taken into account, not only as regards the attainment of truth, which is their common end, but as regards the influence which they exercise upon those whose education consists in the study of them. I have said already, that to give undue prominence to one is to be unjust to another; to neglect or supersede these is to divert those from their proper object. It is to unsettle the boundary lines between science and science, to disturb their action, to destroy the harmony which binds them together. Such a proceeding will have a corresponding effect when introduced into a place of education. There is no science but tells a different tale, when viewed as a portion of a whole, from what it is likely to suggest when taken by itself, without the safeguard, as I may call it, of others. . . .

It is a great point then to enlarge the range of studies which a University professes, even for the sake of the students; and, though they cannot pursue every subject which is open to them, they will be the gainers by living among those and under those who represent the whole circle. This I conceive to be the advantage of a seat of universal learning, considered as a place of education. An assemblage of learned men, zealous for their own sciences, and rivals of each other, are brought, by familiar intercourse and for the sake of intellectual peace, to adjust together the claims and relations of their respective subjects of investigation. They learn to respect, to consult, to aid each other. Thus is created a pure and clear atmosphere of thought, which the student also breathes, though in his own case he only pursues a few sciences out of the multitude. He profits by an intellectual tradition, which is independent of particular teachers, which guides him in his choice of subjects, and duly interprets for him those which he chooses. He apprehends the great outlines of knowledge, the principles on which it rests, the scale of its parts, its lights and its shades, its great points and its little, as he otherwise cannot apprehend them. Hence it is that his education is called "Liberal." A habit of mind is formed which lasts through life, of which the attributes are, freedom, equitableness, calmness, moderation, and wisdom; or what in a former Discourse I have ventured to call a philosophical habit. This then I would assign as the special fruit of the education furnished at a University, as contrasted with other places of teaching or modes of teaching. This is the main purpose of a University in its treatment of its students.

And now the question is asked me, What is the *use* of it? and my answer will constitute the main subject of the Discourses which are to follow.

2

Cautious and practical thinkers, I say, will ask of me, what, after all, is the gain of this Philosophy, of which I make such account, and from which I promise so much. Even supposing it to enable us to exercise the degree of trust exactly due to every science respectively, and to estimate precisely the value of every truth which is anywhere to be found, how are we better for this master view of things, which I have been extolling? Does it not reverse the principle of the division of labour? will practical objects be obtained better or worse by its cultivation? to what then does it lead? where does it end? what does it do? how does it profit? what does it promise? Particular sciences are respectively the basis of definite arts, which carry on to results tangible and beneficial the truths which are the subjects of the knowledge attained; what is the Art of this science of sciences? what is the fruit of such a Philosophy? what are we proposing to effect, what inducements do we hold out to the Catholic community, when we set about the enterprise of founding a University?

I am asked what is the end of University Education, and of the Liberal or Philosophical Knowledge which I conceive it to impart: I answer, that what I have already said has been sufficient to show that it has a very tangible, real, and sufficient end, though the end cannot be divided from that knowledge itself. Knowledge is capable of being its own end. Such is the constitution of the human mind, that any kind of knowledge, if it be really such, is its own reward. And if this is true of all knowledge, it is true also of that special Philosophy, which I have made to consist in a comprehensive view of truth in all its branches, of the relations of science to science, of their mutual bearings, and their respective values. What the worth of such an acquirement is, compared with other objects which we seek,—wealth or power or honour or the conveniences and comforts of life, I do not profess here to discuss; but I would maintain, and mean to show, that it is an object, in its own nature so really and undeniably good, as to be the compensation of a great deal of thought in the compassing, and a great deal of trouble in the attaining. . . .

4

Things, which can bear to be cut off from everything else and yet persist in living, must have life in themselves; pursuits, which issue in nothing, and still maintain their ground for ages, which are regarded as admirable, though they have not as yet proved themselves to be useful, must have their sufficient end in themselves, whatever it turn out to be. And we are brought to the same conclusion by considering the force of the epithet, by which the knowledge under consideration is popularly designated. It is common to speak of "*liberal* knowledge," of the "*liberal* arts and studies," and of a "*liberal* education," as the especial characteristic or property of a University and of a gentleman; what is really meant by the word? Now, first, in its grammatical sense it is opposed to *servile;* and by "servile work" is understood, as our catechisms inform us, bodily labour, mechanical employment, and the like, in which the mind has little or no part. Parallel to such servile works are those arts, if they deserve the name, of which the poet speaks, which owe their origin and their method to hazard, not to skill; as, for instance, the practice and operations of an empiric. As far as this contrast may be considered as a guide into the meaning of the word, liberal education and liberal pursuits are exercises of mind, of reason, of reflection.

But we want something more for its explanation, for there are bodily exercises which are liberal, and mental exercises which are not so. For instance, in ancient times the practitioners in medicine were commonly slaves; yet it was an art as intellectual in its nature, in spite of the pretence, fraud, and quackery with which it might then, as now, be debased, as it was heavenly in its aim. And so in like manner, we contrast a liberal education with a commercial education or a professional; yet no one can deny that commerce and the professions afford scope for the highest and most diversified powers of mind. There is then a great variety of intellectual exercises, which are not technically called "liberal"; on the other hand, I say, there are exercises of the body which do receive that appellation. Such, for instance, was the palaestra, in ancient times; such the Olympic games, in which strength and dexterity of body as well as of mind gained the prize. In Xenophon we read of the young Persian nobility being taught to ride on horseback and to speak the truth; both being among the accomplishments of a gentleman. War, too, however rough a profession, has ever been accounted liberal, unless in cases when it becomes heroic, which would introduce us to another subject.

Now comparing these instances together, we shall have no difficulty in determining the principle of this apparent variation in the application of the term which I am examining. Manly games, or games of skill, or military prowess, though bodily, are, it seems, accounted liberal; on the other hand, what is merely professional, though highly intellectual, nay, though liberal in comparison of trade and manual labour, is not simply called liberal, and mercantile occupations are not liberal at all. Why this distinction? because that alone is liberal knowledge, which stands on its own pretensions, which is independent of sequel, expects no complement, refuses to be *informed* (as it is called) by any end, or absorbed into any art, in order duly to present itself to our contemplation. The most ordinary pursuits have this specific character, if they are self-sufficient and complete; the highest lose it, when they minister to something beyond them. It is absurd to balance, in point of worth and importance, a treatise on reducing fractures with a game of cricket or a fox-chase; yet of the two the bodily exercise has that quality which we call "liberal," and the intellectual has not. And so of the learned professions altogether, considered merely as professions; although one of them be the most popularly beneficial, and another the most politically important, and the third the most intimately divine of all human pursuits, yet the very greatness of their end, the health of the body, or of the commonwealth, or of the soul, diminishes, not increases, their claim to the appellation "liberal," and that still more, if they are cut down to the strict exigencies of that end. If, for instance, Theology, instead of being cultivated as a contemplation, be limited to the purposes of the pulpit or be represented by the catechism, it loses, —not its usefulness, not its divine character, not its meritoriousness (rather it gains a claim upon these titles by such charitable condescension),—but it does lose the particular attribute which I am illustrating; just as a face worn by tears and fasting loses its beauty, or a labourer's hand loses its delicateness;—for Theology thus exercised is not simple knowledge, but rather is an art or a business making use of Theology. And thus it appears that even what is supernatural need not be liberal, nor need a hero be a gentleman, for the plain reason that one idea is not another idea. And in like manner the Baconian Philosophy, by using its physical sciences in the service of man, does thereby transfer them from the order of Liberal Pursuits to, I do not say the inferior, but the distinct class of the Useful. And, to take a different instance, hence again, as is evident, whenever personal gain is the motive, still more distinctive an effect has it upon the character of a given pursuit; thus racing, which was a liberal exercise in

17. the poet speaks. Newman's own note refers to Aristotle's *Nicomachean Ethics,* VI—"Art loves fate, and fate loves art." **20. empiric,** one who relies upon practical experience. **40. palaestra,** wrestling school. **42. Xenophon,** Athenian soldier and historian (*c.* 434–*c.*355 B.C.).

Greece, forfeits its rank in times like these, so far as it is made the occasion of gambling.

All that I have been now saying is summed up in a few characteristic words of the great Philosopher. "Of possessions," he says, "those rather are useful, which bear fruit; those *liberal, which tend to enjoyment.* By fruitful, I mean, which yield revenue; by enjoyable, where *nothing accrues of consequence beyond the using.*" . . .

6

Now bear with me, Gentlemen, if what I am about to say, has at first sight a fanciful appearance. Philosophy, then, or Science, is related to Knowledge in this way:—Knowledge is called by the name of Science or Philosophy, when it is acted upon, informed, or if I may use a strong figure, impregnated by Reason. Reason is the principle of that intrinsic fecundity of Knowledge, which, to those who possess it, is its especial value, and which dispenses with the necessity of their looking abroad for any end to rest upon external to itself. Knowledge, indeed, when thus exalted into a scientific form, is also power; not only is it excellent in itself, but whatever such excellence may be, it is something more, it has a result beyond itself. Doubtless; but that is a further consideration, with which I am not concerned. I only say that, prior to its being a power, it is a good; that it is, not only an instrument, but an end. I know well it may resolve itself into an art, and terminate in a mechanical process, and in tangible fruit; but it also may fall back upon that Reason which informs it, and resolve itself into Philosophy. In one case it is called Useful Knowledge, in the other Liberal. The same person may cultivate it in both ways at once; but this again is a matter foreign to my subject; here I do but say that there are two ways of using Knowledge, and in matter of fact those who use it in one way are not likely to use it in the other, or at least in a very limited measure. You see, then, here are two methods of Education; the end of the one is to be philosophical, of the other to be mechanical; the one rises towards general ideas, the other is exhausted upon what is particular and external. Let me not be thought to deny the necessity, or to decry the benefit, of such attention to what is particular and practical, as belongs to the useful or mechanical arts; life could not go on without them; we owe our daily welfare to them; their exercise is the duty of the many, and we owe to the many a debt of gratitude for fulfilling that duty. I only say that Knowledge, in proportion as it tends more and more to be particular, ceases to be Knowledge. . . . When I speak of Knowledge, I mean something intellectual, something which grasps what it perceives through the senses; something which takes a view of things; which sees more than the senses convey; which reasons upon what it sees, and while it sees; which invests it with an idea. It expresses itself, not in a mere enunciation, but by an enthymeme: it is of the nature of science from the first, and in this consists its dignity. The principle of real dignity in Knowledge, its worth, its desirableness, considered irrespectively of its results, is this germ within it of a scientific or a philosophical process. This is how it comes to be an end in itself; this is why it admits of being called Liberal. Not to know the relative disposition of things is the state of slaves or children; to have mapped out the Universe is the boast, or at least the ambition, of Philosophy.

Moreover, such knowledge is not a mere extrinsic or accidental advantage, which is ours to-day and another's to-morrow, which may be got up from a book, and easily forgotten again, which we can command or communicate at our pleasure, which we can borrow for the occasion, carry about in our hand, and take into the market; it is an acquired illumination, it is a habit, a personal possession, and an inward endowment. And this is the reason, why it is more correct, as well as more usual, to speak of a University as a place of education, than of instruction, though, when knowledge is concerned, instruction would at first sight have seemed the more appropriate word. . . . When, then, we speak of the communication of Knowledge as being Education, we thereby really imply that that Knowledge is a state or condition of mind; and since cultivation of mind is surely worth seeking for its own sake, we are thus brought once more to the conclusion, which the word "Liberal" and the word "Philosophy" have already suggested, that there is a Knowledge, which is desirable, though nothing come of it, as being of itself a treasure, and a sufficient remuneration of years of labour.

7

. . . It may be objected . . . that, when we profess to seek Knowledge for some end or other beyond itself, whatever it be, we speak intelligibly; but that, whatever men may have said, however obstinately the idea may have kept its ground from age to age, still it is simply unmeaning to say that we seek Knowledge for its own sake, and for noth-

5–9. "Of possessions . . . the using." "Aristotle, *Rhetoric*, I, 5." (Newman)

9. enthymeme: an argument with the premise understood; or with only two propositions.

ing else; for that it ever leads to something beyond itself, which therefore is its end, and the cause why it is desirable;—moreover, that this end is two-fold, either of this world or of the next; that all knowledge is cultivated either for secular objects or for eternal; that if it is directed to secular objects, it is called Useful Knowledge, if to eternal, Religious or Christian Knowledge;—in consequence, that if, as I have allowed, this Liberal Knowledge does not benefit the body or estate, it ought to benefit the soul; but if the fact be really so, that it is neither a physical or a secular good on the one hand, nor a moral good on the other, it cannot be a good at all, and is not worth the trouble which is necessary for its acquisition.

And then I may be reminded that the professors of this Liberal or Philosophical Knowledge have themselves, in every age, recognized this exposition of the matter, and have submitted to the issue in which it terminates; for they have ever been attempting to make men virtuous; or, if not, at least have assumed that refinement of mind was virtue, and that they themselves were the virtuous portion of mankind. This they have professed on the one hand; and on the other, they have utterly failed in their professions, so as ever to make themselves a proverb among men, and a laughing-stock both to the grave and the dissipated portion of mankind, in consequence of them. Thus they have furnished against themselves both the ground and the means of their own exposure, without any trouble at all to anyone else. In a word, from the time that Athens was the University of the world, what has Philosophy taught men, but to promise without practising, and to aspire without attaining? What has the deep and lofty thought of its disciples ended in but eloquent words? Nay, what has its teaching ever meditated, when it was boldest in its remedies for human ill, beyond charming us to sleep by its lessons, that we might feel nothing at all? like some melodious air, or rather like those strong and transporting perfumes, which at first spread their sweetness over everything they touch, but in a little while do but offend in proportion as they once pleased us. Did Philosophy support Cicero under the disfavour of the fickle populace, or nerve Seneca to oppose an imperial tyrant? It abandoned Brutus, as he sorrowfully confessed, in his greatest need, and it forced Cato, as his panegyrist strangely boasts, into the false position of defying heaven. How few can be counted among its professors, who, like Polemo, were thereby converted from a profligate course, or like Anaxagoras, thought the world well lost in exchange for its possession? The philosopher in *Rasselas* taught a superhuman doctrine, and then succumbed without an effort to a trial of human affection.

"He discoursed," we are told, "with great energy on the government of the passions. His look was venerable, his action graceful, his pronunciation clear, and his diction elegant. He showed, with great strength of sentiment and variety of illustration, that human nature is degraded and debased, when the lower faculties predominate over the higher. He communicated the various precepts given, from time to time, for the conquest of passion, and displayed the happiness of those who had obtained the important victory, after which man is no longer the slave of fear, nor the fool of hope. . . . He enumerated many examples of heroes immovable by pain or pleasure, who looked with indifference on those modes or accidents to which the vulgar give the names of good and evil."

Rasselas in a few days found the philosopher in a room half darkened, with his eyes misty, and his face pale. "Sir," said he, "you have come at a time when all human friendship is useless; what I suffer cannot be remedied, what I have lost cannot be supplied. My daughter, my only daughter, from whose tenderness I expected all the comforts of my age, died last night of a fever." "Sir," said the prince, "mortality is an event by which a wise man can never be surprised; we know that death is always near, and it should therefore always be expected." "Young man," answered the philosopher, "you speak like one who has never felt the pangs of separation." "Have you, then, forgot the precept," said Rasselas, "which you so powerfully enforced? . . . consider that external things are naturally variable, but truth and reason are always the same." "What comfort," said the mourner, "can truth and reason afford me? Of what effect are they now, but to tell me that my daughter will not be restored?"

8

Better, far better, to make no professions, you will say, than to cheat others with what we are not, and to scandalize them with what we are. The sensualist, or the man of the world, at any rate, is not the

44–48. Cicero . . . Seneca . . . Brutus . . . Cato. Possibly Newman refers to Cicero's compromising course during the contest between Pompey and Julius Caesar. Seneca, Brutus, and Marcus Cato the Younger all committed suicide, Seneca in 65 A.D. when accused of conspiring against Nero, Brutus in 42 B.C. after his defeat by Octavius, following the assassination of Julius Caesar (as in Shakespeare's play), Cato in 46 B.C. to avoid being conquered by Julius Caesar. Cato was praised by Cicero and by Lucan (compare Addison's tragedy, 1713). **2. Polemo,** Greek philosopher of the third century B.C. **3–4. Anaxagoras,** Greek philosopher of the fifth century B.C., who preferred exile to recantation. **5. Rasselas,** Dr. Samuel Johnson's novel of that title, 1759, chap. 18.

victim of fine words, but pursues a reality and gains it. The Philosophy of Utility, you will say, Gentlemen, has at least done its work; and I grant it,—it aimed low, but it has fulfilled its aim. If that man of great intellect who has been its Prophet in the conduct of life played false to his own professions, he was not bound by his philosophy to be true to his friend or faithful in his trust. Moral virtue was not the line in which he undertook to instruct men; and though, as the poet calls him, he were the "meanest" of mankind, he was so in what may be called his private capacity and without any prejudice to the theory of induction. He had a right to be so, if he chose, for anything that the Idols of the den or the theatre had to say to the contrary. His mission was the increase of physical enjoyment and social comfort; and most wonderfully, most awfully has he fulfilled his conception and his design. Almost day by day have we fresh and fresh shoots, and buds, and blossoms, which are to ripen into fruit, on that magical tree of Knowledge which he planted, and to which none of us perhaps, except the very poor, but owes, if not his present life, at least his daily food, his health, and general well-being. He was the divinely provided minister of temporal benefits to all of us so great, that, whatever I am forced to think of him as a man, I have not the heart, from mere gratitude, to speak of him severely. And, in spite of the tendencies of his philosophy, which are, as we see at this day, to depreciate, or to trample on Theology, he has himself, in his writings, gone out of his way, as if with a prophetic misgiving of those tendencies, to insist on it as the instrument of that beneficent Father, who, when He came on earth in visible form, took on Him first and most prominently the office of assuaging the bodily wounds of human nature. And truly, like the old mediciner in the tale, "he sat diligently at his work, and hummed, with cheerful countenance, a pious song"; and then in turn "went out singing into the meadows so gaily, that those who had seen him from afar might well have thought it was a youth gathering flowers for his beloved, instead of an old physician gathering healing herbs in the morning dew."

Alas, that men, in the action of life or in their heart of hearts, are not what they seem to be in their moments of excitement, or in their trances or intoxications of genius,—so good, so noble, so serene! Alas, that Bacon too in his own way should after all be but the fellow of those heathen philosophers who in their disadvantages had some excuse for their inconsistency, and who surprise us rather in what they did say than in what they did not do! Alas, that he too, like Socrates or Seneca, must be stripped of his holy-day coat, which looks so fair, and should be but a mockery amid his most majestic gravity of phrase; and, for all his vast abilities, should, in the littleness of his own moral being, but typify the intellectual narrowness of his school! However, granting all this, heroism after all was not his philosophy:—I cannot deny he has abundantly achieved what he proposed. His is simply a Method whereby bodily discomforts and temporal wants are to be most effectually removed from the greatest number; and already, before it has shown any signs of exhaustion, the gifts of nature, in their most artificial shapes and luxurious profusion and diversity, from all quarters of the earth, are, it is undeniable, by its means brought even to our doors, and we rejoice in them.

9

Useful Knowledge then, I grant, has done its work; and Liberal Knowledge as certainly has not done its work,—that is, supposing, as the objectors assume, its direct end, like Religious Knowledge, is to make men better; but this I will not for an instant allow, and, unless I allow it, those objectors have said nothing to the purpose. I admit, rather I maintain, what they have been urging, for I consider Knowledge to have its end in itself. For all its friends, or its enemies, may say, I insist upon it, that it is as real a mistake to burden it with virtue or religion as with the mechanical arts. Its direct business is not to steel the soul against temptation or to console it in affliction, any more than to set the loom in motion, or to direct the steam carriage; be it ever so much the means or the condition of both material and moral advancement, still, taken by and in itself, it as little mends our hearts as it improves out temporal circumstances. And if its eulogists claim for it such a power, they commit the very same kind of encroachment on a province not their own as the political economist who should maintain that his science educated him for casuistry or diplomacy. Knowledge is one thing, virtue is another; good sense is not conscience, refinement is not humility, nor is largeness and justness of view faith.

5. Prophet, Sir Francis Bacon. See his life and selections from his writings, pages 315–327 of this volume. **10. poet,** Alexander Pope, in "An Essay on Man," Ep. IV, ll. 281–82. **14. Idols.** Bacon classifies the false notions to which the mind is subject as idols of the tribe, of the den, of the market place, and of the theater (*Novum Organum*, I). **31–34. he has himself . . . of that beneficent Father.** Bacon definitely commits himself to belief in God in his essay "Of Atheism," and in many other passages of his writings. **37–44. And truly . . . morning dew."** "Fouqué's *Unknown Patient*." (Newman) Baron de la Motte Fouqué (1777–1843) was a German poet and novelist best known today by his *Undine*, 1811.

Philosophy, however enlightened, however profound, gives no command over the passions, no influential motives, no vivifying principles. Liberal Education makes not the Christian, not the Catholic, but the gentleman. It is well to be a gentleman, it is well to have a cultivated intellect, a delicate taste, a candid, equitable, dispassionate mind, a noble and courteous bearing in the conduct of life;—these are the connatural qualities of a large knowledge; they are the objects of a University; I am advocating, I shall illustrate and insist upon them; but still, I repeat, they are no guarantee for sanctity or even for conscientiousness, they may attach to the man of the world, to the profligate, to the heartless,—pleasant, alas, and attractive as he shows when decked out in them. Taken by themselves, they do but seem to be what they are not; they look like virtue at a distance, but they are detected by close observers, and on the long run; and hence it is that they are popularly accused of pretence and hypocrisy, not, I repeat, from their own fault, but because their professors and their admirers persist in taking them for what they are not, and are officious in arrogating for them a praise to which they have no claim. Quarry the granite rock with razors, or moor the vessel with a thread of silk; then may you hope with such keen and delicate instruments as human knowledge and human reason to contend against those giants, the passion and the pride of man.

Surely we are not driven to theories of this kind in order to vindicate the value and dignity of Liberal Knowledge. Surely the real grounds on which its pretensions rest are not so very subtle or abstruse, so very strange or improbable. Surely it is very intelligible to say, and that is what I say here, that Liberal Education, viewed in itself, is simply the cultivation of the intellect, as such, and its object is nothing more or less than intellectual excellence. Every thing has its own perfection, be it higher or lower in the scale of things; and the perfection of one is not the perfection of another. Things animate, inanimate, visible, invisible, all are good in their kind, and have a *best* of themselves, which is an object of pursuit. Why do you take such pains with your garden or your park? You see to your walks and turf and shrubberies; to your trees and drives; not as if you meant to make an orchard of the one, or corn or pasture land of the other, but because there is a special beauty in all that is goodly in wood, water, plain, and slope, brought all together by art into one shape, and grouped into one whole. Your cities are beautiful, your palaces, your public buildings, your territorial mansions, your churches; and their beauty leads to nothing beyond itself. There is a physical beauty and a moral: there is a beauty of person, there is a beauty of our moral being, which is natural virtue; and in like manner there is a beauty, there is a perfection, of the intellect. There is an ideal perfection in these various subject-matters, towards which individual instances are seen to rise, and which are the standards for all instances whatever. The Greek divinities and demigods, as the statuary has moulded them, with their symmetry of figure and their high forehead and their regular features, are the perfection of physical beauty. The heroes, of whom history tells, Alexander, or Caesar, or Scipio, or Saladin, are the representatives of that magnanimity or self-mastery which is the greatness of human nature. Christianity too has its heroes, and in the supernatural order, and we call them Saints. The artist puts before him beauty of feature and form; the poet, beauty of mind; the preacher, the beauty of grace: then intellect too, I repeat, has its beauty, and it has those who aim at it. To open the mind, to correct it, to refine it, to enable it to know, and to digest, master, rule, and use its knowledge, to give it power over its own faculties, application, flexibility, method, critical exactness, sagacity, resource, address, eloquent expression, is an object as intelligible (for here we are inquiring, not what the object of a Liberal Education is worth, nor what use the Church makes of it, but what it is in itself), I say, an object as intelligible as the cultivation of virtue, while, at the same time, it is absolutely distinct from it.

10

This indeed is but a temporal object, and a transitory possession: but so are other things in themselves which we make much of and pursue. The moralist will tell us that man, in all his functions, is but a flower which blossoms and fades, except so far as a higher principle breathes upon him, and makes him and what he is immortal. Body and mind are carried on into an eternal state of being by the gifts of Divine Munificence; but at first they do but fail in a failing world; and if the powers of intellect decay, the powers of the body have decayed before them, and, as an Hospital or an Almshouse, though its end be ephemeral, may be sanctified to the service of religion, so surely may a University, even were it nothing more than I have as yet described it. We attain to heaven by using this world well,

14. Scipio, the conqueror of Hannibal (c. 237–c. 183 B.C.). **Saladin,** Sultan of Egypt (1137–1193), who opposed the Christians in the Third Crusade. See Scott's novel *The Talisman.*

though it is to pass away; we perfect our nature, not by undoing it, but by adding to it what is more than nature, and directing it towards aims higher than its own. . . .

from APOLOGIA PRO VITA SUA

Cardinal Newman's autobiography, *Apologia pro Vita Sua* (*Justification for His Life*) was occasioned by a controversy with Charles Kingsley (1819–1875), novelist and Anglican divine, who had accused him, and the Roman clergy in general, of little respect for truthtelling. Since not only his honor but the honor of his church was involved, Newman felt bound to reply; the result was both a brilliant piece of controversial writing and a great piece of spiritual autobiography. It was published in 1864.

Kingsley's attack on Newman is usually regarded as his worst failure; the *Apologia* itself was the means of re-establishing its author, after many years of comparative neglect, in the hearts of his countrymen.

from PART VII

General Answer to Mr. Kingsley

From the time that I became a Catholic, of course I have no further history of my religious opinions to narrate. In saying this, I do not mean to say that my mind has been idle, or that I have given up thinking on theological subjects; but that I have had no changes to record, and have had no anxiety of heart whatever. I have been in perfect peace and contentment. I never have had one doubt. I was not conscious to myself, on my conversion, of any difference of thought or of temper from what I had before. I was not conscious of firmer faith in the fundamental truths of revelation, or of more self-command; I had not more fervour; but it was like coming into port after a rough sea; and my happiness on that score remains to this day without interruption.

Nor had I any trouble about receiving those additional articles which are not found in the Anglican Creed. Some of them I believed already, but not any one of them was a trial to me. I made a profession of them upon my reception with the greatest ease, and I have the same ease in believing them now. I am far of course from denying that every article of the Christian Creed, whether as held by Catholics or by Protestants, is beset with intellectual difficulties; and it is simple fact that, for myself, I cannot answer those difficulties. Many persons are very sensitive of the difficulties of religion; I am as sensitive as any one; but I have never been able to see a connexion between apprehending those difficulties, however keenly, and multiplying them to any extent, and doubting the doctrines to which they are attached. Ten thousand difficulties do not make one doubt, as I understand the subject; difficulty and doubt are incommensurate. . . .

But I am going to take upon myself the responsibility of more than the mere Creed of the Church; as the parties accusing me are determined I shall do. They say, that now, in that I am a Catholic, though I may not have offences of my own against honesty to answer for, yet, at least, I am answerable for the offences of others, of my co-religionists, of my brother priests, of the Church herself. I am quite willing to accept the responsibility; and, as I have been able, as I trust, by means of a few words, to dissipate, in the minds of all those who do not begin with disbelieving me, the suspicion with which so many Protestants start, in forming their judgment of Catholics, viz. that our Creed is actually set up in inevitable superstition and hypocrisy, as the original sin of Catholicism; so now I will go on, as before, identifying myself with the Church and vindicating it,—not of course denying the enormous mass of sin and ignorance which exists of necessity in that world-wide multiform Communion,—but going to the proof of this one point, that its system is in no sense dishonest, and that therefore the upholders and teachers of that system, as such, have a claim to be acquitted in their own persons of that odious imputation.

Starting then with the being of a God (which, as I have said, is as certain to me as the certainty of my own existence, though when I try to put the grounds of that certainty into logical shape I find a difficulty in doing so in mood and figure to my satisfaction), I look out of myself into the world of men, and there I see a sight which fills me with unspeakable distress. The world seems simply to give the lie to that great truth, of which my whole being is so full; and the effect upon me is, in consequence, as a matter of necessity, as confusing as if it denied that I am in existence myself. If I looked into a mirror, and did not see my face, I should have the sort of feeling which actually comes upon me, when I look into this living busy world, and see no reflexion of its Creator. This is, to me, one of the great difficulties of this absolute primary truth, to which I referred just now. Were it not for this voice, speaking so clearly in my conscience and my heart, I should be an atheist, or a pantheist, or a polytheist when I looked into the world. . . .

To consider the world in its length and breadth, its various history, the many races of man, their starts, their fortunes, their mutual alienation, their conflicts; and then their ways, habits, governments, forms of worship; their enterprises, their aimless courses, their random achievements and acquirements, the impotent conclusion of long-standing facts, the tokens so faint and broken, of a superintending design, the blind evolution of what turn out to be great powers or truths, the progress of things, as if from unreasoning elements, not towards final causes, the greatness and littleness of man, his far-reaching aims, his short duration, the curtain hung over his futurity, the disappointments of life, the defeat of good, the success of evil, physical pain, mental anguish, the prevalence and intensity of sin, the pervading idolatries, the corruptions, the dreary hopeless irreligion, that condition of the whole race, so fearfully yet exactly described in the Apostle's words, "having no hope and without God in the world,"—all this is a vision to dizzy and appal; and inflicts upon the mind the sense of a profound mystery, which is absolutely beyond human solution.

What shall be said to this heart-piercing, reason-bewildering fact? I can only answer, that either there is no Creator, or this living society of men is in a true sense discarded from His presence. Did I see a boy of good make and mind, with the tokens on him of a refined nature, cast upon the world without provision, unable to say whence he came, his birth-place or his family connexions, I should conclude that there was some mystery connected with his history, and that he was one, of whom, from one cause or other, his parents were ashamed. Thus only should I be able to account for the contrast between the promise and condition of his being. And so I argue about the world;—*if* there be a God, *since* there is a God, the human race is implicated in some terrible aboriginal calamity. It is out of joint with the purposes of its Creator. This is a fact, a fact as true as the fact of its existence; and thus the doctrine of what is theologically called original sin becomes to me almost as certain as that the world exists, and as the existence of God.

And now, supposing it were the blessed and loving will of the Creator to interfere in this anarchical condition of things, what are we to suppose would be the methods which might be necessarily or naturally involved in His object of mercy? Since the world is in so abnormal a state, surely it would be no surprise to me, if the interposition were of necessity equally extraordinary—or what is called miraculous. But that subject does not directly come into the scope of my present remarks. Miracles as evidence, involve an argument; and of course I am thinking of some means which does not immediately run into argument. I am rather asking what must be the face-to-face antagonist, by which to withstand and baffle the fierce energy of passion and the all-corroding, all-dissolving scepticism of the intellect in religious inquiries? I have no intention at all to deny, that truth is the real object of our reason, and that, if it does not attain to truth, either the premiss or the process is in fault; but I am not speaking of right reason, but of reason as it acts in fact and concretely in fallen man. I know that even the unaided reason, when correctly exercised, leads to a belief in God, in the immortality of the soul, and in a future retribution; but I am considering it actually and historically; and in this point of view, I do not think I am wrong in saying that its tendency is towards a simple unbelief in matters of religion. No truth, however sacred, can stand against it, in the long run; and hence it is that in the pagan world, when our Lord came, the last traces of the religious knowledge of former times were all but disappearing from those portions of the world in which the intellect had been active and had had a career.

And in these latter days, in like manner, outside the Catholic Church things are tending, with far greater rapidity than in that old time from the circumstance of the age, to atheism in one shape or other. What a scene, what a prospect, does the whole of Europe present at this day! and not only Europe, but every government and every civilization through the world which is under the influence of the European mind! Especially, for it most concerns us, how sorrowful, in the view of religion, even taken in its most elementary, most attenuated form, is the spectacle presented to us by the educated intellect of England, France, and Germany! Lovers of their country and of their race, religious men, external to the Catholic Church, have attempted various expedients to arrest fierce wilful human nature in its onward course, and to bring it into subjection. The necessity of some form of religion for the interests of humanity, has been generally acknowledged: but where was the concrete representative of things invisible, which would have the force and the toughness necessary to be a breakwater against the deluge? Three centuries ago the establishment of religion, material, legal, and social, was generally adopted as the best expedient for the purpose, in those countries which separated

20–21. "having . . . world," St. Paul, in Ephesians 2:12. **43. original sin,** the hereditary stain inherited by all mankind from Adam.

from the Catholic Church; and for a long time it was successful; but now the crevices of those establishments are admitting the enemy. Thirty years ago, education was relied upon: ten years ago there was a hope that wars would cease for ever, under the influence of commercial enterprise and the reign of the useful and fine arts; but will any one venture to say that there is any thing any where on this earth, which will afford a fulcrum for us, whereby to keep the earth from moving onwards?

The judgment, which experience passes on establishments or education, as a means of maintaining religious truth in this anarchical world, must be extended even to Scripture, though Scripture be divine. Experience proves surely that the Bible does not answer a purpose for which it was never intended. It may be accidentally the means of the conversion of individuals; but a book, after all, cannot make a stand against the wild living intellect of man, and in this day it begins to testify, as regards its own structure and contents, to the power of that universal solvent, which is so successfully acting upon religious establishments.

Supposing then it to be the Will of the Creator to interfere in human affairs, and to make provisions for retaining in the world a knowledge of Himself, so definite and distinct as to be proof against the energy of human scepticism, in such a case,—I am far from saying that there was no other way,—but there is nothing to surprise the mind, if He should think fit to introduce a power into the world, invested with the prerogative of infallibility in religious matters. Such a provision would be a direct, immediate, active, and prompt means of withstanding the difficulty; it would be an instrument suited to the need; and, when I find that this is the very claim of the Catholic Church, not only do I feel no difficulty in admitting the idea, but there is a fitness in it, which recommends it to my mind. And thus I am brought to speak of the Church's infallibility, as a provision, adapted by the mercy of the Creator, to preserve religion in the world, and to restrain that freedom of thought, which of course in itself is one of the greatest of our natural gifts, and to rescue it from its own suicidal excesses. And let it be observed that, neither here nor in what follows, shall I have occasion to speak directly of the revealed body of truths, but only as they bear upon the defence of natural religion. I say, that a power, possessed of infallibility in religious teaching, is happily adapted to be a working instrument, in the course of human affairs, for smiting hard and throwing back the immense energy of the aggressive intellect:—and in saying this, as in the other things that I have to say, it must still be recollected that I am all along bearing in mind my main purpose, which is a defence of myself.

I am defending myself here from a plausible charge brought against Catholics, as will be seen better as I proceed. The charge is this:—that I, as a Catholic, not only make profession to hold doctrines which I cannot possibly believe in my heart, but that I also believe in the existence of a power on earth, which at its own will imposes upon men any new set of *credenda*, when it pleases, by a claim to infallibility; in consequence, that my own thoughts are not my own property; that I cannot tell that to-morrow I may not have to give up what I hold to-day, and that the necessary effect of such a condition of mind must be a degrading bondage, or a bitter inward rebellion relieving itself in secret infidelity, or the necessity of ignoring the whole subject of religion in a sort of disgust, and of mechanically saying every thing that the Church says, and leaving to others the defence of it. As then I have above spoken of the relation of my mind towards the Catholic Creed, so now I shall speak of the attitude which it takes up in the view of the Church's infallibility.

And first, the initial doctrine of the infallible teacher must be an emphatic protest against the existing state of mankind. Man had rebelled against his Maker. It was this that caused the divine interposition: and the first act of the divinely accredited messenger must be to proclaim it. The Church must denounce rebellion as of all possible evils the greatest. She must have no terms with it; if she would be true to her Master, she must ban and anathematize it. This is the meaning of a statement which has furnished matter for one of those special accusations to which I am at present replying: I have, however, no fault at all to confess in regard to it; I have nothing to withdraw, and in consequence I here deliberately repeat it. I said, "The Catholic Church holds it better for the sun and moon to drop from heaven, for the earth to fail, and for all the many millions on it to die of starvation in extremest agony, as far as temporal affliction goes, than that one soul, I will not say, should be lost, but should commit one single venial sin, should tell one wilful untruth, or should steal one poor farthing without excuse." I think the principle here enunciated to be the mere preamble in the formal credentials of the Catholic Church, as an Act of Parliament might begin with a "*Whereas.*" It is because of

5–7. that wars would cease . . . fine arts, as manifested in the Great Exhibition at the Crystal Palace in 1851.

13. credenda, articles of faith.

the intensity of the evil which has possession of mankind, that a suitable antagonist has been provided against it; and the initial act of that divinely-commissioned power is of course to deliver her challenge and to defy the enemy. Such a preamble then gives a meaning to her position in the world, and an interpretation to her whole course of teaching and action.

In like manner she has ever put forth, with most energetic distinctness, those other great elementary truths, which either are an explanation of her mission or give a character to her work. She does not teach that human nature is irreclaimable, else wherefore should she be sent? not that it is to be shattered and reversed, but to be extricated, purified, and restored; not that it is a mere mass of evil, but that it has the promise of great things, and even now has a virtue and a praise proper to itself. But in the next place she knows and she preaches that such a restoration, as she aims at effecting in it, must be brought about, not simply through any outward provision of preaching and teaching, even though it be her own, but from a certain inward spiritual power or grace imparted directly from above, and which is in her keeping. She has it in charge to rescue human nature from its misery, but not simply by raising it upon its own level, but by lifting it up to a higher level than its own. She recognizes in it real moral excellence though degraded, but she cannot set it free from earth except by exalting it towards heaven. It was for this end that a renovating grace was put into her hands, and therefore from the nature of the gift, as well as from the reasonableness of the case, she goes on, as a further point, to insist, that all true conversion must begin with the first springs of thought, and to teach that each individual man must be in his own person one whole and perfect temple of God, while he is also one of the living stones which build up a visible religious community. And thus the distinctions between nature and grace, and between outward and inward religion, become two further articles in what I have called the preamble of her divine commission. . . .

Passing now from what I have called the preamble of that grant of power, with which the Church is invested, to that power itself, Infallibility, I make two brief remarks: on the one hand, I am not here determining anything about the essential seat of that power, because that is a question doctrinal, not historical and practical; nor, on the other hand, am I extending the direct subject-matter, over which that power has jurisdiction, beyond religious opinion:—and now as to the power itself.

This power, viewed in its fulness, is as tremendous as the giant evil which has called for it. It claims, when brought into exercise in the legitimate manner, for otherwise of course it is but dormant, to have for itself a sure guidance into the very meaning of every portion of the Divine Message in detail, which was committed by our Lord to His Apostles. It claims to know its own limits, and to decide what it can determine absolutely and what it cannot. It claims, moreover, to have a hold upon statements not directly religious, so far as this, to determine whether they indirectly relate to religion, and, according to its own definitive judgment, to pronounce whether or not, in a particular case, they are consistent with revealed truth. It claims to decide magisterially, whether infallibly or not, that such and such statements are or are not prejudicial to the Apostolic *depositum* of faith, in their spirit or in their consequences, and to allow them, or condemn and forbid them, accordingly. It claims to impose silence at will on any matters, or controversies, of doctrine, which on its own *ipse dixit* it pronounces to be dangerous, or inexpedient, or inopportune. It claims that whatever may be the judgment of Catholics upon such acts, these acts should be received by them with those outward marks of reverence, submission, and loyalty, which Englishmen, for instance, pay to the presence of their sovereign, without public criticism on them, as being in their matter inexpedient, or in their manner violent or harsh. And lastly, it claims to have the right of inflicting spiritual punishment, of cutting off from the ordinary channels of the divine life, and of simply excommunicating, those who refuse to submit themselves to its formal declarations. Such is the infallibility lodged in the Catholic Church, viewed in the concrete, as clothed and surrounded by the appendages of its high sovereignty: it is, to repeat what I said above, a super-eminent prodigious power sent upon earth to encounter and master a giant evil.

And now, having thus described it, I profess my own absolute submission to its claim. I believe the whole revealed dogma as taught by the Apostles, as committed by the Apostles to the Church, and as declared by the Church to me. I receive it, as it is infallibly interpreted by the authority to whom it is thus committed, and (implicitly) as it shall be, in like manner, further interpreted by that same authority till the end of time. I submit, moreover, to the universally received traditions of the Church, in which lies the matter of those new dogmatic

23–24. ipse dixit, assertion (without proof).

definitions which are from time to time made, and which in all times are the clothing and the illustration of the Catholic dogma as already defined. And I submit myself to those other decisions of the Holy See, theological or not, through the organs which it has itself appointed, which, waiving the question of their infallibility, on the lowest ground come to me with a claim to be accepted and obeyed. Also, I consider that, gradually and in the course of ages, Catholic inquiry has taken certain definite shapes, and has thrown itself into the form of a science, with a method and a phraseology of its own, under the intellectual handling of great minds, such as St. Athanasius, St. Augustine, and St. Thomas; and I feel no temptation at all to break in pieces the great legacy of thought thus committed to us for these latter days.

All this being considered to be a profession *ex animo*, as on my own part, so also on the part of the Catholic body, as far as I know it, it will at first sight be said that the restless intellect of our common humanity is utterly weighed down to the repression of all independent effort and action whatever, so that, if this is to be the mode of bringing it into order, it is brought into order only to be destroyed. But this is far from the result, far from what I conceive to be the intention of that high Providence who has provided a great remedy for a great evil,—far from borne out by the history of the conflict between Infallibility and Reason in the past, and the prospect of it in the future. The energy of the human intellect "does from opposition grow"; it thrives and is joyous, with a tough elastic strength, under the terrible blows of the divinely-fashioned weapon, and is never so much itself as when it has lately been overthrown. It is the custom with Protestant writers to consider that, whereas there are two great principles in action in the history of religion, Authority and Private Judgment, they have all the Private Judgment to themselves, and we have the full inheritance and the superincumbent oppression of Authority. But this is not so; it is the vast Catholic body itself, and it only, which affords an arena for both combatants in that awful, never-dying duel. It is necessary for the very life of religion, viewed in its large operations and its history, that the warfare should be incessantly carried on. Every exercise of Infallibility is brought out into act by an intense and varied operation of the Reason, from within and without, and provokes again a reaction of Reason against it; and, as in a civil polity the State exists and endures by means of the rivalry and collision, the encroachments and defeats of its constituent parts, so in like manner Catholic Christendom is no simple exhibition of religious absolutism, but it presents a continuous picture of Authority and Private Judgment alternately advancing and retreating as the ebb and flow of the tide;—it is a vast assemblange of human beings with wilful intellects and wild passions, brought together into one by the beauty and the majesty of a Superhuman Power—into what may be called a large reformatory or training-school, not to be sent to bed, not to be buried alive, but for the melting, refining, and moulding, as in some moral factory, by an incessant noisy process (if I may proceed to another metaphor), of the raw material of human nature, so excellent, so dangerous, so capable of divine purposes.

St. Paul says in one place that his Apostolical power is given him to edification, and not to destruction. There can be no better account of the Infallibility of the Church. It is a supply for a need, and it does not go beyond that need. Its object is, and its effect also, not to enfeeble the freedom or vigour of human thought in religious speculation, but to resist and control its extravagance. What have been its great works? All of them in the distinct province of theology:—to put down Arianism, Eutychianism, Pelagianism, Manichaeism, Lutheranism, Jansenism. Such is the broad result of its action in the past;—and now as to the securities which are given us that so it ever will act in time to come.

First, Infallibility cannot act outside of a definite circle of thought, and it must in all its decisions, or *definitions*, as they are called, profess to be keeping within it. The great truths of the moral law, of natural religion, and of Apostolical faith, are both its boundary and its foundation. It must not go beyond them, and it must ever appeal to them. Both its subject-matter, and its articles in that subject-matter, are fixed. Thus, in illustration, it does not

14. St. Thomas, St. Thomas Aquinas (c. 1225–1274), whose *Sum of Theology* is the authoritative statement of Catholic doctrine. **19. ex animo,** from the heart.

19. St. Paul says in one place, in 2 Corinthians 10:8. **29–30. Eutychianism,** from Eutyches, a monk of the Greek Church (fifth century), the essence of the view being that Christ had been one nature after the Incarnation. **Pelagianism,** from Pelagius, a British monk (fourth and fifth centuries), who taught a number of heresies, denying the doctrine of original sin, and maintaining the ability of men to save themselves through righteous living, though without the aid of the Gospel. **Manichaeism,** from Mani (c. 216–277), who introduced Persian dualism into Christianity, distinguishing between the spiritual Christ, as divine, and the historical Jesus, as evil. **Lutheranism,** the religious beliefs and ecclesiastical practices of Martin Luther (1483–1546), who headed the Protestant revolt in Germany. **Jansenism,** a many-sided heresy named from Cornelis Jansen (1585–1639), Bishop of Ypres. See the article "Jansenism" in *New International Encyclopaedia.*

extend to statements, however sound and evident, which are mere logical conclusions from the Articles of the Apostolic *Depositum;* again, it can pronounce nothing about the persons of heretics, whose works fall within its legitimate province. It must ever profess to be guided by Scripture and by tradition. It must refer to the particular Apostolic truth which it is enforcing, or (what is called) *defining.* Nothing, then, can be presented to me, in time to come, as part of the faith, but what I ought already to have received, and have not actually received, (if not) merely because it has not been told me. Nothing can be imposed upon me different in kind from what I hold already,—much less contrary to it. The new truth which is promulgated, if it is to be called new, must be at least homogeneous, cognate, implicit, viewed relatively to the old truth. It must be what I may even have guessed, or wished, to be included in the Apostolic revelation; and at least it will be of such a character, that my thoughts readily concur in it or coalesce with it, as soon as I hear it. Perhaps I and others actually have always believed it, and the only question which is now decided in my behalf, is that I am henceforth to believe that I have only been holding what the Apostles held before me.

John Stuart Mill

1806–1873

By blood and training, John Stuart Mill inherited the Utilitarian point of view (see pages 901–902 for background). He himself is still popularly regarded as the great Victorian thinking machine, the high priest of Reason in his generation. But the truth is that Mill also, while clinging in important particulars to the Positivist outlook, modified classical Utilitarianism in important particulars. His study of Wordsworth, Coleridge, and others led him to distinguish between kinds and qualities of pleasure after a fashion that his father, James Mill, had never known, and he found in practice that he could not continue to serve the Utilitarian ideal of "the greatest happiness of the greatest number" without so far abandoning the laissez-faire principle as virtually to advocate a form of State Socialism. The admirable vigor and clarity of his thinking appear in the stirring defense of freedom by which he is represented in this volume; the nobility and disinterested passion of his character are quite as obvious.

The facts of Mill's life are easily summarized. He was born in London, May 20, 1806, entered the service of the East India Company at seventeen, and continued in that service until the dissolution of the company thirty-five years later. He edited the *London and Westminster Review;* married in 1851 Mrs. Harriet Taylor, with whom he had long been intimate, and who had an important influence upon him; became a member of Parliament in 1865, but was defeated three years later. In 1866 he headed a committee to bring Governor Eyre, the Jamaica butcher, to justice, against the opposition of an astonishing number of the great Victorians. He spent his last years in France, and died at Avignon, May 8, 1873.

Mill served many causes. He defended the French revolutionaries in 1830, and supported the Union cause in the Civil War. He supported Charles Bradlaugh's long-contested right to sit in Parliament despite his atheism. He opposed heavy armaments, and advocated a liberal policy toward Ireland. He favored woman suffrage and the extension of the franchise; to escape the rule of ignorance he suggested plural voting for educated persons. Co-operative production, profit-sharing, popular education, and religious toleration all found in him an ardent advocate.

Mill's *On Liberty*, 1859, is still the most influential exposition of the popular idea of liberty in English-speaking countries. Recent political history, however, has shown the fallacy of some of his propositions, and his idea of liberty is open to grave objections with respect both to the relation of the individual to society and to the absolute freedom of the individual will.

from ON LIBERTY

from CHAPTER 2

Of the Liberty of Thought and Discussion

THE time, it is to be hoped, is gone by, when any defence would be necessary of the "liberty of the press" as one of the securities against corrupt or tyrannical government. . . . Though the law of England, on the subject of the press, is as servile to this day as it was in the time of the Tudors, there is little danger of its being actually put in force against political discussion, except during some temporary panic, when fear of insurrection drives ministers and judges from their propriety; and, speaking generally, it is not, in constitutional countries, to be apprehended, that the government, whether completely responsible to the people or not, will often attempt to control the expression of opinion, except when in doing so it makes itself the organ of the general intolerance of the public. Let us suppose, therefore, that the government is entirely at one with the people, and never thinks of exerting any power of coercion unless in agreement with what it conceives to be their voice. But I deny the right of the people to exercise such coercion, either by themselves or by their government. The power itself is illegitimate. The best government has no more title to it than the worst. It is as noxious, or more noxious, when exerted in accordance with public opinion, than when in opposition to it. If all mankind minus one, were of one opinion, and only one person were of the contrary opinion, mankind would be no more justified in silencing that one person, than he, if he had the power, would be justified in silencing mankind. Were an opinion a personal possession of no value except to the owner; if to be obstructed in the enjoyment of it were simply a private injury, it would make some difference whether the injury was inflicted only on a few persons or on many. But the peculiar evil of silencing the expression of an opinion is, that it is robbing the human race; posterity as well as the existing generation; those who dissent from the opinion, still more than those who hold it. If the opinion is right, they are deprived of the opportunity of exchanging error for truth: if wrong, they lose, what is almost as great a benefit, the clearer perception and livelier impression of truth, produced by its collision with error.

It is necessary to consider separately these two hypotheses, each of which has a distinct branch of the argument corresponding to it. We can never be sure that the opinion we are endeavouring to stifle is a false opinion; and if we were sure, stifling it would be an evil still.

First: the opinion which it is attempted to suppress by authority may possibly be true. Those who desire to suppress it, of course deny its truth; but they are not infallible. They have no authority to decide the question for all mankind, and exclude every other person from the means of judging. To refuse a hearing to an opinion, because they are sure that it is false, is to assume that *their* certainty is the same thing as *absolute* certainty. All silencing of discussion is an assumption of infallibility. Its condemnation may be allowed to rest on this common argument, not the worse for being common. . . .

When we consider either the history of opinion, or the ordinary conduct of human life, to what is it to be ascribed that the one and the other are no worse than they are? Not certainly to the inherent force of the human understanding; for, on any matter not self-evident, there are ninety-nine persons totally incapable of judging of it, for one who is capable; and the capacity of the hundredth person is only comparative; for the majority of the eminent men of every past generation held many opinions now known to be erroneous, and did or approved numerous things which no one will now justify. Why is it, then, that there is on the whole a preponderance among mankind of rational opinions and rational conduct? If there really is this preponderance—which there must be unless human affairs are, and have always been, in an almost desperate state—it is owing to a quality of the human mind, the source of everything respectable in man either as an intellectual or as a moral being, namely, that his errors are corrigible. He is capable of rectifying his mistakes, by discussion and experience. Not by experience alone. There must be discussion, to show how experience is to be interpreted. Wrong opinions and practices gradually yield to fact and argument: but facts and arguments, to produce any effect on the mind, must be brought before it. Very few facts are able to tell their own story, without comments to bring out their meaning. The whole strength and value, then, of human judgment, depending on the one property, that it can be set right when it is wrong, reliance can be placed on it only when the means of setting it right are kept constantly at hand. In the case of any person whose judgment is really deserving of confidence, how has it become so? Because he has kept his mind open to criticism of his opinions and conduct. Because it has been his practice to listen to all that could be said against him; to profit by as much of it as was just, and expound to himself, and upon occasion to others, the fallacy of what was fallacious. Because he has felt, that the only way in which a human being can make some

3. the time of the Tudors, Henry VII (1485–1509); Henry VIII (1509–47); Edward VI (1547–53); Mary (1553–58); Elizabeth (1558–1603).

approach to knowing the whole of a subject, is by hearing what can be said about it by persons of every variety of opinion, and studying all modes in which it can be looked at by every character of mind. No wise man ever acquired his wisdom in any mode but this; nor is it in the nature of human intellect to become wise in any other manner. The steady habit of correcting and completing his own opinion by collating it with those of others, so far from causing doubt and hesitation in carrying it into practice, is the only stable foundation for a just reliance on it: for, being cognisant of all that can, at least obviously, be said against him, and having taken up his position against all gainsayers—knowing that he has sought for objections and difficulties, instead of avoiding them, and has shut out no light which can be thrown upon the subject from any quarter—he has a right to think his judgment better than that of any person, or any multitude, who have not gone through a similar process. . . .

Strange it is, that men should admit the validity of the arguments for free discussion, but object to their being "pushed to an extreme"; not seeing that unless the reasons are good for an extreme case, they are not good for any case. Strange that they should imagine that they are not assuming infallibility, when they acknowledge that there should be free discussion on all subjects which can possibly be *doubtful*, but think that some particular principle or doctrine should be forbidden to be questioned because it is so *certain*, that is, because *they are certain* that it is certain. To call any proposition certain, while there is any one who would deny its certainty if permitted, but who is not permitted, is to assume that we ourselves, and those who agree with us, are the judges of certainty, and judges without hearing the other side.

In the present age—which has been described as "destitute of faith, but terrified at scepticism"—in which people feel sure, not so much that their opinions are true, as that they should not know what to do without them—the claims of an opinion to be protected from public attack are rested not so much on its truth, as on its importance to society. There are, it is alleged, certain beliefs, so useful, not to say indispensable to well-being, that it is as much the duty of governments to uphold those beliefs, as to protect any other of the interests of society. In a case of such necessity, and so directly in the line of their duty, something less than infallibility may, it is maintained, warrant, and even bind, governments, to act on their own opinion, confirmed by the general opinion of mankind. It is also often argued, and still oftener thought, that none but bad men would desire to weaken these salutary beliefs; and there can be nothing wrong, it is thought, in restraining bad men, and prohibiting what only such men would wish to practise. This mode of thinking makes the justification of restraints on discussion not a question of the truth of doctrines, but of their usefulness; and flatters itself by that means to escape the responsibility of claiming to be an infallible judge of opinions. But those who thus satisfy themselves, do not perceive that the assumption of infallibility is merely shifted from one point to another. The usefulness of an opinion is itself matter of opinion: as disputable, as open to discussion, and requiring discussion as much, as the opinion itself. There is the same need of an infallible judge of opinions to decide an opinion to be noxious, as to decide it to be false, unless the opinion, condemned has full opportunity of defending itself. . . .

Mankind can hardly be too often reminded that there was once a man named Socrates, between whom and the legal authorities and public opinion of his time there took place a memorable collision. Born in an age and country abounding in individual greatness, this man has been handed down to us by those who best knew both him and the age, as the most virtuous man in it; while *we* know him as the head and prototype of all subsequent teachers of virtue, the source equally of the lofty inspiration of Plato and the judicious utilitarianism of Aristotle, "*i maëstri di color che sanno*," the two headsprings of ethical as of all other philosophy. This acknowledged master of all the eminent thinkers who have since lived—whose fame, still growing after more than two thousand years, all but outweighs the whole remainder of the names which make his native city illustrious—was put to death by his countrymen, after a judicial conviction, for impiety and immorality. Impiety, in denying the gods recognised by the State; indeed his accuser asserted (see the "Apologia") that he believed in no gods at all. Immorality in being, by his doctrines and instructions, a "corruptor of youth." Of these charges the tribunal, there is every ground for believing, honestly found him guilty, and condemned the man who probably of all then born had deserved best of mankind, to be put to death as a criminal.

22. Socrates, Athenian philosopher (469–399 B.C.). **31. Plato** (c. 427–347 B.C.), the principal disciple of Socrates, and author of the *Apologia*, in which the story of his death is told. **Aristotle,** Greek philosopher (384–322 B.C.), one of the most important influences on the thinking of western Europe. **32. "i maëstri di color che sanno,"** "the teachers of those who know." See Dante, *The Divine Comedy*, *Inferno*, Canto IV, l. 131.

To pass from this to the only other instance of judicial iniquity, the mention of which, after the condemnation of Socrates, would not be an anti-climax: the event which took place on Calvary rather more than eighteen hundred years ago. The man who left on the memory of those who witnessed his life and conversation, such an impression of his moral grandeur, that eighteen subsequent centuries have done homage to him as the Almighty in person, was ignominiously put to death, as what? As a blasphemer. Men did not merely mistake their benefactor; they mistook him for the exact contrary of what he was, and treated him as that prodigy of impiety, which they themselves are now held to be, for their treatment of him. The feelings with which mankind now regard these lamentable transactions, especially the later of the two, render them extremely unjust in their judgment of the unhappy actors. These were, to all appearance, not bad men—not worse than men commonly are, but rather the contrary; men who possessed in a full, or somewhat more than a full measure, the religious, moral, and patriotic feelings of their time and people: the very kind of men who, in all times, our own included, have every chance of passing through life blameless and respected. The high-priest who rent his garments when the words were pronounced, which, according to all the ideas of his country, constituted the blackest guilt, was in all probability quite as sincere in his horror and indignation, as the generality of respectable and pious men now are in the religious and moral sentiments they profess; and most of those who now shudder at his conduct, if they had lived in his time, and been born Jews, would have acted precisely as he did. Orthodox Christians who are tempted to think that those who stoned to death the first martyrs must have been worse men than they themselves are, ought to remember that one of those persecutors was Saint Paul. . . .

Let us now pass to the second division of the argument, and dismissing the supposition that any of the received opinions may be false, let us assume them to be true, and examine into the worth of the manner in which they are likely to be held, when their truth is not freely and openly canvassed. . . .

If the intellect and judgment of mankind ought to be cultivated, a thing which Protestants at least do not deny, on what can these faculties be more appropriately exercised by any one, than on the things which concern him so much that it is considered necessary for him to hold opinions on them? If the cultivation of the understanding consists in one thing more than in another, it is surely in learning the grounds of one's own opinions. Whatever people believe, on subjects on which it is of the first importance to believe rightly, they ought to be able to defend against at least the common objections. But, some one may say, "Let them be *taught* the grounds of their opinions. It does not follow that opinions must be merely parroted because they are never heard controverted. Persons who learn geometry do not simply commit the theorems to memory, but understand and learn likewise the demonstrations; and it would be absurd to say that they remain ignorant of the grounds of geometrical truths, because they never hear any one deny, and attempt to disprove them." Undoubtedly: and such teaching suffices on a subject like mathematics, where there is nothing at all to be said on the wrong side of the question. The peculiarity of the evidence of mathematical truths is, that all the argument is on one side. There are no objections, and no answers to objections. But on every subject on which difference of opinion is possible, the truth depends on a balance to be struck between two sets of conflicting reasons. Even in natural philosophy, there is always some other explanation possible of the same facts; some geocentric theory instead of heliocentric, some phlogiston instead of oxygen; and it has to be shown why that other theory cannot be the true one: and until this is shown, and until we know how it is shown, we do not understand the grounds of our opinion. But when we turn to subjects infinitely more complicated, to morals, religion, politics, social relations, and the business of life, three-fourths of the arguments for every disputed opinion consist in dispelling the appearances which favour some opinion different from it. The greatest orator, save one, of antiquity, has left it on record that he always studied his adversary's case with as great, if not with still greater, intensity than even his own. What Cicero practised as the means of forensic success, requires to be imitated by all who study any subject in order to arrive at the truth. He who knows only his own side of the case, knows little of that. His reasons may be good, and no one may have been able to refute them. But if he is equally unable to refute the reasons on the opposite side; if he does not so much as know what they are, he has no ground for preferring either opinion.

26–27. The high-priest . . . garments. See Mark 14:63. **39. Saint Paul,** or Saul (as he was then) guarded the clothes of those who stoned Stephen, the first Christian martyr (Acts 6–7).

44. Cicero, Roman orator, statesman, and writer (106–43 B.C.).

The rational position for him would be suspension of judgment, and unless he contents himself with that, he is either led by authority, or adopts, like the generality of the world, the side to which he feels most inclination. Nor is it enough that he should hear the arguments of adversaries from his own teachers, presented as they state them, and accompanied by what they offer as refutations. That is not the way to do justice to the arguments, or bring them into real contact with his own mind. He must be able to hear them from persons who actually believe them; who defend them in earnest, and do their very utmost for them. He must know them in their most plausible and persuasive form; he must feel the whole force of the difficulty which the true view of the subject has to encounter and dispose of; else he will never really possess himself of the portion of truth which meets and removes that difficulty. Ninety-nine in a hundred of what are called educated men are in this condition; even of those who can argue fluently for their opinions. Their conclusion may be true, but it might be false for anything they know: they have never thrown themselves into the mental position of those who think differently from them, and considered what such persons may have to say; and consequently they do not, in any proper sense of the word, know the doctrine which they themselves profess. They do not know those parts of it which explain and justify the remainder; the considerations which show that a fact which seemingly conflicts with another is reconcilable with it, or that, of two apparently strong reasons, one and not the other ought to be preferred. All that part of the truth which turns the scale, and decides the judgment of a completely informed mind, they are strangers to; nor is it ever really known, but to those who have attended equally and impartially to both sides, and endeavoured to see the reasons of both in the strongest light. So essential is this discipline to a real understanding of moral and human subjects, that if opponents of all important truths do not exist, it is indispensable to imagine them, and supply them with the strongest arguments which the most skilful devil's advocate can conjure up. . . .

If . . . the mischievous operation of the absence of free discussion, when the received opinions are true, were confined to leaving men ignorant of the grounds of those opinions, it might be thought that this, if an intellectual, is no moral evil, and does not affect the worth of the opinions, regarded in their influence on the character. The fact, however, is, that not only the grounds of the opinion are forgotten in the absence of discussion, but too often the meaning of the opinion itself. The words which convey it, cease to suggest ideas, or suggest only a small portion of those they were originally employed to communicate. Instead of a vivid conception and a living belief, there remain only a few phrases retained by rote; or, if any part, the shell and husk only of the meaning is retained, the finer essence being lost. The great chapter in human history which this fact occupies and fills, cannot be too earnestly studied and meditated on.

It is illustrated in the experience of almost all ethical doctrines and religious creeds. They are all full of meaning and vitality to those who originate them, and to the direct disciples of the originators. Their meaning continues to be felt in undiminished strength, and is perhaps brought out into even fuller consciousness, so long as the struggle lasts to give the doctrine or creed an ascendancy over other creeds. At last it either prevails, and becomes the general opinion, or its progress stops; it keeps possession of the ground it has gained, but ceases to spread further. When either of these results has become apparent, controversy on the subject flags, and gradually dies away. The doctrine has taken its place, if not as a received opinion, as one of the admitted sects or divisions of opinion: those who hold it have generally inherited, not adopted it; and conversion from one of these doctrines to another, being now an exceptional fact, occupies little place in the thoughts of their professors. Instead of being, as at first, constantly on the alert either to defend themselves against the world, or to bring the world over to them, they have subsided into acquiescence, and neither listen, when they can help it, to arguments against their creed, nor trouble dissentients (if there be such) with arguments in its favour. From this time may usually be dated the decline in the living power of the doctrine. We often hear the teachers of all creeds lamenting the difficulty of keeping up in the minds of believers a lively apprehension of the truth which they nominally recognise, so that it may penetrate the feelings, and acquire a real mastery over the conduct. No such difficulty is complained of while the creed is still fighting for its existence: even the weaker combatants then know and feel what they are fighting for, and the difference between it and other doctrines; and in that period of every creed's existence, not a few persons may be found, who have realized its fundamental principles in all the forms of thought, have weighed and considered them in all their important bearings, and have experienced the full effect on the character, which belief in that creed ought to produce in a mind thoroughly imbued with it. But when it has come to be an hereditary creed, and to be received passively, not actively—when the mind is no longer compelled, in the same degree as at first, to exercise its vital powers on the questions which its belief presents to it, there is a progressive tendency to forget all of the belief except the formularies, or to give it a dull and torpid assent, as if accepting it on trust dispensed with the necessity of realizing it in consciousness, or testing it by personal experience; until it almost ceases to connect itself at all with the inner life of the human being. Then are seen the cases, so frequent in this age of the world as almost to form the majority, in which the creed remains as it were outside the mind, encrusting and petrifying it against all other influences addressed to the higher parts of our nature; manifesting its power by not suffering any fresh and living conviction to get in, but itself doing nothing for the mind or heart, except standing sentinel over them to keep them vacant. . . .

It still remains to speak of one of the principal causes which make diversity of opinion advantageous, and will continue to do so until mankind shall have entered a stage of intellectual advancement which at present seems at an incalculable distance. We have hitherto considered only two possibilities: that the received opinion may be false, and some other opinion, consequently, true; or that, the received opinion being true, a conflict with the opposite error is essential to a clear apprehension and deep feeling of its truth. But there is a commoner case than either of these; when the conflicting doctrines, instead of being one true and the other false, share the truth between them; and the nonconforming opinion is needed to supply the remainder of the truth, of which the received doctrine embodies only a part. Popular opinions, on subjects not palpable to sense, are often true, but seldom or never the whole truth. They are a part of the truth; sometimes a greater, sometimes a smaller part, but exaggerated, distorted, and disjoined from the truths by which they ought to be accompanied and limited. Heretical opinions, on the other hand, are generally some of these suppressed and neglected truths, bursting the bonds which kept them down, and either seeking reconciliation with the truth contained in the common opinion, or fronting it as enemies, and setting themselves up, with similar exclusiveness, as the whole truth. . . .

Thus, in the eighteenth century, when nearly all the instructed, and all those of the uninstructed who were led by them, were lost in admiration of what is called civilization, and of the marvels of modern science, literature, and philosophy, and while greatly overrating the amount of unlikeness between the men of modern and those of ancient times, indulged the belief that the whole of the difference was in their own favour; with what a salutary shock did the paradoxes of Rousseau explode like bombshells in the midst, dislocating the compact mass of one-sided opinion, and forcing its elements to recombine in a better form and with additional ingredients. Not that the current opinions were on the whole farther from the truth than Rousseau's were; on the contrary, they were nearer to it; they contained more of positive truth, and very much less of error. Nevertheless there lay in Rousseau's doctrine, and has floated down the stream of opinion along with it, a considerable amount of exactly those truths which the popular opinion wanted; and these are the deposit which was left behind when the flood subsided. The superior worth of simplicity of life, the enervating and demoralizing effect of the trammels and hypocrisies of artificial society, are ideas which have never been entirely absent from cultivated minds since Rousseau wrote; and they will in time produce their due effect, though at present needing to be asserted as much as ever, and to be asserted by deeds, for words, on this subject, have nearly exhausted their power.

In politics, again, it is almost a commonplace, that a party of order or stability, and a party of progress or reform, are both necessary elements of a healthy state of political life; until the one or the other shall have so enlarged its mental grasp as to be a party equally of order and of progress, knowing and distinguishing what is fit to be preserved from what ought to be swept away. . . .

Before quitting the subject of freedom of opinion, it is fit to take some notice of those who say, that the free expression of all opinions should be permitted, on condition that the manner be temperate, and do not pass the bounds of fair discussion. Much might be said on the impossibility of fixing where these supposed bounds are to be placed; for if the test be offence to those whose opinion is attacked, I think experience testifies that this offence is given whenever the attack is telling and powerful, and that every opponent who pushes them hard, and whom they find it difficult to answer, appears to them, if he shows any strong feeling on the subject, an in-

8. Rousseau. Rousseau's primitivistic ideas had a tremendous influence on both political and educational theory, and on English literature.

temperate opponent. But this, though an important consideration in a practical point of view, merges in a more fundamental objection. Undoubtedly the manner of asserting an opinion, even though it be a true one, may be very objectionable, and may justly incur severe censure. But the principal offences of the kind are such as it is mostly impossible, unless by accidental self-betrayal, to bring home to conviction. The gravest of them is, to argue sophistically, to suppress facts or arguments, to misstate the elements of the case, or misrepresent the opposite opinion. But all this, even to the most aggravated degree, is so continually done in perfect good faith, by persons who are not considered, and in many other respects may not deserve to be considered, ignorant or incompetent, that it is rarely possible on adequate grounds conscientiously to stamp the misrepresentation as morally culpable; and still less could law presume to interfere with this kind of controversial misconduct. With regard to what is commonly meant by intemperate discussion, namely invective, sarcasm, personality, and the like, the denunciation of these weapons would deserve more sympathy if it were ever proposed to interdict them equally to both sides; but it is only desired to restrain the employment of them against the prevailing opinion: against the unprevailing they may not only be used without general disapproval, but will be likely to obtain for him who uses them the praise of honest zeal and righteous indignation. Yet whatever mischief arises from their use, is greatest when they are employed against the comparatively defenceless; and whatever unfair advantage can be derived by any opinion from this mode of asserting it, accrues almost exclusively to received opinions. The worst offence of this kind which can be committed by a polemic, is to stigmatize those who hold the contrary opinion as bad and immoral men. To calumny of this sort, those who hold any unpopular opinion are peculiarly exposed, because they are in general few and uninfluential, and nobody but themselves feels much interested in seeing justice done them; but this weapon is, from the nature of the case, denied to those who attack a prevailing opinion: they can neither use it with safety to themselves, nor, if they could, would it do anything but recoil on their own cause. In general, opinions contrary to those commonly received can only obtain a hearing by studied moderation of language, and the most cautious avoidance of unnecessary offence, from which they hardly ever deviate even in a slight degree without losing ground: while unmeasured vituperation employed on the side of the prevailing opinion, really does deter people from professing contrary opinions, and from listening to those who profess them. For the interest, therefore, of truth and justice, it is far more important to restrain this employment of vituperative language than the other; and, for example, if it were necessary to choose, there would be much more need to discourage offensive attacks on infidelity, than on religion. It is, however, obvious that law and authority have no business with restraining either, while opinion ought, in every instance, to determine its verdict by the circumstances of the individual case; condemning every one, on whichever side of the argument he places himself, in whose mode of advocacy either want of candour, or malignity, bigotry, or intolerence of feeling manifest themselves; but not inferring these vices from the side which a person takes, though it be the contrary side of the question to our own: and giving merited honour to every one, whatever opinion he may hold, who has calmness to see and honesty to state what his opponents and their opinions really are, exaggerating nothing to their discredit, keeping nothing back which tells, or can be supposed to tell, in their favour. This is the real morality of public discussion: and if often violated, I am happy to think that there are many controversialists who to a great extent observe it, and a still greater number who conscientiously strive towards it.

Alfred, Lord Tennyson
1809–1892

Tennyson was Victoria's poet laureate. During his lifetime his supreme greatness was generally taken for granted, though it is true that he struggled long against public neglect. Later, in the reaction against all things Victorian which occurred, it was inevitable that his reputation should suffer. Of recent years, however, the curve of Tennyson's popularity has risen rapidly. The fiftieth anniversary of his death in 1942 brought forth, in addition to a memorial service in Westminster Abbey, a large number of special articles in the press. In its editorial, the *London Times Literary Supplement* said:

"Events have done so much to prove Tennyson right that from a negligible spinner of pretty sounds and sweet sentiments and delicate respectabilities he has risen to be one of the greatest and most inspiring of our poets. Not a politician nor a preacher, but a poet."

On the technical side Tennyson is clearly one of the greatest poets; his skill with varied verse forms entitles him to that high rank. Those who have attacked him have directed their criticism chiefly at his thought—what they call his pale proprieties, his sentimentality, his shallow optimism. But often he is judged too exclusively from the point of view of a later time. Among his contemporaries, Huxley, who was anything but pious, considered him the modern Lucretius. With the exception of the *Idylls of the King*, Tennyson made no single contribution so original as those of Wordsworth, Coleridge, Byron, Shelley, or Keats, but he had a vastly wider range than any of them. In a sense he sums up all English poetry. And in at least one form, the lyric, he is unsurpassed.

Tennyson was born at Somersby rectory, Lincolnshire, on August 6, 1809. When he was eight, he was sent to school at Louth, where the harsh methods of the master probably helped to determine his lifelong shyness. Later he was tutored at home by his father, and in 1828 he went to Trinity College, Cambridge, but he was not distinguished as a student and never took a degree. The important thing Cambridge did for him was to bring him in contact with the "Twelve Apostles," a company of students which included Richard Monckton Milnes (later Lord Houghton), Frederick Denison Maurice, and Arthur Henry Hallam. As a group they helped to impress him with a sense of the sacredness of his poetic calling; Hallam individually brought him one of the great experiences of his life (see the introductory note to *In Memoriam*).

Tennyson had been writing poetry since he was five years old. In 1827 he and his brother Charles had collaborated in *Poems by Two Brothers* (with a few contributions from a third brother, Frederick). In 1829 he won the Chancellor's medal for poetry at Cambridge. His first proper book, *Poems Chiefly Lyrical*, 1830, was extravagantly puffed by Hallam and his friends, and quite as extravagantly damned by the influential critic "Christopher North" (John Wilson) in *Blackwood's*. Tennyson had the bad judgment to make a rather harsh reply, which, although rightly deserved, may help to account for the venom of John Gibson Lockhart's review of the 1832 volume, *Poems*, in the *Quarterly Review*. Lockhart's review was, in any event, diabolically effective; it destroyed Tennyson's reputation and made him for years an object of derision and a joke. No wonder that when Hallam's death followed hard upon this crushing disappointment, Tennyson should almost have despaired. He did not quite despair, however. He spent the next ten years industriously perfecting his art; when he reappeared in 1842 with *Poems*, in two volumes, he had won his public. In 1846 he was granted a small pension; in 1847 he published *The Princess*.

The year 1850 was a crowning year in Tennyson's life. In the spring he published *In Memoriam;* in June he married Emily Sellwood, to whom he had been engaged through fourteen years of poverty; in November he was appointed poet laureate. In 1853 he built a house at Farringford on the Isle of Wight, in 1868 another at Aldworth in Surrey.

Once he had found his stride, Tennyson's industry never slackened. *Maud, and Other Poems* came out in 1855; *Idylls of the King* in 1859, and subsequently; *Idylls of the Hearth* (*Enoch Arden, and Other Poems*) in 1864. After 1875 he turned his attention to the drama and wrote a number of plays, including *Queen Mary*, *Harold*, and *Becket*. Both *Becket* and *The Cup* were produced by Sir Henry Irving; the latter ran more than one hundred and thirty nights. The most important publications of Tennyson's last years were *Ballads, and Other Poems*, 1880; *Tiresias, and Other Poems*, 1885; *Demeter, and Other Poems*, 1889; *The Death of Oenone, Akbar's Death, and Other Poems*, 1892. He died October 6, 1892, with his Shakespeare on the moonlight-drenched bed beside him, open to the boatman's song in *Cymbeline*.

THE LADY OF SHALOTT

According to Tennyson, the key to the meaning of this, his first Arthurian poem, is to be found in the last four lines of Part II. He explains: "The new-born love for something, for some one in the wide world from which she has been so long secluded, takes her out of the region of shadows into that of realities."

PART I

On either side the river lie
Long fields of barley and of rye,
That clothe the wold and meet the sky;
And through the field the road runs by
  To many-towered Camelot;
And up and down the people go,
Gazing where the lilies blow

3. wold, open, uncultivated country **5. Camelot,** King Arthur's city. **7. blow,** bloom.

Round an island there below,
The island of Shalott.

Willows whiten, aspens quiver,
Little breezes dusk and shiver
Through the wave that runs for ever
By the island in the river
Flowing down to Camelot.
Four gray walls, and four gray towers,
Overlook a space of flowers,
And the silent isle imbowers
The Lady of Shalott.

By the margin, willow-veiled,
Slide the heavy barges trailed
By slow horses; and unhailed
The shallop flitteth silken-sailed
Skimming down to Camelot:
But who hath seen her wave her hand?
Or at the casement seen her stand?
Or is she known in all the land,
The Lady of Shalott?

Only reapers, reaping early
In among the bearded barley,
Hear a song that echoes cheerly
From the river winding clearly,
Down to towered Camelot:
And by the moon the reaper weary,
Piling sheaves in uplands airy,
Listening, whispers "'Tis the fairy
Lady of Shalott."

PART II

There she weaves by night and day
A magic web with colours gay.
She has heard a whisper say,
A curse is on her if she stay
To look down to Camelot.
She knows not what the curse may be,
And so she weaveth steadily,
And little other care hath she,
The Lady of Shalott.

And moving through a mirror clear
That hangs before her all the year,
Shadows of the world appear.
There she sees the highway near
Winding down to Camelot:
There the river eddy whirls,
And there the surly village-churls,
And the red cloaks of market girls,
Pass onward from Shalott.

Sometimes a troop of damsels glad,
An abbot on an ambling pad,
Sometimes a curly shepherd-lad,
Or long-haired page in crimson clad,
Goes by to towered Camelot;
And sometimes through the mirror blue
The knights come riding two and two:
She hath no loyal knight and true,
The Lady of Shalott.

But in her web she still delights
To weave the mirror's magic sights,
For often through the silent nights
A funeral, with plumes and lights
And music, went to Camelot:
Or when the moon was overhead,
Came two young lovers lately wed;
"I am half sick of shadows," said
The Lady of Shalott.

PART III

A bow-shot from her bower-eaves,
He rode between the barley-sheaves,
The sun came dazzling through the leaves,
And flamed upon the brazen greaves
Of bold Sir Lancelot.
A red-cross knight for ever kneeled
To a lady in his shield,
That sparkled on the yellow field,
Beside remote Shalott.

The gemmy bridle glittered free,
Like to some branch of stars we see
Hung in the golden Galaxy.
The bridle bells rang merrily
As he rode down to Camelot:
And from his blazoned baldric slung
A mighty silver bugle hung,
And as he rode his armour rung,
Beside remote Shalott.

All in the blue unclouded weather
Thick-jewelled shone the saddle-leather,
The helmet and the helmet-feather
Burned like one burning flame together,
As he rode down to Camelot;
As often through the purple night,
Below the starry clusters bright,

9. Shalott, from Tennyson's source, the Italian romance *Donna di Scalotta*. Shalott and Astolat, Malory's name for Elaine's home, are the same word. See Tennyson's "Lancelot and Elaine," *Idylls of the King*. **10. Willows whiten.** The white undersides of the leaves are turned up by the wind.

56. pad, easy-paced horse. **84. Galaxy,** the Milky Way.

Some bearded meteor, trailing light,
Moves over still Shalott.

His broad clear brow in sunlight glowed;
On burnished hooves his war-horse trode;
From underneath his helmet flowed
His coal-black curls as on he rode,
As he rode down to Camelot.
From the bank and from the river
He flashed into the crystal mirror,
"Tirra lirra," by the river
Sang Sir Lancelot.

She left the web, she left the loom,
She made three paces through the room,
She saw the water-lily bloom,
She saw the helmet and the plume,
She looked down to Camelot.
Out flew the web and floated wide;
The mirror cracked from side to side;
"The curse is come upon me," cried
The Lady of Shalott.

PART IV

In the stormy east-wind straining,
The pale yellow woods were waning,
The broad stream in his banks complaining,
Heavily the low sky raining
Over towered Camelot;
Down she came and found a boat
Beneath a willow left afloat,
And round about the prow she wrote
The Lady of Shalott.

And down the river's dim expanse
Like some bold seër in a trance,
Seeing all his own mischance—
With a glassy countenance
Did she look to Camelot.
And at the closing of the day
She loosed the chain, and down she lay;
The broad stream bore her far away,
The Lady of Shalott.

Lying, robed in snowy white
That loosely flew to left and right—
The leaves upon her falling light—
Through the noises of the night
She floated down to Camelot:
And as the boat-head wound along
The willowy hills and fields among,
They heard her singing her last song,
The Lady of Shalott.

Heard a carol, mournful, holy,
Chanted loudly, chanted lowly,
Till her blood was frozen slowly,
And her eyes were darkened wholly,
Turned to towered Camelot.
For ere she reached upon the tide
The first house by the water-side,
Singing in her song she died,
The Lady of Shalott.

Under tower and balcony,
By garden-wall and gallery,
A gleaming shape she floated by,
Dead-pale between the houses high,
Silent into Camelot.
Out upon the wharfs they came,
Knight and burgher, lord and dame,
And round the prow they read her name,
The Lady of Shalott.

Who is this? and what is here?
And in the lighted palace near
Died the sound of royal cheer;
And they crossed themselves for fear,
All the knights at Camelot:
But Lancelot mused a little space;
He said, "She has a lovely face;
God in his mercy lend her grace,
The Lady of Shalott."

from THE LOTOS-EATERS

In the course of their wanderings, Ulysses and his companions come to the land of the lotus-eaters, where they are possessed by the lethargy of their hosts. See *Odyssey*, Book IX, ll. 82 ff. and the note to "Ulysses," below. The selection given here comprises the introduction to "The Lotos-Eaters."

"Courage!" he said, and pointed toward the land,
"This mounting wave will roll us shoreward soon."
In the afternoon they came unto a land
In which it seemèd always afternoon.
All round the coast the languid air did swoon,
Breathing like one that hath a weary dream.
Full-faced above the valley stood the moon;
And, like a downward smoke, the slender stream
Along the cliff to fall and pause and fall did seem.

A land of streams! some, like a downward smoke,
Slow-dropping veils of thinnest lawn, did go;
And some through wavering lights and shadows broke,
Rolling a slumbrous sheet of foam below.
They saw the gleaming river seaward flow
From the inner land: far off, three mountain-tops,
Three silent pinnacles of aged snow,

Stood sunset-flushed: and, dewed with showery drops,
Up-clomb the shadowy pine above the woven copse.

The charmèd sunset lingered low adown
In the red West: through mountain clefts the dale
Was seen far inland, and the yellow down
Bordered with palm, and many a winding vale
And meadow, set with slender galingale;
A land where all things always seemed the same!
And round about the keel with faces pale,
Dark faces pale against that rosy flame,
The mild-eyed melancholy Lotos-eaters came.

Branches they bore of that enchanted stem,
Laden with flower and fruit, whereof they gave
To each, but whoso did receive of them,
And taste, to him the gushing of the wave
Far far away did seem to mourn and rave
On alien shores; and if his fellow spake,
His voice was thin, as voices from the grave;
And deep-asleep he seemed, yet all awake,
And music in his ears his beating heart did make.

They sat them down upon the yellow sand,
Between the sun and moon upon the shore;
And sweet it was to dream of Fatherland,
Of child, and wife, and slave; but evermore
Most weary seemed the sea, weary the oar,
Weary the wandering fields of barren foam.
Then some one said, "We will return no more";
And all at once they sang, "Our island home
Is far beyond the wave; we will no longer roam."

ULYSSES

Ulysses is the hero of Homer's *Odyssey*, which relates the ten years' wandering that intervened between his departure from Troy, at the end of the war, and his return to Ithaca, where he slew the insolent suitors of his faithful wife, Penelope, and re-established himself as king. The Greeks were familiar with further wanderings of Ulysses to appease the god Poseidon, whom he had offended. Dante's *Divine Comedy*, Canto XXVI, had already endowed him with what we should call the pioneer spirit. But the conception of his departure from Ithaca, inspired by an irresistible desire for new experiences, is original with Tennyson, for whom the poem had definitely an autobiographical significance. He wrote it soon after the death of Hallam, and he himself said of it that it gave "the feeling about the need of going forward and braving the struggle of life perhaps more simply than anything in *In Memoriam*." It has always been regarded as one of his great achievements; it is interesting, also, to study his use of a form which Browning is often thought of as having made distinctly his own, the dramatic monologue. The speaker is, of course, Ulysses himself.

23. galingale. cypress.

It little profits that an idle king,
By this still hearth, among these barren crags,
Matched with an agèd wife, I mete and dole
Unequal laws unto a savage race,
That hoard, and sleep, and feed, and know not me.
I cannot rest from travel: I will drink
Life to the lees: all times I have enjoyed
Greatly, have suffered greatly, both with those
That loved me, and alone; on shore, and when
Through scudding drifts the rainy Hyades
Vext the dim sea: I am become a name;
For always roaming with a hungry heart
Much have I seen and known; cities of men
And manners, climates, councils, governments,
Myself not least, but honoured of them all;
And drunk delight of battle with my peers,
Far on the ringing plains of windy Troy.
I am a part of all that I have met;
Yet all experience is an arch wherethrough
Gleams that untravelled world, whose margin fades
For ever and for ever when I move.
How dull it is to pause, to make an end,
To rust unburnished, not to shine in use!
As though to breathe were life! Life piled on life
Were all too little, and of one to me
Little remains: but every hour is saved
From that eternal silence, something more,
A bringer of new things; and vile it were
For some three suns to store and hoard myself,
And this gray spirit yearning in desire
To follow knowledge like a sinking star,
Beyond the utmost bound of human thought.
    This is my son, mine own Telemachus,
To whom I leave the sceptre and the isle—
Well-loved of me, discerning to fulfil
This labour, by slow prudence to make mild
A rugged people, and through soft degrees
Subdue them to the useful and the good.
Most blameless is he, centred in the sphere
Of common duties, decent not to fail
In offices of tenderness, and pay
Meet adoration to my household gods,
When I am gone. He works his work, I mine.
    There lies the port; the vessel puffs her sail:
There gloom the dark, broad seas. My mariners,
Souls that have toiled, and wrought, and thought with me—
That ever with a frolic welcome took
The thunder and the sunshine, and opposed

10. rainy Hyades, a cluster of stars in the constellation Taurus, associated with rainy weather.

Free hearts, free foreheads—you and I are old;
Old age hath yet his honour and his toil.
Death closes all: but something ere the end,
Some work of noble note, may yet be done,
Not unbecoming men that strove with Gods.
The lights begin to twinkle from the rocks;
The long day wanes; the slow moon climbs; the deep
Moans round with many voices. Come, my friends,
'Tis not too late to seek a newer world.
Push off, and sitting well in order smite
The sounding furrows; for my purpose holds
To sail beyond the sunset, and the baths
Of all the western stars, until I die.
It may be that the gulfs will wash us down:
It may be we shall touch the Happy Isles,
And see the great Achilles, whom we knew.
Though much is taken, much abides; and though
We are not now that strength which in old days
Moved earth and heaven; that which we are, we are;
One equal temper of heroic hearts,
Made weak by time and fate, but strong in will
To strive, to seek, to find, and not to yield.

LOCKSLEY HALL

"Locksley Hall" is a monologue, expressing a young man's grief and disgust over the loss of his sweetheart, his cousin Amy, who has been induced by her parents to marry a fox-hunting squire, a much wealthier man. Tennyson remarked that the poem "represents young life, its good side, its deficiencies, and its yearnings." He insisted that it was not a self-portrait. He was, nevertheless, much preoccupied with this kind of man—who recurs notably in *Maud*—and the preoccupation indicates a somewhat morbid strain in his genius. In "Locksley Hall Sixty Years After" the hero of the present poem is reintroduced so that we may see what life has taught him. "Locksley Hall" is almost invariably included in anthologies, not so much for its poetic merit, which is considerable, as because of the many interesting references it contains not only to the events of Tennyson's time but, as in ll. 119–30, by anticipation of our own.

Comrades, leave me here a little, while as yet 'tis early morn:
Leave me here, and when you want me, sound upon the bugle-horn.

'Tis the place, and all around it, as of old, the curlews call,
Dreary gleams about the moorland flying over Locksley Hall;

Locksley Hall, that in the distance overlooks the sandy tracts,
And the hollow ocean-ridges roaring into cataracts.

Many a night from yonder ivied casement, ere I went to rest,
Did I look on great Orion sloping slowly to the West.

Many a night I saw the Pleiads, rising through the mellow shade,
Glitter like a swarm of fireflies tangled in a silver braid.

Here about the beach I wandered, nourishing a youth sublime
With the fairy tales of science, and the long result of time;

When the centuries behind me like a fruitful land reposed;
When I clung to all the present for the promise that it closed:

When I dipt into the future far as human eye could see;
Saw the Vision of the world, and all the wonder that would be.—

In the spring a fuller crimson comes upon the robin's breast;
In the spring the wanton lapwing gets himself another crest;

In the spring a livelier iris changes on the burnished dove;
In the spring a young man's fancy lightly turns to thoughts of love.

51–53. Death closes all . . . Gods. Not being a Christian, Ulysses does not believe in immortality; his hunger for life is desperate, for he must soon go down into the darkness. One of Dante's most effective symbols of experience in *The Divine Comedy* is his conception of the heretics who denied immortality, who are enclosed in red-hot tombs upon which the lids are slowly closing. The reference to **the Happy Isles** (l. 63), where Ulysses hopes to see the great hero Achilles, who was slain in the war, must not be taken to contradict any of this. The Islands of the Blessed, described by Hesiod, Pindar, and others as lying toward the edge of the westward ocean, are the abiding-place of certain specially favored mortals who have been rescued by the gods from the common doom of men. **55–56. The long day wanes . . . many voices.** Note the sympathetic natural background. Being an old man, Ulysses sails out into the twilight.

4. Dreary . . . Hall. An absolute construction, Tennyson told Dr. Furness, not an assertion about the curlews. **8. Orion,** the constellation. **9. Pleiads, a cluster of stars.**

Then her cheek was pale and thinner than should be for one so young,
And her eyes on all my motions with a mute observance hung.

And I said, "My cousin Amy, speak, and speak the truth to me,
Trust me, cousin, all the current of my being sets to thee."

On her pallid cheek and forehead came a colour and a light,
As I have seen the rosy red flushing in the northern night.

And she turned—her bosom shaken with a sudden storm of sighs—
All the spirit deeply dawning in the dark of hazel eyes—

Saying, "I have hid my feelings, fearing they should do me wrong";
Saying, "Dost thou love me, cousin?" weeping, "I have loved thee long."

Love took up the glass of Time, and turned it in his glowing hands;
Every moment, lightly shaken, ran itself in golden sands.

Love took up the harp of Life, and smote on all the chords with might;
Smote the chord of Self, that, trembling, passed in music out of sight.

Many a morning on the moorland did we hear the copses ring,
And her whisper thronged my pulses with the fulness of the Spring.

Many an evening by the waters did we watch the stately ships,
And our spirits rushed together at the touching of the lips.

O my cousin, shallow-hearted! O my Amy, mine no more!
O the dreary, dreary moorland! O the barren, barren shore!

Falser than all fancy fathoms, falser than all songs have sung,
Puppet to a father's threat, and servile to a shrewish tongue!

Is it well to wish thee happy?—having known me—to decline
On a range of lower feelings and a narrower heart than mine!

Yet it shall be: thou shalt lower to his level day by day,
What is fine within thee growing coarse to sympathise with clay.

As the husband is, the wife is: thou art mated with a clown,
And the grossness of his nature will have weight to drag thee down.

He will hold thee, when his passion shall have spent its novel force,
Something better than his dog, a little dearer than his horse.

What is this? his eyes are heavy: think not they are glazed with wine.
Go to him, it is thy duty; kiss him, take his hand in thine.

It may be my lord is weary, that his brain is overwrought:
Soothe him with thy finer fancies, touch him with thy lighter thought.

He will answer to the purpose, easy things to understand—
Better thou wert dead before me, though I slew thee with my hand!

Better thou and I were lying, hidden from the heart's disgrace,
Rolled in one another's arms, and silent in a last embrace.

Cursed be the social wants that sin against the strength of youth!
Cursed be the social lies that warp us from the living truth!

Cursed be the sickly forms that err from honest Nature's rule!
Cursed be the gold that gilds the straitened forehead of the fool!

Well—'tis well that I should bluster!—Hadst thou less unworthy proved—
Would to God—for I had loved thee more than ever wife was loved.

24. sets, flows.

Am I mad, that I should cherish that which bears but bitter fruit?
I will pluck it from my bosom, though my heart be at the root.

Never, though my mortal summers to such length of years should come
As the many-wintered crow that leads the clanging rookery home.

Where is comfort? in division of the records of the mind?
Can I part her from herself, and love her, as I knew her, kind?

I remember one that perished: sweetly did she speak and move:
Such a one do I remember, whom to look at was to love.

Can I think of her as dead, and love her for the love she bore?
No—she never loved me truly: love is love for evermore.

Comfort? comfort scorned of devils! this is truth the poet sings,
That a sorrow's crown of sorrow is remembering happier things.

Drug thy memories, lest thou learn it, lest thy heart be put to proof,
In the dead unhappy night, and when the rain is on the roof.

Like a dog, he hunts in dreams, and thou art staring at the wall,
Where the dying night-lamp flickers, and the shadows rise and fall.

Then a hand shall pass before thee, pointing to his drunken sleep,
To thy widowed marriage-pillows, to the tears that thou wilt weep.

Thou shalt hear the "Never, never," whispered by the phantom years,
And a song from out the distance in the ringing of thine ears;

And an eye shall vex thee, looking ancient kindness on thy pain.
Turn thee, turn thee on thy pillow: get thee to thy rest again.

Nay, but Nature brings thee solace; for a tender voice will cry.
'Tis a purer life than thine; a lip to drain thy trouble dry.

Baby lips will laugh me down: my latest rival brings thee rest.
Baby fingers, waxen touches, press me from the mother's breast.

O, the child too clothes the father with a dearness not his due.
Half is thine and half is his: it will be worthy of the two.

O, I see thee old and formal, fitted to thy petty part,
With a little hoard of maxims preaching down a daughter's heart.

"They were dangerous guides the feelings—she herself was not exempt—
Truly, she herself had suffered"—Perish in thy self-contempt!

Overlive it—lower yet—be happy! wherefore should I care?
I myself must mix with action, lest I wither by despair.

What is that which I should turn to, lighting upon days like these?
Every door is barred with gold, and opens but to golden keys.

Every gate is thronged with suitors, all the markets overflow.
I have but an angry fancy: what is that which I should do?

I had been content to perish, falling on the foeman's ground,
When the ranks are rolled in vapour, and the winds are laid with sound.

76. That . . . things. A paraphrase of Dante, *Inferno*, Canto V, ll. 121–23. **79. he,** Amy's husband, who cries out the language of the hunt in his drunken stupor.

95–96. "They . . . suffered." The quotation is given indirectly. **104. winds are laid,** the supposed effect of cannon fire.

But the jingling of the guinea helps the hurt that Honour feels,
And the nations do but murmur, snarling at each other's heels.

Can I but relive in sadness? I will turn that earlier page.
Hide me from my deep emotion, O thou wondrous Mother-Age!

Make me feel the wild pulsation that I felt before the strife,
When I heard my days before me, and the tumult of my life;

Yearning for the large excitement that the coming years would yield,
Eager-hearted as a boy when first he leaves his father's field,

And at night along the dusky highway near and nearer drawn,
Sees in heaven the light of London flaring like a dreary dawn;

And his spirit leaps within him to be gone before him then,
Underneath the light he looks at, in among the throngs of men:

Men, my brothers, men the workers, ever reaping something new:
That which they have done but earnest of the things that they shall do.

For I dipt into the future, far as human eye could see,
Saw the Vision of the world, and all the wonder that would be;

Saw the heavens fill with commerce, argosies of magic sails,
Pilots of the purple twilight, dropping down with costly bales;

Heard the heavens fill with shouting, and there rained a ghastly dew
From the nations' airy navies grappling in the central blue;

Far along the world-wide whisper of the south-wind rushing warm,
With the standards of the peoples plunging through the thunder-storm;

Till the war-drum throbbed no longer, and the battle-flags were furled
In the Parliament of man, the Federation of the world.

There the common sense of most shall hold a fretful realm in awe,
And the kindly earth shall slumber, lapt in universal law.

So I triumphed ere my passion sweeping through me left me dry,
Left me with the palsied heart, and left me with the jaundiced eye;

Eye, to which all order festers, all things here are out of joint.
Science moves, but slowly, slowly, creeping on from point to point:

Slowly comes a hungry people, as a lion creeping nigher,
Glares at one that nods and winks behind a slowly-dying fire.

Yet I doubt not through the ages one increasing purpose runs,
And the thoughts of men are widened with the process of the suns.

What is that to him that reaps not harvest of his youthful joys,
Though the deep heart of existence beat for ever like a boy's?

Knowledge comes, but wisdom lingers, and I linger on the shore,
And the individual withers, and the world is more and more.

Knowledge comes, but wisdom lingers, and he bears a laden breast,
Full of sad experience, moving toward the stillness of his rest.

Hark, my merry comrades call me, sounding on the bugle-horn,
They to whom my foolish passion were a target for their scorn.

135. hungry people, a reference either to contemporary revolutionary activities or to Malthus's theory of population (see page 902). **138. process . . . suns,** the passing years.

Shall it not be scorn to me to harp on such a mouldered string?
I am shamed through all my nature to have loved so slight a thing.

Weakness to be wroth with weakness! woman's pleasure, woman's pain—
Nature made them blinder motions bounded in a shallower brain.

Woman is the lesser man, and all thy passions, matched with mine,
Are as moonlight unto sunlight, and as water unto wine—

Here at least, where nature sickens, nothing. Ah, for some retreat
Deep in yonder shining Orient, where my life began to beat;

Where in wild Mahratta-battle fell my father evil-starred;—
I was left a trampled orphan, and a selfish uncle's ward.

Or to burst all links of habit—there to wander far away,
On from island unto island at the gateways of the day.

Larger constellations burning, mellow moons and happy skies,
Breadths of tropic shade and palms in cluster, knots of Paradise.

Never comes the trader, never floats an European flag,
Slides the bird o'er lustrous woodland, swings the trailer from the crag;

Droops the heavy-blossomed bower, hangs the heavy-fruited tree—
Summer isles of Eden lying in dark-purple spheres of sea.

There methinks would be enjoyment more than in this march of mind,
In the steamship, in the railway, in the thoughts that shake mankind.

There the passions cramped no longer shall have scope and breathing space;
I will take some savage woman, she shall rear my dusky race.

150. motions, impulses. **155. Mahratta-battle,** in India. **162. trailer,** trailing vine.

Iron jointed, supple-sinewed, they shall dive, and they shall run,
Catch the wild goat by the hair, and hurl their lances in the sun;

Whistle back the parrot's call, and leap the rainbows of the brooks,
Not with blinded eyesight poring over miserable books—

Fool, again the dream, the fancy! but I *know* my words are wild,
But I count the gray barbarian lower than the Christian child.

I, to herd with narrow foreheads, vacant of our glorious gains,
Like a beast with lower pleasures, like a beast with lower pains!

Mated with a squalid savage—what to me were sun or clime?
I the heir of all the ages, in the foremost files of time—

I that rather held it better men should perish one by one,
Than that earth should stand at gaze like Joshua's moon in Ajalon!

Not in vain the distance beacons. Forward, forward let us range,
Let the great world spin for ever down the ringing grooves of change.

Through the shadow of the globe we sweep into the younger day:
Better fifty years of Europe than a cycle of Cathay.

Mother-Age (for mine I knew not) help me as when life begun:
Rift the hills, and roll the waters, flash the lightnings, weigh the sun.

Oh, I see the crescent promise of my spirit hath not set.
Ancient founts of inspiration well through all my fancy yet.

180. at gaze . . . Ajalon. Joshua commanded the moon to stand still in the valley of Ajalon until the Israelites had avenged themselves upon their enemies (see Joshua 10: 12–13). **182. grooves,** a reflection of Tennyson's first impression that the wheels of railway trains turned in grooves. **184. cycle of Cathay,** a thousand years of China.

Howsoever these things be, a long farewell to Locksley Hall!
Now for me the woods may wither, now for me the roof-tree fall.

Comes a vapour from the margin, blackening over heath and holt,
Cramming all the blast before it, in its breast a thunderbolt.

Let it fall on Locksley Hall, with rain or hail, or fire or snow;
For the mighty wind arises, roaring seaward, and I go.

SAINT AGNES' EVE

On St. Agnes' Eve (January 21) girls tried to envision their future husbands (see Keats's "The Eve of St. Agnes"). Tennyson has worked the theme out in religious terms; the nun is the bride of Christ.

Deep on the convent-roof the snows
  Are sparkling to the moon;
My breath to heaven like vapour goes;
  May my soul follow soon!
The shadows of the convent-towers
  Slant down the snowy sward,
Still creeping with the creeping hours
  That lead me to my Lord:
Make Thou my spirit pure and clear
  As are the frosty skies,
Or this first snowdrop of the year
  That in my bosom lies.

As these white robes are soiled and dark,
  To yonder shining ground;
As this pale taper's earthly spark,
  To yonder argent round;
So shows my soul before the Lamb,
  My spirit before Thee;
So in mine earthly house I am,
  To that I hope to be.
Break up the heavens, O Lord! and far,
  Through all yon starlight keen,
Draw me, thy bride, a glittering star,
  In raiment white and clean.

He lifts me to the golden doors;
  The flashes come and go;
All heaven bursts her starry floors,
  And strows her lights below,
And deepens on and up! the gates
  Roll back, and far within
For me the Heavenly Bridegroom waits,
  To make me pure of sin.
The Sabbaths of Eternity,
  One Sabbath deep and wide—
A light upon the shining sea—
  The Bridegroom with his bride!

16. yonder argent round, the full moon.

BREAK, BREAK, BREAK

Break, break, break,
  On thy cold gray stones, O Sea!
And I would that my tongue could utter
  The thoughts that arise in me.

O well for the fisherman's boy,
  That he shouts with his sister at play!
O well for the sailor lad,
  That he sings in his boat on the bay!

And the stately ships go on
  To their haven under the hill;
But O for the touch of a vanished hand,
  And the sound of a voice that is still!

Break, break, break,
  At the foot of thy crags, O Sea!
But the tender grace of a day that is dead
  Will never come back to me.

Songs from THE PRINCESS

The Princess, 1847, the story of an abortive attempt to "emancipate" women by educating them completely apart from men, is Tennyson's discussion of the "woman question." The action involves both battle and comic-opera disguises, and the conclusion is that the natural affections must not be repressed. The story is definitely "dated"; Gilbert and Sullivan, indeed, burlesqued it in *Princess Ida* as early as 1884. But the songs Tennyson added in later editions are among the most glorious in English literature. "Sweet and low" was set to music by Sir Joseph Barnby, "Now sleeps the crimson petal" by Roger Quilter.

I. AS THROUGH THE LAND

As through the land at eve we went,
  And plucked the ripened ears,
We fell out, my wife and I,

11–12. hand . . . voice. Hallam's. See notes to "Ulysses" and *In Memoriam*.

O, we fell out, I know not why,
  And kissed again with tears.
And blessings on the falling out
  That all the more endears,
When we fall out with those we love
  And kiss again with tears!
For when we came where lies the child
  We lost in other years,
There above the little grave,
O, there above the little grave,
  We kissed again with tears.

2. SWEET AND LOW

Sweet and low, sweet and low,
  Wind of the western sea,
Low, low, breathe and blow,
  Wind of the western sea!
Over the rolling waters go,
Come from the dying moon, and blow,
  Blow him again to me;
While my little one, while my pretty one, sleeps.

Sleep and rest, sleep and rest,
  Father will come to thee soon;
Rest, rest, on mother's breast,
  Father will come to thee soon;
Father will come to his babe in the nest,
Silver sails all out of the west
  Under the silver moon:
Sleep, my little one, sleep, my pretty one, sleep.

3. THE SPLENDOUR FALLS

The splendour falls on castle walls
  And snowy summits old in story:
The long light shakes across the lakes,
  And the wild cataract leaps in glory.
Blow, bugle, blow, set the wild echoes flying,
Blow, bugle; answer, echoes, dying, dying, dying.

O hark, O hear! how thin and clear,
  And thinner, clearer, farther going!
O sweet and far from cliff and scar
  The horns of Elfland faintly blowing!
Blow, let us hear the purple glens replying:
Blow, bugle; answer, echoes, dying, dying, dying.

O love, they die in yon rich sky,
  They faint on hill or field or river:
Our echoes roll from soul to soul,
  And grow for ever and for ever.
Blow, bugle, blow, set the wild echoes flying,
And answer, echoes, answer, dying, dying, dying.

4. TEARS, IDLE TEARS

Tears, idle tears, I know not what they mean,
Tears from the depth of some divine despair
Rise in the heart, and gather to the eyes,
In looking on the happy autumn-fields,
And thinking of the days that are no more.

Fresh as the first beam glittering on a sail,
That brings our friends up from the underworld,
Sad as the last which reddens over one
That sinks with all we love below the verge;
So sad, so fresh, the days that are no more.

Ah, sad and strange as in dark summer dawns
The earliest pipe of half-awakened birds
To dying ears, when unto dying eyes
The casement slowly grows a glimmering square;
So sad, so strange, the days that are no more.

Dear as remembered kisses after death,
And sweet as those by hopeless fancy feigned
On lips that are for others; deep as love,
Deep as first love, and wild with all regret;
O Death in Life, the days that are no more!

5. HOME THEY BROUGHT

Home they brought her warrior dead;
  She nor swooned, nor uttered cry:
All her maidens, watching, said,
  "She must weep or she will die."

Then they praised him, soft and low,
  Called him worthy to be loved,
Truest friend and noblest foe;
  Yet she neither spoke nor moved.

Stole a maiden from her place,
  Lightly to the warrior stept,
Took the face-cloth from the face;
  Yet she neither moved nor wept.

Rose a nurse of ninety years,
  Set his child upon her knee—
Like summer tempest came her tears—
  "Sweet my child, I live for thee."

6. ASK ME NO MORE

Ask me no more: the moon may draw the sea;
  The cloud may stoop from heaven and take the shape,
  With fold to fold, of mountain or of cape;
But O too fond, when have I answered thee?
    Ask me no more.

Ask me no more: what answer should I give?
  I love not hollow cheek or faded eye:
  Yet, O my friend, I will not have thee die!
Ask me no more, lest I should bid thee live;
    Ask me no more.

Ask me no more: thy fate and mine are sealed;
  I strove against the stream and all in vain;
  Let the great river take me to the main:
No more, dear love, for at a touch I yield;
    Ask me no more.

7. NOW SLEEPS THE CRIMSON PETAL

  Now sleeps the crimson petal, now the white;
Nor waves the cypress in the palace walk;
Nor winks the gold fin in the porphyry font.
The fire-fly wakens: waken thou with me.

  Now droops the milk-white peacock like a ghost,
And like a ghost she glimmers on to me.

  Now lies the Earth all Danaë to the stars,
And all thy heart lies open unto me.

  Now slides the silent meteor on, and leaves
A shining furrow, as thy thoughts in me.

  Now folds the lily all her sweetness up,
And slips into the bosom of the lake:
So fold thyself, my dearest, thou, and slip
Into my bosom and be lost in me.

from IN MEMORIAM A. H. H.

Obiit MDCCCXXXIII

Arthur Henry Hallam, Tennyson's most intimate friend and prospective brother-in-law, died suddenly in Vienna, September 15, 1833. For Tennyson this death marked the beginning of a long period of spiritual struggle; he could never believe in life again until he had explained to himself how, in a world ruled by a good God, such a man could be cut off at the very beginning of his usefulness. He worked on this problem for seventeen years. The result was *In Memoriam*, which is probably his masterpiece and certainly one of the most important of all theological poems.

Milton saw Edward King ("Lycidas"), Shelley saw Keats ("Adonais"), Matthew Arnold saw Clough ("Thyrsis"), less as individuals than as types of unfulfilment. But Alfred Tennyson loved Arthur Henry Hallam. It was natural, therefore, that instead of expressing himself, as these other poets did, in the pastoral elegy (which is a highly artificial form of literature), he should rather, after a long period of gestation, have cast his utterance into a freer and more spacious form. He is careful, to be sure, to prevent our assuming that there has been no artistic rearrangement of materials in his spiritual autobiography. "It must be remembered that this is a poem, *not* an actual biography. . . . The different moods of sorrow as in a drama are dramatically given, and my conviction that fear, doubts, and suffering will find answer and relief only through Faith in a God of Love. 'I' is not always the author speaking of himself, but the voice of the human race speaking through him." It is clear that Tennyson wrote the poem for himself, to serve his own needs; but because the problem with which he grapples must be faced, in some form, by all who lose a loved one, and because, disdaining all factitious comfort, he frankly faced every difficulty in the way of faith that the age presented to his typically Victorian mind, the results he achieved were valuable not only for him but for tens of thousands of his contemporaries. To know *In Memoriam*, consequently, with all its implications, is to know Victorian England.

Though the "*In Memoriam* quatrain" had been used inconspicuously in English poetry before Tennyson, the poet was not aware of this; he consequently invented it anew. In his *Tennyson's "In Memoriam," Its Purpose and Its Structure* (Houghton Mifflin, 1884), John F. Genung outlines suggestively as follows:

PROLOGUE

INTRODUCTORY STAGE, 1–27

Prospect	1–6
Defining-Point—Beginning	7
Arrival and Burial of the Dead	17–20

FIRST CYCLE—28–77

Christmastide	28–30
Springtide	38–39
First Anniversary	72

SECOND CYCLE—78–103

Christmastide	78
New Year	83
Second Anniversary	99

7. **hollow cheek or faded eye.** The battle has necessitated turning the college into a hospital. Pity draws the princess to love.

7. **Danaë,** a princess of Argos imprisoned by her father in a brazen tower. Here Zeus visited her in the form of a golden shower.

THIRD CYCLE—104–131

Christmastide	104–05
New Year	106
Birthday of Deceased (Feb. 1)	107
Springtide	115–16
Defining-Point—End	119
Retrospect and Conclusion	130–31

Genung calls the Prologue the period of overwhelming grief. The First Cycle he calls the cycle of the past. The Second Cycle is the cycle of the present. The Third Cycle is the cycle of the future. Note the use of seasons and anniversaries to mark stages and transitions.

PROLOGUE

Strong Son of God, immortal Love,
Whom we, that have not seen thy face,
By faith, and faith alone, embrace,
Believing where we cannot prove;

Thine are these orbs of light and shade;
Thou madest Life in man and brute;
Thou madest Death; and lo, thy foot
Is on the skull which thou hast made.

Thou wilt not leave us in the dust:
Thou madest man, he knows not why,
He thinks he was not made to die;
And thou hast made him: thou art just.

Thou seemest human and divine,
The highest, holiest manhood, thou:
Our wills are ours, we know not how;
Our wills are ours, to make them thine.

Our little systems have their day;
They have their day and cease to be:
They are but broken lights of thee,
And thou, O Lord, art more than they.

We have but faith: we cannot know;
For knowledge is of things we see;
And yet we trust it comes from thee,
A beam in darkness: let it grow.

Let knowledge grow from more to more,
But more of reverence in us dwell;
That mind and soul, according well,
May make one music as before,

But vaster. We are fools and slight;
We mock thee when we do not fear:
But help thy foolish ones to bear;
Help thy vain worlds to bear thy light.

Forgive what seemed my sin in me;
What seemed my worth since I began;
For merit lives from man to man,
And not from man, O Lord, to thee.

Forgive my grief for one removed,
Thy creature, whom I found so fair.
I trust he lives in thee, and there
I find him worthier to be loved.

Forgive these wild and wandering cries,
Confusions of a wasted youth;
Forgive them where they fail in truth,
And in thy wisdom make me wise.

I

I held it truth, with him who sings
To one clear harp in divers tones,
That men may rise on stepping-stones
Of their dead selves to higher things.

But who shall so forecast the years
And find in loss a gain to match?
Or reach a hand through time to catch
The far-off interest of tears?

Let Love clasp Grief lest both be drowned,
Let darkness keep her raven gloss:
Ah, sweeter to be drunk with loss,
To dance with Death, to beat the ground,

Than that the victor Hours should scorn
The long result of love, and boast,
"Behold the man that loved and lost,
But all he was is overworn."

3

O Sorrow, cruel fellowship,
O Priestess in the vaults of Death,
O sweet and bitter in a breath,
What whispers from thy lying lip?

1–4. Strong Son . . . cannot prove. See John 20:24–29. **5. orbs,** planets. **7–8. thy foot . . . hast made.** Since the Maker of Life made Death, Death cannot have the last word. The Son is not generally thought of as the Creator, but see John 1:3. **15–16. Our wills . . . to make them thine.** Tennyson maintains the freedom of the human will, without which there can be no morality, but perceives the necessity for a voluntary adjustment of the will of the individual to the universe. **25. Let knowledge grow.** Tennyson had no patience with religionists who opposed scientific investigation and experiment.

27. according, agreeing. **28. as before,** before modern science upset previously entertained beliefs. **35–36. merit lives . . . to thee.** Man can impute praise or blame to man, but not to God. **42. wasted,** desolated. *Sec. 1.* **1. him.** In 1891 Tennyson thought he had meant Goethe.

"The stars," she whispers, "blindly run;
  A web is wov'n across the sky;
  From out waste places comes a cry,
And murmurs from the dying sun:

"And all the phantom, Nature, stands—
  With all the music in her tone,
  A hollow echo of my own,—
A hollow form with empty hands."

And shall I take a thing so blind,
  Embrace her as my natural good;
  Or crush her, like a vice of blood,
Upon the threshold of the mind?

5

I sometimes hold it half a sin
  To put in words the grief I feel;
  For words, like Nature, half reveal
And half conceal the Soul within.

But, for the unquiet heart and brain,
  A use in measured language lies;
  The sad mechanic exercise,
Like dull narcotics, numbing pain.

In words, like weeds, I'll wrap me o'er,
  Like coarsest clothes against the cold:
  But that large grief which these enfold
Is given in outline and no more.

6

One writes, that "Other friends remain,"
  That "Loss is common to the race"—
  And common is the commonplace,
And vacant chaff well meant for grain.

That loss is common would not make
  My own less bitter, rather more:
  Too common! Never morning wore
To evening, but some heart did break.

O father, wheresoe'er thou be,
  Who pledgest now thy gallant son;
  A shot, ere half thy draught be done,
Hath stilled the life that beat from thee.

O mother, praying God will save
  Thy sailor,—while thy head is bowed,

Sec. 5. **9. weeds,** garments, as in "widow's weeds." *Sec. 6.* **1–8. One . . . break.** See *Hamlet,* Act I, sc. 2. The Queen brings Hamlet the same shallow comfort of which Tennyson speaks here. The poet, like the prince, replies in effect that the universality of sorrow makes his own situation worse, not better. Through his own sufferings he enters into the experience of all who suffer; imaginatively he bears the burden of all the suffering of the world.

  His heavy-shotted hammock-shroud
Drops in his vast and wandering grave.

Ye know no more than I who wrought
  At that last hour to please him well;
  Who mused on all I had to tell,
And something written, something thought;

Expecting still his advent home;
  And ever met him on his way
  With wishes, thinking, "here to-day,"
Or "here to-morrow will he come."

O somewhere, meek, unconscious dove,
  That sittest ranging golden hair;
  And glad to find thyself so fair,
Poor child, that waitest for thy love!

For now her father's chimney glows
  In expectation of a guest;
  And thinking "this will please him best,"
She takes a riband or a rose;

For he will see them on to-night;
  And with the thought her colour burns;
  And, having left the glass, she turns
Once more to set a ringlet right;

And, even when she turned, the curse
  Had fallen, and her future Lord
  Was drowned in passing through the ford,
Or killed in falling from his horse.

O, what to her shall be the end?
  And what to me remains of good?
  To her, perpetual maidenhood,
And unto me no second friend.

7

Dark house, by which once more I stand
  Here in the long unlovely street,
  Doors, where my heart was used to beat
So quickly, waiting for a hand,

A hand that can be clasped no more—
  Behold me, for I cannot sleep,
  And like a guilty thing I creep
At earliest morning to the door.

He is not here; but far away
  The noise of life begins again,
  And ghastly through the drizzling rain
On the bald street breaks the blank day.

26. ranging, arranging. **1. Dark house,** where Hallam lived. **12. bald . . . breaks . . . blank.** Note the effective alliteration and tone color.

21

I sing to him that rests below,
And, since the grasses round me wave,
I take the grasses of the grave,
And make them pipes whereon to blow.

The traveller hears me now and then,
And sometimes harshly will he speak:
"This fellow would make weakness weak,
And melt the waxen hearts of men."

Another answers: "Let him be,
He loves to make parade of pain,
That with his piping he may gain
The praise that comes to constancy."

A third is wroth: "Is this an hour
For private sorrow's barren song,
When more and more the people throng
The chairs and thrones of civil power?

"A time to sicken and to swoon,
When Science reaches forth her arms
To feel from world to world, and charms
Her secret from the latest moon?"

Behold, ye speak an idle thing;
Ye never knew the sacred dust.
I do but sing because I must,
And pipe but as the linnets sing:

And one is glad; her note is gay,
For now her little ones have ranged;
And one is sad; her note is changed,
Because her brood is stolen away.

27

I envy not in any moods
The captive void of noble rage,
The linnet born within the cage,
That never knew the summer woods:

I envy not the beast that takes
His license in the field of time,
Unfettered by the sense of crime,
To whom a conscience never wakes;

Nor, what may count itself as blest,
The heart that never plighted troth
But stagnates in the weeds of sloth;
Nor any want-begotten rest.

I hold it true, whate'er befall;
I feel it, when I sorrow most;
'Tis better to have loved and lost
Than never to have loved at all.

28

The time draws near the birth of Christ:
The moon is hid, the night is still;
The Christmas bells from hill to hill
Answer each other in the mist.

Four voices of four hamlets round,
From far and near, on mead and moor,
Swell out and fail, as if a door
Were shut between me and the sound;

Each voice four changes on the wind,
That now dilate, and now decrease,
Peace and goodwill, goodwill and peace,
Peace and goodwill, to all mankind.

This year I slept and woke with pain,
I almost wished no more to wake,
And that my hold on life would break
Before I heard those bells again;

But they my troubled spirit rule,
For they controlled me when a boy;
They bring me sorrow touched with joy,
The merry, merry bells of Yule.

30

With trembling fingers did we weave
The holly round the Christmas hearth;
A rainy cloud possessed the earth,
And sadly fell our Christmas-eve.

At our old pastimes in the hall
We gamboled, making vain pretence
Of gladness, with an awful sense
Of one mute Shadow watching all.

We paused: the winds were in the beech:
We heard them sweep the winter land;
And in a circle hand-in-hand
Sat silent, looking each at each.

13–16. an hour . . . power. Probably a reference to the Chartist movement (see page 901 of this volume). **18–20. Science . . . moon.** Neptune was discovered in 1846; the eighth satellite of Saturn, two years later. *Sec. 27.* **9–16. Nor . . . at all.** One of the most interesting points to observe about *In Memoriam* is the poet's consistent refusal to purchase peace at the cost of love, that is, by forgetfulness.

Sec. 28. **1. The time . . . Christ,** the first Christmas after Hallam's death, 1833. **9. Each voice four changes.** Each church had four bells. *Sec. 30.* **4. sadly.** See Sec. 78, l. 4; Sec. 105, l. 4.

Then echo-like our voices rang;
We sung, though every eye was dim.
A merry song we sang with him
Last year; impetuously we sang.

We ceased; a gentler feeling crept
Upon us: surely rest is meet.
"They rest," we said, "their sleep is sweet,"
And silence followed, and we wept.

Our voices took a higher range;
Once more we sang: "They do not die
Nor lose their mortal sympathy,
Nor change to us, although they change;

"Rapt from the fickle and the frail
With gathered power, yet the same,
Pierces the keen seraphic flame
From orb to orb, from veil to veil."

Rise, happy morn, rise, holy morn,
Draw forth the cheerful day from night:
O Father, touch the east, and light
The light that shone when Hope was born.

33

O thou that after toil and storm
Mayst seem to have reached a purer air,
Whose faith has centre everywhere,
Nor cares to fix itself to form,

Leave thou thy sister when she prays,
Her early Heaven, her happy views;
Nor thou with shadowed hint confuse
A life that leads melodious days.

Her faith through form is pure as thine,
Her hands are quicker unto good.
Oh, sacred be the flesh and blood
To which she links a truth divine!

See thou, that countest reason ripe
In holding by the law within,
Thou fail not in a world of sin,
And ev'n for want of such a type.

32. when Hope was born, with Christ, who brought the hope of immortality to men. *Sec. 33.* The poet warns those who have 'emancipated" themselves from "narrow" creeds and ceremonies not to disturb the simple, adequate faith of others and not to hold themselves superior to these others. **9. form,** creeds, ritualistic observances, etc. **11. flesh and blood,** possibly the bread and wine of the sacrament, more probably any symbol that has a spiritual significance for the believer. Tennyson argues that the faith and purity of life fostered by such things makes them sacred, even if they have in themselves no absolute value.

34

My own dim life should teach me this,
That life shall live for evermore,
Else earth is darkness at the core,
And dust and ashes all that is;

This round of green, this orb of flame,
Fantastic beauty; such as lurks
In some wild poet, when he works
Without a conscience or an aim.

What then were God to such as I?
'Twere hardly worth my while to choose
Of things all mortal, or to use
A little patience ere I die;

'Twere best at once to sink to peace,
Like birds the charming serpent draws,
To drop head-foremost in the jaws
Of vacant darkness and to cease.

36

Though truths in manhood darkly join,
Deep-seated in our mystic frame,
We yield all blessing to the name
Of Him that made them current coin;

For Wisdom dealt with mortal powers,
Where truth in closest words shall fail,
When truth embodied in a tale
Shall enter in at lowly doors.

And so the Word had breath, and wrought
With human hands the creed of creeds
In loveliness of perfect deeds,
More strong than all poetic thought;

Which he may read that binds the sheaf,
Or builds the house, or digs the grave,
And those wild eyes that watch the wave
In roarings round the coral reef.

47

That each, who seems a separate whole,
Should move his rounds, and fusing all
The skirts of self again, should fall
Remerging in the general Soul,

Sec. 34. **5. round . . . orb,** earth . . . sun. *Sec. 36.* **1–4. Though . . . coin.** The mature thinker may perceive the harmony of all religions, but we of the western world owe our religion to Jesus Christ. **7–8. a tale . . . doors.** See the parables of Jesus. **9. the Word.** See John 1:1–18. *Sec. 47.* Tennyson here considers a possible compromise between extinction and immortality: the soul survives, but loses its individual identity. He rejects this idea as unsatisfactory.

Is faith as vague as all unsweet:
Eternal form shall still divide
The eternal soul from all beside;
And I shall know him when we meet:

And we shall sit at endless feast,
Enjoying each the other's good:
What vaster dream can hit the mood
Of Love on earth? He seeks at least

Upon the last and sharpest height,
Before the spirits fade away,
Some landing-place, to clasp and say,
"Farewell! We lose ourselves in light."

50

Be near me when my light is low,
When the blood creeps, and the nerves prick
And tingle; and the heart is sick,
And all the wheels of Being slow.

Be near me when the sensuous frame
Is racked with pangs that conquer trust;
And Time, a maniac scattering dust,
And Life, a Fury slinging flame.

Be near me when my faith is dry,
And men the flies of latter spring,
That lay their eggs, and sting and sing
And weave their petty cells and die.

Be near me when I fade away,
To point the term of human strife,
And on the low dark verge of life
The twilight of eternal day.

52

I cannot love thee as I ought,
For love reflects the thing beloved;
My words are only words, and moved
Upon the topmost froth of thought.

"Yet blame not thou thy plaintive song,"
The Spirit of true love replied;
"Thou canst not move me from thy side,
Nor human frailty do me wrong.

"What keeps a spirit wholly true
To that ideal which he bears?
What record? not the sinless years
That breathed beneath the Syrian blue:

Sec. 52. In this section the poet exhorts himself not to permit an oversensitive conscience (Chaucer's "spiced conscience") to deprive him of a sense of fellowship with his departed friend. **11. the sinless years,** the earthly life of Jesus.

"So fret not, like an idle girl,
That life is dashed with flecks of sin.
Abide: thy wealth is gathered in,
When Time hath sundered shell from pearl."

54

Oh yet we trust that somehow good
Will be the final goal of ill,
To pangs of nature, sins of will,
Defects of doubt, and taints of blood;

That nothing walks with aimless feet;
That not one life shall be destroyed,
Or cast as rubbish to the void,
When God hath made the pile complete;

That not a worm is cloven in vain;
That not a moth with vain desire
Is shrivelled in a fruitless fire,
Or but subserves another's gain.

Behold, we know not anything;
I can but trust that good shall fall
At last—far off—at last, to all,
And every winter change to spring.

So runs my dream: but what am I?
An infant crying in the night:
An infant crying for the light:
And with no language but a cry.

55

The wish, that of the living whole
No life may fail beyond the grave,
Derives it not from what we have
The likest God within the soul?

Are God and Nature then at strife,
That Nature lends such evil dreams?
So careful of the type she seems,
So careless of the single life;

That I, considering everywhere
Her secret meaning in her deeds,
And finding that of fifty seeds
She often brings but one to bear,

Sec. 54. This section and Secs. 55–56 are full of references to the evolutionary philosophy, though Darwin's *Origin of Species* was not published until 1859. *Sec. 55.* **1–6. The wish . . . dreams.** Tennyson was no pantheist; "The Higher Pantheism" (page 926) is not pantheistic at all in the ordinary sense. For him the source of our religious convictions was "within ourselves," not in the world of nature. At Cambridge he voted no on the question "Is an intelligible First Cause deducible from the phenomena of the universe?" (See Sec. 124, ll. 5–8.)

I falter where I firmly trod,
And falling with my weight of cares
Upon the great world's altar-stairs
That slope through darkness up to God,

I stretch lame hands of faith, and grope,
And gather dust and chaff, and call
To what I feel is Lord of all,
And faintly trust the larger hope.

56

"So careful of the type?" but no.
From scarpèd cliff and quarried stone
She cries, "A thousand types are gone:
I care for nothing, all shall go.

"Thou makest thine appeal to me:
I bring to life, I bring to death:
The spirit does but mean the breath:
I know no more." And he, shall he,

Man, her last work, who seemed so fair,
Such splendid purpose in his eyes,
Who rolled the psalm to wintry skies,
Who built him fanes of fruitless prayer,

Who trusted God was love indeed
And love Creation's final law—
Though Nature, red in tooth and claw
With ravine, shrieked against his creed—

Who loved, who suffered countless ills,
Who battled for the True, the Just,
Be blown about the desert dust,
Or sealed within the iron hills?

No more? A monster then, a dream,
A discord. Dragons of the prime,
That tare each other in their slime,
Were mellow music matched with him.

O life as futile, then, as frail!
O for thy voice to soothe and bless!
What hope of answer, or redress?
Behind the veil, behind the veil.

Sec. 55. **20. the larger hope,** universal salvation, one of Tennyson's most earnest religious convictions. He said he "would rather know that he was to be lost eternally than not to know that the whole human race was to live eternally." When the Revised Version of the Bible was published, he was greatly disappointed that the revisers had kept the word *eternal* in the passage, "Depart from me, ye cursed, into the eternal fire" (Matthew 25:41). He had hoped that some such word as "Aeonian" might be employed. *Sec. 56.* **3. She,** Nature. **12. fanes,** temples, churches. **22–24. Dragons . . . with him.** If man's spiritual aspirations are doomed to disappointment, then the prehistoric monsters, who had no spiritual aspirations, were more harmoniously adjusted to their environment than he to his. **26. thy,** Hallam's.

78

Again at Christmas did we weave
The holly round the Christmas hearth;
The silent snow possessed the earth,
And calmly fell our Christmas-eve.

The yule-clog sparkled keen with frost,
No wing of wind the region swept,
But over all things brooding slept
The quiet sense of something lost.

As in the winters left behind,
Again our ancient games had place,
The mimic picture's breathing grace,
And dance and song and hoodman-blind.

Who showed a token of distress?
No single tear, no mark of pain:
O sorrow, then can sorrow wane?
O grief, can grief be changed to less?

O last regret, regret can die!
No—mixt with all this mystic frame,
Her deep relations are the same,
But with long use her tears are dry.

94

How pure at heart and sound in head,
With what divine affections bold
Should be the man whose thought would hold
An hour's communion with the dead.

In vain shalt thou, or any, call
The spirits from their golden day,
Except, like them, thou too canst say,
My spirit is at peace with all.

They haunt the silence of the breast,
Imaginations calm and fair,
The memory like a cloudless air,
The conscience as a sea at rest:

But when the heart is full of din,
And doubt beside the portal waits,
They can but listen at the gates,
And hear the household jar within.

96

You say, but with no touch of scorn,
Sweet-hearted, you, whose light-blue eyes

Sec. 78. **1. Christmas,** the second Christmas, 1834. **5. clog,** log. **11. mimic picture,** charades. *Sec. 96.* This section is addressed to a simple believer, evidently feminine, who does not understand the true significance of the poet's experience.

Are tender over drowning flies,
You tell me, doubt is Devil-born.

I know not: one indeed I knew
In many a subtle question versed,
Who touched a jarring lyre at first,
But ever strove to make it true:

Perplext in faith, but pure in deeds,
At last he beat his music out.
There lives more faith in honest doubt,
Believe me, than in half the creeds.

He fought his doubts and gathered strength,
He would not make his judgment blind,
He faced the spectres of the mind
And laid them: thus he came at length

To find a stronger faith his own;
And Power was with him in the night,
Which makes the darkness and the light,
And dwells not in the light alone,

But in the darkness and the cloud,
As over Sinaï's peaks of old,
While Israel made their gods of gold,
Although the trumpet blew so loud.

104

The time draws near the birth of Christ;
The moon is hid, the night is still;
A single church below the hill
Is pealing, folded in the mist.

A single peal of bells below,
That wakens at this hour of rest
A single murmur in the breast,
That these are not the bells I know.

Like strangers' voices here they sound,
In lands where not a memory strays,
Nor landmark breathes of other days,
But all is new unhallowed ground.

105

To-night ungathered let us leave
This laurel, let this holly stand:
We live within the stranger's land,
And strangely falls our Christmas-eve.

Our father's dust is left alone
And silent under other snows:
There in due time the woodbine blows,
The violet comes, but we are gone.

No more shall wayward grief abuse
The genial hour with mask and mime;
For change of place, like growth of time,
Has broke the bond of dying use.

Let cares that petty shadows cast,
By which our lives are chiefly proved,
A little spare the night I loved,
And hold it solemn to the past.

But let no footstep beat the floor,
Nor bowl of wassail mantle warm;
For who would keep an ancient form
Through which the spirit breathes no more?

Be neither song, nor game, nor feast;
Nor harp be touched, nor flute be blown;
No dance, no motion, save alone
What lightens in the lucid east

Of rising worlds by yonder wood.
Long sleeps the summer in the seed;
Run out your measured arcs, and lead
The closing cycle rich in good.

106

Ring out, wild bells, to the wild sky,
The flying cloud, the frosty light:
The year is dying in the night;
Ring out, wild bells, and let him die.

Ring out the old, ring in the new,
Ring, happy bells, across the snow:
The year is going, let him go;
Ring out the false, ring in the true.

Ring out the grief that saps the mind,
For those that here we see no more;
Ring out the feud of rich and poor,
Ring in redress to all mankind.

Ring out a slowly dying cause,
And ancient forms of party strife;
Ring in the nobler modes of life,
With sweeter manners, purer laws.

Ring out the want, the care, the sin,
The faithless coldness of the times;

Sec. 96. 5. **one,** Hallam. 21–24. **But . . . loud.** While Moses was receiving the Ten Commandments from God "in the thick darkness and the cloud" on Mt. Sinai, the Israelites were making and worshiping a golden calf. See Exodus 32. *Sec. 104.* **1. The time,** Christmas of 1837. **3. church,** Waltham Abbey, near Tennyson's home.

Sec. 105. 7. **blows,** blooms. *Sec. 106.* This famous New Year's song has been set to music by Gounod.

Ring out, ring out my mournful rhymes,
But ring the fuller minstrel in.

Ring out false pride in place and blood,
The civic slander and the spite;
Ring in the love of truth and right,
Ring in the common love of good.

Ring out old shapes of foul disease;
Ring out the narrowing lust of gold;
Ring out the thousand wars of old,
Ring in the thousand years of peace.

Ring in the valiant man and free,
The larger heart, the kindlier hand;
Ring out the darkness of the land,
Ring in the Christ that is to be.

107

It is the day when he was born,
A bitter day that early sank
Behind a purple-frosty bank
Of vapour, leaving night forlorn.

The time admits not flowers or leaves
To deck the banquet. Fiercely flies
The blast of North and East, and ice
Makes daggers at the sharpened eaves,

And bristles all the brakes and thorns
To yon hard crescent, as she hangs
Above the wood which grides and clangs
Its leafless ribs and iron horns

Together, in the drifts that pass
To darken on the rolling brine
That breaks the coast. But fetch the wine,
Arrange the board and brim the glass;

Bring in great logs and let them lie,
To make a solid core of heat;
Be cheerful-minded, talk and treat
Of all things ev'n as he were by;

We keep the day. With festal cheer,
With books and music, surely we
Will drink to him, whate'er he be,
And sing the songs he loved to hear.

108

I will not shut me from my kind,
And, lest I stiffen into stone,
I will not eat my heart alone,
Nor feed with sighs a passing wind:

What profit lies in barren faith,
And vacant yearning, though with might
To scale the heaven's highest height,
Or dive below the wells of Death?

What find I in the highest place,
But mine own phantom chanting hymns?
And on the depths of death there swims
The reflex of a human face.

I'll rather take what fruit may be
Of sorrow under human skies:
'Tis held that sorrow makes us wise,
Whatever wisdom sleep with thee.

113

'Tis held that sorrow makes us wise;
Yet how much wisdom sleeps with thee
Which not alone had guided me,
But served the seasons that may rise;

For can I doubt, who knew thee keen
In intellect, with force and skill
To strive, to fashion, to fulfil—
I doubt not what thou wouldst have been:

A life in civic action warm,
A soul on highest mission sent,
A potent voice of Parliament,
A pillar steadfast in the storm,

Should licensed boldness gather force,
Becoming, when the time has birth,
A lever to uplift the earth
And roll it in another course,

With thousand shocks that come and go,
With agonies, with energies,
With overthrowings, and with cries,
And undulations to and fro.

118

Contemplate all this work of Time,
The giant labouring in his youth;
Nor dream of human love and truth,
As dying Nature's earth and lime;

But trust that those we call the dead
Are breathers of an ampler day

28. thousand years of peace. See Revelation 20. *Sec. 107.* **1. day,** February 1. Its brevity is symbolical of Hallam's short life. **11. grides,** scrapes raspingly.

For ever nobler ends. They say,
The solid earth whereon we tread

In tracts of fluent heat began,
And grew to seeming-random forms,
The seeming prey of cyclic storms,
Till at the last arose the man;

Who throve and branched from clime to clime,
The herald of a higher race,
And of himself in higher place,
If so he type this work of time

Within himself, from more to more;
Or, crowned with attributes of woe
Like glories, move his course, and show
That life is not as idle ore,

But iron dug from central gloom,
And heated hot with burning fears,
And dipt in baths of hissing tears,
And battered with the shocks of doom

To shape and use. Arise and fly
The reeling Faun, the sensual feast;
Move upward, working out the beast,
And let the ape and tiger die.

123

There rolls the deep where grew the tree.
O earth, what changes hast thou seen!
There where the long street roars, hath been
The stillness of the central sea.

The hills are shadows, and they flow
From form to form, and nothing stands;
They melt like mist, the solid lands,
Like clouds they shape themselves and go.

But in my spirit will I dwell,
And dream my dream, and hold it true;
For though my lips may breathe adieu,
I cannot think the thing farewell.

124

That which we dare invoke to bless;
Our dearest faith; our ghastliest doubt;
He, They, One, All; within, without;
The Power in darkness whom we guess;

I found Him not in world or sun,
Or eagle's wing, or insect's eye;
Nor through the questions men may try,
The petty cobwebs we have spun.

If e'er when faith had fall'n asleep,
I heard a voice, "Believe no more,"
And heard an ever-breaking shore
That tumbled in the Godless deep,

A warmth within the breast would melt
The freezing reason's colder part,
And like a man in wrath the heart
Stood up and answered "I have felt."

No, like a child in doubt and fear:
But that blind clamour made me wise;
Then was I as a child that cries,
But, crying, knows his father near;

And what I am beheld again
What is, and no man understands;
And out of darkness came the hands
That reach through nature, moulding men.

126

Love is and was my Lord and King,
And in his presence I attend
To hear the tidings of my friend,
Which every hour his couriers bring.

Love is and was my King and Lord,
And will be, though as yet I keep
Within his court on earth, and sleep
Encompassed by his faithful guard,

And hear at times a sentinel
Who moves about from place to place,
And whispers to the worlds of space,
In the deep night, that all is well.

127

And all is well, though faith and form
Be sundered in the night of fear;
Well roars the storm to those that hear
A deeper voice across the storm,

Proclaiming social truth shall spread,
And justice, ev'n though thrice again
The red fool-fury of the Seine
Should pile her barricades with dead.

Sec. 118. **7–15. They say . . . place.** Another interesting reference to nineteenth-century science. **25–28. Arise and fly . . . tiger die.** The evolutionary hypothesis itself seemed to Tennyson to afford a sound scientific basis for morality.

16. "I have felt." To Tennyson, a mystic, man is more than his mind. *Sec. 127.* **6–8. thrice . . . dead.** There were revolutions in France in 1789, 1830, and 1848.

But ill for him that wears a crown,
  And him, the lazar, in his rags:
  They tremble, the sustaining crags;
The spires of ice are toppled down,

And molten up, and roar in flood;
  The fortress crashes from on high,
  The brute earth lightens to the sky,
And the great Aeon sinks in blood,

And compassed by the fires of Hell;
  While thou, dear spirit, happy star,
  O'erlook'st the tumult from afar,
And smilest, knowing all is well.

129

Dear friend, far off, my lost desire,
  So far, so near in woe and weal;
  O loved the most, when most I feel
There is a lower and a higher;

Known and unknown; human, divine;
  Sweet human hand and lips and eye;
  Dear heavenly friend that canst not die,
Mine, mine, for ever, ever mine;

Strange friend, past, present, and to be;
  Loved deeplier, darklier understood;
  Behold, I dream a dream of good,
And mingle all the world with thee.

130

Thy voice is on the rolling air;
  I hear thee where the waters run,
  Thou standest in the rising sun,
And in the setting thou art fair.

What art thou then? I cannot guess;
  But though I seem in star and flower
  To feel thee some diffusive power,
I do not therefore love thee less:

My love involves the love before;
  My love is vaster passion now;
  Though mixed with God and Nature thou,
I seem to love thee more and more.

Far off thou art, but ever nigh;
  I have thee still, and I rejoice;
  I prosper, circled with thy voice;
I shall not lose thee though I die.

131

O living will that shalt endure
  When all that seems shall suffer shock,
  Rise in the spiritual rock,
Flow through our deeds and make them pure,

That we may lift from out of dust
  A voice as unto him that hears,
  A cry above the conquered years
To one that with us works, and trust,

With faith that comes of self-control,
  The truths that never can be proved
  Until we close with all we loved,
And all we flow from, soul in soul.

from EPILOGUE

And rise, O moon, from yonder down,
  Till over down and over dale
  All night the shining vapour sail
And pass the silent-lighted town,

The white-faced halls, the glancing rills,
  And catch at every mountain head,
  And o'er the friths that branch and spread
Their sleeping silver through the hills;

And touch with shade the bridal doors,
  With tender gloom the roof, the wall;
  And breaking let the splendour fall
To spangle all the happy shores

By which they rest, and ocean sounds,
  And, star and system rolling past,
  A soul shall draw from out the vast
And strike his being into bounds,

And, moved through life of lower phase,
  Result in man, be born and think,
  And act and love, a closer link
Betwixt us and the crowning race

Of those that, eye to eye, shall look
  On knowledge; under whose command
  Is Earth and Earth's, and in their hand
Is Nature like an open book;

Sec. 131. **1. living will,** free will. **3. spiritual rock,** Christ. See 1 Corinthians 10:4. *Epilogue.* This is a nuptial song for Cecilia Tennyson and Edmund Low Lushington. Beginning with a funeral, *In Memoriam* ends "cheerfully," as Tennyson intended, with a wedding.

No longer half-akin to brute,
For all we thought and loved and did,
And hoped, and suffered, is but seed
Of what in them is flower and fruit;

Whereof the man, that with me trod
This planet, was a noble type
Appearing ere the times were ripe,
That friend of mine who lives in God,

That God, which ever lives and loves,
One God, one law, one element,
And one far-off divine event,
To which the whole creation moves.

from MAUD

Maud, a Monodrama, 1855, was one of Tennyson's favorites among his poems; "a little *Hamlet*," he called it. He loved to read aloud to his visitors—Henry James says that when he read his poems he took more out of them than he had put into them in writing—and *Maud* was the poem he generally chose. Though the work has some astonishing technical merits, several features—its morbidness, the role insanity plays in it, the jingoism of the Crimean War episode—long kept *Maud* from gaining the critical approval it has more recently been receiving. But, as in the case of *The Princess*, there can be no question as to the lyrics. "Come into the garden, Maud" has been set to music by Balfe.

O LET THE SOLID GROUND

1

O, let the solid ground
Not fail beneath my feet
Before my life has found
What some have found so sweet!
Then let come what come may,
What matter if I go mad,
I shall have had my day.

2

Let the sweet heavens endure,
Not close and darken above me
Before I am quite quite sure
That there is one to love me!
Then let come what come may
To a life that has been so sad,
I shall have had my day.

GO NOT, HAPPY DAY

Go not, happy day,
From the shining fields,
Go not, happy day,
Till the maiden yields.
Rosy is the West,
Rosy is the South,
Roses are her cheeks,
And a rose her mouth.
When the happy Yes
Falters from her lips,
Pass and blush the news
Over glowing ships;
Over blowing seas,
Over seas at rest,
Pass the happy news,
Blush it through the West;
Till the red man dance
By his red cedar-tree,
And the red man's babe
Leap, beyond the sea.
Blush from West to East,
Blush from East to West,
Till the West is East,
Blush it through the West.
Rosy is the West,
Rosy is the South,
Roses are her cheeks,
And a rose her mouth.

COME INTO THE GARDEN, MAUD

1

Come into the garden, Maud,
For the black bat, night, has flown,
Come into the garden, Maud,
I am here at the gate alone;
And the woodbine spices are wafted abroad,
And the musk of the rose is blown,

2

For a breeze of morning moves,
And the planet of Love is on high,
Beginning to faint in the light that she loves
On a bed of daffodil sky,
To faint in the light of the sun she loves,
To faint in his light, and to die.

3

All night have the roses heard
The flute, violin, bassoon;
All night has the casement jessamine stirred
To the dancers dancing in tune;
Till a silence fell with the waking bird,
And a hush with the setting moon.

4

I said to the lily, "There is but one
With whom she has heart to be gay.
When will the dancers leave her alone?
She is weary of dance and play."
Now half to the setting moon are gone,
And half to the rising day;
Low on the sand and loud on the stone
The last wheel echoes away.

5

I said to the rose, "The brief night goes
In babble and revel and wine.
O young lord-lover, what sighs are those,
For one that will never be thine?
But mine, but mine," so I sware to the rose,
"For ever and ever, mine."

6

And the soul of the rose went into my blood,
As the music clashed in the hall;
And long by the garden lake I stood,
For I heard your rivulet fall
From the lake to the meadow and on to the wood,
Our wood, that is dearer than all;

7

From the meadow your walks have left so sweet
That whenever a March-wind sighs
He sets the jewel-print of your feet
In violets blue as your eyes,
To the woody hollows in which we meet
And the valleys of Paradise.

8

The slender acacia would not shake
One long milk-bloom on the tree;
The white lake-blossom fell into the lake
As the pimpernel dozed on the lea;
But the rose was awake all night for your sake,
Knowing your promise to me;
The lilies and roses were all awake,
They sighed for the dawn and thee.

9

Queen rose of the rosebud garden of girls,
Come hither, the dances are done,
In gloss of satin and glimmer of pearls,
Queen lily and rose in one;
Shine out, little head, sunning over with curls,
To the flowers, and be their sun.

10

There has fallen a splendid tear
From the passion-flower at the gate.
She is coming, my dove, my dear;
She is coming, my life, my fate;
The red rose cries, "She is near, she is near";
And the white rose weeps, "She is late";
The larkspur listens, "I hear, I hear";
And the lily whispers, "I wait."

11

She is coming, my own, my sweet;
Were it ever so airy a tread,
My heart would hear her and beat,
Were it earth in an earthy bed;
My dust would hear her and beat,
Had I lain for a century dead;
Would start and tremble under her feet,
And blossom in purple and red.

O THAT 'TWERE POSSIBLE

1

O that 'twere possible
After long grief and pain
To find the arms of my true love
Round me once again!

2

When I was wont to meet her
In the silent woody places
By the home that gave me birth,
We stood tranced in long embraces
Mixt with kisses sweeter, sweeter
Than anything on earth.

3

A shadow flits before me,
Not thou, but like to thee:
Ah Christ, that it were possible
For one short hour to see
The souls we loved, that they might tell us
What and where they be!

4

It leads me forth at evening,
It lightly winds and steals
In a cold white robe before me,
When all my spirit reels
At the shouts, the leagues of lights,
And the roaring of the wheels.

5

Half the night I waste in sighs,
Half in dreams I sorrow after
The delight of early skies;
In a wakeful doze I sorrow
For the hand, the lips, the eyes,
For the meeting of the morrow,
The delight of happy laughter,
The delight of low replies.

6

'Tis a morning pure and sweet,
And a dewy splendour falls
On the little flower that clings
To the turrets and the walls;
'Tis a morning pure and sweet,
And the light and shadow fleet.
She is walking in the meadow,
And the woodland echo rings;
In a moment we shall meet.
She is singing in the meadow,
And the rivulet at her feet
Ripples on in light and shadow
To the ballad that she sings.

7

Do I hear her sing as of old,
My bird with the shining head,
My own dove with the tender eye?
But there rings on a sudden a passionate cry,
There is some one dying or dead,
And a sullen thunder is rolled;
For a tumult shakes the city,
And I wake, my dream is fled.
In the shuddering dawn, behold,
Without knowledge, without pity,
By the curtains of my bed
That abiding phantom cold!

8

Get thee hence, nor come again,
Mix not memory with doubt,
Pass, thou deathlike type of pain,
Pass and cease to move about!
'Tis the blot upon the brain
That *will* show itself without.

9

Then I rise, the eave-drops fall,
And the yellow vapours choke
The great city sounding wide;
The day comes, a dull red ball
Wrapt in drifts of lurid smoke
On the misty river-tide.

10

Through the hubbub of the market
I steal, a wasted frame;
It crosses here, it crosses there,
Through all that crowd confused and loud,
The shadow still the same;
And on my heavy eyelids
My anguish hangs like shame.

11

Alas for her that met me,
That heard me softly call,
Came glimmering through the laurels
At the quiet evenfall,
In the garden by the turrets
Of the old manorial hall!

12

Would the happy spirit descend,
From the realms of light and song,
In the chamber or the street,
As she looks among the blest,
Should I fear to greet my friend
Or to say "Forgive the wrong,"
Or to ask her, "Take me, sweet,
To the regions of thy rest"?

13

But the broad light glares and beats,
And the shadow flits and fleets
And will not let me be;
And I loathe the squares and streets,
And the faces that one meets,
Hearts with no love for me:
Always I long to creep
Into some still cavern deep,
There to weep, and weep, and weep
My whole soul out to thee.

MILTON

Alcaics

One of Tennyson's several "experiments in quantity." This one is an English imitation of a form of prosody invented by the Greek Alcaeus.

O mighty-mouthed inventor of harmonies,
O skilled to sing of Time or Eternity,
God-gifted organ-voice of England,
Milton, a name to resound for ages;
Whose Titan angels, Gabriel, Abdiel,
Starred from Jehovah's gorgeous armouries,

5. Gabriel, Abdiel, champions of God against Satan in Book B of *Paradise Lost.* Tennyson calls them Titans, after the giants of Greek mythology.

Tower, as the deep-domed empyrëan
Rings to the roar of an angel onset—
Me rather all that bowery loneliness,
The brooks of Eden mazily murmuring,
And bloom profuse and cedar arches
Charm, as a wanderer out in ocean,
Where some refulgent sunset of India
Streams o'er a rich ambrosial ocean isle,
And crimson-hued the stately palm-woods
Whisper in odorous heights of even.

THE HIGHER PANTHEISM

Tennyson here sees God in nature, but unlike the pantheist he does not permit his God to be swallowed up in nature; hence the title of this poem. See the note on *In Memoriam*, Sec. 55, and Swinburne's parody, "The Higher Pantheism in a Nutshell," page 1138.

Tennyson was one of the founders of the Metaphysical Society of Great Britain. In his later years he was much interested in occult speculation.

The sun, the moon, the stars, the seas, the hills and the plains—
Are not these, O Soul, the Vision of Him who reigns?

Is not the Vision He? though He be not that which He seems?
Dreams are true while they last, and do we not live in dreams?

Earth, these solid stars, this weight of body and limb,
Are they not sign and symbol of thy division from Him?

Dark is the world to thee: thyself art the reason why;
For is He not all but that which has power to feel "I am I"?

Glory about thee, without thee; and thou fulfillest thy doom,
Making Him broken gleams, and a stifled splendour and gloom.

Speak to Him, thou, for He hears, and Spirit with Spirit can meet—
Closer is He than breathing, and nearer than hands and feet.

God is law, say the wise; O Soul, and let us rejoice,
For if He thunder by law the thunder is yet His voice.

Law is God, say some: no God at all, says the fool;
For all we have power to see is a straight staff bent in a pool;

And the ear of man cannot hear, and the eye of man cannot see;
But if we could see and hear, this Vision—were it not He?

FLOWER IN THE CRANNIED WALL

Flower in the crannied wall,
I pluck you out of the crannies,
I hold you here, root and all, in my hand,
Little flower—but *if* I could understand
What you are, root and all, and all in all,
I should know what God and man is.

from THE IDYLLS OF THE KING

Tennyson's interest in King Arthur went back to his earliest years. "The Lady of Shalott" (page 952) was his first Arthurian poem; it was followed by "Sir Launcelot and Queen Guinevere," "Sir Galahad," and "Morte d'Arthur" (later taken up into "The Passing of Arthur"). At one time he seems to have planned an Arthurian drama. The general plan of the *Idylls* was first mapped out in 1855, and three poems appeared two years later. The other nine followed through the years until the last—"Balin and Balan"—came out in 1885. As they stand, the idylls are intended, in a general way, to trace the progress of the year from January to December.

Malory's *Morte d'Arthur* was the principal source, supplemented later by Lady Charlotte Guest's translation of the *Mabinogion*, a collection of Welsh tales.

The *Idylls* are allegorical, an

"old imperfect tale,
New-old, and shadowing Sense at war with Soul,"

only in a general way. In later years Tennyson complained of the critics: "They have taken my hobby, and ridden it too hard, and have explained some things too allegorically, although there is an allegorical or perhaps rather a parabolic drift in the poem."

Those who dislike Tennyson's Victorianism have generally little use for the *Idylls*. It is true that the inhabitants of Camelot as he presents them never convince us that they lived in the sixth century, but it is equally certain that he never intended them to. Seeing Arthur as the ideal Englishman, an inspiration to his countrymen in any age, the poet saw no reason why he should not present him as an incarnation of the particular ideals which appealed most strongly to Victorian gentlemen. What

The Higher Pantheism. **15. says the fool.** See Psalm 14:1.
Flower in . . . Wall. **6. is.** The singular verb is used because the central idea of the poem is the unity of all life.

one thinks of the result will depend on many factors. For most readers today the appeal of the *Idylls* resides less in the general design or symbolic intent than it does in the pictorial beauty and dramatic interest of such episodes as the one that follows.

THE PASSING OF ARTHUR

That story which the bold Sir Bedivere,
First made and latest left of all the knights,
Told, when the man was no more than a voice
In the white winter of his age, to those
With whom he dwelt, new faces, other minds.

For on their march to westward, Bedivere,
Who slowly paced among the slumbering host,
Heard in his tent the moanings of the King:

"I found Him in the shining of the stars,
I marked Him in the flowering of His fields,
But in His ways with men I find Him not.
I waged His wars, and now I pass and die.
O me! for why is all around us here
As if some lesser god had made the world,
But had not force to shape it as he would,
Till the High God behold it from beyond,
And enter it, and make it beautiful?
Or else as if the world were wholly fair,
But that these eyes of men are dense and dim,
And have not power to see it as it is:
Perchance, because we see not to the close;—
For I, being simple, thought to work His will,
And have but stricken with the sword in vain;
And all whereon I leaned in wife and friend
Is traitor to my peace, and all my realm
Reels back into the beast, and is no more.
My God, thou hast forgotten me in my death!
Nay—God my Christ—I pass but shall not die."

Then, ere that last weird battle in the west,
There came on Arthur sleeping, Gawain killed
In Lancelot's war, the ghost of Gawain blown
Along a wandering wind, and past his ear
Went shrilling: "Hollow, hollow all delight!
Hail, King! to-morrow thou shalt pass away.
Farewell! there is an isle of rest for thee.
And I am blown along a wandering wind,
And hollow, hollow, hollow all delight."
And fainter onward, like wild birds that change
Their season in the night and wail their way
From cloud to cloud, down the long wind the dream
Shrilled; but in going mingled with dim cries
Far in the moonlit haze among the hills,
As of some lonely city sacked by night,
When all is lost, and wife and child with wail
Pass to new lords; and Arthur woke and called:
"Who spake? A dream. O, light upon the wind,
Thine, Gawain, was the voice—are these dim cries
Thine? or doth all that haunts the waste and wild
Mourn, knowing it will go along with me?"

This heard the bold Sir Bedivere and spake:
"O me, my King, let pass whatever will,
Elves, and the harmless glamour of the field;
But in their stead thy name and glory cling
To all high places like a golden cloud
For ever; but as yet thou shalt not pass.
Light was Gawain in life, and light in death
Is Gawain, for the ghost is as the man;
And care not thou for dreams from him, but rise—
I hear the steps of Modred in the west,
And with him many of thy people, and knights
Once thine, whom thou hast loved, but grosser grown
Than heathen, spitting at their vows and thee.
Right well in heart they know thee for the King.
Arise, go forth and conquer as of old."

Then spake King Arthur to Sir Bedivere:
"Far other is this battle in the west
Whereto we move than when we strove in youth,
And brake the petty kings, and fought with Rome,
Or thrust the heathen from the Roman wall,
And shook him through the north. Ill doom is mine
To war against my people and my knights.
The king who fights his people fights himself.
And they my knights, who loved me once, the stroke
That strikes them dead is as my death to me.
Yet let us hence, and find or feel a way
Through this blind haze, which ever since I saw
One lying in the dust at Almesbury,
Hath folded in the passes of the world."

Then rose the King and moved his host by night,
And ever pushed Sir Modred, league by league,
Back to the sunset bound of Lyonnesse—
A land of old upheaven from the abyss
By fire, to sink into the abyss again;
Where fragments of forgotten peoples dwelt,

6. westward, to the battle against the rebel Modred. **24–26. And all . . . is no more.** The end of the noble fellowship of the Knights of the Round Table was marked by Arthur's discovery that his queen, Guinevere, and his trusted friend, Sir Lancelot, had betrayed him. **28. I pass but shall not die."** See ll. 191–92.

77. Almesbury, the nunnery where Guinevere had taken refuge. **81. Lyonnesse,** a fabled country supposed to have embraced the Scilly Islands and part of what is now Cornwall.

And the long mountains ended in a coast
Of ever-shifting sand, and far away
The phantom circle of a moaning sea.
There the pursuer could pursue no more,
And he that fled no further fly the King;
And there, that day when the great light of heaven
Burned at his lowest in the rolling year,
On the waste sand by the waste sea they closed.
Nor ever yet had Arthur fought a fight
Like this last, dim, weird battle of the west.
A death-white mist slept over sand and sea:
Whereof the chill, to him who breathed it, drew
Down with his blood, till all his heart was cold
With formless fear; and ev'n on Arthur fell
Confusion, since he saw not whom he fought.
For friend and foe were shadows in the mist,
And friend slew friend not knowing whom he slew;
And some had visions out of golden youth,
And some beheld the faces of old ghosts
Look in upon the battle; and in the mist
Was many a noble deed, many a base,
And chance and craft and strength in single fights,
And ever and anon with host to host
Shocks, and the splintering spear, the hard mail hewn,
Shield-breakings, and the clash of brands, the crash
Of battle-axes on shattered helms, and shrieks
After the Christ, of those who falling down
Looked up for heaven, and only saw the mist;
And shouts of heathen and the traitor knights,
Oaths, insult, filth, and monstrous blasphemies,
Sweat, writhings, anguish, labouring of the lungs
In that close mist, and cryings for the light,
Moans of the dying, and voices of the dead.

Last, as by some one death-bed after wail
Of suffering, silence follows, or through death
Or death-like swoon, thus over all that shore,
Save for some whisper of the seething seas,
A dead hush fell; but when the dolorous day
Grew drearier toward twilight falling, came
A bitter wind, clear from the North, and blew
The mist aside, and with that wind the tide
Rose, and the pale King glanced across the field
Of battle: but no man was moving there;
Nor any cry of Christian heard thereon,
Nor yet of heathen; only the wan wave
Brake in among dead faces, to and fro
Swaying the helpless hands, and up and down
Tumbling the hollow helmets of the fallen,
And shivered brands that once had fought with Rome,
And rolling far along the gloomy shores
The voice of days of old and days to be.

Then spake King Arthur to Sir Bedivere,
And whiter than the mist that all day long
Had held the field of battle was the King:

"Hearest thou this great voice that shakes the world,
And wastes the narrow realm whereon we move,
And beats upon the faces of the dead,
My dead, as though they had not died for me?—
O Bedivere, for on my heart hath fall'n
Confusion, till I know not what I am,
Nor whence I am, nor whether I be king.
Behold, I seem but king among the dead."

Then spake the bold Sir Bedivere: "My King,
King everywhere! and so the dead have kings,
There also will I worship thee as King.
Yet still thy life is whole, and still I live
Who love thee; but who hates thee, he that brought
The heathen back among us, yonder stands,
Modred, unharmed, the traitor of thine house."

Then spake the King: "My house hath been my doom.
But call not thou this traitor of my house
Who hath but dwelt beneath one roof with me.
My house are rather they who sware my vows,
Yea, even while they brake them, owned me King.
And well for thee, saying in my dark hour,
When all the purport of my throne hath failed,
That quick or dead thou holdest me for King.
King am I, whatsoever be their cry;
And one last act of kinghood shalt thou see
Yet, ere I pass." And uttering this the King
Made at the man: then Modred smote his liege
Hard on that helm which many a heathen sword
Had beaten thin; while Arthur at one blow,
Striking the last stroke with Excalibur,
Slew him, and, all but slain himself, he fell.

So all day long the noise of battle rolled
Among the mountains by the winter sea;
Until King Arthur's Table, man by man,
Had fall'n in Lyonnesse about their lord,
King Arthur. Then, because his wound was deep,
The bold Sir Bedivere uplifted him,
And bore him to a chapel nigh the field,
A broken chancel with a broken cross,
That stood on a dark strait of barren land:
On one side lay the Ocean, and on one
Lay a great water, and the moon was full.

90–91. when . . . lowest, at the winter solstice, about December 22.

Then spake King Arthur to Sir Bedivere:
"The sequel of to-day unsolders all
The goodliest fellowship of famous knights
Whereof this world holds record. Such a sleep
They sleep—the men I loved. I think that we
Shall never more, at any future time,
Delight our souls with talk of knightly deeds,
Walking about the gardens and the halls
Of Camelot, as in the days that were.
I perish by this people which I made,—
Though Merlin sware that I should come again
To rule once more—but, let what will be, be,
I am so deeply smitten through the helm
That without help I cannot last till morn.
Thou therefore take my brand Excalibur,
Which was my pride: for thou rememberest how
In those old days, one summer noon, an arm
Rose up from out the bosom of the lake,
Clothed in white samite, mystic, wonderful,
Holding the sword—and how I rowed across
And took it, and have worn it, like a king;
And, wheresoever I am sung or told
In aftertime, this also shall be known.
But now delay not: take Excalibur,
And fling him far into the middle mere:
Watch what thou seest, and lightly bring me word."

To him replied the bold Sir Bedivere:
"It is not meet, Sir King, to leave thee thus,
Aidless, alone, and smitten through the helm—
A little thing may harm a wounded man;
Yet I thy hest will all perform at full,
Watch what I see, and lightly bring thee word."

So saying, from the ruined shrine he stept,
And in the moon athwart the place of tombs,
Where lay the mighty bones of ancient men,
Old knights, and over them the sea-wind sang
Shrill, chill, with flakes of foam. He, stepping down
By zigzag paths, and juts of pointed rock,
Came on the shining levels of the lake.

There drew he forth the brand Excalibur,
And o'er him, drawing it, the winter moon,
Brightening the skirts of a long cloud, ran forth
And sparkled keen with frost against the hilt;
For all the haft twinkled with diamond sparks,
Myriads of topaz-lights, and jacinth-work
Of subtlest jewellery. He gazed so long
That both his eyes were dazzled as he stood,
This way and that dividing the swift mind,
In act to throw: but at the last it seemed
Better to leave Excalibur concealed
There in the many-knotted water-flags,
That whistled stiff and dry about the marge.
So strode he back slow to the wounded King.

Then spake King Arthur to Sir Bedivere:
"Hast thou performed my mission which I gave?
What is it thou hast seen? or what hast heard?"

And answer made the bold Sir Bedivere:
"I heard the ripple washing in the reeds,
And the wild water lapping on the crag."

To whom replied King Arthur, faint and pale:
"Thou hast betrayed thy nature and thy name,
Not rendering true answer, as beseemed
Thy fealty, nor like a noble knight;
For surer sign had followed, either hand,
Or voice, or else a motion of the mere.
This is a shameful thing for men to lie.
Yet now, I charge thee, quickly go again,
As thou art lief and dear, and do the thing
I bade thee, watch, and lightly bring me word."

Then went Sir Bedivere the second time
Across the ridge, and paced beside the mere,
Counting the dewy pebbles, fixed in thought;
But when he saw the wonder of the hilt,
How curiously and strangely chased, he smote
His palms together, and he cried aloud:

"And if indeed I cast the brand away,
Surely a precious thing, one worthy note,
Should thus be lost for ever from the earth,
Which might have pleased the eyes of many men.
What good should follow this, if this were done?
What harm, undone? Deep harm to disobey,
Seeing obedience is the bond of rule.
Were it well to obey then, if a king demand
An act unprofitable, against himself?
The King is sick, and knows not what he does.
What record, or what relic of my lord
Should be to aftertime, but empty breath
And rumours of a doubt? But were this kept,
Stored in some treasure-house of mighty kings,
Some one might show it at a joust of arms,
Saying: 'King Arthur's sword, Excalibur,
Wrought by the lonely maiden of the Lake.
Nine years she wrought it, sitting in the deeps
Upon the hidden bases of the hills.'
So might some old man speak in the aftertime
To all the people, winning reverence.
But now much honour and much fame were lost."

189. Camelot, the seat of Arthur's court. **205.** mere, lake. **211.** hest, command.

248. lief, beloved.

So spake he, clouded with his own conceit,
And hid Excalibur the second time,
And so strode back slow to the wounded King.

Then spoke King Arthur, breathing heavily:
"What is it thou hast seen? or what hast heard?"

And answer made the bold Sir Bedivere:
"I heard the water lapping on the crag,
And the long ripple washing in the reeds."

To whom replied King Arthur, much in wrath:
"Ah miserable and unkind, untrue,
Unknightly, traitor-hearted! Woe is me!
Authority forgets a dying king,
Laid widowed of the power in his eye
That bowed the will. I see thee what thou art,
For thou, the latest-left of all my knights,
In whom should meet the offices of all,
Thou wouldst betray me for the precious hilt;
Either from lust of gold, or like a girl
Valuing the giddy pleasure of the eyes.
Yet, for a man may fail in duty twice,
And the third time may prosper, get thee hence;
But, if thou spare to fling Excalibur,
I will arise and slay thee with my hands."

Then quickly rose Sir Bedivere, and ran,
And, leaping down the ridges lightly, plunged
Among the bulrush beds, and clutched the sword,
And strongly wheeled and threw it. The great brand
Made lightnings in the splendour of the moon,
And flashing round and round, and whirled in an arch,
Shot like a streamer of the northern morn,
Seen where the moving isles of winter shock
By night, with noises of the Northern Sea.
So flashed and fell the brand Excalibur:
But ere he dipt the surface, rose an arm
Clothed in white samite, mystic, wonderful,
And caught him by the hilt, and brandished him
Three times, and drew him under in the mere.
And lightly went the other to the King.

Then spoke King Arthur, drawing thicker breath:
"Now see I by thine eyes that this is done.
Speak out: what is it thou hast heard, or seen?"

And answer made the bold Sir Bedivere:
"Sir King, I closed mine eyelids, lest the gems

278. conceit, fancy. **307. streamer of the northern morn,** Aurora Borealis. **308. moving isles,** icebergs.

Should blind my purpose, for I never saw,
Nor shall see, here or elsewhere, till I die,
Not though I live three lives of mortal men,
So great a miracle as yonder hilt.
Then with both hands I flung him, wheeling him;
But when I looked again, behold an arm,
Clothed in white samite, mystic, wonderful,
That caught him by the hilt, and brandished him
Three times, and drew him under in the mere."

And answer made King Arthur, breathing hard:
"My end draws nigh; 'tis time that I were gone.
Make broad thy shoulders to receive my weight,
And bear me to the margin; yet I fear
My wound hath taken cold, and I shall die."

So saying, from the pavement he half rose,
Slowly, with pain, reclining on his arm,
And looking wistfully with wide blue eyes
As in a picture. Him Sir Bedivere
Remorsefully regarded through his tears,
And would have spoken, but he found not words;
Then took with care, and kneeling on one knee,
O'er both his shoulders drew the languid hands,
And rising bore him through the place of tombs.

But, as he walked, King Arthur panted hard,
Like one that feels a nightmare on his bed
When all the house is mute. So sighed the King,
Muttering and murmuring at his ear, "Quick, quick!
I fear it is too late, and I shall die."
But the other swiftly strode from ridge to ridge,
Clothed with his breath, and looking, as he walked,
Larger than human on the frozen hills.
He heard the deep behind him, and a cry
Before. His own thought drove him like a goad.
Dry clashed his harness in the icy caves
And barren chasms, and all to left and right
The bare black cliff clanged round him, as he based
His feet on juts of slippery crag that rang
Sharp-smitten with the dint of armèd heels—
And on a sudden, lo, the level lake,
And the long glories of the winter moon!

Then saw they how there hove a dusky barge,
Dark as a funeral scarf from stem to stern,
Beneath them; and descending they were ware
That all the decks were dense with stately forms,
Black-stoled, black-hooded, like a dream—by these
Three Queens with crowns of gold: and from them rose

366. Three Queens. Malory makes them King Arthur's sister, Queen Morgen le Fay; the Queen of Northgales; the Queen of the Waste Lands. When Tennyson was asked

A cry that shivered to the tingling stars,
And, as it were one voice, an agony
Of lamentation, like a wind that shrills
All night in a waste land, where no one comes,
Or hath come, since the making of the world.

Then murmured Arthur, "Place me in the barge."
So to the barge they came. There those three Queens
Put forth their hands, and took the King, and wept.
But she that rose the tallest of them all
And fairest, laid his head upon her lap,
And loosed the shattered casque, and chafed his hands,
And called him by his name, complaining loud,
And dropping bitter tears against a brow
Striped with dark blood: for all his face was white
And colourless, and like the withered moon
Smote by the fresh beam of the springing east;
And all his greaves and cuisses dashed with drops
Of onset; and the light and lustrous curls—
That made his forehead like a rising sun
High from the dais-throne—were parched with dust;
Or, clotted into points and hanging loose,
Mixed with the knightly growth that fringed his lips.
So like a shattered column lay the King;
Not like that Arthur who, with lance in rest,
From spur to plume a star of tournament,
Shot through the lists at Camelot, and charged
Before the eyes of ladies and of kings.

Then loudly cried the bold Sir Bedivere:
"Ah! my Lord Arthur, whither shall I go?
Where shall I hide my forehead and my eyes?
For now I see the true old times are dead,
When every morning brought a noble chance,
And every chance brought out a noble knight.
Such times have been not since the light that led
The holy Elders with the gift of myrrh.
But now the whole Round Table is dissolved
Which was an image of the mighty world;
And I, the last, go forth companionless,
And the days darken round me, and the years,
Among new men, strange faces, other minds."

And slowly answered Arthur from the barge:
"The old order changeth, yielding place to new,
And God fulfils himself in many ways,
Lest one good custom should corrupt the world.
Comfort thyself; what comfort is in me?
I have lived my life, and that which I have done
May He within himself make pure! but thou,
If thou shouldst never see my face again,
Pray for my soul. More things are wrought by prayer
Than this world dreams of. Wherefore, let thy voice
Rise like a fountain for me night and day.
For what are men better than sheep or goats
That nourish a blind life within the brain,
If, knowing God, they lift not hands of prayer
Both for themselves and those who call them friend?
For so the whole round earth is every way
Bound by gold chains about the feet of God.
But now farewell. I am going a long way
With these thou seest—if indeed I go
(For all my mind is clouded with a doubt)—
To the island-valley of Avilion;
Where falls not hail, or rain, or any snow,
Nor ever wind blows loudly; but it lies
Deep-meadowed, happy, fair with orchard lawns
And bowery hollows crowned with summer sea,
Where I will heal me of my grievous wound."

So said he, and the barge with oar and sail
Moved from the brink, like some full-breasted swan
That, fluting a wild carol ere her death,
Ruffles her pure cold plume, and takes the flood
With swarthy webs. Long stood Sir Bedivere
Revolving many memories, till the hull
Looked one black dot against the verge of dawn,
And on the mere the wailing died away.

whether, in the allegorical interpretation, the three queens were to be identified as Faith, Hope, and Charity, he replied: "They mean that and they do not. They are also those three Graces, but they are much more. I hate to be tied down to say, '*This* means *that*,' because the thought within the image is much more than any one interpretation."—Hallam, Lord Tennyson, *Alfred, Lord Tennyson, a Memoir*, Macmillan, 1897. **401. The holy Elders,** the Magi, who brought gold and frankincense and myrrh to the infant Jesus (see Matthew 2:1–12).

THE REVENGE

A Ballad of the Fleet

The sea fight commemorated in this poem took place in 1591; Tennyson's main source was Sir Walter Raleigh's *Report of the Truth of the Fight about the Isles of Azores This Last Summer*. For the hero, see A. L. Rowse, *Sir Richard Grenville of the Revenge* (Houghton Mifflin, 1937).

"The Revenge" is notable as a spirited poem of action. Professor Alden [1] made the following pertinent comment on the verse form Tennyson employed:

408. The old order . . . new. See "The Coming of Arthur" (*Idylls of the King*), l. 508. **427. Avilion,** Avalon. **435. wild carol,** a reference to the old belief that the swan sings just before her death.

[1] Raymond M. Alden, *Alfred Tennyson, How To Know Him*, Bobbs-Merrill, 1917.

"At the height of Tennyson's rhythmical symphonies we should probably place the ballad of 'The Revenge.' No one, so far as I know, has ever instanced this poem under the head of 'free verse,' yet it would be very difficult to name its metrical type. Just as one is prepared to call it 'trochaic' it becomes clearly trisyllabic; just as we are sure it is 'anapaestic' it falls back into the rhythm of twos or fours which carries Sir Richard's final march . . . and the hurrying, windy epilogue which dismisses the whole Armada to destruction. It is all a metrical *tour de force* (not to speak here of its more inward qualities) which defies both conventional critic and uncrafty imitator."

1

At Flores in the Azores Sir Richard Grenville lay,
And a pinnace, like a fluttered bird, came flying from far away:
"Spanish ships of war at sea! we have sighted fifty-three!"
Then sware Lord Thomas Howard: "'Fore God I am no coward;
But I cannot meet them here, for my ships are out of gear,
And the half my men are sick. I must fly, but follow quick.
We are six ships of the line; can we fight with fifty-three?"

2

Then spake Sir Richard Grenville: "I know you are no coward;
You fly them for a moment to fight with them again.
But I've ninety men and more that are lying sick ashore.
I should count myself the coward if I left them, my Lord Howard,
To these Inquisition dogs and the devildoms of Spain."

3

So Lord Howard past away with five ships of war that day,
Till he melted like a cloud in the silent summer heaven;
But Sir Richard bore in hand all his sick men from the land
Very carefully and slow,
Men of Bideford in Devon,
And we laid them on the ballast down below;
For we brought them all aboard,
And they blest him in their pain, that they were not left to Spain,
To the thumbscrew and the stake, for the glory of the Lord.

4

He had only a hundred seamen to work the ship and to fight,
And he sailed away from Flores till the Spaniard came in sight,
With his huge sea-castles heaving upon the weather bow.
"Shall we fight or shall we fly?
Good Sir Richard, tell us now,
For to fight is but to die!
There'll be little of us left by the time this sun be set."
And Sir Richard said again: "We be all good English men.
Let us bang these dogs of Seville, the children of the devil,
For I never turned my back upon Don or devil yet."

5

Sir Richard spoke and he laughed, and we roared a hurrah, and so
The little Revenge ran on sheer into the heart of the foe,
With her hundred fighters on deck, and her ninety sick below;
For half of their fleet to the right and half to the left were seen,
And the little Revenge ran on through the long sea-lane between.

6

Thousands of their soldiers looked down from their decks and laughed,
Thousands of their seamen made mock at the mad little craft
Running on and on, till delayed
By their mountain-like San Philip that, of fifteen hundred tons,
And up-shadowing high above us with her yawning tiers of guns,
Took the breath from our sails, and we stayed.

7

And while now the great San Philip hung above us like a cloud
Whence the thunderbolt will fall
Long and loud,
Four galleons drew away
From the Spanish fleet that day,

7. ships of the line, fighting ships. **12. Inquisition.** The special function of the "holy office" was to deal with cases of heresy. It was especially active in Spain. **17. Bideford,** Grenville's birthplace. It plays a considerable part in Kingsley's novel of the Elizabethan sea rovers, *Westward Ho!*

21. To . . . the Lord, that is, to the Inquisition.

And two upon the larboard and two upon the starboard lay,
And the battle-thunder broke from them all.

8

But anon the great San Philip, she bethought herself and went,
Having that within her womb that had left her ill content;
And the rest they came aboard us, and they fought us hand to hand,
For a dozen times they came with their pikes and musqueteers,
And a dozen times we shook 'em off as a dog that shakes his ears
When he leaps from the water to the land.

9

And the sun went down, and the stars came out far over the summer sea,
But never a moment ceased the fight of the one and the fifty-three.
Ship after ship, the whole night long, their high-built galleons came,
Ship after ship, the whole night long, with her battle-thunder and flame;
Ship after ship, the whole night long, drew back with her dead and her shame.
For some were sunk and many were shattered, and so could fight us no more—
God of battles, was ever a battle like this in the world before?

10

For he said, "Fight on! fight on!"
Though his vessel was all but a wreck;
And it chanced that, when half of the short summer night was gone,
With a grisly wound to be drest he had left the deck,
But a bullet struck him that was dressing it suddenly dead,
And himself he was wounded again in the side and the head,
And he said, "Fight on! fight on!"

11

And the night went down, and the sun smiled out far over the summer sea,
And the Spanish fleet with broken sides lay round us all in a ring;
But they dared not touch us again, for they feared that we still could sting,
So they watched what the end would be.
And we had not fought them in vain,
But in perilous plight were we,
Seeing forty of our poor hundred were slain,
And half of the rest of us maimed for life
In the crash of the cannonades and the desperate strife;
And the sick men down in the hold were most of them stark and cold,
And the pikes were all broken or bent, and the powder was all of it spent;
And the masts and the rigging were lying over the side;
But Sir Richard cried in his English pride,
"We have fought such a fight for a day and a night
As may never be fought again!
We have won great glory, my men!
And a day less or more
At sea or ashore,
We die—does it matter when?
Sink me the ship, Master Gunner—sink her, split her in twain!
Fall into the hands of God, not into the hands of Spain!"

12

And the gunner said "Ay, ay," but the seamen made reply:
"We have children, we have wives,
And the Lord hath spared our lives.
We will make the Spaniard promise, if we yield, to let us go;
We shall live to fight again and to strike another blow."
And the lion there lay dying, and they yielded to the foe.

13

And the stately Spanish men to their flagship bore him then,
Where they laid him by the mast, old Sir Richard caught at last,
And they praised him to his face with their courtly foreign grace;
But he rose upon their decks, and he cried:
"I have fought for Queen and Faith like a valiant man and true;
I have only done my duty as a man is bound to do:
With a joyful spirit I Sir Richard Grenville die!"
And he fell upon their decks, and he died.

14

And they stared at the dead that had been so valiant and true,
And had holden the power and glory of Spain so cheap
That he dared her with one little ship and his English few;
Was he devil or man? He was devil for aught they knew,
But they sank his body with honour down into the deep,
And they manned the Revenge with a swarthier alien crew,
And away she sailed with her loss and longed for her own;
When a wind from the lands they had ruined awoke from sleep,
And the water began to heave and the weather to moan,
And or ever that evening ended a great gale blew,
And a wave like the wave that is raised by an earthquake grew,
Till it smote on their hulls and their sails and their masts and their flags,
And the whole sea plunged and fell on the shot-shattered navy of Spain,
And the little Revenge herself went down by the island crags
To be lost evermore in the main.

RIZPAH

17—

In the Biblical story (2 Samuel 21:1–14), God indicates his disapproval of the wrong King Saul had done the Gibeonites by sending famine upon Israel; David, therefore, is compelled to deliver up the sons of Rizpah to be slain as a sacrifice. "And Rizpah . . . took sackcloth, and spread it for her upon the rock, from the beginning of harvest until water dropped upon them from heaven, and suffered neither the birds of the air to rest on them by day, nor the beasts of the field by night." When the rains fall, it is clear that God has accepted the sacrifice; Rizpah's sons may now be taken down and buried and their souls may find rest in Sheol.

Tennyson sees Rizpah's spirit living again in an English mother of the eighteenth century who collects the bones of her son as they fall from the gallows where he has been hanged in chains for robbing the mail, because she wants him to be able to rise up whole on the Judgment Day and also because she thinks it necessary for his salvation that he should be buried in consecrated ground. He took the suggestion from an incident reported in a current magazine.

"Rizpah" is one of Tennyson's great achievements; it convinced Swinburne that the laureate was a greater poet than Alfred de Musset. The pathos of the situation is deepened by having the heroic mother harassed upon her deathbed by an unsympathetic parish visitor, a fanatical Calvinist.

For another version of the Rizpah story, see Amy Lowell, "Dried Marjoram," in *Legends*, 1921, written independently of Tennyson's poem, which the author did not read until afterward.

1

Wailing, wailing, wailing, the wind over land and sea—
And Willy's voice in the wind, "O mother, come out to me!"
Why should he call me to-night, when he knows that I cannot go?
For the downs are as bright as day, and the full moon stares at the snow.

2

We should be seen, my dear; they would spy us out of the town.
The loud black nights for us, and the storm rushing over the down,
When I cannot see my own hand, but am led by the creak of the chain,
And grovel and grope for my son till I find myself drenched with the rain.

3

Anything fallen again? nay—what was there left to fall?
I have taken them home, I have numbered the bones, I have hidden them all.
What am I saying? and what are *you?* do you come as a spy?
Falls? what falls? who knows? As the tree falls so must it lie.

4

Who let her in? how long has she been? you—what have you heard?
Why did you sit so quiet? you never have spoken a word.
O—to pray with me—yes—a lady—none of their spies—
But the night has crept into my heart, and begun to darken my eyes.

5

Ah—you, that have lived so soft, what should *you* know of the night,

The blast and the burning shame and the bitter frost and the fright?
I have done it, while you were asleep—you were only made for the day.
I have gathered my baby together—and now you may go your way.

6

Nay—for it's kind of you, Madam, to sit by an old dying wife.
But say nothing hard of my boy, I have only an hour of life.
I kissed my boy in the prison, before he went out to die.
"They dared me to do it," he said, and he never has told me a lie.
I whipt him for robbing an orchard once when he was but a child—
"The farmer dared me to do it," he said; he was always so wild—
And idle—and couldn't be idle—my Willy—he never could rest.
The King should have made him a soldier, he would have been one of his best.

7

But he lived with a lot of wild mates, and they never would let him be good;
They swore that he dare not rob the mail, and he swore that he would;
And he took no life, but he took one purse, and when all was done
He flung it among his fellows—"I'll none of it," said my son.

8

I came into court to the Judge and the lawyers. I told them my tale,
God's own truth—but they killed him, they killed him for robbing the mail.
They hanged him in chains for a show—we had always borne a good name—
To be hanged for a thief—and then put away—isn't that enough shame?
Dust to dust—low down—let us hide! but they set him so high
That all the ships of the world could stare at him, passing by.
God 'ill pardon the hell-black raven and horrible fowls of the air,
But not the black heart of the lawyer who killed him and hanged him there.

9

And the jailer forced me away. I had bid him my last good-bye;
They had fastened the door of his cell. "O mother!" I heard him cry.
I couldn't get back though I tried, he had something further to say,
And now I never shall know it. The jailer forced me away.

10

Then since I couldn't but hear that cry of my boy that was dead,
They seized me and shut me up: they fastened me down on my bed.
"Mother, O mother!"—he called in the dark to me year after year—
They beat me for that, they beat me—you know that I couldn't but hear;
And then at the last they found I had grown so stupid and still
They let me abroad again—but the creatures had worked their will.

11

Flesh of my flesh was gone, but bone of my bone was left—
I stole them all from the lawyers—and you, will you call it a theft?—
My baby, the bones that had sucked me, the bones that had laughed and had cried—
Theirs? O no! they are mine—not theirs—they had moved in my side.

12

Do you think I was scared by the bones? I kissed 'em, I buried 'em all—
I can't dig deep, I am old—in the night by the churchyard wall.
My Willy 'ill rise up whole when the trumpet of judgment 'ill sound,
But I charge you never to say that I laid him in holy ground.

13

They would scratch him up—they would hang him again on the cursed tree.
Sin? O, yes—we are sinners, I know—let all that be,
And read me a Bible verse of the Lord's good will toward men—

"Full of compassion and mercy, the Lord"—let me hear it again;
"Full of compassion and mercy—long-suffering." Yes, O yes!
For the lawyer is born but to murder—the Saviour lives but to bless.
He'll never put on the black cap except for the worst of the worst,
And the first may be last—I have heard it in church —and the last may be first.
Suffering—O, long-suffering—yes, as the Lord must know,
Year after year in the mist and the wind and the shower and the snow.

14

Heard, have you? what? they have told you he never repented his sin.
How do they know it? are *they* his mother? are *you* of his kin?
Heard! have you ever heard, when the storm on the downs began,
The wind that 'ill wail like a child and the sea that 'ill moan like a man?

15

Election, Election and Reprobation—it's all very well.
But I go to-night to my boy, and I shall not find him in Hell.
For I cared so much for my boy that the Lord has looked into my care,
And He means me I'm sure to be happy with Willy, I know not where.

16

And if *he* be lost—but to save *my* soul, that is all your desire:
Do you think that I care for *my* soul if my boy be gone to the fire?
I have been with God in the dark—go, go, you may leave me alone—
You never have borne a child—you are just as hard as a stone.

62. "Full . . . the Lord." See Psalm 86:15. **65. black cap,** worn by English judges in pronouncing the death sentence. **66. And the first . . . may be first.** See Matthew 19:30. **73. Election . . . Reprobation,** a reference to the Calvinistic belief that some persons are foreordained to salvation and others to damnation.

17

Madam, I beg your pardon! I think that you mean to be kind,
But I cannot hear what you say for my Willy's voice in the wind—
The snow and the sky so bright—he used but to call in the dark,
And he calls to me now from the church and not from the gibbet—for hark!
Nay—you can hear it yourself—it is coming—shaking the walls—
Willy—the moon's in a cloud—Good-night. I am going. He calls.

CROSSING THE BAR

In this poem, which, at his own request, is placed at the end of his collected poems, Tennyson describes death in terms of a sea voyage. A bar is any bank of sand, gravel, or the like across the mouth of a river; it is generally advisable to take the bar when there is plenty of water over it. The poet is embarking for the other world; the tide is full; but is now ebbing back to the sea. After taking the ship out across the bar the pilot drops off and returns to his station on land; at this time, a passenger might well expect to see him "face to face." Ordinarily no such desire would be felt very strongly, but Tennyson uses the term to indicate "That Divine and Unseen Who is always guiding us."

Sunset and evening star,
  And one clear call for me!
And may there be no moaning of the bar,
  When I put out to sea,

But such a tide as moving seems asleep,
  Too full for sound and foam,
When that which drew from out the boundless deep
  Turns again home.

Twilight and evening bell,
  And after that the dark!
And may there be no sadness of farewell,
  When I embark;

For though from out our bourne of Time and Place
  The flood may bear me far,
I hope to see my Pilot face to face
  When I have crost the bar.

Robert Browning
1812–1889

Robert Browning was born at Camberwell, just across the Thames from London, May 7, 1812. His mother, who was of Scotch and German ancestry, influenced especially his love of music, his interest in fauna and flora, and his religion. The poet's father, having brought displeasure to his family by objecting to the use of slave labor on the family plantation in the West Indies, had been left to make his own way in the Bank of England. This did not prevent him from collecting a library of six thousand well-chosen volumes in many languages, almost all of which his son devoured at an early age. Though Browning had many tutors in language, science, and music, he attended school but seldom. Oxford and Cambridge were not open to Dissenters in his day, and less than a year at the new University of London was enough. "Italy was my university," he once said, but he had another which was more important—his father's library. Browning acquired more learning there than he ever realized, and his celebrated obscurity is due largely to his unawareness of this fact. *Sordello*, for example, alienated English readers for many years because the intimate details of the political struggles in medieval Italy, which were as plain as the palm of his hand to Browning, were not at all familiar to most readers of his poem.

Browning's first poetic passion was for Byron, but of the unpublished volume *Incondita*, which testifies to this influence, little has survived. Byron was superseded by Shelley, who appears clearly in *Pauline*, 1833. In this extremely uncharacteristic work, Browning manifests the very young man's intense preoccupation with himself, conducting, as it were, his spiritual ablutions in public. This was a mistake he was never to make again. *Paracelsus*, 1835, marks the beginning of the true Browning.

In 1837, Browning's play, *Strafford*, was produced by W. C. Macready; five years later, the same great actor-manager brought out *A Blot in the 'Scutcheon.* Browning's plays interest us chiefly as preparation for his dramatic monologues; while he had great skill in developing a situation, he could never have mastered the practical requirements of playwriting. Yet several of his dramas have had modest stage histories.

In 1841 Browning found himself with three plays on his hands—*Pippa Passes*, *King Victor and King Charles*, and *The Return of the Druses*. Edward Moxon agreed to publish these, as well as a series of poems, in cheap pamphlet form. The ensuing series of pamphlets was called *Bells and Pomegranates*, 1841–46. About the time publication was completed Browning married Elizabeth Barrett (see the introductory note to Mrs. Browning's poems) and went to live in Italy.

In 1849 the first edition of Browning's *Collected Poems* came out. This was followed in 1850 by *Christmas Eve and Easter Day*, in 1855 by *Men and Women*. Though *Men and Women* contained some of his very finest poems, Browning had not yet found his public; he did not publish another book for nine years. After the death of Mrs. Browning in 1861, he returned to London with their only child.

Then, after a period of painful readjustment to life, Browning entered upon his final phase as what Henry James called an "accomplished, saturated, sane, sound man of the London world and the world of culture." In 1864 he published *Dramatis Personae*. In 1868, the six-volume edition of his *Collected Poems* appeared, and at the same time he earned a wider hearing with *The Ring and the Book*, his greatest achievement.

Like Tennyson, Browning was immensely productive during his later years, but with the exception of the two series of *Dramatic Idyls*, 1879–80, few of the poems he wrote during this period are now widely read. His work during these years was both increasingly obscure and increasingly filled with metaphysical speculation. *Asolando*, 1889, was his last book.

By this time Browning had received high academic honors from Oxford, and Dr. F. J. Furnivall had founded the famous Browning Society. After long neglect, the poet was now a classic in his own lifetime; he carried his late-won honors lightly. The Browning Society became a veritable symbol of late nineteenth-century culture all over the English-speaking world. At the height of his fame, Browning died in Venice, December 12, 1889.

Although the period of his great personal "vogue" is past, Browning has continued to be one of the most widely read and admired of English poets. And there is reason for thinking his literary reputation actually rests on a solider base today than it did a few decades ago when adulation of Browning was not always discriminating nor always primarily concerned with literary values. His constant and vigorous statement of faith must ever be exhilarating to many readers; Browning remains one of the great affirmative voices of English literature. But it is in his bold energy of expression, the vehicle for remarkable psychological insight into the motives and passions of individual human beings, that his poetic genius makes itself most enduringly felt. Moreover, Browning's psychological method and the unconventional "broken utterance" he often employs have influenced modern poets to an extent they have not always acknowledged or perhaps always realized.

from PIPPA PASSES

The song of the little silk-weaver in the drama *Pippa Passes,* a study in unconscious influence, is generally taken as an expression of Browning's own optimism. Though it is unfair to take any dramatic utterance out of its context and attribute it to the poet personally, the spirit of these lines is not uncharacteristic of Browning.

The year's at the spring
And day's at the morn;
Morning's at seven;
The hill-side's dew-pearled;
The lark's on the wing;
The snail's on the thorn:
God's in his heaven—
All's right with the world!

CAVALIER TUNES

Browning wrote three dramatic lyrics from the point of view of King Charles I's supporters in the English Civil War. The speakers are imaginary characters.

I. MARCHING ALONG

Kentish Sir Byng stood for his King,
Bidding the crop-headed Parliament swing:
And, pressing a troop unable to stoop
And see the rogues flourish and honest folk droop,
Marched them along, fifty-score strong,
Great-hearted gentlemen, singing this song.

God for King Charles! Pym and such carles
To the Devil that prompts 'em their treasonous parles!
Cavaliers, up! Lips from the cup,
Hands from the pasty, nor bite take nor sup
Till you're—
CHORUS.—Marching along, fifty-score strong,
Great-hearted gentlemen, singing this song.

Hampden to hell, and his obsequies' knell.
Serve Hazelrig, Fiennes, and young Harry as well!
England, good cheer! Rupert is near!
Kentish and loyalists, keep we not here,
CHORUS.—Marching along, fifty-score strong,
Great-hearted gentlemen, singing this song?

Then, God for King Charles! Pym and his snarls
To the Devil that pricks on such pestilent carles!
Hold by the right, you double your might;
So, onward to Nottingham, fresh for the fight,
CHORUS.—March we along, fifty-score strong,
Great-hearted gentlemen, singing this song!

2. GIVE A ROUSE

King Charles, and who'll do him right now?
King Charles, and who's ripe for fight now?
Give a rouse: here's, in hell's despite now,
King Charles!
Who gave me the goods that went since?
Who raised me the house that sank once?
Who helped me to gold I spent since?
Who found me in wine you drank once?
CHORUS.—King Charles, and who'll do him right now?
King Charles, and who's ripe for fight now?
Give a rouse: here's, in hell's despite now,
King Charles!

To whom used my boy George quaff else,
By the old fool's side that begot him?
For whom did he cheer and laugh else,
While Noll's damned troopers shot him?
CHORUS.—King Charles, and who'll do him right now?
King Charles, and who's ripe for fight now?
Give a rouse: here's, in hell's despite now,
King Charles!

Marching Along. **2. crop-headed Parliament.** Puritan members of the Long Parliament "bobbed" their hair, instead of wearing it in long curls like the Cavaliers. **7. Pym,** John Pym, Puritan leader along with Cromwell and John Hampden. **8. parles,** debates.

Marching Along. **14. Hazelrig, etc.,** other leaders of the Parliamentary cause. **15. Rupert,** Prince Rupert of Bavaria, the King's nephew. *Give a Rouse.* **3. rouse,** cheer. **16. Noll's,** Oliver Cromwell's.

3. BOOT AND SADDLE

Boot, saddle, to horse, and away!
Rescue my castle before the hot day
Brightens to blue from its silvery grey,
  CHORUS.—*Boot, saddle, to horse, and away!*

Ride past the suburbs, asleep as you'd say;
Many's the friend there, will listen and pray
"God's luck to gallants that strike up the lay—
  CHORUS.—*Boot, saddle, to horse, and away!*"

Forty miles off, like a roebuck at bay,
Flouts Castle Brancepeth the Roundheads' array:
Who laughs, "Good fellows ere this, by my fay,
  CHORUS.—*Boot, saddle, to horse, and away!*"

Who? My wife Gertrude; that, honest and gay,
Laughs when you talk of surrendering, "Nay!
I've better counsellors; what counsel they?
  CHORUS.—*Boot, saddle, to horse, and away!*"

SOLILOQUY OF THE SPANISH CLOISTER

In this shocking and amusing monologue we hear the voice of a man who has "fallen in hate." The easily contented, somewhat puttering, probably not too intelligent Brother Lawrence gets "on the nerves" of the speaker. Being cloistered, he cannot escape from the object of his detestation, and his hatred has poisoned his whole life. In stanza 4 he imputes his own sensuality to Lawrence; in stanza 5 he bolsters his own egoism with the reminder that he is a better formalist than the other man. In stanzas 7 and 8 he speculates on the possibility of tricking Lawrence out of his salvation; note the implicit admission that unless he is tricked, Lawrence is sure of it. Browning leaves the construction in both stanzas incomplete grammatically, the implication being "Do you suppose I could do that?" But by the time we reach stanza 9 our speaker is desperate. He is not playing for high stakes now; he would risk his own soul to be able to destroy a rosebush.

I

Gr-r-r—there go, my heart's abhorrence!
  Water your damned flower-pots, do!
If hate killed men, Brother Lawrence,
  God's blood, would not mine kill you!
What? your myrtle-bush wants trimming?
  Oh, that rose has prior claims—
Needs its leaden vase filled brimming?
  Hell dry you up with its flames!

2

At the meal we sit together:
  Salve tibi! I must hear
Wise talk of the kind of weather,
  Sort of season, time of year:
Not a plenteous cork-crop: scarcely
  Dare we hope oak-galls, I doubt:
What's the Latin name for "parsley"?
What's the Greek name for Swine's Snout?

3

Whew! We'll have our platter burnished,
  Laid with care on our own shelf!
With a fire-new spoon we're furnished,
  And a goblet for ourself,
Rinsed like something sacrificial
  Ere 'tis fit to touch our chaps—
Marked with L for our initial!
  (He-he! There his lily snaps!)

4

Saint, forsooth! While brown Dolores
  Squats outside the Convent bank
With Sanchicha, telling stories,
  Steeping tresses in the tank,
Blue-black, lustrous, thick like horsehairs,
  —Can't I see his dead eye glow,
Bright as 'twere a Barbary corsair's?
  (That is, if he'd let it show!)

5

When he finishes refection,
  Knife and fork he never lays
Cross-wise, to my recollection,
  As do I, in Jesu's praise.
I the Trinity illustrate,
  Drinking watered orange-pulp—
In three sips the Arian frustrate;
  While he drains his at one gulp.

6

Oh, those melons! If he's able
  We're to have a feast! so nice!

Boot and Saddle. **10. Brancepeth,** the castle of the singer of the song. **Roundheads,** the Parliamentarians, so called because they "bobbed" their hair, instead of wearing it in long curls like the Cavaliers.

10. *Salve tibi,* Hail to thee. **31. Barbary corsair,** a privateer or pirate of the Barbary coast (North Africa), not noted for sexual or any other virtues. **39. Arian.** Arius denied the equality of the Son with God the Father. The Council of Nicea (325 A.D.), where he was opposed by Athanasius, condemned his views.

One goes to the Abbot's table,
All of us get each a slice.
How go on your flowers? None double?
Not one fruit-sort can you spy?
Strange!—And I, too, at such trouble,
Keep them close-nipped on the sly!

7

There's a great text in Galatians,
Once you trip on it, entails
Twenty-nine distinct damnations,
One sure, if another fails:
If I trip him just a-dying,
Sure of heaven as sure can be,
Spin him round and send him flying
Off to hell, a Manichee?

8

Or, my scrofulous French novel
On grey paper with blunt type!
Simply glance at it, you grovel
Hand and foot in Belial's gripe:
If I double down its pages
At the woeful sixteenth print,
When he gathers his greengages,
Ope a sieve and slip it in't?

9

Or, there's Satan!—one might venture
Pledge one's soul to him, yet leave
Such a flaw in the indenture
As he'd miss till, past retrieve,
Blasted lay that rose-acacia
We're so proud of! *Hy, Zy, Hine* . . .
'St, there's Vespers! *Plena gratiâ,*
Ave, Virgo! Gr-r-r—you swine!

MY LAST DUCHESS

Ferrara

Browning varies the technique of his monologues: the Spanish monk soliloquizes, but the Duke of Ferrara (a city near Venice) talks to the envoy with whom he is negotiating for a bride and shows him the portrait of his late wife.

49. text in Galatians. Galatians 3:10 (which in turn refers to Deuteronomy 28) and Galatians 5:19–21 have both been suggested. The latter passage enumerates only seventeen sins, one of which is heresy. The Church taught that the eternal state of the soul depends on its spiritual condition at the moment of death. (See Hamlet's reluctance to kill the King at prayer, *Hamlet,* Act. III, sc. 3.) **56. Manichee,** an adherent of the heresy of Manes (3rd century), who taught that Satan is coeternal with God. **60. Belial's,** of the spirit of evil, particularly of lust. **70. Hy, Zy, Hine,** probably indicating the sound of the vesper bells. **71–72. Plena . . . Virgo!** Hail, Virgin, full of grace—a formal prayer.

That's my last Duchess painted on the wall,
Looking as if she were alive. I call
That piece a wonder, now: Frà Pandolf's hands
Worked busily a day, and there she stands.
Will't please you sit and look at her? I said
"Frà Pandolf" by design, for never read
Strangers like you that pictured countenance,
The depth and passion of its earnest glance,
But to myself they turned (since none puts by
The curtain I have drawn for you, but I)
And seemed as they would ask me, if they durst,
How such a glance came there; so, not the first
Are you to turn and ask thus. Sir, 'twas not
Her husband's presence only, called that spot
Of joy into the Duchess' cheek: perhaps
Frà Pandolf chanced to say, "Her mantle laps
Over my lady's wrist too much," or "Paint
Must never hope to reproduce the faint
Half-flush that dies along her throat": such stuff
Was courtesy, she thought, and cause enough
For calling up that spot of joy. She had
A heart—how shall I say?—too soon made glad,
Too easily impressed: she liked whate'er
She looked on, and her looks went everywhere.
Sir, 'twas all one! My favour at her breast,
The dropping of the daylight in the West,
The bough of cherries some officious fool
Broke in the orchard for her, the white mule
She rode with round the terrace—all and each
Would draw from her alike the approving speech,
Or blush, at least. She thanked men,—good! but thanked
Somehow—I know not how—as if she ranked
My gift of a nine-hundred-years-old name
With anybody's gift. Who'd stoop to blame
This sort of trifling? Even had you skill
In speech—(which I have not)—to make your will
Quite clear to such an one, and say, "Just this
Or that in you disgusts me; here you miss,
Or there exceed the mark"—and if she let
Herself be lessoned so, nor plainly set
Her wits to yours, forsooth, and made excuse,
—E'en then would be some stooping; and I choose

3. Frà Pandolf, Brother Pandolf, an imaginary painter, a monk. **8. The depth . . . glance.** Spoken ironically. **9–10. since none . . . but I.** The Duke is a "man of property"; his art treasures are for him alone. Probably it pleases him to know that he has the image of his dead wife—as he never had the original—absolutely under his own control. The important thing is to understand that no sentiment is indicated. **33–34. My gift . . . anybody's gift.** Evidently the social position of the Duchess was inferior to that of her husband.

Never to stoop. Oh sir, she smiled, no doubt,
Whene'er I passed her; but who passed without
Much the same smile? This grew; I gave commands;
Then all smiles stopped together. There she stands
As if alive. Will't please you rise? We'll meet
The company below, then. I repeat,
The Count your master's known munificence
Is ample warrant that no just pretence
Of mine for dowry will be disallowed;
Though his fair daughter's self, as I avowed
At starting, is my object. Nay, we'll go
Together down, sir. Notice Neptune, though,
Taming a sea-horse, thought a rarity,
Which Claus of Innsbruck cast in bronze for me!

MEETING AT NIGHT

The grey sea and the long black land;
And the yellow half-moon large and low;
And the startled little waves that leap
In fiery ringlets from their sleep,
As I gain the cove with pushing prow,
And quench its speed i' the slushy sand.

Then a mile of warm sea-scented beach;
Three fields to cross till a farm appears;
A tap at the pane, the quick sharp scratch
And blue spurt of a lighted match,
And a voice less loud, through its joys and fears,
Than the two hearts beating each to each!

PARTING AT MORNING

Round the cape of a sudden came the sea,
And the sun looked over the mountain's rim:
And straight was a path of gold for him,
And the need of a world of men for me.

45–46. I gave . . . together. When Hiram Corson asked Browning if this meant that the Duchess was put to death, he first replied affirmatively, then added, "or he might have had her shut up in a convent." In any event, he broke her heart and was responsible for her death. **53–54. Nay . . . down, sir.** Too cruel to be aware that his heartlessness has shocked the envoy, the Duke is most condescending. The two men descend the stairs side by side, as if they were equals. **54–56. Notice . . . for me. Neptune** is the god of the sea. **Claus** is an imaginary sculptor. **Innsbruck** in the Tyrol was famous for its statues. This touch completes the revelation of the Duke's character. He can turn without a qualm from one art treasure, the portrait of a woman whose life he ruined, to another which depicts a scene in mythology. **8. farm,** farmhouse, as often in British usage. *Parting at Morning.* **3. him,** the sun.

HOME-THOUGHTS, FROM ABROAD

Oh, to be in England
Now that April's there,
And whoever wakes in England
Sees, some morning, unaware,
That the lowest boughs and the brushwood sheaf
Round the elm-tree bole are in tiny leaf,
While the chaffinch sings on the orchard bough
In England—now!

And after April, when May follows,
And the whitethroat builds, and all the swallows!
Hark, where my blossomed pear-tree in the hedge
Leans to the field and scatters on the clover
Blossoms and dewdrops—at the bent spray's edge—
That's the wise thrush; he sings each song twice over,
Lest you should think he never could recapture
The first fine careless rapture!
And though the fields look rough with hoary dew,
All will be gay when noontide wakes anew
The buttercups, the little children's dower
—Far brighter than this gaudy melon-flower!

HOME-THOUGHTS, FROM THE SEA

Nobly, nobly Cape Saint Vincent to the Northwest died away;
Sunset ran, one glorious blood-red, reeking into Cadiz Bay;
Bluish 'mid the burning water, full in face Trafalgar lay;
In the dimmest Northeast distance dawned Gibraltar grand and grey;
"Here and here did England help me: how can I help England?"—say,
Whoso turns as I, this evening, turn to God to praise and pray,
While Jove's planet rises yonder, silent over Africa.

Home-thoughts, from the Sea. **1. Cape Saint Vincent,** the southwest point of Portugal, scene of an English naval victory over Spain, 1797. **2. Cadiz,** on the southwest coast of Spain, where England defeated the second Spanish Armada, 1596. **3. Trafalgar,** east of Cadiz Bay, the scene of Nelson's great victory, 1805. **4. Gibraltar,** the rock and fortress guarding the entrance to the Mediterranean, owned by England since 1713. **5. say.** Let us say, or suppose we say. Browning's argument is that true patriotism is inseparable from piety, which alone can make a nation great. **7. Jove's planet,** Jupiter.

THE BISHOP ORDERS HIS TOMB AT SAINT PRAXED'S CHURCH

Rome, 15—

"I know of no other piece of modern English, prose or poetry, in which there is so much told, as in these lines, of the Renaissance spirit,—its worldliness, inconsistency, pride, hypocrisy, ignorance of itself, love of art, of luxury, and of good Latin. It is nearly all that I have said of the central Renaissance in thirty pages of the *Stones of Venice*, put into as many lines, Browning's also being the antecedent work."—John Ruskin, *Modern Painters*, Vol. 4.

Vanity, saith the preacher, vanity!
Draw round my bed: is Anselm keeping back?
Nephews—sons mine . . . ah God, I know not! Well—
She, men would have to be your mother once,
Old Gandolf envied me, so fair she was!
What's done is done, and she is dead beside,
Dead long ago, and I am Bishop since,
And as she died so must we die ourselves,
And thence ye may perceive the world's a dream.
Life, how and what is it? As here I lie
In this state-chamber, dying by degrees,
Hours and long hours in the dead night, I ask
"Do I live, am I dead?" Peace, peace seems all.
Saint Praxed's ever was the church for peace;
And so, about this tomb of mine. I fought
With tooth and nail to save my niche, ye know:
—Old Gandolf cozened me, despite my care;
Shrewd was that snatch from out the corner South
He graced his carrion with, God curse the same!
Yet still my niche is not so cramped but thence
One sees the pulpit o' the epistle-side,
And somewhat of the choir, those silent seats,
And up into the aery dome where live
The angels, and a sunbeam's sure to lurk:
And I shall fill my slab of basalt there,
And 'neath my tabernacle take my rest,
With those nine columns round me, two and two,
The odd one at my feet where Anselm stands:
Peach-blossom marble all, the rare, the ripe
As fresh-poured red wine of a mighty pulse.
—Old Gandolf with his paltry onion-stone,
Put me where I may look at him! True peach,
Rosy and flawless: how I earned the prize!
Draw close: that conflagration of my church
—What then? So much was saved if aught were missed!
My sons, ye would not be my death? Go dig
The white-grape vineyard where the oil-press stood,
Drop water gently till the surface sink,
And if ye find . . . Ah God, I know not, I! . . .
Bedded in store of rotten fig-leaves soft,
And corded up in a tight olive-frail,
Some lump, ah God, of *lapis lazuli*,
Big as a Jew's head cut off at the nape,
Blue as a vein o'er the Madonna's breast . . .
Sons, all have I bequeathed you, villas, all,
That brave Frascati villa with its bath,
So, let the blue lump poise between my knees,
Like God the Father's globe on both his hands
Ye worship in the Jesu Church so gay,
For Gandolf shall not choose but see and burst!
Swift as a weaver's shuttle fleet our years:
Man goeth to the grave, and where is he?
Did I say basalt for my slab, sons? Black—
'Twas ever antique-black I meant! How else
Shall ye contrast my frieze to come beneath?
The bas-relief in bronze ye promised me,
Those Pans and Nymphs ye wot of, and perchance
Some tripod, thyrsus, with a vase or so,
The Saviour at his sermon on the mount,
Saint Praxed in a glory, and one Pan
Ready to twitch the Nymph's last garment off,
And Moses with the tables . . . but I know
Ye mark me not! What do they whisper thee,
Child of my bowels, Anselm? Ah, ye hope
To revel down my villas while I gasp
Bricked o'er with beggar's mouldy travertine
Which Gandolf from his tomb-top chuckles at!
Nay, boys, ye love me—all of jasper, then!
'Tis jasper ye stand pledged to, lest I grieve
My bath must needs be left behind, alas!
One block, pure green as a pistachio-nut,
There's plenty jasper somewhere in the world—
And have I not Saint Praxed's ear to pray
Horses for ye, and brown Greek manuscripts,
And mistresses with great smooth marbly limbs?

1. Vanity . . . vanity. See Ecclesiastes 1:2. **3. Nephews,** by a pious fiction, since, of course, they were his illegitimate children. **5. Gandolf,** the Bishop's hated predecessor and rival in love. **21. the epistle-side.** The epistles are read on the right-hand side of the altar as one faces it, the Gospels on the left. **25. basalt,** a dark hard stone. **26. tabernacle,** a canopy over the tomb. **31. onion-stone,** inferior greenish marble.

41. olive-frail, a basket to hold olives. **46. Frascati,** a fashionable district, near Rome. **49. Jesu Church.** There is or was such an image as the Bishop refers to in the Church of the Jesuits in Rome. With characteristic irreverence the Bishop would take upon himself the posture of God. **51. Swift . . . years.** See Job 7:6. **56–62. The bas-relief . . . the tables.** The mingling of Christian and pagan symbolism is characteristic of the Renaissance (see Milton's "Lycidas"). Here it is also intended to show the Bishop's lack of respect for sacred things. **Pan** (l. 57) was the god of the fields. The priestess of Apollo at Delphi sat on a **tripod** (l.58); the worshipers of Dionysos carried a **thyrsus** (l. 58). The **sermon on the mount** (l. 59) is recorded in Matthew 5–7. **Moses** gets **the tables** of the Law (l. 62) from Yahweh on Mount Sinai in Exodus 24 ff. **66. travertine,** cheap limestone.

—That's if ye carve my epitaph aright,
Choice Latin, picked phrase, Tully's every word,
No gaudy ware like Gandolf's second line—
Tully, my masters? Ulpian serves his need!
And then how I shall lie through centuries,
And hear the blessed mutter of the mass,
And see God made and eaten all day long,
And feel the steady candle-flame, and taste
Good, strong, thick, stupefying incense-smoke!
For as I lie here, hours of the dead night,
Dying in state and by such slow degrees,
I fold my arms as if they clasped a crook,
And stretch my feet forth straight as stone can point,
And let the bedclothes, for a mortcloth, drop
Into great laps and folds of sculptor's-work:
And as yon tapers dwindle, and strange thoughts
Grow, with a certain humming in my ears,
About the life before I lived this life,
And this life too, popes, cardinals and priests,
Saint Praxed at his sermon on the mount,
Your tall pale mother with her talking eyes,
And new-found agate urns as fresh as day,
And marble's language, Latin pure, discreet,
—Aha, ELUCESCEBAT quoth our friend?
No Tully, said I, Ulpian at the best!
Evil and brief hath been my pilgrimage.
All *lapis*, all, sons! Else I give the Pope
My villas! Will ye ever eat my heart?
Ever your eyes were as a lizard's quick,
They glitter like your mother's for my soul,
Or ye would heighten my impoverished frieze,
Piece out its starved design, and fill my vase
With grapes, and add a vizor and a term,
And to the tripod ye would tie a lynx
That in his struggle throws the thyrsus down,
To comfort me on my entablature
Whereon I am to lie till I must ask
"Do I live, am I dead?" There, leave me, there!
For ye have stabbed me with ingratitude
To death—ye wish it—God, ye wish it! Stone—
Gritstone, a-crumble! Clammy squares which sweat
As if the corpse they keep were oozing through—
And no more *lapis* to delight the world!
Well, go! I bless ye. Fewer tapers there,
But in a row: and, going, turn your backs
—Ay, like departing altar-ministrants,
And leave me in my church, the church for peace,
That I may watch at leisure if he leers—
Old Gandolf—at me, from his onion-stone,
As still he envied me, so fair she was!

77–79. Choice Latin . . . his need? The Bishop's love of pure Latin is one of the few sincere things about him. **Tully** is Cicero, whom the Bishop takes as setting the standard. He regards **Ulpian,** a Roman jurist (170–228) as far below Tully's level. **80–84. And then how . . . incense-smoke!** These lines contain a reference to the Roman Catholic doctrine of transubstantiation, the belief that every time the mass is celebrated a miracle occurs and the bread and wine on the altar become the body and blood of Christ. But Browning makes even this reference to a sacred mystery point the Bishop's sensuality; the passage is almost cannibalistic. The dying man has no interest in the spiritual significance of the service or of the sacrament, and probably no belief in it; on the other hand, it interests him tremendously as a colorful pageant. **87. crook,** the crosier, or shepherd's staff, symbol of the Bishop's office. **95. Saint Praxed at his sermon.** Saint Praxed (Prassede) was a female saint of first-century Rome. This is one of several indications that the Bishop's mind is wandering. **99. Elucescebat,** he was famous. The Bishop prefers the pure classical form, *elucebat.* **108. term,** a bust on a square block of stone.

116. Gritstone, a kind of coarse sandstone.

SAUL

"Saul" is one of the noblest religious poems in the language. It was suggested by 1 Samuel 16:14–23, which relates how David, the shepherd lad, was called to bring his music to cure King Saul, who was suffering from melancholia, and, as W. C. DeVane has shown, by Christopher Smart's preface to his "Ode to Musick on Saint Cecilia's Day." The poem has had an interesting history. Only the first nine divisions were published in 1845; the rest did not come out until ten years later. The meaning of the poem, as we know it today, inheres in the second part, but, as A. W. Crawford has pointed out, Browning could not achieve the great affirmation it comprises until he had first worked out his own theological problems.

The order of David's procedure is significant. He first appeals to the interests and enthusiasms which man shares with the other animals (stanzas 5–6), from which he passes, first, to what has been called "the help-tunes of the great epochs in human life" (7), then, by way of a transition through that paean in praise of "the wild joys of living" (9), to "songs of human aspiration." On the merely human level one cannot go beyond a great king's hope of deathless glory; at the end of stanza 15, therefore, David has reached an impasse. Deliverance comes through a fresh revelation of the character of God. What David cannot do for Saul can be achieved in God, who is love. Otherwise, the rule which prevails everywhere else in the universe is broken, and the Creator finds himself surpassed by the creature, which is unthinkable.

The ideas expressed in the poem are, of course, much too advanced for David's day. David lived late in the eleventh and early in the tenth century B.C., Hosea, the first prophet to think of God as love, in the eighth century B.C. Actually, Browning goes beyond the range of the Old Testament altogether, expressing, at the end of stanza 18, the Christian doctrine of the Incarnation.

In the poem David, who is alone with his sheep, tells the story of his visit to King Saul.

1

Said Abner, "At last thou art come! Ere I tell, ere thou speak,
Kiss my cheek, wish me well!" Then I wished it, and did kiss his cheek.
And he: "Since the King, O my friend, for thy countenance sent,
Neither drunken nor eaten have we; nor until from his tent
Thou return with the joyful assurance the King liveth yet,
Shall our lip with the honey be bright, with the water be wet.
For out of the black mid-tent's silence, a space of three days,
Not a sound hath escaped to thy servants, of prayer nor of praise,
To betoken that Saul and the Spirit have ended their strife,
And that, faint in his triumph, the monarch sinks back upon life.

2

"Yet now my heart leaps, O belovèd! God's child with his dew
On thy gracious gold hair, and those lilies still living and blue
Just broken to twine round thy harp-strings, as if no wild heat
Were now raging to torture the desert!"

3

Then I, as was meet,
Knelt down to the God of my fathers, and rose on my feet,
And ran o'er the sand burnt to powder. The tent was unlooped;
I pulled up the spear that obstructed, and under I stooped;
Hands and knees on the slippery grass-patch, all withered and gone,
That extends to the second enclosure, I groped my way on
Till I felt where the foldskirts fly open. Then once more I prayed,
And opened the foldskirts and entered, and was not afraid
But spoke, "Here is David, thy servant!" And no voice replied.
At the first I saw nought but the blackness; but soon I descried
A something more black than the blackness—the vast, the upright
Main prop which sustains the pavilion: and slow into sight
Grew a figure against it, gigantic and blackest of all.
Then a sunbeam, that burst through the tent-roof, showed Saul.

4

He stood as erect as that tent-prop, both arms stretched out wide
On the great cross-support in the centre, that goes to each side;
He relaxed not a muscle, but hung there as, caught in his pangs
And waiting his change, the king-serpent all heavily hangs,
Far away from his kind, in the pine, till deliverance come
With the spring-time,—so agonised Saul, drear and stark, blind and dumb.

5

Then I tuned my harp,—took off the lilies we twine round its chords
Lest they snap 'neath the stress of the noontide—those sunbeams like swords!
And I first played the tune all our sheep know, as, one after one,
So docile they come to the pen-door till folding be done.
They are white and untorn by the bushes, for lo, they have fed
Where the long grasses stifle the water within the stream's bed;
And now one after one seeks its lodging, as star follows star
Into eve and the blue far above us,—so blue and so far!

6

—Then the tune, for which quails on the cornland will each leave his mate
To fly after the player; then, what makes the crickets elate
Till for boldness they fight one another; and then, what has weight
To set the quick jerboa a-musing outside his sand house—
There are none such as he for a wonder, half bird and half mouse!

1. Abner, Saul's cousin and commander in chief. **thou,** David. **9. Spirit,** the "evil spirit" of 1 Samuel 16:14. **12. gold hair.** The "ruddy" quality attributed to David in 1 Samuel 16:12 properly refers to skin but has always been popularly applied to his hair.

31. king-serpent, a very large serpent. The particular variety is not specified. **45. jerboa,** a small jumping rodent.

God made all the creatures and gave them our love and our fear,
To give sign, we and they are his children, one family here.

7

Then I played the help-tune of our reapers, their wine-song, when hand
Grasps at hand, eye lights eye in good friendship, and great hearts expand
And grow one in the sense of this world's life.—And then, the last song
When the dead man is praised on his journey—"Bear, bear him along,
With his few faults shut up like dead flowerets! Are balm-seeds not here
To console us? The land has none left such as he on the bier.
Oh, would we might keep thee, my brother!"—And then, the glad chaunt
Of the marriage —first go the young maidens; next, she whom we vaunt
As the beauty, the pride of our dwelling.—And then, the great march
Wherein man runs to man to assist him and buttress an arch
Nought can break; who shall harm them, our friends?—Then, the chorus intoned
As the Levites go up to the altar in glory enthroned.
But I stopped here: for here in the darkness Saul groaned.

8

And I paused, held my breath in such silence, and listened apart;
And the tent shook, for mighty Saul shuddered: and sparkles 'gan dart
From the jewels that woke in his turban, at once with a start,
All its lordly male-sapphires, and rubies courageous at heart.
So the head: but the body still moved not, still hung there erect.
And I bent once again to my playing, pursued it unchecked,
As I sang,—

9

"Oh, our manhood's prime vigour! No spirit feels waste,
Not a muscle is stopped in its playing nor sinew unbraced.
Oh, the wild joys of living! the leaping from rock up to rock,
The strong rending of boughs from the fir-tree, the cool silver shock
Of the plunge in a pool's living water, the hunt of the bear,
And the sultriness showing the lion is couched in his lair.
And the meal, the rich dates yellowed over with gold dust divine,
And the locust-flesh steeped in the pitcher, the full draught of wine,
And the sleep in the dried river-channel where bulrushes tell
That the water was wont to go warbling so softly and well.
How good is man's life, the mere living! how fit to employ
All the heart and the soul and the senses for ever in joy!
Hast thou loved the white locks of thy father, whose sword thou didst guard
When he trusted thee forth with the armies, for glorious reward?
Didst thou see the thin hands of thy mother, held up as men sung
The low song of the nearly-departed, and hear her faint tongue
Joining in while it could to the witness, 'Let one more attest,
I have lived, seen God's hand through a lifetime, and all was for best'?
Then they sung through their tears in strong triumph, not much, but the rest.
And thy brothers, the help and the contest, the working whence grew
Such result as, from seething grape-bundles, the spirit strained true:
And the friends of thy boyhood—that boyhood of wonder and hope,
Present promise and wealth of the future beyond the eye's scope,—
Till lo, thou art grown to a monarch; a people is thine;
And all gifts, which the world offers singly, on one head combine!
On one head, all the beauty and strength, love and rage (like the throe
That, a-work in the rock, helps its labour and lets the gold go),
High ambition and deeds which surpass it, fame crowning them,—all
Brought to blaze on the head of one creature—King Saul!"

60. Levites, priests. See I Chronicles 23:24–32.

10

And lo, with that leap of my spirit,—heart, hand, harp and voice,
Each lifting Saul's name out of sorrow, each bidding rejoice
Saul's fame in the light it was made for—as when, dare I say,
The Lord's army, in rapture of service, strains through its array,
And upsoareth the cherubim-chariot—"Saul!" cried I, and stopped,
And waited the thing that should follow. Then Saul, who hung propped
By the tent's cross-support in the centre, was struck by his name.
Have ye seen when Spring's arrowy summons goes right to the aim,
And some mountain, the last to withstand her, that held (he alone,
While the vale laughed in freedom and flowers) on a broad bust of stone
A year's snow bound about for a breastplate,—leaves grasp of the sheet?
Fold on fold all at once it crowds thunderously down to his feet,
And there fronts you, stark, black, but alive yet, your mountain of old,
With his rents, the successive bequeathings of ages untold—
Yea, each harm got in fighting your battles, each furrow and scar
Of his head thrust 'twixt you and the tempest—all hail, there they are!
—Now again to be softened with verdure, again hold the nest
Of the dove, tempt the goat and its young to the green on his crest
For their food in the ardours of summer. One long shudder thrilled
All the tent till the very air tingled, then sank and was stilled
At the King's self left standing before me, released and aware.
What was gone, what remained? All to traverse, 'twixt hope and despair,
Death was past, life not come: so he waited. Awhile his right hand
Held the brow, helped the eyes left too vacant forthwith to remand
To their place what new objects should enter: 'twas Saul as before.
I looked up and dared gaze at those eyes, nor was hurt any more
Than by slow pallid sunsets in autumn, ye watch from the shore,
At their sad level gaze o'er the ocean—a sun's slow decline
Over hills which, resolved in stern silence, o'erlap and entwine
Base with base to knit strength more intensely: so, arm folded arm
O'er the chest whose slow heavings subsided.

11

What spell or what charm,
(For, awhile there was trouble within me) what next should I urge
To sustain him where song had restored him?—Song filled to the verge
His cup with the wine of this life, pressing all that it yields
Of mere fruitage, the strength and the beauty: beyond, on what fields,
Glean a vintage more potent and perfect to brighten the eye
And bring blood to the lip, and commend them the cup they put by?
He saith, "It is good"; still he drinks not: he lets me praise life,
Gives assent, yet would die for his own part.

12

Then fancies grew rife
Which had come long ago on the pasture, when round me the sheep
Fed in silence—above, the one eagle wheeled slow as in sleep;
And I lay in my hollow and mused on the world that might lie
'Neath his ken, though I saw but the strip 'twixt the hill and the sky:
And I laughed—"Since my days are ordained to be passed with my flocks,
Let me people at least, with my fancies, the plains and the rocks,
Dream the life I am never to mix with, and image the show
Of mankind as they live in those fashions I hardly shall know!
Schemes of life, its best rules and right uses, the courage that gains,
And the prudence that keeps what men strive for." And now these old trains
Of vague thought came again; I grew surer; so, once more the string
Of my harp made response to my spirit, as thus—

13

"Yea, my King,"
I began—"thou dost well in rejecting mere comforts that spring
From the mere mortal life held in common by man and by brute:
In our flesh grows the branch of this life, in our soul it bears fruit.
Thou hast marked the slow rise of the tree,—how its stem trembled first
Till it passed the kid's lip, the stag's antler; then safely outburst
The fan-branches all round; and thou mindest when these too, in turn,
Broke a-bloom and the palm-tree seemed perfect: yet more was to learn,
E'en the good that comes in with the palm-fruit. Our dates shall we slight,
When their juice brings a cure for all sorrow? or care for the plight
Of the palm's self whose slow growth produced them? Not so! stem and branch
Shall decay, nor be known in their place, while the palm-wine shall staunch
Every wound of man's spirit in winter. I pour thee such wine.
Leave the flesh to the fate it was fit for! the spirit be thine!
By the spirit, when age shall o'ercome thee, thou still shalt enjoy
More indeed, than at first when inconscious, the life of a boy.
Crush that life, and behold its wine running! Each deed thou hast done
Dies, revives, goes to work in the world; until e'en as the sun
Looking down on the earth, though clouds spoil him, though tempests efface,
Can find nothing his own deed produced not, must everywhere trace
The results of his past summer-prime,—so, each ray of thy will,
Every flash of thy passion and prowess, long over. shall thrill
Thy whole people, the countless, with ardour, till they too give forth
A like cheer to their sons, who in turn, fill the South and the North
With the radiance thy deed was the germ of. Carouse in the past!
But the license of age has its limit; thou diest at last:
As the lion when age dims his eyeball, the rose at her height,
So with man—so his power and his beauty for ever take flight.
No! Again a long draught of my soul-wine! Look forth o'er the years!
Thou hast done now with eyes for the actual; begin with the seer's!
Is Saul dead? In the depth of the vale make his tomb—bid arise
A grey mountain of marble heaped four-square till, built to the skies,
Let it mark where the great First King slumbers: whose fame would ye know?
Up above see the rock's naked face, where the record shall go
In great characters cut by the scribe,—Such was Saul, so he did;
With the sages directing the work, by the populace chid,—
For not half, they'll affirm, is comprised there! Which fault to amend,
In the grove with his kind grows the cedar, whereon they shall spend
(See, in tablets 'tis level before them) their praise, and record
With the gold of the graver, Saul's story,—the statesman's great word
Side by side with the poet's sweet comment. The river's a-wave
With smooth paper-reeds grazing each other when prophet-winds rave:
So the pen gives unborn generations their due and their part
In thy being! Then, first of the mighty, thank God that thou art!"

14

And behold while I sang . . . but O Thou who didst grant me that day,
And before it not seldom hast granted thy help to essay,
Carry on and complete an adventure,—my shield and my sword
In that act where my soul was thy servant, thy word was my word,—
Still be with me, who then at the summit of human endeavour
And scaling the highest, man's thought could, gazed hopeless as ever
On the new stretch of heaven above me—till, mighty to save,
Just one lift of thy hand cleared that distance—God's throne from man's grave!

188. paper-reeds, papyrus plants.

Let me tell out my tale to its ending—my voice to my heart
Which can scarce dare believe in what marvels last night I took part,
As this morning I gather the fragments, alone with my sheep,
And still fear lest the terrible glory evanish like sleep!
For I wake in the grey dewy covert, while Hebron upheaves
The dawn struggling with night on his shoulder, and Kidron retrieves
Slow the damage of yesterday's sunshine.

15

I say then,—my song
While I sang thus, assuring the monarch, and ever more strong
Made a proffer of good to console him—he slowly resumed
His old motions and habitudes kingly. The right-hand replumed
His black locks to their wonted composure, adjusted the swathes
Of his turban, and see—the huge sweat that his countenance bathes,
He wipes off with the robe; and he girds now his loins as of yore,
And feels slow for the armlets of price, with the clasp set before.
He is Saul, ye remember in glory,—ere error had bent
The broad brow from the daily communion; and still, though much spent
Be the life and the bearing that front you, the same, God did choose,
To receive what a man may waste, desecrate, never quite lose.
So sank he along by the tent-prop till, stayed by the pile
Of his armour and war-cloak and garments, he leaned there awhile,

203. **Hebron,** a hill in Judea with the city of Hebron on it. 204. **Kidron,** a brook near Jerusalem. 213–14. **ere . . . communion.** There are two different versions of the rejection of Saul by Samuel. In 1 Samuel 13, he is rejected because he himself offered sacrifice before a battle instead of waiting for Samuel to come to do it. In 1 Samuel 15, the difficulty is that he spared Agag, king of the Amalekites, and some of the booty, when they ought to have been "devoted." The truth of the matter seems to have been that Saul was, generally speaking, a disappointment to Samuel and the religious party. He was apparently a man capable of great enthusiasm, of a somewhat primitive variety, but his staying power seems to have been weak. Whether his failure was the cause of his melancholia or was itself caused by it, it is impossible to determine at this distance. In any case, the problem was, in part at least, pathological.

And sat out my singing,—one arm round the tent-prop, to raise
His bent head, and the other hung slack—till I touched on the praise
I foresaw from all men in all time, to the man patient there;
And thus ended, the harp falling forward. Then first I was 'ware
That he sat, as I say, with my head just above his vast knees
Which were thrust out on each side around me, like oak-roots which please
To encircle a lamb when it slumbers. I looked up to know
If the best I could do had brought solace: he spoke not, but slow
Lifted up the hand slack at his side, till he laid it with care
Soft and grave, but in mild settled will, on my brow: through my hair
The large fingers were pushed, and he bent back my head, with kind power—
All my face back, intent to peruse it, as men do a flower.
Thus held he me there with his great eyes that scrutinized mine—
And oh, all my heart how it loved him! but where was the sign?
I yearned—"Could I help thee, my father, inventing a bliss,
I would add, to that life of the past, both the future and this;
I would give thee new life altogether, as good, ages hence,
As this moment,—had love but the warrant, love's heart to dispense!"

16

Then the truth came upon me. No harp more—no song more! outbroke—

17

"I have gone the whole round of creation: I saw and I spoke:
I, a work of God's hand for that purpose, received in my brain
And pronounced on the rest of his handwork—returned him again
His creation's approval or censure: I spoke as I saw:
I report, as a man may of God's work—all's love, yet all's law.
Now I lay down the judgeship he lent me. Each faculty tasked

To perceive him, has gained an abyss, where a dew-drop was asked.
Have I knowledge? confounded it shrivels at Wisdom laid bare.
Have I forethought? How purblind, how blank, to the Infinite Care!
Do I task any faculty highest, to imagine success?
I but open my eyes,—and perfection, no more and no less,
In the kind I imagined, full-fronts me, and God is seen God
In the star, in the stone, in the flesh, in the soul, and the clod.
And thus looking within and around me, I ever renew
(With that stoop of the soul which in bending upraises it too)
The submission of man's nothing-perfect to God's all-complete,
As by each new obeisance in spirit, I climb to his feet.
Yet with all this abounding experience, this deity known,
I shall dare to discover some province, some gift of my own.
There's a faculty pleasant to exercise, hard to hoodwink,
I am fain to keep still in abeyance (I laugh as I think),
Lest, insisting to claim and parade in it, wot ye, I worst
E'en the Giver in one gift.—Behold, I could love if I durst!
But I sink the pretension as fearing a man may o'ertake
God's own speed in the one way of love: I abstain for love's sake.
—What, my soul? see thus far and no farther? when doors great and small,
Nine-and-ninety flew ope at our touch, should the hundredth appall?
In the least things have faith, yet distrust in the greatest of all?
Do I find love so full in my nature, God's ultimate gift,
That I doubt his own love can compete with it? Here, the parts shift?
Here, the creature surpass the Creator,—the end, what Began?
Would I fain in my impotent yearning do all for this man,
And dare doubt he alone shall not help him, who yet alone can?
Would it ever have entered my mind, the bare will, much less power,
To bestow on this Saul what I sang of, the marvellous dower
Of the life he was gifted and filled with? to make such a soul,
Such a body, and then such an earth for insphering the whole?
And doth it not enter my mind (as my warm tears attest)
These good things being given, to go on, and give one more, the best?
Ay, to save and redeem and restore him, maintain at the height
This perfection,—succeed with life's day-spring, death's minute of night?
Interpose at the difficult minute, snatch Saul the mistake,
Saul the failure, the ruin he seems now,—and bid him awake
From the dream, the probation, the prelude, to find himself set
Clear and safe in new light and new life,—a new harmony yet
To be run, and continued, and ended—who knows?—or endure!
The man taught enough by life's dream, of the rest to make sure;
By the pain-throb, triumphantly winning intensified bliss,
And the next world's reward and repose, by the struggles in this.

18

"I believe it! 'Tis thou, God, that givest, 'tis I who receive:
In the first is the last, in thy will is my power to believe.
All's one gift: thou canst grant it moreover, as prompt to my prayer
As I breathe out this breath, as I open these arms to the air.
From thy will, stream the worlds, life and nature, thy dread Sabaoth:
I will?—the mere atoms despise me! Why am I not loth
To look that, even that, in the face too? Why is it I dare
Think but lightly of such impuissance? What stops my despair?
This;—'tis not what man Does which exalts him, but what man Would do!

291. Sabaoth, a title applied to God in His manifestation as "Lord of Hosts," first in a military sense, later with a wider meaning.

See the King—I would help him but cannot, the wishes fall through.
Could I wrestle to raise him from sorrow, grow poor to enrich,
To fill up his life, starve my own out, I would—knowing which,
I know that my service is perfect. Oh, speak through me now!
Would I suffer for him that I love? So wouldst thou—so wilt thou!
So shall crown thee the topmost, ineffablest, uttermost crown—
And thy love fill infinitude wholly, nor leave up nor down
One spot for the creature to stand in! It is by no breath,
Turn of eye, wave of hand, that salvation joins issue with death!
As thy Love is discovered almighty, almighty be proved
Thy power, that exists with and for it, of being Beloved!
He who did most, shall bear most; the strongest shall stand the most weak.
'Tis the weakness in strength that I cry for! my flesh, that I seek
In the Godhead! I seek and I find it. O Saul, it shall be
A Face like my face that receives thee; a Man like to me
Thou shalt love and be loved by, for ever: a Hand like this hand
Shall throw open the gates of new life to thee! See the Christ stand!"

19

I know not too well how I found my way home in the night.
There were witnesses, cohorts about me, to left and to right,
Angels, powers, the unuttered, unseen, the alive, the aware:
I repressed, I got through them as hardly, as struggling there,
As a runner beset by the populace famished for news—
Life or death. The whole earth was awakened, hell loosed with her crews;
And the stars of night beat with emotion, and tingled and shot
Out in fire the strong pain of pent knowledge: but I fainted not.
For the Hand still impelled me at once and supported, suppressed
All the tumult, and quenched it with quiet, and holy behest,
Till the rapture was shut in itself, and the earth sank to rest.
Anon at the dawn, all that trouble had withered from earth—
Not so much, but I saw it die out in the day's tender birth;
In the gathered intensity brought to the grey of the hills;
In the shuddering forests' held breath; in the sudden wind-thrills;
In the startled wild beasts that bore off, each with eye sidling still
Though averted with wonder and dread; in the birds stiff and chill
That rose heavily, as I approached them, made stupid with awe:
E'en the serpent that slid away silent,—he felt the new law.
The same stared in the white humid faces upturned by the flowers;
The same worked in the heart of the cedar and moved the vine-bowers:
And the little brooks witnessing murmured, persistent and low,
With their obstinate, all but hushed voices—"E'en so, it is so!"

LOVE AMONG THE RUINS

"Love among the Ruins," one of Browning's most beloved poems, proves that he could write as melodiously as anyone else when he chose. There is a twofold contrast in the poem: between the past and the present (note the careful parallelism within each stanza); between love and glory.

I

Where the quiet-coloured end of evening smiles
Miles and miles
On the solitary pastures where our sheep
Half-asleep
Tinkle homeward through the twilight, stray or stop
As they crop—
Was the site once of a city great and gay,
(So they say)
Of our country's very capital, its prince
Ages since
Held his court in, gathered councils, wielding far
Peace or war.

2

Now,—the country does not even boast a tree,
As you see,
To distinguish slopes of verdure, certain rills
From the hills
Intersect and give a name to, (else they run
Into one)
Where the domed and daring palace shot its spires
Up like fires
O'er the hundred-gated circuit of a wall
Bounding all,
Made of marble, men might march on nor be pressed,
Twelve abreast.

3

And such plenty and perfection, see, of grass
Never was!
Such a carpet as, this summer-time, o'erspreads
And embeds
Every vestige of the city, guessed alone,
Stock or stone—
Where a multitude of men breathed joy and woe
Long ago;
Lust of glory pricked their hearts up, dread of shame
Struck them tame;
And that glory and that shame alike, the gold
Bought and sold.

4

Now,—the single little turret that remains
On the plains,
By the caper overrooted, by the gourd
Overscored,
While the patching houseleek's head of blossom winks
Through the chinks—
Marks the basement whence a tower in ancient time
Sprang sublime,
And a burning ring, all round, the chariots traced
As they raced,
And the monarch and his minions and his dames
Viewed the games.

5

And I know, while thus the quiet-coloured eve
Smiles to leave
To their folding, all our many-tinkling fleece
In such peace.
And the slopes and rills in undistinguished grey
Melt away—
That a girl with eager eyes and yellow hair
Waits me there
In the turret whence the charioteers caught soul
For the goal,
When the king looked, where she looks now, breathless, dumb
Till I come.

6

But he looked upon the city, every side,
Far and wide,
All the mountains topped with temples, all the glades'
Colonnades,
All the causeys, bridges, aqueducts,—and then,
All the men!
When I do come, she will speak not, she will stand,
Either hand
On my shoulder, give her eyes the first embrace
Of my face,
Ere we rush, ere we extinguish sight and speech
Each on each.

7

In one year they sent a million fighters forth
South and North,
And they built their gods a brazen pillar high
As the sky,
Yet reserved a thousand chariots in full force—
Gold, of course.
Oh heart! oh blood that freezes, blood that burns!
Earth's returns
For whole centuries of folly, noise and sin!
Shut them in,
With their triumphs and their glories and the rest!
Love is best.

MEMORABILIA

This poem, "Things Worth Remembering," relates an experience of Browning's own. The speaker, an enthusiast for Shelley, encounters a man who once had the privilege of meeting the poet, but whose appreciation of his own good fortune obviously falls far short of what his present companion's would be. The metaphor Browning employs in the latter two stanzas is one of his most apt and evocative.

I

Ah, did you once see Shelley plain,
And did he stop and speak to you,
And did you speak to him again?
How strange it seems and new!

65. **causeys,** causeways.

2

But you were living before that,
And also you are living after;
And the memory I started at—
My starting moves your laughter!

3

I crossed a moor, with a name of its own
And a certain use in the world no doubt,
Yet a hand's-breadth of it shines alone
'Mid the blank miles round about:

4

For there I picked up on the heather,
And there I put inside my breast
A moulted feather, an eagle-feather!
Well, I forget the rest.

THE LAST RIDE TOGETHER

This poem is one of Browning's great expressions of his favorite doctrines of success in failure and of the superiority of love not only to glory but to art—this last a somewhat unusual point of view for a poet.

1

I said—Then, dearest, since 'tis so,
Since now at length my fate I know,
Since nothing all my love avails,
Since all, my life seemed meant for, fails,
Since this was written and needs must be—
My whole heart rises up to bless
Your name in pride and thankfulness!
Take back the hope you gave,—I claim
Only a memory of the same,
—And this beside, if you will not blame,
Your leave for one more last ride with me.

2

My mistress bent that brow of hers;
Those deep dark eyes where pride demurs
When pity would be softening through,
Fixed me a breathing-while or two
With life or death in the balance: right!
The blood replenished me again;
My last thought was at least not vain:
I and my mistress, side by side
Shall be together, breathe and ride,
So, one day more am I deified.
Who knows but the world may end to-night?

3

Hush! if you saw some western cloud
All billowy-bosomed, over-bowed
By many benedictions—sun's
And moon's and evening-star's at once—
And so, you, looking and loving best,
Conscious grew, your passion drew
Cloud, sunset, moonrise, star-shine too,
Down on you, near and yet more near,
Till flesh must fade for heaven was here!—
Thus leant she and lingered—joy and fear!
Thus lay she a moment on my breast.

4

Then we began to ride. My soul
Smoothed itself out, a long-cramped scroll
Freshening and fluttering in the wind.
Past hopes already lay behind.
What need to strive with a life awry?
Had I said that, had I done this,
So might I gain, so might I miss.
Might she have loved me? just as well
She might have hated, who can tell!
Where had I been now if the worst befell?
And here we are riding, she and I.

5

Fail I alone, in words and deeds?
Why, all men strive, and who succeeds?
We rode; it seemed my spirit flew,
Saw other regions, cities new,
As the world rushed by on either side.
I thought,—All labour, yet no less
Bear up beneath their unsuccess.
Look at the end of work, contrast
The petty done, the undone vast,
This present of theirs with the hopeful past!
I hoped she would love me; here we ride.

6

What hand and brain went ever paired?
What heart alike conceived and dared?
What act proved all its thought had been?
What will but felt the fleshly screen?
We ride and I see her bosom heave.
There's many a crown for who can reach.
Ten lines, a statesman's life in each!
The flag stuck on a heap of bones,
A soldier's doing! what atones?
They scratch his name on the Abbey-stones.
My riding is better, by their leave.

33. **Thus lay she . . . on my breast,** as she mounted her horse.

7

What does it all mean, poet? Well,
Your brains beat into rhythm, you tell
What we felt only; you expressed
You hold things beautiful the best,
  And pace them in rhyme so, side by side.
'Tis something, nay 'tis much: but then,
Have you yourself what's best for men?
Are you—poor, sick, old ere your time—
Nearer one whit your own sublime
Than we who never have turned a rhyme?
  Sing, riding's a joy! For me, I ride.

8

And you, great sculptor—so, you gave
A score of years to Art, her slave,
And that's your Venus, whence we turn
To yonder girl that fords the burn!
  You acquiesce, and shall I repine?
What, man of music, you grown grey
With notes and nothing else to say,
Is this your sole praise from a friend,
"Greatly his opera's strains intend,
But in music we know how fashions end!"
  I gave my youth; but we ride, in fine.

9

Who knows what's fit for us? Had fate
Proposed bliss here should sublimate
My being—had I signed the bond—
Still one must lead some life beyond,
  Have a bliss to die with, dim-descried.
This foot once planted on the goal,
This glory-garland round my soul,
Could I descry such? Try and test!
I sink back shuddering from the quest.
Earth being so good, would heaven seem best?
  Now, heaven and she are beyond this ride.

10

And yet—she has not spoke so long!
What if heaven be that, fair and strong
At life's best, with our eyes upturned
Whither life's flower is first discerned,
  We, fixed so, ever should so abide?
What if we still ride on, we two,
With life for ever old yet new,
Changed not in kind but in degree,
The instant made eternity,—
And heaven just prove that I and she
  Ride, ride together, for ever ride?

81. burn, brook.

"CHILDE ROLAND TO THE DARK TOWER CAME"

(See Edgar's Song in "LEAR")

A masterly interpretation by one of Browning's most enthusiastic critics[1] provides a helpful introduction to a difficult work:

"The poem is an example of the power of creative imagination. Out of one line from an old ballad quoted by Shakespeare, Browning has built up a marvellous succession of vivid pictures. The twilight deepens as Childe Roland advances; one can feel the darkness coming on.

> . . . hands unseen
> Were hanging the night around us fast.

"Although the poem means nothing specifically except a triumphant close to a heart-shaking experience, the close is so solemnly splendid that it is difficult to repress a shout of physical exultation. One lonely man, in the presence of all the powers of the Air, sends out an honest blast of defiance—the individual will against the malignant forces of the whole universe.

"What happened when he blew his horn? Did the awful mountains in the blood-red sunset dissolve as the walls of Jericho fell to a similar sound? Did the round, squat Tower vanish like a dream-phantom? Or was the sound of the horn the last breath of the hero? If we believe the former, then Childe Roland is telling his experience to a listener; it is the song of the man 'who came whither he went.' If the latter, which seems to me more dramatic, and more like Browning, then the monologue is murmured by the solitary knight as he advances on his darkening path.

"Three entirely different interpretations may be made of the poem. First, the Tower is the quest, and Success is found only in the moment of Failure. Second, the Tower is the quest, and when found is worth nothing: the hero has spent his life searching something that in the end is seen to be only a round, squat, blind turret—for such things do men throw away their lives! Third, the Tower is not the quest at all—it is damnation, and when the knight turns *aside* from the true road to seek the Tower, he is a lost soul steadily slipping through increasing darkness to hell."

But the latter two interpretations do not seem characteristic of Browning:

"No, I believe that once upon a time, Roland, Giles, Cuthbert, and other knights in solemn assembly took an oath to go on the quest of the Dark Tower: to find it or perish on the way. All but these three have apparently kept their word; they have never returned, and when Roland is on the last stages of his journey, he sees why; they have died a horrible death. The quest is indeed an unspeakably perilous thing: for all but Giles and Cuth-

[1] William Lyon Phelps, *Robert Browning*, new ed., Bobbs-Merrill, 1932. Copyright, 1915, 1932. Used by special permission of the publishers.

bert are dead, and these two suffered a fate worse than death—the awful fear inspired by something hideous on the march changed these splendid specimens of manhood into craven traitors. . . . Roland alone is left. And he has experienced so many disappointments that now all hope of finding the Tower is dead in his breast. Just one spark of manhood remains. He can not succeed, but God grant that he may be fit to fail.

> . . . just to fail as they, seemed best,
> And all the doubt was now—should I be fit?

"As he advances the country becomes an abomination of desolation; then appear evidences of struggle, the marks of monsters: then the awful, boiling river, with the nerve-shattering shriek from its depths as he thrust in his spear. On the other bank, fresh evidences of fearful combats, followed farther along by the appearance of engines of torture. Those of his companions who had survived the beasts had there perished in this frightful manner. Nevertheless, Roland advances, his eyes on the ground. Suddenly the wide wing of some dreadful bird of the night brushes his cap, and he looks up—to his overwhelming amazement, *he sees the Tower!* He sees it as the sailor sees the rocks on a dark night, only when the ship is lost. He sees it in a sudden glare of hell; the air is full of mocking laughter, the scorn of fiends mingling with the sound of the names of their victims, his peers and comrades all lost! The ugly misshapen mountains look like sinister giants, lying chin upon hand, lazily awaiting his destruction. But this atom of humanity, in the presence of all the material forces of this world and the supernatural powers of darkness, places the horn to his lips, and sends out on the evening air a shrill blast of utter defiance. He that endureth to the end shall be saved. Not his possessions, not his happiness, not his bodily frame—they all succumb: but *he* shall be saved."

1

My first thought was, he lied in every word,
That hoary cripple, with malicious eye
Askance to watch the working of his lie
On mine, and mouth scarce able to afford
Suppression of the glee, that pursed and scored
Its edge, at one more victim gained thereby.

2

What else should he be set for, with his staff?
What, save to waylay with his lies, ensnare
All travellers who might find him posted there,
And ask the road? I guessed what skull-like laugh
Would break, what crutch 'gin write my epitaph
For pastime in the dusty thoroughfare,

3

If at his counsel I should turn aside
Into that ominous tract which, all agree,
Hides the Dark Tower. Yet acquiescingly
I did turn as he pointed: neither pride
Nor hope rekindling at the end descried,
So much as gladness that some end might be.

4

For, what with my whole world-wide wandering,
What with my search drawn out through years, my hope
Dwindled into a ghost not fit to cope
With that obstreperous joy success would bring,—
I hardly tried now to rebuke the spring
My heart made, finding failure in its scope.

5

As when a sick man very near to death
Seems dead indeed, and feels begin and end
The tears, and takes the farewell of each friend,
And hears one bid the other go, draw breath
Freelier outside, ("since all is o'er," he saith,
"And the blow fallen no grieving can amend";)

6

While some discuss if near the other graves
Be room enough for this, and when a day
Suits best for carrying the corpse away,
With care about the banners, scarves and staves:
And still the man hears all, and only craves
He may not shame such tender love and stay.

7

Thus, I had so long suffered in this quest,
Heard failure prophesied so oft, been writ
So many times among "The Band"—to wit,
The knights who to the Dark Tower's search addressed
Their steps—that just to fail as they, seemed best,
And all the doubt was now—should I be fit?

8

So, quiet as despair, I turned from him,
That hateful cripple, out of his highway
Into the path he pointed. All the day
Had been a dreary one at best, and dim
Was settling to its close, yet shot one grim
Red leer to see the plain catch its estray.

48. estray, the one astray; that is, Childe Roland.

9

For mark! no sooner was I fairly found
Pledged to the plain, after a pace or two,
Than, pausing to throw backward a last view
O'er the safe road, 'twas gone; grey plain all round:
Nothing but plain to the horizon's bound.
I might go on; nought else remained to do.

10

So, on I went. I think I never saw
Such starved ignoble nature; nothing throve:
For flowers—as well expect a cedar grove!
But cockle, spurge, according to their law
Might propagate their kind, with none to awe,
You'd think; a burr had been a treasure trove.

11

No! penury, inertness and grimace,
In some strange sort, were the land's portion. "See
Or shut your eyes," said Nature peevishly,
"It nothing skills: I cannot help my case:
'Tis the Last Judgment's fire must cure this place,
Calcine its clods and set my prisoners free."

12

If there pushed any ragged thistle-stalk
Above its mates, the head was chopped; the bents
Were jealous else. What made those holes and rents
In the dock's harsh swarth leaves, bruised as to baulk
All hope of greenness? 'tis a brute must walk
Pashing their life out, with a brute's intents.

13

As for the grass, it grew as scant as hair
In leprosy; thin dry blades pricked the mud
Which underneath looked kneaded up with blood.
One stiff blind horse, his every bone a-stare,
Stood stupefied, however he came there:
Thrust out past service from the devil's stud!

14

Alive? he might be dead for aught I know,
With that red gaunt and colloped neck a-strain,
And shut eyes underneath the rusty mane;
Seldom went such grotesqueness with such woe;
I never saw a brute I hated so;
He must be wicked to deserve such pain.

15

I shut my eyes and turned them on my heart.
As a man calls for wine before he fights,
I asked one draught of earlier, happier sights,
Ere fitly I could hope to play my part.
Think first, fight afterwards—the soldier's art:
One taste of the old time sets all to rights.

16

Not it! I fancied Cuthbert's reddening face
Beneath its garniture of curly gold,
Dear fellow, till I almost felt him fold
An arm in mine to fix me to the place,
That way he used. Alas, one night's disgrace!
Out went my heart's new fire and left it cold.

17

Giles then, the soul of honour—there he stands
Frank as ten years ago when knighted first.
What honest man should dare (he said) he durst.
Good—but the scene shifts—faugh! what hangman hands
Pin to his breast a parchment? His own bands
Read it. Poor traitor, spit upon and curst!

18

Better this present than a past like that;
Back therefore to my darkening path again!
No sound, no sight as far as eye could strain.
Will the night send a howlet or a bat?
I asked: when something on the dismal flat
Came to arrest my thoughts and change their train.

19

A sudden little river crossed my path
As unexpected as a serpent comes.
No sluggish tide congenial to the glooms;
This, as it frothed by, might have been a bath
For the fiend's glowing hoof—to see the wrath
Of its black eddy bespate with flakes and spumes.

20

So petty yet so spiteful! All along,
Low scrubby alders kneeled down over it;
Drenched willows flung them headlong in a fit
Of mute despair, a suicidal throng:
The river which had done them all the wrong,
Whate'er that was, rolled by, deterred no whit.

21

Which, while I forded,—good saints, how I feared
To set my foot upon a dead man's cheek,
Each step, or feel the spear I thrust to seek

68. bents, coarse grasses. **72. pashing,** crushing.

114. bespate, spattered.

For hollows, tangled in his hair or beard!
—It may have been a water-rat I speared,
But, ugh! it sounded like a baby's shriek.

22

Glad was I when I reached the other bank.
Now for a better country. Vain presage!
Who were the strugglers, what war did they wage,
Whose savage trample thus could pad the dank
Soil to a plash? Toads in a poisoned tank,
Or wild cats in a red-hot iron cage—

23

The fight must so have seemed in that fell cirque.
What penned them there, with all the plain to choose?
No foot-print leading to that horrid mews,
None out of it. Mad brewage set to work
Their brains, no doubt, like galley-slaves the Turk
Pits for his pastime, Christians against Jews.

24

And more than that—a furlong on—why, there!
What bad use was that engine for, that wheel,
Or brake, not wheel—that harrow fit to reel
Men's bodies out like silk? with all the air
Of Tophet's tool, on earth left unaware,
Or brought to sharpen its rusty teeth of steel.

25

Then came a bit of stubbed ground, once a wood,
Next a marsh, it would seem, and now mere earth
Desperate and done with; (so a fool finds mirth,
Makes a thing and then mars it, till his mood
Changes and off he goes!) within a rood—
Bog, clay and rubble, sand and stark black dearth.

26

Now blotches rankling, coloured gay and grim,
Now patches where some leanness of the soil's
Broke into moss or substances like boils;
Then came some palsied oak, a cleft in him
Like a distorted mouth that splits its rim
Gaping at death, and dies while it recoils.

27

And just as far as ever from the end!
Nought in the distance but the evening, nought
To point my footstep further! At the thought,
A great black bird, Apollyon's bosom-friend,
Sailed past, nor beat his wide wing dragon-penned
That brushed my cap—perchance the guide I sought.

28

For, looking up, aware I somehow grew,
'Spite of the dusk, the plain had given place
All round to mountains—with such name to grace
Mere ugly heights and heaps now stolen in view.
How thus they had surprised me,—solve it, you!
How to get from them was no clearer case.

29

Yet half I seemed to recognize some trick
Of mischief happened to me, God knows when—
In a bad dream perhaps. Here ended, then,
Progress this way. When, in the very nick
Of giving up, one time more, came a click
As when a trap shuts—you're inside the den!

30

Burningly it came on me all at once,
This was the place! those two hills on the right,
Crouched like two bulls locked horn in horn in fight;
While to the left, a tall scalped mountain . . . Dunce,
Dotard, a-dozing at the very nonce,
After a life spent training for the sight!

31

What in the midst lay but the Tower itself?
The round squat turret, blind as the fool's heart,
Built of brown stone, without a counterpart
In the whole world. The tempest's mocking elf
Points to the shipman thus the unseen shelf
He strikes on, only when the timbers start.

32

Not see? because of night perhaps?—why, day
Came back again for that! before it left,
The dying sunset kindled through a cleft:
The hills, like giants at a hunting, lay,
Chin upon hand, to see the game at bay,—
"Now stab and end the creature—to the heft!"

33

Not hear? when noise was everywhere! it tolled
Increasing like a bell. Names in my ears,
Of all the lost adventurers my peers,—

143. Tophet, here, hell. **160. Apollyon,** the devil. See Revelation 9:11 and the famous scene in *The Pilgrim's Progress.*

161. dragon-penned, feathered like a dragon's wing. **184–86. The tempest's mocking elf . . . the timbers start,** as in "The Tale of Carmilhan," in Longfellow's *Tales of a Wayside Inn.*

How such a one was strong, and such was bold,
And such was fortunate, yet each of old
Lost, lost! one moment knelled the woe of years.

34

There they stood, ranged along the hillsides, met
To view the last of me, a living frame
For one more picture! in a sheet of flame
I saw them and I knew them all. And yet
Dauntless the slug-horn to my lips I set,
And blew. "*Childe Roland to the Dark Tower came.*"

FRA LIPPO LIPPI

Browning derived his information concerning Fra Lippo Lippi (1406–1469) from Vasari and from Filippo Baldinucci, who stresses the artist's break with the manner of his predecessors. In the poem the painter-monk is returning to the house of his patron, Cosimo de' Medici (now the Palazzo Riccardi—scene also of "The Statue and the Bust"), whence he had fled to join a gay carnival crowd, when he is apprehended by the watch. In his monologue he states, among other things, his artistic creed. Art is its own justification; it is not necessary to use it to preach a sermon or to teach a lesson. Nor need the painter add "something more." If he simply employs his skill to reproduce what already exists in nature, so that those who carelessly passed it by at first hand may respond to its beauty on canvas, he has fulfilled his function. Both the "naturalists" and the "art for art's sake" crowd have their points of affinity with Fra Lippo Lippi!

Browning himself was neither a naturalist nor an "art for art's sake" man—nor was he a loose liver—yet it is clear that Fra Lippo Lippi held all his sympathy, as he holds ours also. He was a friar without vocation, and the special circumstances under which he entered the cloister cause us to judge his failings leniently. Browning did think of himself as opposing a certain reality to the febrile idealism of much Victorian poetry, and above all he was an enthusiastic apostle of the strenuous life. He could hardly have failed to admire a man who, whatever other Biblical adjurations he may have disregarded, at least obeyed the command "Whatsoever thy hand findeth to do, do it with thy might."

I am poor brother Lippo, by your leave!
You need not clap your torches to my face.
Zooks, what's to blame? you think you see a monk!
What, 'tis past midnight, and you go the rounds,
And here you catch me at an alley's end
Where sportive ladies leave their doors ajar?
The Carmine's my cloister: hunt it up,
Do,—harry out, if you must show your zeal,
Whatever rat, there, haps on his wrong hole,
And nip each softling of a wee white mouse,
Weke, weke, that's crept to keep him company!
Aha, you know your betters! Then, you'll take
Your hand away that's fiddling on my throat,
And please to know me likewise. Who am I?
Why, one, sir, who is lodging with a friend
Three streets off—he's a certain . . . how d'ye call?
Master—a . . . Cosimo of the Medici,
I' the house that caps the corner. Boh! you were best!
Remember and tell me, the day you're hanged,
How you affected such a gullet's-gripe!
But you, sir, it concerns you that your knaves
Pick up a manner nor discredit you:
Zooks, are we pilchards, that they sweep the streets
And count fair prize what comes into their net?
He's Judas to a tittle, that man is!
Just such a face! Why, sir, you make amends.
Lord, I'm not angry! Bid your hangdogs go
Drink out this quarter-florin to the health
Of the munificent House that harbours me
(And many more beside, lads! more beside!)
And all's come square again. I'd like his face—
His, elbowing on his comrade in the door
With the pike and lantern,—for the slave that holds
John Baptist's head a-dangle by the hair
With one hand ("Look you, now," as who should say)
And his weapon in the other, yet unwiped!
It's not your chance to have a bit of chalk,
A wood-coal or the like? or you should see!
Yes, I'm the painter, since you style me so.
What, brother Lippo's doings, up and down,
You know them and they take you? like enough!
I saw the proper twinkle in your eye—
'Tell you, I liked your looks at very first.
Let's sit and set things straight now, hip to haunch.
Here's spring come, and the nights one makes up bands
To roam the town and sing out carnival,
And I've been three weeks shut within my mew,
A-painting for the great man, saints and saints
And saints again. I could not paint all night—
Ouf! I leaned out of window for fresh air.
There came a hurry of feet and little feet,
A sweep of lute-strings, laughs, and whifts of song,—

203. slug-horn, slogan; that is, trumpet. **3. Zooks,** the oath "Gadzooks." **7. Carmine,** the cloister of the Carmelite friars. See note on ll. 139–40.

18. Boh! you were best! you were best release me. Cosimo's name has frightened the watchman. **20. you,** the captain of the guard. **25. Judas,** the betrayer of Christ. Fra Lippo Lippi sees the watchman who has displeased him with a professional eye. He would like to paint him as Judas. See ll. 31 ff. **34. John Baptist's head,** after Herod had it cut off in fulfillment of his rash promise to Salome. See Matthew 14:1–11. **46. carnival,** the gay season preceding Lent.

Flower o' the broom,
Take away love, and our earth is a tomb!
Flower o' the quince,
I let Lisa go, and what good in life since?
Flower o' the thyme—and so on. Round they went.
Scarce had they turned the corner when a titter
Like the skipping of rabbits by moonlight,—three slim shapes,
And a face that looked up . . . zooks, sir, flesh and blood,
That's all I'm made of! Into shreds it went,
Curtain and counterpane and coverlet,
All the bed-furniture—a dozen knots,
There was a ladder! Down I let myself,
Hands and feet, scrambling somehow, and so dropped,
And after them. I came up with the fun
Hard by Saint Laurence, hail fellow, well met,—
Flower o' the rose,
If I've been merry, what matter who knows?
And so as I was stealing back again
To get to bed and have a bit of sleep
Ere I rise up to-morrow and go work
On Jerome knocking at his poor old breast
With his great round stone to subdue the flesh,
You snap me of the sudden. Ah, I see!
Though your eye twinkles still, you shake your head—
Mine's shaved—a monk, you say—the sting's in that!
If Master Cosimo announced himself,
Mum's the word naturally; but a monk!
Come, what am I a beast for? tell us, now!
I was a baby when my mother died
And father died and left me in the street.
I starved there, God knows how, a year or two
On fig-skins, melon-parings, rinds and shucks,
Refuse and rubbish. One fine frosty day,
My stomach being empty as your hat,
The wind doubled me up and down I went.
Old Aunt Lapaccia trussed me with one hand,
(Its fellow was a stinger as I knew)
And so along the wall, over the bridge,
By the straight cut to the convent. Six words there,
While I stood munching my first bread that month:
"So, boy, you're minded," quoth the good fat father
Wiping his own mouth, 'twas refection-time,—
"To quit this very miserable world?
Will you renounce" . . . "the mouthful of bread?" thought I;
By no means! Brief, they made a monk of me;
I did renounce the world, its pride and greed,
Palace, farm, villa, shop and banking-house,
Trash, such as these poor devils of Medici
Have given their hearts to—all at eight years old.
Well, sir, I found in time, you may be sure,
'Twas not for nothing—the good bellyful,
The warm serge and the rope that goes all round,
And day-long blessed idleness beside!
"Let's see what the urchin's fit for"—that came next.
Not overmuch their way, I must confess.
Such a to-do! They tried me with their books:
Lord, they'd have taught me Latin in pure waste!
Flower o' the clove,
All the Latin I construe is "amo," I love!
But, mind you, when a boy starves in the streets
Eight years together, as my fortune was,
Watching folk's faces to know who will fling
The bit of half-stripped grape-bunch he desires,
And who will curse or kick him for his pains,—
Which gentleman processional and fine,
Holding a candle to the Sacrament,
Will wink and let him lift a plate and catch
The droppings of the wax to sell again,
Or holla for the Eight and have him whipped,—
How say I?—nay, which dog bites, which lets drop
His bone from the heap of offal in the street,—
Why, soul and sense of him grow sharp alike,
He learns the look of things, and none the less
For admonition from the hunger-pinch.
I had a store of such remarks, be sure,
Which, after I found leisure, turned to use.
I drew men's faces on my copy-books,
Scrawled them within the antiphonary's marge,
Joined legs and arms to the long music-notes,
Found eyes and nose and chin for A's and B's,
And made a string of pictures of the world
Betwixt the ins and outs of verb and noun,
On the wall, the bench, the door. The monks looked black.
"Nay," quoth the Prior, "turn him out, d'ye say?
In no wise. Lose a crow and catch a lark.
What if at last we get our man of parts,
We Carmelites, like those Camaldolese
And Preaching Friars, to do our church up fine
And put the front on it that ought to be!"

67. **Hard by Saint Lawrence,** near the Church of San Lorenzo. 73. **Jerome knocking,** St. Jerome (340?–420), often so represented. 88. **trussed,** supported. 94. **refection,** lunch.

117. **gentleman processional and fine,** a gentleman finely attired in churchly garb to march in a religious procession. 120. **wax,** of candles burned in churches. 121. **the Eight,** Florentine magistrates. 127. **remarks,** things noticed. 130. **antiphonary's marge,** margins of the choir book. 139–40. **Carmelites,** an order of friars which derives its name from Mt. Carmel. **Camaldolese,** of the convent of Camaldoli, near Florence. **Preaching Friars, Dominicans.**

And hereupon he bade me daub away.
Thank you! my head being crammed, the walls a blank,
Never was such prompt disemburdening.
First, every sort of monk, the black and white,
I drew them, fat and lean: then, folk at church,
From good old gossips waiting to confess
Their cribs of barrel-droppings, candle-ends,—
To the breathless fellow at the altar-foot,
Fresh from his murder, safe and sitting there
With the little children round him in a row
Of admiration, half for his beard and half
For that white anger of his victim's son
Shaking a fist at him with one fierce arm,
Signing himself with the other because of Christ
(Whose sad face on the cross sees only this
After the passion of a thousand years)
Till some poor girl, her apron o'er her head,
(Which the intense eyes looked through) came at eve
On tiptoe, said a word, dropped in a loaf,
Her pair of earrings and a bunch of flowers
(The brute took growling), prayed, and so was gone.
I painted all, then cried "'Tis ask and have;
Choose, for more's ready!"—laid the ladder flat,
And showed my covered bit of cloister-wall.
The monks closed in a circle and praised loud
Till checked, taught what to see and not to see,
Being simple bodies,—"That's the very man!
Look at the boy who stoops to pat the dog!
That woman's like the Prior's niece who comes
To care about his asthma: it's the life!"
But there my triumph's straw-fire flared and funked;
Their betters took their turn to see and say:
The Prior and the learnèd pulled a face
And stopped all that in no time. "How? what's here?
Quite from the mark of painting, bless us all!
Faces, arms, legs and bodies like the true
As much as pea and pea! it's devil's-game!
Your business is not to catch men with show,
With homage to the perishable clay,
But lift them over it, ignore it all,
Make them forget there's such a thing as flesh.
Your business is to paint the souls of men—
Man's soul, and it's a fire, smoke . . . no, it's not . . .
It's vapour done up like a new-born babe—
(In that shape when you die it leaves your mouth)
It's . . . well, what matters talking, it's the soul!
Give us no more of body than shows soul!
Here's Giotto, with his Saint a-praising God,
That sets us praising,—why not stop with him?
Why put all thoughts of praise out of our head
With wonder at lines, colours, and what not?
Paint the soul, never mind the legs and arms!
Rub all out, try at it a second time.
Oh, that white smallish female with the breasts,
She's just my niece . . . Herodias, I would say,—
Who went and danced and got men's heads cut off!
Have it all out!" Now, is this sense, I ask?
A fine way to paint soul, by painting body
So ill, the eye can't stop there, must go further
And can't fare worse! Thus, yellow does for white
When what you put for yellow's simply black,
And any sort of meaning looks intense
When all beside itself means and looks nought.
Why can't a painter lift each foot in turn,
Left foot and right foot, go a double step,
Make his flesh liker and his soul more like,
Both in their order? Take the prettiest face,
The Prior's niece . . . patron-saint—is it so pretty
You can't discover if it means hope, fear,
Sorrow or joy? won't beauty go with these?
Suppose I've made her eyes all right and blue,
Can't I take breath and try to add life's flash,
And then add soul and heighten them threefold?
Or say there's beauty with no soul at all—
(I never saw it—put the case the same—)
If you get simple beauty and nought else,
You get about the best thing God invents:
That's somewhat: and you'll find the soul you have missed,
Within yourself, when you return him thanks.
"Rub all out!" Well, well, there's my life, in short,
And so the thing has gone on ever since.
I'm grown a man no doubt, I've broken bounds:
You should not take a fellow eight years old
And make him swear to never kiss the girls.
I'm my own master, paint now as I please—
Having a friend, you see, in the Corner-house!
Lord, it's fast holding by the rings in front—
Those great rings serve more purposes than just
To plant a flag in, or tie up a horse!
And yet the old schooling sticks, the old grave eyes
Are peeping o'er my shoulder as I work,
The heads shake still—"It's art's decline, my son!

148. cribs, thefts. **barrel-droppings,** wine. **candle-ends,** see l. 120. **150. safe,** because the civil law could not seize him in a sacred place. **157. passion,** suffering, as in Passion Play.

189. Giotto, the famous painter, architect, and sculptor (1276–1337). His method conformed to the notions of propriety entertained by Fra Lippo Lippi's critics. **196–97. Herodias . . . cut off.** It was Salome, the daughter of Herodias, who danced. See note on l. 34. **229. more purposes,** climbing, in the speaker's case.

You're not of the true painters, great and old;
Brother Angelico's the man, you'll find;
Brother Lorenzo stands his single peer:
Fag on at flesh, you'll never make the third!"
Flower o' the pine,
You keep your mistr . . . manners, and I'll stick to mine!
I'm not the third, then: bless us, they must know!
Don't you think they're the likeliest to know,
They with their Latin? So, I swallow my rage,
Clench my teeth, suck my lips in tight, and paint
To please them—sometimes do and sometimes don't;
For, doing most, there's pretty sure to come
A turn, some warm eve finds me at my saints—
A laugh, a cry, the business of the world—
(*Flower o' the peach,*
Death for us all, and his own life for each!)
And my whole soul revolves, the cup runs over,
The world and life's too big to pass for a dream,
And I do these wild things in sheer despite,
And play the fooleries you catch me at,
In pure rage! The old mill-horse, out at grass
After hard years, throws up his stiff heels so,
Although the miller does not preach to him
The only good of grass is to make chaff.
What would men have? Do they like grass or no—
May they or mayn't they? all I want's the thing
Settled for ever one way. As it is,
You tell too many lies and hurt yourself:
You don't like what you only like too much,
You do like what, if given you at your word,
You find abundantly detestable.
For me, I think I speak as I was taught;
I always see the garden and God there
A-making man's wife: and, my lesson learned,
The value and significance of flesh,
I can't unlearn ten minutes afterwards.

You understand me: I'm a beast, I know.
But see, now—why, I see as certainly
As that the morning-star's about to shine,
What will hap some day. We've a youngster here
Comes to our convent, studies what I do,
Slouches and stares and lets no atom drop:
His name is Guidi—he'll not mind the monks—
They call him Hulking Tom, he lets them talk—
He picks my practice up—he'll paint apace,
I hope so—though I never live so long,
I know what's sure to follow. You be judge!
You speak no Latin more than I, belike;
However, you're my man, you've seen the world
—The beauty and the wonder and the power,
The shapes of things, their colours, lights and shades,
Changes, surprises,—and God made it all!
—For what? Do you feel thankful, ay or no,
For this fair town's face, yonder river's line,
The mountain round it and the sky above,
Much more the figures of man, woman, child,
These are the frame to? What's it all about?
To be passed over, despised? or dwelt upon,
Wondered at? oh, this last of course!—you say.
But why not do as well as say,—paint these
Just as they are, careless what comes of it?
God's works—paint anyone, and count it crime
To let a truth slip. Don't object, "His works
Are here already; nature is complete:
Suppose you reproduce her—(which you can't
There's no advantage! you must beat her, then.)"
For, don't you mark? we're made so that we love
First when we see them painted, things we have passed
Perhaps a hundred times nor cared to see;
And so they are better, painted—better to us,
Which is the same thing. Art was given for that;
God uses us to help each other so,
Lending our minds out. Have you noticed, now,
Your cullion's hanging face? A bit of chalk,
And trust me but you should, though! How much more,
If I drew higher things with the same truth!
That were to take the Prior's pulpit-place,
Interpret God to all of you! Oh, oh,
It makes me mad to see what men shall do
And we in our graves! This world's no blot for us,
Nor blank; it means intensely, and means good:
To find its meaning is my meat and drink.
"Ay, but you don't so instigate to prayer!"
Strikes in the Prior: "when your meaning's plain
It does not say to folk—remember matins,
Or, mind you fast next Friday!" Why, for this
What need of art at all? A skull and bones,
Two bits of stick nailed crosswise, or, what's best,
A bell to chime the hour with, does as well.
I painted a Saint Laurence six months since
At Prato, splashed the fresco in fine style:
"How looks my painting, now the scaffold's down?"
I ask a brother: "Hugely," he returns—
Already not one phiz of your three slaves
Who turn the Deacon off his toasted side,

235. **Brother Angelico,** Fra Angelico, the noted painter (1387–1455). 236. **Brother Lorenzo,** Lorenzo Monaco (c. 1370–1425). 276. **Guidi,** Masaccio (1401–1428), actually Fra Lippo Lippi's predecessor, not his successor.

323–24. **Saint Laurence . . . fine style.** St. Lawrence was martyred in 258 A.D. by being roasted on a gridiron. At one point he asked his tormentors to turn him over; he was "done on one side." **At Prato,** the cathedral at Prato, a town near Florence.

But's scratched and prodded to our heart's content,
The pious people have so eased their own
With coming to say prayers there in a rage:
We get on fast to see the bricks beneath.
Expect another job this time next year,
For pity and religion grow i' the crowd—
Your painting serves its purpose!" Hang the fools!

—That is—you'll not mistake an idle word
Spoke in a huff by a poor monk, God wot,
Tasting the air this spicy night which turns
The unaccustomed head like Chianti wine!
Oh, the church knows! don't misreport me, now!
It's natural a poor monk out of bounds
Should have his apt word to excuse himself:
And hearken how I plot to make amends.
I have bethought me: I shall paint a piece
. . . There's for you! Give me six months, then go, see
Something in Sant' Ambrogio's! Bless the nuns!
They want a cast o' my office. I shall paint
God in the midst, Madonna and her babe,
Ringed by a bowery, flowery angel-brood,
Lilies and vestments and white faces, sweet
As puff on puff of grated orris-root
When ladies crowd to Church at midsummer.
And then i' the front, of course a saint or two—
Saint John, because he saves the Florentines,
Saint Ambrose, who puts down in black and white
The convent's friends and gives them a long day,
And Job, I must have him there past mistake,
The man of Uz (and Us without the z,
Painters who need his patience). Well, all these
Secured at their devotion, up shall come
Out of a corner when you least expect,
As one by a dark stair into a great light,
Music and talking, who but Lippo! I!—
Mazed, motionless, and moonstruck—I'm the man!
Back I shrink—what is this I see and hear?
I, caught up with my monk's-things by mistake,
My old serge gown and rope that goes all round,
I, in this presence, this pure company!
Where's a hole, where's a corner for escape?
Then steps a sweet angelic slip of a thing
Forward, puts out a soft palm—"Not so fast!"
—Addresses the celestial presence, "nay—
He made you and devised you, after all,
Though he's none of you! Could Saint John there draw—
His camel-hair make up a painting-brush?
We come to brother Lippo for all that,
Iste perfecit opus!" So, all smile—
I shuffle sideways with my blushing face
Under the cover of a hundred wings
Thrown like a spread of kirtles when you're gay
And play hot cockles, all the doors being shut,
Till, wholly unexpected, in there pops
The hothead husband! Thus I scuttle off
To some safe bench behind, not letting go
The palm of her, the little lily thing
That spoke the good word for me in the nick,
Like the Prior's niece . . . Saint Lucy, I would say.
And so all's saved for me, and for the church
A pretty picture gained. Go, six months hence!
Your hand, sir, and good-bye: no lights, no lights!
The street's hushed, and I know my own way back,
Don't fear me! There's the grey beginning. Zooks!

339. Chianti wine, wine from Chianti, a region south of Florence. **345. There's for you!** He gives him money. **346. Sant' Ambrogio's,** St. Ambrose's Church in Florence. **347 ff. I shall paint . . .** The picture described in "The Coronation of the Virgin," which now hangs in the Academy of Fine Arts, Florence. **354. Saint John . . . Florentines.** St. John the Baptist is the patron saint of Florence. **355–56. Saint Ambrose . . . long day.** St. Ambrose is to be shown writing down the names of those who have made gifts to the convent. As long as these names can be read, the fame of the donors will endure. **357. Job,** the hero of the Old Testament book which bears his name, popularly regarded as a type of patience. **258. Uz, where Job lived.**

375. camel-hair, the raiment of John the Baptist, according to Mark 1:6. **377. Iste perfecit opus!"** This one did the work. A scroll attached to the artist's portrait in the painting carries this legend. **380. kirtles,** tunics, coats. **381. hot cockles.** The blindfolded player in the old English game of cockles must guess who strikes him. But the reference to "The hothead husband" in l. 383, shows that the monk is thinking also of a less innocent game.

ANDREA DEL SARTO

(CALLED "THE FAULTLESS PAINTER")

John Kenyon, Browning's friend and benefactor, asked for a photograph of Andrea del Sarto's picture of his wife and himself in the Pitti Palace, Florence; Browning, unable to secure one, sent this poem instead. Andrea's pictures often give the impression of something viewed through a kind of white mist; the poet has been wonderfully successful in creating the same effect in another medium. The silvery grayness of this "twilight piece" makes a most interesting contrast with the nervous vitality of "Fra Lippo Lippi." In both cases the style is the man, not the man writing, but the man portrayed.

Andrea d'Agnolo di Francesco di Luca (1486–1531) was the son of a tailor, hence "del Sarto." Browning's sources for the poem were the same as for "Fra Lippo Lippi"—Vasari and Baldinucci. The apostle of the glory of the imperfect could not sympathize with a man who was able to achieve everything he wanted to do—

> "Ah, but a man's reach should exceed his grasp,
> Or what's a heaven for?"

Moreover no true artist ever stops working before he has reached his point of failure. Browning presents Andrea as enslaved to soulless beauty—the complaisant, subservient husband of a faithless wife. And since no man can create anything greater than his own soul, Andrea's pictures, for all their technical perfection, must be essentially meaningless. Some recent writers take a much more favorable view of both Andrea's character and his art.

But do not let us quarrel any more,
No, my Lucrezia; bear with me for once:
Sit down and all shall happen as you wish.
You turn your face, but does it bring your heart?
I'll work then for your friend's friend, never fear,
Treat his own subject after his own way,
Fix his own time, accept too his own price,
And shut the money into this small hand
When next it takes mine. Will it? tenderly?
Oh, I'll content him,—but to-morrow, Love!
I often am much wearier than you think,
This evening more than usual, and it seems
As if—forgive now—should you let me sit
Here by the window with your hand in mine
And look a half-hour forth on Fiesole,
Both of one mind, as married people use,
Quietly, quietly the evening through,
I might get up to-morrow to my work
Cheerful and fresh as ever. Let us try.
To-morrow, how you shall be glad for this!
Your soft hand is a woman of itself,
And mine the man's bared breast she curls inside.
Don't count the time lost, neither; you must serve
For each of the five pictures we require:
It saves a model. So! keep looking so—
My serpentining beauty, rounds on rounds!
—How could you ever prick those perfect ears,
Even to put the pearl there! oh, so sweet—
My face, my moon, my everybody's moon,
Which everybody looks on and calls his,
And, I suppose, is looked on by in turn,
While she looks—no one's: very dear, no less.
You smile? why, there's my picture ready made,
There's what we painters call our harmony!
A common greyness silvers everything,—
All in a twilight, you and I alike
—You, at the point of your first pride in me
(That's gone you know),—but I, at every point;
My youth, my hope, my art, being all toned down
To yonder sober pleasant Fiesole.
There's the bell clinking from the chapel-top;
That length of convent-wall across the way
Holds the trees safer, huddled more inside;
The last monk leaves the garden; days decrease,
And autumn grows, autumn in everything.
Eh? the whole seems to fall into a shape
As if I saw alike my work and self
And all that I was born to be and do,
A twilight-piece. Love, we are in God's hand.
How strange now looks the life he makes us lead;
So free we seem, so fettered fast we are!
I feel he laid the fetter: let it lie!
This chamber for example—turn your head—
All that's behind us! You don't understand
Nor care to understand about my art,
But you can hear at least when people speak:
And that cartoon, the second from the door
—It is the thing, Love! so such thing should be—
Behold Madonna!—I am bold to say.
I can do with my pencil what I know,
What I see, what at bottom of my heart
I wish for, if I ever wish so deep—
Do easily, too—when I say, perfectly,
I do not boast, perhaps: yourself are judge,
Who listened to the Legate's talk last week,
And just as much they used to say in France.
At any rate, 'tis easy, all of it!
No sketches first, no studies, that's long past:
I do what many dream of, all their lives,
—Dream? strive to do, and agonize to do,
And fail in doing. I could count twenty such
On twice your fingers, and not leave this town,
Who strive—you don't know how the others strive
To paint a little thing like that you smeared
Carelessly passing with your robes afloat,—
Yet do much less, so much less, Someone says,
(I know his name, no matter)—so much less!
Well, less is more, Lucrezia: I am judged.
There burns a truer light of God in them,
In their vexed beating stuffed and stopped-up brain,
Heart, or whate'er else, than goes on to prompt
This low-pulsed forthright craftsman's hand of mine.
Their works drop groundward, but themselves, I know,
Reach many a time a heaven that's shut to me,
Enter and take their place there sure enough,
Though they come back and cannot tell the world.
My works are nearer heaven, but I sit here.
The sudden blood of these men! at a word—
Praise them, it boils, or blame them, it boils too.
I, painting from myself and to myself,
Know what I do, am unmoved by men's blame
Or their praise either. Somebody remarks
Morello's outline there is wrongly traced,

2. Lucrezia, wife of the painter. **15. Fiesole,** a suburb of Florence. **16. use,** are accustomed to do.

49–52. Love . . . let it lie! Andrea finds fatalism comforting. If God is responsible for his condition, then he need take no responsibility himself. **82. forthright,** unswerving. **93. Morello,** a peak in the Apennines.

His hue mistaken; what of that? or else,
Rightly traced and well ordered; what of that?
Speak as they please, what does the mountain care?
Ah, but a man's reach should exceed his grasp,
Or what's a heaven for? All is silver-grey,
Placid and perfect with my art: the worse!
I know both what I want and what might gain,
And yet how profitless to know, to sigh
"Had I been two, another and myself,
Our head would have o'erlooked the world!" No
    doubt.
Yonder's a work now, of that famous youth
The Urbinate who died five years ago.
('Tis copied, George Vasari sent it me.)
Well, I can fancy how he did it all,
Pouring his soul, with kings and popes to see,
Reaching, that heaven might so replenish him,
Above and through his art—for it gives way;
That arm is wrongly put—and there again—
A fault to pardon in the drawing's lines,
Its body, so to speak: its soul is right,
He means right—that, a child may understand.
Still, what an arm! and I could alter it:
But all the play, the insight and the stretch—
Out of me, out of me! And wherefore out?
Had you enjoined them on me, given me soul,
We might have risen to Rafael, I and you!
Nay, Love, you did give all I asked, I think—
More than I merit, yes, by many times.
But had you—oh, with the same perfect brow,
And perfect eyes, and more than perfect mouth,
And the low voice my soul hears, as a bird
The fowler's pipe, and follows to the snare—
Had you, with these the same, but brought a mind!
Some women do so. Had the mouth there urged
"God and the glory! never care for gain.
The present by the future, what is that?
Live for fame, side by side with Agnolo!
Rafael is waiting: up to God, all three!"
I might have done it for you. So it seems:
Perhaps not. All is as God overrules.
Besides, incentives come from the soul's self;
The rest avail not. Why do I need you?
What wife had Rafael, or has Agnolo?
In this world, who can do a thing, will not;
And who would do it, cannot, I perceive:
Yet the will's somewhat—somewhat, too, the power—
And thus we half-men struggle. At the end,
God, I conclude, compensates, punishes.
'Tis safer for me, if the award be strict,
That I am something underrated here,
Poor this long while, despised, to speak the truth.
I dared not, do you know, leave home all day,
For fear of chancing on the Paris lords.
The best is when they pass and look aside;
But they speak sometimes; I must bear it all.
Well may they speak! That Francis, that first time,
And that long festal year at Fontainebleau!
I surely then could sometimes leave the ground,
Put on the glory, Rafael's daily wear,
In that humane great monarch's golden look,—
One finger in his beard or twisted curl
Over his mouth's good mark that made the smile,
One arm about my shoulder, round my neck,
The jingle of his gold chain in my ear,
I painting proudly with his breath on me,
All his court round him, seeing with his eyes,
Such frank French eyes, and such a fire of souls
Profuse, my hand kept plying by those hearts,—
And, best of all, this, this, this face beyond,
This in the background, waiting on my work,
To crown the issue with a last reward!
A good time, was it not, my kingly days?
And had you not grown restless . . . but I know—
'Tis done and past; 'twas right, my instinct said;
Too live the life grew, golden and not grey,
And I'm the weak-eyed bat no sun should tempt
Out of the grange whose four walls make his world.
How could it end in any other way?
You called me, and I came home to your heart.
The triumph was—to reach and stay there; since
I reached it ere the triumph, what is lost?
Let my hands frame your face in your hair's gold,
You beautiful Lucrezia that are mine!
"Rafael did this, Andrea painted that;
The Roman's is the better when you pray,
But still the other's Virgin was his wife—"
Men will excuse me. I am glad to judge
Both pictures in your presence; clearer grows
My better fortune, I resolve to think.
For, do you know, Lucrezia, as God lives,
Said one day Agnolo, his very self,
To Rafael . . . I have known it all these years . . .
(When the young man was flaming out his thoughts
Upon a palace-wall for Rome to see,
Too lifted up in heart because of it)
"Friend, there's a certain sorry little scrub

105. Urbinate, Raphael, a native of Urbino. **106. George Vasari,** (1512–1574), who studied under Andrea, and wrote *The Lives of the Most Eminent Painters, Sculptors, and Architects,* an important source for this poem (see the introductory note). **130. Agnolo, Michelangelo** (1475–1564).

149. That Francis, Francis I (1494–1547), king of France. According to the story Browning accepted, Andrea left the King's palace at Fontainebleau in obedience to Lucrezia's call, and bought her a house with the money Francis had entrusted to him for the purchase of art treasures. **178. The Roman's,** Raphael's. **186–88. When . . . it,** when Raphael was painting in the Vatican.

Goes up and down our Florence, none cares how,
Who, were he set to plan and execute
As you are, pricked on by your popes and kings,
Would bring the sweat into that brow of yours!"
To Rafael's!—And indeed the arm is wrong.
I hardly dare . . . yet, only you to see,
Give the chalk here—quick, thus the line should go!
Ay, but the soul! he's Rafael! rub it out!
Still, all I care for, if he spoke the truth
(What he? why, who but Michel Agnolo?
Do you forget already words like those?),
If really there was such a chance, so lost,—
Is, whether you're—not grateful—but more pleased.
Well, let me think so. And you smile indeed!
This hour has been an hour! Another smile?
If you would sit thus by me every night
I should work better, do you comprehend?
I mean that I should earn more, give you more.
See, it is settled dusk now; there's a star;
Morello's gone, the watch-lights show the wall,
The cue-owls speak the name we call them by.
Come from the window, love,—come in, at last,
Inside the melancholy little house
We built to be so gay with. God is just.
King Francis may forgive me: oft at nights
When I look up from painting, eyes tired out,
The walls become illumined, brick from brick
Distinct, instead of mortar, fierce bright gold,
That gold of his I did cement them with!
Let us but love each other. Must you go?
That Cousin here again? he waits outside?
Must see you—you, and not with me? Those loans?
More gaming debts to pay? you smiled for that?
Well, let smiles buy me! have you more to spend?
While hand and eye and something of a heart
Are left me, work's my ware, and what's it worth?
I'll pay my fancy. Only let me sit
The grey remainder of the evening out,
Idle, you call it, and muse perfectly
How I could paint, were I but back in France,
One picture, just one more—the Virgin's face,
Not yours this time! I want you at my side
To hear them—that is, Michel Agnolo—
Judge all I do and tell you of its worth.
Will you? Tomorrow, satisfy your friend.
I take the subjects for his corridor,
Finish the portrait out of hand—there, there,
And throw him in another thing or two
If he demurs; the whole should prove enough
To pay for this same Cousin's freak. Beside,
What's better and what's all I care about,
Get you the thirteen scudi for the ruff!

220. Cousin, lover. **241. scudi.** The scudo is an Italian coin worth about a dollar.

Love, does that please you? Ah, but what does he,
The Cousin! what does he to please you more?

I am grown peaceful as old age to-night.
I regret little, I would change still less.
Since there my past life lies, why alter it?
The very wrong to Francis!—it is true
I took his coin, was tempted and complied,
And built this house and sinned, and all is said.
My father and my mother died of want.
Well, had I riches of my own? you see
How one gets rich! Let each one bear his lot.
They were born poor, lived poor, and poor they died:
And I have laboured somewhat in my time
And not been paid profusely. Some good son
Paint my two hundred pictures—let him try!
No doubt, there's something strikes a balance. Yes,
You loved me quite enough, it seems to-night.
This must suffice me here. What would one have?
In heaven, perhaps, new chances, one more chance—
Four great walls in the New Jerusalem,
Meted on each side by the angel's reed,
For Leonard, Rafael, Agnolo and me
To cover—the three first without a wife,
While I have mine! So—still they overcome
Because there's still Lucrezia,—as I choose.

Again the Cousin's whistle! Go, my Love.

CALIBAN UPON SETEBOS;

OR, NATURAL THEOLOGY IN THE ISLAND

"Thou thoughtest that I was altogether such an one as thyself." [Psalm 50:21]

Caliban is the monster in Shakespeare's play *The Tempest;* Sycorax, his mother; Setebos, his god. The magician Prospero holds him in bondage. The main title of Browning's poem is intentionally ironical. We read Darwin on evolution, Gibbon on the Roman Empire; why not Caliban upon Setebos?

Natural theology—the religious beliefs deducible from the phenomena of nature—stands opposite revealed theology, which presupposes the Deity conveys special knowledge of the Truth to a particular group. In ll. 217–18 Caliban denies the possibility of revelation.

It was Alexander Pope who once declared that: "An

250. My father . . . want. Andrea neglected his own family to lavish benefits on Lucrezia's. **261. New Jerusalem.** See Revelation 21:10–21. **263. Leonard,** Leonardo da Vinci (1452–1519).

honest man's the noblest work of God." Robert G. Ingersoll, the nineteenth-century American agnostic, cynically reversed the saying: "An honest god's the noblest work of man." Anthropomorphism, the well-known human tendency to frame God in our own image, is undoubtedly the object of some of Browning's shafts in this poem; there are passages, such as ll. 98–108, where he is clearly thinking particularly of the Calvinists, whose special faith in foreordination and election he abhorred.

Shakespeare's attitude toward Caliban is nearly as unsympathetic and unpsychological as Prospero's own; Browning, probably finding a suggestion in current speculations concerning the "missing link" of Darwinian evolution, takes us on a tour in Caliban's mind. It proves a very interesting mind.

Some aspects of the monster's life and thought are, indeed, quite revolting. His god is not a god of law but a god of caprice. Setebos is a moon god; he made the world for spite and for sport; he wanted to escape from ennui; there is no suggestion of any higher motive. The only reason Caliban does not hate him is that he knows that if he were God he would behave quite as badly himself!

But this realization itself indicates capacity for development in Caliban, and it does not stand alone. The monster's joy in creative activity (l.188) is significant: so is his feeling that Setebos could not possibly have made the stars. He is too sensitive to accept the consistent dualism of his mother, who believed that the Quiet made the world and Setebos vexed it; the world does not bear the signature of the Quiet! Nor can her son agree with Sycorax that more torture is to be looked for after death; Setebos, he feels sure, has done his worst and his all here. (To get the full force of this we must remember that though Browning's faith in immortality was absolute, he did not believe in eternal damnation; annihilation was, to his way of thinking, infinitely more humane than the Calvinistic view of eternity.)

It will save much trouble in reading this poem if certain matters are cleared up at the outset. In ll. 1–23, Browning sets his stage; Caliban does not "blossom into speech" before l. 24. Note the use of brackets to mark this passage off from the monologue, and compare ll. 284–95. The matter is slightly confusing because the second passage, especially, is more or less in Caliban's own style. The use of an apostrophe before a verb indicates Caliban. He generally speaks of himself in the third person; Caliban refers consistently to Setebos as "He" and to the Quiet as "it."

['Will sprawl, now that the heat of day is best,
Flat on his belly in the pit's much mire,
With elbows wide, fists clenched to prop his chin.
And, while he kicks both feet in the cool slush,
And feels about his spine small eft-things course,
Run in and out each arm, and make him laugh:
And while above his head a pompion-plant,
Coating the cave-top as a brow its eye,
Creeps down to touch and tickle hair and beard,
And now a flower drops with a bee inside,
And now a fruit to snap at, catch and crunch,—
He looks out o'er yon sea which sunbeams cross
And recross till they weave a spider-web,
(Meshes of fire, some great fish breaks at times)
And talks to his own self, howe'er he please,
Touching that other, whom his dam called God.
Because to talk about Him, vexes—ha,
Could He but know! and time to vex is now,
When talk is safer than in winter-time.
Moreover Prosper and Miranda sleep
In confidence he drudges at their task,
And it is good to cheat the pair, and gibe,
Letting the rank tongue blossom into speech.]

Setebos, Setebos, and Setebos!
'Thinketh, He dwelleth i' the cold o' the moon.

'Thinketh He made it, with the sun to match,
But not the stars; the stars came otherwise;
Only made clouds, winds, meteors, such as that:
Also this isle, what lives and grows thereon,
And snaky sea which rounds and ends the same.

'Thinketh, it came of being ill at ease:
He hated that He cannot change His cold,
Nor cure its ache. 'Hath spied an icy fish
That longed to 'scape the rock-stream where she lived,
And thaw herself within the lukewarm brine
O' the lazy sea her stream thrusts far amid,
A crystal spike 'twixt two warm walls of wave;
Only, she ever sickened, found repulse
At the other kind of water, not her life,
(Green-dense and dim-delicious, bred o' the sun,)
Flounced back from bliss she was not born to breathe,
And in her old bounds buried her despair,
Hating and loving warmth alike: so He.

'Thinketh, He made thereat the sun, this isle,
Trees and the fowls here, beast and creeping thing.
Yon otter, sleek-wet, black, lithe as a leech;
Yon auk, one fire-eye in a ball of foam,
That floats and feeds; a certain badger brown
He hath watched hunt with that slant white-wedge eye
By moonlight; and the pie with the long tongue
That pricks deep into oakwarts for a worm,
And says a plain word when she finds her prize,
But will not eat the ants; the ants themselves
That build a wall of seeds and settled stalks
About their hole—He made all these and more,

5. eft-things, newts. **7. pompion-plant,** pumpkin.

19. When talk . . . winter-time. In winter Setebos stays closer to the island. **50. pie,** magpie.

Made all we see, and us, in spite: how else?
He could not, Himself, make a second self
To be His mate; as well have made Himself:
He would not make what he mislikes or slights,
An eyesore to Him, or not worth His pains:
But did, in envy, listlessness or sport,
Make what Himself would fain, in a manner, be—
Weaker in most points, stronger in a few,
Worthy, and yet mere playthings all the while,
Things He admires and mocks too,—that is it.
Because, so brave, so better though they be,
It nothing skills if He begin to plague.
Look now, I melt a gourd-fruit into mash,
And honeycomb and pods, I have perceived,
Which bite like finches when they bill and kiss,—
Then, when froth rises bladdery, drink up all,
Quick, quick, till maggots scamper through my brain;
Last, throw me on my back i' the seeded thyme,
And wanton, wishing I were born a bird.
Put case, unable to be what I wish,
I yet could make a live bird out of clay:
Would not I take clay, pinch my Caliban
Able to fly?—for, there, see, he hath wings,
And great comb like the hoopoe's to admire,
And there, a sting to do his foes offence,
There, and I will that he begin to live,
Fly to yon rock-top, nip me off the horns
Of grigs high up that make the merry din,
Saucy through their veined wings, and mind me not.
In which feat, if his leg snapped, brittle clay,
And he lay stupid-like,—why, I should laugh;
And if he, spying me, should fall to weep,
Beseech me to be good, repair his wrong,
Bid his poor leg smart less or grow again,—
Well, as the chance were, this might take or else
Not take my fancy: I might hear his cry,
And give the manikin three sound legs for one,
Or pluck the other off, leave him like an egg,
And lessoned he was mine and merely clay.
Were this no pleasure, lying in the thyme,
Drinking the mash, with brain become alive,
Making and marring clay at will? So He.

'Thinketh, such shows nor right nor wrong in Him,
Nor kind, nor cruel: He is strong and Lord.
'Am strong myself compared to yonder crabs
That march now from the mountain to the sea;
'Let twenty pass, and stone the twenty-first,
Loving not, hating not, just choosing so.
'Say, the first straggler that boasts purple spots
Shall join the file, one pincer twisted off;
'Say, this bruised fellow shall receive a worm,
And two worms he whose nippers end in red;
As it likes me each time, I do: so He.

Well then, 'supposeth He is good i' the main,
Placable if His mind and ways were guessed,
But rougher than His handiwork, be sure!
Oh, He hath made things worthier than Himself,
And envieth that, so helped, such things do more
Than He who made them! What consoles but this?
That they, unless through Him, do nought at all,
And must submit: What other use in things?
'Hath cut a pipe of pithless elder-joint
That, blown through, gives exact the scream o' the jay
When from her wing you twitch the feathers blue:
Sound this, and little birds that hate the jay
Flock within stone's throw, glad their foe is hurt:
Put case such pipe could prattle and boast forsooth,
"I catch the birds, I am the crafty thing,
I make the cry my maker cannot make
With his great round mouth; he must blow through mine!"
Would not I smash it with my foot? So He.

But wherefore rough, why cold and ill at ease?
Aha, that is a question! Ask, for that,
What knows,—the something over Setebos
That made Him, or He, may be, found and fought,
Worsted, drove off and did to nothing, perchance.
There may be something quiet o'er His head,
Out of His reach, that feels nor joy nor grief,
Since both derive from weakness in some way.
I joy because the quails come; would not joy
Could I bring quails here when I have a mind:
This Quiet, all it hath a mind to, doth.
'Esteemeth stars the outposts of its couch,
But never spends much thought nor care that way.
It may look up, work up,—the worse for those
It works on! 'Careth but for Setebos
The many-handed as a cuttle-fish,
Who, making Himself feared through what He does,
Looks up, first, and perceives he cannot soar
To what is quiet and hath happy life;
Next looks down here, and out of very spite

67. skills, avails. **71. bladdery,** in bubbles. **75. Put case.** Consider this hypothetical case. **82. nip me off,** the ethical dative, common in Shakespeare, sometimes found in formal writing and frequently in popular speech to this day. See l. 262. **83. grigs,** crickets or grasshoppers.

138. its, the Quiet's. **140–41. It may . . . works on!** The Quiet may, for all Caliban knows or cares. He has no evidence that it does; he is not much interested in the matter one way or the other. He "never spends much thought nor care that way"; Caliban "careth but for Setebos"; that is the god he must watch out for! **143. Who,** refers back to Setebos; l. 142 is parenthetical.

Makes this a bauble-world to ape yon real,
These good things to match those as hips do grapes.
'Tis solace making baubles, ay, and sport.
Himself peeped late, eyed Prosper at his books
Careless and lofty, lord now of the isle:
Vexed, 'stitched a book of broad leaves, arrow-shaped,
Wrote thereon, he knows what, prodigious words;
Has peeled a wand and called it by a name;
Weareth at whiles for an enchanter's robe
The eyed skin of a supple oncelot;
And hath an ounce sleeker than youngling mole,
A four-legged serpent he makes cower and couch,
Now snarl, now hold its breath and mind his eye,
And saith she is Miranda and my wife:
'Keeps for his Ariel a tall pouch-bill crane
He bids go wade for fish and straight disgorge;
Also a sea-beast, lumpish, which he snared,
Blinded the eyes of, and brought somewhat tame,
And split its toe-webs, and now pens the drudge
In a hole o' the rock and calls him Caliban;
A bitter heart that bides its time and bites.
'Plays thus at being Prosper in a way,
Taketh his mirth with make-believes: so He.
His dam held that the Quiet made all things
Which Setebos vexed only: 'holds not so.
Who made them weak, meant weakness He might vex.
Had He meant other, while His hand was in,
Why not make horny eyes no thorn could prick,
Or plate my scalp with bone against the snow,
Or overscale my flesh 'neath joint and joint,
Like an orc's armour? Ay,—so spoil His sport!
He is the One now: only He doth all.

'Saith, He may like, perchance, what profits Him.
Ay, himself loves what does him good; but why?
'Gets good no otherwise. This blinded beast
Loves whoso places flesh-meat on his nose,
But, had he eyes, would want no help, but hate
Or love, just as it liked him: He hath eyes.
Also it pleaseth Setebos to work,
Use all His hands, and exercise much craft,
By no means for the love of what is worked.
'Tasteth, himself, no finer good i' the world
When all goes right, in this safe summer-time,
And he wants little, hungers, aches not much,
Than trying what to do with wit and strength.
'Falls to make something: 'piled yon pile of turfs,
And squared and stuck there squares of soft white chalk,
And, with a fish-tooth, scratched a moon on each,
And set up endwise certain spikes of tree,
And crowned the whole with a sloth's skull a-top,
Found dead i' the woods, too hard for one to kill.
No use at all i' the work, for work's sole sake;
'Shall some day knock it down again: so He.

'Saith He is terrible: watch His feats in proof!
One hurricane will spoil six good months' hope.
He hath a spite against me, that I know,
Just as He favours Prosper, who knows why?
So it is, all the same, as well I find.
'Wove wattles half the winter, fenced them firm
With stone and stake to stop she-tortoises
Crawling to lay their eggs here: well, one wave,
Feeling the foot of Him upon its neck,
Gaped as a snake does, lolled out its large tongue,
And licked the whole labour flat: so much for spite.
Saw a ball flame down late (yonder it lies)
Where, half an hour before, I slept i' the shade:
Often they scatter sparkles: there is force!
'Dug up a newt He may have envied once
And turned to stone, shut up inside a stone.
Please Him and hinder this?—What Prosper does?
Aha, if He would tell me how! Not He!
There is the sport: discover how or die!
All need not die, for of the things o' the isle
Some flee afar, some dive, some run up trees;
Those at His mercy,—why, they please Him most
When . . . when . . . well, never try the same way twice!
Repeat what act has pleased, He may grow wroth.
You must not know His ways, and play Him off,
Sure of the issue. 'Doth the like himself:
'Spareth a squirrel that it nothing fears
But steals the nut from underneath my thumb,
And when I threat, bites stoutly in defence:
'Spareth an urchin that contrariwise,
Curls up into a ball, pretending death
For fright at my approach: the two ways please.
But what would move my choler more than this,
That either creature counted on its life
To-morrow and next day and all days to come,
Saying, forsooth, in the inmost of its heart,
"Because he did so yesterday with me,
And otherwise with such another brute,
So must he do henceforth and always."—Ay?

148. hips, false fruit of a rosebush. **150. Himself,** Caliban. **156. oncelot.** Does not appear in the *New English Dictionary.* Perhaps Browning confused "ounce," snow leopard, with "ocelot." **160. Miranda,** not Prospero's wife, but his daughter. Caliban, who (according to Shakespeare) lusts after her, would naturally image her in a sexual aspect. **161. Ariel,** in Shakespeare, the light, airy spirit kept in bondage by Prospero, as Caliban is the gross, earthy spirit.

216. Please Him . . . does? Shall I win his favor, as Prospero does, so that he may not treat me as he treated, for example, the newt? **226. that,** so that.

Would teach the reasoning couple what "must" means!
'Doth as he likes, or wherefore Lord? So He.

'Conceiveth all things will continue thus,
And we shall have to live in fear of Him
So long as He lives, keeps His strength: no change,
If He have done His best, make no new world
To please Him more, so leave off watching this,—
If He surprise not even the Quiet's self
Some strange day,—or, suppose, grow into it
As grubs grow butterflies: else, here we are,
And there is He, and nowhere help at all.

'Believeth with the life, the pain shall stop.
His dam held different, that after death
He both plagued enemies and feasted friends:
Idly! He doth His worst in this our life,
Giving just respite lest we die through pain,
Saving last pain for worst,—with which, an end.
Meanwhile, the best way to escape His ire
Is, not to seem too happy. 'Sees, himself,
Yonder two flies, with purple films and pink,
Bask on the pompion-bell above: kills both.
'Sees two black painful beetles roll their ball
On head and tail as if to save their lives:
Moves them the stick away they strive to clear.
Even so, 'would have Him misconceive, suppose
This Caliban strives hard and ails no less,
And always, above all else, envies Him;
Wherefore he mainly dances on dark nights,
Moans in the sun, gets under holes to laugh,
And never speaks his mind save housed as now:
Outside, 'groans, curses. If He caught me here,
O'erheard this speech, and asked "What chucklest at?"
'Would, to appease Him, cut a finger off,
Or of my three kid yearlings burn the best,
Or let the toothsome apples rot on tree,
Or push my tame beast for the orc to taste:
While myself lit a fire, and made a song
And sung it, "*What I hate, be consecrate*
To celebrate Thee and Thy state, no mate
For Thee; what see for envy in poor me?"
Hoping the while, since evils sometimes mend,
Warts rub away and sores are cured with slime,
That some strange day, will either the Quiet catch
And conquer Setebos, or likelier He
Decrepit may doze, doze, as good as die.

[What, what? A curtain o'er the world at once!
Crickets stop hissing; not a bird—or, yes,
There scuds His raven that has told Him all!
It was fool's play, this prattling! Ha! The wind
Shoulders the pillared dust, death's house o' the move,
And fast invading fires begin! White blaze—
A tree's head snaps—and there, there, there, there, there,
His thunder follows! Fool to gibe at Him!
Lo! 'Lieth flat and loveth Setebos!
'Maketh his teeth meet through his upper lip,
Will let those quails fly, will not eat this month
One little mess of whelks, so he may 'scape!]

244. make, if he make. **252. He,** Setebos. **253. Idly!** His dam held these ideas idly; that is, they are wrong. **254. just . . . pain,** just enough respite so that we do not die under torture. **271 ff. 'Would, to appease him . . .** Browning is thinking of the primitive habit of sacrificing to the gods, also, perhaps, of the idea still prevalent in his own time that God is pleased to have people give up the things that make them happy. See ll. 294–95. **276. What I hate.** Setebos must not suspect Caliban's own attachment to the offering; he is a jealous god. **277–78. no mate for Thee,** there is no mate for Thee; that is, Setebos is unique and incomparable; why, then, should he permit so insignificant a creature as Caliban to rouse his wrath?

283. Decrepit may doze . . . die. This contrasts interestingly with Hardy's hope, in *The Dynasts* and elsewhere, that the Immanent Will behind the universe, now blind, may some day come to wake and understand.

PROSPICE

The title (Latin) means "Look Forward." The poem was written shortly after the death of Mrs. Browning, who is distinctly referred to at the close.

Fear death?—to feel the fog in my throat,
The mist in my face,
When the snows begin, and the blasts denote
I am nearing the place,
The power of the night, the press of the storm,
The post of the foe;
Where he stands, the Arch Fear in a visible form,
Yet the strong man must go:
For the journey is done and the summit attained,
And the barriers fall,
Though a battle's to fight ere the guerdon be gained,
The reward of it all.
I was ever a fighter, so—one fight more,
The best and the last!
I would hate that death bandaged my eyes, and forbore,
And bade me creep past.
No! let me taste the whole of it, fare like my peers
The heroes of old,
Bear the brunt, in a minute pay glad life's arrears
Of pain, darkness and cold.
For sudden the worst turns the best to the brave,

The black minute's at end,
And the elements' rage, the fiend-voices that rave,
Shall dwindle, shall blend,
Shall change, shall become first a peace out of pain,
Then a light, then thy breast,
O thou soul of my soul! I shall clasp thee again,
And with God be the rest!

EPILOGUE

This is the last poem in Browning's last book *Asolando*, published on the day of his death.

At the midnight in the silence of the sleep-time,
When you set your fancies free,
Will they pass to where—by death, fools think, imprisoned—
Low he lies who once so loved you, whom you love so,
—Pity me?

Oh to love so, be so loved, yet so mistaken!
What had I on earth to do
With the slothful, with the mawkish, the unmanly?
Like the aimless, helpless, hopeless, did I drivel
—Being—who?

One who never turned his back but marched breast forward,
Never doubted clouds would break,
Never dreamed, though right were worsted, wrong would triumph,
Held we fall to rise, are baffled to fight better,
Sleep to wake.

No, at noonday in the bustle of man's work-time
Greet the unseen with a cheer!
Bid him forward, breast and back as either should be,
"Strive and thrive!" cry "Speed,—fight on, fare ever
There as here!"

Elizabeth Barrett Browning
1806–1861

To Elizabeth Barrett Browning belongs the double honor of being one of the two or three most distinguished woman poets in English literature and the heroine of the most celebrated romance in English literary history. At fifteen an injury to her spine initiated a period of semi-invalidism, during which she studied Greek and Hebrew, read widely, and wrote and published verse. Her literary career thus began early; romance came to her only in her fortieth year. When her future husband met her (through his admiration for her poetry) in 1845, her reputation was far greater than his; and through the years of their married life most of the money that literature made for the Brownings came through her books. When Wordsworth died in 1850, Mrs. Browning was suggested for the laureateship.

Elizabeth Barrett was considered to be a helpless invalid when, in his first letter to her in January 1845, Browning wrote, "I love your verses with all my heart, dear Miss Barrett," and later in the same letter added, "I love you too." At that time they had never met, and it was not until the following May that Miss Barrett yielded, somewhat in spite of her better judgment, to the young poet's entreaties that he be allowed to call on her. The swift flowering of their love, the renewed vitality it brought to the prisoner in her stern father's home, the elopement of the couple to Italy and lifelong happiness—these are facts of literary history that have become all but legend.

Mrs. Browning brought to her husband not only love and understanding, but also a fine critical sense from which his own work benefited. She shared his active interest in Italian political affairs, and two of her works, *Casa Guidi Windows*, 1851, and *Poems before Congress*, 1860, reflect her passion for Italy. The Brownings lived continuously in Italy, and they had enjoyed fifteen years of ideally happy marriage when she died in Florence in 1861.

Mrs. Browning wrote a great number of poems, but too many are marred by diffuseness and extravagance both in thought and expression. *Sonnets from the Portuguese*, however, is a genuine contribution to English literature. The title of the sonnets, published anonymously, was, of course, a smoke screen. She thrust them into Browning's pocket one day in 1847, telling him to tear them up if he did not like them. The sonnets survive partly because the restraint and compression of the

Italian sonnet form helped her to avoid some, if not all, of her faults; partly because the theme is timeless; and they will continue to be read also because they are the one work which gives us their author in the aspect in which it is most appealing to think of her—as the beloved of Robert Browning.

from SONNETS FROM THE PORTUGUESE

1

I thought once how Theocritus had sung
Of the sweet years, the dear and wished-for years,
Who each one in a gracious hand appears
To bear a gift for mortals, old or young:
And, as I mused it in his antique tongue,
I saw, in gradual vision through my tears,
The sweet, sad years, the melancholy years,
Those of my own life, who by turns had flung
A shadow across me. Straightway I was 'ware,
So weeping, how a mystic Shape did move
Behind me, and drew me backward by the hair,
And a voice said in mastery, while I strove, . . .
"Guess now who holds thee?"—"Death," I said. But, there,
The silver answer rang . . . "Not Death, but Love."

3

Unlike are we, unlike, O princely Heart!
Unlike our uses and our destinies.
Our ministering two angels look surprise
On one another, as they strike athwart
Their wings in passing. Thou, bethink thee, art
A guest for queens to social pageantries,
With gages from a hundred brighter eyes
Than tears even can make mine, to play thy part
Of chief musician. What hast *thou* to do
With looking from the lattice-lights at me,
A poor, tired, wandering singer, . . . singing through
The dark, and leaning up a cypress-tree?
The chrism is on thine head,—on mine, the dew,—
And Death must dig the level where these agree.

7

The face of all the world is changed, I think,
Since first I heard the footsteps of thy soul
Move still, oh, still, beside me, as they stole
Betwixt me and the dreadful outer brink
Of obvious death, where I, who thought to sink,
Was caught up into love, and taught the whole
Of life in a new rhythm. The cup of dole
God gave for baptism, I am fain to drink,
And praise its sweetness, Sweet, with thee anear.
The names of country, heaven, are changed away
For where thou art or shalt be, there or here;
And this . . . this lute and song . . . loved yesterday,
(The singing angels know) are only dear
Because thy name moves right in what they say.

8

What can I give thee back, O liberal
And princely giver, who hast brought the gold
And purple of thine heart, unstained, untold,
And laid them on the outside of the wall
For such as I to take or leave withal,
In unexpected largesse? am I cold,
Ungrateful, that for these most manifold
High gifts, I render nothing back at all?
Not so; not cold,—but very poor instead.
Ask God who knows. For frequent tears have run
The colours from my life, and left so dead
And pale a stuff, it were not fitly done
To give the same as pillow to thy head.
Go farther! let it serve to trample on.

14

If thou must love me, let it be for nought
Except for love's sake only. Do not say
"I love her for her smile . . . her look . . . her way
Of speaking gently, . . . for a trick of thought
That falls in well with mine, and certes brought
A sense of pleasant ease on such a day"—
For these things in themselves, Belovèd, may
Be changed, or change for thee,—and love, so wrought,
May be unwrought so. Neither love me for
Thine own dear pity's wiping my cheeks dry,—
A creature might forget to weep, who bore
Thy comfort long, and lose thy love thereby!
But love me for love's sake, that evermore
Thou may'st love on, through love's eternity.

18

I never gave a lock of hair away
To a man, Dearest, except this to thee,
Which now upon my fingers thoughtfully
I ring out to the full brown length and say
"Take it." My day of youth went yesterday;
My hair no longer bounds to my foot's glee,

1. **Theocritus,** Greek pastoral poet (third century B.C.). *Sec. 3.* *7.* **gages,** pledges. **12. cypress-tree,** traditionally associated with death.

Nor plant I it from rose or myrtle-tree,
As girls do, any more. It only may
Now shade on two pale cheeks the mark of tears,
Taught drooping from the head that hangs aside
Through sorrow's trick. I thought the funeral-shears
Would take this first, but Love is justified,—
Take it thou, . . . finding pure, from all those years,
The kiss my mother left here when she died.

20

Belovèd, my Belovèd, when I think
That thou wast in the world a year ago,
What time I sat alone here in the snow
And saw no footprint, heard the silence sink
No moment at thy voice, . . . but, link by link,
Went counting all my chains as if that so
They never could fall off at any blow
Struck by thy possible hand . . . why, thus I drink
Of life's great cup of wonder! Wonderful,
Never to feel thee thrill the day or night
With personal act or speech,—nor ever cull
Some prescience of thee with the blossoms white
Thou sawest growing! Atheists are as dull,
Who cannot guess God's presence out of sight.

23

Is it indeed so? If I lay here dead,
Wouldst thou miss any life in losing mine?
And would the sun for thee more coldly shine
Because of grave-damps falling round my head?
I marvelled, my Belovèd, when I read
Thy thought so in the letter. I am thine—
But . . . *so* much to thee? Can I pour thy wine
While my hands tremble? Then my soul, instead
Of dreams of death, resumes life's lower range.
Then, love me, Love! Look on me . . . breathe on me!
As brighter ladies do not count it strange,
For love, to give up acres and degree,
I yield the grave for thy sake, and exchange
My near sweet view of Heaven, for earth with thee!

24

Let the world's sharpness like a clasping knife
Shut in upon itself and do no harm
In this close hand of Love, now soft and warm,
And let us hear no sound of human strife
After the click of the shutting. Life to life—

Sec. 18. **7–8. Nor plant . . . any more.** She no longer wears leaves or blossoms in her hair, as she did when she was younger.

I lean upon thee, Dear, without alarm,
And feel as safe as guarded by a charm
Against the stab of worldlings, who if rife
Are weak to injure. Very whitely still
The lilies of our lives may reassure
Their blossoms from their roots, accessible
Alone to heavenly dews that drop not fewer;
Growing straight, out of man's reach, on the hill.
God only, who made us rich, can make us poor.

26

I lived with visions for my company
Instead of men and women, years ago,
And found them gentle mates, nor thought to know
A sweeter music than they played to me.
But soon their trailing purple was not free
Of this world's dust,—their lutes did silent grow,
And I myself grew faint and blind below
Their vanishing eyes. Then THOU didst come . . . to be,
Belovèd, what they seemed. Their shining fronts,
Their songs, their splendours (better, yet the same,
As river-water hallowed into fonts),
Met in thee, and from out thee overcame
My soul with satisfaction of all wants—
Because God's gifts put man's best dreams to shame.

27

My own Belovèd, who hast lifted me
From this drear flat of earth where I was thrown,
And, in betwixt the languid ringlets, blown
A life-breath, till the forehead hopefully
Shines out again, as all the angels see,
Before thy saving kiss! My own, my own,
Who camest to me when the world was gone,
And I who looked for only God found *thee!*
I find thee; I am safe, and strong, and glad.
As one who stands in dewless asphodel
Looks backward on the tedious time he had
In the upper life,—so I, with bosom-swell,
Make witness, here, between the good and bad,
That Love, as strong as Death, retrieves as well.

28

My letters! all dead paper, . . . mute and white!—
And yet they seem alive and quivering
Against my tremulous hands which loose the string
And let them drop down on my knee to-night.
This said, . . . he wished to have me in his sight
Once, as a friend: this fixed a day in spring
To come and touch my hand . . . a simple thing,
Yet I wept for it!—this, . . . the paper's light . . .

Sec. 27. **10. asphodel,** here, a flower in the Greek other-world.

Said, *Dear, I love thee;* and I sank and quailed
As if God's future thundered on my past.
This said, *I am thine*—and so its ink has paled
With lying at my heart that beat too fast.
And this . . . O Love, thy words have ill availed,
If, what this said, I dared repeat at last!

31

Thou comest! all is said without a word.
I sit beneath thy looks, as children do
In the noon-sun, with souls that tremble through
Their happy eyelids from an unaverred
Yet prodigal inward joy. Behold, I erred
In that last doubt! and yet I cannot rue
The sin most, but the occasion—that we two
Should for a moment stand unministered
By a mutual presence. Ah, keep near and close,
Thou dovelike help! and, when my fears would rise,
With thy broad heart serenely interpose;
Brood down with thy divine sufficiencies
These thoughts which tremble when bereft of those,
Like callow birds left desert to the skies.

35

If I leave all for thee, wilt thou exchange
And be all to me? Shall I never miss
Home-talk and blessing and the common kiss
That comes to each in turn, nor count it strange,
When I look up, to drop on a new range
Of walls and floors . . . another home than this?
Nay, wilt thou fill that place by me which is
Filled by dead eyes too tender to know change?
That's hardest. If to conquer love, has tried,
To conquer grief, tries more . . . as all things prove;
For grief indeed is love and grief beside.
Alas, I have grieved so I am hard to love.
Yet love me—wilt thou? Open thine heart wide,
And fold within the wet wings of thy dove.

38

First time he kissed me, he but only kissed
The fingers of this hand wherewith I write;
And, ever since, it more grew clean and white, . . .
Slow to world-greetings . . . quick with its "Oh, list,"
When the angels speak. A ring of amethyst
I could not wear here, plainer to my sight,
Than that first kiss. The second passed in height
The first, and sought the forehead, and half missed,
Half falling on the hair. O beyond meed!
That was the chrism of love, which love's own crown,
With sanctifying sweetness, did precede.
The third upon my lips was folded down
In perfect, purple state: since when, indeed,
I have been proud and said, "My love, my own."

41

I thank all who have loved me in their hearts,
With thanks and love from mine. Deep thanks to all
Who paused a little near the prison-wall
To hear my music in its louder parts
Ere they went onward, each one to the mart's
Or temple's occupation, beyond call.
But thou, who, in my voice's sink and fall,
When the sob took it, thy divinest Art's
Own instrument didst drop down at thy foot,
To hearken what I said between my tears, . . .
Instruct me how to thank thee!—Oh, to shoot
My soul's full meaning into future years,
That *they* should lend it utterance, and salute
Love that endures, from Life that disappears!

43

How do I love thee? Let me count the ways.
I love thee to the depth and breadth and height
My soul can reach, when feeling out of sight
For the ends of Being and ideal Grace.
I love thee to the level of every day's
Most quiet need, by sun and candlelight.
I love thee freely, as men strive for Right;
I love thee purely, as they turn from Praise.
I love thee with the passion put to use
In my old griefs, and with my childhood's faith.
I love thee with a love I seemed to lose
With my lost saints,—I love thee with the breath,
Smiles, tears, of all my life!—and, if God choose,
I shall but love thee better after death.

44

Belovèd, thou hast brought me many flowers
Plucked in the garden, all the summer through
And winter, and it seemed as if they grew
In this close room, nor missed the sun and showers.
So, in the like name of that love of ours,
Take back these thoughts which here unfolded too,
And which on warm and cold days I withdrew
From my heart's ground. Indeed, those beds and bowers
Be overgrown with bitter weeds and rue,
And wait thy weeding; yet here's eglantine,
Here's ivy!—take them, as I used to do
Thy flowers, and keep them where they shall not pine.
Instruct thine eyes to keep their colors true,
And tell thy soul their roots are left in mine.

Emily Brontë
1818–1848

A pseudonymous book called *Poems by Currer, Ellis, and Acton Bell* was published in 1846. Two persons are known to have purchased it; the bulk of the edition was used for trunk-lining. Today such copies as have survived are worth almost their weight in gold.

Three sisters wrote the poems in a lonely parsonage at Haworth, on the edge of the Yorkshire moors. It was a place that knew disease, eccentricity, and (in the person of Branwell, the son of the household) a life-destroying dissipation, but it knew also the glorifying power of the ideal. Two of the "Bells"—Currer (Charlotte Brontë) and Ellis (Emily Brontë)—won fame as novelists, the former with *Jane Eyre*, *Shirley*, and *Villette*, the latter with *Wuthering Heights*, the only English novel before Hardy to achieve a cosmic outlook. Acton (Anne Brontë) also published two novels, but probably nobody would read them today if they had not been written by the sister of Charlotte and Emily.

As a poet Emily is the only Brontë to deserve serious consideration. Her reputation has now advanced to such heights that Christina Rossetti is perhaps her only rival as England's most distinguished woman poet. There is nothing to tell of her life except what she herself told in her poems and her one superb novel, for, in the ordinary sense of the term, nothing ever happened to her. She did go with Charlotte to the Pensionnat Héger in Brussels, but Brussels did not impress her, and she did not impress Brussels. Almost completely independent of outward circumstance, she was one of the most self-sufficient women who ever lived; she died, of tuberculosis, in her thirtieth year. One doubts whether even that need have made any difference to her; as a mystic, she had always been quite at home in eternity.

Emily Brontë's mental and spiritual characteristics are revealed clearly enough in her poems, but the reader must always allow for the fact that, unlike Charlotte's, her genius was not lyrical but dramatic. The Brontë children discovered a strong mythmaking faculty in themselves at an early age. Charlotte and Branwell wrote about an African kingdom called Angria; Emily and Anne chose an island in the Pacific which they named Gondal. The Angrian material has now been printed in part; the Gondal materials, unfortunately, no longer exist. Much ink has been wasted in an attempt to identify the lover of "Remembrance"; we know now that the poem is Rosina's lament for King Julius in the Gondal saga.

REMEMBRANCE

Cold in the earth—and the deep snow piled above thee,
Far, far removed, cold in the dreary grave!
Have I forgot, my only Love, to love thee,
Severed at last by Time's all-severing wave?

Now, when alone, do my thoughts no longer hover
Over the mountains, on that northern shore,
Resting their wings where heath and fern-leaves cover
Thy noble heart for ever, ever more?

Cold in the earth—and fifteen wild Decembers,
From those brown hills, have melted into spring:
Faithful, indeed, is the spirit that remembers
After such years of change and suffering!

Sweet Love of youth, forgive, if I forget thee,
While the world's tide is bearing me along;
Other desires and other hopes beset me,
Hopes which obscure, but cannot do thee wrong!

No later light has lightened up my heaven,
No second moon has ever shone for me;
All my life's bliss from thy dear life was given,
All my life's bliss is in the grave with thee.

But, when the days of golden dreams had perished,
And ev'n Despair was powerless to destroy;
Then did I learn how existence could be cherished,
Strengthened, and fed without the aid of joy.

Then did I check the tears of useless passion—
Weaned my young soul from yearning after thine;
Sternly denied its burning wish to hasten
Down to that tomb already more than mine.

And, even yet, I dare not let it languish,
Dare not indulge in memory's rapturous pain;
Once drinking deep of that divinest anguish,
How could I seek the empty world again?

SONG

The linnet in the rocky dells,
The moor-lark in the air,
The bee among the heather bells
That hide my lady fair:

The wild deer browse above her breast;
The wild birds raise their brood;
And they, her smiles of love caressed,
Have left her solitude.

I ween that, when the grave's dark wall
Did first her form retain,
They thought their hearts could ne'er recall
The light of joy again.

They thought the tide of grief would flow
Unchecked through future years;
But where is all their anguish now,
And where are all their tears?

Well, let them fight for honour's breath,
Or pleasure's shade pursue—
The dweller in the land of death
Is changed and careless too.

And, if their eyes should watch and weep
Till sorrow's source were dry,
She would not, in her tranquil sleep,
Return a single sigh!

Blow, west-wind, by the lonely mound,
And murmur, summer-streams—
There is no need of other sound
To soothe my lady's dreams.

TO IMAGINATION

When weary with the long day's care,
And earthly change from pain to pain,
And lost, and ready to despair,
Thy kind voice calls me back again,
O my true friend! I am not lone,
While thou canst speak with such a tone!

So hopeless is the world without,
The world within I doubly prize;
Thy world, where guile, and hate, and doubt,
And cold suspicion never rise;
Where thou, and I, and Liberty,
Have undisputed sovereignty.

What matters it, that all around
Danger, and guilt, and darkness lie,
If but within our bosom's bound
We hold a bright, untroubled sky,
Warm with ten thousand mingled rays
Of suns that know no winter days?

Reason, indeed, may oft complain
For Nature's sad reality,
And tell the suffering heart how vain
Its cherished dreams must always be;
And Truth may rudely trample down
The flowers of Fancy, newly-blown:

But thou art ever there, to bring
The hovering vision back, and breathe
New glories o'er the blighted spring,
And call a lovelier Life from Death,
And whisper, with a voice divine,
Of real worlds, as bright as thine.

I trust not to thy phantom bliss,
Yet, still, in evening's quiet hour,
With never-failing thankfulness,
I welcome thee, Benignant Power,
Sure solacer of human cares,
And sweeter hope, when hope despairs!

THE OLD STOIC

Riches I hold in light esteem,
And Love I laugh to scorn;
And lust of fame was but a dream
That vanished with the morn:

And if I pray, the only prayer
That moves my lips for me
Is, "Leave the heart that now I bear,
And give me liberty!"

Yes, as my swift days near their goal,
'Tis all that I implore:
In life and death a chainless soul,
With courage to endure.

STANZAS

Often rebuked, yet always back returning
To those first feelings that were born with me,
And leaving busy chase of wealth and learning
For idle dreams of things which cannot be:

To-day, I will seek not the shadowy region:
Its unsustaining vastness waxes drear;
And visions rising, legion after legion,
Bring the unreal world too strangely near.

I'll walk, but not in old heroic traces,
And not in paths of high morality,
And not among the half-distinguished faces,
The clouded forms of long-past history.

I'll walk where my own nature would be leading:
It vexes me to choose another guide:
Where the grey flocks in ferny glens are feeding;
Where the wild wind blows on the mountain-side.

What have those lonely mountains worth revealing?
More glory and more grief than I can tell:
The earth that wakes *one* human heart to feeling
Can centre both the worlds of Heaven and Hell.

I AM THE ONLY BEING

I am the only being whose doom
No tongue would ask, no eye would mourn;
I've never caused a thought of gloom,
A smile of joy, since I was born.

In secret pleasure, secret tears,
This changeful life has slipped away,
As friendless after eighteen years,
As lone as on my natal day.

There have been times I cannot hide,
There have been times when this was drear,
When my sad soul forgot its pride
And longed for one to love me here.

But those were in the early glow
Of feelings, long subdued by care;
And they have died so long ago,
I hardly now believe they were.

First melted off the hope of youth,
Then fancy's rainbow fast withdrew;
And then experience told me truth
In mortal bosoms never grew.

'Twas grief enough to think mankind
All hollow, servile, insincere;
But worse to turn to my own mind,
And find the same corruption there.

LINES BY CLAUDIA

I did not sleep; 'twas noon of day;
I saw the burning sunshine fall,
The long grass bending where I lay,
The blue sky brooding over all.

I heard the mellow hum of bees,
And singing birds and sighing trees,
And, far away, in woody dell
The music of the Sabbath-bell.

I did not dream: remembrance still
Clasped round my heart its fetters chill;
But I am sure the soul is free
To leave its clay a little while,
Or how, in exile-misery,
Could I have seen my country smile?

In English fields my limbs were laid,
With English turf beneath my head;
My spirit wandered o'er that shore
Where nought but it may wander more.

Yet if the soul can thus return,
I need not, and I will not mourn;
And vainly did you drive me far
With leagues of ocean stretched between:
My mortal flesh you might debar,
But not the eternal fire within.

My monarch died to rule for ever
A heart that can forget him never;
And dear to me, ay, doubly dear
Though shut within the silent tomb,
His name shall be for whom I bear
This long-sustained and hopeless doom.

And brighter in the hour of woe
Than in the blaze of victory's pride,
That glory-shedding star shall glow,
For which we fought and bled and died.

LAST LINES

No coward soul is mine,
No trembler in the world's storm-troubled sphere:
I see Heaven's glories shine,
And Faith shines equal, arming me from Fear.

O God within my breast,
Almighty, ever-present Deity!
Life—that in me has rest,
As I—undying Life—have power in thee!

Vain are the thousand creeds
That move men's hearts: unutterably vain;
Worthless as withered weeds,
Or idlest froth amid the boundless main,

To waken doubt in one
Holding so fast by Thine infinity,
So surely anchored on
The steadfast rock of Immortality.

With wide-embracing love
Thy spirit animates eternal years,
Pervades and broods above,
Changes, sustains, dissolves, creates, and rears.

Though earth and man were gone,
And suns and universes ceased to be,
And Thou wert left alone,
Every existence would exist in Thee.

There is not room for Death,
Nor atom that his might could render void:
Thou—Thou art Being and Breath,
And what Thou art may never be destroyed.

Edward FitzGerald
1809–1883

Of the life of Edward FitzGerald, beloved friend of Tennyson and Thackeray, there is little to tell. He was born in 1809, and, after spending some years of his childhood in France, was educated at King Edward the Sixth's School at Bury St. Edmund's and at Cambridge. Then "he walked a little, talked a little, thought a little, scribbled a little as he would have said himself, smoked a great deal, and died."[1]

The "scribbling" took the form of translations from Persian, Greek, and Spanish, of which all except the *Six Dramas from Calderon Freely Translated*, 1853, appeared anonymously. All FitzGerald's translations are "free." He himself said: "I suppose very few people have ever taken such pains in translation as I have: though certainly not to be literal. But at all costs a thing must *live:* with a transfusion of one's own worse life if one can't retain the original's better." To none of his works do his words apply better than to the one which gave him his fame, *The Rubáiyát of Omar Khayyám*.

Omar, called Khayyám (the tent-maker), probably from his father's occupation, was a Persian poet, astronomer, mathematician, unsystematic philosopher, and free-liver who is said to have died in A.D. 1123. There are a hundred and fifty-eight of his multitudinous *rubā'is* (quatrains) in the Bodleian manuscript FitzGerald used, "independent stanzas, consisting each of four lines of equal, though varied, prosody; sometimes *all* rhyming, but oftener (as here imitated) the third line a blank. Somewhat as in the Greek alcaic, where the penultimate line seems to lift and suspend the wave that falls over in the last. As usual with such kind of Oriental verse, the Rubáiyát follow one another according to alphabetic rime—a strange succession of grave and gay" (FitzGerald). The translator combined and arranged to suit himself, imposing his own continuity upon heterogeneous material.

Success was by no means instantaneous. Of the original paper-bound edition of 1859, which contained seventy-five quatrains, most of the copies were offered for sale by a London bookseller at a penny each; fortunately Swinburne and Rossetti came upon them, and their enthusiasm helped to turn the tide. The revised edition of 1868 ran to one hundred and ten stanzas; later editions, 1872 and 1879, reduced the number to one hundred and one, and established a new order. (The fourth edition is reprinted here.) By the seventies, "advanced" spirits in England were already beginning to tire of moral earnestness. Consequently Omar's melancholy, his determination not to miss any of the pleasures of the senses, his agnostic materialism dashed with occasional vagrant gleams of mystic yearning, were destined to endear him to a very large public as the years went by. FitzGerald himself described the mood of the Rubáiyát as "a desperate sort of thing, unfortunately at the bottom of all thinking men's minds, but made music of." The vogue of *The Rubáiyát of Omar Khayyám* lasted at least until the war of 1914–18; in some respects, indeed, it is with us still.

[1] Gamaliel Bradford, *Bare Souls*, Harper, 1924.

THE RUBÁIYÁT OF OMAR KHAYYÁM

1

Wake! For the Sun, who scattered into flight
The Stars before him from the Field of Night,
  Drives Night along with them from Heav'n, and strikes
The Sultán's Turret with a Shaft of Light.

2

Before the phantom of False morning died,
Methought a Voice within the Tavern cried,
  "When all the Temple is prepared within,
Why nods the drowsy Worshipper outside?"

3

And, as the Cock crew, those who stood before
The Tavern shouted—"Open then the Door!
  You know how little while we have to stay,
And, once departed, may return no more."

4

Now the New Year reviving old Desires,
The thoughtful Soul to Solitude retires,
  Where the White Hand of Moses on the Bough
Puts out, and Jesus from the Ground suspires.

5

Iram indeed is gone with all his Rose,
And Jamshyd's Sev'n-ringed Cup where no one knows;
  But still a Ruby kindles in the Vine,
And many a Garden by the Water blows.

6

And David's lips are lockt; but in divine
High-piping Pehleví, with "Wine! Wine! Wine!
  Red Wine!"—the Nightingale cries to the Rose
That sallow cheek of hers to incarnadine.

7

Come, fill the Cup, and in the fire of Spring
Your Winter-garment of Repentance fling:
  The Bird of Time has but a little way
To flutter—and the Bird is on the Wing.

8

Whether at Naíshápúr or Babylon,
Whether the Cup with sweet or bitter run,
  The Wine of Life keeps oozing drop by drop,
The Leaves of Life keep falling one by one.

9

Each Morn a thousand Roses brings, you say;
Yes, but where leaves the Rose of Yesterday?
  And this first Summer month that brings the Rose
Shall take Jamshyd and Kaikobád away.

10

Well, let it take them! What have we to do
With Kaikobád the Great, or Kaikhosrú?
  Let Zál and Rustum bluster as they will,
Or Hátim call to Supper—heed not you.

11

With me along the strip of Herbage strown
That just divides the desert from the sown,
  Where name of Slave and Sultán is forgot—
And Peace to Mahmúd on his golden throne!

12

A Book of Verses underneath the Bough,
A Jug of Wine, a Loaf of Bread—and Thou
  Beside me singing in the Wilderness—
Oh, Wilderness were Paradise enow!

13

Some for the Glories of This World; and some
Sigh for the Prophet's Paradise to come;
  Ah, take the Cash, and let the Credit go,
Nor heed the rumble of a distant Drum!

5. False morning, "a transient light on the horizon about an hour before the . . . true dawn; a well-known phenomenon in the east." (FitzGerald) **13. New Year,** beginning with the vernal equinox. **15–16. White Hand . . . suspires.** "Exodus 4:6; where Moses draws forth his hand—not, according to the Persians, '*leprous as snow*'—but *white*, as our May-blossom in spring perhaps. According to them also the healing power of Jesus resided in his breath." (FitzGerald) **17. Iram,** an ancient Persian garden. **18. Jamshyd's Sev'n-ringed Cup.** Jamshyd was a legendary king of Persia. The seven rings on his divining cup typified the seven heavens, the seven planets, the seven seas, and so on. **21. David,** king of Judah and Israel (*c.* 1033–993 B.C.). **22. Pehleví,** an ancient literary language of Persia.

29. Naíshápúr, Omar's home city in Persia. **36. Kaikobád,** another ancient legendary king. **38. Kaikhosrú,** Cyrus the Great, who overthrew Belshazzar, King of Babylonia, and founded the Persian Empire, 538 B.C. **39. Zál and Rustum,** Zál, King of India, and his son Rustum, chief of the Persian mythical heroes. **40. Hátim** typifies Oriental hospitality. **44. Mahmúd,** the sultan. **50. Prophet's,** Mohammed's. **52. Drum,** "beaten outside of palace." (FitzGerald)

14

Look to the blowing Rose about us—"Lo,
Laughing," she says, "into the world I blow,
At once the silken tassel of my Purse
Tear, and its Treasure on the Garden throw."

15

And those who husbanded the Golden Grain,
And those who flung it to the winds like Rain,
Alike to no such aureate Earth are turned
As, buried once, Men want dug up again.

16

The Worldly Hope men set their Hearts upon
Turns Ashes—or it prospers; and anon,
Like Snow upon the Desert's dusty Face,
Lighting a little hour or two—is gone.

17

Think, in this battered Caravanserai
Whose Portals are alternate Night and Day,
How Sultán after Sultán with his Pomp
Abode his destined Hour, and went his way.

18

They say the Lion and the Lizard keep
The Courts where Jamshyd gloried and drank deep:
And Bahrám, the great Hunter—the Wild Ass
Stamps o'er his Head, but cannot break his Sleep.

19

I sometimes think that never blows so red
The Rose as where some buried Caesar bled;
That every Hyacinth the Garden wears
Dropt in her Lap from some once lovely Head.

20

And this reviving Herb whose tender Green
Fledges the River-Lip on which we lean—
Ah, lean upon it lightly! for who knows
From what once lovely Lip it springs unseen!

21

Ah, my Belovèd, fill the Cup that clears
TO-DAY of past Regrets and future Fears:
To-morrow!—Why, To-morrow I may be
Myself with Yesterday's Sev'n thousand Years.

56. Treasure, "the rose's golden center." (FitzGerald) **57. Golden Grain,** wealth. **71. Bahrám,** a ruler of Persia drowned in a swamp while hunting a wild ass. **75. Hyacinth.** The hyacinth sprang up from the ground watered by the blood of Hyacinthus, who had been accidentally killed by Apollo. **84. Sev'n thousand Years,** "a thousand years to each planet." (FitzGerald)

22

For some we loved, the loveliest and the best
That from his Vintage rolling Time hath prest,
Have drunk their Cup a Round or two before,
And one by one crept silently to rest.

23

And we, that now make merry in the Room
They left, and Summer dresses in new bloom,
Ourselves must we beneath the Couch of Earth
Descend—ourselves to make a Couch—for whom?

24

Ah, make the most of what we yet may spend,
Before we too into the Dust descend;
Dust into Dust, and under Dust, to lie,
Sans Wine, sans Song, sans Singer, and—sans End!

25

Alike for those who for TO-DAY prepare,
And those that after some TO-MORROW stare,
A Muezzín from the Tower of Darkness cries,
"Fools, your Reward is neither Here nor There."

26

Why, all the Saints and Sages who discussed
Of the Two Worlds so wisely—they are thrust
Like foolish Prophets forth; their Words to Scorn
Are scattered, and their Mouths are stopt with Dust.

27

Myself when young did eagerly frequent
Doctor and Saint, and heard great argument
About it and about: but evermore
Came out by the same door where in I went.

28

With them the seed of Wisdom did I sow,
And with mine own hand wrought to make it grow;
And this was all the Harvest that I reaped—
"I came like Water, and like Wind I go."

29

Into this Universe, and *Why* not knowing
Nor *Whence*, like Water willy-nilly flowing;
And out of it, as Wind along the Waste,
I know not *Whither*, willy-nilly blowing.

30

What, without asking, hither hurried *Whence?*
And, without asking, *Whither* hurried hence!

96. Sans, without (French). **99. Muezzín,** a crier who summons Mohammedans to prayer.

Oh, many a Cup of this forbidden Wine
Must drown the memory of that insolence!

31

Up from Earth's Centre through the Seventh Gate
I rose, and on the Throne of Saturn sate,
And many a Knot unravelled by the Road;
But not the Master-knot of Human Fate.

32

There was the Door to which I found no Key;
There was the Veil through which I might not see:
Some little talk awhile of ME and THEE
There was—and then no more of THEE and ME.

33

Earth could not answer; nor the Seas that mourn
In flowing Purple, of their Lord forlorn;
Nor rolling Heaven, with all his Signs revealed
And hidden by the sleeve of Night and Morn.

34

Then of the THEE IN ME who works behind
The Veil, I lifted up my hands to find
A lamp amid the Darkness; and I heard,
As from Without—"THE ME WITHIN THEE BLIND!"

35

Then to the Lip of this poor earthen Urn
I leaned, the Secret of my Life to learn:
And Lip to Lip it murmured—"While you live,
Drink!—for, once dead, you never shall return."

36

I think the Vessel, that with fugitive
Articulation answered, once did live,
And drink; and Ah! the passive Lip I kissed,
How many Kisses might it take—and give!

37

For I remember stopping by the way
To watch a Potter thumping his wet Clay;
And with its all-obliterated Tongue
It murmured—"Gently, Brother, gently, pray!"

38

And has not such a Story from of Old
Down Man's successive generations rolled
Of such a clod of saturated Earth
Cast by the Maker into Human mould?

39

And not a drop that from our Cups we throw
For Earth to drink of, but may steal below
To quench the fire of Anguish in some Eye
There hidden—far beneath, and long ago.

40

As then the Tulip for her morning sup
Of Heav'nly Vintage from the soil looks up,
Do you devoutly do the like, till Heav'n
To Earth invert you—like an empty Cup.

41

Perplext no more with Human or Divine,
To-morrow's tangle to the winds resign,
And lose your fingers in the tresses of
The Cypress-slender Minister of Wine.

42

And if the Wine you drink, the Lip you press,
End in what All begins and ends in—Yes;
Think that you are TO-DAY what YESTERDAY
You were—TO-MORROW you shall not be less.

43

So when the Angel of the darker Drink
At last shall find you by the river-brink,
And offering his Cup, invite your Soul
Forth to your Lips to quaff—you shall not shrink.

44

Why, if the Soul can fling the Dust aside,
And naked on the Air of Heaven ride,
Were't not a Shame—were't not a Shame for him
In this clay carcase crippled to abide?

45

'Tis but a Tent where takes his one day's rest
A Sultán to the realm of Death addrest;
The Sultán rises, and the dark Ferrásh
Strikes, and prepares it for another Guest.

119. forbidden, by the Mohammedan religion. **122. Saturn,** here, lord of the seventh heaven, enthroned in one of the nine concentric spheres which, according to the Ptolemaic system of astronomy, surrounded the earth. **131. Signs,** of the zodiac. **145 ff. For I remember . . .** "One of the Persian poets—Attar, I think—has a pretty story about this. A thirsty traveller dips his hand into a spring of water to drink from. By-and-by comes another and draws up and drinks from an earthen bowl, and then departs, leaving his bowl behind him. The first traveller takes it up for another draught; but is surprised to find that the same water which had tasted sweet from his own hand tastes bitter from the earthen bowl. But a voice—from heaven, I think—tells him the clay from which the bowl is made was once man, and, into whatever shape renewed, can never lose the bitter flavour of mortality." (FitzGerald)

153–54. a drop . . . drink of, a custom in the East, says FitzGerald. **164. Cypress slender . . . Wine,** the girl who passes the wine. **179. Ferrásh,** the servant who takes down the tent.

46

And fear not lest Existence closing your
Account, and mine, should know the like no more;
The Eternal Sákí from that Bowl has poured
Millions of Bubbles like us, and will pour.

47

When You and I behind the Veil are past,
Oh, but the long, long while the World shall last,
Which of our Coming and Departure heeds
As the Sea's self should heed a pebble-cast.

48

A Moment's Halt—a momentary taste
Of Being from the Well amid the Waste—
And Lo!—the phantom Caravan has reached
The Nothing it set out from—Oh, make haste!

49

Would you that spangle of Existence spend
About the secret—quick about it, Friend!
A Hair perhaps divides the False and True—
And upon what, prithee, does life depend?

50

A Hair perhaps divides the False and True—
Yes; and a single Alif were the clue—
Could you but find it—to the Treasure-house,
And peradventure to The Master too;

51

Whose secret Presence, through Creation's veins
Running Quicksilver-like, eludes your pains;
Taking all shapes from Máh to Máhi, and
They change and perish all—but He remains;

52

A moment guessed—then back behind the Fold
Immerst of Darkness round the Drama rolled
Which, for the Pastime of Eternity,
He doth himself contrive, enact, behold.

53

But if in vain, down on the stubborn floor
Of Earth, and up to Heav'n's unopening Door,
You gaze To-day, while You are You—how then
To-morrow, when You shall be You no more?

54

Waste not your Hour, nor in the vain pursuit
Of This and That endeavour and dispute;
Better be jocund with the fruitful Grape
Than sadden after none, or bitter, Fruit.

55

You know, my Friends, with what a brave Carouse
I made a Second Marriage in my house;
Divorced old barren Reason from my Bed,
And took the Daughter of the Vine to Spouse.

56

For "Is" and "Is-not" though with Rule and Line,
And "Up-and-down" by Logic I define,
Of all that one should care to fathom, I
Was never deep in anything but—Wine.

57

Ah, but my Computations, People say,
Reduced the Year to better reckoning?—Nay,
'Twas only striking from the Calendar
Unborn To-morrow, and dead Yesterday.

58

And lately, by the Tavern Door agape,
Came shining through the Dusk an Angel Shape
Bearing a Vessel on his Shoulder; and
He bid me taste of it; and 'twas—the Grape!

59

The Grape that can with Logic absolute
The Two-and-Seventy jarring Sects confute:
The sovereign Alchemist that in a trice
Life's leaden metal into Gold transmute:

60

The mighty Mahmúd, Allah-breathing Lord,
That all the misbelieving and black Horde
Of Fears and Sorrows that infest the Soul
Scatters before him with his whirlwind Sword.

61

Why, be this Juice the growth of God, who dare
Blaspheme the twisted tendril as a Snare?
A Blessing, we should use it, should we not?
And if a Curse—why, then, Who set it there?

62

I must abjure the Balm of Life, I must,
Scared by some After-reckoning ta'en on trust,

183. Sákí, wine-bearer, here used symbolically. **198. Alif,** the first letter of the Arabic alphabet, a single vertical stroke. **203. from Máh to Máhi,** from fish to moon.

225. Computations, Omar, astronomer and mathematician, helped reform the calendar. **234. The Two-and-Seventy jarring Sects,** "The seventy-two religions supposed to divide the world." (FitzGerald) **237–40. The mighty . . . Sword. Mahmúd.** See l. 44. **Allah-breathing,** uttering the name of Allah in adoration. The rest of the passage refers to the conquest of India by Mahmúd the Great. **241. be this Juice,** since the wine is. **242. the twisted tendril,** of the grapevine.

Or lured with Hope of some Diviner Drink,
To fill the Cup—when crumbled into Dust!

63

O threats of Hell and Hopes of Paradise!
One thing at least is certain—*This* Life flies;
One thing is certain and the rest is Lies;
The Flower that once has blown for ever dies.

64

Strange, is it not? that of the myriads who
Before us passed the door of Darkness through,
Not one returns to tell us of the Road,
Which to discover we must travel too.

65

The Revelations of Devout and Learned
Who rose before us, and as Prophets burned,
Are all but Stories, which, awoke from Sleep
They told their comrades, and to Sleep returned.

66

I sent my Soul through the Invisible,
Some letter of that After-life to spell:
And by and by my Soul returned to me,
And answered "I Myself am Heav'n and Hell":

67

Heav'n but the Vision of fulfilled Desire,
And Hell the Shadow from a Soul on fire,
Cast on the Darkness into which Ourselves,
So late emerged from, shall so soon expire.

68

We are no other than a moving row
Of Magic Shadow-shapes that come and go
Round with the Sun-illumined Lantern held
In Midnight by the Master of the Show;

69

But helpless Pieces of the Game He plays
Upon this Chequer-board of Nights and Days;
Hither and thither moves, and checks, and slays,
And one by one back in the Closet lays.

70

The Ball no question makes of Ayes and Noes,
But Here or There as strikes the Player goes;
And He that tossed you down into the Field,
He knows about it all—HE knows—HE knows!

277. Ball, in the polo game.

71

The Moving Finger writes; and, having writ,
Moves on: nor all your Piety nor Wit
Shall lure it back to cancel half a Line,
Nor all your Tears wash out a Word of it.

72

And that inverted Bowl they call the Sky,
Whereunder crawling cooped we live and die,
Lift not your hands to *It* for help—for It
As impotently moves as you or I.

73

With Earth's first Clay They did the Last Man knead,
And there of the Last Harvest sowed the Seed:
And the first Morning of Creation wrote
What the Last Dawn of Reckoning shall read.

74

YESTERDAY *This* Day's Madness did prepare;
TO-MORROW's Silence, Triumph, or Despair:
Drink! for you know not whence you came, nor why:
Drink! for you know not why you go, nor where.

75

I tell you this—When, started from the Goal,
Over the flaming shoulders of the Foal
Of Heav'n Parwín and Mushtarí they flung,
In my predestined Plot of Dust and Soul

76

The Vine had struck a fibre: which about
If clings my Being—let the Dervish flout;
Of my Base metal may be filed a Key,
That shall unlock the Door he howls without.

77

And this I know: whether the one True Light
Kindle to Love, or Wrath consume me quite,
One Flash of It within the Tavern caught
Better than in the Temple lost outright.

78

What! out of senseless Nothing to provoke
A conscious Something to resent the yoke
Of unpermitted Pleasure, under pain
Of Everlasting Penalties, if broke!

298–99. Foal of Heav'n, the constellation Equuleus, the Little Horse. **Parwín and Mushtarí,** the Pleiades and Jupiter. **302. Dervish,** a devotee.

79

What! from his helpless Creature be repaid
Pure Gold for what he lent him dross-allayed—
  Sue for a Debt we never did contract,
And cannot answer—Oh, the sorry trade!

80

O Thou, who didst with pitfall and with gin
Beset the Road I was to wander in,
  Thou wilt not with Predestined Evil round
Enmesh, and then impute my Fall to Sin!

81

O Thou, who Man of baser Earth didst make,
And ev'n with Paradise devise the Snake:
  For all the Sin wherewith the Face of Man
Is blackened—Man's forgiveness give—and take!

82

As under cover of departing Day
Slunk hunger-stricken Ramazán away,
  Once more within the Potter's house alone
I stood, surrounded by the Shapes of Clay.

83

Shapes of all Sorts and Sizes, great and small,
That stood along the floor and by the wall;
  And some loquacious Vessels were; and some
Listened perhaps, but never talked at all.

84

Said one among them—"Surely not in vain
My substance of the common Earth was ta'en
  And to this Figure moulded, to be broke,
Or trampled back to shapeless Earth again."

85

Then said a Second—"Ne'er a peevish Boy
Would break the Bowl from which he drank in joy;
  And He that with his hand the Vessel made
Will surely not in after Wrath destroy."

86

After a momentary silence spake
Some Vessel of a more ungainly Make:
  "They sneer at me for leaning all awry;
What! did the Hand then of the Potter shake?"

87

Whereat some one of the loquacious Lot—
I think a Súfi pipkin—waxing hot—
  "All this of Pot and Potter—Tell me then,
Who is the Potter, pray, and who the Pot?"

88

"Why," said another, "Some there are who tell
Of one who threatens he will toss to Hell
  The luckless Pots he marred in making—Pish!
He's a Good Fellow, and 'twill all be well."

89

"Well," murmured one, "Let whoso make or buy,
My Clay with long Oblivion is gone dry:
  But fill me with the old familiar Juice,
Methinks I might recover by and by."

90

So while the Vessels one by one were speaking,
The little Moon looked in that all were seeking:
  And then they jogged each other, "Brother! Brother!
Now for the Porter's shoulder-knot a-creaking."

91

Ah, with the Grape my fading Life provide,
And wash the Body whence the Life has died,
  And lay me, shrouded in the living Leaf,
By some not unfrequented Garden-side.

92

That ev'n my buried Ashes such a snare
Of Vintage shall fling up into the Air
  As not a True-believer passing by
But shall be overtaken unaware.

93

Indeed the Idols I have loved so long
Have done my credit in this World much wrong:
  Have drowned my Glory in a shallow Cup,
And sold my Reputation for a Song.

94

Indeed, indeed, Repentance oft before
I swore—but was I sober when I swore?
  And then and then came Spring, and Rose-in-hand
My thread-bare Penitence apieces tore.

95

And much as Wine has played the Infidel,
And robbed me of my Robe of Honour—Well,
  I wonder often what the Vintners buy
One half so precious as the stuff they sell.

317. gin, trap. **326. Ramazán,** the fasting month. **327 ff. the Potter's house . . .** With Omar's references to the potter, compare Jeremiah's (18–19) and St. Paul's echo to the same (Romans 9: 21 ff.). **346. Súfi,** a Persian mystic.

358. Moon looked in, marking the end of the fast. **360. Porter's shoulder-knot a-creaking,** as he carries the jars filled with wine.

96

Yet Ah, that Spring should vanish with the Rose!
That Youth's sweet-scented manuscript should close!
  The Nightingale that in the branches sang,
Ah whence, and whither flown again, who knows!

97

Would but the Desert of the Fountain yield
One glimpse—if dimly, yet indeed, revealed,
  To which the fainting Traveller might spring,
As springs the trampled herbage of the field!

98

Would but some wingèd Angel ere too late
Arrest the yet unfolded Roll of Fate,
  And make the stern Recorder otherwise
Enregister, or quite obliterate!

99

Ah Love! could you and I with Him conspire
To grasp this sorry Scheme of Things entire,
  Would not we shatter it to bits—and then
Re-mould it nearer to the Heart's Desire!

100

Yon rising Moon that looks for us again—
How oft hereafter will she wax and wane;
  How oft hereafter rising look for us
Through this same Garden—and for *one* in vain!

101

And when like her, O Sákí, you shall pass
Among the Guests Star-scattered on the Grass,
  And in your joyous errand reach the spot
Where I made One—turn down an empty Glass!

TAMÁM

John Ruskin
1819–1900

John Ruskin was born in London, February 8, 1819. His father was a Scotch Calvinist, a wine merchant, and a millionaire. The boy was educated by his mother and by private tutors, and he traveled widely with his parents, both in Great Britain and on the Continent, developing his passionate love of scenery and his great sensitiveness to beauty. His career at Oxford was broken by ill-health, but he was graduated in 1842, winning the Newdigate Prize for poetry.

Ruskin's first important book was Volume I of *Modern Painters*, 1843. *Modern Painters*, *The Seven Lamps of Architecture*, 1849, and *The Stones of Venice*, 1851–63 (see below) contain his most important art criticism. In 1860 he turned to political economy in *Unto This Last*, and startled England with a furious attack upon Utilitarian economics (see page 902). *Unto This Last* was soon followed by *Sesame and Lilies*, 1865, *The Ethics of the Dust*, 1866, *The Crown of Wild Olive*, 1866 (see page 1046), and *Time and Tide*, 1867. Many of his most important ideas in political economy were expressed also in *Fors Clavigera* (see page 1052), a series of letters addressed to the workingmen of England over the years 1871 to 1884. The Slade Professorship of Art at Oxford, which Ruskin held for a number of years beginning in 1870, produced several books, including *Aratra Pentelici*, 1872, which deals with sculpture, and *Val d'Arno*, 1874, which concerns Florentine art of the thirteenth century, In *The Queen of the Air*, 1869, he wrote of Greek myths of the cloud and storm; in *Love's Meinie*, 1873, 1881, of birds; in *Proserpina*, 1875–86, of wayside flowers; in *Deucalion*, 1875–83, of rocks. This by no means exhausts Ruskin's list; he was a very prolific writer, and his range was immense; he had well over fifty years of authorship.

Ruskin's private life was none too happy. There was a neurotic strain in him; his emotional balance was perhaps adversely affected by the domination of his mother. His ill-advised marriage with Euphemia Gray ended, after six years, in an annulment, and Mrs. Ruskin married the painter John Everett Millais. Later Ruskin had a very unhappy love affair with a girl named Rose La Touche. During his last years, Ruskin's mind was partially deranged; much of his autobiography, *Praeterita*, 1885–89, had to be written during lucid intervals. He died January 20, 1900.

Ruskin's art criticism took hold of people partly because of his luxuriant, highly colored style but more because of the vitality of his ideas. He never concerned himself with mere technicalities. So far as he was concerned, technique was merely the language of art; the all-important question was what the man had to say about life. But as he saw it, a work of art was the product not merely of the artist but also of his times. Great art was national and social; a rotten society could not produce pure art. The art of the Renaissance was inferior to that of the Gothic Middle Ages because the life of the Renaissance had sunk to a lower level; as for contemporary England, capitalism had well-nigh finished art there. "It is the vainest of affectations to try and put beauty into shadows, while all real things that cast them are in deformity and pain. . . . Beautiful art can only be produced by people who have beautiful things about them, and leisure to look at them." The principle he finally arrived at was a simple one: "Life without industry is guilt, and industry without art is brutality."

It will be seen that Ruskin's shift of emphasis from the work of an art critic in his first phase to that of a reformer in his second startled his critics only because they had understood nothing he had said to them. Everything he finally stood for was implicit in his work from the beginning; it is not too much to say that his advocacy of the income tax, of limitation of income, of shorter hours of labor, and of the responsibility of the state to care for the aged and destitute, all resulted, directly or indirectly, from his conception of the nature of beauty.

The importance of Ruskin's influence is difficult to evaluate; like Carlyle, like Dickens on his ideational side, he seemed, in his own time, a voice crying in the wilderness; in ours, many of his ideas have been quietly accepted. Carlyle's influence upon him was perhaps unfortunate; though he never embraced the hero cult in its complete brutality, he went farther than many of us today would have had him go; moreover, because, like Carlyle, he looked backward for his inspiration, he sought to solve social problems in terms of a modified feudalism—society organized into classes, with the rich and the gifted bearing the heavier burdens. This ideal expressed itself notably in the Guild of St. George, which Ruskin organized about himself as "Master" in 1871, and to which (together with various experiments in housing, education, and so on) he gave almost all his money. In this and similar organizations, Ruskin attempted to combine art, science, and industry. No more than Tolstoi did he consider the actual work of the world beneath him; he cleaned streets; on one occasion, he and a group of his students at Oxford built a road—not too well, it is said, but they got it built.

from THE STONES OF VENICE

In *The Stones of Venice*, Ruskin's aim, as he afterwards declared, was "to show that the Gothic architecture of Venice had arisen out of, and indicated in all its features, a state of pure national faith, and of domestic virtue, and that its Renaissance architecture had arisen out of, and in all its features indicated, a state of concealed national infidelity, and of domestic corruption."

from Chapter 6: THE NATURE OF GOTHIC

I believe . . . that the characteristic or moral elements of Gothic are the following . . .:

1. Savageness.
2. Changefulness.
3. Naturalism.
4. Grotesqueness.
5. Rigidity.
6. Redundance. . . .

1. SAVAGENESS. I am not sure when the word "Gothic" was first generically applied to the architecture of the North; but I presume that, whatever the date of its original usage, it was intended to imply reproach, and express the barbaric character of the nations among whom that architecture arose. It never implied that they were literally of Gothic lineage, far less that their architecture had been originally invented by the Goths themselves; but it did imply that they and their buildings together exhibited a degree of sternness and rudeness, which, in contradistinction to the character of Southern and Eastern nations, appeared like a perpetual reflection of the contrast between the Goth and the Roman in their first encounter. And when that fallen Roman, in the utmost impotence of his luxury, and insolence of his guilt, became the model for the imitation of civilized Europe, at the close of the so-called Dark Ages, the word Gothic became a term of unmitigated contempt, not unmixed with aversion. From that contempt, by the exertion of the antiquaries and architects of this century, Gothic architecture has been sufficiently vindicated. . . .

The charts of the world which have been drawn up by modern science have thrown into a narrow space the expression of a vast amount of knowledge, but I have never yet seen any one pictorial enough to enable the spectator to imagine the kind of contrast in physical character which exists between Northern and Southern countries. . . . We know that gentians grow on the Alps, and olives on the Apennines; but we do not enough conceive . . . that difference between the district of the gentian and of the olive which the stork and the swallow see far off, as they lean upon the sirocco wind. Let us, for a moment, try to raise ourselves even above the level of their flight, and imagine the Mediterranean lying beneath us like an irregular lake, and all its ancient promontories sleeping in the sun: here and there an angry spot of thunder, a grey stain of storm, moving upon the burning field; and here and there a fixed wreath of white volcano smoke, surrounded by its circle of ashes; but for the most part a great peacefulness of light, Syria and Greece, Italy and Spain, laid like pieces of a golden pavement into the sea-blue, chased, as we stoop nearer to them, with bossy beaten work of mountain chains, and glowing softly with terraced gardens, and flowers heavy with frankincense, mixed among masses of laurel, and orange, and plumy palm, that abate with their grey-green shadows the burning of the marble rocks, and of the ledges of porphyry sloping under lucent sand. Then let us pass farther towards the north, until we see the orient colours change gradually into a vast belt of rainy green, where the pastures of Switzerland, and poplar valleys of France, and dark forests of the Danube and Carpathians stretch from the mouths of the Loire to those of the Volga, seen through clefts in grey swirls of rain-cloud and flaky veils of the mist of the brooks, spreading low along the pasture lands: and then, farther north still, to see the earth heave into mighty masses of leaden rock and heathy moor, bordering with a broad waste of gloomy purple that belt of field and wood, and splintering into irregular and grisly islands amidst the northern seas, beaten by storm, and chilled by ice-drift, and tormented by furious pulses of contending tide, until the roots of the last forests fail from among the hill ravines, and the hunger of the north wind bites their peaks into barrenness; and, at last, the wall of ice, durable like iron, sets, deathlike, its white teeth against us out of the polar twilight. And, having once traversed in thought this gradation of the zoned iris of the earth in all its material vastness, let us go down nearer to it, and watch the parallel change in the belt of animal life: the multitudes of swift and brilliant creatures that glance in the air and sea, or tread the sands of the southern zone; striped zebras and spotted leopards, glistening serpents, and birds arrayed in purple and scarlet. Let us contrast their delicacy and brilliancy of colour, and swiftness of motion, with the frost-cramped strength, and shaggy covering, and dusky plumage of the northern tribes; contrast the Arabian horse with the Shetland, the tiger and leopard with the wolf and bear, the antelope with the elk, the bird of paradise with the osprey; and then, submissively acknowledging the great laws by which the earth and all that it bears are ruled throughout their being, let us not condemn, but rejoice in the expression by man of his own rest in the statutes of the lands that gave him birth. Let us watch him with reverence as he sets side by side the burning gems, and smooths with soft sculpture the jasper pillars, that are to reflect a ceaseless sunshine, and rise into a cloudless sky: but not with less reverence let us stand by him, when, with rough strength and hurried stroke, he smites an uncouth animation out of the rocks which he has torn from among the moss of the moorland, and heaves into the darkened air the pile of iron buttress and rugged wall, instinct with work of an imagination as wild and wayward as the northern sea; creatures of ungainly shape and rigid limb, but full of wolfish life; fierce as the winds that beat, and changeful as the clouds that shade them.

There is, I repeat, no degradation, no reproach in this, but all dignity and honourableness: and we should err grievously in refusing either to recognize as an essential character of the existing architecture of the North, or to admit as a desirable character in that which it yet may be, this wildness of thought, and roughness of work; this look of mountain brotherhood between the cathedral and the Alp; this magnificence of sturdy power, put forth only the more energetically because the fine finger-touch was chilled away by the frosty wind, and the eye dimmed by the moor-mist, or blinded by the hail; this out-speaking of the strong spirit of men who may not gather redundant fruitage from the earth, nor bask in dreamy benignity of sunshine, but must break the rock for bread, and cleave the forest for fire, and show, even in what they did for their delight, some of the hard habits of the arm and heart that grew on them as they swung the axe or pressed the plough.

If, however, the savageness of Gothic architecture, merely as an expression of its origin among Northern nations, may be considered, in some sort, a noble character, it possesses a higher nobility still, when considered as an index, not of climate, but of religious principle.

In the 13th and 14th paragraphs of Chapter XXI. of the first volume of this work, it was noticed that the systems of architectural ornament, properly so called, might be divided into three:—1. Servile ornament, in which the execution or power of the inferior workman is entirely subjected to the intellect of the higher;—2. Constitutional ornament, in which the executive inferior power is, to a certain point, emancipated and independent, having a will of its own, yet confessing its inferiority and rendering obedience to higher powers;—and

3. Revolutionary ornament, in which no executive inferiority is admitted at all. I must here explain the nature of these divisions at somewhat greater length.

Of Servile ornament, the principal schools are the Greek, Ninevite, and Egyptian; but their servility is of different kinds. The Greek master-workman was far advanced in knowledge and power above the Assyrian or Egyptian. Neither he nor those for whom he worked could endure the appearance of imperfection in anything; and, therefore, what ornament he appointed to be done by those beneath him was composed of mere geometrical forms,—balls, ridges, and perfectly symmetrical foliage,—which could be executed with absolute precision by line and rule, and were as perfect in their way, when completed, as his own figure sculpture. The Assyrian and Egyptian, on the contrary, less cognisant of accurate form in anything, were content to allow their figure sculpture to be executed by inferior workmen, but lowered the method of its treatment to a standard which every workman could reach, and then trained him by discipline so rigid, that there was no chance of his falling beneath the standard appointed. The Greek gave to the lower workman no subject which he could not perfectly execute. The Assyrian gave him subjects which he could only execute imperfectly, but fixed a legal standard for his imperfection. The workman was, in both systems, a slave.

But in the mediaeval, or especially Christian, system of ornament, this slavery is done away with altogether; Christianity having recognized, in small things as well as great, the individual value of every soul. But it not only recognizes its value; it confesses its imperfection, in only bestowing dignity upon the acknowledgment of unworthiness. That admission of lost power and fallen nature, which the Greek or Ninevite felt to be intensely painful, and, as far as might be, altogether refused, the Christian makes daily and hourly, contemplating the fact of it without fear, as tending, in the end, to God's greater glory. Therefore, to every spirit which Christianity summons to her service, her exhortation is: Do what you can, and confess frankly what you are unable to do; neither let your effort be shortened for fear of failure, nor your confession silenced for fear of shame. And it is, perhaps, the principal admirableness of the Gothic schools of architecture, that they thus receive the results of the labour of inferior minds; and out of fragments full of imperfection, and betraying that imperfection in every touch, indulgently raise up a stately and unaccusable whole.

But the modern English mind has this much in common with that of the Greek, that it intensely desires, in all things, the utmost completion or perfection compatible with their nature. This is a noble character in the abstract, but becomes ignoble when it causes us to forget the relative dignities of that nature itself, and to prefer the perfectness of the lower nature to the imperfection of the higher; not considering that as, judged by such a rule, all the brute animals would be preferable to man, because more perfect in their functions and kind, and yet are always held inferior to him, so also in the works of man, those which are more perfect in their kind are always inferior to those which are, in their nature, liable to more faults and shortcomings. . . .

And observe, you are put to stern choice in this matter. You must either make a tool of the creature, or a man of him. You cannot make both. Men were not intended to work with the accuracy of tools, to be precise and perfect in all their actions. If you will have that precision out of them, and make their fingers measure degrees like cog-wheels, and their arms strike curves like compasses, you must unhumanise them. All the energy of their spirits must must be given to make cogs and compasses of themselves. All their attention and strength must go to the accomplishment of the mean act. The eye of the soul must be bent upon the finger-point, and the soul's force must fill all the invisible nerves that guide it, ten hours a day, that it may not err from its steely precision, and so soul and sight be worn away, and the whole human being be lost at last—a heap of sawdust, so far as its intellectual work in this world is concerned; saved only by its Heart, which cannot go into the form of cogs and compasses, but expands, after the ten hours are over, into fireside humanity. On the other hand, if you will make a man of the working creature, you cannot make a tool. Let him but begin to imagine, to think, to try to do anything worth doing; and the engine-turned precision is lost at once. Out come all his roughness, all his dulness, all his incapability; shame upon shame, failure upon failure, pause after pause: but out comes the whole majesty of him also; and we know the height of it only when we see the clouds settling upon him. And, whether the clouds be bright or dark, there will be transfiguration behind and within them.

And now, reader, look round this English room of yours, about which you have been proud so often, because the work of it was so good and strong, and the ornaments of it so finished. Examine again all those accurate mouldings, and perfect polishings, and unerring adjustments of the seasoned wood and tempered steel. Many a time you have exulted over them, and thought how great England was, because her slightest work was done so thoroughly. Alas! if read rightly, these perfectnesses are signs of a slavery in our England a thousand times more bitter and more degrading than that of the scourged African, or helot Greek. Men may be beaten, chained, tormented, yoked like cattle, slaughtered like summer flies, and yet remain in one sense, and the best sense, free. But to smother their souls within them, to blight and hew into rotting pollards the suckling branches of their human intelligence, to make the flesh and skin which, after the worm's work on it, is to see God, into leathern thongs to yoke machinery with,—this it is to be slave-masters indeed; and there might be more freedom in England, though her feudal lords' lightest words were worth men's lives, and though the blood of the vexed husbandman dropped in the furrows of her fields, than there is while the animation of her multitudes is sent like fuel to feed the factory smoke, and the strength of them is given daily to be wasted into the fineness of a web, or racked into the exactness of a line.

And, on the other hand, go forth again to gaze upon the old cathedral front, where you have smiled so often at the fantastic ignorance of the old sculptors: examine once more those ugly goblins, and formless monsters, and stern statues, anatomiless and rigid; but do not mock at them, for they are signs of the life and liberty of every workman who struck the stone; a freedom of thought, and rank in scale of being, such as no laws, no charters, no charities can secure; but which it must be the first aim of all Europe at this day to regain for her children.

Let me not be thought to speak wildly or extravagantly. It is verily this degradation of the operative into a machine, which, more than any other evil of the times, is leading the mass of the nations everywhere into vain, incoherent, destructive struggling for a freedom of which they cannot explain the nature to themselves. Their universal outcry against wealth, and against nobility, is not forced from them either by the pressure of famine, or the sting of mortified pride. These do much, and have done much in all ages; but the foundations of society were never yet shaken as they are at this day. It is not that men are ill fed, but that they have no pleasure in the work by which they make their bread, and therefore look to wealth as the only means of pleasure. It is not that men are pained by the scorn of the upper classes, but they cannot endure their own; for they feel that the kind of labour to which they are condemned is verily a degrading one, and makes them less than men. Never had the upper classes so much sympathy with the lower, or charity for them, as they have at this day, and yet never were they so much hated by them: for, of old, the separation between the noble and the poor was merely a wall built by law; now it is a veritable difference in level of standing, a precipice between upper and lower grounds in the field of humanity, and there is pestilential air at the bottom of it. I know not if a day is ever to come when the nature of right freedom will be understood, and when men will see that to obey another man, to labour for him, yield reverence to him or to his place, is not slavery. It is often the best kind of liberty,—liberty from care. The man who says to one, Go, and he goeth, and to another, Come, and he cometh, has, in most cases, more sense of restraint and difficulty than the man who obeys him. The movements of the one are hindered by the burden on his shoulder; of the other, by the bridle on his lips: there is no way by which the burden may be lightened; but we need not suffer from the bridle if we do not champ at it. To yield reverence to another, to hold ourselves and our lives at his disposal, is not slavery; often it is the noblest state in which a man can live in this world. There is, indeed, a reverence which is servile, that is to say irrational or selfish: but there is also noble reverence, that is to say, reasonable and loving; and a man is never so noble as when he is reverent in this kind; nay, even if the feeling pass the bounds of mere reason, so that it be loving, a man is raised by it. Which had, in reality, most of the serf nature in him,—the Irish peasant who was lying in wait yesterday for his landlord, with his musket muzzle thrust through the ragged hedge; or that old mountain servant, who, 200 years ago, at Inverkeithing, gave up his own life and the lives of his seven sons for his chief?—as each fell, calling forth his brother to the death, "Another for Hector!" And therefore, in all ages and all countries, reverence has been paid and sacrifice made by men to each other, not only without complaint, but rejoicingly; and famine, and peril, and sword, and all evil, and all shame, have been borne willingly in the causes of masters and kings; for all these gifts of the heart ennobled the men who gave, not less than the men who received them, and nature prompted,

6. helot, Spartan serf.

15–16. The man . . . cometh. See Matthew 8:9. **36–40. that old . . . Hector."** "In the battle of Inverkeithing, between the Royalists and Oliver Cromwell's troops, a foster-father and seven brave sons are known to have . . . sacrificed themselves for Sir Hector Maclean of Duart; the old man, whenever one of his boys fell, thrusting forward another to fill his place at the right hand of the beloved chief, with the . . . words . . .—'Another for Hector!' "—Sir Walter Scott, *The Fair Maid of Perth*, Preface.

and God rewarded the sacrifice. But to feel their souls withering within them, unthanked, to find their whole being sunk into an unrecognized abyss, to be counted off into a heap of mechanism, numbered with its wheels, and weighed with its hammer strokes;—this nature bade not,—this God blesses not,—this, humanity for no long time is able to endure.

We have much studied and much perfected, of late, the great civilized invention of the division of labour; only we give it a false name. It is not, truly speaking, the labour that is divided; but the men:—Divided into mere segments of men—broken into small fragments and crumbs of life; so that all the little piece of intelligence that is left in a man is not enough to make a pin, or a nail, but exhausts itself in making the point of a pin, or the head of a nail. Now it is a good and desirable thing, truly, to make many pins in a day; but if we could only see with what crystal sand their points were polished,—sand of human soul, much to be magnified before it can be discerned for what it is,—we should think there might be some loss in it also. And the great cry that rises from all our manufacturing cities, louder than their furnace blast, is all in very deed for this,—that we manufacture everything there except men; we blanch cotton, and strengthen steel, and refine sugar, and shape pottery; but to brighten, to strengthen, to refine, or to form a single living spirit, never enters into our estimate of advantages. And all the evil to which that cry is urging our myriads can be met only in one way: not by teaching nor preaching, for to teach them is but to show them their misery, and to preach to them, if we do nothing more than preach, is to mock at it. It can be met only by a right understanding, on the part of all classes, of what kinds of labour are good for men, raising them, and making them happy; by a determined sacrifice of such convenience, or beauty, or cheapness as is to be got only by the degradation of the workman; and by equally determined demand for the products and results of healthy and ennobling labour. . . .

I should be led far from the matter in hand, if I were to pursue this interesting subject. Enough, I trust, has been said to show the reader that the rudeness or imperfection which at first rendered the term "Gothic" one of reproach is indeed, when rightly understood, one of the most noble characters of Christian architecture, and not only a noble but an *essential* one. It seems a fantastic paradox, but it is nevertheless a most important truth, that no architecture can be truly noble which is *not* imperfect. And this is easily demonstrable. For since the architect, whom we will suppose capable of doing all in perfection, cannot execute the whole with his own hands, he must either make slaves of his workmen in the old Greek, and present English fashion, and level his work to a slave's capacities, which is to degrade it; or else he must take his workmen as he finds them, and let them show their weaknesses together with their strength, which will involve the Gothic imperfection, but render the whole work as noble as the intellect of the age can make it.

But the principle may be stated more broadly still. I have confined the illustration of it to architecture, but I must not leave it as if true of architecture only. Hitherto I have used the words imperfect and perfect merely to distinguish between work grossly unskilful, and work executed with average precision and science; and I have been pleading that any degree of unskilfulness should be admitted, so only that the labourer's mind had room for expression. But, accurately speaking, no good work whatever can be perfect, and *the demand for perfection is always a sign of a misunderstanding of the ends of art.*

This for two reasons, both based on everlasting laws. The first, that no great man ever stops working till he has reached his point of failure: that is to say, his mind is always far in advance of his powers of execution, and the latter will now and then give way in trying to follow it; besides that he will always give to the inferior portions of his work only such inferior attention as they require; and according to his greatness he becomes so accustomed to the feeling of dissatisfaction with the best he can do, that in moments of lassitude or anger with himself he will not care though the beholder be dissatisfied also. I believe there has only been one man who would not acknowledge this necessity, and strove always to reach perfection, Leonardo; the end of his vain effort being merely that he would take ten years to a picture, and leave it unfinished. And therefore, if we are to have great men working at all, or less men doing their best, the work will be imperfect, however beautiful. Of human work none but what is bad can be perfect, in its own bad way.

The second reason is, that imperfection is in some sort essential to all that we know of life. It is the sign of life in a mortal body, that is to say, of a state of progress and change. Nothing that lives is, or can be, rigidly perfect; part of it is decaying, part nascent. The foxglove blossom,—a third part bud, a third part past, a third part in full bloom,—is a type of

39. **Leonardo,** Leonardo da Vinci, the great painter (1452–1519).

the life of this world. And in all things that live there are certain irregularities and deficiencies which are not only signs of life, but sources of beauty. No human face is exactly the same in its lines on each side, no leaf perfect in its lobes, no branch in its symmetry. All admit irregularity as they imply change; and to banish imperfection is to destroy expression, to check exertion, to paralyze vitality. All things are literally better, lovelier, and more beloved for the imperfections which have been divinely appointed, that the law of human life may be Effort, and the law of human judgment, Mercy.

Accept this then for a universal law, that neither architecture nor any other noble work of man can be good unless it be imperfect; and let us be prepared for the otherwise strange fact, which we shall discern clearly as we approach the period of the Renaissance, that the first cause of the fall of the arts of Europe was a relentless requirement of perfection, incapable alike either of being silenced by veneration for greatness, or softened into forgiveness of simplicity.

Thus far then of the Rudeness or Savageness, which is the first mental element of Gothic architecture. It is an element in many other healthy architectures also, as the Byzantine and Romanesque; but true Gothic cannot exist without it.

The second mental element above named was CHANGEFULNESS, or Variety.

I have already enforced the allowing independent operation to the inferior workman, simply as a duty *to him*, and as ennobling the architecture by rendering it more Christian. We have now to consider what reward we obtain for the performance of this duty, namely, the perpetual variety of every feature of the building.

Wherever the workman is utterly enslaved, the parts of the building must of course be absolutely like each other; for the perfection of his execution can only be reached by exercising him in doing one thing, and giving him nothing else to do. The degree in which the workman is degraded may be thus known at a glance, by observing whether the several parts of the building are similar or not; and if, as in Greek work, all the capitals are alike, and all the mouldings unvaried, then the degradation is complete; if, as in Egyptian or Ninevite work, though the manner of executing certain figures is always the same, the order of design is perpetually varied, the degradation is less total; if, as in Gothic work, there is perpetual change both in design and execution, the workman must have been altogether set free.

How much the beholder gains from the liberty of the labourer may perhaps be questioned in England, where one of the strongest instincts in nearly every mind is that Love of Order which makes us desire that our house windows should pair like our carriage horses, and allows us to yield our faith unhesitatingly to architectural theories which fix a form for everything, and forbid variation from it. I would not impeach love of order: it is one of the most useful elements of the English mind; it helps us in our commerce and in all purely practical matters; and it is in many cases one of the foundation stones of morality. Only do not let us suppose that love of order is love of art. It is true that order, in its highest sense, is one of the necessities of art, just as time is a necessity of music; but love of order has no more to do with our right enjoyment of architecture or painting, than love of punctuality with the appreciation of an opera. Experience, I fear, teaches us that accurate and methodical habits in daily life are seldom characteristic of those who either quickly perceive, or richly possess, the creative powers of art; there is, however, nothing inconsistent between the two instincts, and nothing to hinder us from retaining our business habits, and yet fully allowing and enjoying the noblest gifts of Invention. We already do so, in every other branch of art except architecture, and we only do *not* so there because we have been taught that it would be wrong. Our architects gravely inform us that, as there are four rules of arithmetic, there are five orders of architecture; we, in our simplicity, think that this sounds consistent, and believe them. They inform us also that there is one proper form for Corinthian capitals, another for Doric, and another for Ionic. We, considering that there is also a proper form for the letters A, B, and C, think that this also sounds consistent, and accept the proposition. Understanding, therefore, that one form of the said capitals is proper, and no other, and having a conscientious horror of all impropriety, we allow the architect to provide us with the said capitals, of the proper form, in such and such a quantity, and in all other points to take care that the legal forms are observed; which having done, we rest in forced confidence that we are well housed.

But our higher instincts are not deceived. We take no pleasure in the building provided for us, resembling that which we take in a new book or a new picture. We may be proud of its size, complacent in its correctness, and happy in its convenience. We may take the same pleasure in its symmetry and workmanship as in a well-ordered room, or a skilful piece of manufacture. And this we suppose to be all the pleasure that architecture was ever intended to give us. The idea of reading a building as we would read Milton or Dante, and getting the same kind of delight out of the stones as out of the stanzas, never enters our minds for a moment. And for good reason;—There is indeed rhythm in the verses, quite as strict as the symmetries or rhythm of the architecture, and a thousand times more beautiful, but there is something else than rhythm. The verses were neither made to order, nor to match, as the capitals were; and we have therefore a kind of pleasure in them other than a sense of propriety. But it requires a strong effort of common sense to shake ourselves quit of all that we have been taught for the last two centuries, and wake to the perception of a truth just as simple and certain as it is new: that great art, whether expressing itself in words, colours, or stones, does *not* say the same thing over and over again; that the merit of architectural, as of every other art, consists in its saying new and different things; that to repeat itself is no more a characteristic of genius in marble than it is of genius in print; and that we may, without offending any laws of good taste, require of an architect, as we do of a novelist, that he should be not only correct, but entertaining.

Yet all this is true, and self-evident; only hidden from us, as many other self-evident things are, by false teaching. Nothing is a great work of art, for the production of which either rules or models can be given. Exactly so far as architecture works on known rules, and from given models, it is not an art, but a manufacture; and it is, of the two procedures, rather less rational (because more easy) to copy capitals or mouldings from Phidias, and call ourselves architects, than to copy heads and hands from Titian, and call ourselves painters.

Let us then understand at once that change or variety is as much a necessity to the human heart and brain in buildings as in books; that there is no merit, though there is some occasional use, in monotony; and that we must no more expect to derive either pleasure or profit from an architecture whose ornaments are of one pattern, and whose pillars are of one proportion, than we should out of a universe in which the clouds were all of one shape, and the trees all of one size.

And this we confess in deeds, though not in words. All the pleasure which the people of the nineteenth century take in art, is in pictures, sculpture, minor objects of virtù, or mediaeval architecture, which we enjoy under the term picturesque: no pleasure is taken anywhere in modern buildings, and we find all men of true feeling delighting to escape out of modern cities into natural scenery: hence, as I shall hereafter show, that peculiar love of landscape, which is characteristic of the age. It would be well, if in all other matters, we were as ready to put up with what we dislike, for the sake of compliance with established law, as we are in architecture.

How so debased a law ever came to be established, we shall see when we come to describe the Renaissance schools; here we have only to note, as the second most essential element of the Gothic spirit, that it broke through that law wherever it found it in existence; it not only dared, but delighted in, the infringement of every servile principle; and invented a series of forms of which the merit was, not merely that they were new, but that they were *capable of perpetual novelty*. The pointed arch was not merely a bold variation from the round, but it admitted of millions of variations in itself; for the proportions of a pointed arch are changeable to infinity, while a circular arch is always the same. The grouped shaft was not merely a bold variation from the single one, but it admitted of millions of variations in its grouping, and in the proportions resultant from its grouping. The introduction of tracery was not only a startling change in the treatment of window lights, but admitted endless changes in the interlacement of the tracery bars themselves. So that, while in all living Christian architecture the love of variety exists, the Gothic schools exhibited that love in culminating energy; and their influence, wherever it extended itself, may be sooner and farther traced by this character than by any other; the tendency to the adoption of Gothic types being always first shown by greater irregularity, and richer variation in the forms of the architecture it is about to supersede, long before the appearance of the pointed arch or of any other recognizable *outward* sign of the Gothic mind.

We must, however, herein note carefully what distinction there is between a healthy and a diseased love of change; for as it was in healthy love of change that the Gothic architecture rose, it was partly in consequence of diseased love of change that it was destroyed. In order to understand this clearly, it will be necessary to consider the different ways in which change and monotony are presented to us in nature; both having their use, like darkness and light, and the one incapable of being enjoyed without the other: change being most delightful after some prolongation of monotony, as light appears most brilliant after the eyes have been for some time closed. . . .

34. Phidias, Greek sculptor (c. 500–c. 432 B.C.). **36. Titian,** Venetian painter (1477–1576).

. . . The variety of the Gothic schools is the more healthy and beautiful, because in many cases it is entirely unstudied, and results, not from the mere love of change, but from practical necessities. For in one point of view Gothic is not only the best, but the *only rational* architecture, as being that which can fit itself most easily to all services, vulgar or noble. Undefined in its slope of roof, height of shaft, breadth of arch, or disposition of ground plan, it can shrink into a turret, expand into a hall, coil into a staircase, or spring into a spire, with undegraded grace and unexhausted energy; and whenever it finds occasion for change in its form or purpose, it submits to it without the slightest sense of loss either to its unity or majesty,—subtle and flexible like a fiery serpent, but ever attentive to the voice of the charmer. And it is one of the chief virtues of the Gothic builders, that they never suffered ideas of outside symmetries and consistencies to interfere with the real use and value of what they did. If they wanted a window, they opened one; a room, they added one; a buttress, they built one; utterly regardless of any established conventionalities of external appearance, knowing (as indeed it always happened) that such daring interruptions of the formal plan would rather give additional interest to its symmetry than injure it. So that, in the best times of Gothic, a useless window would rather have been opened in an unexpected place for the sake of the surprise, than a useful one forbidden for the sake of symmetry. Every successive architect, employed upon a great work, built the pieces he added in his own way, utterly regardless of the style adopted by his predecessors; and if two towers were raised in nominal correspondence at the sides of a cathedral front, one was nearly sure to be different from the other, and in each the style at the top to be different from the style at the bottom.

These marked variations were, however, only permitted as part of the great system of perpetual change which ran through every member of Gothic design, and rendered it as endless a field for the beholder's inquiry as for the builder's imagination: change, which in the best schools is subtle and delicate, and rendered more delightful by intermingling of a noble monotony; in the more barbaric schools is somewhat fantastic and redundant; but, in all, a necessary and constant condition of the life of the school. Sometimes the variety is in one feature, sometimes in another; it may be in the capitals or crockets, in the niches or the traceries, or in all together, but in some one or other of the features it will be found always. If the mouldings are constant, the surface sculpture will change; if the capitals are of a fixed design, the traceries will change; if the traceries are monotonous, the capitals will change; and if even, as in some fine schools, the early English for example, there is the slightest approximation to an unvarying type of mouldings, capitals, and floral decoration, the variety is found in the disposition of the masses, and in the figure sculpture. . . .

The third constituent element of the Gothic mind was stated to be NATURALISM; that is to say, the love of natural objects for their own sake, and the effort to represent them frankly, unconstrained by artistical laws.

This characteristic of the style partly follows in necessary connection with those named above. For, so soon as the workman is left free to represent what subjects he chooses, he must look to the nature that is round him for material, and will endeavour to represent it as he sees it, with more or less accuracy according to the skill he possesses, and with much play of fancy, but with small respect for law. There is, however, a marked distinction between the imaginations of the Western and Eastern races, even when both are left free; the Western, or Gothic, delighting most in the representation of facts, and the Eastern (Arabian, Persian, and Chinese) in the harmony of colours and forms. Each of these intellectual dispositions has its particular forms of error and abuse, which, though I have often before stated, I must here again briefly explain; and this the rather, because the word Naturalism is, in one of its senses, justly used as a term of reproach, and the questions respecting the real relations of art and nature are so many and so confused throughout all the schools of Europe at this day, that I cannot clearly enunciate any single truth without appearing to admit, in fellowship with it, some kind of error, unless the reader will bear with me in entering into such an analysis of the subject as will serve us for general guidance.

We are to remember, in the first place, that the arrangement of colours and lines is an art analogous to the composition of music, and entirely independent of the representation of facts. Good colouring does not necessarily convey the image of anything but itself. It consists in certain proportions and arrangements of rays of light, but not in likenesses to anything. A few touches of certain greys and purples laid by a master's hand on white paper will be good colouring; as more touches are added beside them, we may find out that they were intended to represent a dove's neck, and we may praise, as the drawing advances, the perfect imitation of the dove's neck. But the good colouring does not consist in that imitation, but in the abstract qualities and relations of the grey and purple.

In like manner, as soon as a great sculptor begins to shape his work out of the block, we shall see that its lines are nobly arranged, and of noble character. We may not have the slightest idea for what the forms are intended, whether they are of man or beast, of vegetation or drapery. Their likeness to anything does not affect their nobleness. They are magnificent forms, and that is all we need care to know of them, in order to say whether the workman is a good or bad sculptor.

Now the noblest art is an exact unison of the abstract value, with the imitative power, of forms and colours. It is the noblest composition, used to express the noblest facts. But the human mind cannot in general unite the two perfections: it either pursues the fact to the neglect of the composition, or pursues the composition to the neglect of the fact.

And it is intended by the Deity that it *should* do this: the best art is not always wanted. Facts are often wanted without art, as in a geological diagram; and art often without facts, as in a Turkey carpet. And most men have been made capable of giving either one or the other, but not both; only one or two, the very highest, can give both.

Observe then. Men are universally divided, as respects their artistical qualifications, into three great classes; a right, a left, and a centre. On the right side are the men of facts, on the left the men of design, in the centre the men of both.

The three classes of course pass into each other by imperceptible gradations. The men of facts are hardly ever altogether without powers of design; the men of design are always in some measure cognizant of facts; and as each class possesses more or less of the powers of the opposite one, it approaches to the character of the central class. Few men, even in that central rank, are so exactly throned on the summit of the crest that they cannot be perceived to incline in the least one way or the other, embracing both horizons with their glance. Now each of these classes has, as I above said, a healthy function in the world, and correlative diseases or unhealthy functions; and, when the work of either of them is seen in its morbid condition, we are apt to find fault with the class of workmen, instead of finding fault only with the particular abuse which has perverted their action. . . .

There is, however, one direction in which the Naturalism of the Gothic workmen is peculiarly manifested; and this direction is even more characteristic of the school than the Naturalism itself; I mean their peculiar fondness for the forms of Vegetation. In rendering the various circumstances of daily life, Egyptian and Ninevite sculpture is as frank and as diffuse as the Gothic. From the highest pomps of state or triumphs of battle, to the most trivial domestic arts and amusements, all is taken advantage of to fill the field of granite with the perpetual interest of a crowded drama; and the early Lombardic and Romanesque sculpture is equally copious in its description of the familiar circumstances of war and the chase. But in all the scenes portrayed by the workmen of these nations, vegetation occurs only as an explanatory accessary; the reed is introduced to mark the course of the river, or the tree to mark the covert of the wild beast, or the ambush of the enemy, but there is no especial interest in the forms of the vegetation strong enough to induce them to make it a subject of separate and accurate study. Again, among the nations who followed the arts of design exclusively, the forms of foliage introduced were meagre and general, and their real intricacy and life were neither admired nor expressed. But to the Gothic workman the living foliage became a subject of intense affection, and he struggled to render all its characters with as much accuracy as was compatible with the laws of his design and the nature of his material, not unfrequently tempted in his enthusiasm to transgress the one and disguise the other.

There is a peculiar significance in this, indicative both of higher civilization and gentler temperament, than had before been manifested in architecture. Rudeness, and the love of change, which we have insisted upon as the first elements of Gothic, are also elements common to all healthy schools. But here is a softer element mingled with them, peculiar to the Gothic itself. The rudeness or ignorance which would have been painfully exposed in the treatment of the human form, are still not so great as to prevent the successful rendering of the wayside herbage; and the love of change, which be comes morbid and feverish in following the haste of the hunter and the rage of the combatant, is at once soothed and satisfied as it watches the wandering of the tendril, and the budding of the flower. Nor is this all: the new direction of mental interest marks an infinite change in the means and the habits of life. The nations whose chief support was in the chase, whose chief interest was in the battle, whose chief pleasure was in the banquet, would take small care respecting the shapes of leaves and flowers; and notice little in the forms of the forest trees which sheltered them, except the signs indicative of the wood which would make the toughest lance, the closest roof, or the clearest fire. The affectionate observation of the grace and outward character of vegetation is the sure sign of a more tranquil and gentle existence, sustained by the gifts, and gladdened by the splendour, of the earth. In that careful distinction of species, and richness of delicate and undisturbed organization, which characterize the Gothic design, there is the history of rural and thoughtful life, influenced by habitual tenderness, and devoted to subtle inquiry; and every discriminating and delicate touch of the chisel, as it rounds the petal or guides the branch, is a prophecy of the development of the entire body of the natural sciences, beginning with that of medicine, of the recovery of literature, and the establishment of the most necessary principles of domestic wisdom and national peace.

I have before alluded to the strange and vain supposition, that the original conception of Gothic architecture had been derived from vegetation,—from the symmetry of avenues, and the interlacing of branches. It is a supposition which never could have existed for a moment in the mind of any person acquainted with early Gothic; but, however idle as a theory, it is most valuable as a testimony to the character of the perfected style. It is precisely because the reverse of this theory is the fact, because the Gothic did not arise out of, but develope itself into, a resemblance to vegetation, that this resemblance is so instructive as an indication of the temper of the builders. It was no chance suggestion of the form of an arch from the bending of a bough, but a gradual and continual discovery of a beauty in natural forms which could be more and more perfectly transferred into those of stone, that influenced at once the heart of the people, and the form of the edifice. The Gothic architecture arose in massy and mountainous strength, axe-hewn, and iron-bound, block heaved upon block by the monk's enthusiasm and the soldier's force; and cramped and stanchioned into such weight of grisly wall, as might bury the anchoret in darkness, and beat back the utmost storm of battle, suffering but by the same narrow crosslet the passing of the sunbeam, or of the arrow. Gradually, as that monkish enthusiasm became more thoughtful, and as the sound of war became more and more intermittent beyond the gates of the convent or the keep, the stony pillar grew slender and the vaulted roof grew light, till they had wreathed themselves into the semblance of the summer woods at their fairest, and of the dead field-flowers, long trodden down in blood, sweet monumental statues were set to bloom for ever, beneath the porch of the temple, or the canopy of the tomb.

Nor is it only as a sign of greater gentleness or refinement of mind, but as a proof of the best possible direction of this refinement, that the tendency of the Gothic to the expression of vegetative life is to be admired. That sentence of Genesis, "I have given thee every green herb for meat," like all the rest of the book, has a profound symbolical as well as a literal meaning. It is not merely the nourishment of the body, but the food of the soul, that is intended. The green herb is, of all nature, that which is most essential to the healthy spiritual life of man. Most of us do not need fine scenery; the precipice and the mountain peak are not intended to be seen by all men,—perhaps their power is greatest over those who are unaccustomed to them. But trees, and fields, and flowers were made for all, and are necessary for all. God has connected the labour which is essential to the bodily sustenance, with the pleasures which are healthiest for the heart; and while He made the ground stubborn, He made its herbage fragrant, and its blossoms fair. The proudest architecture that man can build has no higher honour than to bear the image and recall the memory of that grass of the field which is, at once, the type and the support of his existence; the goodly building is then most glorious when it is sculptured into the likeness of the leaves of Paradise; and the great Gothic spirit, as we showed it to be noble in its disquietude, is also noble in its hold of nature; it is, indeed, like the dove of Noah, in that she found no rest upon the face of the waters,—but like her in this also, "LO, IN HER MOUTH WAS AN OLIVE BRANCH, PLUCKED OFF."

The fourth essential element of the Gothic mind was above stated to be the sense of the GROTESQUE; but I shall defer the endeavour to define this most curious and subtle character until we have occasion to examine one of the divisions of the Renaissance schools, which was morbidly influenced by it. . . . It is the less necessary to insist upon it here, because every reader familiar with Gothic architecture must understand what I mean, and will, I believe, have no hesitation in admitting that the tendency to delight in fantastic and ludicrous, as well as in sublime, images, is a universal instinct of the Gothic imagination.

The fifth element above named was RIGIDITY; and this character I must endeavour carefully to define, for neither the word I have used, nor any other that I can think of, will express it accurately.

7–8. "I have . . . meat." See Genesis 1:30.
34–35. "Lo . . . off." See Genesis 8:11.

For I mean, not merely stable, but *active* rigidity; the peculiar energy which gives tension to movement, and stiffness to resistance, which makes the fiercest lightning forked rather than curved, and the stoutest oak-branch angular rather than bending, and is as much seen in the quivering of the lance as in the glittering of the icicle.

I have before had occasion . . . to note some manifestations of this energy or fixedness; but it must be still more attentively considered here, as it shows itself throughout the whole structure and decoration of Gothic work. Egyptian and Greek buildings stand, for the most part, by their own weight and mass, one stone passively incumbent on another: but in the Gothic vaults and traceries there is a stiffness analogous to that of the bones of a limb, or fibres of a tree; an elastic tension and communication of force from part to part, and also a studious expression of this throughout every visible line of the building. And, in like manner, the Greek and Egyptian ornament is either mere surface engraving, as if the face of the wall had been stamped with a seal, or its lines are flowing, lithe, and luxuriant; in either case, there is no expression of energy in the framework of the ornament itself. But the Gothic ornament stands out in prickly independence, and frosty fortitude, jutting into crockets, and freezing into pinnacles; here starting up into a monster, there germinating into a blossom; anon knitting itself into a branch, alternately thorny, bossy, and bristly, or writhed into every form of nervous entanglement; but, even when most graceful, never for an instant languid, always quickset: erring, if at all, ever on the side of brusquerie. . . .

Last, because the least essential, of the constituent elements of this noble school, was placed that of REDUNDANCE,—the uncalculating bestowal of the wealth of its labour. There is, indeed, much Gothic, and that of the best period, in which this element is hardly traceable, and which depends for its effect almost exclusively on loveliness of simple design and grace of uninvolved proportion; still, in the most characteristic buildings, a certain portion of their effect depends upon accumulation of ornament; and many of those which have most influence on the minds of men, have attained it by means of this attribute alone. And although, by careful study of the school, it is possible to arrive at a condition of taste which shall be better contended by a few perfect lines than by a whole façade covered with fretwork, the building which only satisfies such a taste is not to be considered the best. For the very first requirement of Gothic architecture being, as we saw above, that it shall both admit the aid, and appeal to the admiration, of the rudest as well as the most refined minds, the richness of the work is, paradoxical as the statement may appear, a part of its humility. No architecture is so haughty as that which is simple; which refuses to address the eye, except in a few clear and forceful lines; which implies, in offering so little to our regards, that all it has offered is perfect; and disdains, either by the complexity of the attractiveness of its features, to embarrass our investigation, or betray us into delight. That humility, which is the very life of the Gothic school, is shown not only in the imperfection, but in the accumulation, of ornament. The inferior rank of the workman is often shown as much in the richness, as the roughness, of his work; and if the co-operation of every hand, and the sympathy of every heart, are to be received, we must be content to allow the redundance which disguises the failure of the feeble, and wins the regard of the inattentive. There are, however, far nobler interests mingling, in the Gothic heart, with the rude love of decorative accumulation: a magnificent enthusiasm, which feels as if it never could do enough to reach the fulness of its ideal; and unselfishness of sacrifice, which would rather cast fruitless labour before the altar than stand idle in the market; and, finally, a profound sympathy with the fulness and wealth of the material universe, rising out of that Naturalism whose operation we have already endeavoured to define. The sculptor who sought for his models among the forest leaves, could not but quickly and deeply feel that complexity need not involve the loss of grace, nor richness that of repose; and every hour which he spent in the study of the minute and various work of Nature, made him feel more forcibly the barrenness of what was best in that of man: nor is it to be wondered at, that, seeing her perfect and exquisite creations poured forth in a profusion which conception could not grasp nor calculation sum, he should think that it ill became him to be niggardly of his own rude craftsmanship; and where he saw throughout the universe a faultless beauty lavished on measureless spaces of broidered field and blooming mountain, to grudge his poor and imperfect labour to the few stones that he had raised one upon another, for habitation or memorial. The years of his life passed away before his task was accomplished; but generation succeeded generation with unwearied enthusiasm, and the cathedral front was at last lost in the tapestry of its traceries, like a rock among the thickets and herbage of spring.

from THE CROWN OF WILD OLIVE

The crown of wild olive was the only prize given to winners at the Olympic Games; Ruskin uses it to discourage runners in the race of life from working for material reward.

The four lectures contained in the book thus entitled (1866) were "War," "The Future of England," "Work," and "Traffic." The occasion for "Traffic" was Ruskin's visit to the town of Bradford, in Yorkshire, where the building of a new Exchange was contemplated.

Lecture 2: TRAFFIC

YOU cannot have good architecture merely by asking people's advice on occasion. All good architecture is the expression of national life and character, and it is produced by a prevalent and eager national taste, or desire for beauty. And I want you to think a little of the deep significance of this word "taste"; for no statement of mine has been more earnestly or oftener controverted than that good taste is essentially a moral quality. "No," say many of my antagonists, "taste is one thing, morality is another. Tell us what is pretty: we shall be glad to know that; but we need no sermons—even were you able to preach them, which may be doubted."

Permit me, therefore, to fortify this old dogma of mine somewhat. Taste is not only a part and an index of morality;—it is the ONLY morality. The first, and last, and closest trial question to any living creature is, "What do you like?" Tell me what you like, and I'll tell you what you are. Go out into the street, and ask the first man or woman you meet, what their "taste" is; and if they answer candidly, you know them, body and soul. "You, my friend in the rags, with the unsteady gait, what do *you* like?" "A pipe and a quatern of gin." I know you. "You, good woman, with the quick step and tidy bonnet, what do you like?" "A swept hearth, and a clean tea-table; and my husband opposite me, and a baby at my breast." Good, I know you also. "You, little girl with the golden hair and the soft eyes, what do you like?" "My canary, and a run among the wood hyacinths." "You, little boy with the dirty hands, and the low forehead, what do you like?" "A shy at the sparrows, and a game at pitch farthing." Good; we know them all now. What more need we ask?

"Nay," perhaps you answer; "we need rather to ask what these people and children do, than what they like. If they *do* right, it is no matter that they like what is wrong; and if they *do* wrong, it is no matter that they like what is right. Doing is the great thing; and it does not matter that the man likes drinking, so that he does not drink; nor that the little girl likes to be kind to her canary, if she will not learn her lessons; nor that the little boy likes throwing stones at the sparrows, if he goes to the Sunday school." Indeed, for a short time, and in a provisional sense, this is true. For if, resolutely, people do what is right, in time they come to like doing it. But they only are in a right moral state when they *have* come to like doing it; and as long as they don't like it, they are still in a vicious state. The man is not in health of body who is always thinking of the bottle in the cupboard, though he bravely bears his thirst; but the man who heartily enjoys water in the morning, and wine in the evening, each in its proper quantity and time. And the entire object of true education is to make people not merely *do* the right things, but *enjoy* the right things:—not merely industrious, but to love industry—not merely learned, but to love knowledge—not merely pure, but to love purity—not merely just, but to hunger and thirst after justice.

But you may answer or think, "Is the liking for outside ornaments,—for pictures, or statues, or furniture, or architecture,—a moral quality?" Yes, most surely, if a rightly set liking. Taste for *any* pictures or statues is not a moral quality, but taste for good ones is. Only here again we have to define the word "good." I don't mean by "good," clever—or learned—or difficult in the doing. Take a picture by Teniers, of sots quarrelling over their dice; it is an entirely clever picture; so clever that nothing in its kind has ever been done equal to it; but it is also an entirely base and evil picture. It is an expression of delight in the prolonged contemplation of a vile thing, and delight in that is an "unmannered," or "immoral" quality. It is "bad taste" in the profoundest sense—it is the taste of the devils. On the other hand, a picture of Titian's, or a Greek statue, or a Greek coin, or a Turner landscape, expresses delight in the perpetual contemplation of a good and perfect thing. That is an entirely moral quality—it is the taste of the angels. And all delight in fine art, and all love of it, resolve themselves into simple love of that which deserves love. That deserving is the quality which we call "loveliness"—(we ought to have an opposite word, hateliness, to be said of the things which deserve to be hated); and it is not an indifferent nor optional thing whether we love this or that; but it is just the

21–22. but to hunger . . . justice, see Matthew 5:6.
31. Teniers. There were two famous Dutch painters of this name—David Teniers, the elder (1582–1649) and David Teniers, the younger (1610–1690).

vital function of all our being. What we *like* determines what we *are*, and is the sign of what we are; and to teach taste is inevitably to form character. . . .

And so completely and unexceptionally is this so, that, if I had time to-night, I could show you that a nation cannot be affected by any vice, or weakness, without expressing it, legibly, and for ever, either in bad art, or by want of art; and that there is no national virtue, small or great, which is not manifestly expressed in all the art which circumstances enable the people possessing that virtue to produce. Take, for instance, your great English virtue of enduring and patient courage. You have at present in England only one art of any consequence—that is, iron-working. You know thoroughly well how to cast and hammer iron. Now, do you think, in those masses of lava which you build volcanic cones to melt, and which you forge at the mouths of the Infernos you have created; do you think, on those iron plates, your courage and endurance are not written for ever,—not merely with an iron pen, but on iron parchment? And take also your great English vice—European vice—vice of all the world—vice of all other worlds that roll or shine in heaven, bearing with them yet the atmosphere of hell—the vice of jealousy, which brings competition into your commerce, treachery into your councils, and dishonour into your wars—that vice which has rendered for you, and for your next neighbouring nation, the daily occupations of existence no longer possible, but with the mail upon your breasts and the sword loose in its sheath; so that at last, you have realized for all the multitudes of the two great peoples who lead the so-called civilization of the earth,—you have realized for them all, I say, in person and in policy, what was once true only of the rough Border riders of your Cheviot hills—

> "They carved at the meal
> With gloves of steel,
> And they drank the red wine through the helmet barred";—

do you think that this national shame and dastardliness of heart are not written as legibly on every rivet of your iron armour as the strength of the right hands that forged it?

. . . Believe me, without farther instance, I could show you, in all time, that every nation's vice, or virtue, was written in its art: the soldiership of early Greece; the sensuality of late Italy; the visionary religion of Tuscany; the splendid human energy of Venice. I have no time to do this to-night (I have done it elsewhere before now); but I proceed to apply the principle to ourselves in a more searching manner.

I notice that among all the new buildings which cover your once wild hills, churches and schools are mixed in due, that is to say, in large proportion, with your mills and mansions; and I notice also that the churches and schools are almost always Gothic, and the mansions and mills are never Gothic. May I ask the meaning of this? for, remember, it is peculiarly a modern phenomenon. When Gothic was invented, houses were Gothic as well as churches; and when the Italian style superseded the Gothic, churches were Italian as well as houses. If there is a Gothic spire to the cathedral of Antwerp, there is a Gothic belfry to the Hôtel de Ville at Brussels; if Inigo Jones builds an Italian Whitehall, Sir Christopher Wren builds an Italian St. Paul's. But now you live under one school of architecture, and worship under another. What do you mean by doing this? Am I to understand that you are thinking of changing your architecture back to Gothic; and that you treat your churches experimentally, because it does not matter what mistakes you make in a church? Or am I to understand that you consider Gothic a pre-eminently sacred and beautiful mode of building, which you think, like the fine frankincense, should be mixed for the tabernacle only, and reserved for your religious services? For if this be the feeling, though it may seem at first as if it were graceful and reverent, at the root of the matter, it signifies neither more nor less than that you have separated your religion from your life.

For consider what a wide significance this fact has; and remember that it is not you only, but all the people of England, who are behaving thus, just now.

You have all got into the habit of calling the church "the house of God." I have seen, over the doors of many churches, the legend actually carved, "*This* is the house of God and this is the gate of heaven." Now, note where that legend comes from, and of what place it was first spoken. A boy leaves his father's house to go on a long journey on foot, to visit his uncle: he has to cross a wild hill-desert; just as if one of your own boys had to cross the wolds to visit an uncle at Carlisle. The second or third

40–43. "They carved . . . barred," Scott, *Lay of the Last Minstrel*, I, 31 ff.

19–20. if Inigo Jones . . . St. Paul's. Inigo Jones (1573–1652) designed the banqueting house at Whitehall, 1619–22. **Sir Christopher Wren** (1632–1723) rebuilt St. Paul's Cathedral after the great fire of 1666. **41 ff. You have all got . . . gate of heaven."** See Genesis 28:10–22.

day your boy finds himself somewhere between Hawes and Brough, in the midst of the moors, at sunset. It is stony ground, and boggy; he cannot go one foot farther that night. Down he lies, to sleep, on Wharnside, where best he may, gathering a few of the stones together to put under his head;—so wild the place is, he cannot get anything but stones. And there, lying under the broad night, he has a dream; and he sees a ladder set up on the earth, and the top of it reaches to heaven, and the angels of God are seen ascending and descending upon it. And when he wakes out of his sleep, he says, "How dreadful is this place; surely this is none other than the house of God, and this is the gate of heaven." This PLACE, observe; not this church; not this city; not this stone, even, which he puts up for a memorial—the piece of flint on which his head has lain. But this *place;* this windy slope of Wharnside; this moorland hollow, torrent-bitten, snow-blighted! this *any* place where God lets down the ladder. And how are you to know where that will be? or how are you to determine where it may be, but by being ready for it always? Do you know where the lightning is to fall next? You *do* know that, partly; you can guide the lightning; but you cannot guide the going forth of the Spirit, which is as that lightning when it shines from the east to the west.

But the perpetual and insolent warping of that strong verse to serve a merely ecclesiastical purpose is only one of the thousand instances in which we sink back into gross Judaism. We call our churches "temples." Now, you know perfectly well they are *not* temples. They have never had, never can have, anything whatever to do with temples. They are "synagogues"—"gathering places" where you gather yourselves together as an assembly; and by not calling them so, you again miss the force of another mighty text—"Thou, when thou prayest, shalt not be as the hypocrites are; for they love to pray standing in the *churches*" [we should translate it], "that they may be seen of men. But thou, when thou prayest, enter into thy closet, and when thou hast shut thy door, pray to thy Father,"—which is, not in chancel nor in aisle, but "in secret."

Now, you feel, as I say this to you—I know you feel—as if I were trying to take away the honour of your churches. Not so; I am trying to prove to you the honour of your houses and your hills; not that the Church is not sacred—but that the whole Earth is. I would have you feel what careless, what constant, what infectious sin there is in all modes of thought, whereby, in calling your churches only "holy," you call your hearths and homes "profane"; and have separated yourselves from the heathen by casting all your household gods to the ground, instead of recognizing, in the place of their many and feeble Lares, the presence of your One and Mighty Lord and Lar. . . .

I hope, now, that there is no risk of your misunderstanding me when I come to the gist of what I want to say to-night;—when I repeat, that every great national architecture has been the result and exponent of a great national religion. You can't have bits of it here, bits there—you must have it everywhere or nowhere. It is not the monopoly of a clerical company—it is not the exponent of a theological dogma—it is not the hieroglyphic writing of an initiated priesthood; it is the manly language of a people inspired by resolute and common purpose, and rendering resolute and common fidelity to the legible laws of an undoubted God.

Now there have as yet been three distinct schools of European architecture. I say, European, because Asiatic and African architectures belong so entirely to other races and climates, that there is no question of them here; only, in passing, I will simply assure you that whatever is good or great in Egypt, and Syria, and India, is just as good or great for the same reasons as the buildings on our side of the Bosphorus. We Europeans, then, have had three great religions: the Greek, which was the worship of the God of Wisdom and Power; the Mediaeval, which was the worship of the God of Judgment and Consolation; the Renaissance, which was the worship of the God of Pride and Beauty.

. . . And all these three worships issue in vast temple building. Your Greek worshipped Wisdom, and built you the Parthenon—the Virgin's temple. The Mediaeval worshipped Consolation, and built you Virgin temples also—but to our Lady of Salvation. Then the Revivalist worshipped beauty, of a sort, and built you Versailles and the Vatican. Now, lastly, will you tell me what *we* worship, and what *we* build?

You know we are speaking always of the real, active, continual, national worship; that by which men act, while they live; not that which they talk of, when they die. Now, we have, indeed, a nominal

38–44. "Thou, when thou prayest . . . in secret." See Matthew 6:5–6.

5. Lares, Roman household gods. **36. Parthenon,** built on the Acropolis, Athens, fifth century B.C. **37–39. The Mediaeval . . . Salvation,** see Henry Adams's excellent description of Chartres Cathedral in *Mont Saint Michel and Chartres*, Houghton Mifflin, *c.* 1904, especially chaps. VI, X, XIII. **39. Revivalist,** of classical architecture. **40. Versailles and the Vatican.** The palace at Versailles dates chiefly from 1661; it was restored under Louis-Philippe (1830–48). The beginnings of the Vatican, as we know it today, go back at least to Nicholas V (1447–55).

religion, to which we pay tithes of property and sevenths of time; but we have also a practical and earnest religion, to which we devote nine-tenths of our property and six-sevenths of our time. And we dispute a great deal about the nominal religion: but we are all unanimous about this practical one; of which I think you will admit that the ruling goddess may be best generally described as the "Goddess of Getting-on," or "Britannia of the Market." The Athenians had an "Athena Agoraia," or Athena of the Market; but she was a subordinate type of their goddess, while our Britannia Agoraia is the principal type of ours. And all your great architectural works are, of course, built to her. It is long since you built a great cathedral; and how you would laugh at me if I proposed building a cathedral on the top of one of these hills of yours, to make it an Acropolis! But your railroad mounds, vaster than the walls of Babylon; your railroad stations, vaster than the temple of Ephesus, and innumerable; your chimneys, how much more mighty and costly than cathedral spires! your harbour-piers; your warehouses; your exchanges!—all these are built to your great Goddess of "Getting-on"; and she has formed, and will continue to form, your architecture, as long as you worship her; and it is quite vain to ask me to tell you how to build to *her;* you know far better than I.

There might, indeed, on some theories, be a conceivably good architecture for Exchanges—that is to say, if there were any heroism in the fact or deed of exchange, which might be typically carved on the outside of your building. For, you know, all beautiful architecture must be adorned with sculpture or painting; and for sculpture or painting, you must have a subject. And hitherto it has been a received opinion among the nations of the world that the only right subjects for either, were *heroisms* of some sort. Even on his pots and his flagons, the Greek put a Hercules slaying lions, or an Apollo slaying serpents, or Bacchus slaying melancholy giants, and earthborn despondencies. On his temples, the Greek put contests of great warriors in founding states, or of gods with evil spirits. On his houses and temples alike, the Christian put carvings of angels conquering devils; or of hero-martyrs exchanging this world for another; subject inappropriate, I think, to our direction of exchange here. And the Master of Christians not only left His followers without any orders as to the sculpture of affairs of exchange on the outside of buildings, but gave some strong evidence of His dislike of affairs of exchange within them. And yet there might surely be a heroism in such affairs; and all commerce become a kind of selling of doves, not impious. The wonder has always been great to me, that heroism has never been supposed to be in any wise consistent with the practice of supplying people with food, or clothes; but rather with that of quartering one's self upon them for food, and stripping them of their clothes. Spoiling of armour is an heroic deed in all ages; but the selling of clothes, old or new, has never taken any colour of magnanimity. Yet one does not see why feeding the hungry and clothing the naked should ever become base businesses, even when engaged in on a large scale. If one could contrive to attach the notion of conquest to them anyhow! so that, supposing there were anywhere an obstinate race, who refused to be comforted, one might take some pride in giving them compulsory comfort! and, as it were, "*occupying* a country" with one's gifts, instead of one's armies? If one could only consider it as much a victory to get a barren field sown, as to get an eared field stripped; and contend who should build villages, instead of who should "carry" them! Are not all forms of heroism conceivable in doing these serviceable deeds? You doubt who is strongest? It might be ascertained by push of spade, as well as push of sword. Who is wisest? There are witty things to be thought of in planning other business than campaigns. Who is bravest? There are always the elements to fight with, stronger than men; and nearly as merciless.

The only absolutely and unapproachably heroic element in the soldier's work seems to be—that he is paid little for it—and regularly: while you traffickers, and exchangers, and others occupied in presumably benevolent business, like to be paid much for it—and by chance. I never can make out how it is that a *knight*-errant does not expect to be paid for his trouble, but a *pedlar*-errant always does;—that people are willing to take hard knocks for nothing, but never to sell ribands cheap; that they are ready to go on fervent crusades, to recover the tomb of a buried God, but never on any travels to fulfil the orders of a living one;—that they will go anywhere barefoot to preach their faith, but must be well bribed to practice it, and are perfectly

20. temple of Ephesus, in Asia Minor. The temple was sacred to Diana. **40. Hercules,** the great, half-divine "strong man" of Greek mythology. **Apollo,** the god of manly beauty, poetry, music, etc. **41. Bacchus,** the god of wine. For the particular adventures referred to, see Gayley's *Classic Myths,* or some similar handbook of mythology.

3–4. gave some strong evidence . . . them, when he drove the money-changers out of the Temple; see Matthew 21:12–13. **46–47. to go . . . God,** as western Europe did in the Crusades (11th, 12th, 13th centuries).

ready to give the Gospel gratis, but never the loaves and fishes.

If you chose to take the matter up on any such soldierly principle; to do your commerce, and your feeding of nations, for fixed salaries; and to be as particular about giving people the best food, and the best cloth, as soldiers are about giving them the best gunpowder, I could carve something for you on your exchange worth looking at. But I can only at present suggest decorating its frieze with pendant purses; and making its pillars broad at the base, for the sticking of bills. And in the innermost chambers of it there might be a statue of Britannia of the Market, who may have, perhaps advisably, a partridge for her crest, typical at once of her courage in fighting for noble ideas, and of her interest in game; and round its neck, the inscription in golden letters, "Perdix fovit quae non peperit." Then, for her spear, she might have a weaver's beam; and on her shield, instead of St. George's Cross, the Milanese boar, semi-fleeced, with the town of Gennesaret proper, in the field; and the legend, "In the best market," and her corslet, of leather, folded over her heart in the shape of a purse, with thirty slits in it, for a piece of money to go in at, on each day of the month. And I doubt not but that the people would come to see your exchange, and its goddess, with applause.

Nevertheless, I want to point out to you certain strange characters in this goddess of yours. She differs from the great Greek and Mediaeval deities essentially in two things—first, as to the continuance of her presumed power, secondly, as to the extent of it.

First, as to the Continuance.

The Greek Goddess of Wisdom gave continual increase of wisdom, as the Christian Spirit of Comfort (or Comforter) continual increase of comfort. There was no question, with these, of any limit or cessation of function. But with your Agora Goddess, that is just the most important question. Getting on—but where to? Gathering together—but how much? Do you mean to gather always—never to spend? If so, I wish you joy of your goddess, for I am just as well off as you, without the trouble of worshipping her at all. But if you do not spend, somebody else will—somebody else must. And it is because of this (among many other such errors) that I have fearlessly declared your so-called science of Political Economy to be no science; because, namely, it has omitted the study of exactly the most important branch of the business—the study of *spending*. For spend you must, and as much as you make, ultimately. You gather corn:—will you bury England under a heap of grain; or will you, when you have gathered, finally eat? You gather gold:—will you make your house-roofs of it or pave your streets with it? That is still one way of spending it. But if you keep it, that you may get more, I'll give you more; I'll give you all the gold you want—all you can imagine—if you can tell me what you'll do with it. You shall have thousands of gold pieces;—thousands of thousands—millions—mountains, of gold: where will you keep them? Will you put an Olympus of silver upon a golden Pelion—make Ossa like a wart? Do you think the rain and dew would then come down to you, in the streams from such mountains, more blessedly than they will down the mountains which God has made for you, of moss and whinstone? But it is not gold that you want to gather! What is it? greenbacks? No; not those neither. What is it then—is it ciphers after a capital I? Cannot you practise writing ciphers, and write as many as you want? Write ciphers for an hour every morning, in a big book, and say every evening, I am worth all those naughts more than I was yesterday. Won't that do? Well, what in the name of Plutus is it you want? Not gold, not greenbacks, not ciphers after a capital I? You will have to answer, after all, "No; we want, somehow or other, money's *worth*." Well, what is that? Let your Goddess of Getting-on discover it, and let her learn to stay therein.

But there is yet another question to be asked respecting this Goddess of Getting-on. The first was of the continuance of her power; the second is of its extent.

Pallas and the Madonna were supposed to be all the world's Pallas, and all the world's Madonna. They could teach all men, and they could comfort all men. But, look strictly into the nature of the power of your Goddess of Getting-on; and you will find she is the Goddess—not of everybody's getting on—but only of somebody's getting on. This is a

1–2. the loaves and fishes. See Matthew 14:19, 15:36. **18. "Perdix . . . peperit."** See Jeremiah 17:11—"As the partridge sitteth on eggs, and hatcheth them not; so he that getteth riches, and not by right, shall leave them in the midst of his days, and at his end shall be a fool." **20. St. George's Cross,** worn by Knights of the Garter. **21. Gennesaret.** The "land of Gennesaret" is mentioned twice—in Matthew 14:34–36 and Mark 6:53–56. Neither passage throws any light on what Ruskin may have had in mind in this reference. Perhaps he was thinking of the town of Gadara and the story of the Gadarene swine, Luke 8:26–37. **24. thirty slits,** possibly an allusion to the thirty pieces of silver Judas received for betraying Jesus; see Matthew 26:14–16.

21–22. Olympus, the mountain-home of the Greek pantheon. **Pelion, Ossa,** mountains piled one atop the other by the giants in trying to scale Olympus; see *Hamlet*, Act V, sc. 1, l. 305. **34. Plutus,** the god of riches. **45. Pallas,** Athena, Minerva.

vital, or rather deathful, distinction. Examine it in your own ideal of the state of national life which this Goddess is to evoke and maintain. I asked you what it was, when I was last here;—you have never told me. Now, shall I try to tell you?

Your ideal of human life then is, I think, that it should be passed in a pleasant undulating world, with iron and coal everywhere underneath it. On each pleasant bank of this world is to be a beautiful mansion, with two wings; and stables, and coach-houses; a moderately-sized park; a large garden and hot-houses; and pleasant carriage drives through the shrubberies. In this mansion are to live the favoured votaries of the Goddess; the English gentleman, with his gracious wife, and his beautiful family; he always able to have the boudoir and the jewels for the wife, and the beautiful ball dresses for the daughters, and hunters for the sons, and a shooting in the Highlands for himself. At the bottom of the bank, is to be the mill; not less than a quarter of a mile long, with one steam engine at each end, and two in the middle, and a chimney three hundred feet high. In this mill are to be in constant employment from eight hundred to a thousand workers, who never drink, never strike, always go to church on Sunday, and always express themselves in respectful language.

Is not that, broadly, and in the main features, the kind of thing you propose to yourselves? It is very pretty indeed, seen from above; not at all so pretty, seen from below. For, observe, while to one family this deity is indeed the Goddess of Getting-on, to a thousand families she is the Goddess of *not* Getting-on. "Nay," you say, "they have all their chance." Yes, so has every one in a lottery, but there must always be the same number of blanks. "Ah! but in a lottery it is not skill and intelligence which take the lead, but blind chance." What then! do you think the old practice, that "they should take who have the power, and they should keep who can," is less iniquitous, when the power has become power of brains instead of fist? and that, though we may not take advantage of a child's or a woman's weakness, we may of a man's foolishness? "Nay, but finally, work must be done, and some one must be at the top, some one at the bottom." Granted, my friends. Work must always be, and captains of work must always be; and if you in the least remember the tone of any of my writings, you must know that they are thought unfit for this age, because they are always insisting on need of government, and speaking with scorn of liberty. But I beg you to observe that there is a wide difference between being captains or governors of work, and taking the profits of it. It does not follow, because you are general of an army, that you are to take all the treasure, or land, it wins; (if it fight for treasure or land); neither, because you are king of a nation, that you are to consume all the profits of the nation's work. Real kings, on the contrary, are known invariably by their doing quite the reverse of this—by their taking the least possible quantity of the nation's work for themselves. There is no test of real kinghood so infallible as that. Does the crowned creature live simply, bravely, unostentatiously? probably he *is* a King. Does he cover his body with jewels, and his table with delicates? in all probability he is *not* a King. It is possible he may be, as Solomon was; but that is when the nation shares his splendour with him. Solomon made gold, not only to be in his own palace as stones, but to be in Jerusalem as stones. But, even so, for the most part, these splendid kinghoods expire in ruin, and only the true kinghoods live, which are of royal labourers governing loyal labourers; who, both leading rough lives, establish the true dynasties. Conclusively you will find that because you are king of a nation, it does not follow that you are to gather for yourself all the wealth of that nation; neither, because you are king of a small part of the nation, and lord over the means of its maintenance—over field, or mill, or mine,—are you to take all the produce of that piece of the foundation of national existence for yourself.

You will tell me I need not preach against these things, for I cannot mend them. No, good friends, I cannot; but you can, and you will; or something else can and will. Even good things have no abiding power—and shall these evil things persist in victorious evil? All history shows, on the contrary, that to be the exact thing they never can do. Change *must* come; but it is ours to determine whether change of growth, or change of death. Shall the Parthenon be in ruins on its rock, and Bolton priory in its meadow, but these mills of yours be the consummation of the buildings of the earth, and their wheels be as the wheels of eternity? Think you that "men may come, and men may go," but—mills—go on for ever? Not so; out of these, better or worse shall come; and it is for you to choose which.

I know that none of this wrong is done with deliberate purpose. I know, on the contrary, that you wish your workmen well; that you do much for them, and that you desire to do more for them, if

16. Solomon, King of Israel, 9th century B.C.; for his wealth, see 1 Kings 10:14–23. **41. Bolton priory,** an abbey in Yorkshire. **43–44. "men . . . for ever,"** a reference to Tennyson's poem, "The Brook."

you saw your way to such benevolence safely. I know that even all this wrong and misery are brought about by a warped sense of duty, each of you striving to do his best; but, unhappily, not knowing for whom this best should be done. And all our hearts have been betrayed by the plausible impiety of the modern economist, telling us that, "To do the best for ourselves, is finally to do the best for others." Friends, our great Master said not so; and most absolutely we shall find this world is not made so. Indeed, to do the best for others, is finally to do the best for ourselves; but it will not do to have our eyes fixed on that issue. . . .

from FORS CLAVIGERA

In Letter 2 of *Fors Clavigera* (1871–84), Ruskin presented a detailed explanation of his title. Fors "is the best part of three good English words, Force, Fortitude, and Fortune." Clava means club; clavis, key; clavus, nail. "Clavigera may mean, therefore, either Club-bearer, Key-bearer, or Nail-bearer." Hence "Fors, the Club-bearer, means the strength of Hercules, or of Deed. Fors, the Key-bearer, means the strength of Ulysses, or of Patience. Fors, the Nail-bearer, means the strength of Lycurgus, or of Law."

Letter 58

The Catholic Prayer

"Deus, a quo sancta desideria, recta consilia, et justa sunt opera, da servis tuis illam quam mundus dare non potest pacem, ut et corda nostra mandatis tuis, et, hostium sublata formidine, tempora, sint tuâ protectione tranquilla."

"God, from whom are all holy desires, right counsels, and just works, give to Thy servants that peace which the world cannot, that both our hearts, in Thy commandments, and our times, the fear of enemies being taken away, may be calm under Thy guard."

THE adulteration of this great Catholic prayer in our English church-service (as needless as it was senseless, since the pure form of it contains nothing but absolutely Christian prayer, and is as fit for the most stammering Protestant lips as for Dante's), destroyed all the definite meaning of it, and left merely the vague expression of desire for peace, on quite unregarded terms. For of the millions of people who utter the prayer at least weekly, there is not one in a thousand who is ever taught, or can for themselves find out, either what a holy desire means, or a right counsel means, or a just work means,—or what the world is, or what the peace is which it cannot give. And half-an-hour after they have insulted God by praying to Him in this deadest of all dead languages, not understanded of the people, they leave the church, themselves pacified in their perennial determination to put no check on their natural covetousness; to act on their own opinions, be they right or wrong; to do whatever they can make money by, be it just or unjust; and to thrust themselves, with the utmost of their soul and strength, to the highest, by them attainable, pinnacle of the most bedrummed and betrumpeted booth in the Fair of the World.

The prayer, in its pure text, is essentially, indeed, a monastic one; but it is written for the great Monastery of the Servants of God, whom the world hates. It cannot be uttered with honesty but by these; nor can it ever be answered but with the peace bequeathed to these, "not as the world giveth."

Of which peace, the nature is not to be without war, but undisturbed in the midst of war; and not without enemies, but without fear of them. It is a peace without pain, because desiring only what is holy; without anxiety, because it thinks only what is right; without disappointment, because a just work is always successful; without sorrow, because "great peace have they which love Thy Law, and nothing shall offend them"; and without terror, because the God of all battles is its Guard.

So far as any living souls in the England of this day can use, understandingly, the words of this collect, they are already, consciously or not, companions of all good labourers in the vineyard of God. For those who use it reverently, yet have never set themselves to find out what the commandments of God are, nor how lovable they are, nor how far, instead of those commandments, the laws of the world are the only code they care for, nor how far they still think their own thoughts and speak their own words, it is assuredly time to search out these things. And I believe that, after having searched them out, no sincerely good and religious person would find, whatever his own particular form of belief might be, anything which he could reasonably refuse, or which he ought in anywise to fear to profess before all men, in the following statement of creed and resolution, which must be written with their own hand, and signed, with the solemnity of a vow, by every person received into the St. George's Company.

1. I trust in the Living God, Father Almighty, Maker of heaven and earth, and of all things and creatures visible and invisible.

15–16. "not . . . giveth." See John 14:27. **24–25. "great . . . them."** See Psalms 119:165. **47. St. George's Company,** see general introduction to Ruskin.

I trust in the kindness of His law, and the goodness of His work.

And I will strive to love Him, and keep His law, and see His work, while I live.

II. I trust in the nobleness of human nature, in the majesty of its faculties, the fulness of its mercy, and the joy of its love.

And I will strive to love my neighbour as myself, and, even when I cannot, will act as if I did.

III. I will labour, with such strength and opportunity as God gives me, for my own daily bread; and all that my hand finds to do, I will do with my might.

IV. I will not deceive, or cause to be deceived, any human being for my gain or pleasure; nor hurt, or cause to be hurt, any human being for my gain or pleasure; nor rob, or cause to be robbed, any human being for my gain or pleasure.

V. I will not kill nor hurt any living creature needlessly, nor destroy any beautiful thing, but will strive to save and comfort all gentle life, and guard and perfect all natural beauty, upon the earth.

VI. I will strive to raise my own body and soul daily into higher powers of duty and happiness; not in rivalship or contention with others, but for the help, delight, and honour of others, and for the joy and peace of my own life.

VII. I will obey all the laws of my country faithfully; and the orders of its monarch, and of all persons appointed to be in authority under its monarch, so far as such laws or commands are consistent with what I suppose to be the law of God; and when they are not, or seem in anywise to need change, I will oppose them loyally and deliberately, not with malicious, concealed, or disorderly violence.

VIII. And with the same faithfulness, and under the limits of the same obedience, which I render to the laws of my country, and the commands of its rulers, I will obey the laws of the Society called of St. George, into which I am this day received; and the orders of its masters, and of all persons appointed to be in authority under its masters, so long as I remain a Companion, called of St. George.

Matthew Arnold

1822–1888

Matthew Arnold was born at Laleham, December 24, 1822. His father was Thomas Arnold, who as headmaster of Rugby became one of the great English teachers of his day. Matthew's own education included both Rugby and Oxford; he taught briefly at Rugby, and became a fellow of Oriel College, Oxford, in 1845. For four years he acted as a private secretary; in 1851 he married, and was appointed inspector of schools. This onerous position he held for many years, preparing valuable reports on both English and continental schools with meticulous care. For ten years Arnold was Professor of Poetry at Oxford. In 1883–84 he lectured in the United States. He died of heart failure at Liverpool, April 15, 1888.

Arnold's early poems appeared in *The Strayed Reveller*, 1849, and *Empedocles on Etna*, 1852, both "by A," and both withdrawn from circulation by the author. The first volume to which he put his name was *Poems*, 1853. *Poems, Second Series*, 1855, and *New Poems*, 1867, contained old works as well as new. *Merope*, a classical tragedy, appeared in 1858. After 1867 Arnold wrote little poetry of importance; those volumes that appeared during the last two decades of his life consisted chiefly of recastings and rearrangements of his earlier poems.

From beginning to end the elegiac note is dominant in Arnold's poetry. With pensive, controlled melancholy, but with no sentimentality, he was ever fashioning a memorial for human beings in whom nobility of spirit had conspicuously dwelt, for a world where faith had been an anchor and hope a beacon. To the poetic task Arnold brought a deeply meditative mind, technical skill, sure mastery over his own gravely majestic music—"the tremulous cadence slow"—, and the ability to achieve a delicately modulated balance between feeling and intellect. His most celebrated poem, "Dover Beach," transcends poignant personal emotion to attain true universality of utterance. Modern sensibility has found in Arnold a stoically resigned mood that is often in key with its own. This fact must account for the steady growth of his poetic reputation in our time. His range as a poet is indeed limited; there is astute and disarming self-criticism in his admission that he had "less poetical sentiment than Tennyson, and less intellectual vigor and abundance than Browning." But the somber music of Arnold's lines continues to speak to a generation that is all too aware of "its sick hurry, its divided aims."

Arnold ceased early to write poetry and turned to prose criticism, probably because, by his own standard of self-judgment, writing poetry was not his chief vocation. He had already shown his fine discernment as a critic, not only in the Preface to the 1853 volume but in many of the poems themselves. His first volume of criticism was *On Translating Homer*, 1861; but he first truly found his stride with *Essays in Criticism*, 1865 (*Second Series*, 1888). A later work, *On the Study of Celtic Literature*, 1867, has often been scoffed at; it defined aspects of the Celtic temperament which are generally accepted to this day. (Arnold returned to this theme in *Irish Essays and Others*, 1882.) With *Culture and Anarchy*, 1869, and *Friendship's Garland*, 1871, he turned to the criticism of society. Between 1870 and 1877 he published four books on religious themes—*St. Paul and Protestantism*, 1870; *Literature and Dogma*, 1873; *God and the Bible*, 1875; *Last Essays on Church and Religion*, 1877. *Mixed Essays* appeared in 1879, while *Discourses in America*, 1885, and *Civilization in the United States*, 1888, came out of the American tour.

As a critic Arnold does not rely upon historical or impressionistic judgments. The study of backgrounds he considered mere dilettantism unless it resulted in clearer understanding and greater enjoyment of the literature itself. He derived his standards from the classics, keeping great passages of classical literature in mind to serve as touchstones in estimating work as yet untested. Poetry was for him a "criticism of life," and the value of the poet could not be divorced from the soundness of the criticism he presented. He considered Wordsworth England's chief poet since Milton, but ranked him below Goethe, in his eyes the supremely great poet.

The reader of Arnold's criticism can never fail to be aware that he is in the presence of a mind that is powerful and, at the same time, finely balanced and admirably humane. Our critical attitudes and preconceptions owe more to him than we sometimes realize; his evaluation of the Romantic poets and his depreciation of Dryden and Pope, for example, set a pattern that has only recently met with serious challenge. Yet valuable and stimulating though his individual judgments were, it is probably the generous temper, the cool sanity of his criticism that will remain his lasting contribution. In the company of Ben Jonson, Dryden, Samuel Johnson, Coleridge—and T. S. Eliot in our own century—he speaks with special authority as critic because he is also poet.

In his social criticism Arnold stakes everything upon culture; if we would save society in a day of crumbling standards, we must find the best that men have thought and known and make it prevail. Here, again he finds his ideal in Greece. The England of his day he saw divided among Barbarians, Philistines, and Populace, with no higher ideal than that of doing as one likes, and without any particular consideration of the value of the thing done. Though he never subscribed to Carlyle's worship of the hero, he felt the need for state control of many important phases of civilized life. Arnold found both security and happiness quite impossible in the midst of suffering, but he rejected all socialistic and communistic schemes as too much concerned with mere material well-being.

Religion, for Arnold, was "morality touched by emotion," God, "a stream of tendency, not ourselves, that makes for righteousness." On this basis he hoped to bring religion within the scope of his Goethean naturalism. He was sure that men could neither do without the Christian religion nor do with it as at present constituted; he tried, therefore, to desupernaturalize it. The result was a kind of Christian agnosticism; or, as Gladstone put it, "He combined a sincere devotion to the Christian religion with a faculty for presenting it in such a form as to be recognisable neither by friend or foe." Actually Arnold expected many of the functions of religion to be taken over by poetry: "More and more mankind will discover that we have to turn to poetry to interpret life for us, to console us, to sustain us."

QUIET WORK

One lesson, Nature, let me learn of thee,
One lesson which in every wind is blown,
One lesson of two duties kept at one
Though the loud world proclaim their enmity—

Of toil unsevered from tranquillity!
Of labour, that in lasting fruit outgrows
Far noisier schemes, accomplished in repose,
Too great for haste, too high for rivalry!

Yes, while on earth a thousand discords ring,
Man's fitful uproar mingling with his toil,
Still do thy sleepless ministers move on,

Their glorious tasks in silence perfecting;
Still working, blaming still our vain turmoil,
Labourers that shall not fail, when man is gone.

TO A FRIEND

Who prop, thou ask'st, in these bad days, my mind?—
He much, the old man, who, clearest-souled of men,
Saw The Wide Prospect, and the Asian Fen,
And Tmolus hill, and Smyrna bay, though blind.

Much he, whose friendship I not long since won,
That halting slave, who in Nicopolis
Taught Arrian, when Vespasian's brutal son
Cleared Rome of what most shamed him. But be his

My special thanks, whose even-balanced soul,
From first youth tested up to extreme old age,
Business could not make dull, nor passion wild;

Who saw life steadily, and saw it whole;
The mellow glory of the Attic stage,
Singer of sweet Colonus, and its child.

SHAKESPEARE

Others abide our question. Thou art free.
We ask and ask—Thou smilest and art still,
Out-topping knowledge. For the loftiest hill,
Who to the stars uncrowns his majesty,

Planting his steadfast footsteps in the sea,
Making the heaven of heavens his dwelling-place,
Spares but the cloudy border of his base
To the foiled searching of mortality;

And thou, who didst the stars and sunbeams know,
Self-schooled, self-scanned, self-honoured, self-secure,
Didst tread on earth unguessed at.—Better so!

To a Friend. C. B. Tinker and H. F. Lowry in *The Poetry of Matthew Arnold: A Commentary*, Oxford Press, 1940, conjecture Arthur Hugh Clough (1819–1861), a Victorian poet whose affinity of spirit with Arnold was very close. **2. the old man,** Homer. **3. The Wide Prospect,** Europe, a literal translation of the Greek Εὐρώπη. **Asian Fen,** marshlands in Asia Minor, in the northwest corner of which Troy was situated. **4. Tmolus hill . . . Smyrna bay,** a mountain and a seaport in Asia Minor. **6. halting slave,** Epictetus, Stoic philosopher (*c.* 60–*c.* 120), who was lame and at one time a slave. **7. Arrian,** Greek philosopher and historian, a pupil of Epictetus (B.C. 180). **7–8. Vespasian's . . . him.** Domitian, Roman Emperor from 81 to 96, who banished Epictetus. **8. his,** Sophocles', the great Athenian dramatist (497–406 B.C.). **14. Colonus,** the birthplace of Sophocles.

All pains the immortal spirit must endure,
All weakness which impairs, all griefs which bow,
Find their sole speech in that victorious brow.

IN HARMONY WITH NATURE

TO A PREACHER

"In harmony with Nature?" Restless fool,
Who with such heat dost preach what were to thee,
When true, the last impossibility—
To be like Nature strong, like Nature cool!

Know, man hath all which Nature hath, but more,
And in that *more* lie all his hopes of good.
Nature is cruel, man is sick of blood;
Nature is stubborn, man would fain adore;

Nature is fickle, man hath need of rest;
Nature forgives no debt, and fears no grave;
Man would be mild, and with safe conscience blest.

Man must begin, know this, where Nature ends;
Nature and man can never be fast friends.
Fool, if thou canst not pass her, rest her slave!

THE FORSAKEN MERMAN

Marriage between a human and a creature of the sea is a familiar situation in folklore, but generally it is the female that comes from the sea.

Come, dear children, let us away;
Down and away below!
Now my brothers call from the bay,
Now the great winds shoreward blow,
Now the salt tides seaward flow;
Now the wild white horses play,
Champ and chafe and toss in the spray.
Children dear, let us away!
This way, this way!

Call her once before you go—
Call once yet!
In a voice that she will know:
"Margaret! Margaret!"
Children's voices should be dear
(Call once more) to a mother's ear;
Children's voices, wild with pain—
Surely she will come again!
Call her once and come away;
This way, this way!

"Mother dear, we cannot stay!
The wild white horses foam and fret."
Margaret! Margaret!

Come, dear children, come away down;
Call no more!
One last look at the white-walled town,
And the little grey church on the windy shore;
Then come down!
She will not come though you call all day;
Come away, come away!

Children dear, was it yesterday
We heard the sweet bells over the bay?
In the caverns where we lay,
Through the surf and through the swell,
The far-off sound of a silver bell?
Sand-strewn caverns, cool and deep,
Where the winds are all asleep;
Where the spent lights quiver and gleam,
Where the salt weed sways in the stream,
Where the sea-beasts, ranged all round,
Feed in the ooze of their pasture-ground;
Where the sea-snakes coil and twine,
Dry their mail and bask in the brine;
Where great whales come sailing by,
Sail and sail, with unshut eye,
Round the world for ever and aye?
When did music come this way?
Children dear, was it yesterday?

Children dear, was it yesterday
(Call yet once) that she went away?
Once she sate with you and me,
On a red gold throne in the heart of the sea,
And the youngest sate on her knee.
She combed its bright hair, and she tended it well,
When down swung the sound of a far-off bell.
She sighed, she looked up through the clear green sea;
She said: "I must go, for my kinsfolk pray
In the little grey church on the shore to-day.
'Twill be Easter-time in the world—ah me!
And I lose my poor soul, Merman! here with thee."
I said: "Go up, dear heart, through the waves;
Say thy prayer, and come back to the kind sea-caves!"
She smiled, she went up through the surf in the bay.
Children dear, was it yesterday?

Children dear, were we long alone?
"The sea grows stormy, the little ones moan;
Long prayers," I said, "in the world they say;
Come!" I said; and we rose through the surf in the bay.
We went up the beach, by the sandy down
Where the sea-stocks bloom, to the white-walled town;
Through the narrow paved streets, where all was still,
To the little grey church on the windy hill.
From the church came a murmur of folk at their prayers,
But we stood without in the cold blowing airs.
We climbed on the graves, on the stones worn with rains,
And we gazed up the aisle through the small leaded panes.
She sate by the pillar; we saw her clear:
"Margaret, hist! come quick, we are here!
Dear heart," I said, "we are long alone;
The sea grows stormy, the little ones moan."
But, ah, she gave me never a look,
For her eyes were sealed to the holy book!
Loud prays the priest; shut stands the door.
Come away, children, call no more!
Come away, come down, call no more!

Down, down, down!
Down to the depths of the sea!
She sits at her wheel in the humming town,
Singing most joyfully.
Hark what she sings: "O joy, O joy,
For the humming street, and the child with its toy!
For the priest, and the bell, and the holy well;
For the wheel where I spun,
And the blessed light of the sun!"
And so she sings her fill,
Singing most joyfully,
Till the spindle drops from her hand,
And the whizzing wheel stands still.
She steals to the window, and looks at the sand,
And over the sand at the sea;
And her eyes are set in a stare;
And anon there breaks a sigh,
And anon there drops a tear,
From a sorrow-clouded eye,
And a heart sorrow-laden,
A long, long sigh;
For the cold strange eye of a little Mermaiden
And the gleam of her golden hair.

Come away, away children;
Come children, come down!
The hoarse wind blows coldly;
Lights shine in the town.
She will start from her slumber
When gusts shake the door;
She will hear the winds howling,
Will hear the waves roar.

We shall see, while above us
The waves roar and whirl,
A ceiling of amber,
A pavement of pearl.
Singing: "Here came a mortal,
But faithless was she!
And alone dwell for ever
The kings of the sea."

But, children, at midnight,
When soft the winds blow,
When clear falls the moonlight,
When spring-tides are low;
When sweet airs come seaward
From heaths starred with broom,
And high rocks throw mildly
On the blanched sands a gloom;
Up the still, glistening beaches,
Up the creeks we will hie,
Over banks of bright seaweed
The ebb-tide leaves dry.
We will gaze, from the sand-hills,
At the white, sleeping town;
At the church on the hill-side—
And then come back down.
Singing: "There dwells a loved one,
But cruel is she!
She left lonely for ever
The kings of the sea."

TO MARGUERITE

IN RETURNING A VOLUME OF THE LETTERS OF ORTIS

This is one of a group of six love poems entitled *Switzerland*.

Yes: in the sea of life enisl'd,
With echoing straits between us thrown,
Dotting the shoreless watery wild,
We mortal millions live *alone*.
The islands feel the enclasping flow,
And then their endless bounds they know.

But when the moon their hollows lights
And they are swept by balms of spring,
And in their glens, on starry nights
The nightingales divinely sing,
And lovely notes, from shore to shore,
Across the sounds and channels pour;

Oh then a longing like despair
Is to their farthest caverns sent;
For surely once, they feel, we were
Parts of a single continent.
Now round us spreads the watery plain—
Oh might our marges meet again!

Who order'd, that their longing's fire
Should be, as soon as kindled, cool'd?
Who renders vain their deep desire?
A God, a God their severance rul'd;
And bade betwixt their shores to be
The unplumb'd, salt, estranging sea.

MEMORIAL VERSES

April, 1850

Goethe in Weimar sleeps, and Greece,
Long since, saw Byron's struggle cease.
But one such death remained to come;
The last poetic voice is dumb—
We stand to-day by Wordsworth's tomb.

When Byron's eyes were shut in death,
We bowed our head and held our breath.
He taught us little; but our soul
Had *felt* him like the thunder's roll.
With shivering heart the strife we saw
Of passion with eternal law;
And yet with reverential awe
We watched the fount of fiery life
Which served for that Titanic strife.

When Goethe's death was told, we said:
Sunk, then, is Europe's sagest head.
Physician of the iron age,
Goethe has done his pilgrimage.
He took the suffering human race,
He read each wound, each weakness clear;
And struck his finger on the place,
And said: *Thou ailest here, and here!*
He looked on Europe's dying hour
Of fitful dream and feverish power;
His eye plunged down the weltering strife,
The turmoil of expiring life—
He said: *The end is everywhere,*
Art still has truth, take refuge there!
And he was happy, if to know
Causes of things, and far below
His feet to see the lurid flow

Memorial Verses. **17. iron age,** in classical mythology the fourth, last, and worst of the periods of world history (gold, silver, brass, iron), here applied to the years of war and revolution through which Goethe lived and whose turmoil he ignored to devote himself to art. **29ff. And he . . . happiness.** See Virgil, *Georgics*, II, ll. 490–92.

Of terror, and insane distress,
And headlong fate, be happiness.

And Wordsworth!—Ah, pale ghosts, rejoice!
For never has such soothing voice
Been to your shadowy world conveyed,
Since erst, at morn, some wandering shade
Heard the clear song of Orpheus come
Through Hades, and the mournful gloom.
Wordsworth has gone from us—and ye,
Ah, may ye feel his voice as we!
He too upon a wintry clime
Had fallen—on this iron time
Of doubts, disputes, distractions, fears.
He found us when the age had bound
Our souls in its benumbing round;
He spoke, and loosed our heart in tears.
He laid us as we lay at birth
On the cool flowery lap of earth,
Smiles broke from us and we had ease;
The hills were round us, and the breeze
Went o'er the sun-lit fields again;
Our foreheads felt the wind and rain.
Our youth returned; for there was shed
On spirits that had long been dead,
Spirits dried up and closely furled,
The freshness of the early world.

Ah! since dark days still bring to light
Man's prudence and man's fiery might,
Time may restore us in his course
Goethe's sage mind and Byron's force;
But where will Europe's latter hour
Again find Wordsworth's healing power?
Others will teach us how to dare,
And against fear our breast to steel;
Others will strengthen us to bear—
But who, ah! who, will make us feel?
The cloud of mortal destiny,
Others will front it fearlessly—
But who, like him, will put it by?

Keep fresh the grass upon his grave
O Rotha, with thy living wave!
Sing him thy best! for few or none
Hears thy voice right, now he is gone.

SELF-DEPENDENCE

Weary of myself, and sick of asking
What I am, and what I ought to be,
At this vessel's prow I stand, which bears me
Forwards, forwards, o'er the starlit sea.

And a look of passionate desire
O'er the sea and to the stars I send:
"Ye who from my childhood up have calmed me,
Calm me, ah, compose me to the end!

"Ah, once more," I cried, "ye stars, ye waters,
On my heart your mighty charm renew;
Still, still let me, as I gaze upon you,
Feel my soul becoming vast like you!"

From the intense, clear, star-sown vault of heaven,
Over the lit sea's unquiet way,
In the rustling night-air came the answer:
"Wouldst thou *be* as these are? *Live* as they.

"Unaffrighted by the silence round them,
Undistracted by the sights they see,
These demand not that the things without them
Yield them love, amusement, sympathy.

"And with joy the stars perform their shining,
And the sea its long moon-silvered roll;
For self-poised they live, nor pine with noting
All the fever of some differing soul.

"Bounded by themselves, and unregardful
In what state God's other works may be,
In their own tasks all their powers pouring,
These attain the mighty life you see."

O air-born voice! long since, severely clear,
A cry like thine in mine own heart I hear:
"Resolve to be thyself; and know that he,
Who finds himself, loses his misery!"

THE BURIED LIFE

Light flows our war of mocking words, and yet,
Behold, with tears mine eyes are wet!
I feel a nameless sadness o'er me roll.
Yes, yes, we know that we can jest,
We know, we know that we can smile!
But there's a something in this breast,
To which thy light words bring no rest,
And thy gay smiles no anodyne.
Give me thy hand, and hush awhile,
And turn those limpid eyes on mine,
And let me read there, love! thy inmost soul.

Alas! is even love too weak
To unlock the heart, and let it speak?

38. Orpheus, the legendary Greek musician who invaded Hades in search of his wife Eurydice. **72. Rotha,** a stream near Grasmere, where Wordsworth is buried.

Are even lovers powerless to reveal
To one another what indeed they feel?
I knew the mass of men concealed
Their thoughts, for fear that if revealed
They would by other men be met
With blank indifference, or with blame reproved;
I knew they lived and moved
Tricked in disguises, alien to the rest
Of men, and alien to themselves—and yet
The same heart beats in every human breast!

But we, my love!—doth a like spell benumb
Our hearts, our voices?—must we too be dumb?

Ah! well for us, if even we,
Even for a moment, can get free
Our heart, and have our lips unchained;
For that which seals them hath been deep-ordained!

Fate, which foresaw
How frivolous a baby man would be—
By what distractions he would be possessed,
How he would pour himself in every strife,
And well-nigh change his own identity—
That it might keep from his capricious play
His genuine self, and force him to obey
Even in his own despite his being's law,
Bade through the deep recesses of our breast
The unregarded river of our life
Pursue with indiscernible flow its way;
And that we should not see
The buried stream, and seem to be
Eddying at large in blind uncertainty,
Though driving on with it eternally.

But often, in the world's most crowded streets,
But often, in the din of strife,
There rises an unspeakable desire
After the knowledge of our buried life;
A thirst to spend our fire and restless force
In tracking out our true, original course;
A longing to inquire
Into the mystery of this heart which beats
So wild, so deep in us—to know
Whence our lives come and where they go.
And many a man in his own breast then delves,
But deep enough, alas! none ever mines.
And we have been on many thousand lines,
And we have shown, on each, spirit and power;
But hardly have we, for one little hour,
Been on our own line, have we been ourselves—
Hardly had skill to utter one of all
The nameless feelings that course through our breast,
But they course on for ever unexpressed.
And long we try in vain to speak and act
Our hidden self, and what we say and do
Is eloquent, is well—but 'tis not true!
And then we will no more be racked
With inward striving, and demand
Of all the thousand nothings of the hour
Their stupefying power;
Ah yes, and they benumb us at our call!
Yet still, from time to time, vague and forlorn,
From the soul's subterranean depth upborne
As from an infinitely distant land,
Come airs, and floating echoes, and convey
A melancholy into all our day.

Only—but this is rare—
When a belovèd hand is laid in ours,
When, jaded with the rush and glare
Of the interminable hours,
Our eyes can in another's eyes read clear,
When our world-deafened ear
Is by the tones of a loved voice caressed—
A bolt is shot back somewhere in our breast,
And a lost pulse of feeling stirs again.
The eye sinks inward, and the heart lies plain,
And what we mean, we say, and what we would, we know.
A man becomes aware of his life's flow,
And hears its winding murmur; and he sees
The meadows where it glides, the sun, the breeze.

And there arrives a lull in the hot race
Wherein he doth for ever chase
That flying and elusive shadow, rest.
An air of coolness plays upon his face,
And an unwonted calm pervades his breast.
And then he thinks he knows
The hills where his life rose,
And the sea where it goes.

PHILOMELA

Philomela is the traditional poetic name of the nightingale. According to one version of the ancient legend, an Athenian girl Philomela was violated by King Tereus of Thrace, husband of her sister Procne. Tereus pretended Procne was dead, but in reality he had deprived her of her tongue and forced her into hiding. When Philomela learned this horrible truth (through a web in which Procne had woven her sad story), the two sisters gained revenge by serving up Tereus' son to him in a meal. As they fled from Tereus' palace, Philomela was changed into a nightingale, Procne into a swallow, and the pursuing Tereus into a hawk.

Hark! ah, the nightingale—
The tawny-throated!
Hark, from that moonlit cedar what a burst!
What triumph! hark!—what pain!

O wanderer from a Grecian shore,
Still, after many years, in distant lands,
Still nourishing in thy bewildered brain
That wild, unquenched, deep-sunken, old-world pain—
Say, will it never heal?
And can this fragrant lawn
With its cool trees, and night,
And the sweet, tranquil Thames,
And moonshine, and the dew,
To thy racked heart and brain
Afford no balm?

Dost thou to-night behold,
Here, through the moonlight on this English grass,
The unfriendly palace in the Thracian wild?
Dost thou again peruse
With hot cheeks and seared eyes
The too clear web, and thy dumb sister's shame?
Dost thou once more assay
Thy flight, and feel come over thee,
Poor fugitive, the feathery change
Once more, and once more seem to make resound
With love and hate, triumph and agony,
Lone Daulis, and the high Cephissian vale?
Listen, Eugenia—
How thick the bursts come crowding through the leaves!
Again—thou hearest?
Eternal passion!
Eternal pain!

REQUIESCAT

The person commemorated in this poem, if not imaginary, is unknown. The title is Latin for "May she rest [in peace]."

Strew on her roses, roses,
And never a spray of yew!
In quiet she reposes;
Ah, would that I did too!

Her mirth the world required;
She bathed it in smiles of glee.
But her heart was tired, tired,
And now they let her be.

Her life was turning, turning,
In mazes of heat and sound.
But for peace her soul was yearning,
And now peace laps her round.

Her cabined, ample spirit,
It fluttered and failed for breath.
To-night it doth inherit
The vasty hall of death.

THE SCHOLAR-GIPSY

Go, for they call you, shepherd, from the hill;
Go, shepherd, and untie the wattled cotes!
No longer leave thy wistful flock unfed,
Nor let thy bawling fellows rack their throats,
Nor the cropped herbage shoot another head.
But when the fields are still,
And the tired men and dogs all gone to rest,
And only the white sheep are sometimes seen
Cross and recross the strips of moon-blanched green,
Come, shepherd, and again begin the quest!

Here, where the reaper was at work of late—
In this high field's dark corner, where he leaves
His coat, his basket, and his earthen cruse,
And in the sun all morning binds the sheaves,
Then here, at noon, comes back his stores to use—
Here will I sit and wait,
While to my ear from uplands far away
The bleating of the folded flocks is borne,
With distant cries of reapers in the corn—
All the live murmur of a summer's day.

Screened is this nook o'er the high, half-reaped field,
And here till sun-down, shepherd! will I be.
Through the thick corn the scarlet poppies peep,

27. Daulis, in Phocis, Greece, where Philomela lived. **Cephissian.** Cephissus is a river in Phocis. **28. Eugenia,** an imaginary companion. *Requiescat.* **2. yew,** a tree common in graveyards, often used as a symbol of death.

1. shepherd. Tinker and Lowry (*op. cit.*, pp. 208–09) point out that the function of the shepherd is not quite clear. "What is the quest [l. 10] which is to be renewed by moonlight? Is it the same quest as that of the scholar-gipsy, or merely emblematic of the spiritual quest of the thoughtful soul? And who is the companion that is to share it? 'Thyrsis,' very probably, for Clough and Arnold are naturally associated in the reader's mind with the spiritual and philosophical 'quests' of their time." "Thyrsis" (see page 1064) is an elegy for Arthur Hugh Clough, Victorian poet who gave up much for his spiritual and intellectual integrity. The spirit of the scholar-gipsy is not wholly unlike Clough's. **2. wattled cotes,** sheepfolds made of twigs or withes. **19. corn,** grain, wheat.

And round green roots and yellowing stalks I see
Pale pink convolvulus in tendrils creep;
And air-swept lindens yield
Their scent, and rustle down their perfumed showers
Of bloom on the bent grass where I am laid,
And bower me from the August sun with shade;
And the eye travels down to Oxford's towers.

And near me on the grass lies Glanvil's book—
Come, let me read the oft-read tale again!
The story of the Oxford scholar poor,
Of pregnant parts and quick inventive brain,
Who, tired of knocking at preferment's door,
One summer-morn forsook
His friends, and went to learn the gipsy-lore,
And roamed the world with that wild brother-hood,
And came, as most men deemed, to little good,
But came to Oxford and his friends no more.

But once, years after, in the country-lanes,
Two scholars, whom at college erst he knew,
Met him, and of his way of life inquired;
Whereat he answered, that the gipsy-crew,
His mates, had arts to rule as they desired
The workings of men's brains,
And they can bind them to what thoughts they will.
"And I," he said, "the secret of their art,
When fully learned, will to the world impart;
But it needs heaven-sent moments for this skill."

This said, he left them, and returned no more.—
But rumours hung about the country-side,
That the lost Scholar long was seen to stray,
Seen by rare glimpses, pensive and tongue-tied,
In hat of antique shape, and cloak of grey,
The same the gipsies wore.
Shepherds had met him on the Hurst in spring;
At some lone alehouse in the Berkshire moors,
On the warm ingle-bench, the smock-frocked boors
Had found him seated at their entering,

But, 'mid their drink and clatter, he would fly.
And I myself seem half to know thy looks,
And put the shepherds, wanderer! on thy trace;
And boys who in lone wheatfields scare the rooks
I ask if thou hast passed their quiet place;
Or in my boat I lie
Moored to the cool bank in the summer-heats,
'Mid wide grass meadows which the sunshine fills,
And watch the warm, green-muffled Cumner hills,
And wonder if thou haunt'st their shy retreats.

For most, I know, thou lov'st retired ground!
Thee at the ferry Oxford riders blithe,
Returning home on summer-nights, have met
Crossing the stripling Thames at Bab-lock-hithe,
Trailing in the cool stream thy fingers wet,
As the punt's rope chops round;
And leaning backward in a pensive dream,
And fostering in thy lap a heap of flowers
Plucked in shy fields and distant Wychwood bowers,
And thine eyes resting on the moonlit stream.

And then they land, and thou art seen no more!—
Maidens, who from the distant hamlets come
To dance around the Fyfield elm in May,
Oft through the darkening fields have seen thee roam,
Or cross a stile into the public way.
Oft thou hast given them store
Of flowers—the frail-leafed, white anemone,
Dark bluebells drenched with dews of summer eves,
And purple orchises with spotted leaves—
But none hath words she can report of thee.

And, above Godstow Bridge, when hay-time's here
In June, and many a scythe in sunshine flames,
Men who through those wide fields of breezy grass
Where black-winged swallows haunt the glitter-ing Thames,
To bathe in the abandoned lasher pass,
Have often passed thee near
Sitting upon the river bank o'ergrown;
Marked thine outlandish garb, thy figure spare,
Thy dark vague eyes, and soft abstracted air—
But, when they came from bathing, thou wast gone!

31. Glanvil's book, *The Vanity of Dogmatizing*, 1661, by Joseph Glanvill, in which the story of the scholar who left Oxford to live with the gipsies is told. **57. Hurst,** Cumner Hurst, in the parish of Cumner, near Oxford. **58. Berk-shire,** the county south of Oxford. **59. ingle-bench,** in the chimney corner.

74. Bab-lock-hithe, a ferry near Cumner village. **79. Wychwood,** a forest northwest of Oxford. **83. To dance . . . May,** a reference to the Maypole dance in the village of Fyfield, near Oxford. **91. Godstow Bridge,** about two miles up the Thames from Oxford. **95. lasher pass,** a pool fed by water from a weir.

At some lone homestead in the Cumner hills,
Where at her open door the housewife darns,
Thou hast been seen, or hanging on a gate
To watch the threshers in the mossy barns.
Children, who early range these slopes and late
For cresses from the rills,
Have known thee eying, all an April-day,
The springing pastures and the feeding kine;
And marked thee, when the stars come out and shine,
Through the long dewy grass move slow away.

In autumn, on the skirts of Bagley Wood—
Where most the gipsies by the turf-edged way
Pitch their smoked tents, and every bush you see
With scarlet patches tagged and shreds of grey,
Above the forest-ground called Thessaly—
The blackbird, picking food,
Sees thee, nor stops his meal, nor fears at all;
So often has he known thee past him stray,
Rapt, twirling in thy hand a withered spray,
And waiting for the spark from heaven to fall.

And once, in winter, on the causeway chill
Where home through flooded fields foot-travellers go,
Have I not passed thee on the wooden bridge,
Wrapt in thy cloak and battling with the snow,
Thy face toward Hinksey and its wintry ridge?
And thou hast climbed the hill,
And gained the white brow of the Cumner range;
Turned once to watch, while thick the snow-flakes fall,
The line of festal light in Christ-Church hall—
Then sought thy straw in some sequestered grange.

But what—I dream! Two hundred years are flown
Since first thy story ran through Oxford halls,
And the grave Glanvil did the tale inscribe
That thou wert wandered from the studious walls
To learn strange arts, and join a gipsy-tribe;
And thou from earth art gone
Long since, and in some quiet churchyard laid—
Some country-nook, where o'er thy unknown grave
Tall grasses and white flowering nettles wave,
Under a dark, red-fruited yew-tree's shade.

—No, no, thou hast not felt the lapse of hours!
For what wears out the life of mortal men?
'Tis that from change to change their being rolls;
'Tis that repeated shocks, again, again,
Exhaust the energy of strongest souls
And numb the elastic powers,
Till having used our nerves with bliss and teen,
And tired upon a thousand schemes our wit,
To the just-pausing Genius we remit
Our worn-out life, and are—what we have been.

Thou hast not lived, why should'st thou perish, so?
Thou hadst *one* aim, *one* business, *one* desire;
Else wert thou long since numbered with the dead!
Else hadst thou spent, like other men, thy fire!
The generations of thy peers are fled,
And we ourselves shall go;
But thou possessest an immortal lot,
And we imagine thee exempt from age
And living as thou liv'st on Glanvil's page,
Because thou hadst—what we, alas! have not.

For early didst thou leave the world, with powers
Fresh, undiverted to the world without,
Firm to their mark, not spent on other things;
Free from the sick fatigue, the languid doubt,
Which much to have tried, in much been baffled, brings.
O life unlike to ours!
Who fluctuate idly without term or scope,
Of whom each strives, nor knows for what he strives,
And each half lives a hundred different lives;
Who wait like thee, but not, like thee, in hope.

Thou waitest for the spark from heaven! and we,
Light half-believers of our casual creeds,
Who never deeply felt, nor clearly willed,
Whose insight never has borne fruit in deeds,
Whose vague resolves never have been fulfilled;
For whom each year we see

111. Bagley Wood, southwest of Oxford. **114. With scarlet . . . grey,** hung with the clothes of the gipsies. **115. Thessaly,** near Bagley Wood. **120. spark,** of inspiration. **125. Hinksey.** See note on "Thyrsis," l. 2 (page 1064). **129. Christ-Church hall,** the dining-hall of Christ Church College, Oxford.

147. teen, sorrow. **149–50. To the . . . been.** A **Genius** is a tutelary deity or guiding spirit. The general sense of the passage is not clear.

Breeds new beginnings, disappointments new;
Who hesitate and falter life away,
And lose to-morrow the ground won to-day—
Ah! do not we, wanderer! await it too?

Yes, we await it!—but it still delays,
And then we suffer! and amongst us one,
Who most has suffered, takes dejectedly
His seat upon the intellectual throne;
And all his store of sad experience he
Lays bare of wretched days;
Tells us his misery's birth and growth and signs,
And how the dying spark of hope was fed,
And how the breast was soothed, and how the head,
And all his hourly varied anodynes.

This for our wisest! and we others pine,
And wish the long unhappy dream would end,
And waive all claim to bliss, and try to bear;
With close-lipped patience for our only friend,
Sad patience, too near neighbour to despair—
But none has hope like thine!
Thou through the fields and through the woods dost stray,
Roaming the country-side, a truant boy,
Nursing thy project in unclouded joy,
And every doubt long blown by time away.

O born in days when wits were fresh and clear,
And life ran gaily as the sparkling Thames;
Before this strange disease of modern life,
With its sick hurry, its divided aims,
Its heads o'ertaxed, its palsied hearts, was rife—
Fly hence, our contact fear!
Still fly, plunge deeper in the bowering wood!
Averse, as Dido did with gesture stern
From her false friend's approach in Hades turn,
Wave us away, and keep thy solitude!

Still nursing the unconquerable hope,
Still clutching the inviolable shade,
With a free, onward impulse brushing through,
By night, the silvered branches of the glade—
Far on the forest-skirts, where none pursue,
On some mild pastoral slope
Emerge, and resting on the moonlit pales
Freshen thy flowers as in former years
With dew, or listen with enchanted ears,
From the dark dingles, to the nightingales!

But fly our paths, our feverish contact fly!
For strong the infection of our mental strife,
Which, though it gives no bliss, yet spoils for rest;
And we should win thee from thy own fair life,
Like us distracted, and like us unblest.
Soon, soon thy cheer would die,
Thy hopes grow timorous, and unfixed thy powers,
And thy clear aims be cross and shifting made;
And then thy glad perennial youth would fade,
Fade, and grow old at last, and die like ours.

Then fly our greetings, fly our speech and smiles!
—As some grave Tyrian trader, from the sea,
Descried at sunrise an emerging prow
Lifting the cool-haired creepers stealthily,
The fringes of a southward-facing brow
Among the Aegaean isles;
And saw the merry Grecian coaster come,
Freighted with amber grapes, and Chian wine,
Green, bursting figs, and tunnies steeped in brine—
And knew the intruders on his ancient home,

The young light-hearted masters of the waves—
And snatched his rudder, and shook out more sail;
And day and night held on indignantly
O'er the blue Midland waters with the gale,
Betwixt the Syrtes and soft Sicily,
To where the Atlantic raves
Outside the western straits; and unbent sails
There, where down cloudy cliffs, through sheets of foam,
Shy traffickers, the dark Iberians come;
And on the beach undid his corded bales.

182–90. one. Arnold once declared the reference was to Goethe. Tinker and Lowry (*op. cit.*, pp. 209–11) suggest a number of reasons for believing that he may rather have had Tennyson in mind. If this identification be accepted, the suffering would refer to the death of Hallam; **the intellectual throne** (see Tennyson's "The Palace of Art," l. 216) would have some reference to the laureateship; the **hourly varied anodynes** would be the many poems which make up *In Memoriam*. **208–10. as Dido . . . solitude!** When Aeneas passed through Hades he was spurned by the shade of Dido, who had killed herself for love of him (*Aeneid*, Book VI, ll. 450–71).

232. Tyrian, Phoenician of Tyre. The Phoenicians were the great traders of the Mediterranean area until displaced by the Greeks. For the controversy concerning the suitableness of this figure, see Tinker and Lowry, *op. cit.*, pp. 212–14. **234. cool-haired creepers,** evidently foliage overhanging the entrance to some waterway. **237. come,** a past participle, say Tinker and Lowry. **238. Chian,** from Chios, an island in the Aegean. **244. Midland,** Mediterranean. **245. Syrtes,** Gulf of Sidra, on the northern coast of Africa. **249. Iberians,** inhabitants of the Spanish peninsula, where the Tyrian hopes to find a new market.

THYRSIS

A Monody, *to commemorate the author's friend,* Arthur Hugh Clough, *who died at Florence, 1861.*

"Thyrsis" ranks with Milton's "Lycidas" and Shelley's "Adonais" among the great pastoral elegies of English literature. The tradition traces back to Theocritus, Bion, and Moschus in late Greek literature (more particularly to Theocritus in Arnold's case, though his poem owes more to observation than to reading), and the identification of the poet and his friends with shepherds is conventional. Thyrsis (Clough—see note on l. 1 of "The Scholar-Gipsy," page 1060) and Corydon (Arnold) are traditional names.

How changed is here each spot man makes or fills!
In the two Hinkseys nothing keeps the same;
The village street its haunted mansion lacks,
And from the sign is gone Sibylla's name,
And from the roofs the twisted chimney-stacks—
Are ye too changed, ye hills?
See, 'tis no foot of unfamiliar men
To-night from Oxford up your pathway strays!
Here came I often, often, in old days—
Thyrsis and I; we still had Thyrsis then.

Runs it not here, the track by Childsworth Farm,
Past the high wood, to where the elm-tree crowns
The hill behind whose ridge the sunset flames?
The signal-elm, that looks on Ilsley Downs,
The Vale, the three lone weirs, the youthful Thames?—
This winter-eve is warm,
Humid the air! leafless, yet soft as spring,
The tender purple spray on copse and briers!
And that sweet city with her dreaming spires,
She needs not June for beauty's heightening,

Lovely all times she lies, lovely to-night!—
Only, methinks, some loss of habit's power
Befalls me wandering through this upland dim.
Once passed I blindfold here, at any hour;
Now seldom come I, since I came with him.
That single elm-tree bright
Against the west—I miss it! is it gone?
We prized it dearly; while it stood, we said,
Our friend, the Gipsy-Scholar, was not dead;
While the tree lived, he in these fields lived on.

Too rare, too rare, grow now my visits here,
But once I knew each field, each flower, each stick;
And with the country-folk acquaintance made
By barn in threshing-time, by new-built rick.
Here, too, our shepherd-pipes we first assayed.
Ah me! this many a year
My pipe is lost, my shepherd's holiday!
Needs must I lose them, needs with heavy heart
Into the world and wave of men depart;
But Thyrsis of his own will went away.

It irked him to be here, he could not rest.
He loved each simple joy the country yields,
He loved his mates; but yet he could not keep,
For that a shadow loured on the fields,
Here with the shepherds and the silly sheep.
Some life of men unblest
He knew, which made him droop, and filled his head.
He went; his piping took a troubled sound
Of storms that rage outside our happy ground;
He could not wait their passing, he is dead.

So, some tempestuous morn in early June,
When the year's primal burst of bloom is o'er,
Before the roses and the longest day—
When garden-walks and all the grassy floor
With blossoms red and white of fallen May
And chestnut-flowers are strewn—
So have I heard the cuckoo's parting cry,
From the wet field, through the vext garden-trees,
Come with the volleying rain and tossing breeze:
The bloom is gone, and with the bloom go I!

Too quick despairer, wherefore wilt thou go?
Soon will the high Midsummer pomps come on,
Soon will the musk carnations break and swell,

2. **two Hinkseys,** villages southwest of Oxford. 4. **Sibylla,** the hostess of the Cross Keys Tavern in South Hinksey had actually been Sybella Curr. 11. **Childsworth Farm,** Chilswell Farm near Oxford. 14. **signal-elm.** Topographers are not agreed as to the location of this tree. **Ilsley Downs,** in western Berkshire, the county south of Oxford. 15. **youthful Thames,** because not yet far from its source. 19. **sweet city,** Oxford.

29. **the Gipsy-Scholar.** Compare the preceding poem. 35. **our shepherd-pipes we first assayed,** first attempted poetry. 37. **My pipe is lost.** Arnold was writing very little poetry as he grew older. 40. **Thyrsis . . . went away.** Clough resigned his Oriel fellowship in 1848 because he could no longer profess faith in the Thirty-nine Articles. 45. **silly,** simple. 48–50. **his piping . . . dead.** Clough's poetry reflects the religious, intellectual, and even political struggles of his time. 62. **pomps,** shows, displays.

Soon shall we have gold-dusted snapdragon,
  Sweet-William with his homely cottage-smell,
    And stocks in fragrant blow;
Roses that down the alleys shine afar,
  And open, jasmine-muffled lattices,
  And groups under the dreaming garden-trees,
And the full moon, and the white evening-star.

He hearkens not! light comer, he is flown!
  What matters it? next year he will return,
    And we shall have him in the sweet spring-days,
  With whitening hedges, and uncrumpling fern,
    And bluebells trembling by the forest-ways,
      And scent of hay new-mown.
  But Thyrsis never more we swains shall see;
    See him come back, and cut a smoother reed,
    And blow a strain the world at last shall heed—
  For Time, not Corydon, hath conquered thee!

Alack, for Corydon no rival now!—
  But when Sicilian shepherds lost a mate,
    Some good survivor with his flute would go,
  Piping a ditty sad for Bion's fate;
    And cross the unpermitted ferry's flow,
      And relax Pluto's brow,
  And make leap up with joy the beauteous head
    Of Proserpine, among whose crownèd hair
    Are flowers first opened on Sicilian air,
  And flute his friend, like Orpheus, from the dead.

O easy access to the hearer's grace
  When Dorian shepherds sang to Proserpine!
    For she herself had trod Sicilian fields,
  She knew the Dorian water's gush divine,
    She knew each lily white which Enna yields,
      Each rose with blushing face;
  She loved the Dorian pipe, the Dorian strain.
    But ah, of our poor Thames she never heard!
    Her foot the Cumner cowslips never stirred;
  And we should tease her with our plaint in vain!

Well! wind-dispersed and vain the words will be,
  Yet, Thyrsis, let me give my grief its hour
    In the old haunt, and find our tree-topped hill!
  Who, if not I, for questing here hath power?
    I know the wood which hides the daffodil,
      I know the Fyfield tree,
  I know what white, what purple fritillaries
    The grassy harvest of the river-fields,
    Above by Ensham, down by Sandford, yields,
  And what sedged brooks are Thames's tributaries;

I know these slopes; who knows them if not I?—
  But many a dingle on the loved hill-side,
    With thorns once studded, old, white-blossomed trees,
  Where thick the cowslips grew, and far descried
    High towered the spikes of purple orchises,
      Hath since our day put by
  The coronals of that forgotten time;
    Down each green bank hath gone the plough-boy's team,
    And only in the hidden brookside gleam
  Primroses, orphans of the flowery prime.

Where is the girl, who by the boatman's door,
  Above the locks, above the boating throng,
    Unmoored our skiff when through the Wytham flats,
  Red loosestrife and blond meadow-sweet among
    And darting swallows and light water-gnats,
      We tracked the shy Thames shore?
  Where are the mowers, who, as the tiny swell
    Of our boat passing heaved the river-grass,
    Stood with suspended scythe to see us pass?—
  They all are gone, and thou art gone as well!

Yes, thou art gone! and round me too the night
  In ever-nearing circle weaves her shade.
    I see her veil draw soft across the day,
  I feel her slowly chilling breath invade
    The cheek grown thin, the brown hair sprent with grey;
      I feel her finger light
  Laid pausefully upon life's headlong train;—
    The foot less prompt to meet the morning dew,
    The heart less bounding at emotion new,
  And hope, once crushed, less quick to spring again.

And long the way appears, which seemed so short
  To the less-practised eye of sanguine youth;
    And high the mountain-tops, in cloudy air,

80. Time . . . thee! Competitive singing-matches are common in pastoral poetry. **85. unpermitted ferry,** the river Styx in Hades, crossed only by the spirits of the dead. **86. Pluto,** god of the underworld. **88. Proserpine,** queen of the underworld, whom Pluto carried off while she was gathering flowers in the vale of Enna. **90. Orpheus.** Orpheus, Greek musician, invaded Hades in search of his dead wife Eurydice. **91.** This stanza and those beginning with ll. 121 and 141 were Arnold's favorites. **92. Dorian,** Sicilian. **99. Cumner.** See note on "The Scholar-Gipsy," l. 57.

106. Fyfield tree. See "The Scholar-Gipsy," l. 83 (page 1061). **109. Ensham,** Eynsham, northwest of Oxford. **Sandford,** south of Oxford. **123. Wytham flats,** northwest of Oxford. **135. sprent,** sprinkled. **137. pausefully,** so as to occasion a pause.

The mountain-tops where is the throne of Truth,
Tops in life's morning-sun so bright and bare!
Unbreachable the fort
Of the long-battered world uplifts its wall;
And strange and vain the earthly turmoil grows,
And near and real the charm of thy repose,
And night as welcome as a friend would fall.

But hush! the upland hath a sudden loss
Of quiet!—Look, adown the dusk hill-side,
A troop of Oxford hunters going home,
As in old days, jovial and talking, ride!
From hunting with the Berkshire hounds they come.
Quick! let me fly, and cross
Into yon farther field!—'Tis done; and see,
Backed by the sunset, which doth glorify
The orange and pale violet evening-sky,
Bare on its lonely ridge, the Tree! the Tree!

I take the omen! Eve lets down her veil,
The white fog creeps from bush to bush about,
The west unflushes, the high stars grow bright,
And in the scattered farms the lights come out.
I cannot reach the signal-tree to-night,
Yet, happy omen, hail!
Hear it from thy broad lucent Arno-vale
(For there thine earth-forgetting eyelids keep
The morningless and unawakening sleep
Under the flowery oleanders pale),

Hear it, O Thyrsis, still our tree is there!—
Ah, vain! These English fields, this upland dim,
These brambles pale with mist engarlanded,
That lone, sky-pointing tree, are not for him;
To a boon southern country he is fled,
And now in happier air,
Wandering with the great Mother's train divine
(And purer or more subtle soul than thee,
I trow, the mighty Mother doth not see)
Within a folding of the Apennine,

Thou hearest the immortal chants of old!—
Putting his sickle to the perilous grain
In the hot cornfield of the Phrygian king,
For thee the Lityerses-song again
Young Daphnis with his silver voice doth sing;
Sings his Sicilian fold,
His sheep, his hapless love, his blinded eyes—
And how a call celestial round him rang,
And heavenward from the fountain-brink he sprang,
And all the marvel of the golden skies.

There thou art gone, and me thou leavest here
Sole in these fields! yet will I not despair.
Despair I will not, while I yet descry
'Neath the mild canopy of English air
That lonely tree against the western sky.
Still, still these slopes, 'tis clear,
Our Gipsy-Scholar haunts, outliving thee!
Fields where soft sheep from cages pull the hay,
Woods with anemonies in flower till May,
Know him a wanderer still; then why not me?

A fugitive and gracious light he seeks,
Shy to illumine; and I seek it too.
This does not come with houses or with gold,
With place, with honour, and a flattering crew;
'Tis not in the world's market bought and sold—
But the smooth-slipping weeks
Drop by, and leave its seeker still untired;
Out of the heed of mortals he is gone,
He wends unfollowed, he must house alone;
Yet on he fares, by his own heart inspired.

Thou too, O Thyrsis, on like quest wast bound;
Thou wanderedst with me for a little hour!
Men gave thee nothing; but this happy quest,
If men esteemed thee feeble, gave thee power,
If men procured thee trouble, gave thee rest.
And this rude Cumner ground,
Its fir-topped Hurst, its farms, its quiet fields,
Here cam'st thou in thy jocund youthful time,
Here was thine height of strength, thy golden prime!
And still the haunt beloved a virtue yields.

What though the music of thy rustic flute
Kept not for long its happy, country tone;
Lost it too soon, and learnt a stormy note
Of men contention-tost, of men who groan,
Which tasked thy pipe too sore, and tired thy throat—
It failed, and thou wast mute!

167. Arno-vale. Florence, where Clough died, is on the Arno. **177. great Mother,** Cybele, goddess of nature. **183–84. Phrygian king . . . Lityerses,** who compelled strangers to compete with him in reaping, cut off the heads of the vanquished, and sang as he disposed of their bodies. **Daphnis,** the ideal Sicilian shepherd, entered into this perilous contest to deliver his sweetheart, Piplea, from **Lityerses'** power; he was overcome but delivered by **Hercules.**

217. Hurst. See the note on "The Scholar-Gipsy," l. 57 (page 1061). **221–26. What . . . mute!** Tinker and Lowry (*op. cit.*, p. 217) point out that this statement is not literally true, "for the verse composed at Oxford had its own note of perplexity and melancholy which reflected the religious stirring and controversy within the university. Moreover, in 'The Bothie,' 'Amours de Voyage,' and some of his later satires, Clough's humour and gaiety were at their best."

Yet hadst thou alway visions of our light,
And long with men of care thou couldst not stay,
And soon thy foot resumed its wandering way,
Left human haunt, and on alone till night.

Too rare, too rare, grow now my visits here!
'Mid city-noise, not, as with thee of yore,
Thyrsis! in reach of sheep-bells is my home.
—Then through the great town's harsh, heart-wearying roar,
Let in thy voice a whisper often come,
To chase fatigue and fear:
Why faintest thou? I wandered till I died.
Roam on! The light we sought is shining still.
Dost thou ask proof? Our tree yet crowns the hill,
Our Scholar travels yet the loved hill-side.

DOVER BEACH

This poem has been given an elaborate musical setting by the talented young American composer Samuel Barber.

The sea is calm to-night.
The tide is full, the moon lies fair
Upon the straits;—on the French coast the light
Gleams and is gone; the cliffs of England stand,
Glimmering and vast, out in the tranquil bay.
Come to the window, sweet is the night-air!
Only, from the long line of spray
Where the sea meets the moon-blanched land,
Listen! you hear the grating roar
Of pebbles which the waves draw back, and fling,
At their return, up the high strand,
Begin, and cease, and then again begin,
With tremulous cadence slow, and bring
The eternal note of sadness in.

Sophocles long ago
Heard it on the Aegaean, and it brought
Into his mind the turbid ebb and flow
Of human misery; we
Find also in the sound a thought,
Hearing it by this distant northern sea.

Dover Beach. Dover is in Kent at the eastern end of the English Channel, where England is separated from the continent by only twenty miles. **4–5. the cliffs . . . bay,** a reference to the white chalk cliffs of Dover. **15–18. Sophocles . . . misery.** Arnold is generally believed to have been thinking of the *Antigone*, ll. 583 ff. Tinker and Lowry (*op. cit.*, pp. 177–78) suggest other possibilities.

The Sea of Faith
Was once, too, at the full, and round earth's shore
Lay like the folds of a bright girdle furled.
But now I only hear
Its melancholy, long, withdrawing roar,
Retreating, to the breath
Of the night-wind, down the vast edges drear
And naked shingles of the world.

Ah, love, let us be true
To one another! for the world, which seems
To lie before us like a land of dreams,
So various, so beautiful, so new,
Hath really neither joy, nor love, nor light,
Nor certitude, nor peace, nor help for pain;
And we are here as on a darkling plain
Swept with confused alarms of struggle and flight,
Where ignorant armies clash by night.

THE LAST WORD

Creep into thy narrow bed,
Creep, and let no more be said!
Vain thy onset! all stands fast.
Thou thyself must break at last.

Let the long contention cease!
Geese are swans, and swans are geese.
Let them have it how they will!
Thou art tired; best be still.

They out-talked thee, hissed thee, tore thee?
Better men fared thus before thee;
Fired their ringing shot and passed,
Hotly charged—and sank at last.

Charge once more, then, and be dumb!
Let the victors, when they come,
When the forts of folly fall,
Find thy body by the wall!

RUGBY CHAPEL

November, 1857

The poet's father, Dr. Thomas Arnold, headmaster of Rugby, died of heart failure in 1842, and was buried in the college chapel.

29–37. Ah, love . . . night. Tinker and Lowry (*op. cit.*, pp. 175–76) point out reasons for believing that these lines were written before the rest of the poem. They contain "no reference to the sea or the tides," and may have been suggested by Thucydides' history of the Peloponnesian War, Book VII, Chaps. 43–44.

Coldly, sadly descends
The autumn-evening. The field
Strewn with its dank yellow drifts
Of withered leaves, and the elms,
Fade into dimness apace,
Silent;—hardly a shout
From a few boys late at their play!
The lights come out in the street,
In the school-room windows;—but cold,
Solemn, unlighted, austere,
Through the gathering darkness, arise
The chapel-walls, in whose bound
Thou, my father! art laid.

There thou dost lie, in the gloom
Of the autumn evening. But ah!
That word, *gloom*, to my mind
Brings thee back, in the light
Of thy radiant vigour, again;
In the gloom of November we passed
Days not dark at thy side;
Seasons impaired not the ray
Of thy buoyant cheerfulness clear.
Such thou wast! and I stand
In the autumn evening, and think
Of bygone autumns with thee.

Fifteen years have gone round
Since thou arosest to tread,
In the summer-morning, the road
Of death, at a call unforeseen,
Sudden. For fifteen years,
We who till then in thy shade
Rested as under the boughs
Of a mighty oak, have endured
Sunshine and rain as we might,
Bare, unshaded, alone,
Lacking the shelter of thee.

O strong soul, by what shore
Tarriest thou now? For that force,
Surely, has not been left vain!
Somewhere, surely, afar,
In the sounding labour-house vast
Of being, is practised that strength,
Zealous, beneficent, firm!

Yes, in some far-shining sphere,
Conscious or not of the past,
Still thou performest the word
Of the Spirit in whom thou dost live—
Prompt, unwearied, as here!
Still thou upraisest with zeal
The humble good from the ground,
Sternly repressest the bad!
Still, like a trumpet, dost rouse
Those who with half-open eyes
Tread the border-land dim
'Twixt vice and virtue; revivest,
Succourest!—this was thy work,
This was thy life upon earth.

What is the course of the life
Of mortal men on the earth?—
Most men eddy about
Here and there—eat and drink,
Chatter and love and hate,
Gather and squander, are raised
Aloft, are hurled in the dust,
Striving blindly, achieving
Nothing; and then they die—
Perish;—and no one asks
Who or what they have been,
More than he asks what waves,
In the moonlit solitudes mild
Of the midmost Ocean, have swelled,
Foamed for a moment, and gone.

And there are some, whom a thirst
Ardent, unquenchable, fires,
Not with the crowd to be spent,
Not without aim to go round
In an eddy of purposeless dust,
Effort unmeaning and vain.
Ah yes! some of us strive
Not without action to die
Fruitless, but something to snatch
From dull oblivion, nor all
Glut the devouring grave!
We, we have chosen our path—
Path to a clear-purposed goal,
Path of advance!—but it leads
A long, steep journey, through sunk
Gorges, o'er mountains in snow.
Cheerful, with friends, we set forth—
Then, on the height, comes the storm.
Thunder crashes from rock
To rock, the cataracts reply,
Lightnings dazzle our eyes.
Roaring torrents have breached
The track, the stream-bed descends
In the place where the wayfarer once
Planted his footstep—the spray
Boils o'er its borders! aloft
The unseen snow-beds dislodge
Their hanging ruin; alas,
Havoc is made in our train!
Friends, who set forth at our side,

Falter, are lost in the storm.
We, we only are left!
With frowning foreheads, with lips
Sternly compressed, we strain on,
On—and at nightfall at last
Come to the end of our way,
To the lonely inn 'mid the rocks;
Where the gaunt and taciturn host
Stands on the threshold, the wind
Shaking his thin white hairs—
Holds his lantern to scan
Our storm-beat figures, and asks:
Whom in our party we bring?
Whom we have left in the snow?

Sadly we answer: We bring
Only ourselves! we lost
Sight of the rest in the storm.
Hardly ourselves we fought through,
Stripped, without friends, as we are.
Friends, companions, and train,
The avalanche swept from our side.

But thou would'st not *alone*
Be saved, my father! *alone*
Conquer and come to thy goal,
Leaving the rest in the wild.
We were weary, and we
Fearful, and we in our march
Fain to drop down and to die.
Still thou turnedst, and still
Beckonedst the trembler, and still
Gavest the weary thy hand.

If, in the paths of the world,
Stones might have wounded thy feet,
Toil or dejection have tried
Thy spirit, of that we saw
Nothing—to us thou wast still
Cheerful, and helpful, and firm!
Therefore to thee it was given
Many to save with thyself;
And, at the end of thy day,
O faithful shepherd! to come,
Bringing thy sheep in thy hand.
And through thee I believe
In the noble and great who are gone;
Pure souls honoured and blest
By former ages, who else—
Such, so soulless, so poor,
Is the race of men whom I see—
Seemed but a dream of the heart,
Seemed but a cry of desire.

110. host, Death, or Time. **148. else,** but for thee.

Yes! I believe that there lived
Others like thee in the past,
Not like the men of the crowd
Who all round me to-day
Bluster or cringe, and make life
Hideous, and arid, and vile;
But souls tempered with fire,
Fervent, heroic, and good,
Helpers and friends of mankind.

Servants of God!—or sons
Shall I not call you? because
Not as servants ye knew
Your Father's innermost mind,
His, who unwillingly sees
One of his little ones lost—
Yours is the praise, if mankind
Hath not as yet in its march
Fainted, and fallen, and died!

See! In the rocks of the world
Marches the host of mankind,
A feeble, wavering line.
Where are they tending?—A God
Marshalled them, gave them their goal.
Ah, but the way is so long!
Years they have been in the wild!
Sore thirst plagues them, the rocks,
Rising all round, overawe;
Factions divide them, their host
Threatens to break, to dissolve.
—Ah, keep, keep them combined!
Else, of the myriads who fill
That army, not one shall arrive;
Sole they shall stray; in the rocks
Stagger for ever in vain,
Die one by one in the waste.

Then, in such hour of need
Of your fainting, dispirited race,
Ye, like angels, appear,
Radiant with ardour divine!
Beacons of hope, ye appear!
Languor is not in your heart,
Weakness is not in your word,
Weariness not on your brow.
Ye alight in our van! at your voice,
Panic, despair, flee away.
Ye move through the ranks, recall
The stragglers, refresh the outworn,
Praise, re-inspire the brave!

162–65. Servants . . . mind, see John 15:15. **166–67. His . . . lost,** see Matthew 18:6, 12. **190. Ye,** the servants of God.

Order, courage, return.
Eyes rekindling, and prayers,
Follow your steps as ye go.
Ye fill up the gaps in our files,
Strengthen the wavering line,
Stablish, continue our march,
On, to the bound of the waste,
On, to the City of God.

from ESSAYS IN CRITICISM, FIRST SERIES

from Chapter I: THE FUNCTION OF CRITICISM AT THE PRESENT TIME

MANY objections have been made to a proposition which, in some remarks of mine on translating Homer, I ventured to put forth; a proposition about criticism, and its importance at the present day. I said: "Of the literature of France and Germany, as of the intellect of Europe in general, the main effort, for now many years, has been a critical effort; the endeavour, in all branches of knowledge, theology, philosophy, history, art, science, to see the object as in itself it really is." I added, that owing to the operation in English literature of certain causes, "almost the last thing for which one would come to English literature is just that very thing which now Europe most desires,—criticism"; and that the power and value of English literature was thereby impaired. More than one rejoinder declared that the importance I here assigned to criticism was excessive, and asserted the inherent superiority of the creative effort of the human spirit over its critical effort. And the other day, . . . I found in [Wordsworth] . . . a sentence passed on the critic's business, which seems to justify every possible disparagement of it. . . .

"The writers in these publications [the *Reviews*], while they prosecute their inglorious employment, cannot be supposed to be in a state of mind very favorable for being affected by the finer influences of a thing so pure as genuine poetry."

. . . It is undeniable that the exercise of a creative power, that a free creative activity, is the highest function of man; it is proved to be so by man's finding in it his true happiness. But it is undeniable, also, that men may have the sense of exercising this free creative activity in other ways than in producing great works of literature or art; if it were not so, all but a very few men would be shut out from the true happiness of all men. They may have it in well-doing, they may have it in learning, they may have it even in criticising. This is one thing to be kept in mind. Another is, that the exercise of the creative power in the production of great works of literature or art, however high this exercise of it may rank, is not at all epochs and under all conditions possible; and that therefore labour may be vainly spent in attempting it, which might with more fruit be used in preparing for it, in rendering it possible. This creative power works with elements, with materials; what if it has not those materials, those elements, ready for its use? In that case it must surely wait till they are ready. Now, in literature,—I will limit myself to literature, for it is about literature that the question arises,—the elements with which the creative power works are ideas; the best ideas on every matter which literature touches, current at the time. At any rate we may lay it down as certain that in modern literature no manifestation of the creative power not working with these can be very important or fruitful. And I say *current* at the time, not merely accessible at the time; for creative literary genius does not principally show itself in discovering new ideas, that is rather the business of the philosopher. The grand work of literary genius is a work of synthesis and exposition, not of analysis and discovery; its gift lies in the faculty of being happily inspired by a certain intellectual and spiritual atmosphere, by a certain order of ideas, when it finds itself in them; of dealing divinely with these ideas, presenting them in the most effective and attractive combinations,—making beautiful works with them, in short. But it must have the atmosphere, it must find itself amidst the order of ideas, in order to work freely; and these it is not so easy to command. This is why great creative epochs in literature are so rare, this is why there is so much that is unsatisfactory in the productions of many men of real genius; because, for the creation of a master-work of literature two powers must concur, the power of the man and the power of the moment, and the man is not enough without the moment; the creative power has, for its happy exercise, appointed elements, and those elements are not in its own control.

Nay, they are more within the control of the critical power. It is the business of the critical power, as I said in the words already quoted, "in all branches of knowledge, theology, philosophy, history, art, science, to see the object as in itself it really is." Thus it tends, at last, to make an intellectual situation of which the creative power can profitably avail itself. It tends to establish an order of ideas, if not absolutely true, yet true by comparison with

17–18. in some remarks . . . Homer, at the end of Lecture 2 of ***On Translating Homer.***

that which it displaces; to make the best ideas prevail. Presently these new ideas reach society, the touch of truth is the touch of life, and there is a stir and growth everywhere; out of this stir and growth come the creative epochs of literature.

Or, to narrow our range, and quit these considerations of the general march of genius and of society,—considerations which are apt to become too abstract and impalpable,—every one can see that a poet, for instance, ought to know life and the world before dealing with them in poetry; and life and the world being in modern times very complex things, the creation of a modern poet, to be worth much, implies a great critical effort behind it; else it must be a comparatively poor, barren, and short-lived affair. This is why Byron's poetry had so little endurance in it, and Goethe's so much; both Byron and Goethe had a great productive power, but Goethe's was nourished by a great critical effort providing the true materials for it, and Byron's was not; Goethe knew life and the world, the poet's necessary subjects, much more comprehensively and thoroughly than Byron. . . .

It has long seemed to me that the burst of creative activity in our literature, through the first quarter of this century, had about it in fact something premature; and that from this cause its productions are doomed, most of them, in spite of the sanguine hopes which accompanied and do still accompany them, to prove hardly more lasting than the productions of far less splendid epochs. And this prematureness comes from its having proceeded without having its proper data, without sufficient materials to work with. In other words, the English poetry of the first quarter of this century, with plenty of energy, plenty of creative force, did not know enough. This makes Byron so empty of matter, Shelley so incoherent, Wordsworth even, profound as he is, yet so wanting in completeness and variety. Wordsworth cared little for books, and disparaged Goethe. . . .

But to speak of books and reading may easily lead to a misunderstanding here. It was not really books and reading that lacked to our poetry at this epoch: Shelley had plenty of reading, Coleridge had immense reading. Pindar and Sophocles—as we all say so glibly, and often with so little discernment of the real import of what we are saying—had not many books; Shakspeare was no deep reader. True; but in the Greece of Pindar and Sophocles, in the England of Shakspeare, the poet lived in a current of ideas in the highest degree animating and nourishing to the creative power; society was, in the fullest measure, permeated by fresh thought, intelligent and alive. And this state of things is the true basis for the creative power's exercise, in this it finds its data, its materials, truly ready for its hand; all the books and reading in the world are only valuable as they are helps to this. Even when this does not actually exist, books and reading may enable a man to construct a kind of semblance of it in his own mind, a world of knowledge and intelligence in which he may live and work. This is by no means an equivalent to the artist for the nationally diffused life and thought of the epochs of Sophocles or Shakspeare; but, besides that it may be a means of preparation for such epochs, it does really constitute, if many share in it, a quickening and sustaining atmosphere of great value. Such an atmosphere the many-sided learning and the long and widely combined critical effort of Germany formed for Goethe, when he lived and worked. There was no national glow of life and thought there as in the Athens of Pericles or the England of Elizabeth. That was the poet's weakness. But there was a sort of equivalent for it in the complete culture and unfettered thinking of a large body of Germans. That was his strength. In the England of the first quarter of this century there was neither a national glow of life and thought, such as we had in the age of Elizabeth, nor yet a culture and a force of learning and criticism such as were to be found in Germany. Therefore the creative power of poetry wanted, for success in the highest sense, materials and a basis; a thorough interpretation of the world was necessarily denied to it. . . .

It is of the last importance that English criticism should clearly discern what rule for its course, in order to avail itself of the field now opening to it, and to produce fruit for the future, it ought to take. The rule may be summed up in one word,—*disinterestedness*. And how is criticism to show disinterestedness? By keeping aloof from what is called "the practical view of things"; by resolutely following the law of its own nature, which is to be a free play of the mind on all subjects which it touches. By steadily refusing to lend itself to any of those ulterior, political, practical considerations about ideas, which plenty of people will be sure to attach to them, which perhaps ought often to be attached to them, which in this country at any rate are certain to be attached to them quite sufficiently, but which

48. Pindar, Greek lyric poet (522–*c*. 448 B.C.).

22–23. Pericles, Athenian statesman (*c*. 495–429 B.C.). **Elizabeth,** Queen of England from 1558 to 1603.

criticism has really nothing to do with. Its business is, as I have said, simply to know the best that is known and thought in the world, and by in its turn making this known, to create a current of true and fresh ideas. Its business is to do this with inflexible honesty, with due ability; but its business is to do no more, and to leave alone all questions of practical consequences and applications, questions which will never fail to have due prominence given to them. Else criticism, besides being really false to its own nature, merely continues in the old rut which it has hitherto followed in this country, and will certainly miss the chance now given to it. For what is at present the bane of criticism in this country? It is that practical considerations cling to it and stifle it. It subserves interests not its own. Our organs of criticism are organs of men and parties having practical ends to serve, and with them those practical ends are the first thing and the play of mind the second; so much play of mind as is compatible with the prosecution of those practical ends is all that is wanted. An organ like the *Revue des Deux Mondes*, having for its main function to understand and utter the best that is known and thought in the world, existing, it may be said, as just an organ for a free play of the mind, we have not. But we have the *Edinburgh Review*, existing as an organ of the old Whigs, and for as much play of mind as may suit its being that; we have the *Quarterly Review*, existing as an organ of the Tories, and for as much play of mind as may suit its being that; we have the *British Quarterly Review*, existing as an organ of the political Dissenters, and for as much play of mind as may suit its being that; we have the *Times*, existing as an organ of the common, satisfied, well-to-do Englishman, and for as much play of mind as may suit its being that. And so on through all the various fractions, political and religious, of our society; every fraction has, as such, its organ of criticism, but the notion of combining all fractions in the common pleasure of a free disinterested play of mind meets with no favour. Directly this play of mind wants to have more scope, and to forget the pressure of practical considerations a little, it is checked, it is made to feel the chain. We saw this the other day in the extinction, so much to be regretted, of the *Home and Foreign Review*. Perhaps in no organ of criticism in this country was there so much knowledge, so much play of mind; but these could not save it. The *Dublin Review* subordinates play of mind to the practical business of English and Irish Catholicism, and lives. . . .

It is because criticism has so little kept in the pure intellectual sphere, has so little detached itself from practice, has been so directly polemical and controversial, that it has so ill accomplished, in this country, its best spiritual work; which is to keep man from a self-satisfaction which is retarding and vulgarising, to lead him towards perfection, by making his mind dwell upon what is excellent in itself, and the absolute beauty and fitness of things. A polemical practical criticism makes men blind even to the ideal imperfection of their practice, makes them willingly assert its ideal perfection, in order the better to secure it against attack; and clearly this is narrowing and baneful for them. If they were reassured on the practical side, speculative considerations of ideal perfection they might be brought to entertain, and their spiritual horizon would thus gradually widen. Sir Charles Adderley says to the Warwickshire farmers:—

"Talk of the improvement of breed! Why, the race we ourselves represent, the men and women, the old Anglo-Saxon race, are the best breed in the whole world. . . . The absence of a too enervating climate, too unclouded skies, and a too luxurious nature, has produced so vigorous a race of people, and has rendered us so superior to all the world."

Mr. Roebuck says to the Sheffield cutlers:—

"I look around me and ask what is the state of England? Is not property safe? Is not every man able to say what he likes? Can you not walk from one end of England to the other in perfect security? I ask you whether, the world over or in past history, there is anything like it? Nothing. I pray that our unrivalled happiness may last."

Now obviously there is a peril for poor human nature in words and thoughts of such exuberant self-satisfaction, until we find ourselves safe in the streets of the Celestial City.

"Das wenige verschwindet leicht dem Blicke
Der vorwärts sieht, wie viel noch übrig bleibt—"

says Goethe; "the little that is done seems nothing when we look forward and see how much we have yet to do." Clearly this is a better line of reflection

22–23. Revue des Deux Mondes, Paris, established 1831; still current. **27. Edinburgh Review,** established 1802; discontinued 1929. **29. Quarterly Review,** London, established 1809; still current. **32. British Quarterly Review,** London, 1845–86. **34. Times,** London, established 1788; still current. **47. Home and Foreign Review,** London, 1862–64.

2. Dublin Review, established 1836; still current. **23. Sir Charles Adderley,** first Baron Norton (1814–1905). **32. Mr. Roebuck,** John Arthur Roebuck, M.P. (1801–1879), radical politician, one of Arnold's favorite targets. **47. says Goethe,** in *Iphigenia in Tauris*, Act I, sc. 2, ll. 91–92.

for weak humanity, so long as it remains on this earthly field of labour and trial.

But neither Sir Charles Adderley nor Mr. Roebuck is by nature inaccessible to considerations of this sort. They only lose sight of them owing to the controversial life we all lead, and the practical form which all speculation takes with us. They have in view opponents whose aim is not ideal, but practical; and in their zeal to uphold their own practice against these innovators, they go so far as even to attribute to this practice an ideal perfection. Somebody has been wanting to introduce a six-pound franchise, or to abolish church-rates, or to collect agricultural statistics by force, or to diminish local self-government. How natural, in reply to such proposals, very likely improper or ill-timed, to go a little beyond the mark and to say stoutly, "Such a race of people as we stand, so superior to all the world! The old Anglo-Saxon race, the best breed in the whole world! I pray that our unrivalled happiness may last! I ask you whether, the world over or in past history, there is anything like it?" And so long as criticism answers this dithyramb by insisting that the old Anglo-Saxon race would be still more superior to all others if it had no church-rates, or that our unrivalled happiness would last yet longer with a six-pound franchise, so long will the strain, "The best breed in the whole world!" swell louder and louder, everything ideal and refining will be lost out of sight, and both the assailed and their critics will remain in a sphere, to say the truth, perfectly unvital, a sphere in which spiritual progression is impossible. But let criticism leave church-rates and the franchise alone, and in the most candid spirit, without a single lurking thought of practical innovation, confront with our dithyramb this paragraph on which I stumbled in a newspaper immediately after reading Mr. Roebuck:—

"A shocking child murder has just been committed at Nottingham. A girl named Wragg left the workhouse there on Saturday morning with her young illegitimate child. The child was soon afterwards found dead on Mapperly Hills, having been strangled. Wragg is in custody."

Nothing but that; but, in juxtaposition with the absolute eulogies of Sir Charles Adderley and Mr. Roebuck, how eloquent, how suggestive are those few lines! "Our old Anglo-Saxon breed, the best in the whole world!"—how much that is harsh and ill-favoured there is in this best! *Wragg!* If we are to talk of ideal perfection, of "the best in the whole world," has any one reflected what a touch of grossness in our race, what an original shortcoming in the more delicate spiritual perceptions, is shown by the natural growth amongst us of such hideous names,—Higginbottom, Stiggins, Bugg! In Ionia and Attica they were luckier in this respect than "the best race in the world"; by the Ilissus there was no Wragg, poor thing! And "our unrivalled happiness";—what an element of grimness, bareness, and hideousness mixes with it and blurs it; the workhouse, the dismal Mapperly Hills,—how dismal those who have seen them will remember;—the gloom, the smoke, the cold, the strangled illegitimate child! "I ask you whether, the world over or in past history, there is anything like it?" Perhaps not, one is inclined to answer; but at any rate, in that case, the world is very much to be pitied. And the final touch,—short, bleak, and inhuman: *Wragg is in custody.* The sex lost in the confusion of our unrivalled happiness; or (shall I say?) the superfluous Christian name lopped off by the straightforward vigour of our old Anglo-Saxon breed! There is profit for the spirit in such contrasts as this; criticism serves the cause of perfection by establishing them. By eluding sterile conflict, by refusing to remain in the sphere where alone narrow and relative conceptions have any worth and validity, criticism may diminish its momentary importance, but only in this way has it a chance of gaining admittance for those wider and more perfect conceptions to which all its duty is really owed. Mr. Roebuck will have a poor opinion of an adversary who replies to his defiant songs of triumph only by murmuring under his breath, *Wragg is in custody;* but in no other way will these songs of triumph be induced gradually to moderate themselves, to get rid of what in them is excessive and offensive, and to fall into a softer and truer key.

It will be said that it is a very subtle and indirect action which I am thus prescribing for criticism, and that, by embracing in this manner the Indian virtue of detachment and abandoning the sphere of practical life, it condemns itself to a slow and obscure work. Slow and obscure it may be, but it is the only proper work of criticism. The mass of mankind will never have any ardent zeal for seeing things as they are; very inadequate ideas will always satisfy them. On these inadequate ideas reposes, and must repose, the general practice of the world. That is as much as saying that whoever sets himself to see things as they are will find himself one

12–13. six-pound franchise, a bill to grant the right to vote to all persons owning property worth £6 (instead of £10) per year. **church-rates,** taxes for the support of the Church of England.

6–7. Ionia . . . Attica, districts in ancient Greece. **8. Ilissus,** a river near Athens. **42. Indian,** Hindu, Buddhist.

of a very small circle; but it is only by this small circle resolutely doing its own work that adequate ideas will ever get current at all. The rush and roar of practical life will always have a dizzying and attracting effect upon the most collected spectator, and tend to draw him into its vortex; most of all will this be the case where that life is so powerful as it is in England. But it is only by remaining collected, and refusing to lend himself to the point of view of the practical man, that the critic can do the practical man any service; and it is only by the greatest sincerity in pursuing his own course, and by at last convincing even the practical man of his sincerity, that he can escape misunderstandings which perpetually threaten him. . . .

Do what he will, . . . the critic will still remain exposed to frequent misunderstandings, and nowhere so much as in this country. For here people are particularly indisposed even to comprehend that without this free disinterested treatment of things, truth and the highest culture are out of the question. So immersed are they in practical life, so accustomed to take all their notions from this life and its processes, that they are apt to think that truth and culture themselves can be reached by the processes of this life, and that it is an impertinent singularity to think of reaching them in any other. We are all *terrae filii*," cries their eloquent advocate; "all Philistines together. Away with the notion of proceeding by any other course than the course dear to the Philistines; let us have a social movement, let us organise and combine a party to pursue truth and new thought, let us call it *the liberal party*, and let us all stick to each other, and back each other up. Let us have no nonsense about independent criticism, and intellectual delicacy, and the few and the many. Don't let us trouble ourselves about foreign thought; we shall invent the whole thing for ourselves as we go along. If one of us speaks well, applaud him; if one of us speaks ill, applaud him too; we are all in the same movement, we are all liberals, we are all in pursuit of truth." In this way the pursuit of truth becomes really a social, practical, pleasurable affair, almost requiring a chairman, a secretary, and advertisements; with the excitement of an occasional scandal, with a little resistance to give the happy sense of difficulty overcome; but, in general, plenty of bustle and very little thought. To act is so easy, as Goethe says; to think is so hard! It is true that the critic has many temptations to go with the stream, to make one of the party movement, one of these *terrae filii;* it seems ungracious to refuse to be a *terrae filius*, when so many excellent people are; but the critic's duty is to refuse, or, if resistance is vain, at least to cry with Obermann: *Périssons en résistant*. . . .

I lately heard a man of thought and energy contrasting the want of ardour and movement which he now found amongst young men in this country with what he remembered in his own youth, twenty years ago. "What reformers we were then!" he exclaimed; "What a zeal we had! how we canvassed every institution in Church and State, and were prepared to remodel them all on first principles!" He was inclined to regret, as a spiritual flagging, the lull which he saw. I am disposed rather to regard it as a pause in which the turn to a new mode of spiritual progress is being accomplished. Everything was long seen, by the young and ardent amongst us, in inseparable connection with politics and practical life. We have pretty well exhausted the benefits of seeing things in this connection, we have got all that can be got by so seeing them. Let us try a more disinterested mode of seeing them; let us betake ourselves more to the serener life of the mind and spirit. This life, too, may have its excesses and dangers; but they are not for us at present. Let us think of quietly enlarging our stock of true and fresh ideas, and not, as soon as we get an idea or half an idea, be running out with it into the street, and trying to make it rule there. Our ideas will, in the end, shape the world all the better for maturing a little. . . .

If I have insisted so much on the course which criticism must take where politics and religion are concerned, it is because, where these burning matters are in question, it is most likely to go astray. I have wished, above all, to insist on the attitude which criticism should adopt towards things in general; on its right tone and temper of mind. But then comes another question as to the subject-matter which literary criticism should most seek. Here, in general, its course is determined for it by the idea which is the law of its being; the idea of a disinterested endeavour to learn and propagate the best

29. terrae filii," sons of the earth. **30. Philistines,** one of Arnold's most famous words, used first in "Heinrich Heine" (*Essays in Criticism*), most elaborately in "Barbarians, Philistines, Populace" (*Culture and Anarchy*). By it he indicates an uncultured member of the middle class. Historically, the Philistines were a non-Semitic people in Palestine with whom the Hebrews had considerable friction. They play a considerable part in the story of Samson (Book of Judges).

9. Périssons en résistant. Let us die resisting. See Etienne Pivert de Sénancour (1770–1846), *Obermann*, Letter 90. **39–41. If . . . concerned.** Much of this discussion has been omitted from the present reprint.

that is known and thought in the world, and thus to establish a current of fresh and true ideas. By the very nature of things, as England is not all the world, much of the best that is known and thought in the world cannot be of English growth, must be foreign; by the nature of things, again, it is just this that we are least likely to know, while English thought is streaming in upon us from all sides, and takes excellent care that we shall not be ignorant of its existence. The English critic of literature, therefore, must dwell much on foreign thought, and with particular heed on any part of it, which, while significant and fruitful in itself, is for any reason specially likely to escape him. . . .

But stop, some one will say; all this talk is of no practical use to us whatever; this criticism of yours is not what we have in our minds when we speak of criticism; when we speak of critics and criticism, we mean critics and criticism of the current English literature of the day; when you offer to tell criticism its function, it is to this criticism that we expect you to address yourself. I am sorry for it, for I am afraid I must disappoint these expectations. I am bound by my own definition of criticism: *a disinterested endeavour to learn and propagate the best that is known and thought in the world.* How much of current English literature comes into this "best that is known and thought in the world"? Not very much, I fear; certainly less, at this moment, than of the current literature of France or Germany. Well, then, am I to alter my definition of criticism, in order to meet the requirements of a number of practising English critics, who, after all, are free in their choice of a business? That would be making criticism lend itself just to one of those alien practical considerations, which, I have said, are so fatal to it. One may say, indeed, to those who have to deal with the mass—so much better disregarded—of current English literature, that they may at all events endeavour, in dealing with this, to try it, so far as they can, by the standard of the best that is known and thought in the world; one may say, that to get anywhere near this standard, every critic should try and possess one great literature, at least, besides his own; and the more unlike his own, the better. But, after all, the criticism I am really concerned with, —the criticism which alone can much help us for the future, the criticism which, throughout Europe, is at the present day meant, when so much stress is laid on the importance of criticism and the critical spirit,—is a criticism which regards Europe as being, for intellectual and spiritual purposes, one great confederation, bound to a joint action and working to a common result; and whose members have, for their proper outfit, a knowledge of Greek, Roman, and Eastern antiquity, and of one another. . . .

I conclude with what I said at the beginning: to have the sense of creative activity is the great happiness and the great proof of being alive, and it is not denied to criticism to have it; but then criticism must be sincere, simple, flexible, ardent, ever widening its knowledge. Then it may have, in no contemptible measure, a joyful sense of creative activity; a sense which a man of insight and conscience will prefer to what he might derive from a poor, starved, fragmentary, inadequate creation. And at some epochs no other creation is possible.

Still, in full measure, the sense of creative activity belongs only to genuine creation; in literature we must never forget that. But what true man of letters ever can forget it? It is no such common matter for a gifted nature to come into possession of a current of true and living ideas, and to produce amidst the inspiration of them, that we are likely to underrate it. The epochs of Aeschylus and Shakspeare make us feel their pre-eminence. In an epoch like those is, no doubt, the true life of literature; there is the promised land, towards which criticism can only beckon. That promised land it will not be ours to enter, and we shall die in the wilderness: but to have desired to enter it, to have saluted it from afar, is already, perhaps, the best distinction among contemporaries; it will certainly be the best title to esteem with posterity.

from CULTURE AND ANARCHY

from Chapter I: SWEETNESS AND LIGHT

THE disparagers of culture make its motive curiosity; sometimes, indeed, they make its motive mere exclusiveness and vanity. The culture which is supposed to plume itself on a smattering of Greek and Latin is a culture which is begotten by nothing so intellectual as curiosity; it is valued either out of sheer vanity and ignorance or else as an engine of social and class distinction, separating its holder, like a badge or title, from other people who have not got it. No serious man would call this *culture*, or attach any value to it, as culture, at all. To find the real ground for the very different estimate which serious people will set upon culture, we must find some motive for culture in the terms of which

24. Aeschylus, Greek tragic dramatist (525–456 B.C.).

may lie a real ambiguity; and such a motive the word *curiosity* gives us.

I have before now pointed out that we English do not, like the foreigners, use this word in a good sense as well as in a bad sense. With us the word is always used in a somewhat disapproving sense. A liberal and intelligent eagerness about the things of the mind may be meant by a foreigner when he speaks of curiosity, but with us the word always conveys a certain notion of frivolous and unedifying activity. In the *Quarterly Review*, some little time ago, was an estimate of the celebrated French critic, M. Sainte-Beuve, and a very inadequate estimate it in my judgment was. And its inadequacy consisted chiefly in this: that in our English way it left out of sight the double sense really involved in the word *curiosity*, thinking enough was said to stamp M. Sainte-Beuve with blame if it was said that he was impelled in his operations as a critic by curiosity, and omitting either to perceive that M. Sainte-Beuve himself, and many other people with him, would consider that this was praiseworthy and not blameworthy, or to point out why it ought really to be accounted worthy of blame and not of praise. For as there is a curiosity about intellectual matters which is futile, and merely a disease, so there is certainly a curiosity,—a desire after the things of the mind simply for their own sakes and for the pleasure of seeing them as they are,—which is, in an intelligent being, natural and laudable. Nay, and the very desire to see things as they are implies a balance and regulation of mind which is not often attained without fruitful effort, and which is the very opposite of the blind and diseased impulse of mind which is what we mean to blame when we blame curiosity. . . .

But there is of culture another view, in which not solely the scientific passion, the sheer desire to see things as they are, natural and proper in an intelligent being, appears as the ground of it. There is a view in which all the love of our neighbour, the impulses towards action, help, and beneficence, the desire for removing human error, clearing human confusion, and diminishing human misery, the noble aspiration to leave the world better and happier than we found it,—motives eminently such as are called social,—come in as part of the grounds of culture, and the main and pre-eminent part. Culture is then properly described not as having its origin in curiosity, but as having its origin in the love of perfection; it is *a study of perfection*. . . . As, in the first view of it, we took for its worthy motto Montesquieu's words: "To render an intelligent being yet more intelligent!" so, in the second view of it, there is no better motto which it can have than these words of Bishop Wilson: "To make reason and the will of God prevail!"

Only, whereas the passion for doing good is apt to be overhasty in determining what reason and the will of God say, because its turn is for acting rather than thinking and it wants to be beginning to act; and whereas it is apt to take its own conceptions, which proceed from its own state of development and share in all the imperfections and immaturities of this, for a basis of action; what distinguishes culture is, that it is possessed by the scientific passion as well as by the passion of doing good; that it demands worthy notions of reason and the will of God, and does not readily suffer its own crude conceptions to substitute themselves for them. And knowing that no action or institution can be salutary and stable which is not based on reason and the will of God, it is not so bent on acting and instituting, even with the great aim of diminishing human error and misery ever before its thoughts, but that it can remember that acting and instituting are of little use, unless we know how and what we ought to act and to institute. . . .

The moment this view of culture is seized, the moment it is regarded not solely as the endeavour to see things as they are, to draw towards a knowledge of the universal order which seems to be intended and aimed at in the world, and which it is a man's happiness to go along with or his misery to go counter to,—to learn, in short, the will of God,—the moment, I say, culture is considered not merely as the endeavour to *see* and *learn* this, but as the endeavour, also, to make it *prevail*, the moral, social, and beneficent character of culture becomes manifest. . . .

And religion, the greatest and most important of the efforts by which the human race has manifested its impulse to perfect itself,—religion, that voice of the deepest human experience,—does not only enjoin and sanction the aim which is the great aim of culture, the aim of setting ourselves to ascertain what perfection is and to make it prevail; but also, in determining generally in what human perfection consists, religion comes to a conclusion iden-

13. M. Sainte-Beuve, Charles Augustin Sainte-Beuve (1804–1869).

2. Montesquieu, Charles de Secondat, Baron de la Brède et de Montesquieu (1689–1755), French political philosopher. **5. Bishop Wilson,** Thomas Wilson (1663–1755), Bishop of Sodor and Man.

tical with that which culture,—culture seeking the determination of this question through *all* the voices of human experience which have been heard upon it, of art, science, poetry, philosophy, history, as well as of religion, in order to give a greater fulness and certainty to its solution,—likewise reaches. Religion says: *The kingdom of God is within you;* and culture, in like manner, places human perfection in an *internal* condition, in the growth and predominance of our humanity proper, as distinguished from our animality. It places it in the ever-increasing efficacy and in the general harmonious expansion of those gifts of thought and feeling, which make the peculiar dignity, wealth, and happiness of human nature. As I have said on a former occasion: "It is in making endless additions to itself, in the endless expansion of its powers, in endless growth in wisdom and beauty, that the spirit of the human race finds its ideal. To reach this ideal, culture is an indispensable aid, and that is the true value of culture." Not a having and a resting, but a growing and a becoming, is the character of perfection as culture conceives it; and here, too, it coincides with religion.

And because men are all members of one great whole, and the sympathy which is in human nature will not allow one member to be indifferent to the rest or to have a perfect welfare independent of the rest, the expansion of our humanity, to suit the idea of perfection which culture forms, must be a *general* expansion. Perfection, as culture conceives it, is not possible while the individual remains isolated. The individual is required, under pain of being stunted and enfeebled in his own development if he disobeys, to carry others along with him in his march towards perfection, to be continually doing all he can to enlarge and increase the volume of the human stream sweeping thitherward. And here, once more, culture lays on us the same obligation as religion, which says, as Bishop Wilson has admirably put it, that "to promote the kingdom of God is to increase and hasten one's own happiness."

But, finally, perfection,—as culture from a thorough disinterested study of human nature and human experience learns to conceive it,—is a harmonious expansion of *all* the powers which make the beauty and worth of human nature, and is not consistent with the over-development of any one power at the expense of the rest. Here culture goes beyond religion, as religion is generally conceived by us.

If culture, then, is a study of perfection, and of harmonious perfection, general perfection, and perfection which consists in becoming something rather than in having something, in an inward condition of the mind and spirit, not in an outward set of circumstances,—it is clear that culture, instead of being the frivolous and useless thing which Mr. Bright, and Mr. Frederic Harrison, and many other Liberals are apt to call it, has a very important function to fulfil for mankind. And this function is particularly important in our modern world, of which the whole civilisation is, to a much greater degree than the civilisation of Greece and Rome, mechanical and external, and tends constantly to become more so. But above all in our own country has culture a weighty part to perform, because here that mechanical character, which civilisation tends to take everywhere, is shown in the most eminent degree. Indeed nearly all the characters of perfection, as culture teaches us to fix them, meet in this country with some powerful tendency which thwarts them and sets them at defiance. The idea of perfection as an *inward* condition of the mind and spirit is at variance with the mechanical and material civilisation in esteem with us, and nowhere, as I have said, so much in esteem as with us. The idea of perfection as a *general* expansion of the human family is at variance with our strong individualism, our hatred of all limits to the unrestrained swing of the individual's personality, our maxim of "every man for himself." Above all, the idea of perfection as a *harmonious* expansion of human nature is at variance with our want of flexibility, with our inaptitude for seeing more than one side of a thing, with our intense energetic absorption in the particular pursuit we happen to be following. So culture has a rough task to achieve in this country. Its preachers have, and are likely long to have, a hard time of it, and they will much oftener be regarded, for a great while to come, as elegant or spurious Jeremiahs than as friends and benefactors. That, however, will not prevent their doing in the end good service if they persevere. And, meanwhile, the mode of action they have to pursue, and the sort of habits they must fight against, ought to be made quite clear for

7. The kingdom . . . you. See Luke 17:21. The meaning of the passage is disputed; see any good Bible commentary.

7. Mr. Bright, John Bright (1811–1889), famous Victorian statesman. **8. Mr. Frederic Harrison** (1831–1923), a prominent Victorian writer in varied fields, known especially as a leader of the Positivist movement. **40. elegant or spurious Jeremiahs.** Jeremiah (seventh century B.C.) was probably the greatest of the Hebrew prophets (see Stefan Zweig's play *Jeremiah*, Viking Press, 1923, and Franz Werfel's novel *Hearken to the Voice*, Viking Press, 1938), but from the attribution to him of the Book of Lamentations he enjoys an undeserved reputation as "the weeping prophet." Note the word "jeremiad," a lamenting and denunciatory complaint. Arnold was himself called an "elegant Jeremiah."

every one to see, who may be willing to look at the matter attentively and dispassionately.

Faith in machinery is, I said, our besetting danger; often in machinery most absurdly disproportioned to the end which this machinery, if it is to do any good at all, is to serve; but always in machinery, as if it had a value in and for itself. What is freedom but machinery? what is population but machinery? what is coal but machinery? what are railroads but machinery? what is wealth but machinery? what are, even, religious organisations but machinery? Now almost every voice in England is accustomed to speak of these things as if they were precious ends in themselves, and therefore had some of the characters of perfection indisputably joined to them. . . .

. . . Every one must have observed the strange language current during the late discussions as to the possible failures of our supplies of coal. Our coal, thousands of people were saying, is the real basis of our national greatness; if our coal runs short, there is an end of the greatness of England. But what *is* greatness?—culture makes us ask. Greatness is a spiritual condition worthy to excite love, interest, and admiration; and the outward proof of possessing greatness is that we excite love, interest, and admiration. If England were swallowed up by the sea to-morrow, which of the two, a hundred years hence, would most excite the love, interest, and admiration of mankind,—would most, therefore, show the evidences of having possessed greatness,—the England of the last twenty years, or the England of Elizabeth, of a time of splendid spiritual effort, but when our coal, and our industrial operations depending on coal, were very little developed? Well, then, what an unsound habit of mind it must be which makes us talk of things like coal or iron as constituting the greatness of England, and how salutary a friend is culture, bent on seeing things as they are, and thus dissipating delusions of this kind and fixing standards of perfection that are real!

Wealth, again, that end to which our prodigious works for material advantage are directed,—the commonest of commonplaces tells us how men are always apt to regard wealth as a precious end in itself; and certainly they have never been so apt thus to regard it as they are in England at the present time. Never did people believe anything more firmly than nine Englishmen out of ten at the present day believe that our greatness and welfare are proved by our being so very rich. Now, the use of culture is that it helps us, by means of its spiritual standard of perfection, to regard wealth as but machinery, and not only to say as a matter of words that we regard wealth as but machinery, but really to perceive and feel that it is so. If it were not for this purging effect wrought upon our minds by culture, the whole world, the future as well as the present, would inevitably belong to the Philistines. The people who believe most that our greatness and welfare are proved by our being very rich, and who most give their lives and thoughts to becoming rich, are just the very people whom we call Philistines. Culture says: "Consider these people, then, their way of life, their habits, their manners, the very tones of their voice; look at them attentively; observe the literature they read, the things which give them pleasure, the words which come forth out of their mouths, the thoughts which make the furniture of their minds; would any amount of wealth be worth having with the condition that one was to become just like these people by having it?" . . .

Population, again, and bodily health and vigour, are things which are nowhere treated in such an unintelligent, misleading, exaggerated way as in England. Both are really machinery; yet how many people all around us do we see rest in them and fail to look beyond them! Why, one has heard people, fresh from reading certain articles of the *Times* on the Registrar-General's returns of marriages and births in this country, who would talk of our large English families in quite a solemn strain, as if they had something in itself beautiful, elevating, and meritorious in them; as if the British Philistine would have only to present himself before the Great Judge with his twelve children, in order to be received among the sheep as a matter of right!

But bodily health and vigour, it may be said, are not to be classed with wealth and population as mere machinery; they have a more real and essential value. True; but only as they are more intimately connected with a perfect spiritual condition than wealth or population are. The moment we disjoin them from the idea of a perfect spiritual condition, and pursue them, as we do pursue them, for their own sake and as ends in themselves, our worship of them becomes as mere worship of machinery, as our worship of wealth or population, and as unintelligent and vulgarising a worship as that is. Every one with anything like an adequate idea of human perfection has distinctly marked this subordination to higher and spiritual ends of the

7. **Philistines.** See note 30 on page 1074.

cultivation of bodily vigour and activity. "Bodily exercise profiteth little; but godliness is profitable unto all things," says the author of the Epistle to Timothy. And the utilitarian Franklin says just as explicitly:—"Eat and drink such an exact quantity as suits the constitution of thy body, *in reference to the services of the mind*." But the point of view of culture, keeping the mark of human perfection simply and broadly in view, and not assigning to this perfection, as religion or utilitarianism assigns to it, a special and limited character, this point of view, I say, of culture is best given by these words of Epictetus:—"It is a sign of ἀφυΐα," says he,—that is, of a nature not finely tempered,—"to give yourselves up to things which relate to the body; to make, for instance, a great fuss about exercise, a great fuss about eating, a great fuss about drinking, a great fuss about walking, a great fuss about riding. All these things ought to be done merely by the way: the formation of the spirit and character must be our real concern." This is admirable; and, indeed, the Greek word εὐφυΐα, a finely tempered nature, gives exactly the notion of perfection as culture brings us to conceive it: a harmonious perfection, a perfection in which the characters of beauty and intelligence are both present, which unites "the two noblest of things,"—as Swift, who of one of the two, at any rate, had himself all too little, most happily calls them in his *Battle of the Books*,—"the two noblest of things, *sweetness and light*." The εὐφυής is the man who tends towards sweetness and light; the ἀφυής, on the other hand, is our Philistine. The immense spiritual significance of the Greeks is due to their having been inspired with this central and happy idea of the essential character of human perfection; and Mr. Bright's misconception of culture, as a smattering of Greek and Latin, comes itself, after all, from this wonderful significance of the Greeks having affected the very machinery of our education, and is in itself a kind of homage to it.

In thus making sweetness and light to be characters of perfection, culture is of like spirit with poetry, follows one law with poetry. Far more than on our freedom, our population, and our industrialism, many amongst us rely upon our religious organisations to save us. I have called religion a yet more important manifestation of human nature than poetry, because it has worked on a broader scale for perfection, and with greater masses of men. But the idea of beauty and of a human nature perfect on all its sides, which is the dominant idea of poetry, is a true and invaluable idea, though it has not yet had the success that the idea of conquering the obvious faults of our animality, and of a human nature perfect on the moral side,—which is the dominant idea of religion,—has been enabled to have; and it is destined, adding to itself the religious idea of a devout energy, to transform and govern the other.

The best art and poetry of the Greeks, in which religion and poetry are one, in which the idea of beauty and of a human nature perfect on all sides adds to itself a religious and devout energy, and works in the strength of that, is on this account of such surpassing interest and instructiveness for us, though it was,—as, having regard to the human race in general, and, indeed, having regard to the Greeks themselves, we must own,—a premature attempt, an attempt which for success needed the moral and religious fibre in humanity to be more braced and developed than it had yet been. But Greece did not err in having the idea of beauty, harmony, and complete human perfection, so present and paramount. It is impossible to have this idea too present and paramount; only, the moral fibre must be braced too. And we, because we have braced the moral fibre, are not on that account in the right way, if at the same time the idea of beauty, harmony, and complete human perfection, is wanting or misapprehended amongst us; and evidently it *is* wanting or misapprehended at present. And when we rely as we do on our religious organisations, which in themselves do not and cannot give us this idea, and think we have done enough if we make them spread and prevail, then, I say, we fall into our common fault of overvaluing machinery.

Nothing is more common than for people to confound the inward peace and satisfaction which follows the subduing of the obvious faults of our animality with what I may call absolute inward peace and satisfaction,—the peace and satisfaction which are reached as we draw near to complete spiritual perfection, and not merely to moral perfection, or rather to relative moral perfection. No people in the world have done more and struggled more to attain this relative moral perfection than our English race has. For no people in the world has the command to *resist the devil*, to *overcome the wicked one*, in the nearest and most obvious sense of those words, had such a pressing force and reality. And we have had our reward, not only in the great worldly prosperity which our obedience to this

1–3. "Bodily . . . things." See 1 Timothy, 4:8. The **author** is St. Paul. **5–7. "Eat . . . mind."** Inaccurately quoted from *Poor Richard's Almanack*. **13–21. "It is . . . concern."** Freely translated from the *Encheiridion*. **Epictetus.** See note 6 on page 1055. **29. Battle of the Books,** published 1704. From it, as the context shows, Arnold derived the title of this essay.

49. resist . . . one. See James 4:7.

command has brought us, but also, and far more, in great inward peace and satisfaction. But to me few things are more pathetic than to see people, on the strength of the inward peace and satisfaction which their rudimentary efforts towards perfection have brought them, employ, concerning their incomplete perfection and the religious organisations within which they have found it, language which properly applies only to complete perfection, and is a far-off echo of the human soul's prophecy of it. Religion itself, I need hardly say, supplies them in abundance with this grand language. And very freely do they use it; yet it is really the severest possible criticism of such an incomplete perfection as alone we have yet reached through our religious organisations. . . .

But men of culture and poetry, it will be said, are again and again failing, and failing conspicuously, in the necessary first stage to a harmonious perfection, in the subduing of the great obvious faults of our animality, which it is the glory of these religious organisations to have helped us to subdue. True, they do often so fail. They have often been without the virtues as well as the faults of the Puritan; it has been one of their dangers that they so felt the Puritan's faults that they too much neglected the practice of his virtues. I will not, however, exculpate them at the Puritan's expense. They have often failed in morality, and morality is indispensable. And they have been punished for their failure, as the Puritan has been rewarded for his performance. They have been punished wherein they erred; but their ideal of beauty, of sweetness and light, and a human nature complete on all its sides, remains the true ideal of perfection still; just as the Puritan's ideal of perfection remains narrow and inadequate, although for what he did well he has been richly rewarded. Notwithstanding the mighty results of the Pilgrim Fathers' voyage, they and their standard of perfection are rightly judged when we figure to ourselves Shakspeare or Virgil,—souls in whom sweetness and light, and all that in human nature is most humane, were eminent,—accompanying them on their voyage, and think what intolerable company Shakspeare and Virgil would have found them! . . .

Culture, however, shows its single-minded love of perfection, its desire simply to make reason and the will of God prevail, its freedom from fanaticism, by its attitude towards all this machinery, even while it insists that it *is* machinery. Fanatics, seeing the mischief men do themselves by their blind belief in some machinery or other,—whether it is wealth and industrialism, or whether it is the cultivation of bodily strength and activity, or whether it is a political organisation,—or whether it is a religious organisation,—oppose with might and main the tendency to this or that political and religious organisation, or to games and athletic exercises, or to wealth and industrialism, and try violently to stop it. But the flexibility which sweetness and light give, and which is one of the rewards of culture pursued in good faith, enables a man to see that a tendency may be necessary, and even, as a preparation for something in the future, salutary, and yet that the generations or individuals who obey this tendency are sacrificed to it, that they fall short of the hope of perfection by following it; and that its mischiefs are to be criticised, lest it should take too firm a hold and last after it has served its purpose. . . .

I remember, when I was under the influence of a mind to which I feel the greatest obligations, the mind of a man who was the very incarnation of sanity and clear sense, a man the most considerable, it seems to me, whom America has yet produced,—Benjamin Franklin,—I remember the relief with which, after long feeling the sway of Franklin's imperturbable common-sense, I came upon a project of his for a new version of the Book of Job, to replace the old version, the style of which, says Franklin, has become obsolete, and thence less agreeable. "I give," he continues, "a few verses, which may serve as a sample of the kind of version I would recommend." We all recollect the famous verse in our translation: "Then Satan answered the Lord and said: 'Doth Job fear God for nought?' " Franklin makes this: "Does your Majesty imagine that Job's good conduct is the effect of mere personal attachment and affection?" I well remember how, when first I read that, I drew a deep breath of relief, and said to myself: "After all, there is a stretch of humanity beyond Franklin's victorious good sense!" So, after hearing Bentham cried loudly up as the renovator of modern society, and Bentham's mind and ideas proposed as the rulers of our future, I open the *Deontology*. There I read: "While Xenophon was writing his history and Euclid teaching geometry, Socrates and Plato were talking nonsense under pretence of talking wisdom

41–42. Franklin's victorious good sense!" Harrold and Templeman (*English Prose of the Victorian Era*, Oxford Press, 1938), have pointed out that since Franklin's discussion of the Book of Job is included among his *Bagatelles*, it can hardly have been intended seriously. **45. Deontology,** *Deontology, or, The Science of Morality*, by Jeremy Bentham, edited and arranged for the press, after Bentham's death, by John Bowring, 1834.

and morality. This morality of theirs consisted in words; this wisdom of theirs was the denial of matters known to every man's experience." From the moment of reading that, I am delivered from the bondage of Bentham! the fanaticism of his adherents can touch me no longer. I feel the inadequacy of his mind and ideas for supplying the rule of human society, for perfection.

. . . "The man of culture is in politics," cries Mr. Frederic Harrison, "one of the poorest mortals alive!" Mr. Frederic Harrison wants to be doing business, and he complains that the man of culture stops him with a "turn for small fault-finding, love of selfish ease, and indecision in action." Of what use is culture, he asks, except for "a critic of new books or a professor of *belles-lettres*"? Why, it is of use because, in presence of the fierce exasperation which breathes, or rather, I may say, hisses through the whole production in which Mr. Frederic Harrison asks that question, it reminds us that the perfection of human nature is sweetness and light. It is of use because, like religion,—that other effort after perfection,—it testifies, that, where bitter envying and strife are, there is confusion and every evil work.

The pursuit of perfection, then, is the pursuit of sweetness and light. He who works for sweetness and light, works to make reason and the will of God prevail. He who works for machinery, he who works for hatred, works only for confusion. Culture looks beyond machinery, culture hates hatred; culture has one great passion, the passion for sweetness and light. It has one even yet greater!—the passion for making them *prevail*. It is not satisfied till we *all* come to a perfect man; it knows that the sweetness and light of the few must be imperfect until the raw and unkindled masses of humanity are touched with sweetness and light. If I have not shrunk from saying that we must work for sweetness and light, so neither have I shrunk from saying that we must have a broad basis, must have sweetness and light for as many as possible. Again and again I have insisted how those are the happy moments of humanity, how those are the marking epochs of a people's life, how those are the flowering times for literature and art and all the creative power of genius, when there is a *national* glow of life and thought, when the whole of society is in the fullest measure permeated by thought, sensible to beauty, intelligent and alive. Only it must be *real* thought and *real* beauty; *real* sweetness and *real* light. Plenty of people will try to give the masses, as they call them, an intellectual food prepared and adapted in the way they think proper for the actual condition of the masses. The ordinary popular literature is an example of this way of working on the masses. Plenty of people will try to indoctrinate the masses with the set of ideas and judgments constituting the creed of their own profession or party. Our religious and political organisations give an example of this way of working on the masses. I condemn neither way; but culture works differently. It does not try to teach down to the level of inferior classes; it does not try to win them for this or that sect of its own, with ready-made judgments and watchwords. It seeks to do away with classes; to make the best that has been thought and known in the world current everywhere; to make all men live in an atmosphere of sweetness and light, where they may use ideas, as it uses them itself, freely,—nourished, and not bound by them.

This is the *social idea;* and the men of culture are the true apostles of equality. The great men of culture are those who have had a passion for diffusing, for making prevail, for carrying from one end of society to the other, the best knowledge, the best ideas of their time; who have laboured to divest knowledge of all that was harsh, uncouth, difficult, abstract, professional, exclusive; to humanise it, to make it efficient outside the clique of the cultivated and learned, yet still remaining the *best* knowledge and thought of the time, and a true source, therefore, of sweetness and light. Such a man was Abelard in the Middle Ages, in spite of all his imperfections; and thence the boundless emotion and enthusiasm which Abelard excited. Such were Lessing and Herder in Germany, at the end of the last century; and their services to Germany were in this way inestimably precious. Generations will pass, and literary monuments will accumulate, and works far more perfect than the works of Lessing and Herder will be produced in Germany; and yet the names of these two men will fill a German with a reverence and enthusiasm such as the names of the most gifted masters will hardly awaken. And why? Because they *humanised* knowledge; because they broadened the basis of life and intelligence; because they worked powerfully to diffuse sweetness and light, to make reason and the will of God prevail. With Saint Augustine they said: "Let us not leave thee alone to make in the secret of thy knowledge, as thou didst

30. Abelard, Pierre Abelard (1079–1142), famous French philosopher, known to modern theologians as the first noteworthy proponent of the "moral influence" theory of the Atonement, and to the general reader for *The Love-Letters of Abelard and Héloïse*. **33. Lessing,** Gotthold Ephraim Lessing (1729–1781). **34. Herder,** Johann Gottfried von Herder (1744–1803). **47–12** (*p.* 1082). **"Let . . . yet."** Quoted from the famous *Confessions* by St. Augustine.

before the creation of the firmament, the division of light from darkness; let the children of thy spirit, placed in their firmament, make their light shine upon the earth, mark the division of night and day, and announce the revolution of the times; for the old order is passed, and the new arises; the night is spent, the day is come forth; and thou shalt crown the year with thy blessing, when thou shalt send forth labourers into thy harvest sown by other hands than theirs; when thou shalt send forth new labourers to new seed-times, whereof the harvest shall be not yet."

from ESSAYS IN CRITICISM, SECOND SERIES

from THE STUDY OF POETRY

This essay was first published in 1880 as the general introduction to T. H. Ward's anthology, *The English Poets*. It was reprinted as the first of Arnold's *Essays in Criticism, Second Series*, 1888.

"The future of poetry is immense, because in poetry, where it is worthy of its high destinies, our race, as time goes on, will find an ever surer and surer stay. There is not a creed which is not shaken, not an accredited dogma which is not shown to be questionable, not a received tradition which does not threaten to dissolve. Our religion has materialised itself in the fact, in the supposed fact; it has attached its emotion to the fact, and now the fact is failing it. But for poetry the idea is everything; the rest is a world of illusion, of divine illusion. Poetry attaches its emotion to the idea; the idea *is* the fact. The strongest part of our religion today is its unconscious poetry."

Let me be permitted to quote these words of my own, as uttering the thought which should, in my opinion, go with us and govern us in all our study of poetry. In the present work it is the course of one great contributory stream to the world-river of poetry that we are invited to follow. We are here invited to trace the stream of English poetry. But whether we set ourselves, as here, to follow only one of the several streams that make the mighty river of poetry, or whether we seek to know them all, our governing thought should be the same. We should conceive of poetry worthily, and more highly than it has been the custom to conceive of it. We should conceive of it as capable of higher uses, and called to higher destinies, than those which in general men have assigned to it hitherto. More and more mankind will discover that we have to turn to poetry to interpret life for us, to console us, to sustain us. Without poetry, our science will appear incomplete; and most of what now passes with us for religion and philosophy will be replaced by poetry. Science, I say, will appear incomplete without it. For finely and truly does Wordsworth call poetry "the impassioned expression which is in the countenance of all science"; and what is a countenance without its expression? Again, Wordsworth finely and truly calls poetry "the breath and finer spirit of all knowledge"; our religion, parading evidences such as those on which the popular mind relies now; our philosophy, pluming itself on its reasonings about causation and finite and infinite being; what are they but the shadows and dreams and false shows of knowledge? The day will come when we shall wonder at ourselves for having trusted to them, for having taken them seriously; and the more we perceive their hollowness, the more we shall prize "the breath and finer spirit of knowledge" offered to us by poetry.

But if we conceive thus highly of the destinies of poetry, we must also set our standard for poetry high, since poetry, to be capable of fulfilling such high destinies, must be poetry of a high order of excellence. We must accustom ourselves to a high standard and to a strict judgment. Sainte-Beuve relates that Napoleon one day said, when somebody was spoken of in his presence as a charlatan: "Charlatan as much as you please; but where is there *not* charlatanism?"—"Yes," answers Sainte-Beuve, "in politics, in the art of governing mankind, that is perhaps true. But in the order of thought, in art, the glory, the eternal honour is that charlatanism shall find no entrance; herein lies the inviolableness of that noble portion of man's being." It is admirably said, and let us hold fast to it. In poetry, which is thought and art in one, it is the glory, the eternal honour, that charlatanism shall find no entrance; that this noble sphere be kept inviolate and inviolable. Charlatanism is for confusing or obliterating the distinctions between excellent and inferior, sound and unsound or only half-sound, true and untrue or only half-true. It is charlatanism, conscious or unconscious, whenever we confuse or obliterate these. And in poetry, more than anywhere else, it is unpermissible to confuse or obliterate them. For in poetry the distinction between excellent and inferior, sound and unsound or only half-sound, true and untrue or only half-true, is of paramount importance. It is of paramount importance because of the high destinies of poetry. In poetry, as a criticism of life under the conditions fixed for such a criticism by the laws of poetic truth and poetic beauty, the spirit of our race will find, we have said, as time goes on and as other helps fail, its consolation and stay. But the consolation and stay will be of power in proportion to the power of the criticism of life. And the criticism of life will be of power in proportion as the poetry conveying it is excellent rather than inferior, sound rather than unsound or half-sound, true rather than untrue or half-true.

The best poetry is what we want; the best poetry will be found to have a power of forming, sustaining, and delighting us, as nothing else can. A clearer, deeper sense of the best in poetry, and of the strength and joy to be drawn from it, is the most precious benefit which we can gather from a poetical collection such as the present. And yet in the very nature and conduct of such a collection there is inevitably something which tends to obscure in us the consciousness of what our benefit should be, and to distract us from the pursuit of it. We should therefore steadily set it before our minds at the outset, and should compel ourselves to revert constantly to the thought of it as we proceed.

Yes; constantly in reading poetry, a sense for the best, the really excellent, and of the strength and joy to be drawn from it, should be present in our minds and should govern our estimate of what we read. But this real estimate, the only true one, is liable to be superseded, if we are not watchful, by two other kinds of estimate, the historic estimate and the personal estimate, both of which are fallacious. A poet or a poem may count to us historically, they may count to us on grounds personal to ourselves, and they may count to us really. They may count to us historically. The course of development of a nation's language, thought, and poetry, is profoundly interesting; and by regarding a poet's work as a stage in this course of development we may easily bring ourselves to make it of more importance as poetry than in itself it really is, we may come to use a language of quite exaggerated praise in criticising it; in short, to overrate it. So arises in our poetic judgments the fallacy caused by the estimate which we may call historic. Then, again, a poet or a poem may count to us on grounds personal to ourselves. Our personal affinities, likings, and circumstances, have great power to sway our estimate of this or that poet's work, and to make us attach more importance to it as poetry than in itself it really possesses, because to us it is, or has been, of high importance. Here also we overrate the object of our interest, and apply to it a language of praise which is quite exaggerated. And thus we get the source of a second fallacy in our poetic judgments—the fallacy caused by an estimate which we may call personal.

Both fallacies are natural. It is evident how naturally the study of the history and development of a poetry may incline a man to pause over reputations and works once conspicuous but now obscure, and to quarrel with a careless public for skipping, in obedience to mere tradition and habit, from one famous name or work in its national poetry to another, ignorant of what it misses, and of the reason for keeping what it keeps, and of the whole process of growth in its poetry. . . .

Indeed there can be no more useful help for discovering what poetry belongs to the class of the truly excellent, and can therefore do us most good, than to have always in one's mind lines and expressions of the great masters, and to apply them as a touchstone to other poetry. Of course we are not to require this other poetry to resemble them; it may be very dissimilar. But if we have any tact we shall find them, when we have lodged them well in our minds, an infallible touchstone for detecting the presence or absence of high poetic quality, and also the degree of this quality in all other poetry which we may place beside them. Short passages, even single lines, will serve our turn quite sufficiently. . . . Take of Shakespeare a line or two of Henry the Fourth's expostulation with sleep—

"Wilt thou upon the high and giddy mast
Seal up the ship-boy's eyes, and rock his brains
In cradle of the rude imperious surge . . . ."

and take, as well, Hamlet's dying request to Horatio—

"If thou didst ever hold me in thy heart,
Absent thee from felicity awhile,
And in this harsh world draw thy breath in pain
To tell my story . . ."

Take of Milton that Miltonic passage—

"Darken'd so, yet shone
Above them all the archangel; but his face
Deep scars of thunder had intrench'd, and care
Sat on his faded cheek . . ."

add two such lines as—

16. poetical collection. Arnold is referring to the anthology, *The English Poets,* to which this essay was the introduction.

33–35. "Wilt . . . surge." *Henry IV*, Part II, III, i, 18–20. **40–43. "If . . . story."** *Hamlet*, V, ii, 357–60. **46–49. "Darken'd . . . cheek."** *Paradise Lost*, I, 599–602.

"And courage never to submit or yield
And what is else not to be overcome . . ."

and finish with the exquisite close to the loss of Proserpine, the loss

". . . which cost Ceres all that pain
To seek her through the world."

These few lines, if we have tact and can use them, are enough even of themselves to keep clear and sound our judgments about poetry, to save us from fallacious estimates of it, to conduct us to a real estimate.

The specimens I have quoted differ widely from one another, but they have in common this: the possession of the very highest poetical quality. If we are thoroughly penetrated by their power, we shall find that we have acquired a sense enabling us, whatever poetry may be laid before us, to feel the degree in which a high poetical quality is present or wanting there. Critics give themselves great labour to draw out what in the abstract constitutes the characters of a high quality of poetry. It is much better simply to have recourse to concrete examples;—to take specimens of poetry of the high, the very highest quality, and to say: The characters of a high quality of poetry are what is expressed *there*. They are far better recognised by being felt in the verse of the master, than by being perused in the prose of the critic. Nevertheless if we are urgently pressed to give some critical account of them, we may safely, perhaps, venture on laying down, not indeed how and why the characters arise, but where and in what they arise. They are in the matter and substance of the poetry, and they are in its manner and style. Both of these, the substance and matter on the one hand, the style and manner on the other, have a mark, an accent, of high beauty, worth, and power. But if we are asked to define this mark and accent in the abstract, our answer must be: No, for we should thereby be darkening the question, not clearing it. The mark and accent are as given by the substance and matter of that poetry, by the style and manner of that poetry, and of all other poetry which is akin to it in quality.

Only one thing we may add as to the substance and matter of poetry, guiding ourselves by Aristotle's profound observation that the superiority of poetry over history consists in its possessing a higher truth and a higher seriousness (φιλοσοφώτερον καὶ σπουδαιότερον). Let us add, therefore, to what we have said, this: that the substance and matter of the best poetry acquire their special character from possessing, in an eminent degree, truth and seriousness. We may add yet further, what is in itself evident, that to the style and manner of the best poetry their special character, their accent, is given by their diction, and, even yet more, by their movement. And though we distinguish between the two characters, the two accents, of superiority, yet they are nevertheless vitally connected one with the other. The superior character of truth and seriousness, in the matter and substance of the best poetry, is inseparable from the superiority of diction and movement marking its style and manner. The two superiorities are closely related, and are in steadfast proportion one to the other. So far as high poetic truth and seriousness are wanting to a poet's matter and substance, so far also, we may be sure, will a high poetic stamp of diction and movement be wanting to his style and manner. In proportion as this high stamp of diction and movement, again, is absent from a poet's style and manner, we shall find, also, that high poetic truth and seriousness are absent from his substance and matter. . . .

1–2. "And . . . overcome." *Ibid.*, I, 108–9. **6–7. "which . . . world."** *Ibid.*, IV, 271–72. Ceres, goddess of agriculture and of the fruits of the earth, was the mother of Proserpine, who was carried away by Pluto, god of the underworld. **48 ff. Aristotle's profound observation,** in his *Poetics*, IX. The phrase which Arnold quotes from Aristotle means literally "more philosophic and more serious" (than history).

from DISCOURSES IN AMERICA

from Lecture 2: LITERATURE AND SCIENCE

THE question is raised whether, to meet the needs of our modern life, the predominance ought not now to pass from letters to science; and naturally the question is nowhere raised with more energy than here in the United States. The design of abasing what is called "mere literary instruction and education," and of exalting what is called "sound, extensive, and practical scientific knowledge," is, in this intensely modern world of the United States, even more perhaps than in Europe, a very popular design, and makes great and rapid progress.

I am going to ask whether the present movement for ousting letters from their old predominance in education, and for transferring the predominance in education to the natural sciences, whether this brisk and flourishing movement ought to prevail, and whether it is likely that in the end it really will prevail. . . .

Some of you may possibly remember a phrase of mine which has been the object of a good deal of comment; an observation to the effect that in our culture, the aim being *to know ourselves and the world*, we have, as the means to this end, *to know the best which has been thought and said in the world*. A man of science, who is also an excellent writer and the very prince of debaters, Professor Huxley, in a discourse at the opening of Sir Josiah Mason's college at Birmingham, laying hold of this phrase, expanded it by quoting some more words of mine, which are these: "The civilised world is to be regarded as now being, for intellectual and spiritual purposes, one great confederation, bound to a joint action and working to a common result; and whose members have for their proper outfit a knowledge of Greek, Roman, and Eastern antiquity, and of one another. Special local and temporary advantages being put out of account, that modern nation will in the intellectual and spiritual sphere make most progress which most thoroughly carries out this programme."

Now on my phrase, thus enlarged, Professor Huxley remarks that when I speak of the above-mentioned knowledge as enabling us to know ourselves and the world, I assert *literature* to contain the materials which suffice for thus making us know ourselves and the world. But it is not by any means clear, says he, that after having learnt all which ancient and modern literatures have to tell us, we have laid a sufficiently broad and deep foundation for that criticism of life, that knowledge of ourselves and the world, which constitutes culture. On the contrary, Professor Huxley declares that he finds himself "wholly unable to admit that either nations or individuals will really advance, if their outfit draws nothing from the stores of physical science. An army without weapons of precision, and with no particular base of operations, might more hopefully enter upon a campaign on the Rhine, than a man, devoid of a knowledge of what physical science has done in the last century, upon a criticism of life." . . .

But when we talk of knowing Greek and Roman antiquity, for instance, which is the knowledge people have called the humanities, I for my part mean a knowledge which is something more than a superficial humanism, mainly decorative. . . .

When I speak of knowing Greek and Roman antiquity . . . as a help to knowing ourselves and the world, I mean more than a knowledge of so much vocabulary, so much grammar, so many portions of authors in the Greek and Latin languages; I mean knowing the Greeks and Romans, and their life and genius, and what they were and did in the world; what we get from them, and what is its value. . . .

The same also as to knowing our own and other modern nations. . . . To know the best that has been thought and said by the modern nations, is to know, says Professor Huxley, "only what modern *literatures* have to tell us; it is the criticism of life contained in modern literature." And yet "the distinctive character of our times," he urges, "lies in the vast and constantly increasing part which is played by natural knowledge." And how, therefore, can a man, devoid of knowledge of what physical science has done in the last century, enter hopefully upon a criticism of modern life?

Let us, I say, be agreed about the meaning of the terms we are using. I talk of knowing the best which has been thought and uttered in the world; Professor Huxley says this means knowing *literature*. Literature is a large word; it may mean everything written with letters or printed in a book. Euclid's *Elements* and Newton's *Principia* are thus literature. All knowledge that reaches us through books is literature. But by literature Professor Huxley means *belles lettres*. He means to make me say, that knowing the best which has been thought and said by the modern nations is knowing their *belles lettres* and no more. And this is no sufficient equipment, he argues, for a criticism of modern life. But as I do not mean, by knowing ancient Rome, knowing merely more or less of Latin *belles lettres*, and taking no account of Rome's military, and political, and legal, and administrative work in the world; and as, by knowing ancient Greece, I understand knowing her as the giver of Greek art, and the guide to a free and right use of reason and to scientific method, and the founder of our mathematics and physics and astronomy and biology,—I understand knowing her as all this, and not merely knowing certain Greek poems, and histories, and treatises, and speeches,—so as to the knowledge of modern nations also. By knowing modern nations, I mean not merely knowing their *belles lettres*, but knowing also what has been done by such men as Copernicus, Galileo, Newton, Darwin. . . .

4–6. to know ourselves . . . the world. See Arnold's essay on "The Function of Criticism," page 1070. **8–10. Professor Huxley . . . Birmingham.** See pages 1090–1096 for an account of Huxley and his discourse on "Science and Culture."

27–28. Euclid's Elements, of geometry. **28. Newton's Principia,** *Philosophiae Naturalis Principia Mathematica*, **1687,** by Sir Isaac Newton.

There is, therefore, really no question between Professor Huxley and me as to whether knowing the great results of the modern scientific study of nature is not required as part of our culture, as well as knowing the products of literature and art. But to follow the processes by which those results are reached, ought, say the friends of physical science, to be made the staple of education for the bulk of mankind. And here there does arise a question between those whom Professor Huxley calls with playful sarcasm "the Levites of culture," and those whom the poor humanist is sometimes apt to regard as its Nebuchadnezzars.

The great results of the scientific investigation of nature we are agreed upon knowing, but how much of our study are we bound to give to the processes by which those results are reached? The results have their visible bearing on human life. But all the processes, too, all the items of fact, by which those results are reached and established, are interesting. All knowledge is interesting to a wise man, and the knowledge of nature is interesting to all men. It is very interesting to know, that, from the albuminous white of the egg, the chick in the egg gets the materials for its flesh, bones, blood, and feathers; while, from the fatty yolk of the egg, it gets the heat and energy which enable it at length to break its shell and begin the world. It is less interesting, perhaps, but still it is interesting, to know that when a taper burns, the wax is converted into carbonic acid and water. Moreover, it is quite true that the habit of dealing with facts, which is given by the study of nature, is, as the friends of physical science praise it for being, an excellent discipline. The appeal, in the study of nature, is constantly to observation and experiment; not only is it said that the thing is so, but we can be made to see that it is so. Not only does a man tell us that when a taper burns the wax is converted into carbonic acid and water, as a man may tell us, if he likes, that Charon is punting his ferryboat on the river Styx, or that Victor Hugo is a sublime poet, or Mr. Gladstone the most admirable of statesmen; but we are made to see that the conversion into carbonic acid and water does actually happen. This reality of natural knowledge it is, which makes the friends of physical science contrast it, as a knowledge of things, with the humanist's knowledge, which is, say they, a knowledge of words. And hence Professor Huxley is moved to lay it down that, "for the purpose of attaining real culture, an exclusively scientific education is at least as effectual as an exclusively literary education." And a certain President of the Section for Mechanical Science in the British Association is, in Scripture phrase, "very bold," and declares that if a man, in his mental training, "has substituted literature and history for natural science, he has chosen the less useful alternative." But whether we go these lengths or not, we must all admit that in natural science the habit gained of dealing with facts is a most valuable discipline, and that every one should have some experience of it.

More than this, however, is demanded by the reformers. It is proposed to make the training in natural science the main part of education, for the great majority of mankind at any rate. And here, I confess, I part company with the friends of physical science, with whom up to this point I have been agreeing. . . .

All knowledge is, as I said just now, interesting; and even items of knowledge which from the nature of the case cannot well be related, but must stand isolated in our thoughts, have their interest. Even lists of exceptions have their interest. If we are studying Greek accents, it is interesting to know that *pais* and *pas*, and some other monosyllables of the same form of declension, do not take the circumflex upon the last syllable of the genitive plural, but vary, in this respect, from the common rule. If we are studying physiology, it is interesting to know that the pulmonary artery carries dark blood and the pulmonary vein carries bright blood, departing in this respect from the common rule for the division of labour between the veins and the arteries. But every one knows how we seek naturally to combine the pieces of our knowledge together, to bring them under general rules, to relate them to principles; and how unsatisfactory and tiresome it would be to go on for ever learning lists of exceptions, or accumulating items of fact which must stand isolated.

Well, that same need of relating our knowledge, which operates here within the sphere of our knowledge itself, we shall find operating, also, outside that sphere. We experience, as we go on learning and knowing,—the vast majority of us experience,—the need of relating what we have learnt and known to the sense which we have in us for con-

11. Levites, a subordinate rank of the priesthood in ancient Israel. **12. humanist,** one who believes in the study of the humanities, sometimes especially the Greek and Latin classics, and who opposes the doctrinaire. **13. Nebuchadnezzar,** King of Babylonia, who carried the Jews into captivity 597 and 586 B.C. **40. Charon,** in classical mythology the ferryman who carries the souls of the dead across the River Styx. **41. Victor Hugo,** one of the giant figures in French literature (1802–1885). **42. Mr. Gladstone,** William Ewart Gladstone (1809–1898), the most eminent Liberal leader of Victorian England.

duct, to the sense which we have in us for beauty. . . .

But, no doubt, some kinds of knowledge cannot be made to directly serve the instinct in question, cannot be directly related to the sense for beauty, to the sense for conduct. These are instrument-knowledges; they lead on to other knowledges, which can. A man who passes his life in instrument-knowledges is a specialist. They may be invaluable as instruments to something beyond, for those who have the gift thus to employ them; and they may be disciplines in themselves wherein it is useful for every one to have some schooling. But it is inconceivable that the generality of men should pass all their mental life with Greek accents or with formal logic. . . . Of course this is quite consistent with their being of immense importance as an instrument to something else; but it is the few who have the aptitude for thus using them, not the bulk of mankind.

The natural sciences do not, however, stand on the same footing with these instrument-knowledges. Experience shows us that the generality of men will find more interest in learning that, when a taper burns, the wax is converted into carbonic acid and water, or in learning the explanation of the phenomenon of dew, or in learning how the circulation of the blood is carried on, than they find in learning that the genitive plural of *pais* and *pas* does not take the circumflex on the termination. And one piece of natural knowledge is added to another, and others are added to that, and at last we come to propositions so interesting as Mr. Darwin's famous proposition that "our ancestor was a hairy quadruped furnished with a tail and pointed ears, probably arboreal in his habits." . . .

Interesting, indeed, these results of science are, important they are, and we should all of us be acquainted with them. But what I now wish you to mark is, that we are still, when they are propounded to us and we receive them, we are still in the sphere of intellect and knowledge. And for the generality of men there will be found, I say, to arise, when they have duly taken in the proposition that their ancestor was "a hairy quadruped furnished with a tail and pointed ears, probably arboreal in his habits," there will be found to arise an invincible desire to relate this proposition to the sense in us for conduct, and to the sense in us for beauty. But this the men of science will not do for us, and will hardly even profess to do. They will give us other pieces of knowledge, other facts, about other animals and their ancestors, or about plants, or about stones, or about stars; and they may finally bring us to those great "general conceptions of the universe, which are forced upon us all," says Professor Huxley, "by the progress of physical science." But still it will be *knowledge* only which they give us; knowledge not put for us into relation with our sense for conduct, our sense for beauty, and touched with emotion by being so put; not thus put for us, and therefore, to the majority of mankind, after a certain while, unsatisfying, wearying.

Not to the born naturalist, I admit. But what do we mean by a born naturalist? We mean a man in whom the zeal for observing nature is so uncommonly strong and eminent, that it marks him off from the bulk of mankind. Such a man will pass his life happily in collecting natural knowledge and reasoning upon it, and will ask for nothing, or hardly anything, more. I have heard it said that the sagacious and admirable naturalist whom we lost not very long ago, Mr. Darwin, once owned to a friend that for his part he did not experience the necessity for two things which most men find so necessary to them,—religion and poetry; science and the domestic affections, he thought, were enough. To a born naturalist, I can well understand that this should seem so. So absorbing is his occupation with nature, so strong his love for his occupation, that he goes on acquiring natural knowledge and reasoning upon it, and has little time or inclination for thinking about getting it related to the desire in man for conduct, the desire in man for beauty. He relates it to them for himself as he goes along, so far as he feels the need; and he draws from the domestic affections all the additional solace necessary. But then Darwins are extremely rare. Another great and admirable master of natural knowledge, Faraday, was a Sandemanian. That is to say, he related his knowledge to his instinct for conduct and to his instinct for beauty, by the aid of that respectable Scottish sectary, Robert Sandeman. And so strong, in general, is the demand of religion and poetry to have their share in a man, to associate themselves

21–22. Mr. Darwin . . . did not experience. Arnold was misinformed about Darwin's statement. Darwin regretted the loss, for which he blamed himself, of an interest in poetry and the arts. He concluded: "If I had to live my life again, I would have made a rule to read some poetry or listen to some music at least once every week; for perhaps the parts of my brain now atrophied would thus have kept active through use." (See Darwin's autobiography in *Life and Letters of Charles Darwin*, ed. Francis Darwin, I, 81, D. Appleton and Company, 1919.) **37. Faraday,** Michael Faraday (1791–1867), great physicist and chemist. **38. Sandemanian,** a follower of Robert Sandeman (1718–1771); see arts. "Sandeman, Robert" and "Sandemanians, or Glassites," in *New International Encyclopaedia.*

with his knowing, and to relieve and rejoice it, that, probably, for one man amongst us with the disposition to do as Darwin did in this respect, there are at least fifty with the disposition to do as Faraday.

Education lays hold upon us, in fact, by satisfying this demand. Professor Huxley holds up to scorn mediaeval education, with its neglect of the knowledge of nature, its poverty even of literary studies, its formal logic devoted to "showing how and why that which the Church said was true and must be true." But the great mediaeval Universities were not brought into being, we may be sure, by the zeal for giving a jejune and contemptible education. Kings have been their nursing fathers, and queens have been their nursing mothers, but not for this. The mediaeval Universities came into being, because the supposed knowledge, delivered by Scripture and the Church, so deeply engaged men's hearts, by so simply, easily, and powerfully relating itself to their desire for conduct, their desire for beauty. All other knowledge was dominated by this supposed knowledge and was subordinated to it, because of the surpassing strength of the hold which it gained upon the affections of men, by allying itself profoundly with their sense for conduct, their sense for beauty.

But now, says Professor Huxley, conceptions of the universe fatal to the notions held by our forefathers have been forced upon us by physical science. Grant to him that they are thus fatal, that the new conceptions must and will soon become current everywhere, and that every one will finally perceive them to be fatal to the beliefs of our forefathers. The need of humane letters, as they are truly called, because they serve the paramount desire in men that good should be for ever present to them,—the need of humane letters, to establish a relation between the new conceptions, and our instinct for beauty, our instinct for conduct, is only the more visible. The Middle Age could do without humane letters, as it could do without the study of nature, because its supposed knowledge was made to engage its emotions so powerfully. Grant that the supposed knowledge disappears, its power of being made to engage the emotions will of course disappear along with it,—but the emotions themselves, and their claim to be engaged and satisfied, will remain. Now if we find by experience that humane letters have an undeniable power of engaging the emotions, the importance of humane letters in a man's training becomes not less, but greater, in proportion to the success of modern science in extirpating what it calls "mediaeval thinking."

Have humane letters, then, have poetry and eloquence, the power here attributed to them of engaging the emotions, and do they exercise it? And if they have it and exercise it, *how* do they exercise it, so as to exert an influence upon man's sense for conduct, his sense for beauty? Finally, even if they both can and do exert an influence upon the senses in question, how are they to relate to them the results,—the modern results,—of natural science? All these questions may be asked. First, have poetry and eloquence the power of calling out the emotions? The appeal is to experience. Experience shows that for the vast majority of men, for mankind in general, they have the power. Next, do they exercise it? They do. But then, *how* do they exercise it so as to affect man's sense for conduct, his sense for beauty? And this is perhaps a case for applying the Preacher's words: "Though a man labour to seek it out, yet he shall not find it; yea, farther, though a wise man think to know it, yet shall he not be able to find it." Why should it be one thing, in its effect upon the emotions, to say, "Patience is a virtue," and quite another thing, in its effect upon the emotions, to say with Homer,

τλητὸν γὰρ Μοῖραι θυμὸν θέσαν ἀνθρώποισιν.—

"for an enduring heart have the destinies appointed to the children of men"? Why should it be one thing, in its effect upon the emotions, to say with the philosopher Spinoza, *Felicitas in eo consistit quod homo suum esse conservare potest*—"Man's happiness consists in his being able to preserve his own essence," and quite another thing, in its effect upon the emotions, to say with the Gospel, "What is a man advantaged, if he gain the whole world, and lose himself, forfeit himself"? How does this difference of effect arise? I cannot tell, and I am not much concerned to know; the important thing is that it does arise, and that we can profit by it. But how, finally, are poetry and eloquence to exercise the power of relating the modern results of natural science to man's instinct for conduct, his instinct for beauty? And here again I answer that I do not know *how* they will exercise it, but that they can and will exercise it I am sure. I do not mean that modern philosophical poets and modern philosophical moralists are to come and relate for us, in express terms, the results of modern scientific research to our instinct for conduct, our instinct for beauty. But I mean that we shall find, as a matter of experience,

18–21. "Though . . . it." "Ecclesiastes, 8:17." (Arnold) **25.** τλητὸν . . . ἀνθρώποισιν. "Iliad, xxiv, 49." (Arnold) **30–31. "Man's . . . essence,"** quoted from the *Ethics* of Benedict Spinoza (1632–1677.) **33–35. "What . . . self?"** See Luke 9:25.

if we know the best that has been thought and uttered in the world, we shall find that the art and poetry and eloquence of men who lived, perhaps, long ago, who had the most limited natural knowledge, who had the most erroneous conceptions about many important matters, we shall find that this art, and poetry, and eloquence, have in fact not only the power of refreshing and delighting us, they have also the power,—such is the strength and worth, in essentials, of their authors' criticism of life,—they have a fortifying, and elevating, and quickening, and suggestive power, capable of wonderfully helping us to relate the results of modern science to our need for conduct, our need for beauty. Homer's conceptions of the physical universe were, I imagine, grotesque; but really, under the shock of hearing from modern science that "the world is not subordinated to man's use, and that man is not the cynosure of things terrestrial," I could, for my own part, desire no better comfort than Homer's line which I quoted just now,

> τλητὸν γὰρ Μοῖραι θυμὸν θέσαν ἀνθρώποισιν.—

"for an enduring heart have the destinies appointed to the children of men"!

And the more that men's minds are cleared, the more that the results of science are frankly accepted, the more that poetry and eloquence come to be received and studied as what in truth they really are, —the criticism of life by gifted men, alive and active with extraordinary power at an unusual number of points;—so much the more will the value of humane letters, and of art also, which is an utterance having a like kind of power with theirs, be felt and acknowledged, and their place in education be secured.

Let us therefore, all of us, avoid indeed as much as possible any invidious comparison between the merits of humane letters, as means of education, and the merits of the natural sciences. But when some President of a Section for Mechanical Science insists on making the comparison, and tells us that "he who in his training has substituted literature and history for natural science has chosen the less useful alternative," let us make answer to him that the student of humane letters only, will, at least, know also the great general conceptions brought in by modern physical science; for science, as Professor Huxley says, forces them upon us all. But the student of the natural sciences only, will, by our very hypothesis, know nothing of humane letters; not to mention that in setting himself to be perpetually accumulating natural knowledge, he sets himself to do what only specialists have in general the gift for doing genially. And so he will probably be unsatisfied, or at any rate incomplete, and even more incomplete than the student of humane letters only. . . .

If then there is to be separation and option between humane letters on the one hand, and the natural sciences on the other, the great majority of mankind, all who have not exceptional and overpowering aptitudes for the study of nature, would do well, I cannot but think, to choose to be educated in humane letters rather than in the natural sciences. Letters will call out their being at more points, will make them live more. . . .

Thomas Henry Huxley
1825–1895

Thomas Henry Huxley was born at Ealing, May 4, 1825. He studied medicine, went to Australia in 1846 as assistant surgeon on the British naval vessel *Rattlesnake*, and laid the foundation of his fame by his researches on marine animals during this cruise. Not until 1855, however, did the brilliant young scientist find sufficient economic security to make it possible for him to marry.

It would be tedious to enumerate the positions Huxley held as a teacher, the learned societies with which he was connected, the scientific and scholastic honors which came to him, the royal commissions upon which he sat. When *The Origin of Species* appeared in 1859, he was one of the three men upon whose judgment Darwin offered to rest his case. From then on he was "Darwin's Bulldog," devoting much of his energy to defending Darwinism against its opponents, and often carrying the war into the enemy's country.

Huxley championed a scientific as against a classical education (compare Newman, Arnold), yet did not dislike literature and the classics; he accepted some basic materialistic assumptions, but refused to call himself an infidel; he championed evolution, but, unlike Herbert Spencer, could discern no ethical trend in it. He believed "that a deep sense of religion was compatible with the entire absence of theology," and that "the ethical progress of society depends not on imitating the cosmic process, still less in running away from it, but in combating it." He was interested in many "causes," always on the liberal side; like Mill, he was a feminist, and like him he opposed excesses of English imperialism.

In 1876 Huxley came to the United States to deliver an address at the opening of the Johns Hopkins University in Baltimore. His "Science and Morals" was published in 1886, his "Ethics and Evolution" in 1893. He died in London on June 29, 1895.

Huxley's style, whatever his subject, and whether he is speaking or writing, is always clear and forthright. Scientific facts and theories have perhaps never had such lucid exposition, and even readers who find themselves unable to accept his premises or conclusions cannot fail to admire the clarity, felicity, and courteous manner of his essays and addresses. His grandson, Aldous Huxley, gives an interesting analysis of his style in his essay "T. H. Huxley as a Literary Man," in *The Huxley Memorial Lectures, 1925–1932*, Macmillan, 1932.

Among Huxley's works are *Evidence as to Man's Place in Nature*, 1863; *Lay Sermons, Addresses, and Reviews*, 1870; *Science and Culture*, 1881; *Science and Morals*, 1886; *Ethics and Evolution*, 1893; and his *Autobiography*, 1889. The two sections that follow give (1) his outline sketch of his early life, and (2) one of his most significant utterances on education.

from SCIENCE AND EDUCATION[1]

SCIENCE AND CULTURE

FROM the time that the first suggestion to introduce physical science into ordinary education was timidly whispered, until now, the advocates of scientific education have met with opposition of two kinds. On the one hand, they have been pooh-poohed by the men of business who pride themselves on being the representatives of practicality; while, on the other hand, they have been excommunicated by the classical scholars, in their capacity of Levites in charge of the ark of culture and monopolists of liberal education.

The practical men believed that the idol whom they worship—rule of thumb—has been the source of the past prosperity, and will suffice for the future welfare of the arts and manufactures. They are of opinion that science is speculative rubbish; that theory and practice have nothing to do with one another; and that the scientific habit of mind is an impediment, rather than an aid, in the conduct of ordinary affairs.

I have used the past tense in speaking of the practical men—for although they were very formidable thirty years ago, I am not sure that the pure species has not been extirpated. In fact, so far as mere argument goes, they have been subjected to such a

[1] By Thomas Henry Huxley, reprinted by permission of D. Appleton-Century Company, Inc. **10. Levites in charge of the ark of culture.** Huxley's reference is to Matthew Arnold; see Arnold's "Literature and Science" in this volume. For the Biblical reference, see Joshua 6 and art. "Priests and Levites" in Hastings's *Dictionary of the Bible.*

feu d'enfer that it is a miracle if any have escaped. But I have remarked that your typical practical man has an unexpected resemblance to one of Milton's angels. His spiritual wounds, such as are inflicted by logical weapons, may be as deep as a well and as wide as a church door, but beyond shedding a few drops of ichor, celestial or otherwise, he is no whit the worse. So, if any of these opponents be left, I will not waste time in vain repetition of the demonstrative evidence of the practical value of science; but knowing that a parable will sometimes penetrate where syllogisms fail to effect an entrance, I will offer a story for their consideration.

Once upon a time, a boy, with nothing to depend upon but his own vigorous nature, was thrown into the thick of the struggle for existence in the midst of a great manufacturing population. He seems to have had a hard fight, inasmuch as, by the time he was thirty years of age, his total disposable funds amounted to twenty pounds. Nevertheless, middle life found him giving proof of his comprehension of the practical problems he had been roughly called upon to solve, by a career of remarkable prosperity.

Finally, having reached old age with its well-earned surroundings of "honour, troops of friends," the hero of my story bethought himself of those who were making a like start in life, and how he could stretch out a helping hand to them.

After long and anxious reflection this successful practical man of business could devise nothing better than to provide them with the means of obtaining "sound, extensive, and practical scientific knowledge." And he devoted a large part of his wealth and five years of incessant work to this end.

I need not point the moral of a tale which, as the solid and spacious fabric of the Scientific College assures us, is no fable, nor can anything which I could say intensify the force of this practical answer to practical objections.

We may take it for granted then, that, in the opinion of those best qualified to judge, the diffusion of thorough scientific education is an absolutely essential condition of industrial progress; and that the College which has been opened today will confer an inestimable boon upon those whose livelihood is to be gained by the practice of the arts and manufactures of the district.

The only question worth discussion is, whether the conditions, under which the work of the College is to be carried out, are such as to give it the best possible chance of achieving permanent success.

Sir Josiah Mason, without doubt most wisely, has left very large freedom of action to the trustees, to whom he proposes ultimately to commit the administration of the College, so that they may be able to adjust its arrangements in accordance with the changing conditions of the future. But, with respect to three points, he has laid most explicit injunctions upon both administrators and teachers.

Party politics are forbidden to enter into the minds of either, so far as the work of the College is concerned; theology is as sternly banished from its precincts; and finally, it is especially declared that the College shall make no provision for "mere literary instruction and education."

It does not concern me at present to dwell upon the first two injunctions any longer than may be needful to express my full conviction of their wisdom. But the third prohibition brings us face to face with those other opponents of scientific education, who are by no means in the moribund condition of the practical man, but alive, alert, and formidable.

It is not impossible that we shall hear this express exclusion of "literary instruction and education" from a College which, nevertheless, professes to give a high and efficient education, sharply criticised. Certainly the time was that the Levites of culture would have sounded their trumpets against its walls as against an educational Jericho.

How often have we not been told that the study of physical science is incompetent to confer culture; that it touches none of the higher problems of life; and, what is worse, that the continual devotion to scientific studies tends to generate a narrow and bigoted belief in the applicability of scientific methods to the search after truth of all kinds! How frequently one has reason to observe that no reply to a troublesome argument tells so well as calling its author a "mere scientific specialist." And, as I am afraid it is not permissible to speak of this form of opposition to scientific education in the past tense, may we not expect to be told that this, not only omission, but prohibition, of "mere literary instruction and education" is a patent example of scientific narrow-mindedness?

I am not acquainted with Sir Josiah Mason's reasons for the action which he has taken; but if, as I apprehend is the case, he refers to the ordinary classical course of our schools and universities by the name of "mere literary instruction and education," I venture to offer sundry reasons of my own in support of that action.

1. feu d'enfer, hell-fire; an artillery term meaning heavy gunfire. **4–8. spiritual wounds . . . the worse.** See *Paradise Lost*, Book VI, ll. 327–53. **14. a boy,** Josiah Mason (1795–1881), founder of the Scientific College in Birmingham at whose opening Huxley delivered this address.

30. Jericho. See Judges 6.

For I hold very strongly by two convictions:—The first is, that neither the discipline nor the subject-matter of classical education is of such direct value to the student of physical science as to justify the expenditure of valuable time upon either; and the second is, that for the purpose of attaining real culture, an exclusively scientific education is at least as effectual as an exclusively literary education.

I need hardly point out to you that these opinions, especially the latter, are diametrically opposed to those of the great majority of educated Englishmen, influenced as they are by school and university traditions. In their belief, culture is obtainable only by a liberal education; and a liberal education is synonymous, not merely with education and instruction in literature, but in one particular form of literature, namely, that of Greek and Roman antiquity. They hold that the man who has learned Latin and Greek, however little, is educated; while he who is versed in other branches of knowledge, however deeply, is a more or less respectable specialist, not admissible into the cultured caste. The stamp of the educated man, the University degree, is not for him.

I am too well acquainted with the generous catholicity of spirit, the true sympathy with scientific thought, which pervades the writings of our chief apostle of culture to identify him with these opinions; and yet one may cull from one and another of those epistles to the Philistines, which so much delight all who do not answer to that name, sentences which lend them some support.

Mr. Arnold tells us that the meaning of culture is "to know the best that has been thought and said in the world." It is the criticism of life contained in literature. That criticism regards "Europe as being, for intellectual and spiritual purposes, one great confederation, bound to a joint action and working to a common result; and whose members have, for their common outfit, a knowledge of Greek, Roman, and Eastern antiquity, and of one another. Special local and temporary advantages being put out of account, that modern nation will in the intellectual and spiritual sphere make most progress which most thoroughly carries out this programme. And what is that but saying that we too, all of us, as individuals, the more thoroughly we carry it out, shall make the more progress?"

We have here to deal with two distinct propositions. The first, that a criticism of life is the essence of culture; the second, that literature contains the materials which suffice for the construction of such criticism.

I think that we must all assent to the first proposition. For culture certainly means something quite different from learning or technical skill. It implies the possession of an ideal, and the habit of critically estimating the value of things by comparison with a theoretic standard. Perfect culture should supply a complete theory of life, based upon a clear knowledge alike of its possibilities and of its limitations.

But we may agree to all this, and yet strongly dissent from the assumption that literature alone is competent to supply this knowledge. After having learnt all that Greek, Roman, and Eastern antiquity have thought and said, and all that modern literature have to tell us, it is not self-evident that we have laid a sufficiently broad and deep foundation for that criticism of life which constitutes culture.

Indeed, to any one acquainted with the scope of physical science, it is not at all evident. Considering progress only in the "intellectual and spiritual sphere," I find myself wholly unable to admit that either nations or individuals will really advance, if their common outfit draws nothing from the stores of physical science. I should say that an army, without weapons of precision and with no particular base of operations, might more hopefully enter upon a campaign on the Rhine, than a man, devoid of a knowledge of what physical science has done in the last century, upon a criticism of life.

When a biologist meets with an anomaly, he instinctively turns to the study of development to clear it up. The rationale of contradictory opinions may with equal confidence be sought in history.

It is, happily, no new thing that Englishmen should employ their wealth in building and endowing institutions for educational purposes. But, five or six hundred years ago, deeds of foundation expressed or implied conditions as nearly as possible contrary to those which have been thought expedient by Sir Josiah Mason. That is to say, physical science was practically ignored, while a certain literary training was enjoined as a means to the acquirement of knowledge which was essentially theological.

The reason of this singular contradiction between the actions of men alike animated by a strong and disinterested desire to promote the welfare of their fellows, is easily discovered.

At that time, in fact, if any one desired knowledge beyond such as could be obtained by his own obser-

28. apostle of culture, Arnold. **33–48. Mr. Arnold . . . progress?"** Both the quotations in this paragraph are from Arnold's essay on "The Function of Criticism at the Present Time," which is included in this volume.

vation, or by common conversation, his first necessity was to learn the Latin language, inasmuch as all the higher knowledge of the western world was contained in works written in that language. Hence, Latin grammar, with logic and rhetoric, studied through Latin, were the fundamentals of education. With respect to the substance of the knowledge imparted through this channel, the Jewish and Christian Scriptures, as interpreted and supplemented by the Romish Church, were held to contain a complete and infallibly true body of information.

Theological dicta were, to the thinkers of those days, that which the axioms and definitions of Euclid are to the geometers of these. The business of the philosophers of the Middle Ages was to deduce from the data furnished by the theologians, conclusions in accordance with ecclesiastical decrees. They were allowed the high privilege of showing, by logical process, how and why that which the Church said was true, must be true. And if their demonstrations fell short of or exceeded this limit, the Church was maternally ready to check their aberrations; if need were by the help of the secular arm.

Between the two, our ancestors were furnished with a compact and complete criticism of life. They were told how the world began and how it would end; they learned that all material existence was but a base and insignificant blot upon the fair face of the spiritual world, and that nature was, to all intents and purposes, the play-ground of the devil; they learned that the earth is the centre of the visible universe, and that man is the cynosure of things terrestrial; and more especially was it inculcated that the course of nature had no fixed order, but that it could be, and constantly was, altered by the agency of innumerable spiritual beings, good and bad, according as they were moved by the deeds and prayers of men. The sum and substance of the whole doctrine was to produce the conviction that the only thing really worth knowing in this world was how to secure that place in a better which, under certain conditions, the Church promised.

Our ancestors had a living belief in this theory of life, and acted upon it in their dealings with education, as in all other matters. Culture meant saintliness—after the fashion of the saints of those days; the education that led to it was, of necessity, theological; and the way to theology lay through Latin.

That the study of nature—further than was requisite for the satisfaction of everyday wants—should have any bearing on human life was far from the thoughts of men thus trained. Indeed, as nature had been cursed for man's sake, it was an obvious conclusion that those who meddled with nature were likely to come into pretty close contact with Satan. And, if any born scientific investigator followed his instincts, he might safely reckon upon earning the reputation, and probably upon suffering the fate, of a sorcerer.

Had the western world been left to itself in Chinese isolation, there is no saying how long this state of things might have endured. But, happily, it was not left to itself. Even earlier than the thirteenth century, the development of Moorish civilisation in Spain and the great movement of the Crusades had introduced the leaven which, from that day to this, has never ceased to work. At first, through the intermediation of Arabic translations, afterwards by the study of the originals, the western nations of Europe became acquainted with the writings of the ancient philosophers and poets, and, in time, with the whole of the vast literature of antiquity.

Whatever there was of high intellectual aspiration or dominant capacity in Italy, France, Germany, and England, spent itself for centuries in taking possession of the rich inheritance left by the dead civilisations of Greece and Rome. Marvellously aided by the invention of printing, classical learning spread and flourished. Those who possessed it prided themselves on having attained the highest culture then within the reach of mankind.

And justly. For, saving Dante on his solitary pinnacle, there was no figure in modern literature at the time of the Renascence to compare with the men of antiquity; there was no art to compete with their sculpture; there was no physical science but that which Greece had created. Above all, there was no other example of perfect intellectual freedom—of the unhesitating acceptance of reason as the sole guide to truth and the supreme arbiter of conduct.

The new learning necessarily soon exerted a profound influence upon education. The language of the monks and schoolmen seemed little better than gibberish to scholars fresh from Virgil and Cicero, and the study of Latin was placed upon a new foundation. Moreover, Latin itself ceased to afford the sole key to knowledge. The student who sought the highest thought of antiquity, found only a second-hand reflection of it in Roman literature, and turned his face to the full light of the Greeks. And after a battle, not altogether dissimilar to that which is at present being fought over the teaching of physical science, the study of Greek was recog-

1. as nature . . . sake. See Genesis 3:17. **32. Renascence,** the great revival of learning referred to in the preceding paragraphs.

nised as an essential element of all higher education.

Then the Humanists, as they were called, won the day; and the great reform which they effected was of incalculable service to mankind. But the Nemesis of all reformers is finality; and the reformers of education, like those of religion, fell into the profound, however common, error of mistaking the beginning for the end of the work of reformation.

The representatives of the Humanists, in the nineteenth century, take their stand upon classical education as the sole avenue to culture, as firmly as if we were still in the age of Renascence. Yet, surely, the present intellectual relations of the modern and the ancient worlds are profoundly different from those which obtained three centuries ago. Leaving aside the existence of a great and characteristically modern literature, of modern painting, and, especially, of modern music, there is one feature of the present state of the civilised world which separates it more widely from the Renascence, than the Renascence was separated from the middle ages.

This distinctive character of our own times lies in the vast and constantly increasing part which is played by natural knowledge. Not only is our daily life shaped by it, not only does the prosperity of millions of men depend upon it, but our whole theory of life has long been influenced, consciously or unconsciously, by the general conceptions of the universe, which have been forced upon us by physical science.

In fact, the most elementary acquaintance with the results of scientific investigation shows us that they offer a broad and striking contradiction to the opinion so implicitly credited and taught in the middle ages.

The notions of the beginning and the end of the world entertained by our forefathers are no longer credible. It is very certain that the earth is not the chief body in the material universe, and that the world is not subordinated to man's use. It is even more certain that nature is the expression of a definite order with which nothing interferes, and that the chief business of mankind is to learn that order and govern themselves accordingly. Moreover this scientific "criticism of life" presents itself to us with different credentials from any other. It appeals not to authority, nor to what anybody may have thought or said, but to nature. It admits that all our interpretations of natural fact are more or less imperfect and symbolic, and bids the learner seek for truth not among words but among things. It warns us that the assertion which outstrips evidence is not only a blunder but a crime.

The purely classical education advocated by the representatives of the Humanists in our day gives no inkling of all this. A man may be a better scholar than Erasmus, and know no more of the chief causes of the present intellectual fermentation than Erasmus did. Scholarly and pious persons, worthy of all respect, favour us with allocutions upon the sadness of the antagonism of science to their mediaeval way of thinking, which betray an ignorance of the first principles of scientific investigation, an incapacity for understanding what a man of science means by veracity, and an unconsciousness of the weight of established scientific truths, which is almost comical.

There is no great force in the *tu quoque* argument, or else the advocates of scientific education might fairly enough retort upon the modern Humanists that they may be learned specialists, but that they possess no such sound foundation for a criticism of life as deserves the name of culture. And, indeed, if we were disposed to be cruel, we might urge that the Humanists have brought this reproach upon themselves, not because they are too full of the spirit of the ancient Greek, but because they lack it.

The period of the Renascence is commonly called that of the "Revival of Letters," as if the influences then brought to bear upon the mind of Western Europe had been wholly exhausted in the field of literature. I think it is very commonly forgotten that the revival of science, effected by the same agency, although less conspicuous, was not less momentous.

In fact, the few and scattered students of nature of that day picked up the clue to her secrets exactly as it fell from the hands of the Greeks a thousand years before. The foundations of mathematics were so well laid by them, that our children learn their geometry from a book written for the schools of Alexandria two thousand years ago. Modern astronomy is the natural continuation and development of the work of Hipparchus and of Ptolemy; modern physics of that of Democritus and of Archimedes; it was long before modern biological science outgrew the knowledge bequeathed to us by Aristotle, by Theophrastus, and by Galen.

4. Erasmus, the great Dutch scholar (c. 1466–1536), author of *The Praise of Folly*, a reformer who refused to leave the Church with the Protestants. **15. tu quoque.** "So are you!" **38–39. a book . . . ago.** Euclid's *Elements* (of geometry). **41. Hipparchus,** Greek astronomer (c. 160–c. 125 B.C.). **Ptolemy,** Greco-Egyptian astronomer (second century A.D.). **42–43. Democritus,** Greek natural philosopher (c. 460–c. 362 B.C.). **Archimedes,** Greek mathematician (c. 287–212 B.C.). **45. Theophrastus,** Greek philosopher and botanist (died c. 287 B.C). **Galen,** Greek physician (130–c. 200), long recognized as an authority on medicine.

We cannot know all the best thoughts and sayings of the Greeks unless we know what they thought about natural phenomena. We cannot fully apprehend their criticism of life unless we understand the extent to which that criticism was affected by scientific conceptions. We falsely pretend to be the inheritors of their culture, unless we are penetrated, as the best minds among them were, with an unhesitating faith that the free employment of reason, in accordance with scientific method, is the sole method of reaching truth.

Thus I venture to think that the pretensions of our modern Humanists to the possession of the monopoly of culture and to the exclusive inheritance of the spirit of antiquity must be abated, if not abandoned. But I should be very sorry that anything I have said should be taken to imply a desire on my part to depreciate the value of classical education, as it might be and as it sometimes is. The native capacities of mankind vary no less than their opportunities; and while culture is one, the road by which one man may best reach it is widely different from that which is most advantageous to another. Again, while scientific education is yet inchoate and tentative, classical education is thoroughly well organised upon the practical experience of generations of teachers. So that, given ample time for learning and estimation for ordinary life, or for a literary career, I do not think that a young Englishman in search of culture can do better than follow the course usually marked out for him, supplementing its deficiencies by his own efforts.

But for those who mean to make science their serious occupation; or who intend to follow the profession of medicine; or who have to enter early upon the business of life; for all these, in my opinion, classical education is a mistake; and it is for this reason that I am glad to see "mere literary education and instruction" shut out from the curriculum of Sir Josiah Mason's College, seeing that its inclusion would probably lead to the introduction of the ordinary smattering of Latin and Greek.

Nevertheless, I am the last person to question the importance of genuine literary education, or to suppose that intellectual culture can be complete without it. An exclusively scientific training will bring about a mental twist as surely as an exclusively literary training. The value of the cargo does not compensate for a ship's being out of trim; and I should be very sorry to think that the Scientific College would turn out none but lopsided men.

There is no need, however, that such a catastrophe should happen. Instruction in English, French, and German is provided, and thus the three greatest literatures of the modern world are made accessible to the student.

French and German, and especially the latter language, are absolutely indispensable to those who desire full knowledge in any department of science. But even supposing that the knowledge of these languages acquired is not more than sufficient for purely scientific purposes, every Englishman has, in his native tongue, an almost perfect instrument of literary expression; and, in his own literature, models of every kind of literary excellence. If an Englishman cannot get literary culture out of his Bible, his Shakespeare, his Milton, neither, in my belief, will the profoundest study of Homer and Sophocles, Virgil and Horace, give it to him.

Thus, since the constitution of the College makes sufficient provision for literary as well as for scientific education, and since artistic instruction is also contemplated, it seems to me that a fairly complete culture is offered to all who are willing to take advantage of it.

But I am not sure that at this point the "practical" man, scotched but not slain, may ask what all this talk about culture has to do with an Institution, the object of which is defined to be "to promote the prosperity of the manufactures and the industry of the country." He may suggest that what is wanted for this end is not culture, nor even a purely scientific discipline, but simply a knowledge of applied science.

I often wish that this phrase, "applied science," had never been invented. For it suggests that there is a sort of scientific knowledge of direct practical use, which can be studied apart from another sort of scientific knowledge, which is of no practical utility, and which is termed "pure science." But there is no more complete fallacy than this. What people call applied science is nothing but the application of pure science to particular classes of problems. It consists of deductions from those general principles, established by reasoning and observation, which constitute pure science. No one can safely make these deductions until he has a firm grasp of the principles; and he can obtain that grasp only by personal experience of the operations of observation and of reasoning on which they are founded.

Almost all the processes employed in the arts and manufactures fall within the range either of physics or of chemistry. In order to improve them, one must thoroughly understand them; and no one has a

23. scotched, slashed. Cf. *Macbeth*, Act III, sc. 2, ll. 13–14.

We have scotched the snake, not killed it.
She'll close, and be herself.

chance of really understanding them, unless he has obtained that mastery of principles and that habit of dealing with facts, which is given by long-continued and well-directed purely scientific training in the physical and the chemical laboratory. So that there really is no question as to the necessity of purely scientific discipline, even if the work of the College were limited by the narrowest interpretation of its stated aims.

And, as to the desirableness of a wider culture than that yielded by science alone, it is to be recollected that the improvement of manufacturing processes is only one of the conditions which contribute to the prosperity of industry. Industry is a means and not an end; and mankind work only to get something which they want. What that something is depends partly on their innate, and partly on their acquired, desires.

If the wealth resulting from prosperous industry is to be spent upon the gratification of unworthy desires, if the increasing perfection of manufacturing processes is to be accompanied by an increasing debasement of those who carry them on, I do not see the good of industry and prosperity.

Now it is perfectly true that men's views of what is desirable depend upon their characters; and that the innate proclivities to which we give that name are not touched by any amount of instruction. But it does not follow that even mere intellectual education may not, to an indefinite extent, modify the practical manifestation of the characters of men in their actions, by supplying them with motives unknown to the ignorant. A pleasure-loving character will have pleasure of some sort; but, if you give him the choice, he may prefer pleasures which do not degrade him to those which do. And this choice is offered to every man, who possesses in literary or artistic culture a never-failing source of pleasures, which are neither withered by age, nor staled by custom, nor embittered in the recollection by the pangs of self-reproach.

If the Institution opened today fulfils the intention of its founder, the picked intelligences among all classes of the population of this district will pass through it. No child born in Birmingham, henceforward, if he have the capacity to profit by the opportunities offered to him, first in the primary and other schools, and afterwards in the Scientific College, need fail to obtain, not merely the instruction, but the culture most appropriate to the conditions of his life.

39–40. neither . . . custom. See Shakespeare's *Antony and Cleopatra*, Act II, sc. 2, ll. 240–41.

Within these walls, the future employer and the future artisan may sojourn together for a while, and carry, through all their lives, the stamp of the influences then brought to bear upon them. Hence, it is not beside the mark to remind you, that the prosperity of industry depends not merely upon the improvement of manufacturing processes, not merely upon the ennobling of the individual character, but upon a third condition, namely, a clear understanding of the conditions of social life, on the part of both the capitalist and the operative, and their agreement upon common principles of social action. They must learn that social phenomena are as much the expression of natural laws as any others; that no social arrangements can be permanent unless they harmonise with the requirements of social statics and dynamics; and that, in the nature of things, there is an arbiter whose decisions execute themselves.

But this knowledge is only to be obtained by the application of the methods of investigation adopted in physical researches to the investigation of the phenomena of society. Hence, I confess, I should like to see one addition made to the excellent scheme of education propounded for the College, in the shape of provision for the teaching of Sociology. For though we are all agreed that party politics are to have no place in the instruction of the College; yet in this country, practically governed as it is now by universal suffrage, every man who does his duty must exercise political functions. And, if the evils which are inseparable from the good of political liberty are to be checked, if the perpetual oscillation of nations between anarchy and despotism is to be replaced by the steady march of self-restraining freedom; it will be because men will gradually bring themselves to deal with political, as they now deal with scientific questions; to be as ashamed of undue haste and partisan prejudice in the one case as in the other; and to believe that the machinery of society is at least as delicate as that of a spinning-jenny, and as little likely to be improved by the meddling of those who have not taken the trouble to master the principles of its action.

In conclusion, I am sure that I make myself the mouthpiece of all present in offering to the venerable founder of the Institution, which now commences its beneficent career, our congratulations on the completion of his work; and in expressing the conviction, that the remotest posterity will point to it as a crucial instance of the wisdom which natural piety leads all men to ascribe to their ancestors.

Dante Gabriel Rossetti
1828–1882

Dante Gabriel Rossetti, poet and painter, was born in London, May 12, 1828, the son of an exiled Italian poet, patriot, and lover of liberty who became a professor in King's College, London; his mother was the high-minded daughter of an English mother and an Italian father. Dante Gabriel had a younger brother, William Michael, who gained distinction as editor and critic of art, and a younger sister, Christina, who became one of England's chief women poets.

Rossetti's talents budded early. As a small child he wrote a drama and made pictures for *King Henry VI* and the *Iliad; Hamlet* and Scott's novels were among his literary passions. But he was impatient of formal instruction. His dislike of the "moral" atmosphere and the rough games at King's College School combined with his lack of interest in the curriculum to cause him to leave the school and take up the study of painting. After a short period at Cary's Art Museum he began his studies at the Royal Academy in 1846, but, finding it too conventional, he left the Academy also. In 1848, at the age of twenty, he became a pupil of the artist Ford Madox Brown.

Rossetti's dissatisfaction with academic and conventional standards in art led him to found in 1849 the Pre-Raphaelite Brotherhood, a group consisting at first of himself and two other young painters, John Everett Millais and Holman Hunt. His friend and instructor Brown was attracted and influenced by the Brotherhood although he never joined it. Rossetti's sister and brother, Christina and William Michael, and also William Morris, Swinburne, Ruskin, and Edward Burne-Jones were later connected, in one way or another, with the movement. In January, 1850, the Pre-Raphaelite Brotherhood established a magazine, *The Germ*, of which only four numbers were published. The little magazine set forth the artistic theories of the Brotherhood and contained poems and sketches by the members. Rossetti's "The Blessed Damozel," "My Sister's Sleep," and several others of his best lyrics, as well as his prose tale, "Hand and Soul," were first published in *The Germ.*

The aim of the Pre-Raphaelite Brotherhood was "to divest art of conventionality, to work with sincerity of purpose, to reproduce with fidelity." They took their name from the conviction that painting had declined since Raphael; to achieve sincerity and spontaneity one must stop imitating Raphael and return to the painters who preceded him, the men who created the beautiful frescoes at the Campo Santo in Pisa and who went to life itself for their inspiration. Most Englishmen quite failed to perceive any gleams of mystical idealism in these notions. Dickens, for example, attacked the Brotherhood furiously for its realism, although the Pre-Raphaelites were never interested in realism for its own sake. Ruskin, on the other hand, rushed to their defense. The battle was one of the hottest waged on any artistic front in Victoria's time, and during its course the Pre-Raphaelites had to give ground. Hunt was the only member of the band who remained permanently loyal to the original program. After the Brotherhood had disbanded in 1852, Millais became a member of the hated Royal Academy. But short-lived as it was, the movement made an impression on English painting and poetry. It may fairly be maintained that the members of the Brotherhood found Victorian art at its lowest and restored its soul.

In 1850 Rossetti fell in love with Elizabeth Siddal, a milliner's assistant who had become the favorite model of the Pre-Raphaelites, a girl of some talent both in painting and writing. Elizabeth's ill health and the poet's lack of money delayed their marriage until 1860. In 1861 Mrs. Rossetti was delivered of a stillborn child, and her frail health was permanently shattered. When she died in 1862 of an overdose of laudanum, in his grief and remorse Rossetti buried the manuscript of his unpublished poems with her. Some years later the manuscript was exhumed and from it Rossetti's second volume, *Poems*, was published in 1870. Included were some of the series of sonnets entitled *The House of Life*.

Rossetti's own health declined rapidly after his wife's death. Failing eyesight, hypochondria, and insomnia racked him. To avoid insomnia, he began the use of chloral, and his last days were spent in unhappy seclusion. He was a poet to the end, and among his last compositions were such works as "The Ballad of the White Ship," "Rose Mary," and "The King's Tragedy." His final volume,

Ballads and Sonnets, appeared in 1881, a year before his death.

Rossetti is matchless in his combination of melody, sonority, and color. Much of his poetry breathes also the strange beauty, half spiritual, half sensuous, that distinguishes his painting. There are times when the poet is too exactly the painter, when the very particularity of detail and wealth of color produce an overelaborate effect. But Rossetti's best poems are unusually rich in appeal to the imagination. Some critics, searching for a term to describe Rossetti's fervent devotion to beauty in both its spiritual and its physical aspects, have resorted to the word "mysticism." Yet Rossetti was never a mystic in the true religious sense, for emotional realization and aesthetic delight came first in his artistic creed. The passionate directness of his poetry and its brave affirmation of the validity of the individual experience are perhaps his most precious contributions to the temper of English literature.

THE BLESSED DAMOZEL

"The Blessed Damozel" was suggested by Edgar Allan Poe's "The Raven." "I saw," said Rossetti, "that Poe had done the utmost it was possible to do with the grief of the lover on earth, and I determined to reverse the conditions, and give utterance to the yearning of the loved one in heaven." Debussy composed a setting of "The Blessed Damozel" for female voices and orchestra, after the French text by Gabriel Sarrazin.

The blessed damozel leaned out
  From the gold bar of Heaven;
Her eyes were deeper than the depth
  Of waters stilled at even;
She had three lilies in her hand,
  And the stars in her hair were seven.

Her robe, ungirt from clasp to hem,
  No wrought flowers did adorn,
But a white rose of Mary's gift,
  For service meetly worn;
Her hair that lay along her back
  Was yellow like ripe corn.

Herseemed she scarce had been a day
  One of God's choristers;
The wonder was not yet quite gone
  From that still look of hers;
Albeit, to them she left, her day
  Had counted as ten years.

(To one, it is ten years of years.
  . . . Yet now, and in this place,
Surely she leaned o'er me—her hair
  Fell all about my face. . . .
Nothing: the autumn fall of leaves.
  The whole year sets apace.)

It was the rampart of God's house
  That she was standing on;
By God built over the sheer depth
  The which is Space begun;
So high, that looking downward thence
  She scarce could see the sun.

It lies in Heaven, across the flood
  Of ether, as a bridge.
Beneath, the tides of day and night
  With flame and darkness ridge
The void, as low as where this earth
  Spins like a fretful midge.

Around her, lovers, newly met
  'Mid deathless love's acclaims,
Spoke evermore among themselves
  Their heart-remembered names;
And the souls mounting up to God
  Went by her like thin flames.

And still she bowed herself and stooped
  Out of the circling charm;
Until her bosom must have made
  The bar she leaned on warm,
And the lilies lay as if asleep
  Along her bended arm.

From the fixed place of Heaven she saw
  Time like a pulse shake fierce
Through all the worlds. Her gaze still strove
  Within the gulf to pierce
Its path; and now she spoke as when
  The stars sang in their spheres.

The sun was gone now; the curled moon
  Was like a little feather

10. For . . . worn, suitably worn while serving the Blessed Virgin.

19–24. (To . . . apace.) Here, and elsewhere in the poem, parentheses are used to indicate the shift to the viewpoint of the lover on earth. **54. The stars . . . spheres.** According to the Ptolemaic astronomy, the stars and planets make music as they move about the earth in their concentric spheres. See Job 38:7; *The Merchant of Venice*, Act V, sc. 1, ll. 60–65.

Fluttering far down the gulf; and now
  She spoke through the still weather.
Her voice was like the voice the stars
  Had when they sang together.

(Ah sweet! Even now, in that bird's song,
  Strove not her accents there,
Fain to be hearkened? When those bells
  Possessed the mid-day air,
Strove not her steps to reach my side
  Down all the echoing stair?)

"I wish that he were come to me,
  For he will come," she said.
"Have I not prayed in Heaven?—on earth,
  Lord, Lord, has he not prayed?
Are not two prayers a perfect strength?
  And shall I feel afraid?

"When round his head the aureole clings,
  And he is clothed in white,
I'll take his hand and go with him
  To the deep wells of light;
As unto a stream we will step down,
  And bathe there in God's sight.

"We two will stand beside that shrine,
  Occult, withheld, untrod,
Whose lamps are stirred continually
  With prayer sent up to God;
And see our old prayers, granted, melt
  Each like a little cloud.

"We two will lie i' the shadow of
  That living mystic tree
Within whose secret growth the Dove
  Is sometimes felt to be,
While every leaf that His plumes touch
  Saith His Name audibly.

"And I myself will teach to him,
  I myself, lying so,
The songs I sing here; which his voice
  Shall pause in, hushed and slow,
And find some knowledge at each pause,
  Or some new thing to know."

(Alas! We two, we two, thou say'st!
  Yea, one wast thou with me
That once of old. But shall God lift
  To endless unity
The soul whose likeness with thy soul
  Was but its love for thee?)

"We two," she said, "will seek the groves
  Where the lady Mary is,
With her five handmaidens, whose names
  Are five sweet symphonies,
Cecily, Gertrude, Magdalen,
  Margaret and Rosalys.

"Circlewise sit they, with bound locks
  And foreheads garlanded;
Into the fine cloth white like flame
  Weaving the golden thread,
To fashion the birth-robes for them
  Who are just born, being dead.

"He shall fear, haply, and be dumb:
  Then will I lay my cheek
To his, and tell about our love,
  Not once abashed or weak:
And the dear Mother will approve
  My pride, and let me speak.

"Herself shall bring us, hand in hand,
  To Him round whom all souls
Kneel, the clear-ranged unnumbered heads
  Bowed with their aureoles:
And angels meeting us shall sing
  To their citherns and citoles.

"There will I ask of Christ the Lord
  Thus much for him and me:—
Only to live as once on earth
  With Love,—only to be,
As then awhile, for ever now
  Together, I and he."

She gazed and listened and then said,
  Less sad of speech than mild,—
"All this is when he comes." She ceased.
  The light thrilled towards her, filled
With angels in strong level flight.
  Her eyes prayed, and she smiled.

(I saw her smile.) But soon their path
  Was vague in distant spheres:
And then she cast her arms along
  The golden barriers,
And laid her face between her hands,
  And wept. (I heard her tears.)

86. That living mystic tree. See Revelation 22:2. **87. Dove,** the Holy Spirit. See Luke 3:22.

107–08. Cecily . . . Rosalys, five saints. **112. golden thread,** used in weaving in England as far back as Anglo-Saxon times. Rossetti gives it symbolic religious significance.

SISTER HELEN

This story of black magic is based on the old belief that a person may be injured by what is done to his image. The custom of hanging in effigy originated in this belief, and the primitive fear of having one's features copied or photographed is closely connected with it. An interesting literary parallel is Susan Nunsuch's treatment of Eustacia Vye in *The Return of the Native* by Thomas Hardy.

"Why did you melt your waxen man,
Sister Helen?
To-day is the third since you began."
"The time was long, yet the time ran,
Little brother."
(*O Mother, Mary Mother,*
Three days to-day, between Hell and Heaven!)

"But if you have done your work aright,
Sister Helen,
You'll let me play, for you said I might."
"Be very still in your play to-night,
Little brother."
(*O Mother, Mary Mother,*
Third night, to-night, between Hell and Heaven!)

"You said it must melt ere vesper-bell,
Sister Helen;
If now it be molten, all is well."
"Even so,—nay, peace! you cannot tell,
Little brother."
(*O Mother, Mary Mother,*
O what is this, between Hell and Heaven?)

"Oh the waxen knave was plump to-day,
Sister Helen;
How like dead folk he has dropped away!"
"Nay now, of the dead what can you say,
Little brother?"
(*O Mother, Mary Mother,*
What of the dead, between Hell and Heaven?)

"See, see, the sunken pile of wood,
Sister Helen,
Shines through the thinned wax red as blood!"
"Nay now, when looked you yet on blood,
Little brother?"
(*O Mother, Mary Mother,*
How pale she is, between Hell and Heaven!)

"Now close your eyes, for they're sick and sore,
Sister Helen,
And I'll play without the gallery door."
"Aye, let me rest,—I'll lie on the floor,
Little brother."
(*O Mother, Mary Mother,*
What rest to-night, between Hell and Heaven?)

"Here high up in the balcony,
Sister Helen,
The moon flies face to face with me."
"Aye, look and say whatever you see,
Little brother."
(*O Mother, Mary Mother,*
What sight to-night, between Hell and Heaven?)

"Outside it's merry in the wind's wake,
Sister Helen;
In the shaken trees the chill stars shake."
"Hush, heard you a horse-tread as you spake,
Little brother?"
(*O Mother, Mary Mother,*
What sound to-night, between Hell and Heaven?)

"I hear a horse-tread, and I see,
Sister Helen,
Three horsemen that ride terribly."
"Little brother, whence come the three,
Little brother?"
(*O Mother, Mary Mother,*
Whence should they come, between Hell and Heaven?)

"They come by the hill-verge from Boyne Bar,
Sister Helen,
And one draws nigh, but two are afar."
"Look, look, do you know them who they are,
Little brother?"
(*O Mother, Mary Mother,*
Who should they be, between Hell and Heaven?)

"Oh, it's Keith of Eastholm rides so fast,
Sister Helen,
For I know the white mane on the blast."
"The hour has come, has come at last,
Little brother!"
(*O Mother, Mary Mother,*
Her hour at last, between Hell and Heaven!)

"He has made a sign and called Halloo!
Sister Helen,
And he says that he would speak with you."
"Oh tell him I fear the frozen dew,
Little brother."
(*O Mother, Mary Mother,*
Why laughs she thus, between Hell and Heaven?)

64. Boyne Bar, at the mouth of the Boyne River, **Leinster, Ireland.**

"The wind is loud, but I hear him cry,
Sister Helen,
That Keith of Ewern's like to die."
"And he and thou, and thou and I,
Little brother."
(O Mother, Mary Mother,
And they and we, between Hell and Heaven!)

"Three days ago, on his marriage-morn,
Sister Helen,
He sickened, and lies since then forlorn."
"For bridegroom's side is the bride a thorn,
Little brother?"
(O Mother, Mary Mother,
Cold bridal cheer, between Hell and Heaven!)

"Three days and nights he has lain abed,
Sister Helen,
And he prays in torment to be dead."
"The thing may chance, if he have prayed,
Little brother!"
(O Mother, Mary Mother,
If ye have prayed, between Hell and Heaven!)

"But he has not ceased to cry to-day,
Sister Helen,
That you should take your curse away."
"*My* prayer was heard,—he need but pray,
Little brother!"
(O Mother, Mary Mother,
Shall God not hear, between Hell and Heaven?)

"But he says, till you take back your ban,
Sister Helen,
His soul would pass, yet never can."
"Nay then, shall I slay a living man,
Little brother?"
(O Mother, Mary Mother,
A living soul, between Hell and Heaven!)

"But he calls for ever on your name,
Sister Helen,
And says that he melts before a flame."
"My heart for his pleasure fared the same,
Little brother."
(O Mother, Mary Mother,
Fire at the heart, between Hell and Heaven!)

"Here's Keith of Westholm riding fast,
Sister Helen,
For I know the white plume on the blast."
"The hour, the sweet hour I forecast,
Little brother!"
(O Mother, Mary Mother,
Is the hour sweet, between Hell and Heaven?)

"He stops to speak, and he stills his horse,
Sister Helen;
But his words are drowned in the wind's course."
"Nay hear, nay hear, you must hear perforce,
Little brother!"
(O Mother, Mary Mother,
What word now heard, between Hell and Heaven!)

"Oh he says that Keith of Ewern's cry,
Sister Helen,
Is ever to see you ere he die."
"In all that his soul sees, there am I,
Little brother!"
(O Mother, Mary Mother,
The soul's one sight, between Hell and Heaven!)

"He sends a ring and a broken coin,
Sister Helen,
And bids you mind the banks of Boyne."
"What else he broke will he ever join,
Little brother?"
(O Mother, Mary Mother,
No, never joined, between Hell and Heaven!)

"He yields you these and craves full fain,
Sister Helen,
You pardon him in his mortal pain."
"What else he took will he give again,
Little brother?"
(O Mother, Mary Mother,
Not twice to give, between Hell and Heaven!)

"He calls your name in an agony,
Sister Helen,
That even dead Love must weep to see."
"Hate, born of Love, is blind as he,
Little brother!"
(O Mother, Mary Mother,
Love turned to hate, between Hell and Heaven!)

"Oh, it's Keith of Keith now that rides fast,
Sister Helen,
For I know the white hair on the blast."
"The short, short hour will soon be past,
Little brother!"
(O Mother, Mary Mother,
Will soon be past, between Hell and Heaven!)

87. Keith of Ewern, the false lover whom Sister Helen is destroying.

148. a broken coin, Keith of Ewern's half of the coin that he and Helen broke together when they plighted their troth by the banks of the Boyne.

"He looks at me and he tries to speak,
Sister Helen,
But oh! his voice is sad and weak!"
"What here should the mighty Baron seek,
Little brother?"
(*O Mother, Mary Mother,*
Is this the end, between Hell and Heaven?)

"Oh his son still cries, if you forgive,
Sister Helen,
The body dies but the soul shall live."
"Fire shall forgive me as I forgive,
Little brother!"
(*O Mother, Mary Mother,*
As she forgives, between Hell and Heaven!)

"Oh he prays you, as his heart would rive,
Sister Helen,
To save his dear son's soul alive."
"Fire cannot slay it, it shall thrive,
Little brother!"
(*O Mother, Mary Mother,*
Alas, alas, between Hell and Heaven!)

"He cries to you, kneeling in the road,
Sister Helen,
To go with him for the love of God!"
"The way is long to his son's abode,
Little brother."
(*O Mother, Mary Mother,*
The way is long, between Hell and Heaven!)

"A lady's here, by a dark steed brought,
Sister Helen,
So darkly clad, I saw her not."
"See her now or never see aught,
Little brother!"
(*O Mother, Mary Mother,*
What more to see, between Hell and Heaven?)

"Her hood falls back, and the moon shines fair,
Sister Helen,
On the Lady of Ewern's golden hair."
"Blest hour of my power and her despair,
Little brother!"
(*O Mother, Mary Mother,*
Hour blest and banned, between Hell and Heaven!)

"Pale, pale her cheeks, that in pride did glow,
Sister Helen,
Neath the bridal wreath three days ago."
"One morn for pride and three days for woe,
Little brother!"
(*O Mother, Mary Mother,*
Three days, three nights, between Hell and Heaven!)

"Her clasped hands stretch from her bending head,
Sister Helen;
With the loud wind's wail her sobs are wed."
"What wedding-strains hath her bridal-bed,
Little brother?"
(*O Mother, Mary Mother,*
What strain but death's, between Hell and Heaven?)

"She may not speak, she sinks in a swoon,
Sister Helen,—
She lifts her lips and gasps on the moon."
"Oh! might I but hear her soul's blithe tune,
Little brother!"
(*O Mother, Mary Mother,*
Her woe's dumb cry, between Hell and Heaven!)

"They've caught her to Westholm's saddle-bow,
Sister Helen,
And her moonlit hair gleams white in its flow."
"Let it turn whiter than winter snow,
Little brother!"
(*O Mother, Mary Mother,*
Woe-withered gold, between Hell and Heaven!)

"O Sister Helen, you heard the bell,
Sister Helen!
More loud than the vesper-chime it fell."
"No vesper-chime, but a dying knell,
Little brother!"
(*O Mother, Mary Mother,*
His dying knell, between Hell and Heaven!)

"Alas! but I fear the heavy sound,
Sister Helen;
Is it in the sky or in the ground?"
"Say, have they turned their horses round,
Little brother?"
(*O Mother, Mary Mother,*
What would she more, between Hell and Heaven?)

"They have raised the old man from his knee,
Sister Helen,
And they ride in silence hastily."
"More fast the naked soul doth flee,
Little brother!"
(*O Mother, Mary Mother,*
The naked soul, between Hell and Heaven!)

186. "Fire shall forgive me, probably when she is burned for witchcraft.

"Flank to flank are the three steeds gone,
Sister Helen,
But the lady's dark steed goes alone."
"And lonely her bridegroom's soul hath flown,
Little brother."
(O Mother, Mary Mother,
The lonely ghost, between Hell and Heaven!)

"Oh the wind is sad in the iron chill,
Sister Helen,
And weary sad they look by the hill."
"But he and I are sadder still,
Little brother!"
(O Mother, Mary Mother,
Most sad of all, between Hell and Heaven!)

"See, see, the wax has dropped from its place,
Sister Helen,
And the flames are winning up apace!"
"Yet here they burn but for a space,
Little brother!"
(O Mother, Mary Mother,
Here for a space, between Hell and Heaven!)

"Ah! what white thing at the door has crossed,
Sister Helen?
Ah! what is this that sighs in the frost?"
"A soul that's lost as mine is lost,
Little brother!"
(O Mother, Mary Mother,
Lost, lost, all lost, between Hell and Heaven!)

ON REFUSAL OF AID BETWEEN NATIONS

This poem is a protest against what Rossetti considered the shameful indifference of other nations toward the struggle of Italy and Hungary against Austria.

Not that the earth is changing, O my God!
Nor that the seasons totter in their walk,—
Not that the virulent ill of act and talk
Seethes ever as a winepress ever trod,—
Not therefore are we certain that the rod
Weighs in thine hand to smite thy world; though now
Beneath thine hand so many nations bow,
So many kings:—not therefore, O my God!—

But because Man is parcelled out in men
Today; because, for any wrongful blow,
No man not stricken asks, "I would be told
Why thou dost strike"; but his heart whispers then,
"He is he, I am I." By this we know
That our earth falls asunder, being old.

FIRST LOVE REMEMBERED

Peace in her chamber, wheresoe'er
It be, a holy place:
The thought still brings my soul such grace
As morning meadows wear.

Whether it still be small and light,
A maid's who dreams alone,
As from her orchard-gate the moon
Its ceiling showed at night:

Or whether, in a shadow dense
As nuptial hymns invoke,
Innocent maidenhood awoke
To married innocence:

There still the thanks unheard await
The unconscious gift bequeathed;
For there my soul this hour has breathed
An air inviolate.

SUDDEN LIGHT

I have been here before,
But when or how I cannot tell:
I know the grass beyond the door,
The sweet keen smell,
The sighing sound, the lights around the shore.

You have been mine before,—
How long ago I may not know:
But just when at that swallow's soar
Your neck turned so,
Some veil did fall,—I knew it all of yore.

Has this been thus before?
And shall not thus time's eddying flight
Still with our lives our loves restore
In death's despite,
And day and night yield one delight once more?

from THE HOUSE OF LIFE

"The House of Life" is probably Rossetti's most important single work. It is not exactly a sonnet sequence, for it does not tell a connected story; it is rather a series of sonnets on different aspects of life as love. About half the poems were recovered from Mrs. Rossetti's coffin in 1869; in 1881 the series was completed in *Ballads and Sonnets*. In astrology the first of the "houses" into which the heavens are divided is the "house of life."

THE SONNET

A sonnet is a moment's monument—
Memorial from the Soul's eternity
To one dead deathless hour. Look that it be,
Whether for lustral rite or dire portent,
Of its own arduous fullness reverent.
Carve it in ivory or in ebony,
As Day or Night may rule; and let Time see
Its flowering crest impearled and orient.

A sonnet is a coin; its face reveals
The Soul—its converse, to what Power 'tis due:—
Whether for tribute to the august appeals
Of Life, or dower in Love's high retinue,
It serve; or 'mid the dark wharf's cavernous breath,
In Charon's palm it pay the toll to Death.

Part I. Youth and Change

1. LOVE ENTHRONED

I marked all kindred Powers the heart finds fair:—
Truth, with awed lips; and Hope, with eyes upcast;
And Fame, whose loud wings fan the ashen Past
To signal-fires, Oblivion's flight to scare;
And Youth, with still some single golden hair
Unto his shoulder clinging, since the last
Embrace wherein two sweet arms held him fast;
And Life, still wreathing flowers for Death to wear.

Love's throne was not with these; but far above
All passionate wind of welcome and farewell
He sat in breathless bowers they dream not of;
Though Truth foreknow Love's heart, and Hope foretell,
And Fame be for Love's sake desirable,
And Youth be dear, and Life be sweet to Love.

2. BRIDAL BIRTH

As when desire, long darkling, dawns, and first
The mother looks upon the newborn child,
Even so my Lady stood at gaze and smiled
When her soul knew at length the Love it nursed.
Born with her life, creature of poignant thirst
And exquisite hunger, at her heart Love lay
Quickening in darkness, till a voice that day
Cried on him, and the bonds of birth were burst.

Now, shielded in his wings, our faces yearn
Together, as his full-grown feet now range
The grove, and his warm hands our couch prepare:
Till to his song our bodiless souls in turn
Be born his children, when Death's nuptial change
Leaves us for light the halo of his hair.

4. LOVESIGHT

When do I see thee most, belovèd one?
When in the light the spirits of mine eyes
Before thy face, their altar, solemnize
The worship of that Love through thee made known?
Or when in the dusk hours, (we two alone,)
Close-kissed and eloquent of still replies
Thy twilight-hidden glimmering visage lies,
And my soul only sees thy soul its own?

O love, my love! if I no more should see
Thyself, nor on the earth the shadow of thee,
Nor image of thine eyes in any spring,—
How then should sound upon Life's darkening slope
The ground-whirl of the perished leaves of Hope,
The wind of Death's imperishable wing?

5. HEART'S HOPE

By what word's power, the key of paths untrod,
Shall I the difficult deeps of Love explore,
Till parted waves of Song yield up the shore
Even as that sea which Israel crossed dryshod?
For lo! in some poor rhythmic period,
Lady, I fain would tell how evermore
Thy soul I know not from thy body, nor
Thee from myself, neither our love from God.

Yea, in God's name, and Love's, and thine, would I
Draw from one loving heart such evidence
As to all hearts all things shall signify;
Tender as dawn's first hill-fire, and intense
As instantaneous penetrating sense,
In Spring's birth-hour, of other Springs gone by.

19. SILENT NOON

Your hands lie open in the long, fresh grass,—
The finger-points look through like rosy blooms:
Your eyes smile peace. The pasture gleams and glooms
'Neath billowing skies that scatter and amass.
All round our nest, far as the eye can pass,
Are golden kingcup-fields with silver edge

Where the cow-parsley skirts the hawthorn-hedge.
'Tis visible silence, still as the hour-glass.

Deep in the sun-searched growths the dragon-fly
Hangs like a blue thread loosened from the sky:—
So this winged hour is dropt to us from above.
Oh! clasp we to our hearts, for deathless dower,
This close-companioned inarticulate hour
When twofold silence was the song of love.

24. PRIDE OF YOUTH

Even as a child, of sorrow that we give
The dead, but little in his heart can find,
Since without need of thought to his clear mind
Their turn it is to die and his to live:—
Even so the winged New Love smiles to receive
Along his eddying plumes the auroral wind,
Nor, forward glorying, casts one look behind
Where night-rack shrouds the Old Love fugitive.

There is a change in every hour's recall,
And the last cowslip in the fields we see
On the same day with the first corn-poppy.
Alas for hourly change! Alas for all
The loves that from his hand proud Youth lets fall,
Even as the beads of a told rosary!

28. SOUL-LIGHT

What other woman could be loved like you,
Or how of you should love possess his fill?
After the fullness of all rapture, still,—
As at the end of some deep avenue
A tender glamour of the day,—there comes to view
Far in your eyes a yet more hungering thrill,—
Such fire as Love's soul-winnowing hands distil
Even from his inmost ark of light and dew.

And as the traveller triumphs with the sun,
Glorying in heat's mid-height, yet star tide brings
Wonder new-born, and still fresh transport springs
From limpid lambent hours of day begun;—
Even so, through eyes and voice, your soul doth move
My soul with changeful light of infinite love.

53. WITHOUT HER

What of her glass without her? The blank grey
There where the pool is blind of the moon's face.
Her dress without her? The tossed empty space
Of cloud-rack whence the moon has passed away.
Her paths without her? Day's appointed sway
Usurped by desolate night. Her pillowed place
Without her? Tears, ah me! for love's good grace,
And cold forgetfulness of night or day.

What of the heart without her? Nay, poor heart,
Of thee what word remains ere speech be still?
A wayfarer by barren ways and chill,
Steep ways and weary, without her thou art,
Where the long cloud, the long wood's counterpart,
Sheds double darkness up the labouring hill.

Part II. Change and Fate

77. SOUL'S BEAUTY

(Sibylla Palmifera)

Under the arch of Life, where love and death,
Terror and mystery, guard her shrine, I saw
Beauty enthroned; and though her gaze struck awe,
I drew it in as simply as my breath.
Hers are the eyes which, over and beneath,
The sky and sea bend on thee,—which can draw,
By sea or sky or woman, to one law,
The allotted bondman of her palm and wreath.

This is that Lady Beauty, in whose praise
Thy voice and hand shake still,—long known to thee
By flying hair and fluttering hem,—the beat
Following her daily of thy heart and feet,
How passionately and irretrievably,
In what fond flight, how many ways and days!

78. BODY'S BEAUTY

Of Adam's first wife, Lilith, it is told
(The witch he loved before the gift of Eve,)
That, ere the snake's, her sweet tongue could deceive,
And her enchanted hair was the first gold.
And still she sits, young while the earth is old,
And, subtly of herself contemplative,
Draws men to watch the bright net she can weave,
Till heart and body and life are in its hold.

Sec. 77. Soul's Beauty. **Sibylla Palmifera,** the palm-bearing Sibyl. This sonnet and the next were originally written for paintings. *Sec. 78. Body's Beauty.* **1. Lilith,** according to the Talmud, the first wife of Adam: she was discarded when she became intractable.

The rose and poppy are her flowers; for where
Is he not found, O Lilith, whom shed scent
And soft-shed kisses and soft sleep shall snare?
Lo! as that youth's eyes burned at thine, so went
Thy spell through him, and left his straight neck bent,
And round his heart one strangling golden hair.

101. THE ONE HOPE

When vain desire at last and vain regret
Go hand in hand to death, and all is vain,
What shall assuage the unforgotten pain
And teach the unforgetful to forget?
Shall Peace be still a sunk stream long unmet,—
Or may the soul at once in a green plain
Stoop through the spray of some sweet life-fountain
And cull the dew-drenched flowering amulet?

Ah! when the wan soul in that golden air
Between the scriptured petals softly blown
Peers breathless for the gift of grace unknown,—
Ah! let none other written spell soe'er
But only the one Hope's one name be there,—
Not less nor more, but even that word alone.

ALAS, SO LONG!

Ah! dear one, we were young so long,
It seemed that youth would never go,
For skies and trees were ever in song
And water in singing flow
In the days we never again shall know.
Alas, so long!
Ah! then was it all Spring weather?
Nay, but we were young and together.

Ah! dear one, I've been old so long,
It seems that age is loath to part,
Though days and years have never a song,
And oh! have they still the art
That warmed the pulses of heart to heart?
Alas, so long!
Ah, then was it all Spring weather?
Nay, but we were young and together.

Ah, dear one, you've been dead so long,—
How long until we meet again,
Where hours may never lose their song
Nor flowers forget the rain
In glad moonlight that never shall wane?
Alas, so long!
Ah! shall it be then Spring weather,
And ah! shall we be young together?

Christina Rossetti
1830–1894

Christina Georgina, the youngest of the four Rossetti children, was born in London on December 5, 1830. Closely involved in the beginnings of Pre-Raphaelitism, she served as a model for her brother's pictures and also tried her own hand at drawing. But while she shared Dante Gabriel's marvelous sensitiveness to the sights and sounds of the sensuous world, this side of her nature was balanced (or overbalanced) by a spirit of intense devoutness in harmony with the tenets and standards of that part of the Church of England which the Oxford Movement had regenerated. "I cannot possibly use the word happy without meaning something beyond this present life," she wrote.

One need not look far to discern a conflict between her intensely feminine preoccupation with loving and being loved and her tendency toward asceticism; her passionate Italian nature responded to the lure of the flesh only to crucify it. James Collinson, her first sweetheart, she dismissed because he was a Roman Catholic; Charles Cayley, her second, whom she loved as long as life remained in her, she refused on account of the uncertainty of his religious views. There was physical as well as mental suffering in her life, for she was cursed both with Graves' disease and with cancer, but in spite of all her trials, and what, even in her day, were coming to be regarded as very narrow views, she never lost her gift for charming nonsense. The austerities of her faith she kept for herself; it flowed out toward others in Christian love and an unceasing, unpretentious search for ways of doing good.

Christina Rossetti's first book was published when she was only seventeen years old. In 1861 she contributed some poems to *Macmillan's Magazine;* the next year, *Goblin Market and Other Poems* became the first literary success of the Pre-Raphaelite Movement. This was followed by *The Prince's Progress,*

1866, *Sing-Song*, 1872, and other volumes, all of which have now been collected in her *Poetical Works*, edited by W. M. Rossetti (Macmillan, 1924). She also wrote short stories, tracts, and books for children.

Her poems, unpretentious like herself, are more highly regarded today than they have ever been. "She accepted the conditions which are at the very root of mortal and earthly life," says Walter de La Mare; "and in that acceptance triumphed." But the quality of her poetry is easier to feel than to define. Intensity of feeling and expression accounts for much of its enduring strength.

SONG

When I am dead, my dearest,
  Sing no sad songs for me;
Plant thou no roses at my head,
  Nor shady cypress tree:
Be the green grass above me
  With showers and dewdrops wet;
And if thou wilt, remember,
  And if thou wilt, forget.

I shall not see the shadows,
  I shall not feel the rain;
I shall not hear the nightingale
  Sing on as if in pain:
And dreaming through the twilight
  That doth not rise nor set,
Haply I may remember,
  And haply may forget.

REMEMBER

Remember me when I am gone away,
  Gone far away into the silent land;
  When you can no more hold me by the hand,
Nor I half turn to go yet turning stay.
Remember me when no more day by day
  You tell me of our future that you planned:
  Only remember me; you understand
It will be late to counsel then or pray.
Yet if you should forget me for a while
  And afterwards remember, do not grieve:
  For if the darkness and corruption leave
  A vestige of the thoughts that once I had,
Better by far you should forget and smile
  Than that you should remember and be sad.

Song. **4. cypress tree,** emblem of mourning.

AFTER DEATH

The curtains were half drawn, the floor was swept
  And strewn with rushes, rosemary and may
  Lay thick upon the bed on which I lay,
Where through the lattice ivy-shadows crept.
He leaned above me, thinking that I slept
  And could not hear him; but I heard him say:
  "Poor child, poor child": and as he turned away
Came a deep silence, and I knew he wept.
He did not touch the shroud, or raise the fold
  That hid my face, or take my hand in his,
    Or ruffle the smooth pillows for my head:
    He did not love me living; but once dead
  He pitied me; and very sweet it is
To know he still is warm though I am cold.

PARADISE

This poem is full of references to the description of the City of God in Revelation 21–22.

Once in a dream I saw the flowers
  That bud and bloom in Paradise;
  More fair they are than waking eyes
Have seen in all this world of ours.
And faint the perfume-bearing rose,
  And faint the lily on its stem,
And faint the perfect violet,
    Compared with them.

I heard the songs of Paradise;
  Each bird sat singing in his place;
  A tender song so full of grace
It soared like incense to the skies.
Each bird sat singing to his mate
  Soft cooing notes among the trees:
The nightingale herself were cold
    To such as these.

I saw the fourfold River flow,
  And deep it was, with golden sand;
  It flowed between a mossy land
With murmured music grave and low.
It hath refreshment for all thirst,
  For fainting spirits strength and rest;
Earth holds not such a draught as this
    From east to west.

The Tree of Life stood budding there,
  Abundant with its twelvefold fruits;
  Eternal sap sustains its roots,

Its shadowing branches fill the air.
Its leaves are healing for the world,
  Its fruit the hungry world can feed,
Sweeter than honey to the taste
    And balm indeed.

I saw the Gate called Beautiful,
  And looked, but scarce could look within;
  I saw the golden streets begin,
And outskirts of the glassy pool.
Oh harps, oh crowns of plenteous stars,
  Oh green palm branches many-leaved—
Eye hath not seen, nor ear hath heard,
    Nor heart conceived!

I hope to see these things again,
  But not as once in dreams by night;
  To see them with my very sight,
And touch and handle and attain:
To have all Heaven beneath my feet
  For narrow way that once they trod;
To have my part with all the saints,
    And with my God.

A BETTER RESURRECTION

I have no wit, no words, no tears;
  My heart within me like a stone
Is numbed too much for hopes or fears.
  Look right, look left, I dwell alone;
I lift mine eyes, but dimmed with grief
  No everlasting hills I see;
My life is in the falling leaf:
    O Jesus, quicken me!

My life is like a faded leaf,
  My harvest dwindled to a husk;
Truly my life is void and brief
  And tedious in the barren dusk;
My life is like a frozen thing,
  No bud nor greenness can I see:
Yet rise it shall,—the sap of Spring;
    O Jesus, rise in me!

My life is like a broken bowl,
  A broken bowl that cannot hold
One drop of water for my soul
  Or cordial in the searching cold;
Cast in the fire the perished thing;
  Melt and remould it, till it be
A royal cup for Him, my King:
    O Jesus, drink of me!

39–40. Eye . . . conceived!" See 1 Corinthians 2:9. **46. For . . . trod,** by way of recompense for having traveled the narrow path here. See Matthew 7:14.

A BIRTHDAY

My heart is like a singing bird
  Whose nest is in a watered shoot;
My heart is like an apple-tree
  Whose boughs are bent with thickset fruit;
My heart is like a rainbow shell
  That paddles in a halcyon sea;
My heart is gladder than all these
  Because my love is come to me.

Raise me a dais of silk and down;
  Hang it with vair and purple dyes;
Carve it in doves and pomegranates,
  And peacocks with a hundred eyes;
Work it in gold and silver grapes,
  In leaves and silver fleurs-de-lys;
Because the birthday of my life
  Is come, my love is come to me.

AT HOME

When I was dead, my spirit turned
  To seek the much-frequented house.
I passed the door, and saw my friends
  Feasting beneath green orange-boughs;
From hand to hand they pushed the wine,
  They sucked the pulp of plum and peach;
They sang, they jested, and they laughed,
  For each was loved of each.

I listened to their honest chat.
  Said one: "To-morrow we shall be
Plod plod along the featureless sands,
  And coasting miles and miles of sea."
Said one: "Before the turn of tide
  We will achieve the eyrie-seat."
Said one: "To-morrow shall be like
  To-day, but much more sweet."

"To-morrow," said they, strong with hope,
  And dwelt upon the pleasant way:
"To-morrow," cried they one and all,
  While no one spoke of yesterday.
Their life stood full at blessed noon;
  I, only I, had passed away:
"To-morrow and to-day," they cried;
  I was of yesterday.

I shivered comfortless, but cast
  No chill across the tablecloth;
I all-forgotten shivered, sad
  To stay, and yet to part how loth:

I passed from the familiar room,
I who from love had passed away,
Like the remembrance of a guest
That tarrieth but a day.

UP-HILL

Does the road wind up-hill all the way?
Yes, to the very end.
Will the day's journey take the whole long day?
From morn to night, my friend.

But is there for the night a resting-place?
A roof for when the slow dark hours begin.
May not the darkness hide it from my face?
You cannot miss that inn.

Shall I meet other wayfarers at night?
Those who have gone before.
Then must I knock, or call when just in sight?
They will not keep you standing at that door.

Shall I find comfort, travel-sore and weak?
Of labour you shall find the sum.
Will there be beds for me and all who seek?
Yea, beds for all who come.

from SING-SONG

If I were a Queen,
What would I do?
I'd make you King,
And I'd wait on you.

If I were a King,
What would I do?
I'd make you Queen,
For I'd marry you.

Mother shake the cherry-tree,
Susan catch a cherry;
Oh how funny that will be,
Let's be merry!

One for brother, one for sister,
Two for mother more,
Six for father, hot and tired,
Knocking at the door.

The wind has such a rainy sound
Moaning through the town,
The sea has such a windy sound,—
Will the ships go down?

The apples in the orchard
Tumble from their tree.—
Oh, will the ships go down, go down,
In the windy sea?

Fly away, fly away over the sea,
Sun-loving swallow, for summer is done;
Come again, come again, come back to me,
Bringing the summer and bringing the sun.

Who has seen the wind?
Neither I nor you:
But when the leaves hang trembling
The wind is passing through.

Who has seen the wind?
Neither you nor I:
But when the trees bow down their heads
The wind is passing by.

Boats sail on the rivers,
And ships sail on the seas;
But clouds that sail across the sky
Are prettier far than these.

There are bridges on the rivers,
As pretty as you please;
But the bow that bridges heaven,
And overtops the trees,
And builds a road from earth to sky,
Is prettier far than these.

DE PROFUNDIS[1]

Oh, why is heaven built so far,
Oh, why is earth set so remote?
I cannot reach the nearest star
That hangs afloat.

I would not care to reach the moon,
One round monotonous of change;
Yet even she repeats her tune
Beyond my range.

I never watch the scattered fire
Of stars, or sun's far-trailing train,
But all my heart is one desire,
And all in vain.

For I am bound with fleshly bands,
Joy, beauty, lie beyond my scope;
I strain my heart, I stretch my hands,
And catch at hope.

Up-Hill. **12. standing at that door.** See Revelation 3:20.

[1] *De Profundis.* From the depths.

THE HILLS ARE TIPPED WITH SUNSHINE

The hills are tipped with sunshine, while I walk
 In shadows dim and cold;
The unawakened rose sleeps on her stalk
 In a bud's fold,
 Until the sun flood all the world with gold.

The hills are crowned with glory, and the glow
 Flows widening down apace;
Unto the sunny hilltops I, set low,
 Lift a tired face—
 Ah, happy rose, content to wait for grace!

How tired a face, how tired a brain, how tired
 A heart I lift, who long
For something never felt but still desired;
 Sunshine and song,
 Song where the choirs of sunny heaven stand choired.

SLEEPING AT LAST

This is believed to be the last poem Christina Rossetti wrote.

Sleeping at last, the trouble and tumult over,
 Sleeping at last, the struggle and horror past,
Cold and white, out of sight of friend and of lover,
 Sleeping at last.

 No more a tired heart downcast or overcast,
No more pangs that wring or shifting fears that hover,
 Sleeping at last in a dreamless sleep locked fast.

Fast asleep. Singing birds in their leafy cover
 Cannot wake her, nor shake her the gusty blast.
Under the purple thyme and the purple clover
 Sleeping at last.

William Morris

1834–1896

Poet, craftsman, and publicist, William Morris lived perhaps the fullest life of all the great nineteenth-century poets. The three phases of his work were closely connected; like Ruskin, who influenced him, he perceived that it is futile to achieve beauty in one's dream life while the world of actuality that hems one in on every side is overwhelmingly ugly; later he came to believe that the only way to get rid of this ugliness was to destroy the present economic order.

Morris was born of a well-to-do commercial family at Walthamstow, March 24, 1834. He was brought up on the edge of Epping Forest, which tremendously stimulated his imagination; in art as well as in nature, the glamour of the past soon powerfully enthralled him. One of his great early passions was for Scott's novels.

When Morris went to Oxford in 1853 he was thinking of taking holy orders. Partly as the result of an association with Rossetti and Burne-Jones, his interests shifted from religion to art. He tried architecture, then painting. In the *Oxford and Cambridge Magazine,* which he financed, he published the stories now reprinted in "Everyman's Library" as *The Early Romances of William Morris.* In 1858 he published *The Defence of Guenevere and Other Poems.* The general public did not relish the Pre-Raphaelite, un-Tennysonian spirit of this volume; a more romantic, less psychological, and less obscure treatment of medievalism was still in vogue.

In 1859 Morris married Jane Burden, a beautiful girl who had served as a Pre-Raphaelite model. For her he built the beautiful "Red House" in Kent, and it was because of his inability to buy the things he wanted for it in the open market that the firm of Morris, Marshall, Faulkner, and Company was formed. Among other articles this firm produced furniture, tapestries, embroideries, carpets, tiles, designs for wallpaper and chintzes, and stained-glass windows. Thorough research everywhere was Morris's rule—he studied dyes for two years—and he gave prizes not for designs but for finished articles. "Have nothing in your houses," he cried, "that you do not know to be useful or believe to be beautiful." Actually he made the useful articles beautiful. His employees were not wage slaves but creative artists, and his business was very successful.

Toward the close of his life Morris took up his last craft, printing, and established the Kelmscott Press. Here again ink, paper, everything was made to order. The Kelmscott Chaucer is one of the most famous of printed books. Morris raced against time to complete it, and its appearance only briefly antedated his death.

Morris's most elaborate poems were *The Earthly Paradise*, *The Life and Death of Jason*, and *The Story of Sigurd the Volsung and the Fall of the Niblungs*, 1877, which Bernard Shaw thought the greatest epic since Homer. Before he finished *The Earthly Paradise*, Morris had become tremendously interested in Northern myth; two trips to Iceland (1871 and 1873) did much to increase this interest. In 1873 he published *Love Is Enough*, a morality play based on the *Mabinogion*. He made extensive translations from Scandinavian sources, from the *Odyssey* and the *Aeneid*, *Beowulf*, and other works. His last great literary enterprise was a series of gloriously titled Northern romances—*The House of the Wolfings*, 1889; *The Roots of the Mountains*, 1890; *The Story of the Glittering Plain*, 1890; *The Wood beyond the World*, 1894; *Child Christopher and Goldilind the Fair*, 1895; *The Well at the World's End*, 1896; *The Water of the Wondrous Isles*, 1897; *The Sundering Flood*, 1898.

Morris's public service was in two fields, as a member of the Society for the Protection of Ancient Buildings and as a Socialist. From 1883 to 1890 he gave his energies largely to Socialist propaganda. He did not take up this work primarily because he pitied the unfortunate, but because he was convinced that the heroic race he liked to write about could never breed in England under modern conditions. His Socialistic views are set forth directly in *The Aims of Art*, 1887, in *Signs of Change*, 1888; and artistically in his beautiful story of the fourteenth century Peasants' Revolt, *A Dream of John Ball*, 1888, in his Utopia, *News from Nowhere*, 1891, and in *Poems by the Way*, 1891. Morris died (of trying to live ten men's lives, as somebody has said) in 1896.

Morris was a shaggy, full-bodied man, of abounding vitality. He was restless, impatient, and of violent temper, and he inspired both enthusiasm and repulsion. He hated conventional society and conventional ways—he hated the "modern" both in literature and in life. He wrote very rapidly, sometimes as much as seven hundred lines of poetry in a day, and he disliked revision; when changes were necessary, he rewrote. His work is the bread of poetry; he has few magical lines. But he is a fine storyteller, and the melodious flow of his verse is always agreeable. One senses also the poet's own obvious pleasure in composition. Morris lived intensely every moment of his life, and he did not need prodding to keep him alive. Above all, he is an interesting example of a man whose zealous service of the present flowed directly from his idealization of the past.

THE DEFENCE OF GUENEVERE

Guenevere, King Arthur's queen, on trial for adultery, addresses her judges while she waits for Launcelot to come and deliver her. He had been found in her chamber by a company of knights, all save one of whom he slew.

The poem contains references also to a previous occasion upon which Guenevere had been under sentence. This had followed her imprisonment by Sir Mellyagraunce in his castle, la Fausse Garde, from which Launcelot rescued her. Coming into her chamber, he cut his arm on the window bars, and his blood was found on her bed. Launcelot saved Guenevere from the stake on this occasion by slaying Mellyagraunce in judicial combat.

Malory's *Morte Darthur*, Books 19–20, is Morris's source for this poem. Three other Arthurian poems were published with this one—"King Arthur's Tomb," "Sir Galahad, a Christmas Mystery," and "The Chapel in Lyoness."

But, knowing now that they would have her speak,
She threw her wet hair backward from her brow,
Her hand close to her mouth touching her cheek,

As though she had had there a shameful blow,
And feeling it shameful to feel aught but shame
All through her heart, yet felt her cheek burned so,

She must a little touch it; like one lame
She walked away from Gauwaine, with her head
Still lifted up; and on her cheek of flame

The tears dried quick; she stopped at last and said:
"O knights and lords, it seems but little skill
To talk of well-known things past now and dead.

"God wot I ought to say, I have done ill,
And pray you all forgiveness heartily!
Because you must be right, such great lords—still

"Listen, suppose your time were come to die,
And you were quite alone and very weak;
Yea, laid a-dying, while very mightily

"The wind was ruffling up the narrow streak
Of river through your broad lands running well:
Suppose a hush should come, then some one speak:

" 'One of these cloths is heaven, and one is hell,
Now choose one cloth for ever; which they be,
I will not tell you, you must somehow tell

" 'Of your own strength and mightiness; here, see!'
Yea, yea, my lord, and you to ope your eyes,
At foot of your familiar bed to see

"A great God's angel standing, with such dyes,
Not known on earth, on his great wings, and hands,
Held out two ways, light from the inner skies

"Showing him well, and making his commands
Seem to be God's commands, moreover, too,
Holding within his hands the cloths on wands;

"And one of these strange choosing cloths was blue,
Wavy and long, and one cut short and red;
No man could tell the better of the two.

"After a shivering half-hour you said,
'God help! heaven's colour, the blue'; and he said: 'hell.'
Perhaps you would then roll upon your bed,

"And cry to all good men that loved you well,
'Ah Christ! if only I had known, known, known';
Launcelot went away, then I could tell,

"Like wisest man how all things would be, moan,
And roll and hurt myself, and long to die,
And yet fear much to die for what was sown.

"Nevertheless you, O Sir Gauwaine, lie,
Whatever may have happened through these years,
God knows I speak truth, saying that you lie."

Her voice was low at first, being full of tears,
But as it cleared, it grew full loud and shrill,
Growing a windy shriek in all men's ears,

A ringing in their startled brains, until
She said that Gauwaine lied, then her voice sunk,
And her great eyes began again to fill,

Though still she stood right up, and never shrunk,
But spoke on bravely, glorious lady fair!
Whatever tears her full lips may have drunk,

She stood, and seemed to think, and wrung her hair,
Spoke out at last with no more trace of shame,
With passionate twisting of her body there:

"It chanced upon a day that Launcelot came
To dwell at Arthur's court: at Christmas-time
This happened; when the heralds sung his name,

" 'Son of King Ban of Benwick,' seemed to chime
Along with all the bells that rang that day,
O'er the white roofs, with little change of rhyme.

"Christmas and whitened winter passed away,
And over me the April sunshine came,
Made very awful with black hail-clouds, yea,

"And in the Summer I grew white with flame,
And bowed my head down—Autumn, and the sick
Sure knowledge things would never be the same,

"However often Spring might be most thick
Of blossoms and buds, smote on me, and I grew
Careless of most things, let the clock tick, tick,

"To my unhappy pulse, that beat right through
My eager body; while I laughed out loud,
And let my lips curl up at false or true,

"Seemed cold and shallow without any cloud.
Behold my judges, then the cloths were brought;
While I was dizzied thus, old thoughts would crowd,

"Belonging to the time ere I was bought
By Arthur's great name and his little love;
Must I give up for ever then, I thought,

"That which I deemed would ever round me move
Glorifying all things; for a little word,
Scarce ever meant at all, must I now prove

"Stone-cold for ever? Pray you, does the Lord
Will that all folks should be quite happy and good?
I love God now a little, if this cord

"Were broken, once for all what striving could
Make me love anything in earth or heaven?
So day by day it grew, as if one should

"Slip slowly down some path worn smooth and even,
Down to a cool sea on a summer day;
Yet still in slipping there was some small leaven

"Of stretched hands catching small stones by the way,
Until one surely reached the sea at last,
And felt strange new joy as the worn head lay

46. "Nevertheless. . . . lie. For some unexplained reason, Morris made Gauwaine Guenevere's accuser. In Malory he is her defender.

70. I grew white with flame, that is, fell in love with Launcelot. **75. clock,** of course an anachronism. **80. the cloths were brought.** This symbolism harks back to her parable in ll. 21 ff. **86. a little word,** her marriage vow.

"Back, with the hair like sea-weed; yea all past
Sweat of the forehead, dryness of the lips,
Washed utterly out by the dear waves o'ercast,

"In the lone sea, far off from any ships!
Do I not know now of a day in Spring?
No minute of that wild day ever slips

"From out my memory; I hear thrushes sing,
And wheresoever I may be, straightway
Thoughts of it all come up with most fresh sting:

"I was half mad with beauty on that day,
And went without my ladies all alone,
In a quiet garden walled round every way;

"I was right joyful of that wall of stone,
That shut the flowers and trees up with the sky,
And trebled all the beauty: to the bone,

"Yea right through to my heart, grown very shy
With weary thoughts, it pierced, and made me glad;
Exceedingly glad, and I knew verily,

"A little thing just then had made me mad;
I dared not think, as I was wont to do,
Sometimes, upon my beauty; if I had

"Held out my long hand up against the blue,
And, looking on the tenderly darkened fingers,
Thought that by rights one ought to see quite through,

"There, see you, where the soft still light yet lingers,
Round by the edges; what should I have done,
If this had joined with yellow spotted singers,

"And startling green drawn upward by the sun?
But shouting, loosed out, see now! all my hair,
And trancedly stood watching the west wind run

"With faintest half-heard breathing sound; why there
I lose my head e'en now in doing this;
But shortly listen: In that garden fair

"Came Launcelot walking; this is true, the kiss
Wherewith we kissed in meeting that spring day,
I scarce dare talk of the remembered bliss,

"When both our mouths went wandering in one way,
And aching sorely, met among the leaves;
Our hands being left behind strained far away.

"Never within a yard of my bright sleeves
Had Launcelot come before: and now, so nigh!
After that day why is it Guenevere grieves?

"Nevertheless you, O Sir Gauwaine, lie,
Whatever happened on through all those years,
God knows I speak truth, saying that you lie.

"Being such a lady could I weep these tears
If this were true? A great queen such as I
Having sinned this way, straight her conscience sears;

"And afterwards she liveth hatefully,
Slaying and poisoning, certes never weeps,—
Gauwaine, be friends now, speak me lovingly.

"Do I not see how God's dear pity creeps
All through your frame, and trembles in your mouth?
Remember in what grave your mother sleeps,

"Buried in some place far down in the south,
Men are forgetting as I speak to you;
By her head severed in that awful drouth

"Of pity that drew Agravaine's fell blow,
I pray your pity! let me not scream out
For ever after, when the shrill winds blow

"Through half your castle-locks! let me not shout
For ever after in the winter night
When you ride out alone! in battle-rout

"Let not my rusting tears make your sword light!
Ah! God of mercy, how he turns away!
So, ever must I dress me to the fight,

"So: let God's justice work! Gauwaine, I say,
See me hew down your proofs: yea all men know
Even as you said how Mellyagraunce one day,

"One bitter day in *la Fausse Garde*, for so
All good knights held it after, saw:
Yea, sirs, by cursed unknightly outrage; though

142–44. "Nevertheless . . . lie. The repetition at this point would seem to indicate that Morris did not think Guenevere guilty of any more serious infidelity than her kiss. In his "King Arthur's Tomb," however, her sin is deeper. **153. your mother,** Morgause, Arthur's sister, was slain by her son, Sir Gaheris, not by Agravaine (l. 157), when he found her faithless to his father (Malory, Book X). **171. unknightly outrage,** the entrance of Mellyagraunce into Guenevere's chamber and his thrusting aside the curtains of her bed before she was up.

"You, Gauwaine, held his word without a flaw,
This Mellyagraunce saw blood upon my bed—
Whose blood then pray you? is there any law

"To make a queen say why some spots of red
Lie on her coverlet? or will you say:
'Your hands are white, lady, as when you wed,

" 'Where did you bleed?' and must I stammer out, 'Nay,
I blush indeed, fair lord, only to rend
My sleeve up to my shoulder, where there lay

" 'A knife-point last night': so must I defend
The honour of the Lady Guenevere?
Not so, fair lords, even if the world should end

"This very day, and you were judges here
Instead of God. Did you see Mellyagraunce
When Launcelot stood by him? what white fear

"Curdled his blood, and how his teeth did dance,
His side sink in? as my knight cried and said,
'Slayer of unarmed men, here is a chance!

" 'Setter of traps, I pray you guard your head,
By God, I am so glad to fight with you,
Stripper of ladies, that my hand feels lead

" 'For driving weight; hurrah now! draw and do,
For all my wounds are moving in my breast,
And I am getting mad with waiting so.'

"He struck his hands together o'er the beast,
Who fell down flat, and grovelled at his feet,
And groaned at being slain so young—'at least.'

"My knight said: 'Rise you, sir, who are so fleet
At catching ladies, half-armed will I fight,
My left side all uncovered!' then I weet,

"Up sprang Sir Mellyagraunce with great delight
Upon his knave's face; not until just then
Did I quite hate him, as I saw my knight

"Along the lists look to my stake and pen
With such a joyous smile, it made me sigh
From agony beneath my waist-chain, when

190. "Setter of traps. Launcelot had fallen into a trap while being shown about the castle of Mellyagraunce. **201. uncovered,** unprotected. **weet,** observed, knew.

"The fight began, and to me they drew nigh;
Ever Sir Launcelot kept him on the right,
And traversed warily, and ever high

"And fast leapt caitiff's sword, until my knight
Sudden threw up his sword to his left hand,
Caught it, and swung it; that was all the fight,

"Except a spout of blood on the hot land;
For it was hottest summer; and I know
I wondered how the fire, while I should stand,

"And burn, against the heat, would quiver so,
Yards above my head; thus these matters went;
Which things were only warnings of the woe

"That fell on me. Yet Mellyagraunce was shent,
For Mellyagraunce had fought against the Lord;
Therefore, my lords, take heed lest you be blent

"With all this wickedness; say no rash word
Against me, being so beautiful; my eyes,
Wept all away to grey, may bring some sword

"To drown you in your blood; see my breast rise,
Like waves of purple sea, as here I stand;
And how my arms are moved in wonderful wise,

"Yea also at my full heart's strong command,
See through my long throat how the words go up
In ripples to my mouth; how in my hand

"The shadow lies like wine within a cup
Of marvellously coloured gold; yea now
This little wind is rising, look you up,

"And wonder how the light is falling so
Within my moving tresses: will you dare,
When you have looked a little on my brow,

"To say this thing is vile? or will you care
For any plausible lies of cunning woof,
When you can see my face with no lie there

"For ever? am I not a gracious proof?
'But in your chamber Launcelot was found'—
Is there a good knight then would stand aloof,

"When a queen says with gentle queenly sound:
'O true as steel, come now and talk with me,
I love to see your step upon the ground

220. shent, destroyed. **222. blent,** blinded.

" 'Unwavering, also well I love to see
That gracious smile light up your face, and hear
Your wonderful words, that all mean verily

" 'The thing they seem to mean: good friend, so dear
To me in everything, come here to-night,
Or else the hours will pass most dull and drear;

" 'If you come not, I fear this time I might
Get thinking over much of times gone by,
When I was young, and green hope was in sight:

" 'For no man cares now to know why I sigh;
And no man comes to sing me pleasant songs,
Nor any brings me the sweet flowers that lie

" 'So thick in the gardens; therefore one so longs
To see you, Launcelot; that we may be
Like children once again, free from all wrongs

" 'Just for one night.' Did he not come to me?
What thing could keep true Launcelot away
If I said, 'Come'? There was one less than three

"In my quiet room that night, and we were gay;
Till sudden I rose up, weak, pale, and sick,
Because a bawling broke our dream up, yea

"I looked at Launcelot's face and could not speak,
For he looked helpless too, for a little while;
Then I remember how I tried to shriek,

"And could not, but fell down; from tile to tile
The stones they threw up rattled o'er my head
And made me dizzier; till within a while

"My maids were all about me, and my head
On Launcelot's breast was being soothed away
From its white chattering, until Launcelot said—

"By God! I will not tell you more to-day,
Judge any way you will—what matters it?
You know quite well the story of that fray,

"How Launcelot stilled their bawling, the mad fit
That caught up Gauwaine—all, all, verily,
But just that which would save me; these things flit.

"Nevertheless you, O Sir Gauwaine, lie;
Whatever may have happened these long years,
God knows I speak truth, saying that you lie!

"All I have said is truth, by Christ's dear tears."
She would not speak another word, but stood
Turned sideways; listening, like a man who hears

His brother's trumpet sounding through the wood
Of his foes' lances. She leaned eagerly,
And gave a slight spring sometimes, as she could

At last hear something really; joyfully
Her cheek grew crimson, as the headlong speed
Of the roan charger drew all men to see,
The knight who came was Launcelot at good need.

267. bawling, the coming of the knights with their accusations. **282. that . . . me,** her innocence.

THE HAYSTACK IN THE FLOODS[1]

Had she come all the way for this,
To part at last without a kiss?

Yea, had she borne the dirt and rain
That her own eyes might see him slain
Beside the haystack in the floods?

Along the dripping leafless woods,
The stirrup touching either shoe,
She rode astride as troopers do;
With kirtle kilted to her knee,
To which the mud splashed wretchedly;
And the wet dripped from every tree
Upon her head and heavy hair,
And on her eyelids broad and fair;
The tears and rain ran down her face.

By fits and starts they rode apace,
And very often was his place
Far off from her; he had to ride
Ahead, to see what might betide
When the roads crossed; and sometimes, when
There rose a murmuring from his men,
Had to turn back with promises;
Ah me! she had but little ease;
And often for pure doubt and dread
She sobbed, made giddy in the head
By the swift riding; while, for cold,
Her slender fingers scarce could hold
The wet reins; yea, and scarcely, too,
She felt the foot within her shoe
Against the stirrup: all for this,
To part at last without a kiss
Beside the haystack in the floods.

For when they neared that old soaked hay,
They saw across the only way
That Judas, Godmar, and the three
Red running lions dismally

[1] This and the other selections of William Morris still in copyright are taken from *The Collected Works of William Morris* and reprinted by permission of Longmans, Green & Company.

Grinned from his pennon, under which
In one straight line along the ditch,
They counted thirty heads.
So then,
While Robert turned round to his men,
She saw at once the wretched end,
And, stooping down, tried hard to rend
Her coif the wrong way from her head,
And hid her eyes; while Robert said:
"Nay, love, 'tis scarcely two to one;
At Poictiers where we made them run
So fast: why, sweet my love, good cheer,
The Gascon frontier is so near,
Nought after us."

But: "O!" she said,
"My God! my God! I have to tread
The long way back without you; then
The court at Paris; those six men;
The gratings of the Chatelet;
The swift Seine on some rainy day
Like this, and people standing by,
And laughing, while my weak hands try
To recollect how strong men swim.
All this, or else a life with him,
For which I should be damned at last.
Would God that this next hour were past!"

He answered not, but cried his cry,
"St. George for Marny!" cheerily;
And laid his hand upon her rein.
Alas! no man of all his train
Gave back that cheery cry again;
And, while for rage his thumb beat fast
Upon his sword-hilt, some one cast
About his neck a kerchief long,
And bound him.

Then they went along
To Godmar; who said: "Now, Jehane,
Your lover's life is on the wane
So fast, that, if this very hour
You yield not as my paramour,
He will not see the rain leave off—
Nay, keep your tongue from gibe and scoff
Sir Robert, or I slay you now."

She laid her hand upon her brow,
Then gazed upon the palm, as though
She thought her forehead bled, and—"No!"
She said, and turned her head away,
As there were nothing else to say,
And everything were settled: red
Grew Godmar's face from chin to head:
"Jehane, on yonder hill there stands
My castle, guarding well my lands:
What hinders me from taking you,
And doing that I list to do
To your fair wilful body, while
Your knight lies dead?"

A wicked smile
Wrinkled her face, her lips grew thin,
A long way out she thrust her chin:
"You know that I should strangle you
While you were sleeping; or bite through
Your throat, by God's help: ah!" she said,
"Lord Jesus, pity your poor maid!
For in such wise they hem me in,
I cannot choose but sin and sin,
Whatever happens: yet I think
They could not make me eat or drink,
And so should I just reach my rest."
"Nay, if you do not my behest,
O Jehane! though I love you well,"
Said Godmar, "would I fail to tell
All that I know?" "Foul lies," she said.
"Eh! lies, my Jehane? by God's head,
At Paris folks would deem them true!
Do you know, Jehane, they cry for you:
'Jehane the brown! Jehane the brown!
Give us Jehane to burn or drown!'—
Eh—gag me Robert!—sweet my friend,
This were indeed a piteous end
For those long fingers, and long feet,
And long neck, and smooth shoulders sweet;
An end that few men would forget
That saw it.—So, an hour yet:
Consider, Jehane, which to take
Of life or death!"

So, scarce awake,
Dismounting, did she leave that place,
And totter some yards: with her face
Turned upward to the sky she lay,
Her head on a wet heap of hay,
And fell asleep: and while she slept,
And did not dream, the minutes crept
Round to the twelve again; but she,
Being waked at last, sighed quietly,
And strangely childlike came, and said:

45. Poictiers. At the battle of Poictiers, 1356, the English defeated the French against five-to-one odds. **47. Gascon frontier.** Gascony was English territory. **50–56. then . . . swim.** Jehane, accused of witchcraft, would be imprisoned at Paris in the Chatelet, and finally flung into the Seine. If she sank she would be judged innocent, the theory being that the water would not take a witch to its bosom. **61. "St. George for Marny!"** The name of the hero of the poem is Sir Robert de Marny. St. George is the patron saint of England.

"I will not." Straightway Godmar's head,
As though it hung on strong wires, turned
Most sharply round, and his face burned.

For Robert—both his eyes were dry,
He could not weep, but gloomily
He seemed to watch the rain; yea, too,
His lips were firm; he tried once more
To touch her lips; she reached out, sore
And vain desire so tortured them,
The poor grey lips, and now the hem
Of his sleeve brushed them.

With a start
Up Godmar rose, thrust them apart;
From Robert's throat he loosed the bands
Of silk and mail; with empty hands
Held out, she stood and gazed, and saw
The long bright blade without a flaw
Glide out from Godmar's sheath, his hand
In Robert's hair; she saw him bend
Back Robert's head; she saw him send
The thin steel down; the blow told well,
Right backward the knight Robert fell,
And moaned as dogs do, being half dead,
Unwitting, as I deem: so then
Godmar turned grinning to his men,
Who ran, some five or six, and beat
His head to pieces at their feet.

Then Godmar turned again and said:
"So, Jehane, the first fitte is read!
Take note, my lady, that your way
Lies backward to the Chatelet!"
She shook her head and gazed awhile
At her cold hands with a rueful smile,
As though this thing had made her mad.

This was the parting that they had
Beside the haystack in the floods.

from THE LIFE AND DEATH OF JASON

from BOOK IV

I Know a Little Garden-close

With this song the water nymph sings young Hylas asleep.

I know a little garden-close,
Set thick with lily and red rose,
Where I would wander if I might
From dewy morn to dewy night,
And have one with me wandering.
And though within it no birds sing,
And though no pillared house is there,
And though the apple boughs are bare
Of fruit and blossom, would to God,
Her feet upon the green grass trod,
And I beheld them as before.
There comes a murmur from the shore,
And in the place two fair streams are,
Drawn from the purple hills afar,
Drawn down unto the restless sea:
Dark hills whose flowers ne'er feed the bee,
The shore no ship has ever seen,
Tormented by the billows green,
Whose murmur comes unceasingly
Unto the place for which I cry.
For which I cry both day and night,
For which I let slip all delight,
That maketh me both deaf and blind,
Careless to win, unskilled to find,
And quick to lose what all men seek.
Yet tottering as I am and weak,
Still have I left a little breath
To seek within the jaws of death
An entrance to that happy place,
To seek the unforgotten face,
Once seen, once kissed, once reft from me
Anigh the murmuring of the sea.

153. fitte, canto, division, as of a poem. **1. garden-close,** an enclosed garden.

from BOOK XII

O Death, That Makest Life so Sweet

Orpheus sings this song to encourage his companions on their homeward journey.

O death, that makest life so sweet.
O fear, with mirth before thy feet,
What have ye yet in store for us,
The conquerors, the glorious?
Men say: "For fear that thou shouldst die
To-morrow, let to-day pass by
Flower-crowned and singing"; yet have we
Passed our to-day upon the sea,
Or in a poisonous unknown land,
With fear and death on either hand,
And listless when the day was done
Have scarcely hoped to see the sun
Dawn on the morrow of the earth,
Nor in our hearts have thought of mirth.
And while the world lasts, scarce again
Shall any sons of men bear pain
Like we have borne, yet be alive.

So surely not in vain we strive
Like other men for our reward;
Sweet peace and deep, the chequered sward
Beneath the ancient mulberry-trees,
The smooth-paved gilded palaces,
Where the shy thin-clad damsels sweet
Make music with their gold-ringed feet.
The fountain court amidst of it,
Where the short-haired slave-maidens sit,
While on the veinèd pavement lie
The honied things and spicery
Their arms have borne from out the town.
The dancers on the thymy down
In summer twilight, when the earth
Is still of all things but their mirth,
And echoes borne upon the wind
Of others in like way entwined:
The merchant-town's fair market-place,
Where over many a changing face
The pigeons of the temple flit,
And still the outland merchants sit
Like kings above their merchandise,
Lying to foolish men and wise.
Ah! if they heard that we were come
Into the bay, and bringing home
That which all men have talked about,
Some men with rage, and some with doubt,
Some with desire, and some with praise;
Then would the people throng the ways,
Nor heed the outland merchandise,
Nor any talk, from fools or wise,
But tales of our accomplished quest.
What soul within the house shall rest
When we come home? The wily king
Shall leave his throne to see the thing;
No man shall keep the landward gate,
The hurried traveller shall wait
Until our bulwarks graze the quay;
Unslain the milk-white bull shall be
Beside the quivering altar-flame;
Scarce shall the maiden clasp for shame
Over her breast the raiment thin
The morn that Argo cometh in.
Then cometh happy life again
That payeth well our toil and pain
In that sweet hour, when all our woe
But as a pensive tale we know,
Nor yet remember deadly fear;
For surely now if death be near,
Unthought-of is it, and unseen
When sweet is, that hath bitter been.

30. thymy down, a tract of open upland, covered with thyme. **43. That . . . about,** the Golden Fleece.

from THE EARTHLY PARADISE

AN APOLOGY

Of Heaven or Hell I have no power to sing,
I cannot ease the burden of your fears,
Or make quick-coming death a little thing,
Or bring again the pleasure of past years,
Nor for my words shall ye forget your tears,
Or hope again, for aught that I can say,
The idle singer of an empty day.

But rather, when aweary of your mirth,
From full hearts still unsatisfied ye sigh,
And, feeling kindly unto all the earth,
Grudge every minute as it passes by,
Made the more mindful that the sweet days die—
Remember me a little then, I pray,
The idle singer of an empty day.

The heavy trouble, the bewildering care
That weighs us down who live and earn our bread,
These idle verses have no power to bear;
So let me sing of names rememberèd,
Because they, living not, can ne'er be dead,
Or long time take their memory quite away
From us poor singers of an empty day.

Dreamer of dreams, born out of my due time,
Why should I strive to set the crooked straight?
Let it suffice me that my murmuring rhyme
Beats with light wing against the ivory gate,
Telling a tale not too importunate
To those who in the sleepy region stay,
Lulled by the singer of an empty day.

Folk say, a wizard to a northern king
At Christmas-tide such wondrous things did show,
That through one window men beheld the spring,
And through another saw the summer glow,
And through a third the fruited vines a-row,
While still, unheard, but in its wonted way,
Piped the drear wind of that December day.

So with this Earthly Paradise it is,
If ye will read aright, and pardon me,
Who strive to build a shadowy isle of bliss
Midmost the beating of the steely sea,
Where tossed about all hearts of men must be;
Whose ravening monsters mighty men shall slay,
Not the poor singer of an empty day.

25. the ivory gate, the egress through which purely fanciful dreams issue from the house of Morpheus, god of sleep. Dreams of any significance pass through a gate of horn.

NO MASTER

Saith man to man, We've heard and known
That we no master need
To live upon this earth, our own,
In fair and manly deed.
The grief of slaves long passed away
For us hath forged the chain,
Till now each worker's patient day
Builds up the House of Pain.

And we, shall we too crouch and quail,
Ashamed, afraid of strife,
And lest our lives untimely fail
Embrace the Death in Life?
Nay, cry aloud, and have no fear,
We few against the world;
Awake, arise! the hope we bear
Against the curse is hurled.

It grows and grows—are we the same,
The feeble band, the few?
Or what are these with eyes aflame,
And hands to deal and do?
This is the host that bears the word,
"No Master high or low"—
A lightning flame, a shearing sword,
A storm to overthrow.

George Meredith
1828–1909

Meredith belongs to the small company of English writers who won front rank both as novelist and as poet. He was born in Portsmouth, February 12, 1828, the son of a tailor. Of his unsystematic education two years at a Moravian school in Austria were probably the most significant part. He attempted to study law; he did editorial work alike in the newspaper and the periodical fields; he served in Italy as a war correspondent (see his novels, *Sandra Belloni* and *Vittoria*); for thirty-five years he earned his living as a publisher's reader. In 1849 he was married, most unhappily, to Thomas Love Peacock's daughter, who deserted him in 1858; in 1864 he married Marie Vulliamy. His first book was a collection of *Poems*, 1851; his first real novel was *The Ordeal of Richard Feverel*, 1859. *Evan Harrington*, *Rhoda Fleming*, *Beauchamp's Career*, and *The Egoist* followed, but Meredith did not find a large public until *Diana of the Crossways* appeared in 1885. The death of his wife and his own ill-health darkened his later years. By that time, however, he was at the height of his reputation, and his home at Box Hill, Surrey, had become a literary shrine. In 1892 he became president of the British Society of Authors; in 1905 he received the Order of Merit. He died May 18, 1909.

Though Meredith does not disdain to use the term "God" freely, he was basically a nature-worshiper. He was a romanticist, but he did not ignore the evidence of science; he hated both asceticism and sensuality, and he hated sentimentalism, which he regarded as merely an inverted sensuality. He accepted the evolutionary hypothesis, but he interpreted it optimistically, not pessimistically as Hardy did. But he did not share Spencer's or Macaulay's faith in automatic progress; he believed that to serve the needs of life men must give themselves unselfishly to the purposes of life. Like George Eliot, he saw egoism at the root of all human difficulties.

Disdaining a supernatural solution of the human problem, Meredith found comedy—"the sword of common sense"—a powerful weapon against sentimentalism, egoism, and all their breed: "One excellent test of the civilization of a country . . . I take to be the flourishing of the Comic idea and Comedy; and the test of true Comedy is that it shall awaken thoughtful laughter."

Most of Meredith's later novels reflect his own highly individual brand of "feminism." Fuller recognition of the role of women in society was not only essential to the sanity and sense of proportion he felt were required for civilized living. It was also a vital part of his whole artistic concept. The particular kind of intellectual comedy through which he worked out his ideas could exist only in a society in which men and women mingle on terms of at least approximate equality.

Meredith's novels are among the most brilliant in our language. His examination into the psychology of his characters is minute and searching, his style bristling with wit and imagery. His young people are especially attractive; *The Ordeal of Richard Feverel* and many later novels reveal sympathetic understanding of youth's perplexity in some of its relations with an older generation. Meredith was, however, always rather indifferent to the matter of plot. That lack, and the frequent difficulty of his style and thought, have done much to keep him from reaching a wide popular audience. In his later years Meredith seemed perversely determined to wreak vengeance upon the public for its long neglect of him by making his novels as difficult to read as possible. He would labor what seems a trifling point for pages upon pages, then pass over an important climax in a phrase.

Meredith was a poet by natural endowment, and his attitude toward life was that of a poet even when he was writing prose. Imagery was his everyday idiom, and he was as sensitive to the world of nature as to the world of men and women. Indeed it was part of his philosophy that those two are not different worlds. Much of his poetry is of the earth, its woods and valleys, of the wind and stars. It expresses—sometimes obscurely, but often radiantly—his consciousness of a quickening unity between man and the world he dwells in. Among his titles in this field are *Poems and Lyrics of the Joy of Earth*, *Ballads and Poems of Tragic Life*, *A Reading of Earth*, and *A Reading of Life*.

JUGGLING JERRY[1]

1

Pitch here the tent, while the old horse grazes:
By the old hedge-side we'll halt a stage.
It's nigh my last above the daisies:
My next leaf'll be man's blank page.
Yes, my old girl! and it's no use crying:
Juggler, constable, king, must bow.
One that outjuggles all's been spying
Long to have me, and he has me now.

2

We've travelled times to this old common:
Often we've hung our pots in the gorse.
We've had a stirring life, old woman,
You, and I, and the old grey horse.
Races, and fairs, and royal occasions,
Found us coming to their call:
Now they'll miss us at our stations:
There's a Juggler outjuggles all!

3

Up goes the lark, as if all were jolly!
Over the duck-pond the willow shakes.
Easy to think that grieving's folly,
When the hand's firm as driven stakes!
Ay, when we're strong, and braced, and manful,
Life's a sweet fiddle: but we're a batch
Born to become the Great Juggler's han'ful:
Balls he shies up, and is safe to catch.

4

Here's where the lads of the village cricket:
I was a lad not wide from here:
Couldn't I whip off the bail from the wicket?
Like an old world those days appear!
Donkey, sheep, geese, and thatched ale-house—I know them!
They are old friends of my halts, and seem,
Somehow, as if kind thanks I owe them:
Juggling don't hinder the heart's esteem.

5

Juggling's no sin, for we must have victual:
Nature allows us to bait for the fool.
Holding one's own makes us juggle no little;
But, to increase it, hard juggling's the rule.
You that are sneering at my profession,
Haven't you juggled a vast amount?
There's the Prime Minister, in one Session,
Juggles more games than my sins'll count.

6

I've murdered insects with mock thunder:
Conscience, for that, in men don't quail.
I've made bread from the bump of wonder:
That's my business, and there's my tale.
Fashion and rank all praised the professor:
Ay! and I've had my smile from the Queen:
Bravo, Jerry! she meant: God bless her!
Ain't this a sermon on that scene?

7

I've studied men from my topsy-turvy
Close, and, I reckon, rather true.
Some are fine fellows: some, right scurvy:
Most, a dash between the two.
But it's a woman, old girl, that makes me
Think more kindly of the race:
And it's a woman, old girl, that shakes me
When the Great Juggler I must face.

[1] This and the following selections are from *The Poetical Works of George Meredith*, Charles Scribner's Sons. Reprinted by permission. **10. gorse,** furze, a spiny evergreen shrub.

25. cricket, play cricket. **53–54. But it's . . . race,** a characteristically Meredithian point of view, as all readers of his novels will recognize.

8

We two were married, due and legal:
  Honest we've lived since we've been one.
Lord! I could then jump like an eagle:
  You danced bright as a bit o' the sun.
Birds in a May-bush we were! right merry!
  All night we kissed, we juggled all day.
Joy was the heart of Juggling Jerry!
  Now from his old girl he's juggled away.

9

It's past parsons to console us:
  No, nor no doctor fetch for me:
I can die without my bolus;
  Two of a trade, lass, never agree!
Parson and Doctor!—don't they love rarely,
  Fighting the devil in other men's fields!
Stand up yourself and match him fairly:
  Then see how the rascal yields!

10

I, lass, have lived no gipsy, flaunting
  Finery while this poor helpmate grubs:
Coin I've stored, and you won't be wanting:
  You sha'n't beg from the troughs and tubs.
Nobly you've stuck to me, though in his kitchen
  Many a Marquis would hail you Cook!
Palaces you could have ruled and grown rich in,
  But your old Jerry you never forsook.

11

Hand up the chirper! ripe ale winks in it;
  Let's have comfort and be at peace.
Once a stout draught made me light as a linnet.
  Cheer up! the Lord must have his lease.
May be—for none see in that black hollow—
  It's just a place where we're held in pawn,
And, when the Great Juggler makes as to swallow,
  It's just the sword-trick—I ain't quite gone!

12

Yonder came smells of the gorse, so nutty,
  Gold-like and warm: it's the prime of May.
Better than mortar, brick and putty,
  Is God's house on a blowing day.
Lean me more up the mound; now I feel it:
  All the old heath-smells! Ain't it strange?
There's the world laughing, as if to conceal it,
  But He's by us, juggling the change.

13

I mind it well, by the sea-beach lying,
  Once—it's long gone—when two gulls we beheld,
Which, as the moon got up, were flying
  Down a big wave that sparked and swelled.
Crack, went a gun: one fell: the second
  Wheeled round him twice, and was off for new luck:
There in the dark her white wing beckoned:—
  Drop me a kiss—I'm the bird dead-struck!

81. **chirper,** chirper cup (that is, producing merriment), "the cup that cheers." 95. **it,** the change from life to death.

from MODERN LOVE

Modern Love is often spoken of as a sonnet sequence; actually each stanza is sixteen lines in length. The situation described has some points in common with that in which Meredith found himself after his unfortunate marriage to the daughter of Thomas Love Peacock.

1

By this he knew she wept with waking eyes:
That, at his hand's light quiver by her head,
The strange low sobs that shook their common bed
Were called into her with a sharp surprise,
And strangled mute, like little gaping snakes,
Dreadfully venomous to him. She lay
Stone-still, and the long darkness flowed away
With muffled pulses. Then, as midnight makes
Her giant heart of Memory and Tears
Drink the pale drug of silence, and so beat
Sleep's heavy measure, they from head to feet
Were moveless, looking through their dead black years,
By vain regret scrawled over the blank wall.
Like sculptured effigies they might be seen
Upon their marriage-tomb, the sword between;
Each wishing for the sword that severs all.

13

"I play for Seasons, not Eternities!"
Says Nature, laughing on her way. "So must
All those whose stake is nothing more than dust!"
And lo, she wins, and of her harmonies
She is full sure! Upon her dying rose
She drops a look of fondness, and goes by,
Scarce any retrospection in her eye;
For she the laws of growth most deeply knows,
Whose hands bear, here, a seed-bag—there, an urn.
Pledged she herself to aught, 'twould mark her end!
This lesson of our only visible friend
Can we not teach our foolish hearts to learn?

15. **the sword between,** a reference to the sword often placed between chaste lovers in the medieval romances.

Yes! yes!—but, oh, our human rose is fair
Surpassingly! Lose calmly Love's great bliss,
When the renewed for ever of a kiss
Whirls life within the shower of loosened hair!

16

In our old shipwrecked days there was an hour,
When in the firelight steadily aglow,
Joined slackly, we beheld the red chasm grow
Among the clicking coals. Our library-bower
That eve was left to us; and hushed we sat
As lovers to whom Time is whispering.
From sudden-opened doors we heard them sing;
The nodding elders mixed good wine with chat.
Well knew we that Life's greatest treasure lay
With us, and of it was our talk. "Ah, yes!
Love dies!" I said: I never thought it less.
She yearned to me that sentence to unsay.
Then when the fire domed blackening, I found
Her cheek was salt against my kiss, and swift
Up the sharp scale of sobs her breast did lift:—
Now am I haunted by that taste! that sound!

17

At dinner, she is hostess, I am host.
Went the feast ever cheerfuller? She keeps
The Topic over intellectual deeps
In buoyancy afloat. They see no ghost.
With sparkling surface-eyes we play the ball;
It is in truth a most contagious game:
HIDING THE SKELETON shall be its name.
Such play as this the devils might appal!
But here's the greater wonder: in that we,
Enamoured of an acting naught can tire,
Each other, like true hypocrites, admire;
Warm-lighted looks, Love's ephemerioe,
Shoot gaily o'er the dishes and the wine.
We waken envy of our happy lot.
Fast, sweet, and golden, shows the marriage-knot.
Dear guests, you now have seen Love's corpse-light shine.

29

Am I failing? For no longer can I cast
A glory round about this head of gold.
Glory she wears, but springing from the mould;
Not like the consecration of the Past!
Is my soul beggared? Something more than earth
I cry for still: I cannot be at peace
In having Love upon a mortal lease.
I cannot take the woman at her worth!
Where is the ancient wealth wherewith I clothed
Our human nakedness, and could endow
With spiritual splendour a white brow
That else had grinned at me the fact I loathed?
A kiss is but a kiss now! and no wave
Of a great flood that whirls me to the sea.
But, as you will! we'll sit contentedly,
And eat our pot of honey on the grave.

43

Mark where the pressing wind shoots javelin-like
Its skeleton shadow on the broad-backed wave!
Here is a fitting spot to dig Love's grave;
Here where the ponderous breakers plunge and strike,
And dart their hissing tongues high up the sand:
In hearing of the ocean, and in sight
Of those ribbed wind-streaks running into white.
If I the death of Love had deeply planned,
I never could have made it half so sure,
As by the unblest kisses which upbraid
The full-waked sense; or failing that, degrade!
'Tis morning; but no morning can restore
What we have forfeited. I see no sin;
The wrong is mixed. In tragic life, God wot,
No villain need be! Passions spin the plot;
We are betrayed by what is false within.

44

They say that Pity in Love's service dwells,
A porter at the rosy temple's gate.
I missed him going: but it is my fate
To come upon him now beside his wells;
Whereby I know that I Love's temple leave,
And that the purple doors have closed behind.
Poor soul! if, in those early days unkind,
Thy power to sting had been but power to grieve,
We now might with an equal spirit meet,
And not be matched like innocence and vice.
She for the Temple's worship has paid price,
And takes the coin of Pity as a cheat.
She sees through simulation to the bone:
What's best in her impels her to the worst:
Never, she cries, shall Pity soothe Love's thirst,
Or foul hypocrisy for truth atone!

47

We saw the swallows gathering in the sky,
And in the osier-isle we heard their noise.
We had not to look back on summer joys,
Or forward to a summer of bright dye:
But in the largeness of the evening earth

Sec. 17. **3. The Topic,** of conversation. **4. They,** the guests. **12. ephemerioe,** insects living only a day. **16. corpse-light,** a light like the flame of a candle, sometimes seen in graveyards, and believed to portend death.

Sec. 43. **14. wot,** knows.

Our spirits grew as we went side by side.
The hour became her husband and my bride.
Love, that had robbed us so, thus blessed our dearth!
The pilgrims of the year waxed very loud
In multitudinous chatterings, as the flood
Full brown came from the West, and like pale blood
Expanded to the upper crimson cloud.
Love, that had robbed us of immortal things,
This little moment mercifully gave,
Where I have seen across the twilight wave
The swan sail with her young beneath her wings.

50

Thus piteously Love closed what he begat:
The union of this ever-diverse pair!
These two were rapid falcons in a snare,
Condemned to do the flitting of the bat.
Lovers beneath the singing sky of May,
They wandered once, clear as the dew on flowers,
But they fed not on the advancing hours:
Their hearts held cravings for the buried day.
Then each applied to each that fatal knife,
Deep questioning, which probes to endless dole.
Ah, what a dusty answer gets the soul
When hot for certainties in this our life!—
In tragic hints here see what evermore
Moves dark as yonder midnight ocean's force,
Thundering like ramping hosts of warrior horse,
To throw that faint thin line upon the shore!

LOVE IN THE VALLEY

This beautiful poem is notable for the way in which the rhythm itself is used "to give Meredith's feeling for the exquisite light-hearted, light-footed girl whose nature he is trying to recapture and set in words for us." In the nineteenth stanza we get the impression of a hot, drowsy, summer noon; there are actually nineteen extra stresses in this stanza. Sir Arthur Quiller-Couch said of the poem that "with Spenser's 'Epithalamion,' it shares claim to be the greatest song of human love in our language."

Under yonder beech-tree single on the green-sward,
  Couched with her arms behind her golden head,
Knees and tresses folded to slip and ripple idly,
  Lies my young love sleeping in the shade.
Had I the heart to slide an arm beneath her,
  Press her parting lips as her waist I gather slow,
Waking in amazement she could not but embrace me:
  Then would she hold me and never let me go?

Shy as the squirrel and wayward as the swallow,
  Swift as the swallow along the river's light,
Circleting the surface to meet his mirrored winglets,
  Fleeter she seems in her stay than in her flight.
Shy as the squirrel that leaps among the pine-tops,
  Wayward as the swallow overhead at set of sun,
She whom I love is hard to catch and conquer;
  Hard, but oh, the glory of the winning were she won!

When her mother tends her before the laughing mirror,
  Tying up her laces, looping up her hair,
Often she thinks, were this wild thing wedded,
  More love should I have, and much less care.
When her mother tends her before the lighted mirror,
  Loosening her laces, combing down her curls,
Often she thinks, were this wild thing wedded,
  I should miss but one for many boys and girls.

Heartless she is as the shadow in the meadows
  Flying to the hills on a blue and breezy noon.
No, she is athirst and drinking up her wonder:
  Earth to her is young as the slip of the new moon.
Deals she an unkindness, 'tis but her rapid measure,
  Even as in a dance; and her smile can heal no less:
Like the swinging May-cloud that pelts the flowers with hailstones
  Off a sunny border, she was made to bruise and bless.

Lovely are the curves of the white owl sweeping
  Wavy in the dusk lit by one large star.
Lone on the fir-branch, his rattle-note unvaried,
  Brooding o'er the gloom, spins the brown eve-jar.
Darker grows the valley, more and more forgetting:
  So were it with me if forgetting could be willed.
Tell the grassy hollow that holds the bubbling well-spring,
  Tell it to forget the source that keeps it filled.

Stepping down the hill with her fair companions,
  Arm in arm, all against the raying West,
Boldly she sings, to the merry tune she marches,
  Brave in her shape, and sweeter unpossessed.
Sweeter, for she is what my heart first awaking
  Whispered the world was; morning light is she.
Love that so desires would fain keep her changeless;
  Fain would fling the net, and fain have her free.

36. eve-jar, nightjar.

Happy happy time, when the white star hovers
  Low over dim fields fresh with bloomy dew,
Near the face of dawn, that draws athwart the darkness,
  Threading it with colour, like yewberries the yew.
Thicker crowd the shades as the grave East deepens
  Glowing, and with crimson a long cloud swells.
Maiden still the morn is; and strange she is, and secret;
  Strange her eyes; her cheeks are cold as cold sea-shells.

Sunrays, leaning on our southern hills and lighting
  Wild cloud-mountains that drag the hills along,
Oft ends the day of your shifting brilliant laughter
  Chill as a dull face frowning on a song.
Ay, but shows the South-west a ripple-feathered bosom
  Blown to silver while the clouds are shaken and ascend
Scaling the mid-heavens as they stream, there comes a sunset
  Rich, deep like love in beauty without end.

When at dawn she sighs, and like an infant to the window
  Turns grave eyes craving light, released from dreams,
Beautiful she looks, like a white water-lily
  Bursting out of bud in havens of the streams.
When from bed she rises clothed from neck to ankle
  In her long nightgown sweet as boughs of May,
Beautiful she looks, like a tall garden lily
  Pure from the night, and splendid for the day.

Mother of the dews, dark eye-lashed twilight,
  Low-lidded twilight, o'er the valley's brim,
Rounding on thy breast sings the dew-delighted skylark,
  Clear as though the dewdrops had their voice in him.
Hidden where the rose-flush drinks the rayless planet,
  Fountain-full he pours the spraying fountain-showers.
Let me hear her laughter, I would have her ever
  Cool as dew in twilight, the lark above the flowers.

All the girls are out with their baskets for the primrose;
  Up lanes, woods through, they troop in joyful bands.
My sweet leads: she knows not why, but now she loiters,
  Eyes the bent anemones, and hangs her hands.
Such a look will tell that the violets are peeping,
  Coming the rose: and unaware a cry
Springs in her bosom for odours and for colour,
  Covert and the nightingale; she knows not why.

Kerchiefed head and chin she darts between her tulips,
  Streaming like a willow grey in arrowy rain:
Some bend beaten cheek to gravel, and their angel
  She will be; she lifts them, and on she speeds again.
Black the driving raincloud breasts the iron gateway:
  She is forth to cheer a neighbour lacking mirth.
So when sky and grass met rolling dumb for thunder
  Saw I once a white dove, sole light of earth.

Prim little scholars are the flowers of her garden,
  Trained to stand in rows, and asking if they please.
I might love them well but for loving more the wild ones:
  O my wild ones! they tell me more than these.
You, my wild one, you tell of honied field-rose,
  Violet, blushing eglantine in life; and even as they,
They by the wayside are earnest of your goodness,
  You are of life's, on the banks that line the way.

Peering at her chamber the white crowns the red rose,
  Jasmine winds the porch with stars two and three.
Parted is the window; she sleeps; the starry jasmine
  Breathes a falling breath that carries thoughts of me.
Sweeter unpossessed, have I said of her my sweetest?
  Not while she sleeps: while she sleeps the jasmine breathes,
Luring her to love; she sleeps; the starry jasmine
  Bears me to her pillow under white rose-wreaths.

Yellow with birdfoot-trefoil are the grass-glades;
  Yellow with cinquefoil of the dew-grey leaf;
Yellow with stonecrop; the moss-mounds are yellow;

77. rayless planet, the morning star, whose rays have been quenched by the rising sun.

113. birdfoot-trefoil, a clover-shaped leaf or flower, suggesting the spreading foot of a bird.

Blue-necked the wheat sways, yellowing to the sheaf.
Green-yellow bursts from the copse the laughing yaffle:
Sharp as a sickle is the edge of shade and shine:
Earth in her heart laughs looking at the heavens,
Thinking of the harvest: I look and think of mine.

This I may know: her dressing and undressing
Such a change of light shows as when the skies in sport
Shift from cloud to moonlight; or edging over thunder
Slips a ray of sun; or sweeping into port
White sails furl; or on the ocean borders
White sails lean along the waves leaping green.
Visions of her shower before me, but from eyesight
Guarded she would be like the sun were she seen.

Front door and back of the mossed old farmhouse
Open with the morn, and in a breezy link
Freshly sparkles garden to stripe-shadowed orchard,
Green across a rill where on sand the minnows wink.
Busy in the grass the early sun of summer
Swarms, and the blackbird's mellow fluting notes
Call my darling up with round and roguish challenge:
Quaintest, richest carol of all the singing throats!

Cool was the woodside; cool as her white dairy
Keeping sweet the cream-pan; and there the boys from school,
Cricketing below, rushed brown and red with sunshine;
O the dark translucence of the deep-eyed cool!
Spying from the farm, herself she fetched a pitcher
Full of milk, and tilted for each in turn the beak.
Then a little fellow, mouth up and on tiptoe,
Said, "I will kiss you": she laughed and leaned her cheek.

Doves of the fir-wood walling high our red roof
Through the long noon coo, crooning through the coo.
Loose droop the leaves, and down the sleepy roadway
Sometimes pipes a chaffinch; loose droops the blue.
Cows flap a slow tail knee-deep in the river,
Breathless, given up to sun and gnat and fly.
Nowhere is she seen; and if I see her nowhere,
Lightning may come, straight rains and tiger sky.

O the golden sheaf, the rustling treasure-armful!
O the nutbrown tresses nodding interlaced!
O the treasure-tresses one another over
Nodding! O the girdle slack about the waist!
Slain are the poppies that shot their random scarlet
Quick amid the wheatears: wound about the waist,
Gathered, see these brides of Earth one blush of ripeness!
O the nutbrown tresses nodding interlaced!

Large and smoky red the sun's cold disk drops,
Clipped by naked hills, on violet shaded snow:
Eastward large and still lights up a bower of moonrise,
Whence at her leisure steps the moon aglow.
Nightlong on black print-branches our beech-tree
Gazes in this whiteness: nightlong could I.
Here may life on death or death on life be painted.
Let me clasp her soul to know she cannot die!

Gossips count her faults; they scour a narrow chamber
Where there is no window, read not heaven or her.
"When she was a tiny," one aged woman quavers,
Plucks at my heart and leads me by the ear.
Faults she had once as she learnt to run and tumbled:
Faults of feature some see, beauty not complete.
Yet, good gossips, beauty that makes holy
Earth and air, may have faults from head to feet.

Hither she comes; she comes to me; she lingers,
Deepens her brown eyebrows, while in new surprise
High rise the lashes in wonder of a stranger;
Yet am I the light and living of her eyes.
Something friends have told her fills her heart to brimming,
Nets her in her blushes, and wounds her, and tames.—
Sure of her haven, O like a dove alighting,
Arms up, she dropped: our souls were in our names.

Soon will she lie like a white-frost sunrise.
Yellow oats and brown wheat, barley pale as rye,
Long since your sheaves have yielded to the thresher,

117. yaffle, the green woodpecker. **130. link,** land adjacent to a bend in a stream.

165. print-branches, shadows.

Felt the girdle loosened, seen the tresses fly.
Soon will she lie like a blood-red sunset.
Swift with the to-morrow, green-winged Spring!
Sing from the South-West, bring her back the truants,
Nightingale and swallow, song and dipping wing.

Soft new beech-leaves, up to beamy April
Spreading bough on bough a primrose mountain, you,
Lucid in the moon, raise lilies to the skyfields,
Youngest green transfused in silver shining through:
Fairer than the lily, than the wild white cherry:
Fair as in image my seraph love appears
Borne to me by dreams when dawn is at my eyelids:
Fair as in the flesh she swims to me on tears.

Could I find a place to be alone with heaven,
I would speak my heart out: heaven is my need.
Every woodland tree is flushing like the dogwood,
Flashing like the whitebeam, swaying like the reed.
Flushing like the dogwood crimson in October;
Streaming like the flag-reed South-West blown;
Flashing as in gusts the sudden-lighted whitebeam:
All seem to know what is for heaven alone.

THE LARK ASCENDING

He rises and begins to round,
He drops the silver chain of sound,
Of many links without a break,
In chirrup, whistle, slur and shake,
All intervolved and spreading wide,
Like water-dimples down a tide
Where ripple ripple overcurls
And eddy into eddy whirls;
A press of hurried notes that run
So fleet they scarce are more than one,
Yet changeingly the trills repeat
And linger ringing while they fleet,
Sweet to the quick o' the ear, and dear
To her beyond the handmaid ear,
Who sits beside our inner springs,
Too often dry for this he brings,
Which seems the very jet of earth
At sight of sun, her music's mirth,

14. her, the spirit of Nature within us, which hears that which her handmaid, the ear of clay, cannot hear.

As up he wings the spiral stair,
A song of light, and pierces air
With fountain ardour, fountain play,
To reach the shining tops of day,
And drink in everything discerned
An ecstasy to music turned,
Impelled by what his happy bill
Disperses; drinking, showering still,
Unthinking save that he may give
His voice the outlet, there to live
Renewed in endless notes of glee,
So thirsty of his voice is he,
For all to hear and all to know
That he is joy, awake, aglow,
The tumult of the heart to hear
Through pureness filtered crystal-clear,
And know the pleasure sprinkled bright
By simple singing of delight,
Shrill, irreflective, unrestrained,
Rapt, ringing, on the jet sustained
Without a break, without a fall,
Sweet-silvery, sheer lyrical,
Perennial, quavering up the chord
Like myriad dews of sunny sward
That trembling into fulness shine,
And sparkle dropping argentine;
Such wooing as the ear receives
From zephyr caught in choric leaves
Of aspens when their chattering net
Is flushed to white with shivers wet;
And such the water-spirit's chime
On mountain heights in morning's prime,
Too freshly sweet to seem excess,
Too animate to need a stress;
But wider over many heads
The starry voice ascending spreads,
Awakening, as it waxes thin,
The best in us to him akin;
And every face to watch him raised
Puts on the light of children praised,
So rich our human pleasure ripes
When sweetness on sincereness pipes,
Though nought be promised from the seas,
But only a soft-ruffling breeze
Sweep glittering on a still content,
Serenity in ravishment.

For singing till his heaven fills,
'Tis love of earth that he instils,
And ever winging up and up,
Our valley is his golden cup,
And he the wine which overflows
To lift us with him as he goes:
The woods and brooks, the sheep and kine,

He is, the hill, the human line,
The meadows green, the fallows brown,
The dreams of labour in the town;
He sings the sap, the quickened veins;
The wedding song of sun and rains
He is, the dance of children, thanks
Of sowers, shout of primrose-banks,
And eye of violets while they breathe;
All these the circling song will wreathe,
And you shall hear the herb and tree,
The better heart of men shall see,
Shall feel celestially, as long
As you crave nothing save the song.

Was never voice of ours could say
Our inmost in the sweetest way,
Like yonder voice aloft, and link
All hearers in the song they drink.
Our wisdom speaks from failing blood,
Our passion is too full in flood,
We want the key of his wild note
Of truthful in a tuneful throat,
The song seraphically free
Of taint of personality,
So pure that it salutes the suns,
The voice of one for millions,
In whom the millions rejoice
For giving their one spirit voice.

Yet men have we, whom we revere,
Now names, and men still housing here,
Whose lives, by many a battle-dint
Defaced, and grinding wheels on flint,
Yield substance, though they sing not, sweet
For song our highest heaven to greet:
Whom heavenly singing gives us new,
Enspheres them brilliant in our blue,
From firmest base to farthest leap,
Because their love of Earth is deep,
And they are warriors in accord
With life to serve, and pass reward,
So touching purest and so heard
In the brain's reflex of yon bird:
Wherefore their soul in me, or mine,
Through self-forgetfulness divine,
In them, that song aloft maintains,
To fill the sky and thrill the plains
With showerings drawn from human stores,
As he to silence nearer soars,
Extends the world at wings and dome,
More spacious making more our home,
Till lost on his aërial rings
In light, and then the fancy sings.

91. want, lack. **110. pass,** pass up, disdain.

LUCIFER IN STARLIGHT

On a starred night Prince Lucifer uprose.
Tired of his dark dominion swung the fiend
Above the rolling ball in cloud part screened,
Where sinners hugged their spectre of repose.
Poor prey to his hot fit of pride were those.
And now upon his western wing he leaned,
Now his huge bulk o'er Afric's sands careened,
Now the black planet shadowed Arctic snows.
Soaring through wider zones that pricked his scars
With memory of the old revolt from Awe,
He reached the middle height, and at the stars,
Which are the brain of heaven, he looked, and sank.
Around the ancient track marched, rank on rank,
The army of unalterable law.

ON THE DANGER OF WAR

Avert, High Wisdom, never vainly wooed,
This threat of War, that shows a land brain-sick.
When nations gain the pitch where rhetoric
Seems reason they are ripe for cannon's food.
Dark looms the issue though the cause be good,
But with the doubt 'tis our old devil's trick.
O now the down-slope of the lunatic
Illumine lest we redden of that brood.
For not since man in his first view of thee
Ascended to the heavens giving sign
Within him of deep sky and sounded sea,
Did he unforfeiting thy laws transgress;
In peril of his blood his ears incline
To drums whose loudness is their emptiness.

Lucifer in Starlight. **1. Prince Lucifer.** Lucifer (literally, "light-bringer") is the planet Venus as the morning star. On the basis of Isaiah 14:12—"How art thou fallen from heaven, O Lucifer, son of the morning!"—Lucifer has been popularly identified (as in *Paradise Lost*) with Satan, the rebel archangel. **2. dark dominion,** hell. **3. rolling ball,** the earth. **5. Poor prey . . . those.** If Lucifer had not fallen through pride, he would never have corrupted humanity. **9. scars,** of battle against the heavenly hosts.

Algernon Charles Swinburne
1837–1909

Swinburne was the *enfant terrible* of Victorian poetry. He was born in London on April 5, 1837, of a distinguished and aristocratic family. His early training was largely under his mother, the daughter of the Earl of Ashburnham, and his grandfather, Sir John Edward Swinburne, who in all his habits of thinking and living was a French gentleman of the old school. The boy distinguished himself at Eton and at Oxford by his encyclopedic reading in several languages, and also by his insubordination; he left both places, with the approval of the authorities, before having completed his course. From 1860, when he left Oxford, until 1879, he lived most of the time in London, where he associated with Rossetti, Morris, Burne-Jones, and others whose Pre-Raphaelite ideals he shared.

Swinburne's first publication—a volume containing two romantic plays in blank verse, *The Queen Mother* and *Rosamond*—appeared in 1860. Dedicated to Rossetti, it was a volume that the Pre-Raphaelites approved of, but the public paid it no attention, and Swinburne spoke of it as stillborn. His genius, however, had been nourished not only at the spring of medieval romanticism. He had drunk deeply of the Greek fountain, and perhaps no other English poet of his day had imbibed more of the spirit of the Greek classics. This spirit welled up in his *Atalanta in Calydon*, 1865, a tragedy in the Greek classical form. Something of the variety of Swinburne's interests and the fact that he was as much at home with the Elizabethan dramatists as with the Greeks are indicated by his publishing in the same year his *Chastelard*, the first of a trilogy of romantic dramas dealing with Mary Queen of Scots. The two other plays of the group appeared much later: *Bothwell*, in 1874, and *Mary Stuart*, in 1881.

At the age of twenty-nine he achieved both fame and notoriety when his *Poems and Ballads*, 1866, became at once a poetic triumph and a rousing scandal. No lover of poetry could deny that the lyrics in the volume were full of fresh and enchanting beauty, and no guardian of public or private morality could overlook the pagan sensuality of the poems. A second series of *Poems and Ballads* in the same mood and manner, and containing some exquisite elegies, appeared in 1878, and a third in 1889. Swinburne's reputation as a sensualist is due largely to the three series of *Poems and Ballads*. In point of fact, Swinburne with his small elf-like body, crowned with an amazing shock of red hair, was a frail, nervous creature whose actual experience of sin always lagged behind his imaginative comprehension of it.

By 1879 Swinburne had shown himself clearly incapable of managing his own life. That was when Theodore Watts-Dunton took charge of him. For the last thirty years of Swinburne's life Watts-Dunton handled all his practical affairs and made most of his decisions for him. A steady stream of books flowed from Swinburne during those years, most of which are generally considered inferior to his earlier works. But without Watts-Dunton he would have written nothing. He died at Putney on April 10, 1909.

Among Swinburne's poetic works, in addition to those already mentioned, are *Songs before Sunrise*, 1867; *Tristram of Lyonesse and Other Poems*, 1882; *A Century of Roundels*, 1883; *Astrophel and Other Poems*, 1894; and *Rosamund, Queen of the Lombards*, 1899. He produced extensive critical writings, including studies of Shakespeare and other Elizabethan dramatists, Blake, Victor Hugo, and several Victorian novelists.

The elements of strength in Swinburne's character included his sensitiveness to beauty, his enthusiasm for liberty, and his ability to find satisfaction in "the noble art of praising." His critical writing, however, veers between extravagant praise and equally extravagant censure—he was never pleased or displeased in moderation. Yet he has many sane critical passages, and many that evince his capacity to achieve a fundamentally just assessment of life. The religious indifference of Rossetti and Morris became with him a positive hostility, though the very violence of his reaction probably indicates that the religious view of life had a stronger hold upon him than he would admit.

In Swinburne's style, as in his mind, there is a luscious quality. Matthew Arnold criticized him for using a hundred words when one would have expressed his meaning. He was aware of this mannerism and parodied it in such poems as "Nephelidia." But if in his welter of words it is sometimes hard to find the idea, it is after all true that poetry is written with words, not ideas.

from ATALANTA IN CALYDON

Atalanta in Calydon, 1865, was Swinburne's attempt "to do something original in English which might in some degree reproduce for English readers the likeness of a Greek tragedy with something of its true poetic life and charm." Three beautiful choruses from the play are given here.

1. WHEN THE HOUNDS OF SPRING

When the hounds of spring are on winter's traces,
  The mother of months in meadow or plain
Fills the shadows and windy places
  With lisp of leaves and ripple of rain;
And the brown bright nightingale amorous
Is half assuaged for Itylus,
For the Thracian ships and the foreign faces,
  The tongueless vigil, and all the pain.

Come with bows bent and with emptying of quivers,
  Maiden most perfect, lady of light,
With a noise of winds and many rivers,
  With a clamour of waters, and with might;
Bind on thy sandals, O thou most fleet,
Over the splendour and speed of thy feet;
For the faint east quickens, the wan west shivers,
  Round the feet of the day and the feet of the night.

Where shall we find her, how shall we sing to her,
  Fold our hands round her knees, and cling?
O that man's heart were as fire and could spring to her,
  Fire, or the strength of the streams that spring!
For the stars and the winds are unto her
As raiment, as songs of the harp-player;
For the risen stars and the fallen cling to her,
  And the southwest-wind and the west-wind sing.

For winter's rains and ruins are over,
  And all the season of snows and sins;
The days dividing lover and lover,
  The light that loses, the night that wins;
And time remembered is grief forgotten,
And frosts are slain and flowers begotten,
And in green underwood and cover
  Blossom by blossom the spring begins.

The full streams feed on flower of rushes,
  Ripe grasses trammel a travelling foot,
The faint fresh flame of the young year flushes
  From leaf to flower and flower to fruit;
And fruit and leaf are as gold and fire,
And the oat is heard above the lyre,
And the hoofèd heel of a satyr crushes
  The chestnut-husk at the chestnut-root.

And Pan by noon and Bacchus by night,
  Fleeter of foot than the fleet-foot kid,
Follows with dancing and fills with delight
  The Maenad and the Bassarid;
And soft as lips that laugh and hide
The laughing leaves of the trees divide,
And screen from seeing and leave in sight
  The god pursuing, the maiden hid.

The ivy falls with the Bacchanal's hair
  Over her eyebrows hiding her eyes;
The wild vine slipping down leaves bare
  Her bright breast shortening into sighs;
The wild vine slips with the weight of its leaves,
But the berried ivy catches and cleaves
To the limbs that glitter, the feet that scare
  The wolf that follows, the fawn that flies.

2. **The mother of months,** the moon goddess, Artemis or Diana. 5–8. **And the brown . . . pain.** See the note on Arnold's "Philomela," page 1059 of this volume.

2. BEFORE THE BEGINNING OF YEARS

Before the beginning of years,
  There came to the making of man
Time, with a gift of tears;
  Grief, with a glass that ran;
Pleasure, with pain for leaven;
  Summer, with flowers that fell;
Remembrance fallen from heaven,
  And madness risen from hell;
Strength without hands to smite;
  Love that endures for a breath;
Night, the shadow of light,
  And life, the shadow of death.

And the high gods took in hand
  Fire, and the falling of tears,
And a measure of sliding sand
  From under the feet of the years;
And froth and drift of the sea;
  And dust of the labouring earth;

38. **oat,** the shepherd's pipe, made of oat straw. 39. **satyr,** in Greek mythology half man and half god. Satyrs were often pictured as partly equine in appearance. They were also noted for their lust. 41. **Pan,** god of woods and fields, patron of shepherds and hunters. **Bacchus,** Dionysus, god of wine. 44. **Maenad,** a female devotee of Bacchus. **Bassarid,** a Thracian maenad.

And bodies of things to be
In the houses of death and of birth;
And wrought with weeping and laughter,
And fashioned with loathing and love,
With life before and after
And death beneath and above,
For a day and a night and a morrow,
That his strength might endure for a span
With travail and heavy sorrow,
The holy spirit of man.

From the winds of the north and the south
They gathered as unto strife;
They breathed upon his mouth,
They filled his body with life;
Eyesight and speech they wrought
For the veils of the soul therein,
A time for labour and thought,
A time to serve and to sin;
They gave him light in his ways,
And love, and a space for delight,
And beauty and length of days,
And night, and sleep in the night.
His speech is a burning fire;
With his lips he travaileth;
In his heart is a blind desire,
In his eyes foreknowledge of death;
He weaves, and is clothed with derision;
Sows, and he shall not reap;
His life is a watch or a vision
Between a sleep and a sleep.

3. WE HAVE SEEN THEE, O LOVE

We have seen thee, O Love, thou art fair; thou art goodly, O Love;
Thy wings make light in the air as the wings of a dove.
Thy feet are as winds that divide the stream of the sea;
Earth is thy covering to hide thee, the garment of thee.
Thou art swift and subtle and blind as a flame of fire;
Before thee the laughter, behind thee the tears of desire;
And twain go forth beside thee, a man with a maid;
Her eyes are the eyes of a bride whom delight makes afraid;
As the breath in the buds that stir is her bridal breath:
But Fate is the name of her; and his name is Death.

1–2. We have seen thee . . . of a dove. See Song of Solomon 4:5.

HYMN TO PROSERPINE

(After the Proclamation in Rome of the Christian Faith)

Vicisti, Galilaee

"After the proclamation in Rome of the Christian faith," that is, after Constantine's Edict of Milan, 313, an unconverted pagan laments the passing of the old gods. Proserpine, originally a girl of Sicily, was carried off by Pluto to become the queen of the lower world and therefore of death. "*Vicisti, Galilaee*" means "Thou hast conquered, Galilean," the Galilean being, of course, Jesus; these are the traditional last words of the emperor Julian the Apostate (331–363), who attempted to restore the pagan gods.

The poem is not a dramatic utterance merely; it represents Swinburne's own point of view as well as the speaker's. Historically it is open to grave objection. It was the pagan world that was sad at this time; abounding joy was the distinctive note of Christian experience. The Resurrection, not the Crucifixion (see l. 44) was what particularly interested the early Christians; nor did they stress the sorrows of the Virgin Mary more than her joys (see l. 81). Line 110 prejudges the whole question at issue between paganism and Christianity; it is the very essence of the Christian faith that there is a "God found stronger than death." For a striking interpretation of early Christian experience in which all these points are brought out, see Bernard Shaw's play *Androcles and the Lion.*

Swinburne might be defended, however, on the ground that what really interested him was the religious problem in his own day. He had many contemporaries who seriously presented the Christian religion in terms of the travesty he here combats.

I have lived long enough, having seen one thing; that love hath an end;
Goddess and maiden and queen, be near me now and befriend.
Thou art more than the day or the morrow, the seasons that laugh or that weep;
For these give joy and sorrow; but thou, Proserpina, sleep.
Sweet is the treading of wine, and sweet the feet of the dove;
But a goodlier gift is thine than foam of the grapes or love.
Yea, is not even Apollo, with hair and harpstring of gold,
A bitter God to follow, a beautiful God to behold?
I am sick of singing; the bays burn deep and chafe: I am fain

5. dove, sacred to Venus. **9. singing,** making poems. **bays,** laurel, with which poets were crowned.

To rest a little from praise and grievous pleasure and pain.
For the Gods we know not of, who give us our daily breath,
We know they are cruel as love or life, and lovely as death.
O Gods dethroned and deceased, cast forth, wiped out in a day!
From your wrath is the world released, redeemed from your chains, men say.
New Gods are crowned in the city, their flowers have broken your rods;
They are merciful, clothed with pity, the young compassionate Gods.
But for me their new device is barren, the days are bare;
Things long past over suffice, and men forgotten that were.
Time and the Gods are at strife: ye dwell in the midst thereof,
Draining a little life from the barren breasts of love.
I say to you, cease, take rest; yea, I say to you all, be at peace,
Till the bitter milk of her breast and the barren bosom shall cease.
Wilt thou yet take all, Galilean? but these thou shalt not take,
The laurel, the palms and the paean, the breasts of of the nymphs in the brake;
Breasts more soft than a dove's, that tremble with tenderer breath;
And all the wings of the Loves, and all the joy before death;
All the feet of the hours that sound as a single lyre,
Dropped and deep in the flowers, with strings that flicker like fire.
More than these wilt thou give, things fairer than all these things?
Nay, for a little we live, and life hath mutable wings.
A little while and we die; shall life not thrive as it may?
For no man under the sky lives twice, outliving his day.
And grief is a grievous thing, and a man hath enough of his tears;
Why should he labour, and bring fresh grief to blacken his years?
Thou hast conquered, O pale Galilean; the world has grown grey from thy breath;
We have drunken of things Lethean, and fed on the fulness of death.
Laurel is green for a season, and love is sweet for a day;
But love grows bitter with treason, and laurel outlives not May.
Sleep, shall we sleep after all? for the world is not sweet in the end;
For the old faiths loosen and fall, the new years ruin and rend.
Fate is a sea without shore, and the soul is a rock that abides;
But her ears are vexed with the roar and her face with the foam of the tides.
O lips that the live blood faints in, the leavings of racks and rods!
O ghastly glories of saints, dead limbs of gibbeted Gods!
Though all men abase them before you in spirit, and all knees bend,
I kneel not, neither adore you, but standing, look to the end.
All delicate days and pleasant, all spirits and sorrows are cast
Far out with the foam of the present that sweeps to the surf of the past:
Where beyond the extreme sea-wall, and between the remote sea-gates,
Waste water washes, and tall ships founder, and deep death waits:
Where, mighty with deepening sides, clad about with the seas as with wings,
And impelled of invisible tides, and fulfilled of unspeakable things,
White-eyed and poisonous-finned, shark-toothed and serpentine-curled,
Rolls, under the whitening wind of the future, the wave of the world.
The depths stand naked in sunder behind it, the storms flee away;
In the hollow before it the thunder is taken and snared as a prey;
In its sides is the north-wind bound; and its salt is of all men's tears;
With light of ruin, and sound of changes, and pulse of years:
With travail of day after day, and with trouble of hour upon hour;
And bitter as blood is the spray; and the crests are as fangs that devour:
And its vapour and storm of its steam as the sighing of spirits to be;
And its noise as the noise in a dream; and its depth as the roots of the sea:
And the height of its heads as the height of the utmost stars of the air:

23. Wilt . . . all. Cf. *King Lear*, Act. III, sc. 4, l. 66.

And the ends of the earth at the might thereof tremble, and time is made bare.
Will ye bridle the deep sea with reins, will ye chasten the high sea with rods?
Will ye take her to chain her with chains, who is older than all ye Gods?
All ye as a wind shall go by, as a fire shall ye pass and be past;
Ye are Gods, and behold, ye shall die, and the waves be upon you at last.
In the darkness of time, in the deeps of the years, in the changes of things,
Ye shall sleep as a slain man sleeps, and the world shall forget you for kings.
Though the feet of thine high priests tread where thy lords and our forefathers trod,
Though these that were Gods are dead, and thou being dead art a God,
Though before thee the throned Cytherean be fallen, and hidden her head,
Yet thy kingdom shall pass, Galilean, thy dead shall go down to thee dead.
Of the maiden thy mother men sing as a goddess with grace clad around;
Thou art throned where another was king; where another was queen she is crowned.
Yea, once we had sight of another: but now she is queen, say these.
Not as thine, not as thine was our mother, a blossom of flowering seas,
Clothed round with the world's desire as with raiment, and fair as the foam,
And fleeter than kindled fire, and a goddess, and mother of Rome.
For thine came pale and a maiden, and sister to sorrow; but ours,
Her deep hair heavily laden with odour and colour of flowers,
White rose of the rose-white water, a silver splendour, a flame,
Bent down unto us that besought her, and earth grew sweet with her name.
For thine came weeping, a slave among slaves, and rejected; but she
Came flushed from the full-flushed wave, and imperial, her foot on the sea.
And the wonderful waters knew her, the winds and the viewless ways,
And the roses grew rosier, and bluer the sea-blue stream of the bays.

73. Cytherean, Venus, who, according to Hesiod, was formed of the foam of the sea gathering itself about the mutilated body of Uranus, and came to land at Cythera, in Cyprus. See Botticelli's famous painting "The Birth of Venus."

Ye are fallen, our lords, by what token? we wist that ye should not fall.
Ye were all so fair that are broken; and one more fair than ye all.
But I turn to her still, having seen she shall surely abide in the end;
Goddess and maiden and queen, be near me now and befriend.
O daughter of earth, of my mother, her crown and blossom of birth,
I am also, I also, thy brother; I go as I came unto earth.
In the night where thine eyes are as moons are in heaven, the night where thou art,
Where the silence is more than all tunes, where sleep overflows from the heart,
Where the poppies are sweet as the rose in our world, and the red rose is white,
And the wind falls faint as it blows with the fume of the flowers of the night,
And the murmur of spirits that sleep in the shadow of Gods from afar
Grows dim in thine ears and deep as the deep dim soul of a star,
In the sweet low light of thy face, under heavens untrod by the sun,
Let my soul with their souls find place, and forget what is done and undone.
Thou art more than the Gods who number the days of our temporal breath;
For these give labour and slumber; but thou, Proserpina, death.
Therefore now at thy feet I abide for a season in silence. I know
I shall die as my fathers died, and sleep as they sleep; even so.
For the glass of the years is brittle wherein we gaze for a span;
A little soul for a little bears up this corpse which is man.
So long I endure, no longer; and laugh not again, neither weep.
For there is no God found stronger than death; and death is a sleep.

A MATCH

If love were what the rose is,
And I were like the leaf,
Our lives would grow together

91. her, Prosperine. **97. poppies,** sacred to Proserpine. **108. A little soul . . . man.** Swinburne quotes Epictetus: "Thou art a little soul bearing up a corpse."

In sad or singing weather,
Blown fields or flowerful closes,
Green pleasure or grey grief;
If love were what the rose is,
And I were like the leaf.

If I were what the words are,
And love were like the tune,
With double sound and single
Delight our lips would mingle,
With kisses glad as birds are
That get sweet rain at noon;
If I were what the words are,
And love were like the tune.

If you were life, my darling,
And I your love were death,
We'd shine and snow together
Ere March made sweet the weather
With daffodil and starling
And hours of fruitful breath;
If you were life, my darling,
And I your love were death.

If you were thrall to sorrow,
And I were page to joy,
We'd play for lives and seasons
With loving looks and treasons
And tears of night and morrow
And laughs of maid and boy;
If you were thrall to sorrow,
And I were page to joy.

If you were April's lady,
And I were lord in May,
We'd throw with leaves for hours
And draw for days with flowers,
Till day like night were shady
And night were bright like day;
If you were April's lady,
And I were lord in May.

If you were queen of pleasure,
And I were king of pain,
We'd hunt down love together,
Pluck out his flying-feather,
And teach his feet a measure,
And find his mouth a rein;
If you were queen of pleasure,
And I were king of pain.

5. **closes,** enclosures, here gardens.

THE GARDEN OF PROSERPINE

Here, where the world is quiet,
Here, where all trouble seems
Dead winds' and spent waves' riot
In doubtful dreams of dreams;
I watch the green field growing
For reaping folk and sowing,
For harvest time and mowing,
A sleepy world of streams.

I am tired of tears and laughter,
And men that laugh and weep;
Of what may come hereafter
For men that sow to reap:
I am weary of days and hours,
Blown buds of barren flowers,
Desires and dreams and powers
And everything but sleep.

Here life has death for neighbour,
And far from eye or ear
Wan waves and wet winds labour,
Weak ships and spirits steer;
They drive adrift, and whither
They wot not who make thither;
But no such winds blow hither,
And no such things grow here.

No growth of moor or coppice,
No heather-flower or vine,
But bloomless buds of poppies,
Green grapes of Proserpine,
Pale beds of blowing rushes
Where no leaf blooms or blushes,
Save this whereout she crushes
For dead men deadly wine.

Pale, without name or number,
In fruitless fields of corn,
They bow themselves and slumber
All night till light is born;
And like a soul belated,
In hell and heaven unmated,
By cloud and mist abated
Comes out of darkness morn.

Though one were strong as seven,
He too with death shall dwell,
Nor wake with wings in heaven,
Nor weep for pains in hell;

Proserpine. See the introductory note to "Hymn to Proserpine," page 1130 of this volume. 34. **corn,** grain.

Though one were fair as roses,
His beauty clouds and closes;
And well though love reposes,
In the end it is not well.

Pale, beyond porch and portal,
Crowned with calm leaves, she stands
Who gathers all things mortal
With cold immortal hands;
Her languid lips are sweeter
Than love's who fears to greet her
To men that mix and meet her
From many times and lands.

She waits for each and other,
She waits for all men born;
Forgets the earth her mother,
The life of fruits and corn;
And spring and seed and swallow
Take wing for her and follow
Where summer song rings hollow
And flowers are put to scorn.

There go the loves that wither,
The old loves with wearier wings;
And all dead years draw thither,
And all disastrous things;
Dead dreams of days forsaken,
Blind buds that snows have shaken,
Wild leaves that winds have taken,
Red strays of ruined springs.

We are not sure of sorrow,
And joy was never sure;
To-day will die to-morrow;
Time stoops to no man's lure;
And love, grown faint and fretful,
With lips but half regretful
Sighs, and with eyes forgetful
Weeps that no loves endure.

From too much love of living,
From hope and fear set free,
We thank with brief thanksgiving
Whatever gods may be
That no life lives for ever;
That dead men rise up never;
That even the weariest river
Winds somewhere safe to sea.

Then star nor sun shall waken,
Nor any change of light:
Nor sound of waters shaken,
Nor any sound or sight:
Nor wintry leaves nor vernal,
Nor days nor things diurnal;
Only the sleep eternal
In an eternal night.

TO WALT WHITMAN IN AMERICA

Whitman, the author of *Leaves of Grass*, was regarded by Swinburne, when he wrote this poem, as the voice of American democracy.

Send but a song oversea for us,
Heart of their hearts who are free,
Heart of their singer, to be for us
More than our singing can be;
Ours, in the tempest at error,
With no light but the twilight of terror;
Send us a song oversea!

Sweet-smelling of pine-leaves and grasses,
And blown as a tree through and through
With the winds of the keen mountain-passes,
And tender as sun-smitten dew;
Sharp-tongued as the winter that shakes
The wastes of your limitless lakes,
Wide-eyed as the sea-line's blue.

O strong-winged soul with prophetic
Lips hot with the bloodbeats of song,
With tremor of heartstrings magnetic,
With thoughts as thunders in throng,
With consonant ardours of chords
That pierce men's souls as with swords
And hale them hearing along,

Make us too music, to be with us
As a word from a world's heart warm,
To sail the dark as a sea with us,
Full-sailed, outsinging the storm,
A song to put fire in our ears
Whose burning shall burn up tears,
Whose sign bid battle reform;

A note in the ranks of a clarion,
A word in the wind of cheer,
To consume as with lightning the carrion
That makes time foul for us here;
In the air that our dead things infest
A blast of the breath of the west,
Till east way as west way is clear.

Out of the sun beyond sunset,
From the evening whence morning shall be,

With the rollers in measureless onset,
  With the van of the storming sea,
With the world-wide wind, with the breath
That breaks ships driven upon death,
  With the passion of all things free,

With the sea-steeds footless and frantic,
  White myriads for death to bestride
In the charge of the ruining Atlantic
  Where deaths by regiments ride,
With clouds and clamours of waters,
With a long note shriller than slaughter's
  On the furrowless fields world-wide,

With terror, with ardour and wonder,
  With the soul of the season that wakes
When the weight of a whole year's thunder
  In the tidestream of autumn breaks,
Let the flight of the wide-winged word
Come over, come in and be heard,
  Take form and fire for our sakes.

For a continent bloodless with travail
  Here toils and brawls as it can,
And the web of it who shall unravel
  Of all that peer on the plan;
Would fain grow men, but they grow not,
And fain be free, but they know not
  One name for freedom and man?

One name, not twain for division;
  One thing, not twain, from the birth;
Spirit and substance and vision,
  Worth more than worship is worth;
Unbeheld, unadored, undivined,
The cause, the centre, the mind,
  The secret and sense of the earth.

Here as a weakling in irons,
  Here as a weanling in bands,
As a prey that the stake-net environs,
  Our life that we looked for stands;
And the man-child naked and dear,
Democracy, turns on us here
  Eyes trembling with tremulous hands.

It sees not what season shall bring to it
  Sweet fruit of its bitter desire;
Few voices it hears yet sing to it,
  Few pulses of hearts reaspire;

73. stake-net, a fishing net fastened with stakes.

Foresees not time, nor forehears
The noises of imminent years,
  Earthquake, and thunder, and fire:

When crowned and weaponed and curbless
  It shall walk without helm or shield
The bare burnt furrows and herbless
  Of war's last flame-stricken field,
Till godlike, equal with time,
It stand in the sun sublime,
  In the godhead of man revealed.

Round your people and over them
  Light like raiment is drawn,
Close as a garment to cover them
  Wrought not of mail nor of lawn;
Here, with hope hardly to wear,
Naked nations and bare
  Swim, sink, strike out for the dawn.

Chains are here, and a prison,
  Kings, and subjects, and shame;
If the God upon you be arisen,
  How should our songs be the same?
How, in confusion of change,
How shall we sing, in a strange
  Land, songs praising his name?

God is buried and dead to us,
  Even the spirit of earth,
Freedom; so have they said to us,
  Some with mocking and mirth,
Some with heartbreak and tears;
And a God without eyes, without ears,
  Who shall sing of him, dead in the birth?

The earth-god Freedom, the lonely
  Face lightening, the footprint unshod,
Not as one man crucified only
  Nor scourged with but one life's rod;
The soul that is substance of nations,
Reincarnate with fresh generations;
  The great god Man, which is God.

But in weariest of years and obscurest
  Doth it live not at heart of all things,
The one God and one spirit, a purest
  Life, fed from unstanchable springs?
Within love, within hatred it is,
And its seed in the stripe as the kiss,
  And in slaves is the germ, and in kings.

Freedom we call it, for holier

102–05. How should . . . his name? See Psalm 137.

Name of the soul's there is none;
Surelier it labours, if slowlier,
Than the metres of star or of sun;
Slowlier than life into breath,
Surelier than time into death,
It moves till its labour be done.

Till the motion be done and the measure
Circling through season and clime,
Slumber and sorrow and pleasure,
Vision of virtue and crime;
Till consummate with conquering eyes,
A soul disembodied, it rise
From the body transfigured of time.

Till it rise and remain and take station
With the stars of the world that rejoice;
Till the voice of its heart's exultation
Be as theirs an invariable voice;
By no discord of evil estranged,
By no pause, by no breach in it changed,
By no clash in the chord of its choice.

It is one with the world's generations,
With the spirit, the star, and the sod;
With the kingless and king-stricken nations,
With the cross, and the chain, and the rod;
The most high, the most secret, most lonely,
The earth-soul Freedom, that only
Lives, and that only is God.

A JACOBITE'S FAREWELL
1716

A Scottish Jacobite (sympathizer with the House of Stuart) takes leave of his love following the failure of the rising of 1716 in behalf of the "Old Pretender," son of King James II. See *Rob Roy* by Sir Walter Scott.

There's nae mair lands to tyne, my dear,
And nae mair lives to gie;
Though a man think sair to live nae mair,
There's but one day to die.

For a' things come and a' days gane,
What needs ye rend your hair?
But kiss me till the morn's morrow,
Then I'll kiss ye nae mair.

O lands are lost and life's losing,
And what were they to gie?
Fu' mony a man gives all he can,
But nae man else gives ye.

Our king wons ower the sea's water,
And I in prison sair;
But I'll win out the morn's morrow
And ye'll see me nae mair.

A Jacobite's Farewell. **13. wons,** lives (in France). The Jacobites never acknowledged the right of the house of Hanover to hold the English throne. When they toasted "the King" at banquets, each was careful to carry his wine glass over a tumbler of water.

A BALLAD OF FRANÇOIS VILLON
Prince of All Ballad-Makers

Bird of the bitter bright grey golden morn
Scarce risen upon the dusk of dolorous years,
First of us all and sweetest singer born
Whose far shrill note the world of new men hears
Cleave the cold shuddering shade as twilight clears;
When song new-born put off the old world's attire
And felt its tune on her changed lips expire,
Writ foremost on the roll of them that came
Fresh girt for service of the latter lyre,
Villon, our sad bad glad mad brother's name!

Alas the joy, the sorrow, and the scorn,
That clothed thy life with hopes and sins and fears,
And gave thee stones for bread and tares for corn
And plume-plucked gaol-birds for thy starveling peers
Till death clipt close their flight with shameful shears;
Till shifts came short and loves were hard to hire,
When lilt of song nor twitch of twangling wire
Could buy thee bread or kisses; when light fame
Spurned like a ball and haled through brake and briar,
Villon, our sad bad glad mad brother's name!

Poor splendid wings so frayed and soiled and torn!
Poor kind wild eyes so dashed with light quick tears!
Poor perfect voice, most blithe when most forlorn,
That rings athwart the sea whence no man steers
Like joy-bells crossed with death-bells in our ears!
What far delight has cooled the fierce desire
That like some ravenous bird was strong to tire
On that frail flesh and soul consumed with flame,
But left more sweet than roses to respire,
Villon, our sad bad glad mad brother's name?

ENVOI

Prince of sweet songs made out of tears and fire,
A harlot was thy nurse, a God thy sire;

A Ballad of François Villon. **1. golden morn,** the Renaissance. **2. dolorous years,** the Middle Ages. **13. stones for bread.** See Matthew 7:9.

Shame soiled thy song, and song assoiled thy shame.
But from thy feet now death has washed the mire,
Love reads out first at head of all our quire,
Villon, our sad bad glad mad brother's name.

THE HIGHER PANTHEISM IN A NUTSHELL

This poem, one of Swinburne's most amusing parodies, burlesques "The Higher Pantheism," by Tennyson (page 977 of this volume).

One, who is not, we see: but one, whom we see not, is:
Surely this is not that: but that is assuredly this.

What, and wherefore, and whence? for under is over and under:
If thunder could be without lightning, lightning could be without thunder.

Doubt is faith in the main: but faith, on the whole, is doubt:
We cannot believe by proof: but could we believe without?

Why, and whither, and how? for barley and rye are not clover:
Neither are straight lines curves: yet over is under and over.

Two and two may be four: but four and four are not eight:
Fate and God may be twain: but God is the same thing as fate.

Ask a man what he thinks, and get from a man what he feels:
God, once caught in the fact, shows you a fair pair of heels.

Body and spirit are twins: God only knows which is which:
The soul squats down in the flesh, like a tinker drunk in a ditch.

More is the whole than a part: but half is more than the whole:
Clearly, the soul is the body: but is not the body the soul?

One and two are not one: but one and nothing is two:
Truth can hardly be false, if falsehood cannot be true.

Once the mastodon was: pterodactyls were common as cocks:
Then the mammoth was God: now is He a prize ox.

Parallels all things are: yet many of these are askew:
You are certainly I: but certainly I am not you.

Springs the rock from the plain, shoots the stream from the rock:
Cocks exist for the hen: but hens exist for the cock.

God, whom we see not, is: and God, who is not, we see:
Fiddle, we know, is diddle: and diddle, we take it, is dee.

NEPHELIDIA

Any possible reader who is offended by Swinburne's burlesque of Tennyson (the preceding poem) ought surely to forgive him after reading this consummate burlesque of himself. The title means "Cloudlets."

From the depth of the dreamy decline of the dawn through a notable nimbus of nebulous noonshine,
Pallid and pink as the palm of the flag-flower that flickers with fear of the flies as they float,
Are the looks of our lovers that lustrously lean from a marvel of mystic miraculous moonshine,
These that we feel in the blood of our blushes that thicken and threaten with throbs through the throat?
Thicken and thrill as a theatre thronged at appeal of an actor's appalled agitation,
Fainter with fear of the fires of the future than pale with the promise of pride in the past;
Flushed with the famishing fullness of fever that reddens with radiance of rathe recreation,
Gaunt as the ghastliest of glimpses that gleam through the gloom of the gloaming when ghosts go aghast?
Nay, for the nick of the tick of the time is a tremulous touch on the temples of terror,
Strained as the sinews yet strenuous with strife of the dead who is dumb as the dust-heaps of death:

Surely no soul is it, sweet as the spasm of erotic emotional exquisite error,
Bathed in the balms of beautified bliss, beatific itself by beatitude's breath.
Surely no spirit or sense of a soul that was soft to the spirit and soul of our senses
Sweetens the stress of suspiring suspicion that sobs in the semblance and sound of a sigh;
Only this oracle opens Olympian, in mystical moods and triangular tenses—
"Life is the lust of a lamp for the light that is dark till the dawn of the day when we die."
Mild is the mirk and monotonous music of memory, melodiously mute as it may be,
While the hope in the heart of a hero is bruised by the breach of men's rapiers, resigned to the rod;
Made meed as a mother whose bosom-beats bound with the bliss-bringing bulk of a balm-breathing baby,
As they grope through the grave-yard of creeds, under skies growing green at a groan for the grimness of God.
Blank is the book of his bounty beholden of old, and its binding is blacker than bluer:
Out of blue into black is the scheme of the skies, and their dews are the wine of the bloodshed of things;
Till the darkling desire of delight shall be free as a fawn that is freed from the fangs that pursue her,
Till the heart-beats of hell shall be hushed by a hymn from the hunt that has harried the kennel of kings.

A CHILD'S LAUGHTER

One of the most striking (and most unexpected) developments of Swinburne's later years was a considerable number of poems expressing ecstatic appreciation of childhood. In 1918 these poems were collected by Sir Edmund Gosse in a book called *The Springtide of Life*, with illustrations by Arthur Rackham (Lippincott).

All the bells of heaven may ring,
All the birds of heaven may sing,
All the wells on earth may spring,
All the winds on earth may bring
All sweet sounds together;
Sweeter far than all things heard,
Hand of harper, tone of bird,
Sound of woods at sundawn stirred,
Welling water's winsome word,
Wind in warm wan weather,

One thing yet there is, that none
Hearing ere its chime be done
Knows not well the sweetest one
Heard of man beneath the sun,
Hoped in heaven hereafter;
Soft and strong and loud and light,
Very sound of very light
Heard from morning's rosiest height,
When the soul of all delight
Fills a child's clear laughter.

Golden bells of welcome rolled
Never forth such notes, nor told
Hours so blithe in tones so bold,
As the radiant mouth of gold
Here that rings forth heaven.
If the golden-crested wren
Were a nightingale—why, then,
Something seen and heard of men
Might be half as sweet as when
Laughs a child of seven.

ON THE DEATH OF ROBERT BROWNING

This is the last of a series of seven sonnets inspired by the death of Browning (see pages 988–989 of this volume). Note how, in writing of Browning, Swinburne catches Browning's own strenuous faith and optimism; compare this poem with "The Garden of Proserpine," ll. 81–88 (page 1134 of this volume).

He held no dream worth waking: so he said,
He who stands now on death's triumphal steep,
Awakened out of life wherein we sleep
And dream of what he knows and sees, being dead.
But never death for him was dark or dread:
"Look forth," he bade the soul, and fear not. Weep,
All ye that trust not in his truth, and keep
Vain memory's vision of a vanished head
As all that lives of all that once was he
Save that which lightens from his word: but we,
Who, seeing the sunset-coloured waters roll,
Yet know the sun subdued not of the sea,
Nor weep nor doubt that still the spirit is whole,
And life and death but shadows of the soul.

Walter Pater
1839–1894

Walter Horatio Pater was born in East London, August 4, 1839, the son of a physician. Dr. Pater's early death was especially unfortunate in that it left his son to be reared at Enfield under the exclusively feminine care of mother and grandmother; this circumstance certainly did not tend to encourage the development in young Pater of any of the robuster potentialities that may have existed as elements in his delicately-attuned genius.

Pater attended King's School, Canterbury, and Queen's College, Oxford; he became a fellow of Brasenose College in 1864. He knew the metropolis, and he traveled in Germany, Italy, and France. But for the most part he lived quietly, in modest college rooms, conscientious in the performance of his duties but indifferent to administrative affairs as such, always kindly and accessible, but always conveying the impression that his real life was passed in a world of his own. He died July 30, 1894.

As a writer, Pater concerned himself with the souls of individuals and of civilizations. His first book, *Studies in the History of the Renaissance* (later called simply *The Renaissance*) appeared in 1873. In his second, *Marius the Epicurean*, 1885, which concerns the spiritual life of a sensitive young man of Marcus Aurelius' time, he attempted a kind of novel, but he left *Gaston de Latour*, 1896, which might have been a companion volume to *Marius*, unfinished. The method of *Imaginary Portraits*, 1887, was possibly more congenial to him; in any case it established an individual type of writing ideally suited to his somewhat peculiar genius. In *Appreciations*, 1889, he collected various studies in literary criticism. *Plato and Platonism*, 1893, and *Greek Studies*, 1895, explore several Hellenic themes.

In the development of the Esthetic Movement, Pater stands midway between Ruskin and Arnold, on the one hand, and Wilde on the other. Neither of the older men could have countenanced the somewhat enervating philosophy he expressed in the famous "Conclusion" to his book on the Renaissance, where he urged that in a world of flux we cherish our keenest sensations, "catch at any exquisite passion, or any contribution to knowledge that seems by a lifted horizon to set the spirit free for a moment." It is well to remember that Pater did not wholly countenance this view either; he went so far as to remove it from the second edition of his book. Yet Pater's remains a classic statement of a creed that will always have its adherents. There was nothing of Wilde's immoralism about him; for all his relativity, he disliked being called a hedonist, and his simple, blameless life was about as close to asceticism as anybody has ever come outside a monastery. The increasing uncertainty of a groping age is reflected in Pater, yet he would have carried out his youthful plan to enter the Church if his friends had not prevented him; and though Benjamin Jowett complained with some justice that Pater seemed to think religion was all ritual, in some aspects he was a more spiritual man than Jowett himself. His ideal of burning always "with a hard, gem-like flame" by no means ruled self-sacrifice out of his philosophy of life, and he felt idealistically that the function of all higher education was "to impart the art . . . of so relieving the ideal or poetic traits, the elements of distinction in our every-day life—of so exclusively living in them—that the unadorned remainder of it, the mere drift of *débris* of our days, comes to be as though it were not."

It was, no doubt, inevitable that such a man should see "a certain kind of temperament, the power of being deeply moved by the presence of beautiful objects" as more important for the critic than "a correct abstract definition of beauty"; that his own criticism should be what we call impressionistic, or what Anatole France defines as a record of the adventures of the soul among masterpieces. It is hard to separate his critical from his creative writing; there is as much Pater as Leonardo in his description of the smile of the Mona Lisa; the step from the *Renaissance* to "The Child in the House" and the *Imaginary Portraits* with which it is so closely allied was not a long one. But it was about as long a step as Pater could take. He could never have been a true novelist; the fastidiousness, the exclusiveness—even the morbidness—in his heroes all derive from himself.

He wrote slowly and deliberately; his carefully wrought periods are poetic prose, like De Quincey's, like Sir Thomas Browne's. He fashioned a style that can be artificial and self-conscious, but at its best is a model of subtlety and grace.

THE CHILD IN THE HOUSE[1]

This beautiful piece of writing, almost indefinable as to genre, was subtitled "An Imaginary Portrait" when it first appeared in *Macmillan's Magazine* in 1878, thus anticipating the title of the book with whose contents it has much in common. It is generally regarded as containing autobiographical elements.

As Florian Deleal walked, one hot afternoon, he overtook by the wayside a poor aged man, and, as he seemed weary with the road, helped him on with the burden which he carried, a certain distance. And as the man told his story, it chanced that he named the place, a little place in the neighbourhood of a great city, where Florian had passed his earliest years, but which he had never since seen, and, the story told, went forward on his journey comforted. And that night, like a reward for his pity, a dream of that place came to Florian, a dream which did for him the office of the finer sort of memory, bringing its object to mind with a great clearness, yet, as sometimes happens in dreams, raised a little above itself, and above ordinary retrospect. The true aspect of the place, especially of the house there in which he had lived as a child, the fashion of its doors, its hearths, its windows, the very scent upon the air of it, was with him in sleep for a season; only, with tints more musically blent on wall and floor, and some finer light and shadow running in and out along its curves and angles, and with all its little carvings daintier. He awoke with a sigh at the thought of almost thirty years which lay between him and that place, yet with a flutter of pleasure still within him at the fair light, as if it were a smile, upon it. And it happened that this accident of his dream was just the thing needed for the beginning of a certain design he then had in view, the noting, namely, of some things in the story of his spirit—in that process of brain-building by which we are, each one of us, what we are. With the image of the place so clear and favourable upon him, he fell to thinking of himself therein, and how his thoughts had grown up to him. In that half-spiritualised house he could watch the better, over again, the gradual expansion of the soul which had come to be there—of which indeed, through the law which makes the material objects about them so large an element in children's lives, it had actually become a part; inward and outward being woven through and through each other into one inextricable texture—half, tint and trace and accident of homely colour and form, from the wood and the bricks; half, mere soul-stuff, floated thither from who knows how far. In the house and garden of his dream he saw a child moving, and could divide the main streams at least of the winds that had played on him, and study so the first stage in that mental journey.

The *old house*, as when Florian talked of it afterwards he always called it, (as all children do, who can recollect a change of home, soon enough but not too soon to mark a period in their lives) really was an old house; and an element of French descent in its inmates—descent from Watteau, the old court-painter, one of whose gallant pieces still hung in one of the rooms—might explain, together with some other things, a noticeable trimness and comely whiteness about everything there—the curtains, the couches, the paint on the walls with which the light and shadow played so delicately; might explain also the tolerance of the great poplar in the garden, a tree most often despised by English people, but which French people love, having observed a certain fresh way its leaves have of dealing with the wind, making it sound, in never so slight a stirring of the air, like running water.

The old-fashioned, low wainscoting went round the rooms, and up the staircase with carved balusters and shadowy angles, landing half-way up at a broad window, with a swallow's nest below the sill, and the blossom of an old pear-tree showing across it in late April, against the blue, below which the perfumed juice of the find of fallen fruit in autumn was so fresh. At the next turning came the closet which held on its deep shelves the best china. Little angel faces and reedy flutings stood out round the fireplace of the children's room. And on the top of the house, above the large attic, where the white mice ran in the twilight—an infinite, unexplored wonderland of childish treasures, glass beads, empty scent-bottles still sweet, thrum of coloured silks, among its lumber—a flat space of roof, railed round, gave a view of the neighbouring steeples; for the house, as I said, stood near a great city, which sent up heavenwards, over the twisting weather-vanes, not seldom, its beds of rolling cloud and smoke, touched with storm or sunshine. But the child of whom I am writing did not hate the fog because of the crimson lights which fell from it sometimes upon the chimneys, and the whites which gleamed through its openings, on summer

[1] From *Imaginary Portraits*, The Macmillan Company, 1887. Reprinted by permission.

13. Watteau, Jean Antoine Watteau (1684–1721); see "A Prince of Court Painters," in *Imaginary Portraits*. But Pater was really thinking of his possible relative, Jean Baptiste Pater (1696–1736), who, as Jean Baptiste, also appears in "A Prince of Court Painters."

mornings, on turret or pavement. For it is false to suppose that a child's sense of beauty is dependent on any choiceness or special fineness, in the objects which present themselves to it, though this indeed comes to be the rule with most of us in later life; earlier, in some degree, we see inwardly; and the child finds for itself, and with unstinted delight, a difference for the sense, in those whites and reds through the smoke on very homely buildings, and in the gold of the dandelions at the roadside, just beyond the houses, where not a handful of earth is virgin and untouched, in the lack of better ministries to its desire of beauty.

This house then stood not far beyond the gloom and rumours of the town, among high garden-walls, bright all summer-time with Golden-rod and brown-and-golden Wall-flower—*Flos Parietis*, as the children's Latin-reading father taught them to call it, while he was with them. Tracing back the threads of his complex spiritual habit, as he was used in after years to do, Florian found that he owed to the place many tones of sentiment afterwards customary with him, certain inward lights under which things most naturally presented themselves to him. The coming and going of travellers to the town along the way, the shadow of the streets, the sudden breath of the neighbouring gardens, the singular brightness of bright weather there, its singular darknesses which linked themselves in his mind to certain engraved illustrations in the old big Bible at home, the coolness of the dark, cavernous shops round the great church, with its giddy winding stair up to the pigeons and the bells—a citadel of peace in the heart of the trouble—all this acted on his childish fancy, so that ever afterwards the like aspects and incidents never failed to throw him into a well-recognised imaginative mood, seeming actually to have become a part of the texture of his mind. Also, Florian could trace home to this point a pervading preference in himself for a kind of comeliness and dignity, an *urbanity* literally, in modes of life, which he connected with the pale people of towns, and which made him susceptible to a kind of exquisite satisfaction in the trimness and well-considered grace of certain things and persons he afterwards met with, here and there, in his way through the world.

So the child of whom I am writing lived on there quietly; things without ministering to him, as he sat daily at the window with the birdcage hanging below it, and his mother taught him to read, wondering at the ease with which he learned, and at the quickness of his memory. The perfume of the little flowers of the lime-tree fell through the air upon them like rain; while time seemed to move ever more slowly to the murmur of the bees in it, till it almost stood still on June afternoons. How insignificant, at the moment, seem the influences of the sensible things which are tossed and fall and lie about us, so, or so, in the environment of early childhood. How indelibly, as we afterwards discover, they affect us; with what capricious attractions and associations they figure themselves on the white paper, the smooth wax, of our ingenuous souls, as "with lead in the rock for ever," giving form and feature, and as it were assigned house-room in our memory, to early experiences of feeling and thought, which abide with us ever afterwards, thus, and not otherwise. The realities and passions, the rumours of the greater world without, steal in upon us, each by its own special little passage-way, through the wall of custom about us; and never afterwards quite detach themselves from this or that accident, or trick, in the mode of their first entrance to us. Our susceptibilities, the discovery of our powers, manifold experiences—our various experiences of the coming and going of bodily pain, for instance—belong to this or the other well-remembered place in the material habitation—that little white room with the window across which the heavy blossoms could beat so peevishly in the wind, with just that particular catch or throb, such a sense of teasing in it, on gusty mornings; and the early habitation thus gradually becomes a sort of material shrine or sanctuary of sentiment; a system of visible symbolism interweaves itself through all our thoughts and passions; and irresistibly, little shapes, voices, accidents—the angle at which the sun in the morning fell on the pillow—become parts of the great chain wherewith we are bound.

Thus far, for Florian, what all this had determined was a peculiarly strong sense of home—so forcible a motive with all of us—prompting to us our customary love of the earth, and the larger part of our fear of death, that revulsion we have from it, as from something strange, untried, unfriendly; though life-long imprisonment, they tell you, and final banishment from home is a thing bitterer still; the looking forward to but a short space, a mere childish *goûter* and dessert of it, before the end, being so great a resource of effort to pilgrims and wayfarers, and the soldier in distant quarters, and lending, in lack of that, some power of solace to the

41. urbanity. Note the etymology of the word.

8–12. How indelibly . . . for ever." The **white paper** echoes Locke, the **smooth wax,** Aristotle; the quotation is from Job 19:23, 24. **48. goûter,** lunch, snack.

thought of sleep in the home churchyard, at least—dead cheek by dead cheek, and with the rain soaking in upon one from above.

So powerful is this instinct, and yet accidents like those I have been speaking of so mechanically determine it; its essence being indeed the early familiar, as constituting our ideal, or typical conception, of rest and security. Out of so many possible conditions, just this for you and that for me, brings ever the unmistakeable realisation of the delightful *chez soi;* this for the Englishman, for me and you, with the closely-drawn white curtain and the shaded lamp; that, quite other, for the wandering Arab, who folds his tent every morning, and makes his sleeping-place among haunted ruins, or in old tombs.

With Florian then the sense of home became singularly intense, his good fortune being that the special character of his home was in itself so essentially home-like. As after many wanderings I have come to fancy that some parts of Surrey and Kent are, for Englishmen, the true landscape, true home-counties, by right, partly, of a certain earthy warmth in the yellow of the sand below their gorse-bushes, and of a certain grey-blue mist after rain, in the hollows of the hills there, welcome to fatigued eyes, and never seen farther south; so I think that the sort of house I have described, with precisely those proportions of red-brick and green, and with a just perceptible monotony in the subdued order of it, for its distinguishing note, is for Englishmen at least typically home-like. And so for Florian that general human instinct was reinforced by this special home-likeness in the place his wandering soul had happened to light on, as, in the second degree, its body and earthly tabernacle; the sense of harmony between his soul and its physical environment became, for a time at least, like perfectly played music, and the life led there singularly tranquil and filled with a curious sense of self-possession. The love of security, of an habitually undisputed standing-ground or sleeping-place, came to count for much in the generation and correcting of his thoughts, and afterwards as a salutary principle of restraint in all his wanderings of spirit. The wistful yearning towards home, in absence from it, as the shadows of evening deepened, and he followed in thought what was doing there from hour to hour, interpreted to him much of a yearning and regret he experienced afterwards, towards he knew not what, out of strange ways of feeling and thought in which, from time to time, his spirit found itself alone; and in the tears shed in such absences there seemed always to be some soul-subduing foretaste of what his last tears might be.

And the sense of security could hardly have been deeper, the quiet of the child's soul being one with the quiet of its home, a place "inclosed" and "sealed." But upon this assured place, upon the child's assured soul which resembled it, there came floating in from the larger world without, as at windows left ajar unknowingly, or over the high garden walls, two streams of impressions, the sentiments of beauty and pain—recognitions of the visible, tangible, audible loveliness of things, as a very real and somewhat tyrannous element in them—and of the sorrow of the world, of grown people and children and animals, as a thing not to be put by in them. From this point he could trace two predominant processes of mental change in him—the growth of an almost diseased sensibility to the spectacle of suffering, and, parallel with this, the rapid growth of a certain capacity of fascination by bright colour and choice form—the sweet curvings, for instance, of the lips of those who seemed to him comely persons, modulated in such delicate unison to the things they said or sang,—marking early the activity in him of a more than customary sensuousness, "the lust of the eye," as the Preacher says, which might lead him, one day, how far! Could he have foreseen the weariness of the way! In music sometimes the two sorts of impressions came together, and he would weep, to the surprise of older people. Tears of joy too the child knew, also to older people's surprise; real tears, once, of relief from long-strung, childish expectation, when he found returned at evening, with new roses in her cheeks, the little sister who had been to a place where there was a wood, and brought back for him a treasure of fallen acorns, and black crow's feathers, and his peace at finding her again near him mingled all night with some intimate sense of the distant forest, the rumour of its breezes, with the glossy blackbirds aslant and the branches lifted in them, and of the perfect nicety of the little cups that fell. So those two elementary apprehensions of the tenderness and of the colour in things grew apace in him, and were seen by him afterwards to send their roots back into the beginnings of life.

Let me note first some of the occasions of his recognition of the element of pain in things—incidents, now and again, which seemed suddenly to awake in him the whole force of that sentiment which Goethe has called the *Weltschmerz,* and in

11. chez soi, at home.

26–27. as the Preacher says, not Ecclesiastes, but 1 John 2:16. **51. Weltschmerz,** an expansive, sentimental world-weariness, which often afflicts young people in too comfortable circumstances.

which the concentrated sorrow of the world seemed suddenly to lie heavy upon him. A book lay in an old book-case, of which he cared to remember one picture—a woman sitting, with hands bound behind her, the dress, the cap, the hair, folded with a simplicity which touched him strangely, as if not by her own hands, but with some ambiguous care at the hands of others—Queen Marie Antoinette, on her way to execution—we all remember David's drawing, meant merely to make her ridiculous. The face that had been so high had learned to be mute and resistless; but out of its very resistlessness, seemed now to call on men to have pity, and forbear; and he took note of that, as he closed the book, as a thing to look at again, if he should at any time find himself tempted to be cruel. Again, he would never quite forget the appeal in the small sister's face, in the garden under the lilacs, terrified at a spider lighted on her sleeve. He could trace back to the look then noted a certain mercy he conceived always for people in fear, even of little things, which seemed to make him, though but for a moment, capable of almost any sacrifice of himself. Impressible, susceptible persons, indeed, who had had their sorrows, lived about him; and this sensibility was due in part to the tacit influence of their presence, enforcing upon him habitually the fact that there are those who pass their days, as a matter of course, in a sort of "going quietly." Most poignantly of all he could recall, in unfading minutest circumstance, the cry on the stair, sounding bitterly through the house, and struck into his soul for ever, of an aged woman, his father's sister, come now to announce his death in distant India; how it seemed to make the aged woman like a child again; and, he knew not why, but this fancy was full of pity to him. There were the little sorrows of the dumb animals too—of the white angora, with a dark tail like an ermine's, and a face like a flower, who fell into a lingering sickness, and became quite delicately human in its valetudinarianism, and came to have a hundred different expressions of voice—how it grew worse and worse, till it began to feel the light too much for it, and at last, after one wild morning of pain, the little soul flickered away from the body, quite worn to death already, and now but feebly retaining it.

So he wanted another pet; and as there were starlings about the place, which could be taught to speak, one of them was caught, and he meant to treat it kindly; but in the night its young ones could be heard crying after it, and the responsive cry of the mother-bird towards them; and at last, with the first light, though not till after some debate with himself, he went down and opened the cage, and saw a sharp bound of the prisoner up to her nestlings; and therewith came the sense of remorse,—that he too was become an accomplice in moving, to the limit of his small power, the springs and handles of that great machine in things, constructed so ingeniously to play pain-fugues on the delicate nerve-work of living creatures.

I have remarked how, in the process of our brain-building, as the house of thought in which we live gets itself together, like some airy bird's-nest of floating thistle-down and chance straws, compact at last, little accidents have their consequence; and thus it happened that, as he walked one evening, a garden gate, usually closed, stood open; and lo! within, a great red hawthorn in full flower, embossing heavily the bleached and twisted trunk and branches, so aged that there were but few green leaves thereon—a plumage of tender, crimson fire out of the heart of the dry wood. The perfume of the tree had now and again reached him, in the currents of the wind, over the wall, and he had wondered what might be behind it, and was now allowed to fill his arms with the flowers—flowers enough for all the old blue-china pots along the chimney-piece, making *fête* in the children's room. Was it some periodic moment in the expansion of soul within him, or mere trick of heat in the heavily-laden summer air? But the beauty of the thing struck home to him feverishly; and in dreams at night he loitered along a magic roadway of crimson flowers, which seemed to open ruddily in thick, fresh masses about his feet, and fill softly all the little hollows in the banks on either side. Always afterwards, summer by summer, as the flowers came on, the blossom of the red hawthorn still seemed to him absolutely the reddest of all things; and the goodly crimson, still alive in the works of old Venetian masters or old Flemish tapestries, called out always from afar the recollection of the flame in those perishing little petals, as it pulsed gradually out of them, kept long in the drawers of an old cabinet. Also then, for the first time, he seemed to experience a passionateness in his relation to fair outward objects, an inexplicable excitement in their presence, which disturbed him, and from which he half longed to be free. A touch of regret or desire mingled all night with the remembered presence of the red flowers, and their perfume in the darkness about him: and the longing for some undivined, entire possession of them was the beginning of a revelation to him, growing ever

9. David, Louis David (1748–1825). The picture may be seen in Stefan Zweig's *Marie Antoinette,* Viking Press, 1933.

clearer, with the coming of the gracious summer guise of fields and trees and persons in each succeeding year, of a certain, at times seemingly exclusive, predominance in his interests, of beautiful physical things, a kind of tyranny of the senses over him.

In later years he came upon philosophies which occupied him much in the estimate of the proportion of the sensuous and the ideal elements in human knowledge, the relative parts they bear in it; and, in his intellectual scheme, was led to assign very little to the abstract thought, and much to its sensible vehicle or occasion. Such metaphysical speculation did but reinforce what was instinctive in his way of receiving the world, and for him, everywhere, that sensible vehicle or occasion became, perhaps only too surely, the necessary concomitant of any perception of things, real enough to be of any weight or reckoning, in his house of thought. There were times when he could think of the necessity he was under of associating all thoughts to touch and sight, as a sympathetic link between himself and actual, feeling, living objects; a protest in favour of real men and women against mere grey, unreal abstractions; and he remembered gratefully how the Christian religion, hardly less than the religion of the ancient Greeks, translating so much of its spiritual verity into things that may be seen, condescends in part to sanction this infirmity, if so it be, of our human existence, wherein the world of sense is so much with us, and welcomed this thought as a kind of keeper and sentinel over his soul therein. But certainly, he came more and more to be unable to care for, or think of soul but as in an actual body, or of any world but that wherein are water and trees, and where men and women look so or so, and press actual hands. It was the trick even his pity learned, fastening those who suffered in anywise to his affections by a kind of sensible attachments. He would think of Julian, fallen into incurable sickness, as spoiled in the sweet blossom of his skin like pale amber, and his honey-like hair; of Cecil, early dead, as cut off from the lilies, from golden summer days, from women's voices; and then what comforted him a little was the thought of the turning of the child's flesh to violets in the turf above him. And thinking of the very poor, it was not the things which most men care most for that he yearned to give them; but fairer roses, perhaps, and power to taste quite as they will, at their ease and not task-burdened, a certain desirable, clear light in the new morning, through which sometimes he had noticed them, quite unconscious of it, on their way to their early toil.

So he yielded himself to these things, to be played upon by them like a musical instrument, and began to note with deepening watchfulness, but always with some puzzled, unutterable longing in his enjoyment, the phases of the seasons and of the growing or waning day, down even to the shadowy changes wrought on bare wall or ceiling—the light cast up from the snow, bringing out their darkest angles; the brown light in the cloud, which meant rain; that almost too austere clearness, in the protracted light of the lengthening day, before warm weather began, as if it lingered but to make a severer workday, with the school-books opened earlier and later; that beam of June sunshine, at last, as he lay awake before the time, a way of gold-dust across the darkness; all the humming, the freshness, the perfume of the garden seemed to lie upon it—and coming in one afternoon in September, along the red gravel walk, to look for a basket of yellow crab-apples left in the cool, old parlour, he remembered it the more, and how the colours struck upon him, because a wasp on one bitten apple stung him, and he felt the passion of sudden, severe pain. For this too brought its curious reflexions; and, in relief from it, he would wonder over it—how it had then been with him—puzzled at the depth of the charm or spell over him, which lay, for a little while at least, in the mere absence of pain; once, especially, when an older boy taught him to make flowers of sealing-wax, and he had burnt his hand badly at the lighted taper, and been unable to sleep. He remembered that also afterwards, as a sort of typical thing—a white vision of heat about him, clinging closely, through the languid scent of the ointments put upon the place to make it well.

Also, as he felt this pressure upon him of the sensible world, then, as often afterwards, there would come another sort of curious questioning how the last impressions of eye and ear might happen to him, how they would find him—the scent of the last flower, the soft yellowness of the last morning, the last recognition of some object of affection, hand or voice; it could not be but that the latest look of the eyes, before their final closing, would be strangely vivid; one would go with the hot tears, the cry, the touch of the wistful bystander, impressed how deeply on one! or would it be, perhaps, a mere frail retiring of all things, great or little, away from one, into a level distance?

For with this desire of physical beauty mingled it-

31. the world . . . us, almost certainly an echo of Wordsworth's famous sonnet; see page 724.

self early the fear of death—the fear of death intensified by the desire of beauty. Hitherto he had never gazed upon dead faces, as sometimes, afterwards, at the *Morgue* in Paris, or in that fair cemetery at Munich, where all the dead must go and lie in state before burial, behind glass windows, among the flowers and incense and holy candles—the aged clergy with their sacred ornaments, the young men in their dancing-shoes and spotless white linen—after which visits, those waxen, resistless faces would always live with him for many days, making the broadest sunshine sickly. The child had heard indeed of the death of his father, and how, in the Indian station, a fever had taken him, so that though not in action he had yet died as a soldier; and hearing of the "resurrection of the just," he could think of him as still abroad in the world, somehow, for his protection—a grand, though perhaps rather terrible figure, in beautiful soldier's things, like the figure in the picture of Joshua's Vision in the Bible—and of that, round which the mourners moved so softly, and afterwards with such solemn singing, as but a worn-out garment left at a deserted lodging. So it was, until on a summer day he walked with his mother through a fair churchyard. In a bright dress he rambled among the graves, in the gay weather, and so came, in one corner, upon an open grave for a child—a dark space on the brilliant grass—the black mould heaped up round it, weighing down the little jewelled branches of the dwarf rose-bushes in flower. And therewith came, full-grown, never wholly to leave him, with the certainty that even children do sometimes die, the physical horror of death, with its wholly selfish recoil from the association of lower forms of life, and the suffocating weight above. No benign, grave figure in beautiful soldier's things any longer abroad in the world for his protection! only a few poor, piteous bones; and above them, possibly, a certain sort of figure he hoped not to see. For sitting one day in the garden below an open window, he heard people talking, and could not but listen, how, in a sleepless hour, a sick woman had seen one of the dead sitting beside her, come to call her hence; and from the broken talk evolved with much clearness the notion that not all those dead people had really departed to the churchyard, nor were quite so motionless as they looked, but led a secret, half-fugitive life in their old homes, quite free by night, though sometimes visible in the day, dodging from room to room, with no great goodwill towards those who shared the place with them. All night the figure sat beside him in the reveries of his broken sleep, and was not quite gone in the morning—an odd, irreconcileable new member of the household, making the sweet familiar chambers unfriendly and suspect by its uncertain presence. He could have hated the dead he had pitied so, for being thus. Afterwards he came to think of those poor, home-returning ghosts, which all men have fancied to themselves—the *revenants*—pathetically, as crying, or beating with vain hands at the doors, as the wind came, their cries distinguishable in it as a wilder inner note. But, always making death more unfamiliar still, that old experience would ever, from time to time, return to him; even in the living he sometimes caught its likeness; at any time or place, in a moment, the faint atmosphere of the chamber of death would be breathed around him, and the image with the bound chin, the quaint smile, the straight stiff feet, shed itself across the air upon the bright carpet, amid the gayest company, or happiest communing with himself.

To most children the sombre questionings to which impressions like these attach themselves, if they come at all, are actually suggested by religious books, which therefore they often regard with much secret distaste, and dismiss, as far as possible, from their habitual thoughts as a too depressing element in life. To Florian such impressions, these misgivings as to the ultimate tendency of the years, of the relationship between life and death, had been suggested spontaneously in the natural course of his mental growth by a strong innate sense for the soberer tones in things, further strengthened by actual circumstances; and religious sentiment, that system of biblical ideas in which he had been brought up, presented itself to him as a thing that might soften and dignify, and light up as with a "lively hope," a melancholy already deeply settled in him. So he yielded himself easily to religious impressions, and with a kind of mystical appetite for sacred things; the more as they came to him through a saintly person who loved him tenderly, and believed that this early pre-occupation with them already marked the child out for a saint. He began to love, for their own sakes, church lights, holy days, all that belonged to the comely order of the sanctuary, the secrets of its white linen, and holy vessels, and fonts of pure water; and its hieratic purity and simplicity became the type of something he desired to have about him in actual life. He pored over the pictures in religious books, and knew by heart the exact mode in which the wrestling angel grasped Jacob,

16. "resurrection of the just." See Luke 14:14. **20. Joshua's Vision.** See Joshua 6:13–15.

8. revenants, returners (from the dead). **36. "lively hope."** See I Peter 1:3. **51. the wrestling angel grasped Jacob.** See Genesis 32:24.

how Jacob looked in his mysterious sleep, how the bells and pomegranates were attached to the hem of Aaron's vestment, sounding sweetly as he glided over the turf of the holy place. His way of conceiving religion came then to be in effect what it ever afterwards remained—a sacred history indeed, but still more a sacred ideal, a transcendent version or representation, under intenser and more expressive light and shade, of human life and its familiar or exceptional incidents, birth, death, marriage, youth, age, tears, joy, rest, sleep, waking—a mirror, towards which men might turn away their eyes from vanity and dullness, and see themselves therein as angels, with their daily meat and drink, even, become a kind of sacred transaction—a complementary strain or burden, applied to our every-day existence, whereby the stray snatches of music in it re-set themselves, and fall into the scheme of some higher and more consistent harmony. A place adumbrated itself in his thoughts, wherein those sacred personalities, which are at once the reflex and the pattern of our nobler phases of life, housed themselves; and this region in his intellectual scheme all subsequent experience did but tend still further to realise and define. Some ideal, hieratic persons he would always need to occupy it and keep a warmth there. And he could hardly understand those who felt no such need at all, finding themselves quite happy without such heavenly companionship, and sacred double of their life, beside them.

Thus a constant substitution of the typical for the actual took place in his thoughts. Angels might be met by the way, under English elm or beech-tree; mere messengers seemed like angels, bound on celestial errands; a deep mysticity brooded over real meetings and partings; marriages were made in heaven; and deaths also, with hands of angels thereupon, to bear soul and body quietly asunder, each to its appointed rest. All the acts and accidents of daily life borrowed a sacred colour and significance; the very colours of things became themselves weighty with meanings like the sacred stuffs of Moses' tabernacle, full of penitence or peace. Sentiment, congruous in the first instance only with those divine transactions, the deep, effusive unction of the House of Bethany, was assumed as the due attitude for the reception of our every-day existence; and for a time he walked through the world in a sustained, not unpleasurable awe, generated by the habitual recognition, beside every circumstance and event of life, of its celestial correspondent.

Sensibility—the desire of physical beauty—a strange biblical awe, which made any reference to the unseen act on him like solemn music—these qualities the child took away with him, when, at about the age of twelve years, he left the old house and was taken to live in another place. He had never left his home before, and, anticipating much from this change, had long dreamed over it, jealously counting the days till the time fixed for departure should come; had been a little careless about others even, in his strong desire for it—when Lewis fell sick, for instance, and they must wait still two days longer. At last the morning came, very fine; and all things—the very pavement with its dust, at the roadside—seemed to have a white, pearl-like lustre in them. They were to travel by a favourite road on which he had often walked a certain distance, and on one of those two prisoner days, when Lewis was sick, had walked farther than ever before, in his great desire to reach the new place. They had started and gone a little way when a pet bird was found to have been left behind, and must even now—so it presented itself to him—have already all the appealing fierceness and wild self-pity at heart of one left by others to perish of hunger in a closed house; and he returned to fetch it, himself in hardly less stormy distress. But as he passed in search of it from room to room, lying so pale, with a look of meekness in their denudation, and at last through that little stripped white room, the aspect of the place touched him like the face of one dead; and a clinging back towards it came over him, so intense that he knew it would last long, and spoiling all his pleasure in the realisation of a thing so eagerly anticipated. And so, with the bird found, but himself in an agony of homesickness, thus capriciously sprung up within him, he was driven quickly away, far into the rural distance, so fondly speculated on, of that favourite country-road.

1–4. how Jacob . . . sleep. See Genesis 28:11–15. **how the bells . . . holy place.** See Exodus 39:24–26. **42–43. the sacred stuffs . . . peace.** See Exodus 25–27.

2. House of Bethany. See Matthew 26:6–13.

Gerard Manley Hopkins
1844–1889

Gerard Manley Hopkins was a great Victorian poet of whose existence the Victorians were never made aware; the slender body of his work remained largely in manuscript until, after long delay, his friend Robert Bridges published it in 1918 At Oxford Hopkins was a brilliant student, "the star of Balliol," who had Walter Pater for a tutor, and who came under the influence of the Oxford Movement. He decided to become a Roman Catholic and turned to Newman for guidance. His conversion took place in 1866; eleven years later he entered the priesthood. He served as a missionary in the slums of Liverpool, where his fastidious sensitiveness caused him much suffering. Later he had charge of a church at Oxford, and still later taught Greek in the University of Dublin.

Hopkins was blessed with a variety of gifts. Most important of all, there were combined in him two types, the artist and the saint. His friend Coventry Patmore wrote of him: "A Catholic of the most scrupulous strictness, he could nevertheless see the Holy Spirit in all goodness, truth, and beauty." It is not surprising, therefore, that his poetry should be marked by a "sensualism," as Bridges called it, as strong as Shelley's, at the same time reflecting a mind to which the bewilderingly multiple and desirable beauties of this earth can have significance only as they reflect the unchanging Reality that called them into being. Hopkins coined the word "inscape" to denote the pattern or design that he discerned in natural phenomena, and he was intent on communicating to his reader (or listener) the unified complex of the sensible qualities of that "inscape." The coalescence of these qualities occurs in Hopkins's mind and vision long before it reaches written form; hence the difficulty of much of his verse.

As a poet Hopkins is particularly interesting because his experiments in prosody are on the one hand suggestive of the patterns of the earliest poetry and on the other anticipative of certain twentieth-century trends. Perhaps it is most important to keep in mind the fact that his verse, like that of the ancient poets, was intended for the ear rather than the eye. Poetry he described as "speech framed to be heard for its own sake and interest even over and above its interest of meaning." He employed what he called Sprung [*i.e.*, sudden] Rhythm, the model for which was actual speech. This rhythm allows any kind of foot to follow any other kind, and the scansion runs from the beginning of a stanza to the end. Students of prosody should read Hopkins's own Preface and the discussions of his poetry in *Gerard Manley Hopkins* by the Kenyon Critics (New Directions Books, Norfolk, Conn., 1945). He disregards ordinary grammar and conventional word-sequence, and is much given to telescoping whole groups of words that he welds together inextricably. It would be too much to maintain that Hopkins always avoids clumsiness and always achieves great poetry by his methods. But there is no denying that he has given us some of the most refreshingly original images and rhythms and some of the most startling glimpses of beauty in our literature. Not since George Herbert in the seventeenth century has an English poet wrung so much sweetness from the monosyllables of everyday speech as this Victorian who ends a sonnet, "O thou lord of life, send my roots rain."

HEAVEN–HAVEN[1]

A NUN TAKES THE VEIL

I have desired to go
    Where springs not fail,
To fields where flies no sharp and sided hail
    And a few lilies blow.

And I have asked to be
    Where no storms come,
Where the green swell is in the havens dumb,
    And out of the swing of the sea.

THE HABIT OF PERFECTION

Elected Silence, sing to me
And beat upon my whorlèd ear,
Pipe me to pastures still and be
The music that I care to hear.

[1] This and the following selections are from the *Poems of Gerard Manley Hopkins*, Oxford University Press, 1948. They are reprinted by permission of the Press and the poet's family.

Shape nothing, lips; be lovely-dumb:
It is the shut, the curfew sent
From there where all surrenders come
Which only makes you eloquent.

Be shellèd, eyes, with double dark
And find the uncreated light:
This ruck and reel which you remark
Coils, keeps, and teases simple sight.

Palate, the hutch of tasty lust,
Desire not to be rinsed with wine:
The can must be so sweet, the crust
So fresh that come in fasts divine!

Nostrils, your careless breath that spend
Upon the stir and keep of pride,
What relish shall the censers send
Along the sanctuary side!

O feel-of-primrose hands, O feet
That want the yield of plushy sward,
But you shall walk the golden street
And you unhouse and house the Lord.

And, Poverty, be thou the bride
And now the marriage feast begun,
And lily-coloured clothes provide
Your spouse not laboured-at nor spun.

THE SEA AND THE SKYLARK

On ear and ear two noises too old to end
Trench—right, the tide that ramps against the shore;
With a flood or a fall, low lull-off or all roar,
Frequenting there while moon shall wear and wend.

Left hand, off land, I hear the lark ascend,
His rash-fresh re-winded new-skeinèd score
In crisps of curl off wild winch whirl, and pour
And pelt music, till none's to spill nor spend.

How these two shame this shallow and frail town!
How ring right out our sordid turbid time,
Being pure! We, life's pride and cared-for crown,

Have lost that cheer and charm of earth's past prime:
Our make and making break, are breaking, down
To man's last dust, drain fast towards man's first slime.

The Habit of Perfection. **11. ruck and reel,** the confusion of the world. **23. you,** his feet. **the golden street,** in heaven. **27–28. lily-coloured . . . spun.** See Matthew 6:28–29.

GOD'S GRANDEUR

The world is charged with the grandeur of God.
It will flame out, like shining from shook foil;
It gathers to a greatness, like the ooze of oil
Crushed. Why do men then now not reck his rod?
Generations have trod, have trod, have trod;
And all is seared with trade; bleared, smeared with toil;
And wears man's smudge and shares man's smell: the soil
Is bare now, nor can foot feel, being shod.

And for all this, nature is never spent;
There lives the dearest freshness deep down things;
And though the last lights off the black West went
Oh, morning, at the brown brink eastward, springs—
Because the Holy Ghost over the bent
World broods with warm breast and with ah! bright wings.

HURRAHING IN HARVEST

Summer ends now; now, barbarous in beauty, the stooks arise
Around; up above, what wind-walks! what lovely behaviour
Of silk-sack clouds! has wilder, wilful-wavier
Meal-drift moulded ever and melted across skies?

I walk, I lift up, I lift up heart, eyes,
Down all that glory in the heavens to glean our Saviour;
And, éyes, heárt, what looks, what lips yet gave you a
Rapturous love's greeting of realer, of rounder replies?

And the azurous hung hills are his world-wielding shoulder
Majestic—as a stallion stalwart, very-violet-sweet!—
These things, these things were here and but the beholder
Wanting; which two when they once meet,
The heart rears wings bold and bolder
And hurls for him, O half hurls earth for him off under his feet.

God's Grandeur. **3–4. oil Crushed,** from olives. *Hurrahing in Harvest.* **1. stooks,** shocks of corn.

THE WINDHOVER

To Christ Our Lord

I caught this morning morning's minion, kingdom of daylight's dauphin, dapple-dawn-drawn Falcon, in his riding
  Of the rolling level underneath him steady air, and striding
High there, how he rung upon the rein of a wimpling wing
In his ecstasy! then off, off forth on swing,
  As a skate's heel sweeps smooth on a bow-bend: the hurl and gliding
  Rebuffed the big wind. My heart in hiding
Stirred for a bird,—the achieve of, the mastery of the thing!

Brute beauty and valour and act, oh, air, pride, plume, here
  Buckle! AND the fire that breaks from thee then, a billion
Times told lovelier, more dangerous, O my chevalier!

  No wonder of it: shéer plód makes plough down sillion
Shine, and blue-bleak embers, ah my dear,
  Fall, gall themselves, and gash gold-vermilion.

PIED BEAUTY

Glory be to God for dappled things—
  For skies of couple-colour as a brinded cow;
    For rose-moles all in stipple upon trout that swim;
Fresh-firecoal chestnut-falls; finches' wings;
  Landscape plotted and pieced—fold, fallow, and plough;
    And áll trádes, their gear and tackle and trim.

All things counter, original, spare, strange;
  Whatever is fickle, freckled (who knows how?)
    With swift, slow; sweet, sour; adazzle, dim;
He fathers-forth whose beauty is past change:
                Praise him.

THE CAGED SKYLARK

As a dare-gale skylark scanted in a dull cage
  Man's mounting spirit in his bone-house, mean house, dwells—
  That bird beyond the remembering his free fells;
This in drudgery, day-labouring-out life's age.

Though aloft on turf or perch or poor low stage,
  Both sing sometímes the sweetest, sweetest spells,
  Yet both droop deadly sómetimes in their cells
Or wring their barriers in bursts of fear or rage.

Not that the sweet-fowl, the song-fowl, needs no rest—
Why, hear him, hear him babble and drop down to his nest,
  But his own nest, wild nest, no prison.

Man's spirit will be flesh-bound when found at best,
But uncumbered: meadow-down is not distressed
  For a rainbow footing it nor he for his bónes rísen.

The Windhover. **6. My heart in hiding.** W. H. Gardner in his *Gerard Manley Hopkins*, Yale University Press, 1948, pp. 180–1, comments as follows: "The poet's emotions—sympathy, admiration, love—were ever aroused by all natural or 'mortal' beauty, but principally by the supreme pattern of 'immortal' beauty—the character of Christ. For this ideal, the poet had renounced worldly ambition, the fullest life of the senses; hence his heart was 'in hiding' with Christ, wholly dedicated to His love, praise and service. 'My heart in hiding' is the first giving out of the essential moral theme of the poem. . . . Hopkins holds up to a passionate but critical judgment two conflicting sets of values, one represented by the 'kingdom of daylight's dauphin'—the windhover, the other by the Kingdom of Heaven's 'chevalier'—Christ. . . . The poet's decision is, moreover, cathartic: he finds relief in his reconciliation of opposite, discordant tendencies in the active personality and the consciously controlled character. The reconciliation is between the claims of this life and the claims of the next; between the value and the danger of 'mortal beauty'; between the desire for freedom of expression—the natural function 'wild and self-instressed'—and the will to suffer, to subject oneself to the ascetic rule, to dedicate all one's powers to Christ's employment." *Pied Beauty.* **2. couple-colour,** two colors. **3. rose-moles all in stipple.** The rose-colored dots look as if they had been stippled in. **4. chestnut-falls,** chestnuts stripped of their husks. **6. trim,** equipment. **7. counter,** in opposition. **spare,** rare.

SONNETS

MY OWN HEART LET ME MORE HAVE PITY ON

My own heart let me more have pity on; let
Me live to my sad self hereafter kind,
Charitable; not live this tormented mind
With this tormented mind tormenting yet.
  I cast for comfort I can no more get
By groping round my comfortless, than blind

My Own Heart Let Me More Have Pity On. **6. comfortless.** "I have added the comma after *comfortless;* that word has the same grammatical value as *dark* in the following line. I cast for comfort, (which) I can no more find in my comfortless (world) than a blind man in his dark world, . . .'" (Bridges)

Eyes in their dark can day or thirst can find
Thirst's all-in-all in all a world of wet.

Soul, self; come, poor Jackself, I do advise
You, jaded, let be; call off thoughts awhile
Elsewhere; leave comfort root-room; let joy size
At God knows when to God knows what; whose smile
's not wrung, see you; unforeseen times rather—as skies
Betweenpie mountains—lights a lovely mile.

THOU ART INDEED JUST, LORD

Justus quidem tu es, Domine, si disputem tecum: verumtamen justa loquar ad te: Quare via impiorum prosperatur? &c.

Thou art indeed just, Lord, if I contend
With thee; but, sir, so what I plead is just.
Why do sinners' ways prosper? and why must
Disappointment all I endeavour end?
Wert thou my enemy, O thou my friend,
How wouldst thou worse, I wonder, than thou dost
Defeat, thwart me? Oh, the sots and thralls of lust
Do in spare hours more thrive than I that spend,
Sir, life upon thy cause. See, banks and brakes
Now, leavèd how thick! lacèd they are again
With fretty chervil, look, and fresh wind shakes
Them; birds build—but not I build; no, but strain,
Time's eunuch, and not breed one work that wakes.
Mine, O thou lord of life, send my roots rain.

Robert Louis Stevenson
1850–1894

Robert Louis Stevenson was one of the most versatile writers of his time; beginning with his own experiences in living (*An Inland Voyage*, 1878; *Travels with a Donkey*, 1879) and in reading (*Virginibus Puerisque*, 1881; *Familiar Studies of Men and Books*, 1882), he practiced the literary craft until he had written almost every kind of book that a man can write. His first long fiction was *Treasure Island*, 1883, written ostensibly for the amusement of his stepson, Lloyd Osbourne, and still the finest example in English literature of the "penny dreadful" raised to the level of fine art. R.L.S. won his popularity slowly; *The Strange Case of Dr. Jekyll and Mr. Hyde*, 1886, which is half pseudo-science and half supernaturalism, was his earliest book to enjoy a huge sale. The same year produced *Kidnapped*, a story of adventure in the Highlands and elsewhere; Alan Breck, one of Stevenson's most famous characters, somewhat overshadows David Balfour, the boy hero in this novel. David's adventures were later continued into early manhood in *David Balfour* (entitled *Catriona* in England), which R.L.S. published the year of his death. *The Master of Ballantrae*, 1889, is the most ambitious of his completed novels, but it would probably have been surpassed by *Weir of Hermiston*, 1896, if Stevenson had lived to finish it; as it stands, *Weir of Hermiston* is a magnificent fragment. Less successful experiments included *Prince Otto*, 1885, an imitation of Meredith's *Adventures of Harry Richmond*, and *The Black Arrow*, 1888, a romance of the Wars of the Roses, which is merely a good story for adolescents.

Like his friend Henry James, Stevenson helped English readers begin to take the novel seriously as a work of art, but unlike Henry James, he was a romanticist. His critical essays achieved a stirring restatement of the case for romanticism in terms which his contemporaries could understand; this was his most important critical service. He had an important affinity not only with the Scottish "Kailyard school" of which J. M. Barrie was the most distinguished member, but also with many other romancers. (See the introductory note to "A Gossip on Romance," page 1156.) Stevenson's romanticism was closely associated with his general philosophical attitude.

Stevenson's was a personality of extraordinary complexity and charm, at once Puritan and bohemian. The boy who enjoyed the role of carefree vagabond lived to write the beautiful *Vailima Prayers*. He had been expected to follow the ancestral profession of lighthouse engineer, but ill-health combined with a rebellious spirit to prevent this. His apprenticeship to the law was only half-hearted; he had the writing urge if any man ever had it, and began to write even before he had any-

14. betweenpie, "a strange word, in which *pie* apparently makes a compound verb with *between*, meaning 'as the sky seen between dark mountains is brightly dappled,' the grammar such as *intervariegates* would make. This word might have delighted William Barnes, if the verb 'to pie' existed." (Bridges) *Thou Art Indeed Just, Lord.* **Justus quidem . . .** Jeremiah 12:1, quoted from the Vulgate.

thing to say, training himself by careful imitation of his favorite authors. Like many consumptives, he had a vast hunger for life. He never coddled himself, but his illness drove him to cross the world in search of a favorable climate. The Continent first, and later California and Saranac Lake, afforded only temporary relief before he finally ceased his wanderings to spend the last four years of life in the South Seas. There on his Samoan plantation he quickly won the affection of the natives, to whom he was their Tusitala, Teller of Tales, and their benevolent champion in the political affairs of the islands. Stevenson's charm has always been personal as well as literary; no doubt his dauntless courage is an important element in the spell he has cast over thousands of readers. As a storyteller in the best romantic manner and as an essayist in the tradition of Lamb and Hazlitt he ranks high. He was most gifted as a writer of prose, but a few of his poems also live on; *A Child's Garden of Verses*, written for his stepson, has proved to be an enduring children's classic. It is a proof of his extraordinary versatility that he could, when his fancy chose, adjust his mind and mood to that of children, and contract his adult world to the nursery and the garden.

THRAWN JANET

"Thrawn Janet," written in Lowland Scots, is in the classic tradition of Scottish diablerie, and Janet is "by far the most common of names for witch-wives." Moreover, "There are several cases recorded of warlocks awaiting execution in their cells, who were found with their necks 'thrawn,' hanging by the thinnest of tapes, and with other circumstances that demonstrated beyond a doubt that the Devil had done the deed, either to preclude all possible confessions from the victim or to punish him for confessions or renunciations already made." See Douglas Percy Bliss, *The Devil in Scotland*, Macmillan, 1934.

Stevenson has recorded that when he wrote "Thrawn Janet" it "frightened him to death," and he generally considered it one of his finest achievements.

THE REVEREND MURDOCH SOULIS was long minister of the moorland parish of Balweary, in the vale of Dule. A severe, bleak-faced old man, dreadful to his hearers, he dwelt in the last years of his life, without relative or servant or any human company, in the small and lonely manse under the Hanging Shaw. In spite of the iron composure of his features, his eye was wild, scared, and uncertain; and when he dwelt, in private admonitions, on the future of the impenitent, it seemed as if his eye pierced through the storms of time to the terrors of eternity. Many young persons, coming to prepare themselves against the season of the Holy Communion, were dreadfully affected by his talk. He had a sermon on 1st Peter, v. and 8th, "The devil as a roaring lion," on the Sunday after every seventeenth of August, and he was accustomed to surpass himself upon that text both by the appalling nature of the matter and the terror of his bearing in the pulpit. The children were frightened into fits, and the old looked more than usually oracular, and were, all that day, full of those hints that Hamlet deprecated. The manse itself, where it stood by the water of Dule among some thick trees, with the Shaw overhanging it on the one side, and on the other many cold, moorish hilltops rising towards the sky, had begun, at a very early period of Mr. Soulis's ministry, to be avoided in the dusk hours by all who valued themselves upon their prudence; and guidmen sitting at the clachan alehouse shook their heads together at the thought of passing late by that uncanny neighbourhood. There was one spot, to be more particular, which was regarded with especial awe. The manse stood between the high-road and the water of Dule, with a gable to each; its back was towards the kirktown of Balweary, nearly half a mile away; in front of it, a bare garden, hedged with thorn, occupied the land between the river and the road. The house was two stories high, with two large rooms on each. It opened not directly on the garden, but on a causewayed path, or passage, giving on the road on the one hand, and closed on the other by the tall willows and elders that bordered on the stream. And it was this strip of causeway that enjoyed among the young parishioners of Balweary so infamous a reputation. The minister walked there often after dark, sometimes groaning aloud in the instancy of his unspoken prayers; and when he was far from home, and the manse door was locked, the more daring schoolboys ventured, with beating hearts, to "follow my leader" across that legendary spot.

This atmosphere of terror, surrounding, as it did, a man of God of spotless character and orthodoxy, was a common cause of wonder and subject of inquiry among the few strangers who were led by chance or business into that unknown, outlying country. But many even of the people of the parish

[1] This and the following selections by Robert Louis Stevenson are reprinted by permission of Charles Scribner's Sons.

50. Shaw, wood.

14–15. hints that Hamlet deprecated. Shakespeare's Hamlet (Act I, sc. 5) makes Horatio and the guards swear that they will not even hint that they have seen his father's ghost. **22. clachan,** a small village around a church, a hamlet.

were ignorant of the strange events which had marked the first year of Mr. Soulis's ministrations; and among those who were better informed, some were naturally reticent, and others shy of that particular topic. Now and again, only, one of the older folk would warm into courage over his third tumbler, and recount the cause of the minister's strange looks and solitary life.

Fifty years syne, when Mr. Soulis cam' first into Ba'weary, he was still a young man—a callant, the folk said—fu' o' book-learnin' and grand at the exposition, but, as was natural in sae young a man, wi' nae leevin' experience in religion. The younger sort were greatly taken wi' his gifts and his gab; but auld, concerned, serious men and women were moved even to prayer for the young man, whom they took to be a self-deceiver, and the parish that was like to be sae ill-supplied. It was before the days o' the Moderates—weary fa' them; but ill things are like guid—they baith come bit by bit, a pickle at a time; and there were folk even then that said the Lord had left the college professors to their ain devices, an' the lads that went to study wi' them wad hae done mair and better sittin' in a peat-bog, like their forebears of the persecution, wi' a Bible under their oxter and a speerit o' prayer in their heart. There was nae doubt, onyway, but that Mr. Soulis had been ower lang at the college. He was careful and troubled for mony things besides the ae thing needful. He had a feck o' books wi' him—mair than had ever been seen before in a' that presbytery; and a sair wark the carrier had wi' them, for they were a' like to have smoored in the De'il's Hag between this and Kilmackerlie. They were books o' divinity, to be sure, or so they ca'd them; but the serious were o' opinion there was little service for sae mony, when the hail o' God's Word would gang in the neuk of a plaid. Then he wad sit half the day, an' half the nicht forbye, which was scant decent—writin', nae less; an' first, they were feared he wad read his sermons; and syne it proved he was writin' a book himsel', which was surely no fittin' for ane of his years an' sma' experience.

Onyway it behoved him to get an auld, decent wife to keep the manse for him an' see to his bit denners; an' he was recommended to an auld limmer—Janet M'Clour, they ca'd her—an' sae far left to himsel' as to be ower persuaded. There was mony advised him to the contrar, for Janet was mair than suspeckit by the best folk in Ba'weary. Lang or that, she had had a wean to a dragoon; she hadnae come forrit for maybe thretty year; and bairns had seen her mumblin' to hersel' up on Key's Loan in the gloamin', whilk was an unco time an' place for a God-fearin' woman. Howsoever, it was the laird himsel' that had first tauld the minister o' Janet; and in thae days he wad have gane a far gate to pleesure the laird. When folk tauld him that Janet was sib to the de'il, it was a' superstition by his way o' it; an' when they cast up the Bible to him an' the witch o' Endor, he wad threep it doun their thrapples that thir days were a' gane by, an' the de'il was mercifully restrained.

Weel, when it got about the clachan that Janet M'Clour was to be servant at the manse, the folk were fair mad wi' her an' him thegither; an' some o' the guidwives had nae better to dae than get round her door-cheeks and chairge her wi' a' that was ken't again' her, frae the sodger's bairn to John Tamson's twa kye. She was nae great speaker; folk usually let her gang her ain gate, an' she let them gang theirs, wi' neither Fair-guid-een nor Fair-guid-day; but when she buckled to, she had a tongue to deave the miller. Up she got, an' there wasna an auld story in Ba'weary but she gart somebody lowp for it that day; they couldnae say ae thing but she could say twa to it; till, at the hinder end, the guidwives up and claught haud of her, and clawed the coats aff her back, and pu'd her doun the clachan to the water o' Dule, to see if she were a witch or no, soum or droun. The carline skirled till ye could hear her at the Hangin' Shaw, and she focht like ten; there was mony a guidwife bure the mark of her neist day an' mony a lang day after; and just in the

10. syne, ago. **11. callant,** stripling. **12–13. exposition,** of the Scriptures. **20. Moderates,** a party in the Church of Scotland inclined to look somewhat tolerantly upon beliefs and practices violating strict Calvinistic doctrine and discipline. **20. weary fa' them,** woe befall them. **21. a pickle,** a little. **26. of the persecution,** Calvinists oppressed by non-Calvinists in control of the government. **26–27. under their oxter,** under their armpit. **29–31. He was . . . needful,** an echo of Jesus' rebuke to Martha in Luke 10:41–42. **31. feck,** quantity. **34. smoored,** smothered. **34. Hag,** a pit in moss ground. **38. neuk,** corner (nook). **40. forbye,** besides. **42. syne,** here, then.

1. wife, woman, not a wife for himself. **2–3. limmer,** hussy, jade, a rather loose term of reproach. **7. Lang or that,** long before that. **7. wean,** baby. **8. come forrit,** "to offer oneself as a communicant." (Stevenson) **9. bairns,** children. **10. whilk,** which. **10. unco,** strange, remarkable. **13. he wad have gane a far gate,** he would have gone a great distance. **15. sib to the de'il,** kin to the devil. **17. witch o' Endor.** See 1 Samuel 28:7–25. **17–18. threep it doun their thrapples,** vehemently affirm it and thrust it down their throats. **18. thir days,** that is, of the Old Testament dispensation. **24. cheeks,** sides. **25–26. John Tamson's twa kye,** upon which Janet, being suspected of witchcraft, was no doubt accused of having cast a spell. **27. gang her ain gate,** go her own way. **30. deave,** deafen. **31. gart,** caused. **31. lowp,** jump. **37. soum or droun.** If she "soumed" (swam), she was a witch, the belief being that the water would not receive such a creature unto itself. **37. carline,** beldam. **37. skirled,** screeched.

hettest o' the collieshangie, wha suld come up (for his sins) but the new minister!

"Women," said he (and he had a grand voice), "I charge you in the Lord's name to let her go."

Janet ran to him—she was fair wud wi' terror—an' clang to him, an' prayed him, for Christ's sake, save her frae the cummers; an' they, for their pairt, tauld him a' that was ken't, and maybe mair.

"Woman," says he to Janet, "is this true?"

"As the Lord sees me," says she, "as the Lord made me, no a word o't. Forbye the bairn," says she, "I've been a decent woman a' my days."

"Will you," says Mr. Soulis, "in the name of God, and before me, His unworthy minister, renounce the devil and his works?"

Weel, it wad appear that when he askit that, she gave a girn that fairly frichtit them that saw her, an' they could hear her teeth play dirl thegither in her chafts; but there was naething for't but the ae way or the ither; an' Janet lifted up her hand and renounced the de'il before them a'.

"And now," says Mr. Soulis to the guidwives, "home with ye, one and all, and pray to God for His forgiveness."

An' he gied Janet his arm, though she had little on her but a sark, and took her up the clachan to her ain door like a leddy of the land; an' her screighin' and laughin' as was a scandal to be heard.

There were mony grave folk lang ower their prayers that nicht; but when the morn cam' there was sic a fear fell upon a' Ba'weary that the bairns hid theirsels, and even the men-folk stood and keekit frae their doors. For there was Janet comin' doun the clachan—her or her likeness, nane could tell—wi' her neck thrawn, and her heid on ae side, like a body that has been hangit, and a girn on her face like an unstreakit corp. By an' by they got used wi' it, and even speered at her to ken what was wrang; but frae that day forth she couldna speak like a Christian woman, but slavered and played click wi' her teeth like a pair o' shears; and frae that day forth the name o' God cam' never on her lips. Whiles she wad try to say it, but it michtna be. Them that kenned best said least; but they never gied that Thing the name o' Janet M'Clour; for the auld Janet, by their way o't, was in muckle hell that day. But the minister was neither to haud nor to bind; he preached about naething but the folk's cruelty that had gi'en her a stroke of the palsy; he skelpit the bairns that meddled her; an' he had her up to the manse that same nicht, and dwalled there a' his lane wi' her under the Hangin' Shaw.

Weel, time gaed by: and the idler sort commenced to think mair lichtly o' that black business. The minister was weel thocht o'; he was aye late at the writing, folk wad see his can'le doon by the Dule water after twal' at e'en; an' he seemed pleased wi' himsel' and upsitten as at first, though a'body could see that he was dwining. As for Janet she cam' an' she gaed; if she didna speak muckle afore, it was reason she should speak less then; she meddled naebody; but she was an eldritch thing to see, an' nane wad hae mistrysted wi' her for Ba'weary glebe.

About the end o' July there cam' a spell o' weather, the like o't never was in that countryside; it was lown an' het an' heartless; the herds couldna win up the Black Hill, the bairns were ower weariet to play; an' yet it was gousty too, wi' claps o' het wund that rumm'led in the glens, and bits o' shouers that slockened naething. We aye thocht it büt to thun'er on the morn; but the morn cam, an' the morn's morning, and it was aye the same uncanny weather, sair on folks and bestial. O' a' that were the waur, nane suffered like Mr. Soulis; he could neither sleep nor eat, he tauld his elders; an' when he wasna writin' at his weary book, he wad be stravaguin' ower a' the countryside like a man possessed, when a'body else was blythe to keep caller ben the house.

Abune Hangin' Shaw, in the bield o' the Black Hill, there's a bit enclosed grund wi' an iron yett; an' it seems, in the auld days, that was the kirkyaird o' Ba'weary, an' consecrated by the Papists before the blessed licht shone upon the kingdom. It was a great howff o' Mr. Soulis's, onyway; there he would sit an' consider his sermons; and indeed it's a bieldy bit. Weel, as he cam' ower the wast end o' the Black Hill ae day, he saw first twa, an' syne fower, an' syne seeven corbie craws fleein' round an' round abune the auld kirkyaird. They flew laigh and heavy, an' squawked to ither as they gaed; and it was clear to Mr. Soulis that something had put them frae their ordinar'. He wasna easy fleyed, an' gaed straucht up to the wa's; an' what suld he find there but a man, or the appearance o' a man, sittin'

1. **collieshangie,** squabble. 5. **wud,** mad. 7. **cummers,** women, often used in an uncomplimentary sense. 17. **girn,** grin—showing the teeth in pain or rage, not joy. 18. **play dirl,** vibrate. 19. **chafts,** jaws. 25. **gied,** gave. 26. **sark,** shift. 28. **screighin',** screeching. 33. **keekit,** peeped. 36. **thrawn,** turned, twisted. 38. **unstreakit,** not laid out (unstretched). 39. **speered,** asked. 43. **Whiles,** at times. 47. **muckle,** much. 48. **haud,** hold.

2. **skelpit,** spanked. 12. **dwining,** wasting. 15. **eldritch,** unearthly. 16. **mistrysted,** broken an engagement. 20. **lown,** calm. 24. **slockened,** slaked. 31. **stravaguin',** wandering. 34. **bield,** shelter. 35. **yett,** gate. 39. **howff,** haunt. 43. **corbie,** raven. 44. **laigh,** low. 47. **fleyed,** frightened.

in the inside upon a grave. He was of a great stature, an' black as hell, and his e'en were singular to see. Mr. Soulis had heard tell o' black men, mony's the time; but there was something unco about this black man that daunted him. Het as he was, he took a kind o' cauld grue in the marrow o' his banes; but up he spak for a' that; an' says he: "My friend, are you a stranger in this place?" The black man answered never a word; he got upon his feet, an' begoud to hirsle to the wa' on the far side; but he aye lookit at the minister; an' the minister stood an' lookit back; till a' in a meenit the black man was ower the wa' an' rinnin' for the bield o' the trees. Mr. Soulis, he hardly kenned why, ran after him; but he was sair forjeskit wi' his walk an' the het, unhalesome weather; and rin as he likit, he got nae mair than a glisk o' the black man amang the birks, till he won doun to the foot o' the hillside, an' there he saw him ance mair, gaun, hap-step-an'-lowp ower Dule water to the manse.

Mr. Soulis wasna weel pleased that this fearsome gangrel suld mak' sae free wi' Ba'weary manse; an' he ran the harder, an', wet shoon, ower the burn, an' up the walk; but the deil a black man was there to see. He stepped out upon the road, but there was naebody there; he gaed a' ower the gairden, but na, nae black man. At the hinder end, and a bit feared as was but natural, he lifted the hasp an' into the manse; and there was Janet M'Clour before his een, wi' her thrawn craig, and nane sae pleased to see him. And he aye minded sinsyne, when first he set his een upon her, he had the same cauld and deidly grue.

"Janet," says he, "have you seen a black man?"

"A black man?" quo' she. "Save us a'! Ye're no wise, minister. There's nae black man in a' Ba'weary."

But she didna speak plain, ye maun understand; but yam-yammered, like a powney wi' the bit in its moo.

"Weel," says he, "Janet, if there was nae black man, I have spoken with the Accuser of the Brethren."

And he sat doun like ane wi' a fever, an' his teeth chittered in his heid.

"Hoots," says she, "think shame to yoursel', minister"; an' gied him a drap brandy that she keept aye by her.

Syne Mr. Soulis gaed into his study amang a' his books. It's a lang, laigh, mirk chalmer, perishin' cauld in winter, an' no' very dry even in the tap o' the simmer, for the manse stands near the burn. Sae doun he sat, and thocht o' a' that had come an' gane since he was in Ba'weary, an' his hame, an' the days when he was a bairn an' ran daffin' on the braes; and that black man aye ran in his heid like the owercome o' a sang. Aye the mair he thocht, the mair he thocht o' the black man. He tried the prayer, an' the words wadna come to him; an' he tried, they say, to write at his book, but he couldna mak' nae mair o' that. There was whiles he thocht the black man was at his oxter, an' the swat stood upon him cauld as well-water; and there was other whiles, when he cam' to himsel' like a christened bairn an' minded naething.

The upshot was that he gaed to the window an' stood glowrin' at Dule water. The trees are unco thick, an' the water lies deep an' black under the manse; an' there was Janet washin' the cla'es wi' her coats kilted. She had her back to the minister, an' he, for his pairt, hardly kenned what he was lookin' at. Syne she turned round, an' shawed her face; Mr. Soulis had the same cauld grue as twice that day afore, an' it was borne in upon him what folk said, that Janet was deid lang syne, an' this was a bogle in her clay-cauld flesh. He drew back a pickle and he scanned her narrowly. She was tramp-trampin' in the cla'es, croonin' to hersel'; and eh! Gude guide us, but it was a fearsome face. Whiles she sang louder, but there was nae man born o' woman that could tell the words o' her sang; an' whiles she lookit side-lang doun, but there was naething there for her to look at. There gaed a scunner through the flesh upon his banes; and that was Heeven's advertisement. But Mr. Soulis just blamed himsel', he said, to think sae ill o' a puir, auld afflicted wife that hadna a freend forbye himsel'; an' he put up a bit prayer for him an' her, an' drank a little caller water—for his heart rose again' the meat—an' gaed up to his naked bed in the gloamin'.

That was a nicht that has never been forgotten in Ba'weary, the nicht o' the seventeenth o' August, seventeen hun'er' an' twal'. It had been het afore, as I hae said, but that nicht it was hetter than ever. The sun gaed doun amang unco-lookin' clouds; it fell as mirk as the pit; no' a star, no' a breath o' wund;

1–3. He was . . . to see. "It was a common belief in Scotland that the devil appeared as a black man. This appears in several witch trials and I think in Law's *Memorials*, that delightful store-house of the quaint and grisly." (Stevenson) **6. grue,** goose flesh. **9–10. begoud,** began. **10. hirsle,** rustle. **15. forjeskit,** tired out. **17. glisk,** glance. **17. birks,** birches. **19. gaun, hap-step-an'-lowp,** going hop, step, and jump. **22. gangrel,** vagrant. **23. burn,** brook. **30. craig,** throat. **31. sinsyne,** since then, afterward.

9. daffin', larking. **10. braes,** small hills. **24. coats kilted,** skirts turned up. **37. scunner,** shudder of loathing. **43. caller,** cool.

ye couldna see your han' afore your face, and even the auld folk cuist the covers frae their beds and lay pechin' for their breath. Wi' a' that he had upon his mind, it was geyan unlikely Mr. Soulis wad get muckle sleep. He lay an' he tummled; the gude, caller bed that he got into brunt his very banes; whiles he slept, and whiles he waukened; whiles he heard the time o' nicht, and whiles a tyke yowlin' up the muir, as if somebody was deid; whiles he thocht he heard bogles claverin' in his lug, an' whiles he saw spunkies in the room. He behoved, he judged, to be sick; an' sick he was—little he jaloosed the sickness.

At the hinder end he got a clearness in his mind, sat up in his sark on the bed-side, and fell thinkin' ance mair o' the black man an' Janet. He couldna weel tell how—maybe it was the cauld to his feet—but it cam' in upon him wi' a spate that there was some connection between thir twa, an' that either or baith o' them were bogles. An' just at that moment, in Janet's room, which was neist to his, there cam' a stramp o' feet as if men were wars'lin', an' then a loud bang; an' then a wund gaed reishling round the fower quarters of the house; an' then a' was ance mair as seelent as the grave.

Mr. Soulis was feared for neither man nor deevil. He got his tinder-box, an' lit a can'le, an' made three steps o't ower to Janet's door. It was on the hasp, an' he pushed it open, an' keekit bauldly in. It was a big room, as big as the minister's ain, an' plenished wi' grand, auld, solid gear, for he had naething else. There was a fower-posted bed wi' auld tapestry; and a braw cabinet o' aik, that was fu' o' the minister's divinity books, an' put there to be out o' the gate; an' a wheen duds o' Janet's lying here and there about the floor. But nae Janet could Mr. Soulis see; nor ony sign o' a contention. In he gaed (an' there's few that wad hae followed him) an' lookit a' round, an' listened. But there was naething to be heard, neither inside the manse nor in a' Ba'weary parish, an' naething to be seen but the muckle shadows turnin' round the can'le. An' then a' at aince the minister's heart played dunt an' stood stock-still; an' a cauld wund blew amang the hairs o' his heid. Whaten a weary sicht was that for the puir man's een! For there was Janet hangin' frae a nail beside the auld aik cabinet: her heid aye lay on her shouther, her een were steekit, the tongue projected frae her mouth, an' her heels were twa feet clear abune the floor.

"God forgive us all!" thocht Mr. Soulis; "poor Janet's dead."

He cam' a step nearer to the corp; an' then his heart fair whammled in his inside. For, by what cantrip it wad ill beseem a man to judge, she was hingin' frae a single nail an' by a single wursted thread for darnin' hose.

It's an awfu' thing to be your lane at nicht wi' siccan prodigies o' darkness; but Mr. Soulis was strong in the Lord. He turned an' gaed his ways oot o' that room, and lockit the door ahint him; and step by step, doon the stairs, as heavy as leed; and set doon the can'le on the table at the stairfoot. He couldna pray, he couldna think, he was dreepin' wi' caul' swat, an' naething could he hear but the dunt-dunt-duntin' o' his ain heart. He micht maybe hae stood there an hour, or maybe twa, he minded sae little; when a' o' a sudden, he heard a laigh, uncanny steer upstairs; a foot gaed to an' fro in the chalmer whaur the corp was hingin'; syne the door was opened, though he minded weel that he had lockit it; an' syne there was a step upon the landin', an' it seemed to him as if the corp was lookin' ower the rail and doun upon him whaur he stood.

He took up the can'le again (for he couldna want the licht), an' as saftly as ever he could, gaed straucht out o' the manse an' to the far end o' the causeway. It was aye pit-mirk; the flame o' the can'le, when he set it on the grund, brunt steedy and clear as in a room; naething moved, but the Dule water seepin' and sabbin' doon the glen, an' yon unhaly footstep than cam' ploddin' doun the stairs inside the manse. He kenned the foot ower weel, for it was Janet's; and at ilka step that cam' a wee thing nearer, the cauld got deeper in his vitals. He commended his soul to Him that made an' keepit him; "and, O Lord," said he, "give me strength this night to war against the powers of evil."

By this time the foot was comin' through the passage for the door; he could hear a hand skirt alang the wa', as if the fearsome thing was feelin' for its way. The saughs tossed an' maned thegither, a long sigh cam' ower the hills, the flame o' the can'le was blawn aboot; an' there stood the corp o' Thrawn Janet, wi' her grogram goun an' her black mutch, wi' the heid aye upon the shouther, an' the girn still upon the face o't—leevin', ye wad hae said—deid,

3. **pechin'**, panting. 4. **geyan unlikely**, very unlikely. 8. **tyke**, dog. 10. **claverin'**, gossiping. 10. **lug**, ear. 11. **spunkies**, will-o'-the-wisps. 12. **jaloosed**, suspected. 18. **spate**, flood. 36. **out o' the gate**, out of the way. 36. **wheen duds**, quantity of clothes. 44. **played dunt**, beat hard. 49. **steekit**, shut.

6. **whammled**, turned upside down. 11. **siccan**, such. 21. **steer**, stir. 45. **saughs**, willows. 48. **grogram**, a coarse fabric of silk, mohair, and wool. 48. **mutch**, cap or coif.

as Mr. Soulis weel kenned—upon the threshold o' the manse.

It's a strange thing that the saul o' man should be that thirled into his perishable body; but the minister saw that, an' his heart didna break.

She didna stand there lang; she began to move again an' cam' slowly towards Mr. Soulis whaur he stood under the saughs. A' the life o' his body, a' the strength o' his speerit, were glowerin' frae his een. It seemed she was gaun to speak, but wanted words, an' made a sign wi' the left hand. There cam' a clap o' wund, like a cat's fuff; oot gaed the can'le, the saughs skreighed like folk; an' Mr. Soulis kenned that, live or die, this was the end o't.

"Witch, beldame, devil!" he cried, "I charge you, by the power of God, be gone—if you be dead, to the grave—if you be damned, to hell."

An' at that moment the Lord's ain hand out o' the Heevens struck the Horror whaur it stood; the auld, deid, desecrated corp o' the witch-wife, sae lang keepit frae the grave an' hirsled round by de'ils, lowed up like a brunstane spunk an' fell in ashes to the grund; the thunder followed, peal on dirlin' peal, the rairin' rain upon the back o' that; an' Mr. Soulis lowped through the garden hedge, an' ran, wi' skelloch upon skelloch, for the clachan.

That same mornin', John Christie saw the Black Man pass the Muckle Cairn as it was chappin' six; before eicht he gaed by the change-house at Knockdow; an' no' lang after, Sandy M'Lellan saw him gaun linkin' doun the braes frae Kilmackerlie. There's little doubt but it was him that dwalled sae lang in Janet's body; but he was awa' at last; and sinsyne the de'il has never fashed us in Ba'weary.

But it was a sair dispensation for the minister; lang, lang he lay ravin' in his bed; and frae that hour to this he was the man ye ken the day.

A GOSSIP ON ROMANCE

"The Lantern-Bearers" (in *Across the Plains*), "A Gossip on Romance," and "A Humble Remonstrance" (both in *Memories and Portraits*) are Stevenson's most important attempts as a critic to vindicate his love for romance. This was determined partly by his love of colorful and adventurous materials, but that was not the basic thing. He did not believe it possible for fiction to present life directly; it could only describe how somebody reacts to life. He hated "realism" and "naturalism" because they were based on the assumption that the business of the artist was to describe human experience without passion or prejudice from the outside. Since no life can be lived in this manner, it must necessarily follow that "realism" and "naturalism" are fundamentally and basically untrue.

This reasoned defense of romanticism has had considerable influence upon modern fiction. Stevenson helped make it possible for the romanticist to continue to take himself seriously as a literary artist. He showed that the assumptions at the root of the modern attack on romanticism are basically hostile to all imaginative writing, and helped prevent the theorizers from confusing the novel unduly.

In anything fit to be called by the name of reading, the process itself should be absorbing and voluptuous; we should gloat over a book, be rapt clean out of ourselves, and rise from the perusal, our mind filled with the busiest, kaleidoscopic dance of images, incapable of sleep or of continuous thought. The words, if the book be eloquent, should run thenceforward in our ears like the noise of breakers, and the story, if it be a story, repeat itself in a thousand coloured pictures to the eye. It was for this last pleasure that we read so closely, and loved our books so dearly, in the bright, troubled period of boyhood. Eloquence and thought, character and conversation, were but obstacles to brush aside as we dug blithely after a certain sort of incident, like a pig for truffles. For my part, I liked a story to begin with an old wayside inn where, "towards the close of the year 17—," several gentlemen in three-cocked hats were playing bowls. A friend of mine preferred the Malabar coast in a storm, with a ship beating to windward, and a scowling fellow of Herculean proportions striding along the beach; he, to be sure, was a pirate. This was further afield than my home-keeping fancy loved to travel, and designed altogether for a larger canvas than the tales that I affected. Give me a highwayman and I was full to the brim; a Jacobite would do, but the highwayman was my favourite dish. I can still hear that merry clatter of the hoofs along the moonlit lane; night and the coming of day are still related in my mind with the doings of John Rann or Jerry Abershaw; and the words "post-chaise," the "great North road,"

4. thirled into, drilled into, hence difficult to separate from. **12. fuff,** puff. **22. lowed,** flamed. **26. skelloch,** shrill cry. **28. chappin',** striking. **29. change-house,** an inn where horses were changed. **31. linkin',** tripping. **34. fashed,** troubled.

32–33. Malabar coast, southwestern coast of India. **40. Jacobite,** one loyal to the Stuarts after the revolution of 1688. The Jacobite rebellions of 1715 and 1745 in behalf of the Old Pretender (James III and VIII) and the Young Pretender (Bonnie Prince Charlie) respectively have been the favorite themes of Scotch romancers from Scott to John Buchan. **44. John Rann or Jerry Abershaw,** well-known criminals, executed in 1774 and 1795 respectively. **45. "great North road,"** a road leading out of London. Stevenson tried to catch the magic the phrase had for him in a novel, *The Great North Road,* which remained a fragment.

"ostler," and "nag" still sound in my ears like poetry. One and all, at least, and each with his particular fancy, we read story-books in childhood, not for eloquence or character or thought, but for some quality of the brute incident. That quality was not mere bloodshed or wonder. Although each of these was welcome in its place, the charm for the sake of which we read depended on something different from either. My elders used to read novels aloud; and I can still remember four different passages which I heard, before I was ten, with the same keen and lasting pleasure. One I discovered long afterwards to be the admirable opening of *What will He Do with It?*: it was no wonder that I was pleased with that. The other three still remain unidentified. One is a little vague; it was about a dark, tall house at night, and people groping on the stairs by the light that escaped from the open door of a sickroom. In another, a lover left a ball, and went walking in a cool, dewy park, whence he could watch the lighted windows and the figures of the dancers as they moved. This was the most sentimental impression I think I had yet received, for a child is somewhat deaf to the sentimental. In the last, a poet, who had been tragically wrangling with his wife, walked forth on the sea-beach on a tempestuous night and witnessed the horrors of a wreck. Different as they are, all these early favourites have a common note—they have all a touch of the romantic.

Drama is the poetry of conduct, romance the poetry of circumstance. The pleasure that we take in life is of two sorts—the active and the passive. Now we are conscious of a great command over our destiny; anon we are lifted up by circumstance, as by a breaking wave, and dashed we know not how into the future. Now we are pleased by our conduct, anon merely pleased by our surroundings. It would be hard to say which of these modes of satisfaction is the more effective, but the latter is surely the more constant. Conduct is three parts of life, they say; but I think they put it high. There is a vast deal in life and letters both which is not immoral, but simply non-moral; which either does not regard the human will at all, or deals with it in obvious and healthy relations; where the interest turns, not upon what a man shall choose to do, but on how he manages to do it; not on the passionate slips and hesitations of the conscience, but on the problems of the body and of the practical intelligence, in clean, open-air adventure, the shock of arms or the diplomacy of life. With such material as this it is impossible to build a play, for the serious theatre exists solely on moral grounds, and is a standing proof of the dissemination of the human conscience. But it is possible to build, upon this ground, the most joyous of verses, and the most lively, beautiful, and buoyant tales.

One thing in life calls for another; there is a fitness in events and places. The sight of a pleasant arbour puts it in our mind to sit there. One place suggests work, another idleness, a third early rising and long rambles in the dew. The effect of night, of any flowing water, of lighted cities, of the peep of day, of ships, of the open ocean, calls up in the mind an army of anonymous desires and pleasures. Something, we feel, should happen; we know not what, yet we proceed in quest of it. And many of the happiest hours of life fleet by us in this vain attendance on the genius of the place and moment. It is thus that tracts of young fir, and low rocks that reach into deep soundings, particularly torture and delight me. Something must have happened in such places, and perhaps ages back, to members of my race; and when I was a child I tried in vain to invent appropriate games for them, as I still try, just as vainly, to fit them with the proper story. Some places speak distinctly. Certain dank gardens cry aloud for a murder; certain old houses demand to be haunted; certain coasts are set apart for shipwreck. Other spots again seem to abide their destiny, suggestive and impenetrable, "miching mallecho." The inn at Burford Bridge, with its arbours and green garden and silent, eddying river—though it is known already as the place where Keats wrote some of his *Endymion* and Nelson parted from his Emma—still seems to wait the coming of the appropriate legend. Within these ivied walls, behind these old green shutters, some further business smoulders, waiting for its hour. The old Hawes Inn at the Queen's Ferry makes a similar call upon my fancy. There it stands, apart from the town, beside the pier, in a climate of its own, half inland, half marine—in front, the ferry bubbling with the tide and the guardship swinging to her anchor; behind, the old garden with the trees. Americans seek it already for the sake of Lovel and Oldbuck, who

13–14. **What will He Do with It?** by Sir Edward Bulwer-Lytton, 1858. **24–28. In the last . . . a wreck.** "Since traced by many obliging correspondents to the gallery of Charles Kingsley." (Stevenson) The novel is *Two Years Ago*, 1857. **42. they.** See Matthew Arnold, *Literature and Dogma*, chap. 1.

34–35. "miching mallecho," hidden mischief. See *Hamlet*, Act III, sc. 2, l. 147. **38–39. Nelson parted from his Emma.** Horatio Nelson (1758–1805) loved Lady Hamilton (1761?–1815).

dined there at the beginning of the *Antiquary.* But you need not tell me—that is not all; there is some story, unrecorded or not yet complete, which must express the meaning of that inn more fully. So it is with names and faces; so it is with incidents that are idle and inconclusive in themselves; and yet seem like the beginning of some quaint romance, which the all-careless author leaves untold. How many of these romances have we not seen determine at their birth; how many people have met us with a look of meaning in their eye, and sunk at once into trivial acquaintances; to how many places have we not drawn near, with express intimations—"here my destiny awaits me"—and we have but dined there and passed on! I have lived both at the Hawes and Burford in a perpetual flutter, on the heels, as it seemed, of some adventure that should justify the place; but though the feeling had me to bed at night and called me again at morning in one unbroken round of pleasure and suspense, nothing befell me in either worth remark. The man or the hour had not yet come; but some day, I think, a boat shall put off from the Queen's Ferry, fraught with a dear cargo, and some frosty night a horseman, on a tragic errand, rattle with his whip upon the green shutters of the inn at Burford.

Now this is one of the natural appetites with which any lively literature has to count. The desire for knowledge, I had almost added the desire for meat, is not more deeply seated than this demand for fit and striking incident. The dullest of clowns tells, or tries to tell, himself a story, as the feeblest of children uses invention in his play; and even as the imaginative grown person, joining in the game, at once enriches it with many delightful circumstances, the great creative writer shows us the realisation and the apotheosis of the day-dreams of common men. His stories may be nourished with the realities of life, but their true mark is to satisfy the nameless longings of the reader, and to obey the ideal laws of the day-dream. The right kind of thing should fall out in the right kind of place; the right kind of thing should follow; and not only the characters talk aptly and think naturally, but all the circumstances in a tale answer one to another like notes in music. The threads of a story come from time to time together and make a picture in the web; the characters fall from time to time into some attitude to each other or to nature, which stamps the story home like an illustration. Crusoe recoiling from the footprint, Achilles shouting over against the Trojans, Ulysses bending the great bow, Christian running with his fingers in his ears,—these are each culminating moments in the legend, and each has been printed on the mind's eye for ever. Other things we may forget; we may forget the words, although they are beautiful; we may forget the author's comment, although perhaps it was ingenious and true; but these epoch-making scenes, which put the last mark of truth upon a story, and fill up, at one blow, our capacity for sympathetic pleasure, we so adopt into the very bosom of our mind that neither time nor tide can efface or weaken the impression. This, then, is the plastic part of literature: to embody character, thought, or emotion in some act or attitude that shall be remarkably striking to the mind's eye. This is the highest and hardest thing to do in words; the thing which, once accomplished, equally delights the schoolboy and the sage, and makes, in its own right, the quality of epics. Compared with this, all other purposes in literature, except the purely lyrical or the purely philosophic, are bastard in nature, facile of execution, and feeble in result. It is one thing to write about the inn at Burford, or to describe scenery with the word-painters; it is quite another to seize on the heart of the suggestion and make a country famous with a legend. It is one thing to remark and to dissect, with the most cutting logic, the complications of life, and of the human spirit; it is quite another to give them body and blood in the story of Ajax or of Hamlet. The first is literature, but the second is something besides, for it is likewise art.

English people of the present day are apt, I know not why, to look somewhat down on incident, and reserve their admiration for the clink of teaspoons and the accents of the curate. It is thought clever to write a novel with no story at all, or at least with a very dull one. Reduced even to the lowest terms, a certain interest can be communicated by the art of narrative; a sense of human kinship stirred; and a kind of monotonous fitness, comparable to the words and air of *Sandy's Mull*, preserved among the infinitesimal occurrences recorded. Some people work, in this manner, with even a strong touch. Mr. Trollope's inimitable clergymen naturally arise to the mind in this connection. But even Mr. Trollope does not confine himself to chronicling

1. the Antiquary, by Sir Walter Scott, 1816. **22–27. The man . . . Burford.** "Since the above was written I have tried to launch the boat with my own hand in *Kidnapped*. Some day, perhaps, I may try a rattle at the shutters." (Stevenson)

2–7. Crusoe . . . for ever. Famous moments in Defoe's *Robinson Crusoe*, Homer's *Iliad* and *Odyssey*, Bunyan's *The Pilgrim's Progress*. **33. the story of Ajax,** in the *Iliad*. **50. Mr. Trollope,** Anthony Trollope (1815–1882). See page 908.

small beer. Mr. Crawley's collision with the Bishop's wife, Mr. Melnotte dallying in the deserted banquet-room, are typical incidents, epically conceived, fitly embodying a crisis. Or again look at Thackeray. If Rawdon Crawley's blow were not delivered, *Vanity Fair* would cease to be a work of art. That scene is the chief ganglion of the tale; and the discharge of energy from Rawdon's fist is the reward and consolation of the reader. The end of *Esmond* is a yet wider excursion from the author's customary fields; the scene at Castlewood is pure Dumas; the great and wily English borrower has here borrowed from the great, unblushing French thief; as usual, he has borrowed admirably well, and the breaking of the sword rounds off the best of all his books with a manly, martial note. But perhaps nothing can more strongly illustrate the necessity for marking incident than to compare the living fame of *Robinson Crusoe* with the discredit of *Clarissa Harlowe*. *Clarissa* is a book of a far more startling import, worked out, on a great canvas, with inimitable courage and unflagging art. It contains wit, character, passion, plot, conversations full of spirit and insight, letters sparkling with unstrained humanity; and if the death of the heroine be somewhat frigid and artificial, the last days of the hero strike the only note of what we now call Byronism, between the Elizabethans and Byron himself. And yet a little story of a shipwrecked sailor, with not a tenth part of the style nor a thousandth part of the wisdom, exploring none of the arcana of humanity and deprived of the perennial interest of love, goes on from edition to edition, while *Clarissa* lies upon the shelves unread. A friend of mine, a Welsh blacksmith, was twenty-five years old and could neither read nor write, when he heard a chapter of *Robinson* read aloud in a farm kitchen. Up to that moment he had sat content, huddled in his ignorance, but he left that farm another man. There were day-dreams, it appeared, divine day-dreams, written and printed and bound, and to be bought for money and enjoyed at pleasure. Down he sat that day, painfully learned to read Welsh, and returned to borrow the book. It had been lost, nor could he find another copy but one that was in English. Down he sat once more, learned English, and at length, and with entire delight, read *Robinson*. It is like the story of a love-chase. If he had heard a letter from *Clarissa*, would he have been fired with the same chivalrous ardour? I wonder. Yet *Clarissa* has every quality that can be shown in prose, one alone excepted—pictorial or picture-making romance. While *Robinson* depends, for the most part and with the overwhelming majority of its readers, on the charm of circumstance.

In the highest achievements of the art of words, the dramatic and the pictorial, the moral and romantic interest, rise and fall together by a common and organic law. Situation is animated with passion, passion clothed upon with situation. Neither exists for itself, but each inheres indissolubly with the other. This is high art; and not only the highest art possible in words, but the highest art of all, since it combines the greatest mass and diversity of the elements of truth and pleasure. Such are epics, and the few prose tales that have the epic weight. But as from a school of works, aping the creative, incident and romance are ruthlessly discarded, so may character and drama be omitted or subordinated to romance. There is one book, for example, more generally loved than Shakespeare, that captivates in childhood, and still delights in age—I mean the *Arabian Nights*—where you shall look in vain for moral or for intellectual interest. No human face or voice greets us among that wooden crowd of kings and genies, sorcerers and beggarmen. Adventure, in the most naked terms, furnishes forth the entertainment and is found enough. Dumas approaches perhaps nearest of any modern to these Arabian authors in the purely material charm of some of his romances. The early part of *Monte Cristo*, down to the finding of the treasure, is a piece of perfect story-telling; the man never breathed who shared these moving incidents without a tremor; and yet Faria is a thing of packthread and Dantès little more than a name. The sequel is one long-drawn error, gloomy, bloody, unnatural, and dull; but as for these early chapters, I do not believe there is another volume extant where you can breathe the same unmingled atmosphere of romance. It is very thin and light, to be sure, as on a high mountain; but it is brisk and clear and sunny in proportion. I saw the other day, with envy, an old and very clever lady setting forth on a second or third voyage into *Monte Cristo*. Here are stories which powerfully affect the reader, which can be reperused at any age, and where the characters are no more than puppets. The bony fist of the showman visibly propels them; their springs are an open secret; their faces are of wood, their bellies filled with bran; and yet we thrillingly partake of their adventures. And

1–3. Mr. Crawley's . . . banquet-room. The incidents referred to occur in *The Last Chronicle of Barset*, 1867, and *The Way We Live Now*, 1875, respectively. The second name is properly Melmotte. **19–20. Clarissa Harlowe,** 1747–48, by Samuel Richardson, the longest, and one of the greatest, novels in the English language, but not one of the liveliest. **26–28. the only note . . . Byron himself.** Stevenson's statement is, of course, not true. There is much "Byronism" in the Gothic novels, to adduce no further examples.

the point may be illustrated still further. The last interview between Lucy and Richard Feverel is pure drama; more than that, it is the strongest scene, since Shakespeare, in the English tongue. Their first meeting by the river, on the other hand, is pure romance; it has nothing to do with character; it might happen to any other boy and maiden, and be none the less delightful for the change. And yet I think he would be a bold man who should choose between these passages. Thus in the same book we may have two scenes, each capital in its order: in the one, human passion, deep calling unto deep, shall utter its genuine voice; in the second, according circumstances, like instruments in tune, shall build up a trivial but desirable incident, such as we love to prefigure for ourselves; and in the end, in spite of the critics, we may hesitate to give the preference to either. The one may ask more genius—I do not say it does; but at least the other dwells as clearly in the memory.

True romantic art, again, makes a romance of all things. It reaches into the highest abstraction of the ideal; it does not refuse the most pedestrian realism. *Robinson Crusoe* is as realistic as it is romantic; both qualities are pushed to an extreme, and neither suffers. Nor does romance depend upon the material importance of the incidents. To deal with strong and deadly elements, banditti, pirates, war and murder, is to conjure with great names, and, in the event of failure, to double the disgrace. The arrival of Haydn and Consuelo at the Canon's villa is a very trifling incident; yet we may read a dozen boisterous stories from beginning to end, and not receive so fresh and stirring an impression of adventure. It was the scene of Crusoe at the wreck, if I remember rightly, that so bewitched my blacksmith. Nor is the fact surprising. Every single article the castaway recovers from the hulk is "a joy for ever" to the man who reads of them. They are the things that should be found, and the bare enumeration stirs the blood. I found a glimmer of the same interest the other day in a new book, *The Sailor's Sweetheart*, by Mr. Clark Russell. The whole business of the brig *Morning Star* is very rightly felt and spiritedly written; but the clothes, the books, and the money satisfy the reader's mind like things to eat. We are dealing here with the old cut-and-dry, legitimate interest of treasure-trove. But even treasure-trove can be made dull. There are few people who have not groaned under the plethora of goods that fell to the lot of the *Swiss Family Robinson*, that dreary family. They found article after article, creature after creature, from milk-kine to pieces of ordnance, a whole consignment; but no informing taste had presided over the selection, there was no smack or relish in the invoice; and these riches left the fancy cold. The box of goods in Verne's *Mysterious Island* is another case in point: there was no gusto and no glamour about that; it might have come from a shop. But the two hundred and seventy-eight Australian sovereigns on board the *Morning Star* fell upon me like a surprise that I had expected; whole vistas of secondary stories, besides the one in hand, radiated forth from that discovery, as they radiate from a striking particular in life; and I was made for the moment as happy as a reader has the right to be.

To come at all at the nature of this quality of romance, we must bear in mind the peculiarity of our attitude to any art. No art produces illusion; in the theatre we never forget that we are in the theatre; and while we read a story, we sit wavering between two minds, now merely clapping our hands at the merit of the performance, now condescending to take an active part in fancy with the characters. This last is the triumph of romantic story-telling: when the reader consciously plays at being the hero, the scene is a good scene. Now in character-studies the pleasure that we take is critical; we watch, we approve, we smile at incongruities, we are moved to sudden heats of sympathy for courage, suffering, or virtue. But the characters are still themselves, they are not us; the more clearly they are depicted, the more widely do they stand away from us, the more imperiously do they thrust us back into our place as a spectator. I cannot identify myself with Rawdon Crawley or with Eugène de Rastignac, for I have scarce a hope or fear in common with them. It is not character but incident that woos us out of our reserve. Something happens as we desire to have it happen to ourselves; some situation, that we have long dallied with in fancy, is realised in the story with enticing and appropriate details. Then we forget the characters; then we push the hero aside; then we plunge into the tale in our own person and bathe in fresh experience; and then, and then only, do we say we have been reading a romance. It is not only pleasurable things that we imagine in our day-dreams; there are lights in which we are willing to contemplate even the idea of our own death; ways

1–2. **The last . . . Feverel,** in Meredith's *The Ordeal of Richard Feverel,* 1859. 31–32. **The arrival . . . villa,** in George Sand's *Consuelo,* 1842.

1. **the Swiss Family Robinson,** in Johann Rudolph Wyss's book of that title, 1813. Its continued popularity proves that Stevenson's opinion of it is not accepted universally. 7. **Mysterious Island,** The, 1870, by Jules Verne. 36. **Eugène de Rastignac,** in Balzac's *Père Goriot,* 1834.

in which it seems as if it would amuse us to be cheated, wounded, or calumniated. It is thus possible to construct a story, even of tragic import, in which every incident, detail, and trick of circumstance shall be welcome to the reader's thoughts. Fiction is to the grown man what play is to the child; it is there that he changes the atmosphere and tenor of his life; and when the game so chimes with his fancy that he can join in it with all his heart, when it pleases him at every turn, when he loves to recall it and dwells upon its recollection with entire delight, fiction is called romance.

Walter Scott is out and away the king of the romantics. *The Lady of the Lake* has no indisputable claim to be a poem beyond the inherent fitness and desirability of the tale. It is just such a story as a man would make up for himself, walking, in the best health and temper, through just such scenes as it is laid in. Hence it is that a charm dwells undefinable among these slovenly verses, as the unseen cuckoo fills the mountains with his note; hence, even after we have flung the book aside, the scenery and adventures remain present to the mind, a new and green possession, not unworthy of that beautiful name, *The Lady of the Lake*, or that direct, romantic opening—one of the most spirited and poetical in literature—"The stag at eve had drunk his fill." The same strength and the same weaknesses adorn and disfigure the novels. In that ill-written, ragged book, *The Pirate*, the figure of Cleveland—cast up by the sea on the resounding foreland of Dunrossness—moving, with the blood on his hands and the Spanish words on his tongue, among the simple islanders—singing a serenade under the window of his Shetland mistress—is conceived in the very highest manner of romantic invention. The words of his song, "Through groves of palm," sung in such a scene and by such a lover, clench, as in a nutshell, the emphatic contrast upon which the tale is built.

In *Guy Mannering*, again, every incident is delightful to the imagination; and the scene when Harry Bertram lands at Ellangowan is a model instance of romantic method.

"'I remember the tune well,' he says, 'though I cannot guess what should at present so strongly recall it to my memory.' He took his flageolet from his pocket and played a simple melody. Apparently the tune awoke the corresponding associations of a damsel. . . . She immediately took up the song—

"'Are these the links of Forth,' she said;
'Or are they the crooks of Dee,
Or the bonny woods of Warroch Head
That I so fain would see?'

"'By heaven!' said Bertram, 'it is the very ballad.'"

On this quotation two remarks fall to be made. First, as an instance of modern feeling for romance, this famous touch of the flageolet and the old song is selected by Miss Braddon for omission. Miss Braddon's idea of a story, like Mrs. Todgers's idea of a wooden leg, were something strange to have expounded. As a matter of personal experience, Meg's appearance to old Mr. Bertram on the road, the ruins of Derncleugh, the scene of the flageolet, and the Dominie's recognition of Harry, are the four strong notes that continue to ring in the mind after the book is laid aside. The second point is still more curious. The reader will observe a mark of excision in the passage as quoted by me. Well, here is how it runs in the original: "a damsel who, close behind a fine spring about half-way down the descent, and which had once supplied the castle with water, was engaged in bleaching linen." A man who gave in such copy would be discharged from the staff of a daily paper. Scott has forgotten to prepare the reader for the presence of the "damsel"; he has forgotten to mention the spring and its relation to the ruin; and now, face to face with his omission, instead of trying back and starting fair, crams all this matter, tail foremost, into a single shambling sentence. It is not merely bad English, or bad style; it is abominably bad narrative besides.

Certainly the contrast is remarkable; and it is one that throws a strong light upon the subject of this paper. For here we have a man of the finest creative instinct touching with perfect certainty and charm the romantic junctures of his story; and we find him utterly careless, almost, it would seem, incapable, in the technical matter of style, and not only frequently weak, but frequently wrong in points of drama. In character parts, indeed, and particularly in the Scotch, he was delicate, strong, and truthful; but the trite, obliterated features of too many of his heroes have already wearied two generations of readers. At times his characters will speak with something far beyond propriety—with a true heroic note; but on the next page they will be wading wearily forward with an ungrammatical and undramatic rigmarole of words. The man who could

7. Miss Braddon, Mary Elizabeth Braddon (1837–1915), author of *Lady Audley's Secret*, 1862, and many other best-sellers, was one of the most successful of the followers of Wilkie Collins. She had the bad judgment to try to "edit" Scott. **8. Mrs. Todgers,** the keeper of a London boarding-house in Dickens's *Martin Chuzzlewit*, and a friend of Mr. Pecksniff, who, inebriated, suggests that he would "very much like to see Mrs. Todgers's notion of a wooden leg, if perfectly agreeable to herself."

conceive and write the character of Elspeth of the Craigburnfoot, as Scott has conceived and written it, had not only splendid romantic but splendid tragic gifts. How comes it, then, that he could so often fob us off with languid, inarticulate twaddle? It seems to me that the explanation is to be found in the very quality of his surprising merits. As his books are play to the reader, so were they play to him. He was a great day-dreamer, a seer of fit and beautiful and humorous visions, but hardly a great artist. He conjured up the romantic with delight, but he had hardly patience to describe it. Of the pleasures of his art he tasted fully; but of its cares and scruples never man knew less.

1–2. Elspeth of the Craigburnfoot, in *The Antiquary*.

REQUIEM

This is Stevenson's own epitaph. The last two lines are inscribed on his monument in Samoa.

Under the wide and starry sky,
Dig the grave and let me lie.
Glad did I live and gladly die,
    And I laid me down with a will.

This be the verse you grave for me:
Here he lies where he longed to be;
Home is the sailor, home from sea,
    And the hunter home from the hill.

Francis Thompson 1859–1907

Francis Thompson, whose aim was not "to be the poet of the return to Nature" but rather "the poet of the return to God," came to his destiny by a winding and difficult road. He was born in Lancashire, December 18, 1859, and was first intended for the Roman Catholic priesthood. He failed to qualify, turned next to his father's profession of medicine, and failed quite as ignominiously. From 1885 to 1888 he lived the life of an outcast on the streets of London, suffering both physical agony and mental torture, the latter greatly aggravated by the fact that he had contracted the opium habit during an illness. Wilfrid Meynell, the editor of *Merry England*, and his wife Alice, the distinguished poet, literally snatched him from the jaws of death, and gave him the means of working out his salvation as a man, as an artist, and as a human soul. He spent some time at the Premonstratensian Priory in Sussex, and later at a Capuchin monastery in Wales, where he became an intimate friend of Coventry Patmore. He died of tuberculosis in London, November 13, 1907.

Thompson published three volumes of poetry: *Poems*, 1893; *Sister Songs* (written for the Meynell children, whom he loved), 1895; *New Poems*, 1897. During the last ten years of his life he wrote only prose, including a fine essay on Shelley and a life of St. Ignatius Loyola, and a large body of literary criticism remarkable for its range and perceptiveness. His work shows the influence of Shelley, but more strongly that of the metaphysical poets of the seventeenth century, especially Crashaw. In his own time, when the metaphysicals were less read than they are today, he was much reproached for the difficulty of his verse. Thompson was not, however, basically a derivative poet. His best work shows striking originality of conception and imaginative power.

THE HOUND OF HEAVEN

The theme of this, one of the great poems of religious experience, is the willful, futile flight of the human soul from God's divine grace that tirelessly pursues and overtakes it. G. K. Chesterton has a stimulating essay on the poem in *The Common Man*, Sheed and Ward, 1950. It has been plausibly suggested that the title may have come from Thompson's beloved Shelley, who speaks in *Prometheus Unbound*, l. 34, of "Heaven's wingèd hound."

I fled Him, down the nights and down the days;
  I fled Him, down the arches of the years;
  I fled Him, down the labyrinthine ways
  Of my own mind; and in the mist of tears
I hid from Him, and under running laughter.
          Up vistaed hopes I sped;
          And shot, precipitated,
Adown Titanic glooms of chasmed fears,
  From those strong Feet that followed, followed after.

1. I fled Him. See Psalm 138:7–12.

But with unhurrying chase,
And unperturbèd pace,
Deliberate speed, majestic instancy,
They beat—and a Voice beat
More instant than the Feet—
"All things betray thee, who betrayest Me."

I pleaded, outlaw-wise,
By many a hearted casement, curtained red,
Trellised with intertwining charities;
(For, though I knew His love Who followèd,
Yet was I sore adread
Lest, having Him, I must have naught beside)
But, if one little casement parted wide,
The gust of His approach would clash it to.
Fear wist not to evade, as Love wist to pursue.
Across the margent of the world I fled,
And troubled the gold gateways of the stars,
Smiting for shelter on their clangèd bars;
Fretted to dulcet jars
And silvern chatter the pale ports o' the moon.
I said to Dawn: Be sudden—to Eve: Be soon;
With thy young skiey blossoms heap me over
From this tremendous Lover—
Float thy vague veil about me, lest He see!
I tempted all His servitors, but to find
My own betrayal in their constancy,
In faith to Him their fickleness to me,
Their traitorous trueness, and their loyal deceit.
To all swift things for swiftness did I sue;
Clung to the whistling mane of every wind.
But whether they swept, smoothly fleet,
The long savannahs of the blue;
Or whether, Thunder-driven,
They clanged his chariot 'thwart a heaven,
Plashy with flying lightnings round the spurn o' their feet:—
Fear wist not to evade as Love wist to pursue.
Still with unhurrying chase,
And unperturbèd pace,
Deliberate speed, majestic instancy,
Came on the following Feet,
And a Voice above their beat—
"Naught shelters thee, who wilt not shelter Me."

I sought no more that after which I strayed,
In face of man or maid;
But still within the little children's eyes
Seems something, something that replies.
They at least are for me, surely for me!
I turned me to them very wistfully;
But just as their young eyes grew sudden fair
With dawning answers there,
Their angel plucked them from me by the hair.
"Come then, ye other children, Nature's—share
With me" (said I) "your delicate fellowship;
Let me greet you lip to lip,
Let me twine with you caresses,
Wantoning
With our Lady-Mother's vagrant tresses,
Banqueting
With her in her wind-walled palace,
Underneath her azured daïs,
Quaffing, as your taintless way is,
From a chalice
Lucent-weeping out of the dayspring."
So it was done;
I in their delicate fellowship was one—
Drew the bolt of Nature's secrecies.
I knew all the swift importings
On the wilful face of skies;
I knew how the clouds arise
Spumèd of the wild sea-snortings;
All that's born or dies
Rose and drooped with; made them shapers
Of mine own moods, or wailful or divine—
With them joyed and was bereaven.
I was heavy with the even,
When she lit her glimmering tapers
Round the day's dead sanctities.
I laughed in the morning's eyes.
I triumphed and I saddened with all weather,
Heaven and I wept together,
And its sweet tears were salt with mortal mine;
Against the red throb of its sunset-heart
I laid my own to beat,
And share commingling heat;
But not by that, by that, was eased my human smart.
In vain my tears were wet on Heaven's grey cheek.
For ah! we know not what each other says,
These things and I; in sound *I* speak—

14. instant, pressing, urgent. **16–18. I pleaded . . . charities.** "The casement, being here the human heart, is trellised not merely with the vine of the love of God but also with the love of creatures."—Francis P. LeBuffe, *The Hound of Heaven, An Interpretation,* Macmillan, 1921, page 34. **24. wist,** knew. **25. margent,** margin, boundary. **30. I said . . . Be soon.** See Deuteronomy 28:67. **34–37. I tempted . . . deceit.** Since the poet sought in creatures what can only be found in the Creator, they served God by refusing to satisfy their ill-advised adorer. **41. savannahs of the blue,** plains of the heavens.

60. Their angel, their guardian angel, who did not wish the children to be the innocent means of deflecting the poet from God. In this passage, and in that which immediately follows, Thompson's Catholic dissent from the primitivistic Nature-cult prominent in so many nineteenth-century poets appears clearly. **66. Lady-Mother's.** Nature's. **vagrant,** wandering. **72. Lucent-weeping,** dripping light.

Their sound is but their stir, they speak by silences.
Nature, poor stepdame, cannot slake my drouth;
Let her, if she would owe me,
Drop yon blue bosom-veil of sky, and show me
The breasts o' her tenderness:
Never did any milk of hers once bless
My thirsting mouth.
Nigh and nigh draws the chase.
With unperturbèd pace,
Deliberate speed, majestic instancy,
And past those noisèd Feet
A voice comes yet more fleet—
"Lo! naught contents thee, who content'st not Me."

Naked I wait Thy love's uplifted stroke!
My harness piece by piece Thou hast hewn from me,
And smitten me to my knee;
I am defenceless utterly.
I slept, methinks, and woke,
And, slowly gazing, find me stripped in sleep.
In the rash lustihead of my young powers,
I shook the pillaring hours
And pulled my life upon me; grimed with smears,
I stand amid the dust o' the mounded years—
My mangled youth lies dead beneath the heap.
My days have crackled and gone up in smoke,
Have puffed and burst as sun-starts on a stream.
Yea, faileth now even dream
The dreamer, and the lute the lutanist;
Even the linked fantasies, in whose blossomy twist
I swung the earth a trinket at my wrist,
Are yielding; cords of all too weak account
For earth with heavy griefs so overplussed.
Ah! is Thy love indeed
A weed, albeit an amaranthine weed,
Suffering no flowers except its own to mount?
Ah! must—
Designer infinite!—
Ah! must Thou char the wood ere Thou canst limn with it?
My freshness spent its wavering shower i' the dust;
And now my heart is as a broken fount,
Wherein tear-drippings stagnate, spilt down ever
From the dank thoughts that shiver
Upon the sighful branches of my mind.
Such is; what is to be?
The pulp so bitter, how shall taste the rind?
I dimly guess what Time in mists confounds;
Yet ever and anon a trumpet sounds
From the hid battlements of Eternity,
Those shaken mists a space unsettle, then
Round the half-glimpsèd turrets slowly wash again.
But not ere him who summoneth
I first have seen, enwound
With glooming robes purpureal, cypress-crowned;
His name I know, and what his trumpet saith.
Whether man's heart or life it be which yields
Thee harvest, must Thy harvest fields
Be dunged with rotten death?

Now of that long pursuit
Comes on at hand the bruit;
That Voice is round me like a bursting sea:
"And is thy earth so marred,
Shattered in shard on shard?
Lo, all things fly thee, for thou fliest Me!
Strange, piteous, futile thing!
Wherefore should any set thee love apart?
Seeing none but I makes much of naught" (He said),
"And human love needs human meriting:
How hast thou merited—
Of all man's clotted clay the dingiest clot?
Alack, thou knowest not
How little worthy of any love thou art!
Whom wilt thou find to love ignoble thee,
Save Me, save only Me?
All which I took from thee I did but take,
Not for thy harms,
But just that thou might'st seek it in My arms.
All which thy child's mistake
Fancies as lost, I have stored for thee at home:
Rise, clasp My hand, and come!"
Halts by me that footfall:
Is my gloom, after all,
Shade of His hand, outstretched caressingly?
"Ah, fondest, blindest, weakest,
I am He Whom thou seekest!
Thou dravest love from thee, who dravest Me."

A FALLEN YEW

It seemed corrival of the world's great prime,
Made to un-edge the scythe of Time,
And last with stateliest rhyme.

100. owe, own. **108. noisèd,** making noise. **115–21. I slept . . . heap.** Like Samson, in Judges 16. **122. My days . . . smoke.** See Psalm 101:4–7. **123. sun-starts,** bubbles. **126–27. linked fantasies . . . wrist,** his poetic dreams. **131. A weed,** because it roots out all our loves. **amaranthine,** like the immortal amaranth. See *Paradise Lost,* Book III, ll. 353–57. **135. limn,** draw. **148. him,** "a symbol of death to self in the spirit of Christ."—Terence L. Connolly, in his annotated edition of Thompson's *Poems*, Appleton-Century, 1932. **150. purpureal,** purple. **cypress,** the symbol of death. **152–54. Whether . . . death.** So it was in the sacrifice of Christ, and so it is in the Christian's death to self. **156. bruit,** noise. **179. Shade of His hand.** See Isaiah 49:2. **1. corrival,** companion.

No tender Dryad ever did indue
  That rigid chiton of rough yew,
    To fret her white flesh through:

But some god like to those grim Asgard lords,
  Who walk the fables of the hordes
    From Scandinavian fjords,

Upheaved its stubborn girth, and raised unriven,
  Against the whirl-blast and the levin,
    Defiant arms to Heaven.

When doom puffed out the stars, we might have said,
  It would decline its heavy head,
    And see the world to bed.

For this firm yew did from the vassal leas,
  And rain and air, its tributaries,
    Its revenues increase,

And levy impost on the golden sun,
  Take the blind years as they might run,
    And no fate seek or shun.

But now our yew is strook, is fallen—yea,
  Hacked like dull wood of every day
    To this and that, men say.

Never!—To Hades' shadowy shipyards gone,
  Dim barge of Dis, down Acheron
    It drops, or Lethe wan.

Stirred by its fall—poor destined bark of Dis!—
  Along my soul a bruit there is
    Of echoing images,

Reverberations of mortality:
  Spelt backward from its death, to me
    Its life reads saddenedly.

Its breast was hollowed as the tooth of eld;
  And boys, there creeping unbeheld,
    A laughing moment dwelled.

Yet they, within its very heart so crept,
  Reached not the heart that courage kept
    With winds and years beswept.

4. Dryad, in Greek mythology, a wood nymph inhabiting a tree. **5. chiton,** shift or tunic. **7. Asgard,** the home of the gods in Norse mythology. **11. levin,** lightning. **25. Hades,** the Greek land of the dead. **26. Dis,** Pluto, the ruler of Hades. **Acheron,** the river of sorrow in Hades. **27. Lethe,** the river of forgetfulness.

And in its boughs did close and kindly nest
  The birds, as they within its breast,
    By all its leaves caressed.

But bird nor child might touch by any art
  Each other's or the tree's hid heart,
    A whole God's breadth apart;

The breadth of God, the breadth of death and life!
  Even so, even so, in undreamed strife
    With pulseless Law, the wife,—

The sweetest wife on sweetest marriage-day,—
  Their souls at grapple in mid-way,
    Sweet to her sweet may say:

"I take you to my inmost heart, my true!"
  Ah, fool! but there is one heart you
    Shall never take him to!

The hold that falls not when the town it got,
  The heart's heart, whose immurèd plot
    Hath keys yourself keep not!

Its ports you cannot burst—you are withstood—
  For him that to your listening blood
    Sends precepts as he would.

Its gates are deaf to Love, high summoner;
  Yea, Love's great warrant runs not there:
    You are your prisoner.

Yourself are with yourself the sole consortress
  In that unleaguerable fortress;
    It knows you not for portress.

Its keys are at the cincture hung of God;
  Its gates are trepidant to His nod;
    By Him its floors are trod.

And if His feet shall rock those floors in wrath,
  Or blest aspersion sleek His path,
    Is only choice it hath.

Yea, in that ultimate heart's occult abode
  To lie as in an oubliette of God,
    Or in a bower untrod,

Built by a secret Lover for His Spouse;—
  Sole choice is this your life allows,
    Sad tree, whose perishing boughs
      So few birds house!

68. trepidant, in a state of vibration. **71. aspersion,** sprinkling. **sleek,** make smooth. **76. Lover,** God. **His Spouse,** man's spiritual being.

THE KINGDOM OF GOD

"In no Strange Land"

O world invisible, we view thee,
O world intangible, we touch thee,
O world unknowable, we know thee,
Inapprehensible, we clutch thee!

Does the fish soar to find the ocean,
The eagle plunge to find the air—
That we ask of the stars in motion
If they have rumour of thee there?

Not where the wheeling systems darken,
And our benumbed conceiving soars!—
The drift of pinions, would we hearken,
Beats at our own clay-shuttered doors.

The angels keep their ancient places;—
Turn but a stone and start a wing!
'Tis ye, 'tis your estrangèd faces,
That miss the many-splendoured thing.

But (when so sad thou canst not sadder)
Cry;—and upon thy so sore loss
Shall shine the traffic of Jacob's ladder
Pitched betwixt Heaven and Charing Cross.

Yea, in the night, my Soul, my daughter,
Cry,—clinging Heaven by the hems;
And lo, Christ walking on the water
Not of Gennesareth, but Thames!

"In no Strange Land." See Exodus 2:22; Psalm 137:4.

ENVOY

Go, songs, for ended is our brief, sweet play;
Go, children of swift joy and tardy sorrow:
And some are sung, and that was yesterday,
And some unsung, and that may be to-morrow.

Go forth; and if it be o'er stony way,
Old joy can lend what newer grief must borrow:
And it was sweet, and that was yesterday,
And sweet is sweet, though purchasèd with sorrow.

Go, songs, and come not back from your far way:
And if men ask you why ye smile and sorrow,
Tell them ye grieve, for your hearts know To-day,
Tell them ye smile, for your eyes know To-morrow.

Rudyard Kipling
1865–1936

India, the land with which so much of his writing is identified, saw the birth of Rudyard Kipling, at Bombay, on December 30, 1865. His parents were English; his father, John Lockwood Kipling, was professor of architectural sculpture, curator of the Lahore Museum, a painter, and an illustrator of some note. At six young Kipling was taken to England and educated at Westward Ho, in North Devon, and his experiences at the English school furnished the basis for the amusing *Stalky and Co.*, 1899. Returning to India, he engaged in journalism; at seventeen he became subeditor of the *Lahore Civil and Military Gazette.* At twenty-one he published his first volume, *Departmental Ditties*, 1886, a small book of light and occasional verse. A year later he challenged attention as a storyteller with *Plain Tales from the Hills*, 1887. Before he was twenty-four he had brought out six small collections of stories which showed his mastery in the form; among these early narratives are some of his best: *Under the Deodars*, *Soldiers Three*, *The Phantom 'Rickshaw*, and *Wee Willie Winkie*. They—and the stories which followed in rapid succession—were astonishing in their racy vigor, brilliant color, accurate observation, and, above all, their swift inventiveness. A new method as well as a new province was added to fiction: a realistic *Arabian Nights* transplanted to India and told by an Englishman.

With maturity, Kipling's gift grew in power and range. His soldier stories embodied characters which rank with those of Dickens. His stories for children —*The Jungle Books*, 1894–95; *Captains Courageous*, 1897; and *Just So Stories*, 1902—became contemporary classics. He appealed equally to youth and age with *Kim*, 1901; *Puck of Pook's Hill*, 1906, *Rewards and Fairies*, 1910. His poems, from the early *Barrack-Room Ballads*, 1892, to the full-throated *The Five Nations*, 1903, impressed the craftsman with their skill and captivated the common reader with their gusto.

Between his twenty-third and twenty-sixth year he traveled to China, Japan, India, and America.

In England he found himself famous at twenty-seven. On a return visit to the United States in 1892 Kipling married an American, Caroline Starr Balestier, sister of Wolcott Balestier, with whom he wrote *The Naulahka*, 1891, and lived for a few years in Brattleboro, Vermont. Here he wrote several of his most popular works, including the animal stories in *Jungle Books*, and it seems likely that he would have remained in America if a quarrel with another brother-in-law, Beatty Balestier, and threats of legal action, had not driven him from Vermont back to England. Sensitive to criticism and increasingly wary of social contacts, Kipling withdrew from public life and buried himself in a little Sussex village.

It is a remarkable fact in literary history that, though the latter half of his life fell within the twentieth century, Kipling gained his enormous reputation during the age of Victoria. And with that period he continues to be identified, both as artist and as spokesman of national feeling. Kipling continued to publish in his later years, but his writing never again had the full impact of his earlier works. The death of a son during World War I embittered and almost silenced him. Although he had received the Nobel Prize for literature in 1907, changes in taste caused a reaction, directed chiefly against Kipling's militant "imperialism," which had earlier influenced British sentiment and, to some extent, British policies. Nevertheless, his work continued to grow in subtlety, if not in quantity, and he was at work on a collection of autobiographical notes when he died a few weeks after his seventieth birthday, January 17, 1936.

It has become the fashion in some quarters to belittle Kipling's uncritical affirmations, his "inverted nostalgia" for Mandalay and the exotic regions "somewhere east of Suez," his patriotic fervor, and his "crude force." But if his energy is boisterous, it is irresistible. He not only discovered new scenes and fresh subject matter, he explored strange territories and established the "true romance" of bridge-builders, wireless operators, engineers, people familiar and unfamiliar up and down the world. Henry James was one of the first to feel in Kipling's tales "the irresistible magic of scorching suns, subject empires, uncanny religions, uneasy garrisons," and to point out "the remarkable way in which he makes us aware that he has been put up to the whole thing directly by life." The early story of India included here, "At the End of the Passage," has been praised alike by James and Somerset Maugham for its striking impression of hard reality.

Kipling was one of those rare writers who are equally at home in prose and in verse. His prime quality as poet is his zest, his rich and seemingly inexhaustible enthusiasm. Sometimes this exuberance defeats itself; the drum is often beaten so loudly that the music itself is drowned. But Kipling is important for more than his brisk rhymes and marching rhythms. Coming at a time when poetry was surfeited with delicate languors and pastel imitations of antiquity, he proclaimed the beauty as well as the liveliness of the actual world. Opposed to the affectations of romance, he offered realities which were often more truly romantic than the exaggerations. He invigorated the life-blood of poetry with the simple expressions of men. He revived the ballad; he restored sincerity of tone, which the Pre-Raphaelites had not always taken pains to preserve.

There are signs that Kipling, whose reputation has suffered a decline in recent years, is due for a return to favor. This is not too much to expect when so different a poet and so discerning a critic as Mr. T. S. Eliot has edited, with an introductory essay, *A Choice of Kipling's Verse* (Scribner, 1943).

There is, as yet, no definitive biographical and critical study of Kipling. A year after his death there appeared *Something of Myself*, 1937, a collection of autobiographical notes containing memoirs, a sidelight on an era, and that "something" about the author which Kipling was willing to divulge.

MANDALAY[1]

By the old Moulmein Pagoda, lookin' eastward to the sea,
There's a Burma girl a-settin', an' I know she thinks o' me;
For the wind is in the palm-trees, and the temple-bells they say:
"Come you back, you British soldier; come you back to Mandalay!"
Come you back to Mandalay,
Where the old Flotilla lay:
Can't you 'ear their paddles chunkin' from Rangoon to Mandalay?
On the road to Mandalay,
Where the flyin'-fishes play,
An' the dawn comes up like thunder outer China 'crost the Bay!

'Er petticoat was yaller an' 'er little cap was green,
An' 'er name was Supi-yaw-lat—jes' the same as Theebaw's Queen,

[1] This and the three poems that follow are from *Departmental Ditties, Barrack-Room Ballads and Other Verses*, 1890.

An' I seed her first a-smokin' of a whackin' white cheroot,
An' a-wastin' Christian kisses on an 'eathen idol's foot:
Bloomin' idol made o' mud—
Wot they called the Great Gawd Budd—
Plucky lot she cared for idols when I kissed 'er where she stud!
On the road to Mandalay . . .

When the mist was on the rice-fields an' the sun was droppin' slow,
She'd git 'er little banjo an' she'd sing "*Kulla-lo-lo!*"
With 'er arm upon my shoulder an' her cheek agin my cheek
We useter watch the steamers an' the *hathis* pilin' teak.
Elephints a-pilin' teak
In the sludgy, squdgy creek,
Where the silence 'ung that 'eavy you was 'arf afraid to speak!
On the road to Mandalay . . .

But that's all shove be'ind me—long ago an' fur away,
An' there ain't no 'busses running' from the Bank to Mandalay;
An' I'm learnin' 'ere in London what the ten-year soldier tells:
"If you've 'eard the East a-callin', you won't never 'eed naught else."
No! you won't 'eed nothin' else
But them spicy garlic smells,
An' the sunshine an' the palm-trees an' the tinkly temple-bells;
On the road to Mandalay . . .

I am sick o' wastin' leather on these gritty pavin'-stones,
An' the blasted Henglish drizzle wakes the fever in my bones;
Though I walks with fifty 'ousemaids outer Chelsea to the Strand,
An' they talks a lot o' lovin', but wot do they understand?
Beefy face an' grubby 'and—
Law! wot do they understand?
I've a neater, sweeter maiden in a cleaner, greener land!
On the road to Mandalay . . .

Ship me somewheres east of Suez, where the best is like the worst,
Where there aren't no Ten Commandments an' a man can raise a thirst;
For the temple-bells are callin', an' it's there that I would be—
By the old Moulmein Pagoda, lookin' lazy at the sea;
On the road to Mandalay,
Where the old Flotilla lay,
With our sick beneath the awnings when we went to Mandalay!
On the road to Mandalay,
Where the flyin'-fishes play,
An' the dawn comes up like thunder outer China 'crost the Bay!

FUZZY-WUZZY

(*Soudan Expeditionary Force*)

We've fought with many men acrost the seas,
An' some of 'em was brave an' some was not:
The Paythan an' the Zulu an' Burmese;
But the Fuzzy was the finest o' the lot.
We never got a ha'porth's change of 'im:
'E squatted in the scrub an' 'ocked our 'orses,
'E cut our sentries up at Sua*kim*,
An' 'e played the cat an' banjo with our forces.
So 'ere's *to* you, Fuzzy-Wuzzy, at your 'ome in the Soudan;
You're a pore benighted 'eathen but a first-class fightin' man;
We gives you your certificate, an' if you want it signed
We'll come an' 'ave a romp with you whenever you're inclined.

We took our chanst among the Kyber 'ills,
The Boers knocked us silly at a mile,
The Burman give us Irriwaddy chills,
An' a Zulu *impi* dished us up in style:
But all we ever got from such as they
Was pop to what the Fuzzy made us swaller;
We 'eld our bloomin' own, the papers say,
But man for man the Fuzzy knocked us 'oller.
Then 'ere's *to* you, Fuzzy-Wuzzy, an' the missis and the kid;
Our orders was to break you, an' of course we went an' did.
We sloshed you with Martinis, an' it wasn't 'ardly fair;
But for all the odds agin' you, Fuzzy-Wuz, you broke the square.

'E 'asn't got no papers of 'is own,
'E 'asn't got no medals nor rewards,
So *we* must certify the skill 'e's shown
In usin' of 'is long two-'anded swords;

When 'e's 'oppin' in an' out among the bush
  With 'is coffin-'eaded shield an' shovel-spear,
An 'appy day with Fuzzy on the rush
  Will last an 'ealthy Tommy for a year.
    So 'ere's *to* you, Fuzzy-Wuzzy, an' your friends which are no more,
    If we 'adn't lost some messmates we would 'elp you to deplore;
    But give an' take's the gospel, an' we'll call the bargain fair,
    For if you 'ave lost more than us, you crumpled up the square!

'E rushes at the smoke when we let drive,
  An', before we know, 'e's 'ackin' at our 'ead;
'E's all 'ot sand an' ginger when alive,
  An' 'e's generally shammin' when 'e's dead.
'E's a daisy, 'e's a ducky, 'e's a lamb!
  'E's a injia-rubber idiot on the spree,
'E's a on'y thing that doesn't care a damn
  For the Regiment o' British Infantree!
    So 'ere's *to* you, Fuzzy-Wuzzy, at your 'ome in the Soudan;
    You're a pore benighted 'eathen but a first-class fightin' man;
    An 'ere's *to* you Fuzzy-Wuzzy, with your 'ay-rick 'ead of 'air—
    You big black boundin' beggar—for you broke a British square!

DANNY DEEVER

"What are the bugles blowin' for?" said Files-on-Parade.
"To turn you out, to turn you out," the Color-Sergeant said.
"What makes you look so white, so white?" said Files-on-Parade.
"I'm dreadin' what I've got to watch," the Color-Sergeant said.
  For they're hangin' Danny Deever, you can hear the Dead March play,
  The regiment's in 'ollow square—they're hangin' him to-day;
  They've taken of his buttons off an' cut his stripes away,
  An' they're hangin' Danny Deever in the mornin'.

"What makes the rear-rank breathe so 'ard?" said Files-on-Parade.
"It's bitter cold, it's bitter cold," the Color-Sergeant said.
"What makes that front-rank man fall down?" said Files-on-Parade.
"A touch o' sun, a touch o' sun," the Color-Sergeant said.
  They are hangin' Danny Deever, they are marchin' of 'im round,
  They 'ave 'alted Danny Deever by 'is coffin on the ground;
  An' 'e'll swing in 'arf a minute for a sneakin' shootin' hound—
  O they're hangin' Danny Deever in the mornin'!

"'Is cot was right-'and cot to mine," said Files-on-Parade.
"'E's sleepin' out an' far to-night," the Color-Sergeant said.
"I've drunk 'is beer a score o' times," said Files-on-Parade.
"'E's drinkin' bitter beer alone," the Color-Sergeant said.
  They are hangin' Danny Deever, you must mark 'im to 'is place,
  For 'e shot a comrade sleepin'—you must look 'im in the face;
  Nine 'undred of 'is county an' the regiment's disgrace,
  While they're hangin' Danny Deever in the mornin'.

"What's that so black agin the sun?" said Files-on-Parade.
"It's Danny fightin' 'ard for life," the Color-Sergeant said.
"What's that that whimpers over'ead?" said Files-on-Parade.
"It's Danny's soul that's passin' now," the Color-Sergeant said.
  For they're done with Danny Deever, you can 'ear the quickstep play,
  The regiment's in column, an' they're marchin' us away;
  Ho! the young recruits are shakin', an' they'll want their beer to-day,
  After hangin' Danny Deever in the mornin'!

L'ENVOI

What is the moral? Who rides may read.
  When the night is thick and the tracks are blind
A friend at a pinch is a friend indeed;
  But a fool to wait for the laggard behind;
Down to Gehenna or up to the Throne,
He travels the fastest who travels alone.

White hands cling to the tightened rein,
  Slipping the spur from the booted heel,
Tenderest voices cry "Turn again."

Red lips tarnish the scabbarded steel.
High hopes faint on a warm hearthstone—
He travels the fastest who travels alone.

One may fall but he falls by himself—
Falls by himself with himself to blame;
One may attain and to him is pelf,
Loot of the city in Gold or Fame:
Plunder of earth shall be all his own
Who travels the fastest and travels alone.

Wherefore the more ye be holpen and stayed—
Stayed by a friend in the hour of toil,
Sing the heretical song I have made—
His be the labor and yours be the spoil.
Win by his aid and the aid disown—
He travels the fastest who travels alone.

RECESSIONAL

This poem was published in 1897 in the London *Times* towards the close of the Diamond Jubilee celebration of Queen Victoria's accession to the throne.

God of our fathers, known of old,
Lord of our far-flung battle-line,
Beneath whose awful hand we hold
Dominion over palm and pine—
Lord God of Hosts, be with us yet,
Lest we forget—lest we forget!

The tumult and the shouting dies;
The Captains and the Kings depart;
Still stands Thine ancient sacrifice,
An humble and a contrite heart.
Lord God of Hosts, be with us yet,
Lest we forget—lest we forget!

Far-called, our navies melt away;
On dune and headland sinks the fire:
Lo, all our pomp of yesterday
Is one with Nineveh and Tyre!
Judge of the Nations, spare us yet,
Lest we forget—lest we forget!

If, drunk with sight of power, we loose
Wild tongues that have not Thee in awe—
Such boastings as the Gentiles use,
Or lesser breeds without the Law—
Lord God of Hosts, be with us yet,
Lest we forget—lest we forget!

For heathen heart that puts her trust
In reeking tube and iron shard—
All valiant dust that builds on dust,
And guarding calls not Thee to guard,
For frantic boast and foolish word—
Thy Mercy on Thy People, Lord!

AT THE END OF THE PASSAGE[1]

FOUR men, theoretically entitled to "life, liberty, and the pursuit of happiness," sat at a table playing whist. The thermometer marked—for them—one hundred and one degrees of heat. The room was darkened till it was only just possible to distinguish the pips of the cards and the very white faces of the players. A tattered, rotten punkah of whitewashed calico was puddling the hot air and whining dolefully at each stroke. Outside lay gloom of a November day in London. There was neither sky, sun, nor horizon—nothing but a brown-purple haze of heat. It was as though the earth were dying of apoplexy.

From time to time clouds of tawny dust rose from the ground without wind or warning, flung themselves table-clothwise among the tops of the parched trees, and came down again. Then a whirling dust-devil would scutter across the plain for a couple of miles, break, and fall outward, though there was nothing to check its flight save a long low line of piled railway-sleepers white with the dust, a cluster of huts made of mud, condemned rails and canvas, and the one squat four-roomed bungalow that belonged to the assistant engineer in charge of a section of the Gandhari State line then under construction.

The four men, stripped to the thinnest of sleeping suits, played whist crossly, with wranglings as to leads and returns. It was not the best kind of whist, but they had taken some trouble to arrive at it. Mottram, of the India Survey, had ridden thirty and railed one hundred miles from his lonely post in the desert since the previous night; Lowndes, of the Civil Service, on special duty in the political department, had come as far to escape for an instant the miserable intrigues of an impoverished native state whose king alternately fawned and blustered for more money from the pitiful revenues contributed by hard-wrung peasants and despairing camel-breeders; Spurstow, the doctor of the line, had left a cholera-stricken camp of coolies to look after itself for forty-eight hours while he associated with white men once more. Hummil, the assistant engineer, was the host. He stood fast, and received his friends thus every Sunday if they could come in. When one of them failed to appear, he would send a telegram

[1] From *Life's Handicap*, 1891.

to his last address, in order that he might know whether the defaulter was dead or alive. There be very many places in the East where it is not good or kind to let your acquaintances drop out of sight even for one short week.

The players were not conscious of any special regard for each other. They squabbled whenever they met; but they ardently desired to meet, as men without water desire to drink. They were lonely folk who understood the dread meaning of loneliness. They were all under thirty years of age—which is too soon for any man to possess that knowledge.

"Pilsener," said Spurstow, after the second rubber, mopping his forehead.

"Beer's out, I'm sorry to say, and there's hardly enough soda-water for to-night," said Hummil.

"What filthy bad management!" snarled Spurstow.

"Can't help it. I've written and wired; but the trains don't come through regularly yet. Last week the ice ran out—as Lowndes knows."

"Glad I didn't come. I could ha' sent you some if I had known, though. Phew! it's too hot to go on playing bumblepuppy."

This was a savage growl at Lowndes, who only laughed. He was a hardened offender.

Mottram rose from the table and looked out of a chink in the shutters.

"What a sweet day!" said he.

The company yawned unanimously and betook themselves to an aimless investigation of all Hummil's possessions—guns, tattered novels, saddlery, spurs, and the like. They had fingered them a score of times before, but there was really nothing else to do.

"Got anything fresh?" said Lowndes.

"Last week's 'Gazette of India,' and a cutting from a home paper. My father sent it out. It's rather amusing."

"One of those vestrymen that call 'emselves M. P.'s again, is it?" said Spurstow, who read his newspapers when he could get them.

"Yes. Listen to this. It's to your address, Lowndes. The man was making a speech to his constituents, and he piled it on. Here's a sample: 'And I assert unhesitatingly that the Civil Service in India is the preserve—the pet preserve—of the aristocracy of England. What does the democracy—what do the masses—get from that country, which we have step by step fraudulently annexed? I answer, nothing whatever. It is farmed, with a single eye to their own interest, by the scions of the aristocracy. They take good care to maintain their lavish scale of incomes, to avoid or stifle any inquiries into the nature and conduct of their administration, while they themselves force the unhappy peasant to pay with the sweat of his brow for all the luxuries in which they are lapped.' " Hummil waved the cutting above his head. " 'Ear! 'ear!" said his audience.

Then Lowndes, meditatively: "I'd give—I'd give three months' pay to have that gentleman spend one month with me and see how the free and independent native prince works things. Old Timbersides"—this was his flippant title for an honored and decorated prince—"has been wearing my life out this week past for money. By Jove! his latest performance was to send me one of his women as a bribe!"

"Good for you. Did you accept it?" said Mottram.

"No. I rather wish I had, now. She was a pretty little person, and she yarned away to me about the horrible destitution among the king's women-folk. The darlings haven't had any new clothes for nearly a month, and the old man wants to buy a new drag from Calcutta—solid silver railings and silver lamps, and trifles of that kind. I've tried to make him understand that he has played the deuce with the revenues for the last twenty years, and must go slow. He can't see it."

"But he has the ancestral treasure-vault to draw on. There must be three millions at least in jewels and coin under his palace," said Hummil.

"Catch a native king disturbing the family treasure! The priests forbid it, except as the last resort. Old Timbersides has added something like a quarter of a million to the deposit in his reign."

"Where the mischief does it all come from?" said Mottram.

"The country. The state of the people is enough to make you sick. I've known the tax-men wait by a milch-camel till the foal was born, and then hurry off the mother for arrears. And what can I do? I can't get the court clerks to give me any accounts; I can't raise anything more than a fat smile from the commander-in-chief when I find out the troops are three months in arrears; and old Timbersides begins to weep when I speak to him. He has taken to the king's peg heavily—liqueur brandy for whisky and Heidsieck for soda-water."

"That's what the Rao of Jubela took to. Even a native can't last long at that," said Spurstow. "He'll go out."

"And a good thing, too. Then I suppose we'll have a council of regency, and a tutor for the young prince, and hand him back his kingdom with ten years' accumulations."

"Whereupon that young prince, having been taught all the vices of the English, will play ducks and drakes with the money, and undo ten years' work in eighteen months. I've seen that business before," said Spurstow. "I should tackle the king with a light hand, if I were you, Lowndes. They'll hate you quite enough under any circumstances."

"That's all very well. The man who looks on can talk about the light hand; but you can't clean a pig-sty with a pen dipped in rosewater. I know my risks; but nothing has happened yet. My servant's an old Pathan, and he cooks for me. They are hardly likely to bribe him, and I don't accept food from my true friends, as they call themselves. Oh, but it's weary work! I'd sooner be with you, Spurstow. There's shooting near your camp."

"Would you? I don't think it. About fifteen deaths a day don't incite a man to shoot anything but himself. And the worst of it is that the poor devils look at you as though you ought to save them. Lord knows, I've tried everything. My last attempt was empirical, but it pulled an old man through. He was brought to me apparently past hope, and I gave him gin and Worcester sauce with cayenne. It cured him; but I don't recommend it."

"How do the cases run generally?" said Hummil.

"Very simply indeed. Chlorodyne, opium pill, chlorodyne, collapse, nitre, bricks to the feet, and then—the burning-ghat. The last seems to be the only thing that stops the trouble. It's black cholera, you know. Poor devils! But, I will say, little Bunsee Lal, my apothecary, works like a demon. I've recommended him for promotion if he comes through it all alive."

"And what are your chances, old man?" said Mottram.

"Don't know: don't care much; but I've sent the letter in. What are you doing with yourself generally?"

"Sitting under a table in the tent and spitting on the sextant to keep it cool," said the man of the survey. "Washing my eyes to avoid ophthalmia, which I shall certainly get, and trying to make a sub-surveyor understand that an error of five degrees in an angle isn't quite so small as it looks. I'm altogether alone, y' know, and shall be till the end of the hot weather."

"Hummil's the lucky man," said Lowndes, flinging himself into a long chair. "He has an actual roof—torn as to the ceiling-cloth, but still a roof—over his head. He sees one train daily. He can get beer and soda-water, and ice it when God is good. He has books, pictures"—they were torn from the "Graphic"—"and the society of the excellent sub-contractor Jevins, besides the pleasure of receiving us weekly."

Hummil smiled grimly. "Yes, I'm the lucky man, I suppose. Jevins is luckier."

"How? Not—"

"Yes. Went out. Last Monday."

"*Ap se?*" said Spurstow, quickly, hinting the suspicion that was in everybody's mind. There was no cholera near Hummil's section. Even fever gives a man at least a week's grace, and sudden death generally implied self-slaughter.

"I judge no man this weather," said Hummil. "He had a touch of the sun, I fancy; for last week, after you fellows had left, he came into the veranda and told me that he was going home to see his wife, in Market Street, Liverpool, that evening. I got the apothecary in to look at him, and we tried to make him lie down. After an hour or two he rubbed his eyes and said he believed he had had a fit—hoped he hadn't said anything rude. Jevins had a great idea of bettering himself socially. He was very like Chucks in his language."

"Well?"

"Then he went to his own bungalow and began cleaning a rifle. He told the servant that he was going after buck in the morning. Naturally he fumbled with the trigger, and shot himself through the head accidentally. The apothecary sent in a report to my chief, and Jevins is buried somewhere out there. I'd have wired to you, Spurstow, if you could have done anything."

"You're a queer chap," said Mottram. "If you killed the man yourself you couldn't have been more quiet about the business."

"Good Lord! what does it matter?" said Hummil, calmly. "I've got to do a lot of his overseeing work in addition to my own. I'm the only person that suffers. Jevins is out of it—by pure accident, of course, but out of it. The apothecary was going to write a long screed on suicide. Trust a babu to drivel when he gets the chance."

"Why didn't you let it go in as suicide?" said Lowndes.

"No direct proof. A man hasn't many privileges in this country, but he might at least be allowed to mishandle his own rifle. Besides, some day I may need a man to smother up an accident to myself. Live and let live. Die and let die."

"You take a pill," said Spurstow, who had been watching Hummil's white face narrowly. "Take a pill, and don't be an ass. That sort of talk is skittles. Anyhow, suicide is shirking your work. If I was a Job ten times over, I should be so interested in what was going to happen next that I'd stay on and watch."

"Ah! I've lost that curiosity," said Hummil.

"Liver out of order?" said Lowndes, feelingly.

"No. Can't sleep. That's worse."

"By Jove, it is!" said Mottram. "I'm that way every now and then, and the fit has to wear itself out. What do you take for it?"

"Nothing. What's the use? I haven't had ten minutes' sleep since Friday morning."

"Poor chap! Spurstow, you ought to attend to this," said Mottram. "Now you mention it, your eyes are rather gummy and swollen."

Spurstow, still watching Hummil, laughed lightly. "I'll patch him up later on. Is it too hot, do you think, to go for a ride?"

"Where to?" said Lowndes, wearily. "We shall have to go away at eight, and there'll be riding enough for us then. I hate a horse, when I have to use him as a necessity. Oh, heavens! what is there to do?"

"Begin whist again, at chick points" (a "chick" is supposed to be eight shillings), "and a gold mohur on the rub," said Spurstow promptly.

"Poker. A month's pay all round for the pool—no limit—and fifty-rupee raises. Somebody would be broken before we got up," said Lowndes.

"Can't say that it would give me any pleasure to break any man in this company," said Mottram. "There isn't enough excitement in it, and it's foolish." He crossed over to the worn and battered little camp-piano—wreckage of a married household that had once held the bungalow—and opened the case.

"It's used up long ago," said Hummil. "The servants have picked it to pieces."

The piano was indeed hopelessly out of order, but Mottram managed to bring the rebellious notes into a sort of agreement, and there rose from the ragged keyboard something that might once have been the ghost of a popular music-hall song. The men in the long chairs turned with evident interest as Mottram banged the more lustily.

"That's good!" said Lowndes. "By Jove! the last time I heard that song was in '79, or thereabouts, just before I came out."

"Ah!" said Spurstow, with pride, "I was home in '80." And he mentioned a song of the streets popular at that date.

Mottram executed it indifferently well. Lowndes criticised, and volunteered emendations. Mottram dashed into another ditty, not of the music-hall character, and made as if to rise.

"Sit down," said Hummil. "I didn't know that you had any music in your composition. Go on playing until you can't think of anything more. I'll have that piano tuned up before you come again. Play something festive."

Very simple indeed were the tunes to which Mottram's art and the limitations of the piano could give effect, but the men listened with pleasure, and in the pauses talked all together of what they had seen or heard when they were last at home. A dense duststorm sprang up outside and swept roaring over the house, enveloping it in the choking darkness of midnight, but Mottram continued unheeding, and the crazy tinkle reached the ears of the listeners above the flapping of the tattered ceiling-cloth.

In the silence after the storm he glided from the more directly personal songs of Scotland, half humming them as he played, into the "Evening Hymn."

"Sunday," said he, nodding his head.

"Go on. Don't apologize for it," said Spurstow.

Hummil laughed long and riotously. "Play it, by all means. You're full of surprises to-day. I didn't know you had such a gift of finished sarcasm. How does that thing go?"

Mottram took up the tune.

"Too slow by half. You miss the note of gratitude," said Hummil. "It ought to go to the 'Grasshopper's Polka'—this way." And he chanted, *prestissimo:*

> "'Glory to Thee, my God, this night,
> For all the blessings of the light.'

That shows we really feel our blessings. How does it go on?—

> "'If in the night I sleepless lie,
> My soul with sacred thoughts supply;
> May no ill dreams disturb my rest,'—

Quicker, Mottram!—

> "'Or powers of darkness me molest!'"

"Bah! what an old hypocrite you are."

"Don't be an ass," said Lowndes. "You are at full liberty to make fun of anything else you like, but leave that hymn alone. It's associated in my mind with the most sacred recollections—"

"Summer evenings in the country—stained-glass window—light going out, and you and she jamming your heads together over one hymn-book," said Mottram.

"Yes, and a fat old cockchafer hitting you in the eye when you walked home. Smell of hay, and a moon as big as a band-box sitting on the top of a haycock; bats—roses—milk and midges," said Lowndes.

"Also mothers. I can just recollect my mother singing me to sleep with that when I was a little chap," said Spurstow.

The darkness had fallen on the room. They could hear Hummil squirming in his chair.

"Consequently," said he, testily, "you sing it when you are seven fathoms deep in hell! It's an insult to the intelligence of the Deity to pretend we're anything but tortured rebels."

"Take *two* pills," said Spurstow: "that's tortured liver."

"The usually placid Hummil is in a vile bad temper. I'm sorry for the coolies to-morrow," said Lowndes, as the servants brought in the lights and prepared the table for dinner.

As they were settling into their places about the miserable goat-chops, the curried eggs, and the smoked tapioca pudding, Spurstow took occasion to whisper to Mottram: "Well done, David!"

"Look after Saul, then," was the reply.

"What are you two whispering about?" said Hummil, suspiciously.

"Only saying that you are a d——d poor host. This fowl can't be cut," returned Spurstow, with a sweet smile. "Call this a dinner?"

"I can't help it. You don't expect a banquet, do you?"

Throughout that meal Hummil contrived laboriously to insult directly and pointedly all his guests in succession, and at each insult Spurstow kicked the aggrieved person under the table; but he dared not exchange a glance of intelligence with either of them. Hummil's face was white and pinched, while his eyes were unnaturally large. No man dreamed for a moment of resenting his savage personalities, but as soon as the meal was over they made haste to get away.

"Don't go. You're just getting amusing, you fellows. I hope I haven't said anything that annoyed you. You're such touchy devils." Then, changing the note into one of almost abject entreaty: "I say, you surely aren't going?"

"Where I dines, I sleeps, in the language of the blessed Jorrocks," said Spurstow. "I want to have a look at your coolies to-morrow, if you don't mind. You can give me a place to lie down in, I suppose?"

The others pleaded the urgency of their several employs next day, and, saddling up, departed together, Hummil begging them to come next Sunday. As they jogged off together, Lowndes unbosomed himself to Mottram: ". . . And I never felt so like kicking a man at his own table in my life. Said I cheated at whist, and reminded me I was in debt! Told you you were as good as a liar to your face! You aren't half indignant enough over it."

"Not I," said Mottram. "Poor devil! Did you ever know old Hummy behave like that before? Did you ever know him go within a hundred miles of it?"

"That's no excuse. Spurstow was hacking my shin all the time, so I kept a hand on myself. Else I should have—"

"No, you wouldn't. You'd have done as Hummy did about Jevins; judge no man this weather. By Jove! the buckle of my bridle is hot in my hand! Trot out a bit, and mind the rat-holes."

Ten minutes' trotting jerked out of Lowndes one very sage remark when he pulled up, sweating from every pore:

"Good thing Spurstow's with him to-night."

"Ye-es. Good man, Spurstow. Our roads turn here. See you again next Sunday, if the sun doesn't bowl me over."

"S'pose so, unless old Timbersides' finance minister manages to dress some of my food. Good-night, and—God bless you!"

"What's wrong now?"

"Oh, nothing." Lowndes gathered up his whip, and, as he flicked Mottram's mare on the flank, added: "You're a good little chap—that's all." And the mare bolted half a mile across the sand on the word.

In the assistant engineer's bungalow Spurstow and Hummil smoked the pipe of silence together, each narrowly watching the other. The capacity of a bachelor's establishment is as elastic as its arrangements are simple. A servant cleared away the dining-room table, brought in a couple of rude native bedsteads made of tape strung on a light wood frame, flung a square of cool Calcutta matting over each, set them side by side, pinned two towels to the punkah so that their fringes should just sweep clear of each sleeper's nose and mouth, and announced that the couches were ready.

The men flung themselves down, adjuring the punkah-coolies by all the powers of Eblis to pull. Every door and window was shut, for the outside air was that of an oven. The atmosphere within was only 104°, as the thermometer attested, and heavy with the foul smell of badly trimmed kerosene lamps; and this stench, combined with that of native tobacco, baked brick, and dried earth, sends the heart of many a strong man down to his boots, for it is the smell of the great Indian Empire when she turns herself for six months into a house of torment. Spurstow packed his pillows craftily, so that he reclined rather than lay, his head at a safe elevation above his feet. It is not good to sleep on a low pillow in the hot weather if you happen to be of thick-necked build, for you may pass with lively snores and gurglings from natural sleep into the deep slumber of heat-apoplexy.

"Pack your pillows," said the doctor, sharply, as he saw Hummil preparing to lie down at full length.

The night-light was trimmed; the shadow of the punkah wavered across the room, and the *flick* of the punkah-towel and the soft whine of the rope through the wall-hole followed it. Then the punkah flagged, almost ceased. The sweat poured from Spurstow's brow. Should he go out and harangue the coolie? It started forward again with a savage jerk, and a pin came out of the towels. When this was replaced, a tom-tom in the coolie lines began to beat with the steady throb of a swollen artery inside some brain-fevered skull. Spurstow turned on his side and swore gently. There was no movement on Hummil's part. The man had composed himself as rigidly as a corpse, his hands clinched at his sides. The respiration was too hurried for any suspicion of sleep. Spurstow looked at the set face. The jaws were clinched, and there was a pucker round the quivering eyelids.

"He's holding himself as tightly as ever he can," thought Spurstow. "What a sham it is! and what in the world is the matter with him?—Hummil!"

"Yes."

"Can't you get to sleep?"

"No."

"Head hot? Throat feeling bulgy? or how?"

"Neither, thanks. I don't sleep much, you know."

"Feel pretty bad?"

"Pretty bad, thanks. There is a tom-tom outside, isn't there? I thought it was my head at first. Oh, Spurstow, for pity's sake, give me something that will put me asleep—sound sleep—if it's only for six hours!" He sprung up. "I haven't been able to sleep naturally for days, and I can't stand it!—I can't stand it!"

"Poor old chap!"

"That's no use. Give me something to make me sleep. I tell you I'm nearly mad. I don't know what I say half my time. For three weeks I've had to think and spell out every word that has come through my lips before I dared say it. I had to get my sentences out down to the last word, for fear of talking drivel if I didn't. Isn't that enough to drive a man mad? I can't see things correctly now, and I've lost my sense of touch. Make me sleep. Oh, Spurstow, for the love of God, make me sleep sound. It isn't enough merely to let me dream. Let me sleep!"

"All right, old man, all right. Go slow. You aren't half as bad as you think." The flood-gates of reserve once broken, Hummil was clinging to him like a frightened child.

"You're pinching my arm to pieces."

"I'll break your neck if you don't do something for me. No, I didn't mean that. Don't be angry, old fellow." He wiped the sweat off himself as he fought to regain composure. "As a matter of fact, I'm a bit restless and off my oats, and perhaps you could recommend some sort of sleeping-mixture—bromide of potassium."

"Bromide of skittles! Why didn't you tell me this before? Let go of my arm, and I'll see if there's anything in my cigarette-case to suit your complaint." He hunted among his day-clothes, turned up the lamp, opened a little silver cigarette-case, and advanced on the expectant Hummil with the daintiest of fairy squirts.

"The last appeal of civilization," said he, "and a thing I hate to use. Hold out your arm. Well, your sleeplessness hasn't ruined your muscle; and what a thick hide it is! Might as well inject a buffalo subcutaneously. Now in a few minutes the morphia will begin working. Lie down and wait."

A smile of unalloyed and idiotic delight began to creep over Hummil's face. "I think," he whispered—"I think I'm going off now. Gad! it's positively heavenly! Spurstow, you must give me that case to keep; you—" The voice ceased as the head fell back.

"Not for a good deal," said Spurstow to the unconscious form. "And now, my friend, sleeplessness of your kind being very apt to relax the moral fiber in little matters of life and death, I'll just take the liberty of spiking your guns."

He paddled into Hummil's saddle-room in his bare feet, and uncased a twelve-bore, an express, and a revolver. Of the first he unscrewed the nipples and hid them in the bottom of a saddlery-case; of the second he abstracted the lever, placing it behind a big wardrobe. The third he merely opened, and knocked the doll-head bolt of the grip up with the heel of a riding-boot.

"That's settled," he said, as he shook the sweat off his hands. "These little precautions will at least give you time to turn. You have too much sympathy with gun-room accidents."

And as he rose from his knees, the thick muffled voice of Hummil cried in the doorway: "You fool!"

Such tones they use who speak in the lucid intervals of delirium to their friends a little before they die.

Spurstow jumped with sheer fright. Hummil

stood in the doorway, rocking with helpless laughter.

"That was awf'ly good of you, I'm sure," he said, very slowly, feeling for his words. "I don't intend to go out by my own hand at present. I say, Spurstow, that stuff won't work. What shall I do? What shall I do?" And panic terror stood in his eyes.

"Lie down and give it a chance. Lie down at once."

"I daren't. It will only take me half-way again, and I sha'n't be able to get away this time. Do you know it was all I could do to come out just now? Generally I am as quick as lightning; but you have clogged my feet. I was nearly caught."

"Oh, yes, I understand. Go and lie down."

"No, it isn't delirium; but it was an awfully mean trick to play on me. Do you know I might have died?"

As a sponge rubs a slate clean, so some power unknown to Spurstow had wiped out of Hummil's face all that stamped it for the face of a man, and he stood at the doorway in the expression of his lost innocence. He had slept back into terrified childhood.

"Is he going to die on the spot?" thought Spurstow. Then, aloud: "All right, my son. Come back to bed, and tell me all about it. You couldn't sleep; but what was all the rest of the nonsense?"

"A place—a place down there," said Hummil, with simple sincerity. The drug was acting on him by waves, and he was flung from the fear of a strong man to the fright of a child as his nerves gathered sense or were dulled.

"Good God! I've been afraid of it for months past, Spurstow. It has made every night hell to me; and yet I'm not conscious of having done anything wrong."

"Be still, and I'll give you another dose. We'll stop your nightmares, you unutterable idiot!"

"Yes, but you must give me so much that I can't get away. You must make me quite sleepy—not just a little sleepy. It's so hard to run then."

"I know it; I know it. I've felt it myself. The symptoms are exactly as you describe."

"Oh, don't laugh at me, confound you! Before this awful sleeplessness came to me I've tried to rest on my elbow and put a spur in the bed to sting me when I fell back. Look!"

"By Jove! the man has been roweled like a horse! Ridden by the nightmare with a vengeance! And we all thought him sensible enough. Heaven send us understanding! You like to talk, don't you, old man?"

"Yes, sometimes. Not when I'm frightened. *Then* I want to run. Don't you?"

"Always. Before I give you your second dose, try to tell me exactly what your trouble is."

Hummil spoke in broken whispers for nearly ten minutes, while Spurstow looked into the pupils of his eyes and passed his hand before them once or twice.

At the end of the narrative the silver cigarette-case was produced, and the last words that Hummil said as he fell back for the second time were: "Put me quite to sleep; for if I'm caught, I die—I die!"

"Yes, yes; we all do that sooner or later, thank Heaven! who has set a term to our miseries," said Spurstow, settling the cushions under the head. "It occurs to me that unless I drink something I shall go out before my time. I've stopped sweating, and I wear a seventeen-inch collar." And he brewed himself scalding hot tea, which is an excellent remedy against heat-apoplexy if you take three or four cups of it in time. Then he watched the sleeper.

"A blind face that cries and can't wipe its eyes. H'm! Decidedly, Hummil ought to go on leave as soon as possible; and, sane or otherwise, he undoubtedly did rowel himself most cruelly. Well, Heaven send us understanding!"

At midday Hummil rose, with an evil taste in his mouth, but an unclouded eye and a joyful heart.

"I was pretty bad last night, wasn't I?" said he.

"I have seen healthier men. You must have had a touch of the sun. Look here: if I write you a swinging medical certificate, will you apply for leave on the spot?"

"No."

"Why not? You want it."

"Yes, but I can hold on till the weather's a little cooler."

"Why should you, if you can get relieved on the spot?"

"Burkett is the only man who could be sent; and he's a born fool."

"Oh, never mind about the line. You aren't so important as all that. Wire for leave, if necessary."

Hummil looked very uncomfortable.

"I can hold on till the rains," he said, evasively.

"You can't. Wire to headquarters for Burkett."

"I won't. If you want to know why, particularly, Burkett is married, and his wife's just had a kid, and she's up at Simla, in the cool, and Burkett has a very nice billet that takes him into Simla from Saturday to Monday. That little woman isn't at all well. If Burkett was transferred she'd try to follow him. If she left the baby behind she'd fret herself to death. If she came—and Burkett's one of those selfish little beasts who are always talking about a wife's place being with her husband—she'd die. It's murder to bring a woman here just now. Burkett has got the physique of a rat. If he came here he'd go out; and I know she hasn't any money, and I'm pretty sure she'd go out too. I'm salted in a sort of way, and I'm not married. Wait till the rains, and then Burkett can get thin down here. It'll do him heaps of good."

"Do you mean to say that you intend to face—what you have faced, for the next fifty-six nights?"

"Oh, it won't be so bad, now you've shown me a way out of it. I can always wire to you. Besides, now I've once got into the way of sleeping, it'll be all right. Anyhow, I shan't put in for leave. That's the long and the short of it."

"My great Scott! I thought all that sort of thing was dead and done with."

"Bosh! You'd do the same yourself. I feel a new man, thanks to that cigarette-case. You're going over to camp now, aren't you?"

"Yes; but I'll try to look you up every other day, if I can."

"I'm not bad enough for that. I don't want you to bother. Give the coolies gin and ketchup."

"Then you feel all right?"

"Fit to fight for my life, but not to stand out in the sun talking to you. Go along, old man, and bless you!"

Hummil turned on his heel to face the echoing desolation of his bungalow, and the first thing he saw standing in the veranda was the figure of himself. He had met a similar apparition once before, when he was suffering from overwork and the strain of the hot weather.

"This is bad—already," he said, rubbing his eyes. "If the thing slides away from me all in one piece, like a ghost, I shall know it is only my eyes and stomach that are out of order. If it walks, I shall know that my head is going."

He walked to the figure, which naturally kept at an unvarying distance from him, as is the use of all specters that are born of overwork. It slid through the house and dissolved into swimming specks within the eyeball as soon as it reached the burning light of the garden. Hummil went about his business till even. When he came in to dinner he found himself sitting at the table. The thing rose and walked out hastily.

No living man knows what that week held for Hummil. An increase of the epidemic kept Spurstow in camp among the coolies, and all he could do was to telegraph to Mottram, bidding him go to the bungalow and sleep there. But Mottram was forty miles away from the nearest telegraph, and knew nothing of anything save the needs of the survey till he met early on Sunday morning Lowndes and Spurstow heading toward Hummil's for the weekly gathering.

"Hope the poor chap's in a better temper," said the former, swinging himself off his horse at the door. "I suppose he isn't up yet."

"I'll just have a look at him," said the doctor. "If he's asleep there's no need to wake him."

And an instant later, by the tone of Spurstow's voice calling upon them to enter, the men knew what had happened.

The punkah was still being pulled over the bed, but Hummil had departed this life at least three hours before.

The body lay on its back, hands clinched by the side, as Spurstow had seen it lying seven nights previously. In the staring eyes was written terror beyond the expression of any pen.

Mottram, who had entered behind Lowndes, bent over the dead and touched the forehead lightly with his lips. "Oh, you lucky, lucky devil!" he whispered.

But Lowndes had seen the eyes, and had withdrawn shuddering to the other side of the room.

"Poor chap! poor chap! And the last time I met him I was angry. Spurstow, we should have watched him. Has he—"

Deftly Spurstow continued his investigations, ending by a search round the room.

"No, he hasn't," he snapped. "There's no trace of anything. Call in the servants."

They came, eight or ten of them, whispering and peering over each other's shoulders.

"When did your sahib go to bed?" said Spurstow.

"At eleven or ten, we think," said Hummil's personal servant.

"He was well then? But how should you know?"

"He was not ill, as far as our comprehension extended. But he had slept very little for three nights. This I know, because I saw him walking much, and especially in the heart of the night."

As Spurstow was arranging the sheet, a big, straight-necked hunting-spur tumbled on the ground. The doctor groaned. The personal servant peeped at the body.

"What do you think, Chuma?" said Spurstow, catching the look in the dark face.

"Heaven-born, in my poor opinion, this that was my master has descended into the Dark Places, and there has been caught, because he was not able to escape with sufficient speed. We have the spur for evidence that he fought with Fear. Thus have I seen men of my race do with thorns when a spell was laid upon them to overtake them in their sleeping hours and they dared not sleep."

"Chuma, you're a mud-head. Go out and prepare seals to be set on the sahib's property."

"God has made the heaven-born. God has made me. Who are we, to inquire into the dispensations of God? I will bid the other servants hold aloof while you are reckoning the tale of the sahib's property. They are all thieves, and would steal."

"As far as I can make out, he died from—oh, anything: stopping of the heart's action, heat-apoplexy, or some other visitation," said Spurstow to his companions. "We must make an inventory of his effects, and so on."

"He was scared to death," insisted Lowndes. "Look at those eyes! For pity's sake, don't let him be buried with them open!"

"Whatever it was, he's out of all the trouble now," said Mottram, softly.

Spurstow was peering into the open eyes.

"Come here," said he. "Can you see anything there?"

"I can't face it!" whimpered Lowndes. "Cover up the face! Is there any fear on earth that can turn a man into that likeness? It's ghastly. Oh, Spurstow, cover him up!"

"No fear—on earth," said Spurstow. Mottram leaned over his shoulder and looked intently.

"I see nothing except some gray blurs in the pupil. There can be nothing there, you know."

"Even so. Well, let's think. It'll take half a day to knock up any sort of coffin; and he must have died at midnight. Lowndes, old man, go out and tell the coolies to break ground next to Jevins' grave. Mottram, go round the house with Chuma and see that the seals are put on things. Send a couple of men to me here, and I'll arrange."

The strong-armed servants when they returned to their own kind told a strange story of the doctor sahib vainly trying to call their master back to life by magic arts—to wit, the holding of a little green box opposite each of the dead man's eyes, of a frequent clicking of the same, and of a bewildered muttering on the part of the doctor sahib, who subsequently took the little green box away with him.

The resonant hammering of a coffin-lid is no pleasant thing to hear, but those who have experience maintain that much more terrible is the soft swish of the bed-linen, the reeving and unreeving of the bed-tapes, when he who has fallen by the road-side is appareled for burial, sinking gradually as the tapes are tied over, till the swaddled shape touches the floor and there is no protest against the indignity of hasty disposal.

At the last moment Lowndes was seized with scruples of conscience. "Ought you to read the service—from beginning to end?" said he.

"I intend to. You're my senior as a civilian. You can take it, if you like."

"I didn't mean that for a moment. I only thought if we could get a chaplain from somewhere—I'm willing to ride anywhere—and give poor Hummil a better chance. That's all."

"Bosh!" said Spurstow, as he framed his lips to the tremendous words that stand at the head of the burial service.

After breakfast they smoked a pipe in silence to the memory of the dead. Then said Spurstow, absently:

"'Tisn't in medical science."

"What?"

"Things in a dead man's eyes."

"For goodness' sake, leave that horror alone!" said Lowndes. "I've seen a native die of fright when a tiger chivied him. I know what killed Hummil."

"The deuce you do! I'm going to try to see." And the doctor retreated into the bath-room with a Kodak camera, splashing and grunting for ten minutes. Then there was the sound of something being hammered to pieces, and Spurstow emerged, very white indeed.

"Have you got a picture?" said Mottram. "What does the thing look like?"

"Nothing there. It was impossible, of course. You needn't look, Mottram. I've torn up the films. There was nothing there. It was impossible."

"That," said Lowndes, very distinctly, watching the shaking hand striving to relight the pipe, "is a damned lie."

There was no further speech for a long time. The hot wind whistled without, and the dry trees sobbed. Presently the daily train, winking brass, burnished steel, and spouting steam, pulled up panting in the intense glare. "We'd better go on that," said Spurstow. "Go back to work. I've written my certificate. We can't do any more good here. Come on."

No one moved. It is not pleasant to face railway journeys at midday in June. Spurstow gathered up his hat and whip, and, turning in the doorway, said:

"There may be heaven—there must be hell.
Meantime, there is our life here. We-ell?"

But neither Mottram nor Lowndes had any answer to the question.

SUGGESTIONS FOR FURTHER READING

This list is to be supplemented by the brief lists of books given in the General Bibliography and in the various introductions to specific authors and works.

HISTORICAL AND POLITICAL BACKGROUND

Bolitho, Hector. *The Reign of Queen Victoria*, Macmillan, 1948. A sympathetic study of the period and its monarch.

Brinton, Crane. *English Political Thought in the Nineteenth Century*, Longmans, 1922. The best brief study of the subject.

Dickinson, G. L. *The Development of Parliament during the Nineteenth Century*, Longmans, 1895. A standard work.

Dietz, F. C. *A Political and Social History of England*, Macmillan, 1937. Valuable for its section on the nineteenth century.

Egerton, H. E. *Short History of British Colonial Policy*, Macmillan, 1915. A useful source of information.

Evans, R. J. *The Victorian Age, 1815–1914*, Longmans, 1950. A recent and illuminating study.

Gretton, R. H. *A Modern History of the English People: 1880–1922*, Dial Press, 1930.

Lunt, W. E. *History of England*, 3rd ed., Harper, 1945. Contains a valuable survey of the period.

Trevelyan, G. M. *British History in the Nineteenth Century*, Longmans, 1922. A standard work.

Ward, Sir A. W., Prothero, G. W., and Leathes, Stanley, *The Cambridge Modern History*, Cambridge University Press, 1934. Vols. VIII–XII are invaluable for a study of the Age of Victoria.

Willcox, W. S. *Star of Empire: A Study of Britain as a World Power, 1485–1945*, Knopf, 1950. A clear, forceful, and sound study of British history in its world-wide setting. Especially valuable for its treatment of the nineteenth century.

CULTURAL AND SOCIAL BACKGROUND

Brown, A. W. *The Metaphysical Society: Victorian Minds in Crisis, 1869–1880*, Columbia University Press, 1947. A comprehensive study of the conflict between religion and science in Victorian England.

Clapham, J. H. *Economic History of Modern Britain*, Cambridge University Press, 1926–38.

Cunningham, William. *Growth of English Industry and Commerce*, rev. ed., Cambridge University Press, 1925–29. Vol. VI contains a valuable study of *laissez faire*.

Guedalla, Philip. *The Hundred Years, 1837–1937*, Doubleday, Doran, 1937. A lively panorama of men and events.

Heaton, Herbert. *Economic History of Europe*, rev. ed., Harper, 1948. Valuable for its survey of British economy in its world-wide setting.

Lichten, Frances. *Decorative Art of Victoria's Era*, Scribner, 1950. A fascinating panorama of the Victorian way of life, with abundant illustrations.

Metz, Rudolf. *A Hundred Years of British Philosophy*, ed. by J. H. Muirhead, Macmillan, 1938. A standard work.

Quennell, Peter. *Victorian Panorama: A Survey of Life and Fashion from Contemporary Photographs*, Scribner, 1937.

Randall, J. H. *The Making of the Modern Mind*, Houghton Mifflin, 1926.

Routh, H. V. *Towards the Twentieth Century*, Macmillan, 1937.

Sitwell, Edith. *Victoria of England*, Houghton Mifflin, 1936. A brilliant and fair-minded book.

Somervell, D. C. *English Thought in the Nineteenth Century*, Longmans, 1936.

Strachey, Lytton. *Queen Victoria*, Harcourt, Brace, 1921. A fine work of art, but the author's anti-Victorian bias must be allowed for.

——— *Eminent Victorians*, Penguin Books. Brilliant but biased studies of Thomas Arnold, Cardinal Manning, "Chinese" Gordon, and Florence Nightingale.

Willey, Basil. *Nineteenth Century Studies*, Chatto and Windus, 1949. An important examination of nineteenth-century thought, traced in the writings of Coleridge, Carlyle, Mill, Newman, George Eliot, and Matthew Arnold.

Wingfield-Stratford, Esmé. *The Victorian Cycle*, Morrow, 1935. An omnibus comprising the author's illuminating studies *Those Earnest Victorians*, *The Victorian Sunset*, and *The Victorian Aftermath*.

Young, G. M., ed. *Early Victorian England*, Oxford University Press, 1934. A valuable collection of essays.

LITERATURE OF THE PERIOD

COLLECTIONS

Brown, E. K., ed. *Victorian Poetry*, Ronald Press, 1942.

Harold, Charles F., and Templeman, William D., eds. *English Prose of the Victorian Era*, Oxford University Press, 1938.

Moses, Montrose J., ed. *Representative British Dramas, Victorian and Modern*, rev. ed., Little, Brown, 1939.

Woods, George B., ed. *Poetry of the Victorian Period*, Scott, Foresman, 1930.

CRITICISM

Chesterton, G. K. *The Victorian Age in Literature*, Home University Library, Oxford University Press. An excellent brief survey.

Cooke, J. D., and Stevenson, Lionel. *English Literature of the Victorian Period*, Appleton-Century-Crofts, 1949. A valuable companion to studies of the period.

Cruse, Amy. *The Victorians and Their Reading*, Houghton Mifflin, 1935. A delightful account of the literary and intellectual tastes of the Victorians.

Elton, Oliver. *A Survey of English Literature, 1780–1880*, Macmillan, 1920. Volumes III and IV contain the best detailed survey of the literature of the period.

Hicks, Granville. *Figures of Transition*, Macmillan, 1940. Excellent criticism.

Hough, Graham. *The Last Romantics*, Macmillan, 1949. A fresh assessment of the important personalities and movements of the literary scene from Ruskin to Yeats.

Leavis, F. R. *The Great Tradition*, Chatto and Windus, 1948. A recent and stimulating study of Victorian thought and expression.

McCullough, Bruce. *Representative English Novelists: Defoe to Conrad*, Harper, 1946.

Schilling, B. N. *Human Dignity and the Great Victorians*, Columbia University Press, 1947. An interpretation of seven writers whose work is unified by a common concern—Coleridge, Southey, Carlyle, Kingsley, Arnold, Ruskin, and Morris.

Warren, A. H., Jr. *English Poetic Theory, 1825–1865*, Princeton University Press, 1951.

ARNOLD

Poetical Works, with introduction by Sir A. T. Quiller-Couch, Oxford University Press, 1942.

Poetry and Prose, with introduction and notes by E. K. Chambers and essays by Lionel Johnson and H. W. Garrod, Oxford University Press, 1939.

The Portable Matthew Arnold, ed. by Lionel Trilling, Viking, 1949. Includes *Empedocles on Etna*, *Culture and Anarchy* (abridged), other poems, essays, and letters.

Chambers, E. K. *Matthew Arnold: A Study*, Oxford University Press, 1947.

Tinker, C. B., and Lowry, H. F. *The Poetry of Matthew Arnold: A Commentary*, Oxford University Press, 1940. The standard commentary on the poems.

Trilling, Lionel. *Matthew Arnold*, new ed., Columbia University Press, 1949. A penetrating critical study.

EMILY BRONTË

Complete Poems, ed. by C. W. Hatfield, Columbia University Press, 1941.

Bentley, Phyllis. *The Brontës*, English Novelists Series, Alan Swallow, Denver, 1948.

Hanson, Lawrence, and E. M. *The Four Brontës*, Oxford University Press, 1949.

Hinkley, Laura L. *Charlotte and Emily: the Brontës*, Hastings House, 1945.

ELIZABETH BARRETT BROWNING

The Complete Poetical Works, Cambridge Edition, Houghton Mifflin.

Burdett, Osbert. *The Brownings*, Houghton Mifflin, 1929. A very readable biographical study.

Woolf, Virginia. *Flush; a Biography*, Harcourt, Brace, 1933. The most delightful of all Browning books; a picture of the famous courtship seen through the eyes of Miss Barrett's dog.

ROBERT BROWNING

The Complete Poetical Works, Cambridge Edition, Houghton Mifflin.

Poetical Works, Oxford Standard Authors, Oxford University Press, 1940.

DeVane, W. C. *A Browning Handbook*, Crofts, 1935. An indispensable repository of information.

Dowden, Edward. *The Life of Robert Browning*, Everyman's Library, Dutton, 1915. Combines biography and excellent criticism.

Griffin, W. H., and Minchin, H. C. *Robert Browning*, Macmillan, 1910. The standard biography.

Phelps, William Lyon. *Browning*, Bobbs-Merrill, 1932.

CARLYLE

Selections from Carlyle, ed. by A. H. R. Ball, Cambridge University Press, 1929.

Sartor Resartus, ed. by C. F. Harrold, Odyssey, 1937. An inexpensive and well-annotated edition.

Lehman, B. H. *Carlyle's Theory of the Hero*, Duke University Press, 1928.

Neff, Emery. *Carlyle and Mill*, Columbia University Press, 1926. Compares, contrasts, and relates the personality and thought of two prophets of the Victorian era.

FITZGERALD

Polnay, Peter de. *Into an Old Room*, Creative Age, 1949. An interpretation of FitzGerald's life and work.

Terhune, A. M. *The Life of Edward FitzGerald*, Oxford University Press, 1947. An interesting account of "Old Fitz," containing his letters to Tennyson, Thackeray, Carlyle, and others.

HOPKINS

Poems, 3rd ed., ed. by W. H. Gardner, Oxford University Press, 1948. Contains the "Author's Preface," in which Hopkins explains his prosody, the preface and notes by Robert Bridges from the first edition, and additional poems, notes, and a biographical introduction.

Gardner, W. H. *Gerard Manley Hopkins*, Secker and Warburg, 1944; Yale University Press, 1948. The most thorough and valuable study of Hopkins's "poetic idiosyncrasy in relation to poetic tradition."

Iyengar, K. R. S. *Gerard Manley Hopkins, the Man and the Poet*, Oxford University Press, 1949.

Peters, W. A. M. *Gerard Manley Hopkins*, Oxford University Press, 1948.

Pick, John. *Gerard Manley Hopkins, Priest and Poet*, Oxford University Press, 1948. A critical essay toward the understanding of his poetry.

Wayand, Norman, S. J., ed. *Immortal Diamond: Studies in Gerard Manley Hopkins*, Sheed and Ward, 1949. A group of Jesuits interprets Hopkins.

HUXLEY

Readings from Huxley, rev. ed., ed. by C. Rinaker, Harcourt, Brace, 1934.

Selections from the Essays, ed. by Alburey Castell, Crofts Classics, Crofts, 1948.

Touchstone for Ethics, with Julian Huxley, Harper, 1947. Two essays, one by Huxley and one by his grandson, discuss the ethical implications of science.

Huxley, Aldous. "T. H. Huxley as a Literary Man," in *The Huxley Memorial Lectures, 1925–32*, Macmillan, 1932. Huxley's other famous grandson analyzes his literary style.

KIPLING

Selected Prose and Poetry of Rudyard Kipling, Garden City, 1937. A one-volume edition including *Barrack-Room Ballads, The Light That Failed, Plain Tales from the Hills, Soldiers Three, The Phantom 'Rickshaw and Other Ghost Stories, Wee Willie Winkie*, and *The Story of the Gadsbys*.

A Choice of Kipling's Verse with an Essay on Rudyard Kipling, ed. by T. S. Eliot, Faber and Faber, 1941. An examination of Kipling's verse by a present-day poet, critic, and admirer of Kipling.

Brown, Hilton. *Rudyard Kipling: A New Appreciation*, with a foreword by Frank Swinnerton, Hamilton, 1945.

Shanks, Edward. *Rudyard Kipling: A Study in Literature and Political Ideas*, Doubleday, Doran, 1940. A useful book of facts about Kipling.

Wilson, Edmund. "The Kipling That Nobody Read," in *The Wound and the Bow*, Houghton Mifflin, 1941. One of the most discerning essays on Kipling.

MACAULAY

Selected Writings, ed. by Harold Hobson, Falcon Prose Classics, Falcon Press, 1948.

Beatty, R. C. *Lord Macaulay: Victorian Liberal*, University of Oklahoma Press, 1938. The best brief biography.

Trevelyan, G. O. *Life and Letters of Lord Macaulay*, two vols., Oxford World's Classics, Oxford University Press, 1932. The standard biography, by Macaulay's nephew.

MEREDITH

Poetical Works, ed. by G. M. Trevelyan, Scribner, 1912.

Essay on Comedy, ed. by Lane Cooper, Scribner, 1918. Contains an excellent introduction and notes.

Sassoon, Siegfried. *Meredith*, Viking, 1948. The most recent and thorough biography and analysis of Meredith's works.

MORRIS

Selected Writings, ed. by William Gaunt, Falcon Prose Classics, Falcon Press, 1948.

Cameron, William. *The Day Is Coming*, Macmillan, 1944. An absorbing account in the form of a novel of Morris's social and economic theories from 1887 to 1938.

Grennan, Margaret. *William Morris: Medievalist and Revolutionary*, Columbia University Press, 1945. An excellent and well-written study.

Meynell, Esther. *Portrait of William Morris*, Chapman and Hall, 1948. Another new biography, handled with critical and sympathetic understanding.

Shaw, Bernard. *William Morris As I Knew Him*, Dodd, Mead, 1936. A Shavian treatment of Morris.

NEWMAN

Works, ed. by C. F. Harrold, three vols., Longmans, 1947. Includes the *Apologia, Grammar of Assent*, and *Idea of a University*.

A Newman Treasury, ed. by C. F. Harrold, Longmans, 1943. Selections from the prose works.

Harrold, C. F. *John Henry Newman*, Longmans, 1945. The most thorough study of Newman's mind, thought, and art.

Middleton, R. D. *Newman and Bloxam, an Oxford Friendship*, Oxford University Press, 1947.

Przywara, Erich. *A Newman Synthesis*, Sheed and Ward, 1945.

PATER

Selected Works, ed. by Richard Aldington, Duell, Sloan and Pearce, 1948. An excellent compendium with a valuable introduction.

The Renaissance, Modern Library.

Appreciations, with An Essay on Style, New Eversley Series, Macmillan.

Symons, Arthur. *A Study of Walter Pater*, Sawyer, 1932. An informative and very readable study.

CHRISTINA ROSSETTI

Poetical Works, ed. by W. M. Rossetti, Macmillan, 1906. With memoir and annotations.

Goblin Market, The Prince's Progress, and Other Poems, Oxford World's Classics, Oxford University Press.

Thomas, Eleanor W. *Christina Georgina Rossetti*, Columbia University Press, 1931. The most thorough study of her life and art.

Zaturenska, Marya. *Christina Rossetti: A Portrait with Background*, Macmillan, 1949. An intelligent and sympathetic study by a contemporary lyric poet.

DANTE GABRIEL ROSSETTI

Complete Poetical Works, ed. by W. M. Rossetti, Little, Brown, 1903.

Poems, Ballads, and Sonnets, ed. by P. F. Baum, Doubleday, Doran, 1937. An excellent one-volume edition of Rossetti's chief works.

Doughty, Oswald. *Dante Gabriel Rossetti*, Yale, 1949. A reconstruction of the pageant of the Pre-Raphaelite brotherhood.

Gaunt, William. *The Pre-Raphaelite Tragedy*, Harcourt, Brace, 1942.

RUSKIN

Selections, ed. by A. C. Benson, Cambridge University Press, 1923.

Modern Painters (5 vols.); *Crown of Wild Olive and Cestus of Aglaia; Elements of Drawing and Perspective; Ethics of the Dust; Pre-Raphaelitism; Sesame and Lilies, The Two Paths and The King of the Golden River; Seven Lamps of Architecture; Stones of Venice* (3 vols.); *Time and Tide with Other Essays; and Unto this Last, The Political Economy of Art*, are available in Everyman's Library, Dutton.

Praeterita, with a valuable interpretative introduction by Sir Kenneth Clark, Hart-Davis, 1949.

Ball, A. H. R. *Ruskin as Literary Critic*, Macmillan, 1928. Selections from Ruskin's literary criticism, with introduction and notes.

Leon, Derrick. *Ruskin: the Great Victorian*, Routledge and Kegan Paul, 1949. The best portrait of Ruskin; reflecting his thought on art, economics, and religion.

Livingstone, R. W. *Ruskin*, Oxford University Press, 1946. A recent and very illuminating lecture.

TENNYSON

Poems, sel. and ed. by Sir Herbert Warren, with introduction by Stephen Gwynn, Oxford World's Classics, Oxford University Press.

Baum, P. F. *Tennyson Sixty Years After*, University of North Carolina Press, 1948. A twentieth-century analytical and critical appraisal of the poet, with some freshly gathered biographical material.

Lounsbury, T. R. *The Life and Times of Tennyson*, Yale University Press, 1916. An unsurpassed study of Tennyson before 1850.

Nicolson, Harold. *Tennyson: Aspects of His Life, Character, and Poetry*, Houghton Mifflin, 1925; new ed. 1949. A brilliant biographical and critical study.

Tennyson, Charles. *Alfred Tennyson*, Macmillan, 1949. The latest biography, by the poet's grandson.

THOMPSON

Collected Works, ed. by Wilfrid Meynell, three vols. in one, Newman, 1947.

Complete Poetical Works, Modern Library.

Selected Poems, with biographical note by Wilfrid Meynell, Scribner, 1930.

The Hound of Heaven, ed. by Rev. F. P. LeBuffe, S. J., Macmillan, 1921. The most complete study of the poem.

Literary Criticisms by Francis Thompson, ed. by Rev. T. L. Connolly, S. J., Dutton, 1948.

NOVELS

Almost all Victorian novels are interesting reading. Nothing more has been attempted here than to mention a number of the most distinguished novelists, together with the titles of a few good books to begin on in getting acquainted with each. The date given after each title is that of original publication.

Most of the great Victorian novels are available in Everyman's Library, Dutton; World's Classics, Oxford University Press; Pocket Classics, Macmillan; and similar inexpensive editions. The editions mentioned specifically below are particularly attractive.

Brontë, Charlotte. *Jane Eyre*, 1847. Represents the triumph of Romanticism in Victorian fiction.

Brontë, Emily. *Wuthering Heights*, 1847; Heritage Press, 1940, illustrated by Barnett Freedman. The only English novel of cosmic scope before Hardy.

Butler, Samuel. *The Way of All Flesh*, 1903. This young man's repudiation of his conventional environment has influenced the naturalistic novels of our century.

Collins, Wilkie. *The Moonstone*, 1868, and *The Woman in White*, 1860; Modern Library Giant. The first English "mysteries" and still the best.

Dickens, Charles. *David Copperfield*, 1849–50; Heritage Press, 1935, illustrated by John Austen. Probably the most beloved novel in the language. Among the many great novels of Dickens, mention should also be made of *Pickwick Papers*, 1837, *Martin Chuzzlewit*, 1843, *Bleak House*, 1852–53, and *Great Expectations*, 1860–61.

Gaskell, Mrs. *Cranford*, 1853. Genteel people in English village life. A perfect idyll.

Eliot, George, pseud. *Adam Bede*, 1859; *The Mill on the Floss*, 1860; *Silas Marner*, 1861; *Romola*, 1862–63; Modern Library Giant, an omnibus volume of some of the author's best books.

Hardy, Thomas. *The Return of the Native*, 1878; Harper, 1929, illustrated by Clare Leighton. One of the greatest "landscape novels" and the best expression of Hardy's feeling of the determinative effect of environment on character. *Far from the Madding Crowd*, 1874; *The Mayor of Casterbridge*, 1884–85; and *Tess of the D'Urbervilles*, 1891, also rank high.

Kingsley, Charles. *Westward Ho!* 1855; Scribner, 1920, illustrated by N. C. Wyeth. Elizabethan sea rovers on the Spanish Main.

Kipling, Rudyard. *Kim*, 1901. This story of an Irish boy's adventures provides a brilliant panorama of life in India.

Meredith, George. *The Ordeal of Richard Feverel*, 1859. One of the most touching love stories in modern literature.

Stevenson, Robert Louis. *The Master of Ballantrae*, 1889. An exciting if somber historical romance laid in eighteenth-century Scotland.

Thackeray, William Makepeace. *Vanity Fair*, 1847–48; Heritage Press, 1940, with Thackeray's own illustrations. A picture and a criticism of English society at the time of Waterloo, with Becky Sharp, one of the grandest adventuresses in fiction. *Henry Esmond*, 1852, is a splendid historical novel laid in the time of Queen Anne and Marlborough's campaigns.

Trollope, Anthony. *The Warden*, 1855, and *Barchester Towers*, 1857. The first two novels, often published together, in a deservedly famous series. Trollope delights with his minutely faithful and gently satirical pictures of life in a small-town cathedral community.

THE TWENTIETH CENTURY

PLATE XXV

A THE CORONATION OF GEORGE VI IN 1937 (*Combine*)

The Coronation procession is seen passing through the Admiralty Arch on the way to Westminster Abbey. Shown here is the State Coach, built for George III in 1761, in which are riding King George VI and Queen Elizabeth.

England is a land hallowed by tradition. Throughout the year, hardly a week goes by in which an antique rite or ceremonial of historic and symbolic significance is not celebrated in some corner of the island. Whether this takes the form of a pancake race on Shrove Tuesday or the investiture of a monarch, it serves to reaffirm the continuity of English life and affords the English people a sense of stability and unity with the past.

The Coronation is both the most important and the most colorful of the English ceremonies, and every step in its elaborate ritual evokes some phase of English history. When the King enters Westminster Abbey where the peers are assembled to begin the ceremony, the Archbishop of Canterbury asks for *recognition* by the people—a reminder of the centuries-long conflicts over succession. The Archbishop says:

> Sirs, I here present unto you King George, your undoubted King: Wherefore all you who are come this day to do your homage and service, Are you willing to do the same?

It is in the act of anointing that the deepest symbolism of the Coronation lies, for this rite signifies the spiritual nature of the King's office: he is not just a secular leader of his people, but their spiritual sovereign as well. Later in the ceremony the act of crowning further emphasizes this sacred nature of the kingly office: the crown lies on the altar; it is taken thence by the Archbishop of Canterbury and placed by him on the head of the King, thus demonstrating that the power of the monarch comes from God, not from the King himself.

A relic of the days of chivalry is the presentation to the King of spurs and sword—symbols of his knighthood; and the homage which is offered by all the peers of the realms, both spiritual and temporal, after the crowning recalls the feudal relationship of King and liegeman.

B A CRICKET MATCH AT WORCESTER (*British Information*)

No one has yet definitely established the date of the origin of cricket in England, but there is mention of the game in the sixteenth century; more frequent references occur in the seventeenth century; and, by the eighteenth century, cricket had acquired a permanent place in the first rank of English sports. This interest continues undiminished today. Nearly every village and town has its cricket green where, on a Saturday or Sunday afternoon, one can sit comfortably in the shade and watch the leisurely progress of white-flanneled players on the grass.

A single game may last four hours (or days), but there is always a pleasant interlude for both players and spectators at teatime. During the Test Matches (annual competitions between an all-England team and a team from the Commonwealth) excitement runs high, and the members of the team, like our baseball and football players, are national heroes.

C THE RIVER LIFFEY, DUBLIN (*Combine*)

The city of Dublin has played an important part in the development of twentieth-century literature. There the Irish literary revival came into being; *The Playboy of the Western World* had its first performances at the Abbey Theater, and the early work of Yeats, George Moore, Lady Gregory, and "AE" is closely associated with Dublin. Although James Joyce left Ireland for the Continent, the setting of most of his writing continued to be his native Dublin. The River Liffey flows on as "Anna Livia Plurabelle" in *Finnegans Wake*.

PLATE XXVI

A THE PERSISTENCE OF MEMORY, BY SALVADOR DALI (*Collection The Museum of Modern Art, New York*)

The present age has been one of experiment in all the arts. Nowhere is this truer than in painting. Surrealism, which has been one of the most striking of the "new directions," has drawn its concepts and materials largely from the subconscious world of dreams. In this respect it shows the influence of the psychological theories of

PLATE XXV

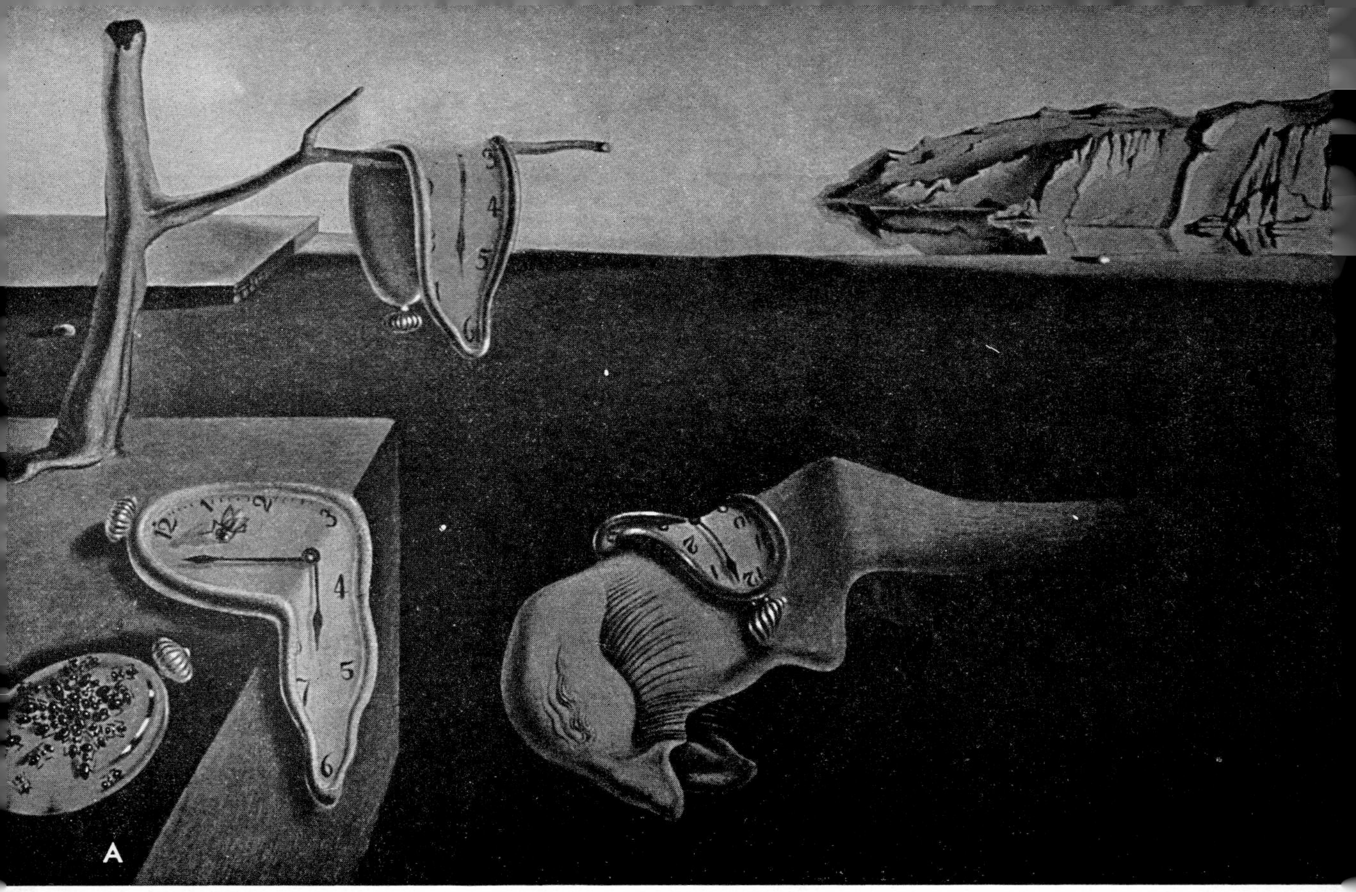

A

B

C

PLATE XXVI

PLATE XXVII

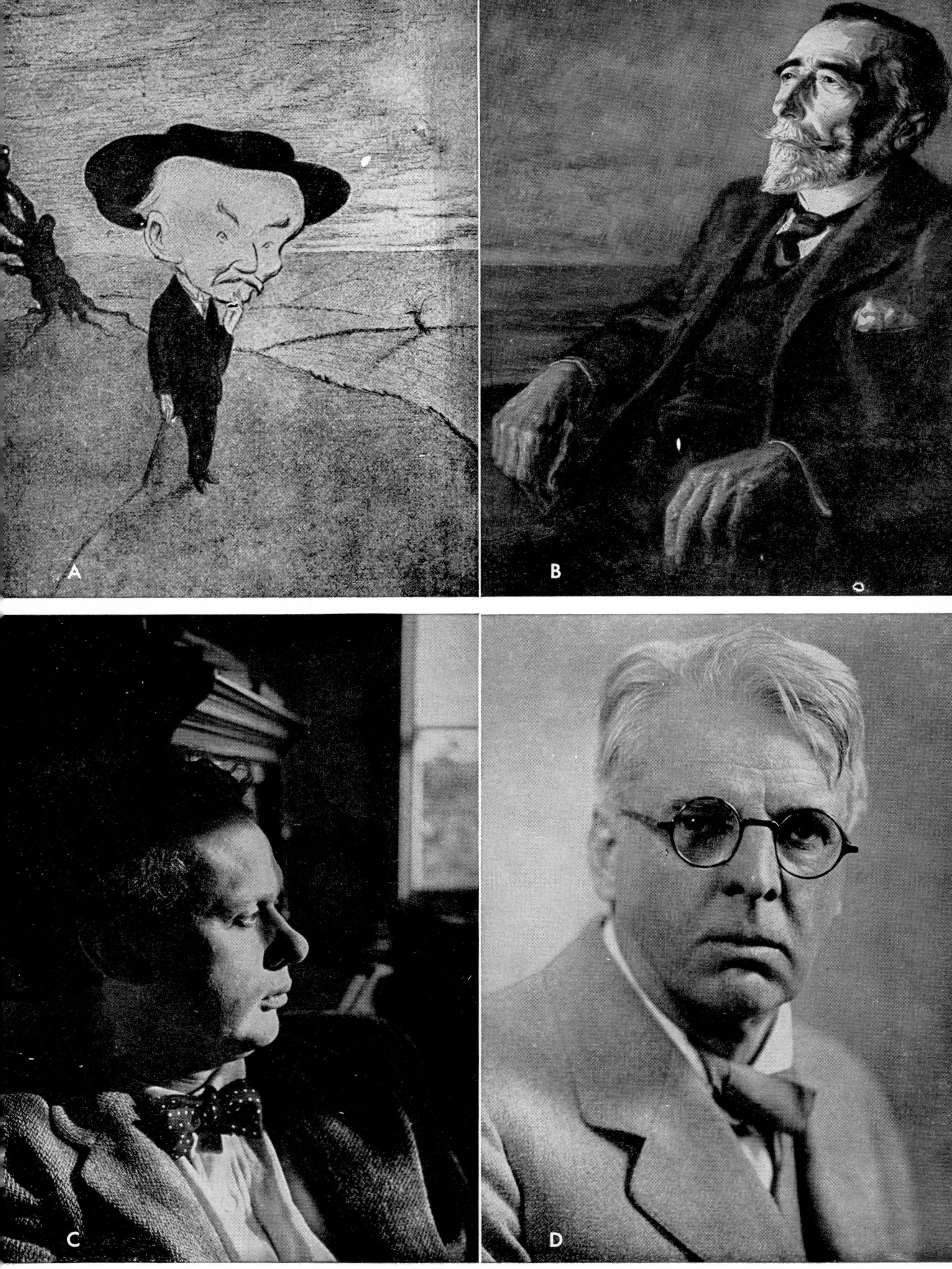

PLATE XXVIII

Sigmund Freud, and as an artistic movement it has obvious parallels with literature. Dali's *Persistence of Memory*, a notable example of the surrealist manner, shows the inquiring preoccupation with the nature of time which in this age of Einstein has also fascinated the literary artist—witness the poetry of Eliot, the novels of Joyce and Virginia Woolf, Proust and Thomas Mann.

B THE SHROPSHIRE TOWN OF LUDLOW (*Ewing Galloway*)

When smoke stood up from Ludlow,
And mist blew off from Teme . . .

So begins one of A. E. Housman's poems. The quiet Shropshire town of Ludlow, with its tower and its castle on the hill, occurs again and again in Housman's poetry. Wenlock, Clee, Clunbury, and other towns closely associated with *A Shropshire Lad* and *Last Poems* are but a few miles away from it. Ludlow has also an earlier poetic association, for it was in Ludlow Castle that Milton's *Comus* was first performed as part of the ceremony to welcome the Earl of Bridgewater, newly made Lord President of Wales.

C THE SHAKESPEARE MEMORIAL THEATER, STRATFORD-ON-AVON (*British Information*)

From April to October each year thousands of tourists and native Englishmen flock to the Memorial Theater at Stratford to see Shakespeare's plays produced with all the advantages of modern stage techniques. Although the modern playhouse is in striking contrast to the Globe and the Swan, the audiences are no less attentive, and probably much more reverent, than they were in Shakespeare's own day.

PLATE XXVII

A THE HANGED MAN FROM A DECK OF TAROT CARDS

The deck to which this card belongs is known as the Tarot of Charles VI and is attributed to a fourteenth-century French painter.

"Tarot" is the French version of the Italian word, *tarocchi*, the derivation of which is obscure. It is applied both to a card game and to the deck of cards used in that game. Although most playing cards were introduced into Europe from the East, the tarot cards apparently originated in Italy. At least, the twenty-one numbered picture cards, the *attutti* or trumps, and the joker known as *il matto* or the fool, are native to Italy. These twenty-two cards comprised only one-fourth of the original tarot deck; there were fifty-six other cards in it, arranged in four suits each consisting of ten numbered cards and four picture cards.

The hanged man is one of the twenty-one *attutti*. Like several of the other *attutti*, its significance is difficult to explain, but it may represent Judas Iscariot, holding a bag of money in each hand. Throughout their history, playing cards have been used for divination as well as for gaming. Around the tarots there exists a wealth of occult lore. For example, a book published in 1947 on the mysteries of tarot identifies the hanged man as Mem, the element of water and reflection (because the figure is upside down). Its name means "suspended mind" and also refers to the "dependence of the human personality upon the cosmic life."

B MAY DAY DEMONSTRATION, LONDON, 1927 (*Wide World Photos*)

This demonstration was one of the preliminaries to the General Strike of 1926 which completely paralyzed England for eight days. On May 4, two million five hundred thousand English workers left their jobs. All activity was immediately brought to a standstill except for such emergency services as were performed by the Army and volunteer workers, mostly bright young college men who considered the strike a gay adventure. Even the newspapers ceased to function, and the workers expected the government to fall. But the government remained firm, and the strikers, not having a definite program of action or dynamic leadership, were forced to abandon their effort. May 12 saw the end of the walkout, and the defeat of many of the hopes of labor as well.

C LONDON AFIRE DURING WORLD WAR II (*Press Association*)

The dome of St. Paul's dominates this spectacular view of the London skyline taken during an air raid. The destruction by German bombs in World War II changed a good deal of the face of London —sometimes for the better by eliminating slum areas, but often by obliterating some of the city's cherished landmarks. St. Paul's and Westminster

Abbey both suffered damage, as did many of the historic buildings that were not completely destroyed. The work of repairing and rebuilding is still going on and promises to continue for years to come. Indeed, the job of preserving England's ancient monuments is a never-ending one, for what is spared by the war is ravaged by time. Old stone crumbles; the deathwatch beetle riddles old timber. But, in spite of time and decay, England's architecture remains one of her chief glories.

D THE TOMB OF OLIVER GOLDSMITH IN THE INNER TEMPLE (*Acme*)

This grimly amusing photograph shows the eighteenth-century writer placidly contemplating the bomb destruction which surrounds him in another age. For many Englishmen such a sight as this in wartime symbolized the enduring strength of the English spirit.

E A LONDON FAMILY AT DINNER

Austerity has been the keynote of postwar English living as the nation has tried to recover from the tremendous material and financial drain of two major wars. The wartime program of rationing and controlled distribution of consumer goods has continued up to the present time, with little or no immediate prospect of relief. Yet, with characteristic stolidity, the English people have "carried on," grumbling but patiently "making do" with their scraps of meat and buckets of coal in the hope of a more plentiful future.

PLATE XXVIII

A MR. THOMAS HARDY COMPOSING A LYRIC, BY MAX BEERBOHM (*From* Fifty Caricatures, *courtesy E. P. Dutton and Co.*)

The thoughtful melancholy of much of Hardy's poetry is here suggested, mischievously, but reverently, by England's most accomplished literary caricaturist. Max Beerbohm (1872–) was a London dandy at the turn of the century. Dramatic critic and author of the brilliant fantasy, *Zuleika Dobson*, he has been an urbane and gifted essayist for over half a century. His drawings (*Fifty Caricatures*, *The Poet's Corner*, *Rossetti and His Circle*) and his prose writings (*Seven Men*, *The Happy Hypocrite*, *And Even Now*) show Beerbohm as a delightfully deft and comprehending satirist. His "Sequelula to *The Dynasts*" an effective parody of Hardy, is included in *A Christmas Garland* along with a dozen or so other amusing imitations of the literary styles of Conrad, Henry James, Kipling, Chesterton, and others.

B JOSEPH CONRAD (*Courtesy of the Yale University Library*)

This portrait was painted by Walter Tittle in 1924 and is now in the Yale University Library.

C DYLAN THOMAS (*Deakin from Black Star*)

D WILLIAM BUTLER YEATS (*Martin Vos, New York*)

THE TWENTIETH CENTURY

Decline of an Empire

THE contemporary period has been variously characterized as "the age of anxiety," "the era of nerves," "the time of reparation and repudiation," and "the world against itself." But such phrases, though provocative, are not conclusive. It is impossible to impose a pattern upon a period in flux. The nature of our age is violent and complex and increasingly confused. The first quarter of the twentieth century was experimental in every sense—politically, socially, culturally; the second quarter, from 1925 to 1950, was explosive. It went to every extreme. It expressed itself in an eruption of opposing schools of thought and differing canons of art; every form, fashion, and tendency was matched by its opposite.

The half century following the Victorian era presented not only an abrupt contrast to the preceding period but an almost complete contradiction of all its values. Against alleged Victorian complacency it pitted a determined rebelliousness. The once sanctified aura of "sweetness and light" was dispelled by darkening doubts; the undisputed standards of conduct, glorifying "high seriousness," the "genteel tradition," and "good taste" were challenged, reappraised, and rejected. The dominance of the aristocracy had given way before the rising power of the middle classes; now the middle classes were on the defensive. Within fifty years England had changed from a triumphant imperialism to a troubled socialism. In world affairs the proud Empire shrank from confident expansion and extension of influence to ever-tightening limitations and ultimate loss of power. The slogan "There'll always be an England" took on an accent that was both wistful and bewildered.

The turn of the century was marked by the death of Queen Victoria in 1901, the formation that same year of a distinct and independent Labor Party, and the continuance of the South African War which had broken out in 1899. The war was the climax of a series of conflicts, raids, revolts, and massacres, involving the native Zulus and Kaffirs, the Dutch (Boer) cattlemen and farmers, and the colonizing British. The discovery of gold and diamonds intensified the struggle. The Boers were convinced that the British planned to take over the whole rich Transvaal; the British were certain that their opponents thought the time propitious to drive all Englishmen out of South Africa. It took almost three years for the greatly superior English forces to gain a decision through ruthless warfare—120,000 Boer women and children had been crowded into concentration camps and 20,000 of them had died of brutality—and, though the Boers accepted British rule in May, 1902, England suffered a serious loss in prestige.

Victoria's successor, Edward VII, had been a popular, pleasure-loving, almost nonpolitical Prince of Wales. He retained these characteristics when, nearing sixty, he became King. A devoted sportsman, he was quite willing to let his ministers run the country. On the whole, they did it well.

For the first time control of secondary education was assumed by the government; there were wide tariff reforms; and, in 1906, a liberal program, which included a pioneering Workman's Compensation Act, went into effect. Five years later the powers of the House of Lords were curtailed and that hitherto aristocratic body was crippled; but a protracted battle between the Liberals and Conservatives was going on when Edward VII died and was succeeded in 1910 by the sound, devoted George V. A greater number of Englishmen now understood what Kipling had meant when, at the height of Victoria's Diamond Jubilee, he warned them in "Recessional":

For heathen heart that puts her trust
  In reeking tube and iron shard,
All valiant dust that builds on dust,
  And, guarding, calls not Thee to guard,
For frantic boast and foolish word,
Thy mercy on Thy people, Lord!

The "reeking tube and iron shard," the latest in guns and best in bullets, had won foreign wars and given rise to "frantic boasts and foolish words," but as the first decade of the new century ended there was little reason for complacency at home. A three-cornered struggle involving the House of Lords, the Commons, and the leaders of the Irish Nationalist movement was increasing in pitch. While the Liberal program of social reform was bringing benefits to the working class, suffragettes were busily breaking plate glass windows.

Meanwhile abroad a series of crises, largely caused by the struggle for overseas markets following upon colonial expansion, made a tense and explosive Europe. England could not but be involved, and behind the flimsy façade of leagues and alliances the armaments race was on. By 1914 Anglo-European relations were growing steadily worse, and only the provocative incident was needed to set off a general conflict. On June 28, 1914, an Austrian archduke was assassinated by a member of a Serbian terrorist organization. Germany backed up Austria; Russia egged on Serbia; France deliberated and hesitated, but mobilized; German troops, threatening Paris, invaded Belgium; England declared war on Germany. In the next two years twenty declarations of war were issued from the chancelleries; all Europe was embroiled, and this First World War threw all the normal and fruitful patterns of life, prominent among them the arts, sciences, and professions, into a state of chaos. From 1914 to 1918 Europe wore a shirt of fire. Only a few years earlier the Reverend Newell Dwight Hillis had hailed the brave new century in these confident words: "For the first time government, invention, art, industry, and religion have served all the people." Now all the people were served by propaganda and poison gas, and war was followed by a scorn of traditional faiths and a reckless pursuit of novelty, by suppressed depravity and unconcealed violence. Truth was a broken convention. David Daiches summarized the postwar disillusionment in *The Novel and the Modern World:* "One by one the preconceptions of our fathers have been shattered, and instead of being replaced naturally with new beliefs as they die, they have been replaced by nothing. In terms of ethics and theory of value generally, if not with complete literalness, what ought to have been a brave new world has turned out a wasteland."

When the Allied Powers at last achieved victory, the treaty of Versailles in 1919 brought no real peace. Many danger spots on the map of Europe remained unerased. Badgered by new fears the politicians turned to temporary reforms, and public conscience blundered into social consciousness. Strikes were prevalent after the end of the war. Since such troubles at home kept England sufficiently occupied, her support of the newly formed League of Nations was not firm. "Security pacts" signed by seven powers at Locarno in 1925 betrayed the League's impotence and did little to check the reviving tide of German nationalism. In 1926 a General Strike involved more than two and a half million British trade-unionists. In 1928 women were belatedly and reluctantly allowed to vote on the same terms as men. The ever-vexing Irish problem was not eased but aggravated when the British government granted Dominion status to Southern Ireland as the Irish Free State, while North Ireland retained its former status. The world depression of 1929 shook England's gold reserves so severely that, shortly after the formation of a coalition government two years later, it proved necessary to abandon the gold standard. George V's Silver Jubilee in 1935 was followed swiftly by his death the following January. Three kings occupied the throne that historic year. The popular Prince of Wales succeeded his father only to abdicate before his coronation in order to marry a commoner, an American divorcee; his brother, King George VI, succeeded him.

Conditions abroad had rapidly grown more alarming. World-wide collapse ended all efforts at international co-operation; the problems of reparation and war debts proved insoluble. The period of depression and repudiation was followed by aggression. England and the democracies were afflicted by a crippling apathy. The militaristic states grew into unchecked dictatorships, headed by Hitler in Germany, Mussolini in Italy, and Hirohito in Japan. In 1936 the Republican government of Spain was overthrown by General Franco and his monarchist army officers. After Spain had become a bloody testing ground—a dress rehearsal for a world conflict with Germany and Italy on the side of the Royalists and Russia supporting the Republicans—a dictatorship was set up with Franco as its head. Appeasement of the totalitarian states did not insure peace. It provoked fresh aggressions. On September 1, 1939, Germany invaded Poland, and the Second World War began in Europe. Poland could not stand up long under Hitler's savage attack, and then after a winter lull first Denmark and Norway, then Holland, Belgium, and finally France fell before the Nazi onslaught. Britain, behind her indomitable leader, Winston Churchill, braced herself and with incredible fortitude endured through late summer the bombardment by the German Luftwaffe. By June Italy had jumped in for the kill; exactly a year later Hitler turned on another ostensible ally, Russia, and in so doing made one of his gravest blunders. On December 7, 1941, during peace negotiations, Japan bombed Pearl Harbor, the United States was forced into the conflict, and the war became literally a global war.

Eventually the tide of war began to turn against the Fascist powers. The Russians stood fast at Stalingrad, Italy gave way in 1943, and the tremendous Allied invasion of the Continent the following June spelled the end. Germany surrendered in May, 1945; Japan, already crumbling, collapsed utterly when two atomic bombs were dropped on her cities in August. After six years of interminable air raids, devastating long-range missiles, and incalculable destruction, a war-racked world could hardly believe it was at peace. With grim resolution most nations addressed themselves to the task of preventing future catastrophe. The idea of "One World," as opposed to embittered countries in continual conflict, prepared the way for the United Nations. But the terms of peace were fought over with increasing suspicion, bad feeling, and the threat of rearmament. Russia speedily revealed her determination to obstruct any and all efforts at international co-operation; an "iron curtain" descended between Eastern and Western Europe. England, under a badgered Labor government, became a Socialist, though not a Communist, state. With food scarce, and a practically bankrupt economy, the once rich Empire turned to a program of "austerity," a rigorous denial of luxuries and almost everything except necessities. As new war threatened in the Far East, the situation was grim for an England which could no longer hope to dominate but had to struggle merely to survive.

New Challenges, Shifting Values

In an era darkened by two world wars, there was a continual shifting of values. Under a barrage of psychological and social challenges, orthodox standards were through the early twentieth century re-examined, resisted, and finally, many of them repudiated. Moral earnestness declined in favor of amoral curiosity; the Victorian virtues were laughed at by the experimenting Edwardians. Such imponderables as the soul, a sustaining belief in "the good, the beautiful, and the true," a deep concern with God and the Hereafter, which had already been losing their hold in late Victorian days, concerned the artist far less than did a materialistic philosophy, the threat (or promise) of a new political order, and a general preoccupation with the daily life of all-too-mortal man.

The rise of materialism, speeded up by the enormously growing power of the machine, shifted attention from the spiritual universe to the world of science and physical sensation. Failing to find security in creeds and questionable faiths, men turned to research. They looked to psychoanalysis and various brands of socialism in the hope of finding a way of life which could be integrated and controlled through the exercise of the intelligence. The "machine age" was no longer a figure of speech. More and more mechanisms were assuming the functions of human beings and taking the place of thinking men, and the inflexible authoritarian state, predicted by political economists and such novelists as George Orwell (in the frightening *Nineteen Eighty-Four*), threatened to become a reality.

The opening years of the new century had presaged this succession of hectic reactions and reappraisals. With each succeeding decade the pendulum swung fiercely from one extremity to another. The 1920's, characterized as the "Roaring Twenties," was the period of "flaming youth," knee-length dresses, and unlimited audacity. Women's hair, skirts, and morals were worn outrageously short. Any kind of conformity was scorned as "bourgeois" and "Philistine." The 1930's, the decade of the great depression, often called the Threadbare Thirties, was a glum succession of stock market crashes, sit-down strikes, torn-up treaties, the cynical flouting of national commitments and international law. The 1940's were concerned almost wholly with war.

The spread of mass education, sensational and simplified journalism—the "tabloids" originated in England—the intensified realism of motion pictures, and such new means of communication as phonograph records, radio, and television profoundly altered the social-intellectual framework as the twentieth century grew older. The background of everyday living and thinking was further affected by the doctrine of William James and the pragmatists, who maintained the chief criterion of truth to be experience; James, exploring within the human mind, found not any logical order but instead a "stream of thought, or consciousness," while Henri Bergson in France also challenged the reality of scientific exactitude. A powerful immediate effect was made by the spread of psychoanalysis—part philosophy, part therapy. The Viennese founder of psychoanalysis, Sigmund Freud, cast new light on the unconscious workings of the human mind; Carl Jung and Alfred Adler developed divergent theories, and such terms as id and ego, Oedipus complex, inhibition and defense-mechanism came into common currency.

The artistic conflict was on two levels: between a culture which gave promise of a democratic art, and mass entertainment which distracted people from the real problems of life; between a groping individualism and a grasping industrialism. This conflict continued without a decision. The reading, listening, and looking habits of the nation underwent a gradual and almost complete transformation. Painters deserted Romanticism for Impressionism; Realism was superseded by Abstractionism, a complete departure from reality. Readers were seldom soothed now by pretty romances and comfortable finalities. Only a few writers were devoted to easy escapes and elaborate assurances. Many artists, caught between creation and frustration, tried to make their exasperation articulate, to substitute disbelief and even disgust for faith, to give formlessness a form. An uneasy literature of nerves became apparent.

This restless literature was, at times, expressive and eloquent, but its main expression was confusion. Here the artist was a true, if puzzled, recorder of his period. He attempted to depict a world assaulted by the midnight radio and the morning headlines, by the revaluations of the psychoanalyst and the wish fulfillments of the cinema, by all the isms from Socialism to Imagism, from Militarism to Cubism, Vorticism, Dadaism, Surrealism, and the other extremes of artistic expression. The consequence was dislocation and disruption. Logic gave way to a free association of ideas; purposeful dissonances jarred the expected harmonies. On canvas the human figure was distorted beyond recognition. The once orderly metaphor was forced to run wild, and the customary plausible progression was broken by startling chain images and interruptions abrupt as chain lightning.

The "modern temper" was always at fever pitch; it was riddled with apprehension and universal suspicion. It had been cheated by "causes," betrayed by slogans. Its symbols changed overnight. The airplane, which upon its trial flights only yesterday seemed the symbol of liberation from earth, an image of free adventuring in the heavens, became a symbol of fear, of death that dropped casually and horribly from the unperturbed skies.

Space shrank with the airplane; radio and television annihilated man's geographical and mental boundaries. But governments grew more nationalistic and men less neighborly than ever. There were those who hoped to see a new society rise from the ashes of the old. Brought up in the midst of tragedy, ill-nourished on tension, the period cried out for inspired leadership. The world was divided, and at mid-century the hope of a prolonged and creative peace became a dwindling dream.

The Irish Movement

It is notable that the first and perhaps the most powerful single movement in contemporary English literature developed in Ireland. Already at the beginning of the new century a vigorous literary and nationalist movement known as the Celtic Revival was in full swing. William Butler Yeats, George W. Russell ("AE"), Douglas Hyde, and George Moore were separated by taste and tradition, but they had a common aim: they proposed to create a national literature, which, though written in English, would express the unique spirit of Ireland and, founded upon Irish lore and legendry, would create an independent tradition of its own.

Two movements for social and economic reform in Ireland had sprung to life. The first, the Gaelic League (founded in 1893 by Douglas Hyde), had as its object the study of ancient Irish literature and the preservation of Irish as the racial language. The second, organized about six years later as the Irish Agricultural Organization Society by Horace Plunkett and abetted by George Russell, was a co-operative movement with a simple slogan: "Better farming; better business; better living." The social economy implicit in both movements strengthened the national culture. George Russell successfully combined agrarianism and mysticism; Douglas Hyde was able to unite a love of folklore and continual warfare against the survival of the feudal system; William Butler Yeats dealt simultaneously in magic and politics. The movements joined and became steadily more radical. Insurrections, suddenly rising and severely put down, grew increasingly violent; rebellion flamed everywhere; the hope of a few dreamers became the battle flag of an embittered nation. The Irish renaissance ended in revolution; Eire was born of the blood of its poets. A poet, Douglas Hyde, became its President in 1938.

Much of the activity centered about the independent Irish Literary Theater, later to be known as the Abbey Players because of the stirring performances in the Abbey Theater in Dublin. For this theater Yeats wrote his plays—plays that were atmospheric but compelling, symbolic but deeply emotional. The best of them communicated a sense of trance, a depth beyond ordinary reality. *Cathleen ni Houlihan*, a prose play first performed in 1902, lifted allegory to a plane of high patriotism. Even the most literal-minded members of the audience could not fail to see in the poor harried woman who had lost her fields and for whom men gladly died—a woman who never aged and who had "the walk of a queen"—the figure of Ireland. Among the other plays of Yeats which became famous for their summoning of the past in terms of the present are *The Land of Heart's Desire*, 1899; *Where There Is Nothing*, 1903; *The Hour Glass*, 1903; and *The King's Threshold*, 1904. Yeats's plays were but a part of the artistic achievement of one who later grew to be a major poet of his age.

Lady Gregory (1859–1932) was the most prolific of the Abbey playwrights. Besides various translations she wrote twenty-four plays, racily characteristic in setting and idiom. Yet the most powerful as well as the most original dramatist of the group was J. M. Synge (1871–1909). Synge's plays were few in number. But the longer pieces, such as *The Playboy of the Western World*, 1907, are rich in texture, and the one-act plays (especially *The Shadow of the Glen*, 1903, and *Riders to the Sea*, 1904) are masterpieces, classic in form and noble in conception. Synge's language alone would have made a reputation for any writer. It was the language of simple people, peasants mostly, lifted into natural picturesqueness and spiced with fresh imagery "to show that what is exalted for tender is not made by feeble blood." "I have thought," Synge wrote in an introduction to his bare and peat-flavored poems, "that at the side of the poetic diction, which everyone condemns, modern verse contains a great deal of poetic material, using poetic in the same special sense. The poetry of exaltation will be always the highest; but when men lose their poetic feeling for ordinary life, and cannot write of ordinary things, their exalted poetry is likely to lose its strength of exaltation, in the way men cease to build beautiful churches when they have lost happiness in building shops." No one recorded the Irish scene more graphically yet more colorfully; he not only crystallized it, he transfigured it. Lennox Robinson followed Synge as a director of the Abbey Theater. An account of the drama of the Irish Movement must include his comedy, *The Whiteheaded Boy*, 1916, the realistic plays of St. John Ervine, and also the even more realistic, somber plays of Sean O'Casey—particularly *Juno and the Paycock*, 1924, and *The Plough and the Stars*, 1926.

Although the Irish renaissance began as a literary movement, it became a social synthesis which called forth every expression of creative and political thought. Poetry and drama were the forms which first attracted the writers of the group, but it was not long before wider experiences were embodied in a prose which varied from polemics to portraiture, from bitter wisdom to shrewd fancy. The important contribution of James Joyce, transcending national boundaries in its influence, will be taken up in the general section dealing with the novel. Outstanding Irish writers of fiction and essays were George Moore (whose *Hail and Farewell*, 1911–1914, is a rather mordant reflection of the Revival), Daniel Corkery, St. John Ervine, James Stephens, and Liam O'Flaherty. O'Flaherty's *The Informer*, 1926, won an English prize as a memorable piece of fiction and the Motion Picture Academy Award as a film. The novels of the gifted and independent-minded Sean O'Faolain remain to be mentioned; his short stories, and those of Frank O'Connor, show the influence of the Russian masters, but they speak in the rhythms and moods of Ireland.

The Changing Novel

The rapidly changing social and economic values during the early decades of the century were reflected in the changed character and implications of the printed word. Journalism became more candid and direct. Undisguised facts prompted in particular a more honest fiction. With the chief Edwardian novelists (such as H. G. Wells, Arnold Bennett, and John Galsworthy) the plot, scrupulously recorded, was still the thing. With the Georgians (such as D. H. Lawrence, James Joyce, Virginia Woolf, E. M. Forster, and Aldous Huxley) there was so much analysis, impressionism, experimentation, and intimate "atmosphere" that the plot almost disappeared. A new kind of novel came into being. Subtleties of style and odd techniques took the place of the traditional tightly constructed plot and neatly ordered development of events. The rigid form became increasingly flexible and free.

The most interesting forerunner of the twentieth-century "naturalistic" novelist was Samuel Butler. *The Way of All Flesh*, 1903, which was part autobiography, part fiction, and part essay, was a devastating attack on the theological absurdities and domestic hypocrisies of Butler's generation. Its freedom of form and range of interest prepared the way for the more realistic plays and novels of the following quarter of a century. On the other hand, the more recent analytical emphasis has not seemed especially new to readers of Henry James, whose fiction and observations on his craft reached the height of critical acclaim at mid-century.

The work of H. G. Wells (1866–1946) mingled naturalism and romanticism; it combined carefully assembled data and imagination with inexhaustible enthusiasm. The most voluminous writer of the time, he was also the most versatile. Before he died at eighty, Wells was the author of almost a hundred volumes and thirty pamphlets; his fertility ranged from such full-length novels as *Kipps*, 1905, and *Tono-Bungay*, 1909 (which, like Butler's *The Way of All Flesh*, was a mixture of autobiography and invention), to a comprehensive review of humanity, *The Outline of History*, 1920; from the fantastic short stories of *Tales of Space and Time*, 1899 (forerunners of today's vogue for science-fiction), to prophecies of social reconstruction (*Men Like Gods*, 1928, *The World Set Free*, 1914, and others)—from the library to the laboratory and back again. There can be no doubt that many of Wells's prophecies have been fulfilled, that his short stories are often as dynamic as they are surprising, and that the best of his novels are adroit in lifting the casual to the pitch of the extraordinary. A product of the English liberal-rationalist movement, Wells was a passionate believer in a dynamic conception of a changing society, a society that would evolve into a brotherhood of peoples because of the good will and "infinite perfectibility of man."

Celebration of the commonplace was achieved by Arnold Bennett (1867–1931). As well as being the author of many novels, short stories, essays, and memoirs, Bennett was a playwright, a musician, and a water-colorist. Bennett's novels differed from those of Wells not only in being more objective, more painstaking, and less passionate, but also in being far more slowly and solidly built. Bennett loved the minute, even the sordid, details of everyday existence. At the worst he was, as one of his critics complained, a "literary bricklayer," adding one small block of facts upon another. At his best—in *The Old Wives' Tale*, 1908, and the *Clayhanger* trilogy, 1910–1916—Bennett was a painter in the Dutch manner; in a cleanly built prose he revealed an unsurpassed picture of the hard-working, unimaginative, and dominating middle class of England.

What *The Old Wives' Tale* did for the lower middle classes, John Galsworthy's *The Forsyte Saga*, 1922, accomplished for the upper class. Galsworthy (1867–1933) devoted himself to the genteel propertied society. Sensitive, sane, liberal without being radical, Galsworthy might have stepped out of one of his own novels. In the early Forsyte novels Galsworthy looked with the eye of a realist upon the limitations of the property-conscious caste, but as he grew older the satirist became the all too gentle observer of a new generation he could not understand.

Joseph Conrad (1857–1924) differed from Galsworthy and Wells in being forceful with less deliberate ethical purpose. Conrad (born Teodor Jozef Konrad Korzeniowski in the Ukraine) learned English through translations of Dickens and Shakespeare and the help of Ford Madox Ford, with whom he collaborated. His most characteristic tales are flung out against a panorama of dangerous waters, heavy skies, and mysterious reaches of space. Conrad employed a strange manner of narration which, in its very complication, allowed him to introduce "asides" and interpretations impossible in straightforward storytelling; but the very interruptions and digressions gave his fiction the air of scrupulous reality. Reality and artistry were Conrad's chief concern. In his novels and in his shorter fiction he was eager, first of all, "to make you *feel*, to make you *see*," and his force as well as his manner of telling a story or drawing a character succeeded in bringing "the light of magic suggestiveness to play for an evanescent instant over the commonplace surface of words worn thin by ages of careless usage."

E. M. Forster (1879–) deals with the powers of a machine-driven civilization without worshiping them. On the contrary, he shows man beaten by brute conquest but, somehow, triumphing over ruthlessness. In "The Machine Stops," a vividly imaginative novelette, Forster envisioned the breakdown of the deified state with its dehumanized and submissive slaves. He pitted the individual against limitless size, and made size seem small. To Forster the physical events of life are less important than the personal relationship, the intricate human affections, the clash between basic passions and man's private integrities. ("Centuries of embracement, yet man is no nearer to understanding man.") His best novel, *A Passage to India*, 1925, is superficially a social-political tract; but it is first of all a subtle analysis of humanity, of the people of one race by a person of another. It renders no judgment, points no moral, but when it is finished the reader finds life larger and richer than before. In Forster's *Aspects of the Novel* are to be found this master practitioner's engaging, perceptive observations on the dominant literary form of our era.

D. H. Lawrence (1885–1930) represented an extreme if not final revolt against Victorianism. He continually fought the standards of society, challenged the ideal of democracy, and questioned civilization itself. An impassioned and maladjusted spirit, he was both realist and mystic, puritan and prophet. Forster wrote that Lawrence was "the only prophetic novelist writing to-day—all the rest are fantasists or preachers: the only living novelist in whom the song predominates, who has the rapt bardic quality. . . . What is valuable about him cannot be put into words; it is color, gesture, and outline in people and things." Lawrence was fascinated by the nonreasonable (and even irrational) elements of human nature. He had an ideal of pure "mindlessness"; he never ceased to be fascinated by the role of the unconscious, which Freud was making so vital. It was an unconscious with a conscience which compelled Lawrence in *Sons and Lovers*, 1913, and *The Rainbow*, 1915. Lashed by his self-contradictions, he tore himself to death. He worried flesh and spirit; he never ceased to agonize over dark and mystical demands which turned out to be twisted ethical problems. Essentially a poet, he wrote prose with "the hot blood's blindfold art."

James Joyce (1882–1941), who grew up in the most exhilarating years of the Irish renaissance, carried the unconscious much further than Lawrence; he let its energy loose in the nightmare power and confusion of *Ulysses*. Joyce seemed to glory in the dissolution of ordinary human values without attempting to create new ones. He was not so much an explorer as an exploder. *Ulysses*, 1922, preceded by orderly and organized earlier works—the fine short stories called *Dubliners*, 1914, and the autobiographical *Portrait of the Artist as a Young Man*, 1916—is an explosive work disruptive in style, detonating with quasi-mythological allusions, immense knowledge, and private meanings. It abounds in verbal and musical brilliance, exuberance, and creative power, and its influence upon a literary generation has been enormous. Yet as sympathetic a critic as Virginia Woolf had with reluctance to call *Ulysses* a magnificent failure artistically. *Finnegans Wake*, 1939, a conglomerate discharge of myths, puns, dreams, and violences of language, carries distortion to such a pitch that, though magnificently resonant, it is, for the most part, unintelligible to the average intelligent reader. Joyce now stands very high among twentieth-century writers, and only time can tell how serious an obstacle the obscurity of his later work will be to his permanent reputation.

In the works of Virginia Woolf (1882–1941) the unconscious, with its outlet in the "stream of consciousness," was acknowledged, but it was strictly controlled. As a critic, she was, in her *The Common Reader*, 1925, and *A Room of One's Own*, 1929, cleanly penetrating, witty without being malicious, and fairly orthodox in manner. Her novels—notably *Mrs. Dalloway*, 1925, *To the Lighthouse*, 1927, *Orlando*, 1928, and *The Waves*, 1931—were far more experimental. They progressed through a growing series of bold and successful techniques. Mrs. Woolf triumphed in impressionism: in the stylization of *Orlando*, a fantasy which is partly a history of the national spirit and partly a parody of literary styles; in the "interior monologue" of *The Waves*, a stylized soliloquy gradually revealing events and characters; in an almost complete abandonment of plot; and in a kind of writing which fluctuated between prose and poetry. Mrs. Woolf's quality was not so much a steady sequence of experiences as a burst of unexpected flashes, a brilliant shower of actions and reactions.

The novels of Aldous Huxley (1894–   ) show the gifted grandson of the illustrious Victorian scientist as a hard-driven and disillusioned interpreter of a not too brave new world. Like his grandfather, Aldous Huxley is skeptical about the moral sense, questions Christianity as a civilizing agency, and never ceases to wage war upon orthodox beliefs. He has turned, with equal loathing, from the ethics of the past and the standards of the present. The high spirits, witty satire, and sophisticated irony of his first novels, *Crome Yellow*, 1921, and *Antic Hay*, 1923, rightly won him fame, but they also reflected in themselves the intellectual and moral confusion of their times. His characters luxuriated in the disembodied pleasures of the intellect and plunged into sexuality only to be cheated by the mind and betrayed by the body. Even in the later novels, where Huxley attempts to repudiate the negativism of the early work, his characters live in a world of discontent and self-disgust. Finding no help in sensation, no faith in religion, and little hope in science, Huxley has more recently turned for sustaining power to the mysticism of the East. It is in Huxley's short stories, such as "The Tillotson Banquet," "The Gioconda Smile," and "Young Archimedes," rather than in his full-length and more satirical novels, that he reveals his greatest ability as a writer of fiction.

At seventy-five W. Somerset Maugham (1874–) had published so many short stories that his reputation as a novelist suffered. Appraisers have had a hard time keeping Maugham in a convenient category. In his early period, as he observes, they said he was brutal, in his middle years they called him cynical, and in his later phase they dismissed him as superficial. Yet few novels of the time have surpassed the probing and poignant *Of Human Bondage*, 1915; and the tempestuous *The Moon and Sixpence*, 1919, and the delightfully malicious *Cakes and Ale*, 1930, rank high. The complex self-analysis in *The Summing Up*, 1938, is as tolerant as it is wise. In whatever role he has cared to assume as creator and commentator, Maugham has always been conceded to be "the prince of entertainers."

Among living British writers Graham Greene (1904–) is as popular as he is prolific. Critics differ whether to rate his nine novels above or below what he has called his "entertainments," but all agree that Greene is a superb storyteller whose works combine realism and spirituality, tenderness and tension, extraordinary symbolism and psychological insight. Among Greene's novels the most praised are *The Man Within*, 1929, *Brighton Rock*, 1938, and *The Heart of the Matter*, 1948; the best of his "entertainments" and "mysteries" are *Orient Express*, 1933, *The Ministry of Fear*, 1943, and *The Third Man*, 1950. Evelyn Waugh (1903–) constructs his books with a unique combination of hot anger and cold satire. "Hectic," "blistering," "supersophisticated" are a few of the characteristic adjectives which have been pinned upon Waugh's *Decline and Fall*, 1928, *Vile Bodies*, 1930, *A Handful of Dust*, 1934, and *The Loved One*, 1948, although, after Catholicism became his major interest, his writings display an increasing aversion to our own confused times and, as in *Helena*, 1950, a devotion to the legendary past. The Anglo-Irish novelist, Elizabeth Bowen (1899–) has been paired with Virginia Woolf as the most distinguished of contemporary women novelists. If they are constricted and limited in scope, Miss Bowen's *The Hotel*, 1927, *The House in Paris*, 1935, *The Death of the Heart*, 1938, and *The Heat of the Day*, 1949, are nevertheless marked by a wide emotional range and psychological intensity. Ford Madox Ford (1873–1939) made and lost a reputation during his life and recovered it eleven years after his death. *Parade's End*, 1950, consisted of four closely related novels—*Some Do Not*, *No More Parades*, *A Man Could Stand Up*, and *The Last Post*—brought together in one volume a quarter of a century after they first appeared. Ford presented a panorama of a collapsing society, a sprawling picture of "the last English Tory" lost in a ruined world.

George Orwell (1903–1950) was one of the most original intelligences of the period. Before his untimely death Orwell had written novels, essays, reviews, and autobiographical reminiscences, all of them in a style "as bare and sharp as a winter tree." Although humor and toleration were implicit in everything he wrote, Orwell loathed any curtailment of personal freedom. A passion for the individual flares through *Animal Farm*, 1946, a satiric fable directed against the dehumanization of man. It is intensified in *Nineteen Eighty-Four*, 1949, which is a terrifying protest, and perhaps a prophecy, aimed at a civilization regimented and ridden by thought control, victimized and destroyed by authoritarian oppression. In promising first novels Humphrey Slater (*The Heretics*, 1947) and Patrick Bair (*Faster, Faster!*, 1950) reflect this nightmare mood.

A less prophetic but equally truthful author, who had published for years before given his rightful recognition, is Joyce Cary (1888–). Although *A House of Children*, 1941, won the James Tait Black Memorial Prize, Cary is best known and most himself in the tart and amoral trilogy of recent English life: *Herself Surprised*, 1941, *To Be a Pilgrim*, 1942, and *The Horse's Mouth*, 1944. Like Cary, Henry Green (1905–) deals wittily with serious matters. A British industrialist with a penchant for anonymity, "Green" is known almost entirely because of a series of sensitive novels which have been called "fairy tales for adults." Each of his slim, simple, yet vividly poetic books has for title a single symbolic word: *Living*, 1942, *Caught*, 1944, *Loving*, 1945, *Back*, 1946, *Concluding*, 1948.

The Short Story

The short story achieved a new richness and variety during the first half of the twentieth century. The reason for this is not far to seek. The tempo of life had changed. The increasingly rapid pace, the feverish alteration of standards, the flux of quickly accepted and quickly discarded ideas, demanded a condensed form of fiction. The times called for narratives which could be read between tasks at a single setting. The short story served both as a stimulant and as an anodyne. It had always been a favorite medium of entertainment as a transcription of life and as a dramatization of it. But now the tellers of tales began to record many and significant deviations. It may be said that in the twentieth century the short story came of age.

A comparison of the short stories of the present with those written during the last century reveals an evolution not only of feeling but of form. The short story of the past moved quickly. It was firm in construction; it had a definite beginning and a climactic (and often unexpected) end; it permitted no irrelevant details; it emphasized adroitness and surprise even at the expense of plausibility. To be sure, some twentieth-century narrators continued in this manner, but many were not satisfied with the old formulas. They insisted on new techniques to achieve new and more realistic effects. The elegant tone gave way to a colloquial manner; the tale frequently began in the very midst of things and often came to no particular conclusion; significant details were introduced not only for "atmosphere" but for characterizing elements; carefully "arranged" incidents were sacrificed for a pervading sense of actuality. Often, indeed, there was no "story" element. Instead there was presented a situation which, on the surface, seemed trivial but which was charged with tension and untold possibilities.

The tradition of Poe and Maupassant, with its manipulated drama and skillfully patterned effects, clashed with the more recent tradition of the Russian master, Anton Chekhov, and the American-turned-Englishman, Henry James, in which no precise pattern was discernible. In the stories of James Joyce, D. H. Lawrence, and Katherine Mansfield the manner is deceptively casual; instead of a tight and orderly progress there is maintained a flexibility of mood and a looseness which suggest the haphazard mystery of existence. Situation is the first requisite to the writers who, like Chekhov, preferred a study of character rather than a plot. Sensibility is the touchstone. There is less of a prearranged dramatic "development" and more of an actual transcript, "a slice of life."

W. Somerset Maugham, a critical compiler as well as an expert writer of short stories, summed up the differences. In an analytical introduction to his anthology, *Tellers of Tales*, Maugham wrote: "People grow tired even of good things. They want change. . . . It is hard to invent such a story as Poe wrote and, as we know, even he, in his small output, more than once repeated himself. There is a good deal of trickiness in a narrative of this kind, and when, with the appearance and immediate popularity of the monthly magazine, the demand for such narratives became great, authors were not slow to learn the tricks. Craftsmen rather than artists, in order to make their stories effective they forced upon them a conventional design and presently deviated so far from plausibility in their delineation of life that their readers rebelled. They grew weary of stories written to a pattern they knew only too well. They demanded greater realism."

Thus the characteristics of the short story adapted themselves not only to the fashion of the moment but also to the basic spirit of the age. Prompted by Poe, Maugham originally defined a short story as "a piece of fiction dealing with a single incident; it must sparkle, excite or impress; it must have unity of effect; it should move in an even line from its exposition to its close." Later tendencies, however, amended the definition to a formula which is not derived from Poe and permits the compiler to include stories which depend less on narration and more on implication. Maugham finally concluded that his definition could be simpler and more comprehensive: "I should define a short story as a piece of fiction that has unity of impression and that can be read at a single sitting. I should be inclined to say that the only test of its excellence is that it interests."

Most of the novelists already mentioned also excelled in the writing of short stories. Besides these, several other authors developed an extraordinary subtlety. Among those who followed the Poe-Maupassant tradition, the most notable were Maugham himself with dozens of famous stories that were effectively adapted to the stage, screen, and television; Leonard Merrick (1864–1939); H. H. Munro ("Saki") (1870–1916); A. E. Coppard (1878–); G. K. Chesterton (1874–1936); J. B. Priestley (1894–); and James Hilton (1900–). The influence of Chekhov was apparent in the short stories of James Joyce, Virginia Woolf, Elizabeth Bowen, and other experimental writers, notably Katherine Mansfield (1888–1923), whose studies of a cultured middle-class society were precise and almost painful in their extreme sensitivity. In the work of Conrad both methods were discernible.

The Critical Biography

Perhaps the greatest change in tone and attitude during the middle decades was manifest in the writing of biography. True children of their age, the new biographers dedicated themselves to a lively skepticism. They were concerned with more than the facts of history; they probed behind the carefully assembled data to the living, disconcerting, and often disillusioning spirit. They felt that the account of a man and his age should be at least as interesting as fiction, and they knew that without creative imagination there could be no sense of reality.

The most remarkable biographer of the period was Lytton Strachey (1880–1932). Strachey may be said to have founded a whole school. It was a school of reappraisal which did not hesitate to apply relentless analysis, even psychoanalysis, to legendary heroes, saintly heroines, and rulers who had been considered sacrosanct. Strachey cut through the pietism, the swaddled sentiment, the prudish reticences. His method was vivacious, his technique was new. His was a search for unsuspected truths, not for a restatement of recorded facts; his aim was esthetic, not ethical. For this he was equipped with an inquisitive subtlety, a devastating wit, and a bewildering, brilliant style—he was "half butterfly and half gadfly."

Philip Guedalla (1889–1944) outlived Strachey in years, though not in popularity. Guedalla, frequently considered Strachey's rival, was consistently sharp and a little too determinedly epigrammatic. His scrutiny was closer than Strachey's, but Strachey was the finer stylist. Guedalla specialized in figures and backgrounds of the nineteenth century, and he dealt with them in a manner that was alternately suave and savage. Guedalla's full-length *Wellington*, 1931, and *The Hundred Years*, 1936, are a necessary complement to the grace and malice of Strachey's *Eminent Victorians*, 1918, and *Portraits in Miniature*, 1931. It should be added that the biographers of this period were often more dogmatic than their more guarded predecessors. They forgot Chesterton's reminder that our own time is only a time, and not the Day of Judgment. In an effort to avoid dullness at any cost, they sometimes sacrificed accuracy for brilliance and facts for prejudices. The cleverness of Guedalla produced shoddy imitations, and the wit of Strachey did not prevent this portraitist from being frequently unfair to his sitter.

Besides revaluing history, the biographer also played the part of the essayist; often he became essayist and autobiographer in one. Among those who made the transition most skillfully were the older conservatives Hilaire Belloc (1870–), G. K. Chesterton (1874–1936), and Maurice Baring (1874–); the younger appraisers Lord David Cecil (1902–) and Harold Nicolson (1886–). Thomas Edward Lawrence (1888–1935), soldier, archeologist, and adventurer, in his *The Seven Pillars of Wisdom*, wrote a contemporary classic; Osbert Sitwell (1892–), balanced his enthusiasms and irritations in a series of autobiographical volumes that began with *Left Hand, Right Hand*, 1944; and the poets Edmund Blunden (1896–), Robert Graves (1895–), and Siegfried Sassoon (1886–), all turned to prose for their autobiographical records of the First World War and its crushing effects on sensibility.

The speeches and memoirs of Winston Churchill (1874–) acted—literally with acts accompanying the words—not only as an autobiography of the man but of his times. Statesman and Prime Minister, Churchill composed in a style which was rhetorical and resounding, graceful yet vigorous, literary yet lively. A profound devotion to tradition did not prevent Churchill from recreating and invigorating the records of a recent past in a language both living and lasting. In a prose gusty and resonant, reflecting a restless, incisive, and indomitable spirit, a great Englishman wrote—and created—history in the grand manner.

As essayist Aldous Huxley took an entirely different attitude from that of Huxley the novelist. The bloodless satirist of *Point Counter Point*, 1928, and *Brave New World*, 1932, became the sympathetic humanist of *The Perennial Philosophy*, 1945. The heartless cynic turned to his fellow-sufferers and, with the passion of the earnest moralist, attempted to find ways which would not only save himself but them. The more disinterested familiar essay in the English tradition continued to flourish in the writings of H. M. Tomlinson (1873–), W. H. Hudson (1841–1922), E. V. Lucas (1868–1948), and especially in the nimble, polished prose of Max Beerbohm (1872–)—"the incomparable Max."

Tendencies in the Drama

As the Irish theater was on the point of bursting forth with the fresh energy we have been observing, the drama elsewhere experienced a complete transition toward the end of the nineteenth century. The play of contrived situations and facile romanticism gave way to half-serious, half-superficial social dramas, which, in turn, were supplanted by dramas of real social criticism and protest. The continental "tailor-made" plays of Victorien Sardou and the younger Dumas had dominated the English theater as late as the 1880's, and when the realistic work of Henrik Ibsen was first performed in London he was howled down as "immoral," "bestial," and "a chronicler of the abnormal." Yet it was not long before Ibsen became an influence. The social problems he posed were adapted and Anglicized by Henry Arthur Jones (1851–1929) and Arthur Wing Pinero (1855–1934), both of whom, nevertheless, retained the technique of Sardou with its emphasis on calculated tension, manufactured complications, and "the big scene." Jones and Pinero kept themselves well within the proprieties. They presumed to question that arbitress of propriety, Mrs. Grundy, but not actually to dispute her dictates; they were willing to be unconventional, but not unpopular.

Oscar Wilde had amused and shocked society without seriously challenging it. George Bernard Shaw (1856–1950) was a dynamo in the theater, an electric storm in the academies, and one of the most energizing forces in contemporary culture. His early plays, notably *Widowers' Houses*, 1892, and *Mrs. Warren's Profession*, 1898, bear the mark of Ibsen — Shaw's first critical study was entitled *The Quintessence of Ibsenism*, 1891—but his later work resembles in no way that of the grim Norwegian dramatist. Shaw succeeded in adding the dazzling repartee of Wilde to the iconoclasm of Samuel Butler and in superimposing a bristling personality of his own. Shaw's manner was impertinent and paradoxical, defiant, and diabolically mocking, but his purpose was serious. He took nothing for granted; instead, he looked askance at institutions, attacked current mores, and combated the status quo all along the line. He queried everything and, without waiting for a reply, supplied answers that were more embarrassing than the questions. So great was Shaw's vitality that at seventy he won the Nobel Prize for Literature, at eighty-two he wrote his fiftieth play (*Geneva*, 1938), and on the eve of his death at ninety-four he was still astonishing the world with the audacity of his ideas. His continual attacks on enshrined convention and pious sham—from the romantic *Caesar and Cleopatra*, 1899, to the untheatrical *Misalliance*, 1910, and *Heartbreak House*, 1917, which are dramatized discussions—helped not only to change the form of the drama but to mold the social sense of the times. Shaw's particular combination of brilliance and unexpected beauty distinguished *Major Barbara*, 1905, *Pygmalion*, 1912, *Back to Methuselah*, 1921, a sequence of five full-length dramas, which range from the Garden of Eden to a time thirty thousand years from now; and *Saint Joan*, 1923, is a masterpiece of poetic reappraisal.

Shaw's own birthplace was Dublin, but he had left for London long before the Abbey Theater began to contribute so conspicuously to twentieth-century British drama. Another who sought out the London literary scene was J. M. Barrie, who spiritually, however, never left his native Scotland. Before the First World War Barrie was looked upon as one of the literary giants of his era; his reputation faded—probably none other has suffered such eclipse—with the violent reaction against sentimentality that has characterized the postwar attitude. But Barrie was not all whimsy, and if *Peter Pan*, 1904, is destined to remain a children's classic, *The Admirable Crichton*, 1902, *Dear Brutus*, 1917, and *What Every Woman Knows*, 1908, are valuable contributions to the theater. As Allardyce Nicoll observes, in *World Drama*, "In a civilization highly conscious of economic conditions and dominated by behavioristic psychology his is a lonely figure, yet no other dramatist of his time was more adroit than he, no other fixed his gaze so intimately upon the vagaries of human nature viewed, not at moments of tempestuous passion, but by the light of the desert island's camp-fire, the gentle glow of the parlour fire, or the moonlight of the enchanted forest."

Although one thinks of John Galsworthy primarily as a novelist, he was successful and, for the most part, convincing as a dramatist. More critical of society in his plays than in his novels, he dealt with the struggles of the weak and the unfortunate caught in the industrial machine. Such plays as *Strife*, 1909, *Justice*, 1910, and *Loyalties*, 1922, balance themselves on ethical and social problems; and, though Galsworthy impartially presented the just claims of the opposing points of view, there is no doubt that his sympathy was with the losers. His mastery of the naturalistic method rarely failed him on the stage.

Harley Granville-Barker (1877–1946), carrying the realistic method even farther than Galsworthy, distinguished himself equally as playwright, producer, and critic of the theater. The whimsical manner of Barrie was carried on in the pleasant comedies of A. A. Milne (1882–). Somerset Maugham first attained prominence as a dramatist, and at least two or three of his sophisticated comedies have sufficient point and brilliance to endure. Through the twenties and thirties, following upon John Drinkwater's *Abraham Lincoln*, 1918, and Shaw's *Saint Joan*, historical drama enjoyed a vogue; Rudolph Besier's *The Barretts of Wimpole Street*, 1931, and Laurence Housman's *Victoria Regina*, 1935, were representative of this trend.

Noel Coward early abandoned serious drama for the bright and facile. Always skillful and often refreshingly clever, most of Coward's plays have delighted without in any way disturbing. In *Private Lives*, 1930, and *Blithe Spirit*, 1941, Coward was at his diverting best. *Cavalcade*, 1931, an impressive play, was an even better motion picture; several other first-rate films have revealed Coward in more serious mood. J. B. Priestley has been more ambitious and experimental, piercing with insight and theatrical effect into the imaginative world of his characters. Perhaps the most promising talent at mid-century was that of Terence Rattigan, who in such plays as *The Winslow Boy*, 1946, was turning from slender farces to work of more serious intent.

The purely poetic play was fitfully revived by the blank verse dramas of Stephen Phillips (1868–1915) and Lascelles Abercrombie (1881–). But poetry returned seriously and successfully to the theater with T. S. Eliot (1888–) and Christopher Fry (1907–). Mirroring Eliot's poetic development, his plays (*The Rock*, 1934, *Murder in the Cathedral*, 1935, *The Family Reunion*, 1939, and *The Cocktail Party*, 1949) express a deepening religious sense. At first Eliot availed himself freely of the conventions of the Greek theater—the chorus in *Murder in the Cathedral*, and the Eumenides in *The Family Reunion*, for example—and used them to good advantage. But he has been steadily developing a dramatic technique and symbolism of his own for dealing with the complexities of modern life. Increasingly the stage materials have been wedded to poetry of evocative but unobtrusive beauty. The plays of Christopher Fry (especially *A Phoenix Too Frequent*, 1946, *The Lady's Not for Burning*, 1949, and *Venus Observed*, 1950) restore the pure magic of the spoken word to the stage. Fry's vocabulary is spectacular; it runs the gamut of English speech from the rugged forthrightness of Chaucer to the elaborate double images of Auden. The effect is breathless; and the bravura poet triumphs over the playwright who has not found a theme worthy of his eloquence.

Poetry of Frustration and Fulfillment

Between 1900 and 1950, the course of poetry fluctuated even more than the other mediums of communication. Beginning with echoes of "the great tradition," it ranged through experimentation and revolt to writing so extreme as to seem willfully complicated and, at times, incomprehensible. A few poets served as a "bridge" between the Victorian and the modern period, chiefly the self-immolated Thomas Hardy (1840–1928), Robert Bridges (1844–1930), A. E. Housman (1859–1936), and Arthur Symons (1865–1945). William Butler Yeats, already an important literary figure in the nineties, reached the height of his reputation as a poet in the twentieth century.

Hardy had written his great novels by the end of the nineteenth century, but his career as a poet had barely begun. Always a questioner of the conventions and certainties which Victoria's Age sanctified, Hardy acknowledged the shifting backgrounds, the increased tempo, and the dictates of modern science, but he accepted them without joy and without hope. Belonging spiritually to the new century rather than the old, he took no pleasure in the bleakness of the human picture, nor on the other hand did he allow it to embitter him. Actually the poet was an unorthodox moralist whose heart went out to the things, people, and elements he loved. W. H. Auden, acknowledging a great debt to Hardy in the technical aspects of the poet's craft, has also praised "his hawk's vision, his way of looking at life from a very great height." At first acquaintance, the rhythms of Hardy's poetry are irritatingly crude; syntax is often clumsy, language involved, archaic, and harsh. But underneath the surface crudities—and many of them are efforts to achieve particular effects—the poetry is as disciplined as it is original. Hardy's resources are seemingly endless; most readers prefer him in that curiously lyric-narrative style which he perfected, but his intensities escape category. *The Dynasts*, a vast panorama of the Napoleonic wars and human destiny, is his most ambitious effort in verse, but the reader probably approaches his poetry most rewardingly through his individual, intense, and often sharply ironic shorter poems.

A similar note was sounded by A. E. Housman in three small volumes of verse, one of which was posthumously published. Housman's was a quiet pessimism, achieved partly by the actuality of his Shropshire background, partly by his terse, almost epigrammatic, idiom. A cloistered Latin scholar, Housman wrote with detachment about murder and suicide, personal betrayal and cosmic evil. His stanzas are miracles of incongruity; the most horrendous happenings shape themselves into measures which are a cross between a jig and a hymn tune. His heroism is a far cry from the good world of the Victorians or the cheerful jingoism of Kipling. Evil is a constant, but it must be borne. Cruelty is natural to the physical world, but it can be endured. This was a peculiar hardness, a kind of tonic bitterness. It acknowledged a sense of suffering, real but manfully restrained; a pervasive ill which, if gradually absorbed, creates an immunity against pain. Meanwhile there is love and laughter and enough liquor to go round. These, says the English poet, grimly echoing the Persian pleasure-seeker who wrote the *Rubiáyát*, are better than thinking—

> And malt does more than Milton can
> To justify God's ways to man.

William Butler Yeats was already a poet of note when at the turn of the century he threw his energies into the Irish literary movement. In early years his was the poetry of delicate effects and romantic loveliness, musical almost to a fault. The younger Yeats steeped himself in mysticism and occultism, in the folklore of his native land; for a while, in the words of a discerning critic, he "escaped into the tapestry land of legend." But the search for a pattern or ordering that would relate the abstract world of imagination to the concrete world of actuality soon absorbed him, and he evolved a set of poetic images to communicate his own "vision" of man. Yeats gradually turned away from the poetry of incantation to a plain-speaking verse, from the mystic rose and wild swans to a more personal symbolism of swords and towers and winding stairs. His later work grew firmer in thought, more complex in harmony. "The Second Coming," "Sailing to Byzantium," and "Leda and the Swan"—to name but a few of Yeats's richest poems—belong among the undoubted masterpieces of twentieth-century poetry.

The group of poets known as the Georgians was so called because their work, presented in a series of biennial collections entitled *Georgian Poetry*, was produced in the decade between 1912 and 1922 during the reign of George V. Critics accused the poetry of resembling the monarch: pleasant and almost nonpolitical. But, if the Georgians lacked a cohered philosophy and an intellectual core, their attitude was spirited, the tone was fresh. If the technique was not startling, it was interesting. The idiom was generally patterned on the accents of everyday speech; old-fashioned inversions were shunned; apostrophes were taboo; "poetic diction" was discarded in favor of an easily communicated language.

At first the spirit of the Georgian poets was as resolute as their speech. They seized on the commonplace with ardor. John Masefield (1874–) wrote about sailors, laborers, hunters, and murderers in such vigorous narratives as *The Widow in the Bye Street*, 1912, *Dauber*, 1913, *The Daffodil Fields*, 1913, and *Reynard the Fox*, 1919. Wilfrid Wilson Gibson (1878–) dramatized stonecutters, farmers, and ferrymen in *Daily Bread*, 1910, and *Livelihood*, 1917. D. H. Lawrence (1885–1930) put the almost inarticulate colliers and the overworked townspeople of his native Nottinghamshire into his early *Love Poems and Others*, 1913. But gathering complexities bewildered the Georgians; war defeated and scattered them. As though betrayed by the upheaval, Masefield retreated into vague generalities about life and platitudes about beauty; Gibson fled to the security of remote associations and familiar stereotypes; Lawrence gave himself up to an increasingly baffled contemplation of the psyche. Perplexity grew; the movement became a movement of escape. The Georgians withdrew to the consoling English countryside, to a tender and prettified Nature, to the false solace of dreams. In their decline they staged a whole series of retreats; they attempted to return to romantic primitivism, to the belief that Nature was full of loving-kindness, that man was instinctively good, and that the nearer man got to Nature, the better he became. Man is a child of Nature; therefore, argued the Georgians, goodness and beauty will attend him as long as he shuns the evil city. They forgot that as early as 1845 Matthew Arnold had cautioned nature worshipers:

> Man must begin, know this, where Nature ends;
> Nature and man can never be fast friends.

The genuinely naïve and artless W. H. Davies (1871–1940) was followed by poets who adopted the bucolic attitude. Theirs was an almost studied simplicity, a determined thoughtlessness. Ralph Hodgson (1871–) turned the pastoral note to a music old in form but fresh in utterance; truly simple, Hodgson avoided mediocrity by the vitality of his emotion and the vigor of his imagination. Harold Monro (1879–1932) protected his hurt sensitivity by fantasies about ordinary objects and half-whimsical, half-metaphysical speculations about man's place in a mechanical world. Walter De La Mare (1873–) was obsessed by the mysteries of the unconscious mind, a mind half awake and faintly stirring beneath the conscious will. De La Mare did not altogether forget the active world, but he saw it as in a reverie, a dream within a dream.

The First World War inhibited and practically stopped the progress of poetry. It killed such brilliant singers as Edward Thomas (1878–1918), Rupert Brooke (1887–1915), James Elroy Flecker

(1884–1915), Wilfred Owen (1893–1918), Isaac Rosenberg (1890–1918), Francis Ledwidge (1891–1917), and the amazing boy, Charles Hamilton Sorley (1895–1915), dead at twenty. The impetus of the Georgians was spent; the physical and intellectual lifeblood had been drained. Ironically enough, it took the threat of a new war to bring on a new vitalizing impulse.

Readers and writers suffered from a violent disillusion. Personal romanticism was suspect and pastoral scenes gave no assurance of peace. The younger poets tried to create out of disbelief; wherever they turned they found scorn instead of serenity, frustration instead of fulfillment.

The Sitwells were among the first to revolt against the romantic and vague promises of the Georgians. There were three of them: Edith Sitwell (1887–), Osbert Sitwell (1892–), and Sacheverell Sitwell (1897–). Mocking what they considered the false ingenuousness of their contemporaries, they created an even more artificial art. They specialized in grotesque unrealities, in a purposely overcolored rhetoric, in an approximation of the formalism of the ballet and the slapstick of the music hall. They advertised themselves impudently; they even exploited their own absurdities. Until they turned to deeper realities later in life, they distorted sense-effects and built a series of ivory towers inhabited (seemingly) by children and neurotics. Edith Sitwell grew into a poet of power, concerned with deeply human values.

T. S. Eliot, the most influential poet and critic of our time, has been the high priest of the new sensibility. In the long and difficult *The Waste Land*, 1922, and in his other early poems, Eliot mirrored an age shellshocked by war and assaulted by economic uncertainty, an age in which faiths had been shattered and foundations crumbled. To communicate states of feeling that were complicated and often highly personal, Eliot employed a complex verse, combining trivial and tawdry pictures with traditionally poetic subject matter, linking the banalities of conversation to rich rhetoric and interrupting the sordid present with "flash-backs" to the more fruitful past. Eliot's readers recognized his remarkable lyric gift and metrical mastery, but they were often puzzled by imagery that followed an emotional rather than a logical sequence and derived from a vast reservoir of literature, philosophy, and recondite learning. This was poetry for the few, but for those few it was poetry that stirred them deeply.

Although the average man could detect no sense in the wandering of the new literature, it soon became evident that it was mad only north-northwest and that it had something significant if not pleasurable to say. The literature of nerves indicated another readjustment of values; it placarded new slogans and relied on eccentric efforts to show man's relation to a changing environment. Every means was used to evoke a disturbed mood or represent a shaken condition of the mind. No tenet seemed too extreme. Herbert Read (1893–), professor of fine arts as well as poet and critic, wrote: "Prose is constructive expression; poetry is creative expression. We now see that poetry may inhere in a single word, in a single syllable, and may therefore in an extreme case be without rhythm." The critics thundered; prophets of doom were heard on every side. There was renewed talk of the disintegration of literature. But the literary conservatives and radicals continued in their opposed camps.

Aftermath of War

A new group of writers, chiefly poets, rose in the thirties and immediately challenged attention. The new men had more than youth and poetry in common; they shared the conviction that most of their generation were born in one war and seemed fated to die in another. Their predilections, their tastes, their social and political convictions, were equally opposed to those of the Georgians and the Sitwellians. They owed much of their technique to three experimental predecessors: Gerald Manley Hopkins, that fervent, richly associative, and most original poet who was neglected during his lifetime; William Butler Yeats, and particularly his later, more probing poems; and T. S. Eliot, who influenced all poetry written in English after 1925. Eliot prepared the way for the younger men; he celebrated and satirized the end of a cycle, the cultural decay of a period, and the approaching dissolution of a system. But when Eliot, unable to proceed further with doubt, turned to Anglo-Catholicism, the younger school broke with him; they refused to follow his apparent defeatism and questioned the "esoteric mysticism," which many others feel inspired, in *Ash Wednesday* and *Four Quartets*, his most moving poetry.

The postwar group faced their world with suspicion rather than with confidence, with fearful intuition instead of calm experience. They came forward with hopeful gestures in place of certainties; they voiced prophecies rather than deliberate dogmas. The most notable of the group were W. H. Auden (1907–), Stephen Spender (1909–), Louis MacNeice (1907–), C. Day Lewis (1904–

), Christopher Isherwood (1904–), and Dylan Thomas (1914–).

Auden was the most intellectually daring, the most experimental in idea, and most brilliant in execution. His popularity was limited because of his very excess of energy, his willfullness and private satire, his rough improvisations and elaborate angers, his mixture of clear beauty and allegory. Nevertheless, in the mid-forties Auden was recognized as, after Eliot, the most influential poet of the period. He was acclaimed as a versatile originator, a superb maker of images, equally adept at persiflage and pure enchantment.

Stephen Spender was less versatile but more intense. A genuine romantic as well as a rebel, Spender's emotion was fixed and forthright. He did not mask his passions or preoccupations; he translated the machine into poetry, announcing "the first powerful plain manifesto, the black statement of pistons," and placed his emphasis on social consciousness.

Dylan Thomas, on the other hand, was so bemused by the pure color and sheer sound of words that, instead of controlling them, he seemed sometimes to let the syllables control him. His lines pitch and toss, fling, shout, and seem to leave the printed page in an excess of abandon. Thomas surpasses all his contemporaries in an irrepressible outpouring of speech, a rich and improvised rhetoric, a compulsive rush of feeling. If Thomas's language is often intuitional rather than logical, the sense of life is so strong, the passion so spontaneous, that no reader can resist it.

Although the postwar poets held to a belief in mankind, they refused to accept worn-out platitudes and panaceas. They could not, like the Georgians, turn to fancy for forgetfulness or to Nature for healing. "The poet," wrote Alastair Miller for them in *The Saturday Review of Literature*, "no longer looks out of his window in the country and, blinding himself to the railway track, sees a beneficent Providence creating the pleasures and necessities of men: he sees electric pylons conveying imprisoned power, telegraph wires defying distance, motorploughs forcing fertility into the soil. There is no disrespect, as is sometimes maintained, for primroses and budding trees; but they are not accepted as a solution of, or consolation for, human misery."

To accomplish their ends, the postwar writers developed distinctive methods and technical innovations. They substituted rapid allusions for definite statements. They proceeded from one image to another by inference and association rather than by natural sequence. Logic ceased to rule; often it was carelessly disdained, sometimes it was consciously discarded in favor of "the logic of the emotions." The legendary "hero" continued to fascinate, but he was suspect; an idealized common man became "the coming man." Spender, in particular, celebrated

The names of those who in their lives fought for life,
Who wore at their hearts the fire's center.
Born of the sun they travelled a short while towards the sun,
And left the vivid air signed with their honour.

Faced by the specter of continuing wars and a grim increase of tensions, the writers of the period did not resign themselves to a doomed existence. Though disorder almost overwhelmed the world, they knew that chaos was not a constant. Theirs was a literature of protest, a piercing and often painful record of swift change, a transition between a disappearing and an emerging culture. If anger prompted many of their pages, it was a necessary and even noble outcry against the terrorization of thought and the debasing of the spirit. Turning away from cynicism and despair, they looked toward a time when men could once again express "the palpable and obvious love of man," when not only poets but ordinary people could leave "the vivid air signed with their honour."

Thomas Hardy
1840–1928

As a novelist and writer of short stories, Hardy belongs to the Age of Victoria; as a poet, chiefly to the twentieth century. And Hardy and Meredith alone among English writers achieved front rank both as novelist and poet. Hardy was born, the son of a stonemason, June 2, 1840, in Dorsetshire in southern England. His native district, with which his prose and verse are mainly concerned, he called Wessex in his writings, reviving the ancient Anglo-Saxon name for the region. His rather irregular schooling was over by the time he reached sixteen, when he was apprenticed to a Dorsetshire architect. Until he was twenty-one he worked at his profession, studied Greek and Latin at odd hours, and became acquainted with English poetry. From his twenty-second to his twenty-sixth year he continued his architectural studies in London and also engaged in the active practice of an ecclesiastical architect. That he was not without abilities in the profession is indicated by his having won two prizes before he gave up architecture for literature. Most of his books were written in the house at Max Gate in Dorchester which he designed and built for himself and his wife.

Hardy began his literary career as a poet and wrote only poetry until 1870, when his engagement to Emma Gifford made it seem advisable that he turn his efforts to a more remunerative kind of writing. His first novel, *Desperate Remedies*, 1871, published anonymously, was a failure, but his second and third, *Under the Greenwood Tree*, 1872, and *A Pair of Blue Eyes*, 1873, made it apparent that a major novelist had arrived. Until the end of the century he continued to produce novels, of which the best are *Far From the Madding Crowd*, 1874, *The Return of the Native*, 1878, *The Mayor of Casterbridge*, 1886, and *Tess of the D'Urbervilles*, 1891. His three collections of short stories are, in general, below the level of his best work. His last novel, *Jude the Obscure*, 1896, was attacked so violently by the critics that he abandoned novel writing at the height of his powers, and from then on until the end of his long life he devoted himself exclusively to his first love, poetry. His first volume of verse, *Wessex Poems*, 1898, illustrated with his own drawings, was a collection of pieces written during thirty years. It excited no enthusiasm from the critics, and a second volume, *Poems of the Past and Present*, 1902, likewise drew little applause. In his sixty-fourth year, 1904, Hardy published the first part of his vast epic-drama of the Napoleonic Wars, *The Dynasts*, which he carried through to completion in 1908. No other poem of the twentieth century is so monumental in structure: it is in three books, nineteen acts, and one hundred and thirty scenes. Hardy is almost unique in English literature in that both the number and the quality of his poems increased with his years. Three volumes of his best verse appeared after he was eighty. His last volume, *Winter Words*, was published posthumously. When he died, in his eighty-eighth year, January 11, 1928, he was the outstanding English writer of his generation. His heart was buried, in accordance with his wishes, in his native Dorset; his ashes were placed in the Poets' Corner of Westminster Abbey.

Though Hardy is often regarded as an iconoclast, no writer was ever more imbued with a sense of the past. As a child in Dorset he heard the country folk still discussing Napoleon's threatened invasion of England half a century before, and Roman and British ruins still standing carried his imagination back eighteen hundred years before Napoleon. According to Hardy's view, whatever has been lives on forever in one form or other. The body has its resurrection in trees and flowers; less materially, the hands of the dead hover over the knobs of "Old Furniture," and the lineaments of the family project themselves through the generations. To purely human concerns the dead are quite indifferent, yet they retain a consciousness of human affairs. English soldiers leave their bodies in an alien clime, but their souls come home on the wings of the wind to an England quite indifferent to their military glory but happy to remember their quiet household ways in days gone by.

Men are so much like Nature in Hardy's world that an old woman's life will be likened to the leaves she rakes up in the park. Yet Nature is perfectly indifferent to human beings, and they must enjoy the myriad beauties she presents without any thought that these were designed for human delectation. And Hardy's God is as indifferent as his Nature. God has forgotten that He ever made the world. It was one of His failures, and He lost interest in it almost from the beginning. For that matter, God knows nothing of values. Values are a human invention. The very thing that Browning (in "Saul") said could not happen has happened in Hardy's world. In such a world no "private joy" is possible; even as one sits down by the Christmas fire, a starving bird comes to the window, to suggest all the underprivileged who are shut out in the cold. Over everything hovers the threat of war, once honorable, now utterly ruthless, senseless, stripped of every value war may once have possessed. Yet somehow life goes on—love goes on. And, somehow, hope goes on in the world, as in "The Darkling Thrush," and even in Hardy's own heart, at least on Christmas Eve.

Somber as is Hardy's conception of life and the world—and it should be remembered that he presents it suggestively, as a poet, not dogmatically, as a philosopher—it serves him well. It is challenging, it is original, and it furnishes a complete standard of reference. His technique as an artist, as varied almost as any in English, is adequate to his conceptions. When, as in his most characteristic poems, he is plain, angular, austere, it is because he no more desires the sensuous harmonies of a Spenser or a Tennyson in his verse than he desires the sophisticated completeness of a Henry James in his prose fiction. But whatever he may lose in grace he more than makes up in rugged power.

THE SOULS OF THE SLAIN [1]

The thick lids of Night closed upon me
  Alone at the Bill
  Of the Isle by the Race—
Many-cavernèd, bald, wrinkled of face—
And with darkness and silence the spirit was on me
  To brood and be still.

No wind fanned the flats of the ocean,
  Or promontory sides,
  Or the ooze by the strand,
Or the bent-bearded slope of the land,
Whose base took its rest amid everlong motion
  Of criss-crossing tides.

Soon from out of the Southward seemed nearing
  A whirr, as of wings
  Waved by mighty-vanned flies,
Or by night-moths of measureless size,
And in softness and smoothness well-nigh beyond hearing
  Of corporal things.

And they bore to the bluff, and alighted—
  A dim-discerned train
  Of sprites without mould,
Frameless souls none might touch or might hold—
On the ledge by the turreted lantern, far-sighted
  By men of the main.

And I heard them say "Home!" and I knew them
  For souls of the felled
  On the earth's nether bord
Under Capricorn, whither they'd warred,
And I neared in my awe, and gave heedfulness to them
  With breathings inheld.

Then, it seemed, there approached from the northward
  A senior soul-flame
  Of the like filmy hue:
And he met them and spake: "Is it you,
O my men?" Said they, "Aye! We bear homeward and hearthward
  To feast on our fame!"

"I've flown there before you," he said then:
  "Your households are well;
  But—your kin linger less
On your glory and war-mightiness
Than on dearer things."—"Dearer?" cried these from the dead then,
  "Of what do they tell?"

"Some mothers muse sadly, and murmur
  Your doings as boys—
  Recall the quaint ways
Of your babyhood's innocent days.
Some pray that, ere dying, your faith had grown firmer,
  And higher your joys.

"A father broods: 'Would I had set him
  To some humble trade,
  And so slacked his high fire,
And his passionate martial desire;
Had told him no stories to woo him and whet him
  To this dire crusade!' "

"And, General, how hold out our sweethearts,
  Sworn loyal as doves?"
  —"Many mourn; many think
It is not unattractive to prink

[1] This and the following poems by Thomas Hardy are from *The Collected Poems of Thomas Hardy*, copyright, 1925, by The Macmillan Company. Reprinted by permission of The Macmillan Company and of Macmillan & Co. Ltd. and the Trustees of the Hardy Estate.

Them in sables for heroes. Some fickle and fleet hearts
Have found them new loves."

"And our wives?" quoth another resignedly,
"Dwell they on our deeds?"
—"Deeds of home; that live yet
Fresh as new—deeds of fondness or fret;
Ancient words that were kindly expressed or unkindly,
These, these have their heeds."

—"Alas! then it seems that our glory
Weighs less in their thought
Than our old homely acts,
And the long-ago commonplace facts
Of our lives—held by us as scarce part of our story,
And rated as nought!"

Then bitterly some: "Was it wise now
To raise the tomb-door
For such knowledge? Away!"
But the rest: "Fame we prized till to-day;
Yet that hearts keep us green for old kindness we prize now
A thousand times more!"

Thus speaking, the trooped apparitions
Began to disband
And resolve them in two:
Those whose record was lovely and true
Bore to northward for home: those of bitter traditions
Again left the land,

And, towering to seaward in legions,
They paused at a spot
Overbending the Race—
That engulphing, ghast, sinister place—
Whither headlong they plunged, to the fathomless regions
Of myriads forgot.

And the spirits of those who were homing
Passed on, rushingly,
Like the Pentecost Wind;
And the whirr of their wayfaring thinned
And surceased on the sky, and but left in the gloaming
Sea-mutterings and me.

93. Pentecost Wind. See Acts 2:2.

THE DARKLING THRUSH

I leant upon a coppice gate
When Frost was spectre-gray,
And Winter's dregs made desolate
The weakening eye of day.
The tangled vine-stems scored the sky
Like strings of broken lyres,
And all mankind that haunted nigh
Had sought their household fires.

The land's sharp features seemed to be
The Century's corpse outleant,
His crypt the cloudy canopy,
The wind his death-lament.
The ancient pulse of germ and birth
Was shrunken hard and dry,
And every spirit upon earth
Seemed fervourless as I.

At once a voice arose among
The bleak twigs overhead
In a full-hearted evensong
Of joy illimited;
An aged thrush, frail, gaunt, and small,
In blast-beruffled plume,
Had chosen thus to fling his soul
Upon the growing gloom.

So little cause for carolings
Of such ecstatic sound
Was written on terrestrial things
Afar or nigh around,
That I could think there trembled through
His happy good-night air
Some blessed Hope, whereof he knew
And I was unaware.

SHELLEY'S SKYLARK

(The Neighbourhood of Leghorn: March 1887)

Somewhere afield here something lies
In Earth's oblivious eyeless trust
That moved a poet to prophecies—
A pinch of unseen, unguarded dust:

The dust of the lark that Shelley heard,
And made immortal through times to be;—
Though it only lived like another bird,
And knew its immortality:

Lived its meek life; then, one day, fell—
A little ball of feather and bone;
And how it perished, when piped farewell,
And where it wastes, are alike unknown.

Maybe it rests in the loam I view,
Maybe it throbs in a myrtle's green,
Maybe it sleeps in the coming hue
Of a grape on the slopes of yon inland scene.

Go find it, faeries, go and find
That tiny pinch of priceless dust,
And bring a casket silver-lined,
And framed of gold that gems encrust;

And we will lay it safe therein,
And consecrate it to endless time;
For it inspired a bard to win
Ecstatic heights in thought and rhyme.

THE TO-BE-FORGOTTEN

I heard a small sad sound,
And stood awhile among the tombs around:
"Wherefore, old friends," said I, "are you distrest,
Now, screened from life's unrest?"

—"O not at being here;
But that our future second death is near;
When, with the living, memory of us numbs,
And blank oblivion comes!

"These, our sped ancestry,
Lie here embraced by deeper death than we;
Nor shape nor thought of theirs can you descry
With keenest backward eye.

"They count as quite forgot;
They are as men who have existed not;
Theirs is a loss past loss of fitful breath;
It is the second death.

"We here, as yet, each day
Are blest with dear recall; as yet, can say
We hold in some soul loved continuance
Of shape and voice and glance.

"But what has been will be—
First memory, then oblivion's swallowing sea;
Like men foregone, shall we merge into those
Whose story no one knows.

"For which of us could hope
To show in life that world-awakening scope
Granted the few whose memory none lets die,
But all men magnify?

"We were but Fortune's sport;
Things true, things lovely, things of good report
We neither shunned nor sought . . . We see our bourne,
And seeing it we mourn."

THE NIGHT OF TRAFALGÁR

from THE DYNASTS

In the wild October night-time, when the wind raved round the land,
And the Back-sea met the Front-sea, and our doors were blocked with sand,
And we heard the drub of Dead-man's Bay, where bones of thousands are,
We knew not what the day had done for us at Trafalgár.
Had done,
Had done,
For us at Trafalgár!

"Pull hard, and make the Nothe, or down we go!" one says, says he.
We pulled; and bedtime brought the storm; but snug at home slept we.
Yet all the while our gallants after fighting through the day,
Were beating up and down the dark, sou'-west of Cadiz Bay.
The dark,
The dark,
Sou'-west of Cadiz Bay!

The victors and the vanquished then the storm it tossed and tore,
As hard they strove, those worn-out men, upon that surly shore;
Dead Nelson and his half-dead crew, his foes from near and far,
Were rolled together on the deep that night at Trafalgár!
The deep,
The deep,
That night at Trafalgár!

30. Things . . . report. See Philippians 4:8.

AT CASTERBRIDGE FAIR

I. THE BALLAD-SINGER

Sing, Ballad-singer, raise a hearty tune;
Make me forget that there was ever a one
I walked with in the meek light of the moon
  When the day's work was done.

Rhyme, Ballad-rhymer, start a country song;
Make me forget that she whom I loved well
Swore she would love me dearly, love me long,
  Then—what I cannot tell!

Sing, Ballad-singer, from your little book;
Make me forget those heart-breaks, achings, fears;
Make me forget her name, her sweet sweet look—
  Make me forget her tears.

2. FORMER BEAUTIES

These market-dames, mid-aged, with lips thin-drawn,
  And tissues sere,
Are they the ones we loved in years agone,
  And courted here?

Are these the muslined pink young things to whom
  We vowed and swore
In nooks on summer Sundays by the Froom,
  Or Budmouth shore?

Do they remember those gay tunes we trod
  Clasped on the green;
Aye; trod till moonlight set on the beaten sod
  A satin sheen?

They must forget, forget! They cannot know
  What once they were,
Or memory would transfigure them, and show
  Them always fair.

3. AFTER THE CLUB-DANCE

Black'on frowns east on Maidon,
  And westward to the sea,
But on neither is his frown laden
  With scorn, as his frown on me!

At dawn my heart grew heavy,
  I could not sip the wine,
I left the jocund bevy
  And that young man o' mine.

The roadside elms pass by me,—
  Why do I sink with shame
When the birds a-perch there eye me?
  They, too, have done the same!

4. THE MARKET-GIRL

Nobody took any notice of her as she stood on the causey kerb,
All eager to sell her honey and apples and bunches of garden herb;
And if she had offered to give her wares and herself with them too that day,
I doubt if a soul would have cared to take a bargain so choice away.

But chancing to trace her sunburnt grace that morning as I passed nigh,
I went and I said "Poor maidy dear!—and will none of the people buy?"
And so it began; and soon we knew what the end of it all must be,
And I found that though no others had bid, a prize had been won by me.

5. THE INQUIRY

And are ye one of Hermitage—
Of Hermitage, by Ivel Road,
And do ye know, in Hermitage
A thatch-roofed house where sengreens grow?
And does John Waywood live there still—
He of the name that there abode
When father hurdled on the hill
    Some fifteen years ago?

Does he now speak o' Patty Beech,
The Patty Beech he used to—see,
Or ask at all if Patty Beech
Is known or heard of out this way?
—Ask if ever she's living yet,
And where her present home may be,
And how she bears life's fag and fret
    After so long a day?

In years agone at Hermitage
This faded face was counted fair,
None fairer; and at Hermitage

Casterbridge, Hardy's name for Dorchester, Dorsetshire, as in his novel *The Mayor of Casterbridge*. *Former Beauties*. 7. **Froom,** the river Frome. 8. **Budmouth,** Weymouth. *After the Club-Dance*. 1. **Black'on,** Blackdown Hill. **Maidon,** Maiden Castle, an ancient British fort near Dorchester.

The Inquiry. 1. **Hermitage,** a village near Dorchester. 2. **Ivel Road,** the road to Yeovil. 4. **sengreens,** plants growing in the walls of houses. 7. **hurdled,** made hurdles for enclosing farm or pasture land.

We swore to wed when he should thrive.
But never a chance had he or I,
And waiting made his wish outwear,
And Time, that dooms man's love to die,
Preserves a maid's alive.

6. A WIFE WAITS

Will's at the dance in the Club-room below,
Where the tall liquor-cups foam;
I on the pavement up here by the Bow,
Wait, wait, to steady him home.

Will and his partner are treading a tune,
Loving companions they be;
Willy, before we were married in June,
Said he loved no one but me;

Said he would let his old pleasures all go
Ever to live with his Dear.
Will's at the dance in the Club-room below,
Shivering I wait for him here.

7. AFTER THE FAIR

The singers are gone from the Cornmarket-place
With their broadsheets of rhymes,
The street rings no longer in treble and bass
With their skits on the times,
And the Cross, lately thronged, is a dim naked space
That but echoes the stammering chimes.

From Clock-corner steps, as each quarter ding-dongs,
Away the folk roam
By the "Hart" and Grey's Bridge into byways and "drongs,"
Or across the ridged loam;
The younger ones shrilling the lately heard songs,
The old saying, "Would we were home."

The shy-seeming maiden so mute in the fair
Now rattles and talks,
And that one who looked the most swaggering there
Grows sad as she walks,
And she who seemed eaten by cankering care
In statuesque sturdiness stalks.

And midnight clears High Street of all but the ghosts
Of its buried burghees,
From the latest far back to those old Roman hosts
Whose remains one yet sees,
Who loved, laughed, and fought, hailed their friends, drank their toasts
At their meeting-times here, just as these!

A Wife Waits. **3. the Bow.** "The old name for a curved corner by the cross-streets in the middle of Casterbridge." (Hardy) *After the Fair.* **1. Cornmarket-place,** the central market in Dorchester. **5. Cross,** the intersection of two streets at Cornmarket-place. **7. Clock-corner,** in Dorchester, near St. Peter's Church. **9. "Hart,"** the White Hart, an inn. **Grey's Bridge,** across a branch of the Frome. **"drongs,"** narrow lanes between walls.

After the Fair. **19. High Street,** the chief street of Dorchester. **20. burghees,** citizens. **21. Roman hosts,** Dorchester was an important walled town during the Roman occupation of Britain.

THE MAN HE KILLED

"Had he and I but met
By some old ancient inn,
We should have sat us down to wet
Right many a nipperkin!

"But ranged as infantry,
And staring face to face,
I shot at him as he at me,
And killed him in his place.

"I shot him dead because—
Because he was my foe,
Just so: my foe of course he was;
That's clear enough; although

"He thought he'd 'list, perhaps,
Off-hand like—just as I—
Was out of work—had sold his traps—
No other reason why.

"Yes; quaint and curious war is!
You shoot a fellow down
You'd treat if met where any bar is,
Or help to half-a-crown."

NEW YEAR'S EVE

"I have finished another year," said God,
"In grey, green, white, and brown;
I have strewn the leaf upon the sod,
Sealed up the worm within the clod,
And let the last sun down."

"And what's the good of it?" I said,
"What reasons made you call
From formless void this earth we tread,
When nine-and-ninety can be read
Why nought should be at all?

"Yea, Sire; why shaped you us, 'who in
This tabernacle groan'—
If ever a joy be found herein,
Such joy no man had wished to win
If he had never known!"

Then he: "My labours—logicless—
You may explain; not I:
Sense-sealed I have wrought, without a guess
That I evolved a Consciousness
To ask for reasons why.

"Strange that ephemeral creatures who
By my own ordering are,
Should see the shortness of my view,
Use ethic tests I never knew,
Or made provision for!"

He sank to raptness as of yore,
And opening New Year's Day
Wove it by rote as theretofore,
And went on working evermore
In his unweeting way.

IN TIME OF "THE BREAKING OF NATIONS" [1]

Only a man harrowing clods
In a slow silent walk
With an old horse that stumbles and nods
Half asleep as they stalk.

Only thin smoke without flame
From the heaps of couch-grass;
Yet this will go onward the same
Though Dynasties pass.

Yonder a maid and her wight
Come whispering by:
War's annals will fade into night
Ere their story die.

WHEN I SET OUT FOR LYONNESSE

When I set out for Lyonnesse,
A hundred miles away,
The rime was on the spray,
And starlight lit my lonesomeness
When I set out for Lyonnesse
A hundred miles away.

What would bechance at Lyonnesse
While I should sojourn there
No prophet durst declare,
Nor did the wisest wizard guess
What would bechance at Lyonnesse
While I should sojourn there.

When I came back from Lyonnesse
With magic in my eyes,
All marked with mute surmise
My radiance rare and fathomless,
When I came back from Lyonnesse
With magic in my eyes!

11–12. 'who . . . groan.' See 2 Corinthians 5:4. [1] Cf. Jeremiah 51:20, "Thou art my battle-axe and weapons of war: for with thee will I break in pieces the nations, and with thee will I destroy kingdoms."

THE OXEN [1]

Christmas Eve, and twelve of the clock.
"Now they are all on their knees,"
An elder said as we sat in a flock
By the embers in hearthside ease.

We pictured the meek mild creatures where
They dwelt in their strawy pen,
Nor did it occur to one of us there
To doubt they were kneeling then.

So fair a fancy few would weave
In these years! Yet, I feel,
If someone said on Christmas Eve,
"Come; see the oxen kneel,

"In the lonely barton by yonder coomb
Our childhood used to know,"
I should go with him in the gloom,
Hoping it might be so.

TO THE MOON

"What have you looked at, Moon,
In your time,
Now long past your prime?"
"O, I have looked at, often looked at
Sweet, sublime,
Sore things, shudderful, night and noon
In my time."

"What have you mused on, Moon,
In your day,
So aloof, so far away?"

[1] "The Oxen" is based on the old popular belief that cattle kneel at midnight of Christmas Eve, following the example of the animals in the stable of Bethlehem on the night of Christ's birth. **13. barton,** farmyard. **coomb,** a valley on the flank of a hill.

"O, I have mused on, often mused on
Growth, decay,
Nations alive, dead, mad, aswoon,
In my day!"

"Have you much wondered, Moon,
On your rounds,
Self-wrapt, beyond Earth's bounds?"
"Yea, I have wondered, often wondered
At the sounds
Reaching me of the human tune
On my rounds."

"What do you think of it, Moon,
As you go?
Is Life much, or no?"
"O, I think of it, often think of it
As a show
God ought surely to shut up soon,
As I go."

OLD FURNITURE

I know not how it may be with others
Who sit amid relics of householdry
That date from the days of their mothers' mothers,
But well I know how it is with me
Continually.

I see the hands of the generations
That owned each shiny familiar thing
In play on its knobs and indentations,
And with its ancient fashioning
Still dallying:

Hands behind hands, growing paler and paler,
As in a mirror a candle-flame
Shows images of itself, each frailer
As it recedes, though the eye may frame
Its shape the same.

On the clock's dull dial a foggy finger,
Moving to set the minutes right
With tentative touches that lift and linger
In the wont of a moth on a summer night,
Creeps to my sight.

On this old viol, too, fingers are dancing—
As whilom—just over the strings by the nut,
The tip of a bow receding, advancing
In airy quivers, as if it would cut
The plaintive gut.

And I see a face by that box for tinder,
Glowing forth in fits from the dark,
And fading again, as the linten cinder
Kindles to red at the flinty spark,
Or goes out stark.

Well, well. It is best to be up and doing,
The world has no use for one to-day
Who eyes things thus—no aim pursuing!
He should not continue in this stay,
But sink away.

Joseph Conrad
1857–1924

Incongruous as it may seem, one of the greatest of modern British writers was by birth a Pole. Joseph Conrad was born Teodor Jozef Konrad Korzeniowski in 1857, in the Ukraine, then part of Russia. His parents were well-to-do Polish exiles with a broad cultural background; his father not only wrote poetry, but translated Shakespeare. After the death of his parents Conrad was brought up by an uncle, who made it possible for him to enter the University of Cracow. Although a comfortable and gentlemanly career was planned for him, the boy decided to become a sailor and shipped as a seaman at sixteen. It was a strange choice for the son of Polish aristocrats whose homeland did not even touch the sea, but the lad had already determined to be an Englishman, and, what is more, an English sailor. Before he was twenty-seven he had become a Master in the British Marine and a naturalized British subject, and had changed his name to Joseph Conrad.

He remained at sea for twenty years, not because he was sentimental about the element romanticized by landsmen, but because he was fascinated by the conflict between a sophisticated civilization and incalculable forces which can never be civilized. It seemed to him that men were most themselves when freed from the effects of organized society and pitted against a hostile universe. Sometimes this universe was actively threatening, sometimes it was cruelly apathetic; but it usually called forth man's integrity and, not infrequently, brought a submerged heroism to the surface.

The essentially tragic struggle between nobility and despair, high hope and defeat, is sounded in Conrad's first novel *Almayer's Folly*, 1895. Conrad was almost forty when he wrote it. Within the next twenty years he perfected a prose style and became one of the great masters of modern English fiction. The books which elicited the most praise were the novels *The Nigger of the "Narcissus,"* 1898; *Lord Jim*, 1900; *Victory*, 1915; and the shorter tales *Typhoon*, 1902, *Youth*, 1902, *Heart of Darkness*, 1902, and *Within the Tides*, 1915. (A book of the complete short stories of Conrad was posthumously issued in 1933.) His first volume was published a few months after he left the sea (in 1894), married an Englishwoman, and settled in England. Although he learned the nuances of his adopted language, from the simplest idioms to the most ornate figures of speech, he spoke with a foreign accent until the day of his death, August 3, 1924.

Conrad's attitude to life and art has been the subject of much controversy. It is an intellectual rather than a philosophical attitude. The spectacle of life fills him with pessimism—"if you take it to heart it becomes an unendurable tragedy"—but it is as a spectacle that he regards life. "I would fondly believe that its purpose is purely spectacular," he wrote, and such a conclusion explains Conrad's passion for observation and aloofness. Existence, to him, is full of terror and hidden evil, but he devotes himself to a magic suggestiveness and "the few particles of truth floating in an ocean of insignificance." His indirect method of narration is famous and characteristic. Conrad is so anxious to appear objective, to avoid any possibility of being identified with his characters, that he goes to some length to remain outside of his work. Often he tells a story within the frame of another story or employs a narrator as disinterested agent and recording eye. Two of his most notable tales, *Youth* and *Heart of Darkness*, unfortunately too long to include here, are related through Marlow, a character used for no other purpose than to restrict the author's personal "point of view."

The story-within-a-story method, employed in "The Tale" and elsewhere, results in a roundabout approach, a somewhat rambling beginning, and a tendency to slow up the narrative. But it makes for an almost complete detachment, and a sense of actuality of the thing recorded and retold rather than invented. "The Tale" is one of Conrad's later stories. In its exploration of the human heart in time of inner crisis, as well as in manner of telling, it illustrates the distinctive qualities of its author.

A small literature has grown up about Conrad and his work. Perhaps the most important are his own critical studies, *Notes on Life and Letters*, 1921, and *Notes on My Books*, 1921. A biography was published by Conrad's widow in 1935. Conrad's reputation, very high at the time of his death, suffered an inevitable decline in the thirties. There are now signs, however, of his return to critical esteem. A literary generation that sets much value on the uses of symbolism, an important artistic device in Conrad's method, also looks with favor on the moral centrality of his work.

THE TALE[1]

OUTSIDE the large single window the crepuscular light was dying out slowly in a great square gleam without colour, framed rigidly in the gathering shades of the room.

It was a long room. The irresistible tide of the night ran into the most distant part of it, where the whispering of a man's voice, passionately interrupted and passionately renewed, seemed to plead against the answering murmurs of infinite sadness.

At last no answering murmur came. His movement when he rose slowly from his knees by the side of the deep, shadowy couch holding the shadowy suggestion of a reclining woman revealed him tall under the low ceiling, and somber all over except for the crude discord of the white collar under the shape of his head and the faint, minute spark of a brass button here and there on his uniform.

He stood over her a moment, masculine and mysterious in his immobility, before he sat down on a chair near by. He could see only the faint oval of her upturned face and, extended on her black dress, her pale hands, a moment before abandoned to his kisses, and now as if too weary to move.

He dared not make a sound, shrinking as a man would do from the prosaic necessities of existence. As usual, it was the woman who had the courage. Her voice was heard first—almost conventional while her being vibrated yet with conflicting emotions.

"Tell me something," she said.

The darkness hid his surprise and then his smile. Had he not just said to her everything worth saying in the world—and that not for the first time!

"What am I to tell you?" he asked, in a voice

[1] From *Tales of Hearsay*, 1925. Reprinted by permission of J. M. Dent & Sons Ltd.

credibly steady. He was beginning to feel grateful to her for that something final in her tone which had eased the strain.

"Why not tell me a tale?"

"A tale!" He was really amazed.

"Yes. Why not?"

These words came with a slight petulance, the hint of a loved woman's capricious will, which is capricious only because it feels itself to be a law, embarrassing sometimes and always difficult to elude.

"Why not?" he repeated, with a slightly mocking accent, as though he had been asked to give her the moon. But now he was feeling a little angry with her for that feminine mobility that slips out of an emotion as easily as out of a splendid gown.

He had heard her say, a little unsteadily, with a sort of fluttering intonation which made him think suddenly of a butterfly's flight:

"You used to tell—your—your simple and—and professional—tales very well at one time. Or well enough to interest me. You had a—a sort of art—in the days—the days before the war."

"Really?" he said, with involuntary gloom. "But now, you see, the war is going on," he continued in such a dead, equable tone that she felt a slight chill fall over her shoulders. And yet she persisted. For there's nothing more unswerving in the world than a woman's caprice.

"It could be a tale not of this world," she explained.

"You want a tale of the other, the better world?" he asked, with a matter-of-fact surprise. "You must evoke for that task those who have already gone there."

"No. I don't mean that. I mean another—some other—world. In the universe—not in heaven."

"I am relieved. But you forget that I have only five days' leave."

"Yes. And I've also taken five days' leave from —from my duties."

"I like that word."

"What word?"

"Duty."

"It is horrible—sometimes."

"Oh, that's because you think it's narrow. But it isn't. It contains infinities, and—and so——"

"What is this jargon?"

He disregarded the interjected scorn. "An infinity of absolution, for instance," he continued. "But as to this 'another world'—who's going to look for it and for the tale that is in it?"

"You," she said, with a strange, almost rough, sweetness of assertion.

He made a shadowy movement of assent in his chair, the irony of which not even the gathered darkness could render mysterious.

"As you will. In that world, then, there was once upon a time a Commanding Officer and a Northman. Put in the capitals, please, because they had no other names. It was a world of seas and continents and islands——"

"Like the earth," she murmured, bitterly.

"Yes. What else could you expect from sending a man made of our common, tormented clay on a voyage of discovery? What else could he find? What else could you understand or care for, or feel the existence of, even? There was comedy in it, and slaughter."

"Always like the earth," she murmured.

"Always. And since I could find in the universe only what was deeply rooted in the fibres of my being, there was love in it, too. But we won't talk of that."

"No. We won't," she said, in a neutral tone which concealed perfectly her relief—or her disappointment. Then after a pause she added: "It's going to be a comic story."

"Well——" he paused, too. "Yes. In a way. In a very grim way. It will be human, and, as you know, comedy is but a matter of the visual angle. And it won't be a noisy story. All the long guns in it will be dumb—as dumb as so many telescopes."

"Ah, there are guns in it, then! And may I ask—where?"

"Afloat. You remember that the world of which we speak had its seas. A war was going on in it. It was a funny world and terribly in earnest. Its war was being carried on over the land, over the water, under the water, up in the air, and even under the ground. And many young men in it, mostly in wardrooms and messrooms, used to say to each other—pardon the unparliamentary word —they used to say, 'It's a damned bad war, but it's better than no war at all.' Sounds flippant, doesn't it?"

He heard a nervous, impatient sigh in the depths of the couch while he went on without a pause.

"And yet there is more in it than meets the eye. I mean more wisdom. Flippancy, like comedy, is but a matter of visual first-impression. That world was not very wise. But there was in it a certain amount of common working sagacity. That, however, was mostly worked by the neutrals in diverse ways, public and private, which had to be watched; watched by acute minds and also by actual sharp eyes. They had to be very sharp indeed, too, I assure you."

"I can imagine," she murmured, appreciatively.

"What is there that you can't imagine?" he pronounced, soberly. "You have the world in you. But let us go back to our Commanding Officer, who, of course, commanded a ship of a sort. My tales, if often professional (as you remarked just now), have never been technical. So I'll just tell you that the ship was of a very ornamental sort once, with lots of grace and elegance and luxury about her. Yes, once! She was like a pretty woman who had suddenly put on a suit of sackcloth and stuck revolvers in her belt. But she floated lightly, she moved nimbly, she was quite good enough."

"That was the opinion of the Commanding Officer?" said the voice from the couch.

"It was. He used to be sent out with her along certain coasts to see—what he could see. Just that. And sometimes he had some preliminary information to help him, and sometimes he had not. And it was all one, really. It was about as useful as information trying to convey the locality and intentions of a cloud, of a phantom taking shape here and there and impossible to seize, would have been.

"It was in the early days of the war. What at first used to amaze the Commanding Officer was the unchanged face of the waters, with its familiar expression, neither more friendly nor more hostile. On fine days the sun strikes sparks upon the blue; here and there a peaceful smudge of smoke hangs in the distance, and it is impossible to believe that the familiar clear horizon traces the limit of one great circular ambush.

"Yes, it is impossible to believe, till some day you see a ship not your own ship (that isn't so impressive), but some ship in company, blow up all of a sudden and plop under her almost before you know what has happened to her. Then you begin to believe. Henceforth you go out for the work to see—what you can see, and you keep on at it with the conviction that some day you will die from something you have not seen. One envies the soldiers at the end of the day, wiping the sweat and blood from their faces, counting the dead fallen to their hands, looking at the devastated fields, the torn earth that seems to suffer and bleed with them. One does, really. The final brutality of it—the taste of primitive passion—the ferocious frankness of the blow struck with one's hand—the direct call and the straight response. Well, the sea gave you nothing of that, and seemed to pretend that there was nothing the matter with the world."

She interrupted, stirring a little.

"Oh, yes. Sincerity—frankness—passion—three words of your gospel. Don't I know them!"

"Think! Isn't it ours—believed in common?" he asked, anxiously, yet without expecting an answer, and went on at once: "Such were the feelings of the Commanding Officer. When the night came trailing over the sea, hiding what looked like the hypocrisy of an old friend, it was a relief. The night blinds you frankly—and there are circumstances when the sunlight may grow as odious to one as falsehood itself. Night is all right.

"At night the Commanding Officer could let his thoughts get away—I won't tell you where. Somewhere where there was no choice but between truth and death. But thick weather, though it blinded one, brought no such relief. Mist is deceitful, the dead luminosity of the fog is irritating. It seems that you *ought* to see.

"One gloomy, nasty day the ship was steaming along her beat in sight of a rocky, dangerous coast that stood out intensely black like an India-ink drawing on grey paper. Presently the second in command spoke to his chief. He thought he saw something on the water, to seaward. Small wreckage, perhaps.

" 'But there shouldn't be any wreckage here, sir,' he remarked.

" 'No,' said the Commanding Officer. 'The last reported submarined ships were sunk a long way to the westward. But one never knows. There may have been others since then not reported nor seen. Gone with all hands.'

"That was how it began. The ship's course was altered to pass the object close; for it was necessary to have a good look at what one could see. Close, but without touching; for it was not advisable to come in contact with objects of any form whatever floating casually about. Close, but without stopping or even diminishing speed; for in those times it was not prudent to linger on any particular spot, even for a moment. I may tell you at once that the object was not dangerous in itself. No use in describing it. It may have been nothing more remarkable than, say, a barrel of a certain shape and colour. But it was significant.

"The smooth bow-wave hove it up as if for a closer inspection, and then the ship, brought again to her course, turned her back on it with indifference, while twenty pairs of eyes on her deck stared in all directions trying to see—what they could see.

"The Commanding Officer and his second in command discussed the object with understanding. It appeared to them to be not so much a proof of the sagacity as of the activity of certain neutrals. This activity had in many cases taken the form of replenishing the stores of certain submarines at sea. This was generally believed, if not absolutely known. But the very nature of things in those early days pointed that way. The object, looked at closely and turned away from with apparent indifference, put it beyond doubt that something of the sort had been done somewhere in the neighbourhood.

"The object in itself was more than suspect. But the fact of its being left in evidence roused other suspicions. Was it the result of some deep and devilish purpose? As to that, all speculation soon appeared to be a vain thing. Finally the two officers came to the conclusion that it was left there most likely by accident, complicated possibly by some unforeseen necessity; such, perhaps, as the sudden need to get away quickly from the spot, or something of that kind.

"Their discussion had been carried on in curt, weighty phrases, separated by long, thoughtful silences. And all the time their eyes roamed about the horizon in an everlasting, almost mechanical effort of vigilance. The younger man summed up grimly:

" 'Well, it's evidence. That's what this is. Evidence of what we were pretty certain of before. And plain, too.'

" 'And much good it will do to us,' retorted the Commanding Officer. 'The parties are miles away; the submarine, devil only knows where, ready to kill; and the noble neutral slipping away to the eastward, ready to lie!'

"The second in command laughed a little at the tone. But he guessed that the neutral wouldn't even have to lie very much. Fellows like that, unless caught in the very act, felt themselves pretty safe. They could afford to chuckle. That fellow was probably chuckling to himself. It's very possible he had been before at the game and didn't care a rap for the bit of evidence left behind. It was a game in which practice made one bold and successful, too.

"And again he laughed faintly. But his Commanding Officer was in revolt against the murderous stealthiness of methods and the atrocious callousness of complicities that seemed to taint the very source of men's deep emotions and noblest activities; to corrupt their imagination which builds up the final conceptions of life and death. He suffered——"

The voice from the sofa interrupted the narrator.

"How well I can understand that in him!"

He bent forward slightly.

"Yes. I, too. Everything should be open in love and war. Open as the day, since both are the call of an ideal which it is so easy, so terribly easy, to degrade in the name of Victory."

He paused; then went on:

"I don't know that the Commanding Officer delved so deep as that into his feelings. But he did suffer from them—a sort of disenchanted sadness. It is possible, even, that he suspected himself of folly. Man is various. But he had no time for much introspection, because from the southwest a wall of fog had advanced upon his ship. Great convolutions of vapours flew over, swirling about masts and funnel, which looked as if they were beginning to melt. Then they vanished.

"The ship was stopped, all sounds ceased, and the very fog became motionless, growing denser and as if solid in its amazing dumb immobility. The men at their stations lost sight of each other. Footsteps sounded stealthy; rare voices, impersonal and remote, died out without resonance. A blind, white stillness took possession of the world.

"It looked, too, as if it would last for days. I don't mean to say that the fog did not vary a little in its density. Now and then it would thin out mysteriously, revealing to the men a more or less ghostly presentment of their ship. Several times the shadow of the coast itself swam darkly before their eyes through the fluctuating opaque brightness of the great white cloud clinging to the water.

"Taking advantage of these moments, the ship had been moved cautiously nearer the shore. It was useless to remain out in such thick weather. Her officers knew every nook and cranny of the coast along their beat. They thought that she would be much better in a certain cove. It wasn't a large place, just ample room for a ship to swing at her anchor. She would have an easier time of it till the fog lifted up.

"Slowly, with infinite caution and patience, they crept closer and closer, seeing no more of the cliffs than an evanescent dark loom with a narrow border of angry foam at its foot. At the moment of anchoring the fog was so thick that for all they could see they might have been a thousand miles out in the open sea. Yet the shelter of the land could be felt. There was a peculiar quality in the stillness of the air. Very faint, very elusive, the wash of the ripple against the encircling land reached their ears, with mysterious sudden pauses.

"The anchor dropped, the leads were laid in. The Commanding Officer went below into his cabin. But he had not been there very long when a voice outside his door requested his presence on deck. He thought to himself: 'What is it now?' He felt some impatience at being called out again to face the wearisome fog.

"He found that it had thinned again a little

and had taken on a gloomy hue from the dark cliffs which had no form, no outline, but asserted themselves as a curtain of shadows all round the ship, except in one bright spot, which was the entrance from the open sea. Several officers were looking that way from the bridge. The second in command met him with the breathlessly whispered information that there was another ship in the cove.

“She had been made out by several pairs of eyes only a couple of minutes before. She was lying at anchor very near the entrance—a mere vague blot on the fog's brightness. And the Commanding Officer, by staring in the direction pointed out to him by eager hands, ended by distinguishing it at last himself. Indubitably a vessel of some sort.

“ ‘It's a wonder we didn't run slap into her when coming in,’ observed the second in command.

“ ‘Send a boat on board before she vanishes,’ said the Commanding Officer. He surmised that this was a coaster. It could hardly be anything else. But another thought came into his head suddenly. ‘It is a wonder,’ he said to his second in command, who had rejoined him after sending the boat away.

“By that time both of them had been struck by the fact that the ship so suddenly discovered had not manifested her presence by ringing her bell.

“ ‘We came in very quietly, that's true,’ concluded the younger officer. ‘But they must have heard our leadsmen at least. We couldn't have passed her more than fifty yards off. The closest shave! They may even have made us out, since they were aware of something coming in. And the strange thing is that we never heard a sound from her. The fellows on board must have been holding their breath.’

“ ‘Aye,’ said the Commanding Officer, thoughtfully.

“In due course the boarding-boat returned, appearing suddenly alongside, as though she had burrowed her way under the fog. The officer in charge came up to make his report, but the Commanding Officer didn't give him time to begin. He cried from a distance:

“ ‘Coaster, isn't she?’

“ ‘No, sir. A stranger—a neutral,’ was the answer.

“ ‘No. Really! Well, tell us all about it. What is she doing here?’

“The young man stated then that he had been told a long and complicated story of engine troubles. But it was plausible enough from a strictly professional point of view, and it had the usual features: disablement, dangerous drifting along the shore, weather more or less thick for days, fear of a gale, ultimately a resolve to go in and anchor anywhere on the coast, and so on. Fairly plausible.

“ ‘Engines still disabled?’ inquired the Commanding Officer.

“ ‘No, sir. She has steam on them.’

“The Commanding Officer took his second aside. ‘By Jove!’ he said, ‘you were right! They were holding their breaths as we passed them. They were.’

“But the second in command had his doubts now.

“ ‘A fog like this does muffle small sounds, sir,’ he remarked. ‘And what could his object be, after all?’

“ ‘To sneak out unnoticed,’ answered the Commanding Officer.

“ ‘Then why didn't he? He might have done it, you know. Not exactly unnoticed, perhaps. I don't suppose he could have slipped his cable without making some noise. Still, in a minute or so he would have been lost to view—clean gone before we had made him out fairly. Yet he didn't.’

“They looked at each other. The Commanding Officer shook his head. Such suspicions as the one which had entered his head are not defended easily. He did not even state it openly. The boarding officer finished his report. The cargo of the ship was a harmless and useful character. She was bound to an English port. Papers and everything in perfect order. Nothing suspicious to be detected anywhere.

“Then passing to the men, he reported the crew on deck as the usual lot. Engineers of the well-known type, and very full of their achievement in repairing the engines. The mate surly. The master rather a fine specimen of a Northman, civil enough, but appeared to have been drinking. Seemed to be recovering from a regular bout of it.

“ ‘I told him I couldn't give him permission to proceed. He said he wouldn't dare to move his ship her own length out in such weather as this, permission or no permission. I left a man on board, though.’

“ ‘Quite right.’

“The Commanding Officer, after communing with his suspicions for a time, called his second aside.

“ ‘What if she were the very ship which had been feeding some infernal submarine or other?’ he said in an undertone.

“The other started. Then, with conviction:

“ ‘She would get off scot-free. You couldn't prove it, sir.’

" 'I want to look into it myself.'

" 'From the report we've heard I am afraid you couldn't even make a case for reasonable suspicion, sir.'

" 'I'll go on board all the same.'

"He had made up his mind. Curiosity is the great motive power of hatred and love. What did he expect to find? He could not have told anybody—not even himself.

"What he really expected to find there was the atmosphere, the atmosphere of gratuitous treachery, which in his view nothing could excuse; for he thought that even a passion of unrighteousness for its own sake could not excuse that. But could he detect it? Sniff it? Taste it? Receive some mysterious communication which would turn his invincible suspicions into a certitude strong enough to provoke action with all its risks?

"The master met him on the after-deck, looming up in the fog amongst the blurred shapes of the usual ship's fittings. He was a robust Northman, bearded, and in the force of his age. A round leather cap fitted his head closely. His hands were rammed deep into the pockets of his short leather jacket. He kept them there while he explained that at sea he lived in the chart-room, and led the way there, striding carelessly. Just before reaching the door under the bridge he staggered a little, recovered himself, flung it open, and stood aside, leaning his shoulder as if involuntarily against the side of the house, and staring vaguely into the fog-filled space. But he followed the Commanding Officer at once, flung the door to, snapped on the electric light, and hastened to thrust his hands back into his pockets, as though afraid of being seized by them either in friendship or in hostility.

"The place was stuffy and hot. The usual chart-rack overhead was full, and the chart on the table was kept unrolled by an empty cup standing on a saucer half-full of some spilt dark liquid. A slightly nibbled biscuit reposed on the chronometer-case. There were two settees, and one of them had been made up into a bed with a pillow and some blankets, which were now very much tumbled. The Northman let himself fall on it, his hands still in his pockets.

" 'Well, here I am,' he said, with a curious air of being surprised at the sound of his own voice.

"The Commanding Officer from the other settee observed the handsome, flushed face. Drops of fog hung on the yellow beard and moustache of the Northman. The much darker eyebrows ran together in a puzzled frown, and suddenly he jumped up.

" 'What I mean is that I don't know where I am. I really don't,' he burst out, with extreme earnestness. 'Hang it all! I got turned around somehow. The fog has been after me for a week. More than a week. And then my engines broke down. I will tell you how it was.'

"He burst out into loquacity. It was not hurried, but it was insistent. It was not continuous, for all that. It was broken by the most queer, thoughtful pauses. Each of these pauses lasted no more than a couple of seconds, and each had the profundity of an endless meditation. When he began again nothing betrayed in him the slightest consciousness of these intervals. There was the same fixed glance, the same unchanged earnestness of tone. He didn't know. Indeed, more than one of these pauses occurred in the middle of a sentence.

"The Commanding Officer listened to the tale. It struck him as more plausible than simple truth is in the habit of being. But that, perhaps, was prejudice. All the time the Northman was speaking the Commanding Officer had been aware of an inward voice, a grave murmur in the depth of his very own self, telling another tale, as if on purpose to keep alive in him his indignation and his anger with that baseness of greed or of mere outlook which lies often at the root of simple ideas.

"It was the story that had been already told to the boarding officer an hour or so before. The Commanding Officer nodded slightly at the Northman from time to time. The latter came to an end and turned his eyes away. He added, as an afterthought:

" 'Wasn't it enough to drive a man out of his mind with worry? And it's my first voyage to this part, too. And the ship's my own. Your officer has seen the papers. She isn't much, as you can see for yourself. Just an old cargo-boat. Bare living for my family.'

"He raised a big arm to point at a row of photographs plastering the bulkhead. The movement was ponderous, as if the arm had been made of lead. The Commanding Officer said, carelessly:

" 'You will be making a fortune yet for your family with this old ship.'

" 'Yes, if I don't lose her,' said the Northman, gloomily.

" 'I mean—out of this war,' added the Commanding Officer.

"The Northman stared at him in a curiously unseeing and at the same time interested manner, as only eyes of a particular blue shade can stare.

" 'And you wouldn't be angry at it,' he said,

'would you? You are too much of a gentleman. We didn't bring this on you. And suppose we sat down and cried. What good would that be? Let those cry who made the trouble,' he concluded, with energy. 'Time's money, you say. Well—*this* time *is* money. Oh! isn't it!'

"The Commanding Officer tried to keep under the feeling of immense disgust. He said to himself that it was unreasonable. Men were like that—moral cannibals feeding on each other's misfortunes. He said aloud:

" 'You have made it perfectly plain how it is that you are here. Your log-book confirms you very minutely. Of course, a log-book may be cooked. Nothing easier.'

"The Northman never moved a muscle. He was gazing at the floor; he seemed not to have heard. He raised his head after a while.

" 'But you can't suspect me of anything,' he muttered, negligently.

"The Commanding Officer thought: 'Why should he say this?'

"Immediately afterwards the man before him added: 'My cargo is for an English port.'

"His voice had turned husky for the moment. The Commanding Officer reflected: 'That's true. There can be nothing. I can't suspect him. Yet why was he lying with steam up in this fog—and then, hearing us come in, why didn't he give some sign of life? Why? Could it be anything else but a guilty conscience? He could tell by the leadsmen that this was a man-of-war.'

"Yes—why? The Commanding Officer went on thinking: 'Suppose I ask him and then watch his face. He will betray himself in some way. It's perfectly plain that the fellow *has* been drinking. Yes, he has been drinking; but he will have a lie ready all the same.' The Commanding Officer was one of those men who are made morally and almost physically uncomfortable by the mere thought of having to beat down a lie. He shrank from the act in scorn and disgust, which were invincible because more temperamental than moral.

"So he went out on deck instead and had the crew mustered formally for his inspection. He found them very much what the report of the boarding officer had led him to expect. And from their answers to his questions he could discover no flaw in the log-book story.

"He dismissed them. His impression of them was—a picked lot; have been promised a fistful of money each if this came off; all slightly anxious, but not frightened. Not a single one of them likely to give the show away. They don't feel in danger of their life. They know England and English ways too well!

"He felt alarmed at catching himself thinking as if his vaguest suspicions were turning into a certitude. For, indeed, there was no shadow of reason for his inferences. There was nothing to give away.

"He returned to the chart-room. The Northman had lingered behind there; and something subtly different in his bearing, more bold in his blue, glassy stare, induced the Commanding Officer to conclude that the fellow had snatched at the opportunity to take another swig at the bottle he must have had concealed somewhere.

"He noticed, too, that the Northman on meeting his eyes put on an elaborately surprised expression. At least, it seemed elaborated. Nothing could be trusted. And the Englishman felt himself with astonishing conviction faced by an enormous lie, solid like a wall, with no way round to get at the truth, whose ugly murderous face he seemed to see peeping over at him with a cynical grin.

" 'I dare say,' he began, suddenly, 'you are wondering at my proceedings, though I am not detaining you, am I? You wouldn't dare to move in this fog?'

" 'I don't know where I am,' the Northman ejaculated, earnestly. 'I really don't.'

"He looked around as if the very chart-room fittings were strange to him. The Commanding Officer asked him whether he had not seen any unusual objects floating about while he was at sea.

" 'Objects! What objects? We were groping blind in the fog for days.'

" 'We had a few clear intervals,' said the Commanding Officer. 'And I'll tell you what we have seen and the conclusion I've come to about it.'

"He told him in a few words. He heard the sound of a sharp breath indrawn through closed teeth. The Northman with his hand on the table stood absolutely motionless and dumb. He stood as if thunderstruck. Then he produced a fatuous smile.

"Or at least so it appeared to the Commanding Officer. Was this significant, or of no meaning whatever? He didn't know, he couldn't tell. All the truth had departed out of the world as if drawn in, absorbed in this monstrous villainy this man was—or was not—guilty of.

" 'Shooting's too good for people that conceive neutrality in this pretty way,' remarked the Commanding Officer, after a silence.

" 'Yes, yes, yes,' the Northman assented, hurriedly

—then added an unexpected and dreamy-voiced 'Perhaps.'

"Was he pretending to be drunk, or only trying to appear sober? His glance was straight, but it was somewhat glazed. His lips outlined themselves firmly under his yellow moustache. But they twitched. Did they twitch? And why was he drooping like this in his attitude?

" 'There's no perhaps about it,' pronounced the Commanding Officer sternly.

"The Northman had straightened himself. And unexpectedly he looked stern, too.

" 'No. But what about the tempters? Better kill that lot off. There's about four, five, six million of them,' he said, grimly; but in a moment changed into a whining key. 'But I had better hold my tongue. You have some suspicions.'

" 'No, I've no suspicions,' declared the Commanding Officer.

"He never faltered. At that moment he had the certitude. The air of the chart-room was thick with guilt and falsehood braving the discovery, defying simple right, common decency, all humanity of feeling, every scruple of conduct.

"The Northman drew a long breath. 'Well, we know that you English are gentlemen. But let us speak the truth. Why should we love you so very much? You haven't done anything to be loved. We don't love the other people, of course. They haven't done anything for that, either. A fellow comes along with a bag of gold . . . I haven't been in Rotterdam my last voyage for nothing.'

" 'You may be able to tell something interesting, then, to our people when you come into port,' interjected the officer.

" 'I might. But you keep some people in your pay at Rotterdam. Let them report. I am a neutral—am I not? . . . Have you ever seen a poor man on one side and a bag of gold on the other? Of course, I couldn't be tempted. I haven't the nerve for it. Really I haven't. It's nothing to me. I am just talking openly for once.'

" 'Yes. And I am listening to you,' said the Commanding Officer, quietly.

"The Northman leaned forward over the table. 'Now that I know you have no suspicions, I talk. You don't know what a poor man is. I do. I am poor myself. This old ship, she isn't much, and she is mortgaged, too. Bare living, no more. Of course, I wouldn't have the nerve. But a man who has nerve! See. The stuff he takes aboard looks like any other cargo—packages, barrels, tins, copper tubes—what not. He doesn't see it work. It isn't real to him. But he sees the gold. That's real. Of course, nothing could induce me. I suffer from an internal disease. I would either go crazy from anxiety—or—or—take to drink or something. The risk is too great. Why—ruin!'

" 'It should be death.' The Commanding Officer got up, after this curt declaration, which the other received with a hard stare oddly combined with an uncertain smile. The officer's gorge rose at the atmosphere of murderous complicity which surrounded him, denser, more impenetrable, more acrid than the fog outside.

" 'It's nothing to me,' murmured the Northman, swaying visibly.

" 'Of course not,' assented the Commanding Officer, with a great effort to keep his voice calm and low. The certitude was strong within him. 'But I am going to clear all you fellows off this coast at once. And I will begin with you. You must leave in half an hour.'

"By that time the officer was walking along the deck with the Northman at his elbow.

" 'What! In this fog?' the latter cried out, huskily.

" 'Yes, you will have to go in this fog.'

" 'But I don't know where I am. I really don't.'

"The Commanding Officer turned round. A sort of fury possessed him. The eyes of the two men met. Those of the Northman expressed a profound amazement.

" 'Oh, you don't know how to get out.' The Commanding Officer spoke with composure, but his heart was beating with anger and dread. 'I will give you your course. Steer south-by-east-half-east for about four miles and then you will be clear to haul to the eastward for your port. The weather will clear up before very long.'

" 'Must I? What could induce me? I haven't the nerve.'

" 'And yet you must go. Unless you want to——'

" 'I don't want to,' panted the Northman. 'I've enough of it.'

"The Commanding Officer got over the side. The Northman remained still, as if rooted to the deck. Before his boat reached his ship the Commanding Officer heard the steamer beginning to pick up her anchor. Then, shadowy in the fog, she steamed out on the given course.

" 'Yes,' he said to his officers, 'I let him go.' "

The narrator bent forward toward the couch, where no movement betrayed the presence of a living person.

"Listen," he said, forcibly. "That course would lead the Northman straight on a deadly ledge of rock. And the Commanding Officer gave it to him. He steamed out—ran on it—and went down. So he had spoken the truth. He did not know where he was. But it proves nothing. Nothing either way. It may have been the only truth in all his story. And yet. . . . He seems to have been driven out by a menacing stare—nothing more."

He abandoned all pretence.

"Yes, I gave that course to him. It seemed to me a supreme test. I believe—no, I don't believe. I don't know. At the time I was certain. They all went down; and I don't know whether I have done stern retribution—or murder; whether I have added to the corpses that litter the bed of the unreadable sea the bodies of men completely innocent or basely guilty. I don't know. I shall never know."

He rose. The woman on the couch got up and threw her arms round his neck. Her eyes put two gleams in the deep shadow of the room. She knew his passion for truth, his horror of deceit, his humanity.

"Oh, my poor, poor——"

"I shall never know," he repeated, sternly, disengaged himself, pressed her hands to his lips, and went out.

A. E. Housman

1859–1936

No English writer has ever been more closely identified with the border county of Shropshire than A. E. Housman. Born there in the village of Bromsgrove on March 26, 1859, Housman made Shropshire the scene of practically all his verse. He was educated at Oxford and became a Higher Division Clerk in the British Patent Office for ten years. In 1892 he left the Office, where he said he "did as little as possible," to become a teacher. As a professor of Latin (first at University College, London, later at Cambridge) he became one of the great scholars of his day. Shy in his personal life, in his scholarly papers he wrote with confident authority and often with sarcasm and cold invective. The introductions to his editions of Manilius, Juvenal, and Lucan reveal Housman's admiration for chiseled form and his contempt for carelessness. But these were the preoccupations of the Latinist; as a person Housman discouraged controversies and avoided intimacies. A fellow poet, Wilfrid Scawen Blunt, wrote of him, "He does not smoke, drinks little, and would, I think, be quite silent if he were allowed to be." Housman said wryly that the description seemed accurate, except that Blunt offered him little to drink.

Housman's edition of Manilius, published in 1932, represents an analysis of that author which occupied him for a full quarter of a century. A year after completion of this work, Housman's health began to fail. Nevertheless he continued to attend classes. Arguing that lecturing was a pleasure as well as a duty, he gave two lectures on Horace during the Lent term in 1936. He never completed the course. He died on April 30, 1936.

It is not, however, Housman's work as scholar and editor which spread his reputation beyond classical circles. He became internationally famous as the poet of *A Shropshire Lad*, 1896. His entire literary output during his life consisted of two small volumes of poetry and one or two essays, of which *The Name and Nature of Poetry*, 1933, is the most trenchant and controversial. More than twenty-five years elapsed between the publication of *A Shropshire Lad* and an equally small volume significantly entitled *Last Poems*, 1922. A posthumous *More Poems*, edited by his brother Laurence, was published in 1936.

With the exception of Fitzgerald's translation of *The Rubáiyát of Omar Khayyám* no book of poetry of the period was more popular than *A Shropshire Lad;* none was so widely quoted. Although the former is Oriental and the latter Occidental, both books voice the same basic philosophy. It is a negative philosophy, a pessimistic extension of the theme, "Eat, drink, and be merry, for tomorrow we die." Housman's fatalism is the darker of the two. Omar rejects a difficult and unjust world and comforts himself with a life of sheer sensation; Housman's lads escape only by suicide. That these volumes should have elicited so enthusiastic a response—especially from young people—is not a strange phenomenon. Readers were captivated by the quick turn of phrase, the charming sophistications and deceptive simplicities, the brisk rhythms, the appeal of easy recklessness, the subdued melancholy.

Housman's infectious verse presents a queer paradox. In the blithest measures he assures us that the world is evil, that men and girls are untrue, that we are roused to struggles that have no reason, and that Nature is only a little more inhuman than human nature. Train for ill and not for good, Housman warns us with fierce stoicism and bright jog-trot tunes. There is joy and beauty to be snatched, but there is endless injustice to be endured. The quiet countryside teaches us fortitude in its haphazard cruelty. "Luck's a chance, but trouble's sure," Housman repeats like a cheerful prophet of doom; men are noblest when, realizing the futility of their efforts, they still struggle against frustration. Housman, remembering his favorite classics, ironically reminds us that we must be patient even in our disbelief; our tragedy is an ancient one: "The troubles of our proud and angry dust are from eternity, and shall not fail."

Grim this undoubtedly is; but the music is gay. With unsurpassed artistry Housman composed stanza after stanza which echoes in the ear and cannot be shaken from the mind. His is a stripped verse, almost bare of decoration. But the spareness gives it precision, and the elimination of ornament gives it strength. Not since the Elizabethans have there been lyrics so delicate and yet so firm, so seemingly casual yet so inevitable. "Loveliest of Trees," "When I Was One-and-Twenty," "Reveille," "Is My Team Ploughing?" "To an Athlete Dying Young"—to name only a few of the favorites—have the authority that comes with age and tradition. Although written in our own period, they seem part of the permanent literature of the English language. They are small; they are limited in range and sometimes inflexible because of their overdisciplined line. But many of them are as nearly perfect as lyrics can be.

LOVELIEST OF TREES[1]

Loveliest of trees, the cherry now
Is hung with bloom along the bough,
And stands about the woodland ride
Wearing white for Eastertide.

[1] This and the following poems by A. E. Housman are from *The Collected Poems of A. E. Housman*. Copyright, 1922, 1940, by Henry Holt and Company, Inc. Copyright, 1936, 1950, by Barclays Bank, Ltd. Used by permission of the publishers and of The Society of Authors as the Literary Representative of the Trustees of the Estate of the late A. E. Housman, and Messrs. Jonathan Cape, Ltd., publishers of A. E. Housman's Collected Poems. *Loveliest of Trees.* **3. woodland ride,** a narrow forest road.

Now, of my threescore years and ten,
Twenty will not come again,
And take from seventy springs a score,
It only leaves me fifty more.

And since to look at things in bloom
Fifty springs are little room,
About the woodlands I will go
To see the cherry hung with snow.

WHEN SMOKE STOOD UP FROM LUDLOW

When smoke stood up from Ludlow,
  And mist blew off from Teme,
And blithe afield to ploughing
  Against the morning beam
  I strode beside my team,

The blackbird in the coppice
  Looked out to see me stride,
And hearkened as I whistled
  The trampling team beside,
  And fluted and replied:

"Lie down, lie down, young yeoman;
  What use to rise and rise?
Rise man a thousand mornings
  Yet down at last he lies,
  And then the man is wise."

I heard the tune he sang me,
  And spied his yellow bill;
I picked a stone and aimed it
  And threw it with a will:
  Then the bird was still.

Then my soul within me
  Took up the blackbird's strain,
And still beside the horses
  Along the dewy lane
  It sang the song again:

"Lie down, lie down, young yeoman;
  The sun moves always west;
The road one treads to labour
  Will lead one home to rest,
  And that will be the best."

REVEILLE

Wake: the silver dusk returning
  Up the beach of darkness brims,

When Smoke Stood Up. **6. coppice,** a thicket, copse, underbrush.

And the ship of sunrise burning
 Strands upon the eastern rims.

Wake: the vaulted shadow shatters,
 Trampled to the floor it spanned,
And the tent of night in tatters
 Straws the sky-pavilioned land.

Up, lad, up, 'tis late for lying:
 Hear the drums of morning play;
Hark, the empty highways crying
 "Who'll beyond the hills away?"

Towns and countries woo together,
 Forelands beacon, belfries call;
Never lad that trod on leather
 Lived to feast his heart with all.

Up, lad: thews that lie and cumber
 Sunlit pallets never thrive;
Morns abed and daylight slumber
 Were not meant for man alive.

Clay lies still, but blood's a rover;
 Breath's a ware that will not keep.
Up, lad: when the journey's over
 There'll be time enough to sleep.

WHEN I WAS ONE-AND-TWENTY

When I was one-and-twenty
 I heard a wise man say,
"Give crowns and pounds and guineas,
 But not your heart away;
Give pearls away and rubies
 But keep your fancy free."
But I was one-and-twenty,
 No use to talk to me.

When I was one-and-twenty
 I heard him say again,
"The heart out of the bosom
 Was never given in vain;
'Tis paid with sighs a plenty
 And sold for endless rue."
And I am two-and-twenty,
 And oh, 'tis true, 'tis true.

TO AN ATHLETE DYING YOUNG

The time you won your town the race
We chaired you through the market-place;
Man and boy stood cheering by,
And home we brought you shoulder-high.

To-day, the road all runners come,
Shoulder-high we bring you home,
And set you at your threshold down,
Townsman of a stiller town.

Smart lad, to slip betimes away
From fields where glory does not stay,
And early though the laurel grows
It withers quicker than the rose.

Eyes the shady night has shut
Cannot see the record cut,
And silence sounds no worse than cheers
After earth has stopped the ears:

Now you will not swell the rout
Of lads that wore their honours out,
Runners whom renown outran
And the name died before the man.

So set, before its echoes fade,
The fleet foot on the sill of shade,
And hold to the low lintel up
The still-defended challenge-cup.

And round that early-laurelled head
Will flock to gaze the strengthless dead,
And find unwithered on its curls
The garland briefer that a girl's.

IS MY TEAM PLOUGHING?

"Is my team ploughing,
 That I was used to drive
And hear the harness jingle
 When I was man alive?"

Ay, the horses trample,
 The harness jingles now;
No change though you lie under
 The land you used to plough.

"Is football playing
 Along the river shore,
With lads to chase the leather,
 Now I stand up no more?"

Ay, the ball is flying,
 The lads play heart and soul;
The goal stands up, the keeper
 Stands up to keep the goal.

"Is my girl happy,
 That I thought hard to leave,
And has she tired of weeping
 As she lies down at eve?"

Ay, she lies down lightly,
She lies not down to weep:
Your girl is well contented.
Be still, my lad, and sleep.

"Is my friend hearty,
Now I am thin and pine,
And has he found to sleep in
A better bed than mine?"

Yes, lad, I lie easy,
I lie as lads would choose;
I cheer a dead man's sweetheart,
Never ask me whose.

BE STILL, MY SOUL, BE STILL

Be still, my soul, be still; the arms you bear are brittle,
Earth and high heaven are fixt of old and founded strong.
Think rather,—call to thought, if now you grieve a little,
The days when we had rest, O soul, for they were long.

Men loved unkindness then, but lightless in the quarry
I slept and saw not; tears fell down, I did not mourn;
Sweat ran and blood sprang out and I was never sorry:
Then it was well with me, in days ere I was born.

Now, and I muse for why and never find the reason,
I pace the earth, and drink the air, and feel the sun.
Be still, be still, my soul; it is but for a season:
Let us endure an hour and see injustice done.

Ay, look: high heaven and earth ail from the prime foundation;
All thoughts to rive the heart are here, and all are vain:
Horror and scorn and hate and fear and indignation—
Oh why did I awake? when shall I sleep again?

THE ISLE OF PORTLAND

The star-filled seas are smooth to-night
From France to England strown;
Black towers above the Portland light
The felon-quarried stone.

On yonder island, not to rise,
Never to stir forth free,
Far from his folk a dead lad lies
That once was friends with me.

Lie you easy, dream you light,
And sleep you fast for aye;
And luckier may you find the night
Than ever you found the day.

TERENCE, THIS IS STUPID STUFF

"Terence, this is stupid stuff:
You eat your victuals fast enough;
There can't be much amiss, 'tis clear,
To see the rate you drink your beer.
But oh, good Lord, the verse you make,
It gives a chap the belly-ache.
The cow, the old cow, she is dead;
It sleeps well, the hornèd head:
We poor lads, 'tis our turn now
To hear such tunes as killed the cow.
Pretty friendship 'tis to rhyme
Your friends to death before their time
Moping melancholy mad:
Come, pipe a tune to dance to, lad."

Why, if 'tis dancing you would be,
There's brisker pipes than poetry.
Say, for what were hop-yards meant,
Or why was Burton built on Trent?
Oh many a peer of England brews
Livelier liquor than the Muse,
And malt does more than Milton can
To justify God's way to man.
Ale, man, ale's the stuff to drink
For fellows whom it hurts to think:
Look into the pewter pot
To see the world as the world's not.
And faith, 'tis pleasant till 'tis past:
The mischief is that 'twill not last.
Oh I have been to Ludlow fair
And left my necktie God knows where,
And carried half-way home, or near
Pints and quarts of Ludlow beer:
Then the world seemed none so bad,
And I myself a sterling lad;
And down in lovely muck I've lain,
Happy till I woke again.
Then I saw the morning sky:
Heigho, the tale was all a lie;

18. Burton, Burton-on-Trent, site of England's most famous breweries.

The world, it was the old world yet,
I was I, my things were wet,
And nothing now remained to do
But begin the game anew.

Therefore, since the world has still
Much good, but much less good than ill,
And while the sun and moon endure
Luck's a chance, but trouble's sure,
I'd face it as a wise man would,
And train for ill and not for good.
'Tis true, the stuff I bring for sale
Is not so brisk a brew as ale:
Out of a stem that scored the hand
I wrung it in a weary land.
But take it: if the smack is sour,
The better for the embittered hour;
It should do good to heart and head
When your soul is in my soul's stead;
And I will friend you, if I may,
In the dark and cloudy day.

There was a king reigned in the East:
There, when kings will sit to feast,
They got their fill before they think
With poisoned meat and poisoned drink.
He gathered all that springs to birth
From the many-venomed earth;
First a little, thence to more,
He sampled all her killing store;
And easy, smiling, seasoned sound,
Sate the king when healths went round.
They put arsenic in his meat
And stared aghast to watch him eat;
They poured strychnine in his cup
And shook to see him drink it up:
They shook, they stared as white's their shirt:
Them it was their poison hurt.
—I tell the tale that I heard told.
Mithridates, he died old.

THE CHESTNUT CASTS HIS FLAMBEAUX

The chestnut casts his flambeaux, and the flowers
Stream from the hawthorn on the wind away,
The doors clap to, the pane is blind with showers,
Pass me the can, lad; there's an end of May.

There's one spoilt spring to scant our mortal lot,
One season ruined of our little store.
May will be fine next year as like as not:
Oh ay, but then we shall be twenty-four.

We for a certainty are not the first
Have sat in taverns while the tempest hurled
Their hopeful plans to emptiness, and cursed
Whatever brute and blackguard made the world.

It is in truth iniquity on high
To cheat our sentenced souls of aught they crave,
And mar the merriment as you and I
Fare on our long fool's errand to the grave.

Iniquity it is; but pass the can.
My lad, no pair of kings our mothers bore;
Our only portion is the estate of man:
We want the moon, but we shall get no more.

If here to-day the cloud of thunder lours,
To-morrow it will hie on far behests;
The flesh will grieve on other bones than ours
Soon, and the soul will mourn in other breasts.

The troubles of our proud and angry dust
Are from eternity, and shall not fail.
Bear them we can, and if we can we must.
Shoulder the sky, my lad, and drink your ale.

1. **flambeaux,** torches, sometimes decorated candlesticks; in this instance the torchlike flowering clusters of the chestnut tree.

EIGHT O'CLOCK

He stood, and heard the steeple
Sprinkle the quarters on the morning town.
One, two, three, four, to market-place and people
It tossed them down.

Strapped, noosed, nighing his hour,
He stood and counted them and cursed his luck;
And then the clock collected in the tower
Its strength, and struck.

WHEN FIRST MY WAY TO FAIR I TOOK

When first my way to fair I took
Few pence in purse had I,
And long I used to stand and look
At things I could not buy.

Now times are altered: if I care
To buy a thing, I can;
The pence are here and here's the fair,
But where's the lost young man?

—To think that two and two are four
And neither five nor three
The heart of man has long been sore
And long 'tis like to be.

EPITAPH ON AN ARMY OF MERCENARIES

These, in the day when heaven was falling,
The hour when earth's foundations fled,
Followed their mercenary calling
And took their wages and are dead.

Their shoulders held the sky suspended;
They stood, and earth's foundations stay;
What God abandoned, these defended,
And saved the sum of things for pay.

EPIGRAPH TO *MORE POEMS*

They say my verse is sad: no wonder;
Its narrow measure spans
Tears of eternity, and sorrow,
Not mine, but man's.

This is for all ill-treated fellows
Unborn and unbegot,
For them to read when they're in trouble
And I am not.

William Butler Yeats
1865–1939

The family of William Butler Yeats was a distinguished one: his father was a well-known artist; his brother became a landscape-painter; one of his sisters established the Cuala Press, which presented many of the new writers of the Irish revival. Yeats was born June 13, 1865, at Sandymount, near Dublin, Ireland. When he was still a boy, his parents moved to London, and the child was sent to Godolphin School, but much of his youth was spent in the wilds of County Sligo. At fifteen, he returned to Ireland to attend the Erasmus Smith School in Dublin, and his vacations found him in the countryside sitting by turf fires and listening to folk tales.

At twenty-one Yeats published his first book, *Mosada: A Poem*, 1886. Immediately after its publication he went to London, became a contributor to the *Yellow Book*, formed the group known as the Rhymers' Club, and identified himself with those who made the 1890's a period of elegantly mannered affectation. But Yeats's native integrity prevented him from associating himself with the cult of the bizarre. Although he traveled abroad, he was rooted in Ireland. He helped found the Irish literary theater, dreamed of a national poetry that would be English in words but Irish in spirit, persuaded J. M. Synge to leave Paris and write for the Abbey Theater in Dublin, and continued to direct as well as to inspire the multiple activities of the Irish Renaissance. The experimental poet grew into the national patriot. He was made Senator and served the Free State from 1922 to 1928. His influence grew in every field: as folklorist, playwright, champion of new tendencies (he was one of the first to hail such "strange" American phenomena as Vachel Lindsay and Ezra Pound), as essayist, and, perhaps most of all, as seer. The Nobel Prize for Literature was awarded to him in 1924. The last years of his life were spent on the French and Italian Riviera. He died, after a brief illness, at Roquebrune, near Nice, January 28, 1939, and was buried there. But in September, 1948, an Irish corvette brought his body back to his native Ireland where it was re-interred, in accordance with his wishes, in Drumcliff graveyard in Sligo.

Although his essays and autobiography show him as an unusually intuitive spirit and a critic of the first order, it is as a poet that Yeats commands the reader's chief attention. His was a passion not only for poetry but for perfection. He was never fully satisfied with his work; it is said that he rewrote even more than he wrote. In continual attempts to refine and clarify his communication, he published many different editions of his *Collected Poems*, each edition completely superseding the previous volume.

The poetry of Yeats is of two sorts: the early verse, which charms because of its music, and the later poetry, which arrests because of its masterful imagery and metaphysical strength. *The Wanderings of Oisin*, 1889, *The Wind among the Reeds*, 1899, and *In the Seven Woods*, 1903, are extraordinary in their mixture of folk tone and personal fancy, of a music which is vague and a mythology which is both abstract and allusive. Sacrificing strength of thought to delicacy of phrase, Yeats first dealt with a small set of symbols, symbols that were colorful but which tended to become rhetorical and facile.

Responsibilities, 1914, *The Wild Swans at Coole*, 1917, and *Later Poems*, 1922, disclose a sudden change. The tone is sharper; the phrasing is direct rather than decorative. Even more significant is the poet's attitude to his subject matter. Yeats acknowledges this change implicitly in the poem wherein he declares that originally he had made his songs wear a romantic disguise, a coat

> Covered with embroideries
> Out of old mythologies.

He says it explicitly in a dedication to his *Essays*, 1924: "My friends and I loved symbols, popular beliefs. and old scraps of verse that made Ireland romantic to herself; but the new Ireland, overwhelmed by responsibility, begins to long for psychological truth."

It is "psychological truth" which Yeats probed for, discovered, and revealed in his later writings. The artfully constructed fairylands and the elaborately allegorical gods of his youth are discarded for real people, immediate events, and the stripped facts of actual life. Pretty fancy is exchanged for mature imagination; the leaping fire is taught to burn slowly, but no less fiercely. "It is only when the intellect has wrought the whole of life to drama, to crisis, that we may live for contemplation, yet keep our intensity," he says. "I am content to follow to its source every event in action or in thought," Yeats wrote in "A Dialogue of Self and Soul," and he concluded the poem with a Blake-like divination:

> When such as I cast out remorse
> So great a sweetness flows into the breast
> We must laugh and we must sing,
> We are blest by everything,
> Everything we look upon is blest.

As Yeats grew old his intellectual power increased. *The Tower*, 1928, *The Winding Stair*, 1932, *The King of the Great Clock Tower*, 1935, published in Yeats's seventieth year, and the posthumous *Last Poems and Plays*, 1940, contain magnificent expressions of "pure mind" or a clarification which is the completion of the partial mind. They also contain the utterances of a man not afraid to taste unpalatable truths and even less afraid to say that they are bitter. The later poems are weighted with a sense of isolation, with the disillusionments of the age—and of old age—with defeated dreams, with the decay of beauty (as reflected in Yeats's constant evocation of Maud Gonne, the beautiful Irish actress and revolutionary), with the death of friends and the degeneration of the contemporary world. Yet, though Yeats voiced his horror and even disgust in the later poems and plays, he did not despair. The ladder of happy fantasy was gone, but, even at the end, he was willing to begin the long ascent again.

> I must lie down where all the ladders start,
> In the foul rag-and-bone shop of the heart.

Yeats separated his rational and intuitive self just as, in life, he separated the spiritual (and impersonal) poet from the violent (and personal) radicalism of Maud Gonne. The mysticism is not, however, an "escape"; it seems to be an extension of Yeats's theory that "nature, races, and individual men are unified by an image," that when men desert one myth they will substitute another. This is cumulatively proved by the verse. If Yeats's symbolism is complicated and questionable, the directness of his best poetry, the burning vision, "simple as flame," is undeniable.

THE STOLEN CHILD[1]

Where dips the rocky highland
Of Sleuth Wood in the lake,
There lies a leafy island
Where flapping herons wake
The drowsy water-rats;
There we've hid our faery vats,
Full of berries
And of reddest stolen cherries.
Come away, O human child!
To the waters and the wild
With a faery, hand in hand,
For the world's more full of weeping than you can understand.

Where the wave of moonlight glosses
The dim grey sands with light,
Far off by furthest Rosses
We foot it all the night,
Weaving olden dances,
Mingling hands and mingling glances
Till the moon has taken flight;
To and fro we leap
And chase the frothy bubbles,
While the world is full of troubles
And is anxious in its sleep.

[1] This and the following poems by W. B. Yeats are from *Collected Poems of W. B. Yeats*, copyright, 1933, by The Macmillan Company. Reprinted by permission of The Macmillan Company, Mrs. W. B. Yeats, and The Macmillan Company of Canada.

Come away, O human child!
To the waters and the wild
With a faery, hand in hand,
For the world's more full of weeping than you can understand.

Where the wandering water gushes
From the hills above Glen-Car,
In pools among the rushes
That scarce could bathe a star,
We seek for slumbering trout
And whispering in their ears
Give them unquiet dreams;
Leaning softly out
From ferns that drop their tears
Over the young streams.
Come away, O human child!
To the waters and the wild
With a faery, hand in hand,
For the world's more full of weeping than you can understand.

Away with us he's going,
The solemn-eyed:
He'll hear no more the lowing
Of the calves on the warm hillside
Or the kettle on the hob
Sing peace into his breast,
Or see the brown mice mob
Round and round the oatmeal-chest.
For he comes, the human child,
To the waters and the wild
With a faery, hand in hand,
From a world more full of weeping than he can understand.

DOWN BY THE SALLEY GARDENS

Down by the salley gardens my love and I did meet;
She passed the salley gardens with little snow-white feet.
She bid me take love easy, as the leaves grow on the tree;
But I, being young and foolish, with her would not agree.

In a field by the river my love and I did stand,
And on my leaning shoulder she laid her snow-white hand.
She bid me take life easy, as the grass grows on the weirs;
But I was young and foolish, and now am full of tears.

Down by the Salley Gardens. **Salley,** willow. "This," Yeats wrote in a footnote in one of the early editions (titled "An Old Song Resung") "is an extension of three lines sung to me by an old woman of Ballisodare."

THE ROSE OF THE WORLD [1]

Who dreamed that beauty passes like a dream?
For these red lips, with all their mournful pride,
Mournful that no new wonder may betide,
Troy passed away in one high funeral gleam,
And Usna's children died.

We and the labouring world are passing by:
Amid men's souls, that waver and give place
Like the pale waters in their wintry race,
Under the passing stars, foam of the sky,
Lives on this lonely face.

Bow down, archangels, in your dim abode:
Before you were, or any hearts to beat,
Weary and kind one lingered by His seat;
He made the world to be a grassy road
Before her wandering feet.

THE LAKE ISLE OF INNISFREE

I will arise and go now, and go to Innisfree,
And a small cabin build there, of clay and wattles made:
Nine bean-rows will I have there, a hive for the honey-bee,
And live alone in the bee-loud glade.

And I shall have some peace there, for peace comes dropping slow,
Dropping from the veils of the morning to where the cricket sings;
There midnight's all a glimmer, and noon a purple glow,
And evening full of the linnet's wings.

I will arise and go now, for always night and day
I hear lake water lapping with low sounds by the shore;
While I stand on the roadway, or on the pavements grey,
I hear it in the deep heart's core.

[1] The "rose" is the traditional symbol of love. **2, 4, 5. red lips . . . Troy . . . Usna's children.** The love of Paris for Helen led to the Trojan War and the burning of Troy. The love of Naoise, son of Usna, for Deirdre, the most beautiful heroine of Irish legends, led, through the treachery of a rival lover, King Conchobar of Ulster, to the slaughter of Naoise and his two brothers. Deirdre killed herself in her grief for Naoise. **1. Innisfree,** an island in Lough Gill, County Sligo, Ireland, where Yeats lived in his young days.

WHEN YOU ARE OLD

When you are old and grey and full of sleep,
And nodding by the fire, take down this book,
And slowly read, and dream of the soft look
Your eyes had once, and of their shadows deep;

How many loved your moments of glad grace,
And loved your beauty with love false or true;
But one man loved the pilgrim soul in you,
And loved the sorrows of your changing face.

And bending down beside the glowing bars,
Murmur, a little sadly, how Love fled
And paced upon the mountains overhead
And hid his face amid a crowd of stars.

FAIRY SONG

from THE LAND OF HEART'S DESIRE

The wind blows out of the gates of the day,
The wind blows over the lonely of heart,
And the lonely of heart is withered away,
While the faëries dance in a place apart,
Shaking their milk-white feet in a ring,
Tossing their milk-white arms in the air:
For they hear the wind laugh and murmur and sing
Of a land where even the old are fair,
And even the wise are merry of tongue;
But I heard a reed of Coolaney say,
"When the wind has laughed and murmured and sung,
The lonely of heart is withered away!"

THE LOVER TELLS OF THE ROSE IN HIS HEART

All things uncomely and broken, all things worn out and old,
The cry of a child by the roadway, the creak of a lumbering cart,
The heavy steps of the ploughman, splashing the wintry mould,
Are wronging your image that blossoms a rose in the deeps of my heart.

The wrong of unshapely things is a wrong too great to be told;
I hunger to build them anew and sit on a green knoll apart,
With the earth and the sky and the water, re-made, like a casket of gold
For my dreams of your image that blossoms a rose in the deeps of my heart.

THE SONG OF WANDERING AENGUS [1]

I went out to the hazel wood,
Because a fire was in my head,
And cut and peeled a hazel wand,
And hooked a berry to a thread;
And when white moths were on the wing,
And moth-like stars were flickering out,
I dropped the berry in a stream
And caught a little silver trout.

When I had laid it on the floor
I went to blow the fire a-flame,
But something rustled on the floor,
And some one called me by my name:
It had become a glimmering girl
With apple blossom in her hair
Who called me by my name and ran
And faded through the brightening air.

Though I am old with wandering
Through hollow lands and hilly lands,
I will find out where she has gone,
And kiss her lips and take her hands;
And walk among long dappled grass,
And pluck till time and times are done
The silver apples of the moon
The golden apples of the sun.

HE WISHES FOR THE CLOTHS OF HEAVEN

Had I the heavens' embroidered cloths,
Enwrought with golden and silver light,
The blue and the dim and the dark cloths
Of night and light and the half-light,
I would spread the cloths under your feet:
But I, being poor, have only my dreams;
I have spread my dreams under your feet;
Tread softly because you tread on my dreams.

THE WILD SWANS AT COOLE

The trees are in their autumn beauty,
The woodland paths are dry,

[1] *The Song of Wandering Aengus.* Aengus is the Celtic god of love.

Under the October twilight the water
Mirrors a still sky;
Upon the brimming water among the stones
Are nine-and-fifty swans.

The nineteenth autumn has come upon me
Since I first made my count;
I saw, before I had well finished,
All suddenly mount
And scatter wheeling in great broken rings
Upon their clamorous wings.

I have looked upon those brilliant creatures,
And now my heart is sore.
All's changed since I, hearing at twilight,
The first time on this shore,
The bell-beat of their wings above my head,
Trod with a lighter tread.

Unwearied still, lover by lover,
They paddle in the cold
Companionable streams or climb the air;
Their hearts have not grown old;
Passion or conquest, wander where they will,
Attend upon them still.

But now they drift on the still water
Mysterious, beautiful;
Among what rushes will they build,
By what lake's edge or pool
Delight men's eyes when I awake some day
To find they have flown away?

AN IRISH AIRMAN FORESEES HIS DEATH

I know that I shall meet my fate
Somewhere among the clouds above;
Those that I fight I do not hate,
Those that I guard I do not love;
My country is Kiltartan Cross,
My countrymen Kiltartan's poor,
No likely end could bring them loss
Or leave them happier than before.
Nor law, nor duty bade me fight,
Nor public men, nor cheering crowds,
A lonely impulse of delight
Drove to this tumult in the clouds;
I balanced all, brought all to mind,
The years to come seemed waste of breath,
A waste of breath the years behind
In balance with this life, this death.

THE SECOND COMING

In this powerful poem Yeats moves from awareness of contemporary discord to a mood, boldly imaged, of terrifying prophecy.

Turning and turning in the widening gyre
The falcon cannot hear the falconer;
Things fall apart; the centre cannot hold;
Mere anarchy is loosed upon the world,
The blood-dimmed tide is loosed, and everywhere
The ceremony of innocence is drowned;
The best lack all conviction, while the worst
Are full of passionate intensity.

Surely some revelation is at hand;
Surely the Second Coming is at hand.
The Second Coming! Hardly are those words out
When a vast image out of *Spiritus Mundi*
Troubles my sight: somewhere in sands of the desert
A shape with lion body and the head of a man,
A gaze blank and pitiless as the sun,
Is moving its slow thighs, while all about it
Reel shadows of the indignant desert birds.
The darkness drops again; but now I know
That twenty centuries of stony sleep
Were vexed to nightmare by a rocking cradle,
And what rough beast, its hour come round at last,
Slouches toward Bethlehem to be born?

SAILING TO BYZANTIUM

Ancient Byzantium, ancestress of the modern Constantinople (Istanbul), is used symbolically to represent the ideal fusion of flesh and mind and spirit in old age, in contrast to mere sensuous experience. See the illuminating discussion of this poem in Cleanth Brooks's *Modern Poetry and the Tradition*, University of North Carolina Press, 1939, pp. 89–202.

I

That is no country for old men. The young
In one another's arms, birds in the trees,
—Those dying generations—at their song,
The salmon-falls, the mackerel-Crowded seas,
Fish, flesh, or fowl, commend all summer long
Whatever is begotten, born, and dies.
Caught in that sensual music all neglect
Monuments of unaging intellect.

12. ***Spiritus Mundi,*** Spirit of the World. It was Yeats's belief that all experience belongs to a great collective spirit or memory, which men can perceive only intuitively.

II

An aged man is but a paltry thing,
A tattered coat upon a stick, unless
Soul clap its hands and sing, and louder sing
For every tatter in its mortal dress,
Nor is there singing school but studying
Monuments of its own magnificence;
And therefore I have sailed the seas and come
To the holy city of Byzantium.

III

O sages standing in God's holy fire
As in the gold mosaic of a wall,
Come from the holy fire, perne in a gyre,
And be the singing-masters of my soul.
Consume my heart away; sick with desire
And fastened to a dying animal
It knows not what it is; and gather me
Into the artifice of eternity.

IV

Once out of nature I shall never take
My bodily form from any natural thing,
But such a form as Grecian goldsmiths make
Of hammered gold and gold enamelling
To keep a drowsy Emperor awake;
Or set upon a golden bough to sing
To lords and ladies of Byzantium
Of what is past, or passing, or to come.

THE NEW FACES

If you, that have grown old, were the first dead,
Neither catalpa tree nor scented lime
Should hear my living feet, nor would I tread
Where we wrought that shall break the teeth of Time,
Let the new faces play what tricks they will
In the old rooms; night can outbalance day,
Our shadows rove the garden gravel still,
The living seem more shadowy than they.

19. perne in a gyre. A pern is a species of the hawk family, specifically the honey-buzzard. "Yeats imagined that the whole world, at the present time, was whirling at great velocity in the manner of a gyre, i.e. like a tornado, spirally about its axis. By *perne* Yeats probably means to move in the manner of a hawk, i.e. circling and then swooping. The image thus conveys the idea of moving in such a manner as to pierce through the gyre in order to reach the poet who is caught in it by the accident of having been born into the present-day world." (Wright Thomas and Stuart G. Brown, *Reading Poems: An Introduction to Critical Study*, Oxford University Press, 1941, p. 713) **28–30. hammered gold . . . sing.** "I have read somewhere that in the Emperor's palace at Byzantium was a tree made of gold and silver, and artificial birds that sang." (Yeats)

LEDA AND THE SWAN

Zeus, enamored of Leda, visited her in the form of a swan, and begot upon her the Helen whose fatal beauty brought about the destruction of Troy—"The broken wall, the burning roof and tower, And Agamemnon dead." The poem first appeared in Yeats's essay on his symbolic system, *A Vision*, 1925.

A sudden blow: the great wings beating still
Above the staggering girl, her thighs caressed
By the dark webs, her nape caught in his bill,
He holds her helpless breast upon his breast.

How can those terrified vague fingers push
The feathered glory from her loosening thighs?
And how can body, laid in that white rush,
But feel the strange heart beating where it lies?

A shudder in the loins engenders there
The broken wall, the burning roof and tower
And Agamemnon dead.
Being so caught up,
So mastered by the brute blood of the air,
Did she put on his knowledge with his power
Before the indifferent beak could let her drop?

AMONG SCHOOL CHILDREN

In the course of his duties as a Senator in later years, Yeats occasionally paid official visits to the primary schools. Such a visit is here the point of departure for one of his most mature and searching poems.

I

I walk through the long schoolroom questioning;
A kind old nun in a white hood replies;
The children learn to cipher and to sing,
To study reading-books and histories,
To cut and sew, be neat in everything
In the best modern way—the children's eyes
In momentary wonder stare upon
A sixty-year-old smiling public man.

II

I dream of a Ledaean body, bent
Above a sinking fire, a tale that she
Told of a harsh reproof, or trivial event
That changed some childish day to tragedy—
Told, and it seemed that our two natures blent
Into a sphere from youthful sympathy,
Or else, to alter Plato's parable,
Into the yolk and white of the one shell.

9. Ledaean, like Leda's. (See headnote to "Leda and the Swan.") **15. Plato's parable.** According to Plato's parable of the origin of love, Zeus divided human beings in two, with the result that they were ever after trying to reunite.

III

And thinking of that fit of grief or rage
I look upon one child or t'other there
And wonder if she stood so at that age—
For even daughters of the swan can share
Something of every paddler's heritage—
And had that colour upon cheek or hair,
And thereupon my heart is driven wild:
She stands before me as a living child.

IV

Her present image floats into the mind—
Did Quattrocento finger fashion it
Hollow of cheek as though it drank the wind
And took a mess of shadows for its meat?
And I though never of Ledaean kind
Had pretty plumage once—enough of that,
Better to smile on all that smile, and show
There is a comfortable kind of old scarecrow.

V

What youthful mother, a shape upon her lap
Honey of generation had betrayed,
And that must sleep, shriek, struggle to escape
As recollection or the drug decide,
Would think her son, did she but see that shape
With sixty or more winters on its head,
A compensation for the pang of his birth,
Or the uncertainty of his setting forth?

VI

Plato thought nature but a spume that plays
Upon a ghostly paradigm of things;
Soldier Aristotle played the taws
Upon the bottom of a king of kings;
World-famous golden-thighed Pythagoras
Fingered upon a fiddle-stick or strings
What a star sang and careless Muses heard:
Old clothes upon old sticks to scare a bird.

VII

Both nuns and mothers worship images,
But those the candles light are not as those
That animate a mother's reveries,
But keep a marble or a bronze repose.
And yet they too break hearts—O Presences
That passion, piety or affection knows,
And that all heavenly glory symbolise—
O self-born mockers of man's enterprise;

VIII

Labour is blossoming or dancing where
The body is not bruised to pleasure soul,
Nor beauty born out of its own despair,
Nor blear-eyed wisdom out of midnight oil.
O chestnut-tree, great-rooted blossomer,
Are you the leaf, the blossom or the bole?
O body swayed to music, O brightening glance,
How can we know the dancer from the dance?

26. Quattrocento, fifteenth century. **43. taws,** birch rods. **44. king of kings,** Alexander the Great. Aristotle did not hesitate to whip his most illustrious pupil. **45. Pythagoras.** The metaphysics of the Greek philosopher were based on music and mathematics.

from UNDER BEN BULBEN

A few months before his death Yeats wrote this personal epitaph, which forms the final section of a longer poem affirming for the last time his indomitable sense of the high purpose of art and his deep love for Ireland.

Under bare Ben Bulben
In Drumcliff churchyard Yeats is laid.
An ancestor was rector there
Long years ago, a church stands near,
By the road an ancient cross.
No marble, no conventional phrase;
On limestone quarried near the spot
By his command these words are cut.

Cast a cold eye
On life, on death,
Horseman, pass by!

G. K. Chesterton

1874–1936

The man often called the master of paradox, G. K. Chesterton, was born at Campden Hill, Kensington, now part of London, on May 29, 1874. After graduating from St. Paul's School and the Slade School of Art, he wavered between a career in art and a future in literature. He began by uniting both desires: he reviewed books of art. He never wholly discontinued his fondness for drawing; he illustrated several of his works, and about ten of the novels of his friend Hilaire Belloc. He delighted in debates, and the First World War intensified his passion for controversy. Aware that something was wrong with the economic system, he revolted against both capitalism and socialism, and proclaimed a new order which was curiously like an old disorder: a confused and romanticized medievalism. Chesterton often wrote like an adult who lived in a world of childish fantasy, a serious thinker who thought only in terms of paradox, a philosopher who defended the obvious with the zeal of a fanatic crucified for his heresies.

His versatility matched his vigor. He traveled and lectured extensively; he became chief columnist on the *Daily News and Leader*, editor of *G. K.'s Weekly*, Fellow of the Royal Society of Literature, president of the Distributists League. In 1922 he was converted to Catholicism. When he died on June 14, 1936, he was the author of more than one hundred volumes of fiction, poetry, plays, biographies, criticisms, essays, and studies. His robust Englishness is evidenced by his choice of Chaucer, Browning, and Dickens as subjects for his most ambitious literary studies.

As a writer of fiction Chesterton delighted in high-flying surprise. His most characteristic novel, *The Man Who Was Thursday*, 1908, was subtitled "A Nightmare," and his Father Brown narratives—beginning with *The Innocence of Father Brown*, 1911, and ending with *The Scandal of Father Brown*, 1935—were a set of detective stories incongruously full of Christian symbols and faintly disguised sermons. A clue to Chesterton's humor is contained in some of the other titles: *The Club of Queer Trades*, 1905; *The Unthinkable Theory of Professor Green*, 1925; *The Moderate Murderer*, 1929; *The Poet and the Lunatics*, 1929.

In all these works there is a tremendous zest, a zest for the common people and the uncommon poet. Chesterton accomplishes new and dexterous combinations; he turns out journalistic articles which become poetic allegories, essays (like "A Piece of Chalk") which are parables. The Chestertonian gusto plays with rhetoric, with winning but artificial simplicity, with a brilliant but calculated extravagance—all in a witty topsy-turvy land. His criticism of Mrs. Browning's style might well be applied to him:

"Whenever her verse is bad, it is bad from some violence of comparison, some kind of debauch of cleverness. Her nonsense never arises from weakness, but from a confusion of powers. . . . She cannot leave anything alone, she cannot write a line, without a conceit. She gives the reader the impression that she never declined a fancy."

Chesterton's liveliness and energy are at their best in his poetry—*New and Collected Poems*, 1929—in the tramping measures of "The rolling English drunkard who made the rolling English road," in the trumpeting rhymes and pounding rhythms of "Lepanto" and those other vigorous poems, "The Wild Knight" and "The Ballad of the White Horse." But he is likely to be remembered chiefly as a determined wielder of paradox, an author whose most characteristic volume was significantly entitled *Tremendous Trifles*, 1909.

A biography, *G. K. Chesterton*, was written by Maurice Evans and published in 1939. Chesterton's *Autobiography*, 1936, is written with characteristic enthusiasm.

A PIECE OF CHALK [1]

I REMEMBER one splendid morning, all blue and silver, in the summer holidays, when I reluctantly tore myself away from the task of doing nothing in particular, and put on a hat of some sort and picked up a walking-stick, and put six very bright-coloured chalks in my pocket. I then went

[1] From *Tremendous Trifles* by G. K. Chesterton, copyright, 1909, by Dodd, Mead & Company. Used by permission of the publishers, of Miss Collins, executrix of the late G. K. Chesterton, and of Methuen & Co. Ltd.

into the kitchen (which, along with the rest of the house, belonged to a very square and sensible old woman in a Sussex village), and asked the owner and occupant of the kitchen if she had any brown paper. She had a great deal; in fact, she had too much; and she mistook the purpose and the rationale of the existence of brown paper. She seemed to have an idea that if a person wanted brown paper he must be wanting to tie up parcels; which was the last thing I wanted to do; indeed, it is a thing which I have found to be beyond my mental capacity. Hence she dwelt very much on the varying qualities of toughness and endurance in the material. I explained to her that I only wanted to draw pictures on it, and that I did not want them to endure in the least; and that from my point of view, therefore, it was a question not of tough consistency, but of responsive surface, a thing comparatively irrelevant in a parcel. When she understood that I wanted to draw she offered to overwhelm me with note-paper, apparently supposing that I did my notes and correspondence on old brown paper wrappers from motives of economy.

I then tried to explain the rather delicate logical shade, that I not only liked brown paper, but liked the quality of brownness in paper, just as I liked the quality of brownness in October woods, or in beer, or in the peat-streams of the North. Brown paper represents the primal twilight of the first toil of creation, and with a bright-coloured chalk or two you can pick out points of fire in it, sparks of gold, and blood-red, and sea-green, like the first fierce stars that sprang out of divine darkness. All this I said (in an off-hand way) to the old woman; and I put the brown paper in my pocket along with the chalks, and possibly other things. I suppose every one must have reflected how primeval and how poetical are the things that one carries in one's pocket; the pocket-knife, for instance, the type of all human tools, the infant of the sword. Once I planned to write a book of poems entirely about the things in my pocket. But I found it would be too long; and the age of the great epics is past.

With my stick and my knife, my chalks and my brown paper, I went out on to the great downs. I crawled across those colossal contours that express the best quality of England, because they are at the same time soft and strong. The smoothness of them has the same meaning as the smoothness of great cart-horses, or the smoothness of the beech-tree; it declares in the teeth of our timid and cruel theories that the mighty are merciful. As my eye swept the landscape, the landscape was as kindly as any of its cottages, but for power it was like an earthquake. The villages in the immense valley were safe, one could see, for centuries; yet the lifting of the whole land was like the lifting of one enormous wave to wash them all away.

I crossed one swell of living turf after another, looking for a place to sit down and draw. Do not, for heaven's sake, imagine I was going to sketch from Nature. I was going to draw devils and seraphim, and blind old gods that men worshipped before the dawn of right, and saints in robes of angry crimson, and seas of strange green, and all the sacred or monstrous symbols that look so well in bright colours on brown paper. They are much better worth drawing than Nature; also they are much easier to draw. When a cow came slouching by in the field next to me, a mere artist might have drawn it; but I always get wrong in the hind legs of quadrupeds. So I drew the soul of the cow; which I saw there plainly walking before me in the sunlight; and the soul was all purple and silver, and had seven horns and the mystery that belongs to all the beasts. But though I could not with a crayon get the best out of the landscape, it does not follow that the landscape was not getting the best out of me. And this, I think, is the mistake that people make about the old poets who lived before Wordsworth, and were supposed not to care very much about Nature because they did not describe it much.

They preferred writing about great men to writing about great hills; but they sat on the great hills to write it. They gave out much less about Nature, but they drank in, perhaps, much more. They painted the white robes of their holy virgins with the blinding snow, at which they stared all day. They blazoned the shields of their paladins with the purple and gold of many heraldic sunsets. The greenness of a thousand green leaves clustered into the live green figure of Robin Hood. The blueness of a score of forgotten skies became the blue robes of the Virgin. The inspiration went in like sunbeams and came out like Apollo.

But as I sat scrawling these silly figures on the brown paper, it began to dawn on me, to my great disgust, that I had left one chalk, and that a most exquisite and essential chalk, behind. I searched all my pockets, but I could not find any white chalk. Now, those who are acquainted with all the philosophy (nay, religion) which is typified in the art of drawing on brown paper, know that white is positive and essential. I cannot avoid remarking here upon a moral significance. One of the wise and awful truths which this brown-paper art reveals, is this, that white is a colour. It is not a mere absence of colour; it is a shining and affirmative thing, as fierce as red, as definite as black. When (so to speak) your pencil grows red-hot, it draws roses; when it grows white-hot, it draws stars. And one of the two or three defiant verities of the best religious morality, of real Christianity for example, is exactly this same thing; the chief assertion of religious morality is that white is a colour. Virtue is not the absence of vices or the avoidance of moral danger; virtue is a vivid and separate thing, like pain or a particular smell. Mercy does not mean not being cruel or sparing people revenge or punishment; it means a plain and positive thing like the sun, which one has either seen or not seen. Chastity does not mean abstention from sexual wrong; it means something flaming, like Joan of Arc. In a word, God paints in many colours; but He never paints so gorgeously, I had almost said gaudily, as when He paints in white. In a sense our age has realized this fact, and expressed it in our sullen costume. For if it were really true that white was a blank and colourless thing, negative and non-committal, then white would be used instead of black and grey for the funeral dress of this pessimistic period. We should see city gentlemen in frock coats of spotless silver linen, with top hats as white as wonderful arum lilies. Which is not the case.

Meanwhile, I could not find my chalk.

I sat on the hill in a sort of despair. There was no town nearer than Chichester at which it was even remotely probable that there would be such a thing as an artist's colourman. And yet, without white, my absurd little pictures would be as pointless as the world would be if there were no good people in it. I stared stupidly round, racking my brain for expedients. Then I suddenly stood up and roared with laughter, again and again, so that the cows stared at me and called a committee. Imagine a man in the Sahara regretting that he had no sand for his hour-glass. Imagine a gentleman in mid-ocean wishing that he had brought some salt water with him for his chemical experiments. I was sitting on an immense warehouse of white chalk. The landscape was made entirely out of white chalk. White chalk was piled mere miles until it met the sky. I stooped and broke a piece off the rock I sat on: it did not mark so well as the shop chalks do; but it gave the effect. And I stood there in a trance of pleasure, realizing that this Southern England is not only a grand peninsula, and a tradition and a civilization; it is something even more admirable. It is a piece of chalk.

LEPANTO [1]

In this poem, one of his most artistic and vigorous, Chesterton communicates the excitement throughout Europe that was engendered by the naval battle fought in the Gulf of Lepanto, or Corinth, Greece, on October 5, 1571. The Turkish fleet, under the Sultan Selim II, was almost obliterated by the allied squadrons of the Holy League, which comprised Pope Pius V, Philip II of Spain, the Venetian Republic, and other Italian states. Don John of Austria, illegitimate son of the Emperor Charles V, was in command of the forces of the Holy League. Chesterton appropriately describes the expedition in terms of a Crusade.

White founts falling in the Courts of the Sun,
And the Soldan of Byzantium is smiling as they run;
There is laughter like the fountains in that face of all men feared,
It stirs the forest darkness, the darkness of his beard.
It curls the blood-red crescent, the crescent of his lips,
For the inmost sea of all the earth is shaken with his ships.
They have dared the white republics up the capes of Italy,
They have dashed the Adriatic round the Lion of the Sea,
And the Pope has cast his arms abroad for agony and loss,
And called the kings of Christendom for swords about the Cross.
The cold queen of England is looking in the glass;
The shadow of the Valois is yawning at the Mass;
From evening isles fantastical rings faint the Spanish gun,
And the Lord upon the Golden Horn is laughing in the sun.

Dim drums throbbing, in the hills half heard,
Where only on a nameless throne a crownless prince has stirred,
Where, risen from a doubtful seat and half-attainted stall,

[1] Printed by permission from *The Collected Poems of G. K. Chesterton*, copyright, 1932, by Dodd, Mead and Company, Inc. Also by permission of Miss Collins, executrix of the late G. K. Chesterton. **8. Lion of the Sea,** Venice, whose emblem is the lion of St. Mark. **11. cold queen,** Elizabeth, who, as a Protestant, had no part in the expedition. **12. shadow of the Valois,** Charles IX of France, who was dominated by his mother, Catherine de' Medici, Duchess of Valois. **14. Lord . . . Horn,** the Sultan. The harbor of Constantinople (Byzantium) is an arm of the Bosporus, known as the Golden Horn. **16–17. crownless prince . . . half attainted.** Don John was an illegitimate son.

The last knight of Europe takes weapons from the wall,
The last and lingering troubadour to whom the bird has sung,
That once went singing southward when all the world was young.
In that enormous silence, tiny and unafraid,
Comes up along a winding road the noise of the Crusade.
Strong gongs groaning as the guns boom far,
Don John of Austria is going to the war.
Stiff flags straining in the night-blasts cold,
In the gloom black-purple, in the glint old-gold,
Torchlight crimson on the copper kettledrums,
Then the tuckets, then the trumpets, then the cannon, and he comes.
Don John laughing in the brave beard curled,
Spurning of his stirrups like the thrones of all the world,
Holding his head up for a flag of all the free.
Love-light of Spain—hurrah!
Death-light of Africa!
Don John of Austria
Is riding to the sea.

Mahound is in his paradise above the evening star.
(*Don John of Austria is going to the war.*)
He moves a mighty turban on the timeless houri's knees,
His turban that is woven of the sunsets and the seas.
He shakes the peacock gardens as he rises from his ease,
And he strides among the tree-tops and is taller than the trees;
And his voice through all the garden is a thunder sent to bring
Black Azrael and Ariel and Ammon on the wing.
Giants and the Genii,
Multiplex of wing and eye,
Whose strong obedience broke the sky
When Solomon was king.

They rush in red and purple from the red clouds of the morn,
From the temples where the yellow gods shut up their eyes in scorn;
They rise in green robes roaring from the green hells of the sea
Where fallen skies and evil hues and eyeless creatures be;
On them the sea-valves cluster and the grey sea-forests curl,
Splashed with a splendid sickness, the sickness of the pearl;
They swell in sapphire smoke out of the blue cracks of the ground,—
They gather and they wonder and give worship to Mahound.
And he saith, "Break up the mountains where the hermit-folk may hide,
And sift the red and silver sands lest bone of saint abide,
And chase the Giaours flying night and day, not giving rest,
For that which was our trouble comes again out of the west.
We have set the seal of Solomon on all things under sun,
Of knowledge and of sorrow and endurance of things done.
But a noise is in the mountains, in the mountains, and I know
The voice that shook our palaces—four hundred years ago;
It is he that saith not 'Kismet'; it is he that knows not Fate;
It is Richard, it is Raymond, it is Godfrey at the gate!
It is he whose loss is laughter when he counts the wager worth,
Put down your feet upon him, that our peace be on the earth."
For he heard drums groaning and he heard guns jar,
(*Don John of Austria is going to the war.*)
Sudden and still—hurrah!
Bolt from Iberia!
Don John of Austria
Is gone by Alcalar.

St. Michael's on his Mountain in the sea-roads of the North
(*Don John of Austria is girt and going forth.*)

36. Mahound, Mahomet. **38. houri,** one of the nymphs of the Mahometan Paradise. **43. Azrael and Ariel and Ammon.** Azrael is the Mahometan angel of death. Ariel is one of the chief spirits in late Jewish and Mahometan legends. Ammon or Amon was an ancient Egyptian deity, but here the name Ammon is given to a spirit doubtless because of the reference, in I Kings 11: 5, 7, 33, to Solomon's having built a high place for Milcom (Molech) the god of Ammon or the Ammonites.

58. Giaours, unbelievers, i.e., Christians. **63. four hundred years ago,** in the time of the early Crusades. **64. 'Kismet,'** Fate. **65. Richard . . . Raymond . . . Godfrey.** Richard I of England, Raymond IV, Count of Toulouse, and Godfrey of Bouillon, Duke of Lower Lorraine, were leaders of the early Crusades. **71. Iberia,** Spain. **74. St. Michael's . . . Mountain.** Mont-Saint-Michel, a rocky isle off the northern coast of France, is surmounted by the celebrated Benedictine abbey of St. Michael.

Where the grey seas glitter and the sharp tides shift,
And the sea-folk labour and the red sails lift.
He shakes his lance of iron and he claps his wings of stone;
The noise is gone through Normandy; the noise is gone alone;
The North is full of tangled things and texts and aching eyes,
And dead is all the innocence of anger and surprise,
And Christian killeth Christian in a narrow dusty room,
And Christian dreadeth Christ that hath a newer face of doom,
And Christian hateth Mary that God kissed in Galilee,—
But Don John of Austria is riding to the sea.
Don John calling through the blast and the eclipse,
Crying with the trumpet, with the trumpet of his lips,
Trumpet that sayeth *ha!*
Domino Gloria!
Don John of Austria
Is shouting to the ships.

King Philip's in his closet with the Fleece about his neck
(*Don John of Austria is armed upon the deck.*)
The walls are hung with velvet that is black and soft as sin,
And little dwarfs creep out of it and little dwarfs creep in.
He holds a crystal phial that has colours like the moon;
He touches, and it tingles, and he trembles very soon,
And his face is as a fungus of a leprous white and grey
Like plants in the high houses, that are shuttered from the day,
And death is in the phial and the end of noble work,
But Don John of Austria has fired upon the Turk.
Don John's hunting, and his hounds have bayed—
Booms away past Italy the rumour of his raid.
Gun upon gun, ha! ha!
Gun upon gun, hurrah!
Don John of Austria
Has loosed the cannonade.

The Pope was in his chapel before day or battle broke,
(*Don John of Austria is hidden in the smoke.*)
The hidden room in a man's house where God sits all the year,
The secret window whence the world looks small and very dear.
He sees as in a mirror on the monstrous twilight sea
The crescent of his cruel ships whose name is mystery;
They fling great shadows foe-wards, making Cross and Castle dark,
They veil the plumèd lions on the galleys of St. Mark;
And above the ships are palaces of brown, black-bearded chiefs,
And below the ships are prisons, where with multitudinous griefs,
Christian captives sick and sunless, all a labouring race repines
Like a race in sunken cities, like a nation in the mines.
They are lost like slaves that swat, and in the skies of morning hung
The stairways of the tallest gods when tyranny was young.
They are countless, voiceless, hopeless as those fallen or fleeing on
Before the high Kings' horses in the granite of Babylon.
And many a one grows witless in his quiet room in hell
Where a yellow face looks inward through the lattice of his cell,
And he finds his God forgotten, and he seeks no more a sign—
(*But Don John of Austria has burst the battle-line!*)
Don John pounding from the slaughter-painted poop,
Purpling all the ocean like a bloody pirate's sloop,
Scarlet running over on the silvers and the golds,
Breaking of the hatches up and bursting of the holds,
Thronging of the thousands up that labour under sea,
White for bliss and blind for sun and stunned for liberty.
Vivat Hispania!
Domino Gloria!
Don John of Austria
Has set his people free!

92. King Philip's . . . Fleece, Philip II of Spain with the collar of the Order of the Golden Fleece.

118. captives, galley slaves in the Turkish fleet. **137. Has set his people free.** "The thrill of the stanza describing the setting free of the Christian captives in the galleys is a little spoiled for those readers who remember Motley's estimate that at least 7,200 Turkish slaves were distributed among the Christian princes (Don John himself receiving 174 as a present from the Pope). But it would be unfair to allow the historical fact—if it is a fact—to spoil one's pleasure in a poem which is a romantic expression of a romantic abandonment to emotion." (Charles Williams, in his essay on Chesterton in *Poetry at Present*, Oxford, 1930.)

Cervantes on his galley sets the sword back in the sheath
(*Don John of Austria rides homeward with a wreath.*)
And he sees across a weary land a straggling road in Spain,
Up which a lean and foolish knight for ever rides in vain.
And he smiles, but not as Sultans smile, and settles back the blade. . . .
(*But Don John of Austria rides home from the Crusade.*)

W. Somerset Maugham

1874–

It was in Paris, where his father was connected with the British Embassy, that W(illiam) Somerset Maugham was born, January 25, 1874. He was, it seems, born to be a cosmopolitan, an inveterate traveler, and an insatiable reader. He had read all of Scott by the time he was ten; he taught himself to write by copying whole sections of the English classics. He was educated at King's School, Canterbury, and Heidelberg University. His father wanted him to be a doctor, and he dutifully took his degree at St. Thomas' Hospital in London, but he never practiced medicine. His first novel, *Liza of Lambeth*, 1897, written before he was twenty-three and while he was a medical student, grew out of his hospital experiences. Its frank revelation of slum conditions was considered sordid, even revolting, but it marked the advent of a new and extremely gifted apostle of candor.

Maugham wrote eighteen works between *Liza of Lambeth* and his next success. There were seven novels, a collection of short stories, a melodrama, several comedies and farces; but none of them made any particular impression. It was *Of Human Bondage*, 1915, which forced the critics to take Maugham seriously. *Of Human Bondage*, perhaps Maugham's most important contribution to the period, is semi-autobiographical; it returns to his days at the hospital and presents without mawkishness or false indignation a panorama of everyday, working-class existence. Superficially disinterested and detached, the author goes deep into ordinary life to realize extraordinary scenes. Passages of extreme brutality are followed by moments of great pity and tenderness. *The Moon and Sixpence*, 1919, was a sudden and enormously popular change. Adapting the life story of the French artist Paul Gauguin in Tahiti, Maugham discovered the South Seas. For many years he luxuriated in the Orient, in actuality as well as in fiction. The mood of the public was "escapist," and Maugham, an unusually skilled craftsman, exploited that mood to the full. Some books of short stories of this period are *The Trembling of a Leaf*, 1921, which contained "Miss Thompson," a story that was successfully adapted for the stage and screen in *Rain; The Casuarina Tree*, 1929, in which appeared "The Letter," one of Maugham's greatest stage and screen successes; and *Ah King*, 1933. The East also yielded such a tense novel as *The Painted Veil*, 1925, and such an original play as *East of Suez*, 1922.

By the time he was seventy-five, the number of Maugham's published volumes had almost reached that of his years, and most of them had enlarged his audience, enhanced his reputation, and swelled his fortune. His plays were brilliant and financially dependable; among the dramatic "hits" of the London stage were *The Circle*, 1921; *Our Betters*, 1923; *The Letter*, 1925; and *The Constant Wife*, 1926. Maugham is probably one of the few contemporary authors who have served their country as a spy—see *Ashenden, or, The British Agent*, 1928—and whose garret was a magnificent villa on the Riviera. For a while in later middle life, Maugham occupied himself largely with reminiscences and reappraisal. *Cakes and Ale, or, The Skeleton in the Cupboard*, 1930, is part fact, part fiction, and part caricature of a Grand Old Man of English letters (supposedly Thomas Hardy), a facile literary opportunist (obviously the novelist Hugh Walpole), and a gallery of shamelessly public "private lives." *The Summing Up*, 1938, is a frank and revealing "mental autobiography." *East and West*, 1934, reassembles Maugham's collected short stories, many of which are delicate but penetrating explorations of the intricacies and contrasts of human character. As an anthologist, the selection in *Tellers of Tales*, 1939, proves his taste; the volume also contains a long and stimulating introductory essay on the art of writing. He has recently returned

138. Cervantes, the author of *Don Quixote*, who fought and was wounded in the battle of Lepanto.

141. a lean and foolish knight, Don Quixote.

to fiction, and his latest works include the novels, *The Razor's Edge*, 1944, and *Catalina*, 1948, and a volume of short stories, *Creatures of Circumstance*, 1947.

In 1949, at the age of seventy-five, in the prologue to a motion picture called *Quartet*, made up of four of his short stories, Maugham summed up the critics' appraisal of his career as follows: "In my twenties the critics said I was brutal, in my thirties they said I was flippant, in my forties they said I was cynical, and in my fifties they said I was competent, and then in my sixties they said I was superficial. I have gone my own way, with a shrug of the shoulders, following the path I have traced, trying with my work to fill out the pattern of life that I have made for myself." *A Writer's Notebook*, published in the same year, contains hints for "copy" and sketches of men, women, and incidents jotted down over fifty years.

"Successful," "cosmopolitan," "accomplished" are the words usually employed to characterize Maugham. If they are not altogether critical, they are fairly accurate descriptions of one who is, first and last, a teller of tales. "Red," the story given here, is reminiscent of *The Moon and Sixpence* in its haunting romantic mood and its poetic tone intermixed with blunt cynicism.

RED[1]

THE skipper thrust his hand into one of his trouser pockets and with difficulty, for they were not at the sides but in front and he was a portly man, pulled out a large silver watch. He looked at it and then looked again at the declining sun. The Kanaka at the wheel gave him a glance, but did not speak. The skipper's eyes rested on the island they were approaching. A white line of foam marked the reef. He knew there was an opening large enough to get his ship through, and when they came a little nearer he counted on seeing it. They had nearly an hour of daylight still before them. In the lagoon the water was deep and they could anchor comfortably. The chief of the village which he could already see among the coconut trees was a friend of the mate's, and it would be pleasant to go ashore for the night. The mate came forward at that minute and the skipper turned to him.

"We'll take a bottle of booze along with us and get some girls in to dance," he said.

"I don't see the opening," said the mate.

He was a Kanaka, a handsome swarthy fellow, with somewhat the look of a later Roman emperor, inclined to stoutness; but his face was fine and clean-cut.

"I'm dead sure there's one right here," said the captain, looking through his glasses. "I can't understand why I can't pick it up. Send one of the boys up the mast to have a look."

The mate called one of the crew and gave him the order. The captain watched the Kanaka climb and waited for him to speak. But the Kanaka shouted down that he could see nothing but the unbroken line of foam. The captain spoke Samoan like a native, and he cursed him freely.

"Shall he stay up there?" asked the mate.

"What the hell good does that do?" answered the captain. "The blame fool can't see worth a cent. You bet your sweet life I'd find the opening if I was up there."

He looked at the slender mast with anger. It was all very well for a native who had been used to climbing up coconut trees all his life. He was fat and heavy.

"Come down," he shouted. "You're no more use than a dead dog. We'll just have to go along the reef till we find the opening."

It was a seventy-ton schooner with paraffin auxiliary, and it ran, when there was no head wind, between four and five knots an hour. It was a bedraggled object; it had been painted white a very long time ago, but it was now dirty, dingy, and mottled. It smelt strongly of paraffin and of the copra which was its usual cargo. They were within a hundred feet of the reef now and the captain told the steersman to run along it till they came to the opening, But when they had gone a couple of miles he realised that they had missed it. He went about and slowly worked back again. The white foam of the reef continued without interruption and now the sun was setting. With a curse at the stupidity of the crew the skipper resigned himself to waiting till next morning.

"Put her about," he said. "I can't anchor here."

They went out to sea a little and presently it was quite dark. They anchored. When the sail was furled the ship began to roll a good deal. They said in Apia that one day she would roll right over; and the owner, a German-American who managed one of the largest stores, said that no money was big enough to induce him to go out in her. The cook, a Chinese in white trousers, very dirty and ragged, and a thin white tunic, came to say that supper was ready, and when the skipper went into the cabin he

[1] From *East and West* by W. Somerset Maugham. Copyright, 1934, by Doubleday, Doran and Company, Inc., and used by their permission. Also from *Altogether*, used by permission of Mr. Maugham and William Heinemann Ltd.

found the engineer already seated at table. The engineer was a long lean man with a scraggy neck. He was dressed in blue overalls and a sleeveless jersey which showed his thin arms tattooed from elbow to wrist.

"Hell, having to spend the night outside," said the skipper.

The engineer did not answer, and they ate their supper in silence. The cabin was lit by a dim oil lamp. When they had eaten the canned apricots with which the meal finished, the Chink brought them a cup of tea. The skipper lit a cigar and went on the upper deck. The island now was only a darker mass against the night. The stars were very bright. The only sound was the ceaseless breaking of the surf. The skipper sank into a deck-chair and smoked idly. Presently three or four members of the crew came up and sat down. One of them had a banjo and another a concertina. They began to play, and one of them sang. The native song sounded strange on these instruments. Then to the singing a couple began to dance. It was a barbaric dance, savage and primeval, rapid, with quick movements of the hands and feet and contortions of the body; it was sensual, sexual even, but sexual without passion. It was very animal, direct, weird without mystery, natural in short, and one might almost say childlike. At last they grew tired. They stretched themselves on the deck and slept, and all was silent. The skipper lifted himself heavily out of his chair and clambered down the companion. He went into his cabin and got out of his clothes. He climbed into his bunk and lay there. He panted a little in the heat of the night.

But next morning, when the dawn crept over the tranquil sea, the opening in the reef which had eluded them the night before was seen a little to the east of where they lay. The schooner entered the lagoon. There was not a ripple on the surface of the water. Deep down among the coral rocks you saw little coloured fish swim. When he had anchored his ship the skipper ate his breakfast and went on deck. The sun shone from an unclouded sky, but in the early morning the air was grateful and cool. It was Sunday, and there was a feeling of quietness, a silence as though nature were at rest, which gave him a peculiar sense of comfort. He sat, looking at the wooded coast, and felt lazy and well at ease. Presently a slow smile moved his lips and he threw the stump of his cigar into the water.

"I guess I'll go ashore," he said. "Get the boat out."

He climbed stiffly down the ladder and was rowed to a little cove. The coconut trees came down to the water's edge, not in rows, but spaced out with an ordered formality. They were like a ballet of spinsters, elderly but flippant, standing in affected attitudes with the simpering graces of a bygone age. He sauntered idly through them, along a path that could be just seen winding its tortuous way, and it led him presently to a broad creek. There was a bridge across it, but a bridge constructed of single trunks of coconut trees, a dozen of them, placed end to end and supported where they met by a forked branch driven into the bed of the creek. You walked on a smooth, round surface, narrow and slippery, and there was no support for the hand. To cross such a bridge required sure feet and a stout heart. The skipper hesitated. But he saw on the other side, nestling among the trees, a white man's house; he made up his mind and, rather gingerly, began to walk. He watched his feet carefully, and where one trunk joined on to the next and there was a difference of level, he tottered a little. It was with a gasp of relief that he reached the last tree and finally set his feet on the firm ground of the other side. He had been so intent on the difficult crossing that he never noticed any one was watching him, and it was with surprise that he heard himself spoken to.

"It takes a bit of nerve to cross these bridges when you're not used to them."

He looked up and saw a man standing in front of him. He had evidently come out of the house which he had seen.

"I saw you hesitate," the man continued, with a smile on his lips, "and I was watching to see you fall in."

"Not on your life," said the captain, who had now recovered his confidence.

"I've fallen in myself before now. I remember, one evening I came back from shooting, and I fell in, gun and all. Now I get a boy to carry my gun for me."

He was a man no longer young, with a small beard, now somewhat grey, and a thin face. He was dressed in a singlet, without arms, and a pair of duck trousers. He wore neither shoes nor socks. He spoke English with a slight accent.

"Are you Neilson?" asked the skipper.

"I am."

"I've heard about you. I thought you lived somewheres round here."

The skipper followed his host into the little bungalow and sat down heavily in the chair which the other motioned him to take. While Neilson went out to fetch whisky and glasses he took a look round the room. It filled him with amazement. He had never seen so many books. The shelves reached from floor to ceiling on all four walls, and they were closely packed. There was a grand piano littered with music, and a large table on which books and magazines lay in disorder. The room made him feel embarrassed. He remembered that Neilson was a queer fellow. No one knew very much about him, although he had been in the islands for so many years, but those who knew him agreed that he was queer. He was a Swede.

"You've got one big heap of books here," he said, when Neilson returned.

"They do no harm," answered Neilson with a smile.

"Have you read them all?" asked the skipper.

"Most of them."

"I'm a bit of a reader myself. I have the *Saturday Evening Post* sent me regler."

Neilson poured his visitor a good stiff glass of whisky and gave him a cigar. The skipper volunteered a little information.

"I got in last night, but I couldn't find the opening, so I had to anchor outside. I never been this run before, but my people had some stuff they wanted to bring over here. Gray, d'you know him?"

"Yes, he's got a store a little way along."

"Well, there was a lot of canned stuff that he wanted over, an' he's got some copra. They thought I might just as well come over as lie idle at Apia. I run between Apia and Pago-Pago mostly, but they've got smallpox there just now, and there's nothing stirring."

He took a drink of his whisky and lit a cigar. He was a taciturn man, but there was something in Neilson that made him nervous, and his nervousness made him talk. The Swede was looking at him with large dark eyes in which there was an expression of faint amusement.

"This is a tidy little place you've got here."

"I've done my best with it."

"You must do pretty well with your trees. They look fine. With copra at the price it is now. I had a bit of a plantation myself once, in Upolu it was, but I had to sell it."

He looked round the room again, where all those books gave him a feeling of something incomprehensible and hostile.

"I guess you must find it a bit lonesome here though," he said.

"I've got used to it. I've been here for twenty-five years."

Now the captain could think of nothing more to say, and he smoked in silence. Neilson had apparently no wish to break it. He looked at his guest with a meditative eye. He was a tall man, more than six feet high, and very stout. His face was red and blotchy, with a network of little purple veins on the cheeks, and his features were sunk into its fatness. His eyes were bloodshot. His neck was buried in rolls of fat. But for a fringe of long curly hair, nearly white, at the back of his head, he was quite bald; and that immense, shiny surface of forehead, which might have given him a false look of intelligence, on the contrary gave him one of peculiar imbecility. He wore a blue flannel shirt, open at the neck and showing his fat chest covered with a mat of reddish hair, and a very old pair of blue serge trousers. He sat in his chair in a heavy ungainly attitude, his great belly thrust forward and his fat legs uncrossed. All elasticity had gone from his limbs. Neilson wondered idly what sort of man he had been in his youth. It was almost impossible to imagine that this creature of vast bulk had ever been a boy who ran about. The skipper finished his whisky, and Neilson pushed the bottle towards him.

"Help yourself."

The skipper leaned forward and with his great hand seized it.

"And how come you in these parts anyways?" he said.

"Oh, I came out to the islands for my health. My lungs were bad and they said I hadn't a year to live. You see they were wrong."

"I meant, how come you to settle down right here?"

"I am a sentimentalist."

"Oh!"

Neilson knew that the skipper had not an idea what he meant, and he looked at him with an ironical twinkle in his dark eyes. Perhaps just because the skipper was so gross and dull a man the whim seized him to talk further.

"You were too busy keeping your balance to notice, when you crossed the bridge, but this spot is generally considered rather pretty."

"It's a cute little house you've got here."

"Ah, that wasn't here when I first came. There was a native hut, with its beehive roof and its pillars, overshadowed by a great tree with red flowers; and the croton bushes, their leaves yellow and red and golden, made a pied fence around it. And then all about were the coconut trees, as fanciful as women, and as vain. They stood at the water's edge and spent all day looking at their reflections. I was a young man then—Good Heavens, it's a quarter of a century ago—and I wanted to enjoy all the loveliness of the world in the short time allotted to me before I passed into the darkness. I thought it was the most beautiful spot I had ever seen. The first time I saw it I had a catch at my heart, and I was afraid I was going to cry. I wasn't more than twenty-five, and though I put the best face I could on it, I didn't want to die. And somehow it seemed to me that the very beauty of this place made it easier for me to accept my fate. I felt when I came here that all my past life had fallen away, Stockholm and its University, and then Bonn: it all seemed the life of somebody else, as though now at last I had achieved the reality which our doctors of philosophy—I am one myself, you know—had discussed so much. 'A year,' I cried to myself. To have a year. I will spend it here and then I am content to die.'

"We are foolish and sentimental and melodramatic at twenty-five, but if we weren't perhaps we should be less wise at fifty.

"Now drink, my friend. Don't let the nonsense I talk interfere with you."

He waved his thin hand towards the bottle, and the skipper finished what remained in his glass.

"You ain't drinking nothin'," he said, reaching for the whisky.

"I am of a sober habit," smiled the Swede. "I intoxicate myself in ways which I fancy are more subtle. But perhaps that is only vanity. Anyhow, the effects are more lasting and the results less deleterious."

"They say there's a deal of cocaine taken in the States now," said the captain.

Neilson chuckled.

"But I do not see a white man often," he continued, "and for once I don't think a drop of whisky can do me any harm."

He poured himself out a little, added some soda, and took a sip.

"And presently I found out why the spot had such an unearthly loveliness. Here love had tarried for a moment like a migrant bird that happens on a ship in mid-ocean and for a little while folds its tired wings. The fragrance of a beautiful passion hovered over it like the fragrance of hawthorn in May in the meadows of my home. It seems to me that the places where men have loved or suffered keep about them always some faint aroma of something that has not wholly died. It is as though they had acquired a spiritual significance which mysteriously affects those who pass. I wish I could make myself clear." He smiled a little. "Though I cannot imagine that if I did you would understand."

He paused.

"I think this place was beautiful because here I had been loved beautifully." And now he shrugged his shoulders. "But perhaps it is only that my aesthetic sense is gratified by the happy conjunction of young love and a suitable setting."

Even a man less thick-witted than the skipper might have been forgiven if he were bewildered by Neilson's words. For he seemed faintly to laugh at what he said. It was as though he spoke from emotion which his intellect found ridiculous. He had said himself that he was a sentimentalist, and when sentimentality is joined with scepticism there is often the devil to pay.

He was silent for an instant and looked at the captain with eyes in which there was a sudden perplexity.

"You know, I can't help thinking that I've seen you before somewhere or other," he said.

"I couldn't say as I remember you," returned the skipper.

"I have a curious feeling as though your face were familiar to me. It's been puzzling me for some time. But I can't situate my recollection in any place or at any time."

The skipper massively shrugged his heavy shoulders.

"It's thirty years since I first came to the islands. A man can't figure on remembering all the folk he meets in a while like that."

The Swede shook his head.

"You know how one sometimes has the feeling that a place one has never been to before is strangely familiar. That's how I seem to see you." He gave a whimsical smile. Perhaps I knew you in some past existence. Perhaps, perhaps you were the master of a galley in ancient Rome and I was a slave at the oar. Thirty years have you been here?"

"Every bit of thirty years."

"I wonder if you knew a man called Red?"

"Red?"

"That is the only name I've ever known him by. I never knew him personally. I never even set eyes on him. And yet I seem to see him more clearly than many men, my brothers, for instance, with whom I passed my daily life for many years. He lives in my imagination with the distinctness of a Paolo Malatesta or a Romeo. But I daresay you have never read Dante or Shakespeare?"

"I can't say as I have," said the captain.

Neilson, smoking a cigar, leaned back in his chair and looked vacantly at the ring of smoke which floated in the still air. A smile played on his lips, but his eyes were grave. Then he looked at the captain. There was in his gross obesity something extraordinarily repellent. He had the plethoric self-satisfaction of the very fat. It was an outrage. It set

Neilson's nerves on edge. But the contrast between the man before him and the man he had in mind was pleasant.

"It appears that Red was the most comely thing you ever saw. I've talked to quite a number of people who knew him in those days, white men, and they all agree that the first time you saw him his beauty just took your breath away. They called him Red on account of his flaming hair. It had a natural wave and he wore it long. It must have been of that wonderful colour that the pre-Raphaelites raved over. I don't think he was vain of it, he was much too ingenuous for that, but no one could have blamed him if he had been. He was tall, six feet and an inch or two—in the native house that used to stand here was the mark of his height cut with a knife on the central trunk that supported the roof—and he was made like a Greek god, broad in the shoulders and thin in the flanks; he was like Apollo, with just that soft roundness which Praxiteles gave him, and that suave, feminine grace which has in it something troubling and mysterious. His skin was dazzling white, milky, like satin; his skin was like a woman's."

"I had kind of a white skin myself when I was a kiddie," said the skipper, with a twinkle in his bloodshot eyes.

But Neilson paid no attention to him. He was telling his story now and interruption made him impatient.

"And his face was just as beautiful as his body. He had large blue eyes, very dark, so that some say they were black, and unlike most red-haired people he had dark eyebrows and long dark lashes. His features were perfectly regular and his mouth was like a scarlet wound. He was twenty."

On these words the Swede stopped with a certain sense of the dramatic. He took a sip of whisky.

"He was unique. There never was any one more beautiful. There was no more reason for him than for a wonderful blossom to flower on a wild plant. He was a happy accident of nature.

"One day he landed at that cove into which you must have put this morning. He was an American sailor, and he had deserted from a man-of-war in Apia. He had induced some good-humoured native to give him a passage on a cutter that happened to be sailing from Apia to Safoto, and he had been put ashore here in a dug-out. I do not know why he deserted. Perhaps life on a man-of-war with its restrictions irked him, perhaps he was in trouble, and perhaps it was the South Seas and these romantic islands that got into his bones. Every now and then they take a man strangely, and he finds himself like a fly in a spider's web. It may be that there was a softness of fibre in him, and these green hills with their soft airs, this blue sea, took the northern strength from him as Delilah took the Nazarite's. Anyhow, he wanted to hide himself, and he thought he would be safe in this secluded nook till his ship had sailed from Samoa.

"There was a native hut at the cove and as he stood there, wondering where exactly he should turn his steps, a young girl came out and invited him to enter. He knew scarcely two words of the native tongue and she as little English. But he understood well enough what her smiles meant, and her pretty gestures, and he followed her. He sat down on a mat and she gave him slices of pineapple to eat. I can speak of Red only from hearsay, but I saw the girl three years after he first met her, and she was scarcely nineteen then. You cannot imagine how exquisite she was. She had the passionate grace of the hibiscus and the rich colour. She was rather tall, slim, with the delicate features of her race, and large eyes like pools of still water under the palm trees; her hair, black and curling, fell down her back, and she wore a wreath of scented flowers. Her hands were lovely. They were so small, so exquisitely formed, they gave your heart-strings a wrench. And in those days she laughed easily. Her smile was so delightful that it made your knees shake. Her skin was like a field of ripe corn on a summer day. Good Heavens, how can I describe her? She was too beautiful to be real.

"And these two young things, she was sixteen and he was twenty, fell in love with one another at first sight. That is the real love, not the love that comes from sympathy, common interests, or intellectual community, but love pure and simple. That is the love that Adam felt for Eve when he awoke and found her in the garden gazing at him with dewy eyes. That is the love that draws the beasts to one another, and the Gods. That is the love that makes the world a miracle. That is the love which gives life its pregnant meaning. You have never heard of the wise, cynical French duke who said that with two lovers there is always one who loves and one who lets himself be loved; it is a bitter truth to which most of us have to resign ourselves; but now and then there are two who love and two who let themselves be loved. Then one might fancy that the sun stands still as it stood when Joshua prayed to the God of Israel.

"And even now after all these years, when I think of these two, so young, so fair, so simple, and of their love, I feel a pang. It tears my heart just as my heart is torn when on certain nights I watch the full moon shining on the lagoon from an unclouded sky. There is always pain in the contemplation of perfect beauty.

"They were children. She was good and sweet and kind. I know nothing of him, and I like to think that then at all events he was ingenuous and frank. I like to think that his soul was as comely as his body. But I daresay he had no more soul than the creatures of the woods and forests who made pipes from reeds and bathed in the mountain streams when the world was young, and you might catch sight of little fauns galloping through the glade on the back of a bearded centaur. A soul is a troublesome possession and when man developed it he lost the Garden of Eden.

"Well, when Red came to the island it had recently been visited by one of those epidemics which the white man has brought to the South Seas, and one-third of the inhabitants had died. It seems that the girl had lost all her near kin and she lived now in the house of distant cousins. The household consisted of two ancient crones, bowed and wrinkled, two younger women, and a man and a boy. For a few days he stayed there. But perhaps he felt himself too near the shore, with the possibility that he might fall in with white men who would reveal his hiding-place; perhaps the lovers could not bear that the company of others should rob them for an instant of the delight of being together. One morning they set out, the pair of them, with the few things that belonged to the girl, and walked along a grassy path under the coconuts, till they came to the creek you see. They had to cross the bridge you crossed, and the girl laughed gleefully because he was afraid. She held his hand till they came to the end of the first tree, and then his courage failed him and he had to go back. He was obliged to take off all his clothes before he could risk it, and she carried them over for him on her head. They settled down in the empty hut that stood here. Whether she had any rights over it (land tenure is a complicated business in the islands), or whether the owner had died during the epidemic, I do not know, but anyhow no one questioned them, and they took possession. Their furniture consisted of a couple of grass mats on which they slept, a fragment of looking-glass, and a bowl or two. In this pleasant land that is enough to start housekeeping on.

"They say that happy people have no history, and certainly a happy love has none. They did nothing all day long and yet the days seemed all too short. The girl had a native name, but Red called her Sally. He picked up the easy language very quickly, and he used to lie on the mat for hours while she chattered gaily to him. He was a silent fellow, and perhaps his mind was lethargic. He smoked incessantly the cigarettes which she made him out of the native tobacco and pandanus leaf, and he watched her while with deft fingers she made grass mats. Often natives would come in and tell long stories of the old days when the island was disturbed by tribal wars. Sometimes he would go fishing on the reef, and bring home a basket full of coloured fish. Sometimes at night he would go out with a lantern to catch lobster. There were plantains round the hut and Sally would roast them for their frugal meal. She knew how to make delicious messes from coconuts, and the breadfruit tree by the side of the creek gave them its fruit. On feast-days they killed a little pig and cooked it on hot stones. They bathed together in the creek; and in the evening they went down to the lagoon and paddled about in a dug-out, with its great outrigger. The sea was deep blue, wine-coloured at sundown, like the sea of Homeric Greece; but in the lagoon the colour had an infinite variety, aquamarine and amethyst and emerald; and the setting sun turned it for a short moment to liquid gold. Then there was the colour of the coral, brown, white, pink, red, purple; and the shapes it took were marvellous. It was like a magic garden, and the hurrying fish were like butterflies. It strangely lacked reality. Among the coral were pools with a floor of white sand and here, where the water was dazzling clear, it was very good to bathe. Then, cool and happy, they wandered back in the gloaming over the soft grass road to the creek, walking hand in hand, and now the mynah birds filled the coconut trees with their clamour. And then the night, with that great sky shining with gold, that seemed to stretch more widely than the skies of Europe, and the soft airs that blew gently through the open hut, the long night again was all too short. She was sixteen and he was barely twenty. The dawn crept in among the wooden pillars of the hut and looked at those lovely children sleeping in one another's arms. The sun hid behind the great tattered leaves of the plantains so that it might not disturb them, and then, with playful malice, shot a golden ray, like the outstretched paw of a Persian cat, on their faces. They opened their sleepy eyes and they smiled to welcome another day. The weeks lengthened into months, and a year passed. They seemed to love one another as—I hesitate to say passionately, for passion has in it always a shade of sadness, a touch of bitterness or anguish, but as whole-heartedly, as simply and naturally as on that first day on which, meeting, they had recognized that a god was in them.

"If you had asked them I have no doubt that they would have thought it impossible to suppose their love could ever cease. Do we not know that the essential element of love is a belief in its own eternity? And yet perhaps in Red there was already a very little seed, unknown to himself and unsuspected by the girl, which would in time have grown to weariness. For one day one of the natives from the cove told them that some way down the coast at the anchorage was a British whaling-ship.

" 'Gee,' he said, 'I wonder if I could make a trade of some nuts and plantains for a pound or two of tobacco.'

"The pandanus cigarettes that Sally made him with untiring hands were strong and pleasant enough to smoke, but they left him unsatisfied; and he yearned on a sudden for real tobacco, hard, rank, and pungent. He had not smoked a pipe for many months. His mouth watered at the thought of it. One would have thought some premonition of harm would have made Sally seek to dissuade him, but love possessed her so completely that it never occurred to her any power on earth could take him from her. They went up into the hills together and gathered a great basket of wild oranges, green, but sweet and juicy; and they picked plantains from around the hut, and coconuts from their trees, and breadfruit and mangoes; and they carried them down to the cove. They loaded the unstable canoe with them, and Red and the native boy who had brought them the news of the ship paddled along outside the reef.

"It was the last time she ever saw him.

"Next day the boy came back alone. He was all in tears. This is the story he told. When after their long paddle they reached the ship and Red hailed it, a white man looked over the side and told them to come on board. They took the fruit they had brought with them and Red piled it up on the deck. The white man and he began to talk, and they seemed to come to some agreement. One of them went below and brought up tobacco. Red took some at once and lit a pipe. The boy imitated the zest with which he blew a great cloud of smoke from his mouth. Then they said something to him and he went into the cabin. Through the open door the boy, watching curiously, saw a bottle brought out and glasses. Red drank and smoked. They seemed to ask him something, for he shook his head and laughed. The man, the first man who had spoken to them, laughed too, and he filled Red's glass once more. They went on talking and drinking, and presently, growing tired of watching a sight that meant nothing to him, the boy curled himself up on the deck and slept. He was awakened by a kick; and, jumping to his feet, he saw that the ship was slowly sailing out of the lagoon. He caught sight of Red seated at the table, with his head resting heavily on his arms, fast asleep. He made a movement towards him, intending to wake him, but a rough hand seized his arm, and a man, with a scowl and words which he did not understand, pointed to the side. He shouted to Red, but in a moment he was seized and flung overboard. Helpless, he swam around to his canoe which was drifting a little way off, and pushed it on to the reef. He climbed in and, sobbing all the way, paddled back to shore.

"What had happened was obvious enough. The whaler, by desertion or sickness, was short of hands, and the captain when Red came aboard had asked him to sign on; on his refusal he had made him drunk and kidnapped him.

"Sally was beside herself with grief. For three days she screamed and cried. The natives did what they could to comfort her, but she would not be comforted. She would not eat. And then, exhausted, she sank into a sullen apathy. She spent long days at the cove, watching the lagoon, in the vain hope that Red somehow or other would manage to escape. She sat on the white sand, hour after hour, with the tears running down her cheeks, and at night dragged herself wearily back across the creek to the little hut where she had been happy. The people with whom she had lived before Red came to the island wished her to return to them, but she would not; she was convinced that Red would come back, and she wanted him to find her where he had left her. Four months later she was delivered of a still-born child, and the old woman who had come to help her through her confinement remained with her in the hut. All joy was taken from her life. If her anguish with time became less intolerable it was replaced by a settled melancholy. You would not have thought that among these people, whose emotions, though so violent, are very transient, a woman could be found capable of so enduring a passion. She never lost the profound conviction that sooner or later Red would come back. She watched for him, and every time some one crossed this slender little bridge of coconut trees she looked. It might at last be he."

Neilson stopped talking and gave a faint sigh.

"And what happened to her in the end?" asked the skipper.

Neilson smiled bitterly.

"Oh, three years afterwards she took up with another white man."

The skipper gave a fat, cynical chuckle.

"That's generally what happens to them," he said.

The Swede shot him a look of hatred. He did not know why that gross, obese man excited in him so violent a repulsion. But his thoughts wandered and he found his mind filled with memories of the past. He went back five-and-twenty years. It was when he first came to the island, weary of Apia, with its heavy drinking, its gambling and coarse sensuality, a sick man, trying to resign himself to the loss of the career which had fired his imagination with ambitious thoughts. He set behind him resolutely all his hopes of making a great name for himself and strove to content himself with the few poor months of careful life which was all that he could count on. He was boarding with a half-caste trader who had a store a couple of miles along the coast at the edge of a native village; and one day, wandering aimlessly along the grassy paths of the coconut groves, he had come upon the hut in which Sally lived. The beauty of the spot had filled him with a rapture so great that it was almost painful, and then he had seen Sally. She was the loveliest creature he had ever seen, and the sadness in those dark, magnificent eyes of hers affected him strangely. The Kanakas were a handsome race, and beauty was not rare among them, but it was the beauty of shapely animals. It was empty. But those tragic eyes were dark with mystery, and you felt in them the bitter complexity of the groping, human soul. The trader told him the story and it moved him.

"Do you think he'll ever come back?" asked Neilson.

"No fear. Why, it'll be a couple of years before the ship is paid off, and by then he'll have forgotten all about her. I bet he was pretty mad when he woke up and found he'd been shanghaied, and I shouldn't wonder but he wanted to fight somebody. But he'd got to grin and bear it, and I guess in a month he was thinking it the best thing that had ever happened to him that he got away from the island."

But Neilson could not get the story out of his head. Perhaps because he was sick and weakly, the radiant health of Red appealed to his imagination. Himself an ugly man, insignificant of appearance, he prized very highly comeliness in others. He had never been passionately in love, and certainly he had never been passionately loved. The mutual attraction of those two young things gave him a singular delight. It had the ineffable beauty of the Absolute. He went again to the little hut by the creek. He had a gift for languages and an energetic mind, accustomed to work, and he had already given much time to the study of the local tongue. Old habit was strong in him and he was gathering together material for a paper on the Samoan speech. The old crone who shared the hut with Sally invited him to come in and sit down. She gave him *kava* to drink and cigarettes to smoke. She was glad to have some one to chat with and while she talked he looked at Sally. She reminded him of the Psyche in the museum at Naples. Her features had the same clear purity of line, and though she had borne a child she had still a virginal aspect.

It was not till he had seen her two or three times that he induced her to speak. Then it was only to ask him if he had seen in Apia a man called Red. Two years had passed since his disappearance, but it was plain that she still thought of him incessantly.

It did not take Neilson long to discover that he was in love with her. It was only by an effort of will now that he prevented himself from going every day to the creek, and when he was not with Sally his thoughts were. At first, looking upon himself as a dying man, he asked only to look at her, and occasionally hear her speak, and his love gave him a wonderful happiness. He exulted in its purity. He wanted nothing from her but the opportunity to weave around her graceful person a web of beautiful fancies. But the open air, the equable temperature, the rest, the simple fare, began to have an unexpected effect on his health. His temperature did not soar at night to such alarming heights, he coughed less and began to put on weight; six months passed without his having a haemorrhage; and on a sudden he saw the possibility that he might live. He had studied his disease carefully, and the hope dawned upon him that with great care he might arrest its course. It exhilarated him to look forward once more to the future. He made plans. It was evident that any active life was out of the question, but he could live on the islands, and the small income he had, insufficient elsewhere, would be ample to keep him. He could grow coconuts; that would give him an occupation; and he would send for his books and a piano; but his quick mind saw that in all this he was merely trying to conceal for himself the desire which obsessed him.

He wanted Sally. He loved not only her beauty, but that dim soul which he divined behind her suffering eyes. He would intoxicate her with his passion. In the end he would make her forget. And in an ecstasy of surrender he fancied himself giving her too the happiness which he had thought never to know again, but had now so miraculously achieved.

He asked her to live with him. She refused. He had expected that and did not let it depress him, for he was sure that sooner or later she would yield.

His love was irresistible. He told the old woman of his wishes, and found somewhat to his surprise that she and the neighbours, long aware of them, were strongly urging Sally to accept his offer. After all, every native was glad to keep house for a white man, and Neilson according to the standards of the island was a rich one. The trader with whom he boarded went to her and told her not to be a fool; such an opportunity would not come again, and after so long she could not still believe that Red would ever return. The girl's resistance only increased Neilson's desire, and what had been a very pure love now became an agonizing passion. He was determined that nothing should stand in his way. He gave Sally no peace. At last, worn out by his persistence and the persuasions, by turns pleading and angry, of every one around her, she consented. But the day after when, exultant, he went to see her he found that in the night she had burnt down the hut in which she and Red had lived together. The old crone ran towards him full of angry abuse of Sally, but he waved her aside; it did not matter; they would build a bungalow on the place where the hut had stood. A European house would really be more convenient if he wanted to bring out a piano and a vast number of books.

And so the little wooden house was built in which he had now lived for many years, and Sally became his wife. But after the first few weeks of rapture, during which he was satisfied with what she gave him, he had known little happiness. She had yielded to him, through weariness, but she had only yielded what she set no store on. The soul which he had dimly glimpsed escaped him. He knew that she cared nothing for him. She still loved Red, and all the time she was waiting for his return. At a sign from him, Neilson knew that, notwithstanding his love, his tenderness, his sympathy, his generosity, she would leave him without a moment's hesitation. She would never give a thought to his distress. Anguish seized him and he battered at that impenetrable self of hers which sullenly resisted him. His love became bitter. He tried to melt her heart with kindness, but it remained as hard as before; he feigned indifference, but she did not notice it. Sometimes he lost his temper and abused her, and then she wept silently. Sometimes he thought she was nothing but a fraud, and that soul simply an invention of his own, and that he could not get into the sanctuary of her heart because there was no sanctuary there. His love became a prison from which he longed to escape, but he had not the strength merely to open the door—that was all it needed—and walk out into the open air. It was torture and at last he became numb and hopeless. In the end the fire burnt itself out and, when he saw her eyes rest for an instant on the slender bridge, it was no longer rage that filled his heart but impatience. For many years now they had lived together bound by the ties of habit and convenience, and it was with a smile that he looked back on his old passion. She was an old woman, for the women on the islands age quickly, and if he had no love for her any more he had tolerance. She left him alone. He was contented with his piano and his books.

His thoughts led him to a desire for words.

"When I look back now and reflect on that brief passionate love of Red and Sally, I think that perhaps they should thank the ruthless fate that separated them when their love seemed still to be at its height. They suffered, but they suffered in beauty. They were spared the real tragedy of love."

"I don't know exactly as I get you," said the skipper.

"The tragedy of love is not death or separation. How long do you think it would have been before one or other of them ceased to care? Oh, it is dreadfully bitter to look at a woman whom you have loved with all your heart and soul, so that you felt you could not bear to let her out of your sight, and realize that you would not mind if you never saw her again. The tragedy of love is indifference."

But while he was speaking a very extraordinary thing happened. Though he had been addressing the skipper he had not been talking to him, he had been putting his thoughts into words for himself, and with his eyes fixed on the man in front of him he had not seen him. But now an image presented itself to them, an image not of the man he saw, but of another man. It was as though he were looking into one of those distorting mirrors that make you extraordinarily squat or outrageously elongate, but here exactly the opposite took place, and in the obese, ugly old man he caught the shadowy glimpse of a stripling. He gave him now a quick, searching scrutiny. Why had a haphazard stroll brought him just to this place? A sudden tremor of his heart made him slightly breathless. An absurd suspicion seized him. What had occurred to him was impossible, and yet it might be a fact.

"What is your name?" he asked abruptly.

The skipper's face puckered and he gave a cunning chuckle. He looked then malicious and horribly vulgar.

"It's such a damned long time since I heard it that I almost forget it myself. But for thirty years now in the islands they've always called me Red."

His huge form shook as he gave a low, almost

silent laugh. It was obscene. Neilson shuddered. Red was hugely amused, and from his bloodshot eyes tears ran down his cheeks.

Neilson gave a gasp, for at that moment a woman came in. She was a native, a woman of somewhat commanding presence, stout without being corpulent, dark, for the natives grow darker with age, with very grey hair. She wore a black Mother Hubbard, and its thinness showed her heavy breasts. The moment had come.

She made an observation to Neilson about some household matter and he answered. He wondered if his voice sounded as unnatural to her as it did to himself. She gave the man who was sitting in the chair by the window an indifferent glance, and went out of the room. The moment had come and gone.

Neilson for a moment could not speak. He was strangely shaken. Then he said:

"I'd be very glad if you'd stay and have a bit of dinner with me. Pot luck."

"I don't think I will," said Red. "I must go after this fellow Gray. I'll give him his stuff and then I'll get away. I want to be back in Apia to-morrow."

"I'll send a boy along with you to show you the way."

"That'll be fine."

Red heaved himself out of his chair, while the Swede called one of the boys who worked on the plantation. He told him where the skipper wanted to go, and the boy stepped along the bridge. Red prepared to follow him.

"Don't fall in," said Neilson.

"Not on your life."

Neilson watched him make his way across and when he had disappeared among the coconuts he looked still. Then he sank heavily in his chair. Was that the man who had prevented him from being happy? Was that the man whom Sally had loved all these years and for whom she had waited so desperately? It was grotesque. A sudden fury seized him so that he had an instinct to spring up and smash everything around him. He had been cheated. They had seen each other at last and had not known it. He began to laugh, mirthlessly, and his laughter grew till it became hysterical. The Gods had played him a cruel trick. And he was old now.

At last Sally came in to tell him dinner was ready. He sat down in front of her and tried to eat. He wondered what she would say if he told her now that the fat old man sitting in the chair was the lover whom she remembered still with the passionate abandonment of her youth. Years ago, when he hated her because she made him so unhappy, he would have been glad to tell her. He wanted to hurt her then as she hurt him, because his hatred was only love. But now he did not care. He shrugged his shoulders listlessly.

"What did that man want?" she asked presently.

He did not answer at once. She was old too, a fat old native woman. He wondered why he had ever loved her so madly. He had laid at her feet all the treasures of his soul, and she had cared nothing for them. Waste, what waste! And now, when he looked at her, he felt only contempt. His patience was at last exhausted. He answered her question.

"He's the captain of a schooner. He's come from Apia."

"Yes."

"He brought me news from home. My eldest brother is very ill and I must go back."

"Will you be gone long?"

He shrugged his shoulders.

John Masefield
1878–

John Masefield was born June 1, 1878, at Ledbury, Herefordshire. His father, a lawyer, died while Masefield was still a boy, and the lad was indentured to a merchant ship at fourteen. The first twenty years of his life were hard; after several rough years at sea his wanderings took him to America, where he worked for a while in a Greenwich Village saloon in New York City and in a carpet factory in Yonkers. Masefield's unpretentious autobiographical volume, *In the Mill*, 1941, describes his years as an American industrial worker, during which for the first time he read Chaucer, Malory, and the Romantics, and determined to be a poet.

Five years after his return to England he published *Salt-Water Ballads*, 1902, a collection of swinging lyrics of sailors and the sea. It did not attract much attention, but the volume contained many of Masefield's most quoted verses. *The Everlasting Mercy*, 1911, was the first volume to achieve popular success; it was praised by the critics for its "Chaucerian vigor," relished by the lay reader for its plain speech and rhythmical heartiness. *The Widow in the Bye Street*, 1912, and *Dauber*, 1913, enlarged the author's reputation and increased his audience. Masefield's sympathy with ordinary workers and "common characters" often brought him to the verge of sentimentality—his dramatis personae usually "got religion" and reformed—but he was one of the first to make the Georgian movement seem a movement of innovation, even of protest. Moreover he succeeded (if only temporarily) in bringing narrative verse back to favor. The popularity of his rude and sometimes shocking story-poems was great; they were liked for their gusto; they achieved a blend of personal strength and abstract vigor. But the First World War did not stimulate a literature of violence. On the contrary, force lost its power and gave way to a literature of exhaustion. Immediately after the war, the poets with few exceptions turned from bugle calls to pastorals. Masefield joined the movement of escape and began writing "classic" sonnets, religious verse, and new versions of old myths such as *King Cole*, 1921, and *A Tale of Troy*, 1932. But in sacrificing his early vigor of epithet and plot he also sacrificed his individuality. Critical opinion changed. It began to be suspected that the rebellious Georgian was little more than a roughened Victorian.

Besides his poetry, the best of which can be found in *Collected Poems*, 1932, Masefield wrote more than a dozen plays (including translations from Racine); about twelve volumes of essays and studies which range from *Sea Life in Nelson's Time*, 1905, through *The Battle of the Somme*, 1919, to *Chaucer*, 1931; several books for boys; and "adventure" novels which capture his early robustness.

In 1930 Masefield succeeded Robert Bridges as poet laureate. It was said that *Reynard the Fox*, 1919, which vigorously expresses the spirit of rural England, did more than any other work to win him the honor. Producing little beyond the perfunctory laureate verse expected of him, Masefield has remained totally unaffected by the poetic movements and fashions of recent decades. When in 1950 he published an anthology of his favorite poems, characteristically enough he included no poet more recent than Dante Gabriel Rossetti. He has been most content in the company of Chaucer, Shakespeare, Milton, and the Romantic poets, especially Shelley, although he makes no claim to approaching their achievements. In his later unproductive years it has perhaps been too easy to ignore a poet capable of delicate lyricism as well as narrative power who, in a time of experimentation and new directions, has preferred to follow the traditional path, and who, in the early years of the century, brought a new and startlingly elemental vigor into English poetry.

SEA-FEVER [1]

I must go down to the seas again, to the lonely sea and the sky,
And all I ask is a tall ship and a star to steer her by,
And the wheel's kick and the wind's song and the white sail's shaking,
And a gray mist on the sea's face and a gray dawn breaking.

I must go down to the seas again, for the call of the running tide
Is a wild call and a clear call that may not be denied;
And all I ask is a windy day with the white clouds flying,
And the flung spray and the blown spume, and the sea-gulls crying.

I must go down to the seas again to the vagrant gypsy life,
To the gull's way and the whale's way where the wind's like a whetted knife;
And all I ask is a merry yarn from a laughing fellow-rover,
And quiet sleep and a sweet dream when the long trick's over.

A WANDERER'S SONG

A wind's in the heart of me, a fire's in my heels,
I am tired of brick and stone and rumbling wagon-wheels;
I hunger for the sea's edge, the limits of the land,
Where the wild old Atlantic is shouting on the sand.

Oh I'll be going, leaving the noises of the street,
To where a lifting foresail-foot is yanking at the sheet;
To a windy, tossing anchorage where yawls and ketches ride,
Oh I'll be going, going, until I meet the tide.

[1] This and the following poems by John Masefield are from *The Collected Poems of John Masefield*, copyright, 1923, by The Macmillan Company and used with their permission.

And first I'll hear the sea-wind, the mewing of the gulls,
The clucking, sucking of the sea about the rusty hulls,
The songs at the capstan in the hooker warping out,
And then the heart of me'll know I'm there or thereabout.

Oh I am sick of brick and stone, the heart of me is sick,
For windy green, unquiet sea, the realm of Moby Dick;
And I'll be going, going, from the roaring of the wheels,
For a wind's in the heart of me, a fire's in my heels.

THE WEST WIND

It's a warm wind, the west wind, full of birds' cries;
I never hear the west wind but tears are in my eyes.
For it comes from the west lands, the old brown hills,
And April's in the west wind, and daffodils.

It's a fine land, the west land, for hearts as tired as mine,
Apple orchards blossom there, and the air's like wine.
There is cool green grass there, where men may lie at rest,
And the thrushes are in song there, fluting from the nest.

"Will you not come home, brother? you have been long away,
It's April, and blossom time, and white is the spray;
And bright is the sun, brother, and warm is the rain—
Will you not come, brother, home to us again?

"The young corn is green, brother, where the rabbits run,
It's blue sky, and white clouds, and warm rain and sun.
It's song to a man's soul, brother, fire to a man's brain,
To hear the wild bees and see the merry spring again.

"Larks are singing in the west, brother, above the green wheat,
So will you not come home, brother, and rest your tired feet?
I've a balm for bruised hearts, brother, sleep for aching eyes,"
Says the warm wind, the west wind, full of birds' cries.

It's the white road westwards is the road I must tread
To the green grass, the cool grass, and rest for heart and head,
To the violets and the brown brooks and the thrushes' song,
In the fine land, the west land, the land where I belong.

3. **brown hills.** One of the many references in Masefield's poetry to the landscape of his native Herefordshire, in the west of England.

CARGOES

Quinquireme of Nineveh from distant Ophir,
Rowing home to haven in sunny Palestine,
With a cargo of ivory,
And apes and peacocks,
Sandalwood, cedarwood, and sweet white wine.

Stately Spanish galleon coming from the Isthmus,
Dipping through the Tropics by the palm-green shores,
With a cargo of diamonds,
Emeralds, amethysts,
Topazes, and cinnamon, and gold moidores.

Dirty British coaster with a salt-caked smoke stack,
Butting through the Channel in the mad March days,
With a cargo of Tyne coal,
Road-rails, pig-lead,
Firewood, iron-ware, and cheap tin trays.

BEAUTY

I have seen dawn and sunset on moors and windy hills
Coming in solemn beauty like slow old tunes of Spain;
I have seen the lady April bringing the daffodils,
Bringing the springing grass, and the soft warm April rain.

1. **Quinquireme,** an ancient galley with five banks of oars. **Nineveh,** the capital of ancient Assyria. **Ophir,** a district famous in Old Testament days for its gold and other precious merchandise. See I Kings 9:28 and 10:11. **6. Isthmus,** of Panama. **10. moidores,** Portuguese gold coins, worth about five dollars each. **13. Tyne coal,** coal carried from Newcastle down the Tyne River, in Northumberland, England.

I have heard the song of the blossoms and the old chant of the sea,
And seen strange lands from under the arched white sails of ships;
But the loveliest things of beauty God ever has showed to me
Are her voice, and her hair, and eyes, and the dear red curve of her lips.

from LOLLINGDON DOWNS

8

The Kings go by with jewelled crowns;
Their horses gleam, their banners shake, their spears are many.
The sack of many-peopled towns
Is all their dream;
The way they take
Leaves but a ruin in the brake,
And, in the furrow that the ploughmen make,
A stampless penny: a tale, a dream.

The merchants reckon up their gold;
Their letters come, their ships arrive, their freights are glories;
The profits of their treasure sold
They tell and sum:
The foremen drive
Their servants, starved to half-alive,
Whose labours do but make the earth a hive
Of stinking stories: a tale, a dream.

The priests are singing in their stalls;
Their singing lifts, their incense burns, their praying clamours;
Yet God is as the sparrow falls;
The ivy drifts,
The votive urns
Are all left void when Fortune turns;
The god is but a marble for the kerns
To break with hammers: a tale, a dream.

O Beauty, let me know again
The green earth cold, the April rain, the quiet waters figuring sky,
The one star risen.
So shall I pass into the feast
Not touched by King, merchant, or priest;
Know the red spirit of the beast,
Be the green grain;
Escape from prison.

31

Flesh, I have knocked at many a dusty door,
Gone down full many a windy midnight lane,
Probed in old walls and felt along the floor,
Pressed in blind hope the lighted window-pane,
But useless all, though sometimes when the moon
Was full in heaven and the sea was full,
Along my body's alleys came a tune
Played in the tavern by the Beautiful.
Then for an instant I have felt at point
To find and seize her, whosoe'er she be,
Whether some saint whose glory doth anoint
Those whom she loves, or but a part of me,
Or something that the things not understood
Make for their uses out of flesh and blood.

41

Roses are beauty, but I never see
Those blood drops from the burning heart of June
Glowing like thought upon the living tree,
Without a pity that they die so soon,
Die into petals, like those roses old,
Those women, who were summer in men's hearts
Before the smile upon the Sphinx was cold,
Or sand had hid the Syrian and his arts.
O myriad dust of beauty that lies thick
Under our feet that not a single grain
But stirred and moved in beauty and was quick
For one brief moon and died nor lived again;
But, when the moon rose, lay upon the grass,
Pasture to living beauty, life that was.

ON GROWING OLD

Be with me, Beauty, for the fire is dying,
My dog and I are old, too old for roving.
Man, whose young passion sets the spindrift flying,
Is soon too lame to march, too cold for loving.

I take the book and gather to the fire,
Turning old yellow leaves; minute by minute
The clock ticks to my heart; a withered wire
Moves a thin ghost of music in the spinet.

I cannot sail your seas, I cannot wander
Your cornland, nor your hill-land, nor your valleys
Ever again, nor share the battle yonder
Where the young knight the broken squadron rallies.

Only stay quiet while my mind remembers
The beauty of fire from the beauty of embers.

Beauty, have pity, for the young have power,
The rich their wealth, the beautiful their grace,
Summer of man its sunlight and its flower,
Springtime of man all April in a face.

Only, as in the jostling in the Strand,
Where the mob thrusts or loiters or is loud,
The beggar with the saucer in his hand
Asks only a penny from the passing crowd,

So, from this glittering world with all its fashion,
Its fire and play of men, its stir, its march,
Let me have wisdom, Beauty, wisdom and passion,
Bread to the soul, rain where the summers parch.

Give me but these, and though the darkness close,
Even the night will blossom as the rose.

E. M. Forster
1879–

Edward Morgan Forster was born in London on January 1, 1879, and went as a day-boy to the boarding school at Tonbridge in Kent. The town and the school, under the name of Sawston, were to receive severe treatment in his first two novels. He was much happier at King's College, Cambridge, to which he went when he was eighteen and to which he pays a glorious tribute in *The Longest Journey* and elsewhere. At Cambridge he acquired an enthusiasm for ancient Greece and Italy which sent him off on travels to the Mediterranean shortly after he left college. He visited Greece and lived for a while in Italy, which furnished the setting for his earliest novels. His interest in people and the complexities of human relationships began to express itself in short stories during his early twenties. He made his first appearance in print at twenty-four, and his first novel, *Where Angels Fear to Tread*, was published in 1905, two years later. Three more novels followed within a few years—*The Longest Journey*, 1907; *A Room with a View*, 1908; and *Howards End*, 1910. Fourteen years and a world war were to intervene between *Howards End* and his fifth and best known novel, *A Passage to India*, 1924. In 1911 he brought out a collection of his early stories in *The Celestial Omnibus*, most of them in the vein of fantasy and mythology, and dealing in one way or another with the theme which was to preoccupy him in all his work—the ceaseless struggle between the world of spirit and the everyday world of conventions and compromise.

In 1912 Forster sailed with his friends G. Lowes Dickinson, the Cambridge philosopher, and R. C. Trevelyan for India, where he was to gather the materials for his most famous novel. The war years between 1914 and 1918 he spent in non-combatant service in Egypt, chiefly in Alexandria. Here he found time to write *Alexandria: A History and a Guide*, 1922, one of the best books of its kind, and a volume of sketches of Alexandrian history, customs, and local color, *Pharos and Pharillon*, 1923. In 1922, ten years after his first visit, he made a second journey to India, where he became greatly interested in Anglo-Indian relationships, and studied at first hand the complexities of the problem of British rule in the great sub-continent and the conflicts and diversities among the Indians themselves. Out of his studies and reflections came his novel, *A Passage to India*, which achieved instant success. Since 1924 no fiction has come from his pen, although he reprinted six of his short stories in a volume, *The Eternal Moment*, in 1928.

Forster's fiction has those qualities of intelligence, critical insight, and perceptiveness and a grace of style which make a special appeal to skillful practitioners of the art of writing and to the critically minded. Lionel Trilling, for example, begins his study of Forster thus: "E. M. Forster is for me the only living novelist who can be read again and again and who, after each reading, gives me what few writers can give us after our first days of novel-reading, the sensation of having learned something."[1] Two discerning novelists and critics, Rose Macaulay[2] and Virginia Woolf,[3] have discussed his work in detail. The corpus of his fiction is small, and, as has been noted, one predominant theme runs through all of it: the conflict in various aspects and forms between the real and the sham, between the free world of nature and the spirit and the middle-class world of conventions and compromises

[1] Lionel Trilling, *E. M. Forster*, New Directions, 1943.
[2] Rose Macaulay, *The Writings of E. M. Forster*, Hogarth Press, 1938. [3] Virginia Woolf, *The Death of the Moth and Other Essays*, Harcourt, Brace, 1942.

and snobberies. Of the pretensions and affectations and cruelties of that world Forster has never ceased to be an acute, relentless, but withal gay and genial critic. In *Where Angels Fear to Tread* and *A Room with a View* the scene is Italy, and the conflict is between Anglo-Saxon and Italian temperaments and mores. In *The Longest Journey* Cambridge supplies the setting and a sensitive English lad is pitted against his Philistine companions. In *Howards End* prewar London is the arena in which a complicated series of conflicts involving personal relationships, economic and social philosophies, the fate of England and the Empire, are brought into play. The nature of the conflict and the factors involved in *A Passage to India* have been intimated.

Forster's productions during the past twenty-five years have consisted of critical essays and lectures. A pamphlet of ingenious literary speculation called *Anonymity, An Enquiry* was brought out in 1925, and in 1927 he delivered the Clark Lectures at Cambridge. They were published under the title *Aspects of the Novel*. The lecture on fantasy which is printed below is taken from this series. A generous collection of Forster's essays and reviews was published in the volume *Abinger Harvest* in 1936. In 1934 he produced a biography, remarkable for its objectiveness as well as for its brilliance, of his friend G. Lowes Dickinson. In 1941, as Rede Lecturer at Cambridge, he commemorated his friend Virginia Woolf, who had just died. The lecture was published in 1942.

Forster is one of the most companionable of writers, and the master of one of the most natural and unforced styles in the language. As novelist, interpreter of the art of the novel, commentator, and social critic, his rank as one of the greatest English writers of the first half of the twentieth century seems assured.

from ASPECTS OF THE NOVEL [1]

Fantasy

A COURSE of lectures, if it is to be more than a collection of remarks, must have an idea running through it. It must also have a subject, and the idea ought to run through the subject too. This is so obvious as to sound foolish, but any one who has tried to lecture will realize that here is a genuine difficulty. A course, like any other collection of words, generates an atmosphere. It has its own apparatus—a lecturer, an audience or provision for one, it occurs at regular intervals, it is announced by printed notices, and it has a financial side, though this last is tactfully concealed. Thus it tends in its parasitic way to lead a life of its own, and it and the idea running through it are apt to move in one direction while the subject steals off in the other.

The idea running through these lectures is by now plain enough: that there are in the novel two forces: human beings and a bundle of various things not human beings, and that it is the novelist's business to adjust two forces and conciliate their claims. That is plain enough, but does it run through the novel too? Perhaps our subject, namely the books we have read, has stolen away from us while we theorize, like a shadow from an ascending bird. The bird is all right—it climbs, it is consistent and eminent. The shadow is all right—it has flickered across roads and gardens. But the two things resemble one another less and less, they do not touch as they did when the bird rested its toes on the ground. Criticism, especially a critical course, is so misleading. However lofty its intentions and sound its method, its subject slides away from beneath it, imperceptibly away, and lecturer and audience may awake with a start to find that they are carrying on in a distinguished and intelligent manner, but in regions which have nothing to do with anything they have read.

It was this that was worrying Gide, or rather one of the things that was worrying him, for he has an anxious mind. When we try to translate truth out of one sphere into another, whether from life into books or from books into lectures, something happens to truth, it goes wrong, not suddenly when it might be detected, but slowly. . . . There is more in the novel than time or people or logic or any of their derivatives, more even than Fate. And by "more" I do not mean something that excludes these aspects nor something that includes them, embraces them. I mean something that cuts across them like a bar of light, that is intimately connected with them at one place and patiently illumines all their problems, and at another place shoots over or through them as if they did not exist. We shall give that bar of light two names, fantasy and prophecy.

The novels we have now to consider all tell a story, contain characters, and have plots or bits of plots, so we could apply to them the apparatus

[1] *Aspects of the Novel* by E. M. Forster, copyright, 1927, by Harcourt, Brace and Company, Inc. Reprinted by permission of Harcourt, Brace and Company and Edward Arnold and Company, London.

30. Gide. André Gide, 1869–1951, was one of the most distinguished French novelists and leaders of French liberal thought. Forster refers frequently to Gide's best known novel, *Les Faux-Monnayeurs* (*The Counterfeiters*), 1927.

suited for Fielding or Arnold Bennett. But when I say two of their names—*Tristram Shandy* and *Moby Dick*—it is clear that we must stop and think a moment. The bird and the shadow are too far apart. A new formula must be found: the mere fact that one can mention Tristram and Moby in a single sentence shows it. What an impossible pair! As far apart as the poles. Yes. And like the poles they have one thing in common, which the lands round the equator do not share: an axis. What is essential in Sterne and Melville belongs to this new aspect of fiction: the fantastic-prophetical axis. George Meredith touched it: he was somewhat fantastic. So did Charlotte Brontë: she was a prophetess occasionally. But in neither of these was it essential. Deprive them of it, and a book remains which still resembles *Harry Richmond* or *Shirley*. Deprive Sterne or Melville of it, deprive Peacock or Max Beerbohm or Virginia Woolf or Walter de la Mare or William Beckford or James Joyce or D. H. Lawrence or Swift, and nothing is left at all.

Our easiest approach to a definition of any aspect of fiction is always by considering the sort of demand it makes of the reader. Curiosity for the story, human feelings and a sense of value for the characters, intelligence and memory for the plot. What does fantasy ask of us? It asks us to pay something extra. It compels us to an adjustment that is different to an additional adjustment. The other novelists say "Here is something that might occur in your lives," the fantasist says "Here's something that could not occur. I must ask you first to accept my book as a whole, and secondly to accept certain things in my book." Many readers can grant the first request, but refuse the second. "One knows a book isn't real," they say, "still one does expect it to be natural, and this angel or midget or ghost or silly delay about the child's birth—no, it's too much." They either retract their original concession and stop reading, or if they do go on it is with complete coldness, and they watch the gambols of the author without realizing how much they may mean to him.

No doubt the above approach is not critically sound. We all know that a work of art is an entity, etc., etc.; it has its own laws which are not those of daily life, anything that suits it is true, so why should any question arise about the angel, etc., except whether it is suitable to its book? Why place an angel on a different basis from a stockbroker? Once in the realm of the fictitious, what difference is there between an apparition and a mortgage? I see the soundness of this argument, but my heart refuses to assent. The general tone of novels is so literal that when the fantastic is introduced it produces a special effect: some readers are thrilled, others choked off: it demands an additional adjustment because of the oddness of its method or subject matter—like a sideshow in an exhibition where you have to pay sixpence as well as the original entrance fee. Some readers pay with delight, it is only for the sideshows that they entered the exhibition, and it is only to them I can now speak. Others refuse with indignation, and these have our sincere regards, for to dislike the fantastic in literature is not to dislike literature. It does not even imply poverty of imagination, only a disinclination to meet certain demands that are made on it. Mr. Asquith (if gossip is correct) could not meet the demands made on him by *Lady into Fox*. He should not have objected, he said, if the fox had become a lady again, but as it was he was left with an uncomfortable dissatisfied feeling. This feeling reflects no discredit either upon an eminent politician or a charming book. It merely means that Mr. Asquith, though a genuine lover of literature, could not pay the additional sixpence—or rather he was willing to pay it but hoped to get it back again at the end.

So fantasy asks us to pay something extra.

Let us now distinguish between fantasy and prophecy.

They are alike in having gods, and unlike in the gods they have. There is in both the sense of mythology which differentiates them from other aspects of our subject. An invocation is again possible, therefore on behalf of fantasy let us now

1. **Fielding.** Henry Fielding, 1707–1754, English novelist, author of *Joseph Andrews*, 1743, *Tom Jones* (his masterpiece), 1748, and *Amelia*, 1751. **Arnold Bennett,** English novelist (1867–1931), whose best novel is *The Old Wives' Tale*, 1908. 2. ***Tristram Shandy,*** the masterpiece of Laurence Sterne, 1713–1768, English clergyman and novelist. 3. ***Moby Dick,*** the great novel by the American author, Herman Melville, 1819–1891. 17. ***Harry Richmond,*** Meredith's novel, *The Adventures of Harry Richmond*, 1871. 18. ***Shirley,*** a novel by Charlotte Brontë, 1849. 19. **Peacock.** Thomas Love Peacock, 1785–1866, English poet and author of witty, satirical novels such as *Headlong Hall*, 1816, and *Nightmare Abbey*, 1818, of which Shelley is the hero. **Max Beerbohm,** 1872– , English essayist and author of the novel, *Zuleika Dobson*, which Forster later discusses. **Virginia Woolf.** See p. 1268, below. 20. **Walter de la Mare,** 1873– , English poet. **William Beckford,** 1760–1844, English author of the Oriental fantasy, *Vathek*, 1786. 20–21. **James Joyce.** See p. 1261, below. 21. **D. H. Lawrence.** See p. 1273, below. **Swift.** See p. 498, above.

32. **Mr. Asquith.** Herbert Henry Asquith, first Earl of Oxford and Asquith, 1852–1928, British statesman and prime minister, 1908–1916. 33. ***Lady into Fox,*** a novel by David Garnett, published by Knopf, 1922.

invoke all beings who inhabit the lower air, the shallow water, and the smaller hills, all Fauns and Dryads and slips of the memory, all verbal coincidences, Pans and puns, all that is mediaeval this side of the grave. When we come to prophecy, we shall utter no invocation, but it will have been to whatever transcends our abilities, even when it is human passion that transcends them, to the deities of India, Greece, Scandinavia and Judaea, to all that is mediaeval beyond the grave and to Lucifer son of the morning. By their mythologies we shall distinguish these two sorts of novels.

A number of rather small gods then should haunt us today—I would call them fairies if the word were not consecrated to imbecility. (Do you believe in fairies? No, not under any circumstances.) The stuff of daily life will be tugged and strained in various directions, the earth will be given little tilts mischievous or pensive, spot lights will fall on objects that have no reason to anticipate or welcome them, and tragedy herself, though not excluded, will have a fortuitous air as if a word would disarm her. The power of fantasy penetrates into every corner of the universe, but not into the forces that govern it—the stars that are the brain of heaven, the army of unalterable law, remain untouched—and novels of this type have an improvised air, which is the secret of their force and charm. They may contain solid character-drawing, penetrating and bitter criticism of conduct and civilization; yet our simile of the beam of light must remain, and if one god must be invoked specially, let us call upon Hermes—messenger, thief, and conductor of souls to a not too terrible hereafter.

You will expect me now to say that a fantastic book asks us to accept the supernatural. I will say it, but reluctantly, because any statement as to their subject matter brings these novels into the claws of critical apparatus, from which it is important that they should be saved. It is truer of them than of most books that we can only know what is in them by reading them, and their appeal is specially personal—they are sideshows inside the main show. So I would rather hedge as much as possible, and say that they ask us to accept either the supernatural or its absence.

A reference to the greatest of them—*Tristram Shandy*—will make this point clear. The supernatural is absent from the Shandy ménage, yet a thousand incidents suggest that it is not far off. It would not be really odd, would it, if the furniture in Mr. Shandy's bedroom, where he retired in despair after hearing the omitted details of his son's birth, should come alive like Belinda's toilette in *The Rape of the Lock*, or that Uncle Toby's drawbridge should lead into Lilliput? There is a charmed stagnation about the whole epic—the more the characters do, the less gets done; the less they have to say, the more they talk; the harder they think, the softer they get; facts have an unholy tendency to unwind and trip up the past instead of begetting the future, as in well-conducted books, and the obstinacy of inanimate objects, like Dr. Slop's bag, is most suspicious. Obviously a god is hidden in *Tristram Shandy*, his name is Muddle, and some readers cannot accept him. Muddle is almost incarnate—quite to reveal his awful features was not Sterne's intention; that is the deity that lurks behind his masterpiece—the army of unutterable muddle, the universe as a hot chestnut. Small wonder that another divine muddler, Dr. Johnson, writing in 1776, should remark, "Nothing odd will do long: *Tristram Shandy* did not last!" Doctor Johnson was not always happy in his literary judgments, but the appropriateness of this one passes belief.

Well, that must serve as our definition of fantasy. It implies the supernatural, but need not express it. Often it does express it, and were that type of classification helpful, we could make a list of the devices which writers of a fantastic turn have used—such as the introduction of a god, ghost, angel, monkey, monster, midget, witch, into ordinary life; or the introduction of ordinary men into no man's land, the future, the past, the interior of the earth, the fourth dimension; or divings into and dividings of personality; or finally the device of parody or adaptation. These devices need never grow stale; they will occur naturally to writers of a certain temperament, and be put to fresh use; but the fact that their number is strictly limited is of interest; and suggests that the beam of light can only be manipulated in certain ways.

I will select, as a typical example, a recent book about a witch: *Flecker's Magic*, by Norman Matson. It seemed to me good and I recommended it to a friend whose judgment I respect. He thought it poor. That is what is so tiresome about new books; they never give us that restful feeling which we

10–11. Lucifer son of the morning. See Isaiah 14:12. **26. the army of unalterable law.** See Meredith's poem, "Lucifer in Starlight," p. 1127, above.

4. *The Rape of the Lock*, the mock-epic poem by Alexander Pope. See p. 549. **4–5. Uncle Toby's drawbridge . . . Lilliput.** Uncle Toby is a whimsical old soldier in Sterne's *Tristram Shandy*. Lilliput is the diminutive kingdom described in Swift's *Gulliver's Travels*. See p. 501. **13. Dr. Slop's bag.** Dr. Slop is a choleric and bungling physician in Sterne's *Tristram Shandy*. **44. *Flecker's Magic*,** published in 1926 by Boni and Liveright, New York.

have when perusing the classics. *Flecker's Magic* contains scarcely anything that is new—fantasies cannot: only the old old story of the wishing ring which brings either misery or nothing at all. Flecker, an American boy who is learning to paint in Paris, is given the ring by a girl in a café; she is a witch, she tells him; he has only to be sure what he wants and he will get it. To prove her power, a motorbus rises slowly from the street and turns upside down in the air. The passengers, who do not fall out, try to look as if nothing was happening. The driver, who is standing on the pavement at the moment, cannot conceal his surprise, but when his bus returns safe to earth again he thinks it wiser to get into his seat and drive off as usual. Motorbuses do not revolve slowly through the air—so they do not. Flecker now accepts the ring. His character, though slightly sketched, is individual, and this definiteness causes the book to grip.

It proceeds with a growing tension, a series of little shocks. The method is Socratic. The boy starts by thinking of something obvious, like a Rolls-Royce. But where shall he put the beastly thing? Or a beautiful lady. But what about her *carte d'identité?* Or money? Ah, that's more like it—he is almost a beggar. Say a million dollars. He prepares to turn the ring for this wish—except while one's about it two millions seem safer—or ten—or—and money blares out into madness, and the same thing happens when he thinks of long life: to die in forty years—no, in fifty—in one hundred —horrible, horrible. Then a solution occurs. He has always wanted to be a great painter. Well, he'll be it at once. But what kind of greatness? Giotto's? Cézanne's? Certainly not; his own kind, and he does not know what that is, so this wish likewise is impossible.

And now a horrible old woman begins to haunt his days and dreams. She reminds him vaguely of the girl who gave him the ring. She knows his thoughts and she is always sidling up to him in the streets and saying, "Dear boy—darling boy—wish for happiness." We learn in time that she is the real witch—the girl was a human acquaintance whom she used to get into touch with Flecker. The last of the witches—very lonely. The rest have committed suicide during the eighteenth century—they could not endure to survive into the world of Newton where two and two make four, and even the world of Einstein is not sufficiently decentralised to revive them. She has hung on in the hope of smashing this world, and she wants the boy to ask for happiness because such a wish has never been made in all the history of the ring.

"Perhaps Flecker was the first modern man to find himself in this predicament? The people of the old world had so little they knew surely what they wanted. They knew about Almighty God, who wore a beard and sat in an armchair about a mile above the fields, and life was very short and very long too, for the days were so full of unthinking effort.

"The people of the recorded olden times wished for a beautiful castle on a high hill and lived therein until death. But the hill was not so high one might see from the windows back along thirty centuries—as one may from a bungalow. In the castle there were no great volumes filled with words and pictures of things dug up by man's relentless curiosity from sand and soil in all corners of the world; there was a sentimental half-belief in dragons, but no knowledge that once upon a time only dragons had lived on the earth—that man's grandfather and grandmother were dragons; there were no movies flickering like thoughts against a white wall, no phonograph, no machinery with which to achieve the sensation of speed; no diagrams of the fourth dimension, no contrasts in life like that of Waterville, Minn., and Paris, France. In the castle the light was weak and flickering, hallways were dark, rooms deeply shadowed. The little outside world was full of shadow, and on the very top of the mind of him who lived in the castle played a dim light—underneath were shadows, fear, ignorance, will-to-ignorance. Most of all, there was not in the castle on the hill the breathless sense of imminent revelation—that today or surely tomorrow Man would at a stroke double his power and change the world again.

"The ancient tales of magic were the mumbling thoughts of a distant shabby little world—so, at least, thought Flecker, offended. The tales gave him no guidance. There was too much difference between his world and theirs.

"He wondered if he hadn't dismissed the wish for happiness rather heedlessly? He seemed to get nowhere thinking about it. He was not wise enough. In the old tales a wish for happiness was never made! He wondered why.

"He might chance it—just to see what would happen. The thought made him tremble. He leaped from his bed and paced the red-tiled floor, rubbing his hands together.

" 'I want to be happy for ever,' he whispered, to hear the words, careful not to touch the ring. '*Happy . . . for ever*'—the two syllables of the first word, like hard little pebbles, struck musically against the bell of his imagination, but the second was a sigh. *For ever*—his spirit sank under the soft heavy impact of it. Held in his thought the word made a dreary music, fading. '*Happy for ever*'—NO! ! ' "

Thus again and again—the mark of the true fantasist—does Norman Matson merge the kingdoms of magic and common sense by using words that apply to both, and the mixture he has created comes alive. I will not tell the end of the story. You will have guessed its essentials, but there are always surprises in the working of a fresh mind, and to the end of time good literature will be made round this notion of a wish.

To turn from this simple example of the supernatural to a more complicated one—to a highly accomplished and superbly written book whose spirit is farcical: *Zuleika Dobson* by Max Beerbohm. You all know Miss Dobson—not personally, or you would not be here now. She is the damsel for love of whom all the undergraduates of Oxford except one drowned themselves during Eights week, and he threw himself out of a window.

A superb theme for a fantasy, but all will depend on the handling. It is treated with a mixture of realism, wittiness, charm and mythology, and the mythology is most important. Max has borrowed or created a number of supernatural machines—to have entrusted Zuleika to one of them would be inept; the fantasy would become heavy or thin. But we pass from the sweating emperors to the black and pink pearls, the hooting owls, the interference of the Muse Clio, the ghosts of Chopin and George Sand, of Nellie O'Mora; just as one fails another starts, to uphold this gayest and most exquisite of funeral palls.

"Through the square, across the High, down Grove Street they passed. The Duke looked up at the tower of Merton, ὡς οὔποτ' αὖθις ἀλλὰ νῦν πανύστατον. Strange that tonight it would still be standing here, in all its sober and solid beauty—still be gazing, over the roofs and chimneys, at the tower of Magdalen, its rightful bride. Through untold centuries of the future it would stand thus, gaze thus. He winced. Oxford walls have a way of belittling us; and the Duke was loth to regard his doom as trivial.

"Aye, by all minerals we are mocked. Vegetables, yearly deciduous, are far more sympathetic. The lilac and laburnum, making lovely now the railed pathway to Christ Church meadow, were all a-swaying and nodding to the Duke as he passed by. 'Adieu, adieu, your Grace,' they were whispering. 'We are very sorry for you, very sorry indeed. We never dared suppose you would predecease us. We think your death a very great tragedy. Adieu! Perhaps we shall meet in another world—that is, if the members of the animal kingdom have immortal souls, as we have.'

"The Duke was little versed in their language; yet, as he passed between these gently garrulous blooms, he caught at the least the drift of their salutation, and smiled a vague but courteous acknowledgment, to the right and left alternately, creating a very favourable impression."

Has not a passage like this—with its freedom of invocation—a beauty unattainable by serious literature? It is so funny and charming, so iridescent yet so profound. Criticisms of human nature fly through the book, not like arrows but upon the wings of sylphs. Towards the end—that dreadful end often so fatal to fiction—the book rather flags: the suicide of all the undergraduates of Oxford is not as delightful as it ought to be when viewed at close quarters, and the defenestration of Noaks almost nasty. Still it is a great work—the most consistent achievement of fantasy in our time, and the closing scene in Zuleika's bedroom with its menace of further disasters is impeccable.

"And now with pent breath and fast-beating heart, she stared at the lady of the mirror, without seeing her; and now she wheeled round and swiftly glided to that little table on which stood her two books. She snatched Bradshaw.

"We always intervene between Bradshaw and any one whom we see consulting him. 'Mademoiselle will permit me to find that which she seeks?' asked Mélisande.

" 'Be quiet,' said Zuleika. We always repulse, at first, any one who intervenes between us and Bradshaw.

"We always end by accepting the intervention. 'See if it is possible to go direct from here to Cambridge,' said Zuleika, handing the book on. 'If it isn't, then—well, see how one *does* get there.'

' We never have any confidence in the intervener. Nor is the intervener, when it comes to the point,

23. Eights week, the week of the boat races between Oxford and Cambridge. **41–42.** ὡς . . . πανύστατον. "since never again, but now for the last time of all [shall I look upon the beam and orb of the sun]." Part of the farewell speech of Polyxena to her mother Hecuba in Euripides' *Hecuba*, 409–12.

39. Bradshaw, the standard railway guide and timetable in Great Britain.

sanguine. With mistrust mounting to exasperation Zuleika sat watching the faint and frantic researches of her maid.

" 'Stop!' she said suddenly. 'I have a much better idea. Go down very early to the station. See the stationmaster. Order me a special train. For ten o'clock, say.'

"Rising, she stretched her arms above her head. Her lips parted in a yawn, met in a smile. With both hands she pushed back her hair from her shoulders, and twisted it into a loose knot. Very lightly she slipped up into bed, and very soon she was asleep."

So Zuleika ought to have come on to this place. She does not seem ever to have arrived and we can only suppose that through the intervention of the gods her special train failed to start, or, more likely, is still in a siding at Bletchley.

Among the devices in my list I mentioned "parody" or "adaptation" and would now examine this further. The fantasist here adopts for his mythology some earlier work and uses it as a framework or quarry for his own purposes. There is an aborted example of this in *Joseph Andrews*. Fielding set out to use *Pamela* as a comic mythology. He thought it would be fun to invent a brother to Pamela, a pure-minded footman, who should repulse Lady Booby's attentions just as Pamela had repulsed Mr. B.'s, and he made Lady Booby Mr. B.'s aunt. Thus he would be able to laugh at Richardson, and incidentally express his own views of life. Fielding's view of life however was of the sort that only rests content with the creation of solid round characters, and with the growth of Parson Adams and Mrs. Slipslop the fantasy ceases, and we get an independent work. *Joseph Andrews* (which is also important historically) is interesting to us as an example of a false start. Its author begins by playing the fool in a Richardsonian world, and ends by being serious in a world of his own—the world of Tom Jones and Amelia.

Parody or adaptation has enormous advantages to certain novelists, particularly to those who may have a great deal to say and plenty of literary genius, but who do not see the world in terms of individual men and women—who do not, in other words, take easily to creating characters. How are such men to start writing? An already existing book or literary tradition may inspire them—they may find high up in its cornices a pattern that will serve as a beginning, they may swing about in its rafters and gain strength. That fantasy of Lowes Dickinson, *The Magic Flute*, seems to be created thus: it has taken as its mythology the world of Mozart. Tamino, Sarastro, and the Queen of the Night stand in their enchanted kingdom ready for the author's thoughts, and when these are poured in they become alive and a new and exquisite work is born. And the same is true of another fantasy, anything but exquisite—James Joyce's *Ulysses*. That remarkable affair—perhaps the most interesting literary experiment of our day—could not have been achieved unless Joyce had had, as his guide and butt, the world of the *Odyssey*.

I am only touching on one aspect of *Ulysses:* it is of course more than a fantasy—it is a dogged attempt to cover the universe with mud, it is an inverted Victorianism, an attempt to make crossness and dirt succeed where sweetness and light failed, a simplification of the human character in the interests of Hell. All simplifications are fascinating, all lead us away from the truth (which lies far nearer the muddle of *Tristram Shandy*), and *Ulysses* must not detain us on the ground that it contains a morality—otherwise we shall also have to discuss Mrs. Humphry Ward. We are concerned with it because, through a mythology, Joyce has been able to create the peculiar stage and characters he required.

The action of those 400,000 words occupies a single day, the scene is Dublin, the theme is a journey—the modern man's journey from morn to midnight, from bed to the squalid tasks of mediocrity, to a funeral, newspaper office, library, pub, lavatory, lying-in hospital, a saunter by the beach, brothel, coffee stall, and so back to bed. And it coheres because it depends from the journey of a hero through the seas of Greece, like a bat hanging to a cornice.

Ulysses himself is Mr. Leopold Bloom—a converted Jew—greedy, lascivious, timid, undignified, desultory, superficial, kindly and always at his lowest when he pretends to aspire. He tries to explore life through the body. Penelope is Mrs. Marion Bloom, an overblown soprano, by no means harsh to her suitors. The third character is young Stephen Dedalus, whom Bloom recognizes as his spiritual son much as Ulysses recognizes Telemachus as his actual son. Stephen tries to

26. *Pamela.* *Pamela, or Virtue Rewarded,* 1740, a novel by Samuel Richardson, in which the heroine, Pamela Andrews, an unsophisticated country girl, resists innumerable temptations by a young squire, called Mr. B., and eventually marries and reforms him.

27. Mrs. Humphry Ward, niece of Matthew Arnold and author of popular novels, interested in philanthropy and social work. Her best known novel, *Robert Elsmere,* 1888, is concerned with the "higher criticism" of the Bible.

explore life through the intellect—we have met him before in *The Portrait of the Artist as a Young Man*, and now he is worked into this epic of grubbiness and disillusion. He and Bloom meet half way through in Night Town (which corresponds partly to Homer's Palace of Circe, partly to his Descent into Hell) and in its supernatual and filthy alleys they strike up their slight but genuine friendship. This is the crisis of the book, and here—and indeed throughout—smaller mythologies swarm and pullulate, like vermin between the scales of a poisonous snake. Heaven and earth fill with infernal life, personalities melt, sexes interchange, until the whole universe, including poor, pleasure-loving Mr. Bloom, is involved in one joyless orgy.

Does it come off? No, not quite. Indignation in literature never quite comes off either in Juvenal or Swift of Joyce; there is something in words that is alien to its simplicity. The Night Town scene does not come off except as a superfetation of fantasies, a monstrous coupling of reminiscences. Such satisfaction as can be attained in this direction is attained, and all through the book we have similar experiments—the aim of which is to degrade all things, and more particularly civilization and art, by turning them inside out and upside down. Some enthusiasts may think that *Ulysses* ought to be mentioned not here but later on, under the heading of prophecy, and I understand this criticism. But I prefer to mention it today with *Tristram Shandy*, *Flecker's Magic*, *Zuleika Dobson*, and *The Magic Flute*, because the raging of Joyce, like the happier or calmer moods of the other writers, seems essentially fantastic, and lacks the note for which we shall be listening soon.

Lytton Strachey
1880–1932

Lytton Strachey was born in London in 1880. He was the son of General Sir Richard and Lady Jane Strachey; his cousin was St. Loe Strachey, editor of the *Spectator*. He was educated at Trinity College, Cambridge, where he won the Chancellor's Medal with a poem entitled *Ely*, a celebration of Cambridge and its poets. Strachey was then in his twenty-second year, and the judges who awarded the prize for the eminently traditional verses with their overtones of Tennyson and Arnold could scarcely have predicted Strachey would become one of the period's most famous tradition-smashers.

Strachey was an intellectual undergraduate but not a prodigy. His first book, *Landmarks in French Literature*, 1912, was published when he was thirty-two, and caused little comment and practically no surprise. It was not until Strachey was nearly forty that his *Eminent Victorians*, 1918, occasioned something of a furor. This was a strange sort of biography, brilliant, caustic, and dramatic; it bewildered the worshipers of tradition and delighted the rebels. Here was a historian who was making an art of biography—"that ill-digested mass of material, slipshod style, tedious panegyric"—and applying the psychoanalytical method to popular figures which had resisted analysis of any kind. With uninhibited candor and irrepressible curiosity, Strachey tore veil after veil from the shrines. It was not a rude iconoclasm but a cool elegance which accomplished such ironic reappraisals in *Queen Victoria*, 1921, *Books and Characters*, 1922, *Elizabeth and Essex*, 1928, and *Portraits in Miniature*, 1931.

Before he died, on January 21, 1932, Strachey had brought not only an unexpected verve but a critical selectiveness to biography. He wrote history like a novelist; his imaginative speculations, his acid skepticism, and his flair for epigrams started a vogue. The new type of biography found many disciples, but none could match Strachey in brilliance of execution. It has been charged against him that his forte was malicious attack, that he dipped his pen in vitriol to write poisonous letters about the defenseless dead. But Strachey's best work is neither vicious nor destructive; he knew gold wherever he might find it, and he makes the true metal of his effigies shine through their gilded reputations.

Strachey's successes and failures are bound up in his desire to humanize famous and little-known "names." The essay on "Lady Hester Stanhope" is as typical as it is quotable. The defects and the mannerisms are obvious; Strachey tended to cultivate a style for style's sake. Moreover, his sense of drama tempted him to impose undue significance upon small facts; and, though he prided himself upon his restraint, his irony compelled him to distort details. Yet it is only necessary to compare Strachey's *Queen Victoria* with Sir Sidney Lee's book on the same subject to see what Strachey accomplished. Lee's book is dull; Strachey's is dazzling. At first there had probably been the temptation on Strachey's part to seize too readily on the satirical possibilities, but he managed to remain agreeably amused while he was still illuminating and respectful. In the words of the novelist Frank Swinnerton, who has written wisely of the Georgian scene, "As the months passed, and Strachey found out more and more about the queen who was to be his subject, he found laughter fade before a growing respect, admiration, affection. . . . He found her a queen after all, a real person surrounded by Teutonic artists, governesses, husbands, and uncles."[1] Strachey was always bookish; he drew from the pages rather than from immediate impressions of life—and he was not really at ease in so vibrant and full-bodied an age past and recorded as Elizabeth's.

Whether or not Strachey's reputation will survive is a question that cannot yet be answered. It is not to be doubted, however, that, though his direct influence may have been harmful, Strachey indirectly changed the historian's entire approach. He brought to the writing of biography a dramatic incisiveness, a challenging imagination, and a fine prose rhythm. An anti-traditionalist, he wrote in the tradition of those biographers who achieved a freedom of spirit, sharp revaluation, sudden brilliance, and, at times, a magnificence which can be accomplished only by the artist who has all his powers—factual and fictive—under strict control.

[1] *The Georgian Literary Scene*, Farrar, Straus and Young, 1951.

LADY HESTER STANHOPE[1]

THE Pitt nose has a curious history. One can watch its transmigrations through three lives. The tremendous hook of old Lord Chatham, under whose curve Empires came to birth, was succeeded by the bleak upward-pointing nose of William Pitt the younger—the rigid symbol of an indomitable *hauteur*. With Lady Hester Stanhope came the final stage. The nose, still with an upward tilt in it, had lost its masculinity; the hard bones of the uncle and the grandfather had disappeared. Lady Hester's was a nose of wild ambitions, of pride grown fantastical, a nose that scorned the earth, shooting off, one fancies, towards some eternally eccentric heaven. It was a nose, in fact, altogether in the air.

Noses, of course, are aristocratic things; and Lady Hester was the child of a great aristocracy. But, in her case, the aristocratic impulse, which had carried her predecessors to glory, had less fortunate results. There has always been a strong strain of extravagance in the governing families of England; from time to time they throw off some peculiarly ill-balanced member, who performs a strange meteoric course. A century earlier, Lady Mary Wortley Montagu was an illustrious example of this tendency: that splendid comet, after filling half the heavens, vanished suddenly into desolation and darkness. Lady Hester Stanhope's spirit was still more uncommon; and she met with a most uncommon fate.

She was born in 1776, the eldest daughter of that extraordinary Earl Stanhope, Jacobin and inventor, who made the first steamboat and the first calculating machine, who defended the French Revolution in the House of Lords and erased the armorial bearings—"damned aristocratical nonsense"—from his carriages and his plate. Her mother, Chatham's daughter and the favourite sister of Pitt, died when she was four years old. The second Lady Stanhope, a frigid woman of fashion, left her stepdaughters to the care of futile governesses, while "Citizen Stanhope" ruled the household from his laboratory with the violence of a tyrant. It was not until Lady Hester was twenty-four that she escaped from the slavery of her father's house, by going to live with her grandmother, Lady Chatham. On Lady Chatham's death, three years later, Pitt offered her his protection, and she remained with him until his death in 1806.

Her three years with Pitt, passed in the very centre of splendid power, were brilliant and exciting. She flung herself impetuously into the movement and the passion of that vigorous society; she ruled her uncle's household with high vivacity; she was liked and courted; if not beautiful, she was fascinating—very tall, with a very fair and clear complexion, and dark-blue eyes, and a countenance of wonderful expressiveness. Her talk, full of the trenchant nonchalance of those days, was both amusing and alarming: "My dear Hester, what are you saying?" Pitt would call out to her from across the room. She was devoted to her uncle, who warmly returned her affection. She was devoted, too—but in a more dangerous fashion—to the intoxicating Antinous, Lord Granville Leveson Gower. The reckless manner in which she carried on this love-affair was the first indication of something overstrained, something wild and unaccountable, in her temperament. Lord Granville, after flirting with her outrageously, declared that he could never marry her, and went off on an embassy to St. Petersburg. Her distraction was extreme: she hinted that she would follow him to Russia; she threatened, and perhaps attempted, suicide; she went about telling everybody that he had jilted her. She was taken ill, and then there were rumours of an accouchement, which, it was said, she took care to *afficher*, by appearing without rouge and fainting on the slightest provocation. In the midst of these excursions and alarums there was a terrible and unexpected catastrophe. Pitt died. And Lady Hester suddenly found herself a dethroned princess, living in a small house in Montagu Square on a pension of £1,200 a year.

She did not abandon society, however, and the tongue of gossip continued to wag. Her immediate marriage with a former lover, Mr. Hill, was announced: "il est bien bon," said Lady Bessborough. Then it was whispered that Canning was "le régnant"—that he was with her "not only all day, but almost all night." She quarrelled with Canning and became attached to Sir John Moore. Whether she was actually engaged to marry him—as she seems to have asserted many years later—is doubtful; his letters to her, full as they are of respectful tenderness, hardly warrant the conclusion; but it is certain that he died with her name on his lips. Her favourite brother, Charles, was killed beside him; and it was natural that under this double blow she

[1] From *Books and Characters* by Lytton Strachey, copyright, 1922, by Harcourt, Brace and Company, Inc.

39. Canning, George Canning (1770–1827), British statesman, orator, and wit; he favored the liberal movements and a foreign policy of nonintervention. **42. Sir John Moore,** British general (1761–1809), especially famous for his Spanish campaign against Napoleon.

should have retired from London. She buried herself in Wales; but not for long. In 1810 she set sail for Gibraltar with her brother James, who was rejoining his regiment in the Peninsula. She never returned to England.

There can be no doubt that at the time of her departure the thought of a lifelong exile was far from her mind. It was only gradually, as she moved further and further eastward, that the prospect of life in England—at last even in Europe—grew distasteful to her; as late as 1816 she was talking of a visit to Provence. Accompanied by two or three English fellow travellers, her English maid, Mrs. Fry, her private physician, Dr. Meryon, and a host of servants, she progressed, slowly and in a great state, through Malta and Athens, to Constantinople. She was conveyed in battleships, and lodged with governors and ambassadors. After spending many months in Constantinople, Lady Hester discovered that she was "dying to see Napoleon with her own eyes," and attempted accordingly to obtain passports to France. The project was stopped by Stratford Canning, the English Minister, upon which she decided to visit Egypt, and, chartering a Greek vessel, sailed for Alexandria in the winter of 1811. Off the island of Rhodes a violent storm sprang up; the whole party were forced to abandon the ship, and to take refuge upon a bare rock, where they remained without food or shelter for thirty hours. Eventually, after many severe privations, Alexandria was reached in safety; but this disastrous voyage was a turning-point in Lady Hester's career. At Rhodes she was forced to exchange her torn and dripping raiment for the attire of a Turkish gentleman—a dress which she never afterwards abandoned. It was the first step in her orientalization.

She passed the next two years in a triumphal progress. Her appearance in Cairo caused the greatest sensation, and she was received in state by the Pasha, Mehemet Ali. Her costume on this occasion was gorgeous: she wore a turban of cashmere, a brocaded waistcoat, a priceless pelisse, and a vast pair of purple velvet pantaloons embroidered all over in gold. She was ushered by chamberlains with silver wands through the inner courts of the palace to a pavilion in the harem, where the Pasha, rising to receive her, conversed with her for an hour. From Cairo she turned northwards, visiting Jaffa, Jerusalem, Acre, and Damascus. Her travelling dress was of scarlet cloth trimmed with gold, and, when on horseback, she wore over the whole a white-hooded and tasselled burnous. Her maid, too, was forced, protesting, into trousers, though she absolutely refused to ride astride. Poor Mrs. Fry had gone through various and dreadful sufferings—shipwreck and starvation, rats and blackbeetles unspeakable—but she retained her equanimity. Whatever her Ladyship might think fit to be, *she* was an Englishwoman to the last, and Philippaki was Philip Parker and Mustapha Mr. Farr.

Outside Damascus, Lady Hester was warned that the town was the most fanatical in Turkey, and that the scandal of a woman entering it in man's clothes, unveiled, would be so great as to be dangerous. She was begged to veil herself, and to make her entry under cover of darkness. "I must take the bull by the horns," she replied, and rode into the city unveiled at midday. The population were thunderstruck; but at last their amazement gave way to enthusiasm, and the incredible lady was hailed everywhere as Queen, crowds followed her, coffee was poured out before her, and the whole bazaar rose as she passed. Yet she was not satisfied with her triumphs; she would do something still more glorious and astonishing; she would plunge into the desert and visit the ruins of Palmyra, which only half-a-dozen of the boldest travellers had ever seen. The Pasha of Damascus offered her a military escort, but she preferred to throw herself upon the hospitality of the Bedouin Arabs, who, overcome by her horsemanship, her powers of sight, and her courage, enrolled her a member of their tribe. After a week's journey in their company, she reached Palmyra, where the inhabitants met her with wild enthusiasm, and under the Corinthian columns of Zenobia's temple crowned her head with flowers. This happened in March, 1813; it was the apogee of Lady Hester's life. Henceforward her fortunes gradually but steadily declined.

The rumour of her exploits had spread through Syria, and from the year 1813 onwards, her reputation was enormous. She was received everywhere as a royal, almost as a supernatural, personage: she progressed from town to town amid official prostrations and popular rejoicings. But she herself was in a state of hesitation and discontent. Her future was uncertain; she had grown scornful of the West—must she return to it? The East alone was sympathetic, the East alone was tolerable—but could she cut herself off for ever from the past? At Laodicea she was suddenly struck down by the plague, and, after months of illness, it was borne in upon her that all was vanity. She rented an empty monastery on the slopes of Mount Lebanon, not far from Sayda (the ancient Sidon), and took up her abode there. Then her mind took a new surprising turn; she dashed to Ascalon, and, with the permission of the Sultan, began excavations in a ruined temple with the object of discovering a hidden treasure of three million pieces of gold. Having unearthed nothing but an antique statue, which, in order to prove her disinterestedness, she ordered her appalled doctor to break into little bits, she returned to her monastery. Finally, in 1816, she moved to another house, further up Mount Lebanon, and near the village of Djoun; and at Djoun she remained until her death, more than twenty years later.

Thus, almost accidentally as it seems, she came to the end of her wanderings, and the last, long, strange, mythical period of her existence began. Certainly the situation that she had chosen was sublime. Her house, on the top of a high bare hill among great mountains, was a one-storied group of buildings, with many ramifying courts and outhouses, and a garden of several acres surrounded by a rampart wall. The garden, which she herself had planted and tended with the utmost care, commanded a glorious prospect. On every side but one the vast mountains towered, but to the west there was an opening, through which, in the far distance, the deep blue Mediterranean was revealed. From this romantic hermitage, her singular renown spread over the world. European travellers who had been admitted to her presence brought back stories full of Eastern mystery; they told of a peculiar grandeur, a marvellous prestige, an imperial power. The precise nature of Lady Hester's empire was, indeed, dubious; she was in fact merely the tenant of her Djoun establishment, for which she paid a rent of £20 a year. But her dominion was not subject to such limitations. She ruled imaginatively, transcendentally; the solid glory of Chatham had been transmuted into the phantasy of an Arabian Night. No doubt she herself believed that she was something more than a chimerical Empress. When a French traveller was murdered in the desert, she issued orders for the punishment of the offenders; punished they were, and Lady Hester actually received the solemn thanks of the French Chamber. It seems probable, however, that it was the Sultan's orders rather than Lady Hester's which produced the desired effect. In her feud with her terrible neighbour, the Emir Beshyr, she maintained an undaunted front. She kept the tyrant at bay; but perhaps the Emir, who, so far as physical force was concerned, held her in the hollow of his hand, might have proceeded to extremities if he had not received a severe admonishment from Stratford Canning at Constantinople. What is certain is that the ignorant and superstitious populations around her feared and loved her, and that she, reacting to her own mysterious prestige, became at last even as they. She plunged into astrology and divination; she awaited the moment when, in accordance with prophecy, she should enter Jerusalem side by side with Mahdi, the Messiah; she kept two sacred horses, destined, by sure signs, to carry her and him to their last triumph. The Orient had mastered her utterly. She was no longer an Englishwoman, she declared; she loathed England; she would never go there again; if she went anywhere it would be to Arabia, to "her own people."

Her expenses were immense—not only for herself but for others, for she poured out her hospitality with a noble hand. She ran into debt, and was swindled by the moneylenders; her steward cheated her, her servants pilfered her; her distress was at last acute. She fell into fits of terrible depression, bursting into dreadful tears and savage cries. Her habits grew more and more eccentric. She lay in bed all day, and sat up all night, talking unceasingly for hour upon hour to Dr. Meryon, who, alone of her English attendants, remained with her, Mrs. Fry having withdrawn to more congenial scenes long since. The doctor was a poor-spirited and muddle-headed man, but he was a good listener; and there he sat while that extraordinary talk flowed on—talk that scaled the heavens and ransacked the earth, talk in which memories of an abolished past—stories of Mr. Pitt and of George III., vituperations against Mr. Canning, mimicries of the Duchess of Devonshire—mingled phantasmagorically with doctrines of Fate and planetary influence, and speculations on the Arabian origin of the Scottish clans, and lamentations over the wickedness of servants; till the unaccountable figure, with its robes and its long pipe, loomed through the tobacco-smoke like some vision of a Sibyl in a dream. She might be robbed and ruined, her house might crumble over her head; but she talked on. She grew ill and desperate; yet still she talked. Did she feel that the time was coming when she should talk no more?

Her melancholy deepened into a settled gloom when the news came of her brother James's death. She had quarrelled with all her English friends, except Lord Hardwicke—with her eldest brother, with her sister, whose kind letters she left unanswered; she was at daggers drawn with the Eng-

36. £20, about $100.

lish consul at Alexandria, who worried her about her debts. Ill and harassed, she hardly moved from her bedroom, while her servants rifled her belongings and reduced the house to a condition of indescribable disorder and filth. Three dozen hungry cats ranged through the rooms, filling the courts with frightful noises. Dr. Meryon, in the midst of it all, knew not whether to cry or laugh. At moments the great lady regained her ancient fire; her bells pealed tumultuously for hours together; or she leapt up, and arraigned the whole trembling household before her, with her Arab war-mace in her hand. Her finances grew more and more involved —grew at length irremediable. It was in vain that the faithful Lord Hardwicke pressed her to return to England to settle her affairs. Return to England, indeed! To England, that ungrateful, miserable country, where, so far as she could see, they had forgotten the very name of Mr. Pitt! The final blow fell when a letter came from the English authorities threatening to cut off her pension for the payment of her debts. Upon that, after dispatching a series of furious missives to Lord Palmerston, to Queen Victoria, to the Duke of Wellington, she renounced the world. She commanded Dr. Meryon to return to Europe, and he—how could he have done it?—obeyed her. Her health was broken, she was over sixty, and, save for her vile servants, absolutely alone. She lived for nearly a year after he left her —we know no more. She had vowed never again to pass through the gate of her house; but did she sometimes totter to her garden—that beautiful garden which she had created, with its roses and its fountains, its alleys and its bowers—and look westward at the sea? The end came in June, 1839. Her servants immediately possessed themselves of every movable object in the house. But Lady Hester cared no longer: she was lying back in her bed—inexplicable, grand, preposterous, with her nose in the air.

James Joyce
1882–1941

James Joyce was born in Dublin on February 2, 1882, and educated for the priesthood. For thirteen years he attended the best Jesuit schools in Ireland; his mind was thoroughly disciplined, but not his spirit. At twenty he wrote a blasphemous broadside, left his country, and repudiated his countrymen, "the most belated race in Europe."

From that time his life (according to Herbert Gorman, Joyce's official biographer) became "a constant struggle against terrific odds, prejudices, mob smugness, poverty, and physical disability." His work was censored, officially banned, and even burned; his books, forbidden by several governments, were illicitly published all over the world, and Joyce received no royalties from the pirated publications. He studied medicine in Paris; almost became a professional singer; taught languages in Trieste and Switzerland; wandered about the Continent until he finally settled in Paris. Illness and overwork necessitated ten eye operations in twenty years; Joyce was nearly blind after 1920. Writing was a painful effort for him; a few lines at a time scrawled on a large sheet of paper was all he could manage.

Joyce's literary debut was quiet and undistinguished. *Chamber Music*, 1907, was a small volume of pseudo-Elizabethan verse in the traditional lyric manner. His next book marked the beginning of the artist's twofold struggle for recognition and for the right to pursue his own methods—methods which, depending upon the point of view, were lauded as pioneering or attacked as mere arrogance. A contract had been signed for a volume of short stories, *Dubliners*, in Joyce's twenty-fourth year. It was not until 1914 (eight years after the manuscript had been accepted) that *Dubliners* was published—in England, not in Ireland.

Such an incident suggests at least one reason for Joyce's self-imposed exile in France and his refusal to join the Celtic movement which was exploiting the "liberation" of Irish culture. *Dubliners*, like Synge's *The Playboy of the Western World*, was too frankly naturalistic for romantic folklorists and myth-lovers. It is significant that though Joyce was an ardent linguist and spoke Italian, German, French, and ten other languages, he never studied Gaelic. Contemplating the subject matter which Joyce transfuses into "the twilight sleep of his novels," Alfred Kazin wrote, "we have the extraordinary spectacle of an Irishman who hates Ireland, and can write of nothing else; a renegade Catholic whose novels owe their exaltation of blasphemy, their convoluted speech and scholastic imagery, to Irish catholicism; a member of the great nationalistic generation who has always despised Ireland's literary nationalism and the cult of the Gaelic, but whose novels, along with the poetry of Yeats, may yet be considered modern Ireland's finest literary testament."[1]

In his early thirties Joyce achieved full independence. *A Portrait of the Artist as a Young Man*, 1916, definitely breaks with tradition. It is a welter of moods and theories, a kaleidoscope of scenes which are both weird and commonplace. Yet Stephen Dedalus' rejection of his environment is realized with fine honesty and artistic control. Rarely have painful autobiographical elements been put so effectively to the purposes of fiction.

The central character of the *Artist as a Young Man*, Stephen Dedalus, becomes one of the chief figures in Joyce's *Ulysses*, 1922, banned until 1933 in the United States. *Ulysses*, another autobiographical extension of reality is one of the strangest novels ever written and one of the most extraordinary works of the age. It is amazingly complex, yet compact. The protean "action," which involves many lives and runs to more than seven hundred crowded pages, takes place in a single day. In style and structure it is unlike anything which preceded it. Although the time background is eighteen hours in Dublin, the associations are epic. *Ulysses* is a macabre transformation of Homer's *Odyssey:* Leopold Bloom is Ulysses, Bloom's father is Tiresias, Paddy Dignam is Elpenor, Mr. Deasy is Nestor, Father Coffey is Cerberus, Mrs. Bloom is Penelope, Gerty MacDowell is Nausicaä, the newspaper office is the Cave of the Winds, the brothel is the court of Circe, the gluttons in the Burton are the Lestrygonians, and so on to the smallest detail of metamorphosis. The book itself is a mammoth exhibition of scholarliness and pornographic caricature, tragedy and horseplay, perverse obscurity and accomplished burlesque—one incredible chapter is composed of parodies of every style of English writing, from Anglo-Saxon to current journalese. Above all, *Ulysses* shows an unprecedented power of scrutiny joined to an insatiable thirst for analysis. As Herbert Gorman discovered in his first biography (*James Joyce*, 1924), "He left no stone unturned in Dublin, no scandal unexploited, no important personage ignored. Nothing has been left unsaid. It is all there to take or to leave as the reader will. Rabelais is pale beside it." Gorman failed to add that, while Rabelais constructed a world common to all humanity, Joyce created a world where the crowd was unwelcome and the individual had turned within himself. This was art for the few.

Technically *Ulysses* is still a battleground of controversy. It violates all the conventional laws of unity, dispenses with quotation marks, jams together description and conversation, interrupts narratives with abrupt "interior monologues." The last forty-two pages are one long, unpunctuated sentence, an unbroken "stream of consciousness." Concerning this uninhibited record of a common woman's musings, Arnold Bennett wrote, "I have never read anything to surpass it, and I doubt if I have ever read anything to equal it." With all its difficulties, Joyce's minute exploration of the workings of the mind and the psychology of human personality in *Ulysses* has with little doubt made it the most influential prose work of the second quarter of the twentieth century.

Ulysses was crystal-clear compared to the book which followed: *Finnegans Wake*, 1939, a work in which nothing at first seemed clear except its confusion. Apparently *Finnegans Wake* was a head-on collision with the language of speech and literature, a colossal series of telescoped expressions that communicate little or nothing to the average reader, a crazy pattern of unknown words that Joyce had made up out of other words. A patient dissection revealed a set of characters who divide into multiple personalities; figures which dissolve into allusions; a nightmare distortion of history and legend, time and space; and a constant irruption of elaborate puns. After more than a decade *Finnegans Wake* continues to fascinate and to puzzle, but it seems to be on its way to becoming recognized as a work of art—a twentieth-century version of the ancient story of death and resurrection, comprehending in many forms and phases and idioms and on many levels the history of mankind's fall and redemption, from the tragedy of the Garden of Eden to that of the modern world.

Dubliners, from which our selection is taken, is a naturalistic and impersonal collection in the best tradition of short-story writing. These stories, written by a man in his early twenties, are a proof of the inarticulate made articulate. Most of the people in *Dubliners*, wrote Padraic Colum, "live in little terraces and face the world with a certain gentility. And those whose stories are the most memorable

[1] From a review of Herbert Gorman's *James Joyce* in the *New York Herald Tribune: Books*, Feb. 18, 1940.

have been stirred by a look they have taken into the darkness."[1] "Counterparts" and "Ivy Day in the Committee Room" are "bridges" to Joyce's later work. The scenes in Davy Byrne's and Mulligan's pub (in "Counterparts") anticipate similar but more violent episodes in *Ulysses*.

Joyce died in Zurich, January 13, 1941. A small library of reference has already grown up about him and his books. The following studies will be found particularly illuminating: Herbert Gorman's *James Joyce*, a full and intimate accounting (including extracts from Joyce's notebooks and letter files), revised edition, Rinehart, 1949; Stuart Gilbert's *James Joyce's Ulysses: A Study*, Knopf, 1934; Harry Levin's *James Joyce, A Critical Introduction*, New Directions, 1941; and W. Y. Tindall's *James Joyce*, Scribner, 1950.

COUNTERPARTS [2]

THE bell rang furiously and, when Miss Parker went to the tube, a furious voice called out in a piercing North of Ireland accent:

"Send Farrington here!"

Miss Parker returned to her machine, saying to a man who was writing at a desk:

"Mr. Alleyne wants you upstairs."

The man muttered "*Blast* him!" under his breath and pushed back his chair to stand up. When he stood up he was tall and of great bulk. He had a hanging face, dark wine-coloured, with fair eyebrows and moustache: his eyes bulged forward slightly and the whites of them were dirty. He lifted up the counter and, passing by the clients, went out of the office with a heavy step.

He went heavily upstairs until he came to the second landing, where a door bore a brass plate with the inscription *Mr. Alleyne*. Here he halted, puffing with labour and vexation, and knocked. The shrill voice cried:

"Come in!"

The man entered Mr. Alleyne's room. Simultaneously Mr. Alleyne, a little man wearing gold-rimmed glasses on a clean-shaven face, shot his head up over a pile of documents. The head itself was so pink and hairless it seemed like a large egg reposing on the papers. Mr. Alleyne did not lose a moment:

"Farrington? What is the meaning of this? Why have I always to complain of you? May I ask you why you haven't made a copy of that contract between Bodley and Kirwan? I told you it must be ready by four o'clock."

"But Mr. Shelley said, sir—"

"*Mr. Shelley said, sir*. . . . Kindly attend to what I say and not to what *Mr. Shelley says, sir*. You have always some excuse or another for shirking work. Let me tell you that if the contract is not copied before this evening I'll lay the matter before Mr. Crosbie. . . . Do you hear me now?"

"Yes, sir."

"Do you hear me now? . . . Ay and another little matter! I might as well be talking to the wall as talking to you. Understand once for all that you get a half an hour for your lunch and not an hour and a half. How many courses do you want, I'd like to know. . . . Do you mind me now?"

"Yes, sir."

Mr. Alleyne bent his head again upon his pile of papers. The man stared fixedly at the polished skull which directed the affairs of Crosbie & Alleyne, gauging its fragility. A spasm of rage gripped his throat for a few moments and then passed, leaving after it a sharp sensation of thirst. The man recognized the sensation and felt that he must have a good night's drinking. The middle of the month was passed and, if he could get the copy done in time, Mr. Alleyne might give him an order on the cashier. He stood still, gazing fixedly at the head upon the pile of papers. Suddenly Mr. Alleyne began to upset all the papers, searching for something. Then, as if he had been unaware of the man's presence till that moment, he shot up his head again, saying:

"Eh? Are you going to stand there all day? Upon my word, Farrington, you take things easy!"

"I was waiting to see . . ."

"Very good, you needn't wait to see. Go downstairs and do your work."

The man walked heavily towards the door and, as he went out of the room, he heard Mr. Alleyne cry after him that if the contract was not copied by evening Mr. Crosbie would hear of the matter.

He returned to his desk in the lower office and counted the sheets which remained to be copied. He took up his pen and dipped it in the ink, but he continued to stare stupidly at the last words he had written: *In no case shall the said Bernard Bodley be* . . . The evening was falling and in a few minutes they would be lighting the gas: then he could write. He felt that he must slake the thirst in his throat. He stood up from his desk and, lifting the counter as before, passed out of the office. As he was passing out the chief clerk looked at him inquiringly.

"It's all right, Mr. Shelley," said the man, point-

[1] *Introduction to Dubliners*, Modern Library Edition, 1926.
[2] From *Dubliners* by James Joyce by permission of The Viking Press, Inc.

ing with his finger to indicate the objective of his journey.

The chief clerk glanced at the hat-rack, but, seeing the row complete, offered no remark. As soon as he was on the landing the man pulled a shepherd's plaid cap out of his pocket, put it on his head and ran quickly down the rickety stairs. From the street door he walked on furtively on the inner side of the path towards the corner and all at once dived into a doorway. He was now safe in the dark snug of O'Neill's shop, and, filling up the little window that looked into the bar with his inflamed face, the colour of dark wine or dark meat, he called out:

"Here, Pat, give us a g.p., like a good fellow."

The curate brought him a glass of plain porter. The man drank it at a gulp and asked for a caraway seed. He put his penny on the counter and, leaving the curate to grope for it in the gloom, retreated out of the snug as furtively as he had entered it.

Darkness, accompanied by a thick fog, was gaining upon the dusk of February and the lamps in Eustace Street had been lit. The man went up by the houses until he reached the door of the office, wondering whether he could finish his copy in time. On the stairs a moist pungent odour of perfumes saluted his nose: evidently Miss Delacour had come while he was out in O'Neill's. He crammed his cap back again into his pocket and re-entered the office, assuming an air of absent-mindedness.

"Mr. Alleyne has been calling for you," said the chief clerk severely. "Where were you?"

The man glanced at the two clients who were standing at the counter as if to intimate that their presence prevented him from answering. As the clients were both male the chief clerk allowed himself a laugh.

"I know that game," he said. "Five times in one day is a little bit. . . . Well, you better look sharp and get a copy of our correspondence in the Delacour case for Mr. Alleyne."

This address in the presence of the public, his run upstairs and the porter he had gulped down so hastily confused the man and, as he sat down at his desk to get what was required, he realized how hopeless was the task of finishing his copy of the contract before half-past five. The dark damp night was coming and he longed to spend it in the bars, drinking with his friends amid the glare of gas and the clatter of glasses. He got out the Delacour correspondence and passed out of the office. He hoped Mr. Alleyne would not discover that the last two letters were missing.

The moist pungent perfume lay all the way up to Mr. Alleyne's room. Miss Delacour was a middle-aged woman of Jewish appearance. Mr. Alleyne was said to be sweet on her or on her money. She came to the office often and stayed a long time when she came. She was sitting beside his desk now in an aroma of perfumes, smoothing the handle of her umbrella and nodding the great black feather in her hat. Mr. Alleyne had swivelled his chair round to face her and thrown his right foot jauntily upon his left knee. The man put the correspondence on the desk and bowed respectfully but neither Mr. Alleyne nor Miss Delacour took any notice of his bow. Mr. Alleyne tapped a finger on the correspondence and then flicked it towards him as if to say: "*That's all right: you can go.*"

The man returned to the lower office and sat down again at his desk. He stared intently at the incomplete phrase: *In no case shall the said Bernard Bodley be* . . . and thought how strange it was that the last three words began with the same letter. The chief clerk began to hurry Miss Parker, saying she would never have the letters typed in time for post. The man listened to the clicking of the machine for a few minutes and then set to work to finish his copy. But his head was not clear and his mind wandered away to the glare and rattle of the public-house. It was a night for hot punches. He struggled on with his copy, but when the clock struck five he had still fourteen pages to write. Blast it! He couldn't finish it in time. He longed to execrate aloud, to bring his fist down on something violently. He was so enraged that he wrote *Bernard Bernard* instead of *Bernard Bodley* and had to begin again on a clean sheet.

He felt strong enough to clear out the whole office single-handed. His body ached to do something, to rush out and revel in violence. All the indignities of his life enraged him. . . . Could he ask the cashier privately for an advance? No, the cashier was no good, no damn good: he wouldn't give an advance. . . . He knew where he would meet the boys: Leonard and O'Halloran and Nosey Flynn. The barometer of his emotional nature was set for a spell of riot.

His imagination had so abstracted him that his name was called twice before he answered. Mr. Alleyne and Miss Delacour were standing outside the counter and all the clerks had turned round in anticipation of something. The man got up from his desk. Mr. Alleyne began a tirade of abuse, saying that two letters were missing. The man an-

16. curate, ironic slang for bartender. **17–18. caraway seed**, used, like cloves, to disguise the breath.

swered that he knew nothing about them, that he had made a faithful copy. The tirade continued: it was so bitter and violent that the man could hardly restrain his fist from descending upon the head of the manikin before him.

"I know nothing about any other two letters," he said stupidly.

"*You—know—nothing*. Of course you know nothing," said Mr. Alleyne. "Tell me," he added, glancing first for approval to the lady beside him, "do you take me for a fool? Do you think me an utter fool?"

The man glanced from the lady's face to the little egg-shaped head and back again; and, almost before he was aware of it, his tongue had found a felicitous moment:

"I don't think, sir," he said, "that that's a fair question to put to me."

There was a pause in the very breathing of the clerks. Every one was astounded (the author of the witticism no less than his neighbours) and Miss Delacour, who was a stout amiable person, began to smile broadly. Mr. Alleyne flushed to the hue of a wild rose and his mouth twitched with a dwarf's passion. He shook his fist in the man's face till it seemed to vibrate like the knob of some electric machine:

"You impertinent ruffian! You impertinent ruffian! I'll make short work of you! Wait till you see! You'll apologize to me for your impertinence or you'll quit the office instanter! You'll quit this, I'm telling you, or you'll apologize to me!"

He stood in a doorway opposite the office, watching to see if the cashier would come out alone. All the clerks passed out and finally the cashier came out with the chief clerk. It was no use trying to say a word to him when he was with the chief clerk. The man felt that his position was bad enough. He had been obliged to offer an abject apology to Mr. Alleyne for his impertinence, but he knew what a hornet's nest the office would be for him. He could remember the way in which Mr. Alleyne had hounded little Peake out of the office in order to make room for his own nephew. He felt savage and thirsty and revengeful, annoyed with himself and with every one else. Mr. Alleyne would never give him an hour's rest; his life would be a hell to him. He had made a proper fool of himself this time. Could he not keep his tongue in his cheek? But they had never pulled together from the first, he and Mr. Alleyne, ever since the day Mr. Alleyne had overheard him mimicking his North of Ireland accent to amuse Higgins and Miss Parker: that had been the beginning of it. He might have tried Higgins for the money, but sure Higgins never had anything for himself. A man with two establishments to keep up, of course he couldn't. . . .

He felt his great body again aching for the comfort of the public-house. The fog had begun to chill him and he wondered could he touch Pat in O'Neill's. He could not touch him for more than a bob—and a bob was no use. Yet he must get money somewhere or other: he had spent his last penny for the g.p. and soon it would be too late for getting money anywhere. Suddenly, as he was fingering his watch chain, he thought of Terry Kelly's pawn-office in Fleet Street. That was the dart! Why didn't he think of it sooner?

He went through the narrow alley of Temple Bar quickly, muttering to himself that they could all go to hell, because he was going to have a good night of it. The clerk in Terry Kelly's said *A crown!* but the consignor held out for six shillings; and in the end the six shillings was allowed him literally. He came out of the pawn-office joyfully, making a little cylinder of the coins between his thumb and fingers. In Westmoreland Street the footpaths were crowded with young men and women returning from business, and ragged urchins ran here and there yelling out the names of the evening editions. The man passed through the crowd, looking on the spectacle generally with proud satisfaction and staring masterfully at the office-girls. His head was full of the noises of tram-gongs and swishing trolleys and his nose already sniffed the curling fumes of punch. As he walked on he preconsidered the terms in which he would narrate the incident to the boys:

"So, I just looked at him—coolly, you know, and looked at her. Then I looked back at him again—taking my time you know. 'I don't think that that's a fair question to put to me,' says I."

Nosey Flynn was sitting up in his usual corner of Davy Byrne's and, when he heard the story, he stood Farrington a half-one, saying it was as smart a thing as ever he heard. Farrington stood a drink in his turn. After a while O'Halloran and Paddy Leonard came in and the story was repeated to them. O'Halloran stood tailors of malt, hot, all round and told the story of the retort he had made to the chief clerk when he was in Callan's of Fownes's Street; but, as the retort was after the manner of the liberal shepherds in the eclogues, he had to admit that it was not as clever as Farrington's retort. At this Farrington told the boys to polish off that and have another.

Just as they were naming their poisons who should come in but Higgins! Of course he had to join in with the others. The men asked him to give his version of it, and he did so with great vivacity, for the sight of five small hot whiskies was very exhilarating. Every one roared laughing when he showed the way in which Mr. Alleyne shook his fist in Farrington's face. Then he imitated Farrington, saying, "*And here was my nabs, as cool as you please*," while Farrington looked at the company out of his heavy dirty eyes, smiling and at times drawing forth stray drops of liquor from his moustache with the aid of his lower lip.

When that round was over there was a pause. O'Halloran had money, but neither of the other two seemed to have any; so the whole party left the shop somewhat regretfully. At the corner of Duke Street Higgins and Nosey Flynn bevelled off to the left while the other three turned back towards the city. Rain was drizzling down on the cold streets and, when they reached the Ballast Office, Farrington suggested the Scotch House. The bar was full of men and loud with the noise of tongues and glasses. The three men pushed past the whining matchsellers at the door and formed a little party at the corner of the counter. They began to exchange stories. Leonard introduced them to a young fellow named Weathers who was performing at the Tivoli as an acrobat and knockabout *artiste*. Farrington stood a drink all around. Weathers said he would take a small Irish and Apollinaris. Farrington, who had definite notions of what was what, asked the boys would they have an Apollinaris too; but the boys told Tim to make theirs hot. The talk became theatrical. O'Halloran stood a round and then Farrington stood another round, Weathers protesting that the hospitality was too Irish. He promised to get them in behind the scenes and introduce them to some nice girls. O'Halloran said that he and Leonard would go, but that Farrington wouldn't go because he was a married man; and Farrington's heavy dirty eyes leered at the company in token that he understood he was being chaffed. Weathers made them all have just one little tincture at his expense and promised to meet them later on at Mulligan's in Poolbeg Street.

When the Scotch House closed they went round to Mulligan's. They went into the parlour at the back and O'Halloran ordered small hot specials all round. They were all beginning to feel mellow. Farrington was just standing another round when Weathers came back. Much to Farrington's relief he drank a glass of bitter this time. Funds were getting low, but they had enough to keep them going. Presently two young women with big hats and a young man in a check suit came in and sat at a table close by. Weathers saluted them and told the company that they were out of the Tivoli. Farrington's eyes wandered at every moment in the direction of one of the young women. There was something striking in her appearance. An immense scarf of peacock-blue muslin was wound round her hat and knotted in a great bow under her chin; and she wore bright yellow gloves, reaching to the elbow. Farrington gazed admiringly at the plump arm which she moved very often and with much grace; and when, after a little time, she answered his gaze he admired still more her large dark brown eyes. The oblique staring expression in them fascinated him. She glanced at him once or twice and, when the party was leaving the room, she brushed against his chair and said "*O, pardon!*" in a London accent. He watched her leave the room in the hope that she would look back at him, but he was disappointed. He cursed his want of money and cursed all the rounds he had stood, particularly all the whiskies and Apollinaris which he had stood to Weathers. If there was one thing that he hated it was a sponge. He was so angry that he lost count of the conversation of his friends.

When Paddy Leonard called him he found that they were talking about feats of strength. Weathers was showing his biceps muscle to the company and boasting so much that the other two had called on Farrington to uphold the national honour. Farrington pulled up his sleeve accordingly and showed his biceps muscle to the company. The two arms were examined and compared and finally it was agreed to have a trial of strength. The table was cleared and the two men rested their elbows on it, clasping hands. When Paddy Leonard said "Go!" each was to try to bring down the other's hand on to the table. Farrington looked very serious and determined.

The trial began. After about thirty seconds Weathers brought his opponent's hand slowly down on to the table. Farrington's dark wine-coloured face flushed darker still with anger and humiliation at having been defeated by such a stripling.

"You're not to put the weight of your body behind it. Play fair," he said.

"Who's not playing fair?" said the other.

"Come on again. The two best out of three."

The trial began again. The veins stood out on Farrington's forehead, and the pallor of Weathers' complexion changed to peony. Their hands and arms trembled under the stress. After a long struggle Weathers again brought his opponent's hand slowly on to the table. There was a murmur of applause from the spectators. The curate, who was standing beside the table, nodded his red head towards the victor and said with stupid familiarity:

"Ah! that's the knock!"

"What the hell do you know about it?" said Farrington fiercely, turning on the man. "What do you put in your gab for?"

"Sh, sh!" said O'Halloran, observing the violent expression of Farrington's face. "Pony up, boys. We'll have just one little smahan more and then we'll be off."

A very sullen-faced man stood at the corner of O'Connell Bridge waiting for the little Sandymount tram to take him home. He was full of smouldering anger and revengefulness. He felt humiliated and discontented; he did not even feel drunk; and he had only twopence in his pocket. He cursed everything. He had done for himself in the office, pawned his watch, spent all his money; and he had not even got drunk. He began to feel thirsty again and he longed to be back again in the hot, reeking public-house. He had lost his reputation as a strong man, having been defeated twice by a mere boy. His heart swelled with fury and, when he thought of the woman in the big hat who had brushed against him and said *Pardon!* his fury nearly choked him.

His tram let him down at Shelbourne Road and he steered his great body along in the shadow of the wall of the barracks. He loathed returning to his home. When he went in by the side-door he found the kitchen empty and the kitchen fire nearly out. He bawled upstairs:

"Ada! Ada!"

His wife was a little sharp-faced woman who bullied her husband when he was sober and was bullied by him when he was drunk. They had five children. A little boy came running down the stairs.

"Who is that?" said the man, peering through the darkness.

"Me, pa."

"Who are you? Charlie?"

"No, pa. Tom."

"Where's your mother?"

"She's out at the chapel."

"That's right. . . . Did she think of leaving any dinner for me?"

"Yes, pa. I——"

"Light the lamp. What do you mean by having the place in darkness? Are the other children in bed?"

The man sat down heavily on one of the chairs while the little boy lit the lamp. He began to mimic his son's flat accent, saying half to himself: "*At the chapel. At the chapel, if you please!*" When the lamp was lit he banged his fist on the table and shouted:

"What's for my dinner?"

"I'm going . . . to cook it, pa," said the little boy.

The man jumped up furiously and pointed to the fire.

"On that fire! You let the fire out! By God, I'll teach you to do that again!"

He took a step to the door and seized the walking-stick which was standing behind it.

"I'll teach you to let the fire out!" he said, rolling up his sleeve in order to give his arm free play.

The little boy cried "*O, pa!*" and ran whimpering round the table, but the man followed him and caught him by the coat. The little boy looked about him wildly but, seeing no way of escape, fell upon his knees.

"Now, you'll let the fire out the next time!" said the man, striking at him vigorously with the stick. "Take that, you little whelp!"

The boy uttered a squeal of pain as the stick cut his thigh. He clasped his hands together in the air and his voice shook with fright.

"O, pa," he cried. "Don't beat me, pa! And I'll . . . I'll say a *Hail Mary* for you. . . . I'll say a *Hail Mary* for you, pa, if you don't beat me. . . . I'll say a *Hail Mary*. . . ."

9. smahan, nip.

Virginia Woolf
1882–1941

The third of four children of the eminent biographer and critic Sir Leslie Stephen by his second marriage, Virginia (Stephen) Woolf was born in London in 1882. Stephen's first wife was a daughter of Thackeray, and the Stephens were related to the Darwins, the Macaulays, the Trevelyans, the Stracheys and other distinguished families. Her father's home, where Virginia Stephen received a thorough if informal education, was a focal point of culture. After her elder sister, Vanessa, married the art critic Clive Bell, Virginia married the author and publisher Leonard Woolf, in 1912, and became a member of the "Bloomsbury Group." This group, so called from the district of London in which most of them lived, included (besides the Woolfs and the Bells) the biographer Lytton Strachey, the economist John Maynard Keynes, the novelist E. M. Forster, and the painter Roger Fry. The members of the group, devoting themselves to "a pursuit of truth and a contemplation of beauty," opposed the genteel tradition; "in a gentlemanly society, they were ruthless . . . passionate in their devotion to what they thought good, brutal in their rejection of what they thought second-rate, resolute in their refusal to compromise."

Shortly after their marriage Leonard and Virginia Woolf began printing limited editions from a small hand press; their publications were in demand, the editions grew larger, and the Hogarth Press was founded. Meanwhile, Virginia Woolf had been experimenting in the novel, the short story, and the essay. From her first published book, *The Voyage Out*, 1915, it was evident that a refined and highly sensitive intelligence was at work. *Night and Day*, 1919, struggled against the restrictions of the conventional novel; *Monday or Tuesday*, 1921, a set of short stories, alternated between prose statement and poetic implication; *Mrs. Dalloway*, 1925, imposed the past upon the present, and illumined a whole series of lives in eighteen hours of one woman's life.

Mrs. Dalloway marked the turning-point of Virginia Woolf's creative power. Here her gifts were fused; she combined a "stream of consciousness" technique, the current scientific inquiries regarding space and time as "fourth dimensions," and her own minute perceptions. Character, environment, and action were revealed in "the atoms as they fall upon the mind . . . by tracing the pattern, however disconnected and incoherent it appears, which each sight or incident scores upon the unconscious." This fusion was emphasized in *To the Lighthouse*, 1927, in which the atmosphere is even finer and more transparent than in the preceding work; in *Orlando*, 1928, which is an absorbing tour de force, a fantasy in which time is treated arbitrarily, the heroine nonchalantly changes her sex, and the author romps through English literature with stylistic bravura; in *The Waves*, 1931, and *The Years*, 1937, in which characters develop in terms of images, and in which Mrs. Woolf's gifts of observation and sensibility attain what seems to be an abstract virtuosity.

But Mrs. Woolf is not always experimental and involved. There is *Flush*, 1933, the "biography" of Elizabeth Barrett Browning's cocker spaniel, which is as sympathetic as it is shrewd; there are the delightful straightforward and pointed feminist writings *A Room of One's Own*, 1929, and *Three Guineas*, 1938; there are the apt and uncomplicated essays in *The Common Reader*, 1925, and *The Second Common Reader*, 1932. In her last novel, *Between the Acts*, 1941, which was published after her death, she provides a simple synthesis of English history through the medium of a village pageant watched by a group of persons from a terrace on a summer afternoon a few months before the world was again at war. The horror of that war and the dreaded return of illness proved too much for her sensitive spirit, and in March, 1941, she took her life.

It may be that Mrs. Woolf will be remembered longest as one of the novelists who wrote during a suspension of faith and an unhappy search for new beliefs. The more serious novelists faced the situation with courage, if without solutions. "Joyce met the problem by retreating into a realm without values; Katherine Mansfield met it by endeavoring to cultivate an impossible purity of vision; Aldous Huxley met it by denunciation followed by romantic compensation; Virginia Woolf met it by trying to refine all life into a problem for the meditative intellect."[1]

[1] David Daiches, *The Novel and the Modern World*, University of Chicago Press, 1939.

It is too early to estimate Mrs. Woolf's status; it is impossible to decide whether she will achieve permanence as a novelist, an essayist, or a poetic analyst who used prose as a searching medium.

Before her death Mrs. Woolf had planned a volume of her collected short stories. Her intention was carried out by Leonard Woolf, and from the volume, *A Haunted House and Other Stories*, 1944, is taken the story printed below. It was first published in *Harper's Bazaar* in 1938, and illustrates as well as any one piece could what E. M. Forster calls that combination in her of a humorous appreciation of the muddle of life with a keen sense of its beauty and its tragedy.

LAPPIN AND LAPINOVA [1]

THEY were married. The wedding march pealed out. The pigeons fluttered. Small boys in Eton jackets threw rice; a fox terrier sauntered across the path; and Ernest Thorburn led his bride to the car through that small inquisitive crowd of complete strangers which always collects in London to enjoy other people's happiness or unhappiness. Certainly he looked handsome and she looked shy. More rice was thrown, and the car moved off.

That was on Tuesday. Now it was Saturday. Rosalind had still to get used to the fact that she was Mrs. Ernest Thorburn. Perhaps she would never get used to the fact that she was Mrs. Ernest Anybody, she thought, as she sat in the bow window of the hotel looking over the lake to the mountains, and waited for her husband to come down to breakfast. Ernest was a difficult name to get used to. It was not the name she would have chosen. She would have preferred Timothy, Antony, or Peter. He did not look like Ernest either. The name suggested the Albert Memorial, mahogany sideboards, steel engravings of the Prince Consort with his family—her mother-in-law's dining-room in Porchester Terrace in short.

But here he was. Thank goodness he did not look like Ernest—no. But what did he look like? She glanced at him sideways. Well, when he was eating toast he looked like a rabbit. Not that anyone else would have seen a likeness to a creature so diminutive and timid in this spruce, muscular young man with the straight nose, the blue eyes, and the very firm mouth. But that made it all the more amusing. His nose twitched very slightly when he ate. So did her pet rabbit's. She kept watching his nose twitch; and then she had to explain, when he caught her looking at him, why she laughed.

"It's because you're like a rabbit, Ernest," she said. "Like a wild rabbit," she added, looking at him. "A hunting rabbit; a King Rabbit; a rabbit that makes laws for all the other rabbits."

Ernest had no objection to being that kind of rabbit, and since it amused her to see him twitch his nose—he had never known that his nose twitched—he twitched it on purpose. And she laughed and laughed; and he laughed too, so that the maiden ladies and the fishing man and the Swiss waiter in his greasy black jacket all guessed right; they were very happy. But how long does such happiness last? they asked themselves; and each answered according to his own circumstances.

At lunch time, seated on a clump of heather beside the lake, "Lettuce, rabbit?" said Rosalind, holding out the lettuce that had been provided to eat with the hard-boiled eggs. "Come and take it out of my hand," she added, and he stretched out and nibbled the lettuce and twitched his nose.

"Good rabbit, nice rabbit," she said, patting him, as she used to pat her tame rabbit at home. But that was absurd. He was not a tame rabbit, whatever he was. She turned it into French. "Lapin," she called him. But whatever he was, he was not a French rabbit. He was simply and solely English—born at Porchester Terrace, educated at Rugby; now a clerk in His Majesty's Civil Service. So she tried "Bunny" next; but that was worse. "Bunny" was someone plump and soft and comic; he was thin and hard and serious. Still, his nose twitched. "Lappin," she exclaimed suddenly; and gave a little cry as if she had found the very word she looked for.

"Lappin, Lappin, King Lappin," she repeated. It seemed to suit him exactly; he was not Ernest, he was King Lappin. Why? She did not know.

When there was nothing new to talk about on their long solitary walks—and it rained, as everyone had warned them that it would rain; or when they were sitting over the fire in the evening, for it was cold, and the maiden ladies had gone and the fishing man, and the waiter only came if you rang the bell for him, she let her fancy play with the story of the Lappin tribe. Under her hands—she was sewing; he was reading—they became very real, very vivid, very amusing. Ernest put down the paper and helped her. There were the black rabbits and the red; there were the enemy rabbits and the friendly. There were the wood in which they lived and the outlying prairies and

[1] From *A Haunted House and Other Stories* by Virginia Woolf, copyright, 1944, by Harcourt, Brace and Company, Inc. Reprinted by permission of Harcourt, Brace and Company and The Hogarth Press Ltd.

the swamp. Above all there was King Lappin, who, far from having only the one trick—that he twitched his nose—became as the days passed an animal of the greatest character; Rosalind was always finding new qualities in him. But above all he was a great hunter.

"And what," said Rosalind, on the last day of the honeymoon, "did the King do today?"

In fact they had been climbing all day; and she had worn a blister on her heel; but she did not mean that.

"Today," said Ernest, twitching his nose as he bit the end off his cigar, "he chased a hare." He paused; struck a match, and twitched again.

"A woman hare," he added.

"A white hare!" Rosalind exclaimed, as if she had been expecting this. "Rather a small hare; silver grey; with big bright eyes?"

"Yes," said Ernest, looking at her as she had looked at him, "a smallish animal; with eyes popping out of her head, and two little front paws dangling." It was exactly how she sat, with her sewing dangling in her hands; and her eyes, that were so big and bright, were certainly a little prominent.

"Ah, Lapinova," Rosalind murmured.

"Is that what she's called?" said Ernest—"the real Rosalind?" He looked at her. He felt very much in love with her.

"Yes; that's what she's called," said Rosalind. "Lapinova." And before they went to bed that night it was all settled. He was King Lappin; she was Queen Lapinova. They were the opposite of each other; he was bold and determined; she wary and undependable. He ruled over the busy world of rabbits; her world was a desolate, mysterious place, which she ranged mostly by moonlight. All the same, their territories touched; they were King and Queen.

Thus when they came back from their honeymoon they possessed a private world, inhabited, save for the one white hare, entirely by rabbits. No one guessed that there was such a place, and that of course made it all the more amusing. It made them feel, more even than most young married couples, in league together against the rest of the world. Often they looked slyly at each other when people talked about rabbits and woods and traps and shooting. Or they winked furtively across the table when Aunt Mary said that she could never bear to see a hare in a dish—it looked so like a baby: or when John, Ernest's sporting brother, told them what price rabbits were fetching that autumn in Wiltshire, skins and all. Sometimes when they wanted a gamekeeper, or a poacher or a Lord of the Manor, they amused themselves by distributing the parts among their friends. Ernest's mother, Mrs. Reginald Thorburn, for example, fitted the part of the Squire to perfection. But it was all secret—that was the point of it; nobody save themselves knew that such a world existed.

Without that world, how, Rosalind wondered, that winter could she have lived at all? For instance, there was the golden-wedding party, when all the Thorburns assembled at Porchester Terrace to celebrate the fiftieth anniversary of that union which had been so blessed—had it not produced Ernest Thorburn?—and so fruitful—had it not produced nine other sons and daughters into the bargain, many themselves married and also fruitful? She dreaded that party. But it was inevitable. As she walked upstairs she felt bitterly that she was an only child and an orphan at that; a mere drop among all those Thorburns assembled in the great drawing-room with the shiny satin wallpaper and the lustrous family portraits. The living Thorburns much resembled the painted; save that instead of painted lips they had real lips; out of which came jokes; jokes about schoolrooms, and how they had pulled the chair from under the governess; jokes about frogs and how they had put them between the virgin sheets of maiden ladies. As for herself, she had never even made an apple-pie bed. Holding her present in her hand she advanced toward her mother-in-law sumptuous in yellow satin; and toward her father-in-law decorated with a rich yellow carnation. All round them on tables and chairs there were golden tributes, some nestling in cotton wool; others branching resplendent—candlesticks; cigar boxes; chains; each stamped with the goldsmith's proof that it was solid gold, hall-marked, authentic. But her present was only a little pinchbeck box pierced with holes; an old sand caster, an eighteenth-century relic, once used to sprinkle sand over wet ink. Rather a senseless present she felt—in an age of blotting paper; and as she proffered it, she saw in front of her the stubby black handwriting in which her mother-in-law when they were engaged had expressed the hope that "My son will make you happy." No, she was not happy. Not at all happy. She looked at Ernest, straight as a ramrod with a nose like all the noses in the family portraits; a nose that never twitched at all.

Then they went down to dinner. She was half hidden by the great chrysanthemums that curled their red and gold petals into large tight balls.

Everything was gold. A gold-edged card with gold initials intertwined recited the list of all the dishes that would be set one after another before them. She dipped her spoon in a plate of clear golden fluid. The raw white fog outside had been turned by the lamps into a golden mesh that blurred the edges of the plates and gave the pineapples a rough golden skin. Only she herself in her white wedding dress peering ahead of her with her prominent eyes seemed insoluble as an icicle.

As the dinner wore on, however, the room grew steamy with heat. Beads of perspiration stood out on the men's foreheads. She felt that her icicle was being turned to water. She was being melted; dispersed; dissolved into nothingness; and would soon faint. Then through the surge in her head and the din in her ears she heard a woman's voice exclaim, "But they breed so!"

The Thorburns—yes; they breed so, she echoed; looking at all the round red faces that seemed doubled in the giddiness that overcame her; and magnified in the gold mist that enhaloed them. "They breed so." Then John bawled:

"Little devils! . . . Shoot 'em! Jump on 'em with big boots! That's the only way to deal with 'em . . . rabbits!"

At that word, that magic word, she revived. Peeping between the chrysanthemums she saw Ernest's nose twitch. It rippled, it ran with successive twitches. And at that a mysterious catastrophe befell the Thorburns. The golden table became a moor with the gorse in full bloom; the din of voices turned to one peal of lark's laughter ringing down from the sky. It was a blue sky—clouds passed slowly. And they had all been changed—the Thorburns. She looked at her father-in-law, a furtive little man with dyed moustaches. His foible was collecting things—seals, enamel boxes, trifles from eighteenth-century dressing tables which he hid in the drawers of his study from his wife. Now she saw him as he was—a poacher, stealing off with his coat bulging with pheasants and partridges to drop them stealthily into a three-legged pot in his smoky little cottage. That was her real father-in-law—a poacher. And Celia, the unmarried daughter, who always nosed out other people's secrets, the little things they wished to hide—she was a white ferret with pink eyes, and a nose clotted with earth from her horrid underground nosings and pokings. Slung round men's shoulders, in a net, and thrust down a hole—it was a pitiable life—Celia's; it was none of her fault. So she saw Celia. And then she looked at her mother-in-law—whom they dubbed The Squire. Flushed, coarse, a bully—she was all that, as she stood returning thanks, but now that Rosalind—that is Lapinova—saw her, she saw behind her the decayed family mansion, the plaster peeling off the walls, and heard her, with a sob in her voice, give thanks to her children (who hated her) for a world that had ceased to exist. There was a sudden silence. They all stood with their glasses raised; they all drank; then it was over.

"Oh, King Lappin!" she cried as they went home together in the fog, "if your nose hadn't twitched just at that moment, I should have been trapped!"

"But you're safe," said King Lappin, pressing her paw.

"Quite safe," she answered.

And they drove back through the Park, King and Queen of the marsh, of the mist, and of the gorse-scented moor.

Thus time passed; one year; two years of time. And on a winter's night, which happened by a coincidence to be the anniversary of the golden-wedding party—but Mrs. Reginald Thorburn was dead; the house was to let; and there was only a caretaker in residence—Ernest came home from the office. They had a nice little home; half a house above a saddler's shop in South Kensington, not far from the Tube station. It was cold, with fog in the air, and Rosalind was sitting over the fire, sewing.

"What d'you think happened to me today?" she began as soon as he had settled himself down with his legs stretched to the blaze. "I was crossing the stream when—"

"What stream?" Ernest interrupted her.

"The stream at the bottom, where our wood meets the black wood," she explained.

Ernest looked completely blank for a moment.

"What the deuce are you talking about?" he asked.

"My dear Ernest!" she cried in dismay. "King Lappin," she added, dangling her little front paws in the firelight. But his nose did not twitch. Her hands—they turned to hands—clutched the stuff she was holding; her eyes popped half out of her head. It took him five minutes at least to change from Ernest Thorburn to King Lappin; and while she waited she felt a load on the back of her neck, as if somebody were about to wring it. At last he changed to King Lappin; his nose twitched; and they spent the evening roaming the woods much as usual.

But she slept badly. In the middle of the night she woke, feeling as if something strange had happened to her. She was stiff and cold. At last she turned on the light and looked at Ernest lying beside her. He was sound asleep. He snored. But even though he snored, his nose remained perfectly still. It looked as if it had never twitched at all. Was it possible that he was really Ernest; and that she was really married to Ernest? A vision of her mother-in-law's dining-room came before her; and there they sat, she and Ernest, grown old, under the engravings, in front of the sideboard. . . . It was their golden-wedding day. She could not bear it.

"Lappin, King Lappin!" she whispered, and for a moment his nose seemed to twitch of its own accord. But he still slept. "Wake up, Lappin, wake up!" she cried.

Ernest woke; and seeing her sitting bolt upright beside him he asked:

"What's the matter?"

"I thought my rabbit was dead!" she whimpered. Ernest was angry.

"Don't talk such rubbish, Rosalind," he said. "Lie down and go to sleep."

He turned over. In another moment he was sound asleep and snoring.

But she could not sleep. She lay curled up on her side of the bed, like a hare in its form. She had turned out the light, but the street lamp lit the ceiling faintly, and the trees outside made a lacy network over it as if there were a shadowy grove on the ceiling in which she wandered, turning, twisting, in and out, round and round, hunting, being hunted, hearing the bay of hounds and horns; flying, escaping . . . until the maid drew the blinds and brought their early tea.

Next day she could settle to nothing. She seemed to have lost something. She felt as if her body had shrunk; it had grown small, and black and hard. Her joints seemed stiff too, and when she looked in the glass, which she did several times as she wandered about the flat, her eyes seemed to burst out of her head, like currants in a bun. The rooms also seemed to have shrunk. Large pieces of furniture jutted out at odd angles and she found herself knocking against them. At last she put on her hat and went out. She walked along the Cromwell Road; and every room she passed and peered into seemed to be a dining-room where people sat eating under steel engravings, with thick yellow lace curtains, and mahogany sideboards. At last she reached the Natural History Museum; she used to like it when she was a child. But the first thing she saw when she went in was a stuffed hare standing on sham snow with pink glass eyes. Somehow it made her shiver all over. Perhaps it would be better when dusk fell. She went home and sat over the fire, without a light, and tried to imagine that she was out alone on a moor; and there was a stream rushing; and beyond the stream a dark wood. But she could get no further than the stream. At last she squatted down on the bank on the wet grass, and sat crouched in her chair, with her hands dangling empty, and her eyes glazed, like glass eyes, in the firelight. Then there was the crack of a gun. . . . She started as if she had been shot. It was only Ernest, turning his key in the door. She waited, trembling. He came in and switched on the light. There he stood tall, handsome, rubbing his hands that were red with cold.

"Sitting in the dark?" he said.

"Oh, Ernest, Ernest!" she cried, starting up in her chair.

"Well, what's up, now?" he asked briskly, warming his hands at the fire.

"It's Lapinova . . ." she faltered, glancing wildly at him out of her great startled eyes. "She's gone, Ernest. I've lost her!"

Ernest frowned. He pressed his lips tight together. "Oh, that's what's up, is it?" he said, smiling rather grimly at his wife. For ten seconds he stood there, silent; and she waited, feeling hands tightening at the back of her neck.

"Yes," he said at length. "Poor Lapinova . . ." He straightened his tie at the looking-glass over the mantelpiece.

"Caught in a trap," he said, "killed," and sat down and read the newspaper.

So that was the end of that marriage.

D. H. Lawrence
1885–1930

David Herbert Lawrence was born on September 11, 1885, at Eastwood, Nottinghamshire. Eastwood is a small colliery town, and Lawrence's father was an intemperate coal-miner, who not infrequently beat his wife and bullied his son. It is little wonder that the child developed an inordinate attachment to his mother, an attachment which is reflected in the autobiographical *Sons and Lovers*, 1913, one of Lawrence's early novels. Escaping the harshness of his environment, he took refuge in books and won a scholarship in the Nottingham high school. At sixteen he became a clerk; at eighteen, while he was still studying, he became a teacher in an elementary school; at nineteen he won another scholarship, but his poverty was such that he could not take advantage of it. At twenty-four a friend, who figures as "Miriam" in *Sons and Lovers*, copied out some of his poems and submitted them for publication. Five of the poems were accepted by Ford Madox Ford, who printed them in the *English Review*. Two years later, sponsored by Ford, Lawrence published his first novel, *The White Peacock*, 1911.

Lawrence had met and fallen in love with a married woman, Mrs. Ernest Weekley, born Baroness Frieda von Richthofen. The two eloped, lived abroad, were married, and came back to England to suffer through the World War. Lawrence was rejected for war service because of his tubercular condition; Frieda was suspected of being a German spy, and the couple were harried and hounded throughout the war.

When peace came Lawrence left England and, except for occasional visits, never returned to his homeland. He tried to establish himself in many parts of the world, but nowhere in the universe was he at home. He was alternately—and inconsistently—seeking a new world and the poet's lost security, the demolished ivory tower. He yearned for them in Florence, Sicily, Ceylon, Australia, Tahiti, Taos, Mexico, the Riviera—around the world and back again.

Meanwhile, during his futile quest for "ultima Thule," Lawrence wrote thirteen novels, including *The Rainbow*, 1915, the most intensely poetic, and *Lady Chatterley's Lover*, 1928, the most openly scandalous; a dozen volumes of short stories; thirteen collections of poems, including a two-volume *Collected Poems*, 1928; four plays, twelve books of essays, three of travel, and a half-dozen translations. Three of the novels were suppressed; an exhibition of his paintings was raided by the police in London (1929); several of his canvases were not only banned but confiscated. Worn out by controversy, weary of travel, undermined in health, he died at Vence, near Nice, on March 2, 1930.

Lawrence's life, his letters, and his creative work are inextricably interknit. In everything he wrote and said his unhappy obsessions persist. He was possessed by and preoccupied with sex; he celebrated an almost fanatic primitivism and worshiped "the hot blood's blindfold art." A prophet of the "dark" subconscious, he glorified mindlessness with all his intellectuality. Suffering is rarely absent from his pages; the books reveal sexual torment and social defeat. The intensity is almost more than the reader can bear. Yet Lawrence's revolt against the intelligence is raised to a pitch of eloquence not attained by any writer of his generation. His great power is the articulation of blind instinct and his exploration of levels touched only by the probing psychoanalyst. One critic observed:

> "His spirit is exalted only when it takes fire from his senses; his mind follows the fluctuations of his desires, intellectualizing them, not operating in its own right. . . . And that is because he is on the side of the instincts, and against all the forms, emasculated or deformed, in which they can be manifested in a civilized society." [1]

It is generally conceded that, as a novelist, Lawrence never surpassed *Sons and Lovers* and *The Rainbow*. Elsewhere in the prose of this very gifted but very uneven writer there are many pages of imaginative richness and strength. His short stories rank among the finest in the language. In direct, concentrated form the best of these arrest human consciousness in moments of intense revelation. Of "The Blind Man," Lawrence wrote to Katherine Mansfield: "It seems to me, if one is to do fiction now, one must cross the threshold of the human people. . . . I've done 'The Blind Man'—the end queer and ironical."

In the course of his fertile career Lawrence grew

[1] Edwin Muir, *Transition*, The Viking Press, 1926.

also into a poet of considerable power. His letters, edited by Aldous Huxley in *The Letters of D. H. Lawrence*, are fresh with insight and vitality. A balanced selection of his prose and poetry is obtainable in *The Portable D. H. Lawrence*, Viking, 1950, edited by Diana Trilling.

Lawrence became a legend in his day. He appeared, faintly disguised, in Osbert Sitwell's *Miracle on Sinai*, 1933; he is "Mark Rampion" in Aldous Huxley's *Point Counter Point*, 1928. After his death a whole library of controversial books was written about him; Lawrence seems to have attracted a small army of warring biographers. Of the numerous biographies and reminiscences that have been printed, the most illuminating are Frieda Lawrence's *Not I, But the Wind*, 1934; Mabel Dodge Luhan's *Lorenzo in Taos*, 1932; Hugh Kingsmill's *The Life of D. H. Lawrence*, 1938; and Richard Aldington's *D. H. Lawrence: Portrait of a Genius But—*, 1950.

THE BLIND MAN[1]

ISABEL PERVIN was listening for two sounds—for the sound of wheels on the drive outside and for the noise of her husband's footsteps in the hall. Her dearest and oldest friend, a man who seemed almost indispensable to her living, would drive up in the rainy dusk of the closing November day. The trap had gone to fetch him from the station. And her husband, who had been blinded in Flanders, and who had a disfiguring mark on his brow, would be coming in from the outhouses.

He had been home for a year now. He was totally blind. Yet they had been very happy. The Grange was Maurice's own place. The back was a farmstead, and the Wernhams, who occupied the rear premises, acted as farmers. Isabel lived with her husband in the handsome rooms in front. She and he had been almost entirely alone together since he was wounded. They talked and sang and read together in a wonderful and unspeakable intimacy. Then she reviewed books for a Scottish newspaper, carrying on her old interest, and he occupied himself a good deal with the farm. Sightless, he could still discuss everything with Wernham, and he could also do a good deal of work about the place—menial work, it is true, but it gave him satisfaction. He milked the cows, carried in the pails, turned the separator, attended to the pigs and horses. Life was still very full and strangely serene for the blind man, peaceful with the almost incomprehensible peace of immediate contact in darkness. With his wife he had a whole world, rich and real and invisible.

They were newly and remotely happy. He did not even regret the loss of his sight in these times of dark, palpable joy. A certain exultance swelled his soul.

But as time wore on, sometimes the rich glamour would leave them. Sometimes, after months of this intensity, a sense of burden overcame Isabel, a weariness, a terrible *ennui*, in that silent house approached between a colonnade of tall-shafted pines. Then she felt she would go mad, for she could not bear it. And sometimes he had devastating fits of depression, which seemed to lay waste his whole being. It was worse than depression—a black misery, when his own life was a torture to him, and when his presence was unbearable to his wife. The dread went down to the roots of her soul as these black days recurred. In a kind of panic she tried to wrap herself up still further in her husband. She forced the old spontaneous cheerfulness and joy to continue. But the effort it cost her was almost too much. She knew she could not keep it up. She felt she would scream with the strain, and would give anything, anything, to escape. She longed to possess her husband utterly; it gave her inordinate joy to have him entirely to herself. And yet, when again he was gone in a black and massive misery, she could not bear him, she could not bear herself; she wished she could be snatched away off the earth altogether, anything rather than live at this cost.

Dazed, she schemed for a way out. She invited friends, she tried to give him some further connection with the outer world. But it was no good. After all their joy and suffering, after their dark, great year of blindness and solitude and unspeakable nearness, other people seemed to them both shallow, rattling, rather impertinent. Shallow prattle seemed presumptuous. He became impatient and irritated, she was wearied. And so they lapsed into their solitude again. For they preferred it.

But now, in a few weeks' time, her second baby would be born. The first had died, an infant, when her husband first went out to France. She looked with joy and relief to the coming of the second. It would be her salvation. But also she felt some anxiety. She was thirty years old, her husband was a year younger. They both wanted the child very much. Yet she could not help feeling afraid. She had her husband on her hands, a terrible joy to her, and a terrifying burden. The child would occupy her love and attention. And then, what of Maurice? What would he do? If only she could feel that he,

[1] From *The Portable D. H. Lawrence*. Copyright, 1922, by Thos. Seltzer, Inc., 1950, by Frieda Lawrence. Reprinted by permission of The Viking Press, Inc., New York.

too, would be at peace and happy when the child came! She did so want to luxuriate in a rich, physical satisfaction of maternity. But the man, what would he do? How could she provide for him, how avert those shattering black moods of his, which destroyed them both?

She sighed with fear. But at this time Bertie Reid wrote to Isabel. He was her old friend, a second or third cousin, a Scotchman, as she was a Scotchwoman. They had been brought up near to one another, and all her life he had been her friend, like a brother, but better than her own brothers. She loved him—though not in the marrying sense. There was a sort of kinship between them, an affinity. They understood one another instinctively. But Isabel would never have thought of marrying Bertie. It would have seemed like marrying in her own family.

Bertie was a barrister and a man of letters, a Scotchman of the intellectual type, quick, ironical, sentimental, and on his knees before the woman he adored but did not want to marry. Maurice Pervin was different. He came of a good old country family—the Grange was not a very great distance from Oxford. He was passionate, sensitive, perhaps oversensitive, wincing—a big fellow with heavy limbs and a forehead that flushed painfully. For his mind was slow, as if drugged by the strong provincial blood that beat in his veins. He was very sensitive to his own mental slowness, his feelings being quick and acute. So that he was just the opposite to Bertie, whose mind was much quicker than his emotions, which were not so very fine.

From the first the two men did not like each other. Isabel felt that they *ought* to get on together. But they did not. She felt that if only each could have the clue to the other there would be such a rare understanding between them. It did not come off, however. Bertie adopted a slightly ironical attitude, very offensive to Maurice, who returned the Scotch irony with English resentment, a resentment which deepened sometimes into stupid hatred.

This was a little puzzling to Isabel. However, she accepted it in the course of things. Men were made freakish and unreasonable. Therefore, when Maurice was going out to France for the second time, she felt that, for her husband's sake, she must discontinue her friendship with Bertie. She wrote to the barrister to this effect. Bertram Reid simply replied that in this, as in all other matters, he must obey her wishes, if these were indeed her wishes.

For nearly two years nothing had passed between the two friends. Isabel rather gloried in the fact; she had no compunction. She had one great article of faith, which was, that husband and wife should be so important to one another, that the rest of the world simply did not count. She and Maurice were husband and wife. They loved one another. They would have children. Then let everybody and everything else fade into insignificance outside this connubial felicity. She professed herself quite happy and ready to receive Maurice's friends. She was happy and ready: the happy wife, the ready woman in possession. Without knowing why, the friends retired abashed, and came no more. Maurice, of course, took as much satisfaction in this connubial absorption as Isabel did.

He shared in Isabel's literary activities, she cultivated a real interest in agriculture and cattle-raising. For she, being at heart perhaps an emotional enthusiast, always cultivated the practical side of life and prided herself on her mastery of practical affairs. Thus the husband and wife had spent the five years of their married life. The last had been one of blindness and unspeakable intimacy. And now Isabel felt a great indifference coming over her, a sort of lethargy. She wanted to be allowed to bear her child in peace, to nod by the fire and drift vaguely, physically, from day to day. Maurice was like an ominous thunder-cloud. She had to keep waking up to remember him.

When a little note came from Bertie, asking if he were to put up a tombstone to their dead friendship, and speaking of the real pain he felt on account of her husband's loss of sight, she felt a pang, a fluttering agitation of re-awakening. And she read the letter to Maurice.

"Ask him to come down," he said.

"Ask Bertie to come here!" she re-echoed.

"Yes—if he wants to."

Isabel paused for a few moments.

"I know he wants to—he'd only be too glad," she replied. "But what about you, Maurice? How would you like it?"

"I should like it."

"Well—in that case—— But I thought you didn't care for him——"

"Oh, I don't know. I might think differently of him now," the blind man replied. It was rather abstruse to Isabel.

"Well, dear," she said, "if you're quite sure——"

"I'm sure enough. Let him come," said Maurice.

So Bertie was coming, coming this evening, in the November rain and darkness. Isabel was agitated, racked with her old restlessness and indecision. She had always suffered from this pain of doubt, just an agonizing sense of uncertainty. It had begun to pass off, in the lethargy of maternity.

Now it returned, and she resented it. She struggled as usual to maintain her calm, composed, friendly bearing, a sort of mask she wore over all her body.

A woman had lighted a tall lamp beside the table and spread the cloth. The long dining-room was dim, with its elegant but rather severe pieces of old furniture. Only the round table glowed softly under the light. It had a rich, beautiful effect. The white cloth glistened and dropped its heavy, pointed lace corners almost to the carpet, the china was old and handsome, creamy-yellow, with a blotched pattern of harsh red and deep blue, the cups large and bell-shaped, the teapot gallant. Isabel looked at it with superficial appreciation.

Her nerves were hurting her. She looked automatically again at the high, uncurtained windows. In the last dusk she could just perceive outside a huge fir-tree swaying its boughs: it was as if she thought it rather than saw it. The rain came flying on the window-panes. Ah, why had she no peace? These two men, why did they tear at her? Why did they not come—why was there this suspense?

She sat in a lassitude that was really suspense and irritation. Maurice, at least, might come in—there was nothing to keep him out. She rose to her feet. Catching sight of her reflection in a mirror, she glanced at herself with a slight smile of recognition, as if she were an old friend to herself. Her face was oval and calm, her nose a little arched. Her neck made a beautiful line down to her shoulder. With hair knotted loosely behind, she had something of a warm, maternal look. Thinking this of herself, she arched her eyebrows and her rather heavy eyelids, with a little flicker of a smile, and for a moment her grey eyes looked amused and wicked, a little sardonic, out of her transfigured Madonna face.

Then, resuming her air of womanly patience—she was really fatally self-determined—she went with a little jerk towards the door. Her eyes were slightly reddened.

She passed down the wide hall and through a door at the end. Then she was in the farm premises. The scent of dairy, and of farm-kitchen, and of farm-yard and of leather almost overcame her: but particularly the scent of dairy. They had been scalding out the pans. The flagged passage in front of her was dark, puddled, and wet. Light came out from the open kitchen door. She went forward and stood in the doorway. The farm-people were at tea, seated at a little distance from her, round a long, narrow table, in the centre of which stood a white lamp. Ruddy faces, ruddy hands holding food, red mouths working, heads bent over the tea-cups: men, land-girls, boys: it was tea-time, feeding-time. Some faces caught sight of her. Mrs. Wernham, going round behind the chairs with a large black teapot, halting slightly in her walk, was not aware of her for a moment. Then she turned suddenly.

"Oh, is it Madam!" she exclaimed. "Come in, then, come in! We're at tea." And she dragged forward a chair.

"No, I won't come in," said Isabel. "I'm afraid I interrupt your meal."

"No—no—not likely, Madam, not likely."

"Hasn't Mr. Pervin come in, do you know?"

"I'm sure I couldn't say! Missed him, have you, Madam?"

"No, I only wanted him to come in," laughed Isabel, as if shyly.

"Wanted him, did ye? Get up, boy—get up, now——"

Mrs. Wernham knocked one of the boys on the shoulder. He began to scrape to his feet, chewing largely.

"I believe he's in top stable," said another face from the table.

"Ah! No, don't get up. I'm going myself," said Isabel.

"Don't you go out of a dirty night like this. Let the lad go. Get along wi' ye, boy," said Mrs. Wernham.

"No, no," said Isabel, with a decision that was always obeyed. "Go on with your tea, Tom. I'd like to go across to the stable, Mrs. Wernham."

"Did ever you hear tell!" exclaimed the woman.

"Isn't the trap late?" asked Isabel.

"Why, no," said Mrs. Wernham, peering into the distance at the tall, dim clock. "No, Madam—we can give it another quarter or twenty minutes yet, good—yes, every bit of a quarter."

"Ah! It seems late when darkness falls so early," said Isabel.

"It do, that it do. Bother the days, that they draw in so," answered Mrs. Wernham. "Proper miserable!"

"They are," said Isabel, withdrawing.

She pulled on her overshoes, wrapped a large tartan shawl around her, put on a man's felt hat, and ventured out along the causeways of the first yard. It was very dark. The wind was roaring in the great elms behind the outhouses. When she came to the second yard the darkness seemed deeper. She was unsure of her footing. She wished she had brought a lantern. Rain blew against her. Half she liked it, half she felt unwilling to battle.

She reached at last the just visible door of the stable. There was no sign of a light anywhere.

Opening the upper half, she looked in: into a simple well of darkness. The smell of horses, and ammonia, and of warmth was startling to her, in that full night. She listened with all her ears but could hear nothing save the night, and the stirring of a horse.

"Maurice!" she called, softly and musically, though she was afraid. "Maurice—are you there?"

Nothing came from the darkness. She knew the rain and wind blew in upon the horses, the hot animal life. Feeling it wrong, she entered the stable and drew the lower half of the door shut, holding the upper part close. She did not stir, because she was aware of the presence of the dark hind-quarters of the horses, though she could not see them, and she was afraid. Something wild stirred in her heart.

She listened intensely. Then she heard a small noise in the distance—far away, it seemed—the chink of a pan, and a man's voice speaking a brief word. It would be Maurice, in the other part of the stable. She stood motionless, waiting for him to come through the partition door. The horses were so terrifyingly near to her, in the invisible.

The loud jarring of the inner door-latch made her start; the door was opened. She could hear and feel her husband entering and invisibly passing among the horses near to her, darkness as they were, actively intermingled. The rather low sound of his voice as he spoke to the horses came velvety to her nerves. How near he was, and how invisible! The darkness seemed to be in a strange swirl of violent life, just upon her. She turned giddy.

Her presence of mind made her call, quietly and musically:

"Maurice! Maurice—dea-ar!"

"Yes," he answered. "Isabel?"

She saw nothing, and the sound of his voice seemed to touch her.

"Hello!" she answered cheerfully, straining her eyes to see him. He was still busy, attending to the horses near her, but she saw only darkness. It made her almost desperate.

"Won't you come in, dear?" she said.

"Yes, I'm coming. Just half a minute. *Stand over—now!* Trap's not come, has it?"

"Not yet," said Isabel.

His voice was pleasant and ordinary, but it had a slight suggestion of the stable to her. She wished he would come away. Whilst he was so utterly invisible, she was afraid of him.

"How's the time?" he asked.

"Not yet six," she replied. She disliked to answer into the dark. Presently he came very near to her, and she retreated out of doors.

"The weather blows in here," he said, coming steadily forward, feeling for the doors. She shrank away. At last she could dimly see him.

"Bertie won't have much of a drive," he said, as he closed the doors.

"He won't indeed!" said Isabel calmly, watching the dark shape at the door.

"Give me your arm, dear," she said.

She pressed his arm close to her, as she went. But she longed to see him, to look at him. She was nervous. He walked erect, with face rather lifted, but with a curious tentative movement of his powerful, muscular legs. She could feel the clever, careful, strong contact of his feet with the earth, as she balanced against him. For a moment he was a tower of darkness to her, as if he rose out of the earth.

In the house-passage he wavered and went cautiously, with a curious look of silence about him as he felt for the bench. Then he sat down heavily. He was a man with rather sloping shoulders, but with heavy limbs, powerful legs that seemed to know the earth. His head was small, usually carried high and light. As he bent down to unfasten his gaiters and boots he did not look blind. His hair was brown and crisp, his hands were large, reddish, intelligent, the veins stood out in the wrists; and his thighs and knees seemed massive. When he stood up his face and neck were surcharged with blood, the veins stood out on his temples. She did not look at his blindness.

Isabel was always glad when they had passed through the dividing door into their own regions of repose and beauty. She was a little afraid of him, out there in the animal grossness of the back. His bearing also changed, as he smelt the familiar indefinable odour that pervaded his wife's surroundings, a delicate, refined scent, very faintly spicy. Perhaps it came from the potpourri bowls.

He stood at the foot of the stairs, arrested, listening. She watched him, and her heart sickened. He seemed to be listening to fate.

"He's not here yet," he said. "I'll go up and change."

"Maurice," she said, "you're not wishing he wouldn't come, are you?"

"I couldn't quite say," he answered. "I feel myself rather on the qui vive."

"I can see you are," she answered. And she reached up and kissed his cheek. She saw his mouth relax into a slow smile.

"What are you laughing at?" she said roguishly.

"You consoling me," he answered.

"Nay," she answered. "Why should I console

you? You know we love each other—you know *how* married we are! What does anything else matter?"

"Nothing at all, my dear."

He felt for her face and touched it, smiling.

"*You're* all right, aren't you?" he asked anxiously.

"I'm wonderfully all right, love," she answered. "It's you I am a little troubled about, at times."

"Why me?" he said, touching her cheeks delicately with the tips of his fingers. The touch had an almost hypnotizing effect on her.

He went away upstairs. She saw him mount into the darkness, unseeing and unchanging. He did not know that the lamps on the upper corridor were unlighted. He went on into the darkness with unchanging step. She heard him in the bath-room.

Pervin moved about almost unconsciously in his familiar surroundings, dark though everything was. He seemed to know the presence of objects before he touched them. It was a pleasure to him to rock thus through a world of things, carried on the flood in a sort of blood-prescience. He did not think much or trouble much. So long as he kept this sheer immediacy of blood-contact with the substantial world he was happy, he wanted no intervention of visual consciousness. In this state there was a certain rich positivity, bordering sometimes on rapture. Life seemed to move in him like a tide lapping, lapping, and advancing, enveloping all things darkly. It was a pleasure to stretch forth the hand and meet the unseen object, clasp it, and possess it in pure contact. He did not try to remember, to visualize. He did not want to. The new way of consciousness substituted itself in him.

The rich suffusion of this state generally kept him happy, reaching its culmination in the consuming passion for his wife. But at times the flow would seem to be checked and thrown back. Then it would beat inside him like a tangled sea, and he was tortured in the shattered chaos of his own blood. He grew to dread this arrest, this throw-back, this chaos inside himself, when he seemed merely at the mercy of his own powerful and conflicting elements. How to get some measure of control or surety, this was the question. And when the question rose maddening in him, he would clench his fists as if he would *compel* the whole universe to submit to him. But it was in vain. He could not even compel himself.

Tonight, however, he was still serene, though little tremors of unreasonable exasperation ran through him. He had to handle the razor very carefully, as he shaved, for it was not at one with him, he was afraid of it. His hearing also was too much sharpened. He heard the woman lighting the lamps on the corridor, and attending to the fire in the visitors' room. And then, as he went to his room, he heard the trap arrive. Then came Isabel's voice, lifted and calling, like a bell ringing:

"Is it you, Bertie? Have you come?"

And a man's voice answered out of the wind:

"Hello, Isabel! There you are."

"Have you had a miserable drive? I'm so sorry we couldn't send a closed carriage. I can't see you at all, you know."

"I'm coming. No, I liked the drive—it was like Perthshire. Well, how are you? You're looking fit as ever, as far as I can see."

"Oh, yes," said Isabel. "I'm wonderfully well. How are you? Rather thin, I think——"

"Worked to death—everybody's old cry. But I'm all right, Ciss. How's Pervin?—isn't he here?"

"Oh, yes, he's upstairs changing. Yes, he's awfully well. Take off your wet things; I'll send them to be dried."

"And how are you both, in spirits? He doesn't fret?"

"No—no, not at all. No, on the contrary, really. We've been wonderfully happy, incredibly. It's more than I can understand—so wonderful: the nearness, and the peace——"

"Ah! Well, that's awfully good news——"

They moved away. Pervin heard no more. But a childish sense of desolation had come over him, as he heard their brisk voices. He seemed shut out—like a child that is left out. He was aimless and excluded, he did not know what to do with himself. The helpless desolation came over him. He fumbled nervously as he dressed himself, in a state almost of childishness. He disliked the Scotch accent in Bertie's speech, and the slight response it found on Isabel's tongue. He disliked the slight purr of complacency in the Scottish speech. He disliked intensely the glib way in which Isabel spoke of their happiness and nearness. It made him recoil. He was fretful and beside himself like a child, he had almost a childish nostalgia to be included in the life circle. And at the same time he was a man, dark and powerful and infuriated by his own weakness. By some fatal flaw, he could not be by himself, he had to depend on the support of another. And this very dependence enraged him. He hated Bertie Reid, and at the same time he knew the hatred was nonsense, he knew it was the outcome of his own weakness.

He went downstairs. Isabel was alone in the dining-room. She watched him enter, head erect, his feet tentative. He looked so strong-blooded and healthy and, at the same time, cancelled. Cancelled

—that was the word that flew across her mind. Perhaps it was his scar suggested it.

"You heard Bertie come, Maurice?" she said.

"Yes—isn't he here?"

"He's in his room. He looks very thin and worn."

"I suppose he works himself to death."

A woman came in with a tray—and after a few minutes Bertie came down. He was a little dark man, with a very big forehead, thin, wispy hair, and sad, large eyes. His expression was inordinately sad—almost funny. He had odd, short legs.

Isabel watched him hesitate under the door, and glance nervously at her husband. Pervin heard him and turned.

"Here you are, now," said Isabel. "Come, let us eat."

Bertie went across to Maurice.

"How are you, Pervin?" he said, as he advanced.

The blind man stuck his hand out into space, and Bertie took it.

"Very fit. Glad you've come," said Maurice.

Isabel glanced at them, and glanced away, as if she could not bear to see them.

"Come," she said. "Come to table. Aren't you both awfully hungry? I am, tremendously."

"I'm afraid you waited for me," said Bertie, as they sat down.

Maurice had a curious monolithic way of sitting in a chair, erect and distant. Isabel's heart always beat when she caught sight of him thus.

"No," she replied to Bertie. "We're very little later than usual. We're having a sort of high tea, not dinner. Do you mind? It gives us such a nice long evening, uninterrupted."

"I like it," said Bertie.

Maurice was feeling, with curious little movements, almost like a cat kneading her bed, for his plate, his knife and fork, his napkin. He was getting the whole geography of his cover into his consciousness. He sat erect and inscrutable, remote-seeming. Bertie watched the static figure of the blind man, the delicate tactile discernment of the large, ruddy hands, and the curious mindless silence of the brow, above the scar. With difficulty he looked away, and without knowing what he did, picked up a little crystal bowl of violets from the table, and held them to his nose.

"They are sweet-scented," he said. "Where do they come from?"

"From the garden—under the windows," said Isabel.

"So late in the year—and so fragrant! Do you remember the violets under Aunt Bell's south wall?"

The two friends looked at each other and exchanged a smile, Isabel's eyes lighting up.

"Don't I?" she replied. "*Wasn't* she queer!"

"A curious old girl," laughed Bertie. "There's a streak of freakishness in the family, Isabel."

"Ah—but not in you and me, Bertie," said Isabel. "Give them to Maurice, will you?" she added, as Bertie was putting down the flowers. "Have you smelled the violets, dear? Do!—they are so scented."

Maurice held out his hand, and Bertie placed the tiny bowl against his large, warm-looking fingers. Maurice's hand closed over the thin white fingers of the barrister. Bertie carefully extricated himself. Then the two watched the blind man smelling the violets. He bent his head and seemed to be thinking. Isabel waited.

"Aren't they sweet, Maurice?" she said at last, anxiously.

"Very," he said. And he held out the bowl. Bertie took it. Both he and Isabel were a little afraid, and deeply disturbed.

The meal continued. Isabel and Bertie chatted spasmodically. The blind man was silent. He touched his food repeatedly, with quick, delicate touches of his knife-point, then cut irregular bits. He could not bear to be helped. Both Isabel and Bertie suffered: Isabel wondered why. She did not suffer when she was alone with Maurice. Bertie made her conscious of a strangeness.

After the meal the three drew their chairs to the fire, and sat down to talk. The decanters were put on a table near at hand. Isabel knocked the logs on the fire, and clouds of brilliant sparks went up the chimney. Bertie noticed a slight weariness in her bearing.

"You will be glad when your child comes now, Isabel?" he said.

She looked up to him with a quick wan smile.

"Yes, I shall be glad," she answered. "It begins to seem long. Yes, I shall be very glad. So will you, Maurice, won't you?" she added.

"Yes, I shall," replied her husband.

"We are both looking forward so much to having it," she said.

"Yes, of course," said Bertie.

He was a bachelor, three or four years older than Isabel. He lived in beautiful rooms overlooking the river, guarded by a faithful Scottish man-servant. And he had his friends among the fair sex—not lovers, friends. So long as he could avoid any danger of courtship or marriage, he adored a few good women with constant and unfailing homage, and he was chivalrously fond of quite a number. But if they seemed to encroach on him, he withdrew and detested them.

Isabel knew him very well, knew his beautiful constancy, and kindness, also his incurable weakness, which made him unable ever to enter into close contact of any sort. He was ashamed of himself because he could not marry, could not approach women physically. He wanted to do so. But he could not. At the centre of him he was afraid, helplessly and even brutally afraid. He had given up hope, had ceased to expect any more that he could escape his own weakness. Hence he was a brilliant and successful barrister, also a *littérateur* of high repute, a rich man, and a great social success. At the centre he felt himself neuter, nothing.

Isabel knew him well. She despised him even while she admired him. She looked at his sad face, his little short legs, and felt contempt of him. She looked at his dark grey eyes, with their uncanny, almost childlike, intuition, and she loved him. He understood amazingly—but she had no fear of his understanding. As a man she patronized him.

And she turned to the impassive, silent figure of her husband. He sat leaning back, with folded arms, and face a little uptilted. His knees were straight and massive. She sighed, picked up the poker, and again began to prod the fire, to rouse the clouds of soft brilliant sparks.

"Isabel tells me," Bertie began suddenly, "that you have not suffered unbearably from the loss of sight."

Maurice straightened himself to attend but kept his arms folded.

"No," he said, "not unbearably. Now and again one struggles against it, you know. But there are compensations."

"They say it is much worse to be stone deaf," said Isabel.

"I believe it is," said Bertie. "Are there compensations?" he added, to Maurice.

"Yes. You cease to bother about a great many things." Again Maurice stretched his figure, stretched the strong muscles of his back, and leaned backwards, with uplifted face.

"And that is a relief," said Bertie. "But what is there in place of the bothering? What replaces the activity?"

There was a pause. At length the blind man replied, as out of a negligent, unattentive thinking:

"Oh, I don't know. There's a good deal when you're not active."

"Is there?" said Bertie. "What, exactly? It always seems to me that when there is no thought and no action, there is nothing."

Again Maurice was slow in replying.

"There is something," he replied. "I couldn't tell you what it is."

And the talk lapsed once more, Isabel and Bertie chatting gossip and reminiscence, the blind man silent.

At length Maurice rose restlessly, a big obtrusive figure. He felt tight and hampered. He wanted to go away.

"Do you mind," he said, "if I go and speak to Wernham?"

"No—go along, dear," said Isabel.

And he went out. A silence came over the two friends. At length Bertie said:

"Nevertheless, it is a great deprivation, Cissie."

"It is, Bertie. I know it is."

"Something lacking all the time," said Bertie.

"Yes, I know. And yet—and yet—Maurice is right. There is something else, something *there*, which you never knew was there, and which you can't express."

"What is there?" asked Bertie.

"I don't know—it's awfully hard to define it—but something strong and immediate. There's something strange in Maurice's presence—indefinable—but I couldn't do without it. I agree that it seems to put one's mind to sleep. But when we're alone I miss nothing; it seems awfully rich, almost splendid, you know."

"I'm afraid I don't follow," said Bertie.

They talked desultorily. The wind blew loudly outside, rain chattered on the window-panes, making a sharp drum-sound because of the closed, mellow-golden shutters inside. The logs burned slowly, with hot, almost invisible small flames. Bertie seemed uneasy, there were dark circles round his eyes. Isabel, rich with her approaching maternity, leaned looking into the fire. Her hair curled in odd, loose strands, very pleasing to the man. But she had a curious feeling of old woe in her heart, old, timeless night-woe.

"I suppose we're all deficient somewhere," said Bertie.

"I suppose so," said Isabel wearily.

"Damned, sooner or later."

"I don't know," she said, rousing herself. "I feel quite all right, you know. The child coming seems to make me indifferent to everything, just placid. I can't feel that there's anything to trouble about, you know."

"A good thing, I should say," he replied slowly.

"Well, there it is. I suppose it's just Nature. If only I felt I needn't trouble about Maurice, I should be perfectly content——"

"But you feel you must trouble about him?"

"Well—I don't know——" She even resented this much effort.

The night passed slowly. Isabel looked at the clock. "I say," she said. "It's nearly ten o'clock. Where can Maurice be? I'm sure they're all in bed at the back. Excuse me a moment."

She went out, returning almost immediately.

"It's all shut up and in darkness," she said. "I wonder where he is. He must have gone out to the farm——"

Bertie looked at her.

"I suppose he'll come in," he said.

"I suppose so," she said. "But it's unusual for him to be out now."

"Would you like me to go out and see?"

"Well—if you wouldn't mind. I'd go, but——" She did not want to make the physical effort.

Bertie put on an old overcoat and took a lantern. He went out from the side door. He shrank from the wet and roaring night. Such weather had a nervous effect on him: too much moisture everywhere made him feel almost imbecile. Unwilling, he went through it all. A dog barked violently at him. He peered in all the buildings. At last, as he opened the upper door of a sort of intermediate barn, he heard a grinding noise, and looking in, holding up his lantern, saw Maurice, in his shirt-sleeves, standing listening, holding the handle of a turnip-pulper. He had been pulping sweet roots, a pile of which lay dimly heaped in a corner behind him.

"That you, Wernham?" said Mauriee, listening.

"No, it's me," said Bertie.

A large, half-wild grey cat was rubbing at Maurice's leg. The blind man stooped to rub its sides. Bertie watched the scene, then unconsciously entered and shut the door behind him. He was in a high sort of barn-place, from which, right and left, ran off the corridors in front of the stalled cattle. He watched the slow, stooping motion of the other man, as he caressed the great cat.

Maurice straightened himself.

"You came to look for me?" he said.

"Isabel was a little uneasy," said Bertie.

"I'll come in. I like messing about doing these jobs."

The cat had reared her sinister, feline length against his leg, clawing at his thigh affectionately. He lifted her claws out of his flesh.

"I hope I'm not in your way at all at the Grange here," said Bertie, rather shy and stiff.

"My way? No, not a bit. I'm glad Isabel has somebody to talk to. I'm afraid it's I who am in the way. I know I'm not very lively company. Isabel's all right, don't you think? She's not unhappy, is she?"

"I don't think so."

"What does she say?"

"She says she's very content—only a little troubled about you."

"Why me?"

"Perhaps afraid that you might brood," said Bertie, cautiously.

"She needn't be afraid of that." He continued to caress the flattened grey head of the cat with his fingers. "What I am a bit afraid of," he resumed, "is that she'll find me a dead weight, always alone with me down here."

"I don't think you need think that," said Bertie, though this was what he feared himself.

"I don't know," said Maurice. "Sometimes I feel it isn't fair that she's saddled with me." Then he dropped his voice curiously. "I say," he asked, secretly struggling, "is my face much disfigured? Do you mind telling me?"

"There is the scar," said Bertie, wondering. "Yes, it is a disfigurement. But more pitiable than shocking."

"A pretty bad scar, though," said Maurice.

"Oh, yes."

There was a pause.

"Sometimes I feel I am horrible," said Maurice, in a low voice, talking as if to himself. And Bertie actually felt a quiver of horror.

"That's nonsense," he said.

Maurice again straightened himself, leaving the cat.

"There's no telling," he said. Then again, in an odd tone, he added: "I don't really know you, do I?"

"Probably not," said Bertie.

"Do you mind if I touch you?"

The lawyer shrank away instinctively. And yet, out of very philanthropy, he said, in a small voice: "Not at all."

But he suffered as the blind man stretched out a strong, naked hand to him. Maurice accidentally knocked off Bertie's hat.

"I thought you were taller," he said, starting. Then he laid his hand on Bertie Reid's head, closing the dome of the skull in a soft, firm grasp, gathering it, as it were; then, shifting his grasp and softly closing again, with a fine, close pressure, till he had covered the skull and the face of the smaller man, tracing the brows, and touching the full, closed eyes, touching the small nose and the nostrils, the rough, short moustache, the mouth, the rather strong chin. The hand of the blind man grasped the shoulder, the arm, the hand of the other man. He seemed to take him, in the soft, travelling grasp.

"You seem young," he said quietly, at last.

The lawyer stood almost annihilated, unable to answer.

"Your head seems tender, as if you were young," Maurice repeated. "So do your hands. Touch my eyes, will you?—touch my scar."

Now Bertie quivered with revulsion. Yet he was under the power of the blind man, as if hypnotized. He lifted his hand, and laid the fingers on the scar, on the scarred eyes. Maurice suddenly covered them with his own hand, pressed the fingers of the other man upon his disfigured eye-sockets, trembling in every fibre, and rocking slightly, slowly, from side to side. He remained thus for a minute or more, whilst Bertie stood as if in a swoon, unconscious, imprisoned.

Then suddenly Maurice removed the hand of the other man from his brow, and stood holding it in his own.

"Oh, my God," he said, "we shall know each other now, shan't we? We shall know each other now."

Bertie could not answer. He gazed mute and terror-struck, overcome by his own weakness. He knew he could not answer. He had an unreasonable fear, lest the other man should suddenly destroy him. Whereas Maurice was actually filled with hot, poignant love, the passion of friendship. Perhaps it was this very passion of friendship which Bertie shrank from most,

"We're all right together now, aren't we?" said Maurice. "It's all right now, as long as we live, so far as we're concerned?"

"Yes," said Bertie, trying by any means to escape.

Maurice stood with head lifted, as if listening. The new delicate fulfilment of mortal friendship had come as a revelation and surprise to him, something exquisite and unhoped-for. He seemed to be listening to hear if it were real.

Then he turned for his coat.

"Come," he said, "we'll go to Isabel."

Bertie took the lantern and opened the door. The cat disappeared. The two men went in silence along the causeways. Isabel, as they came, thought their footsteps sounded strange. She looked up pathetically and anxiously for their entrance. There seemed a curious elation about Maurice. Bertie was haggard, with sunken eyes.

"What is it?" she asked.

"We've become friends," said Maurice, standing with his feet apart, like a strange colossus.

"Friends!" re-echoed Isabel. And she looked again at Bertie. He met her eyes with a furtive, haggard look; his eyes were as if glazed with misery.

"I'm so glad," she said, in sheer perplexity.

"Yes," said Maurice.

He was indeed so glad. Isabel took his hand with both hers, and held it fast.

"You'll be happier now, dear," she said.

But she was watching Bertie. She knew that he had one desire—to escape from this intimacy, this friendship, which had been thrust upon him. He could not bear it that he had been touched by the blind man, his insane reserve broken in. He was like a mollusc whose shell is broken.

T. S. Eliot
1888–

On the occasion of Eliot's sixtieth birthday in 1948, more than one of his appraisers remarked that he had become an institution; many did not hesitate to call him the authentic voice of our complex civilization; and none disagreed with the distinguished French critic Denis Saurat, who declared that, since the death of Paul Valéry, Eliot had become undoubtedly the most famous poet of our time and the most potent influence on English, American, and perhaps European poetry of the twentieth century. "For once in our history," wrote the critic of the London *Sunday Times*, "a living English poet has exerted a fruitful influence on poets and readers in France, Germany, Italy, Greece, and India." In his sixtieth year Mr. Eliot was awarded the highest formal literary honor, the Nobel Prize for Literature, and the most distinguished of British awards of honor, the Order of Merit. A symposium of forty-six contributions from poets and critics of many nationalities was presented to him as a birthday present, and newspapers and journals over the world paid him such tributes as have rarely been showered upon a living artist.

This most famous of living poets and critics, Thomas Stearns Eliot, was born in St. Louis, Missouri, September 26, 1888, the grandson of the founder of Washington University in that city. He came of a family that had a distinguished New England tradition and an English ancestry with origins in Somerset and Devon. He studied at the Smith Academy in St. Louis and at Harvard, where he had among his teachers Irving Babbitt and George Santayana and where he was graduated in 1910. He continued his studies at the Sorbonne in Paris in 1910–11, and returned to Harvard where he was again a student and an assistant in philosophy. The summer of 1914, which ended with the outbreak of the First World War, he spent in Germany on a traveling fellowship, and in the autumn of that year he went to study Greek philosophy at Merton College, Oxford. In 1915 he began a long residence in London where he was to view the world from various desks as schoolmaster, bank official, editor, and publisher, as well as poet and critic. After having helped to edit a magazine, *The Egoist*, he established in 1922 the quarterly review, *The Criterion*, which was one of the most stimulating of literary and critical journals until it fell a victim to the Second World War. He assumed British nationality in 1927. In 1932 he returned for the first time to the United States, where he held a year's lectureship at Harvard and delivered a series of lectures at the University of Virginia. Since then Eliot has frequently crossed the Atlantic, and in 1948 he was a resident member of the Institute for Advanced Study at Princeton.

Eliot's literary career may be said to have begun at Harvard, where he published several poems in the *Advocate*, of which he was an editor. He began to attract attention with his first mature poems, "The Love Song of J. Alfred Prufrock" and "Preludes," in 1915. It was clear that a new genius with a startlingly fresh manner of expression and technical facility had arrived. His first volume of verse, *Prufrock and Other Observations*, appeared in England in 1917, and a second volume, *Poems*, was brought out in 1919. He further upset the world of poetry by the production of his remarkable poem *The Waste Land* in 1922. His admirers and imitators as well as his denouncers increased as other notable poems followed: "The Hollow Men," 1925; "The Journey of the Magi," 1927; "A Song for Simeon," 1928; "Ash-Wednesday," 1930; and the unfinished "Sweeney Agonistes," 1932.

Meanwhile Eliot's development as a critic was keeping pace with his progress as a poet. His poetic attitude has always been a reflection of his critical theories, and it was inevitable that the poet who shunned and castigated the contemporary world in which he saw only chaos and defeat should as a critic of life and letters emphasize tradition, restraint, and an inner serenity. In 1917, the year in which his first volume of verse appeared, he published what is perhaps his most important critical essay, "Tradition and the Individual Talent." In 1920 came *The Sacred Wood*, a volume of essays on poetry and criticism. There followed during the next quarter of a century essays on a great variety of subjects, ancient and modern, literary, dramatic, religious, moral, and political. The volumes of his collected prose include *Selected Essays*, 1932; *The Use of Poetry and the Use of Criticism*, 1933; *After Strange Gods*, 1934; *Elizabethan Essays*, 1934; *Essays,*

Ancient and Modern, 1936. One of his most recent and most provocative books is his *Notes towards the Definition of Culture*, 1948. Something of the versatility of Eliot's mind and work is indicated by the fact that in 1939 he published both *The Idea of a Christian Society* and *Old Possum's Book of Practical Cats*, a collection of humorous verse for children, and that he has written introductions to selections from the works of such different writers as Tennyson, Kipling, and James Joyce.

In addition to creating the chief poetic style of the twentieth century and, as poet and critic, revitalizing the whole conception of poetry and the ways in which we write and read it, Eliot has to his credit the feat of founding a new poetic tradition in the theater. In *The Sacred Wood* he discussed the possibility of a poetic drama, and in 1934 he composed choruses for a religious pageant, *The Rock*. In 1935 his *Murder in the Cathedral*, a play in blank verse, was as great a success in theatrical as in literary circles. A second verse drama, *The Family Reunion*, followed in 1939. In these plays both Greek tragedy and medieval miracle plays furnish the author with models and devices for presenting to the audience moral, spiritual, and psychological problems of the modern world. In 1949 the first performance of his latest play, *The Cocktail Party*, was given at the Edinburgh Festival before an enthusiastic audience, and the following year that brilliant, cerebral comedy in verse was a hit of the Broadway season.

It is not altogether possible to explain Eliot's unique role in the literary and cultural life of the twentieth century. It is a matter of common knowledge that he voiced the disillusion and the disgust of sensitive persons as they contemplated the world between the wars, and in such poems as *The Waste Land* and "The Hollow Men" he presented better than any other poet of his time the spectacle of a spiritually bankrupt world. One secret of his power in these poems was that he came to the writing of poetry and the work of castigation thoroughly prepared by deep and wide reading in philosophy, in Dante, the Elizabethan dramatists, the seventeenth-century poets, and the French Symbolists. He had also an imaginative sensibility and a technical expertness that attracted admirers and imitators, and impressed even those who did not share his philosophy or his critical theories.

The spiritual odyssey of Eliot from a world of despair and denial to a world of faith and affirmation may be traced through his poems. "Ash-Wednesday" and "Sweeney Agonistes" represent the turning-point in his development as a poet and as a man of faith. Along with the plays, his later poetic work has consisted chiefly of religious meditations, published in 1943 as *Four Quartets*. In his maturer years he has defined his position generally as that of a royalist in politics, a classicist in literature, and an Anglo-Catholic in religion. The closing words of his Theodore Spencer lecture at Harvard in 1950 reveal his conviction that it is the ultimate function of art "in imposing a credible order upon ordinary reality, and thereby eliciting some perception of an order *in* reality, to bring us to a condition of serenity, stillness and reconciliation; and then leave us, as Virgil left Dante, to proceed toward a region where that guide can avail us no farther."

Of Eliot's importance in the history of contemporary literature there can be no doubt, but of the exact nature and quality of his influence and of the absolute and lasting merit of his work it is too early to judge. The slender corpus of his verse and prose has been surrounded and almost swamped by a mass of commentary, and he has become the subject of more discussion and the center of more controversies than any other literary man of the century. Meanwhile the consensus of his readers is that if, by its very nature, his art presents great difficulties, it also offers great rewards.

TRADITION AND THE INDIVIDUAL TALENT [1]

I

IN English writing we seldom speak of tradition, though we occasionally apply its name in deploring its absence. We cannot refer to "the tradition" or to "a tradition"; at most, we employ the adjective in saying that the poetry of So-and-so is "traditional" or even "too traditional." Seldom, perhaps, does the word appear except in a phrase of censure. If otherwise, it is vaguely approbative, with the implication, as to the work approved, of some pleasing archæological reconstruction. You can hardly make the word agreeable to English ears without this comfortable reference to the reassuring science of archæology.

Certainly the word is not likely to appear in our appreciations of living or dead writers. Every nation, every race, has not only its own creative, but its own critical turn of mind; and is even more oblivious of the shortcomings and limitations of its critical habits than of those of its creative genius.

[1] From *Selected Essays, 1917–1932*, by T. S. Eliot, copyright, 1932, by Harcourt, Brace and Company, Inc. Reprinted by permission of Harcourt, Brace and Company and Faber and Faber Limited.

We know, or think we know, from the enormous mass of critical writing that has appeared in the French language the critical method or habit of the French; we only conclude (we are such unconscious people) that the French are "more critical" than we, and sometimes even plume ourselves a little with the fact, as if the French were the less spontaneous. Perhaps they are; but we might remind ourselves that criticism is as inevitable as breathing, and that we should be none the worse for articulating what passes in our minds when we read a book and feel an emotion about it, for criticizing our own minds in their work of criticism. One of the facts that might come to light in this process is our tendency to insist, when we praise a poet, upon those aspects of his work in which he least resembles any one else. In these aspects or parts of his work we pretend to find what is individual, what is the peculiar essence of the man. We dwell with satisfaction upon the poet's difference from his predecessors, especially his immediate predecessors; we endeavour to find something that can be isolated in order to be enjoyed. Whereas if we approach a poet without this prejudice we shall often find that not only the best, but the most individual parts of his work may be those in which the dead poets, his ancestors, assert their immortality most vigorously. And I do not mean the impressionable period of adolescence, but the period of full maturity.

Yet if the only form of tradition, of handing down, consisted in following the ways of the immediate generation before us in a blind or timid adherence to its successes, "tradition" should positively be discouraged. We have seen many such simple currents soon lost in the sand; and novelty is better than repetition. Tradition is a matter of much wider significance. It cannot be inherited, and if you want it you must obtain it by great labour. It involves, in the first place, the historical sense, which we may call nearly indispensable to any one who would continue to be a poet beyond his twenty-fifth year; and the historical sense involves a perception, not only of the pastness of the past, but of its presence; the historical sense compels a man to write not merely with his own generation in his bones, but with a feeling that the whole of the literature of Europe from Homer and within it the whole of the literature of his own country has a simultaneous existence and composes a simultaneous order. This historical sense, which is a sense of the timeless as well as of the temporal and of the timeless and of the temporal together, is what makes a writer traditional. And it is at the same time what makes a writer most acutely conscious of his place in time, of his own contemporaneity.

No poet, no artist of any art, has his complete meaning alone. His significance, his appreciation is the appreciation of his relation to the dead poets and artists. You cannot value him alone; you must set him, for contrast and comparison, among the dead. I mean this as a principle of æsthetic, not merely historical, criticism. The necessity that he shall conform, that he shall cohere, is not onesided; what happens when a new work of art is created is something that happens simultaneously to all the works of art which preceded it. The existing monuments form an ideal order among themselves, which is modified by the introduction of the new (the really new) work of art among them. The existing order is complete before the new work arrives; for order to persist after the supervention of novelty, the *whole* existing order must be, if ever so slightly, altered; and so the relations, proportions, values of each work of art toward the whole are readjusted; and this is conformity between the old and the new. Whoever has approved this idea of order, of the form of European, of English literature will not find it preposterous that the past should be altered by the present as much as the present is directed by the past. And the poet who is aware of this will be aware of great difficulties and responsibilities.

In a peculiar sense he will be aware also that he must inevitably be judged by the standards of the past. I say judged, not amputated, by them; not judged to be as good as, or worse or better than, the dead; and certainly not judged by the canons of dead critics. It is a judgment, a comparison, in which two things are measured by each other. To conform merely would be for the new work not really to conform at all; it would not be new, and would therefore not be a work of art. And we do not quite say that the new is more valuable because it fits in; but its fitting in is a test of its value—a test, it is true, which can only be slowly and cautiously applied, for we are none of us infallible judges of conformity. We say: it appears to conform, and is perhaps individual, or it appears individual, and may conform; but we are hardly likely to find that it is one and not the other.

To proceed to a more intelligible exposition of the relation of the poet to the past: he can neither take the past as a lump, an indiscriminate bolus, nor can he form himself wholly on one or two private admirations, nor can he form himself wholly upon one preferred period. The first course is inadmissible, the second is an important experience of youth, and the third is a pleasant and highly desirable supplement. The poet must be very conscious of the main current, which does not at all flow invariably through the most distinguished reputations. He must be quite aware of the obvious fact that art never improves, but that the material of art is never quite the same. He must be aware that the mind of Europe—the mind of his own country—a mind which he learns in time to be much more important than his own private mind—is a mind which changes, and that this change is a development which abandons nothing *en route*, which does not superannuate either Shakespeare, or Homer, or the rock drawing of the Magdalenian draughtsmen. That this development, refinement perhaps, complication certainly, is not, from the point of view of the artist, any improvement. Perhaps not even an improvement from the point of view of the psychologist or not to the extent which we imagine; perhaps only in the end based upon a complication in economics and machinery. But the difference between the present and the past is that the conscious present is an awareness of the past in a way and to an extent which the past's awareness of itself cannot show.

Some one said: "The dead writers are remote from us because we *know* so much more than they did." Precisely, and they are that which we know.

I am alive to a usual objection to what is clearly part of my programme for the *métier* of poetry. The objection is that the doctrine requires a ridiculous amount of erudition (pedantry), a claim which can be rejected by appeal to the lives of poets in any pantheon. It will even be affirmed that much learning deadens or perverts poetic sensibility. While, however, we persist in believing that a poet ought to know as much as will not encroach upon his necessary receptivity and necessary laziness, it is not desirable to confine knowledge to whatever can be put into a useful shape for examinations, drawing-rooms, or the still more pretentious modes of publicity. Some can absorb knowledge, the more tardy must sweat for it. Shakespeare acquired more essential history from Plutarch than most men could from the whole British Museum. What is to be insisted upon is that the poet must develop or procure the consciousness of the past and that he should continue to develop this consciousness throughout his career.

What happens is a continual surrender of himself as he is at the moment to something which is more valuable. The progress of an artist is a continual self-sacrifice, a continual extinction of personality.

There remains to define this process of depersonalization and its relation to the sense of tradition. It is in this depersonalization that art may be said to approach the condition of science. I, therefore, invite you to consider, as a suggestive analogy, the action which takes place when a bit of finely filiated platinum is introduced into a chamber containing oxygen and sulphur dioxide.

II

Honest criticism and sensitive appreciation are directed not upon the poet but upon the poetry. If we attend to the confused cries of the newspaper critics and the *susurrus* of popular repetition that follows, we shall hear the names of poets in great numbers; if we seek not Bluebook knowledge but the enjoyment of poetry, and ask for a poem, we shall seldom find it. I have tried to point out the importance of the relation of the poem to other poems by other authors, and suggested the conception of poetry as a living whole of all the poetry that has ever been written. The other aspect of this Impersonal theory of poetry is the relation of the poem to its author. And I hinted, by an analogy, that the mind of the mature poet differs from that of the immature one not precisely in any valuation of "personality," not being necessarily more interesting, or having "more to say," but rather by being a more finely perfected medium in which special, or very varied, feelings are at liberty to enter into new combinations.

The analogy was that of the catalyst. When the two gases previously mentioned are mixed in the presence of a filament of platinum, they form sulphurous acid. This combination takes place only if the platinum is present; nevertheless the newly formed acid contains no trace of platinum, and the platinum itself is apparently unaffected; has remained inert, neutral, and unchanged. The mind of the poet is the shred of platinum. It may partly or exclusively operate upon the experience of the man himself; but, the more perfect the artist, the more completely separate in him will be the man who suffers and the mind which creates; the more perfectly will the mind digest and transmute the passions which are its material.

The experience, you will notice, the elements which enter the presence of the transforming catalyst, are of two kinds: emotions and feelings. The effect of a work of art upon the person who enjoys it is an experience different in kind from any experience not of art. It may be formed out of one emotion, or may be a combination of several; and

14. susurrus, murmuring.

various feelings, inhering for the writer in particular words or phrases or images, may be added to compose the final result. Or great poetry may be made without the direct use of any emotion whatever: composed out of feelings solely. Canto XV of the *Inferno* (Brunetto Latini) is a working up of the emotion evident in the situation; but the effect, though single as that of any work of art, is obtained by considerable complexity of detail. The last quatrain gives an image, a feeling attaching to an image, which "came," which did not develop simply out of what precedes, but which was probably in suspension in the poet's mind until the proper combination arrived for it to add itself to. The poet's mind is in fact a receptacle for seizing and storing up numberless feelings, phrases, images, which remain there until all the particles which can unite to form a new compound are present together.

If you compare several representative passages of the greatest poetry you see how great is the variety of types of combination, and also how completely any semi-ethical criterion of "sublimity" misses the mark. For it is not the "greatness," the intensity, of the emotions, the components, but the intensity of the artistic process, the pressure, so to speak, under which the fusion takes place, that counts. The episode of Paolo and Francesca employs a definite emotion, but the intensity of the poetry is something quite different from whatever intensity in the supposed experience it may give the impression of. It is no more intense, furthermore, than Canto XXVI, the voyage of Ulysses, which has not the direct dependence upon an emotion. Great variety is possible in the process of transmutation of emotion: the murder of Agamemnon, or the agony of Othello, gives an artistic effect apparently closer to a possible original than the scenes from Dante. In the *Agamemnon*, the artistic emotion approximates to the emotion of an actual spectator; in *Othello* to the emotion of the protagonist himself. But the difference between art and the event is always absolute; the combination which is the murder of Agamemnon is probably as complex as that which is the voyage of Ulysses. In either case there has been a fusion of elements. The ode of Keats contains a number of feelings which have nothing particular to do with the nightingale, but which the nightingale, partly, perhaps, because of its attractive name, and partly because of its reputation, served to bring together.

The point of view which I am struggling to attack is perhaps related to the metaphysical theory of the substantial unity of the soul: for my meaning is, that the poet has, not a "personality" to express, but a particular medium, which is only a medium and not a personality, in which impressions and experiences combine in peculiar and unexpected ways. Impressions and experiences which are important for the man may take no place in the poetry, and those which become important in the poetry may play quite a negligible part in the man, the personality.

I will quote a passage which is unfamiliar enough to be regarded with fresh attention in the light—or darkness—of these observations:

And now methinks I could e'en chide myself
For doating on her beauty, though her death
Shall be revenged after no common action.
Does the silkworm expend her yellow labours
For thee? For thee does she undo herself?
Are lordships sold to maintain ladyships
For the poor benefit of a bewildering minute?
Why does yon fellow falsify highways,
And put his life between the judge's lips,
To refine such a thing—keep horse and men
To beat their valours for her? . . .

In this passage (as is evident if it is taken in its context) there is a combination of positive and negative emotions: an intensely strong attraction toward beauty and an equally intense fascination by the ugliness which is contrasted with it and which destroys it. This balance of contrasted emotion is in the dramatic situation to which the speech is pertinent, but that situation alone is inadequate to it. This is, so to speak, the structural emotion, provided by the drama. But the whole effect, the dominant tone, is due to the fact that a number of floating feelings, having an affinity to this emotion by no means superficially evident, have combined to give us a new art emotion.

It is not in his personal emotions, the emotions provoked by particular events in his life, that the poet is in any way remarkable or interesting. His particular emotions may be simple, or crude, or flat. The emotion in his poetry will be a very complex thing, but not with the complexity of the emotions of people who have very complex or unusual emotions in life. One error, in fact, of eccentricity in poetry is to seek for new human emotions to express; and in this search for novelty in the wrong place it discovers the perverse. The business of the poet is not to find new emotions, but to use the ordinary ones and, in working them up into poetry, to express feelings which are not in actual

25. this passage. From *The Revenger's Tragedy*, III, v, by the Elizabethan dramatist, Cyril Tourneur.

emotions at all. And emotions which he has never experienced will serve his turn as well as those familiar to him. Consequently, we must believe that "emotion recollected in tranquillity" is an inexact formula. For it is neither emotion, nor recollection, nor, without distortion of meaning, tranquillity. It is a concentration, and a new thing resulting from the concentration, of a very great number of experiences which to the practical and active person would not seem to be experiences at all; it is a concentration which does not happen consciously or of deliberation. These experiences are not "recollected," and they finally unite in an atmosphere which is "tranquil" only in that it is a passive attending upon the event. Of course this is not quite the whole story. There is a great deal, in the writing of poetry, which must be conscious and deliberate. In fact, the bad poet is usually unconscious where he ought to be conscious, and conscious where he ought to be unconscious. Both errors tend to make him "personal." Poetry is not a turning loose of emotion, but an escape from emotion; it is not the expression of personality, but an escape from personality. But, of course, only those who have personality and emotions know what it means to want to escape from these things.

III

ὁ δὲ νοῦς ἴσως θειότερόν τι καὶ ἀπαθές ἐστιν.

This essay proposes to halt at the frontier of metaphysics or mysticism, and confine itself to such practical conclusions as can be applied by the reasonable person interested in poetry. To divert interest from the poet to the poetry is a laudable aim: for it would conduce to a juster estimation of actual poetry, good and bad. There are many people who appreciate the expression of sincere emotion in verse, and there is a smaller number of people who can appreciate technical excellence. But very few know when there is an expression of *significant* emotion, emotion which has its life in the poem and not in the history of the poet. The emotion of art is impersonal. And the poet cannot reach this impersonality without surrendering himself wholly to the work to be done. And he is not likely to know what is to be done unless he lives in what is not merely the present, but the present moment of the past, unless he is conscious, not of what is dead, but of what is already living.

27. From Aristotle's *On the Soul*. W. S. Hett translates it: "Possibly the mind is too divine, and is therefore unaffected."

PORTRAIT OF A LADY[1]

In this poem Eliot skillfully evokes the appropriate atmosphere for the development—or, more correctly, the nondevelopment—of an artificial and unproductive relationship between the speaker and the cultivated lady whose remarks he weaves into his soliloquy. The epigraph from Marlowe's play provides ironic focus.

Thou hast committed—
Fornication: but that was in another country,
And besides, the wench is dead.

THE JEW OF MALTA

I

Among the smoke and fog of a December afternoon
You have the scene arrange itself—as it will seem to do—
With "I have saved this afternoon for you";
And four wax candles in the darkened room,
Four rings of light upon the ceiling overhead,
And atmosphere of Juliet's tomb
Prepared for all the things to be said, or left unsaid.
We have been, let us say, to hear the latest Pole
Transmit the Preludes, through his hair and finger-tips.
"So intimate, this Chopin, that I think his soul
Should be resurrected only among friends
Some two or three, who will not touch the bloom
That is rubbed and questioned in the concert room."
—And so the conversation slips
Among velleities and carefully caught regrets
Through attenuated tones of violins
Mingled with remote cornets
And begins.
"You do not know how much they mean to me, my friends,
And how, how rare and strange it is, to find
In a life composed so much, so much of odds and ends
(For indeed I do not love it . . . you knew?
You are not blind!
How keen you are!)
To find a friend who has these qualities,
Who has, and gives
Those qualities upon which friendship lives.
How much it means that I say this to you—
Without these friendships—life, what *cauchemar!*"
Among the windings of the violins
And the ariettes

[1] This and the following poems by T. S. Eliot are from *Collected Poems 1909–1935*, by T. S. Eliot, copyright, 1936, by Harcourt, Brace and Company, Inc. Reprinted by permission of Harcourt, Brace and Company and Faber and Faber Limited. **15. velleities,** slight wishes. **29. cauchemar,** nightmare.

Of cracked cornets
Inside my brain a dull tom-tom begins
Absurdly hammering a prelude of its own,
Capricious monotone
That is at least one definite "false note."
—Let us take the air, in a tobacco trance,
Admire the monuments,
Discuss the late events,
Correct our watches by the public clocks;
Then sit for half an hour and drink our bocks.

II

Now that lilacs are in bloom
She has a bowl of lilacs in her room
And twists one in her fingers while she talks.
"Ah, my friend, you do not know, you do not know
What life is, you who hold it in your hands";
(Slowly twisting the lilac stalks)
"You let it flow from you, you let it flow,
And youth is cruel, and has no remorse
And smiles at situations which it cannot see."
I smile, of course,
And go on drinking tea.
"Yet with these April sunsets, that somehow recall
My buried life, and Paris in the Spring,
I feel immeasurably at peace, and find the world
To be wonderful and youthful, after all."

The voice returns like the insistent out-of-tune
Of a broken violin on an August afternoon:
"I am always sure that you understand
My feelings, always sure that you feel,
Sure that across the gulf you reach your hand.

You are invulnerable, you have no Achilles' heel.
You will go on, and when you have prevailed
You can say: at this point many a one has failed.
"But what have I, but what have I, my friend,
To give you, what can you receive from me?
Only the friendship and the sympathy
Of one about to reach her journey's end.

I shall sit here, serving tea to friends. . . ."

I take my hat: how can I make a cowardly amends
For what she has said to me?
You will see me any morning in the park
Reading the comics and the sporting page.
Particularly I remark
An English countess goes upon the stage.
A Greek was murdered at a Polish dance,
Another bank defaulter has confessed.
I keep my countenance,
I remain self-possessed
Except when a street piano, mechanical and tired,
Reiterates some worn-out common song
With the smell of hyacinths across the garden,
Recalling things that other people have desired.
Are these ideas right or wrong?

III

The October night comes down; returning as before
Except for a slight sensation of being ill at ease
I mount the stairs and turn the handle of the door
And feel as if I had mounted on my hands and knees.

"And so you are going abroad; and when do you return?
But that's a useless question.
You hardly know when you are coming back;
You will find so much to learn."
My smile falls heavily among the bric-à-brac.

"Perhaps you can write to me."
My self-possession flares up for a second:
This is as I had reckoned.
"I have been wondering frequently of late
(But our beginnings never know our ends!)
Why we have not developed into friends."
I feel like one who smiles, and turning shall remark
Suddenly, his expression in a glass.
My self-possession gutters; we are really in the dark.

"For everybody said so, all our friends,
They all were sure our feelings would relate
So closely! I myself can hardly understand.
We must leave it now to fate.
You will write, at any rate.
Perhaps it is not too late.
I shall sit here, serving tea to friends."

And I must borrow every changing shape
To find expression . . . dance, dance
Like a dancing bear,
Cry like a parrot, chatter like an ape.
Let us take the air, in a tobacco trance—

Well! and what if she should die some afternoon,
Afternoon grey and smoky, evening yellow and rose;
Should die and leave me sitting pen in hand
With the smoke coming down above the housetops;
Doubtful, for a while
Not knowing what to feel or if I understand
Or whether wise or foolish, tardy or too soon . . .
Would she not have the advantage, after all?
This music is successful with a "dying fall"
Now that we talk of dying—
And should I have the right to smile?

THE WASTE LAND

The Waste Land, thanks to its direct pertinence to the spiritual temper of the modern world and to its brilliant and original structure and imagery, has achieved the distinction of being perhaps the most widely discussed and most influential poem of the first half of the twentieth century. It is one of the most admired and one of the most severely criticized poems of our time.

Of its general nature and background, Eliot writes as follows: "Not only the title, but the plan and a good deal of the incidental symbolism of the poem were suggested by Miss Jessie L. Weston's book on the Grail legend: *From Ritual to Romance* (Cambridge). Indeed, so deeply am I indebted, Miss Weston's book will elucidate the difficulties of the poem much better than my notes can do; and I recommend it (apart from the great interest of the book itself) to any who think such elucidation of the poem worth the trouble. To another work of anthropology I am indebted in general, one which has influenced our generation profoundly; I mean *The Golden Bough;* I have used especially the two volumes *Adonis, Attis, Osiris*. Anyone who is acquainted with these works will immediately recognize in the poem certain references to vegetation ceremonies."

In the legends of the Holy Grail, with which Miss Weston's book deals, the Waste Land is under a curse of sterility. It is ruled over by the Fisher King, who has also been rendered impotent. The land and its king will remain in this condition until they are restored by a knight of purity. This primitive legend came in time to be connected with the Arthurian cycle of stories, particularly with the legend of the Holy Grail, the cup supposed to have been used at the Last Supper and later to have received the blood of Christ. The quest of the Grail is undertaken by a knight, who sets forth for the Waste Land, encountering many adventures and dangers to both body and soul. The knight meets the severest tests of all in the horrors of the Perilous Chapel in the Waste Land. If he can pass successfully these final tests of his courage, he will reach the Grail Castle, and through the means of the Grail will heal the Fisher King and release him and his land from the curse. Miss Weston's book demonstrates the connection between the later Grail legends and the primitive fertility cults having to do with the seasons, the rain and the sun, the bringing of spring out of winter and of life out of death.

It will be apparent from Eliot's note quoted above that in the poem he conceives of the contemporary world as a waste land, spiritually dry and barren, and inhabited by people who have lost the knowledge of good and evil and whose very life is a kind of death.

The poem is not, as will be seen, a narrative. The author's method is that of the impressionists, and at times suggests that of the cinema, with its flashbacks and closeups, its "dissolving-view" technique, and its free association of ideas and images, all related more or less to the basic symbols of the Grail legend. In his analysis of the poem in his *Modern Poetry and the Tradition* (University of North Carolina Press, 1939), Cleanth Brooks says: "*The Waste Land* is built on a major contrast—a device which is a favorite of Eliot's and to be found in many of his poems, particularly his later poems. The contrast is between two kinds of life and two kinds of death. Life devoid of meaning is death; sacrifice, even the sacrificial death, may be life-giving, an awakening to life. The poem occupies itself to a great extent with this paradox, and with a number of variations on it."

For other useful analyses and discussions of the poem see F. O. Matthiessen, *The Achievement of T. S. Eliot*, Houghton Mifflin, 1935; revised and enlarged edition, Oxford University Press, 1947; F. R. Leavis, *New Bearings in English Poetry*, Chatto and Windus, London, 1932, 1942; and Elizabeth Drew, *T. S. Eliot: The Design of His Poetry*, Scribner, 1949. Eliot has himself contributed notes to the poem, which are given below and marked (E.).

"NAM Sibyllam quidem Cumis ego ipse oculis meis vidi in ampulla pendere, et cum illi pueri dicerent: Σίβυλλα τί θέλεις; respondebat illa: ἀποθανεῖν θέλω."[1]

I. THE BURIAL OF THE DEAD

April is the cruellest month, breeding
Lilacs out of the dead land, mixing
Memory and desire, stirring
Dull roots with spring rain.
Winter kept us warm, covering
Earth in forgetful snow, feeding
A little life with dried tubers.
Summer surprised us, coming over the Starnbergersee
With a shower of rain; we stopped in the colonnade,
And went on in sunlight, into the Hofgarten,
And drank coffee, and talked for an hour.
Bin gar keine Russin, stamm' aus Litauen, echt deutsch.

[1] **"NAM . . . . θέλω."** From a satirical prose romance, *Satyricon*, by Petronius Arbiter (died about A.D. 66), director of pleasures at the court of the Emperor Nero. The passage is part of a scoffing account of an earlier and more heroic age. The Sibyl of Cumae, who had once uttered divine wisdom, is now withered, exhibited in a cage, full of despair, and the sport of boys. The passage reads: "Yes, and I myself saw with my own eyes the Sibyl of Cumae hanging in a cage; and when the boys cried to her, 'Sibyl, what do you want?' she used to reply, 'I would that I were dead.'"
1. April, the month of rebirth. With the opening of the poem compare Eliot's lines in "Journey of the Magi":

"this Birth was
Hard and bitter agony for us, like Death, our Death."

8–18. Summer . . . winter. Snatches of trivial conversation from the gadabout near-fashionables of the "lost generation." The scene is Munich and its environs.
12. Bin . . . deutsch, I am no Russian, I come from Lithuania, true German.

And when we were children, staying at the archduke's,
My cousin's, he took me out on a sled,
And I was frightened. He said, Marie,
Marie, hold on tight. And down we went.
In the mountains, there you feel free.
I read, much of the night, and go south in the winter.

What are the roots that clutch, what branches grow
Out of this stony rubbish? Son of man,
You cannot say, or guess, for you know only
A heap of broken images, where the sun beats,
And the dead tree gives no shelter, the cricket no relief,
And the dry stone no sound of water. Only
There is shadow under this red rock,
(Come in under the shadow of this red rock),
And I will show you something different from either
Your shadow at morning striding behind you
Or your shadow at evening rising to meet you;
I will show you fear in a handful of dust.
Frisch weht der Wind
Der Heimat zu
Mein Irisch Kind,
Wo weilest du?
"You gave me hyacinths first a year ago;
"They called me the hyacinth girl."
—Yet when we came back, late, from the Hyacinth garden,
Your arms full, and your hair wet, I could not
Speak, and my eyes failed, I was neither
Living nor dead, and I knew nothing,
Looking into the heart of light, the silence.
Oed' und leer das Meer.

Madame Sosostris, famous clairvoyante,
Had a bad cold, nevertheless
Is known to be the wisest woman in Europe,
With a wicked pack of cards. Here, said she,
Is your card, the drowned Phoenician Sailor,
(Those are pearls that were his eyes. Look!)
Here is Belladonna, the Lady of the Rocks,
The lady of situations.
Here is the man with three staves, and here the Wheel,
And here is the one-eyed merchant, and this card,
Which is blank, is something he carries on his back,
Which I am forbidden to see. I do not find
The Hanged Man. Fear death by water.
I see crowds of people, walking round in a ring.
Thank you. If you see dear Mrs. Equitone,
Tell her I bring the horoscope myself:
One must be so careful these days.

Unreal City,

20. Out . . . man. Cf. Ezekiel 2:1. (E.) See also the verses that follow and Ezekiel 37:1–14 (the vision of the valley of dry bones). **23. And . . . relief.** Cf. Ecclesiastes 12:5. (E.) **31–34. *Frisch . . . du?*** See Wagner's *Tristan und Isolde*, I, verses 5–8. (E.) "Fresh blows the wind to the homeland; my Irish child, where do you tarry?" The words are sung by a sailor in the rigging of the ship that is bringing the Irish Isolde to Cornwall. The love song calls to mind, in the passage that follows, another experience of love that ended unhappily. **42. *Oed' . . . Meer.*** Cf. *Tristan und Isolde*, I, verses 5–8. (E.) "Desolate and empty the sea." These are the words of the watcher to the dying Tristan as he waits for the appearance of Isolde's ship.

46–55. pack of cards . . . Hanged Man. "I am not familiar with the exact constitution of the Tarot pack of cards, from which I have obviously departed to suit my own convenience. The Hanged Man, a member of the traditional pack, fits my purpose in two ways: because he is associated in my mind with the Hanged God of Frazer, and because I associate him with the hooded figure in the passage of the disciples to Emmaus in Part V. The Phoenician Sailor and the Merchant appear later; also the 'crowds of people,' and Death by Water is executed in Part IV. The Man with Three Staves (an authentic member of the Tarot pack) I associate, quite arbitrarily, with the Fisher King himself." (E.) The Tarot pack of cards, used by fortune tellers, is of very primitive and very obscure origin. It was used in ancient vegetation rituals in predicting the rising of the waters. Its suits, Cup, Lance, Sword, Dish, are symbols found in the Grail legend itself. The Phoenician Sailor is a type of the fertility god whose image was thrown annually into the sea to symbolize the death of summer. **48. Those . . . eyes.** See *The Tempest*, I, ii, 396, and Part II, line 126 below. **52. one-eyed merchant,** as seen in profile on the card. **60. Unreal City.** Cf. Baudelaire:

"Fourmillante cité, cité pleine de rêves,
Où le spectre en plein jour raccroche le passant." (E.)

"Swarming city, city full of dreams,
Where the spectre in broad daylight buttonholes the passer-by."

(From Charles Baudelaire's *Fleurs du Mal*, No. 90, "The Seven Old Men.") **63. I had . . . so many.** Cf. *Inferno*, III, 55–57:

"si lunga tratta
di gente, ch'io non avrei mai creduto
che morte tanta n'avesse disfatta." (E.)

"so long a train
of people that I scarce could have believed
death had undone so many."

The passages from Baudelaire and Dante describe respectively a great modern city, in which the inhabitants live a spectre-like existence, and the Limbo of Dante's *Inferno*, where are seen those who on earth had lived without praise or blame and without hope of death, and who had been, as it were, dead while they were alive. Such a place the waste land of the modern world, and particularly the great modern city, seems to the poet. The crowd flowing over London Bridge is the crowd of businessmen, office workers, and the miscellaneous group of people who, morning after morning, travel like so many automata to London by railway from suburban sections—the army of commuters in any great modern city.

Under the brown fog of a winter dawn,
A crowd flowed over London Bridge, so many,
I had not thought death had undone so many.
Sighs, short and infrequent, were exhaled,
And each man fixed his eyes before his feet.
Flowed up the hill and down King William Street,
To where Saint Mary Woolnoth kept the hours
With a dead sound on the final stroke of nine.
There I saw one I knew, and stopped him, crying: "Stetson!
"You who were with me in the ships at Mylae!
"That corpse you planted last year in the garden,
"Has it begun to sprout? Will it bloom this year?
"Or has the sudden frost disturbed its bed?
"Oh keep the Dog far hence, that's friend to men,
"Or with his nails he'll dig it up again!
"You! hypocrite lecteur!—mon semblable,—mon frère!"

66. King William Street, a street in the heart of the "City," the financial and commercial district of London. **67. Saint Mary Woolnoth,** a beautiful eighteenth-century City church at the corner of King William and Lombard Streets. **68. dead sound . . . nine.** "A phenomenon which I have often noticed." (E.) **69. There I saw one I knew.** Dante, after describing the crowd undone by death, in the third canto of the *Inferno*, says: "After I had recognized some amongst them, I saw and knew the shade of him who, through cowardice, made the great refusal." The name "Stetson" presumably has no particular significance, although it has been suggested that the well-known American hat of that name, often worn by well-to-do businessmen, may have supplied the term. **70. Mylae,** the scene of the great naval victory of the Romans over the Carthaginians in the First Punic War—a trade war comparable to the war of 1914–18. Ancient wars and modern wars, like other human experiences ancient and modern, tend to become one and the same. **71–75. That corpse . . . again.** A much-disputed passage in which, however, the basic allusion to the buried god of the fertility rites is clear, as is also that to Stetson's suburban gardening operations. Eliot refers the reader to the dirge in John Webster's play, *The White Devil* (*c.* 1608):

> "Call for the robin red-breast and the wren,
> Since o'er shady groves they hover,
> And with leaves and flowers do cover
> The friendless bodies of unburied men.
> Call unto his funeral dole
> The ant, the field-mouse, and the mole,
> To rear him hillocks that shall keep him warm,
> And, when gay tombs are robbed, sustain no harm;
> But keep the wolf far thence, that's foe to men,
> For with his nails he'll dig them up again."

This song is sung by the mad Cornelia to her son Flamineo, while she is preparing for burial the corpse of another son, Marcello, who has been murdered by Flamineo.

76. You! hypocrite lecteur! Eliot refers the reader to Baudelaire's prefatory poem to the *Fleurs du Mal*. After describing the monstrous "menagerie" of human vices, Baudelaire turns to the ugliest monster of all—Boredom:

> "Boredom!—his eye full of involuntary tears—
> He dreams of gallows, smoking his pipe.
> You know him, reader, this dainty monster.
> —Hypocrite reader,—my double,—my brother!"

II. A GAME OF CHESS

The Chair she sat in, like a burnished throne,
Glowed on the marble, where the glass
Held up by standards wrought with fruited vines
From which a golden Cupidon peeped out
(Another hid his eyes behind his wing)
Doubled the flames of sevenbranched candelabra
Reflecting light upon the table as
The glitter of her jewels rose to meet it,
From satin cases poured in rich profusion;
In vials of ivory and coloured glass
Unstoppered, lurked her strange synthetic perfumes,
Unguent, powdered, or liquid—troubled, confused
And drowned the sense in odours; stirred by the air
That freshened from the window, these ascended
In fattening the prolonged candle-flames,
Flung their smoke into the laquearia,
Stirring the pattern on the coffered ceiling.
Huge sea-wood fed with copper
Burned green and orange, framed by the coloured stone,
In which sad light a carvèd dolphin swam.
Above the antique mantel was displayed
As though a window gave upon the sylvan scene

II. A Game of Chess. The first part of the poem has indicated in a general way the pain that must accompany the awakening of life and has presented a panorama of the death-in-life of the unreal city in the waste land. The second part emphasizes more particularly and concretely the lack of significance of that life on two levels of society—that of the wealthy class, sterile and surfeited with luxury, and that of the drab but more vital poor, as seen in the vulgar dreariness of a London "pub." On both levels life is without love and meaning. **77. The Chair she sat in.** Eliot refers the reader to *Antony and Cleopatra*, II, ii, 190, the beginning of the description of Cleopatra when she first met Antony upon the River Cydnus. The contrast between the abundant life and love and infinite variety of Shakespeare's queen, who is an integral and interested part of all her surroundings, and the thin and frustrated existence of the rich lady in the midst of a too ornate luxury, which has no meaning for her, is apparent and striking. **80. Cupidon,** Cupid. **92. laquearia.** Eliot quotes Virgil's *Aeneid*, I, 726–27:

> "dependent lychni laquearibus aureis incensi,
> et noctem flammis funalia vincunt."

("Lighted lamps hang from the gilded ceiling, and torches with their flames dispel the night.") The scene is the palace of Dido, Queen of Carthage, who is giving an elaborate banquet to Aeneas. Venus has sent Cupid to the feast to smite Dido with love for Aeneas. Later, when Aeneas leaves Carthage, Dido, one of the great lovers of legend, destroys herself in despair on a funeral pile. **98. sylvan scene.** Eliot refers to *Paradise Lost*, IV, 140 ff., the description of Paradise, the abode of the first pair of lovers, whose perfect love Milton celebrates in the hymn, "Hail wedded love" (IV, 750 ff.).

The change of Philomel, by the barbarous king
So rudely forced; yet there the nightingale
Filled all the desert with inviolable voice
And still she cried, and still the world pursues,
"Jug Jug" to dirty ears.
And other withered stumps of time
Were told upon the walls; staring forms
Leaned out, leaning, hushing the room enclosed.
Footsteps shuffled on the stair.
Under the firelight, under the brush, her hair
Spread out in fiery points
Glowed into words, then would be savagely still.

"My nerves are bad to-night. Yes, bad. Stay with me.
"Speak to me. Why do you never speak. Speak.
"What are you thinking of? What thinking? What?
"I never know what you are thinking. Think."

I think we are in rats' alley
Where the dead men lost their bones.

"What is that noise?"
The wind under the door.
"What is that noise now? What is the wind doing?"
Nothing again nothing.

"Do
"You know nothing? Do you see nothing? Do you remember
"Nothing?"

I remember
Those are pearls that were his eyes.
"Are you alive, or not? Is there nothing in your head?"

But

O O O O that Shakespeherian Rag—
It's so elegant
So intelligent
"What shall I do now? What shall I do?"
"I shall rush out as I am, and walk the street
"With my hair down, so. What shall we do to-morrow?
"What shall we ever do?"
The hot water at ten.
And if it rains, a closed car at four.
And we shall play a game of chess,
Pressing lidless eyes and waiting for a knock upon the door.

When Lil's husband got demobbed, I said—
I didn't mince my words, I said to her myself,
HURRY UP PLEASE ITS TIME
Now Albert's coming back, make yourself a bit smart.
He'll want to know what you done with that money he gave you
To get yourself some teeth. He did, I was there.
You have them all out, Lil, and get a nice set,
He said, I swear, I can't bear to look at you.
And no more can't I, I said, and think of poor Albert,
He's been in the army four years, he wants a good time,

99. The change of Philomel. The story of Philomela, for which Eliot refers us to Ovid's *Metamorphoses*, VI, is briefly as follows: Procne, the wife of Tereus, king of Thrace, was sister to Philomela, of whom Tereus became violently enamored and whom he violated and deprived of her tongue. He informed Procne that her sister was dead, but Philomela, by weaving a few words into a cloth, made the truth known to Procne. The latter thereupon killed her own son, Itys, and served up his flesh to his father. Procne and Philomela then fled and were pursued by Tereus. When the sisters were overtaken, they prayed to the gods to change them into birds. Procne became a swallow, Philomela a nightingale. Tereus was changed into a hawk. (In some versions it is Procne who becomes the nightingale and Philomela the swallow.) The elements of the story—lust, violated chastity, the transformation of suffering into beauty, etc.—are important themes and symbols throughout the poem, and recur in various connections. **103. "Jug, Jug,"** the nightingale's notes as frequently and somewhat indelicately represented in Elizabethan literature. See below, Part III, lines 203–06. **115. rats' alley.** Cf. below, Part III, lines 194–195. **125. Those . . . eyes.** Cf. above, Part I, line 48. This line from Ariel's song in *The Tempest*, which echoes in several sections of the poem, suggests one of the principal themes of the poem, "death by water"—the "sea-change into something rich and strange"—the death which is an awakening into a new life. The reader will recall the vegetation ritual involving the throwing of the effigy of the god into the water and the retrieving of it therefrom. **128. that Shakespeherian Rag.** Eliot is here, as frequently, travestying a popular song, like "O that Indiana Rag" (ragtime). The implication is, of course, that in the waste land Shakespeare, like the other artists and sources of beauty and inspiration referred to previously, has become a mere name, suggesting merely something "elegant" and "intelligent," but without real meaning or significance. **137. a game of chess.** Eliot refers to the game of chess in Act II, scene ii of Thomas Middleton's *Women Beware Women* (*c.* 1626) which is used to distract a woman's attention while her daughter-in-law is being seduced. The theme of ravishment, announced in the story of Philomela, is central to Part II of the poem, in both a physical and a spiritual sense. **139. demobbed,** demobilized, discharged from the army. In the lines that follow, in which two cockney women in a London pub discuss a third one, Eliot displays a remarkable sense of control of rhythm even while he is giving what seems to be the ordinary speech of vulgar people. **141. Hurry up please its time,** the insistent call of the barmaid as the moment for closing the pub approaches. The sense of the urgency of time is expressed in various ways throughout the poem. Cf. Part III, line 185 below, and note.

And if you don't give it him, there's others will, I said.
Oh is there, she said. Something o' that, I said.
Then I'll know who to thank, she said, and give me a straight look.
HURRY UP PLEASE ITS TIME
If you don't like it you can get on with it, I said.
Others can pick and choose if you can't.
But if Albert makes off, it won't be for lack of telling.
You ought to be ashamed, I said, to look so antique.
(And her only thirty-one.)
I can't help it, she said, pulling a long face,
It's them pills I took, to bring it off, she said.
(She's had five already, and nearly died of young George.)
The chemist said it would be all right, but I've never been the same.
You *are* a proper fool, I said.
Well, if Albert won't leave you alone, there it is, I said,
What you get married for if you don't want children?
HURRY UP PLEASE ITS TIME
Well, that Sunday Albert was home, they had a hot gammon,
And they asked me in to dinner, to get the beauty of it hot—
HURRY UP PLEASE ITS TIME
HURRY UP PLEASE ITS TIME
Goonight Bill. Goonight Lou. Goonight May. Goonight.
Ta ta. Goonight. Goonight.
Good night, ladies, good night, sweet ladies, good night, good night.

III. THE FIRE SERMON

The river's tent is broken: the last fingers of leaf
Clutch and sink into the wet bank. The wind
Crosses the brown land, unheard. The nymphs are departed.
Sweet Thames, run softly, till I end my song.
The river bears no empty bottles, sandwich papers,
Silk handkerchiefs, cardboard boxes, cigarette ends
Or other testimony of summer nights. The nymphs are departed.
And their friends, the loitering heirs of city directors;
Departed, have left no addresses.
By the waters of Leman I sat down and wept . . .
Sweet Thames, run softly till I end my song,
Sweet Thames, run softly, for I speak not loud or long.
But at my back in a cold blast I hear
The rattle of the bones, and chuckle spread from ear to ear.
A rat crept softly through the vegetation
Dragging its slimy belly on the bank
While I was fishing in the dull canal
On a winter evening round behind the gashouse
Musing upon the king my brother's wreck
And on the king my father's death before him.
White bodies naked on the low damp ground
And bones cast in a little low dry garret,
Rattled by the rat's foot only, year to year.
But at my back from time to time I hear

161. chemist, druggist. **166. gammon,** a cut of bacon containing the hind leg. **172. Good night, ladies . . . good night.** The poet here makes a remarkably deft transition from the vulgar farewells of the cockney women to the pathetic adieus of the insane Ophelia (cf. *Hamlet*, V, v, 71) to the ladies of the court of Denmark. Ophelia has also come to distraction through the failure of human relationships, and, like Philomela, if not like Lil, has come to tragic beauty through suffering. ***III. The Fire Sermon.*** In his "sermon" the poet presents a broader panorama of the waste land and its inhabitants, depicting them chiefly in terms of two symbols, fire and water. The fire symbolizes the consuming and sterile nature of lust. The water—appearing variously as the Thames River, Lake Leman, the canal, the English Channel, etc.—and the waterside scenes and episodes connect us again with the Grail legend, in which the castle of the Fisher King stands by the water, and with the ancient fertility symbol of the fish.

176. Sweet Thames . . . song. Eliot quotes the refrain of Spenser's *Prothalamion* (see p. 253), and thus provides an ironic contrast between Spenser's noble wedding party of nymphs and knights "along the shore of silver streaming Thames" and the holiday trippers and excursionists seen along the present-day Thames. **182. By the waters of Leman.** Cf. Psalm 137, the lament of the Jewish captives in Babylon: "By the rivers of Babylon, there we sat down; yea, we wept when we remembered Zion. We hanged our harps upon the willows in the midst thereof." **185. at my back . . . I hear.** Here and in line 196 Eliot alludes ironically to lines 21–22 of Andrew Marvell's poem "To His Coy Mistress" (see p. 435):

"But at my back I always hear
Time's wingèd chariot hurrying near."

189–92. While I was fishing . . . my father's death. Eliot has adapted to the circumstances of the story of the Fisher King, wounded and impotent, a passage from Shakespeare's *The Tempest*, I, ii, 387–404, from which he has already quoted a line in Ariel's song (line 48 of Part I above), which Prince Ferdinand hears as he is

"Sitting on a bank,
Weeping again the king my father's wreck."

194–95. bones . . . rattled by the rat's foot. Cf. lines 115–16 in Part II above. **196. at my back . . . I hear.** Eliot has fused the passage from Marvell with a quotation from John Day's masque-like play *The Parliament of Bees* (*c.* 1607):

"When of the sudden, listening, you shall hear,
A noise of horns and hunting, which shall bring
Actaeon to Diana in the spring,
Where all shall see her naked skin . . ."

(Actaeon, a celebrated huntsman, during a chase saw Diana with her nymphs bathing, whereupon the goddess changed him into a stag, in which form he was killed by his own dogs.)

The sound of horns and motors, which shall bring
Sweeney to Mrs. Porter in the spring.
O the moon shone bright on Mrs. Porter
And on her daughter
They wash their feet in soda water
Et O ces voix d'enfants, chantant dans la coupole!

Twit twit twit
Jug jug jug jug jug jug
So rudely forc'd.
Tereu

Unreal City
Under the brown fog of a winter noon
Mr. Eugenides, the Smyrna merchant
Unshaven, with a pocket full of currants
C. i. f. London: documents at sight,
Asked me in demotic French
To luncheon at the Cannon Street Hotel
Followed by a weekend at the Metropole.

At the violet hour, when the eyes and back
Turn upward from the desk, when the human
    engine waits
Like a taxi throbbing waiting,
I Tiresias, though blind, throbbing between two
    lives,
Old man with wrinkled female breasts, can see
At the violet hour, the evening hour that strives
Homeward, and brings the sailor home from sea,
The typist home at teatime, clears her breakfast,
    lights
Her stove, and lays out food in tins.
Out of the window perilously spread
Her drying combinations touched by the sun's last
    rays,
On the divan are piled (at night her bed)
Stockings, slippers, camisoles, and stays.
I Tiresias, old man with wrinkled dugs
Perceived the scene, and foretold the rest—
I too awaited the expected guest.
He, the young man carbuncular, arrives,
A small house agent's clerk, with one bold stare,
One of the low on whom assurance sits

198. Sweeney, Eliot's favorite name for the type of the vulgar bourgeois. Cf. his "Sweeney Erect" and *Sweeney Agonistes.* **199. O the moon . . . on Mrs. Porter.** "I do not know the origin of the ballad from which these lines are taken: it was reported to me from Sydney, Australia." (E.) **202.** ***Et O ces voix . . . coupole!*** Eliot refers to Paul Verlaine's *Parsifal,* in which Parsifal achieves the quest of the Holy Grail. In his devotions in the Grail chapel thereafter he hears "the voices of children singing in the dome," at the ceremony of the foot-washing (cf. John 13:1–15) that precedes the healing of Anfortas (the Fisher King) by Parsifal, and the lifting of the curse from the waste land. **203–4. Twit twit . . . jug jug.** Such onomatopoeic words as these were frequently used in Elizabethan poetry to suggest the song of birds. Cf. Thomas Nashe's *Summer's Last Will and Testament* (1600):

> "In every street these tunes our ears do greet:
> Cuckoo, jug-jug, pu-we, to-witta-woo!
> Spring, the sweet spring!"

205–6. So rudely forc'd. Tereu. Cf. lines 99–100 in Part II above. "Tereu" represents the nightingale's complaint upon the name of the Thracian king who wronged Philomela. **207. Unreal City.** Cf. Part I, lines 60–61, above. **209. Mr. Eugenides . . . merchant.** Cf. Part I, line 52 above. Mr. Eugenides is the unworthy modern representative of the Syrian merchants who, as Miss Weston's book informs us, were the carriers of the ancient mysteries of the Grail legends. **211. C. i. f. London.** Eliot, who was once employed in the foreign exchange department of Lloyd's, appends the note: "The currants were quoted at a price 'carriage and insurance free to London'; and the Bill of Lading, etc., were to be handed to the buyer upon payment of the sight draft." **213. Cannon Street Hotel.** The hotel attached to the Cannon Street Railway Station in the heart of the City was formerly a favorite rendezvous of foreign businessmen and their English clients. **214. the Metropole,** a "grand hotel" at Brighton, the once fashionable and still popular seaside resort, one hour from London, on the English Channel. The Metropole is notorious for weekend pleasure parties. **215. the violet hour,** the evening hour. The poet alludes ironically to the lines of Sappho, the ancient Greek poetess: "Evening, thou that bringest all that bright morning scattered: thou bringest the sheep, the goat, the child back to its mother."

218. Tiresias. Eliot comments: "Tiresias, although a mere spectator and not indeed a 'character,' is yet the most important personage in the poem, uniting all the rest. Just as the one-eyed merchant, seller of currants, melts into the Phoenician Sailor, and the latter is not wholly distinct from Prince Ferdinand of Naples, so all the women are one woman, and the two sexes meet in Tiresias. What Tiresias *sees,* in fact, is the substance of the poem. The whole passage from Ovid [*Metamorphoses,* III, 322 ff.] is of great anthropological interest:

> 'it chanced that Jove (as the story goes), while warmed with wine, put care aside and bandied good-humored jests with Juno in an idle hour. "I maintain," said he, "that your pleasure in love is greater than that which we [male gods] enjoy." She held the opposite view. And so they decided to ask the judgment of wise Tiresias. He knew both sides of love. For once, with a blow of his staff, he had outraged two huge serpents mating in the green forest; and, wonderful to relate, from man he was changed into a woman, and in that form spent seven years. In the eighth year he saw the same serpents again and said: "Since in striking you there is such magic power as to change the nature of the giver of the blow, now will I strike you once again." So saying, he struck the serpents, and his former state was restored, and he became as he had been born. He, therefore, being asked to arbitrate the playful dispute of the gods, took sides with Jove. Saturnia [Juno], they say, grieved more deeply than she should and than the issue warranted, and condemned the arbitrator to perpetual blindness. But the Almighty Father (for no god may undo what another god has done) in return for his loss of sight gave Tiresias the power to know the future, lightening the penalty by the honour.'" (Translation by Frank Justus Miller in the Loeb Classical Library, published by Harvard University Press.)

Tiresias, a Theban, was one of the most renowned soothsayers of antiquity. Even in the lower world he was believed to retain the powers of perception and the use of his golden staff. Cf. Tennyson's poem "Tiresias."

221. Homeward . . . from sea. "This may not appear as exact as Sappho's lines, but I had in mind the 'longshore' or 'dory' fisherman, who returns at nightfall." (E.)

As a silk hat on a Bradford millionaire.
The time is now propitious, as he guesses,
The meal is ended, she is bored and tired,
Endeavours to engage her in caresses
Which still are unreproved, if undesired.
Flushed and decided, he assaults at once;
Exploring hands encounter no defence;
His vanity requires no response,
And makes a welcome of indifference.
(And I Tiresias have foresuffered all
Enacted on this same divan or bed;
I who have sat by Thebes below the wall
And walked among the lowest of the dead.)
Bestows one final patronising kiss,
And gropes his way, finding the stairs unlit . . .

She turns and looks a moment in the glass,
Hardly aware of her departed lover;
Her brain allows one half-formed thought to pass:
"Well now that's done: and I'm glad it's over."
When lovely woman stoops to folly and
Paces about her room again, alone,
She smoothes her hair with automatic hand,
And puts a record on the gramophone.

"This music crept by me upon the waters"
And along the Strand, up Queen Victoria Street.
O City city, I can sometimes hear
Beside a public bar in Lower Thames Street,
The pleasant whining of a mandoline
And a clatter and a chatter from within
Where fishmen lounge at noon: where the walls
Of Magnus Martyr hold
Inexplicable splendour of Ionian white and gold.

The river sweats
Oil and tar
The barges drift
With the turning tide
Red sails
Wide
To leeward, swing on the heavy spar.
The barges wash
Drifting logs
Down Greenwich reach
Past the Isle of Dogs.
Weialala leia
Wallala leialala

Elizabeth and Leicester
Beating oars
The stern was formed
A gilded shell
Red and gold
The brisk swell
Rippled both shores
Southwest wind
Carried down stream
The peal of bells
White towers
Weialala leia
Wallala leialala

234. Bradford, a manufacturing city in Yorkshire. During the war of 1914–18 it produced a great many "war profiteers" and "newly rich" men. **253–56. When lovely woman . . . gramophone.** By way of suggesting the breakdown of traditional standards and attitudes, Eliot alludes to a song in Goldsmith's *Vicar of Wakefield:*

> "When lovely woman stoops to folly
> And finds too late that men betray,
> What charm can soothe her melancholy,
> What art can wash her guilt away?
>
> The only art her guilt to cover,
> To hide her shame from every eye,
> To give repentance to her lover
> And wring his bosom—is to die."

257. "This music . . . waters." Another line from Ariel's song in *The Tempest*, I, ii, 387–404, to which allusions have already been made. The music of the typist's gramophone and the circumstances of its playing are contrasted ironically with the song and the circumstances in Shakespeare's play. **258. the Strand.** The modern "Strand" provides, like its Victorian neighbors, a striking contrast with the road that ran along the shore of the Thames, bordered by the palaces and gardens of Elizabethan nobles. See Spenser's *Prothalamion*, to which Eliot has alluded at the beginning of Part III above, for a lyrical description of the Strand and the Thames in the days of Elizabeth and Essex and Leicester. **261–63. pleasant whining . . . fishmen.** Probably a reference to the cheery music of the itinerant musicians or actors called "buskers," who play at certain London bars. The mention of the fishmen (from Billingsgate Market) recalls the ancient use of the fish as a life symbol.

264. Magnus Martyr. "The interior of St. Magnus Martyr is to my mind one of the finest among Wren's interiors. See *The Proposed Demolition of Nineteen City Churches* (P. S. King & Son, Ltd.)." (E.) The abundant, if vulgar, vitality of the bar affords a striking contrast with the deserted beauty of a city church. **266–306.** "The song of the (three) Thames-daughters begins here. From line 292 to 306 inclusive they speak in turn. See *Götterdämmerung*, III, i: the Rhine-daughters." (E.) The first song of the Rhine-daughters at the opening of Wagner's *Das Rheingold*, with its refrain of "Weialala," is a joyous one of the gold they are guarding. In *Götterdämmerung*, III, their song is one of lamentation over the loss of the gold, of the beauty of the Rhine, and of their own former joy. The reader will detect the contrast in the first two songs between the modern Thames, bearing barges of "black gold" (oil, tar, etc.), and the Elizabethan Thames, whose shores were rippled by a "gilded shell." **279. Elizabeth and Leicester.** "See Froude, *Elizabeth*, Vol. I, ch. iv, letter of De Quadra to Philip of Spain: 'In the afternoon we were in a barge, watching the games on the river. (The queen) was alone with Lord Robert [Leicester] and myself on the poop, when they began to talk nonsense, and went so far that Lord Robert at last said, as I was on the spot [De Quadra was a bishop] there was no reason why they should not be married if the queen pleased.'" (E.) **281–83. The stern . . . gold.** Eliot alludes again to the passage in Shakespeare's *Antony and Cleopatra* which he has used at the beginning of Part II above. **289. White towers,** of the Tower of London.

"Trams and dusty trees.
Highbury bore me. Richmond and Kew
Undid me. By Richmond I raised my knees
Supine on the floor of a narrow canoe."

"My feet are at Moorgate, and my heart
Under my feet. After the event
He wept. He promised 'a new start.'
I made no comment. What should I resent?"

"On Margate Sands.
I can connect
Nothing with nothing.
The broken fingernails of dirty hands.
My people humble people who expect
Nothing."
                la la

To Carthage then I came
Burning burning burning burning
O Lord Thou pluckest me out

293–94. Highbury bore me. Eliot refers to Dante's *Purgatorio*, V, 133. Among the souls whom Dante meets as he begins the ascent of the Mount of Purgatory is "La Pia." According to legend she was the wife of a nobleman who, in order to rid himself of her so that he might marry another woman, forced her to live in a house in the marshes of Maremma until she died of malaria. The third Thames-daughter, in her song of unhappy and sordid love, paraphrases part of La Pia's words to Dante:

> "ricorditi di me, che son la Pia;
> Siena mi fe', disfecemi Maremma:
> salsi colui che innanellata, pria
>
> disposando, m' avea con la sua gemma."

(Remember me, who am La Pia; Siena made me, Maremma unmade me: 'tis known to him who, first plighting troth, had wedded me with his gem.) **293. Highbury,** a middle-class parish in the northeast section of metropolitan London. **Richmond,** once the seat of a royal residence, and **Kew,** famous for its botanical gardens, are within easy reach of the city proper. **296. Moorgate,** in the financial center of London, is occupied by office buildings and slum dwellings. **300. Margate,** a popular seaside resort to the east of London. **307. To Carthage.** "See St. Augustine's *Confessions:* 'to Carthage then I came, where a cauldron of unholy loves sang all about mine ears.'" (E.) These words of St. Augustine come at the opening of Book III of the *Confessions.* At the end of Book II he confesses that in his youth he had gone astray from God, and had become to himself "a land of want." The first chapter of Book III deals with the sexual indulgence that was an illusory and vicious substitute for the love of God: "I had a famine within me, even of that inward food (thyself, O God), though that famine made me not hungry." Sensual desire appears constantly in the *Confessions* as a distraction from the good life. **308. Burning . . . burning.** "The complete text of the Buddha's Fire Sermon (which corresponds in importance to the Sermon on the Mount) from which these words are taken, will be found translated in the late Henry Clarke Warren's *Buddhism in Translation* (Harvard Oriental Series)." (E.) **309–10. O Lord . . . Thou pluckest.** "From St. Augustine's *Confessions* again. The collocation of these two representatives of eastern and western asceticism, as the culmination of this part of the poem, is not an accident." (E.)

O Lord Thou pluckest

burning

IV. DEATH BY WATER

Phlebas the Phoenician, a fortnight dead,
Forgot the cry of gulls, and the deep sea swell
And the profit and loss.
                                A current under sea
Picked his bones in whispers. As he rose and fell
He passed the stages of his age and youth
Entering the whirlpool.
                                Gentile or Jew
O you who turn the wheel and look to windward,
Consider Phlebas, who was once handsome and tall as you.

V. WHAT THE THUNDER SAID

After the torchlight red on sweaty faces
After the frosty silence in the gardens
After the agony in stony places
The shouting and the crying
Prison and palace and reverberation
Of thunder of spring over distant mountains
He who was living is now dead
We who were living are now dying
With a little patience

311. burning. Buddha states that all things are on fire, the bodily senses and whatever consciousness depends on sense impressions. "With the fire of passion, say I, with the fire of hatred, with the fire of infatuation; with birth, old age, death, sorrow, lamentation, misery, grief, and despair are they on fire." The Buddha advises his disciple to conceive an aversion for sense-impressions and thus to free himself from passion and from the endless reincarnation which the Buddhist fears, and, in knowing that he has done this, to know that he has lived a holy life and is no more for this world. **312. Phlebas the Phoenician.** Phlebas, the drowned sailor, as Eliot indicates in his notes, is to be associated with the drowned god of the fertility cults. The effigy of the head of the god, as Miss Weston's book informs us, was thrown into the water to symbolize the death of the powers of nature and later raised from the water to symbolize the rebirth of the god and of nature. See Eliot's note to line 218 of Part III above. It will be noticed that water (symbolizing the losing of one's life in order to save it) is as important a symbol in Part IV as is the destroying fire of lust in Part III. **318, 320. the whirlpool, the wheel.** These symbols, employed frequently by Eliot, doubtless have to do with the cycle of the seasons and of death and resurrection. ***V. What the Thunder Said.*** "In the first part of Part V three themes are employed: the journey to Emmaus, the approach to the Chapel Perilous (see Miss Weston's book) and the present decay of eastern Europe." (E.) **322–26. After the torchlight . . . palace.** The passage alludes to the agony of Christ in the Garden of Gethsemane and to his trial before the Crucifixion. See John 18:1–40. The sacrifice of Christ is associated with that of the hanged gods of the ancient legends. **329. We . . . are now dying.** The theme of death-in-life (cf. Part I, lines 62–65 above) is reintroduced.

Here is no water but only rock
Rock and no water and the sandy road
The road winding above among the mountains
Which are mountains of rock without water
If there were water we should stop and drink
Amongst the rock one cannot stop or think
Sweat is dry and feet are in the sand
If there were only water amongst the rock
Dead mountain mouth of carious teeth that cannot spit
Here one can neither stand nor lie nor sit
There is not even silence in the mountains
But dry sterile thunder without rain
There is not even solitude in the mountains
But red sullen faces sneer and snarl
From doors of mudcracked houses
If there were water
And no rock
If there were rock
And also water
And water
A spring
A pool among the rock
If there were the sound of water only
Not the cicada
And dry grass singing
But sound of water over a rock
Where the hermit-thrush sings in the pine trees
Drip drop drip drop drop drop drop
But there is no water

Who is the third who walks always beside you?
When I count, there are only you and I together
But when I look ahead up the white road
There is always another one walking beside you
Gliding wrapt in a brown mantle, hooded
I do not know whether a man or a woman
—But who is that on the other side of you?

What is that sound high in the air
Murmur of maternal lamentation
Who are those hooded hordes swarming
Over endless plains, stumbling in cracked earth
Ringed by the flat horizon only
What is the city over the mountains
Cracks and reforms and bursts in the violet air
Falling towers
Jerusalem Athens Alexandria
Vienna London
Unreal

A woman drew her long black hair out tight
And fiddled whisper music on those strings
And bats with baby faces in the violet light
Whistled, and beat their wings
And crawled head downward down a blackened wall
And upside down in air were towers
Tolling reminiscent bells, that kept the hours
And voices singing out of empty cisterns and exhausted wells.

In this decayed hole among the mountains
In the faint moonlight, the grass is singing
Over the tumbled graves, about the chapel
There is the empty chapel, only the wind's home.
It has no windows, and the door swings,
Dry bones can harm no one.
Only a cock stood on the rooftree
Co co rico co co rico
In a flash of lightning. Then a damp gust
Bringing rain

Ganga was sunken, and the limp leaves
Waited for rain, while the black clouds
Gathered far distant, over Himavant.
The jungle crouched, humped in silence.
Then spoke the thunder

331. Here is no water. In lines 331–58 the theme of the sterility of the waste land is reintroduced. **344–45. red sullen faces . . . houses.** The scene has shifted from Palestine to Central Asia, presumably Tibet. **356–57. the hermit-thrush . . . drop drop.** This is the hermit-thrush which I have heard in Quebec County. . . . Its 'water-dripping song' is justly celebrated." (E.) **359. Who is the third . . . beside you?** For the account of the journey to Emmaus by Christ and his disciples see Luke 24:1–32. **360–65. When I count . . . the other side of you?** "The following lines," says Eliot, "were stimulated by the account of one of the Antarctic expeditions (I forget which, but I think one of Shackleton's): it was related that the party of explorers, at the extremity of their strength, had the constant delusion that there was *one more member* than could actually be counted." **367. maternal lamentation.** Cf. Matthew 2:17, 18 and Luke 23:27–31.

368–76. Who are those hooded hordes . . . Unreal. Eliot quotes a passage from Herman Hesse's *Blick ins Chaos* (*A Glimpse into Chaos*): "Already half of Europe, already at least half of Eastern Europe, is on the way to chaos, traveling drunken in holy illusion along the edge of the abyss, and, as she goes, sings drunken hymns, as Dmitri Karamazov [cf. Dostoevsky's *The Brothers Karamazov*] sang. Over these songs the outraged burgher laughs scornfully, the saint and seer hears them with tears." **377–84. A woman . . . wells.** In this passage are involved, as in a horrible dream, figures, scenes, and episodes which have already appeared or been alluded to in the poem. Cf. Part I, lines 108–10; Part III, lines 202, 255, and 288. The entire passage is projected against the background of Ecclesiastes 12, which Eliot alludes to in connection with Part I, line 23. **385–94. In this decayed hole . . . rain.** The second of the themes that Eliot mentions at the beginning of Part V, the approach to the Chapel Perilous, is developed in this passage. The last of the labors and obstacles which the Grail Knight must overcome as a test of fitness to accomplish his quest of the Holy Grail is a night of terrors at the Chapel Perilous. **391. a cock . . . rooftree.** At the coming of the dawn and the crowing of the cock, spirits were supposed to take their departure. Cf. Genesis 32:24–26 and *Hamlet*, I, i, 157–64.

Da
Datta: what have we given?
My friend, blood shaking my heart
The awful daring of a moment's surrender
Which an age of prudence can never retract
By this, and this only, we have existed
Which is not to be found in our obituaries
Or in memories draped by the beneficent spider
Or under seals broken by the lean solicitor
In our empty rooms
Da
Dayadhvam: I have heard the key
Turn in the door once and turn once only
We think of the key, each in his prison
Thinking of the key, each confirms a prison
Only at nightfall, aethereal rumours
Revive for a moment a broken Coriolanus
Da
Damyata: The boat responded
Gaily, to the hand expert with sail and oar
The sea was calm, your heart would have responded
Gaily, when invited, beating obedient
To controlling hands

I sat upon the shore
Fishing, with the arid plain behind me
Shall I at least set my lands in order?
London Bridge is falling down falling down falling down
Poi s'ascose nel foco che gli affina
Quando fiam uti chelidon—O swallow swallow
Le Prince d'Aquitaine à la tour abolie
These fragments I have shored against my ruins
Why then Ile fit you. Hieronymo's mad againe.
Datta. Dayadhvam. Damyata.
Shantih shantih shantih

401, 411, 417. *Datta . . . Dayadhvam . . . Damyata.* Eliot translates the three Sanskrit words "Give," "Sympathize," "Control," and adds: "The fable of the meaning of the Thunder is found in the *Brihadaranyaka-Upanishad*, 5, 1. A translation is found in Deussen's *Sechzig Upanishads des Veda*, p. 489." The Upanishads are the philosophic portion of the Vedic Books, the sacred books of wisdom of the Hindus, for the most part between 1000 and 500 B.C., the earliest literature in the Indo-European (Aryan) languages. In R. E. Hume's *The Thirteen Principal Upanishads*, Oxford, 1921, p. 150, is an account of how the Lord of Creation (Prajapati) spoke three times the syllable "Da" (evidently a sound representing thunder). His pupils interpreted this syllable in three ways, according to three Sanskrit words that began with it. Hence the *datta* ("give"), *dayadhvam* ("sympathize" or "be compassionate"), *damyata* ("control" or "restrain yourselves") that Eliot inserts in his poem. The fable concludes: "This same thing does the divine voice here thunder, repeat: *Da! Da! Da!* . . . One should practise this same triad: self-restraint, giving, compassion." **407. memories . . . spider.** Eliot alludes again to John Webster's play, *The White Devil*, V, 6:

> ". . . they'll remarry
> Ere the worm pierce your winding-sheet, ere the spider
> Make a thin curtain for your epitaphs."

411–412. heard the key . . . door. The allusion is to Dante's *Inferno*, XXXIII, 46, 47:

> "ed io sentii chiavar l' uscio di sotto
> all' orribile torre":

(and below I heard the outlet of the horrible tower locked up). The words are from the story told to Dante by Count Ugolino of Pisa, one of the traitors whom Dante finds in the lowest circle of Hell, in Canto XXXIII of the *Inferno*. The significance of the locking of the tower with respect to the divine command *Dayadhvam* is suggested by Eliot in lines 413–14 and in the following passage which he quotes from F. H. Bradley's *Appearance and Reality*, p. 346: "My external sensations are no less private to myself than are my thoughts or my feelings. In either case my experience falls within my own circle, a circle closed on the outside; and, with all its elements alike, every sphere is opaque to the others which surround it. . . . In brief, regarded as an existence which appears in a soul, the whole world for each is peculiar and private to that soul." **416. Coriolanus,** the Roman general whose pride destroyed him.

423–24. I sat upon the shore Fishing. Cf. Part III, lines 189–93 and the chapter on the Fisher King in Miss Weston's book referred to above. **426. London Bridge.** Cf. the well-known nursery rime. **427. *Poi . . . affina*** Eliot so quotes Dante's *Purgatorio*, XXVI, 148 (Then he hid himself in the fire which refines them). In his journey through Purgatory, Dante meets a group of souls who while on earth failed to restrain their carnal appetites. Among them is the troubadour Arnaut Daniel, who tells of his condition, and implores Dante's prayers: "I am Arnaut that weep and go a-singing; in thought I see my past madness, and I see with joy the day which I await before me. Now I pray you, by that Goodness which guideth you to the summit of the stairway, be mindful in due time of my pain." Then he hid himself in the fire. **428. *Quando . . . chelidon,*** When shall I be like the swallow? (Cf. Philomela in Parts II and III.) The quotation is from *Pervigilium Veneris*, an anonymous Latin poem of the second or third century A.D. On the "Vigil of Venus," all nature rejoices. Even the nightingale sings as if she had forgotten the wrong done her by Tereus. Only the poet is silent, and only for him has the joy of springtime not come. When shall he, too, sing like the swallow, regain his lost Muse, and be heeded by Apollo? **O swallow swallow.** Cf. Swinburne's "Itylus," in which the nightingale asks the swallow how she can be so cheerful, so forgetful of the bitter experience they have shared:

> "Swallow, my sister, O sister swallow,
> How can thine heart be full of the spring?"

429. Le Prince d'Aquitaine. In his sonnet "*El Desdichado*" (The Disinherited), Gérard de Nerval (1808–55) dramatizes himself as the frustrated descendant of the ancient nobility of Aquitania in Southern France, the land of princely troubadours and fabulous castles. In a spirit of dejection he calls himself "the prince of Aquitaine, of the ruined tower." (*El Desdichado* is the Spanish motto on the shield of Scott's Ivanhoe when he fights in disguise at the tournament of Ashby-de-la-Zouche.) **431. Why then . . . mad againe.** The allusion is to Thomas Kyd's *Spanish Tragedy* (1584), IV, i, 67, a play which has many resemblances to Shakespeare's *Hamlet*. In Kyd's play the ghost of the murdered son of the hero, Hieronymo, relates his story, the hero feigns madness, presents a play at court ("Why then Ile fit you"), his scheme succeeds, he bites off his own tongue to avoid confessing, and at the close of the play innocent and guilty alike are involved in the catastrophes. **433. Shantih.** "Repeated, as here, a formal ending to an Upanishad. 'The Peace which passeth understanding' is our equivalent to this word." (E.)

MARINA

This intensely lyrical poem is one of four published in 1931 as the *Ariel Poems.* The mood and situation were suggested by the scene toward the end of Shakespeare's *Pericles*, where, after years of searching on land and sea, Pericles is joyously and almost unbelievingly reunited with his daughter Marina whom he had believed dead.

Quis hic locus, quae regio, quae mundi plaga? [1]

What seas what shores what grey rocks and what islands
What water lapping the bow
And scent of pine and the woodthrush singing through the fog
What images return
O my daughter.

Those who sharpen the tooth of the dog, meaning
Death
Those who glitter with the glory of the humming-bird, meaning
Death
Those who sit in the stye of contentment, meaning
Death
Those who suffer the ecstasy of the animals, meaning
Death

Are become unsubstantial, reduced by a wind,
A breath of pine, and the woodsong fog
By this grace dissolved in place

What is this face, less clear and clearer
The pulse in the arm, less strong and stronger—
Given or lent? more distant than stars and nearer than the eye

Whispers and small laughter between leaves and hurrying feet
Under sleep, where all the waters meet.

Bowsprit cracked with ice and paint cracked with heat.
I made this, I have forgotten
And remember.
The rigging weak and the canvas rotten
Between one June and another September.
Made this unknowing, half conscious, unknown, my own.
The garboard strake leaks, the seams need caulking.
This form, this face, this life
Living to live in a world of time beyond me; let me
Resign my life for this life, my speech for that unspoken,
The awakened, lips parted, the hope, the new ships.

What seas what shores what granite islands towards my timbers
And woodthrush calling through the fog
My daughter.

[1] In Seneca's play, *Hercules Furens*, Hercules awakens to the awful realization that, in a crazed mood and unknowingly, he has killed his own children.

LANDSCAPES

I. NEW HAMPSHIRE

Children's voices in the orchard
Between the blossom- and the fruit-time:
Golden head, crimson head,
Between the green tip and the root.
Black wing, brown wing, hover over;
Twenty years and the spring is over;
To-day grieves, to-morrow grieves,
Cover me over, light-in-leaves;
Golden head, black wing,
Cling, swing,
Spring, sing,
Swing up into the apple-tree.

II. VIRGINIA

Red river, red river,
Slow flow heat is silence
No will is still as a river
Still. Will heat move
Only through the mocking-bird
Heard once? Still hills
Wait. Gates wait. Purple trees,
White trees, wait, wait,
Delay, decay. Living, living,
Never moving. Ever moving
Iron thoughts came with me
And go with me:
Red river, river, river.

III. USK

Do not suddenly break the branch, or
Hope to find
The white hart behind the white well.
Glance aside, not for lance, do not spell
Old enchantments. Let them sleep.
"Gently dip, but not too deep,"
Lift your eyes
Where the roads dip and where the roads rise
Seek only there
Where the grey light meets the green air
The hermit's chapel, the pilgrim's prayer.

JOURNEY OF THE MAGI

This is one of the *Ariel Poems*, 1931. It is, in form, a monologue spoken in old age by one of the Magi (the "wise men from the East") who were guided by a star to the birthplace of Christ. The opening lines are taken almost verbatim from a sermon preached in 1622 by Bishop Lancelot Andrewes, one of the translators of the King James Bible, and the style and mood of the poem echo those of Andrewes' seventeenth-century prose.

"A cold coming we had of it,
Just the worst time of the year
For a journey, and such a long journey:
The ways deep and the weather sharp,
The very dead of winter."
And the camels galled, sore-footed, refractory,
Lying down in the melting snow.
There were times we regretted
The summer palaces on slopes, the terraces,
And the silken girls bringing sherbet.
Then the camel men cursing and grumbling
And running away, and wanting their liquor and women,
And the night-fires going out, and the lack of shelters,
And the cities hostile and the towns unfriendly
And the villages dirty and charging high prices:
A hard time we had of it.
At the end we preferred to travel all night,
Sleeping in snatches,
With the voices singing in our ears, saying
That this was all folly.

Then at dawn we came down to a temperate valley,
Wet, below the snow line, smelling of vegetation;
With a running stream and a water-mill beating the darkness,
And three trees on the low sky,
And an old white horse galloped away in the meadow.
Then we came to a tavern with vine-leaves over the lintel,
Six hands at an open door dicing for pieces of silver,
And feet kicking the empty wine-skins.
But there was no information, and so we continued
And arrived at evening, not a moment too soon
Finding the place; it was (you may say) satisfactory.

All this was a long time ago, I remember,
And I would do it again, but set down
This set down
This: were we led all that way for
Birth or Death? There was a Birth, certainly,
We had evidence and no doubt. I had seen birth and death,
But had thought they were different; this Birth was
Hard and bitter agony for us, like Death, our death.
We returned to our places, these Kingdoms,
But no longer at ease here, in the old dispensation,
With an alien people clutching their gods.
I should be glad of another death.

8. regretted, felt keenly the loss of.

BURNT NORTON

τοῦ λόγου δ'ἐόντος ξυνοῦ ζώουσιν οἱ πολλοί
ὡς ἰδίαν ἔχοντες φρόνησιν.
I. p. 77. Fr. 2.[1]

ὁδὸς ἄνω κάτω μία καὶ ὡυτή.
I. p. 89. Fr. 60.[2]

Diels: *Die Fragmente der Vorsokratiker* (Herakleitos).

This poem takes its title from the name of a Gloucestershire manor house which apparently had enduring associations for the poet. *Burnt Norton* first appeared in Eliot's *Collected Poems*, 1936. In 1943 it was republished as the first of *Four Quartets*, a group of related poems, each of which in structure and development showed analogies with musical composition. Like the other "quartets," *Burnt Norton* is a poem of religious meditation. A helpful guide into its rich imaginative world is Professor F. O. Matthiessen's statement that "The chief contrast around which Eliot constructs this poem is that between the view of time as a mere continuum, and the difficult paradoxical Christian view of how man lives 'in and out of time,' how he is immersed in the flux and yet can penetrate to the eternal by apprehending timeless existence within time and above it." (*The Achievement of T. S. Eliot*, Oxford University Press, 1947)

I

Time present and time past
Are both perhaps present in time future,
And time future contained in time past.
If all time is eternally present
All time is unredeemable.
What might have been is an abstraction
Remaining a perpetual possibility
Only in a world of speculation.
What might have been and what has been
Point to one end, which is always present.

[1] Although the Word is common to all, the majority live as if they had intelligence peculiarly their own. [2] The journey up and down is one and the same. (Heraclitus)

Footfalls echo in the memory
Down the passage which we did not take
Towards the door we never opened
Into the rose-garden. My words echo
Thus, in your mind.
But to what purpose
Disturbing the dust on a bowl of rose-leaves
I do not know.
Other echoes
Inhabit the garden. Shall we follow?
Quick, said the bird, find them, find them,
Round the corner. Through the first gate,
Into our first world, shall we follow
The deception of the thrush? Into our first world.
There they were, dignified, invisible,
Moving without pressure, over the dead leaves,
In the autumn heat, through the vibrant air,
And the bird called, in response to
The unheard music hidden in the shrubbery,
And the unseen eyebeam crossed, for the roses
Had the look of flowers that are looked at.
There they were as our guests, accepted and accepting.
So we moved, and they, in a formal pattern,
Along the empty alley, into the box circle,
To look down into the drained pool.
Dry the pool, dry concrete, brown edged,
And the pool was filled with water out of sunlight,
And the lotos rose, quietly, quietly,
The surface glittered out of heart of light,
And they were behind us, reflected in the pool.
Then a cloud passed, and the pool was empty.
Go, said the bird, for the leaves were full of children,
Hidden excitedly, containing laughter.
Go, go, go, said the bird: human kind
Cannot bear very much reality.
Time past and time future
What might have been and what has been
Point to one end, which is always present.

II[1]

Garlic and sapphires in the mud
Clot the bedded axle-tree.
The trilling wire in the blood
Sings below inveterate scars
And reconciles forgotten wars.
The dance along the artery
The circulation of the lymph
Are figured in the drift of stars
Ascend to summer in the tree
We move above the moving tree
In light upon the figured leaf
And hear upon the sodden floor
Below, the boarhound and the boar
Pursue their pattern as before
But reconciled among the stars.
At the still point of the turning world. Neither flesh nor fleshless;
Neither from nor towards; at the still point, there the dance is,
But neither arrest nor movement. And do not call it fixity.
Where past and future are gathered. Neither movement from nor towards,
Neither ascent nor decline. Except for the point, the still point,
There would be no dance, and there is only the dance.
I can only say, *there* we have been: but I cannot say where.
And I cannot say, how long, for that is to place it in time.

The inner freedom from the practical desire,
The release from action and suffering, release from the inner
And the outer compulsion, yet surrounded
By a grace of sense, a white light still and moving,
Erhebung without motion, concentration
Without elimination, both a new world
And the old made explicit, understood
In the completion of its partial ecstasy,
The resolution of its partial horror.
Yet the enchainment of past and future
Woven in the weakness of the changing body,
Protects mankind from heaven and damnation
Which flesh cannot endure.
Time past and time future
Allow but a little consciousness.
To be conscious is not to be in time
But only in time can the moment in the rose-garden,
The moment in the arbour where the rain beat,
The moment in the draughty church at smoke-fall
Be remembered; involved with past and future.
Only through time time is conquered.

III

Here is a place of disaffection

14. rose-garden. The rose-garden is a favorite symbol of Eliot's, often linked with poignant emotional experience.
[1] In her valuable study, *T. S. Eliot: The Design of his Poetry* (Scribner, 1949), Elizabeth Drew observes: "The lovely dancing lyric at the opening of the second movement is obviously based on the Heraclitean idea of the perpetual strife which resolves itself into beautiful harmony."

76. Erhebung, elevation. **93. place of disaffection.** In this section the London underground railway furnishes the foreground image for descent into the dark regions of the soul.

Time before and time after
In a dim light: neither daylight
Investing form with lucid stillness
Turning shadow into transient beauty
With slow rotation suggesting permanence
No darkness to purify the soul
Emptying the sensual with deprivation
Cleansing affection from the temporal.
Neither plenitude nor vacancy. Only a flicker
Over the strained time-ridden faces
Distracted from distraction by distraction
Filled with fancies and empty of meaning
Tumid apathy with no concentration
Men and bits of paper, whirled by the cold wind
That blows before and after time,
Wind in and out of unwholesome lungs
Time before and time after.
Eructation of unhealthy souls
Into the faded air, the torpid
Driven on the wind that sweeps the gloomy hills of London,
Hampstead and Clerkenwell, Campden and Putney,
Highgate, Primrose and Ludgate. Not here
Not here the darkness, in this twittering world.

Descend lower, descend only
Into the world of perpetual solitude,
World not world, but that which is not world,
Internal darkness, deprivation
And destitution of all property,
Desiccation of the world of sense,
Evacuation of the world of fancy,
Inoperancy of the world of spirit;
This is the one way, and the other
Is the same, not in movement
But abstention from movement; while the world moves
In appetency, on its metalled ways
Of time past and time future.

IV

Time and the bell have buried the day,
The black cloud carries the sun away.
Will the sunflower turn to us, will the clematis
Stray down, bend to us; tendril and spray
Clutch and cling?
Chill
Fingers of yew be curled
Down on us? After the kingfisher's wing
Has answered light to light, and is silent, the light is still
At the still point of the turning world.

V

Words move, music moves
Only in time; but that which is only living
Can only die. Words, after speech, reach
Into the silence. Only by the form, the pattern,
Can words or music reach
The stillness, as a Chinese jar still
Moves perpetually in its stillness.
Not the stillness of the violin, while the note lasts,
Not that only, but the co-existence,
Or say that the end precedes the beginning,
And the end and the beginning were always there
Before the beginning and after the end.
And all is always now. Words strain,
Crack and sometimes break, under the burden,
Under the tension, slip, slide, perish,
Decay with imprecision, will not stay in place,
Will not stay still. Shrieking voices
Scolding, mocking, or merely chattering,
Always assail them. The Word in the desert
Is most attacked by voices of temptation,
The crying shadow in the funeral dance,
The loud lament of the disconsolate chimera.

The detail of the pattern is movement,
As in the figure of the ten stairs.
Desire itself is movement
Not in itself desirable;
Love is itself unmoving,
Only the cause and end of movement,
Timeless, and undesiring
Except in the aspect of time
Caught in the form of limitation
Between un-being and being.
Sudden in a shaft of sunlight
Even while the dust moves
There rises the hidden laughter
Of children in the foliage
Quick now, here, now, always—
Ridiculous the waste sad time
Stretching before and after.

130–39. "The images are handled with the utmost tact as symbols of divine gifts which may be bestowed—but it is not in our power to draw them towards us." (Raymond Preston, *'Four Quartets' Rehearsed*, Sheed and Ward, 1947.)

163. ten stairs. The sixteenth-century Spanish mystic, St. John of the Cross, described the discipline of purgative contemplation as a ladder of ten stairs, which the soul continually ascends and descends until, perfected, it becomes united with God.

Katherine Mansfield
1888–1923

Katherine Mansfield was born Kathleen Beauchamp near Wellington, New Zealand, on October 14, 1888. Third daughter of an eminent banker, Sir Harold Beauchamp, she was brought up in more than ordinary comfort. (Several charming episodes of her New Zealand childhood are recorded in *The Scrapbook of Katherine Mansfield*, 1940, which her husband published sixteen years after her death.) Even before she reached her teens, it was apparent that she would be a writer; her first story appeared in the magazine of Wellington Girls' College when she was nine. A little later she "published" a school magazine which she wrote out in longhand. Between her fourteenth and eighteenth years she was in England, where she attended Queen's College and edited the college paper. She returned to New Zealand in 1906 and, adopting the pseudonym by which she became known, contributed a series of articles to *The Native Companion*. But she was not happy. The hypersensitivity and restlessness which grew with the years was already taking possession of her. An inadequate allowance from her father increased her sense of lack; she craved isolation and dreaded it; she wanted opposites with stubborn intensity.

In her twentieth year she was allowed to return to England. But she would not stay in London. An excellent amateur musician, she joined a traveling opera company. But the hardships of "the road" were too much for her. The first of her breakdowns occurred, and, from that time on, she struggled between physical and mental distress, between actual illness and brooding neuroticism. She went to Germany for her health, and there she wrote "In a German Pension," which was printed by A. R. Orage in *The New Age*, 1911. Through Orage she met J. Middleton Murry, with whom she became associated on a literary review entitled *Rhythm*. Two years later (in 1913) she and Murry were married. With him and D. H. Lawrence she founded *Signature*, to which she made many contributions under a new pseudonym: "Matilda Berry."

By this time she was working under great stress. World War I intensified her nervous fears; she continually diagnosed herself for heart disease; the death of her brother at the front almost killed her, and she lived, she said, to write and justify him. Her *Journal* declared:

"I want to write about my own country till I simply exhaust my store. Not only because it is a 'sacred debt' that I pay to my country because my brother and I were born there, but also because in my thoughts I range with him over all the remembered places."

She wandered unhappily about Europe, coughing and changing one unpleasant lodging for another. She identified herself with two literary fellow sufferers, Chekhov and Keats, both of them tubercular, and, "reading between the lines" of their letters, she found affinities of thought and a conviction of doom. She fluctuated between England and France, finding peace nowhere. She was lonely, disillusioned in love, full of dread. She became overobservant and, in consequence, overwrought. She felt lost without Murry, and she was miserable with him.

"A day passed in the usual violent agitation such as J. only can fling me into. . . . At such times I feel I could never get well with him. It's like having a cannon-ball tied to one's feet when one is trying not to drown."

She retreated to Bandol, the Riviera, Italy, Switzerland, all to no avail. From Orage she learned of a place where her illness might be cured by "spiritual discipline." She attempted a kind of regeneration at the "brotherhood" in France, a final effort to purge herself of "the last trace of earthly degradation." She wanted to win back health in every sense—"to be rooted in life; to learn, to desire, to know, to feel, to think, to act." Here, at this combination of school and nursing home, following a way of life prescribed by Gurdjeff, she became calmer, but her physical condition grew worse. Her already wasted energy suddenly deserted her. She died of a violent hemorrhage January 9, 1923, at Fontainebleau.

The posthumous *Journal of Katherine Mansfield*, 1927, and *Letters of Katherine Mansfield*, 1928, both of which were edited by J. Middleton Murry, betray the sick woman whose illness exaggerated her intuitive state and intensified overwrought sensibilities. But they also reveal the tenderness and poignance which made her so sensitive. Hers was an understanding spirit, delicate, keen, seemingly detached and deeply emotional. She knew "the moment of direct feeling when we are most ourselves and least personal."

The person and the author were inseparable. She had a passion for perfection and destroyed much of her work, including the records of several years in "huge complaining diaries." Like her spirit, her work was frail but exquisite. She understood her limitations, but she was not inhibited by them. Following Chekhov, her greatest influence, she aimed at a literature which would be "an initiation into truth."

Almost all of Katherine Mansfield's work shows this dedication to truth in the smallest details of phrase and gesture. One remembers the evocations of mood and "atmosphere," the sharp stroke of characterization, rather than the narratives, in *Bliss*, 1920; *The Garden Party*, 1922; *The Doves' Nest*, 1923. Nowhere is her subtlety more skillfully employed than in "The Daughters of the Late Colonel." Here neurotic reality is achieved by fine nuances of implications, by the very blurring of the actual event and the train of memories it sets in motion. By suggestion and flashes into the past—flashes that are unprepared but perfectly convincing—a series of lives are revealed: the fluttering sisters living on frustrated dreams and genteel poverty; Kate, the domestic dragon, whom they dare not discharge; Nurse Andrews, whose affectations "point" the scene and whose concern with the butter emphasizes the situation; Cyril, the grandson, whose embarrassed casualness contrasts with the painful ceremoniousness of his worried aunts; and the old Colonel who, even in death, irascibly dominates them all. A tragicomic novel has been condensed into significant episodes and expressed in states of poignant sensibility.

Katherine Mansfield died prematurely at thirty-four; but she was not defeated. The woman struggled and lost; the artist survived. Her intensity triumphed in a few books which startle the reader with their swift illuminations. Her work as a writer, summarized Louis Kronenberger, "was an endless stalking of feelings, perceptions, language; it revealed—whatever its limitations, either in impulse or achievement—that amoral integrity which is the peculiar mark of the artist." [1]

[1] "Katherine Mansfield, a Review," *Nation*, Feb. 10, 1940.

THE DAUGHTERS OF THE LATE COLONEL [1]

I

THE week after was one of the busiest weeks of their lives. Even when they went to bed it was only their bodies that lay down and rested; their minds went on, thinking things out, talking things over, wondering, deciding, trying to remember where . . .

Constantia lay like a statue, her hands by her sides, her feet just overlapping each other, the sheet up to her chin. She stared at the ceiling.

"Do you think father would mind if we gave his top-hat to the porter?"

"The porter?" snapped Josephine. "Why ever the porter? What a very extraordinary idea!"

"Because," said Constantia slowly, "he must often have to go to funerals. And I noticed at—at the cemetery that he only had a bowler." She paused. "I thought then how very much he'd appreciate a top-hat. We ought to give him a present, too. He was always very nice to father."

"But," cried Josephine, flouncing on her pillow and staring across the dark at Constantia, "father's head!" And suddenly, for one awful moment, she nearly giggled. Not, of course, that she felt in the least like giggling. It must have been habit. Years ago, when they had stayed awake at night talking, their beds had simply heaved. And now the porter's head, disappearing, popped out, like a candle, under father's hat. . . . The giggle mounted, mounted; she clenched her hands; she fought it down; she frowned fiercely at the dark and said "Remember" terribly sternly.

"We can decide to-morrow," she sighed.

Constantia had noticed nothing; she sighed.

"Do you think we ought to have our dressing-gowns dyed as well?"

"Black?" almost shrieked Josephine.

"Well, what else?" said Constantia. "I was thinking—it doesn't seem quite sincere, in a way, to wear black out of doors and when we're fully dressed, and then when we're at home——"

"But nobody sees us," said Josephine. She gave the bedclothes such a twitch that both her feet became uncovered, and she had to creep up the pillows to get them well under again.

"Kate does," said Constantia. "And the postman very well might."

Josephine thought of her dark-red slippers, which

[1] From *The Garden Party* by Katherine Mansfield, copyright, 1922, by Alfred A. Knopf, Inc.

matched her dressing-gown, and of Constantia's favourite indefinite green ones which went with hers. Black! Two black dressing-gowns and two pairs of black woolly slippers, creeping off to the bathroom like black cats.

"I don't think it's absolutely necessary," said she.

Silence. Then Constantia said, "We shall have to post the papers with the notice in them to-morrow to catch the Ceylon mail. . . . How many letters have we had up till now?"

"Twenty-three."

Josephine had replied to them all, and twenty-three times when she came to "We miss our dear father so much" she had broken down and had to use her handkerchief, and on some of them even to soak up a very light-blue tear with an edge of blotting-paper. Strange! She couldn't have put it on—but twenty-three times. Even now, though, when she said over to herself sadly, "We miss our dear father *so* much" she could have cried if she'd wanted to.

"Have you got enough stamps?" came from Constantia.

"Oh, how can I tell?" said Josephine crossly. "What's the good of asking me that now?"

"I was just wondering," said Constantia mildly.

Silence again. There came a little rustle, a scurry, a hop.

"A mouse," said Constantia.

"It can't be a mouse because there aren't any crumbs," said Josephine.

"But it doesn't know there aren't," said Constantia.

A spasm of pity squeezed her heart. Poor little thing! She wished she'd left a tiny piece of biscuit on the dressing-table. It was awful to think of it not finding anything. What would it do?

"I can't think how they manage to live at all," she said slowly.

"Who?" demanded Josephine.

And Constantia said more loudly than she meant to, "Mice."

Josephine was furious. "Oh, what nonsense, Con!" she said. "What have mice got to do with it? You're asleep."

"I don't think I am," said Constantia. She shut her eyes to make sure. She was.

Josephine arched her spine, pulled up her knees, folded her arms so that her fists came under her ears, and pressed her cheek hard against the pillow.

2

Another thing which complicated matters was they had Nurse Andrews staying on with them that week. It was their own fault; they had asked her. It was Josephine's idea. On the morning—well, on the last morning, when the doctor had gone, Josephine had said to Constantia, "Don't you think it would be rather nice if we asked Nurse Andrews to stay on for a week as our guest?"

"Very nice," said Constantia.

"I thought," went on Josephine quickly, "I should just say this afternoon, after I've paid her, 'My sister and I would be very pleased, after all you've done for us, Nurse Andrews, if you would stay on for a week as our guest.' I'd have to put that in about being our guest in case——"

"Oh, but she could hardly expect to be paid!" cried Constantia.

"One never knows," said Josephine sagely.

Nurse Andrews had, of course, jumped at the idea. But it was a bother. It meant they had to have regular sit-down meals at the proper times, whereas if they'd been alone they could just have asked Kate if she wouldn't have minded bringing them a tray wherever they were. And meal-times now that the strain was over were rather a trial.

Nurse Andrews was simply fearful about butter. Really they couldn't help feeling that about butter, at least, she took advantage of their kindness. And she had that maddening habit of asking for just an inch more bread to finish what she had on her plate, and then, at the last mouthful, absent-mindedly—of course it wasn't absent-mindedly—taking another helping. Josephine got very red when this happened, and she fastened her small, bead-like eyes on the tablecloth as if she saw a minute strange insect creeping through the web of it. But Constantia's long, pale face lengthened and set, and she gazed away—away—far over the desert, to where that line of camels unwound like a thread of wool. . . .

"When I was with Lady Tukes," said Nurse Andrews, "she had such a dainty little contrayvance for the buttah. It was a silvah Cupid balanced on the—on the bordah of a glass dish, holding a tayny fork. And when you wanted some buttah you simply pressed his foot and he bent down and speared you a piece. It was quite a gayme."

Josephine could hardly bear that. But "I think those things are very extravagant" was all she said.

"But whey?" asked Nurse Andrews, beaming through her eyeglasses. "No one, surely, would take more buttah than one wanted—would one?"

"Ring, Con," cried Josephine. She couldn't trust herself to reply.

And proud young Kate, the enchanted princess, came in to see what the old tabbies wanted now. She snatched away their plates of mock something or other and slapped down a white, terrified blanc-mange.

"Jam, please, Kate," said Josephine kindly.

Kate knelt and burst open the sideboard, lifted the lid of the jam-pot, saw it was empty, put it on the table, and stalked off.

"I'm afraid," said Nurse Andrews a moment later, "there isn't any."

"Oh, what a bother!" said Josephine. She bit her lip. "What had we better do?"

Constantia looked dubious. "We can't disturb Kate again," she said softly.

Nurse Andrews waited, smiling at them both. Her eyes wandered, spying at everything behind her eye-glasses. Constantia in despair went back to her camels. Josephine frowned heavily—concentrated. If it hadn't been for this idiotic woman she and Con would, of course, have eaten their blanc-mange without. Suddenly the idea came.

"I know," she said. "Marmalade. There's some marmalade in the sideboard. Get it, Con."

"I hope," laughed Nurse Andrews, and her laugh was like a spoon tinkling against a medicine-glass—"I hope it's not very bittah marmalayde."

3

But, after all, it was not long now, and then she'd be gone for good. And there was no getting over the fact that she had been very kind to father. She had nursed him day and night at the end. Indeed, both Constantia and Josephine felt privately she had rather overdone the not leaving him at the very last. For when they had gone in to say good-bye Nurse Andrews had sat beside his bed the whole time, holding his wrist and pretending to look at her watch. It couldn't have been necessary. It was so tactless, too. Supposing father had wanted to say something—something private to them. Not that he had. Oh, far from it! He lay there, purple, a dark, angry purple in the face, and never even looked at them when they came in. Then, as they were standing there, wondering what to do, he had suddenly opened one eye. Oh, what a difference it would have made, what a difference to their memory of him, how much easier to tell people about it, if he had only opened both! But no—one eye only. It glared at them a moment and then . . . went out.

4

It had made it very awkward for them when Mr. Farolles, of St. John's, called the same afternoon.

"The end was quite peaceful, I trust?" were the first words he said as he glided towards them through the dark drawing-room.

"Quite," said Josephine faintly. They both hung their heads. Both of them felt certain that eye wasn't at all a peaceful eye.

"Won't you sit down?" said Josephine.

"Thank you, Miss Pinner," said Mr. Farolles gratefully. He folded his coat-tails and began to lower himself into father's arm-chair, but just as he touched it he almost sprang up and slid into the next chair instead.

He coughed. Josephine clasped her hands; Constantia looked vague.

"I want you to feel, Miss Pinner," said Mr. Farolles, "and you, Miss Constantia, that I'm trying to be helpful. I want to be helpful to you both, if you will let me. These are the times," said Mr. Farolles, very simply and earnestly, "when God means us to be helpful to one another."

"Thank you very much, Mr. Farolles," said Josephine and Constantia.

"Not at all," said Mr. Farolles gently. He drew his kid gloves through his fingers and leaned forward. "And if either of you would like a little Communion, either or both of you, here *and* now, you have only to tell me. A little Communion is often very help—a great comfort," he added tenderly.

But the idea of a little Communion terrified them. What! In the drawing-room by themselves—with no—no altar or anything! The piano would be much too high, thought Constantia, and Mr. Farolles could not possibly lean over it with the chalice. And Kate would be sure to come bursting in and interrupt them, thought Josephine. And supposing the bell rang in the middle? It might be somebody important—about their mourning. Would they get up reverently and go out, or would they have to wait . . . in torture?

"Perhaps you will send round a note by your good Kate if you would care for it later," said Mr. Farolles.

"Oh yes, thank you very much!" they both said.

Mr. Farolles got up and took his black straw hat from the round table.

"And about the funeral," he said softly. "I may arrange that—as your dear father's old friend and yours, Miss Pinner—and Miss Constantia?"

Josephine and Constantia got up too.

"I should like it to be quite simple," said Josephine firmly, "and not too expensive. At the same time, I should like——"

"A good one that will last," thought dreamy Constantia, as if Josephine were buying a nightgown. But of course Josephine didn't say that. "One suitable to our father's position." She was very nervous.

"I'll run round to our good friend Mr. Knight," said Mr. Farolles soothingly. "I will ask him to come and see you. I am sure you will find him very helpful indeed."

5

Well, at any rate, all that part of it was over, though neither of them could possibly believe that father was never coming back. Josephine had had a moment of absolute terror at the cemetery, while the coffin was lowered, to think that she and Constantia had done this thing without asking his permission. What would father say when he found out? For he was bound to find out sooner or later. He always did. "Buried. You two girls had me *buried!*" She heard his stick thumping. Oh, what would they say? What possible excuse could they make? It sounded such an appallingly heartless thing to do. Such a wicked advantage to take of a person because he happened to be helpless at the moment. The other people seemed to treat it all as a matter of course. They were strangers; they couldn't be expected to understand that father was the very last person for such a thing to happen to. No, the entire blame for it all would fall on her and Constantia. And the expense, she thought, stepping into the tight-buttoned cab. When she had to show him the bills. What would he say then?

She heard him absolutely roaring, "And do you expect me to pay for this gimcrack excursion of yours?"

"Oh," groaned poor Josephine aloud, "we shouldn't have done it, Con!"

And Constantia, pale as a lemon in all that blackness, said in a frightened whisper, "Done what, Jug?"

"Let them bu-bury father like that," said Josephine, breaking down and crying into her new, queer-smelling mourning handkerchief.

"But what else could we have done?" asked Constantia wonderingly. "We couldn't have kept him, Jug—we couldn't have kept him unburied. At any rate, not in a flat that size."

Josephine blew her nose; the cab was dreadfully stuffy.

"I don't know," she said forlornly. "It is all so dreadful. I feel we ought to have tried to, just for a time at least. To make perfectly sure. One thing's certain"—and her tears sprang out again—"father will never forgive us for this—never!"

6

Father would never forgive them. That was what they felt more than ever when, two mornings later, they went into his room to go through his things. They had discussed it quite calmly. It was even down on Josephine's list of things to be done. *Go through father's things and settle about them.* But that was a very different matter from saying after breakfast:

"Well, are you ready, Con?"

"Yes, Jug—when you are."

"Then I think we'd better get it over."

It was dark in the hall. It had been a rule for years never to disturb father in the morning, whatever happened. And now they were going to open the door without knocking even. . . . Constantia's eyes were enormous at the idea; Josephine felt weak in the knees.

"You—you go first," she gasped, pushing Constantia.

But Constantia said, as she always had said on those occasions, "No, Jug, that's not fair. You're eldest."

Josephine was just going to say—what at other times she wouldn't have owned to for the world—what she kept for her very last weapon, "But you're tallest," when they noticed that the kitchen door was open, and there stood Kate. . . .

"Very stiff," said Josephine, grasping the door-handle and doing her best to turn it. As if anything ever deceived Kate!

It couldn't be helped. That girl was . . . Then the door was shut behind them, but—but they weren't in father's room at all. They might have suddenly walked through the wall by mistake into a different flat altogether. Was the door just behind them? They were too frightened to look. Josephine knew that if it was it was holding itself tight shut. Constantia felt that, like the doors in dreams, it hadn't any handle at all. It was the coldness which made it so awful. Or the whiteness—which? Everything was covered. The blinds were down, a cloth hung over the mirror, a sheet hid the bed; a huge fan of white paper filled the fireplace. Constantia timidly put out her hand; she almost expected a snowflake to fall. Josephine felt a queer tingling in her nose, as if her nose was freezing. Then a cab klop-klopped over the cobbles below, and the quiet seemed to shake into little pieces.

"I had better pull up a blind," said Josephine bravely.

"Yes, it might be a good idea," whispered Constantia.

They only gave the blind a touch, but it flew up

and the cord flew after, rolling round the blind-stick, and the little tassel tapped as if trying to get free. That was too much for Constantia.

"Don't you think—don't you think we might put it off for another day?" she whispered.

"Why?" snapped Josephine, feeling, as usual, much better now that she knew for certain that Constantia was terrified. "It's got to be done. But I do wish you wouldn't whisper, Con."

"I didn't know I was whispering," whispered Constantia.

"And why do you keep on staring at the bed?" said Josephine, raising her voice almost defiantly.

"Oh, Jug, don't say so!" said poor Connie. "At any rate, not so loudly."

Josephine felt herself that she had gone too far. She took a wide swerve over to the chest of drawers, put out her hand, but quickly drew it back again.

"Connie!" she gasped, and she wheeled round and leaned with her back against the chest of drawers.

"Oh, Jug—what?"

Josephine could only glare. She had the most extraordinary feeling that she had just escaped something simply awful. But how could she explain to Constantia that father was in the chest of drawers? He was in the top drawer with his handkerchiefs and neckties, or in the next with his shirts and pyjamas, or in the lowest of all with his suits. He was watching there, hidden away—just behind the door-handle—ready to spring.

She pulled a funny old-fashioned face at Constantia, just as she used to in the old days when she was going to cry.

"I can't open," she nearly wailed.

"No, don't, Jug," whispered Constantia earnestly. "It's much better not to. Don't let's open anything. At any rate, not for a long time."

"But—but it seems so weak," said Josephine, breaking down.

"But why not be weak for once, Jug?" argued Constantia, whispering quite fiercely. "If it is weak." And her pale stare flew from the locked writing-table—so safe—to the huge glittering wardrobe, and she began to breathe in a queer, panting way. "Why shouldn't we be weak for once in our lives, Jug? It's quite excusable. Let's be weak—be weak, Jug. It's much nicer to be weak than to be strong."

And then she did one of those amazingly bold things that she'd done about twice before in their lives; she marched over to the wardrobe, turned the key, and took it out of the lock. Took it out of the lock and held it up to Josephine, showing Josephine by her extraordinary smile that she knew what she'd done, she'd risked deliberately father being in there among his overcoats.

If the huge wardrobe had lurched forward, had crashed down on Constantia, Josephine wouldn't have been surprised. On the contrary, she would have thought it the only suitable thing to happen. But nothing happened. Only the room seemed quieter than ever, and bigger flakes of cold air fell on Josephine's shoulders and knees. She began to shiver.

"Come, Jug," said Constantia, still with that awful callous smile, and Josephine followed just as she had that last time, when Constantia had pushed Benny into the round pond.

7

But the strain told on them when they were back in the dining-room. They sat down, very shaky, and looked at each other.

"I don't feel I can settle to anything," said Josephine, "until I've had something. Do you think we could ask Kate for two cups of hot water?"

"I really don't see why we shouldn't," said Constantia carefully. She was quite normal again. "I won't ring. I'll go to the kitchen door and ask her."

"Yes, do," said Josephine, sinking down into a chair. "Tell her, just two cups, Con, nothing else—on a tray."

"She needn't even put the jug on, need she?" said Constantia, as though Kate might very well complain if the jug had been there.

"Oh no, certainly not! The jug's not at all necessary. She can pour it direct out of the kettle," cried Josephine, feeling that would be a labour-saving indeed.

Their cold lips quivered at the greenish brims. Josephine curved her small red hands round the cup; Constantia sat up and blew on the wavy stream, making it flutter from one side to the other.

"Speaking of Benny," said Josephine.

And though Benny hadn't been mentioned Constantia immediately looked as though he had.

"He'll expect us to send him something of father's, of course. But it's so difficult to know what to send to Ceylon."

"You mean things get unstuck so on the voyage," murmured Constantia.

"No, lost," said Josephine sharply. "You know there's no post. Only runners."

Both paused to watch a black man in white linen drawers running through the pale fields for dear life, with a large brown-paper parcel in his hands. Josephine's black man was tiny; he scurried along glistening like an ant. But there was something blind and tireless about Constantia's tall, thin fellow, which made him, she decided, a very unpleasant person indeed. . . . On the veranda, dressed all in white and wearing a cork helmet, stood Benny. His right hand shook up and down, as father's did when he was impatient. And behind him, not in the least interested, sat Hilda, the unknown sister-in-law. She swung in a cane rocker and flicked over the leaves of the *Tatler*.

"I think his watch would be the most suitable present," said Josephine.

Constantia looked up; she seemed surprised.

"Oh, would you trust a gold watch to a native?"

"But of course I'd disguise it," said Josephine. "No one would know it was a watch." She liked the idea of having to make a parcel such a curious shape that no one could possibly guess what it was. She even thought for a moment of hiding the watch in a narrow cardboard corset-box that she'd kept by her for a long time, waiting for it to come in for something. It was such beautiful firm cardboard. But, no, it wouldn't be appropriate for this occasion. It had lettering on it: *Medium Women's 28. Extra Firm Busks.* It would be almost too much of a surprise for Benny to open that and find father's watch inside.

"And of course it isn't as though it would be going—ticking, I mean," said Constantia, who was still thinking of the native love of jewellery. "At least," she added, "it would be very strange if after all that time it was."

8

Josephine made no reply. She had flown off on one of her tangents. She had suddenly thought of Cyril. Wasn't it more usual for the only grandson to have the watch? And then dear Cyril was so appreciative, and a gold watch meant so much to a young man. Benny, in all probability, had quite got out of the habit of watches; men so seldom wore waistcoats in those hot climates. Whereas Cyril in London wore them from year's end to year's end. And it would be so nice for her and Constantia, when he came to tea, to know it was there. "I see you've got on grandfather's watch, Cyril." It would be somehow so satisfactory.

Dear boy! What a blow his sweet, sympathetic little note had been! Of course they quite understood; but it was most unfortunate.

"It would have been such a point, having him," said Josephine.

"And he would have enjoyed it so," said Constantia, not thinking what she was saying.

However, as soon as he got back he was coming to tea with his aunties. Cyril to tea was one of their rare treats.

"Now, Cyril, you mustn't be frightened of our cakes. Your Auntie Con and I bought them at Buszard's this morning. We know what a man's appetite is. So don't be ashamed of making a good tea."

Josephine cut recklessly into the rich dark cake that stood for her winter gloves or the soling and heeling of Constantia's only respectable shoes. But Cyril was most unmanlike in appetite.

"I say, Aunt Josephine, I simply can't. I've only just had lunch, you know."

"Oh, Cyril, that can't be true! It's after four," cried Josephine. Constantia sat with her knife poised over the chocolate-roll.

"It is, all the same," said Cyril. "I had to meet a man at Victoria, and he kept me hanging about till . . . there was only time to get lunch and to come on here. And he gave me—phew"—Cyril put his hand to his forehead—"a terrific blow-out," he said.

It was disappointing—to-day of all days. But still he couldn't be expected to know.

"But you'll have a meringue, won't you, Cyril?" said Aunt Josephine. "These meringues were bought specially for you. Your dear father was so fond of them. We were sure you are, too."

"I *am*, Aunt Josephine," cried Cyril ardently. "Do you mind if I take half to begin with?"

"Not at all, dear boy; but we mustn't let you off with that."

"Is your dear father still so fond of meringues?" asked Auntie Con gently. She winced faintly as she broke through the shell of hers.

"Well, I don't quite know, Auntie Con," said Cyril breezily.

At that they both looked up.

"Don't know?" almost snapped Josephine. "Don't know a thing like that about your own father, Cyril?"

"Surely," said Aunty Con softly.

Cyril tried to laugh it off. "Oh, well," he said, "it's such a long time since——" He faltered. He stopped. Their faces were too much for him.

"Even *so*," said Josephine.

And Auntie Con looked.

Cyril put down his teacup. "Wait a bit," he cried. "Wait a bit, Aunt Josephine. What am I thinking of?"

He looked up. They were beginning to brighten. Cyril slapped his knee.

"Of course," he said, "it was meringues. How

18. Victoria, one of the chief railroad stations of London.

could I have forgotten? Yes, Aunt Josephine, you're perfectly right. Father's most frightfully keen on meringues."

They didn't only beam. Aunt Josephine went scarlet with pleasure; Auntie Con gave a deep, deep sigh.

"And now, Cyril, you must come and see father," said Josephine. "He knows you were coming to-day."

"Right," said Cyril, very firmly and heartily. He got up from his chair; suddenly he glanced at the clock.

"I say, Auntie Con, isn't your clock a bit slow? I've got to meet a man at—at Paddington just after five. I'm afraid I shan't be able to stay very long with grandfather."

"Oh, he won't expect you to stay *very* long!" said Aunt Josephine.

Constantia was still gazing at the clock. She couldn't make up her mind if it was fast or slow. It was one or the other, she felt almost certain of that. At any rate, it had been.

Cyril still lingered. "Aren't you coming along, Auntie Con?"

"Of course," said Josephine, "we shall all go. Come on, Con."

9

They knocked at the door, and Cyril followed his aunts into grandfather's hot, sweetish room.

"Come on," said Grandfather Pinner. "Don't hang about. What is it? What've you been up to?"

He was sitting in front of a roaring fire, clasping his stick. He had a thick rug over his knees. On his lap there lay a beautiful pale yellow silk handkerchief.

"It's Cyril, father," said Josephine shyly. And she took Cyril's hand and led him forward.

"Good afternoon, grandfather," said Cyril, trying to take his hand out of Aunt Josephine's. Grandfather Pinner shot his eyes at Cyril in the way he was famous for. Where was Auntie Con? She stood on the other side of Aunt Josephine; her long arms hung down in front of her; her hands were clasped. She never took her eyes off grandfather.

"Well," said Grandfather Pinner, beginning to thump, "what have you got to tell me?"

What had he, what had he got to tell him? Cyril felt himself smiling like a perfect imbecile. The room was stifling, too.

But Aunt Josephine came to his rescue. She cried brightly, "Cyril says his father is still very fond of meringues, father dear."

"Eh?" said Grandfather Pinner, curving his hand like a purple meringue-shell over one ear.

Josephine repeated, "Cyril says his father is still very fond of meringues."

"Can't hear," said old Colonel Pinner. And he waved Josephine away with his stick, then pointed with his stick to Cyril. "Tell me what she's trying to say," he said.

(My God!) "Must I?" said Cyril, blushing and staring at Aunt Josephine.

"Do, dear," she smiled. "It will please him so much."

"Come on, out with it!" cried Colonel Pinner testily, beginning to thump again.

And Cyril leaned forward and yelled, "Father's still very fond of meringues."

At that Grandfather Pinner jumped as though he had been shot.

"Don't shout!" he cried. "What's the matter with the boy? *Meringues!* What about 'em?"

"Oh, Aunt Josephine, must we go on?" groaned Cyril desperately.

"It's quite all right, dear boy," said Aunt Josephine, as though he and she were at the dentist's together. "He'll understand in a minute." And she whispered to Cyril, "He's getting a bit deaf, you know." Then she leaned forward and really bawled at Grandfather Pinner, "Cyril only wanted to tell you, father dear, that *his* father is still very fond of meringues."

Colonel Pinner heard that time, heard and brooded, looking Cyril up and down.

"What an esstrordinary thing!" said old Grandfather Pinner. "What an esstrordinary thing to come all this way here to tell me!"

And Cyril felt it *was*.

"Yes, I shall send Cyril the watch," said Josephine.

"That would be very nice," said Constantia. "I seem to remember last time he came there was some little trouble about the time."

10

They were interrupted by Kate bursting through the door in her usual fashion, as though she had discovered some secret panel in the wall.

"Fried or boiled?" asked the bold voice.

Fried or boiled? Josephine and Constantia were quite bewildered for the moment. They could hardly take it in.

"Fried or boiled what, Kate?" asked Josephine, trying to begin to concentrate.

Kate gave a loud sniff. "Fish."

"Well, why didn't you say so immediately?" Josephine reproached her gently. "How could you expect us to understand, Kate? There are a great many things in this world, you know, which are fried or boiled." And after such a display of courage she said quite brightly to Constantia, "Which do you prefer, Con?"

"I think it might be nice to have it fried," said Constantia. "On the other hand, of course boiled fish is very nice. I think I prefer both equally well . . . Unless you . . . In that case——"

"I shall fry it," said Kate, and she bounced back, leaving their door open and slamming the door of her kitchen.

Josephine gazed at Constantia; she raised her pale eyebrows until they rippled away into her pale hair. She got up. She said in a very lofty, imposing way, "Do you mind following me into the drawing-room, Constantia? I've something of great importance to discuss with you."

For it was always to the drawing-room they retired when they wanted to talk over Kate.

Josephine closed the door meaningly. "Sit down, Constantia," she said, still very grand. She might have been receiving Constantia for the first time. And Con looked round vaguely for a chair, as though she felt indeed quite a stranger.

"Now the question is," said Josephine, bending forward, "whether we shall keep her or not."

"That is the question," agreed Constantia.

"And this time," said Josephine firmly, "we must come to a definite decision."

Constantia looked for a moment as though she might begin going over all the other times, but she pulled herself together and said, "Yes, Jug."

"You see, Con," explained Josephine, "everything is so changed now." Constantia looked up quickly. "I mean," went on Josephine, "we're not dependent on Kate as we were." And she blushed faintly. "There's not father to cook for."

"That is perfectly true," agreed Constantia. "Father certainly doesn't want any cooking now, whatever else——"

Josephine broke in sharply, "You're not sleepy, are you, Con?"

"Sleepy, Jug?" Constantia was wide-eyed.

"Well, concentrate more," said Josephine sharply, and she returned to the subject. "What it comes to is, if we did"—and this she barely breathed, glancing at the door—"give Kate notice"—she raised her voice again—"we could manage our own food."

"Why not?" cried Constantia. She couldn't help smiling. The idea was so exciting. She clasped her hands. "What should we live on, Jug?"

"Oh, eggs in various forms!" said Jug, lofty again. "And, besides, there are all the cooked foods."

"But I've always heard," said Constantia, "they are considered so very expensive."

"Not if one buys them in moderation," said Josephine. But she tore herself away from this fascinating bypath and dragged Constantia after her.

"What we've got to decide now, however, is whether we really do trust Kate or not."

Constantia leaned back. Her flat little laugh flew from her lips.

"Isn't it curious, Jug," said she, "that just on this one subject I've never been able to quite make up my mind?"

II

She never had. The whole difficulty was to prove anything. How did one prove things, how could one? Suppose Kate had stood in front of her and deliberately made a face. Mightn't she very well have been in pain? Wasn't it impossible, at any rate, to ask Kate if she was making a face at her? If Kate answered "No"—and of course she would say "No"—what a position! How undignified! Then again Constantia suspected, she was almost certain that Kate went to her chest of drawers when she and Josephine were out, not to take things but to spy. Many times she had come back to find her amethyst cross in the most unlikely places, under her lace ties or on top of her evening Bertha. More than once she had laid a trap for Kate. She had arranged things in a special order and then called Josephine to witness.

"You see, Jug?"

"Quite, Con."

"Now we shall be able to tell."

But, oh dear, when she did go to look, she was as far off from a proof as ever! If anything was displaced, it might so very well have happened as she closed the drawer; a jolt might have done it so easily.

"You come, Jug, and decide. I really can't. It's too difficult."

But after a pause and a long glare Josephine would sigh, "Now you've put the doubt into my mind, Con, I'm sure I can't tell myself."

"Well, we can't postpone it again," said Josephine. "If we postpone it this time——"

12

But at that moment in the street below a barrel-rgan struck up. Josephine and Constantia sprang ɔ their feet together.

"Run, Con," said Josephine. "Run quickly. 'here's sixpence on the——"

Then they remembered. It didn't matter. They ʋould never have to stop the organ-grinder again. ſever again would she and Constantia be told to ıake that monkey take his noise somewhere else. 'ever would sound that loud, strange bellow when ıther thought they were not hurrying enough. The rgan-grinder might play there all day and the stick 'ould not thump.

It never will thump again,
It never will thump again,

layed the barrel-organ.

What was Constantia thinking? She had such a range smile; she looked different. She couldn't be ɔing to cry.

"Jug, Jug," said Constantia softly, pressing her ands together. "Do you know what day it is? It's aturday. It's a week to-day, a whole week."

A week since father died,
A week since father died,

·ied the barrel-organ. And Josephine, too, forgot to ɛ practical and sensible; she smiled faintly, rangely. On the Indian carpet there fell a square sunlight, pale red; it came and went and came—ıd stayed, deepened—until it shone almost ɔlden.

"The sun's out," said Josephine, as though it ·ally mattered.

A perfect fountain of bubbling notes shook from ıe barrel-organ, round, bright notes, carelessly attered.

Constantia lifted her big, cold hands as if to catch ıem, and then her hands fell again. She walked ʋer to the mantelpiece to her favourite Buddha. nd the stone and gilt image, whose smile always ıve her such a queer feeling, almost a pain and yet pleasant pain, seemed to-day to be more than ıiling. He knew something; he had a secret. "I ıow something that you don't know," said her ıddha. Oh, what was it, what could it be? And ·t she had always felt there was . . . something.

The sunlight pressed through the windows, ıieved its way in, flashed its light over the furniture ıd the photographs. Josephine watched it. When it came to mother's photograph, the enlargement over the piano, it lingered as though puzzled to find so little remained of mother, except the earrings shaped like tiny pagodas and a black feather boa. Why did the photographs of dead people always fade so? wondered Josephine. As soon as a person was dead their photograph died too. But, of course, this one of mother was very old. It was thirty-five years old. Josephine remembered standing on a chair and pointing out that feather boa to Constantia and telling her that it was a snake that had killed their mother in Ceylon. . . . Would everything have been different if mother hadn't died? She didn't see why. Aunt Florence had lived with them until they had left school, and they had moved three times and had their yearly holiday and . . . and there'd been changes of servants, of course.

Some little sparrows, young sparrows they sounded, chirped on the window-ledge. *Yeep—eyeep—yeep*. But Josephine felt they were not sparrows, not on the window-ledge. It was inside her, that queer little crying noise. *Yeep—eyeep—yeep*. Ah, what was it crying, so weak and forlorn?

If mother had lived, might they have married? But there had been nobody for them to marry. There had been father's Anglo-Indian friends before he quarrelled with them. But after that she and Constantia never met a single man except clergymen. How did one meet men? Or even if they'd met them, how could they have got to know men well enough to be more than strangers? One read of people having adventures, being followed, and so on. But nobody had ever followed Constantia and her. Oh yes, there had been one year at Eastbourne a mysterious man at their boarding-house who had put a note on the jug of hot water outside their bedroom door! But by the time Connie had found it the steam had made the writing too faint to read; they couldn't even make out to which of them it was addressed. And he had left next day. And that was all. The rest had been looking after father, and at the same time keeping out of father's way. But now? But now? The thieving sun touched Josephine gently. She lifted her face. She was drawn over to the window by gentle beams. . . .

Until the barrel-organ stopped playing Constantia stayed before the Buddha, wondering, but not as usual, not vaguely. This time her wonder was like longing. She remembered the times she had come in here, crept out of bed in her nightgown when the moon was full, and lain on the floor with her arms outstretched, as though she was crucified. Why? The big, pale moon had made her do it. The horrible dancing figures on the carved screen had leered at her and she hadn't minded. She remembered too how, whenever they were at the seaside, she had gone off by herself and got as close to the sea as she could, and sung something, something she had made up, while she gazed all over that restless water. There had been this other life, running out, bringing things home in bags, getting things on approval, discussing them with Jug, and taking them back to get more things on approval, and arranging father's trays and trying not to annoy father. But it all seemed to have happened in a kind of tunnel. It wasn't real. It was only when she came out of the tunnel into the moonlight or by the sea or into a thunderstorm that she really felt herself. What did it mean? What was it she was always wanting? What did it all lead to? Now? Now?

She turned away from the Buddha with one of her vague gestures. She went over to where Josephine was standing. She wanted to say something to Josephine, something frightfully important, about—about the future and what . . .

"Don't you think perhaps——" she began.

But Josephine interrupted her. "I was wondering if now——" she murmured. They stopped; they waited for each other.

"Go on, Con," said Josephine.

"No, no, Jug; after you," said Constantia.

"No, say what you were going to say. You began," said Josephine.

"I . . . I'd rather hear what you were going to say first," said Constantia.

"Don't be absurd, Con."

"Really, Jug."

"Connie!"

"Oh, *Jug!*"

A pause. Then Constantia said faintly, "I can't say what I was going to say, Jug, because I've forgotten what it was . . . that I was going to say."

Josephine was silent for a moment. She stared at a big cloud where the sun had been. Then she replied shortly, "I've forgotten too."

Aldous Huxley

1894–

Aldous (Leonard) Huxley was born at Godalming on July 26, 1894. His father was the well-known writer, editor, and Greek scholar Leonard Huxley; his grandfather was the famous scientist Thomas Huxley; his great-uncle was Matthew Arnold. Yet from so rich an inheritance Aldous Huxley could find, in a new age, no support in the classicist's standard of values nor in the scientist's faith in science. Educated at Eton and at Balliol College, Oxford, Huxley intended to become a doctor, but serious trouble with his eyes prohibited the study of medicine, and, perfecting himself in touch-typing, he turned to literature.

Huxley's first publication was a book of verse, *The Burning Wheel*, 1916, and he has never quite relinquished his interest in poetic form; there have been five subsequent volumes of facile but undistinguished poetry. It was not until he was twenty-seven that Huxley devoted himself almost entirely to prose. A book of short stories, *Limbo*, 1920, and a novel, *Crome Yellow*, 1921, showed a new attitude, brilliant, erudite, and unhappy. In the thirty years between 1920 and 1950 Huxley published more than thirty-five volumes. Among the novels those which made the greatest impression are *Antic Hay*, 1923; *Point Counter Point*, 1928; *Brave New World*, 1932; and *After Many a Summer Dies the Swan*, 1940. The best of his short stories are in *Mortal Coils*, 1922, *Two or Three Graces*, 1926, and *Brief Candles*, 1930. His nonfictional prose, which some critics consider his most characteristic, includes the essays in *Proper Studies*, 1927; *Vulgarity in Literature*, 1930; *Music At Night*, 1931; and the travel pieces in *Jesting Pilate*, 1926, and *Beyond the Mexique Bay*, 1934. Huxley, who was an intimate of D. H. Lawrence, Katherine Mansfield, and J. Middleton Murry—he joined Murry on the editorial staff of the *Athenaeum*—also edited *The Letters of D. H. Lawrence*, 1932.

Ends and Means, 1937, was concerned with the problems of a society facing collapse as it drifted towards war. Huxley's later works, most of which are discussions of various aspects of mysticism, include: *Grey Eminence*, 1941, a study of religion and politics in the life of the Capuchin Friar Joseph of Paris; *Time Must Have a Stop*, 1944; *The Perennial Philosophy*, 1945, an anthology, with explanatory comments, of sacred writings, chiefly from Eastern sources; *Science, Liberty, and Peace*, 1946; *Ape and Essence*, 1948; and *Theme and Variations*, 1950.

In Huxley's works of fiction as well as in the

other earlier volumes, there is revealed a curious kind of writing: writing which disguises itself as entertainment in order to interest, but which neither respects the entertainment nor believes in the instruction. The aim, it seems, is satire, yet this is satire which frustrates itself. It begins to criticize life, then falters, then, disgusted with the human animal, turns away both from criticism and from life. Contemptuous of those who live on a "time-bound" plane, Huxley contemplates an "algebra of spiritual existence," yet he indicates no salvation for humanity in a Nirvana of abstract mathematics. His is a distortion of the mystic's way of thinking: he redeems the world in order to reject it.

The mystical vein—romantic, pacifist, nonresistant—increases in the later work; the early novels and stories are sufficiently realistic and cynical. Like Swift, to whom he is frequently compared, Huxley takes a sadistic delight in exposing human weakness and stripping the last rag of illusion from his own shabby and bewildered creatures. This savage disgust is, in itself, a confession of a personal hurt translated into a cosmic despair.

Huxley himself defends his disinclination to accept the suffering world on its own terms. In *After Many a Summer Dies the Swan* Huxley creates Mr. Propter, a mystical philosopher who echoes Huxley's deepest fears and his most devastating finalities. For example, Mr. Propter concludes that one of the enormous defects of so-called good literature was its acceptance of the conventional scale of values: "it treated as though they were reasonable the mainly lunatic preoccupations of statesmen, lovers, business men, social climbers, parents. In a word, it took seriously the causes of suffering as well as the suffering. . . . So that even when a tragedy ended badly, the reader was hypnotized by the eloquence of the piece into imagining that it was all somehow noble and worth while. . . . No, a good satire was much more deeply truthful and, of course, much more profitable than good tragedy."

And good satire has probably been Huxley's most important contribution to the literature of his time. *Crome Yellow, Antic Hay, Point Counter Point, Brave New World*—these novels may now seem dated in some respects, yet they retain a brilliant fancy that makes their negativism tolerable if unattractive. Ironically, the Huxley who of late has concerned himself almost exclusively with man's spiritual nature seems to have least to say artistically. Since ideas have always been the stuff of Huxley's writing, a mystic attitude involving withdrawal from ideas and even from personality leaves him without the normal ingredients of his literary expression.

"The Tillotson Banquet" is one of the best of Huxley's short stories, displaying his keen sense of comedy without the virulence that sometimes mars his work. Huxley himself has admitted that behind his story "hovers the ghost" of Benjamin Robert Haydon, early nineteenth-century painter and friend of Keats, Lamb, and Wordsworth—Haydon who, according to Huxley, "possessed all the characteristics of great genius except talent."

THE TILLOTSON BANQUET [1]

YOUNG Spode was not a snob; he was too intelligent for that, too fundamentally decent. Not a snob; but all the same he could not help feeling very well pleased at the thought that he was dining, alone and intimately, with Lord Badgery. It was a definite event in his life, a step forward, he felt, towards that final success, social, material, and literary, which he had come to London with the fixed intention of making. The conquest and capture of Badgery was an almost essential strategical move in the campaign.

Edmund, forty-seventh Baron Badgery, was a lineal descendant of that Edmund, surnamed Le Blayreau, who landed on English soil in the train of William the Conqueror. Ennobled by William Rufus, the Badgerys had been one of the very few baronial families to survive the Wars of the Roses and all the other changes and chances of English history. They were a sensible and philoprogenitive race. No Badgery had ever fought in any war, no Badgery had ever engaged in any kind of politics. They had been content to live and quietly to propagate their species in a huge machicolated Norman castle, surrounded by a triple moat, only sallying forth to cultivate their property and to collect their rents. In the eighteenth century, when life had become relatively secure, the Badgerys began to venture forth into civilised society. From boorish squires they blossomed into *grands seigneurs*, patrons of the arts, virtuosi. Their property was large, they were rich; and with the growth of industrialism their riches also grew. Villages on their estate turned into manufacturing towns, unsuspected coal was discovered beneath the surface of their barren moorlands. By the middle of the nineteenth century the Badgerys were among the richest of English noble families. The forty-seventh baron disposed of an income of at least two hundred

[1] From *Mortal Coils* by Aldous Huxley. Copyright, 1921, 1949, by Aldous Huxley. Reprinted by permission of Harper & Brothers.

thousand pounds a year. Following the great Badgery tradition, he had refused to have anything to do with politics or war. He occupied himself by collecting pictures; he took an interest in theatrical productions; he was the friend and patron of men of letters, of painters, and musicians. A personage, in a word, of considerable consequence in that particular world in which young Spode had elected to make his success.

Spode had only recently left the university. Simon Gollamy, the editor of the *World's Review* (the "Best of all possible Worlds"), had got to know him—he was always on the lookout for youthful talent—had seen possibilities in the young man, and appointed him art critic of his paper. Gollamy liked to have young and teachable people about him. The possession of disciples flattered his vanity, and he found it easier, moreover, to run his paper with docile collaborators than with men grown obstinate and case-hardened with age. Spode had not done badly at his new job. At any rate, his articles had been intelligent enough to arouse the interest of Lord Badgery. It was, ultimately, to them that he owed the honour of sitting tonight in the dining-room of Badgery House.

Fortified by several varieties of wine and a glass of aged brandy, Spode felt more confident and at ease than he had done the whole evening. Badgery was rather a disquieting host. He had an alarming habit of changing the subject of any conversation that had lasted for more than two minutes. Spode had found it, for example, horribly mortifying when his host, cutting across what was, he prided himself, a particularly subtle and illuminating disquisition on baroque art, had turned a wandering eye about the room and asked him abruptly whether he liked parrots. He had flushed and glanced suspiciously towards him, fancying that the man was trying to be offensive. But no; Badgery's white, fleshy, Hanoverian face wore an expression of perfect good faith. There was no malice in his small greenish eyes. He evidently did genuinely want to know if Spode liked parrots. The young man swallowed his irritation and replied that he did. Badgery then told a good story about parrots. Spode was on the point of capping it with a better story, when his host began to talk about Beethoven. And so the game went on. Spode cut his conversation to suit his host's requirements. In the course of ten minutes he had made a more or less witty epigram on Benvenuto Cellini, Queen Victoria, sport, God, Stephen Phillips, and Moorish architecture. Lord Badgery thought him the most charming young man, and so intelligent.

"If you've quite finished your coffee," he said, rising to his feet as he spoke, "we'll go and look at the pictures."

Spode jumped up with alacrity, and only then realised that he had drunk just ever so little too much. He would have to be careful, talk deliberately, plant his feet consciously, one after the other.

"This house is quite cluttered up with pictures," Lord Badgery complained. "I had a whole wagon-load taken away to the country last week; but there are still far too many. My ancestors would have their portraits painted by Romney. Such a shocking artist, don't you think? Why couldn't they have chosen Gainsborough, or even Reynolds? I've had all the Romneys hung in the servants' hall now. It's such a comfort to know that one can never possibly see them again. I suppose you know all about the ancient Hittites?"

"Well . . ." the young man replied, with befitting modesty.

"Look at that, then." He indicated a large stone head which stood in a case near the dining-room door. "It's not Greek, or Egyptian, or Persian, or anything else; so if it isn't ancient Hittite, I don't know what it is. And that reminds me of that story about Lord George Sanger, the Circus King . . ." and, without giving Spode time to examine the Hittite relic, he led the way up the huge staircase, pausing every now and then in his anecdote to point out some new object of curiosity or beauty.

"I suppose you know Deburau's pantomimes?" Spode rapped out as soon as the story was over. He was in an itch to let out his information about Deburau. Badgery had given him a perfect opening with his ridiculous Sanger. "What a perfect man, isn't he? He used to . . ."

"This is my main gallery," said Lord Badgery, throwing open one leaf of a tall folding door. "I must apologise for it. It looks like a roller-skating rink." He fumbled with the electric switches and there was suddenly light—light that revealed an enormous gallery, duly receding into distance according to all the laws of perspective. "I dare say you've heard of my poor father," Lord Badgery continued. "A little insane, you know; sort of mechanical genius with a screw loose. He used to have a toy railway in this room. No end of fun he had, crawling about the floor after his trains. And all the pictures were stacked in the cellars. I can't tell you what they were like when I found them: mushrooms growing out of the Botticellis. Now I'm rather proud of this Poussin; he painted it for Scarron."

"Exquisite!" Spode exclaimed, making with his

hand a gesture as though he were modelling a pure form in the air. "How splendid the onrush of those trees and leaning figures is! And the way they're caught up, as it were, and stemmed by that single godlike form opposing them with his contrary movement! And the draperies . . ."

But Lord Badgery had moved on, and was standing in front of a little fifteenth-century Virgin of carved wood.

"School of Rheims," he explained.

They "did" the gallery at high speed. Badgery never permitted his guest to halt for more than forty seconds before any work of art. Spode would have liked to spend a few moments of recollection and tranquillity in front of some of these lovely things. But it was not permitted.

The gallery done, they passed into a little room leading out of it. At the sight of what the lights revealed, Spode gasped.

"It's like something out of Balzac," he exclaimed. "Un de ces salons dorés où se déploie un luxe insolent. You know."

"My nineteenth-century chamber," Badgery explained. "The best thing of its kind, I flatter myself, outside the State Apartments at Windsor."

Spode tiptoed round the room, peering with astonishment at all the objects in glass, in gilded bronze, in china, in feathers, in embroidered and painted silk, in beads, in wax, objects of the most fantastic shapes and colours, all the queer products of a decadent tradition, with which the room was crowded. There were paintings on the walls—a Martin, a Wilkie, an early Landseer, several Ettys, a big Haydon, a slight pretty water-colour of a girl by Wainewright, the pupil of Blake and arsenic poisoner, a score of others. But the picture which arrested Spode's attention was a medium sized canvas representing Troilus riding into Troy among the flowers and plaudits of an admiring crowd, and oblivious (you could see from his expression) of everything but the eyes of Cressida, who looked down at him from a window, with Pandarus smiling over her shoulder.

"What an absurd and enchanting picture!" Spode exclaimed.

"Ah, you've spotted my Troilus." Lord Badgery was pleased.

"What bright harmonious colours! Like Etty's, only stronger, not so obviously pretty. And there's an energy about it that reminds one of Haydon. Only Haydon could never have done anything so impeccable in taste. Who is it by?" Spode turned to his host inquiringly.

"You were right in detecting Haydon," Lord Badgery answered. "It's by his pupil, Tillotson. I wish I could get hold of more of his work. But nobody seems to know anything about him. And he seems to have done so little."

This time it was the younger man who interrupted.

"Tillotson, Tillotson . . ." He put his hand to his forehead. A frown incongruously distorted his round, floridly curved face. "No . . . yes, I have it." He looked up triumphantly with serene and childish brows. "Tillotson, Walter Tillotson—the man's still alive."

Badgery smiled. "This picture was painted in 1846, you know."

"Well, that's all right. Say he was born in 1820, painted his masterpiece when he was twenty-six, and it's 1913 now; that's to say he's only ninety-three. Not as old as Titian yet."

"But he's not been heard of since 1860," Lord Badgery protested.

"Precisely. Your mention of his name reminded me of the discovery I made the other day when I was looking through the obituary notices in the archives of the *World's Review*. (One has to bring them up to date every year or so for fear of being caught napping if one of these old birds chooses to shuffle off suddenly.) Well, there, among them—I remember my astonishment at the time—there I found Walter Tillotson's biography. Pretty full to 1860, and then a blank, except for a pencil note in the early nineteen hundreds to the effect that he had returned from the East. The obituary has never been used or added to. I draw the obvious conclusion: the old chap isn't dead yet. He's just been overlooked somehow."

"But this is extraordinary," Lord Badgery exclaimed. "You must find him, Spode—you must find him. I'll commission him to paint frescoes round this room. It's just what I've always vainly longed for—a real nineteenth-century artist to decorate this place for me. Oh, we must find him at once—at once."

Lord Badgery strode up and down in a state of great excitement.

"I can see how this room could be made quite perfect," he went on. "We'd clear away all these cases and have the whole of that wall filled by a heroic fresco of Hector and Andromache, or 'Distraining for Rent,' or Fanny Kemble as Belvidera in 'Venice Preserved'—anything like that, provided it's in the grand manner of the 'thirties and 'forties. And here I'd have a landscape with lovely receding perspectives, or else something architectural and grand in the style of Belshazzar's feast. Then we'll have this Adam fireplace taken down and replaced by something Mauro-Gothic. And on these walls I'll have mirrors, or no! let me see . . ."

He sank into meditative silence, from which he finally roused himself to shout:

"The old man, the old man! Spode, we must find this astonishing old creature. And don't breathe a word to anybody. Tillotson shall be our secret. Oh, it's too perfect, it's incredible! Think of the frescoes."

Lord Badgery's face had become positively animated. He had talked of a single subject for nearly a quarter of an hour.

2

Three weeks later Lord Badgery was aroused from his usual after-luncheon somnolence by the arrival of a telegram. The message was a short one. "Found.—Spode." A look of pleasure and intelligence made human Lord Badgery's clayey face of surfeit. "No answer," he said. The footman padded away on noiseless feet.

Lord Badgery closed his eyes and began to contemplate. Found! What a room he would have! There would be nothing like it in the world. The frescoes, the fireplace, the mirrors, the ceiling. . . . And a small, shrivelled old man clambering about the scaffolding, agile and quick like one of those whiskered little monkeys at the Zoo, painting away, painting away. . . . Fanny Kemble as Belvidera, Hector and Andromache, or why not the Duke of Clarence in the Butt, the Duke of Malmsey, the Butt of Clarence. . . . Lord Badgery was asleep.

Spode did not lag long behind his telegram. He was at Badgery House by six o'clock. His lordship was in the nineteenth-century chamber, engaged in clearing away with his own hands the bric-à-brac. Spode found him looking hot and out of breath.

"Ah, there you are," said Lord Badgery. "You see me already preparing for the great man's coming. Now you must tell me all about him."

"He's older even than I thought," said Spode. "He's ninety-seven this year. Born in 1816. Incredible, isn't it! There, I'm beginning at the wrong end."

"Begin where you like," said Badgery genially.

"I won't tell you all the incidents of the hunt. You've no idea what a job I had to run him to earth. It was like a Sherlock Holmes story, immensely elaborate, too elaborate. I shall write a book about it some day. At any rate, I found him at last."

"Where?"

"In a sort of respectable slum in Holloway, older and poorer and lonelier than you could have believed possible, I found out how it was he came to be forgotten, how he came to drop out of life in the way he did. He took it into his head, somewhere about the 'sixties, to go to Palestine to get local colour for his religious pictures—scapegoats and things, you know. Well, he went to Jerusalem and then on to Mount Lebanon and on and on, and then, somewhere in the middle of Asia Minor, he got stuck. He got stuck for about forty years."

"But what did he do all that time?"

"Oh, he painted, and started a mission, and converted three Turks, and taught the local Pashas the rudiments of English, Latin, and perspective, and God knows what else. Then, in about 1904, it seems to have occurred to him that he was getting rather old and had been away from home for rather a long time. So he made his way back to England, only to find that everyone he had known was dead, that the dealers had never heard of him and wouldn't buy his pictures, that he was simply a ridiculous old figure of fun. So he got a job as a drawing-master in a girls' school in Holloway, and there he's been ever since, growing older and older, and feebler and feebler, and blinder and deafer, and generally more gaga, until finally the school has given him the sack. He had about ten pounds in the world when I found him. He lives in a kind of black hole in a basement full of beetles. When his ten pounds are spent, I suppose he'll just quietly die there."

Badgery held up a white hand. "No more, no more. I find literature quite depressing enough. I insist that life at least shall be a little gayer. Did you tell him I wanted him to paint my room?"

"But he can't paint. He's too blind and palsied."

"Can't paint?" Badgery exclaimed in horror. "Then what's the good of the old creature?"

"Well, if you put it like that . . ." Spode began.

"I shall never have my frescoes. Ring the bell, will you?"

Spode rang.

"What right has Tillotson to go on existing if he can't paint?" went on Lord Badgery petulantly. "After all, that was his only justification for occupying a place in the sun."

"He doesn't have much sun in his basement."

The footman appeared at the door.

"Get someone to put all these things back in their places," Lord Badgery commanded, indicating with a wave of the hand the ravaged cases, the confusion of glass and china with which he had littered the floor, the pictures unhooked. "We'll go to the library, Spode; it's more comfortable there."

He led the way through the long gallery and down the stairs.

"I'm sorry old Tillotson has been such a disappointment," said Spode sympathetically.

"Let us talk about something else; he ceases to interest me."

"But don't you think we ought to do something about him? He's only got ten pounds between him and the workhouse. And if you'd seen the blackbeetles in his basement!"

"Enough—enough. I'll do everything you think fitting."

"I thought we might get up a subscription amongst lovers of the arts."

"There aren't any," said Badgery.

"No; but there are plenty of people who will subscribe out of snobbism."

"Not unless you give them something for their money."

"That's true. I hadn't thought of that." Spode was silent for a moment. "We might have a dinner in his honour. The Great Tillotson Banquet. Doyen of the British Art. A Link with the Past. Can't you see it in the papers? I'd make a stunt of it in the *World's Review*. That ought to bring in the snobs."

"And we'll invite a lot of artists and critics—all the ones who can't stand one another. It will be fun to see them squabbling." Badgery laughed. Then his face darkened once again. "Still," he added, "it'll be a very poor second best to my frescoes. You'll stay to dinner, of course."

"Well, since you suggest it. Thanks very much."

3

The Tillotson Banquet was fixed to take place about three weeks later. Spode, who had charge of the arrangements, proved himself an excellent organiser. He secured the big banqueting-room at the Café Bomba, and was successful in bullying and cajoling the manager into giving fifty persons dinner at twelve shillings a head, including wine. He sent out invitations and collected subscriptions. He wrote an article on Tillotson in the *World's Review*—one of those charming, witty articles couched in the tone of amused patronage and contempt with which one speaks of the great men of 1840. Nor did he neglect Tillotson himself. He used to go to Holloway almost every day to listen to the old man's endless stories about Asia Minor and the Great Exhibition of '51 and Benjamin Robert Haydon. He was sincerely sorry for this relic of another age.

Mr. Tillotson's room was about ten feet below the level of the soil of South Holloway. A little grey light percolated through the area bars, forced a difficult passage through panes opaque with dirt, and spent itself, like a drop of milk that falls into an inkpot, among the inveterate shadows of the dungeon. The place was haunted by the sour smell of damp plaster and of woodwork that has begun to moulder secretly at the heart. A little miscellaneous furniture, including a bed, a washstand and chest of drawers, a table and one or two chairs, lurked in the obscure corners of the den or ventured furtively out into the open. Hither Spode now came almost every day, bringing the old man news of the progress of the banquet scheme. Every day he found Mr. Tillotson sitting in the same place under the window, bathing, as it were, in his tiny puddle of light. "The oldest man that ever wore grey hairs," Spode reflected as he looked at him. Only there were very few hairs left on that bald, unpolished head. At the sound of the visitor's knock Mr. Tillotson would turn in his chair, stare in the direction of the door with blinking, uncertain eyes. He was always full of apologies for being so slow in recognising who was there.

"No discourtesy meant," he would say, after asking. "It's not as if I had forgotten who you were. Only it's so dark and my sight isn't what it was."

After that he never failed to give a little laugh, and, pointing out of the window at the area railings, would say:

"Ah, this is the place for somebody with good sight. It's the place for looking at ankles. It's the grand stand."

It was the day before the great event. Spode came as usual, and Mr. Tillotson punctually made his little joke about the ankles, and Spode, as punctually, laughed.

"Well, Mr. Tillotson," he said, after the reverberation of the joke had died away, "tomorrow you make your re-entry into the world of art and fashion. You'll find some changes."

"I've always had such extraordinary luck," said Mr. Tillotson, and Spode could see by his expression that he genuinely believed it, that he had forgotten the black hole and the blackbeetles and the almost exhausted ten pounds that stood between him and the workhouse. "What an amazing piece of good fortune, for instance, that you should have found me just when you did. Now, this dinner will bring me back to my place in the world. I shall have money, and in a little while—who knows?—I shall be able to see well enough to paint again. I believe my eyes are getting better, you know. Ah, the future is very rosy."

Mr. Tillotson looked up, his face puckered into a smile, and nodded his head in affirmation of his words.

"You believe in the life to come?" said Spode, and immediately flushed for shame at the cruelty of the words.

But Mr. Tillotson was in far too cheerful a mood to have caught their significance.

"Life to come," he repeated. "No, I don't believe in any of that stuff—not since 1859. The 'Origin of Species' changed my views, you know. No life to come for me, thank you! You don't remember the excitement of course. You're very young, Mr. Spode."

"Well, I'm not so old as I was," Spode replied. "You know how middle-aged one is as a schoolboy and undergraduate. Now I'm old enough to know I'm young."

Spode was about to develop this little paradox further, but he noticed that Mr. Tillotson had not been listening. He made a note of the gambit for use in companies that were more appreciative of the subleties.

"You were talking about the 'Origin of Species'," he said.

"Was I?" said Mr. Tillotson, waking from reverie.

"About its effect on your faith, Mr. Tillotson."

"To be sure, yes. It shattered my faith. But I remember a fine thing by the Poet Laureate, something about there being more faith in honest doubt, believe me, than in all the . . . all the . . . I forget exactly what; but you see the train of thought. Oh, it was a bad time for religion. I am glad my master Haydon never lived to see it. He was a man of fervour. I remember him pacing up and down his studio in Lisson Grove, singing and shouting and praying all at once. It used almost to frighten me. Oh, but he was a wonderful man, a great man. Take him for all in all, we shall not look upon his like again. As usual, the Bard is right. But it was all very long ago, before your time, Mr. Spode."

"Well, I'm not as old as I was," said Spode, in the hope of having his paradox appreciated this time. But Mr. Tillotson went on without noticing the interruption.

"It's a very, very long time. And yet, when I look back on it, it all seems but a day or two ago. Strange that each day should seem so long and that many days added together should be less than an hour. How clearly I can see old Haydon pacing up and down! Much more clearly, indeed, than I see you, Mr. Spode. The eyes of memory don't grow dim. But my sight is improving, I assure you; it's improving daily. I shall soon be able to see those ankles." He laughed, like a cracked bell—one of those little old bells, Spode fancied, that ring, with much rattling of wires, in the far-off servants' quarters of ancient houses. "And very soon," Mr. Tillotson went on, "I shall be painting again. Ah, Mr. Spode, my luck is extraordinary. I believe in it, I trust in it. And after all, what is luck? Simply another name for Providence, in spite of the 'Origin of Species' and the rest of it. How right the Laureate was when he said that there was more faith in honest doubt, believe me, than in all the . . . er, the . . . er . . . well, you know. I regard you, Mr. Spode, as the emissary of Providence. Your coming marked a turning-point in my life and the beginning, for me, of happier days. Do you know, one of the first things I shall do when my fortunes are restored will be to buy a hedgehog."

"A hedgehog, Mr. Tillotson?"

"For the blackbeetles. There's nothing like a hedgehog for beetles. It will eat blackbeetles till it's sick, till it dies of surfeit. That reminds me of the time when I told my poor great master Haydon—in joke, of course—that he ought to send in a cartoon of King John dying of a surfeit of lampreys for the frescoes in the new Houses of Parliament. As I told him, it's a most notable event in the annals of British liberty—the providential and exemplary removal of a tyrant."

Mr. Tillotson laughed again—the little bell in the deserted house; a ghostly hand pulling the cord in the drawing-room, and phantom footmen responding to the thin, flawed note.

"I remember he laughed, laughed like a bull in his old grand manner. But oh, it was a terrible blow when they rejected his design, a terrible blow. It was the first and fundamental cause of his suicide."

Mr. Tillotson paused. There was a long silence. Spode felt strangely moved, he hardly knew why, in the presence of this man, so frail, so ancient, in body three parts dead, in the spirit so full of life and hopeful patience. He felt ashamed. What was the use of his own youth and cleverness? He saw himself suddenly as a boy with a rattle scaring birds—rattling his noisy cleverness, waving his arms in ceaseless and futile activity, never resting in his efforts to scare away the birds that were always trying to settle in his mind. And what birds! wide-winged and beautiful, all those serene thoughts and faiths and emotions that only visit minds that have humbled themselves to quiet. Those gracious visitants he was for ever using all his energies to drive away. But this old man, with his hedgehogs and his honest doubts and all the rest of it—his mind was like a field made beautiful by the free coming and going, the unafraid alightings of a multitude of white, bright-winged creatures. He felt ashamed. But then, was it possible to alter one's life? Wasn't it a little absurd to risk a conversion? Spode shrugged his shoulders.

"I'll get you a hedgehog at once," he said. "They're sure to have some at Whiteley's."

Before he left that evening Spode made an alarming discovery. Mr. Tillotson did not possess a dress-suit. It was hopeless to think of getting one made at this short notice, and, besides, what an unnecessary expense!

"We shall have to borrow a suit, Mr. Tillotson. I ought to have thought of that before."

"Dear me, dear me." Mr. Tillotson was a little chagrined by this unlucky discovery. "Borrow a suit?"

Spode hurried away for counsel to Badgery House, Lord Badgery surprisingly rose to the occasion. "Ask Boreham to come and see me," he told the footman who answered his ring.

Boreham was one of those immemorial butlers who linger on, generation after generation, in the houses of the great. He was over eighty now, bent, dried up, shrivelled with age.

"All old men are about the same size," said Lord Badgery. It was a comforting theory. "Ah, here he is. Have you got a spare suit of evening clothes, Boreham?"

"I have an old suit, my lord, that I stopped wearing in—let me see—was it nineteen seven or eight?"

"That's the very thing. I should be most grateful, Boreham, if you could lend it to me for Mr. Spode here for a day."

The old man went out, and soon reappeared carrying over his arm a very old black suit. He held up the coat and trousers for inspection. In the light of day they were deplorable.

"You've no idea, sir," said Boreham deprecatingly to Spode—"you've no idea how easy things get stained with grease and gravy and what not. However careful you are, sir—however careful."

"I should imagine so." Spode was sympathetic.

"However careful, sir."

"But in artificial light they'll look all right."

"Perfectly all right," Lord Badgery repeated. "Thank you, Boreham; you shall have them back on Thursday."

"You're welcome, my lord, I'm sure." And the old man bowed and disappeared.

On the afternoon of the great day Spode carried up to Holloway a parcel containing Boreham's retired evening-suit and all the necessary appurtenances in the way of shirts and collars. Owing to the darkness and his own feeble sight Mr. Tillotson was happily unaware of the defects in the suit. He was in a state of extreme nervous agitation. It was with some difficulty that Spode could prevent him, although it was only three o'clock, from starting his toilet on the spot.

"Take it easy, Mr. Tillotson, take it easy. We needn't start till half-past seven, you know."

Spode left an hour later, and as soon as he was safely out of the room Mr. Tillotson began to prepare himself for the banquet. He lighted the gas and a couple of candles, and, blinking myopically at the image that fronted him in the tiny looking-glass that stood on his chest of drawers, he set to work, with all the ardour of a young girl preparing for her first ball. At six o'clock, when the last touches had been given, he was not unsatisfied.

He marched up and down his cellar, humming to himself the gay song which had been so popular in his middle years:

Oh, oh, Anna Maria Jones!
Queen of the tambourine, the cymbals, and the
  bones!

Spode arrived an hour later in Lord Badgery's second Rolls-Royce. Opening the door of the old man's dungeon, he stood for a moment, wide-eyed with astonishment, on the threshold. Mr. Tillotson was standing by the empty grate, one elbow resting on the mantelpiece, one leg crossed over the other in a jaunty and gentlemanly attitude. The effect of the candlelight shining on his face was to deepen every line and wrinkle with intense black shadow; he looked immeasurably old. It was a noble and pathetic head. On the other hand, Boreham's outworn evening-suit was simply buffoonish. The coat was too long in the sleeves and the tail; the trousers bagged in elephantine creases about his ankles. Some of the grease-spots were visible even in candlelight. The white tie, over which Mr. Tillotson had taken infinite pains and which he believed in his purblindness to be perfect, was fantastically lop-sided. He had buttoned up his waistcoat in such a fashion that one button was widowed of its hole and one hole of its button. Across his shirt front lay the broad green ribbon of some unknown Order.

"Queen of the tambourine, the cymbals, and the bones," Mr. Tillotson concluded in a gnat-like voice before welcoming his visitor.

"Well, Spode, here you are. I'm dressed already, you see. The suit, I flatter myself, fits very well, almost as though it had been made for me. I am all gratitude to the gentleman who was kind enough to lend it to me; I shall take the greatest care of it. It's a dangerous thing to lend clothes. For loan oft loseth both itself and friend. The Bard is always right."

"Just one thing," said Spode. "A touch to your waistcoat." He unbuttoned the dissipated garment and did it up again more symmetrically.

Mr. Tillotson was a little piqued at being found so absurdly in the wrong.

"Thanks, thanks," he said, protestingly, trying to edge away from his valet. "It's all right, you know; I can do it myself. Foolish oversight. I flatter myself the suit fits very well."

"And perhaps the tie might . . ." Spode began tentatively. But the old man would not hear of it.

"No, no. The tie's all right. I can tie a tie, Mr. Spode. The tie's all right. Leave it as it is, I beg."

"I like your Order."

Mr. Tillotson looked down complacently at his shirt front. "Ah, you've noticed my Order. It's a long time since I wore that. It was given me by the Grand Porte, you know, for services rendered in the Russo-Turkish War. It's the Order of Chastity, the second class. They only give the first class to crowned heads, you know—crowned heads and ambassadors. And only Pashas of the highest rank get the second. Mine's the second. They only give the first class to crowned heads . . ."

"Of course, of course," said Spode.

"Do you think I look all right, Mr. Spode?" Mr. Tillotson asked, a little anxiously.

"Splendid, Mr. Tillotson—splendid. The Order's magnificent."

The old man's face brightened once more. "I flatter myself," he said, "that this borrowed suit fits me very well. But I don't like borrowing clothes. For loan oft loseth both itself and friend, you know. And the Bard is always right."

"Ugh, there's one of those horrible beetles!" Spode exclaimed.

Mr. Tillotson bent down and stared at the floor. "I see it," he said, and stamped on a small piece of coal, which crunched to powder under his foot. "I shall certainly buy a hedgehog."

It was time for them to start. A crowd of little boys and girls had collected round Lord Badgery's enormous car. The chauffeur, who felt that honour and dignity were at stake, pretended not to notice the children, but sat gazing, like a statue, into eternity. At the sight of Spode and Mr. Tillotson emerging from the house a yell of mingled awe and derision went up. It subsided to an astonished silence as they climbed into the car. "Bomba's," Spode directed. The Rolls-Royce gave a faintly stertorous sigh and began to move. The children yelled again, and ran along beside the car, waving their arms in a frenzy of excitement. It was then that Mr. Tillotson, with an incomparably noble gesture, leaned forward and tossed among the seething crowd of urchins his three last coppers.

4

In Bomba's big room the company was assembling. The long gilt-edged mirrors reflected a singular collection of people. Middle-aged Academicians shot suspicious glances at youths whom they suspected, only too correctly, of being iconoclasts, organisers of Post-Impressionist Exhibitions. Rival art critics, brought suddenly face to face, quivered with restrained hatred. Mrs. Nobes, Mrs. Cayman, and Mrs. Mandragore, those indefatigable hunters of artistic big game, came on one another all unawares in this well-stored menagerie, where each had expected to hunt alone, and were filled with rage. Through this crowd of mutually repellent vanities Lord Badgery moved with a suavity that seemed unconscious of all the feuds and hatreds. He was enjoying himself immensely. Behind the heavy waxen mask of his face, ambushed behind the Hanoverian nose, the little lustreless pig's eyes, the pale thick lips, there lurked a small devil of happy malice that rocked with laughter.

"So nice of you to have come, Mrs. Mandragore, to do honour to England's artistic past. And I'm so glad to see you've brought dear Mrs. Cayman. And is that Mrs. Nobes, too? So it is! I hadn't noticed her before. How delightful! I knew we could depend on your love of art."

And he hurried away to seize the opportunity of introducing that eminent sculptor, Sir Herbert Herne, to the bright young critic who had called him, in the public prints, a monumental mason.

A moment later the Maître d'Hôtel came to the door of the gilded saloon and announced, loudly and impressively, "Mr. Walter Tillotson." Guided from behind by young Spode, Mr. Tillotson came into the room slowly and hesitatingly. In the glare of the lights his eyelids beat heavily, painfully, like the wings of an imprisoned moth, over his filmy eyes. Once inside the door he halted and drew himself up with a conscious assumption of dignity. Lord Badgerly hurried forward and seized his hand.

"Welcome, Mr. Tillotson—welcome in the name of English art!"

Mr. Tillotson inclined his head in silence. He was too full of emotion to be able to reply.

"I should like to introduce you to a few of your younger colleagues, who have assembled here to do you honour."

Lord Badgery presented everyone in the room to the old painter, who bowed, shook hands, made little noises in his throat, but still found himself unable to speak. Mrs. Nobes, Mrs. Cayman, and Mrs. Mandragore all said charming things.

Dinner was served; the party took their places. Lord Badgery sat at the head of the table, with Mr. Tillotson on his right hand and Sir Herbert Herne on his left. Confronted with Bomba's succulent cooking and Bomba's wines, Mr. Tillotson ate and drank a good deal. He had the appetite of one who has lived on greens and potatoes for ten years among the blackbeetles. After the second glass of wine he began to talk, suddenly and in a flood, as though a sluice had been pulled up.

"In Asia Minor," he began, "it is the custom when one goes to dinner, to hiccough as a sign of appreciative fullness. *Eructavit cor meum*, as the Psalmist has it; he was an Oriental himself."

Spode had arranged to sit next to Mrs. Cayman; he had designs upon her. She was an impossible woman, of course, but rich and useful; he wanted to bamboozle her into buying some of his young friends' pictures.

"In a cellar?" Mrs. Cayman was saying, "with blackbeetles? Oh, how dreadful! Poor old man! And he's ninety-seven, didn't you say? Isn't that shocking! I only hope the subscription will be a large one. Of course, one wishes one could have given more oneself. But then, you know, one has so many expenses, and things are so difficult now."

"I know, I know," said Spode, with feeling.

"It's all because of Labour," Mrs. Cayman explained. "Of course, I should simply love to have him in to dinner sometimes. But, then, I feel he's really too old, too *farouche* and *gâteux;* it would not be doing a kindness to him, would it? And so you are working with Mr. Gollamy now? What a charming man, so talented, such conversation . . ."

"*Eructavit cor meum*," said Mr. Tillotson for the third time. Lord Badgery tried to head him off the subject of Turkish etiquette, but in vain.

By half-past nine a kinder vinolent atmosphere had put to sleep the hatreds and suspicions of before dinner. Sir Herbert Herne had discovered that the young Cubist sitting next him was not insane and actually knew a surprising amount about the Old Masters. For their part these young men had realised that their elders were not at all malignant; they were just very stupid and pathetic. It was only in the bosoms of Mrs. Nobes, Mrs. Cayman, and Mrs. Mandragore that hatred still reigned undiminished. Being ladies and old-fashioned, they had drunk almost no wine.

The moment for speech-making arrived. Lord Badgery rose to his feet, said what was expected of him, and called upon Sir Herbert to propose the toast of the evening. Sir Herbert coughed, smiled and began. In the course of a speech that lasted twenty minutes he told anecdotes of Mr. Gladstone, Lord Leighton, Sir Alma Tadema, and the late Bishop of Bombay; he made three puns, he quoted Shakespeare and Whittier, he was playful, he was eloquent, he was grave. . . . At the end of his harangue Sir Herbert handed to Mr. Tillotson a silk purse containing fifty-eight pounds ten shillings, the total amount of the subscription. The old man's health was drunk with acclamation.

Mr. Tillotson rose with difficulty to his feet. The dry, snake-like skin of his face was flushed; his tie was more crooked than ever; the green ribbon of the Order of Chastity of the second class had somehow climbed up his crumpled and maculate shirt front.

"My lords, ladies, and gentlemen," he began in a choking voice, and then broke down completely. It was a very painful and pathetic spectacle. A feeling of intense discomfort afflicted the minds of all who looked upon that trembling relic of a man, as he stood there weeping and stammering. It was as though a breath of the wind of death had blown suddenly through the room, lifting the vapours of wine and tobacco-smoke, quenching the laughter and the candle flames. Eyes floated uneasily, not knowing where to look. Lord Badgery, with great presence of mind, offered the old man a glass of wine. Mr. Tillotson began to recover. The guests heard him murmur a few disconnected words.

"This great honour . . . overwhelmed with kindness . . . this magnificent banquet . . . not used to it . . . in Asia Minor . . . *eructavit cor meum*."

At this point Lord Badgery plucked sharply at one of his long coat tails. Mr. Tillotson paused, took another sip of wine, and then went on with a newly won coherence and energy.

"The life of the artist is a hard one. His work is unlike other men's work, which may be done mechanically, by rote and almost, as it were, in sleep. It demands from him a constant expense of spirit. He gives continually of his best life, and in return he receives much joy, it is true—much fame, it may be—but of material blessings, very few. It is eighty years since first I devoted my life to the service of art; eighty years, and almost every one of those years has brought me fresh and painful proof of what I have been saying: the artist's life is a hard one."

This unexpected deviation into sense increased the general feeling of discomfort. It became necessary to take the old man seriously, to regard him as a human being. Up till then he had been no more than an object of curiosity, a mummy in an absurd suit of evening-clothes with a green ribbon across the shirt front. People could not help wishing that they had subscribed a little more. Fifty-eight pounds ten—it wasn't enormous. But happily for the peace of mind of the company, Mr. Tillotson paused again, took another sip of wine, and began to live up to his proper character by talking absurdly.

"When I consider the life of that great man, Benjamin Robert Haydon, one of the greatest men England has ever produced . . ." The audience heaved a sigh of relief; this was all as it should be. There was a burst of loud bravoing and clapping. Mr. Tillotson turned his dim eyes round the room, and smiled gratefully at the misty figures he beheld. "That great man, Benjamin Robert Haydon," he continued, "whom I am proud to call my master and who, it rejoices my heart to see, still lives in your memory and esteem,—that great man, one of the greatest that England has ever produced, led a life so deplorable that I cannot think of it without a tear."

And with infinite repetitions and divagations, Mr. Tillotson related the history of B. R. Haydon, his imprisonments for debt, his battle with the Academy, his triumphs, his failures, his despair, his suicide. Half-past ten struck. Mr. Tillotson was declaiming against the stupid and prejudiced judges who had rejected Haydon's designs for the decoration of the new Houses of Parliament in favour of the paltriest German scribblings.

"That great man, one of the greatest England has ever produced, that great Benjamin Robert Haydon, whom I am proud to call my master and who, it rejoices me to see, still lives on in your memory and esteem—at that affront his great heart burst; it was the unkindest cut of all. He who had worked all his life for the recognition of the artist by the State, he who had petitioned every Prime Minister, including the Duke of Wellington, for thirty years, begging them to employ artists to decorate public buildings, he to whom the scheme for decorating the Houses of Parliament was undeniably due . . ." Mr. Tillotson lost a grip on his syntax and began a new sentence. "It was the unkindest cut of all, it was the last straw. The artist's life is a hard one."

At eleven Mr. Tillotson was talking about the pre-Raphaelites. At a quarter past he had begun to tell the story of B. R. Haydon all over again. At twenty-five minutes to twelve he collapsed quite speechless into his chair. Most of the guests had already gone away; the few who remained made haste to depart. Lord Badgery led the old man to the door and packed him into the second Rolls-Royce. The Tillotson Banquet was over; it had been a pleasant evening, but a little too long.

Spode walked back to his rooms in Bloomsbury, whistling as he went. The arc lamps of Oxford Street reflected in the polished surface of the road; canals of dark bronze. He would have to bring that into an article some time. The Cayman woman had been very successfully nobbled. "Voi che sapete," he whistled—somewhat out of tune, but he could not hear that.

When Mr. Tillotson's landlady came in to call him on the following morning, she found the old man lying fully dressed on his bed. He looked very ill and very, very old; Boreham's dress-suit was in a terrible state, and the green ribbon of the Order of Chastity was ruined. Mr. Tillotson lay very still, but he was not asleep. Hearing the sound of footsteps, he opened his eyes a little and faintly groaned. His landlady looked down at him menacingly.

"Disgusting!" she said; "disgusting, I call it. At your age."

Mr. Tillotson groaned again. Making a great effort, he drew out of his trouser pocket a large silk purse, opened it, and extracted a sovereign.

"The artist's life is a hard one, Mrs. Green," he said, handing her the coin. "Would you mind sending for the doctor? I don't feel very well. And oh, what shall I do about these clothes? What shall I say to the gentleman who was kind enough to lend them to me? Loan oft loseth both itself and friend. The Bard is always right."

W. H. Auden

1907–

Wystan Hugh Auden is the most brilliant and the most influential of the group of younger poets who helped to revivify English poetry in the fourth decade of the twentieth century. The group includes C. Day Lewis, Louis MacNeice, and Stephen Spender, and all were friends and contemporaries at the Universities of Oxford and Cambridge. By the force of their social convictions and the freshness and strength of their vocabulary they aroused readers from the listlessness induced by the tired repetitions and stock gestures into which much of the poetry of the time had lapsed.

The careers of these poets began after the First World War, and their writing reflects the social, moral, and political unrest and instability of the period following the war. The social theories of Karl Marx and the psychological teachings of Freud and Jung are much in evidence in their work. They have been critical of contemporary conditions and institutions, and Auden in particular has been unsparing in his parody and satire of the prevailing theories and practices of the modern world. At times the poet and the artist in each of them has been too much submerged in the propagandist and the social philosopher, angry at the injustices and inequalities of a world he never made, and fervently believing in the poet's duty to face his responsibilities as a citizen of the modern world. They accepted the modern scene with all its implications; they did not shrink from the necessity of the machine, nor did they sentimentalize it. They saw "electric pylons conveying imprisoned power, telegraph wires defying distance, motor ploughs forcing fertility into the soil."

The change in subject matter was matched by a change in technique. These young poets rejected the traditional and conventional language and atmosphere of English poetry, and chose rather the idioms and esthetic experiments of such English authors as Hopkins, Yeats, Eliot, and Joyce, foreign authors like Kierkegaard, Kafka, Proust, and Thomas Mann. Their lyricism was enlivened by colloquialisms, and, like Gerard Manley Hopkins, they speeded up their verse with rapidly leaping images, enriched the line by unexpected internal rime, and achieved tension by strange syntactical ellipses. Auden, the most accomplished technician of the group, has mingled eloquence with banality, high rhetoric with the quick appeal of popular songs, and technical terms from factory, farm, and barroom with the jargon of air force pilots and psychologists.

Auden was born at York on February 21, 1907, and was educated at St. Edmund's School, at Gresham's School, Holt, and at Christ Church, Oxford. At the university he was specially interested in biology and in English literature, and he began his career as a poet while he was an undergraduate. His first volume, *Poems*, was published in 1930. This was followed in 1932 by *The Orators*, a book of social and political propaganda containing both poetry and prose, the latter rather the more successful. In 1933 came an allegorical satire, *The Dance of Death*, likewise concerned with social problems. He had meanwhile become a teacher in a preparatory school at Malvern, Worcestershire, where summer festivals of drama are held yearly. He was engaged by the G. P. O. Film Unit in 1935 and 1936, and with his friend Christopher Isherwood, the novelist and critic, he collaborated in three poetic dramas, *The Dog Beneath the Skin*, 1935, *The Ascent of F6*, 1936, and *On the Frontier*, 1938. The plays are technically interesting as experiments in modern verse drama and in the adaptation of the art of the theater to the inventions of the films and the radio. Another book of verse, *Look Stranger* (published in the United States as *On This Island*), had appeared in 1936, and evinced more mature thought and artistry.

In collaboration with his friend and fellow poet Louis MacNeice, Auden produced in 1937 a book of *Letters from Iceland*, the result of a visit by the two poets to that northern outpost of civilization. Auden, MacNeice, and Spender went to Spain during the Spanish Civil War, and Auden's poem *Spain*, 1937, is the climax of this phase of his life and philosophy. With Isherwood he made another journey, this time to the scene of a longer and greater struggle, the China of the late 1930's, and the two collaborated in a prose volume, *Journey to a War*, 1939. Just before the outbreak of the Second World War, Auden came to New York, and has since then been a resident of the United States.

Auden's first American volume of verse, *Another*

Time, 1940, is the least political of his books. In *The Double Man* (called in England *New Year Letter*), 1941, he writes movingly of what England means to him. His later publications include *For the Time Being*, 1944, *The Age of Anxiety: A Baroque Eclogue*, 1947, *Nones*, 1951, and a volume of essays, *The Enchafèd Flood*, 1950. In the United States he has engaged in the teaching as well as the writing of poetry. He edited a volume of selections from Tennyson in 1946, and has served as Associate Professor of English Literature at the University of Michigan. In 1948 he was awarded the Pulitzer Prize for Poetry.

It is too early to assess Auden's work as a poet or to venture suggestions with respect to his further achievements. He has changed to some extent both his social and his poetic philosophy during his sojourn in America. He is one of the most constantly discussed poets of the day, and, as with Eliot, critical opinion is divided about his work. Of his versatility and his brilliant accomplishments as a technician in verse, as well as of his influence on younger poets in both England and America, there is no doubt.

CONSIDER [1]

Consider this and in our time
As the hawk sees it or the helmeted airman:
The clouds rift suddenly—look there
At cigarette-end smouldering on a border
At the first garden party of the year.
Pass on, admire the view of the massif
Through plate-glass windows of the Sport Hotel;
Join there the insufficient units
Dangerous, easy, in furs, in uniform
And constellated at reserved tables
Supplied with feelings by an efficient band
Relayed elsewhere to farmers and their dogs
Sitting in kitchens in the stormy fens.

Long ago, supreme Antagonist,
More powerful than the great northern whale
Ancient and sorry at life's limiting defect,
In Cornwall, Mendip, or the Pennine moor
Your comments on the highborn mining-captains,
Found they no answer, made them wish to die
—Lie since in barrows out of harm.
You talk to your admirers every day
By silted harbours, derelict works,
In strangled orchards, and the silent comb
Where dogs have worried or a bird was shot.
Order the ill that they attack at once:
Visit the ports and, interrupting
The leisurely conversation in the bar
Within a stone's throw of the sunlit water,
Beckon your chosen out. Summon
Those handsome and diseased youngsters, those women
Your solitary agents in the country parishes;
And mobilize the powerful forces latent
In soils that make the farmer brutal
In the infected sinus, and the eyes of stoats.
Then, ready, start your rumour, soft
But horrifying in its capacity to disgust
Which, spreading magnified, shall come to be
A polar peril, a prodigious alarm,
Scattering the people, as torn-up paper
Rags and utensils in a sudden gust,
Seized with immeasurable neurotic dread.

Seekers after happiness, all who follow
The convolutions of your simple wish,
It is later than you think; nearer that day
Far other than that distant afternoon
Amid rustle of frocks and stamping feet
They gave the prizes to the ruined boys.
You cannot be away, then, no
Not though you pack to leave within an hour,
Escaping humming down arterial roads:
The date was yours; the prey to fugues,
Irregular breathing and alternate ascendancies
After some haunted migratory years
To disintegrate on an instant in the explosion of mania
Or lapse for ever into a classic fatigue.

THE SECRET AGENT

Control of the passes was, he saw, the key
To this new district, but who would get it?
He, the trained spy, had walked into the trap
For a bogus guide, seduced with the old tricks.

At Greenhearth was a fine site for a dam
And easy power, had they pushed the rail
Some stations nearer. They ignored his wires.
The bridges were unbuilt and trouble coming.

The street music seemed gracious now to one
For weeks up in the desert. Woken by water
Running away in the dark, he often had
Reproached the night for a companion
Dreamed of already. They would shoot, of course,
Parting easily who were never joined.

[1] This and the following poems by W. H. Auden are from *The Collected Poetry of W. H. Auden*, copyright, 1945, by W. H. Auden. Reprinted by permission of Random House, Inc.

SOMETHING IS BOUND TO HAPPEN

Doom is dark and deeper than any sea-dingle.
Upon what man it fall
In spring, day-wishing flowers appearing,
Avalanche sliding, white snow from rock-face,
That he should leave his house,
No cloud-soft hand can hold him, restraint by women;
But ever that man goes
Through place-keepers, through forest trees,
A stranger to strangers over undried sea,
Houses for fishes, suffocating water,
Or lonely on fell as chat,
By pot-holed becks
A bird stone-haunting, an unquiet bird.

There head falls forward, fatigued at evening,
And dreams of home,
Waving from window, spread of welcome,
Kissing of wife under single sheet;
But waking sees
Bird-flocks nameless to him, through doorway voices
Of new men making another love.

Save him from hostile capture,
From sudden tiger's spring at corner;
Protect his house,
His anxious house where days are counted
From thunderbolt protect,
From gradual ruin spreading like a stain;
Converting number from vague to certain,
Bring joy, bring day of his returning,
Lucky with day approaching, with leaning dawn.

SEPTEMBER 1, 1939

I sit in one of the dives
On Fifty-second Street
Uncertain and afraid
As the clever hopes expire
Of a low dishonest decade:
Waves of anger and fear
Circulate over the bright
And darkened lands of the earth,
Obsessing our private lives;
The unmentionable odour of death
Offends the September night.

Accurate scholarship can
Unearth the whole offence
From Luther until now
That has driven a culture mad,
Find what occurred at Linz,
What huge imago made
A psychopathic god:
I and the public know
What all schoolchildren learn,
Those to whom evil is done
Do evil in return.

Exiled Thucydides knew
All that a speech can say
About Democracy,
And what dictators do,
The elderly rubbish they talk
To an apathetic grave;
Analysed all in his book,
The enlightenment driven away,
The habit-forming pain,
Mismanagement and grief:
We must suffer them all again.

Into this neutral air
Where blind skyscrapers use
Their full height to proclaim
The strength of Collective Man,
Each language pours its vain
Competitive excuse:
But who can live for long
In an euphoric dream;
Out of the mirror they stare,
Imperialism's face
And the international wrong.

Faces along the bar
Cling to their average day:
The lights must never go out,
The music must always play,
All the conventions conspire
To make this fort assume
The furniture of home;
Lest we should see where we are,
Lost in a haunted wood,
Children afraid of the night
Who have never been happy or good.

The windiest militant trash
Important Persons shout
Is not so crude as our wish:
What mad Nijinsky wrote
About Diaghilev
Is true of the normal heart;
For the error bred in the bone
Of each woman and each man

Craves what it cannot have,
Not universal love
But to be loved alone.

From the conservative dark
Into the ethical life
The dense commuters come,
Repeating their morning vow;
"I *will* be true to the wife,
I'll concentrate more on my work,"
And helpless governors wake
To resume their compulsory game:
Who can release them now,
Who can reach the deaf,
Who can speak for the dumb?

Defenceless under the night
Our world in stupor lies;
Yet, dotted everywhere,
Ironic points of light
Flash out wherever the Just
Exchange their messages:
May I, composed like them
Or Eros and of dust,
Beleaguered by the same
Negation and despair,
Show an affirming flame.

PETITION

Sir, no man's enemy, forgiving all
But will its negative inversion, be prodigal:
Send to us power and light, a sovereign touch
Curing the intolerable neural itch,
The exhaustion of weaning, the liar's quinsy,
And the distortions of ingrown virginity.
Prohibit sharply the rehearsed response
And gradually correct the coward's stance;
Cover in time with beams those in retreat
That, spotted, they turn though the reverse were great;
Publish each healer that in city lives
Or country houses at the end of drives;
Harrow the house of the dead; look shining at
New styles of architecture, a change of heart.

WHO'S WHO

A shilling life will give you all the facts:
How Father beat him, how he ran away,
What were the struggles of his youth, what acts
Made him the greatest figure of his day:
Of how he fought, fished, hunted, worked all night,
Though giddy, climbed new mountains; named a sea:
Some of the last researchers even write
Love made him weep his pints like you and me.

With all his honours on, he sighed for one
Who, say astonished critics, lived at home;
Did little jobs about the house with skill
And nothing else; could whistle; would sit still
Or potter round the garden; answered some
Of his long marvellous letters but kept none.

Petition. See Cleanth Brooks's discussion of this poem in *Modern Poetry and the Tradition*, pp. 1–3, and the further explications of it in *The Explicator* for March, 1945 (III, 38) and May, 1945 (III, 51).

PAYSAGE MORALISÉ

Hearing of harvests rotting in the valleys,
Seeing at end of street the barren mountains,
Round corners coming suddenly on water,
Knowing them shipwrecked who were launched for islands,
We honour founders of these starving cities
Whose honour is the image of our sorrow,

Which cannot see its likeness in their sorrow
That brought them desperate to the brink of valleys;
Dreaming of evening walks through learned cities
They reined their violent horses on the mountains,
Those fields like ships to castaways on islands,
Visions of green to them who craved for water.

They built by rivers and at night the water
Running past windows comforted their sorrow;
Each in his little bed conceived of islands
Where every day was dancing in the valleys
And all the green trees blossomed on the mountains
Where love was innocent, being far from cities.

But dawn came back and they were still in cities;
No marvellous creature rose up from the water;
There was still gold and silver in the mountains
But hunger was a more immediate sorrow,
Although to moping villagers in valleys
Some waving pilgrims were describing islands . . .

"The gods," they promised, "visit us from islands,
Are stalking, head-up, lovely, through our cities;
Now is the time to leave your wretched valleys

Paysage Moralisé. This poem is written in the complex verse form called *sestina*, consisting of six stanzas of six lines each and a concluding tercet, invented by the celebrated troubadour Arnaut Daniel in the thirteenth century. The ingenious difficulty of the form may be discovered by a careful study of the arrangement of the words in the different stanzas and the tercet.

And sail with them across the lime-green water,
Sitting at their white sides, forget your sorrow,
The shadow cast across your lives by mountains"

So many, doubtful, perished in the mountains,
Climbing up crags to get a view of islands,
So many, fearful, took with them their sorrow
Which stayed them when they reached unhappy cities,
So many, careless, dived and drowned in water,
So many, wretched, would not leave their valleys.

It is our sorrow. Shall it melt? Ah, water
Would gush, flush, green these mountains and these valleys,
And we rebuild our cities, not dream of islands.

LOOK, STRANGER, ON THIS ISLAND NOW

Look, stranger, on this island now
The leaping light for your delight discovers,
Stand stable here
And silent be,
That through the channels of the ear
May wander like a river
The swaying sound of the sea.

Here at the small field's ending pause
When the chalk wall falls to the foam and its tall ledges
Oppose the pluck
And knock of the tide,
And the shingle scrambles after the sucking surf,
And the gull lodges
A moment on its sheer side.

Far off like floating seeds the ships
Diverge on urgent voluntary errands,
And the full view
Indeed may enter
And move in memory as now these clouds do,
That pass the harbour mirror
And all the summer through the water saunter.

AS I WALKED OUT ONE EVENING

As I walked out one evening,
  Walking down Bristol Street,
The crowds upon the pavement
  Were fields of harvest wheat.

And down by the brimming river
  I heard a lover sing
Under an arch of the railway:
  "Love has no ending.

"I'll love you, dear, I'll love you
  Till China and Africa meet,
And the river jumps over the mountain
  And the salmon sing in the street.

"I'll love you till the ocean
  Is folded and hung up to dry,
And the seven stars go squawking
  Like geese about the sky.

"The years shall run like rabbits,
  For in my arms I hold
The Flower of the Ages,
  And the first love of the world."

But all the clocks in the city
  Began to whirr and chime:
"O let not Time deceive you,
  You cannot conquer Time.

"In the burrows of the Nightmare
  Where Justice naked is,
Time watches from the shadow
  And coughs when you would kiss.

"In headaches and in worry
  Vaguely life leaks away,
And Time will have his fancy
  Tomorrow or today.

"Into many a green valley
  Drifts the appalling snow;
Time breaks the threaded dances
  And the diver's brilliant bow.

"O plunge your hands in water,
  Plunge them in up to the wrist;
Stare, stare in the basin
  And wonder what you've missed.

"The glacier knocks in the cupboard,
  The desert sighs in the bed,
And the crack in the tea-cup opens
  A lane to the land of the dead.

"Where the beggars raffle the banknotes
  And the Giant is enchanting to Jack,
And the Lily-white Boy is a Roarer,
  And Jill goes down on her back.

"O look, look in the mirror,
  O look in your distress;
Life remains a blessing
  Although you cannot bless

"O stand, stand at the window
As the tears scald and start;
You shall love your crooked neighbour
With your crooked heart."

It was late, late in the evening,
The lovers they were gone;
The clocks had ceased their chiming,
And the deep river ran on.

CRISIS

Where do They come from? Those whom we so much dread
As on our dearest location falls the chill
Of their crooked wing and endangers
The melting friend, the aqueduct, the flower.

Terrible Presences that the ponds reflect
Back at the famous, and when the blond boy
Bites eagerly into the shining
Apple, emerge in their shocking fury.

And we realise the woods are deaf and the sky
Nurses no one, and we are awake and these
Like farmers have purpose and knowledge,
And towards us their hate is directed.

We are the barren pastures to which they bring
The resentment of outcasts; on us they work
Out their despair; they wear our weeping
As the disgraceful badge of their exile.

O we conjured them here like a lying map;
Desiring the extravagant joy of life
We lured with a mirage of orchards
Fat in the lazy climate of refuge.

Our money sang like streams on the aloof peaks
Of our thinking that beckoned them on like girls;
Our culture like a West of wonder
Shone a solemn promise in their faces.

We expected the beautiful or the wise
Ready to see a charm in our childish fib,
Pleased to find nothing but stones and
Able at once to create a garden.

But those who come are not even children with
The big indiscriminate eyes we had lost,
Occupying our narrow spaces
With their anarchist vivid abandon.

They arrive, already adroit, having learned
Restraint at the table of a father's rage;
In a mother's distorting mirror
They discovered the Meaning of Knowing.

These pioneers have long adapted themselves
To the night and the nightmare; they come equipped
To reply to terror with terror,
With lies to unmask the least deception.

For a future of marriage nevertheless
The bed is prepared; though all our whiteness shrinks
From the hairy and clumsy bridegroom,
We conceive in the shuddering instant.

For the barren must wish to bear though the Spring
Punish; and the crooked that dreads to be straight
Cannot alter its prayer but summons
Out of the dark a horrible rector.

O the striped and vigorous tiger can move
With style through the borough of murder; the ape
Is really at home in the parish
Of grimacing and licking: but we have

Failed as their pupils. Our tears well from a love
We have never outgrown; our cities predict
More than we hope; even our armies
Have to express our need of forgiveness.

IN MEMORY OF W. B. YEATS

(d. Jan. 1939)

I

He disappeared in the dead of winter:
The brooks were frozen, the airports almost deserted,
And snow disfigured the public statues;
The mercury sank in the mouth of the dying day.
O all the instruments agree
The day of his death was a dark cold day.

Far from his illness
The wolves ran on through the evergreen forests,

The peasant river was untempted by the fashionable quays;
By mourning tongues
The death of the poet was kept from his poems.

But for him it was his last afternoon as himself,
An afternoon of nurses and rumours;
The provinces of his body revolted,
The squares of his mind were empty,
Silence invaded the suburbs,
The current of his feeling failed: he became his admirers.

Now he is scattered among a hundred cities
And wholly given over to unfamiliar affections;
To find his happiness in another kind of wood
And be punished under a foreign code of conscience.
The words of a dead man
Are modified in the guts of the living.

But in the importance and noise of tomorrow
When the brokers are roaring like beasts on the floor of the Bourse,
And the poor have the sufferings to which they are fairly accustomed,
And each in the cell of himself is almost convinced of his freedom,
A few thousand will think of this day
As one thinks of a day when one did something slightly unusual.
O all the instruments agree
The day of his death was a dark cold day.

2

You were silly like us: your gift survived it all;
The parish of rich women, physical decay,
Yourself; mad Ireland hurt you into poetry.
Now Ireland has her madness and her weather still,
For poetry makes nothing happen: it survives
In the valley of its saying where executives
Would never want to tamper; it flows south
From ranches of isolation and the busy griefs,
Raw towns that we believe and die in; it survives,
A way of happening, a mouth.

3

Earth, receive an honoured guest;
William Yeats is laid to rest:
Let the Irish vessel lie
Emptied of its poetry.

Time that is intolerant
Of the brave and innocent,
And indifferent in a week
To a beautiful physique,

Worships language and forgives
Everyone by whom it lives;
Pardons cowardice, conceit,
Lays its honours at their feet.

Time that with this strange excuse
Pardoned Kipling and his views,
And will pardon Paul Claudel,
Pardons him for writing well.

In the nightmare of the dark
All the dogs of Europe bark,
And the living nations wait,
Each sequestered in its hate;

Intellectual disgrace
Stares from every human face,
And the seas of pity lie
Locked and frozen in each eye.

Follow, poet, follow right
To the bottom of the night,
With your unconstraining voice
Still persuade us to rejoice;

With the farming of a verse
Make a vineyard of the curse,
Sing of human unsuccess
In a rapture of distress;

In the deserts of the heart
Let the healing fountain start,
In the prison of his days
Teach the free man how to praise.

Stephen Spender

1909–

Stephen Spender was born near London, February 28, 1909. His mother was Violet Schuster; his father was Harold Spender, a well-known journalist. As a child Spender showed remarkable precocity; he interested himself in painting as well as poetry. At seventeen he revolted from formal education and tried to support himself; he bought a hand press and hoped to earn a living by printing chemists' labels. On this press Spender set up and printed in 1928 a paper-bound pamphlet of verse, *Nine Experiments*, which he had written in his seventeenth and eighteenth years. At nineteen he attended University College, Oxford, but did not wait to complete his course. *Twenty Poems*, 1930, was printed while he was an undergraduate, but Spender's name was unknown to America until the publication of *Poems*, 1933, which made something of a sensation in both England and America.

One of the reasons for this favorable reception was the quality of Spender's poetry, and another was the evidence it gave that new and vigorous poetry was again being written in England. Spender was less adroit and far less versatile technically, but far more intense, than Auden. An almost Shelleyan fervor is apparent in such poems as "Not Palaces," "The Express," "The Funeral," and the exalted lines beginning "I think continually of those who were truly great." This last poem is one of the age's finest tributes to those

"Who wore at their hearts the fire's centre.
Born of the sun they travelled a short while towards the sun,
And left the vivid air signed with their honour."

Francis Scarfe, in his *Auden and After*, says that Spender stands in very much the same relation to Auden as Shelley did to Byron. His poetry is more introspective than Auden's, and he is a far more sensitive poet, often painfully so, than Auden or MacNeice or Day Lewis, with whom he has been associated. There is also about his verse a quiet lyrical and romantic quality that distinguishes it from the verse of his fellow poets.

"Not Palaces" is typical of Spender's idiom and the quick transit of his imagination. Here, in an abrupt set of images and half-evoked associations, is a call to youth, a call to co-operate with the changes taking place in a shifting world. The palaces are down; it is too late, the poet says, to sentimentalize over the past, too late for family pride and outworn prettiness, "beauty's filtered dusts." He insists that we must draw energy "As from the electric charge of a battery" if we are to be active spirits of our time. All our faculties must co-operate to appreciate this change—the eye, that quickly darting, delicately wandering gazelle; the ear, which "suspends on a chord The spirit drinking timelessness"; touch that intensifies all senses. These must equip us to realize a greater humanity, a humanity which will no longer be in love with war and death ("the programme of the antique Satan"), but which will proclaim death to the killers, "bringing light to life."

After the slim volume of *Poems*, 1933, came in the next year a long didactic poem, *Vienna*, which was occasioned by the murder of the Austrian Socialists. In this poem lyrical passages alternate with abstract philosophical discussions, and the poem fails as a sustained piece. Another poem of a political nature, *Trial of a Judge*, 1938, is an allegorical verse drama based on outrages committed by the Nazis in Germany. *Poems from Spain* and *The Still Centre*, 1939, were inspired by the Spanish Civil War, and are examples of Spender's more meditative but no less impassioned verse, although they reveal also the tendency towards didacticism and speculation that mar much of his work. Two later volumes of verse, *Ruins and Visions*, 1943, and *Poems of Dedication*, 1947, show an increase in his mastery of imagery but are less felicitous in their lyrics and almost morbid in their sensitivity and introspection. His most recent volume, *The Edge of Being*, 1949, contains some poems in his best lyrical style and others that are merely speculative. It contains evidence also that he is still concerned with the social and moral problems of a sensitive man in the contemporary world as well as with the technical problems of the modern poet and artist.

Besides his poetry Spender has written several volumes of prose, among the most distinguished of which are *The Destructive Element*, 1935, a study of modern writers and beliefs written from a politico-moral standpoint; *The Burning Cactus*, 1936, a collection of five introspective short stories; and *Life and the Poet*, 1942, a book of criticism. In the autobiographical volume, *World Within World*, 1951,

Spender found as "the only true hope for civilization—the conviction of the individual that his inner life can affect outward events and that, whether or not he does so, he is responsible for them."

HE WILL WATCH THE HAWK[1]

He will watch the hawk with an indifferent eye
Or pitifully;
Nor on those eagles that so feared him, now
Will strain his brow;
Weapons men use, stone, sling and strong-thewed bow
He will not know.

This aristocrat, superb of all instinct,
With death close linked
Had paced the enormous cloud, almost had won
War on the sun;
Till now, like Icarus mid-ocean-drowned,
Hands, wings, are found.

BEETHOVEN'S DEATH MASK

I imagine him still with heavy brow.
Huge, black, with bent head and falling hair
He ploughs the landscape. His face
Is this hanging mask transfigured,
This mask of death which the white lights make stare.

I see the thick hands clasped; the scare-crow coat;
The light strike upwards at the holes for eyes;
The beast squat in that mouth, whose opening is
The hollow opening of an organ pipe:
There the wind sings and the harsh longing cries.

He moves across my vision like a ship.
What else is iron but he? The fields divide
And, heaving, are changing waters of the sea.
He is prisoned, masked, shut off from being;
Life like a fountain he sees leap—outside.

Yet, in that head there twists the roaring cloud
And coils, as in a shell, the roaring wave.
The damp leaves whisper; bending to the rain
The April rises in him, chokes his lungs
And climbs the torturing passage of his brain.

[1] This and the following poems by Stephen Spender are from *Poems of Stephen Spender*, copyright, 1934, by Modern Library. Reprinted by permission of Random House, Inc.

Then the drums move away, the Distance shows;
Now cloudy peaks are bared; the mystic One
Horizons haze, as the blue incense heaven.
Peace, peace . . . Then splitting skull and dream, there comes,
Blotting our lights, the trumpeter, the sun.

OH YOUNG MEN OH YOUNG COMRADES

oh young men oh young comrades
it is too late now to stay in those houses
your fathers built where they built you to build to breed
money on money it is too late
to make or even to count what has been made
Count rather those fabulous possessions
which begin with your body and your fiery soul:—
the hairs on your head the muscles extending
in ranges with their lakes across your limbs
Count your eyes as jewels and your valued sex
then count the sun and the innumerable coined light
sparkling on waves and spangled under trees
It is too late to stay in great houses where the ghosts are prisoned
—those ladies like flies perfect in amber
those financiers like fossils of bones in coal.
Oh comrades, step beautifully from the solid wall
advance to rebuild and sleep with friend on hill
advance to rebel and remember what you have
no ghost ever had, immured in his hall.

THE FUNERAL

Death is another milestone on their way.
With laughter on their lips and with winds blowing round them
They record simply
How this one excelled all others in making driving-belts.

This is festivity, it is the time of statistics
When they record what one unit contributed:
They are glad as they lay him back in the earth
And thank him for what he gave them.

They walk home remembering the straining red flags,
And with pennons of song still fluttering through their blood
They speak of the world state
With its towns like brain-centres and its pulsing arteries.

They think how one life hums, revolves and toils,
One cog in a golden and singing hive:
Like spark from fire, its task happily achieved,
It falls away quietly.

No more are they haunted by the individual grief
Nor the crocodile tears of European genius,
The decline of a culture
Mourned by scholars who dream of the ghosts of Greek boys.

THE EXPRESS

After the first powerful plain manifesto
The black statement of pistons, without more fuss
But gliding like a queen, she leaves the station.
Without bowing and with restrained unconcern
She passes the houses which humbly crowd outside,
The gasworks and at last the heavy page
Of death, printed by gravestones in the cemetery.
Beyond the town there lies the open country
Where, gathering speed, she acquires mystery,
The luminous self-possession of ships on ocean.
It is now she begins to sing—at first quite low
Then loud, and at last with a jazzy madness—
The song of her whistle screaming at curves,
Of deafening tunnels, brakes, innumerable bolts.
And always light, aerial, underneath
Goes the elate metre of her wheels.
Steaming through metal landscape on her lines
She plunges new eras of wild happiness
Where speed throws up strange shapes, broad curves
And parallels clean like the steel of guns.
At last, further than Edinburgh or Rome,
Beyond the crest of the world, she reaches night
Where only a low streamline brightness
Of phosphorus on the tossing hills is white.
Ah, like a comet through flame she moves entranced
Wrapt in her music no bird song, no, nor bough
Breaking with honey buds, shall ever equal.

THE LANDSCAPE NEAR AN AERODROME

More beautiful and soft than any moth
With burring, furred antennae feeling its huge path
Through dusk, the air-liner with shut-off engines
Glides over suburbs and the sleeves set trailing tall
To point the wind. Gently, broadly, she falls,
Scarcely disturbing charted currents of air.

Lulled by descent, the travellers across sea
And across feminine land indulging its easy limbs
In miles of softness, now let their eyes trained by watching
Penetrate through dusk the outskirts of this town
Here where industry shows a fraying edge.
Here they may see what is being done.

Beyond the winking masthead light
And the landing-ground, they observe the outposts
Of work: chimneys like lank black fingers
Or figures frightening and mad: and squat buildings
With their strange air behind trees, like women's faces
Shattered by grief. Here where few houses
Moan with faint light behind their blinds
They remark the unhomely sense of complaint, like a dog
Shut out and shivering at the foreign moon.

In the last sweep of love, they pass over fields
Behind the aerodrome, where boys play all day
Hacking dead grass: whose cries, like wild birds,
Settle upon the nearest roofs
But soon are hid under the loud city.

Then, as they land, they hear the tolling bell
Reaching across the landscape of hysteria
To where, larger than all the charcoaled batteries
And imaged towers against that dying sky,
Religion stands, the church blocking the sun.

NOT PALACES

Not palaces, an era's crown
Where the mind dwells, intrigues, rests;
The architectural gold-leaved flower
From people ordered like a single mind,
I build. This only what I tell:
It is too late for rare accumulation
For family pride, for beauty's filtered dusts;
I say, stamping the words with emphasis,
Drink from here energy and only energy,
As from the electric charge of a battery,
To will this Time's change.
Eye, gazelle, delicate wanderer,
Drinker of horizon's fluid line;
Ear that suspends on a chord
The spirit drinking timelessness;
Touch, love, all senses;
Leave your gardens, your singing feasts,
Your dreams of suns circling before our sun,
Of heaven after our world.
Instead, watch images of flashing brass
That strike the outward sense, the polished will
Flag of our purpose which the wind engraves.
No spirit seek here rest. But this: No man

Shall hunger: Man shall spend equally.
Our goal which we compel: Man shall be man.

—That programme of the antique Satan
Bristling with guns on the indented page
With battleship towering from hilly waves:
For what? Drive of a ruining purpose
Destroying all but its age-long exploiters.
Our programme like this, yet opposite,
Death to the killers, bringing light to life.

I THINK CONTINUALLY OF THOSE

I think continually of those who were truly great.
Who, from the womb, remembered the soul's history
Through corridors of light where the hours are suns
Endless and singing. Whose lovely ambition
Was that their lips, still touched with fire,
Should tell of the Spirit clothed from head to foot in song.
And who hoarded from the Spring branches
The desires falling across their bodies like blossoms.

What is precious is never to forget
The delight of the blood drawn from ageless springs
Breaking through rocks in worlds before our earth.
Never to deny its pleasure in the simple morning light
Nor its grave evening demand for love.
Never to allow gradually the traffic to smother
With noise and fog the flowering of the spirit.

Near the snow, near the sun, in the highest fields
See how these names are fêted by the waving grass
And by the streamers of white cloud,
And whispers of wind in the listening sky.
The names of those who in their lives fought for life
Who wore at their hearts the fire's centre.
Born of the sun they travelled a short while towards the sun,
And left the vivid air signed with their honour.

Dylan Thomas 1914–1953

Dylan Marlais Thomas was born in Carmarthenshire, Wales. His *Portrait of the Artist as a Young Dog* (1940), a collection of autobiographical sketches, tells of his youth in the coal-mining district and of those holidays on the farm that, if we may judge by his later poems, captivated his imagination. He attended Swansea Grammar School, but other than this he had no formal education. For several years he earned his living by broadcasting for the British Broadcasting Corporation. In 1950 he toured the United States, reading his poetry to college audiences but generally refusing to discuss it. An excellent reader, he recorded many of his poems for the Library of Congress.

His earliest work, *18 poems*, appeared in 1934. This was followed by *Twenty-Five Poems* (1936), *The Map of Love* (1939), which contains not only poems but short stories, *Deaths and Entrances* (1945), and *Twenty-Six Poems*, 1949. In America his poems and stories have been collected as *The World I Breathe* (1939) and *Selected Writings* (1946).

Thomas's work differs in many ways from that of Eliot or Auden, his immediate predecessors. At first glance his poetry seems a rich and almost mad confusion of images. It becomes clear, however, that this surface confusion is the result of deliberate craft. Progressions and interlinking of sounds, repetitions of words and phrases, and sequences of images evince a conscious control that distinguishes Thomas from the Surrealists, with whom at first he seems to have much in common. Astounding images such as "a face of hands" or "the sea-legged deck" are neither echoes of the Surrealists nor translations from the Welsh as some critics have supposed. Brought up in an English-speaking district, Thomas knows little Welsh. His literary antecedents include Hopkins, Joyce, the Metaphysical poets of the seventeenth century, and the French Symbolists, especially Rimbaud. Although he writes within these traditions, his images owe more to Freud and the Bible, the two most common stocks of imagery in our time.

Taking an image from Freud, the Bible, or his own unconscious, Thomas allows it to suggest its opposite. The interaction of these opposites produces a third image, and the third a fourth. The resultant of this dialectical process is what Thomas calls "that momentary peace which is a poem," the synthesis in which the contradictory images have a meaningful relationship. As confusing on the surface as the manifest level of a dream, the resulting system of images may be translated into prose sense by the aid of Freud and one's memories of Sunday school. Thomas's poetry grows out of his concern, on the one hand, with the cycle of sex, birth, and growth, and, on the other, with the force of death. In his line "From limbs that had the measure of the worm," Freud and the Bible are united. The line implies birth, death, the story of the serpent in the Garden of Eden, the Fall of Man, and his Redemption. Such richness of implication is common enough in Thomas. Take as another example his phrase "the kissproof world." Kissproof is the name of a lipstick. Coming at the end of an early poem about life and death, this image presents not only adolescent frustration and despair, but, by its wit, a kind of gaiety.

Thomas's systems of images may, as has been said, be translated into prose, but such translation proves only that Thomas is concerned with love, religion, and death. The prose sense of his poetry is neither its meaning nor its value, which lie rather in the interaction of the sense and the rich surface or in interactions among the audible images. He has remarkable gifts of incantatory rhythm and metaphor. Perhaps the best way to read him is to surrender oneself to the magical surface without worrying too much about meanings. That is why Thomas reads but almost never explains his poems.

His early verse, in which he was absorbed in self-contemplation and concerned with the mysteries of womb and tomb, yielded gradually to the light of day. The later poetry deals with the growing years of childhood, about which some of his happiest and most beautiful verse has been written, and with the tragedy of war. In his later work Thomas is more concerned with the art of poetic communication, and although it lacks the strangeness of the early poems, it has retained their magic. At times in the collection *Deaths and Entrances* he seems, through the use of religious symbols, to attain an almost mystical desire to enter from a death of the self into communion with God. "Fern Hill," perhaps the best of his mature works, is one of the outstanding poems of our time.

Thomas has been the chief influence on a group of younger poets, including J. F. Hendry and Henry Treece, who call themselves the Apocalyptics, and who emphasize the importance of the myth as a means of integrating poetry. Their political philosophy exalts the small organic community as most conducive to individual freedom.

THE FORCE THAT THROUGH THE GREEN FUSE DRIVES [1]

The force that through the green fuse drives the flower
Drives my green age; that blasts the roots of trees
Is my destroyer.
And I am dumb to tell the crooked rose
My youth is bent by the same wintry fever.

The force that drives the water through the rocks
Drives my red blood; that dries the mouthing streams
Turns mine to wax.
And I am dumb to mouth unto my veins
How at the mountain spring the same mouth sucks.

The hand that whirls the water in the pool
Stirs the quicksand; that ropes the blowing wind
Hauls my shroud sail.
And I am dumb to tell the hanging man
How of my clay is made the hangman's lime.

The lips of time leech to the fountain head;
Love drips and gathers, but the fallen blood
Shall calm her sores.
And I am dumb to tell a weather's wind
How time has ticked a heaven round the stars.

And I am dumb to tell the lover's tomb
How at my sheet goes the same crooked worm.

IN MEMORY OF ANN JONES

After the funeral, mule praises, brays,
Windshake of sailshaped ears, muffle-toed tap
Tap happily of one peg in the thick
Grave's foot, blinds down the lids, the teeth in black,
The spittled eyes, the salt ponds in the sleeves,
Morning smack of the spade that wakes up sleep,
Shakes a desolate boy who slits his throat
In the dark of the coffin and sheds dry leaves,
That breaks one bone to light with a judgment clout,
After the feast of tear-stuffed time and thistles
In a room with a stuffed fox and a stale fern,
I stand, for this memorial's sake, alone
In the snivelling hours with dead, humped Ann
Whose hooded, fountain heart once fell in puddles

[1] This and the following poems by Dylan Thomas are from *Selected Writings*, copyright, 1939, 1946, by New Directions and used with their permission.

Round the parched worlds of Wales and drowned each sun
(Though this for her is a monstrous image blindly
Magnified out of praise; her death was a still drop;
She would not have me sinking in the holy
Flood of her heart's fame; she would lie dumb and deep
And need no druid of her broken body).
But I, Ann's bard on a raised hearth, call all
The seas to service that her wood-tongued virtue
Babble like a bellbuoy over the hymning heads,
Bow down the walls of the ferned and foxy woods
That her love sing and swing through a brown chapel,
Bless her bent spirit with four, crossing birds.
Her flesh was meek as milk, but this skyward statue
With the wild breast and blessed and giant skull
Is carved from her in a room with a wet window
In a fiercely mourning house in a crooked year.
I know her scrubbed and sour humble hands
Lie with religion in their cramp, her threadbare
Whisper in a damp word, her wits drilled hollow,
Her fist of a face died clenched on a round pain;
And sculptured Ann is seventy years of stone.
These cloud-sopped, marble hands, this monumental
Argument of the hewn voice, gesture and psalm
Storm me forever over her grave until
The stuffed lung of the fox twitch and cry Love
And the strutting fern lay seeds on the black sill.

THE HAND THAT SIGNED THE PAPER

The hand that signed the paper felled a city;
Five sovereign fingers taxed the breath,
Doubled the globe of dead and halved a country;
These five kings did a king to death.

The mighty hand leads to a sloping shoulder,
The finger joints are cramped with chalk;
A goose's quill has put an end to murder
That put an end to talk.

The hand that signed the treaty bred a fever,
And famine grew, and locusts came;
Great is the hand that holds dominion over
Man by a scribbled name.

The five kings count the dead but do not soften
The crusted wound nor pat the brow;
A hand rules pity as a hand rules heaven;
Hands have no tears to flow.

AND DEATH SHALL HAVE NO DOMINION

And death shall have no dominion.
Dead men naked they shall be one
With the man in the wind and the west moon;
When their bones are picked clean and the clean bones gone,
They shall have stars at elbow and foot;
Though they go mad they shall be sane,
Though they sink through the sea they shall rise again;
Though lovers be lost love shall not;
And death shall have no dominion.

And death shall have no dominion.
Under the windings of the sea
They lying long shall not die windily;
Twisting on racks when sinews give way,
Strapped to a wheel, yet they shall not break;
Faith in their hands shall snap in two,
And the unicorn evils run them through;
Split all ends up they shan't crack;
And death shall have no dominion.

And death shall have no dominion.
No more may gulls cry at their ears
Or waves break loud on the seashores;
Where blew a flower may a flower no more
Lift its head to the blows of the rain;
Though they be mad and dead as nails,
Heads of the characters hammer through daisies;
Break in the sun till the sun breaks down,
And death shall have no dominion.

FERN HILL

Now as I was young and easy under the apple boughs
About the lilting house and happy as the grass was green,
The night above the dingle starry,
Time let me hail and climb
Golden in the heydays of his eyes,
And honoured among wagons I was prince of the apple towns
And once below a time I lordly had the trees and leaves
Trail with daisies and barley
Down the rivers of the windfall light.

And as I was green and carefree, famous among the barns

About the happy yard and singing as the farm was home,
In the sun that is young once only,
Time let me play and be
Golden in the mercy of his means,
And green and golden I was huntsman and herdsman, the calves
Sang to my horn, the foxes on the hills barked clear and cold,
And the sabbath rang slowly
In the pebbles of the holy streams.

All the sun long it was running, it was lovely, the hay-
Fields high as the house, the tunes from the chimneys, it was air
And playing, lovely and watery
And fire green as grass.
And nightly under the simple stars
As I rode to sleep the owls were bearing the farm away,
All the moon long I heard, blessed among stables, the night-jars
Flying with the ricks, and the horses
Flashing into the dark.

And then to awake, and the farm, like a wanderer white
With the dew, come back, the cock on his shoulder; it was all
Shining, it was Adam and maiden,
The sky gathered again
And the sun grew round that very day.
So it must have been after the birth of the simple light
In the first, spinning place, the spellbound horses walking warm
Out of the whinnying green stable
On to the fields of praise.

And honoured among foxes and pheasants by the gay house
Under the new made clouds and happy as the heart was long,
In the sun born over and over
I ran my heedless ways,
My wishes raced through the house-high hay
And nothing I cared, at my sky blue trades, that time allows
In all his tuneful turning so few and such morning songs
Before the children green and golden
Follow him out of grace,

Nothing I cared, in the lamb white days, that time would take me
Up to the swallow thronged loft by the shadow of my hand,
In the moon that is always rising,
Nor that riding to sleep
I should hear him fly with the high fields
And wake to the farm forever fled from the childless land.
Oh as I was young and easy in the mercy of his means,
Time held me green and dying
Though I sang in my chains like the sea.

SUGGESTIONS FOR FURTHER READING

This list is to be supplemented by the brief lists of books given in the General Bibliography and in the various introductions to specific authors and works.

HISTORICAL AND POLITICAL BACKGROUND

Churchill, Winston S. *The Second World War*, Houghton Mifflin, 1948—. The classic study of the subject by Britain's great war leader.

Cruttwell, C. R. M. F. *A History of the Great War, 1914–1918*, Oxford University Press, 1936.

Dietz, F. C. *A Political and Social History of England*, Macmillan, 1937.

Gretton, R. H. *A Modern History of the English People: 1880–1922*, Dial Press, 1930.

Guedalla, Philip. *The Hundred Years, 1837–1937*, Doubleday, Doran, 1937.

Hodson, H. V. *Twentieth-Century Empire*, Faber and Faber, 1949.

Kohn, Hans. *The Twentieth Century: A Mid-Way Account of the Western World*, Macmillan, 1949. An excellent survey of the first half of the century.

Somervell, D. C. *British Politics since 1900*, Oxford University Press, 1950.

CULTURAL AND SOCIAL BACKGROUND

Cole, G. D. H., and Postgate, Raymond. *The British Common People, 1746–1938*, Knopf, 1939.

Collier, John, and Lang, Iain. *Just the Other Day: An Informal History of Great Britain since the War*, Harper, 1932.

Copland, Aaron. *Our New Music: Leading Composers in Europe and America*, McGraw-Hill, 1941.

Davidson, Morris. *An Approach to Modern Painting*, Coward-McCann, 1948.

Desmond, Shaw. *The Edwardian Story*, Macmillan, 1951. A vivid panorama of the first decade of the twentieth century.

Graves, Robert, and Hodge, Alan. *The Long Weekend: A Social History of Britain, 1918–1939*, Macmillan, 1941.

Jeans, Sir James. *The Growth of Physical Science*, Cambridge University Press, 1947. An excellent history for the general reader of the evolution of the physical sciences.

Whitehead, A. N. *Science and the Modern World*, Macmillan, 1925. A standard work.

LITERATURE OF THE PERIOD

COLLECTIONS

Cordell, R. A., ed. *Twentieth-Century Plays (British)*, Ronald Press, 1947. An excellent collection, with introduction and notes on the playwrights and their works.

Five Great Modern Irish Plays, Modern Library. (Synge: *The Playboy of the Western World* and *Riders to the Sea;* O'Casey: *Juno and the Paycock;* Lady Gregory: *Spreading the News;* Carroll: *Shadow and Substance.*)

Heilman, Robert B., ed. *Modern Short Stories: A Critical Anthology*, Harcourt, Brace, 1950.

Kreymborg, Alfred, ed. *Poetic Drama: An Anthology of Plays in Verse.* Modern Age Books, 1941.

Rexroth, Kenneth. *New British Poets, An Anthology*, New Directions, 1949.

Schorer, Mark, Miles, Josephine, and McKenzie, Gordon, eds. *Criticism: The Foundations of Modern Literary Judgment*, Harcourt, Brace, 1948. A collection representing the scope of modern literary criticism.

Selected Modern English Essays, First and Second Series, World's Classics, Oxford University Press.

Short, R. W., and Sewall, R. B., eds. *Short Stories for Study: An Anthology*, Holt, 1941.

Untermeyer, Louis, ed. *Modern British Poetry* (Mid-Century Edition), Harcourt, Brace, 1949. A generous selection of twentieth-century British poetry.

Yeats, William Butler, ed. *The Oxford Book of Modern Verse, 1892–1935*, Oxford University Press, 1936.

CRITICISM

Connolly, Cyril. *Enemies of Promise*, Little, Brown, 1939. A study of the artistic and moral problems of contemporary English writers.

Cunliffe, J. W. *English Literature in the Twentieth Century*, Macmillan, 1934.

Foerster, Norman, ed. *The Humanities after the War*, Princeton University Press, 1949. An excellent symposium of the problems and possibilities of artists, authors, and students of the humanities today.

Millett, F. B., Manly, J. M., and Rickert, Edith. *Contemporary British Literature: A Critical Survey and 232 Author-bibliographies*, Harcourt, Brace, 1935.

Routh, H. V. *English Literature and Ideas in the Twentieth Century: An Inquiry into Present Difficulties and Future Prospects*, Longmans, 1948.

Swinnerton, Frank. *The Georgian Literary Scene, 1910–1935*, Farrar, Straus, and Young, 1951. Reissue of an urbane and enlightening volume.

Tindall, William Y. *Forces in Modern British Literature, 1885–1946*, Knopf, 1947. Witty and very readable.

Vines, Sherard. *Movements in Modern English Poetry and Prose*, Oxford, 1927.

Bailey, Ruth. *A Dialogue on Modern Poetry*, Oxford, 1939.

Brooks, Cleanth. *Modern Poetry and the Tradition*, University of North Carolina Press, 1939. A valuable discussion of contemporary verse in the light of traditional forms.

Daiches, David. *Poetry and the Modern World*, University of Chicago Press, 1940.

Hulme, T. E. *Speculations*, Harcourt, Brace, 1924. This has influenced twentieth-century poets more, perhaps, than any other single work of modern philosophy.

Leavis, F. R. *New Bearings in English Poetry*, Chatto and Windus, 1942.

Lewis, Cecil Day. *A Hope for Poetry*, printed with his *Collected Poems, 1929–33*, Random House, 1935. An appraisal of the younger poets in the early 1930's.

—— *The Poetic Image*, Oxford, 1947.

O'Connor, William Van. *Sense and Sensibility in Modern Poetry*, Chicago University Press, 1948.

Sparrow, John. *Sense and Poetry*, Yale University Press, 1934. Studies in the place of meaning in contemporary verse; an attack on the "obscurity" of much modern poetry.

Weygandt, Cornelius. *The Time of Yeats: English Poetry of Today against an American Background*, Appleton-Century, 1937.

Beach, J. W. *The Twentieth-Century Novel: Studies in Technique*, Appleton-Century, 1932.

Forster, E. M. *Aspects of the Novel*, Harcourt, Brace, 1927.

James, Henry. *Notes on Novelists*, Scribner, 1914. See especially the chapter on "The New Novel."

Leavis, F. R. *The Great Tradition*, George W. Stewart, 1949. Stimulating, provocative discussions of George Eliot, Henry James, Conrad, D. H. Lawrence, etc.

Lubbock, Percy. *The Craft of Fiction*, Cape, 1921. Perhaps the best single book on the novel.

O'Connor, William Van, compiler. *Forms of Modern Fiction*, University of Minnesota Press, 1948. A stimulating symposium on aspects of contemporary fiction.

Bates, H. E. *The Modern Short Story: A Survey*, Nelson, 1942.

Classe, André. *The Rhythm of English Prose*, Oxford, 1939.

Dobrée, Bonamy. *Modern Prose Style*, Oxford, 1934.

Longaker, Mark. *Contemporary Biography*, University of Pennsylvania Press, 1934.

Archer, William. *The Old Drama and the New*, Dodd, Mead, 1923.

Bentley, Eric R. *The Playwright as Thinker, A Study of Drama in Modern Times*, Reynal and Hitchcock, 1946.

Clark, B. H. *A Study of the Modern Drama*, Appleton, 1925.

Dickinson, T. H. *The Contemporary Drama of England*, Little, Brown, 1931.

Eliot, T. S. *The Sacred Wood*, Methuen, 1920. Contains

two important essays, "The Possibility of a Poetic Drama," and "Rhetoric and Poetic Drama."

—— *Poetry and Drama*, Harvard University Press, 1951.

Ellis-Fermor, Una. *The Frontiers of Drama*, Methuen, 1946.

Malone, A. E. *The Irish Drama*, Scribner, 1929.

Nicoll, Allardyce. *The Development of the Theatre*, Harcourt, Brace, 1948.

AUDEN

The Collected Poetry of W. H. Auden, Random House, 1945.

The Age of Anxiety, a Baroque Eclogue, Random House, 1947.

Scarfe, Francis. *Auden and After: The Liberation of Poetry, 1930–1941*, Transatlantic Press, 1945.

CHESTERTON

Tremendous Trifles, Dodd, Mead, 1918. Essays.

New and Collected Poems, Dodd, Mead, 1929.

A Father Brown Omnibus, Dodd, Mead, 1935. Ingenious and entertaining short detective stories.

Autobiography, Sheed and Ward, 1936.

Ward, Maisie. *Gilbert Keith Chesterton*, Sheed and Ward, 1944.

CONRAD

The Portable Conrad, Viking Press, 1947. Includes *The Nigger of the Narcissus*, *Youth*, *Typhoon*, short stories, and letters.

Ford, Ford Madox. *Joseph Conrad, a Personal Reminiscence*, Little, Brown, 1924.

Gordan, J. D. *Joseph Conrad: The Making of a Novelist*, Harvard University Press, 1940.

Guérard, A. J. *Joseph Conrad*, New Directions, 1947. Perhaps the most stimulating study of Conrad.

ELIOT

Collected Poems, 1909–1935; Murder in the Cathedral, 1935; *The Family Reunion*, 1939; *Four Quartets*, 1943; *The Cocktail Party*, 1950, Harcourt, Brace.

Selected Essays, rev. ed., Harcourt, Brace, 1950.

Matthiessen, F. O. *The Achievement of T. S. Eliot: An Essay on the Nature of Poetry*, 2nd ed., rev., Oxford University Press, 1947. Widely regarded as the best single book on Eliot.

Rajan, Balachandra, ed. *T. S. Eliot: A Study of His Writings by Several Hands*, D. Dobson, 1948.

Unger, Leonard, ed. *T. S. Eliot: A Selected Critique*, Rinehart, 1948.

Drew, Elizabeth. *T. S. Eliot: The Design of His Poetry*, Scribner, 1949.

Gardner, Helen. *The Art of T. S. Eliot*, Cresset Press, 1949.

FORSTER

Abinger Harvest, Harcourt, Brace, 1936. Essays.

Collected Tales, Knopf, 1947.

Macaulay, Rose. *The Writings of E. M. Forster*, Hogarth Press, 1938.

Trilling, Lionel. *E. M. Forster*, New Directions, 1943. The standard study of Forster.

HARDY

Collected Poems, Macmillan, 1926.

Weber, C. J. *Hardy of Wessex*, Columbia University Press, 1940.

Blunden, Edmund. *Thomas Hardy*, Macmillan, 1942.

Chakravarty, Amirya. "*The Dynasts*" *and the Post-War Age in Poetry: A Study in Modern Ideas*, Oxford, 1938.

Southworth, J. G. *The Poetry of Thomas Hardy*, Columbia University Press, 1947.

Webster, H. C. *On a Darkling Plain, The Art and Thought of Thomas Hardy*, University of Chicago Press, 1948. The influence of Hardy's life on his thought and writing.

Guérard, A. J. *Thomas Hardy: The Novels and Stories*, Harvard University Press, 1949. A reappraisal of Hardy the storyteller.

HOUSMAN

Collected Poems, Holt, 1940.

The Name and Nature of Poetry, Cambridge University Press, 1933. Vigorous statement of a romantic view of poetry. Leslie Stephen Lecture.

Gow, A. S. F. *A. E. Housman; a sketch, together with a list of his writings and indexes to his classical papers*, Cambridge University Press, 1936.

HUXLEY

The World of Aldous Huxley; an omnibus of his fiction and nonfiction over three decades, Harper, 1947.

Music at Night and Other Essays, Harper, 1931.

JOYCE

Collected Poems, 1937; *Finnegans Wake*, 1947, Viking Press.

The Portable James Joyce, Viking Press, 1947. Includes *Dubliners*, *Portrait of the Artist as a Young Man*, *Exiles*, *Collected Poems*, and parts of *Ulysses* and *Finnegans Wake*.

Leven, Harry. *James Joyce*, New Directions, 1941. The best general study of Joyce.

Givens, Seon. *James Joyce: Two Decades of Criticism*, Vanguard Press, 1948.

Gorman, Herbert. *James Joyce, His Life and Work*, Rinehart, 1949.

Strong, L. A. G. *The Sacred River: An Approach to James Joyce*, Methuen, 1949.

Tindall, W. Y. *James Joyce: His Way of Interpreting the Modern World*, Scribner, 1949.

LAWRENCE

Selected Poems, New Directions, 1948. A generally good selection from Lawrence's very uneven poetry.

The Portable D. H. Lawrence, Viking Press, 1947. Includes selections from *The Rainbow* and *Women in Love*, novelettes, stories, poems, travel sketches, essays, letters.

Aldington, Richard. *D. H. Lawrence*, Chatto and Windus, 1927.

Gregory, Horace. *Pilgrim of the Apocalypse*, Viking Press, 1933.

MANSFIELD

The Short Stories of Katherine Mansfield, Knopf, 1937.

The Poems of Katherine Mansfield, Knopf, 1924.

The Letters of Katherine Mansfield, Knopf, 1929.
Berkman, Sylvia. *Katherine Mansfield*, Yale University Press, 1951. Biography and criticism.
Mantz, Ruth E., and Murry, J. M. *The Life of Katherine Mansfield*, Constable, 1933.

MASEFIELD

Collected Poems, Macmillan, 1935.
Recent Prose, Macmillan, 1933.
In the Mill, Macmillan, 1941. An autobiographical account of early years.
Hamilton, W. H. *John Masefield*, Macmillan, 1922.

MAUGHAM

East and West, the Collected Short Stories of W. Somerset Maugham, Garden City, 1934.
A Writer's Notebook, Doubleday, 1949. A collection of jottings kept during a half century of writing.
Aldington, Richard. *W. Somerset Maugham: An Appreciation*, Doubleday, Doran, 1939.

SPENDER

Poems, Random House, 1934.
Ruins and Visions, Random House, 1942. Later poems.
The Destructive Element, A Study of Modern Writers and Beliefs, Houghton, Mifflin, 1935. Treats chiefly James, Yeats, Eliot, and Lawrence.
World within World, Harcourt, Brace, 1951. Chapters of sensitive autobiography.

STRACHEY

Eminent Victorians, Modern Library.
Queen Victoria, Harbrace Modern Classics, Harcourt, Brace.
Beerbohm, Max. *Lytton Strachey*, Cambridge University Press, 1943. The Rede Lecture.
Lehman, B. H. *The Art of Lytton Strachey*, University of California Press, 1929.

THOMAS

Selected Writings, introduction by J. L. Sweeney, New Directions, 1946.

WOOLF

The Haunted House and Other Stories, Harcourt, Brace, 1942
The Common Reader, First and Second Series, Harcourt, Brace, 1948. The best of Virginia Woolf's essays.
Forster, E. M. *Virginia Woolf*, Harcourt, Brace, 1942.
Daiches, David. *Virginia Woolf*, New Directions, 1942. Perhaps the best study of her work.
Blackstone, Bernard. *Virginia Woolf; a Commentary*, Harcourt, Brace, 1949.

YEATS

Collected Poems, Macmillan, 1947.
Collected Plays, Macmillan, 1934.
Autobiography, Macmillan, 1938.
Hone, Joseph. *W. B. Yeats*, Macmillan, 1943.
Ellman, Richard. *Yeats: The Man and the Masks*, Macmillan, 1948. Based on personal papers of Yeats recently made available to scholars.
Stauffer, D. A. *The Golden Nightingale: Essays on Some Principles of Poetry in the Lyrics of William Butler Yeats*, Macmillan, 1949. Clear, compressed, and enthusiastic criticism.
Hall, James, and Steinmann, Martin, eds. *The Permanence of Yeats*, Macmillan, 1949. The best of the criticism of Yeats's work.

NOVELS

The following is a list of representative novels of the twentieth century, many of which may be obtained in inexpensive editions:

Beerbohm, Max. *Zuleika Dobson*, 1911. Modern Library.
Bennett, Arnold. *The Old Wives' Tale*, 1908. Modern Library.
Bowen, Elizabeth. *The Death of the Heart*, Knopf, 1939.
Cary, Joyce. *The Horse's Mouth*, Harper, 1950.
Chesterton, G. K. *The Flying Inn*, John Lane, 1914.
Compton-Burnett, Ivy. *Two Worlds and Their Ways*, Knopf, 1949.
Conrad, Joseph. *Lord Jim*, 1900; *Victory*, 1915. Modern Library.
de la Mare, Walter. *Memoirs of a Midget*, Knopf, 1921.
Douglas, Norman. *South Wind*, 1917. Modern Library.
Ford, Ford Madox. *Parade's End*, Knopf, 1950. Four novels of the Tietjens series.
Forster, E. M. *A Passage to India*, 1924. Harbrace Modern Classics. *The Longest Journey*, *A Room with a View*, New Directions, 1943.
Galsworthy, John. *The Forsyte Saga*, Scribner, 1922.
Green, Henry. *Loving*, Viking Press, 1949.
Greene, Graham. *The Heart of the Matter*, Viking Press, 1948.
Herbert, A. P. *The Water Gipsies*, Doubleday, Doran, 1930.
Hudson, W. H. *Green Mansions, A Romance of the Tropical Forest*, 1904. Modern Library.
Huxley, Aldous. *Point Counter Point*, 1928. Modern Library.
James, Henry. *The Wings of a Dove*, 1902. Modern Library.
Joyce, James. *Portrait of the Artist as a Young Man*, 1917. Modern Library. *Ulysses*, 1922. Random House.
Lawrence, D. H. *Sons and Lovers*, 1913. Modern Library.
Lehmann, Rosamond. *The Ballad and the Source*, Reynal and Hitchcock, 1945.
Maugham, W. Somerset. *Of Human Bondage*, 1915. Modern Library.
Newby, P. H. *Journey into the Interior*, Doubleday, 1946.
Orwell, George. *Nineteen Eighty-Four*, Harcourt, Brace, 1949.
Priestley, J. B. *The Good Companions*, Harper, 1929.
Richardson, Henry Handel (Henrietta). *The Fortunes of Richard Mahony*, Norton, 1930.
Walpole, Hugh. *Fortitude*, 1913. Modern Library.
Wells, H. G. *Tono-Bungay*, 1909. Modern Library.
Woolf, Virginia. *Mrs. Dalloway*, 1925; *To the Lighthouse*, 1927. Harbrace Modern Classics, Harcourt, Brace.

THE RULERS OF ENGLAND

Ecgbert	802–839	Richard II	1377–1399
Aethelwulf	839–858	Henry IV	1399–1413
Aethelbald	858–860	Henry V	1413–1422
Aethelbert	860–866	Henry VI	1422–1461
Aethelred I	866–871	Edward IV	1461–1483
Alfred	871–901	Edward V	1483
Edward the Elder	901–925	Richard III	1483–1485
Aethelstan	925–940	Henry VII	1485–1509
Edmund I	940–946	Henry VIII	1509–1547
Edred	946–955	Edward VI	1547–1553
Eadwig	955–959	Mary	1553–1558
Edgar	959–975	Elizabeth I	1558–1603
Edward the Martyr	975–978	James I	1603–1625
Aethelred the Unready	978–1016	Charles I	1625–1649
Edmund Ironside	1016	Oliver Cromwell	1653–1658
Canute	1016–1035	Richard Cromwell	1658–1659
Harold I	1035–1040	Charles II	1660–1685
Hardicanute	1040–1042	James II	1685–1688
Edward the Confessor	1042–1066	William III	1688–1702
Harold II	1066	Anne	1702–1714
William I	1066–1087	George I	1714–1727
William II	1087–1100	George II	1727–1760
Henry I	1100–1135	George III	1760–1820
Stephen	1135–1154	George IV	1820–1830
Henry II	1154–1189	William IV	1830–1837
Richard I	1189–1199	Victoria	1837–1901
John	1199–1216	Edward VII	1901–1910
Henry III	1216–1272	George V	1910–1936
Edward I	1272–1307	Edward VIII	1936
Edward II	1307–1327	George VI	1936–1952
Edward III	1327–1377	Elizabeth II	1952–

Poetic Forms and Patterns

ALTHOUGH drastically condensed and limited, this appendix presents the chief poetic designs and devices. It is by no means a complete outline, but rather a brief explanation of the principal forms of poetry and the common properties of versification. The definitions are general, not inclusive, popular (in the sense that they do not list exceptions to the rules) rather than pedagogic. However, most of the traditional forms have been included and only the rare or archaic terms have been omitted.

FEET AND METERS

The problems of rhythm and accent, of duration and pause, have been variously interpreted. The very nature of accent has given rise to controversy, some scholars maintaining it is due to a change in pitch of the voice, others to an increase of volume of tone. It is, however, generally accepted as *stress*, and in the following paragraphs it will be so regarded.

In English verse the rhythm is based upon this stress or accent, "the measured undulation of accented and unaccented syllables being its essential feature without which it becomes prose" (Brewer). Although classical prosody lists about thirty combinations of stressed and unstressed syllables (divided into accented and unaccented "feet"), the fundamental ones in English verse are five.

1. The *iambic foot* is an unaccented syllable followed by an accented one. It is commonly expressed thus: ˘ ´; such words as *oppose*, *delight*, *amuse* being, in themselves, iambic feet. English verse is founded on the iambic beat; it might be said that our very speech tends to fall into iambics. An illustrative couplet:

> A book of verses underneath the bough,
> A jug of wine, a loaf of bread—and thou.

2. The *trochaic foot* is an accented syllable followed by an unaccented one. It is commonly expressed thus: ´ ˘; such words as *gather*, *heartless*, *feeling* being in themselves trochaic feet. It is second in importance to the iambic measure. An illustrative example:

> Soft and easy is thy cradle
> Coarse and hard thy Saviour lay.

It should be noted that the majority of trochaic lines in English show a deficient last foot; that is to say, the last syllable is often omitted, as in the second line of the example quoted.

3. The *dactylic foot* is an accented syllable followed by two unaccented ones. It is commonly expressed thus: ´ ˘ ˘; such words as *happiness*, *sentiment*, *merrily* being in themselves dactylic feet. Grace and a lilting movement are achieved by its use. An illustrative example:

> Love again, song again, nest again, young again.

4. The *anapestic foot* consists of two unaccented syllables followed by an accented syllable. It is commonly expressed thus: ˘ ˘ ´; such words as *interrupt*, *supersede*, *disappear* being, in themselves, anapestic feet. It is a speedy and propulsive rhythm. An illustrative example:

> With the sheep in the fold and the cows in their stalls.

Both dactylic and anapestic measures tend to become monotonous, and therefore most poets who employ them vary the measures by introducing two-syllable (iambic or trochaic) feet.

5. The *spondee* consists of two equally accented syllables expressed thus: ´ ´; compound words like *heartbreak*, *childhood*, *wineglass* being perfect spondees. It is mostly found in classic poetry and is used chiefly for grave and strong emphasis. An illustrative example:

> Slow spondee stalks; strong foot.

It should be added that there are few poems in the English language which adhere absolutely to one foot or accent; most poems of any length reveal a variety of feet. Pope has illustrated this variation, this change of pace, in his lines on the craft of verse in "An Essay on Criticism":

> True ease in writing comes from art, not chance,
> As those move easiest who have learned to dance.
> 'Tis not enough no harshness gives offence,
> The sound must seem an echo to the sense.
> Soft is the strain when Zephyr gently blows,
> And the smooth stream in smoother numbers flows;
> But when loud surges lash the sounding shore,
> The hoarse, rough verse should like the torrent roar:
> When Ajax strives some rock's vast weight to throw,
> The line too labours, and the words move slow;
> Not so, when swift Camilla scours the plain,
> Flies o'er the unbending corn, and skims along the main.

The *meter* or measure of a verse is determined by the number of feet in the line. The terms explain themselves: *monometer*—one foot; *dimeter*—two feet; *trimeter*—three feet; *tetrameter*—four feet; *pentameter*—five feet; *hexameter*—six feet; *heptameter*—seven feet; *octameter*—eight feet. Thus the following line:

To hear | the lark | begin | his flight

is a line of four feet. Since it is a compound of four iambic feet, it would be classified as *iambic tetrameter.*

STANZA FORMS

In the same way that feet are combined into the structure of a line, lines are combined into the pattern of a poem. These patterns, or stanzas, have certain distinct characteristics and are usually classified as follows:

The *couplet* consists of two lines of matched verse in immediate succession. It has always been popular, especially for sharp or epigrammatic effect. The form has been a favorite since the time of Chaucer's *Canterbury Tales.* Dryden brought it to a kind of perfection, and Pope tightened it into a "thought couplet," each couplet being a unit in itself.

Behold the child, by nature's kindly law,
Pleased with a rattle, tickled with a straw:
Some livelier plaything gives his youth delight,
A little louder, but as empty quite:
Scarfs, garters, gold, amuse his riper stage,
And beads and prayer-books are the toys of age:
Pleased with this bauble still, as that before,
Till tired he sleeps, and life's poor play is o'er.
—*Essay on Man*

The *tercet* (sometimes known as the *triplet*) is a stanza of three lines rhyming together. Examples of this pattern may be found in Crashaw's "Wishes to His Supposed Mistress," Herrick's "Upon Julia's Clothes," Herbert's "Paradise." A further illustration is Browning's

Boot, saddle, to horse, and away! a
Rescue my castle before the hot day a
Brightens to blue from its silvery gray. a

The *quatrain,* the commonest stanza form, consists of four lines rhymed in a variety of ways. Perhaps the most familiar arrangement is in the ballad meter, in which the second and fourth lines are rhymed while the first and third are unrhymed. See "Sir Patrick Spens," "Johnie Armstrong," and "The Wife of Usher's Well" (all of which you will find in the ballad section, pages 134–146). Almost as well known is the quatrain in which the rhymes are *a-b-a-b,* as, for example, Drayton's

Clear had the day been from the dawn, a
All chequered was the sky, b
Thin clouds, like scarfs of cobweb lawn, a
Veiled heaven's most glorious eye. b

A form of quatrain somewhat less familiar is one in which the lines rhyme *a-b-b-a,* as, for example, Tennyson's

Our little systems have their day; a
They have their day and cease to be: b
They are but broken lights of Thee, b
And thou, O Lord, art more than they. a

An even more unusual form of quatrain is one in which all four lines have only one rhyme. Although this single-sounding rhyme tends toward monotony it can be used with great effectiveness, as in Dante Gabriel Rossetti's "The Woodspurge":

My eyes, wide open, had the run a
Of some ten weeds to fix upon; a
Among those few, out of the sun, a
The woodspurge flowered, three cups in one. a

The variations are great and range from the clipped stanzas of Herbert's "Discipline" to the long measure of Gray's "Elegy." The quatrain itself, in its various shapes, appears throughout this volume too frequently to be listed.

The *quintet* is a five-line stanza variously rhymed, although the favorite formula seems to be *a-b-a-b-b.* Swinburne's "Hertha" is written in this form, a particularly fluent example, with its long-rolling last line:

I the grain and the furrow, a
The plough-cloven clod b
And the ploughshare drawn thorough, a
The germ and the sod, b
The deed and the doer, the seed and the sower, the dust which is God. b

Shelley's "To a Skylark," Waller's "Go, Lovely Rose," and Christina Rossetti's "Weary in Well-Doing" are among the more famous poems built on the quintet.

The *sestet* is a six-line stanza in which the possibilities of line and rhyme arrangement are almost endless. It may be made of a quatrain and an added couplet (*a-b-a-b-c-c*), as in Edward Dyer's "My Mind to Me a Kingdom Is":

My mind to me a kingdom is, a
Such present joys therein I find, b
That it excels all other bliss a
That earth affords or grows by kind: b

Though much I want which most would have, c
Yet still my mind forbids to crave. c

The sestet may also be composed of interlacing couplets, as in Shakespeare's "O Mistress Mine" from *Twelfth Night:*

O mistress mine! where are you roaming? a
O! stay and hear; your true love's coming, a
  That can sing both high and low. b
Trip no further, pretty sweeting; a
Journeys end in lovers meeting, a
  Every wise man's son doth know. b

The sestet may be a mingling of rhymed and unrhymed lines, as in D. G. Rossetti's "The Blessed Damozel," or the quaint arrangement which Robert Burns made his own in "To a Mouse" and "The Hermit."

The blessed damozel leaned out
  From the gold bar of Heaven;
Her eyes were deeper than the depth
  Of waters stilled at even;
She had three lilies in her hand,
  And the stars in her hair were seven.

The term "sestet" is also used to designate the last six lines of the sonnet.

The *septet*, a rather uncommon but flexible seven-line form, is chiefly esteemed in the variation known as *rime royal*, so called because it was supposedly first employed by King James I of Scotland. Chaucer was fond of using it (see his "Prioress's Tale," "Troilus and Criseyde" and "Parliament of Fowls"); Masefield erected his "The Widow in the Bye Street," "Dauber," and others on this design.

Among thise children was a wydwes sone, a
A litel clergeoun, seven yeer of age, b
That day by day to scole was his wone, a
And eek also, wher as he say th'ymage b
Of Cristes moder, hadde he in usage, b
As hym was taught, to knele adoun and seye c
His *Ave Marie*, as he goth by the weye. c
—*Prioress's Tale*

The *octave*, a stanza of eight lines, presents infinite possibilities for the poet. It may be composed of the linking of two quatrains (*a-b-a-b-c-d-c-d*) or two triplets with an intervening pair of rhyming lines (*a-a-a-b-c-c-c-b*), as in the first example quoted below, or a quatrain, a triplet and an extra, final rhyme (*a-b-a-b-c-c-c-b*), as in the second example. William Butler Yeats' "Sailing to Byzantium" presents still another arrangement (*a-b-a-b-a-c-d-d*).

Upon Saint Crispin's Day a
Fought was this noble fray, a
Which fame did not delay a
  To England to carry. b
O when shall English men c
With such acts fill a pen? c
Or England breed again c
  Such a King Harry? b
—*Drayton, Agincourt*

From too much love of living, a
  From hope and fear set free, b
We thank with brief thanksgiving a
  Whatever gods may be b
That no life lives for ever; c
That dead men rise up never; c
That even the weariest river c
  Winds somewhere safe to sea. b
—*Swinburne, The Garden of Proserpine*

That is no country for old men. The young a
In one another's arms, birds in the trees, b
—Those dying generations—at their song, a
The salmon-falls, the mackerel-crowded seas, b
Fish, flesh, or fowl, commend all summer long a
Whatever is begotten, born, and dies. c
Caught in that sensual music all neglect d
Monuments of unaging intellect. d
—*Yeats, Sailing to Byzantium*

A particular form of the eight-line stanza is know as *ottava rima*, since it was adapted from the Italian. The arrangement is *a-b-a-b-a-b-c-c*, and examples of it are found in Byron's "Don Juan" and "The Vision of Judgment." An octave from the former:

I can't but say it is an awkward sight a
  To see one's native land receding through b
The growing waters; it unmans one quite, a
  Especially when life is rather new: b
I recollect Great Britain's coast looks white, a
  But almost every other country's blue, b
When gazing on them, mystified by distance, c
We enter on our nautical existence. c

The term "octave" is also used to designate the first eight lines of the sonnet.

The *Spenserian stanza* is a solemn, nine-line stanza, invented by Spenser. Its rhyme scheme is intricate (*a-b-a-b-b-c-b-c-c*) and the ninth line (called the *Alexandrine*) is one foot longer than the others, rounding out the stanza with an impressive sonority. Among the poems built on Spenserian stanza are Byron's "Childe Harold," Keats's "The Eve of St. Agnes," Shelley's "Adonais," and Spenser's own *The Faerie Queene*, one stanza of which follows:

And more, to lulle him in his slumber soft, a
A trickling streame from high rocke tumbling downe b
And ever-drizling raine upon the loft, a
Mixt with a murmuring winde, much like the sowne b
Of swarming Bees, did cast him in a swowne: b
No other noyse, nor peoples troublous cryes, c
As still are wont t' annoy the wallèd towne, b
Might there be heard: but carelesse Quiet lyes, c
Wrapt in eternall silence farre from enemyes. c

The ten-, eleven-, and twelve-line stanzas are combinations of smaller units and are rather uncommon. The fourteen-line stanza (the sonnet) has developed into one of the richest patterns in English poetry and must be considered separately.

THE BALLAD

Webster defines the *ballad* as follows: "A popular short narrative poem, especially a romantic poem characterized by simplicity of structure . . . usually founded on folk legend or tradition." There are, moreover, five features which characterize the ballad, no matter whether it is long or short.

1. The action is swift. There is no introduction and practically no explanation. No time is wasted in exposition; the characters leap at once into life.

2. The tale is simple and direct. The tone is straightforward and without elaboration; the language is the language of the people.

3. The story is moving. Whether it concerns an event of the day or something supernatural, the verses stir the emotion and the imagination.

4. The attitude is impersonal. The ballad-maker is a born storyteller, especially in the sense that he is outside of the story. He rarely comments or philosophizes upon the event; he scarcely ever renders judgment upon the characters.

5. With few exceptions, the story is concentrated upon one incident; it does not attempt to give all the events leading up to it, nor does it enlarge upon the consequences.

THE SONNET

The sonnets in this volume are easily recognized. Although they show a variety of rhyme schemes, their basic structure is identical. All sonnets are built on fourteen lines, the lines themselves (with few exceptions) being composed of ten syllables—iambic pentameter. These fourteen lines are usually divided into the first eight (the octave) and the second six (the sestet). The three main types are the Petrarchan (or Italian), the Shakespearean, and the Miltonic sonnet.

The *Petrarchan sonnet* is the strictest; it permits only two rhymes in the octave and not more than three (often two) in the sestet. The octave is rhymed *a-b-b-a-a-b-b-a*. The sestet allows a variation in the line arrangement, the favorite pattern being either *c-d-e-c-d-e* or *c-d-c-d-c-d*. An example of the Petrarchan sonnet follows:

O Earth, lie heavily upon her eyes; a
Seal her sweet eyes weary of watching, Earth; b
Lie close around her; leave no room for mirth b
With its harsh laughter, nor for sound of sighs. a
She hath no questions, she hath no replies, a
Hush'd in and curtain'd with a blessed dearth b
Of all that irk'd her from the hour of birth; b
With stillness that is almost Paradise. a

Darkness more clear than noonday holdeth her, c
Silence more musical than any song; d
Even her very heart has ceased to stir: c
Until the morning of Eternity e
Her rest shall not begin nor end, but be; e
And when she wakes she will not think it long. d

—*Christina Rossetti, Rest*

The *Shakespearean sonnet*, perfected but not invented by Shakespeare, completely departs from the finely interwoven Italian model. It is actually nothing more than a set of three quatrains concluded and cemented by a couplet. An example:

No longer mourn for me when I am dead a
Than you shall hear the surly sullen bell b
Give warning to the world that I am fled a
From this vile world with vilest worms to dwell; b
Nay, if you read this line, remember not c
The hand that writ it, for I love you so d
That I in your sweet thoughts would be forgot c
If thinking on me then should make you woe. d
O if, I say, you look upon this verse e
When I perhaps compounded am with clay, f
Do not so much as my poor name rehearse, e
But let your love even with my life decay, f
Lest the wise world should look into your moan g
And mock you with me after I am gone. g

—*Shakespeare*

The *Miltonic sonnet* is an adaptation of the Petrarchan with a striking difference. The Italian model separated the octave and sestet by a break in thought; the octave usually presented a general idea while the sestet pointed it and made it particular. Instead of dividing his sonnets in two parts, Milton unrolled his thought and his rich music without interruption through the fourteen lines:

Avenge, O Lord, thy slaughtered Saints, whose bones a
Lie scattered on the Alpine mountains cold; b
Even them who kept thy truth so pure of old, b
When all our fathers worshipped stocks and stones, a
Forget not: in thy book record their groans a
Who were thy sheep, and in their ancient fold b
Slain by the bloody Piemontese, that rolled b
Mother with infant down the rocks. Their moans a
The vales redoubled to the hills, and they c
To heaven. Their martyred blood and ashes sow d
O'er all the Italian fields, where still doth sway c
The triple Tyrant; that from these may grow d
A hundredfold, who, having learnt thy way, c
Early may fly the Babylonian woe. d

The green land's name that a charm encloses, a
It never was writ in the traveller's chart, b
And sweet on its trees as the fruit that grows is; a
It never was sold in the merchant's mart. b
The swallows of dreams through its dim fields dart, b
And sleep's are the tunes in its tree-tops heard; c
No hound's note wakens the wildwood hart, b
Only the song of a secret bird. c

ENVOI

In the world of dreams I have chosen my part, b
To sleep for a season and hear no word c
Of true love's truth or of light love's art, b
Only the song of a secret bird. c

—*Swinburne, A Ballade of Dreamland*

THE BALLADE

The *ballade* (not to be confused with the ballad) is the most popular as well as the most important of the strict forms brought over from France. Villon immortalized the form and Chaucer used it in England as early as the fourteenth century—see his "Ballade of Good Counsel." It is composed of three stanzas of eight lines and a half-stanza (the *envoy*) of four lines. The rhymes of the first stanza are arranged in the order *a-b-a-b-b-c-b-c*, and this arrangement is repeated in all the other stanzas—the envoy (or "message") being *b-c-b-c*. Only three rhymes are used throughout the entire ballade, and no rhyme word may be repeated.

The outstanding feature of the ballade is its *refrain*. The refrain is the line which ends all the stanzas and the envoy; it is repeated in its entirety and gives a unity to the poem.

I hid my heart in a nest of roses, a
Out of the sun's way, hidden apart; b
In a softer bed than the soft white snow's is, a
Under the roses I hid my heart. b
Why would it sleep not? Why should it start, b
When never a leaf of the rose-tree stirred? c
What made sleep flutter his wings and part? b
Only the song of a secret bird. c

Lie still, I said, for the wind's wing closes, a
And mild leaves muffle the keen sun's dart; b
Lie still, for the wind on the warm seas dozes, a
And the wind is unquieter yet than thou art. b
Does a thought in thee still as a thorn's wound smart? b
Does the fang still fret thee of hope deferred? c
What bids the lips of thy sleep dispart? b
Only the song of a secret bird. c

THE RONDEAU

The *rondeau* is a nimbler form usually employed for sprightly themes, although it can be used gravely. It is composed of thirteen lines built on only two rhymes, the refrain being a repetition of the first part of the first line. Using *R* to represent the refrain, the rhyme scheme would be *Ra-a-b-b-a*, *a-a-b-R*, *a-a-b-b-a-R*. Here is Austin Dobson's skillful paraphrase of a famous French rondeau:

You bid me try, blue eyes, to write Ra
A rondeau. What!—forthwith—to-night? a
Reflect. Some skill I have, 'tis true; b
But thirteen lines—and rhymed on two! b
"Refrain," as well. Ah, hapless plight! a

Still, here are five lines—ranged aright. a
These Gallic bonds, I feared, would fright a
My easy Muse. They did till you— b
You bid me try! R

This makes them nine. The port's in sight; a
'Tis all because your eyes are bright! a
Now, just a pair to end with "oo"— b
When maids command, what can't we do? b
Behold! the rondeau—tasteful, light— a
You bid me try! R

THE TRIOLET

In common with the ballade, the rondeau, and other forms imported from France, the *triolet* is founded on a strict rhyme scheme and constructed by skillful repetition. The smallest and shortest of the French forms, it consists of only eight lines—and three of the eight are repeated. The first line

(*Ra*) is repeated to make the fourth and seventh lines; the second line (*Rb*) is repeated to make the eighth line. An example of the triolet's nimbleness:

Under the sun Ra
There's nothing new; Rb
Poem or pun, a
Under the sun, Ra
Said Solomon, a
And he said true. b
"Under the sun Ra
There's nothing new." Rb

—*H. C. Beeching*

THE VILLANELLE

Originally used for pastoral subjects, the *villanelle* has become so stylized that its simplicity is quite artificial. It is composed of five three-line stanzas and a concluding stanza of four lines, each stanza ending with an alternating line of the first verse. In the last stanza both of these lines appear together as a concluding couplet. Only two rhymes are permitted throughout the verses. W. H. Auden has used this form. Henley has described its very essence as follows:

A dainty thing's the Villanelle. a 1
Sly, musical, a jewel in rhyme, b
It serves its purpose passing well. a 2

A double-clappered silver bell a
That must be made to clink in chime, b
A dainty thing's the Villanelle; a 1

And if you wish to flute a spell, a
Or ask a meeting 'neath the lime, b
It serves its purpose passing well. a 2

You must not ask of it the swell a
Of organs grandiose and sublime— b
A dainty thing's the Villanelle; a 1

And, filled with sweetness, as a shell a
Is filled with sound, and launched in time, b
It serves its purpose passing well. a 2

Still fair to see and good to smell a
As in the quaintness of its prime, b
A dainty thing's the Villanelle; a 1
It serves its purpose passing well. a 2

THE ODE

Derived from a Greek word meaning "song," the *ode*, according to the lexicographers, became "a form of stately and elaborate verse." Originally chanted, the ode was built on a set of themes and responses and sung by divided choirs, half the singers intoning the strophe, the other half replying with the antistrophe, and both uniting with the epode. Most of the odes in English verse depart from the Greek model, although Swinburne's "Athens" and some of his political odes preserve the antique mode, while Dryden's "Alexander's Feast" blends the responsive voices in the classical manner. Cowley invented a variation on the form which he called the *Pindaric ode*—an irregular, passionate declamation in which the form is swept aside on a wave of emotion—Cowley failing to comprehend that Pindar varied the verse arrangement of his odes but that each was consistently and strictly patterned.

Since Cowley, the shape of the ode has grown more and more uncertain. The odes of Coleridge, Wordsworth, and Tennyson, though eloquent, are irregular. The magnificent odes of Keats and Shelley are, in reality, extended and sustained lyrics. The term itself has been broadened; strophe and antistrophe have disappeared; the length and the stanza pattern are unpredictable. Today the ode may be recognized not by its form at all, but rather by its tone: an intense, richly elaborated, and often profound apostrophe.

BLANK VERSE

Blank verse may be defined as (1) any unrhymed regular measure or (2) unrhymed verse in iambic pentameter. But the term "blank verse" seems attached to the iambic five-accented line first employed in English by Henry Howard, Earl of Surrey, and glorified by Shakespeare's dramas, Milton's epics, and Wordsworth's meditations. Along with its sonority, its great strength lies in its flexibility. It can deviate from strict metrical regularity without injuring the rolling line—in fact the departures, the endless variety of effects, reveal its never-exhausted power. Every master of blank verse has given the measure new modulations and stamped it with his characteristic idiom.

From the countless examples of eloquent blank verse five illustrative segments, ranging from the sixteenth to the twentieth century, have been chosen.

The stars move still, time runs, the clock will strike,
The devil will come, and Faustus must be damned.
O, I'll leap up to heaven!—Who pulls me down?—
See, where Christ's blood streams in the firmament!
One drop of blood will save me: O my Christ!—

Rend not my heart for naming of my Christ;
Yet will I call on him: O, spare me, Lucifer!—
Where is it now? 'tis gone:
And, see, a threatening arm, an angry brow!
Mountains and hills, come, come, and fall on me,
And hide me from the heavy wrath of heaven!

—*Marlowe, Dr. Faustus*

There is a tide in the affairs of men,
Which, taken at the flood, leads on to fortune;
Omitted, all the voyage of their life
Is bound in shallows and in miseries.
On such a full sea are we now afloat;
And we must take the current when it serves,
Or lose our ventures. . . .

—*Shakespeare, Julius Caesar*

These are thy glorious works, Parent of good,
Almighty, Thine this universal frame,
Thus wondrous fair: Thyself how wondrous then!
Unspeakable, who sitt'st above these heavens
To us invisible, or dimly seen
In these thy lowest works; yet these declare
Thy goodness beyond thought, and power divine.
Speak, ye who best can tell, ye sons of light,
Angels, for ye behold Him, and with songs
And choral symphonies, day without night,
Circle His throne rejoicing, ye, in heaven,
On earth join all ye creatures to extol
Him first, Him last, Him midst, and without end.

—*Milton, Paradise Lost*

. . . That time is past,
And all its aching joys are now no more,
And all its dizzy raptures. Not for this
Faint I, nor mourn nor murmur; other gifts
Have followed; for such loss, I would believe,
Abundant recompence. For I have learned
To look on nature, not as in the hour
Of thoughtless youth; but hearing oftentimes
The still, sad music of humanity.

—*Wordsworth, Tintern Abbey*

See how these names are fêted by the waving grass . . .
The names of those who in their lives fought for life,
Who wore at their hearts the fire's centre.
Born of the sun they travelled a short while towards the sun,
And left the vivid air signed with their honour.

—*Spender, I Think Continually of Those*

FREE VERSE

It has been characteristic of many twentieth-century poets to abandon the devices of rhyme and regular verse form in the interests of freer expression. The result is a poetry, sometimes known as *free verse*, that is founded on a *general* rather than on a precise meter. However, though free verse dispenses with any decided meter, it employs all the other assets of poetry: assonance, alliteration, balance. In fact, it differs from formal poetry only in its irregularity of rhythm. Nor is this freer verse form really a new development. When in the Bible we read the Psalms, the Song of Solomon, and the Book of Job, we are reading the greatest free verse that has ever been written. And examples are to be found throughout the long course of English poetry. But never was the departure from traditional poetic patterns and restrictions so pronounced and deliberate as in the 1920's and 1930's. At mid-century there are signs of some return toward orthodoxy. The following lines from T. S. Eliot's "Burnt Norton" well illustrate the merits of the free verse form:

Will the sunflower turn to us, will the clematis
Stray down, bend to us; tendril and spray
Clutch and cling?
Chill
Fingers of yew be curled
Down on us?

VARIOUS DEVICES

Besides the patterns already defined, the poet has recourse to various devices. Some of the most easily recognizable are *alliteration*, *rhyme*, *assonance*, *onomatopoeia*, *metonymy*, *synecdoche*, *epithet*, *simile*, and *metaphor*.

Devices of Sound

Alliteration is the repetition of the same consonant sound in words or syllables succeeding each other at close intervals. Usually it refers to the repetition of a sound or letter at the beginning of words, as in

Fields ever fresh and groves ever green.

But, besides the repetition of *f* and *g* in this line, there is alliteration of the *v* sounds, half buried in the midst of the words. It is the most recognizable of devices, often overused—Swinburne carried it to the point of parody—but it is extremely effective as an enrichment of rhyme, even a substitute for it, as in Anglo-Saxon poetry. A famous example is Tennyson's

The moan of doves in immemorial elms,
And murmuring of innumerable bees.

In our time the poetry of Dylan Thomas is rich in alliteration:

And death shall have no dominion.
Dead men naked they shall be one
With the man in the wind and the west moon.

Rhyme, sometimes spelled *rime*, has been variously defined. However, the principle laid down by Thomas Hood still holds: "A rhyme must commence on an accented syllable. From the accented vowel of that syllable to the end, the words intended to rhyme must be *identical* in sound, but the letter or letters preceding the accented vowel must be *unlike* in sound." "Night" and "fight," for example, are true rhymes, but "night" and "knight" do not rhyme, there being nothing unlike in the sound preceding the vowel. Neither can "night" and "ride" be said to rhyme, for though the sound preceding the vowel is different, the sound *following* the vowel is not identical, as it should be to constitute a true rhyme. "Night" and "ride" is an instance of assonance.

Assonance is the matching of the vowel sound alone, irrespective of the consonant (or sound) which follows it. Thus "base" and "face" would be true rhyme, whereas "base" and "fade" would be assonance. The old ballads and folk poetry are full of assonance, sometimes purposeful, sometimes accidental, as in "Sir Patrick Spens":

The anchor broke, the topmast *split*,
'Twas such a deadly *storm*.
The waves came over the broken *ship*
Till all her sides were *torn*.

Onomatopoeia is the formation of words by the imitation of sounds; the words thus formed vividly suggest the object or action producing the sound. Such words are found in the cradle of the individual as well as in the infancy of the race: *bow-wow*, *ding-dong*, *hum*, *buzz*, and so on. Though not confined to verse, words like *whiz*, *crash*, *crunch*, *crackle*, *jangle*, *squeal*, *honk*, *hiss* have become properties of the poet.

When Keats wrote

The murmurous haunt of flies on summer eves

he not only suggested the presence of flies, he *imitated* the drone and buzzing of insects on a sultry evening.

Devices of Sense

Metonymy and *synecdoche* are related to metaphor and simile, being forms of comparison. Metonymy (literally "name change") is the substitution of one thing to represent another. Thus when Byron, describing the ball on the night before Waterloo says:

And Belgium's capital had gathered then
Her beauty and her chivalry—

the word "beauty" represents "fair women" and the word "chivalry" symbolizes "brave men."

Synecdoche (literally, "receiving together") is a figure of speech in which a part represents the whole: in the cry

"A sail! A sail!"

the word "sail" symbolizes the entire ship. Both metonymy and synecdoche are "figures of association," and there is little real difference in the way they are used today.

An *epithet* is a word (usually an adjective) which describes its object with unusual exactness. It is the arresting term which not only points a description but reveals how imagination intensifies observation. This exactness and fancy may be seen in such epithets as: "*smooth-sliding* Mincius," "*brittle* beauty," "lazy, *leaden-stepping* hours," "the river *sweats* oil and tar," "the *strong* crust of *friendly* bread," "the *green hells* of the sea," "*full-throated* ease," "*embalmed* darkness."

Simile and *metaphor* are poetry's most constant properties. The power of each lies in establishing a kinship between two (usually unrelated) objects, and fixing the attention on one object by comparing it to another. When the comparison is direct and introduced by *like* or *as*, it is a simile; when the comparison is indirect or implied, without the use of *like* or *as*, it is a metaphor.

Among the many familiar similes, these may be listed:

My luve is like a red, red rose (*Burns*)

I wandered lonely as a cloud (*Wordsworth*)

I have seen old ships sail like swans alseep (*Flecker*)

As a dare-gale skylark scanted in a dull cage
Man's mounting spirit in his bone-house, mean house, dwells (*Hopkins*)

The following are vivid examples of metaphor:

There is a garden in her face (*Campion*)

Life's but a walking shadow, a poor player (*Shakespeare*)

My life is measured out with coffee spoons (*Eliot*)

Without simile and metaphor the image would lose its swiftness and strength; poetry is founded on the vigor and range of the metaphorical mind. Its element is surprise. To relate the hitherto unrelated, to make the strange seem familiar and the familiar seem strange, is the aim of metaphor. Through this heightened awareness, poetry, though variously defined, is invariably pronounced and unmistakably perceived.

L. U.

INDEXES

GENERAL INDEX

The names of the authors whose selections are represented are shown in CAPITALS and SMALL CAPITALS.

The titles of selections quoted are shown in **bold face.**

The **bold-face** numbers refer to the pages on which authors are discussed in detail, and to the pages on which the quoted selections appear.

INDEX OF FIRST LINES

W 3
X 4
Y 5
Z 6

A LITERARY MAP OF ENGLAND
Scale of English Miles
0
20
40
60
ISLAY
JURA
KINTYRE
ARRAN
BUTE
Bute
THE HIGH
Loch Lomond
Dundee
Scone
Dunfermline
Firth of Forth
Edinburgh
Prestonpans
Hawthornden
Dumbarton
Greenock
Glasgow
Clyde R.
Kilmarnock
LAMMERMOOR HILLS
Berwick-upon-Tweed
LINDISFARNE
FARNE IS.
Dryburgh Abbey
Ednam
Tweed R.
FLODDEN FIELD
Abbotsford
Melrose Abbey
Yarrow R.
Selkirk
Ettrick
Ayr
Alloway
Auchinleck
Firth of Clyde
Doon R.
R. Afton
R. Nith
CHEVIOT HILLS
Warkworth Castle
Otterburn
NORTHUMBERLAND
Blyth
Tynemouth
Newcastle
Tyne R.
Craigenputtock
Ecclefechan
Gretna Green
Annan
Dumfries
Kirkcudbright
Carlisle
Derwent R.
Jarrow
Wearmouth
Durham
DURHAM
Wear
Hartlepool
Tees R.
CUMBERLAND
CUMBRIAN MTS.
Solway Firth
Cockermouth
MT. SKIDDAW
Keswick
Rydal Mt.
Derwent Water
Ullswater
Appleby
MT. HELVELLYN
WESTMORLAND
PENNINE
Grasmere
Hawkshead
Brantwood
NORTH CHANNEL
Belfast
MULL OF GALLOWAY
ST. BEES HEAD
ISLE OF MAN
Douglas
Castletown
Swale R.
Hipswell
Whitby
NORTH YORK MOORS
Scarborough
Coxwold
Stillington
Sutton-on-the-Forest
FLAMBOROUGH HEAD
Ure R.
MARSTON MOOR
YORK
York
Elvington
Ouse R.
THE
Hull
Lancaster
Morecambe Bay
Haworth
Leeds
Bradford
Halifax
Pomfret Castle
Wakefield
Humber R.
WOLDS
Great Grimsby
IRISH SEA
LANCASTER
FORMBY POINT
Manchester
Don R.
Liverpool
Sheffield
LINCOLN
Dublin
Holyhead
HOLY I.
ANGLESEY
Menai Strait
St. Asaph
Birkenhead
Mersey R.
THE PEAK
SHERWOOD FOREST
NOTTINGHAM
Bangor
Caernarvon
Denbigh
FLINT
Chester
Hawarden
CHESTER
DERBY
Trent R.
Lincoln
Somersby
Witham R.
SNOWDON
DENBIGH
Crewe
Derwent
Newstead Abbey
AERNARVON
Wrexham
Dee
STAFFORD
Newark
Swineshead
Boston
Wash
Wells next
NNEL